SELECTED FEDERAL TAXATION STATUTES AND REGULATIONS

1987 EDITION

Selected and Edited

by

MICHAEL D. ROSE

Professor of Law, The Ohio State University

WEST PUBLISHING CO.
ST. PAUL, MINN., 1987

Sel.Fed.Tax. 1987 Ed.
1st Reprint—1987

PREFACE

This volume is for student use. It contains selected and edited provisions of the Internal Revenue Code (Title 26 of the United States Code) and the Treasury Regulations (Title 26 of the Code of Federal Regulations).

The purpose of the volume is to provide a reasonably compact, convenient, and economical set of materials. Thus, it is not a complete source of the Internal Revenue Code and Treasury Regulations. The entire text of the Code and Regulations is over 8,000 pages, the bulk of which students do not use.

This 1987 edition is current through October 31, 1986. Consequently, it reflects the Tax Reform Act of 1986, Public Law 99–514, signed by the President on October 22, 1986. Regulations that have been promulgated since May 15, 1986, the cut-off date for the 1986 edition, are contained in this edition. Included are those under § 704(b), relating to allocations of loss and deduction attributable to nonrecourse debt of a partnership, and new §§ 25.2518–1, 25.2518–2, and 25.2518–3, relating to disclaimer of property transferred by gift or inheritance. Sections 311, 333, 336, and 337 prior to amendment or repeal by the Tax Reform Act of 1986 are in the Appendix along with the transitional rule for small corporations.

The comments and suggestions about the materials are appreciated. They were helpful in preparing this edition. Again, ideas for improvement are invited.

MICHAEL D. ROSE

Columbus, Ohio
December, 1986

*

SUMMARY OF CONTENTS

*

SELECTED FEDERAL TAXATION STATUTES AND REGULATIONS

*

INTERNAL REVENUE TITLE

TABLE OF SUBTITLES

TABLE OF CHAPTERS IN SUBTITLES

Subtitle A. Income Taxes

Subtitle B. Estate and Gift Taxes

Subtitle C. Employment Taxes *

Subtitle D. Miscellaneous Excise Taxes *

* Omitted entirely.

Subtitle E. Alcohol, Tobacco, and Certain Other Excise Taxes *

Subtitle F. Procedure and Administration

Subtitle G. The Joint Committee on Taxation *

Subtitle H. Financing of Presidential Election Campaigns *

Subtitle I. Trust Fund Code *

* Omitted entirely.

TABLE OF SUBCHAPTERS, PARTS AND SUBPARTS IN CHAPTERS

SUBTITLE A. INCOME TAXES

* Omitted entirely.

4

INCOME TAXES

* Omitted entirely.

INCOME TAXES

* Omitted entirely.

INCOME TAXES

* Omitted entirely.

SUBTITLE B. ESTATE AND GIFT TAXES

* Omitted entirely.

SUBTITLE C. EMPLOYMENT TAXES *

SUBTITLE D. MISCELLANEOUS EXCISE TAXES *

* * *

SUBTITLE E. ALCOHOL, TOBACCO, AND CERTAIN OTHER EXCISE TAXES*

* * *

* Omitted entirely.

SUBTITLE F. PROCEDURE AND ADMINISTRATION

* Omitted entirely.

INCOME TAXES

* Omitted entirely.

SUBTITLE G. THE JOINT COMMITTEE ON TAXATION*

SUBTITLE H. FINANCING OF PRESIDENTIAL ELECTION CAMPAIGNS*

SUBTITLE I. TRUST FUND CODE*

* Omitted entirely.

INTERNAL REVENUE TITLE

SUBTITLE A—INCOME TAXES

Chapter
1. Normal taxes and surtaxes.
2. Tax on self-employment income.*
3. Withholding of tax on nonresident aliens and foreign corporations.*
4. Rules applicable to recovery of excessive profits on government contracts.*
5. Tax on transfers to avoid income tax.*
6. Consolidated returns.

CHAPTER 1—NORMAL TAXES AND SURTAXES

Subchapter
A. Determination of tax liability.
B. Computation of taxable income.
C. Corporate distributions and adjustments.
D. Deferred compensation, etc.
E. Accounting periods and methods of accounting.
F. Exempt organizations.
G. Corporations used to avoid income tax on shareholders.
H. Banking institutions.*
I. Natural resources.
J. Estates, trusts, beneficiaries, and decedents.
K. Partners and partnerships.
L. Insurance companies.*
M. Regulated investment companies and real estate investment trusts.*
N. Tax based on income from sources within or without the United States.*
O. Gain or loss on disposition of property.
P. Capital gains and losses.
Q. Readjustment of tax between years and special limitations.
[R. Repealed]
S. Tax treatment of S corporations and their shareholders.
T. Cooperatives and their patrons.*
[U. Repealed]
V. Title 11 cases.*

SUBCHAPTER A—DETERMINATION OF TAX LIABILITY

Part
I. Tax on individuals.
II. Tax on corporations.
III. Changes in rates during a taxable year.*
IV. Credits against tax.
* Omitted entirely.

Part
[V. Repealed]
VI. Alternative minimum tax.

PART I—TAX ON INDIVIDUALS

§ 1. Tax imposed

(a) **Married individuals filing joint returns and surviving spouses.**—There is hereby imposed on the taxable income of—

(1) every married individual (as defined in section 7703) who makes a single return jointly with his spouse under section 6013, and

(2) every surviving spouse (as defined in section 2(a)),

a tax determined in accordance with the following table:

If taxable income is	The tax is:
Not over $29,750	15% of taxable income.
Over $29,750	$4,462.50, plus 28% of the excess over $29,750.

(b) **Heads of households.**—There is hereby imposed on the taxable income of every head of a household (as defined in section 2(b)) a tax determined in accordance with the following table:

If taxable income is	The tax is:
Not over $23,900	15% of taxable income.
Over $23,900	$3,585, plus 28% of the excess over $23,900.

(c) **Unmarried individuals (other than surviving spouses and heads of households).**—There is hereby imposed on the taxable income of every individual (other than a surviving spouse as defined in section 2(a) or the head of a household as defined in section 2(b)) who is not a married individual (as defined in section 7703) a tax determined in accordance with the following table:

If taxable income is	The tax is:
Not over $17,850	15% of taxable income.
Over $17,850	$2,677.50, plus 28% of the excess over $17,850.

(d) **Married individuals filing separate returns.**—There is hereby imposed on the taxable income of every married individual (as defined in section 7703) who does not make a single return jointly with his spouse under section 6013, a tax determined in accordance with the following table:

If taxable income is	The tax is:
Not over $14,875	15% of taxable income.
Over $14,875	$2,231.25, plus 28% of the excess over $14,875.

(e) **Estates and trusts.**—There is hereby imposed on the taxable income of—

(1) every estate, and

(2) every trust,

taxable under this subsection a tax determined in accordance with the following table:

14

If taxable income is	The tax is:
Not over $5,000	15% of taxable income.
Over $5,000	$750, plus 28% of the excess over $5,000.

(f) Adjustments in tax tables so that inflation will not result in tax increases.—

(1) In general.—Not later than December 15 of 1988, and each subsequent calendar year, the Secretary shall prescribe tables which shall apply in lieu of the tables contained in subsections (a), (b), (c), (d), and (e) with respect to taxable years beginning in the succeeding calendar year.

(2) Method of prescribing tables.—The table which under paragraph (1) is to apply in lieu of the table contained in subsection (a), (b), (c), (d), or (e), as the case may be, with respect to taxable years beginning in any calendar year shall be prescribed—

(A) by increasing the minimum and maximum dollar amounts for each rate bracket for which a tax is imposed under such table by the cost-of-living adjustment for such calendar year,

(B) by not changing the rate applicable to any rate bracket as adjusted under subparagraph (A), and

(C) by adjusting the amounts setting forth the tax to the extent necessary to reflect the adjustments in the rate brackets.

(3) Cost-of-living adjustment.—For purposes of paragraph (2), the cost-of-living adjustment for any calendar year is the percentage (if any) by which—

(A) the CPI for the preceding calendar year, exceeds

(B) the CPI for the calendar year 1987.

(4) CPI for any calendar year.—For purposes of paragraph (3), the CPI for any calendar year is the average of the Consumer Price Index as of the close of the 12-month period ending on August 31 of such calendar year.

(5) Consumer price index.—For purposes of paragraph (4), the term "Consumer Price Index" means the last Consumer Price Index for all-urban consumers published by the Department of Labor. For purposes of the preceding sentence, the revision of the Consumer Price Index which is most consistent with the Consumer Price Index for calendar year 1986 shall be used.

(6) Rounding.—

(A) In general.—If any increase determined under paragraph (2)(A), subsection (g)(4), section 63(c)(4), or section 151(d)(3) is not a multiple of $50, such increase shall be rounded to the next lowest multiple of $50.

(B) Table for married individuals filing separately.—In the case of a married individual filing a separate return, subparagraph (A) (other than with respect to section 63(c)(4)) shall be applied by substituting "$25" for "$50" each place it appears.

(g) Phaseout of 15-percent rate and personal exemptions.—

(1) In general.—The amount of tax imposed by this section (determined without regard to this subsection) shall be increased by 5 percent of the excess (if any) of—

(A) taxable income, over

(B) the applicable dollar amount.

15

(2) **Limitation.**—The increase determined under paragraph (1) with respect to any taxpayer for any taxable year shall not exceed the sum of—

(A) 13 percent of the maximum amount of taxable income to which the 15-percent rate applies under the table contained in subsection (a), (b), (c), or (e) (whichever applies), and

(B) 28 percent of the deductions for personal exemptions allowable to the taxpayer for the taxable year under section 151.

In the case of any individual taxable under subsection (d), subparagraph (A) shall apply as if such individual were taxable under subsection (a).

(3) **Applicable dollar amount.**—For purposes of paragraph (1), the applicable dollar amount shall be determined under the following table:

In the case of a taxpayer to which the following subsection of this section applies:	The applicable dollar amount is:
Subsection (a)	$71,900
Subsection (b)	61,650
Subsection (c)	43,150
Subsection (d)	35,950
Subsection (e)	13,000

(4) **Adjustment for inflation.**—In the case of any taxable year beginning in a calendar year after 1988, each dollar amount contained in paragraph (3) shall be increased by an amount equal to—

(A) such dollar amount, multiplied by

(B) the cost-of-living adjustment determined under subsection (f)(3) for the calendar year in which the taxable year begins.

(h) **Tax schedules for taxable years beginning in 1987.**—In the case of any taxable year beginning in 1987—

(1) subsection (g) shall not apply, and

(2) the following tables shall apply in lieu of the tables set forth in subsections (a), (b), (c), (d), and (e):

(A) **Married individuals filing joint returns and surviving spouses.**—The table to apply for purposes of subsection (a) is as follows:

If taxable income is	The tax is:
Not over $3,000	11% of taxable income.
Over $3,000 but not over $28,000	$330, plus 15% of the excess over $3,000.
Over $28,000 but not over $45,000	$4,080, plus 28% of the excess over $28,000.
Over $45,000 but not over $90,000	$8,840, plus 35% of the excess over $45,000.
Over $90,000	$24,590, plus 38.5% of the excess over $90,000.

(B) **Heads of households.**—The table to apply for purposes of subsection (b) is as follows:

If taxable income is	The tax is:
Not over $2,500	11% of taxable income.
Over $2,500 but not over $23,000	$275, plus 15% of the excess over $2,500.
Over $23,000 but not over $38,000	$3,350, plus 28% of the excess over $23,000.
Over $38,000 but not over $80,000	$7,550, plus 35% of the excess over $38,000.
Over $80,000	$22,250, plus 38.5% of the excess over $80,000.

(C) **Unmarried individuals other than surviving spouses and heads of households.**—The table to apply for purposes of subsection (c) is as follows:

If taxable income is	The tax is:
Not over $1,800	11% of taxable income.
Over $1,800 but not over $16,800	$198, plus 15% of the excess over $1,800.
Over $16,800 but not over $27,000	$2,448, plus 28% of the excess over $16,800.
Over $27,000 but not over $54,000	$5,304, plus 35% of the excess over $27,000.
Over $54,000	$14,754, plus 38.5% of the excess over $54,000.

(D) Married individuals filing separate returns.—The table to apply for purposes of subsection (d) is as follows:

If taxable income is	The tax is:
Not over $1,500	11% of taxable income.
Over $1,500 but not over $14,000	$165, plus 15% of the excess over $1,500.
Over $14,000 but not over $22,500	$2,040, plus 28% of the excess over $14,000.
Over $22,500 but not over $45,000	$4,420, plus 35% of the excess over $22,500.
Over $45,000	$12,295, plus 38.5% of the excess over $45,000.

(E) Estates and trusts.—The table to apply for purposes of subsection (e) is as follows:

If taxable income is	The tax is:
Not over $500	11% of taxable income.
Over $500 but not over $4,700	$55, plus 15% of the excess over $500.
Over $4,700 but not over $7,550	$685, plus 28% of the excess over $4,700.
Over $7,550 but not over $15,150	$1,483, plus 35% of the excess over $7,550.
Over $15,150	$4,143, plus 38.5% of the excess over $15,150.

(i) Certain unearned income of minor children taxed as if parent's income.—

(1) In general.—In the case of any child to whom this subsection applies, the tax imposed by this section shall be equal to the greater of—

(A) the tax imposed by this section without regard to this subsection, or

(B) the sum of—

(i) the tax which would be imposed by this section if the taxable income of such child for the taxable year were reduced by the net unearned income of such child, plus

(ii) such child's share of the allocable parental tax.

(2) Child to whom subsection applies.—This subsection shall apply to any child for any taxable year if—

(A) such child has not attained age 14 before the close of the taxable year, and

(B) either parent of such child is alive at the close of the taxable year.

(3) Allocable parental tax.—For purposes of this subsection—

(A) In general.—The term "allocable parental tax" means the excess of—

(i) the tax which would be imposed by this section on the parent's taxable income if such income included the net unearned income of all children of the parent to whom this subsection applies, over

(ii) the tax imposed by this section on the parent without regard to this subsection.

For purposes of clause (i), net unearned income of all children of the parent shall not be taken into account in computing any deduction or credit of the parent.

(B) **Child's share.**—A child's share of any allocable parental tax of a parent shall be equal to an amount which bears the same ratio to the total allocable parental tax as the child's net unearned income bears to the aggregate net unearned income of all children of such parent to whom this subsection applies.

(4) **Net unearned income.**—For purposes of this subsection—

(A) **In general.**—The term "net unearned income" means the excess of—

(i) the portion of the gross income for the taxable year which is not earned income (as defined in section 911(d)(2)), over

(ii) the sum of—

(I) the amount in effect for the taxable year under section 63(c)(5)(A) (relating to limitation on standard deduction in the case of certain dependents), plus

(II) the greater of the amount described in subclause (I) or, if the child itemizes his deduction for the taxable year, the amount of the deductions allowed by this chapter for the taxable year which are directly connected with the production of the portion of gross income referred to in clause (i).

(B) **Limitation based on taxable income.**—The amount of the net unearned income for any taxable year shall not exceed the individual's taxable income for such taxable year.

(5) **Special rules for determining parent to whom subsection applies.**—For purposes of this subsection, the parent whose taxable income shall be taken into account shall be—

(A) in the case of parents who are not married (within the meaning of section 7703), the custodial parent of the child, and

(B) in the case of married individuals filing separately, the individual with the greater taxable income.

(6) **Providing of parent's TIN.**—The parent of any child to whom this subsection applies for any taxable year shall provide the TIN of such parent to such child and such child shall include such TIN on the child's return of tax imposed by this section for such taxable year.

(j) **Maximum capital gains rate.**—

(1) **In general.**—If a taxpayer has a net capital gain for any taxable year to which this subsection applies, then the tax imposed by this section shall not exceed the sum of—

(A) a tax computed at the rates and in the same manner as if this subsection had not been enacted on the greater of—

(i) the taxable income reduced by the amount of net capital gain, or

(ii) the amount of taxable income taxed at a rate below 28 percent, plus

(B) a tax of 28 percent of the amount of taxable income in excess of the amount determined under subparagraph (A), plus

(C) the amount of increase determined under subsection (g).

(2) **Years to which subsection applies.**—This subsection shall apply to—

(A) any taxable year beginning in 1987, and

(B) any taxable year beginning after 1987 if the highest rate of tax set forth in subsection (a), (b), (c), (d), or (e) (whichever applies) for such taxable year exceeds 28 percent.

§ 2. Definitions and special rules

(a) Definition of surviving spouse.—

(1) **In general.**—For purposes of section 1, the term "surviving spouse" means a taxpayer—

(A) whose spouse died during either of his two taxable years immediately preceding the taxable year, and

(B) who maintains as his home a household which constitutes for the taxable year the principal place of abode (as a member of such household) of a dependent (i) who (within the meaning of section 152) is a son, stepson, daughter, or stepdaughter of the taxpayer, and (ii) with respect to whom the taxpayer is entitled to a deduction for the taxable year under section 151.

For purposes of this paragraph, an individual shall be considered as maintaining a household only if over half of the cost of maintaining the household during the taxable year is furnished by such individual.

(2) **Limitations.**—Notwithstanding paragraph (1), for purposes of section 1 a taxpayer shall not be considered to be a surviving spouse—

(A) if the taxpayer has remarried at any time before the close of the taxable year, or

(B) unless, for the taxpayer's taxable year during which his spouse died, a joint return could have been made under the provisions of section 6013 (without regard to subsection (a) (3) thereof).

* * *

(b) Definition of head of household.—

(1) **In general.**—For purposes of this subtitle, an individual shall be considered a head of a household if, and only if, such individual is not married at the close of his taxable year, is not a surviving spouse (as defined in subsection (a)), and either—

(A) maintains as his home a household which constitutes for more than one-half of such taxable year the principal place of abode, as a member of such household, of—

(i) a son, stepson, daughter, or stepdaughter of the taxpayer, or a descendant of a son or daughter of the taxpayer, but if such son, stepson, daughter, stepdaughter, or descendant is married at the close of the taxpayer's taxable year, only if the taxpayer is entitled to a deduction for the taxable year for such person under section 151 (or would be so entitled but for paragraph (2) or (4) of section 152(e)) or

(ii) any other person who is a dependent of the taxpayer, if the taxpayer is entitled to a deduction for the taxable year for such person under section 151, or

(B) maintains a household which constitutes for such taxable year the principal place of abode of the father or mother of the taxpayer, if the taxpayer is entitled to a deduction for the taxable year for such father or mother under section 151.

For purposes of this paragraph, an individual shall be considered as maintaining a household only if over half of the cost of maintaining the household during the taxable year is furnished by such individual.

(2) **Determination of status.**—For purposes of this subsection—

(A) a legally adopted child of a person shall be considered a child of such person by blood;

(B) an individual who is legally separated from his spouse under a decree of divorce or of separate maintenance shall not be considered as married;

(C) a taxpayer shall be considered as not married at the close of his taxable year if at any time during the taxable year his spouse is a nonresident alien; and

(D) a taxpayer shall be considered as married at the close of his taxable year if his spouse (other than a spouse described in subparagraph (C)) died during the taxable year.

(3) **Limitations.**—Notwithstanding paragraph (1), for purposes of this subtitle a taxpayer shall not be considered to be a head of a household—

(A) if at any time during the taxable year he is a nonresident alien; or

(B) by reason of an individual who would not be a dependent for the taxable year but for—

(i) paragraph (9) of section 152(a), or

(ii) subsection (c) of section 152.

(c) **Certain married individuals living apart.**—For purposes of this part, an individual shall be treated as not married at the close of the taxable year if such individual is so treated under the provisions of section 7703(b).

* * *

(e) **Cross reference.**—

For definition of taxable income, see section 63.

§ 3.   Tax tables for individuals

(a) **Imposition of tax table tax.**—

(1) **In general.**—In lieu of the tax imposed by section 1, there is hereby imposed for each taxable year on the taxable income of every individual—

(A) who does not itemize his deductions for the taxable year, and

(B) whose taxable income for such taxable year does not exceed the ceiling amount,

a tax determined under tables, applicable to such taxable year, which shall be prescribed by the Secretary and which shall be in such form as he determines appropriate. In the table so prescribed, the amounts of the tax shall be computed on the basis of the rates prescribed by section 1.

(2) **Ceiling amount defined.**—For purposes of paragraph (1), the term "ceiling amount" means, with respect to any taxpayer, the amount (not less than $20,000) determined by the Secretary for the tax rate category in which such taxpayer falls.

(3) **Authority to prescribe tables for taxpayers who itemize deductions.** —The Secretary may provide that this section shall apply also for any taxable year to individuals who itemize their deductions. Any tables prescribed under the preceding sentence shall be on the basis of taxable income.

(b) **Section inapplicable to certain individuals.**—This section shall not apply to—

(1) an individual making a return under section 443(a)(1) for a period of less than 12 months on account of a change in annual accounting period, and

(2) an estate or trust.

(c) **Tax treated as imposed by section 1.**—For purposes of this title, the tax imposed by this section shall be treated as tax imposed by section 1.

(d) **Taxable income.**—Whenever it is necessary to determine the taxable income of an individual to whom this section applies, the taxable income shall be determined under section 63.

PART II—TAX ON CORPORATIONS

§ 11. Tax imposed

(a) **Corporations in general.**—A tax is hereby imposed for each taxable year on the taxable income of every corporation.

(b) **Amount of tax.**—The amount of the tax imposed by subsection (a) shall be the sum of—

(1) 15 percent (16 percent for taxable years beginning in 1982) of so much of the taxable income as does not exceed $25,000;

(2) 18 percent (19 percent for taxable years beginning in 1982) of so much of the taxable income as exceeds $25,000 but does not exceed $50,000;

(3) 30 percent of so much of the taxable income as exceeds $50,000 but does not exceed $75,000;

(4) 40 percent of so much of the taxable income as exceeds $75,000 but does not exceed $100,000; plus

(5) 46 percent of so much of the taxable income as exceeds $100,000.

In the case of a corporation with taxable income in excess of $1,000,000 for any taxable year, the amount of tax determined under the preceding sentence for such taxable year shall be increased by the lesser of (A) 5 percent of such excess, or (B) $20,250.

* * *

Amendment of Subsec. (b)

Pub.L. 99–514, Title VI, § 601(a), (b)(1), Oct. 22, 1986, 100 Stat. ——, provided that, applicable to taxable years beginning on or after July 1, 1987, subsec. (b) of this section is amended to read as follows:

(b) **Amount of tax.**—The amount of the tax imposed by subsection (a) shall be the sum of—

(1) 15 percent of so much of the taxable income as does not exceed $50,000,

(2) 25 percent of so much of the taxable income as exceeds $50,000 but does not exceed $75,000, and

(3) 34 percent of so much of the taxable income as exceeds $75,000.

In the case of a corporation which has taxable income in excess of $100,000 for any taxable year, the amount of tax determined under the preceding sentence for such taxable year shall be increased by the lesser of (A) 5 percent of such excess, or (B) $11,750.

§ 12. Cross references relating to tax on corporations

(1) For tax on the unrelated business income of certain charitable and other corporations exempt from tax under this chapter, see section 511.

(2) For accumulated earnings tax and personal holding company tax, see parts I and II of subchapter G (sec. 531 and following).

* * *

(4) For alternative tax in case of capital gains, see section 1201(a).

* * *

(6) For limitation on benefits of graduated rate schedule provided in section 11(b), see section 1551.

(7) For alternative minimum tax, see section 55.

PART IV—CREDITS AGAINST TAX

Subpart
- A. Nonrefundable personal credits.
- B. Foreign tax credit, etc.*
- C. Refundable credits.*
- D. Business-related credits.
- E. Rules for computing credit for investment in certain depreciable property.
- F. Rules for computing targeted jobs credit.*

Subpart A—Nonrefundable Personal Credits

§ 21. Expenses for household and dependent care services necessary for gainful employment

(a) Allowance of credit.—

(1) **In general.**—In the case of an individual who maintains a household which includes as a member one or more qualifying individuals (as defined in subsection (b)(1)), there shall be allowed as a credit against the tax imposed by this chapter for the taxable year an amount equal to the applicable percentage of the employment-related expenses (as defined in subsection (b)(2)) paid by such individual during the taxable year.

(2) **Applicable percentage defined.**—For purposes of paragraph (1), the term "applicable percentage" means 30 percent reduced (but not below 20 percent) by 1 percentage point for each $2,000 (or fraction thereof) by which the taxpayer's adjusted gross income for the taxable year exceeds $10,000.

(b) Definitions of qualifying individual and employment-related expenses. —For purposes of this section—

(1) **Qualifying individual.**—The term "qualifying individual" means—

(A) a dependent of the taxpayer who is under the age of 15 and with respect to whom the taxpayer is entitled to a deduction under section 151(c),

(B) a dependent of the taxpayer who is physically or mentally incapable of caring for himself, or

(C) the spouse of the taxpayer, if he is physically or mentally incapable of caring for himself.

(2) **Employment-related expenses.—**

(A) **In general.**—The term "employment-related expenses" means amounts paid for the following expenses, but only if such expenses are incurred to enable the taxpayer to be gainfully employed for any period for which there are 1 or more qualifying individuals with respect to the taxpayer:

(i) expenses for household services, and

* Omitted entirely.

(ii) expenses for the care of a qualifying individual.

(B) Exception.—Employment-related expenses described in subparagraph (A) which are incurred for services outside the taxpayer's household shall be taken into account only if incurred for the care of—

(i) a qualifying individual described in paragraph (1)(A), or

(ii) a qualifying individual (not described in paragraph (1)(A)) who regularly spends at least 8 hours each day in the taxpayer's household.

(C) Dependent care centers.—Employment-related expenses described in subparagraph (A) which are incurred for services provided outside the taxpayer's household by a dependent care center (as defined in subparagraph (D)) shall be taken into account only if—

(i) such center complies with all applicable laws and regulations of a State or unit of local government, and

(ii) the requirements of subparagraph (B) are met.

(D) Dependent care center defined.—For purposes of this paragraph, the term "dependent care center" means any facility which—

(i) provides care for more than six individuals (other than individuals who reside at the facility), and

(ii) receives a fee, payment, or grant for providing services for any of the individuals (regardless of whether such facility is operated for profit).

(c) Dollar limit on amount creditable.—The amount of the employment-related expenses incurred during any taxable year which may be taken into account under subsection (a) shall not exceed—

(1) $2,400 if there is 1 qualifying individual with respect to the taxpayer for such taxable year, or

(2) $4,800 if there are 2 or more qualifying individuals with respect to the taxpayer for such taxable year.

(d) Earned income limitation.—

(1) In general.—Except as otherwise provided in this subsection, the amount of the employment-related expenses incurred during any taxable year which may be taken into account under subsection (a) shall not exceed—

(A) in the case of an individual who is not married at the close of such year, such individual's earned income for such year, or

(B) in the case of an individual who is married at the close of such year, the lesser of such individual's earned income or the earned income of his spouse for such year.

(2) Special rule for spouse who is a student or incapable of caring for himself.—In the case of a spouse who is a student or a qualifying individual described in subsection (b)(1)(C), for purposes of paragraph (1), such spouse shall be deemed for each month during which such spouse is a full-time student at an educational institution, or is such a qualifying individual, to be gainfully employed and to have earned income of not less than—

(A) $200 if subsection (c)(1) applies for the taxable year, or

(B) $400 if subsection (c)(2) applies for the taxable year.

In the case of any husband and wife, this paragraph shall apply with respect to only one spouse for any one month.

(e) Special rules.—For purposes of this section—

(1) Maintaining household.—An individual shall be treated as maintaining a household for any period only if over half the cost of maintaining the household for such period is furnished by such individual (or, if such individual is married during such period, is furnished by such individual and his spouse).

(2) Married couples must file joint return.—If the taxpayer is married at the close of the taxable year, the credit shall be allowed under subsection (a) only if the taxpayer and his spouse file a joint return for the taxable year.

(3) Marital status.—An individual legally separated from his spouse under a decree of divorce or of separate maintenance shall not be considered as married.

(4) Certain married individuals living apart.—If—

(A) an individual who is married and who files a separate return—

(i) maintains as his home a household which constitutes for more than one-half of the taxable year the principal place of abode of a qualifying individual, and

(ii) furnishes over half of the cost of maintaining such household during the taxable year, and

(B) during the last 6 months of such taxable year such individual's spouse is not a member of such household,

such individual shall not be considered as married.

(5) Special dependency test in case of divorced parents, etc.—If—

(A) paragraph (2) or (4) of section 152(e) applies to any child with respect to any calendar year, and

(B) such child is under the age of 15 or is physically or mentally incapable of caring for himself,

in the case of any taxable year beginning in such calendar year, such child shall be treated as a qualifying individual described in subparagraph (A) or (B) of subsection (b)(1) (whichever is appropriate) with respect to the custodial parent (within the meaning of section 152(e)(1)), and shall not be treated as a qualifying individual with respect to the noncustodial parent.

(6) Payments to related individuals.—No credit shall be allowed under subsection (a) for any amount paid by the taxpayer to an individual—

(A) with respect to whom, for the taxable year, a deduction under section 151(c) (relating to deduction for personal exemptions for dependents) is allowable either to the taxpayer or his spouse, or

(B) who is a child of the taxpayer (within the meaning of section 151(c)(3)) who has not attained the age of 19 at the close of the taxable year.

For purposes of this paragraph, the term "taxable year" means the taxable year of the taxpayer in which the service is performed.

(7) Student.—The term "student" means an individual who during each of 5 calendar months during the taxable year is a full-time student at an educational organization.

(8) Educational organization.—The term "educational organization" means an educational organization described in section 170(b)(1)(A)(ii).

(f) Regulations.—The Secretary shall prescribe such regulations as may be necessary to carry out the purposes of this section.

§ 22. Credit for the elderly and the permanently and totally disabled

(a) General rule.—In the case of a qualified individual, there shall be allowed as a credit against the tax imposed by this chapter for the taxable year an amount equal to 15 percent of such individual's section 22 amount for such taxable year.

(b) Qualified individual.—For purposes of this section, the term "qualified individual" means any individual—

(1) who has attained age 65 before the close of the taxable year, or

(2) who retired on disability before the close of the taxable year and who, when he retired, was permanently and totally disabled.

(c) Section 22 amount.—For purposes of subsection (a)—

(1) In general.—An individual's section 22 amount for the taxable year shall be the applicable initial amount determined under paragraph (2), reduced as provided in paragraph (3) and in subsection (d).

(2) Initial amount.—

(A) In general.—Except as provided in subparagraph (B), the initial amount shall be—

(i) $5,000 in the case of a single individual, or a joint return where only one spouse is a qualified individual,

(ii) $7,500 in the case of a joint return where both spouses are qualified individuals, or

(iii) $3,750 in the case of a married individual filing a separate return.

(B) Limitation in case of individuals who have not attained age 65.—

(i) **In general.**—In the case of a qualified individual who has not attained age 65 before the close of the taxable year, except as provided in clause (ii), the initial amount shall not exceed the disability income for the taxable year.

(ii) **Special rules in case of joint return.**—In the case of a joint return where both spouses are qualified individuals and at least one spouse has not attained age 65 before the close of the taxable year—

(I) if both spouses have not attained age 65 before the close of the taxable year, the initial amount shall not exceed the sum of such spouses' disability income, or

(II) if one spouse has attained age 65 before the close of the taxable year, the initial amount shall not exceed the sum of $5,000 plus the disability income for the taxable year of the spouse who has not attained age 65 before the close of the taxable year.

(iii) **Disability income.**—For purposes of this subparagraph, the term "disability income" means the aggregate amount includable in the gross income of the individual for the taxable year under section 72 or 105(a) to the extent such amount constitutes wages (or payments in lieu of wages) for the period during which the individual is absent from work on account of permanent and total disability.

(3) Reduction.—

(A) In general.—The reduction under this paragraph is an amount equal to the sum of the amounts received by the individual (or, in the case of a joint return, by either spouse) as a pension or annuity or as a disability benefit—

(i) which is excluded from gross income and payable under—

(I) title II of the Social Security Act,

(II) the Railroad Retirement Act of 1974, or

(III) a law administered by the Veterans' Administration, or

(ii) which is excluded from gross income under any provision of law not contained in this title.

No reduction shall be made under clause (i)(III) for any amount described in section 104(a)(4).

(B) Treatment of certain workmen's compensation benefits.—For purposes of subparagraph (A), any amount treated as a social security benefit under section 86(d)(3) shall be treated as a disability benefit received under title II of the Social Security Act.

(d) Adjusted gross income limitation.—If the adjusted gross income of the taxpayer exceeds—

(1) $7,500 in the case of a single individual,

(2) $10,000 in the case of a joint return, or

(3) $5,000 in the case of a married individual filing a separate return,

the section 22 amount shall be reduced by one-half of the excess of the adjusted gross income over $7,500, $10,000, or $5,000, as the case may be.

(e) Definitions and special rules.—For purposes of this section—

(1) Married couple must file joint return.—Except in the case of a husband and wife who live apart at all times during the taxable year, if the taxpayer is married at the close of the taxable year, the credit provided by this section shall be allowed only if the taxpayer and his spouse file a joint return for the taxable year.

(2) Marital status.—Marital status shall be determined under section 7703.

(3) Permanent and total disability defined.—An individual is permanently and totally disabled if he is unable to engage in any substantial gainful activity by reason of any medically determinable physical or mental impairment which can be expected to result in death or which has lasted or can be expected to last for a continuous period of not less than 12 months. An individual shall not be considered to be permanently and totally disabled unless he furnishes proof of the existence thereof in such form and manner, and at such times, as the Secretary may require.

* * *

§ 24. Contributions to candidates for public office [Repealed.]

§ 26. Limitation based on tax liability; definition of tax liability

(a) Limitation based on amount of tax.—The aggregate amount of credits allowed by this subpart for the taxable year shall not exceed the excess (if any) of—

(1) the taxpayer's regular tax liability for the taxable year, over

(2) the tentative minimum tax for the taxable year (determined without regard to the alternative minimum tax foreign tax credit).

(b) Regular tax liability.—For purposes of this part—

(1) In general.—The term "regular tax liability" means the tax imposed by this chapter for the taxable year.

(2) **Exception for certain taxes.**—For purposes of paragraph (1), any tax imposed by any of the following provisions shall not be treated as tax imposed by this chapter:

(A) section 55 (relating to minimum tax),

(B) section 59A (relating to environmental tax),

(C) subsection (m)(5)(B), (o)(2), or (q) of section 72 (relating to additional tax on certain distributions),

(D) section 408(f) (relating to additional tax on income from certain retirement accounts),

(E) section 531 (relating to accumulated earnings tax),

(F) section 541 (relating to personal holding company tax),

(G) section 1351(d)(1) (relating to recoveries of foreign expropriation losses),

(H) section 1374 (relating to tax on certain built-in gains of S corporations),

* * *

(c) **Tentative minimum tax.**—For purposes of this part, the term "tentative minimum tax" means the amount determined under section 55(b)(1).

Subpart D—Business Related Credits

§ 38. General business credit

(a) **Allowance of credit.**—There shall be allowed as a credit against the tax imposed by this chapter for the taxable year an amount equal to the sum of—

(1) the business credit carryforwards carried to such taxable year,

(2) the amount of the current year business credit, plus

(3) the business credit carrybacks carried to such taxable year.

(b) **Current year business credit.**—For purposes of this subpart, the amount of the current year business credit is the sum of the following credits determined for the taxable year:

(1) the investment credit determined under section 46(a),

(2) the targeted jobs credit determined under section 51(a),

(3) the alcohol fuels credit determined under section 40(a),

(4) the research credit determined under section 41(a), plus

(5) the low-income housing credit determined under section 42(a).

(c) **Limitation based on amount of tax.**—

(1) **In general.**—The credit allowed under subsection (a) for any taxable year shall not exceed the lesser of—

(A) the allowable portion of the taxpayer's net regular tax liability for the taxable year, or

(B) the excess (if any) of the taxpayer's net regular tax liability for the taxable year over the tentative minimum tax for the taxable year.

(2) **Allowable portion of net regular tax liability.**—For purposes of this subsection, the allowable portion of the taxpayer's net regular tax liability for the taxable year is the sum of—

(A) so much of the taxpayer's net regular tax liability for the taxable year as does not exceed $25,000, plus

(B) 75 percent of so much of the taxpayer's net regular tax liability for the taxable year as exceeds $25,000.

For purposes of the preceding sentence, the term "net regular tax liability" means the regular tax liability reduced by the sum of the credits allowable under subparts A and B of this part.

(3) Regular investment tax credit may offset 25 percent of minimum tax.—In the case of any C corporation, to the extent the credit under subsection (a) is attributable to the application of the regular percentage under section 46, the limitation of paragraph (1) shall be the greater of—

(A) the lesser of—

(i) the allowable portion of the taxpayer's net regular tax liability for the taxable year, or

(ii) the excess (if any) of the taxpayer's net regular tax liability for the taxable year over 75 percent of the tentative minimum tax for the taxable year, or

(B) 25 percent of the taxpayer's tentative minimum tax for the year.

In no event shall this paragraph permit the allowance of a credit which (in combination with the alternative tax net operating loss deduction and the alternative minimum tax foreign tax credit) would reduce the tax payable under section 55 below an amount equal to 10 percent of the amount which would be determined under section 55(b) without regard to the alternative tax net operating loss deduction and the alternative minimum tax foreign tax credit.

* * *

§ 39. Carryback and carryforward of unused credits

(a) In general.—

(1) 3-year carryback and 15-year carryforward.—If the sum of the business credit carryforwards to the taxable year plus the amount of the current year business credit for the taxable year exceeds the amount of the limitation imposed by subsection (c) of section 38 for such taxable year (hereinafter in this section referred to as the "unused credit year"), such excess (to the extent attributable to the amount of the current year business credit) shall be—

(A) a business credit carryback to each of the 3 taxable years preceding the unused credit year, and

(B) a business credit carryforward to each of the 15 taxable years following the unused credit year,

and, subject to the limitations imposed by subsections (b) and (c), shall be taken into account under the provisions of section 38(a) in the manner provided in section 38(a).

(2) Amount carried to each year.—

(A) Entire amount carried to first year.—The entire amount of the unused credit for an unused credit year shall be carried to the earliest of the 18 taxable years to which (by reason of paragraph (1)) such credit may be carried.

(B) Amount carried to other 17 years.—The amount of the unused credit for the unused credit year shall be carried to each of the other 17 taxable years to the extent that such unused credit may not be taken into account under section 38(a) for a prior taxable year because of the limitations of subsections (b) and (c).

(b) Limitation on carrybacks.—The amount of the unused credit which may be taken into account under section 38(a)(3) for any preceding taxable year shall not exceed the amount by which the limitation imposed by section 38(c) for such taxable year exceeds the sum of—

(1) the amounts determined under paragraphs (1) and (2) of section 38(a) for such taxable year, plus

(2) the amounts which (by reason of this section) are carried back to such taxable year and are attributable to taxable years preceding the unused credit year.

(c) Limitation on carryforwards.—The amount of the unused credit which may be taken into account under section 38(a)(1) for any succeeding taxable year shall not exceed the amount by which the limitation imposed by section 38(c) for such taxable year exceeds the sum of the amounts which, by reason of this section, are carried to such taxable year and are attributable to taxable years preceding the unused credit year.

* * *

Subpart E—Rules for Computing Credit for Investment in Certain Depreciable Property

§ 46. Amount of credit

(a) Amount of investment credit.—For purposes of section 38, the amount of the investment credit determined under this section for any taxable year shall be an amount equal to the sum of the following percentages of the qualified investment (as determined under subsections (c) and (d)):

(1) the regular percentage,

(2) in the case of energy property, the energy percentage, and

(3) in the case of that portion of the basis of any property which is attributable to qualified rehabilitation expenditures, the rehabilitation percentage.

(b) Determination of percentages.—For purposes of subsection (a)—

(1) **Regular percentage.**—The regular percentage is 10 percent.

* * *

(c) Qualified investment.—

(1) **In general.**—For purposes of this subpart, the term "qualified investment" means, with respect to any taxable year, the aggregate of—

(A) the applicable percentage of the basis of each new section 38 property (as defined in section 48(b)) placed in service by the taxpayer during such taxable year, plus

(B) the applicable percentage of the cost of each used section 38 property (as defined in section 48(c) (1)) placed in service by the taxpayer during such taxable year.

(2) **Applicable percentage in certain cases.**—Except as provided in paragraphs (3), (6), and (7), the applicable percentage for purposes of paragraph (1) for any property shall be determined under the following table:

If the useful life is—	The applicable percentage is—
3 years or more but less than 5 years	33⅓
5 years or more but less than 7 years	66⅔
7 years or more	100

For purposes of this subpart, the useful life of any property shall be the useful life used in computing the allowance for depreciation under section 167 for the taxable year in which the property is placed in service.

* * *

§ 47. Certain dispositions, etc., of section 38 property

(a) General rule.—Under regulations prescribed by the Secretary—

(1) Early disposition, etc.—If during any taxable year any property is disposed of, or otherwise ceases to be section 38 property with respect to the taxpayer, before the close of the useful life which was taken into account in computing the credit under section 38, then the tax under this chapter for such taxable year shall be increased by an amount equal to the aggregate decrease in the credits allowed under section 38 for all prior taxable years which would have resulted solely from substituting, in determining qualified investment, for such useful life the period beginning with the time such property was placed in service by the taxpayer and ending with the time such property ceased to be section 38 property.

* * *

(5) Special rules for recovery property.—

(A) General rule.—If, during any taxable year, section 38 recovery property is disposed of, or otherwise ceases to be section 38 property with respect to the taxpayer before the close of the recapture period, then, except as provided in subparagraph (D), the tax under this chapter for such taxable year shall be increased by the recapture percentage of the aggregate decrease in the credits allowed under section 38 for all prior taxable years which would have resulted solely from reducing to zero the qualified investment taken into account with respect to such property.

(B) Recapture percentage.—For purposes of subparagraph (A), the recapture percentage shall be determined in accordance with the following table:

If the recovery property ceases to be section 38 property within—	The recapture percentage is:	
	For property other than 3-year property	For 3-year property
One full year after placed in service	100	100
One full year after the close of the period described in clause (i)	80	66
One full year after the close of the period described in clause (ii)	60	33
One full year after the close of the period described in clause (iii)	40	0
One full year after the close of the period described in clause (iv)	20	0

* * *

(E) Definitions and special rules.—

(i) Section 38 recovery property.—For purposes of this paragraph, the term "section 38 recovery property" means any section 38 property which is recovery property (within the meaning of section 168).

(ii) Recapture period.—For purposes of this paragraph, the term "recapture period" means, with respect to any recovery property, the period consisting of the first full year after the property is placed in service and the 4 succeeding full years (the 2 succeeding full years in the case of 3-year property).

(iii) Classification of property.—For purposes of this paragraph, property shall be classified as provided in section 168(c).

(iv) Paragraph (1) not to apply.—Paragraph (1) shall not apply with respect to any recovery property.

(6) Carrybacks and carryovers adjusted.—In the case of any cessation described in paragraph (1), (3), or (5) or any change in use described in paragraph (2) or (4), the carrybacks and carryovers under section 39 shall be adjusted by reason of such cessation (or change in use).

* * *

(b) Section not to apply in certain cases.—Subsection (a) shall not apply to—

(1) a transfer by reason of death,

(2) a transaction to which section 381(a) applies, or

* * *

For purposes of subsection (a), property shall not be treated as ceasing to be section 38 property with respect to the taxpayer by reason of a mere change in the form of conducting the trade or business so long as the property is retained in such trade or business as section 38 property and the taxpayer retains a substantial interest in such trade or business.

(c) Special rule.—Any increase in tax under subsection (a) shall not be treated as tax imposed by this chapter for purposes of determining the amount of any credit allowable under subpart A, B, or D.

(d) Increases in nonqualified nonrecourse financing.—

(1) In general.—If, as of the close of the taxable year, there is a net increase with respect to the taxpayer in the amount of nonqualified nonrecourse financing (within the meaning of section 46(c)(8)) with respect to any property to which section 46(c)(8) applied, then the tax under this chapter for such taxable year shall be increased by an amount equal to the aggregate decrease in credits allowed under section 38 for all prior taxable years which would have resulted from reducing the credit base (as defined in section 48(c)(8)(C)) taken into account with respect to such property by the amount of such net increase. "For purposes of determining the amount of credit subject to the early disposition or cessation rules of subsection (a), the net increase in the amount of the nonqualified nonrecourse financing with respect to the property shall be treated as reducing the property's credit base (and correspondingly reducing the qualified investment in the property) in the year in which the property was first placed in service."

(2) Transfers of debt more than 1 year after initial borrowing not treated as increasing nonqualified nonrecourse financing.—For purposes of paragraph

31

(1), the amount of nonqualified nonrecourse financing (within the meaning of section 46(c)(8)(D)) with respect to the taxpayer shall not be treated as increased by reason of a transfer of (or agreement to transfer) any evidence of an indebtedness if such transfer occurs (or such agreement is entered into) more than 1 year after the date such indebtedness was incurred.

* * *

(e) Transfers between spouses or incident to divorce.—In the case of any transfer described in subsection (a) of section 1041—

(1) subsection (a) of this section shall not apply, and

(2) the same tax treatment under this section with respect to the transferred property shall apply to the transferee as would have applied to the transferor.

§ 48.　Definitions; special rules

(a) Section 38 property.—

(1) In general.—Except as provided in this subsection, the term "section 38 property" means—

(A) tangible personal property (other than an air conditioning or heating unit), or

(B) other tangible property (not including a building and its structural components) but only if such property—

(i) is used as an integral part of manufacturing, production, or extraction or of furnishing transportation, communications, electrical energy, gas, water, or sewage disposal services, or

(ii) constitutes a research facility used in connection with any of the activities referred to in clause (i), or

(iii) constitutes a facility used in connection with any of the activities referred to in clause (i) for the bulk storage of fungible commodities (including commodities in a liquid or gaseous state), or

(C) elevators and escalators, but only if—

(i) the construction, reconstruction, or erection of the elevator or escalator is completed by the taxpayer after June 30, 1963, or

(ii) the elevator or escalator is acquired after June 30, 1963, and the original use of such elevator or escalator commences with the taxpayer and commences after such date, or

(D) single purpose agricultural or horticultural structures; or

(E) in the case of a qualified rehabilitated building, that portion of the basis which is attributable to qualified rehabilitation expenditures (within the meaning of subsection (g)), or

(F) in the case of qualified timber property (within the meaning of section 194(c)(1)), that portion of the basis of such property constituting the amortizable basis acquired during the taxable year (other than that portion of such amortizable basis attributable to property which otherwise qualifies as section 38 property) and taken into account under section 194 (after the application of section 194(b)(1)), or

(G) a storage facility (not including a building and its structural components) used in connection with the distribution of petroleum or any primary product of petroleum.

Such term includes only recovery property (within the meaning of section 168 without regard to any useful life) and any other property with respect to which depreciation (or amortization in lieu of depreciation) is allowable and having a useful life (determined as of the time such property is placed in service) of 3 years or more. The preceding sentence shall not apply to property described in subparagraph (F) and, for purposes of this subpart, the useful life of such property shall be treated as its normal growing period.

* * *

(b) New section 38 property.—For purposes of this subpart—

(1) In general.—The term "new section 38 property" means section 38 property the original use of which commences with the taxpayer. Such term includes any section 38 property the reconstruction of which is completed by the taxpayer, buy only with respect to that portion of the basis which is properly attributable to such reconstruction.

(2) Special rule for sale-leasebacks.—For purposes of the first sentence of paragraph (1), in the case of any section 38 property which—

(A) is originally placed in service by a person, and

(B) is sold and leased back by such person, or is leased to such person, within 3 months after the date such property was originally placed in service,

such property shall be treated as originally placed in service not earlier than the date on which such property is used under the leaseback (or lease) referred to in subparagraph (B). The preceding sentence shall not apply to any property if the lessee and lessor of such property make an election under this sentence. Such an election, once made, may be revoked only with the consent of the Secretary.

(3) Special rule for energy property.—The principles of paragraph (2) shall be applicable in determining whether the original use of property commences with the taxpayer for purposes of section 48(*l*)(2)(B)(ii).

(c) Used section 38 property.—

(1) In general.—For purposes of this subpart, the term "used section 38 property" means section 38 property acquired by purchase after December 31, 1961, which is not new section 38 property. Property shall not be treated as "used section 38 property" if, after its acquisition by the taxpayer, it is used by a person who used such property before such acquisition (or by a person who bears a relationship described in section 179(d) (2) (A) or (B) to a person who used such property before such acquisition).

(2) Dollar limitation.—

(A) In general.—The cost of used section 38 property taken into account under section 46(c)(1)(B) for any taxable year shall not exceed $125,000 ($150,000 for taxable years beginning after 1987). If such cost exceeds $125,000 (or $150,000 as the case may be), the taxpayer shall select (at such time and in such manner as the Secretary shall by regulations prescribe) the items to be taken into account, but only to the extent of an aggregate cost of $125,000 (or $150,000). Such a selection, once made, may be changed only in the manner, and to the extent, provided by such regulations.

(B) Married individuals.—In the case of a husband or wife who files a separate return, the limitation under subparagraph (A) shall be $62,500 ($75,000 for taxable years beginning after 1987.) This subparagraph shall not apply if the spouse of the taxpayer has no used section 38 property which may be taken into account as qualified investment for the taxable year of such spouse which ends within or with the taxpayer's taxable year.

(C) **Controlled groups.**—In the case of a controlled group, the amount specified under subparagraph (A) shall be reduced for each component member of the group by apportioning such amount among the component members of such group in accordance with their respective amounts of used section 38 property which may be taken into account.

(D) **Partnerships and S corporations.**—In the case of a partnership, the limitation contained in subparagraph (A) shall apply with respect to the partnership and with respect to each partner. A similar rule shall apply in the case of an S corporation and its shareholders.

(3) **Definitions.**—For purposes of this subsection—

(A) **Purchase.**—The term "purchase" has the meaning assigned to such term by section 179(d) (2).

(B) **Cost.**—The cost of used section 38 property does not include so much of the basis of such property as is determined by reference to the adjusted basis of other property held at any time by the person acquiring such property. If property is disposed of (other than by reason of its destruction or damage by fire, storm, shipwreck, or other casualty, or its theft) and used section 38 property similar or related in service or use is acquired as a replacement therefor in a transaction to which the preceding sentence does not apply, the cost of the used section 38 property acquired shall be its basis reduced by the adjusted basis of the property replaced. The cost of used section 38 property shall not be reduced with respect to the adjusted basis of any property disposed of if, by reason of section 47, such disposition involved an increase of tax or a reduction of the unused credit carrybacks or carryovers described in section 39.

(C) **Controlled group.**—The term "controlled group" has the meaning assigned to such term by section 1563(a), except that the phrase "more than 50 percent" shall be substituted for the phrase "at least 80 percent" each place it appears in section 1563(a) (1).

* * *

(8) **Certain nonrecourse financing excluded from credit base.**—

* * *

(D) **Nonqualified nonrecourse financing.**—

* * *

(iv) **Qualified person.**—For purposes of this paragraph, the term "qualified person" means any person which is actively and regularly engaged in the business of lending money and which is not—

(I) a related person with respect to the taxpayer,

(II) a person from which the taxpayer acquired the property (or a related person to such person), or

(III) a person who receives a fee with respect to the taxpayer's investment in the property (or a related person to such person).

* * *

(q) **Basis adjustment to section 38 property.**—

(1) **In general.**—For purposes of this subtitle, if a credit is determined under section 46(a) with respect to section 38 property, the basis of such property shall be reduced by 50 percent of the amount of the credit so determined.

(2) Certain dispositions.—If during any taxable year there is a recapture amount determined with respect to any section 38 property the basis of which was reduced under paragraph (1), the basis of such property (immediately before the event resulting in such recapture) shall be increased by an amount equal to 50 percent of such recapture amount. For purposes of the preceding sentence, the term "recapture amount" means any increase in tax (or adjustment in carrybacks or carryovers) determined under section 47.

(3) Special rule for qualified rehabilitated buildings.—In the case of any credit determined under section 46(a) for any qualified rehabilitation expenditure in connection with a qualified rehabilitated building, paragraphs (1) and (2) of this subsection and paragraph (5) of subsection (d) shall be applied without regard to the phrase "50 percent of".

(4) Election of reduced credit in lieu of basis adjustment for regular percentage.—

(A) In general.—If the taxpayer elects to have this paragraph apply with respect to any recovery property—

(i) paragraphs (1) and (2) shall not apply to so much of the credit determined under section 46(a) with respect to such property as is attributable to the regular percentage set forth in section 46(b)(1); and

(ii) the amount of the credit allowable under section 38 with respect to such property shall be determined under subparagraph (B).

(B) Reduction in credit.—In the case of any recovery property to which an election under subparagraph (A) applies—

(i) solely for the purposes of applying the regular percentage, the applicable percentage under subsection (c) or (d) of section 46 shall be deemed to be 100 percent, and

(ii) notwithstanding section 46(b)(1), the regular percentage shall be—

(I) 8 percent in the case of recovery property other than 3-year property, or

(II) 4 percent in the case of recovery property which is 3-year property.

For purposes of the preceding sentence, RRB replacement property (within the meaning of section 168(f)(3)(B)) shall be treated as property which is not 3-year property.

(C) Time and manner of making election.—

(i) **In general.**—An election under this subsection with respect to any property shall be made on the taxpayer's return of the tax imposed by this chapter for the taxpayer's taxable year in which such property is placed in service (or in the case of property to which an election under section 46(d) applies, for the first taxable year for which qualified progress expenditures were taken into account with respect to such property).

(ii) **Revocable only with consent.**—An election under this subsection with respect to any property, once made, may be revoked only with the consent of the Secretary.

(5) Recapture of reductions.—

(A) In general.—For purposes of sections 1245 and 1250, any reduction under this subsection shall be treated as a deduction allowed for depreciation.

(B) Special rule for section 1250.—For purposes of section 1250(b), the determination of what would have been the depreciation adjustments under the straight line method shall be made as if there had been no reduction under this section.

* * *

§ 49. Termination of regular percentage

(a) **General rule.**—For purposes of determining the amount of the investment tax credit determined under section 46, the regular percentage shall not apply to any property placed in service after December 31, 1985.

(b) **Exceptions.**—Subject to the provisions of subsections (c) and (d), subsection (a) shall not apply to the following:

(1) **Transition property.**—Property which is transition property (within the meaning of subsection (e)).

(2) **Qualified progress expenditure for periods before January 1, 1986.**—In the case of any taxpayer who has made an election under section 46(d)(6), the portion of the adjusted basis of any progress expenditure property attributable to qualified progress expenditures for periods before January 1, 1986.

* * *

(c) **35-Percent reduction in credit for taxable years after 1986.**—

(1) **Reduction in current year investment credit.**—Any portion of the current year business credit under section 38(b) for any taxable year beginning after June 30, 1987, which is attributable to the regular investment credit shall be reduced by 35 percent.

(2) **Unexpired carryforwards to 1st taxable year beginning after June 30, 1987.**—Any portion of the business credit carryforward under section 38(a)(1) attributable to the regular investment credit which has not expired as of the close of the taxable year preceding the 1st taxable year of the taxpayer beginning after June 30, 1987, shall be reduced by 35 percent.

PART VI—ALTERNATIVE MINIMUM TAX

§ 53. Credit for prior year minimum tax liability

(a) **Allowance of credit.**—There shall be allowed as a credit against the tax imposed by this chapter for any taxable year an amount equal to the minimum tax credit for such taxable year.

(b) **Minimum tax credit.**—For purposes of subsection (a), the minimum tax credit for any taxable year is the excess (if any) of—

(1) the adjusted net minimum tax imposed for all prior taxable years beginning after 1986, over

(2) the amount allowable as a credit under subsection (a) for such prior taxable years.

(c) **Limitation.**—The credit allowable under subsection (a) for any taxable year shall not exceed the excess (if any) of—

(1) the regular tax liability of the taxpayer for such taxable year reduced by the sum of the credits allowable under subparts A, B, D, E, and F of this part, over

(2) the tentative minimum tax for the taxable year.

(d) **Definitions.**—For purposes of this section—

(1) **Net minimum tax.**—

(A) **In general.**—The term "net minimum tax" means the tax imposed by section 55.

(B) **Credit not allowed for exclusion preferences.**—

(i) **Adjusted net minimum tax.**—The adjusted net minimum tax for any taxable year is—

(I) the amount of the net minimum tax for such taxable year, reduced by

(II) the amount which would be the net minimum tax for such taxable year if the only adjustments and items of tax preference taken into account were those specified in clause (ii).

(ii) **Specified items.**—The following are specified in this clause—

(I) the adjustments provided for in subsections (b)(1) and (c)(3) of section 56, and

(II) the items of tax preference described in paragraphs (1), (5), and (6) of section 57(a).

In the case of taxable years beginning after 1989, the adjustments provided in section 56(g) shall be treated as specified in this clause to the extent attributable to items which are excluded from gross income for any taxable year for purposes of the regular tax, or are not deductible for any taxable year under the adjusted earnings and profits method of section 56(g).

(2) **Tentative minimum tax.**—The term "tentative minimum tax" has the meaning given to such term by section 55(b).

§ 55. Alternative minimum tax imposed

(a) **General rule.**—There is hereby imposed (in addition to any other tax imposed by this subtitle) a tax equal to the excess (if any) of—

(1) the tentative minimum tax for the taxable year, over

(2) the regular tax for the taxable year.

(b) **Tentative minimum tax.**—For purposes of this part—

(1) **In general.**—The tentative minimum tax for the taxable year is—

(A) 20 percent (21 percent in the case of a taxpayer other than a corporation) of so much of the alternative minimum taxable income for the taxable year as exceeds the exemption amount, reduced by

(B) the alternative minimum tax foreign tax credit for the taxable year.

(2) **Alternative minimum taxable income.**—The term "alternative minimum taxable income" means the taxable income of the taxpayer for the taxable year—

(A) determined with the adjustments provided in section 56 and section 58, and

(B) increased by the amount of the items of tax preference described in section 57.

(c) **Regular tax.**—

(1) **In general.**—For purposes of this section, the term "regular tax" means the regular tax liability for the taxable year (as defined in section 26(b)) reduced by the foreign tax credit allowable under section 27(a). Such term shall not include any tax imposed by section 402(e) and shall not include any increase in tax under section 47 or section 42(j).

(2) Cross references.—

For provisions providing that certain credits are not allowable against the tax imposed by this section, see sections 26(a), 28(d)(2), 29(b)(5), and 38(c).

(d) Exemption amount.—For purposes of this section—

(1) Exemption amount for taxpayers other than corporations.—In the case of a taxpayer other than a corporation, the term "exemption amount" means—

(A) $40,000 in the case of—

(i) a joint return, or

(ii) a surviving spouse,

(B) $30,000 in the case of an individual who—

(i) is not a married individual, and

(ii) is not a surviving spouse, and

(C) $20,000 in the case of—

(i) a married individual who files a separate return, or

(ii) an estate or trust.

For purposes of this paragraph, the term "surviving spouse" has the meaning given to such term by section 2(a), and marital status shall be determined under section 7703.

(2) Corporations.—In the case of a corporation, the term "exemption amount" means $40,000.

(3) Phase-out of exemption amount.—The exemption amount of any taxpayer shall be reduced (but not below zero) by an amount equal to 25 percent of the amount by which the alternative minimum taxable income of the taxpayer exceeds—

(A) $150,000 in the case of a taxpayer described in paragraph (1)(A) or (2),

(B) $112,500 in the case of a taxpayer described in paragraph (1)(B), and

(C) $75,000 in the case of a taxpayer described in paragraph (1)(C).

§ 56. Adjustments in computing alternative minimum taxable income

(a) Adjustments applicable to all taxpayers.—In determining the amount of the alternative minimum taxable income for any taxable year the following treatment shall apply (in lieu of the treatment applicable for purposes of computing the regular tax):

(1) Depreciation.—

(A) In general.—

(i) Property other than certain real property.—Except as provided in clause (ii), the depreciation deduction allowable under section 167 with respect to any tangible property placed in service after December 31, 1986, shall be determined under the alternative system of section 168(g).

(ii) 150–percent declining balance method for certain property.—The method of depreciation used shall be—

(I) the 150 percent declining balance method,

(II) switching to the straight line method for the 1st taxable year for which using the straight line method with respect to the adjusted basis as of the beginning of the year will yield a higher allowance.

The preceding sentence shall not apply to any section 1250 property (as defined in section 1250(c)) or to any other property if the depreciation deduction determined under section 168 with respect to such other property for purposes of the regular tax is determined by using the straight line method.

(B) Exception for certain property.—This paragraph shall not apply to property described in paragraph (1), (2), (3), or (4) of section 168(f).

(C) Coordination with transitional rules.—

(i) In general.—This paragraph shall not apply to property placed in service after December 31, 1986, to which the amendments made by section 201 of the Tax Reform Act of 1986 do not apply.

(ii) Treatment of certain property placed in service before 1987.—This paragraph shall apply to any property to which the amendments made by section 201 of the Tax Reform Act of 1986 apply by reason of an election under section 203(a)(1)(B) of such Act without regard to the requirement of subparagraph (A) that the property be placed in service after December 31, 1986.

(D) Normalization rules.—With respect to public utility property described in section 167(1)(3)(A), the Secretary shall prescribe the requirements of a normalization method of accounting for this section.

(2) Mining exploration and development costs.—

(A) In general.—With respect to each mine or other natural deposit (other than an oil, gas, or geothermal well) of the taxpayer, the amount allowable as a deduction under section 616(a) or 617(a) (determined without regard to section 291(b)) in computing the regular tax for costs paid or incurred after December 31, 1986, shall be capitalized and amortized ratably over the 10-year period beginning with the taxable year in which the expenditures were made.

(B) Loss allowed.—If a loss is sustained with respect to any property described in subparagraph (A), a deduction shall be allowed for the expenditures described in subparagraph (A) for the taxable year in which such loss is sustained in an amount equal to the lesser of—

(i) the amount allowable under section 165(a) for the expenditures if they had remained capitalized, or

(ii) the amount of such expenditures which have not previously been amortized under subparagraph (A).

(3) Treatment of certain long-term contracts.—In the case of any long-term contract entered into by the taxpayer on or after March 1, 1986, the taxable income from such contract shall be determined under the percentage of completion method of accounting (as modified by section 460(b)).

(4) Alternative tax net operating loss deduction.—The alternative tax net operating loss deduction shall be allowed in lieu of the net operating loss deduction allowed under section 172.

(5) Pollution control facilities.—In the case of any certified pollution control facility placed in service after December 31, 1986, the deduction allowable under section 169 (without regard to section 291) shall be determined under the alternative system of section 168(g).

(6) Installment sales of certain property.—In the case of any—

(A) disposition after March 1, 1986, of property described in section 1221(1), or

(B) other disposition if an obligation arising from such disposition would be an applicable installment obligation (as defined in section 453C(e)) to which section 453C applies,

income from such disposition shall be determined without regard to the installment method under section 453 or 453A and all payments to be received for the disposition shall be deemed received in the taxable year of the disposition. This paragraph shall not apply to any disposition with respect to which an election is in effect under section 453C(e)(4).

(7) Adjusted basis.—The adjusted basis of any property to which paragraph (1) or (5) applies (or with respect to which there are any expenditures to which paragraph (2) or subsection (b)(2) applies) shall be determined on the basis of the treatment prescribed in paragraph (1), (2), or (5), or subsection (b)(2), whichever applies.

(b) Adjustments applicable to individuals.—In determining the amount of the alternative minimum taxable income of any taxpayer (other than a corporation), the following treatment shall apply (in lieu of the treatment applicable for purposes of computing the regular tax):

(1) Limitation on itemized deductions.—

(A) In general.—

(i) for any miscellaneous itemized deduction (as defined in section 67(b)), or

(ii) for any taxes described in paragraph (1), (2), or (3) of section 164(a).

Clause (ii) shall not apply to any amount allowable in computing adjusted gross income.

(B) Medical expenses.—In determining the amount allowable as a deduction under section 213, subsection (a) of section 213 shall be applied by substituting "10 percent" for "7.5 percent".

(C) Interest.—In determining the amount allowable as a deduction for interest, subsections (d) and (h) of section 163 shall apply, except that—

(i) in lieu of the exception under section 163(h)(2)(D), the term "personal interest" shall not include any qualified housing interest (as defined in subsection (e)),

(ii) sections 163(d)(6) and 163(h)(6) (relating to phase-ins) shall not apply, and

(iii) interest on any specified private activity bond (and any amount treated as interest on a specified activity bond under section 56(a)(5)(B)), and any deduction referred to in section 57(a)(5)(A), shall be treated as includible in gross income (or as deductible) for purposes of applying section 163(d).

(D) Treatment of certain recoveries.—No recovery of any tax to which subparagraph (A)(ii) applied shall be included in gross income for purposes of determining alternative minimum taxable income.

(E) Standard deduction not allowed.—The standard deduction provided in section 63(c) shall not be allowed.

(2) Circulation and research and experimental expenditures.—

(A) In general.—The amount allowable as a deduction under section 173 or 174(a) in computing the regular tax for amounts paid or incurred after December 31, 1986, shall be capitalized and—

(i) in the case of circulation expenditures described in section 173, shall be amortized ratably over the 3–year period beginning with the taxable year in which the expenditures were made, or

(ii) in the case of research and experimental expenditures described in section 174(a), shall be amortized ratably over the 10–year period beginning with the taxable year in which the expenditures were made.

(B) **Loss allowed.**—If a loss is sustained with respect to any property described in subparagraph (A), a deduction shall be allowed for the expenditures described in subparagraph (A) for the taxable year in which such loss is sustained in an amount equal to the lesser of—

(i) the amount allowable under section 165(a) for the expenditures if they had remained capitalized, or

(ii) the amount of such expenditures which have not previously been amortized under subparagraph (A).

(C) **Special rule for personal holding companies.**—In the case of circulation expenditures described in section 173, the adjustments provided in this paragraph shall apply also to a personal holding company (as defined in section 542).

(c) **Adjustments applicable to corporations.**—In determining the amount of the alternative minimum taxable income of a corporation, the following treatment shall apply:

(1) **Adjustment for book income or adjusted earnings and profits.**—

(A) **Book income adjustment.**—For taxable years beginning in 1987, 1988, and 1989, alternative minimum taxable income shall be adjusted as provided under subsection (f).

(B) **Adjusted earnings and profits.**—For taxable years beginning after 1989, alternative minimum taxable income shall be adjusted as provided under subsection (g).

(2) **Merchant marine capital construction funds.**—In the case of a capital construction fund established under section 607 of the Merchant Marine Act, 1936 (46 U.S.C. 1177)—

(A) subparagraphs (A), (B), and (C) of section 7518(c)(1) (and the corresponding provisions of such section 607) shall not apply to—

(i) any amount deposited in such fund after December 31, 1986, or

(ii) any earnings (including gains and losses) after December 31, 1986, on amounts in such fund, and

(B) no reduction in basis shall be made under section 7518(f) (or the corresponding provisions of such section 607) with respect to the withdrawal from the fund of any amount to which subparagraph (A) applies.

For purposes of this paragraph, any withdrawal of deposits or earnings from the fund shall be treated as allocable first to deposits made before (and earnings received or accrued before) January 1, 1987.

(d) **Alternative tax net operating loss deduction defined.**—

(1) **In general.**—For purposes of subsection (a)(4), the term "alternative tax net operating loss deduction" means the net operating loss deduction allowable for the taxable year under section 172, except that—

(A) the amount of such deduction shall not exceed 90 percent of alternative minimum taxable income determined without regard to such deduction, and

41

(B) in determining the amount of such deduction—

(i) the net operating loss (within the meaning of section 172(c)) for any loss year shall be adjusted as provided in paragraph (2), and

(ii) in the case of taxable years beginning after December 31, 1986, section 172(b)(2) shall be applied by substituting "90 percent of alternative minimum taxable income determined without regard to the alternative tax net operating loss deduction" for "taxable income" each place it appears.

(2) Adjustments to net operating loss computation.—

(A) Post–1986 loss years.—In the case of a loss year beginning after December 31, 1986, the net operating loss for such year under section 172(c) shall—

(i) be determined with the adjustments provided in this section and section 58, and

(ii) be reduced by the items of tax preference determined under section 57 for such year (other than subsection (a)(6) thereof).

(B) Pre–1987 years.—In the case of loss years beginning before January 1, 1987, the amount of the net operating loss which may be carried over to taxable years beginning after December 31, 1986, for purposes of paragraph (2), shall be equal to the amount which may be carried from the loss year to the first taxable year of the taxpayer beginning after December 31, 1986.

(e) Qualified housing interest.—For purposes of this part—

(1) In general.—The term "qualified housing interest" means interest which is paid or accrued during the taxable year on indebtedness which is incurred in acquiring, constructing, or substantially rehabilitating any property which—

(A) is the principal residence (within the meaning of section 1034) of the taxpayer at the time such interest accrues or is paid, or

(B) is a qualified dwelling which is a qualified residence (within the meaning of section 163(h)(3)).

Such term also includes interest on any indebtedness resulting from the refinancing of indebtedness meeting the requirements of the preceding sentence; but only to the extent that the amount of the indebtedness resulting from such refinancing does not exceed the amount of the refinanced indebtedness immediately before the refinancing.

(2) Qualified dwelling.—The term "qualified dwelling" means any—

(A) house,

(B) apartment,

(C) condominium, or

(D) mobile home not used on a transient basis (within the meaning of section 7701(a)(19)(C)(v)),

including all structures or other property appurtenant thereto.

(3) Special rule for indebtedness incurred before July 1, 1982.—The term "qualified housing interest" includes interest paid or accrued on indebtedness which—

(A) was incurred by the taxpayer before July 1, 1982, and

(B) is secured by property which, at the time such indebtedness was incurred, was—

(i) the principal residence (within the meaning of section 1034) of the taxpayer, or

(ii) a qualified dwelling used by the taxpayer (or any member of his family (within the meaning of section 267(c)(4))).

(f) Adjustments for book income of corporations.—

(1) In general.—The alternative minimum taxable income of any corporation for any taxable year beginning in 1987, 1988, or 1989 shall be increased by 50 percent of the amount (if any) by which—

(A) the adjusted net book income of the corporation, exceeds

(B) the alternative minimum taxable income for the taxable year (determined without regard to this subsection and the alternative tax net operating loss deduction).

(2) Adjusted net book income.—For purposes of this subsection—

(A) In general.—The term "adjusted net book income" means the net income or loss of the taxpayer set forth on the taxpayer's applicable financial statement, adjusted as provided in this paragraph.

(B) Adjustments for certain taxes.—The amount determined under subparagraph (A) shall be appropriately adjusted to disregard any Federal income taxes, or income, war profits, or excess profits taxes imposed by any foreign country or possession of the United States, which are directly or indirectly taken into account on the taxpayer's applicable financial statement. The preceding sentence shall not apply to any such taxes imposed by a foreign country or possession of the United States if the taxpayer does not choose to take, to any extent, the benefits of section 901.

(C) Special rules for related corporations.—

(i) Consolidated returns.—If the taxpayer files a consolidated return for any taxable year, adjusted net book income for such taxable year shall take into account items on the taxpayer's applicable financial statement which are properly allocable to members of such group included on such return.

(ii) Treatment of dividends.—In the case of any corporation which is not included on a consolidated return with the taxpayer, adjusted net book income shall take into account the earnings of such other corporation only to the extent of the sum of the dividends received from such other corporation and other amounts required to be included in gross income under this chapter in respect of the earnings of such other corporation.

(D) Statements covering different periods.—Appropriate adjustments shall be made in adjusted net book income in any case in which an applicable financial statement covers a period other than the taxable year.

(E) Special rule for cooperatives.—In the case of a cooperative to which section 1381 applies, the amount determined under subparagraph (A) shall be reduced by the amounts referred to in section 1382(b) (relating to patronage dividends and per-unit retain allocations) to the extent such amounts were not otherwise taken into account in determining adjusted net book income.

(F) Treatment of dividends from 936 corporations.—

(i) In general.—In determining the amount of adjusted net book income, any dividend received from a corporation eligible for the credit provided by section 936 shall be increased by the amount of any withholding tax paid to a possession of the United States with respect to such dividend.

(ii) Treatment as foreign taxes.—

(I) In general.—50 percent of any withholding tax paid to a possession of the United States with respect to dividends referred to in clause (i) (to the extent such dividends do not exceed the excess referred to in paragraph (1), determined without regard to clause (i)) shall, for purposes of this part, be treated as a tax paid by the corporation receiving the dividend to a foreign country.

(II) Treatment of taxes imposed on 936 corporation.—For purposes of this subparagraph, taxes paid by any corporation eligible for the credit provided by section 936 to a possession of the United States, shall be treated as a withholding tax paid with respect to any dividend paid by such corporation to the extent such taxes would be treated as paid by the corporation receiving the dividend under rules similar to the rules of section 902.

(G) Rules for Alaska native corporations.—The amount determined under subparagraph (A) shall be appropriately adjusted to allow:

(i) cost recovery and depletion attributable to property the basis of which is determined under section 21(c) of the Alaska Native Claims Settlement Act (43 U.S.C. 1620(c)), and

(ii) deductions for amounts payable made pursuant to section 7(i) or section 7(j) of such Act (43 U.S.C. 1606(i) and 1606(j)) only at such time as the deductions are allowed for tax purposes.

(H) Secretarial authority to adjust items.—Under regulations, adjusted net book income shall be properly adjusted to prevent the omission or duplication of any item.

(3) Applicable financial statement.—For purposes of this subsection—

(A) In general.—The term "applicable financial statement" means, with respect to any taxable year, any statement covering such taxable year—

(i) which is required to be filed with the Securities and Exchange Commission,

(ii) which is a certified audited income statement to be used for the purposes of a statement or report—

(I) for credit purposes,

(II) to shareholders, or

(III) for any other substantial nontax purpose,

(iii) which is an income statement required to be provided to—

(I) the Federal Government or any agency thereof,

(II) a State government or any agency thereof, or

(III) a political subdivision of a State or any agency thereof, or

(iv) which is an income statement to be used for the purposes of a statement or report—

(I) for credit purposes,

(II) to shareholders, or

(III) for any other substantial nontax purpose.

(B) Earnings and profits used in certain cases.—If—

(i) a taxpayer has no applicable financial statement, or

(ii) a taxpayer has only a statement described in subparagraph (A)(iv) and the taxpayer elects the application of this subparagraph,

the net income or loss set forth on the taxpayer's applicable financial statement shall, for purposes of paragraph (3)(A), be treated as being equal to the taxpayer's earnings and profits for the taxable year (without diminution by reason of distributions during the tax year). Such election, once made, shall remain in effect for any taxable year for which the taxpayer is described in this subparagraph unless revoked with the consent of the Secretary.

(C) **Special rule where more than 1 statement.**—For purposes of subparagraph (A), if a taxpayer has a statement described in more than 1 clause or subclause, the applicable financial statement shall be the statement described in the clause or subclause with the lowest number designation.

(4) **Exception for certain corporations.**—This subsection shall not apply to any S corporation, regulated investment company, real estate investment trust, or REMIC.

(g) **Adjustments based on adjusted current earnings.—**

(1) **In general.**—The alternative minimum taxable income of any corporation for any taxable year beginning after 1989 shall be increased by 75 percent of the excess (if any) of—

(A) the adjusted current earnings of the corporation, over

(B) the alternative minimum taxable income (determined without regard to this subsection and the alternative tax net operating loss deduction).

(2) **Allowance of negative adjustments.—**

(A) **In general.**—The alternative minimum taxable income for any corporation of any taxable year beginning after 1989, shall be reduced by 75 percent of the excess (if any) of—

(i) the amount referred to in subparagraph (B) of paragraph (1), over

(ii) the amount referred to in subparagraph (A) of paragraph (1).

(B) **Limitation.**—The reduction under subparagraph (A) for any taxable year shall not exceed the excess (if any) of—

(i) the aggregate increases in alternative minimum taxable income under paragraph (1) for prior taxable years, over

(ii) the aggregate reductions under subparagraph (A) of this paragraph for prior taxable years.

(3) **Adjusted current earnings.**—For purposes of this subsection, the term "adjusted current earnings" means the alternative minimum taxable income for the taxable year—

(A) determined with the adjustments provided in paragraph (4), and

(B) determined without regard to this subsection and the alternative tax net operating loss deduction.

(4) **Adjustments.**—In determining adjusted current earnings, the following adjustments shall apply:

(A) **Depreciation.—**

(i) **Property placed in service after 1989.**—The depreciation deduction with respect to any property placed in service in a taxable year beginning after 1989 shall be determined under whichever of the following methods yields deductions with a smaller present value:

(I) The alternative system of section 168(g), or

(II) The method used for book purposes.

(ii) **Property to which new ACRS system applies.**—In the case of any property to which the amendments made by section 201 of the Tax Reform Act of 1986 apply and which is placed in service in a taxable year beginning before 1990, the depreciation deduction shall be determined—

(I) by taking into account the adjusted basis of such property (as determined for purposes of computing alternative minimum taxable income) as of the close of the last taxable year beginning before January 1, 1990, and

(II) by using the straight-line method over the remainder of the recovery period applicable to such property under the alternative system of section 168(g).

(iii) **Property to which original ACRS system applies.**—In the case of any property to which section 168 (as in effect on the day before the date of the enactment of the Tax Reform Act of 1986 and without regard to subsection (d)(1)(A)(ii) thereof) applies, the depreciation deduction shall be determined—

(I) by taking into account the adjusted basis of such property (as determined for purposes of computing the regular tax) as of the close of the last taxable year beginning before January 1, 1990, and

(II) by using the straight line method over the remainder of the recovery period which would apply to such property under the alternative system of section 168(g).

(iv) **Property placed in service before 1981.**—In the case of any property not described in clause (i), (ii), or (iii), the amount allowable as depreciation or amortization with respect to such property shall be determined in the same manner as for purposes of computing taxable income.

(v) **Slower method used if used for book purposes.**—In the case of any property to which clause (ii), (iii), or (iv) applies, if the depreciation method used for book purposes yields deductions for taxable years beginning after 1989 with a smaller present value than the method which would otherwise be used under such clause, the method used for book purposes shall be used in lieu of the method which would otherwise be used under such clause.

(B) **Inclusion of items included for purposes of computing earnings and profits.**—

(i) **In general.**—In the case of any amount which is excluded from gross income for purposes of computing alternative minimum taxable income but is taken into account in determining the amount of earnings and profits—

(I) such amount shall be included in income in the same manner as if such amount were includible in gross income for purposes of computing alternative minimum taxable income, and

(II) the amount of such income shall be reduced by any deduction which would have been allowable in computing alternative minimum taxable income if such amount were includible in gross income.

(ii) **Inclusion of buildup in life insurance contracts.**—In the case of any life insurance contract—

(I) the income on such contract (as determined under section 7702(g)) for any taxable year shall be, treated as includible in gross income for such year, and

(II) there shall be allowed as a deduction that portion of any premium which is attributable to insurance coverage.

(iii) Inclusion of income on annuity contract.—In the case of any annuity contract, the income on such contract (as determined under section 72(u)(2)) shall be treated as includible in gross income for such year

(C) Disallowance of items not deductible in computing earnings and profits.—

(i) In general.—A deduction shall not be allowed for any item if such item would not be deductible for any taxable year for purposes of computing earnings and profits.

(ii) Special rule for 100–percent dividends.—Clause (i) shall not apply to any deduction allowable under section 243 or 245 for a 100–percent dividend—

(I) if the corporation receiving such dividend and the corporation paying such dividend could not be members of the same affiliated group under section 1504 by reason of section 1504(b),

(II) but only to the extent such dividend is attributable to income of the paying corporation which is subject to tax under this chapter (determined after the application of sections 936 and 921).

For purposes of the preceding sentence, the term "100 percent dividend" means any dividend if the percentage used for purposes of determining the amount allowable as a deduction under section 243 or 245 with respect to such dividend is 100 percent.

(iii) Special rule for dividends from section 936 companies.—In the case of any dividend received from a corporation eligible for the credit provided by section 936, rules similar to the rules of subparagraph (F) of subsection (f)(1) shall apply, except that "75 percent" shall be substituted for "50 percent" in clause (ii)(I) thereof.

(D) Certain other earnings and profits adjustments.—

(i) In general.—The adjustments provided in section 312(n) shall apply; except that—

(I) paragraphs (1), (2), and (3) shall apply only to amounts paid or incurred in taxable years beginning after December 31, 1989,

(II) paragraph (4) shall apply only to taxable years beginning after December 31, 1989,

(III) paragraph (5) shall apply only to installment sales in taxable years beginning after December 31, 1989,

(IV) paragraph (6) shall apply only to contracts entered into on or after March 1, 1986, and

(V) paragraphs (7) and (8) shall not apply.

(ii) Special rule for intangible drilling costs and mineral exploration and development costs.—If—

(I) the present value of the deductions provided under subparagraph (A)(ii) or (B)(ii) of section 312(n)(2) with respect to amounts paid or incurred in taxable years beginning after December 31, 1989, exceeds

(II) the present value of the deductions for such amounts under the method used for book purposes, such amounts shall be deductible under the method used for book purposes in lieu of that provided in such subparagraph.

(E) **Disallowance of loss on exchange of debt pools.**—No loss shall be recognized on the exchange of any pool of debt obligations for another pool of debt obligations having substantially the same effective interest rates and maturities.

(F) **Acquisition expenses of life insurance companies.**—Acquisition expenses of life insurance companies shall be capitalized and amortized in accordance with the treatment generally required under generally accepted accounting principles as if this subparagraph applied to all taxable years.

(G) **Depletion.**—The allowances for depletion with respect to any property placed in service in a taxable year beginning after 1989, shall be determined under whichever of the following methods yields deductions with a smaller present value:

(i) cost depletion determined under section 611, or

(ii) the method used for book purposes.

(H) **Treatment of certain ownership changes.**—If—

(i) there is an ownership change (within the meaning of section 382) after the date of the enactment of the Tax Reform Act of 1986 with respect to any corporation, and

(ii)(I) the aggregate adjusted bases of the assets of such corporation (immediately after the change), exceed

(II) the value of the stock of such corporation (as determined for purposes of section 382), properly adjusted for liabilities and other relevant items,

then the adjusted basis of each asset of such corporation (as of such time) shall be its proportionate share (determined on the basis of respective fair market values) of the amount referred to in clause (ii)(II).

(5) **Other definitions.**—For purposes of paragraph (4)—

(A) **Book purposes.**—The term "book purposes" means the treatment for purposes of preparing the applicable financial statement referred to in subsection (f).

(B) **Earnings and profits.**—The term 'earnings and profits' means earnings and profits computed for purposes of subchapter C.

(C) **Present value.**—Present value shall be determined as of the time the property is placed in service (or, if later, as of the beginning of the first taxable year beginning after 1989) and under regulations prescribed by the Secretary.

(D) **Treatment of alternative minimum taxable income.**—The treatment of any item for purposes of computing alternative minimum taxable income shall be determined without regard to this subsection.

(6) **Exception for certain corporations.**—This subsection shall not apply to any S corporation, regulated investment company, real estate investment trust, or REMIC.

§ 57. Items of tax preference

(a) **General rule.**—For purposes of this part, the items of tax preference determined under this section are—

(1) Depletion.—With respect to each property (as defined in section 614), the excess of the deduction for depletion allowable under section 611 for the taxable year over the adjusted basis of the property at the end of the taxable year (determined without regard to the depletion deduction for the taxable year).

(2) Intangible drilling costs.—

(A) In general.—With respect to all oil, gas, and geothermal properties of the taxpayer, the amount (if any) by which the amount of the excess intangible drilling costs arising in the taxable year is greater than 65 percent of the net income of the taxpayer from oil, gas, and geothermal properties for the taxable year.

(B) Excess intangible drilling costs.—For purposes of subparagraph (A), the amount of the excess intangible drilling costs arising in the taxable year is the excess of—

(i) the intangible drilling and development costs paid or incurred in connection with oil, gas, and geothermal wells (other than costs incurred in drilling a nonproductive well) allowable under section 263(c) or 291(b) for the taxable year, over

(ii) the amount which would have been allowable for the taxable year if such costs had been capitalized and straight line recovery of intangibles (as defined in subsection (b)) had been used with respect to such costs.

(C) Net income from oil, gas, and geothermal properties.—For purposes of subparagraph (A), the amount of the net income of the taxpayer from oil, gas, and geothermal properties for the taxable year is the excess of—

(i) the aggregate amount of gross income (within the meaning of section 613(a)) from all oil, gas, and geothermal properties of the taxpayer received or accrued by the taxpayer during the taxable year, over

(ii) the amount of any deductions allocable to such properties reduced by the excess described in subparagraph (B) for such taxable year.

(D) Paragraph applied separately with respect to geothermal properties and oil and gas properties.—This paragraph shall be applied separately with respect to—

(i) all oil and gas properties which are not described in clause (ii), and

(ii) all properties which are geothermal deposits (as defined in section 613(e)(3)).

(3) Incentive stock options.—

(A) In general.—With respect to the transfer of a share of stock pursuant to the exercise of an incentive stock option (as defined in section 422A), the amount by which the fair market value of the share at the time of exercise exceeds the option price. For purposes of this paragraph, the fair market value of a share of stock shall be determined without regard to any restriction other than a restriction which, by its terms, will never lapse.

(B) Basis adjustment.—In determining the amount of gain or loss recognized for purposes of this part on any disposition of a share of stock acquired pursuant to an exercise (in a taxable year beginning after December 31, 1986) of an incentive stock option, the basis of such stock shall be increased by the amount of the excess referred to in subparagraph (A).

(4) Reserves for losses on bad debts of financial institutions.—In the case of a financial institution to which section 585 or 593 applies, the amount by which the deduction allowable for the taxable year for a reasonable addition to a reserve for bad debts exceeds the amount that would have been allowable had the institution maintained its bad debt reserve for all taxable years on the basis of actual experience.

(5) Tax-exempt interest.—

(A) In general.—Interest on specified private activity bonds reduced by any deduction (not allowable in computing the regular tax) which would have been allowable if such interest were includible in gross income.

(B) Treatment of exempt-interest dividends.—Under regulations prescribed by the Secretary, any exempt-interest dividend (as defined in section 852(b)(5)(A)) shall be treated as interest on a specified private activity bond to the extent of its proportionate share of the interest on such bonds received by the company paying such dividend.

(C) Specified private activity bonds.—

(i) In general.—For purposes of this part, the term "specified private activity bonds" means any private activity bond (as defined in section 141) issued after August 7, 1986.

(ii) Exception for qualified 501(c)(3) bonds.—For purposes of clause (i), the term "private activity bond" shall not include any qualified 501(c)(3) bond (as defined in section 145).

(iii) Exception for refundings.—For purposes of clause (i), the term "private activity bond" shall not include any refunding bond if the refunded bond (or in the case of a series of refundings, the original bond) was issued before August 8, 1986.

(iv) Certain bonds issued before September 1, 1986.—For purposes of this subparagraph, a bond issued before September 1, 1986, shall be treated as issued before August 8, 1986, unless such bond would be a private activity bond if—

(I) paragraphs (1) and (2) of section 141(b) were applied by substituting "25 percent" for "10 percent" each place it appears,

(II) paragraphs (3), (4), and (5) of section 141(b) did not apply, and

(III) subparagraph (B) of section 141(c)(1) did not apply.

(6) Appreciated property charitable deduction.—

(A) In general.—The amount by which the deduction allowable under section 170 would be reduced if all capital gain property were taken into account at its adjusted basis.

(B) Capital gain property.—For purposes of subparagraph (A), the term "capital gain property" has the meaning given to such term by section 170(b)(1)(C)(iv). Such term shall not include any property to which an election under section 170(b)(1)(C)(iii) applies.

(7) Accelerated depreciation or amortization on certain property placed in service before January 1, 1987.—The amounts which would be treated as items of tax preference with respect to the taxpayer under paragraphs (2), (3), (4), and (12) of this subsection (as in effect on the day before the date of the enactment of the Tax Reform Act of 1986). The preceding sentence shall not apply to any property to which section 56(a)(1) or (5) applies.

(b) Straight line recovery of intangibles defined.—For purposes of paragraph (2) of subsection (a)—

(1) **In general.**—The term "straight line recovery of intangibles", when used with respect to intangible drilling and development costs for any well, means (except in the case of an election under paragraph (2)) ratable amortization of such costs over the 120–month period beginning with the month in which production from such well begins.

(2) **Election.**—If the taxpayer elects with respect to the intangible drilling and development costs for any well, the term "straight line recovery of intangibles" means any method which would be permitted for purposes of determining cost depletion with respect to such well and which is selected by the taxpayer for purposes of subsection (a)(2).

§ 58. Denial of certain losses

(a) **Denial of farm loss.**—

(1) **In general.**—For purposes of computing the amount of the alternative minimum taxable income for any taxable year of a taxpayer other than a corporation—

(A) **Disallowance of farm loss.**—No loss of the taxpayer for such taxable year from any tax shelter farm activity shall be allowed.

(B) **Deduction in succeeding taxable year.**—Any loss from a tax shelter farm activity disallowed under subparagraph (A) shall be treated as a deduction allocable to such activity in the 1st succeeding taxable year.

(2) **Tax shelter farm activity.**—For purposes of this subsection, the term "tax shelter farm activity" means—

(A) any farming syndicate as defined in section 464(c) (as modified by section 461(i)(4)(A)), and

(B) any other activity consisting of farming which is a passive activity (within the meaning of section 469(d), without regard to paragraph (1)(B) thereof).

(3) **Application to personal service corporations.**—For purposes of paragraph (1), a personal service corporation (within the meaning of section 469(g)(1)(C)) shall be treated as a taxpayer other than a corporation.

(b) **Disallowance of passive activity loss.**—In computing the alternative minimum taxable income of the taxpayer for any taxable year, section 469 shall apply, except that in applying section 469—

(1) the adjustments of section 56 shall apply,

(2) any deduction to the extent such deduction is an item of tax preference under section 57(a) shall not be taken into account, and

(3) the provisions of section 469(*l*) (relating to phase-in of disallowance) shall not apply.

(c) **Special rules.**—For purposes of this section—

(1) **Special rule for insolvent taxpayers.**—

(A) **In general.**—The amount of losses to which subsection (a) or (b) applies shall be reduced by the amount (if any) by which the taxpayer is insolvent as of the close of the taxable year.

(B) **Insolvent.**—For purposes of this paragraph, the term "insolvent" means the excess of liabilities over the fair market value of assets.

(2) **Loss allowed for year of disposition of farm shelter activity.**—If the taxpayer disposes of his entire interest in any tax shelter farm activity during any

taxable year, the amount of the loss attributable to such activity (determined after carryovers under subsection (a)(1)(B)) shall (to the extent otherwise allowable) be allowed for such taxable year in computing alternative minimum taxable income and not treated as a loss from a tax shelter farm activity.

§ 59. Other definitions and special rules

(a) **Alternative minimum tax foreign tax credit.**—For purposes of this part—

(1) **In general.**—The alternative minimum tax foreign tax credit for any taxable year shall be the credit which would be determined under section 27(a) for such taxable year if—

(A) the amount determined under section 55(b)(1)(A) were the tax against which such credit was taken for purposes of section 904 for the taxable year and all prior taxable years beginning after December 31, 1986,

(B) section 904 were applied on the basis of alternative minimum taxable income instead of taxable income, and

(C) for purposes of section 904, any increase in alternative minimum taxable income by reason of section 56(c)(1)(A) (relating to adjustment for book income) shall have the same proportionate source (and character) as alternative minimum taxable income determined without regard to such increase.

(2) **Limitation to 90 percent of tax.**—

(A) **In general.**—The alternative minimum tax foreign tax credit for any taxable year shall not exceed the excess (if any) of—

(i) the amount determined under section 55(b)(1)(A) for the taxable year, over

(ii) 10 percent of the amount which would be determined under section 55(b)(1)(A) without regard to the alternative tax net operating loss deduction.

(B) **Carryback and carryforward.**—If the alternative minimum tax foreign tax credit exceeds the amount determined under subparagraph (A), such excess shall, for purposes of this part, be treated as an amount to which section 904(c) applies.

(b) **Minimum tax not to apply to income eligible for section 936 credit.**—In the case of any corporation for which a credit is allowable for the taxable year under section 936, alternative minimum taxable income shall not include any amount with respect to which the requirements of subparagraph (A) or (B) of section 936(a)(1) are met.

(c) **Treatment of estates and trusts.**—In the case of any estate or trust, the alternative minimum taxable income of such estate or trust and any beneficiary thereof shall be determined by applying part I of subchapter J with the adjustments provided in this part.

(d) **Apportionment of differently treated items in case of certain entities.**—

(1) **In general.**—The differently treated items for the taxable year shall be apportioned (in accordance with regulations prescribed by the Secretary)—

(A) **Regulated investment companies and real estate investment trusts.** —In the case of a regulated investment company to which part I of subchapter M applies or a real estate investment company to which part II of subchapter M applies, between such company or trust and shareholders and holders of beneficial interest in such company or trust.

(B) **Common trust funds.**—In the case of a common trust fund (as defined in section 584(a)), pro rata among the participants of such fund.

(2) **Differently treated items.**—For purposes of this section, the term "differently treated item" means any item of tax preference or any other item which is treated differently for purposes of this part than for purposes of computing the regular tax.

(e) **Optional 10-year writeoff of certain tax preferences.**—

(1) **In general.**—For purposes of this title, any qualified expenditure to which an election under this paragraph applies shall be allowed as a deduction ratably over the 10-year period (3-year period in the case of circulation expenditures described in section 173) beginning with the taxable year in which such expenditure was made.

(2) **Qualified expenditure.**—For purposes of this subsection, the term "qualified expenditure" means any amount which, but for an election under this subsection, would have been allowable as a deduction for the taxable year in which paid or incurred under—

(A) section 173 (relating to circulation expenditures),

(B) section 174(a) (relating to research and experimental expenditures),

(C) section 263(c) (relating to intangible drilling and development expenditures),

(D) section 616(a) (relating to development expenditures), or

(E) section 617(a) (relating to mining exploration expenditures).

(3) **Other sections not applicable.**—Except as provided in this subsection, no deduction shall be allowed under any other section for any qualified expenditure to which an election under this subsection applies.

(4) **Election.**—

(A) **In general.**—An election may be made under paragraph (1) with respect to any portion of any qualified expenditure.

(B) **Revocable only with consent.**—Any election under this subsection may be revoked only with the consent of the Secretary.

(C) **Partners and shareholders of S corporations.**—In the case of a partnership, any election under paragraph (1) shall be made separately by each partner with respect to the partner's allocable share of any qualified expenditure. A similar rule shall apply in the case of an S corporation and its shareholders.

(5) **Dispositions.**—

(A) **Application of section 1254.**—In the case of any disposition of property to which section 1254 applies (determined without regard to this section), any deduction under paragraph (1) with respect to amounts which are allocable to such property shall, for purposes of section 1254, be treated as a deduction allowable under section 263(c), 616(a), or 617(a), whichever is appropriate.

(B) **Application of section 617(d).**—In the case of any disposition of mining property to which section 617(d) applies (determined without regard to this subsection), any deduction under paragraph (1) with respect to amounts which are allocable to such property shall, for purposes of section 617(d), be treated as a deduction allowable under section 617(a).

(6) **Amounts to which election apply not treated as tax preference.**—Any portion of any qualified expenditure to which an election under paragraph (1)

53

applies shall not be treated as an item of tax preference under section 57(a) and section 56 shall not apply to such expenditure.

(f) Coordination with section 291.—Except as otherwise provided in this part, section 291 (relating to cutback of corporate preferences) shall apply before the application of this part.

(g) Tax benefit rule.—The Secretary may prescribe regulations under which differently treated items shall be properly adjusted where the tax treatment giving rise to such items will not result in the reduction of the taxpayer's regular tax for any taxable year.

(h) Coordination with certain limitations.—The limitations of sections 704(d), 465, and 1366(d) (and such other provisions as may be specified in regulations) shall be applied for purposes of computing the alternative minimum taxable income of the taxpayer for the taxable year—

(1) with the adjustments of section 56, and

(2) by not taking into account any deduction to the extent such deduction is an item of tax preference under section 57(a).

(i) Special rule for interest treated as tax preference.—For purposes of this subtitle, interest shall not fail to be treated as wholly exempt from tax imposed by this title solely by reason of being included in alternative minimum taxable income.

SUBCHAPTER B—COMPUTATION OF TAXABLE INCOME

Part

PART I—DEFINITION OF GROSS INCOME, ADJUSTED GROSS INCOME, TAXABLE INCOME, ETC.

§ 61. Gross income defined

(a) General definition.—Except as otherwise provided in this subtitle, gross income means all income from whatever source derived, including (but not limited to) the following items:

(1) Compensation for services, including fees, commissions, fringe benefits, and similar items;

* Omitted entirely.

(2) Gross income derived from business;

(3) Gains derived from dealings in property;

(4) Interest;

(5) Rents;

(6) Royalties;

(7) Dividends;

(8) Alimony and separate maintenance payments;

(9) Annuities;

(10) Income from life insurance and endowment contracts;

(11) Pensions;

(12) Income from discharge of indebtedness;

(13) Distributive share of partnership gross income;

(14) Income in respect of a decedent; and

(15) Income from an interest in an estate or trust.

(b) Cross references.—

For items specifically included in gross income, see part II (sec. 71 and following). For items specifically excluded from gross income, see part III (sec. 101 and following).

§ 62. Adjusted gross income defined

(a) General rule.—For purposes of this subtitle, the term "adjusted gross income" means, in the case of an individual, gross income minus the following deductions:

(1) Trade and business deductions.—The deductions allowed by this chapter (other than by part VII of this subchapter) which are attributable to a trade or business carried on by the taxpayer, if such trade or business does not consist of the performance of services by the taxpayer as an employee.

(2) Certain trade and business deductions of employees.—

(A) Reimbursed expenses.—The deductions allowed by part VI (sec. 161 and following) which consist of expenses paid or incurred by the taxpayer, in connection with the performance by him of services as an employee, under a reimbursement or other expense allowance arrangement with his employer.

(B) Certain expenses of performing artists.—The deductions allowed by section 162 which consist of expenses paid or incurred by a qualified performing artist in connection with the performances by him of services in the performing arts as an employee.

(3) Losses from sale or exchange of property.—The deductions allowed by part VI (sec. 161 and following) as losses from the sale or exchange of property.

(4) Deductions attributable to rents and royalties.—The deductions allowed by part VI (sec. 161 and following), by section 212 (relating to expenses for production of income), and by section 611 (relating to depletion) which are attributable to property held for the production of rents or royalties.

(5) Certain deductions of life tenants and income beneficiaries of property. —In the case of a life tenant of property, or an income beneficiary of property held in trust, or an heir, legatee, or devisee of an estate, the deduction for depreciation allowed by section 167 and the deduction allowed by section 611.

(6) Pension, profit-sharing, and annuity plans of self-employed individuals.
—In the case of an individual who is an employee within the meaning of section 401(c)(1).

(7) Retirement savings.—The deduction allowed by section 219 (relating to deduction of certain retirement savings).

(8) Certain portion of lump-sum distributions from pension plans taxed under section 402(e).—The deduction allowed by section 402(e) (3).

(9) Penalties forfeited because of premature withdrawal of funds from time savings accounts or deposits.—The deductions allowed by section 165 for losses incurred in any transaction entered into for profit, though not connected with a trade or business to the extent that such losses include amounts forfeited to a bank, mutual savings bank, savings and loan association, building and loan association, cooperative bank or homestead association as a penalty for premature withdrawal of funds from a time savings account, certificate of deposit, or similar class of deposit.

(10) Alimony.—The deduction allowed by section 215.

(11) Reforestation expenses.—The deduction allowed by section 194.

(12) Certain required repayments of supplemental unemployment compensation benefits.—The deduction allowed by section 165 for the repayment to a trust described in paragraph (9) or (17) of section 501(c) of supplemental unemployment compensation benefits received from such trust if such repayment is required because of the receipt of trade readjustment allowances under section 231 or 232 of the Trade Act of 1974 (19 U.S.C. 2291 and 2292).

(b) Qualified performing artist.—

(1) In general.—For purposes of subsection (a)(2)(B), the term "qualified performing artist" means, with respect to any taxable year, any individual if—

(A) such individual performed services in the performing arts as an employee during the taxable year for at least 2 employers,

(B) the aggregate amount allowable as a deduction under section 162 in connection with the performance of such services exceeds 10 percent of such individual's gross income attributable to the performance of such services, and

(C) the adjusted gross income of such individual for the taxable year (determined without regard to subsection (a)(2)(B)) does not exceed $16,000.

(2) Nominal employer not taken into account.—An individual shall not be treated as performing services in the performing arts as an employee for any employer during any taxable year unless the amount received by such individual from such employer for the performance of such services during the taxable year equals or exceeds $200.

(3) Special rules for married couples.—

(A) In general.—Except in the case of a husband and wife who lived apart at all times during the taxable year, if the taxpayer is married at the close of the taxable year, subsection (a)(2)(B) shall apply only if the taxpayer and his spouse file a joint return for the taxable year.

(B) Application of paragraph (1).—In the case of a joint return—

(i) paragraph (1) (other than subparagraph (C) thereof) shall be applied separately with respect to each spouse, but

(ii) paragraph (1)(C) shall be applied with respect to their combined adjusted gross income.

(C) Determination of marital status.—For purposes of this subsection, marital status shall be determined under section 7703(a).

(D) Joint return.—For purposes of this subsection, the term "joint return" means the joint return of a husband and wife made under section 6013.

Nothing in this section shall permit the same item to be deducted more than once.

§ 63. Taxable income defined

(a) **In general.**—Except as provided in subsection (b), for purposes of this subtitle, the term "taxable income" means gross income minus the deductions allowed by this chapter (other than the standard deduction).

(b) **Individuals who do not itemize their deductions.**—In the case of an individual who does not elect to itemize his deductions for the taxable year, for purposes of this subtitle, the term "taxable income" means adjusted gross income, minus—

(1) the standard deduction, and

(2) the deduction for personal exemptions provided in section 151.

(c) **Standard deduction.**—For purposes of this subtitle—

(1) **In general.**—Except as otherwise provided in this subsection, the term "standard deduction" means the sum of—

(A) the basic standard deduction, and

(B) the additional standard deduction.

(2) **Basic standard deduction.**—For purposes of paragraph (1), the basic standard deduction is—

(A) $5,000 in the case of—

(i) a joint return, or

(ii) a surviving spouse (as defined in section 2(a)),

(B) $4,400 in the case of a head of household (as defined in section 2(b)),

(C) $3,000 in the case of an individual who is not married and who is not a surviving spouse or head of household, or

(D) $2,500 in the case of a married individual filing a separate return.

(3) **Additional standard deduction for aged and blind.**—For purposes of paragraph (1), the additional standard deduction is the sum of each additional amount to which the taxpayer is entitled under subsection (f).

(4) **Adjustments for inflation.**—In the case of any taxable year beginning in a calendar year after 1988, each dollar amount contained in paragraph (2) or (5)(A) or subsection (f) shall be increased by an amount equal to—

(A) such dollar amount, multiplied by

(B) the cost-of-living adjustment determined under section 1(f)(3) for the calendar year in which the taxable year begins.

(5) **Limitation on standard deduction in the case of certain dependents.**—In the case of an individual with respect to whom a deduction under section 151 is allowable to another taxpayer for a taxable year beginning in the calendar year in which the individual's taxable year begins, the standard deduction applicable to such individual for such individual's taxable year shall not exceed the greater of—

(A) $500, or

(B) such individual's earned income.

(6) **Certain individuals, etc., not eligible for standard deduction.**—In the case of—

(A) a married individual filing a separate return where either spouse itemizes deductions,

(B) a nonresident alien individual,

(C) an individual making a return under section 443(a)(1) for a period of less than 12 months on account of a change in his annual accounting period, or

(D) an estate or trust, common trust fund, or partnership,

the standard deduction shall be zero.

(d) **Itemized deductions.**—For purposes of this subtitle, the term "itemized deductions" means the deductions allowable under this chapter other than—

(1) the deductions allowable in arriving at adjusted gross income, and

(2) the deduction for personal exemptions provided by section 151.

(e) **Election to itemize.**—

(1) **In general.**—Unless an individual makes an election under this subsection for the taxable year, no itemized deduction shall be allowed for the taxable year. For purposes of this subtitle, the determination of whether a deduction is allowable under this chapter shall be made without regard to the preceding sentence.

(2) **Time and manner of election.**—Any election under this subsection shall be made on the taxpayer's return, and the Secretary shall prescribe the manner of signifying such election on the return.

(3) **Change of election.**—Under regulations prescribed by the Secretary, a change of election with respect to itemized deductions for any taxable year may be made after the filing of the return for such year. If the spouse of the taxpayer filed a separate return for any taxable year corresponding to the taxable year of the taxpayer, the change shall not be allowed unless, in accordance with such regulations—

(A) the spouse makes a change of election with respect to itemized deductions, for the taxable year covered in such separate return, consistent with the change of treatment sought by the taxpayer, and

(B) the taxpayer and his spouse consent in writing to the assessment (within such period as may be agreed on with the Secretary) of any deficiency, to the extent attributable to such change of election, even though at the time of the filing of such consent the assessment of such deficiency would otherwise be prevented by the operation of any law or rule of law.

This paragraph shall not apply if the tax liability of the taxpayer's spouse for the taxable year corresponding to the taxable year of the taxpayer has been compromised under section 7122.

(f) **Aged or blind additional amounts.**—

(1) **Additional amounts for the aged.**—The taxpayer shall be entitled to an additional amount of $600—

(A) for himself if he has attained age 65 before the close of his taxable year, and

(B) for the spouse of the taxpayer if the spouse has attained age 65 before the close of the taxable year and an additional exemption is allowable to the taxpayer for such spouse under section 151(b).

(2) Additional amount for blind.—The taxpayer shall be entitled to an additional amount of $600—

    (A) for himself if he is blind at the close of the taxable year, and

    (B) for the spouse of the taxpayer if the spouse is blind as of the close of the taxable year and an additional exemption is allowable to the taxpayer for such spouse under section 151(b).

For purposes of subparagraph (B), if the spouse dies during the taxable year the determination of whether such spouse is blind shall be made as of the time of such death.

    (4) Blindness defined.—For purposes of this subsection, an individual is blind only if his central visual acuity does not exceed 20/200 in the better eye with correcting lenses, or if his visual acuity is greater than 20/200 but is accompanied by a limitation in the fields of vision such that the widest diameter of the visual field subtends an angle no greater than 20 degrees.

    (3) Higher amount for certain unmarried individuals.—In the case of an individual who is not married and is not a surviving spouse, paragraphs (1) and (2) shall be applied by substituting "$750" for "$600".

    (g) Marital status.—For purposes of this section, marital status shall be determined under section 7703.

    (h) Transitional rule for taxable years beginning in 1987.—In the case of any taxable year beginning in 1987, paragraph (2) of subsection (c) shall be applied—

    (1) by substituting "$3,760" for "$5,000",

    (2) by substituting "$2,540" for "$4,400",

    (3) by substituting "$2,540" for "$3,000", and

    (4) by substituting "$1,880" for "$2,500".

The preceding sentence shall not apply if the taxpayer is entitled to an additional amount determined under subsection (f) (relating to additional amount for aged and blind) for the taxable year.

§ 64. Ordinary income defined

For purposes of this subtitle, the term "ordinary income" includes any gain from the sale or exchange of property which is neither a capital asset nor property described in section 1231(b). Any gain from the sale or exchange of property which is treated or considered, under other provisions of this subtitle, as "ordinary income" shall be treated as gain from the sale or exchange of property which is neither a capital asset nor property described in section 1231(b).

§ 65. Ordinary loss defined

For purposes of this subtitle, the term "ordinary loss" includes any loss from the sale or exchange of property which is not a capital asset. Any loss from the sale or exchange of property which is treated or considered, under other provisions of this subtitle, as "ordinary loss" shall be treated as loss from the sale or exchange of property which is not a capital asset.

§ 66. Treatment of community income

(a) Treatment of community income where spouses live apart.—If—

    (1) 2 individuals are married to each other at any time during a calendar year;

(2) such individuals—

(A) live apart at all times during the calendar year, and

(B) do not file a joint return under section 6013 with each other for a taxable year beginning or ending in the calendar year;

(3) one or both of such individuals have earned income for the calendar year which is community income; and

(4) no portion of such earned income is transferred (directly or indirectly) between such individuals before the close of the calendar year,

then, for purposes of this title, any community income of such individuals for the calendar year shall be treated in accordance with the rules provided by section 879(a).

(b) Secretary may disregard community property laws where spouse not notified of community income.—The Secretary may disallow the benefits of any community property law to any taxpayer with respect to any income if such taxpayer acted as if solely entitled to such income and failed to notify the taxpayer's spouse before the due date (including extensions) for filing the return for the taxable year in which the income was derived of the nature and amount of such income.

(c) Spouse relieved of liability in certain other cases.—Under regulations prescribed by the Secretary, if—

(1) an individual does not file a joint return for any taxable year,

(2) such individual does not include in gross income for such taxable year an item of community income properly includible therein which, in accordance with the rules contained in section 879(a), would be treated as the income of the other spouse,

(3) the individual establishes that he or she did not know of, and had no reason to know of, such item of community income, and

(4) taking into account all facts and circumstances, it is inequitable to include such item of community income in such individual's gross income,

then, for purposes of this title, such item of community income shall be included in the gross income of the other spouse (and not in the gross income of the individual).

(d) Definitions.—For purposes of this section—

(1) **Earned income.**—The term "earned income" has the meaning given to such term by section 911(b).

(2) **Community income.**—The term "community income" means income which, under applicable community property laws, is treated as community income.

(3) **Community property laws.**—The term "community property laws" means the community property laws of a State, a foreign country, or a possession of the United States.

§ 67.　2–Percent floor on miscellaneous itemized deductions

(a) General Rule.—In the case of an individual, the miscellaneous itemized deductions for any taxable year shall be allowed only to the extent that the aggregate of such deductions exceeds 2 percent of adjusted gross income.

(b) Miscellaneous itemized deductions.—For purposes of this section, the term "miscellaneous itemized deductions" means the itemized deductions other than—

(1) the deduction under section 163 (relating to interest),

(2) the deduction under section 164 (relating to taxes),

(3) the deduction under section 165(a) for losses described in subsection (c)(3) or (d) of section 165,

(4) the deduction under section 170 (relating to charitable, etc., contributions and gifts),

(5) the deduction under section 213 (relating to medical, dental, etc., expenses),

(6) the deduction under section 217 (relating to moving expenses),

(7) any deduction allowable for impairment-related work expenses,

(8) the deduction under section 691(c) (relating to deduction for estate tax in case of income in respect of the decedent),

(9) any deduction allowable in connection with personal property used in a short sale,

(10) the deduction under section 1341 (relating to computation of tax where taxpayer restores substantial amount held under claim of right),

(11) the deduction under section 72(b)(3) (relating to deduction where annuity payments cease before investment recovered),

(12) the deduction under section 171 (relating to deduction for amortizable bond premium), and

(13) the deduction under section 216 (relating to deductions in connection with cooperative housing corporations).

(c) **Disallowance of indirect deduction through pass-thru entity.**—The Secretary shall prescribe regulations which prohibit the indirect deduction through pass-thru entities of amounts which are not allowable as a deduction if paid or incurred directly by an individual and which contain such reporting requirements as may be necessary to carry out the purposes of this subsection. The preceding sentence shall not apply with respect to estates, trusts, cooperatives, and real estate investment trusts.

(d) **Impairment-related work expenses.**—For purposes of this section, the term "impairment-related work expenses" means expenses—

(1) of a handicapped individual (as defined in section 190(b)(3)) for attendant care services at the individual's place of employment and other expenses in connection with such place of employment which are necessary for such individual to be able to work, and

(2) with respect to which a deduction is allowable under section 162 (determined without regard to this section).

(e) **Determination of adjusted gross income in case of estates and trusts.** —For purposes of this section, the adjusted gross income of an estate or trust shall be computed in the same manner as in the case of an individual, except that the deductions for costs which are paid or incurred in connection with the administration of the estate or trust and would not have been incurred if the property were not held in such trust or estate shall be treated as allowable in arriving at adjusted gross income.

(Added Pub.L. 99–514, Title I, § 132(a), Oct. 22, 1986, 100 Stat. ——.)

PART II—ITEMS SPECIFICALLY INCLUDED IN GROSS INCOME

§ 71. Alimony and separate maintenance payments

(a) General rule.—Gross income includes amounts received as alimony or separate maintenance payments.

(b) Alimony or separate maintenance payments defined.—For purposes of this section—

(1) In general.—The term "alimony or separate maintenance payment" means any payment in cash if—

(A) such payment is received by (or on behalf of) a spouse under a divorce or separation instrument,

(B) the divorce or separation instrument does not designate such payment as a payment which is not includible in gross income under this section and not allowable as a deduction under section 215,

(C) in the case of an individual legally separated from his spouse under a decree of divorce or of separate maintenance, the payee spouse and the payor spouse are not members of the same household at the time such payment is made, and

(D) there is no liability to make any such payment for any period after the death of the payee spouse and there is no liability to make any payment (in cash or property) as a substitute for such payments after the death of the payee spouse.

(2) Divorce or separation instrument.—The term "divorce or separation instrument" means—

(A) a decree of divorce or separate maintenance or a written instrument incident to such a decree,

(B) a written separation agreement, or

(C) a decree (not described in subparagraph (A)) requiring a spouse to make payments for the support or maintenance of the other spouse.

(c) Payments to support children.—

(1) In general.—Subsection (a) shall not apply to that part of any payment which the terms of the divorce or separation instrument fix (in terms of an amount of money or a part of the payment) as a sum which is payable for the support of children of the payor spouse.

(2) Treatment of certain reductions related to contingencies involving child.—For purposes of paragraph (1), if any amount specified in the instrument will be reduced—

(A) on the happening of a contingency specified in the instrument relating to a child (such as attaining a specified age, marrying, dying, leaving school, or a similar contingency), or

(B) at a time which can clearly be associated with a contingency of a kind specified in subparagraph (A),

an amount equal to the amount of such reduction will be treated as an amount fixed as payable for the support of children of the payor spouse.

(3) Special rule where payment is less than amount specified in instrument.—For purposes of this subsection, if any payment is less than the amount specified in the instrument, then so much of such payment as does not exceed the sum payable for support shall be considered a payment for such support.

(d) Spouse.—For purposes of this section, the term "spouse" includes a former spouse.

(e) Exception for joint returns.—This section and section 215 shall not apply if the spouses make a joint return with each other.

(f) Recomputation where excess front-loading of alimony payments—

(1) In general.—If there are excess alimony payments—

(A) the payor spouse shall include the amount of such excess payments in gross income for the payor spouse's taxable year beginning in the 3rd post-separation year, and

(B) the payee spouse shall be allowed a deduction in computing adjusted gross income for the amount of such excess payments for the payee's taxable year beginning in the 3rd post-separation year.

(2) Excess alimony payments.—For purposes of this subsection, the term "excess alimony payments" mean the sum of—

(A) the excess payments for the 1st post-separation year, and

(B) the excess payments for the 2nd post-separation year.

(3) Excess payments for 1st post-separation year.—For purposes of this subsection, the amount of the excess payments for the 1st post-separation year is the excess (if any) of—

(A) the amount of the alimony or separate maintenance payments paid by the payor spouse during the 1st post-separation year, over

(B) the sum of—

(i) the average of—

(I) the alimony or separate maintenance payments paid by the payor spouse during the 2nd post-separation year, reduced by the excess payments for the 2nd post-separation year, and

(II) the alimony or separate maintenance payments paid by the payor spouse during the 3rd post-separation year, plus

(ii) $15,000.

(4) Excess payments for 2nd post-separation year.—For purposes of this subsection, the amount of the excess payments for the 2nd post-separation year is the excess (if any) of—

(A) the amount of the alimony or separate maintenance payments paid by the payor spouse during the 2nd post-separation year, over

(B) the sum of—

(i) the amount of the alimony or separate maintenance payments paid by the payor spouse during the 3rd post-separation year, plus

(ii) $15,000.

(5) Exceptions.—

(A) Where payment ceases by reason of death or remarriage.—Paragraph (1) shall not apply if—

(i) either spouse dies before the close of the 3rd post-separation year, or the payee spouse remarries before the close of the 3rd post-separation year, and

(ii) the alimony or separate maintenance payments cease by reason of such death or remarriage.

(B) Support payments.—For purposes of this subsection, the term "alimony or separate maintenance payment" shall not include any payment received under a decree described in subsection (b)(2)(C).

(C) Fluctuating payments not within control of payor spouse.—For purposes of this subsection, the term "alimony or separate maintenance payment" shall not include any payment to the extent it is made pursuant to a continuing liability (over a period of not less than 3 years) to pay a fixed portion or portions of the income from a business or property or from compensation for employment or self-employment.

(6) Post-separation years.—For purposes of this subsection, the term "1st post-separation years" means the 1st calendar year in which the payor spouse paid to the payee spouse alimony or separate maintenance payments to which this section applies. The 2nd and 3rd post-separation years shall be the 1st and 2nd succeeding calendar years, respectively.

(g) Cross references.—

(1) For deduction of alimony or separate maintenance payments, see section 215.

(2) For taxable status of income of an estate or trust in the case of divorce, etc., see section 682.

§ 72.   Annuities; certain proceeds of endowment and life insurance contracts

(a) General rule for annuities.—Except as otherwise provided in this chapter, gross income includes any amount received as an annuity (whether for a period certain or during one or more lives) under an annuity, endowment, or life insurance contract.

(b) Exclusion ratio.—

(1) In general.—Gross income does not include that part of any amount received as an annuity under an annuity, endowment, or life insurance contract which bears the same ratio to such amount as the investment in the contract (as of the annuity starting date) bears to the expected return under the contract (as of such date).

(2) Exclusion limited to investment.—The portion of any amount received as an annuity which is excluded from gross income under paragraph (1) shall not exceed the unrecovered investment in the contract immediately before the receipt of such amount.

(3) Deduction where annuity payments cease before entire investment recovered.—

(A) In general.—If—

(i) after the annuity starting date, payments as an annuity under the contract cease by reason of the death of an annuitant, and

(ii) as of the date of such cessation, there is unrecovered investment in the contract,

the amount of such unrecovered investment (in excess of any amount specified in subsection (e)(5) which was not included in gross income) shall be allowed as a deduction to the annuitant for his last taxable year.

(B) Payments to other persons.—In the case of any contract which provides for payments meeting the requirements of subparagraphs (B) and (C) of subsection (c)(2), the deduction under subparagraph (A) shall be allowed to the person entitled to such payments for the taxable year in which such payments are received.

(C) Net operating loss deductions provided.—For purposes of section 172, a deduction allowed under this paragraph shall be treated as if it were attributable to a trade or business of the taxpayer.

(4) Unrecovered investment.—For purposes of this subsection, the unrecovered investment in the contract as of any date is—

(A) the investment in the contract as of the annuity starting date, reduced by

(B) the aggregate amount received under the contract on or after such annuity starting date and before the date as of which the determination is being made, to the extent such amount was excludable from gross income under this subtitle.

(c) Definitions.—

(1) Investment in the contract.—For purposes of subsection (b), the investment in the contract as of the annuity starting date is—

(A) the aggregate amount of premiums or other consideration paid for the contract, minus

(B) the aggregate amount received under the contract before such date, to the extent that such amount was excludable from gross income under this subtitle or prior income tax laws.

(2) Adjustment in investment where there is refund feature.—If—

(A) the expected return under the contract depends in whole or in part on the life expectancy of one or more individuals;

(B) the contract provides for payments to be made to a beneficiary (or to the estate of an annuitant) on or after the death of the annuitant or annuitants; and

(C) such payments are in the nature of a refund of the consideration paid,

then the value (computed without discount for interest) of such payments on the annuity starting date shall be subtracted from the amount determined under paragraph (1). Such value shall be computed in accordance with actuarial tables prescribed by the Secretary. For purposes of this paragraph and of subsection (e)(2)(A), the term "refund of the consideration paid" includes amounts payable after the death of an annuitant by reason of a provision in the contract for a life annuity with minimum period of payments certain, but (if part of the consideration was contributed by an employer) does not include that part of any payment to a beneficiary (or to the estate of the annuitant) which is not attributable to the consideration paid by the employee for the contract as determined under paragraph (1)(A).

(3) Expected return.—For purposes of subsection (b), the expected return under the contract shall be determined as follows:

(A) Life expectancy.—If the expected return under the contract, for the period on and after the annuity starting date, depends in whole or in part on the life expectancy of one or more individuals, the expected return shall be computed with reference to actuarial tables prescribed by the Secretary.

(B) Installment payments.—If subparagraph (A) does not apply, the expected return is the aggregate of the amounts receivable under the contract as an annuity.

(4) Annuity starting date.—For purposes of this section, the annuity starting date in the case of any contract is the first day of the first period for which an amount is received as an annuity under the contract; except that if such date was before January 1, 1954, then the annuity starting date is January 1, 1954.

[(d) Employees' annuities.—Repealed.]

(e) Amounts not received as annuities.—

   (1) Application of subsection.—

      (A) In general.—This subsection shall apply to any amount which—

         (i) is received under an annuity, endowment, or life insurance contract, and

         (ii) is not received as an annuity,

if no provision of this subtitle (other than this subsection) applies with respect to such amount.

      (B) Dividends.—For purposes of this section, any amount received which is in the nature of a dividend or similar distribution shall be treated as an amount not received as an annuity.

   (2) General rule.—Any amount to which this subsection applies—

      (A) if received on or after the annuity starting date, shall be included in gross income, or

      (B) if received before the annuity starting date—

         (i) shall be included in gross income to the extent allocable to income on the contract, and

         (ii) shall not be included in gross income to the extent allocable to the investment in the contract.

   (3) Allocation of amounts to income and investment.—For purposes of paragraph (2)(B)—

      (A) Allocation to income.—Any amount to which this subsection applies shall be treated as allocable to income on the contract to the extent that such amount does not exceed the excess (if any) of—

         (i) the cash value of the contract (determined without regard to any surrender charge) immediately before the amount is received, over

         (ii) the investment in the contract at such time.

      (B) Allocation to investment.—Any amount to which this subsection applies shall be treated as allocable to investment in the contract to the extent that such amount is not allocated to income under subparagraph (A).

   (4) Special rules for application of paragraph (2)(B).—For purposes of paragraph (2)(B)—

      (A) Loans treated as distributions.—If, during any taxable year, an individual—

         (i) receives (directly or indirectly) any amount as a loan under any contract to which this subsection applies, or

         (ii) assigns or pledges (or agrees to assign or pledge) any portion of the value of any such contract,

such amount or portion shall be treated as received under the contract as an amount not received as an annuity.

(B) Treatment of policyholder dividends.—Any amount described in paragraph (1)(B) shall not be included in gross income under paragraph (2)(B)(i) to the extent such amount is retained by the insurer as a premium or other consideration paid for the contract.

(C) Certain life insurance and endowment contracts.—Except to the extent prescribed by the Secretary by regulations, this paragraph shall apply to any amount not received as an annuity which is received under a life insurance or endowment contract.

(5) Retention of existing rules in certain cases.—

(A) In general.—In any case to which this paragraph applies—

(i) paragraphs (2)(B) and (4)(A) shall not apply, and

(ii) if paragraph (2)(A) does not apply,

the amount shall be included in gross income, but only to the extent it exceeds the investment in the contract.

(B) Existing contracts.—This paragraph shall apply to contracts entered into before August 14, 1982. Any amount allocable to investment in the contract after August 13, 1982, shall be treated as from a contract entered into after such date.

(C) Certain life insurance and endowment contracts.—Except to the extent prescribed by the Secretary by regulations, this paragraph shall apply to any amount not received as an annuity which is received under a life insurance or endowment contract.

(D) Contracts under qualified plans.—Except as provided in paragraphs (7) and (8), this paragraph shall apply to any amount received—

(i) from a trust described in section 401(a) which is exempt from tax under section 501(a),

(ii) from a contract—

(I) purchased by a trust described in clause (i),

(II) purchased as part of a plan described in section 403(a),

(III) described in section 403(b), or

(IV) provided for employees of a life insurance company under a plan described in section 818(a)(3), or

(iii) from an individual retirement account or an individual retirement annuity.

Any dividend described in section 404(k) which is received by a participant or beneficiary shall, for purposes of this subparagraph, be treated as paid under a separate contract to which clause (ii)(I) applies.

(E) Full refunds, surrenders, redemptions, and maturities.—This paragraph shall apply to—

(i) any amount received, whether in a single sum or otherwise, under a contract in full discharge of the obligation under the contract which is in the nature of a refund of the consideration paid for the contract, and

(ii) any amount received under a contract on its complete surrender, redemption, or maturity.

In the case of any amount to which the preceding sentence applies, the rule of paragraph (2)(A) shall not apply.

(6) Investment in the contract.—For purposes of this subsection, the investment in the contract as of any date is—

(A) the aggregate amount of premiums or other consideration paid for the contract before such date, minus

(B) the aggregate amount received under the contract before such date, to the extent that such amount was excludable from gross income under this subtitle or prior income tax laws.

(7) Special rules for plans where substantially all contributions are employee contributions.—

(A) In general.—In the case of any plan or contract to which this paragraph applies, subparagraph (D) of paragraph (5) shall not apply to any amount received from such plan or contract.

(B) Plans or contracts to which this paragraph applies.—This paragraph shall apply to any plan or contract—

(i) which is described in clause (i) or subclause (I), (II), or (III) of clause (ii) of paragraph (5)(D), and

(ii) with respect to which 85 percent or more of the total contributions during a representative period are derived from employee contributions.

For purposes of clause (ii), deductible employee contributions (as defined in subsection (o)(5)(A)) shall not be taken into account.

(C) Special rule for certain federal plans.—If the Federal Government or an instrumentality thereof maintains more than 1 plan, subparagraph (B) shall be applied by aggregating all such plans which are actively administered by the Federal Government or such instrumentality.

* * *

(f) Special rules for computing employees' contributions.—In computing, for purposes of subsection (c) (1) (A), the aggregate amount of premiums or other consideration paid for the contract, for purposes of subsections (d)(1) and (e)(7), the consideration for the contract contributed by the employee, and for purposes of subsection (e)(6) the aggregate premiums or other consideration paid, amounts contributed by the employer shall be included, but only to the extent that—

(1) such amounts were includible in the gross income of the employee under this subtitle or prior income tax laws; or

(2) if such amounts had been paid directly to the employee at the time they were contributed, they would not have been includible in the gross income of the employee under the law applicable at the time of such contribution.

Paragraph (2) shall not apply to amounts which were contributed by the employer after December 31, 1962, and which would not have been includible in the gross income of the employee by reason of the application of section 911 if such amounts had been paid directly to the employee at the time of contribution. The preceding sentence shall not apply to amounts which were contributed by the employer, as determined under regulations prescribed by the Secretary, to provide pension or annuity credits, to the extent such credits are attributable to services performed before January 1, 1963, and are provided pursuant to pension or annuity plan provisions in existence on March 12, 1962, and on that date applicable to such services.

(g) Rules for transferee where transfer was for value.—Where any contract (or any interest therein) is transferred (by assignment or otherwise) for a valuable consideration, to the extent that the contract (or interest therein) does not, in the hands of the transferee, have a basis which is determined by reference to the basis in the hands of the transferor, then—

(1) for purposes of this section, only the actual value of such consideration, plus the amount of the premiums and other consideration paid by the transferee after the transfer, shall be taken into account in computing the aggregate amount of the premiums or other consideration paid for the contract;

(2) for purposes of subsection (c) (1) (B), there shall be taken into account only the aggregate amount received under the contract by the transferee before the annuity starting date, to the extent that such amount was excludable from gross income under this subtitle or prior income tax laws; and

(3) the annuity starting date is January 1, 1954, or the first day of the first period for which the transferee received an amount under the contract as an annuity, whichever is the later.

For purposes of this subsection, the term "transferee" includes a beneficiary of, or the estate of, the transferee.

(h) Option to receive annuity in lieu of lump sum.—If—

(1) a contract provides for payment of a lump sum in full discharge of an obligation under the contract, subject to an option to receive an annuity in lieu of such lump sum;

(2) the option is exercised within 60 days after the day on which such lump sum first became payable; and

(3) part or all of such lump sum would (but for this subsection) be includible in gross income by reason of subsection (e) (1),

then, for purposes of this subtitle, no part of such lump sum shall be considered as includible in gross income at the time such lump sum first became payable.

[(i) Repealed.]

(j) Interest.—Notwithstanding any other provision of this section, if any amount is held under an agreement to pay interest thereon, the interest payments shall be included in gross income.

[(k) Repealed.]

* * *

(m) Special rules applicable to employee annuities and distributions under employee plans.—

[(1) Repealed.]

(2) Computation of consideration paid by the employee.—In computing—

(A) the aggregate amount of premiums or other consideration paid for the contract for purposes of subsection (c) (1) (A) (relating to the investment in the contract),

(B) the consideration for the contract contributed by the employee for purposes of subsection (d) (1) (relating to employee's contributions recoverable in 3 years) and subsection (e)(7) (relating to plans where substantially all contributions are employee contributions), and

(C) the aggregate premiums or other consideration paid for purposes of subsection (e)(6) (relating to certain amounts not received as an annuity),

any amount allowed as a deduction with respect to the contract under section 404 which was paid while the employee was an employee within the meaning of section 401(c) (1) shall be treated as consideration contributed by the employer, and there

69

shall not be taken into account any portion of the premiums or other consideration for the contract paid while the employee was an owner-employee which is properly allocable (as determined under regulations prescribed by the Secretary) to the cost of life, accident, health, or other insurance.

(3) Life insurance contracts.—

(A) This paragraph shall apply to any life insurance contract—

(i) purchased as a part of a plan described in section 403(a), or

(ii) purchased by a trust described in section 401(a) which is exempt from tax under section 501(a) if the proceeds of such contract are payable directly or indirectly to a participant in such trust or to a beneficiary of such participant.

(B) Any contribution to a plan described in subparagraph (A) (i) or a trust described in subparagraph (A) (ii) which is allowed as a deduction under section 404, and any income of a trust described in subparagraph (A) (ii), which is determined in accordance with regulations prescribed by the Secretary to have been applied to purchase the life insurance protection under a contract described in subparagraph (A), is includible in the gross income of the participant for the taxable year when so applied.

(C) In the case of the death of an individual insured under a contract described in subparagraph (A), an amount equal to the cash surrender value of the contract immediately before the death of the insured shall be treated as a payment under such plan or a distribution by such trust, and the excess of the amount payable by reason of the death of the insured over such cash surrender value shall not be includible in gross income under this section and shall be treated as provided in section 101.

[(4) Repealed.]

(5) Penalties applicable to certain amounts received by 5-percent owners.—

(A) This paragraph applies to amounts which are received from a qualified trust described in section 401(a) or under a plan described in section 403(a) at any time by an individual who is, or has been, a 5-percent owner, or by a successor of such an individual, but only to the extent such amounts are determined, under regulations prescribed by the Secretary, to exceed the benefits provided for such individual under the plan formula.

(B) If a person receives an amount to which this paragraph applies, his tax under this chapter for the taxable year in which such amount is received shall be increased by an amount equal to 10 percent of the portion of the amount so received which is includible in his gross income for such taxable year.

(C) For purposes of this paragraph, the term "5-percent owner" means any individual who, at any time during the 5 plan years preceding the plan year ending in the taxable year in which the amount is received, is a 5-percent owner (as defined in section 416(i)(1)(B)).

(6) Owner-employee defined.—For purposes of this subsection, the term "owner-employee" has the meaning assigned to it by section 401(c) (3) and includes an individual for whose benefit an individual retirement account or annuity described in section 408(a) or (b) is maintained. For purposes of the preceding sentence, the term "owner-employee" shall include an employee within the meaning of section 401(c)(1).

(7) Meaning of disabled.—For purposes of this section, an individual shall be considered to be disabled if he is unable to engage in any substantial gainful activity by reason of any medically determinable physical or mental impairment which can be expected to result in death or to be of long-continued and indefinite duration. An individual shall not be considered to be disabled unless he furnishes proof of the existence thereof in such form and manner as the Secretary may require.

[(8) Repealed.]

[(9) Repealed.]

(10) Determination of investment in the contract in the case of qualified domestic relations orders.—Under regulations prescribed by the Secretary, in the case of a distribution or payment made to an alternative payee who is the spouse or former spouse of a participant pursuant to a qualified domestic relations order (as defined in section 414(p)), the investment in the contract as of the date prescribed in such regulations shall be allocated on a pro rata basis between the present value of such distribution or payment and the present value of all other benefits payable with respect to the participant to which such order relates.

* * *

(o) Special rules for distributions from qualified plans to which employee made deductible contributions.—

(1) Treatment of contributions.—For purposes of this section and sections 402 and 403, notwithstanding section 414(h), any deductible employee contribution made to a qualified employer plan or government plan shall be treated as an amount contributed by the employer which is not includible in the gross income of the employee.

(2) Additional tax if amount received before age 59½.—If—

(A) any accumulated deductible employee contributions are received from a qualified employer plan or government plan,

(B) such amount is received by the employee before the employee attains the age of 59½, and

(C) such amount is not attributable to such employee's becoming disabled (within the meaning of subsection (m)(7)),

then the employee's tax under this chapter for the taxable year in which such amount is received shall be increased by an amount equal to 10 percent of the amount so received to the extent that such amount is includible in gross income. For purposes of this title, any tax imposed by this paragraph shall be treated as a tax imposed by subsection (m)(5)(B).

(3) Amounts constructively received.—

(A) In general.—For purposes of this subsection, rules similar to the rules provided by subsection (p) (other than the exception contained in paragraph (2) thereof) shall apply.

(B) Purchase of life insurance.—To the extent any amount of accumulated deductible employee contributions of an employee are applied to the purchase of life insurance contracts, such amount shall be treated as distributed to the employee in the year so applied.

(4) Special rule for treatment of rollover amounts.—For purposes of sections 402(a)(5), 402(a)(7), 403(a)(4), and 408(d)(3), the Secretary shall prescribe regulations providing for such allocations of amounts attributable to accumulated deductible employee contributions, and for such other rules, as may be necessary to insure that such accumulated deductible employee contributions do not become eligible for additional tax benefits (or freed from limitations) through the use of rollovers.

(5) Definitions and special rules.—For purposes of this subsection—

(A) Deductible employee contributions.—The term "deductible employee contributions" means any qualified voluntary employee contribution (as defined in section 219(e)(2)) made after December 31, 1981, in a taxable year beginning after such date and made for a taxable year beginning before January 1, 1987, and allowable as a deduction under section 219(a) for such taxable year.

(B) Accumulated deductible employee contributions.—The term "accumulated deductible employee contributions" means the deductible employee contributions—

(i) increased by the amount of income and gain allocable to such contributions, and

(ii) reduced by the sum of the amount of loss and expense allocable to such contributions and the amounts distributed with respect to the employee which are attributable to such contributions (or income or gain allocable to such contributions).

(C) Qualified employer plan.—The term "qualified employer plan" has the meaning given to such term by subsection (p)(3)(A)(i).

(D) Government plan.—The term "government plan" has the meaning given such term by subsection (p)(3)(B).

(6) Ordering rules.—Unless the plan specifies otherwise, any distribution from such plan shall not be treated as being made from the accumulated deductible employee contributions until all other amounts to the credit of the employee have been distributed.

(p) Loans treated as distributions.—For purposes of this section—

(1) Treatment as distributions.—

(A) Loans.—If during any taxable year a participant or beneficiary receives (directly or indirectly) any amount as a loan from a qualified employer plan, such amount shall be treated as having been received by such individual as a distribution under such plan.

(B) Assignments or pledges.—If during any taxable year a participant or beneficiary assigns (or agrees to assign) or pledges (or agrees to pledge) any portion of his interest in a qualified employer plan, such portion shall be treated as having been received by such individual as a loan from such plan.

(2) Exception for certain loans.—

(A) General rule.—Paragraph (1) shall not apply to any loan to the extent that such loan (when added to the outstanding balance of all other loans from such plan whether made on, before, or after August 13, 1982), does not exceed the lesser of—

(i) $50,000, reduced by the excess (if any) of—

(I) the highest outstanding balance of loans from the plan during the 1–year period ending on the day before the date on which such loan was made, over

(II) the outstanding balance of loans from the plan on the date on which such loan was made, or

(ii) the greater of (I) one-half of the present value of the nonforfeitable accrued benefit of the employee under the plan, or (II) $10,000.

For purposes of clause (ii), the present value of the nonforfeitable accrued benefit shall be determined without regard to any accumulated deductible employee contributions (as defined in subsection (o)(5)(B)).

(B) Requirement that loan be repayable within 5 years.—

(i) In general.—Subparagraph (A) shall not apply to any loan unless such loan, by its terms, is required to be repaid within 5 years.

(ii) Exception for home loans.—Clause (i) shall not apply to any loan used to acquire any dwelling unit which within a reasonable time is to be used (determined at the time the loan is made) as the principal residence of the participant.

(C) Requirement of level amortization.—Except as provided in regulations, this paragraph shall not apply to any loan unless substantially level amortization of such loan (with payments not less frequently than quarterly) is required over the term of the loan.

(D) Related employers and related plans.—For purposes of this paragraph—

(i) the rules of subsections (b), (c), and (m) of section 414 shall apply, and

(ii) all plans of an employer (determined after the application of such subsections) shall be treated as 1 plan.

(3) Denial of interest deductions in certain cases.—

(A) In general.—No deduction otherwise allowable under this chapter shall be allowed under this chapter for any interest paid or accrued on any loan described in subparagraph (B).

(B) Loans to which subparagraph (A) applies.—

For purposes of subparagraph (A), a loan is described in this subparagraph—

(i) if paragraph (1) does not apply to such loan by reason of paragraph (2), and

(ii) if—

(I) such loan is made to a key employee (as defined in section 416(i)), or

(II) such loan is secured by amounts attributable to elective 401(k) or 403(b) deferrals (as defined in section 402(g)(3)).

(4) Qualified employer plan, etc.—For purposes of this subsection—

(A) Qualified employer plan.—

(i) In general.—The term "qualified employer plan" means—

(I) a plan described in section 401(a) which includes a trust exempt from tax under section 501(a),

(II) an annuity plan described in section 403(a), and

(III) a plan under which amounts are contributed by an individual's employer for an annuity contract described in section 403(b).

(ii) Special rules.—The term "qualified employer plan"—

(I) shall include any plan which was (or was determined to be) a qualified employer plan or a government plan, but

(II) shall not include a plan described in subsection (e)(7).

(B) Government plan.—The term "government plan" means any plan, whether or not qualified, established and maintained for its employees by the

United States, by a State or political subdivision thereof, or by an agency or instrumentality of any of the foregoing.

(5) Special rules for loans, etc., from certain contracts.—For purposes of this subsection, any amount received as a loan under a contract purchased under a qualified employer plan (and any assignment or pledge with respect to such a contract) shall be treated as a loan under such employer plan.

(q) 10-percent penalty for premature distributions from annuity contracts.—

(1) Imposition of penalty.—If any taxpayer receives any amount under an annuity contract, the taxpayer's tax under this chapter for the taxable year in which such amount is received shall be increased by an amount equal to 10 percent of the portion of such amount which is includible in gross income.

(2) Subsection not to apply to certain distributions.—Paragraph (1) shall not apply to any distribution—

(A) made on or after the date on which the taxpayer attains age 59½,

(B) made to a beneficiary (or to the estate of an annuitant) on or after the death of an annuitant,

(C) attributable to the taxpayer's becoming disabled within the meaning of subsection (m)(7),

(D) which is a part of a series of substantially equal periodic payments (not less frequently than annually) made for the life (or life expectancy) of the taxpayer or the joint lives (or joint life expectancies) of such taxpayer and his beneficiary.

(E) from a plan, contract, account, trust, or annuity described in subsection (e)(5)(D) (determined without regard to subsection (e)(7)),

(F) allocable to investment in the contract before August 14, 1982, or

(G) under a qualified funding asset (within the meaning of section 130(d), but without regard to whether there is a qualified assignment).

(I)[1] under an immediate annuity contract (within the meaning of section 72(u)(4)), or

(J)[2] which is purchased by an employer upon the termination of a plan described in section 401(a) or 403(a) and which is held by the employer until such time as the employee separates from service.

(3) Change in substantially equal payments.—If—

(A) paragraph (1) does not apply to a distribution by reason of paragraph (2)(D), and

(B) the series of payments under such paragraph are subsequently modified (other than by reason of death or disability)—

(i) before the close of the 5–year period beginning on the date of the first payment and after the employee attains age 59½, or

(ii) before the employee attains age 59½,

the taxpayer's tax for the 1st taxable year in which such modification occurs shall be increased by an amount, determined under regulations, equal to the tax which (but for paragraph (2)(D)) would have been imposed, plus interest for the deferral period (within the meaning of subsection (t)(4)(B)).

* * *

[1] Editor's note: Probably should read "(H)".

[2] Editor's note: Probably should read "(I)".

(s) Required distributions where holder dies before entire interest is distributed.—

(1) In general.—A contract shall not be treated as an annuity contract for purposes of this title unless it provides that—

(A) if the holder of such contract dies on or after the annuity starting date and before the entire interest in such contract has been distributed, the remaining portion of such interest will be distributed at least as rapidly as under the method of distributions being used as of the date of his death, and

(B) if the holder of such contract dies before the annuity starting date, the entire interest in such contract will be distributed within 5 years after the death of such holder.

(2) Exception for certain amounts payable over life of beneficiary.—If—

(A) any portion of the holder's interest is payable to (or for the benefit of) a designated beneficiary,

(B) such portion will be distributed (in accordance with regulations) over the life of such designated beneficiary (or over a period not extending beyond the life expectancy of such beneficiary), and

(C) such distributions begin not later than 1 year after the date of the holder's death or such later date as the Secretary may by regulations prescribe,

then for purposes of paragraph (1), the portion referred to in subparagraph (A) shall be treated as distributed on the day on which such distributions begin.

(3) Special rule where surviving spouse beneficiary.—If the designated beneficiary referred to in paragraph (2)(A) is the surviving spouse of the holder of the contract, paragraphs (1) and (2) shall be applied by treating such spouse as the holder of such contract.

(4) Designated beneficiary.—For purposes of this subsection, the term "designated beneficiary" means any individual designated a beneficiary by the holder of the contract.

(5) Exception for annuity contracts which are part of qualified plans. —This subsection shall not apply to any annuity contract—

(A) which is provided—

(i) under a plan described in section 401(a) which includes a trust exempt from tax under section 501, or

(ii) under a plan described in section 403(a),

(B) which is described in section 403(b), or

(C) which is an individual retirement annuity or provided under an individual retirement account or annuity.

(6) Special rule where holder is corporation or other non-individual.—

(A) In general.—For purposes of this subsection, if the holder of the contract is not an individual, the primary annuitant shall be treated as the holder of the contract.

(B) Primary annuitant.—For purposes of subparagraph (A), the term "primary annuitant" means the individual, the events in the life of whom are of primary importance in affecting the timing or amount of the payout under the contract.

(7) Treatment of changes in primary annuitant where holder of contract is not an individual.—For purposes of this subsection, in the case of a holder of an annuity contract which is not an individual, if there is a change in a primary annuity (as defined in paragraph (6)(B)), such change shall be treated as the death of the holder.

Amendment of Subsec. (s)(1)

Pub.L. 99–514, Title XVIII, § 1826(b)(2), (4), Oct. 22, 1986, 100 Stat. ——, provided that, applicable to contracts issued after the date which is 6 months after Oct. 22, 1986, in taxable years ending after such date, subsec. (s)(1) of this section is amended by striking out "the holder of such contract" each place it appears and inserting in lieu thereof "any holder of such contract".

(t) 10–percent additional tax on early distributions from qualified retirement plans.—

(1) Imposition of additional tax.—If any taxpayer receives any amount from a qualified retirement plan (as defined in section 4974(c)), the taxpayer's tax under this chapter for the taxable year in which such amount is received shall be increased by an amount equal to 10 percent of the portion of such amount which is includible in gross income.

(2) Subsection not to apply to certain distributions.—Except as provided in paragraphs (3) and (4), paragraph (1) shall not apply to any of the following distributions:

(A) In general.—Distributions which are—

(i) made on or after the date on which the employee attains age 59½,

(ii) made to a beneficiary (or to the estate of the employee) on or after the death of the employee,

(iii) attributable to the employee's being disabled within the meaning of subsection (m)(7),

(iv) part of a series of substantially equal periodic payments (not less frequently than annually) made for the life (or life expectancy) of the employee or the joint lives (or joint life expectancies) of such employee and his beneficiary,

(v) made to an employee after separation from service on account of early retirement under the plan after attainment of age 55, or

(vi) dividends paid with respect to stock of a corporation which are described in section 404(k).

(B) Medical expenses.—Distributions made to the employee (other than distributions described in subparagraph (A) or (C)) to the extent such distributions do not exceed the amount allowable as a deduction under section 213 to the employee for amounts paid during the taxable year for medical care (determined without regard to whether the employee itemizes deductions for such taxable year).

(C) Certain plans.—

(i) In general.—Except as provided in clause (ii), any distribution made before January 1, 1990, to an employee from an employee stock ownership plan defined in section 4975(e)(7) to the extent that, on average, a majority of assets in the plan have been invested in employer securities (as defined in section 409(*l*)) for the 5–plan-year period preceding the plan year in which the distribution is made.

(ii) Benefits distributed must be invested in employer securities for 5 years.—Clause (i) shall not apply to any distribution which is attributable to assets which have not been invested in employer securities at all times during the period referred to in clause (i).

(D) Payments to alternate payees pursuant to qualified domestic relations orders.—Any distribution to an alternate payee pursuant to a qualified domestic relations order (within the meaning of section 414(p)(1)).

(3) Limitations.—

(A) Certain exceptions not to apply to individual retirement plans.—Subparagraphs (A)(v), (B), and (C) of paragraph (2) shall not apply to distributions from an individual retirement plan.

(B) Periodic payments under qualified plans must begin after separation.—Paragraph (2)(A)(iv) shall not apply to any amount paid from a trust described in section 401(a) which is exempt from tax under section 501(a) or from a contract described in section 72(e)(5)(D)(ii) unless the series of payments begins after the employee separates from service.

(4) Change in substantially equal payments.—

(A) In general.—If—

(i) paragraph (1) does not apply to a distribution by reason of paragraph (2)(A)(iv), and

(ii) the series of payments under such paragraph are subsequently modified (other than by reason of death or disability)—

(I) before the close of the 5–year period beginning with the date of the first payment and after the employee attains age 59½, or

(II) before the employee attains age 59½, the taxpayer's tax for the 1st taxable year in which such modification occurs shall be increased by an amount, determined under regulations, equal to the tax which (but for paragraph (2)(A)(iv)) would have been imposed, plus interest for the deferral period.

(B) Deferral period.—For purposes of this paragraph, the term 'deferral period' means the period beginning with the taxable year in which (without regard to paragraph (2)(A)(iv)) the distribution would have been includible in gross income and ending with the taxable year in which the modification described in subparagraph (A) occurs.

(5) Employee.—For purposes of this subsection, the term "employee" includes any participant, and in the case of an individual retirement plan, the individual for whose benefit such plan was established.

§ 73. Services of child

(a) Treatment of amounts received.—Amounts received in respect of the services of a child shall be included in his gross income and not in the gross income of the parent, even though such amounts are not received by the child.

(b) Treatment of expenditures.—All expenditures by the parent or the child attributable to amounts which are includible in the gross income of the child (and not of the parent) solely by reason of subsection (a) shall be treated as paid or incurred by the child.

(c) Parent defined.—For purposes of this section, the term "parent" includes an individual who is entitled to the services of a child by reason of having parental rights and duties in respect of the child.

(d) Cross reference.—

For assessment of tax against parent in certain cases, see section 6201(c).

§ 74.   Prizes and awards

(a) General rule.—Except as otherwise provided in this section or in section 117 (relating to qualified scholarships), gross income includes amounts received as prizes and awards.

(b) Exception for certain prizes and awards transferred to charities.—Gross income does not include amounts received as prizes and awards made primarily in recognition of religious, charitable, scientific, educational, artistic, literary, or civic achievement, but only if—

(1) the recipient was selected without any action on his part to enter the contest or proceeding;

(2) the recipient is not required to render substantial future services as a condition to receiving the prize or award; and

(3) the prize or award is transferred by the payor to a governmental unit or organization described in paragraph (1) or (2) of section 170(c) pursuant to a designation made by the recipient.

* * *

(c) Exception for certain employee achievement awards.—

(1) In general.—Gross income shall not include the value of an employee achievement award (as defined in section 274(j)) received by the taxpayer if the cost to the employer of the employee achievement award does not exceed the amount allowable as a deduction to the employer for the cost of the employee achievement award.

(2) Excess deduction award.—If the cost to the employer of the employee achievement award received by the taxpayer exceeds the amount allowable as a deduction to the employer, then gross income includes the greater of—

(A) an amount equal to the portion of the cost to the employer of the award that is not allowable as a deduction to the employer (but not in excess of the value of the award), or

(B) the amount by which the value of the award exceeds the amount allowable as a deduction to the employer.

The remaining portion of the value of such award shall not be included in the gross income of the recipient.

(3) Treatment of tax-exempt employers.—In the case of an employer exempt from taxation under this subtitle, any reference in this subsection to the amount allowable as a deduction to the employer shall be treated as a reference to the amount which would be allowable as a deduction to the employer if the employer were not exempt from taxation under this subtitle.

(4) Cross reference.—

For provisions excluding certain de minimis fringes from gross income, see section 132(e).

§ 79.   Group-term life insurance purchased for employees

(a) General rule.—There shall be included in the gross income of an employee for the taxable year an amount equal to the cost of group-term life insurance on his life provided for part or all of such year under a policy (or policies) carried directly or indirectly by his employer (or employers); but only to the extent that such cost exceeds the sum of—

(1) the cost of $50,000 of such insurance, and

(2) the amount (if any) paid by the employee toward the purchase of such insurance.

(b) **Exceptions.**—Subsection (a) shall not apply to—

(1) the cost of group-term life insurance on the life of an individual which is provided under a policy carried directly or indirectly by an employer after such individual has terminated his employment with such employer and is disabled (within the meaning of section 72(m)(7)),

(2) the cost of any portion of the group-term life insurance on the life of an employee provided during part or all of the taxable year of the employee under which—

(A) the employer is directly or indirectly the beneficiary, or

(B) a person described in section 170(c) is the sole beneficiary, for the entire period during such taxable year for which the employee receives such insurance, and

(3) the cost of any group-term life insurance which is provided under a contract to which section 72(m) (3) applies.

(c) **Determination of cost of insurance.**—For purposes of this section and section 6052, the cost of group-term insurance on the life of an employee provided during any period shall be determined on the basis of uniform premiums (computed on the basis of 5-year age brackets) prescribed by regulations by the Secretary. In the case of an employee who has attained age 64, the cost prescribed shall not exceed the cost with respect to such individual if he were age 63.

(d) **Nondiscrimination requirements.**—

(1) **In general.**—In the case of a discriminatory group-term life insurance plan—

(A) subsection (a)(1) shall not apply with respect to any key employee, and

(B) the cost of group-term life insurance on the life of any key employee shall be the greater of—

(i) such cost determined without regard to subsection (c), or

(ii) such cost determined with regard to subsection (c).

(2) **Discriminatory group-term life insurance plan.**—For purposes of this subsection, the term "discriminatory group-term life insurance plan" means any plan of an employer for providing group-term life insurance unless—

(A) the plan does not discriminate in favor of key employees as to eligibility to participate, and

(B) the type and amount of benefits available under the plan do not discriminate in favor of participants who are key employees.

(3) **Nondiscriminatory eligibility classification.**—

(A) **In general.**—A plan does not meet requirements of subparagraph (A) of paragraph (2) unless—

(i) such plan benefits 70 percent or more of all employees of the employer,

(ii) at least 85 percent of all employees who are participants under the plan are not key employees,

(iii) such plan benefits such employees as qualify under a classification set up by the employer and found by the Secretary not to be discriminatory in favor of key employees, or

(iv) in the case of a plan which is part of a cafeteria plan, the requirements of section 125 are met.

(B) **Exclusion of certain employees.**—For purposes of subparagraph (A), there may be excluded from consideration—

(i) employees who have not completed 3 years of service;

(ii) part-time or seasonal employees;

(iii) employees not included in the plan who are included in a unit of employees covered by an agreement between employee representatives and one or more employers which the Secretary finds to be a collective bargaining agreement, if the benefits provided under the plan were the subject of good faith bargaining between such employee representatives and such employer or employers; and

* * *

(4) **Nondiscriminatory benefits.**—A plan does not meet the requirements of paragraph (2)(B) unless all benefits available to participants who are key employees are available to all other participants.

(5) **Special rule.**—A plan shall not fail to meet the requirements of paragraph (2)(B) merely because the amount of life insurance on behalf of the employees under the plan bears a uniform relationship to the total compensation or the basic or regular rate of compensation of such employees.

(6) **Key employee defined.**—For purposes of this subsection, the term "key employee" has the meaning given to such term by paragraph (1) of section 416(i). Such term also includes any retired employee if such employee when he retired or separated from service was a key employee.

(7) **Certain controlled groups, etc.**—All employees who are treated as employed by a single employer under subsection (b), (c), or (m) of section 414 shall be treated as employed by a single employer for purposes of this section.

(8) **Treatment of former employees.**—To the extent provided in regulations, this subsection shall be applied separately with respect to former employees.

Amendment of Subsec. (d)

Pub.L. 95–514, Title XI, § 1151(c)(1), (k), Oct. 22, 1986, 100 Stat. ——, provided that except as otherwise provided, applicable to years beginning after the later of Dec. 31, 1987, or the earlier of date three months after date Secretary of Treasury issues regulations necessary to carry out section 89 of Title 26, Internal Revenue Code, or Dec. 31, 1988, subsec. (d) is amended to read as follows:

(d) **Nondiscrimination Requirements.**—In the case of a group-term life insurance plan which is a discriminatory employee benefit plan, subsection (a)(1) shall apply only to the extent provided in section 89.

(e) **Employee includes former employee.**—For purposes of this section the term "employee" includes a former employee.

§ 82.   Reimbursement for expenses of moving

There shall be included in gross income (as compensation for services) any amount received or accrued, directly or indirectly, by an individual as a payment for or reimbursement of expenses of moving from one residence to another residence which is attributable to employment or self-employment.

§ 83. Property transferred in connection with performance of services

(a) **General rule.**—If, in connection with the performance of services, property is transferred to any person other than the person for whom such services are performed, the excess of—

(1) the fair market value of such property (determined without regard to any restriction other than a restriction which by its terms will never lapse) at the first time the rights of the person having the beneficial interest in such property are transferable or are not subject to a substantial risk of forfeiture, whichever occurs earlier, over

(2) the amount (if any) paid for such property,

shall be included in the gross income of the person who performed such services in the first taxable year in which the rights of the person having the beneficial interest in such property are transferable or are not subject to a substantial risk of forfeiture, whichever is applicable. The preceding sentence shall not apply if such person sells or otherwise disposes of such property in an arm's length transaction before his rights in such property become transferable or not subject to a substantial risk of forfeiture.

(b) **Election to include in gross income in year of transfer.**—

(1) **In general.**—Any person who performs services in connection with which property is transferred to any person may elect to include in his gross income, for the taxable year in which such property is transferred, the excess of—

(A) the fair market value of such property at the time of transfer (determined without regard to any restriction other than a restriction which by its terms will never lapse), over

(B) the amount (if any) paid for such property.

If such election is made, subsection (a) shall not apply with respect to the transfer of such property, and if such property is subsequently forfeited, no deduction shall be allowed in respect of such forfeiture.

(2) **Election.**—An election under paragraph (1) with respect to any transfer of property shall be made in such manner as the Secretary prescribes and shall be made not later than 30 days after the date of such transfer. Such election may not be revoked except with the consent of the Secretary.

(c) **Special rules.**—For purposes of this section—

(1) **Substantial risk of forfeiture.**—The rights of a person in property are subject to a substantial risk of forfeiture if such person's rights to full enjoyment of such property are conditioned upon the future performance of substantial services by any individual.

(2) **Transferability of property.**—The rights of a person in property are transferable only if the rights in such property of any transferee are not subject to a substantial risk of forfeiture.

(3) **Sales which may give rise to suit under section 16(b) of the Securities Exchange Act of 1934.**—So long as the sale of property at a profit could subject a person to suit under section 16(b) of the Securities Exchange Act of 1934, such person's rights in such property are—

(A) subject to a substantial risk of forfeiture, and

(B) not transferable.

(d) Certain restrictions which will never lapse.—

(1) Valuation.—In the case of property subject to a restriction which by its terms will never lapse, and which allows the transferee to sell such property only at a price determined under a formula, the price so determined shall be deemed to be the fair market value of the property unless established to the contrary by the Secretary, and the burden of proof shall be on the Secretary with respect to such value.

(2) Cancellation.—If, in the case of property subject to a restriction which by its terms will never lapse, the restriction is canceled, then, unless the taxpayer establishes—

(A) that such cancellation was not compensatory, and

(B) that the person, if any, who would be allowed a deduction if the cancellation were treated as compensatory, will treat the transaction as not compensatory, as evidenced in such manner as the Secretary shall prescribe by regulations,

the excess of the fair market value of the property (computed without regard to the restrictions) at the time of cancellation over the sum of—

(C) the fair market value of such property (computed by taking the restriction into account) immediately before the cancellation, and

(D) the amount, if any, paid for the cancellation,

shall be treated as compensation for the taxable year in which such cancellation occurs.

(e) Applicability of section.—This section shall not apply to—

(1) a transaction to which section 421 applies,

(2) a transfer to or from a trust described in section 401(a) or a transfer under an annuity plan which meets the requirements of section 404(a) (2),

(3) the transfer of an option without a readily ascertainable fair market value,

(4) the transfer of property pursuant to the exercise of an option with a readily ascertainable fair market value at the date of grant, or

(5) group-term life insurance to which section 79 applies.

(f) Holding period.—In determining the period for which the taxpayer has held property to which subsection (a) applies, there shall be included only the period beginning at the first time his rights in such property are transferable or are not subject to a substantial risk of forfeiture, whichever occurs earlier.

(g) Certain exchanges.—If property to which subsection (a) applies is exchanged for property subject to restrictions and conditions substantially similar to those to which the property given in such exchange was subject, and if section 354, 355, 356, or 1036 (or so much of section 1031 as relates to section 1036) applied to such exchange, or if such exchange was pursuant to the exercise of a conversion privilege—

(1) such exchange shall be disregarded for purposes of subsection (a), and

(2) the property received shall be treated as property to which subsection (a) applies.

(h) Deduction by employer.—In the case of a transfer of property to which this section applies or a cancellation of a restriction described in subsection (d), there shall be allowed as a deduction under section 162, to the person for whom were performed the services in connection with which such property was transferred, an amount equal to the amount included under subsection (a), (b), or (d) (2) in the gross income of the person who performed such services. Such deduction shall be allowed for the taxable year of such person in which or with which ends the taxable year in which such amount is included in the gross income of the person who performed such services.

* * *

§ 84. Transfer of appreciated property to political organization

(a) **General rule.**—If—

(1) any person transfers property to a political organization, and

(2) the fair market value of such property exceeds its adjusted basis,

then for purposes of this chapter the transferor shall be treated as having sold such property to the political organization on the date of the transfer, and the transferor shall be treated as having realized an amount equal to the fair market value of such property on such date.

(b) **Basis of property.**—In the case of a transfer of property to a political organization to which subsection (a) applies, the basis of such property in the hands of the political organization shall be the same as it would be in the hands of the transferor, increased by the amount of gain recognized to the transferor by reason of such transfer.

(c) **Political organization defined.**—For purposes of this section, the term "political organization" has the meaning given to such term by section 527(e)(1).

§ 85. Unemployment compensation

(a) **General rule.**—In the case of an individual, gross income includes unemployment compensation.

(b) **Unemployment compensation defined.**—For purposes of this section, the term "unemployment compensation" means any amount received under a law of the United States or of a State which is in the nature of unemployment compensation.

§ 86. Social security and tier 1 railroad retirement benefits

(a) **In general.**—Gross income for the taxable year of any taxpayer described in subsection (b) (notwithstanding section 207 of the Social Security Act) includes social security benefits in an amount equal to the lesser of—

(1) one-half of the social security benefits received during the taxable year, or

(2) one-half of the excess described in subsection (b)(1).

(b) **Taxpayers to whom subsection (a) applies.**—

(1) **In general.**—A taxpayer is described in this subsection if—

(A) the sum of—

(i) the modified adjusted gross income of the taxpayer for the taxable year, plus

(ii) one-half of the social security benefits received during the taxable year, exceeds

(B) the base amount.

(2) **Modified adjusted gross income.**—For purposes of this subsection, the term "modified adjusted gross income" means adjusted gross income—

(A) determined without regard to this section and sections 911, 931, and 933, and

(B) increased by the amount of interest received or accrued by the taxpayer during the taxable year which is exempt from tax.

(c) **Base amount.**—For purposes of this section, the term "base amount" means—

(1) except as otherwise provided in this subsection, $25,000,

(2) $32,000, in the case of a joint return, and

(3) zero, in the case of a taxpayer who—

(A) is married at the close of the taxable year (within the meaning of section 7703) but does not file a joint return for such year, and

(B) does not live apart from his spouse at all times during the taxable year.

(d) **Social security benefit.**—

(1) **In general.**—For purposes of this section, the term "social security benefit" means any amount received by the taxpayer by reason of entitlement to—

(A) a monthly benefit under title II of the Social Security Act, or

(B) a tier 1 railroad retirement benefit.

For purposes of the preceding sentence, the amount received by any taxpayer shall be determined as if the Social Security Act did not contain section 203(i) thereof.

(2) **Adjustment for repayments during year.**—

(A) **In general.**—For purposes of this section, the amount of social security benefits received during any taxable year shall be reduced by any repayment made by the taxpayer during the taxable year of a social security benefit previously received by the taxpayer (whether or not such benefit was received during the taxable year).

(B) **Denial of deduction.**—If (but for this subparagraph) any portion of the repayments referred to in subparagraph (A) would have been allowable as a deduction for the taxable year under section 165, such portion shall be allowable as a deduction only to the extent it exceeds the social security benefits received by the taxpayer during the taxable year (and not repaid during such taxable year).

(3) **Workmen's compensation benefits substituted for social security benefits.**—For purposes of this section, if, by reason of section 224 of the Social Security Act (or by reason of section 3(a)(1) of the Railroad Retirement Act of 1974), any social security benefit is reduced by reason of the receipt of a benefit under a workmen's compensation act, the term "social security benefit" includes that portion of such benefit received under the workmen's compensation act which equals such reduction.

(4) **Tier 1 railroad retirement benefit.**—For purposes of paragraph (1), the term "tier 1 railroad retirement benefit" means—

(A) the amount of the annuity under the Railroad Retirement Act of 1974 equal to the amount of the benefit to which the taxpayer would have been entitled under the Social Security Act if all of the service after December 31, 1936, of the employee (on whose employment record the annuity is being paid) had been included in the term "employment" as defined in the Social Security Act, and

(B) a monthly annuity amount under section 3(f)(3) of the Railroad Retirement Act of 1974.

(5) Effect of early delivery of benefit checks.—For purposes of subsection (a), in any case where section 708 of the Social Security Act causes social security benefit checks to be delivered before the end of the calendar month for which they are issued, the benefits involved shall be deemed to have been received in the succeeding calendar month.

* * *

(g) Operating rules.—

(1) Aggregation of comparable health plans.—In the case of health plans maintained by an employer—

(A) In general.—An employer may treat a group of comparable plans as 1 plan for purposes of applying subsections (d)(1)(B), (d)(2) and (f).

(B) Comparable plans.—For purposes of subparagraph (A), a group of comparable plans is any group (selected by the employer) of plans of the same type if the smallest employer-provided benefit available to any participant in any such plan is at least 95 percent of the largest employer-provided benefit available to any participant in any such plan.

(2) Special rules for applying benefit requirements to health plan.—

(A) Election.—For purposes of determining whether the requirements of subsection (e) are met with respect to health plans, the employer may elect—

(i) to disregard any employee if such employee and his spouse and dependents (if any) are covered by a health plan providing core benefits maintained by another employer, and

(ii) to apply subsection (e) separately with respect to coverage of spouses or dependents by such plans and to take into account with respect to such coverage only employees with a spouse or dependents who are not covered by a health plan providing core benefits maintained by another employer.

(B) Sworn statements.—Any employer who elects the application of subparagraph (A) shall obtain and maintain, in such manner as the Secretary may prescribe, adequate sworn statements to demonstrate whether individuals have—

(i) a spouse or dependents, and

(ii) core health benefits under a plan of another employer.

The Secretary shall provide a method for meeting the requirements of this subparagraph through the use of valid sampling techniques.

(C) Presumption where no statement.—In the absence of a statement described in subparagraph (B)—

(i) an employee who is not a highly compensated employee shall be treated—

(I) as not covered by another plan of another employer providing core benefits, and

(II) as having a spouse and dependents not covered by another plan of another employer providing core benefits, and

(ii) a highly compensated employee shall be treated—

(I) as covered by another plan of another employer providing core benefits, and

(II) as not having a spouse or dependents.

(D) Certain individuals may not be disregarded.—In the case of a highly compensated employee who receives employer-provided benefits under all health plans of the employer which are more than 133⅓ percent of the average employer-provided benefit under such plan for employees other than highly compensated employees, the employer may not disregard such employee, or his spouse or dependents for purposes of clause (i) or (ii) of subparagraph (A).

(3) Employer-provided benefit.—For purposes of this section—

(A) In general.—Except as provided in subsection (k), an employee's employer-provided benefit under any statutory employee benefit plan is—

(i) in the case of any health or group-term life insurance plan, the value of the coverage, or

(ii) in the case of any other plan, the value of the benefits,

provided during the plan year to or on behalf of such employee to the extent attributable to contributions made by the employer.

(B) Special rule for health plans.—The value of the coverage provided by any health plan shall be determined under procedures prescribed by the Secretary which shall—

(i) set forth the values of various standard types of coverage involving a representative group, and

(ii) provide for adjustments to take into account the specific coverage and group involved.

(C) Special rule for group-term life plans.—

(i) In general.—Except as provided in clause (ii), in determining the value of coverage under a group-term life insurance plan, the amount taken into account for any employee shall be based on the cost of the insurance determined under section 79(c) for an employee who is age 40.

(ii) Excess benefit.—For purposes of subsection (b), the excess benefit with respect to coverage under a group-term life insurance plan shall be equal to the greater of—

(I) the cost of such excess benefit (expressed as dollars of coverage) determined without regard to section 79(c), or

(II) such cost determined with regard to section 79(c).

(D) Salary reductions.—Except for purposes of subsections (d)(1)(A)(ii) and (j)(5), any salary reduction shall be treated as an employer-provided benefit.

(4) Election to test plans of different types together.—

(A) In general.—Except as provided in subparagraph (B), the employer may elect to treat all plans of the types specified in such election as plans of the same type for purposes of applying subsection (e).

(B) Exception for health plans.—Subparagraph (A) shall not apply for purposes of determining whether any health plan meets the requirements of subsection (e); except that benefits provided under health plans which meet such requirements may be taken into account in determining whether plans of other types meet the requirements of subsection (e).

(5) Separate line of business exception.—If, under section 414(r), an employer is treated as operating separate lines of business for a year, the employer may apply the preceding provisions of this section separately with respect to employees in each such separate line of business. The preceding sentence shall not apply to any plan unless such plan is available to a group of employees as qualify under a classification set up by the employer and found by the Secretary not to be discriminatory in favor of highly compensated employees.

(6) Special rule for applying eligibility requirements and 80–percent test to health plans.—For purposes of determining whether the requirements of subsection (d)(1)(A)(ii) or of subsection (f) are met with respect to health plans, the employer may elect—

(A) to apply this section separately with respect to coverage of spouses and dependents by such plans, and

(B) to take into account with respect to such coverage only those employees with a spouse or dependent (determined under rules similar to the rules of paragraphs (2)(B) and (C)).

(h) Excluded employees.—

(1) In general.—The following employees shall be excluded from consideration under this section:

(A) Employees who have not completed 1 year of service (or in the case of core benefits under a health plan, 6 months of service). An employee shall be excluded from consideration until the 1st day of the 1st month beginning after completion of the period of service required under the preceding sentence.

(B) Employees who normally work less than 17½ hours per week.

(C) Employees who normally work during not more than 6 months during any year.

(D) Employees who have not attained age 21.

(E) Employees who are included in a unit of employees covered by an agreement which the Secretary finds to be a collective bargaining agreement between employee representatives and 1 or more employers if there is evidence that the type of benefits provided under the plan was the subject of good faith bargaining between the employee representatives and such employer or employers.

(F) Employees who are nonresident aliens and who receive no earned income (within the meaning of section 911(d)(2)) from the employer which constitutes income from sources within the United States (within the meaning of section 861(a)(3)).

Subparagraphs (A), (B), (C), and (D) shall be applied by substituting a shorter period of service, smaller number of hours or months, or lower age specified in the plan for the period of service, number of hours or months, or age (as the case may be) specified in such subparagraph.

(2) Certain exclusions not to apply if excluded employees covered.—Except to the extent provided in regulations, employees shall not be excluded from consideration under any subparagraph of paragraph (1) (other than subparagraph (F)) unless no employee described in such subparagraph (determined with regard to the last sentence of paragraph (1)) is eligible under the plan.

(3) Exclusion must apply to all plans.—

(A) In general.—An exclusion shall apply under any subparagraph of paragraph (1) (other than subparagraph (F) thereof) only if the exclusion applies to all statutory employee benefit plans of the employer of the same type. In the case of a cafeteria plan, all benefits under the cafeteria plan shall be treated as provided under plans of the same type.

(B) Exception.—Subparagraph (A) shall not apply to any difference in waiting periods for core and noncore benefits provided by health plans.

(4) Exception for separate line of business.—If any line of business is treated separately under subsection (h)(5), then paragraphs (2) and (3) shall be applied separately to such line of business.

(5) Requirements may be met separately with respect to excluded group. —Notwithstanding paragraphs (2) and (3), if employees do not meet minimum age or service requirements described in paragraph (1) (without regard to the last sentence thereof) and are covered under a plan of the employer which meets the requirements of this section separately with respect to such employees, such employees may be excluded from consideration in determining whether any plan of the employer meets the requirements of this section.

(i) Statutory employee benefit plan.—For purposes of this section—

(1) In general.—The term "statutory employee benefit plan" means—

(A) an accident or health plan (within the meaning of section 105(e)), and

(B) any plan of an employer for providing group-term life insurance (within the meaning of section 79).

(2) Employer may elect to treat other plans as statutory employee benefit plan.—An employer may elect to treat any of the following plans as statutory employee benefit plans:

(A) A qualified group legal services plan (within the meaning of section 120(b)).

(B) An educational assistance program (within the meaning of section 127(b)).

(C) A dependent care assistance program (within the meaning of section 129(d)).

An election under this paragraph with respect to any plan shall apply with respect to all plans of the same type as such plan.

(3) Plans of the same type.—2 or more plans shall be treated as of the same type if such plans are described in the same subparagraph of paragraph (1) or (2).

(j) Other definitions and special rules.—For purposes of this section—

(1) Highly compensated employee.—The term "highly compensated employee" has the meaning given such term by section 414(q).

(2) Health plan.—The term "health plan" means any plan described in paragraph (1)(A) of subsection (i).

(3) Treatment of former employees.—Except to the extent provided in regulations, this section shall be applied separately to former employees under requirements similar to the requirements that apply to employees.

(4) Group-term life insurance plans.—

(A) In general.—Any group-term life insurance plan shall not be treated as 2 or more separate plans merely because the amount of life insurance under the plan on behalf of employees bears a uniform relationship to the compensation (within the meaning of section 414(s)) of such employees.

(B) Limitation on compensation.—For purposes of subparagraph (A), compensation in excess of the amount applicable under section 401(a)(17) shall not be taken into account.

(C) Limitation.—This paragraph shall not apply to any plan if such plan is combined with plans of other types pursuant to an election under subsection (g)(4).

(5) Special rule for employees working less than 30 hours per week.—Any health plan shall not fail to meet the requirements of this section merely because the employer-provided benefit is proportionately reduced for employees who normally work less than 30 hours per week. The preceding sentence shall apply only where the average work week of employees who are not highly compensated employees is 30 hours or more.

(6) Treatment of self-employed individuals.—In the case of a statutory employee benefit plan described in subparagraph (A), (B), or (C) of subsection (i)(2)—

(A) Treatment as employee, etc.—The term "employee" includes any self-employed individual (as defined in section 401(c)(1)), and the term "compensation" includes such individual's earned income (as defined in section 401(c)(2)).

(B) Employer.—An individual who owns the entire interest in an unincorporated trade or business shall be treated as his own employer. A partnership shall be treated as the employer of each partner who is treated as an employee under subparagraph (A).

(7) Certain plans treated as meeting other nondiscrimination requirements.—If an employer makes an election under subsection (i)(2) to have this section apply to any plan and such plan meets the requirements of this section, such plan shall be treated as meeting any other nondiscrimination requirement imposed on such plan (other than any requirement under section 120(c)(3), 127(b)(3), or 129(d)(4)).

(8) Special rules for certain dispositions or acquisitions.—

(A) In general.—If a person becomes, or ceases to be, a member of a group described in subsection (b), (c), (m), or (o) of section 414, then the requirements of this section shall be treated as having been met during the transition period with respect to any plan covering employees of such person or any other member of such group if—

(i) such requirements were met immediately before each such change, and

(ii) the coverage under such plan is not significantly changed during the transition period (other than by reason of the change in members of a group).

(B) Transition period.—For purposes of subparagraph (A), the term "transition period" means the period—

(i) beginning on the date of the change in members of a group, and

(ii) ending on the last day of the 1st plan year beginning after the date of such change.

(9) Coordination with Medicare, etc.—If a plan may be coordinated with health benefits provided under any Federal, State, or foreign law or under any other health plan covering the employee or family member of the employee, such plan shall not fail to meet the requirements of this section with respect to health benefits merely because the amount of such benefits provided to any employee or family member of any employee are coordinated in a manner which does not discriminate in favor of highly compensated employees.

(10) Disability benefits.—

(A) In general.—If a plan may be coordinated with disability benefits provided under any Federal, State, or foreign law or under any other plan covering the employee, such plan shall not fail to meet the requirements of this section with

89

respect to disability benefits merely because the amount of such benefits provided to an employee are coordinated in a manner which does not discriminate in favor of highly compensated employees.

(B) Certain disability plans exempt from nondiscrimination rules.—Subsection (a) shall not apply to any disability coverage other than disability coverage the benefits of which are excludable from gross income under section 105(b) or (c).

(11) Separate application in the case of options.—Each option or different benefit shall be treated as a separate plan.

(k) Requirement that plan be in writing, etc.—

(1) In general.—Notwithstanding any provision of part III of this subchapter, gross income of an employee shall include an amount equal to such employee's employer-provided benefit for the taxable year under an employee benefit plan to which this subsection applies unless, except to the extent provided in regulations—

(A) such plan is in writing,

(B) the employees' rights under such plan are legally enforceable,

(C) employees are provided reasonable notification of benefits available in the plan,

(D) such plan is maintained for the exclusive benefit of employees, and

(E) such plan was established with the intention of being maintained for an indefinite period of time.

Such inclusion shall be in lieu of any inclusion under subsection (a) with respect to such plan.

(2) Plans to which subsection applies.—This subsection shall apply to—

(A) any statutory employee benefit plan,

(B) a qualified tuition reduction program (within the meaning of section 117(d)),

(C) a cafeteria plan (within the meaning of section 125),

(D) a fringe benefit program providing no-additional-cost services, qualified employee discounts, or employer-operated eating facilities which are excludable from gross income under section 132, and

(E) a plan to which section 505 applies.

(3) Special rule for determining inclusion.—For purposes of paragraph (1), an employee's employer-provided benefit shall be the value of the benefits provided to the employee.

(4) Plans to which contributions are made by more than 1 employer.—For purposes of paragraph (1)(D), in the case of a plan to which contributions are made by more than 1 employer, each employer shall be treated as employing employees of all other employers.

§ 89. Benefits provided under certain employee benefit plans

(a) Benefits under discriminatory plans.—

(1) In general.—Notwithstanding any provision of part III of this subchapter, gross income of a highly compensated employee who is a participant in a discriminatory employee benefit plan during any plan year shall include an amount equal to such employee's excess benefit under such plan for such plan year.

(2) **Year of inclusion.**—Any amount included in gross income under paragraph (1) shall be taken into account for the taxable year of the employee with or within which the plan year ends.

(b) **Excess benefit.**—For purposes of this section—

(1) **In general.**—The excess benefit of any highly compensated employee is the excess of such employee's employer-provided benefit under the plan over the highest permitted benefit.

(2) **Highest permitted benefit.**—For purposes of paragraph (1), the highest permitted benefit under any plan shall be determined by reducing the nontaxable benefits of highly compensated employees (beginning with the employees with the greatest nontaxable benefits) until such plan would not be treated as a discriminatory employee benefit plan if such reduced benefits were taken into account.

(3) **Plans of same type.**—In computing the excess benefit with respect to any benefit, there shall be taken into account all plans of the employer of the same type.

(4) **Nontaxable benefits.**—For purposes of this subsection, the term "nontaxable benefit" means any benefit provided under a plan to which this section applies which (without regard to subsection (a)(1)) is excludable from gross income under this chapter.

(c) **Discriminatory employee benefit plan.**—For purposes of this section, the term "discriminatory employee benefit plan" means any statutory employee benefit plan unless such plan meets the—

(1) eligibility requirements of subsection (d), and

(2) benefit requirements of subsection (e).

(d) **Eligibility requirements.**—

(1) **In general.**—A plan meets the eligibility requirements of this subsection for any plan year if—

(A) at least 90 percent of all employees who are not highly compensated employees—

(i) are eligible to participate in such plan (or in any other plan of the employer of the same type), and

(ii) would (if they participated) have available under such plans an employer-provided benefit which is at least 50 percent of the largest employer-provided benefit available under all such plans of the employer to any highly compensated employee,

(B) at least 50 percent of the employees eligible to participate in such plan are not highly compensated employees, and

(C) such plan does not contain any provision relating to eligibility to participate which (by its terms or otherwise) discriminates in favor of highly compensated employees.

(2) **Alternative eligibility percentage test.**—A plan shall be treated as meeting the requirements of paragraph (1)(B) if—

(A) the percentage determined by dividing the number of highly compensated employees eligible to participate in the plan by the total number of highly compensated employees, does not exceed

(B) the percentage similarly determined with respect to employees who are not highly compensated employees.

(e) Benefit requirements.—

(1) In general.—A plan meets the benefit requirements of this subsection for any plan year if the average employer-provided benefit received by employees other than highly compensated employees under all plans of the employer of the same type is at least 75 percent of the average employer-provided benefit received by highly compensated employees under all plans of the employer of the same type.

(2) Average employer-provided benefit.—For purposes of this subsection, the term "average employer-provided benefit" means, with respect to highly compensated employees, an amount equal to—

(A) the aggregate employer-provided benefits received by highly compensated employees under all plans of the type being tested, divided by

(B) the number of highly compensated employees (whether or not covered under such plans).

The average employer-provided benefit with respect to employees other than highly compensated employees shall be determined in the same manner as the average employer-provided benefit for highly compensated employees.

(f) Special rule where health or group-term plan meets 80–percent coverage test.—If at least 80 percent of the employees who are not highly compensated employees are covered under a health plan or group-term life insurance plan during the plan year, such plan shall be treated as meeting the requirements of subsections (d) and (e) for such year. The preceding sentence shall not apply if the plan does not meet the requirements of subsection (d)(1)(C) (relating to nondiscriminatory provisions).

(g) Operating rules.—

(1) Aggregation of comparable health plans.—In the case of health plans maintained by an employer—

(A) In general.—An employer may treat a group of comparable plans as 1 plan for purposes of applying subsections (d)(1)(B), (d)(2) and (f).

(B) Comparable plans.—For purposes of subparagraph (A), a group of comparable plans is any group (selected by the employer) of plans of the same type if the smallest employer-provided benefit available to any participant in any such plan is at least 95 percent of the largest employer-provided benefit available to any participant in any such plan.

(2) Special rules for applying benefit requirements to health plans.—

(A) Election.—For purposes of determining whether the requirements of subsection (e) are met with respect to health plans, the employer may elect—

(i) to disregard any employee if such employee and his spouse and dependents (if any) are covered by a health plan providing core benefits maintained by another employer, and

(ii) to apply subsection (e) separately with respect to coverage of spouses or dependents by such plans and to take into account with respect to such coverage only employees with a spouse or dependents who are not covered by a health plan providing core benefits maintained by another employer.

(B) Sworn statements.—Any employer who elects the application of subparagraph (A) shall obtain and maintain, in such manner as the Secretary may prescribe, adequate sworn statements to demonstrate whether individuals have—

(i) a spouse or dependents, and

(ii) core health benefits under a plan of another employer.

The Secretary shall provide a method for meeting the requirements of this subparagraph through the use of valid sampling techniques.

(C) Presumption where no statement.—In the absence of a statement described in subparagraph (B)—

(i) an employee who is not a highly compensated employee shall be treated—

(I) as not covered by another plan of another employer providing core benefits, and

(II) as having a spouse and dependents not covered by another plan of another employer providing core benefits, and

(ii) a highly compensated employee shall be treated—

(I) as covered by another plan of another employer providing core benefits, and

(II) as not having a spouse or dependents.

(D) Certain individuals may not be disregarded.—In the case of a highly compensated employee who receives employer-provided benefits under all health plans of the employer which are more than $133\frac{1}{3}$ percent of the average employer-provided benefit under such plan for employees other than highly compensated employees, the employer may not disregard such employee, or his spouse or dependents for purposes of clause (i) or (ii) of subparagraph (A).

(3) Employer-provided benefit.—For purposes of this section—

(A) In general.—Except as provided in subsection (k), an employee's employer-provided benefit under any statutory employee benefit plan is—

(i) in the case of any health or group-term life insurance plan, the value of the coverage, or

(ii) in the case of any other plan, the value of the benefits,

provided during the plan year to or on behalf of such employee to the extent attributable to contributions made by the employer.

(B) Special rule for health plans.—The value of the coverage provided by any health plan shall be determined under procedures prescribed by the Secretary which shall—

(i) set forth the values of various standard types of coverage involving a representative group, and

(ii) provide for adjustments to take into account the specific coverage and group involved.

(C) Special rule for group-term life plans.—

(i) **In general.**—Except as provided in clause (ii), in determining the value of coverage under a group-term life insurance plan, the amount taken into account for any employee shall be based on the cost of the insurance determined under section 79(c) for an employee who is age 40.

(ii) **Excess benefit.**—For purposes of subsection (b), the excess benefit with respect to coverage under a group-term life insurance plan shall be equal to the greater of—

(I) the cost of such excess benefit (expressed as dollars of coverage) determined without regard to section 79(c), or

(II) such cost determined with regard to section 79(c).

(D) Salary reductions.—Except for purposes of subsections (d)(1)(A)(ii) and (j)(5), any salary reduction shall be treated as an employer-provided benefit.

(4) Election to test plans of different types together.—

(A) In general.—Except as provided in subparagraph (B), the employer may elect to treat all plans of the types specified in such election as plans of the same type for purposes of applying subsection (e).

(B) Exception for health plans.—Subparagraph (A) shall not apply for purposes of determining whether any health plan meets the requirements of subsection (e); except that benefits provided under health plans which meet such requirements may be taken into account in determining whether plans of other types meet the requirements of subsection (e).

(5) Separate line of business exception.—If, under section 414(r), an employer is treated as operating separate lines of business for a year, the employer may apply the preceding provisions of this section separately with respect to employees in each such separate line of business. The preceding sentence shall not apply to any plan unless such plan is available to a group of employees as qualify under a classification set up by the employer and found by the Secretary not to be discriminatory in favor of highly compensated employees.

(6) Special rule for applying eligibility requirements and 80–percent test to health plans.—For purposes of determining whether the requirements of subsection (d)(1)(A)(ii) or of subsection (f) are met with respect to health plans, the employer may elect—

(A) to apply this section separately with respect to coverage of spouses and dependents by such plans, and

(B) to take into account with respect to such coverage only those employees with a spouse or dependent (determined under rules similar to the rules of paragraphs (2)(B) and (C)).

(h) Excluded employees.—

(1) In general.—The following employees shall be excluded from consideration under this section:

(A) Employees who have not completed 1 year of service (or in the case of core benefits under a health plan, 6 months of service). An employee shall be excluded from consideration until the 1st day of the 1st month beginning after completion of the period of service required under the preceding sentence.

(B) Employees who normally work less than 17½ hours per week.

(C) Employees who normally work during not more than 6 months during any year.

(D) Employees who have not attained age 21.

(E) Employees who are included in a unit of employees covered by an agreement which the Secretary finds to be a collective bargaining agreement between employee representatives and 1 or more employers if there is evidence that the type of benefits provided under the plan was the subject of good faith bargaining between the employee representatives and such employer or employers.

(F) Employees who are nonresident aliens and who receive no earned income (within the meaning of section 911(d)(2)) from the employer which constitutes income from sources within the United States (within the meaning of section 861(a)(3)).

Subparagraphs (A), (B), (C), and (D) shall be applied by substituting a shorter period of service, smaller number of hours or months, or lower age specified in the plan for the period of service, number of hours or months, or age (as the case may be) specified in such subparagraph.

(2) **Certain exclusions not to apply if excluded employees covered.**—Except to the extent provided in regulations, employees shall not be excluded from consideration under any subparagraph of paragraph (1) (other than subparagraph (F)) unless no employee described in such subparagraph (determined with regard to the last sentence of paragraph (1)) is eligible under the plan.

(3) **Exclusion must apply to all plans.**—

(A) **In general.**—An exclusion shall apply under any subparagraph of paragraph (1) (other than subparagraph (F) thereof) only if the exclusion applies to all statutory employee benefit plans of the employer of the same type. In the case of a cafeteria plan, all benefits under the cafeteria plan shall be treated as provided under plans of the same type.

(B) **Exception.**—Subparagraph (A) shall not apply to any difference in waiting periods for core and noncore benefits provided by health plans.

(4) **Exception for separate line of business.**—If any line of business is treated separately under subsection (h)(5), then paragraphs (2) and (3) shall be applied separately to such line of business.

(5) **Requirements may be met separately with respect to excluded group.**—Notwithstanding paragraphs (2) and (3), if employees do not meet minimum age or service requirements described in paragraph (1) (without regard to the last sentence thereof) and are covered under a plan of the employer which meets the requirements of this section separately with respect to such employees, such employees may be excluded from consideration in determining whether any plan of the employer meets the requirements of this section.

(i) **Statutory employee benefit plan.**—For purposes of this section—

(1) **In general.**—The term "statutory employee benefit plan" means—

(A) an accident or health plan (within the meaning of section 105(e)), and

(B) any plan of an employer for providing group-term life insurance (within the meaning of section 79).

(2) **Employer may elect to treat other plans as statutory employee benefit plan.**—An employer may elect to treat any of the following plans as statutory employee benefit plans:

(A) A qualified group legal services plan (within the meaning of section 120(b)).

(B) An educational assistance program (within the meaning of section 127(b)).

(C) A dependent care assistance program (within the meaning of section 129(d)).

An election under this paragraph with respect to any plan shall apply with respect to all plans of the same type as such plan.

(3) **Plans of the same type.**—2 or more plans shall be treated as of the same type if such plans are described in the same subparagraph of paragraph (1) or (2).

(j) **Other definitions and special rules.**—For purposes of this section—

(1) **Highly compensated employee.**—The term "highly compensated employee" has the meaning given such term by section 414(q).

(2) Health plan.—The term "health plan" means any plan described in paragraph (1)(A) of subsection (i).

(3) Treatment of former employees.—Except to the extent provided in regulations, this section shall be applied separately to former employees under requirements similar to the requirements that apply to employees.

(4) Group-term life insurance plans.—

(A) In general.—Any group-term life insurance plan shall not be treated as 2 or more separate plans merely because the amount of life insurance under the plan on behalf of employees bears a uniform relationship to the compensation (within the meaning of section 414(s)) of such employees.

(B) Limitation on compensation.—For purposes of subparagraph (A), compensation in excess of the amount applicable under section 401(a)(17) shall not be taken into account.

(C) Limitation.—This paragraph shall not apply to any plan if such plan is combined with plans of other types pursuant to an election under subsection (g)(4).

(5) Special rule for employees working less than 30 hours per week.—Any health plan shall not fail to meet the requirements of this section merely because the employer-provided benefit is proportionately reduced for employees who normally work less than 30 hours per week. The preceding sentence shall apply only where the average work week of employees who are not highly compensated employees is 30 hours or more.

(6) Treatment of self-employed individuals.—In the case of a statutory employee benefit plan described in subparagraph (A), (B), or (C) of subsection (i)(2)—

(A) Treatment as employee, etc.—The term "employee" includes any self-employed individual (as defined in section 401(c)(1)), and the term "compensation" includes such individual's earned income (as defined in section 401(c)(2)).

(B) Employer.—An individual who owns the entire interest in an unincorporated trade or business shall be treated as his own employer. A partnership shall be treated as the employer of each partner who is treated as an employee under subparagraph (A).

(7) Certain plans treated as meeting other nondiscrimination requirements.—If an employer makes an election under subsection (i)(2) to have this section apply to any plan and such plan meets the requirements of this section, such plan shall be treated as meeting any other nondiscrimination requirement imposed on such plan (other than any requirement under section 120(c)(3), 127(b)(3), or 129(d)(4)).

(8) Special rules for certain dispositions or acquisitions.—

(A) In general.—If a person becomes, or ceases to be, a member of a group described in subsection (b), (c), (m), or (o) of section 414, then the requirements of this section shall be treated as having been met during the transition period with respect to any plan covering employees of such person or any other member of such group if—

(i) such requirements were met immediately before each such change, and

(ii) the coverage under such plan is not significantly changed during the transition period (other than by reason of the change in members of a group).

(B) Transition period.—For purposes of subparagraph (A), the term "transition period" means the period—

(i) beginning on the date of the change in members of a group, and

(ii) ending on the last day of the 1st plan year beginning after the date of such change.

(9) Coordination with Medicare, etc.—If a plan may be coordinated with health benefits provided under any Federal, State, or foreign law or under any other health plan covering the employee or family member of the employee, such plan shall not fail to meet the requirements of this section with respect to health benefits merely because the amount of such benefits provided to any employee or family member of any employee are coordinated in a manner which does not discriminate in favor of highly compensated employees.

(10) Disability benefits.—

(A) In general.—If a plan may be coordinated with disability benefits provided under any Federal, State, or foreign law or under any other plan covering the employee, such plan shall not fail to meet the requirements of this section with respect to disability benefits merely because the amount of such benefits provided to an employee are coordinated in a manner which does not discriminate in favor of highly compensated employees.

(B) Certain disability plans exempt from nondiscrimination rules.—Subsection (a) shall not apply to any disability coverage other than disability coverage the benefits of which are excludable from gross income under section 105(b) or (c).

(11) Separate application in the case of options.—Each option or different benefit shall be treated as a separate plan.

(k) Requirement that plan be in writing, etc.—

(1) In general.—Notwithstanding any provision of part III of this subchapter, gross income of an employee shall include an amount equal to such employee's employer-provided benefit for the taxable year under an employee benefit plan to which this subsection applies unless, except to the extent provided in regulations—

(A) such plan is in writing,

(B) the employees' rights under such plan are legally enforceable,

(C) employees are provided reasonable notification of benefits available in the plan,

(D) such plan is maintained for the exclusive benefit of employees, and

(E) such plan was established with the intention of being maintained for an indefinite period of time.

Such inclusion shall be in lieu of any inclusion under subsection (a) with respect to such plan.

(2) Plans to which subsection applies.—This subsection shall apply to—

(A) any statutory employee benefit plan,

(B) a qualified tuition reduction program (within the meaning of section 117(d)),

(C) a cafeteria plan (within the meaning of section 125),

(D) a fringe benefit program providing no-additional-cost services, qualified employee discounts, or employer-operated eating facilities which are excludable from gross income under section 132, and

(E) a plan to which section 505 applies.

(3) Special rule for determining inclusion.—For purposes of paragraph (1), an employee's employer-provided benefit shall be the value of the benefits provided to the employee.

(4) Plans to which contributions are made by more than 1 employer.—For purposes of paragraph (1)(D), in the case of a plan to which contributions are made by more than 1 employer, each employer shall be treated as employing employees of all other employers.

(*l*) Reporting requirements.—

(1) In general.—If an employee of an employer maintaining a plan is required to include any amount in gross income under this section for any plan year ending with or within a calendar year, the employer shall separately include such amount on the statement which the employer is required to provide the employee under section 6051(a) (and any statement required to be furnished under section 6051(d)).

(2) Penalty.—

> For penalty for failing to report, see section 6652(1).

(m) Regulations.—The Secretary shall prescribe such regulations as may be necessary or appropriate to carry out the purposes of this section, including regulations providing for appropriate adjustments in case of individuals not employees of the employer throughout the plan year.

(Added Pub.L. 99–514, Title XI, § 1151(a), Oct. 22, 1986, 100 Stat. ——)

PART III—ITEMS SPECIFICALLY EXCLUDED FROM GROSS INCOME

§ 101. Certain death benefits

(a) Proceeds of life insurance contracts payable by reason of death.—

(1) General rule.—Except as otherwise provided in paragraph (2), subsection (d), and subsection (f), gross income does not include amounts received (whether in a single sum or otherwise) under a life insurance contract, if such amounts are paid by reason of the death of the insured.

(2) Transfer for valuable consideration.—In the case of a transfer for a valuable consideration, by assignment or otherwise, of a life insurance contract or any interest therein, the amount excluded from gross income by paragraph (1) shall not exceed an amount equal to the sum of the actual value of such consideration and the premiums and other amounts subsequently paid by the transferee. The preceding sentence shall not apply in the case of such a transfer—

(A) if such contract or interest therein has a basis for determining gain or loss in the hands of a transferee determined in whole or in part by reference to such basis of such contract or interest therein in the hands of the transferor, or

(B) if such transfer is to the insured, to a partner of the insured, to a partnership in which the insured is a partner, or to a corporation in which the insured is a shareholder or officer.

(b) Employees' death benefits.—

(1) General rule.—Gross income does not include amounts received (whether in a single sum or otherwise) by the beneficiaries or the estate of an employee, if such amounts are paid by or on behalf of an employer and are paid by reason of the death of the employee.

(2) Special rules for paragraph (1).—

(A) $5,000 limitation.—The aggregate amounts excludable under paragraph (1) with respect to the death of any employee shall not exceed $5,000.

(B) Nonforfeitable rights.—Paragraph (1) shall not apply to amounts with respect to which the employee possessed, immediately before his death, a nonforfeitable right to receive the amounts while living. This subparagraph shall not apply to a lump sum distribution (as defined in section 402(e) (4))—

(i) by a stock bonus, pension, or profit-sharing trust described in section 401(a) which is exempt from tax under section 501(a),

(ii) under an annuity contract under a plan described in section 403(a), or

(iii) under an annuity contract purchased by an employer which is an organization referred to in section 170(b) (1) (A) (ii) or (vi) or which is a religious organization (other than a trust) and which is exempt from tax under section 501(a), but only with respect to that portion of such total distributions payable which bears the same ratio to the amount of such total distributions payable which is (without regard to this subsection) includible in gross income, as the amounts contributed by the employer for such annuity contract which are excludable from gross income under section 403(b) bear to the total amounts contributed by the employer for such annuity contract.

(C) Joint and survivor annuities.—Paragraph (1) shall not apply to amounts received by a surviving annuitant under a joint and survivor's annuity contract after the first day of the first period for which an amount was received as an annuity by the employee (or would have been received if the employee had lived).

(D) Other annuities.—In the case of any amount to which section 72 (relating to annuities, etc.) applies, the amount which is excludable under paragraph (1) (as modified by the preceding subparagraphs of this paragraph) shall be determined by reference to the value of such amount as of the day on which the employee died. Any amount so excludable under paragraph (1) shall, for purposes of section 72, be treated as additional consideration paid by the employee. Paragraph (1) shall not apply in the case of an annuity under chapter 73 of title 10 of the United States Code if the member or former member of the uniformed services by reason of whose death such annuity is payable died after attaining retirement age.

(3) Treatment of self-employed individuals.—For purposes of this subsection—

(A) Self-employed individual not considered employee.—Except as provided in subparagraph (B), the term "employee" does not include a self-employed individual described in section 401(c)(1).

(B) Special rule for certain distributions.—In the case of any amount paid or distributed—

(i) by a trust described in section 401(a) which is exempt from tax under section 501(a),

(ii) under a plan described in section 403(a),

the term "employee" includes a self-employed individual described in section 401(c)(1).

(c) Interest.—If any amount excluded from gross income by subsection (a) or (b) is held under an agreement to pay interest thereon, the interest payments shall be included in gross income.

(d) Payment of life insurance proceeds at a date later than death.—

(1) **General rule.**—The amounts held by an insurer with respect to any beneficiary shall be prorated (in accordance with such regulations as may be prescribed by the Secretary) over the period or periods with respect to which such payments are to be made. There shall be excluded from the gross income of such beneficiary in the taxable year received any amount determined by such proration. Gross income includes, to the extent not excluded by the preceding sentence, amounts received under agreements to which this subsection applies.

(2) **Amount held by an insurer.**—An amount held by an insurer with respect to any beneficiary shall mean an amount to which subsection (a) applies which is—

(A) held by any insurer under an agreement provided for in the life insurance contract, whether as an option or otherwise, to pay such amount on a date or dates later than the death of the insured, and

(B) equal to the value of such agreement to such beneficiary

(i) as of the date of death of the insured (as if any option exercised under the life insurance contract were exercised at such time), and

(ii) as discounted on the basis of the interest rate used by the insurer in calculating payments under the agreement and mortality tables prescribed by the Secretary.

(3) **Application of subsection.**—This subsection shall not apply to any amount to which subsection (c) is applicable.

[**(e) Repealed.**]

(f) Proceeds of flexible premium contracts issued before January 1, 1985 payable by reason of death.—

(1) **In general.**—Any amount paid by reason of the death of the insured under a flexible premium life insurance contract issued before January 1, 1985 shall be excluded from gross income only if—

(A) under such contract—

(i) the sum of the premiums paid under such contract does not at any time exceed the guideline premium limitation as of such time, and

(ii) any amount payable by reason of the death of the insured (determined without regard to any qualified additional benefit) is not at any time less than the applicable percentage of the cash value of such contract at such time, or

(B) by the terms of such contract, the cash value of such contract may not at any time exceed the net single premium with respect to the amount payable by reason of the death of the insured (determined without regard to any qualified additional benefit) at such time.

(2) **Guideline premium limitation.**—For purposes of this subsection—

(A) **Guideline premium limitation.**—The term "guideline premium limitation" means, as of any date, the greater of—

(i) the guideline single premium, or

(ii) the sum of the guideline level premiums to such date.

(B) **Guideline single premium.**—The term "guideline single premium" means the premium at issue with respect to future benefits under the contract (without regard to any qualified additional benefit), and with respect to any charges for qualified additional benefits, at the time of a determination under subparagraph (A) or (E) and which is based on—

(i) the mortality and other charges guaranteed under the contract, and

(ii) interest at the greater of an annual effective rate of 6 percent or the minimum rate or rates guaranteed upon issue of the contract.

(C) Guideline level premium.—The term "guideline level premium" means the level annual amount, payable over the longest period permitted under the contract (but ending not less than 20 years from date of issue or not later than age 95, if earlier), computed on the same basis as the guideline single premium, except that subparagraph (B)(ii) shall be applied by substituting "4 percent" for "6 percent".

(D) Computational rules.—In computing the guideline single premium or guideline level premium under subparagraph (B) or (C)—

(i) the excess of the amount payable by reason of the death of the insured (determined without regard to any qualified additional benefit) over the cash value of the contract shall be deemed to be not greater than such excess at the time the contract was issued,

(ii) the maturity date shall be the latest maturity date permitted under the contract, but not less than 20 years after the date of issue or (if earlier) age 95, and

(iii) the amount of any endowment benefit (or sum of endowment benefits) shall be deemed not to exceed the least amount payable by reason of the death of the insured (determined without regard to any qualified additional benefit) at any time under the contract.

(E) Adjustments.—The guideline single premium and guideline level premium shall be adjusted in the event of a change in the future benefits or any qualified additional benefit under the contract which was not reflected in any guideline single premiums or guideline level premium previously determined.

(3) Other definitions and special rules.—For purposes of this subsection—

(A) Flexible premium life insurance contract.—The terms "flexible premium life insurance contract" and "contract" mean a life insurance contract (including any qualified additional benefits) which provides for the payment of one or more premiums which are not fixed by the insurer as to both timing and amount. Such terms do not include that portion of any contract which is treated under State law as providing any annuity benefits other than as a settlement option.

(B) Premiums paid.—The term "premiums paid" means the premiums paid under the contract less any amounts (other than amounts includible in gross income) to which section 72(e) applies. If, in order to comply with the requirements of paragraph (1)(A), any portion of any premium paid during any contract year is returned by the insurance company (with interest) within 60 days after the end of a contract year—

(i) the amount so returned (excluding interest) shall be deemed to reduce the sum of the premiums paid under the contract during such year, and

(ii) notwithstanding the provisions of section 72(e), the amount of any interest so returned shall be includible in the gross income of the recipient.

(C) Applicable percentage.—The term "applicable percentage" means—

(i) 140 percent in the case of an insured with an attained age at the beginning of the contract year of 40 or less, and

(ii) in the case of an insured with an attained age of more than 40 as of the beginning of the contract year, 140 percent reduced (but not below 105 percent) by one percent for each year in excess of 40.

(D) **Cash value.**—The cash value of any contract shall be determined without regard to any deduction for any surrender charge or policy loan.

(E) **Qualified additional benefits.**—The term "qualified additional benefits" means any—

(i) guaranteed insurability,

(ii) accidental death benefit,

(iii) family term coverage, or

(iv) waiver of premium.

(F) **Premium payments not disqualifying contract.**—The payment of a premium which would result in the sum of the premiums paid exceeding the guideline premium limitation shall be disregarded for purposes of paragraph (1)(A)(i) if the amount of such premium does not exceed the amount necessary to prevent the termination of the contract without cash value on or before the end of the contract year.

(G) **Net single premium.**—In computing the net single premium under paragraph (1)(B)—

(i) the mortality basis shall be that guaranteed under the contract (determined by reference to the most recent mortality table allowed under all State laws on the date of issuance),

(ii) interest shall be based on the greater of—

(I) an annual effective rate of 4 percent (3 percent for contracts issued before July 1, 1983), or

(II) the minimum rate or rates guaranteed upon issue of the contract, and

(iii) the computational rules of paragraph (2)(D) shall apply, except that the maturity date referred to in clause (ii) thereof shall not be earlier than age 95.

(H) **Correction of errors.**—If the taxpayer establishes to the satisfaction of the Secretary that—

(i) the requirements described in paragraph (1) for any contract year was not satisfied due to reasonable error, and

(ii) reasonable steps are being taken to remedy the error,

the Secretary may waive the failure to satisfy such requirements.

(I) **Regulations.**—The Secretary shall prescribe such regulations as may be necessary or appropriate to carry out the purposes of this subsection.

§ 102.   Gifts and inheritances

(a) **General rule.**—Gross income does not include the value of property acquired by gift, bequest, devise, or inheritance.

(b) **Income.**—Subsection (a) shall not exclude from gross income—

(1) the income from any property referred to in subsection (a); or

(2) where the gift, bequest, devise, or inheritance is of income from property, the amount of such income.

Where, under the terms of the gift, bequest, devise, or inheritance, the payment, crediting, or distribution thereof is to be made at intervals, then, to the extent that it is paid or credited or to be distributed out of income from property, it shall be treated for purposes of paragraph (2) as a gift, bequest, devise, or inheritance of income from property. Any amount included in the gross income of a beneficiary under subchapter J shall be treated for purposes of paragraph (2) as a gift, bequest, devise, or inheritance of income from property.

(2) Cross references.—

For provisions excluding certain employee achievement awards from gross income, see section 74(c).

For provisions excluding certain de minimis fringes from gross income, see section 132(e).

(C) Gross Inc. shall not exclude any inc. to an employee from employer

§ 103. Interest on state and local bonds

(a) Exclusion.—Except as provided in subsection (b), gross income does not include interest on any State or local bond.

(b) Exceptions.—Subsection (a) shall not apply to—

(1) Private activity bond which is not a qualified bond.—Any private activity bond which is not a qualified bond (within the meaning of section 141).

(2) Arbitrage bond.—Any arbitrage bond (within the meaning of section 148).

(3) Bond not in registered form, etc.—Any bond unless such bond meets the applicable requirements of section 149.

(c) Definitions.—For purposes of this section and part IV—

(1) State or local bond.—The term "State or local bond" means an obligation of a State or political subdivision thereof.

(2) State.—The term "State" includes the District of Columbia and any possession of the United States.

§ 104. Compensation for injuries or sickness

(a) In general.—Except in the case of amounts attributable to (and not in excess of) deductions allowed under section 213 (relating to medical, etc., expenses) for any prior taxable year, gross income does not include—

(1) amounts received under workmen's compensation acts as compensation for personal injuries or sickness;

(2) the amount of any damages received (whether by suit or agreement and whether as lump sums or as periodic payments) on account of personal injuries or sickness;

(3) amounts received through accident or health insurance for personal injuries or sickness (other than amounts received by an employee, to the extent such amounts (A) are attributable to contributions by the employer which were not includible in the gross income of the employee, or (B) are paid by the employer);

(4) amounts received as a pension, annuity, or similar allowance for personal injuries or sickness resulting from active service in the armed forces of any country or in the Coast and Geodetic Survey or the Public Health Service, or as a disability annuity payable under the provisions of section 808 of the Foreign Service Act of 1980; and

(5) amounts received by an individual as disability income attributable to injuries incurred as a direct result of a violent attack which the Secretary of State determines to be a terrorist attack and which occurred while such individual was an employee of the United States engaged in the performance of his official duties outside the United States.

For purposes of paragraph (3), in the case of an individual who is, or has been, an employee within the meaning of section 401(c) (1) (relating to self-employed individuals), contributions made on behalf of such individual while he was such an employee to a trust described in section 401(a) which is exempt from tax under section 501(a), or under a plan described in section 403(a), shall, to the extent allowed as deductions under section 404, be treated as contributions by the employer which were not includible in the gross income of the employee.

(b) Termination of application of subsection (a) (4) in certain cases.—

(1) In general.—Subsection (a) (4) shall not apply in the case of any individual who is not described in paragraph (2).

(2) Individuals to whom subsection (a) (4) continues to apply.—An individual is described in this paragraph if—

(A) on or before September 24, 1975, he was entitled to receive any amount described in subsection (a) (4),

(B) on September 24, 1975, he was a member of any organization (or reserve component thereof) referred to in subsection (a) (4) or under a binding written commitment to become such a member,

(C) he receives an amount described in subsection (a) (4) by reason of a combat-related injury, or

(D) on application therefor, he would be entitled to receive disability compensation from the Veterans' Administration.

(3) Special rules for combat-related injuries.—For purposes of this subsection, the term "combat-related injury" means personal injury or sickness—

(A) which is incurred—

(i) as a direct result of armed conflict,

(ii) while engaged in extrahazardous service, or

(iii) under conditions simulating war; or

(B) which is caused by an instrumentality of war.

In the case of an individual who is not described in subparagraph (A) or (B) of paragraph (2), except as provided in paragraph (4), the only amounts taken into account under subsection (a) (4) shall be the amounts which he receives by reason of a combat-related injury.

(4) Amount excluded to be not less than veterans' disability compensation.—In the case of any individual described in paragraph (2), the amounts excludable under subsection (a) (4) for any period with respect to any individual shall not be less than the maximum amount which such individual, on application therefor, would be entitled to receive as disability compensation from the Veterans' Administration.

(c) Cross references.—

(1) For exclusion from employee's gross income of employer contributions to accident and health plans, see section 106.

(2) For exclusion of part of disability retirement pay from the application of subsection (a)(4) of this section, see section 1403 of title 10, United States Code (relating to career compensation laws).

§ 105. Amounts received under accident and health plans

(a) Amounts attributable to employer contributions.—Except as otherwise provided in this section, amounts received by an employee through accident or health insurance for personal injuries or sickness shall be included in gross income to the extent such amounts (1) are attributable to contributions by the employer which were not includible in the gross income of the employee, or (2) are paid by the employer.

(b) Amounts expended for medical care.—Except in the case of amounts attributable to (and not in excess of) deductions allowed under section 213 (relating to medical, etc., expenses) for any prior taxable year, gross income does not include amounts referred to in subsection (a) if such amounts are paid, directly or indirectly, to the taxpayer to reimburse the taxpayer for expenses incurred by him for the medical care (as defined in section 213(d)) of the taxpayer, his spouse, and his dependents (as defined in section 152). Any child to whom section 152(e) applies shall be treated as a dependent of both parents for purposes of this subsection.

(c) Payments unrelated to absence from work.—Gross income does not include amounts referred to in subsection (a) to the extent such amounts—

(1) constitute payment for the permanent loss or loss of use of a member or function of the body, or the permanent disfigurement, of the taxpayer, his spouse, or a dependent (as defined in section 152), and

(2) are computed with reference to the nature of the injury without regard to the period the employee is absent from work.

[(d) Repealed.]

(e) Accident and health plans.—For purposes of this section and section 104—

(1) amounts received under an accident or health plan for employees, and

(2) amounts received from a sickness and disability fund for employees maintained under the law of a State or the District of Columbia,

shall be treated as amounts received through accident or health insurance.

(f) Rules for application of section 213.—For purposes of section 213(a) (relating to medical, dental, etc., expenses) amounts excluded from gross income under subsection (c) or (d) shall not be considered as compensation (by insurance or otherwise) for expenses paid for medical care.

(g) Self-employed individual not considered an employee.—For purposes of this section, the term "employee" does not include an individual who is an employee within the meaning of section 401(c) (1) (relating to self-employed individuals).

(h) Amount paid to highly compensated individuals under a discriminatory self-insured medical expense reimbursement plan.—

(1) In general.—In the case of amounts paid to a highly compensated individual under a self-insured medical reimbursement plan which does not satisfy the requirements of paragraph (2) for a plan year, subsection (b) shall not apply to such amounts to the extent they constitute an excess reimbursement of such highly compensated individual.

(2) Prohibition of discrimination.—A self-insured medical reimbursement plan satisfies the requirements of this paragraph only if—

(A) the plan does not discriminate in favor of highly compensated individuals as to eligibility to participate; and

(B) the benefits provided under the plan do not discriminate in favor of participants who are highly compensated individuals.

(3) Nondiscriminatory eligibility classifications.—

(A) **In general.**—A self-insured medical reimbursement plan does not satisfy the requirements of subparagraph (A) of paragraph (2) unless such plan benefits—

(i) 70 percent or more of all employees, or 80 percent or more of all the employees who are eligible to benefit under the plan if 70 percent or more of all employees are eligible to benefit under the plan; or

(ii) such employees as qualify under a classification set up by the employer and found by the Secretary not to be discriminatory in favor of highly compensated individuals.

(B) Exclusion of certain employees.—For purposes of subparagraph (A), there may be excluded from consideration—

(i) employees who have not completed 3 years of service;

(ii) employees who have not attained age 25;

(iii) part-time or seasonal employees;

(iv) employees not included in the plan who are included in a unit of employees covered by an agreement between employee representatives and one or more employers which the Secretary finds to be a collective bargaining agreement, if accident and health benefits were the subject of good faith bargaining between such employee representatives and such employer or employers; and

(v) employees who are nonresident aliens and who receive no earned income (within the meaning of section 911(d)(2)) from the employer which constitutes income from sources within the United States (within the meaning of section 861(a)(3)).

(4) Nondiscriminatory benefits.—A self-insured medical reimbursement plan does not meet the requirements of subparagraph (B) of paragraph (2) unless all benefits provided for participants who are highly compensated individuals are provided for all other participants.

(5) Highly compensated individual defined.—For purposes of this subsection, the term "highly compensated individual" means an individual who is—

(A) one of the 5 highest paid officers,

(B) a shareholder who owns (with the application of section 318) more than 10 percent in value of the stock of the employer, or

(C) among the highest paid 25 percent of all employees (other than employees described in paragraph (3)(B) who are not participants).

(6) Self-insured medical reimbursement plan.—The term "self-insured medical reimbursement plan" means a plan of an employer to reimburse employees for expenses referred to in subsection (b) for which reimbursement is not provided under a policy of accident and health insurance.

(7) Excess reimbursement of highly compensated individual.—For purposes of this section, the excess reimbursement of a highly compensated individual which is attributable to a self-insured medical reimbursement plan is—

(A) in the case of a benefit available to highly compensated individuals but not to all other participants (or which otherwise fails to satisfy the requirements of paragraph (2)(B)), the amount reimbursed under the plan to the employee with respect to such benefit, and

(B) in the case of benefits ([1] other than benefits described in subparagraph (A) paid to a highly compensated individual by a plan which fails to satisfy the requirements of paragraph (2), the total amount reimbursed to the highly compensated individual for the plan year multiplied by a fraction—

(i) the numerator of which is the total amount reimbursed to all participants who are highly compensated individuals under the plan for the plan year, and

(ii) the denominator of which is the total amount reimbursed to all employees under the plan for such plan year.

In determining the fraction under subparagraph (B), there shall not be taken into account any reimbursement which is attributable to a benefit described in subparagraph (A).

(8) **Certain controlled groups, etc.**—All employees who are treated as employed by a single employer under subsection (b), (c), or (m) of section 414 shall be treated as employed by a single employer for purposes of this section.

(9) **Regulations.**—The Secretary shall prescribe such regulations as may be necessary to carry out the provisions of this section.

(10) **Time of inclusion.**—Any amount paid for a plan year that is included in income by reason of this subsection shall be treated as received or accrued in the taxable year of the participant in which the plan year ends.

* * *

Amendment of Section

Pub.L. 99–514, Title XI, § 1151(c)(2), (k), Oct. 22, 1986, 100 Stat. ——, provided that, except as otherwise provided, applicable to years beginning after the later of Dec. 31, 1987, or the earlier of date three months after date Secretary of Treasury issues regulations necessary to carry out section 89 of Title 26, Internal Revenue Code, or Dec. 31, 1988, section 105 is amended by striking out subsection (h) and by redesignating subsection (i) as subsection (h).

§ 106. Contributions by employer to accident and health plans

(a) **In general.**—Gross income does not include contributions by the employer to accident or health plans for compensation (through insurance or otherwise) to his employees for personal injuries or sickness.

(b) **Exception for highly compensated individuals where plan fails to provide certain continuation coverage.**—

(1) **In general.**—Subsection (a) shall not apply to any amount contributed by an employer on behalf of a highly compensated employee (within the meaning of section 414(q)) to a group health plan maintained by such employer unless all such plans maintained by such employer meet the continuing coverage requirements of section 162(k).

(2) **Exception for certain plans.**—Paragraph (1) shall not apply to any—

(A) group health plan for any calendar year if all employers maintaining such plan normally employed fewer than 20 employees on a typical business day during the preceding calendar year,

(B) governmental plan (within the meaning of section 414(d)), or

(C) church plan (within the meaning of section 414(e)).

Under regulations, rules similar to the rules of subsections (a) and (b) of section 52 (relating to employers under common control) shall apply for purposes of subparagraph (A).

(3) **Group health plan.**—for purposes of this subsection, the term "group health plan" has the meaning given such term by section 162(i)(3).

Amendment of Subsec. (a)

Pub.L. 99–514, Title XI, § 1151(j)(2), (k), Oct. 22, 1986, 100 Stat. ——, provided that, except as otherwise provided, applicable to years beginning after the later of Dec. 31, 1987, or the earlier of date three months after date Secretary of Treasury issues regulations necessary to carry out section 89 of Title 26, Internal Revenue Code, or Dec. 31, 1988, subsec. (a) is amended to read as follows:

(a) **In General.**—Gross income of an employee does not include employer-provided coverage under an accident or health plan.

§ 107. Rental value of parsonages

In the case of a minister of the gospel, gross income does not include—

(1) the rental value of a home furnished to him as part of his compensation; or

(2) the rental allowance paid to him as part of his compensation, to the extent used by him to rent or provide a home.

§ 108. Income from discharge of indebtedness

(a) **Exclusion from gross income.**—

(1) **In general.**—Gross income does not include any amount which (but for this subsection) would be includible in gross income by reason of the discharge (in whole or in part) of indebtedness of the taxpayer if—

(A) the discharge occurs in a title 11 case, or

(B) the discharge occurs when the taxpayer is insolvent.

(2) **Coordination of exclusions.**—Subparagraph (B) of paragraph (1) shall not apply to a discharge which occurs in a title 11 case.

(3) **Insolvency exclusion limited to amount of insolvency.**—In the case of a discharge to which paragraph (1)(B) applies, the amount excluded under paragraph (1)(B) shall not exceed the amount by which the taxpayer is insolvent.

(b) **Reduction of tax attributes in title 11 case or insolvency.**—

(1) **In general.**—The amount excluded from gross income under subparagraph (A) or (B) of subsection (a)(1) shall be applied to reduce the tax attributes of the taxpayer as provided in paragraph (2).

(2) **Tax attributes affected; order of reduction.**—Except as provided in paragraph (5), the reduction referred to in paragraph (1) shall be made in the following tax attributes in the following order:

(A) **NOL.**—Any net operating loss for the taxable year of the discharge, and any net operating loss carryover to such taxable year.

(B) **General business credit.**—Any carryover to or from the taxable year of a discharge of an amount for purposes for determining the amount allowable as a credit under section 38 (relating to general business credit).

(C) **Capital loss carryovers.**—Any net capital loss for the taxable year of the discharge, and any capital loss carryover to such taxable year under section 1212.

(D) **Basis reduction.**—

(i) **In general.**—The basis of the property of the taxpayer.

(ii) **Cross reference.**—

For provisions for making the reduction described in clause (i), see section 1017.

* * *

(3) Amount of reduction.—

(A) In general.—Except as provided in subparagraph (B), the reductions described in paragraph (2) shall be one dollar for each dollar excluded by subsection (a).

(B) Credit carryover reduction.—The reductions described in subparagraphs (B) and (E) of paragraph (2) shall be 33$\frac{1}{3}$ cents for each dollar excluded by subsection (a).

(4) Ordering rules.—

(A) Reductions made after determination of tax for year.—The reductions described in paragraph (2) shall be made after the determination of the tax imposed by this chapter for the taxable year of the discharge.

(B) Reductions under subparagraph (A) or (C) of paragraph (2).—The reductions described in subparagraph (A) or (C) of paragraph (2) (as the case may be) shall be made first in the loss for the taxable year of the discharge and then in the carryovers to such taxable year in the order of the taxable years from which each such carryover arose.

(C) Reductions under subparagraphs (B) and (E) of paragraph (2).—The reductions described in subparagraphs (B) and (E) of paragraph (2) shall be made in the order in which carryovers are taken into account under this chapter for the taxable year of the discharge.

(5) Election to apply reduction first against depreciable property.—

(A) In general.—The taxpayer may elect to apply any portion of the reduction referred to in paragraph (1) to the reduction under section 1017 of the basis of the depreciable property of the taxpayer.

(B) Limitation.—The amount to which an election under subparagraph (A) applies shall not exceed the aggregate adjusted bases of the depreciable property held by the taxpayer as of the beginning of the taxable year following the taxable year in which the discharge occurs.

(C) Other tax attributes not reduced.—Paragraph (2) shall not apply to any amount to which an election under this paragraph applies.

(c) [Repealed.]

(d) Meaning of terms; special rules relating to subsections (a) and (b).—

(1) Indebtedness of taxpayer.—For purposes of this section, the term "indebtedness of the taxpayer" means any indebtedness—

(A) for which the taxpayer is liable, or

(B) subject to which the taxpayer holds property.

(2) Title 11 case.—For purposes of this section, the term "title 11 case" means a case under title 11 of the United States Code (relating to bankruptcy), but only if the taxpayer is under the jurisdiction of the court in such case and the discharge of indebtedness is granted by the court or is pursuant to a plan approved by the court.

(3) Insolvent.—For purposes of this section, the term "insolvent" means the excess of liabilities over the fair market value of assets. With respect to any discharge, whether or not the taxpayer is insolvent, and the amount by which the taxpayer is insolvent, shall be determined on the basis of the taxpayer's assets and liabilities immediately before the discharge.

(4) [Repealed.]

(5) Depreciable property.—The term "depreciable property" has the same meaning as when used in section 1017.

(6) Subsections (a) and (b) to be applied at partner level.—In the case of a partnership, subsections (a) and (b) shall be applied at the partner level.

(7) Special rules for S corporation.—

(A) Subsections (a) and (b) to be applied at corporate level.—In the case of an S corporation, subsections (a) and (b) shall be applied at the corporate level.

(B) Reduction in carryover of disallowed losses and deductions.—In the case of an S corporation, for purposes of subparagraph (A) of subsection (b)(2), any loss or deduction which is disallowed for the taxable year of the discharge under section 1366(d)(1) shall be treated as a net operating loss for such taxable year.

(C) Coordination with basis adjustments under section 1367(b)(2).—For purposes of subsection (e)(6), a shareholder's adjusted basis in indebtedness of an S corporation shall be determined without regard to any adjustments made under section 1367(b)(2).

(8) Reductions of tax attributes in title 11 cases of individuals to be made by estate.—In any case under chapter 7 or 11 of title 11 of the United States Code to which section 1398 applies, for purposes of paragraphs (1) and (5) of subsection (b) the estate (and not the individual) shall be treated as the taxpayer. The preceding sentence shall not apply for purposes of applying section 1017 to property transferred by the estate to the individual.

(9) Time for making election, etc.—

(A) Time.—An election under paragraph (5) of subsection (b) shall be made on the taxpayer's return for the taxable year in which the discharge occurs or at such other time as may be permitted in regulations prescribed by the Secretary.

(B) Revocation only with consent.—An election referred to in subparagraph (A), once made, may be revoked only with the consent of the Secretary.

(C) Manner.—An election referred to in subparagraph (A) shall be made in such manner as the Secretary may by regulations prescribe.

(10) Cross reference.—

For provision that no reduction is to be made in the basis of exempt property of an individual debtor, see section 1017(c)(1).

(e) General rules for discharge of indebtedness (including discharges not in title 11 cases or insolvency).—For purposes of this title—

(1) No other insolvency exception.—Except as otherwise provided in this section, there shall be no insolvency exception from the general rule that gross income includes income from the discharge of indebtedness.

(2) Income not realized to extent of lost deductions.—No income shall be realized from the discharge of indebtedness to the extent that payment of the liability would have given rise to a deduction.

(3) Adjustments for unamortized premium and discount.—The amount taken into account with respect to any discharge shall be properly adjusted for unamortized premium and unamortized discount with respect to the indebtedness discharged.

(4) Acquisition of indebtedness by person related to debtor.—

(A) Treated as acquisition by debtor.—For purposes of determining income of the debtor from discharge of indebtedness, to the extent provided in regulations prescribed by the Secretary, the acquisition of outstanding indebtedness by a person bearing a relationship to the debtor specified in section 267(b) or 707(b)(1) from a person who does not bear such a relationship to the debtor shall be treated as the acquisition of such indebtedness by the debtor. Such regulations shall provide for such adjustments in the treatment of any subsequent transactions involving the indebtedness as may be appropriate by reason of the application of the preceding sentence.

(B) **Members of family.**—For purposes of this paragraph, sections 267(b) and 707(b)(1) shall be applied as if section 267(c)(4) provided that the family of an individual consists of the individual's spouse, the individual's children, grandchildren, and parents, and any spouse of the individual's children or grandchildren.

(C) **Entities under common control treated as related.**—For purposes of this paragraph, two entities which are treated as a single employer under subsection (b) or (c) of section 414 shall be treated as bearing a relationship to each other which is described in section 267(b).

(5) **Purchase-money debt reduction for solvent debtor treated as price reduction.**—If—

(A) the debt of a purchaser of property to the seller of such property which arose out of the purchase of such property is reduced,

(B) such reduction does not occur—

(i) in a title 11 case, or

(ii) when the purchaser is insolvent, and

(C) but for this paragraph, such reduction would be treated as income to the purchaser from the discharge of indebtedness,

then such reduction shall be treated as a purchase price adjustment.

(6) **Indebtedness contributed to capital.**—For purposes of determining income of the debtor from discharge of indebtedness, if a debtor corporation acquires its indebtedness from a shareholder as a contribution to capital—

(A) section 118 shall not apply, but

(B) such corporation shall be treated as having satisfied the indebtedness with an amount of money equal to the shareholder's adjusted basis in the indebtedness.

(7) **Recapture of gain on subsequent sale of stock.**—

(A) **In general.**—If a creditor acquires stock of a debtor corporation in satisfaction of such corporation's indebtedness, for purposes of section 1245—

(i) such stock (and any other property the basis of which is determined in whole or in part by reference to the adjusted basis of such stock) shall be treated as section 1245 property,

(ii) the aggregate amount allowed to the creditor—

(I) as deductions under subsection (a) or (b) of section 166 (by reason of the worthlessness or partial worthlessness of the indebtedness), or

(II) as an ordinary loss on the exchange,

shall be treated as an amount allowed as a deduction for depreciation, and

(iii) an exchange of such stock qualifying under section 354(a), 355(a), or 356(a) shall be treated as an exchange to which section 1245(b)(3) applies.

The amount determined under clause (ii) shall be reduced by the amount (if any) included in the creditor's gross income on the exchange.

(B) Special rule for cash basis taxpayers.—In the case of any creditor who computes his taxable income under the cash receipts and disbursements method, proper adjustment shall be made in the amount taken into account under clause (ii) of subparagraph (A) for any amount which was not included in the creditor's gross income but which would have been included in such gross income if such indebtedness had been satisfied in full.

(C) Stock of parent corporation.—For purposes of this paragraph, stock of a corporation in control (within the meaning of section 368(c)) of the debtor corporation shall be treated as stock of the debtor corporation.

(D) Treatment of successor corporation.—For purposes of this paragraph, the term "debtor corporation" includes a successor corporation.

(E) Partnership rule.—Under regulations prescribed by the Secretary, rules similar to the rules of the foregoing subparagraphs of this paragraph shall apply with respect to the indebtedness of a partnership.

(8) Stock for debt exception not to apply in de minimis cases.—For purposes of determining income of the debtor from discharge of indebtedness, the stock for debt exception shall not apply—

(A) to the issuance of nominal or token shares, or

(B) with respect to an unsecured creditor, where the ratio of the value of the stock received by such unsecured creditor to the amount of his indebtedness cancelled or exchanged for stock in the workout is less than 50 percent of a similar ratio computed for all unsecured creditors participating in the workout.

* * *

(10) Indebtedness satisfied by corporation's stock.—

(A) In general.—For purposes of determining income of a debtor from discharge of indebtedness, if a debtor corporation transfers stock to a creditor in satisfaction of its indebtedness, such corporation shall be treated as having satisfied the indebtedness with an amount of money equal to the fair market value of the stock.

(B) Exception for title 11 cases and insolvent debtors.—Subparagraph (A) shall not apply in the case of a debtor in a title 11 case or to the extent the debtor is insolvent.

(C) Exception for transfers in certain workouts.—

(i) **In general.**—Subparagraph (A) shall not apply to any transfer of stock in a qualified workout.

(ii) **Qualified workout.**—For purposes of clause (i), the term "qualified workout" means any plan under which stock is transferred to creditors in satisfaction of indebtedness if—

(I) because of cash flow and credit problems, the corporation making such transfer will have trouble in meeting liabilities coming due during the next 12 months to such an extent that there is a substantial threat of involuntary proceedings relating to insolvency or bankruptcy,

(II) such corporation in any report to its shareholders for the period during which such transfer occurs includes a statement that such corporation believes it meets the requirement of subclause (I) and that it is availing itself of the workout provisions of this subparagraph,

(III) the holders of more than 50 percent of the total indebtedness of the corporation approve such plan, and

(IV) at least 25 percent of the total indebtedness of the corporation is extinguished by transfers pursuant to such plan.

(f) Student loans.—

(1) **In general.**—In the case of an individual, gross income does not include any amount which (but for this subsection) would be includible in gross income by reason of the discharge (in whole or in part) of any student loan if such discharge was pursuant to a provision of such loan under which all or part of the indebtedness of the individual would be discharged if the individual worked for a certain period of time in certain professions for any of a broad class of employers.

(2) **Student loan.**—For purposes of this subsection, the term "student loan" means any loan to an individual to assist the individual in attending an educational organization described in section 170(b)(1)(A)(ii) made by—

(A) the United States, or an instrumentality or agency thereof,

(B) a State, territory, or possession of the United States, or the District of Columbia, or any political subdivision thereof, or

(C) a public benefit corporation—

(i) which is exempt from taxation under section 501(c)(3),

(ii) which has assumed control over a State, county, or municipal hospital, and

(iii) whose employees have been deemed to be public employees under State law, or

(D) any educational organization so described pursuant to an agreement with any entity described in subparagraph (A), (B), or (C) under which the funds from which the loan was made were provided to such educational organization.

(g) Special rules for discharge of qualified farm indebtedness of solvent farmers.—

(1) **In general.**—For purposes of this section and section 1017, the discharge by a qualified person of qualified farm indebtedness of a taxpayer who is not insolvent at the time of the discharge shall be treated in the same manner as if the discharge had occurred when the taxpayer was insolvent.

(2) **Qualified farm indebtedness.**—For purposes of this subsection, indebtedness of a taxpayer shall be treated as qualified farm indebtedness if—

(A) such indebtedness was incurred directly in connection with the operation by the taxpayer of the trade or business of farming, and

(B) 50 percent or more of the average annual gross receipts of the taxpayer for the 3 taxable years preceding the taxable year in which the discharge of such indebtedness occurs is attributable to the trade or business of farming.

(3) **Qualified person.**—For purposes of this subsection, the term "qualified person" means a person described in section 46(c)(8)(D)(iv).

§ 109. Improvements by lessee on lessor's property

Gross income does not include income (other than rent) derived by a lessor of real property on the termination of a lease, representing the value of such property attributable to buildings erected or other improvements made by the lessee.

§ 111. Recovery of tax benefit items

(a) Deductions.—Gross income does not include income attributable to the recovery during the taxable year of any amount deducted in any prior taxable year to the extent such amount did not reduce the amount of tax imposed by this chapter.

(b) Credits.—

(1) In general.—If—

(A) a credit was allowable with respect to any amount for any prior taxable year, and

(B) during the taxable year there is a downward price adjustment or similar adjustment,

the tax imposed by this chapter for the taxable year shall be increased by the amount of the credit attributable to the adjustment.

(2) Exception where credit did not reduce tax.—Paragraph (1) shall not apply to the extent that the credit allowable for the recovered amount did not reduce the amount of tax imposed by this chapter.

(3) Exception for investment tax credit and foreign tax credit.—This subsection shall not apply with respect to the credit determined under section 46 and the foreign tax credit.

(c) Treatment of carryovers.—For purposes of this section, an increase in a carryover which has not expired before the beginning of the taxable year in which the recovery or adjustment takes place shall be treated as reducing tax imposed by this chapter.

(d) Special rules for accumulated earnings tax and for personal holding company tax.—In applying subsection (a) for the purpose of determining the accumulated earnings tax under section 531 or the tax under section 541 (relating to personal holding companies)—

(1) any excluded amount under subsection (a) allowed for the purposes of this subtitle (other than section 531 or section 541) shall be allowed whether or not such amount resulted in a reduction of the tax under section 531 or the tax under section 541 for the prior taxable year; and

(2) where any excluded amount under subsection (a) was not allowable as a deduction for the prior taxable year for purposes of this subtitle other than of section 531 or section 541 but was allowable for the same taxable year under section 531 or section 541, then such excluded amount shall be allowable if it did not result in a reduction of the tax under section 531 or the tax under section 541.

§ 115. Income of states, municipalities, etc.

Gross income does not include—

(1) income derived from any public utility or the exercise of any essential governmental function and accruing to a State or any political subdivision thereof, or the District of Columbia; or

(2) income accruing to the government of any possession of the United States, or any political subdivision thereof.

§ 116. Partial exclusion of dividends received by individuals [Repealed.]

§ 117. Qualified scholarships

(a) General rule.—Gross income does not include any amount received as a qualified scholarship by an individual who is a candidate for a degree at an educational organization described in section 170(b)(1)(A)(ii).

(b) Qualified scholarship.—For purposes of this section—

(1) In general.—The term "qualified scholarship" means any amount received by an individual as a scholarship or fellowship grant to the extent the individual establishes that, in accordance with the conditions of the grant, such amount was used for qualified tuition and related expenses.

(2) Qualified tuition and related expenses.—For purposes of paragraph (1), the term "qualified tuition and related expenses" means—

(A) tuition and fees required for the enrollment or attendance of a student at an educational organization described in section 170(b)(1)(A)(ii), and

(B) fees, books, supplies, and equipment required for courses of instruction at such an educational organization.

(c) Limitation.—Subsections (a) and (d) shall not apply to that portion of any amount received which represents payment for teaching, research, or other services by the student required as a condition for receiving the qualified scholarship or qualified tuition reduction.

(d) Qualified tuition reduction.—

(1) In general.—Gross income shall not include any qualified tuition reduction.

(2) Qualified tuition reduction.—For purposes of this subsection, the term "qualified tuition reduction" means the amount of any reduction in tuition provided to an employee of an organization described in section 170(b)(1)(A)(ii) for the education (below the graduate level) at such organization (or another organization described in section 170(b)(1)(A)(ii)) of—

(A) such employee, or

(B) any person treated as an employee (or whose use is treated as an employee use) under the rules of section 132(f).

(3) Reduction must not discriminate in favor of highly compensated, etc. —Paragraph (1) shall apply with respect to any qualified tuition reduction provided with respect to any officer, owner, or highly compensated employee only if such reduction is available on substantially the same terms to each member of a group of employees which is defined under a reasonable classification set up by the employer which does not discriminate in favor of officers, owners, or highly compensated employees (within the meaning of section 414(q)).

Amendment of subsec. (d)

Pub. L. 99–514, Title XI, § 1114(b)(2), (c)(2), Oct. 22, 1986, 100 Stat. ——, provided that, applicable to years beginning after December 31, 1987, subsec. (d)(3) of this section is amended—

(A) by striking out "officer, owner, or",

(B) by striking out "officers, owners, or", and

(C) by inserting at the end thereof the following new sentence: "For purposes of this paragraph, the term 'highly compensated employee' has the meaning given such term by section 414(q)."

Pub.L. 99–514, Title XI, § 1151(g)(2), (k), Oct. 22, 1986, 100 Stat. ——, provided that, except as otherwise provided, applicable to years beginning after the later of Dec. 31, 1987, or the earlier of date three months after date Secretary of Treasury issues regulations necessary to carry out section 89 of Title 26, Internal Revenue Code, or Dec. 31, 1988, subsec. (d) is amended by adding at the end thereof the following new paragraph:

(4) Exclusion of Certain Employees.—For purposes of this subsection, there may be excluded from consideration employees who may be excluded from consideration under section 89(h).

§ 118. Contributions to the capital of a corporation

(a) General rule.—In the case of a corporation, gross income does not include any contribution to the capital of the taxpayer.

(b) Contributions in aid of construction, etc.—For purposes of subsection (a), the term "contribution to the capital of the taxpayer" does not include any contribution in aid of construction or any other contribution as a customer or potential customer.

(c) Cross references.—

(1) For basis of property acquired by a corporation through a contribution to its capital, see section 362.

(2) For special rules in the case of contributions of indebtedness, see section 108(e)(6).

§ 119. Meals or lodging furnished for the convenience of the employer

(a) Meals and lodging furnished to employee, his spouse, and his dependents, pursuant to employment.—There shall be excluded from gross income of an employee the value of any meals or lodging furnished to him, his spouse, or any of his dependents by or on behalf of his employer for the convenience of the employer, but only if—

(1) in the case of meals, the meals are furnished on the business premises of the employer, or

(2) in the case of lodging, the employee is required to accept such lodging on the business premises of his employer as a condition of his employment.

(b) Special rules.—For purposes of subsection (a)—

(1) Provisions of employment contract or state statute not to be determinative.—In determining whether meals or lodging are furnished for the convenience of the employer, the provisions of an employment contract or of a State statute fixing terms of employment shall not be determinative of whether the meals or lodging are intended as compensation.

(2) Certain factors not taken into account with respect to meals.—In determining whether meals are furnished for the convenience of the employer, the fact that a charge is made for such meals, and the fact that the employee may accept or decline such meals, shall not be taken into account.

(3) Certain fixed charges for meals.—

(A) In general.—If—

(i) an employee is required to pay on a periodic basis a fixed charge for his meals, and

(ii) such meals are furnished by the employer for the convenience of the employer,

there shall be excluded from the employee's gross income an amount equal to such fixed charge.

(B) Application of subparagraph (A).—Subparagraph (A) shall apply—

(i) whether the employee pays the fixed charge out of his stated compensation or out of his own funds, and

(ii) only if the employee is required to make the payment whether he accepts or declines the meals.

* * *

(d) Lodging furnished by certain educational institutions to employees.—

(1) In general.—In the case of an employee of an educational institution, gross income shall not include the value of qualified campus lodging furnished to such employee during the taxable year.

(2) Exception in cases of inadequate rent.—Paragraph (1) shall not apply to the extent of the excess of—

(A) the lesser of—

(i) 5 percent of the appraised value (as of the close of the calendar year in which the taxable year begins) of the qualified campus lodging, or

(ii) the average of the rentals paid by individuals (other than employees or students of the educational institution) during such calendar year for lodging provided by the educational institution which is comparable to the qualified campus lodging provided to the employee, over

(B) the rent paid by the employee for the qualified campus lodging during such calendar year.

(3) Qualified campus lodging.—For purposes of this subsection, the term "qualified campus lodging" means lodging to which subsection (a) does not apply and which is—

(A) located on, or in the proximity of, a campus of the educational institution, and

(B) furnished to the employee, his spouse, and any of his dependents by or on behalf of such institution for use as a residence.

(4) Educational institution.—For purposes of this paragraph, the term "educational institution" means an institution described in section 170(b)(1)(A)(ii).

§ 121. One-time exclusion of gain from sale of principal residence by individual who has attained age 55

(a) General rule.—At the election of the taxpayer, gross income does not include gain from the sale or exchange of property if—

(1) the taxpayer has attained the age of 55 before the date of such sale or exchange, and

(2) during the 5-year period ending on the date of the sale or exchange, such property has been owned and used by the taxpayer as his principal residence for periods aggregating 3 years or more.

(b) Limitations.—

(1) **Dollar limitation.**—The amount of the gain excluded from gross income under subsection (a) shall not exceed $125,000 ($62,500 in the case of a separate return by a married individual).

(2) **Application to only 1 sale or exchange.**—Subsection (a) shall not apply to any sale or exchange by the taxpayer if an election by the taxpayer or his spouse under subsection (a) with respect to any other sale or exchange is in effect.

(3) **Additional election if prior sale was made on or before July 26, 1978.** —In the case of any sale or exchange after July 26, 1978, this section shall be applied by not taking into account any election made with respect to a sale or exchange on or before such date.

(c) Election.—An election under subsection (a) may be made or revoked at any time before the expiration of the period for making a claim for credit or refund of the tax imposed by this chapter for the taxable year in which the sale or exchange occurred, and shall be made or revoked in such manner as the Secretary shall by regulations prescribe. In the case of a taxpayer who is married, an election under subsection (a) or a revocation thereof may be made only if his spouse joins in such election or revocation.

(d) Special rules.—

(1) **Property held jointly by husband and wife.**—For purposes of this section, if—

(A) property is held by a husband and wife as joint tenants, tenants by the entirety, or community property,

(B) such husband and wife make a joint return under section 6013 for the taxable year of the sale or exchange, and

(C) one spouse satisfies the age, holding, and use requirements of subsection (a) with respect to such property,

then both husband and wife shall be treated as satisfying the age, holding, and use requirements of subsection (a) with respect to such property.

(2) **Property of deceased spouse.**—For purposes of this section, in the case of an unmarried individual whose spouse is deceased on the date of the sale or exchange of property, if—

(A) the deceased spouse (during the 5-year period ending on the date of the sale or exchange) satisfied the holding and use requirements of subsection (a) (2) with respect to such property, and

(B) no election by the deceased spouse under subsection (a) is in effect with respect to a prior sale or exchange,

then such individual shall be treated as satisfying the holding and use requirements of subsection (a) (2) with respect to such property.

(3) **Tenant-stockholder in cooperative housing corporation.**—For purposes of this section, if the taxpayer holds stock as a tenant-stockholder (as defined in section 216) in a cooperative housing corporation (as defined in such section), then—

(A) the holding requirements of subsection (a) (2) shall be applied to the holding of such stock, and

(B) the use requirements of subsection (a) (2) shall be applied to the house or apartment which the taxpayer was entitled to occupy as such stockholder.

(4) Involuntary conversions.—For purposes of this section, the destruction, theft, seizure, requisition, or condemnation of property shall be treated as the sale of such property.

(5) Property used in part as principal residence.—In the case of property only a portion of which, during the 5-year period ending on the date of the sale or exchange, has been owned and used by the taxpayer as his principal residence for periods aggregating 3 years or more, this section shall apply with respect to so much of the gain from the sale or exchange of such property as is determined, under regulations prescribed by the Secretary, to be attributable to the portion of the property so owned and used by the taxpayer.

(6) Determination of marital status.—In the case of any sale or exchange, for purposes of this section—

(A) the determination of whether an individual is married shall be made as of the date of the sale or exchange; and

(B) an individual legally separated from his spouse under a decree of divorce or of separate maintenance shall not be considered as married.

(7) Application of sections 1033 and 1034.—In applying sections 1033 (relating to involuntary conversions) and 1034 (relating to sale or exchange of residence), the amount realized from the sale or exchange of property shall be treated as being the amount determined without regard to this section, reduced by the amount of gain not included in gross income pursuant to an election under this section.

* * *

§ 123. Amounts received under insurance contracts for certain living expenses

(a) General rule.—In the case of an individual whose principal residence is damaged or destroyed by fire, storm, or other casualty, or who is denied access to his principal residence by governmental authorities because of the occurrence or threat of occurrence of such a casualty, gross income does not include amounts received by such individual under an insurance contract which are paid to compensate or reimburse such individual for living expenses incurred for himself and members of his household resulting from the loss of use or occupancy of such residence.

(b) Limitation.—Subsection (a) shall apply to amounts received by the taxpayer for living expenses incurred during any period only to the extent the amounts received do not exceed the amount by which—

(1) the actual living expenses incurred during such period for himself and members of his household resulting from the loss of use or occupancy of their residence, exceed

(2) the normal living expenses which would have been incurred for himself and members of his household during such period.

§ 125. Cafeteria plans

(a) In general.—Except as provided in subsection (b), no amount shall be included in the gross income of a participant in a cafeteria plan solely because, under the plan, the participant may choose among the benefits of the plan.

(b) Exception for highly compensated participants and key employees.—

(1) **Highly compensated participants.**—In the case of a highly compensated participant, subsection (a) shall not apply to any benefit attributable to a plan year for which the plan discriminates in favor of—

(A) highly compensated individuals as to eligibility to participate, or

(B) highly compensated participants as to contributions and benefits.

(2) **Key employees.**—In the case of a key employee (within the meaning of section 416(i)(1)), subsection (a) shall not apply to any benefit attributable to a plan for which the statutory nontaxable benefits provided to key employees exceed 25 percent of the aggregate of such benefits provided for all employees under the plan. For purposes of the preceding sentence, statutory nontaxable benefits shall be determined without regard to the last sentence of subsection (f).

(3) **Year of inclusion.**—For purposes of determining the taxable year of inclusion, any benefit described in paragraph (1) or (2) shall be treated as received or accrued in the taxable year of the participant or key employee in which the plan year ends.

(c) **Discrimination as to benefits or contributions.**—For purposes of subparagraph (B) of subsection (b)(1), a cafeteria plan does not discriminate where qualified benefits and total benefits (or employer contributions allocable to qualified benefits and employer contributions for total benefits) do not discriminate in favor of highly compensated participants.

(d) **Cafeteria plan defined.**—For purposes of this section—

(1) **In general.**—The term "cafeteria plan" means a written plan under which—

(A) all participants are employees, and

(B) the participants may choose among two or more benefits consisting of cash and qualified benefits.

(2) **Deferred compensation plans excluded.**—The term "cafeteria plan" does not include any plan which provides for deferred compensation. The preceding sentence shall not apply in the case of a profit-sharing or stock bonus plan which includes a qualified cash or deferred arrangement (as defined in section 401(k)(2)) to the extent of amounts which a covered employee may elect to have the employer pay as contributions to a trust under such plan on behalf of the employee.

(e) **Highly compensated participant and individual defined.**—For purposes of this section—

(1) **Highly compensated participant.**—The term "highly compensated participant" means a participant who is—

(A) an officer,

(B) a shareholder owning more than 5 percent of the voting power or value of all classes of stock of the employer,

(C) highly compensated, or

(D) a spouse or dependent (within the meaning of section 152) of an individual described in subparagraph (A), (B), or (C).

(2) **Highly compensated individual.**—The term "highly compensated individual" means an individual who is described in subparagraphs (A), (B), (C), or (D) of paragraph (1).

(f) **Qualified benefits defined.**—For purposes of this section, the term "qualified benefit" means any benefit which, with the application of subsection (a), is not includible in the gross income of the employee by reason of an express provision of this chapter (other than section 117, 124, 127, or 132). Such term includes any group term life insurance which is includible in gross income only because it exceeds the dollar limitation of section 79 and such term includes any other benefit permitted under regulations.

(g) Special rules.—

(1) Collectively bargained plan not considered discriminatory.—For purposes of this section, a plan shall not be treated as discriminatory if the plan is maintained under an agreement which the Secretary finds to be a collective bargaining agreement between employee representatives and one or more employers.

(2) Health benefits.—For purposes of subparagraph (B) of subsection (b) (1), a cafeteria plan which provides health benefits shall not be treated as discriminatory if—

(A) contributions under the plan on behalf of each participant include an amount which—

(i) equals 100 percent of the cost of the health benefit coverage under the plan of the majority of the highly compensated participants similarly situated, or

(ii) equals or exceeds 75 percent of the cost of the health benefit coverage of the participant (similarly situated) having the highest cost health benefit coverage under the plan, and

(B) contributions or benefits under the plan in excess of those described in subparagraph (A) bear a uniform relationship to compensation.

(3) Certain participation eligibility rules not treated as discriminatory.—For purposes of subparagraph (A) of subsection (b) (1), a classification shall not be treated as discriminatory if the plan—

(A) benefits a group of employees described in subparagraph (B) of section 410(b) (1), and

(B) meets the requirements of clauses (i) and (ii):

(i) No employee is required to complete more than 3 years of employment with the employer or employers maintaining the plan as a condition of participation in the plan, and the employment requirement for each employee is the same.

(ii) Any employee who has satisfied the employment requirement of clause (i) and who is otherwise entitled to participate in the plan commences participation no later than the first day of the first plan year beginning after the date the employment requirement was satisfied unless the employee was separated from service before the first day of that plan year.

(4) Certain controlled groups, etc.—All employees who are treated as employed by a single employer under subsection (b), (c), or (m) of section 414 shall be treated as employed by a single employer for purposes of this section.

(h) Cross Reference.—

For reporting and recordkeeping requirements, see section 6039D.

(i) Regulations.—The Secretary shall prescribe such regulations as may be necessary to carry out the provisions of this section.

Amendment of Section

Pub.L. 99–514, Title XI, § 1151(d)(1), (k), Oct. 22, 1986, 100 Stat. ——, ——, provided that, except as otherwise provided, applicable to years beginning after the later of Dec. 31, 1987, or the earlier of date three months after date Secretary of

Treasury issues regulations necessary to carry out section 89 of Title 26, Internal Revenue Code, or Dec. 31, 1988, section 125 is amended to read as follows:

§ 125. Cafeteria plans

(a) **General rule.**—In the case of a cafeteria plan—

(1) amounts shall not be included in gross income of a participant in such plan solely because, under the plan, the participant may choose among the benefits of the plan, and

(2) if the plan fails to meet the requirements of subsection (b) for any plan year—

(A) paragraph (1) shall not apply, and

(B) notwithstanding any other provision of part III of this subchapter, any qualified benefits received under such cafeteria plan by a highly compensated employee for such plan year shall be included in the gross income of such employee for the taxable year with or within which such plan year ends.

(b) **Prohibition against discrimination as to eligibility to participate.**—

(1) **Highly compensated employees.**—A plan shall be treated as failing to meet the requirements of this subsection unless the plan is available to a group of employees as qualify under a classification set up by the employer and which the Secretary find not to be discriminatory in favor of highly compensated employees.

(2) **Key employees.**—In the case of a key employee (within the meaning of section 416(i)(1)), a plan shall be treated as failing to meet the requirements of this subsection if the qualified benefits provided to key employees under the plan exceed 25 percent of the aggregate of such benefits provided for all employees under the plan. For purposes of the preceding sentence, qualified benefits shall be determined without regard to the last sentence of subsection (e).

(3) **Excludable employees.**—For purposes of this subsection, there may be excluded from consideration employees who may be excluded from consideration under section 89(h).

(c) **Cafeteria plan defined.**—For purposes of this section—

(1) **In general.**—The term "cafeteria plan" means a plan which meets the requirements of section 89(k) and under which—

(A) all participants are employees, and

(B) the participants may choose—

(i) among 2 or more benefits consisting of cash and qualified benefits, or

(ii) among 2 or more qualified benefits.

(2) **Deferred compensation plans excluded.**—

(A) **In general.**—The term "cafeteria plan" does not include any plan which provides for deferred compensation.

(B) **Exception for cash and deferred arrangements.**—Subparagraph (A) shall not apply to a profit-sharing or stock bonus plan which includes a qualified cash or deferred arrangement (as defined in section 401(k)(2)) to the extent of amounts which a covered employee may elect to have the employer pay as contributions to a trust under such plan on behalf of the employee.

(C) **Exception for certain plans maintained by educational institutions.**—Subparagraph (A) shall not apply to a plan maintained by an educational organization described in section 170(b)(1)(A)(ii) to the extent of amounts which a covered employee may elect to have the employer pay as contributions for post-retirement group life insurance if—

(i) all contributions for such insurance must be made before retirement, and

(ii) such life insurance does not have a cash surrender value at any time.

For purposes of section 79, any life insurance described in the preceding sentence shall be treated as group-term life insurance.

(d) **Highly compensated employee.**—For purposes of this section, the term "highly compensated employee" has the meaning given such term by section 414(q).

(e) **Qualified benefits defined.**—For purposes of this section—

(1) **In general.**—The term "qualified benefit" means any benefit which, with the application of subsection (a), is not includible in the gross income of the employee by reason of an express provision of this chapter (other than section 117, 124, 127, or 132).

(2) **Certain benefits included.**—The term "qualified benefits" includes—

(A) any group-term life insurance which is includible in gross income only because it exceeds the dollar limitation of section 79, and

(B) any other benefit permitted under regulations.

(f) **Collectively bargained plan not considered discriminatory.**—For purposes of this section, a plan shall not be treated as discriminatory if the plan is maintained under an agreement which the Secretary finds to be a collective bargaining agreement between employee representatives and one or more employers.

(g) **Cross references.**—

For reporting and recordkeeping requirements, see section 6039D.

§ **126.** Certain cost-sharing payments

(a) **General rule.**—Gross income does not include the excludable portion of payments received under—

(1) The rural clean water program authorized by section 208(j) of the Federal Water Pollution Control Act (33 U.S.C. 1288(j)).

(2) The rural abandoned mine program authorized by section 406 of the Surface Mining Control and Reclamation Act of 1977 (30 U.S.C. 1236).

(3) The water bank program authorized by the Water Bank Act (16 U.S.C. 1301 et seq.)

(4) The emergency conservation measures program authorized by title IV of the Agricultural Credit Act of 1978.

(5) The agricultural conservation program authorized by section 16 of the Soil Conservation and Domestic Allotment Act (16 U.S.C. 590a).

(6) The great plains conservation program authorized by section 16 of the Soil Conservation and Domestic Policy Act (16 U.S.C. 590p(b)).

(7) The resource conservation and development program authorized by the Bankhead-Jones Farm Tenant Act and by the Soil Conservation and Domestic Allotment Act (7 U.S.C. 1010; 16 U.S.C. 590a et seq.).

(8) The forestry incentives program authorized by section 4 of the Cooperative Forestry Assistance Act of 1978 (16 U.S.C. 2103).

(9) Any small watershed program administered by the Secretary of Agriculture which is determined by the Secretary of the Treasury or his delegate to be

substantially similar to the type of programs described in paragraphs (1) through (8).

(10) Any program of a State, possession of the United States, a political subdivision of any of the foregoing, or the District of Columbia under which payments are made to individuals primarily for the purpose of conserving soil, protecting or restoring the environment, improving forests, or providing a habitat for wildlife.

(b) Excludable portion.—For purposes of this section—

(1) In general.—The term "excludable portion" means that portion (or all) of a payment made to any person under any program described in subsection (a) which—

(A) is determined by the Secretary of Agriculture to be made primarily for the purpose of conserving soil and water resources, protecting or restoring the environment, improving forests, or providing a habitat for wildlife, and

(B) is determined by the Secretary of the Treasury or his delegate as not increasing substantially the annual income derived from the property.

(2) Payments not chargeable to capital account.—The term "excludable portion" does not include that portion of any payment which is properly associated with an amount which is allowable as a deduction for the taxable year in which such amount is paid or incurred.

(c) Election for section not to apply.—

(1) In general.—The taxpayer may elect not to have this section (and section 1255) apply to any excludable portion (or portion thereof).

(2) Manner and time for making election.—Any election under paragraph (1) shall be made in the manner prescribed by the Secretary by regulations and shall be made not later than the due date prescribed by law (including extensions) for filing the return of tax under this chapter for the taxable year in which the payment was received or accrued.

(d) Denial of double benefits.—No deduction or credit shall be allowed with respect to any expenditure which is properly associated with any amount excluded from gross income under subsection (a).

(e) Basis of property not increased by reason of excludable payments.—Notwithstanding any provision of section 1016 to the contrary, no adjustment to basis shall be made with respect to property acquired or improved through the use of any payment, to the extent that such adjustment would reflect any amount which is excluded from gross income under subsection (a).

§ 127. Educational assistance programs

(a) Exclusion from gross income.—

(1) In general.—Gross income of an employee does not include amounts paid or expenses incurred by the employer for educational assistance to the employee if the assistance is furnished pursuant to a program which is described in subsection (b).

(2) $5,000 Maximum exclusion.—If, but for this paragraph, this section would exclude from gross income more than $5,250 of educational assistance furnished to an individual during a calendar year, this section shall apply only to the first $5,250 of such assistance so furnished.

(b) Educational assistance program.—

(1) In general.—For purposes of this section an educational assistance program is a separate written plan of an employer for the exclusive benefit of his employees to provide such employees with educational assistance. The program must meet the requirements of paragraphs (2) through (6) of this subsection.

(2) Eligibility.—The program shall benefit employees who qualify under a classification set up by the employer and found by the Secretary not to be discriminatory in favor of employees who are officers, owners, or highly compensated, or their dependents. For purposes of this paragraph, there shall be excluded from consideration employees not included in the program who are included in a unit of employees covered by an agreement which the Secretary of Labor finds to be a collective bargaining agreement between employee representatives and one or more employers, if there is evidence that educational assistance benefits were the subject of good faith bargaining between such employee representatives and such employer or employers.

(3) Principal shareholders or owners.—Not more than 5 percent of the amounts paid or incurred by the employer for educational assistance during the year may be provided for the class of individuals who are shareholders or owners (or their spouses or dependents), each of whom (on any day of the year) owns more than 5 percent of the stock or of the capital or profits interest in the employer.

(4) Other benefits as an alternative.—A program must not provide eligible employees with a choice between educational assistance and other remuneration includible in gross income. For purposes of this section, the business practices of the employer (as well as the written program) will be taken into account.

(5) No funding required.—A program referred to in paragraph (1) is not required to be funded.

(6) Notification of employees.—Reasonable notification of the availability and terms of the program must be provided to eligible employees.

(c) Definitions; special rules.—For purposes of this section—

(1) Educational assistance.—The term "educational assistance" means—

(A) the payment, by an employer, of expenses incurred by or on behalf of an employee for education of the employee (including, but not limited to, tuition, fees, and similar payments, books, supplies, and equipment), and

(B) the provision, by an employer, of courses of instruction for such employee (including books, supplies, and equipment),

but does not include payment for, or the provision of, tools or supplies which may be retained by the employee after completion of a course of instruction, or meals, lodging, or transportation. The term "educational assistance" also does not include any payment for, or the provision of any benefits with respect to, any course or other education involving sports, games, or hobbies.

(2) Employee.—The term "employee" includes, for any year, an individual who is an employee within the meaning of section 401(c)(1) (relating to self-employed individuals).

(3) Employer.—An individual who owns the entire interest in an unincorporated trade or business shall be treated as his own employer. A partnership shall be treated as the employer of each partner who is an employee within the meaning of paragraph (2).

(4) Attribution rules.—

(A) Ownership of stock.—Ownership of stock in a corporation shall be determined in accordance with the rules provided under subsections (d) and (e) of section 1563 (without regard to section 1563(e)(3)(C)).

(B) Interest in unincorporated trade or business.—The interest of an employee in a trade or business which is not incorporated shall be determined in accordance with regulations prescribed by the Secretary, which shall be based on principles similar to the principles which apply in the case of subparagraph (A).

(5) Certain tests not applicable.—An educational assistance program shall not be held or considered to fail to meet any requirements of subsection (b) merely because—

(A) of utilization rates for the different types of educational assistance made available under the program; or

(B) successful completion, or attaining a particular course grade, is required for or considered in determining reimbursement under the program.

(6) Relationship to current law.—This section shall not be construed to affect the deduction or inclusion in income of amounts (not within the exclusion under this section) which are paid or incurred, or received as reimbursement, for educational expenses under section 117, 162 or 212.

(7) Disallowance of excluded amounts as credit or deduction.—No deduction or credit shall be allowed to the employee under any other section of this chapter for any amount excluded from income by reason of this section.

(8) Coordination with section 117(d).—In the case of the education of an individual who is a graduate student at an educational organization described in section 170(b)(1)(A)(ii) and who is engaged in teaching or research activities for such organization, section 117(d)(2) shall be applied as if it did not contain the phrase "(below the graduate level)".

(d) Termination.—This section shall not apply to taxable years beginning after December 31, 1987.

* * *

§ 132.   Certain fringe benefits

(a) Exclusion from gross income.—Gross income shall not include any fringe benefit which qualifies as a—

(1) no-additional-cost service,

(2) qualified employee discount,

(3) working condition fringe, or

(4) de minimis fringe.

(b) No-additional-cost service defined.—For purposes of this section, the term "no-additional-cost service" means any service provided by an employer to an employee for use by such employee if—

(1) such service is offered for sale to customers in the ordinary course of the line of business of the employer in which the employee is performing services, and

(2) the employer incurs no substantial additional cost (including forgone revenue) in providing such service to the employee (determined without regard to any amount paid by the employee for such service).

(c) Qualified employee discount defined.—For purposes of this section—

(1) Qualified employee discount.—The term "qualified employee discount" means any employee discount with respect to qualified property or services to the extent such discount does not exceed—

(A) in the case of property, the gross profit percentage of the price at which the property is being offered by the employer to customers, or

(B) in the case of services, 20 percent of the price at which the services are being offered by the employer to customers.

(2) Gross profit percentage.—

(A) In general.—The term "gross profit percentage" means the percent which—

(i) the excess of the aggregate sales price of property sold by the employer to customers over the aggregate cost of such property to the employer, is of

(ii) the aggregate sale price of such property.

(B) Determination of gross profit percentage.—Gross profit percentage shall be determined on the basis of—

(i) all property offered to customers in the ordinary course of the line of business of the employer in which the employee is performing services (or a reasonable classification of property selected by the employer), and

(ii) the employer's experience during a representative period.

(3) Employee discount defined.—The term "employee discount" means the amount by which—

(A) the price at which the property or services are provided by the employer to an employee for use by such employee, is less than

(B) the price at which such property or services are being offered by the employer to customers.

(4) Qualified property or services.—The term "qualified property or services" means any property (other than real property and other than personal property of a kind held for investment) or services which are offered for sale to customers in the ordinary course of the line of business of the employer in which the employee is performing services.

(d) Working condition fringe defined.—For purposes of this section, the term "working condition fringe" means any property or services provided to an employee of the employer to the extent that, if the employee paid for such property or services, such payment would be allowable as a deduction under section 162 or 167.

(e) De minimis fringe defined.—For purposes of this section—

(1) In general.—The term "de minimis fringe" means any property or service the value of which is (after taking into account the frequency with which similar fringes are provided by the employer to the employer's employees) so small as to make accounting for it unreasonable or administratively impracticable.

(2) Treatment of certain eating facilities.—The operation by an employer of any eating facility for employees shall be treated as a de minimis fringe if—

(A) such facility is located on or near the business premises of the employer, and

(B) revenue derived from such facility normally equals or exceeds the direct operating costs of such facility.

The preceding sentence shall apply with respect to any officer, owner, or highly compensated employee only if access to the facility is available on substantially the same terms to each member of a group of employees which is defined under a reasonable classification set up by the employer which does not discriminate in favor of officers, owners, or highly compensated employees.

Amendment of subsec. (e)(2)

Pub.L. 99–514, Title XI, § 1114(b)(5)(A), (c)(2), Oct. 22, 1986, 100 Stat. ——, provided that, applicable to years beginning after December 31, 1987, subsec. (e)(2) of this section is amended by striking out "officer, owner, or" and by striking out "officers, owners, or" in the provisions following subpar. (B).

(f) Certain individuals treated as employees for purposes of subsections (a)(1) and (2).—For purposes of paragraphs (1) and (2) of subsection (a)—

(1) Retired and disabled employees and surviving spouse of employee treated as employee.—With respect to a line of business of an employer, the term "employee" includes—

(A) any individual who was formerly employed by such employer in such line of business and who separated from service with such employer in such line of business by reason of retirement or disability, and

(B) any widow or widower of any individual who died while employed by such employer in such line of business or while an employee within the meaning of subparagraph (A).

(2) Spouse and dependent children.—

(A) In general.—Any use by the spouse or a dependent child of the employee shall be treated as use by the employee.

(B) Dependent child.—For purposes of subparagraph (A), the term "dependent child" means any child (as defined in section 151(e)(3)) of the employee—

(i) who is a dependent of the employee, or

(ii) both of whose parents are deceased and who has not attained age 25.

For purposes of the preceding sentence, any child to whom section 152(e) applies shall be treated as the dependent of both parents.

(3) Special rule for parents in the case of air transportation.—Any use of air transportation by a parent of an employee (determined without regard to paragraph (1)(B)) shall be treated as use by the employee.

(g) Special rules relating to employer.—For purposes of this section—

(1) Controlled groups, etc.—All employees treated as employed by a single employer under subsection (b), (c), or (m) of section 414 shall be treated as employed by a single employer for purposes of this section.

(2) Reciprocal agreements.—For purposes of paragraph (1) of subsection (a), any service provided by an employer to an employee of another employer shall be treated as provided by the employer of such employee if—

(A) such service is provided pursuant to a written agreement between such employers, and

(B) neither of such employers incurs any substantial additional cost (including forgone revenue) in providing such service or pursuant to such agreement.

Amendment of Subsec. (g)

Pub.L. 99–514, Title XI, § 1151(e)(2), (k), Oct. 22, 1986, 100 Stat. ——, ——, provided that, except as otherwise provided, applicable to years beginning after the later of Dec. 31, 1987, or the earlier of date three months after date Secretary of Treasury issues regulations necessary to carry out section 89 of Title 26, Internal Revenue Code, or Dec. 31, 1988, subsec. (g) is amended to read as follows:

(g) Reciprocal agreements.—For purposes of paragraph (1) of subsection (a), any service provided by an employer to an employee of another employer shall be treated as provided by the employer of such employee if—

(1) such service is provided pursuant to a written agreement between such employers, and

(2) neither of such employers incurs any substantial additional costs (including foregone revenue) in providing such service or pursuant to such agreement.

(h) Special rules.—

(1) Exclusions under subsection (a)(1) and (2) apply to officers, etc., only if no discrimination.—Paragraphs (1) and (2) of subsection (a) shall apply with respect to any fringe benefit described therein provided with respect to any officer, owner, or highly compensated employee only if such fringe benefit is available on substantially the same terms to each member of a group of employees which is defined under a reasonable classification set up by the employer which does not discriminate in favor of officers, owners, or highly compensated employees.

Amendment of subsec. (h)(1)

Pub.L. 99–514, Title XI, § 1114(b)(5)(A), (c)(2), Oct. 22, 1986, 100 Stat. ——, provided that, applicable to years beginning after December 31, 1987, subsec. (h)(1) of this section is amended by striking out "officer, owner, or" and by striking out "officers, owners, or".

Pub.L. 99–514, Title XI, § 1151(g)(5), (k), Oct. 22, 1986, 100 Stat. ——, ——, provided that, except as otherwise provided, applicable to years beginning after the later of Dec. 31, 1987, or the earlier of date three months after date Secretary of Treasury issues regulations necessary to carry out section 89 of Title 26, Internal Revenue Code, or Dec. 31, 1988, subsec. (h)(1) is amended by adding at the end thereof the following new sentence: "For purposes of this paragraph and subsection (e), there may be excluded from consideration employees who may be excluded from consideration under section 89(h)."

(2) Special rule for leased sections of department stores.—

(A) In general.—For purposes of paragraph (2) of subsection (a), in the case of a leased section of a department store—

(i) such section shall be treated as part of the line of business of the person operating the department store, and

(ii) employees in the leased section shall be treated as employees of the person operating the department store.

(B) Leased section of department store.—For purposes of subparagraph (A), a leased section of a department store is any part of a department store where over-the-counter sales of property are made under a lease or similar arrangement where it appears to the general public that individuals making such sales are employed by the person operating the department store.

(3) Auto salesmen.—

(A) In general.—For purposes of subsection (a)(3), qualified automobile demonstration use shall be treated as a working condition fringe.

(B) Qualified automobile demonstration use.—For purposes of subparagraph (A), the term "qualified automobile demonstration use" means any use of an automobile by a full-time automobile salesman in the sales area in which the automobile dealer's sales office is located if—

(i) such use is provided primarily to facilitate the salesman's performance of services for the employer, and

(ii) there are substantial restrictions on the personal use of such automobile by such salesman.

(4) **Parking.**—The term "working condition fringe" includes parking provided to an employee on or near the business premises of the employer.

(5) **On-premises gyms and other athletic facilities.—**

(A) **In general.**—Gross income shall not include the value of any on-premises athletic facility provided by an employer to his employees.

(B) **On-premises athletic facility.**—For purposes of this paragraph, the term "on-premises athletic facility" means any gym or other athletic facility—

(i) which is located on the premises of the employer,

(ii) which is operated by the employer, and

(iii) substantially all the use of which is by employees of the employer, their spouses, and their dependent children (within the meaning of subsection (f)).

(6) **Special rule for affiliates of airlines.—**

(A) **In general.**—If—

(i) a qualified affiliate is a member of an affiliated group another member of which operates an airline, and

(ii) employees of the qualified affiliate who are directly engaged in providing airline-related services are entitled to no-additional-cost service with respect to air transportation provided by such other member,

then, for purposes of applying paragraph (1) of subsection (a) to such no-additional-cost service provided to such employees, such qualified affiliate shall be treated as engaged in the same line of business as such other member.

(B) **Qualified affiliate.**—For purposes of this paragraph, the term "qualified affiliate" means any corporation which is predominantly engaged in airline-related services.

(C) **Airline-related services.**—For purposes of this paragraph, the term "airline-related services" means any of the following services provided in connection with air transportation:

(i) Catering.

(ii) Baggage handling.

(iii) Ticketing and reservations.

(iv) Flight planning and weather analysis.

(v) Restaurants and gift shops located at an airport.

(vi) Such other similar services provided to the airline as the Secretary may prescribe.

(D) **Affiliated group.**—For purposes of this paragraph, the term "affiliated group" has the meaning given such term by section 1504(a).

Enactment of subsec. (h)(7)

Pub.L. 99–514, Title XI, § 1114(b)(5)(B), (c)(2), Oct. 22, 1986, 100 Stat. ——, provided that, applicable to years beginning after December 31, 1987, subsec. (h) of this section is amended by adding at the end thereof the following new paragraph:

"(7) **Highly compensated employee.**—For purposes of this section, the term 'highly compensated employee' has the meaning given such term by section 414(q)."

(i) **Customers not to include employees.**—For purposes of this section (other than subsection (c)(2)), the term "customers" shall only include customers who are not employees.

(j) **Section not to apply to fringe benefits expressly provided for elsewhere.** —This section (other than subsection (e)) shall not apply to any fringe benefits of a type the tax treatment of which is expressly provided for in any other section of this chapter.

(k) **Regulations.**—The Secretary shall prescribe such regulations as may be necessary or appropriate to carry out the purposes of this section.

§ 134. Certain military benefits

(a) **General rule.**—Gross income shall not include any qualified military benefit.

(b) **Qualified military benefit.**—For purposes of this section—

(1) **In general.**—The term "qualified military benefit" means any allowance or in-kind benefit which—

(A) is received by any member or former member of the uniformed services of the United States or any dependent of such member by reason of such member's status or service as a member of such uniformed services, and

(B) was excludable from gross income on September 9, 1986, under any provision of law or regulation thereunder which was in effect on such date (other than a provision of this title).

(2) **No other benefit to be excludable except as provided by this title.** —Notwithstanding any other provision of law, no benefit shall be treated as a qualified military benefit unless such benefit—

(A) is a benefit described in paragraph (1), or

(B) is excludable from gross income under this title without regard to any provision of law which is not contained in this title and which is not contained in a revenue Act.

(3) **Limitations on modifications.—**

(A) **In general.**—Except as provided in subparagraph (B), no modification or adjustment of any qualified military benefit after September 9, 1986, under any provision of law or regulation described in paragraph (1) shall be taken into account.

(B) **Exception for certain adjustments to cash benefits.**—Subparagraph (A) shall not apply to any adjustment to any qualified military benefit payable in cash which—

(i) is pursuant to a provision of law or regulation (as in effect on September 9, 1986), and

(ii) is determined by reference to any fluctuation in cost, price, currency, or other similar index.

(Added Pub.L. 99–514, Title XI, § 1168(a), Oct. 22, 1986, 100 Stat. ——.)

PART IV—TAX EXEMPTION REQUIREMENTS FOR STATE AND LOCAL BONDS

Subpart
A. Private activity bonds.
B. Requirements applicable to all state and local bonds.
C. Definitions and special rules.

Subpart A—Private Activity Bonds

§ 141. Private activity bond; qualified bond

(a) **Private Activity Bond.**—For purposes of this title, the term "private activity bond" means any bond issued as part of an issue—

(1) which meets—

(A) the private business use test of paragraph (1) of subsection (b), and

(B) the private security or payment test of paragraph (2) of subsection (b), or

(2) which meets the private loan financing test of subsection (c).

(b) **Private business tests.**—

(1) **Private business use test.**—Except as otherwise provided in this subsection, an issue meets the test of this paragraph if more than 10 percent of the proceeds of the issue are to be used for any private business use.

(2) **Private security or payment test.**—Except as otherwise provided in this subsection, an issue meets the test of this paragraph if the payment of the principal of, or the interest on, more than 10 percent of the proceeds of such issue is (under the terms of such issue or any underlying arrangement) directly or indirectly—

(A) secured by any interest in—

(i) property used or to be used for a private business use, or

(ii) payments in respect of such property, or

(B) to be derived from payments (whether or not to the issuer) in respect of property, or borrowed money, used or to be used for a private business use.

(3) **5 percent test for private business use not related o disproportionate to government use financed by the issue.**—

(A) **In general.**—An issue shall be treated as meeting the tests of paragraphs (1) and (2) if such tests would be met if such paragraphs were applied—

(i) by substituting "5 percent" for "10 percent" each place it appears, and

(ii) by taking into account only—

(I) the proceeds of the issue which are to be used for any private business use which is not related to any government use of such proceeds,

(II) the disproportionate related business use proceeds of the issue, and

(III) payments, property, and borrowed money with respect to any use of proceeds described in subclause (I) or (II).

(B) **Disproportionate related business use proceeds.**—For purposes of subparagraph (A), the disproportionate related business use proceeds of an issue is an amount equal to the aggregate of the excesses (determined under the following sentence) for each private business use of the proceeds of an issue which is

132

related to a government use of such proceeds. The excess determined under this sentence is the excess of—

(i) the proceeds of the issue which are to be used for the private business use, over

(ii) the proceeds of the issue which are to be used for the government use to which such private business use relates.

(4) Lower limitation for certain output facilities.—An issue 5 percent or more of the proceeds of which are to be used with respect to any output facility (other than a facility for the furnishing of water) shall be treated as meeting the tests of paragraphs (1) and (2) if the nonqualified amount with respect to such issue exceeds the excess of—

(A) $15,000,000, over

(B) the aggregate nonqualified amounts with respect to all prior tax-exempt issues 5 percent or more of the proceeds of which are or will be used with respect to such facility (or any other facility which is part of the same project).

There shall not be taken into account under subparagraph (B) any bond which is not outstanding at the time of the later issue or which is to be redeemed (other than in an advance refunding) from the net proceeds of the later issue.

(5) Coordination with volume cap where nonqualified amount exceeds $15,000,000.—If the nonqualified amount with respect to an issue—

(A) exceeds $15,000,000, but

(B) does not exceed the amount which would cause bond which is part of such issue to be treated as a private activity bond without regard to this paragraph,

such bond shall nonetheless be treated as a private activity bond unless the issuer allocates a portion of its volume cap under section 146 to such issue in an amount equal to the excess of such nonqualified amount over $15,000,000.

(6) Private business use defined.—

(A) In general.—For purposes of this subsection, the term "private business use" means use (directly or indirectly) in a trade or business carried on by any person other than a governmental unit. For purposes of the preceding sentence, use as a member of the general public shall not be taken into account.

(B) Clarification of trade or business.—For purposes of the 1st sentence of subparagraph (A), any activity carried on by a person other than a natural person shall be treated as a trade or business.

(7) Government use.—The term "government use" means any use other than a private business use.

(8) Nonqualified amount.—For purposes of this subsection, the term "nonqualified amount" means, with respect to an issue, the lesser of—

(A) the proceeds of such issue which are to be used for any private business use, or

(B) the proceeds of such issue with respect to which there are payments (or property or borrowed money) described in paragraph (2).

(9) Exception for qualified 501(c)(3) bonds.—There shall not be taken into account under this subsection or subsection (c) the portion of the proceeds of an issue which (if issued as a separate issue) would be treated as a qualified 501(c)(3) bond if the issuer elects to treat such portion as a qualified 501(c)(3) bond.

(c) Private loan financing test.—

(1) In general.—An issue meets the test of this subsection if the amount of the proceeds of the issue which are to be used (directly or indirectly) to make or finance loans (other than loans described in paragraph (2)) to persons other than governmental units exceeds the lesser of—

(A) 5 percent of such proceeds, or

(B) $5,000,000.

(2) Exception for tax assessment, etc., loans.—For purposes of paragraph (1), a loan is described in this paragraph if such loan—

(A) enables the borrower to finance any governmental tax or assessment of general application for a specific essential governmental function, or

(B) is a nonpurpose investment (within the meaning of section 148(f)(6)(A)).

(d) Qualified bond.—For purposes of this part, the term "qualified bond" means any private activity bond if—

(1) In general.—Such bond is—

(A) an exempt facility bond,

(B) a qualified mortgage bond,

(C) a qualified veterans' mortgage bond,

(D) a qualified small issue bond,

(E) a qualified student loan bond,

(F) a qualified redevelopment bond, or

(G) a qualified 501(c)(3) bond.

(2) Volume cap.—Such bond is issued as part of an issue which meets the applicable requirements of section 146, and

(3) Other requirements.—Such bond meets the applicable requirements of each subsection of section 147.

(Added Pub.L. 99–514, Title XIII, § 1301(b), Oct. 22, 1986, 100 Stat. ——.)

§ 142. Exempt facility bond

(a) General rule.—For purposes of this part, the term "exempt facility bond" means any bond issued as part of an issue 95 percent or more of the net proceeds of which are to be used to provide—

(1) airports,

(2) docks and wharves,

(3) mass commuting facilities,

(4) facilities for the furnishing of water,

(5) sewage facilities,

(6) solid waste disposal facilities,

(7) qualified residential rental projects,

(8) facilities for the local furnishing of electric energy or gas,

(9) local district heating or cooling facilities, or

(10) qualified hazardous waste facilities.

(b) Special exempt facility bond rules.—For purposes of subsection (a)—

(1) Certain facilities must be governmentally owned.—

(A) In general.—A facility shall be treated as described in paragraph (1), (2), or (3) of subsection (a) only if all of the property to be financed by the net proceeds of the issue is to be owned by a governmental unit.

(B) Safe harbor for leases and management contracts.—For purposes of subparagraph (A), property leased by a governmental unit shall be treated as owned by such governmental unit if—

(i) the lessee makes an irrevocable election (binding on the lessee and all successors in interest under the lease) not to claim depreciation or an investment credit with respect to such property,

(ii) the lease term (as defined in 168(i)(3)) is not more than 80 percent of the reasonably expected economic life of the property (as determined under section 147(b)), and

(iii) the lessee has no option to purchase the property other than at fair market value (as of the time such option is exercised).

Rules similar to the rules of the preceding sentence shall apply to management contracts and similar types of operating agreements.

(2) Limitation on office space.—An office shall not be treated as described in a paragraph of subsection (a) unless—

(A) the office is located on the premises of a facility described in such a paragraph, and

(B) not more than a de minimis amount of the functions to be performed at such office is not directly related to the day-to-day operations at such facility.

(c) Airports, docks and wharves, and mass commuting facilities.—For purposes of subsection (a)—

(1) Storage and training facilities.—Storage or training facilities directly related to a facility described in paragraph (1), (2), or (3) of subsection (a) shall be treated as described in the paragraph in which such facility is described.

(2) Exception for certain private facilities.—Property shall not be treated as described in paragraph (1), (2), or (3) of subsection (a) if such property is described in any of the following subparagraphs and is to be used for any private business use (as defined in section 141(b)(6)).

(A) Any lodging facility.

(B) Any retail facility (including food and beverage facilities) in excess of a size necessary to serve passengers and employees at the exempt facility.

(C) Any retail facility (other than parking) for passengers or the general public located outside the exempt facility terminal.

(D) Any office building for individuals who are not employees of a governmental unit or of the operating authority for the exempt facility.

(E) Any industrial park or manufacturing facility.

(d) Qualified residential rental project.—For purposes of this section—

(1) In general.—The term "qualified residential rental project" means any project for residential rental property if, at all times during the qualified project period, such project meets the requirements of subparagraph (A) or (B), whichever is elected by the issuer at the time of the issuance of the issue with respect to such project:

(A) **20–50 test.**—The project meets the requirements of this subparagraph if 20 percent or more of the residential units in such project are occupied by individuals whose income is 50 percent or less of area median gross income.

(B) **40–60 test.**—The project meets the requirements of this subparagraph if 40 percent or more of the residential units in such project are occupied by individuals whose income is 60 percent or less of area median gross income.

For purposes of this paragraph, any property shall not be treated as failing to be residential rental property merely because part of the building in which such property is located is used for purposes other than residential rental purposes.

(2) **Definitions and special rules.**—For purposes of this subsection—

(A) **Qualified project period.**—The term "qualified project period" means the period beginning on the 1st day on which 10 percent of the residential units in the project are occupied and ending on the latest of—

(i) the date which is 15 years after the date on which 50 percent of the residential units in the project are occupied,

(ii) the 1st day on which no tax-exempt private activity bond issued with respect to the project is outstanding, or

(iii) the date on which any assistance provided with respect to the project under section 8 of the United States Housing Act of 1937 terminates.

(B) **Income of individuals; area median gross income.**—The income of individuals and area median gross income shall be determined by the Secretary in a manner consistent with determinations of lower income families and area median gross income under section 8 of the United States Housing Act of 1937 (or, if such program is terminated, under such program as in effect immediately before such termination). Determinations under the preceding sentence shall include adjustments for family size.

(3) **Current income determinations.**—For purposes of this subsection—

(A) **In general.**—The determination of whether the income of a resident of a unit in a project exceeds the applicable income limit shall be made at least annually on the basis of the current income of the resident.

(B) **Continuing resident's income may increase above the applicable limit.**—If the income of a resident of a unit in a project did not exceed the applicable income limit upon commencement of such resident's occupancy of such unit (or as of any prior determination under subparagraph (A)), the income of such resident shall be treated as continuing to not exceed the applicable income limit. The preceding sentence shall cease to apply to any resident whose income as of the most recent determination under subparagraph (A) exceeds 140 percent of the applicable income limit if after such determination, but before the next determination, any residential unit of comparable or smaller size in the same project is occupied by a new resident whose income exceeds the applicable income limit.

(4) **Special rule in case of deep rent skewing.**—

(A) **In general.**—In the case of any project described in subparagraph (B), the 2d sentence of subparagraph (B) of paragraph (3) shall be applied by substituting—

(i) "170 percent" for "140 percent", and

(ii) "any low-income unit in the same project is occupied by a new resident whose income exceeds 40 percent of area median gross income" for "any residential unit of comparable or smaller size in the same project is occupied by a new resident whose income exceeds the applicable income limit".

(B) Deep rent skewed project.—A project is described in this subparagraph if the owner of the project elects to have this paragraph apply and, at all times during the qualified project period, such project meets the requirements of clauses (i), (ii), and (iii):

(i) The project meets the requirements of this clause if 15 percent or more of the low-income units in the project are occupied by individuals whose income is 40 percent or less of area median gross income.

(ii) The project meets the requirements of this clause if the gross rent with respect to each low-income unit in the project does not exceed 30 percent of the applicable income limit which applies to individuals occupying the unit.

(iii) The project meets the requirements of this clause if the gross rent with respect to each low-income unit in the project does not exceed ⅓ of the average rent with respect to units of comparable size which are not occupied by individuals who meet the applicable income limit.

(C) Definitions applicable to subparagraph (B).—For purposes of subparagraph (B)—

(i) Low-income unit.—The term "low-income unit" means any unit which is required to be occupied by individuals who meet the applicable income limit.

(ii) Gross rent.—The term "gross rent" includes—

(I) any payment under section 8 of the United States Housing Act of 1937, and

(II) any utility allowance determined by the Secretary after taking into account such determinations under such section 8.

(5) Applicable income limit.—For purposes of paragraphs (3) and (4), the term "applicable income limit" means—

(A) the limitation under subparagraph (A) or (B) of paragraph (1) which applies to the project, or

(B) in the case of a unit to which paragraph (4)(B)(i) applies, the limitation which applies to such unit.

(6) Special rule for certain high cost housing area.—In the case of a project located in a city having 5 boroughs and a population in excess of 5,000,000, subparagraph (B) of paragraph (1) shall be applied by substituting "25 percent" for "40 percent".

(7) Certification to secretary.—The operator of any project with respect to which an election was made under this subsection shall submit to the Secretary (at such time and in such manner as the Secretary shall prescribe) an annual certification as to whether such project continues to meet the requirements of this subsection. Any failure to comply with the provisions of the preceding sentence shall not affect the tax-exempt status of any bond but shall subject the operator to penalty, as provided in section 6652(j).

(e) Facilities for the furnishing of water.—For purposes of subsection (a)(4), the term "facilities for the furnishing of water" means any facility for the furnishing of water if—

(1) the water is or will be made available to members of the general public (including electric utility, industrial, agricultural, or commercial users), and

(2) either the facility is operated by a governmental unit or the rates for the furnishing or sale of the water have been established or approved by a State or political subdivision thereof, by an agency or instrumentality of the United States, or by a public service or public utility commission or other similar body of any State or political subdivision thereof.

(f) Local furnishing of electric energy or gas.—For purposes of subsection (a)(8), the local furnishing of electric energy or gas from a facility shall only include furnishing solely within the area consisting of—

(1) a city and 1 contiguous county, or

(2) 2 contiguous counties.

(g) Local district heating or cooling facility.—

(1) **In general.**—For purposes of subsection (a)(9), the term "local district heating or cooling facility" means property used as an integral part of a local district heating or cooling system.

(2) **Local district heating or cooling system.—**

(A) **In general.**—For purposes of paragraph (1), the term "local district heating or cooling system" means any local system consisting of a pipeline or network (which may be connected to a heating or cooling source) providing hot water, chilled water, or steam to 2 or more users for—

(i) residential, commercial, or industrial heating or cooling, or

(ii) process steam.

(B) **Local system.**—For purposes of this paragraph, a local system includes facilities furnishing heating and cooling to an area consisting of a city and 1 contiguous county.

(h) Qualified hazardous waste facilities.—For purposes of subsection (a)(10), the term "qualified hazardous waste facility" means any facility for the disposal of hazardous waste by incineration or entombment but only if—

(1) the facility is subject to final permit requirements under subtitle C of title II of the Solid Waste Disposal Act (as in effect on the date of the enactment of the Tax Reform Act of 1986), and

(2) the portion of such facility which is to be provided by the issue does not exceed the portion of the facility which is to be used by persons other than—

(A) the owner or operator of such facility, and

(B) any related person (within the meaning of section 144(a)(3)) to such owner or operator.

(Added Pub.L. 99–514, Title XIII, § 1301(b), Oct. 22, 1986, 100 Stat. ——.)

§ 143. Mortgage revenue bonds: qualified mortgage bond and qualified veterans' mortgage bond

(a) Qualified mortgage bond.—

(1) **Qualified mortgage bond defined.—**

(A) **In general.**—For purposes of this title, the term "qualified mortgage bond" means a bond which is issued as part of a qualified mortgage issue.

(B) **Termination on December 31, 1988.**—No bond issued after December 31, 1988, may be treated as a qualified mortgage bond.

(2) **Qualified mortgage issue defined.—**

(A) Definition.—For purposes of this title, the term "qualified mortgage issue" means an issue by a State or political subdivision thereof of 1 or more bonds, but only if—

(i) all proceeds of such issue (exclusive of issuance costs and a reasonably required reserve) are to be used to finance owner-occupied residences,

(ii) such issue meets the requirements of subsections (c), (d), (e), (f), (g), (h), and (i), and

(iii) no bond which is part of such issue meets the private business tests of paragraphs (1) and (2) of section 141(b).

(B) Good faith effort to comply with mortgage eligibility requirements. —An issue which fails to meet 1 or more of the requirements of subsections (c), (d), (e), (f), and (i) shall be treated as meeting such requirements if—

(i) the issuer in good faith attempted to meet all such requirements before the mortgages were executed,

(ii) 95 percent or more of the proceeds devoted to owner-financing was devoted to residences with respect to which (at the time the mortgages were executed) all such requirements were met, and

(iii) any failure to meet the requirements of such subsections is corrected within a reasonable period after such failure is first discovered.

(C) Good faith effort to comply with other requirements.—An issue which fails to meet 1 or more of the requirements of subsections (g) and (h) shall be treated as meeting such requirements if—

(i) the issuer in good faith attempted to meet all such requirements, and

(ii) any failure to meet such requirements is due to inadvertent error after taking reasonable steps to comply with such requirements.

(b) Qualified veterans' mortgage bond defined.—For purposes of this part, the term "qualified veterans' mortgage bond" means any bond—

(1) which is issued as part of an issue 95 percent or more of the net proceeds of which are to be used to provide residences for veterans,

(2) the payment of the principal and interest on which is secured by the general obligation of a State,

(3) which is part of an issue which meets the requirements of subsections (c), (g), (i)(1), and (*l*), and

(4) which does not meet the private business tests of paragraphs (1) and (2) of section 141(b).

Rules similar to the rules of subparagraphs (B) and (C) of subsection (a)(2) shall apply to the requirements specified in paragraph (3) of this subsection.

(c) Residence requirements.—

(1) For a residence.—A residence meets the requirements of this subsection only if—

(A) it is a single-family residence which can reasonably be expected to become the principal residence of the mortgagor within a reasonable time after the financing is provided, and

(B) it is located within the jurisdiction of the authority issuing the bond.

(2) **For an issue.**—An issue meets the requirements of this subsection only if all of the residences for which owner-financing is provided under the issue meet the requirements of paragraph (1).

(d) **3–year requirement.**—

(1) **In general.**—An issue meets the requirements of this subsection only if 95 percent or more of the net proceeds of such issue are used to finance the residences of mortgagors who had no present ownership interest in their principal residences at any time during the 3–year period ending on the date their mortgage is executed.

(2) **Exceptions.**—For purposes of paragraph (1), the proceeds of an issue which are used to provide—

(A) financing with respect to targeted area residences, and

(B) qualified home improvement loans and qualified rehabilitation loans, shall be treated as used as described in paragraph (1).

(3) **Mortgagor's interest in residence being financed.**—For purposes of paragraph (1), a mortgagor's interest in the residence with respect to which the financing is being provided shall not be taken into account.

(e) **Purchase price requirement.**—

(1) **In general.**—An issue meets the requirements of this subsection only if the acquisition cost of each residence the owner-financing of which is provided under the issue does not exceed 90 percent of the average area purchase price applicable to such residence.

(2) **Average area purchase price.**—For purposes of paragraph (1), the term "average area purchase price" means, with respect to any residence, the average purchase price of single family residences (in the statistical area in which the residence is located) which were purchased during the most recent 12–month period for which sufficient statistical information is available. The determination under the preceding sentence shall be made as of the date on which the commitment to provide the financing is made (or, if earlier, the date of the purchase of the residence).

(3) **Separate application to new residences and old residences.**—For purposes of this subsection, the determination of average area purchase price shall be made separately with respect to—

(A) residences which have not been previously occupied, and

(B) residences which have been previously occupied.

(4) **Special rule for 2 to 4 family residences.**—For purposes of this subsection, to the extent provided in regulations, the determination of average area purchase price shall be made separately with respect to 1 family, 2 family, 3 family, and 4 family residences.

(5) **Special rule for targeted area residences.**—In the case of a targeted area residence, paragraph (1) shall be applied by substituting "110 percent" for "90 percent".

(6) **Exception for qualified home improvement loans.**—Paragraph (1) shall not apply with respect to any qualified home improvement loan.

(f) **Income requirements.**—

(1) **In general.**—An issue meets the requirements of this subsection only if all owner-financing provided under the issue is provided for mortgagors whose family income is 115 percent or less of the applicable median family income.

(2) **Determination of family income.**—For purposes of this subsection, the family income of mortgagors, and area median gross income, shall be determined by the Secretary after taking into account the regulations prescribed under section 8 of the United States Housing Act of 1937 (or, if such program is terminated, under such program as in effect immediately before such termination).

(3) **Special rule for applying paragraph (1) in the case of targeted area residences.**—In the case of any financing provided under any issue for targeted area residences—

(A) ⅓ of the amount of such financing may be provided without regard to paragraph (1), and

(B) paragraph (1) shall be treated as satisfied with respect to the remainder of the owner financing if the family income of the mortgagor is 140 percent or less of the applicable median family income.

(4) **Applicable median family income.**—For purposes of this subsection, the term "applicable median family income" means, with respect to a residence, whichever of the following is the greater:

(A) the area median gross income for the area in which such residence is located, or

(B) the statewide median gross income for the State in which such residence is located.

(g) **Requirements related to arbitrage.**—

(1) **In general.**—An issue meets the requirements of this subsection only if such issue meets the requirements of paragraphs (2) and (3) of this subsection. Such requirements shall be in addition to the requirements of section 148 (other than subsection (f) thereof).

(2) **Effective rate of mortgage interest cannot exceed bond yield by more than 1.125 percentage points.**—

(A) **In general.**—An issue shall be treated as meeting the requirements of this paragraph only if the excess of—

(i) the effective rate of interest on the mortgages provided under the issue, over

(ii) the yield on the issue,

is not greater than 1.125 percentage points.

(B) **Effective rate of mortgage interest.**—

(i) **In general.**—In determining the effective rate of interest on any mortgage for purposes of this paragraph, there shall be taken into account all fees, charges, and other amounts borne by the mortgagor which are attributable to the mortgage or to the bond issue.

(ii) **Specification of some of the amounts to be treated as borne by the mortgagor.**—For purposes of clause (i), the following items (among others) shall be treated as borne by the mortgagor:

(I) all points or similar charges paid by the seller of the property, and

(II) the excess of the amounts received from any person other than the mortgagor by any person in connection with the acquisition of the mortgagor's interest in the property over the usual and reasonable acquisition costs of a person acquiring like property where owner-financing is not provided through the use of qualified mortgage bonds or qualified veterans' mortgage bonds.

(iii) Specification of some of the amounts to be treated as not borne by the mortgagor.—For purposes of clause (i), the following items shall not be taken into account:

(I) any expected rebate of arbitrage profits, and

(II) any application fee, survey fee, credit report fee, insurance charge, or similar amount to the extent such amount does not exceed amounts charged in such area in cases where owner-financing is not provided through the use of qualified mortgage bonds or qualified veterans' mortgage bonds.

Subclause (II) shall not apply to origination fees, points, or similar amounts.

(iv) Prepayment assumptions.—In determining the effective rate of interest—

(I) it shall be assumed that the mortgage prepayment rate will be the rate set forth in the most recent applicable mortgage maturity experience table published by the Federal Housing Administration, and

(II) prepayments of principal shall be treated as received on the last day of the month in which the issuer reasonably expects to receive such prepayments.

(C) Yield on the issue.—For purposes of this subsection, the yield on an issue shall be determined on the basis of—

(i) the issue price (within the meaning of sections 1273 and 1274), and

(ii) an expected maturity for the bonds which is consistent with the assumptions required under subparagraph (B)(iv).

(3) Arbitrage and investment gains to be used to reduce costs of owner-financing.—

(A) In general.—An issue shall be treated as meeting the requirements of this paragraph only if an amount equal to the sum of—

(i) the excess of—

(I) the amount earned on all nonpurpose investments (other than investments attributable to an excess described in this clause), over

(II) the amount which would have been earned if such investments were invested at a rate equal to the yield on the issue, plus

(ii) any income attributable to the excess described in clause (i),

is paid or credited to the mortgagors as rapidly as may be practicable.

(B) Investment gains and losses.—For purposes of subparagraph (A), in determining the amount earned on all nonpurpose investments, any gain or loss on the disposition of such investments shall be taken into account.

(C) Reduction where issuer does not use full 1.125 percentage points under paragraph (2).—

(i) In general.—The amount required to be paid or credited to mortgagors under subparagraph (A) (determined under this paragraph without regard to this subparagraph) shall be reduced by the unused paragraph (2) amount.

(ii) Unused paragraph (2) amount.—For purposes of clause (i), the unused paragraph (2) amount is the amount which (if it were treated as an interest payment made by mortgagors) would result in the excess referred to in paragraph (2)(A) being equal to 1.125 percentage points. Such amount shall be fixed and determined as of the yield determination date.

(D) Election to pay United States.—Subparagraph (A) shall be satisfied with respect to any issue if the issuer elects before issuing the bonds to pay over to the United States—

(i) not less frequently than once each 5 years after the date of issue, an amount equal to 90 percent of the aggregate amount which would be required to be paid or credited to mortgagors under subparagraph (A) (and not theretofore paid to the United States), and

(ii) not later than 60 days after the redemption of the last bond, 100 percent of such aggregate amount not theretofore paid to the United States.

(E) Simplified accounting.—The Secretary shall permit any simplified system of accounting for purposes of this paragraph which the issuer establishes to the satisfaction of the Secretary will assure that the purposes of this paragraph are carried out.

(F) Nonpurpose investment.—For purposes of this paragraph, the term "nonpurpose investment" has the meaning given such term by section 148(f)(6)(A).

(h) Portion of loans required to be placed in targeted areas.—

(1) In general.—An issue meets the requirements of this subsection only if at least 20 percent of the proceeds of the issue which are devoted to providing owner-financing is made available (with reasonable diligence) for owner-financing of targeted area residences for at least 1 year after the date on which owner-financing is first made available with respect to targeted area residences.

(2) Limitation.—Nothing in paragraph (1) shall be treated as requiring the making available of an amount which exceeds 40 percent of the average annual aggregate principal amount of mortgages executed during the immediately preceding 3 calendar years for single-family, owner-occupied residences located in targeted areas within the jurisdiction of the issuing authority.

(i) Other requirements.—

(1) Mortgages must be new mortgages.—

(A) In general.—An issue meets the requirements of this subsection only if no part of the proceeds of such issue is used to acquire or replace existing mortgages.

(B) Exceptions.—Under regulations prescribed by the Secretary, the replacement of—

(i) construction period loans,

(ii) bridge loans or similar temporary initial financing, and

(iii) in the case of a qualified rehabilitation, an existing mortgage,

shall not be treated as the acquisition or replacement of an existing mortgage for purposes of subparagraph (A).

(2) Certain requirements must be met where mortgage is assumed.—An issue meets the requirements of this subsection only if each mortgage with respect to which owner-financing has been provided under such issue may be assumed only if the requirements of subsections (c), (d), and (e), and the requirements of paragraph (1) or (3)(B) of subsection (f) (whichever applies), are met with respect to such assumption.

(j) Targeted area residences.—

(1) In general.—For purposes of this section, the term "targeted area residence" means a residence in an area which is either—

(A) a qualified census tract, or

(B) an area of chronic economic distress.

(2) Qualified census tract.—

(A) In general.—For purposes of paragraph (1), the term "qualified census tract" means a census tract in which 70 percent or more of the families have income which is 80 percent or less of the statewide median family income.

(B) Data used.—The determination under subparagraph (A) shall be made on the basis of the most recent decennial census for which data are available.

(3) Area of chronic economic distress.—

(A) In general.—For purposes of paragraph (1), the term "area of chronic economic distress" means an area of chronic economic distress—

(i) designated by the State as meeting the standards established by the State for purposes of this subsection, and

(ii) the designation of which has been approved by the Secretary and the Secretary of Housing and Urban Development.

(B) Criteria to be used in approving state designations.—The criteria used by the Secretary and the Secretary of Housing and Urban Development in evaluating any proposed designation of an area for purposes of this subsection shall be—

(i) the condition of the housing stock, including the age of the housing and the number of abandoned and substandard residential units,

(ii) the need of area residents for owner-financing under this section, as indicated by low per capita income, a high percentage of families in poverty, a high number of welfare recipients, and high unemployment rates,

(iii) the potential for use of owner-financing under this section to improve housing conditions in the area, and

(iv) the existence of a housing assistance plan which provides a displacement program and a public improvements and services program.

(k) Other definitions and special rules.—For purposes of this section—

(1) Mortgage.—The term "mortgage" means any owner-financing.

(2) Statistical area.—

(A) In general.—The term "statistical area" means—

(i) a metropolitan statistical area, and

(ii) any county (or the portion thereof) which is not within a metropolitan statistical area.

(B) Metropolitan statistical area.—The term "metropolitan statistical area" includes the area defined as such by the Secretary of Commerce.

(C) Designation where adequate statistical information not available. —For purposes of this paragraph, if there is insufficient recent statistical information with respect to a county (or portion thereof) described in subparagraph (A)(ii), the Secretary may substitute for such county (or portion thereof) another area for which there is sufficient recent statistical information.

(D) Designation where no county.—In the case of any portion of a State which is not within a county, subparagraphs (A)(ii) and (C) shall be applied by substituting for "county" an area designated by the Secretary which is the equivalent of a county.

(3) Acquisition cost.—

(A) In general.—The term "acquisition cost" means the cost of acquiring the residence as a completed residential unit.

(B) Exceptions.—The term "acquisition cost" does not include—

(i) usual and reasonable settlement or financing costs,

(ii) the value of services performed by the mortgagor or members of his family in completing the residence, and

(iii) the cost of land which has been owned by the mortgagor for at least 2 years before the date on which construction of the residence begins.

(C) Special rule for qualified rehabilitation loans.—In the case of a qualified rehabilitation loan, for purposes of subsection (e), the term "acquisition cost" includes the cost of the rehabilitation.

(4) Qualified home improvement loan.—The term "qualified home improvement loan" means the financing (in an amount which does not exceed $15,000)—

(A) of alterations, repairs, and improvements on or in connection with an existing residence by the owner thereof, but

(B) only of such items as substantially protect or improve the basic livability or energy efficiency of the property.

(5) Qualified rehabilitation loan.—

(A) In general.—The term "qualified rehabilitation loan" means any owner-financing provided in connection with—

(i) a qualified rehabilitation, or

(ii) the acquisition of a residence with respect to which there has been a qualified rehabilitation,

but only if the mortgagor to whom such financing is provided is the first resident of the residence after the completion of the rehabilitation.

(B) Qualified rehabilitation.—For purposes of subparagraph (A), the term "qualified rehabilitation" means any rehabilitation of a building if—

(i) there is a period of at least 20 years between the date on which the building was first used and the date on which the physical work on such rehabilitation begins,

(ii) in the rehabilitation process—

(I) 50 percent or more of the existing external walls of such building are retained in place as external walls,

(II) 75 percent or more of the existing external walls of such building are retained in place as internal or external walls, and

(III) 75 percent or more of the existing internal structural framework of such building is retained in place, and

(iii) the expenditures for such rehabilitation are 25 percent or more of the mortgagor's adjusted basis in the residence.

For purposes of clause (iii), the mortgagor's adjusted basis shall be determined as of the completion of the rehabilitation or, if later, the date on which the mortgagor acquires the residence.

(6) Determinations on actuarial basis.—All determinations of yield, effective interest rates, and amounts required to be paid or credited to mortgagors or paid to the United States under subsection (g) shall be made on an actuarial basis taking into account the present value of money.

(7) Single-family and owner-occupied residences include certain residences with 2 to 4 units.—Except for purposes of subsection (h)(2), the terms "single-family" and "owner-occupied", when used with respect to residences, include 2, 3, or 4 family residences—

(A) one unit of which is occupied by the owner of the units, and

(B) which were first occupied at least 5 years before the mortgage is executed.

(8) Cooperative housing corporations.—

(A) **In general.**—In the case of any cooperative housing corporation—

(i) each dwelling unit shall be treated as if it were actually owned by the person entitled to occupy such dwelling unit by reason of his ownership of stock in the corporation, and

(ii) any indebtedness of the corporation allocable to the dwelling unit shall be treated as if it were indebtedness of the shareholder entitled to occupy the dwelling unit.

(B) **Adjustment to targeted area requirement.**—In the case of any issue to provide financing to a cooperative housing corporation with respect to cooperative housing not located in a targeted area, to the extent provided in regulations, such issue may be combined with 1 or more other issues for purposes of determining whether the requirements of subsection (h) are met.

(C) **Cooperative housing corporation.**—The term "cooperative housing corporation" has the meaning given to such term by section 216(b)(1).

(9) Treatment of limited equity cooperative housing.—

(A) **Treatment as residential rental property.**—Except as provided in subparagraph (B), for purposes of this part—

(i) any limited equity cooperative housing shall be treated as residential rental property and not as owner-occupied housing, and

(ii) bonds issued to provide such housing shall be subject to the same requirements and limitations as bonds the proceeds of which are to be used to provide qualified residential rental projects (as defined in section 142(d)).

(B) **Bonds subject to qualified mortgage bond termination date.**—Subparagraph (A) shall not apply to any bond issued after the date specified in subsection (a)(1)(B).

(C) **Limited equity cooperative housing.**—For purposes of this paragraph, the term "limited equity cooperative housing" means any dwelling unit which a person is entitled to occupy by reason of his ownership of stock in a qualified cooperative housing corporation.

(D) **Qualified cooperative housing corporation.**—For purposes of this paragraph, the term "qualified cooperative housing corporation" means any cooperative housing corporation (as defined in section 216(b)(1)) if—

(i) the consideration paid for stock held by any stockholder entitled to occupy any house or apartment in a building owned or leased by the corporation may not exceed the sum of—

(I) the consideration paid for such stock by the first such stockholder, as adjusted by a cost-of-living adjustment determined by the Secretary,

(II) payments made by any stockholder for improvements to such house or apartment, and

(III) payments (other than amounts taken into account under subclause (I) or (II)) attributable to any stockholder to amortize the principal of the corporation's indebtedness arising from the acquisition or development of real property, including improvements thereof,

(ii) the value of the corporation's assets (reduced by any corporate liabilities), to the extent such value exceeds the combined transfer values of the outstanding corporate stock, shall be used only for public benefit or charitable purposes, or directly to benefit the corporation itself, and shall not be used directly to benefit any stockholder, and

(iii) at the time of issuance of the issue, such corporation makes an election under this paragraph.

(E) **Effect of election.**—If a cooperative housing corporation makes an election under this paragraph, section 216 shall not apply with respect to such corporation (or any successor thereof) during the qualified project period (as defined in section 142(d)(2)).

(F) **Corporation must continue to be qualified cooperative.**—Subparagraph (A)(i) shall not apply to limited equity cooperative housing unless the cooperative housing corporation continues to be a qualified cooperative housing corporation at all times during the qualified project period (as defined in section 142(d)(2)).

(G) **Election irrevocable.**—Any election under this paragraph, once made, shall be irrevocable.

(*l*) **Additional requirements for qualified veterans' mortgage bonds.**—An issue meets the requirements of this subsection only if it meets the requirements of paragraphs (1), (2), and (3).

(1) **Veterans to whom financing may be provided.**—An issue meets the requirements of this paragraph only if each mortgagor to whom financing is provided under the issue is a qualified veteran.

(2) **Requirement that state program be in effect before June 22, 1984.**—An issue meets the requirements of this paragraph only if it is a general obligation of a State which issued qualified veterans' mortgage bonds before June 22, 1984.

(3) **Volume limitation.**—

(A) **In general.**—An issue meets the requirements of this paragraph only if the aggregate amount of bonds issued pursuant thereto (when added to the aggregate amount of qualified veterans' mortgage bonds previously issued by the State during the calendar year) does not exceed the State veterans limit for such calendar year.

(B) **State veterans limit.**—A State veterans limit for any calendar year is the amount equal to—

(i) the aggregate amount of qualified veterans bonds issued by such State during the period beginning on January 1, 1979, and ending on June 22, 1984 (not including the amount of any qualified veterans bond issued by such State during the calendar year (or portion thereof) in such period for which the amount of such bonds so issued was the lowest), divided by

(ii) the number (not to exceed 5) of calendar years after 1979 and before 1985 during which the State issued qualified veterans bonds (determined by only taking into account bonds issued on or before June 22, 1984).

(C) Treatment of refunding issues.—

(i) In general.—For purposes of subparagraph (A), the term "qualified veterans' mortgage bond" shall not include any bond issued to refund another bond but only if the maturity date of the refunding bond is not later than the later of—

(I) the maturity date of the bond to be refunded, or

(II) the date 32 years after the date on which the refunded bond was issued (or in the case of a series of refundings, the date on which the original bond was issued).

The preceding sentence shall apply only to the extent that the amount of the refunding bond does not exceed the outstanding amount of the refunded bond.

(ii) Exception for advance refunding.—Clause (i) shall not apply to any bond issued to advance refund another bond.

(4) Qualified veteran.—For purposes of this subsection, the term "qualified veteran" means any veteran—

(A) who served on active duty at some time before January 1, 1977, and

(B) who applied for the financing before the later of—

(i) the date 30 years after the last date on which such veteran left active service, or

(ii) January 31, 1985.

(5) Special rule for certain short-term bonds.—In the case of any bond—

(A) which has a term of 1 year or less,

(B) which is authorized to be issued under O.R.S. 407.435 (as in effect on the date of the enactment of this subsection), to provide financing for property taxes, and

(C) which is redeemed at the end of such term,

the amount taken into account under this subsection with respect to such bond shall be $1/15$ of its principal amount.

Subpart B—Requirements Applicable to All State and Local Bonds

§ 149. Bonds must be registered to be tax exempt; other requirements

(a) Bonds must be registered to be tax exempt.—

(1) General rule.—Nothing in section 103(a) or in any other provision of law shall be construed to provide an exemption from Federal income tax for interest on any registration-required bond unless such bond is in registered form.

(2) Registration-required bond.—For purposes of paragraph (1), the term "registration-required bond" means any bond other than a bond which—

(A) is not of a type offered to the public,

(B) has a maturity (at issue) of not more than 1 year, or

(C) is described in section 163(f)(2)(B).

(3) Special rules.—

(A) Book entries permitted.—For purposes of paragraph (1), a book entry bond shall be treated as in registered form if the right to the principal of, and stated interest on, such bond may be transferred only through a book entry consistent with regulations prescribed by the Secretary.

(B) Nominees.—The Secretary shall prescribe such regulations as may be necessary to carry out the purpose of paragraph (1) where there is a nominee or chain of nominees.

(b) Federally guaranteed bond is not tax exempt.—

(1) In general.—Section 103(a) shall not apply to any State or local bond if such bond is federally guaranteed.

(2) Federally guaranteed defined.—For purposes of paragraph (1), a bond is federally guaranteed if—

(A) the payment of principal or interest with respect to such bond is guaranteed (in whole or in part) by the United States (or any agency or instrumentality thereof),

(B) such bond is issued as part of an issue and 5 percent or more of the proceeds of such issue is to be—

(i) used in making loans the payment of principal or interest with respect to which are to be guaranteed (in whole or in part) by the United States (or any agency or instrumentality thereof), or

(ii) invested (directly or indirectly) in federally insured deposits or accounts, or

(C) the payment of principal or interest on such bond is otherwise indirectly guaranteed (in whole or in part) by the United States (or an agency or instrumentality thereof).

(3) Exceptions.—

(A) Certain insurance programs.—A bond shall not be treated as federally guaranteed by reason of—

(i) any guarantee by the Federal Housing Administration, the Veterans' Administration, the Federal National Mortgage Association, the Federal Home Loan Mortgage Corporation, or the Government National Mortgage Association,

(ii) any guarantee of student loans and any guarantee by the Student Loan Marketing Association to finance student loans, or

(iii) any guarantee by the Bonneville Power Authority pursuant to the Northwest Power Act (16 U.S.C. 839d) as in effect on the date of the enactment of the Tax Reform Act of 1984 with respect to any bond issued before July 1, 1989.

(B) Debt service, etc.—Paragraph (1) shall not apply to—

(i) proceeds of the issue invested for an initial temporary period until such proceeds are needed for the purpose for which such issue was issued,

(ii) investments of a bona fide debt service fund,

(iii) investments of a reserve which meet the requirements of section 148(d),

(iv) investments in bonds issued by the United States Treasury, or

(v) other investments permitted under regulations.

(C) Exception for housing programs.—

149

(i) **In general.**—Except as provided in clause (ii), paragraph (1) shall not apply to—

(I) a private activity bond for a qualified residential rental project or a housing program obligation under section 11(b) of the United States Housing Act of 1937,

(II) a qualified mortgage bond, or

(III) a qualified veterans' mortgage bond.

(ii) **Exception not to apply where bond invested in federally insured deposits or accounts.**—Clause (i) shall not apply to any bond which is federally guaranteed within the meaning of paragraph (2)(B)(ii).

(D) **Loans to, or guarantees by, financial institutions.**—Except as provided in paragraph (2)(B)(ii), a bond which is issued as part of an issue shall not be treated as federally guaranteed merely by reason of the fact that the proceeds of such issue are used in making loans to a financial institution or there is a guarantee by a financial institution unless such guarantee constitutes a federally insured deposit or account.

(4) **Definitions.**—For purposes of this subsection—

(A) **Treatment of certain entities with authority to borrow from United States.**—To the extent provided in regulations prescribed by the Secretary, any entity with statutory authority to borrow from the United States shall be treated as an instrumentality of the United States. Except in the case of an exempt facility bond, a qualified small issue bond, a qualified student loan bond, and a qualified redevelopment bond, nothing in the preceding sentence shall be construed as treating the District of Columbia or any possession of the United States as an instrumentality of the United States.

(B) **Federally insured deposit or account.**—The term "federally insured deposit or account" means any deposit or account in a financial institution to the extent such deposit or account is insured under Federal law by the Federal Deposit Insurance Corporation, the Federal Savings and Loan Insurance Corporation, the National Credit Union Administration, or any similar federally chartered corporation.

(c) **Tax exemption must be derived from this title.**—

(1) **General rule.**—Except as provided in paragraph (2), no interest on any bond shall be exempt from taxation under this title unless such interest is exempt from tax under this title without regard to any provision of law which is not contained in this title and which is not contained in a revenue Act.

(2) **Certain prior exemptions.**—

(A) **Prior exemptions continued.**—For purposes of this title, notwithstanding any provision of this part, any bond the interest on which is exempt from taxation under this title by reason of any provision of law (other than a provision of this title) which is in effect on January 6, 1983, shall be treated as a bond described in section 103(a).

(B) **Additional requirements for bonds issued after 1983.**—Subparagraph (A) shall not apply to a bond (not described in subparagraph (C)) issued after 1983 if the appropriate requirements of this part (or the corresponding provisions of prior law) are not met with respect to such bond.

(C) **Description of bond.**—A bond is described in this subparagraph (and treated as described in subparagraph (A)) if—

(i) such bond is issued pursuant to the Northwest Power Act (16 U.S.C. 839d), as in effect on July 18, 1984;

(ii) such bond is issued pursuant to section 608(a)(6)(A) of Public Law 97–468, as in effect on the date of the enactment of the Tax Reform Act of 1986; or

(iii) such bond is issued before June 19, 1984 under section 11(b) of the United States Housing Act of 1937.

(d) Advance refundings.—

(1) In general.—Nothing in section 103(a) or in any other provision of law shall be construed to provide an exemption from Federal income tax for interest on any bond issued as part of an issue described in paragraph (2), (3), or (4).

(2) Certain private activity bonds.—An issue is described in this paragraph if any bond (issued as part of such issue) is issued to advance refund a private activity bond (other than a qualified 501(c)(3) bond).

(3) Other bonds.—

(A) In general.—An issue is described in this paragraph if any bond (issued as part of such issue), hereinafter in this paragraph referred to as the "refunding bond", is issued to advance refund a bond unless—

(i) the refunding bond is only—

(I) the 1st advance refunding of the original bond if the original bond is issued after 1985, or

(II) the 1st or 2nd advance refunding of the original bond if the original bond was issued before 1986,

(ii) in the case of refunded bonds issued before 1986, the refunded bond is redeemed not later than the earliest date on which such bond may be redeemed at par or at a premium of 3 percent or less,

(iii) in the case of refunded bonds issued after 1985, the refunded bond is redeemed not later than the earliest date on which such bond may be redeemed,

(iv) the initial temporary period under section 148(c) ends—

(I) with respect to the proceeds of the refunding bond not later than 30 days after the date of issue of such bond, and

(II) with respect to the proceeds of the refunded bond on the date of issue of the refunding bond, and

(v) in the case of refunded bonds to which section 148(e) did not apply, on and after the date of issue of the refunding bond, the amount of proceeds of the refunded bond invested in higher yielding investments (as defined in section 148(b)) which are nonpurpose investments (as defined in section 148(f)(6)(A)) does not exceed—

(I) the amount so invested as part of a reasonably required reserve or replacement fund or during an allowable temporary period, and

(II) the amount which is equal to the lesser of 5 percent of the proceeds of the issue of which the refunded bond is a part or $100,000 (to the extent such amount is allocable to the refunded bond).

(B) Special rules for redemptions.—

(i) Issuer must redeem only if debt service savings.—Clause (ii) and (iii) of subparagraph (A) shall apply only if the issuer may realize present value debt service savings (determined without regard to administrative expenses) in connection with the issue of which the refunding bond is a part.

(ii) Redemptions not required before 90th day.—For purposes of clauses (ii) and (iii) of subparagraph (A), the earliest date referred to in such clauses shall not be earlier than the 90th day after the date of issuance of the refunding bond.

(4) Abusive transactions prohibited.—An issue is described in this paragraph if any bond (issued as part of such issue) is issued to advance refund another bond and a device is employed in connection with the issuance of such issue to obtain a material financial advantage (based on arbitrage) apart from savings attributable to lower interest rates.

(5) Advance refunding.—For purposes of this part, a bond shall be treated as issued to advance refund another bond if it is issued more than 90 days before the redemption of the refunded bond.

(6) Special rules for purposes of paragraph (3).—For purposes of paragraph (3), bonds issued before the date of the enactment of this subsection shall be taken into account under subparagraph (A)(i) thereof except—

(A) a refunding which occurred before 1986 shall be treated as an advance refunding only if the refunding bond was issued more than 180 days before the redemption of the refunded bond, and

(B) a bond issued before 1986, shall be treated as advance refunded no more than once before March 15, 1986.

(7) Regulations.—The Secretary shall prescribe such regulations as may be necessary or appropriate to carry out the purposes of this subsection.

(e) Information reporting.—

(1) In general.—Nothing in section 103(a) or any other provision of law shall be construed to provide an exemption from Federal income tax for interest on any bond unless such bond satisfies the requirements of paragraph (2).

(2) Information reporting requirements.—A bond satisfies the requirements of this paragraph if the issuer submits to the Secretary, not later than the 15th day of the 2d calendar month after the close of the calendar quarter in which the bond is issued (or such later time as the Secretary may prescribe with respect to any portion of the statement), a statement concerning the issue of which the bond is a part which contains—

(A) the name and address of the issuer,

(B) the date of issue, the amount of net proceeds of the issue, the stated interest rate, term, and face amount of each bond which is part of the issue, the amount of issuance costs of the issue, and the amount of reserves of the issue,

(C) where required, the name of the applicable elected representative who approved the issue, or a description of the voter referendum by which the issue was approved,

(D) the name, address, and employer identification number of—

(i) each initial principal user of any facility provided with the proceeds of the issue,

(ii) the common parent of any affiliated group of corporations (within the meaning of section 1504(a)) of which such initial principal user is a member, and

(iii) if the issue is treated as a separate issue under section 144(a)(6)(A), any person treated as a principal user under section 144(a)(6)(B),

(E) a description of any property to be financed from the proceeds of the issue,

(F) a certification by a State official designated by State law (or, where there is no such official, the Governor) that the bond meets the requirements of section 146 (relating to cap on private activity bonds), if applicable, and

(G) such other information as the Secretary may require.

Subparagraphs (C) and (D) shall not apply to any bond which is not a private activity bond. The Secretary may provide that certain information specified in the 1st sentence need not be included in the statement with respect to an issue where the inclusion of such information is not necessary to carry out the purposes of this subsection.

(3) **Extension of time.**—The Secretary may grant an extension of time for the filing of any statement required under paragraph (2) if there is reasonable cause for the failure to file such statement in a timely fashion.

(Added Pub.L. 99–514, Title XIII, § 1301(b), Oct. 22, 1986, 100 Stat. ——.)

Subpart C—Definitions and Special Rules

§ 150. Definitions and special rules

(a) **General rule.**—For purposes of this part—

(1) **Bond.**—The term "bond" includes any obligation.

(2) **Governmental unit not to include federal government.**—The term "governmental unit" does not include the United States or any agency or instrumentality thereof.

(3) **Net proceeds.**—The term "net proceeds" means, with respect to any issue, the proceeds of such issue reduced by amounts in a reasonably required reserve or replacement fund.

(4) **501(c)(3) organization.**—The term "501(c)(3) organization" means any organization described in section 501(c)(3) and exempt from tax under section 501(a).

(5) **Ownership of property.**—Property shall be treated as owned by a governmental unit if it is owned on behalf of such unit.

(6) **Tax-exempt bond.**—The term "tax-exempt" means, with respect to any bond (or issue), that the interest on such bond (or on the bonds issued as part of such issue) is excluded from gross income.

(b) **Change in use of facilities financed with tax-exempt private activity bonds.—**

(1) **Mortgage revenue bonds.—**

(A) **In general.**—In the case of any residence with respect to which financing is provided from the proceeds of a qualified mortgage bond or qualified veterans' mortgage bond, if there is a continuous period of at least 1 year during which such residence is not the principal residence of at least 1 of the mortgagors who received such financing, then no deduction shall be allowed under this chapter for interest on such financing which accrues on or after the date such period began.

(B) **Exception.**—Subparagraph (A) shall not apply to the extent the Secretary determines that its application would result in undue hardship and that the failure to meet the requirements of subparagraph (A) resulted from circumstances beyond the mortgagor's control.

(2) Qualified residential rental projects.—In the case of any project for residential rental property—

(A) with respect to which financing is provided from the proceeds of any private activity bond which, when issued, purported to be a tax-exempt bond described paragraph (7) of section 142(a), and

(B) which does not meet the requirements of section 142(d),

no deduction shall be allowed under this chapter for interest on such financing which accrues during the period beginning on the 1st day of the taxable year in which such project fails to meet such requirements and ending on the date such project meets such requirements.

(3) Qualified 501(c)(3) bonds.—

(A) In general.—In the case of any facility with respect to which financing is provided from the proceeds of any private activity bond which, when issued, purported to be a tax-exempt qualified 501(c)(3) bond, if any portion of such facility—

    (i) is used in a trade or business of any person other than a 501(c)(3) organization or a governmental unit, but

    (ii) continues to be owned by a 501(c)(3) organization,

then the owner of such portion shall be treated for purposes of this title as engaged in an unrelated trade or business (as defined in section 513) with respect to such portion. The amount of gross income attributable to such portion for any period shall not be less than the fair rental value of such portion for such period.

(B) Denial of deduction for interest.—No deduction shall be allowed under this chapter for interest on financing described in subparagraph (A) which accrues during the period beginning on the date such facility is used as described in subparagraph (A)(i) and ending on the date such facility is not so used.

(4) Certain exempt facility bonds.—

(A) In general.—In the case of any facility with respect to which financing is provided from the proceeds of any private activity bond to which this paragraph applies, if such facility is not used for a purpose for which a tax-exempt bond could be issued on the date of such issue, no deduction shall be allowed under this chapter for interest on such financing which accrues during the period beginning on the date such facility is not so used and ending on the date such facility is so used.

(B) Bonds to which paragraph applies.—This paragraph applies to any private activity bond which, when issued, purported to be a tax-exempt exempt facility bond described in a paragraph (other than paragraph (7)) of section 142(a).

(5) Facilities required to be owned by governmental units or 501(c)(3) organizations.—If—

(A) financing is provided with respect to any facility from the proceeds of any private activity bond which, when issued, purported to be a tax-exempt bond,

(B) such facility is required to be owned by a governmental unit or a 501(c)(3) organization as a condition of such tax exemption, and

    (C) such facility is not so owned,

then no deduction shall be allowed under this chapter for interest on such financing which accrues during the period beginning on the date such facility is not so owned and ending on the date such facility is so owned.

(c) **Exception and special rules for purposes of subsection (b).**—For purposes of subsection (b)—

(1) **Exception.**—Any use with respect to facilities financed with proceeds of an issue which are not required to be used for the exempt purpose of such issue shall not be taken into account.

(2) **Treatment of amounts other than interest.**—If the amounts payable for the use of a facility are not interest, subsection (b) shall apply to such amounts as if they were interest but only to the extent such amounts for any period do not exceed the amount of interest accrued on the bond financing for such period.

(3) **Use of portion of facility.**—In the case of any person which uses only a portion of the facility, only the interest accruing on the financing allocable to such portion shall be taken into account by such person.

(4) **Cessation with respect to portion of facility.**—In the case of any facility where part but not all of the facility is not used for an exempt purpose, only the interest accruing on the financing allocable to such part shall be taken into account.

(5) **Regulations.**—The Secretary shall prescribe such regulations as may be necessary or appropriate to carry out the purposes of this subsection and subsection (b).

(d) **Qualified scholarship funding bond.**—For purposes of this part and section 103—

(1) **Treatment as State or local bond.**—A qualified scholarship funding bond shall be treated as a State or local bond.

(2) **Qualified scholarship funding bond defined.**—The term "qualified scholarship funding bond" means a bond issued by a corporation which—

(A) is a corporation not for profit established and operated exclusively for the purpose of acquiring student loan notes incurred under the Higher Education Act of 1965, and

(B) is organized at the request of the State or 1 or more political subdivisions thereof or is requested to exercise such power by 1 or more political subdivisions and required by its corporate charter and bylaws, or required by State law, to devote any income (after payment of expenses, debt service, and the creation of reserves for the same) to the purchase of additional student loan notes or to pay over any income to the United States.

(e) **Bonds of certain volunteer fire departments.**—For purposes of this part and section 103—

(1) **In general.**—A bond of a volunteer fire department shall be treated as a bond of a political subdivision of a State if—

(A) such department is a qualified volunteer fire department with respect to an area within the jurisdiction of such political subdivision, and

(B) such bond is issued as part of an issue 95 percent or more of the net proceeds of which are to be used for the acquisition, construction, reconstruction, or improvement of a firehouse or firetruck used or to be used by such department.

(2) **Qualified volunteer fire department.**—For purposes of this subsection, the term "qualified volunteer fire department" means, with respect to a political subdivision of a State, any organization—

(A) which is organized and operated to provide firefighting or emergency medical services for persons in an area (within the jurisdiction of such political subdivision) which is not provided with any other firefighting services, and

(B) which is required (by written agreement) by the political subdivision to furnish firefighting services in such area.

(Added Pub.L. 99–514, Title XIII, § 1301(b), Oct. 22, 1986, 100 Stat. ——.)

PART V—DEDUCTIONS FOR PERSONAL EXEMPTIONS

§ 151. Allowance of deductions for personal exemptions

(a) **Allowance of deductions.**—In the case of an individual, the exemptions provided by this section shall be allowed as deductions in computing taxable income.

(b) **Taxpayer and spouse.**—An exemption of the exemption amount for the taxpayer; and an additional exemption of the exemption amount for the spouse of the taxpayer if a joint return is not made by the taxpayer and his spouse, and if the spouse, for the calendar year in which the taxable year of the taxpayer begins, has no gross income and is not the dependent of another taxpayer.

(c) **Additional Exemption for Dependents.**—

(1) **In general.**—An exemption for the exemption amount for each dependent (as defined in section 152)—

(A) whose gross income for the calendar year in which the taxable year of the taxpayer begins is less than the exemption amount or

(B) who is a child of the taxpayer and who (i) has not attained the age of 19 at the close of the calendar year in which the taxable year of the taxpayer begins, or (ii) is a student.

(2) **Exemption denied in case of certain married dependents.**—No exemption shall be allowed under this subsection for any dependent who has made a joint return with his spouse under section 6013 for the taxable year beginning in the calendar year in which the taxable year of the taxpayer begins.

(3) **Child defined.**—For purposes of paragraph (1) (B), the term "child" means an individual who (within the meaning of section 152) is a son, stepson, daughter, or stepdaughter of the taxpayer.

(4) **Student defined.**—For purposes of paragraph (1) (B) (ii), the term "student" means an individual who during each of 5 calendar months during the calendar year in which the taxable year of the taxpayer begins—

(A) is a full-time student at an educational organization described in section 170(b) (1) (A) (ii); or

(B) is pursuing a full-time course of institutional on-farm training under the supervision of an accredited agent of an educational organization described in section 170(b) (1) (A) (ii) or of a State or political subdivision of a State.

(5) **Certain income of handicapped dependents not taken into account.**—

(A) **In general.**—For purposes of paragraph (1)(A), the gross income of an individual who is permanently and totally disabled shall not include income attributable to services performed by the individual at a sheltered workshop if—

(i) the availability of medical care at such workshop is the principal reason for his presence there, and

(ii) the income arises solely from activities at such workshop which are incident to such medical care.

(B) Sheltered workshop defined.—For purposes of subparagraph (A), the term "sheltered workshop" means a school—

(i) which provides special instruction or training designed to alleviate the disability of the individual, and

(ii) which is operated by—

(I) an organization described in section 501(c)(3) and exempt from tax under section 501(a), or

(II) a State, a possession of the United States, any political subdivision of any of the foregoing, the United States, or the District of Columbia.

(C) Permanent and total disability defined.—An individual shall be treated as permanently and totally disabled for purposes of this paragraph if such individual would be so treated under paragraph (3) of section 22(e).

(d) Exemption amount.—For purposes of this section—

(1) In general.—Except as provided in paragraph (2), the term "exemption amount" means—

(A) $1,900 for taxable years beginning during 1987,

(B) $1,950 for taxable years beginning during 1988, and

(C) $2,000 for taxable years beginning after December 31, 1988.

(2) Exemption amount disallowed in the case of certain dependents.—In the case of an individual with respect to whom a deduction under this section is allowable to another taxpayer for a taxable year beginning in the calendar year in which the individual's taxable year begins, the exemption amount applicable to such individual for such individual's taxable year shall be zero.

(3) Inflation adjustment for years after 1989.—In the case of any taxable year beginning in a calendar year after 1989, the dollar amount contained in paragraph (1)(C) shall be increased by an amount equal to—

(A) such dollar amount, multiplied by

(B) the cost-of-living adjustment determined under section 1(f)(3), for the calendar year in which the taxable year begins, by substituting "calendar year 1988" for "calendar year 1987" in subparagraph (B) thereof.

§ 152. Dependent defined

(a) General definition.—For purposes of this subtitle, the term "dependent" means any of the following individuals over half of whose support, for the calendar year in which the taxable year of the taxpayer begins, was received from the taxpayer (or is treated under subsection (c) or (e) as received from the taxpayer):

(1) A son or daughter of the taxpayer, or a descendant of either,

(2) A stepson or stepdaughter of the taxpayer,

(3) A brother, sister, stepbrother, or stepsister of the taxpayer,

(4) The father or mother of the taxpayer, or an ancestor of either,

(5) A stepfather or stepmother of the taxpayer,

(6) A son or daughter of a brother or sister of the taxpayer,

(7) A brother or sister of the father or mother of the taxpayer,

(8) A son-in-law, daughter-in-law, father-in-law, mother-in-law, brother-in-law, or sister-in-law of the taxpayer, or

(9) An individual (other than an individual who at any time during the taxable year was the spouse, determined without regard to section 7703, of the taxpayer) who, for the taxable year of the taxpayer, has as his principal place of abode the home of the taxpayer and is a member of the taxpayer's household.

(b) Rules relating to general definition.—For purposes of this section—

(1) The terms "brother" and "sister" include a brother or sister by the halfblood.

(2) In determining whether any of the relationships specified in subsection (a) or paragraph (1) of this subsection exists, a legally adopted child of an individual (and a child who is a member of an individual's household, if placed with such individual by an authorized placement agency for legal adoption by such individual), or a foster child of an individual (if such child satisfies the requirements of subsection (a) (9) with respect to such individual), shall be treated as a child of such individual by blood.

(3) The term "dependent" does not include any individual who is not a citizen or national of the United States unless such individual is a resident of the United States or of a country contiguous to the United States. The preceding sentence shall not exclude from the definition of "dependent" any child of the taxpayer legally adopted by him, if, for the taxable year of the taxpayer, the child has as his principal place of abode the home of the taxpayer and is a member of the taxpayer's household, and if the taxpayer is a citizen or national of the United States.

(4) A payment to a wife which is includible in the gross income of the wife under section 71 or 682 shall not be treated as a payment by her husband for the support of any dependent.

(5) An individual is not a member of the taxpayer's household if at any time during the taxable year of the taxpayer the relationship between such individual and the taxpayer is in violation of local law.

(c) Multiple support agreements.—For purposes of subsection (a), over half of the support of an individual for a calendar year shall be treated as received from the taxpayer if—

(1) no one person contributed over half of such support;

(2) over half of such support was received from persons each of whom, but for the fact that he did not contribute over half of such support, would have been entitled to claim such individual as a dependent for a taxable year beginning in such calendar year;

(3) the taxpayer contributed over 10 percent of such support; and

(4) each person described in paragraph (2) (other than the taxpayer) who contributed over 10 percent of such support files a written declaration (in such manner and form as the Secretary may by regulations prescribe) that he will not claim such individual as a dependent for any taxable year beginning in such calendar year.

(d) Special support test in case of students.—For purposes of subsection (a), in the case of any individual who is—

(1) a son, stepson, daughter, or stepdaughter of the taxpayer (within the meaning of this section), and

(2) a student (within the meaning of section 151(c) (4)),

amounts received as scholarships for study at an educational organization described in section 170(b) (1) (A) (ii) shall not be taken into account in determining whether such individual received more than half of his support from the taxpayer.

(e) Support test in case of child of divorced parents, etc.—

(1) Custodial parent gets exemption.—Except as otherwise provided in this subsection, if—

(A) a child (as defined in section 151(c)(3)) receives over half of his support during the calendar year from his parents—

(i) who are divorced or legally separated under a decree of divorce or separate maintenance,

(ii) who are separated under a written separation agreement, or

(iii) who live apart at all times during the last 6 months of the calendar year, and

(B) such child is in the custody of one or both of his parents for more than one-half of the calendar year,

such child shall be treated, for purposes of subsection (a), as receiving over half of his support during the calendar year from the parent having custody for a greater portion of the calendar year (hereinafter in this subsection referred to as the "custodial parent").

(2) Exception where custodial parent releases claim to exemption for the year.—A child of parents described in paragraph (1) shall be treated as having received over half of his support during a calendar year for the noncustodial parent if—

(A) the custodial parent signs a written declaration (in such manner and form as the Secretary may by regulations prescribe) that such custodial parent will not claim such child as a dependent for any taxable year beginning in such calendar year, and

(B) the noncustodial parent attaches such written declaration to the noncustodial parent's return for the taxable year beginning during such calendar year.

For purposes of this subsection, the term "noncustodial parent" means the parent who is not the custodial parent.

(3) Exception for multiple-support agreement.—This subsection shall not apply to any case where over half of the support of the child is treated as having been received from a taxpayer under the provisions of subsection (c).

(4) Exception for certain pre-1985 instruments.—

(A) In general.—A child of parents described in paragraph (1) shall be treated as having received over half his support during a calendar year from the noncustodial parent if—

(i) a qualified pre-1985 instrument between the parents applicable to the taxable year beginning in such calendar year provides that the noncustodial parent shall be entitled to any deduction allowable under section 151 for such child, and

(ii) the noncustodial parent provides at least $600 for the support of such child during such calendar year.

For purposes of this subparagraph, amounts expended for the support of a child or children shall be treated as received from the noncustodial parent to the extent that such parent provided amounts for such support.

(B) Qualified pre-1985 instrument.—For purposes of this paragraph, the term "qualified pre-1985 instrument" means any decree of divorce or separate maintenance or written agreement—

(i) which is executed before January 1, 1985,

(ii) which on such date contains the provision described in subparagraph (A)(i), and

(iii) which is not modified on or after such date in a modification which expressly provides that this paragraph shall not apply to such decree or agreement.

(5) Special rule for support received from new spouse of parent.—For purposes of this subsection, in the case of the remarriage of a parent, support of a child received from the parent's spouse shall be treated as received from the parent.

(6) Cross reference.—

For provision treating child as dependent of both parents for purposes of medical expense deduction, see section 213(d)(5).

§ 153. Cross references

(1) For definitions of "husband" and "wife", as used in section 152(b) (4), see section 7701(a) (17).

(2) For deductions of estates and trusts, in lieu of the exemptions under section 151, see section 642(b).

* * *

(4) For determination of marital status, see section 7703.

PART VI—ITEMIZED DEDUCTIONS FOR INDIVIDUALS AND CORPORATIONS

§ 161. Allowance of deductions

In computing taxable income under section 63, there shall be allowed as deductions the items specified in this part, subject to the exceptions provided in part IX (sec. 261 and following, relating to items not deductible).

§ 162. Trade or business expenses

(a) **In general.**—There shall be allowed as a deduction all the ordinary and necessary expenses paid or incurred during the taxable year in carrying on any trade or business, including—

(1) a reasonable allowance for salaries or other compensation for personal services actually rendered;

(2) traveling expenses (including amounts expended for meals and lodging other than amounts which are lavish or extravagant under the circumstances) while away from home in the pursuit of a trade or business; and

(3) rentals or other payments required to be made as a condition to the continued use or possession, for purposes of the trade or business, of property to which the taxpayer has not taken or is not taking title or in which he has no equity.

For purposes of the preceding sentence, the place of residence of a Member of Congress (including any Delegate and Resident Commissioner) within the State, congressional district, or possession which he represents in Congress shall be considered his home, but amounts expended by such Members within each taxable year for living expenses shall not be deductible for income tax purposes in excess of $3,000.

(b) Charitable contributions and gifts excepted.—No deduction shall be allowed under subsection (a) for any contribution or gift which would be allowable as a deduction under section 170 were it not for the percentage limitations, the dollar limitations, or the requirements as to the time of payment, set forth in such section.

(c) Illegal bribes, kickbacks, and other payments.—

(1) Illegal payments to government officials or employees.—No deduction shall be allowed under subsection (a) for any payment made, directly or indirectly, to an official or employee of any government, or of any agency or instrumentality of any government, if the payment constitutes an illegal bribe or kickback or, if the payment is to an official or employee of a foreign government, the payment is unlawful under the Foreign Corrupt Practices Act of 1977. The burden of proof in respect of the issue, for the purposes of this paragraph, as to whether a payment constitutes an illegal bribe or kickback (or is unlawful under the Foreign Corrupt Practices Act of 1977) shall be upon the Secretary to the same extent as he bears the burden of proof under section 7454 (concerning the burden of proof when the issue relates to fraud).

(2) Other illegal payments.—No deduction shall be allowed under subsection (a) for any payment (other than a payment described in paragraph (1)) made, directly or indirectly, to any person, if the payment constitutes an illegal bribe, illegal kickback, or other illegal payment under any law of the United States, or under any law of a State (but only if such State law is generally enforced), which subjects the payor to a criminal penalty or the loss of license or privilege to engage in a trade or business. For purposes of this paragraph, a kickback includes a payment in consideration of the referral of a client, patient, or customer. The burden of proof in respect of the issue, for purposes of this paragraph, as to whether a payment constitutes an illegal bribe, illegal kickback, or other illegal payment shall be upon the Secretary to the same extent as he bears the burden of proof under section 7454 (concerning the burden of proof when the issue relates to fraud).

(3) Kickbacks, rebates, and bribes under medicare and medicaid.—No deduction shall be allowed under subsection (a) for any kickback, rebate, or bribe made by any provider of services, supplier, physician, or other person who furnishes items or services for which payment is or may be made under the Social Security Act, or in whole or in part out of Federal funds under a State plan approved under such Act, if such kickback, rebate, or bribe is made in connection with the furnishing of such items or services or the making or receipt of such payments. For purposes of this paragraph, a kickback includes a payment in consideration of the referral of a client, patient, or customer.

* * *

(e) Appearances, etc., with respect to legislation.—

(1) In general.—The deduction allowed by subsection (a) shall include all the ordinary and necessary expenses (including, but not limited to, traveling expenses described in subsection (a) (2) and the cost of preparing testimony) paid or incurred during the taxable year in carrying on any trade or business—

(A) in direct connection with appearances before, submission of statements to, or sending communications to, the committees, or individual members, of Congress or of any legislative body of a State, a possession of the United States, or a political subdivision of any of the foregoing with respect to legislation or proposed legislation of direct interest to the taxpayer,

(B) in direct connection with communication of information between the taxpayer and an organization of which he is a member with respect to legislation or proposed legislation of direct interest to the taxpayer and to such organization,

and that portion of the dues so paid or incurred with respect to any organization of which the taxpayer is a member which is attributable to the expenses of the activities described in subparagraphs (A) and (B) carried on by such organization.

(2) **Limitation.**—The provisions of paragraph (1) shall not be construed as allowing the deduction of any amount paid or incurred (whether by way of contribution, gift, or otherwise)—

(A) for participation in, or intervention in, any political campaign on behalf of any candidate for public office, or

(B) in connection with any attempt to influence the general public, or segments thereof, with respect to legislative matters, elections, or referendums.

(f) **Fines and penalties.**—No deduction shall be allowed under subsection (a) for any fine or similar penalty paid to a government for the violation of any law.

(g) **Treble damage payments under the antitrust laws.**—If in a criminal proceeding a taxpayer is convicted of a violation of the antitrust laws, or his plea of guilty or nolo contendere to an indictment or information charging such a violation is entered or accepted in such a proceeding, no deduction shall be allowed under subsection (a) for two-thirds of any amount paid or incurred—

(1) on any judgment for damages entered against the taxpayer under section 4 of the Act entitled "An Act to supplement existing laws against unlawful restraints and monopolies, and for other purposes", approved October 15, 1914 (commonly known as the Clayton Act), on account of such violation or any related violation of the antitrust laws which occurred prior to the date of the final judgment of such conviction, or

(2) in settlement of any action brought under such section 4 on account of such violation or related violation.

* * *

(h) **State legislators' travel expenses away from home.**—

(1) **In general.**—For purposes of subsection (a), in the case of any individual who is a State legislator at any time during the taxable year and who makes an election under this subsection for the taxable year—

(A) the place of residence of such individual within the legislative district which he represented shall be considered his home,

(B) he shall be deemed to have expended for living expenses (in connection with his trade or business as a legislator) an amount equal to the sum of the amounts determined by multiplying each legislative day of such individual during the taxable year by the greater of—

(i) the amount generally allowable with respect to such day to employees of the State of which he is a legislator for per diem while away from home, to the extent such amount does not exceed 110 percent of the amount described in clause (ii) with respect to such day, or

(ii) the amount generally allowable with respect to such day to employees of the executive branch of the Federal Government for per diem while away from home but serving in the United States, and

(C) he shall be deemed to be away from home in the pursuit of a trade or business on each legislative day.

(2) Legislative days.—For purposes of paragraph (1), a legislative day during any taxable year for any individual shall be any day during such year on which—

(A) the legislature was in session (including any day in which the legislature was not in session for a period of 4 consecutive days or less), or

(B) the legislature was not in session but the physical presence of the individual was formally recorded at a meeting of a committee of such legislature.

(3) Election.—An election under this subsection for any taxable year shall be made at such time and in such manner as the Secretary shall by regulations prescribe.

(4) Section not to apply to legislators who reside near capitol.—For taxable years beginning after December 31, 1980, this subsection shall not apply to any legislator whose place of residence within the legislative district which he represents is 50 or fewer miles from the capitol building of the State.

(i) Group health plans.—

(1) Coverage relating to end stage renal disease.—The expenses paid or incurred by an employer for a group health plan shall not be allowed as a deduction under this section if the plan differentiates in the benefits it provides between individuals having end stage renal disease and other individuals covered by such plan on the basis of the existence of end stage renal disease, the need for renal dialysis, or in any other manner.

(2) Plans must provide continuation coverage to certain individuals.—

(A) In general.—No deduction shall be allowed under this section for expenses paid or incurred by an employer for any group health plan maintained by such employer unless all such plans maintained by such employer meet the continuing coverage requirements of subsection (k).

(B) Exception for certain small employers, etc.—Subparagraph (A) shall not apply to any plan described in section 106(b)(2).

(3) Group health plan.—For purposes of this subsection the term "group health plan" means any plan of, or contributed to by, an employer to provide medical care (as defined in section 213(d)) to his employees, former employees, or the families of such employees or former employees, directly or through insurance, reimbursement, or otherwise.

(j) Certain foreign advertising expenses.—

(1) In general.—No deduction shall be allowed under subsection (a) for any expenses of an advertisement carried by a foreign broadcast undertaking and directed primarily to a market in the United States. This paragraph shall apply only to foreign broadcast undertakings located in a country which denies a similar deduction for the cost of advertising directed primarily to a market in the foreign country when placed with a United States broadcast undertaking.

(2) Broadcast undertaking.—For purposes of paragraph (1), the term "broadcast undertaking" includes (but is not limited to) radio and television stations.

(k) Continuation coverage requirements of group health plans.—

(1) In general.—For purposes of subsection (i)(2) and section 106(b)(1), a group health plan meets the requirements of this subsection only if each qualified beneficiary who would lose coverage under the plan as a result of a qualifying event is entitled to elect, within the election period, continuation coverage under the plan.

(2) Continuation coverage.—For purposes of paragraph (1), the term "continuation coverage" means coverage under the plan which meets the following requirements:

(A) Type of benefit coverage.—The coverage must consist of coverage which, as of the time the coverage is being provided, is identical to the coverage provided under the plan to similarly situated beneficiaries under the plan with respect to whom a qualifying event has not occurred. If coverage under the plan is modified for any group of similarly situated beneficiaries, the coverage shall also be modified in the same manner for all individuals who are qualified beneficiaries under the plan pursuant to this subsection in connection with such group.

(B) Period of coverage.—The coverage must extend for at least the period beginning on the date of the qualifying event and ending not earlier than the earliest of the following:

(i) Maximum required period—

(I) General rule for terminations and reduced hours.—In the case of a qualifying event described in paragraph (3)(B), except as provided in subclause (II), the date which is 18 months after the date of the qualifying event.

(II) Special rule for multiple qualifying events.—If a qualifying event (other than a qualifying event described in paragraph (3)(F)) occurs during the 18 months after the date of a qualifying event described in paragraph (3)(B), the date which is 36 months after the date of the qualifying event described in paragraph (3)(B).

(ii) End of plan.—The date on which the employer ceases to provide any group health plan to any employee.

(III) Special rule for certain bankruptcy proceedings.—In the case of a qualifying event described in paragraph (3)(F) (relating to bankruptcy proceedings), the date of the death of the covered employee or qualified beneficiary (described in paragraph (7)(B)(iv)(III), or in the case of the surviving spouse or dependent children of the covered employee, 36 months after the date of the death of the covered employee.

(IV) General rule for other qualifying events.—In the case of a qualifying event not described in paragraph (3)(B) or (3)(F), the date which is 36 months after the date of the qualifying event.

(iii) Failure to pay premium.—The date on which coverage ceases under the plan by reason of a failure to make timely payment of any premium required under the plan with respect to the qualified beneficiary. The payment of any premium (other than any payment referred to in the last sentence of subparagraph (C)) shall be considered to be timely if made within 30 days after the date due or within such longer period as applies to or under the plan.

(iv) Group health plan coverage or medicare eligibility.—The date on which the qualified beneficiary first becomes, after the date of the election—

(I) covered under any other group health plan (as an employee or otherwise), or

(II) entitled in the case of a qualified beneficiary other than a qualified beneficiary described in paragraph (7)(B)(iv), to benefits under title XVIII of the Social Security Act.

(C) Premium requirements.—The plan may require payment of a premium for any period of continuation coverage, except that such premium—

(i) shall not exceed 102 percent of the applicable premium for such period, and

(ii) may, at the election of the payor, be made in monthly installments.

If an election is made after the qualifying event, the plan shall permit payment for continuation coverage during the period preceding the election to be made within 45 days of the date of the election.

(D) No requirement of insurability.—The coverage may not be conditioned upon, or discriminate on the basis of lack of, evidence of insurability.

(E) Conversion option.—In the case of a qualified beneficiary whose period of continuation coverage expires under subparagraph (B)(i), the plan must, during the 180-day period ending on such expiration date, provide to the qualified beneficiary the option of enrollment under a conversion health plan otherwise generally available under the plan.

(3) Qualifying event.—For purposes of this subsection, the term "qualifying event" means, with respect to any covered employee, any of the following events which, but for the continuation coverage required under this subsection, would result in the loss of coverage of a qualified beneficiary:

(A) The death of the covered employee.

(B) The termination (other than by reason of such employee's gross misconduct), or reduction of hours, of the covered employee's employment.

(C) The divorce or legal separation of the covered employee from the employee's spouse.

(D) The covered employee becoming entitled to benefits under title XVIII of the Social Security Act.

(E) A dependent child ceasing to be a dependent child under the generally applicable requirements of the plan.

(F) A proceeding in a case under title 11, United States Code, commencing on or after July 1, 1986, with respect to the employer from whose employment the covered employee retired at any time.

In the case of an event described in subparagraph (F), a loss of coverage includes a substantial elimination of coverage with respect to a qualified beneficiary described in paragraph (7)(B)(iv) within one year before or after the date of commencement of the proceeding.

(4) Applicable premium.—For purposes of this subsection—

(A) In general.—The term "applicable premium" means, with respect to any period of continuation coverage of qualified beneficiaries, the cost to the plan for such period of the coverage for similarly situated beneficiaries with respect to whom a qualifying event has not occurred (without regard to whether such cost is paid by the employer or employee).

(B) Special rule for self-insured plans.—To the extent that a plan is a self-insured plan—

(i) **In general.**—Except as provided in clause (ii), the applicable premium for any period of continuation coverage of qualified beneficiaries shall be equal to a reasonable estimate of the cost of providing coverage for such period for similarly situated beneficiaries which—

(I) is determined on an actuarial basis, and

(II) takes into account such factors as the Secretary may prescribe in regulations.

(ii) Determination on basis of past cost.—If a plan administrator elects to have this clause apply, the applicable premium for any period of continuation coverage of qualified beneficiaries shall be equal to—

(I) the cost to the plan for similarly situated beneficiaries for the same period occurring during the preceding determination period under subparagraph (C), adjusted by

(II) the percentage increase or decrease in the implicit price deflator of the gross national product (calculated by the Department of Commerce and published in the Survey of Current Business) for the 12-month period ending on the last day of the sixth month of such preceding determination period.

(iii) Clause (ii) not to apply where significant change.—A plan administrator may not elect to have clause (ii) apply in any case in which there is any significant difference, between the determination period and the preceding determination period, in coverage under, or in employees covered by, the plan. The determination under the preceding sentence for any determination period shall be made at the same time as the determination under subparagraph (C).

(C) Determination period.—The determination of any applicable premium shall be made for a period of 12 months and shall be made before the beginning of such period.

(5) Election.—For purposes of this subsection—

(A) Election period.—The term "election period" means the period which—

(i) begins not later than the date on which coverage terminates under the plan by reason of a qualifying event,

(ii) is of at least 60 days' duration, and

(iii) ends not earlier than 60 days after the later of—

(I) the date described in clause (i), or

(ii) in the case of any qualified beneficiary who receives notice under paragraph (6)(D), the date of such notice.

(B) Effect of election on other beneficiaries.—Except as otherwise specified in an election, any election of continuation coverage by a qualified beneficiary described in clause (i)(I) or (ii) of paragraph (7)(B) shall be deemed to include an election of continuation coverage on behalf of any other qualified beneficiary who would lose coverage under the plan by reason of the qualifying event. If there is a choice among types of coverage under the plan, each qualified beneficiary is entitled to make a separate selection among such types of coverage.

(6) Notice requirements.—In accordance with regulations prescribed by the Secretary—

(A) the group health plan shall provide, at the time of commencement of coverage under the plan, written notice to each covered employee and spouse of the employee (if any) of the rights provided under this subsection,

(B) the employer of an employee under a plan must notify the plan administrator of a qualifying event described in subparagraph (A), (B), (D), or (F) of paragraph (3) with respect to such employee within 30 days of the date of the qualifying event,

(C) each covered employee or qualified beneficiary is responsible for notifying the plan administrator of the occurrence of any qualifying event described in subparagraph (C) or (E) of paragraph (3) within 60 days after the date of the qualifying event, and

(D) the plan administrator shall notify—

(i) in the case of a qualifying event described in subparagraph (A), (B), (D) or (F) of paragraph (3), any qualified beneficiary with respect to such event, and

(ii) in the case of a qualifying event described in subparagraph (C) or (E) of paragraph (3) where the covered employee notifies the plan administrator under subparagraph (C), any qualified beneficiary with respect to such event,

of such beneficiary's rights under this subsection.

For purposes of subparagraph (D), any notification shall be made within 14 days of the date on which the plan administrator is notified under subparagraph (B) or (C), whichever is applicable, and any such notification to an individual who is a qualified beneficiary as the spouse of the covered employee shall be treated as notification to all other qualified beneficiaries residing with such spouse at the time such notification is made.

(7) **Definitions.**—For purposes of this subsection—

(A) **Covered employee.**—The term "covered employee" means an individual who is (or was) provided coverage under a group health plan by virtue of the individual's employment or previous employment with an employer

(B) **Qualified beneficiary.**—

(i) **In general.**—The term "qualified beneficiary" means, with respect to a covered employee under a group health plan, any other individual who, on the day before the qualifying event for that employee, is a beneficiary under the plan—

(I) as the spouse of the covered employee, or

(II) as the dependent child of the employee.

(ii) **Special rule for terminations and reduced employment.**—In the case of a qualifying event described in paragraph (3)(B), the term "qualified beneficiary" includes the covered employee.

* * *

(C) **Plan administrator.**—The term "plan administrator" has the meaning given the term "administrator" by section 3(16)(A) of the Employee Retirement Income Security Act of 1974.

(*l*) **Stock redemption expenses.**—

(1) **In general.**—Except as provided in paragraph (2), no deduction otherwise allowable shall be allowed under this chapter for any amount paid or incurred by a corporation in connection with the redemption of its stock.

(2) **Exceptions.**—Paragraph (1) shall not apply to—

(A) **Certain specific deductions.**—Any—

(i) deduction allowable under section 163 (relating to interest), or

(ii) deduction for dividends paid (within the meaning of section 561).

(B) Stock of certain regulated investment companies.—Any amount paid or incurred in connection with the redemption of any stock in a regulated investment company which issues only stock which is redeemable upon the demand of the shareholder.

(n) Cross references.—

* * *

(1) For special rule relating to expenses in connection with subdividing real property for sale, see section 1237.

(2) For special rule relating to the treatment of payments by a transferee of a franchise, trademark, or trade name, see section 1253.

(3) For special rules relating to—

  (A) funded welfare benefit plans, see section 419, and

  (B) deferred compensation and other deferred benefits, see section 404.

§ 163.   Interest

(a) General rule.—There shall be allowed as a deduction all interest paid or accrued within the taxable year on indebtedness.

(b) Installment purchases where interest charge is not separately stated.—

(1) **General rule.**—If personal property or educational services are purchased under a contract—

  (A) which provides that payment of part or all of the purchase price is to be made in installments, and

  (B) in which carrying charges are separately stated but the interest charge cannot be ascertained,

then the payments made during the taxable year under the contract shall be treated for purposes of this section as if they included interest equal to 6 percent of the average unpaid balance under the contract during the taxable year. For purposes of the preceding sentence, the average unpaid balance is the sum of the unpaid balance outstanding on the first day of each month beginning during the taxable year, divided by 12. For purposes of this paragraph, the term "educational services" means any service (including lodging) which is purchased from an educational organization described in section 170(b)(1)(A)(ii) and which is provided for a student of such organization.

(2) **Limitation.**—In the case of any contract to which paragraph (1) applies, the amount treated as interest for any taxable year shall not exceed the aggregate carrying charges which are properly attributable to such taxable year.

(c) Redeemable ground rents.—For purposes of this subtitle, any annual or periodic rental under a redeemable ground rent (excluding amounts in redemption thereof) shall be treated as interest on an indebtedness secured by a mortgage.

(d) Limitation on investment interest.—

(1) **In general.**—In the case of a taxpayer other than a corporation, the amount allowed as a deduction under this chapter for investment interest for any taxable year shall not exceed the net investment income of the taxpayer for the taxable year.

(2) **Carryforward of disallowed interest.**—The amount not allowed as a deduction for any taxable year by reason of paragraph (1) shall be treated as investment interest paid or accrued by the taxpayer in the succeeding taxable year.

(3) Investment interest.—For purposes of this subsection—

(A) In general.—The term "investment interest" means any interest allowable as a deduction under this chapter (determined without regard to paragraph (1)) which is paid or accrued on indebtedness incurred or continued to purchase or carry property held for investment.

(B) Exceptions.—The term "investment interest" shall not include—

(i) any qualified residence interest (as defined in subsection (h)(3)), or

(ii) any interest which is taken into account under section 469 in computing income or loss from a passive activity of the taxpayer.

(C) Personal property used in short sale.—For purposes of this paragraph, the term "interest" includes any amount allowable as a deduction in connection with personal property used in a short sale.

(4) Net investment income.—For purposes of this subsection—

(A) In general.—The term "net investment income" means the excess of—

(i) investment income, over

(ii) investment expenses.

(B) Investment income.—The term "investment income" means the sum of—

(i) gross income (other than gain described in clause (ii)) from property held for investment, and

(ii) any net gain attributable to the disposition of property held for investment,

but only to the extent such amounts are not derived from the conduct of a trade or business.

(C) Investment expenses.—The term "investment expenses" means the deductions allowed under this chapter (other than for interest) which are directly connected with the production of investment income.

(D) Income and expenses from passive activities.—Investment income and investment expenses shall not include any income or expenses taken into account under section 469 in computing income or loss from a passive activity.

(E) Reduction in investment income during phase-in of passive loss rules.—Investment income of the taxpayer for any taxable year shall be reduced by the amount of the passive activity loss to which section 469(a) does not apply for such taxable year by reason of section 469(*l*). The preceding sentence shall not apply to any portion of such passive activity loss which is attributable to a rental real estate activity with respect to which the taxpayer actively participates (within the meaning of section 469(i)(6)) during such taxable year.

(5) Property held for investment.—For purposes of this subsection—

(A) In general.—The term "property held for investment" shall include—

(i) any property which produces income of a type described in section 469(e)(1), and

(ii) any interest held by a taxpayer in an activity involving the conduct of a trade or business—

(I) which is not a passive activity, and

(II) with respect to which the taxpayer does not materially participate.

(B) Investment expenses.—In the case of property described in subparagraph (A)(i), expenses shall be allocated to such property in the same manner as under section 469.

(C) Terms.—For purposes of this paragraph, the terms "activity", "passive activity", and "materially participate" have the meanings given such terms by section 469.

(6) Phase-in of disallowance.—In the case of any taxable year beginning in calendar years 1987 through 1990—

(A) In general.—The amount of interest disallowed under this subsection for any such taxable year shall be equal to the sum of—

(i) the applicable percentage of the amount which (without regard to this paragraph) is not allowed as a deduction under this subsection for the taxable year to the extent such amount does not exceed the ceiling amount,

(ii) the amount which (without regard to this paragraph) is not allowed as a deduction under this subsection in excess of the ceiling amount, plus

(iii) the amount of any carryforward to such taxable year under paragraph (2) with respect to which a deduction was disallowed under this subsection for a preceding taxable year.

For purposes of this subparagraph, the amount under clause (i) or (ii) shall be computed without regard to the amount described in clause (iii).

(B) Applicable percentage.—For purposes of this paragraph, the applicable percentage shall be determined in accordance with the following table:

In the case of taxable years beginning in:	The applicable percentage is:
1987	35
1988	60
1989	80
1990	90

(C) Ceiling amount.—For purposes of this paragraph, the term "ceiling amount" means—

(i) $10,000 in the case of a taxpayer not described in clause (ii) or (iii),

(ii) $5,000 in the case of a married individual filing a separate return, and

(iii) zero in the case of a trust.

(e) Original issue discount.—

(1) In general.—In the case of any debt instrument issued after July 1, 1982, the portion of the original issue discount with respect to such debt instrument which is allowable as a deduction to the issuer for any taxable year shall be equal to the aggregate daily portions of the original issue discount for days during such taxable year.

(2) Definitions and special rules.—For purposes of this subsection—

(A) Debt instrument.—The term "debt instrument" has the meaning given such term by section 1275(a)(1).

(B) Daily portions.—The daily portion of the original issue discount for any day shall be determined under section 1272(a) (without regard to paragraph (6) thereof and without regard to section 1273(a)(3)).

(C) Short-term obligations.—In the case of an obligor of a short-term obligation (as defined in section 1283(a)(1)(A)) who uses the cash receipts and disbursements method of accounting, the original issue discount (and any other interest payable) on such obligation shall be deductible only when paid.

(4) Exceptions.—This subsection shall not apply to any debt instrument described in—

(A) subparagraph (D) of section 1272(a)(2) (relating to obligations issued by natural persons before March 2, 1984), and

(B) subparagraph (E) of section 1272(a)(2) (relating to loans between natural persons).

(f) Denial of deduction for interest on certain obligations not in registered form.—

(1) In general.—Nothing in subsection (a) or in any other provision of law shall be construed to provide a deduction for interest on any registration-required obligation unless such obligation is in registered form.

(2) Registration-required obligation.—For purposes of this section—

(A) In general.—The term "registration-required obligation" means any obligation (including any obligation issued by a governmental entity) other than an obligation which—

(i) is issued by a natural person,

(ii) is not of a type offered to the public,

(iii) has a maturity (at issue) of not more than 1 year, or

(iv) is described in subparagraph (B).

(B) Certain obligations not included.—An obligation is described in this subparagraph if—

(i) there are arrangements reasonably designed to ensure that such obligation will be sold (or resold in connection with the original issue) only to a person who is not a United States person, and

(ii) in the case of an obligation not in registered form—

(I) interest on such obligation is payable only outside the United States and its possessions, and

(II) on the face of such obligation there is a statement that any United States person who holds such obligation will be subject to limitations under the United States income tax laws.

(C) Authority to include other obligations.—Clauses (ii) and (iii) of subparagraph (A), and subparagraph (B), shall not apply to any obligation if—

(i) in the case of—

(I) subparagraph (A), such obligation is of a type which the Secretary has determined by regulations to be used frequently in avoiding Federal taxes, or

(II) subparagraph (B), such obligation is of a type specified by the Secretary in regulations, and

(ii) such obligation is issued after the date on which the regulations referred to in clause (i) take effect.

(3) Book entries permitted, etc.—For purposes of this subsection, rules similar to the rules of section 149(a)(3) shall apply.

* * *

(h) Disallowance of deduction for personal interest.—

(1) **In general.**—In the case of a taxpayer other than a corporation, no deduction shall be allowed under this chapter for personal interest paid or accrued during the taxable year.

(2) **Personal interest.**—For purposes of this subsection, the term "personal interest" means any interest allowable as a deduction under this chapter other than—

(A) interest paid or accrued on indebtedness incurred or continued in connection with the conduct of a trade or business (other than the trade or business of performing services as an employee),

(B) any investment interest (within the meaning of subsection (d)),

(C) any interest which is taken into account under section 469 in computing income or loss from a passive activity of the taxpayer,

(D) any qualified residence interest (within the meaning of paragraph (3)), and

(E) any interest payable under section 6601 on any unpaid portion of the tax imposed by section 2001 for the period during which an extension of time for payment of such tax is in effect under section 6163 or 6166.

(3) **Qualified residence interest.**—For purposes of this subsection—

(A) **In general.**—The term "qualified residence interest" means interest which is paid or accrued during the taxable year on indebtedness which is secured by any property which (at the time such interest is paid or accrued) is a qualified residence of the taxpayer.

(B) **Limitation on amount of interest.**—The term "qualified residence interest" shall not include any interest paid or accrued on indebtedness secured by any qualified residence which is allocable to that portion of the principal amount of such indebtedness which, when added to the outstanding aggregate principal amount of all other indebtedness previously incurred and secured by such qualified residence, exceeds the lesser of—

(i) the fair market value of such qualified residence, or

(ii) the sum of—

(I) the taxpayer's basis in such qualified residence (adjusted only by the cost of any improvements to such residence), plus

(II) the aggregate amount of qualified indebtedness of the taxpayer with respect to such qualified residence.

(C) **Cost not less than balance of indebtedness incurred on or before August 16, 1986.**—The amount under subparagraph (B)(ii)(I) at any time after August 16, 1986, shall not be less than the outstanding aggregate principal amount (as of such time) of indebtedness which was incurred on or before August 16, 1986, and which was secured by the qualified residence on August 16, 1986.

(D) **Time for determination.**—Except as provided in regulations, any determination under subparagraph (B) shall be made as of the time the indebtedness is incurred.

(4) **Qualified indebtedness.**—For purposes of this subsection—

(A) **In general.**—The term "qualified indebtedness" means indebtedness secured by a qualified residence of the taxpayer which is incurred after August 16, 1986, to pay for—

(i) qualified medical expenses, or

(ii) qualified educational expenses, which are paid or incurred within a reasonable period of time before or after such indebtedness is incurred.

(B) Qualified medical expenses.—For purposes of this paragraph, the term "qualified medical expenses" means amounts, not compensated for by insurance or otherwise, incurred for medical care (within the meaning of subparagraphs (A) and (B) of section 213(d)(1)) for the taxpayer, his spouse, or a dependent.

(C) Qualified educational expenses.—For purposes of this paragraph—

(i) In general.—The term "qualified educational expenses" means qualified tuition and related expenses of the taxpayer, his spouse, or a dependent for attendance at an educational institution described in section 170(b)(1)(A)(ii).

(ii) Qualified tuition and related expenses.—The term "qualified tuition and related expenses" has the meaning given such term by section 117(b), except that such term shall include any reasonable living expenses while away from home.

(D) Dependent.—For purposes of this paragraph, the term "dependent" has the meaning given such term by section 152.

(5) Other definitions and special rules.—

(A) Qualified residence.—For purposes of this subsection—

(i) In general.—The term "qualified residence" means—

(I) the principal residence (within the meaning of section 1034) of the taxpayer, and

(II) 1 other residence of the taxpayer which is selected by the taxpayer for purposes of this subsection for the taxable year and which is used by the taxpayer as a residence (within the meaning of section 280A(d)(1)).

(ii) Married individuals filing separate returns.—If a married couple does not file a joint return for the taxable year—

(I) such couple shall be treated as 1 taxpayer for purposes of clause (i), and

(II) each individual shall be entitled to take into account 1 residence unless both individuals consent in writing to 1 individual taking into account the principal residence and 1 other residence.

(iii) Residence not used or rented.—For purposes of clause (i)(II), notwithstanding section 280A(d)(1), if the taxpayer does not rent or use a dwelling unit at any time during a taxable year, such unit may be treated as a residence for such taxable year.

(B) Special rule for cooperative housing corporations.—For purposes of this paragraph, any indebtedness secured by stock held by the taxpayer as a tenant-stockholder (as defined in section 216) in a cooperative housing corporation (as so defined) shall be treated as secured by the house or apartment which the taxpayer is entitled to occupy as such a tenant-stockholder. If stock described in the preceding sentence may not be used to secure indebtedness, indebtedness shall be treated as so secured if the taxpayer establishes to the satisfaction of the Secretary that such indebtedness was incurred to acquire such stock.

(6) Phase-in of limitation.—In the case of any taxable year beginning in calendar years 1987 through 1990, the amount of interest with respect to which a deduction is disallowed under this subsection shall be equal to the applicable percentage (within the meaning of subsection (d)(6)(B)) of the amount which (but for this subsection) would have been so disallowed.

(i) Cross references.—

(1) For disallowance of certain amounts paid in connection with insurance, endowment, or annuity contracts, see section 264.

(2) For disallowance of deduction for interest relating to tax-exempt income, see section 265(2).

(3) For disallowance of deduction for carrying charges chargeable to capital account, see section 266.

(4) For disallowance of interest with respect to transactions between related taxpayers, see section 267.

* * *

§ 164. Taxes

(a) General rule.—Except as otherwise provided in this section, the following taxes shall be allowed as a deduction for the taxable year within which paid or accrued:

(1) State and local, and foreign, real property taxes.

(2) State and local personal property taxes.

(3) State and local, and foreign, income, war profits, and excess profits taxes.

(4) The environmental tax imposed by section 59A.

(5) The GST tax imposed on income distributions.

In addition, there shall be allowed as a deduction State and local, and foreign, taxes not described in the preceding sentence which are paid or accrued within the taxable year in carrying on a trade or business or an activity described in section 212 (relating to expenses for production of income). Notwithstanding the preceding sentence, any tax (not described in the first sentence of this subsection) which is paid or accrued by the taxpayer in connection with an acquisition or disposition of property shall be treated as part of the cost of the acquired property or, in the case of a disposition, as a reduction in the amount realized on the disposition.

(b) Definitions and special rules.—For purposes of this section—

(1) Personal property taxes.—The term "personal property tax" means an ad valorem tax which is imposed on an annual basis in respect of personal property.

(2) State or local taxes.—A State or local tax includes only a tax imposed by a State, a possession of the United States, or a political subdivision of any of the foregoing, or by the District of Columbia.

(3) Foreign taxes.—A foreign tax includes only a tax imposed by the authority of a foreign country.

(4) Special rules for GST tax.—

(A) In general.—The GST tax imposed on income distributions is—

(i) the tax imposed by section 2601, and

(ii) any State tax described in section 2604,

but only to the extent such tax is imposed on a transfer which is included in the gross income of the distributee and to which section 666 does not apply.

(B) Special rule for tax paid before due date.—Any tax referred to in subparagraph (A) imposed with respect to a transfer occurring during the taxable year of the distributee (or, in the case of a taxable termination, the trust) which is paid not later than the time prescribed by law (including extensions) for filing the return with respect to such transfer shall be treated as having been paid on the last day of the taxable year in which the transfer was made.

(c) Deduction denied in case of certain taxes.—No deduction shall be allowed for the following taxes:

(1) Taxes assessed against local benefits of a kind tending to increase the value of the property assessed; but this paragraph shall not prevent the deduction of so much of such taxes as is properly allocable to maintenance or interest charges.

(2) Taxes on real property, to the extent that subsection (d) requires such taxes to be treated as imposed on another taxpayer.

(d) Apportionment of taxes on real property between seller and purchaser.—

(1) General rule.—For purposes of subsection (a), if real property is sold during any real property tax year, then—

(A) so much of the real property tax as is properly allocable to that part of such year which ends on the day before the date of the sale shall be treated as a tax imposed on the seller, and

(B) so much of such tax as is properly allocable to that part of such year which begins on the date of the sale shall be treated as a tax imposed on the purchaser.

(2) Special rules.—

(A) In the case of any sale of real property, if—

(i) a taxpayer may not, by reason of his method of accounting, deduct any amount for taxes unless paid, and

(ii) the other party to the sale is (under the law imposing the real property tax) liable for the real property tax for the real property tax year,

then for purposes of subsection (a) the taxpayer shall be treated as having paid, on the date of the sale, so much of such tax as, under paragraph (1) of this subsection, is treated as imposed on the taxpayer. For purposes of the preceding sentence, if neither party is liable for the tax, then the party holding the property at the time the tax becomes a lien on the property shall be considered liable for the real property tax for the real property tax year.

(B) In the case of any sale of real property, if the taxpayer's taxable income for the taxable year during which the sale occurs is computed under an accrual method of accounting, and if no election under section 461(c) (relating to the accrual of real property taxes) applies, then, for purposes of subsection (a), that portion of such tax which—

(i) is treated, under paragraph (1) of this subsection, as imposed on the taxpayer, and

(ii) may not, by reason of the taxpayer's method of accounting, be deducted by the taxpayer for any taxable year,

shall be treated as having accrued on the date of the sale.

(e) Taxes of shareholder paid by corporation.—Where a corporation pays a tax imposed on a shareholder on his interest as a shareholder, and where the shareholder does not reimburse the corporation, then—

(1) the deduction allowed by subsection (a) shall be allowed to the corporation; and

(2) no deduction shall be allowed the shareholder for such tax.

(f) Deduction for one-half of self-employment taxes.—

(1) In general.—In the case of an individual, in addition to the taxes described in subsection (a), there shall be allowed as a deduction for the taxable year an amount equal to one-half of the taxes imposed by section 1401 for such taxable year.

(2) Deduction treated as attributable to trade or business.—For purposes of this chapter, the deduction allowed by paragraph (1) shall be treated as attributable to a trade or business carried on by the taxpayer which does not consist of the performance of services by the taxpayer as an employee.

(g) Cross references.—

(1) For provisions disallowing any deduction for certain taxes, see section 275.

* * *

§ 165. Losses

(a) General rule.—There shall be allowed as a deduction any loss sustained during the taxable year and not compensated for by insurance or otherwise.

(b) Amount of deduction.—For purposes of subsection (a), the basis for determining the amount of the deduction for any loss shall be the adjusted basis provided in section 1011 for determining the loss from the sale or other disposition of property.

(c) Limitation on losses of individuals.—In the case of an individual, the deduction under subsection (a) shall be limited to—

(1) losses incurred in a trade or business;

(2) losses incurred in any transaction entered into for profit, though not connected with a trade or business; and

(3) except as provided in subsection (h), losses of property not connected with a trade or business or a transaction entered into for profit, if such losses arise from fire, storm, shipwreck, or other casualty, or from theft.

(d) Wagering losses.—Losses from wagering transactions shall be allowed only to the extent of the gains from such transactions.

(e) Theft losses.—For purposes of subsection (a), any loss arising from theft shall be treated as sustained during the taxable year in which the taxpayer discovers such loss.

(f) Capital losses.—Losses from sales or exchanges of capital assets shall be allowed only to the extent allowed in sections 1211 and 1212.

(g) Worthless securities.—

(1) General rule.—If any security which is a capital asset becomes worthless during the taxable year, the loss resulting therefrom shall, for purposes of this subtitle, be treated as a loss from the sale or exchange, on the last day of the taxable year, of a capital asset.

(2) Security defined.—For purposes of this subsection, the term "security" means—

(A) a share of stock in a corporation;

(B) a right to subscribe for, or to receive, a share of stock in a corporation; or

(C) a bond, debenture, note, or certificate, or other evidence of indebtedness, issued by a corporation or by a government or political subdivision thereof, with interest coupons or in registered form.

(3) Securities in affiliated corporation.—For purposes of paragraph (1), any security in a corporation affiliated with a taxpayer which is a domestic corporation shall not be treated as a capital asset. For purposes of the preceding sentence, a corporation shall be treated as affiliated with the taxpayer only if—

(A) stock possessing at least 80 percent of the voting power of all classes of its stock and at least 80 percent of each class of its nonvoting stock is owned directly by the taxpayer, and

(B) more than 90 percent of the aggregate of its gross receipts for all taxable years has been from sources other than royalties, rents (except rents derived from rental of properties to employees of the corporation in the ordinary course of its operating business), dividends, interest (except interest received on deferred purchase price of operating assets sold), annuities, and gains from sales or exchanges of stocks and securities.

In computing gross receipts for purposes of the preceding sentence, gross receipts from sales or exchanges of stocks and securities shall be taken into account only to the extent of gains therefrom. As used in subparagraph (A), the term "stock" does not include nonvoting stock which is limited and preferred as to dividends.

(h) Treatment of casualty gains and losses.—

(1) $100 limitation per casualty.—Any loss of an individual described in subsection (c)(3) shall be allowed only to the extent that the amount of the loss to such individual arising from each casualty, or from each theft, exceeds $100.

(2) Net casualty loss allowed only to the extent it exceeds 10 percent of adjusted gross income.—

(A) In general.—If the personal casualty losses for any taxable year exceed the personal casualty gains for such taxable year, such losses shall be allowed for the taxable year only to the extent of the sum of—

(i) the amount of the personal casualty gains for the taxable year, plus

(ii) so much of such excess as exceeds 10 percent of the adjusted gross income of the individual.

(B) Special rule where personal casualty gains exceed personal casualty losses.—If the personal casualty gains for any taxable year exceed the personal casualty losses for such taxable year—

(i) all such gains shall be treated as gains from sales or exchanges of capital assets, and

(ii) all such losses shall be treated as losses from sales or exchanges of capital assets.

(3) Definitions of personal casualty gain and personal casualty loss.—For purposes of this subsection—

(A) Personal casualty gain.—The term "personal casualty gain" means the recognized gain from any involuntary conversion of property which is described in subsection (c)(3) arising from fire, storm, shipwreck, or other casualty, or from theft.

(B) Personal casualty loss.—The term "personal casualty loss" means any loss described in subsection (c)(3). For purposes of paragraph (2), the amount of any personal casualty loss shall be determined after the application of paragraph (1).

(4) Special rules.—

(A) Personal casualty losses allowable in computing adjusted gross income to the extent of personal casualty gains.—In any case to which paragraph (2)(A) applies, the deduction for personal casualty losses for any

177

taxable year shall be treated as a deduction allowable in computing adjusted gross income to the extent such losses do not exceed the personal casualty gains for the taxable year.

(B) Joint returns.—For purposes of this subsection, a husband and wife making a joint return for the taxable year shall be treated as 1 individual.

(C) Determination of adjusted gross income in case of estates and trusts.—For purposes of paragraph (2), the adjusted gross income of an estate or trust shall be computed in the same manner as in the case of an individual, except that the deductions for costs paid or incurred in connection with the administration of the estate or trust shall be treated as allowable in arriving at adjusted gross income.

(D) Coordination with estate tax.—No loss described in subsection (c)(3) shall be allowed if, at the time of filing the return, such loss has been claimed for estate tax purposes in the estate tax return.

(E) Claim required to be filed in certain cases.—Any loss of an individual described in subsection (c)(3) to the extent covered by insurance shall be taken into account under this section only if the individual files a timely insurance claim with respect to such loss.

(i) Disaster losses.—

(1) Election to take deduction for preceding year.—Notwithstanding the provisions of subsection (a), any loss attributable to a disaster occurring in an area subsequently determined by the President of the United States to warrant assistance by the Federal Government under the Disaster Relief Act of 1974 may, at the election of the taxpayer, be taken into account for the taxable year immediately preceding the taxable year in which the disaster occurred.

(2) Year of loss.—If an election is made under this subsection, the casualty resulting in the loss shall be treated for purposes of this title as having occurred in the taxable year for which the deduction is claimed.

(3) Amount of loss.—The amount of the loss taken into account in the preceding taxable year by reason of paragraph (1) shall not exceed the uncompensated amount determined on the basis of the facts existing at the date the taxpayer claims the loss.

(j) Denial of deduction for losses on certain obligations not in registered form.—

(1) In general.—Nothing in subsection (a) or in any other provision of law shall be construed to provide a deduction for any loss sustained on any registration-required obligation unless such obligation is in registered form (or the issuance of such obligation was subject to tax under section 4701).

(2) Definitions.—For purposes of this subsection—

(A) Registration-required obligation.—The term "registration-required obligation" has the meaning given to such term by section 163(f)(2) except that clause (iv) of subparagraph (A), and subparagraph (B), of such section shall not apply.

(B) Registered form.—The term "registered form" has the same meaning as when used in section 163(f).

(3) Exceptions.—The Secretary may, by regulations, provide that this subsection and section 1287 shall not apply with respect to obligations held by any person if—

(A) such person holds such obligations in connection with a trade or business outside the United States,

(B) such person holds such obligations as a broker dealer (registered under Federal or State law) for sale to customers in the ordinary course of his trade or business,

(C) such person complies with reporting requirements with respect to ownership, transfers, and payments as the Secretary may require, or

(D) such person promptly surrenders the obligation to the issuer for the issuance of a new obligation in registered form,

but only if such obligations are held under arrangements provided in regulations or otherwise which are designed to assure that such obligations are not delivered to any United States person other than a person described in subparagraph (A), (B), or (C).

(k) Treatment as disaster loss where taxpayer ordered to demolish or relocate residence in disaster area because of disaster.—In the case of a taxpayer whose residence is located in an area which has been determined by the President of the United States to warrant assistance by the Federal Government under the Disaster Relief Act of 1974, if—

(1) not later than the 120th day after the date of such determination, the taxpayer is ordered, by the government of the State or any political subdivision thereof in which such residence is located, to demolish or relocate such residence, and

(2) the residence has been rendered unsafe for use as a residence by reason of the disaster,

any loss attributable to such disaster shall be treated as a loss which arises from a casualty and which is described in subsection (i).

* * *

§ 166. Bad debts.

(a) General Rule.—

(1) Wholly worthless debts.—There shall be allowed as a deduction any debt which becomes worthless within the taxable year.

(2) Partially worthless debts.—When satisfied that a debt is recoverable only in part, the Secretary may allow such debt, in an amount not in excess of the part charged off within the taxable year, as a deduction.

(b) Amount of Deduction.—For purposes of subsection (a), the basis for determining the amount of the deduction for any bad debt shall be the adjusted basis provided in section 1011 for determining the loss from the sale or other disposition of property.

[(c) Repealed.] — Used to allow loss deduction in Advance - doubtful Accounts

(d) Nonbusiness Debts.—

(1) General rule.—In the case of a taxpayer other than a corporation—

(A) subsections (a) and (c) shall not apply to any nonbusiness debt; and

(B) where any nonbusiness debt becomes worthless within the taxable year, the loss resulting therefrom shall be considered a loss from the sale or exchange, during the taxable year, of a capital asset held for not more than 6 months.

(2) Nonbusiness debt defined.—For purposes of paragraph (1), the term "nonbusiness debt" means a debt other than—

 (A) a debt created or acquired (as the case may be) in connection with a trade or business of the taxpayer; or

 (B) a debt the loss from the worthlessness of which is incurred in the taxpayer's trade or business.

 (e) Worthless Securities.—This section shall not apply to a debt which is evidenced by a security as defined in section 165(g)(2)(C).

* * *

§ 167. Depreciation

 (a) General rule.—There shall be allowed as a depreciation deduction a reasonable allowance for the exhaustion, wear and tear (including a reasonable allowance for obsolescence)—

 (1) of property used in the trade or business, or

 (2) of property held for the production of income.

In the case of recovery property (within the meaning of section 168), the deduction allowable under section 168 shall be deemed to constitute the reasonable allowance provided by this section, except with respect to that portion of the basis of such property to which subsection (k) applies.

 (b) Use of certain methods and rates.—For taxable years ending after December 31, 1953, the term "reasonable allowance" as used in subsection (a) shall include (but shall not be limited to) an allowance computed in accordance with regulations prescribed by the Secretary, under any of the following methods:

 (1) the straight line method,

 (2) the declining balance method, using a rate not exceeding twice the rate which would have been used had the annual allowance been computed under the method described in paragraph (1),

 (3) the sum of the years-digits method, and

 (4) any other consistent method productive of an annual allowance which, when added to all allowances for the period commencing with the taxpayer's use of the property and including the taxable year, does not, during the first two-thirds of the useful life of the property, exceed the total of such allowances which would have been used had such allowances been computed under the method described in paragraph (2).

Nothing in this subsection shall be construed to limit or reduce an allowance otherwise allowable under subsection (a).

 (c) Limitations on use of certain methods and rates.—Paragraphs (2), (3), and (4) of subsection (b) shall apply only in the case of property (other than intangible property) described in subsection (a) with a useful life of 3 years or more—

 (1) the construction, reconstruction, or erection of which is completed after December 31, 1953, and then only to that portion of the basis which is properly attributable to such construction, reconstruction, or erection after December 31, 1953, or

 (2) acquired after December 31, 1953, if the original use of such property commences with the taxpayer and commences after such date.

 (d) Agreement as to useful life on which depreciation rate is based.—Where, under regulations prescribed by the Secretary, the taxpayer and the Secretary have, after August 16, 1954, entered into an agreement in writing specifically dealing with the useful life and rate of depreciation of any property, the rate so agreed upon shall be binding on both the taxpayer and the Secretary in the absence of facts or circumstances not taken into consideration in the adoption of such agreement. The responsibility of establishing the existence of such facts and circumstances shall rest with the party initiating the modification. Any change in the agreed rate and useful life specified in the agreement shall not be effective for taxable years before the taxable year in which notice in writing by certified mail or registered mail is served by the party to the agreement initiating such change. This subsection shall not apply with respect to recovery property defined in section 168.

(e) Change in method.—

(1) Change from declining balance method.—In the absence of an agreement under subsection (d) containing a provision to the contrary, a taxpayer may at any time elect in accordance with regulations prescribed by the Secretary to change from the method of depreciation described in subsection (b) (2) to the method described in subsection (b) (1).

(2) Change with respect to section 1245 property.—A taxpayer may, on or before the last day prescribed by law (including extensions thereof) for filing his return for his first taxable year beginning after December 31, 1962, and in such manner as the Secretary shall by regulations prescribe, elect to change his method of depreciation in respect of section 1245 property (as defined in section 1245(a) (3)) from any declining balance or sum of the years-digits method to the straight line method. An election may be made under this paragraph notwithstanding any provision to the contrary in an agreement under subsection (d).

(3) Change with respect to section 1250 property.—A taxpayer may, on or before the last day prescribed by law (including extensions thereof) for filing his return for his first taxable year beginning after December 31, 1975, and in such manner as the Secretary shall by regulation prescribe, elect to change his method of depreciation in respect of section 1250 property (as defined in section 1250(c)) from any declining balance or sum of the years-digits method to the straight line method. An election may be made under this paragraph notwithstanding any provision to the contrary in an agreement under subsection (d).

(f) Salvage value.—

(1) General rule.—Under regulations prescribed by the Secretary, a taxpayer may, for purposes of computing the allowance under subsection (a) with respect to personal property, reduce the amount taken into account as salvage value by an amount which does not exceed 10 percent of the basis of such property (as determined under subsection (g) as of the time as of which such salvage value is required to be determined).

(2) Personal property defined.—For purposes of this subsection, the term "personal property" means depreciable personal property (other than livestock) with a useful life of 3 years or more acquired after October 16, 1962.

(g) Basis for depreciation.—The basis on which exhaustion, wear and tear, and obsolescence are to be allowed in respect of any property shall be the adjusted basis provided in section 1011 for the purpose of determining the gain on the sale or other disposition of such property.

(h) Life tenants and beneficiaries of trusts and estates.—In the case of property held by one person for life with remainder to another person, the deduction shall be computed as if the life tenant were the absolute owner of the property and shall be allowed to the life tenant. In the case of property held in trust, the allowable deduction shall be apportioned between the income beneficiaries and the trustee in accordance with the pertinent provisions of the instrument creating the trust, or, in the absence of such provisions, on the basis of the trust income allocable to each. In the case of an estate, the allowable deduction shall be apportioned between the estate and the heirs, legatees, and devisees on the basis of the income of the estate allocable to each.

[(i) Repealed.]

(j) Special rules for section 1250 property.—

(1) General rule.—Except as provided in paragraphs (2) and (3), in the case of section 1250 property, subsection (b) shall not apply and the term "reasonable allowance" as used in subsection (a) shall include an allowance computed in accordance with regulations prescribed by the Secretary, under any of the following methods:

(A) the straight line method,

(B) the declining balance method, using a rate not exceeding 150 percent of the rate which would have been used had the annual allowance been computed under the method described in subparagraph (A), or

(C) any other consistent method productive of an annual allowance which, when added to all allowances for the period commencing with the taxpayer's use of the property and including the taxable year, does not, during the first two-thirds of the useful life of the property, exceed the total of such allowances which would have been used had such allowances been computed under the method described in subparagraph (B).

Nothing in this paragraph shall be construed to limit or reduce an allowance otherwise allowable under subsection (a) except where allowable solely by reason of paragraph (2), (3), or (4) of subsection (b).

(2) Residential rental property.—

(A) In general.—Paragraph (1) of this subsection shall not apply, and subsection (b) shall apply in any taxable year, to a building or structure—

(i) which is residential rental property located within the United States or any of its possessions, or located within a foreign country if a method of depreciation for such property comparable to the method provided in subsection (b) (2) or (3) is provided by the laws of such country, and

(ii) the original use of which commences with the taxpayer.

In the case of residential rental property located within a foreign country, the original use of which commences with the taxpayer, if the allowance for depreciation provided under the laws of such country for such property is greater than that provided under paragraph (1) of this subsection, but less than that provided under subsection (b), the allowance for depreciation under subsection (b) shall be limited to the amount provided under the laws of such country.

(B) Definition.—For purposes of subparagraph (A), a building or structure shall be considered to be residential rental property for any taxable year only if 80 percent or more of the gross rental income from such building or structure for such year is rental income from dwelling units (within the meaning of subsection (k) (3) (C)). For purposes of the preceding sentence, if any portion of such building or structure is occupied by the taxpayer, the gross rental income from such building or structure shall include the rental value of the portion so occupied.

(C) Change in method of depreciation.—Any change in the computation of the allowance for depreciation for any taxable year, permitted or required by reason of the application of subparagraph (A), shall not be considered a change in a method of accounting.

(3) Property constructed, etc., before July 25, 1969.—Paragraph (1) of this subsection shall not apply, and subsection (b) shall apply, in the case of property—

(A) the construction, reconstruction, or erection of which was begun before July 25, 1969, or

(B) for which a written contract entered into before July 25, 1969, with respect to any part of the construction, reconstruction, or erection or for the permanent financing thereof, was on July 25, 1969, and at all times thereafter, binding on the taxpayer.

(4) Used section 1250 property.—Except as provided in paragraph (5), in the case of section 1250 property acquired after July 24, 1969, the original use of which does not commence with the taxpayer, the allowance for depreciation under this section shall be limited to an amount computed under—

(A) the straight line method, or

(B) any other method determined by the Secretary to result in a reasonable allowance under subsection (a), not including—

(i) any declining balance method,

(ii) the sum of the years-digits method, or

(iii) any other method allowable solely by reason of the application of subsection (b) (4) or paragraph (1) (C) of this subsection.

(5) Used residential rental property.—In the case of section 1250 property which is residential rental property (as defined in paragraph (2) (B)) acquired after July 24, 1969, having a useful life of 20 years or more, the original use of which does not commence with the taxpayer, the allowance for depreciation under this section shall be limited to an amount computed under—

(A) the straight line method,

(B) the declining balance method, using a rate not exceeding 125 percent of the rate which would have been used had the annual allowance been computed under the method described in subparagraph (A), or

(C) any other method determined by the Secretary to result in a reasonable allowance under subsection (a), not including—

(i) the sum of the years-digits method,

(ii) any declining balance method using a rate in excess of the rate permitted under subparagraph (B), or

(iii) any other method allowable solely by reason of the application of subsection (b) (4) or paragraph (1) (C) of this subsection.

(6) Special rules.—

(A) Under regulations prescribed by the Secretary, rules similar to the rules provided in paragraphs (5), (9), (10), and (13) of section 48(h) shall be applied for purposes of paragraphs (3), (4), and (5) of this subsection.

(B) For purposes of paragraphs (2), (4), and (5), if section 1250 property which is not property described in subsection (a) when its original use commences, becomes property described in subsection (a) after July 24, 1969, such property shall not be treated as property the original use of which commences with the taxpayer.

(C) Paragraphs (4) and (5) shall not apply in the case of section 1250 property acquired after July 24, 1969, pursuant to a written contract for the acquisition of such property or for the permanent financing thereof, which was, on July 24, 1969, and at all times thereafter, binding on the taxpayer.

(k) Depreciation of expenditures to rehabilitate low-income rental housing.—

(1) **60-month rule.**—The taxpayer may elect, in accordance with regulations prescribed by the Secretary, to compute the depreciation deduction provided by subsection (a) attributable to rehabilitation expenditures incurred with respect to low-income rental housing after July 24, 1969, and before January 1, 1987, under the straight line method using a useful life of 60 months and no salvage value. Such method shall be in lieu of any other method of computing the depreciation deduction under subsection (a), and in lieu of any deduction for amortization, for such expenditures.

(2) **Limitations.—**

(A) Except as provided in subparagraph (B), the aggregate amount of rehabilitation expenditures paid or incurred by the taxpayer with respect to any dwelling unit in any low-income rental housing which may be taken into account under paragraph (1) shall not exceed $20,000.

(B) The aggregate amount of rehabilitation expenditures paid or incurred by the taxpayer with respect to any dwelling unit in any low-income rental housing which may be taken into account under paragraph (1) may exceed $20,000, but shall not exceed $40,000, if the rehabilitation is conducted pursuant to a program certified by the Secretary of Housing and Urban Development, or his delegate, or by the government of a State or political subdivision of the United States and if:

(i) the certification of development costs is required;

(ii) the tenants occupy units in the property as their principal residence and the program provides for sale of the units to tenants demonstrating home ownership responsibility; and

(iii) the leasing and sale of such units are pursuant to a program in which the sum of the taxable income, if any, from leasing of each such unit, for the entire period of such leasing, and the amount realized from sale or other disposition of a unit, if sold, normally does not exceed the excess of the taxpayer's cost basis for such unit of property, before adjustment under section 1016 for deductions under section 167, over the net tax benefits realized by the taxpayer, consisting of the tax benefits from such deductions under section 167 minus the tax incurred on such taxable income from leasing, if any.

(C) Rehabilitation expenditures paid or incurred by the taxpayer in any taxable year with respect to any dwelling unit in any low-income rental housing shall be taken into account under paragraph (1) only if over a period of two consecutive years, including the taxable year, the aggregate amount of such expenditures exceeds $3,000.

(3) **Definitions.**—For purposes of this subsection—

(A) **Rehabilitation expenditures.**—The term "rehabilitation expenditures" means amounts chargeable to capital account and incurred for property or additions or improvements to property (or related facilities) with a useful life of 5 years or more, in connection with the rehabilitation of an existing building for low-income rental housing; but such term does not include the cost of acquisition of such building or any interest therein.

(B) **Low-income rental housing.**—The term "low-income rental housing" means any building the dwelling units in which are held for occupancy on a rental basis by families and individuals of low or moderate income, as deter-

(I) the amount allowable as a deduction under this section (as in effect before the date of the enactment of this paragraph) with respect to such property is greater than

(II) the amount allowable as a deduction under this section (as in effect on or after such date and using the half-year convention) for such taxable year.

(g) Alternative depreciation system for certain property.—

(1) In general.—In the case of—

(A) any tangible property which during the taxable year is used predominantly outside the United States,

(B) any tax-exempt use property,

(C) any tax-exempt bond financed property,

(D) any imported property covered by an Executive order under paragraph (6), and

(E) any property to which an election under paragraph (7) applies,

the depreciation deduction provided by section 167(a) shall be determined under the alternative depreciation system.

(2) Alternative depreciation system.—For purposes of paragraph (1), the alternative depreciation system is depreciation determined by using—

(A) the straight line method (without regard to salvage value),

(B) the applicable convention determined under subsection (d), and

(C) a recovery period determined under the following table:

In the case of:	The recovery period shall be:
(i) Property not described in clause (ii) or (iii)	The class life
(ii) Personal property with no class life	12 years
(iii) Nonresidential real and residential rental property	40 years

(3) Special rules for determining class life.—

(A) Tax-exempt use property subject to lease.—In the case of any tax-exempt use property subject to a lease, the recovery period used for purposes of paragraph (2) shall in no event be less than 125 percent of the lease term.

(B) Special rule for certain property assigned to classes.—For purposes of paragraph (2), in the case of property described in any of the following subparagraphs of subsection (e)(3), the class life shall be determined as follows:

If property is described in subparagraph:	The class life is:
(B)(ii)	5
(B)(iii)	9.5
(C)(i)	10
(C)(ii)	15
(D)(i)	24
(D)(ii)	24
(E)	50

(C) Qualified technological equipment.—In the case of any qualified technological equipment, the recovery period used for purposes of paragraph (2) shall be 5 years.

(D) **Automobiles, etc.**—In the case of any automobile or light general purpose truck, the recovery period used for purposes of paragraph (2) shall be 5 years.

(E) **Certain real property.**—In the case of any section 1245 property which is real property with no class life, the recovery period used for purposes of paragraph (2) shall be 40 years.

(4) **Property used predominantly outside the United States.**—For purposes of this subsection, rules similar to the rules under section 48(a)(2) (including the exceptions contained in subparagraph (B) thereof) shall apply in determining whether property is used predominantly outside the United States. In addition to the exceptions contained in such subparagraph (B), there shall be excepted any satellite or other spacecraft (or any interest therein) held by a United States person if such satellite or spacecraft was launched from within the United States.

(5) **Tax-exempt bond financed property.**—For purposes of this subsection—

(A) **In general.**—Except as otherwise provided in this paragraph, the term "tax-exempt bond financed property" means any property to the extent such property is financed (directly or indirectly) by an obligation the interest on which is exempt from tax under section 103(a).

(B) **Allocation of bond proceeds.**—For purposes of subparagraph (A), the proceeds of any obligation shall be treated as used to finance property acquired in connection with the issuance of such obligation in the order in which such property is placed in service.

(C) **Qualified residential rental projects.**—The term "tax-exempt bond financed property" shall not include any qualified residential rental project (within the meaning of section 142(a)(7)).

(6) **Imported property.**—

(A) **Countries maintaining trade restrictions or engaging in discriminatory acts.**—If the President determines that a foreign country—

(i) maintains nontariff trade restrictions, including variable import fees, which substantially burden United States commerce in a manner inconsistent with provisions of trade agreements, or

(ii) engages in discriminatory or other acts (including tolerance of international cartels) or policies unjustifiably restricting United States commerce,

the President may by Executive order provide for the application of paragraph (1)(D) to any article or class of articles manufactured or produced in such foreign country for such period as may be provided by such Executive order. Any period specified in the preceding sentence shall not apply to any property ordered before (or the construction, reconstruction, or erection of which began before) the date of the Executive order unless the President determines an earlier date to be in the public interest and specifies such date in the Executive order.

(B) **Imported property.**—For purposes of this subsection, the term "imported property" means any property if—

(i) such property was completed outside the United States, or

(ii) less than 50 percent of the basis of such property is attributable to value added within the United States.

For purposes of this subparagraph, the term "United States" includes the Commonwealth of Puerto Rico and the possessions of the United States.

(7) **Election to use alternative depreciation system.**—

(A) In general.—If the taxpayer makes an election under this paragraph with respect to any class of property for any taxable year, the alternative depreciation system under this subsection shall apply to all property in such class placed in service during such taxable year. Notwithstanding the preceding sentence, in the case of nonresidential real property or residential rental property, such election may be made separately with respect to each property.

(B) Election irrevocable.—An election under subparagraph (A), once made, shall be irrevocable.

(h) Tax-exempt use property.—

(1) In general.—For purposes of this section—

(A) Property other than nonresidential real property.—Except as otherwise provided in this subsection, the term "tax-exempt use property" means that portion of any tangible property (other than nonresidential real property) leased to a tax-exempt entity.

(B) Nonresidential real property.—

(i) In general.—In the case of nonresidential real property, the term "tax-exempt use property" means that portion of the property leased to a tax-exempt entity in a disqualified lease.

(ii) Disqualified lease.—For purposes of this subparagraph, the term "disqualified lease" means any lease of the property to a tax-exempt entity, but only if—

(I) part or all of the property was financed (directly or indirectly) by an obligation the interest on which is exempt from tax under section 103(a) and such entity (or a related entity) participated in such financing,

(II) under such lease there is a fixed or determinable price purchase or sale option which involves such entity (or a related entity) or there is the equivalent of such an option,

(III) such lease has a lease term in excess of 20 years, or

(IV) such lease occurs after a sale (or other transfer) of the property by, or lease of the property from, such entity (or a related entity) and such property has been used by such entity (or a related entity) before such sale (or other transfer) or lease.

(iii) 35-percent threshold test.—Clause (i) shall apply to any property only if the portion of such property leased to tax-exempt entities in disqualified leases is more than 35 percent of the property.

(iv) Treatment of improvements.—For purposes of this subparagraph, improvements to a property (other than land) shall not be treated as a separate property.

(v) Leasebacks during 1st 3 months of use not taken into account.—Subclause (IV) of clause (ii) shall not apply to any property which is leased within 3 months after the date such property is first used by the tax-exempt entity (or a related entity).

(C) Exception for short-term leases.—

(i) In general.—Property shall not be treated as tax-exempt use property merely by reason of a short-term lease.

(ii) Short-term lease.—For purposes of clause (i), the term "short-term lease" means any lease the term of which is—

(I) less than 3 years, and

(II) less than the greater of 1 year or 30 percent of the property's present class life.

In the case of nonresidential real property and property with no present class life, subclause (II) shall not apply.

(D) Exception where property used in unrelated trade or business.—The term "tax-exempt use property" shall not include any portion of a property if such portion is predominantly used by the tax-exempt entity (directly or through a partnership of which such entity is a partner) in an unrelated trade or business the income of which is subject to tax under section 511. For purposes of subparagraph (B)(iii), any portion of a property so used shall not be treated as leased to a tax-exempt entity in a disqualified lease.

(E) Nonresidential real property defined.—For purposes of this paragraph, the term "nonresidential real property" includes residential rental property.

(2) Tax-exempt entity.—

(A) In general.—For purposes of this subsection, the term "tax-exempt entity" means—

(i) the United States, any State or political subdivision thereof, any possession of the United States, or any agency or instrumentality of any of the foregoing,

(ii) an organization (other than a cooperative described in section 521) which is exempt from tax imposed by this chapter, and

(iii) any foreign person or entity.

(B) Exceptions for certain property subject to United States tax and used by foreign person or entity.—

(i) Income from property subject to United States tax.—Clause (iii) of subparagraph (A) shall not apply with respect to any property if more than 50 percent of the gross income for the taxable year derived by the foreign person or entity from the use of such property is—

(I) subject to tax under this chapter, or

(II) included under section 951 in the gross income of a United States shareholder for the taxable year with or within which ends the taxable year of the controlled foreign corporation in which such income was derived.

For purposes of the preceding sentence, any exclusion or exemption shall not apply for purposes of determining the amount of the gross income so derived, but shall apply for purposes of determining the portion of such gross income subject to tax under this chapter.

(ii) Movies and sound recordings.—Clause (iii) of subparagraph (A) shall not apply with respect to any qualified film (as defined in section 48(k)(1)(B)) or any sound recording (as defined in section 48(r)(5)).

(C) Foreign person or entity.—For purposes of this paragraph, the term "foreign person or entity" means—

(i) any foreign government, any international organization, or any agency or instrumentality of any of the foregoing, and

(ii) any person who is not a United States person.

Such term does not include any foreign partnership or other foreign pass-thru entity.

(D) Treatment of certain taxable instrumentalities.—For purposes of this subsection, a corporation shall not be treated as an instrumentality of the United States or of any State or political subdivision thereof if—

(i) all of the activities of such corporation are subject to tax under this chapter, and

(ii) a majority of the board of directors of such corporation is not selected by the United States or any State or political subdivision thereof.

(E) Certain previously tax-exempt organizations.—

(i) **In general.**—For purposes of this subsection, an organization shall be treated as an organization described in subparagraph (A)(ii) with respect to any property (other than property held by such organization) if such organization was an organization (other than a cooperative described in section 521) exempt from tax imposed by this chapter at any time during the 5-year period ending on the date such property was first used by such organization. The preceding sentence and subparagraph (D)(ii) shall not apply to the Federal Home Loan Mortgage Corporation.

(ii) **Election not to have clause (I) apply.**—

(I) **In general.**—In the case of an organization formerly exempt from tax under section 501(a) as an organization described in section 501(c)(12), clause (i) shall not apply to such organization with respect to any property if such organization elects not to be exempt from tax under section 501(a) during the tax-exempt use period with respect to such property.

(II) **Tax-exempt use period.**—For purposes of subclause (I), the term "tax-exempt use period" means the period beginning with the taxable year in which the property described in subclause (I) is first used by the organization and ending with the close of the 15th taxable year following the last taxable year of the applicable recovery period of such property.

(III) **Election.**—Any election under subclause (I), once made, shall be irrevocable.

(iii) **Treatment of successor organizations.**—Any organization which is engaged in activities substantially similar to those engaged in by a predecessor organization shall succeed to the treatment under this subparagraph of such predecessor organization.

(iv) **First used.**—For purposes of this subparagraph, property shall be treated as first used by the organization—

(I) when the property is first placed in service under a lease to such organization, or

(II) in the case of property leased to (or held by) a partnership (or other pass-thru entity) in which the organization is a member, the later of when such property is first used by such partnership or pass-thru entity or when such organization is first a member of such partnership or pass-thru entity.

(3) Special rules for certain high technology equipment.—

(A) Exemption where lease term is 5 years or less.—For purposes of this section, the term "tax-exempt use property" shall not include any qualified technological equipment if the lease to the tax-exempt entity has a lease term of 5 years or less.

(B) Exception for certain property.—

(i) **In general.**—For purposes of subparagraph (A), the term "qualified technological equipment" shall not include any property leased to a tax-exempt entity if—

(I) part or all of the property was financed (directly or indirectly) by an obligation the interest on which is exempt from tax under section 103(a),

(II) such lease occurs after a sale (or other transfer) of the property by, or lease of such property from, such entity (or related entity) and such property has been used by such entity (or a related entity) before such sale (or other transfer) or lease, or

(III) such tax-exempt entity is the United States or any agency or instrumentality of the United States.

(ii) **Leasebacks during 1st 3 months of use not taken into account.**—Subclause (II) of clause (i) shall not apply to any property which is leased within 3 months after the date such property is first used by the tax-exempt entity (or a related entity).

(4) **Related entities.**—For purposes of this subsection—

(A)(i) Each governmental unit and each agency or instrumentality of a governmental unit is related to each other such unit, agency, or instrumentality which directly or indirectly derives its powers, rights, and duties in whole or in part from the same sovereign authority.

(ii) For purposes of clause (i), the United States, each State, and each possession of the United States shall be treated as a separate sovereign authority.

(B) Any entity not described in subparagraph (A)(i) is related to any other entity if the 2 entities have—

(i) significant common purposes and substantial common membership, or

(ii) directly or indirectly substantial common direction or control.

(C)(i) An entity is related to another entity if either entity owns (directly or through 1 or more entities) a 50 percent or greater interest in the capital or profits of the other entity.

(ii) For purposes of clause (i), entities treated as related under subparagraph (A) or (B) shall be treated as 1 entity.

(D) An entity is related to another entity with respect to a transaction if such transaction is part of an attempt by such entities to avoid the application of this subsection.

(5) **Tax-exempt use of property leased to partnerships, etc., determined at partner level.**—For purposes of this subsection—

(A) **In general.**—In the case of any property which is leased to a partnership, the determination of whether any portion of such property is tax-exempt use property shall be made by treating each tax-exempt entity partner's proportionate share (determined under paragraph (6)(C)) of such property as being leased to such partner.

(B) **Other pass-thru entities; tiered entities.**—Rules similar to the rules of subparagraph (A) shall also apply in the case of any pass-thru entity other than a partnership and in the case of tiered partnerships and other entities.

(C) **Presumption with respect to foreign entities.**—Unless it is otherwise established to the satisfaction of the Secretary, it shall be presumed that the partners of a foreign partnership (and the beneficiaries of any other foreign pass-thru entity) are persons who are not United States persons.

(6) Treatment of property owned by partnerships, etc.—

(A) In general.—For purposes of this subsection, if—

(i) any property which (but for this subparagraph) is not tax-exempt use property is owned by a partnership which has both a tax-exempt entity and a person who is not a tax-exempt entity as partners, and

(ii) any allocation to the tax-exempt entity of partnership items is not a qualified allocation,

an amount equal to such tax-exempt entity's proportionate share of such property shall (except as provided in paragraph (1)(D)) be treated as tax-exempt use property.

(B) Qualified allocation.—For purposes of subparagraph (A), the term "qualified allocation" means any allocation to a tax-exempt entity which—

(i) is consistent with such entity's being allocated the same distributive share of each item of income, gain, loss, deduction, credit, and basis and such share remains the same during the entire period the entity is a partner in the partnership, and

(ii) has substantial economic effect within the meaning of section 704(b)(2).

For purposes of this subparagraph, items allocated under section 704(c) shall not be taken into account.

(C) Determination of proportionate share.—

(i) **In general.**—For purposes of subparagraph (A), a tax-exempt entity's proportionate share of any property owned by a partnership shall be determined on the basis of such entity's share of partnership items of income or gain (excluding gain allocated under section 704(c)), whichever results in the largest proportionate share.

(ii) **Determination where allocations vary.**—For purposes of clause (i), if a tax-exempt entity's share of partnership items of income or gain (excluding gain allocated under section 704(c)) may vary during the period such entity is a partner in the partnership, such share shall be the highest share such entity may receive.

(D) Determination of whether property used in unrelated trade or business.—For purposes of this subsection, in the case of any property which is owned by a partnership which has both a tax-exempt entity and a person who is not a tax-exempt entity as partners, the determination of whether such property is used in an unrelated trade or business of such an entity shall be made without regard to section 514.

(E) Other pass-thru entities; tiered entities.—Rules similar to the rules of subparagraphs (A), (B), (C), and (D) shall also apply in the case of any pass-thru entity other than a partnership and in the case of tiered partnerships and other entities.

(F) Treatment of certain taxable entities.—

(i) **In general.**—For purposes of this paragraph and paragraph (5), except as otherwise provided in this subparagraph, any tax-exempt controlled entity shall be treated as a tax-exempt entity.

(ii) **Election.**—If a tax-exempt controlled entity makes an election under this clause—

(I) such entity shall not be treated as a tax-exempt entity for purposes of this paragraph and paragraph (5), and

(II) any gain recognized by a tax-exempt entity on any disposition of an interest in such entity (and any dividend or interest received or accrued by a tax-exempt entity from such tax-exempt controlled entity) shall be treated as unrelated business taxable income for purposes of section 511.

Any such election shall be irrevocable and shall bind all tax-exempt entities holding interests in such tax-exempt controlled entity. For purposes of subclause (II), there shall only be taken into account dividends which are properly allocable to income of the tax-exempt controlled entity which was not subject to tax under this chapter.

(iii) **Tax-exempt controlled entity.—**

(I) **In general.—**The term "tax-exempt controlled entity" means any corporation (which is not a tax-exempt entity determined without regard to this subparagraph and paragraph (2)(E)) if 50 percent or more (in value) of the stock in such corporation is held by 1 or more tax-exempt entities (other than a foreign person or entity).

(II) **Only 5-percent shareholders taken into account in case of publicly traded stock.—**For purposes of subclause (I), in the case of a corporation the stock of which is publicly traded on an established securities market, stock held by a tax-exempt entity shall not be taken into account unless such entity holds at least 5 percent (in value) of the stock in such corporation. For purposes of this subclause, related entities (within the meaning of paragraph (4)) shall be treated as 1 entity.

(III) **Section 318 to apply.—**For purposes of this clause, a tax-exempt entity shall be treated as holding stock which it holds through application of section 318 (determined without regard to the 50–percent limitation contained in subsection (a)(2)(C) thereof).

(G) **Regulations.—**For purposes of determining whether there is a qualified allocation under subparagraph (B), the regulations prescribed under paragraph (8) for purposes of this paragraph—

(i) shall set forth the proper treatment for partnership guaranteed payments, and

(ii) may provide for the exclusion or segregation of items.

(7) **Lease.—**For purposes of this subsection, the term "lease" includes any grant of a right to use property.

(8) **Regulations.—**The Secretary shall prescribe such regulations as may be necessary or appropriate to carry out the purposes of this subsection.

(i) **Definitions and Special Rules.—**For purposes of this section—

(1) **Class life.—**

(A) **In general.—**Except as provided in this section, the term "class life" means the class life (if any) which would be applicable with respect to any property as of January 1, 1986, under subsection (m) of section 167 (determined without regard to paragraph (4) thereof and as if the taxpayer had made an election under such subsection).

(B) **Secretarial authority.—**The Secretary, through an office established in the Treasury—

(i) shall monitor and analyze actual experience with respect to all depreciable assets, and

(ii) except in the case of residential rental property or nonresidential real property—

(I) may prescribe a new class life for any property,

(II) in the case of assigned property, may modify any assigned item, or

(III) may prescribe a class life for any property which does not have a class life within the meaning of subparagraph (A).

Any class life or assigned item prescribed or modified under the preceding sentence shall reasonably reflect the anticipated useful life, and the anticipated decline in value over time, of the property to the industry or other group.

(C) Effect of modification.—Any class life or assigned item with respect to any property prescribed or modified under subparagraph (B) shall be used in classifying such property under subsection (e) and in applying subsection (g).

(D) No modification of assigned property before January 1, 1992.—

(i) In general.—Except as otherwise provided in this subparagraph, the Secretary may not modify an assigned item under subparagraph (B)(ii)(II) for any assigned property which is placed in service before January 1, 1992.

(ii) Exception for shorter class life.—In the case of assigned property which is placed in service before January 1, 1992, and for which the assigned item reflects a class life which is shorter than the class life under subparagraph (A), the Secretary may modify such assigned item under subparagraph (B)(ii)(II) if such modification results in an item which reflects a shorter class life than such assigned item.

(E) Assigned property and item.—For purposes of this paragraph—

(i) Assigned Property.—The term "assigned property" means property for which a class life, classification, or recovery period is assigned under subsection (e)(3) or subparagraph (B), (C), or (D) of subsection (g)(3).

(ii) Assigned item.—The term "assigned item" means the class life, classification, or recovery period assigned under subsection (e)(3) or subparagraph (B), (C), or (D) of subsection (g)(3).

(2) Qualified technological equipment.—

(A) In general.—The term "qualified technological equipment" means—

(i) any computer or peripheral equipment,

(ii) any high technology telephone station equipment installed on the customer's premises, and

(iii) any high technology medical equipment.

(B) Computer or peripheral equipment defined.—For purposes of this paragraph—

(i) In general.—The term "computer or peripheral equipment" means—

(I) any computer, and

(II) any related peripheral equipment.

(ii) Computer.—The term "computer" means a programmable electronically activated device which—

(I) is capable of accepting information, applying prescribed processes to the information, and supplying the results of these processes with or without human intervention, and

(II) consists of a central processing unit containing extensive storage, logic, arithmetic, and control capabilities.

(iii) **Related peripheral equipment.**—The term "related peripheral equipment" means any auxiliary machine (whether on-line or off-line) which is designed to be placed under the control of the central processing unit of a computer.

(iv) **Exceptions.**—The term "computer or peripheral equipment" shall not include—

(I) any equipment which is an integral part of other property which is not a computer,

(II) typewriters, calculators, adding and accounting machines, copiers, duplicating equipment, and similar equipment, and

(III) equipment of a kind used primarily for amusement or entertainment of the user.

(C) **High technology medical equipment.**—For purposes of this paragraph, the term "high technology medical equipment" means any electronic, electromechanical, or computer-based high technology equipment used in the screening, monitoring, observation, diagnosis, or treatment of patients in a laboratory, medical, or hospital environment.

(3) **Lease term.**—

(A) **In general.**—In determining a lease term—

(i) there shall be taken into account options to renew, and

(ii) 2 or more successive leases which are part of the same transaction (or a series of related transactions) with respect to the same or substantially similar property shall be treated as 1 lease.

(B) **Special rule for fair rental options on nonresidential real property or residential rental property.**—For purposes of clause (i) of subparagraph (A), in the case of nonresidential real property or residential rental property, there shall not be taken into account any option to renew at fair market value, determined at the time of renewal.

(4) **General asset accounts.**—Under regulations, a taxpayer may maintain 1 or more general asset accounts for any property to which this section applies. Except as provided in regulations, all proceeds realized on any disposition of property in a general asset account shall be included in income as ordinary income.

(5) **Changes in use.**—The Secretary shall, by regulations, provide for the method of determining the deduction allowable under section 167(a) with respect to any tangible property for any taxable year (and the succeeding taxable years) during which such property changes status under this section but continues to be held by the same person.

(6) **Treatments of additions or improvements to property.**—In the case of any addition to (or improvement of) any property—

(A) any deduction under subsection (a) for such addition or improvement shall be computed in the same manner as the deduction for such property would be computed if such property had been placed in service at the same time as such addition or improvement, and

(B) the applicable recovery period for such addition or improvement shall begin on the later of—

(i) the date on which such addition (or improvement) is placed in service, or

(ii) the date on which the property with respect to which such addition (or improvement) was made is placed in service.

(7) Treatment of certain transferees.—

(A) In general.—In the case of any property transferred in a transaction described in subparagraph (B), the transferee shall be treated as the transferor for purposes of computing the depreciation deduction determined under this section with respect to so much of the basis in the hands of the transferee as does not exceed the adjusted basis in the hands of the transferor.

(B) Transactions covered.—The transactions described in this subparagraph are any transaction described in section 332, 351, 361, 371(a), 374(a), 721, or 731. Subparagraph (A) shall not apply in the case of a termination of a partnership under section 708(b)(1)(B).

(C) Property reacquired by the taxpayer.—Under regulations, property which is disposed of and then reacquired by the taxpayer shall be treated for purposes of computing the deduction allowable under subsection (a) as if such property had not been disposed of.

(D) Exception.—This paragraph shall not apply to any transaction to which subsection (f)(5) applies (relating to churning transactions).

(8) Treatment of leasehold improvements.—In the case of any building erected (or improvements made) on leased property, if such building or improvement is property to which this section applies, the depreciation deduction shall be determined under the provisions of this section.

(9) Normalization rules.—

(A) In general.—In order to use a normalization method of accounting with respect to any public utility property for purposes of subsection (f)(2)—

(i) the taxpayer must, in computing its tax expense for purposes of establishing its cost of service for rate-making purposes and reflecting operating results in its regulated books of account, use a method of depreciation with respect to such property that is the same as, and a depreciation period for such property that is no shorter than, the method and period used to compute its depreciation expense for such purposes; and

(ii) if the amount allowable as a deduction under this section with respect to such property differs from the amount that would be allowable as a deduction under section 167 (determined without regard to section 167(l)) using the method (including the period, first and last year convention, and salvage value) used to compute regulated tax expense under clause (i), the taxpayer must make adjustments to a reserve to reflect the deferral of taxes resulting from such difference.

(B) Use of inconsistent estimates and projections, etc.—

(i) In general.—One way in which the requirements of subparagraph (A) are not met is if the taxpayer, for ratemaking purposes, uses a procedure or adjustment which is inconsistent with the requirements of subparagraph (A).

(ii) Use of inconsistent estimates and projections.—The procedures and adjustments which are to be treated as inconsistent for purposes of clause (i) shall include any procedure or adjustment for ratemaking purposes which uses an estimate or projection of the taxpayer's tax expense, depreciation expense, or reserve for deferred taxes under subparagraph (A)(ii) unless such estimate or projection is also used, for ratemaking purposes, with respect to the other 2 such items and with respect to the rate base.

(iii) **Regulatory authority.**—The Secretary may by regulations prescribe procedures and adjustments (in addition to those specified in clause (ii)) which are to be treated as inconsistent for purposes of clause (i).

(C) **Public utility property which does not meet normalization rules.**—In the case of any public utility property to which this section does not apply by reason of subsection (f)(2), the allowance for depreciation under section 167(a) shall be an amount computed using the method and period referred to in subparagraph (A)(i).

(10) **Public utility property.**—The term "public utility property" has the meaning given such term by section 167(*l*)(3)(A).

(11) **Research and experimentation.**—The term "research and experimentation" has the same meaning as the term research and experimental has under section 174.

(12) **Section 1245 and 1250 property.**—The terms "section 1245 property" and "section 1250 property" have the meanings given such terms by sections 1245(a)(3) and 1250(c), respectively.

§ 170. Charitable, etc., contributions and gifts

(a) **Allowance of deduction.**—

(1) **General rule.**—There shall be allowed as a deduction any charitable contribution (as defined in subsection (c)) payment of which is made within the taxable year. A charitable contribution shall be allowable as a deduction only if verified under regulations prescribed by the Secretary.

(2) **Corporations on accrual basis.**—In the case of a corporation reporting its taxable income on the accrual basis, if—

(A) the board of directors authorizes a charitable contribution during any taxable year, and

(B) payment of such contribution is made after the close of such taxable year and on or before the 15th day of the third month following the close of such taxable year,

then the taxpayer may elect to treat such contribution as paid during such taxable year. The election may be made only at the time of the filing of the return for such taxable year, and shall be signified in such manner as the Secretary shall by regulations prescribe.

(3) **Future interests in tangible personal property.**—For purposes of this section, payment of a charitable contribution which consists of a future interest in tangible personal property shall be treated as made only when all intervening interests in, and rights to the actual possession or enjoyment of, the property have expired or are held by persons other than the taxpayer or those standing in a relationship to the taxpayer described in section 267(b) or 707(b). For purposes of the preceding sentence, a fixture which is intended to be severed from the real property shall be treated as tangible personal property.

(b) **Percentage limitations.**—

(1) **Individuals.**—In the case of an individual, the deduction provided in subsection (a) shall be limited as provided in the succeeding subparagraphs.

(A) **General rule.**—Any charitable contribution to—

(i) a church or a convention or association of churches,

(ii) an educational organization which normally maintains a regular faculty and curriculum and normally has a regularly enrolled body of pupils or students in attendance at the place where its educational activities are regularly carried on,

(iii) an organization the principal purpose or functions of which are the providing of medical or hospital care or medical education or medical research, if the organization is a hospital, or if the organization is a medical research organization directly engaged in the continuous active conduct of medical research in conjunction with a hospital, and during the calendar year in which the contribution is made such organization is committed to spend such contributions for such research before January 1 of the fifth calendar year which begins after the date such contribution is made,

(iv) an organization which normally receives a substantial part of its support (exclusive of income received in the exercise or performance by such organization of its charitable, educational, or other purpose or function constituting the basis for its exemption under section 501(a)) from the United States or any State or political subdivision thereof or from direct or indirect contributions from the general public, and which is organized and operated exclusively to receive, hold, invest, and administer property and to make expenditures to or for the benefit of a college or university which is an organization referred to in clause (ii) of this subparagraph and which is an agency or instrumentality of a State or political subdivision thereof, or which is owned or operated by a State or political subdivision thereof or by an agency or instrumentality of one or more States or political subdivisions,

(v) a governmental unit referred to in subsection (c) (1),

(vi) an organization referred to in subsection (c) (2) which normally receives a substantial part of its support (exclusive of income received in the exercise or performance by such organization of its charitable, educational, or other purpose or function constituting the basis for its exemption under section 501(a)) from a governmental unit referred to in subsection (c) (1) or from direct or indirect contributions from the general public,

(vii) a private foundation described in subparagraph (E), or

(viii) an organization described in section 509(a) (2) or (3),

shall be allowed to the extent that the aggregate of such contributions does not exceed 50 percent of the taxpayer's contribution base for the taxable year.

(B) Other contributions.—Any charitable contribution other than a charitable contribution to which subparagraph (A) applies shall be allowed to the extent that the aggregate of such contributions does not exceed the lesser of—

(i) 30 percent of the taxpayer's contribution base for the taxable year, or

(ii) the excess of 50 percent of the taxpayer's contribution base for the taxable year over the amount of charitable contributions allowable under subparagraph (A) (determined without regard to subparagraph (C)).

If the aggregate of such contributions exceeds the limitation of the preceding sentence, such excess shall be treated (in a manner consistent with the rules of subsection (d)(1)) as a charitable contribution (to which subparagraph (A) does not apply) in each of the 5 succeeding taxable years in order of time.

(C) Special limitation with respect to contributions described in subparagraph (A) of certain capital gain property.—

(i) In the case of charitable contributions described in subparagraph (A) of capital gain property to which subsection (e)(1)(B) does not apply, the total amount of contributions of such property which may be taken into account under subsection (a) for any taxable year shall not exceed 30 percent of the taxpayer's contribution base for such year. For purposes of this subsection, contributions of capital gain property to which this subparagraph applies shall be taken into account after all other charitable contributions (other than charitable contributions to which subparagraph (D) applies).

(ii) If charitable contributions described in subparagraph (A) of capital gain property to which clause (i) applies exceeds 30 percent of the taxpayer's contribution base for any taxable year, such excess shall be treated, in a manner consistent with the rules of subsection (d) (1), as a charitable contribution of capital gain property to which clause (i) applies in each of the 5 succeeding taxable years in order of time.

(iii) At the election of the taxpayer (made at such time and in such manner as the Secretary prescribes by regulations), subsection (e) (1) shall apply to all contributions of capital gain property (to which subsection (e) (1) (B) does not otherwise apply) made by the taxpayer during the taxable year. If such an election is made, clauses (i) and (ii) shall not apply to contributions of capital gain property made during the taxable year, and, in applying subsection (d) (1) for such taxable year with respect to contributions of capital gain property made in any prior contribution year for which an election was not made under this clause, such contributions shall be reduced as if subsection (e) (1) had applied to such contributions in the year in which made.

(iv) For purposes of this paragraph, the term "capital gain property" means, with respect to any contribution, any capital asset the sale of which at its fair market value at the time of the contribution would have resulted in gain which would have been long-term capital gain. For purposes of the preceding sentence, any property which is property used in the trade or business (as defined in section 1231(b)) shall be treated as a capital asset.

(D) Special limitation with respect to contributions of capital gain property to organizations not described in subparagraph (A).—

(i) **In general.**—In the case of charitable contributions (other than charitable contributions to which subparagraph (A) applies) of capital gain property, the total amount of such contributions of such property taken into account under subsection (a) for any taxable year shall not exceed the lesser of—

(I) 20 percent of the taxpayer's contribution base for the taxable year, or

(II) the excess of 30 percent of the taxpayer's contribution base for the taxable year over the amount of the contributions of capital gain property to which subparagraph (C) applies.

For purposes of this subsection, contributions of capital gain property to which this subparagraph applies shall be taken into account after all other charitable contributions.

(ii) **Carryover.**—If the aggregate amount of contributions described in clause (i) exceeds the limitation of clause (i), such excess shall be treated (in a manner consistent with the rules of subsection (d)(1)) as a charitable contribution of capital gain property to which clause (i) applies in each of the 5 succeeding taxable years in order of time.

* * *

(F) **Contribution base defined.**—For purposes of this section, the term "contribution base" means adjusted gross income (computed without regard to any net operating loss carryback to the taxable year under section 172).

(2) **Corporations.**—In the case of a corporation, the total deductions under subsection (a) for any taxable year shall not exceed 10 percent of the taxpayer's taxable income computed without regard to—

(A) this section,

(B) part VIII (except section 248),

(C) any net operating loss carryback to the taxable year under section 172, and

(D) any capital loss carryback to the taxable year under section 1212(a) (1).

(c) **Charitable contribution defined.**—For purposes of this section, the term "charitable contribution" means a contribution or gift to or for the use of—

(1) A State, a possession of the United States, or any political subdivision of any of the foregoing, or the United States or the District of Columbia, but only if the contribution or gift is made for exclusively public purposes.

(2) A corporation, trust, or community chest, fund, or foundation—

(A) created or organized in the United States or in any possession thereof, or under the law of the United States, any State, the District of Columbia, or any possession of the United States;

(B) organized and operated exclusively for religious, charitable, scientific, literary, or educational purposes, or to foster national or international amateur sports competition (but only if no part of its activities involve the provision of athletic facilities or equipment), or for the prevention of cruelty to children or animals;

(C) no part of the net earnings of which inures to the benefit of any private shareholder or individual; and

(D) which is not disqualified for tax exemption under section 501(c) (3) by reason of attempting to influence legislation, and which does not participate in, or intervene in (including the publishing or distributing of statements), any political campaign on behalf of any candidate for public office.

A contribution or gift by a corporation to a trust, chest, fund, or foundation shall be deductible by reason of this paragraph only if it is to be used within the United States or any of its possessions exclusively for purposes specified in subparagraph (B). Rules similar to the rules of section 501(j) shall apply for purposes of this paragraph.

(3) A post or organization of war veterans, or an auxiliary unit or society of, or trust or foundation for, any such post or organization—

(A) organized in the United States or any of its possessions, and

(B) no part of the net earnings of which inures to the benefit of any private shareholder or individual.

(4) In the case of a contribution or gift by an individual, a domestic fraternal society, order, or association, operating under the lodge system, but only if such contribution or gift is to be used exclusively for religious, charitable, scientific, literary, or educational purposes, or for the prevention of cruelty to children or animals.

(5) A cemetery company owned and operated exclusively for the benefit of its members, or any corporation chartered solely for burial purposes as a cemetery corporation and not permitted by its charter to engage in any business not

necessarily incident to that purpose, if such company or corporation is not operated for profit and no part of the net earnings of such company or corporation inures to the benefit of any private shareholder or individual.

For purposes of this section, the term "charitable contribution" also means an amount treated under subsection (g) as paid for the use of an organization described in paragraph (2), (3), or (4).

(d) Carryovers of excess contributions.—

(1) Individuals.—

(A) In general.—In the case of an individual, if the amount of charitable contributions described in subsection (b) (1) (A) payment of which is made within a taxable year (hereinafter in this paragraph referred to as the "contribution year") exceeds 50 percent of the taxpayer's contribution base for such year, such excess shall be treated as a charitable contribution described in subsection (b) (1) (A) paid in each of the 5 succeeding taxable years in order of time, but, with respect to any such succeeding taxable year, only to the extent of the lesser of the two following amounts:

(i) the amount by which 50 percent of the taxpayer's contribution base for such succeeding taxable year exceeds the sum of the charitable contributions described in subsection (b) (1) (A) payment of which is made by the taxpayer within such succeeding taxable year (determined without regard to this subparagraph) and the charitable contributions described in subsection (b) (1) (A) payment of which was made in taxable years before the contribution year which are treated under this subparagraph as having been paid in such succeeding taxable year; or

(ii) in the case of the first succeeding taxable year, the amount of such excess, and in the case of the second, third, fourth, or fifth succeeding taxable year, the portion of such excess not treated under this subparagraph as a charitable contribution described in subsection (b) (1) (A) paid in any taxable year intervening between the contribution year and such succeeding taxable year.

(B) Special rule for net operating loss carryovers.—In applying subparagraph (A), the excess determined under subparagraph (A) for the contribution year shall be reduced to the extent that such excess reduces taxable income (as computed for purposes of the second sentence of section 172(b) (2)) and increases the net operating loss deduction for a taxable year succeeding the contribution year.

(2) Corporations.—

(A) In general.—Any contribution made by a corporation in a taxable year (hereinafter in this paragraph referred to as the "contribution year") in excess of the amount deductible for such year under subsection (b) (2) shall be deductible for each of the 5 succeeding taxable years in order of time, but only to the extent of the lesser of the two following amounts: (i) the excess of the maximum amount deductible for such succeeding taxable year under subsection (b) (2) over the sum of the contributions made in such year plus the aggregate of the excess contributions which were made in taxable years before the contribution year and which are deductible under this subparagraph for such succeeding taxable year; or (ii) in the case of the first succeeding taxable year, the amount of such excess contribution, and in the case of the second, third, fourth, or fifth succeeding taxable year, the portion of such excess contribution not deductible under this subparagraph for any taxable year intervening between the contribution year and such succeeding taxable year.

(B) Special rule for net operating loss carryovers.—For purposes of sub-paragraph (A), the excess of—

(i) the contributions made by a corporation in a taxable year to which this section applies, over

(ii) the amount deductible in such year under the limitation in subsection (b) (2),

shall be reduced to the extent that such excess reduces taxable income (as computed for purposes of the second sentence of section 172(b) (2)) and increases a net operating loss carryover under section 172 to a succeeding taxable year.

(e) Certain contributions of ordinary income and capital gain property.—

(1) General rule.—The amount of any charitable contribution of property other-wise taken into account under this section shall be reduced by the sum of—

(A) the amount of gain which would not have been long-term capital gain if the property contributed had been sold by the taxpayer at its fair market value (determined at the time of such contribution), and

(B) in the case of a charitable contribution—

(i) of tangible personal property, if the use by the donee is unrelated to the purpose or function constituting the basis for its exemption under section 501 (or, in the case of a governmental unit, to any purpose or function described in subsection (c)), or

(ii) to or for the use of a private foundation (as defined in section 509(a)), other than a private foundation described in subsection (b)(1)(E),

the amount of gain which would have been long-term capital gain if the property contributed had been sold by the taxpayer at its fair market value (determined at the time of such contribution).

For purposes of applying this paragraph (other than in the case of gain to which section 617(d)(1), 1245(a), 1250(a), 1252(a), or 1254(a) applies), property which is property used in the trade or business (as defined in section 1231(b)) shall be treated as a capital asset.

(2) Allocation of basis.—For purposes of paragraph (1), in the case of a charitable contribution of less than the taxpayer's entire interest in the property contributed, the taxpayer's adjusted basis in such property shall be allocated between the interest contributed and any interest not contributed in accordance with regulations prescribed by the Secretary.

(3) Special rule for certain contributions of inventory and other proper-ty.—

(A) Qualified contributions.—For purposes of this paragraph, a qualified contribution shall mean a charitable contribution of property described in paragraph (1) or (2) of section 1221, by a corporation (other than a corporation which is an S corporation) to an organization which is described in section 501(c) (3) and is exempt under section 501(a) (other than a private foundation, as defined in section 509(a), which is not an operating foundation, as defined in section 4942(j) (3)), but only if—

(i) the use of the property by the donee is related to the purpose or function constituting the basis for its exemption under section 501 and the property is to be used by the donee solely for the care of the ill, the needy, or infants;

(ii) the property is not transferred by the donee in exchange for money, other property, or services;

(iii) the taxpayer receives from the donee a written statement representing that its use and disposition of the property will be in accordance with the provisions of clauses (i) and (ii); and

(iv) in the case where the property is subject to regulation under the Federal Food, Drug, and Cosmetic Act, as amended, such property must fully satisfy the applicable requirements of such Act and regulations promulgated thereunder on the date of transfer and for one hundred and eighty days prior thereto.

(B) Amount of reduction.—The reduction under paragraph (1) (A) for any qualified contribution (as defined in subparagraph (A)) shall be no greater than the sum of—

(i) one-half of the amount computed under paragraph (1) (A) (computed without regard to this paragraph), and

(ii) the amount (if any) by which the charitable contribution deduction under this section for any qualified contribution (computed by taking into account the amount determined in clause (i), but without regard to this clause) exceeds twice the basis of such property.

(C) This paragraph shall not apply to so much of the amount of the gain described in paragraph (1)(A) which would be long-term capital gain but for the application of sections 617, 1245, 1250, or 1252.

* * *

(f) Disallowance of deduction in certain cases and special rules.—

(1) In general.—No deduction shall be allowed under this section for a contribution to or for the use of an organization or trust described in section 508(d) or 4948(c) (4) subject to the conditions specified in such sections.

(2) Contributions of property placed in trust.—

(A) Remainder interest.—In the case of property transferred in trust, no deduction shall be allowed under this section for the value of a contribution of a remainder interest unless the trust is a charitable remainder annuity trust or a charitable remainder unitrust (described in section 664), or a pooled income fund (described in section 642(c) (5)).

(B) Income interests, etc.—No deduction shall be allowed under this section for the value of any interest in property (other than a remainder interest) transferred in trust unless the interest is in the form of a guaranteed annuity or the trust instrument specifies that the interest is a fixed percentage distributed yearly of the fair market value of the trust property (to be determined yearly) and the grantor is treated as the owner of such interest for purposes of applying section 671. If the donor ceases to be treated as the owner of such an interest for purposes of applying section 671, at the time the donor ceases to be so treated, the donor shall for purposes of this chapter be considered as having received an amount of income equal to the amount of any deduction he received under this section for the contribution reduced by the discounted value of all amounts of income earned by the trust and taxable to him before the time at which he ceases to be treated as the owner of the interest. Such amounts of income shall be discounted to the date of the contribution. The Secretary shall prescribe such regulations as may be necessary to carry out the purposes of this subparagraph.

(C) Denial of deduction in case of payments by certain trusts.—In any case in which a deduction is allowed under this section for the value of an interest in property described in subparagraph (B), transferred in trust, no deduction shall be allowed under this section to the grantor or any other person for the amount of any contribution made by the trust with respect to such interest.

(D) Exception.—This paragraph shall not apply in a case in which the value of all interests in property transferred in trust are deductible under subsection (a).

(3) Denial of deduction in case of certain contributions of partial interests in property.—

(A) In general.—In the case of a contribution (not made by a transfer in trust) of an interest in property which consists of less than the taxpayer's entire interest in such property, a deduction shall be allowed under this section only to the extent that the value of the interest contributed would be allowable as a deduction under this section if such interest had been transferred in trust. For purposes of this subparagraph, a contribution by a taxpayer of the right to use property shall be treated as a contribution of less than the taxpayer's entire interest in such property.

(B) Exceptions.—Subparagraph (A) shall not apply to—

(i) a contribution of a remainder interest in a personal residence or farm,

(ii) a contribution of an undivided portion of the taxpayer's entire interest in property, and

(iii) a qualified conservation contribution.

(4) Valuation of remainder interest in real property.—For purposes of this section, in determining the value of a remainder interest in real property, depreciation (computed on the straight line method) and depletion of such property shall be taken into account, and such value shall be discounted at a rate of 6 percent per annum, except that the Secretary may prescribe a different rate.

(5) Reduction for certain interest.—If, in connection with any charitable contribution, a liability is assumed by the recipient or by any other person, or if a charitable contribution is of property which is subject to a liability, then, to the extent necessary to avoid the duplication of amounts, the amount taken into account for purposes of this section as the amount of the charitable contribution—

(A) shall be reduced for interest (i) which has been paid (or is to be paid) by the taxpayer, (ii) which is attributable to the liability, and (iii) which is attributable to any period after the making of the contribution, and

(B) in the case of a bond, shall be further reduced for interest (i) which has been paid (or is to be paid) by the taxpayer on indebtedness incurred or continued to purchase or carry such bond, and (ii) which is attributable to any period before the making of the contribution.

The reduction pursuant to subparagraph (B) shall not exceed the interest (including interest equivalent) on the bond which is attributable to any period before the making of the contribution and which is not (under the taxpayer's method of accounting) includible in the gross income of the taxpayer for any taxable year. For purposes of this paragraph, the term "bond" means any bond, debenture, note, or certificate or other evidence of indebtedness.

(6) Deductions for out-of-pocket expenditures.—No deduction shall be allowed under this section for an out-of-pocket expenditure made by any person on behalf of an organization described in subsection (c) (other than an organization described in section 501(h) (5) (relating to churches, etc.)) if the expenditure is made for the purpose of influencing legislation (within the meaning of section 501(c) (3)).

(7) Reformations to comply with paragraph (2).—

(A) In general. A deduction shall be allowed under subsection (a) in respect of any qualified reformation (within the meaning of section 2055(e)(3)(B)).

(B) Rules similar to section 2055(e)(3) to apply.—For purposes of this paragraph, rules similar to the rules of section 2055(e)(3) shall apply.

* * *

(i) Rule for nonitemization of deductions.—

(1) In general.—In the case of an individual who does not itemize his deductions for the taxable year, the applicable percentage of the amount allowable under subsection (a) for the taxable year shall be taken into account as a direct charitable deduction under section 63.

(2) Applicable percentage.—For purposes of paragraph (1), the applicable percentage shall be determined under the following table:

For taxable years beginning in—	The applicable percentage is—
1982, 1983 or 1984	25
1985	50
1986 or thereafter	100

(3) Limitation for taxable years beginning before 1985.—In the case of a taxable year beginning before 1985, the portion of the amount allowable under subsection (a) to which the applicable percentage shall be applied—

(A) shall not exceed $100 for taxable years beginning in 1982 or 1983, and

(B) shall not exceed $300 for taxable years beginning in 1984.

In the case of a married individual filing a separate return, the limit under subparagraph (A) shall be $50, and the limit under subparagraph (B) shall be $150.

(4) Termination.—The provisions of this subsection shall not apply to contributions made after December 31, 1986.

(j) Standard mileage rate for use of passenger automobile.—For purposes of computing the deduction under this section for use of a passenger automobile the standard mileage rate shall be 12 cents per mile.

(k) Denial of deduction for certain travel expenses.—No deduction shall be allowed under this section for traveling expenses (including amounts expended for meals and lodging) while away from home, whether paid directly or by reimbursement, unless there is no significant element of personal pleasure, recreation, or vacation in such travel.

* * *

§ 172. Net operating loss deduction

(a) Deduction allowed.—There shall be allowed as a deduction for the taxable year an amount equal to the aggregate of (1) the net operating loss carryovers to such year, plus (2) the net operating loss carrybacks to such year. For purposes of this subtitle, the term "net operating loss deduction" means the deduction allowed by this subsection.

(b) Net operating loss carrybacks and carryovers.—

(1) Years to which loss may be carried.—

(A) Except as provided in subparagraphs (D), (E), (F), (G), (H), (I), (J), (K), (L), and (M), a net operating loss for any taxable year shall be a net operating loss carryback to each of the 3 taxable years preceding the taxable year of such loss.

(B) Except as provided in subparagraphs (C), (D), and (E), a net operating loss for any taxable year ending after December 31, 1955, shall be a net operating loss carryover to each of the 5 taxable years following the taxable year of such loss. Except as provided in subparagraphs (C), (D), (E), (F), (G), (H), (J), (L), and (M), a net operating loss for any taxable year ending after December 31, 1975, shall be a net operating loss carryover to each of the 15 taxable years following the taxable year of such loss.

* * *

(I) **Product liability losses.**—In the case of a taxpayer which has a product liability loss (as defined in subsection (j)) for a taxable year beginning after September 30, 1979 (referred to in this subparagraph as the "loss year"), the product liability loss shall be a net operating loss carryback to each of the 10 taxable years preceding the loss year.

(J) **Special rule for deferred statutory or tort liability losses.**—In the case of a taxpayer which has a deferred statutory or tort liability loss (as defined in subsection (k)) for any taxable year beginning after December 31, 1983, the deferred statutory or tort liability loss shall be a net operating loss carryback to each of the 10 taxable years preceding the taxable year of such loss.

* * *

(2) **Amount of carrybacks and carryovers.**—Except as provided in subsection (g), the entire amount of the net operating loss for any taxable year (hereinafter in this section referred to as the "loss year") shall be carried to the earliest of the taxable years to which (by reason of paragraph (1)) such loss may be carried. The portion of such loss which shall be carried to each of the other taxable years shall be the excess, if any, of the amount of such loss over the sum of the taxable income for each of the prior taxable years to which such loss may be carried. For purposes of the preceding sentence, the taxable income for any such prior taxable year shall be computed—

(A) with the modifications specified in subsection (d) other than paragraphs (1), (4), and (5) thereof; and

(B) by determining the amount of the net operating loss deduction—

(i) without regard to the net operating loss for the loss year or for any taxable year thereafter, and

(ii) without regard to that portion, if any, of a net operating loss for a taxable year attributable to a foreign expropriation loss, if such portion may not, under paragraph (1) (D), be carried back to such prior taxable year,

and the taxable income so computed shall not be considered to be less than zero.
* * *

(3) **Special rules.**—

* * *

(C) Any taxpayer entitled to a carryback period under paragraph (1) may elect to relinquish the entire carryback period with respect to a net operating loss for any taxable year ending after December 31, 1975. Such election shall be made in such manner as may be prescribed by the Secretary, and shall be made by the due date (including extensions of time) for filing the taxpayer's return for the taxable year of the net operating loss for which the election is to be in effect. Such election, once made for any taxable year, shall be irrevocable for that taxable year.

(c) Net operating loss defined.—For purposes of this section, the term "net operating loss" means the excess of the deductions allowed by this chapter over the gross income. Such excess shall be computed with the modifications specified in subsection (d).

(d) Modifications.—The modifications referred to in this section are as follows:

(1) Net operating loss deduction.—No net operating loss deduction shall be allowed.

(2) Capital gains and losses of taxpayers other than corporations.—In the case of a taxpayer other than a corporation, the amount deductible on account of losses from sales or exchanges of capital assets shall not exceed the amount includible on account of gains from sales or exchanges of capital assets.

(3) Deduction for personal exemptions.—No deduction shall be allowed under section 151 (relating to personal exemptions). No deduction in lieu of any such deduction shall be allowed.

(4) Nonbusiness deductions of taxpayers other than corporations.—In the case of a taxpayer other than a corporation, the deductions allowable by this chapter which are not attributable to a taxpayer's trade or business shall be allowed only to the extent of the amount of the gross income not derived from such trade or business. For purposes of the preceding sentence—

(A) any gain or loss from the sale or other disposition of—

(i) property, used in the trade or business, of a character which is subject to the allowance for depreciation provided in section 167, or

(ii) real property used in the trade or business,

shall be treated as attributable to the trade or business;

(B) the modifications specified in paragraphs (1), (2) (B), and (3) shall be taken into account;

(C) any deduction allowable under section 165(c) (3) (relating to casualty losses) shall not be taken into account; and

(D) any deduction allowed under section 404 to the extent attributable to contributions which are made on behalf of an individual who is an employee within the meaning of section 401(c)(1) shall not be treated as attributable to the trade or business of such individual.

* * *

(e) Law applicable to computations.—In determining the amount of any net operating loss carryback or carryover to any taxable year, the necessary computations involving any other taxable year shall be made under the law applicable to such other taxable year.

[(f) Repealed.]

* * *

(j) Rules relating to product liability losses.—For purposes of this section—

(1) Product liability loss.—The term "product liability loss" means, for any taxable year, the lesser of—

(A) the net operating loss for such year reduced by any portion thereof which is attributable to a foreign expropriation loss, or

(B) the sum of the amounts allowable as deductions under sections 162 and 165 which are attributable to—

(i) product liability, or

(ii) expenses incurred in the investigation or settlement of, or opposition to, claims against the taxpayer on account of product liability.

(2) Product liability.—The term "product liability" means—

(A) liability of the taxpayer for damages on account of physical injury or emotional harm to individuals, or damage to or loss of the use of property, on account of any defect in any product which is manufactured, leased, or sold by the taxpayer, but only if

(B) such injury, harm, or damage arises after the taxpayer has completed or terminated operations with respect to, and has relinquished possession of, such product.

(3) Election.—Any taxpayer entitled to a 10-year carryback under subsection (b)(1)(I) from any loss year may elect to have the carryback period with respect to such loss year determined without regard to subsection (b)(1)(I). Such election shall be made in such manner as may be prescribed by the Secretary and shall be made by the due date (including extensions of time) for filing the taxpayer's return for the taxable year of the net operating loss. Such election, once made for any taxable year, shall be irrevocable for that taxable year.

(k) Definitions and special rules relating to deferred statutory or tort liability losses.—For purposes of this section—

(1) Deferred statutory or tort liability loss.—The term "deferred statutory or tort liability loss" means, for any taxable year, the lesser of—

(A) the net operating loss for such taxable year, reduced by any portion thereof attributable to—

(i) a foreign expropriation loss, or

(ii) a product liability loss, or

(B) the sum of the amounts allowable as a deduction under this chapter (other than any deduction described in subsection (j)(1)(B)) which—

(i) is taken into account in computing the net operating loss for such taxable year, and

(ii) is for an amount incurred with respect to a liability which arises under a Federal or State law or out of any tort of the taxpayer and—

(I) in the case of a liability arising out of a Federal or State law, the act (or failure to act) giving rise to such liability occurs at least 3 years before the beginning of such taxable year, or

(II) in the case of a liability arising out of a tort, such liability arises out of a series of actions (or failures to act) over an extended period of time a substantial portion of which occurs at least 3 years before the beginning of such taxable year.

A liability shall not be taken into account under the preceding sentence unless the taxpayer used an accrual method of accounting throughout the period or periods during which the acts or failures to act giving rise to such liability occurred.

* * *

(4) No carryback to taxable years beginning before January 1, 1984.—No deferred statutory or tort liability loss may be carried back to a taxable year beginning before January 1, 1984, unless such loss may be carried back to such year without regard to subsection (b)(1)(J).

(*l*) **Rules relating to bad debt losses of commercial banks.**—For purposes of this section—

(m) **Cross references.**—

(1) For treatment of net operating loss carryovers in certain corporate acquisitions, see section 381.

(2) For special limitation on net operating loss carryovers in case of a corporate change of ownership, see section 382.

§ 173. Circulation expenditures

(a) **General rule.**—

Notwithstanding section 263, all expenditures (other than expenditures for the purchase of land or depreciable property or for the acquisition of circulation through the purchase of any part of the business of another publisher of a newspaper, magazine, or other periodical) to establish, maintain, or increase the circulation of a newspaper, magazine or other periodical shall be allowed as a deduction; except that the deduction shall not be allowed with respect to the portion of such expenditures as, under regulations prescribed by the Secretary, is chargeable to capital account if the taxpayer elects, in accordance with such regulations, to treat such portion as so chargeable. Such election, if made, must be for the total amount of such portion of the expenditures which is so chargeable to capital account, and shall be binding for all subsequent taxable years unless, upon application by the taxpayer, the Secretary permits a revocation of such election subject to such conditions as he deems necessary.

* * *

§ 174. Research and experimental expenditures

(a) **Treatment as expenses.**—

(1) **In general.**—A taxpayer may treat research or experimental expenditures which are paid or incurred by him during the taxable year in connection with his trade or business as expenses which are not chargeable to capital account. The expenditures so treated shall be allowed as a deduction.

(2) **When method may be adopted.**—

(A) **Without consent.**—A taxpayer may, without the consent of the Secretary, adopt the method provided in this subsection for his first taxable year—

(i) which begins after December 31, 1953, and ends after August 16, 1954, and

(ii) for which expenditures described in paragraph (1) are paid or incurred.

(B) **With consent.**—A taxpayer may, with the consent of the Secretary, adopt at any time the method provided in this subsection.

(3) **Scope.**—The method adopted under this subsection shall apply to all expenditures described in paragraph (1). The method adopted shall be adhered to in computing taxable income for the taxable year and for all subsequent taxable years unless, with the approval of the Secretary, a change to a different method is authorized with respect to part or all of such expenditures.

(b) **Amortization of certain research and experimental expenditures.**—

(1) **In general.**—At the election of the taxpayer, made in accordance with regulations prescribed by the Secretary, research or experimental expenditures which are—

(A) paid or incurred by the taxpayer in connection with his trade or business,

(B) not treated as expenses under subsection (a), and

(C) chargeable to capital account but not chargeable to property of a character which is subject to the allowance under section 167 (relating to allowance for depreciation, etc.) or section 611 (relating to allowance for depletion),

may be treated as deferred expenses. In computing taxable income, such deferred expenses shall be allowed as a deduction ratably over such period of not less than 60 months as may be selected by the taxpayer (beginning with the month in which the taxpayer first realizes benefits from such expenditures). Such deferred expenses are expenditures properly chargeable to capital account for purposes of section 1016(a) (1) (relating to adjustments to basis of property).

(2) **Time for and scope of election.**—The election provided by paragraph (1) may be made for any taxable year beginning after December 31, 1953, but only if made not later than the time prescribed by law for filing the return for such taxable year (including extensions thereof). The method so elected, and the period selected by the taxpayer, shall be adhered to in computing taxable income for the taxable year for which the election is made and for all subsequent taxable years unless, with the approval of the Secretary, a change to a different method (or to a different period) is authorized with respect to part or all of such expenditures. The election shall not apply to any expenditure paid or incurred during any taxable year before the taxable year for which the taxpayer makes the election.

(c) **Land and other property.**—This section shall not apply to any expenditure for the acquisition or improvement of land, or for the acquisition or improvement of property to be used in connection with the research or experimentation and of a character which is subject to the allowance under section 167 (relating to allowance for depreciation, etc.) or section 611 (relating to allowance for depletion); but for purposes of this section allowances under section 167, and allowances under section 611, shall be considered as expenditures.

(d) **Exploration expenditures.**—This section shall not apply to any expenditure paid or incurred for the purpose of ascertaining the existence, location, extent, or quality of any deposit of ore or other mineral (including oil and gas).

(e) **Cross references.—**

(1) **For adjustments to basis of property for amounts allowed as deductions as deferred expenses under subsection (b), see section 1016(a)(14).**

(2) **For election of 10-year amortization of expenditures allowable as a deduction under subsection (a), see section 59(d).**

§ 175. Soil and water conservation expenditures

(a) **In general.**—A taxpayer engaged in the business of farming may treat expenditures which are paid or incurred by him during the taxable year for the purpose of soil or water conservation in respect of land used in farming, or for the prevention of erosion of land used in farming, as expenses which are not chargeable to capital account. The expenditures so treated shall be allowed as a deduction.

(b) **Limitation.**—The amount deductible under subsection (a) for any taxable year shall not exceed 25 percent of the gross income derived from farming during the taxable year. If for any taxable year the total of the expenditures treated as expenses which are not chargeable to capital account exceeds 25 percent of the gross income derived from farming during the taxable year, such excess shall be deductible for succeeding taxable years in order of time; but the amount deductible under this section for any one such succeeding taxable year (including the expenditures actually paid or incurred during the taxable year) shall not exceed 25 percent of the gross income derived from farming during the taxable year.

(c) **Definitions.**—For purposes of subsection (a)—

(1) The term "expenditures which are paid or incurred by him during the taxable year for the purpose of soil or water conservation in respect of land used in farming, or for the prevention of erosion of land used in farming" means expenditures paid or incurred for the treatment or moving of earth, including (but not limited to) leveling, grading and terracing, contour furrowing, the construction, control, and protection of diversion channels, drainage ditches, earthen dams, watercourses, outlets, and ponds, the eradication of brush, and the planting of windbreaks. Such term does not include—

(A) the purchase, construction, installation, or improvement of structures, appliances, or facilities which are of a character which is subject to the allowance for depreciation provided in section 167, or

(B) any amount paid or incurred which is allowable as a deduction without regard to this section.

Notwithstanding the preceding sentences, such term also includes any amount, not otherwise allowable as a deduction, paid or incurred to satisfy any part of an assessment levied by a soil or water conservation or drainage district to defray expenditures made by such district (i) which, if paid or incurred by the taxpayer, would without regard to this sentence constitute expenditures deductible under this section, or (ii) for property of a character subject to the allowance for depreciation provided in section 167 and used in the soil or water conservation or drainage district's business as such (to the extent that the taxpayer's share of the assessment levied on the members of the district for such property does not exceed 10 percent of such assessment).

(2) The term "land used in farming" means land used (before or simultaneously with the expenditures described in paragraph (1)) by the taxpayer or his tenant for the production of crops, fruits, or other agricultural products or for the sustenance of livestock.

(3) **Additional limitations.—**

(A) **Expenditures must be consistent with soil conservation plan.**—Notwithstanding any other provision of this section, subsection (a) shall not apply to any expenditures unless such expenditures are consistent with—

(i) the plan (if any) approved by the Soil Conservation Service of the Department of Agriculture for the area in which the land is located, or

(ii) if there is no plan described in clause (i), any soil conservation plan of a comparable State agency.

(B) **Certain wetland, etc., activities not qualified.**—Subsection (a) shall not apply to any expenditures in connection with the draining or filling of wetlands or land preparation for center pivot irrigation systems.

(d) **When method may be adopted.—**

(1) **Without consent.**—A taxpayer may, without the consent of the Secretary, adopt the method provided in this section for his first taxable year—

(A) which begins after December 31, 1953, and ends after August 16, 1954, and

(B) for which expenditures described in subsection (a) are paid or incurred.

(2) **With consent.**—A taxpayer may, with the consent of the Secretary, adopt at any time the method provided in this section.

(e) Scope.—The method adopted under this section shall apply to all expenditures described in subsection (a). The method adopted shall be adhered to in computing taxable income for the taxable year and for all subsequent taxable years unless, with the approval of the Secretary, a change to a different method is authorized with respect to part or all of such expenditures.

§ 177. Trademark and trade name expenditures [Repealed]

§ 178. Amortization of cost of acquiring a lease

(a) General rule.—In determining the amount of the deduction allowable to a lessee of a lease for any taxable year for amortization under section 167, 169, 179, 185, 190, 193, or 194 in respect of any cost of acquiring the lease, the term of the lease shall be treated as including all renewal options (and any other period for which the parties reasonably expect the lease to be renewed) if less than 75 percent of such cost is attributable to the period of the term of the lease remaining on the date of its acquisition.

(b) Certain periods excluded.—For purposes of subsection (a), in determining the period of the term of the lease remaining on the date of acquisition, there shall not be taken into account any period for which the lease may subsequently be renewed, extended, or continued pursuant to an option exercisable by the lessee.

§ 179. Election to expense certain depreciable business assets

(a) Treatment as expenses.—A taxpayer may elect to treat the cost of any section 179 property as an expense which is not chargeable to capital account. Any cost so treated shall be allowed as a deduction for the taxable year in which the section 179 property is placed in service.

(b) Limitations.—

(1) Dollar limitation.—The aggregate cost which may be taken into account under subsection (a) for any taxable year shall not exceed $10,000.

(2) Reduction in limitation.—The limitation under paragraph (1) for any taxable year shall be reduced (but not below zero) by the amount by which the cost of section 179 property placed in service during such taxable year exceeds $200,000.

(3) Limitation based on income from trade or business.—

(A) In general.—The aggregate cost of section 179 property taken into account under subsection (a) for any taxable year shall not exceed the aggregate amount of taxable income of the taxpayer for such taxable year which is derived from the active conduct by the taxpayer of any trade or business during such taxable year.

(B) Carryover of unused cost.—The amount of any cost which (but for subparagraph (A)) would have been allowed as a deduction under subsection (a) for any taxable year shall be carried to the succeeding taxable year and added to the amount allowable as a deduction under subsection (a) for such succeeding taxable year.

(C) Computation of taxable income.—For purposes of this paragraph, taxable income derived from the conduct of a trade or business shall be computed without regard to the cost of any section 179 property.

(4) Married individuals filing separately.—In the case of a husband and wife filing separate returns for the taxable year—

(A) such individuals shall be treated as 1 taxpayer for purposes of paragraphs (1) and (2), and

(B) unless such individuals elect otherwise, 50 percent of the cost which may be taken into account under subsection (a) for such taxable year (before application of paragraph (3)) shall be allocated to each such individual.

(c) Election.—

(1) In general.—An election under this section for any taxable year shall—

(A) specify the items of section 179 property to which the election applies and the portion of the cost of each of such items which is to be taken into account under subsection (a), and

(B) be made on the taxpayer's return of the tax imposed by this chapter for the taxable year.

Such election shall be made in such manner as the Secretary may by regulations prescribe.

(2) Election irrevocable.—Any election made under this section, and any specification contained in any such election, may not be revoked except with the consent of the Secretary.

(d) Definitions and special rules.—

(1) Section 179 property.—For purposes of this section, the term "section 179 property" means any recovery property which is section 38 property and which is acquired by purchase for use in the active conduct of a trade or business.

(2) Purchase defined.—For purposes of paragraph (1), the term "purchase" means any acquisition of property, but only if—

(A) the property is not acquired from a person whose relationship to the person acquiring it would result in the disallowance of losses under section 267 or 707(b) (but, in applying section 267(b) and (c) for purposes of this section, paragraph (4) of section 267(c) shall be treated as providing that the family of an individual shall include only his spouse, ancestors, and lineal descendants),

(B) the property is not acquired by one component member of a controlled group from another component member of the same controlled group, and

(C) the basis of the property in the hands of the person acquiring it is not determined—

(i) in whole or in part by reference to the adjusted basis of such property in the hands of the person from whom acquired, or

(ii) under section 1014(a) (relating to property acquired from a decedent).

(3) Cost.—For purposes of this section, the cost of property does not include so much of the basis of such property as is determined by reference to the basis of other property held at any time by the person acquiring such property.

(4) Section not to apply to estates and trusts.—This section shall not apply to estates and trusts.

(5) Section not to apply to certain noncorporate lessors.—This section shall not apply to any section 179 property purchased by any person described in section 46(e)(3) unless the credit under section 38 is allowable with respect to such person for such property (determined without regard to this section).

(6) Dollar limitation of controlled group.—For purposes of subsection (b) of this section—

(A) all component members of a controlled group shall be treated as one taxpayer, and

(B) the Secretary shall apportion the dollar limitation contained in subsection (b) (1) among the component members of such controlled group in such manner as he shall by regulations prescribe.

(7) Controlled group defined.—For purposes of paragraphs (2) and (6), the term "controlled group" has the meaning assigned to it by section 1563(a), except that, for such purposes, the phrase "more than 50 percent" shall be substituted for the phrase "at least 80 percent" each place it appears in section 1563(a) (1).

(8) Treatment of partnerships and s corporations.—In the case of a partnership, the limitations of subsection (b) shall apply with respect to the partnership and with respect to each partner. A similar rule shall apply in the case of an S corporation and its shareholders.

(9) Coordination with section 38.—No credit shall be allowed under section 38 with respect to any amount for which a deduction is allowed under subsection (a).

(10) Recapture in certain cases.—The Secretary shall, by regulations, provide for recapturing the benefit under any deduction allowable under subsection (a) with respect to any property which is not used predominantly in a trade or business at any time.

§ 182. Expenditures by farmers for clearing land [Repealed]

§ 183. Activities not engaged in for profit

(a) General rule.—In the case of an activity engaged in by an individual or an S corporation, if such activity is not engaged in for profit, no deduction attributable to such activity shall be allowed under this chapter except as provided in this section.

(b) Deductions allowable.—In the case of an activity not engaged in for profit to which subsection (a) applies, there shall be allowed—

(1) the deductions which would be allowable under this chapter for the taxable year without regard to whether or not such activity is engaged in for profit, and

(2) a deduction equal to the amount of the deductions which would be allowable under this chapter for the taxable year only if such activity were engaged in for profit, but only to the extent that the gross income derived from such activity for the taxable year exceeds the deductions allowable by reason of paragraph (1).

(c) Activity not engaged in for profit defined.—For purposes of this section, the term "activity not engaged in for profit" means any activity other than one with respect to which deductions are allowable for the taxable year under section 162 or under paragraph (1) or (2) of section 212.

(d) Presumption.—If the gross income derived from an activity for 3 or more of the taxable years in the period of 5 consecutive taxable years which ends with the taxable year exceeds the deductions attributable to such activity (determined without regard to whether or not such activity is engaged in for profit), then, unless the Secretary establishes to the contrary, such activity shall be presumed for purposes of this chapter for such taxable year to be an activity engaged in for profit. In the case of an activity which consists in major part of the breeding, training, showing, or racing of horses, the preceding sentence shall be applied by substituting "2" for "3" and "7" for "5".

(e) Special rule.—

(1) In general.—A determination as to whether the presumption provided by subsection (d) applies with respect to any activity shall, if the taxpayer so elects, not be made before the close of the fourth taxable year (sixth taxable year, in the case of an activity described in the last sentence of such subsection) following the taxable year in which the taxpayer first engages in the activity. For purposes of the preceding sentence, a taxpayer shall be treated as not having engaged in an activity during any taxable year beginning before January 1, 1970.

(2) Initial period.—If the taxpayer makes an election under paragraph (1), the presumption provided by subsection (d) shall apply to each taxable year in the 5-taxable year (or 7-taxable year) period beginning with the taxable year in which the taxpayer first engages in the activity, if the gross income derived from the activity for 2 or more of the taxable years in such period exceeds the deductions attributable to the activity (determined without regard to whether or not the activity is engaged in for profit).

(3) Election.—An election under paragraph (1) shall be made at such time and manner, and subject to such terms and conditions, as the Secretary may prescribe.

(4) Time for assessing deficiency attributable to activity.—If a taxpayer makes an election under paragraph (1) with respect to an activity, the statutory period for the assessment of any deficiency attributable to such activity shall not expire before the expiration of 2 years after the date prescribed by law (determined without extensions) for filing the return of tax under chapter 1 for the last taxable year in the period of 5 taxable years (or 7 taxable years) to which the election relates. Such deficiency may be assessed notwithstanding the provisions of any law or rule of law which would otherwise prevent such an assessment.

§ 186.   Recoveries of damages for antitrust violations, etc.

(a) Allowance of deduction.—If a compensatory amount which is included in gross income is received or accrued during the taxable year for a compensable injury, there shall be allowed as a deduction for the taxable year an amount equal to the lesser of—

(1) the amount of such compensatory amount, or

(2) the amount of the unrecovered losses sustained as a result of such compensable injury.

(b) Compensable injury.—For purposes of this section, the term "compensable injury" means—

(1) injuries sustained as a result of an infringement of a patent issued by the United States,

(2) injuries sustained as a result of a breach of contract or a breach of fiduciary duty or relationship, or

(3) injuries sustained in business, or to property, by reason of any conduct forbidden in the antitrust laws for which a civil action may be brought under section 4 of the Act entitled "An Act to supplement existing laws against unlawful restraints and monopolies, and for other purposes", approved October 15, 1914 (commonly known as the Clayton Act).

(c) Compensatory amount.—For purposes of this section, the term "compensatory amount" means the amount received or accrued during the taxable year as damages as a result of an award in, or in settlement of, a civil action for recovery for a compensable injury, reduced by any amounts paid or incurred in the taxable year in securing such award or settlement.

(d) Unrecovered losses.—

(1) In general.—For purposes of this section, the amount of any unrecovered loss sustained as a result of any compensable injury is—

(A) the sum of the amount of the net operating losses (as determined under section 172) for each taxable year in whole or in part within the injury period, to the extent that such net operating losses are attributable to such compensable injury, reduced by

(B) the sum of—

(i) the amount of the net operating losses described in subparagraph (A) which were allowed for any prior taxable year as a deduction under section 172 as a net operating loss carryback or carryover to such taxable year, and

(ii) the amounts allowed as a deduction under subsection (a) for any prior taxable year for prior recoveries of compensatory amounts for such compensable injury.

(2) Injury period.—For purposes of paragraph (1), the injury period is—

(A) with respect to any infringement of a patent, the period in which such infringement occurred,

(B) with respect to a breach of contract or breach of fiduciary duty or relationship, the period during which amounts would have been received or accrued but for the breach of contract or breach of fiduciary duty or relationship, and

(C) with respect to injuries sustained by reason of any conduct forbidden in the antitrust laws, the period in which such injuries were sustained.

(3) Net operating losses attributable to compensable injuries.—For purposes of paragraph (1)—

(A) a net operating loss for any taxable year shall be treated as attributable to a compensable injury to the extent of the compensable injury sustained during such taxable year, and

(B) if only a portion of a net operating loss for any taxable year is attributable to a compensable injury, such portion shall (in applying section 172 for purposes of this section) be considered to be a separate net operating loss for such year to be applied after the other portion of such net operating loss.

(e) Effect on net operating loss carryovers.—If for the taxable year in which a compensatory amount is received or accrued any portion of a net operating loss carryover to such year is attributable to the compensable injury for which such amount is received or accrued, such portion of such net operating loss carryover shall be reduced by an amount equal to—

(1) the deduction allowed under subsection (a) with respect to such compensatory amount, reduced by

(2) any portion of the unrecovered losses sustained as a result of the compensable injury with respect to which the period for carryover under section 172 has expired.

§ 189. Amortization of real property construction period interest and taxes [Repealed.]

§ 195. Start-up expenditures

(a) Capitalization of expenditures.—Except as otherwise provided in this section, no deduction shall be allowed for start-up expenditures.

(b) Election to amortize.—

(1) In general.—Start-up expenditures may, at the election of the taxpayer, be treated as deferred expenses. Such deferred expenses shall be allowed as a deduction prorated equally over such period of not less than 60 months as may be selected by the taxpayer (beginning with the month in which the active trade or business begins).

(2) Dispositions before close of amortization period.—In any case in which a trade or business is completely disposed of by the taxpayer before the end of the period to which paragraph (1) applies, any deferred expenses attributable to such trade or business which were not allowed as a deduction by reason of this section may be deducted to the extent allowable under section 165.

(c) Definitions.—For purposes of this section—

(1) Start-up expenditures.—The term "start-up expenditure" means any amount—

(A) paid or incurred in connection with—

(i) investigating the creation or acquisition of an active trade or business, or

(ii) creating an active trade or business, or

(iii) any activity engaged in for profit and for the production of income before the date on which the active trade or business begins, in anticipation of such activity becoming an active trade or business, and

(B) which, if paid or incurred in connection with the operation of an existing active trade or business (in the same field as the trade or business referred to in subparagraph (A)), would be allowable as a deduction for the taxable year in which paid or incurred.

The term "start-up expenditure" does not include any amount with respect to which a deduction is allowable under section 163(a), 164, or 174.

(2) Beginning of trade or business.—

(A) In general.—Except as provided in subparagraph (B), the determination of when an active trade or business begins shall be made in accordance with such regulations as the Secretary may prescribe.

(B) Acquired trade or business.—An acquired active trade or business shall be treated as beginning when the taxpayer acquires it.

(d) Election.—

(1) Time for making election.—An election under subsection (b) shall be made not later than the time prescribed by law for filing the return for the taxable year in which the trade or business begins (including extensions thereof).

(2) Scope of election.—The period selected under subsection (b) shall be adhered to in computing taxable income for the taxable year for which the election is made and all subsequent taxable years.

§ 196. Deduction for certain unused business credits

(a) Allowance of deduction.—If any portion of the qualified business credits determined for any taxable year has not, after the application of section 38(c), been allowed to the taxpayer as a credit under section 38 for any taxable year, an amount equal to the credit not so allowed shall be allowed to the taxpayer as a deduction for the first taxable year following the last taxable year for which such credit could, under section 39, have been allowed as a credit.

(b) Taxpayer's dying or ceasing to exist.—If a taxpayer dies or ceases to exist before the first taxable year following the last taxable year for which the qualified business credits could, under section 39, have been allowed as a credit, the amount described in subsection (a) (or the proper portion thereof) shall, under regulations prescribed by the Secretary, be allowed to the taxpayer as a deduction for the taxable year in which such death or cessation occurs.

(c) Qualified business credits.—For purposes of this section, the term "qualified business credits" means—

(1) the investment credit determined under section 46(a) (but only to the extent attributable to property the basis of which is reduced by section 48(q)),

(2) the targeted jobs credit determined under section 51(a), and

(3) the alcohol fuels credit determined under section 40(a).

(d) Special rule for investment tax credit.—In the case of the investment credit determined under section 46(a) (other than a credit to which section 48(q)(3) applies), subsection (a) shall be applied by substituting "an amount equal to 50 percent of" for "an amount equal to".

PART VII—ADDITIONAL ITEMIZED DEDUCTIONS FOR INDIVIDUALS

§ 211. Allowance of deductions

In computing taxable income under section 63, there shall be allowed as deductions the items specified in this part, subject to the exceptions provided in part IX (section 261 and following, relating to items not deductible).

§ 212. Expenses for production of income

In the case of an individual, there shall be allowed as a deduction all the ordinary and necessary expenses paid or incurred during the taxable year—

(1) for the production or collection of income;

(2) for the management, conservation, or maintenance of property held for the production of income; or

(3) in connection with the determination, collection, or refund of any tax.

§ 213. Medical, dental, etc., expenses

(a) Allowance of deduction.—There shall be allowed as a deduction the expenses paid during the taxable year, not compensated for by insurance or otherwise, for medical care of the taxpayer, his spouse, or a dependent (as defined in section 152), to the extent that such expenses exceed 7.5 percent of adjusted gross income.

(b) Limitation with respect to medicine and drugs

An amount paid during the taxable year for medicine or a drug shall be taken into account under subsection (a) only if such medicine or drug is a prescribed drug or is insulin.

(c) Special rule for decedents.—

(1) Treatment of expenses paid after death.—For purposes of subsection (a), expenses for the medical care of the taxpayer which are paid out of his estate during the 1-year period beginning with the day after the date of his death shall be treated as paid by the taxpayer at the time incurred.

(2) **Limitation.**—Paragraph (1) shall not apply if the amount paid is allowable under section 2053 as a deduction in computing the taxable estate of the decedent, but this paragraph shall not apply if (within the time and in the manner and form prescribed by the Secretary) there is filed—

(A) a statement that such amount has not been allowed as a deduction under section 2053, and

(B) a waiver of the right to have such amount allowed at any time as a deduction under section 2053.

(d) **Definitions.**—For purposes of this section—

(1) The term "medical care" means amounts paid—

(A) for the diagnosis, cure, mitigation, treatment, or prevention of disease, or for the purpose of affecting any structure or function of the body,

(B) for transportation primarily for and essential to medical care referred to in subparagraph (A), or

(C) for insurance (including amounts paid as premiums under part B of title XVIII of the Social Security Act, relating to supplementary medical insurance for the aged) covering medical care referred to in subparagraphs (A) and (B).

(2) **Amounts paid for certain lodging away from home treated as paid for medical care.**—Amounts paid for lodging (not lavish or extravagant under the circumstances) while away from home primarily for and essential to medical care referred to in paragraph (1)(A) shall be treated as amounts paid for medical care if—

(A) the medical care referred to in paragraph (1)(A) is provided by a physician in a licensed hospital (or in a medical care facility which is related to, or the equivalent of, a licensed hospital), and

(B) there is no significant element of personal pleasure, recreation, or vacation in the travel away from home.

The amount taken into account under the preceding sentence shall not exceed $50 for each night for each individual.

(3) **Prescribed drug.**—The term "prescribed drug" means a drug or biological which requires a prescription of a physician for its use by an individual.

(4) **Physician.**—The term "physician" has the meaning given to such term by section 1861(r) of the Social Security Act (42 U.S.C. 1395x(r)).

(5) **Special rule in the case of child of divorced parents, etc.**—Any child to whom section 152(e) applies shall be treated as a dependent of both parents for purposes of this section.

(6) In the case of an insurance contract under which amounts are payable for other than medical care referred to in subparagraphs (A) and (B) of paragraph (1)—

(A) no amount shall be treated as paid for insurance to which paragraph (1) (C) applies unless the charge for such insurance is either separately stated in the contract, or furnished to the policyholder by the insurance company in a separate statement,

(B) the amount taken into account as the amount paid for such insurance shall not exceed such charge, and

(C) no amount shall be treated as paid for such insurance if the amount specified in the contract (or furnished to the policyholder by the insurance company in a separate statement) as the charge for such insurance is unreasonably large in relation to the total charges under the contract.

(7) Subject to the limitations of paragraph (6), premiums paid during the taxable year by a taxpayer before he attains the age of 65 for insurance covering medical care (within the meaning of subparagraphs (A) and (B) of paragraph (1)) for the taxpayer, his spouse, or a dependent after the taxpayer attains the age of 65 shall be treated as expenses paid during the taxable year for insurance which constitutes medical care if premiums for such insurance are payable (on a level payment basis) under the contract for a period of 10 years or more or until the year in which the taxpayer attains the age of 65 (but in no case for a period of less than 5 years).

(8) The determination of whether an individual is married at any time during the taxable year shall be made in accordance with the provisions of section 6013(d) (relating to determination of status as husband and wife).

(e) Exclusion of amounts allowed for care of certain dependents.—Any expense allowed as a credit under section 21 shall not be treated as an expense paid for medical care.

§ 215. Alimony, etc., payments

(a) General rule.—In the case of an individual, there shall be allowed as a deduction an amount equal to the alimony or separate maintenance payments paid during such individual's taxable year.

(b) Alimony or separate maintenance payments defined.—For purposes of this section, the term "alimony or separate maintenance payment" means any alimony or separate maintenance payment (as defined in section 71(b)) which is includible in the gross income of the recipient under section 71.

(c) Requirement of identification number.—The Secretary may prescribe regulations under which—

(1) any individual receiving alimony or separate maintenance payments is required to furnish such individual's taxpayer identification number to the individual making such payments, and

(2) the individual making such payments is required to include such taxpayer identification number on such individual's return for the taxable year in which such payments are made.

(d) Coordination with section 682.—No deduction shall be allowed under this section with respect to any payment if, by reason of section 682 (relating to income of alimony trusts), the amount thereof is not includible in such individual's gross income.

§ 217. Moving expenses

(a) Deduction allowed.—There shall be allowed as a deduction moving expenses paid or incurred during the taxable year in connection with the commencement of work by the taxpayer as an employee or as a self-employed individual at a new principal place of work.

(b) Definition of moving expenses.—

(1) In general.—For purposes of this section, the term "moving expenses" means only the reasonable expenses—

(A) of moving household goods and personal effects from the former residence to the new residence,

(B) of traveling (including meals and lodging) from the former residence to the new place of residence,

(C) of traveling (including meals and lodging), after obtaining employment, from the former residence to the general location of the new principal place of work and return, for the principal purpose of searching for a new residence,

(D) of meals and lodging while occupying temporary quarters in the general location of the new principal place of work during any period of 30 consecutive days after obtaining employment, or

(E) constituting qualified residence sale, purchase, or lease expenses.

(2) Qualified residence sale, etc., expenses.—For purposes of paragraph (1) (E), the term "qualified residence sale, purchase, or lease expenses" means only reasonable expenses incident to—

(A) the sale or exchange by the taxpayer or his spouse of the taxpayer's former residence (not including expenses for work performed on such residence in order to assist in its sale) which (but for this subsection and subsection (e)) would be taken into account in determining the amount realized on the sale or exchange,

(B) the purchase by the taxpayer or his spouse of a new residence in the general location of the new principal place of work which (but for this subsection and subsection (e)) would be taken into account in determining—

(i) the adjusted basis of the new residence, or

(ii) the cost of a loan (but not including any amounts which represent payments or prepayments of interest),

(C) the settlement of an unexpired lease held by the taxpayer or his spouse on property used by the taxpayer as his former residence, or

(D) the acquisition of a lease by the taxpayer or his spouse on property used by the taxpayer as his new residence in the general location of the new principal place of work (not including amounts which are payments or prepayments of rent).

(3) Limitations.—

(A) Dollar limits.—The aggregate amount allowable as a deduction under subsection (a) in connection with a commencement of work which is attributable to expenses described in subparagraph (C) or (D) of paragraph (1) shall not exceed $1,500. The aggregate amount allowable as a deduction under subsection (a) which is attributable to qualified residence sale, purchase, or lease expenses shall not exceed $3,000, reduced by the aggregate amount so allowable which is attributable to expenses described in subparagraph (C) or (D) of paragraph (1).

(B) Husband and wife.—If a husband and wife both commence work at a new principal place of work within the same general location, subparagraph (A) shall be applied as if there was only one commencement of work. In the case of a husband and wife filing separate returns, subparagraph (A) shall be applied by substituting "$750" for "$1,500", and by substituting "$1,500" for "$3,000".

(C) Individuals other than taxpayer.—In the case of any individual other than the taxpayer, expenses referred to in subparagraphs (A) through (D) of paragraph (1) shall be taken into account only if such individual has both the former residence and the new residence as his principal place of abode and is a member of the taxpayer's household.

(c) Conditions for allowance.—No deduction shall be allowed under this section unless—

(1) the taxpayer's new principal place of work—

(A) is at least 35 miles farther from his former residence than was his former principal place of work, or

(B) if he had no former principal place of work, is at least 35 miles from his former residence, and

(2) either—

(A) during the 12-month period immediately following his arrival in the general location of his new principal place of work, the taxpayer is a full-time employee, in such general location, during at least 39 weeks, or

(B) during the 24-month period immediately following his arrival in the general location of his new principal place of work, the taxpayer is a full-time employee or performs services as a self-employed individual on a full-time basis, in such general location, during at least 78 weeks, of which not less than 39 weeks are during the 12-month period referred to in subparagraph (A).

For purposes of paragraph (1), the distance between two points shall be the shortest of the more commonly traveled routes between such two points.

(d) Rules for application of subsection (c) (2).—

(1) The condition of subsection (c) (2) shall not apply if the taxpayer is unable to satisfy such condition by reason of—

(A) death or disability, or

(B) involuntary separation (other than for willful misconduct) from the service of, or transfer for the benefit of, an employer after obtaining full-time employment in which the taxpayer could reasonably have been expected to satisfy such condition.

(2) If a taxpayer has not satisfied the condition of subsection (c) (2) before the time prescribed by law (including extensions thereof) for filing the return for the taxable year during which he paid or incurred moving expenses which would otherwise be deductible under this section, but may still satisfy such condition, then such expenses may (at the election of the taxpayer) be deducted for such taxable year notwithstanding subsection (c) (2).

(3) If—

(A) for any taxable year moving expenses have been deducted in accordance with the rule provided in paragraph (2), and

(B) the condition of subsection (c) (2) cannot be satisfied at the close of a subsequent taxable year,

then an amount equal to the expenses which were so deducted shall be included in gross income for the first such subsequent taxable year.

(e) Denial of double benefit.—The amount realized on the sale of the residence described in subparagraph (A) of subsection (b) (2) shall not be decreased by the amount of any expenses described in such subparagraph which are allowed as a deduction under subsection (a), and the basis of a residence described in subparagraph (B) of subsection (b) (2) shall not be increased by the amount of any expenses described in such subparagraph which are allowed as a deduction under subsection (a). This subsection shall not apply to any expenses with respect to which an amount is included in gross income under subsection (d) (3).

(f) Rules for self-employed individuals.—

(1) Definition.—For purposes of this section, the term "self-employed individual" means an individual who performs personal services—

(A) as the owner of the entire interest in an unincorporated trade or business, or

(B) as a partner in a partnership carrying on a trade or business.

(2) **Rule for application of subsections (b) (1) (C) and (D).**—For purposes of subparagraphs (C) and (D) of subsection (b) (1), an individual who commences work at a new principal place of work as a self-employed individual shall be treated as having obtained employment when he has made substantial arrangements to commence such work.

(g) **Rules for members of the Armed Forces of the United States.**—In the case of a member of the Armed Forces of the United States on active duty who moves pursuant to a military order and incident to a permanent change of station—

(1) the limitations under subsection (c) shall not apply;

(2) any moving and storage expenses which are furnished in kind (or for which reimbursement or an allowance is provided, but only to the extent of the expenses paid or incurred) to such member, his spouse, or his dependents, shall not be includible in gross income, and no reporting with respect to such expenses shall be required by the Secretary of Defense or the Secretary of Transportation, as the case may be; and

(3) if moving and storage expenses are furnished in kind (or if reimbursement or an allowance for such expenses is provided) to such member's spouse and his dependents with regard to moving to a location other than the one to which such member moves (or from a location other than the one from which such member moves), this section shall apply with respect to the moving expenses of his spouse and dependents—

(A) as if his spouse commenced work as an employee at a new principal place of work at such location;

(B) for purposes of subsection (b) (3), as if such place of work was within the same general location as the member's new principal place of work, and

(C) without regard to the limitations under subsection (c).

* * *

(j) **Regulations.**—The Secretary shall prescribe such regulations as may be necessary to carry out the purposes of this section.

§ 219. Retirement savings

(a) **Allowance of deduction.**—In the case of an individual, there shall be allowed as a deduction an amount equal to the qualified retirement contributions of the individual for the taxable year.

(b) **Maximum amount of deduction.**—

(1) **In general.**—The amount allowable as a deduction under subsection (a) to any individual for any taxable year shall not exceed the lesser of—

(A) $2,000, or

(B) an amount equal to the compensation includible in the individual's gross income for such taxable year.

* * *

(c) **Special rules for certain married individuals.**—

(1) **In general.**—In the case of any individual with respect to whom a deduction is otherwise allowable under subsection (a)—

(A) who files a joint return under section 6013 for a taxable year, and

there shall be allowed as a deduction any amount paid in cash for the taxable year by or on behalf of the individual to an individual retirement plan established for the benefit of his spouse.

(2) **Limitation.**—The amount allowable as a deduction under paragraph (1) shall not exceed the excess of—

(A) the lesser of—

(i) $2,250, or

(ii) an amount equal to the compensation includible in the individual's gross income for the taxable year, over

(B) the amount allowable as a deduction under subsection (a) for the taxable year

In no event shall the amount allowable as a deduction under paragraph (1) exceed $2,000.

(d) Other limitations and restrictions.—

(1) **Beneficiary must be under age 70½.**—No deduction shall be allowed under this section with respect to any qualified retirement contribution for the benefit of an individual if such individual has attained age 70½ before the close of such individual's taxable year for which the contribution was made.

(2) **Recontributed amounts.**—No deduction shall be allowed under this section with respect to a rollover contribution described in section 402(a)(5), 402(a)(7), 403(a)(4), 403(b)(8), or 408(d)(3).

(3) **Amounts contributed under endowment contract.**—In the case of an endowment contract described in section 408(b), no deduction shall be allowed under this section for that portion of the amounts paid under the contract for the taxable year which is properly allocable, under regulations prescribed by the Secretary, to the cost of life insurance.

(4) **Denial of deduction for amount contributed to inherited annuities or accounts.**—No deduction shall be allowed under this section with respect to any amount paid to an inherited individual retirement account or individual retirement annuity (within the meaning of section 408(d)(3)(C)(ii)).

(e) Qualified retirement contribution.—For purposes of this section, the term "qualified retirement contribution" means—

(1) any amount paid in cash for the taxable year by or on behalf of an individual to an individual retirement plan for such individual's benefit, and

(2) any amount contributed on behalf of any individual to a plan described in section 501(c)(18).

(f) Other definitions and special rules.—

(1) **Compensation.**—For purposes of this section, the term "compensation" includes earned income (as defined in section 401(c)(2)). The term "compensation" does not include any amount received as a pension or annuity and does not include any amount received as deferred compensation. The term "compensation" shall include any amount includible in the individual's gross income under section 71 with respect to a divorce or separation instrument described in subparagraph (A) of section 71(b)(2).

(2) **Married individuals.**—The maximum deduction under subsections (b) and (c) shall be computed separately for each individual, and this section shall be applied without regard to any community property laws.

(3) Time when contributions deemed made.—For purposes of this section, a taxpayer shall be deemed to have made a contribution to an individual retirement plan on the last day of the preceding taxable year if the contribution is made on account of such taxable year and is made not later than the time prescribed by law for filing the return for such taxable year (not including extensions thereof).

(g) Limitation on deduction for active participants in certain pension plans.—

(1) In general.—If (for any part of any plan year ending with or within a taxable year) an individual or the individual's spouse is an active participant, each of the dollar limitations contained in subsections (b)(1)(A) and (c)(2) for such taxable year shall be reduced (but not below zero) by the amount determined under paragraph (2).

(2) Amount of reduction.—

(A) In general.—The amount determined under this paragraph with respect to any dollar limitation shall be the amount which bears the same ratio to such limitation as—

    (i) the excess of—

        (I) the taxpayer's adjusted gross income for such taxable year, over

        (II) the applicable dollar amount, bears to

    (ii) $10,000.

(B) No reduction below $200 until complete phaseout.—No dollar limitation shall be reduced below $200 under paragraph (1) unless (without regard to this subparagraph) such limitation is reduced to zero.

(C) Rounding.—Any amount determined under this paragraph which is not a multiple of $10 shall be rounded to the next lowest $10.

(3) Adjusted gross income; applicable dollar amount.—For purposes of this subsection—

(A) Adjusted gross income.—Adjusted gross income of any taxpayer shall be determined—

    (i) after application of sections 86 and 469, and

    (ii) without regard to section 911 or the deduction allowable under this section.

(B) Applicable dollar amount.—The term "applicable dollar amount" means—

    (i) in the case of a taxpayer filing a joint return, $40,000,

    (ii) in the case of any other taxpayer (other than a married individual filing a separate return), $25,000, and

    (iii) in the case of a married individual filing a separate return, zero.

(4) Special rule for married individuals filing separately.—In the case of a married individual filing a separate return for any taxable year, paragraph (1) shall be applied without regard to whether such individual's spouse is an active participant for any plan year ending with or within such taxable year.

(5) Active participant.—For purposes of this subsection, the term "active participant" means, with respect to any plan year, an individual—

**(A) who is an active participant in—

(i) a plan described in section 401(a) which includes a trust exempt from tax under section 501(a),

(ii) an annuity plan described in section 403(a),

(iii) a plan established for its employees by the United States, by a State or political subdivision thereof, or by an agency or instrumentality of any of the foregoing,

(iv) an annuity contract described in section 403(b), or

(v) a simplified employee pension (within the meaning of section 408(k)), or

(B) who makes deductible contributions to a trust described in section 501(c)(18).

The determination of whether an individual is an active participant shall be made without regard to whether or not such individual's rights under a plan, trust, or contract are nonforfeitable. An eligible deferred compensation plan (within the meaning of section 457(b)) shall not be treated as a plan described in subparagraph (A)(iii).

(6) **Certain individuals not treated as active participants.**—For purposes of this subsection, any individual described in any of the following subparagraphs shall not be treated as an active participant for any taxable year solely because of any participation so described:

(A) **Members of reserve components.**—Participation in a plan described in subparagraph (A)(iii) of paragraph (5) by reason of service as a member of a reserve component of the Armed Forces (as defined in section 261(a) of title 10), unless such individual has served in excess of 90 days on active duty (other than active duty for training) during the year.

(B) **Volunteer firefighters.**—A volunteer firefighter—

(i) who is a participant in a plan described in subparagraph (A)(iii) of paragraph (5) based on his activity as a volunteer firefighter, and

(ii) whose accrued benefit as of the beginning of the taxable year is not more than an annual benefit of $1,800 (when expressed as a single life annuity commencing at age 65).

(4) **Reports.**—The Secretary shall prescribe regulations which prescribe the time and the manner in which reports to the Secretary and plan participants shall be made by the plan administrator of a qualified employer or government plan receiving qualified voluntary employee contributions.

(5) **Employer payments.**—For purposes of this title, any amount paid by an employer to an individual retirement plan shall be treated as payment of compensation to the employee (other than a self-employed individual who is an employee within the meaning of section 401(c)(1)) includible in his gross income in the taxable year for which the amount was contributed, whether or not a deduction for such payment is allowable under this section to the employee.

(6) **Excess contributions treated as contribution made during subsequent year for which there is an unused limitation.**—

(A) **In general.**—If for the taxable year the maximum amount allowable as a deduction under this section for contributions to an individual retirement plan exceeds the amount contributed, then the taxpayer shall be treated as having made an additional contribution for the taxable year in an amount equal to the lesser of—

(i) the amount of such excess, or

(ii) the amount of the excess contributions for such taxable year (determined under section 4973(b)(2) without regard to subparagraph (C) thereof).

(B) **Amount contributed.**—For purposes of this paragraph, the amount contributed—

(i) shall be determined without regard to this paragraph, and

(ii) shall not include any rollover contribution.

(C) **Special rule where excess deduction was allowed for closed year.**—Proper reduction shall be made in the amount allowable as a deduction by reason of this paragraph for any amount allowed as a deduction under this section for a prior taxable year for which the period for assessing deficiency has expired if the amount so allowed exceeds the amount which should have been allowed for such prior taxable year.

§ 221. Deduction for two-earner married couples [Repealed.]

PART VIII—SPECIAL DEDUCTIONS FOR CORPORATIONS

§ 241. Allowance of special deductions

In addition to the deductions provided in part VI (sec. 161 and following), there shall be allowed as deductions in computing taxable income the items specified in this part.

§ 243. Dividends received by corporations

(a) **General rule.**—In the case of a corporation, there shall be allowed as a deduction an amount equal to the following percentages of the amount received as dividends from a domestic corporation which is subject to taxation under this chapter:

(1) 80 percent, in the case of dividends other than dividends described in paragraph (2) or (3);

(2) 100 percent, in the case of dividends received by a small business investment company operating under the Small Business Investment Act of 1958 (15 U.S.C. 661 and following); and

(3) 100 percent, in the case of qualifying dividends (as defined in subsection (b) (1)).

(b) **Qualifying dividends.**—

(1) **Definition.**—For purposes of subsection (a) (3), the term "qualifying dividends" means dividends received by a corporation which, at the close of the day the dividends are received, is a member of the same affiliated group of corporations (as defined in paragraph (5)) as the corporation distributing the dividends, if—

(A) such affiliated group has made an election under paragraph (2) which is effective for the taxable years of its members which include such day, and either

(B) such dividends are distributed out of earnings and profits of a taxable year of the distributing corporation ending after December 31, 1963—

(i) on each day of which the distributing corporation and the corporation receiving the dividends were members of such affiliated group, and

(ii) for which an election under section 1562 (relating to election of multiple surtax exemptions) is not effective, or

* * *

(2) Election.—An election under this paragraph shall be made for an affiliated group by the common parent corporation, and shall be made for any taxable year of the common parent corporation at such time and in such manner as the Secretary by regulations prescribes. Such election may not be made for an affiliated group for any taxable year of the common parent corporation for which an election under section 1562 is effective. Each corporation which is a member of such group at any time during its taxable year which includes the last day of such taxable year of the common parent corporation must consent to such election at such time and in such manner as the Secretary by regulations prescribes. An election under this paragraph shall be effective—

(A) for the taxable year of each member of such affiliated group which includes the last day of the taxable year of the common parent corporation with respect to which the election is made, and

(B) for the taxable year of each member of such affiliated group which ends after the last day of such taxable year of the common parent corporation but which does not include such date, unless the election is terminated under paragraph (4).

(3) Effect of election.—If an election by an affiliated group is effective with respect to a taxable year of the common parent corporation, then under regulations prescribed by the Secretary—

(A) no member of such affiliated group may consent to an election under section 1562 for such taxable year,

(B) the members of such affiliated group shall be treated as one taxpayer for purposes of making the election under section 901(a) (relating to allowance of foreign tax credit), and

(C) the members of such affiliated group shall be limited to one—

(i) $250,000 minimum accumulated earnings credit under section 535(c)(2) or (3), and

(ii) surtax exemption, and one amount under section 6154(c)(2) and section 6655(e)(2), for purposes of estimated tax payment requirements under section 6154 and the addition to the tax under section 6655 for failure to pay estimated tax.

(4) Termination.—An election by an affiliated group under paragraph (2) shall terminate with respect to the taxable year of the common parent corporation and with respect to the taxable years of the members of such affiliated group which include the last day of such taxable year of the common parent corporation if—

(A) Consent of members.—Such affiliated group files a termination of such election (at such time and in such manner as the Secretary by regulations prescribes) with respect to such taxable year of the common parent corporation, and each corporation which is a member of such affiliated group at any time during its taxable year which includes the last day of such taxable year of the common parent corporation consents to such termination, or

(B) Refusal by new member to consent.—During such taxable year of the common parent corporation such affiliated group includes a member which—

(i) was not a member of such group during such common parent corporation's immediately preceding taxable year, and

(ii) such member files a statement that it does not consent to the election at such time and in such manner as the Secretary by regulations prescribes.

(5) Definition of affiliated group.—For purposes of this subsection, the term "affiliated group" has the meaning assigned to it by section 1504(a), except that for such purposes sections 1504(b) (2), 1504(b) (4), and 1504(c) shall not apply.

* * *

§ 246A. Dividends received deduction reduced where portfolio stock is debt financed

(a) General rule.—In the case of any dividend on debt-financed portfolio stock, there shall be substituted for the percentage which (but for this subsection) would be used in determining the amount of the deduction allowable under section 243, 244, or 245(a) a percentage equal to the product of—

(1) 80 percent, and

(2) 100 percent minus the average indebtedness percentage.

(b) Section not to apply to dividends for which 100 percent dividends received deduction allowable.—Subsection (a) shall not apply to—

(1) qualifying dividends (as defined in section 243(b) without regard to section 243(c)(4)), and

(2) dividends received by a small business investment company operating under the Small Business Investment Act of 1958.

(c) Debt financed portfolio stock.—For purposes of this section—

(1) **In general.**—The term "debt financed portfolio stock" means any portfolio stock if at some time during the base period there is portfolio indebtedness with respect to such stock.

(2) **Portfolio stock.**—The term "portfolio stock" means any stock of a corporation unless—

(A) as of the beginning of the ex-dividend date, the taxpayer owns stock of such corporation—

(i) possessing at least 50 percent of the total voting power of the stock of such corporation, and

(ii) having a value equal to at least 50 percent of the total value of the stock of such corporation, or

(B) as of the beginning of the ex-dividend date—

(i) the taxpayer owns stock of such corporation which would meet the requirements of subparagraph (A) if "20 percent" were substituted for "50 percent" each place it appears in such subparagraph, and

(ii) stock meeting the requirements of subparagraph (A) is owned by 5 or fewer corporate shareholders.

* * *

(4) **Treatment of certain preferred stock.**—For purposes of determining whether the requirements of subparagraph (A) or (B) of paragraph (2) or of subparagraph (A) of paragraph (3) are met, stock described in section 1504(a)(4) shall not be taken into account.

(d) Average indebtedness percentage.—For purposes of this section—

(1) **In general.**—Except as provided in paragraph (2), the term "average indebtedness percentage" means the percentage obtained by dividing—

(A) the average amount (determined under regulations prescribed by the Secretary) of the portfolio indebtedness with respect to the stock during the base period, by

(B) the average amount (determined under regulations prescribed by the Secretary) of the adjusted basis of the stock during the base period.

(2) **Special rule where stock not held throughout base period.**—In the case of any stock which was not held by the taxpayer throughout the base period, paragraph (1) shall be applied as if the base period consisted only of that portion of the base period during which the stock was held by the taxpayer.

(3) **Portfolio indebtedness.**—

(A) **In general.**—The term "portfolio indebtedness" means any indebtedness directly attributable to investment in the portfolio stock.

(B) **Certain amounts received from short sale treated as indebtedness.**—For purposes of subparagraph (A), any amount received from a short sale shall be treated as indebtedness for the period beginning on the day on which such amount is received and ending on the day the short sale is closed.

(4) **Base period.**—The term "base period" means, with respect to any dividend, the shorter of—

(A) the period beginning on the ex-dividend date for the most recent previous dividend on the stock and ending on the day before the ex-dividend date for the dividend involved, or

(B) the 1-year period ending on the day before the ex-dividend date for the dividend involved.

(e) **Reduction in dividends received deduction not to exceed allocable interest.**—Under regulations prescribed by the Secretary, any reduction under this section in the amount allowable as a deduction under section 243, 244, or 245 with respect to any dividend shall not exceed the amount of any interest deduction (including any deductible short sale expense) allocable to such dividend.

(f) **Regulations.**—The regulations prescribed for purposes of this section under section 7701(f) shall include regulations providing for the disallowance of interest deductions or other appropriate treatment (in lieu of reducing the dividend received deduction) where the obligor of the indebtedness is a person other than the person receiving the dividend.

§ 248. Organizational expenditures

(a) **Election to amortize.**—The organizational expenditures of a corporation may, at the election of the corporation (made in accordance with regulations prescribed by the Secretary), be treated as deferred expenses. In computing taxable income, such deferred expenses shall be allowed as a deduction ratably over such period of not less than 60 months as may be selected by the corporation (beginning with the month in which the corporation begins business).

(b) **Organizational expenditures defined.**—The term "organizational expenditures" means any expenditure which—

(1) is incident to the creation of the corporation;

(2) is chargeable to capital account; and

(3) is of a character which, if expended incident to the creation of a corporation having a limited life, would be amortizable over such life.

233

(c) **Time for and scope of election.**—The election provided by subsection (a) may be made for any taxable year beginning after December 31, 1953, but only if made not later than the time prescribed by law for filing the return for such taxable year (including extensions thereof). The period so elected shall be adhered to in computing the taxable income of the corporation for the taxable year for which the election is made and all subsequent taxable years. The election shall apply only with respect to expenditures paid or incurred on or after August 16, 1954.

PART IX—ITEMS NOT DEDUCTIBLE

§ 261. General rule for disallowance of deductions

In computing taxable income no deduction shall in any case be allowed in respect of the items specified in this part.

§ 262. Personal, living, and family expenses

Except as otherwise expressly provided in this chapter, no deduction shall be allowed for personal, living, or family expenses.

§ 263. Capital expenditures

(a) **General rule.**—No deduction shall be allowed for—

(1) Any amount paid out for new buildings or for permanent improvements or betterments made to increase the value of any property or estate. This paragraph shall not apply to—

(A) expenditures for the development of mines or deposits deductible under section 616,

(B) research and experimental expenditures deductible under section 174,

(C) soil and water conservation expenditures deductible under section 175,

(D) expenditures by farmers for fertilizer, etc., deductible under section 180,

(E) expenditures for removal of architectural and transportation barriers to the handicapped and elderly which the taxpayer elects to deduct under section 190,

(F) expenditures for tertiary injectants with respect to which a deduction is allowed under section 193; or

(G) expenditures for which a deduction is allowed under section 179.

(2) Any amount expended in restoring property or in making good the exhaustion thereof for which an allowance is or has been made.

* * *

(c) **Intangible drilling and development costs in the case of oil and gas wells and geothermal wells.**—Notwithstanding subsection (a), and except as provided in subsection (i), regulations shall be prescribed by the Secretary under this subtitle corresponding to the regulations which granted the option to deduct as expenses intangible drilling and development costs in the case of oil and gas wells and which were recognized and approved by the Congress in House Concurrent Resolution 50, Seventy-ninth Congress. Such regulations shall also grant the option to deduct as expenses intangible drilling and development costs in the case of wells drilled for any geothermal deposit (as defined in section 613(e)(3)) to the same extent and in the same manner as such expenses are deductible in the case of oil and gas wells. This subsection shall not apply with respect to any costs to which any deduction is allowed under section 59(d) or 291.

* * *

§ 263A. Capitalization and inclusion in inventory costs of certain expenses

(a) Nondeductibility of certain direct and indirect costs.—

(1) In general.—In the case of any property to which this section applies, any costs described in paragraph (2)—

(A) in the case of property which is inventory in the hands of the taxpayer, shall be included in inventory costs, and

(B) in the case of any other property, shall be capitalized.

(2) Allocable costs.—The costs described in this paragraph with respect to any property are—

(A) the direct costs of such property, and

(B) such property's proper share of those indirect costs (including taxes) part or all of which are allocable to such property.

(b) Property to which section applies.—Except as otherwise provided in this section, this section shall apply to—

(1) Property produced by taxpayer.—Real or tangible personal property produced by the taxpayer.

(2) Property acquired for resale.—

(A) In general.—Real or personal property described in section 1221(1) which is acquired by the taxpayer for resale.

(B) Exception for taxpayer with gross receipts of $10,000,000 or less. —Subparagraph (A) shall not apply to any personal property acquired during any taxable year by the taxpayer for resale if the average annual gross receipts of the taxpayer (or any predecessor) for the 3–taxable year period ending with the taxable year preceding such taxable year do not exceed $10,000,000.

(C) Aggregation rules, etc.—For purposes of subparagraph (B), rules similar to the rules of paragraphs (2) and (3) of section 448(c) shall apply.

For purposes of paragraph (1), the term "tangible personal property" shall include a film, sound recording, video tape, book, or similar property.

(c) General exceptions.—

(1) Personal use property.—This section shall not apply to any property produced by the taxpayer for use by the taxpayer other than in a trade or business or an activity conducted for profit.

(2) Research and experimental expenditures.—This section shall not apply to any amount allowable as a deduction under section 174.

(3) Certain development and other costs of oil and gas wells or other mineral property.—This section shall not apply to any cost allowable as a deduction under section 263(c), 616(a), or 617(a).

(4) Coordination with long-term contract rules.—This section shall not apply to any property produced by the taxpayer pursuant to a long-term contract.

(5) Timber and certain ornamental trees.—This section shall not apply to—

(A) trees raised, harvested, or grown by the taxpayer other than trees described in clause (ii) of subsection (e)(4)(B) (after application of the last sentence thereof), and

(B) any real property underlying such trees.

(d) Exception for farming businesses.—

(1) Section to apply only if preproductive period is more than 2 years.—

(A) In general.—This section shall not apply to any plant or animal which is produced by the taxpayer in a farming business and which has a preproductive period of 2 years or less.

(B) Exception for taxpayers required to use accrual method.—Subparagraph (A) shall not apply to any corporation, partnership, or tax shelter required to use an accrual method of accounting under section 447 or 448(a)(3).

(2) Treatment of certain plants lost by reason of casualty.—

(A) In general.—If plants bearing an edible crop for human consumption were lost or damaged (while in the hands of the taxpayer) by reason of freezing temperatures, disease, drought, pests, or casualty, this section shall not apply to any costs of the taxpayer of replanting plants bearing the same type of crop (whether on the same parcel of land on which such lost or damaged plants were located or any other parcel of land of the same acreage in the United States).

(B) Special rule for person with minority interest who materially participates.—Subparagraph (A) shall apply to amounts paid or incurred by a person (other than the taxpayer described in subparagraph (A)) if—

(i) the taxpayer described in subparagraph (A) has an equity interest of more than 50 percent in such grove, orchard, or vineyard, and

(ii) such other person holds any part of the remaining equity interest and materially participates in the planting, maintenance, cultivation, or development of such grove, orchard, or vineyard during the 4–taxable year period beginning with the taxable year in which the grove, orchard or vineyard was lost or damaged.

The determination of whether an individual materially participates in any activity shall be made in a manner similar to the manner in which such determination is made under section 2032A(e)(6).

(3) Election to have this section not apply.—

(A) In general.—If a taxpayer makes an election under this paragraph, this section shall not apply to any plant or animal produced in any farming business carried on by such taxpayer.

(B) Certain persons not eligible.—No election may be made under this paragraph—

(i) by a corporation, partnership, or tax shelter, if such corporation, partnership, or tax shelter is required to use an accrual method of accounting under section 447 or 448(a)(3), or

(ii) with respect to the planting, cultivation, maintenance, or development of pistachio trees.

(C) Special rule for citrus and almond growers.—An election under this paragraph shall not apply with respect to any item which is attributable to the planting, cultivation, maintenance, or development of any citrus or almond grove (or part thereof) and which is incurred before the close of the 4th taxable year beginning with the taxable year in which the trees were planted. For purposes of the preceding sentence, the portion of a citrus or almond grove planted in 1 taxable year shall be treated separately from the portion of such grove planted in another taxable year.

(D) Election.—Unless the Secretary otherwise consents, an election under this paragraph may be made only for the taxpayer's 1st taxable year which begins after December 31, 1986, and during which the taxpayer engages in a farming business. Any such election, once made, may be revoked only with the consent of the Secretary.

(e) Definitions and special rules for purposes of subsection (d).—

(1) Recapture of expensed amounts on disposition.—

(A) In general.—In the case of any plant or animal with respect to which amounts would have been capitalized under subsection (a) but for an election under subsection (d)(3)—

(i) such plant or animal (if not otherwise section 1245 property) shall be treated as section 1245 property, and

(ii) for purposes of section 1245, the recapture amount shall be treated as a deduction allowed for depreciation with respect to such property.

(B) Recapture amount.—For purposes of subparagraph (A), the term "recapture amount" means any amount allowable as a deduction to the taxpayer which, but for an election under subsection (d)(3), would have been capitalized with respect to the plant or animal.

(2) Effects of election on depreciation.—

(A) In general.—If the taxpayer (or any related person) makes an election under subsection (d)(3), the provisions of section 168(g)(2) (relating to alternative depreciation) shall apply to all property of the taxpayer used predominantly in the farming business and placed in service in any taxable year during which any such election is in effect.

(B) Related person.—For purposes of subparagraph (A), the term "related person" means—

(i) the taxpayer and members of the taxpayer's family,

(ii) any corporation (including an S corporation) if 50 percent or more (in value) of the stock of such corporation is owned (directly or through the application of section 318) by the taxpayer or members of the taxpayer's family,

(iii) a corporation and any other corporation which is a member of the same controlled group described in section 1563(a)(1), and

(iv) any partnership if 50 percent or more (in value) of the interests in such partnership is owned directly or indirectly by the taxpayer or members of the taxpayer's family.

(C) Members of family.—For purposes of this paragraph, the term "family" means the taxpayer, the spouse of the taxpayer, and any of their children who have not attained age 18 before the close of the taxable year.

(3) Preproductive period.—

(A) In general.—For purposes of this section, the term "preproductive period" means—

(i) in the case of a plant or animal which will have more than 1 crop or yield, the period before the 1st marketable crop or yield from such plant or animal, or

(ii) in the case of any other plant or animal, the period before such plant or animal is reasonably expected to be disposed of.

For purposes of this subparagraph, use by the taxpayer in a farming business of any supply produced in such business shall be treated as a disposition.

(B) Rule for determining period.—In the case of a plant grown in commercial quantities in the United States, the preproductive period for such plant if grown in the United States shall be based on the nationwide weighted average preproductive period for such plant.

(4) Farming business.—For purposes of this section—

(A) In general.—The term "farming business" means the trade or business of farming.

(B) Certain trades and businesses included.—The term "farming business" shall include the trade or business of—

(i) operating a nursery or sod farm, or

(ii) the raising or harvesting of trees bearing fruit, nuts, or other crops, or ornamental trees.

For purposes of clause (ii), an evergreen tree which is more than 6 years old at the time severed from the roots shall not be treated as an ornamental tree.

(5) Certain inventory valuation methods permitted.—The Secretary shall by regulations permit the taxpayer to use reasonable inventory valuation methods to compute the amount required to be capitalized under subsection (a) in the case of any plant or animal.

(f) Special rules for allocation of interest to property produced by the taxpayer.—

(1) Interest capitalized only in certain cases.—Subsection (a) shall only apply to interest costs which are—

(A) paid or incurred during the production period, and

(B) allocable to property which is described in subsection (B)(1) and which has—

(i) a long useful life,

(ii) an estimated production period exceeding 2 years, or

(iii) an estimated production period exceeding 1 year and a cost exceeding $1,000,000.

(2) Allocation rules.—

(A) In general.—In determining the amount of interest required to be capitalized under subsection (a) with respect to any property—

(i) interest on any indebtedness directly attributable to production expenditures with respect to such property shall be assigned to such property, and

(ii) interest on any other indebtedness shall be assigned to such property to the extent that the taxpayer's interest costs could have been reduced if production expenditures (not attributable to indebtedness described in clause (i)) had not been incurred.

(B) Exception for qualified residence interest.—Subparagraph (A) shall not apply to any qualified residence interest (within the meaning of section 163(h)).

(C) Special rule for flow-through entities.—Except as provided in regulations, in the case of any flow-through entity, this paragraph shall be applied first at the entity level and then at the beneficiary level.

(3) Interest relating to property used to produce property.—This subsection shall apply to any interest on indebtedness incurred or continued in connection with property used to produce property to which this subsection applies to the extent such interest is allocable to the produced property.

(4) Definitions.—For purposes of this subsection—

(A) Long useful life.—Property has a long useful life if such property is—

(i) real property, or

(ii) property with a class life of 20 years or more (as determined under section 168).

(B) Production period.—The term "production period" means, when used with respect to any property, the period—

(i) beginning on the date on which production of the property begins, and

(ii) ending on the date on which the property is ready to be placed in service or is ready to be held for sale.

(C) Production expenditures.—The term "production expenditures" means the costs (whether or not incurred during the production period) required to be capitalized under subsection (a) with respect to the property.

(g) Production.—For purposes of this section—

(1) In general.—The term "produce" includes construct, build, install, manufacture, develop, or improve.

(2) Treatment of property produced under contract for the taxpayer.—The taxpayer shall be treated as producing any property produced for the taxpayer under a contract with the taxpayer; except that only costs paid or incurred by the taxpayer (whether under such contract or otherwise) shall be taken into account in applying subsection (a) to the taxpayer.

(h) Regulations.—The Secretary shall prescribe such regulations as may be necessary or appropriate to carry out the purposes of this section, including—

(1) regulations to prevent the use of related parties, pass-thru entities, or intermediaries to avoid the application of this section, and

(2) regulations providing for simplified procedures for the application of this section in the case of property described in subsection (b)(2).

(Added Pub.L. 99–514, Title VIII, § 803(a), Oct. 22, 1986, 100 Stat. ——.)

§ 264. Certain amounts paid in connection with insurance contracts

(a) General rule.—No deduction shall be allowed for—

(1) Premiums paid on any life insurance policy covering the life of any officer or employee, or of any person financially interested in any trade or business carried on by the taxpayer, when the taxpayer is directly or indirectly a beneficiary under such policy.

(2) Any amount paid or accrued on indebtedness incurred or continued to purchase or carry a single premium life insurance, endowment, or annuity contract.

(3) Except as provided in subsection (c), any amount paid or accrued on indebtedness incurred or continued to purchase or carry a life insurance, endowment, or annuity contract (other than a single premium contract or a contract treated as a single premium contract) pursuant to a plan of purchase which contemplates the systematic direct or indirect borrowing of part or all of the increases in the cash value of such contract (either from the insurer or otherwise).

(4) Any interest paid or accrued on any indebtedness with respect to 1 or more life insurance policies owned by the taxpayer covering the life of any individual who—

    (A) is an officer or employee of, or

    (B) is financially interested in,

any trade or business carried on by the taxpayer to the extent that the aggregate amount of such indebtedness with respect to policies covering such individual exceeds $50,000.

Paragraph (2) shall apply in respect of annuity contracts only as to contracts purchased after March 1, 1954. Paragraph (3) shall apply only in respect of contracts purchased after August 6, 1963. Paragraph (4) shall apply with respect to contracts purchased after June 20, 1986.

(b) Contracts treated as single premium contracts.—For purposes of subsection (a) (2), a contract shall be treated as a single premium contract—

(1) if substantially all the premiums on the contract are paid within a period of 4 years from the date on which the contract is purchased, or

(2) if an amount is deposited after March 1, 1954, with the insurer for payment of a substantial number of future premiums on the contract.

(c) Exceptions.—Subsection (a) (3) shall not apply to any amount paid or accrued by a person during a taxable year on indebtedness incurred or continued as part of a plan referred to in subsection (a) (3)—

(1) if no part of 4 of the annual premiums due during the 7-year period (beginning with the date the first premium on the contract to which such plan relates was paid) is paid under such plan by means of indebtedness,

(2) if the total of the amounts paid or accrued by such person during such taxable year for which (without regard to this paragraph) no deduction would be allowable by reason of subsection (a) (3) does not exceed $100,

(3) if such amount was paid or accrued on indebtedness incurred because of an unforeseen substantial loss of income or unforeseen substantial increase in his financial obligations, or

(4) if such indebtedness was incurred in connection with his trade or business.

For purposes of applying paragraph (1), if there is a substantial increase in the premiums on a contract, a new 7-year period described in such paragraph with respect to such contract shall commence on the date the first such increased premium is paid.

§ 265. Expenses and interest relating to tax-exempt income

(a) General rule.—No deduction shall be allowed for—

(1) **Expenses.**—Any amount otherwise allowable as a deduction which is allocable to one or more classes of income other than interest (whether or not any amount of income of that class or classes is received or accrued) wholly exempt from the taxes imposed by this subtitle, or any amount otherwise allowable under

section 212 (relating to expenses for production of income) which is allocable to interest (whether or not any amount of such interest is received or accrued) wholly exempt from the taxes imposed by this subtitle.

(2) Interest.—Interest on indebtedness incurred or continued to purchase or carry obligations the interest on which is wholly exempt from the taxes imposed by this subtitle, or to purchase or carry any certificate to the extent the interest on such certificate is excludable under section 128.

* * *

(6) Section not to apply with respect to parsonage and military housing allowances.—No deduction shall be denied under this section for interest on a mortgage on, or real property taxes on, the home of the taxpayer by reason of the receipt of an amount as—

(A) a military housing allowance, or

(B) a parsonage allowance excludable from gross income under section 107.

* * *

§ 266. Carrying charges

No deduction shall be allowed for amounts paid or accrued for such taxes and carrying charges as, under regulations prescribed by the Secretary, are chargeable to capital account with respect to property, if the taxpayer elects, in accordance with such regulations, to treat such taxes or charges as so chargeable.

§ 267. Losses, expenses, and interest with respect to transactions between related taxpayers

(a) In general.—

(1) Deduction for losses disallowed.—No deduction shall be allowed in respect of any loss from the sale or exchange of property (other than a loss in case of a distribution in corporate liquidation), directly or indirectly, between persons specified in any of the paragraphs of subsection (b).

(2) Matching of deduction and payee income item in the case of expenses and interest.—If—

(A) by reason of the method of accounting of the person to whom the payment is to be made, the amount thereof is not (unless paid) includible in the gross income of such person, and

(B) at the close of the taxable year of the taxpayer for which (but for this paragraph) the amount would be deductible under this chapter, both the taxpayer and the person to whom the payment is to be made are persons specified in any of the paragraphs of subsection (b),

then any deduction allowable under this chapter in respect of such amount shall be allowable as of the day as of which such amount is includible in the gross income of the person to whom the payment is made (or, if later, as of the day on which it would be so allowable but for this paragraph). "For purposes of this paragraph, in the case of a personal service corporation (within the meaning of section 441(i)(2)), such corporation and any employee-owner (within the meaning of section 269A(b)(2), as modified by section 441(i)(2)) shall be treated as persons specified in subsection (b)."

(3) **Payments to foreign persons.**—The Secretary shall by regulations apply the matching principle of paragraph (2) in cases in which the person to whom the payment is to be made is not a United States person.

For purposes of this paragraph, in the case of a personal service corporation (within the meaning of section 441(i)(2)), such corporation and any employee-owner (within the meaning of section 269A(b)(2), as modified by section 441(i)(2)) shall be treated as persons specified in subsection (b).

(b) **Relationships.**—The persons referred to in subsection (a) are:

(1) Members of a family, as defined in subsection (c) (4);

(2) An individual and a corporation more than 50 percent in value of the outstanding stock of which is owned, directly or indirectly, by or for such individual;

(3) Two corporations which are members of the same controlled group (as defined in subsection (f));

(4) A grantor and a fiduciary of any trust;

(5) A fiduciary of a trust and a fiduciary of another trust, if the same person is a grantor of both trusts;

(6) A fiduciary of a trust and a beneficiary of such trust;

(7) A fiduciary of a trust and a beneficiary of another trust, if the same person is a grantor of both trusts;

(8) A fiduciary of a trust and a corporation more than 50 percent in value of the outstanding stock of which is owned, directly or indirectly, by or for the trust or by or for a person who is a grantor of the trust;

(9) A person and an organization to which section 501 (relating to certain educational and charitable organizations which are exempt from tax) applies and which is controlled directly or indirectly by such person or (if such person is an individual) by members of the family of such individual;

(10) A corporation and a partnership if the same persons own—

(A) more than 50 percent in value of the outstanding stock of the corporation, and

(B) more than 50 percent of the capital interest, or the profits interest, in the partnership;

(11) An S corporation and another S corporation if the same persons own more than 50 percent in value of the outstanding stock of each corporation; or

(12) An S corporation and a C corporation, if the same persons own more than 50 percent in value of the outstanding stock of each corporation.

(c) **Constructive ownership of stock.**—For purposes of determining, in applying subsection (b), the ownership of stock—

(1) Stock owned, directly or indirectly, by or for a corporation, partnership, estate, or trust shall be considered as being owned proportionately by or for its shareholders, partners, or beneficiaries;

(2) An individual shall be considered as owning the stock owned, directly or indirectly, by or for his family;

(3) An individual owning (otherwise than by the application of paragraph (2)) any stock in a corporation shall be considered as owning the stock owned, directly or indirectly, by or for his partner;

(4) The family of an individual shall include only his brothers and sisters (whether by the whole or half blood), spouse, ancestors, and lineal descendants; and

(5) Stock constructively owned by a person by reason of the application of paragraph (1) shall, for the purpose of applying paragraph (1), (2), or (3), be treated as actually owned by such person, but stock constructively owned by an individual by reason of the application of paragraph (2) or (3) shall not be treated as owned by him for the purpose of again applying either of such paragraphs in order to make another the constructive owner of such stock.

(d) Amount of gain where loss previously disallowed.—If—

(1) in the case of a sale or exchange of property to the taxpayer a loss sustained by the transferor is not allowable to the transferor as a deduction by reason of subsection (a) (1) (or by reason of section 24(b) of the Internal Revenue Code of 1939); and

(2) after December 31, 1953, the taxpayer sells or otherwise disposes of such property (or of other property the basis of which in his hands is determined directly or indirectly by reference to such property) at a gain,

then such gain shall be recognized only to the extent that it exceeds so much of such loss as is properly allocable to the property sold or otherwise disposed of by the taxpayer. This subsection applies with respect to taxable years ending after December 31, 1953. This subsection shall not apply if the loss sustained by the transferor is not allowable to the transferor as a deduction by reason of section 1091 (relating to wash sales) or by reason of section 118 of the Internal Revenue Code of 1939.

(e) Special rules for pass-thru entities.—

(1) **In general.**—In the case of any amount paid or incurred by, to, or on behalf of, a pass-thru entity, for purposes of applying subsection (a)(2)—

(A) such entity,

(B) in the case of—

(i) a partnership, any person who owns (directly or indirectly) any capital interest or profits interest of such partnership, or

(ii) an S corporation, any person who owns (directly or indirectly) any of the stock of such corporation,

(C) any person who owns (directly or indirectly) any capital interest or profits interest of a partnership in which such entity owns (directly or indirectly) any capital interest or profits interest, and

(D) any person related (within the meaning of subsection (b) of this section or section 707(b)(1)) to a person described in subparagraph (B) or (C),

shall be treated as persons specified in a paragraph of subsection (b). Subparagraph (C) shall apply to a transaction only if such transaction is related either to the operations of the partnership described in such subparagraph or to an interest in such partnership.

(2) **Pass-thru entity.**—For purposes of this section, the term "pass-thru entity" means—

(A) a partnership, and

(B) an S corporation.

(3) **Constructive ownership in the case of partnerships.**—For purposes of determining ownership of a capital interest or profits interest of a partnership, the principles of subsection (c) shall apply, except that—

(A) paragraph (3) of subsection (c) shall not apply, and

(B) interests owned (directly or indirectly) by or for a C corporation shall be considered as owned by or for any shareholder only if such shareholder owns (directly or indirectly) 5 percent or more in value of the stock of such corporation.

(4) Subsection (a)(2) not to apply to certain guaranteed payments of partnerships.—In the case of any amount paid or incurred by a partnership, subsection (a)(2) shall not apply to the extent that section 707(c) applies to such amount.

(5) Exception for certain expenses and interest of partnerships owning low-income housing.—

(A) In general.—This subsection shall not apply with respect to qualified expenses and interest paid or incurred by a partnership owning low-income housing to—

(i) any qualified 5-percent or less partner of such partnership, or

(ii) any person related (within the meaning of subsection (b) of this section or section 707(b)(1)) to any qualified 5-percent or less partner of such partnership.

(B) Qualified 5-percent or less partner.—For purposes of this paragraph, the term "qualified 5-percent or less partner" means any partner who has (directly or indirectly) an interest of 5 percent or less in the aggregate capital and profits interests of the partnership but only if—

(i) such partner owned the low-income housing at all times during the 2-year period ending on the date such housing was transferred to the partnership, or

(ii) such partnership acquired the low-income housing pursuant to a purchase, assignment, or other transfer from the Department of Housing and Urban Development or any State or local housing authority.

For purposes of the preceding sentence, a partner shall be treated as holding any interest in the partnership which is held (directly or indirectly) by any person related (within the meaning of subsection (b) of this section or section 707(b)(1)) to such partner.

(C) Qualified expenses and interest.—For purpose of this paragraph, the term "qualified expenses and interest" means any expense or interest incurred by the partnership with respect to low-income housing held by the partnership but—

(i) only if the amount of such expense or interest (as the case may be) is unconditionally required to be paid by the partnership not later than 10 years after the date such amount was incurred, and

(ii) in the case of such interest, only if such interest is incurred at an annual rate not in excess of 12 percent.

(D) Low-income housing.—For purposes of this paragraph, the term "low-income housing" means—

(i) any interest in property described in clause (i), (ii), (iii), or (iv) of section 1250(a)(1)(B), and

(ii) any interest in a partnership owning such property.

(6) Cross reference.—

For additional rules relating to partnerships, see section 707(b).

(f) Controlled group defined; special rules applicable to controlled groups.—

(1) Controlled group defined.—For purposes of this section, the term "controlled group" has the meaning given to such term by section 1563(a), except that—

(A) "more than 50 percent" shall be substituted for "at least 80 percent" each place it appears in section 1563(a), and

(B) the determination shall be made without regard to subsections (a)(4) and (e)(3)(C) of section 1563.

(2) Deferral (rather than denial) of loss from sale or exchange between members.—In the case of any loss from the sale or exchange of property which is between members of the same controlled group and to which subsection (a)(1) applies (determined without regard to this paragraph but with regard to paragraph (3))—

(A) subsections (a)(1) and (d) shall not apply to such loss, but

(B) such loss shall be deferred until the property is transferred outside such controlled group and there would be recognition of loss under consolidated return principles or until such other time as may be prescribed in regulations.

(3) Loss deferral rules not to apply in certain cases.—

(A) Transfer to DISC.—For purposes of applying subsection (a)(1), the term "controlled group" shall not include a DISC.

(B) Certain sales of inventory.—Except to the extent provided in regulations prescribed by the Secretary, subsection (a)(1) shall not apply to the sale or exchange of property between members of the same controlled group (or persons described in subsection (b)(10)) if—

(i) such property in the hands of the transferor is property described in section 1221(1),

(ii) such sale or exchange is in the ordinary course of the transferor's trade or business,

(iii) such property in the hands of the transferee is property described in section 1221(1), and

(iv) the transferee or the transferor is a foreign corporation.

(C) Certain foreign currency losses.—To the extent provided in regulations, subsection (a)(1) shall not apply to any loss sustained by a member of a controlled group on the repayment of a loan made to another member of such group if such loan is payable in a foreign currency or is denominated in such a currency and such loss is attributable to a reduction in value of such foreign currency.

(g) Coordination with section 1041.—Subsection (a)(1) shall not apply to any transfer described in section 1041(a) (relating to transfers of property between spouses or incident to divorce).

§ 268. Sale of land with unharvested crop

Where an unharvested crop sold by the taxpayer is considered under the provisions of section 1231 as "property used in the trade or business", in computing taxable income no deduction (whether or not for the taxable year of the sale and whether for expenses, depreciation, or otherwise) attributable to the production of such crop shall be allowed.

§ 269. Acquisitions made to evade or avoid income tax

(a) In general.—If—

(1) any person or persons acquire, or acquired on or after October 8, 1940, directly or indirectly, control of a corporation, or

(2) any corporation acquires, or acquired on or after October 8, 1940, directly or indirectly, property of another corporation, not controlled, directly or indirectly, immediately before such acquisition, by such acquiring corporation or its stockholders, the basis of which property, in the hands of the acquiring corporation, is determined by reference to the basis in the hands of the transferor corporation,

and the principal purpose for which such acquisition was made is evasion or avoidance of Federal income tax by securing the benefit of a deduction, credit, or other allowance which such person or corporation would not otherwise enjoy, then the Secretary may disallow such deduction, credit, or other allowance. For purposes of paragraphs (1) and (2), control means the ownership of stock possessing at least 50 percent of the total combined voting power of all classes of stock entitled to vote or at least 50 percent of the total value of shares of all classes of stock of the corporation.

(b) Certain liquidations after qualified stock purchases.—

(1) In general.—If—

(A) there is a qualified stock purchase by a corporation of another corporation,

(B) an election is not made under section 338 with respect to such purchase,

(C) the acquired corporation is liquidated pursuant to a plan of liquidation adopted not more than 2 years after the acquisition date, and

(D) the principal purpose for such liquidation is the evasion or avoidance of Federal income tax by securing the benefit of a deduction, credit, or other allowance which the acquiring corporation would not otherwise enjoy,

then the Secretary may disallow such deduction, credit, or other allowance.

(2) Meaning of terms.—For purposes of paragraph (1), the terms "qualified stock purchase" and "acquisition date" have the same respective meanings as when used in section 338.

(c) Power of Secretary to allow deduction, etc., in part.—In any case to which subsection (a) or (b) applies the Secretary is authorized—

(1) to allow as a deduction, credit, or allowance any part of any amount disallowed by such subsection, if he determines that such allowance will not result in the evasion or avoidance of Federal income tax for which the acquisition was made; or

(2) to distribute, apportion, or allocate gross income, and distribute, apportion, or allocate the deductions, credits, or allowances the benefit of which was sought to be secured, between or among the corporations, or properties, or parts thereof, involved, and to allow such deductions, credits, or allowances so distributed, apportioned, or allocated, but to give effect to such allowance only to such extent as he determines will not result in the evasion or avoidance of Federal income tax for which the acquisition was made; or

(3) to exercise his powers in part under paragraph (1) and in part under paragraph (2).

§ 269A.   Personal service corporations formed or availed of to avoid or evade income tax

(a) General rule—If—

(1) substantially all of the services of a personal service corporation are performed for (or on behalf of) 1 other corporation, partnership, or other entity, and

(2) the principal purpose for forming, or availing of, such personal service corporation is the avoidance or evasion of Federal income tax by reducing the income of, or securing the benefit of any expense, deduction, credit, exclusion, or other allowance for, any employee-owner which would not otherwise be available,

then the Secretary may allocate all income, deductions, credits, exclusions, and other allowances between such personal service corporation and its employee-owners, if such allocation is necessary to prevent avoidance or evasion of Federal income tax or clearly to reflect the income of the personal service corporation or any of its employee-owners.

(b) Definitions.—For purposes of this section—

(1) **Personal service corporation.**—The term "personal service corporation" means a corporation the principal activity of which is the performance of personal services and such services are substantially performed by employee-owners.

(2) **Employee-owner.**—The term "employee-owner" means any employee who owns, on any day during the taxable year, more than 10 percent of the outstanding stock of the personal service corporation. For purposes of the preceding sentence, section 318 shall apply, except that "5 percent" shall be substituted for "50 percent" in section 318(a)(2)(C).

(3) **Related persons.**—All related persons (within the meaning of section 144(a)(3)) shall be treated as 1 entity.

§ 271.   Debts owed by political parties, etc.

(a) General rule.—In the case of a taxpayer (other than a bank as defined in section 581) no deduction shall be allowed under section 166 (relating to bad debts) or under section 165(g) (relating to worthlessness of securities) by reason of the worthlessness of any debt owed by a political party.

(b) Definitions.—

(1) **Political party.**—For purposes of subsection (a), the term "political party" means—

(A) a political party;

(B) a national, State, or local committee of a political party; or

(C) a committee, association, or organization which accepts contributions or makes expenditures for the purpose of influencing or attempting to influence the election of presidential or vice-presidential electors or of any individual whose name is presented for election to any Federal, State, or local elective public office, whether or not such individual is elected.

(2) **Contributions.**—For purposes of paragraph (1) (C), the term "contributions" includes a gift, subscription, loan, advance, or deposit, of money, or anything of value, and includes a contract, promise, or agreement to make a contribution, whether or not legally enforceable.

(3) **Expenditures.**—For purposes of paragraph (1) (C), the term "expenditures" includes a payment, distribution, loan, advance, deposit, or gift, of money, or

anything of value, and includes a contract, promise, or agreement to make an expenditure, whether or not legally enforceable.

(c) **Exception.**—In the case of a taxpayer who uses an accrual method of accounting, subsection (a) shall not apply to a debt which accrued as a receivable on a bona fide sale of goods or services in the ordinary course of the taxpayer's trade or business if—

(1) for the taxable year in which such receivable accrued, more than 30 percent of all receivables which accrued in the ordinary course of the trades and businesses of the taxpayer were due from political parties, and

(2) the taxpayer made substantial continuing efforts to collect on the debt.

§ 273.　Holders of life or terminable interest

Amounts paid under the laws of a State, the District of Columbia, a possession of the United States, or a foreign country as income to the holder of a life or terminable interest acquired by gift, bequest, or inheritance shall not be reduced or diminished by any deduction for shrinkage (by whatever name called) in the value of such interest due to the lapse of time.

§ 274.　Disallowance of certain entertainment, etc., expenses

(a) **Entertainment, amusement, or recreation.**—

(1) **In general.**—No deduction otherwise allowable under this chapter shall be allowed for any item—

(A) **Activity.**—With respect to an activity which is of a type generally considered to constitute entertainment, amusement, or recreation, unless the taxpayer establishes that the item was directly related to, or, in the case of an item directly preceding or following a substantial and bona fide business discussion (including business meetings at a convention or otherwise), that such item was associated with, the active conduct of the taxpayer's trade or business, or

(B) **Facility.**—With respect to a facility used in connection with an activity referred to in subparagraph (A).

In the case of an item described in subparagraph (A), the deduction shall in no event exceed the portion of such item which meets the requirements of subparagraph (A).

(2) **Special rules.**—For purposes of applying paragraph (1)—

(A) Dues or fees to any social, athletic, or sporting club or organization shall be treated as items with respect to facilities.

(B) An activity described in section 212 shall be treated as a trade or business.

(C) In the case of a club, paragraph (1) (B) shall apply unless the taxpayer establishes that the facility was used primarily for the furtherance of the taxpayer's trade or business and that the item was directly related to the active conduct of such trade or business.

(b) **Gifts.**—

(1) **Limitation.**—No deduction shall be allowed under section 162 or section 212 for any expense for gifts made directly or indirectly to any individual to the extent that such expense, when added to prior expenses of the taxpayer for gifts made to such individual during the same taxable year, exceeds $25. For purposes of this section, the term "gift" means any item excludable from gross income of the

recipient under section 102 which is not excludable from his gross income under any other provision of this chapter, but such term does not include—

(A) an item having a cost to the taxpayer not in excess of $4.00 on which the name of the taxpayer is clearly and permanently imprinted and which is one of a number of identical items distributed generally by the taxpayer, or

(B) a sign, display rack, or other promotional material to be used on the business premises of the recipient.

(2) Special rules.—

(A) In the case of a gift by a partnership, the limitation contained in paragraph (1) shall apply to the partnership as well as to each member thereof.

(B) For purposes of paragraph (1), a husband and wife shall be treated as one taxpayer.

(c) Certain foreign travel.—

(1) In general.—In the case of any individual who travels outside the United States away from home in pursuit of a trade or business or in pursuit of an activity described in section 212, no deduction shall be allowed under section 162 or section 212 for that portion of the expenses of such travel otherwise allowable under such section which, under regulations prescribed by the Secretary, is not allocable to such trade or business or to such activity.

(2) Exception.—Paragraph (1) shall not apply to the expenses of any travel outside the United States away from home if—

(A) such travel does not exceed one week, or

(B) the portion of the time of travel outside the United States away from home which is not attributable to the pursuit of the taxpayer's trade or business or an activity described in section 212 is less than 25 percent of the total time on such travel.

(3) Domestic travel excluded.—For purposes of this subsection, travel outside the United States does not include any travel from one point in the United States to another point in the United States.

(d) Substantiation Required.—No deduction or credit shall be allowed—

(1) under section 162 or 212 for any traveling expense (including meals and lodging while away from home),

(2) for any item with respect to an activity which is of a type generally considered to constitute entertainment, amusement, or recreation, or with respect to a facility used in connection with such an activity,

(3) any expense for gifts, or

(4) with respect to any listed property (as defined in section 280F(d)(4)),

unless the taxpayer substantiates by adequate records or by sufficient evidence corroborating the taxpayer's own statement (A) the amount of such expense or other item, (B) the time and place of the travel, entertainment, amusement, recreation or use of the facility or property, or the date and description of the gift, (C) the business purpose of the expense or other item, and (D) the business relationship to the taxpayer of persons entertained, using the facility or property, or receiving the gift. The Secretary may by regulations provide that some or all of the requirements of the preceding sentence shall not apply in the case of an expense which does not exceed an amount prescribed pursuant to such regulations. This subsection shall not apply to any qualified nonpersonal use vehicle (as defined in subsection (i)).

(e) Specific exceptions to application of subsection (a).—Subsection (a) shall not apply to—

(1) Food and beverages for employees.—Expenses for food and beverages (and facilities used in connection therewith) furnished on the business premises of the taxpayer primarily for his employees.

(2) Expenses treated as compensation.—Expenses for goods, services, and facilities, to the extent that the expenses are treated by the taxpayer, with respect to the recipient of the entertainment, amusement, or recreation, as compensation to an employee on the taxpayer's return of tax under this chapter and as wages to such employee for purposes of chapter 24 (relating to withholding of income tax at source on wages).

(3) Reimbursed expenses.—Expenses paid or incurred by the taxpayer, in connection with the performance by him of services for another person (whether or not such other person is his employer), under a reimbursement or other expense allowance arrangement with such other person, but this paragraph shall apply—

(A) where the services are performed for an employer, only if the employer has not treated such expenses in the manner provided in paragraph (2), or

(B) where the services are performed for a person other than an employer, only if the taxpayer accounts (to the extent provided by subsection (d)) to such person.

(4) Recreational, etc., expenses for employees.—Expenses for recreational, social, or similar activities (including facilities therefor) primarily for the benefit of employees (other than employees who are highly compensated employees (within the meaning of section 414(q)). For purposes of this paragraph, an individual owning less than a 10-percent interest in the taxpayer's trade or business shall not be considered a shareholder or other owner, and for such purposes an individual shall be treated as owning any interest owned by a member of his family (within the meaning of section 267(c) (4)).

(5) Employee, stockholder, etc., business meetings.—Expenses incurred by a taxpayer which are directly related to business meetings of his employees, stockholders, agents, or directors.

(6) Meetings of business leagues, etc.—Expenses directly related and necessary to attendance at a business meeting or convention of any organization described in section 501(c) (6) (relating to business leagues, chambers of commerce, real estate boards, and boards of trade) and exempt from taxation under section 501(a).

(7) Items available to public.—Expenses for goods, services, and facilities made available by the taxpayer to the general public.

(8) Entertainment sold to customers.—Expenses for goods or services (including the use of facilities) which are sold by the taxpayer in a bona fide transaction for an adequate and full consideration in money or money's worth.

(9) Expenses includible in income of persons who are not employees.—Expenses paid or incurred by the taxpayer for goods, services, and facilities to the extent that the expenses are includible in the gross income of a recipient of the entertainment, amusement, or recreation who is not an employee of the taxpayer as compensation for services rendered or as a prize or award under section 74. The preceding sentence shall not apply to any amount paid or incurred by the taxpayer if such amount is required to be included (or would be so required except that the amount is less than $600) in any information return filed by such taxpayer under part III of subchapter A of chapter 61 and is not so included.

For purposes of this subsection, any item referred to in subsection (a) shall be treated as an expense.

(f) Interest, taxes, casualty losses, etc.—This section shall not apply to any deduction allowable to the taxpayer without regard to its connection with his trade or business (or with his income-producing activity). In the case of a taxpayer which is not an individual, the preceding sentence shall be applied as if it were an individual.

(g) Treatment of entertainment, etc., type facility.—For purposes of this chapter, if deductions are disallowed under subsection (a) with respect to any portion of a facility, such portion shall be treated as an asset which is used for personal, living, and family purposes (and not as an asset used in the trade or business).

(h) Attendance at conventions, etc.—

(1) In general.—In the case of any individual who attends a convention, seminar, or similar meeting which is held outside the North American area, no deduction shall be allowed under section 162 for expenses allocable to such meeting unless the taxpayer establishes that the meeting is directly related to the active conduct of his trade or business and that, after taking into account in the manner provided by regulations prescribed by the Secretary—

(A) the purpose of such meeting and the activities taking place at such meeting,

(B) the purposes and activities of the sponsoring organizations or groups,

(C) the residences of the active members of the sponsoring organization and the places at which other meetings of the sponsoring organization or groups have been held or will be held, and

(D) such other relevant factors as the taxpayer may present,

it is as reasonable for the meeting to be held outside the North American area as within the North American area.

(2) Conventions on cruise ships.—In the case of any individual who attends a convention, seminar, or other meeting which is held on any cruise ship, no deduction shall be allowed under section 162 for expenses allocable to such meeting, unless the taxpayer meets the requirements of paragraph (5) and establishes that the meeting is directly related to the active conduct of his trade or business and that—

(A) the cruise ship is a vessel registered in the United States; and

(B) all ports of call of such cruise ship are located in the United States or in possessions of the United States.

With respect to cruises beginning in any calendar year, not more than $2,000 of the expenses attributable to an individual attending one or more meetings may be taken into account under section 162 by reason of the preceding sentence.

(3) Definitions.—For purposes of this subsection—

(A) **North American area.**—The term "North American area" means the United States, its possessions, and the Trust Territory of the Pacific Islands, and Canada and Mexico.

(B) **Cruise ship.**—The term "cruise ship" means any vessel sailing within or without the territorial waters of the United States.

(4) Subsection to apply to employer as well as to traveler.—

(A) Except as provided in subparagraph (B), this subsection shall apply to deductions otherwise allowable under section 162 to any person, whether or not such person is the individual attending the convention, seminar, or similar meeting.

(B) This subsection shall not deny a deduction to any person other than the individual attending the convention, seminar, or similar meeting with respect to any amount paid by such person to or on behalf of such individual if includible in the gross income of such individual. The preceding sentence shall not apply if the amount is required to be included in any information return filed by such person under part III of subchapter A of chapter 61 and is not so included.

(5) **Reporting requirements.**—No deduction shall be allowed under section 162 for expenses allocable to attendance at a convention, seminar, or similar meeting on any cruise ship unless the taxpayer claiming the deduction attaches to the return of tax on which the deduction is claimed—

(A) a written statement signed by the individual attending the meeting which includes—

(i) information with respect to the total days of the trip, excluding the days of transportation to and from the cruise ship port, and the number of hours of each day of the trip which such individual devoted to scheduled business activities,

(ii) a program of the scheduled business activities of the meeting, and

(iii) such other information as may be required in regulations prescribed by the Secretary; and

(B) a written statement signed by an officer of the organization or group sponsoring the meeting which includes—

(i) a schedule of the business activities of each day of the meeting,

(ii) the number of hours which the individual attending the meeting attended such scheduled business activities, and

(iii) such other information as may be required in regulations prescribed by the Secretary.

(6) **Treatment of conventions in certain Caribbean countries.**—

(A) **In general.**—For purposes of this subsection, the term "North American area" includes, with respect to any convention, seminar, or similar meeting, any beneficiary country if (as of the time such meeting begins)—

(i) there is in effect a bilateral or multilateral agreement described in subparagraph (C) between such country and the United States providing for the exchange of information between the United States and such country, and

(ii) there is not in effect a finding by the Secretary that the tax laws of such country discriminate against conventions held in the United States.

(B) **Beneficiary country.**—For purposes of this paragraph, the term "beneficiary country" has the meaning given to such term by section 212(a)(1)(A) of the Caribbean Basin Economic Recovery Act; except that such term shall include Bermuda.

(C) **Authority to conclude exchange of information agreements.**—

(i) **In general.**—The Secretary is authorized to negotiate and conclude an agreement for the exchange of information with any beneficiary country. Except as provided in clause (ii), an exchange of information agreement shall provide for the exchange of such information (not limited to information concerning nationals or residents of the United States or the beneficiary country) as may be necessary or appropriate to carry out and enforce the tax laws of the United States and the beneficiary country (whether criminal or civil proceedings), including information which may otherwise be subject to nondisclosure provisions of the local law of the beneficiary country such as provisions respecting bank secrecy and bearer shares. The exchange of information agreement shall be terminable by either country on reasonable notice and shall provide that information received by either country will be disclosed only to persons or authorities (including courts and administrative bodies) involved in the administration or oversight of, or in the determination of appeals in respect of, taxes of the United States or the beneficiary country and will be used by such persons or authorities only for such purposes.

(ii) Nondisclosure of qualified confidential information sought for civil tax purposes.—An exchange of information agreement need not provide for the exchange of qualified confidential information which is sought only for civil tax purposes if—

(I) the Secretary of the Treasury, after making all reasonable efforts to negotiate an agreement which includes the exchange of such information, determines that such an agreement cannot be negotiated but that the agreement which was negotiated will significantly assist in the administration and enforcement of the tax laws of the United States, and

(II) the President determines that the agreement as negotiated is in the national security interest of the United States.

(iii) Qualified confidential information defined.—For purposes of this subparagraph, the term "qualified confidential information" means information which is subject to the nondisclosure provisions of any local law of the beneficiary country regarding bank secrecy or ownership of bearer shares.

(iv) Civil tax purposes.—For purposes of this subparagraph, the determination of whether information is sought only for civil tax purposes shall be made by the requesting party.

(D) Coordination with section 6103.—Any exchange of information agreement negotiated under subparagraph (C) shall be treated as an income tax convention for purposes of section 6103(k)(4). The Secretary may exercise his authority under subchapter A of chapter 78 to carry out any obligation of the United States under an agreement referred to in subparagraph (C).

(E) Determinations published in the federal register.—The following shall be published in the Federal Register—

(i) any determination by the President under subparagraph (C)(ii) (including the reasons for such determination),

(ii) any determination by the Secretary under subparagraph (C)(ii) (including the reasons for such determination), and

(iii) any finding by the Secretary under subparagraph (A)(ii) (and any termination thereof).

(7) Seminars, etc. for section 212 purposes.—No deduction shall be allowed under section 212 for expenses allocable to a convention, seminar, or similar meeting.

(j) Employee achievement awards.—

(1) General rule.—No deduction shall be allowed under section 162 or section 212 for the cost of an employee achievement award except to the extent that such cost does not exceed the deduction limitations of paragraph (2).

(2) Deduction limitations.—The deduction for the cost of an employee achievement award made by an employer to an employee—

(A) which is not a qualified plan award, when added to the cost to the employer for all other employee achievement awards made to such employee during the taxable year which are not qualified plan awards, shall not exceed $400, and

(B) which is a qualified plan award, when added to the cost to the employer for all other employee achievement awards made to such employee during the taxable year (including employee achievement awards which are not qualified plan awards), shall not exceed $1,600.

(3) Definitions.—For purposes of this subsection—

(A) Employee achievement award.—The term "employee achievement award" means an item of tangible personal property which is—

(i) transferred by an employer to an employee for length of service achievement or safety achievement,

(ii) awarded as part of a meaningful presentation, and

(iii) awarded under conditions and circumstances that do not create a significant likelihood of the payment of disguised compensation.

(B) Qualified plan award.—

(i) **In general.**—The term "qualified plan award" means an employee achievement award awarded as part of an established written plan or program of the taxpayer which does not discriminate in favor of highly compensated employees (within the meaning of section 414(q)) as to eligibility or benefits.

(ii) **Limitation.**—An employee achievement award shall not be treated as a qualified plan award for any taxable year if the average cost of all employee achievement awards which are provided by the employer during the year, and which would be qualified plan awards but for this subparagraph, exceeds $400. For purposes of the preceding sentence, average cost shall be determined by including the entire cost of qualified plan awards, without taking into account employee achievement awards of nominal value.

(4) Special rules.—For purposes of this subsection—

(A) Partnerships.—In the case of an employee achievement award made by a partnership, the deduction limitations contained in paragraph (2) shall apply to the partnership as well as to each member thereof.

(B) Length of service awards.—An item shall not be treated as having been provided for length of service achievement if the item is received during the recipient's 1st 5 years of employment or if the recipient received a length of service achievement award (other than an award excludable under section 132(e)(1)) during that year or any of the prior 4 years.

(C) Safety achievement awards.—An item provided by an employer to an employee shall not be treated as having been provided for safety achievement if—

(i) during the taxable year, employee achievement awards (other than awards excludable under section 132(e)(1)) for safety achievement have previously been awarded by the employer to more than 10 percent of the employees of the employer (excluding employees described in clause (ii)), or

(ii) such item is awarded to a manager, administrator, clerical employee, or other professional employee.

(i) **Qualified nonpersonal use vehicle.**—For purposes of subsection (d), the term "qualified nonpersonal use vehicle" means any vehicle which, by reason of its nature, is not likely to be used more than a de minimis amount for personal purposes.

(k) **Business meals.—**

(1) **In general.**—No deduction shall be allowed under this chapter for the expense of any food or beverages unless—

(A) such expense is not lavish or extravagant under the circumstances, and

(B) the taxpayer (or an employee of the taxpayer) is present at the furnishing of such food or beverages.

(2) **Exceptions.**—Paragraph (1) shall not apply to any expense if subsection (a) does not apply to such expense by reason of paragraph (2), (3), (4), (7), (8), or (9) of subsection (e).

(*l*) **Additional limitations on entertainment tickets.—**

(1) **Entertainment tickets.—**

(A) **In general.**—In determining the amount allowable as a deduction under this chapter for any ticket for any activity or facility described in subsection (d)(2), the amount taken into account shall not exceed the face value of such ticket.

(B) **Exception for certain charitable sports events.**—Subparagraph (A) shall not apply to any ticket for any sports event—

(i) which is organized for the primary purpose of benefiting an organization which is described in section 501(c)(3) and exempt from tax under section 501(a),

(ii) all of the net proceeds of which are contributed to such organization, and

(iii) which utilizes volunteers for substantially all of the work performed in carrying out such event.

(2) **Skyboxes, etc.—**

(A) **In general.**—In the case of a skybox or other private luxury box leased for more than 1 event, the amount allowable as a deduction under this chapter with respect to such events shall not exceed the sum of the face value of non-luxury box seat tickets for the seats in such box covered by the lease. For purposes of the preceding sentence, 2 or more related leases shall be treated as 1 lease.

(B) **Phasein.**—In the case of—

(i) a taxable year beginning in 1987, the amount disallowed under subparagraph (A) shall be 1/3 of the amount which would be disallowed without regard to this subparagraph, and

(ii) in the case of a taxable year beginning in 1988, the amount disallowed under subparagraph (A) shall be 2/3 of the amount which would have been disallowed without regard to this subparagraph.

(m) **Additional limitations on travel expenses.—**

(1) **Luxury water transportation.—**

(A) **In general.**—No deduction shall be allowed under this chapter for expenses incurred for transportation by water to the extent such expenses exceed twice the aggregate per diem amounts for days of such transportation. For purposes of the preceding sentence, the term "per diem amounts" means the highest amount generally allowable with respect to a day to employees of the executive branch of the Federal Government for per diem while away from home but serving in the United States.

(B) **Exceptions.**—Subparagraph (A) shall not apply to—

(i) any expense allocable to a convention, seminar, or other meeting which is held on any cruise ship, and

(ii) any expense to which subsection (a) does not apply by reason of paragraph (2), (3), (4), (7), (8), or (9) of subsection (e).

(2) **Travel as form of education.**—No deduction shall be allowed under this chapter for expenses for travel as a form of education.

(n) **Only 80 percent of meal and entertainment expenses allowed as deduction.**—

(1) **In general.**—The amount allowable as a deduction under this chapter for—

(A) any expense for food or beverages, and

(B) any item with respect to an activity which is of a type generally considered to constitute entertainment, amusement, or recreation, or with respect to a facility used in connection with such activity,

shall not exceed 80 percent of the amount of such expense or item which would (but for this paragraph) be allowable as a deduction under this chapter.

(2) **Exceptions.**—Paragraph (1) shall not apply to any expense if—

(A) subsection (a) does not apply to such expense by reason of paragraph (2), (3), (4), (7), (8), or (9) of subsection (e),

(B) in the case of an expense for food or beverages, such expense is excludable from the gross income of the recipient under section 132 by reason of subsection (e) thereof (relating to de minimis fringes),

(C) such expense is covered by a package involving a ticket described in subsection (l)(1)(B), or

(D) in the case of an expense for food or beverages before January 1, 1989, such expense is an integral part of a qualified meeting.

(3) **Qualified meeting.**—For purposes of paragraph (2)(D), the term "qualified meeting" means any convention, seminar, annual meeting, or similar business program with respect to which—

(A) an expense for food or beverages is not separately stated,

(B) more than 50 percent of the participants are away from home,

(C) at least 40 individuals attend, and

(D) such food and beverages are part of a program which includes a speaker.

(o) **Regulatory authority.**—The Secretary shall prescribe such regulations as he may deem necessary to carry out the purposes of this section, including regulations prescribing whether subsection (a) or subsection (b) applies in cases where both such subsections would otherwise apply.

§ 275. Certain taxes

(a) **General rule.**—No deduction shall be allowed for the following taxes:

(1) Federal income taxes, including—

(A) the tax imposed by section 3101 (relating to the tax on employees under the Federal Insurance Contributions Act);

(B) the taxes imposed by sections 3201 and 3211 (relating to the taxes on railroad employees and railroad employee representatives); and

(C) the tax withheld at source on wages under section 3402.

(2) Federal war profits and excess profits taxes.

(3) Estate, inheritance, legacy, succession, and gift taxes.

* * *

(5) Taxes on real property, to the extent that section 164(d) requires such taxes to be treated as imposed on another taxpayer.

* * *

(b) Cross reference.—

For disallowance of certain other taxes, see section 164(c).

§ 279. Interest on indebtedness incurred by corporation to acquire stock or assets of another corporation

(a) General rule.—No deduction shall be allowed for any interest paid or incurred by a corporation during the taxable year with respect to its corporate acquisition indebtedness to the extent that such interest exceeds—

(1) $5,000,000, reduced by

(2) the amount of interest paid or incurred by such corporation during such year on obligations (A) issued after December 31, 1967, to provide consideration for an acquisition described in paragraph (1) of subsection (b), but (B) which are not corporate acquisition indebtedness.

(b) Corporate acquisition indebtedness.—For purposes of this section, the term "corporate acquisition indebtedness" means any obligation evidenced by a bond, debenture, note, or certificate or other evidence of indebtedness issued after October 9, 1969, by a corporation (hereinafter in this section referred to as "issuing corporation") if—

(1) such obligation is issued to provide consideration for the acquisition of—

(A) stock in another corporation (hereinafter in this section referred to as "acquired corporation"), or

(B) assets of another corporation (hereinafter in this section referred to as "acquired corporation") pursuant to a plan under which at least two-thirds (in value) of all the assets (excluding money) used in trades and businesses carried on by such corporation are acquired,

(2) such obligation is either—

(A) subordinated to the claims of trade creditors of the issuing corporation generally, or

(B) expressly subordinated in right of payment to the payment of any substantial amount of unsecured indebtedness, whether outstanding or subsequently issued, of the issuing corporation,

(3) the bond or other evidence of indebtedness is either—

(A) convertible directly or indirectly into stock of the issuing corporation, or

(B) part of an investment unit or other arrangement which includes, in addition to such bond or other evidence of indebtedness, an option to acquire, directly or indirectly, stock in the issuing corporation, and

(4) as of a day determined under subsection (c)(1), either—

(A) the ratio of debt to equity (as defined in subsection (c)(2) of the issuing corporation exceeds 2 to 1, or

(B) the projected earnings (as defined in subsection (c)(3)) do not exceed 3 times the annual interest to be paid or incurred (determined under subsection (c)(4)).

(c) Rules for application of subsection (b)(4).—For purposes of subsection (b)(4)—

(1) Time of determination.—Determinations are to be made as of the last day of any taxable year of the issuing corporation in which it issues any obligation to provide consideration for an acquisition described in subsection (b)(1) of stock in, or assets of, the acquired corporation.

(2) Ratio of debt to equity.—The term "ratio of debt to equity" means the ratio which the total indebtedness of the issuing corporation bears to the sum of its money and all its other assets (in an amount equal to their adjusted basis for determining gain) less such total indebtedness.

(3) Projected earnings.—

(A) The term "projected earnings" means the "average annual earnings" (as defined in subparagraph (B)) of—

(i) the issuing corporation only, if clause (ii) does not apply, or

(ii) both the issuing corporation and the acquired corporation, in any case where the issuing corporation has acquired control (as defined in section 368(c)), or has acquired substantially all of the properties, of the acquired corporation.

(B) The average annual earnings referred to in subparagraph (A) is, for any corporation, the amount of its earnings and profits for any 3-year period ending with the last day of a taxable year of the issuing corporation described in paragraph (1), computed without reduction for—

(i) interest paid or incurred,

(ii) depreciation or amortization allowed under this chapter,

(iii) liability for tax under this chapter, and

(iv) distributions to which section 301(c)(1) applies (other than such distributions from the acquired to the issuing corporation),

and reduced to an annual average for such 3-year period pursuant to regulations prescribed by the Secretary. Such regulations shall include rules for cases where any corporation was not in existence for all of such 3-year period or such period includes only a portion of a taxable year of any corporation.

(4) Annual interest to be paid or incurred.—The term "annual interest to be paid or incurred" means—

(A) if subparagraph (B) does not apply, the annual interest to be paid or incurred by the issuing corporation only, determined by reference to its total indebtedness outstanding, or

(B) if projected earnings are determined under clause (ii) of paragraph (3)(A), the annual interest to be paid or incurred by both the issuing corporation and the acquired corporation, determined by reference to their combined total indebtedness outstanding.

(5) Special rules for banks and lending or finance companies.—With respect to any corporation which is a bank (as defined in section 581) or is primarily engaged in a lending or finance business—

(A) in determining under paragraph (2) the ratio of debt to equity of such corporation (or of the affiliated group of which such corporation is a member), the total indebtedness of such corporation (and the assets of such corporation) shall be reduced by an amount equal to the total indebtedness owed to such corporation which arises out of the banking business of such corporation, or out of the lending or finance business of such corporation, as the case may be;

(B) in determining under paragraph (4) the annual interest to be paid or incurred by such corporation (or by the issuing and acquired corporations referred to in paragraph (4)(B) or by the affiliated group of which such corporation is a member) the amount of such interest (determined without regard to this paragraph) shall be reduced by an amount which bears the same ratio to the amount of such interest as the amount of the reduction for the taxable year under subparagraph (A) bears to the total indebtedness of such corporation; and

(C) in determining under paragraph (3)(B) the average annual earnings, the amount of the earnings and profits for the 3-year period shall be reduced by the sum of the reductions under subparagraph (B) for such period.

For purposes of this paragraph, the term "lending or finance business" means a business of making loans or purchasing or discounting accounts receivable, notes, or installment obligations.

(d) Table years to which applicable.—In applying this section—

(1) First year of disallowance.—The deduction of interest on any obligation shall not be disallowed under subsection (a) before the first taxable year of the issuing corporation as of the last day of which the application of either subparagraph (A) or subparagraph (B) of subsection (b)(4) results in such obligation being corporate acquisition indebtedness.

(2) General rule for succeeding years.—Except as provided in paragraphs (3), (4), and (5), if an obligation is determined to be corporate acquisition indebtedness as of the last day of any taxable year of the issuing corporation, it shall be corporate acquisition indebtedness for such taxable year and all subsequent taxable years.

(3) Redetermination where control, etc., is acquired.—If an obligation is determined to be corporate acquisition indebtedness as of the close of a taxable year of the issuing corporation in which clause (i) of subsection (c)(3)(A) applied, but would not be corporate acquisition indebtedness if the determination were made as of the close of the first taxable year of such corporation thereafter in which clause (ii) of subsection (c)(3)(A) could apply, such obligation shall be considered not to be corporate acquisition indebtedness for such later taxable year and all taxable years thereafter.

(4) Special 3-year rule.—If an obligation which has been determined to be corporate acquisition indebtedness for any taxable year would not be such indebtedness for each of any 3 consecutive taxable years thereafter if subsection (b)(4) were applied as of the close of each of such 3 years, then such obligation shall not be corporate acquisition indebtedness for all taxable years after such 3 consecutive taxable years.

(5) 5 percent stock rule.—In the case of obligations issued to provide consideration for the acquisition of stock in another corporation, such obligations shall be corporate acquisition indebtedness for a taxable year only if at some time after October 9, 1969, and before the close of such year the issuing corporation owns 5 percent or more of the total combined voting power of all classes of stock entitled to vote of such other corporation.

(e) **Certain nontaxable transactions.**—An acquisition of stock of a corporation of which the issuing corporation is in control (as defined in section 368(c)) in a transaction in which gain or loss is not recognized shall be deemed an acquisition described in paragraph (1) of subsection (b) only if immediately before such transaction (1) the acquired corporation was in existence, and (2) the issuing corporation was not in control (as defined in section 368(c)) of such corporation.

(f) **Exemption for certain acquisitions of foreign corporations.**—For purposes of this section, the term "corporate acquisition indebtedness" does not include any indebtedness issued to any person to provide consideration for the acquisition of stock in, or assets of, any foreign corporation substantially all of the income of which, for the 3-year period ending with the date of such acquisition or for such part of such period as the foreign corporation was in existence, is from sources without the United States.

(g) **Affiliated groups.**—In any case in which the issuing corporation is a member of an affiliated group, the application of this section shall be determined, pursuant to regulations prescribed by the Secretary, by treating all of the members of the affiliated group in the aggregate as the issuing corporation, except that the ratio of debt to equity of, projected earnings of, and annual interest to be paid or incurred by any corporation (other than the issuing corporation determined without regard to this subsection) shall be included in the determinations required under subparagraphs (A) and (B) of subsection (b)(4) as of any day only if such corporation is a member of the affiliated group on such day, and, in determining projected earnings of such corporation under subsection (c)(3), there shall be taken into account only the earnings and profits of such corporation for the period during which it was a member of the affiliated group. For purposes of the preceding sentence, the term "affiliated group" has the meaning assigned to such term by section 1504(a), except that all corporations other than the acquired corporation shall be treated as includible corporations (without any exclusion under section 1504(b)) and the acquired corporation shall not be treated as an includible corporation.

(h) **Changes in obligation.**—For purposes of this section—

(1) Any extension, renewal, or refinancing of an obligation evidencing a preexisting indebtedness shall not be deemed to be the issuance of a new obligation.

(2) Any obligation which is corporate acquisition indebtedness of the issuing corporation is also corporate acquisition indebtedness of any corporation which becomes liable for such obligation as guarantor, endorser, or indemnitor or which assumes liability for such obligation in any transaction.

(i) **Certain obligations issued after October 9, 1969.**—For purposes of this section, an obligation shall not be corporate acquisition indebtedness if issued after October 9, 1969, to provide consideration for the acquisition of—

(1) stock or assets pursuant to a binding written contract which was in effect on October 9, 1969, and at all times thereafter before such acquisition, or

(2) stock in any corporation where the issuing corporation, on October 9, 1969, and at all times thereafter before such acquisition, owned at least 50 percent of the total combined voting power of all classes of stock entitled to vote of the acquired corporation.

(j) **Effect on other provisions.**—No inference shall be drawn from any provision in this section that any instrument designated as a bond, debenture, note, or certificate or other evidence of indebtedness by its issuer represents an obligation or indebtedness of such issuer in applying any other provision of this title.

§ 280A. Disallowance of certain expenses in connection with business use of home, rental of vacation homes, etc.

(a) General rule.—Except as otherwise provided in this section, in the case of a taxpayer who is an individual or an S corporation, no deduction otherwise allowable under this chapter shall be allowed with respect to the use of a dwelling unit which is used by the taxpayer during the taxable year as a residence.

(b) Exception for interest, taxes, casualty losses, etc.—Subsection (a) shall not apply to any deduction allowable to the taxpayer without regard to its connection with his trade or business (or with his income-producing activity).

(c) Exceptions for certain business or rental use; limitation on deductions for such use.—

(1) Certain business use.—Subsection (a) shall not apply to any item to the extent such item is allocable to a portion of the dwelling unit which is exclusively used on a regular basis—

(A) the principal place of business for any trade or business of the taxpayer.

(B) as a place of business which is used by patients, clients, or customers in meeting or dealing with the taxpayer in the normal course of his trade or business, or

(C) in the case of a separate structure which is not attached to the dwelling unit, in connection with the taxpayer's trade or business.

In the case of an employee, the preceding sentence shall apply only if the exclusive use referred to in the preceding sentence is for the convenience of his employer.

(2) Certain storage use.—Subsection (a) shall not apply to any item to the extent such item is allocable to space within the dwelling unit which is used on a regular basis as a storage unit for the inventory of the taxpayer held for use in the taxpayer's trade or business of selling products at retail or wholesale, but only if the dwelling unit is the sole fixed location of such trade or business.

(3) Rental use.—Subsection (a) shall not apply to any item which is attributable to the rental of the dwelling unit or portion thereof (determined after the application of subsection (e)).

(4) Use in providing day care services.—

(A) In general.—Subsection (a) shall not apply to any item to the extent that such item is allocable to the use of any portion of the dwelling unit on a regular basis in the taxpayer's trade or business of providing day care for children, for individuals who have attained age 65, or for individuals who are physically or mentally incapable of caring for themselves.

(B) Licensing, etc., requirement.—Subparagraph (A) shall apply to items accruing for a period only if the owner or operator of the trade or business referred to in subparagraph (A)—

(i) has applied for (and such application has not been rejected),

(ii) has been granted (and such granting has not been revoked), or

(iii) is exempt from having,

a license, certification, registration, or approval as a day care center or as a family or group day care home under the provisions of any applicable State law. This subparagraph shall apply only to items accruing in periods beginning on or after the first day of the first month which begins more than 90 days after the date of the enactment of the Tax Reduction and Simplification Act of 1977.

(C) Allocation formula.—If a portion of the taxpayer's dwelling unit used for the purposes described in subparagraph (A) is not used exclusively for those purposes, the amount of the expenses attributable to that portion shall not exceed an amount which bears the same ratio to the total amount of the items allocable to such portion as the number of hours the portion is used for such purposes bears to the number of hours the portion is available for use.

(5) Limitation on deductions.—In the case of a use described in paragraph (1), (2), or (4), and in the case of a use described in paragraph (3) where the dwelling unit is used by the taxpayer during the taxable year as a residence, the deductions allowed under this chapter for the taxable year by reason of being attributed to such use shall not exceed the excess of—

(A) the gross income derived from such use for the taxable year, over

(B) the sum of—

(i) the deductions allocable to such use which are allowable under this chapter for the taxable year whether or not such unit (or portion thereof) was so used, and

(ii) the deductions allocable to the trade or business in which such use occurs (but which are not allocable to such use) for such taxable year.

Any amount not allowable as a deduction under this chapter by reason of the preceding sentence shall be taken into account as a deduction (allocable to such use) under this chapter for the succeeding taxable year.

(6) Treatment of rental to employer.—Paragraphs (1) and (3) shall not apply to any item which is attributable to the rental of the dwelling unit (or any portion thereof) by the taxpayer to his employer during any period in which the taxpayer uses the dwelling unit (or portion) in performing services as an employee of the employer.

(d) Use as residence.—

(1) In general.—For purposes of this section, a taxpayer uses a dwelling unit during the taxable year as a residence if he uses such unit (or portion thereof) for personal purposes for a number of days which exceeds the greater of—

(A) 14 days, or

(B) 10 percent of the number of days during such year for which such unit is rented at a fair rental.

For purposes of subparagraph (B), a unit shall not be treated as rented at a fair rental for any day for which it is used for personal purposes.

(2) Personal use of unit.—For purposes of this section, the taxpayer shall be deemed to have used a dwelling unit for personal purposes for a day if, for any part of such day, the unit is used—

(A) for personal purposes by the taxpayer or any other person who has an interest in such unit, or by any member of the family (as defined in section 267(c)(4)) of the taxpayer or such other person;

(B) by any individual who uses the unit under an arrangement which enables the taxpayer to use some other dwelling unit (whether or not a rental is charged for the use of such other unit); or

(C) by any individual (other than an employee with respect to whose use section 119 applies), unless for such day the dwelling unit is rented for a rental which, under the facts and circumstances, is fair rental.

The Secretary shall prescribe regulations with respect to the circumstances under which use of the unit for repairs and annual maintenance will not constitute personal use under this paragraph, except that if the taxpayer is engaged in repair and maintenance on a substantially full time basis for any day, such authority shall not allow the Secretary to treat a dwelling unit as being used for personal use by the taxpayer on such day merely because other individuals who are on the premises on such day are not so engaged.

(3) Rental to family member, etc., for use as principal residence.—

(A) In general.—A taxpayer shall not be treated as using a dwelling unit for personal purposes by reason of a rental arrangement for any period if for such period such dwelling unit is rented, at a fair rental, to any person for use as such person's principal residence.

(B) Special rules for rental to person having interest in unit.—

(i) Rental must be pursuant to shared equity financing agreement. —Subparagraph (A) shall apply to a rental to a person who has an interest in the dwelling unit only if such rental is pursuant to a shared equity financing agreement.

(ii) Determination of fair rental.—In the case of a rental pursuant to a shared equity financing agreement, fair rental shall be determined as of the time the agreement is entered into and by taking into account the occupant's qualified ownership interest.

(C) Shared equity financing agreement.—For purposes of this paragraph, the term "shared equity financing agreement" means an agreement under which—

(i) 2 or more persons acquire qualified ownership interests in a dwelling unit, and

(ii) the person (or persons) holding 1 or more of such interests—

(I) is entitled to occupy the dwelling unit for use as a principal residence, and

(II) is required to pay rent to 1 or more other persons holding qualified ownership interests in the dwelling unit.

(D) Qualified ownership interest.—For purposes of this paragraph, the term "qualified ownership interest" means an undivided interest for more than 50 years in the entire dwelling unit and appurtenant land being acquired in the transaction to which the shared equity financing agreement relates.

(4) Rental of principal residence.—

(A) In general.—For purposes of applying subsection (c) (5) to deductions allocable to a qualified rental period, a taxpayer shall not be considered to have used a dwelling unit for personal purposes for any day during the taxable year which occurs before or after a qualified rental period described in subparagraph (B) (i), or before a qualified rental period described in subparagraph (B) (ii), if with respect to such day such unit constitutes the principal residence (within the meaning of section 1034) of the taxpayer.

(B) Qualified rental period.—For purposes of subparagraph (A), the term "qualified rental period" means a consecutive period of—

(i) 12 or more months which begins or ends in such taxable year, or

(ii) less than 12 months which begins in such taxable year and at the end of which such dwelling unit is sold or exchanged, and

for which such unit is rented, or is held for rental, at a fair rental.

(e) Expenses attributable to rental.—

(1) In general.—In any case where a taxpayer who is an individual or an S corporation uses a dwelling unit for personal purposes on any day during the taxable year (whether or not he is treated under this section as using such unit as a residence), the amount deductible under this chapter with respect to expenses attributable to the rental of the unit (or portion thereof) for the taxable year shall not exceed an amount which bears the same relationship to such expenses as the number of days during each year that the unit (or portion thereof) is rented at a fair rental bears to the total number of days during such year that the unit (or portion thereof) is used.

(2) Exception for deductions otherwise allowable.—This subsection shall not apply with respect to deductions which would be allowable under this chapter for the taxable year whether or not such unit (or portion thereof) was rented.

(f) Definitions and special rules.—

(1) Dwelling unit defined.—For purposes of this section—

(A) In general.—The term "dwelling unit" includes a house, apartment, condominium, mobile home, boat, or similar property, and all structures or other property appurtenant to such dwelling unit.

(B) Exception.—The term "dwelling unit" does not include that portion of a unit which is used exclusively as a hotel, motel, inn, or similar establishment.

(2) Personal use by shareholders of S corporation.—In the case of an S corporation, subparagraphs (A) and (B) of subsection (d) (2) shall be applied by substituting "any shareholder of the S corporation" for "the taxpayer" each place it appears.

(3) Coordination with section 183.—If subsection (a) applies with respect to any dwelling unit (or portion thereof) for the taxable year—

(A) section 183 (relating to activities not engaged in for profit) shall not apply to such unit (or portion thereof) for such year, but

(B) such year shall be taken into account as a taxable year for purposes of applying subsection (d) of section 183 (relating to 5-year presumption).

(4) Coordination with section 162(a)(2).—Nothing in this section shall be construed to disallow any deduction allowable under section 162(a)(2) (or any deduction which meets the tests of section 162(a)(2) but is allowable under another provision of this title) by reason of the taxpayer's being away from home in the pursuit of a trade or business (other than the trade or business of renting dwelling units).

(g) Special rule for certain rental use.—

Notwithstanding any other provision of this section or section 183, if a dwelling unit is used during the taxable year by the taxpayer as a residence and such dwelling unit is actually rented for less than 15 days during the taxable year, then—

(1) no deduction otherwise allowable under this chapter because of the rental use of such dwelling unit shall be allowed, and

(2) the income derived from such use for the taxable year shall not be included in the gross income of such taxpayer under section 61.

§ 280B. Demolition of structures

In the case of the demolition of any structure—

(1) no deduction otherwise allowable under this chapter shall be allowed to the owner or lessee of such structure for—

(A) any amount expended for such demolition, or

(B) any loss sustained on account of such demolition; and

(2) amounts described in paragraph (1) shall be treated as properly chargeable to capital account with respect to the land on which the demolished structure was located.

* * *

§ 280E. Expenditures in connection with the illegal sale of drugs

No deduction or credit shall be allowed for any amount paid or incurred during the taxable year in carrying on any trade or business if such trade or business (or the activities which comprise such trade or business) consists of trafficking in controlled substances (within the meaning of schedule I and II of the Controlled Substances Act) which is prohibited by Federal law or the law of any State in which such trade or business is conducted.

§ 280F. Limitation on investment tax credit and depreciation for luxury automobiles; limitation where certain property used for personal purposes

(a) Limitation on amount of investment tax credit and depreciation for luxury automobiles.—

(1) **Investment tax credit.**—The amount of the credit determined under section 46(a) for any passenger automobile shall not exceed $675.

(2) **Depreciation.**—

(A) **Limitation.**—The amount of the depreciation deduction for any taxable year for any passenger automobile shall not exceed—

(i) $2,560 for the 1st taxable year in the recovery period,

(ii) $4,100 for the 2nd taxable year in the recovery period,

(iii) $2,450 for the 3rd taxable year in the recovery period, and

(iv) $1,475 for each succeeding taxable year in the recovery period.

(B) **Disallowed deductions allowed for years after recovery period.**—

(i) **In general.**—Except as provided in clause (ii), the unrecovered basis of any passenger automobile shall be treated as an expense for the 1st taxable year after the recovery period. Any excess of the unrecovered basis over the limitation of clause (ii) shall be treated as an expense in the succeeding taxable year.

(ii) **$1,475 limitation.**—The amount treated as an expense under clause (i) for any taxable year shall not exceed $1,475.

(iii) **Property must be depreciable.**—No amount shall be allowable as a deduction by reason of this subparagraph with respect to any property for any taxable year unless a depreciation deduction would be allowable with respect to such property for such taxable year.

(iv) **Amount treated as recovery deduction.**—For purposes of this subtitle, any amount allowable as a deduction by reason of this subparagraph shall be treated as a depreciation deduction allowable under section 168.

(3) Coordination with reductions in amount allowable by reason of personal use, etc.—This subsection shall be applied before—

(A) the application of subsection (b), and

(B) the application of any other reduction in the amount of the credit determined under section 46(a) or any depreciation deduction allowable under section 168 by reason of any use not qualifying the property for such credit or depreciation deduction.

(4) Special rule where election of reduced credit in lieu of the basis adjustment.—In the case of any election under section 48(q)(4) with respect to any passenger automobile, the limitation of paragraph (1) applicable to such passenger automobile shall be $\frac{2}{3}$ of the amount which would be so applicable but for this paragraph.

(b) Limitation where business use of listed property not greater than 50 percent.—

(1) Investment tax credit.—For purposes of this subtitle, any listed property shall not be treated as section 38 property for any taxable year unless such property is predominantly used in a qualified business use for such taxable year.

(2) Depreciation.—If any listed property is not predominantly used in a qualified business use for any taxable year, the deduction allowed under section 168 with respect to such property for such taxable year and any subsequent taxable year shall be determined under section 168(g) (relating to alternative depreciation system).

(3) Recapture.—

(A) Where business use percentage does not exceed 50 percent.—If—

(i) property is predominantly used in a qualified business use in a taxable year in which it is placed in service, and

(ii) such property is not predominantly used in a qualified business use for any subsequent taxable year,

then any excess depreciation shall be included in gross income for the taxable year referred to in clause (ii), and the depreciation deduction for the taxable year referred to in clause (ii) and any subsequent taxable years shall be determined under section 168(g) (relating to alternative depreciation system).

(B) Excess depreciation.—For purposes of subparagraph (A), the term "excess depreciation" means the excess (if any) of—

(i) the amount of the recovery deductions [1] allowable with respect to the property for taxable years before the 1st taxable year in which the property was not predominantly used in a qualified business use, over

(ii) the amount which would have been so allowable if the property had not been predominantly used in a qualified business use for the taxable year in which it was placed in service.

(4) Property predominantly used in qualified business use.—For purposes of this subsection, property shall be treated as predominantly used in a qualified business use for any taxable year if the business use percentage for such taxable year exceeds 50 percent.

(c) Treatment of leases.—

---

[1] Probably should be "depreciation deductions".

(1) Lessor's credits and deductions not affected.—This section shall not apply to any listed property leased or held for leasing by any person regularly engaged in the business of leasing such property.

(2) Lessee's deductions reduced.—For purposes of determining the amount allowable as a deduction under this chapter for rentals or other payments under a lease for a period of 30 days or more of listed property, only the allowable percentage of such payments shall be taken into account.

(3) Allowable percentage.—For purposes of paragraph (2), the allowable percentage shall be determined under tables prescribed by the Secretary. Such tables shall be prescribed so that the reduction in the deduction under paragraph (2) is substantially equivalent to the applicable restrictions contained in subsections (a) and (b).

(4) Lease term.—In determining the term of any lease for purposes of paragraph (2), the rules of section 168(i)(3)(A) shall apply.

(5) Lessee recapture.—Under regulations prescribed by the Secretary, rules similar to the rules of subsection (b)(3) shall apply to any lessee to which paragraph (2) applies.

(d) Definitions and special rules.—For purposes of this section—

(1) Coordination with section 179.—Any deduction allowable under section 179 with respect to any listed property shall be subject to the limitations of subsections (a) and (b) in the same manner as if it were a depreciation deduction allowable under section 168.

(2) Subsequent depreciation deductions reduced for deductions allocable to personal use.—Solely for purposes of determining the amount of the depreciation deduction for subsequent taxable years, if less than 100 percent of the use of any listed property during any taxable year is use in a trade or business (including the holding for the production of income), all of the use of such property during such taxable year shall be treated as use so described.

(3) Deductions of employee.—

(A) In general.—Any employee use of listed property shall not be treated as use in a trade or business for purposes of determining the amount of any credit allowable under section 38 to the employee or the amount of any recovery deduction allowable to the employee (or the amount of any deduction allowable to the employee for rentals or other payments under a lease of listed property) unless such use is for the convenience of the employer and required as a condition of employment.

(B) Employee use.—For purposes of subparagraph (A), the term "employee use" means any use in connection with the performance of services as an employee.

(4) Listed property.—

(A) In general.—Except as provided in subparagraph (B), the term "listed property" means—

(i) any passenger automobile,

(ii) any other property used as a means of transportation,

(iii) any property of a type generally used for purposes of entertainment, recreation, or amusement,

(iv) any computer or peripheral equipment (as defined in section 168(i)(2)(B)), and

(v) any other property of a type specified by the Secretary by regulations.

(B) **Exception for certain computers.**—The term "listed property" shall not include any computer or peripheral equipment (as so defined) used exclusively at a regular business establishment and owned or leased by the person operating such establishment. For purposes of the preceding sentence, any portion of a dwelling unit shall be treated as a regular business establishment if (and only if) the requirements of section 280A(c)(1) are met with respect to such portion.

(C) **Exception for property used in business of transporting persons or property.**—Except to the extent provided in regulations, clause (ii) of subparagraph (A) shall not apply to any property substantially all of the use of which is in a trade or business of providing to unrelated persons services consisting of the transportation of persons or property for compensation or hire.

(5) **Passenger automobile.**—

(A) **In general.**—Except as provided in subparagraph (B), the term "passenger automobile" means any 4-wheeled vehicle—

(i) which is manufactured primarily for use on public streets, roads, and highways, and

(ii) which is rated at 6,000 pounds unloaded gross vehicle weight or less.

In the case of a truck or van, clause (ii) shall be applied by substituting "gross vehicle weight" for "unloaded gross vehicle weight".

(B) **Exception for certain vehicles.**—The term "passenger automobile" shall not include—

(i) any ambulance, hearse, or combination ambulance-hearse used by the taxpayer directly in a trade or business,

(ii) any vehicle used by the taxpayer directly in the trade or business of transporting persons or property for compensation or hire, and

(iii) under regulations, any truck or van.

(6) **Business use percentage.**—

(A) **In general.**—The term "business use percentage" means the percentage of the use of any listed property during any taxable year which is a qualified business use.

(B) **Qualified business use.**—Except as provided in subparagraph (C), the term "qualified business use" means any use in a trade or business of the taxpayer.

(C) **Exception for certain use by 5-percent owners and related persons.**—

(i) **In general.**—The term "qualified business use" shall not include—

(I) leasing property to any 5-percent owner or related person,

(II) use of property provided as compensation for the performance of services by a 5-percent owner or related person, or

(II) use of property provided as compensation for the performance of services by any person not described in subclause (II) unless an amount is included in the gross income of such person with respect to such use, and, where required, there was withholding under chapter 24.

(ii) **Special rule for aircraft.**—Clause (i) shall not apply with respect to any aircraft if at least 25 percent of the total use of the aircraft during the taxable year consists of qualified business use not described in clause (i).

(D) Definitions.—For purposes of this paragraph—

(i) 5-percent owner.—The term "5-percent owner" means any person who is a 5-percent owner with respect to the taxpayer (as defined in section 416(i)(1)(B)(i)).

(ii) Related person.—The term "related person" means any person related to the taxpayer (within the meaning of section 267(b)).

(7) Automobile price inflation adjustment.—

(A) In general.—In the case of any passenger automobile placed in service after 1988, subsection (a) shall be applied by increasing each dollar amount contained in such subsection by the automobile price inflation adjustment for the calendar year in which such automobile is placed in service. Any increase under the preceding sentence shall be rounded to the nearest multiple of $100 (or if the increase is a multiple of $50, such increase shall be increased to the next higher multiple of $100).

(B) Automobile price inflation adjustment.—For purposes of this paragraph—

(i) In general.—The automobile price inflation adjustment for any calendar year is the percentage (if any) by which—

(I) the CPI automobile component for October of the preceding calendar year, exceeds

(II) the CPI automobile component for October of 1987.

(ii) CPI automobile component.—The term "CPI automobile component" means the automobile component of the Consumer Price Index for All Urban Consumers published by the Department of Labor.

(8) Unrecovered basis.—For purposes of subsection (a)(2), the term "unrecovered basis" means the adjusted basis of the passenger automobile determined after the application of subsection (a) and as if all use during the recovery period were use in a trade or business (including the holding of property for the production of income).

(9) All taxpayers holding interests in passenger automobile treated as 1 taxpayer.—All taxpayers holding interests in any passenger automobile shall be treated as 1 taxpayer for purposes of applying subsection (a) to such automobile, and the limitations of subsection (a) shall be allocated among such taxpayers in proportion to their interests in such automobile.

(10) Special rule for property acquired in nonrecognition transactions.—For purposes of subsection (a)(2) any property acquired in a nonrecognition transaction shall be treated as a single property originally placed in service in the taxable year in which it was placed in service after being so acquired.

(e) Regulations.—The Secretary shall prescribe such regulations as may be necessary or appropriate to carry out the purposes of this section, including regulations with respect to items properly included in, or excluded from, the adjusted basis of any listed property.

§ 280G. Golden parachute payments

(a) General rule.—No deduction shall be allowed under this chapter for any excess parachute payment.

(b) Excess parachute payment.—For purposes of this section—

(1) In general.—The term "excess parachute payment" means an amount equal to the excess of any parachute payment over the portion of the base amount allocated to such payment.

(2) Parachute payment defined.—

(A) In general.—The term "parachute payment" means any payment in the nature of compensation to (or for the benefit of) a disqualified individual if—

(i) such payment is contingent on a change—

(I) in the ownership or effective control of the corporation, or

(II) in the ownership of a substantial portion of the assets of the corporation, and

(ii) the aggregate present value of the payments in the nature of compensation to (or for the benefit of) such individual which are contingent on such change equals or exceeds an amount equal to 3 times the base amount.

For purposes of clause (ii), payments not treated as parachute payments under paragraph (4)(A), (5), or (6) shall not be taken into account.

(B) Agreements.—The term "parachute payment" shall also include any payment in the nature of compensation to (or for the benefit of) a disqualified individual if such payment is made pursuant to an agreement which violates any generally enforced securities laws or regulations. In any proceeding involving the issue of whether any payment made to a disqualified individual is a parachute payment on account of a violation of any generally enforced securities laws or regulations, the burden of proof with respect to establishing the occurrence of a violation of such a law or regulation shall be upon the Secretary.

(C) Treatment of certain agreements entered into within 1 year before change of ownership.—For purposes of subparagraph (A)(i), any payment pursuant to—

(i) an agreement entered into within 1 year before the change described in subparagraph (A)(i), or

(ii) an amendment made within such 1-year period of a previous agreement,

shall be presumed to be contingent on such change unless the contrary is established by clear and convincing evidence.

(3) Base amount.—

(A) In general.—The term "base amount" means the individual's annualized includible compensation for the base period.

(B) Allocation.—The portion of the base amount allocated to any parachute payment shall be an amount which bears the same ratio to the base amount as—

(i) the present value of such payment, bears to

(ii) the aggregate present value of all such payments.

(4) Treatment of amounts which taxpayer establishes as reasonable compensation.—In the case of any payment described in paragraph (2)(A)—

(A) the amount treated as a parachute payment shall not include the portion of such payment which the taxpayer establishes by clear and convincing evidence is reasonable compensation for personal services to be rendered on or after the date of the change described in paragraph (2)(A)(i), and

(B) the amount treated as an excess parachute payment shall be reduced by the portion of such payment which the taxpayer establishes by clear and convincing evidence is reasonable compensation for personal services actually rendered before the date of the change described in paragraph (2)(A)(i).

For purposes of subparagraph (B), reasonable compensation for services actually rendered before the date of the change described in paragraph (2)(A)(i) shall be first offset against the base amount.

(5) Exemption for small business corporations, etc.—

(A) In general.—Notwithstanding paragraph (2), the term "parachute payment" does not include—

(i) any payment to a disqualified individual with respect to a corporation which (immediately before the change described in paragraph (2)(A)(i)) was a small business corporation (as defined in section 1361(b)), and

(ii) any payment to a disqualified individual with respect to a corporation (other than a corporation described in clause (i)) if—

(I) immediately before the change described in paragraph (2)(A)(i), no stock in such corporation was readily tradeable on an established securities market or otherwise, and

(II) the shareholder approval requirements of subparagraph (B) are met with respect to such payment.

The Secretary may, by regulations, prescribe that the requirements of subclause (I) of clause (ii) are not met where a substantial portion of the assets of any entity consists (directly or indirectly) of stock in such corporation and interests in such other entity are readily tradeable on an established securities market, or otherwise.

(B) Shareholder approval requirements.—The shareholder approval requirements of this subparagraph are met with respect to any payment if—

(i) such payment was approved by a vote of the persons who owned, immediately before the change described in paragraph (2)(A)(i), more than 75 percent of the voting power of all outstanding stock of the corporation, and

(ii) there was adequate disclosure to shareholders of all material facts concerning all payments which (but for this paragraph) would be parachute payments with respect to a disqualified individual."

(6) Exemption for payments under qualified plans.—Notwithstanding paragraph (2), the term "parachute payment" shall not include any payment to or from—

(A) a plan described in section 401(a) which includes a trust exempt from tax under section 501(a),

(B) an annuity plan described in section 403(a), or

(C) a simplified employee pension (as defined in section 408(k)).

(c) Disqualified individuals.—For purposes of this section, the term "disqualified individual" means any individual who is—

(1) an employee, independent contractor, or other person specified in regulations by the Secretary who performs personal services for any corporation, and

(2) is an officer, shareholder, or highly-compensated individual.

For purposes of this section, a personal service corporation (or similar entity) shall be treated as an individual. For purposes of paragraph (2), the term 'highly compensated individual' only includes an individual who is (or would be if the individual were an employee) a member of the group consisting of the highest paid 1 percent of the employees of the corporation or, if less, the highest paid 250 employee of the corporation.

(d) Other definitions and special rules.—For purposes of this section—

(1) Annualized includible compensation for base period.—The term "annualized includible compensation for the base period" means the average annual compensation which—

(A) was payable by the corporation with respect to which the change in ownership or control described in paragraph (2)(A) of subsection (b) occurs, and

(B) was includible in the gross income of the disqualified individual for taxable years in the base period.

(2) Base period.—The term "base period" means the period consisting of the most recent 5 taxable years ending before the date on which the change in ownership or control described in paragraph (2)(A) of subsection (b) occurs (or such portion of such period during which the disqualified individual performed personal services for the corporation).

(3) Property transfers.—Any transfer of property—

(A) shall be treated as a payment, and

(B) shall be taken into account as its fair market value.

(4) Present value.—Present value shall be determined by using a discount rate equal to 120 percent of the applicable Federal rate (determined under section 1274(d)), compounded semiannually."

(5) Treatment of affiliated groups.—Except as otherwise provided in regulations, all members of the same affiliated group (as defined in section 1504, determined without regard to section 1504(b)) shall be treated as 1 corporation for purposes of this section. Any person who is an officer or any member of such group shall be treated as an officer of such 1 corporation.

(e) Regulations.—The Secretary shall prescribe such regulations as may be necessary or appropriate to carry out the purposes of this section (including regulations for the application of this section in the case of related corporations and in the case of personal service corporations).

PART XI—SPECIAL RULES RELATING TO CORPORATE PREFERENCE ITEMS

§ 291. Special rules relating to corporate preference items

(a) reduction [1] in certain preference items, etc.—For purposes of this subtitle, in the case of a corporation—

(1) Section 1250 capital gain treatment.—In the case of section 1250 property which is disposed of during the taxable year, 20 percent of the excess (if any) of—

(A) the amount which would be treated as ordinary income if such property was section 1245 property, over

(B) the amount treated as ordinary income under section 1250 (determined without regard to this paragraph),

shall be treated as gain which is ordinary income under section 1250 and shall be recognized notwithstanding any other provision of this title. Under regulations prescribed by the Secretary, the provisions of this paragraph shall not apply to the

[1] Editor's Note: Probably should be "Reduction".

disposition of any property to the extent section 1250(a) does not apply to such disposition by reason of section 1250(d).

(2) Reduction in percentage depletion.—In the case of iron ore and coal (including lignite), the amount allowable as a deduction under section 613 with respect to any property (as defined in section 614) shall be reduced by 20 percent of the amount of the excess (if any) of—

(A) the amount of the deduction allowable under section 613 for the taxable year (determined without regard to this paragraph), over

(B) the adjusted basis of the property at the close of the taxable year (determined without regard to the depletion deduction for the taxable year).

* * *

(b) Special rules for treatment of intangible drilling costs and mineral exploration and development costs.—For purposes of this subtitle, in the case of a corporation—

(1) In general.—The amount allowable as a deduction for any taxable year (determined without regard to this section)—

(A) under section 263(c) in the case of an integrated oil company, or

(B) under section 616(a) or 617(a).

shall be reduced by 30 percent.

(2) Amortization of amounts not allowable as deductions under paragraph (1).—The amount not allowable as a deduction under section 263(c), 616(a), or 617(a) (as the case may be) for any taxable year by reason of paragraph (1) shall be allowable as a deduction ratably over the 60–month period beginning with the month in which the costs are paid or incurred.

(3) Dispositions.—For purposes of section 1254, any deduction under paragraph (2) shall be treated as a deduction allowable under section 263(c), 616(a), or 617(a) (whichever is appropriate).

(4) Integrated oil company defined.—For purposes of this subsection, the term "integrated oil company" means, with respect to any taxable year, any producer (within the meaning of section 4996(a)(1)) of crude oil other than an independent producer (within the meaning of section 4992(b)).

(5) Coordination with cost depletion.—The portion of the adjusted basis of any property which is attributable to amounts to which paragraph (1) applied shall not be taken into account for purposes of determining depletion under section 611.

* * *

SUBCHAPTER C—CORPORATE DISTRIBUTIONS AND ADJUSTMENTS

PART I—DISTRIBUTIONS BY CORPORATIONS

* Omitted entirely.

Subpart
A. Effects on recipients.
B. Effects on corporation.
C. Definitions; constructive ownership of stock.

Subpart A—Effects on Recipients

§ 301. Distributions of property

(a) **In general.**—Except as otherwise provided in this chapter, a distribution of property (as defined in section 317(a)) made by a corporation to a shareholder with respect to its stock shall be treated in the manner provided in subsection (c).

(b) **Amount distributed.**—

(1) **General rule.**—For purposes of this section, the amount of any distribution shall be—

(A) **Noncorporate distributees.**—If the shareholder is not a corporation, the amount of money received, plus the fair market value of the other property received.

(B) **Corporate distributees.**—If the shareholder is a corporation, unless subparagraph (D) applies, the amount of money received, plus whichever of the following is the lesser:

(i) the fair market value of the other property received; or

(ii) the adjusted basis (in the hands of the distributing corporation immediately before the distribution) of the other property received, increased in the amount of gain recognized to the distributing corporation on the distribution.

* * *

(2) **Reduction for liabilities.**—The amount of any distribution determined under paragraph (1) shall be reduced (but not below zero) by—

(A) the amount of any liability of the corporation assumed by the shareholder in connection with the distribution, and

(B) the amount of any liability to which the property received by the shareholder is subject immediately before, and immediately after, the distribution.

(3) **Determination of fair market value.**—For purposes of this section, fair market value shall be determined as of the date of the distribution.

(c) **Amount taxable.**—In the case of a distribution to which subsection (a) applies—

(1) **Amount constituting dividend.**—That portion of the distribution which is a dividend (as defined in section 316) shall be included in gross income.

(2) **Amount applied against basis.**—That portion of the distribution which is not a dividend shall be applied against and reduce the adjusted basis of the stock.

(3) **Amount in excess of basis.**—

(A) **In general.**—Except as provided in subparagraph (B), that portion of the distribution which is not a dividend, to the extent that it exceeds the adjusted basis of the stock, shall be treated as gain from the sale or exchange of property.

(B) **Distributions out of increase in value accrued before March 1, 1913.** —That portion of the distribution which is not a dividend, to the extent that it exceeds the adjusted basis of the stock and to the extent that it is out of increase in value accrued before March 1, 1913, shall be exempt from tax.

(d) Basis.—The basis of property received in a distribution to which subsection (a) applies shall be—

(1) Noncorporate distributees.—If the shareholder is not a corporation, the fair market value of such property.

(2) Corporate distributees.—If the shareholder is a corporation, unless paragraph (3) applies, whichever of the following is the lesser:

(A) the fair market value of such property; or

(B) the adjusted basis (in the hands of the distributing corporation immediately before the distribution) of such property, increased in the amount of gain recognized to the distributing corporation on the distribution.

* * *

(e) Special rule for holding period of appreciated property distributed to corporation.—For purposes of this subtitle—

(1) Where gain recognized under section 311(d).—If—

(A) property is distributed to a corporation, and

(B) gain is recognized on such distribution under paragraph (1) of section 311(d),

then such corporation's holding period in the distributed property shall begin on the date of such distribution.

(2) Where gain not recognized under section 311(d).—If—

(A) property is distributed to a corporation,

(B) gain is not recognized on such distribution under paragraph (1) of section 311(d), and

(C) the basis of such property in the hands of such corporation is determined under subsection (d)(2)(B),

then (except for purposes of section 1248) such corporation shall not be treated as holding the distributed property during any period before the date on which such corporation's holding period in the stock began.

(f) Special rule for certain distributions received by 20 percent corporate shareholder.—

(1) In general.—Except to the extent otherwise provided in regulations, solely for purposes of determining the taxable income of any 20 percent corporate shareholder (and its adjusted basis in the stock of the distributing corporation), section 312 shall be applied with respect to the distributing corporation as if it did not contain subsection (n) thereof.

(2) 20 percent corporate shareholder.—For purposes of this subsection, the term "20 percent corporate shareholder" means, with respect to any distribution, any corporation which owns (directly or through the application of section 318)—

(A) stock in the corporation making the distribution possessing at least 20 percent of the total combined voting power of all classes of stock entitled to vote, or

(B) at least 20 percent of the total value of all stock of the distributing corporation (except nonvoting stock which is limited and preferred as to dividends), but only if, but for this subsection, the distributee corporation would be entitled to a deduction under section 243, 244, or 245 with respect to such distribution.

(3) Regulations.—The Secretary shall prescribe such regulations as may be necessary or appropriate to carry out the purposes of this subsection.

(g) Special rules.—

(1) For distributions in redemption of stock, see section 302.

(2) For distributions in complete liquidation, see part II (sec. 331 and following).

(3) For distributions in corporate organizations and reorganizations, see part III (sec. 351 and following).

(4) [Repealed.]

§ 302. Distributions in redemption of stock

(a) General rule.—If a corporation redeems its stock (within the meaning of section 317(b)), and if paragraph (1), (2), (3), or (4) of subsection (b) applies, such redemption shall be treated as a distribution in part or full payment in exchange for the stock.

(b) Redemptions treated as exchanges.—

(1) Redemptions not equivalent to dividends.—Subsection (a) shall apply if the redemption is not essentially equivalent to a dividend.

(2) Substantially disproportionate redemption of stock.—

(A) In general.—Subsection (a) shall apply if the distribution is substantially disproportionate with respect to the shareholder.

(B) Limitation.—This paragraph shall not apply unless immediately after the redemption the shareholder owns less than 50 percent of the total combined voting power of all classes of stock entitled to vote.

(C) Definitions.—For purposes of this paragraph, the distribution is substantially disproportionate if—

(i) the ratio which the voting stock of the corporation owned by the shareholder immediately after the redemption bears to all of the voting stock of the corporation at such time,

is less than 80 percent of—

(ii) the ratio which the voting stock of the corporation owned by the shareholder immediately before the redemption bears to all of the voting stock of the corporation at such time.

For purposes of this paragraph, no distribution shall be treated as substantially disproportionate unless the shareholder's ownership of the common stock of the corporation (whether voting or nonvoting) after and before redemption also meets the 80 percent requirement of the preceding sentence. For purposes of the preceding sentence, if there is more than one class of common stock, the determinations shall be made by reference to fair market value.

(D) Series of redemptions.—This paragraph shall not apply to any redemption made pursuant to a plan the purpose or effect of which is a series of redemptions resulting in a distribution which (in the aggregate) is not substantially disproportionate with respect to the shareholder.

(3) Termination of shareholder's interest.—Subsection (a) shall apply if the redemption is in complete redemption of all of the stock of the corporation owned by the shareholder.

(4) Redemption from noncorporate shareholder in partial liquidation. —Subsection (a) shall apply to a distribution if such distribution is—

(A) in redemption of stock held by a shareholder who is not a corporation, and

(B) in partial liquidation of the distributing corporation.

(5) Application of paragraphs.—In determining whether a redemption meets the requirements of paragraph (1), the fact that such redemption fails to meet the requirements of paragraph (2), (3) or (4) shall not be taken into account. If a redemption meets the requirements of paragraph (3) and also the requirements of paragraph (1), (2), or (4), then so much of subsection (c) (2) as would (but for this sentence) apply in respect of the acquisition of an interest in the corporation within the 10-year period beginning on the date of the distribution shall not apply.

(c) Constructive ownership of stock.—

(1) In general.—Except as provided in paragraph (2) of this subsection, section 318(a) shall apply in determining the ownership of stock for purposes of this section.

(2) For determining termination of interest.—

(A) In the case of a distribution described in subsection (b) (3), section 318(a) (1) shall not apply if—

(i) immediately after the distribution the distributee has no interest in the corporation (including an interest as officer, director, or employee), other than an interest as a creditor,

(ii) the distributee does not acquire any such interest (other than stock acquired by bequest or inheritance) within 10 years from the date of such distribution, and

(iii) the distributee, at such time and in such manner as the Secretary by regulations prescribes, files an agreement to notify the Secretary of any acquisition described in clause (ii) and to retain such records as may be necessary for the application of this paragraph.

If the distributee acquires such an interest in the corporation (other than by bequest or inheritance) within 10 years from the date of the distribution, then the periods of limitation provided in sections 6501 and 6502 on the making of an assessment and the collection by levy or a proceeding in court shall, with respect to any deficiency (including interest and additions to the tax) resulting from such acquisition, include one year immediately following the date on which the distributee (in accordance with regulations prescribed by the Secretary) notifies the Secretary of such acquisition; and such assessment and collection may be made notwithstanding any provision of law or rule of law which otherwise would prevent such assessment and collection.

(B) Subparagraph (A) of this paragraph shall not apply if—

(i) any portion of the stock redeemed was acquired, directly or indirectly, within the 10-year period ending on the date of the distribution by the distributee from a person the ownership of whose stock would (at the time of distribution) be attributable to the distributee under section 318(a), or

(ii) any person owns (at the time of the distribution) stock the ownership of which is attributable to the distributee under section 318(a) and such person acquired any stock in the corporation, directly or indirectly, from the distributee within the 10-year period ending on the date of the distribution, unless such stock so acquired from the distributee is redeemed in the same transaction.

The preceding sentence shall not apply if the acquisition (or, in the case of clause (ii), the disposition) by the distributee did not have as one of its principal purposes the avoidance of Federal income tax.

(C) Special rule for waivers by entities.—

(i) In general.—Subparagraph (A) shall not apply to a distribution to any entity unless—

(I) such entity and each related person meet the requirements of clauses (i), (ii), and (iii) of subparagraph (A), and

(II) each related person agrees to be jointly and severally liable for any deficiency (including interest and additions to tax) resulting from an acquisition described in clause (ii) of subparagraph (A).

In any case to which the preceding sentence applies, the second sentence of subparagraph (A) and subparagraph (B)(ii) shall be applied by substituting "distributee or any related person" for "distributee" each place it appears.

(ii) Definitions.—For purposes of this subparagraph—

(I) the term "entity" means a partnership, estate, trust, or corporation; and

(II) the term "related person" means any person to whom ownership of stock in the corporation is (at the time of the distribution) attributable under section 318(a)(1) if such stock is further attributable to the entity under section 318(a)(3).

(d) Redemptions treated as distributions of property.—Except as otherwise provided in this subchapter, if a corporation redeems its stock (within the meaning of section 317(b)), and if subsection (a) of this section does not apply, such redemption shall be treated as a distribution of property to which section 301 applies.

(e) Partial liquidation defined.—

(1) In general.—For purposes of subsection (b)(4), a distribution shall be treated as in partial liquidation of a corporation if—

(A) the distribution is not essentially equivalent to a dividend (determined at the corporate level rather than at the shareholder level), and

(B) the distribution is pursuant to a plan and occurs within the taxable year in which the plan is adopted or within the succeeding taxable year.

(2) Termination of business.—The distributions which meet the requirements of paragraph (1)(A) shall include (but shall not be limited to) a distribution which meets the requirements of subparagraphs (A) and (B) of this paragraph:

(A) The distribution is attributable to the distributing corporation's ceasing to conduct, or consists of the assets of, a qualified trade or business.

(B) Immediately after the distribution, the distributing corporation is actively engaged in the conduct of a qualified trade or business.

(3) Qualified trade or business.—For purposes of paragraph (2), the term "qualified trade or business" means any trade or business which—

(A) was actively conducted throughout the 5-year period ending on the date of the redemption, and

(B) was not acquired by the corporation within such period in a transaction in which gain or loss was recognized in whole or in part.

(4) Redemption may be pro rata.—Whether or not a redemption meets the requirements of subparagraphs (A) and (B) of paragraph (2) shall be determined without regard to whether or not the redemption is pro rata with respect to all of the shareholders of the corporation.

(5) Treatment of certain pass-thru entities.—For purposes of determining under subsection (b)(4) whether any stock is held by a shareholder who is not a corporation, any stock held by a partnership, estate, or trust shall be treated as if it were actually held proportionately by its partners or beneficiaries.

(f) Cross references.—

For special rules relating to redemption—

(1) **Death Taxes.**—Of stock to pay death taxes, see section 303.

(2) **Section 306 Stock.**—Of section 306 stock, see section 306.

(3) **Liquidations.**—Of stock in complete liquidation, see section 331.

§ 303. Distributions in redemption of stock to pay death taxes

(a) In general.—A distribution of property to a shareholder by a corporation in redemption of part or all of the stock of such corporation which (for Federal estate tax purposes) is included in determining the gross estate of a decedent, to the extent that the amount of such distribution does not exceed the sum of—

(1) the estate, inheritance, legacy, and succession taxes (including any interest collected as a part of such taxes) imposed because of such decedent's death, and

(2) the amount of funeral and administration expenses allowable as deductions to the estate under section 2053 (or under section 2106 in the case of the estate of a decedent nonresident, not a citizen of the United States),

shall be treated as a distribution in full payment in exchange for the stock so redeemed.

(b) Limitations on application of subsection (a).—

(1) Period for distribution.—Subsection (a) shall apply only to amounts distributed after the death of the decedent and—

(A) within the period of limitations provided in section 6501(a) for the assessment of the Federal estate tax (determined without the application of any provision other than section 6501(a)), or within 90 days after the expiration of such period,

(B) if a petition for redetermination of a deficiency in such estate tax has been filed with the Tax Court within the time prescribed in section 6213, at any time before the expiration of 60 days after the decision of the Tax Court becomes final, or

(C) if an election has been made under section 6166 and if the time prescribed by this subparagraph expires at a later date than the time prescribed by subparagraph (B) of this paragraph, within the time determined under section 6166 for the payment of the installments.

(2) Relationship of stock to decedent's estate.—

(A) In general.—Subsection (a) shall apply to a distribution by a corporation only if the value (for Federal estate tax purposes) of all of the stock of such corporation which is included in determining the value of the decedent's gross estate exceeds 35 percent of the excess of—

(i) the value of the gross estate of such decedent, over

(ii) the sum of the amounts allowable as a deduction under section 2053 or 2054.

(B) Special rule for stock in 2 or more corporations.—For purposes of subparagraph (A), stock of 2 or more corporations, with respect to each of which there is included in determining the value of the decedent's gross estate 20 percent or more in value of the outstanding stock, shall be treated as the stock of a single corporation. For purposes of the 20-percent requirement of the preceding sentence, stock which, at the decedent's death, represents the surviving spouse's interest in property held by the decedent and the surviving spouse as community property or as joint tenants, tenants by the entirety, or tenants in common shall be treated as having been included in determining the value of the decedent's gross estate.

(3) Relationship of shareholder to estate tax.—Subsection (a) shall apply to a distribution by a corporation only to the extent that the interest of the shareholder is reduced directly (or through a binding obligation to contribute) by any payment of an amount described in paragraph (1) or (2) of subsection (a).

(4) Additional requirements for distributions made more than 4 years after decedent's death.—In the case of amounts distributed more than 4 years after the date of the decedent's death, subsection (a) shall apply to a distribution by a corporation only to the extent of the lesser of—

(A) the aggregate of the amounts referred to in paragraph (1) or (2) of subsection (a) which remained unpaid immediately before the distribution, or

(B) the aggregate of the amounts referred to in paragraph (1) or (2) of subsection (a) which are paid during the 1-year period beginning on the date of such distribution.

(c) Stock with substituted basis.—If—

(1) a shareholder owns stock of a corporation (referred to in this subsection as "new stock") the basis of which is determined by reference to the basis of stock of a corporation (referred to in this subsection as "old stock"),

(2) the old stock was included (for Federal estate tax purposes) in determining the gross estate of a decedent, and

(3) subsection (a) would apply to a distribution of property to such shareholder in redemption of the old stock,

then, subject to the limitations specified in subsection (b), subsection (a) shall apply in respect of a distribution in redemption of the new stock.

(d) Special rules for generation-skipping transfers.—Where stock in a corporation is the subject of a generation-skipping transfer (within the meaning of section 2611(a)) occurring at the same time as and as a result of the death of an individual—

(1) the stock shall be deemed to be included in the gross estate of such individual;

(2) taxes of the kind referred to in subsection (a)(1) which are imposed because of the generation-skipping transfer shall be treated as imposed because of such individual's death (and for this purpose the tax imposed by section 2601 shall be treated as an estate tax);

(3) the period of distribution shall be measured from the date of the generation-skipping transfer; and

(4) the relationship of stock to the decedent's estate shall be measured with reference solely to the amount of the generation-skipping transfer.

§ 304. Redemption through use of related corporations

(a) Treatment of certain stock purchases.—

(1) Acquisition by related corporation (other than subsidiary).—For purposes of sections 302 and 303, if—

(A) one or more persons are in control of each of two corporations, and

(B) in return for property, one of the corporations acquires stock in the other corporation from the person (or persons) so in control,

then (unless paragraph (2) applies) such property shall be treated as a distribution in redemption of the stock of the corporation acquiring such stock. To the extent that such distribution is treated as a distribution to which section 301 applies, the stock so acquired shall be treated as having been transferred by the person from whom acquired, and as having been received by the corporation acquiring it, as a contribution to the capital of such corporation.

(2) Acquisition by subsidiary.—For purposes of sections 302 and 303, if—

(A) in return for property, one corporation acquires from a shareholder of another corporation stock in such other corporation, and

(B) the issuing corporation controls the acquiring corporation,

then such property shall be treated as a distribution in redemption of the stock of the issuing corporation.

(b) Special rules for application of subsection (a).—

(1) Rule for determinations under section 302(b).—In the case of any acquisition of stock to which subsection (a) of this section applies, determinations as to whether the acquisition is, by reason of section 302(b), to be treated as a distribution in part or full payment in exchange for the stock shall be made by reference to the stock of the issuing corporation. In applying section 318(a) (relating to constructive ownership of stock) with respect to section 302(b) for purposes of this paragraph, sections 318(a) (2) (C) and 318(a) (3) (C) shall be applied without regard to the 50 percent limitation contained therein.

(2) Amount constituting dividend.—In the case of any acquisition of stock to which subsection (a) applies, the determination of the amount which is a dividend (and the source thereof) shall be made as if the property were distributed—

(A) by the acquiring corporation to the extent of its earnings and profits, and

(B) then by the issuing corporation to the extent of its earnings and profits.

(3) Coordination with section 351.—

(A) Property treated as received in redemption.—Except as otherwise provided in this paragraph, subsection (a) (and not section 351 and not so much of sections 357 and 358 as relates to section 351) shall apply to any property received in a distribution described in subsection (a).

(B) Certain assumptions of liability, etc.—

(i) In general.—In the case of an acquisition described in section 351, subsection (a) shall not apply to any liability—

(I) assumed by the acquiring corporation, or

(II) to which the stock is subject,

if such liability was incurred by the transferor to acquire the stock. For purposes of the preceding sentence, the term "stock" means stock referred to in paragraph (1)(B) or (2)(A) of subsection (a).

281

(ii) **Extension of obligations, etc.**—For purposes of clause (i), an extension, renewal, or refinancing of a liability which meets the requirements of clause (i) shall be treated as meeting such requirements.

(iii) **Clause (i) does not apply to stock acquired from related person except where complete termination.**—Clause (i) shall apply only to stock acquired by the transferor from a person—

(I) none of whose stock is attributable to the transferor under section 318(a) (other than paragraph (4) thereof), or

(II) who satisfies rules similar to the rules of section 302(c)(2) with respect to both the acquiring and the issuing corporations (determined as if such person were a distributee of each such corporation).

* * *

(c) Control.—

(1) In general.—For purposes of this section, control means the ownership of stock possessing at least 50 percent of the total combined voting power of all classes of stock entitled to vote, or at least 50 percent of the total value of shares of all classes of stock. If a person (or persons) is in control (within the meaning of the preceding sentence) of a corporation which in turn owns at least 50 percent of the total combined voting power of all stock entitled to vote of another corporation, or owns at least 50 percent of the total value of the shares of all classes of stock of another corporation, then such person (or persons) shall be treated as in control of such other corporation.

(2) Stock acquired in the transaction.—For purposes of subsection (a)(1)—

(A) **General rule.**—Where 1 or more persons in control of the issuing corporation transfer stock of such corporation in exchange for stock of the acquiring corporation, the stock of the acquiring corporation received shall be taken into account in determining whether such person or persons are in control of the acquiring corporation.

(B) **Definition of control group.**—Where 2 or more persons in control of the issuing corporation transfer stock of such corporation to the acquiring corporation and, after the transfer, the transferors are in control of the acquiring corporation, the person or persons in control of each corporation shall include each of the persons who so transfer stock.

(3) Constructive ownership.—

(A) **In general.**—Section 318(a) (relating to constructive ownership of stock) shall apply for purposes of determining control under this section.

(B) **Modification of 50-percent limitations in section 318.**—For purposes of subparagraph (A)—

(i) paragraph (2)(C) of section 318(a) shall be applied by substituting "5 percent" for "50 percent", and

(ii) paragraph (3)(C) of section 318(a) shall be applied—

(I) by substituting "5 percent" for "50 percent", and

(II) in any case where such paragraph would not apply but for subclause (I), by considering a corporation as owning the stock (other than stock in such corporation) owned by or for any shareholder of such corporation in that proportion which the value of the stock which such shareholder owned in such corporation bears to the value of all stock in such corporation.

§ 305. Distributions of stock and stock rights

(a) General rule.—Except as otherwise provided in this section, gross income does not include the amount of any distribution of the stock of a corporation made by such corporation to its shareholders with respect to its stock.

(b) Exceptions.—Subsection (a) shall not apply to a distribution by a corporation of its stock, and the distribution shall be treated as a distribution of property to which section 301 applies—

(1) Distributions in lieu of money.—If the distribution is, at the election of any of the shareholders (whether exercised before or after the declaration thereof), payable either—

(A) in its stock, or

(B) in property.

(2) Disproportionate distributions.—If the distribution (or a series of distributions of which such distribution is one) has the result of—

(A) the receipt of property by some shareholders, and

(B) an increase in the proportionate interests of other shareholders in the assets or earnings and profits of the corporation.

(3) Distributions of common and preferred stock.—If the distribution (or a series of distributions of which such distribution is one) has the result of—

(A) the receipt of preferred stock by some common shareholders, and

(B) the receipt of common stock by other common shareholders.

(4) Distributions on preferred stock.—If the distribution is with respect to preferred stock, other than an increase in the conversion ratio of convertible preferred stock made solely to take account of a stock dividend or stock split with respect to the stock into which such convertible stock is convertible.

(5) Distributions of convertible preferred stock.—If the distribution is of convertible preferred stock, unless it is established to the satisfaction of the Secretary that such distribution will not have the result described in paragraph (2).

(c) Certain transactions treated as distributions.—For purposes of this section and section 301, the Secretary shall prescribe regulations under which a change in conversion ratio, a change in redemption price, a difference between redemption price and issue price, a redemption which is treated as a distribution to which section 301 applies, or any transaction (including a recapitalization) having a similar effect on the interest of any shareholder shall be treated as a distribution with respect to any shareholder whose proportionate interest in the earnings and profits or assets of the corporation is increased by such change, difference, redemption, or similar transaction.

(d) Definitions.—

(1) Rights to acquire stock.—For purposes of this section (other than subsection (e)), the term "stock" includes rights to acquire such stock.

(2) Shareholders.—For purposes of subsections (b) and (c), the term "shareholder" includes a holder of rights or of convertible securities.

* * *

(f) Cross references.—

For special rules—

(1) Relating to the receipt of stock and stock rights in corporate organizations and reorganizations, see part III (sec. 351 and following).

(2) In the case of a distribution which results in a gift, see section 2501 and following.

(3) In the case of a distribution which has the effect of the payment of compensation, see section 61(a) (1).

§ 306. Dispositions of certain stock

(a) **General rule.**—If a shareholder sells or otherwise disposes of section 306 stock (as defined in subsection (c))—

(1) **Dispositions other than redemptions.**—If such disposition is not a redemption (within the meaning of section 317(b))—

(A) The amount realized shall be treated as ordinary income. This subparagraph shall not apply to the extent that—

(i) the amount realized, exceeds

(ii) such stock's ratable share of the amount which would have been a dividend at the time of distribution if (in lieu of section 306 stock) the corporation had distributed money in an amount equal to the fair market value of the stock at the time of distribution.

(B) Any excess of the amount realized over the sum of—

(i) the amount treated under subparagraph (A) as ordinary income, plus

(ii) the adjusted basis of the stock,

shall be treated as gain from the sale of such stock.

(C) No loss shall be recognized.

(2) **Redemption.**—If the disposition is a redemption, the amount realized shall be treated as a distribution of property to which section 301 applies.

(b) **Exceptions.**—Subsection (a) shall not apply—

(1) **Termination of shareholder's interest, etc.—**

(A) **Not in redemption.**—If the disposition—

(i) is not a redemption;

(ii) is not, directly or indirectly, to a person the ownership of whose stock would (under section 318 (a)) be attributable to the shareholder; and

(iii) terminates the entire stock interest of the shareholder in the corporation (and for purposes of this clause, section 318(a) shall apply).

(B) **In redemption.**—If the disposition is a redemption and paragraph (3) or (4) of section 302(b) applies.

(2) **Liquidations.**—If the section 306 stock is redeemed in a distribution in complete liquidation to which part II (sec. 331 and following) applies.

(3) **Where gain or loss is not recognized.**—To the extent that, under any provision of this subtitle, gain or loss to the shareholder is not recognized with respect to the disposition of the section 306 stock.

(4) **Transactions not in avoidance.**—If it is established to the satisfaction of the Secretary—

(A) that the distribution, and the disposition or redemption, or

(B) in the case of a prior or simultaneous disposition (or redemption) of the stock with respect to which the section 306 stock disposed of (or redeemed) was issued, that the disposition (or redemption) of the section 306 stock,

was not in pursuance of a plan having as one of its principal purposes the avoidance of Federal income tax.

(c) Section 306 stock defined.—

(1) In general.—For purposes of this subchapter, the term "section 306 stock" means stock which meets the requirements of subparagraph (A), (B), or (C) of this paragraph.

(A) Distributed to seller.—Stock (other than common stock issued with respect to common stock) which was distributed to the shareholder selling or otherwise disposing of such stock if, by reason of section 305(a), any part of such distribution was not includible in the gross income of the shareholder.

(B) Received in a corporate reorganization or separation.—Stock which is not common stock and—

(i) which was received, by the shareholder selling or otherwise disposing of such stock, in pursuance of a plan of reorganization (within the meaning of section 368(a)), or in a distribution or exchange to which section 355 (or so much of section 356 as relates to section 355) applied, and

(ii) with respect to the receipt of which gain or loss to the shareholder was to any extent not recognized by reason of part III, but only to the extent that either the effect of the transaction was substantially the same as the receipt of a stock dividend, or the stock was received in exchange for section 306 stock.

For purposes of this section, a receipt of stock to which the foregoing provisions of this subparagraph apply shall be treated as a distribution of stock.

(C) Stock having transferred or substituted basis.—Except as otherwise provided in subparagraph (B), stock the basis of which (in the hands of the shareholder selling or otherwise disposing of such stock) is determined by reference to the basis (in the hands of such shareholder or any other person) of section 306 stock.

(2) Exception where no earnings and profits.—For purposes of this section, the term "section 306 stock" does not include any stock no part of the distribution of which would have been a dividend at the time of the distribution if money had been distributed in lieu of the stock.

(3) Certain stock acquired in section 351 exchange.—The term "section 306 stock" also includes any stock which is not common stock acquired in an exchange to which section 351 applied if receipt of money (in lieu of the stock) would have been treated as a dividend to any extent. Rules similar to the rules of section 304(b)(2) shall apply—

(A) for purposes of the preceding sentence, and

(B) for purposes of determining the application of this section to any subsequent disposition of stock which is section 306 stock by reason of an exchange described in the preceding sentence.

(4) Application of attribution rules for certain purposes.—For purposes of paragraphs (1)(B)(ii) and (3), section 318(a) shall apply. For purposes of applying the preceding sentence to paragraph (3), the rules of section 304(c)(3)(B) shall apply.

(d) Stock rights.—For purposes of this section—

(1) stock rights shall be treated as stock, and

(2) stock acquired through the exercise of stock rights shall be treated as stock distributed at the time of the distribution of the stock rights, to the extent of the fair market value of such rights at the time of the distribution.

(e) Convertible stock.—For purposes of subsection (c)—

(1) if section 306 stock was issued with respect to common stock and later such section 306 stock is exchanged for common stock in the same corporation (whether or not such exchange is pursuant to a conversion privilege contained in the section 306 stock), then (except as provided in paragraph (2)) the common stock so received shall not be treated as section 306 stock; and

(2) common stock with respect to which there is a privilege of converting into stock other than common stock (or into property), whether or not the conversion privilege is contained in such stock, shall not be treated as common stock.

* * *

(g) Change in terms and conditions of stock.—If a substantial change is made in the terms and conditions of any stock, then, for purposes of this section—

(1) the fair market value of such stock shall be the fair market value at the time of the distribution or at the time of such change, whichever such value is higher;

(2) such stock's ratable share of the amount which would have been a dividend if money had been distributed in lieu of stock shall be determined as of the time of distribution or as of the time of such change, whichever such ratable share is higher; and

(3) subsection (c) (2) shall not apply unless the stock meets the requirements of such subsection both at the time of such distribution and at the time of such change.

* * *

§ 307. Basis of stock and stock rights acquired in distributions

(a) General rule.—If a shareholder in a corporation receives its stock or rights to acquire its stock (referred to in this subsection as "new stock") in a distribution to which section 305(a) applies, then the basis of such new stock and of the stock with respect to which it is distributed (referred to in this section as "old stock"), respectively, shall, in the shareholder's hands, be determined by allocating between the old stock and the new stock the adjusted basis of the old stock. Such allocation shall be made under regulations prescribed by the Secretary.

(b) Exception for certain stock rights.—

(1) In general.—If—

(A) a corporation distributes rights to acquire its stock to a shareholder in a distribution to which section 305(a) applies, and

(B) the fair market value of such rights at the time of the distribution is less than 15 percent of the fair market value of the old stock at such time,

then subsection (a) shall not apply and the basis of such rights shall be zero, unless the taxpayer elects under paragraph (2) of this subsection to determine the basis of the old stock and of the stock rights under the method of allocation provided in subsection (a).

(2) Election.—The election referred to in paragraph (1) shall be made in the return filed within the time prescribed by law (including extensions thereof) for the taxable year in which such rights were received. Such election shall be made in such manner as the Secretary may by regulations prescribe, and shall be irrevocable when made.

* * *

Subpart B—Effects on Corporation

§ 311. Taxability of corporation on distribution

(a) **General rule.**—Except as provided in subsection (b), no gain or loss shall be recognized to a corporation on the distribution, with respect to its stock, of—

(1) its stock (or rights to acquire its stock), or

(2) property.

(b) **Distributions of appreciated property.**—

(1) **In general.**—If—

(A) a corporation distributes property (other than an obligation of such corporation) to a shareholder in a distribution to which subpart A applies, and

(B) the fair market value of such property exceeds its adjusted basis (in the hands of the distributing corporation),

then gain shall be recognized to the distributing corporation as if such property were sold to the distributee at its fair market value.

(2) **Treatment of liabilities in excess of basis.**—Rules similar to the rules of section 336(b) shall apply for purposes of this subsection.

§ 312. Effect on earnings and profits

(a) **General rule.**—Except as otherwise provided in this section, on the distribution of property by a corporation with respect to its stock, the earnings and profits of the corporation (to the extent thereof) shall be decreased by the sum of—

(1) the amount of money,

(2) the principal amount of the obligations of such corporation (or, in the case of obligations having original issue discount, the aggregate issue price of such obligations), and

(3) the adjusted basis of the other property, so distributed.

(b) **Distributions of appreciated property.**—On the distribution by a corporation, with respect to its stock, of any property the fair market value of which exceeds the adjusted basis thereof—

(1) the earnings and profits of the corporation shall be increased by the amount of such excess, and

(2) subsection (a)(3) shall be applied by substituting "fair market value" for "adjusted basis".

For purposes of this subsection and subsection (a), the adjusted basis of any property is its adjusted basis as determined for purposes of computing earnings and profits.

(c) **Adjustments for liabilities.**—In making the adjustments to the earnings and profits of a corporation under subsection (a) or (b), proper adjustment shall be made for—

(1) the amount of any liability to which the property distributed is subject, and

(2) the amount of any liability of the corporation assumed by a shareholder in connection with the distribution.

(d) Certain distributions of stock and securities.—

(1) In general.—The distribution to a distributee by or on behalf of a corporation of its stock or securities, of stock or securities in another corporation, or of property, in a distribution to which this title applies, shall not be considered a distribution of the earnings and profits of any corporation—

(A) if no gain to such distributee from the receipt of such stock or securities, or property, was recognized under this title, or

(B) if the distribution was not subject to tax in the hands of such distributee by reason of section 305(a).

(2) Prior distributions.—In the case of a distribution of stock or securities, or property, to which section 115(h) of the Internal Revenue Code of 1939 (or the corresponding provision of prior law) applied, the effect on earnings and profits of such distribution shall be determined under such section 115(h), or the corresponding provision of prior law, as the case may be.

(3) Stock or securities.—For purposes of this subsection, the term "stock or securities" includes rights to acquire stock or securities.

[(e)   Repealed.]

(f) Effect on earnings and profits of gain or loss and of receipt of tax-free distributions.—

(1) Effect on earnings and profits of gain or loss.—The gain or loss realized from the sale or other disposition (after February 28, 1913) of property by a corporation—

(A) for the purpose of the computation of the earnings and profits of the corporation, shall (except as provided in subparagraph (B)) be determined by using as the adjusted basis the adjusted basis (under the law applicable to the year in which the sale or other disposition was made) for determining gain, except that no regard shall be had to the value of the property as of March 1, 1913; but

(B) for purposes of the computation of the earnings and profits of the corporation for any period beginning after February 28, 1913, shall be determined by using as the adjusted basis the adjusted basis (under the law applicable to the year in which the sale or other disposition was made) for determining gain.

Gain or loss so realized shall increase or decrease the earnings and profits to, but not beyond, the extent to which such a realized gain or loss was recognized in computing taxable income under the law applicable to the year in which such sale or disposition was made. Where, in determining the adjusted basis used in computing such realized gain or loss, the adjustment to the basis differs from the adjustment proper for the purpose of determining earnings and profits, then the latter adjustment shall be used in determining the increase or decrease above provided. For purposes of this subsection, a loss with respect to which a deduction is disallowed under section 1091 (relating to wash sales of stock or securities), or the corresponding provision of prior law, shall not be deemed to be recognized.

(2) Effect on earnings and profits of receipt of tax-free distributions.—Where a corporation receives (after February 28, 1913) a distribution from a second corporation which (under the law applicable to the year in which the distribution was made) was not a taxable dividend to the shareholders of the second corporation, the amount of such distribution shall not increase the earnings and profits of the first corporation in the following cases:

(A) no such increase shall be made in respect of the part of such distribution which (under such law) is directly applied in reduction of the basis of the stock in respect of which the distribution was made; and

(B) no such increase shall be made if (under such law) the distribution causes the basis of the stock in respect of which the distribution was made to be allocated between such stock and the property received (or such basis would, but for section 307(b), be so allocated).

* * *

(h) Allocation in certain corporate separations and reorganizations.—

(1) **Section 355.**—In the case of a distribution or exchange to which section 355 (or so much of section 356 as relates to section 355) applies, proper allocation with respect to the earnings and profits of the distributing corporation and the controlled corporation (or corporations) shall be made under regulations prescribed by the Secretary.

(2) **Section 368(a)(1)(C) or (D).**—In the case of a reorganization described in subparagraph (C) or (D) of section 368(a)(1), proper allocation with respect to the earnings and profits of the acquired corporation shall, under regulations prescribed by the Secretary, be made between the acquiring corporation and the acquired corporation (or any corporation which had control of the acquired corporation before the reorganization).

* * *

(k) Effect of depreciation on earnings and profits.—

(1) **General rule.**—For purposes of computing the earnings and profits of a corporation for any taxable year beginning after June 30, 1972, the allowance for depreciation (and amortization, if any) shall be deemed to be the amount which would be allowable for such year if the straight line method of depreciation had been used for each taxable year beginning after June 30, 1972.

(2) **Exception.**—If for any taxable year beginning after June 30, 1972, a method of depreciation was used by the taxpayer which the Secretary has determined results in a reasonable allowance under section 167(a), and which is not—

(A) a declining balance method,

(B) the sum of the years-digits method, or

(C) any other method allowable solely by reason of the application of subsection (b) (4) or (j) (1) (C) of section 167,

then the adjustment to earnings and profits for depreciation for such year shall be determined under the method so used (in lieu of under the straight line method).

(3) **Exception for tangible property.—**

(A) **In general.**—Except as provided in subparagraph (B), in the case of tangible property to which section 168 applies, the adjustment to earnings and profits for depreciation for any taxable year shall be determined under the alternative depreciation system (within the meaning of section 168(g)(2)).

(B) **Treatment of amounts deductible under section 179.**—For purposes of computing the earnings and profits of a corporation, any amount deductible under section 179 shall be allowed as a deduction ratably over the period of 5 taxable years (beginning with the taxable year for which such amount is deductible under section 179).

* * *

(5) **Basis adjustment not taken into account.**—In computing the earnings and profits of a corporation for any taxable year, the allowance for depreciation (and amortization, if any) shall be computed without regard to any basis adjustment under section 48(q).

(*l*) **Discharge of indebtedness income.**—

(1) **Does not increase earnings and profits if applied to reduce basis.**—The earnings and profits of a corporation shall not include income from the discharge of indebtedness to the extent of the amount applied to reduce basis under section 1017.

(2) **Reduction of deficit in earnings and profits in certain cases.**—If—

(A) the interest of any shareholder of a corporation is terminated or extinguished in a title 11 or similar case (within the meaning of section 368(a)(3)(A)), and

(B) there is a deficit in the earnings and profits of the corporation,

then such deficit shall be reduced by an amount equal to the paid-in capital which is allocable to the interest of the shareholder which is so terminated or extinguished.

(m) **No adjustment for interest paid on certain registration-required obligations not in registered form.**—The earnings and profits of any corporation shall not be decreased by any interest with respect to which a deduction is not or would not be allowable by reason of section 163(f), unless at the time of issuance the issuer is a foreign corporation that is not a controlled foreign corporation (within the meaning of section 957), a foreign investment company (within the meaning of section 1246(b)), or a foreign personal holding company (within the meaning of section 552) and the issuance did not have as a purpose the avoidance of section 163(f) or this subsection.

(n) **Adjustments to earnings and profits to more accurately reflect economic gain and loss.**—For purposes of computing the earnings and profits of a corporation, the following adjustments shall be made:

(1) **Construction period carrying charges.**—

(A) **In general.**—In the case of any amount paid or incurred for construction period carrying charges—

(i) no deduction shall be allowed with respect to such amount, and

(ii) the basis of the property with respect to which such charges are allocable shall be increased by such amount.

(B) **Construction period carrying charges defined.**—For purposes of this paragraph, the term "construction period carrying charges" means all—

(i) interest paid or accrued on indebtedness incurred or continued to acquire, construct, or carry property,

(ii) property taxes, and

(iii) similar carrying charges,

to the extent such interest, taxes, or charges are attributable to the construction period for such property and would be allowable as a deduction in determining taxable income under this chapter for the taxable year in which paid or incurred.

(C) **Construction period.**—The term "construction period" has the meaning given the term production period under section 263A(f)(4)(B).

(2) Intangible drilling costs and mineral exploration and development costs.—

(A) Intangible drilling costs.—Any amount allowable as a deduction under section 263(c) in determining taxable income (other than costs incurred in connection with a nonproductive well)—

(i) shall be capitalized, and

(ii) shall be allowed as a deduction ratably over the 60-month period beginning with the month in which the production from the well begins.

(B) Mineral exploration and development costs.—Any amount allowable as a deduction under section 616(a) or 617 in determining taxable income—

(i) shall be capitalized, and

(ii) shall be allowed as a deduction ratably over the 120-month period beginning with the later of—

(I) the month in which production from the deposit begins, or

(II) the month in which such amount was paid or incurred.

(3) Certain amortization provisions not to apply.—Sections 173 and 248 shall not apply.

(4) LIFO inventory adjustments.—

(A) In general.—Earnings and profits shall be increased or decreased by the amount of any increase or decrease in the LIFO recapture amount as of the close of each taxable year; except that any decrease below the LIFO recapture amount as of the close of the taxable year preceding the 1st taxable year to which this paragraph applies to the taxpayer shall be taken into account only to the extent provided in regulations prescribed by the Secretary.

(B) LIFO recapture amount.—For purposes of this paragraph, the term "LIFO recapture amount" means the amount (if any) by which—

(i) the inventory amount of the inventory assets under the first-in, first-out method authorized by section 471, exceeds

(ii) the inventory amount of such assets under the LIFO method.

(C) Definitions.—For purposes of this paragraph—

(i) LIFO method.—The term "LIFO method" means the method authorized by section 472 (relating to last-in, first-out inventories).

(ii) Inventory assets.—The term "inventory assets" means stock in trade of the corporation, or other property of a kind which would properly be included in the inventory of the corporation if on hand at the close of the taxable year.

(iii) Inventory amount.—The inventory amount of assets under the first-in, first-out method authorized by section 471 shall be determined—

(I) if the corporation uses the retail method of valuing inventories under section 472, by using such method, or

(II) if subclause (I) does not apply, by using cost or market, whichever is lower.

(5) Installment sales.—In the case of any installment sale, earnings and profits shall be computed as if the corporation did not use the installment method.

(6) Completed contract method of accounting.—In the case of a taxpayer who uses the completed contract method of accounting, earnings and profits shall be computed as if such taxpayer used the percentage of completion method of accounting.

(7) Redemptions.—If a corporation distributes amounts in a redemption to which section 302(a) or 303 applies, the part of such distribution which is properly chargeable to earnings and profits shall be an amount which is not in excess of the ratable share of the earnings and profits of such corporation accumulated after February 28, 1913, attributable to the stock so redeemed.

* * *

(o) Definition of original issue discount and issue price for purposes of subsection (a)(2).—For purposes of subsection (a)(2), the terms "original issue discount" and "issue price" have the same respective meanings as when used in subpart A of part V of subchapter P of this chapter.

Subpart C—Definitions; Constructive Ownership of Stock

§ 316. Dividend defined

(a) General rule.—For purposes of this subtitle, the term "dividend" means any distribution of property made by a corporation to its shareholders—

(1) out of its earnings and profits accumulated after February 28, 1913, or

(2) out of its earnings and profits of the taxable year (computed as of the close of the taxable year without diminution by reason of any distributions made during the taxable year), without regard to the amount of the earnings and profits at the time the distribution was made.

Except as otherwise provided in this subtitle, every distribution is made out of earnings and profits to the extent thereof, and from the most recently accumulated earnings and profits. To the extent that any distribution is under any provision of this subchapter, treated as a distribution of property to which section 301 applies, such distribution shall be treated as a distribution of property for purposes of this subsection.

(b) Special rules.—

(1) Certain insurance company dividends.—The definition in subsection (a) shall not apply to the term "dividend" as used in subchapter L in any case where the reference is to dividends of insurance companies paid to policyholders as such.

(2) Distributions by personal holding companies.—

(A) In the case of a corporation which—

(i) under the law applicable to the taxable year in which the distribution is made, is a personal holding company (as defined in section 542), or

(ii) for the taxable year in respect of which the distribution is made under section 563(b) (relating to dividends paid after the close of the taxable year), or section 547 (relating to deficiency dividends), or the corresponding provisions of prior law, is a personal holding company under the law applicable to such taxable year,

the term "dividend" also means any distribution of property (whether or not a dividend as defined in subsection (a)) made by the corporation to its shareholders, to the extent of its undistributed personal holding company income (determined under section 545 without regard to distributions under this paragraph) for such year.

(B) For purposes of subparagraph (A), the term "distribution of property" includes a distribution in complete liquidation occurring within 24 months after the adoption of a plan of liquidation, but—

(i) only to the extent of the amounts distributed to distributees other than corporate shareholders, and

(ii) only to the extent that the corporation designates such amounts as a dividend distribution and duly notifies such distributees of such designation, under regulations prescribed by the Secretary, but

(iii) not in excess of the sum of such distributees' allocable share of the undistributed personal holding company income for such year, computed without regard to this subparagraph or section 562(b).

* * *

§ 317. Other definitions

(a) **Property.**—For purposes of this part, the term "property" means money, securities, and any other property; except that such term does not include stock in the corporation making the distribution (or rights to acquire such stock).

(b) **Redemption of stock.**—For purposes of this part, stock shall be treated as redeemed by a corporation if the corporation acquires its stock from a shareholder in exchange for property, whether or not the stock so acquired is cancelled, retired, or held as treasury stock.

§ 318. Constructive ownership of stock

(a) **General rule.**—For purposes of those provisions of this subchapter to which the rules contained in this section are expressly made applicable—

(1) **Members of family.**—

(A) **In general.**—An individual shall be considered as owning the stock owned, directly or indirectly, by or for—

(i) his spouse (other than a spouse who is legally separated from the individual under a decree of divorce or separate maintenance), and

(ii) his children, grandchildren, and parents.

(B) **Effect of adoption.**—For purposes of subparagraph (A) (ii), a legally adopted child of an individual shall be treated as a child of such individual by blood.

(2) **Attribution from partnerships, estates, trusts, and corporations.**—

(A) **From partnerships and estates.**—Stock owned, directly or indirectly, by or for a partnership or estate shall be considered as owned proportionately by its partners or beneficiaries.

(B) **From trusts.**—

(i) Stock owned, directly or indirectly, by or for a trust (other than an employees' trust described in section 401(a) which is exempt from tax under section 501(a)) shall be considered as owned by its beneficiaries in proportion to the actuarial interest of such beneficiaries in such trust.

(ii) Stock owned, directly or indirectly, by or for any portion of a trust of which a person is considered the owner under subpart E of part I of subchapter J (relating to grantors and others treated as substantial owners) shall be considered as owned by such person.

(C) From corporations.—If 50 percent or more in value of the stock in a corporation is owned, directly or indirectly, by or for any person, such person shall be considered as owning the stock owned, directly or indirectly, by or for such corporation, in that proportion which the value of the stock which such person so owns bears to the value of all the stock in such corporation.

(3) Attribution to partnerships, estates, trusts, and corporations.—

(A) To partnerships and estates.—Stock owned, directly or indirectly, by or for a partner or a beneficiary of an estate shall be considered as owned by the partnership or estate.

(B) To trusts.—

(i) Stock owned, directly or indirectly, by or for a beneficiary of a trust (other than an employees' trust described in section 401(a) which is exempt from tax under section 501(a)) shall be considered as owned by the trust, unless such beneficiary's interest in the trust is a remote contingent interest. For purposes of this clause, a contingent interest of a beneficiary in a trust shall be considered remote if, under the maximum exercise of discretion by the trustee in favor of such beneficiary, the value of such interest, computed actuarially, is 5 percent or less of the value of the trust property.

(ii) Stock owned, directly or indirectly, by or for a person who is considered the owner of any portion of a trust under subpart E of part I of subchapter J (relating to grantors and others treated as substantial owners) shall be considered as owned by the trust.

(C) To corporations.—If 50 percent or more in value of the stock in a corporation is owned, directly or indirectly, by or for any person, such corporation shall be considered as owning the stock owned, directly or indirectly, by or for such person.

(4) Options.—If any person has an option to acquire stock, such stock shall be considered as owned by such person. For purposes of this paragraph, an option to acquire such an option, and each one of a series of such options, shall be considered as an option to acquire such stock.

(5) Operating rules.—

(A) In general.—Except as provided in subparagraphs (B) and (C), stock constructively owned by a person by reason of the application of paragraph (1), (2), (3), or (4), shall, for purposes of applying paragraphs (1), (2), (3), and (4), be considered as actually owned by such person.

(B) Members of family.—Stock constructively owned by an individual by reason of the application of paragraph (1) shall not be considered as owned by him for purposes of again applying paragraph (1) in order to make another the constructive owner of such stock.

(C) Partnerships, estates, trusts, and corporations.—Stock constructively owned by a partnership, estate, trust, or corporation by reason of the application of paragraph (3) shall not be considered as owned by it for purposes of applying paragraph (2) in order to make another the constructive owner of such stock.

(D) Option rule in lieu of family rule.—For purposes of this paragraph, if stock may be considered as owned by an individual under paragraph (1) or (4), it shall be considered as owned by him under paragraph (4).

(E) S corporation treated as partnership.—For purposes of this subsection—

(i) an S corporation shall be treated as a partnership, and

(ii) any shareholder of the S corporation shall be treated as a partner of such partnership.

The preceding sentence shall not apply for purposes of determining whether stock in the S corporation is constructively owned by any person.

(b) Cross references.—

For provisions to which the rules contained in subsection (a) apply, see—

(1) section 302 (relating to redemption of stock);

(2) section 304 (relating to redemption by related corporations);

(3) section 306(b) (1) (A) (relating to disposition of section 306 stock);

(4) section 338(h)(3) (defining purchase);

(5) section 382(*l*)(3) (relating to special limitations on net operating loss carryovers);

* * *

PART II—CORPORATE LIQUIDATIONS

Subpart
  A. Effects on recipients.
  B. Effects on corporation.
  C. Collapsible corporations.
  D. Definition and special rule.

Subpart A—Effects on Recipients

§ 331. Gain or loss to shareholders in corporate liquidations

(a) Distributions in complete liquidation treated as exchanges.—Amounts received by a shareholder in a distribution in complete liquidation of a corporation shall be treated as in full payment in exchange for the stock.

(b) Nonapplication of section 301.—Section 301 (relating to effects on shareholder of distributions of property) shall not apply to any distribution of property (other than a distribution referred to in paragraph (2) (B) of section 316(b)) in complete liquidation.

(c) Cross reference.—

For general rule for determination of the amount of gain or loss recognized, see section 1001.

§ 332. Complete liquidations of subsidiaries

(a) General rule.—No gain or loss shall be recognized on the receipt by a corporation of property distributed in complete liquidation of another corporation.

(b) Liquidations to which section applies.—For purposes of subsection (a), a distribution shall be considered to be in complete liquidation only if—

(1) the corporation receiving such property was, on the date of the adoption of the plan of liquidation, and has continued to be at all times until the receipt of the property, the owner of stock (in such other corporation) meeting the requirements of section 1504(a)(2); and either

(2) the distribution is by such other corporation in complete cancellation or redemption of all its stock, and the transfer of all the property occurs within the taxable year; in such case the adoption by the shareholders of the resolution under which is authorized the distribution of all the assets of such corporation in

complete cancellation or redemption of all its stock shall be considered an adoption of a plan of liquidation, even though no time for the completion of the transfer of the property is specified in such resolution; or

(3) such distribution is one of a series of distributions by such other corporation in complete cancellation or redemption of all its stock in accordance with a plan of liquidation under which the transfer of all the property under the liquidation is to be completed within 3 years from the close of the taxable year during which is made the first of the series of distributions under the plan, except that if such transfer is not completed within such period, or if the taxpayer does not continue qualified under paragraph (1) until the completion of such transfer, no distribution under the plan shall be considered a distribution in complete liquidation.

If such transfer of all the property does not occur within the taxable year, the Secretary may require of the taxpayer such bond, or waiver of the statute of limitations on assessment and collection, or both, as he may deem necessary to insure, if the transfer of the property is not completed within such 3-year period, or if the taxpayer does not continue qualified under paragraph (1) until the completion of such transfer, the assessment and collection of all income taxes then imposed by law for such taxable year or subsequent taxable years, to the extent attributable to property so received. A distribution otherwise constituting a distribution in complete liquidation within the meaning of this subsection shall not be considered as not constituting such a distribution merely because it does not constitute a distribution or liquidation within the meaning of the corporate law under which the distribution is made; and for purposes of this subsection a transfer of property of such other corporation to the taxpayer shall not be considered as not constituting a distribution (or one of a series of distributions) in complete cancellation or redemption of all the stock of such other corporation, merely because the carrying out of the plan involves (A) the transfer under the plan to the taxpayer by such other corporation of property, not attributable to shares owned by the taxpayer, on an exchange described in section 361, and (B) the complete cancellation or redemption under the plan, as a result of exchanges described in section 354, of the shares not owned by the taxpayer.

§ 333. Election as to recognition of gain in certain liquidations [Repealed.]

§ 334. Basis of property received in liquidations

(a) **General rule.**—If property is received in a distribution in complete liquidation, and if gain or loss is recognized on receipt of such property, then the basis of the property in the hands of the distributee shall be the fair market value of such property at the time of the distribution.

(b) **Liquidation of subsidiary.**—

(1) **Distribution in complete liquidation.**—If property is received by a corporation in a distribution in a complete liquidation to which section 332(a) applies, the basis of the property in the hands of the distributee shall be the same as it would be in the hands of the transferor.

(2) **Transfers to which section 332(c) applies.**—If property is received by a corporation in a transfer to which section 332(c) applies, the basis of the property in the hands of the transferee shall be the same as it would be in the hands of the transferor.

(3) **Distributee defined.**—For purposes of this subsection, the term "distributee" means only the corporation which meets the 80-percent stock ownership requirements specified in section 332(b).

Subpart B—Effects on Corporation

§ 336. Gain or loss recognized on property distributed in complete liquidation

(a) General rule.—Except as otherwise provided in this section or section 337, gain or loss shall be recognized to a liquidating corporation on the distribution of property in complete liquidation as if such property were sold to the distributee at its fair market value.

(b) Treatment of liabilities in excess of basis.—If any property distributed in the liquidation is subject to a liability or the shareholder assumes a liability of the liquidating corporation in connection with the distribution, for purposes of subsection (a) and section 337, the fair market value of such property shall be treated as not less than the amount of such liability.

(c) Exception for certain liquidations to which part III applies.—This section shall not apply with respect to any distribution of property to the extent there is nonrecognition of gain or loss with respect to such property to the recipient under part III.

(d) Limitations on recognition of loss.—

(1) No loss recognized in certain distributions to related persons.—

(A) In general.—No loss shall be recognized to a liquidating corporation on the distribution of any property to a related person (within the meaning of section 267) if—

(i) such distribution is not pro rata, or

(ii) such property is disqualified property.

(B) Disqualified property.—For purposes of subparagraph (A), the term "disqualified property" means any property which is acquired by the liquidating corporation in a transaction to which section 351 applied, or as a contribution to capital, during the 5–year period ending on the date of the distribution. Such term includes any property if the adjusted basis of such property is determined (in whole or in part) by reference to the adjusted basis of property described in the preceding sentence.

(2) Special rule for certain property acquired in certain carryover basis transactions.—

(A) In general.—For purposes of determining the amount of loss recognized by any liquidating corporation on any sale, exchange, or distribution of property described in subparagraph (B), the adjusted basis of such property shall be reduced (but not below zero) by the excess (if any) of—

(i) the adjusted basis of such property immediately after its acquisition by such corporation, over

(ii) the fair market value of such property as of such time.

(B) Description of property.—

(i) **In general.**—For purposes of subparagraph (A), property is described in this subparagraph if—

(I) such property is acquired by the liquidating corporation in a transaction to which section 351 applied or as a contribution to capital, and

(**II**) the acquisition of such property by the liquidating corporation was part of a plan a principal purpose of which was to recognize loss by the liquidating corporation with respect to such property in connection with the liquidation.

Other property shall be treated as so described if the adjusted basis of such other property is determined (in whole or in part) by reference to the adjusted basis of property described in the preceding sentence.

(**ii**) **Certain acquisitions treated as part of plan.**—For purposes of clause (i), any property described in clause (i)(I) acquired by the liquidating corporation during the 2–year period ending on the date of the adoption of the plan of complete liquidation shall, except as provided in regulations, be treated as part of a plan described in clause (i)(II).

(**C**) **Recapture in lieu of disallowance.**—The Secretary may prescribe regulations under which, in lieu of disallowing a loss under subparagraph (A) for a prior taxable year, the gross income of the liquidating corporation for the taxable year in which the plan of complete liquidation is adopted shall be increased by the amount of the disallowed loss.

(**3**) **Special rule in case of liquidation to which section 332 applies.**—In the case of any liquidation to which section 332 applies, no loss shall be recognized to the liquidating corporation on any distribution in such liquidation.

(**e**) **Certain stock sales and distributions may be treated as asset transfers.**—Under regulations prescribed by the Secretary, if—

(**1**) a corporation owns stock in another corporation meeting the requirements of section 1504(a)(2), and

(**2**) such corporation sells, exchanges, or distributes all of such stock,

such corporation may elect to treat such sale, exchange, or distribution as a disposition of all of the assets of such other corporation, and no gain or loss shall be recognized on the sale, exchange, or distribution of such stock.

(Pub.L. 99–514, Title VI, § 631(a), Oct. 22, 1986, 100 Stat. ____.)

§ 337. Nonrecognition for property distributed to parent in complete liquidation of subsidiary

(**a**) **In general.**—No gain or loss shall be recognized to the liquidating corporation on the distribution to the 80-percent distributee of any property in a complete liquidation to which section 332 applies.

(**b**) **Treatment of indebtedness of subsidiary, etc.—**

(**1**) **Indebtedness of subsidiary to parent.**—If—

(**A**) a corporation is liquidated in a liquidation to which section 332 applies, and

(**B**) on the date of the adoption of the plan of liquidation, such corporation was indebted to the 80-percent distributee,

for purposes of this section and section 336, any transfer of property to the 80-percent distributee in satisfaction of such indebtedness shall be treated as a distribution to such distributee in such liquidation.

(**2**) **Treatment of tax-exempt distributee.—**

(**A**) **In general.**—Except as provided in subparagraph (B), paragraph (1) and subsection (a) shall not apply where the 80-percent distributee is an organization (other than a cooperative described in section 521) which is exempt from the tax imposed by this chapter.

(B) Exception where property will be used in unrelated business.—

(i) In general.—Subparagraph (A) shall not apply to any distribution of property to an organization described in section 511(a)(2) or 511(b)(2) if, immediately after such distribution, such organization uses such property in an unrelated trade or business (as defined in section 513).

(ii) Later disposition or change in use.—If any property to which clause (i) applied is disposed of by the organization acquiring such property, notwithstanding any other provision of law, any gain (not in excess of the amount not recognized by reason of clause (i) shall be included in such organization's unrelated business taxable income. For purposes of the preceding sentence, if such property ceases to be used in an unrelated trade or business of such organization, such organization shall be treated as having disposed of such property on the date of such cessation.

(c) 80-percent distributee.—For purposes of this section, the term "80-percent distributee" means only the corporation which meets the 80-percent stock ownership requirements specified in section 332(b).

(d) Regulations.—The Secretary shall prescribe such regulations as may be necessary or appropriate to carry out the purposes of the amendments made to this subpart by the Tax Reform Act of 1986, including—

(1) regulations to ensure that such purposes may not be circumvented through the use of any provision of law or regulations (including the consolidated return regulations and part III of this subchapter), and

(2) regulations providing for appropriate coordination of the provisions of this section with the provisions of this title relating to taxation of foreign corporations and their shareholders.

(Pub.L. 99–514, Title VI, § 631(a), Oct. 22, 1986, 100 Stat. ____.)

§ 338. Certain stock purchases treated as asset acquisitions

(a) General rule.—For purposes of this subtitle, if a purchasing corporation makes an election under this section (or is treated under subsection (e) as having made such an election), then, in the case of any qualified stock purchase, the target corporation—

(1) shall be treated as having sold all of its assets at the close of the acquisition date at fair market value in a single transaction, and

(2) shall be treated as a new corporation which purchased all of the assets referred to in paragraph (1) as of the beginning of the day after the acquisition date.

(b) Basis of assets after deemed purchase.—

(1) In general.—For purposes of subsection (a), the assets of the target corporation shall be treated as purchased for an amount equal to the sum of—

(A) the grossed-up basis of the purchasing corporation's recently purchased stock, and

(B) the basis of the purchasing corporation's nonrecently purchased stock.

(2) Adjustment for liabilities and other relevant items.—The amount described in paragraph (1) shall be adjusted under regulations prescribed by the Secretary for liabilities of the target corporation and other relevant items.

(3) Election to step-up the basis of certain target stock.—

(A) In general.—Under regulations prescribed by the Secretary, the basis of the purchasing corporation's nonrecently purchased stock shall be the basis amount determined under subparagraph (B) of this paragraph if the purchasing corporation makes an election to recognize gain as if such stock were sold on the acquisition date for an amount equal to the basis amount determined under subparagraph (B).

(B) Determination of basis amount.—For purposes of subparagraph (A), the basis amount determined under this subparagraph shall be an amount equal to the grossed-up basis determined under subparagraph (A) of paragraph (1) multiplied by a fraction—

(i) the numerator of which is the percentage of stock (by value) in the target corporation attributable to the purchasing corporation's nonrecently purchased stock, and

(ii) the denominator of which is 100 percent minus the percentage referred to in clause (i).

(4) Grossed-up basis.—For purposes of paragraph (1), the grossed-up basis shall be an amount equal to the basis of the corporation's recently purchased stock, multiplied by a fraction—

(A) the numerator of which is 100 percent, minus the percentage of stock (by value) in the target corporation attributable to the purchasing corporation's nonrecently purchased stock, and

(B) the denominator of which is the percentage of stock (by value) in the target corporation attributable to the purchasing corporation's recently purchased stock.

(5) Allocation among assets.—The amount determined under paragraphs (1) and (2) shall be allocated among the assets of the target corporation under regulations prescribed by the Secretary.

(6) Definitions of recently purchased stock and nonrecently purchased stock.—For purposes of this subsection—

(A) Recently purchased stock.—The term "recently purchased stock" means any stock in the target corporation which is held by the purchasing corporation on the acquisition date and which was purchased by such corporation during the 12-month acquisition period.

(B) Nonrecently purchased stock.—The term "nonrecently purchased stock" means any stock in the target corporation which is held by the purchasing corporation on the acquisition date and which is not recently purchased stock.

[(c) **Special rules.**—Repealed]

(d) **Purchasing corporation; target corporation; qualified stock purchase.** —For purposes of this section—

(1) Purchasing corporation.—The term "purchasing corporation" means any corporation which makes a qualified stock purchase of stock of another corporation.

(2) Target corporation.—The term "target corporation" means any corporation the stock of which is acquired by another corporation in a qualified stock purchase.

(3) Qualified stock purchase.—The term "qualified stock purchase" means any transaction or series of transactions in which stock (meeting the requirements of section 1504(a)(2)) of 1 corporation is acquired by another corporation by purchase during the 12–month acquisition period.

(e) Deemed election where purchasing corporation acquires asset of target corporation.—

(1) **In general.—**A purchasing corporation shall be treated as having made an election under this section with respect to any target corporation if, at any time during the consistency period, it acquires any asset of the target corporation (or a target affiliate).

(2) **Exceptions.—**Paragraph (1) shall not apply with respect to any acquisition by the purchasing corporation if—

(A) such acquisition is pursuant to a sale by the target corporation (or the target affiliate) in the ordinary course of its trade or business,

(B) the basis of the property acquired is determined (wholly) by reference to the adjusted basis of such property in the hands of the person from whom acquired,

(C) such acquisition was before September 1, 1982, or

(D) such acquisition is described in regulations prescribed by the Secretary and meets such conditions as such regulations may provide.

(3) **Anti-avoidance rule.—**Whenever necessary to carry out the purpose of this subsection and subsection (f), the Secretary may treat stock acquisitions which are pursuant to a plan and which meet the 80 percent requirements of subparagraphs (A) and (B) of subsection (d)(3) as qualified stock purchases.

(f) Consistency required for all stock acquisitions from same affiliated group.—If a purchasing corporation makes qualified stock purchases with respect to the target corporation and 1 or more target affiliates during any consistency period, then (except as otherwise provided in subsection (e))—

(1) any election under this section with respect to the first such purchase shall apply to each other such purchase, and

(2) no election may be made under this section with respect to the second or subsequent such purchase if such an election was not made with respect to the first such purchase.

(g) Election.—

(1) **When made.—**Except as otherwise provided in regulations, an election under this section shall be made not later than the 15th day of the 9th month beginning after the month in which the acquisition date occurs.

(2) **Manner.—**An election by the purchasing corporation under this section shall be made in such manner as the Secretary shall by regulations prescribe.

(3) **Election irrevocable.—**An election by a purchasing corporation under this section, once made, shall be irrevocable.

(h) Definitions and special rules.—For purposes of this section—

(1) **12-month acquisition period.—**The term "12-month acquisition period" means the 12-month period beginning with the date of the first acquisition by purchase of stock included in a qualified stock purchase (or, if any of such stock was acquired in an acquisition which is a purchase by reason of subparagraph (C) of paragraph (3), the date on which the acquiring corporation is first considered under section 318(a) (other than paragraph (4) thereof) as owning stock owned by the corporation from which such acquisition was made).

(2) Acquisition date.—The term "acquisition date" means, with respect to any corporation, the first day on which there is a qualified stock purchase with respect to the stock of such corporation.

(3) Purchase.—

(A) In general.—The term "purchase" means any acquisition of stock, but only if—

(i) the basis of the stock in the hands of the purchasing corporation is not determined (I) in whole or in part by reference to the adjusted basis of such stock in the hands of the person from whom acquired, or (II) under section 1014(a) (relating to property acquired from a decedent),

(ii) the stock is not acquired in an exchange to which section 351, 354, 355, or 356 applies and is not acquired in any other transaction described in regulations in which the transferor does not recognize the entire amount of the gain or loss realized on the transaction, and

(iii) the stock is not acquired from a person the ownership of whose stock would, under section 318(a) (other than paragraph (4) thereof), be attributed to the person acquiring such stock.

(B) Deemed purchase under subsection (a).—The term "purchase" includes any deemed purchase under subsection (a)(2). The acquisition date for a corporation which is deemed purchased under subsection (a)(2) shall be determined under regulations prescribed by the Secretary.

(C) Certain stock acquisitions from related corporations.—

(i) In general.—Clause (iii) of subparagraph (A) shall not apply to an acquisition of stock from a related corporation if at least 50 percent in value of the stock of such related corporation was acquired by purchase (within the meaning of subparagraphs (A) and (B)).

(ii) Certain distributions.—Clause (i) of subparagraph (A) shall not apply to an acquisition of stock described in clause (i) of this subparagraph if the corporation acquiring such stock—

(I) made a qualified stock purchase of stock of the related corporation, and

(II) made an election under this section (or is treated under subsection (e) as having made such an election) with respect to such qualified stock purchase.

(iii) Related corporation defined.—For purposes of this subparagraph, a corporation is a related corporation if stock owned by such corporation is treated (under section 318(a) other than paragraph (4) thereof) as owned by the corporation acquiring the stock.

(4) Consistency period.—

(A) In general.—Except as provided in subparagraph (B), the term "consistency period" means the period consisting of—

(i) the 1-year period before the beginning of the 12-month acquisition period for the target corporation,

(ii) such acquisition period (up to and including the acquisition date), and

(iii) the 1-year period beginning on the day after the acquisition date.

(B) Extension where there is plan.—The period referred to in subparagraph (A) shall also include any period during which the Secretary determines that there was in effect a plan to make a qualified stock purchase plus 1 or more other qualified stock purchases (or asset acquisitions described in subsection (e)) with respect to the target corporation or any target affiliate.

(5) Affiliated group.—The term "affiliated group" has the meaning given to such term by section 1504(a) (determined without regard to the exceptions contained in section 1504(b)).

(6) Target affiliate.—

(A) In general.—A corporation shall be treated as a target affiliate of the target corporation if each of such corporations was, at any time during so much of the consistency period as ends on the acquisition date of the target corporation, a member of an affiliated group which had the same common parent.

* * *

(7) Additional percentage must be attributable to purchase, etc.—For purposes of subsection (c)(1), any increase in the maximum percentage of stock taken into account over the percentage of stock (by value) of the target corporation held by the purchasing corporation on the acquisition date shall be taken into account only to the extent such increase is attributable to—

(A) purchase, or

(B) a redemption of stock of the target corporation—

(i) to which section 302(a) applies, or

(ii) in the case of a shareholder who is not a corporation, to which section 301 applies.

(8) Acquisitions by affiliated group treated as made by 1 corporation. —Except as provided in regulations prescribed by the Secretary, stock and asset acquisitions made by members of the same affiliated group shall be treated as made by 1 corporation.

(9) Target not treated as member of affiliated group.—Except as otherwise provided in paragraph (10) or in regulations prescribed under this paragraph, the target corporation shall not be treated as a member of an affiliated group with respect to the sale described in subsection (a)(1).

(10) Elective recognition of gain or loss by target corporation, together with nonrecognition of gain or loss on stock sold by selling consolidated group.—

(A) In general.—Under regulations prescribed by the Secretary, an election may be made under which if—

(i) the target corporation was, before the transaction, a member of the selling consolidated group, and

(ii) the target corporation recognizes gain or loss with respect to the transaction as if it sold all of its assets in a single transaction,

then the target corporation shall be treated as a member of the selling consolidated group with respect to such sale, and (to the extent provided in regulations) no gain or loss will be recognized on stock sold or exchanged in the transaction by members of the selling consolidated group.

(B) Selling consolidated group.—For purposes of subparagraph (A), the term "selling consolidated group" means any group of corporations which (for the taxable period which includes the transaction)—

(i) includes the target corporation, and

(ii) files a consolidated return.

To the extent provided in regulations, such term also includes any affiliated group of corporations which includes the target corporation (whether or not such group files a consolidated return).

(11) Elective formula for determining fair market value.—For purposes of subsection (a)(1), fair market value may be determined on the basis of a formula provided in regulations prescribed by the Secretary which takes into account liabilities and other relevant items.

[**(12) Repealed:**]

(13) Tax on deemed sale not taken into account for estimated tax purposes.—For purposes of section 6655, tax attributable to the sale described in subsection (a)(1) shall not be taken into account.

(14) Coordination with section 341.—For purposes of determining whether section 341 applies to a disposition within 1 year after the acquisition date of stock by a shareholder (other than the acquiring corporation) who held stock in the target corporation on the acquisition date, section 341 shall be applied without regard to this section.

(15) Combined deemed sale return.—Under regulations prescribed by the Secretary, a combined deemed sale return may be filed by all target corporations acquired by a purchasing corporation on the same acquisition date if such target corporations were members of the same selling consolidated group (as defined in subparagraph (B) of paragraph (10)).

(i) Regulations.—The Secretary shall prescribe such regulations as may be necessary or appropriate to carry out the purposes of this section, including—

(1) regulations to ensure that the purpose of this section to require consistency of treatment of stock and asset sales and purchases may not be circumvented through the use of any provision of law or regulations (including the consolidated return regulations) and

(2) regulations providing for the coordination of the provisions of this section with the provision of this title relating to foreign corporations and their shareholders.

Subpart C—Collapsible Corporations

§ 341. Collapsible corporations

(a) Treatment of gain to shareholders.—Gain from—

(1) the sale or exchange of stock of a collapsible corporation,

(2) a distribution—

(A) in complete liquidation of a collapsible corporation if such distribution is treated under this part as in part or full payment in exchange for stock, or

(B) in partial liquidation (within the meaning of section 302(e)) of a collapsible corporation if such distribution is treated under section 302(b)(4) as in part or full payment in exchange for the stock, and

(3) a distribution made by a collapsible corporation which, under section 301(c)(3)(A), is treated, to the extent it exceeds the basis of the stock, in the same manner as a gain from the sale or exchange of property,

to the extent that it would be considered (but for the provisions of this section) as gain from the sale or exchange of a capital asset shall, except as otherwise provided in this section, be considered as ordinary income.

(b) Definitions.—

(1) Collapsible corporation.—For purposes of this section, the term "collapsible corporation" means a corporation formed or availed of principally for the manufacture, construction, or production of property, for the purchase of property which (in the hands of the corporation) is property described in paragraph (3), or for the holding of stock in a corporation so formed or availed of, with a view to—

    (A) the sale or exchange of stock by its shareholders (whether in liquidation or otherwise), or a distribution to its shareholders, before the realization by the corporation manufacturing, constructing, producing, or purchasing the property of ⅔ of the taxable income to be derived from such property, and

    (B) the realization by such shareholders of gain attributable to such property.

(2) Production or purchase of property.—For purposes of paragraph (1), a corporation shall be deemed to have manufactured, constructed, produced, or purchased property, if—

    (A) it engaged in the manufacture, construction, or production of such property to any extent,

    (B) it holds property having a basis determined, in whole or in part, by reference to the cost of such property in the hands of a person who manufactured, constructed, produced, or purchased the property, or

    (C) it holds property having a basis determined, in whole or in part, by reference to the cost of property manufactured, constructed, produced, or purchased by the corporation.

(3) Section 341 assets.—For purposes of this section, the term "section 341 assets" means property held for a period of less than 3 years which is—

    (A) stock in trade of the corporation, or other property of a kind which would properly be included in the inventory of the corporation if on hand at the close of the taxable year;

    (B) property held by the corporation primarily for sale to customers in the ordinary course of its trade or business;

    (C) unrealized receivables or fees, except receivables from sales of property other than property described in this paragraph; or

    (D) property described in section 1231(b) (without regard to any holding period therein provided), except such property which is or has been used in connection with the manufacture, construction, production, or sale of property described in subparagraph (A) or (B).

In determining whether the 3-year holding period specified in this paragraph has been satisfied, section 1223 shall apply, but no such period shall be deemed to begin before the completion of the manufacture, construction, production, or purchase.

(4) Unrealized receivables.—For purposes of paragraph (3)(C), the term "unrealized receivables or fees" means, to the extent not previously includible in income under the method of accounting used by the corporation, any rights (contractual or otherwise) to payment for—

    (A) goods delivered, or to be delivered, to the extent the proceeds therefrom would be treated as amounts received from the sale or exchange of property other than a capital asset, or

    (B) services rendered or to be rendered.

(c) Presumption in certain cases.—

(1) **In general.**—For purposes of this section, a corporation shall, unless shown to the contrary, be deemed to be a collapsible corporation if (at the time of the sale or exchange, or the distribution, described in subsection (a)) the fair market value of its section 341 assets (as defined in subsection (b) (3)) is—

(A) 50 percent or more of the fair market value of its total assets, and

(B) 120 percent or more of the adjusted basis of such section 341 assets.

Absence of the conditions described in subparagraphs (A) and (B) shall not give rise to a presumption that the corporation was not a collapsible corporation.

(2) **Determination of total assets.**—In determining the fair market value of the total assets of a corporation for purposes of paragraph (1) (A), there shall not be taken into account—

(A) cash,

(B) obligations which are capital assets in the hands of the corporation, and

(C) stock in any other corporation.

(d) **Limitations on application of section.**—In the case of gain realized by a shareholder with respect to his stock in a collapsible corporation, this section shall not apply—

(1) unless, at any time after the commencement of the manufacture, construction, or production of the property, or at the time of the purchase of the property described in subsection (b) (3) or at any time thereafter, such shareholder (A) owned (or was considered as owning) more than 5 percent in value of the outstanding stock of the corporation, or (B) owned stock which was considered as owned at such time by another shareholder who then owned (or was considered as owning) more than 5 percent in value of the outstanding stock of the corporation;

(2) to the gain recognized during a taxable year, unless more than 70 percent of such gain is attributable to the property described in subsection (b)(1); and

(3) to gain realized after the expiration of 3 years following the completion of such manufacture, construction, production, or purchase.

For purposes of paragraph (1), the ownership of stock shall be determined in accordance with the rules prescribed in paragraphs (1), (2), (3), (5), and (6) of section 544(a) (relating to personal holding companies); except that, in addition to the persons prescribed by paragraph (2) of that section, the family of an individual shall include the spouses of that individual's brothers and sisters (whether by the whole or half blood) and the spouses of that individual's lineal descendants. In determining whether property is described in subsection (b)(1) for purposes of applying paragraph (2), all property described in section 1221(1) shall, to the extent provided in regulations prescribed by the Secretary, be treated as one item of property.

(e) **Exceptions to application of section.**—

(1) **Sales or exchanges of stock.**—For purposes of subsection (a) (1), a corporation shall not be considered to be a collapsible corporation with respect to any sale or exchange of stock of the corporation by a shareholder, if, at the time of such sale or exchange, the sum of—

(A) the net unrealized appreciation in subsection (e) assets of the corporation (as defined in paragraph (5) (A)), plus

(B) if the shareholder owns more than 5 percent in value of the outstanding stock of the corporation, the net unrealized appreciation in assets of the corporation (other than assets described in subparagraph (A)) which would be subsection

306

(e) assets under clauses (i) and (iii) of paragraph (5) (A) if the shareholder owned more than 20 percent in value of such stock, plus

(C) if the shareholder owns more than 20 percent in value of the outstanding stock of the corporation and owns, or at any time during the preceding 3-year period owned, more than 20 percent in value of the outstanding stock of any other corporation more than 70 percent in value of the assets of which are, or were at any time during which such shareholder owned during such 3-year period more than 20 percent in value of the outstanding stock, assets similar or related in service or use to assets comprising more than 70 percent in value of the assets of the corporation, the net unrealized appreciation in assets of the corporation (other than assets described in subparagraph (A)) which would be subsection (e) assets under clauses (i) and (iii) of paragraph (5) (A) if the determination whether the property, in the hands of such shareholder, would be property gain from the sale or exchange of which would under any provision of this chapter be considered in whole or in part as ordinary income, were made—

(i) by treating any sale or exchange by such shareholder of stock in such other corporation within the preceding 3-year period (but only if at the time of such sale or exchange the shareholder owned more than 20 percent in value of the outstanding stock in such other corporation) as a sale or exchange by such shareholder of his proportionate share of the assets of such other corporation, and

(ii) by treating any sale or exchange of property by such other corporation within such 3-year period (but only if at the time of such sale or exchange the shareholder owned more than 20 percent in value of the outstanding stock in such other corporation), gain or loss on which was not recognized to such other corporation under section 337(a), as a sale or exchange by such shareholder of his proportionate share of the property sold or exchanged,

does not exceed an amount equal to 15 percent of the net worth of the corporation. This paragraph shall not apply to any sale or exchange of stock to the issuing corporation or, in the case of a shareholder who owns more than 20 percent in value of the outstanding stock of the corporation, to any sale or exchange of stock by such shareholder to any person related to him (within the meaning of paragraph (8)).

* * *

(5) Subsection (e) asset defined.—

(A) For purposes of paragraph (1), the term "subsection (e) asset" means, with respect to property held by any corporation—

(i) property (except property used in the trade or business, as defined in paragraph (9)) which in the hands of the corporation is, or, in the hands of a shareholder who owns more than 20 percent in value of the outstanding stock of the corporation, would be, property gain from the sale or exchange of which would under any provision of this chapter be considered in whole or in part as ordinary income;

(ii) property used in the trade or business (as defined in paragraph (9)), but only if the unrealized depreciation on all such property on which there is unrealized depreciation exceeds the unrealized appreciation on all such property on which there is unrealized appreciation;

(iii) if there is net unrealized appreciation on all property used in the trade or business (as defined in paragraph (9)), property used in the trade or business (as defined in paragraph (9)) which, in the hands of a shareholder who owns more than 20 percent in value of the outstanding stock of the corporation, would be property gain from the sale or exchange of which would under any provision of this chapter be considered in whole or in part as ordinary income; and

(iv) property (unless included under clause (i), (ii), or (iii)) which consists of a copyright, a literary, musical, or artistic composition, a letter or memorandum, or similar property, or any interest in any such property, if the property was created in whole or in part by the personal efforts of, or (in the case of a letter, memorandum, or similar property) was prepared, or produced in whole or in part for, any individual who owns more than 5 percent in value of the stock of the corporation.

The determination as to whether property of the corporation in the hands of the corporation is, or in the hands of a shareholder would be, property gain from the sale or exchange of which would under any provision of this chapter be considered in whole or in part as ordinary income shall be made as if all property of the corporation had been sold or exchanged to one person in one transaction.

* * *

(6) Net unrealized appreciation defined.—

(A) For purposes of this subsection, the term "net unrealized appreciation" means, with respect to the assets of a corporation, the amount by which—

(i) the unrealized appreciation in such assets on which there is unrealized appreciation, exceeds

(ii) the unrealized depreciation in such assets on which there is unrealized depreciation.

(B) For purposes of subparagraph (A) and paragraph (5) (A), the term "unrealized appreciation" means, with respect to any asset, the amount by which—

(i) the fair market value of such asset, exceeds

(ii) the adjusted basis for determining gain from the sale or other disposition of such asset.

(C) For purposes of subparagraph (A) and paragraph (5) (A), the term "unrealized depreciation" means, with respect to any asset, the amount by which—

(i) the adjusted basis for determining gain from the sale or other disposition of such asset, exceeds

(ii) the fair market value of such asset.

(D) For purposes of this paragraph (but not paragraph (5) (A)), in the case of any asset on the sale or exchange of which only a portion of the gain would under any provision of this chapter be considered as ordinary income, there shall be taken into account only an amount of the unrealized appreciation in such asset which is equal to such portion of the gain.

(7) Net worth defined.—For purposes of this subsection, the net worth of a corporation, as of any day, is the amount by which—

(A) (i) the fair market value of all its assets at the close of such day, plus

(ii) the amount of any distribution in complete liquidation made by it on or before such day, exceeds

(B) all its liabilities at the close of such day.

For purposes of this paragraph, the net worth of a corporation as of any day shall not take into account any increase in net worth during the one-year period ending on such day to the extent attributable to any amount received by it for stock, or as a contribution to capital or as paid-in surplus, if it appears that there was not a bona fide business purpose for the transaction in respect of which such amount was received.

(8) **Related person defined.**—For purposes of paragraphs (1) and (4), the following persons shall be considered to be related to a shareholder:

(A) If the shareholder is an individual—

(i) his spouse, ancestors, and lineal descendants, and

(ii) a corporation which is controlled by such shareholder.

(B) If the shareholder is a corporation—

(i) a corporation which controls, or is controlled by, the shareholder, and

(ii) if more than 50 percent in value of the outstanding stock of the shareholder is owned by any person, a corporation more than 50 percent in value of the outstanding stock of which is owned by the same person.

For purposes of determining the ownership of stock in applying subparagraphs (A) and (B), the rules of section 267(c) shall apply, except that the family of an individual shall include only his spouse, ancestors, and lineal descendants. For purposes of this paragraph, control means the ownership of stock possessing at least 50 percent of the total combined voting power of all classes of stock entitled to vote or at least 50 percent of the total value of shares of all classes of stock of the corporation.

(9) **Property used in the trade or business.**—For purposes of this subsection, the term "property used in the trade or business" means property described in section 1231(b), without regard to any holding period therein provided.

(10) **Ownership of stock.**—For purposes of this subsection (other than paragraph (8)), the ownership of stock shall be determined in the manner prescribed in subsection (d).

(11) **Corporations and shareholders not meeting requirements.**—In determining whether or not any corporation is a collapsible corporation within the meaning of subsection (b), the fact that such corporation, or such corporation with respect to any of its shareholders, does not meet the requirements of paragraph (1), (2), (3), or (4) of this subsection shall not be taken into account, and such determination, in the case of a corporation which does not meet such requirements, shall be made as if this subsection had not been enacted.

(12) **Nonapplication of section 1245(a), etc.**—For purposes of this subsection, the determination of whether gain from the sale or exchange of property would under any provision of this chapter be considered as ordinary income shall be made without regard to the application of sections 617(d)(1), 1245(a), 1250(a), 1252(a), 1254(a), and 1276(a).

(f) Certain sales of stock of consenting corporations.—

(1) **In general.**—Subsection (a) (1) shall not apply to a sale of stock of a corporation (other than a sale to the issuing corporation) if such corporation (hereinafter in this subsection referred to as "consenting corporation") consents (at such time and in such manner as the Secretary may by regulations prescribe) to have the provisions of paragraph (2) apply. Such consent shall apply with respect to each sale of stock of such corporation made within the 6-month period beginning with the date on which such consent is filed.

(2) **Recognition of gain.**—Except as provided in paragraph (3), if a subsection (f) asset (as defined in paragraph (4)) is disposed of at any time by a consenting

corporation (or, if paragraph (3) applies, by a transferee corporation), then the amount by which—

(A) in the case of a sale, exchange, or involuntary conversion, the amount realized, or

(B) in the case of any other disposition, the fair market value of such asset,

exceeds the adjusted basis of such asset shall be treated as gain from the sale or exchange of such asset. Such gain shall be recognized notwithstanding any other provision of this subtitle, but only to the extent such gain is not recognized under any other provision of this subtitle.

(3) **Exception for certain tax-free transactions.**—If the basis of a subsection (f) asset in the hands of a transferee is determined by reference to its basis in the hands of the transferor by reason of the application of section 332, 351, 361, 371(a), or 374(a), then the amount of gain taken into account by the transferor under paragraph (2) shall not exceed the amount of gain recognized to the transferor on the transfer of such asset (determined without regard to this subsection). This paragraph shall apply only if the transferee—

(A) is not an organization which is exempt from tax imposed by this chapter, and

(B) agrees (at such time and in such manner as the Secretary may by regulations prescribe) to have the provisions of paragraph (2) apply to any disposition by it of such subsection (f) asset.

(4) **Subsection (f) asset defined.**—For purposes of this subsection—

(A) **In general.**—The term "subsection (f) asset" means any property which, as of the date of any sale of stock referred to in paragraph (1), is not a capital asset and is property owned by, or subject to an option to acquire held by, the consenting corporation. For purposes of this subparagraph, land or any interest in real property (other than a security interest), and unrealized receivables or fees (as defined in subsection (b) (4)), shall be treated as property which is not a capital asset.

(B) **Property under construction.**—If manufacture, construction, or production with respect to any property described in subparagraph (A) has commenced before any date of sale described therein, the term "subsection (f) asset" includes the property resulting from such manufacture, construction, or production.

(C) **Special rule for land.**—In the case of land or any interest in real property (other than a security interest) described in subparagraph (A), the term "subsection (f) asset" includes any improvements resulting from construction with respect to such property if such construction is commenced (by the consenting corporation or by a transferee corporation which has agreed to the application of paragraph (2)) within 2 years after the date of any sale described in subparagraph (A).

(5) **5-year limitation as to shareholder.**—Paragraph (1) shall not apply to the sale of stock of a corporation by a shareholder if, during the 5-year period ending on the date of such sale, such shareholder (or any related person within the meaning of subsection (e) (8) (A)) sold any stock of another consenting corporation within any 6-month period beginning on a date on which a consent was filed under paragraph (1) by such other corporation.

(6) **Special rule for stock ownership in other corporations.**—If a corporation (hereinafter in this paragraph referred to as "owning corporation") owns 5 percent or more in value of the outstanding stock of another corporation on the date of any sale of stock of the owning corporation during a 6-month period with respect to

which a consent under paragraph (1) was filed by the owning corporation, such consent shall not be valid with respect to such sale unless such other corporation has (within the 6-month period ending on the date of such sale) filed a valid consent under paragraph (1) with respect to sales of its stock. For purposes of applying paragraph (4) to such other corporation, a sale of stock of the owning corporation to which paragraph (1) applies shall be treated as a sale of stock of such other corporation. In the case of a chain of corporations connected by the 5-percent ownership requirements of this paragraph, rules similar to the rules of the two preceding sentences shall be applied.

(7) Adjustments to basis.—The Secretary shall prescribe such regulations as he may deem necessary to provide for adjustments to the basis of property to reflect gain recognized under paragraph (2).

* * *

Subpart D—Definition and Special Rule

§ 346. Definition and special rule

(a) Complete liquidation.—For purposes of this subchapter, a distribution shall be treated as in complete liquidation of a corporation if the distribution is one of a series of distributions in redemption of all of the stock of the corporation pursuant to a plan.

(b) Transactions which might reach same result as partial liquidations.—The Secretary shall prescribe such regulations as may be necessary to ensure that the purposes of subsections (a) and (b) of section 222 of the Tax Equity and Fiscal Responsibility Act of 1982 (which repeal the special tax treatment for partial liquidations) may not be circumvented through the use of section 355, 351, or any other provision of law or regulations (including the consolidated return regulations).

PART III—CORPORATE ORGANIZATIONS AND REORGANIZATIONS

Subpart
A. Corporate organizations.
B. Effects on shareholders and security holders.
C. Effects on corporation.
D. Special rule; definitions.

Subpart A—Corporate Organizations

§ 351. Transfer to corporation controlled by transferor

(a) General rule.—No gain or loss shall be recognized if property is transferred to a corporation by one or more persons solely in exchange for stock or securities in such corporation and immediately after the exchange such person or persons are in control (as defined in section 368(c)) of the corporation.

(b) Receipt of property.—If subsection (a) would apply to an exchange but for the fact that there is received, in addition to the stock or securities permitted to be received under subsection (a), other property or money, then—

(1) gain (if any) to such recipient shall be recognized, but not in excess of—

(A) the amount of money received, plus

(B) the fair market value of such other property received; and

(2) no loss to such recipient shall be recognized.

(c) **Special rule.**—In determining control, for purposes of this section, the fact that any corporate transferor distributes part or all of the stock which it receives in the exchange to its shareholders shall not be taken into account.

(d) **Services, certain indebtedness, and accrued interest not treated as property.**—For purposes of this section, stock or securities issued for—

(1) services,

(2) indebtedness of the transferee corporation which is not evidenced by a security, or

(3) interest on indebtedness of the transferee corporation which accrued on or after the beginning of the transferor's holding period for the debt,

shall not be considered as issued in return for property.

(e) **Exceptions.**—This section shall not apply to—

(1) **Transfer of property to an investment company.**—A transfer of property to an investment company.

(2) **Title 11 or similar case.**—A transfer of property of a debtor pursuant to a plan while the debtor is under the jurisdiction of a court in a title 11 or similar case (within the meaning of section 368(a)(3)(A)), to the extent that the stock or securities received in the exchange are used to satisfy the indebtedness of such debtor.

(f) **Cross references.—**

(1) For special rule where another party to the exchange assumes a liability, or acquires property subject to a liability, see section 357.

(2) For the basis of stock, securities, or property received in an exchange to which this section applies, see sections 358 and 362.

(3) For special rule in the case of an exchange described in this section but which results in a gift, see section 2501 and following.

(4) For special rule in the case of an exchange described in this section but which has the effect of the payment of compensation by the corporation or by a transferor, see section 61(a)(1).

(5) For coordination of this section with section 304, see section 304(b)(3).

Subpart B—Effects on Shareholders and Security Holders

§ 354. Exchanges of stock and securities in certain reorganizations

(a) **General rule.—**

(1) **In general.**—No gain or loss shall be recognized if stock or securities in a corporation a party to a reorganization are, in pursuance of the plan of reorganization, exchanged solely for stock or securities in such corporation or in another corporation a party to the reorganization.

(2) **Limitations.—**

(A) **Excess principal amount.**—Paragraph (1) shall not apply if—

(i) the principal amount of any such securities received exceeds the principal amount of any such securities surrendered, or

(ii) any such securities are received and no such securities are surrendered.

(B) Property attributable to accrued interest.—Neither paragraph (1) nor so much of section 356 as relates to paragraph (1) shall apply to the extent that any stock, securities, or other property received is attributable to interest which has accrued on securities on or after the beginning of the holder's holding period.

(3) Cross references.—

(A) For treatment of the exchange if any property is received which is not permitted to be received under this subsection (including an excess principal amount of securities received over securities surrendered, but not including property to which paragraph (2)(B) applies), see section 356.

(B) For treatment of accrued interest in the case of an exchange described in paragraph (2)(B), see section 61.

(b) Exception.—

(1) In general.—Subsection (a) shall not apply to an exchange in pursuance of a plan of reorganization within the meaning of subparagraph (D) or (G) of section 368(a)(1), unless—

(A) the corporation to which the assets are transferred acquires substantially all of the assets of the transferor of such assets; and

(B) the stock, securities, and other properties received by such transferor, as well as the other properties of such transferor, are distributed in pursuance of the plan of reorganization.

(2) Cross reference.—

For special rules for certain exchanges in pursuance of plans of reorganization within the meaning of subparagraph (D) or (G) of section 368(a)(1), see section 355.

* * *

§ 355. Distribution of stock and securities of a controlled corporation

(a) Effect on distributees.—

(1) General rule.—If—

(A) a corporation (referred to in this section as the "distributing corporation")—

(i) distributes to a shareholder, with respect to its stock, or

(ii) distributes to a security holder, in exchange for its securities,

solely stock or securities of a corporation (referred to in this section as "controlled corporation") which it controls immediately before the distribution,

(B) the transaction was not used principally as a device for the distribution of the earnings and profits of the distributing corporation or the controlled corporation or both (but the mere fact that subsequent to the distribution stock or securities in one or more of such corporations are sold or exchanged by all or some of the distributees (other than pursuant to an arrangement negotiated or agreed upon prior to such distribution) shall not be construed to mean that the transaction was used principally as such a device),

(C) the requirements of subsection (b) (relating to active businesses) are satisfied, and

(D) as part of the distribution, the distributing corporation distributes—

(i) all of the stock and securities in the controlled corporation held by it immediately before the distribution, or

(ii) an amount of stock in the controlled corporation constituting control within the meaning of section 368(c), and it is established to the satisfaction of the Secretary that the retention by the distributing corporation of stock (or stock and securities) in the controlled corporation was not in pursuance of a plan having as one of its principal purposes the avoidance of Federal income tax,

then no gain or loss shall be recognized to (and no amount shall be includible in the income of) such shareholder or security holder on the receipt of such stock or securities.

(2) **Non pro rata distributions, etc.**—Paragraph (1) shall be applied without regard to the following:

(A) whether or not the distribution is pro rata with respect to all of the shareholders of the distributing corporation,

(B) whether or not the shareholder surrenders stock in the distributing corporation, and

(C) whether or not the distribution is in pursuance of a plan of reorganization (within the meaning of section 368(a) (1) (D)).

(3) **Limitations.**—

(A) **Excess principal amount.**—Paragraph (1) shall not apply if—

(i) the principal amount of the securities in the controlled corporation which are received exceeds the principal amount of the securities which are surrendered in connection with such distribution, or

(ii) securities in the controlled corporation are received and no securities are surrendered in connection with such distribution.

(B) **Stock acquired in taxable transactions within 5 years treated as boot.**—For purposes of this section (other than paragraph (1)(D) of this subsection) and so much of section 356 as relates to this section, stock of a controlled corporation acquired by the distributing corporation by reason of any transaction—

(i) which occurs within 5 years of the distribution of such stock, and

(ii) in which gain or loss was recognized in whole or in part,

shall not be treated as stock of such controlled corporation, but as other property.

(C) **Property attributable to accrued interest.**—Neither paragraph (1) nor so much of section 356 as relates to paragraph (1) shall apply to the extent that any stock, securities, or other property received is attributable to interest which has accrued on securities on or after the beginning of the holder's holding period.

(4) **Cross references.**—

(A) For treatment of the exchange if any property is received which is not permitted to be received under this subsection (including an excess principal amount of securities received over securities surrendered, but not including property to which paragraph (3)(C) applies), see section 356.

(B) For treatment of accrued interest in the case of an exchange described in paragraph (3)(C), see section 61.

(b) Requirements as to active business.—

(1) **In general.**—Subsection (a) shall apply only if either—

(A) the distributing corporation, and the controlled corporation (or, if stock of more than one controlled corporation is distributed, each of such corporations), is engaged immediately after the distribution in the active conduct of a trade or business, or

(B) immediately before the distribution, the distributing corporation had no assets other than stock or securities in the controlled corporations and each of the controlled corporations is engaged immediately after the distribution in the active conduct of a trade or business.

(2) Definition.—For purposes of paragraph (1), a corporation shall be treated as engaged in the active conduct of a trade or business if and only if—

(A) it is engaged in the active conduct of a trade or business, or substantially all of its assets consist of stock and securities of a corporation controlled by it (immediately after the distribution) which is so engaged,

(B) such trade or business has been actively conducted throughout the 5-year period ending on the date of the distribution,

(C) such trade or business was not acquired within the period described in subparagraph (B) in a transaction in which gain or loss was recognized in whole or in part, and

(D) control of a corporation which (at the time of acquisition of control) was conducting such trade or business—

(i) was not acquired directly (or through one or more corporations) by another corporation within the period described in subparagraph (B), or

(ii) was so acquired by another corporation within such period, but such control was so acquired only by reason of transactions in which gain or loss was not recognized in whole or in part, or only by reason of such transactions combined with acquisitions before the beginning of such period.

§ 356. Receipt of additional consideration

(a) Gain on exchanges.—

(1) Recognition of gain.—If—

(A) section 354 or 355 would apply to an exchange but for the fact that

(B) the property received in the exchange consists not only of property permitted by section 354 or 355 to be received without the recognition of gain but also of other property or money,

then the gain, if any, to the recipient shall be recognized, but in an amount not in excess of the sum of such money and the fair market value of such other property.

(2) Treatment as dividend.—If an exchange is described in paragraph (1) but has the effect of the distribution of a dividend (determined with the application of section 318(a)), then there shall be treated as a dividend to each distributee such an amount of the gain recognized under paragraph (1) as is not in excess of his ratable share of the undistributed earnings and profits of the corporation accumulated after February 28, 1913. The remainder, if any, of the gain recognized under paragraph (1) shall be treated as gain from the exchange of property.

(b) Additional consideration received in certain distributions.—If—

(1) section 355 would apply to a distribution but for the fact that

(2) the property received in the distribution consists not only of property permitted by section 355 to be received without the recognition of gain, but also of other property or money, then an amount equal to the sum of such money and the fair market value of such other property shall be treated as a distribution of property to which section 301 applies.

(c) **Loss.**—If—

(1) section 354 would apply to an exchange, or section 355 would apply to an exchange or distribution, but for the fact that

(2) the property received in the exchange or distribution consists not only of property permitted by section 354 or 355 to be received without the recognition of gain or loss, but also of other property or money,

then no loss from the exchange or distribution shall be recognized.

(d) **Securities as other property.**—For purposes of this section—

(1) **In general.**—Except as provided in paragraph (2), the term "other property" includes securities.

(2) **Exceptions.**—

(A) **Securities with respect to which nonrecognition of gain would be permitted.**—The term "other property" does not include securities to the extent that, under section 354 or 355, such securities would be permitted to be received without the recognition of gain.

(B) **Greater principal amount in section 354 exchange.**—If—

(i) in an exchange described in section 354 (other than subsection (c) or (d) thereof), securities of a corporation a party to the reorganization are surrendered and securities of any corporation a party to the reorganization are received, and

(ii) the principal amount of such securities received exceeds the principal amount of such securities surrendered,

then, with respect to such securities received, the term "other property" means only the fair market value of such excess. For purposes of this subparagraph and subparagraph (C), if no securities are surrendered, the excess shall be the entire principal amount of the securities received.

(C) **Greater principal amount in section 355 transaction.**—If, in an exchange or distribution described in section 355, the principal amount of the securities in the controlled corporation which are received exceeds the principal amount of the securities in the distributing corporation which are surrendered, then, with respect to such securities received, the term "other property" means only the fair market value of such excess.

(e) **Exchanges for section 306 stock.**—Notwithstanding any other provision of this section, to the extent that any of the other property (or money) is received in exchange for section 306 stock, an amount equal to the fair market value of such other property (or the amount of such money) shall be treated as a distribution of property to which section 301 applies.

(f) **Transactions involving gift or compensation.**—

For special rules for a transaction described in section 354, 355, or this section, but which—

(1) **results in a gift, see section 2501 and following, or**

(2) **has the effect of the payment of compensation, see section 61(a)(1).**

§ 357. Assumption of liability

(a) General rule.—Except as provided in subsections (b) and (c), if—

(1) the taxpayer receives property which would be permitted to be received under section 351, 361, 371, or 374 without the recognition of gain if it were the sole consideration, and

(2) as part of the consideration, another party to the exchange assumes a liability of the taxpayer, or acquires from the taxpayer property subject to a liability,

then such assumption or acquisition shall not be treated as money or other property, and shall not prevent the exchange from being within the provisions of section 351, 361, 371, or 374, as the case may be.

(b) Tax avoidance purpose.—

(1) In general.—If, taking into consideration the nature of the liability and the circumstances in the light of which the arrangement for the assumption or acquisition was made, it appears that the principal purpose of the taxpayer with respect to the assumption or acquisition described in subsection (a)—

(A) was a purpose to avoid Federal income tax on the exchange, or

(B) if not such purpose, was not a bona fide business purpose,

then such assumption or acquisition (in the total amount of the liability assumed or acquired pursuant to such exchange) shall, for purposes of section 351, 361, 371, or 374 (as the case may be), be considered as money received by the taxpayer on the exchange.

(2) Burden of proof.—In any suit or proceeding where the burden is on the taxpayer to prove such assumption or acquisition is not to be treated as money received by the taxpayer, such burden shall not be considered as sustained unless the taxpayer sustains such burden by the clear preponderance of the evidence.

(c) Liabilities in excess of basis.—

(1) In general.—In the case of an exchange—

(A) to which section 351 applies, or

(B) to which section 361 applies by reason of a plan of reorganization within the meaning of section 368(a) (1) (D),

if the sum of the amount of the liabilities assumed, plus the amount of the liabilities to which the property is subject, exceeds the total of the adjusted basis of the property transferred pursuant to such exchange, then such excess shall be considered as a gain from the sale or exchange of a capital asset or of property which is not a capital asset, as the case may be.

(2) Exceptions.—Paragraph (1) shall not apply to any exchange—

(A) to which subsection (b)(1) of this section applies,

(B) to which section 371 or 374 applies, or

(C) which is pursuant to a plan of reorganization within the meaning of section 368(a)(1)(G) where no former shareholder of the transferor corporation receives any consideration for his stock.

(3) Certain liabilities excluded.—

(A) In general.—If a taxpayer transfers, in an exchange to which section 351 applies, a liability the payment of which either—

(i) would give rise to a deduction, or

(ii) would be described in section 736(a),

then, for purposes of paragraph (1), the amount of such liability shall be excluded in determining the amount of liabilities assumed or to which the property transferred is subject.

(B) Exception.—Subparagraph (A) shall not apply to any liability to the extent that the incurrence of the liability resulted in the creation of, or an increase in, the basis of any property.

§ 358. Basis to distributees

(a) General rule.—In the case of an exchange to which section 351, 354, 355, 356, 361, 371(b), or 374 applies—

(1) Nonrecognition property.—The basis of the property permitted to be received under such section without the recognition of gain or loss shall be the same as that of the property exchanged—

(A) decreased by—

(i) the fair market value of any other property (except money) received by the taxpayer,

(ii) the amount of any money received by the taxpayer, and

(iii) the amount of loss to the taxpayer which was recognized on such exchange, and

(B) increased by—

(i) the amount which was treated as a dividend, and

(ii) the amount of gain to the taxpayer which was recognized on such exchange (not including any portion of such gain which was treated as a dividend).

(2) Other property.—The basis of any other property (except money) received by the taxpayer shall be its fair market value.

(b) Allocation of basis.—

(1) In general.—Under regulations prescribed by the Secretary, the basis determined under subsection (a) (1) shall be allocated among the properties permitted to be received without the recognition of gain or loss.

(2) Special rule for section 355.—In the case of an exchange to which section 355 (or so much of section 356 as relates to section 355) applies, then in making the allocation under paragraph (1) of this subsection, there shall be taken into account not only the property so permitted to be received without the recognition of gain or loss, but also the stock or securities (if any) of the distributing corporation which are retained, and the allocation of basis shall be made among all such properties.

* * *

(c) Section 355 transactions which are not exchanges.—For purposes of this section, a distribution to which section 355 (or so much of section 356 as relates to section 355) applies shall be treated as an exchange, and for such purposes the stock and securities of the distributing corporation which are retained shall be treated as surrendered, and received back, in the exchange.

(d) Assumption of liability.—

(1) In general.—Where, as part of the consideration to the taxpayer, another party to the exchange assumed a liability of the taxpayer or acquired from the taxpayer property subject to a liability, such assumption or acquisition (in the amount of the liability) shall, for purposes of this section, be treated as money received by the taxpayer on the exchange.

(2) **Exception.**—Paragraph (1) shall not apply to the amount of any liability excluded under section 357(c) (3).

(e) **Exception.**—This section shall not apply to property acquired by a corporation by the exchange of its stock or securities (or the stock or securities of a corporation which is in control of the acquiring corporation) as consideration in whole or in part for the transfer of the property to it.

Subpart C—Effects on Corporation

§ 361. Nonrecognition of gain or loss to transferor corporation; other treatment of transferor corporation; etc.

(a) **General rule.**—No gain or loss shall be recognized to a transferor corporation which is a party to a reorganization on any exchange of property pursuant to the plan of reorganization.

(b) **Other treatment of transferor corporation.**—In the case of a transferor corporation which is a party to a reorganization—

(1) sections 336 and 337 shall not apply with respect to any liquidation of such corporation pursuant to the plan of reorganization,

(2) the basis of the property (other than stock and securities described in paragraph (3)) received by the corporation pursuant to such plan of reorganization shall be the same as it would be in the hands of the transferor of such property, adjusted by the amount of gain or loss recognized to such transferor on such transfer, and

(3) no gain or loss shall be recognized by such corporation on any disposition (pursuant to the plan of reorganization) of stock or securities which were received pursuant to such plan and which are in another corporation which is a party to such reorganization.

For purposes of paragraph (3), if the transferor corporation is merged, consolidated, or liquidated pursuant to the plan of reorganization, or if a transaction meets the requirements of section 368(a)(1)(C) pursuant to a waiver granted by the Secretary under section 368(a)(2)(G)(ii), any distribution of such stock or securities by the transferor corporation to its creditors in connection with such transaction shall be treated as pursuant to such plan of reorganization.

(c) **Treatment of distributions of appreciated property.**—Notwithstanding any other provision of this subtitle, gain shall be recognized on the distribution of property (other than property permitted by section 354, 355, or 356 to be received without the recognition of gain) pursuant to a plan of reorganization in the same manner as if such property had been sold to the distributee at its fair market value.

§ 362. Basis to corporations

(a) **Property acquired by issuance of stock or as paid-in surplus.**—If property was acquired on or after June 22, 1954, by a corporation—

(1) in connection with a transaction to which section 351 (relating to transfer of property to corporation controlled by transferor) applies, or

(2) as paid-in surplus or as a contribution to capital,

then the basis shall be the same as it would be in the hands of the transferor, increased in the amount of gain recognized to the transferor on such transfer.

(b) Transfers to corporations.—If property was acquired by a corporation in connection with a reorganization to which this part applies, then the basis shall be the same as it would be in the hands of the transferor, increased in the amount of gain recognized to the transferor on such transfer. This subsection shall not apply if the property acquired consists of stock or securities in a corporation a party to the reorganization, unless acquired by the exchange of stock or securities of the transferee (or of a corporation which is in control of the transferee) as the consideration in whole or in part for the transfer.

(c) Special rule for certain contributions to capital.—

(1) **Property other than money.**—Notwithstanding subsection (a) (2), if property other than money—

(A) is acquired by a corporation, on or after June 22, 1954, as a contribution to capital, and

(B) is not contributed by a shareholder as such,

then the basis of such property shall be zero.

(2) **Money.**—Notwithstanding subsection (a) (2), if money—

(A) is received by a corporation, on or after June 22, 1954, as a contribution to capital, and

(B) is not contributed by a shareholder as such,

then the basis of any property acquired with such money during the 12-month period beginning on the day the contribution is received shall be reduced by the amount of such contribution. The excess (if any) of the amount of such contribution over the amount of the reduction under the preceding sentence shall be applied to the reduction (as of the last day of the period specified in the preceding sentence) of the basis of any other property held by the taxpayer. The particular properties to which the reductions required by this paragraph shall be allocated shall be determined under regulations prescribed by the Secretary.

Subpart D—Special Rule; Definitions

§ 368. Definitions relating to corporate reorganizations

(a) Reorganization.—

(1) **In general.**—For purposes of parts I and II and this part, the term "reorganization" means—

(A) a statutory merger or consolidation;

(B) the acquisition by one corporation, in exchange solely for all or a part of its voting stock (or in exchange solely for all or a part of the voting stock of a corporation which is in control of the acquiring corporation), of stock of another corporation if, immediately after the acquisition, the acquiring corporation has control of such other corporation (whether or not such acquiring corporation had control immediately before the acquisition);

(C) the acquisition by one corporation, in exchange solely for all or a part of its voting stock (or in exchange solely for all or a part of the voting stock of a corporation which is in control of the acquiring corporation), of substantially all of the properties of another corporation, but in determining whether the exchange is solely for stock the assumption by the acquiring corporation of a liability of the other, or the fact that property acquired is subject to a liability, shall be disregarded;

(D) a transfer by a corporation of all or a part of its assets to another corporation if immediately after the transfer the transferor, or one or more of its shareholders (including persons who were shareholders immediately before the transfer), or any combination thereof, is in control of the corporation to which the assets are transferred; but only if, in pursuance of the plan, stock or securities of the corporation to which the assets are transferred are distributed in a transaction which qualifies under section 354, 355, or 356;

(E) a recapitalization;

(F) a mere change in identity, form, or place of organization of one corporation, however effected; or

(G) a transfer by a corporation of all or part of its assets to another corporation in a title 11 or similar case; but only if, in pursuance of the plan, stock or securities of the corporation to which the assets are transferred are distributed in a transaction which qualifies under section 354, 355, or 356.

(2) Special rules relating to paragraph (1).—

(A) Reorganizations described in both paragraph (1) (C) and paragraph (1) (D).—If a transaction is described in both paragraph (1) (C) and paragraph (1) (D), then, for purposes of this subchapter (other than for purposes of subparagraph (c)), such transaction shall be treated as described only in paragraph (1) (D).

(B) Additional consideration in certain paragraph (1) (C) cases.—If—

(i) one corporation acquires substantially all of the properties of another corporation,

(ii) the acquisition would qualify under paragraph (1) (C) but for the fact that the acquiring corporation exchanges money or other property in addition to voting stock, and

(iii) the acquiring corporation acquires, solely for voting stock described in paragraph (1) (C), property of the other corporation having a fair market value which is at least 80 percent of the fair market value of all of the property of the other corporation,

then such acquisition shall (subject to subparagraph (A) of this paragraph) be treated as qualifying under paragraph (1) (C). Solely for the purpose of determining whether clause (iii) of the preceding sentence applies, the amount of any liability assumed by the acquiring corporation, and the amount of any liability to which any property acquired by the acquiring corporation is subject, shall be treated as money paid for the property.

(C) Transfers of assets or stock to subsidiaries in certain paragraph (1)(A), (1)(B), (1)(C), and (1)(G) cases.—A transaction otherwise qualifying under paragraph (1)(A), (1)(B), or (1)(C) shall not be disqualified by reason of the fact that part or all of the assets or stock which were acquired in the transaction are transferred to a corporation controlled by the corporation acquiring such assets or stock. A similar rule shall apply to a transaction otherwise qualifying under paragraph (1)(G) where the requirements of subparagraphs (A) and (B) of section 354(b)(1) are met with respect to the acquisition of the assets.

(D) Use of stock of controlling corporation in paragraph (1)(A) and (1)(G) cases.—The acquisition by one corporation, in exchange for stock of a corporation (referred to in this subparagraph as "controlling corporation") which is in control of the acquiring corporation, of substantially all of the properties of another corporation shall not disqualify a transaction under paragraph (1)(A) or (1)(G) if—

(i) no stock of the acquiring corporation is used in the transaction, and

(ii) in the case of a transaction under paragraph (1)(A), such transaction would have qualified under paragraph (1)(A) had the merger been into the controlling corporation.

(E) Statutory merger using voting stock of corporation controlling merged corporation.—A transaction otherwise qualifying under paragraph (1)(A) shall not be disqualified by reason of the fact that stock of a corporation (referred to in this subparagraph as the "controlling corporation") which before the merger was in control of the merged corporation is used in the transaction, if—

(i) after the transaction, the corporation surviving the merger holds substantially all of its properties and of the properties of the merged corporation (other than stock of the controlling corporation distributed in the transaction); and

(ii) in the transaction, former shareholders of the surviving corporation exchanged, for an amount of voting stock of the controlling corporation, an amount of stock in the surviving corporation which constitutes control of such corporation.

(F) Certain transactions involving 2 or more investment companies.—

(i) If immediately before a transaction described in paragraph (1) (other than subparagraph (E) thereof), 2 or more parties to the transaction were investment companies, then the transaction shall not be considered to be a reorganization with respect to any such investment company (and its shareholders and security holders) unless it was a regulated investment company, a real estate investment trust, or a corporation which meets the requirements of clause (ii).

(ii) A corporation meets the requirements of this clause if not more than 25 percent of the value of its total assets is invested in the stock and securities of any one issuer (other than stock in a regulated investment company, a real estate investment trust, or an investment company which meets the requirements of this clause (ii)), and not more than 50 percent of the value of its total assets is invested in the stock and securities of 5 or fewer issuers (other than stock in a regulated investment company, a real estate investment trust, or an investment company which meets the requirements of this clause (ii)). For purposes of this clause, all members of a controlled group of corporations (within the meaning of section 1563(a)) shall be treated as one issuer.

* * *

(G) Distribution requirement for paragraph (1)(C).—

(i) **In general.**—A transaction shall fail to meet the requirements of paragraph (1)(C) unless the acquired corporation distributes the stock, securities, and other properties it receives, as well as its other properties, in pursuance of the plan of reorganization. "For purposes of the preceding sentence, if the acquired corporation is liquidated pursuant to the plan of reorganization, any distribution to its creditors in connection with such liquidation shall be treated as pursuant to the plan of reorganization.

(ii) **Exception.**—The Secretary may waive the application of clause (i) to any transaction subject to any conditions the Secretary may prescribe.

(H) Special rule for determining whether certain transactions are qualified under paragraph (1)(D).—In the case of any transaction with respect to which the requirements of subparagraphs (A) and (B) of section 354(b)(1) are met, for purposes of determining whether such transaction qualifies under subparagraph (D) of paragraph (1), the term "control" has the meaning given to such term by section 304(c).

(3) Additional rules relating to title 11 and similar cases.—

(A) Title 11 or similar case defined.—For purposes of this part, the term "title 11 or similar case" means—

(i) a case under title 11 of the United States Code, or

(ii) a receivership, foreclosure, or similar proceeding in a Federal or State court.

(B) Transfer of assets in a title 11 or similar case.—In applying paragraph (1)(G), a transfer of the assets of a corporation shall be treated as made in a title 11 or similar case if and only if—

(i) any party to the reorganization is under the jurisdiction of the court in such case, and

(ii) the transfer is pursuant to a plan of reorganization approved by the court.

(C) Reorganizations qualifying under paragraph (1)(G) and another provision.—If a transaction would (but for this subparagraph) qualify both—

(i) under subparagraph (G) of paragraph (1), and

(ii) under any other subparagraph of paragraph (1) or under section 332 or 351,

then, for purposes of this subchapter (other than section 357(c)(1)), such transaction shall be treated as qualifying only under subparagraph (G) of paragraph (1).

* * *

(E) Application of paragraph (2)(E)(ii).—In the case of a title 11 or similar case, the requirement of clause (ii) of paragraph (2)(E) shall be treated as met if—

(i) no former shareholder of the surviving corporation received any consideration for his stock, and

(ii) the former creditors of the surviving corporation exchanged, for an amount of voting stock of the controlling corporation, debt of the surviving corporation which had a fair market value equal to 80 percent or more of the total fair market value of the debt of the surviving corporation.

(b) Party to a reorganization.—For purposes of this part, the term "a party to a reorganization" includes—

(1) a corporation resulting from a reorganization, and

(2) both corporations, in the case of a reorganization resulting from the acquisition by one corporation of stock or properties of another.

In the case of a reorganization qualifying under paragraph (1) (B) or (1) (C) of subsection (a), if the stock exchanged for the stock or properties is stock of a corporation which is in control of the acquiring corporation, the term "a party to a reorganization" includes the corporation so controlling the acquiring corporation. In the case of a reorganization qualifying under paragraph (1) (A), (1) (B), (1) (C), or (1) (G) of subsection (a) by reason of paragraph (2) (C) of subsection (a), the term "a party to a reorganization" includes the corporation controlling the corporation to which the acquired assets or stock are transferred. In the case of a reorganization qualifying under paragraph (1) (A) or (1) (G) of subsection (a) by reason of paragraph (2) (D) of that subsection, the term "a party to a reorganization" includes the controlling corporation referred to in such paragraph (2) (D). In the case of a reorganization qualifying under subsection (a) (1) (A) by reason of subsection (a) (2) (E), the term "party to a reorganization" includes the controlling corporation referred to in subsection (a) (2) (E).

(c) **Control defined.**—For purposes of part I (other than section 304), part II, and this part, the term "control" means the ownership of stock possessing at least 80 percent of the total combined voting power of all classes of stock entitled to vote and at least 80 percent of the total number of shares of all other classes of stock of the corporation.

PART V—CARRYOVERS

§ 381. Carryovers in certain corporate acquisitions

(a) **General rule.**—In the case of the acquisition of assets of a corporation by another corporation—

(1) in a distribution to such other corporation to which section 332 (relating to liquidations of subsidiaries) applies; or

(2) in a transfer to which section 361 (relating to nonrecognition of gain or loss to corporations) applies, but only if the transfer is in connection with a reorganization described in subparagraph (A), (C), (D), (F), or (G) of section 368(a) (1),

the acquiring corporation shall succeed to and take into account, as of the close of the day of distribution or transfer, the items described in subsection (c) of the distributor or transferor corporation, subject to the conditions and limitations specified in subsections (b) and (c). For purposes of the preceding sentence, a reorganization shall be treated as meeting the requirements of subparagraph (D) or (G) of section 368(a)(1) only if the requirements of subparagraphs (A) and (B) of section 354(b)(1) are met.

(b) **Operating rules.**—Except in the case of an acquisition in connection with a reorganization described in subparagraph (F) of section 368(a) (1)—

(1) The taxable year of the distributor or transferor corporation shall end on the date of distribution or transfer.

(2) For purposes of this section, the date of distribution or transfer shall be the day on which the distribution or transfer is completed; except that, under regulations prescribed by the Secretary, the date when substantially all of the property has been distributed or transferred may be used if the distributor or transferor corporation ceases all operations, other than liquidating activities, after such date.

(3) The corporation acquiring property in a distribution or transfer described in subsection (a) shall not be entitled to carry back a net operating loss or a net capital loss for a taxable year ending after the date of distribution or transfer to a taxable year of the distributor or transferor corporation.

(c) **Items of the distributor or transferor corporation.**—The items referred to in subsection (a) are:

(1) **Net operating loss carryovers.**—The net operating loss carryovers determined under section 172, subject to the following conditions and limitations:

(A) The taxable year of the acquiring corporation to which the net operating loss carryovers of the distributor or transferor corporation are first carried shall be the first taxable year ending after the date of distribution or transfer.

(B) In determining the net operating loss deduction, the portion of such deduction attributable to the net operating loss carryovers of the distributor or transferor corporation to the first taxable year of the acquiring corporation ending after the date of distribution or transfer shall be limited to an amount which bears the same ratio to the taxable income (determined without regard to a net operating loss deduction) of the acquiring corporation in such taxable year as the number of days in the taxable year after the date of distribution or transfer bears to the total number of days in the taxable year.

(C) For the purpose of determining the amount of the net operating loss carryovers under section 172(b) (2), a net operating loss for a taxable year (hereinafter in this subparagraph referred to as the "loss year") of a distributor or transferor corporation which ends on or before the end of a loss year of the acquiring corporation shall be considered to be a net operating loss for a year prior to such loss year of the acquiring corporation. For the same purpose, the taxable income for a "prior taxable year" (as the term is used in section 172(b) (2)) shall be computed as provided in such section; except that, if the date of distribution or transfer is on a day other than the last day of a taxable year of the acquiring corporation—

(i) such taxable year shall (for the purpose of this subparagraph only) be considered to be 2 taxable years (hereinafter in this subparagraph referred to as the "pre-acquisition part year" and the "post-acquisition part year");

(ii) the pre-acquisition part year shall begin on the same day as such taxable year begins and shall end on the date of distribution or transfer;

(iii) the post-acquisition part year shall begin on the day following the date of distribution or transfer and shall end on the same day as the end of such taxable year;

(iv) the taxable income for such taxable year (computed with the modifications specified in section 172(b) (2) (A) but without a net operating loss deduction) shall be divided between the pre-acquisition part year and the post-acquisition part year in proportion to the number of days in each;

(v) the net operating loss deduction for the pre-acquisition part year shall be determined as provided in section 172(b) (2) (B), but without regard to a net operating loss year of the distributor or transferor corporation; and

(vi) the net operating loss deduction for the post-acquisition part year shall be determined as provided in section 172(b) (2) (B).

(2) Earnings and profits.—In the case of a distribution or transfer described in subsection (a)—

(A) the earnings and profits or deficit in earnings and profits, as the case may be, of the distributor or transferor corporation shall, subject to subparagraph (B), be deemed to have been received or incurred by the acquiring corporation as of the close of the date of the distribution or transfer; and

(B) a deficit in earnings and profits of the distributor, transferor, or acquiring corporation shall be used only to offset earnings and profits accumulated after the date of transfer. For this purpose, the earnings and profits for the taxable year of the acquiring corporation in which the distribution or transfer occurs shall be deemed to have been accumulated after such distribution or transfer in an amount which bears the same ratio to the undistributed earnings and profits of the acquiring corporation for such taxable year (computed without regard to any earnings and profits received from the distributor or transferor corporation, as described in subparagraph (A) of this paragraph) as the number of days in the taxable year after the date of distribution or transfer bears to the total number of days in the taxable year.

(3) **Capital loss carryover.**—The capital loss carryover determined under section 1212, subject to the following conditions and limitations:

(A) The taxable year of the acquiring corporation to which the capital loss carryover of the distributor or transferor corporation is first carried shall be the first taxable year ending after the date of distribution or transfer.

(B) The capital loss carryover shall be a short-term capital loss in the taxable year determined under subparagraph (A) but shall be limited to an amount which bears the same ratio to the capital gain net income (determined without regard to a short-term capital loss attributable to capital loss carryover), if any, of the acquiring corporation in such taxable year as the number of days in the taxable year after the date of distribution or transfer bears to the total number of days in the taxable year.

(C) For purposes of determining the amount of such capital loss carryover to taxable years following the taxable year determined under subparagraph (A), the capital gain net income in the taxable year determined under subparagraph (A) shall be considered to be an amount equal to the amount determined under subparagraph (B).

(4) **Method of accounting.**—The acquiring corporation shall use the method of accounting used by the distributor or transferor corporation on the date of distribution or transfer unless different methods were used by several distributor or transferor corporations or by a distributor or transferor corporation and the acquiring corporation. If different methods were used, the acquiring corporation shall use the method or combination of methods of computing taxable income adopted pursuant to regulations prescribed by the Secretary.

(5) **Inventories.**—In any case in which inventories are received by the acquiring corporation, such inventories shall be taken by such corporation (in determining its income) on the same basis on which such inventories were taken by the distributor or transferor corporation, unless different methods were used by several distributor or transferor corporations or by a distributor or transferor corporation and the acquiring corporation. If different methods were used, the acquiring corporation shall use the method or combination of methods of taking inventory adopted pursuant to regulations prescribed by the Secretary.

(6) **Method of computing depreciation allowance.**—The acquiring corporation shall be treated as the distributor or transferor corporation for purposes of computing the depreciation allowance under subsections (b), (j), and (k) of section 167 on property acquired in a distribution or transfer with respect to so much of the basis in the hands of the acquiring corporation as does not exceed the adjusted basis in the hands of the distributor or transferor corporation.

[(7) **Repealed.**]

(8) **Installment method.**—If the acquiring corporation acquires installment obligations (the income from which the distributor or transferor corporation reports on the installment basis under section 453 or 453A) the acquiring corporation shall, for purposes of section 453 or 453A, be treated as if it were the distributor or transferor corporation.

(9) **Amortization of bond discount or premium.**—If the acquiring corporation assumes liability for bonds of the distributor or transferor corporation issued at a discount or premium, the acquiring corporation shall be treated as the distributor or transferor corporation after the date of distribution or transfer for purposes of

determining the amount of amortization allowable or includible with respect to such discount or premium.

(10) Treatment of certain mining development and exploration expenses of distributor or transferor corporation.—The acquiring corporation shall be entitled to deduct, as if it were the distributor or transferor corporation, expenses deferred under section 616 (relating to certain development expenditures) if the distributor or transferor corporation has so elected.

(11) Contributions to pension plans, employees' annuity plans, and stock bonus and profit-sharing plans.—The acquiring corporation shall be considered to be the distributor or transferor corporation after the date of distribution or transfer for the purpose of determining the amounts deductible under section 404 with respect to pension plans, employees' annuity plans, and stock bonus and profit-sharing plans.

(12) Recovery of tax benefit items.—If the acquiring corporation is entitled to the recovery of any amounts previously deducted by (or allowable as credits to) the distributor or transferor corporation, the acquiring corporation shall succeed to the treatment under section 111 which would apply to such amounts in the hands of the distributor or transferor corporation.

(13) Involuntary conversions under section 1033.—The acquiring corporation shall be treated as the distributor or transferor corporation after the date of distribution or transfer for purposes of applying section 1033.

(14) Dividend carryover to personal holding company.—The dividend carryover (described in section 564) to taxable years ending after the date of distribution or transfer.

(15) Indebtedness of certain personal holding companies.—The acquiring corporation shall be considered to be the distributor or transferor corporation for the purpose of determining the applicability of subsection (c) of section 545, relating to deduction with respect to payment of certain indebtedness.

(16) Certain obligations of distributor or transferor corporation.—If the acquiring corporation—

    (A) assumes an obligation of the distributor or transferor corporation which, after the date of the distribution or transfer, gives rise to a liability, and

    (B) such liability, if paid or accrued by the distributor or transferor corporation, would have been deductible in computing its taxable income,

the acquiring corporation shall be entitled to deduct such items when paid or accrued, as the case may be, as if such corporation were the distributor or transferor corporation. A corporation which would have been an acquiring corporation under this section if the date of distribution or transfer had occurred on or after the effective date of the provisions of this subchapter applicable to a liquidation or reorganization, as the case may be, shall be entitled, even though the date of distribution or transfer occurred before such effective date, to apply this paragraph with respect to amounts paid or accrued in taxable years beginning after December 31, 1953, on account of such obligations of the distributor or transferor corporation. This paragraph shall not apply if such obligations are reflected in the amount of stock, securities, or property transferred by the acquiring corporation to the transferor corporation for the property of the transferor corporation.

(17) Deficiency dividend of personal holding company.—If the acquiring corporation pays a deficiency dividend (as defined in section 547(d)) with respect to the distributor or transferor corporation, such distributor or transferor corporation shall, with respect to such payments, be entitled to the deficiency dividend deduction provided in section 547.

(18) Percentage depletion on extraction of ores or minerals from the waste or residue of prior mining.—The acquiring corporation shall be considered to be the distributor or transferor corporation for the purpose of determining the applicability of section 613(c) (3) (relating to extraction of ores or minerals from the ground).

(19) Charitable contributions in excess of prior years' limitations.—Contributions made in the taxable year ending on the date of distribution or transfer and the 4 prior taxable years by the distributor or transferor corporation in excess of the amount deductible under section 170(b) (2) for such taxable years shall be deductible by the acquiring corporation for its taxable years which begin after the date of distribution or transfer, subject to the limitations imposed in section 170(b) (2). In applying the preceding sentence, each taxable year of the distributor or transferor corporation beginning on or before the date of distribution or transfer shall be treated as a prior taxable year with reference to the acquiring corporation's taxable years beginning after such date.

* * *

(24) Method of computing recovery allowance for recovery property.—The acquiring corporation shall be treated as the distributor or transferor corporation for purposes of computing the deduction allowable under section 168(a) on property acquired in a distribution or transfer with respect to so much of the basis in the hands of the acquiring corporation as does not exceed the adjusted basis in the hands of the distributor or transferor corporation.

(25) Credit under section 38.—The acquiring corporation shall take into account (to the extent proper to carry out the purposes of this section and section 38, and under such regulations as may be prescribed by the Secretary) the items required to be taken into account for purposes of section 38 in respect of the distributor or transferor corporation.

(27) Credit under section 53.—The acquiring corporation shall take into account (to the extent proper to carry out the purposes of this section and section 53, and under such regulations as may be prescribed by the Secretary) the items required to be taken into account for purposes of section 53 in respect of the distributor or transferor corporation.

* * *

§ 382. Limitation on net operating loss carryforwards and certain built-in losses following ownership change

(a) General rule.—The amount of the taxable income of any new loss corporation for any post-change year which may be offset by pre-change losses shall not exceed the section 382 limitation for such year.

(b) Section 382 limitation.—For purposes of this section—

(1) In general.—Except as otherwise provided in this section, the section 382 limitation for any post-change year is an amount equal to—

(A) the value of the old loss corporation, multiplied by

(B) the long-term tax-exempt rate.

(2) Carryforward of unused limitation.—If the section 382 limitation for any post-change year exceeds the taxable income of the new loss corporation for such year which was offset by pre-change losses, the section 382 limitation for the next post-change year shall be increased by the amount of such excess.

(3) Special rule for post-change year which includes change date.—In the case of any post-change year which includes the change date—

(A) Limitation does not apply to taxable income before change.—Subsection (a) shall not apply to the portion of the taxable income for such year which is allocable to the period in such year on or before the change date. Except as provided in subsection (h)(5) and in regulations, taxable income shall be allocated ratably to each day in the year.

(B) Limitation for period after change.—For purposes of applying the limitation of subsection (a) to the remainder of the taxable income for such year, the section 382 limitation shall be an amount which bears the same ratio to such limitation (determined without regard to this paragraph) as—

(i) the number of days in such year after the change date, bears to

(ii) the total number of days in such year.

(c) Carryforwards disallowed if continuity of business requirements not met.—

(1) In general.—Except as provided in paragraph (2), if the new loss corporation does not continue the business enterprise of the old loss corporation at all times during the 2–year period beginning on the change date, the section 382 limitation for any post-change year shall be zero.

(2) Exception for certain gains.—The section 382 limitation for any post-change year shall not be less than the sum of—

(A) any increase in such limitation under—

(i) subsection (h)(1)(A) for recognized built-in gains for such year, and

(ii) subsection (h)(1)(C) for gain recognized by reason of an election under section 338, plus

(B) any increase in such limitation under subsection (b)(2) for amounts described in subparagraph (A) which are carried forward to such year.

(d) Pre-change loss and post-change year.—For purposes of this section—

(1) Pre-change loss.—The term "pre-change loss" means—

(A) any net operating loss carryforward of the old loss corporation to the taxable year ending with the ownership change or in which the change date occurs, and

(B) the net operating loss of the old loss corporation for the taxable year in which the ownership change occurs to the extent such loss is allocable to the period in such year on or before the change date.

Except as provided in subsection (h)(5) and in regulations, the net operating loss shall, for purposes of subparagraph (B), be allocated ratably to each day in the year.

(2) Post-change year.—The term "post-change year" means any taxable year ending after the change date.

(e) Value of old loss corporation.—For purposes of this section—

(1) In general.—Except as otherwise provided in this subsection, the value of the old loss corporation is the value of the stock of such corporation (including any stock described in section 1504(a)(4)) immediately before the ownership change.

(2) Special rule in the case of redemption.—If a redemption occurs in connection with an ownership change, the value under paragraph (1) shall be determined after taking such redemption into account.

(f) Long-term tax-exempt rate.—For purposes of this section—

(1) In general.—The long-term tax-exempt rate shall be the highest of the adjusted Federal long-term rates in effect for any month in the 3–calendar-month period ending with the calendar month in which the change date occurs.

(2) Adjusted federal long-term rate.—For purposes of paragraph (1), the term "adjusted Federal long-term rate" means the Federal long-term rate determined under section 1274(d), except that—

(A) paragraphs (2) and (3) thereof shall not apply, and

(B) such rate shall be properly adjusted for differences between rates on long-term taxable and tax-exempt obligations.

(g) Ownership change.—For purposes of this section—

(1) In general.—There is an ownership change if, immediately after any owner shift involving a 5–percent shareholder or any equity structure shift—

(A) the percentage of the stock of the new loss corporation owned by 1 or more 5–percent shareholders has increased by more than 50 percentage points, over

(B) the lowest percentage of stock of the old loss corporation (or any predecessor corporation) owned by such shareholders at any time during the testing period.

(2) Owner shift involving 5–percent shareholder.—There is an owner shift involving a 5–percent shareholder if—

(A) there is any change in the respective ownership of stock of a corporation, and

(B) such change affects the percentage of stock of such corporation owned by any person who is a 5–percent shareholder before or after such change.

(3) Equity structure shift defined.—

(A) In general.—The term "equity structure shift" means any reorganization (within the meaning of section 368). Such term shall not include—

(i) any reorganization described in subparagraph (D) or (G) of section 368(a)(1) unless the requirements of section 354(b)(1) are met, and

(ii) any reorganization described in subparagraph (F) of section 368(a)(1).

(B) Taxable reorganization-type transactions, etc.—To the extent provided in regulations, the term "equity structure shift" includes taxable reorganization-type transactions, public offerings, and similar transactions.

(4) Special rules for application of subsection.—

(A) Treatment of less than 5–percent shareholders.—Except as provided in subparagraphs (B)(i) and (C), in determining whether an ownership change has occurred, all stock owned by shareholders of a corporation who are not 5–percent shareholders of such corporation shall be treated as stock owned by 1 5–percent shareholder of such corporation.

(B) Coordination with equity structure shifts.—For purposes of determining whether an equity structure shift (or subsequent transaction) is an ownership change—

(i) **Less than 5–percent shareholders.**—Subparagraph (A) shall be applied separately with respect to each group of shareholders (immediately before such equity structure shift) of each corporation which was a party to the reorganization involved in such equity structure shift.

(ii) **Acquisitions of stock.**—Unless a different proportion is established, acquisitions of stock after such equity structure shift shall be treated as being made proportionately from all shareholders immediately before such acquisition.

(C) **Coordination with other owner shifts.**—Except as provided in regulations, the rules of subparagraph (B) shall apply in determining whether there has been an owner shift involving a 5–percent shareholder and whether such shift (or subsequent transaction) results in an ownership change.

(h) **Special rules for built-in gains and losses and section 338 gains.**—For purposes of this section—

(1) **In general.**—

(A) **Net unrealized built-in gain.**—

(i) **In general.**—If the old loss corporation has a net unrealized built-in gain, the section 382 limitation for any recognition period taxable year shall be increased by the recognized built-in gains for such taxable year.

(ii) **Limitation.**—The increase under clause (i) for any recognition period taxable year shall not exceed—

(I) the net unrealized built-in gain, reduced by

(II) recognized built-in gains for prior years ending in the recognition period.

(B) **Net unrealized built-in loss.**—

(i) **In general.**—If the old loss corporation has a net unrealized built-in loss, the recognized built-in loss for any recognition period taxable year shall be subject to limitation under this section in the same manner as if such loss were a pre-change loss.

(ii) **Limitation.**—Clause (i) shall apply to recognized built-in losses for any recognition period taxable year only to the extent such losses do not exceed—

(I) the net unrealized built-in loss, reduced by

(II) recognized built-in losses for prior taxable years ending in the recognition period.

(C) **Section 338 gain.**—The section 382 limitation for any taxable year in which gain is recognized by reason of an election under section 338 shall be increased by the excess of—

(i) the amount of such gain, over

(ii) the portion of such gain taken into account in computing recognized built-in gains for such taxable year.

(2) **Recognized built-in gain and loss.**—

(A) **Recognized built-in gain.**—The term "recognized built-in gain" means any gain recognized during the recognition period on the disposition of any asset to the extent the new loss corporation establishes that—

(i) such asset was held by the old loss corporation immediately before the change date, and

(ii) such gain does not exceed the excess of—

(I) the fair market value of such asset on the change date, over

(II) the adjusted basis of such asset on such date.

(B) **Recognized built-in loss.**—The term "recognized built-in loss" means any loss recognized during the recognition period on the disposition of any asset except to the extent the new loss corporation establishes that—

(i) such asset was not held by the old loss corporation immediately before the change date, or

(ii) such loss exceeds the excess of—

(I) the adjusted basis of such asset on the change date, over

(II) the fair market value of such asset on such date.

(3) **Net unrealized built-in gain and loss defined.**—

(A) **Net unrealized built-in gain and loss.**—

(i) **In general.**—The terms "net unrealized built-in gain" and "net unrealized built-in loss" mean, with respect to any old loss corporation, the amount by which—

(I) the fair market value of the assets of such corporation immediately before an ownership change is more or less, respectively, than

(II) the aggregate adjusted basis of such assets at such time.

(ii) **Special rule for redemptions.**—If a redemption occurs in connection with an ownership change, determinations under clause (i) shall be made after taking such redemption into account.

(B) **Threshold requirement.**—

(i) If the amount of the net unrealized built-in gain or net unrealized built-in loss (determined without regard to this subparagraph) of any old loss corporation is not greater than 25 percent of the amount determined for purposes of subparagraph (A)(i)(I), the net unrealized built-in gain or net unrealized built-in loss shall be zero.

(ii) **Cash and cash items not taken into account.**—In computing any net unrealized built-in gain or net unrealized built-in loss under clause (i), there shall not be taken into account—

(I) any cash or cash item, or

(II) any marketable security which has a value which does not substantially differ from adjusted basis.

(4) **Disallowed loss treated as a net operating loss.**—If a deduction for any portion of a recognized built-in loss is disallowed for any post-change year, such portion—

(A) shall be carried forward to subsequent taxable years under rules similar to the rules for the carrying forward of net operating losses, but

(B) shall be subject to limitation under this section in the same manner as a pre-change loss.

(5) **Special rules for post-change year which includes change date.**—For purposes of subsection (b)(3)—

(A) in applying subparagraph (A) thereof, taxable income shall be computed without regard to recognized built-in gains and losses, and gain described in paragraph (1)(C), for the year, and

(B) in applying subparagraph (B) thereof, the section 382 limitation shall be computed without regard to recognized built-in gains, and gain described in paragraph (1)(C), for the year.

(6) Secretary may treat certain deductions as built-in losses.—The Secretary may by regulation treat amounts which accrue on or before the change date but which are allowable as a deduction after such date as recognized built-in losses.

(7) Recognition period, etc.—

(A) Recognition period.—The term "recognition period" means, with respect to any ownership change, the 5–year period beginning on the change date.

(B) Recognition period taxable year.—The term "recognition period taxable year" means any taxable year any portion of which is in the recognition period.

(8) Determination of fair market value in certain cases.—If 80 percent or more in value of the stock of a corporation is acquired in 1 transaction (or in a series of related transactions during any 12–month period), for purposes of determining the net unrealized built-in loss, the fair market value of the assets of such corporation shall not exceed the grossed up amount paid for such stock properly adjusted for indebtedness of the corporation and other relevant items.

(9) Tax-free exchanges or transfers.—The Secretary shall prescribe such regulations as may be necessary to carry out the purposes of this subsection where property held on the change date is transferred in a transaction where gain or loss is not recognized (in whole or in part).

(i) Testing period.—For purposes of this section—

(1) 3–year period.—Except as otherwise provided in this section, the testing period is the 3–year period ending on the day of any owner shift involving a 5–percent shareholder or equity structure shift.

(2) Shorter period where there has been recent ownership change.—If there has been an ownership change under this section, the testing period for determining whether a 2nd ownership change has occurred shall not begin before the 1st day following the change date for such earlier ownership change.

(3) Shorter period where all losses arise after 3–year period begins.—The testing period shall not begin before the 1st day of the 1st taxable year from which there is a carryforward of a loss or of an excess credit to the 1st post-change year. Except as provided in regulations, this paragraph shall not apply to any loss corporation which has a net unrealized built-in loss (determined after application of subsection (h)(3)(B)).

(j) Change date.—For purposes of this section, the change date is—

(1) in the case where the last component of an ownership change is an owner shift involving a 5–percent shareholder, the date on which such shift occurs, and

(2) in the case where the last component of an ownership change is an equity structure shift, the date of the reorganization.

(k) Definitions and special rules.—For purposes of this section—

(1) Loss corporation.—The term "loss corporation" means a corporation entitled to use a net operating loss carryover. Except to the extent provided in regulations, such term includes any corporation with a net unrealized built-in loss.

(2) Old loss corporation.—The term "old loss corporation" means any corporation with respect to which there is an ownership change—

(A) which (before the ownership change) was a loss corporation, or

333

(B) with respect to which there is a pre-change loss described in subsection (d)(1)(B).

(3) New loss corporation.—The term "new loss corporation" means a corporation which (after an ownership change) is a loss corporation. Nothing in this section shall be treated as implying that the same corporation may not be both the old loss corporation and the new loss corporation.

(4) Taxable income.—Taxable income shall be computed with the modifications set forth in section 172(d).

(5) Value.—The term "value" means fair market value.

(6) Rules relating to stock.—

(A) Preferred stock.—Except as provided in regulations and subsection (e), the term "stock" means stock other than stock described in section 1504(a)(4).

(B) Treatment of certain rights, etc.—The Secretary shall prescribe such regulations as may be necessary—

(i) to treat warrants, options, contracts to acquire stock, convertible debt interests, and other similar interests as stock, and

(ii) to treat stock as not stock.

(C) Determinations on basis of value.—Determinations of the percentage of stock of any corporation held by any person shall be made on the basis of value.

(7) 5–percent shareholder.—The term "5–percent shareholder" means any person holding 5 percent or more of the stock of the corporation at any time during the testing period.

(*l*) Certain additional operating rules.—For purposes of this section—

(1) Certain capital contributions not taken into account.—

(A) in general.—Any capital contribution received by an old loss corporation as part of a plan a principal purpose of which is to avoid or increase any limitation under this section shall not be taken into account for purposes of this section.

(B) Certain contributions treated as part of plan.—For purposes of subparagraph (A), any capital contribution made during the 2–year period ending on the change date shall, except as provided in regulations, be treated as part of a plan described in subparagraph (A).

(2) Ordering rules for application of section.—

(A) Coordination with section 172(b) carryover rules.—In the case of any pre-change loss for any taxable year (hereinafter in this subparagraph referred to as the "loss year") subject to limitation under this section, for purposes of determining under the 2nd sentence of section 172(b)(2) the amount of such loss which may be carried to any taxable year, taxable income for any taxable year shall be treated as not greater than—

(i) the section 382 limitation for such taxable year, reduced by

(ii) the unused pre-change losses for taxable years preceding the loss year.

Similar rules shall apply in the case of any credit or loss subject to limitation under section 383.

(B) Ordering rule for losses carried from same taxable year.—In any case in which—

334

   (i) a pre-change loss of a loss corporation for any taxable year is subject to a section 382 limitation, and

   (ii) a net operating loss of such corporation from such taxable year is not subject to such limitation,

taxable income shall be treated as having been offset first by the loss subject to such limitation.

(3) Operating rules relating to ownership of stock.—

   (A) Constructive ownership.—Section 318 (relating to constructive ownership of stock) shall apply in determining ownership of stock, except that—

   (i) paragraphs (1) and (5)(B) of section 318(a) shall not apply and an individual and all members of his family described in paragraph (1) of section 318(a) shall be treated as 1 individual for purposes of applying this section,

   (ii) paragraph (2) of section 318(a) shall be applied—

     (I) without regard to the 50–percent limitation contained in subparagraph (C) thereof, and

     (II) except as provided in regulations, by treating stock attributed thereunder as no longer being held by the entity from which attributed,

   (iii) paragraph (3) of section 318(a) shall be applied only to the extent provided in regulations, and

   (iv) except to the extent provided in regulations, paragraph (4) of section 318(a) shall apply to an option if such application results in an ownership change.

A rule similar to the rule of clause (iv) shall apply in the case of any contingent purchase, warrant, convertible debt, put, stock subject to a risk of forfeiture, contract to acquire stock, or similar interests.

   (B) Stock acquired by reason of death, gift, divorce, separation, etc.—If—

   (i) the basis of any stock in the hands of any person is determined—

     (I) under section 1014 (relating to property acquired from a decedent),

     (II) section 1015 (relating to property acquired by a gift or transfer in trust), or

     (III) section 1041(b)(2) (relating to transfers of property between spouses or incident to divorce,

   (ii) stock is received by any person in satisfaction of a right to receive a pecuniary bequest, or

   (iii) stock is acquired by a person pursuant to any divorce or separation instrument (within the meaning of section 71(b)(2)),

such person shall be treated as owning such stock during the period such stock was owned by the person from whom it was acquired.

   (C) Special rule for employee stock ownership plans.—

   (i) **In general.—**Except as provided in clause (ii), the acquisition of employer securities (within the meaning of section 409(l)) by—

     (I) a tax credit employee stock ownership plan or an employee stock ownership plan (within the meaning of section 4975(e)(7)), or

     (II) a participant of any such plan pursuant to the requirements of section 409(h), shall not be taken into account in determining whether an ownership change has occurred.

(ii) **Ownership and allocation requirements.**—Subclause (I) of clause (i) shall not apply to any acquisition unless—

(I) immediately after such acquisition the plan holds stock meeting the requirements of section 1042(b)(2), except that such section shall be applied by substituting "50 percent" for "30 percent", and

(II) the plan meets requirements similar to the requirements of section 409(n).

(D) **Certain changes in percentage ownership which are attributable to fluctuations in value not taken into account.**—Except as provided in regulations, any change in proportionate ownership which is attributable solely to fluctuations in the relative fair market values of different classes of stock shall not be taken into account.

(4) **Reduction in value where substantial nonbusiness assets.**—

(A) **In general.**—If, immediately after an ownership change, the new loss corporation has substantial nonbusiness assets, the value of the old loss corporation shall be reduced by the excess (if any) of—

(i) the fair market value of the nonbusiness assets of the old loss corporation, over

(ii) the nonbusiness asset share of indebtedness for which such corporation is liable.

(B) **Corporation having substantial nonbusiness assets.**—For purposes of subparagraph (A)—

(i) **In general.**—The old loss corporation shall be treated as having substantial nonbusiness assets if at least ⅓ of the value of the total assets of such corporation consists of nonbusiness assets.

(ii) **Exception for certain investment entities.**—A regulated investment company to which part I of subchapter M applies, a real estate investment trust to which part II of subchapter M applies, or a real estate mortgage pool to which part IV of subchapter M applies, shall not be treated as a new loss corporation having substantial nonbusiness assets.

(C) **Nonbusiness assets.**—For purposes of this paragraph, the term "nonbusiness assets" means assets held for investment.

(D) **Nonbusiness asset share.**—For purposes of this paragraph, the nonbusiness asset share of the indebtedness of the corporation is an amount which bears the same ratio to such indebtedness as—

(i) the fair market value of the nonbusiness assets of the corporation, bears to

(ii) the fair market value of all assets of such corporation.

(E) **Treatment of subsidiaries.**—For purposes of this paragraph, stock and securities in any subsidiary corporation shall be disregarded and the parent corporation shall be deemed to own its ratable share of the subsidiary's assets. For purposes of the preceding sentence, a corporation shall be treated as a subsidiary if the parent owns 50 percent or more of the combined voting power of all classes of stock entitled to vote, and 50 percent or more of the total value of shares of all classes of stock.

(5) **Title 11 or similar case.**—

(A) In general.—Subsection (a) shall not apply to any ownership change if—

(i) the old loss corporation is (immediately before such ownership change) under the jurisdiction of the court in a title 11 or similar case, and

(ii) the shareholders and creditors of the old loss corporation (determined immediately before such ownership change) own (immediately after such ownership change) stock of the new loss corporation (or stock of controlling corporation if also in bankruptcy) which meets the requirements of section 1504(a)(2) (determined by substituting "50 percent" for "80 percent" each place it appears).

(B) Reduction for interest payments to creditors becoming shareholders. —In any case to which subparagraph (A) applies, the net operating loss deduction under section 172(a) for any post-change year shall be determined as if no deduction was allowable under this chapter for the interest paid or accrued by the old loss corporation on indebtedness which was converted into stock pursuant to title 11 or similar case during—

(i) any taxable year ending during the 3–year period preceding the taxable year in which the ownership change occurs, and

(ii) the period of the taxable year in which the ownership change occurs on or before the change date.

(C) Reduction of carryforwards where discharge of indebtedness.—In any case to which subparagraph (A) applies, the pre-change losses and excess credits (within the meaning of section 383(a)(2)) which may be carried to a post-change year shall be computed as if 50 percent of the amount which, but for the application of section 108(e)(10)(B), would have been includible in gross income for any taxable year had been so included.

(D) Section 382 limitation zero if another change within 2 years.—If, during the 2–year period immediately following an ownership change to which this paragraph applies, an ownership change of the new loss corporation occurs, this paragraph shall not apply and the section 382 limitation with respect to the 2nd ownership change for any post-change year ending after the change date of the 2nd ownership change shall be zero.

(E) Only certain stock of creditors taken into account.—For purposes of subparagraph (A)(ii), stock transferred to a creditor in satisfaction of indebtedness shall be taken into account only if such indebtedness—

(i) was held by the creditor at least 18 months before the date of the filing of the title 11 or similar case, or

(ii) arose in the ordinary course of the trade or business of the old loss corporation and is held by the person who at all times held the beneficial interest in such indebtedness.

(F) Special rule for certain financial institutions.—

(i) **In general.**—In the case of any ownership change to which this subparagraph applies, this paragraph shall be applied—

(I) by substituting "20 percent" for "50 percent" in subparagraph (A)(ii), and

(II) without regard to subparagraphs (B) and (C).

(ii) **Special rule for depositors.**—For purposes of applying this paragraph to an ownership change to which this subparagraph applies—

(I) a depositor in the old loss corporation shall be treated as a stockholder in such loss corporation immediately before the change,

(II) deposits which, after the change, become deposits of the new loss corporation shall be treated as stock of the new loss corporation, and

(III) the fair market value of the outstanding stock of the new loss corporation shall include deposits described in subclause (II).

(iii) **Changes to which subparagraph applies.**—This subparagraph shall apply to—

(I) an equity structure shift which is a reorganization described in section 368(a)(3)(D)(ii), or

(II) any other equity structure shift (or transaction to which section 351 applies) which occurs as an integral part of a transaction involving a change to which subclause (I) applies.

This subparagraph shall not apply to any equity structure shift or transaction occurring after December 31, 1988.

(G) **Title 11 or similar case.**—For purposes of this paragraph, the term "title 11 or similar case" has the meaning given such term by section 368(a)(3)(A).

(H) **Election not to have paragraph apply.**—A new loss corporation may elect, subject to such terms and conditions as the Secretary may prescribe, not to have the provisions of this paragraph apply.

(6) **Special rule for insolvency transactions.**—If paragraph (5) does not apply to any reorganization described in subparagraph (G) of section 368(a)(1) or any exchange of debt for stock in a title 11 or similar case (as defined in section 368(a)(3)(A)), the value under subsection (e) shall be the value of the new loss corporation immediately after the ownership change.

(7) **Coordination with alternative minimum tax.**—The Secretary shall by regulation provide for the application of this section to the alternative tax net operating loss deduction under section 56(d).

(m) **Regulations.**—The Secretary shall prescribe such regulations as may be necessary or appropriate to carry out the purposes of this section and section 383, including (but not limited to) regulations—

(1) providing for the application of this section and section 383 where an ownership change with respect to the old loss corporation is followed by an ownership change with respect to the new loss corporation, and

(2) providing for the application of this section and section 383 in the case of a short taxable year,

(3) providing for such adjustments to the application of this section and section 383 as is necessary to prevent the avoidance of the purposes of this section and section 383, including the avoidance of such purposes through the use of related persons, pass-thru entities, or other intermediaries,

(4) providing for the treatment of corporate contractions as redemptions for purposes of subsections (e)(2) and (h)(3)(A), and

(5) providing for the application of subsection (g)(4) where there is only 1 corporation involved.

(Pub.L. 99–514, Title VI, § 621(a), Oct. 22, 1986, 100 Stat. _____.)

§ 383. Special limitations on certain excess credits, etc.

(a) Excess credits.—

(1) In general.—Under regulations, if an ownership change occurs with respect to a corporation, the amount of any excess credit for any taxable year which may be used in any post-change year shall be limited to an amount determined on the basis of the tax liability which is attributable to so much of the taxable income as does not exceed the section 382 limitation for such post-change year to the extent available after the application of section 382 and subsections (b) and (c) of this section.

(2) Excess credit.—For purposes of paragraph (1), the term "excess credit" means—

(A) any unused general business credit of the corporation under section 39, and

(B) any unused minimum tax credit of the corporation under section 53.

(b) Limitation on net capital loss.—If an ownership change occurs with respect to a corporation, the amount of any net capital loss under section 1212 for any taxable year before the 1st post-change year which may be used in any post-change year shall be limited under regulations which shall be based on the principles applicable under section 382. Such regulations shall provide that any such net capital loss used in a post-change year shall reduce the section 382 limitation which is applied to pre-change losses under section 382 for such year.

(c) Foreign tax credits.—If an ownership change occurs with respect to a corporation, the amount of any excess foreign taxes under section 904(c) for any taxable year before the 1st post-change taxable year shall be limited under regulations which shall be consistent with purposes of this section and section 382.

(d) Pro ration rules for year which includes change.—For purposes of this section, rules similar to the rules of subsections (b)(3) and (d)(1)(B) of section 382 shall apply.

(e) Definitions.—Terms used in this section shall have the same respective meanings as when used in section 382, except that appropriate adjustments shall be made to take into account that the limitations of this section apply to credits and net capital losses.

(Pub.L. 99–514, Title VI, § 621(b), Oct. 22, 1986, 100 Stat. _____.)

PART VI—TREATMENT OF CERTAIN CORPORATE INTERESTS AS STOCK OR INDEBTEDNESS

§ 385. Treatment of certain interests in corporations as stock or indebtedness

(a) Authority to prescribe regulations.—The Secretary is authorized to prescribe such regulations as may be necessary or appropriate to determine whether an interest in a corporation is to be treated for purposes of this title as stock or indebtedness.

(b) Factors.—The regulations prescribed under this section shall set forth factors which are to be taken into account in determining with respect to a particular factual situation whether a debtor-creditor relationship exists or a corporation-shareholder relationship exists. The factors so set forth in the regulations may include among other factors:

(1) whether there is a written unconditional promise to pay on demand or on a specified date a sum certain in money in return for an adequate consideration in money or money's worth, and to pay a fixed rate of interest,

(2) whether there is subordination to or preference over any indebtedness of the corporation,

(3) the ratio of debt to equity of the corporation,

(4) whether there is convertibility into the stock of the corporation, and

(5) the relationship between holdings of stock in the corporation and holdings of the interest in question.

PART VII—MISCELLANEOUS CORPORATE PROVISIONS

§ 386. Transfers of partnership and trust interests by corporations

(a) **Corporate distributions.**—For purposes of determining the amount (and character) of gain recognized by a corporation on any distribution of an interest in a partnership, the distribution shall be treated in the same manner as if it included a property distribution consisting of the corporation's proportionate share of the recognition property of such partnership.

(b) **Sales or exchange to which section 337 applies.**—For purposes of determining the amount (and character) of gain recognized on a sale or exchange described in section 337, any sale or exchange by a corporation of an interest in a partnership shall be treated as a sale or exchange of the corporation's proportionate share of the recognition property of such partnership.

(c) **Recognition property.**—For purposes of this section, the term "recognition property" means any property with respect to which gain would be recognized to the corporation if such property—

(1) were distributed by the corporation in a distribution described in section 311 or 336, or

(2) were sold in a sale described in section 337,

whichever is appropriate. In determining whether property of a partnership is recognition property, such partnership shall be treated as owning its proportionate share of the property of any other partnership in which it is a partner.

(d) **Limitation on amount of gain recognized in case of non-liquidating distributions.**—In the case of any distribution by a corporation to which section 311 applies, the amount of any gain recognized by reason of subsection (a) shall not exceed the amount of the gain which would have been recognized if the partnership interest had been sold. The Secretary may by regulations provide that the amount of such gain shall be computed without regard to any loss attributable to property contributed to the partnership for the principal purpose of recognizing such loss on the distribution.

(e) **Extension to trusts.**—Under regulations, rules similar to the rules of this section shall also apply in the case of the distribution or sale or exchange by a corporation of an interest in a trust.

SUBCHAPTER D—DEFERRED COMPENSATION, ETC.

Part

Part
II. Certain stock options.*

PART I—PENSION, PROFIT–SHARING, STOCK BONUS PLANS, ETC.

Subpart
A. General rule.
B. Special rules.
C. Special rules for multiemployer plans.*
D. Treatment of welfare benefit funds.

Subpart A—General Rule

§ 401. Qualified pension, profit-sharing, and stock bonus plans

(a) **Requirements for qualification.**—A trust created or organized in the United States and forming part of a stock bonus, pension, or profit-sharing plan of an employer for the exclusive benefit of his employees or their beneficiaries shall constitute a qualified trust under this section—

(1) if contributions are made to the trust by such employer, or employees, or both, or by another employer who is entitled to deduct his contributions under section 404(a) (3) (B) (relating to deduction for contributions to profit-sharing and stock bonus plans), for the purpose of distributing to such employees or their beneficiaries the corpus and income of the fund accumulated by the trust in accordance with such plan;

(2) if under the trust instrument it is impossible, at any time prior to the satisfaction of all liabilities with respect to employees and their beneficiaries under the trust, for any part of the corpus or income to be (within the taxable year or thereafter) used for, or diverted to, purposes other than for the exclusive benefit of his employees or their beneficiaries (but this paragraph shall not be construed, in the case of a multiemployer plan, to prohibit the return of a contribution within 6 months after the plan administrator determines that the contribution was made by a mistake of fact or law (other than a mistake relating to whether the plan is described in section 401(a) or the trust which is part of such plan is exempt from taxation under section 501(a), or the return of any withdrawal liability payment determined to be an overpayment within 6 months of such determination));

(3) if the plan of which such trust is a part satisfies the requirements of section 410 (relating to minimum participation standards); and

(4) if the contributions or the benefits provided under the plan do not discriminate in favor of employees who are—

(A) officers,

(B) shareholders, or

(C) highly compensated.

For purposes of this paragraph, there shall be excluded from consideration employees described in section 410(b) (3) (A) and (C).

Amendment of Subsec. (a)(4)

Pub.L. 99–514, Title XI, § 1114(b)(7), (c) Oct. 22, 1986, 100 Stat. ——, ——, provided that, applicable to taxable years beginning after Dec. 31, 1988, with special rule for determining highly compensated employees, subsec. (a)(4) is amended to read as follows:

* Omitted entirely.

(4) if the contributions or benefits provided under the plan do not discriminate in favor of highly compensated employees (within the meaning of section 414(q)). For purposes of this paragraph, there shall be excluded from consideration employees described in section 410(b)(3)(A) and (C).

(5) A classification shall not be considered discriminatory within the meaning of paragraph (4) or section 410(b) (without regard to paragraph (1) (A) thereof) merely because it excludes employees the whole of whose remuneration constitutes "wages" under section 3121(a) (1) (relating to the Federal Insurance Contributions Act) or merely because it is limited to salaried or clerical employees. Neither shall a plan be considered discriminatory within the meaning of such provisions merely because the contributions or benefits of or on behalf of the employees under the plan bear a uniform relationship to the total compensation, or the basic or regular rate of compensation, of such employees, or merely because the contributions or benefits based on that part of an employee's remuneration which is excluded from "wages" by section 3121(a) (1) differ from the contributions or benefits based on employee's remuneration not so excluded, or differ because of any retirement benefits created under State or Federal law. For purposes of this paragraph and paragraph (10), the total compensation of an individual who is an employee within the meaning of subsection (c) (1) means such individual's earned income (as defined in subsection (c) (2)), and the basic or regular rate of compensation of such an individual shall be determined, under regulations prescribed by the Secretary, with respect to that portion of his earned income which bears the same ratio to his earned income as the basic or regular compensation of the employees under the plan bears to the total compensation of such employees. For purposes of determining whether two or more plans of an employer satisfy the requirements of paragraph (4) when considered as a single plan, if the amount of contributions on behalf of the employees allowed as a deduction under section 404 for the taxable year with respect to such plans, taken together, bears a uniform relationship to the total compensation, or the basic or regular rate of compensation, of such employees, the plans shall not be considered discriminatory merely because the rights of employees to, or derived from, the employer contributions under the separate plans do not become nonforfeitable at the same rate. For the purposes of determining whether two or more plans of an employer satisfy the requirements of paragraph (4) when considered as a single plan, if the employees' rights to benefits under the separate plans do not become nonforfeitable at the same rate, but the levels of benefits provided by the separate plans satisfy the requirements of regulations prescribed by the Secretary to take account of the differences in such rates, the plans shall not be considered discriminatory merely because of the difference in such rates. For purposes of determining whether one or more plans of an employer satisfy the requirements of paragraph (4) and of section 410(b), an employer may take into account all simplified employee pensions to which only the employer contributes.

Amendment of Subsec. (a)(5)

Pub.L. 99–514, Title XI, § 1111(b), (c)(2), (3), Oct. 22, 1986, 100 Stat. ——, provided that, applicable to years beginning after December 31, 1988, and subject to special rules with regard to benefits in specified plan years pursuant to collective bargaining agreements ratified before March 1, 1986, subsec. (a)(5) of this section is amended to read as follows:

(5) Special rules relating to nondiscrimination requirements.—

(A) Salaried or clerical employees.—A classification shall not be considered discriminatory within the meaning of paragraph (4) or section 410(b)(2)(A)(i) merely because it is limited to salaried or clerical employees.

(B) Contributions and benefits may bear uniform relationship to compensation.—A plan shall not be considered discriminatory within the meaning of paragraph (4) merely because the contributions or benefits of, or on behalf of, the employees under the plan bear a uniform relationship to the compensation (within the meaning of section 414(s)) of such employees.

(C) Certain disparity permitted.—A plan shall not be considered discriminatory within the meaning of paragraph (4) merely because the contributions or benefits of, or on behalf of, the employees under the plan favor highly compensated employees (as defined in section 414(q)) in the manner permitted under subsection (*l*).

(D) Integrated defined benefit plan.—

(i) In general.—A defined benefit plan shall not be considered discriminatory within the meaning of paragraph (4) merely because the plan provides that the employer-derived accrued retirement benefit for any participant under the plan may not exceed the excess (if any) of—

(I) the participant's final pay with the employer, over

(II) the employer-derived retirement benefit created under Federal law attributable to service by the participant with the employer.

For purposes of this clause, the employer-derived retirement benefit created under Federal law shall be treated as accruing ratably over 35 years.

(ii) Final pay.—For purposes of this subparagraph, the participant's final pay is the compensation (as defined in section 414(q)(7)) paid to the participant by the employer for any year—

(I) which ends during the 5–year period ending with the year in which the participant separated from service for the employer, and

(II) for which the participant's total compensation from the employer was highest.

(E) 2 or more plans treated as single plan.—For purposes of determining whether 2 or more plans of an employer satisfy the requirements of paragraph (4) when considered as a single plan—

(i) Contributions.—If the amount of contributions on behalf of the employees allowed as a deduction under section 404 for the taxable year with respect to such plans, taken together, bears a uniform relationship to the compensation (within the meaning of section 414(s)) of such employees, the plans shall not be considered discriminatory merely because the rights of employees to, or derived from, the employer contributions under the separate plans do not become nonforfeitable at the same rate.

(ii) Benefits.—If the employees' rights to benefits under the separate plans do not become nonforfeitable at the same rate, but the levels of benefits provided by the separate plans satisfy the requirements of regulations prescribed by the Secretary to take account of the differences in such rates, the plans shall not be considered discriminatory merely because of the difference in such rates.

(6) A plan shall be considered as meeting the requirements of paragraph (3) during the whole of any taxable year of the plan if on one day in each quarter it satisfied such requirements.

(7) A trust shall not constitute a qualified trust under this section unless the plan of which such trust is a part satisfies the requirements of section 411 (relating to minimum vesting standards).

343

(8) A trust forming part of a defined benefit plan shall not constitute a qualified trust under this section unless the plan provides that forfeitures must not be applied to increase the benefits any employee would otherwise receive under the plan.

(9) **Required distributions.—**

(A) **In general.**—A trust shall not constitute a qualified trust under this subsection unless the plan provides that the entire interest of each employee—

(i) will be distributed to such employee not later than the required beginning date, or

(ii) will be distributed, beginning not later than the required beginning date, in accordance with regulations, over the life of such employee or over the lives of such employee and a designated beneficiary (or over a period not extending beyond the life expectancy of such employee or the life expectancy of such employee and a designated beneficiary).

(B) **Required distribution where employee dies before entire interest is distributed.**—

(i) **Where distributions have begun under subparagraph (A)(ii).**—A trust shall not constitute a qualified trust under this section unless the plan provides that if—

(I) the distribution of the employee's interest has begun in accordance with subparagraph (A)(ii), and

(II) the employee dies before his entire interest has been distributed to him,

the remaining portion of such interest will be distributed at least as rapidly as under the method of distributions being used under subparagraph (A)(ii) as of the date of his death.

(ii) **5-year rule for other cases.**—A trust shall not constitute a qualified trust under this section unless the plan provides that, if an employee dies before the distribution of the employee's interest has begun in accordance with subparagraph (A)(ii), the entire interest of the employee will be distributed within 5 years after the death of such employee.

(iii) **Exception to 5-year rule for certain amounts payable over life of beneficiary.**—If—

(I) any portion of the employee's interest is payable to (or for the benefit of) a designated beneficiary,

(II) such portion will be distributed (in accordance with regulations) over the life of such designated beneficiary (or over a period not extending beyond the life expectancy of such beneficiary), and

(III) such distributions begin not later than a year after the date of the employee's death or such later date as the Secretary may by regulations prescribe,

for purposes of clause (ii), the portion referred to in subclause (I) shall be treated as distributed on the date on which such distributions begin.

(iv) **Special rule for surviving spouse of employee.**—If the designated beneficiary referred to in clause (iii)(I) is the surviving spouse of the employee—

(I) the date on which the distributions are required to begin under clause (iii)(III) shall not be earlier than the date on which the employee would have attained age 70½, and

(II) if the surviving spouse dies before the distributions to such spouse begin, this subparagraph shall be applied as if the surviving spouse were the employee.

(C) Required beginning date.—For purposes of this paragraph, the term "required beginning date" means April 1 of the calendar year following the later of—

(i) the calendar year in which the employee attains age 70½, or

(ii) the calendar year in which the employee retires.

Clause (ii) shall not apply in the case of an employee who is a 5-percent owner (as defined in section 416(i)(1)(B)) at any time during the 5-plan-year period ending in the calendar year in which the employee attains age 70½. If the employee becomes a 5-percent owner during any subsequent plan year, the required beginning date shall be April 1 of the calendar year following the calendar year in which such subsequent plan year ends.

Amendment of Subsec. (a)(9)(C)

Pub.L. 99–514, Title XI, § 1121(b), (d), Oct. 22, 1986, 100 Stat. ——, provided that, applicable to years beginning after December 31, 1988, with enumerated transition rules and other provisions relating to collective bargaining agreements ratified before Mar. 1, 1986, subparagraph (C) of subsec. (a)(9) of this section is amended to read as follows:

(C) Required beginning date.—For purposes of this paragraph, the term "required beginning date" means April 1 of the calendar year following the calendar year in which the employee attains age 70½.

(D) Life expectancy.—For purposes of this paragraph, the life expectancy of an employee and the employee's spouse (other than in the case of a life annuity) may be redetermined but not more frequently than annually.

(E) Designated beneficiary.—For purposes of this paragraph, the term "designated beneficiary" means any individual designated as a beneficiary by the employee.

(F) Treatment of payments to children.—Under regulations prescribed by the Secretary, for purposes of this paragraph, any amount paid to a child shall be treated as if it had been paid to the surviving spouse if such amount will become payable to the surviving spouse upon such child reaching majority (or other designated event permitted under regulations).

(G) Treatment of incidental death benefit distributions.—For purposes of this title, any distribution required under the incidental death benefit requirements of this subsection shall be treated as a distribution required under this paragraph.

(10) Other requirements.—

(A) Plans benefiting owner-employees.—In the case of any plan which provides contributions or benefits for employees some or all of whom are owner-employees (as defined in subsection (c)(3)), a trust forming part of such plan shall constitute a qualified trust under this section only if the requirements of subsection (d) are also met.

(B) Top-heavy plans.—

(i) In general.—In the case of any top-heavy plan, a trust forming part of such plan shall constitute a qualified trust under this section only if the requirements of section 416 are met.

(ii) Plans which may become top-heavy.—Except to the extent provided in regulations, a trust forming part of a plan (whether or not a top-heavy plan) shall constitute a qualified trust under this section only if such plan contains provisions—

(I) which will take effect if such plan becomes a top-heavy plan, and

(II) which meet the requirements of section 416.

(iii) Exemption for governmental plans.—This subparagraph shall not apply to any governmental plan.

(11) Requirement of joint and survivor annuity and preretirement survivor annuity.—

(A) In general.—In the case of any plan to which this paragraph applies, except as provided in section 417, a trust forming part of such plan shall not constitute a qualified trust under this section unless—

(i) in the case of a vested participant who does not die before the annuity starting date, the accrued benefit payable to such participant is provided in the form of a qualified joint and survivor annuity, and

(ii) in the case of a vested participant who dies before the annuity starting date and who has a surviving spouse, a qualified preretirement survivor annuity is provided to the surviving spouse of such participant.

(B) Plans to which paragraph applies.—This paragraph shall apply to—

(i) any defined benefit plan,

(ii) any defined contribution plan which is subject to the funding standards of section 412, and

(iii) any participant under any other defined contribution plan unless—

(I) such plan provides that the participant's nonforfeitable accrued benefit (reduced by any security interest held by the plan by reason of a loan outstanding to such participant) is payable in full, on the death of the participant, to the participant's surviving spouse (or, if there is no surviving spouse or the surviving spouse consents in the manner required under section 417(a)(2), to a designated beneficiary),

(II) Such participant does not elect a payment of benefits in the form of a life annuity, and

(III) with respect to such participant, such plan is not a direct or indirect transferee (in a transfer after December 31, 1984) of a plan which is described in clause (i) or (ii) or to which this clause applied with respect to the participant.

Clause (iii)(III) shall apply only with respect to the transferred assets (and income therefrom) if the plan separately accounts for such assets and any income therefrom.

* * *

(D) Special rule where participant and spouse married less than 1 year. —A plan shall not be treated as failing to meet the requirements of subparagraphs (B)(iii) or (C) merely because the plan provides that benefits will not be payable to the surviving spouse of the participant unless the participant and such spouse had been married throughout the 1–year period ending on the earlier of the participant's annuity starting date or the date of the participant's death.

(12) A trust shall not constitute a qualified trust under this section unless the plan of which such trust is a part provides that in the case of any merger or consolidation with, or transfer of assets or liabilities to, any other plan after September 2, 1974, each participant in the plan would (if the plan then terminated) receive a benefit immediately after the merger, consolidation, or transfer which is equal to or greater than the benefit he would have been entitled to receive immediately before the merger, consolidation, or transfer (if the plan had then terminated). The preceding sentence does not apply to any multiemployer plan with respect to any transaction to the extent that participants either before or after the transaction are covered under a multiemployer plan to which title IV of the Employee Retirement Income Security Act of 1974 applies.

(13) Assignment and alienation.—

(A) In general.—A trust shall not constitute a qualified trust under this section unless the plan of which such trust is a part provides that benefits provided under the plan may not be assigned or alienated. For purposes of the preceding sentence, there shall not be taken into account any voluntary and revocable assignment of not to exceed 10 percent of any benefit payment made by any participant who is receiving benefits under the plan unless the assignment or alienation is made for purposes of defraying plan administration costs. For purposes of this paragraph a loan made to a participant or beneficiary shall not be treated as an assignment or alienation if such loan is secured by the participant's accrued nonforfeitable benefit and is exempt from the tax imposed by section 4975 (relating to tax on prohibited transactions) by reason of section 4975(d)(1). This paragraph shall take effect on January 1, 1976 and shall not apply to assignments which were irrevocable on September 2, 1974.

(B) Special rules for domestic relations orders.—Subparagraph (A) shall apply to the creation, assignment, or recognition of a right to any benefit payable with respect to a participant pursuant to a domestic relations order, except that subparagraph (A) shall not apply if the order is determined to be a qualified domestic relations order.

(14) A trust shall not constitute a qualified trust under this section unless the plan of which such trust is a part provides that, unless the participant otherwise elects, the payment of benefits under the plan to the participant will begin not later than the 60th day after the latest of the close of the plan year in which—

(A) the date on which the participant attains the earlier of age 65 or the normal retirement age specified under the plan,

(B) occurs the 10th anniversary of the year in which the participant commenced participation in the plan, or

(C) the participant terminates his service with the employer.

In the case of a plan which provides for the payment of an early retirement benefit, a trust forming a part of such plan shall not constitute a qualified trust under this section unless a participant who satisfied the service requirements for such early retirement benefit, but separated from the service (with any nonforfeitable right to an accrued benefit) before satisfying the age requirement for such early retirement benefit, is entitled upon satisfaction of such age requirement to receive a benefit not less than the benefit to which he would be entitled at the normal retirement age, actuarially reduced under regulations prescribed by the Secretary.

(15) A trust shall not constitute a qualified trust under this section unless under the plan of which such trust is a part—

(A) in the case of a participant or beneficiary who is receiving benefits under such plan, or

(B) in the case of a participant who is separated from the service and who has nonforfeitable rights to benefits,

such benefits are not decreased by reason of any increase in the benefit levels payable under title II of the Social Security Act or any increase in the wage base under such title II, if such increase takes place after September 2, 1974, or (if later) the earlier of the date of first receipt of such benefits or the date of such separation, as the case may be.

(16) A trust shall not constitute a qualified trust under this section if the plan of which such trust is a part provides for benefits or contributions which exceed the limitations of section 415.

[(17), (18) Repealed. Pub.L. 97–248, Title II, § 237(b), Sept. 3, 1982, 96 Stat. 511]

(19) A trust shall not constitute a qualified trust under this section if under the plan of which such trust is a part any part of a participant's accrued benefit derived from employer contributions (whether or not otherwise nonforfeitable), is forfeitable solely because of withdrawal by such participant of any amount attributable to the benefit derived from contributions made by such participant. The preceding sentence shall not apply to the accrued benefit of any participant unless, at the time of such withdrawal, such participant has a nonforfeitable right to at least 50 percent of such accrued benefit (as determined under section 411). The first sentence of this paragraph shall not apply to the extent that an accrued benefit is permitted to be forfeited in accordance with section 411(a) (3) (D) (iii) (relating to proportional forfeitures of benefits accrued before September 2, 1974, in the event of withdrawal of certain mandatory contributions).

* * *

(22) If a defined contribution plan (other than a profit-sharing plan)—

(A) is established by an employer whose stock is not publicly traded, and

(B) after acquiring securities of the employer, more than 10 percent of the total assets of the plan are securities of the employer,

any trust forming part of such plan shall not constitute a qualified trust under this section unless the plan meets the requirements of subsection (e) of section 409.

The requirements of subsection (e) of section 409 shall not apply to any employees of an employer who are participants in any defined contribution plan established and maintained by such employer if the stock of such employer is not publicly traded and the trade or business of such employer consists of publishing on a regular basis a newspaper for general circulation.

(23) A stock bonus plan shall not be treated as meeting the requirements of this section unless such plan meets the requirements of subsections (h) and (o) of section 409, except that in applying section 409(h) for purposes of this paragraph, the term "employer securities" shall include any securities of the employer held by the plan.

* * *

(25) Requirement that actuarial assumptions be specified.—A defined benefit plan shall not be treated as providing definitely determinable benefits unless, whenever the amount of any benefit is to be determined on the basis of actuarial assumptions, such assumptions are specified in the plan in a way which precludes employer discretion.

Enactment of Subsec. (a)(26)

Pub.L. 99–514, Title XI, § 1112(b), (e), Oct. 22, 1986, 100 Stat. ——, provided that, applicable to plan years beginning after December 31, 1988, with special rules regarding collective bargaining agreements ratified before March 1, 1986, and with provision for a waiver of the excise tax on reversions, subsec. (a) of this section is amended by enacting a new par. (26) to read as follows:

(26) Additional participation requirements.—

(A) In general.—A trust shall not constitute a qualified trust under this subsection unless such trust is part of a plan which on each day of the plan year benefits the lesser of—

(i) 50 employees of the employer, or

(ii) 40 percent or more of all employees of the employer.

(B) Treatment of excludable employees.—

(i) **In general.—**A plan may exclude from consideration under this paragraph employees described in paragraphs (3) and (4)(A) of section 410(b).

(ii) **Separate application for certain excludable employees.—**If employees described in section 410(b)(4)(B) are covered under a plan which meets the requirements of subparagraph (A) separately with respect to such employees, such employees may be excluded from consideration in determining whether any plan of the employer meets such requirements if—

(I) the benefits for such employees are provided under the same plan as benefits for other employees

(II) the benefits provided to such employees are not greater than comparable benefits provided to other employees under the plan, and

(III) no highly compensated employee (within the meaning of section 414(q)) is included in the group of such employees for more than 1 year.

(C) Eligibility to participate.—In the case of contributions under section 401(k) or 401(m), employees who are eligible to contribute (or may elect to have contributions made on their behalf) shall be treated as benefiting under the plan.

(D) Special rule for collective bargaining units.—Except to the extent provided in regulations, a plan covering only employees described in section 410(b)(3)(A) may exclude from consideration any employees who are not included in the unit or units in which the covered employees are included.

(E) Paragraph not to apply to multiemployer plans.—Except to the extent provided in regulations, this paragraph shall not apply to employees in a multiemployer plan (within the meaning of section 414(f)) who are covered by collective bargaining agreements.

(F) Regulations.—The Secretary may by regulation provide that any separate benefit structure, any separate trust, or any other separate arrangement is to be treated as a separate plan for purposes of applying this paragraph.

(27) The determination of whether the plan under which any contributions are made is a profit-sharing plan shall be made without regard to current or accumulated profits of the employer and without regard to whether the employer is a tax-exempt organization.

Paragraphs (11), (12), (13), (14), (15), (19), and (20) shall apply only in the case of a plan to which section 411 (relating to minimum vesting standards) applies without regard to subsection (e)(2) of such section.

(b) **Certain retroactive changes in plan.**—A stock bonus, pension, profit-sharing, or annuity plan shall be considered as satisfying the requirements of subsection (a) for the period beginning with the date on which is was put into effect, or for the period beginning with the earlier of the date on which there was adopted or put into effect any amendment which caused the plan to fail to satisfy such requirements, and ending with the time prescribed by law for filing the return of the employer for his taxable year in which such plan or amendment was adopted (including extensions thereof) or such later time as the Secretary may designate, if all provisions of the plan which are necessary to satisfy such requirements are in effect by the end of such period and have been made effective for all purposes for the whole of such period.

(c) **Definitions and rules relating to self-employed individuals and owner-employees.**—For purposes of this section—

(1) **Self-employed individual treated as employee.**—

(A) **In general.**—The term "employee" includes, for any taxable year, an individual who is a self-employed individual for such taxable year.

(B) **Self-employed individual.**—The term "self-employed individual" means, with respect to any taxable year, an individual who has earned income (as defined in paragraph (2)) for such taxable year. To the extent provided in regulations prescribed by the Secretary, such term also includes, for any taxable year—

(i) an individual who would be a self-employed individual within the meaning of the preceding sentence but for the fact that the trade or business carried on by such individual did not have net profits for the taxable year, and

(ii) an individual who has been a self-employed individual within the meaning of the preceding sentence for any prior taxable year.

(2) **Earned income.**—

(A) **In general.**—The term "earned income" means the net earnings from self-employment (as defined in section 1402(a)), but such net earnings shall be determined—

(i) only with respect to a trade or business in which personal services of the taxpayer are a material income-producing factor,

(ii) without regard to paragraphs (4) and (5) of section 1402(c),

(iii) in the case of any individual who is treated as an employee under sections 3121(d) (3) (A), (C), or (D), without regard to paragraph (2) of section 1402(c),

(iv) without regard to items which are not included in gross income for purposes of this chapter, and the deductions properly allocable to or chargeable against such items,

(v) with regard to the deductions allowed by section 404 to the taxpayer, and

(vi) with regard to the deduction allowed to the taxpayer by section 164(f).

For purposes of this subparagraph, section 1402, as in effect for a taxable year ending on December 31, 1962, shall be treated as having been in effect for all taxable years ending before such date.

[(B) Repealed.]

(C) **Income from disposition of certain property.**—For purposes of this section, the term "earned income" includes gains (other than any gain which is treated under any provision of this chapter as gain from the sale or exchange of a capital asset) and net earnings derived from the sale or other disposition of, the transfer of any interest in, or the licensing of the use of property (other than good will) by an individual whose personal efforts created such property.

(3) **Owner-employee.**—The term "owner-employee" means an employee who—

(A) owns the entire interest in an unincorporated trade or business, or

(B) in the case of a partnership, is a partner who owns more than 10 percent of either the capital interest or the profits interest in such partnership.

To the extent provided in regulations prescribed by the Secretary, such term also means an individual who has been an owner-employee within the meaning of the preceding sentence.

(4) **Employer.**—An individual who owns the entire interest in an unincorporated trade or business shall be treated as his own employer. A partnership shall be treated as the employer of each partner who is an employee within the meaning of paragraph (1).

(5) **Contributions on behalf of owner-employees.**—The term "contribution on behalf of an owner-employee" includes, except as the context otherwise requires, a contribution under a plan—

(A) by the employer for an owner-employee, and

(B) by an owner-employee as an employee.

* * *

(d) **Additional requirements for qualification of trusts and plans benefiting owner-employees.**—A trust forming part of a pension or profit-sharing plan which provides contributions or benefits for employees some or all of whom are owner-employees shall constitute a qualified trust under this section only if, in addition to meeting the requirements of subsection (a), the following requirements of this subsection are met by the trust and by the plan of which such trust is a part:

(1)(A) If the plan provides contributions or benefits for an owner-employee who controls, or for two or more owner-employees who together control, the trade or business with respect to which the plan is established, and who also control as an owner-employee or as owner-employees one or more other trades or businesses, such plan and the plans established with respect to such other trades or businesses, when coalesced, constitute a single plan which meets the requirements of subsection (a) (including paragraph (10) thereof) and of this subsection with respect to the employees of all such trades or businesses (including the trade or business with respect to which the plan intended to qualify under this section is established).

(B) For purposes of subparagraph (A), an owner-employee, or two or more owner-employees, shall be considered to control a trade or business if such owner-employee, or such two or more owner-employees together—

(i) own the entire interest in an unincorporated trade or business, or

(ii) in the case of a partnership, own more than 50 percent of either the capital interest or the profits interest in such partnership.

For purposes of the preceding sentence, an owner-employee, or two or more owner-employees, shall be treated as owning any interest in a partnership which is owned, directly or indirectly, by a partnership which such owner-employee, or such two or more owner-employees, are considered to control within the meaning of the preceding sentence.

(2) The plan does not provide contributions or benefits for any owner-employee who controls (within the meaning of paragraph (1)(B)), or for two or more owner-employees who together control, as an owner-employee or as owner-employees, any other trade or business, unless the employees of each trade or business which such owner-employee or such owner-employees control are included under a plan which meets the requirements of subsection (a) (including paragraph (10) thereof) and of this subsection, and provides contributions and benefits for employees which are not less favorable than contributions and benefits provided for owner-employees under the plan.

(3) Under the plan, contributions on behalf of any owner-employee may be made only with respect to the earned income of such owner-employee which is derived from the trade or business with respect to which such plan is established.

* * *

(f) Certain custodial accounts and contracts.—For purposes of this title, a custodial account, an annuity contract, or a contract (other than a life, health or accident, property, casualty, or liability insurance contract) issued by an insurance company qualified to do business in a State shall be treated as a qualified trust under this section if—

(1) the custodial account or contract would, except for the fact that it is not a trust, constitute a qualified trust under this section, and

(2) in the case of a custodial account the assets thereof are held by a bank (as defined in section 408(n)) or another person who demonstrates, to the satisfaction of the Secretary, that the manner in which he will hold the assets will be consistent with the requirements of this section.

For purposes of this title, in the case of a custodial account or contract treated as a qualified trust under this section by reason of this subsection, the person holding the assets of such account or holding such contract shall be treated as the trustee thereof.

* * *

(h) Medical, etc., benefits for retired employees and their spouses and dependents.—Under regulations prescribed by the Secretary, a pension or annuity plan may provide for the payment of benefits for sickness, accident, hospitalization, and medical expenses of retired employees, their spouses and their dependents, but only if—

(1) such benefits are subordinate to the retirement benefits provided by the plan,

(2) a separate account is established and maintained for such benefits,

(3) the employer's contributions to such separate account are reasonable and ascertainable,

(4) it is impossible, at any time prior to the satisfaction of all liabilities under the plan to provide such benefits, for any part of the corpus or income of such separate account to be (within the taxable year or thereafter) used for, or diverted to, any purpose other than the providing of such benefits,

(5) notwithstanding the provisions of subsection (a)(2), upon the satisfaction of all liabilities under the plan to provide such benefits, any amount remaining in such separate account must, under the terms of the plan, be returned to the employer, and

(6) in the case of an employee who is a key employee, a separate account is established and maintained for such benefits payable to such employee (and his spouse and dependents) and such benefits (to the extent attributable to plan years beginning after March 31, 1984, for which the employee is a key employee) are only

payable to such employee (and his spouse and dependents) from such separate account.

For purposes of paragraph (6), the term 'key employee' means any employee, who at any time during the plan year or any preceding plan year during which contributions were made on behalf of such employee, is or was a key employee as defined in section 416(i).

* * *

(k) Cash or deferred arrangements.—

(1) General rule.—A profit-sharing or stock bonus plan, a pre-ERISA money purchase plan, or a rural electric cooperative plan shall not be considered as not satisfying the requirements of subsection (a) merely because the plan includes a qualified cash or deferred arrangement.

(2) Qualified cash or deferred arrangement.—A qualified cash or deferred arrangement is any arrangement which is part of a profit-sharing or stock bonus plan, a pre-ERISA money purchase plan, or a rural electric cooperative plan which meets the requirements of subsection (a)—

(A) under which a covered employee may elect to have the employer make payments as contributions to a trust under the plan on behalf of the employee, or to the employee directly in cash;

(B) under which—

(i) amounts held by the trust which are attributable to employer contributions made pursuant to the employee's election may not be distributable to participants or other beneficiaries earlier than—

(I) separation from service, death, or disability,

(II) termination of the plan without establishment of a successor plan,

(III) the date of the sale by a corporation of substantially all of the assets (within the meaning of section 409(d)(2)) used by such corporation in a trade or business of such corporation with respect to an employee who continues employment with the corporation acquiring such assets,

(IV) the date of the sale by a corporation of such corporation's interest in a subsidiary (within the meaning of section 409(d)(3)) with respect to an employee who continues employment with such subsidiary,

(V) in the case of a profit-sharing or stock bonus plan, the attainment of age 59½, or

(VI) in the case of contributions to a profit-sharing or stock bonus plan to which section 402(a)(8) applies, upon hardship of the employee, and

(ii) amounts will not be distributable merely by reason of the completion of a stated period of participation or the lapse of a fixed number of years; and

(C) which provides that an employee's right to his accrued benefit derived from employer contributions made to the trust pursuant to his election is nonforfeitable.

(3) Application of participation and discrimination standards.—

(A) A cash or deferred arrangement shall not be treated as a qualified cash or deferred arrangement unless—

(i) those employees eligible to benefit under the arrangement satisfy the provisions of subparagraph (A) or (B) of section 410(b)(1), and

Amendment of Subsec. (k)(3)(A)(i)

Pub.L. 99–514, Title XI, § 1112(d)(1), (e), Oct. 22, 1986, 100 Stat. ——, provided that, applicable to plan years beginning after December 31, 1988, subsec. (k)(3)(A)(i) of this section is amended by striking out "subparagraph (A) or (B) of" before "section 410(b)(1)".

(ii) the actual deferral percentage for highly compensated employees (as defined in paragraph (5)) for such year bears a relationship to the actual deferral percentage for all other eligible employees for such plan year which meets either of the following tests:

(I) The actual deferral percentage for the group of highly compensated employees is not more than the actual deferral percentage of all other eligible employees multiplied by 1.25.

(II) The excess of the actual deferral percentage for the group of highly compensated employees over that of all other eligible employees is not more than 2 percentage points, and the actual deferral percentage for the group of highly compensated employees is not more than the actual deferral percentage of all other eligible employees multiplied by 2.

If an employee is a participant under 2 or more cash or deferred arrangements of the employer, for purposes of determining the deferral percentage with respect to such employee, all such cash or deferred arrangements shall be treated as 1 cash or deferred arrangement.

(B) For purposes of subparagraph (A), the actual deferral percentage for a specified group of employees for a plan year shall be the average of the ratios (calculated separately for each employee in such group) of—

(i) the amount of employer contributions actually paid over to the trust on behalf of each such employee for such plan year, to

(ii) the employee's compensation for such plan year.

(C) [5] For purposes of subparagraph (B), the employer contributions on behalf of any employee—

(i) shall include any employer contributions made pursuant to the employee's election under paragraph (2), and

(ii) under such rules as the Secretary may prescribe, may, at the election of the employer, include—

(I) matching contributions (as defined in 401(m)(4)(A)) which meets the requirements of paragraph (2)(B) and (C), and

(II) qualified nonelective contributions (within the meaning of section 401(m)(4)(C)).

(C) [6] A cash or deferred arrangement shall be treated as meeting the requirements of subsection (a)(4) with respect to contributions if the requirements of subparagraph (A)(ii) are met.

(4) Other requirements.—

(A) Benefits (other than matching contributions) must not be contingent on election to defer.—A cash or deferred arrangement of any employer shall not be treated as a qualified cash or deferred arrangement if any other benefit provided by such employer is conditioned (directly or indirectly) on the employee electing to have the employer make or not make contributions under the arrangement in lieu of receiving cash. The preceding sentence shall not apply to

---

[5] Added by Pub.L. 99–514, Title XI, § 1116(c), October 22, 1986, 100 Stat. ——.

[6] Added by Pub.L. 99–514, Title XVIII, § 1852(g)(1), October 22, 1986, 100 Stat. ——. Editor's Note: Probably should read "(D)".

any matching contribution (as defined in section 401(m)) made by reason of such an election.

(B) State and local governments and tax-exempt organizations not eligible.—A cash or deferred arrangement shall not be treated as a qualified cash or deferred arrangement if it is part of a plan maintained by—

(i) a State or local government or political subdivision thereof, or any agency or instrumentality thereof, or

(ii) any organization exempt from tax under this subtitle.

(C) Coordination with other plans.—Except as provided in section 401(m), any employer contribution made pursuant to an employee's election under a qualified cash or deferred arrangement shall not be taken into account for purposes of determining whether any other plan meets the requirements of section 401(a) or 410(b). This subparagraph shall not apply for purposes of determining whether a plan meets the average benefit requirement of section 410(b)(2)(A)(ii).

(5) Highly compensated employee.—For purposes of this subsection, the term "highly compensated employee" has the meaning given such term by section 414(q).

(8) Arrangement not disqualified if excess contributions distributed.—

(A) In general.—A cash or deferred arrangement shall not be treated as failing to meet the requirements of clause (ii) of paragraph (3)(A) for any plan year if, before the close of the following plan year—

(i) the amount of the excess contributions for such plan year (and any income allocable to such contributions) is distributed, or

(ii) to the extent provided in regulations, the employee elects to treat the amount of the excess contributions as an amount distributed to the employee and then contributed by the employee to the plan.

Any distribution of excess contributions (and income) may be made without regard to any other provision of law.

(B) Excess contributions.—For purposes of subparagraph (A), the term "excess contributions" means, with respect to any plan year, the excess of—

(i) the aggregate amount of employer contributions actually paid over to the trust on behalf of highly compensated employees for such plan year, over

(ii) the maximum amount of such contributions permitted under the limitations of clause (ii) of paragraph (3)(A) (determined by reducing contributions made on behalf of highly compensated employees in order of the actual deferral percentages beginning with the highest of such percentages).

(C) Method of distributing excess contributions.—Any distribution of the excess contributions for any plan year shall be made to highly compensated employees on the basis of the respective portions of the excess contributions attributable to each of such employees.

(D) Additional tax under section 72(t) not to apply.—No tax shall be imposed under section 72(t) on any amount required to be distributed under this paragraph.

(E) Cross reference.—

For excise tax on certain excess contributions, see section 4979.

(9) Compensation.—For purposes of this subsection, the term "compensation" has the meaning given such term by section 414(s).

(*l*) Nondiscriminatory coordination of defined contribution plans with OAS-DI.—

(1) In general.—Notwithstanding subsection (a)(5), the coordination of a defined contribution plan with OASDI meets the requirements of subsection (a)(4) only if the total contributions with respect to each participant, when increased by the OASDI contributions, bear a uniform relationship—

(A) to the total compensation of such employee, or

(B) to the basic or regular rate of compensation of such employee.

(2) Definitions.—For purposes of paragraph (1)—

(A) OASDI contributions.—The term "OASDI contributions" means the product of—

(i) so much of the remuneration paid by the employer to the employee during the plan year as—

(I) constitutes wages (within the meaning of section 3121(a) without regard to paragraph (1) thereof), and

(II) does not exceed the contribution and benefit base applicable under OASDI at the beginning of the plan year, multiplied by

(ii) the rate of tax applicable under section 3111(a) (relating to employer's OASDI tax) at the beginning of the plan year.

In the case of an individual who is an employee within the meaning of subsection (c)(1), the preceding sentence shall be applied by taking into account his earned income (as defined in subsection (c)(2)).

(B) OASDI.—The term "OASDI" means the system of old-age, survivors, and disability insurance established under title II of the Social Security Act and the Federal Insurance Contributions Act.

(C) Remuneration.—The term "remuneration" means—

(i) total compensation, or

(ii) basic or regular rate of compensation,

whichever is used in determining contributions or benefits under the plan.

(3) Determination of compensation, etc., of self-employed individuals.—For purposes of this subsection, in the case of an individual who is an employee within the meaning of subsection (c)(1)—

(A) his total compensation shall include his earned income (as defined in subsection (c)(2)), and

(B) his basic or regular rate of compensation shall be determined (under regulations prescribed by the Secretary) with respect to that portion of his earned income which bears the same ratio to his earned income as the basic or regular compensation of the employees under the plan (other than employees within the meaning of subsection (c)(1)) bears to the total compensation of such employees.

Amendment of Subsec. (*l*)

Pub.L. 99–514, Title XI, § 1111(a), (c)(1), (3), Oct. 22, 1986, 100 Stat. ——, provided that, applicable to benefits attributable to plan years beginning after December 31, 1988, and subject to special rules with regard to benefits in specified plan years pursuant to collective bargaining agreements ratified before March 1, 1986, subsec. (*l*) of this section is amended to read as follows:

(*l*) **Permitted disparity in plan contributions or benefits.—**

(1) **In general.—**The requirements of this subsection are met with respect to a plan if—

(A) in the case of a defined contribution plan, the requirements of paragraph (2) are met, and

(B) in the case of a defined benefit plan, the requirements of paragraph (3) are met.

(2) **Defined contribution plan.—**

(A) **In general.—**A defined contribution plan meets the requirements of this paragraph if the excess contribution percentage does not exceed the base contribution percentage by more than the lesser of—

(i) the base contribution percentage, or

(ii) the greater of—

(I) 5.7 percentage points, or

(II) the percentage equal to the portion of the rate of tax under section 3111(a) (in effect as of the beginning of the year) which is attributable to old-age insurance.

(B) **Contribution percentages.—**For purposes of this paragraph—

(i) **Excess contribution percentage.—**The term "excess contribution percentage" means the percentage of compensation which is contributed under the plan with respect to that portion of each participant's compensation in excess of the integration level.

(ii) **Base contribution percentage.—**The term "base contribution percentage" means the percentage of compensation contributed under the plan with respect to that portion of each participant's compensation not in excess of the integration level.

(3) **Defined benefit plan.—**A defined benefit plan meets the requirements of this paragraph if—

(A) **Excess plans.—**

(i) **In general.—**In the case of a plan other than an offset plan—

(I) the excess benefit percentage does not exceed the base benefit percentage by more than the maximum excess allowance,

(II) any optional form of benefit, preretirement benefit, actuarial factor, or other benefit or feature provided with respect to compensation in excess of the integration level is provided with respect to compensation not in excess of such level, and

(III) benefits are based on average annual compensation.

(ii) **Benefit percentages.—**For purposes of this subparagraph, the excess and base benefit percentages shall be computed in the same manner as the excess and base contribution percentages under paragraph (2)(B), except that such determination shall be made on the basis of benefits rather than contributions.

(B) **Offset plans.—**In the case of an offset plan, the plan provides that—

(i) a participant's accrued benefit attributable to employer contributions (within the meaning of section 411(c)(1)) may not be reduced (by reason of the offset) by more than the maximum offset allowance, and

(ii) benefits are based on average annual compensation.

(4) Definitions relating to paragraph (3).—For purposes of paragraph (3)—

(A) Maximum excess allowance.—The maximum excess allowance is equal to—

(i) in the case of benefits attributable to any year of service with the employer taken into account under the plan, ¾ of a percentage point, and

(ii) in the case of total benefits, ¾ of a percentage point, multiplied by the participant's years of service (not in excess of 35) with the employer taken into account under the plan.

In no event shall the maximum excess allowance exceed the base benefit percentage.

(B) Maximum offset allowance.—The maximum offset allowance is equal to—

(i) in the case of benefits attributable to any year of service with the employer taken into account under the plan, ¾ percent of the participant's final average compensation, and

(ii) in the case of total benefits, ¾ percent of the participant's final average compensation, multiplied by the participant's years of service (not in excess of 35) with the employer taken into account under the plan.

In no event shall the maximum offset allowance exceed 50 percent of the benefit which would have accrued without regard to the offset reduction.

(C) Reductions.—

(i) **In general.**—The Secretary shall prescribe regulations requiring the reduction of the ¾ percentage factor under subparagraph (A) or (B)—

(I) in the case of a plan other than an offset plan which has an integration level in excess of covered compensation, or

(II) with respect to any participant in an offset plan who has final average compensation in excess of covered compensation.

(ii) **Basis of reductions.**—Any reductions under clause (i) shall be based on the percentages of compensation replaced by the employer-derived portions of primary insurance amounts under the Social Security Act for participants with compensation in excess of covered compensation.

(D) Offset plan.—The term "offset plan" means any plan with respect to which the benefit attributable to employer contributions for each participant is reduced by an amount specified in the plan.

(5) Other definitions and special rules.—For purposes of this subsection—

(A) Integration level.—

(i) **In general.**—The term "integration level" means the amount of compensation specified under the plan (by dollar amount or formula) at or below which the rate at which contributions or benefits are provided (expressed as a percentage) is less than such rate above such amount.

(ii) **Limitation.**—The integration level for any year may not exceed the contribution and benefit base in effect under section 230 of the Social Security Act for such year.

(iii) **Level to apply to all participants.**—A plan's integration level shall apply with respect to all participants in the plan.

(iv) Multiple integration levels.—Under rules prescribed by the Secretary, a defined benefit plan may specify multiple integration levels.

(B) Compensation.—The term "compensation" has the meaning given such term by section 414(s).

(C) Average annual compensation.—The term "average annual compensation" means the greater of—

(i) the participant's final average compensation (determined without regard to subparagraph (D)(ii)), or

(ii) the participant's highest average annual compensation for any other period of at least 3 consecutive years.

(D) Final average compensation.—

(i) **In general.**—The term "final average compensation" means the participant's average annual compensation for—

(I) the 3-consecutive year period ending with the current year, or

(II) if shorter, the participant's full period of service.

(ii) **Limitation.**—A participant's final average compensation shall be determined by not taking into account in any year compensation in excess of the contribution and benefit base in effect under section 230 of the Social Security Act for such year.

(E) Covered compensation.—

(i) **In general.**—The term "covered compensation" means, with respect to an employee, the average of the contribution and benefit bases in effect under section 230 of the Social Security Act for each year in the 35-year period ending with the year in which the employee attains age 65.

(ii) **Computation for any year.**—For purposes of clause (i), the determination for any year preceding the year in which the employee attains age 65 shall be made by assuming that there is no increase in the bases described in clause (i) after the determination year and before the employee attains age 65.

(F) Regulations.—The Secretary shall prescribe such regulations as are necessary or appropriate to carry out the purposes of this subsection, including—

(i) in the case of a defined benefit plan which provides for unreduced benefits commencing before the social security retirement age (as defined in section 415(b)(8)), rules providing for the reduction of the maximum excess allowance and the maximum offset allowance, and

(ii) in the case of an employee covered by 2 or more plans of the employer which fail to meet the requirements of subsection (a)(4) (without regard to this subsection), rules preventing the multiple use of the disparity permitted under this subsection with respect to any employee.

For purposes of clause (i), unreduced benefits shall not include benefits for disability (within the meaning of section 223(d) of the Social Security Act).

(6) Special rule for plan maintained by railroads.—In determining whether a plan which includes employees of a railroad employer who are entitled to benefits under the Railroad Retirement Act of 1974 meets the requirements of this subsection, rules similar to the rules set forth in this subsection shall apply. Such rules shall take into account the employer-derived portion of the employees' tier 2 railroad retirement benefits and any supplemental annuity under the Railroad Retirement Act of 1974.

(m) Nondiscrimination test for matching contributions and employee contributions.—

(1) In general.—A plan shall be treated as meeting the requirements of subsection (a)(4) with respect to the amount of any matching contribution or employee contribution for any plan year only if the contribution percentage requirement of paragraph (2) of this subsection is met for such plan year.

(2) Requirements.—

(A) Contribution percentage requirement.—A plan meets the contribution percentage requirement of this paragraph for any plan year only if the contribution percentage for eligible highly compensated employees does not exceed the greater of—

(i) 125 percent of such percentage for all other eligible employees, or

(ii) the lesser of 200 percent of such percentage for all other eligible employees, or such percentage for all other eligible employees plus 2 percentage points.

(B) Multiple plans treated as a single plan.—If two or more plans of an employer to which matching contributions, employee contributions, or elective deferrals are made are treated as one plan for purposes of section 410(b), such plans shall be treated as one plan for purposes of this subsection. If a highly compensated employee participates in two or more plans of an employer to which such contributions are made, all such contributions shall be aggregated for purposes of this subsection.

(3) Contribution percentage.—For purposes of paragraph (2), the contribution percentage for a specified group of employees for a plan year shall be the average of the ratios (calculated separately for each employee in such group) of—

(A) the sum of the matching contributions and employee contributions paid under the plan on behalf of each such employee for such plan year, to

(B) the employee's compensation (within the meaning of section 414(s)) for such plan year.

Under regulations, an employer may elect to take into account (in computing the contribution percentage) elective deferrals and qualified nonelective contributions under the plan or any other plan of the employer.

(4) Definitions.—For purposes of this subsection—

(A) Matching contribution.—The term "matching contribution" means—

(i) any employer contribution made to the plan on behalf of an employee on account of an employee contribution made by such employee, and

(ii) any employer contribution made to the plan on behalf of an employee on account of an employee's elective deferral.

(B) Elective deferral.—The term "elective deferral" means any employer contribution described in section 402(g)(3)(A).

(C) Qualified nonelective contributions.—The term "qualified nonelective contribution" means any employer contribution (other than a matching contribution) with respect to which—

(i) the employee may not elect to have the contribution paid to the employee in cash instead of being contributed to the plan, and

(ii) the requirements of subparagraphs (B) and (C) of subsection (k)(2) are met.

(5) Employees taken into consideration.—

(A) In general.—Any employee who is eligible to make an employee contribution (or, if the employer takes elective contributions into account, elective contributions) or to receive a matching contribution under the plan being tested under paragraph (1) shall be considered an eligible employee for purposes of this subsection.

(B) Certain nonparticipants.—If an employee contribution is required as a condition of participation in the plan, any employee who would be a participant in the plan if such employee made such a contribution shall be treated as an eligible employee on behalf of whom no employer contributions are made.

(6) Plan not disqualified if excess aggregate contributions distributed before end of following plan year.—

(A) In general.—A plan shall not be treated as failing to meet the requirements of paragraph (1) for any plan year if, before the close of the following plan year, the amount of the excess aggregate contributions for such plan year (and any income allocable to such contributions) is distributed (or, if forfeitable, is forfeited). Such contributions (and such income) may be distributed without regard to any other provision of law.

(B) Excess aggregate contributions.—For purposes of subparagraph (A), the term "excess aggregate contributions" means, with respect to any plan year, the excess of—

(i) the aggregate amount of the matching contributions and employee contributions (and any qualified nonelective contribution or elective contribution taken into account in computing the contribution percentage) actually made on behalf of highly compensated employees for such plan year, over

(ii) the maximum amount of such contributions permitted under the limitations of paragraph (2)(A) (determined by reducing contributions made on behalf of highly compensated employees in order of their contribution percentages beginning with the highest of such percentages).

(C) Method of distributing excess contributions.—Any distribution of the excess aggregate contributions for any plan year shall be made to highly compensated employees on the basis of the respective portions of such amounts attributable to each of such employees. Forfeitures of excess aggregate contributions may not be allocated to participants whose contributions are reduced under this paragraph.

(D) Coordination with subsection (k) and 402(g).—The determination of the amount of excess aggregate contributions with respect to a plan shall be made after—

(i) first determining the excess deferrals (within the meaning of section 402(g)), and

(ii) then determining the excess contributions under subsection (k).

(7) Treatment of distributions.—

(A) Additional tax of section 72(t) not applicable.—No tax shall be imposed under section 72(t) on any amount required to be distributed under paragraph (8).

(B) Exclusion of employee contributions.—Any distribution attributable to employee contributions shall not be included in gross income except to the extent attributable to income on such contributions.

(8) Highly compensated employee.—For purposes of this subsection, the term "highly compensated employee" has the meaning given to such term by section 414(q).

(9) Regulations.—The Secretary shall prescribe such regulations as may be necessary to carry out the purposes of this subsection and subsection (k) including—

    (A) such regulations as may be necessary to prevent the multiple use of the alternative limitation with respect to any highly compensated employee, and

    (B) regulations permitting appropriate aggregation of plans and contributions.

For purposes of the preceding sentence, the term "alternative limitation" means the limitation of section 401(k)(3)(A)(ii)(II) and the limitation of paragraph (2)(A)(ii) of this subsection.

(10) Cross reference.—

For excise tax on certain excess contributions, see section 4979.

(n) Cross reference.—

For exemption from tax of a trust qualified under this section, see section 501(a).

§ 402. Taxability of beneficiary of employees' trust

(a) Taxability of beneficiary of exempt trust.—

(1) General rule.—Except as provided in paragraphs (2) and (4), the amount actually distributed to any distributee by any employees' trust described in section 401(a) which is exempt from tax under section 501(a) shall be taxable to him, in the year in which so distributed, under section 72 (relating to annuities). The amount actually distributed to any distributee shall not include net unrealized appreciation in securities of the employer corporation attributable to the amount contributed by the employee (other than deductible employee contributions within the meaning of section 72(o)(5)). Such net unrealized appreciation and the resulting adjustments to basis of such securities shall be determined in accordance with regulations prescribed by the Secretary.

* * *

(7) Rollover where spouse receives distributions after death of employee. —If any distribution attributable to an employee is paid to the spouse of the employee after the employee's death, paragraph (5) shall apply to such distribution in the same manner as if the spouse were the employee; except that a trust or plan described in subclause (III) or (IV) of paragraph (5)(E)(iv) shall not be treated as an eligible retirement plan with respect to such distribution.

(8) Cash or deferred arrangements.—For purposes of this title, contributions made by an employer on behalf of an employee to a trust which is a part of a qualified cash or deferred arrangement (as defined in section 401(k) (2)) shall not be treated as distributed or made available to the employee nor as contributions made to the trust by the employee merely because the arrangement includes provisions under which the employee has an election whether the contribution will be made to the trust or received by the employee in cash.

(9) Alternate payee under qualified domestic relations order treated as distributee.—For purposes of subsection (a)(1) and section 72, any alternate payee who is the spouse or former spouse of the participant shall be treated as the distributee of any distribution or payment made to the alternate payee under a qualified domestic relations order (as defined in section 414(p)).

(b) Taxability of beneficiary of nonexempt trust.—Contributions to an employees' trust made by an employer during a taxable year of the employer which ends within or with a taxable year of the trust for which the trust is not exempt from tax under section 501(a) shall be included in the gross income of the employee in accordance with section 83 (relating to property transferred in connection with performance of services), except that the value of the employee's interest in the trust shall be substituted for the fair market value of the property for purposes of applying such section. The amount actually distributed or made available to any distributee by any such trust shall be taxable to him in the year in which so distributed or made available, under section 72 (relating to annuities), except that distributions of income of such trust before the annuity starting date (as defined in section 72(c) (4)) shall be included in the gross income of the employee without regard to section 72(e) (5) (relating to amount not received as annuities). A beneficiary of any such trust shall not be considered the owner of any portion of such trust under subpart E of part I of subchapter J (relating to grantors and others treated as substantial owners).

Amendment of Subsec. (b)

Pub.L. 99–514, Title XI, § 1112(c), (e), Oct. 22, 1986, 100 Stat. ——, provided that, applicable to plan years beginning after December 31, 1988, with special rules regarding collective bargaining agreements ratified before March 1, 1986, and with provisions for a waiver of the excise tax on reversions, subsec. (b) of this section is amended as follows:

(1) The heading of subsec. (b) is amended to read as follows:

(b) Taxability of Beneficiary of Nonexempt Trust.—

(1) In General—

(2) A new paragraph is added at the end thereof to read as follows:

(2) Failure to meet requirements of section 410(b).—

(A) In general.—In the case of a trust which is not exempt from tax under section 501(a) solely because such trust is part of a plan which fails to meet the requirements of section 410(b)—

(i) such trust shall be treated as exempt from tax under section 501(a) for purposes of applying paragraph (1) to employees who are not highly compensated employees, and

(ii) paragraph (1) shall be applied to the vested accrued benefit (other than employee contributions) of any highly compensated employee as of the close of the employer's taxable year described in paragraph (1) (rather than contributions made during such year).

(B) Failure in more than 1 year.—If a plan fails to meet the requirements of section 410(b) for more than 1 taxable year, any portion of the vested accrued benefit to which subparagraph (A) applies shall be included in gross income only once.

(C) Highly compensated employee.—For purposes of this paragraph, the term "highly compensated employee" has the meaning given such term by section 414(q).

* * *

(e) Tax on lump sum distributions.—

(1) Imposition of separate tax on lump sum distributions.—

(A) Separate tax.—There is hereby imposed a tax (in the amount determined under subparagraph (B)) on the ordinary income portion of a lump sum distribution.

(B) Amount of tax.—The amount of tax imposed by subparagraph (A) for any taxable year is an amount equal to 5 times the tax which would be imposed by subsection (c) of section 1 if the recipient were an individual referred to in such subsection and the taxable income were an amount equal to $\frac{1}{5}$ of the excess of—

(C) Minimum distribution allowance.—For purposes of this paragraph, the minimum distribution allowance for the taxable year is an amount equal to—

(D) Liability for tax.—The recipient shall be liable for the tax imposed by this paragraph.

(2) Multiple distributions and distributions of annuity contracts.—In the case of any recipient of a lump sum distribution for the taxable year with respect to whom during the 6-taxable-year period ending on the last day of the taxable year there has been one or more other lump sum distributions after December 31, 1973, or if the distribution (or any part thereof) is an annuity contract, in computing the tax imposed by paragraph (1)(A), the total taxable amounts of all such distributions during such 6-taxable-year period shall be aggregated, but the amount of tax so computed shall be reduced (but not below zero) by the sum of—

(A) the amount of the tax imposed by paragraph (1)(A) paid with respect to such other distributions, plus

(B) that portion of the tax on the aggregated total taxable amounts which is attributable to annuity contracts.

For purposes of this paragraph, a beneficiary of a trust to which a lump sum distribution is made shall be treated as the recipient of such distribution if the beneficiary is an employee (including an employee within the meaning of section 401(c)(1)) with respect to the plan under which the distribution is made or if the beneficiary is treated as the owner of such trust for purposes of subpart E of part I of subchapter J. In the case of the distribution of an annuity contract, the taxable amount of such distribution shall be deemed to be the current actuarial value of the contract, determined on the date of such distribution. In the case of a lump sum distribution with respect to any individual which is made only to two or more trusts, the tax imposed by paragraph (1)(A) shall be computed as if such distribution was made to a single trust, but the liability for such tax shall be apportioned among such trusts according to the relative amounts received by each. The Secretary shall prescribe such regulations as may be necessary to carry out the purposes of this paragraph.

(3) Allowance of deduction.—The total taxable amount of a lump sum distribution for the taxable year shall be allowed as a deduction from gross income for such taxable year, but only to the extent included in the taxpayer's gross income for such taxable year.

(4) Definitions and special rules.—

(A) Lump sum distribution.—For purposes of this section and section 403, the term "lump sum distribution" means the distribution or payment within one taxable year of the recipient of the balance to the credit of an employee which becomes payable to the recipient—

(i) on account of the employee's death,

(ii) after the employee attains age 59½,

(iii) on account of the employee's separation from the service, or

(iv) after the employee has become disabled (within the meaning of section 72(m)(7))

from a trust which forms a part of a plan described in section 401(a) and which is exempt from tax under section 501 or from a plan described in section 403(a). Clause (iii) of this subparagraph shall be applied only with respect to an individual who is an employee without regard to section 401(c)(1), and clause (iv) shall within the meaning of section 401(c)(1). Except for purposes of subsection (a)(2) and section 403(a)(2), a distribution of an annuity contract from a trust or annuity plan referred to in the first sentence of this subparagraph shall be treated as a lump sum distribution. For purposes of this subparagraph, a distribution to two or more trusts shall be treated as a distribution to one recipient. For purposes of this subsection, subsection (a)(2) of this section, and subsection (a)(2) of section 403, the balance to the credit of the employee does not include the accumulated deductible employee contributions under the plan (within the meaning of section 72(o)(5)).

(B) Averaging to apply to 1 lump sum distribution after age 59½.—Paragraph (1) shall apply to a lump sum distribution with respect to an employee under subparagraph (A) only if—

(i) such amount is received on or after the taxpayer has attained age 59½, and

(ii) the taxpayer elects for the taxable year to have all such amounts received during such taxable year so treated.

Not more than 1 election may be made under this subparagraph by any taxpayer with respect to any employee. No election may be made under this subparagraph by any taxpayer other than an individual, an estate, or a trust. In the case of a lump sum distribution made with respect to an employee to 2 or more trusts, the election under this subparagraph shall be made by the personal representative of the taxpayer.

(C) Aggregation of certain trusts and plans.—For purposes of determining the balance to the credit of an employee under subparagraph (A)—

(i) all trusts which are part of a plan shall be treated as a single trust, all pension plans maintained by the employer shall be treated as a single plan, all profit-sharing plans maintained by the employer shall be treated as a single plan, and all stock bonus plans maintained by the employer shall be treated as a single plan, and

(ii) trusts which are not qualified trusts under section 401(a) and annuity contracts which do not satisfy the requirements of section 404(a)(2) shall not be taken into account.

(D) Total taxable amount.—For purposes of this section and section 403, the term "total taxable amount" means, with respect to a lump sum distribution, the amount of such distribution which exceeds the sum of—

(i) the amounts considered contributed by the employee (determined by applying section 72(f)), which employee contributions shall be reduced by any amounts theretofore distributed to him which were not includible in gross income, and

(ii) the net unrealized appreciation attributable to that part of the distribution which consists of the securities of the employer corporation so distributed.

[(E) and (F) Repealed.]

(G) Community property laws.—The provisions of this subsection, other than paragraph (3), shall be applied without regard to community property laws.

(H) Minimum period of service.—For purposes of this subsection, no amount distributed to an employee from or under a plan may be treated as a lump sum distributed under subparagraph (A) unless he has been a participant in the plan for 5 or more taxable years before the taxable year in which such amounts are distributed.

(I) Amounts subject to penalty.—This subsection shall not apply to amounts described in clause (ii) of subparagraph (A) of section 72(m)(5) to the extent that section 72(m)(5) applies to such amounts.

(J) Unrealized appreciation of employer securities.—In the case of any distribution including securities of the employer corporation which, without regard to the requirement of subparagraph (H), would be treated as a lump sum distribution under subparagraph (A), there shall be excluded from gross income the net unrealized appreciation attributable to that part of the distribution which consists of securities of the employer corporation so distributed. In the case of any such distribution or any lump sum distribution including securities of the employer corporation, the amount of net unrealized appreciation of such securities and the resulting adjustments to the basis of such securities shall be determined under regulations prescribed by the Secretary. This subparagraph shall not apply to distributions of accumulated deductible employee contributions (within the meaning of section 72(*o*)(5)). To the extent provided by the Secretary, a taxpayer may elect before any distribution not to have this paragraph apply with respect to such distribution.

(K) Securities.—For purposes of this subsection, the terms "securities" and "securities of the employer corporation" have the respective meanings provided by subsection (a)(3).

(L) Election to treat pre-1974 participation as post-1973 participation. —For purposes of subparagraph (E), subsection (a)(2), and section 403(a)(2), if a taxpayer elects (at the time and in the manner provided under regulations prescribed by the Secretary), all calendar years of an employee's active participation in all plans in which the employee has been an active participant shall be considered years of active participation by such employee after December 31, 1973. An election made under this subparagraph, once made, shall be irrevocable and shall apply to all lump-sum distributions received by the taxpayer with respect to the employee. This subparagraph shall not apply if the taxpayer received a lump-sum distribution in a previous taxable year of the employee beginning after December 31, 1975, unless no portion of such lump-sum distribution was treated under subsection (a)(2) or section 403(a)(2) as gain from the sale or exchange of a capital asset held for more than 6 months.

* * *

(f) Written explanation to recipients of distributions eligible for rollover treatment.—

(1) In general.—The plan administrator of any plan shall, when making a eligible rollover distribution, provide a written explanation to the recipient—

(2) Definitions.—For purposes of this subsection—

(A) Eligible rollover distribution.—The term "eligible rollover distribution" means any distribution any portion of which may be excluded from gross income under subsection (a)(5) of this section or subsection (a)(4) of section 403 if transferred to an eligible retirement plan in accordance with the requirements of such subsection.

(B) Eligible retirement plan.—The term "eligible retirement plan" has the meaning given such term by subsection (a)(5)(E)(iv).

(g) Treatment of self-employed individuals.—For purposes of this section, except as otherwise provided in subparagraph (A) of subsection (e)(4), the term "employee" includes a self-employed individual (as defined in section 401(c)(1)(B)) and the employer of such individual shall be the person treated as his employer under section 401(c)(4).

(g) [1] Effect of disposition of stock by plan on net unrealized appreciation.—

(1) In general.—For purposes of subsection (a)(1) or (e)(4)(J), in the case of any transaction to which this subsection applies, the determination of net unrealized appreciation shall be made without regard to such transaction.

(2) Transaction to which subsection applies.—This subsection shall apply to any transaction in which—

(A) the plan trustee exchanges the plan's securities of the employer corporation for other such securities, or

(B) the plan trustee disposes of securities of the employer corporation and uses the proceeds of such disposition to acquire securities of the employer corporation within 90 days (or such longer period as the Secretary may prescribe), except that this subparagraph shall not apply to any employee with respect to whom a distribution of money was made during the period after such disposition and before such acquisition.

(g) [2] Limitation on exclusion for elective deferrals.—

(1) In general.—Notwithstanding subsections (a)(8) and (h)(1)(B), the elective deferrals of any individual for any taxable year shall be included in such individual's gross income to the extent the amount of such deferrals for the taxable year exceeds $7,000.

(2) Required distribution of excess deferrals.—

(A) In general.—If any amount (hereinafter in this paragraph referred to as "excess deferrals") is included in the gross income of an individual under paragraph (1) for any taxable year—

(i) not later than the 1st March 1 following the close of the taxable year, the individual may allocate the amount of such excess deferrals among the plans under which the deferrals were made and may notify each such plan of the portion allocated to it, and

(ii) not later than the 1st April 15 following the close of the taxable year, each such plan may distribute to the individual the amount allocated to it under clause (i) (and any income allocable to such amount).

The distribution described in clause (ii) may be made notwithstanding any other provision of law.

(B) Treatment of distribution under section 401(k).—Except to the extent provided under rules prescribed by the Secretary, notwithstanding the distribution of any portion of an excess deferral from a plan under subparagraph (A)(ii),

[1] Editor's Note: Probably should read "h". Pub.L. 99–514, Title XVIII, § 1852(b), Oct. 22, 1986, 100 Stat. ___.

[2] Editor's Note: Probably should read "i". Pub.L. 99–514, Title XI, § 1105(a), Oct. 22, 1986, 100 Stat. ___.

such portion shall, for purposes of applying section 401(k)(3)(A)(ii), be treated as an employer contribution.

(C) Taxation of distribution.—In the case of a distribution to which subparagraph (A) applies—

(i) except as provided in clause (ii), such distribution shall not be included in gross income (and no tax shall be imposed under section 72(t)), and

(ii) any income on the excess deferral shall, for purposes of this chapter, be treated as earned and received in the taxable year in which such excess deferral is made.

(3) Elective deferrals.—For purposes of this paragraph, the term "elective deferrals" means, with respect to any taxable year, the sum of—

(A) any employer contribution under a qualified cash or deferred arrangement (as defined in section 401(k)) to the extent not includible in gross income for the taxable year under subsection (a)(8) (determined without regard to this subsection),

(B) any employer contribution to the extent not includible in gross income for the taxable year under subsection (h)(1)(B) (determined without regard to this subsection), and

(C) any employer contribution to purchase an annuity contract under section 403(b) under a salary reduction agreement (within the meaning of section 3121(a)(5)(D)).

(4) Increase in limit for amounts contributed under section 403(b) contracts.—The limitation under paragraph (1) shall be increased (but not to an amount in excess of $9,500) by the amount of any employer contributions for the taxable year described in paragraph (3)(C).

(5) Cost-of-living adjustment.—The Secretary shall adjust the $7,000 amount under paragraph (1) at the same time and in the same manner as under section 415(d).

(6) Disregard of community property laws.—This subsection shall be applied without regard to community property laws.

(7) Coordination with section 72.—For purposes of applying section 72, any amount includible in gross income for any taxable year under this subsection but which is not distributed from the plan during such taxable year shall not be treated as investment in the contract.

(8) Special rule for certain organizations.—

(A) In general.—In the case of a qualified employee of a qualified organization, with respect to employer contributions described in paragraph (3)(C) made by such organization, the limitation of paragraph (1) for any taxable year shall be increased by whichever of the following is the least:

(i) $3,000,

(ii) $15,000 reduced by amounts not included in gross income for prior taxable years by reason of this paragraph, or

(iii) the excess of $5,000 multiplied by the number of years of service of the employee with the qualified organization over the employer contributions described in paragraph (3) made by the organization on behalf of such employee for prior taxable years.

(B) Qualified organization.—For purposes of this paragraph, the term "qualified organization" means any educational organization, hospital, home health service agency, health and welfare service agency, church, or convention or association of churches. Such term includes any organization described in section 414(e)(3)(B)(ii). Terms used in this subparagraph shall have the same meaning as when used in section 415(c)(4).

(C) **Qualified employee.**—For purposes of this paragraph, the term "qualified employee" means any employee who has completed 15 years of service with the qualified organization.

* * *

§ 403. Taxation of employee annuities

(a) Taxability of beneficiary under a qualified annuity plan.—

(1) **Distributee taxable under section 72.**—If an annuity contract is purchased by an employer for an employee under a plan which meets the requirements of section 404(a)(2) (whether or not the employer deducts the amounts paid for the contract under such section), the amount actually distributed to any distributee under the contract shall be taxable to the distributee (in the year in which so distributed) under section 72 (relating to annuities).

[(2) **Capital gains treatment for certain distributions.—Repealed.**]

(3) **Self-employed individuals.**—For purposes of this subsection, the term "employee" includes an individual who is an employee within the meaning of section 401(c) (1), and the employer of such individual is the person treated as his employer under section 401(c) (4).

(4) **Rollover amounts.—**

(A) **General rule.**—If—

(i) any portion of the balance to the credit of an employee in an employee annuity described in paragraph (1) is paid to him,

(ii) the employee transfers any portion of the property he receives in such distribution to an eligible retirement plan, and

(iii) in the case of a distribution of property other than money, the amount so transferred consists of the property distributed,

then such distribution (to the extent so transferred) shall not be includible in gross income for the taxable year in which paid.

(B) **Certain rules made applicable.**—Rules similar to the rules of subparagraphs (B) through (G) of section 402(a) (5) and of paragraphs (6) and (7) of section 402(a) shall apply for purposes of subparagraph (A).

* * *

(c) Taxability of beneficiary under nonqualified annuities or under annuities purchased by exempt organizations.—Premiums paid by an employer for an annuity contract which is not subject to subsection (a) shall be included in the gross income of the employee in accordance with section 83 (relating to property transferred in connection with performance of services), except that the value of such contract shall be substituted for the fair market value of the property for purposes of applying such section. The preceding sentence shall not apply to that portion of the premiums paid which is excluded from gross income under subsection (b). In the case of any portion of any contract which is attributable to premiums to which this subsection applies, the amount actually paid or made available under such contract to any beneficiary which is attributable to such premiums shall be taxable to the beneficiary (in the year in which so paid or made available) under section 72 (relating to annuities).

§ 404. Deduction for contributions of an employer to an employees' trust or annuity plan and compensation under a deferred-payment plan

(a) **General rule.**—If contributions are paid by an employer to or under a stock bonus, pension, profit-sharing, or annuity plan, or if compensation is paid or accrued on account of any employee under a plan deferring the receipt of such compensation, such contributions or compensation shall not be deductible under this chapter; but, if they would otherwise be deductible, they shall be deductible under section, subject, however, to the following limitations as to the amounts deductible in any year:

(1) **Pension trusts.**—

(A) **In general.**—In the taxable year when paid, if the contributions are paid into a pension trust, and if such taxable year ends within or with a taxable year of the trust for which the trust is exempt under section 501(a), in an amount determined as follows:

(i) the amount necessary to satisfy the minimum funding standard provided by section 412(a) for plan years ending within or with such taxable year (or for any prior plan year), if such amount is greater than the amount determined under clause (ii) or (iii) (whichever is applicable with respect to the plan),

(ii) the amount necessary to provide with respect to all of the employees under the trust the remaining unfunded cost of their past and current service credits distributed as a level amount, or a level percentage of compensation, over the remaining future service of each such employee, as determined under regulations prescribed by the Secretary, but if such remaining unfunded cost with respect to any 3 individuals is more than 50 percent of such remaining unfunded cost, the amount of such unfunded cost attributable to such individuals shall be distributed over a period of at least 5 taxable years.

(iii) an amount equal to the normal cost of the plan, as determined under regulations prescribed by the Secretary, plus, if past service or other supplementary pension or annuity credits are provided by the plan, an amount necessary to amortize such credits in equal annual payments (until fully amortized) over 10 years, as determined under regulations prescribed by the Secretary.

In determining the amount deductible in such year under the foregoing limitations the funding method and the actuarial assumptions used shall be those used for such year under section 412, and the maximum amount deductible for such year shall be an amount equal to the full funding limitation for such year determined under section 412.

* * *

(D) **Carryover.**—Any amount paid in a taxable year in excess of the amount deductible in such year under the foregoing limitations shall be deductible in the succeeding taxable years in order of time to the extent of the difference between the amount paid and deductible in each such succeeding year and the maximum amount deductible for such year under the foregoing limitations.

(2) **Employees' annuities.**—In the taxable year when paid, in an amount determined in accordance with paragraph (1), if the contributions are paid toward the purchase of retirement annuities, or retirement annuities and medical benefits as described in section 401(h), and such purchase is a part of a plan which meets

the requirements of section 401(a) (3), (4), (5), (6), (7), (8), (9), (11), (12), (13), (14), (15), (16), (17), (18), (19), (20), and (22), (26) and (27) and, if applicable, the requirements of section 401(a)(10) and of section 401(d), and if refunds of premiums, if any, are applied within the current taxable year or next succeeding taxable year towards the purchase of such retirement annuities, or such retirement annuities and medical benefits.

Amendment of Subsec. (a)(2)

Pub.L. 99–514, Title XI, §§ 1112(d)(2), (e), 1136(b), (c), Oct. 22, 1986, 100 Stat. ——, struck out "and (22)" and inserted in lieu thereof "(22), (26), and (27)", resulting in the insertion of a reference to section 401(a)(26), which applies to years beginning after December 31, 1988, subject to a special rule for collective bargaining agreements ratified before March 1, 1986, and a reference to section 401(a)(27), which applies to years beginning after December 31, 1985.

(3) Stock bonus and profit-sharing trusts.—

(A) Limits on deductible contributions.—

(i) In general.—In the taxable year when paid, if the contributions are paid into a stock bonus or profit-sharing trust, and if such taxable year ends within or with a taxable year of the trust with respect to which the trust is exempt under section 501(a), in an amount not in excess of 15 percent of the compensation otherwise paid or accrued during the taxable year to the beneficiaries under the stock bonus or profit-sharing plan.

(ii) Carryover of excess contributions.—Any amount paid into the trust in any taxable year in excess of the limitation of clause (i) (or the corresponding provision of prior law) shall be deductible in the succeeding taxable years in order of time, but the amount so deductible under this clause in any 1 such succeeding taxable year together with the amount allowable under clause (i) shall not exceed 15 percent of the compensation otherwise paid or accrued during such taxable year to the beneficiaries under the plan.

(iii) Certain retirement plans excluded.—For purposes of this subparagraph, the term "stock bonus or profit-sharing trust" shall not include any trust designed to provided benefits upon retirement and covering a period of years, if under the plan the amounts to be contributed by the employer can be determined actuarially as provided in paragraph (1).

(iv) 2 or more trusts treated as 1 trust.—If the contributions are made to 2 or more stock bonus or profit-sharing trusts, such trusts shall be considered a single trust for purposes of applying the limitations in this subparagraph.

(v) Pre-87 limitation carryforwards.—

(I) In general.—The limitation of clause (i) for any taxable year shall be increased by the unused pre-87 limitation carryforwards (but not to an amount in excess of 25 percent of the compensation described in clause (i)).

(II) Unused pre-87 limitation carryforwards.—For purposes of subclause (I), the term 'unused pre-87 limitation carryforwards' means the amount by which the limitation of the first sentence of this subparagraph (as in effect on the day before the date of the enactment of the Tax Reform Act of 1986) for any taxable year beginning before January 1, 1987, exceeded the amount paid to the trust for such taxable year (to the extent such excess was not taken into account in prior taxable years).

* * *

(5) Other plans.—If the plan is not one included in paragraph (1), (2), or (3), in the taxable year in which an amount attributable to the contribution is includible in the gross income of employees participating in the plan, but, in the case of a plan in which more than one employee participates only if separate accounts are maintained for each employee.

(6) Time when contributions deemed made.—For purposes of paragraphs (1), (2), and (3), a taxpayer shall be deemed to have made a payment on the last day of the preceding taxable year if the payment is on account of such taxable year and is made not later than the time prescribed by law for filing the return for such taxable year (including extensions thereof).

(7) Limitation on deductions where combination of defined contribution plan and defined benefit plan.—

(A) In general.—If amounts are deductible under the foregoing provisions of this subsection (other than paragraph (5)) in connection with 1 or more defined contribution plans and 1 or more defined benefit plans, the total amount deductible in a taxable year under such plans shall not exceed the greater of—

(i) 25 percent of the compensation otherwise paid or accrued during the taxable year to the beneficiaries under such plans, or

(ii) the amount of contributions made to or under the defined benefit plans to the extent such contributions do not exceed the amount of employer contributions necessary to satisfy the minimum funding standard provided by section 412 with respect to any such defined benefit plans for the plan year which ends with or within such taxable year (or for any prior plan year).

A defined contribution plan which is a pension plan shall not be treated as failing to provide definitely determinable benefits merely by limiting employer contributions to amounts deductible under this section.

(B) Carryover of contributions in excess of the deductible limit.—Any amount paid under the plans in any taxable year in excess of the limitation of subparagraph (A) shall be deductible in the succeeding taxable years in order of time, but the amount so deductible under this subparagraph in any 1 such succeeding taxable year together with the amount allowable under subparagraph (A) shall not exceed 25 percent of the compensation otherwise paid or accrued during such taxable year to the beneficiaries under the plans.

(C) Paragraph not to apply in certain cases.—This paragraph shall not have the effect of reducing the amount otherwise deductible under paragraphs (1), (2), and (3), if no employee is a beneficiary under more than 1 trust or under a trust and an annuity plan.

(D) Section 412(i) plans.—For purposes of this paragraph, any plan described in section 412(i) shall be treated as a defined benefit plan.

(8) Self-employed individuals.—In the case of a plan included in paragraph (1), (2), or (3) which provides contributions or benefits for employees some or all of whom are employees within the meaning of section 401(c)(1), for purposes of this section—

(A) the term "employee" includes an individual who is an employee within the meaning of section 401(c)(1), and the employer of such individual is the person treated as his employer under section 401(c)(4);

(B) the term "earned income" has the meaning assigned to it by section 401(c)(2);

(C) the contributions to such plan on behalf of an individual who is an employee within the meaning of section 401(c)(1) shall be considered to satisfy the conditions of section 162 or 212 to the extent that such contributions do not exceed the earned income of such individual (determined without regard to the deductions allowed by this section) derived from the trade or business with respect to which such plan is established, and to the extent that such contributions are not allocable (determined in accordance with regulations prescribed by the Secretary) to the purchase of life, accident, health, or other insurance; and

(D) any reference to compensation shall, in the case of an individual who is an employee within the meaning of section 401(c)(1), be considered to be a reference to the earned income of such individual (determined without regard to the deduction allowed by this section) derived from the trade or business with respect to which the plan is established.

(9) Certain contributions to employee stock ownership plans.—

(A) Principal payments.—Notwithstanding the provisions of paragraphs (3) and (7), if contributions are paid into a trust which forms a part of an employee stock ownership plan (as described in section 4975(e)(7)), and such contributions are, on or before the time prescribed in paragraph (6), applied by the plan to the repayment of the principal of a loan incurred for the purpose of acquiring qualifying employer securities (as described in section 4975(e)(8)), such contributions shall be deductible under this paragraph for the taxable year determined under paragraph (6). The amount deductible under this paragraph shall not, however, exceed 25 percent of the compensation otherwise paid or accrued during the taxable year to the employees under such employee stock ownership plan. Any amount paid into such trust in any taxable year in excess of the amount deductible under this paragraph shall be deductible in the succeeding taxable years in order of time to the extent of the difference between the amount paid and deductible in each such succeeding year and the maximum amount deductible for such year under the preceding sentence.

(B) Interest payment.—Notwithstanding the provisions of paragraphs (3) and (7), if contributions are made to an employee stock ownership plan (described in subparagraph (A)) and such contributions are applied by the plan to the repayment of interest on a loan incurred for the purpose of acquiring qualifying employer securities (as described in subparagraph (A)), such contributions shall be deductible for the taxable year with respect to which such contributions are made as determined under paragraph (6).

(b) Method of contributions, etc., having the effect of a plan; certain deferred benefits.—

(1) Method of contributions, etc., having the effect of a plan.—If—

(A) there is no plan, but

(B) there is a method or arrangement of employer contributions or compensation which has the effect of a stock bonus, pension, profit-sharing, or annuity plan, or other plan deferring the receipt of compensation (including a plan described in paragraph (2)),

subsection (a) shall apply as if there were such a plan.

(2) Plans providing certain deferred benefits.—

(A) In general.—For purposes of this section, any plan providing for deferred benefits (other than compensation) for employees, their spouses, or their dependents shall be treated as a plan deferring the receipt of compensation. In the case of such a plan, for purposes of this section, the determination of when an amount is includible in gross income shall be made without regard to any provisions of this chapter excluding such benefits from gross income.

(B) Exception for certain benefits.—Subparagraph (A) shall not apply to—

(i) any benefit provided through a welfare benefit fund (as defined in section 419(e)), or

(ii) any benefit with respect to which an election under section 463 applies.

* * *

(j) Special rules relating to application with section 415.—

(1) No deduction in excess of section 415 limitation.—In computing the amount of any deduction allowable under paragraph (1), (2), (3), (4), (7), or (10) of subsection (a) for any year—

(A) in the case of a defined benefit plan, there shall not be taken into account any benefits for any year in excess of any limitation on such benefits under section 415 for such year, or

(B) in the case of a defined contribution plan, the amount of any contributions otherwise taken into account shall be reduced by any annual additions in excess of the limitation under section 415 for such year.

(2) No advance funding of cost-of-living adjustments.—For purposes of clause (i), (ii) or (iii) of subsection (a)(1)(A), and in computing the full funding limitation, there shall not be taken into account any adjustments under section 415(d)(1) for any year before the year for which such adjustment first takes effect.

* * *

§ 408. Individual retirement accounts

(a) Individual retirement account.—For purposes of this section, the term "individual retirement account" means a trust created or organized in the United States for the exclusive benefit of an individual or his beneficiaries, but only if the written governing instrument creating the trust meets the following requirements:

(1) Except in the case of a rollover contribution described in subsection (d) (3) in section 402(a)(5), 402(a)(7), 403(a)(4) or 403(b)(8), no contribution will be accepted unless it is in cash, and contributions will not be accepted for the taxable year in excess of $2,000 on behalf of any individual.

(2) The trustee is a bank (as defined in subsection (n)) or such other person who demonstrates to the satisfaction of the Secretary that the manner in which such other person will administer the trust will be consistent with the requirements of this section.

(3) No part of the trust funds will be invested in life insurance contracts.

(4) The interest of an individual in the balance in his account is nonforfeitable.

(5) The assets of the trust will not be commingled with other property except in a common trust fund or common investment fund.

* * *

(d) Tax treatment of distributions.—

(1) In general.—Except as otherwise provided in this subsection, any amount paid or distributed out of an individual retirement plan shall be included in gross income by the payee or distributee, as the case may be, in the manner provided under section 72.

(2) Special rules for applying section 72.—For purposes of applying section 72 to any amount described in paragraph (1)—

(A) all individual retirement plans shall be treated as 1 contract,

(B) all distributions during any taxable year shall be treated as 1 distribution, and

(C) the value of the contract, income on the contract, and investment in the contract shall be computed as of the close of the calendar year with or within which the taxable year ends.

For purposes of subparagraph (C), the value of the contract shall be increased by the amount of any distributions during the calendar year.

(3) Rollover contribution.—An amount is described in this paragraph as a rollover contribution if it meets the requirements of subparagraphs (A) and (B).

(A) In general.—Paragraph (1) does not apply to any amount paid or distributed out of an individual retirement account or individual retirement annuity to the individual for whose benefit the account or annuity is maintained if—

(i) the entire amount received (including money and any other property) is paid into an individual retirement account or individual retirement annuity (other than an endowment contract) for the benefit of such individual not later than the 60th day after the day on which he receives the payment or distribution;

(ii) the entire amount received (including money and any other property) represents the entire amount in the account or the entire value of the annuity and no amount in the account and no part of the value of the annuity is attributable to any source other than a rollover contribution of a qualified total distribution (as defined in section 402(a)(5)(E)(i)) from an employee's trust described in section 401(a) which is exempt from tax under section 501(a), or an annuity plan described in section 403(a) and any earnings on such sums and the entire amount thereof is paid into another such trust (for the benefit of such individual) or annuity plan not later than the 60th day on which he receives the payment or distribution; or

(iii) (I) the entire amount received (including money and other property) represents the entire interest in the account or the entire value of the annuity,

(II) no amount in the account and no part of the value of the annuity is attributable to any source other than a rollover contribution from an annuity contract described in section 403(b) and any earnings on such rollover, and

(III) the entire amount thereof is paid into another annuity contract described in section 403(b) (for the benefit of such individual) not later than the 60th day after he receives the payment or distribution.

Clause (ii) shall not apply during the 5-year period beginning on the date of the qualified total distribution referred to in such clause if the individual was treated as a 5-percent owner with respect to such distribution under section 402(a)(5)(F)(ii).

(B) Limitation.—This paragraph does not apply to any amount described in subparagraph (A)(i) received by an individual from an individual retirement account, or individual retirement annuity if at any time during the 1-year period ending on the day of such receipt such individual received any other amount described in that subparagraph from an individual retirement account, or an individual retirement annuity which was not includible in his gross income because of the application of this paragraph. Clause (ii) of subparagraph (A) shall not apply to any amount paid or distributed out of an individual retirement account or an individual retirement annuity to which an amount was contributed which was treated as a rollover contribution by section 402(a) (7) (or in the case of an individual retirement annuity, such section as made applicable by section 403(a) (4) (B)).

(C) Denial of rollover treatment for inherited accounts, etc.—

(i) In general.—In the case of an inherited individual retirement account or individual retirement annuity—

(I) this paragraph shall not apply to any amount received by an individual from such an account or annuity (and no amount transferred from such account or annuity to another individual retirement account or annuity shall be excluded from gross income by reason of such transfer), and

(II) such inherited account or annuity shall not be treated as an individual retirement account or annuity for purposes of determining whether any other amount is a rollover contribution.

(ii) Inherited individual retirement account or annuity.—An individual retirement account or individual retirement annuity shall be treated as inherited if—

(I) the individual for whose benefit the account or annuity is maintained acquired such account by reason of a death of another individual, and

(II) such individual was not the surviving spouse of such other individual.

(D) Partial rollovers permitted.—

(i) In general.—If any amount paid or distributed out of an individual retirement account or individual retirement annuity would meet the requirements of subparagraph (A) but for the fact that the entire amount was not paid into an eligible plan as required by clause (i), (ii), or (iii) of subparagraph (A), such amount shall be treated as meeting the requirements of subparagraph (A) to the extent it is paid into an eligible plan referred to in such clause not later than the 60th day referred to in such clause.

(ii) Eligible plan.—For purposes of clause (i), the term "eligible plan" means any account, annuity, contract, or plan referred to in subparagraph (A).

* * *

(6) Transfer of account incident to divorce.—The transfer of an individual's interest in an individual retirement account or an individual retirement annuity to his former spouse under a divorce decree or under a written instrument incident to such divorce is not to be considered a taxable transfer made by such individual notwithstanding any other provision of this subtitle, and such interest at the time of the transfer is to be treated as an individual retirement account of such spouse, and not of such individual. Thereafter such account or annuity for purposes of this subtitle is to be treated as maintained for the benefit of such spouse.

(e) Tax treatment of accounts and annuities.—

(1) Exemption from tax.—Any individual retirement account is exempt from taxation under this subtitle unless such account has ceased to be an individual retirement account by reason of paragraph (2) or (3). Notwithstanding the preceding sentence, any such account is subject to the taxes imposed by section 511 (relating to imposition of tax on unrelated business income of charitable, etc. organizations).

* * *

Subpart B—Special Rules

§ 410. Minimum participation standards

(a) Participation.—

(1) Minimum age and service conditions.—

(A) **General rule.**—A trust shall not constitute a qualified trust under section 401(a) if the plan of which it is a part requires, as a condition of participation in the plan, that an employee complete a period of service with the employer or employers maintaining the plan extending beyond the later of the following dates—

(i) the date on which the employee attains the age of 21; or

(ii) the date on which he completes 1 year of service.

(B) **Special rules for certain plans.**—

(i)[1]In the case of any plan which provides that after not more than 3 years of service each participant has a right to 100 percent of his accrued benefit under the plan which is nonforfeitable (within the meaning of section 411) at the time such benefit accrues, clause (ii) of subparagraph (A) shall be applied by substituting "3 years of service" for "1 year of service".

(ii) In the case of any plan maintained exclusively for employees of an educational institution (as defined in section 170(b) (1) (A) (ii)) by an employer which is exempt from tax under section 501(a) which provides that each participant having at least 1 year of service has a right to 100 percent of his accrued benefit under the plan which is nonforfeitable (within the meaning of section 411) at the time such benefit accrues, clause (i) of subparagraph (A) shall be applied by substituting "26" for "21". This clause shall not apply to any plan to which clause (i) applies.

(2) Maximum age conditions.—A trust shall not constitute a qualified trust under section 401(a) if the plan of which it is a part excludes from participation (on the basis of age) employees who have attained a specified age.

(3) Definition of year of service.—

(A) **General rule.**—For purposes of this subsection, the term "year of service" means a 12-month period during which the employee has not less than 1,000 hours of service. For purposes of this paragraph, computation of any 12-month period shall be made with reference to the date on which the employee's employment commenced, except that, under regulations prescribed by the Secretary of Labor, such computation may be made by reference to the first day of a plan year in the case of an employee who does not complete 1,000 hours of service during the 12-month period beginning on the date his employment commenced.

* * *

(C) **Hours of service.**—For purposes of this subsection, the term "hour of service" means a time of service determined under regulations prescribed by the Secretary of Labor.

* * *

(4) Time of participation.—A plan shall be treated as not meeting the requirements of paragraph (1) unless it provides that any employee who has satisfied the

[1] Editor's Note: See end of subsec. (a) for amendment.

minimum age and service requirements specified in such paragraph, and who is otherwise entitled to participate in the plan, commences participation in the plan no later than the earlier of—

(A) the first day of the first plan year beginning after the date on which such employee satisfied such requirements, or

(B) the date 6 months after the date on which he satisfied such requirements,

unless such employee was separated from the service before the date referred to in subparagraph (A) or (B), whichever is applicable.

(5) Breaks in service.—

(A) General rule.—Except as otherwise provided in subparagraphs (B), (C), and (D), all years of service with the employer or employers maintaining the plan shall be taken into account in computing the period of service for purposes of paragraph (1).

(B)[1]Employees under 3-year 100 percent vesting.—In the case of any employee who has any 1-year break in service (as defined in section 411(a) (6) (A)) under a plan to which the service requirements of clause (i) of paragraph (1) (B) apply, if such employee has not satisfied such requirements, service before such break shall not be required to be taken into account.

(C) 1-year break in service.—In computing an employee's period of service for purposes of paragraph (1) in the case of any participant who has any 1-year break in service (as defined in section 411(a) (6) (A)), service before such break shall not be required to be taken into account under the plan until he has completed a year of service (as defined in paragraph (3)) after his return.

(D) Nonvested participants.—

(i) In general.—For purposes of paragraph (1), in the case of a nonvested participant, years of service with the employer or employers maintaining the plan before any period of consecutive 1-year breaks in service shall not be required to be taken into account in computing the period of service if the number of consecutive 1-year breaks in service within such period equals or exceeds the greater of—

(I) 5, or

(II) the aggregate number of years of service before such period.

(ii) Years of service not taken into account.—If any years of service are not required to be taken into account by reason of a period of breaks in service to which clause (i) applies, such years of service shall not be taken into account in applying clause (i) to a subsequent period of breaks in service.

(iii) Nonvested participant defined.—For purposes of clause (i), the term "nonvested participant" means a participant who does not have any nonforfeitable right under the plan to an accrued benefit derived from employer contributions.

(E) Special rule for maternity or paternity absences.—

(i) General rule.—In the case of each individual who is absent from work for any period—

(I) by reason of the pregnancy of the individual,

(II) by reason of the birth of a child of the individual,

[1] Editor's Note: See end of Subsec. (a) for amendment.

(III) by reason of the placement of a child with the individual in connection with the adoption of such child by such individual, or

(IV) for purposes of caring for such child for a period beginning immediately following such birth or placement,

the plan shall treat as hours of service, solely for purposes of determining under this paragraph whether a 1-year break in service (as defined in section 411(a)(6)(A)) has occurred, the hours described in clause (ii).

(ii) **Hours treated as hours of service.**—The hours described in this clause are—

(I) the hours of service which otherwise would normally have been credited to such individual but for such absence, or

(II) in any case in which the plan is unable to determine the hours described in subclause (I), 8 hours of service per day of such absence,

except that the total number of hours treated as hours of service under this clause by reason of any such pregnancy or placement shall not exceed 501 hours.

(iii) **Year to which hours are credited.**—The hours described in clause (ii) shall be treated as hours of service as provided in this subparagraph—

(I) only in the year in which the absence from work begins, if a participant would be prevented from incurring a 1-year break in service in such year solely because the period of absence is treated as hours of service as provided in clause (i); or

(II) in any other case, in the immediately following year.

(iv) **Year defined.**—For purposes of this subparagraph, the term "year" means the period used in computations pursuant to paragraph (3).

(v) **Information required to be filed.**—A plan shall not fail to satisfy the requirements of this subparagraph solely because it provides that no credit will be given pursuant to this subparagraph unless the individual furnishes to the plan administrator such timely information as the plan may reasonably require to establish—

(I) that the absence from work is for reasons referred to in clause (i), and

(II) the number of days for which there was such an absence.

Amendment of Subsec. (a)(1)(B)(i) and (a)(5)(B)

Pub.L. 99–514, Title XI, § 1113(c), (d)(A), (e), Oct. 22, 1986, 100 Stat. ——, provided that, applicable to plan years beginning after December 31, 1988, with special rules with regard to plans maintained pursuant to collective bargaining agreements ratified before March 1, 1986, and with regard to employees who do not have 1 hour of service in any plan year to which the amendment applies, subsec. (a)(1)(B)(i) of this section is amended by striking out "3 years" each place it appears and inserting in lieu thereof "2 years" and the heading of subsec. (a)(5)(B) is amended by striking out "3-year" and inserting in lieu thereof "2-year".

(b) Eligibility.—

(1) **In general.**—A trust shall not constitute a qualified trust under section 401(a) unless the trust, or two or more trusts, or the trust or trusts and annuity plan or plans are designated by the employer as constituting parts of a plan intended to qualify under section 401(a) which benefits either—

(A) 70 percent or more of all employees, or 80 percent or more of all the employees who are eligible to benefit under the plan if 70 percent or more of all the employees are eligible to benefit under the plan, excluding in each case employees who have not satisfied the minimum age and service requirements, if any, prescribed by the plan as a condition of participation, or

(B) such employees as qualify under a classification set up by the employer and found by the Secretary not to be discriminatory in favor of employees who are officers, shareholders, or highly compensated.

* * *

(3) Exclusion of certain employees.—For purposes of paragraphs (1) and (2), there shall be excluded from consideration—

(A) employees not included in the plan who are included in a unit of employees covered by an agreement which the Secretary of Labor finds to be a collective bargaining agreement between employee representatives and one or more employers, if there is evidence that retirement benefits were the subject of good faith bargaining between such employee representatives and such employer or employers,

(B) in the case of a trust established or maintained pursuant to an agreement which the Secretary of Labor finds to be a collective bargaining agreement between air pilots represented in accordance with title II of the Railway Labor Act and one or more employers, all employees not covered by such agreement, and

(C) employees who are nonresident aliens and who receive no earned income (within the meaning of section 911(d)(2)) from the employer which constitutes income from sources within the United States (within the meaning of section 861(a)(3)).

Subparagraph (B) shall not apply in the case of a plan which provides contributions or benefits for employees whose prinicipal duties are not customarily performed aboard aircraft in flight.

* * *

Amendment of Subsec. (b)

Pub.L. 99–514, Title XI, § 1112(a), (e), Oct. 22, 1986, 100 Stat. ——, provided that, applicable to plan years beginning after December 31, 1988, with special rules regarding collective bargaining agreements ratified before March 1, 1986, and with provision for a waiver of the excise tax on reversions, subsec. (b) of this section is amended to read as follows:

(b) Minimum coverage requirements.—

(1) In general.—A trust shall not constitute a qualified trust under section 401(a) unless such trust is designated by the employer as part of a plan which meets 1 of the following requirements:

(A) The plan benefits at least 70 percent of employees who are not highly compensated employees.

(B) The plan benefits—

(i) a percentage of employees who are not highly compensated employees which is at least 70 percent of

(ii) the percentage of highly compensated employees benefiting under the plan.

(C) The plan meets the requirements of paragraph (2).

(2) Average benefit percentage test.—

(A) **In general.**—A plan shall be treated as meeting the requirements of this paragraph if—

(i) the plan benefits such employees as qualify under a classification set up by the employer and found by the Secretary not to be discriminatory in favor of highly compensated employees, and

(ii) the average benefit percentage for employees who are not highly compensated employees is at least 70 percent of the average benefit percentage for highly compensated employees.

(B) Average benefit percentage.—For purposes of this paragraph, the term "average benefit percentage" means, with respect to any group, the average of the benefit percentages calculated separately with respect to each employee in such group (whether or not a participant in any plan).

(C) Benefit percentage.—For purposes of this paragraph—

(i) **In general.**—The term "benefit percentage" means the employer-provided contribution or benefit of an employee under all qualified plans maintained by the employer, expressed as a percentage of such employee's compensation (within the meaning of section 414(s)).

(ii) **Period for computing percentage.**—At the election of an employer, the benefit percentage for any plan year shall be computed on the basis of contributions or benefits for—

(I) such plan year, or

(II) any consecutive plan year period (not greater than 3 years) which ends with such plan year and which is specified in such election.

An election under this clause, once made, may be revoked or modified only with the consent of the Secretary.

(D) Employees taken into account.—For purposes of determining who is an employee for purposes of determining the average benefit percentage under subparagraph (B)—

(i) except as provided in clause (ii), paragraph (4)(A) shall not apply, or

(ii) if the employer elects, paragraph (4)(A) shall be applied by using the lowest age and service requirements of all qualified plans maintained by the employer.

(E) Qualified plan.—For purposes of this paragraph, the term "qualified plan" means any plan which (without regard to this subsection) meets the requirements of section 401(a).

(3) Exclusion of certain employees.—For purposes of this subsection, there shall be excluded from consideration—

(A) employees who are included in a unit of employees covered by an agreement which the Secretary of Labor finds to be a collective bargaining agreement between employee representatives and one or more employers, if there is evidence that retirement benefits were the subject of good faith bargaining between such employee representatives and such employer or employers,

(B) in the case of a trust established or maintained pursuant to an agreement which the Secretary of Labor finds to be a collective bargaining agreement between air pilots represented in accordance with title II of the Railway Labor Act and one or more employers, all employees not covered by such agreement, and

(C) employees who are nonresident aliens and who receive no earned income (within the meaning of section 911(d)(2)) from the employer which constitutes income from sources within the United States (within the meaning of section 861(a)(3)).

Subparagraph (A) shall not apply with respect to coverage of employees under a plan pursuant to an agreement under such subparagraph. Subparagraph (B) shall not apply in the case of a plan which provides contributions or benefits for employees whose principal duties are not customarily performed aboard aircraft in flight.

(4) Exclusion of employees not meeting age and service requirements.—

(A) In general.—If a plan—

(i) prescribes minimum age and service requirements as a condition of participation, and

(ii) excludes all employees not meeting such requirements from participation,

then such employees shall be excluded from consideration for purposes of this subsection.

(B) Requirements may be met separately with respect to excluded group.—If employees do not meet the minimum age or service requirements of subsection (a)(1) (without regard to subparagraph (B) thereof) and are covered under a plan of the employer which meets the requirements of paragraph (1) separately with respect to such employees, such employees may be excluded from consideration in determining whether any plan of the employer meets the requirements of paragraph (1).

(5) Line of business exception.—

(A) In general.—If, under section 414(r), an employer is treated as operating separate lines of business for a year, the employer may apply the requirements of this subsection for such year separately with respect to employees in each separate line of business.

(B) Plan must be nondiscriminatory.—Subparagraph (A) shall not apply with respect to any plan maintained by an employer unless such plan benefits such employees as qualify under a classification set up by the employer and found by the Secretary not to be discriminatory in favor of highly compensated employees.

(6) Definitions and special rules.—For purposes of this subsection—

(A) Highly compensated employee.—The term "highly compensated employee" has the meaning given such term by section 414(q).

(B) Aggregation rules.—An employer may elect to designate—

(i) 2 or more trusts,

(ii) 1 or more trusts and 1 or more annuity plans, or

(iii) 2 or more annuity plans,

as part of 1 plan intended to qualify under section 401(a) to determine whether the requirements of this subsection are met with respect to such trusts or annuity plans. If an employer elects to treat any trusts or annuity plans as 1 plan under this subparagraph, such trusts or annuity plans shall be treated as 1 plan for purposes of section 401(a)(4).

(C) Special rules for certain dispositions or acquisitions.—

(i) **In general.**—If a person becomes, or ceases to be, a member of a group described in subsection (b), (c), (m), or (o) of section 414, then the requirements of this subsection shall be treated as having been met during the transition period with respect to any plan covering employees of such person or any other member of such group if—

(I) such requirements were met immediately before each such change, and

(II) the coverage under such plan is not significantly changed during the transition period (other than by reason of the change in members of a group).

(ii) **Transition period.**—For purposes of clause (i), the term "transition period" means the period—

(I) beginning on the date of the change in members of a group, and

(II) ending on the last day of the 1st plan year beginning after the date of such change.

(D) **Special rule for certain employee stock ownership plans.**—A trust which is part of a tax credit employee stock ownership plan which is the only plan of an employer intended to qualify under section 401(a) shall not be treated as not a qualified trust under section 401(a) solely because it fails to meet the requirements of this subsection if—

(i) such plan benefits 50 percent or more of all the employees who are eligible under a nondiscriminatory classification under the plan, and

(ii) the sum of the amounts allocated to each participant's account for the year does not exceed 2 percent of the compensation of that participant for the year.

(E) **Eligibility to contribute.**—In the case of contributions which are subject to section 401(k) or 401(m), employees who are eligible to contribute (or elect to have contributions made on their behalf) shall be treated as benefiting under the plan (other than for purposes of paragraph (2)(A)(ii)).

(F) **Regulations.**—The Secretary shall prescribe such regulations as may be necessary or appropriate to carry out the purposes of this subsection.

§ 411. Minimum vesting standards

(a) **General rule.**—A trust shall not constitute a qualified trust under section 401(a) unless the plan of which such trust is a part provides that an employee's right to his normal retirement benefit is nonforfeitable upon the attainment of normal retirement age (as defined in paragraph (8)) and in addition satisfies the requirements of paragraphs (1), (2), and (11) of this subsection and the requirements of subsection (b)(3), and also satisfies, in the case of a defined benefit plan, the requirements of subsection (b)(1) and, in the case of a defined contribution plan, the requirements of subsection (b)(2).

(1) **Employee contributions.**—A plan satisfies the requirements of this paragraph if an employee's rights in his accrued benefit derived from his own contributions are nonforfeitable.

(2) **Employer contributions.**—A plan satisfies the requirements of this paragraph if it satisfies the requirements of subparagraph (A), (B), or (C).

(A) **10-year vesting.**—A plan satisfies the requirements of this subparagraph if an employee who has at least 10 years of service has a nonforfeitable right to 100 percent of his accrued benefit derived from employer contributions.

(B) **5- to 15-year vesting.**—A plan satisfies the requirements of this subparagraph if an employee who has completed at least 5 years of service has a nonforfeitable right to a percentage of his accrued benefit derived from employer contributions which percentage is not less than the percentage determined under the following table:

Years of service:	The nonforfeitable percentage is:
3	20
4	40
5	60
6	80
7 or more	100.

(3) Certain permitted forfeitures, suspensions, etc.—For purposes of this subsection—

(A) Forfeiture on account of death.—A right to an accrued benefit derived from employer contributions shall not be treated as forfeitable solely because the plan provides that it is not payable if the participant dies (except in the case of a survivor annuity which is payable as provided in section 401(a) (11)).

(B) Suspension of benefits upon reemployment of retiree.—A right to an accrued benefit derived from employer contributions shall not be treated as forfeitable solely because the plan provides that the payment of benefits is suspended for such period as the employee is employed, subsequent to the commencement of payment of such benefits—

(i) in the case of a plan other than a multiemployer plan, by the employer who maintains the plan under which such benefits were being paid; and

(ii) in the case of a multiemployer plan, in the same industry, the same trade or craft, and the same geographic area covered by the plan as when such benefits commenced.

The Secretary of Labor shall prescribe such regulations as may be necessary to carry out the purposes of this subparagraph, including regulations with respect to the meaning of the term "employed".

(C) Effect of retroactive plan amendments.—A right to an accrued benefit derived from employer contributions shall not be treated as forfeitable solely because plan amendments may be given retroactive application as provided in section 412(c) (8).

(D) Withdrawal of mandatory contribution.—

(i) A right to an accrued benefit derived from employer contributions shall not be treated as forfeitable solely because the plan provides that, in the case of a participant who does not have a nonforfeitable right to at least 50 percent of his accrued benefit derived from employer contributions, such accrued benefit may be forfeited on account of the withdrawal by the participant of any amount attributable to the benefit derived from mandatory contributions (as defined in subsection (c) (2) (C)) made by such participant.

(ii) Clause (i) shall not apply to a plan unless the plan provides that any accrued benefit forfeited under a plan provision described in such clause shall be restored upon repayment by the participant of the full amount of the withdrawal described in such clause plus, in the case of a defined benefit plan, interest. Such interest shall be computed on such amount at the rate determined for purposes of subsection (c)(2)(C) on the date of such repayment (computed annually from the date of such withdrawal). The plan provision required under this clause may provide that such repayment must be made (I) in the case of a withdrawal on account of separation from service, before the earlier of 5 years after the first date on which the participant is subsequently re-employed by the employer, or the close of the first period of 5 consecutive 1-year breaks in service commencing after the withdrawal; or (II) in the case of any other withdrawal, 5 years after the date of the withdrawal.

(iii) In the case of accrued benefits derived from employer contributions which accrued before September 2, 1974, a right to such accrued benefit derived from employer contributions shall not be treated as forfeitable solely because the plan provides that an amount of such accrued benefit may be forfeited on account of the withdrawal by the participant of an amount attributable to the benefit derived from mandatory contributions (as defined in subsection (c) (2) (C)) made by such participant before September 2, 1974 if such amount forfeited is proportional to such amount withdrawn. This clause shall not apply to any plan to which any mandatory contribution is made after September 2, 1974. The Secretary shall prescribe such regulations as may be necessary to carry out the purposes of this clause.

(iv) For purposes of this subparagraph, in the case of any class-year plan, a withdrawal of employee contributions shall be treated as a withdrawal of such contributions on a plan year by plan year basis in succeeding order of time.

(v) For nonforfeitability where the employee has a nonforfeitable right to at least 50 percent of his accrued benefit, see section 401(a) (19).

* * *

(4) Service included in determination of nonforfeitable percentage.—In computing the period of service under the plan for purposes of determining the nonforfeitable percentage under paragraph (2), all of an employee's years of service with the employer or employers maintaining the plan shall be taken into account, except that the following may be disregarded:

(A) years of service before age 18, except that in the case of a plan which does not satisfy subparagraph (A) or (B) of paragraph (2), the plan may not disregard any such year of service during which the employee was a participant;

(B) years of service during a period for which the employee declined to contribute to a plan requiring employee contributions;

(C) years of service with an employer during any period for which the employer did not maintain the plan or a predecessor plan (as defined under regulations prescribed by the Secretary);

(D) service not required to be taken into account under paragraph (6);

(E) years of service before January 1, 1971, unless the employee has had at least 3 years of service after December 31, 1970;

(F) years of service before the first plan year to which this section applies, if such service would have been disregarded under the rules of the plan with regard to breaks in service as in effect on the applicable date; and

* * *

(5) Year of service.—

(A) General rule.—For purposes of this subsection, except as provided in subparagraph (C), the term "year of service" means a calendar year, plan year, or other 12-consecutive month period designated by the plan (and not prohibited under regulations prescribed by the Secretary of Labor) during which the participant has completed 1,000 hours of service.

(B) Hours of service.—For purposes of this subsection, the term "hours of service" has the meaning provided by section 410(a) (3) (C).

* * *

(6) Breaks in service.—

(A) Definition of 1-year break in service.—For purposes of this paragraph, the term "1-year break in service" means a calendar year, plan year, or other 12-consecutive-month period designated by the plan (and not prohibited under regulations prescribed by the Secretary of Labor) during which the participant has not completed more than 500 hours of service.

(B) 1 year of service after 1-year break in service.—For purposes of paragraph (4), in the case of any employee who has any 1-year break in service, years of service before such break shall not be required to be taken into account until he has completed a year of service after his return.

* * *

(7) Accrued benefit.—

(A) In general.—For purposes of this section, the term "accrued benefit" means—

(i) in the case of a defined benefit plan, the employee's accrued benefit determined under the plan and, except as provided in subsection (c) (3), expressed in the form of an annual benefit commencing at normal retirement age, or

(ii) in the case of a plan which is not a defined benefit plan, the balance of the employee's account.

(B) Effect of certain distributions.—Notwithstanding paragraph (4), for purposes of determining the employee's accrued benefit under the plan, the plan may disregard service performed by the employee with respect to which he has received—

(i) a distribution of the present value of his entire nonforfeitable benefit if such distribution was in an amount (not more than $1,750) permitted under regulations prescribed by the Secretary, or

(ii) a distribution of the present value of his nonforfeitable benefit attributable to such service which he elected to receive.

Clause (i) of this subparagraph shall apply only if such distribution was made on termination of the employee's participation in the plan. Clause (ii) of this subparagraph shall apply only if such distribution was made on termination of the employee's participation in the plan or under such other circumstances as may be provided under regulations prescribed by the Secretary.

(C) Repayment of subparagraph (B) distributions.—For purposes of determining the employee's accrued benefit under a plan, the plan may not disregard service as provided in subparagraph (B) unless the plan provides an opportunity for the participant to repay the full amount of the distribution described in such subparagraph (B) with, in the case of a defined benefit plan, interest at the rate determined for purposes of subsection (c)(2)(C) and provides that upon such repayment the employee's accrued benefit shall be recomputed by taking into account service so disregarded. This subparagraph shall apply only in the case of a participant who—

(i) received such a distribution in any plan year to which this section applies, which distribution was less than the present value of his accrued benefit,

(ii) resumes employment covered under the plan, and

(iii) repays the full amount of such distribution with, in the case of a defined benefit plan, interest at the rate determined for purposes of subsection (c)(2)(C).

The plan provision required under this subparagraph may provide that such repayment must be made (I) in the case of a withdrawal on account of separation from service, before the earlier of 5 years after the first date on which the participant is subsequently re-employed by the employer, or the close of the first period of 5 consecutive 1-year breaks in service commencing after the withdrawal; or (II) in the case of any other withdrawal, 5 years after the date of the withdrawal.

(8) **Normal retirement age.**—For purposes of this section, the term "normal retirement age" means the earlier of—

(A) the time a plan participant attains normal retirement age under the plan, or

(B) the latest of—

(ii) in the case of a plan participant who commences participation in the plan within 5 years before attaining normal retirement age under the plan, the 5th anniversary of the time the plan participant commences participation in the plan, or

(iii) in the case of a plan participant not described in clause (ii), the 10th anniversary of the time the plan participant commences participation in the plan.

(9) **Normal retirement benefit.**—For purposes of this section, the term "normal retirement benefit" means the greater of the early retirement benefit under the plan, or the benefit under the plan commencing at normal retirement age. The normal retirement benefit shall be determined without regard to—

(A) medical benefits, and

(B) disability benefits not in excess of the qualified disability benefit.

For purposes of this paragraph, a qualified disability benefit is a disability benefit provided by a plan which does not exceed the benefit which would be provided for the participant if he separated from the service at normal retirement age. For purposes of this paragraph, the early retirement benefit under a plan shall be determined without regard to any benefits commencing before benefits payable under title II of the Social Security Act become payable which—

(i) do not exceed such social security benefits, and

(ii) terminate when such social security benefits commence.

(10) **Changes in vesting schedule.**—

(A) **General rule.**—A plan amendment changing any vesting schedule under the plan shall be treated as not satisfying the requirements of paragraph (2) if the nonforfeitable percentage of the accrued benefit derived from employer contributions (determined as of the later of the date such amendment is adopted, or the date such amendment becomes effective) of any employee who is a participant in the plan is less than such nonforfeitable percentage computed under the plan without regard to such amendment.

(B) **Election of former schedule.**—A plan amendment changing any vesting schedule under the plan shall be treated as not satisfying the requirements of paragraph (2) unless each participant having not less than 5 years of service is permitted to elect, within a reasonable period after the adoption of such amendment, to have his nonforfeitable percentage computed under the plan without regard to such amendment.

(11) Restrictions on certain mandatory distributions.—

(A) In general.—If the present value of any vested accrued benefit exceeds $3,500, a plan meets the requirements of this paragraph only if such plan provides that such benefit may not be immediately distributed without the consent of the participant.

(B) Determination of present value.—

(i) **In general.—**For purposes of subparagraph (A), the present value shall be calculated—

(I) by using an interest rate no greater than the applicable interest rate if the vested accrued benefit (using such rate) is not in excess of $25,000, and

(II) by using an interest rate no greater than 120 percent of the applicable interest rate if the vested accrued benefit exceeds $25,000 (as determined under subclause (I)).

In no event shall the present value determined under subclause (II) be less than $25,000.

(ii) **Applicable interest rate.—**For purposes of clause (i), the term "applicable interest rate" means the interest rate which would be used (as of the date of the distribution) by the Pension Benefit Guaranty Corporation for purposes of determining the present value of a lump sum distribution on plan termination.

(C) Dividend distributions of ESOPS arrangement.—This paragraph shall not apply to any distribution of dividends to which section 404(k) applies.

Amendment of Subsec. (a)

Pub.L. 99–509, Title IX, §§ 9202(b)(3), 9203(b)(2), 9204, applicable only with respect to plan years beginning on or after Jan. 1, 1988, and only with respect to employees who have one hour of service in any plan year to which amendments apply, and further applicable with respect to amendments required to amend plans, provided that this section is amended as follows:

The first sentence of section 411(a) of such Code (relating to minimum vesting standards) is amended by striking out "paragraph (2) of subsection (b), and" and all that follows through the end thereof and inserting in lieu thereof "subsection (b)(3), and also satisfies, in the case of a defined benefit plan, the requirements of subsection (b)(1) and, in the case of a defined contribution plan, the requirements of subsection (b)(2).".

Amendment of Subsec. (a)(2)

Pub.L. 99–514, Title XI, § 1113(a), (e), Oct. 22, 1986, 100 Stat. ——, provided that, applicable to plan years beginning after December 31, 1988, with special rules with regard to plans maintained pursuant to collective bargaining agreements ratified before March 1, 1986, and with regard to employees who do not have 1 hour of service in any plan year to which the amendments apply, subsec. (a)(2) of this section is amended to read as follows:

(2) **Employer contributions.—**A plan satisfies the requirements of this paragraph if it satisfies the requirements of subparagraph (A), (B), or (C).

(A) 5–year vesting.—A plan satisfies the requirements of this subparagraph if an employee who has completed at least 5 years of service has a nonforfeitable right to 100 percent of the employee's accrued benefit derived from employer contributions.

(B) 3 to 7 year vesting.—A plan satisfies the requirements of this subparagraph if an employee has a nonforfeitable right to a percentage of the employee's accrued benefit derived from employer contributions determined under the following table:

Years of service:	The nonforfeitable percentage is:
3	20
4	40
5	60
6	80
7 or more	100.

(C) Multiemployer plans.—A plan satisfies the requirements of this subparagraph if—

(i) the plan is a multiemployer plan (within the meaning of section 414(f)), and

(ii) under the plan—

(I) an employee who is covered pursuant to a collective bargaining agreement described in section 414(f)(1)(B) and who has completed at least 10 years of service has a nonforfeitable right to 100 percent of the employee's accrued benefit derived from employer contributions, and

(II) the requirements of subparagraph (A) or (B) are met with respect to employees not described in subclause (I).

Amendment of Subsec. (a)(10)(B)

Pub.L. 99–514, Title XI, § 1113(d)(B), (e), Oct. 22, 1986, 100 Stat. ——, provided that, applicable to plan years beginning after December 31, 1988, with special rules with regard to plans maintained pursuant to collective bargaining agreements ratified before March 1, 1986, and with regard to employees who do not have 1 hour of service in any plan to which the amendment applies, subsec. (a)(10)(B) of this section is amended by striking out "5 years" and inserting in lieu thereof "3 years".

(b) Accrued benefit requirements.—

(1) Defined benefit plans.—

(A) 3-percent method.—A defined benefit plan satisfies the requirements of this paragraph if the accrued benefit to which each participant is entitled upon his separation from the service is not less than—

(i) 3 percent of the normal retirement benefit to which he would be entitled if he commenced participation at the earliest possible entry age under the plan and served continuously until the earlier of age 65 or the normal retirement age specified under the plan, multiplied by

(ii) the number of years (not in excess of $33\frac{1}{3}$) of his participation in the plan.

In the case of a plan providing retirement benefits based on compensation during any period, the normal retirement benefit to which a participant would be entitled shall be determined as if he continued to earn annually the average rate of compensation which he earned during consecutive years of service, not in excess of 10, for which his compensation was the highest. For purposes of this subparagraph, social security benefits and all other relevant factors used to compute benefits shall be treated as remaining constant as of the current year for all years after such current year.

(B) 133⅓ percent rule.—A defined benefit plan satisfies the requirements of this paragraph for a particular plan year if under the plan the accrued benefit payable at the normal retirement age is equal to the normal retirement benefit and the annual rate at which any individual who is or could be a participant can accrue the retirement benefits payable at normal retirement age under the plan for any later plan year is not more than 133⅓ percent of the annual rate at which he can accrue benefits for any plan year beginning on or after such particular plan year and before such later plan year. For purposes of this subparagraph—

(i) any amendment to the plan which is in effect for the current year shall be treated as in effect for all other plan years;

(ii) any change in an accrual rate which does not apply to any individual who is or could be a participant in the current year shall be disregarded;

(iii) the fact that benefits under the plan may be payable to certain employees before normal retirement age shall be disregarded; and

(iv) social security benefits and all other relevant factors used to compute benefits shall be treated as remaining constant as of the current year for all years after the current year.

(C) Fractional rule.—A defined benefit plan satisfies the requirements of this paragraph if the accrued benefit to which any participant is entitled upon his separation from the service is not less than a fraction of the annual benefit commencing at normal retirement age to which he would be entitled under the plan as in effect on the date of his separation if he continued to earn annually until normal retirement age the same rate of compensation upon which his normal retirement benefit would be computed under the plan, determined as if he had attained normal retirement age on the date on which any such determination is made (but taking into account no more than the 10 years of service immediately preceding his separation from service). Such fraction shall be a fraction, not exceeding 1, the numerator of which is the total number of his years of participation in the plan (as of the date of his separation from the service) and the denominator of which is the total number of years he would have participated in the plan if he separated from the service at the normal retirement age. For purposes of this subparagraph, social security benefits and all other relevant factors used to compute benefits shall be treated as remaining constant as of the current year for all years after such current year.

(D) Accrual for service before effective date.—Subparagraphs (A), (B), and (C) shall not apply with respect to years of participation before the first plan year to which this section applies, but a defined benefit plan satisfies the requirements of this subparagraph with respect to such years of participation only if the accrued benefit of any participant with respect to such years of participation is not less than the greater of—

(i) his accrued benefit determined under the plan, as in effect from time to time prior to September 2, 1974, or

(ii) an accrued benefit which is not less than one-half of the accrued benefit to which such participant would have been entitled if subparagraph (A), (B), or (C) applied with respect to such years of participation.

(E) **First two years of service.**—Notwithstanding subparagraphs (A), (B), and (C) of this paragraph, a plan shall not be treated as not satisfying the requirements of this paragraph solely because the accrual of benefits under the plan does not become effective until the employee has two continuous years of service. For purposes of this subparagraph, the term "years of service" has the meaning provided by section 410(a) (3) (A).

(F) **Certain insured defined benefit plans.**—Notwithstanding subparagraphs (A), (B), and (C), a defined benefit plan satisfies the requirements of this paragraph if such plan—

(i) is funded exclusively by the purchase of insurance contracts, and

(ii) satisfies the requirements of paragraphs (2) and (3) of section 412(i) (relating to certain insurance contract plans),

but only if an employee's accrued benefit as of any applicable date is not less than the cash surrender value his insurance contracts would have on such applicable date if the requirements of paragraphs (4), (5), and (6) of section 412(i) were satisfied.

(G) **Accrued benefit may not decrease on account of increasing age or service.**—Notwithstanding the preceding subparagraphs, a defined benefit plan shall be treated as not satisfying the requirements of this paragraph if the participant's accrued benefit is reduced on account of any increase in his age or service. The preceding sentence shall not apply to benefits under the plan commencing before entitlement to benefits payable under title II of the Social Security Act which benefits under the plan—

(i) do not exceed such social security benefits, and

(ii) terminate when such social security benefits commence.

(H) **Continued accrual beyond normal retirement age.**—

(i) **In general.**—Notwithstanding the preceding subparagraphs, a defined benefit plan shall be treated as not satisfying the requirements of this paragraph if, under the plan, an employee's benefit accrual is ceased, or the rate of an employee's benefit accrual is reduced, because of the attainment of any age.

(ii) **Certain limitations permitted.**—A plan shall not be treated as failing to meet the requirements of this subparagraph solely because the plan imposes (without regard to age) a limitation on the amount of benefits that the plan provides or a limitation on the number of years of service or years of participation which are taken into account for purposes of determining benefit accrual under the plan.

(iii) **Adjustments under plan for delayed retirement taken into account.**—In the case of any employee who, as of the end of any plan year under a defined benefit plan, has attained normal retirement age under such plan—

(I) if distribution of benefits under such plan with respect to such employee has commenced as of the end of such plan year, then any requirement of this subparagraph for continued accrual of benefits under such plan with respect to such employee during such plan year shall be treated as satisfied to the extent of the actuarial equivalent of in-service distribution of benefits, and

(II) if distribution of benefits under such plan with respect to such employee has not commenced as of the end of such year in accordance with section 401(a)(14)(C), and the payment of benefits under such plan with respect to such employee is not suspended during such plan year pursuant to subsection (a)(3)(B), then any requirement of this subparagraph for continued accrual of benefits under such plan with respect to such employee during such plan year shall be treated as satisfied to the extent of any adjustment in the benefit payable under the plan during such plan year attributable to the delay in the distribution of benefits after the attainment of normal retirement age.

The preceding provisions of this clause shall apply in accordance with regulations of the Secretary. Such regulations may provide for the application of the preceding provisions of this clause, in the case of any such employee, with respect to any period of time within a plan year.

(iv) **Disregard of subsidized portion of early retirement benefit.**—A plan shall not be treated as failing to meet the requirements of clause (i) solely because the subsidized portion of any early retirement benefit is disregarded in determining benefit accruals.

(v) **Coordination with other requirements.**—The Secretary shall provide by regulation for the coordination of the requirements of this subparagraph with the requirements of subsection (a), sections 404, 410, and 415, and the provisions of this subchapter precluding discrimination in favor of highly compensated employees.

(2) **Defined contribution plans.**—

(A) **In general.**—A defined contribution plan satisfies the requirements of this paragraph if, under the plan, allocations to the employee's account are not ceased, and the rate at which amounts are allocated to the employee's account is not reduced, because of the attainment of any age.

(B) **Disregard of subsidized portion of early retirement benefit.**—A plan shall not be treated as failing to meet the requirements of subparagraph (A) solely because the subsidized portion of any early retirement benefit is disregarded in determining benefit accruals.

(C) **Application to target benefit plans.**—The Secretary shall provide by regulation for the application of the requirements of this paragraph to target benefit plans.

(D) **Coordination with other requirements.**—The Secretary may provide by regulation for the coordination of the requirements of this subparagraph with the requirements of subsection (a), sections 404, 410, and 415, and the provisions of this subchapter precluding discrimination in favor of highly compensated employees.

(3) **Separate accounting required in certain cases.**—A plan satisfies the requirements of this paragraph if—

(A) in the case of a defined benefit plan, the plan requires separate accounting for the portion of each employee's accrued benefit derived from any voluntary employee contributions permitted under the plan; and

(B) in the case of any plan which is not a defined benefit plan, the plan requires separate accounting for each employee's accrued benefit.

(4) **Year of participation.**—

(A) **Definition.**—For purposes of determining an employee's accrued benefit, the term "year of participation" means a period of service (beginning at the earliest date on which the employee is a participant in the plan and which is included in a period of service required to be taken into account under section 410(a)(5), determined without regard to section 410(a)(5)(E)) as determined under regulations prescribed by the Secretary of Labor which provide for the calculation of such period on any reasonable and consistent basis.

(B) **Less than full time service.**—For purposes of this paragraph, except as provided in subparagraph (C), in the case of any employee whose customary employment is less than full time, the calculation of such employee's service on any basis which provides less than a ratable portion of the accrued benefit to which he would be entitled under the plan if his customary employment were full time shall not be treated as made on a reasonable and consistent basis.

(C) **Less than 1,000 hours of service during year.**—For purposes of this paragraph, in the case of any employee whose service is less than 1,000 hours during any calendar year, plan year or other 12-consecutive month period designated by the plan (and not prohibited under regulations prescribed by the Secretary of Labor) the calculation of his period of service shall not be treated as not made on a reasonable and consistent basis solely because such service is not taken into account.

* * *

(c) **Allocation of accrued benefits between employer and employee contributions.**—

(1) **Accrued benefit derived from employer contributions.**—For purposes of this section, an employee's accrued benefit derived from employer contributions as of any applicable date is the excess, if any, of the accrued benefit for such employee as of such applicable date over the accrued benefit derived from contributions made by such employee as of such date.

(2) **Accrued benefit derived from employee contributions.**—

(A) **Plans other than defined benefit plans.**—In the case of a plan other than a defined benefit plan, the accrued benefit derived from contributions made by an employee as of any applicable date is—

(i) except as provided in clause (ii), the balance of the employee's separate account consisting only of his contributions and the income, expenses, gains, and losses attributable thereto, or

(ii) if a separate account is not maintained with respect to an employee's contributions under such a plan, the amount which bears the same ratio to his total accrued benefit as the total amount of the employee's contributions (less withdrawals) bears to the sum of such contributions and the contributions made on his behalf by the employer (less withdrawals).

(B) **Defined benefit plans.**—

(i) **In general.**—In the case of a defined benefit plan providing an annual benefit in the form of a single life annuity (without ancillary benefits) commencing at normal retirement age, the accrued benefit derived from contributions made by an employee as of any applicable date is the annual benefit equal to the employee's accumulated contributions multiplied by the appropriate conversion factor.

(ii) **Appropriate conversion factor.**—For purposes of clause (i), the term "appropriate conversion factor" means the factor necessary to convert an amount equal to the accumulated contributions to a single life annuity (without ancillary benefits) commencing at normal retirement age and shall be 10 percent for a normal retirement age of 65 years. For other normal retirement ages the conversion factor shall be determined in accordance with regulations prescribed by the Secretary.

(C) Definition of accumulated contributions.—For purposes of this subsection, the term "accumulated contributions" means the total of—

(i) all mandatory contributions made by the employee,

(ii) interest (if any) under the plan to the end of the last plan year to which subsection (a)(2) does not apply (by reason of the applicable effective date), and

(iii) interest on the sum of the amounts determined under clauses (i) and (ii) compounded annually at the rate of 5 percent per annum from the beginning of the first plan year to which subsection (a)(2) applies (by reason of the applicable effective date) to the date upon which the employee would attain normal retirement age.

For purposes of this subparagraph, the term "mandatory contributions" means amounts contributed to the plan by the employee which are required as a condition of employment, as a condition of participation in such plan, or as a condition of obtaining benefits under the plan attributable to employer contributions.

(D) Adjustments.—The Secretary is authorized to adjust by regulation the conversion factor described in subparagraph (B), the rate of interest described in clause (iii) of subparagraph (C), or both, from time to time as he may deem necessary. The rate of interest shall bear the relationship to 5 percent which the Secretary determines to be comparable to the relationship which the long-term money rates and investment yields for the last period of 10 calendar years ending at least 12 months before the beginning of the plan year bear to the long-term money rates and investment yields for the 10-calendar year period 1964 through 1973. No such adjustment shall be effective for a plan year beginning before the expiration of 1 year after such adjustment is determined and published.

(E) Limitation.—The accrued benefit derived from employee contributions shall not exceed the greater of—

(i) the employee's accrued benefit under the plan, or

(ii) the accrued benefit derived from employee contributions determined as though the amounts calculated under clauses (ii) and (iii) of subparagraph (C) were zero.

(3) Actuarial adjustment.—For purposes of this section, in the case of any defined benefit plan, if an employee's accrued benefit is to be determined as an amount other than an annual benefit commencing at normal retirement age, or if the accrued benefit derived from contributions made by an employee is to be determined with respect to a benefit other than an annual benefit in the form of a single life annuity (without ancillary benefits) commencing at normal retirement age, the employee's accrued benefit, or the accrued benefits derived from contributions made by an employee, as the case may be, shall be the actuarial equivalent of such benefit or amount determined under paragraph (1) or (2).

(d) Special rules.—

(1) Coordination with section 401(a) (4).—A plan which satisfies the requirements of this section shall be treated as satisfying any vesting requirements resulting from the application of section 401(a) (4) unless—

(A) there has been a pattern of abuse under the plan (such as a dismissal of employees before their accrued benefits become nonforfeitable) tending to discriminate in favor of employees who are officers, shareholders, or highly compensated, or

(B) there have been, or there is reason to believe there will be, an accrual of benefits or forfeitures tending to discriminate in favor of employees who are officers, shareholders, or highly compensated.

(2) Prohibited discrimination.—Subsection (a) shall not apply to benefits which may not be provided for designated employees in the event of early termination of the plan under provisions of the plan adopted pursuant to regulations prescribed by the Secretary to preclude the discrimination prohibited by section 401(a) (4).

(3) Termination or partial termination; discontinuance of contributions. —Notwithstanding the provisions of subsection (a), a trust shall not constitute a qualified trust under section 401(a) unless the plan of which such trust is a part provides that—

(A) upon its termination or partial termination, or

(B) in the case of a plan to which section 412 does not apply, upon complete discontinuance of contributions under the plan,

the rights of all affected employees to benefits accrued to the date of such termination, partial termination, or discontinuance, to the extent funded as of such date, or the amounts credited to the employees' accounts, are nonforfeitable. This paragraph shall not apply to benefits or contributions which, under provisions of the plan adopted pursuant to regulations prescribed by the Secretary to preclude the discrimination prohibited by section 401(a) (4), may not be used for designated employees in the event of early termination of the plan.

(4) Class-year plans.—

Years of service:	Nonforfeitable percentage
5	25
6	30
7	35
8	40
9	45
10	50
11	60
12	70
13	80
14	90
15 or more	100.

Amendment of Subsec. (d)(1)(A) and (B)

Pub.L. 99–514, Title XI, § 1114(b)(10), (c)(3), Oct. 22, 1986, 100 Stat. ——, provided that, applicable to years beginning after December 31, 1988, subpars. (A) and (B) of subsec. (d) of this section are each amended by striking out "officers, shareholders, or highly compensated" and inserting in lieu thereof "highly compensated employees (within the meaning of section 414(q))".

Repeal of Subsec. (d)(4)

Pub.L. 99–514, Title XI, § 1113(b), (e), Oct. 22, 1986, 100 Stat. ——, repealed subsec. (d)(4) effective to plan years beginning after Dec. 31, 1988, except as otherwise provided.

§ 412. Minimum funding standards

(a) General rule.—Except as provided in subsection (h), this section applies to a plan if, for any plan year beginning on or after the effective date of this section for such plan—

(1) such plan included a trust which qualified (or was determined by the Secretary to have qualified) under section 401(a), or

(2) such plan satisfied (or was determined by the Secretary to have satisfied) the requirements of section 403(a).

A plan to which this section applies shall have satisfied the minimum funding standard for such plan for a plan year if as of the end of such plan year, the plan does not have an accumulated funding deficiency. For purposes of this section and section 4971, the term "accumulated funding deficiency" means for any plan the excess of the total charges to the funding standard account for all plan years (beginning with the first plan year to which this section applies) over the total credits to such account for such years or, if less, the excess of the total charges to the alternative minimum funding standard account for such plan years over the total credits to such account for such years. In any plan year in which a multiemployer plan is in reorganization, the accumulated funding deficiency of the plan shall be determined under section 418B.

(b) Funding standard account.—

(1) Account required.—Each plan to which this section applies shall establish and maintain a funding standard account. Such account shall be credited and charged solely as provided in this section.

(2) Charges to account.—For a plan year, the funding standard account shall be charged with the sum of—

(A) the normal cost of the plan for the plan year,

(B) the amounts necessary to amortize in equal annual installments (until fully amortized)—

(i) in the case of a plan in existence on January 1, 1974, the unfunded past service liability under the plan on the first day of the first plan year to which this section applies, over a period of 40 plan years,

(ii) in the case of a plan which comes into existence after January 1, 1974, the unfunded past service liability under the plan on the first day of the first plan year to which this section applies, over a period of 30 plan years,

(iii) separately, with respect to each plan year, the net increase (if any) in unfunded past service liability under the plan arising from plan amendments adopted in such year, over a period of 30 plan years,

(iv) separately, with respect to each plan year, the net experience loss (if any) under the plan, over a period of 15 plan years, and

(v) separately, with respect to each plan year, the net loss (if any) resulting from changes in actuarial assumptions used under the plan, over a period of 30 plan years,

(C) the amount necessary to amortize each waived funding deficiency (within the meaning of subsection (d) (3)) for each prior plan year in equal annual installments (until fully amortized) over a period of 15 plan years, and

(D) the amount necessary to amortize in equal annual installments (until fully amortized) over a period of 5 plan years any amount credited to the funding standard account under paragraph (3) (D).

(3) **Credits to account.**—For a plan year, the funding standard account shall be credited with the sum of—

(A) the amount considered contributed by the employer to or under the plan for the plan year,

(B) the amount necessary to amortize in equal annual installments (until fully amortized)—

(i) separately, with respect to each plan year, the net decrease (if any) in unfunded past service liability under the plan arising from plan amendments adopted in such year, over a period of 30 plan years,

(ii) separately, with respect to each plan year, the net experience gain (if any) under the plan, over a period of 15 plan years, and

(iii) separately, with respect to each plan year, the net gain (if any) resulting from changes in actuarial assumptions used under the plan, over a period of 30 plan years,

(C) the amount of the waived funding deficiency (within the meaning of subsection (d) (3)) for the plan year, and

(D) in the case of a plan year for which the accumulated funding deficiency is determined under the funding standard account if such plan year follows a plan year for which such deficiency was determined under the alternative minimum funding standard, the excess (if any) of any debit balance in the funding standard account (determined without regard to this subparagraph) over any debit balance in the alternative minimum funding standard account.

(4) **Combining and offsetting amounts to be amortized.**—Under regulations prescribed by the Secretary, amounts required to be amortized under paragraph (2) or paragraph (3), as the case may be—

(A) may be combined into one amount under such paragraph to be amortized over a period determined on the basis of the remaining amortization period for all items entering into such combined amount, and

(B) may be offset against amounts required to be amortized under the other such paragraph, with the resulting amount to be amortized over a period determined on the basis of the remaining amortization periods for all items entering into whichever of the two amounts being offset is the greater.

(5) **Interest.**—The funding standard account (and items therein) shall be charged or credited (as determined under regulations prescribed by the Secretary) with interest at the appropriate rate consistent with the rate or rates of interest used under the plan to determine costs.

* * *

(c) **Special rules.**—

(1) **Determinations to be made under funding method.**—For purposes of this section, normal costs, accrued liability, past service liabilities, and experience gains and losses shall be determined under the funding method used to determine costs under the plan.

(2) **Valuation of assets.**—

(A) **In general.**—For purposes of this section, the value of the plan's assets shall be determined on the basis of any reasonable actuarial method of valuation which takes into account fair market value and which is permitted under regulations prescribed by the Secretary.

(B) Election with respect to bonds.—The value of a bond or other evidence of indebtedness which is not in default as to principal or interest may, at the election of the plan administrator, be determined on an amortized basis running from initial cost at purchase to par value at maturity or earliest call date. Any election under this subparagraph shall be made at such time and in such manner as the Secretary shall by regulations provide, shall apply to all such evidences of indebtedness, and may be revoked only with the consent of the Secretary.

(3) Actuarial assumptions must be reasonable.—For purposes of this section, all costs, liabilities, rates of interest, and other factors under the plan shall be determined on the basis of actuarial assumptions and methods which, in the aggregate, are reasonable (taking into account the experience of the plan and reasonable expectations) and which, in combination, offer the actuary's best estimate of anticipated experience under the plan.

(4) Treatment of certain changes as experience gain or loss.—For purposes of this section, if—

(A) a change in benefits under the Social Security Act or in other retirement benefits created under Federal or State law, or

(B) a change in the definition of the term "wages" under section 3121, or a change in the amount of such wages taken into account under regulations prescribed for purposes of section 401(a)(5),

results in an increase or decrease in accrued liability under a plan, such increase or decrease shall be treated as an experience loss or gain.

(5) Change in funding method or in plan year requires approval.—If the funding method for a plan is changed, the new funding method shall become the funding method used to determine costs and liabilities under the plan only if the change is approved by the Secretary. If the plan year for a plan is changed, the new plan year shall become the plan year for the plan only if the change is approved by the Secretary.

(6) Full funding.—If, as of the close of a plan year, a plan would (without regard to this paragraph) have an accumulated funding deficiency (determined without regard to the alternative minimum funding standard account permitted under subsection (g)) in excess of the full funding limitation—

(A) the funding standard account shall be credited with the amount of such excess, and

(B) all amounts described in paragraphs (2)(B), (C), and (D) and (3)(B) of subsection (b) which are required to be amortized shall be considered fully amortized for purposes of such paragraphs.

(7) Full funding limitation.—For purposes of paragraph (6), the term "full funding limitation" means the excess (if any) of—

(A) the accrued liability (including normal cost) under the plan (determined under the entry age normal funding method if such accrued liability cannot be directly calculated under the funding method used for the plan), over

(B) the lesser of the fair market value of the plan's assets or the value of such assets determined under paragraph (2).

(8) Certain retroactive plan amendments.—For purposes of this section, any amendment applying to a plan year which—

(A) is adopted after the close of such plan year but no later than 2 and one-half months after the close of the plan year (or, in the case of a multiemployer plan, no later than 2 years after the close of such plan year),

(B) does not reduce the accrued benefit of any participant determined as of the beginning of the first plan year to which the amendment applies, and

(C) does not reduce the accrued benefit of any participant determined as of the time of adoption except to the extent required by the circumstances,

shall, at the election of the plan administrator, be deemed to have been made on the first day of such plan year. No amendment described in this paragraph which reduces the accrued benefits of any participant shall take effect unless the plan administrator files a notice with the Secretary of Labor notifying him of such amendment and the Secretary of Labor has approved such amendment, or within 90 days after the date on which such notice was filed, failed to disapprove such amendment. No amendment described in this subsection shall be approved by the Secretary of Labor unless he determines that such amendment is necessary because of a substantial business hardship (as determined under subsection (d)(2)) and that a waiver under subsection (d)(1) is unavailable or inadequate.

(9) **3-year valuation.**—For purposes of this section, a determination of experience gains and losses and a valuation of the plan's liability shall be made not less frequently than once every 3 years, except that such determination shall be made more frequently to the extent required in particular cases under regulations prescribed by the Secretary.

(10) **Time when certain contributions deemed made.**—For purposes of this section, any contributions for a plan year made by an employer after the last day of such plan year, but not later than two and one-half months after such day, shall be deemed to have been made on such last day. For purposes of this paragraph, such two and one-half month period may be extended for not more than six months under regulations prescribed by the Secretary.

(d) **Variance from minimum funding standard.**—

(1) **Waiver in case of substantial business hardship.**—If an employer or in the case of a multiemployer plan, 10 percent or more of the number of employers contributing to or under the plan, are unable to satisfy the minimum funding standard for a plan year without substantial business hardship and if application of the standard would be adverse to the interests of plan participants in the aggregate, the Secretary may waive the requirements of subsection (a) for such year with respect to all or any portion of the minimum funding standard other than the portion thereof determined under subsection (b)(2)(C). The Secretary shall not waive the minimum funding standard with respect to a plan for more than 5 of any 15 consecutive plan years. The interest rate used for purposes of computing the amortization charge described in section 412(b)(2)(C) for a variance granted under this subsection shall be the rate determined under section 6621(b).

(2) **Determination of substantial business hardship.**—For purposes of this section, the factors taken into account in determining substantial business hardship shall include (but shall not be limited to) whether or not—

(A) the employer is operating at an economic loss,

(B) there is substantial unemployment or underemployment in the trade or business and in the industry concerned,

(C) the sales and profits of the industry concerned are depressed or declining, and

(D) it is reasonable to expect that the plan will be continued only if the waiver is granted.

(3) **Waived funding deficiency.**—For purposes of this section, the term "waived funding deficiency" means the portion of the minimum funding standard (deter-

mined without regard to subsection (b)(3)(C)) for a plan year waived by the Secretary and not satisfied by employer contributions.

(e) Extension of amortization periods.—The period of years required to amortize any unfunded liability (described in any clause of subsection (b)(2)(B)) of any plan may be extended by the Secretary of Labor for a period of time (not in excess of 10 years) if he determines that such extension would carry out the purposes of the Employee Retirement Income Security Act of 1974 and would provide adequate protection for participants under the plan and their beneficiaries and if he determines that the failure to permit such extension would—

(1) result in—

(A) a substantial risk to the voluntary continuation of the plan, or

(B) a substantial curtailment of pension benefit levels or employee compensation, and

(2) be adverse to the interests of plan participants in the aggregate.

The interest rate applicable under any arrangement entered into by the Secretary in connection with an extension granted under this subsection shall be the rate determined under section 6621(b).

(f) Requirements relating to waivers and extensions.—

(1) Benefits may not be increased during waiver or extension period.—No amendment of the plan which increases the liabilities of the plan by reason of any increase in benefits, any change in the accrual of benefits, or any change in the rate at which benefits become nonforfeitable under the plan shall be adopted if a waiver under subsection (d)(1) or an extension of time under subsection (e) is in effect with respect to the plan, or if a plan amendment described in subsection (c)(8) has been made at any time in the preceding 12 months (24 months for multiemployer plans). If a plan is amended in violation of the preceding sentence, any such waiver or extension of time shall not apply to any plan year ending on or after the date on which such amendment is adopted.

(2) Exception.—Paragraph (1) shall not apply to any plan amendment which—

(A) the Secretary of Labor determines to be reasonable and which provides for only de minimis increases in the liabilities of the plan,

(B) only repeals an amendment described in subsection (c)(8), or

(C) is required as a condition of qualification under this part.

(3) Security for waivers and extensions; consultations.—

(A) Security may be required.—

(i) In general.—Except as provided in subparagraph (C), the Secretary may require an employer maintaining a defined benefit plan which is a single-employer plan (within the meaning of section 4001(a)(15) of the Employee Retirement Income Security Act of 1974) to provide security to such plan as a condition for granting or modifying a waiver under subsection (d) or an extension under subsection (e).

(ii) Special rules.—Any security provided under clause (i) may be perfected and enforced only by the Pension Benefit Guaranty Corporation, or at the direction of the Corporation, by a contributing sponsor (within the meaning of section 4001(a)(13) of such Act), or a member of such sponsor's controlled group (within the meaning of section 4001(a)(14) of such Act).

(B) Consultation with the pension benefit guaranty corporation.—Except as provided in subparagraph (C), the Secretary shall, before granting or modifying a waiver under subsection (d) or an extension under subsection (e) with respect to a plan described in subparagraph (A)(i)—

(i) provide the Pension Benefit Guaranty Corporation with—

(I) notice of the completed application for any waiver, extension, or modification, and

(II) an opportunity to comment on such application within 30 days after receipt of such notice, and

(ii) consider—

(I) any comments of the Corporation under clause (i)(II), and

(II) any views of any employee organization (within the meaning of section 3(4) of the Employee Retirement Income Security Act of 1974) representing participants in the plan which are submitted in writing to the Secretary in connection with such application.

Information provided to the corporation under this subparagraph shall be considered tax return information and subject to the safeguarding and reporting requirements of section 6103(p).

(C) Exception for certain waivers and extensions.—

(i) In general.—The preceding provisions of this paragraph shall not apply to any plan with respect to which the sum of—

(I) the outstanding balance of the accumulated funding deficiencies (within the meaning of subsection (a) and section 302(a) of such Act) of the plan,

(II) the outstanding balance of the amount of waived funding deficiencies of the plan waived under subsection (d) or section 303 of such Act, and

(III) the outstanding balance of the amount of decreases in the minimum funding standard allowed under subsection (e) or section 304 of such Act,

is less than $2,000,000.

(ii) Accumulated funding deficiencies.—For purposes of clause (i)(I), accumulated funding deficiencies shall include any increase in such amount which would result if all applications for waivers of the minimum funding standard under subsection (d) or section 303 of such Act and for extensions of the amortization period under subsection (e) or section 304 of such Act which are pending with respect to such plan were denied.

(4) Additional requirements.—

(A) Advance notice.—The Secretary shall, before granting a waiver under subsection (d) or an extension under subsection (e), require each applicant to provide evidence satisfactory to the Secretary that the applicant has provided notice of the filing of the application for such waiver or extension to each employee organization representing employees covered by the affected plan.

(B) Consideration of relevant information.—The Secretary shall consider any relevant information provided by a person to whom notice was given under subparagraph (A).

(g) Alternative minimum funding standard.—

(1) In general.—A plan which uses a funding method that requires contributions in all years not less than those required under the entry age normal funding method may maintain an alternative minimum funding standard account for any plan year. Such account shall be credited and charged solely as provided in this subsection.

(2) Charges and credits to account.—For a plan year the alternative minimum funding standard account shall be—

(A) charged with the sum of—

(i) the lesser of normal cost under the funding method used under the plan or normal cost determined under the unit credit method,

(ii) the excess, if any, of the present value of accrued benefits under the plan over the fair market value of the assets, and

(iii) an amount equal to the excess (if any) of credits to the alternative minimum standard account for all prior plan years over charges to such account for all such years, and

(B) credited with the amount considered contributed by the employer to or under the plan for the plan year.

(3) Special rules.—The alternative minimum funding standard account (and items therein) shall be charged or credited with interest in the manner provided **under** subsection (b)(5) with respect to the funding standard account.

* * *

§ 413. Collectively bargained plans, etc.

(a) Application of subsection (b).—Subsection (b) applies to—

(1) a plan maintained pursuant to an agreement which the Secretary of Labor finds to be a collective-bargaining agreement between employee representatives and one or more employers, and

(2) each trust which is a part of such plan.

(b) General rule.—If this subsection applies to a plan, notwithstanding any other provision of this title—

(1) Participation.—Section 410 shall be applied as if all employees of each of the employers who are parties to the collective-bargaining agreement and who are subject to the same benefit computation formula under the plan were employed by a single employer.

(2) Discrimination, etc.—Sections 401(a)(4) and 411(d)(3) shall be applied as if all participants who are subject to the same benefit computation formula and who are employed by employers who are parties to the collective bargaining agreement were employed by a single employer.

(3) Exclusive benefit.—For purposes of section 401(a), in determining whether the plan of an employer is for the exclusive benefit of his employees and their beneficiaries, all plan participants shall be considered to be his employees.

(4) Vesting.—Section 411 (other than subsection (d)(3)) shall be applied as if all employers who have been parties to the collective-bargaining agreement constituted a single employer, except that the application of any rules with respect to breaks in service shall be made under regulations prescribed by the Secretary of Labor.

(5) Funding.—The minimum funding standard provided by section 412 shall be determined as if all participants in the plan were employed by a single employer.

(6) Liability for funding tax.—For a plan year the liability under section 4971 of each employer who is a party to the collective bargaining agreement shall be determined in a reasonable manner not inconsistent with regulations prescribed by the Secretary—

(A) first on the basis of their respective delinquencies in meeting required employer contributions under the plan, and

(B) then on the basis of their respective liabilities for contributions under the plan.

For purposes of this subsection and the last sentence of section 4971(a), an employer's withdrawal liability under part 1 of subtitle E of title IV of the Employee Retirement Income Security Act of 1974 shall not be treated as a liability for contributions under the plan.

(7) Deduction limitations.—Each applicable limitation provided by section 404(a) shall be determined as if all participants in the plan were employed by a single employer. The amounts contributed to or under the plan by each employer who is a party to the agreement, for the portion of his taxable year which is included within such a plan year, shall be considered not to exceed such a limitation if the anticipated employer contributions for such plan year (determined in a manner consistent with the manner in which actual employer contributions for such plan year are determined) do not exceed such limitation. If such anticipated contributions exceed such a limitation, the portion of each such employer's contributions which is not deductible under section 404 shall be determined in accordance with regulations prescribed by the Secretary.

(8) Employees of labor unions.—For purposes of this subsection, employees of employee representatives shall be treated as employees of an employer described in subsection (a)(1) if such representatives meet the requirements of sections 401(a)(4) and 410 with respect to such employees.

(c) Plans maintained by more than one employer.—In the case of a plan maintained by more than one employer—

(1) Participation.—Section 410(a) shall be applied as if all employees of each of the employers who maintain the plan were employed by a single employer.

(2) Exclusive benefit.—For purposes of section 401(a), in determining whether the plan of an employer is for the exclusive benefit of his employees and their beneficiaries all plan participants shall be considered to be his employees.

(3) Vesting.—Section 411 shall be applied as if all employers who maintain the plan constituted a single employer, except that the application of any rules with respect to breaks in service shall be made under regulations prescribed by the Secretary of Labor.

(4) Funding.—The minimum funding standard provided by section 412 shall be determined as if all participants in the plan were employed by a single employer.

(5) Liability for funding tax.—For a plan year the liability under section 4971 of each employer who maintains the plan shall be determined in a reasonable manner not inconsistent with regulations prescribed by the Secretary—

(A) first on the basis of their respective delinquencies in meeting required employer contributions under the plan, and

(B) then on the basis of their respective liabilities for contributions under the plan.

(6) Deduction limitations.—Each applicable limitation provided by section 404(a) shall be determined as if all participants in the plan were employed by a single employer. The amounts contributed to or under the plan by each employer who maintains the plan, for the portion of this taxable year which is included within such a plan year, shall be considered not to exceed such a limitation if the anticipated employer contributions for such plan year (determined in a reasonable manner not inconsistent with regulations prescribed by the Secretary) do not exceed such limitation. If such anticipated contributions exceed such a limitation, the portion of each such employer's contributions which is not deductible under section 404 shall be determined in accordance with regulations prescribed by the Secretary.

Allocations of amounts under paragraphs (4), (5), and (6), among the employers maintaining the plan, shall not be inconsistent with regulations prescribed for this purpose by the Secretary.

* * *

§ 414. Definitions and special rules

(a) **Service for predecessor employer.**—For purposes of this part—

(1) in any case in which the employer maintains a plan of a predecessor employer, service for such predecessor shall be treated as service for the employer, and

(2) in any case in which the employer maintains a plan which is not the plan maintained by a predecessor employer, service for such predecessor shall, to the extent provided in regulations prescribed by the Secretary, be treated as service for the employer.

(b) **Employees of controlled group of corporations.**—For purposes of sections 401, 408(k), 410, 411, 415, and 416 all employees of all corporations which are members of a controlled group of corporations (within the meaning of section 1563(a), determined without regard to section 1563(a) (4) and (e) (3) (C)) shall be treated as employed by a single employer. With respect to a plan adopted by more than one such corporation, the minimum funding standard of section 412, the tax imposed by section 4971, and the applicable limitations provided by section 404(a) shall be determined as if all such employers were a single employer, and allocated to each employer in accordance with regulations prescribed by the Secretary.

(c) **Employees of partnerships, proprietorships, etc., which are under common control.**—For purposes of sections 401, 408(k), 410, 411, 415, and 416 under regulations prescribed by the Secretary, all employees of trades or businesses (whether or not incorporated) which are under common control shall be treated as employed by a single employer. The regulations prescribed under this subsection shall be based on principles similar to the principles which apply in the case of subsection (b).

* * *

(i) **Defined contribution plan.**—For purposes of this part, the term "defined contribution plan" means a plan which provides for an individual account for each participant and for benefits based solely on the amount contributed to the participant's account, and any income, expenses, gains and losses, and any forfeitures of accounts of other participants which may be allocated to such participant's account.

(j) **Defined benefit plan.**—For purposes of this part, the term "defined benefit plan" means any plan which is not a defined contribution plan.

(k) **Certain plans.**—A defined benefit plan which provides a benefit derived from employer contributions which is based partly on the balance of the separate account of a participant shall—

(1) for purposes of section 410 (relating to minimum participation standards), be treated as a defined contribution plan,

(2) for purposes of sections 411(a) (7) (A) (relating to minimum vesting standards), 415 (relating to limitations on benefits and contributions under qualified plans),

and 401(m) (relating to nondiscrimination tests for matching requirements and employee contributions) be treated as consisting of a defined contribution plan to the extent benefits are based on the separate account of a participant and as a defined benefit plan with respect to the remaining portion of benefits under the plan, and

(3) for purposes of section 4975 (relating to tax on prohibited transactions), be treated as a defined benefit plan.

* * *

(m) Employees of an affiliated service group.—

(1) In general.—For purposes of the employee benefit requirements listed in paragraph (4), except to the extent otherwise provided in regulations, all employees of the members of an affiliated service group shall be treated as employed by a single employer.

(2) Affiliated service group.—For purposes of this subsection, the term "affiliated service group" means a group consisting of a service organization (hereinafter in this paragraph referred to as the "first organization") and one or more of the following:

(A) any service organization which—

(i) is a shareholder or partner in the first organization, and

(ii) regularly performs services for the first organization or is regularly associated with the first organization in performing services for third persons, and

(B) any other organization if—

(i) a significant portion of the business of such organization is the performance of services (for the first organization, for organizations described in subparagraph (A), or for both) of a type historically performed in such service field by employees, and

(ii) 10 percent or more of the interests in such organization is held by persons who are officers, highly compensated employees, or owners of the first organization or an organization described in subparagraph (A).

Amendment of Subsec. (m)(2)(B)(ii)

Pub.L. 99–514, Title XI, § 1114(b)(11), (c)(3), Oct. 22, 1986, 100 Stat. ——, provided that, applicable to years beginning after December 31, 1988, subsec. (m)(2)(B)(ii) of this section is amended by striking out "officers, highly compensated employees, or owners" and inserting in lieu thereof "highly compensated employees (within the meaning of section 414(q))".

(3) Service organizations.—For purposes of this subsection, the term "service organization" means an organization the principal business of which is the performance of services.

(4) Employee benefit requirements.—For purposes of this subsection, the employee benefit requirements listed in this paragraph are—

(A) paragraphs (3), (4), (7), and (16) of section 401(a),

(B) sections 408(k), 410, 411, 415, and 416,

(C) section 105(h), and

(D) section 125.

(5) **Certain organizations performing management functions.**—For purposes of this subsection, the term "affiliated service group" also includes a group consisting of—

(A) an organization the principal business of which is performing, on a regular and continuing basis, management functions for 1 organization (or for 1 organization and other organizations related to such 1 organization), and

(B) the organization (and related organizations) for which such functions are so performed by the organization described in subparagraph (A).

For purposes of this paragraph, the term "related organizations" has the same meaning as the term "related persons" when used in section 144(a)(3).

(6) **Other definitions.**—For purposes of this subsection—

(A) Organization defined.—The term "organization" means a corporation, partnership, or other organization.

(B) Ownership.—In determining ownership, the principles of section 318(a) shall apply.

[(7) **Repealed.**]

(n) **Employee leasing.**—

(1) **In general.**—For purposes of the pension requirements listed in paragraph (3), with respect to any person (hereinafter in this subsection referred to as the "recipient") for whom a leased employee performs services—

(A) the leased employee shall be treated as an employee of the recipient, but

(B) contributions or benefits provided by the leasing organization which are attributable to services performed for the recipient shall be treated as provided by the recipient.

(2) **Leased employee.**—For purposes of paragraph (1), the term "leased employee" means any person who is not an employee of the recipient and who provides services to the recipient if—

(A) such services are provided pursuant to an agreement between the recipient and any other person (in this subsection referred to as the ⅛ "leasing organization"),

(B) such person has performed such services for the recipient (or for the recipient and related persons) on a substantially full-time basis for a period of at least 1 year, and

(C) such services are of a type historically performed, in the business field of the recipient, by employees.

(3) **Pension requirements.**—For purposes of this subsection, the pension requirements listed in this paragraph are—

(A) paragraphs (3), (4), (7), and (16) of section 401(a), and

(B) sections 408(k), 410, 411, 415, and 416.

(4) **Time when first considered as employee.**—

(A) In general.—In the case of any leased employee, paragraph (1) shall apply only for purposes of determining whether the requirements listed in paragraph (3) are met for periods after the close of the period referred to in paragraph (2)(B).

(B) Years of service.—In the case of a person who is an employee of the recipient (whether by reason of this subsection or otherwise), for purposes of the requirements listed in paragraph (3), years of service for the recipient shall be determined by taking into account any period for which such employee would have been a leased employee but for the requirements of paragraph (2)(B).

(5) Safe harbor.—

(A) In general.—In the case of requirements described in subparagraphs (A) and (B) of paragraph (3), this subsection shall not apply to any leased employee with respect to services performed for a recipient if—

(i) such employee is covered by a plan which is maintained by the leasing organization and meets the requirements of subparagraph (B), and

(ii) leased employees (determined without regard to this paragraph) do not constitute more than 20 percent of the recipient's nonhighly compensated work force.

(B) Plan requirements.—A plan meets the requirements of this subparagraph if—

(i) such plan is a money purchase pension plan with a nonintegrated employer contribution rate for each participant of at least 10 percent of compensation,

(ii) such plan provides for full and immediate vesting, and

(iii) each employee of the leasing organization (other than employees who perform substantially all of their services for the leasing organization) immediately participates in such plan.

Clause (iii) shall not apply to any individual whose compensation from the leasing organization in each plan year during the 4–year period ending with the plan year is less than $1,000.

(C) Definitions.—For purposes of this paragraph—

(i) **Highly compensated employee.**—The term "highly compensated employee" has the meaning given such term by section 414(q).

(ii) **Nonhighly compensated work force.**—The term "nonhighly compensated work force" means the aggregate number of individuals (other than highly compensated employees)—

(I) who are employees of the recipient (without regard to this subsection) and have performed services for the recipient (or for the recipient and related persons) on a substantially full-time basis for a period of at least 1 year, or

(II) who are leased employees with respect to the recipient (determined without regard to this paragraph).

(iii) **Compensation.**—The term "compensation" has the same meaning as when used in section 415; except that such term shall include—

(I) any employer contribution under a qualified cash or deferred arrangement to the extent not included in gross income under section 402(a)(8) or 402(h)(1)(B),

(II) any amount which the employee would have received in cash but for an election under a cafeteria plan (within the meaning of section 125), and

(III) any amount contributed to an annuity contract described in section 403(b) pursuant to a salary reduction agreement (within the meaning of section 3121(a)(5)(D)).

(6) Other rules.—For purposes of this subsection—

(A) Related persons.—The term "related persons" has the same meaning as when used in section 144(a)(3).

(B) Employees of entities under common control.—The rules of subsections (b), (c), (m), and (o) shall apply.

Amendment of Subsec. (n)

Pub.L. 99–514, Title XI, § 1151(i), (k), Oct. 22, 1986, 100 Stat. ——, provided that, except as otherwise provided, applicable to years beginning after the later of Dec. 31, 1987, or the earlier of date three months after date Secretary of Treasury issues regulations necessary to carry out section 89 of Title 26, Internal Revenue Code, or Dec. 31, 1988, section 414(n) is amended as follows:

(1) Paragraph (1) of section 414(n) is amended by striking out "pension requirements" and inserting in lieu thereof "requirements".

(2) Subparagraph (B) of section 414(n)(2) is amended by inserting "(6 months in the case of core health benefits)" after "1 year".

(3) Paragraph (3) of section 414(n) is amended—

(A) by striking out "PENSION REQUIREMENTS" and inserting in lieu thereof "REQUIREMENTS",

(B) by striking out "pension requirements" and inserting in lieu thereof "requirements".

(o) Regulations.—The Secretary shall prescribe such regulations (which may provide rules in addition to the rules contained in subsections (m) and (n)) as may be necessary to prevent the avoidance of any employee benefit requirement listed in subsection (m)(4) or (n)(3) through the use of—

(1) separate organizations,

(2) employee leasing, or

(3) other arrangements.

The regulations prescribed under subsection (n) shall include provisions to minimize the recordkeeping requirements of subsection (n) in the case of an employer which has no top-heavy plans (within the meaning of section 416(g)) and which uses the services of persons (other than employees) for an insignificant percentage of the employer's total workload.

(p) Qualified domestic relations order defined.—For purposes of this subsection and section 401(a)(13)—

(1) In general.—

(A) Qualified domestic relations order.—The term "qualified domestic relations order" means a domestic relations order—

(i) which creates or recognizes the existence of an alternate payee's right to, or assigns to an alternate payee the right to, receive all or a portion of the benefits payable with respect to a participant under a plan, and

(ii) with respect to which the requirements of paragraphs (2) and (3) are met.

(B) Domestic relations order.—The term "domestic relations order" means any judgment, decree, or order (including approval of a property settlement agreement) which—

(i) relates to the provision of child support, alimony payments, or marital property rights to a spouse, former spouse, child, or other dependent of a participant, and

408

(ii) is made pursuant to a State domestic relations law (including a community property law).

(2) Order must clearly specify certain facts.—A domestic relations order meets the requirements of this paragraph only if such order clearly specifies—

(A) the name and the last known mailing address (if any) of the participant and the name and mailing address of each alternate payee covered by the order,

(B) the amount or percentage of the participant's benefits to be paid by the plan to each such alternate payee, or the manner in which such amount or percentage is to be determined,

(C) the number of payments or period to which such order applies, and

(D) each plan to which such order applies.

(3) Order may not alter amount, form, etc., of benefits.—A domestic relations order meets the requirements of this paragraph only if such order—

(A) does not require a plan to provide any type or form of benefit, or any option, not otherwise provided under the plan,

(B) does not require the plan to provide increased benefits (determined on the basis of actuarial value), and

(C) does not require the payment of benefits to an alternate payee which are required to be paid to another alternate payee under another order previously determined to be a qualified domestic relations order.

(4) Exception for certain payments made after earliest retirement age.—

(A) In general.—domestic relations order shall not be treated as failing to meet the requirements of subparagraph (A) of paragraph (3) solely because such order requires that payment of benefits be made to an alternate payee—

(i) on or in the case of any payment before a participant has separated from service, before the date on which the participant attains (or would have attained) the earliest retirement age,

(ii) as if the participant had retired on the date on which such payment is to begin under such order (but taking into account only the present value of the benefits actually accrued and not taking into account the present value of any employer subsidy for early retirement), and

(iii) in any form in which such benefits may be paid under the plan to the participant (other than in the form of a joint and survivor annuity with respect to the alternate payee and his or her subsequent spouse).

For purposes of clause (ii), the interest rate assumption used in determining the present value shall be the interest rate specified in the plan or, if no rate is specified, 5 percent.

(B) Earliest retirement age.—For purposes of this paragraph, the term "earliest retirement age" means earlier of—

(i) in the date on which the participant is entitled to a distribution under the plan, or

(ii) in the later of—

(I) the date the participant attains age 50, or

(II) the earliest date on which the participant could begin receiving benefits under the plan if the participant separated from service.

(5) Treatment of former spouse as surviving spouse for purposes of determining survivor benefits.—To the extent provided in any qualified domestic relations order—

(A) the former spouse of a participant shall be treated as a surviving spouse of such participant for purposes of sections 401(a)(11) and 417 (and any spouse of the participant shall not be treated as a spouse of the participant for such purposes), and

(B) if married for at least 1 year, the surviving former spouse shall be treated as meeting the requirements of section 417(d).

(6) Plan procedures with respect to orders.—

(A) **Notice and determination by administrator.**—In the case of any domestic relations order received by a plan—

(i) the plan administrator shall promptly notify the participant and each alternate payee of the receipt of such order and the plan's procedures for determining the qualified status of domestic relations orders, and

(ii) within a reasonable period after receipt of such order, the plan administrator shall determine whether such order is a qualified domestic relations order and notify the participant and each alternate payee of such determination.

(B) **Plan to establish reasonable procedures.**—Each plan shall establish reasonable procedures to determine the qualified status of domestic relations orders and to administer distributions under such qualified orders.

(7) Procedures for period during which determination is being made.—

(A) **In general.**—During any period in which the issue of whether a domestic relations order is a qualified domestic relations order is being determined (by the plan administrator, by a court a competent jurisdiction, or otherwise), the plan administrator shall separately account for the amounts (hereinafter in this paragraph referred to as the "segregated amounts") which would have been payable to the alternate payee during such period if the order had been determined to be a qualified domestic relations order.

(B) **Payment to alternate payee if order determined to be qualified domestic relations order.**—If within the 18-month period described in subparagraph (E) the order (or modification thereof) is determined to be a qualified domestic relations order, the plan administrator shall pay the segregated amounts (including any interest thereon) to the person or persons entitled thereto.

(C) **Payment to plan participant in certain cases.**—If within the 18-month period described in subparagraph (E)—

(i) it is determined that the order is not a qualified domestic relations order, or

(ii) the issue as to whether such order is a qualified domestic relations order is not resolved,

then the plan administrator shall pay the segregated amounts (including any interest thereon) to the person or persons who would have been entitled to such amounts if there had been no order.

(D) **Subsequent determination or order to be applied prospectively only.** —Any determination that an order is a qualified domestic relations order which is made after the close of the 18-month period described in subparagraph (E) period shall be applied prospectively only.

(E) **Determination of 18–month period.**—For purposes of this paragraph, the 18–month period described in this subparagraph is the 18–month period beginning with the date on which the first payment would be required to be made under the domestic relations order.

(8) **Alternate payee defined.**—The term "alternate payee" means any spouse, former spouse, child or other dependent of a participant who is recognized by a domestic relations order as having a right to receive all, or a portion of, the benefits payable under a plan with respect to such participant.

(9) **Subsection not to apply to plans to which section 401(a)(13) does not apply.**—This subsection shall not apply to any plan to which section 401(a)(13) does not apply.

(10) **Waiver of certain distribution requirements.**—With respect to the requirements of subsections (a) and (k) of section 401 and section 409(d), a plan shall not be treated as failing to meet such requirements solely by reason of payments to an alternative payee pursuant to a qualified domestic relations order.

* * *

(q) **Highly compensated employee.**—

(1) **In general.**—The term "highly compensated employee" means any employee who, during the year or the preceding year—

(A) was at any time a 5–percent owner,

(B) received compensation from the employer in excess of $75,000,

(C) received compensation from the employer in excess of $50,000 and was in the top-paid group of employees for such year, or

(D) was at any time an officer and received compensation greater than 150 percent of the amount in effect under section 415(c)(1)(A) for such year.

(2) **Special rule for current year.**—In the case of the year for which the relevant determination is being made, an employee not described in subparagraph (B), (C), or (D) of paragraph (1) for the preceding year (without regard to this paragraph) shall not be treated as described in subparagraph (B), (C), or (D) of paragraph (1) unless such employee is a member of the group consisting of the 100 employees paid the greatest compensation during the year for which such determination is being made.

(3) **5–percent owner.**—An employee shall be treated as a 5–percent owner for any year if at any time during such year such employee was a 5–percent owner (as defined in section 416(i)(1)) of the employer.

(4) **Top-paid group.**—An employee is in the top-paid group of employees for any year if such employee is in the group consisting of the top 20 percent of the employees when ranked on the basis of compensation paid during such year.

(5) **Special rules for treatment of officers.**—

(A) **Not more than 50 officers taken into account.**—For purposes of paragraph (1)(D), no more than 50 employees (or, if lesser, the greater of 3 employees or 10 percent of the employees) shall be treated as officers.

(B) **At least 1 officer taken into account.**—If for any year no officer of the employer is described in paragraph (1)(D), the highest paid officer of the employer for such year shall be treated as described in such paragraph.

(6) **Treatment of certain family members.**—

(A) **In general.**—If any individual is a member of the family of a 5–percent owner or of a highly compensated employee in the group consisting of the 10 highly compensated employees paid the greatest compensation during the year, then—

(i) such individual shall not be considered a separate employee, and

(ii) any compensation paid to such individual (and any applicable contribution or benefit on behalf of such individual) shall be treated as if it were paid to (or on behalf of) the 5-percent owner or highly compensated employee.

(B) Family.—For purposes of subparagraph (A), the term "family" means, with respect to any employee, such employee's spouse and lineal ascendants or descendants and the spouses of such lineal ascendants or descendants.

(7) Compensation.—For purposes of this subsection—

(A) In general.—The term "compensation" means compensation within the meaning of section 415(c)(3).

(B) Certain provisions not taken into account.—The determination under subparagraph (A) shall be made—

(i) without regard to sections 125, 402(a)(8), and 402(h)(1)(B), and

(ii) in the case of employer contributions made pursuant to a salary reduction agreement, without regard to section 403(b).

(8) Excluded employees.—For purposes of subsection (r) and for purposes of determining the number of employees in the top-paid group under paragraph (4), the following employees shall be excluded—

(A) employees who have not completed 6 months of service,

(B) employees who normally work less than 17½ hours per week,

(C) employees who normally work during not more than 6 months during any year,

(D) employees who have not attained age 21,

(E) except to the extent provided in regulations, employees who are included in a unit of employees covered by an agreement which the Secretary of Labor finds to be a collective bargaining agreement between employee representatives and the employer, and

(F) employees who are nonresident aliens and who receive no earned income (within the meaning of section 911(d)(2)) from the employer which constitutes income from sources within the United States (within the meaning of section 861(a)(3)).

The employer may elect to apply subparagraph (A), (B), (C), or (D) by substituting a shorter period of service, smaller number of hours or months, or lower age for the period of service, number of hours or months, or age (as the case may be) than that specified in such subparagraph.

(9) Former employees.—A former employee shall be treated as a highly compensated employee if—

(A) such employee was a highly compensated employee when such employee separated from service, or

(B) such employee was a highly compensated employee at any time after attaining age 55.

(10) Coordination with other provisions.—Subsections (b), (c), (m), (n), and (o) shall be applied before the application of this section.

(r) Special rules for separate line of business.—

(1) **In general.**—For purposes of sections 89 and 410(b), an employer shall be treated as operating separate lines of business during any year if the employer for bona fide business reasons operates separate lines of business.

(2) **Line of business must have 50 employees, etc.**—A line of business shall not be treated as separate under paragraph (1) unless—

(A) such line of business has at least 50 employees who are not excluded under subsection (q)(8),

(B) the employer notifies the Secretary that such line of business is being treated as separate for purposes of paragraph (1), and

(C) such line of business meets guidelines prescribed by the Secretary or the employer receives a determination from the Secretary that such line of business may be treated as separate for purposes of paragraph (1).

(3) **Safe harbor rule.**—The requirements of subparagraph (C) of paragraph (2) shall not apply to any line of business if the highly compensated employee percentage with respect to such line of business is—

(A) not less than one-half, and

(B) not more than twice,

the percentage which highly compensated employees are of all employees of the employer. An employer shall be treated as meeting the requirements of subparagraph (A) if at least 10 percent of all highly compensated employees of the employer perform services solely for such line of business.

(4) **Highly compensated employee percentage defined.**—For purposes of this subsection, the term "highly compensated employee percentage" means the percentage which highly compensated employees performing services for the line of business are of all employees performing services for the line of business.

(5) **Allocation of benefits to line of business.**—For purposes of this subsection, benefits which are attributable to services provided to a line of business shall be treated as provided by such line of business.

(6) **Headquarters personnel, etc.**—The Secretary shall prescribe rules providing for—

(A) the allocation of headquarters personnel among the lines of business of the employer, and

(B) the treatment of other employees providing services for more than 1 line of business of the employer or not in lines of business meeting the requirements of paragraph (2).

(7) **Separate operating units.**—For purposes of this subsection, the term "separate line of business" includes an operating unit in a separate geographic area separately operated for a bona fide business reason.

(8) **Affiliated service groups.**—This subsection shall not apply in the case of any affiliated service group (within the meaning of section 414(m)).

(s) **Compensation.**—For purposes of this part—

(1) **In general.**—The term "compensation" means compensation for service performed for an employer which (taking into account the provisions of this chapter) is currently includible in gross income.

(2) **Self-employed individuals.**—The Secretary shall prescribe regulations for the determination of the compensation of an employee who is a self-employed individual (within the meaning of section 401(c)(1)) which are based on the principles of paragraph (1).

(3) **Employer may elect to treat certain deferrals as compensation.**—An employer may elect to include as compensation any amount which is contributed by the employer pursuant to a salary reduction agreement and which is not includible in the gross income of an employee under section 125, 402(a)(8), 402(h), or 403(b).

(4) **Alternative determination of compensation.**—The Secretary shall by regulation provide for alternative methods of determining compensation which may be used by an employer, except that such regulations shall provide that an employer may not use an alternative method if the use of such method discriminates in favor of highly compensated employees (within the meaning of subsection (q)).

Enactment of Subsec. (t)

Pub.L. 99–514, Title XI, § 1151(e)(1), (k), Oct. 22, 1986, 100 Stat. ——, provided that, except as otherwise provided, applicable to years beginning after the later of Dec. 31, 1987, or the earlier of date three months after date Secretary of Treasury issues regulations necessary to carry out section 89 of Title 26, Internal Revenue Code, or Dec. 31, 1988, section 414 is amended by adding at the end thereof the following new subsection:

(t) **Application of controlled group rules to certain employee benefits.**—

(1) **In general.**—All employees who are treated as employed by a single employer under subsection (b), (c), or (m) of section 414 shall be treated as employed by a single employer for purposes of an applicable section. The provisions of subsection (o) of section 414 shall apply with respect to the requirements of an applicable section.

(2) **Applicable section.**—For purposes of this subsection, the term "applicable section" means section 79, 89, 106, 117(d), 120, 125, 127, 129, 132, 274(j), or 505.

§ 415. Limitations on benefits and contribution under qualified plans

(a) **General rule.**—

(1) **Trusts.**—A trust which is a part of a pension, profit-sharing, or stock bonus plan shall not constitute a qualified trust under section 401(a) if—

(A) in the case of a defined benefit plan, the plan provides for the payment of benefits with respect to a participant which exceed the limitation of subsection (b),

(B) in the case of a defined contribution plan, contributions and other additions under the plan with respect to any participant for any taxable year exceed the limitation of subsection (c), or

(C) in any case in which an individual is a participant in both a defined benefit plan and a defined contribution plan maintained by the employer, the trust has been disqualified under subsection (g).

(2) **Section applies to certain annuities and accounts.**—In the case of—

(A) an employee annuity plan described in section 403(a),

(B) an annuity contract described in section 403(b), or

(C) a simplified employee pension described in section 408(k),

such a contract, plan, or pension shall not be considered to be described in section 403(a), 403(b), or 408(k), as the case may be, unless it satisfies the requirements of subparagraph (A) or subparagraph (B) of paragraph (1), whichever is appropriate, and has not been disqualified under subsection (g). In the case of an annuity contract described in section 403(b), the preceding sentence shall apply only to the portion of the annuity contract which exceeds the limitation of subsection (b) or the limitation of subsection (c), whichever is appropriate, and the amount of the contribution for such portion shall reduce the exclusion allowance as provided in section 403(b)(2).

(b) Limitation for defined benefit plans.—

(1) In general.—Benefits with respect to a participant exceed the limitation of this subsection if, when expressed as an annual benefit (within the meaning of paragraph (2)), such annual benefit is greater than the lesser of—

(A) $90,000, or

(B) 100 percent of the participant's average compensation for his high 3 years.

(2) Annual benefit.—

(A) In general.—For purposes of paragraph (1), the term "annual benefit" means a benefit payable annually in the form of a straight life annuity (with no ancillary benefits) under a plan to which employees do not contribute and under which no rollover contributions (as defined in sections 402(a)(5), 403(a)(4), and 408(d)(3)) are made.

(B) Adjustment for certain other forms of benefit.—If the benefit under the plan is payable in any form other than the form described in subparagraph (A), or if the employees contribute to the plan or make rollover contributions (as defined in sections 402(a)(5), 403(a)(4), and 408(d)(3)), the determinations as to whether the limitation described in paragraph (1) has been satisfied shall be made, in accordance with regulations prescribed by the Secretary, by adjusting such benefit so that it is equivalent to the benefit described in subparagraph (A). For purposes of this subparagraph, any ancillary benefit which is not directly related to retirement income benefits shall not be taken into account; and that portion of any joint and survivor annuity which constitutes a qualified joint and survivor annuity (as defined in section 417) shall not be taken into account.

(C) Adjustment to $90,000 limit where benefit begins before the social security retirement age.—If the retirement income benefit under the plan begins before the social security retirement age, the determination as to whether the $90,000 limitation set forth in paragraph (1)(A) has been satisfied shall be made, in accordance with regulations prescribed by the Secretary, by reducing the limitation of paragraph (1)(A) so that such limitation (as so reduced) equals an annual benefit (beginning when such retirement income benefit begins) which is equivalent to a $90,000 annual benefit beginning at the social security retirement age. The reduction under this subparagraph shall be made in such manner as the Secretary may prescribe which is consistent with the reduction for old-age insurance benefits commencing before the social security retirement age under the Social Security Act.

(D) Adjustment to $90,000 limit where benefit begins after the social security retirement age.—If the retirement income benefit under the plan begins after the social security retirement age, the determination as to whether the $90,000 limitation set forth in paragraph (1)(A) has been satisfied shall be made, in accordance with regulations prescribed by the Secretary, by increasing the limitation of paragraph (1)(A) so that such limitation (as so increased) equals an annual benefit (beginning when such retirement income benefit begins) which is equivalent to a $90,000 annual benefit beginning at the social security retirement age.

(E) Limitation on certain assumptions.—

(i) For purposes of adjusting any benefit or limitation under subparagraph (B) or (C), the interest rate assumption shall not be less than the greater of 5 percent or the rate specified in the plan.

(ii) For purposes of adjusting any limitation under subparagraph (D), the interest rate assumption shall not be greater than the lesser of 5 percent or the rate specified in the plan.

(iii) For purposes of this subsection, no adjustments under subsection (d)(1) shall be taken into account before the year for which such adjustment first takes effect.

* * *

(3) **Average compensation for high 3 years.**—For purposes of paragraph (1), a participant's high 3 years shall be the period of consecutive calendar years (not more than 3) during which the participant both was an active participant in the plan and had the greatest aggregate compensation from the employer. In the case of an employee within the meaning of section 401(c) (1), the preceding sentence shall be applied by substituting for "compensation from the employer" the following: "the participant's earned income (within the meaning of section 401(c) (2) but determined without regard to any exclusion under section 911)".

(4) **Total annual benefits not in excess of $10,000.**—Notwithstanding the preceding provisions of this subsection, the benefits payable with respect to a participant under any defined benefit plan shall be deemed not to exceed the limitation of this subsection if—

(A) the retirement benefits payable with respect to such participant under such plan and under all other defined benefit plans of the employer do not exceed $10,000 for the plan year, or for any prior plan year, and

(B) the employer has not at any time maintained a defined contribution plan in which the participant participated.

(5) **Reduction for participation or service of less than 10 years.—**

(A) **Dollar limitation.**—In the case of an employee who has less than 10 years of participation in a defined benefit plan, the limitation referred to in paragraph (1)(A) shall be the limitation determined under such paragraph (without regard to this paragraph) multiplied by a fraction—

(i) the numerator of which is the number of years (or part thereof) of participation in the defined benefit plan of the employer, and

(ii) the denominator of which is 10.

(B) **Compensation and benefits limitations.**—The provisions of subparagraph (A) shall apply to the limitations under paragraphs (1)(B) and (4), except that such subparagraph shall be applied with respect to years of service with an employer rather than years of participation in a plan.

(C) **Limitation on reduction.**—In no event shall subparagraph (A) or (B) reduce the limitations referred to in paragraphs (1) and (4) to an amount less than $\frac{1}{10}$ of such limitation (determined without regard to this paragraph).

(D) **Application to changes in benefit structure.**—To the extent provided in regulations, this paragraph shall be applied separately with respect to each change in the benefit structure of a plan.

(6) **Computation of benefits and contributions.**—The computation of—

(A) benefits under a defined contribution plan, for purposes of section 401(a) (4),

(B) contributions made on behalf of a participant in a defined benefit plan, for purposes of section 401(a) (4), and

(C) contributions and benefits provided for a participant in a plan described in section 414(k), for purposes of this section

shall not be made on a basis inconsistent with regulations prescribed by the Secretary.

(7) Benefits under certain collectively bargained plans.—For a year, the limitation referred to in paragraph (1) (B) shall not apply to benefits with respect to a participant under a defined benefit plan—

(A) which is maintained for such year pursuant to a collective bargaining agreement between employee representatives and one or more employers,

(B) which, at all times during such year, has at least 100 participants,

(C) under which benefits are determined solely by reference to length of service, the particular years during which service was rendered, age at retirement, and date of retirement,

(D) which provides that an employee who has at least 4 years of service has a nonforfeitable right to 100 percent of his accrued benefit derived from employer contributions, and

(E) which requires, as a condition of participation in the plan, that an employee complete a period of not more than 60 consecutive days of service with the employer or employers maintaining the plan.

This paragraph shall not apply to a participant whose compensation for any 3 years during the 10-year period immediately preceding the year in which he separates from service exceeded the average compensation for such 3 years of all participants in such plan. This paragraph shall not apply to a participant for any period for which he is a participant under another plan to which this section applies which is maintained by an employer maintaining this plan. For any year for which the paragraph applies to benefits with respect to a participant, paragraph (1) (A) and subsection (d) (1) (A) shall be applied with respect to such participant by substituting the greater of $68,212 or one-half the amount otherwise applicable for such year under paragraph (1)(A) for "$90,000".

(8) Social security retirement age defined.—For purposes of this subsection, the term "social security retirement age" means the age used as the retirement age under section 216(l) of the Social Security Act, except that such section shall be applied—

(A) without regard to the age increase factor, and

(B) as if the early retirement age under section 216(l)(2) of such Act were 62.

(9) Special rule for commercial airline pilots.—

(A) In general.—Except as provided in subparagraph (B), in the case of any participant who is a commercial airline pilot—

(i) the rule of paragraph (2)(F)(i)(II) shall apply, and

(ii) if, as of the time of the participant's retirement, regulations prescribed by the Federal Aviation Administration require an individual to separate from service as a commercial airline pilot after attaining any age occurring on or after age 60 and before the social security retirement age, paragraph (2)(C) (after application of clause (i)) shall be applied by substituting such age for the social security retirement age.

(B) Individuals who separate from service before age 60.—If a participant described in subparagraph (A) separates from service before age 60, the rules of paragraph (2)(F) shall apply.

(c) Limitation for defined contribution plans.—

(1) In general.—Contributions and other additions with respect to a participant exceed the limitation of this subsection if, when expressed as an annual addition (within the meaning of paragraph (2)) to the participant's account, such annual addition is greater than the lesser of—

(A) $30,000 (or, if greater, ¼ of the dollar limitation in effect under subsection (b)(1)(A)), or

(B) 25 percent of the participant's compensation.

(2) Annual addition.—For purposes of paragraph (1), the term "annual addition" means the sum for any year of—

(A) employer contributions,

(B) the employee contributions, and

(i) the amount of the employee contributions in excess of 6 percent of his compensation, or

(ii) one-half of the employee contributions, and

(C) forfeitures.

For the purposes of this paragraph, employee contributions under subparagraph (B) are determined without regard to any rollover contributions (as defined in sections 402(a)(5), 403(a)(4), 403(b)(8), and 408(d)(3)) without regard to employee contributions to a simplified employee pension which are excludable from gross income under section 408(k)(6). Subparagraph (B) of paragraph (1) shall not apply to any contribution for medical benefits (within the meaning of section 419A(f)(2)) after separation from service which is treated as an annual addition.

(3) Participant's compensation.—For purposes of paragraph (1)

(A) In general.—The term "participant's compensation" means the compensation of the participant from the employer for the year.

(B) Special rule for self-employed individuals.—In the case of an employee within the meaning of section 401(c)(1), subparagraph (A) shall be applied by substituting "the participant's earned income (within the meaning of section 401(c)(2) but determined without regard to any exclusion under section 911)" for "compensation of the participant from the employer".

(C) Special rules for permanent and total disability.—In the case of a participant in any defined contribution plan—

(i) who is permanently and totally disabled (as defined in section 22(e)(3),

(ii) who is not an officer, owner, or highly compensated, and

(iii) with respect to whom the employer elects, at such time and in such manner as the Secretary may prescribe, to have this subparagraph apply,

the term "participant's compensation" means the compensation the participant would have received for the year if the participant was paid at the rate of compensation paid immediately before becoming permanently and totally disabled. This subparagraph shall apply only if contributions made with respect to amounts treated as compensation under this subparagraph are nonforfeitable when made.

* * *

(e) Limitation in case of defined benefit plan and defined contribution plan for same employee.—

(1) In general.—In any case in which an individual is a participant in both a defined benefit plan and a defined contribution plan maintained by the same employer, the sum of the defined benefit plan fraction and the defined contribution plan fraction for any year may not exceed 1.0.

(2) Defined benefit plan fraction.—For purposes of this subsection, the defined benefit plan fraction for any year is a fraction—

(A) the numerator of which is the projected annual benefit of the participant under the plan (determined as of the close of the year), and

(B) the denominator of which is the lesser of—

(i) the product of 1.25, multiplied by the dollar limitation in effect under subsection (b)(1)(A) for such year, or

(ii) the product of—

(I) 1.4, multiplied by

(II) the amount which may be taken into account under subsection (b)(1)(B) with respect to such individual under the plan for such year.

(3) Defined contribution plan fraction.—For purposes of this subsection, the defined contribution plan fraction for any year is a fraction—

(A) the numerator of which is the sum of the annual additions to the participant's account as of the close of the year, and

(B) the denominator of which is the sum of the lesser of the following amounts determined for such year and for each prior year of service with the employer:

(i) the product of 1.25, multiplied by the dollar limitation in effect under subsection (c)(1)(A) for such year (determined without regard to subsection (c)(6)), or

(ii) the product of—

(I) 1.4, multiplied by—

(II) the amount which may be taken into account under subsection (c)(1)(B) (or subsection (c)(7), if applicable) with respect to such individual under such plan for such year.

* * *

(f) Combining of plans.—

(1) In general.—For purposes of applying the limitations of subsections (b), (c), and (e)—

(A) all defined benefit plans (whether or not terminated) of an employer are to be treated as one defined benefit plan, and

(B) all defined contribution plans (whether or not terminated) of an employer are to be treated as one defined contribution plan.

(2) Annual compensation taken into account for defined benefit plans.—If the employer has more than one defined benefit plan—

(A) subsection (b) (1) (B) shall be applied separately with respect to each such plan, but

(B) in applying subsection (b) (1) (B) to the aggregate of such defined benefit plans for purposes of this subsection, the high 3 years of compensation taken into account shall be the period of consecutive calendar years (not more than 3)

during which the individual had the greatest aggregate compensation from the employer.

(g) Aggregation of plans.—The Secretary, in applying the provisions of this section to benefits or contributions under more than one plan maintained by the same employer, and to any trusts, contracts, accounts, or bonds referred to in subsection (a) (2), with respect to which the participant has the control required under section 414(b) or (c), as modified by subsection (h), shall, under regulations prescribed by the Secretary, disqualify one or more trusts, plans, contracts, accounts, or bonds, or any combination thereof until such benefits or contributions do not exceed the limitations contained in this section. In addition to taking into account such other factors as may be necessary to carry out the purposes of subsections (e) and (f), the regulations prescribed under this paragraph shall provide that no plan which has been terminated shall be disqualified until all other trusts, plans, contracts, accounts, or bonds have been disqualified.

(h) 50 percent control.—For purposes of applying subsections (b) and (c) of section 414 to this section, the phrase "more than 50 percent" shall be substituted for the phrase "at least 80 percent" each place it appears in section 1563(a) (1).

* * *

§ 416. Special rules for top-heavy plans

(a) General rule.—A trust shall not constitute a qualified trust under section 401(a) for any plan year if the plan of which it is a part is a top-heavy plan for such plan year unless such plan meets—

(1) the vesting requirements of subsection (b),

(2) the minimum benefit requirements of subsection (c), and

(3) the limitation on compensation requirement of subsection (d).

(b) Vesting requirements.—

(1) In general.—A plan satisfies the requirements of this subsection if it satisfies the requirements of either of the following subparagraphs:

(A) 3-year vesting.—A plan satisfies the requirements of this subparagraph if an employee who has completed at least 3 years of service with the employer or employers maintaining the plan has a nonforfeitable right to 100 percent of his accrued benefit derived from employer contributions.

(B) 6-year graded vesting.—A plan satisfies the requirements of this subparagraph if an employee has a nonforfeitable right to a percentage of his accrued benefit derived from employer contributions determined under the following table:

Years of service	The nonforfeitable percentage is:
2	20
3	40
4	60
5	80
6 or more	100

(2) Certain rules made applicable.—Except to the extent inconsistent with the provisions of this subsection, the rules of section 411 shall apply for purposes of this subsection.

(c) Plan must provide minimum benefits.—

(1) Defined benefit plans.—

(A) In general.—A defined benefit plan meets the requirements of this subsection if the accrued benefit derived from employer contributions of each participant who is a non-key employee, when expressed as an annual retirement benefit, is not less than the applicable percentage of the participant's average compensation for years in the testing period.

(B) Applicable percentage.—For purposes of subparagraph (A), the term "applicable percentage" means the lesser of—

(i) 2 percent multiplied by the number of years of service with the employer, or

(ii) 20 percent.

(C) Years of service.—For purposes of this paragraph—

(i) In general.—Except as provided in clause (ii), years of service shall be determined under the rules of paragraphs (4), (5), and (6) of section 411(a).

(ii) Exception for years during which plan was not top-heavy.—A year of service with the employer shall not be taken into account under this paragraph if—

(I) the plan was not a top-heavy plan for any plan year ending during such year of service, or

(II) such year of service was completed in a plan year beginning before January 1, 1984.

(D) Average compensation for high 5 years.—For purposes of this paragraph—

(i) In general.—A participant's testing period shall be the period of consecutive years (not exceeding 5) during which the participant had the greatest aggregate compensation from the employer.

(ii) Year must be included in year of service.—The years taken into account under clause (i) shall be properly adjusted for years not included in a year of service.

(iii) Certain years not taken into account.—Except to the extent provided in the plan, a year shall not be taken into account under clause (i) if—

(I) such year ends in a plan year beginning before January 1, 1984, or

(II) such year begins after the close of the last year in which the plan was a top-heavy plan.

(E) Annual retirement benefit.—For purposes of this paragraph, the term "annual retirement benefit" means a benefit payable annually in the form of a single life annuity (with no ancillary benefits) beginning at the normal retirement age under the plan.

(2) Defined contribution plans.—

(A) In general.—A defined contribution plan meets the requirements of the subsection if the employer contribution for the year for each participant who is a non-key employee is not less than 3 percent of such participant's compensation (within the meaning of section 415).

(B) Special rule where maximum contribution less than 3 percent.—

(i) In general.—The percentage referred to in subparagraph (A) for any year shall not exceed the percentage at which contributions are made (or required to be made) under the plan for the year for the key employee for whom such percentage is the highest for the year.

(ii) Determination of percentage.—The determination referred to in clause (i) shall be determined for each key employee by dividing the contributions for such employee by so much of his total compensation for the year as does not exceed $200,000.

(iii) Treatment of aggregation groups.—

(I) For purposes of this subparagraph, all defined contribution plans required to be included in an aggregation group under subsection (g)(2)(A)(i) shall be treated as one plan.

(II) This subparagraph shall not apply to any plan required to be included in an aggregation group if such plan enables a defined benefit plan required to be included in such group to meet the requirements of section 401(a)(4) or 410.

(d) Not more than $200,000 in annual compensation taken into account.—

(1) In general.—A plan meets the requirements of this subsection if the annual compensation of each employee taken into account under the plan does not exceed the first $200,000.

* * *

(e) Plan must meet requirements without taking into account social security and similar contributions and benefits.—A top-heavy plan shall not be treated as meeting the requirement of subsection (b) or (c) unless such plan meets such requirement without taking into account contributions or benefits under chapter 2 (relating to tax on self-employment income), chapter 21 (relating to Federal Insurance Contributions Act), title II of the Social Security Act, or any other Federal or State law.

(f) Coordination where employer has 2 or more plans.—The Secretary shall prescribe such regulations as may be necessary or appropriate to carry out the purposes of this section where the employer has 2 or more plans including (but not limited to) regulations to prevent inappropriate omissions or required duplication of minimum benefits or contributions.

(g) Top-heavy plan defined.—For purposes of this section—

(1) In general.—

(A) Plans not required to be aggregated.—Except as provided in subparagraph (B), the term "top-heavy plan" means, with respect to any plan year—

(i) any defined benefit plan if, as of the determination date, the present value of the cumulative accrued benefits under the plan for key employees exceeds 60 percent of the present value of the cumulative accrued benefits under the plan for all employees, and

(ii) any defined contribution plan if, as of the determination date, the aggregate of the accounts of key employees under the plan exceeds 60 percent of the aggregate of the accounts of all employees under such plan.

(B) Aggregated plans.—Each plan of an employer required to be included in an aggregation group shall be treated as a top-heavy plan if such group is a top-heavy group.

(2) Aggregation.—For purposes of this subsection—

(A) Aggregation group.—

(i) Required aggregation.—The term "aggregation group" means—

(I) each plan of the employer in which a key employee is a participant, and

(II) each other plan of the employer which enables any plan described in subclause (I) to meet the requirements of section 401(a)(4) or 410.

(ii) **Permissive aggregation.**—The employer may treat any plan not required to be included in an aggregation group under clause (i) as being part of such group if such group would continue to meet the requirements of sections 401(a)(4) and 410 with such plan being taken into account.

(B) **Top-heavy group.**—The term "top-heavy group" means any aggregation group if—

(i) the sum (as of the determination date) of—

(I) the present value of the cumulative accrued benefits for key employees under all defined benefit plans included in such group, and

(II) the aggregate of the accounts of key employees under all defined contribution plans included in such group,

(ii) exceeds 60 percent of a similar sum determined for all employees.

(3) **Distributions during last 5 years taken into account.**—For purposes of determining—

(A) the present value of the cumulative accrued benefit for any employee, or

(B) the amount of the account of any employee, such present value or amount shall be increased by the aggregate distributions made with respect to such employee under the plan during the 5-year period ending on the determination date. The preceding sentence shall also apply to distributions under a terminated plan which if it had not been terminated would have been required to be included in an aggregation group.

(4) **Other special rules.**—For purposes of this subsection—

(A) **Rollover contributions to plan not taken into account.**—Except to the extent provided in regulations, any rollover contribution (or similar transfer) initiated by the employee and made after December 31, 1983, to a plan shall not be taken into account with respect to the transferee plan for purposes of determining whether such plan is a top-heavy plan (or whether any aggregation group which includes such plan is a top-heavy group).

(B) **Benefits not taken into account if employee ceases to be key employee.**—If any individual is a non-key employee with respect to any plan for any plan year, but such individual was a key employee with respect to such plan for any prior plan year, any accrued benefit for such employee (and the account of such employee) shall not be taken into account.

(C) **Determination date.**—The term "determination date" means, with respect to any plan year—

(i) the last day of the preceding plan year, or

(ii) in the case of the first plan year of any plan, the last day of such plan year.

(D) **Years.**—To the extent provided in regulations, this section shall be applied on the basis of any year specified in such regulations in lieu of plan years.

(E) **Benefits not taken into account if employee not employed for last 5 years.**—If any individual has not performed services for the employer maintaining the plan at any time during the 5–year period ending on the determination

423

date, any accrued benefit for such individual (and the account of such individual) shall not be taken into account.

(h) Adjustments in section 415 limits for top-heavy plans.—

(1) In general.—In the case of any top-heavy plan, paragraphs (2)(B) and (3)(B) of section 415(e) shall be applied by substituting "1.0" for "1.25".

(2) Exception where benefits for key employees do not exceed 90 percent of total benefits and additional contributions are made for non-key employees.—Paragraph (1) shall not apply with respect to any top-heavy plan if the requirements of subparagraphs (A) and (B) of this paragraph are met with respect to such plan.

(A) Minimum benefit requirements.—

(i) In general.—The requirements of this subparagraph are met with respect to any top-heavy plan if such plan (and any plan required to be included in an aggregation group with such plan) meets the requirements of subsection (c) as modified by clause (ii).

(ii) Modifications.—For purposes of clause (i)—

(I) paragraph (1)(B) of subsection (c) shall be applied by substituting "3 percent" for "2 percent", and by increasing (but not by more than 10 percentage points) 20 percent by 1 percentage point for each year for which such plan was taken into account under this subsection, and

(II) paragraph (2)(A) shall be applied by substituting "4 percent" for "3 percent".

(B) Benefits for key employees cannot exceed 90 percent of total benefits.—A plan meets the requirements of this subparagraph if such plan would not be a top-heavy plan if "90 percent" were substituted for "60 percent" each place it appears in paragraphs (1)(A) and (2)(B) of subsection (g).

(3) Transition rule.—If, but for this paragraph, paragraph (1) would begin to apply with respect to any top-heavy plan, the application of paragraph (1) shall be suspended with respect to any individual so long as there are no—

(A) employer contributions, forfeitures, or voluntary nondeductible contributions allocated to such individual, or

(B) accruals for such individual under the defined benefit plan.

* * *

(i) Definitions.—For purposes of this section—

(1) Key employee.—

(A) In general.—The term "key employee" means an employee who, at any time during the plan year or any of the 4 preceding plan years, is—

(i) an officer of the employer having an annual compensation greater than 150 percent of the amount in effect under section 415(c)(1)(A) for any such plan year,

(ii) 1 of the 10 employees having annual compensation from the employer of more than the limitation in effect under section 415(c)(1)(A) and owning (or considered as owning within the meaning of section 318) the largest interests in the employer,

(iii) a 5-percent owner of the employer, or

(iv) a 1-percent owner of the employer having an annual compensation from the employer of more than $150,000.

For purposes of clause (i), no more than 50 employees (or, if lesser, the greater of 3 or 10 percent of the employees) shall be treated as officers. For purposes of clause (ii), if 2 employees have the same interest in the employer, the employee having greater annual compensation from the employer shall be treated as having a larger interest. Such term shall not include any officer or employee of an entity referred to in section 414(d) (relating to governmental plans).

(B) Percentage owners.—

(i) 5-percent owner.—For purposes of this paragraph, the term "5-percent owner" means—

(I) if the employer is a corporation, any person who owns (or is considered as owning within the meaning of section 318) more than 5 percent of the outstanding stock of the corporation or stock possessing more than 5 percent of the total combined voting power of all stock of the corporation, or

(II) if the employer is not a corporation, any person who owns more than 5 percent of the capital or profits interest in the employer.

(ii) 1-percent owner.—For purposes of this paragraph, the term "1-percent owner" means any person who would be described in clause (i) if "1 percent" were substituted for "5 percent" each place it appears in clause (i).

(iii) Constructive ownership rules.—For purposes of this subparagraph and subparagraph (A)(ii)—

(I) subparagraph (C) of section 318(a)(2) shall be applied by substituting "5 percent" for "50 percent", and

(II) in the case of any employer which is not a corporation, ownership in such employer shall be determined in accordance with regulations prescribed by the Secretary which shall be based on principles similar to the principles of section 318 (as modified by subclause (I)).

(C) Aggregation rules do not apply for purposes of determining ownership in the employer.—The rules of subsections (b), (c), and (m) of section 414 shall not apply for purposes of determining ownership in the employer.

(2) Non-key employee.—The term "non-key employee" means any employee who is not a key employee.

(3) Self-employed individuals.—In the case of a self-employed individual described in section 401(c)(1)—

(A) such individual shall be treated as an employee, and

(B) such individual's earned income (within the meaning of section 401(c)(2)) shall be treated as compensation.

* * *

(5) Treatment of beneficiaries.—The terms "employee" and "key employee" include their beneficiaries.

(6) Treatment of simplified employee pensions.—

(A) Treatment as defined contribution plans.—A simplified employee pension shall be treated as a defined contribution plan.

(B) Election to have determinations based on employer contributions. —In the case of a simplified employee pension, at the election of the employer, paragraphs (1)(A)(ii) and (2)(B) of subsection (g) shall be applied by taking into account aggregate employer contributions in lieu of the aggregate of the accounts of employees.

Amendment of Section

Pub.L. 99–514, Title XI, § 1106(d)(3)(A), (B), Oct. 22, 1986, 100 Stat. ——, provided that, except as otherwise provided, applicable to benefits accruing in years beginning after Dec. 31, 1988, this section is amended as follows:

(A) Subsection (a) of section 416 is amended by inserting "and" at the end of paragraph (1), by striking out ", and" at the end of paragraph (2) and inserting in lieu thereof a period, and by striking out paragraph (3).

(B)(i) Subsection (d) of section 416 is hereby repealed.

(ii) Section 416(c)(2)(B) is amended by striking out clause (ii) and by redesignating clause (iii) as clause (ii).

§ 417. Definitions and special rules for purposes of minimum survivor annuity requirements

(a) Election to waive qualified joint and survivor annuity or qualified preretirement survivor annuity.—

(1) In general.—A plan meets the requirements of section 401(a)(11) only if—

(A) under the plan, each participant—

(i) may elect at any time during the applicable election period to waive the qualified joint and survivor annuity form of benefit or the qualified preretirement survivor annuity form of benefit (or both), and

(ii) may revoke any such election at any time during the applicable election period, and

(B) the plan meets the requirements of paragraphs (2), (3), and (4) of this subsection.

(2) Spouse must consent to election.—Each plan shall provide that an election under paragraph (1)(A)(i) shall not take effect unless—

(A)(i) the spouse of the participant consents in writing to such election, (ii) such election designates a beneficiary (or a form of benefits) which may not be changed without spousal consent (or the consent of the spouse expressly permits designations by the participant without any requirement of further consent by the spouse), and (iii) the spouse's consent acknowledges the effect of such election and is witnessed by a plan representative or a notary public, or

(B) it is established to the satisfaction of a plan representative that the consent required under subparagraph (A) may not be obtained because there is no spouse, because the spouse cannot be located, or because of such other circumstances as the Secretary may by regulations prescribe.

Any consent by a spouse (or establishment that the consent of a spouse may not be obtained) under the preceding sentence shall be effective only with respect to such spouse.

(3) Plan to provide written explanations.—

(A) Explanation of joint and survivor annuity.—Each plan shall provide to each participant, within a reasonable period of time before the annuity starting date (and consistent with such regulations as the Secretary may prescribe), a written explanation of—

(i) the terms and conditions of the qualified joint and survivor annuity,

(ii) the participant's right to make, and the effect of, an election under paragraph (1) to waive the joint and survivor annuity form of benefit,

(iii) the rights of the participant's spouse under paragraph (2), and

(iv) the right to make, and the effect of, a revocation of an election under paragraph (1).

(B) Explanation of qualified preretirement survivor annuity.—

(i) In general.—Each plan shall provide to each participant, within the applicable period with respect to such participant (and consistent with such regulations as the Secretary may prescribe), a written explanation with respect to the qualified preretirement survivor annuity comparable to that required under subparagraph (A).

(ii) Applicable period.—For purposes of clause (i), the term "applicable period" means, with respect to a participant, whichever of the following periods ends last:

(I) The period beginning with the first day of the plan year in which the participant attains age 32 and ending with the close of the plan year preceding the plan year in which the participant attains age 35.

(II) A reasonable period after the individual becomes a participant.

(III) A reasonable period ending after paragraph (5) ceases to apply to the participant.

(IV) A reasonable period ending after section 401(a)(11) applies to the participant.

(V) A reasonable period after separation from service in case of a participant who separates before attaining age 35.

(4) Requirement of spousal consent for using plan assets as security for loans.—Each plan shall provide that, if section 401(a)(11) applies to a participant when part or all of the participant's accrued benefit is to be used as security for a loan, no portion of the participant's accrued benefit may be used as security for such loan unless—

(A) the spouse of the participant (if any) consents in writing to such use during the 90-day period ending on the date on which the loan is to be so secured, and

(B) requirements comparable to the requirements of paragraph (2) are met with respect to such consent.

(5) Special rules where plan fully subsidizes costs.—

(A) In general.—The requirements of this subsection shall not apply with respect to the qualified joint and survivor annuity form of benefit or the qualified preretirement survivor annuity form of benefit, as the case may be, if such benefit may not be waived (or another beneficiary selected and if the plan fully subsidizes the costs of such benefit.

(B) Definition.—For purposes of subparagraph (A), a plan fully subsidizes the costs of a benefit if under the plan the failure to waive such benefit by a participant would not result in a decrease in any plan benefits with respect to such participant and would not result in increased contributions from such participant.

(6) Applicable election period defined.—For purposes of this subsection, the term "applicable election period" means—

(A) in the case of an election to waive the qualified joint and survivor annuity form of benefit, the 90-day period ending on the annuity starting date, or

(B) in the case of an election to waive the qualified preretirement survivor annuity, the period which begins on the first day of the plan year in which the participant attains age 35 and ends on the date of the participant's death.

In the case of a participant who is separated from service, the applicable election period under subparagraph (B) with respect to benefits accrued before the date of such separation from service shall not begin later than such date.

(b) Definition of qualified joint and survivor annuity.—For purposes of this section and section 401(a)(11), the term "qualified joint and survivor annuity" means an annuity—

(1) for the life of the participant with a survivor annuity for the life of the spouse which is not less than 50 percent of (and is not greater than 100 percent of) the amount of the annuity which is payable during the joint lives of the participant and the spouse, and

(2) which is the actuarial equivalent of a single annuity for the life of the participant.

Such term also includes any annuity in a form having the effect of an annuity described in the preceding sentence.

(c) Definition of qualified preretirement survivor annuity.—For purposes of this section and section 401(a)(11)—

(1) In general.—Except as provided in paragraph (2), the term "qualified preretirement survivor annuity" means a survivor annuity for the life of the surviving spouse of the participant if—

(A) the payments to the surviving spouse under such annuity are not less than the amounts which would be payable as a survivor annuity under the qualified joint and survivor annuity under the plan (or the actuarial equivalent thereof) if—

(i) in the case of a participant who dies after the date on which the participant attained the earliest retirement age, such participant had retired with an immediate qualified joint and survivor annuity on the day before the participant's date of death, or

(ii) in the case of a participant who dies on or before the date on which the participant would have attained the earliest retirement age, such participant had—

(I) separated from service on the date of death,

(II) survived to the earliest retirement age,

(III) retired with an immediate qualified joint and survivor annuity at the earliest retirement age, and

(IV) died on the day after the day on which such participant would have attained the earliest retirement age, and

(B) under the plan, the earliest period for which the surviving spouse may receive a payment under such annuity is not later than the month in which the participant would have attained the earliest retirement age under the plan.

In the case of an individual who separated from service before the date of such individual's death, subparagraph (A)(ii)(I) shall not apply.

(2) Special rule for defined contribution plans.—In the case of any defined contribution plan or participant described in clause (ii) or (iii) of section 401(a)(11)(B), the term "qualified preretirement survivor annuity" means an annuity for the life of the surviving spouse the actuarial equivalent of which is not less than 50 percent of the portion of the account balance of the participant (as of the date of death) to which the participant had a nonforfeitable right (within the meaning of section 411(a)).

(3) Security interests taken into account.—For purposes of paragraphs (1) and (2), any security interest held by the plan by reason of a loan outstanding to the participant shall be taken into account in determining the amount of the qualified preretirement survivor annuity.

(d) Survivor annuities need not be provided if participant and spouse married less than 1 year.--

(1) In general.—Except as provided in paragraph (2), a plan shall not be treated as failing to meet the requirements of section 401(a)(11) merely because the plan provides that a qualified joint and survivor annuity (or a qualified preretirement survivor annuity) will not be provided unless the participant and spouse had been married throughout the 1-year period ending on the earlier of—

(A) the participant's annuity starting date, or

(B) the date of the participant's death.

(2) Treatment of certain marriages within 1 year of annuity starting date for purposes of qualified joint and survivor annuities.—For purposes of paragraph (1), if—

(A) a participant marries within 1 year before the annuity starting date, and

(B) the participant and the participant's spouse in such marriage have been married for at least a 1-year period ending on or before the date of the participant's death,

such participant and such spouse shall be treated as having been married throughout the 1-year period ending on the participant's annuity starting date.

(e) Restrictions on cash-outs.—

(1) Plan may require distribution if present value not in excess of $3,500. —A plan may provide that the present value of a qualified joint and survivor annuity or a qualified preretirement survivor annuity will be immediately distributed if such value does not exceed $3,500. No distribution may be made under the preceding sentence after the annuity starting date unless the participant and the spouse of the participant (or where the participant has died, the surviving spouse) consents in writing to such distribution.

(2) Plan may distribute benefit in excess of $3,500 only with consent.—If—

(A) the present value of the qualified joint and survivor annuity or the qualified preretirement survivor annuity exceeds $3,500, and

(B) the participant and the spouse of the participant (or where the participant has died, the surviving spouse) consent in writing to the distribution,

the plan may immediately distribute the present value of such annuity.

(3) Determination of present value.—

(A) In general.—For purposes of paragraphs (1) and (2), the present value shall be calculated—

(i) by using an interest rate no greater than the applicable interest rate if the vested accrued benefit (using such rate) is not in excess of $25,000, and

(ii) by using an interest rate no greater than 120 percent of the applicable interest rate if the vested accrued benefit exceeds $25,000 (as determined under clause (i)).

In no event shall the present value determined under subclause (II) be less than $25,000.

(B) Applicable interest rate.—For purposes of subparagraph (A), the term "applicable interest rate" means the interest rate which would be used (as of the date of the distribution) by the Pension Benefit Guaranty Corporation for purposes of determining the present value of a lump sum distribution on plan termination.

(f) Other definitions and special rules.—For purposes of this section and section 401(a)(11)—

(1) Vested participant.—The term "vested participant" means any participant who has a nonforfeitable right (within the meaning of section 411(a)) to any portion of such participant's accrued benefit.

(2) Annuity starting date.—

(A) In general.—The term "annuity starting date" means—

(i) the first day of the first period for which an amount is payable as an annuity, or

(ii) in the case of a benefit not payable in the form of an annuity, the first day on which all events have occurred which entitle the participant to such benefit.

(B) Special rule for disability benefits.—For purposes of subparagraph (A), the first day of the first period for which a benefit is to be received by reason of disability shall be treated as the annuity starting date only if such benefit is not an auxiliary benefit.

(3) Earliest retirement age.—The term "earliest retirement age" means the earliest date on which, under the plan, the participant could elect to receive retirement benefits.

(4) Plan may take into account increased costs.—A plan may take into account in any equitable manner (as determined by the Secretary) any increased costs resulting from providing a qualified joint or survivor annuity or a qualified preretirement survivor annuity.

(5) Distributions by reason of security interests.—If the use of any participant's accrued benefit (or any portion thereof) as security for a loan meets the requirements of subsection (a)(4), nothing in this section or section 411(a)(11) shall prevent any distribution required by reason of a failure to comply with the terms of such loan.

(6) Requirements for certain spousal consents.—No consent of a spouse shall be effective for purposes of subsection (e)(1) or (e)(2) (as the case may be) unless requirements comparable to the requirements for spousal consent to an election under subsection (a)(1)(A) are met.

Subpart D—Treatment of Welfare Benefit Funds

§ 419. Treatment of funded welfare benefit plans

(a) General rule.—Contributions paid or accrued by an employer to a welfare benefit fund—

(1) shall not be deductible under this subchapter, but

(2) if they would otherwise be deductible, shall (subject to the limitation of subsection (b)) be deductible under this section for the taxable year in which paid.

(b) Limitation.—The amount of the deduction allowable under subsection (a)(2) for any taxable year shall not exceed the welfare benefit fund's qualified cost for the taxable year.

(c) Qualified cost.—For purposes of this section—

(1) In general.—Except as otherwise provided in this subsection, the term "qualified cost" means, with respect to any taxable year, the sum of—

(A) the qualified direct cost for such taxable year, and

(B) subject to the limitation of section 419A(b), any addition to a qualified asset account for the taxable year.

(2) Reduction for funds after-tax income.—In the case of any welfare benefit fund, the qualified cost for any taxable year shall be reduced by such fund's after-tax income for such taxable year.

(3) Qualified direct cost.—

(A) In general.—The term "qualified direct cost" means, with respect to any taxable year, the aggregate amount (including administrative expenses) which would have been allowable as a deduction to the employer with respect to the benefits provided during the taxable year, if—

(i) such benefits were provided directly by the employer, and

(ii) the employer used the cash receipts and disbursements method of accounting.

(B) Time when benefits provided.—For purposes of subparagraph (A), a benefit shall be treated as provided when such benefit would be includible in the gross income of the employee if provided directly by the employer (or would be so includible but for any provision of this chapter excluding such benefit from gross income).

(C) 60-month amortization of child care facilities.—

(i) In general.—In determining qualified direct costs with respect to any child care facility for purposes of subparagraph (A), in lieu of depreciation the adjusted basis of such facility shall be allowable as a deduction ratably over a period of 60 months beginning with the month in which the facility is placed in service.

(ii) Child care facility.—The term "child care facility" means any tangible property which qualifies under regulations prescribed by the Secretary as a child care center primarily for children of employees of the employer; except that such term shall not include any property—

(I) not of a character subject to depreciation; or

(II) located outside the United States.

(4) After-tax income.—

(A) In general.—The term "after-tax income" means, with respect to any taxable year, the gross income of the welfare benefit fund reduced by the sum of—

(i) the deductions allowed by this chapter which are directly connected with the production of such gross income, and

(ii) the tax imposed by this chapter on the fund for the taxable year.

(B) Treatment of certain amounts.—In determining the gross income of any welfare benefit fund—

431

(i) contributions and other amounts received from employees shall be taken into account, but

(ii) contributions from the employer shall not taken into account.

(5) Item only taken into account once.—No item may be taken into account more than once in determining the qualified cost of any welfare benefit fund.

(d) Carryover of excess contributions.—If—

(1) the amount of the contributions paid (or deemed paid under this subsection) by the employer during any taxable year to a welfare benefit fund, exceeds

(2) the limitation of subsection (b),

such excess shall be treated as an amount paid by the employer to such fund during the succeeding taxable year.

(e) Welfare benefit fund.—For purposes of this section—

(1) In general.—The term "welfare benefit fund" means any fund—

(A) which is part of a plan of an employer, and

(B) through which the employer provides welfare benefits to employees or their beneficiaries.

(2) Welfare benefit.—The term "welfare benefit" means any benefit other than a benefit with respect to which—

(A) section 83(h) applies,

(B) section 404 applies (determined without regard to section 404(b)(2))

(C) section 404A applies, or

(D) an election under section 463 applies.

(3) Fund.—The term "fund" means—

(A) any organization described in paragraph (7), (9), (17), or (20) of section 501(c),

(B) any trust, corporation, or other organization not exempt from the tax imposed by this chapter, and

(C) to the extent provided in regulations, any account held for an employer by any person.

(f) Method of contributions, etc., having the effect of a plan.—If—

(1) there is no plan, but

(2) there is a method or arrangement of employer contributions or benefits which has the effect of a plan,

this section shall apply as if there were a plan.

(g) Extension to plans for independent contractors.—If any fund would be a welfare benefit fund (as modified by subsection (f)) but for the fact that there is no employee-employer relationship—

(1) this section shall apply as if there were such a relationship, and

(2) any reference in this section to the employer shall be treated as a reference to the person for whom services are provided, and any reference in this section to an employee shall be treated as a reference to the person providing the services.

SUBCHAPTER E—ACCOUNTING PERIODS AND METHODS OF ACCOUNTING

Part

PART I—ACCOUNTING PERIODS

§ 441. Period for computation of taxable income

(a) Computation of taxable income.—Taxable income shall be computed on the basis of the taxpayer's taxable year.

(b) Taxable year.—For purposes of this subtitle, the term "taxable year" means—

(1) the taxpayer's annual accounting period, if it is a calendar year or a fiscal year;

(2) the calendar year, if subsection (g) applies;

(3) the period for which the return is made, if a return is made for a period of less than 12 months; or

* * *

(c) Annual accounting period.—For purposes of this subtitle, the term "annual accounting period" means the annual period on the basis of which the taxpayer regularly computes his income in keeping his books.

(d) Calendar year.—For purposes of this subtitle, the term "calendar year" means a period of 12 months ending on December 31.

(e) Fiscal year.—For purposes of this subtitle, the term "fiscal year" means a period of 12 months ending on the last day of any month other than December. In the case of any taxpayer who has made the election provided by subsection (f), the term means the annual period (varying from 52 to 53 weeks) so elected.

(f) Election of year consisting of 52–53 weeks.—

(1) **General rule.**—A taxpayer who, in keeping his books, regularly computes his income on the basis of an annual period which varies from 52 to 53 weeks and ends always on the same day of the week and ends always—

(A) on whatever date such same day of the week last occurs in a calendar month, or

(B) on whatever date such same day of the weeks falls which is nearest to the last day of a calendar month,

may (in accordance with the regulations prescribed under paragraph (3)) elect to compute his taxable income for purposes of this subtitle on the basis of such annual period. This paragraph shall apply to taxable years ending after the date of the enactment of this title.

(2) **Special rules for 52–53-week year.—**

(A) **Effective dates.**—In any case in which the effective date or the applicability of any provision of this title is expressed in terms of taxable years beginning, including, or ending with reference to a specified date which is the first or last day of a month, a taxable year described in paragraph (1) shall (except for purposes of the computation under section 15) be treated—

    (i) as beginning with the first day of the calendar month beginning nearest to the first day of such taxable year, or

    (ii) as ending with the last day of the calendar month ending nearest to the last day of such taxable year,

as the case may be.

(B) Change in accounting period.—In the case of a change from or to a taxable year described in paragraph (1)—

    (i) if such change results in a short period (within the meaning of section 443) of 359 days or more, or of less than 7 days, section 443(b) (relating to alternative tax computation) shall not apply;

    (ii) if such change results in a short period of less than 7 days, such short period shall, for purposes of this subtitle, be added to and deemed a part of the following taxable year; and

    (iii) if such change results in a short period to which subsection (b) of section 443 applies, the taxable income for such short period shall be placed on an annual basis for purposes of such subsection by multiplying the gross income for such short period (minus the deductions allowed by this chapter for the short period, but only the adjusted amount of the deductions for personal exemptions as described in section 443(c)) by 365, by dividing the result by the number of days in the short period, and the tax shall be the same part of the tax computed on the annual basis as the number of days in the short period is of 365 days.

(3) Special rule for partnerships, S corporations, and personal service corporations.—The Secretary may by regulation provide terms and conditions for the application of this subsection to a partnership, S corporation, or personal service corporation (within the meaning of section 441(i)(2)).

(4) Regulations.—The Secretary shall prescribe such regulations as he deems necessary for the application of this subsection.

(g) No books kept; no accounting period.—Except as provided in section 443 (relating to returns for periods of less than 12 months), the taxpayer's taxable year shall be the calendar year if—

    (1) the taxpayer keeps no books;

    (2) the taxpayer does not have an annual accounting period; or

    (3) the taxpayer has an annual accounting period, but such period does not qualify as a fiscal year.

* * *

(i) Taxable year of personal service corporations.—

(1) In general.—For purposes of this subtitle, the taxable year of any personal service corporation shall be the calendar year unless the corporation establishes, to the satisfaction of the Secretary, a business purpose for having a different period for its taxable year. For purposes of this paragraph, any deferral of income to shareholders shall not be treated as a business purpose.

(2) Personal service corporation.—For purposes of this subsection, the term "personal service corporation" has the meaning given such term by section 269A(b)(1), except that section 269A(b)(2) shall be applied—

    (A) by substituting "any" for "more than 10 percent", and

(B) by substituting "any" for "50 percent or more in value" in section 318(a)(2)(C).

§ 442. Change of annual accounting period

If a taxpayer changes his annual accounting period, the new accounting period shall become the taxpayer's taxable year only if the change is approved by the Secretary. For purposes of this subtitle, if a taxpayer to whom section 441(g) applies adopts an annual accounting period (as defined in section 441(c)) other than a calendar year, the taxpayer shall be treated as having changed his annual accounting period.

§ 443. Returns for a period of less than 12 months

(a) **Returns for short period.**—A return for a period of less than 12 months (referred to in this section as "short period") shall be made under any of the following circumstances:

(1) **Change of annual accounting period.**—When the taxpayer, with the approval of the Secretary, changes his annual accounting period. In such a case, the return shall be made for the short period beginning on the day after the close of the former taxable year and ending at the close of the day before the day designated as the first day of the new taxable year.

(2) **Taxpayer not in existence for entire taxable year.**—When the taxpayer is in existence during only part of what would otherwise be his taxable year.

(b) **Computation of tax on change of annual accounting period.**—

(1) **General rule.**—If a return is made under paragraph (1) of subsection (a), the taxable income for the short period shall be placed on an annual basis by multiplying the modified taxable income for such short period by 12, dividing the result by the number of months in the short period. The tax shall be the same part of the tax computed on the annual basis as the number of months in the short period is of 12 months.

(2) **Exception.**—

(A) **Computation based on 12-month period.**—If the taxpayer applies for the benefits of this paragraph and establishes the amount of his taxable income for the 12-month period described in subparagraph (B), computed as if that period were a taxable year and under the law applicable to that year, then the tax for the short period, computed under paragraph (1), shall be reduced to the greater of the following:

(i) an amount which bears the same ratio to the tax computed on the taxable income for the 12-month period as the modified taxable income computed on the basis of the short period bears to the modified taxable income for the 12-month period; or

(ii) the tax computed on the modified taxable income for the short period.

The taxpayer (other than a taxpayer to whom subparagraph (B)(ii) applies) shall compute the tax and file his return without the application of this paragraph.

435

(B) 12-month period.—The 12-month period referred to in subparagraph (A) shall be—

(i) the period of 12 months beginning on the first day of the short period, or

(ii) the period of 12 months ending at the close of the last day of the short period, if at the end of the 12 months referred to in clause (i) the taxpayer is not in existence or (if a corporation) has theretofore disposed of substantially all of its assets.

(C) Application for benefits.—Application for the benefits of this paragraph shall be made in such manner and at such time as the regulations prescribed under subparagraph (D) may require; except that the time so prescribed shall not be later than the time (including extensions) for filing the return for the first taxable year which ends on or after the day which is 12 months after the first day of the short period. Such application, in case the return was filed without regard to this paragraph, shall be considered a claim for credit or refund with respect to the amount by which the tax is reduced under this paragraph.

(D) Regulations.—The Secretary shall prescribe such regulations as he deems necessary for the application of this paragraph.

(3) Modified taxable income defined.—For purposes of this subsection the term "modified taxable income" means, with respect to any period, the gross income for such period minus the deductions allowed by this chapter for such period (but, in the case of a short period, only the adjusted amount of the deductions for personal exemptions).

(c) Adjustment in deduction for personal exemption.—In the case of a taxpayer other than a corporation, if a return is made for a short period by reason of subsection (a)(1) and if the tax is not computed under subsection (b)(2), then the exemptions allowed as a deduction under section 151 (and any deduction in lieu thereof) shall be reduced to amounts which bear the same ratio to the full exemptions as the number of months in the short period bears to 12.

(d) Adjustment in computing minimum tax and tax preferences.—If a return is made for a short period by reason of subsection (a)—

(1) the alternative minimum taxable income for the short period shall be placed on an annual basis by multiplying such amount by 12 and dividing the result by the number of months in the short period, and

(2) the amount computed under paragraph (1) of section 55(a) shall bear the same relation to the tax computed on the annual basis as the number of months in the short period bears to 12.

* * *

PART II—METHODS OF ACCOUNTING

Subpart
A. Methods of accounting in general.
B. Taxable year for which items of gross income included.
C. Taxable year for which deductions taken.
D. Inventories.

§ 446. General rule for methods of accounting

(a) **General rule.**—Taxable income shall be computed under the method of accounting on the basis of which the taxpayer regularly computes his income in keeping his books.

(b) **Exceptions.**—If no method of accounting has been regularly used by the taxpayer, or if the method used does not clearly reflect income, the computation of taxable income shall be made under such method as, in the opinion of the Secretary, does clearly reflect income.

(c) **Permissible methods.**—Subject to the provisions of subsections (a) and (b), a taxpayer may compute taxable income under any of the following methods of accounting—

    (1) the cash receipts and disbursements method;

    (2) an accrual method;

    (3) any other method permitted by this chapter; or

    (4) any combination of the foregoing methods permitted under regulations prescribed by the Secretary.

(d) **Taxpayer engaged in more than one business.**—A taxpayer engaged in more than one trade or business may, in computing taxable income, use a different method of accounting for each trade or business.

(e) **Requirement respecting change of accounting method.**—Except as otherwise expressly provided in this chapter, a taxpayer who changes the method of accounting on the basis of which he regularly computes his income in keeping his books shall, before computing his taxable income under the new method, secure the consent of the Secretary.

(f) **Failure to request change of method of accounting.**—If the taxpayer does not file with the Secretary a request to change the method of accounting, the absence of the consent of the Secretary to a change in the method of accounting shall not be taken into account—

    (1) to prevent the imposition of any penalty, or the addition of any amount to tax, under this title, or

    (2) to diminish the amount of such penalty or addition to tax.

§ 448. Limitation on use of cash method of accounting

(a) **General rule.**—Except as otherwise provided in this section, in the case of a—

    (1) C corporation,

    (2) partnership which has a C corporation as a partner, or

    (3) tax shelter,

taxable income shall not be computed under the cash receipts and disbursements method of accounting.

(b) **Exceptions.—**

    (1) **Farming business.**—Paragraphs (1) and (2) of subsection (a) shall not apply to any farming business.

(2) Qualified personal service corporations.—Paragraphs (1) and (2) of subsection (a) shall not apply to a qualified personal service corporation, and such a corporation shall be treated as an individual for purposes of determining whether paragraph (2) of subsection (a) applies to any partnership.

(3) Entities with gross receipts of not more than $5,000,000.—Paragraphs (1) and (2) of subsection (a) shall not apply to any corporation or partnership for any taxable year if, for all prior taxable years beginning after December 31, 1985, such entity (or any predecessor) met the $5,000,000 gross receipts test of subsection (c).

(c) $5,000,000 gross receipts test.—For purposes of this section—

(1) In general.—A corporation or partnership meets the $5,000,000 gross receipts test of this subsection for any prior taxable year if the average annual gross receipts of such entity for the 3–taxable-year period ending with such prior taxable year does not exceed $5,000,000.

(2) Aggregation rules.—All persons treated as a single employer under subsection (a) or (b) of section 52 or subsection (m) or (o) of section 414 shall be treated as one person for purposes of paragraph (1).

(3) Special rules.—For purposes of this subsection—

(A) Not in existence for entire 3–year period.—If the entity was not in existence for the entire 3–year period referred to in paragraph (1), such paragraph shall be applied on the basis of the period during which such entity (or trade or business) was in existence.

(B) Short taxable years.—Gross receipts for any taxable year of less than 12 months shall be annualized by multiplying the gross receipts for the short period by 12 and dividing the result by the number of months in the short period.

(C) Gross receipts.—Gross receipts for any taxable year shall be reduced by returns and allowances made during such year.

(d) Definitions and special rules.—For purposes of this section—

(1) Farming business.—

(A) In general.—The term "farming business" means the trade or business of farming (within the meaning of section 263A(e)(4)).

(B) Timber and ornamental trees.—The term "farming business" includes the raising, harvesting, or growing of trees to which section 263A(c)(5) applies.

(2) Qualified personal service corporation.—The term "qualified personal service corporation" means any corporation—

(A) substantially all of the activities of which involve the performance of services in the fields of health, law, engineering, architecture, accounting, actuarial science, performing arts, or consulting, and

(B) substantially all of the stock of which (by value) is held directly or indirectly by—

(i) employees performing services for such corporation in connection with the activities involving a field referred to in subparagraph (A),

(ii) retired employees who had performed such services for such corporation,

(iii) the estate of any individual described in clause (i) or (ii), or

(iv) any other person who acquired such stock by reason of the death of an individual described in clause (i) or (ii) (but only for the 2–year period beginning on the date of the death of such individual).

(3) **Tax shelter defined.**—The term "tax shelter" has the meaning given such term by section 461(i)(3) (determined after application of paragraph (4) thereof).

(4) **Special rules for application of paragraph (2).**—For purposes of paragraph (2)—

(A) community property laws shall be disregarded,

(B) stock held by a plan described in section 401(a) which is exempt from tax under section 501(a) shall be treated as held by an employee described in paragraph (2)(B)(i), and

(C) at the election of the common parent of an affiliated group (within the meaning of section 1504(a)), all members of such group may be treated as 1 taxpayer for purposes of paragraph (2)(B) if substantially all of the activities of all such members involve the performance of services in the same field described in paragraph (2)(A).

(5) **Special rule for services.**—In the case of any person using an accrual method of accounting with respect to amounts to be received for the performance of services by such person, such person shall not be required to accrue any portion of such amounts which (on the basis of experience) will not be collected. This paragraph shall not apply to any amount if interest is required to be paid on such amount or there is any penalty for failure to timely pay such amount.

(6) **Treatment of certain trusts subject to tax on unrelated business income.**—For purposes of this section, a trust subject to tax under section 511(b) shall be treated as a C corporation with respect to its activities constituting an unrelated trade or business.

(7) **Coordination with section 481.**—In the case of any taxpayer required by this section to change its method of accounting for any taxable year—

(A) such change shall be treated as initiated by the taxpayer,

(B) such change shall be treated as made with the consent of the Secretary, and

(C) the period for taking into account the adjustments under section 481 by reason of such change—

(i) except as provided in clause (ii), shall not exceed 4 years, and

(ii) in the case of a hospital, shall be 10 years.

(Added Pub.L. 99–514, Title VIII, § 801(a), Oct. 22, 1986, 100 Stat. ——.)

Subpart B—Taxable Year for Which Items of Gross Income Included

§ 451. General rule for taxable year of inclusion

(a) **General rule.**—The amount of any item of gross income shall be included in the gross income for the taxable year in which received by the taxpayer, unless, under the method of accounting used in computing taxable income, such amount is to be properly accounted for as of a different period.

(b) **Special rule in case of death.**—In the case of the death of a taxpayer whose taxable income is computed under an accrual method of accounting, any amount accrued only by reason of the death of the taxpayer shall not be included in computing taxable income for the period in which falls the date of the taxpayer's death.

(c) **Special rule for employee tips.**—For purposes of subsection (a), tips included in a written statement furnished an employer by an employee pursuant to section

6053(a) shall be deemed to be received at the time the written statement including such tips is furnished to the employer.

(d) Special rule for crop insurance proceeds or disaster payments.—In the case of insurance proceeds received as a result of destruction or damage to crops, a taxpayer reporting on the cash receipts and disbursements method of accounting may elect to include such proceeds in income for the taxable year following the taxable year of destruction or damage, if he establishes that, under his practice, income from such crops would have been reported in a following taxable year. For purposes of the preceding sentence, payments received under the Agricultural Act of 1949, as amended, as a result of (1) destruction or damage to crops caused by drought, flood, or any other natural disaster, or (2) the inability to plant crops because of such a natural disaster shall be treated as insurance proceeds received as a result of destruction or damage to crops. An election under this subsection for any taxable year shall be made at such time and in such manner as the Secretary prescribes.

* * *

(f) Special rule for utility services.—

(1) In general.—In the case of a taxpayer the taxable income of which is computed under an accrual method of accounting, any income attributable to the sale or furnishing of utility services to customers shall be included in gross income not later than the taxable year in which such services are provided to such customers.

(2) Definition and special rule.—For purposes of this subsection—

(A) Utility services.—The term "utility services" includes—

(i) the providing of electrical energy, water, or sewage disposal,

(ii) the furnishing of gas or steam through a local distribution system,

(iii) telephone or other communication services, and

(iv) the transporting of gas or steam by pipeline.

(B) Year in which services provided.—The taxable year in which services are treated as provided to customers shall not, in any manner, be determined by reference to—

(i) the period in which the customers' meters are read, or

(ii) the period in which the taxpayer bills (or may bill) the customers for such service.

(f)[1] Treatment of interest on frozen deposits in certain financial institutions.—

(1) In general.—In the case of interest credited during any calendar year on a frozen deposit in a qualified financial institution, the amount of such interest includible in the gross income of a qualified individual shall not exceed the sum of—

(A) the net amount withdrawn by such individual from such deposit during such calendar year, and

(B) the amount of such deposit which is withdrawable as of the close of the taxable year (determined without regard to any penalty for premature withdrawals of a time deposit).

(2) Interest tested each year.—Any interest not included in gross income by reason of paragraph (1) shall be treated as credited in the next calendar year.

[1] Editor's Note: Probably should read "(g)".

§ 453. Installment method

(a) General rule.—Except as otherwise provided in this section, income from an installment sale shall be taken info account for purposes of this title under the installment method.

(b) Installment sale defined.—For purposes of this section—

(1) In general.—The term "installment sale" means a disposition of property where at least 1 payment is to be received after the close of the taxable year in which the disposition occurs.

(2) Exceptions.—The term "installment sale" does not include—

(A) Dealer disposition of personal property.—A disposition of personal property on the installment plan by a person who regularly sells or otherwise disposes of personal property on the installment plan.

(B) Inventories of personal property.—A disposition of personal property of a kind which is required to be included in the inventory of the taxpayer if on hand at the close of the taxable year.

(c) Installment method defined.—For purposes of this section, the term "installment method" means a method under which the income recognized for any taxable year from a disposition is that proportion of the payments received in that year which the gross profit (realized or to be realized when payment is completed) bears to the total contract price.

(d) Election out.—

(1) In general.—Subsection (a) shall not apply to any disposition if the taxpayer elects to have subsection (a) not apply to such disposition.

(2) Time and manner for making election.—Except as otherwise provided by regulations, an election under paragraph (1) with respect to a disposition may be made only on or before the due date prescribed by law (including extensions) for filing the taxpayer's return of the tax imposed by this chapter for the taxable year in which the disposition occurs. Such an election shall be made in the manner prescribed by regulations.

(3) Election revocable only with consent.—An election under paragraph (1) with respect to any disposition may be revoked only with the consent of the Secretary.

(e) Second dispositions by related persons.—

(1) In general.—If—

(A) any person disposes of property to a related person (hereinafter in this subsection referred to as the "first disposition"), and

(B) before the person making the first disposition receives all payments with respect to such disposition, the related person disposes of the property (hereinafter in this subsection referred to as the "second disposition"),

then, for purposes of this section, the amount realized with respect to such second disposition shall be treated as received at the time of the second disposition by the person making the first disposition.

(2) 2-year cutoff for property other than marketable securities.—

(A) In general.—Except in the case of marketable securities, paragraph (1) shall apply only if the date of the second disposition is not more than 2 years after the date of the first disposition.

(B) Substantial diminishing of risk of ownership.—The running of the 2-year period set forth in subparagraph (A) shall be suspended with respect to any property for any period during which the related person's risk of loss with respect to the property is substantially diminished by—

(i) the holding of a put with respect to such property (or similar property),

(ii) the holding by another person of a right to acquire the property, or

(iii) a short sale or any other transaction.

(3) Limitation on amount treated as received.—The amount treated for any taxable year as received by the person making the first disposition by reason of paragraph (1) shall not exceed the excess of—

(A) the lesser of—

(i) the total amount realized with respect to any second disposition of the property occurring before the close of the taxable year, or

(ii) the total contract price for the first disposition, over

(B) the sum of—

(i) the aggregate amount of payments received with respect to the first disposition before the close of such year, plus

(ii) the aggregate amount treated as received with respect to the first disposition for prior taxable years by reason of this subsection.

(4) Fair market value where disposition is not sale or exchange.—For purposes of this subsection, if the second disposition is not a sale or exchange, an amount equal to the fair market value of the property disposed of shall be substituted for the amount realized.

(5) Later payments treated as receipt of tax paid amounts.—If paragraph (1) applies for any taxable year, payments received in subsequent taxable years by the person making the first disposition shall not be treated as the receipt of payments with respect to the first disposition to the extent that the aggregate of such payments does not exceed the amount treated as received by reason of paragraph (1).

(6) Exception for certain dispositions.—For purposes of this subsection—

(A) Reacquisitions of stock by issuing corporation not treated as first dispositions.—Any sale or exchange of stock to the issuing corporation shall not be treated as a first disposition.

(B) Involuntary conversions not treated as second dispositions.—A compulsory or involuntary conversion (within the meaning of section 1033) and any transfer thereafter shall not be treated as a second disposition if the first disposition occurred before the threat or imminence of the conversion.

(C) Dispositions after death.—Any transfer after the earlier of—

(i) the death of the person making the first disposition, or

(ii) the death of the person acquiring the property in the first disposition,

and any transfer thereafter shall not be treated as a second disposition.

(7) Exception where tax avoidance not a principal purpose.—This subsection shall not apply to a second disposition (and any transfer thereafter) if it is established to the satisfaction of the Secretary that neither the first disposition nor the second disposition had as one of its principal purposes the avoidance of Federal income tax.

(8) Extension of statute of limitations.—The period for assessing a deficiency with respect to a first disposition (to the extent such deficiency is attributable to the application of this subsection) shall not expire before the day which is 2 years after the date on which the person making the first disposition furnishes (in such manner as the Secretary may by regulations prescribe) a notice that there was a second disposition of the property to which this subsection may have applied. Such deficiency may be assessed notwithstanding the provisions of any law or rule of law which would otherwise prevent such assessment.

(f) Definitions and special rules.—For purposes of this section—

(1) Related person.—Except for purposes of subsection (g) and (h), the term "related person" means—

(A) a person whose stock would be attributed under section 318(a) (other than paragraph (4) thereof) to the person first disposing of the property, or

(B) a person who bears a relationship described in section 267(b) to the person first disposing of the property.

(2) Marketable securities.—The term "marketable securities" means any security for which, as of the date of the disposition, there was a market on an established securities market or otherwise.

(3) Payment.—Except as provided in paragraph (4), the term "payment" does not include the receipt of evidences of indebtedness of the person acquiring the property (whether or not payment of such indebtedness is guaranteed by another person).

(4) Purchaser evidences of indebtedness payable on demand or readily tradable.—Receipt of a bond or other evidence of indebtedness which—

(A) is payable on demand, or

(B) is issued by a corporation or a government or political subdivision thereof and is readily tradable,

shall be treated as receipt of payment.

(5) Readily tradable defined.—For purposes of paragraph (4), the term "readily tradable" means a bond or other evidence of indebtedness which is issued—

(A) with interest coupons attached or in registered form (other than one in registered form which the taxpayer establishes will not be readily tradable in an established securities market), or

(B) in any other form designed to render such bond or other evidence of indebtedness readily tradable in an established securities market.

(6) Like-kind exchanges.—In the case of any exchange described in section 1031(b)—

(A) the total contract price shall be reduced to take into account the amount of any property permitted to be received in such exchange without recognition of gain,

(B) the gross profit from such exchange shall be reduced to take into account any amount not recognized by reason of section 1031(b), and

(C) the term "payment", when used in any provision of this section other than subsection (b)(1), shall not include any property permitted to be received in such exchange without recognition of gain.

Similar rules shall apply in the case of an exchange which is described in section 356(a) and is not treated as a dividend.

(7) **Depreciable property.**—The term "depreciable property" means property of a character which (in the hands of the transferee) is subject to the allowance for depreciation provided in section 167.

(8) **Payments to be received defined.**—The term "payment to be received" includes—

(A) the aggregate amount of all payments which are not contingent as to amount, and

(B) the fair market value of any payments which are contingent as to amount.

(g) **Sale of depreciable property to controlled entity.**—

(1) **In general.**—In the case of an installment sale of depreciable property between related persons (within the meaning of section 1239(b))—

(A) subsection (a) shall not apply, and

(B) for purposes of this title—

(i) except as provided in clause (ii), all payments to be received shall be treated as received in the year of the disposition, and

(ii) in the case of any payments which are contingent as to amount but with respect to which the fair market value may not be reasonably ascertained—

(I) the basis shall be recovered ratably, and

(II) the purchaser may not increase the basis of any property acquired in such sale by any amount before such time as the seller includes such amount in income.

(2) **Exception where tax avoidance not a principal purpose.**—Paragraph (1) shall not apply if it is established to the satisfaction of the Secretary that the disposition did not have as one of its principal purposes the avoidance of Federal income tax.

(h) **Use of installment method by shareholders in certain liquidations.**—

(1) **Receipt of obligations not treated as receipt of payment.**—

(A) **In general.**—If, in a liquidation to which section 331 applies, the shareholder receives (in exchange for the shareholder's stock) an installment obligation acquired in respect of a sale or exchange by the corporation during the 12-month period beginning on the date a plan of complete liquidation is adopted and the liquidation is completed during such 12-month period, then, for purposes of this section, the receipt of payments under such obligation (but not the receipt of such obligation) by the shareholder shall be treated as the receipt of payment for the stock.

(B) **Obligations attributable to sale of inventory must result from bulk sale.**—Subparagraph (A) shall not apply to an installment obligation acquired in respect of a sale or exchange of—

(i) stock in trade of the corporation,

(ii) other property of a kind which would properly be included in the inventory of the corporation if on hand at the close of the taxable year, and

(iii) property held by the corporation primarily for sale to customers in the ordinary course of its trade or business,

unless such sale or exchange is to one person and involves substantially all of such property attributable to a trade or business of the corporation.

(C) Special rule where obligor and shareholder are related persons.—If the obligor of any installment obligation and the shareholder are married to each other or are related persons (within the meaning of section 1239(b)), to the extent such installment obligation is attributable to the disposition by the corporation of depreciable property—

(i) subparagraph (A) shall not apply to such obligation, and

(ii) for purposes of this title, all payments to be received by the shareholder shall be deemed received in the year the shareholder receives the obligation.

(D) Coordination with subsection (e)(1)(A).—For purposes of subsection (e)(1)(A), disposition of property by the corporation shall be treated also as disposition of such property by the shareholder.

(E) Sales by liquidating subsidiaries.—For purposes of subparagraph (A), in the case of a controlling corporate shareholder (within the meaning of section 368(c)(1)) of a selling corporation, an obligation acquired in respect of a sale or exchange by the selling corporation shall be treated as so acquired by such controlling corporate shareholder. The preceding sentence shall be applied successively to each controlling corporate shareholder above such controlling corporate shareholder.

(2) Distributions received in more than 1 taxable year of shareholder.—If—

(A) paragraph (1) applies with respect to any installment obligation received by a shareholder from a corporation, and

(B) by reason of the liquidation such shareholder receives property in more than 1 taxable year,

then, on completion of the liquidation, basis previously allocated to property so received shall be reallocated for all such taxable years so that the shareholder's basis in the stock of the corporation is properly allocated among all property received by such shareholder in such liquidation.

(i) Recognition of recapture income in year of disposition.—

(1) In general.—In the case of any installment sale of property to which subsection (a) applies—

(A) notwithstanding subsection (a), any recapture income shall be recognized in the year of the disposition, and

(B) any gain in excess of the recapture income shall be taken into account under the installment method.

(2) Recapture income.—For purposes of paragraph (1), the term "recapture income" means, with respect to any installment sale, the aggregate amount which would be treated as ordinary income under section 1245 or 1250 (or so much of section 751 as relates to section 1245 or 1250) for the taxable year of the disposition if all payments to be received were received in the taxable year of disposition.

(j) Regulations.—

(1) In general.—The Secretary shall prescribe such regulations as may be necessary or appropriate to carry out the provisions of this section.

(2) Selling price not readily ascertainable.—The regulations prescribed under paragraph (1) shall include regulations providing for ratable basis recovery in transactions where the gross profit or the total contract price (or both) cannot be readily ascertained.

(j) [1] Current inclusion in case of revolving credit plans, etc.—In the case of—

[1] Two subsecs. (j) have been enacted.

(1) any disposition of personal property under a revolving credit plan, or

(2) any installment obligation arising out of a sale of—

(A) stock or securities which are traded on an established securities market, or

(B) to the extent provided in regulations, property (other than stock or securities) of a kind regularly traded on an established market,

§ 453A. Installment method for dealers in personal property

(a) General rule.—

(1) In general.—Under regulations prescribed by the Secretary, a person who regularly sells or otherwise disposes of personal property on the installment plan may return as income therefrom in any taxable year that proportion of the installment payments actually received in that year which the gross profit, realized or to be realized when payment is completed, bears to the total contract price.

(2) Total contract price.—For purposes of paragraph (1), the total contract price of all sales of personal property on the installment plan includes the amount of carrying charges or interest which is determined with respect to such sales and is added on the books of account of the seller to the established cash selling price of such property.

(b) Carrying charges not included in total contract price.—If the carrying charges or interest with respect to sales of personal property, the income from which is returned under subsection (a)(1), is not included in the total contract price, payments received with respect to such sales shall be treated as applying first against such carrying charges or interest.

§ 453B. Gain or loss disposition of installment obligations

(a) General rule.—If an installment obligation is satisfied at other than its face value or distributed, transmitted, sold, or otherwise disposed of, gain or loss shall result to the extent of the difference between the basis of the obligation and—

(1) the amount realized, in the case of satisfaction at other than face value or a sale or exchange, or

(2) the fair market value of the obligation at the time of distribution, transmission, or disposition, in the case of the distribution, transmission, or disposition otherwise than by sale or exchange.

Any gain or loss so resulting shall be considered as resulting from the sale or exchange of the property in respect of which the installment obligation was received.

(b) Basis of obligation.—The basis of an installment obligation shall be the excess of the face value of the obligation over an amount equal to the income which would be returnable were the obligation satisfied in full.

(c) Special rule for transmission at death.—Except as provided in section 691 (relating to recipients of income in respect of decedents), this section shall not apply to the transmission of installment obligations at death.

(d) Effect of distribution in liquidations to which section 332 applies.—If—

(1) an installment obligation is distributed in a liquidation to which section 332 (relating to complete liquidations of subsidiaries) applies, and

(2) the basis of such obligation in the hands of the distributee is determined under section 334(b)(1),

then no gain or loss with respect to the distribution of such obligation shall be recognized by the distributing corporation.

* * *

(f) Obligation becomes unenforceable.—For purposes of this section, if any installment obligation is canceled or otherwise becomes unenforceable—

(1) the obligation shall be treated as if it were disposed of in a transaction other than a sale or exchange, and

(2) if the obligor and obligee are related persons (within the meaning of section 453(f)(1)), the fair market value of the obligation shall be treated as not less than its face amount.

(g) Transfers between spouses or incident to divorce.—In the case of any transfer described in subsection (a) of section (other than a transfer in trust)—

(1) subsection (a) of this section shall not apply, and

(2) the same tax treatment with respect to the transferred installment obligation shall apply to the transferee as would have applied to the transferor.

§ 453C. Certain indebtedness treated as payment on installment obligations

(a) General rule.—For purposes of sections 453 and 453A, if a taxpayer has allocable installment indebtedness for any taxable year, such indebtedness—

(1) shall be allocated on a pro rata basis to any applicable installment obligation of the taxpayer which—

(A) arises in such taxable year, and

(B) is outstanding as of the close of such taxable year, and

(2) shall be treated as a payment received on such obligation as of the close of such taxable year.

(b) Allocable installment indebtedness.—For purposes of this section—

(1) **In general.**—The term "allocable installment indebtedness" means, with respect to any taxable year, the excess (if any) of—

(A) the installment percentage of the taxpayer's average quarterly indebtedness for such taxable year, over

(B) the aggregate amount treated as allocable installment indebtedness with respect to applicable installment obligations which—

(i) are outstanding as of the close of such taxable year, but

(ii) did not arise during such taxable year.

(2) **Installment percentage.**—The term "installment percentage" means the percentage (not in excess of 100 percent) determined by dividing—

(A) the face amount of all applicable installment obligations of the taxpayer outstanding as of the close of the taxable year, by

(B) the sum of—

(i) the aggregate adjusted bases of all assets not described in clause (ii) held as of the close of the taxable year, and

(ii) the face amount of all installment obligations outstanding as of such time.

For purposes of subparagraph (B)(i), a taxpayer may elect to compute the aggregate adjusted bases of all assets using the deduction for depreciation which is used in computing earnings and profits under section 312(k).

(3) Special rules for personal use property.—For purposes of this subsection—

(A) for purposes of paragraph (2)(B), there shall not be taken into account any personal use property (within the meaning of section 1275(b)(3)) held by an individual or any installment obligation arising from the sale of such property, and

(B) for purposes of computing the taxpayer's average quarterly indebtedness under paragraph (1)(A), there shall not be taken into account any indebtedness with respect to which substantially all of the property securing such indebtedness is property described in subparagraph (A).

(4) Special rule for casual sales.—If the taxpayer has no applicable installment obligations described in subclause (I) or (II) of subsection (e)(1)(A)(i) outstanding at any time during the taxable year, then the taxpayer's allocable installment indebtedness for such taxable year shall be computed by using the taxpayer's indebtedness as of the close of such taxable year in lieu of the taxpayer's average quarterly indebtedness.

(c) Treatment of subsequent payments.—

(1) Payments treated as receipt of tax paid amounts.—If any amount is treated as received under subsection (a) (after application of subsection (d)(2)) with respect to any applicable installment obligation, subsequent payments received on such obligation shall not be taken into account for purposes of sections 453 and 453A to the extent that the aggregate amount of such subsequent payments does not exceed the aggregate amount treated as received on such obligation under subsection (a).

(2) Reduction of allocable installment indebtedness.—For purposes of applying subsection (b)(1)(B) for the taxable year in which any payment to which paragraph (1) of this subsection applies was received (and for any subsequent taxable year), the allocable installment indebtedness with respect to the applicable installment obligation shall be reduced (but not below zero) by the amount of such payment not taken into account by reason of paragraph (1).

(d) Limitation based on total contract price.—

(1) In general.—The amount treated as received under subsection (a) (after application of paragraph (2)) with respect to any applicable installment obligation for any taxable year shall not exceed the excess (if any) of—

(A) the total contract price, over

(B) any portion of the total contract price received under the contract before the close of such taxable year—

(i) including amounts so treated under subsection (a) for all preceding taxable years (after application of paragraph (2)), but

(ii) not including amounts not taken into account by reason of subsection (c).

(2) Excess allocable installment indebtedness.—If, after application of paragraph (1), the allocable installment indebtedness for any taxable year exceeds the amount which may be allocated to applicable installment obligations arising in (and outstanding as of the close of) such taxable year, such excess shall—

(A) subject to the limitations of paragraph (1), be allocated to applicable installment obligations outstanding as of the close of such taxable year which arose in preceding taxable years, beginning with applicable installment obligations arising in the earliest preceding taxable year, and

(B) be treated as a payment under subsection (a)(2).

(e) Definitions and special rules.—For purposes of this section—

(1) Applicable installment obligation.—

(A) In general.—The term "applicable installment obligation" means any obligation—

(i) which arises from the disposition—

(I) after February 28, 1986, of personal property under the installment method by a person who regularly sells or otherwise disposes of personal property of the same type on the installment plan,

(II) after February 28, 1986, of real property under the installment method which is held by the taxpayer for sale to customers in the ordinary course of the taxpayer's trade or business, or

(III) after August 16, 1986, of real property under the installment method which is property used in the taxpayer's trade or business or property held for the production of rental income, but only if the sales price of such property exceeds $150,000 (determined after application of the rule under the last sentence of section 1274(c)(3)(A)(ii)), and

(ii) which is held by the seller or a member of the same affiliated group (within the meaning of section 1504(a), but without regard to section 1504(b)) as the seller.

(B) Exception for personal use and farm property.—The term "applicable installment obligation" shall not include any obligation which arises from the disposition—

(i) by an individual of personal use property (within the meaning of section 1275(b)(3)), or

(ii) of any property used or produced in the trade or business of farming (within the meaning of section 2032A(e)(4) or (5)).

(2) Aggregation rules.—For purposes of this section, all persons treated as a single employer under section 52 shall be treated as 1 taxpayer. The Secretary shall prescribe regulations for the treatment under this section of transactions between such persons.

(3) Aggregation of obligations.—The Secretary may by regulations provide that all (or any portion of) applicable installment obligations of a taxpayer may be treated as 1 obligation.

(4) Exception for sales of timeshares and residential lots.—

(A) In general.—If a taxpayer elects the application of this paragraph, this section shall not apply to any installment obligation which—

(i) arises from a sale in the ordinary course of the taxpayer's trade or business to an individual of—

(I) a timeshare right to use or a timeshare ownership interest in residential real property for not more than 6 weeks, or a right to use specified campgrounds for recreational purposes, or

(II) any residential lot but only if the taxpayer (or any related person) is not to make any improvements with respect to such lot, and

(ii) which is not guaranteed by any person other than an individual.

For purposes of clause (i)(I), a timeshare right to use (or timeshare ownership interest in) property held by the spouse, children, grandchildren, or parents of an individual shall be treated as held by such individual.

(B) Interest on deferred tax.—If subparagraph (A) applies to any installment obligation, interest shall be paid on the portion of any tax for any taxable year (determined without regard to any deduction allowable for such interest) which is attributable to the receipt of payments on such obligation in such year (other than payments received in the taxable year of the sale). Such interest shall be computed for the period from the date of the sale to the date on which the payment is received using the applicable Federal rate under section 1274 (without regard to subsection (d)(2) or (3) thereof) in effect at the time of the sale, compounded semiannually.

(C) Time for payment.—Any interest payable under this paragraph with respect to a payment shall be treated as an addition to tax for the taxable year in which the payment is received, except that the amount of such interest shall be taken into account in computing the amount of any deduction allowable to the **taxpayer** for interest paid or accrued during such taxable year.

(5) Regulations.—The Secretary shall prescribe regulations as may be necessary to carry out the purposes of this section, including regulations—

(A) disallowing the use of the installment method in whole or in part for transactions in which the rules of this section otherwise would be avoided through the use of related parties, pass-through entities, or intermediaries,

(B) providing for the proper treatment of reserves (including consistent treatment with assets held in the reserves), and

(C) providing that subsection (b)(4) shall not apply where necessary to prevent the avoidance of the application of this section.

(Added Pub.L. 99–514, Title VIII, § 811(a), Oct. 22, 1986, 100 Stat. ——.)

§ 454. Obligations issued at discount

(a) Non-interest-bearing obligations issued at a discount.—If, in the case of a taxpayer owning any non-interest-bearing obligation issued at a discount and redeemable for fixed amounts increasing at stated intervals or owning an obligation described in paragraph (2) of subsection (c), the increase in the redemption price of such obligation occurring in the taxable year does not (under the method of accounting used in computing his taxable income) constitute income to him in such year, such taxpayer may, at his election made in his return for any taxable year, treat such increase as income received in such taxable year. If any such election is made with respect to any such obligation, it shall apply also to all such obligations owned by the taxpayer at the beginning of the first taxable year to which it applies and to all such obligations thereafter acquired by him and shall be binding for all subsequent taxable years, unless on application by the taxpayer the Secretary permits him, subject to such conditions as the Secretary deems necessary, to change to a different method. In the case of any such obligations owned by the taxpayer at the beginning of the first taxable year to which his election applies, the increase in the redemption price of such obligations occurring between the date of acquisition (or, in the case of an obligation described in paragraph (2) of subsection (c), the date of acquisition of the series E bond involved) and the first day of such taxable year shall also be treated as income received in such taxable year.

(b) Short-term obligations issued on discount basis.—In the case of any obligation—

(1) of the United States; or

(2) of a State or a possession of the United States, or any political subdivision of any of the foregoing, or of the District of Columbia,

which is issued on a discount basis and payable without interest at a fixed maturity date not exceeding 1 year from the date of issue, the amount of discount at which such obligation is originally sold shall not be considered to accrue until the date on which such obligation is paid at maturity, sold, or otherwise disposed of.

* * *

§ 455. Prepaid subscription income

(a) **Year in which included.**—Prepaid subscription income to which this section applies shall be included in gross income for the taxable years during which the liability described in subsection (d)(2) exists.

(b) **Where taxpayer's liability ceases.**—In the case of any prepaid subscription income to which this section applies—

(1) If the liability described in subsection (d)(2) ends, then so much of such income as was not includible in gross income under subsection (a) for preceding taxable years shall be included in gross income for the taxable year in which the liability ends.

(2) If the taxpayer dies or ceases to exist, then so much of such income as was not includible in gross income under subsection (a) for preceding taxable years shall be included in gross income for the taxable year in which such death, or such cessation of existence, occurs.

(c) **Prepaid subscription income to which this section applies.**—

(1) **Election of benefits.**—This section shall apply to prepaid subscription income if and only if the taxpayer makes an election under this section with respect to the trade or business in connection with which such income is received. The election shall be made in such manner as the Secretary may by regulations prescribe. No election may be made with respect to a trade or business if in computing taxable income the cash receipts and disbursements method of accounting is used with respect to such trade or business.

(2) **Scope of election.**—An election made under this section shall apply to all prepaid subscription income received in connection with the trade or business with respect to which the taxpayer has made the election; except that the taxpayer may, to the extent permitted under regulations prescribed by the Secretary, include in gross income for the taxable year of receipt the entire amount of any prepaid subscription income if the liability from which it arose is to end within 12 months after the date of receipt. An election made under this section shall not apply to any prepaid subscription income received before the first taxable year for which the election is made.

(3) **When election may be made.**—

(A) **With consent.**—A taxpayer may, with the consent of the Secretary, make an election under this section at any time.

(B) **Without consent.**—A taxpayer may, without the consent of the Secretary, make an election under this section for his first taxable year in which he receives prepaid subscription income in the trade or business. Such election shall be made not later than the time prescribed by law for filing the return for the taxable year (including extensions thereof) with respect to which such election is made.

(4) Period to which election applies.—An election under this section shall be effective for the taxable year with respect to which it is first made and for all subsequent taxable years, unless the taxpayer secures the consent of the Secretary to the revocation of such election. For purposes of this title, the computation of taxable income under an election made under this section shall be treated as a method of accounting.

(d) Definitions.—For purposes of this section—

(1) Prepaid subscription income.—The term "prepaid subscription income" means any amount (includible in gross income) which is received in connection with, and is directly attributable to, a liability which extends beyond the close of the taxable year in which such amount is received, and which is income from a subscription to a newspaper, magazine, or other periodical.

(2) Liability.—The term "liability" means a liability to furnish or deliver a newspaper, magazine, or other periodical.

(3) Receipt of prepaid subscription income.—Prepaid subscription income shall be treated as received during the taxable year for which it is includible in gross income under section 451 (without regard to this section).

(e) Deferral of income under established accounting procedures.—Notwithstanding the provisions of this section, any taxpayer who has, for taxable years prior to the first taxable year to which this section applies, reported his income under an established and consistent method or practice of accounting for prepaid subscription income (to which this section would apply if an election were made) may continue to report his income for taxable years to which this title applies in accordance with such method or practice.

§ 456. Prepaid dues income of certain membership organizations

(a) Year in which included.—Prepaid dues income to which this section applies shall be included in gross income for the taxable years during which the liability described in subsection (e)(2) exists.

(b) Where taxpayer's liability ceases.—In the case of any prepaid dues income to which this section applies—

(1) If the liability described in subsection (e)(2) ends, then so much of such income as was not includible in gross income under subsection (a) for preceding taxable years shall be included in gross income for the taxable year in which the liability ends.

(2) If the taxpayer ceases to exist, then so much of such income as was not includible in gross income under subsection (a) for preceding taxable years shall be included in gross income for the taxable year in which such cessation of existence occurs.

(c) Prepaid dues income to which this section applies.—

(1) Election of benefits.—This section shall apply to prepaid dues income if and only if the taxpayer makes an election under this section with respect to the trade or business in connection with which such income is received. The election shall be made in such manner as the Secretary may by regulations prescribe. No election may be made with respect to a trade or business if in computing taxable income the cash receipts and disbursements method of accounting is used with respect to such trade or business.

(2) Scope of election.—An election made under this section shall apply to all prepaid dues income received in connection with the trade or business with respect to which the taxpayer has made the election; except that the taxpayer may, to the extent permitted under regulations prescribed by the Secretary, include in gross income for the taxable year of receipt the entire amount of any prepaid dues income if the liability from which it arose is to end within 12 months after the date of receipt. Except as provided in subsection (d), an election made under this section shall not apply to any prepaid dues income received before the first taxable year for which the election is made.

(3) When election may be made.—

(A) With consent.—A taxpayer may, with the consent of the Secretary, make an election under this section at any time.

(B) Without consent.—A taxpayer may, without the consent of the Secretary, make an election under this section for its first taxable year in which it receives prepaid dues income in the trade or business. Such election shall be made not later than the time prescribed by law for filing the return for the taxable year (including extensions thereof) with respect to which such election is made.

(4) Period to which election applies.—An election under this section shall be effective for the taxable year with respect to which it is first made and for all subsequent taxable years, unless the taxpayer secures the consent of the Secretary to the revocation of such election. For purposes of this title, the computation of taxable income under an election made under this section shall be treated as a method of accounting.

(d) Transitional rule.—

(1) Amount includible in gross income for election years.—If a taxpayer makes an election under this section with respect to prepaid dues income, such taxpayer shall include in gross income, for each taxable year to which such election applies, not only that portion of prepaid dues income received in such year otherwise includible in gross income for such year under this section, but shall also include in gross income for such year an additional amount equal to the amount of prepaid dues income received in the 3 taxable years preceding the first taxable year to which such election applies which would have been included in gross income in the taxable year had the election been effective 3 years earlier.

(2) Deductions of amounts included in income more than once.—A taxpayer who makes an election with respect to prepaid dues income, and who includes in gross income for any taxable year to which the election applies an additional amount computed under paragraph (1), shall be permitted to deduct, for such taxable year and for each of the 4 succeeding taxable years, an amount equal to one-fifth of such additional amount, but only to the extent that such additional amount was also included in the taxpayer's gross income during any of the 3 taxable years preceding the first taxable year to which such election applies.

(e) Definitions.—For purposes of this section—

(1) Prepaid dues income.—The term "prepaid dues income" means any amount (includible in gross income) which is received by a membership organization in connection with, and is directly attributable to, a liability to render services or make available membership privileges over a period of time which extends beyond the close of the taxable year in which such amount is received.

(2) Liability.—The term "liability" means a liability to render services or make available membership privileges over a period of time which does not exceed 36 months, which liability shall be deemed to exist ratably over the period of time that such services are required to be rendered, or that such membership privileges are required to be made available.

(3) Membership organization.—The term "membership organization" means a corporation, association, federation, or other organization—

(A) organized without capital stock of any kind, and

(B) no part of the net earnings of which is distributable to any member.

(4) Receipt of prepaid dues income.—Prepaid dues income shall be treated as received during the taxable year for which it is includible in gross income under section 451 (without regard to this section).

§ 458. Magazines, paperbacks, and records returned after the close of the taxable year

(a) Exclusion from gross income.—A taxpayer who is on an accrual method of accounting may elect not to include in the gross income for the taxable year the income attributable to the qualified sale of any magazine, paperback, or record which is returned to the taxpayer before the close of the merchandise return period.

(b) Definitions and special rules.—For purposes of this section—

(1) Magazine.—The term "magazine" includes any other periodical.

(2) Paperback.—The term "paperback" means any book which has a flexible outer cover and the pages of which are affixed directly to such outer cover. Such term does not include a magazine.

(3) Record.—The term "record" means a disc, tape, or similar object on which musical, spoken, or other sounds are recorded.

(4) Separate application with respect to magazines, paperbacks, and records.—If a taxpayer makes qualified sales of more than one category of merchandise in connection with the same trade or business, this section shall be applied as if the qualified sales of each such category were made in connection with a separate trade or business. For purposes of the preceding sentence, magazines, paperbacks, and records shall each be treated as a separate category of merchandise.

(5) Qualified sale.—A sale of a magazine, paperback, or record is a qualified sale if—

(A) at the time of sale, the taxpayer has a legal obligation to adjust the sales price of such magazine, paperback, or record if it is not resold, and

(B) the sales price of such magazine, paperback, or record is adjusted by the taxpayer because of a failure to resell it.

(6) Amount excluded.—The amount excluded under this section with respect to any qualified sale shall be the lesser of—

(A) the amount covered by the legal obligation described in paragraph (5)(A), or

(B) the amount of the adjustment agreed to by the taxpayer before the close of the merchandise return period.

(7) Merchandise return period.—

(A) Except as provided in subparagraph (B), the term "merchandise return period" means, with respect to any taxable year—

(i) in the case of magazines, the period of 2 months and 15 days first occurring after the close of taxable year, or

(ii) in the case of paperbacks and records, the period of 4 months and 15 days first occurring after the close of the taxable year.

(B) The taxpayer may select a shorter period than the applicable period set forth in subparagraph (A).

(C) Any change in the merchandise return period shall be treated as a change in the method of accounting.

(8) Certain evidence may be substituted for physical return of merchandise.—Under regulations prescribed by the Secretary, the taxpayer may substitute, for the physical return of magazines, paperbacks, or records required by subsection (a), certification or other evidence that the magazine, paperback, or record has not been resold and will not be resold if such evidence—

(A) is in the possession of the taxpayer at the close of the merchandise return period, and

(B) is satisfactory to the Secretary.

(9) Repurchased [1] by the taxpayer not treated as resale.—A repurchase by the taxpayer shall be treated as an adjustment of the sales price rather than as a resale.

(c) Qualified sales to which section applies.—

(1) Election of benefits.—This section shall apply to qualified sales of magazines, paperbacks, or records, as the case may be, if and only if the taxpayer makes an election under this section with respect to the trade or business in connection with which such sales are made. An election under this section may be made without the consent of the Secretary. The election shall be made in such manner as the Secretary may by regulations prescribed [2] and shall be made for any taxable year not later than the time prescribed by law for filing the return for such taxable year (including extensions thereof).

(2) Scope of election.—An election made under this section shall apply to all qualified sales of magazines, paperbacks, or records, as the case may be, made in connection with the trade or business with respect to which the taxpayer has made the election.

(3) Period to which election applies.—An election under this section shall be effective for the taxable year for which it is made and for all subsequent taxable years, unless the taxpayer secures the consent of the Secretary to the revocation of such election.

(4) Treatment as method of accounting.—Except to the extent inconsistent with the provisions of this section, for purposes of this subtitle, the computation of taxable income under an election made under this section shall be treated as a method of accounting.

(d) 5-year spread of transitional adjustments for magazines.—In applying section 481(c) with respect to any election under this section which applies to magazines, the period for taking into account any decrease in taxable income resulting from the application of section 481(a)(2) shall be the taxable year for which the election is made and the 4 succeeding taxable years.

(e) Suspense account for paperbacks and records.—

(1) In general.—In the case of any election under this section which applies to paperbacks or records, in lieu of applying section 481, the taxpayer shall establish a suspense account for the trade or business for the taxable year for which the election is made.

[1] So in original. Probably should be "repurchase".
[2] So in original. Probably should be "prescribe".

(2) Initial opening balance.—The opening balance of the account described in paragraph (1) for the first taxable year to which the election applies shall be the largest dollar amount of returned merchandise which would have been taken into account under this section for any of the 3 immediately preceding taxable years if this section had applied to such preceding 3 taxable years. This paragraph and paragraph (3) shall be applied by taking into account only amounts attributable to the trade or business for which such account is established.

(3) Adjustments in suspense account.—At the close of each taxable year the suspense account shall be—

(A) reduced the excess (if any) of—

(i) the opening balance of the suspense account for the taxable year, over

(ii) the amount excluded from gross income for the taxable year under subsection (a), or

(B) increased (but not in excess of the initial opening balance) by the excess (if any) of—

(i) the amount excluded from gross income for the taxable year under subsection (a), over

(ii) the opening balance of the account for the taxable year.

(4) Gross income adjustments.—

(A) Reductions excluded from gross income.—In the case of any reduction under paragraph (3)(A) in the account for the taxable year, an amount equal to such reduction shall be excluded from gross income for such taxable year.

(B) Increases added to gross income.—In the case of any increase under paragraph (3)(B) in the account for the taxable year, an amount equal to such increase shall be included in gross income for such taxable year.

If the initial opening balance exceeds the dollar amount of returned merchandise which would have been taken into account under subsection (a) for the taxable year preceding the first taxable year for which the election is effective if this section had applied to such preceding taxable year, then an amount equal to the amount of such excess shall be included in gross income for such first taxable year.

(5) Subchapter C transactions.—The application of this subsection with respect to a taxpayer which is a party to any transaction with respect to which there is nonrecognition of gain or loss to any party to the transaction by reason of subchapter C shall be determined under regulations prescribed by the Secretary.

Subpart C—Taxable Year for Which Deductions Taken

§ 460.   Special rules for long-term contracts

(a) Percentage of completion-capitalized cost method.—

(1) In general.—In the case of any long-term contract—

(A) 40 percent of the items with respect to such contract shall be taken into account under the percentage of completion method (as modified by subsection (b)), and

(B) 60 percent of the items with respect to such contract shall be taken into account under the taxpayer's normal method of accounting.

(2) 40 percent look-back method to apply.—Upon completion of any long-term contract, the taxpayer shall pay (or shall be entitled to receive) interest determined by applying the look-back method of subsection (b)(3) to 40 percent of the items with respect to the contract.

(b) Percentage of completion method.—

(1) Subsection (a) not to apply where percentage of completion method used.—Subsection (a) shall not apply to any long-term contract with respect to which amounts includible in gross income are determined under the percentage of completion method.

(2) Requirements of percentage of completion method.—In the case of any long-term contract with respect to which the percentage of completion method is used—

(A) the percentage of completion shall be determined by comparing costs allocated to the contract under subsection (c) and incurred before the close of the taxable year with the estimated total contract costs, and

(B) upon completion of the contract, the taxpayer shall pay (or shall be entitled to receive) interest computed under the look-back method of paragraph (3).

(3) Look-back method.—The interest computed under the look-back method of this subparagraph shall be determined by—

(A) first allocating income under the contract among taxable years before the year in which the contract is completed on the basis of the actual contract price and costs instead of the estimated contract price and costs,

(B) second, determining (solely for purposes of computing such interest) the overpayment or underpayment of tax for each taxable year referred to in paragraph (1) which would result solely from the application of paragraph (1), and

(C) then using the overpayment rate established by section 6621, compounded daily, on the overpayment or underpayment determined under paragraph (1).

(c) Allocation of costs to contract.—

(1) Direct and certain indirect costs.—In the case of a long-term contract, all costs (including research and experimental costs) which directly benefit, or are incurred by reason of, the long-term contract activities of the taxpayer shall be allocated to such contract in the same manner as costs are allocated to extended period long-term contracts under section 451 and the regulations thereunder.

(2) Costs identified under cost-plus and certain federal contracts.—In the case of a cost-plus long-term contract or a Federal long-term contract, any cost not allocated to such contract under paragraph (1) shall be allocated to such contract if such cost is identified by the taxpayer (or a related person), pursuant to the contract or Federal, State, or local law or regulation, as being attributable to such contract.

(3) Allocation of production period interest to contract.—

(A) In general.—Except as provided in subparagraphs (B) and (C), in the case of a long-term contract, interest costs shall be allocated to the contract in the same manner as interest costs are allocated to property produced by the taxpayer under section 263A(f).

(B) Production period.—In applying section 263A(f) for purposes of subparagraph (A), the production period shall be the period—

(i) beginning on the later of—

(I) the contract commencement date, or

(II) in the case of a taxpayer who uses an accrual method with respect to long-term contracts, the date by which at least 5 percent of the total estimated costs (including design and planning costs) under the contract have been incurred, and

(ii) ending on the contract completion date.

(C) **Application of de minimis rule.**—In applying section 263A(f) for purposes of subparagraph (A), paragraph (1)(B)(iii) of such section shall be applied on a contract-by-contract basis; except that, in the case of a taxpayer described in subparagraph (B)(i)(II) of this paragraph, paragraph (1)(B)(iii) of section 263A(f) shall be applied on a property-by-property basis.

(4) **Certain costs not included.**—This subsection shall not apply to any—

(A) independent research and development expenses,

(B) expenses for unsuccessful bids and proposals, and

(C) marketing, selling, and advertising expenses.

(5) **Independent research and development expenses.**—For purposes of paragraph (4), the term "independent research and development expenses" means any expenses incurred in the performance of research or development, except that such term shall not include—

(A) any expenses which are directly attributable to a long-term contract in existence when such expenses are incurred, or

(B) any expenses under an agreement to perform research or development.

(d) **Federal long-term contract.**—For purposes of this section—

(1) **In general.**—The term "Federal long-term contract" means any long-term contract—

(A) to which the United States (or any agency or instrumentality thereof) is a party, or

(B) which is a subcontract under a contract described in subparagraph (A).

(2) **Special rules for certain taxable entities.**—For purposes of paragraph (1), the rules of section 168(h)(2)(D) (relating to certain taxable entities not treated as instrumentalities) shall apply.

(e) **Exception for certain construction contracts.**—

(1) **In general.**—Subsections (a), (b), and (c)(1) and (2) shall not apply to any construction contract entered into by a taxpayer—

(A) who estimates (at the time such contract is entered into) that such contract will be completed within the 2–year period beginning on the contract commencement date of such contract, and

(B) whose average annual gross receipts for the 3 taxable years preceding the taxable year in which such contract is entered into do not exceed $10,000,000.

(2) **Determination of taxpayer's gross receipts.**—For purposes of paragraph (1), the gross receipts of—

(A) all trades or businesses (whether or not incorporated) which are under common control with the taxpayer (within the meaning of section 52(b)), and

(B) all members of any controlled group of corporations of which the taxpayer is a member,

for the 3 taxable years of such persons preceding the taxable year in which the contract described in paragraph (1) is entered into shall be included in the gross receipts of the taxpayer for the period described in paragraph (1)(B). The Secretary shall prescribe regulations which provide attribution rules that take into account, in addition to the persons and entities described in the preceding sentence, taxpayers who engage in construction contracts through partnerships, joint ventures, and corporations.

(3) Controlled group of corporations.—For purposes of this subsection, the term "controlled group of corporations" has the meaning given to such term by section 1563(a), except that—

(A) "more than 50 percent" shall be substituted for "at least 80 percent" each place it appears in section 1563(a)(1), and

(B) the determination shall be made without regard to subsections (a)(4) and (e)(3)(C) of section 1563.

(4) Construction contract.—For purposes of this subsection, the term "construction contract" means any contract for the building, construction, reconstruction, or rehabilitation of, or the installation of any integral component to, or improvements of, real property.

(f) Long-term contract.—For purposes of this section—

(1) In general.—The term "long-term contract" means any contract for the manufacture, building, installation, or construction of property if such contract is not completed within the taxable year in which such contract is entered into.

(2) Special rule for manufacturing contracts.—A contract for the manufacture of property shall not be treated as a long-term contract unless such contract involves the manufacture of—

(A) any unique item of a type which is not normally included in the finished goods inventory of the taxpayer, or

(B) any item which normally requires more than 12 calendar months to complete (without regard to the period of the contract).

(3) Aggregation, etc.—For purposes of this subsection, under regulations prescribed by the Secretary—

(A) 2 or more contracts which are interdependent (by reason of pricing or otherwise) may be treated as 1 contract, and

(B) a contract which is properly treated as an aggregation of separate contracts may be so treated.

(g) Contract commencement date.—For purposes of this section, the term "contract commencement date" means, with respect to any contract, the first date on which any costs (other than bidding expenses or expenses incurred in connection with negotiating the contract) allocable to such contract are incurred.

(Added Pub.L. 99–514, Title VIII, § 804(a), Oct. 22, 1986, 100 Stat. ——.)

§ 461. General rule for taxable year of deduction

(a) General rule.—The amount of any deduction or credit allowed by this subtitle shall be taken for the taxable year which is the proper taxable year under the method of accounting used in computing taxable income.

(b) Special rule in case of death.—In the case of the death of a taxpayer whose taxable income is computed under an accrual method of accounting, any amount accrued as a deduction or credit only by reason of the death of the taxpayer shall not be allowed in computing taxable income for the period in which falls the date of the taxpayer's death.

(c) Accrual of real property taxes.—

(1) In general.—If the taxable income is computed under an accrual method of accounting, then, at the election of the taxpayer, any real property tax which is related to a definite period of time shall be accrued ratably over that period.

(2) When election may be made.—

(A) Without consent.—A taxpayer may, without the consent of the Secretary, make an election under this subsection for his first taxable year in which he incurs real property taxes. Such an election shall be made not later than the time prescribed by law for filing the return for such year (including extensions thereof).

(B) With consent.—A taxpayer may, with the consent of the Secretary, make an election under this subsection at any time.

(d) Limitation on acceleration of accrual of taxes.—

(1) General rule.—In the case of a taxpayer whose taxable income is computed under an accrual method of accounting, to the extent that the time for accruing taxes is earlier than it would be but for any action of any taxing jurisdiction taken after December 31, 1960, then, under regulations prescribed by the Secretary, such taxes shall be treated as accruing at the time they would have accrued but for such action by such taxing jurisdiction.

(2) Limitation.—Under regulations prescribed by the Secretary, paragraph (1) shall be inapplicable to any item of tax to the extent that its application would (but for this paragraph) prevent all persons (including successors in interest) from ever taking such item into account.

(e) Dividends or interest paid on certain deposits or withdrawable accounts. —Except as provided in regulations prescribed by the Secretary, amounts paid to, or credited to the accounts of, depositors or holders of accounts as dividends or interest on their deposits or withdrawable accounts (if such amounts paid or credited are withdrawable on demand subject only to customary notice to withdraw) by a mutual savings bank not having capital stock represented by shares, a domestic building and loan association, or a cooperative bank shall not be allowed as a deduction for the taxable year to the extent such amounts are paid or credited for periods representing more than 12 months. Any such amount not allowed as a deduction as the result of the application of the preceding sentence shall be allowed as a deduction for such other taxable year as the Secretary determines to be consistent with the preceding sentence.

(f) Contested liabilities.—If—

(1) the taxpayer contests an asserted liability,

(2) the taxpayer transfers money or other property to provide for the satisfaction of the asserted liability,

(3) the contest with respect to the asserted liability exists after the time of the transfer, and

(4) but for the fact that the asserted liability is contested, a deduction would be allowed for the taxable year of the transfer (or for an earlier taxable year) determined after application of subsection (h),

then the deduction shall be allowed for the taxable year of the transfer. This subsection shall not apply in respect of the deduction for income, war profits, and excess profits taxes imposed by the authority of any foreign country or possession of the United States.

(g) Prepaid interest.—

460

(1) In general.—If the taxable income of the taxpayer is computed under the cash receipts and disbursements method of accounting, interest paid by the taxpayer which, under regulations prescribed by the Secretary, is properly allocable to any period—

(A) with respect to which the interest represents a charge for the use or forbearance of money, and

(B) which is after the close of the taxable year in which paid,

shall be charged to capital account and shall be treated as paid in the period to which so allocable.

(2) Exception.—This subsection shall not apply to points paid in respect of any indebtedness incurred in connection with the purchase or improvement of, and secured by, the principal residence of the taxpayer to the extent that, under regulations prescribed by the Secretary, such payment of points is an established business practice in the area in which such indebtedness is incurred, and the amount of such payment does not exceed the amount generally charged in such area.

(h) Certain liabilities not incurred before economic performance.—

(1) In general.—For purposes of this title, in determining whether an amount has been incurred with respect to any item during any taxable year, the all events test shall not be treated as met any earlier than when economic performance with respect to such item occurs.

(2) Time when economic performance occurs.—Except as provided in regulations prescribed by the Secretary, the time when economic performance occurs shall be determined under the following principles:

(A) Services and property provided to the taxpayer.—If the liability of the taxpayer arises out of—

(i) the providing of services to the taxpayer by another person, economic performance occurs as such person provides such services,

(ii) the providing of property to the taxpayer by another person, economic performance occurs as the person provides such property, or

(iii) the use of the property by the taxpayer, economic performance occurs as the taxpayer uses such property.

(B) Services and property provided by the taxpayer.—If the liability of the taxpayer requires the taxpayer to provide property or services, economic performance occurs as the taxpayer provides such property or services.

(C) Workers compensation and tort liabilities of the taxpayer.—If the liability of the taxpayer requires a payment to another person and—

(i) arises under any workers compensation act, or

(ii) arises out of any tort,

economic performance occurs as the payments to such person are made. Subparagraphs (A) and (B) shall not apply to any liability described in the preceding sentence.

(D) Other items.—In the case of any other liability of the taxpayer, economic performance occurs at the time determined under regulations prescribed by the Secretary.

(3) Exception for certain recurring items.—

461

(A) In general.—Notwithstanding paragraph (1) an item shall be treated as incurred during any taxable year if—

(i) the all events test with respect to such item is met during such taxable year (determined without regard to paragraph (1)),

(ii) economic performance with respect to such item occurs within the shorter of—

(I) a reasonable period after the close of such taxable year, or

(II) 8½ months after the close of such taxable year,

(iii) such item is recurring in nature and the taxpayer consistently treats items of such kind as incurred in the taxable year in which the requirements of clause (i) are met, and

(iv) either—

(I) such item is not a material item, or

(II) the accrual of such item in the taxable year in which the requirements of clause (i) are met results in a more proper match against income than accruing such item in the taxable year in which economic performance occurs.

(B) Financial statements considered under subparagraph (A)(iv).—In making a determination under subparagraph (A)(iv), the treatment of such item on financial statements shall be taken into account.

(C) Paragraph not to apply to workers compensation and tort liabilities.—This paragraph shall not apply to any item described in subparagraph (C) of paragraph (2).

(4) All events test.—For purposes of this subsection, the all events test is met with respect to any item if all events have occurred which determine the fact of liability and the amount of such liability can be determined with reasonable accuracy.

(5) Subsection not to apply to certain cases to which other provisions of this title specifically apply.—This subsection shall not apply to any item to which any of the following provisions apply:

(A) Section 463 (relating to vacation pay).

(B) Section 466 (relating to discount coupons).

(C) Any other provisions of this title which specifically provides for a deduction for a reserve for estimated expenses.

(i) Special rules for tax shelters.—

(1) Recurring item exception not to apply.—In the case of a tax shelter, economic performance shall be determined without regard to paragraph (3) of subsection (h).

(2) Special rule for spudding of oil or gas wells.—In the case of a tax shelter, economic performance with respect to the act of drilling an oil or gas well shall be treated as having occurred within a taxable year if drilling of the well commences before the close of the 90th day after the close of the taxable year.

(3) Tax shelter defined.—For purposes of this subsection, the term "tax shelter" means—

(A) any enterprise (other than a C corporation) if at any time interests in such enterprise have been offered for sale in any offering required to be registered with any Federal or State agency having the authority to regulate the offering of securities for sale,

(B) any syndicate (within the meaning of section 1256(e)(3)(B)), and

(C) any tax shelter (within the meaning of section 6661(b)(2)(C)(ii)).

(4) Special rules for farming.—In the case of the trade or business of farming (as defined in section 464(e)), in determining whether an entity is a tax shelter, the definition of farming syndicate in section 464(c) shall be substituted for subparagraphs (A) and (B) of paragraph (3).

(5) Economic performance.—For purposes of this subsection, the term "economic performance" has the meaning given such term by subsection (h).

§ 465. Deductions limited to amount at risk

(a) Limitation to amount at risk.—

(1) In general.—In the case of—

(A) an individual, and

(B) a C corporation with respect to which the stock ownership requirement of paragraph (2) of section 542(a) is met,

engaged in an activity to which this section applies, any loss from such activity for the taxable year shall be allowed only to the extent of the aggregate amount with respect to which the taxpayer is at risk (within the meaning of subsection (b)) for such activity at the close of the taxable year.

(2) Deduction in succeeding year.—Any loss from an activity to which this section applies not allowed under this section for the taxable year shall be treated as a deduction allocable to such activity in the first succeeding taxable year.

(3) Special rules for applying paragraph (1)(B).—For purposes of paragraph (1)(B)—

(A) section 544(a)(2) shall be applied as if such section did not contain the phrase "or by or for his partner"; and

(B) sections 544(a)(4)(A) and 544(b)(1) shall be applied by substituting "the corporation meet the stock ownership requirements of section 542(a)(2)" for "the corporation a personal holding company".

(b) Amounts considered at risk.—

(1) In general.—For purposes of this section, a taxpayer shall be considered at risk for an activity with respect to amounts including—

(A) the amount of money and the adjusted basis of other property contributed by the taxpayer to the activity, and

(B) amounts borrowed with respect to such activity (as determined under paragraph (2)).

(2) Borrowed amounts.—For purposes of this section, a taxpayer shall be considered at risk with respect to amounts borrowed for use in an activity to the extent that he—

(A) is personally liable for the repayment of such amounts, or

(B) has pledged property, other than property used in such activity, as security for such borrowed amount (to the extent of the net fair market value of the taxpayer's interest in such property).

No property shall be taken into account as security if such property is directly or indirectly financed by indebtedness which is secured by property described in paragraph (1).

(3) Certain borrowed amounts excluded.—

(A) In general.—Except to the extent provided in regulations, for purposes of paragraph (1)(B), amounts borrowed shall not be considered to be at risk with respect to an activity if such amounts are borrowed from any person who has an interest in such activity or from a related person to a person (other than the taxpayer) having such an interest.

(B) Exceptions.—

(i) Interest as creditor.—Subparagraph (A) shall not apply to an interest as a creditor in the activity.

(ii) Interest as shareholder with respect to amounts borrowed by corporation.—In the case of amounts borrowed by a corporation from a shareholder, subparagraph (A) shall not apply to an interest as a shareholder.

(C) Related person.—For purposes of this subsection, a person (hereinafter in this paragraph referred to as the "related person") is related to any person if—

(i) the related person bears a relationship to such person specified in section 267(b) or section 707(b)(1), or

(ii) the related person and such person are engaged in trades or business under common control (within the meaning of subsections (a) and (b) of section 52).

For purposes of clause (i), in applying section 267(b) or 707(b)(1), "10 percent" shall be substituted for "50 percent".

(4) Exception.—Notwithstanding any other provision of this section, a taxpayer shall not be considered at risk with respect to amounts protected against loss through nonrecourse financing, guarantees, stop loss agreements, or other similar arrangements.

(5) Amounts at risk in subsequent years.—If in any taxable year the taxpayer has a loss from an activity to which subsection (a) applies, the amount with respect to which a taxpayer is considered to be at risk (within the meaning of subsection (b)) in subsequent taxable years with respect to that activity shall be reduced by that portion of the loss which (after the application of subsection (a)) is allowable as a deduction.

(6) Qualified nonrecourse financing treated as amount at risk.—For purposes of this section—

(A) In general.—Notwithstanding any other provision of this subsection, in the case of an activity of holding real property, a taxpayer shall be considered at risk with respect to the taxpayer's share of any qualified nonrecourse financing which is secured by real property used in such activity.

(B) Qualified nonrecourse financing.—For purposes of this paragraph, the term "qualified nonrecourse financing" means any financing—

(i) which is borrowed by the taxpayer with respect to the activity of holding real property,

(ii) which is borrowed by the taxpayer from a qualified person or represents a loan from any Federal, State, or local government or instrumentality thereof, or is guaranteed by any Federal, State, or local government,

(iii) except to the extent provided in regulations, with respect to which no person is personally liable for repayment, and

(iv) which is not convertible debt.

(C) **Special rule for partnerships.**—In the case of a partnership, a partner's share of any qualified nonrecourse financing of such partnership shall be determined on the basis of the partner's share of liabilities of such partnership incurred in connection with such financing (within the meaning of section 752).

(D) **Qualified person defined.**—For purposes of this paragraph—

(i) **In general.**—The term "qualified person" has the meaning given such term by section 46(c)(8)(D)(iv).

(ii) **Certain commercially reasonable financing from related persons.**—For purposes of clause (i), section 46(c)(8)(D)(iv) shall be applied without regard to subclause (I) thereof (relating to financing from related persons) if the financing from the related person is commercially reasonable and on substantially the same terms as loans involving unrelated persons.

(E) **Activity of holding real property.**—For purposes of this paragraph—

(i) **Incidental personal property and services.**—The activity of holding real property includes the holding of personal property and the providing of services which are incidental to making real property available as living accommodations.

(ii) **Mineral property.**—The activity of holding real property shall not include the holding of mineral property.

(c) **Activities to which section applies.**—

(1) **Types of activities.**—This section applies to any taxpayer engaged in the activity of—

(A) holding, producing, or distributing motion picture films or video tapes,

(B) farming (as defined in section 464(e)),

(C) leasing any section 1245 property (as defined in section 1245(a) (3)),

(D) exploring for, or exploiting, oil and gas resources as a trade or business or for the production of income, or

(E) exploring for, or exploiting, geothermal deposits (as defined in section 613(e) (3)),

as a trade or business for the production of income.

(2) **Separate activities.**—For purposes of this section—

(A) **In general.**—Except as provided in subparagraph (B), a taxpayer's activity with respect to each—

(i) film or video tape,

(ii) section 1245 property which is leased or held for leasing,

(iii) farm,

(iv) oil and gas property (as defined under section 614), or

(v) geothermal property (as defined under section 614),

shall be treated as a separate activity.

(B) **Aggregation rules.**—

(i) Special rule for leases of section 1245 property by partnerships or S corporations.—In the case of any partnership or S corporation, all activities with respect to section 1245 properties which—

(I) are leased or held for lease, and

(II) are placed in service in any taxable year of the partnership or S corporation,

shall be treated as a single activity.

(ii) Other aggregation rules.—Rules similar to the rules of subparagraphs (B) and (C) of paragraph (3) shall apply for purposes of this paragraph.

(3) Extension to other activities.—

(A) In general.—In the case of taxable years beginning after December 31, 1978, this section also applies to each activity—

(i) engaged in by the taxpayer in carrying on a trade or business or for the production of income, and

(ii) which is not described in paragraph (1).

(B) Aggregation of activities where taxpayer actively participates in management of trade or business.—Except as provided in subparagraph (C), for purposes of this section, activities described in subparagraph (A) which constitute a trade or business shall be treated as one activity if—

(i) the taxpayer actively participates in the management of such trade or business, or

(ii) such trade or business is carried on by a partnership or an S corporation and 65 percent or more of the losses for the taxable year is allocable to persons who actively participate in the management of the trade or business.

(C) Aggregation or separation of activities under regulations.—The Secretary shall prescribe regulations under which activities described in subparagraph (A) shall be aggregated or treated as separate activities.

(D) Application of subsection (b)(3).—In the case of an activity described in subparagraph (A), subsection (b)(3) shall apply only to the extent provided in regulations prescribed by the Secretary.

(4) Exclusion for certain equipment leasing by closely-held corporations.—

(A) In general.—In the case of a corporation described in subsection (a)(1)(B) actively engaged in equipment leasing—

(i) the activity of equipment leasing shall be treated as a separate activity, and

(ii) subsection (a) shall not apply to losses from such activity.

(B) 50-percent gross receipts test.—For purposes of subparagraph (A), a corporation shall not be considered to be actively engaged in equipment leasing unless 50 percent or more of the gross receipts of the corporation for the taxable year is attributable, under regulations prescribed by the Secretary, to equipment leasing.

(C) Component members of controlled group treated as a single corporation.—For purposes of subparagraph (A), the component members of a controlled group of corporations shall be treated as a single corporation.

(5) Waiver of controlled group rule where there is substantial leasing activity.—

(A) In general.—In the case of the component members of a qualified leasing group, paragraph (4) shall be applied—

(i) by substituting "80 percent" for "50 percent" in subparagraph (B) thereof, and

(ii) as if paragraph (4) did not include subparagraph (C) thereof.

(B) Qualified leasing group.—For purposes of this paragraph, the term "qualified leasing group" means a controlled group of corporations which, for the taxable year and each of the 2 immediately preceding taxable years, satisfied each of the following 3 requirements:

(i) At least 3 employees.—During the entire year, the group had at least 3 full-time employees substantially all of the services of whom were services directly related to the equipment leasing activity of the qualified leasing members.

(ii) At least 5 separate leasing transactions.—During the year, the qualified leasing members in the aggregate entered into at least 5 separate equipment leasing transactions.

(iii) At least $1,000,000 equipment leasing receipts.—During the year, the qualified leasing members in the aggregate had at least $1,000,000 in gross receipts from equipment leasing.

The term "qualified leasing group" does not include any controlled group of corporations to which, without regard to this paragraph, paragraph (4) applies.

(C) Qualified leasing member.—For purposes of this paragraph, a corporation shall be treated as a qualified leasing member for the taxable year only if for each of the taxable years referred to in subparagraph (B)—

(i) it is a component member of the controlled group of corporations, and

(ii) it meets the requirements of paragraph (4)(B) (as modified by subparagraph (A)(i) of this paragraph).

(6) Definitions relating to paragraphs (4) and (5).—For purposes of paragraphs (4) and (5)—

(A) Equipment leasing.—The term "equipment leasing" means—

(i) the leasing of equipment which is section 1245 property, and

(ii) the purchasing, servicing, and selling of such equipment.

(B) Leasing of master sound recordings, etc., excluded.—The term "equipment leasing" does not include the leasing of master sound recordings, and other similar contractual arrangements with respect to tangible or intangible assets associated with literary, artistic, or musical properties.

(C) Controlled group of corporations; component member.—The terms "controlled group of corporations" and "component member" have the same meanings as when used in section 1563. The determination of the taxable years taken into account with respect to any controlled group of corporations shall be made in a manner consistent with the manner set forth in section 1563.

(7) Exclusion of active businesses of qualified C corporations.—

(A) In general.—In the case of a taxpayer which is a qualified C corporation—

(i) each qualifying business carried on by such taxpayer shall be treated as a separate activity, and

(ii) subsection (a) shall not apply to losses from such business.

(B) Qualified C corporation.—For purposes of subparagraph (A), the term "qualified C corporation" means any corporation described in subparagraph (B) of subsection (a)(1) which is not—

(i) a personal holding company (as defined in section 542(a)),

(ii) a foreign personal holding company (as defined in section 552(a)), or

(iii) a personal service corporation (as defined in section 269A(b) but determined by substituting "5 percent" for "10 percent" in section 269A(b)(2)).

(C) Qualifying business.—For purposes of this paragraph, the term "qualifying business" means any active business if—

(i) during the entire 12-month period ending on the last day of the taxable year, such corporation had at least 1 full-time employee substantially all the services of whom were in the active management of such business,

(ii) during the entire 12-month period ending on the last day of the taxable year, such corporation had at least 3 full-time, nonowner employees substantially all of the services of whom were services directly related to such business,

(iii) the amount of the deductions attributable to such business which are allowable to the taxpayer solely by reason of sections 162 and 404 for the taxable year exceeds 15 percent of the gross income from such business for such year, and

(iv) such business is not an excluded business.

(D) Special rules for application of subparagraph (C).—

(i) **Partnerships in which taxpayer is a qualified corporate partner.** —In the case of an active business of a partnership, if—

(I) the taxpayer is a qualified corporate partner in the partnership, and

(II) during the entire 12-month period ending on the last day of the partnership's taxable year, there was at least 1 full-time employee of the partnership (or of a qualified corporate partner) substantially all the services of whom were in the active management of such business,

then the taxpayer's proportionate share (determined on the basis of its profits interest) of the activities of the partnership in such business shall be treated as activities of the taxpayer (and clause (i) of subparagraph (C) shall not apply in determining whether such business is a qualifying business of the taxpayer).

(ii) **Qualified corporate partner.**—For purposes of clause (i), the term "qualified corporate partner" means any corporation if—

(I) such corporation is a general partner in the partnership,

(II) such corporation has an interest of 10 percent or more in the profits and losses of the partnership, and

(III) such corporation has contributed property to the partnership in an amount not less than the lesser of $500,000 or 10 percent of the net worth of the corporation.

For purposes of subclause (III), any contribution of property other than money shall be taken into account at its fair market value.

(iii) **Deduction for owner employee compensation not taken into account.**—For purposes of clause (iii) of subparagraph (C), there shall not be taken into account any deduction in respect of compensation for personal services rendered by any employee (other than a non-owner employee) of the taxpayer or any member of such employee's family (within the meaning of section 318(a)(1)).

* * *

(v) Special rule for life insurance companies.—

(I) In general.—Clause (iii) of subparagraph (C) shall not apply to any insurance business of a qualified life insurance company.

(II) Insurance business.—For purposes of subclause (I), the term "insurance business" means any business which is not a noninsurance business (within the meaning of section 806(b)(3)).

(III) Qualified life insurance company.—For purposes of subclause (I), the term "qualified life insurance company" means any company which would be a life insurance company as defined in section 816 if unearned premiums were not taken into account under subsections (a)(2) and (c)(2) of section 816.

* * *

(E) Definitions.—For purposes of this paragraph—

(i) Non-owner employee.—The term "non-owner employee" means any employee who does not own, at any time during the taxable year, more than 5 percent in value of the outstanding stock of the taxpayer. For purposes of the preceding sentence, section 318 shall apply, except that "5 percent" shall be substituted for "50 percent" in section 318(a)(2)(C).

(ii) Excluded business.—The term "excluded business" means—

(I) equipment leasing (as defined in paragraph (6)), and

(II) any business involving the use, exploitation, sale, lease, or other disposition of master sound recordings, motion picture films, video tapes, or tangible or intangible assets associated with literary, artistic, musical, or similar properties.

(iii) Special rules relating to communications industry, etc.—

(I) Business not excluded where taxpayer not completely at risk.—A business involving the use, exploitation, sale, lease, or other disposition of property described in subclause (II) of clause (ii) shall not constitute an excluded business by reason of such subclause if the taxpayer is at risk with respect to all amounts paid or incurred (or chargeable to capital account) in such business.

(II) Certain licensed businesses not excluded.—For purposes of subclause (II) of clause (ii), the provision of radio, television, cable television, or similar services pursuant to a license or franchise granted by the Federal Communications Commission or any other Federal, State, or local authority shall not constitute an excluded business by reason of such subclause.

(F) Affiliated group treated as 1 taxpayer.—For purposes of this paragraph—

(i) In general.—Except as provided in subparagraph (G), the component members of an affiliated group of corporations shall be treated as a single taxpayer.

(ii) Affiliated group of corporations.—The term "affiliated group of corporations" means an affiliated group (as defined in section 1504(a)) which files or is required to file consolidated income tax returns.

(iii) **Component member.**—The term "component member" means an includible corporation (as defined in section 1504) which is a member of the affiliated group.

(G) Loss of 1 member of affiliated group may not offset income of personal holding company or personal service corporation.—Nothing in this paragraph shall permit any loss of a member of an affiliated group to be used as an offset against the income of any other member of such group which is a personal holding company (as defined in section 542(a)) or a personal service corporation (as defined in section 269A(b) but determined by substituting "5 percent" for "10 percent" in section 269A(b)(2)).

(d) Definition of loss.—For purposes of this section, the term "loss" means the excess of the deductions allowable under this chapter for the taxable year (determined without regard to the first sentence of subsection (a)) and allocable to an activity to which this section applies over the income received or accrued by the taxpayer during the taxable year from such activity (determined without regard to subsection (e)(1)(A)).

(e) Recapture of losses where amount at risk is less than zero.—

(1) In general.—If zero exceeds the amount for which the taxpayer is at risk in any activity at the close of any taxable year—

(A) the taxpayer shall include in his gross income for such taxable year (as income from such activity) an amount equal to such excess, and

(B) an amount equal to the amount so included in gross income shall be treated as a deduction allocable to such activity for the first succeeding taxable year.

(2) Limitation.—The excess referred to in paragraph (1) shall not exceed—

(A) the aggregate amount of the reductions required by subsection (b) (5) with respect to the activity by reason of losses for all prior taxable years beginning after December 31, 1978, reduced by

(B) the amounts previously included in gross income with respect to such activity under this subsection.

§ 467. Certain payments for the use of property or services

(a) Accrual method on present value basis.—In the case of the lessor or lessee under any section 467 rental agreement, there shall be taken into account for purposes of this title for any taxable year the sum of—

(1) the amount of the rent which accrues during such taxable year as determined under subsection (b), and

(2) interest for the year on the amounts which were taken into account under this subsection for prior taxable years and which are unpaid.

(b) Accrual of rental payments.—

(1) Allocation follows agreement.—Except as provided in paragraph (2), the determination of the amount of the rent under any section 467 rental agreement which accrues during any taxable year shall be made—

(A) by allocating rents in accordance with the agreement, and

(B) by taking into account any rent to be paid after the close of the period in an amount determined under regulations which shall be based on present value concepts.

(2) Constant rental accrual in case of certain tax avoidance transactions, etc.—In the case of any section 467 rental agreement to which this paragraph applies, the portion of the rent which accrues during any taxable year shall be that portion of the constant rental amount with respect to such agreement which is allocable to such taxable year.

(3) Agreements to which paragraph (2) applies.—Paragraph (2) applies to any rental payment agreement if—

(A) such agreement is a disqualified leaseback or long-term agreement, or

(B) such agreement does not provide for the allocation referred to in paragraph (1)(A).

(4) Disqualified leaseback or long-term agreement.—For purposes of this subsection, the term "disqualified leaseback or long-term agreement" means any section 467 rental agreement if—

(A) such agreement is part of a leaseback transaction or such agreement is for a term in excess of 75 percent of the statutory recovery period for the property, and

(B) a principal purpose for providing increasing rents under the agreement is the avoidance of tax imposed by this subtitle.

(5) Exceptions to disqualification in certain cases.—The Secretary shall prescribe regulations setting forth circumstances under which agreements will not be treated as disqualified leaseback or long-term agreements, including circumstances relating to—

(A) changes in amounts paid determined by reference to price indices,

(B) rents based on a fixed percentage of lessee receipts or similar amounts,

(C) reasonable rent holidays, or

(D) changes in amounts paid to unrelated 3rd parties.

(c) Recapture of prior understated inclusions under leaseback or long-term agreements.—

(1) In general.—If—

(A) the lessor under any section 467 rental agreement disposes of any property subject to such agreement during the term of such agreement, and

(B) such agreement is a leaseback or long-term agreement to which paragraph (2) of subsection (b) did not apply,

the recapture amount shall be treated as ordinary income. Such gain shall be recognized notwithstanding any other provision of this subtitle.

(2) Recapture Amount.—For purposes of paragraph (1), the term "recapture amount" means the lesser of—

(A) the prior understated inclusions, or

(B) the excess of the amount realized (or in the case of a disposition other than a sale, exchange, or involuntary conversion, the fair market value of the property) over the adjusted basis of such property.

The amount determined under subparagraph (B) shall be reduced by the amount of any gain treated as ordinary income on the disposition under any other provision of this subtitle.

(3) Prior understated inclusions.—For purposes of this subsection, the term "prior understated inclusion" means the excess (if any) of—

(A) the amount which would have been taken into account by the lessor under subsection (a) for periods before the disposition if subsection (b)(2) had applied to the agreement, over

(B) the amount taken into account under subsection (a) by the lessor for periods before the disposition.

(4) Leaseback or long-term agreement.—For purposes of this subsection, the term "leaseback or long-term agreement" means any agreement described in subsection (b)(4)(A).

(5) Special rules.—Under regulations prescribed by the Secretary—

(A) exceptions similar to the exceptions applicable under section 1245 or 1250 (whichever is appropriate) shall apply for purposes of this subsection,

(B) any transferee in a disposition excepted by reason of subparagraph (A) who has a transferred basis in the property shall be treated in the same manner as the transferor, and

(C) for purposes of sections 170(e), 341(e)(12), and 751(c), amounts treated as ordinary income under this section shall be treated in the same manner as amounts treated as ordinary income under section 1245 or 1250.

(d) Section 467 rental agreements.—

(1) In general.—Except as otherwise provided in this subsection, the term "section 467 rental agreements" means any rental agreement for the use of tangible property under which—

(A) there is at least one amount allocable to the use of property during a calendar year which is to be paid after the close of the calendar year following the calendar year in which such use occurs, or

(B) there are increases in the amount to be paid as rent under the agreement.

(2) Section not to apply to agreements involving payments of $250,000 or less.—This section shall not apply to any amount to be paid for the use of property if the sum of the following amounts does not exceed $250,000—

(A) the aggregate amount of payments received as consideration for such use of property, and

(B) the aggregate value of any other consideration to be received for such use of property.

For purposes of the preceding sentence, rules similar to the rules of clauses (ii) and (iii) of section 1274(c)(4)(C) shall apply.

(e) Definitions.—For purposes of this section—

(1) Constant rental amount.—The term "constant rental amount" means, with respect to any section 467 rental agreement, the amount which, if paid as of the close of each lease period under the agreement, would result in an aggregate present value equal to the present value of the aggregate payments required under the agreement.

(2) Leaseback transaction.—A transaction is a leaseback transaction if it involves a leaseback to any person who had an interest in such property at any time within 2 years before such leaseback (or to a related person).

(3) Statutory recovery period.—

(A) In general.—

In the case of property which is:	The statutory recovery period is:
3-year property	3 years
5-year property	5 years
7-year property	7 years
10-year property	10 years
15-year and 20-year property	15 years
Residential rental property and nonresidential real property	19 years

(B) Special rule for property not depreciable under section 168.—In the case of property to which section 168 does not apply, subparagraph (A) shall be applied as if section 168 applies to such property.

(4) Discount and interest rate.—For purposes of computing present value and interest under subsection (a)(2), the rate used shall be equal to 110 percent of the applicable Federal rate determined under section 1274(d) (compounded semiannually) which is in effect at the time the agreement is entered into with respect to debt instruments having a maturity equal to the term of the agreement.

(5) Related person.—The term "related person" has the meaning given to such term by section 465(b)(3)(C).

(6) Certain options of lessee to renew not taken into account.—Except as provided in regulations prescribed by the Secretary, there shall not be taken into account in computing the term of any agreement for purposes of this section any extension which is solely at the option of the lessee.

(f) Comparable rules where agreement for decreasing payments.—Under regulations prescribed by the Secretary, rules comparable to the rules of this section shall also apply in the case of any agreement where the amount paid under the agreement for the use of property decreases during the term of the agreement.

(g) Comparable rules for services.—Under regulations prescribed by the Secretary, rules comparable to the rules of subsection (a)(2) shall also apply in the case of payments for services which meet requirements comparable to the requirements of subsection (d). The preceding sentence shall not apply to any amount to which section 404 or 404A (or any other provision specified in regulations) applies.

(h) Regulations.—The Secretary shall prescribe such regulations as may be appropriate to carry out the purposes of this section, including regulations providing for the application of this section in the case of contingent payments.

§ 468B. Special rules for designated settlement funds

(a) In general.—For purposes of section 461(h), economic performance shall be deemed to occur as qualified payments are made by the taxpayer to a designated settlement fund.

(b) Taxation of designated settlement fund.—

(1) In general.—There is imposed on the gross income of any designated settlement fund for any taxable year a tax at a rate equal to the maximum rate in effect for such taxable year under section 1(e).

(2) Certain expenses allowed.—For purposes of paragraph (1), gross income for any taxable year shall be reduced by the amount of any administrative costs (including State and local taxes) and other incidental expenses of the designated settlement fund (including legal, accounting, and actuarial expenses)—

(A) which are incurred in connection with the operation of the fund, and

(B) which would be deductible under this chapter for purposes of determining the taxable income of the corporation,

no other deduction shall be allowed to the fund.

(3) Transfers to the fund.—In the case of any qualified payment made to the fund—

(A) the amount of such payment shall not be treated as income of the designated settlement fund,

(B) the basis of the fund in any property which constitutes a qualified payment shall be equal to the fair market value of such property at the time of payment, and

(C) the fund shall be treated as the owner of the property in the fund (and any earnings thereon).

(4) Tax in lieu of other taxation.—The tax imposed by paragraph (1) shall be in lieu of any other taxation under this subtitle of income from assets in the designated settlement fund.

(5) Coordination with subtitle F.—For purposes of subtitle F—

(A) a designated settlement fund shall be treated as a corporation, and

(B) any tax imposed by this subsection shall be treated as a tax imposed by section 11.

(c) Deductions not allowed for transfer of insurance amounts.—No deduction shall be allowable for any qualified payment by the taxpayer of any amounts received from the settlement of any insurance claim to the extent such amounts are excluded from the gross income of the taxpayer.

(d) Definitions.—For purposes of this section—

(1) Qualified payment.—The term "qualified payment" means any money or property which is transferred to any designated settlement fund pursuant to a court order, other than—

(A) any amount which may be transferred from the fund to the taxpayer, or

(B) the transfer of any stock or indebtedness of the taxpayer (or any related person).

(2) Designated settlement fund.—The term "designated settlement fund" means any fund—

(A) which is established pursuant to a court order,

(B) with respect to which no amounts may be transferred other than in the form of qualified payments,

(C) which is administered by persons a majority of whom are independent of the taxpayer,

(D) which is established for the principal purpose of resolving and satisfying present and future claims against the taxpayer (or any related person or formerly related person) arising out of personal injury, death, or property damage,

(E) under the terms of which the taxpayer may not hold any beneficial interest in the income or corpus of the fund, and

(F) with respect to which an election is made under this section by the taxpayer.

An election under this section shall be made at such time and in such manner as the Secretary shall by regulation prescribe. Such an election, once made, may be revoked only with the consent of the Secretary.

(3) **Related person.**—The term "related person" means a person related to the taxpayer within the meaning of section 267(b).

(e) **Nonapplicability of section.**—This section shall not apply with respect to any liability of the taxpayer arising under any workers' compensation Act or any contested liability of the taxpayer within the meaning of section 461(f).

(f) **Other funds.**—Except as provided in regulations, any payment in respect of a liability described in subsection (d)(2)(D) (and not described in subsection (e)) to a trust fund or escrow fund which is not a designated settlement fund shall not be treated as constituting economic performance.

(Added Pub.L. 99–514, Title XVIII, § 1807(a)(7)(A), Oct. 22, 1986, 100 Stat. ——.)

§ 469. Passive activity losses and credits limited

(a) **Disallowance.**—

(1) **In general.**—If for any taxable year the taxpayer is described in paragraph (2), neither—

(A) the passive activity loss, nor

(B) the passive activity credit,

for the taxable year shall be allowed.

(2) **Persons described.**—The following are described in this paragraph:

(A) any individual, estate, or trust,

(B) any closely held C corporation, and

(C) any personal service corporation.

(b) **Disallowed loss or credit carried to next year.**—Except as otherwise provided in this section, any loss or credit from an activity which is disallowed under subsection (a) shall be treated as a deduction or credit allocable to such activity in the next taxable year.

(c) **Passive activity defined.**—For purposes of this section—

(1) **In general.**—The term "passive activity" means any activity—

(A) which involves the conduct of any trade or business, and

(B) in which the taxpayer does not materially participate.

(2) **Passive activity includes any rental activity.**—The term "passive activity" includes any rental activity.

(3) **Working interests in oil and gas property.**—

(A) **In general.**—The term "passive activity" shall not include any working interest in any oil or gas property which the taxpayer holds directly or through an entity which does not limit the liability of the taxpayer with respect to such interest.

(B) **Income in subsequent years.**—If any taxpayer has any loss for any taxable year from a working interest in any oil or gas property which is treated as a loss which is not from a passive activity, then any net income from such property (or any property the basis of which is determined in whole or in part by reference to the basis of such property) for any succeeding taxable year shall be treated as income of the taxpayer which is not from a passive activity.

(4) Material participation not required for paragraphs (2) and (3).—Paragraphs (2) and (3) shall be applied without regard to whether or not the taxpayer materially participates in the activity.

(5) Trade or business includes research and experimentation activity.—For purposes of paragraph (1)(A), the term "trade or business" includes any activity involving research or experimentation (within the meaning of section 174).

(6) Activity in connection with trade or business or production of income.—To the extent provided in regulations, for purposes of paragraph (1)(A), the term "trade or business" includes—

(A) any activity in connection with a trade or business, or

(B) any activity with respect to which expenses are allowable as a deduction under section 212.

(d) Passive activity loss and credit defined.—For purposes of this section—

(1) Passive activity loss.—The term "passive activity loss" means the amount (if any) by which—

(A) the aggregate losses from all passive activities for the taxable year, exceed

(B) the aggregate income from all passive activities for such year.

(2) Passive activity credit.—The term "passive activity credit" means the amount (if any) by which—

(A) the sum of the credits from all passive activities allowable for the taxable year under—

(i) subpart D of part IV of subchapter A, or

(ii) subpart B (other than section 27(a)) of such part IV, exceeds

(B) the regular tax liability of the taxpayer for the taxable year allocable to all passive activities.

(e) Special rules for determining income or loss from a passive activity.—For purposes of this section—

(1) Certain income not treated as income from passive activity.—In determining the income or loss from any activity—

(A) In general.—There shall not be taken into account—

(i) any—

(I) gross income from interest, dividends, annuities, or royalties not derived in the ordinary course of a trade or business,

(II) expenses (other than interest) which are clearly and directly allocable to such gross income, and

(III) interest expense properly allocable to such gross income, and

(ii) gain or loss attributable to the disposition of property—

(I) producing income of a type described in clause (i), or

(II) held for investment.

For purposes of clause (ii), any interest in a passive activity shall not be treated as property held for investment.

(B) Return on working capital.—For purposes of subparagraph (A), any income, gain, or loss which is attributable to an investment of working capital shall be treated as not derived in the ordinary course of a trade or business.

(2) Passive losses of certain closely held corporations may offset active income.—

(A) In general.—If a closely held C corporation (other than a personal service corporation) has net active income for any taxable year, the passive activity loss of such taxpayer for such taxable year (determined without regard to this paragraph)—

(i) shall be allowable as a deduction against net active income, and

(ii) shall not be taken into account under subsection (a) to the extent so allowable as a deduction.

A similar rule shall apply in the case of any passive activity credit of the taxpayer.

(B) Net active income.—For purposes of this paragraph, the term "net active income" means the taxable income of the taxpayer for the taxable year determined without regard to—

(i) any income or loss from a passive activity, and

(ii) any item of gross income, expense, gain, or loss described in paragraph (1)(A).

(3) Compensation for personal services.—Earned income (within the meaning of section 911(d)(2)(A)) shall not be taken into account in computing the income or loss from a passive activity for any taxable year.

(4) Dividends reduced by dividends received deduction.—For purposes of paragraphs (1) and (2), income from dividends shall be reduced by the amount of any dividends received deduction under section 243, 244, or 245.

(f) Treatment of former passive activities.—For purposes of this section—

(1) In general.—If an activity is a former passive activity for any taxable year—

(A) any unused deduction allocable to such activity under subsection (b) shall be offset against the income from such activity for the taxable year,

(B) any unused credit allocable to such activity under subsection (b) shall be offset against the regular tax liability (computed after the application of paragraph (1)) allocable to such activity for the taxable year, and

(C) any such deduction or credit remaining after the application of subparagraphs (A) and (B) shall continue to be treated as arising from a passive activity.

(2) Change in status of closely held C corporation or personal service corporation.—If a taxpayer ceases for any taxable year to be a closely held C corporation or personal service corporation, this section shall continue to apply to losses and credits to which this section applied for any preceding taxable year in the same manner as if such taxpayer continued to be a closely held C corporation or personal service corporation, whichever is applicable.

(3) Former passive activity.—The term "former passive activity" means any activity which, with respect to the taxpayer—

(A) is not a passive activity for the taxable year, but

(B) was a passive activity for any prior taxable year.

(g) Dispositions of entire interest in passive activity.—If during the taxable year a taxpayer disposes of his entire interest in any passive activity (or former passive activity), the following rules shall apply:

(1) Fully taxable transaction.—

(A) In general.—If all gain or loss realized on such disposition is recognized, any loss from such activity which has not previously been allowed as a deduction (and in the case of a passive activity for the taxable year, any loss realized on such disposition) shall not be treated as a passive activity loss and shall be allowable as a deduction against income in the following order:

(i) Income or gain from the passive activity for the taxable year (including any gain recognized on the disposition).

(ii) Net income or gain for the taxable year from all passive activities.

(iii) Any other income or gain.

(B) Subparagraph (A) not to apply to disposition involving related party. —If the taxpayer and the person acquiring the interest bear a relationship to each other described in section 267(b) or section 707(b)(1), then subparagraph (A) shall not apply to any loss of the taxpayer until the taxable year in which such interest is acquired (in a transaction described in subparagraph (A)) by another person who does not bear such a relationship to the taxpayer.

(C) Coordination with section 1211.—In the case of any loss realized on the disposition of an interest in a passive activity, section 1211 shall be applied before subparagraph (A) is applied.

(2) Disposition by death.—If an interest in the activity is transferred by reason of the death of the taxpayer—

(A) paragraph (1) shall apply to such losses to the extent such losses are greater than the excess (if any) of—

(i) the basis of such property in the hands of the transferee, over

(ii) the adjusted basis of such property immediately before the death of the taxpayer, and

(B) any losses to the extent of the excess described in subparagraph (A) shall not be allowed as a deduction for any taxable year.

(3) Installment sale of entire interest.—In the case of an installment sale of an entire interest in an activity to which section 453 applies, paragraph (1) shall apply to the portion of such losses for each taxable year which bears the same ratio to all such losses as the gain recognized on such sale during such taxable year bears to the gross profit from such sale realized (or to be realized) when payment is completed.

(h) Material participation defined.—For purposes of this section—

(1) In general.—A taxpayer shall be treated as materially participating in an activity only if the taxpayer is involved in the operations of the activity on a basis which is—

(A) regular,

(B) continuous, and

(C) substantial.

(2) Interests in limited partnerships.—Except as provided in regulations, no interest in a limited partnership as a limited partner shall be treated as an interest with respect to which a taxpayer materially participates.

(3) Treatment of certain retired individuals and surviving spouses.—A taxpayer shall be treated as materially participating in any farming activity for a taxable year if paragraph (4) or (5) of section 2032A(b) would cause the requirements of section 2032A(b)(1)(C)(ii) to be met with respect to real property used in such activity if such taxpayer had died during the taxable year.

(4) Certain closely held C corporations and personal service corporations. —A closely held C corporation or personal service corporation shall be treated as materially participating in an activity if—

(A) 1 or more shareholders holding stock representing more than 50 percent (by value) of the outstanding stock of such corporation materially participate in such activity, or

(B) in the case of a closely held C corporation (other than a personal service corporation), the requirements of section 465(c)(7)(C) (without regard to clause (iv)) are met with respect to such activity.

(5) Participation by spouse.—In determining whether a taxpayer materially participates, the participation of the spouse of the taxpayer shall be taken into account.

(i) $25,000 Offset for rental real estate activities.—

(1) In general.—In the case of any natural person, subsection (a) shall not apply to that portion of the passive activity loss or the deduction equivalent (within the meaning of subsection (j)(5)) of the passive activity credit for any taxable year which is attributable to all rental real estate activities with respect to which such individual actively participated in the taxable year in which such portion of such loss or credit arose.

(2) Dollar limitation.—The aggregate amount to which paragraph (1) applies for any taxable year shall not exceed $25,000.

(3) Phase-out of exemption.—

(A) In general.—In the case of any taxpayer, the $25,000 amount under paragraph (2) shall be reduced (but not below zero) by 50 percent of the amount by which the adjusted gross income of the taxpayer for the taxable year exceeds $100,000.

(B) Special phase-out of low-income housing and rehabilitation credits. —In the case of any portion of the passive activity credit for any taxable year which is attributable to any credit to which paragraph (6)(B) applies, subparagraph (A) shall be applied by substituting "$200,000" for "$100,000".

(C) Ordering rule to reflect separate phase-outs.—If subparagraph (B) applies for any taxable year, paragraph (1) shall be applied—

(i) first to the passive activity loss,

(ii) second to the portion of the passive activity credit to which subparagraph (B) does not apply, and

(iii) then to the portion of such credit to which subparagraph (B) applies.

(D) Adjusted gross income.—For purposes of this paragraph, adjusted gross income shall be determined without regard to—

(i) any amount includible in gross income under section 86,

(ii) any amount allowable as a deduction under section 219, and

(iii) any passive activity loss.

(4) Special rule for estates.—

(A) In general.—In the case of taxable years of an estate ending less than 2 years after the date of the death of the decedent, this subsection shall apply to all rental real estate activities with respect to which such decedent actively participated before his death.

(B) Reduction for surviving spouse's exemption.—For purposes of subparagraph (A), the $25,000 amount under paragraph (2) shall be reduced by the amount of the exemption under paragraph (1) (without regard to paragraph (3)) allowable to the surviving spouse of the decedent for the taxable year ending with or within the taxable year of the estate.

(5) Married individuals filing separately.—

(A) In general.—Except as provided in subparagraph (B), in the case of any married individual filing a separate return, this subsection shall be applied by substituting—

(i) "$12,500" for "$25,000" each place it appears,

(ii) "$50,000" for "$100,000" in paragraph (3)(A), and

(iii) "$100,000" for "$200,000" in paragraph (3)(B).

(B) Taxpayers not living apart.—This subsection shall not apply to a taxpayer who—

(i) is a married individual filing a separate return for any taxable year, and

(ii) does not live apart from his spouse at all times during such taxable year.

(6) Active participation.—

(A) In general.—An individual shall not be treated as actively participating with respect to any interest in any rental real estate activity for any period if, at any time during such period, such interest (including any interest of the spouse of the individual) is less than 10 percent (by value) of all interests in such activity.

(B) No participation requirement for low-income housing or rehabilitation credit.—Paragraphs (1) and (4)(A) shall be applied without regard to the active participation requirement in the case of—

(i) any credit determined under section 42 for any taxable year, or

(ii) any rehabilitation investment credit (within the meaning of section 48(o)).

(C) Interest as a limited partner.—No interest as a limited partner in a limited partnership shall be treated as an interest with respect to which the taxpayer actively participates.

(D) Participation by spouse.—In determining whether a taxpayer actively participates, the participation of the spouse of the taxpayer shall be taken into account.

(j) Other definitions and special rules.—For purposes of this section—

(1) Closely held C corporation.—The term "closely held C corporation" means any C corporation described in section 465(a)(1)(B).

(2) Personal service corporation.—The term "personal service corporation" has the meaning given such term by section 269A(b)(1), except that section 269A(b)(2) shall be applied—

(A) by substituting "any" for "more than 10 percent", and

(B) by substituting "any" for "50 percent or more in value" in section 318(a)(2)(C).

A corporation shall not be treated as a personal service corporation unless more than 10 percent of the stock (by value) in such corporation is held by employee-owners (within the meaning of section 269A(b)(2), as modified by the preceding sentence).

(3) Regular tax liability.—The term "regular tax liability" has the meaning given such term by section 26(b).

(4) Allocation of passive activity loss and credit.—The passive activity loss and the passive activity credit (and the $25,000 amount under subsection (i)) shall be allocated to activities, and within activities, on a pro rata basis in such manner as the Secretary may prescribe.

(5) Deduction equivalent.—The deduction equivalent of credits from a passive activity for any taxable year is the amount which (if allowed as a deduction) would reduce the regular tax liability for such taxable year by an amount equal to such credits.

(6) Special rule for gifts.—In the case of a disposition of any interest in a passive activity by gift—

  (A) the basis of such interest immediately before the transfer shall be increased by the amount of any passive activity losses allocable to such interest, and

  (B) such losses shall not be allowable as a deduction for any taxable year.

(7) Qualified residence interest.—The passive activity loss of a taxpayer shall be computed without regard to qualified residence interest (within the meaning of section 163(h)(3)).

(8) Rental activity.—The term "rental activity" means any activity where payments are principally for the use of tangible property.

(9) Election to increase basis of property by amount of disallowed credit.—For purposes of determining gain or loss from a disposition of any property to which subsection (g)(1) applies, the transferor may elect to increase the basis of such property immediately before the transfer by an amount equal to the portion of any unused credit allowable under this chapter which reduced the basis of such property for the taxable year in which such credit arose. If the taxpayer elects the application of this paragraph, such portion of the passive activity credit of such taxpayer shall not be allowed for any taxable year.

(k) Regulations.—The Secretary shall prescribe such regulations as may be necessary or appropriate to carry out provisions of this section, including regulations—

  (1) which specify what constitutes an activity, material participation, or active participation for purposes of this section,

  (2) which provide that certain items of gross income will not be taken into account in determining income or loss from any activity (and the treatment of expenses allocable to such income),

  (3) requiring net income or gain from a limited partnership or other passive activity to be treated as not from a passive activity,

  (4) which provide for the determination of the allocation of interest expense for purposes of this section, and

  (5) which deal with changes in marital status and changes between joint returns and separate returns.

(*l*) Phase-in of disallowance of losses and credits for interests held before date of enactment.—

  (1) In general.—In the case of any passive activity loss or credit for any taxable year beginning in calendar years 1987 through 1990 which—

(A) is attributable to a pre-enactment interest, but

(B) is not attributable to a carryforward to such taxable year of any loss or credit which was disallowed under this section for a preceding taxable year,

there shall be disallowed under subsection (a) only the applicable percentage of the amount which (but for this subsection) would have been disallowed under subsection (a) for such taxable year.

(2) Applicable percentage.—For purposes of this subsection, the applicable percentage shall be determined in accordance with the following table:

In the case of taxable years beginning in:	The applicable percentage is:
1987	35
1988	60
1989	80
1990	90.

(3) Portion of loss or credit attributable to pre-enactment interests.—For purposes of this subsection—

(A) In general.—The portion of the passive activity loss for any taxable year which is attributable to pre-enactment interests shall be equal to the lesser of—

(i) the passive activity loss for such taxable year, or

(ii) the passive activity loss for such taxable year determined by taking into account only pre-enactment interests.

For purposes of this subparagraph, the deduction equivalent (within the meaning of subsection (j)(5)) of a passive activity credit shall be taken into account.

(B) Pre-enactment interest.—

(i) In general.—The term "pre-enactment interest" means any interest in a passive activity held by a taxpayer on the date of the enactment of the Tax Reform Act of 1986, and at all times thereafter.

(ii) Binding contract exception.—For purposes of clause (i), any interest acquired after such date of enactment pursuant to a written binding contract in effect on such date, and at all times thereafter, shall be treated as held on such date.

(iii) Interest in activities.—The term "pre-enactment interest" shall not include an interest in a passive activity unless such activity was being conducted on such date of enactment. The preceding sentence shall not apply to an activity commencing after such date if—

(I) the property used in such activity is acquired pursuant to a written binding contract in effect on August 16, 1986, and at all times thereafter, or

(II) construction of property used in such activity began on or before August 16, 1986.

(Added Pub.L. 99–514, Title V, § 501(a), Oct. 22, 1986, 100 Stat. ——.)

Subpart D—Inventories

§ 471. General rule for inventories

(a) General rule.—Whenever in the opinion of the Secretary the use of inventories is necessary in order clearly to determine the income of any taxpayer, inventories shall be taken by such taxpayer on such basis as the Secretary may prescribe as conforming as nearly as may be to the best accounting practice in the trade or business and as most clearly reflecting the income.

(b) Cross reference.—

For rules relating to capitalization of direct and indirect costs of property, see section 263A.

§ 472. Last-in, first-out inventories

(a) Authorization.—A taxpayer may use the method provided in subsection (b) (whether or not such method has been prescribed under section 471) in inventorying goods specified in an application to use such method filed at such time and in such manner as the Secretary may prescribe. The change to, and the use of, such method shall be in accordance with such regulations as the Secretary may prescribe as necessary in order that the use of such method may clearly reflect income.

(b) Method applicable.—In inventorying goods specified in the application described in subsection (a), the taxpayer shall:

(1) Treat those remaining on hand at the close of the taxable year as being: First, those included in the opening inventory of the taxable year (in the order of acquisition) to the extent thereof; and second, those acquired in the taxable year;

(2) Inventory them at cost; and

(3) Treat those included in the opening inventory of the taxable year in which such method is first used as having been acquired at the same time and determine their cost by the average cost method.

(c) Condition.—Subsection (a) shall apply only if the taxpayer establishes to the satisfaction of the Secretary that the taxpayer has used no procedure other than that specified in paragraphs (1) and (3) of subsection (b) in inventorying such goods to ascertain the income, profit, or loss of the first taxable year for which the method described in subsection (b) is to be used, for the purpose of a report or statement covering such taxable year—

(1) to shareholders, partners, or other proprietors, or to beneficiaries, or

(2) for credit purposes.

(d) 3-year averaging for increases in inventory value.—The beginning inventory for the first taxable year for which the method described in subsection (b) is used shall be valued at cost. Any change in the inventory amount resulting from the application of the preceding sentence shall be taken into account ratably in each of the 3 taxable years beginning with the first taxable year for which the method described in subsection (b) is first used.

(e) Subsequent inventories.—If a taxpayer, having complied with subsection (a), uses the method described in subsection (b) for any taxable year, then such method shall be used in all subsequent taxable years unless—

(1) with the approval of the Secretary a change to a different method is authorized; or,

(2) the Secretary determines that the taxpayer has used for any such subsequent taxable year some procedure other than that specified in paragraph (1) of subsection (b) in inventorying the goods specified in the application to ascertain the income, profit, or loss of such subsequent taxable year for the purpose of a report or statement covering such taxable year (A) to shareholders, partners, or other proprietors, or beneficiaries, or (B) for credit purposes; and requires a change to a

method different from that prescribed in subsection (b) beginning with such subsequent taxable year or any taxable year thereafter.

If paragraph (1) or (2) of this subsection applies, the change to, and the use of, the different method shall be in accordance with such regulations as the Secretary may prescribe as necessary in order that the use of such method may clearly reflect income.

(f) Use of government price indexes in pricing inventory.—The Secretary shall prescribe regulations permitting the use of suitable published governmental indexes in such manner and circumstances as determined by the Secretary for purposes of the method described in subsection (b).

(g) Conformity rules applied on controlled group basis.—

(1) **In general.**—Except as otherwise provided in regulations, all members of the same group of financially related corporations shall be treated as 1 taxpayer for purposes of subsections (c) and (e)(2).

(2) **Group of financially related corporations.**—For purposes of paragraph (1), the term "group of financially related corporations" means—

(A) any affiliated group as defined in section 1504 determined by substituting "50 percent" for "80 percent" each place it appears in section 1504(a) and without regard to section 1504(b), and

(B) any other group of corporations which consolidate or combine for purposes of financial statements.

PART III—ADJUSTMENTS

§ 481. Adjustments required by changes in method of accounting

(a) General rule.—In computing the taxpayer's taxable income for any taxable year (referred to in this section as the "year of the change")—

(1) if such computation is under a method of accounting different from the method under which the taxpayer's taxable income for the preceding taxable year was computed, then

(2) there shall be taken into account those adjustments which are determined to be necessary solely by reason of the change in order to prevent amounts from being duplicated or omitted, except there shall not be taken into account any adjustment in respect of any taxable year to which this section does not apply unless the adjustment is attributable to a change in the method of accounting initiated by the taxpayer.

(b) Limitation on tax where adjustments are substantial.—

(1) **Three year allocation.**—If—

(A) the method of accounting from which the change is made was used by the taxpayer in computing his taxable income for the 2 taxable years preceding the year of the change, and

(B) the increase in taxable income for the year of the change which results solely by reason of the adjustments required by subsection (a) (2) exceeds $3,000,

then the tax under this chapter attributable to such increase in taxable income shall not be greater than the aggregate increase in the taxes under this chapter (or under the corresponding provisions of prior revenue laws) which would result if one-third of such increase in taxable income were included in taxable income for the year of the change and one-third of such increase were included for each of the 2 preceding taxable years.

(2) Allocation under new method of accounting.—If—

(A) the increase in taxable income for the year of the change which results solely by reason of the adjustments required by subsection (a) (2) exceeds $3,000, and

(B) the taxpayer establishes his taxable income (under the new method of accounting) for one or more taxable years consecutively preceding the taxable year of the change for which the taxpayer in computing taxable income used the method of accounting from which the change is made,

then the tax under this chapter attributable to such increase in taxable income shall not be greater than the net increase in the taxes under this chapter (or under the corresponding provisions of prior revenue laws) which would result if the adjustments required by subsection (a) (2) were allocated to the taxable year or years specified in subparagraph (B) to which they are properly allocable under the new method of accounting and the balance of the adjustments required by subsection (a) (2) was allocated to the taxable year of the change.

(3) Special rules for computations under paragraphs (1) and (2).—For purposes of this subsection—

(A) There shall be taken into account the increase or decrease in tax for any taxable year preceding the year of the change to which no adjustment is allocated under paragraph (1) or (2) but which is affected by a net operating loss (as defined in section 172) or by a capital loss carryback or carryover (as defined in section 1212), determined with reference to taxable years with respect to which adjustments under paragraph (1) or (2) are allocated.

(B) The increase or decrease in the tax for any taxable year for which an assessment of any deficiency, or a credit or refund of any overpayment, is prevented by any law or rule of law, shall be determined by reference to the tax previously determined (within the meaning of section 1314(a)) for such year.

(C) In applying section 7807(b) (1), the provisions of chapter 1 (other than subchapter E, relating to self-employment income) and chapter 2 of the Internal Revenue Code of 1939 shall be treated as the corresponding provisions of the Internal Revenue Code of 1939.

(c) Adjustments under regulations.—In the case of any change described in subsection (a), the taxpayer may, in such manner and subject to such conditions as the Secretary may by regulations prescribe, take the adjustments required by subsection (a) (2) into account in computing the tax imposed by this chapter for the taxable year or years permitted under such regulations.

§ 482. Allocation of income and deductions among taxpayers

In any case of two or more organizations, trades, or businesses (whether or not incorporated, whether or not organized in the United States, and whether or not affiliated) owned or controlled directly or indirectly by the same interests, the Secretary may distribute, apportion, or allocate gross income, deductions, credits, or allowances between or among such organizations, trades, or businesses, if he determines that such distribution, apportionment, or allocation is necessary in order to prevent evasion of taxes or clearly to reflect the income of any of such organizations, trades, or businesses. In the case of any transfer (or license) of intangible property (within the meaning of section 936(h)(3)(B)), the income with respect to such transfer or license shall be commensurate with the income attributable to the intangible.

§ 483.   Interest on certain deferred payments

(a) Amount constituting interest.—For purposes of this title, in the case of any payment—

(1) under any contract for the sale or exchange of any property, and

(2) to which this section applies,

there shall be treated as interest that portion of the total unstated interest under such contract which, as determined in a manner consistent with the method of computing interest under section 1272(a), is properly allocable to such payment.

(b) Total unstated interest.—For purposes of this section, the term "total unstated interest" means, with respect to a contract for the sale or exchange of property, an amount equal to the excess of—

(1) the sum of the payments to which this section applies which are due under the contract, over

(2) the sum of the present values of such payments and the present values of any interest payments due under the contract.

For purposes of the preceding sentence, the present value of a payment shall be determined under the rules of section 1274(b)(2) using a discount rate equal to the applicable Federal rate determined under section 1274(d).

(c) Payments to which subsection (a) applies.—

(1) In general.—Except as provided in subsection (d), this section shall apply to any payment on account of the sale or exchange of property which constitutes part or all of the sales price and which is due more than 6 months after the date of such sale or exchange under a contract—

(A) under which some or all of the payments are due more than 1 year after the date of such sale or exchange, and

(B) under which there is total unstated interest.

(2) Treatment of other debt instruments.—For purposes of this section, a debt instrument of the purchaser which is given in consideration for the sale or exchange of property shall not be treated as a payment, and any payment due under such debt instrument shall be treated as due under the contract for the sale or exchange.

(3) Debt instrument defined.—For purposes of this subsection, the term "debt instrument" has the meaning given such term by section 1275(a)(1).

(d) Exceptions and limitations.—

(1) Coordination with original issue discount rules.—This section shall not apply to any debt instrument for which an issue price is determined under section 1273(b) (other than paragraph (4) thereof) or section 1274.

(2) Sales prices of $3,000 or less.—This section shall not apply to any payment on account of the sale or exchange of property if it can be determined at the time of such sale or exchange that the sales price cannot exceed $3,000.

(3) Carrying charges.—In the case of the purchaser, the tax treatment of amounts paid on account of the sale or exchange of property shall be made without regard to this section if any such amounts are treated under section 163(b) as if they included interest.

(4) Certain sales of patents.—In the case of any transfer described in section 1235(a) (relating to sale or exchange of patents), this section shall not apply to any amount contingent on the productivity, use, or disposition of the property transferred.

(e) Maximum rate of interest on certain transfers of land between related parties.—

(1) In general.—In the case of any qualified sale, the discount rate used in determining the total unstated interest rate under subsection (b) shall not exceed 6 percent, compounded semiannually.

(2) Qualified sale.—For purposes of this subsection, the term "qualified sale" means any sale or exchange of land by an individual to a member of such individual's family (within the meaning of section 267(c)(4)).

(3) $500,000 limitation.—Paragraph (1) shall not apply to any qualified sale between individuals made during any calendar year to the extent that the sales price for such sale (when added to the aggregate sales price for prior qualified sales between such individuals during the calendar year) exceeds $500,000.

(4) Nonresident alien individuals.—Paragraph (1) shall not apply to any sale or exchange if any party to such sale or exchange is a nonresident alien individual.

(f) Regulations.—The Secretary shall prescribe such regulations as may be necessary or appropriate to carry out the purposes of this section including regulations providing for the application of this section in the case of—

(1) any contract for the sale or exchange of property under which the liability for, or the amount or due date of, a payment cannot be determined at the time of the sale or exchange, or

(2) any change in the liability for, or the amount or due date of, any payment (including interest) under a contract for the sale or exchange of property.

(g) Cross References.—

(1) For treatment of assumptions, see section 1274(c)(4).

(2) For special rules for certain transactions where stated principal amount does not exceed $2,800,000, see section 1274A.

(3) For special rules in case of the borrower under certain loans for personal use, see section 1275(b).

SUBCHAPTER F—EXEMPT ORGANIZATIONS

Part

PART I—GENERAL RULE

§ 501. Exemption from tax on corporations, certain trusts, etc.

(a) Exemption from taxation.—An organization described in subsection (c) or (d) or section 401(a) shall be exempt from taxation under this subtitle unless such exemption is denied under section 502 or 503.

* Omitted entirely.

(b) Tax on unrelated business income and certain other activities.—An organization exempt from taxation under subsection (a) shall be subject to tax to the extent provided in parts II, III, and VI of this subchapter, but (notwithstanding parts II, III, and VI of this subchapter) shall be considered an organization exempt from income taxes for the purpose of any law which refers to organizations exempt from income taxes.

(c) List of exempt organizations.—The following organizations are referred to in subsection (a):

* * *

(3) Corporations, and any community chest, fund, or foundation, organized and operated exclusively for religious, charitable, scientific, testing for public safety, literary, or educational purposes, or to foster national or international amateur sports competition (but only if no part of its activities involve the provision of athletic facilities or equipment), or for the prevention of cruelty to children or animals, no part of the net earnings of which inures to the benefit of any private shareholder or individual, no substantial part of the activities of which is carrying on propaganda, or otherwise attempting, to influence legislation (except as otherwise provided in subsection (h)), and which does not participate in, or intervene in (including the publishing or distributing of statements), any political campaign on behalf of any candidate for public office.

(4) Civic leagues or organizations not organized for profit but operated exclusively for the promotion of social welfare, or local associations of employees, the membership of which is limited to the employees of a designated person or persons in a particular municipality, and the net earnings of which are devoted exclusively to charitable, educational, or recreational purposes.

(5) Labor, agricultural, or horticultural organizations.

(6) Business leagues, chambers of commerce, real-estate boards, boards of trade, or professional football leagues (whether or not administering a pension fund for football players), not organized for profit and no part of the net earnings of which inures to the benefit of any private shareholder or individual.

(7) Clubs organized for pleasure, recreation, and other nonprofitable purposes, substantially all of the activities of which are for such purposes and no part of the net earnings of which inures to the benefit of any private shareholder.

* * *

(9) Voluntary employees' beneficiary associations providing for the payment of life, sick, accident, or other benefits to the members of such association or their dependents or designated beneficiaries, if no part of the net earnings of such association inures (other than through such payments) to the benefit of any private shareholder or individual.

* * *

(h) Expenditures by public charities to influence legislation.—

(1) **General rule.**—In the case of an organization to which this subsection applies, exemption from taxation under subsection (a) shall be denied because a substantial part of the activities of such organization consists of carrying on propaganda, or otherwise attempting, to influence legislation, but only if such organization normally—

(A) makes lobbying expenditures in excess of the lobbying ceiling amount for such organization for each taxable year, or

(B) makes grass roots expenditures in excess of the grass roots ceiling amount for such organization for each taxable year.

(2) **Definitions.**—For purposes of this subsection—

(A) **Lobbying expenditures.**—The term "lobbying expenditures" means expenditures for the purpose of influencing legislation (as defined in section 4911(d)).

(B) **Lobbying ceiling amount.**—The lobbying ceiling amount for any organization for any taxable year is 150 percent of the lobbying nontaxable amount for such organization for such taxable year, determined under section 4911.

(C) **Grass roots expenditures.**—The term "grass roots expenditures" means expenditures for the purpose of influencing legislation (as defined in section 4911(d) without regard to paragraph (1) (B) thereof).

(D) **Grass roots ceiling amount.**—The grass roots ceiling amount for any organization for any taxable year is 150 percent of the grass roots nontaxable amount for such organization for such taxable year, determined under section 4911.

(3) **Organizations to which this subsection applies.**—This subsection shall apply to any organization which has elected (in such manner and at such time as the Secretary may prescribe) to have the provisions of this subsection apply to such organization and which, for the taxable year which includes the date the election is made, is described in subsection (c) (3) and—

(A) is described in paragraph (4), and

(B) is not a disqualified organization under paragraph (5).

(4) **Organizations permitted to elect to have this subsection apply.**—An organization is described in this paragraph if it is described in—

(A) section 170(b) (1) (A) (ii) (relating to educational institutions),

(B) section 170(b) (1) (A) (iii) (relating to hospitals and medical research organizations),

(C) section 170(b) (1) (A) (iv) (relating to organizations supporting government schools),

(D) section 170(b) (1) (A) (vi) (relating to organizations publicly supported by charitable contributions),

(E) section 509(a) (2) (relating to organizations publicly supported by admissions, sales, etc.), or

(F) section 509(a) (3) (relating to organizations supporting certain types of public charities) except that for purposes of this subparagraph, section 509(a) (3) shall be applied without regard to the last sentence of section 509(a).

(5) **Disqualified organizations.**—For purposes of paragraph (3) an organization is a disqualified organization if it is—

(A) described in section 170(b) (1) (A) (i) (relating to churches),

(B) an integrated auxiliary of a church or of a convention or association of churches, or

* * *

(i) **Prohibition of discrimination by certain social clubs.**—Notwithstanding subsection (a), an organization which is described in subsection (c) (7) shall not be exempt from taxation under subsection (a) for any taxable year if, at any time during such taxable year, the charter, bylaws, or other governing instrument, of such organization or any written policy statement of such organization contains a provision which provides for discrimination against any person on the basis of race, color, or religion. The preceding sentence to the extent it relates to discrimination on the basis of religion shall not apply to—

(1) an auxiliary of a fraternal beneficiary society if such society—

(A) is described in subsection (c)(8) and exempt from tax under subsection (a), and

(B) limits its membership to the members of a particular religion, or

(2) a club which in good faith limits its membership to the members of a particular religion in order to further the teachings or principles of that religion, and not to exclude individuals of a particular race or color.

* * *

(k) Treatment of certain organizations providing child care.—For purposes of subsection (c)(3) of this section and sections 170(c)(2), 2055(a)(2), and 2522(a)(2), the term "educational purposes includes the providing of care of children away from their homes if—

(1) substantially all of the care provided by the organization is for purposes of enabling individuals to be gainfully employed, and

(2) the services provided by the organization are available to the general public.

* * *

§ 505. Additional requirements for organizations described in paragraph (9), (17), or (20) of section 501(c)

(a) Certain requirements must be met in the case of organizations described in paragraph (9) or (20) of section 501(c).—

(1) Voluntary employees' beneficiary associations, etc.—An organization described in paragraph (9) or (20) of subsection (c) of section 501 which is part of a plan shall not be exempt from tax under section 501(a) unless such plan meets the requirements of subsection (b) of this section.

(2) Exception for collective bargaining agreements.—Paragraph (1) shall not apply to any organization which is part of a plan maintained pursuant to 1 or more collective bargaining agreements between 1 or more employee organizations and 1 or more employers.

(b) Nondiscrimination requirements.—

(1) In general.—Except a plan meets the requirements of this subsection only if—

(A) each class of benefits under the plan is provided under a classification of employees which is set forth in the plan and which is found by the Secretary not to be discriminatory in favor of employees who are highly compensated individuals, and

(B) in the case of each class of benefits, such benefits do not discriminate in favor of employees who are highly compensated individuals.

A life insurance, disability, severance pay, or supplemental unemployment compensation benefit shall not be considered to fail to meet the requirements of subparagraph (B) merely because the benefits available bear a uniform relationship to the total compensation, or the basic or regular rate of compensation, of employees covered by the plan.

(2) Exclusion of certain employees.—For purposes of paragraph (1), there may be excluded from consideration—

(A) employees who have not completed 3 years of service,

(B) employees who have not attained age 21,

(C) seasonal employees or less than half-time employees,

(D) employees not included in the plan who are included in a unit of employees covered by an agreement between employee representatives and 1 or more employers which the Secretary finds to be a collective bargaining agreement if the class of benefits involved was the subject of good faith bargaining between such employee representatives and such employer or employers, and

(E) employees who are nonresident aliens and who receive no earned income (within the meaning of section 911(d)(2)) from the employer which constitutes income from sources within the United States (within the meaning of section 861(a)(3)).

* * *

(3) Application of subsection where other nondiscrimination rules provided.—In the case of any benefit for which a provision of this chapter other than this subsection provides nondiscrimination rules, paragraph (1) shall not apply but the requirements of this subsection shall be met only if the nondiscrimination rules so provided are satisfied with respect to such benefit.

(4) Aggregation rules.—For purposes of this subsection—

(A) Aggregation of plans.—At the election of the employer, 2 or more plans of such employer may be treated as 1 plan.

(B) Treatment of related employers.—Rules similar to the rules of subsections (b), (c), (m), and (n) of section 414 shall apply. For purposes of the preceding sentence, section 414(n) shall be applied without regard to paragraph (5).

(5) Highly compensated individual.—For purposes of this subsection, the term "highly compensated individual" has the meaning given such term by section 105(h)(5). For purposes of the preceding sentence, section 105(h)(5) shall be applied by substituting "10 percent" for "25 percent".

(c) Requirement that organization notify Secretary that it is applying for tax-exempt status.—

(1) In general.—An organization shall not be treated as an organization described in paragraph (9), (17), or (20) of section 501(c)—

(A) unless it has given notice to the Secretary, in such manner as the Secretary may by regulations prescribed, that it is applying for recognition of such status, or

(B) for any period before the giving of such notice, if such notice is given after the time prescribed by the Secretary by regulations for giving notice under this subsection.

(2) Special rule for existing organizations.—In the case of any organization in existence on the date of the enactment of the Tax Reform Act of 1984, the time for giving notice under paragraph (1) shall not expire before the date 1 year after such date of the enactment.

SUBCHAPTER G—CORPORATIONS USED TO AVOID INCOME TAX ON SHAREHOLDERS

PART I—CORPORATIONS IMPROPERLY ACCUMULATING SURPLUS

§ 531. Imposition of accumulated earnings tax

In addition to other taxes imposed by this chapter, there is hereby imposed for each taxable year on the accumulated taxable income (as defined in section 535) of every corporation described in section 532, an accumulated earnings tax equal to the sum of—

(1) 27½ percent of the accumulated taxable income not in excess of $100,000, plus

(2) 38½ percent of the accumulated taxable income in excess of $100,000.

§ 532. Corporations subject to accumulated earnings tax

(a) **General rule.**—The accumulated earnings tax imposed by section 531 shall apply to every corporation (other than those described in subsection (b)) formed or availed of for the purpose of avoiding the income tax with respect to its shareholders or the shareholders of any other corporation, by permitting earnings and profits to accumulate instead of being divided or distributed.

(b) **Exceptions.**—The accumulated earnings tax imposed by section 531 shall not apply to—

(1) a personal holding company (as defined in section 542),

(2) a foreign personal holding company (as defined in section 552),

(3) a corporation exempt from tax under subchapter F (section 501 and following), or

* * *

(c) **Application determined without regard to number of shareholders.**—The application of this part to a corporation shall be determined without regard to the number of shareholders of such corporation.

§ 533. Evidence of purpose to avoid income tax

(a) **Unreasonable accumulation determinative of purpose.**—For purposes of section 532, the fact that the earnings and profits of a corporation are permitted to accumulate beyond the reasonable needs of the business shall be determinative of the purpose to avoid the income tax with respect to shareholders, unless the corporation by the preponderance of the evidence shall prove to the contrary.

(b) **Holding or investment company.**—The fact that any corporation is a mere holding or investment company shall be prima facie evidence of the purpose to avoid the income tax with respect to shareholders.

  * Omitted entirely.

§ 534. Burden of proof

(a) General rule.—In any proceeding before the Tax Court involving a notice of deficiency based in whole or in part on the allegation that all or any part of the earnings and profits have been permitted to accumulate beyond the reasonable needs of the business, the burden of proof with respect to such allegation shall—

(1) if notification has not been sent in accordance with subsection (b), be on the Secretary, or

(2) if the taxpayer has submitted the statement described in subsection (c), be on the Secretary with respect to the grounds set forth in such statement in accordance with the provisions of such subsection.

(b) Notification by Secretary.—Before mailing the notice of deficiency referred to in subsection (a), the Secretary may send by certified mail or registered mail a notification informing the taxpayer that the proposed notice of deficiency includes an amount with respect to the accumulated earnings tax imposed by section 531.

(c) Statement by taxpayer.—Within such time (but not less than 30 days) after the mailing of the notification described in subsection (b) as the Secretary may prescribe by regulations, the taxpayer may submit a statement of the grounds (together with facts sufficient to show the basis thereof) on which the taxpayer relies to establish that all or any part of the earnings and profits have not been permitted to accumulate beyond the reasonable needs of the business.

* * *

§ 535. Accumulated taxable income

(a) Definition.—For purposes of this subtitle, the term "accumulated taxable income" means the taxable income, adjusted in the manner provided in subsection (b), minus the sum of the dividends paid deduction (as defined in section 561) and the accumulated earnings credit (as defined in subsection (c)).

(b) Adjustments to taxable income.—For purposes of subsection (a), taxable income shall be adjusted as follows:

(1) Taxes.—There shall be allowed as a deduction Federal income and excess profits taxes and income, war profits, and excess profits taxes of foreign countries and possessions of the United States (to the extent not allowable as a deduction under section 275(a) (4)), accrued during the taxable year or deemed to be paid by a domestic corporation under section 902(a) or 960(a) (1) for the taxable year, but not including the accumulated earnings tax imposed by section 531, the personal holding company tax imposed by section 541, or the taxes imposed by corresponding sections of a prior income tax law.

(2) Charitable contributions.—The deduction for charitable contributions provided under section 170 shall be allowed without regard to section 170(b) (2).

(3) Special deductions disallowed.—The special deductions for corporations provided in part VIII (except section 248) of subchapter B (section 241 and following, relating to the deduction for dividends received by corporations, etc.) shall not be allowed.

(4) Net operating loss.—The net operating loss deduction provided in section 172 shall not be allowed.

(5) Capital losses.—

(A) In general.—Except as provided in subparagraph (B), there shall be allowed as a deduction an amount equal to the net capital loss for the taxable year (determined without regard to paragraph (7)(A)).

(B) Recapture of previous deductions for capital gains.—The aggregate amount allowable as a deduction under subparagraph (A) for any taxable year shall be reduced by the lesser of—

(i) the nonrecaptured capital gains deductions, or

(ii) the amount of the accumulated earnings and profits of the corporation as of the close of the preceding taxable year.

(C) Nonrecaptured capital gains deductions.—For purposes of subparagraph (B), the term "nonrecaptured capital gains deductions" means the excess of—

(i) the aggregate amount allowable as a deduction under paragraph (6) for preceding taxable years beginning after July 18, 1984, over

(ii) the aggregate of the reductions under subparagraph (B) for preceding taxable years.

(6) Net capital gains.—

(A) In general.—There shall be allowed as a deduction—

(i) the net capital gain for the taxable year (determined with the application of paragraph (7)), reduced by

(ii) the taxes attributable to such net capital gain.

(B) Attributable taxes.—For purposes of subparagraph (A), the taxes attributable to the net capital gain shall be an amount equal to the difference between—

(i) the taxes imposed by this subtitle (except the tax imposed by this part) for the taxable year, and

(ii) such taxes computed for such year without including in taxable income the net capital gain for the taxable year (determined without the application of paragraph (7)).

(7) Capital loss carryovers.—

(A) Unlimited carryforward.—The net capital loss for any taxable year shall be treated as a short-term capital loss in the next taxable year.

(B) Section 1212 inapplicable.—No allowance shall be made for the capital loss carryback or carryforward provided in section 1212.

(8) Special rules for mere holding or investment companies.—In the case of a mere holding or investment company—

(A) Capital loss deduction, etc., not allowed.—Paragraphs (5) and (7)(A) shall not apply.

(B) Deduction for certain offsets.—There shall be allowed as a deduction the net short-term capital gain for the taxable year to the extent such gain does not exceed the amount of any capital loss carryover to such taxable year under section 1212 (determined without regard to paragraph (7)(B)).

(C) Earnings and profits.—For purposes of subchapter C, the accumulated earnings and profits at any time shall not be less than they would be if this subsection had applied to the computation of earnings and profits for all taxable years beginning after July 18, 1984.

(c) Accumulated earnings credit.—

(1) General rule.—For purposes of subsection (a), in the case of a corporation other than a mere holding or investment company the accumulated earnings credit is (A) an amount equal to such part of the earnings and profits for the taxable year as are retained for the reasonable needs of the business, minus (B) the deduction allowed by subsection (b)(6). For purposes of this paragraph, the amount of the earnings and profits for the taxable year which are retained is the amount by which the earnings and profits for the taxable year exceed the dividends paid deduction (as defined in section 561) for such year.

(2) Minimum credit.—

(A) In general.—The credit allowable under paragraph (1) shall in no case be less than the amount by which $250,000 exceeds the accumulated earnings and profits of the corporation at the close of the preceding taxable year.

(B) Certain service corporations.—In the case of a corporation the principal function of which is the performance of services in the field of health, law, engineering, architecture, accounting, actuarial science, performing arts, or consulting, subparagraph (A) shall be applied by substituting "$150,000" for "$250,000".

(3) Holding and investment companies.—In the case of a corporation which is a mere holding or investment company, the accumulated earnings credit is the amount (if any) by which $250,000 exceeds the accumulated earnings and profits of the corporation at the close of the preceding taxable year.

(4) Accumulated earnings and profits.—For purposes of paragraphs (2) and (3), the accumulated earnings and profits at the close of the preceding taxable year shall be reduced by the dividends which under section 563(a) (relating to dividends paid after the close of the taxable year) are considered as paid during such taxable year.

(5) Cross reference.—

For denial of credit provided in paragraph (2) or (3) where multiple corporations are formed to avoid tax, see section 1551, and for limitation on such credit in the case of certain controlled corporations, see sections 1561 and 1564.

* * *

§ 537. Reasonable needs of the business

(a) General rule.—For purposes of this part, the term "reasonable needs of the business" includes—

(1) the reasonably anticipated needs of the business,

(2) the section 303 redemption needs of the business, and

(3) the excess business holdings redemption needs of the business.

(b) Special rules.—For purposes of subsection (a)—

(1) Section 303 redemption needs.—The term "section 303 redemption needs" means, with respect to the taxable year of the corporation in which a shareholder of the corporation died or any taxable year thereafter, the amount needed (or reasonably anticipated to be needed) to make a redemption of stock included in the gross estate of the decedent (but not in excess of the maximum amount of stock to which section 303(a) may apply).

(2) Excess business holdings redemption needs.—The term "excess business holdings redemption needs" means the amount needed (or reasonably anticipated to be needed) to redeem from a private foundation stock which—

(A) such foundation held on May 26, 1969 (or which was received by such foundation pursuant to a will or irrevocable trust to which section 4943(c) (5) applies), and

(B) constituted excess business holdings on May 26, 1969, or would have constituted excess business holdings as of such date if there were taken into account (i) stock received pursuant to a will or trust described in subparagraph (A), and (ii) the reduction in the total outstanding stock of the corporation which would have resulted solely from the redemption of stock held by the private foundation.

(3) Obligations incurred to make redemptions.—In applying paragraphs (1) and (2), the discharge of any obligation incurred to make a redemption described in such paragraphs shall be treated as the making of such redemption.

(4) Product liability loss reserves.—The accumulation of reasonable amounts for the payment of reasonably anticipated product liability losses (as defined in section 172(i)), as determined under regulations prescribed by the Secretary, shall be treated as accumulated for the reasonably anticipated needs of the business.

(5) No inference as to prior taxable years.—The application of this part to any taxable year before the first taxable year specified in paragraph (1) shall be made without regard to the fact that distributions in redemption coming within the terms of such paragraphs were subsequently made.

PART II—PERSONAL HOLDING COMPANIES

§ 541. Imposition of personal holding company tax

In addition to other taxes imposed by this chapter, there is hereby imposed for each taxable year on the undistributed personal holding company income (as defined in section 545) of every personal holding company (as defined in section 542) a personal holding company tax equal to 28 percent (38.5 percent in the case of taxable years beginning in 1987) of the undistributed personal holding company income.

§ 542. Definition of personal holding company

(a) General rule.—For purposes of this subtitle, the term "personal holding company" means any corporation (other than a corporation described in subsection (c)) if—

(1) Adjusted ordinary gross income requirement.—At least 60 percent of its adjusted ordinary gross income (as defined in section 543(b) (2)) for the taxable year is personal holding company income (as defined in section 543(a)), and

(2) Stock ownership requirement.—At any time during the last half of the taxable year more than 50 percent in value of its outstanding stock is owned, directly or indirectly, by or for not more than 5 individuals. For purposes of this paragraph, an organization described in section 401(a), 501(c) (17), or 509(a) or a portion of a trust permanently set aside or to be used exclusively for the purposes described in section 642(c) or a corresponding provision of a prior income tax law shall be considered an individual.

(b) Corporations filing consolidated returns.—

(1) **General rule.**—In the case of an affiliated group of corporations filing or required to file a consolidated return under section 1501 for any taxable year, the adjusted ordinary gross income requirement of subsection (a) (1) of this section shall, except as provided in paragraphs (2) and (3), be applied for such year with respect to the consolidated adjusted ordinary gross income and the consolidated personal holding company income of the affiliated group. No member of such an affiliated group shall be considered to meet such adjusted ordinary gross income requirement unless the affiliated group meets such requirement.

(2) **Ineligible affiliated group.**—Paragraph (1) shall not apply to an affiliated group of corporations if—

(A) any member of the affiliated group of corporations (including the common parent corporation) derived 10 percent or more of its adjusted ordinary gross income for the taxable year from sources outside the affiliated group, and

(B) 80 percent or more of the amount described in subparagraph (A) consists of personal holding company income (as defined in section 543).

For purposes of this paragraph, section 543 shall be applied as if the amount described in subparagraph (A) were the adjusted ordinary gross income of the corporation.

(3) **Excluded corporations.**—Paragraph (1) shall not apply to an affiliated group of corporations if any member of the affiliated group (including the common parent corporation) is a corporation excluded from the definition of personal holding company under subsection (c).

(4) **Certain dividend income received by a common parent.**—In applying paragraph (2) (A) and (B), personal holding company income and adjusted ordinary gross income shall not include dividends received by a common parent corporation from another corporation if—

(A) the common parent corporation owns, directly or indirectly, more than 50 percent of the outstanding voting stock of such other corporation, and

(B) such other corporation is not a personal holding company for the taxable year in which the dividends are paid.

* * *

(c) **Exceptions.**—The term "personal holding company" as defined in subsection (a) does not include—

(1) a corporation exempt from tax under subchapter F (sec. 501 and following);

(2) a bank as defined in section 581, or a domestic building and loan association within the meaning of section 7701(a) (19);

(3) a life insurance company;

(4) a surety company;

(5) a foreign personal holding company as defined in section 552;

(6) a lending or finance company if—

(A) 60 percent or more of its ordinary gross income (as defined in section 543(b) (1)) is derived directly from the active and regular conduct of a lending or finance business;

(B) the personal holding company income for the taxable year (computed without regard to income described in subsection (d) (3) and income derived directly from the active and regular conduct of a lending or finance business, and computed by including as personal holding company income the entire amount of the gross income from rents, royalties, produced film rents, and compensation for use of corporate property by shareholders) is not more than 20 percent of the ordinary gross income;

(C) the sum of the deductions which are directly allocable to the active and regular conduct of its lending or finance business equals or exceeds the sum of—

(i) 15 percent of so much of the ordinary gross income derived therefrom as does not exceed $500,000, plus

(ii) 5 percent of so much of the ordinary gross income derived therefrom as exceeds $500,000; and

(D) the loans to a person who is a shareholder in such company during the taxable year by or for whom 10 percent or more in value of its outstanding stock is owned directly or indirectly (including, in the case of an individual, stock owned by members of his family as defined in section 544(a) (2)), outstanding at any time during such year do not exceed $5,000 in principal amount;

* * *

(9) a corporation which is subject to the jurisdiction of the court in a title 11 or similar case (within the meaning of section 368(a)(3)(A)) unless a major purpose of instituting or continuing such case is the avoidance of the tax imposed by section 541; and

* * *

(d) Special rules for applying subsection (c) (6).—

(1) Lending or finance business defined.—

(A) In general.—Except as provided in subparagraph (B), for purposes of subsection (c) (6), the term "lending or finance business" means a business of—

(i) making loans,

(ii) purchasing or discounting accounts receivable, notes, or installment obligations,

(iii) rendering services or making facilities available in connection with activities described in clauses (i) and (ii) carried on by the corporation rendering services or making facilities available, or

(iv) rendering services or making facilities available to another corporation which is engaged in the lending or finance business (within the meaning of this paragraph), if such services or facilities are related to the lending or finance business (within such meaning) of such other corporation and such other corporation and the corporation rendering services or making facilities available are members of the same affiliated group (as defined in section 1504).

* * *

§ 543. Personal holding company income

(a) General rule.—For purposes of this subtitle, the term "personal holding company income" means the portion of the adjusted ordinary gross income which consists of:

(1) Dividends, etc.—Dividends, interest, royalties (other than mineral, oil, or gas royalties or copyright royalties), and annuities. This paragraph shall not apply to—

(A) interest constituting rent (as defined in subsection (b)(3)),

* * *

(C) active business computer software royalties (within the meaning of subsection (d)).

(2) **Rents.**—The adjusted income from rents; except that such adjusted income shall not be included if—

(A) such adjusted income constitutes 50 percent or more of the adjusted ordinary gross income, and

(B) the sum of—

(i) the dividends paid during the taxable year (determined under section 562),

(ii) the dividends considered as paid on the last day of the taxable year under section 563(c) (as limited by the second sentence of section 563(b)), and

(iii) the consent dividends for the taxable year (determined under section 565),

equals or exceeds the amount, if any, by which the personal holding company income for the taxable year (computed without regard to this paragraph and paragraph (6), and computed by including as personal holding company income copyright royalties and the adjusted income from mineral, oil, and gas royalties) exceeds 10 percent of the ordinary gross income.

(3) **Mineral, oil, and gas royalties.**—The adjusted income from mineral, oil, and gas royalties; except that such adjusted income shall not be included if—

(A) such adjusted income constitutes 50 percent or more of the adjusted ordinary gross income,

(B) the personal holding company income for the taxable year (computed without regard to this paragraph, and computed by including as personal holding company income copyright royalties and the adjusted income from rents) is not more than 10 percent of the ordinary gross income, and

(C) the sum of the deductions which are allowable under section 162 (relating to trade or business expenses) other than—

(i) deductions for compensation for personal services rendered by the shareholders, and

(ii) deductions which are specifically allowable under sections other than section 162,

equals or exceeds 15 percent of the adjusted ordinary gross income.

(4) **Copyright royalties.**—Copyright royalties; except that copyright royalties shall not be included if—

(A) such royalties (exclusive of royalties received for the use of, or right to use, copyrights or interests in copyrights on works created in whole, or in part, by any shareholder) constitute 50 percent or more of the ordinary gross income,

(B) the personal holding company income for the taxable year computed—

(i) without regard to copyright royalties, other than royalties received for the use of, or right to use, copyrights or interests in copyrights in works created in whole, or in part, by any shareholder owning more than 10 percent of the total outstanding capital stock of the corporation,

(ii) without regard to dividends from any corporation in which the taxpayer owns at least 50 percent of all classes of stock entitled to vote and at least 50 percent of the total value of all classes of stock and which corporation meets the requirements of this subparagraph and subparagraphs (A) and (C), and

(iii) by including as personal holding company income the adjusted income from rents and the adjusted income from mineral, oil, and gas royalties,

is not more than 10 percent of the ordinary gross income, and

(C) the sum of the deductions which are properly allocable to such royalties and which are allowable under section 162, other than—

(i) deductions for compensation for personal services rendered by the shareholders,

(ii) deductions for royalties paid or accrued, and

(iii) deductions which are specifically allowable under sections other than section 162,

equals or exceeds 25 percent of the amount by which the ordinary gross income exceeds the sum of the royalties paid or accrued and the amounts allowable as deductions under section 167 (relating to depreciation) with respect to copyright royalties.

For purposes of this subsection, the term "copyright royalties" means compensation, however designated, for the use of, or the right to use, copyrights in works protected by copyright issued under title 17 of the United States Code and to which copyright protection is also extended by the laws of any country other than the United States of America by virtue of any international treaty, convention, or agreement, or interests in any such copyrighted works, and includes payments from any person for performing rights in any such copyrighted work and payments (other than produced film rents as defined in paragraph (5) (B)) received for the use of, or right to use, films. For purposes of this paragraph, the term "shareholder" shall include any person who owns stock within the meaning of section 544. This paragraph shall not apply to active business computer software royalties.".

(5) Produced film rents.—

(A) Produced film rents; except that such rents shall not be included if such rents constitute 50 percent or more of the ordinary gross income.

(B) For purposes of this section, the term "produced film rents" means payments received with respect to an interest in a film for the use of, or right to use, such film, but only to the extent that such interest was acquired before substantial completion of production of such film. In the case of a producer who actively participates in the production of the film, such term includes an interest in the proceeds or profits from the film, but only to the extent such interest is attributable to such active participation.

(6) Use of corporate property by shareholder.—

(A) Amounts received as compensation (however designated and from whomever received) for the use of, or the right to use, tangible property of the corporation in any case where, at any time during the taxable year, 25 percent or more in value of the outstanding stock of the corporation is owned, directly or indirectly, by or for an individual entitled to the use of the property (whether such right is obtained directly from the corporation or by means of a sublease or other arrangement).

(B) Subparagraph (A) shall apply only to a corporation which has personal holding company income in excess of 10 percent of its ordinary gross income.

(C) For purposes of the limitation in subparagraph (B), personal holding company income shall be computed—

(i) without regard to subparagraph (A) or paragraph (2),

(ii) by excluding amounts received as compensation for the use of (or right to use) intangible property (other than mineral, oil, or gas royalties or copyright royalties) if a substantial part of the tangible property used in connection with such intangible property is owned by the corporation and all such tangible and intangible property is used in the active conduct of a trade or business by an individual or individuals described in subparagraph (A), and

(iii) by including copyright royalties and adjusted income from mineral, oil, and gas royalties.

(7) Personal service contracts.—

(A) Amounts received under a contract under which the corporation is to furnish personal services; if some person other than the corporation has the right to designate (by name or by description) the individual who is to perform the services, or if the individual who is to perform the services is designated (by name or by description) in the contract; and

(B) amounts received from the sale or other disposition of such a contract.

This paragraph shall apply with respect to amounts received for services under a particular contract only if at some time during the taxable year 25 percent or more in value of the outstanding stock of the corporation is owned, directly or indirectly, by or for the individual who has performed, is to perform, or may be designated (by name or by description) as the one to perform, such services.

(8) Estates and trusts.—Amounts includible in computing the taxable income of the corporation under part I of subchapter J (sec. 641 and following, relating to estates, trusts, and beneficiaries).

(b) Definitions.—For purposes of this part—

(1) Ordinary gross income.—The term "ordinary gross income" means the gross income determined by excluding—

(A) all gains from the sale or other disposition of capital assets,

(B) all gains (other than those referred to in subparagraph (A)) from the sale or other disposition of property described in section 1231(b), and

* * *

(2) Adjusted ordinary gross income.—The term "adjusted ordinary gross income" means the ordinary gross income adjusted as follows:

(A) Rents.—From the gross income from rents (as defined in the second sentence of paragraph (3) of this subsection) subtract the amount allowable as deductions for—

(i) exhaustion, wear and tear, obsolescence, and amortization of property other than tangible personal property which is not customarily retained by any one lessee for more than three years,

(ii) property taxes,

(iii) interest, and

(iv) rent,

to the extent allocable, under regulations prescribed by the Secretary, to such gross income from rents. The amount subtracted under this subparagraph shall not exceed such gross income from rents.

(B) Mineral royalties, etc.—From the gross income from mineral, oil, and gas royalties described in paragraph (4), and from the gross income from working interests in an oil or gas well, subtract the amount allowable as deductions for—

(i) exhaustion, wear and tear, obsolescence, amortization, and depletion,

(ii) property and severance taxes,

(iii) interest, and

(iv) rent,

to the extent allocable, under regulations prescribed by the Secretary, to such gross income from royalties or such gross income from working interests in oil or gas wells. The amount subtracted under this subparagraph with respect to royalties shall not exceed the gross income from such royalties, and the amount subtracted under this subparagraph with respect to working interests shall not exceed the gross income from such working interests.

(C) **Interest.**—There shall be excluded—

(i) interest received on a direct obligation of the United States held for sale to customers in the ordinary course of trade or business by a regular dealer who is making a primary market in such obligations, and

(ii) interest on a condemnation award, a judgment, and a tax refund.

(D) **Certain excluded rents.**—From the gross income consisting of compensation described in subparagraph (D) of paragraph (3) subtract the amount allowable as deductions for the items described in clauses (i), (ii), (iii), and (iv) of subparagraph (A) to the extent allocable, under regulations prescribed by the Secretary, to such gross income. The amount subtracted under this subparagraph shall not exceed such gross income.

(3) **Adjusted income from rents.**—The term "adjusted income from rents" means the gross income from rents, reduced by the amount subtracted under paragraph (2) (A) of this subsection. For purposes of the preceding sentence, the term "rents" means compensation, however designated, for the use of, or right to use, property, and the interest on debts owed to the corporation, to the extent such debts represent the price for which real property held primarily for sale to customers in the ordinary course of its trade or business was sold or exchanged by the corporation; but such term does not include—

(A) amounts constituting personal holding company income under subsection (a) (6),

(B) copyright royalties (as defined in subsection (a) (4)),

(C) produced film rents (as defined in subsection (a) (5) (B)),

(D) compensation, however designated, for the use of, or the right to use, any tangible personal property manufactured or produced by the taxpayer, if during the taxable year the taxpayer is engaged in substantial manufacturing or production of tangible personal property of the same type, or

* * *

(4) **Adjusted income from mineral, oil, and gas royalties.**—The term "adjusted income from mineral, oil, and gas royalties" means the gross income from mineral, oil, and gas royalties (including production payments and overriding royalties), reduced by the amount subtracted under paragraph (2) (B) of this subsection in respect of such royalties.

* * *

(d) **Active business computer software royalties.**—

(1) **In general.**—For purposes of this section, the term "active business computer software royalties" means any royalties—

(A) received by any corporation during the taxable year in connection with the licensing of computer software, and

(B) with respect to which the requirements of paragraphs (2), (3), (4), and (5) are met.

(2) Royalties must be received by corporation actively engaged in computer software business.—The requirements of this paragraph are met if the royalties described in paragraph (1)—

(A) are received by a corporation engaged in the active conduct of the trade or business of developing, manufacturing or producing computer software, and

(B) are attributable to computer software which—

(i) is developed, manufactured, or produced by such corporation (or its predecessor) in connection with the trade or business described in subparagraph (A), or

(ii) is directly related to such trade or business.

(3) Royalties must constitute at least 50 percent of income.—The requirements of this paragraph are met if the royalties described in paragraph (1) constitute at least 50 percent of the ordinary gross income of the corporation for the taxable year.

(4) Deductions under sections 162 and 174 relating to royalties must equal or exceed 25 percent of ordinary gross income.—

(A) In general.—The requirements of this paragraph are met if—

(i) the sum of the deductions allowable to the corporation under sections 162, 174, and 195 for the taxable year which are properly allocable to the trade or business described in paragraph (2) equals or exceeds 25 percent of the ordinary gross income of such corporation for such taxable year, or

(ii) the average of such deductions for the 5-taxable year period ending with such taxable year equals or exceeds 25 percent of the average ordinary gross income of such corporation for such period.

If a corporation has not been in existence during the 5-taxable year period described in clause (ii), then the period of existence of such corporation shall be substituted for such 5-taxable year period.

(B) Deductions allowable under section 162.—For purposes of subparagraph (A), a deduction shall not be treated as allowable under section 162 if it is specifically allowable under another section.

(C) Limitation on allowable deductions.—For purposes of subparagraph (A), no deduction shall be taken into account with respect to compensation for personal services rendered by the 5 individual shareholders holding the largest percentage (by value) of the outstanding stock of the corporation. For purposes of the preceding sentence—

(i) individuals holding less than 5 percent (by value) of the stock of such corporation shall not be taken into account, and

(ii) stock deemed to be owned by a shareholder solely by attribution from a partner under section 544(a)(2) shall be disregarded.

(5) Dividends must equal or exceed excess of personal holding company income over 10 percent of ordinary gross income.—

(A) In general.—The requirements of this paragraph are met if the sum of—

(i) the dividends paid during the taxable year (determined under section 562),

(ii) the dividends considered as paid on the last day of the taxable year under section 563(c) (as limited by the second sentence of section 563(b)), and

(iii) the consent dividends for the taxable year (determined under section 565),

equals or exceeds the amount, if any, by which the personal holding company income for the taxable year exceeds 10 percent of the ordinary gross income of such corporation for such taxable year.

(B) Computation of personal holding company income.—For purposes of this paragraph, personal holding company income shall be computed—

(i) without regard to amounts described in subsection (a)(1)(C),

(ii) without regard to interest income during any taxable year—

(I) which is in the 5–taxable year period beginning with the later of the 1st taxable year of the corporation or the 1st taxable year in which the corporation conducted the trade or business described in paragraph (2)(A), and

(II) during which the corporation meets the requirements of paragraphs (2), (3), and (4), and

(iii) by including adjusted income from rents and adjusted income from mineral, oil, and gas royalties (within the meaning of paragraphs (2) and (3) of subsection (a)).

(6) Special rules for affiliated group members.—

(A) In general.—In any case in which—

(i) the taxpayer receives royalties in connection with the licensing of computer software, and

(ii) another corporation which is a member of the same affiliated group as the taxpayer meets the requirements of paragraphs (2), (3), (4), and (5) with respect to such computer software,

the taxpayer shall be treated as having met such requirements.

(B) Affiliated group.—For purposes of this paragraph, the term "affiliated group" has the meaning given such term by section 1504(a).

* * *

§ 544. Rules for determining stock ownership

(a) Constructive ownership.—For purposes of determining whether a corporation is a personal holding company, insofar as such determination is based on stock ownership under section 542(a) (2), section 543(a) (7), section 543(a) (6), or section 543(a) (4)—

(1) Stock not owned by individual.—Stock owned, directly or indirectly, by or for a corporation, partnership, estate, or trust shall be considered as being owned proportionately by its shareholders, partners, or beneficiaries.

(2) Family and partnership ownership.—An individual shall be considered as owning the stock owned, directly or indirectly, by or for his family or by or for his partner. For purposes of this paragraph, the family of an individual includes only his brothers and sisters (whether by the whole or half blood), spouse, ancestors, and lineal descendants.

(3) Options.—If any person has an option to acquire stock, such stock shall be considered as owned by such person. For purposes of this paragraph, an option to acquire such an option, and each one of a series of such options, shall be considered as an option to acquire such stock.

(4) Application of family-partnership and option rules.—Paragraphs (2) and (3) shall be applied—

(A) for purposes of the stock ownership requirement provided in section 542(a) (2), if, but only if, the effect is to make the corporation a personal holding company;

(B) for purposes of section 543(a) (7) (relating to personal service contracts), of section 543(a) (6) (relating to use of property by shareholders), or of section 543(a) (4) (relating to copyright royalties), if, but only if, the effect is to make the amounts therein referred to includible under such paragraph as personal holding company income.

(5) Constructive ownership as actual ownership.—Stock constructively owned by a person by reason of the application of paragraph (1) or (3) shall, for purposes of applying paragraph (1) or (2), be treated as actually owned by such person; but stock constructively owned by an individual by reason of the application of paragraph (2) shall not be treated as owned by him for purposes of again applying such paragraph in order to make another the constructive owner of such stock.

(6) Option rule in lieu of family and partnership rule.—If stock may be considered as owned by an individual under either paragraph (2) or (3) it shall be considered as owned by him under paragraph (3).

(b) Convertible securities.—Outstanding securities convertible into stock (whether or not convertible during the taxable year) shall be considered as outstanding stock—

(1) for purposes of the stock ownership requirement provided in section 542(a) (2), but only if the effect of the inclusion of all such securities is to make the corporation a personal holding company;

(2) for purposes of section 543(a) (7) (relating to personal service contracts), but only if the effect of the inclusion of all such securities is to make the amounts therein referred to includible under such paragraph as personal holding company income;

(3) for purposes of section 543(a) (6) (relating to the use of property by shareholders), but only if the effect of the inclusion of all such securities is to make the amounts therein referred to includible under such paragraph as personal holding company income; and

(4) for purposes of section 543(a) (4) (relating to copyright royalties), but only if the effect of the inclusion of all such securities is to make the amounts therein referred to includible under such paragraph as personal holding company income.

The requirement in paragraphs (1), (2), (3), and (4) that all convertible securities must be included if any are to be included shall be subject to the exception that, where some of the outstanding securities are convertible only after a later date than in the case of others, the class having the earlier conversion date may be included although the others are not included, but no convertible securities shall be included unless all outstanding securities having a prior conversion date are also included.

§ 545. Undistributed personal holding company income

(a) Definition.—For purposes of this part, the term "undistributed personal holding company income" means the taxable income of a personal holding company adjusted in the manner provided in subsections (b), (c), and (d), minus the dividends paid deduction as defined in section 561. In the case of a personal holding company which is a foreign corporation, not more than 10 percent in value of the outstanding stock of which is owned (within the meaning of section 958(a)) during the last half of the taxable year by United States persons, the term "undistributed personal holding company income" means the amount determined by multiplying the undistributed personal holding company income (determined without regard to this sentence) by the percentage in value of its outstanding stock which is the greatest percentage in value of its outstanding stock so owned by United States persons on any one day during such period.

(b) Adjustments to taxable income.—For the purposes of subsection (a), the taxable income shall be adjusted as follows:

(1) Taxes.—There shall be allowed as a deduction Federal income and excess profits taxes and income, war profits and excess profits taxes of foreign countries and possessions of the United States (to the extent not allowable as a deduction under section 275(a) (4)), accrued during the taxable year or deemed to be paid by a domestic corporation under section 902(a) or 960(a) (1) for the taxable year, but not including the accumulated earnings tax imposed by section 531, the personal holding company tax imposed by section 541, or the taxes imposed by corresponding sections of a prior income tax law.

(2) Charitable contributions.—The deduction for charitable contributions provided under section 170 shall be allowed, but in computing such deduction the limitations in section 170(b)(1)(A), (B), and (D) shall apply, and section 170(b)(2) and (d)(1) shall not apply. For purposes of this paragraph, the term "contribution base" when used in section 170(b)(1) means the taxable income computed with the adjustments (other than the 10-percent limitation) provided in section 170(b)(2) and (d)(1) and without deduction of the amount disallowed under paragraph (6) of this subsection.

(3) Special deductions disallowed.—The special deductions for corporations provided in part VIII (except section 248) of subchapter B (section 241 and following, relating to the deduction for dividends received by corporations, etc.) shall not be allowed.

(4) Net operating loss.—The net operating loss deduction provided in section 172 shall not be allowed, but there shall be allowed as a deduction the amount of the net operating loss (as defined in section 172(c)) for the preceding taxable year computed without the deductions provided in part VIII (except section 248) of subchapter B.

(5) Net capital gains.—There shall be allowed as a deduction the net capital gain for the taxable year, minus the taxes imposed by this subtitle attributable to such net capital gain. The taxes attributable to such net capital gain shall be an amount equal to the difference between—

(A) the taxes imposed by this subtitle (except the tax imposed by this part) for such year, and

(B) such taxes computed for such year without including such net capital gain in taxable income.

(6) Expenses and depreciation applicable to property of the taxpayer. —The aggregate of the deductions allowed under section 162 (relating to trade or business expenses) and section 167 (relating to depreciation), which are allocable to the operation and maintenance of property owned or operated by the corporation, shall be allowed only in an amount equal to the rent or other compensation received for the use of, or the right to use, the property, unless it is established (under regulations prescribed by the Secretary) to the satisfaction of the Secretary—

(A) that the rent or other compensation received was the highest obtainable, or, if none was received, that none was obtainable;

(B) that the property was held in the course of a business carried on bona fide for profit; and

(C) either that there was reasonable expectation that the operation of the property would result in a profit, or that the property was necessary to the conduct of the business.

* * *

§ 547. Deduction for deficiency dividends

(a) **General rule.**—If a determination (as defined in subsection (c)) with respect to a taxpayer establishes liability for personal holding company tax imposed by section 541 (or by a corresponding provision of a prior income tax law) for any taxable year, a deduction shall be allowed to the taxpayer for the amount of deficiency dividends (as defined in subsection (d)) for the purpose of determining the personal holding company tax for such year, but not for the purpose of determining interest, additional amounts, or assessable penalties computed with respect to such personal holding company tax.

(b) **Rules for application of section.**—

(1) **Allowance of deduction.**—The deficiency dividend deduction shall be allowed as of the date the claim for the deficiency dividend deduction is filed.

(2) **Credit or refund.**—If the allowance of a deficiency dividend deduction results in an overpayment of personal holding company tax for any taxable year, credit or refund with respect to such overpayment shall be made as if on the date of the determination 2 years remained before the expiration of the period of limitation on the filing of claim for refund for the taxable year to which the overpayment relates. No interest shall be allowed on a credit or refund arising from the application of this section.

(c) **Determination.**—For purposes of this section, the term "determination" means—

(1) a decision by the Tax Court or a judgment, decree, or other order by any court of competent jurisdiction, which has become final;

(2) a closing agreement made under section 7121; or

(3) under regulations prescribed by the Secretary, an agreement signed by the Secretary and by, or on behalf of, the taxpayer relating to the liability of such taxpayer for personal holding company tax.

(d) **Deficiency dividends.**—

(1) **Definition.**—For purposes of this section, the term "deficiency dividends" means the amount of the dividends paid by the corporation on or after the date of the determination and before filing claim under subsection (e), which would have been includible in the computation of the deduction for dividends paid under section 561 for the taxable year with respect to which the liability for personal holding company tax exists, if distributed during such taxable year. No dividends

shall be considered as deficiency dividends for purposes of subsection (a) unless distributed within 90 days after the determination.

(2) Effect on dividends paid deduction.—

(A) For taxable year in which paid.—Deficiency dividends paid in any taxable year (to the extent of the portion thereof taken into account under subsection (a) in determining personal holding company tax) shall not be included in the amount of dividends paid for such year for purposes of computing the dividends paid deduction for such year and succeeding years.

(B) For prior taxable year.—Deficiency dividends paid in any taxable year (to the extent of the portion thereof taken into account under subsection (a) in determining personal holding company tax) shall not be allowed for purposes of section 563(b) in the computation of the dividends paid deduction for the taxable year preceding the taxable year in which paid.

(e) Claim required.—No deficiency dividend deduction shall be allowed under subsection (a) unless (under regulations prescribed by the Secretary) claim therefor is filed within 120 days after the determination.

(f) Suspension of statute of limitations and stay of collection.—

(1) Suspension of running of statute.—If the corporation files a claim, as provided in subsection (e), the running of the statute of limitations provided in section 6501 on the making of assessments, and the bringing of distraint or a proceeding in court for collection, in respect of the deficiency and all interest, additional amounts, or assessable penalties, shall be suspended for a period of 2 years after the date of the determination.

(2) Stay of collection.—In the case of any deficiency with respect to the tax imposed by section 541 established by a determination under this section—

(A) the collection of the deficiency and all interest, additional amounts, and assessable penalties shall, except in cases of jeopardy, be stayed until the expiration of 120 days after the date of the determination, and

(B) if claim for deficiency dividend deduction is filed under subsection (e), the collection of such part of the deficiency as is not reduced by the deduction for deficiency dividends provided in subsection (a) shall be stayed until the date the claim is disallowed (in whole or in part), and if disallowed in part collection shall be made only with respect to the part disallowed.

No distraint or proceeding in court shall be begun for the collection of an amount the collection of which is stayed under subparagraph (A) or (B) during the period for which the collection of such amount is stayed.

(g) Deduction denied in case of fraud, etc.—No deficiency dividend deduction shall be allowed under subsection (a) if the determination contains a finding that any part of the deficiency is due to fraud with intent to evade tax, or to wilful failure to file an income tax return within the time prescribed by law or prescribed by the Secretary in pursuance of law.

PART IV—DEDUCTION FOR DIVIDENDS PAID

§ 561. Definition of deduction for dividends paid

(a) General rule.—The deduction for dividends paid shall be the sum of—

(1) the dividends paid during the taxable year,

(2) the consent dividends for the taxable year (determined under section 565), and

(3) in the case of a personal holding company, the dividend carryover described in section 564.

(b) Special rules applicable.—In determining the deduction for dividends paid, the rules provided in section 562 (relating to rules applicable in determining dividends eligible for dividends paid deduction) and section 563 (relating to dividends paid after the close of the taxable year) shall be applicable.

§ 562. Rules applicable in determining dividends eligible for dividends paid deduction

(a) General rule.—For purposes of this part, the term "dividend" shall, except as otherwise provided in this section, include only dividends described in section 316 (relating to definition of dividends for purposes of corporate distributions).

(b) Distributions in liquidation.—

(1) Except in the case of a personal holding company described in section 542 or a foreign personal holding company described in section 552—

(A) in the case of amounts distributed in liquidation, the part of such distribution which is properly chargeable to earnings and profits accumulated after February 28, 1913, shall be treated as a dividend for purposes of computing the dividends paid deduction, and

(B) in the case of a complete liquidation occurring within 24 months after the adoption of a plan of liquidation, any distribution within such period pursuant to such plan shall, to the extent of the earnings and profits (computed without regard to capital losses) of the corporation for the taxable year in which such distribution is made, be treated as a dividend for purposes of computing the dividends paid deduction.

Except to the extent provided in regulations, the preceding sentence shall not apply in the case of any mere holding or investment company which is not a regulated investment company.

(2) In the case of a complete liquidation of a personal holding company, occurring within 24 months after the adoption of a plan of liquidation, the amount of any distribution within such period pursuant to such plan shall be treated as a dividend for purposes of computing the dividends paid deduction, to the extent that such amount is distributed to corporate distributees and represents such corporate distributees' allocable share of the undistributed personal holding company income for the taxable year of such distribution computed without regard to this paragraph and without regard to subparagraph (B) of section 316(b) (2).

(c) Preferential dividends.—The amount of any distribution shall not be considered as a dividend for purposes of computing the dividends paid deduction, unless such distribution is pro rata, with no preference to any share of stock as compared with other shares of the same class, and with no preference to one class of stock as compared with another class except to the extent that the former is entitled (without reference to waivers of their rights by shareholders) to such preference. In the case of a distribution by a regulated investment company to a shareholder who made an initial investment of at least $10,000,000 in such company, such distribution shall not be treated as not being pro rata or as being preferential solely by reason of an increase in the distribution by reason of reductions in administrative expenses of the company.

(d) Distributions by a member of an affiliated group.—In the case where a corporation which is a member of an affiliated group of corporations filing or required to file a consolidated return for a taxable year is required to file a separate personal holding company schedule for such taxable year, a distribution by such corporation to another member of the affiliated group shall be considered as a dividend for purposes of computing the dividends paid deduction if such distribution would constitute a dividend under the other provisions of this section to a recipient which is not a member of an affiliated group.

* * *

§ 563.   Rules relating to dividends paid after close of taxable year

(a) Accumulated earnings tax.—In the determination of the dividends paid deduction for purposes of the accumulated earnings tax imposed by section 531, a dividend paid after the close of any taxable year and on or before the 15th day of the third month following the close of such taxable year shall be considered as paid during such taxable year.

(b) Personal holding company tax.—In the determination of the dividends paid deduction for purposes of the personal holding company tax imposed by section 541, a dividend paid after the close of any taxable year and on or before the 15th day of the third month following the close of such taxable year shall, to the extent the taxpayer elects in its return for the taxable year, be considered as paid during such taxable year. The amount allowed as a dividend by reason of the application of this subsection with respect to any taxable year shall not exceed either—

(1) The undistributed personal holding company income of the corporation for the taxable year, computed without regard to this subsection, or

(2) 20 percent of the sum of the dividends paid during the taxable year, computed without regard to this subsection.

(c) Dividends considered as paid on last day of taxable year.—For the purpose of applying section 562(a), with respect to distributions under subsection (a) or (b) of this section, a distribution made after the close of a taxable year and on or before the 15th day of the third month following the close of the taxable year shall be considered as made on the last day of such taxable year.

§ 564.   Dividend carryover

(a) General rule.—For purposes of computing the dividends paid deduction under section 561, in the case of a personal holding company the dividend carryover for any taxable year shall be the dividend carryover to such taxable year, computed as provided in subsection (b), from the two preceding taxable years.

(b) Computation of dividend carryover.—The dividend carryover to the taxable year shall be determined as follows:

(1) For each of the 2 preceding taxable years there shall be determined the taxable income computed with the adjustments provided in section 545 (whether or not the taxpayer was a personal holding company for either of such preceding taxable years), and there shall also be determined for each such year the deduction for dividends paid during such year as provided in section 561 (but determined without regard to the dividend carryover to such year).

(2) There shall be determined for each such taxable year whether there is an excess of such taxable income over such deduction for dividends paid or an excess of such deduction for dividends paid over such taxable income, and the amount of each such excess.

(3) If there is an excess of such deductions for dividends paid over such taxable income for the first preceding taxable year, such excess shall be allowed as a dividend carryover to the taxable year.

(4) If there is an excess of such deduction for dividends paid over such taxable income for the second preceding taxable year, such excess shall be reduced by the amount determined in paragraph (5), and the remainder of such excess shall be allowed as a dividend carryover to the taxable year.

(5) The amount of the reduction specified in paragraph (4) shall be the amount of the excess of the taxable income, if any, for the first preceding taxable year over such deduction for dividends paid, if any, for the first preceding taxable year.

§ 565. Consent dividends

(a) **General rule.**—If any person owns consent stock (as defined in subsection (f) (1)) in a corporation on the last day of the taxable year of such corporation, and such person agrees, in a consent filed with the return of such corporation in accordance with regulations prescribed by the Secretary, to treat as a dividend the amount specified in such consent, the amount so specified shall, except as provided in subsection (b), constitute a consent dividend for purposes of section 561 (relating to the deduction for dividends paid).

(b) **Limitations.**—A consent dividend shall not include—

(1) an amount specified in a consent which, if distributed in money, would constitute, or be part of, a distribution which would be disqualified for purposes of the dividends paid deduction under section 562(c) (relating to preferential dividends), or

(2) an amount specified in a consent which would not constitute a dividend (as defined in section 316) if the total amounts specified in consents filed by the corporation had been distributed in money to shareholders on the last day of the taxable year of such corporation.

(c) **Effect of consent.**—The amount of a consent dividend shall be considered, for purposes of this title—

(1) as distributed in money by the corporation to the shareholder on the last day of the taxable year of the corporation, and

(2) as contributed to the capital of the corporation by the shareholder on such day.

(d) **Consent dividends and other distributions.**—If a distribution by a corporation consists in part of consent dividends and in part of money or other property, the entire amount specified in the consents and the amount of such money or other property shall be considered together for purposes of applying this title.

* * *

(f) **Definitions.—**

(1) **Consent stock.**—Consent stock, for purposes of this section, means the class or classes of stock entitled, after the payment of preferred dividends, to a share in the distribution (other than in complete or partial liquidation) within the taxable year of all the remaining earnings and profits, which share constitutes the same proportion of such distribution regardless of the amount of such distribution.

(2) **Preferred dividends.**—Preferred dividends, for purposes of this section, means a distribution (other than in complete or partial liquidation), limited in amount, which must be made on any class of stock before a further distribution

(other than in complete or partial liquidation) of earnings and profits may be made within the taxable year.

SUBCHAPTER H—BANKING INSTITUTIONS

PART I—RULES OF GENERAL APPLICATION TO BANKING INSTITUTIONS

§ 582. Bad debts, losses, and gains with respect to securities held by financial institutions

* * *

(c) Bond, etc., losses and gains of financial institutions.—

* * *

(5) Financial institutions to which paragraph (1) applies.—

(A) In general.—For purposes of paragraph (1), the financial institutions referred to in this paragraph are—

(i) any bank (and any corporation which would be a bank except for the fact it is a foreign corporation),

(ii) any financial institution referred to in section 591,

(iii) any small business investment company operating under the Small Business Investment Act of 1958, and

(iv) any business development corporation.

(B) Business development corporation.—For purposes of subparagraph (A), the term "business development corporation" means a corporation which was created by or pursuant to an act of a State legislature for purposes of promoting, maintaining, and assisting the economy and industry within such State on a regional or statewide basis by making loans to be used in trades and businesses which would generally not be made by banks within such region or State in the ordinary course of their business (except on the basis of a partial participation), and which is operated primarily for such purposes.

(C) Limitations on foreign banks.—In the case of a foreign corporation referred to in subparagraph (A)(i), paragraph (1) shall only apply to gains and losses which are effectively connected with the conduct of a banking business in the United States.

* * *

§ 584. Common trust funds

* * *

(c) Income of participants in fund.—Each participant in the common trust fund in computing its taxable income shall include, whether or not distributed and whether or not distributable—

(1) as part of its gains and losses from sales or exchanges of capital assets held for not more than 6 months, its proportionate share of the gains and losses of the common trust fund from sales or exchanges of capital assets held for not more than 6 months,

(2) as part of its gains and losses from sales or exchanges of capital assets held for more than 6 months, its proportionate share of the gains and losses of the common trust fund from sales or exchanges of capital assets held for more than 6 months, and

(3) its proportionate share of the ordinary taxable income or the ordinary net loss of the common trust fund, computed as provided in subsection (d).

* * *

SUBCHAPTER I—NATURAL RESOURCES

Part
  I. Deductions.
  II. Exclusions from gross income.*
  III. Sales and exchanges.
  IV. Mineral production payments.
  V. Continental shelf areas.*

PART I—DEDUCTIONS

§ 611. Allowance of deduction for depletion

(a) General rule.—In the case of mines, oil and gas wells, other natural deposits, and timber, there shall be allowed as a deduction in computing taxable income a reasonable allowance for depletion and for depreciation of improvements, according to the peculiar conditions in each case; such reasonable allowance in all cases to be made under regulations prescribed by the Secretary. For purposes of this part, the term "mines" includes deposits of waste or residue, the extraction of ores or minerals from which is treated as mining under section 613(c). In any case in which it is ascertained as a result of operations or of development work that the recoverable units are greater or less than the prior estimate thereof, then such prior estimate (but not the basis for depletion) shall be revised and the allowance under this section for subsequent taxable years shall be based on such revised estimate.

(b) Special rules.—

(1) Leases.—In the case of a lease, the deduction under this section shall be equitably apportioned between the lessor and lessee.

(2) Life tenant and remainderman.—In the case of property held by one person for life with remainder to another person, the deduction under this section shall be computed as if the life tenant were the absolute owner of the property and shall be allowed to the life tenant.

(3) Property held in trust.—In the case of property held in trust, the deduction under this section shall be apportioned between the income beneficiaries and the trustee in accordance with the pertinent provisions of the instrument creating the trust, or, in the absence of such provisions, on the basis of the trust income allocable to each.

(4) Property held by estate.—In the case of an estate, the deduction under this section shall be apportioned between the estate and the heirs, legatees, and devisees on the basis of the income of the estate allocable to each.

* * *

§ 612. Basis for cost depletion

Except as otherwise provided in this subchapter, the basis on which depletion is to be allowed in respect of any property shall be the adjusted basis provided in section

* Omitted entirely.

1011 for the purpose of determining the gain upon the sale or other disposition of such property.

§ 613. Percentage depletion

(a) General rule.—In the case of the mines, wells, and other natural deposits listed in subsection (b), the allowance for depletion under section 611 shall be the percentage, specified in subsection (b), of the gross income from the property excluding from such gross income an amount equal to any rents or royalties paid or incurred by the taxpayer in respect of the property. Such allowance shall not exceed 50 percent of the taxpayer's taxable income from the property (computed without allowance for depletion). For purposes of the preceding sentence, the allowable deductions taken into account with respect to expenses of mining in computing the taxable income from the property shall be decreased by an amount equal to so much of any gain which (1) is treated under section 1245 (relating to gain from disposition of certain depreciable property) as ordinary income, and (2) is properly allocable to the property. In no case shall the allowance for depletion under section 611 be less than it would be if computed without reference to this section.

(b) Percentage depletion rates.—The mines, wells, and other natural deposits, and the percentages, referred to in subsection (a) are as follows:

(1) **22 percent**—

(A) sulphur and uranium; and

(B) if from deposits in the United States—anorthosite, clay, laterite, and nephelite syenite (to the extent that alumina and aluminum compounds are extracted therefrom), asbestos, bauxite, celestite, chromite, corundum, fluorspar, graphite, ilmenite, kyanite, mica, olivine, quartz crystals (radio grade), rutile, block steatite talc, and zircon, and ores of the following metals: antimony, beryllium, bismuth, cadmium, cobalt, columbium, lead, lithium, manganese, mercury, molybdenum, nickel, platinum and platinum group metals, tantalum, thorium, tin, titanium, tungsten, vanadium, and zinc.

(2) **15 percent**—If from deposits in the United States—

(A) gold, silver, copper, and iron ore, and

(B) oil shale (except shale described in paragraph (5)).

(3) **14 percent**—

(A) metal mines (if paragraph (1) (B) or (2) (A) does not apply), rock asphalt, and vermiculite; and

(B) if paragraph (1) (B), (5), or (6) (B) does not apply, ball clay, bentonite, china clay, sagger clay, and clay used or sold for use for purposes dependent on its refractory properties.

(4) **10 percent**—asbestos (if paragraph (1) (B) does not apply), brucite, coal, lignite, perlite, sodium chloride, and wollastonite.

(5) **7½ percent**—clay and shale used or sold for use in the manufacture of sewer pipe or brick, and clay, shale, and slate used or sold for use as sintered or burned lightweight aggregates.

(6) **5 percent**—

(A) gravel, peat, pumice, sand, scoria, shale (except shale described in paragraph (2) (B) or (5)), and stone (except stone described in paragraph (7));

(B) clay used, or sold for use, in the manufacture of drainage and roofing tile, flower pots, and kindred products; and

(C) if from brine wells—bromine, calcium chloride, and magnesium chloride.

(7) 14 percent—all other minerals, including, but not limited to, aplite, barite, borax, calcium carbonates, diatomaceous earth, dolomite, feldspar, fullers earth, garnet, gilsonite, granite, limestone, magnesite, magnesium carbonates, marble, mollusk shells (including clam shells and oyster shells), phosphate rock, potash, quartzite, slate, soapstone, stone (used or sold for use by the mine owner or operator as dimension stone or ornamental stone), thenardite, tripoli, trona, and (if paragraph (1) (B) does not apply) bauxite, flake graphite, fluorspar, lepidolite, mica, spodumene, and talc (including pyrophyllite), except that, unless sold on bid in direct competition with a bona fide bid to sell a mineral listed in paragraph (3), the percentage shall be 5 percent for any such other mineral (other than slate to which paragraph (5) applies) when used, or sold for use, by the mine owner or operator as rip rap, ballast, road material, rubble, concrete aggregates, or for similar purposes. For purposes of this paragraph, the term "all other minerals" does not include—

(A) soil, sod, dirt, turf, water, or mosses;

(B) minerals from sea water, the air, or similar inexhaustible sources; or

(C) oil and gas wells.

For the purposes of this subsection, minerals (other than sodium chloride) extracted from brines pumped from a saline perennial lake within the United States shall not be considered minerals from an inexhaustible source.

(c) Definition of gross income from property.—For purposes of this section—

(1) Gross income from the property.—The term "gross income from the property" means, in the case of a property other than an oil or gas well, and other than a geothermal deposit the gross income from mining.

(2) Mining.—The term "mining" includes not merely the extraction of the ores or minerals from the ground but also the treatment processes considered as mining described in paragraph (4) (and the treatment processes necessary or incidental thereto), and so much of the transportation of ores or minerals (whether or not by common carrier) from the point of extraction from the ground to the plants or mills in which such treatment processes are applied thereto as is not in excess of 50 miles unless the Secretary finds that the physical and other requirements are such that the ore or mineral must be transported a greater distance to such plants or mills.

(3) Extraction of the ores or minerals from the ground.—The term "extraction of the ores or minerals from the ground" includes the extraction by mine owners or operators of ores or minerals from the waste or residue of prior mining. The preceding sentence shall not apply to any such extraction of the mineral or ore by a purchaser of such waste or residue or of the rights to extract ores or minerals therefrom.

(4) Treatment processes considered as mining.—The following treatment processes where applied by the mine owner or operator shall be considered as mining to the extent they are applied to the ore or mineral in respect of which he is entitled to a deduction for depletion under section 611:

(A) in the case of coal—cleaning, breaking, sizing, dust allaying, treating to prevent freezing, and loading for shipment;

(B) in the case of sulfur recovered by the Frasch process—cleaning, pumping to vats, cooling, breaking, and loading for shipment;

(C) in the case of iron ore, bauxite, ball and sagger clay, rock asphalt, and ores or minerals which are customarily sold in the form of a crude mineral product—

sorting, concentrating, sintering, and substantially equivalent processes to bring to shipping grade and form, and loading for shipment;

(D) in the case of lead, zinc, copper, gold, silver, uranium, or fluorspar ores, potash, and ores or minerals which are not customarily sold in the form of the crude mineral product—crushing, grinding, and beneficiation by concentration (gravity, flotation, amalgamation, electrostatic, or magnetic), cyanidation, leaching, crystallization, precipitation (but not including electrolytic deposition, roasting, thermal or electric smelting, or refining), or by substantially equivalent processes or combination of processes used in the separation or extraction of the product or products from the ore or the mineral or minerals from other material from the mine or other natural deposit;

(E) the pulverization of talc, the burning of magnesite, the sintering and nodulizing of phosphate rock, the decarbonation of trona, and the furnacing of quicksilver ores;

(F) in the case of calcium carbonates and other minerals when used in making cement—all processes (other than preheating of the kiln feed) applied prior to the introduction of the kiln feed into the kiln, but not including any subsequent process;

(G) in the case of clay to which paragraph (5) or (6) (B) of subsection (b) applies—crushing, grinding, and separating the mineral from waste, but not including any subsequent process;

(H) in the case of oil shale—extraction from the ground, crushing, loading into the retort, and retorting, but not hydrogenation, refining, or any other process subsequent to retorting; and

(I) any other treatment process provided for by regulations prescribed by the Secretary which, with respect to the particular ore or mineral, is not inconsistent with the preceding provisions of this paragraph.

(5) Treatment processes not considered as mining.—Unless such processes are otherwise provided for in paragraph (4) (or are necessary or incidental to processes so provided for), the following treatment processes shall not be considered as "mining": electrolytic deposition, roasting, calcining, thermal or electric smelting, refining, polishing, fine pulverization, blending with other materials, treatment effecting a chemical change, thermal action, and molding or shaping.

(d) Denial of percentage depletion in case of oil and gas wells.—Except as provided in section 613A, in the case of any oil or gas well, the allowance for depletion shall be computed without reference to this section.

(e) Percentage depletion for geothermal deposits.—

(1) In general.—In the case of geothermal deposits located in the United States or in a possession of the United States, for purposes of subsection (a)—

(A) such deposits shall be treated as listed in subsection (b), and

(B) the applicable percentage (determined under the table contained in paragraph (2)) shall be deemed to be the percentage specified in subsection (b).

(2) Applicable percentage.—For purposes of paragraph (1)—

In the case of taxable years beginning in calendar year—	The applicable percentage is—
1978, 1979, or 1980	22
1981	20
1982	18
1983	16
1984 and thereafter	15

(3) Geothermal deposit defined.—For purposes of paragraph (1), the term "geothermal deposit" means a geothermal reservoir consisting of natural heat which is stored in rocks or in an aqueous liquid or vapor (whether or not under pressure). Such a deposit shall in no case be treated as a gas well for purposes of this section or section 613A, and this section shall not apply to a geothermal deposit which is located outside the United States or its possessions.

§ 613A. Limitations on percentage depletion in case of oil and gas wells

(a) General rule.—Except as otherwise provided in this section, the allowance for depletion under section 611 with respect to any oil or gas well shall be computed without regard to section 613.

(b) Exemption for certain domestic gas wells.—

(1) In general.—The allowance for depletion under section 611 shall be computed in accordance with section 613 with respect to—

(A) regulated natural gas, and

(B) natural gas sold under a fixed contract,

and 22 percent shall be deemed to be specified in subsection (b) of section 613 for purposes of subsection (a) of that section.

* * *

(c) Exemption for independent producers and royalty owners.—

(1) In general.—Except as provided in subsection (d), the allowance for depletion under section 611 shall be computed in accordance with section 613 with respect to—

(A) so much of the taxpayer's average daily production of domestic crude oil as does not exceed the taxpayer's depletable oil quantity; and

(B) so much of the taxpayer's average daily production of domestic natural gas as does not exceed the taxpayer's depletable natural gas quantity;

and the applicable percentage (determined in accordance with the table contained in paragraph (5)) shall be deemed to be specified in subsection (b) of section 613 for purposes of subsection (a) of that section.

(2) Average daily production.—For purposes of paragraph (1)—

(A) the taxpayer's average daily production of domestic crude oil or natural gas for any taxable year, shall be determined by dividing his aggregate production of domestic crude oil or natural gas, as the case may be, during the taxable year by the number of days in such taxable year, and

(B) in the case of a taxpayer holding a partial interest in the production from any property (including an interest held in a partnership) such taxpayer's production shall be considered to be that amount of such production determined by multiplying the total production of such property by the taxpayer's percentage participation in the revenues from such property.

(3) Depletable oil quantity.—

(A) **In general.**—For purposes of paragraph (1), the taxpayer's depletable oil quantity shall be equal to—

(i) the tentative quantity determined under the table contained in subparagraph (B), reduced (but not below zero) by

(ii) the taxpayer's average daily secondary or tertiary production for the taxable year.

Clause (ii) shall not apply after December 31, 1983.

(B) Phase-out table.—For purposes of subparagraph (A)—

In the case of production during the calendar year:	The tentative quantity in barrels is:
1975	2,000
1976	1,800
1977	1,600
1978	1,400
1979	1,200
1980 and thereafter	1,000

(4) Daily depletable natural gas quantity.—For purposes of paragraph (1), the depletable natural gas quantity of any taxpayer for any taxable year shall be equal to 6,000 cubic feet multiplied by the number of barrels of the taxpayer's depletable oil quantity to which the taxpayer elects to have this paragraph apply. The taxpayer's depletable oil quantity for any taxable year shall be reduced by the number of barrels with respect to which an election under this paragraph applies. Such election shall be made at such time and in such manner as the Secretary shall by regulations prescribe.

(5) Applicable percentage.—For purposes of paragraph (1)—

In the case of production during the calendar year:	The applicable percentage is:
1975	22
1976	22
1977	22
1978	22
1979	22
1980	22
1981	20
1982	18
1983	16
1984 and thereafter	15

* * *

(7) Special rules.—

(A) Production of crude oil in excess of depletable oil quantity.—If the taxpayer's average daily production of domestic crude oil exceeds his depletable oil quantity, the allowance under paragraph (1)(A) with respect to oil produced during the taxable year from each property in the United States shall be that amount which bears the same ratio to the amount of depletion which would have been allowable under section 613(a) for all of the taxpayer's oil produced from such property during the taxable year (computed as if section 613 applied to all of such production at the rate specified in paragraph (5) or (6), as the case may be) as his depletable oil quantity bears to the aggregate number of barrels representing the average daily production of domestic crude oil of the taxpayer for such year.

(B) Production of natural gas in excess of depletable natural gas quantity.—If the taxpayer's average daily production of domestic natural gas exceeds his depletable natural gas quantity, the allowance under paragraph (1)(B) with respect to natural gas produced during the taxable year from each property in the United States shall be that amount which bears the same ratio to the amount of depletion which would have been allowable under section 613(a) for all of the taxpayer's natural gas produced from such property during the taxable year (computed as if section 613 applied to all of such production at the rate specified in paragraph (5) or (6), as the case may be) as the amount of his depletable natural gas quantity in cubic feet bears to the aggregate number of cubic feet representing the average daily production of domestic natural gas of the taxpayer for such year.

(C) Taxable income from the property.—If both oil and gas are produced from the property during the taxable year, for purposes of subparagraphs (A) and (B) the taxable income from the property, in applying the 50-percent limitation in section 613(a), shall be allocated between the oil production and the gas production in proportion to the gross income during the taxable year from each.

(D) Partnerships.—In the case of a partnership, the depletion allowance shall be computed separately by the partners and not by the partnership. The partnership shall allocate to each partner his proportionate share of the adjusted basis of each partnership oil or gas property. The allocation is to be made as of the later of the date of acquisition of the oil or gas property by the partnership, or January 1, 1975. A partner's proportionate share of the adjusted basis of partnership property shall be determined in accordance with his interest in partnership capital or income and, in the case of property contributed to the partnership by a partner, section 704(c) (relating to contributed property) shall apply in determining such share. Each partner shall separately keep records of his share of the adjusted basis in each oil and gas property of the partnership, adjust such share of the adjusted basis for any depletion taken on such property, and use such adjusted basis each year in the computation of his cost depletion or in the computation of his gain or loss on the disposition of such property by the partnership. For purposes of section 732 (relating to basis of distributed property other than money), the partnership's adjusted basis in mineral property shall be an amount equal to the sum of the partners' adjusted basis in such property as determined under this paragraph.

* * *

(8) Businesses under common control; members of the same family.—

(A) Component members of controlled group treated as one taxpayer. —For purposes of this subsection, persons who are members of the same controlled group of corporations shall be treated as one taxpayer.

(B) Aggregation of business entities under common control.—If 50 percent or more of the beneficial interest in two or more corporations, trusts, or estates is owned by the same or related persons (taking into account only persons who own at least 5 percent of such beneficial interest), the tentative quantity determined under the table in paragraph (3)(B) shall be allocated among all such entities in proportion to the respective production of domestic crude oil during the period in question by such entities.

(C) Allocation among members of the same family.—In the case of individuals who are members of the same family, the tentative quantity determined under the table in paragraph (3)(B) shall be allocated among such individuals in proportion to the respective production of domestic crude oil during the period in question by such individuals.

(D) Definition and special rules.—For purposes of this paragraph—

(i) the term "controlled group of corporations" has the meaning given to such term by section 1563(a), except that section 1563(b)(2) shall not apply and except that "more than 50 percent" shall be substituted for "at least 80 percent" each place it appears in section 1563(a),

(ii) a person is a related person to another person if such persons are members of the same controlled group of corporations or if the relationship between such persons would result in a disallowance of losses under section 267 or 707(b), except that for this purpose the family of an individual includes only his spouse and minor children,

(iii) the family of an individual includes only his spouse and minor children, and

(iv) each 6,000 cubic feet of domestic natural gas shall be treated as 1 barrel of domestic crude oil.

(9) Transfer of oil or gas property.—

(A) In the case of a transfer (including the subleasing of a lease) after December 31, 1974 of an interest (including an interest in a partnership or trust) in any proven oil or gas property, this subsection shall not apply to the transferee (or sublessee) with respect to production of crude oil or natural gas attributable to such interest, and such production shall not be taken into account for any computation by the transferee (or sublessee) under this subsection. A property shall be treated as a proven oil or gas property if at the time of the transfer the principal value of the property has been demonstrated by prospecting or exploration or discovery work.

(B) Subparagraph (A) shall not apply in the case of—

(i) a transfer of property at death,

(ii) the transfer in an exchange to which section 351 applies if following the exchange the tentative quantity determined under the table contained in paragraph (3) (B) is allocated under paragraph (8) between the transferor and transferee,

(iii) a change of beneficiaries of a trust by reason of the death, birth, or adoption of any vested beneficiary if the transferee was a beneficiary of such trust or is a lineal descendant of the settlor or any other vested beneficiary of such trust, except in the case of any trust where any beneficiary of such trust is a member of the family (as defined in section 267(c) (4)) of a settlor who created inter vivos and testamentary trusts for members of the family and such settlor died within the last six days of the fifth month in 1970, and the law in the jurisdiction in which such trust was created requires all or a portion of the gross or net proceeds of any royalty or other interest in oil, gas, or other mineral representing any percentage depletion allowance to be allocated to the principal of the trust,

(iv) a transfer of property between corporations which are members of the same controlled group of corporations (as defined in paragraph (8) (D) (i)), or

(v) a transfer of property between business entities which are under common control (within the meaning of paragraph (8) (B)) or between related persons in the same family (within the meaning of paragraph (8) (C)), or

(vi) a transfer of property between a trust and related persons in the same family (within the meaning of paragraph (8) (C)) to the extent that the beneficiaries of that trust are and continue to be related persons in the family that transferred the property, and to the extent that the tentative oil quantity is allocated among the members of the family (within the meaning of paragraph (8) (C)).

Clause (iv) or (v) shall apply only so long as the tentative oil quantity determined under the table contained in paragraph (3) (B) is allocated under paragraph (8) between the transferor and transferee.

(10) Transfers by individuals to corporations.—

(A) In general.—Paragraph (9)(A) shall not apply to a transfer by an individual of qualified property to a qualified transferee corporation solely in exchange for stock in such corporation.

(B) 1,000-barrel limit for corporation.—A tentative quantity shall be determined for the qualified transferee corporation under this subsection.

(C) Transferor's tentative quantity reduced.—

(i) In general.—The tentative quantity for the transferor (and his family) for any period shall be reduced by the transferor's pro rata share of the corporation's depletable quantity for such period.

(ii) Pro rata share.—For purposes of clause (i), a transferor's pro rata share for any period shall be—

(I) in the case of production from property to which subparagraph (A) applies, that portion of the corporation's depletable quantity which is allocable to production from such property, and

(II) in the case of production from all other property, that portion of the corporation's depletable quantity which is allocable to the production from such property, multiplied by a fraction the numerator of which is the fair market value of the transferor's stock in the corporation, and the denominator of which is the fair market value of all stock in the corporation.

(iii) Depletable quantity.—For purposes of this paragraph, a corporation's depletable quantity for any period in [2] the lesser of—

(I) such corporation's tentative quantity for such period (determined under paragraphs (3) and (8)), or

(II) such corporation's average daily production for such period.

(D) Qualified transferee corporation defined.—For purposes of this paragraph, the term "qualified transferee corporation" means a corporation all of the outstanding stock of which has been issued to individuals solely in exchange for qualified property held by such individuals.

(E) Qualified property defined.—For purposes of this paragraph, the term "qualified property" means oil or gas property with respect to which—

(i) there has been no prior transfer to which paragraph (9)(A) applied, and

(ii) the transferor has made an election to have this paragraph apply.

The term also includes cash (not to exceed $1,000 in the aggregate) which one or more individuals transfer to the corporation and, in the case of any property, also includes necessary production equipment for such property which is in place when the property is transferred.

(F) Transferor must retain stock during lifetime.—If at any time during his lifetime any transferor disposes of stock in the corporation (other than to a member of his family), then the depletable quantity of the corporation (determined without regard to this subparagraph) shall be reduced (for all periods on or after the date of the disposition) by an amount which bears the same ratio to such quantity as the fair market value of the stock so disposed of bears to the aggregate fair market value of all stock of the corporation on such date of disposition.

(G) Special rules relating to family of transferor.—

(i) In general.—For purposes of this paragraph—

(I) the issuance of stock to a member of the family of the transferor shall be treated as issuance of stock to the transferor, and

(II) during the lifetime of the transferor, stock transferred to a member of the family of the transferor shall be treated as held by the transferor.

If stock described in the preceding sentence ceases to be held by a member of the family of the transferor, the transferor shall be treated as having disposed of such stock at the time of such cessation.

(ii) Family defined.—For purposes of this paragraph, the members of the family of an individual include only his spouse and minor children.

(H) Property subject to liabilities.—For purposes of this paragraph, section 357 shall be applied as if—

(i) references to section 351 include references to subparagraph (A) of this paragraph, and

(ii) the reference in subsection (a)(1) of section 357 to the nonrecognition of gain includes a reference to the nonapplication of paragraph (9)(A) of this subsection.

(I) Election.—A transferor may make an election under this paragraph only in such manner as the Secretary may by regulations prescribe and only on or before the due date (including extensions) for filing the return of the corporation of the taxes imposed by this chapter for the corporation's first taxable year ending after the date of the transfer (or, if later, after the date of the enactment of this paragraph).

(J) Regulations.—The Secretary shall prescribe such regulations as may be necessary to carry out the purposes of this paragraph.

(11) Special rule for fiscal year taxpayers.—In applying this subsection to a taxable year which is not a calendar year, each portion of such taxable year which occurs during a single calendar year shall be treated as if it were a short taxable year.

(12) Certain production not taken into account.—In applying this subsection, there shall not be taken into account the production of natural gas with respect to which subsection (b) applies.

(13) Subchapter S corporations.—

(A) Computation of depletion allowance at shareholder level.—In the case of an S corporation, the allowance for depletion with respect to any oil or gas property shall be computed separately by each shareholder.

(B) Allocation of basis.—The S corporation shall allocate to each shareholder his pro rata share of the adjusted basis of the S corporation in each oil or gas property held by the S corporation. The allocation shall be made as of the later of the date of acquisition of the property by the S corporation, or the first day of the first taxable year of the S corporation to which the Subchapter S Revision Act of 1982 applies. Each shareholder shall separately keep records of his share of the adjusted basis in each oil and gas property of the S corporation, adjust such share of the adjusted basis for any depletion taken on such property, and use such adjusted basis each year in the computation of his cost depletion or in the computation of his gain or loss on the disposition of such property by the S corporation. In the case of any distribution of oil or gas property to its shareholders by the S corporation, the corporation's adjusted basis in the property shall be an amount equal to the sum of the shareholders' adjusted bases in such property, as determined under this subparagraph.

(C) Coordination with transfer rule of paragraph (9).—For purposes of paragraph (9)—

(i) an S corporation shall be treated as a partnership, and the shareholders of the S corporation shall be treated as partners, and

(ii) an election by a C corporation to become an S corporation shall be treated as a transfer of all its properties effective on the day on which such election first takes effect.

(D) Coordination with transfer rule of paragraph (10).—For purposes of paragraphs (9) and (10), if an S corporation becomes a C corporation, each shareholder shall be treated as having transferred to such corporation his pro rata share of all the assets of the S corporation.

(d) Limitations on application of subsection (c).—

(1) Limitation based on taxable income.—The deduction for the taxable year attributable to the application of subsection (c) shall not exceed 65 percent of the taxpayer's taxable income for the year computed without regard to—

(A) any depletion on production from an oil or gas property which is subject to the provisions of subsection (c),

(B) any net operating loss carryback to the taxable year under section 172,

(C) any capital loss carryback to the taxable year under section 1212, and

(D) in the case of a trust, any distributions to its beneficiary, except in the case of any trust where any beneficiary of such trust is a member of the family (as defined in section 267(c) (4)) of a settlor who created inter vivos and testamentary trusts for members of the family and such settlor died within the last six days of the fifth month in 1970, and the law in the jurisdiction in which such trust was created requires all or a portion of the gross or net proceeds of any royalty or other interest in oil, gas, or other mineral representing any percentage depletion allowance to be allocated to the principal of the trust.

If an amount is disallowed as a deduction for the taxable year by reason of application of the preceding sentence, the disallowed amount shall be treated as an amount allowable as a deduction under subsection (c) for the following taxable year, subject to the application of the preceding sentence to such taxable year. For purposes of basis adjustments and determining whether cost depletion exceeds percentage depletion with respect to the production from a property, any amount disallowed as a deduction on the application of this paragraph shall be allocated to the respective properties from which the oil or gas was produced in proportion to the percentage depletion otherwise allowable to such properties under subsection (c).

* * *

§ 614. Definition of property

(a) General rule.—For the purpose of computing the depletion allowance in the case of mines, wells, and other natural deposits, the term "property" means each separate interest owned by the taxpayer in each mineral deposit in each separate tract or parcel of land.

* * *

§ 616. Development expenditures

(a) In general.—Except as provided in subsections (b) and (d), there shall be allowed as a deduction in computing taxable income all expenditures paid or incurred during the taxable year for the development of a mine or other natural deposit (other than an oil or gas well) if paid or incurred after the existence of ores or minerals in commercially marketable quantities has been disclosed. This section shall not apply to expenditures for the acquisition or improvement of property of a character which is subject to the allowance for depreciation provided in section 167, but allowances for depreciation shall be considered, for purposes of this section, as expenditures.

(b) Election of taxpayer.—At the election of the taxpayer, made in accordance with regulations prescribed by the Secretary, expenditures described in subsection (a) paid or incurred during the taxable year shall be treated as deferred expenses and shall be deductible on a ratable basis as the units of produced ores or minerals benefited by such expenditures are sold. In the case of such expenditures paid or incurred during the development stage of the mine or deposit, the election shall apply only with respect to the excess of such expenditures during the taxable year over the net receipts during the taxable year from the ores or minerals produced from such mine or deposit. The election under this subsection, if made, must be for the total amount of such expenditures, or the total amount of such excess, as the case may be, with respect to the mine or deposit, and shall be binding for such taxable year.

(c) Adjusted basis of mine or deposit.—The amount of expenditures which are treated under subsection (b) as deferred expenses shall be taken into account in computing the adjusted basis of the mine or deposit, except that such amount, and the adjustments to basis provided in section 1016(a) (9), shall be disregarded in determining the adjusted basis of the property for the purpose of computing a deduction for depletion under section 611.

(d) Special rules for foreign development.—In the case of any expenditures paid or incurred with respect to the development of a mine or other natural deposit (other than an oil, gas, or geothermal well) located outside of the United States—

(1) subsections (a) and (b) shall not apply, and

(2) such expenditures shall—

(A) at the election of the taxpayer, be included in adjusted basis for purposes of computing the amount of any deduction allowable under section 611 (without regard to section 613), or

(B) if subparagraph (A) does not apply, be allowed as a deduction ratably over the 10-taxable year period beginning with the taxable year in which such expenditures were paid or incurred.

* * *

§ 617. Deduction and recapture of certain mining exploration expenditures

(a) Allowance of deduction.—

(1) **General rule.**—At the election of the taxpayer, expenditures paid or incurred during the taxable year for the purpose of ascertaining the existence, location, extent, or quality of any deposit of ore or other mineral, and paid or incurred before the beginning of the development stage of the mine, shall be allowed as a deduction in computing taxable income. This subsection shall apply only with respect to the amount of such expenditures which, but for this subsec-

tion, would not be allowable as a deduction for the taxable year. This subsection shall not apply to expenditures for the acquisition or improvement of property of a character which is subject to the allowance for depreciation provided in section 167, but allowances for depreciation shall be considered, for purposes of this subsection, as expenditures paid or incurred. In no case shall this subsection apply with respect to amounts paid or incurred for the purpose of ascertaining the existence, location, extent, or quality of any deposit of oil or gas or of any mineral with respect to which a deduction for percentage depletion is not allowable under section 613.

(2) Elections.—

(A) Method.—Any election under this subsection shall be made in such manner as the Secretary may by regulations prescribe.

(B) Time and scope.—The election provided by paragraph (1) for the taxable year may be made at any time before the expiration of the period prescribed for making a claim for credit or refund of the tax imposed by this chapter for the taxable year. Such an election for the taxable year shall apply to all expenditures described in paragraph (1) paid or incurred by the taxpayer during the taxable year or during any subsequent taxable year. Such an election may not be revoked unless the Secretary consents to such revocation.

(C) Deficiencies.—The statutory period for the assessment of any deficiency for any taxable year, to the extent such deficiency is attributable to an election or revocation of an election under this subsection, shall not expire before the last day of the 2-year period beginning on the day after the date on which such election or revocation of election is made; and such deficiency may be assessed at any time before the expiration of such 2-year period, notwithstanding any law or rule of law which would otherwise prevent such assessment.

(b) Recapture on reaching producing stage.—

(1) Recapture.—If, in any taxable year, any mine with respect to which expenditures were deducted pursuant to subsection (a) reaches the producing stage, then—

(A) If the taxpayer so elects with respect to all such mines reaching the producing stage during the taxable year, he shall include in gross income for the taxable year an amount equal to the adjusted exploration expenditures with respect to such mines, and the amount so included in income shall be treated for purposes of this subtitle as expenditures which (i) are paid or incurred on the respective dates on which the mines reach the producing stage, and (ii) are properly chargeable to capital account.

(B) If subparagraph (A) does not apply with respect to any such mine, then the deduction for depletion under section 611 with respect to the property shall be disallowed until the amount of depletion which would be allowable but for this subparagraph equals the amount of the adjusted exploration expenditures with respect to such mine.

(2) Elections.—

(A) Method.—Any election under this subsection shall be made in such manner as the Secretary may by regulations prescribe.

(B) Time and scope.—The election provided by paragraph (1) for any taxable year may be made or changed not later than the time prescribed by law for filing the return (including extensions thereof) for such taxable year.

(c) Recapture in case of bonus or royalty.—If an election has been made under subsection (a) with respect to expenditures relating to a mining property and the taxpayer receives or accrues a bonus or a royalty with respect to such property, then the deduction for depletion under section 611 with respect to the bonus or royalty shall be disallowed until the amount of depletion which would be allowable but for this subsection equals the amount of the adjusted exploration expenditures with respect to the property to which the bonus or royalty relates.

(d) Gain from dispositions of certain mining property.—

(1) General rule.—Except as otherwise provided in this subsection, if mining property is disposed of the lower of—

(A) the adjusted exploration expenditures with respect to such property, or

(B) the excess of—

(i) the amount realized (in the case of a sale, exchange, or involuntary conversion), or the fair market value (in the case of any other disposition), over

(ii) the adjusted basis of such property,

shall be treated as ordinary income. Such gain shall be recognized notwithstanding any other provision of this subtitle.

(2) Disposition of portion of property.—For purposes of paragraph (1)—

(A) In the case of the disposition of a portion of a mining property (other than an undivided interest), the entire amount of the adjusted exploration expenditures with respect to such property shall be treated as attributable to such portion to the extent of the amount of the gain to which paragraph (1) applies.

(B) In the case of the disposition of an undivided interest in a mining property (or a portion thereof), a proportionate part of the adjusted exploration expenditures with respect to such property shall be treated as attributable to such undivided interest to the extent of the amount of the gain to which paragraph (1) applies.

This paragraph shall not apply to any expenditure to the extent the taxpayer establishes to the satisfaction of the Secretary that such expenditure relates neither to the portion (or interest therein) disposed of nor to any mine, in the property held by the taxpayer before the disposition, which has reached the producing stage.

(3) Exceptions and limitations.—Paragraphs (1), (2), and (3) of section 1245(b) (relating to exceptions and limitations with respect to gain from disposition of certain depreciable property) shall apply in respect of this subsection in the same manner and with the same effect as if references in section 1245(b) to section 1245 or any provision thereof were references to this subsection or the corresponding provisions of this subsection and as if references to section 1245 property were references to mining property.

(4) Application of subsection.—This subsection shall apply notwithstanding any other provision of this subtitle.

(5) Coordination with section 1254.—This subsection shall not apply to any disposition to which section 1254 applies.

(e) Basis of property.—

(1) Basis.—The basis of any property shall not be reduced by the amount of any depletion which would be allowable but for the application of this section.

(2) Adjustments.—The Secretary shall prescribe such regulations as he may deem necessary to provide for adjustments to the basis of property to reflect gain recognized under subsection (d) (1).

* * *

(g) Special rules relating to partnership property.—

(1) Property distributed to partner.—In the case of any property or mine received by the taxpayer in a distribution with respect to part or all of his interest in a partnership, the adjusted exploration expenditures with respect to such property or mine include the adjusted exploration expenditures (not otherwise included under subsection (f) (1)) with respect to such property or mine immediately prior to such distribution, but the adjusted exploration expenditures with respect to any such property or mine shall be reduced by the amount of gain to which section 751(b) applied realized by the partnership (as constituted after the distribution) on the distribution of such property or mine.

(2) Property retained by partnership.—In the case of any property or mine held by a partnership after a distribution to a partner to which section 751(b) applied, the adjusted exploration expenditures with respect to such property or mine shall, under regulations prescribed by the Secretary, be reduced by the amount of gain to which section 751(b) applied realized by such partner with respect to such distribution on account of such property or mine.

* * *

PART III—SALES AND EXCHANGES

§ 631. Gain or loss in the case of timber, coal, or domestic iron ore

(a) Election to consider cutting as sale or exchange.—If the taxpayer so elects on his return for a taxable year, the cutting of timber (for sale or for use in the taxpayer's trade or business) during such year by the taxpayer who owns, or has a contract right to cut, such timber (providing he has owned such timber or has held such contract right on the first day of such year and for a period of more than 6 months before such cutting) shall be considered as a sale or exchange of such timber cut during such year. If such election has been made, gain or loss to the taxpayer shall be recognized in an amount equal to the difference between the fair market value of such timber, and the adjusted basis for depletion of such timber in the hands of the taxpayer. Such fair market value shall be the fair market value as of the first day of the taxable year in which such timber is cut, and shall thereafter be considered as the cost of such cut timber to the taxpayer for all purposes for which such cost is a necessary factor. If a taxpayer makes an election under this subsection, such election shall apply with respect to all timber which is owned by the taxpayer or which the taxpayer has a contract right to cut and shall be binding on the taxpayer for the taxable year for which the election is made and for all subsequent years, unless the Secretary, on showing of undue hardship, permits the taxpayer to revoke his election; such revocation, however, shall preclude any further elections under this subsection except with the consent of the Secretary. For purposes of this subsection and subsection (b), the term "timber" includes evergreen trees which are more than 6 years old at the time severed from the roots and are sold for ornamental purposes.

(b) Disposal of timber with a retained economic interest.—In the case of the disposal of timber held for more than 6 months before such disposal, by the owner thereof under any form or type of contract by virtue of which such owner retains an economic interest in such timber, the difference between the amount realized from the disposal of such timber and the adjusted depletion basis thereof, shall be considered as though it were a gain or loss, as the case may be, on the sale of such timber. In determining the gross income, the adjusted gross income, or the taxable income of the lessee, the deductions allowable with respect to rents and royalties shall be determined without regard to the provisions of this subsection. The date of disposal of such timber shall be deemed to be the date such timber is cut, but if payment is made to the owner under the contract before such timber is cut the owner may elect to treat the date of such payment as the date of disposal of such timber. For purposes of this subsection, the term "owner" means any person who owns an interest in such timber, including a sublessor and a holder of a contract to cut timber.

(c) Disposal of coal or domestic iron ore with a retained economic interest.—In the case of the disposal of coal (including lignite), or iron ore mined in the United States, held for more than 6 months before such disposal, by the owner thereof under any form of contract by virtue of which such owner retains an economic interest in such coal or iron ore, the difference between the amount realized from the disposal of such coal or iron ore and the adjusted depletion basis thereof plus the deductions disallowed for the taxable year under section 272 shall be considered as though it were a gain or loss, as the case may be, on the sale of such coal or iron ore. If for the taxable year of such gain or loss the maximum rate of tax imposed by this chapter on any net capital gain is less than such maximum rate for ordinary income, such owner shall not be entitled to the allowance for percentage depletion provided in section 613 with respect to such coal or iron ore. This subsection shall not apply to income realized by any owner as a co-adventurer, partner, or principal in the mining of such coal or iron ore, and the word "owner" means any person who owns an economic interest in coal or iron ore in place, including a sublessor. The date of disposal of such coal or iron ore shall be deemed to be the date such coal or iron ore is mined. In determining the gross income, the adjusted gross income, or the taxable income of the lessee, the deductions allowable with respect to rents and royalties shall be determined without regard to the provisions of this subsection. This subsection shall have no application, for purposes of applying subchapter G, relating to corporations used to avoid income tax on shareholders (including the determinations of the amount of the deductions under section 535(b)(6) or section 545(b)(5)). This subsection shall not apply to any disposal of iron ore or coal—

(1) to a person whose relationship to the person disposing of such iron ore would result in the disallowance of losses under section 267 or 707(b), or

(2) to a person owned or controlled directly or indirectly by the same interests which own or control the person disposing of such iron ore or coal.

PART IV—MINERAL PRODUCTION PAYMENTS

§ 636. Income tax treatment of mineral production payments

(a) **Carved-out production payment.**—A production payment carved out of mineral property shall be treated, for purposes of this subtitle, as if it were a mortgage loan on the property, and shall not qualify as an economic interest in the mineral property. In the case of a production payment carved out for exploration or development of a mineral property, the preceding sentence shall apply only if and to the extent gross income from the property (for purposes of section 613) would be realized, in the absence of the application of such sentence, by the person creating the production payment.

(b) **Retained production payment on sale of mineral property.**—A production payment retained on the sale of a mineral property shall be treated, for purposes of this subtitle, as if it were a purchase money mortgage loan and shall not qualify as an economic interest in the mineral property.

(c) **Retained production payment on lease of mineral property.**—A production payment retained in a mineral property by the lessor in a leasing transaction shall be treated, for purposes of this subtitle, insofar as the lessee (or his successors in interest) is concerned, as if it were a bonus granted by the lessee to the lessor payable in installments. The treatment of the production payment in the hands of the lessor shall be determined without regard to the provisions of this subsection.

(d) **Definition.**—As used in this section, the term "mineral property" has the meaning assigned to the term "property" in section 614(a).

(e) **Regulations.**—The Secretary shall prescribe such regulations as may be necessary to carry out the purposes of this section.

SUBCHAPTER J—ESTATES, TRUSTS, BENEFICIARIES, AND DECEDENTS

Part
  I. Estates, trusts, and beneficiaries.
  II. Income in respect of decedents.

PART I—ESTATES, TRUSTS, AND BENEFICIARIES

Subpart
  A. General rules for taxation of estates and trusts.
  B. Trusts which distribute current income only.
  C. Estates and trusts which may accumulate income or which distribute corpus.
  D. Treatment of excess distributions by trusts.
  E. Grantors and others treated as substantial owners.
  F. Miscellaneous.

Subpart A—General Rules for Taxation of Estates and Trusts

§ 641. Imposition of tax

(a) **Application of tax.**—The tax imposed by section 1(e) shall apply to the taxable income of estates or of any kind of property held in trust, including—

(1) income accumulated in trust for the benefit of unborn or unascertained persons or persons with contingent interests, and income accumulated or held for future distribution under the terms of the will or trust;

(2) income which is to be distributed currently by the fiduciary to the beneficiaries, and income collected by a guardian of an infant which is to be held or distributed as the court may direct;

(3) income received by estates of deceased persons during the period of administration or settlement of the estate; and

(4) income which, in the discretion of the fiduciary, may be either distributed to the beneficiaries or accumulated.

(b) **Computation and payment.**—The taxable income of an estate or trust shall be computed in the same manner as in the case of an individual, except as otherwise provided in this part. The tax shall be computed on such taxable income and shall be paid by the fiduciary.

(c) **Exclusion of includible gain from taxable income.**—

(1) **General rule.**—For purposes of this part, the taxable income of a trust does not include the amount of any includible gain as defined in section 644(b) reduced by any deductions properly allocable thereto.

(2) **Cross reference.**—

For the taxation of any includible gain, see section 644.

§ 642. Special rules for credits and deductions

(a) **Foreign tax credit allowed.**—An estate or trust shall be allowed the credit against tax for taxes imposed by foreign countries and possessions of the United States, to the extent allowed by section 901, only in respect of so much of the taxes described in such section as is not properly allocable under such section to the beneficiaries.

(b) **Deduction for personal exemption.**—An estate shall be allowed a deduction of $600. A trust which, under its governing instrument, is required to distribute all of its income currently shall be allowed a deduction of $300. All other trusts shall be allowed a deduction of $100. The deductions allowed by this subsection shall be in lieu of the deductions allowed under section 151 (relating to deduction for personal exemption).

(c) **Deduction for amounts paid or permanently set aside for a charitable purpose.**—

(1) **General rule.**—In the case of an estate or trust (other than a trust meeting the specifications of subpart B), there shall be allowed as a deduction in computing its taxable income (in lieu of the deduction allowed by section 170(a), relating to deduction for charitable, etc., contributions and gifts) any amount of the gross income, without limitation, which pursuant to the terms of the governing instrument is, during the taxable year, paid for a purpose specified in section 170(c) (determined without regard to section 170(c) (2) (A)). If a charitable contribution is paid after the close of such taxable year and on or before the last day of the year following the close of such taxable year, then the trustee or administrator may elect to treat such contribution as paid during such taxable year. The election shall be made at such time and in such manner as the Secretary prescribes by regulations.

(2) **Amounts permanently set aside.**—In the case of an estate, and in the case of a trust (other than a trust meeting the specifications of subpart B) required by the terms of its governing instrument to set aside amounts which was—

(A) created on or before October 9, 1969, if—

(i) an irrevocable remainder interest is transferred to or for the use of an organization described in section 170(c), or

(ii) the grantor is at all times after October 9, 1969, under a mental disability to change the terms of the trust; or

(B) established by a will executed on or before October 9, 1969, if—

(i) the testator dies before October 9, 1972, without having republished the will after October 9, 1969, by codicil or otherwise,

(ii) the testator at no time after October 9, 1969, had the right to change the portions of the will which pertain to the trust, or

(iii) the will is not republished by codicil or otherwise before October 9, 1972, and the testator is on such date and at all times thereafter under a mental disability to republish the will by codicil or otherwise, there shall also be allowed as a deduction in computing its taxable income any amount of the gross income, without limitation, which pursuant to the terms of the governing instrument is, during the taxable year, permanently set aside for a purpose specified in section 170(c), or is to be used exclusively for religious, charitable, scientific, literary, or educational purposes, or for the prevention of cruelty to children or animals, or for the establishment, acquisition, maintenance, or operation of a public cemetery not operated for profit. In the case of a trust, the preceding sentence shall apply only to gross income earned with respect to amounts transferred to the trust before October 9, 1969, or transferred under a will to which subparagraph (B) applies.

(3) **Pooled income funds.**—In the case of a pooled income fund (as defined in paragraph (5)), there shall also be allowed as a deduction in computing its taxable income any amount of the gross income attributable to gain from the sale of a capital asset held for more than 6 months, without limitation, which pursuant to the terms of the governing instrument is, during the taxable year, permanently set aside for a purpose specified in section 170(c).

(4) **Coordination with section 621.**—In the case of a trust, the deduction allowed by this subsection shall be subject to section 681 (relating to unrelated business income).

(5) **Definition of pooled income fund.**—For purposes of paragraph (3), a pooled income fund is a trust—

(A) to which each donor transfers property, contributing an irrevocable remainder interest in such property to or for the use of an organization described in section 170(b) (1) (A) (other than in clauses (vii) or (viii)), and retaining an income interest for the life of one or more beneficiaries (living at the time of such transfer),

(B) in which the property transferred by each donor is commingled with property transferred by other donors who have made or make similar transfers,

(C) which cannot have investments in securities which are exempt from the taxes imposed by this subtitle,

(D) which includes only amounts received from transfers which meet the requirements of this paragraph,

(E) which is maintained by the organization to which the remainder interest is contributed and of which no donor or beneficiary of an income interest is a trustee, and

(F) from which each beneficiary of an income interest receives income, for each year for which he is entitled to receive the income interest referred to in subparagraph (A), determined by the rate of return earned by the trust for such year.

For purposes of determining the amount of any charitable contribution allowable by reason of a transfer of property to a pooled fund, the value of the income interest shall be determined on the basis of the highest rate of return earned by the fund for any of the 3 taxable years immediately preceding the taxable year of the fund in which the transfer is made. In the case of funds in existence less than 3 taxable years preceding the taxable year of the fund in which a transfer is made, the rate of return shall be deemed to be 6 percent per annum, except that the Secretary may prescribe a different rate of return.

(6) **Taxable private foundations.**—In the case of a private foundation which is not exempt from taxation under section 501(a) for the taxable year, the provisions of this subsection shall not apply and the provisions of section 170 shall apply.

(d) Net operating loss deduction.—The benefit of the deduction for net operating losses provided by section 172 shall be allowed to estates and trusts under regulations prescribed by the Secretary.

(e) Deduction for depreciation and depletion.—An estate or trust shall be allowed the deduction for depreciation and depletion only to the extent not allowable to beneficiaries under sections 167(h) and 611(b).

(f) Amortization deductions.—The benefit of the deductions for amortization provided by sections 169, 184, 187, and 188 shall be allowed to estates and trusts in the same manner as in the case of an individual. The allowable deduction shall be apportioned between the income beneficiaries and the fiduciary under regulations prescribed by the Secretary.

(g) Disallowance of double deductions.—Amounts allowable under section 2053 or 2054 as a deduction in computing the taxable estate of a decedent shall not be allowed as a deduction (or as an offset against the sales price of property in determining gain or loss) in computing the taxable income of the estate or of any other person, unless there is filed, within the time and in the manner and form prescribed by the Secretary, a statement that the amounts have not been allowed as deductions under section 2053 or 2054 and a waiver of the right to have such amounts allowed at any time as deductions under section 2053 or 2054. This subsection shall not apply with respect to deductions allowed under part II (relating to income in respect of decedents).

(h) Unused loss carryovers and excess deductions on termination available to beneficiaries.—If on the termination of an estate or trust, the estate or trust has—

(1) a net operating loss carryover under section 172 or a capital loss carryover under section 1212, or

(2) for the last taxable year of the estate or trust deductions (other than the deductions allowed under subsections (b) or (c)) in excess of gross income for such year,

then such carryover or such excess shall be allowed as a deduction, in accordance with regulations prescribed by the Secretary, to the beneficiaries succeeding to the property of the estate or trust.

* * *

§ 643.   Definitions applicable to subparts A, B, C, and D

(a) Distributable net income.—For purposes of this part, the term "distributable net income" means, with respect to any taxable year, the taxable income of the estate or trust computed with the following modifications—

(1) **Deduction for distributions.**—No deduction shall be taken under sections 651 and 661 (relating to additional deductions).

(2) **Deduction for personal exemption.**—No deduction shall be taken under section 642(b) (relating to deduction for personal exemptions).

(3) **Capital gains and losses.**—Gains from the sale or exchange of capital assets shall be excluded to the extent that such gains are allocated to corpus and are not (A) paid, credited, or required to be distributed to any beneficiary during the taxable year, or (B) paid, permanently set aside, or to be used for the purposes specified in section 642(c). Losses from the sale or exchange of capital assets shall be excluded, except to the extent such losses are taken into account in determining

the amount of gains from the sale or exchange of capital assets which are paid, credited, or required to be distributed to any beneficiary during the taxable year.

(4) **Extraordinary dividends and taxable stock dividends.**—For purposes only of subpart B (relating to trusts which distribute current income only), there shall be excluded those items of gross income constituting extraordinary dividends or taxable stock dividends which the fiduciary, acting in good faith, does not pay or credit to any beneficiary by reason of his determination that such dividends are allocable to corpus under the terms of the governing instrument and applicable local law.

(5) **Tax-exempt interest.**—There shall be included any tax-exempt interest to which section 103 applies, reduced by any amounts which would be deductible in respect of disbursements allocable to such interest but for the provisions of section 265 (relating to disallowance of certain deductions).

* * *

(b) **Income.**—For purposes of this subpart and subparts B, C, and D, the term "income", when not preceded by the words "taxable", "distributable net", "undistributed net", or "gross", means the amount of income of the estate or trust for the taxable year determined under the terms of the governing instrument and applicable local law. Items of gross income constituting extraordinary dividends or taxable stock dividends which the fiduciary, acting in good faith, determines to be allocable to corpus under the terms of the governing instrument and applicable local law shall not be considered income.

(c) **Beneficiary.**—For purposes of this part, the term "beneficiary" includes heir, legatee, devisee.

* * *

(e) **Treatment of property distributed in kind.**—

(1) **Basis of beneficiary.**—The basis of any property received by a beneficiary in a distribution from an estate or trust shall be—

(A) the adjusted basis of such property in the hands of the estate or trust immediately before the distribution, adjusted for

(B) any gain or loss recognized to the estate or trust on the distribution.

(2) **Amount of distribution.**—In the case of any distribution of property (other than cash), the amount taken into account under sections 661(a)(2) and 662(a)(2) shall be the lesser of—

(A) the basis of such property in the hands of the beneficiary (as determined under paragraph (1)), or

(B) the fair market value of such property.

(3) **Election to recognize gain.**—

(A) **In general.**—In the case of any distribution of property (other than cash) to which an election under this paragraph applies—

(i) paragraph (2) shall not apply,

(ii) gain or loss shall be recognized by the estate or trust in the same manner as if such property had been sold to the distributee at its fair market value, and

(iii) the amount taken into account under sections 661(a)(2) and 662(a)(2) shall be the fair market value of such property.

533

(B) **Election.**—Any election under this paragraph shall apply to all distributions made by the estate or trust during a taxable year and shall be made on the return of such estate or trust for such taxable year.

Any such election, once made, may be revoked only with the consent of the Secretary.

(4) **Exception for distributions described in section 663(a).**—This subsection shall not apply to any distribution described in section 663(a).

* * *

(f) **Treatment of multiple trusts.**—For purposes of this subchapter, under regulations prescribed by the Secretary, 2 or more trusts shall be treated as 1 trust if—

(1) such trusts have substantially the same grantor or grantors and substantially the same primary beneficiary or beneficiaries, and

(2) a principal purpose of such trusts is the avoidance of the tax imposed by this chapter.

For purposes of the preceding sentence, a husband and wife shall be treated as 1 person.

(g) **Certain payments of estimated tax treated as paid by beneficiary.**—

(1) **In general.**—In the case of a trust—

(A) the trustee may elect to treat any portion of a payment of estimated tax made by such trust for any taxable year of the trust as a payment made by a beneficiary of such trust,

(B) any amount so treated shall be treated as paid or credited to the beneficiary on the last day of such taxable year, and

(C) for purposes of subtitle F, the amount so treated—

(i) shall not be treated as a payment of estimated tax made by the trust, but

(ii) shall be treated as a payment of estimated tax made by such beneficiary on January 15 following the taxable year.

The preceding sentence shall apply only to the extent the payments of estimated tax made by the trust for the taxable year exceed the tax imposed by this chapter shown on its return for the taxable year.

(2) **Time for making election.**—An election under paragraph (1) may be made—

(A) only on the trust's return of the tax imposed by this chapter for the taxable year, and

(B) only if such return is filed on or before the 65th day after the close of the taxable year.

§ 644. Special rule for gain on property transferred to trust at less than fair market value

(a) **Imposition of tax.**—

(1) **In general.**—If—

(A) a trust (or another trust to which the property is distributed) sells or exchanges property at a gain not more than 2 years after the date of the initial transfer of the property in trust by the transferor, and

(B) the fair market value of such property at the time of the initial transfer in trust by the transferor exceeds the adjusted basis of such property immediately after such transfer,

there is hereby imposed a tax determined in accordance with paragraph (2) on the includible gain recognized on such sale or exchange.

(2) **Amount of tax.**—The amount of the tax imposed by paragraph (1) on any includible gain recognized on the sale or exchange of any property shall be equal to the sum of—

(A) the excess of—

(i) the tax which would have been imposed under this chapter for the taxable year of the transferor in which the sale or exchange of such property occurs had the amount of the includible gain recognized on such sale or exchange, reduced by any deductions properly allocable to such gain, been included in the gross income of the transferor for such taxable year, over

(ii) the tax actually imposed under this chapter for such taxable year on the transferor, plus

(B) if such sale or exchange occurs in a taxable year of the transferor which begins after the beginning of the taxable year of the trust in which such sale or exchange occurs, an amount equal to the amount determined under subparagraph (A) multiplied by the underpayment rate established under section 6621.

The determination of tax under clause (i) of subparagraph (A) shall be made by not taking into account any carryback, and by not taking into account any loss or deduction to the extent that such loss or deduction may be carried by the transferor to any other taxable year.

(3) **Taxable year for which tax imposed.**—The tax imposed by paragraph (1) shall be imposed for the taxable year of the trust which begins with or within the taxable year of the transferor in which the sale or exchange occurs.

(4) **Tax to be in addition to other taxes.**—The tax imposed by this subsection for any taxable year of the trust shall be in addition to any other tax imposed by this chapter for such taxable year.

(b) **Definition of includible gain.**—For purposes of this section, the term "includible gain" means the lesser of—

(1) the gain recognized by the trust on the sale or exchange of any property, or

(2) the excess of the fair market value of such property at the time of the initial transfer in trust by the transferor over the adjusted basis of such property immediately after such transfer.

(c) **Character of includible gain.**—For purposes of subsection (a)—

(1) The character of the includible gain shall be determined as if the property had actually been sold or exchanged by the transferor, and any activities of the trust with respect to the sale or exchange of the property shall be deemed to be activities of the transferor, and

(2) the portion of the includible gain subject to the provisions of section 1245 and section 1250 shall be determined in accordance with regulations prescribed by the Secretary.

(d) **Special rules.**—

(1) **Short sales.**—If the trust sells the property referred to in subsection (a) in a short sale within the 2-year period referred to in such subsection, such 2-year period shall be extended to the date of the closing of such short sale.

(2) **Substituted basis property.**—For purposes of this section, in the case of any property held by the trust which has a basis determined in whole or in part by reference to the basis of any other property which was transferred to the trust—

(A) the initial transfer of such property in trust by the transferor shall be treated as having occurred on the date of the initial transfer in trust of such other property,

(B) subsections (a) (1) (B) and (b) (2) shall be applied by taking into account the fair market value and the adjusted basis of such other property, and

(C) the amount determined under subsection (b) (2) with respect to such other property shall be allocated (under regulations prescribed by the Secretary) among such other property and all properties held by the trust which have a basis determined in whole or in part by reference to the basis of such other property.

(e) **Exceptions.**—Subsection (a) shall not apply to property—

(1) acquired by the trust from a decedent or which passed to a trust from a decedent (within the meaning of section 1014), or

(2) acquired by a pooled income fund (as defined in section 642(c) (5)), or

(3) acquired by a charitable remainder annuity trust (as defined in section 664(d) (1)) or a charitable remainder unitrust (as defined in sections 664(d) (2) and (3)), or

(4) if the sale or exchange of the property occurred after the death of the transferor.

(f) **Special rule for installment sales.**—If the trust reports income under section 453 on any sale or exchange to which subsection (a) applies, under regulations prescribed by the Secretary—

(1) subsection (a) (other than the 2-year requirement of paragraph (1) (A) thereof) shall be applied as if each installment were a separate sale or exchange of property to which such subsection applies, and

(2) the term "includible gain" shall not include any portion of an installment received by the trust after the death of the transferor.

§ 645. Taxable year of trusts

(a) **In general.**—For purposes of this subtitle, the taxable year of any trust shall be the calendar year.

(b) **Exception for trusts exempt from tax and charitable trusts.**—Subsection (a) shall not apply to a trust exempt from taxation under section 501(a) or to a trust described in section 4947(a)(1).

(Added Pub.L. 99–514, Title XIV, § 1403(a), Oct. 22, 1986, 100 Stat. ——.)

Subpart B—Trusts Which Distribute Current Income Only

§ 651. Deduction for trusts distributing current income only

(a) **Deduction.**—In the case of any trust the terms of which—

(1) provide that all of its income is required to be distributed currently, and

(2) do not provide that any amounts are to be paid, permanently set aside, or used for the purposes specified in section 642(c) (relating to deduction for charitable, etc., purposes),

there shall be allowed as a deduction in computing the taxable income of the trust the amount of the income for the taxable year which is required to be distributed currently. This section shall not apply in any taxable year in which the trust distributes amounts other than amounts of income described in paragraph (1).

(b) Limitation on deduction.—If the amount of income required to be distributed currently exceeds the distributable net income of the trust for the taxable year, the deduction shall be limited to the amount of the distributable net income. For this purpose, the computation of distributable net income shall not include items of income which are not included in the gross income of the trust and the deductions allocable thereto.

§ 652. Inclusion of amounts in gross income of beneficiaries of trusts distributing current income only

(a) Inclusion.—Subject to subsection (b), the amount of income for the taxable year required to be distributed currently by a trust described in section 651 shall be included in the gross income of the beneficiaries to whom the income is required to be distributed, whether distributed or not. If such amount exceeds the distributable net income, there shall be included in the gross income of each beneficiary an amount which bears the same ratio to distributable net income as the amount of income required to be distributed to such beneficiary bears to the amount of income required to be distributed to all beneficiaries.

(b) Character of amounts.—The amounts specified in subsection (a) shall have the same character in the hands of the beneficiary as in the hands of the trust. For this purpose, the amounts shall be treated as consisting of the same proportion of each class of items entering into the computation of distributable net income of the trust as the total of each class bears to the total distributable net income of the trust, unless the terms of the trust specifically allocate different classes of income to different beneficiaries. In the application of the preceding sentence, the items of deduction entering into the computation of distributable net income shall be allocated among the items of distributable net income in accordance with regulations prescribed by the Secretary.

(c) Different taxable years.—If the taxable year of a beneficiary is different from that of the trust, the amount which the beneficiary is required to include in gross income in accordance with the provisions of this section shall be based upon the amount of income of the trust for any taxable year or years of the trust ending within or with his taxable year.

Subpart C—Estates and Trusts Which May Accumulate Income or Which Distribute Corpus

§ 661. Deduction for estates and trusts accumulating income or distributing corpus

(a) Deduction.—In any taxable year there shall be allowed as a deduction in computing the taxable income of an estate or trust (other than a trust to which subpart B applies), the sum of—

(1) any amount of income for such taxable year required to be distributed currently (including any amount required to be distributed which may be paid out of income or corpus to the extent such amount is paid out of income for such taxable year); and

(2) any other amounts properly paid or credited or required to be distributed for such taxable year;

but such deduction shall not exceed the distributable net income of the estate or trust.

(b) Character of amounts distributed.—The amount determined under subsection (a) shall be treated as consisting of the same proportion of each class of items entering into the computation of distributable net income of the estate or trust as the total of each class bears to the total distributable net income of the estate or trust in the absence of the allocation of different classes of income under the specific terms of the governing instrument. In the application of the preceding sentence, the items of deduction entering into the computation of distributable net income (including the deduction allowed under section 642(c)) shall be allocated among the items of distributable net income in accordance with regulations prescribed by the Secretary.

(c) Limitation on deduction.—No deduction shall be allowed under subsection (a) in respect of any portion of the amount allowed as a deduction under that subsection (without regard to this subsection) which is treated under subsection (b) as consisting of any item of distributable net income which is not included in the gross income of the estate or trust.

§ 662. Inclusion of amounts in gross income of beneficiaries of estates and trusts accumulating income or distributing corpus

(a) Inclusion.—Subject to subsection (b), there shall be included in the gross income of a beneficiary to whom an amount specified in section 661(a) is paid, credited, or required to be distributed (by an estate or trust described in section 661), the sum of the following amounts:

(1) Amounts required to be distributed currently.—The amount of income for the taxable year required to be distributed currently to such beneficiary, whether distributed or not. If the amount of income required to be distributed currently to all beneficiaries exceeds the distributable net income (computed without the deduction allowed by section 642(c), relating to deduction for charitable, etc., purposes) of the estate or trust, then, in lieu of the amount provided in the preceding sentence, there shall be included in the gross income of the beneficiary an amount which bears the same ratio to distributable net income (as so computed) as the amount of income required to be distributed currently to such beneficiary bears to the amount required to be distributed currently to all beneficiaries. For purposes of this section, the phrase "the amount of income for the taxable year required to be distributed currently" includes any amount required to be paid out of income or corpus to the extent such amount is paid out of income for such taxable year.

(2) Other amounts distributed.—All other amounts properly paid, credited, or required to be distributed to such beneficiary for the taxable year. If the sum of—

(A) the amount of income for the taxable year required to be distributed currently to all beneficiaries, and

(B) all other amounts properly paid, credited, or required to be distributed to all beneficiaries

exceeds the distributable net income of the estate or trust, then, in lieu of the amount provided in the preceding sentence, there shall be included in the gross income of the beneficiary an amount which bears the same ratio to distributable net income (reduced by the amounts specified in (A)) as the other amounts properly paid, credited or required to be distributed to the beneficiary bear to the other amounts properly paid, credited, or required to be distributed to all beneficiaries.

(b) Character of amounts.—The amounts determined under subsection (a) shall have the same character in the hands of the beneficiary as in the hands of the estate or trust. For this purpose, the amounts shall be treated as consisting of the same proportion of each class of items entering into the computation of distributable net income as the total of each class bears to the total distributable net income of the estate or trust unless the terms of the governing instrument specifically allocate different classes of income to different beneficiaries. In the application of the preceding sentence, the items of deduction entering into the computation of distributable net income (including the deduction allowed under section 642(c)) shall be allocated among the items of distributable net income in accordance with regulations prescribed by the Secretary. In the application of this subsection to the amount determined under paragraph (1) of subsection (a), distributable net income shall be computed without regard to any portion of the deduction under section 642(c) which is not attributable to income of the taxable year.

(c) Different taxable years.—If the taxable year of a beneficiary is different from that of the estate or trust, the amount to be included in the gross income of the beneficiary shall be based on the distributable net income of the estate or trust and the amounts properly paid, credited, or required to be distributed to the beneficiary during any taxable year or years of the estate or trust ending within or with his taxable year.

§ 663. Special rules applicable to sections 661 and 662

(a) Exclusions.—There shall not be included as amounts falling within section 661(a) or 662(a)—

(1) Gifts, bequests, etc.—Any amount which, under the terms of the governing instrument, is properly paid or credited as a gift or bequest of a specific sum of money or of specific property and which is paid or credited all at once or in not more than 3 installments. For this purpose an amount which can be paid or credited only from the income of the estate or trust shall not be considered as a gift or bequest of a specific sum of money.

(2) Charitable, etc., distributions.—Any amount paid or permanently set aside or otherwise qualifying for the deduction provided in section 642(c) (computed without regard to sections 508(d), 681, and 4948(c) (4)).

(3) Denial of double deduction.—Any amount paid, credited, or distributed in the taxable year, if section 651 or section 661 applied to such amount for a preceding taxable year of an estate or trust because credited or required to be distributed in such preceding taxable year.

(b) Distributions in first sixty-five days of taxable year.—

(1) General rule.—If within the first 65 days of any taxable year of a trust, an amount is properly paid or credited, such amount shall be considered paid or credited on the last day of the preceding taxable year.

(2) Limitation.—Paragraph (1) shall apply with respect to any taxable year of a trust only if the fiduciary of such trust elects, in such manner and at such time as the Secretary prescribes by regulations, to have paragraph (1) apply for such taxable year.

(c) Separate shares treated as separate trusts.—For the sole purpose of determining the amount of distributable net income in the application of sections 661 and 662, in the case of a single trust having more than one beneficiary, substantially separate and independent shares of different beneficiaries in the trust shall be treated as separate trusts. The existence of such substantially separate and independent shares and the manner of treatment as separate trusts, including the application of subpart D, shall be determined in accordance with regulations prescribed by the Secretary.

§ 664. Charitable remainder trusts

(a) **General rule.**—Notwithstanding any other provision of this subchapter, the provisions of this section shall, in accordance with regulations prescribed by the Secretary, apply in the case of a charitable remainder annuity trust and a charitable remainder unitrust.

(b) **Character of distributions.**—Amounts distributed by a charitable remainder annuity trust or by a charitable remainder unitrust shall be considered as having the following characteristics in the hands of a beneficiary to whom is paid the annuity described in subsection (d) (1) (A) or the payment described in subsection (d) (2) (A):

(1) First, as amounts of income (other than gains, and amounts treated as gains, from the sale or other disposition of capital assets) includible in gross income to the extent of such income of the trust for the year and such undistributed income of the trust for prior years;

(2) Second, as a capital gain to the extent of the capital gain of the trust for the year and the undistributed capital gain of the trust for prior years;

(3) Third, as other income to the extent of such income of the trust for the year and such undistributed income of the trust for prior years; and

(4) Fourth, as a distribution of trust corpus.

For purposes of this section, the trust shall determine the amount of its undistributed capital gain on a cumulative net basis.

(c) **Exemption from income taxes.**—A charitable remainder annuity trust and a charitable remainder unitrust shall, for any taxable year, not be subject to any tax imposed by this subtitle, unless such trust, for such year, has unrelated business taxable income (within the meaning of section 512, determined as if part III of subchapter F applied to such trust).

(d) **Definitions.**—

(1) **Charitable remainder annuity trust.**—For purposes of this section, a charitable remainder annuity trust is a trust—

(A) from which a sum certain (which is not less than 5 percent of the initial net fair market value of all property placed in trust) is to be paid, not less often than annually, to one or more persons (at least one of which is not an organization described in section 170(c) and, in the case of individuals, only to an individual who is living at the time of the creation of the trust) for a term of years (not in excess of 20 years) or for the life or lives of such individual or individuals,

(B) from which no amount other than the payments described in subparagraph (A) may be paid to or for the use of any person other than an organization described in section 170(c), and

(C) following the termination of the payments described in subparagraph (A), the remainder interest in the trust is to be transferred to, or for the use of, an organization described in section 170(c) or is to be retained by the trust for such a use.

(2) **Charitable remainder unitrust.**—For purposes of this section, a charitable remainder unitrust is a trust—

(A) from which a fixed percentage (which is not less than 5 percent) of the net fair market value of its assets, valued annually, is to be paid, not less often than annually, to one or more persons (at least one of which is not an organization described in section 170(c) and, in the case of individuals, only to an individual who is living at the time of the creation of the trust) for a term of years (not in excess of 20 years) or for the life or lives of such individual or individuals,

(B) from which no amount other than the payments described in subparagraph (A) may be paid to or for the use of any person other than an organization described in section 170(c), and

(C) following the termination of the payments described in subparagraph (A), the remainder interest in the trust is to be transferred to, or for the use of, an organization described in section 170(c) or is to be retained by the trust for such a use.

(3) Exception.—Notwithstanding the provisions of paragraphs (2) (A) and (B), the trust instrument may provide that the trustee shall pay the income beneficiary for any year—

(A) the amount of the trust income, if such amount is less than the amount required to be distributed under paragraph (2) (A), and

(B) any amount of the trust income which is in excess of the amount required to be distributed under paragraph (2) (A), to the extent that (by reason of subparagraph (A)) the aggregate of the amounts paid in prior years was less than the aggregate of such required amounts.

(e) Valuation for purposes of charitable contribution.—For purposes of determining the amount of any charitable contribution, the remainder interest of a charitable remainder annuity trust or charitable remainder unitrust shall be computed on the basis that an amount equal to 5 percent of the net fair market value of its assets (or a greater amount, if required under the terms of the trust instrument) is to be distributed each year.

(f) Certain contingencies permitted.—

(1) General rule.—If a trust would, but for a qualified contingency, meet the requirements of paragraph (1)(A) or (2)(A) of subsection (d), such trust shall be treated as meeting such requirements.

(2) Value determined without regard to qualified contingency.—For purposes of determining the amount of any charitable contribution (or the actuarial value of any interest), a qualified contingency shall not be taken into account.

(3) Qualified contingency.—For purposes of this subsection, the term "qualified contingency" means any provision of a trust which provides that, upon the happening of a contingency, the payments described in paragraph (1)(A) or (2)(A) of subsection (d) (as the case may be) will terminate not later than such payments would otherwise terminate under the trust.

Subpart D—Treatment of Excess Distributions by Trusts

§ **665.** Definitions applicable to subpart D

(a) Undistributed net income.—For purposes of this subpart, the term "undistributed net income" for any taxable year means the amount by which the distributable net income of the trust for such taxable year exceeds the sum of—

(1) the amounts for such taxable year specified in paragraphs (1) and (2) of section 661(a), and

(2) the amount of taxes imposed on the trust attributable to such distributable net income.

(b) Accumulation distribution.—For purposes of this subpart, the term "accumulation distribution" means, for any taxable year of the trust, the amount by which—

(1) the amounts specified in paragraph (2) of section 661(a) for such taxable year, exceed

(2) distributable net income for such year reduced (but not below zero) by the amounts specified in paragraph (1) of section 661(a).

For purposes of section 667 (other than subsection (c) thereof, relating to multiple trusts), the amounts specified in paragraph (2) of section 661(a) shall not include amounts properly paid, credited, or required to be distributed to a beneficiary from a trust (other than a foreign trust) as income accumulated before the birth of such beneficiary or before such beneficiary attains the age of 21. If the amounts properly paid, credited, or required to be distributed by the trust for the taxable year do not exceed the income of the trust for such year, there shall be no accumulation distribution for such year.

* * *

(d) Taxes imposed on the trust.—For purposes of this subpart—

(1) In general.—The term "taxes imposed on the trust" means the amount of the taxes which are imposed for any taxable year of the trust under this chapter (without regard to this subpart or part IV of subchapter A) and which, under regulations prescribed by the Secretary, are properly allocable to the undistributed portions of distributable net income and gains in excess of losses from sales or exchanges of capital assets. The amount determined in the preceding sentence shall be reduced by any amount of such taxes deemed distributed under section 666(b) and (c) or 669(d) and (e) to any beneficiary.

* * *

(e) Preceding taxable year.—For purposes of this subpart—

(1) in the case of a trust (other than a foreign trust created by a United States person), the term "preceding taxable year" does not include any taxable year of the trust—

(A) which precedes by more than 5 years the taxable year of the trust in which an accumulation distribution is made, if it is made in a taxable year beginning before January 1, 1974, or

(B) which begins before January 1, 1969, in the case of an accumulation distribution made during a taxable year beginning after December 31, 1973; and

(2) in the case of a foreign trust created by a United States person, such term does not include any taxable year of the trust to which this part does not apply.

In the case of a preceding taxable year with respect to which a trust qualifies (without regard to this subpart) under the provisions of subpart B, for purposes of the application of this subpart to such trust for such taxable year, such trust shall, in accordance with regulations prescribed by the Secretary, be treated as a trust to which subpart C applies.

§ 666. Accumulation distribution allocated to preceding years

(a) Amount allocated.—In the case of a trust which is subject to subpart C, the amount of the accumulation distribution of such trust for a taxable year shall be deemed to be an amount within the meaning of paragraph (2) of section 661(a) distributed on the last day of each of the preceding taxable years, commencing with the earliest of such years, to the extent that such amount exceeds the total of any undistributed net income for all earlier preceding taxable years. The amount deemed to be distributed in any such preceding taxable year under the preceding sentence shall not exceed the undistributed net income for such preceding taxable year. For purposes of this subsection, undistributed net income for each of such preceding taxable years shall be computed without regard to such accumulation distribution and without regard to any accumulation distribution determined for any succeeding taxable year.

(b) Total taxes deemed distributed.—If any portion of an accumulation distribution for any taxable year is deemed under subsection (a) to be an amount within the meaning of paragraph (2) of section 661(a) distributed on the last day of any preceding taxable year, and such portion of such distribution is not less than the undistributed net income for such preceding taxable year, the trust shall be deemed to have distributed on the last day of such preceding taxable year an additional amount within the meaning of paragraph (2) of section 661(a). Such additional amount shall be equal to the taxes (other than the tax imposed by section 55) imposed on the trust for such preceding taxable year attributable to the undistributed net income. For purposes of this subsection, the undistributed net income and the taxes imposed on the trust for such preceding taxable year attributable to such undistributed net income shall be computed without regard to such accumulation distribution and without regard to any accumulation distribution determined for any succeeding taxable year.

(c) Pro rata portion of taxes deemed distributed.—If any portion of an accumulation distribution for any taxable year is deemed under subsection (a) to be an amount within the meaning of paragraph (2) of section 661(a) distributed on the last day of any preceding taxable year and such portion of the accumulation distribution is less than the undistributed net income for such preceding taxable year, the trust shall be deemed to have distributed on the last day of such preceding taxable year an additional amount within the meaning of paragraph (2) of section 661(a). Such additional amount shall be equal to the taxes (other than the tax imposed by section 55) imposed on the trust for such taxable year attributable to the undistributed net income multiplied by the ratio of the portion of the accumulation distribution to the undistributed net income of the trust for such year. For purposes of this subsection, the undistributed net income and the taxes imposed on the trust for such preceding taxable year attributable to such undistributed net income shall be computed without regard to the accumulation distribution and without regard to any accumulation distribution determined for any succeeding taxable year.

(d) Rule when information is not available.—If adequate records are not available to determine the proper application of this subpart to an amount distributed by a trust, such amount shall be deemed to be an accumulation distribution consisting of undistributed net income earned during the earliest preceding taxable year of the trust in which it can be established that the trust was in existence.

(e) Denial of refund to trusts and beneficiaries.—No refund or credit shall be allowed to a trust or a beneficiary of such trust for any preceding taxable year by reason of a distribution deemed to have been made by such trust in such year under this section.

§ 667. Treatment of amounts deemed distributed by trust in preceding years

(a) General rule.—The total of the amounts which are treated under section 666 as having been distributed by a trust in a preceding taxable year shall be included in the income of a beneficiary of the trust when paid, credited, or required to be distributed to the extent that such total would have been included in the income of such beneficiary under section 662(a) (2) (and, with respect to any tax-exempt interest to which section 103 applies, under section 662(b)) if such total had been paid to such beneficiary on the last day of such preceding taxable year. The tax imposed by this subtitle on a beneficiary for a taxable year in which any such amount is included in his income shall be determined only as provided in this section and shall consist of the sum of—

(1) a partial tax computed on the taxable income reduced by an amount equal to the total of such amounts, at the rate and in the manner as if this section had not been enacted,

(2) a partial tax determined as provided in subsection (b) of this section, and

(3) in the case of a foreign trust, the interest charge determined as provided in section 668.

(b) Tax on distribution.—

(1) In general.—The partial tax imposed by subsection (a) (2) shall be determined—

(A) by determining the number of preceding taxable years of the trust on the last day of which an amount is deemed under section 666(a) to have been distributed,

(B) by taking from the 5 taxable years immediately preceding the year of the accumulation distribution the 1 taxable year for which the beneficiary's taxable income was the highest and the 1 taxable year for which his taxable income was the lowest,

(C) by adding to the beneficiary's taxable income for each of the 3 taxable years remaining after the application of subparagraph (B) an amount determined by dividing the amount deemed distributed under section 666 and required to be included in income under subsection (a) by the number of preceding taxable years determined under subparagraph (A), and

(D) by determining the average increase in tax for the 3 taxable years referred to in subparagraph (C) resulting from the application of such subparagraph.

The partial tax imposed by subsection (a) (2) shall be the excess (if any) of the average increase in tax determined under subparagraph (D), multiplied by the number of preceding taxable years determined under subparagraph (A), over the amount of taxes (other than the amount of taxes described in section 665(d) (2)) deemed distributed to the beneficiary under sections 666(b) and (c).

(2) Treatment of loss years.—For purposes of paragraph (1), the taxable income of the beneficiary for any taxable year shall be deemed to be not less than zero.

(3) Certain preceding taxable years not taken into account.—For purposes of paragraph (1), if the amount of the undistributed net income deemed distributed in any preceding taxable year of the trust is less than 25 percent of the amount of the accumulation distribution divided by the number of preceding taxable years to which the accumulation distribution is allocated under section 666(a), the number of preceding taxable years of the trust with respect to which an amount is deemed distributed to a beneficiary under section 666(a) shall be determined without regard to such year.

(4) Effect of other accumulation distributions.—In computing the partial tax under paragraph (1) for any beneficiary, the income of such beneficiary for each of his prior taxable years shall include amounts previously deemed distributed to such beneficiary in such year under section 666 as a result of prior accumulation distributions (whether from the same or another trust).

(5) Multiple distributions in the same taxable year.—In the case of accumulation distributions made from more than one trust which are includible in the income of a beneficiary in the same taxable year, the distributions shall be deemed to have been made consecutively in whichever order the beneficiary shall determine.

(6) Adjustment in partial tax for estate and generation-skipping transfer taxes attributable to partial tax.—

(A) In general.—The partial tax shall be reduced by an amount which is equal to the pre-death portion of the partial tax multiplied by a fraction—

(i) the numerator of which is that portion of the tax imposed by chapter 11 or 13, as the case may be, which is attributable (on a proportionate basis) to amounts included in the accumulation distribution, and

(ii) the denominator of which is the amount of the accumulation distribution which is subject to the tax imposed by chapter 11 or 13, as the case may be.

(B) Partial tax determined without regard to this paragraph.—For purposes of this paragraph, the term "partial tax" means the partial tax imposed by subsection (a) (2) determined under this subsection without regard to this paragraph.

(C) Pre-death portion.—For purposes of this paragraph, the pre-death portion of the partial tax shall be an amount which bears the same ratio to the partial tax as the portion of the accumulation distribution which is attributable to the period before the date of the death of the decedent or the date of the generation-skipping transfer bears to the total accumulation distribution.

(c) Special rule for multiple trusts.—

(1) In general.—If, in the same prior taxable year of the beneficiary in which any part of the accumulation distribution from a trust (hereinafter in this paragraph referred to as "third trust") is deemed under section 666(a) to have been distributed to such beneficiary, some part of prior distributions by each of 2 or more other trusts is deemed under section 666(a) to have been distributed to such beneficiary, then subsections (b) and (c) of section 666 shall not apply with respect to such part of the accumulation distribution from such third trust.

(2) Accumulation distributions from trust not taken into account unless they equal or exceed $1,000.—For purposes of paragraph (1), an accumulation distribution from a trust to a beneficiary shall be taken into account only if such distribution, when added to any prior accumulation distributions from such trust which are deemed under section 666(a) to have been distributed to such beneficiary for the same prior taxable year of the beneficiary, equals or exceeds $1,000.

(d) Special rules for foreign trust.—

(1) Foreign tax deemed paid by beneficiary.—

(A) In general.—In determining the increase in tax under subsection (b) (1) (D) for any computation year, the taxes described in section 665(d) (2) which are deemed distributed under section 666(b) or (c) and added under subsection (b) (1) (C) to the taxable income of the beneficiary for any computation year shall, except as provided in subparagraphs (B) and (C), be treated as a credit against the increase in tax for such computation year under subsection (b) (1) (D).

(B) Deduction in lieu of credit.—If the beneficiary did not choose the benefits of subpart A of part III of subchapter N with respect to the computation year, the beneficiary may in lieu of treating the amounts described in subparagraph (A) (without regard to subparagraph (C)) as a credit may treat such amounts as a deduction in computing the beneficiary's taxable income under subsection (b) (1) (C) for the computation year.

(C) Limitation on credit; retention of character.—

(i) Limitation on credit.—For purposes of determining under subparagraph (A) the amount treated as a credit for any computation year, the limitations under subpart A of part III of subchapter N shall be applied separately with respect to amounts added under subsection (b) (1) (C) to the taxable income of the beneficiary for such computation year. For purposes of computing the increase in tax under subsection (b) (1) (D) for any computation year for which the beneficiary did not choose the benefits of subpart A of part III of subchapter N, the beneficiary shall be treated as having chosen such benefits for such computation year.

(ii) Retention of character.—The items of income, deduction, and credit of the Trust shall retain their character (subject to the application of section 904(f) (5)) to the extent necessary to apply this paragraph.

(D) Computation year.—For purposes of this paragraph, the term "computation year" means any of the three taxable years remaining after application of subsection (b) (1) (B).

* * *

Subpart E—Grantors and Others Treated as Substantial Owners

§ 671.   Trust income, deductions, and credits attributable to grantors and others as substantial owners

Where it is specified in this subpart that the grantor or another person shall be treated as the owner of any portion of a trust, there shall then be included in computing the taxable income and credits of the grantor or the other person those items of income, deductions, and credits against tax of the trust which are attributable to that portion of the trust to the extent that such items would be taken into account under this chapter in computing taxable income or credits against the tax of an individual. Any remaining portion of the trust shall be subject to subparts A through D. No items of a trust shall be included in computing the taxable income and credits of the grantor or of any other person solely on the grounds of his dominion and control over the trust under section 61 (relating to definition of gross income) or any other provision of this title, except as specified in this subpart.

§ 672.   Definitions and rules

(a) Adverse party.—For purposes of this subpart, the term "adverse party" means any person having a substantial beneficial interest in the trust which would be adversely affected by the exercise or nonexercise of the power which he possesses respecting the trust. A person having a general power of appointment over the trust property shall be deemed to have a beneficial interest in the trust.

(b) Nonadverse party.—For purposes of this subpart, the term "nonadverse party" means any person who is not an adverse party.

(c) Related or subordinate party.—For purposes of this subpart, the term "related or subordinate party" means any nonadverse party who is—

(1) the grantor's spouse if living with the grantor;

(2) any one of the following: The grantor's father, mother, issue, brother or sister; an employee of the grantor; a corporation or any employee of a corporation in which the stock holdings of the grantor and the trust are significant from the viewpoint of voting control; a subordinate employee of a corporation in which the grantor is an executive.

For purposes of sections 674 and 675, a related or subordinate party shall be presumed to be subservient to the grantor in respect of the exercise or nonexercise of the powers conferred on him unless such party is shown not to be subservient by a preponderance of the evidence.

(d) Rule where power is subject to condition precedent.—A person shall be considered to have a power described in this subpart even though the exercise of the power is subject to a precedent giving of notice or takes effect only on the expiration of a certain period after the exercise of the power.

(e) Grantor treated as holding any power or interest of grantor's spouse. —For purposes of this subpart, if a grantor's spouse is living with the grantor at the time of the creation of any power or interest held by such spouse, the grantor shall be treated as holding such power or interest.

§ 673. Reversionary interests

(a) General rule.—The grantor shall be treated as the owner of any portion of a trust in which he has a reversionary interest in either the corpus or the income therefrom, if, as of the inception of that portion of the trust, the value of such interest exceeds 5 percent of the value of such portion.

(b) Reversionary interest taking effect at death of minor lineal descendant beneficiary.—In the case of any beneficiary who—

(1) is a lineal descendant of the grantor, and

(2) holds all of the present interests in any portion of a trust,

the grantor shall not be treated under subsection (a) as the owner of such portion solely by reason of a reversionary interest in such portion which takes effect upon the death of such beneficiary before such beneficiary attains age 21.

§ 674. Power to control beneficial enjoyment

(a) General rule.—The grantor shall be treated as the owner of any portion of a trust in respect of which the beneficial enjoyment of the corpus or the income therefrom is subject to a power of disposition, exercisable by the grantor or a nonadverse party, or both, without the approval or consent of any adverse party.

(b) Exceptions for certain powers.—Subsection (a) shall not apply to the following powers regardless of by whom held:

(1) **Power to apply income to support of a dependent.**—A power described in section 677(b) to the extent that the grantor would not be subject to tax under that section.

(2) **Power affecting beneficial enjoyment only after occurrence of events.** —A power, the exercise of which can only affect the beneficial enjoyment of the income for a period commencing after the occurrence of an event such that a grantor would not be treated as the owner under section 673 if the power were a reversionary interest; but the grantor may be treated as the owner after the occurrence of the event unless the power is relinquished.

(3) **Power exercisable only by will.**—A power exercisable only by will, other than a power in the grantor to appoint by will the income of the trust where the

income is accumulated for such disposition by the grantor or may be so accumulated in the discretion of the grantor or a nonadverse party, or both, without the approval or consent of any adverse party.

(4) Power to allocate among charitable beneficiaries.—A power to determine the beneficial enjoyment of the corpus or the income therefrom if the corpus or income is irrevocably payable for a purpose specified in section 170(c) (relating to definition of charitable contributions).

(5) Power to distribute corpus.—A power to distribute corpus either—

(A) to or for a beneficiary or beneficiaries or to or for a class of beneficiaries (whether or not income beneficiaries) provided that the power is limited by a reasonably definite standard which is set forth in the trust instrument; or

(B) to or for any current income beneficiary, provided that the distribution of corpus must be chargeable against the proportionate share of corpus held in trust for the payment of income to the beneficiary as if the corpus constituted a separate trust.

A power does not fall within the powers described in this paragraph if any person has a power to add to the beneficiary or beneficiaries or to a class of beneficiaries designated to receive the income or corpus, except where such action is to provide for after-born or after-adopted children.

(6) Power to withhold income temporarily.—A power to distribute or apply income to or for any current income beneficiary or to accumulate the income for him, provided that any accumulated income must ultimately be payable—

(A) to the beneficiary from whom distribution or application is withheld, to his estate, or to his appointees (or persons named as alternate takers in default of appointment) provided that such beneficiary possesses a power of appointment which does not exclude from the class of possible appointees any person other than the beneficiary, his estate, his creditors, or the creditors of his estate, or

(B) on termination of the trust, or in conjunction with a distribution of corpus which is augmented by such accumulated income, to the current income beneficiaries in shares which have been irrevocably specified in the trust instrument.

Accumulated income shall be considered so payable although it is provided that if any beneficiary does not survive a date of distribution which could reasonably have been expected to occur within the beneficiary's lifetime, the share of the deceased beneficiary is to be paid to his appointees or to one or more designated alternate takers (other than the grantor or the grantor's estate) whose shares have been irrevocably specified. A power does not fall within the powers described in this paragraph if any person has a power to add to the beneficiary or beneficiaries or to a class of beneficiaries designated to receive the income or corpus except where such action is to provide for after-born or after-adopted children.

(7) Power to withhold income during disability of a beneficiary.—A power exercisable only during—

(A) the existence of a legal disability of any current income beneficiary, or

(B) the period during which any income beneficiary shall be under the age of 21 years,

to distribute or apply income to or for such beneficiary or to accumulate and add the income to corpus. A power does not fall within the powers described in this paragraph if any person has a power to add to the beneficiary or beneficiaries or to a class of beneficiaries designated to receive the income or corpus, except where such action is to provide for after-born or after-adopted children.

(8) **Power to allocate between corpus and income.**—A power to allocate receipts and disbursements as between corpus and income, even though expressed in broad language.

(c) **Exception for certain powers of independent trustees.**—Subsection (a) shall not apply to a power solely exercisable (without the approval or consent of any other person) by a trustee or trustees, none of whom is the grantor, and no more than half of whom are related or subordinate parties who are subservient to the wishes of the grantor—

(1) to distribute, apportion, or accumulate income to or for a beneficiary or beneficiaries, or to, for, or within a class of beneficiaries; or

(2) to pay out corpus to or for a beneficiary or beneficiaries or to or for a class of beneficiaries (whether or not income beneficiaries).

A power does not fall within the powers described in this subsection if any person has a power to add to the beneficiary or beneficiaries or to a class of beneficiaries designated to receive the income or corpus, except where such action is to provide for after-born or after-adopted children.

(d) **Power to allocate income if limited by a standard.**—Subsection (a) shall not apply to a power solely exercisable (without the approval or consent of any other person) by a trustee or trustees, none of whom is the grantor or spouse living with the grantor, to distribute, apportion, or accumulate income to or for a beneficiary or beneficiaries, or to, for, or within a class of beneficiaries, whether or not the conditions of paragraph (6) or (7) of subsection (b) are satisfied, if such power is limited by a reasonably definite external standard which is set forth in the trust instrument. A power does not fall within the powers described in this subsection if any person has a power to add to the beneficiary or beneficiaries or to a class of beneficiaries designated to receive the income or corpus except where such action is to provide for after-born or after-adopted children.

§ 675. Administrative powers

The grantor shall be treated as the owner of any portion of a trust in respect of which—

(1) **Power to deal for less than adequate and full consideration.**—A power exercisable by the grantor or a nonadverse party, or both, without the approval or consent of any adverse party enables the grantor or any person to purchase, exchange, or otherwise deal with or dispose of the corpus or the income therefrom for less than an adequate consideration in money or money's worth.

(2) **Power to borrow without adequate interest or security.**—A power exercisable by the grantor or a nonadverse party, or both, enables the grantor to borrow the corpus or income, directly or indirectly, without adequate interest or without adequate security except where a trustee (other than the grantor) is authorized under a general lending power to make loans to any person without regard to interest or security.

(3) **Borrowing of the trust funds.**—The grantor has directly or indirectly borrowed the corpus or income and has not completely repaid the loan, including any interest, before the beginning of the taxable year. The preceding sentence shall not apply to a loan which provides for adequate interest and adequate security, if such loan is made by a trustee other than the grantor and other than a related or subordinate trustee subservient to the grantor.

(4) **General powers of administration.**—A power of administration is exercisable in a nonfiduciary capacity by any person without the approval or consent of

549

any person in a fiduciary capacity. For purposes of this paragraph, the term "power of administration" means any one or more of the following powers: (A) a power to vote or direct the voting of stock or other securities of a corporation in which the holdings of the grantor and the trust are significant from the viewpoint of voting control; (B) a power to control the investment of the trust funds either by directing investments or reinvestments, or by vetoing proposed investments or reinvestments, to the extent that the trust funds consist of stocks or securities of corporations in which the holdings of the grantor and the trust are significant from the viewpoint of voting control; or (C) a power to reacquire the trust corpus by substituting other property of an equivalent value.

§ 676. Power to revoke

(a) **General rule.**—The grantor shall be treated as the owner of any portion of a trust, whether or not he is treated as such owner under any other provision of this part, where at any time the power to revest in the grantor title to such portion is exercisable by the grantor or a non-adverse party, or both.

(b) **Power affecting beneficial enjoyment only after occurrence of event.**—Subsection (a) shall not apply to a power the exercise of which can only affect the beneficial enjoyment of the income for a period commencing after the occurrence of an event such that a grantor would not be treated as the owner under section 673 if the power were a reversionary interest. But the grantor may be treated as the owner after the occurrence of such event unless the power is relinquished.

§ 677. Income for benefit of grantor

(a) **General rule.**—The grantor shall be treated as the owner of any portion of a trust, whether or not he is treated as such owner under section 674, whose income without the approval or consent of any adverse party is, or, in the discretion of the grantor or a nonadverse party, or both, may be—

(1) distributed to the grantor or the grantor's spouse;

(2) held or accumulated for future distribution to the grantor or the grantor's spouse; or

(3) applied to the payment of premiums on policies of insurance on the life of the grantor or the grantor's spouse (except policies of insurance irrevocably payable for a purpose specified in section 170(c) (relating to definition of charitable contributions)).

This subsection shall not apply to a power the exercise of which can only affect the beneficial enjoyment of the income for a period commencing after the occurrence of an event such that the grantor would not be treated as the owner under section 673 if the power were a reversionary interest; but the grantor may be treated as the owner after the occurrence of the event unless the power is relinquished.

(b) **Obligations of support.**—Income of a trust shall not be considered taxable to the grantor under subsection (a) or any other provision of this chapter merely because such income in the discretion of another person, the trustee, or the grantor acting as trustee or co-trustee, may be applied or distributed for the support or maintenance of a beneficiary (other than the grantor's spouse) whom the grantor is legally obligated to support or maintain, except to the extent that such income is so applied or distributed. In cases where the amounts so applied or distributed are paid out of corpus or out of other than income for the taxable year, such amounts shall be considered to be an amount paid or credited within the meaning of paragraph (2) of section 661(a) and shall be taxed to the grantor under section 662.

§ 678. Person other than grantor treated as substantial owner

(a) **General rule.**—A person other than the grantor shall be treated as the owner of any portion of a trust with respect to which:

(1) such person has a power exercisable solely by himself to vest the corpus or the income therefrom in himself, or

(2) such person has previously partially released or otherwise modified such a power and after the release or modification retains such control as would, within the principles of sections 671 to 677, inclusive, subject a grantor of a trust to treatment as the owner thereof.

(b) **Exception where grantor is taxable.**—Subsection (a) shall not apply with respect to a power over income, as originally granted or thereafter modified, if the grantor of the trust or a transferor (to whom section 679 applies) is otherwise treated as the owner under the provisions of this subpart other than this section.

(c) **Obligations of support.**—Subsection (a) shall not apply to a power which enables such person, in the capacity of trustee or co-trustee, merely to apply the income of the trust to the support or maintenance of a person whom the holder of the power is obligated to support or maintain except to the extent that such income is so applied. In cases where the amounts so applied or distributed are paid out of corpus or out of other than income of the taxable year, such amounts shall be considered to be an amount paid or credited within the meaning of paragraph (2) of section 661(a) and shall be taxed to the holder of the power under section 662.

(d) **Effect of renunciation or disclaimer.**—Subsection (a) shall not apply with respect to a power which has been renounced or disclaimed within a reasonable time after the holder of the power first became aware of its existence.

(e) **Cross Reference.—**

For provision under which beneficiary of trust is treated as owner of the portion of the trust which consists of stock in an electing small business corporation, see section 1361(d).

Subpart F—Miscellaneous

§ 681. Limitation on charitable deduction

(a) **Trade or business income.**—In computing the deduction allowable under section 642(c) to a trust, no amount otherwise allowable under section 642(c) as a deduction shall be allowed as a deduction with respect to income of a taxable year which is allocable to its unrelated business income for such year. For purposes of the preceding sentence, the term "unrelated business income" means an amount equal to the amount which, if such trust were exempt from tax under section 501(a) by reason of section 501(c) (3), would be computed as its unrelated business taxable income under section 512 (relating to income derived from certain business activities and from certain property acquired with borrowed funds).

* * *

§ 682. Income of an estate or trust in case of divorce, etc.

(a) **Inclusion in gross income of wife.**—There shall be included in the gross income of a wife who is divorced or legally separated under a decree of divorce or of separate maintenance (or who is separated from her husband under a written separation agreement) the amount of the income of any trust which such wife is entitled to receive and which, except for this section, would be includible in the gross income of her husband, and such amount shall not, despite any other provision of this subtitle, be includible in the gross income of such husband. This subsection shall not apply to that part of any such income of the trust which the terms of the decree, written separation agreement, or trust instrument fix, in terms of an amount of money or a portion of such income, as a sum which is payable for the support of minor children of such husband. In case such income is less than the amount specified in the decree, agreement, or instrument, for the purpose of applying the preceding sentence, such income, to the extent of such sum payable for such support, shall be considered a payment for such support.

(b) Wife considered a beneficiary.—For purposes of computing the taxable income of the estate or trust and the taxable income of a wife to whom subsection (a) applies, such wife shall be considered as the beneficiary specified in this part.

(c) Cross reference.—

For definitions of "husband" and "wife", as used in this section, see section 7701(a) (17).

PART II—INCOME IN RESPECT OF DECEDENTS

§ 691. Recipients of income in respect of decedents

(a) Inclusion in gross income.—

(1) General rule.—The amount of all items of gross income in respect of a decedent which are not properly includible in respect of the taxable period in which falls the date of his death or a prior period (including the amount of all items of gross income in respect of a prior decedent, if the right to receive such amount was acquired by reason of the death of the prior decedent or by bequest, devise, or inheritance from the prior decedent) shall be included in the gross income, for the taxable year when received, of:

(A) the estate of the decedent, if the right to receive the amount is acquired by the decedent's estate from the decedent;

(B) the person who, by reason of the death of the decedent, acquires the right to receive the amount, if the right to receive the amount is not acquired by the decedent's estate from the decedent; or

(C) the person who acquires from the decedent the right to receive the amount by bequest, devise, or inheritance, if the amount is received after a distribution by the decedent's estate of such right.

(2) Income in case of sale, etc.—If a right, described in paragraph (1), to receive an amount is transferred by the estate of the decedent or a person who received such right by reason of the death of the decedent or by bequest, devise, or inheritance from the decedent, there shall be included in the gross income of the estate or such person, as the case may be, for the taxable period in which the transfer occurs, the fair market value of such right at the time of such transfer plus the amount by which any consideration for the transfer exceeds such fair market value. For purposes of this paragraph, the term "transfer" includes sale, exchange, or other disposition, or the satisfaction of an installment obligation at other than face value, but does not include transmission at death to the estate of the decedent or a transfer to a person pursuant to the right of such person to receive such amount by reason of the death of the decedent or by bequest, devise, or inheritance from the decedent.

(3) Character of income determined by reference to decedent.—The right, described in paragraph (1), to receive an amount shall be treated, in the hands of the estate of the decedent or any person who acquired such right by reason of the death of the decedent, or by bequest, devise, or inheritance from the decedent, as if it had been acquired by the estate or such person in the transaction in which the right to receive the income was originally derived and the amount includible in gross income under paragraph (1) or (2) shall be considered in the hands of the estate or such person to have the character which it would have had in the hands of the decedent if the decedent had lived and received such amount.

(4) Installment obligations acquired from decedent.—In the case of an installment obligation reportable by the decedent on the installment method under section 453 or 453A, if such obligation is acquired by the decedent's estate from the decedent or by any person by reason of the death of the decedent or by bequest, devise, or inheritance from the decedent—

(A) an amount equal to the excess of the face amount of such obligation over the basis of the obligation in the hands of the decedent (determined under section 453B) shall, for the purpose of paragraph (1), be considered as an item of gross income in respect of the decedent; and

(B) such obligation shall, for purposes of paragraphs (2) and (3), be considered a right to receive an item of gross income in respect of the decedent, but the amount includible in gross income under paragraph (2) shall be reduced by an amount equal to the basis of the obligation in the hands of the decedent (determined under section 453B).

(5) Other rules relating to installment obligations.—

(A) **In general.**—In the case of an installment obligation reportable by the decedent on the installment method under section 453 or 453A, for purposes of paragraph (2)—

(i) the second sentence of paragraph (2) shall be applied by inserting "(other than the obligor)" after "or a transfer to a person",

(ii) any cancellation of such an obligation shall be treated as a transfer, and

(iii) any cancellation of such an obligation occurring at the death of the decedent shall be treated as a transfer by the estate of the decedent (or, if held by a person other than the decedent before the death of the decedent, by such person).

(B) **Face amount treated as fair market value in certain cases.**—In any case to which the first sentence of paragraph (2) applies by reason of subparagraph (A), if the decedent and the obligor were related persons (within the meaning of section 453(f)(1)), the fair market value of the installment obligation shall be treated as not less than its face amount.

(C) **Cancellation includes becoming unenforceable.**—For purposes of subparagraph (A), an installment obligation which becomes unenforceable shall be treated as if it were canceled.

(b) Allowance of deductions and credit.—The amount of any deduction specified in section 162, 163, 164, 212, or 611 (relating to deductions for expenses, interest, taxes, and depletion) or credit specified in section 27 (relating to foreign tax credit), in respect of a decedent which is not properly allowable to the decedent in respect of the taxable period in which falls the date of his death, or a prior period, shall be allowed:

(1) Expenses, interest, and taxes.—In the case of a deduction specified in section 162, 163, 164, or 212 and a credit specified in section 27, in the taxable year when paid—

(A) to the estate of the decedent; except that

(B) if the estate of the decedent is not liable to discharge the obligation to which the deduction or credit relates, to the person who, by reason of the death of the decedent or by bequest, devise, or inheritance acquires, subject to such obligation, from the decedent an interest in property of the decedent.

(2) **Depletion.**—In the case of the deduction specified in section 611, to the person described in subsection (a) (1) (A), (B), or (C) who, in the manner described therein, receives the income to which the deduction relates, in the taxable year when such income is received.

(c) **Deduction for estate tax.**—

(1) **Allowance of deduction.**—

(A) **General rule.**—A person who includes an amount in gross income under subsection (a) shall be allowed, for the same taxable year, as a deduction an amount which bears the same ratio to the estate tax attributable to the net value for estate tax purposes of all the items described in subsection (a) (1) as the value for estate tax purposes of the items of gross income or portions thereof in respect of which such person included the amount in gross income (or the amount included in gross income, whichever is lower) bears to the value for estate tax purposes of all the items described in subsection (a) (1).

(B) **Estates and trusts.**—In the case of an estate or trust, the amount allowed as a deduction under subparagraph (A) shall be computed by excluding from the gross income of the estate or trust the portion (if any) of the items described in subsection (a) (1) which is properly paid, credited, or to be distributed to the beneficiaries during the taxable year.

(2) **Method of computing deduction.**—For purposes of paragraph (1)—

(A) The term "estate tax" means the tax imposed on the estate of the decedent or any prior decedent under section 2001 or 2101, reduced by the credits against such tax.

(B) The net value for estate tax purposes of all the items described in subsection (a) (1) shall be the excess of the value for estate tax purposes of all the items described in subsection (a) (1) over the deductions from the gross estate in respect of claims which represent the deductions and credit described in subsection (b). Such net value shall be determined with respect to the provisions of section 421(c) (2), relating to the deduction for estate tax with respect to stock options to which part II of subchapter D applies.

(C) The estate tax attributable to such net value shall be an amount equal to the excess of the estate tax over the estate tax computed without including in the gross estate such net value.

(3) **Special rule for generation-skipping transfers.**—In the case of any tax imposed by chapter 13 on a taxable termination or a direct skip occurring as a result of the death of the transferor, there shall be allowed a deduction (under principles similar to the principles of this subsection) for the portion of such tax attributable to items of gross income of the trust which were not properly includible in the gross income of the trust for periods before the date of such termination.

(4) **Coordination with capital gain provisions**—For purposes of sections 1(j), 1201, and 1211, the amount of any gain taken into account with respect to any item described in subsection (a)(1) shall be reduced (but not below zero) by the amount of the deduction allowable under paragraph (1) of this subsection with respect to such item.

(5) Coordination with section 402(e).—For purposes of section 402(e) (other than paragraph (1) (D) thereof), the total taxable amount of any lump sum distribution shall be reduced by the amount of the deduction allowable under paragraph (1) of this subsection which is attributable to the total taxable amount (determined without regard to this paragraph).

(d) Amounts received by surviving annuitant under joint and survivor annuity contract.—

(1) Deduction for estate tax.—For purposes of computing the deduction under subsection (c) (1) (A), amounts received by a surviving annuitant—

(A) as an annuity under a joint and survivor annuity contract where the decedent annuitant died after December 31, 1953, and after the annuity starting date (as defined in section 72(c) (4)), and

(B) during the surviving annuitant's life expectancy period,

shall, to the extent included in gross income under section 72, be considered as amounts included in gross income under subsection (a).

(2) Net value for estate tax purposes.—In determining the net value for estate tax purposes under subsection (c) (2) (B) for purposes of this subsection, the value for estate tax purposes of the items described in paragraph (1) of this subsection shall be computed—

(A) by determining the excess of the value of the annuity at the date of the death of the deceased annuitant over the total amount excludable from the gross income of the surviving annuitant under section 72 during the surviving annuitant's life expectancy period, and

(B) by multiplying the figure so obtained by the ratio which the value of the annuity for estate tax purposes bears to the value of the annuity at the date of the death of the deceased.

(3) Definitions.—For purposes of this subsection—

(A) The term "life expectancy period" means the period beginning with the first day of the first period for which an amount is received by the surviving annuitant under the contract and ending with the close of the taxable year with or in which falls the termination of the life expectancy of the surviving annuitant. For purposes of this subparagraph, the life expectancy of the surviving annuitant shall be determined, as of the date of the death of the deceased annuitant, with reference to actuarial tables prescribed by the Secretary.

(B) The surviving annuitant's expected return under the contract shall be computed, as of the death of the deceased annuitant, with reference to actuarial tables prescribed by the Secretary.

(e) Cross reference.—

For application of this section to income in respect of a deceased partner, see section 753.

SUBCHAPTER K—PARTNERS AND PARTNERSHIPS

Part

PART I—DETERMINATION OF TAX LIABILITY

§ 701. Partners, not partnership, subject to tax

A partnership as such shall not be subject to the income tax imposed by this chapter. Persons carrying on business as partners shall be liable for income tax only in their separate or individual capacities.

§ 702. Income and credits of partner

(a) General rule.—In determining his income tax, each partner shall take into account separately his distributive share of the partnership's—

(1) gains and losses from sales or exchanges of capital assets held for not more than 6 months,

(2) gains and losses from sales or exchanges of capital assets held for more than 6 months,

(3) gains and losses from sales or exchanges of property described in section 1231 (relating to certain property used in a trade or business and involuntary conversions),

(4) charitable contributions (as defined in section 170(c)),

(5) dividends with respect to which there is a deduction under part VIII of subchapter B,

(6) taxes, described in section 901, paid or accrued to foreign countries and to possessions of the United States,

(7) other items of income, gain, loss, deduction, or credit, to the extent provided by regulations prescribed by the Secretary, and

(8) taxable income or loss, exclusive of items requiring separate computation under other paragraphs of this subsection.

(b) Character of items constituting distributive share.—The character of any item of income, gain, loss, deduction, or credit included in a partner's distributive share under paragraphs (1) through (7) of subsection (a) shall be determined as if such item were realized directly from the source from which realized by the partnership, or incurred in the same manner as incurred by the partnership.

(c) Gross income of a partner.—In any case where it is necessary to determine the gross income of a partner for purposes of this title, such amount shall include his distributive share of the gross income of the partnership.

(d) Cross reference.—

For rules relating to procedures for determining the tax treatment of partnership items see subchapter C of chapter 63 (section 6221 and following).

§ 703. Partnership computations

(a) Income and deductions.—The taxable income of a partnership shall be computed in the same manner as in the case of an individual except that—

(1) the items described in section 702(a) shall be separately stated, and

(2) the following deductions shall not be allowed to the partnership:

(A) the deductions for personal exemptions provided in section 151,

(B) the deduction for taxes provided in section 164(a) with respect to taxes, described in section 901, paid or accrued to foreign countries and to possessions of the United States,

(C) the deduction for charitable contributions provided in section 170,

(D) the net operating loss deduction provided in section 172,

(E) the additional itemized deductions for individuals provided in part VII of subchapter B (sec. 211 and following), and

(F) the deduction for depletion under section 611 with respect to oil and gas wells.

(b) Elections of the partnership.—Any election affecting the computation of taxable income derived from a partnership shall be made by the partnership, except that any election under—

(1) subsection (b)(5) or (d)(4) of section 108 (relating to income from discharge of indebtedness),

(2) section 617 (relating to deduction and recapture of certain mining exploration expenditures), or

(3) section 901 (relating to taxes of foreign countries and possessions of the United States),

shall be made by each partner separately.

§ 704. Partner's distributive share

(a) Effect of partnership agreement.—A partner's distributive share of income, gain, loss, deduction, or credit shall, except as otherwise provided in this chapter, be determined by the partnership agreement.

(b) Determination of distributive share.—A partner's distributive share of income, gain, loss, deduction, or credit (or item thereof) shall be determined in accordance with the partner's interest in the partnership (determined by taking into account all facts and circumstances), if—

(1) the partnership agreement does not provide as to the partner's distributive share of income, gain, loss, deduction, or credit (or item thereof), or

(2) the allocation to a partner under the agreement of income, gain, loss, deduction, or credit (or item thereof) does not have substantial economic effect.

(c) Contributed property.—Under regulations prescribed by the Secretary, income, gain, loss, and deduction with respect to property contributed to the partnership by a partner shall be shared among partners so as to take account of the variation between the basis of the property to the partnership and its fair market value at the time of contribution. Under regulations prescribed by the Secretary, rules similar to the rules of the preceding sentence shall apply to contributions by a partner (using the cash receipts and disbursements method of accounting) of accounts payable and other accrued but unpaid items.

(d) Limitation on allowance of losses.—A partner's distributive share of partnership loss (including capital loss) shall be allowed only to the extent of the adjusted basis of such partner's interest in the partnership at the end of the partnership year in which such loss occurred. Any excess of such loss over such basis shall be allowed as a deduction at the end of the partnership year in which such excess is repaid to the partnership.

(e) Family partnerships.—

(1) Recognition of interest created by purchase or gift.—A person shall be recognized as a partner for purposes of this subtitle if he owns a capital interest in a partnership in which capital is a material income-producing factor, whether or not such interest was derived by purchase or gift from any other person.

(2) Distributive share of donee includible in gross income.—In the case of any partnership interest created by gift, the distributive share of the donee under the partnership agreement shall be includible in his gross income, except to the extent that such share is determined without allowance of reasonable compensation for services rendered to the partnership by the donor, and except to the extent that the portion of such share attributable to donated capital is proportionately greater than the share of the donor attributable to the donor's capital. The distributive share of a partner in the earnings of the partnership shall not be diminished because of absence due to military service.

(3) Purchase of interest by member of family.—For purposes of this section, an interest purchased by one member of a family from another shall be considered to be created by gift from the seller, and the fair market value of the purchased interest shall be considered to be donated capital. The "family" of any individual shall include only his spouse, ancestors, and lineal descendants, and any trusts for the primary benefit of such persons.

(f) Cross reference.—

For rules in the case of the sale, exchange, liquidation, or reduction of a partner's interest, see section 706(c) (2).

§ 705.   Determination of basis of partner's interest

(a) General rule.—The adjusted basis of a partner's interest in a partnership shall, except as provided in subsection (b), be the basis of such interest determined under section 722 (relating to contributions to a partnership) or section 742 (relating to transfers of partnership interests)—

(1) increased by the sum of his distributive share for the taxable year and prior taxable years of—

(A) taxable income of the partnership as determined under section 703(a),

(B) income of the partnership exempt from tax under this title, and

(C) the excess of the deductions for depletion over the basis of the property subject to depletion;

(2) decreased (but not below zero) by distributions by the partnership as provided in section 733 and by the sum of his distributive share for the taxable year and prior taxable years of—

(A) losses of the partnership, and

(B) expenditures of the partnership not deductible in computing its taxable income and not properly chargeable to capital account; and

(3) decreased (but not below zero) by the amount of the partner's deduction for depletion for any partnership oil and gas property to the extent such deduction does not exceed the proportionate share of the adjusted basis of such property allocated to such partner under section 613A(c)(7)(D).

(b) Alternative rule.—The Secretary shall prescribe by regulations the circumstances under which the adjusted basis of a partner's interest in a partnership may be determined by reference to his proportionate share of the adjusted basis of partnership property upon a termination of the partnership.

§ 706. Taxable years of partner and partnership

(a) **Year in which partnership income is includible.**—In computing the taxable income of a partner for a taxable year, the inclusions required by section 702 and section 707(c) with respect to a partnership shall be based on the income, gain, loss, deduction, or credit of the partnership for any taxable year of the partnership ending within or with the taxable year of the partner.

(b) **Taxable year.**—

(1) **Partnership's taxable year.**—

(A) **Partnership treated as taxpayer.**—The taxable year of a partnership shall be determined as though the partnership were a taxpayer.

(B) **Taxable year determined by reference to partners.**—Except as provided in subparagraph (C), a partnership shall not have a taxable year other than—

(i) the taxable year of 1 or more of its partners who have an aggregate interest in partnership profits and capital of greater than 50 percent,

(ii) if there is no taxable year described in clause (i), the taxable year of all the principal partners of the partnership, or

(iii) if there is no taxable year described in clause (i) or (ii), the calendar year or such other period as the Secretary may prescribe in regulations.

(C) **Business purpose.**—A partnership may have a taxable year not described in subparagraph (B) if it establishes, to the satisfaction of the Secretary, a business purpose therefor. For purposes of this subparagraph, any deferral of income to partners shall not be treated as a business purpose.

(2) **Partner's taxable year.**—A partner may not change to a taxable year other than that of a partnership in which he is a principal partner unless he establishes, to the satisfaction of the Secretary, a business purpose therefor.

(3) **Principal partner.**—For the purpose of this subsection, a principal partner is a partner having an interest of 5 percent or more in partnership profits or capital.

(4) **Application of majority interest rule.**—Clause (i) of paragraph (1)(B) shall not apply to any taxable year of a partnership unless the period which constitutes the taxable year of 1 or more of its partners who have an aggregate interest in partnership profits and capital of greater than 50 percent has been the same for—

(A) the 3–taxable year period of such partner or partners ending on or before the beginning of such taxable year of the partnership, or

(B) if the partnership has not been in existence during all of such 3–taxable year period, the taxable years of such partner or partners ending with or within the period of existence.

This paragraph shall apply without regard to whether the same partners or interests are taken into account in determining the 50 percent interest during any period.

(c) **Closing of partnership year.**—

(1) **General rule.**—Except in the case of a termination of a partnership and except as provided in paragraph (2) of this subsection, the taxable year of a partnership shall not close as the result of the death of a partner, the entry of a new partner, the liquidation of a partner's interest in the partnership, or the sale or exchange of a partner's interest in the partnership.

(2) **Partner who retires or sells interest in partnership.**—

(A) **Disposition of entire interest.**—The taxable year of a partnership shall close—

(i) with respect to a partner who sells or exchanges his entire interest in a partnership, and

(ii) with respect to a partner whose interest is liquidated, except that the taxable year of a partnership with respect to a partner who dies shall not close prior to the end of the partnership's taxable year.

(B) **Disposition of less than entire interest.**—The taxable year of a partnership shall not close (other than at the end of a partnership's taxable year as determined under subsection (b)(1)) with respect to a partner who sells or exchanges less than his entire interest in the partnership or with respect to a partner whose interest is reduced (whether by entry of a new partner, partial liquidation of a partner's interest, gift, or otherwise).

(d) Determination of distributive share when partner's interest changes.—

(1) In general.—Except as provided in paragraphs (2) and (3), if during any taxable year of the partnership there is a change in any partner's interest in the partnership, each partner's distributive share of any item of income, gain, loss, deduction, or credit of the partnership for such taxable year shall be determined by the use of any method prescribed by the Secretary by regulations which takes into account the varying interests of the partners in the partnership during such taxable year.

(2) Certain cash basis items prorated over period to which attributable.—

(A) **In general.**—If during any taxable year of the partnership there is a change in any partner's interest in the partnership, then (except to the extent provided in regulations) each partner's distributive share of any allocable cash basis item shall be determined—

(i) by assigning the appropriate portion of such item to each day in the period to which it is attributable, and

(ii) by allocating the portion assigned to any such day among the partners in proportion to their interests in the partnership at the close of such day.

(B) **Allocable cash basis item.**—For purposes of this paragraph, the term "allocable cash basis item" means any of the following items with respect to which the partnership uses the cash receipts and disbursements method of accounting:

(i) Interest.

(ii) Taxes.

(iii) Payments for services or for the use of property.

(iv) Any other item of a kind specified in regulations prescribed by the Secretary as being an item with respect to which the application of this paragraph is appropriate to avoid significant misstatements of the income of the partners.

(C) **Items attributable to periods not within taxable year.**—If any portion of any allocable cash basis item is attributable to—

(i) any period before the beginning of the taxable year, such portion shall be assigned under subparagraph (A)(i) to the first day of the taxable year, or

(ii) any period after the close of the taxable year, such portion shall be assigned under subparagraph (A)(i) to the last day of the taxable year.

(D) Treatment of deductible items attributable to prior periods.—If any portion of a deductible cash basis item is assigned under subparagraph (C)(i) to the first day of any taxable year—

(i) such portion shall be allocated among persons who are partners in the partnership during the period to which such portion is attributable in accordance with their varying interests in the partnership during such period, and

(ii) any amount allocated under clause (i) to a person who is not a partner in the partnership on such first day shall be capitalized by the partnership and treated in the manner provided for in section 755.

(3) Items attributable to interest in lower tier partnership prorated over entire taxable year.—If—

(A) during any taxable year of the partnership there is a change in any partner's interest in the partnership (hereinafter in this paragraph referred to as the "upper tier partnership"), and

(B) such partnership is a partner in another partnership (hereinafter in this paragraph referred to as the "lower tier partnership"),

then (except to the extent provided in regulations) each partner's distributive share of any item of the upper tier partnership attributable to the lower tier partnership shall be determined by assigning the appropriate portion (determined by applying principles similar to the principles of subparagraphs (C) and (D) of paragraph (2)) of each such item to the appropriate days during which the upper tier partnership is a partner in the lower tier partnership and by allocating the portion assigned to any such day among the partners in proportion to their interests in the upper tier partnership at the close of such day.

(4) Taxable year determined without regard to subsection (c)(2)(A).—For purposes of this subsection, the taxable year of a partnership shall be determined without regard to subsection (c)(2)(A).

§ 707. Transactions between partner and partnership

(a) Partner not acting in capacity as partner.—

(1) In general.—If a partner engages in a transaction with a partnership other than in his capacity as a member of such partnership, the transaction shall, except as otherwise provided in this section, be considered as occurring between the partnership and one who is not a partner.

(2) Treatment of payments to partners for property or services.—Under regulations prescribed by the Secretary—

(A) Treatment of certain services and transfers of property.—If—

(i) a partner performs services for a partnership or transfers property to a partnership,

(ii) there is a related direct or indirect allocation and distribution to such partner, and

(iii) the performance of such services (or such transfer) and the allocation and distribution, when viewed together, are properly characterized as a transaction occurring between the partnership and a partner acting other than in his capacity as a member of the partnership,

such allocation and distribution shall be treated as a transaction described in paragraph (1).

(B) Treatment of certain property transfers.—If—

(i) there is a direct or indirect transfer of money or other property by a partner to a partnership,

(ii) there is a related direct or indirect transfer of money or other property by the partnership to such partner (or another partner), and

(iii) the transfers described in clauses (i) and (ii), when viewed together, are properly characterized as a sale or exchange of property,

such transfers shall be treated either as a transaction described in paragraph (1) or as a transaction between 2 or more partners acting other than in their capacity as members of the partnership.

(b) Certain sales or exchanges of property with respect to controlled partnerships.—

(1) Losses disallowed.—No deduction shall be allowed in respect of losses from sales or exchanges of property (other than an interest in the partnership), directly or indirectly, between—

(A) a partnership and a person owning, directly or indirectly, more than 50 percent of the capital interest, or the profits interest, in such partnership, or

(B) two partnerships in which the same persons own, directly or indirectly, more than 50 percent of the capital interests or profits interests.

In the case of a subsequent sale or exchange by a transferee described in this paragraph, section 267(d) shall be applicable as if the loss were disallowed under section 267(a)(1). For purposes of section 267(a)(2), partnerships described in subparagraph (B) of this paragraph shall be treated as persons specified in section 267(b).

(2) Gains treated as ordinary income.—In the case of a sale or exchange, directly or indirectly, of property, which in the hands of the transferee, is property other than a capital asset as defined in section 1221—

(A) between a partnership and a person owning, directly or indirectly, more than 50 percent of the capital interest, or profits interest, in such partnership, or

(B) between two partnerships in which the same persons own, directly or indirectly, more than 50 percent of the capital interests or profits interests,

any gain recognized shall be considered as ordinary income.

(3) Ownership of a capital or profits interest.—For purposes of paragraphs (1) and (2) of this subsection, the ownership of a capital or profits interest in a partnership shall be determined in accordance with the rules for constructive ownership of stock provided in section 267(c) other than paragraph (3) of such section.

(c) Guaranteed payments.—To the extent determined without regard to the income of the partnership, payments to a partner for services or the use of capital shall be considered as made to one who is not a member of the partnership, but only for the purposes of section 61(a) (relating to gross income) and, subject to section 263, for purposes of section 162(a) (relating to trade or business expenses).

§ 708. Continuation of partnership

(a) General rule.—For purposes of this subchapter, an existing partnership shall be considered as continuing if it is not terminated.

(b) Termination.—

(1) General rule.—For purposes of subsection (a), a partnership shall be considered as terminated only if—

(A) no part of any business, financial operation, or venture of the partnership continues to be carried on by any of its partners in a partnership, or

(B) within a 12-month period there is a sale or exchange of 50 percent or more of the total interest in partnership capital and profits.

(2) Special rules.—

(A) Merger or consolidation.—In the case of the merger or consolidation of two or more partnerships, the resulting partnership shall, for purposes of this section, be considered the continuation of any merging or consolidating partnership whose members own an interest of more than 50 percent in the capital and profits of the resulting partnership.

(B) Division of a partnership.—In the case of a division of a partnership into two or more partnerships, the resulting partnerships (other than any resulting partnership the members of which had an interest of 50 percent or less in the capital and profits of the prior partnership) shall, for purposes of this section, be considered a continuation of the prior partnership.

§ 709. Treatment of organization and syndication fees

(a) General rule.—Except as provided in subsection (b), no deduction shall be allowed under this chapter to the partnership or to any partner for any amounts paid or incurred to organize a partnership or to promote the sale of (or to sell) an interest in such partnership.

(b) Amortization of organization fees.—

(1) Deduction.—Amounts paid or incurred to organize a partnership may, at the election of the partnership (made in accordance with regulations prescribed by the Secretary), be treated as deferred expenses. Such deferred expenses shall be allowed as a deduction ratably over such period of not less than 60 months as may be selected by the partnership (beginning with the month in which the partnership begins business), or if the partnership is liquidated before the end of such 60-month period, such deferred expenses (to the extent not deducted under this section) may be deducted to the extent provided in section 165.

(2) Organizational expenses defined.—The organizational expenses to which paragraph (1) applies, are expenditures which—

(A) are incident to the creation of the partnership;

(B) are chargeable to capital account; and

(C) are of a character which, if expended incident to the creation of a partnership having an ascertainable life, would be amortized over such life.

PART II—CONTRIBUTIONS, DISTRIBUTIONS, AND TRANSFERS

Subpart
A. Contributions to a partnership.
B. Distributions by a partnership.
C. Transfers of interest in a partnership.
D. Provisions common to other subparts.

Subpart A—Contributions to a Partnership

§ 721. Nonrecognition of gain or loss on contribution

(a) General rule.—No gain or loss shall be recognized to a partnership or to any of its partners in the case of a contribution of property to the partnership in exchange for an interest in the partnership.

(b) Special rule.—Subsection (a) shall not apply to gain realized on a transfer of property to a partnership which would be treated as an investment company (within the meaning of section 351) if the partnership were incorporated.

§ 722. Basis of contributing partner's interest

The basis of an interest in a partnership acquired by a contribution of property, including money, to the partnership shall be the amount of such money and the adjusted basis of such property to the contributing partner at the time of the contribution increased by the amount (if any) of gain recognized under section 721(b) to the contributing partner at such time.

§ 723. Basis of property contributed to partnership

The basis of property contributed to a partnership by a partner shall be the adjusted basis of such property to the contributing partner at the time of the contribution increased by the amount (if any) of gain recognized under section 721(b) to the contributing partner at such time.

§ 724. Character of gain or loss on contributed unrealized receivables, inventory items, and capital loss property

(a) Contributions of unrealized receivables.—In the case of any property which—

    (1) was contributed to the partnership by a partner, and

    (2) was an unrealized receivable in the hands of such partner immediately before such contribution,

any gain or loss recognized by the partnership on the disposition of such property shall be treated as ordinary income or ordinary loss, as the case may be.

(b) Contributions of inventory items.—In the case of any property which—

    (1) was contributed to the partnership by a partner, and

    (2) was an inventory item in the hands of such partner immediately before such contribution,

any gain or loss recognized by the partnership on the disposition of such property during the 5-year period beginning on the date of such contribution shall be treated as ordinary income or ordinary loss, as the case may be.

(c) Contributions of capital loss property.—In the case of any property which—

    (1) was contributed by a partner to the partnership, and

    (2) was a capital asset in the hands of such partner immediately before such contribution,

any loss recognized by the partnership on the disposition of such property during the 5-year period beginning on the date of such contribution shall be treated as a loss from the sale of a capital asset to the extent that, immediately before such contribution, the adjusted basis of such property in the hands of the partner exceeded the fair market value of such property.

(d) Definitions.—For purposes of this section—

(1) Unrealized receivable.—The term "unrealized receivable" has the meaning given such term by section 751(c) (determined by treating any reference to the partnership as referring to the partner).

(2) Inventory item.—The term "inventory item" has the meaning given such term by section 751(d)(2) (determined by treating any reference to the partnership as referring to the partner and by applying section 1231 without regard to any holding period therein provided).

(3) Substituted basis property.—

(A) In general.—If any property described in subsection (a), (b), or (c) is disposed of in a nonrecognition transaction, the tax treatment which applies to such property under such subsection shall also apply to any substituted basis property resulting from such transaction. A similar rule shall also apply in the case of a series of non-recognition transactions.

(B) Exception for stock in C corporation.—Subparagraph (A) shall not apply to any stock in a C corporation received in an exchange described in section 351.

Subpart B—Distributions by a Partnership

§ 731. Extent of recognition of gain or loss on distribution

(a) Partners.—In the case of a distribution by a partnership to a partner—

(1) gain shall not be recognized to such partner, except to the extent that any money distributed exceeds the adjusted basis of such partner's interest in the partnership immediately before the distribution, and

(2) loss shall not be recognized to such partner, except that upon a distribution in liquidation of a partner's interest in a partnership where no property other than that described in subparagraph (A) or (B) is distributed to such partner, loss shall be recognized to the extent of the excess of the adjusted basis of such partner's interest in the partnership over the sum of—

(A) any money distributed, and

(B) the basis to the distributee, as determined under section 732, of any unrealized receivables (as defined in section 751(c)) and inventory (as defined in section 751(d) (2)).

Any gain or loss recognized under this subsection shall be considered as gain or loss from the sale or exchange of the partnership interest of the distributee partner.

(b) Partnerships.—No gain or loss shall be recognized to a partnership on a distribution to a partner of property, including money.

(c) Exceptions.—This section shall not apply to the extent otherwise provided by section 736 (relating to payments to a retiring partner or a deceased partner's successor in interest) and section 751 (relating to unrealized receivables and inventory items).

§ 732. Basis of distributed property other than money

(a) Distributions other than in liquidation of a partner's interest.—

(1) **General rule.**—The basis of property (other than money) distributed by a partnership to a partner other than in liquidation of the partner's interest shall, except as provided in paragraph (2), be its adjusted basis to the partnership immediately before such distribution.

(2) **Limitation.**—The basis to the distributee partner of property to which paragraph (1) is applicable shall not exceed the adjusted basis of such partner's interest in the partnership reduced by any money distributed in the same transaction.

(b) **Distributions in liquidation.**—The basis of property (other than money) distributed by a partnership to a partner in liquidation of the partner's interest shall be an amount equal to the adjusted basis of such partner's interest in the partnership reduced by any money distributed in the same transaction.

(c) **Allocation of basis.**—The basis of distributed properties to which subsection (a) (2) or subsection (b) is applicable shall be allocated—

(1) first to any unrealized receivables (as defined in section 751(c)) and inventory items (as defined in section 751(d) (2)) in an amount equal to the adjusted basis of each such property to the partnership (or if the basis to be allocated is less than the sum of the adjusted bases of such properties to the partnership, in proportion to such bases), and

(2) to the extent of any remaining basis, to any other distributed properties in proportion to their adjusted bases to the partnership.

(d) **Special partnership basis to transferee.**—For purposes of subsections (a), (b), and (c), a partner who acquired all or a part of his interest by a transfer with respect to which the election provided in section 754 is not in effect, and to whom a distribution of property (other than money) is made with respect to the transferred interest within 2 years after such transfer, may elect, under regulations prescribed by the Secretary, to treat as the adjusted partnership basis of such property the adjusted basis such property would have if the adjustment provided in section 743(b) were in effect with respect to the partnership property. The Secretary may by regulations require the application of this subsection in the case of a distribution to a transferee partner, whether or not made within 2 years after the transfer, if at the time of the transfer the fair market value of the partnership property (other than money) exceeded 110 percent of its adjusted basis to the partnership.

(e) **Exception.**—This section shall not apply to the extent that a distribution is treated as a sale or exchange of property under section 751(b) (relating to unrealized receivables and inventory items).

§ 733.   Basis of distributee partner's interest

In the case of a distribution by a partnership to a partner other than in liquidation of a partner's interest, the adjusted basis to such partner of his interest in the partnership shall be reduced (but not below zero) by—

(1) the amount of any money distributed to such partner, and

(2) the amount of the basis to such partner of distributed property other than money, as determined under section 732.

§ 734.   Optional adjustment to basis of undistributed partnership property

(a) **General rule.**—The basis of partnership property shall not be adjusted as the result of a distribution of property to a partner unless the election, provided in section 754 (relating to optional adjustment to basis of partnership property), is in effect with respect to such partnership.

(b) Method of adjustment.—In the case of a distribution of property to a partner, a partnership, with respect to which the election provided in section 754 is in effect, shall—

(1) increase the adjusted basis of partnership property by—

(A) the amount of any gain recognized to the distributee partner with respect to such distribution under section 731(a) (1), and

(B) in the case of distributed property to which section 732(a) (2) or (b) applies, the excess of the adjusted basis of the distributed property to the partnership immediately before the distribution (as adjusted by section 732(d)) over the basis of the distributed property to the distributee, as determined under section 732, or

(2) decrease the adjusted basis of partnership property by—

(A) the amount of any loss recognized to the distributee partner with respect to such distribution under section 731(a) (2), and

(B) in the case of distributed property to which section 732(b) applies, the excess of the basis of the distributed property to the distributee, as determined under section 732, over the adjusted basis of the distributed property to the partnership immediately before such distribution (as adjusted by section 732(d)).

Paragraph (1)(B) shall not apply to any distributed property which is an interest in another partnership with respect to which the election provided in section 754 is not in effect.

(c) Allocation of basis.—The allocation of basis among partnership properties where subsection (b) is applicable shall be made in accordance with the rules provided in section 755.

§ 735. Character of gain or loss on disposition of distributed property

(a) Sale or exchange of certain distributed property.—

(1) **Unrealized receivables.**—Gain or loss on the disposition by a distributee partner of unrealized receivables (as defined in section 751(c)) distributed by a partnership, shall be considered as ordinary income or as ordinary loss, as the case may be.

(2) **Inventory items.**—Gain or loss on the sale or exchange by a distributee partner of inventory items (as defined in section 751(d) (2)) distributed by a partnership shall, if sold or exchanged within 5 years from the date of the distribution, be considered as ordinary income or as ordinary loss, as the case may be.

(b) Holding period for distributed property.—In determining the period for which a partner has held property received in a distribution from a partnership (other than for purposes of subsection (a) (2)), there shall be included the holding period of the partnership, as determined under section 1223, with respect to such property.

(c) Special rules.—

(1) **Waiver of holding periods contained in section 1231.**—For purposes of this section, section 751(d)(2) (defining inventory item) shall be applied without regard to any holding period in section 1231(b).

(2) **Substituted basis property.**—

(A) **In general.**—If any property described in subsection (a) is disposed of in a nonrecognition transaction, the tax treatment which applies to such property under such subsection shall also apply to any substituted basis property resulting from such transaction. A similar rule shall also apply in the case of a series of nonrecognition transactions.

(B) **Exception for stock in C corporation.**—Subparagraph (A) shall not apply to any stock in a C corporation received in an exchange described in section 351.

§ 736. Payments to a retiring partner or a deceased partner's successor in interest

(a) **Payments considered as distributive share or guaranteed payment.**—Payments made in liquidation of the interest of a retiring partner or a deceased partner shall, except as provided in subsection (b), be considered—

(1) as a distributive share to the recipient of partnership income if the amount thereof is determined with regard to the income of the partnership, or

(2) as a guaranteed payment described in section 707(c) if the amount thereof is determined without regard to the income of the partnership.

(b) **Payments for interest in partnership.**—

(1) **General rule.**—Payments made in liquidation of the interest of a retiring partner or a deceased partner shall, to the extent such payments (other than payments described in paragraph (2)) are determined, under regulations prescribed by the Secretary, to be made in exchange for the interest of such partner in partnership property, be considered as a distribution by the partnership and not as a distributive share or guaranteed payment under subsection (a).

(2) **Special rules.**—For purposes of this subsection, payments in exchange for an interest in partnership property shall not include amounts paid for—

(A) unrealized receivables of the partnership (as defined in section 751(c)), or

(B) good will of the partnership, except to the extent that the partnership agreement provides for a payment with respect to good will.

(c) **Cross reference.**—

For limitation on the tax attributable to certain gain connected with section 1248 stock, see section 751(e).

Subpart C—Transfers of Interests in a Partnership

§ 741. Recognition and character of gain or loss on sale or exchange

In the case of a sale or exchange of an interest in a partnership, gain or loss shall be recognized to the transferor partner. Such gain or loss shall be considered as gain or loss from the sale or exchange of a capital asset, except as otherwise provided in section 751 (relating to unrealized receivables and inventory items which have appreciated substantially in value).

§ 742. Basis of transferee partner's interest

The basis of an interest in a partnership acquired other than by contribution shall be determined under part II of subchapter O (sec. 1011 and following).

§ 743. Optional adjustment to basis of partnership property

(a) **General rule.**—The basis of partnership property shall not be adjusted as the result of a transfer of an interest in a partnership by sale or exchange or on the death of a partner unless the election provided by section 754 (relating to optional adjustment to basis of partnership property) is in effect with respect to such partnership.

(b) **Adjustment to basis of partnership property.**—In the case of a transfer of an interest in a partnership by sale or exchange or upon the death of a partner, a partnership with respect to which the election provided in section 754 is in effect shall—

(1) increase the adjusted basis of the partnership property by the excess of the basis to the transferee partner of his interest in the partnership over his proportionate share of the adjusted basis of the partnership property, or

(2) decrease the adjusted basis of the partnership property by the excess of the transferee partner's proportionate share of the adjusted basis of the partnership property over the basis of his interest in the partnership.

Under regulations prescribed by the Secretary, such increase or decrease shall constitute an adjustment to the basis of partnership property with respect to the transferee partner only. A partner's proportionate share of the adjusted basis of partnership property shall be determined in accordance with his interest in partnership capital and, in the case of property contributed to the partnership by a partner, section 704(c) (relating to contributed property) shall apply in determining such share. In the case of an adjustment under this subsection to the basis of partnership property subject to depletion, any depletion allowable shall be determined separately for the transferee partner with respect to his interest in such property.

(c) **Allocation of basis.**—The allocation of basis among partnership properties where subsection (b) is applicable shall be made in accordance with the rules provided in section 755.

Subpart D—Provisions Common to Other Subparts

§ 751. Unrealized receivables and inventory items

(a) **Sale or exchange of interest in partnership.**—The amount of any money, or the fair market value of any property, received by a transferor partner in exchange for all or a part of his interest in the partnership attributable to—

(1) unrealized receivables of the partnership, or

(2) inventory items of the partnership which have appreciated substantially in value,

shall be considered as an amount realized from the sale or exchange of property other than a capital asset.

(b) **Certain distributions treated as sales or exchanges.**—

(1) **General rule.**—To the extent a partner receives in a distribution—

(A) partnership property described in subsection (a) (1) or (2) in exchange for all or a part of his interest in other partnership property (including money), or

(B) partnership property (including money) other than property described in subsection (a) (1) or (2) in exchange for all or a part of his interest in partnership property described in subsection (a) (1) or (2), such transactions shall, under regulations prescribed by the Secretary, be considered as a sale or exchange of such property between the distributee and the partnership (as constituted after the distribution).

(2) Exceptions.—Paragraph (1) shall not apply to—

(A) a distribution of property which the distributee contributed to the partnership, or

(B) payments, described in section 736(a), to a retiring partner or successor in interest of a deceased partner.

(c) Unrealized receivables.—For purposes of this subchapter, the term "unrealized receivables" includes, to the extent not previously includible in income under the method of accounting used by the partnership, any rights (contractual or otherwise) to payment for—

(1) goods delivered, or to be delivered, to the extent the proceeds therefrom would be treated as amounts received from the sale or exchange of property other than a capital asset, or

(2) services rendered, or to be rendered.

For purposes of this section and sections 731, 736, and 741, such term also includes mining property (as defined in section 617(f)(2)), stock in a DISC (as described in section 992(a)), section 1245 property (as defined in section 1245(a)(3)), stock in certain foreign corporations (as described in section 1248), section 1250 property (as defined in section 1250(c)), farm land (as defined in section 1252(a)), franchises, trademarks, or trade names (referred to in section 1253(a)), and an oil, gas, or geothermal property (described in section 1254) but only to the extent of the amount which would be treated as gain to which section 617(d)(1), 995(c), 1245(a), 1248(a), 1250(a), 1252(a), 1253(a), or 1254(a) would apply if (at the time of the transaction described in this section or sections 731, 736, or 741, as the case may be) such property had been sold by the partnership at its fair market value. For purposes of this section and sections 731, 736, and 741, such term also includes any market discount bond (as defined in section 1278) and any short-term obligation (as defined in section 1283) but only to the extent of the amount which would be treated as ordinary income if (at the time of the transaction described in this section or section 731, 736, or 741, as the case may be) such property had been sold by the partnership.

(d) Inventory items which have appreciated substantially in value.—

(1) Substantial appreciation.—Inventory items of the partnership shall be considered to have appreciated substantially in value if their fair market value exceeds—

(A) 120 percent of the adjusted basis to the partnership of such property, and

(B) 10 percent of the fair market value of all partnership property, other than money.

(2) Inventory items.—For purposes of this subchapter the term "inventory items" means—

(A) property of the partnership of the kind described in section 1221(1),

(B) any other property of the partnership which, on sale or exchange by the partnership, would be considered property other than a capital asset and other than property described in section 1231,

* * *

(D) any other property held by the partnership which, if held by the selling or distributee partner, would be considered property of the type described in subparagraph (A), (B), or (C).

* * *

(f) Special rules in the case of tiered partnerships, etc.—In determining whether property of a partnership is—

(1) an unrealized receivable, or

(2) an inventory item,

such partnership shall be treated as owning its proportionate share of the property of any other partnership in which it is a partner. Under regulations, rules similar to the rules of the preceding sentence shall also apply in the case of interests in trusts.

§ 752. Treatment of certain liabilities

(a) Increase in partner's liabilities.—Any increase in a partner's share of the liabilities of a partnership, or any increase in a partner's individual liabilities by reason of the assumption by such partner of partnership liabilities, shall be considered as a contribution of money by such partner to the partnership.

(b) Decrease in partner's liabilities.—Any decrease in a partner's share of the liabilities of a partnership, or any decrease in a partner's individual liabilities by reason of the assumption by the partnership of such individual liabilities, shall be considered as a distribution of money to the partner by the partnership.

(c) Liability to which property is subject.—For purposes of this section, a liability to which property is subject shall, to the extent of the fair market value of such property, be considered as a liability of the owner of the property.

(d) Sale or exchange of an interest.—In the case of a sale or exchange of an interest in a partnership, liabilities shall be treated in the same manner as liabilities in connection with the sale or exchange of property not associated with partnerships.

§ 753. Partner receiving income in respect of decedent

The amount includible in the gross income of a successor in interest of a deceased partner under section 736(a) shall be considered income in respect of a decedent under section 691.

§ 754. Manner of electing optional adjustment to basis of partnership property

If a partnership files an election, in accordance with regulations prescribed by the Secretary, the basis of partnership property shall be adjusted, in the case of a distribution of property, in the manner provided in section 734 and, in the case of a transfer of a partnership interest, in the manner provided in section 743. Such an election shall apply with respect to all distributions of property by the partnership and to all transfers of interests in the partnership during the taxable year with respect to which such election was filed and all subsequent taxable years. Such election may be revoked by the partnership, subject to such limitations as may be provided by regulations prescribed by the Secretary.

§ 755. Rules for allocation of basis

(a) General rule.—Any increase or decrease in the adjusted basis of partnership property under section 734(b) (relating to the optional adjustment to the basis of undistributed partnership property) or section 743(b) (relating to the optional adjustment to the basis of partnership property in the case of a transfer of an interest in a partnership) shall, except as provided in subsection (b), be allocated—

(1) in a manner which has the effect of reducing the difference between the fair market value and the adjusted basis of partnership properties, or

(2) in any other manner permitted by regulations prescribed by the Secretary.

(b) **Special rule.**—In applying the allocation rules provided in subsection (a), increases or decreases in the adjusted basis of partnership property arising from a distribution of, or a transfer of an interest attributable to, property consisting of—

(1) capital assets and property described in section 1231(b), or

(2) any other property of the partnership,

shall be allocated to partnership property of a like character except that the basis of any such partnership property shall not be reduced below zero. If, in the case of a distribution, the adjustment to basis of property described in paragraph (1) or (2) is prevented by the absence of such property or by insufficient adjusted basis for such property, such adjustment shall be applied to subsequently acquired property of a like character in accordance with regulations prescribed by the Secretary.

PART III—DEFINITIONS

§ 761. Terms defined

(a) **Partnership.**—For purposes of this subtitle, the term "partnership" includes a syndicate, group, pool, joint venture, or other unincorporated organization through or by means of which any business, financial operation, or venture is carried on, and which is not, within the meaning of this title, a corporation or a trust or estate. Under regulations the Secretary may, at the election of all the members of an unincorporated organization, exclude such organization from the application of all or part of this subchapter, if it is availed of—

(1) for investment purposes only and not for the active conduct of a business,

(2) for the joint production, extraction, or use of property, but not for the purpose of selling services or property produced or extracted, or

(3) by dealers in securities for a short period for the purpose of underwriting, selling, or distributing a particular issue of securities,

if the income of the members of the organization may be adequately determined without the computation of partnership taxable income.

(b) **Partner.**—For purposes of this subtitle, the term "partner" means a member of a partnership.

(c) **Partnership agreement.**—For purposes of this subchapter, a partnership agreement includes any modifications of the partnership agreement made prior to, or at, the time prescribed by law for the filing of the partnership return for the taxable year (not including extensions) which are agreed to by all the partners, or which are adopted in such other manner as may be provided by the partnership agreement.

(d) **Liquidation of a partner's interest.**—For purposes of this subchapter, the term "liquidation of a partner's interest" means the termination of a partner's entire interest in a partnership by means of a distribution, or a series of distributions, to the partner by the partnership.

(e) **Distributions partnership interests treated as exchanges.**—Except as otherwise provided in regulations, for purposes of—

(1) section 708 (relating to continuation of partnership),

(2) section 743 (relating to optional adjustment to basis of partnership property), and

(3) any other provision of this subchapter specified in regulations prescribed by the Secretary,

any distribution of an interest in a partnership (not otherwise treated as an exchange) shall be treated as an exchange.

(f) Cross reference.—

For rules in the case of the sale, exchange, liquidation, or reduction of a partner's interest, see sections 704(b) and 706(c)(2).

SUBCHAPTER O—GAIN OR LOSS ON DISPOSITION OF PROPERTY

Part
I. Determination of amount of and recognition of gain or loss.
II. Basis rules of general application.
III. Common nontaxable exchanges.
IV. Special rules.
V. Changes to effectuate F.C.C. policy.*
VI. Exchanges in obedience to S.E.C. orders.*
VII. Wash sales; Straddles.
VIII. Distributions pursuant to Bank Holding Company Act of 1956.*

PART I—DETERMINATION OF AMOUNT OF AND RECOGNITION OF GAIN OR LOSS

§ 1001. Determination of amount of and recognition of gain or loss

(a) Computation of gain or loss.—The gain from the sale or other disposition of property shall be the excess of the amount realized therefrom over the adjusted basis provided in section 1011 for determining gain, and the loss shall be the excess of the adjusted basis provided in such section for determining loss over the amount realized.

(b) Amount realized.—The amount realized from the sale or other disposition of property shall be the sum of any money received plus the fair market value of the property (other than money) received. In determining the amount realized—

(1) there shall not be taken into account any amount received as reimbursement for real property taxes which are treated under section 164(d) as imposed on the purchaser, and

(2) there shall be taken into account amounts representing real property taxes which are treated under section 164(d) as imposed on the taxpayer if such taxes are to be paid by the purchaser.

(c) Recognition of gain or loss.—Except as otherwise provided in this subtitle, the entire amount of the gain or loss, determined under this section, on the sale or exchange of property shall be recognized.

(d) Installment sales.—Nothing in this section shall be construed to prevent (in the case of property sold under contract providing for payment in installments) the taxation of that portion of any installment payment representing gain or profit in the year in which such payment is received.

* Omitted entirely.

(e) Certain term interests.—

(1) In general.—In determining gain or loss from the sale or other disposition of a term interest in property, that portion of the adjusted basis of such interest which is determined pursuant to section 1014, 1015, or 1041 (to the extent that such adjusted basis is a portion of the entire adjusted basis of the property) shall be disregarded.

(2) Term interest in property defined.—For purposes of paragraph (1), the term "term interest in property" means—

(A) a life interest in property,

(B) an interest in property for a term of years, or

(C) an income interest in a trust.

(3) Exception.—Paragraph (1) shall not apply to a sale or other disposition which is a part of a transaction in which the entire interest in property is transferred to any person or persons.

(f) Cross reference.—

For treatment of certain expenses incident to the sale of a residence which were deducted as moving expenses by the taxpayer or his spouse under section 217(a), see section 217(e).

PART II—BASIS RULES OF GENERAL APPLICATION

§ 1011. Adjusted basis for determining gain or loss

(a) General rule.—The adjusted basis for determining the gain or loss from the sale or other disposition of property, whenever acquired, shall be the basis (determined under section 1012 or other applicable sections of this subchapter and subchapters C (relating to corporate distributions and adjustments), K (relating to partners and partnerships), and P (relating to capital gains and losses)), adjusted as provided in section 1016.

(b) Bargain sale to a charitable organization.—If a deduction is allowable under section 170 (relating to charitable contributions) by reason of a sale, then the adjusted basis for determining the gain from such sale shall be that portion of the adjusted basis which bears the same ratio to the adjusted basis as the amount realized bears to the fair market value of the property.

§ 1012. Basis of property—cost

The basis of property shall be the cost of such property, except as otherwise provided in this subchapter and subchapters C (relating to corporate distributions and adjustments), K (relating to partners and partnerships), and P (relating to capital gains and losses). The cost of real property shall not include any amount in respect of real property taxes which are treated under section 164(d) as imposed on the taxpayer.

§ 1013. Basis of property included in inventory

If the property should have been included in the last inventory, the basis shall be the last inventory value thereof.

§ 1014. Basis of property acquired from a decedent

(a) In general.—Except as otherwise provided in this section, the basis of property in the hands of a person acquiring the property from a decedent or to whom the property passed from a decedent shall, if not sold, exchanged, or otherwise disposed of before the decedent's death by such person, be—

(1) the fair market value of the property at the date of the decedent's death, or

(2) in the case of an election under either section 2032 or section 811(j) of the Internal Revenue Code of 1939 where the decedent died after October 21, 1942, its value at the applicable valuation date prescribed by those sections, or

(3) in the case of an election under section 2032A, its value determined under such section.

(b) Property acquired from the decedent.—For purposes of subsection (a), the following property shall be considered to have been acquired from or to have passed from the decedent:

(1) Property acquired by bequest, devise, or inheritance, or by the decedent's estate from the decedent;

(2) Property transferred by the decedent during his lifetime in trust to pay the income for life to or on the order or direction of the decedent, with the right reserved to the decedent at all times before his death to revoke the trust;

(3) In the case of decedents dying after December 31, 1951, property transferred by the decedent during his lifetime in trust to pay the income for life to or on the order or direction of the decedent with the right reserved to the decedent at all times before his death to make any change in the enjoyment thereof through the exercise of a power to alter, amend, or terminate the trust;

(4) Property passing without full and adequate consideration under a general power of appointment exercised by the decedent by will;

(5) In the case of decedents dying after August 26, 1937, property acquired by bequest, devise, or inheritance or by the decedent's estate from the decedent, if the property consists of stock or securities of a foreign corporation, which with respect to its taxable year next preceding the date of the decedent's death was, under the law applicable to such year, a foreign personal holding company. In such case, the basis shall be the fair market value of such property at the date of the decedent's death or the basis in the hands of the decedent, whichever is lower;

(6) In the case of decedents dying after December 31, 1947, property which represents the surviving spouse's one-half share of community property held by the decedent and the surviving spouse under the community property laws of any State, or possession of the United States or any foreign country, if at least one-half of the whole of the community interest in such property was includible in determining the value of the decedent's gross estate under chapter 11 of subtitle B (section 2001 and following, relating to estate tax) or section 811 of the Internal Revenue Code of 1939;

* * *

(9) In the case of decedents dying after December 31, 1953, property acquired from the decedent by reason of death, form of ownership, or other conditions (including property acquired through the exercise or non-exercise of a power of appointment), if by reason thereof the property is required to be included in determining the value of the decedent's gross estate under chapter 11 of subtitle B or under the Internal Revenue Code of 1939. In such case, if the property is acquired before the death of the decedent, the basis shall be the amount determined under subsection (a) reduced by the amount allowed to the taxpayer as deductions in computing taxable income under this subtitle or prior income tax laws for exhaustion, wear and tear, obsolescence, amortization, and depletion on such property before the death of the decedent. Such basis shall be applicable to

the property commencing on the death of the decedent. This paragraph shall not apply to—

(A) annuities described in section 72;

(B) property to which paragraph (5) would apply if the property had been acquired by bequest; and

(C) property described in any other paragraph of this subsection.

(10) Property includible in the gross estate of the decedent under section 2044 (relating to certain property for which marital deduction was previously allowed). In any such case, the last 3 sentences of paragraph (9) shall apply as if such property were described in the first sentence of paragraph (9).

(c) Property representing income in respect of a decedent.—This section shall not apply to property which constitutes a right to receive an item of income in respect of a decedent under section 691.

* * *

(e) Appreciated property acquired by decedent by gift within 1 year of death.—

(1) **In general.**—In the case of a decedent dying after December 31, 1981, if—

(A) appreciated property was acquired by the decedent by gift during the 1-year period ending on the date of the decedent's death, and

(B) such property is acquired from the decedent by (or passes from the decedent to) the donor of such property (or the spouse of such donor),

the basis of such property in the hands of such donor (or spouse) shall be the adjusted basis of such property in the hands of the decedent immediately before the death of the decedent.

(2) **Definitions.**—For purposes of paragraph (1)—

(A) **Appreciated property.**—The term "appreciated property" means any property if the fair market value of such property on the day it was transferred to the decedent by gift exceeds its adjusted basis.

(B) **Treatment of certain property sold by estate.**—In the case of any appreciated property described in subparagraph (A) of paragraph (1) sold by the estate of the decedent or by a trust of which the decedent was the grantor, rules similar to the rules of paragraph (1) shall apply to the extent the donor of such property (or the spouse of such donor) is entitled to the proceeds from such sale.

§ 1015.   Basis of property acquired by gifts and transfers in trust

(a) Gifts after December 31, 1920.—If the property was acquired by gift after December 31, 1920, the basis shall be the same as it would be in the hands of the donor or the last preceding owner by whom it was not acquired by gift, except that if such basis (adjusted for the period before the date of the gift as provided in section 1016) is greater than the fair market value of the property at the time of the gift, then for the purpose of determining loss the basis shall be such fair market value. If the facts necessary to determine the basis in the hands of the donor or the last preceding owner are unknown to the donee, the Secretary shall, if possible, obtain such facts from such donor or last preceding owner, or any other person cognizant thereof. If the Secretary finds it impossible to obtain such facts, the basis in the hands of such donor or last preceding owner shall be the fair market value of such property as found by the Secretary as of the date or approximate date at which, according to the best information that the Secretary is able to obtain, such property was acquired by such donor or last preceding owner.

(b) Transfer in trust after December 31, 1920.—If the property was acquired after December 31, 1920, by a transfer in trust (other than by a transfer in trust by a gift, bequest, or devise), the basis shall be the same as it would be in the hands of the grantor increased in the amount of gain or decreased in the amount of loss recognized to the grantor on such transfer under the law applicable to the year in which the transfer was made.

* * *

(d) Increased basis for gift tax paid.—

(1) In general.—If—

(A) the property is acquired by gift on or after September 2, 1958, the basis shall be the basis determined under subsection (a), increased (but not above the fair market value of the property at the time of the gift) by the amount of gift tax paid with respect to such gift, or

(B) the property was acquired by gift before September 2, 1958, and has not been sold, exchanged, or otherwise disposed of before such date, the basis of the property shall be increased on such date by the amount of gift tax paid with respect to such gift, but such increase shall not exceed an amount equal to the amount by which the fair market value of the property at the time of the gift exceeded the basis of the property in the hands of the donor at the time of the gift.

(2) Amount of tax paid with respect to gift.—For purposes of paragraph (1), the amount of gift tax paid with respect to any gift is an amount which bears the same ratio to the amount of gift tax paid under chapter 12 with respect to all gifts made by the donor for the calendar year (or preceding calendar period) in which such gift is made as the amount of such gift bears to the taxable gifts (as defined in section 2503(a) but computed without the deduction allowed by section 2521) made by the donor during such calendar year or period. For purposes of the preceding sentence, the amount of any gift shall be the amount included with respect to such gift in determining (for the purposes of section 2503(a)) the total amount of gifts made during the calendar year or period, reduced by the amount of any deduction allowed with respect to such gift under section 2522 (relating to charitable deduction) or under section 2523 (relating to marital deduction).

(3) Gifts treated as made one-half by each spouse.—For purposes of paragraph (1), where the donor and his spouse elected, under section 2513 to have the gift considered as made one-half by each, the amount of gift tax paid with respect to such gift under chapter 12 shall be the sum of the amounts of tax paid with respect to each half of such gift (computed in the manner provided in paragraph (2)).

(4) Treatment as adjustment to basis.—For purposes of section 1016(b), an increase in basis under paragraph (1) shall be treated as an adjustment under section 1016(a).

* * *

(6) Special rule for gifts made after December 31, 1976.—

(A) In general.—In the case of any gift made after December 31, 1976, the increase in basis provided by this subsection with respect to any gift for the gift tax paid under chapter 12 shall be an amount (not in excess of the amount of tax so paid) which bears the same ratio to the amount of tax so paid as—

577

(i) the net appreciation in value of the gift, bears to

(ii) the amount of the gift.

(B) Net appreciation.—For purposes of paragraph (1), the net appreciation in value of any gift is the amount by which the fair market value of the gift exceeds the donor's adjusted basis immediately before the gift.

(e) Gifts between spouses.—In the case of any property acquired by gift in a transfer described in section 1041(a), the basis of such property in the hands of the transferee shall be determined under section 1041(b)(2) and not this section.

§ 1016. Adjustments to basis

(a) General rule.—Proper adjustment in respect of the property shall in all cases be made—

(1) for expenditures, receipts, losses, or other items, properly chargeable to capital account, but no such adjustment shall be made—

(A) for taxes or other carrying charges described in section 266, or

(B) for expenditures described in section 173 (relating to circulation expenditures),

for which deductions have been taken by the taxpayer in determining taxable income for the taxable year or prior taxable years;

(2) in respect of any period since February 28, 1913, for exhaustion, wear and tear, obsolescence, amortization, and depletion, to the extent of the amount—

(A) allowed as deductions in computing taxable income under this subtitle or prior income tax laws, and

(B) resulting (by reason of the deductions so allowed) in a reduction for any taxable year of the taxpayer's taxes under this subtitle (other than chapter 2, relating to tax on self-employment income), or prior income, war-profits, or excess-profits tax laws,

but not less than the amount allowable under this subtitle or prior income tax laws. Where no method has been adopted under section 167 (relating to depreciation deduction), the amount allowable shall be determined under section 167(b) (1). Subparagraph (B) of this paragraph shall not apply in respect of any period since February 28, 1913, and before January 1, 1952, unless an election has been made under section 1020 (as in effect before the date of the enactment of the Tax Reform Act of 1976). Where for any taxable year before the taxable year 1932 the depletion allowance was based on discovery value or a percentage of income, then the adjustment for depletion for such year shall be based on the depletion which would have been allowable for such year if computed without reference to discovery value or a percentage of income;

* * *

(7) in the case of a residence the acquisition of which resulted, under section 1034, in the nonrecognition of any part of the gain realized on the sale, exchange, or involuntary conversion of another residence, to the extent provided in section 1034(e);

* * *

(9) for amounts allowed as deductions as deferred expenses under section 616(b) (relating to certain expenditures in the development of mines) and resulting in a reduction of the taxpayer's taxes under this subtitle, but not less than the amounts allowable under such section for the taxable year and prior years;

[(10) Repealed.]

(11) for deductions to the extent disallowed under section 268 (relating to sale of land with unharvested crops), notwithstanding the provisions of any other paragraph of this subsection;

* * *

(14) for amounts allowed as deductions as deferred expenses under section 174(b) (1) (relating to research and experimental expenditures) and resulting in a reduction of the taxpayers' taxes under this subtitle, but not less than the amounts allowable under such section for the taxable year and prior years;

(15) for deductions to the extent disallowed under section 272 (relating to disposal of coal or domestic iron ore), notwithstanding the provisions of any other paragraph of this subsection;

(16) in the case of any evidence of indebtedness referred to in section 811(b) (relating to amortization of premium and accrual of discount in the case of life insurance companies), to the extent of the adjustments required under section 811(b) (or the corresponding provisions of prior income tax laws) for the taxable year and all prior taxable years;

(17) to the extent provided in section 1376 in the case of stock of, and indebtedness owed to, shareholders of an S corporation;

(18) to the extent provided in section 961 in the case of stock in controlled foreign corporations (or foreign corporations which were controlled foreign corporations) and of property by reason of which a person is considered as owning such stock;

(19) for amounts allowed as deductions for payments made on account of transfers of franchises, trademarks, or trade names under section 1253(d) (2);

(20) to the extent provided in section 23(e), in the case of property with respect to which a credit has been allowed under section 23;

* * *

(23) to the extent provided in section 48(q), in the case of expenditures with respect to which a credit has been allowed under section 38,

(24) for amounts allowed as deductions under section 59(d) (relating to optional 10-year writeoff of certain tax preferences);

(25) to the extent provided in section 1059 (relating to reduction in basis for extraordinary dividends); and

* * *

(b) **Substituted basis.**—Whenever it appears that the basis of property in the hands of the taxpayer is a substituted basis, then the adjustments provided in subsection (a) shall be made after first making in respect of such substituted basis proper adjustments of a similar nature in respect of the period during which the property was held by the transferor, donor, or grantor, or during which the other property was held by the person for whom the basis is to be determined. A similar rule shall be applied in the case of a series of substituted bases.

(c) **Increase in basis of property on which additional estate tax is imposed.**—

(1) **Tax imposed with respect to entire interest.**—If an additional estate tax is imposed under section 2032A(c)(1) with respect to any interest in property and the qualified heir makes an election under this subsection with respect to the imposition of such tax, the adjusted basis of such interest shall be increased by an amount equal to the excess of—

(A) the fair market value of such interest on the date of the decedent's death (or the alternate valuation date under section 2032, if the executor of the decedent's estate elected the application of such section), over

(B) the value of such interest determined under section 2032A(a).

(2) Partial dispositions.—

(A) In general.—In the case of any partial disposition for which an election under this subsection is made, the increase in basis under paragraph (1) shall be an amount—

(i) which bears the same ratio to the increase which would be determined under paragraph (1) (without regard to this paragraph) with respect to the entire interest, as

(ii) the amount of the tax imposed under section 2032A(c)(1) with respect to such disposition bears to the adjusted tax difference attributable to the entire interest (as determined under section 2032A(c)(2)(B)).

(B) Partial disposition.—For purposes of subparagraph (A), the term "partial disposition" means any disposition or cessation to which subsection (c)(2)(D), (h)(1)(B), or (i)(1)(B) of section 2032A applies.

(3) Time adjustment made.—Any increase in basis under this subsection shall be deemed to have occurred immediately before the disposition or cessation resulting in the imposition of the tax under section 2032A(c)(1).

(4) Special rule in the case of substituted property.—If the tax under section 2032A(c)(1) is imposed with respect to qualified replacement property (as defined in section 2032A(h)(3)(B)) or qualified exchange property (as defined in section 2032A(i)(3)), the increase in basis under paragraph (1) shall be made by reference to the property involuntarily converted or exchanged (as the case may be).

(5) Election.—

(A) In general.—An election under this subsection shall be made at such time and in such manner as the Secretary shall by regulations prescribe. Such an election, once made, shall be irrevocable.

(B) Interest on recaptured amount.—If an election is made under this subsection with respect to any additional estate tax imposed under section 2032A(c)(1), for purposes of section 6601 (relating to interest on underpayments), the last date prescribed for payment of such tax shall be deemed to be the last date prescribed for payment of the tax imposed by section 2001 with respect to the estate of the decedent (as determined for purposes of section 6601).

* * *

§ 1017. Discharge of indebtedness

(a) General rule.—If—

(1) an amount is excluded from gross income under subsection (a) of section 108 (relating to discharge of indebtedness), and

(2) under subsection (b)(2)(D) or (b)(5) of section 108, any portion of such amount is to be applied to reduce basis,

then such portion shall be applied in reduction of the basis of any property held by the taxpayer at the beginning of the taxable year following the taxable year in which the discharge occurs.

(b) Amount and properties determined under regulations.—

(1) **In general.**—The amount of reduction to be applied under subsection (a) (not in excess of the portion referred to in subsection (a)), and the particular properties the bases of which are to be reduced, shall be determined under regulations prescribed by the Secretary.

(2) **Limitation in Title 11 case or insolvency.**—In the case of a discharge to which subparagraph (A) or (B) of section 108(a)(1) applies, the reduction in basis under subsection (a) of this section shall not exceed the excess of—

(A) the aggregate of the bases of the property held by the taxpayer immediately after the discharge, over

(B) the aggregate of the liabilities of the taxpayer immediately after the discharge.

The preceding sentence shall not apply to any reduction in basis by reason of an election under section 108(b)(5).

(3) **Certain reductions may only be made in the basis of depreciable property.**—

(A) **In general.**—Any amount which under subsection (b)(5) of section 108 is to be applied to reduce basis shall be applied only to reduce the basis of depreciable property held by the taxpayer.

(B) **Depreciable property.**—For purposes of this section, the term "depreciable property" means any property of a character subject to the allowance for depreciation, but only if a basis reduction under subsection (a) will reduce the amount of depreciation or amortization which otherwise would be allowable for the period immediately following such reduction.

(C) **Special rule for partnership interests.**—For purposes of this section, any interest of a partner in a partnership shall be treated as depreciable property to the extent of such partner's proportionate interest in the depreciable property held by such partnership. The preceding sentence shall apply only if there is a corresponding reduction in the partnership's basis in depreciable property with respect to such partner.

(D) **Special rule in case of affiliated group.**—For purposes of this section, if—

(i) a corporation holds stock in another corporation (hereinafter in this subparagraph referred to as the "subsidiary"), and

(ii) such corporations are members of the same affiliated group which file a consolidated return under section 1501 for the taxable year in which the discharge occurs,

then such stock shall be treated as depreciable property to the extent that such subsidiary consents to a corresponding reduction in the basis of its depreciable property.

(E) **Election to treat certain inventory as depreciable property.**—

(i) **In general.**—At the election of the taxpayer, for purposes of this section, the term "depreciable property" includes any real property which is described in section 1221(1).

(ii) **Election.**—An election under clause (i) shall be made on the taxpayer's return for the taxable year in which the discharge occurs or at such other time as may be permitted in regulations prescribed by the Secretary. Such an election, once made, may be revoked only with the consent of the Secretary.

(4) Ordering rule in the case of qualified farm indebtedness.—Any amount which is excluded from gross income under section 108(a) by reason of the discharge of qualified farm indebtedness (within the meaning of section 108(g)(2)) and which under subsection (b) of section 108 is to be applied to reduce basis shall be applied—

(A) first to reduce the tax attributes described in section 108(b)(2) (other than subparagraph (D) thereof),

(B) then to reduce basis of property other than property described in subparagraph (C), and

(C) then to reduce the basis of land used or held for use in the trade or business of farming.

(c) Special rules.—

(1) Reduction not to be made in exempt property.—In the case of an amount excluded from gross income under section 108(a)(1)(A), no reduction in basis shall be made under this section in the basis of property which the debtor treats as exempt property under section 522 of title 11 of the United States Code.

(2) Reductions in basis not treated as dispositions.—For purposes of this title, a reduction in basis under this section shall not be treated as a disposition.

(d) Recapture of reductions.—

(1) In general.—For purposes of sections 1245 and 1250—

(A) any property the basis of which is reduced under this section and which is neither section 1245 property nor section 1250 property shall be treated as section 1245 property, and

(B) any reduction under this section shall be treated as a deduction allowed for depreciation.

(2) Special rule for section 1250.—For purposes of section 1250(b), the determination of what would have been the depreciation adjustments under the straight line method shall be made as if there had been no reduction under this section.

§ 1019.   Property on which lessee has made improvements

Neither the basis nor the adjusted basis of any portion of real property shall, in the case of the lessor of such property, be increased or diminished on account of income derived by the lessor in respect of such property and excludable from gross income under section 109 (relating to improvements by lessee on lessor's property). If an amount representing any part of the value of real property attributable to buildings erected or other improvements made by a lessee in respect of such property was included in gross income of the lessor for any taxable year beginning before January 1, 1942, the basis of each portion of such property shall be properly adjusted for the amount so included in gross income.

§ 1023.   Cross references

(1) For certain distributions by corporation which are applied in reduction of basis of stock, see section 301(c) (2).

* * *

PART III—COMMON NONTAXABLE EXCHANGES

§ 1031. Exchange of property held for productive use or investment

(a) Nonrecognition of gain or loss from exchanges solely in kind.—

(1) In general.—No gain or loss shall be recognized on the exchange of property held for productive use in a trade or business or for investment if such property is exchanged solely for property of like kind which is to be held either for productive use in a trade or business or for investment.

(2) Exception.—This subsection shall not apply to any exchange of—

(A) stock in trade or other property held primarily for sale,

(B) stocks, bonds, or notes,

(C) other securities or evidences of indebtedness or interest,

(D) interests in a partnership,

(E) certificates of trust or beneficial interests, or

(F) choses in action.

(3) Requirement that property be identified and that exchange be completed not more than 180 days after transfer of exchanged property.—For purposes of this subsection, any property received by the taxpayer shall be treated as property which is not like-kind property if—

(A) such property is not identified as property to be received in the exchange on or before the day which is 45 days after the date on which the taxpayer transfers the property relinquished in the exchange, or

(B) such property is received after the earlier of—

(i) the day which is 180 days after the date on which the taxpayer transfers the property relinquished in the exchange, or

(ii) the due date (determined with regard to extension) for the transferor's return of the tax imposed by this chapter for the taxable year in which the transfer of the relinquished property occurs.

(b) Gain from exchanges not solely in kind.—If an exchange would be within the provisions of subsection (a), of section 1035(a), of section 1036(a), or of section 1037(a), if it were not for the fact that the property received in exchange consists not only of property permitted by such provisions to be received without the recognition of gain, but also of other property or money, then the gain, if any, to the recipient shall be recognized, but in an amount not in excess of the sum of such money and the fair market value of such other property.

(c) Loss from exchanges not solely in kind.—If an exchange would be within the provisions of subsection (a), of section 1035(a), of section 1036(a), or of section 1037(a), if it were not for the fact that the property received in exchange consists not only of property permitted by such provisions to be received without the recognition of gain or loss, but also of other property or money, then no loss from the exchange shall be recognized.

(d) Basis.—If property was acquired on an exchange described in this section, section 1035(a), section 1036(a), or section 1037(a), then the basis shall be the same as that of the property exchanged, decreased in the amount of any money received by the taxpayer and increased in the amount of gain or decreased in the amount of loss to the taxpayer that was recognized on such exchange. If the property so acquired consisted in part of the type of property permitted by this section, section 1035(a), section 1036(a), or section 1037(a), to be received without the recognition of gain or loss, and in part of other property, the basis provided in this subsection shall be allocated between the properties (other than money) received, and for the purpose of the allocation there shall be assigned to such other property an amount equivalent to its fair market value at the date of the exchange. For purposes of this section, section 1035(a), and section 1036(a), where as part of the consideration to the taxpayer another party to the exchange assumed a liability of the taxpayer or acquired from the taxpayer property subject to a liability, such assumption or acquisition (in the amount of the liability) shall be considered as money received by the taxpayer on the exchange.

(e) **Exchanges of livestock of different sexes.**—For purposes of this section, livestock of different sexes are not property of a like kind.

§ 1032. Exchange of stock for property

(a) **Nonrecognition of gain or loss.**—No gain or loss shall be recognized to a corporation on the receipt of money or other property in exchange for stock (including treasury stock) of such corporation. No gain or loss shall be recognized by a corporation with respect to any lapse or acquisition of an option to buy or sell its stock (including treasury stock).

(b) **Basis.**—

For basis of property acquired by a corporation in certain exchanges for its stock, see section 362.

§ 1033. Involuntary conversions

(a) **General rule.**—If property (as a result of its destruction in whole or in part, theft, seizure, or requisition or condemnation or threat or imminence thereof) is compulsorily or involuntarily converted—

(1) **Conversion into similar property.**—Into property similar or related in service or use to the property so converted, no gain shall be recognized.

(2) **Conversion into money.**—Into money or into property not similar or related in service or use to the converted property, the gain (if any) shall be recognized except to the extent hereinafter provided in this paragraph:

(A) **Nonrecognition of gain.**—If the taxpayer during the period specified in subparagraph (B), for the purpose of replacing the property so converted, purchases other property similar or related in service or use to the property so converted, or purchases stock in the acquisition of control of a corporation owning such other property, at the election of the taxpayer the gain shall be recognized only to the extent that the amount realized upon such conversion (regardless of whether such amount is received in one or more taxable years) exceeds the cost of such other property or such stock. Such election shall be made at such time and in such manner as the Secretary may by regulations prescribe. For purposes of this paragraph—

(i) no property or stock acquired before the disposition of the converted property shall be considered to have been acquired for the purpose of replacing such converted property unless held by the taxpayer on the date of such disposition; and

(ii) the taxpayer shall be considered to have purchased property or stock only if, but for the provisions of subsection (b) of this section, the unadjusted basis of such property or stock would be its cost within the meaning of section 1012.

(B) Period within which property must be replaced.—The period referred to in subparagraph (A) shall be the period beginning with the date of the disposition of the converted property, or the earliest date of the threat or imminence of requisition or condemnation of the converted property, whichever is the earlier, and ending—

(i) 2 years after the close of the first taxable year in which any part of the gain upon the conversion is realized, or

(ii) subject to such terms and conditions as may be specified by the Secretary, at the close of such later date as the Secretary may designate on application by the taxpayer. Such application shall be made at such time and in such manner as the Secretary may by regulations prescribe.

(C) Time for assessment of deficiency attributable to gain upon conversion.—If a taxpayer has made the election provided in subparagraph (A), then—

(i) the statutory period for the assessment of any deficiency, for any taxable year in which any part of the gain on such conversion is realized, attributable to such gain shall not expire prior to the expiration of 3 years from the date the Secretary is notified by the taxpayer (in such manner as the Secretary may by regulations prescribe) of the replacement of the converted property or of an intention not to replace, and

(ii) such deficiency may be assessed before the expiration of such 3-year period notwithstanding the provisions of section 6212(c) or the provisions of any other law or rule of law which would otherwise prevent such assessment.

(D) Time for assessment of other deficiencies attributable to election.—If the election provided in subparagraph (A) is made by the taxpayer and such other property or such stock was purchased before the beginning of the last taxable year in which any part of the gain upon such conversion is realized, any deficiency, to the extent resulting from such election, for any taxable year ending before such last taxable year may be assessed (notwithstanding the provisions of section 6212(c) or 6501 or the provisions of any other law or rule of law which would otherwise prevent such assessment) at any time before the expiration of the period within which a deficiency for such last taxable year may be assessed.

(E) Definitions.—For purposes of this paragraph—

(i) Control.—The term "control" means the ownership of stock possessing at least 80 percent of the total combined voting power of all classes of stock entitled to vote and at least 80 percent of the total number of shares of all other classes of stock of the corporation.

(ii) Disposition of the converted property.—The term "disposition of the converted property" means the destruction, theft, seizure, requisition, or condemnation of the converted property, or the sale or exchange of such property under threat or imminence of requisition or condemnation.

(b) Basis of property acquired through involuntary conversion.—If the property was acquired, after February 28, 1913, as the result of a compulsory or involuntary conversion described in subsection (a) (1) or section 112(f) (2) of the Internal Revenue Code of 1939, the basis shall be the same as in the case of the property so converted, decreased in the amount of any money received by the taxpayer which was not expended in accordance with the provisions of law (applicable to the year in which such conversion was made) determining the taxable status of the gain or loss upon such conversion, and increased in the amount of gain or decreased in the amount of loss to the taxpayer recognized upon such conversion under the law applicable to the year in which such conversion was made. This subsection shall not apply in respect of property acquired as a result of a compulsory or involuntary conversion of property used by the taxpayer as his principal residence if the destruction, theft, seizure, requisition, or condemnation of such residence, or the sale or exchange of such residence under threat or imminence thereof, occurred after December 31, 1950, and before January 1, 1954. In the case of property purchased by the taxpayer in a transaction described in subsection (a) (3)* which resulted in the nonrecognition of any part of the gain realized as the result of a compulsory or involuntary conversion, the basis shall be the cost of such property decreased in the amount of the gain not so recognized; and if the property purchased consists of more than one piece of property, the basis determined under this sentence shall be allocated to the purchased properties in proportion to their respective costs.

(c) **Property sold pursuant to reclamation laws.**—For purposes of this subtitle, if property lying within an irrigation project is sold or otherwise disposed of in order to conform to the acreage limitation provisions of Federal reclamation laws, such sale or disposition shall be treated as an involuntary conversion to which this section applies.

(d) **Livestock destroyed by disease.**—For purposes of this subtitle, if livestock are destroyed by or on account of disease, or are sold or exchanged because of disease, such destruction or such sale or exchange shall be treated as an involuntary conversion to which this section applies.

(e) **Livestock sold on account of drought.**—For purposes of this subtitle, the sale or exchange of livestock (other than poultry) held by a taxpayer for draft, breeding, or dairy purposes in excess of the number the taxpayer would sell if he followed his usual business practices shall be treated as an involuntary conversion to which this section applies if such livestock are sold or exchanged by the taxpayer solely on account of drought.

(f) **Replacement of livestock with other farm property where there has been environmental contamination.**—For purposes of subsection (a), if, because of soil contamination or other environmental contamination, it is not feasible for the taxpayer to reinvest the proceeds from compulsorily or involuntarily converted livestock in property similar or related in use to the livestock so converted, other property (including real property) used for farming purposes shall be treated as property similar or related in service or use to the livestock so converted.

(g) **Condemnation of real property held for productive use in trade or business or for investment.**—

(1) **Special rule.**—For purposes of subsection (a), if real property (not including stock in trade or other property held primarily for sale) held for productive use in trade or business or for investment is (as the result of its seizure, requisition, or condemnation, or threat or imminence thereof) compulsorily or involuntarily converted, property of a like kind to be held either for productive use in trade or business or for investment shall be treated as property similar or related in service or use to the property so converted.

(2) **Limitation.**—Paragraph (1) shall not apply to the purchase of stock in the acquisition of control of a corporation described in subsection (a) (2) (A).

* * *

(4) **Special rule.**—In the case of a compulsory or involuntary conversion described in paragraph (1), subsection (a) (2) (B) (i) shall be applied by substituting "3 years" for "2 years".

* Subsection (a)(3) was redesignated (a)(2).

(h) Cross references.—

(1) For determination of the period for which the taxpayer has held property involuntarily converted, see section 1223.

(2) For treatment of gains from involuntary conversions as capital gains in certain cases, see section 1231(a).

(3) For one-time exclusion from gross income of gain from involuntary conversion of principal residence by individual who has attained age 55, see section 121.

§ 1034. Rollover of gain on sale of principal residence

(a) Nonrecognition of gain.—If property (in this section called "old residence") used by the taxpayer as his principal residence is sold by him and, within a period beginning 2 years before the date of such sale and ending 2 years after such date, property (in this section called "new residence") is purchased and used by the taxpayer as his principal residence, gain (if any) from such sale shall be recognized only to the extent that the taxpayer's adjusted sales price (as defined in subsection (b)) of the old residence exceeds the taxpayer's cost of purchasing the new residence.

(b) Adjusted sales price defined.—

(1) In general.—For purposes of this section, the term "adjusted sales price" means the amount realized, reduced by the aggregate of the expenses for work performed on the old residence in order to assist in its sale.

(2) Limitations.—The reduction provided in paragraph (1) applies only to expenses—

    (A) for work performed during the 90-day period ending on the day on which the contract to sell the old residence is entered into;

    (B) which are paid on or before the 30th day after the date of the sale of the old residence; and

    (C) which are—

        (i) not allowable as deductions in computing taxable income under section 63 (defining taxable income), and

        (ii) not taken into account in computing the amount realized from the sale of the old residence.

(c) Rules for application of section.—For purposes of this section:

(1) An exchange by the taxpayer of his residence for other property shall be treated as a sale of such residence, and the acquisition of a residence on the exchange of property shall be treated as a purchase of such residence.

(2) A residence any part of which was constructed or reconstructed by the taxpayer shall be treated as purchased by the taxpayer. In determining the taxpayer's cost of purchasing a residence, there shall be included only so much of his cost as is attributable to the acquisition, construction, reconstruction, and improvements made which are properly chargeable to capital account, during the period specified in subsection (a).

(3) If a residence is purchased by the taxpayer before the date of his sale of the old residence, the purchased residence shall not be treated as his new residence if sold or otherwise disposed of by him before the date of the sale of the old residence.

(4) If the taxpayer, during the period described in subsection (a), purchases more than one residence which is used by him as his principal residence at some time within 2 years after the date of the sale of the old residence, only the last of such residences so used by him after the date of such sale shall constitute the new residence. If a principal residence is sold in a sale to which subsection (d) (2) applies within 2 years after the sale of the old residence, for purposes of applying the preceding sentence with respect to the old residence, the principal residence so sold shall be treated as the last residence used during such 2-year period.

(d) Limitation.—

(1) In general.—Subsection (a) shall not apply with respect to the sale of the taxpayer's residence if within 2 years before the date of such sale the taxpayer sold at a gain other property used by him as his principal residence, and any part of such gain was not recognized by reason of subsection (a).

(2) Subsequent sale connected with commencing work at new place. —Paragraph (1) shall not apply with respect to the sale of the taxpayer's residence if—

(A) such sale was in connection with the commencement of work by the taxpayer as an employee or as a self-employed individual at a new principal place of work, and

(B) if the residence so sold is treated as the former residence for purposes of section 217 (relating to moving expenses), the taxpayer would satisfy the conditions of subsection (c) of section 217 (as modified by the other subsections of such section).

(e) Basis of new residence.—Where the purchase of a new residence results, under subsection (a) or under section 112(n) of the Internal Revenue Code of 1939, in the nonrecognition of gain on the sale of an old residence, in determining the adjusted basis of the new residence as of any time following the sale of the old residence, the adjustments to basis shall include a reduction by an amount equal to the amount of the gain not so recognized on the sale of the old residence. For this purpose, the amount of the gain not so recognized on the sale of the old residence includes only so much of such gain as is not recognized by reason of the cost, up to such time, of purchasing the new residence.

(f) Tenant-stockholder in a cooperative housing corporation.—For purposes of this section, section 1016 (relating to adjustments to basis), and section 1223 (relating to holding period), references to property used by the taxpayer as his principal residence, and references to the residence of a taxpayer, shall include stock held by a tenant-stockholder (as defined in section 216, relating to deduction for amounts representing taxes and interest paid to a cooperative housing corporation) in a cooperative housing corporation (as defined in such section) if—

(1) in the case of stock sold, the house or apartment which the taxpayer was entitled to occupy as such stockholder was used by him as his principal residence, and

(2) in the case of stock purchased, the taxpayer used as his principal residence the house or apartment which he was entitled to occupy as such stockholder.

(g) Husband and wife.—If the taxpayer and his spouse, in accordance with regulations which shall be prescribed by the Secretary pursuant to this subsection, consent to the application of paragraph (2) of this subsection, then—

(1) for purposes of this section—

(A) the taxpayer's adjusted sales price of the old residence is the adjusted sales price (of the taxpayer, or of the taxpayer and his spouse) of the old residence, and

(B) the taxpayer's cost of purchasing the new residence is the cost (to the taxpayer, his spouse, or both) of purchasing the new residence (whether held by the taxpayer, his spouse, or the taxpayer and his spouse); and

(2) so much of the gain on the sale of the old residence as is not recognized solely by reason of this subsection, and so much of the adjustment under subsection (e) to the basis of the new residence as results solely from this subsection shall be allocated between the taxpayer and his spouse as provided in such regulations.

This subsection shall apply only if the old residence and the new residence are each used by the taxpayer and his spouse as their principal residence. In case the taxpayer and his spouse do not consent to the application of paragraph (2) of this subsection then the recognition of gain on the sale of the old residence shall be determined under this section without regard to the rules provided in this subsection.

(h) Members of Armed Forces.—

(1) In general.—The running of any period of time specified in subsection (a) or (c) (other than the 2 years referred to in subsection (c)(4)) shall be suspended during any time that the taxpayer (or his spouse if the old residence and the new residence are each used by the taxpayer and his spouse as their principal residence) serves on extended active duty with the Armed Forces of the United States after the date of the sale of the old residence, except that any such period of time as so suspended shall not extend beyond the date 4 years after the date of the sale of the old residence.

(2) Members stationed outside the United States or required to reside in government quarters.—In the case of any taxpayer who, during any period of time the running of which is suspended by paragraph (1)—

(A) is stationed outside of the United States, or

(B) after returning from a tour of duty outside of the United States and pursuant to a determination by the Secretary of Defense that adequate off-base housing is not available at a remote base site, is required to reside in on-base Government quarters,

any such period of time as so suspended shall not expire before the day which is one year after the last day described in subparagraph (A) or (B), as the case may be, except that any such period of time as so suspended shall not extend beyond the date which is 8 years after the date of the sale of the old residence.

(3) Extended active duty defined.—For purposes of this subsection, the term "extended active duty" means any period of active duty pursuant to a call or order to such duty for a period in excess of 90 days or for an indefinite period.

(i) Special rule for condemnation.—In the case of the seizure, requisition, or condemnation of a residence, or the sale or exchange of a residence under threat or imminence thereof, the provisions of this section, in lieu of section 1033 (relating to involuntary conversions), shall be applicable if the taxpayer so elects. If such election is made, such seizure, requisition, or condemnation shall be treated as the sale of the residence. Such election shall be made at such time and in such manner as the Secretary shall prescribe by regulations.

(j) Statute of limitations.—If the taxpayer during a taxable year sells at a gain property used by him as his principal residence, then—

(1) the statutory period for the assessment of any deficiency attributable to any part of such gain shall not expire before the expiration of 3 years from the date the Secretary is notified by the taxpayer (in such manner as the Secretary may by regulations prescribe) of—

(A) the taxpayer's cost of purchasing the new residence which the taxpayer claims results in nonrecognition of any part of such gain,

(B) the taxpayer's intention not to purchase a new residence within the period specified in subsection (a), or

(C) a failure to make such purchase within such period; and

(2) such deficiency may be assessed before the expiration of such 3-year period notwithstanding the provisions of any other law or rule of law which would otherwise prevent such assessment.

(k) Individual whose tax home is outside the United States.—The running of any period of time specified in subsection (a) or (c) (other than the 2 years referred to in subsection (c) (4)) shall be suspended during any time that the taxpayer (or his spouse if the old residence and the new residence are each used by the taxpayer and his spouse as their principal residence) has a tax home (as defined in section 911(d)(3)) outside the United States after the date of the sale of the old residence; except that any such period of time as so suspended shall not extend beyond the date 4 years after the date of the sale of the old residence.

(*l*) Cross reference.—

For one-time exclusion from gross income of gain from sale of principal residence by individual who has attained age 55, see section 121.

§ 1035. Certain exchanges of insurance policies

(a) General rules.—No gain or loss shall be recognized on the exchange of—

(1) a contract of life insurance for another contract of life insurance or for an endowment or annuity contract; or

(2) a contract of endowment insurance (A) for another contract of endowment insurance which provides for regular payments beginning at a date not later than the date payments would have begun under the contract exchanged, or (B) for an annuity contract; or

(3) an annuity contract for an annuity contract.

(b) Definitions.—For the purpose of this section—

(1) Endowment contract.—A contract of endowment insurance is a contract with an insurance company which depends in part on the life expectancy of the insured, but which may be payable in full in a single payment during his life.

(2) Annuity contract.—An annuity contract is a contract to which paragraph (1) applies but which may be payable during the life of the annuitant only in installments.

(3) Life insurance contract.—A contract of life insurance is a contract to which paragraph (1) applies but which is not ordinarily payable in full during the life of the insured.

(c) Cross references.—

(1) For rules relating to recognition of gain or loss where an exchange is not solely in kind, see subsections (b) and (c) of section 1031.

(2) For rules relating to the basis of property acquired in an exchange described in subsection (a), see subsection (d) of section 1031.

§ 1036. Stock for stock of same corporation

(a) General rule.—No gain or loss shall be recognized if common stock in a corporation is exchanged solely for common stock in the same corporation, or if preferred stock in a corporation is exchanged solely for preferred stock in the same corporation.

(b) Cross references.—

(1) For rules relating to recognition of gain or loss where an exchange is not solely in kind, see subsections (b) and (c) of section 1031.

(2) For rules relating to the basis of property acquired in an exchange described in subsection (a), see subsection (d) of section 1031.

§ 1038. Certain reacquisitions of real property

(a) General rule.—If—

(1) a sale of real property gives rise to indebtedness to the seller which is secured by the real property sold, and

(2) the seller of such property reacquires such property in partial or full satisfaction of such indebtedness,

then, except as provided in subsections (b) and (d), no gain or loss shall result to the seller from such reacquisition, and no debt shall become worthless or partially worthless as a result of such reacquisition.

(b) Amount of gain resulting.—

(1) In general.—In the case of a reacquisition of real property to which subsection (a) applies, gain shall result from such reacquisition to the extent that—

(A) the amount of money and the fair market value of other property (other than obligations of the purchaser) received, prior to such reacquisition, with respect to the sale of such property, exceeds

(B) the amount of the gain on the sale of such property returned as income for periods prior to such reacquisition.

(2) Limitation.—The amount of gain determined under paragraph (1) resulting from a reacquisition during any taxable year beginning after the date of the enactment of this section shall not exceed the amount by which the price at which the real property was sold exceeded its adjusted basis, reduced by the sum of—

(A) the amount of the gain on the sale of such property returned as income for periods prior to the reacquisition of such property, and

(B) the amount of money and the fair market value of other property (other than obligations of the purchaser received with respect to the sale of such property) paid or transferred by the seller in connection with the reacquisition of such property.

For purposes of this paragraph, the price at which real property is sold is the gross sales price reduced by the selling commissions, legal fees, and other expenses incident to the sale of such property which are properly taken into account in determining gain or loss on such sale.

(3) Gain recognized.—Except as provided in this section, the gain determined under this subsection resulting from a reacquisition to which subsection (a) applies shall be recognized, notwithstanding any other provision of this subtitle.

(c) Basis of reacquired real property.—If subsection (a) applies to the reacquisition of any real property, the basis of such property upon such reacquisition shall be the adjusted basis of the indebtedness to the seller secured by such property (determined as of the date of reacquisition), increased by the sum of—

(1) the amount of the gain determined under subsection (b) resulting from such reacquisition, and

(2) the amount described in subsection (b) (2) (B).

If any indebtedness to the seller secured by such property is not discharged upon the reacquisition of such property, the basis of such indebtedness shall be zero.

(d) Indebtedness treated as worthless prior to reacquisition.—If, prior to a reacquisition of real property to which subsection (a) applies, the seller has treated indebtedness secured by such property as having become worthless or partially worthless—

(1) such seller shall be considered as receiving, upon the reacquisition of such property, an amount equal to the amount of such indebtedness treated by him as having become worthless, and

(2) the adjusted basis of such indebtedness shall be increased (as of the date of reacquisition) by an amount equal to the amount so considered as received by such seller.

(e) Principal residences.—If—

(1) subsection (a) applies to a reacquisition of real property with respect to the sale of which—

(A) an election under section 121 (relating to one-time exclusion of gain from sale of principal residence by individual who has attained age 55) is in effect, or

(B) gain was not recognized under section 1034 (relating to rollover of gain on sale of principal residence); and

(2) within one year after the date of the reacquisition of such property by the seller, such property is resold by him,

then, under regulations prescribed by the Secretary, subsections (b), (c), and (d) of this section shall not apply to the reacquisition of such property and, for purposes of applying sections 121 and 1034, the resale of such property shall be treated as a part of the transaction constituting the original sale of such property.

* * *

(g) Acquisition by estate, etc., of seller.—Under regulations prescribed by the Secretary, if an installment obligation is indebtedness to the seller which is described in subsection (a), and if such obligation is, in the hands of the taxpayer, an obligation with respect to which section 691(a)(4)(B) applies, then—

(1) for purposes of subsection (a), acquisition of real property by the taxpayer shall be treated as reacquisition by the seller, and

(2) the basis of the real property acquired by the taxpayer shall be increased by an amount equal to the deduction under section 691(c) which would (but for this subsection) have been allowable to the taxpayer with respect to the gain on the exchange of the obligation for the real property.

§ 1039. Certain sales of low-income housing projects

(a) Nonrecognition of gain.—If—

(1) a qualified housing project is sold or disposed of by the taxpayer in an approved disposition, and

(2) within the reinvestment period the taxpayer constructs, reconstructs, or acquires another qualified housing project,

then, at the election of the taxpayer, gain from such approved disposition shall be recognized only to the extent that the net amount realized on such approved disposition exceeds the cost of such other qualified housing project. An election under this subsection shall be made at such time and in such manner as the Secretary prescribes by regulations.

(b) Definitions.—For purposes of this section—

(1) Qualified housing project.—The term "qualified housing project" means a project to provide rental or cooperative housing for lower income families—

(A) with respect to which a mortgage is insured under section 221(d) (3) or 236 of the National Housing Act, and

(B) with respect to which the owner is, under such sections or regulations issued thereunder—

(i) limited as to the rate of return on his investment in the project, and

(ii) limited as to rentals or occupancy charges for units in the project.

(2) Approved disposition.—The term "approved disposition" means a sale or other disposition of a qualified housing project to the tenants or occupants of units in such project, or to a cooperative or other nonprofit organization formed solely for the benefit of such tenants or occupants, which sale or disposition is approved by the Secretary of Housing and Urban Development under section 221(d) (3) or 236 of the National Housing Act or regulations issued under such sections.

(3) Reinvestment period.—The reinvestment period, with respect to an approved disposition of a qualified housing project, is the period beginning one year before the date of such approved disposition and ending—

(A) one year after the close of the first taxable year in which any part of the gain from such approved disposition is realized, or

(B) subject to such terms and conditions as may be specified by the Secretary, at the close of such later date as the Secretary may designate on application by the taxpayer. Such application shall be made at such time and in such manner as the Secretary prescribes by regulations.

(4) Net amount realized.—The net amount realized on an approved disposition of a qualified housing project is the amount realized reduced by—

(A) the expenses paid or incurred which are directly connected with such approved disposition, and

(B) the amount of taxes (other than income taxes) paid or incurred which are attributable to such approved disposition.

(c) Special rules.—For purposes of applying subsection (a) (2) with respect to an approved disposition—

(1) no property acquired by the taxpayer before the date of the approved disposition shall be taken into account unless such property is held by the taxpayer on such date, and

(2) no property acquired by the taxpayer shall be taken into account unless, except as provided in subsection (d), the unadjusted basis of such property is its cost within the meaning of section 1012.

(d) Basis of other qualified housing project.—If the taxpayer makes an election under subsection (a) with respect to an approved disposition, the basis of the qualified housing project described in subsection (a) (2) shall be its cost reduced by an amount equal to the amount of gain not recognized by reason of the application of subsection (a).

(e) Assessment of deficiencies.—

(1) Deficiency attributable to gain.—If the taxpayer has made an election under subsection (a) with respect to an approved disposition—

(A) the statutory period for the assessment of any deficiency, for any taxable year in which any part of the gain on such approved disposition is realized, attributable to the gain on such approved disposition shall not expire prior to the expiration of 3 years from the date the Secretary is notified by the taxpayer (in such manner as the Secretary may by regulations prescribe) of the construction, reconstruction, or acquisition of another qualified housing project or of the failure to construct, reconstruct, or acquire another qualified housing project, and

(B) such deficiency may be assessed before the expiration of such 3-year period notwithstanding the provisions of section 6212(c) or the provision of any other law or rule of law which would otherwise prevent such assessment.

(2) Time for assessment of other deficiencies attributable to election.—If a taxpayer has made an election under subsection (a) with respect to an approved disposition and another qualified housing project is constructed, reconstructed, or acquired before the beginning of the last taxable year in which any part of the gain upon such approved disposition is realized, any deficiency, to the extent resulting from such election, for any taxable year ending before such last taxable year may be assessed (notwithstanding the provisions of section 6212(c) or 6501 or the provisions of any other law or rule of law which would otherwise prevent such assessment) at any time before the expiration of the period within which a deficiency for such last taxable year may be assessed.

§ 1040. Transfer of certain farm, etc., real property

(a) General rule.—If the executor of the estate of any decedent transfers to a qualified heir (within the meaning of section 2032A(e)(1)) any property with respect to which an election was made under section 2032A, then gain on such transfer shall be recognized to the estate only to the extent that, on the date of such transfer, the fair market value of such property exceeds the value of such property for purposes of chapter 11 (determined without regard to section 2032A).

(b) Similar rule for certain trusts.—To the extent provided in regulations prescribed by the Secretary, a rule similar to the rule provided in subsection (a) shall apply where the trustee of a trust (any portion of which is included in the gross estate of the decedent) transfers property with respect to which an election was made under section 2032A.

(c) Basis of property acquired in transfer described in subsection (a) or (b). —The basis of property acquired in a transfer with respect to which gain realized is not recognized by reason of subsection (a) or (b) shall be the basis of such property immediately before the transfer increased by the amount of the gain recognized to the estate or trust on the transfer.

(d) Application to Section 2032A Property.—For purposes of this section, references to carryover basis property shall be treated as including a reference to property the valuation of which is determined under section 2032A.

§ 1041. Transfers of property between spouses or incident to divorce

(a) General rule.—No gain or loss shall be recognized on a transfer of property from an individual to (or in trust for the benefit of)—

(1) a spouse, or

(2) a former spouse, but only if the transfer is incident to the divorce.

(b) Transfer treated as gift; transferee has transferor's basis.—In the case of any transfer of property described in subsection (a)—

(1) for purposes of this subtitle, the property shall be treated as acquired by the transferee by gift, and

(2) the basis of the transferee in the property shall be the adjusted basis of the transferor.

(c) Incident to divorce.—For purposes of subsection (a)(2), a transfer of property is incident to the divorce if such transfer—

(1) occurs within 1 year after the date on which the marriage ceases, or

(2) is related to the cessation of the marriage.

(d) Special rule where spouse is nonresident alien.—Paragraph (1) of subsection (a) shall not apply if the spouse of the individual making the transfer is a nonresident alien.

PART IV—SPECIAL RULES

§ 1059. Corporate shareholder's basis in stock reduced by non-taxed portion of extraordinary dividends

(a) General rule.—If any corporation receives any extraordinary dividend with respect to any share of stock and such corporation has not held such stock for more than 2 years before the dividend announcement date—

(1) **Reduction in basis.**—The basis of such corporation in such stock shall be reduced (but not below zero) by the nontaxed portion of such dividends.

(2) **Recognition upon sale or disposition in certain cases.**—In addition to any gain recognized under this chapter, there shall be treated as gain from the sale or exchange of any stock for the taxable year in which the sale or disposition of such stock occurs an amount equal to the aggregate nontaxed portions of any extraordinary dividends with respect to such stock which did not reduce the basis of such stock by reason of the limitation on reducing basis below zero.

(b) Nontaxed portion.—For purposes of this section—

(1) **In general.**—The nontaxed portion of any dividend is the excess (if any) of—

(A) the amount of such dividend, over

(B) the taxable portion of such dividend.

(2) **Taxable portion.**—The taxable portion of any dividend is—

(A) the portion of such dividend includible in gross income, reduced by

(B) the amount of any deduction allowable with respect to such dividend under section 243, 244, or 245.

(c) Extraordinary dividend defined.—For purposes of this section—

(1) **In general.**—The term "extraordinary dividend" means any dividend with respect to a share of stock if the amount of such dividend equals or exceeds the threshold percentage of the taxpayer's adjusted basis in such share of stock.

(2) **Threshold percentage.**—The term "threshold percentage" means—

(A) 5 percent in the case of stock which is preferred as to dividends, and

(B) 10 percent in the case of any other stock.

(3) **Aggregation of dividends.**—

(A) **Aggregation within 85-day period.**—All dividends—

(i) which are received by the taxpayer (or a person described in subparagraph (C)) with respect to any share of stock, and

(ii) which have ex-dividend dates within the same period of 85 consecutive days,

shall be treated as 1 dividend.

(B) **Aggregation within 1 year where dividends exceed 20 percent of adjusted basis.**—All dividends—

(i) which are received by the taxpayer (or a person described in subparagraph (C)) with respect to any share of stock, and

(ii) which have ex-dividend dates during the same period of 365 consecutive days,

shall be treated as extraordinary dividends if the aggregate of such dividends exceeds 20 percent of the taxpayer's adjusted basis in such stock (determined without regard to this section).

(C) **Substituted basis transactions.**—In the case of any stock, a person is described in this subparagraph if—

(i) the basis of such stock in the hands of such person is determined in whole or in part by reference to the basis of such stock in the hands of the taxpayer, or

(ii) the basis of such stock in the hands of the taxpayer is determined in whole or in part by reference to the basis of such stock in the hands of such person.

(4) **Fair market value determination.**—If the taxpayer establishes to the satisfaction of the Secretary the fair market value of any share of stock as of the day before the ex-dividend date, the taxpayer may elect to apply paragraphs (1) and (3) by substituting such value for the taxpayer's adjusted basis.

(d) **Special rules.**—For purposes of this section—

(1) **Time for reduction.**—

(A) **In general.**—Except as provided in subparagraph (B), any reduction in basis under subsection (a)(1) shall occur immediately before any sale or disposition of the stock.

(B) **Special rule for computing extraordinary dividend.**—In determining a taxpayer's adjusted basis for purposes of subsection (c)(1), any reduction in basis under subsection (a)(1) by reason of a prior distribution which was an extraordinary dividend shall be treated as occurring at the beginning of the ex-dividend date for such distribution.

(2) **Distributions in kind.**—To the extent any dividend consists of property other than cash, the amount of such dividend shall be treated as the fair market value of such property (as of the date of the distribution) reduced as provided in section 301(b)(2).

(3) **Determination of holding period.**—For purposes of determining the holding period of stock under subsection (a)(2), rules similar to the rules of paragraphs (3) and (4) of section 246(c) shall apply; except that "2 years" shall be substituted for the number of days specified in subparagraph (B) of section 246(c)(3).

(4) **Ex-dividend date.**—The term "ex-dividend date" means the date on which the share of stock becomes ex-dividend.

(5) Extension to certain property distributions.—In the case of any distribution of property (other than cash) to which section 301 applies—

(A) such distribution shall be treated as a dividend without regard to whether the corporation has earnings and profits, and

(B) the amount so treated shall be reduced by the amount of any reduction in basis under section 301(c)(2) by reason of such distribution.

(6) Dividend announcement date.—The term "dividend announcement date" means, with respect to any dividend, the date on which the corporation declares, announces, or agrees to the payment of such dividend, whichever is the earliest.

(7) Exception where stock held during entire existence of corporation.—Subsection (a) shall not apply to any extraordinary dividend with respect to any share of stock of a corporation if—

(A) such stock was held by the taxpayer during the entire period such corporation (and any predecessor corporation) was in existence,

(B) except as provided in regulations, the only earnings and profits of such corporation were earnings and profits accumulated by such corporation (or any predecessor corporation) during such period, and

(C) the application of this paragraph to such dividend is not inconsistent with the purposes of this section.

(e) Special rules for certain distributions.—

(1) Treatment of partial liquidations and non-pro rata redemptions.—Except as otherwise provided in regulations, in the case of any redemption of stock which is—

(A) part of a partial liquidation (within the meaning of section 302(e)) of the redeeming corporation, or

(B) not pro rata as to all shareholders,

any amount treated as a dividend under section 301 with respect to such redemption shall be treated as an extraordinary dividend for purposes of this section (without regard to the holding period of the stock).

(2) Qualifying dividends.—Except as provided in regulations, the term "extraordinary dividend" shall not include any qualifying dividend (within the meaning of section 243(b)(1)).

(3) Qualified preferred dividends.—

(A) In general.—A qualified preferred dividend shall be treated as an extraordinary dividend—

(i) only if the actual rate of return of the taxpayer on the stock with respect to which such dividend was paid exceeds 15 percent, or

(ii) if clause (i) does not apply, and the taxpayer disposes of such stock before the taxpayer has held such stock for more than 5 years, only to the extent the actual rate of return exceeds the stated rate of return.

(B) Rate of return.—For purposes of subparagraph (A)—

(i) Actual rate of return.—The actual rate of return shall be the rate of return for the period for which the taxpayer held the stock, determined—

(I) by only taking into account dividends during such period, and

(II) by using the lesser of the adjusted basis of the taxpayer in such stock or the liquidation preference of such stock.

(ii) Stated rate of return.—The stated rate of return shall be the annual rate of the qualified preferred dividend payable with respect to any share of stock (expressed as a percentage of the amount described in subparagraph (B)(i)(II)).

(C) Definitions and special rules.—For purposes of this paragraph—

(i) Qualified preferred dividend.—The term "qualified preferred dividend" means any dividend payable with respect to any share of stock which—

(I) provides for fixed preferred dividends payable not less frequently than annually, and

(II) is not in arrears as to dividends at the time the taxpayer acquires the stock.

(ii) Holding period.—In determining the holding period for purposes of subparagraph (A)(ii), subsection (d)(3) shall be applied by substituting "5 years" for "2 years".

(f) Regulations.—The Secretary shall prescribe such regulations as may be appropriate to carry out the purposes of this section, including regulations providing for the application of this section in the case of stock dividends, stock splits, reorganizations, and other similar transactions.

§ 1060.   Special allocation rules for certain asset acquisitions

(a) General rule.—In the case of any applicable asset acquisition, for purposes of determining both—

(1) the transferee's basis in such assets, and

(2) the gain or loss of the transferor with respect to such acquisition,

the consideration received for such assets shall be allocated among such assets acquired in such acquisition in the same manner as amounts are allocated to assets under section 338(b)(5).

(b) Information required to be furnished to secretary.—Under regulations, the transferor and transferee in an applicable asset acquisition shall, at such times and in such manner as may be provided in such regulations, furnish to the Secretary the following information:

(1) The amount of the consideration received for the assets which is allocated to goodwill or going concern value.

(2) Any modification of the amount described in paragraph (1).

(3) Any other information with respect to other assets transferred in such acquisition as the Secretary may find necessary to carry out the provisions of this section.

(c) Applicable asset acquisition.—For purposes of this section, the term "applicable asset acquisition" means any transfer (whether directly or indirectly)—

(1) of assets which constitute a trade or business, and

(2) with respect to which the transferee's basis in such assets is determined wholly by reference to the consideration paid for such assets.

A transfer shall not be treated as failing to be an applicable asset acquisition merely because section 1031 applies to a portion of the assets transferred.

(Added Pub.L. 99–514, Title VI, § 641(a), Oct. 22, 1986, 100 Stat. ——.)

PART VII—WASH SALES; STRADDLES

§ 1091. Loss from wash sales of stock or securities

(a) **Disallowance of loss deduction.**—In the case of any loss claimed to have been sustained from any sale or other disposition of shares of stock or securities where it appears that, within a period beginning 30 days before the date of such sale or disposition and ending 30 days after such date, the taxpayer has acquired (by purchase or by an exchange on which the entire amount of gain or loss was recognized by law), or has entered into a contract or option so to acquire, substantially identical stock or securities, then no deduction shall be allowed under section 165 unless the taxpayer is a dealer in stock or securities and the loss is sustained in a transaction made in the ordinary course of such business.

(b) **Stock acquired less than stock sold.**—If the amount of stock or securities acquired (or covered by the contract or option to acquire) is less than the amount of stock or securities sold or otherwise disposed of, then the particular shares of stock or securities the loss from the sale or other disposition of which is not deductible shall be determined under regulations prescribed by the Secretary.

(c) **Stock acquired not less than stock sold.**—If the amount of stock or securities acquired (or covered by the contract or option to acquire) is not less than the amount of stock or securities sold or otherwise disposed of, then the particular shares of stock or securities the acquisition of which (or the contract or option to acquire which) resulted in the nondeductibility of the loss shall be determined under regulations prescribed by the Secretary.

(d) **Unadjusted basis in case of wash sale of stock.**—If the property consists of stock or securities the acquisition of which (or the contract or option to acquire which) resulted in the nondeductibility (under this section or corresponding provisions of prior internal revenue laws) of the loss from the sale or other disposition of substantially identical stock or securities, then the basis shall be the basis of the stock or securities so sold or disposed of, increased or decreased, as the case may be, by the difference, if any, between the price at which the property was acquired and the price at which such substantially identical stock or securities were sold or otherwise disposed of.

(e) **Certain short sales of stock or securities.**—Rules similar to the rules of subsection (a) shall apply to any loss realized on the closing of a short sale of stock or securities if, within a period beginning 30 days before the date of such closing and ending 30 days after such date—

(1) substantially identical stock or securities were sold, or

(2) another short sale of substantially identical stock or securities was entered into.

* * *

SUBCHAPTER P—CAPITAL GAINS AND LOSSES

PART I—TREATMENT OF CAPITAL GAINS

§ 1201.   Alternative tax for corporations

(a) **Corporations.**—If for any taxable year a corporation has a net capital gain and any rate of tax imposed by section 11, 511, or 831(a) (whichever is applicable) exceeds 34 percent (determined without regard to the last sentence of section 11(b)), then, in lieu of any such tax there is hereby imposed a tax (if such tax is less than the tax imposed by such sections) which shall consist of the sum of—

(1) a tax computed on the taxable income reduced by the amount of the net capital gain, at the rates and in the manner as if this subsection had not been enacted, plus

(2) a tax of 34 percent of the net capital gain.

* * *

§ 1202.   Deduction for capital gains [Repealed.]

PART II—TREATMENT OF CAPITAL LOSSES

§ 1211.   Limitation on capital losses

(a) **Corporations.**—In the case of a corporation, losses from sales or exchanges of capital assets shall be allowed only to the extent of gains from such sales or exchanges.

(b) **Other taxpayers.**—In the case of a taxpayer other than a corporation, losses from sales or exchanges of capital assets shall be allowed only to the extent of the gains from such sales or exchanges, plus (if such losses exceed such gains) the lower of—

§ 1212.   Capital loss carrybacks and carryovers

(a) **Corporations.**—

(1) **In general.**—If a corporation has a net capital loss for any taxable year (hereinafter in this paragraph referred to as the "loss year"), the amount thereof shall be—

(A) a capital loss carryback to each of the 3 taxable years preceding the loss year, but only to the extent—

* * *

(ii) the carryback of such loss does not increase or produce a net operating loss (as defined in section 172(c)) for the taxable year to which it is being carried back;

(B) except as provided in subparagraph (C), a capital loss carryover to each of the 5 taxable years succeeding the loss year; and

* * *

and shall be treated as a short-term capital loss in each such taxable year. The entire amount of the net capital loss for any taxable year shall be carried to the earliest of the taxable years to which such loss may be carried, and the portion of such loss which shall be carried to each of the other taxable years to which such loss may be carried shall be the excess, if any, of such loss over the total of the capital gain net income for each of the prior taxable years to which such loss may be carried. For purposes of the preceding sentence, the capital gain net income for any such prior taxable year shall be computed without regard to the net capital loss for the loss year or for any taxable year thereafter. In the case of any net capital loss which cannot be carried back in full to a preceding taxable year by reason of clause (ii) of subparagraph (A), the capital gain net income for such prior taxable year shall in no case be treated as greater than the amount of such loss which can be carried back to such preceding taxable year upon the application of such clause (ii).

* * *

(b) Other taxpayers.—

(1) **In general.**—If a taxpayer other than a corporation has a net capital loss for any taxable year—

(A) the excess of the net short-term capital loss over the net long-term capital gain for such year shall be a short-term capital loss in the succeeding taxable year, and

(B) the excess of the net long-term capital loss over the net short-term capital gain for such year shall be a long-term capital loss in the succeeding taxable year.

(2) **Special rule.**—For purposes of determining the excess referred to in subparagraph (A) or (B) of paragraph (1), an amount equal to the amount allowed for the taxable year under paragraph (1) or (2) of section 1211(b) shall be treated as a short-term capital gain in such year.

PART III—GENERAL RULES FOR DETERMINING CAPITAL GAINS AND LOSSES

§ 1221. Capital asset defined

For purposes of this subtitle, the term "capital asset" means property held by the taxpayer (whether or not connected with his trade or business), but does not include—

(1) stock in trade of the taxpayer or other property of a kind which would properly be included in the inventory of the taxpayer if on hand at the close of the taxable year, or property held by the taxpayer primarily for sale to customers in the ordinary course of his trade or business;

(2) property, used in his trade or business, of a character which is subject to the allowance for depreciation provided in section 167, or real property used in his trade or business;

(3) a copyright, a literary, musical, or artistic composition, a letter or memorandum, or similar property, held by—

(A) a taxpayer whose personal efforts created such property,

(B) in the case of a letter, memorandum, or similar property, a taxpayer for whom such property was prepared or produced, or

(C) a taxpayer in whose hands the basis of such property is determined, for purposes of determining gain from a sale or exchange, in whole or part by reference to the basis of such property in the hands of a taxpayer described in subparagraph (A) or (B);

(4) accounts or notes receivable acquired in the ordinary course of trade or business for services rendered or from the sale of property described in paragraph (1);

(5) a publication of the United States Government (including the Congressional Record) which is received from the United States Government or any agency thereof, other than by purchase at the price at which it is offered for sale to the public, and which is held by—

(A) a taxpayer who so received such publication, or

(B) a taxpayer in whose hands the basis of such publication is determined, for purposes of determining gain from a sale or exchange, in whole or in part by reference to the basis of such publication in the hands of a taxpayer described in subparagraph (A).

§ 1222.   Other terms relating to capital gains and losses

For purposes of this subtitle—

(1) **Short-term capital gain.**—The term "short-term capital gain" means gain from the sale or exchange of a capital asset held for not more than 6 months, if and to the extent such gain is taken into account in computing gross income.

(2) **Short-term capital loss.**—The term "short-term capital loss" means loss from the sale or exchange of a capital asset held for not more than 6 months, if and to the extent that such loss is taken into account in computing taxable income.

(3) **Long-term capital gain.**—The term "long-term capital gain" means gain from the sale or exchange of a capital asset held for more than 6 months, if and to the extent such gain is taken into account in computing gross income.

(4) **Long-term capital loss.**—The term "long-term capital loss" means loss from the sale or exchange of a capital asset held for more than 6 months, if and to the extent that such loss is taken into account in computing taxable income.

(5) **Net short-term capital gain.**—The term "net short-term capital gain" means the excess of short-term capital gains for the taxable year over the short-term capital losses for such year.

(6) **Net short-term capital loss.**—The term "net short-term capital loss" means the excess of short-term capital losses for the taxable year over the short-term capital gains for such year.

(7) **Net long-term capital gain.**—The term "net long-term capital gain" means the excess of long-term capital gains for the taxable year over the long-term capital losses for such year.

(8) **Net long-term capital loss.**—The term "net long-term capital loss" means the excess of long-term capital losses for the taxable year over the long-term capital gains for such year.

(9) **Capital gain net income.**—The term "capital gain net income" means the excess of the gains from sales or exchanges of capital assets over the losses from such sales or exchanges.

(10) **Net capital loss.**—The term "net capital loss" means the excess of the losses from sales or exchanges of capital assets over the sum allowed under section 1211. In the case of a corporation, for the purpose of determining losses under this paragraph, amounts which are short-term capital losses under section 1212 shall be excluded.

(11) **Net capital gain.**—The term "net capital gain" means the excess of the net long-term capital gain for the taxable year over the net short-term capital loss for such year.

For purposes of this subtitle, in the case of futures transactions in any commodity subject to the rules of a board of trade or commodity exchange, the length of the holding period taken into account under this section or under any other section amended by section 1402 of the Tax Reform Act of 1976 shall be determined without regard to the amendments made by subsections (a) and (b) of such section 1402.

§ 1223. Holding period of property

For purposes of this subtitle—

(1) In determining the period for which the taxpayer has held property received in an exchange, there shall be included the period for which he held the property exchanged if, under this chapter, the property has, for the purpose of determining gain or loss from a sale or exchange, the same basis in whole or in part in his hands as the property exchanged, and, in the case of such exchanges after March 1, 1954, the property exchanged at the time of such exchange was a capital asset as defined in section 1221 or property described in section 1231. For purposes of this paragraph—

(A) an involuntary conversion described in section 1033 shall be considered an exchange of the property converted for the property acquired, and

(B) a distribution to which section 355 (or so much of section 356 as relates to section 355) applies shall be treated as an exchange.

(2) In determining the period for which the taxpayer has held property however acquired there shall be included the period for which such property was held by any other person, if under this chapter such property has, for the purpose of determining gain or loss from a sale or exchange, the same basis in whole or in part in his hands as it would have in the hands of such other person.

* * *

(4) In determining the period for which the taxpayer has held stock or securities the acquisition of which (or the contract or option to acquire which) resulted in the nondeductibility (under section 1091 relating to wash sales) of the loss from the sale or other disposition of substantially identical stock or securities, there shall be included the period for which he held the stock or securities the loss from the sale or other disposition of which was not deductible.

(5) In determining the period for which the taxpayer has held stock or rights to acquire stock received on a distribution, if the basis of such stock or rights is determined under section 307 (or under so much of section 1052(c) as refers to section 113(a) (23) of the Internal Revenue Code of 1939), there shall (under regulations prescribed by the Secretary) be included the period for which he held the stock in the distributing corporation before the receipt of such stock or rights upon such distribution.

(6) In determining the period for which the taxpayer has held stock or securities acquired from a corporation by the exercise of rights to acquire such stock or securities, there shall be included only the period beginning with the date on which the right to acquire was exercised.

(7) In determining the period for which the taxpayer has held a residence, the acquisition of which resulted under section 1034 in the nonrecognition of any part of the gain realized on the sale or exchange of another residence, there shall be included the period for which such other residence had been held as of the date of

such sale or exchange. For purposes of this paragraph, the term "sale or exchange" includes an involuntary conversion occurring after December 31, 1950, and before January 1, 1954.

(8) In determining the period for which the taxpayer has held a commodity acquired in satisfaction of a commodity futures contract (other than a commodity futures contract to which section 1256 applies) there shall be included the period for which he held the commodity futures contract if such commodity futures contract was a capital asset in his hands.

* * *

(11) In the case of a person acquiring property from a decedent or to whom property passed from a decedent (within the meaning of section 1014(b)), if—

(A) the basis of such property in the hands of such person is determined under section 1014, and

(B) such property is sold or otherwise disposed of by such person within 6 months after the decedent's death,

then such person shall be considered to have held such property for more than 6 months.

(12) If—

(A) property is acquired by any person in a transfer to which section 1040 applies,

(B) such property is sold or otherwise disposed of by such person within 6 months after the decedent's death, and

(C) such sale or disposition is to a person who is a qualified heir (as defined in section 2032A(e)(1)) with respect to the decedent,

then the person making such sale or other disposition shall be considered to have held such property for more than 6 months.

* * *

(14) Cross references.—

(A) For special holding period provision relating to certain partnership distributions, see section 735(b).

(B) For special holding period provision relating to distributions of appreciated property to corporations, see section 301(e).

PART IV—SPECIAL RULES FOR DETERMINING CAPITAL GAINS AND LOSSES

§ 1231. Property used in the trade or business and involuntary conversions

(a) General rule.—

(1) Gains exceed losses.—If—

(A) the section 1231 gains for any taxable year, exceed

(B) the section 1231 losses for such taxable year,

such gains and losses shall be treated as long-term capital gains or long-term capital losses, as the case may be.

(2) Gains do not exceed losses.—If—

(A) the section 1231 gains for any taxable year, do not exceed

(B) the section 1231 losses for such taxable year,

such gains and losses shall not be treated as gains and losses from sales or exchanges of capital assets.

(3) Section 1231 gains and losses.—For purposes of this subsection—

(A) Section 1231 gain.—The term "section 1231 gain" means—

(i) any recognized gain on the sale or exchange of property used in the trade or business, and

(ii) any recognized gain from the compulsory or involuntary conversion (as a result of destruction in whole or in part, theft or seizure, or an exercise of the power of requisition or condemnation or the threat or imminence thereof) into other property or money of—

(I) property used in the trade or business, or

(II) any capital asset which is held for more than 6 months and is held in connection with a trade or business or a transaction entered into for profit.

(B) Section 1231 loss.—The term "section 1231 loss" means any recognized loss from a sale or exchange or conversion described in subparagraph (A).

(4) Special rules.—For purposes of this subsection—

(A) In determining under this subsection whether gains exceed losses—

(i) the section 1231 gains shall be included only if and to the extent taken into account in computing gross income, and

(ii) the section 1231 losses shall be included only if and to the extent taken into account in computing taxable income, except that section 1211 shall not apply.

(B) Losses (including losses not compensated for by insurance or otherwise) on the destruction, in whole or in part, theft or seizure, or requisition or condemnation of—

(i) property used in the trade or business, or

(ii) capital assets which are held for more than 6 months and are held in connection with a trade or business or a transaction entered into for profit,

shall be treated as losses from a compulsory or involuntary conversion.

(C) In the case of any involuntary conversion (subject to the provisions of this subsection but for this sentence) arising from fire, storm, shipwreck, or other casualty, or from theft, of any—

(i) property used in the trade or business, or

(ii) any capital asset which is held for more than 6 months and is held in connection with a trade or business or a transaction entered into for profit,

this subsection shall not apply to such conversion (whether resulting in gain or loss) if during the taxable year the recognized losses from such conversions exceed the recognized gains from such conversions.

(b) Definition of property used in the trade or business.—For purposes of this section—

(1) General rule.—The term "property used in the trade or business" means property used in the trade or business, of a character which is subject to the allowance for depreciation provided in section 167, held for more than 6 months, and real property used in the trade or business, held for more than 6 months, which is not—

(A) property of a kind which would properly be includible in the inventory of the taxpayer if on hand at the close of the taxable year,

(B) property held by the taxpayer primarily for sale to customers in the ordinary course of his trade or business,

(C) a copyright, a literary, musical, or artistic composition, a letter or memorandum, or similar property, held by a taxpayer described in paragraph (3) of section 1221, or

(D) a publication of the United States Government (including the Congressional Record) which is received from the United States Government, or any agency thereof, other than by purchase at the price at which it is offered for sale to the public, and which is held by a taxpayer described in paragraph (5) of section 1221.

(2) **Timber, coal, or domestic iron ore.**—Such term includes timber, coal, and iron ore with respect to which section 631 applies.

(3) **Livestock.**—Such term includes—

(A) cattle and horses, regardless of age, held by the taxpayer for draft, breeding, dairy, or sporting purposes, and held by him for 24 months or more from the date of acquisition, and

(B) other livestock, regardless of age, held by the taxpayer for draft, breeding, dairy, or sporting purposes, and held by him for 12 months or more from the date of acquisition.

Such term does not include poultry.

(4) **Unharvested crop.**—In the case of an unharvested crop on land used in the trade or business and held for more than 6 months, if the crop and the land are sold or exchanged (or compulsorily or involuntarily converted) at the same time and to the same person, the crop shall be considered as "property used in the trade or business."

(c) **Recapture of net ordinary losses.**—

(1) **In general.**—The net section 1231 gain for any taxable year shall be treated as ordinary income to the extent such gain does not exceed the non-recaptured net section 1231 losses.

(2) **Non-recaptured net section 1231 losses.**—For purposes of this subsection, the term "non-recaptured net section 1231 losses" means the excess of—

(A) the aggregate amount of the net section 1231 losses for the 5 most recent preceding taxable years beginning after December 31, 1981, over

(B) the portion of such losses taken into account under paragraph (1) for such preceding taxable years.

(3) **Net section 1231 gain.**—For purposes of this subsection, the term "net section 1231 gain" means the excess of—

(A) the section 1231 gains, over

(B) the section 1231 losses.

(4) **Net section 1231 loss.**—For purposes of this subsection, the term "net section 1231 loss" means the excess of—

(A) the section 1231 losses, over

(B) the section 1231 gains.

(5) Special rules.—For purposes of determining the amount of the net section 1231 gain or loss for any taxable year, the rules of paragraph (4) of subsection (a) shall apply.

§ 1233. Gains and losses from short sales

(a) Capital assets.—For purposes of this subtitle, gain or loss from the short sale of property shall be considered as gain or loss from the sale or exchange of a capital asset to the extent that the property, including a commodity future, used to close the short sale constitutes a capital asset in the hands of the taxpayer.

(b) Short-term gains and holding periods.—If gain or loss from a short sale is considered as gain or loss from the sale or exchange of a capital asset under subsection (a) and if on the date of such short sale substantially identical property has been held by the taxpayer for not more than 6 months (determined without regard to the effect, under paragraph (2) of this subsection, of such short sale on the holding period), or if substantially identical property is acquired by the taxpayer after such short sale and on or before the date of the closing thereof—

(1) any gain on the closing of such short sale shall be considered as a gain on the sale or exchange of a capital asset held for not more than 6 months (notwithstanding the period of time any property used to close such short sale has been held); and

(2) the holding period of such substantially identical property shall be considered to begin (notwithstanding section 1223, relating to the holding period of property) on the date of the closing of the short sale, or on the date of a sale, gift, or other disposition of such property, whichever date occurs first. This paragraph shall apply to such substantially identical property in the order of the dates of the acquisition of such property, but only to so much of such property as does not exceed the quantity sold short.

For purposes of this subsection, the acquisition of an option to sell property at a fixed price shall be considered as a short sale, and the exercise or failure to exercise such option shall be considered as a closing of such short sale.

(c) Certain options to sell.—Subsection (b) shall not include an option to sell property at a fixed price acquired on the same day on which the property identified as intended to be used in exercising such option is acquired and which, if exercised, is exercised through the sale of the property so identified. If the option is not exercised, the cost of the option shall be added to the basis of the property with which the option is identified. This subsection shall apply only to options acquired after August 16, 1954.

(d) Long-term losses.—If on the date of such short sale substantially identical property has been held by the taxpayer for more than 6 months, any loss on the closing of such short sale shall be considered as a loss on the sale or exchange of a capital asset held for more than 6 months (notwithstanding the period of time any property used to close such short sale has been held, and notwithstanding section 1234).

* * *

(g) Hedging transactions.—This section shall not apply in the case of a hedging transaction in commodity futures.

§ 1234. Options to buy or sell

(a) Treatment of gain or loss in the case of the purchaser.—

607

(1) General rule.—Gain or loss attributable to the sale or exchange of, or loss attributable to failure to exercise, an option to buy or sell property shall be considered gain or loss from the sale or exchange of property which has the same character as the property to which the option relates has in the hands of the taxpayer (or would have in the hands of the taxpayer if acquired by him).

(2) Special rule for loss attributable to failure to exercise option.—For purposes of paragraph (1), if loss is attributable to failure to exercise an option, the option shall be deemed to have been sold or exchanged on the day it expired.

(3) Nonapplication of subsection.—This subsection shall not apply to—

(A) an option which constitutes property described in paragraph (1) of section 1221;

(B) in the case of gain attributable to the sale or exchange of an option, any income derived in connection with such option which, without regard to this subsection, is treated as other than gain from the sale or exchange of a capital asset; and

(C) a loss attributable to failure to exercise an option described in section 1233(c).

(b) Treatment of grantor of option in the case of stock, securities, or commodities.—

(1) General rule.—In the case of the grantor of the option, gain or loss from any closing transaction with respect to, and gain on lapse of, an option in property shall be treated as a gain or loss from the sale or exchange of a capital asset held not more than 6 months.

(2) Definitions.—For purposes of this subsection—

(A) Closing transaction.—The term "closing transaction" means any termination of the taxpayer's obligation under an option in property other than through the exercise or lapse of the option.

(B) Property.—The term "property" means stocks and securities (including stocks and securities dealt with on a "when issued" basis), commodities, and commodity futures.

(3) Nonapplication of subsection.—This subsection shall not apply to any option granted in the ordinary course of the taxpayer's trade or business of granting options.

(c) Treatment of options on section 1256 contracts and cash settlement options.—

(1) Section 1256 contracts.—Gain or loss shall be recognized on the exercise of an option on a section 1256 contract (within the meaning of section 1256(b)).

(2) Treatment of cash settlement options.—

(A) In general.—For purposes of subsections (a) and (b), a cash settlement option shall be treated as an option to buy or sell property.

(B) Cash settlement option.—For purposes of subparagraph (A), the term "cash settlement option" means any option which on exercise settles in (or could be settled in) cash or property other than the underlying property.

§ 1235. Sale or exchange of patents

(a) General.—A transfer (other than by gift, inheritance, or devise) of property consisting of all substantial rights to a patent, or an undivided interest therein which includes a part of all such rights, by any holder shall be considered the sale or exchange of a capital asset held for more than 6 months, regardless of whether or not payments in consideration of such transfer are—

(1) payable periodically over a period generally coterminous with the transferee's use of the patent, or

(2) contingent on the productivity, use, or disposition of the property transferred.

(b) "Holder" defined.—For purposes of this section, the term "holder" means—

(1) any individual whose efforts created such property, or

(2) any other individual who has acquired his interest in such property in exchange for consideration in money or money's worth paid to such creator prior to actual reduction to practice of the invention covered by the patent, if such individual is neither—

(A) the employer of such creator, nor

(B) related to such creator (within the meaning of subsection (d)).

* * *

(d) Related persons.—Subsection (a) shall not apply to any transfer, directly or indirectly, between persons specified within any one of the paragraphs of section 267(b) or persons described in section 707(b); except that, in applying section 267(b) and (c) and section 707(b) for purposes of this section—

(1) the phrase "25 percent or more" shall be substituted for the phrase "more than 50 percent" each place it appears in section 267(b) or 707(b), and

(2) paragraph (4) of section 267(c) shall be treated as providing that the family of an individual shall include only his spouse, ancestors, and lineal descendants.

* * *

§ 1236. Dealers in securities

(a) Capital gains.—Gain by a dealer in securities from the sale or exchange of any security shall in no event be considered as gain from the sale or exchange of a capital asset unless—

(1) the security was, before the close of the day on which it was acquired (or such earlier time as the Secretary may prescribe by regulations), clearly identified in the dealer's records as a security held for investment; and

(2) the security was not, at any time after the close of such day (or such earlier time), held by such dealer primarily for sale to customers in the ordinary course of his trade or business.

(b) Ordinary losses.—Loss by a dealer in securities from the sale or exchange of any security shall, except as otherwise provided in section 582(c), (relating to bond, etc., losses of banks), in no event be considered as ordinary loss if at any time after November 19, 1951, the security was clearly identified in the dealer's records as a security held for investment.

(c) Definition of security.—For purposes of this section, the term "security" means any share of stock in any corporation, certificate of stock or interest in any corporation, note, bond, debenture, or evidence of indebtedness, or any evidence of an interest in or right to subscribe to or purchase any of the foregoing.

§ 1237. Real property subdivided for sale

(a) General.—Any lot or parcel which is part of a tract of real property in the hands of a taxpayer other than a corporation shall not be deemed to be held primarily for sale to customers in the ordinary course of trade or business at the time of sale solely because of the taxpayer having subdivided such tract for purposes of sale or because of any activity incident to such subdivision or sale, if—

(1) such tract, or any lot or parcel thereof, had not previously been held by such taxpayer primarily for sale to customers in the ordinary course of trade or business (unless such tract at such previous time would have been covered by this section) and, in the same taxable year in which the sale occurs, such taxpayer does not so hold any other real property; and

(2) no substantial improvement that substantially enhances the value of the lot or parcel sold is made by the taxpayer on such tract while held by the taxpayer or is made pursuant to a contract of sale entered into between the taxpayer and the buyer. For purposes of this paragraph, an improvement shall be deemed to be made by the taxpayer if such improvement was made by—

(A) the taxpayer or members of his family (as defined in section 267(c) (4)), by a corporation controlled by the taxpayer, or by a partnership which included the taxpayer as a partner; or

(B) a lessee, but only if the improvement constitutes income to the taxpayer; or

(C) Federal, State, or local government, or political subdivision thereof, but only if the improvement constitutes an addition to basis for the taxpayer; and

(3) such lot or parcel, except in the case of real property acquired by inheritance or devise, is held by the taxpayer for a period of 5 years.

(b) Special rules for application of section.—

(1) Gains.—If more than 5 lots or parcels contained in the same tract of real property are sold or exchanged, gain from any sale or exchange (which occurs in or after the taxable year in which the sixth lot or parcel is sold or exchanged) of any lot or parcel which comes within the provisions of paragraphs (1), (2) and (3) of subsection (a) of this section shall be deemed to be gain from the sale of property held primarily for sale to customers in the ordinary course of the trade or business to the extent of 5 percent of the selling price.

(2) Expenditures of sale.—For the purpose of computing gain under paragraph (1) of this subsection, expenditures incurred in connection with the sale or exchange of any lot or parcel shall neither be allowed as a deduction in computing taxable income, nor treated as reducing the amount realized on such sale or exchange; but so much of such expenditures as does not exceed the portion of gain deemed under paragraph (1) of this subsection to be gain from the sale of property held primarily for sale to customers in the ordinary course of trade or business shall be so allowed as a deduction, and the remainder, if any, shall be treated as reducing the amount realized on such sale or exchange.

(3) Necessary improvements.—No improvement shall be deemed a substantial improvement for purposes of subsection (a) if the lot or parcel is held by the taxpayer for a period of 10 years and if—

(A) such improvement is the building or installation of water, sewer, or drainage facilities or roads (if such improvement would except for this paragraph constitute a substantial improvement);

(B) it is shown to the satisfaction of the Secretary that the lot or parcel, the value of which was substantially enhanced by such improvement, would not have been marketable at the prevailing local price for similar building sites without such improvement; and

(C) the taxpayer elects, in accordance with regulations prescribed by the Secretary, to make no adjustment to basis of the lot or parcel, or of any other property owned by the taxpayer, on account of the expenditures for such improvements. Such election shall not make any item deductible which would not otherwise be deductible.

(c) Tract defined.—For purposes of this section, the term "tract of real property" means a single piece of real property, except that 2 or more pieces of real property shall be considered a tract if at any time they were contiguous in the hands of the taxpayer or if they would be contiguous except for the interposition of a road, street, railroad, stream, or similar property. If, following the sale or exchange of any lot or parcel from a tract of real property, no further sales or exchanges of any other lots or parcels from the remainder of such tract are made for a period of 5 years, such remainder shall be deemed a tract.

§ 1239. Gain from sale of depreciable property between certain related taxpayers

(a) Treatment of gain as ordinary income.—In the case of a sale or exchange of property, directly or indirectly, between related persons, any gain recognized to the transferor shall be treated as ordinary income if such property is, in the hands of the transferee, of a character which is subject to the allowance for depreciation provided in section 167.

(b) Related persons.—For purposes of subsection (a), the term "related persons" means—

(1) a person and all entities which are controlled entities with respect to such person,

(2) a taxpayer and any trust in which such taxpayer (or his spouse) is a beneficiary, unless such beneficiary's interest in the trust is a remote contingent interest (within the meaning of section 318(a)(3)(B)(i)).

(c) Controlled entity defined.—

(1) **General rule.**—For purposes of this section, the term "controlled entity" means, with respect to any person—

(A) a corporation more than 50 percent of the value of the outstanding stock of which is owned (directly or indirectly) by or for such person,

(B) a partnership more than 50 percent of the capital interest or profits interest in which is owned (directly or indirectly) by or for such person, and

(C) any entity which is a related person to such person under paragraph (3), (10), (11), or (12) of section 267(b).

(2) **Constructive ownership.**—For purposes of this section, ownership shall be determined in accordance with rules similar to the rules under section 267(c) (other than paragraph (3) thereof).

(d) Employer and related employee association.—For purposes of subsection (a), the term "related person" also includes—

(1) an employer and any person related to the employer (within the meaning of subsection (b)), and

(2) a welfare benefit fund (within the meaning of section 419(e)) which is controlled directly or indirectly by persons referred to in paragraph (1).

(e) Patent applications treated as depreciable property.—For purposes of this section, a patent application shall be treated as property which, in the hands of the transferee, is of a character which is subject to the allowance for depreciation provided in section 167.

§ 1241. Cancellation of lease or distributor's agreement

Amounts received by a lessee for the cancellation of a lease, or by a distributor of goods for the cancellation of a distributor's agreement (if the distributor has a substantial capital investment in the distributorship), shall be considered as amounts received in exchange for such lease or agreement.

§ 1244. Losses on small business stock

(a) **General rule.**—In the case of an individual, a loss on section 1244 stock issued to such individual or to a partnership which would (but for this section) be treated as a loss from the sale or exchange of a capital asset shall, to the extent provided in this section, be treated as an ordinary loss.

(b) **Maximum amount for any taxable year.**—For any taxable year the aggregate amount treated by the taxpayer by reason of this section as an ordinary loss shall not exceed—

(1) $50,000, or

(2) $100,000, in the case of a husband and wife filing a joint return for such year under section 6013.

(c) **Section 1244 stock defined.**—

(1) **In general.**—For purposes of this section, the term "section 1244 stock" means stock in a domestic corporation if—

(A) at the time such stock is issued, such corporation was a small business corporation,

(B) such stock was issued by such corporation for money or other property (other than stock and securities), and

(C) such corporation, during the period of its 5 most recent taxable years ending before the date the loss on such stock was sustained, derived more than 50 percent of its aggregate gross receipts from sources other than royalties, rents, dividends, interests, annuities, and sales or exchanges of stocks or securities.

(2) **Rules for application of paragraph (1) (C).**—

(A) **Period taken into account with respect to new corporations.**—For purposes of paragraph (1) (C), if the corporation has not been in existence for 5 taxable years ending before the date the loss on the stock was sustained, there shall be substituted for such 5-year period—

(i) the period of the corporation's taxable years ending before such date, or

(ii) if the corporation has not been in existence for 1 taxable year ending before such date, the period such corporation has been in existence before such date.

(B) **Gross receipts from sales of securities.**—For purposes of paragraph (1) (C), gross receipts from the sales or exchanges of stock or securities shall be taken into account only to the extent of gains therefrom.

(C) **Nonapplication where deductions exceed gross income.**—Paragraph (1) (C) shall not apply with respect to any corporation if, for the period taken into account for purposes of paragraph (1) (C), the amount of the deductions allowed by this chapter (other than by sections 172, 243, 244, and 245) exceeds the amount of gross income.

(3) **Small business corporation defined.—**

(A) **In general.**—For purposes of this section, a corporation shall be treated as a small business corporation if the aggregate amount of money and other property received by the corporation for stock, as a contribution to capital, and as paid-in surplus, does not exceed $1,000,000. The determination under the preceding sentence shall be made as of the time of the issuance of the stock in question but shall include amounts received for such stock and for all stock theretofore issued.

(B) **Amount taken into account with respect to property.**—For purposes of subparagraph (A), the amount taken into account with respect to any property other than money shall be the amount equal to the adjusted basis to the corporation of such property for determining gain, reduced by any liability to which the property was subject or which was assumed by the corporation. The determination under the preceding sentence shall be made as of the time the property was received by the corporation.

(d) **Special rules.—**

(1) **Limitations on amount of ordinary loss.—**

(A) **Contributions of property having basis in excess of value.**—If—

(i) section 1244 stock was issued in exchange for property,

(ii) the basis of such stock in the hands of the taxpayer is determined by reference to the basis in his hands of such property, and

(iii) the adjusted basis (for determining loss) of such property immediately before the exchange exceeded its fair market value at such time,

then in computing the amount of the loss on such stock for purposes of this section the basis of such stock shall be reduced by an amount equal to the excess described in clause (iii).

(B) **Increases in basis.**—In computing the amount of the loss on stock for purposes of this section, any increase in the basis of such stock (through contributions to the capital of the corporation, or otherwise) shall be treated as allocable to stock which is not section 1244 stock.

(2) **Recapitalizations, changes in name, etc.**—To the extent provided in regulations prescribed by the Secretary, stock in a corporation, the basis of which (in the hands of a taxpayer) is determined in whole or in part by reference to the basis in his hands of stock in such corporation which meets the requirements of subsection (c)(1) (other than subparagraph (C) thereof); or which is received in a reorganization described in section 368(a)(1)(F) in exchange for stock which meets such requirements, shall be treated as meeting such requirements. For purposes of paragraphs (1)(C) and (3)(A) of subsection (c), a successor corporation in a reorganization described in section 368(a)(1)(F) shall be treated as the same corporation as its predecessor.

(3) **Relationship to net operating loss deduction.**—For purposes of section 172 (relating to the net operating loss deduction), any amount of loss treated by reason of this section as an ordinary loss shall be treated as attributable to a trade or business of the taxpayer.

(4) **Individual defined.**—For purposes of this section, the term "individual" does not include a trust or estate.

(e) **Regulations.**—The Secretary shall prescribe such regulations as may be necessary to carry out the purposes of this section.

§ 1245. Gain from dispositions of certain depreciable property

(a) General rule.—

(1) Ordinary income.—Except as otherwise provided in this section, if section 1245 property is disposed of the amount by which the lower of—

(A) the recomputed basis of the property, or

(B) (i) in the case of a sale, exchange, or involuntary conversion, the amount realized, or

(ii) in the case of any other disposition, the fair market value of such property,

exceeds the adjusted basis of such property shall be treated as ordinary income. Such gain shall be recognized notwithstanding any other provision of this subtitle.

(2) Recomputed basis.—For purposes of this section—

(A) In general.—The term "recomputed basis" means, with respect to any property, its adjusted basis recomputed by adding thereto all adjustments reflected in such adjusted basis on account of deductions (whether in respect of the same or other property) allowed or allowable to the taxpayer or to any other person for depreciation or amortization.

(B) Taxpayer may establish amount allowed.—For purposes of subparagraph (A), if the taxpayer can establish by adequate records or other sufficient evidence that the amount allowed for depreciation or amortization for any period was less than the amount allowable, the amount added for such period shall be the amount allowed.

(C) Certain deductions treated as amortization.—Any deduction allowable under section 179, 190, or 193 shall be treated as if it were a deduction allowable for amortization.

(3) Section 1245 property.—For purposes of this section, the term "section 1245 property" means any property which is or has been property of a character subject to the allowance for depreciation provided in section 167 (or subject to the allowance of amortization provided in section 185) and is either—

(A) personal property,

(B) other property (not including a building or its structural components) but only if such other property is tangible and has an adjusted basis in which there are reflected adjustments described in paragraph (2) for a period in which such property (or other property)—

(i) was used as an integral part of manufacturing, production, or extraction or of furnishing transportation, communications, electrical energy, gas, water, or sewage disposal services,

(ii) constituted a research facility used in connection with any of the activities referred to in clause (i), or

(iii) constituted a facility used in connection with any of the activities referred to in clause (i) for the bulk storage of fungible commodities (including commodities in a liquid or gaseous state),

(C) so much of any real property (other than any property described in subparagraph (B)) which has an adjusted basis in which there are reflected adjustments for amortization under section 169, 179, 185, 188, 190, 193, or 194,

(D) a single purpose agricultural or horticultural structure (as defined in section 48(p)), or

(E) a storage facility (not including a building or its structural components) used in connection with the distribution of petroleum or any primary product of petroleum.

(4) Special rule for player contracts.—

(A) In general.—For purposes of this section, if a franchise to conduct any sports enterprise is sold or exchanged, and if, in connection with such sale or exchange, there is a transfer of any player contracts, the recomputed basis of such player contracts in the hands of the transferor shall be the adjusted basis of such contracts increased by the greater of—

(i) the previously unrecaptured depreciation with respect to player contracts acquired by the transferor at the time of acquisition of such franchise, or

(ii) the previously unrecaptured depreciation with respect to the player contracts involved in such transfer.

(B) Previously unrecaptured depreciation with respect to initial contracts.—For purposes of subparagraph (A) (i), the term "previously unrecaptured depreciation" means the excess (if any) of—

(i) the sum of the deduction allowed or allowable to the taxpayer transferor for the depreciation attributable to periods after December 31, 1975, of any player contracts acquired by him at the time of acquisition of such franchise, plus the deduction allowed or allowable for losses incurred after December 31, 1975, with respect to such player contracts acquired at the time of such acquisition, over

(ii) the aggregate of the amounts described in clause (i) treated as ordinary income by reason of this section with respect to prior dispositions of such player contracts acquired upon acquisition of the franchise.

(C) Previously unrecaptured depreciation with respect to contracts transferred.—For purposes of subparagraph (A) (ii), the term "previously unrecaptured depreciation" means the amount of any deduction allowed or allowable to the taxpayer transferor for the depreciation of any contracts involved in such transfer.

(D) Player contract.—For purposes of this paragraph, the term "player contract" means any contract for the services of an athlete which, in the hands of the taxpayer, is of a character subject to the allowance for depreciation provided in section 167.

* * *

(b) Exceptions and limitations.—

(1) Gifts.—Subsection (a) shall not apply to a disposition by gift.

(2) Transfers at death.—Except as provided in section 691 (relating to income in respect of a decedent), subsection (a) shall not apply to a transfer at death.

(3) Certain tax-free transactions.—If the basis of property in the hands of a transferee is determined by reference to its basis in the hands of the transferor by reason of the application of section 332, 351, 361, 371(a), 374(a), 721, or 731, then the amount of gain taken into account by the transferor under subsection (a) (1) shall not exceed the amount of gain recognized to the transferor on the transfer of such property (determined without regard to this section). Except as provided in paragraph (7), this paragraph shall not apply to a disposition to an organization (other than a cooperative described in section 521) which is exempt from the tax imposed by this chapter.

(4) **Like kind exchanges; involuntary conversions, etc.**—If property is disposed of and gain (determined without regard to this section) is not recognized in whole or in part under section 1031 or 1033, then the amount of gain taken into account by the transferor under subsection (a) (1) shall not exceed the sum of—

(A) the amount of gain recognized on such disposition (determined without regard to this section), plus

(B) the fair market value of property acquired which is not section 1245 property and which is not taken into account under subparagraph (A).

* * *

(6) **Property distributed by a partnership to a partner.**—

(A) **In general.**—For purposes of this section, the basis of section 1245 property distributed by a partnership to a partner shall be deemed to be determined by reference to the adjusted basis of such property to the partnership.

(B) **Adjustments added back.**—In the case of any property described in subparagraph (A), for purposes of computing the recomputed basis of such property the amount of the adjustments added back for periods before the distribution by the partnership shall be—

(i) the amount of the gain to which subsection (a) would have applied if such property had been sold by the partnership immediately before the distribution at its fair market value at such time, reduced by

(ii) the amount of such gain to which section 751(b) applied.

(7) **Transfers to tax-exempt organization where property will be used in unrelated business.**—

(A) **In general.**—The second sentence of paragraph (3) shall not apply to a disposition of section 1245 property to an organization described in section 511(a) (2) or 511(b) (2) if, immediately after such disposition, such organization uses such property in an unrelated trade or business (as defined in section 513).

(B) **Later change in use.**—If any property with respect to the disposition of which gain is not recognized by reason of subparagraph (A) ceases to be used in an unrelated trade or business of the organization acquiring such property, such organization shall be treated for purposes of this section as having disposed of such property on the date of such cessation.

(8) **Timber property.**—In determining, under subsection (a)(2), the recomputed basis of property with respect to which a deduction under section 194 was allowed for any taxable year, the taxpayer shall not take into account adjustments under section 194 to the extent such adjustments are attributable to the amortizable basis of the taxpayer acquired before the 10th taxable year preceding the taxable year in which gain with respect to the property is recognized.

(c) **Adjustments to basis.**—The Secretary shall prescribe such regulations as he may deem necessary to provide for adjustments to the basis of property to reflect gain recognized under subsection (a).

(d) **Application of section.**—This section shall apply notwithstanding any other provision of this subtitle.

§ 1250. Gain from dispositions of certain depreciable realty

(a) **General rule.**—Except as otherwise provided in this section—

(1) **Additional depreciation after December 31, 1975.**—

(A) In general.—If section 1250 property is disposed of after December 31, 1975, then the applicable percentage of the lower of—

(i) that portion of the additional depreciation (as defined in subsection (b) (1) or (4)) attributable to periods after December 31, 1975, in respect of the property, or

(ii) the excess of the amount realized (in the case of a sale, exchange, or involuntary conversion), or the fair market value of such property (in the case of any other disposition), over the adjusted basis of such property,

shall be treated as gain which is ordinary income. Such gain shall be recognized notwithstanding any other provision of this subtitle.

(B) Applicable percentage.—For purposes of subparagraph (A), the term "applicable percentage" means—

(i) in the case of section 1250 property with respect to which a mortgage is insured under section 221(d) (3) or 236 of the National Housing Act, or housing financed or assisted by direct loan or tax abatement under similar provisions of State or local laws and with respect to which the owner is subject to the restrictions described in section 1039(b) (1) (B), 100 percent minus 1 percentage point for each full month the property was held after the date the property was held 100 full months;

(ii) in the case of dwelling units which, on the average, were held for occupancy by families or individuals eligible to receive subsidies under section 8 of the United States Housing Act of 1937, as amended, or under the provisions of State or local law authorizing similar levels of subsidy for lower-income families, 100 percent minus 1 percentage point for each full month the property was held after the date the property was held 100 full months;

(iii) in the case of section 1250 property with respect to which a depreciation deduction for rehabilitation expenditures was allowed under section 167(k), 100 percent minus 1 percentage point for each full month in excess of 100 full months after the date on which such property was placed in service;

(iv) in the case of section 1250 property with respect to which a loan is made or insured under title V of the Housing Act of 1949, 100 percent minus 1 percentage point for each full month the property was held after the date the property was held 100 full months; and

(v) in the case of all other section 1250 property, 100 percent.

In the case of a building (or a portion of a building devoted to dwelling units), if, on the average, 85 percent or more of the dwelling units contained in such building (or portion thereof) are units described in clause (ii), such building (or portion thereof) shall be treated as property described in clause (ii). Clauses (i), (ii), and (iv) shall not apply with respect to the additional depreciation described in subsection (b) (4) which was allowed under section 167(k).

(2) Additional depreciation after December 31, 1969, and before January 1, 1976.—

(A) In general.—If section 1250 property is disposed of after December 31, 1969, and the amount determined under paragraph (1) (A) (ii) exceeds the amount determined under paragraph (1) (A) (i), then the applicable percentage of the lower of—

(i) that portion of the additional depreciation attributable to periods after December 31, 1969, and before January 1, 1976, in respect of the property, or

(ii) the excess of the amount determined under paragraph (1) (A) (ii) over the amount determined under paragraph (1) (A) (i),

shall also be treated as gain which is ordinary income. Such gain shall be recognized notwithstanding any other provision of this subtitle.

(B) Applicable percentage.—For purposes of subparagraph (A), the term "applicable percentage" means—

(i) in the case of section 1250 property disposed of pursuant to a written contract which was, on July 24, 1969, and at all times thereafter, binding on the owner of the property, 100 percent minus 1 percentage point for each full month the property was held after the date the property was held 20 full months;

(ii) in the case of section 1250 property with respect to which a mortgage is insured under section 221(d) (3) or 236 of the National Housing Act, or housing financed or assisted by direct loan or tax abatement under similar provisions of State or local laws, and with respect to which the owner is subject to the restrictions described in section 1039(b) (1) (B), 100 percent minus 1 percentage point for each full month the property was held after the date the property was held 20 full months;

(iii) in the case of residential rental property (as defined in section 167(j) (2) (B)) other than that covered by clauses (i) and (ii), 100 percent minus 1 percentage point for each full month the property was held after the date the property was held 100 full months;

(iv) in the case of section 1250 property with respect to which a depreciation deduction for rehabilitation expenditures was allowed under section 167(k), 100 percent minus 1 percentage point for each full month in excess of 100 full months after the date on which such property was placed in service; and

(v) in the case of all other section 1250 property, 100 percent.

Clauses (i), (ii), and (iii) shall not apply with respect to the additional depreciation described in subsection (b) (4).

(3) Additional depreciation before January 1, 1970.—

(A) In general.—If section 1250 property is disposed of after December 31, 1963, and the amount determined under paragraph (1) (A) (ii) exceeds the sum of the amounts determined under paragraphs (1) (A) (i) and (2) (A) (i), then the applicable percentage of the lower of—

(i) that portion of the additional depreciation attributable to periods before January 1, 1970, in respect of the property, or

(ii) the excess of the amount determined under paragraph (1) (A) (ii) over the sum of the amounts determined under paragraphs (1) (A) (i) and (2) (A) (i),

shall also be treated as gain which is ordinary income. Such gain shall be recognized notwithstanding any other provision of this subtitle.

(B) Applicable percentage.—For purposes of subparagraph (A), the term "applicable percentage" means 100 percent minus 1 percentage point for each full month the property was held after the date on which the property was held for 20 full months.

(4) Cross reference.—

For reduction in the case of corporations on capital gain treatment under this section, see section 291(a)(1).

(b) Additional depreciation defined.—For purposes of this section—

(1) **In general.**—The term "additional depreciation" means, in the case of any property, the depreciation adjustments in respect of such property; except that, in the case of property held more than one year, it means such adjustments only to the extent that they exceed the amount of the depreciation adjustments which would have resulted if such adjustments had been determined for each taxable year under the straight line method of adjustment.

(2) **Property held by lessee.**—In the case of a lessee, in determining the depreciation adjustments which would have resulted in respect of any building erected (or other improvement made) on the leased property, or in respect of any cost of acquiring the lease, the lease period shall be treated as including all renewal periods. For purposes of the preceding sentence—

(A) the term "renewal period" means any period for which the lease may be renewed, extended, or continued pursuant to an option exercisable by the lessee, but

(B) the inclusion of renewal periods shall not extend the period taken into account by more than $\frac{2}{3}$ of the period on the basis of which the depreciation adjustments were allowed.

(3) **Depreciation adjustments.**—The term "depreciation adjustments" means, in respect of any property, all adjustments attributable to periods after December 31, 1963, reflected in the adjusted basis of such property on account of deductions (whether in respect of the same or other property) allowed or allowable to the taxpayer or to any other person for exhaustion, wear and tear, obsolescence, or amortization (other than amortization under section 168 (as in effect before its repeal by the Tax Reform Act of 1976), 169, 185 (as in effect before its repeal by the Tax Reform Act of 1986), 188, 190, or 193). For purposes of the preceding sentence, if the taxpayer can establish by adequate records or other sufficient evidence that the amount allowed as a deduction for any period was less than the amount allowable, the amount taken into account for such period shall be the amount allowed.

(4) **Additional depreciation attributable to rehabilitation expenditures.**—The term "additional depreciation" also means, in the case of section 1250 property with respect to which a depreciation or amortization deduction for rehabilitation expenditures was allowed under section 167(k) or 191 (as in effect before its repeal by the Economic Recovery Tax Act of 1981), the depreciation or amortization adjustments allowed under such section to the extent attributable to such property, except that, in the case of such property held for more than one year after the rehabilitation expenditures so allowed were incurred, it means such adjustments only to the extent that they exceed the amount of the depreciation adjustments which would have resulted if such adjustments had been determined under the straight line method of adjustment without regard to the useful life permitted under section 167(k) or 191 (as in effect before its repeal by the Economic Recovery Tax Act of 1981).

(5) **Method of computing straight line adjustments.**—For purposes of paragraph (1), the depreciation adjustments which would have resulted for any taxable year under the straight line method shall be determined—

(A) in the case of recovery property, by determining the adjustments which would have resulted for such year if the taxpayer had elected the straight line method for such year using the recovery period applicable to such property, and

(B) in the case of any property which is not recovery property, if a useful life (or salvage value) was used in determining the amount allowable as a deduction for any taxable year, by using such life (or value).

(c) Section 1250 property.—For purposes of this section, the term "section 1250 property" means any real property (other than section 1245 property, as defined in section 1245(a) (3)) which is or has been property of a character subject to the allowance for depreciation provided in section 167.

(d) Exceptions and limitations.—

(1) **Gifts.**—Subsection (a) shall not apply to a disposition by gift.

(2) **Transfers at death.**—Except as provided in section 691 (relating to income in respect of a decedent), subsection (a) shall not apply to a transfer at death.

(3) **Certain tax-free transactions.**—If the basis of property in the hands of a transferee is determined by reference to its basis in the hands of the transferor by reason of the application of section 332, 351, 361, 371(a), 374(a), 721, or 731, then the amount of gain taken into account by the transferor under subsection (a) shall not exceed the amount of gain recognized to the transferor on the transfer of such property (determined without regard to this section). Except as provided in paragraph (9), this paragraph shall not apply to a disposition to an organization (other than a cooperative described in section 521) which is exempt from the tax imposed by this chapter.

(4) **Like kind exchanges; involuntary conversions, etc.**—

(A) **Recognition limit.**—If property is disposed of and gain (determined without regard to this section) is not recognized in whole or in part under section 1031 or 1033, then the amount of gain taken into account by the transferor under subsection (a) shall not exceed the greater of the following:

(i) the amount of gain recognized on the disposition (determined without regard to this section), increased as provided in subparagraph (B), or

(ii) the amount determined under subparagraph (C).

(B) **Increase for certain stock.**—With respect to any transaction, the increase provided by this subparagraph is the amount equal to the fair market value of any stock purchased in a corporation which (but for this paragraph) would result in nonrecognition of gain under section 1033(a) (2) (A).

(C) **Adjustment where insufficient section 1250 property is acquired.**—With respect to any transaction, the amount determined under this subparagraph shall be the excess of—

(i) the amount of gain which would (but for this paragraph) be taken into account under subsection (a), over

(ii) the fair market value (or cost in the case of a transaction described in section 1033(a) (2)) of the section 1250 property acquired in the transaction.

(D) **Basis of property acquired.**—In the case of property purchased by the taxpayer in a transaction described in section 1033(a) (2), in applying the last sentence of section 1033(b), such sentence shall be applied—

(i) first solely to section 1250 properties and to the amount of gain not taken into account under subsection (a) by reason of this paragraph, and

(ii) then to all purchased properties to which such sentence applies and to the remaining gain not recognized on the transaction as if the cost of the section 1250 properties were the basis of such properties computed under clause (i).

In the case of property acquired in any other transaction to which this paragraph applies, rules consistent with the preceding sentence shall be applied under regulations prescribed by the Secretary.

(E) Additional depreciation with respect to property disposed of.—In the case of any transaction described in section 1031 or 1033, the additional depreciation in respect of the section 1250 property acquired which is attributable to the section 1250 property disposed of shall be an amount equal to the amount of the gain which was not taken into account under subsection (a) by reason of the application of this paragraph.

* * *

(6) Property distributed by a partnership to a partner.—

(A) In general.—For purposes of this section, the basis of section 1250 property distributed by a partnership to a partner shall be deemed to be determined by reference to the adjusted basis of such property to the partnership.

(B) Additional depreciation.—In respect of any property described in subparagraph (A), the additional depreciation attributable to periods before the distribution by the partnership shall be—

(i) the amount of the gain to which subsection (a) would have applied if such property had been sold by the partnership immediately before the distribution at its fair market value at such time and the applicable percentage for the property had been 100 percent, reduced by

(ii) if section 751(b) applied to any part of such gain, the amount of such gain to which section 751(b) would have applied if the applicable percentage for the property had been 100 percent.

(7) Disposition of principal residence.—Subsection (a) shall not apply to a disposition of—

(A) property to the extent used by the taxpayer as his principal residence (within the meaning of section 1034, relating to rollover of gain on sale of principal residence), and

(B) property in respect of which the taxpayer meets the age and ownership requirements of section 121 (relating to one-time exclusion of gain from sale of principal residence by individual who has attained age 55) but only to the extent that he meets the use requirements of such section in respect of such property.

(8) Disposition of qualified low-income housing.—If section 1250 property is disposed of and gain (determined without regard to this section) is not recognized in whole or in part under section 1039, then—

(A) Recognition limit.—The amount of gain recognized by the transferor under subsection (a) shall not exceed the greater of—

(i) the amount of gain recognized on the disposition (determined without regard to this section), or

(ii) the amount determined under subparagraph (B).

(B) Adjustment where insufficient section 1250 property is acquired.—With respect to any transaction, the amount determined under this subparagraph shall be the excess of—

(i) the amount of gain which would (but for this paragraph) be taken into account under subsection (a), over

(ii) the cost of the section 1250 property acquired in the transaction.

(C) Basis of property acquired.—The basis of property acquired by the taxpayer, determined under section 1039(d), shall be allocated—

(i) first to the section 1250 property described in subparagraph (E) (i), in the amount determined under such subparagraph, reduced by the amount of gain not recognized attributable to the section 1250 property disposed of,

(ii) then to any property (other than section 1250 property) to which section 1039 applies, in the amount of its cost, reduced by the amount of gain not recognized except to the extent taken into account under clause (i), and

(iii) then to the section 1250 property described in subparagraph (E) (ii), in the amount determined thereunder, reduced by the amount of gain not recognized except to the extent taken into account under clauses (i) and (ii).

(D) **Additional depreciation with respect to property disposed of.**—The additional depreciation with respect to any property acquired shall include the additional depreciation with respect to the corresponding section 1250 property disposed of, reduced by the amount of gain recognized attributable to such property.

(E) **Property consisting of more than one element.**—There shall be treated as a separate element of section 1250 property—

(i) that portion of the section 1250 property acquired the cost of which does not exceed the net amount realized (as defined in section 1039(b)) attributable to the section 1250 property disposed of, reduced by the amount of gain recognized (if any) attributable to such property, and

(ii) that portion of the section 1250 property acquired the cost of which exceeds the net amount realized (as defined in section 1039(b)) attributable to the section 1250 property disposed of.

(F) **Allocation rules.**—For purposes of this paragraph—

(i) the amount of gain recognized attributable to the section 1250 property disposed of shall be the net amount realized with respect to such property, reduced by the greater of the adjusted basis of the section 1250 property disposed of or the cost of the section 1250 property acquired, but shall not exceed the gain recognized in the transaction, and

(ii) if any section 1250 property is treated as consisting of more than one element by reason of the application of subparagraph (E) to a prior transaction, then the amount of gain recognized, the net amount realized, and the additional depreciation, with respect to each such element shall be allocated in accordance with regulations prescribed by the Secretary.

(9) **Transfers to tax-exempt organization where property will be used in unrelated business.**—

(A) **In general.**—The second sentence of paragraph (3) shall not apply to a disposition of section 1250 property to an organization described in section 511(a) (2) or 511(b) (2) if, immediately after such disposition, such organization uses such property in an unrelated trade or business (as defined in section 513).

(B) **Later change in use.**—If any property with respect to the disposition of which gain is not recognized by reason of subparagraph (A) ceases to be used in an unrelated trade or business of the organization acquiring such property, such organization shall be treated for purposes of this section as having disposed of such property on the date of such cessation.

(10) **Foreclosure dispositions.**—If any section 1250 property is disposed of by the taxpayer pursuant to a bid for such property at foreclosure or by operation of an agreement or of process of law after there was a default on indebtedness which such property secured, the applicable percentage referred to in paragraph (1) (B),

(2) (B), or (3) (B) of subsection (a), as the case may be, shall be determined as if the taxpayer ceased to hold such property on the date of the beginning of the proceedings pursuant to which the disposition occurred, or, in the event there are no proceedings, such percentage shall be determined as if the taxpayer ceased to hold such property on the date, determined under regulations prescribed by the Secretary, on which such operation of an agreement or process of law, pursuant to which the disposition occurred, began.

(11) Section 1245 recovery property.—Subsection (a) shall not apply to the disposition of property which is section 1245 recovery property (as defined in section 1245(a)(5)).

(e) Holding period.—For purposes of determining the applicable percentage under this section, the provisions of section 1223 shall not apply, and the holding period of section 1250 property shall be determined under the following rules:

(1) Beginning of holding period.—The holding period of section 1250 property shall be deemed to begin—

(A) in the case of property acquired by the taxpayer, on the day after the date of acquisition, or

(B) in the case of property constructed, reconstructed, or erected by the taxpayer, on the first day of the month during which the property is placed in service.

(2) Property with transferred basis.—If the basis of property acquired in a transaction described in paragraph (1), (2), (3), or (5) of subsection (d) is determined by reference to its basis in the hands of the transferor, then the holding period of the property in the hands of the transferee shall include the holding period of the property in the hands of the transferor.

(3) Principal residence.—If the basis of property acquired in a transaction described in paragraph (7) of subsection (d) is determined by reference to the basis in the hands of the taxpayer of other property, then the holding period of the property acquired shall include the holding period of such other property.

(4) Qualified low-income housing.—The holding period of any section 1250 property acquired which is described in subsection (d) (8) (E) (i) shall include the holding period of the corresponding element of section 1250 property disposed of.

(f) Special rules for property which is substantially improved.—

(1) Amount treated as ordinary income.—If, in the case of a disposition of section 1250 property, the property is treated as consisting of more than one element by reason of paragraph (3), then the amount taken into account under subsection (a) in respect of such section 1250 property as ordinary income shall be the sum of the amounts determined under paragraph (2).

(2) Ordinary income attributable to an element.—For purposes of paragraph (1), the amount taken into account for any element shall be the sum of a series of amounts determined for the periods set forth in subsection (a), with the amount for any such period being determined by multiplying—

(A) the amount which bears the same ratio to the lower of the amounts specified in clause (i) or (ii) of subsection (a) (1) (A), in clause (i) or (ii) of subsection (a) (2) (A), or in clause (i) or (ii) of subsection (a) (3) (A), as the case may be, for the section 1250 property as the additional depreciation for such element attributable to such period bears to the sum of the additional depreciation for all elements attributable to such period, by

(B) the applicable percentage for such element for such period.

For purposes of this paragraph, determinations with respect to any element shall be made as if it were a separate property.

(3) Property consisting of more than one element.—In applying this subsection in the case of any section 1250 property, there shall be treated as a separate element—

(A) each separate improvement,

(B) if, before completion of section 1250 property, units thereof (as distinguished from improvements) were placed in service, each such unit of section 1250 property, and

(C) the remaining property which is not taken into account under subparagraphs (A) and (B).

(4) Property which is substantially improved.—For purposes of this subsection—

(A) In general.—The term "separate improvement" means each improvement added during the 36-month period ending on the last day of any taxable year to the capital account for the property, but only if the sum of the amounts added to such account during such period exceeds the greatest of—

(i) 25 percent of the adjusted basis of the property,

(ii) 10 percent of the adjusted basis of the property, determined without regard to the adjustments provided in paragraphs (2) and (3) of section 1016(a), or

(iii) $5,000.

For purposes of clauses (i) and (ii), the adjusted basis of the property shall be determined as of the beginning of the first day of such 36-month period, or of the holding period of the property (within the meaning of subsection (e)), whichever is the later.

(B) Exception.—Improvements in any taxable year shall be taken into account for purposes of subparagraph (A) only if the sum of the amounts added to the capital account for the property for such taxable year exceeds the greater of—

(i) $2,000, or

(ii) one percent of the adjusted basis referred to in subparagraph (A) (ii), determined, however, as of the beginning of such taxable year.

For purposes of this section, if the amount added to the capital account for any separate improvement does not exceed the greater of clause (i) or (ii), such improvement shall be treated as placed in service on the first day, of a calendar month, which is closest to the middle of the taxable year.

(C) Improvement.—The term "improvement" means, in the case of any section 1250 property, any addition to capital account for such property after the initial acquisition or after completion of the property.

(g) Special rules for qualified low-income housing.—

(1) Amount treated as ordinary income.—If, in the case of a disposition of section 1250 property, the property is treated as consisting of more than one element by reason of the application of subsection (d) (8) (E), and gain is recognized in whole or in part, then the amount taken into account under subsection (a) as ordinary income shall be the sum of the amounts determined under paragraph (2).

(2) Ordinary income attributable to an element.—For purposes of paragraph (1), the amount taken into account for any element shall be determined in a manner similar to that provided by subsection (f) (2).

(h) Adjustments to basis.—The Secretary shall prescribe such regulations as he may deem necessary to provide for adjustments to the basis of property to reflect gain recognized under subsection (a).

(i) Application of section.—This section shall apply notwithstanding any other provision of this subtitle.

§ 1252.   Gain from disposition of farm land

(a) General rule.—

(1) Ordinary income.—Except as otherwise provided in this section, if farm land which the taxpayer has held for less than 10 years is disposed of during a taxable year beginning after December 31, 1969, the lower of—

    (A) the applicable percentage of the aggregate of the deductions allowed under sections 175 (relating to soil and water conservation expenditures) and 182 (as in effect on the day before the date of the enactment of the Tax Reform Act of 1986) for expenditures made by the taxpayer after December 31, 1969, with respect to the farm land or

    (B) the excess of—

        (i) the amount realized (in the case of a sale, exchange, or involuntary conversion), or the fair market value of the farm land (in the case of any other disposition), over

        (ii) the adjusted basis of such land,

shall be treated as ordinary income. Such gain shall be recognized notwithstanding any other provision of this subtitle.

(2) Farm land.—For purposes of this section, the term "farm land" means any land with respect to which deductions have been allowed under sections 175 (relating to soil and water conservation expenditures) or 182 (relating to expenditures by farmers for clearing land).

(3) Applicable percentage.—For purposes of this section—

If the farm land is disposed of—	The applicable percentage is—
Within 5 years after the date it was acquired	100 percent.
Within the sixth year after it was acquired	80 percent.
Within the seventh year after it was acquired	60 percent.
Within the eighth year after it was acquired	40 percent.
Within the ninth year after it was acquired	20 percent.
10 years or more years after it was acquired	0 percent.

(b) Special rules.—Under regulations prescribed by the Secretary, rules similar to the rules of section 1245 shall be applied for purposes of this section.

§ 1253.   Transfers of franchises, trademarks, and trade names

(a) General rule.—A transfer of a franchise, trademark, or trade name shall not be treated as a sale or exchange of a capital asset if the transferor retains any significant power, right, or continuing interest with respect to the subject matter of the franchise, trademark, or trade name.

(b) Definitions.—For purposes of this section—

(1) **Franchise.**—The term "franchise" includes an agreement which gives one of the parties to the agreement the right to distribute, sell, or provide goods, services, or facilities, within a specified area.

(2) **Significant power, right, or continuing interest.**—The term "significant power, right, or continuing interest" includes, but is not limited to, the following rights with respect to the interest transferred:

(A) A right to disapprove any assignment of such interest, or any part thereof.

(B) A right to terminate at will.

(C) A right to prescribe the standards of quality of products used or sold, or of services furnished, and of the equipment and facilities used to promote such products or services.

(D) A right to require that the transferee sell or advertise only products or services of the transferor.

(E) A right to require that the transferee purchase substantially all of his supplies and equipment from the transferor.

(F) A right to payments contingent on the productivity, use, or disposition of the subject matter of the interest transferred, if such payments constitute a substantial element under the transfer agreement.

(3) **Transfer.**—The term "transfer" includes the renewal of a franchise, trademark, or trade name.

(c) **Treatment of contingent payments by transferor.**—Amounts received or accrued on account of a transfer, sale, or other disposition of a franchise, trademark, or trade name which are contingent on the productivity, use, or disposition of the franchise, trademark, or trade name transferred shall be treated as amounts received or accrued from the sale or other disposition of property which is not a capital asset.

(d) **Treatment of payments by transferee.**—

(1) **Contingent payments.**—Amounts paid or incurred during the taxable year on account of a transfer, sale, or other disposition of a franchise, trademark, or trade name which are contingent on the productivity, use, or disposition of the franchise, trademark, or trade name transferred shall be allowed as a deduction under section 162(a) (relating to trade or business expenses).

(2) **Other payments.**—If a transfer of a franchise, trademark, or trade name is not (by reason of the application of subsection (a)) treated as a sale or exchange of a capital asset, any payment not described in paragraph (1) which is made in discharge of a principal sum agreed upon in the transfer agreement shall be allowed as a deduction—

(A) in the case of a single payment made in discharge of such principal sum, ratably over the taxable years in the period beginning with the taxable year in which the payment is made and ending with the ninth succeeding taxable year or ending with the last taxable year beginning in the period of the transfer agreement, whichever period is shorter;

(B) in the case of a payment which is one of a series of approximately equal payments made in discharge of such principal sum, which are payable over—

(i) the period of the transfer agreement, or

(ii) a period of more than 10 taxable years, whether ending before or after the end of the period of the transfer agreement,

in the taxable year in which the payment is made; and

(C) in the case of any other payment, in the taxable year or years specified in regulations prescribed by the Secretary, consistently with the preceding provisions of this paragraph.

(e) Exception.—This section shall not apply to the transfer of a franchise to engage in professional football, basketball, baseball, or other professional sport.

§ 1254. Gain from disposition of interest in oil, gas, geothermal, or other mineral properties

(a) General rule.—

(1) Ordinary income.—If any section 1254 property is disposed of, the lesser of—

(A) the aggregate amount of—

(i) expenditures which have been deducted by the taxpayer or any person under section 263, 616, or 617 with respect to such property and which, but for such deduction, would have been included in the adjusted basis of such property, and

(ii) the deductions for depletion under section 611 which reduced the adjusted basis of such property, or

(B) the excess of—

(i) in the case of—

(I) a sale, exchange, or involuntary conversion, the amount realized, or

(II) in the case of any other disposition, the fair market value of such property, over

(ii) the adjusted basis of such property,

shall be treated as gain which is ordinary income. Such gain shall be recognized notwithstanding any other provision of this subtitle.

(2) Disposition of portion of property.—For purposes of paragraph (1)—

(A) In the case of the disposition of a portion of section 1254 property (other than an undivided interest), the entire amount of the aggregate expenditures or deductions described in paragraph (1)(A) with respect to such property shall be treated as allocable to such portion to the extent of the amount of the gain to which paragraph (1) applies.

(B) In the case of the disposition of an undivided interest in a section 1254 property (or a portion thereof), a proportionate part of the expenditures or deductions described in paragraph (1)(A) with respect to such property shall be treated as allocable to such undivided interest to the extent of the amount of the gain to which paragraph (1) applies.

This paragraph shall not apply to any expenditures to the extent the taxpayer establishes to the satisfaction of the Secretary that such expenditures do not relate to the portion (or interest therein) disposed of.

(3) Section 1254 property.—The term "section 1254 property" means any property (within the meaning of section 614) if—

(A) any expenditures described in paragraph (1)(A) are properly chargeable to such property, or

(B) the adjusted basis of such property includes adjustments for deductions for depletion under section 611.

(b) Special rules under regulations.—Under regulations prescribed by the Secretary—

(1) rules similar to the rule of subsection (g) of section 617 and to the rules of subsections (b) and (c) of section 1245 shall be applied for purposes of this section; and

(2) in the case of the sale or exchange of stock in an S corporation, rules similar to the rules of section 751 shall be applied to that portion of the excess of the amount realized over the adjusted basis of the stock which is attributable to expenditures referred to in subsection (a)(1)(A) of this section.

§ 1255. Gain from disposition of section 126 property

(a) General rule.—

(1) Ordinary income.—Except as otherwise provided in this section, if section 126 property is disposed of, the lower of—

(A) the applicable percentage of the aggregate payments, with respect to such property, excluded from gross income under section 126, or

(B) the excess of—

(i) the amount realized (in the case of a sale, exchange, or involuntary conversion), or the fair market value of such section 126 property (in the case of any other disposition), over

(ii) the adjusted basis of such property,

shall be treated as ordinary income. Such gain shall be recognized notwithstanding any other provision of this subtitle, except that this section shall not apply to the extent such gain is recognized as ordinary income under any other provision of this part.

(2) Section 126 property.—For purposes of this section, "section 126 property" means any property acquired, improved, or otherwise modified by the application of payments excluded from gross income under section 126.

(3) Applicable percentage.—For purposes of this section, if section 126 property is disposed of less than 10 years after the date of receipt of payments excluded from gross income under section 126, the applicable percentage is 100 percent. If section 126 property is disposed of more than 10 years after such date, the applicable percentage is 100 percent reduced (but not below zero) by 10 percent for each year or part thereof in excess of 10 years such property was held after the date of receipt of the payments.

(b) Special rules.—Under regulations prescribed by the Secretary—

(1) rules similar to the rules applicable under section 1245 shall be applied for purposes of this section, and

(2) for purposes of sections 170(e), 341(e)(12), and 751(c), amounts treated as ordinary income under this section shall be treated in the same manner as amounts treated as ordinary income under section 1245.

§ 1256. Section 1256 contracts marked to market

(a) General rule.—For purposes of this subtitle—

(1) each section 1256 contract held by the taxpayer at the close of the taxable year shall be treated as sold for its fair market value on the last business day of such taxable year (and any gain or loss shall be taken into account for the taxable year),

(2) proper adjustment shall be made in the amount of any gain or loss subsequently realized for gain or loss taken into account by reason of paragraph (1),

(3) any gain or loss with respect to a section 1256 contract shall be treated as—

(A) short-term capital gain or loss, to the extent of 40 percent of such gain or loss, and

(B) long-term capital gain or loss, to the extent of 60 percent of such gain or loss, and

(4) if all the offsetting positions making up any straddle consist of section 1256 contracts to which this section applies (and such straddle is not part of a larger straddle), sections 1092 and 263(g) shall not apply with respect to such straddle.

(b) Section 1256 contract defined.—For purposes of this section, the term "section 1256 contract" means—

(1) any regulated futures contract,

(2) any foreign currency contract,

(3) any nonequity option, and

(4) any dealer equity option.

* * *

(e) Mark to market not to apply to hedging transactions.—

(1) Section not to apply.—Subsection (a) shall not apply in the case of a hedging transaction.

* * *

(3) Special rule for syndicates.—

(A) In general.—Notwithstanding paragraph (2), the term "hedging transaction" shall not include any transaction entered into by or for a syndicate.

(B) Syndicate defined.—For purposes of subparagraph (A), the term "syndicate" means any partnership or other entity (other than a corporation which is not an S corporation) if more than 35 percent of the losses of such entity during the taxable year are allocable to limited partners or limited entrepreneurs (within the meaning of section 464(e)(2)).

* * *

PART V—SPECIAL RULES FOR BONDS AND OTHER DEBT INSTRUMENTS

Subpart
A. Original issue discount.
B. Market discount.
C. Discount on short-term obligations.
D. Miscellaneous provisions.

Subpart A—Original Issue Discount

§ 1271. Treatment of amounts received on retirement or sale or exchange of debt instruments

(a) General rule.—For purposes of this title—

(1) Retirement.—Amounts received by the holder on retirement of any debt instrument shall be considered as amounts received in exchange therefor.

(2) Ordinary income on sale or exchange where intention to call before maturity.—

(A) In general.—If at the time of original issue there was an intention to call a debt instrument before maturity, any gain realized on the sale or exchange thereof which does not exceed an amount equal to—

(i) the original issue discount, reduced by

(ii) the portion of original issue discount previously includible in the gross income of any holder (without regard to subsection (a)(6) or (b)(4) of section 1272 (or the corresponding provisions of prior law)),

shall be treated as ordinary income.

(B) Exceptions.—This paragraph (and paragraph (2) of subsection (c)) shall not apply to—

(i) any tax-exempt obligation, or

(ii) any holder who has purchased the debt instrument at a premium.

(3) Certain short-term Government obligations.—

(A) In general.—On the sale or exchange of any short-term Government obligation, any gain realized which does not exceed an amount equal to the ratable share of the acquisition discount shall be treated as ordinary income.

(B) Short-term government obligation.—For purposes of this paragraph, the term "short-term Government obligation" means any obligation of the United States or any of its possessions, or of a State or any political subdivision thereof, or of the District of Columbia, which has a fixed maturity date not more than 1 year from the date of issue. Such term does not include any tax-exempt obligation.

(C) Acquisition discount.—For purposes of this paragraph, except as provided in subparagraph (E), the term "acquisition discount" means the excess of the stated redemption price at maturity over the taxpayer's basis for the obligation.

(D) Ratable share.—For purposes of this paragraph, the ratable share of the acquisition discount is an amount which bears the same ratio to such discount as—

(i) the number of days which the taxpayer held the obligation, bears to

(ii) the number of days after the date the taxpayer acquired the obligation and up to (and including) the date of its maturity.

(E) Election of accrual on basis of constant interest rate.—At the election of the taxpayer with respect to any obligation, the ratable share of the acquisition discount is the portion of the acquisition discount accruing while the taxpayer held the obligation determined (under regulations prescribed by the Secretary) on the basis of—

(i) the taxpayer's yield to maturity based on the taxpayer's cost of acquiring the obligation, and

(ii) compounding daily.

An election under this subparagraph, once made with respect to any obligation, shall be irrevocable.

(b) Exceptions.—This section shall not apply to—

(1) Natural persons.—Any obligation issued by a natural person.

(2) Obligations issued before July 2, 1982, by certain issuers.—Any obligation issued before July 2, 1982, by an issuer which—

    (A) is not a corporation, and

    (B) is not a government or political subdivision thereof.

(c) Transition rules.—

(1) Special rule for certain obligations issued before January 1, 1955. —Paragraph (1) of subsection (a) shall apply to a debt instrument issued before January 1, 1955, only if such instrument was issued with interest coupons or in registered form, or was in such form on March 1, 1954.

(2) Special rule for certain obligations with respect to which original issue discount not currently includible.—

    (A) In general.—On the sale or exchange of debt instruments issued by a government or political subdivision thereof after December 31, 1954, and before July 2, 1982, or by a corporation after December 31, 1954, and on or before May 27, 1969, any gain realized which does not exceed—

        (i) an amount equal to the original issue discount, or

        (ii) if at the time of original issue there was no intention to call the debt instrument before maturity, an amount which bears the same ratio to the original issue discount as the number of complete months that the debt instrument was held by the taxpayer bears to the number of complete months from the date of original issue to the date of maturity,

shall be considered as ordinary income.

    (B) Subsection (a)(2)(A) not to apply.—Subsection (a)(2)(A) shall not apply to any debt instrument referred to in subparagraph (A) of this paragraph.

    (C) Cross reference.—

For current inclusion of original issue discount, see section 1272.

(d) Double inclusion in income not required.—This section and sections 1272 and 1286 shall not require the inclusion of any amount previously includible in gross income.

§ 1272. Current inclusion in income of original issue discount

(a) Original issue discount on debt instruments issued after July 1, 1982, included in income on basis of constant interest rate.—

    (1) General rule.—For purposes of this title, there shall be included in the gross income of the holder of any debt instrument having original issue discount issued after July 1, 1982, an amount equal to the sum of the daily portions of the original issue discount for each day during the taxable year on which such holder held such debt instrument.

    (2) Exceptions.—Paragraph (1) shall not apply to—

        (A) Tax-exempt obligations.—Any tax-exempt obligation.

        (B) United States savings bonds.—Any United States savings bond.

        (C) Short-term obligations.—Any debt instrument which has a fixed maturity date not more than 1 year from the date of issue.

        (D) Obligations issued by natural persons before March 2, 1984.—Any obligation issued by a natural person before March 2, 1984.

        (E) Loans between natural persons.—

(i) **In general.**—Any loan made by a natural person to another natural person if—

(I) such loan is not made in the course of a trade or business of the lender, and

(II) the amount of such loan (when increased by the outstanding amount of prior loans by such natural person to such other natural person) does not exceed $10,000.

(ii) **Clause (i) not to apply where tax avoidance a principal purpose.**—Clause (i) shall not apply if the loan has as 1 of its principal purposes the avoidance of any Federal tax.

(iii) **Treatment of husband and wife.**—For purposes of this subparagraph, a husband and wife shall be treated as 1 person. The preceding sentence shall not apply where the spouses lived apart at all times during the taxable year in which the loan is made.

(3) **Determination of daily portions.**—For purposes of paragraph (1), the daily portion of the original issue discount on any debt instrument shall be determined by allocating to each day in any accrual period its ratable portion of the increase during such accrual period in the adjusted issue price of the debt instrument. For purposes of the preceding sentence, the increase in the adjusted issue price for any accrual period shall be an amount equal to the excess (if any) of—

(A) the product of—

(i) the adjusted issue price of the debt instrument at the beginning of such accrual period, and

(ii) the yield to maturity (determined on the basis of compounding at the close of each accrual period and properly adjusted for the length of the accrual period), over

(B) the sum of the amounts payable as interest on such debt instrument during such accrual period.

(4) **Adjusted issue price.**—For purposes of this subsection, the adjusted issue price of any debt instrument at the beginning of any accrual period is the sum of—

(A) the issue price of such debt instrument, plus

(B) the adjustments under this subsection to such issue price for all periods before the first day of such accrual period.

(5) **Accrual period.**—Except as otherwise provided in regulations prescribed by the Secretary, the term "accrual period" means a 6-month period (or shorter period from the date of original issue of the debt instrument) which ends on a day in the calendar year corresponding to the maturity date of the debt instrument or the date 6 months before such maturity date.

(6) **Determination of daily portions where principal subject to acceleration.—**

(A) **In general.**—In the case of any debt instrument to which this paragraph applies, the daily portion of the original issue discount shall be determined by allocating to each day in any accrual period its ratable portion of the excess (if any) of—

(i) the sum of (I) the present value determined under subparagraph (B) of all remaining payments under the debt instrument as of the close of such period, and (II) the payments during the accrual period of amounts included in the stated redemption price of the debt instrument, over

(ii) the adjusted issue price of such debt instrument at the beginning of such period.

(B) Determination of present value.—For purposes of subparagraph (A), the present value shall be determined on the basis of—

(i) the original yield to maturity (determined on the basis of compounding at the close of each accrual period and properly adjusted for the length of the accrual period),

(ii) events which have occurred before the close of the accrual period, and

(iii) a prepayment assumption determined in the manner prescribed by regulations.

(C) Debt instruments to which paragraph applies.—This paragraph applies to—

(i) any regular interest in a REMIC or qualified mortgage held by a REMIC, or

(ii) any other debt instrument if payments under such debt instrument may be accelerated by reason of prepayments of other obligations securing such debt instrument (or, to the extent provided in regulations, by reason of other events).

(7) Reduction where subsequent holder pays acquisition premium.—

(A) Reduction.—For purposes of this subsection, in the case of any purchase after its original issue of a debt instrument to which this subsection applies, the daily portion for any day shall be reduced by an amount equal to the amount which would be the daily portion for such day (without regard to this paragraph) multiplied by the fraction determined under subparagraph (B).

(B) Determination of fraction.—For purposes of subparagraph (A), the fraction determined under this subparagraph is a fraction—

(i) the numerator of which is the excess (if any) of—

(I) the cost of such debt instrument incurred by the purchaser, over

(II) the issue price of such debt instrument, increased by the portion of original issue discount previously includible in the gross income of any holder (computed without regard to this paragraph), and

(ii) the denominator of which is the sum of the daily portions for such debt instrument for all days after the date of such purchase and ending on the stated maturity date (computed without regard to this paragraph).

(b) Ratable inclusion retained for corporate debt instruments issued before July 2, 1982.—

(1) General rule.—There shall be included in the gross income of the holder of any debt instrument issued by a corporation after May 27, 1969, and before July 2, 1982—

(A) the ratable monthly portion of original issue discount, multiplied by

(B) the number of complete months (plus any fractional part of a month determined under paragraph (3)) such holder held such debt instrument during the taxable year.

(2) Determination of ratable monthly portion.—Except as provided in paragraph (4), the ratable monthly portion of original issue discount shall equal—

(A) the original issue discount, divided by

(B) the number of complete months from the date of original issue to the stated maturity date of the debt instruments.

(3) Month defined.—For purposes of this subsection—

(A) Complete month.—A complete month commences with the date of original issue and the corresponding day of each succeeding calendar month (or the last day of a calendar month in which there is no corresponding day).

(B) Transfers during month.—In any case where a debt instrument is acquired on any day other than a day determined under subparagraph (A), the ratable monthly portion of original issue discount for the complete month (or partial month) in which such acquisition occurs shall be allocated between the transferor and the transferee in accordance with the number of days in such complete (or partial) month each held the debt instrument.

(4) Reduction where subsequent holder pays acquisition premium.—

(A) Reduction.—For purposes of this subsection, the ratable monthly portion of original issue discount shall not include its share of the acquisition premium.

(B) Share of acquisition premium.—For purposes of subparagraph (A), any month's share of the acquisition premium is an amount (determined at the time of the purchase) equal to—

(i) the excess of—

(I) the cost of such debt instrument incurred by the holder, over

(II) the issue price of such debt instrument, increased by the portion of original issue discount previously includible in the gross income of any holder (computed without regard to this paragraph),

(ii) divided by the number of complete months (plus any fractional part of a month) from the date of such purchase to the stated maturity date of such debt instrument.

(c) Exceptions.—This section shall not apply to any holder—

(1) who has purchased the debt instrument at a premium, or

(2) which is a life insurance company to which section 811(b) applies.

(d) Definition and special rule.—

(1) Purchase defined.—For purposes of this section, the term "purchase" means—

(A) any acquisition of a debt instrument, where

(B) the basis of the debt instrument is not determined in whole or in part by reference to the adjusted basis of such debt instrument in the hands of the person from whom acquired.

(2) Basis adjustment.—The basis of any debt instrument in the hands of the holder thereof shall be increased by the amount included in his gross income pursuant to this section.

§ 1273. Determination of amount of original issue discount

(a) General rule.—For purposes of this subpart—

(1) In general.—The term "original issue discount" means the excess (if any) of—

(A) the stated redemption price at maturity, over

(B) the issue price.

(2) **Stated redemption price at maturity.**—The term "stated redemption price at maturity" means the amount fixed by the last modification of the purchase agreement and includes interest and other amounts payable at that time (other than any interest based on a fixed rate, and payable unconditionally at fixed periodic intervals of 1 year or less during the entire term of the debt instrument).

(3) **¼ of 1 percent de minimis rule.**—If the original issue discount determined under paragraph (1) is less than—

(A) ¼ of 1 percent of the stated redemption price at maturity, multiplied by

(B) the number of complete years to maturity,

then the original issue discount shall be treated as zero.

(b) **Issue price.**—For purposes of this subpart—

(1) **Publicly offered debt instruments not issued for property.**—In the case of any issue of debt instruments—

(A) publicly offered, and

(B) not issued for property,

the issue price is the initial offering price to the public (excluding bond houses and brokers) at which price a substantial amount of such debt instruments was sold.

(2) **Other debt instruments not issue for property.**—In the case of any issue of debt instruments not issued for property and not publicly offered, the issue price of each such instrument is the price paid by the first buyer of such debt instrument.

(3) **Debt instruments issued for property where there is public trading.**—In the case of a debt instrument which is issued for property and which—

(A) is part of an issue a portion of which is traded on an established securities market, or

(B)(i) is issued for stock or securities which are traded on an established securities market, or

(ii) to the extent provided in regulations, is issued for property (other than stock or securities) of a kind regularly traded on an established market,

the issue price of such debt instrument shall be the fair market value of such property.

(4) **Other cases.**—Except in any case—

(A) to which paragraph (1), (2), or (3) of this subsection applies, or

(B) to which section 1274 applies,

the issue price of a debt instrument which is issued for property shall be the stated redemption price at maturity.

(5) **Property.**—In applying this subsection, the term "property" includes services and the right to use property, but such term does not include money.

(c) **Special rules for applying subsection (b).**—For purposes of subsection (b)—

(1) **Initial offering price; price paid by the first buyer.**—The terms "initial offering price" and "price paid by the first buyer" include the aggregate payments made by the purchaser under the purchase agreement, including modifications thereof.

(2) **Treatment of investment units.**—In the case of any debt instrument and an option, security, or other property issued together as an investment unit—

(A) the issue price for such unit shall be determined in accordance with the rules of this subsection and subsection (b) as if it were a debt instrument,

(B) the issue price determined for such unit shall be allocated to each element of such unit on the basis of the relationship of the fair market value of such element to the fair market value of all elements in such unit, and

(C) the issue price of any debt instrument included in such unit shall be the portion of the issue price of the unit allocated to the debt instrument under subparagraph (B).

§ 1274. Determination of issue price in the case of certain debt instruments issued for property

(a) In general.—In the case of any debt instrument to which this section applies, for purposes of this subpart, the issue price shall be—

(1) where there is adequate stated interest, the stated principal amount, or

(2) in any other case, the imputed principal amount.

(b) Imputed principal amount.—For purposes of this section—

(1) In general.—Except as provided in paragraph (3), the imputed principal amount of any debt instrument shall be equal to the sum of the present values of all payments due under such debt instrument.

(2) Determination of present value.—For purposes of paragraph (1), the present value of a payment shall be determined in the manner provided by regulations prescribed by the Secretary—

(A) as of the date of the sale or exchange, and

(B) by using a discount rate equal to the applicable Federal rate, compounded semiannually.

(3) Fair market value rule in potentially abusive situations.—

(A) In general.—In the case of any potentially abusive situation, the imputed principal amount of any debt instrument received in exchange for property shall be the fair market value of such property adjusted to take into account other consideration involved in the transaction.

(B) Potentially abusive situation defined.—For purposes of subparagraph (A), the term "potentially abusive situation" means—

(i) a tax shelter (as defined in section 6661(b)(2)(C)(ii)), and

(ii) any other situation which, by reason of—

(I) recent sales transactions,

(II) nonrecourse financing,

(III) financing with a term in excess of the economic life of the property, or

(IV) other circumstances,

is of a type which the Secretary specifies by regulations as having potential for tax avoidance.

(c) Debt instruments to which section applies.—

(1) In general.—Except as otherwise provided in this subsection, this section shall apply to any debt instrument given in consideration for the sale or exchange of property if—

(A) the stated redemption price at maturity for such debt instrument exceeds—

(i) where there is adequate stated interest, the stated principal amount, or

(ii) in any other case, the imputed principal amount of such debt instrument determined under subsection (b), and

(B) some or all of the payments due under such debt instrument are due more than 6 months after the date of such sale or exchange.

(2) Adequate stated interest.—For purposes of this section, there is adequate stated interest with respect to any debt instrument if the stated principal amount for such debt instrument is less than or equal to the imputed principal amount of such debt instrument determined under subsection (b).

(3) Exceptions.—This section shall not apply to—

(A) Sales for $1,000,000 or less of farms by individuals or small businesses.—

(i) **In general.**—Any debt instrument arising from the sale or exchange of a farm (within the meaning of section 6420(c)(2))—

(I) by an individual, estate, or testamentary trust,

(II) by a corporation which as of the date of the sale or exchange is a small business corporation (as defined in section 1244(c)(3)), or

(III) by a partnership which as of the date of the sale or exchange meets requirements similar to those of section 1244(c)(3).

(ii) **$1,000,000 limitation.**—Clause (i) shall apply only if it can be determined at the time of the sale or exchange that the sales price cannot exceed $1,000,000. For purposes of the preceding sentence, all sales and exchanges which are part of the same transaction (or a series of related transactions) shall be treated as 1 sale or exchange.

(B) Sales of principal residences.—Any debt instrument arising from the sale or exchange by an individual of his principal residence (within the meaning of section 1034).

(C) Sales involving total payments of $250,000 or less.—

(i) **In general.**—Any debt instrument arising from the sale or exchange of property if the sum of the following amounts does not exceed $250,000:

(I) the aggregate amount of the payments due under such debt instrument and all other debt instruments received as consideration for the sale or exchange, and

(II) the aggregate amount of any other consideration to be received for the sale or exchange.

(ii) **Consideration other than debt instrument taken into account at fair market value.**—For purposes of clause (i), any consideration (other than a debt instrument) shall be taken into account at its fair market value.

(iii) **Aggregation of transactions.**—For purposes of this subparagraph, all sales and exchanges which are part of the same transaction (or a series of related transactions) shall be treated as 1 sale or exchange.

(D) Debt instruments which are publicly traded or issued for publicly traded property.—Any debt instrument to which section 1273(b)(3) applies.

(E) **Certain sales of patents.**—In the case of any transfer described in section 1235(a) (relating to sale or exchange of patents), any amount contingent on the productivity, use, or disposition of the property transferred.

(F) **Sales or exchanges to which section 483(e) applies.**—Any debt instrument to the extent section 483(e) (relating to certain land transfers between related persons) applies to such instrument.

(4) **Exception for assumptions.**—If any person—

(A) in connection with the sale or exchange of property, assumes any debt instrument, or

(B) acquires any property subject to any debt instrument,

in determining whether this section or section 483 applies to such debt instrument, such assumption (or such acquisition) shall not be taken into account unless the terms and conditions of such debt instrument are modified (or the nature of the transaction is changed) in connection with the assumption (or acquisition).

(d) **Determination of applicable federal rate.**—For purposes of this section—

(1) **Applicable federal rate.**—

(A) **In general.**—

In the case of a debt instrument with a term of:	The applicable Federal rate is:
Not over 3 years	The Federal short-term rate.
Over 3 years but not over 9 years	The Federal mid-term rate.
Over 9 years	The Federal long-term rate.

(B) **Determination of rates.**—During each calendar month, the Secretary shall determine the Federal short-term rate, mid-term rate, and long-term rate which shall apply during the following calendar month.

(C) **Federal rate for any calendar month.**—For purposes of this paragraph—

(i) **Federal short-term rate.**—The Federal short-term rate shall be the rate determined by the Secretary based on the average market yield (during any 1-month period selected by the Secretary and ending in the calendar month in which the determination is made) on outstanding marketable obligations of the United States with remaining periods to maturity of 3 years or less.

(ii) **Federal mid-term and long-term rates.**—The Federal mid-term and long-term rate shall be determined in accordance with the principles of clause (i).

(D) **Lower rate permitted in certain cases.**—The Secretary may by regulations permit a rate to be used with respect to any debt instrument which is lower than the applicable Federal rate if the taxpayer establishes to the satisfaction of the Secretary that such lower rate is based on the same principles as the applicable Federal rate and is appropriate for the term of such instrument.

(2) **Lowest 3-month rate applicable to any sale or exchange.**—

(A) **In general.**—In the case of any sale or exchange, the applicable Federal rate shall be the lowest 3-month rate.

(B) **Lowest 3-month rate.**—For purposes of subparagraph (A), the term "lowest 3-month rate" means the lowest of the applicable Federal rates in effect for any month in the 3-calendar-month period ending with the 1st calendar month in which there is a binding contract in writing for such sale or exchange.

(3) Term of debt instrument.—In determining the term of a debt instrument for purposes of this subsection, under regulations prescribed by the Secretary, there shall be taken into account options to renew or extend.

(e) 110 Percent rate where sale-leaseback involved.—

(1) In general.—In the case of any debt instrument to which this subsection applies, the discount rate used under subsection (b)(2)(B) or section 483(b) shall be 110 percent of the applicable Federal rate, compounded semiannually.

(2) Lower discount rates shall not apply.—Section 1274A shall not apply to any debt instrument to which this subsection applies.

(3) Debt instruments to which this subsection applies.—This subsection shall apply to any debt instrument given in consideration for the sale or exchange of any property if, pursuant to a plan, the transferor or any related person leases a portion of such property after such sale or exchange.

§ 1274A. Special rules for certain transactions where stated principal amount does not exceed $2,800,000

(a) Lower discount rate.—In the case of any qualified debt instrument, the discount rate used for purposes of sections 483 and 1274 shall not exceed 9 percent, compounded semiannually.

(b) Qualified debt instrument defined.—For purposes of this section, the term "qualified debt instrument" means any debt instrument given in consideration for the sale or exchange of property (other than new section 38 property within the meaning of section 48(b)) if the stated principal amount of such instrument does not exceed $2,800,000.

(c) Election to use cash method where stated principal amount does not exceed $2,000,000.—

(1) In general.—In the case of any cash method debt instrument—

(A) section 1274 shall not apply, and

(B) interest on such debt instrument shall be taken into account by both the borrower and the lender under the cash receipts and disbursements method of accounting.

(2) Cash method debt instrument.—For purposes of paragraph (1), the term "cash method debt instrument" means any qualified debt instrument if—

(A) the stated principal amount does not exceed $2,000,000,

(B) the lender does not use an accrual method of accounting and is not a dealer with respect to the property sold or exchanged,

(C) section 1274 would have applied to such instrument but for an election under this subsection, and

(D) an election under this subsection is jointly made with respect to such debt instrument by the borrower and lender.

(3) Successors bound by election.—

(A) In general.—Except as provided in subparagraph (B), paragraph (1) shall apply to any successor to the borrower or lender with respect to a cash method debt instrument.

(B) Exception where lender transfers debt instrument to accrual method taxpayer.—If the lender (or any successor) transfers any cash method debt instrument to a taxpayer who uses an accrual method of accounting, this paragraph shall not apply with respect to such instrument for periods after such transfer.

(4) Fair market value rule in potentially abusive situations.—In the case of any cash method debt instrument, section 483 shall be applied as if it included provisions similar to the provisions of section 1274(b)(3).

(d) Other special rules.—

(1) Aggregation rules.—For purposes of this section—

(A) all sales or exchanges which are part of the same transaction (or a series of related transactions) shall be treated as 1 sale or exchange, and

(B) all debt instruments arising from the same transaction (or a series of related transactions) shall be treated as 1 debt instrument.

(2) Inflation adjustments.—

(A) In general.—In the case of any debt instrument arising out of a sale or exchange during any calendar year after 1989, each dollar amount contained in the preceding provisions of this section shall be increased by the inflation adjustment for such calendar year. Any increase under the preceding sentence shall be rounded to the nearest multiple of $100 (or, if such increase is multiple of $50, such increase shall be increased to the nearest multiple of $100).

(B) Inflation adjustment.—For purposes of subparagraph (A), the inflation adjustment for any calendar year is the percentage (if any) by which—

(i) the CPI for the preceding calendar year exceeds

(ii) the CPI for calendar year 1988.

For purposes of the preceding sentence, the CPI for any calendar year is the average of the Consumer Price Index as of the close of the 12-month period ending on September 30 of such calendar year.

(e) Regulations.—The Secretary shall prescribe such regulations as may be necessary to carry out the purposes of this subsection, including—

(1) regulations coordinating the provisions of this section with other provisions of this title,

(2) regulations necessary to prevent the avoidance of tax through the abuse of the provisions of subsection (c), and

(3) regulations relating to the treatment of transfers of cash method debt instruments.

§ 1275. Other definitions and special rules

(a) Definitions.—For purposes of this subpart—

(1) Debt instrument.—

(A) In general.—Except as provided in subparagraph (B), the term "debt instrument" means a bond, debenture, note, or certificate or other evidence of indebtedness.

(B) Exception for certain annuity contracts.—The term "debt instrument" shall not include any annuity contract to which section 72 applies and which—

(i) depends (in whole or in substantial part) on the life expectancy of 1 or more individuals, or

(ii) is issued by an insurance company subject to tax under subchapter L—

(I) in a transaction in which there is no consideration other than cash or another annuity contract meeting the requirements of this clause,

(II) pursuant to the exercise of an election under an insurance contract by a beneficiary thereof on the death of the insured party under such contract, or

(III) in a transaction involving a qualified pension or employee benefit plan.

(2) Issue date.—

(A) Publicly offered debt instruments.—In the case of any debt instrument which is publicly offered, the term "date of original issue" means the date on which the issue was first issued to the public.

(B) Issues not publicly offered and not issued for property.—In the case of any debt instrument to which section 1273(b)(2) applies, the term "date of original issue" means the date on which the debt instrument was sold by the issuer.

(C) Other debt instruments.—In the case of any debt instrument not described in subparagraph (A) or (B), the term "date of original issue" means the date on which the debt instrument was issued in a sale or exchange.

(3) Tax-exempt obligation.—The term "tax-exempt obligation" means any obligation if—

(A) the interest on such obligation is not includible in gross income under section 103, or

(B) the interest on such obligation is exempt from tax (without regard to the identity of the holder) under any other provision of law.

(4) Special rule for determination of issue price in case of exchange of debt instruments in reorganizations.—

(A) In general.—If—

(i) any debt instrument is issued pursuant to a plan of reorganization (within the meaning of section 368(a)(1)) for another debt instrument (hereinafter in this paragraph referred to as the "old debt instrument"), and

(ii) the amount which (but for this paragraph) would be the issue price of the debt instrument so issued is less than the adjusted issue price of the old debt instrument,

then the issue price of the debt instrument so issued shall be treated as equal to the adjusted issue price of the old debt instrument.

(B) Definitions.—For purposes of this paragraph—

(i) Debt instrument.—The term "debt instrument" includes an investment unit.

(ii) Adjusted issue price.—

(I) In general.—The adjusted issue price of the old debt instrument is its issue price, increased by the portion of any original issue discount previously includible in the gross income of any holder (without regard to subsection (a)(6) or (b)(4) of section 1272 (or the corresponding provisions of prior law)).

(II) Special rule for applying section 163(e).—For purposes of section 163(e), the adjusted issue price of the old debt instrument is its issue price, increased by any original issue discount previously allowed as a deduction.

(5) Treatment of obligations distributed by corporations.—Any debt obligation of a corporation distributed by such corporation with respect to its stock shall be treated as if it had been issued by such corporation for property.

(b) Treatment of borrower in the case of certain loans for personal use.—

(1) Sections 1274 and 483 not to apply.—In the case of the obligor under any debt instrument given in consideration for the sale or exchange of property, sections 1274 and 483 shall not apply if such property is personal use property.

(2) Original issue discount deducted on cash basis in certain cases.—In the case of any debt instrument, if—

(A) such instrument—

(i) is incurred in connection with the acquisition or carrying of personal use property, and

(ii) has original issue discount (determined after the application of paragraph (1)), and

(B) the obligor under such instrument uses the cash receipts and disbursements method of accounting,

notwithstanding section 163(e), the original issue discount on such instrument shall be deductible only when paid.

(3) Personal use property.—For purposes of this subsection, the term "personal use property" means any property substantially all of the use of which by the taxpayer is not in connection with a trade or business of the taxpayer or an activity described in section 212. The determination of whether property is described in the preceding sentence shall be made as of the time of issuance of the debt instrument.

(c) Information requirements.—

(1) Information required to be set forth on instrument.—

(A) In general.—In the case of any debt instrument having original issue discount, the Secretary may by regulations require that—

(i) the amount of the original issue discount, and

(ii) the issue date,

be set forth on such instrument.

(B) Special rule for instruments not publicly offered.—In the case of any issue of debt instruments not publicly offered, the regulations prescribed under subparagraph (A) shall not require the information to be set forth on the debt instrument before any disposition of such instrument by the first buyer.

(2) Information required to be submitted to secretary.—In the case of any issue of publicly offered debt instruments having original issue discount, the issuer shall (at such time and in such manner as the Secretary shall by regulation prescribe) furnish the Secretary the following information:

(A) The amount of the original issue discount.

(B) The issue date.

(C) Such other information with respect to the issue as the Secretary may by regulations require.

For purposes of the preceding sentence, any person who makes a public offering of stripped bonds (or stripped coupons) shall be treated as the issuer of a publicly offered debt instrument having original issue discount.

(3) **Exceptions.**—This subsection shall not apply to any obligation referred to in section 1272(a)(2) (relating to exceptions from current inclusion of original issue discount).

(4) **Cross reference.**—

For civil penalty for failure to meet requirements of this subsection, see section 6706.

(d) **Regulation authority.**—The Secretary may prescribe regulations providing that where, by reason of varying rates of interest, put or call options, indefinite maturities, contingent payments, assumptions of debt instruments, or other circumstances, the tax treatment under this subpart (or section 163(e)) does not carry out the purposes of this subpart (or section 163(e)), such treatment shall be modified to the extent appropriate to carry out the purposes of this subpart (or section 163(e)).

Subpart B—Market Discount on Bonds

§ 1276. Disposition gain representing accrued market discount treated as ordinary income

(a) **Ordinary income.**—

(1) **In general.**—Except as otherwise provided in this section, gain on the disposition of any market discount bond shall be treated as ordinary income to the extent it does not exceed the accrued market discount on such bond. Such gain shall be recognized notwithstanding any other provision of this subtitle.

(2) **Dispositions other than sales, etc.**—For purposes of paragraph (1), a person disposing of any market discount bond in any transaction other than a sale, exchange, or involuntary conversion shall be treated as realizing an amount equal to the fair market value of the bond.

(3) **Treatment of partial principal payments.**—

(A) **In general.**—Any partial principal payment on a market discount bond shall be included in gross income as ordinary income to the extent such payment does not exceed the accrued market discount on such bond.

(B) **Adjustment.**—If subparagraph (A) applies to any partial principal payment on any market discount bond, for purposes of applying this section to any disposition of (or subsequent partial principal payment on) such bond, the amount of accrued market discount shall be reduced by the amount of such partial principal payment included in gross income under subparagraph (A)."

(b) **Accrued market discount.**—For purposes of this section—

(1) **Ratable accrual.**—Except as otherwise provided in this subsection or subsection (c), the accrued market discount on any bond shall be an amount which bears the same ratio to the market discount on such bond as—

(A) the number of days which the taxpayer held the bond, bears to

(B) the number of days after the date the taxpayer acquired the bond and up to (and including) the date of its maturity.

(2) **Election of accrual on basis of constant interest rate (in lieu of ratable accrual).**—

(A) **In general.**—At the election of the taxpayer with respect to any bond, the accrued market discount on such bond shall be the aggregate amount which would have been includible in the gross income of the taxpayer under section 1272(a) (determined without regard to paragraph (2) thereof) with respect to such bond for all periods during which the bond was held by the taxpayer if such bond had been—

(i) originally issued on the date on which such bond was acquired by the taxpayer,

(ii) for an issue price equal to the basis of the taxpayer in such bond immediately after its acquisition.

(B) Coordination where bond has original issue discount.—In the case of any bond having original issue discount, for purposes of applying subparagraph (A)—

(i) the stated redemption price at maturity of such bond shall be treated as equal to its revised issue price, and

(ii) the determination of the portion of the original issue discount which would have been includible in the gross income of the taxpayer under section 1272(a) shall be made under regulations prescribed by the Secretary.

(C) Election irrevocable.—An election under subparagraph (A), once made with respect to any bond, shall be irrevocable.

Special rule where partial principal payments. In the case of a bond the principal of which may be paid in 2 or more payments, the amount of accrued market discount shall be determined under regulations prescribed by the Secretary

(c) Treatment of nonrecognition transactions.—Under regulations prescribed by the Secretary—

(1) Transferred basis property.—If a market discount bond is transferred in a nonrecognition transaction and such bond is transferred basis property in the hands of the transferee, for purposes of determining the amount of the accrued market discount with respect to the transferee—

(A) the transferee shall be treated as having acquired the bond on the date on which it was acquired by the transferor for an amount equal to the basis of the transferor, and

(B) proper adjustments shall be made for gain recognized by the transferor on such transfer (and for any original issue discount or market discount included in the gross income of the transferor).

(2) Exchanged basis property.—If any market discount bond is disposed of by the taxpayer in a nonrecognition transaction and paragraph (1) does not apply to such transaction, any accrued market discount determined with respect to the property disposed of to the extent not theretofore treated as ordinary income under subsection (a)—

(A) shall be treated as accrued market discount with respect to the exchanged basis property received by the taxpayer in such transaction if such property is a market discount bond, and

(B) shall be treated as ordinary income on the disposition of the exchanged basis property received by the taxpayer in such exchange if such property is not a market discount bond.

(3) Paragraph (1) to apply to certain distributions by corporations or partnerships.—For purposes of paragraph (1), if the basis of any market discount bond in the hands of a transferee is determined under section 732(a), or 732(b), such property shall be treated as transferred basis property in the hands of such transferee.

(d) Special rules.—Under regulations prescribed by the Secretary—

(1) rules similar to the rules of subsection (b) of section 1245 shall apply for purposes of this section; except that—

(A) paragraph (1) of such subsection shall not apply,

(B) an exchange qualifying under section 354(a), 355(a), or 356(a) (determined without regard to subsection (a) of this section) shall be treated as an exchange described in paragraph (3) of such subsection, and

* * *

(2) appropriate adjustments shall be made to the basis of any property to reflect gain recognized under subsection (a).

(e) **Section not to apply to market discount bonds issued on or before date of enactment of section.**—This section shall not apply to any market discount bond issued on or before July 18, 1984.

§ 1277. Deferral of interest deduction allocable to accrued market discount

(a) **General rule.**—Except as otherwise provided in this section, the net direct interest expense with respect to any market discount bond shall be allowed as a deduction for the taxable year only to the extent that such expense exceeds the portion of the market discount allocable to the days during the taxable year on which such bond was held by the taxpayer (as determined under the rules of section 1276(b)).

(b) **Disallowed deduction allowed for later years.**—

(1) **Election to take into account in later year where net interest income from bond.**—

(A) **In general.**—If—

(i) there is net interest income for any taxable year with respect to any market discount bond, and

(ii) the taxpayer makes an election under this subparagraph with respect to such bond, any disallowed interest expense with respect to such bond shall be treated as interest paid or accrued by the taxpayer during such taxable year to the extent such disallowed interest expense does not exceed the net interest income with respect to such bond.

(B) **Determination of disallowed interest expense.**—For purposes of subparagraph (A), the amount of the disallowed interest expense—

(i) shall be determined as of the close of the preceding taxable year, and

(ii) shall not include any amount previously taken into account under subparagraph (A).

(C) **Net interest income.**—For purposes of this paragraph, the term "net interest income" means the excess of the amount determined under paragraph (2) of subsection (c) over the amount determined under paragraph (1) of subsection (c).

(2) **Remainder of disallowed interest expense allowed for year of disposition.**—

(A) **In general.**—Except as otherwise provided in this paragraph, the amount of the disallowed interest expense with respect to any market discount bond shall be treated as interest paid or accrued by the taxpayer in the taxable year in which such bond is disposed of.

(B) Nonrecognition transactions.—If any market discount bond is disposed of in a nonrecognition transaction—

(i) the disallowed interest expense with respect to such bond shall be treated as interest paid or accrued in the year of disposition only to the extent of the amount of gain recognized on such disposition, and

(ii) the disallowed interest expense with respect to such property (to the extent not so treated) shall be treated as disallowed interest expense—

(I) in the case of a transaction described in section 1276(c)(1), of the transferee with respect to the transferee basis property, or

(II) in the case of a transaction described in section 1276(c)(2), with respect to the exchanged basis property.

(C) Disallowed interest expense reduced for amounts previously taken into account under paragraph (1).—For purposes of this paragraph, the amount of the disallowed interest expense shall not include any amount previously taken into account under paragraph (1).

(3) Disallowed interest expense.—For purposes of this subsection, the term "disallowed interest expense" means the aggregate amount disallowed under subsection (a) with respect to the market discount bond.

(c) Net direct interest expense.—For purposes of this section, the term "net direct interest expense" means, with respect to any market discount bond, the excess (if any) of—

(1) the amount of interest paid or accrued during the taxable year on indebtedness which is incurred or continued to purchase or carry such bond, over

(2) the aggregate amount of interest (including original issue discount) includible in gross income for the taxable year with respect to such bond.

In the case of any financial institution which is a bank (as defined in section 585(a)(2)) or to which section 593 applies, the determination of whether interest is described in paragraph (1) shall be made under principles similar to the principles of section 291(e)(1)(B)(ii). Under rules similar to the rules of section 265(a)(5), short sale expenses shall be treated as interest for purposes of determining net direct interest expense.

(d) Special rule for gain recognized on disposition of market discount bonds issued on or before date of enactment of section.—In the case of a market discount bond issued on or before July 18, 1984, any gain recognized by the taxpayer on any disposition of such bond shall be treated as ordinary income to the extent the amount of such gain does not exceed the amount allowable with respect to such bond under subsection (b)(2) for the taxable year in which such bond is disposed of.

§ 1278. Definitions and special rules

(a) In general.—For purposes of this part—

(1) Market discount bond.—

(A) In general.—Except as provided in subparagraph (B), the term "market discount bond" means any bond having market discount.

(B) Exceptions.—The term "market discount bond" shall not include—

(i) Short-term obligations.—Any obligation with a fixed maturity date not exceeding 6 months from the date of issue.

(ii) Tax-exempt obligations.—Any tax-exempt obligation (as defined in section 1275(a)(3)).

(iii) United States savings bonds.—Any United States savings bond.

(iv) Installment obligations.—Any installment obligation to which section 453B applies.

(C) Treatment of bonds acquired at original issue.—

(i) In general.—Except as otherwise provided in this subparagraph or in regulations, the term "market discount bond" shall not include any bond acquired by the taxpayer at its original issue.

(ii) Treatment of bonds acquired for less than issue price.—Clause (i) shall not apply to any bond if—

(I) the basis of the taxpayer in such bond is determined under section 1012, and

(II) such basis is less than the issue price of such bond determined under subpart A of this part.

(iii) Bonds acquired in certain reorganizations.—Clause (i) shall not apply to any bond issued pursuant to a plan of reorganization (within the meaning of section 368(a)(1)) in exchange for another bond having market discount. Solely for purposes of section 1276, the preceding sentence shall not apply if such other bond was issued on or before July 18, 1984 (the date of the enactment of section 1276) and if the bond issued pursuant to such plan of reorganization has the same term and the same interest rate as such other bond had.

(iv) Treatment of certain transferred basis property.—For purposes of clause (i), if the adjusted basis of any bond in the hands of the taxpayer is determined by reference to the adjusted basis of such bond in the hands of a person who acquired such bond at its original issue, such bond shall be treated as acquired by the taxpayer at its original issue.

(2) Market discount.—

(A) In general.—The term "market discount" means the excess (if any) of—

(i) the stated redemption price of the bond at maturity, over

(ii) the basis of such bond immediately after its acquisition by the taxpayer.

(B) Coordination where bond has original issue discount.—In the case of any bond having original issue discount, for purposes of subparagraph (A), the stated redemption price of such bond at maturity shall be treated as equal to its revised issue price.

(C) De minimis rule.—If the market discount is less than ¼ of 1 percent of the stated redemption price of the bond at maturity multiplied by the number of complete years to maturity (after the taxpayer acquired the bond), then the market discount shall be considered to be zero.

(3) Bond.—The term "bond" means any bond, debenture, note, certificate, or other evidence of indebtedness.

(4) Revised issue price.—The term "revised issue price" means the sum of—

(A) the issue price of the bond, and

(B) the aggregate amount of the original issue discount includible in the gross income of all holders for periods before the acquisition of the bond by the taxpayer (determined without regard to section 1272(a)(6) or (b)(4)).

(5) Original issue discount, etc.—The terms "original issue discount", "stated redemption price at maturity", and "issue price" have the respective meanings given such terms by subpart A of this part.

(b) Election to include market discount currently.—

(1) In general.—If the taxpayer makes an election under this subsection—

(A) sections 1276 and 1277 shall not apply, and

(B) market discount on any market discount bond shall be included in the gross income of the taxpayer for the taxable years to which it is attributable (as determined under the rules of subsection (b) of section 1276).

Except for purposes of sections 871(a), 881, 1441, 1442, and 6049 (and such other provisions as may be specified in regulations), any amount included in gross income under subparagraph (B) shall be treated as interest for purposes of this title.

(2) Scope of election.—An election under this subsection shall apply to all market discount bonds acquired by the taxpayer on or after the 1st day of the 1st taxable year to which such election applies.

(3) Period to which election applies.—An election under this subsection shall apply to the taxable year for which it is made and for all subsequent taxable years, unless the taxpayer secures the consent of the Secretary to the revocation of such election.

(c) Regulations.—The Secretary shall prescribe such regulations as may be necessary to carry out the purposes of this subpart.

Subpart C—Discount on Short–Term Obligations

§ 1281. Current inclusion in income of discount on certain short-term obligations

(a) General rule.—In the case of any short-term obligation to which this section applies, for purposes of this title—

(1) there shall be included in the gross income of the holder an amount equal to the sum of the daily portions of the acquisition discount for each day during the taxable year on which such holder held such obligation, and

(2) any interest payable on the obligation (other than interest taken into account in determining the amount of the acquisition discount) shall be included in gross income as it accrues.

(b) Short-term obligations to which section applies.—

(1) In general.—This section shall apply to any short-term obligation which—

(A) is held by a taxpayer using an accrual method of accounting,

(B) is held primarily for sale to customers in the ordinary course of the taxpayer's trade or business,

(C) is held by a bank (as defined in section 581),

(D) is held by a regulated investment company or a common trust fund,

(E) is identified by the taxpayer under section 1256(e)(2) as being part of a hedging transaction, or

* * *

(2) Treatment of obligations held by pass-thru entities.—

(A) In general.—This section shall apply also to—

(i) any short-term obligation which is held by a pass-thru entity which is formed or availed of for purposes of avoiding the provisions of this section, and

(ii) any short-term obligation which is acquired by a pass-thru entity (not described in clause (i)) during the required accrual period.

(B) Required accrual period.—For purposes of subparagraph (A), the term "required accrual period" means the period—

(i) which begins with the first taxable year for which the ownership test of subparagraph (C) is met with respect to the pass-thru entity (or a predecessor), and

(ii) which ends with the first taxable year after the taxable year referred to in clause (i) for which the ownership test of subparagraph (C) is not met and with respect to which the Secretary consents to the termination of the required accrual period.

(C) Ownership test.—The ownership test of this subparagraph is met for any taxable year if, on at least 90 days during the taxable year, 20 percent or more of the value of the interests in the pass-thru entity are held by persons described in paragraph (1) or by other pass-thru entities to which subparagraph (A) applies.

(D) Pass-thru entity.—The term "pass-thru entity" means any partnership, S corporation, trust, or other pass-thru entity.

(c) Cross reference.—

For special rules limiting the application of this section to original issue discount in the case of nongovernmental obligations, see section 1283(c).

§ 1282. Deferral of interest deduction allocable to accrued discount

(a) General rule.—Except as otherwise provided in this section, the net direct interest expense with respect to any short-term obligation shall be allowed as a deduction for the taxable year only to the extent such expense exceeds the sum of—

(1) the daily portions of the acquisition discount for each day during the taxable year on which the taxpayer held such obligation, and

(2) the amount of any interest payable on the obligation (other than interest taken into account in determining the amount of the acquisition discount) which accrues during the taxable year while the taxpayer held such obligation (and is not included in the gross income of the taxpayer for such taxable year by reason of the taxpayer's method of accounting).

(b) Section not to apply to obligations to which section 1281 applies.—

(1) **In general.**—This section shall not apply to any short-term obligation to which section 1281 applies.

(2) **Election to have section 1281 apply to all obligations.—**

(A) In general.—A taxpayer may make an election under this paragraph to have section 1281 apply to all short-term obligations acquired by the taxpayer on or after the 1st day of the 1st taxable year to which such election applies.

(B) Period to which election applies.—An election under this paragraph shall apply to the taxable year for which it is made and for all subsequent taxable years, unless the taxpayer secures the consent of the Secretary to the revocation of such election.

(c) Certain rules made applicable.—Rules similar to the rules of subsections (b) and (c) of section 1277 shall apply for purposes of this section.

(d) Cross reference.—

For special rules limiting the application of this section to original issue discount in the case of nongovernmental obligations, see section 1283(c).

§ 1283.   Definitions and special rules

(a) Definitions.—For purposes of this subpart—

(1) Short-term obligation.—

(A) In general.—Except as provided in subparagraph (B), the term "short-term obligation" means any bond, debenture, note, certificate, or other evidence of indebtedness which has a fixed maturity date not more than 1 year from the date of issue.

(B) Exceptions for tax-exempt obligations.—The term "short-term obligation" shall not include any tax-exempt obligation (as defined in section 1275(a)(3)).

(2) Acquisition discount.—The term "acquisition discount" means the excess of—

(A) the stated redemption price at maturity (as defined in section 1273), over

(B) the taxpayer's basis for the obligation.

(b) Daily portion.—For purposes of the subpart—

(1) Ratable accrual.—Except as otherwise provided in this subsection, the daily portion of the acquisition discount is an amount equal to—

(A) the amount of such discount, divided by

(B) the number of days after the day on which the taxpayer acquired the obligation and up to (and including) the day of its maturity.

(2) Election of accrual on basis of constant interest rate (in lieu of ratable accrual).—

(A) In general.—At the election of the taxpayer with respect to any obligation, the daily portion of the acquisition discount for any day is the portion of the acquisition discount accruing on such day determined (under regulations prescribed by the Secretary) on the basis of—

(i) the taxpayer's yield to maturity based on the taxpayer's cost of acquiring the obligation, and

(ii) compounding daily.

(B) Election irrevocable.—An election under subparagraph (A), once made with respect to any obligation, shall be irrevocable.

(c) Special rules for nongovernmental obligations.—

(1) In general.—In the case of any short-term obligation which is not a short-term Government obligation (as defined in section 1271(a)(3)(B))—

(A) sections 1281 and 1282 shall be applied by taking into account original issue discount in lieu of acquisition discount, and

(B) appropriate adjustments shall be made in the application of subsection (b) of this section.

(2) Election to have paragraph (1) not apply.—

(A) In general.—A taxpayer may make an election under this paragraph to have paragraph (1) not apply to all obligations acquired by the taxpayer on or after the first day of the first taxable year to which such election applies.

(B) Period to which election applies.—An election under this paragraph shall apply to the taxable year for which it is made and for all subsequent taxable years, unless the taxpayer secures the consent of the Secretary to the revocation of such election.

(d) Other special rules.—

(1) Basis adjustments.—The basis of any short-term obligation in the hands of the holder thereof shall be increased by the amount included in his gross income pursuant to section 1281.

(2) Double inclusion in income not required.—Section 1281 shall not require the inclusion of any amount previously includible in gross income.

(3) Coordination with other provisions.—Section 454(b) and paragraphs (3) and (4) of section 1271(a) shall not apply to any short-term obligation to which section 1281 applies.

Subpart D—Miscellaneous Provisions

§ 1286. Tax treatment of stripped bonds

(a) Inclusion in income as if bond and coupons were original issue discount bonds.—If any person purchases after July 1, 1982, a stripped bond or a stripped coupon, then such bond or coupon while held by such purchaser (or by any other person whose basis is determined by reference to the basis in the hands of such purchaser) shall be treated for purposes of this part as a bond originally issued on the purchase date and having an original issue discount equal to the excess (if any) of—

(1) the stated redemption price at maturity (or, in the case of coupon, the amount payable on the due date of such coupon), over

(2) such bond's or coupon's ratable share of the purchase price.

For purposes of paragraph (2), ratable shares shall be determined on the basis of their respective fair market values on the date of purchase.

(b) Tax treatment of person stripping bond.—For purposes of this subtitle, if any person strips 1 or more coupons from a bond and after July 1, 1982, disposes of the bond or such coupon—

(1) such person shall include in gross income an amount equal to the sum of—

(A) the interest accrued on such bond while held by such person and before the time such coupon or bond was disposed of (to the extent such interest has not theretofore been included in such person's gross income), and

(B) the accrued market discount on such bond determined as of the time such coupon or bond was disposed of (to the extent such discount has not theretofore been included in such person's gross income),

(2) the basis of the bond and coupons shall be increased by the amount included in gross income under paragraph (1),

(3) the basis of the bond and coupons immediately before the disposition (as adjusted pursuant to paragraph (2)) shall be allocated among the items retained by such person and the items disposed of by such person on the basis of their respective fair market values, and

(4) for purposes of subsection (a), such person shall be treated as having purchased on the date of such disposition each such item which he retains for an amount equal to the basis allocated to such item under paragraph (3).

A rule similar to the rule of paragraph (4) shall apply in the case of any person whose basis in any bond or coupon is determined by reference to the basis of the person described in the preceding sentence.

(c) Retention of existing law for stripped bonds purchased before July 2, 1982.—If a bond issued at any time with interest coupons—

(1) is purchased after August 16, 1954, and before January 1, 1958, and the purchaser does not receive all the coupons which first become payable more than 12 months after the date of the purchase, or

(2) is purchased after December 31, 1957, and before July 2, 1982, and the purchaser does not receive all the coupons which first become payable after the date of the purchase,

then the gain on the sale or other disposition of such bond by such purchaser (or by a person whose basis is determined by reference to the basis in the hands of such purchaser) shall be considered as ordinary income to the extent that the fair market value (determined as of the time of the purchase) of the bond with coupons attached exceeds the purchase price. If this subsection and section 1271(a)(2)(A) apply with respect to gain realized on the sale or exchange of any evidence of indebtedness, then section 1271(a)(2)(A) shall apply with respect to that part of the gain to which this subsection does not apply.

(d) Special rules for tax-exempt obligations.—In the case of any tax-exempt obligation (as defined in section 1275(a)(3)) from which 1 or more coupons have been stripped—

(1) the amount of original issue discount determined under subsection (a) with respect to any stripped bond or stripped coupon from such obligation shall be the amount which produces a yield to maturity (as of the purchase date) equal to the lower of—

(A) the coupon rate of interest on such obligation before the separation of coupons, or

(B) the yield to maturity (on the basis of purchase price) of the stripped obligation or coupon,

(2) the amount of original issue discount determined under paragraph (1) shall be taken into account in determining the adjusted basis of the holder under section 1288,

(3) subsection (b)(1) shall not apply, and

(4) subsection (b)(2) shall be applied by increasing the basis of the bond or coupon by the interest accrued but not paid before the time such bond or coupon was disposed of (and not previously reflected in basis).

(e) Definitions and special rules.—For purposes of this section—

(1) **Bond.**—The term "bond" means a bond, debenture, note, or certificate or other evidence of indebtedness.

(2) **Stripped bond.**—The term "stripped bond" means a bond issued at any time with interest coupons where there is a separation in ownership between the bond and any coupon which has not yet become payable.

(3) **Stripped coupon.**—The term "stripped coupon" means any coupon relating to a stripped bond.

(4) **Stated redemption price at maturity.**—The term "stated redemption price at maturity" has the meaning given such term by section 1273(a)(2).

(5) Coupon.—The term "coupon" includes any right to receive interest on a bond (whether or not evidenced by a coupon). This paragraph shall apply for purposes of subsection (c) only in the case of purchases after July 1, 1982.

(6) Purchase.—The term "purchase" has the meaning given such term by section 1272(d)(1).

(f) Regulation authority.—The Secretary may prescribe regulations providing that where, by reason of varying rates of interest, put or call options, or other circumstances, the tax treatment under this section does not accurately reflect the income of the holder of a stripped coupon or stripped bond, or of the person disposing of such bond or coupon, as the case may be, for any period, such treatment shall be modified to require that the proper amount of income be included for such period.

§ 1287. Denial of capital gain treatment for gains on certain obligations not in registered form

(a) In general.—If any registration-required obligation is not in registered form, any gain on the sale or other disposition of such obligation shall be treated as ordinary income (unless the issuance of such obligation was subject to tax under section 4701).

Definitions.—For purposes of subsection (a)—

(1) Registration-required obligation.—The term "registration-required obligation" has the meaning given to such term by section 163(f)(2) except that clause (iv) of subparagraph (A), and subparagraph (B), of such section shall not apply.

(2) Registered form.—The term "registered form" has the same meaning as when used in section 163(f).

§ 1288. Treatment of original issue discount on tax-exempt obligations

(a) General rule.—Original issue discount on any tax-exempt obligation shall be treated as accruing—

(1) for purposes of section 163, in the manner provided by section 1272(a) (determined without regard to paragraph (6) thereof), and

(2) for purposes of determining the adjusted basis of the holder, in the manner provided by section 1272(a) (determined with regard to paragraph (6) thereof).

(b) Definitions and special rules.—For purposes of this section—

(1) Original issue discount.—The term "original issue discount" has the meaning given to such term by section 1273(a) without regard to paragraph (3) thereof. In applying section 483 or 1274, under regulations prescribed by the Secretary, appropriate adjustments shall be made to the applicable Federal rate to take into account the tax exemption for interest on the obligation.

(2) Tax-exempt obligation.—The term "tax-exempt obligation" has the meaning given to such term by section 1275(a)(3).

(3) Short-term obligations.—In applying this section to obligations with maturity of 1 year or less, rules similar to the rules of section 1283(b) shall apply.

SUBCHAPTER Q—READJUSTMENT OF TAX BETWEEN YEARS AND SPECIAL LIMITATIONS

Part
  [I.   Repealed]
   II.   Mitigation of effect of limitations and other provisions.
  [III. Repealed]
  [IV.   Repealed]
   V.   Claim of right.
  [VI.   Repealed]
   VII. Recoveries or foreign expropriation losses.*

PART II—MITIGATION OF EFFECT OF LIMITATIONS AND OTHER PROVISIONS

§ 1311.   Correction of error

(a) General rule.—If a determination (as defined in section 1313) is described in one or more of the paragraphs of section 1312 and, on the date of the determination, correction of the effect of the error referred to in the applicable paragraph of section 1312 is prevented by the operation of any law or rule of law, other than this part and other than section 7122 (relating to compromises), then the effect of the error shall be corrected by an adjustment made in the amount and in the manner specified in section 1314.

(b) Conditions necessary for adjustment.—

(1) Maintenance of an inconsistent position.—Except in cases described in paragraphs (3) (B) and (4) of section 1312, an adjustment shall be made under this part only if—

(A) in case the amount of the adjustment would be credited or refunded in the same manner as an overpayment under section 1314, there is adopted in the determination a position maintained by the Secretary, or

(B) in case the amount of the adjustment would be assessed and collected in the same manner as a deficiency under section 1314, there is adopted in the determination a position maintained by the taxpayer with respect to whom the determination is made,

and the position maintained by the Secretary in the case described in subparagraph (A) or maintained by the taxpayer in the case described in subparagraph (B) is inconsistent with the erroneous inclusion, exclusion, omission, allowance, disallowance, recognition, or nonrecognition, as the case may be.

(2) Correction not barred at time of erroneous action.—

(A) Determination described in section 1312(3) (B).—In the case of a determination described in section 1312(3) (B) (relating to certain exclusions from income), adjustment shall be made under this part only if assessment of a deficiency for the taxable year in which the item is includible or against the related taxpayer was not barred, by any law or rule of law, at the time the Secretary first maintained, in a notice of deficiency sent pursuant to section 6212 or before the Tax Court, that the item described in section 1312(3) (B) should be included in the gross income of the taxpayer for the taxable year to which the determination relates.

* Omitted entirely.

(B) Determination described in section 1312(4).—In the case of a determination described in section 1312(4) (relating to disallowance of certain deductions and credits), adjustment shall be made under this part only if credit or refund of the overpayment attributable to the deduction or credit described in such section which should have been allowed to the taxpayer or related taxpayer was not barred, by any law or rule of law, at the time the taxpayer first maintained before the Secretary or before the Tax Court, in writing, that he was entitled to such deduction or credit for the taxable year to which the determination relates.

(3) Existence of relationship.—In case the amount of the adjustment would be assessed and collected in the same manner as a deficiency (except for cases described in section 1312(3) (B)), the adjustment shall not be made with respect to a related taxpayer unless he stands in such relationship to the taxpayer at the time the latter first maintains the inconsistent position in a return, claim for refund, or petition (or amended petition) to the Tax Court for the taxable year with respect to which the determination is made, or if such position is not so maintained, then at the time of the determination.

§ 1312. Circumstances of adjustment

The circumstances under which the adjustment provided in section 1311 is authorized are as follows:

(1) Double inclusion of an item of gross income.—The determination requires the inclusion in gross income of an item which was erroneously included in the gross income of the taxpayer for another taxable year or in the gross income of a related taxpayer.

(2) Double allowance of a deduction or credit.—The determination allows a deduction or credit which was erroneously allowed to the taxpayer for another taxable year or to a related taxpayer.

(3) Double exclusion of an item of gross income.—

(A) Items included in income.—The determination requires the exclusion from gross income of an item included in a return filed by the taxpayer or with respect to which tax was paid and which was erroneously excluded or omitted from the gross income of the taxpayer for another taxable year, or from the gross income of a related taxpayer; or

(B) Items not included in income.—The determination requires the exclusion from gross income of an item not included in a return filed by the taxpayer and with respect to which the tax was not paid but which is includible in the gross income of the taxpayer for another taxable year or in the gross income of a related taxpayer.

(4) Double disallowance of a deduction or credit.—The determination disallows a deduction or credit which should have been allowed to, but was not allowed to, the taxpayer for another taxable year, or to a related taxpayer.

(5) Correlative deductions and inclusions for trusts or estates and legatees, beneficiaries, or heirs.—The determination allows or disallows any of the additional deductions allowable in computing the taxable income of estates or trusts, or requires or denies any of the inclusions in the computation of taxable income of beneficiaries, heirs, or legatees, specified in subparts A to E, inclusive (secs. 641 and following, relating to estates, trusts and beneficiaries) of part I of subchapter J of this chapter, or corresponding provisions of prior internal revenue laws, and the correlative inclusion or deduction, as the case may be, has been erroneously excluded, omitted, or included, or disallowed, omitted, or allowed, as the case may be, in respect of the related taxpayer.

(6) Correlative deductions and credits for certain related corporations.—The determination allows or disallows a deduction (including a credit) in computing the taxable income (or, as the case may be, net income, normal tax net income, or surtax net income) of a corporation, and a correlative deduction or credit has been erroneously allowed, omitted, or disallowed, as the case may be, in respect of a related taxpayer described in section 1313(c) (7).

(7) Basis of property after erroneous treatment of a prior transaction.—

(A) General rule.—The determination determines the basis of property, and in respect of any transaction on which such basis depends, or in respect of any transaction which was erroneously treated as affecting such basis, there occurred, with respect to a taxpayer described in subparagraph (B) of this paragraph, any of the errors described in subparagraph (C) of this paragraph.

(B) Taxpayers with respect to whom the erroneous treatment occurred.—The taxpayer with respect to whom the erroneous treatment occurred must be—

(i) the taxpayer with respect to whom the determination is made,

(ii) a taxpayer who acquired title to the property in the transaction and from whom, mediately or immediately, the taxpayer with respect to whom the determination is made derived title, or

(iii) a taxpayer who had title to the property at the time of the transaction and from whom, mediately or immediately, the taxpayer with respect to whom the determination is made derived title, if the basis of the property in the hands of the taxpayer with respect to whom the determination is made is determined under section 1015(a) (relating to the basis of property acquired by gift).

(C) Prior erroneous treatment.—With respect to a taxpayer described in subparagraph (B) of this paragraph—

(i) there was an erroneous inclusion in, or omission from, gross income,

(ii) there was an erroneous recognition, or nonrecognition, of gain or loss, or

(iii) there was an erroneous deduction of an item properly chargeable to capital account or an erroneous charge to capital account of an item properly deductible.

§ 1313.   Definitions

(a) Determination.—For purposes of this part, the term "determination" means—

(1) a decision by the Tax Court or a judgment, decree, or other order by any court of competent jurisdiction, which has become final;

(2) a closing agreement made under section 7121;

(3) a final disposition by the Secretary of a claim for refund. For purposes of this part, a claim for refund shall be deemed finally disposed of by the Secretary—

(A) as to items with respect to which the claim was allowed, on the date of allowance of refund or credit or on the date of mailing notice of disallowance (by reason of offsetting items) of the claim for refund, and

(B) as to items with respect to which the claim was disallowed, in whole or in part, or as to items applied by the Secretary in reduction of the refund or credit, on expiration of the time for instituting suit with respect thereto (unless suit is instituted before the expiration of such time); or

(4) under regulations prescribed by the Secretary, an agreement for purposes of this part, signed by the Secretary and by any person, relating to the liability of such person (or the person for whom he acts) in respect of a tax under this subtitle for any taxable period.

(b) Taxpayer.—Notwithstanding section 7701(a) (14), the term "taxpayer" means any person subject to a tax under the applicable revenue law.

(c) Related taxpayer.—For purposes of this part, the term "related taxpayer" means a taxpayer who, with the taxpayer with respect to whom a determination is made, stood, in the taxable year with respect to which the erroneous inclusion, exclusion, omission, allowance, or disallowance was made, in one of the following relationships:

(1) husband and wife,

(2) grantor and fiduciary,

(3) grantor and beneficiary,

(4) fiduciary and beneficiary, legatee, or heir,

(5) decedent and decedent's estate,

(6) partner, or

(7) member of an affiliated group of corporations (as defined in section 1504).

§ 1314. Amount and method of adjustment

(a) Ascertainment of amount of adjustment.—In computing the amount of an adjustment under this part there shall first be ascertained the tax previously determined for the taxable year with respect to which the error was made. The amount of the tax previously determined shall be the excess of—

(1) the sum of—

(A) the amount shown as the tax by the taxpayer on his return (determined as provided in section 6211(b) (1), (3), and (4), relating to the definition of deficiency), if a return was made by the taxpayer and an amount was shown as the tax by the taxpayer thereon, plus

(B) the amounts previously assessed (or collected without assessment) as a deficiency, over—

(2) the amount of rebates, as defined in section 6211(b) (2), made.

There shall then be ascertained the increase or decrease in tax previously determined which results solely from the correct treatment of the item which was the subject of the error (with due regard given to the effect of the item in the computation of gross income, taxable income, and other matters under this subtitle). A similar computation shall be made for any other taxable year affected, or treated as affected, by a net operating loss deduction (as defined in section 172) or by a capital loss carryback or carryover (as defined in section 1212), determined with reference to the taxable year with respect to which the error was made. The amount so ascertained (together with any amounts wrongfully collected as additions to the tax or interest, as a result of such error) for each taxable year shall be the amount of the adjustment for that taxable year.

(b) Method of adjustment.—The adjustment authorized in section 1311(a) shall be made by assessing and collecting, or refunding or crediting, the amount thereof in the same manner as if it were a deficiency determined by the Secretary with respect to the taxpayer as to whom the error was made or an overpayment claimed by such taxpayer, as the case may be, for the taxable year or years with respect to which an amount is ascertained under subsection (a), and as if on the date of the determination one year remained before the expiration of the periods of limitation upon assessment or filing claim for refund for such taxable year or years. If, as a result of a determination described in section 1313(a) (4), an adjustment has been made by the assessment and collection of a deficiency or the refund or credit of an overpayment, and subsequently such determination is altered or revoked, the amount of the adjustment ascertained under subsection (a) of this section shall be redetermined on the basis of such alteration or revocation and any overpayment or deficiency resulting from such redetermination shall be refunded or credited, or assessed and collected, as the case may be, as an adjustment under this part. In the case of an adjustment resulting from an increase or decrease in a net operating loss or net capital loss which is carried back to the year of adjustment, interest shall not be collected or paid for any period prior to the close of the taxable year in which the net operating loss or net capital loss arises.

(c) **Adjustment unaffected by other items.**—The amount to be assessed and collected in the same manner as a deficiency, or to be refunded or credited in the same manner as an overpayment, under this part, shall not be diminished by any credit or set-off based upon any item other than the one which was the subject of the adjustment. The amount of the adjustment under this part, if paid, shall not be recovered by a claim or suit for refund or suit for erroneous refund based upon any item other than the one which was the subject of the adjustment.

* * *

PART V—CLAIM OF RIGHT

§ 1341. Computation of tax where taxpayer restores substantial amount held under claim of right

(a) **General rule.**—If—

(1) an item was included in gross income for a prior taxable year (or years) because it appeared that the taxpayer had an unrestricted right to such item;

(2) a deduction is allowable for the taxable year because it was established after the close of such prior taxable year (or years) that the taxpayer did not have an unrestricted right to such item or to a portion of such item; and

(3) the amount of such deduction exceeds $3,000,

then the tax imposed by this chapter for the taxable year shall be the lesser of the following:

(4) the tax for the taxable year computed with such deduction; or

(5) an amount equal to—

(A) the tax for the taxable year computed without such deduction, minus

(B) the decrease in tax under this chapter (or the corresponding provisions of prior revenue laws) for the prior taxable year (or years) which would result solely from the exclusion of such item (or portion thereof) from gross income for such prior taxable year (or years).

* * *

(b) **Special rules.**—

(1) If the decrease in tax ascertained under subsection (a) (5) (B) exceeds the tax imposed by this chapter for the taxable year (computed without the deduction) such excess shall be considered to be a payment of tax on the last day prescribed by law for the payment of tax for the taxable year, and shall be refunded or credited in the same manner as if it were an overpayment for such taxable year.

(2) Subsection (a) does not apply to any deduction allowable with respect to an item which was included in gross income by reason of the sale or other disposition of stock in trade of the taxpayer (or other property of a kind which would properly have been included in the inventory of the taxpayer if on hand at the close of the prior taxable year) or property held by the taxpayer primarily for sale to customers in the ordinary course of his trade or business. This paragraph shall not apply if the deduction arises out of refunds or repayments with respect to rates made by a regulated public utility (as defined in section 7701(a) (33) without regard to the limitation contained in the last two sentences thereof) if such refunds or repayments are required to be made by the Government, political subdivision, agency, or instrumentality referred to in such section, or by an order of a court, or are made in settlement of litigation or under threat or imminence of litigation.

* * *

(4) For purposes of determining whether paragraph (4) or paragraph (5) of subsection (a) applies—

(A) in any case where the deduction referred to in paragraph (4) of subsection (a) results in a net operating loss, such loss shall, for purposes of computing the tax for the taxable year under such paragraph (4), be carried back to the same extent and in the same manner as is provided under section 172; and

(B) in any case where the exclusion referred to in paragraph (5) (B) of subsection (a) results in a net operating loss or capital loss for the prior taxable year (or years), such loss shall, for purposes of computing the decrease in tax for the prior taxable year (or years) under such paragraph (5) (B), be carried back and carried over to the same extent and in the same manner as is provided under section 172 or section 1212, except that no carryover beyond the taxable year shall be taken into account.

(5) For purposes of this chapter, the net operating loss described in paragraph (4) (A) of this subsection, or the net operating loss or capital loss described in paragraph (4) (B) of this subsection, as the case may be, shall (after the application of paragraph (4) or (5) (B) of subsection (a) for the taxable year) be taken into account under section 172 or 1212 for taxable years after the taxable year to the same extent and in the same manner as—

(A) a net operating loss sustained for the taxable year, if paragraph (4) of subsection (a) applied, or

(B) a net operating loss or capital loss sustained for the prior taxable year (or years), if paragraph (5) (B) of subsection (a) applied.

SUBCHAPTER S—TAX TREATMENT OF S CORPORATIONS AND THEIR SHAREHOLDERS

Part

§ 1361. S corporation defined

(a) S corporation defined.—

(1) In general.—For purposes of this title, the term "S corporation" means, with respect to any taxable year, a small business corporation for which an election under section 1362(a) is in effect for such year.

(2) C corporation.—For purposes of this title, the term "C corporation" means, with respect to any taxable year, a corporation which is not an S corporation for such year.

(b) Small business corporation.—

(1) In general.—For purposes of this subchapter, the term "small business corporation" means a domestic corporation which is not an ineligible corporation and which does not—

(A) have more than 35 shareholders,

(B) have as a shareholder a person (other than an estate and other than a trust described in subsection (c)(2)) who is not an individual,

(C) have a nonresident alien as a shareholder, and

(D) have more than 1 class of stock.

(2) Ineligible corporation defined.—For purposes of paragraph (1), the term "ineligible corporation" means any corporation which is—

(A) a member of an affiliated group (determined under section 1504 without regard to the exceptions contained in subsection (b) thereof),

(B) a financial institution which is a bank (as defined in section 585(a)(2)) or to which section 593 applies,

(C) an insurance company subject to tax under subchapter L,

(D) a corporation to which an election under section 936 applies, or

(E) a DISC or former DISC.

(c) Special rules for applying subsection (b).—

(1) Husband and wife treated as 1 shareholder.—For purposes of subsection (b)(1)(A), a husband and wife (and their estates) shall be treated as 1 shareholder.

(2) Certain trusts permitted as shareholders.—

(A) **In general.**—For purposes of subsection (b)(1)(B), the following trusts may be shareholders:

(i) A trust all of which is treated (under subpart E of part I of subchapter J of this chapter) as owned by an individual who is a citizen or resident of the United States.

(ii) A trust which was described in clause (i) immediately before the death of the deemed owner and which continues in existence after such death, but only for the 60-day period beginning on the day of the deemed owner's death. If a trust is described in the preceding sentence and if the entire corpus of the trust is includible in the gross estate of the deemed owner, the preceding sentence shall be applied by substituting "2-year period" for "60-day period".

(iii) A trust with respect to stock transferred to it pursuant to the terms of a will, but only for the 60-day period beginning on the day on which such stock is transferred to it.

(iv) A trust created primarily to exercise the voting power of stock transferred to it.

This subparagraph shall not apply to any foreign trust.

(B) Treatment as shareholders.—For purposes of subsection (b)(1)—

(i) In the case of a trust described in clause (i) of subparagraph (A), the deemed owner shall be treated as the shareholder.

(ii) In the case of a trust described in clause (ii) of subparagraph (A), the estate of the deemed owner shall be treated as the shareholder.

(iii) In the case of a trust described in clause (iii) of subparagraph (A), the estate of the testator shall be treated as the shareholder.

(iv) In the case of a trust described in clause (iv) of subparagraph (A), each beneficiary of the trust shall be treated as a shareholder.

(3) Estate of individual in bankruptcy may be shareholder.—For purposes of subsection (b)(1)(B), the term "estate" includes the estate of an individual in a case under title 11 of the United States Code.

(4) Differences in common stock voting rights disregarded.—For purposes of subsection (b)(1)(D), a corporation shall not be treated as having more than 1 class of stock solely because there are differences in voting rights among the shares of common stock.

(5) Straight debt safe harbor.—

(A) In general.—For purposes of subsection (b)(1)(D), straight debt shall not be treated as a second class of stock.

(B) Straight debt defined.—For purposes of this paragraph, the term "straight debt" means any written unconditional promise to pay on demand or on a specified date a sum certain in money if—

(i) the interest rate (and interest payment dates) are not contingent on profits, the borrower's discretion, or similar factors,

(ii) there is no convertibility (directly or indirectly) into stock, and

(iii) the creditor is an individual (other than a nonresident alien), an estate, or a trust described in paragraph (2).

(C) Regulations.—The Secretary shall prescribe such regulations as may be necessary or appropriate to provide for the proper treatment of straight debt under this subchapter and for the coordination of such treatment with other provisions of this title.

(6) Ownership of stock in certain inactive corporations.—For purposes of subsection (b)(2)(A), a corporation shall not be treated as a member of an affiliated group during any period within a taxable year by reason of the ownership of stock in another corporation if such other corporation—

(A) has not begun business at any time on or before the close of such period, and

(B) does not have gross income for such period.

(d) Special rule for qualified subchapter S trust.—

(1) **In general.**—In the case of a qualified subchapter S trust with respect to which a beneficiary makes an election under paragraph (2)—

(A) such trust shall be treated as a trust described in subsection (c)(2)(A)(i), and

(B) for purposes of section 678(a), the beneficiary of such trust shall be treated as the owner of that portion of the trust which consists of stock in an S corporation with respect to which the election under paragraph (2) is made.

(2) **Election.**—

(A) **In general.**—A beneficiary of a qualified subchapter S trust (or his legal representative) may elect to have this subsection apply.

(B) **Manner and time of election.**—

(i) **Separate election with respect to each corporation.**—An election under this paragraph shall be made separately with respect to each corporation the stock of which is held by the trust.

(ii) **Elections with respect to successive income beneficiaries.**—If there is an election under this paragraph with respect to any beneficiary, an election under this paragraph shall be treated as made by each successive beneficiary unless such beneficiary affirmatively refuses to consent to such election.

(iii) **Time, manner, and form of election.**—Any election, or refusal, under this paragraph shall be made in such manner and form, and at such time, as the Secretary may prescribe.

(C) **Election irrevocable.**—An election under this paragraph, once made, may be revoked only with the consent of the Secretary.

(D) **Grace period.**—An election under this paragraph shall be effective up to 15 days and 2 months before the date of the election.

(3) **Qualified subchapter S trust.**—For purposes of this subsection, the term "qualified subchapter S trust" means a trust—

(A) the terms of which require that—

(i) during the life of the current income beneficiary, there shall be only 1 income beneficiary of the trust,

(ii) any corpus distributed during the life of the current income beneficiary may be distributed only to such beneficiary,

(iii) the income interest of the current income beneficiary in the trust shall terminate on the earlier of such beneficiary's death or the termination of the trust, and

(iv) upon the termination of the trust during the life of the current income beneficiary, the trust shall distribute all of its assets to such beneficiary, and

(B) all of the income (within the meaning of section 643(b)) of which is distributed (or required to be distributed) currently to 1 individual who is a citizen or resident of the United States.

A substantially separate and independent share of a trust treated as a separate trust under section 663(c) shall be treated as a separate trust for purposes of this subsection and subsection (c).

(4) **Trust ceasing to be qualified.**—

(A) **Failure to meet requirements of paragraph (3)(A).**—If a qualified subchapter S trust ceases to meet any requirement of paragraph (3)(A), the provisions of this subsection shall not apply to such trust as of the date it ceases to meet such requirement.

(B) Failure to meet requirements of paragraph (3)(B).—If any qualified subchapter S trust ceases to meet any requirement of paragraph (3)(B) but continues to meet the requirements of paragraph (3)(A), the provisions of this subsection shall not apply to such trust as of the first day of the first taxable year beginning after the first taxable year for which it failed to meet the requirements of paragraph (3)(B).

§ 1362. Election; revocation; termination

(a) Election.—

(1) In general.—Except as provided in subsection (g), a small business corporation may elect, in accordance with the provisions of this section, to be an S corporation.

(2) All shareholders must consent to election.—An election under this subsection shall be valid only if all persons who are shareholders in such corporation on the day on which such election is made consent to such election.

(b) When made.—

(1) In general.—An election under subsection (a) may be made by a small business corporation for any taxable year—

(A) at any time during the preceding taxable year, or

(B) at any time during the taxable year and on or before the 15th day of the 3d month of the taxable year.

(2) Certain elections made during 1st 2½ months treated as made for next taxable year.—If—

(A) an election under subsection (a) is made for any taxable year during such year and on or before the 15th day of the 3d month of such year, but

(B) either—

(i) on 1 or more days in such taxable year before the day on which the election was made the corporation did not meet the requirements of subsection (b) of section 1361, or

(ii) 1 or more of the persons who held stock in the corporation during such taxable year and before the election was made did not consent to the election,

then such election shall be treated as made for the following taxable year.

(3) Election made after 1st 2½ months treated as made for following taxable year.—If—

(A) a small business corporation makes an election under subsection (a) for any taxable year, and

(B) such election is made after the 15th day of the 3d month of the taxable year and on or before the 15th day of the 3rd month of the following taxable year,

then such election shall be treated as made for the following taxable year.

(4) Taxable years of 2½ months or less.—For purposes of this subsection, an election for a taxable year made not later than 2 months and 15 days after the first day of the taxable year shall be treated as timely made during such year.

(c) Years for which effective.—An election under subsection (a) shall be effective for the taxable year of the corporation for which it is made and for all succeeding taxable years of the corporation, until such election is terminated under subsection (d).

(d) Termination.—

(1) By revocation.—

(A) In general.—An election under subsection (a) may be terminated by revocation.

(B) More than one-half of shares must consent to revocation.—An election may be revoked only if shareholders holding more than one-half of the shares of stock of the corporation on the day on which the revocation is made consent to the revocation.

(C) When effective.—Except as provided in subparagraph (D)—

(i) a revocation made during the taxable year and on or before the 15th day of the 3d month thereof shall be effective on the 1st day of such taxable year, and

(ii) a revocation made during the taxable year but after such 15th day shall be effective on the 1st day of the following taxable year.

(D) Revocation may specify prospective date.—If the revocation specifies a date for revocation which is on or after the day on which the revocation is made, the revocation shall be effective on and after the date so specified.

(2) By corporation ceasing to be small business corporation.—

(A) In general.—An election under subsection (a) shall be terminated whenever (at any time on or after the 1st day of the 1st taxable year for which the corporation is an S corporation) such corporation ceases to be a small business corporation.

(B) When effective.—Any termination under this paragraph shall be effective on and after the date of cessation.

(3) Where passive investment income exceeds 25 percent of gross receipts for 3 consecutive taxable years and corporation has subchapter C earnings and profits.—

(A) Termination.—

(i) **In general.**—An election under subsection (a) shall be terminated whenever the corporation—

(I) has subchapter C earnings and profits at the close of each of 3 consecutive taxable years, and

(II) has gross receipts for each of such taxable years more than 25 percent of which are passive investment income.

(ii) **When effective.**—Any termination under this paragraph shall be effective on and after the first day of the first taxable year beginning after the third consecutive taxable year referred to in clause (i).

(iii) **Years taken into account.**—A prior taxable year shall not be taken into account under clause (i) unless—

(I) such taxable year began after December 31, 1981, and

(II) the corporation was an S corporation for such taxable year.

(B) Subchapter C earnings and profits.—For purposes of subparagraph (A), the term "subchapter C earnings and profits" means earnings and profits of any corporation for any taxable year with respect to which an election under section 1362(a) (or under section 1372 of prior law) was not in effect.

(C) Gross receipts from sales of capital assets (other than stock and securities).—For purposes of this paragraph, in the case of dispositions of capital assets (other than stock and securities), gross receipts from such dispositions shall be taken into account only to the extent of the capital gain net income therefrom.

(D) Passive investment income defined.—For purposes of this paragraph—

(i) In general.—Except as otherwise provided in this subparagraph, the term "passive investment income" means gross receipts derived from royalties, rents, dividends, interest, annuities, and sales or exchanges of stock or securities (gross receipts from such sales or exchanges being taken into account for purposes of this paragraph only to the extent of gains therefrom).

(ii) Exception for interest on notes from sales of inventory.—The term "passive investment income" shall not include interest on any obligation acquired in the ordinary course of the corporation's trade or business from its sale of property described in section 1221(1).

(iii) Treatment of certain lending or finance companies.—If the S corporation meets the requirements of section 542(c)(6) for the taxable year, the term "passive investment income" shall not include gross receipts for the taxable year which are derived directly from the active and regular conduct of a lending or finance business (as defined in section 542(d)(1)).

(iv) Treatment of certain liquidations.—Gross receipts derived from sales or exchanges of stock or securities shall not include amounts received by an S corporation which are treated under section 331 (relating to corporate liquidations) as payments in exchange for stock where the S corporation owned more than 50 percent of each class of stock of the liquidating corporation.

(v) Special rule for options and commodities dealers.—In the case of any options or commodities dealer, passive investment income shall be determined by not taking into account any gain or loss described in section 1374(c)(4)(A).

(e) Treatment of S termination year.—

(1) In general.—In the case of an S termination year, for purposes of this title—

(A) S short year.—The portion of such year ending before the 1st day for which the termination is effective shall be treated as a short taxable year for which the corporation is an S corporation.

(B) C short year.—The portion of such year beginning on such 1st day shall be treated as a short taxable year for which the corporation is a C corporation.

(2) Pro rata allocation.—Except as provided in paragraph (3) and subparagraphs (C) and (D) of paragraph (6), the determination of which items are to be taken into account for each of the short taxable years referred to in paragraph (1) shall be made—

(A) first by determining for the S termination year—

(i) the amount of each of the items of income, loss, deduction, or credit described in section 1366(a)(1)(A), and

(ii) the amount of the nonseparately computed income or loss, and

(B) then by assigning an equal portion of each amount determined under subparagraph (A) to each day of the S termination year.

(3) Election to have items assigned to each short taxable year under normal tax accounting rules.—

(A) In general.—A corporation may elect to have paragraph (2) not apply.

(B) Shareholders must consent to election.—An election under this subsection shall be valid only if all persons who are shareholders in the corporation at any time during the S short year and all persons who are shareholders in the corporation on the first day of the C short year consent to such election.

(4) S termination year.—For purposes of this subsection, the term "S termination year" means any taxable year of a corporation (determined without regard to this subsection) in which a termination of an election made under subsection (a) takes effect (other than on the 1st day thereof).

(5) Tax for C short year determined on annualized basis.—

(A) In general.—The taxable income for the short year described in subparagraph (B) of paragraph (1) shall be placed on an annual basis by multiplying the taxable income for such short year by the number of days in the S termination year and by dividing the result by the number of days in the short year. The tax shall be the same part of the tax computed on the annual basis as the number of days in such short year is of the number of days in the S termination year.

* * *

(6) Other special rules.—For purposes of this title—

(A) Short years treated as 1 year for carryover purposes.—The short taxable year described in subparagraph (A) of paragraph (1) shall not be taken into account for purposes of determining the number of taxable years to which any item may be carried back or carried forward by the corporation.

(B) Due date for S year.—The due date for filing the return for the short taxable year described in subparagraph (A) of paragraph (1) shall be the same as the due date for filing the return for the short taxable year described in subparagraph (B) of paragraph (1) (including extensions thereof).

(C) Paragraph (2) not to apply to items resulting from section 338. —Paragraph (2) shall not apply with respect to any item resulting from the application of section 338.

(D) Pro rata allocation for S termination year not to apply if 50-percent change in ownership.—Paragraph (2) shall not apply to an S termination year if there is a sale or exchange of 50 percent or more of the stock in such corporation during such year.

(f) Inadvertent terminations.—If—

(1) an election under subsection (a) by any corporation was terminated under paragraph (2) or (3) of subsection (d),

(2) the Secretary determines that the termination was inadvertent,

(3) no later than a reasonable period of time after discovery of the event resulting in such termination, steps were taken so that the corporation is once more a small business corporation, and

(4) the corporation, and each person who was a shareholder of the corporation at any time during the period specified pursuant to this subsection, agrees to make such adjustments (consistent with the treatment of the corporation as an S corporation) as may be required by the Secretary with respect to such period,

then, notwithstanding the terminating event, such corporation shall be treated as continuing to be an S corporation during the period specified by the Secretary.

(g) Election after termination.—If a small business corporation has made an election under subsection (a) and if such election has been terminated under subsection (d), such corporation (and any successor corporation) shall not be eligible to make an election under subsection (a) for any taxable year before its 5th taxable year which begins after the 1st taxable year for which such termination is effective, unless the Secretary consents to such election.

§ 1363. Effect of election on corporation

(a) **General rule.**—Except as otherwise provided in this subchapter, an S corporation shall not be subject to the taxes imposed by this chapter.

(b) **Computation of corporation's taxable income.**—The taxable income of an S corporation shall be computed in the same manner as in the case of an individual, except that—

(1) the items described in section 1366(a)(1)(A) shall be separately stated,

(2) the deductions referred to in section 703(a)(2) shall not be allowed to the corporation,

(3) section 248 shall apply, and

(4) section 291 shall apply if the S corporation (or any predecessor) was a C corporation for any of the 3 immediately preceding taxable years.

(c) **Elections of the S corporation.—**

(1) **In general.**—Except as provided in paragraph (2), any election affecting the computation of items derived from an S corporation shall be made by the corporation.

(2) **Exceptions.**—In the case of an S corporation, elections under the following provisions shall be made by each shareholder separately—

(A) section 617 (relating to deduction and recapture of certain mining exploration expenditures), and

(B) section 901 (relating to taxes of foreign countries and possessions of the United States).

(d) **Distributions of appreciated property.**—Except as provided in subsection (e), if—

(1) an S corporation makes a distribution of property (other than an obligation of such corporation) with respect to its stock, and

(2) the fair market value of such property exceeds its adjusted basis in the hands of the S corporation,

then, notwithstanding any other provision of this subtitle, gain shall be recognized to the S corporation on the distribution in the same manner as if it had sold such property to the distributee at its fair market value.

(e) **Subsection (d) not to apply to reorganizations, etc.**—Subsection (d) shall not apply to any distribution to the extent it consists of property permitted by section 354, 355, or 356 to be received without the recognition of gain.

PART II—TAX TREATMENT OF SHAREHOLDERS

§ 1366. Pass-thru of items to shareholders

(a) **Determination of shareholder's tax liability.—**

(1) **In general.**—In determining the tax under this chapter of a shareholder for the shareholder's taxable year in which the taxable year of the S corporation ends (or for the final taxable year of a shareholder who dies before the end of the

corporation's taxable year), there shall be taken into account the shareholder's pro rata share of the corporation's—

(A) items of income (including tax-exempt income), loss, deduction, or credit the separate treatment of which could affect the liability for tax of any shareholder, and

(B) nonseparately computed income or loss.

For purposes of the preceding sentence, the items referred to in subparagraph (A) shall include amounts described in paragraph (4) or (6) of section 702(a).

(2) **Nonseparately computed income or loss defined.**—For purposes of this subchapter, the term "nonseparately computed income or loss" means gross income minus the deductions allowed to the corporation under this chapter, determined by excluding all items described in paragraph (1)(A).

(b) **Character passed thru.**—The character of any item included in a shareholder's pro rata share under paragraph (1) of subsection (a) shall be determined as if such item were realized directly from the source from which realized by the corporation, or incurred in the same manner as incurred by the corporation.

(c) **Gross income of a shareholder.**—In any case where it is necessary to determine the gross income of a shareholder for purposes of this title, such gross income shall include the shareholder's pro rata share of the gross income of the corporation.

(d) **Special rules for losses and deductions.**—

(1) **Cannot exceed shareholder's basis in stock and debt.**—The aggregate amount of losses and deductions taken into account by a shareholder under subsection (a) for any taxable year shall not exceed the sum of—

(A) the adjusted basis of the shareholder's stock in the S corporation (determined with regard to paragraph (1) of section 1367(a) for the taxable year), and

(B) the shareholder's adjusted basis of any indebtedness of the S corporation to the shareholder (determined without regard to any adjustment under paragraph (2) of section 1367(b) for the taxable year).

(2) **Indefinite carryover of disallowed losses and deductions.**—Any loss or deduction which is disallowed for any taxable year by reason of paragraph (1) shall be treated as incurred by the corporation in the succeeding taxable year with respect to that shareholder.

(3) **Carryover of disallowed losses and deductions to post-termination transition period.**—

(A) **In general.**—If for the last taxable year of a corporation for which it was an S corporation a loss or deduction was disallowed by reason of paragraph (1), such loss or deduction shall be treated as incurred by the shareholder on the last day of any post-termination transition period.

(B) **Cannot exceed shareholder's basis in stock.**—The aggregate amount of losses and deductions taken into account by a shareholder under subparagraph (A) shall not exceed the adjusted basis of the shareholder's stock in the corporation (determined at the close of the last day of the post-termination transition period and without regard to this paragraph).

(C) **Adjustment in basis of stock.**—The shareholder's basis in the stock of the corporation shall be reduced by the amount allowed as a deduction by reason of this paragraph.

(e) Treatment of family group.—If an individual who is a member of the family (within the meaning of section 704(e)(3)) of one or more shareholders of an S corporation renders services for the corporation or furnishes capital to the corporation without receiving reasonable compensation therefor, the Secretary shall make such adjustments in the items taken into account by such individual and such shareholders as may be necessary in order to reflect the value of such services or capital.

(f) Special rules.—

(1) **Subsection (a) not to apply to credit allowable under section 34.**—Subsection (a) shall not apply with respect to any credit allowable under section 34 (relating to certain uses of gasoline and special fuels.

(2) **Reduction in pass-thru for tax imposed on built-in gains.**—If any tax is imposed under section 1374 for any taxable year on an S corporation, for purposes of subsection (a), the amount of each recognized built-in gain (as defined in section 1374(d)(2)) for such taxable year shall be reduced by its proportionate share of such tax.

(3) **Reduction in pass-thru for tax imposed on excess net passive income.**—If any tax is imposed under section 1375 for any taxable year on an S corporation, for purposes of subsection (a), each item of passive investment income shall be reduced by an amount which bears the same ratio to the amount of such tax as—

(A) the amount of such item, bears to

(B) the total passive investment income for the taxable year.

(g) Cross reference.—

For rules relating to procedures for determining the tax treatment of subchapter S items, see subchapter D of chapter 63.

§ 1367. Adjustments to basis of stock of shareholders, etc.

(a) General rule.—

(1) **Increases in basis.**—The basis of each shareholder's stock in an S corporation shall be increased for any period by the sum of the following items determined with respect to that shareholder for such period:

(A) the items of income described in subparagraph (A) of section 1366(a)(1),

(B) any nonseparately computed income determined under subparagraph (B) of section 1366(a)(1), and

(C) the excess of the deductions for depletion over the basis of the property subject to depletion.

(2) **Decreases in basis.**—The basis of each shareholder's stock in an S corporation shall be decreased for any period (but not below zero) by the sum of the following items determined with respect to the shareholder for such period:

(A) distributions by the corporation which were not includible in the income of the shareholder by reason of section 1368,

(B) the items of loss and deduction described in subparagraph (A) of section 1366(a)(1),

(C) any nonseparately computed loss determined under subparagraph (B) of section 1366(a)(1),

(D) any expense of the corporation not deductible in computing its taxable income and not properly chargeable to capital account, and

(E) the amount of the shareholder's deduction for depletion for any oil and gas property held by the S corporation to the extent such deduction does not exceed the proportionate share of the adjusted basis of such property allocated to such shareholder under section 613A(c)(13)(B).

(b) Special rules.—

(1) Income items.—An amount which is required to be included in the gross income of a shareholder and shown on his return shall be taken into account under subparagraph (A) or (B) of subsection (a)(1) only to the extent such amount is included in the shareholder's gross income on his return, increased or decreased by any adjustment of such amount in a redetermination of the shareholder's tax liability.

(2) Adjustments in basis of indebtedness.—

(A) Reduction of basis.—If for any taxable year the amounts specified in subparagraphs (B), (C), (D), and (E) of subsection (a)(2) exceed the amount which reduces the shareholder's basis to zero, such excess shall be applied to reduce (but not below zero) the shareholder's basis in any indebtedness of the S corporation to the shareholder.

(B) Restoration of basis.—If for any taxable year beginning after December 31, 1982, there is a reduction under subparagraph (A) in the shareholder's basis in the indebtedness of an S corporation to a shareholder, any net increase (after the application of paragraphs (1) and (2) of subsection (a)) for any subsequent taxable year shall be applied to restore such reduction in basis before any of it may be used to increase the shareholder's basis in the stock of the S corporation.

(3) Coordination with sections 165(g) and 166(d).—This section and section 1366 shall be applied before the application of sections 165(g) and 166(d) to any taxable year of the shareholder or the corporation in which the security or debt becomes worthless.

§ 1368. Distributions

(a) General rule.—A distribution of property made by an S corporation with respect to its stock to which (but for this subsection) section 301(c) would apply shall be treated in the manner provided in subsection (b) or (c), whichever applies.

(b) S corporation having no earnings and profits.—In the case of a distribution described in subsection (a) by an S corporation which has no accumulated earnings and profits—

(1) Amount applied against basis.—The distribution shall not be included in gross income to the extent that it does not exceed the adjusted basis of the stock.

(2) Amount in excess of basis.—If the amount of the distribution exceeds the adjusted basis of the stock, such excess shall be treated as gain from the sale or exchange of property.

(c) S corporation having earnings and profits.—In the case of a distribution described in subsection (a) by an S corporation which has accumulated earnings and profits—

(1) Accumulated adjustments account.—That portion of the distribution which does not exceed the accumulated adjustments account shall be treated in the manner provided by subsection (b).

(2) Dividend.—That portion of the distribution which remains after the application of paragraph (1) shall be treated as a dividend to the extent it does not exceed the accumulated earnings and profits of the S corporation.

(3) Treatment of remainder.—Any portion of the distribution remaining after the application of paragraph (2) of this subsection shall be treated in the manner provided by subsection (b).

Except to the extent provided in regulations, if the distributions during the taxable year exceed the amount in the accumulated adjustments account at the close of the taxable year, for purposes of this subsection, the balance of such account shall be allocated among such distributions in proportion to their respective sizes.

(d) Certain adjustments taken into account.—Subsections (b) and (c) shall be applied by taking into account (to the extent proper)—

(1) the adjustments to the basis of the shareholder's stock described in section 1367, and

(2) the adjustments to the accumulated adjustments account which are required by subsection (e)(1).

(e) Definitions and special rules.—For purposes of this section—

(1) Accumulated adjustments account.—

(A) In general.—Except as provided in subparagraph (B), the term "accumulated adjustments account" means an account of the S corporation which is adjusted for the S period in a manner similar to the adjustments under section 1367 (except that no adjustment shall be made for income (and related expenses) which is exempt from tax under this title and the phrase "(but not below zero)" shall be disregarded in section 1367(b)(2)(A)) and no adjustment shall be made for Federal taxes attributable to any taxable year in which the corporation was a C corporation.

(B) Amount of adjustment in the case of redemptions.—In the case of any redemption which is treated as an exchange under section 302(a) or 303(a), the adjustment in the accumulated adjustments account shall be an amount which bears the same ratio to the balance in such account as the number of shares redeemed in such redemption bears to the number of shares of stock in the corporation immediately before such redemption.

(2) S period.—The term "S period" means the most recent continuous period during which the corporation has been an S corporation. Such period shall not include any taxable year beginning before January 1, 1983.

(3) Election to distribute earnings first.—

(A) In general.—An S corporation may, with the consent of all of its affected shareholders, elect to have paragraph (1) of subsection (c) not apply to all distributions made during the taxable year for which the election is made.

(B) Affected shareholder.—For purposes of subparagraph (A), the term "affected shareholder" means any shareholder to whom a distribution is made by the S corporation during the taxable year.

PART III—SPECIAL RULES

§ 1371. Coordination with subchapter C

(a) Application of subchapter C rules.—

(1) In general.—Except as otherwise provided in this title, and except to the extent inconsistent with this subchapter, subchapter C shall apply to an S corporation and its shareholders.

(2) S corporation as shareholder treated like individual.—For purposes of subchapter C, an S corporation in its capacity as a shareholder of another corporation shall be treated as an individual.

(b) No carryover between C year and S year.—

(1) From C year to S year.—No carryforward, and no carryback, arising for a taxable year for which a corporation is a C corporation may be carried to a taxable year for which such corporation is an S corporation.

(2) No carryover from S year.—No carryforward, and no carryback, shall arise at the corporate level for a taxable year for which a corporation is an S corporation.

(3) Treatment of S year as elapsed year.—Nothing in paragraphs (1) and (2) shall prevent treating a taxable year for which a corporation is an S corporation as a taxable year for purposes of determining the number of taxable years to which an item may be carried back or carried forward.

(c) Earnings and profits.—

(1) In general.—Except as provided in paragraphs (2) and (3) and subsection (d)(3), no adjustment shall be made to the earnings and profits of an S corporation.

(2) Adjustments for redemptions, liquidations, reorganizations, divisives, etc.—In the case of any transaction involving the application of subchapter C to any S corporation, proper adjustment to any accumulated earnings and profits of the corporation shall be made.

(3) Adjustments in case of distributions treated as dividends under section 1368(c)(2).—Paragraph (1) shall not apply with respect to that portion of a distribution which is treated as a dividend under section 1368(c)(2).

(d) Coordination with investment credit recapture.—

(1) No recapture by reason of election.—Any election under section 1362 shall be treated as a mere change in the form of conducting a trade or business for purposes of the second sentence of section 47(b).

(2) Corporation continues to be liable.—Notwithstanding an election under section 1362, an S corporation shall continue to be liable for any increase in tax under section 47 attributable to credits allowed for taxable years for which such corporation was not an S corporation.

(3) Adjustment to earnings and profits for amount of recapture.—Paragraph (1) of subsection (c) shall not apply to any increase in tax under section 47 for which the S corporation is liable.

(e) Cash distributions during post-termination transition period.—

(1) In general.—Any distribution of money by a corporation with respect to its stock during a post-termination transition period shall be applied against and reduce the adjusted basis of the stock, to the extent that the amount of the distribution does not exceed the accumulated adjustments account (within the meaning of section 1368(e)).

(2) Election to distribute earnings first.—An S corporation may elect to have paragraph (1) not apply to all distributions made during a post-termination transition period described in section 1377(b)(1)(A). Such election shall not be effective unless all shareholders of the S corporation to whom distributions are made by the S corporation during such post-termination transition period consent to such election.

§ 1372. Partnership rules to apply for fringe benefit purposes

(a) General rule.—For purposes of applying the provisions of this subtitle which relate to employee fringe benefits—

(1) the S corporation shall be treated as a partnership, and

(2) any 2-percent shareholder of the S corporation shall be treated as a partner of such partnership.

(b) 2-percent shareholder defined.—For purposes of this section, the term "2-percent shareholder" means any person who owns (or is considered as owning within the meaning of section 318) on any day during the taxable year of the S corporation more than 2 percent of the outstanding stock of such corporation or stock possessing more than 2 percent of the total combined voting power of all stock of such corporation.

§ 1373. Foreign income

(a) S corporation treated as partnership, etc.—For purposes of subparts A and F of part III, and part V, of subchapter N (relating to income from sources without the United States)—

(1) an S corporation shall be treated as a partnership, and

(2) the shareholders of such corporation shall be treated as partners of such partnership.

(b) Recapture of overall foreign loss.—For purposes of section 904(f) (relating to recapture of overall foreign loss), the making or termination of an election to be treated as an S corporation shall be treated as a disposition of the business.

§ 1374. Tax imposed on certain built-in gains

(a) General Rule.—If for any taxable year beginning in the recognition period an S corporation has a recognized built-in gain, there is hereby imposed a tax (computed under subsection (b)) on the income of such corporation for such taxable year.

(b) Amount of tax.—

(1) **In general.**—The tax imposed by subsection (a) shall be a tax computed by applying the highest rate of tax specified in section 11(b) to the lesser of—

(A) the recognized built-in gains of the S corporation for the taxable year, or

(B) the amount which would be the taxable income of the corporation for such taxable year if such corporation were not an S corporation.

(2) **Net operating loss carryforwards from C years allowed.**—Notwithstanding section 1371(b)(1), any net operating loss carryforward arising in a taxable year for which the corporation was a C corporation shall be allowed as a deduction against the lesser of the amounts referred to in subparagraph (A) or (B) of paragraph (1). For purposes of determining the amount of any such loss which may be carried to subsequent taxable years, the lesser of the amounts referred to in subparagraph (A) or (B) of paragraph (1) shall be treated as taxable income.

(3) **Credits.**—

(A) **In general.**—Except as provided in subparagraph (B), no credit shall be allowable under part IV of subchapter A of this chapter (other than under section 34) against the tax imposed by subsection (a).

(B) **Business credit carryforwards from C years allowed.**—Notwithstanding section 1371(b)(1), any business credit carryforward under section 39 arising in a taxable year for which the corporation was a C corporation shall be allowed as a credit against the tax imposed by subsection (a) in the same manner as if it were imposed by section 11.

(4) **Coordination with section 1201(a).**—For purposes of section 1201(a)—

(A) the tax imposed by subsection (a) shall be treated as if it were imposed by section 11, and

(B) the lower of the amounts specified in subparagraphs (A) and (B) of paragraph (1) shall be treated as the taxable income.

(c) Limitations.—

(1) Corporations which were always S corporations.—Subsection (a) shall not apply to any corporation if an election under section 1362(a) has been in effect with respect to such corporation for each of its taxable years. Except as provided in regulations, an S corporation and any predecessor corporation shall be treated as 1 corporation for purposes of the preceding sentence.

(2) Limitation on amount of recognized built-in gains.—The amount of the recognized built-in gains taken into account under this section for any taxable year shall not exceed the excess (if any) of—

(A) the net unrealized built-in gain, over

(B) the recognized built-in gains for prior taxable years beginning in the recognition period.

(d) Definitions and special rules.—For purposes of this section—

(1) Net unrealized built-in gain.—The term "net unrealized built-in gain" means the amount (if any) by which—

(A) the fair market value of the assets of the S corporation as of the beginning of its 1st taxable year for which an election under section 1362(a) is in effect, exceeds

(B) the aggregate adjusted bases of such assets at such time.

(2) Recognized built-in gain.—The term "recognized built-in gain" means any gain recognized during the recognition period on the disposition of any asset except to the extent that the S corporation establishes that—

(A) such asset was not held by the S corporation as of the beginning of the 1st taxable year referred to in paragraph (1), or

(B) such gain exceeds the excess (if any) of—

(i) the fair market value of such asset as of the beginning of such 1st taxable year, over

(ii) the adjusted basis of the asset as of such time.

(3) Recognition period.—The term "recognition period" means the 10–year period beginning with the 1st day of the 1st taxable year for which the corporation was an S corporation.

(4) Taxable income.—Taxable income of the corporation shall be determined under section 63(a)—

(A) without regard to the deductions allowed by part VIII of subchapter B (other than the deduction allowed by section 248, relating to organization expenditures), and

(B) without regard to the deduction under section 172.

§ 1375. Tax imposed when passive investment income of corporation having subchapter C earnings and profits exceeds 25 percent of gross receipts

(a) General rule.—If for the taxable year an S corporation has—

(1) subchapter C earnings and profits at the close of such taxable year, and

(2) gross receipts more than 25 percent of which are passive investment income,

then there is hereby imposed a tax on the income of such corporation for such taxable year. Such tax shall be computed by multiplying the excess net passive income by the highest rate of tax specified in section 11(b).

(b) **Definitions.**—For purposes of this section—

(1) **Excess net passive income.**—

(A) **In general.**—Except as provided in subparagraph (B), the term "excess net passive income" means an amount which bears the same ratio to the net passive income for the taxable year as—

(i) the amount by which the passive investment income for the taxable year exceeds 25 percent of the gross receipts for the taxable year, bears to

(ii) the passive investment income for the taxable year.

(B) **Limitation.**—The amount of the excess net passive income for any taxable year shall not exceed the corporation's taxable income for the taxable year (determined in accordance with section 1374(d)(4)).

(2) **Net passive income.**—The term "net passive income" means—

(A) passive investment income, reduced by

(B) the deductions allowable under this chapter which are directly connected with the production of such income (other than deductions allowable under section 172 and part VIII of subchapter B).

(3) **Passive investment income; etc.**—The terms "subchapter C earnings and profits", "passive investment income", and "gross receipts" shall have the same respective meanings as when used in paragraph (3) of section 1362(d).

(c) **Special rules.**—

(1) **Disallowance of credit.**—No credit shall be allowed under part IV of subchapter A of this chapter (other than section 34) against the tax imposed by subsection (a).

(2) **Coordination with section 1374.**—If any gain—

(A) is taken into account in determining passive income for purposes of this section, and

(B) is taken into account under section 1374,

the amount of such gain taken into account under section 1374 shall be reduced by the portion of the excess net passive income for the taxable year which is attributable (on a pro rata basis) to such gain.

(d) **Waiver of tax in certain cases.**—If the S corporation establishes to the satisfaction of the Secretary that—

(1) it determined in good faith that it had no subchapter C earnings and profits at the close of a taxable year, and

(2) during a reasonable period of time after it was determined that it did have subchapter C earnings and profits at the close of such taxable year such earnings and profits were distributed,

the Secretary may waive the tax imposed by subsection (a) for such taxable year.

PART IV—DEFINITIONS; MISCELLANEOUS

§ 1377.   Definitions and special rule

(a) **Pro rata share.**—For purposes of this subchapter—

(1) **In general.**—Except as provided in paragraph (2), each shareholder's pro rata share of any item for any taxable year shall be the sum of the amounts determined with respect to the shareholder—

(A) by assigning an equal portion of such item to each day of the taxable year, and

(B) then by dividing that portion pro rata among the shares outstanding on such day.

(2) **Election to terminate year.**—Under regulations prescribed by the Secretary, if any shareholder terminates his interest in the corporation during the taxable year and all persons who are shareholders during the taxable year agree to the application of this paragraph, paragraph (1) shall be applied as if the taxable year consisted of 2 taxable years the first of which ends on the date of the termination.

(b) **Post-termination transition period.**—

(1) **In general.**—For purposes of this subchapter, the term "post-termination transition period" means—

(A) the period beginning on the day after the last day of the corporation's last taxable year as an S corporation and ending on the later of—

(i) the day which is 1 year after such last day, or

(ii) the due date for filing the return for such last year as an S corporation (including extensions), and

(B) the 120-day period beginning on the date of a determination that the corporation's election under section 1362(a) had terminated for a previous taxable year.

(2) **Determination defined.**—For purposes of paragraph (1), the term "determination" means—

(A) a court decision which becomes final,

(B) a closing agreement, or

(C) an agreement between the corporation and the Secretary that the corporation failed to qualify as an S corporation.

(c) **Manner of making elections, etc.**—Any election under this subchapter, and any revocation under section 1362(d)(1), shall be made in such manner as the Secretary shall by regulations prescribe.

§ 1378.   Taxable year of S corporation

(a) **General rule.**—For purposes of this subtitle, the taxable year of an S corporation shall be a permitted year.

(b) **Permitted year defined.**—For purposes of this section, the term "permitted year" means a taxable year which—

(1) is a year ending December 31, or

(2) is any other accounting period for which the corporation establishes a business purpose to the satisfaction of the Secretary.

For purposes of paragraph (2), any defend of income to shareholders shall not be treated as a business purpose.

CHAPTER 6—CONSOLIDATED RETURNS

Subchapter
  A. Returns and payment of tax.
  B. Related rules.

SUBCHAPTER A—RETURNS AND PAYMENT OF TAX

§ 1501. Privilege to file consolidated returns

An affiliated group of corporations shall, subject to the provisions of this chapter, have the privilege of making a consolidated return with respect to the income tax imposed by chapter 1 for the taxable year in lieu of separate returns. The making of a consolidated return shall be upon the condition that all corporations which at any time during the taxable year have been members of the affiliated group consent to all the consolidated return regulations prescribed under section 1502 prior to the last day prescribed by law for the filing of such return. The making of a consolidated return shall be considered as such consent. In the case of a corporation which is a member of the affiliated group for a fractional part of the year, the consolidated return shall include the income of such corporation for such part of the year as it is a member of the affiliated group.

§ 1502. Regulations

The Secretary shall prescribe such regulations as he may deem necessary in order that the tax liability of any affiliated group of corporations making a consolidated return and of each corporation in the group, both during and after the period of affiliation, may be returned, determined, computed, assessed, collected, and adjusted, in such manner as clearly to reflect the income-tax liability and the various factors necessary for the determination of such liability, and in order to prevent avoidance of such tax liability.

§ 1503. Computation and payment of tax

[(a) General rule.—*] In any case in which a consolidated return is made or is required to be made, the tax shall be determined, computed, assessed, collected, and adjusted in accordance with the regulations under section 1502 prescribed before the last day prescribed by law for the filing of such return.

* * *

(d) Dual consolidated Loss.—

(1) **In general.**—The dual consolidated loss for any taxable year of any corporation shall not be allowed to reduce the taxable income of any other member of the affiliated group for the taxable year or any other taxable year.

(2) **Dual consolidated loss.**—For purposes of this section—

* Editorially supplied.

(A) **In general.**—Except as provided in subparagraph (B), the term "dual consolidated loss" means any net operating loss of a domestic corporation which is subject to an income tax of a foreign country on its income without regard to whether such income is from sources in or outside of such foreign country, or is subject to such a tax on a residence basis.

(B) **Special rule where loss not used under foreign law.**—To the extent provided in regulations, the term "dual consolidated loss" shall not include any loss which, under the foreign income tax law, does not offset the income of any foreign corporation.

§ 1504.   Definitions

(a) **Affiliated group defined.**—For purposes of this subtitle—

(1) **In general.**—The term "affiliated group" means—

(A) 1 or more chains of includible corporations connected through stock ownership with a common parent corporation which is an includible corporation, but only if—

(B)(i) the common parent owns directly stock meeting the requirements of paragraph (2) in at least 1 of the other includible corporations, and

(ii) stock meeting the requirements of paragraph (2) in each of the includible corporations (except the common parent) is owned directly by 1 or more of the other includible corporations.

(2) **80-percent voting and value test.**—The ownership of stock of any corporation meets the requirements of this paragraph if it—

(A) possesses at least 80 percent of the total voting power of the stock of such corporation, and

(B) has a value equal to at least 80 percent of the total value of the stock of such corporation.

(3) **5 years must elapse before reconsolidation.**—

(A) **In general.**—If—

(i) a corporation is included (or required to be included) in a consolidated return filed by an affiliated group for a taxable year which includes any period after December 31, 1984, and

(ii) such corporation ceases to be a member of such group in a taxable year beginning after December 31, 1984,

with respect to periods after such cessation, such corporation (and any successor of such corporation) may not be included in any consolidated return filed by the affiliated group (or by another affiliated group with the same common parent or a successor of such common parent) before the 61st month beginning after its first taxable year in which it ceased to be a member of such affiliated group.

(B) **Secretary may waive application of subparagraph (A).**—The Secretary may waive the application of subparagraph (A) to any corporation for any period subject to such conditions as the Secretary may prescribe.

(4) **Stock not to include certain preferred stock.**—For purposes of this subsection, the term "stock" does not include any stock which—

(A) is not entitled to vote,

(B) is limited and preferred as to dividends and does not participate in corporate growth to any significant extent,

(C) has redemption and liquidation rights which do not exceed the issue price of such stock (except for a reasonable redemption or liquidation premium), and

(D) is not convertible into another class of stock.

(5) **Regulations.**—The Secretary shall prescribe such regulations as may be necessary or appropriate to carry out the purposes of this subsection, including (but not limited to) regulations—

(A) which treat warrants, obligations convertible into stock, and other similar interests as stock, and stock as not stock,

(B) which treat options to acquire or sell stock as having been exercised,

(C) which provide that the requirements of paragraph (2)(B) shall be treated as met if the affiliated group, in reliance on a good faith determination of value, treated such requirements as met,

(D) which disregard an inadvertent ceasing to meet the requirements of paragraph (2)(B) by reason of changes in relative values of different classes of stock,

(E) which provide that transfers of stock within the group shall not be taken into account in determining whether a corporation ceases to be a member of an affiliated group, and

(F) which disregard changes in voting power to the extent such changes are disproportionate to related changes in value.

(b) Definition of "includible corporation".—As used in this chapter, the term "includible corporation" means any corporation except—

(1) Corporations exempt from taxation under section 501.

(2) Insurance companies subject to taxation under section 801.

(3) Foreign corporations.

* * *

(c) Includible insurance companies

Notwithstanding the provisions of paragraph (2) of subsection (b)—

* * *

(2)(A) If an affiliated group (determined without regard to subsection (b)(2)) includes one or more domestic insurance companies taxed under section 801, the common parent of such group may elect (pursuant to regulations prescribed by the Secretary) to treat all such companies as includible corporations for purposes of applying subsection (a) except that no such company shall be so treated until it has been a member of the affiliated group for the 5 taxable years immediately preceding the taxable year for which the consolidated return is filed.

* * *

(d) Subsidiary formed to comply with foreign law.—In the case of a domestic corporation owning or controlling, directly or indirectly, 100 percent of the capital stock (exclusive of directors' qualifying shares) of a corporation organized under the laws of a contiguous foreign country and maintained solely for the purpose of complying with the laws of such country as to title and operation of property, such foreign corporation may, at the option of the domestic corporation, be treated for the purpose of this subtitle as a domestic corporation.

(e) Includible tax-exempt organizations.—Despite the provisions of paragraph (1) of subsection (b), two or more organizations exempt from taxation under section 501, one or more of which is described in section 501(c) (2) and the others of which derive income from such 501(c) (2) organizations, shall be considered as includible corporations for the purpose of the application of subsection (a) to such organizations alone.

§ 1505. Cross references

(1) **For suspension of running of statute of limitations when notice in respect of a deficiency is mailed to one corporation, see section 6503(a) (1).**

(2) **For allocation of income and deductions of related trades or businesses, see section 482.**

SUBCHAPTER B—RELATED RULES

Part
  I. In general.
 II. Certain controlled corporations.

PART I—IN GENERAL

§ 1551. Disallowance of the benefits of the graduated corporate rates and accumulated earnings credit

(a) **In general.**—If—

(1) any corporation transfers, on or after January 1, 1951, and on or before June 12, 1963, all or part of its property (other than money) to a transferee corporation,

(2) any corporation transfers, directly or indirectly, after June 12, 1963, all or part of its property (other than money) to a transferee corporation, or

(3) five or fewer individuals who are in control of a corporation transfer, directly or indirectly, after June 12, 1963, property (other than money) to a transferee corporation,

and the transferee corporation was created for the purpose of acquiring such property or was not actively engaged in business at the time of such acquisition, and if after such transfer the transferor or transferors are in control of such transferee corporation during any part of the taxable year of such transferee corporation, then for such taxable year of such transferee corporation the Secretary may (except as may be otherwise determined under subsection (c)) disallow the benefits of the rates contained in section 11(b) which are lower than the highest rate specified in such section, or the accumulated earnings credit provided in paragraph (2) or (3) of section 535(c), unless such transferee corporation shall establish by the clear preponderance of the evidence that the securing of such benefits or credit was not a major purpose of such transfer.

(b) **Control.**—For purposes of subsection (a), the term "control" means—

(1) With respect to a transferee corporation described in subsection (a) (1) or (2), the ownership by the transferor corporation, its shareholders, or both, of stock possessing at least 80 percent of the total combined voting power of all classes of stock entitled to vote or at least 80 percent of the total value of shares of all classes of the stock; or

(2) With respect to each corporation described in subsection (a) (3), the ownership by the five or fewer individuals described in such subsection of stock possessing—

(A) at least 80 percent of the total combined voting power of all classes of stock entitled to vote or at least 80 percent of the total value of shares of all classes of the stock of each corporation, and

(B) more than 50 percent of the total combined voting power of all classes of stock entitled to vote or more than 50 percent of the total value of shares of all classes of stock of each corporation, taking into account the stock ownership of each such individual only to the extent such stock ownership is identical with respect to each such corporation.

For purposes of this subsection, section 1563(e) shall apply in determining the ownership of stock.

(c) Authority of the Secretary under this section.—The provisions of section 269(c), and the authority of the Secretary under such section, shall, to the extent not inconsistent with the provisions of this section, be applicable to this section.

§ 1552. Earnings and profits

(a) General rule.—Pursuant to regulations prescribed by the Secretary the earnings and profits of each member of an affiliated group required to be included in a consolidated return for such group filed for a taxable year shall be determined by allocating the tax liability of the group for such year among the members of the group in accord with whichever of the following methods the group shall elect in its first consolidated return filed for such a taxable year:

(1) The tax liability shall be apportioned among the members of the group in accordance with the ratio which that portion of the consolidated taxable income attributable to each member of the group having taxable income bears to the consolidated taxable income.

(2) The tax liability of the group shall be allocated to the several members of the group on the basis of the percentage of the total tax which the tax of such member if computed on a separate return would bear to the total amount of the taxes for all members of the group so computed.

(3) The tax liability of the group (excluding the tax increases arising from the consolidation) shall be allocated on the basis of the contribution of each member of the group to the consolidated taxable income of the group. Any tax increases arising from the consolidation shall be distributed to the several members in direct proportion to the reduction in tax liability resulting to such members from the filing of the consolidated return as measured by the difference between their tax liabilities determined on a separate return basis and their tax liabilities based on their contributions to the consolidated taxable income.

* * *

PART II—CERTAIN CONTROLLED CORPORATIONS

§ 1561. Limitations on certain multiple tax benefits in the case of certain controlled corporations

(a) General rule.—The component members of a controlled group of corporations on a December 31 shall, for their taxable years which include such December 31, be limited for purposes of this subtitle to—

(1) amounts in each taxable income bracket in the tax table in section 11(b) which do not aggregate more than the maximum amount in such bracket to which a corporation which is not a component member of a controlled group is entitled,

(2) one $250,000 ($150,000 if any component member is a corporation described in section 535(c)(2)(B)) amount for purposes of computing the accumulated earnings credit under section 535(c)(2) and (3),

(3) one $40,000 exemption amount for purposes of computing the amount of the minimum tax, and

(4) one $2,000,000 amount for purposes of computing the tax imposed by section 59A.

The amounts specified in paragraph (1), the amount specified in paragraph (3), and the amount specified in paragraph (4) shall be divided equally among the component members of such group on such December 31 unless all of such component members consent (at such time and in such manner as the Secretary shall by regulations prescribe) to an apportionment plan providing for an unequal, allocation of such amounts. The amounts specified in paragraph (2) shall be divided equally among the component members of such group on such December 31 unless the Secretary prescribes regulations permitting an unequal allocation of such amounts. Notwithstanding paragraph (1), in applying the last sentence of section 11(b) to such component members, the taxable income of all such component members shall be taken into account and any increase in tax under such last sentence shall be divided among such component members in the same manner as amounts under paragraph (1). In applying section 55(d)(3), the alternative minimum taxable income of all component members shall be taken into account and any decrease in the exemption amount shall be allocated to the component members in the same manner as under paragraph (3).

(b) Certain short taxable years.—If a corporation has a short taxable year which does not include a December 31 and is a component member of a controlled group of corporations with respect to such taxable year, then for purposes of this subtitle—

(1) the amount in each taxable income bracket in the tax table in section 11(b), and

(2) the amount to be used in computing the accumulated earnings credit under section 535(c) (2) and (3),

of such corporation for such taxable year shall be the amount specified in subsection (a)(1) or (2) as the case may be, divided by the number of corporations which are component members of such group on the last day of such taxable year. For purposes of the preceding sentence, section 1563(b) shall be applied as if such last day were substituted for December 31.

§ 1563.　Definitions and special rules

(a) **Controlled group of corporations.**—For purposes of this part, the term "controlled group of corporations" means any group of—

(1) **Parent-subsidiary controlled group.**—One or more chains of corporations connected through stock ownership with a common parent corporation if—

(A) stock possessing at least 80 percent of the total combined voting power of all classes of stock entitled to vote or at least 80 percent of the total value of shares of all classes of stock of each of the corporations, except the common parent corporation, is owned (within the meaning of subsection (d) (1)) by one or more of the other corporations; and

(B) the common parent corporation owns (within the meaning of subsection (d) (1)) stock possessing at least 80 percent of the total combined voting power of all classes of stock entitled to vote or at least 80 percent of the total value of shares of all classes of stock of at least one of the other corporations, excluding, in computing such voting power or value, stock owned directly by such other corporations.

(2) Brother-sister controlled group.—Two or more corporations if 5 or fewer persons who are individuals, estates, or trusts own (within the meaning of subsection (d) (2)) stock possessing—

(A) at least 80 percent of the total combined voting power of all classes of stock entitled to vote or at least 80 percent of the total value of shares of all classes of the stock of each corporation, and

(B) more than 50 percent of the total combined voting power of all classes of stock entitled to vote or more than 50 percent of the total value of shares of all classes of stock of each corporation, taking into account the stock ownership of each such person only to the extent such stock ownership is identical with respect to each such corporation.

(3) Combined group.—Three or more corporations each of which is a member of a group of corporations described in paragraph (1) or (2), and one of which—

(A) is a common parent corporation included in a group of corporations described in paragraph (1), and also

(B) is included in a group of corporations described in paragraph (2).

* * *

(b) Component member.—

(1) General rule.—For purposes of this part, a corporation is a component member of a controlled group of corporations on a December 31 of any taxable year (and with respect to the taxable year which includes such December 31) if such corporation—

(A) is a member of such controlled group of corporations on the December 31 included in such year and is not treated as an excluded member under paragraph (2), or

(B) is not a member of such controlled group of corporations on the December 31 included in such year but is treated as an additional member under paragraph (3).

(2) Excluded members.—A corporation which is a member of a controlled group of corporations on December 31 of any taxable year shall be treated as an excluded member of such group for the taxable year including such December 31 if such corporation—

(A) is a member of such group for less than one-half the number of days in such taxable year which precede such December 31,

(B) is exempt from taxation under section 501(a) (except a corporation which is subject to tax on its unrelated business taxable income under section 511) for such taxable year,

(C) is a foreign corporation subject to tax under section 881 for such taxable year,

(D) is an insurance company subject to taxation under section 801 (other than an insurance company which is a member of a controlled group described in subsection (a)(4)), or

(E) is a franchised corporation, as defined in subsection (f) (4).

(3) Additional members.—A corporation which—

683

(A) was a member of a controlled group of corporations at any time during a calendar year,

(B) is not a member of such group on December 31 of such calendar year, and

(C) is not described, with respect to such group, in subparagraph (B), (C), (D), or (E) of paragraph (2),

shall be treated as an additional member of such group on December 31 for its taxable year including such December 31 if it was a member of such group for one-half (or more) of the number of days in such taxable year which precede such December 31.

(4) Overlapping groups.—If a corporation is a component member of more than one controlled group of corporations with respect to any taxable year, such corporation shall be treated as a component member of only one controlled group. The determination as to the group of which such corporation is a component member shall be made under regulations prescribed by the Secretary which are consistent with the purposes of this part.

(c) Certain stock excluded.—

(1) General rule.—For purposes of this part, the term "stock" does not include—

(A) nonvoting stock which is limited and preferred as to dividends,

(B) treasury stock, and

(C) stock which is treated as "excluded stock" under paragraph (2).

(2) Stock treated as "excluded stock".—

(A) Parent-subsidiary controlled group.—For purposes of subsection (a) (1), if a corporation (referred to in this paragraph as "parent corporation") owns (within the meaning of subsections (d) (1) and (e) (4)), 50 percent or more of the total combined voting power of all classes of stock entitled to vote or 50 percent or more of the total value of shares of all classes of stock in another corporation (referred to in this paragraph as "subsidiary corporation"), the following stock of the subsidiary corporation shall be treated as excluded stock—

(i) stock in the subsidiary corporation held by a trust which is part of a plan of deferred compensation for the benefit of the employees of the parent corporation or the subsidiary corporation,

(ii) stock in the subsidiary corporation owned by an individual (within the meaning of subsection (d) (2)) who is a principal stockholder or officer of the parent corporation. For purposes of this clause, the term "principal stockholder" of a corporation means an individual who owns (within the meaning of subsection (d) (2)) 5 percent or more of the total combined voting power of all classes of stock entitled to vote or 5 percent or more of the total value of shares of all classes of stock in such corporation,

(iii) stock in the subsidiary corporation owned (within the meaning of subsection (d) (2)) by an employee of the subsidiary corporation if such stock is subject to conditions which run in favor of such parent (or subsidiary) corporation and which substantially restrict or limit the employee's right (or if the employee constructively owns such stock, the direct owner's right) to dispose of such stock, or

(iv) stock in the subsidiary corporation owned (within the meaning of subsection (d) (2)) by an organization (other than the parent corporation) to which section 501 (relating to certain educational and charitable organizations which are exempt from tax) applies and which is controlled directly or indirectly by the parent corporation or subsidiary corporation, by an individual, estate, or trust that is a principal stockholder (within the meaning of clause (ii)) of the parent corporation, by an officer of the parent corporation, or by any combination thereof.

(B) Brother-sister controlled group.—For purposes of subsection (a) (2), if 5 or fewer persons who are individuals, estates, or trusts (referred to in this subparagraph as "common owners") own (within the meaning of subsection (d) (2)), 50 percent or more of the total combined voting power of all classes of stock entitled to vote or 50 percent or more of the total value of shares of all classes of stock in a corporation, the following stock of such corporation shall be treated as excluded stock—

(i) stock in such corporation held by an employees' trust described in section 401(a) which is exempt from tax under section 501(a), if such trust is for the benefit of the employees of such corporation,

(ii) stock in such corporation owned (within the meaning of subsection (d) (2)) by an employee of the corporation if such stock is subject to conditions which run in favor of any of such common owners (or such corporation) and which substantially restrict or limit the employee's right (or if the employee constructively owns such stock, the direct owner's right) to dispose of such stock. If a condition which limits or restricts the employee's right (or the direct owner's right) to dispose of such stock also applies to the stock held by any of the common owners pursuant to a bona fide reciprocal stock purchase arrangement, such condition shall not be treated as one which restricts or limits the employee's right to dispose of such stock, or

(iii) stock in such corporation owned (within the meaning of subsection (d) (2)) by an organization to which section 501 (relating to certain educational and charitable organizations which are exempt from tax) applies and which is controlled directly or indirectly by such corporation, by an individual, estate, or trust that is a principal stockholder (within the meaning of subparagraph (A) (ii)) of such corporation, by an officer of such corporation, or by any combination thereof.

(d) Rules for determining stock ownership.—

(1) Parent-subsidiary controlled group.—For purposes of determining whether a corporation is a member of a parent-subsidiary controlled group of corporations (within the meaning of subsection (a) (1)), stock owned by a corporation means—

(A) stock owned directly by such corporation, and

(B) stock owned with the application of subsection (e) (1).

(2) Brother-sister controlled group.—For purposes of determining whether a corporation is a member of a brother-sister controlled group of corporations (within the meaning of subsection (a) (2)), stock owned by a person who is an individual, estate, or trust means—

(A) stock owned directly by such person, and

(B) stock owned with the application of subsection (e).

(e) Constructive ownership.—

(1) Options.—If any person has an option to acquire stock, such stock shall be considered as owned by such person. For purposes of this paragraph, an option to acquire such an option, and each one of a series of such options, shall be considered as an option to acquire such stock.

(2) **Attribution from partnerships.**—Stock owned, directly or indirectly, by or for a partnership shall be considered as owned by any partner having an interest of 5 percent or more in either the capital or profits of the partnership in proportion to his interest in capital or profits, whichever such proportion is the greater.

(3) **Attribution from estates or trusts.**—

(A) Stock owned, directly or indirectly, by or for an estate or trust shall be considered as owned by any beneficiary who has an actuarial interest of 5 percent or more in such stock, to the extent of such actuarial interest. For purposes of this subparagraph, the actuarial interest of each beneficiary shall be determined by assuming the maximum exercise of discretion by the fiduciary in favor of such beneficiary and the maximum use of such stock to satisfy his rights as a beneficiary.

(B) Stock owned, directly or indirectly, by or for any portion of a trust of which a person is considered the owner under subpart E of part I of subchapter J (relating to grantors and others treated as substantial owners) shall be considered as owned by such person.

(C) This paragraph shall not apply to stock owned by any employees' trust described in section 401(a) which is exempt from tax under section 501(a).

(4) **Attribution from corporations.**—Stock owned, directly or indirectly, by or for a corporation shall be considered as owned by any person who owns (within the meaning of subsection (d)) 5 percent or more in value of its stock in that proportion which the value of the stock which such person so owns bears to the value of all the stock in such corporation.

(5) **Spouse.**—An individual shall be considered as owning stock in a corporation owned, directly or indirectly, by or for his spouse (other than a spouse who is legally separated from the individual under a decree of divorce whether interlocutory or final, or a decree of separate maintenance), except in the case of a corporation with respect to which each of the following conditions is satisfied for its taxable year—

(A) The individual does not, at any time during such taxable year, own directly any stock in such corporation;

(B) The individual is not a director or employee and does not participate in the management of such corporation at any time during such taxable year;

(C) Not more than 50 percent of such corporation's gross income for such taxable year was derived from royalties, rents, dividends, interest, and annuities; and

(D) Such stock in such corporation is not, at any time during such taxable year, subject to conditions which substantially restrict or limit the spouse's right to dispose of such stock and which run in favor of the individual or his children who have not attained the age of 21 years.

(6) **Children, grandchildren, parents, and grandparents.**—

(A) **Minor children.**—An individual shall be considered as owning stock owned, directly or indirectly, by or for his children who have not attained the age of 21 years, and, if the individual has not attained the age of 21 years, the stock owned, directly or indirectly, by or for his parents.

(B) **Adult children and grandchildren.**—An individual who owns (within the meaning of subsection (d) (2), but without regard to this subparagraph) more than 50 percent of the total combined voting power of all classes of stock entitled to vote or more than 50 percent of the total value of shares of all classes of stock in a corporation shall be considered as owning the stock in such corporation owned, directly or indirectly, by or for his parents, grandparents, grandchildren, and children who have attained the age of 21 years.

(C) Adopted child.—For purposes of this section, a legally adopted child of an individual shall be treated as a child of such individual by blood.

(f) Other definitions and rules.—

(1) Employee defined.—For purposes of this section the term "employee" has the same meaning such term is given by paragraphs (1) and (2) of section 3121(d).

(2) Operating rules.—

(A) In general.—Except as provided in subparagraph (B), stock constructively owned by a person by reason of the application of paragraph (1), (2), (3), (4), (5), or (6) of subsection (e) shall, for purposes of applying such paragraphs, be treated as actually owned by such person.

(B) Members of family.—Stock constructively owned by an individual by reason of the application of paragraph (5) or (6) of subsection (e) shall not be treated as owned by him for purposes of again applying such paragraphs in order to make another the constructive owner of such stock.

(3) Special rules.—For purposes of this section—

(A) If stock may be considered as owned by a person under subsection (e) (1) and under any other paragraph of subsection (e), it shall be considered as owned by him under subsection (e) (1).

(B) If stock is owned (within the meaning of subsection (d)) by two or more persons, such stock shall be considered as owned by the person whose ownership of such stock results in the corporation being a component member of a controlled group. If by reason of the preceding sentence, a corporation would (but for this sentence) become a component member of two controlled groups, it shall be treated as a component member of one controlled group. The determination as to the group of which such corporation is a component member shall be made under regulations prescribed by the Secretary which are consistent with the purposes of this part.

(C) If stock is owned by a person within the meaning of subsection (d) and such ownership results in the corporation being a component member of a controlled group, such stock shall not be treated as excluded stock under subsection (c) (2), if by reason of treating such stock as excluded stock the result is that such corporation is not a component member of a controlled group of corporations.

(4) Franchised corporation.—If—

(A) a parent corporation (as defined in subsection (c) (2) (A)), or a common owner (as defined in subsection (c) (2) (B)), of a corporation which is a member of a controlled group of corporations is under a duty (arising out of a written agreement) to sell stock of such corporation (referred to in this paragraph as "franchised corporation") which is franchised to sell the products of another member, or the common owner, of such controlled group;

(B) such stock is to be sold to an employee (or employees) of such franchised corporation pursuant to a bona fide plan designed to eliminate the stock ownership of the parent corporation or of the common owner in the franchised corporation;

(C) such plan—

(i) provides a reasonable selling price for such stock, and

(ii) requires that a portion of the employee's share of the profits of such corporation (whether received as compensation or as a dividend) be applied to the purchase of such stock (or the purchase of notes, bonds, debentures or other similar evidence of indebtedness of such franchised corporation held by such parent corporation or common owner);

(D) such employee (or employees) owns directly more than 20 percent of the total value of shares of all classes of stock in such franchised corporation;

(E) more than 50 percent of the inventory of such franchised corporation is acquired from members of the controlled group, the common owner, or both; and

(F) all of the conditions contained in subparagraphs (A), (B), (C), (D), and (E) have been met for one-half (or more) of the number of days preceding the December 31 included within the taxable year (or if the taxable year does not include December 31, the last day of such year) of the franchised corporation,

then such franchised corporation shall be treated as an excluded member of such group, under subsection (b) (2), for such taxable year.

SUBTITLE B—ESTATE AND GIFT TAXES

CHAPTER 11—ESTATE TAX

SUBCHAPTER A—ESTATES OF CITIZENS OR RESIDENTS

PART I—TAX IMPOSED

§ 2001. Imposition and rate of tax

(a) **Imposition.**—A tax is hereby imposed on the transfer of the taxable estate of every decedent who is a citizen or resident of the United States.

(b) **Computation of tax.**—The tax imposed by this section shall be the amount equal to the excess (if any) of—

(1) a tentative tax computed in accordance with the rate schedule set forth in subsection (c) on the sum of—

(A) the amount of the taxable estate, and

(B) the amount of the adjusted taxable gifts, over

(2) the aggregate amount of tax which would have been payable under chapter 12 with respect to gifts made by the decedent after December 31, 1976, if the rate schedule set forth in subsection (c) (as in effect at the decedent's death) had been applicable at the time of such gifts.

For purposes of paragraph (1) (B), the term "adjusted taxable gifts" means the total amount of the taxable gifts (within the meaning of section 2503) made by the decedent after December 31, 1976, other than gifts which are includible in the gross estate of the decedent.

(c) **Rate schedule.—**

(1) **In general.—**

* Omitted entirely.

If the amount with respect to
 which the tentative tax to be
 computed is: The tentative tax is:

Not over $10,000	18 percent of such amount.
Over $10,000 but not over $20,000	$1,800, plus 20 percent of the excess of such amount over $10,000.
Over $20,000 but not over $40,000	$3,800, plus 22 percent of the excess of such amount over $20,000.
Over $40,000 but not over $60,000	$8,200, plus 24 percent of the excess of such amount over $40,000.
Over $60,000 but not over $80,000	$13,000, plus 26 percent of the excess of such amount over $60,000.
Over $80,000 but not over $100,000	$18,200, plus 28 percent of the excess of such amount over $80,000.
Over $100,000 but not over $150,000	$23,800, plus 30 percent of the excess of such amount over $100,000.
Over $150,000 but not over $250,000	$38,800, plus 32 percent of the excess of such amount over $150,000.
Over $250,000 but not over $500,000	$70,800, plus 34 percent of the excess of such amount over $250,000.
Over $500,000 but not over $750,000	$155,800, plus 37 percent of the excess of such amount over $500,000.
Over $750,000 but not over $1,000,000	$248,300, plus 39 percent of the excess of such amount over $750,000.
Over $1,000,000 but not over $1,250,000	$345,800, plus 41 percent of the excess of such amount over $1,000,000.
Over $1,250,000 but not over $1,500,000	$448,300, plus 43 percent of the excess of such amount over $1,250,000.
Over $1,500,000 but not over $2,000,000	$555,800, plus 45 percent of the excess of such amount over $1,500,000.
Over $2,000,000 but not over $2,500,000	$780,800, plus 49 percent of the excess of such amount over $2,000,000.
Over $2,500,000	$1,025,800, plus 50% of the excess over $2,500,000.

(2) **Phase-in of 50 percent maximum rate.—**

(A) **In general.**—In the case of decedents dying, and gifts made, before 1988, there shall be substituted for the last item in the schedule contained in paragraph (1) the items determined under this paragraph.

(B) **For 1982.**—In the case of decedents dying, and gifts made, in 1982, the substitution under this paragraph shall be as follows:

Over $2,500,000 but not over $3,000,000	$1,025,800, plus 53% of the excess over $2,500,000.
Over $3,000,000 but not over $3,500,000	$1,290,800, plus 57% of the excess over $3,000,000.
Over $3,500,000 but not over $4,000,000	$1,575,800, plus 61% of the excess over $3,500,000.
Over $4,000,000	$1,880,800, plus 65% of the excess over $4,000,000.

(C) **For 1983.**—In the case of decedents dying, and gifts made, in 1983, the substitution under this paragraph shall be as follows:

Over $2,500,000 but not over $3,000,000	$1,025,800, plus 53% of the excess over $2,500,000.
Over $3,000,000 but not over $3,500,000	$1,290,800, plus 57% of the excess over $3,000,000.
Over $3,500,000	$1,575,800, plus 60% of the excess over $3,500,000.

(D) For 1984, 1985, 1986, or 1987.—In the case of decedents dying, and gifts made, in 1984, 1985, 1986, or 1987, the substitution under this paragraph shall be as follows:

Over $2,500,000 but not over $3,000,000 . . . . . .$1,025,800, plus 53% of the excess over $2,500,000.

Over $3,000,000 . . . .$1,290,800, plus 55% of the excess over $3,000,000.

(d) Adjustment for gift tax paid by spouse.—For purposes of subsection (b) (2), if—

(1) the decedent was the donor of any gift one-half of which was considered under section 2513 as made by the decedent's spouse, and

(2) the amount of such gift is includible in the gross estate of the decedent,

any tax payable by the spouse under chapter 12 on such gift (as determined under section 2012(d)) shall be treated as a tax payable with respect to a gift made by the decedent.

(e) Coordination of sections 2513 and 2035.—If—

(1) the decedent's spouse was the donor of any gift one-half of which was considered under section 2513 as made by the decedent, and

(2) the amount of such gift is includible in the gross estate of the decedent's spouse by reason of section 2035,

such gift shall not be included in the adjusted taxable gifts of the decedent for purposes of subsection (b) (1) (B), and the aggregate amount determined under subsection (b) (2) shall be reduced by the amount (if any) determined under subsection (d) which was treated as a tax payable by the decedent's spouse with respect to such gift.

§ 2002. Liability for payment

Except as provided in section 2210, the tax imposed by this chapter shall be paid by the executor.

PART II—CREDITS AGAINST TAX

§ 2010. Unified credit against estate tax

(a) General rule.—A credit of $192,800 shall be allowed to the estate of every decedent against the tax imposed by section 2001.

(b) Phase-in of credit.—

In the case of decedents dying in:	Subsection (a) shall be applied by substituting for "$192,800" the following amount:
1982	$62,800
1983	79,300
1984	96,300
1985	121,800
1986	155,800

(c) Adjustment to credit for certain gifts made before 1977.—The amount of the credit allowable under subsection (a) shall be reduced by an amount equal to 20 percent of the aggregate amount allowed as a specific exemption under section 2521 (as in effect before its repeal by the Tax Reform Act of 1976) with respect to gifts made by the decedent after September 8, 1976.

(d) Limitation based on amount of tax.—The amount of the credit allowed by subsection (a) shall not exceed the amount of the tax imposed by section 2001.

§ 2011. Credit for State death taxes

(a) In general.—The tax imposed by section 2001 shall be credited with the amount of any estate, inheritance, legacy, or succession taxes actually paid to any State or the District of Columbia, in respect of any property included in the gross estate (not including any such taxes paid with respect to the estate of a person other than the decedent).

(b) Amount of credit.—The credit allowed by this section shall not exceed the appropriate amount stated in the following table:

If the adjusted taxable estate is:	The maximum tax credit shall be:
Not over $90,000	8/10ths of 1% of the amount by which the taxable estate exceeds $40,000.
Over $90,000 but not over $140,000	$400 plus 1.6% of the excess over $90,000.
Over $140,000 but not over $240,000	$1,200 plus 2.4% of the excess over $140,000.
Over $240,000 but not over $440,000	$3,600 plus 3.2% of the excess over $240,000.
Over $440,000 but not over $640,000	$10,000 plus 4% of the excess over $440,000.
Over $640,000 but not over $840,000	$18,000 plus 4.8% of the excess over $640,000.
Over $840,000 but not over $1,040,000	$27,600 plus 5.6% of the excess over $840,000.
Over $1,040,000 but not over $1,540,000	$38,800 plus 6.4% of the excess over $1,040,000.
Over $1,540,000 but not over $2,040,000	$70,800 plus 7.2% of the excess over $1,540,000.
Over $2,040,000 but not over $2,540,000	$106,800 plus 8% of the excess over $2,040,000.
Over $2,540,000 but not over $3,040,000	$146,800 plus 8.8% of the excess over $2,540,000.
Over $3,040,000 but not over $3,540,000	$190,800 plus 9.6% of the excess over $3,040,000.
Over $3,540,000 but not over $4,040,000	$238,800 plus 10.4% of the excess over $3,540,000.
Over $4,040,000 but not over $5,040,000	$290,800 plus 11.2% of the excess over $4,040,000.
Over $5,040,000 but not over $6,040,000	$402,800 plus 12% of the excess over $5,040,000.
Over $6,040,000 but not over $7,040,000	$522,800 plus 12.8% of the excess over $6,040,000.
Over $7,040,000 but not over $8,040,000	$650,800 plus 13.6% of the excess over $7,040,000.
Over $8,040,000 but not over $9,040,000	$786,800 plus 14.4% of the excess over $8,040,000.
Over $9,040,000 but not over $10,040,000 ...	$930,800 plus 15.2% of the excess over $9,040,000.
Over $10,040,000	$1,082,800 plus 16% of the excess over $10,040,000.

For purposes of this section, the term "adjusted taxable estate" means the taxable estate reduced by $60,000.

(c) Period of limitations on credit.—The credit allowed by this section shall include only such taxes as were actually paid and credit therefor claimed within 4 years after the filing of the return required by section 6018, except that—

(1) If a petition for redetermination of a deficiency has been filed with the Tax Court within the time prescribed in section 6213(a), then within such 4-year period

or before the expiration of 60 days after the decision of the Tax Court becomes final.

(2) If, under section 6161 or 6166, an extension of time has been granted for payment of the tax shown on the return, or of a deficiency, then within such 4-year period or before the date of the expiration of the period of the extension.

(3) If a claim for refund or credit of an overpayment of tax imposed by this chapter has been filed within the time prescribed in section 6511, then within such 4-year period or before the expiration of 60 days from the date of mailing by certified mail or registered mail by the Secretary to the taxpayer of a notice of the disallowance of any part of such claim, or before the expiration of 60 days after a decision by any court of competent jurisdiction becomes final with respect to a timely suit instituted upon such claim, whichever is later.

Refund based on the credit may (despite the provisions of sections 6511 and 6512) be made if claim therefor is filed within the period above provided. Any such refund shall be made without interest.

(d) **Basic estate tax.**—The basic estate tax and the estate tax imposed by the Revenue Act of 1926 shall be 125 percent of the amount determined to be the maximum credit provided by subsection (b). The additional estate tax shall be the difference between the tax imposed by section 2001 or 2101 and the basic estate tax.

(e) **Limitation in cases involving deduction under section 2053(d).**—In any case where a deduction is allowed under section 2053(d) for an estate, succession, legacy, or inheritance tax imposed by a State or the District of Columbia upon a transfer for public, charitable, or religious uses described in section 2055 or 2106(a)(2), the allowance of the credit under this section shall be subject to the following conditions and limitations:

(1) The taxes described in subsection (a) shall not include any estate, succession, legacy, or inheritance tax for which such deduction is allowed under section 2053(d).

(2) The credit shall not exceed the lesser of—

(A) the amount stated in subsection (b) on a[1] adjusted taxable estate determined by allowing such deduction authorized by section 2053(d), or

(B) that proportion of the amount stated in subsection (b) on a[1] adjusted taxable estate determined without regard to such deduction authorized by section 2053(d) as (i) the amount of the taxes described in subsection (a), as limited by the provisions of paragraph (1) of this subsection, bears to (ii) the amount of the taxes described in subsection (a) before applying the limitation contained in paragraph (1) of this subsection.

(3) If the amount determined under subparagraph (B) of paragraph (2) is less than the amount determined under subparagraph (A) of that paragraph, then for purposes of subsection (d) such lesser amount shall be the maximum credit provided by subsection (b).

(f) **Limitation based on amount of tax.**—The credit provided by this section shall not exceed the amount of the tax imposed by section 2001, reduced by the amount of the unified credit provided by section 2010.

§ 2012. Credit for gift tax

(a) **In general.**—If a tax on a gift has been paid under chapter 12 (sec. 2501 and following), or under corresponding provisions of prior laws, and thereafter on the

[1] So in original. Probably should read "an".

death of the donor any amount in respect of such gift is required to be included in the value of the gross estate of the decedent for purposes of this chapter, then there shall be credited against the tax imposed by section 2001 the amount of the tax paid on a gift under chapter 12, or under corresponding provisions of prior laws, with respect to so much of the property which constituted the gift as is included in the gross estate, except that the amount of such credit shall not exceed an amount which bears the same ratio to the tax imposed by section 2001 (after deducting from such tax the credit for State death taxes provided by section 2011 and the unified credit provided by section 2010) as the value (at the time of the gift or at the time of the death, whichever is lower) of so much of the property which constituted the gift as is included in the gross estate bears to the value of the entire gross estate reduced by the aggregate amount of the charitable and marital deductions allowed under sections 2055, 2056, and 2106(a) (2).

(b) **Valuation reductions.**—In applying, with respect to any gift, the ratio stated in subsection (a), the value at the time of the gift or at the time of the death, referred to in such ratio, shall be reduced—

(1) by such amount as will properly reflect the amount of such gift which was excluded in determining (for purposes of section 2503(a)), or of corresponding provisions of prior laws, the total amount of gifts made during the calendar quarter (or calendar year if the gift was made before January 1, 1971) in which the gift was made;

(2) if a deduction with respect to such gift is allowed under section 2056(a) (relating to marital deduction), then by the amount of such value, reduced as provided in paragraph (1); and

(3) if a deduction with respect to such gift is allowed under sections 2055 or 2106(a) (2) (relating to charitable deduction), then by the amount of such value, reduced as provided in paragraph (1) of this subsection.

(c) **Where gift considered made one-half by spouse.**—Where the decedent was the donor of the gift but, under the provisions of section 2513, or corresponding provisions of prior laws, the gift was considered as made one-half by his spouse—

(1) the term "the amount of the tax paid on a gift under chapter 12", as used in subsection (a), includes the amounts paid with respect to each half of such gift, the amount paid with respect to each being computed in the manner provided in subsection (d); and

(2) in applying, with respect to such gift, the ratio stated in subsection (a), the value at the time of the gift or at the time of the death, referred to in such ratio, includes such value with respect to each half of such gift, each such value being reduced as provided in paragraph (1) of subsection (b).

(d) **Computation of amount of gift tax paid.**—

(1) **Amount of tax.**—For purposes of subsection (a), the amount of tax paid on a gift under chapter 12, or under corresponding provisions of prior laws, with respect to any gift shall be an amount which bears the same ratio to the total tax paid for the calendar quarter (or calendar year if the gift was made before January 1, 1971) in which the gift was made as the amount of such gift bears to the total amount of taxable gifts (computed without deduction of the specific exemption) for such quarter or year.

(2) **Amount of gift.**—For purposes of paragraph (1), the "amount of such gift" shall be the amount included with respect to such gift in determining (for the purposes of section 2503(a), or of corresponding provisions of prior laws) the total amount of gifts made during such quarter or year, reduced by the amount of any

deduction allowed with respect to such gift under section 2522, or under corresponding provisions of prior laws (relating to charitable deduction), or under section 2523 (relating to marital deduction).

(e) **Section inapplicable to gifts made after December 31, 1976.**—No credit shall be allowed under this section with respect to the amount of any tax paid under chapter 12 on any gift made after December 31, 1976.

§ 2013. Credit for tax on prior transfers

(a) **General rule.**—The tax imposed by section 2001 shall be credited with all or a part of the amount of the Federal estate tax paid with respect to the transfer of property (including property passing as a result of the exercise or non-exercise of a power of appointment) to the decedent by or from a person (herein designated as a "transferor") who died within 10 years before, or within 2 years after, the decedent's death. If the transferor died within 2 years of the death of the decedent, the credit shall be the amount determined under subsections (b) and (c). If the transferor predeceased the decedent by more than 2 years, the credit shall be the following percentage of the amount so determined—

(1) 80 percent, if within the third or fourth years preceding the decedent's death;

(2) 60 percent, if within the fifth or sixth years preceding the decedent's death;

(3) 40 percent, if within the seventh or eighth years preceding the decedent's death; and

(4) 20 percent, if within the ninth or tenth years preceding the decedent's death.

(b) **Computation of credit.**—Subject to the limitation prescribed in subsection (c), the credit provided by this section shall be an amount which bears the same ratio to the estate tax paid (adjusted as indicated hereinafter) with respect to the estate of the transferor as the value of the property transferred bears to the taxable estate of the transferor (determined for purposes of the estate tax) decreased by any death taxes paid with respect to such estate. For purposes of the preceding sentence, the estate tax paid shall be the Federal estate tax paid increased by any credits allowed against such estate tax under section 2012, or corresponding provisions of prior laws, on account of gift tax, and for any credits allowed against such estate tax under this section on account of prior transfers where the transferor acquired property from a person who died within 10 years before the death of the decedent.

(c) **Limitation on credit.**—

(1) **In general.**—The credit provided in this section shall not exceed the amount by which—

(A) the estate tax imposed by section 2001 or section 2101 (after deducting the credits provided for in sections 2010, 2011, 2012, and 2014) computed without regard to this section, exceeds

(B) such tax computed by excluding from the decedent's gross estate the value of such property transferred and, if applicable, by making the adjustment hereinafter indicated.

If any deduction is otherwise allowable under section 2055 or section 2106(a) (2) (relating to charitable deduction) then, for the purpose of the computation indicated in subparagraph (B), the amount of such deduction shall be reduced by that part of such deduction which the value of such property transferred bears to the decedent's entire gross estate reduced by the deductions allowed under sections 2053 and 2054, or section 2106(a) (1) (relating to deduction for expenses, losses, etc.).

For purposes of this section, the value of such property transferred shall be the value as provided for in subsection (d) of this section.

(2) Two or more transferors.—If the credit provided in this section relates to property received from 2 or more transferors, the limitation provided in paragraph (1) of this subsection shall be computed by aggregating the value of the property so transferred to the decedent. The aggregate limitation so determined shall be apportioned in accordance with the value of the property transferred to the decedent by each transferor.

(d) Valuation of property transferred.—The value of property transferred to the decedent shall be the value used for the purpose of determining the Federal estate tax liability of the estate of the transferor but—

(1) there shall be taken into account the effect of the tax imposed by section 2001 or 2101, or any estate, succession, legacy, or inheritance tax, on the net value to the decedent of such property;

(2) where such property is encumbered in any manner, or where the decedent incurs any obligation imposed by the transferor with respect to such property, such encumbrance or obligation shall be taken into account in the same manner as if the amount of a gift to the decedent of such property was being determined; and

(3) if the decedent was the spouse of the transferor at the time of the transferor's death, the net value of the property transferred to the decedent shall be reduced by the amount allowed under section 2056 (relating to marital deductions) as a deduction from the gross estate of the transferor.

(e) Property defined.—For purposes of this section, the term "property" includes any beneficial interest in property, including a general power of appointment (as defined in section 2041).

(f) Treatment of additional tax imposed under section 2032A.—If section 2032A applies to any property included in the gross estate of the transferor and an additional tax is imposed with respect to such property under section 2032A(c) before the date which is 2 years after the date of the decedent's death, for purposes of this section—

(1) the additional tax imposed by section 2032A(c) shall be treated as a Federal estate tax payable with respect to the estate of the transferor; and

(2) the value of such property and the amount of the taxable estate of the transferor shall be determined as if section 2032A did not apply with respect to such property.

§ 2014.   Credit for foreign death taxes

(a) In general.—The tax imposed by section 2001 shall be credited with the amount of any estate, inheritance, legacy, or succession taxes actually paid to any foreign country in respect of any property situated within such foreign country and included in the gross estate (not including any such taxes paid with respect to the estate of a person other than the decedent). The determination of the country within which property is situated shall be made in accordance with the rules applicable under subchapter B (sec. 2101 and following) in determining whether property is situated within or without the United States.

(b) Limitations on credit.—The credit provided in this section with respect to such taxes paid to any foreign country—

(1) shall not, with respect to any such tax, exceed an amount which bears the same ratio to the amount of such tax actually paid to such foreign country as the value of property which is—

(A) situated within such foreign country,

(B) subjected to such tax, and

(C) included in the gross estate

bears to the value of all property subjected to such tax; and

(2) shall not, with respect to all such taxes, exceed an amount which bears the same ratio to the tax imposed by section 2001 (after deducting from such tax the credits provided by sections 2010, 2011, and 2012) as the value of property which is—

(A) situated within such foreign country,

(B) subjected to the taxes of such foreign country, and

(C) included in the gross estate

bears to the value of the entire gross estate reduced by the aggregate amount of the deductions allowed under sections 2055 and 2056.

(c) Valuation of property.—

(1) The values referred to in the ratio stated in subsection (b) (1) are the values determined for purposes of the tax imposed by such foreign country.

(2) The values referred to in the ratio stated in subsection (b) (2) are the values determined under this chapter; but, in applying such ratio, the value of any property described in subparagraphs (A), (B), and (C) thereof shall be reduced by such amount as will properly reflect, in accordance with regulations prescribed by the Secretary, the deductions allowed in respect of such property under sections 2055 and 2056 (relating to charitable and marital deductions).

(d) Proof of credit.—The credit provided in this section shall be allowed only if the taxpayer establishes to the satisfaction of the Secretary—

(1) the amount of taxes actually paid to the foreign country,

(2) the amount and date of each payment thereof,

(3) the description and value of the property in respect of which such taxes are imposed, and

(4) all other information necessary for the verification and computation of the credit.

(e) Period of limitation.—The credit provided in this section shall be allowed only for such taxes as were actually paid and credit therefor claimed within 4 years after the filing of the return required by section 6018, except that—

(1) If a petition for redetermination of a deficiency has been filed with the Tax Court within the time prescribed in section 6213(a), then within such 4-year period or before the expiration of 60 days after the decision of the Tax Court becomes final.

(2) If, under section 6161, an extension of time has been granted for payment of the tax shown on the return, or of a deficiency, then within such 4-year period or before the date of the expiration of the period of the extension.

Refund based on such credit may (despite the provisions of sections 6511 and 6512) be made if claim therefor is filed within the period above provided. Any such refund shall be made without interest.

(f) Additional limitation in cases involving a deduction under section 2053(d).—In any case where a deduction is allowed under section 2053(d) for an estate, succession, legacy, or inheritance tax imposed by and actually paid to any foreign country upon a transfer by the decedent for public, charitable, or religious uses described in section 2055, the property described in subparagraphs (A), (B), and (C) of paragraphs (1) and (2) of subsection (b) of this section shall not include any property in respect of which such deduction is allowed under section 2053(d).

(g) Possession of United States deemed a foreign country.—For purposes of the credits authorized by this section, each possession of the United States shall be deemed to be a foreign country.

(h) Similar credit required for certain alien residents.—Whenever the President finds that—

(1) a foreign country, in imposing estate, inheritance, legacy, or succession taxes, does not allow to citizens of the United States resident in such foreign country at the time of death a credit similar to the credit allowed under subsection (a),

(2) such foreign country, when requested by the United States to do so has not acted to provide such a similar credit in the case of citizens of the United States resident in such foreign country at the time of death, and

(3) it is in the public interest to allow the credit under subsection (a) in the case of citizens or subjects of such foreign country only if it allows such a similar credit in the case of citizens of the United States resident in such foreign country at the time of death,

the President shall proclaim that, in the case of citizens or subjects of such foreign country dying while the proclamation remains in effect, the credit under subsection (a) shall be allowed only if such foreign country allows such a similar credit in the case of citizens of the United States resident in such foreign country at the time of death.

§ 2015. Credit for death taxes on remainders

Where an election is made under section 6163(a) to postpone payment of the tax imposed by section 2001 or 2101, such part of any estate, inheritance, legacy, or succession taxes allowable as a credit under section 2011 or 2014, as is attributable to a reversionary or remainder interest may be allowed as a credit against the tax attributable to such interest, subject to the limitations on the amount of the credit contained in such sections, if such part is paid, and credit therefor claimed, at any time before the expiration of the time for payment of the tax imposed by section 2001 or 2101 as postponed and extended under section 6163.

§ 2016. Recovery of taxes claimed as credit

If any tax claimed as a credit under section 2011 or 2014 is recovered from any foreign country, any State, any possession of the United States, or the District of Columbia, the executor, or any other person or persons recovering such amount, shall give notice of such recovery to the Secretary at such time and in such manner as may be required by regulations prescribed by him, and the Secretary shall (despite the provisions of section 6501) redetermine the amount of the tax under this chapter and the amount, if any, of the tax due on such redetermination, shall be paid by the executor or such person or persons, as the case may be, on notice and demand. No interest shall be assessed or collected on any amount of tax due on any redetermination by the Secretary, resulting from a refund to the executor of tax claimed as a credit under section 2014, for any period before the receipt of such refund, except to the extent interest was paid by the foreign country on such refund.

PART III—GROSS ESTATE

§ 2031. Definition of gross estate

(a) **General.**—The value of the gross estate of the decedent shall be determined by including to the extent provided for in this part, the value at the time of his death of all property, real or personal, tangible or intangible, wherever situated.

(b) **Valuation of unlisted stock and securities.**—In the case of stock and securities of a corporation the value of which, by reason of their not being listed on an exchange and by reason of the absence of sales thereof, cannot be determined with reference to bid and asked prices or with reference to sales prices, the value thereof shall be determined by taking into consideration, in addition to all other factors, the value of stock or securities of corporations engaged in the same or a similar line of business which are listed on an exchange.

(c) **Cross reference.**—

For executor's right to be furnished on request a statement regarding any valuation made by the Secretary within the gross estate, see section 7517.

§ 2032. Alternate valuation

(a) **General.**—The value of the gross estate may be determined, if the executor so elects, by valuing all the property included in the gross estate as follows:

(1) In the case of property distributed, sold, exchanged, or otherwise disposed of, within 6 months after the decedent's death such property shall be valued as of the date of distribution, sale, exchange, or other disposition.

(2) In the case of property not distributed, sold, exchanged, or otherwise disposed of, within 6 months after the decedent's death such property shall be valued as of the date 6 months after the decedent's death.

(3) Any interest or estate which is affected by mere lapse of time shall be included at its value as of the time of death (instead of the later date) with adjustment for any difference in its value as of the later date not due to mere lapse of time.

(b) **Special rules.**—No deduction under this chapter of any item shall be allowed if allowance for such item is in effect given by the alternate valuation provided by this section. Wherever in any other subsection or section of this chapter reference is made to the value of property at the time of the decedent's death, such reference shall be deemed to refer to the value of such property used in determining the value of the gross estate. In case of an election made by the executor under this section, then—

(1) for purposes of the charitable deduction under section 2055 or 2106(a) (2), any bequest, legacy, devise, or transfer enumerated therein, and

(2) for the purpose of the marital deduction under section 2056, any interest in property passing to the surviving spouse,

shall be valued as of the date of the decedent's death with adjustment for any difference in value (not due to mere lapse of time or the occurrence or nonoccurrence of a contingency) of the property as of the date 6 months after the decedent's death (substituting, in the case of property distributed by the executor or trustee, or sold, exchanged, or otherwise disposed of, during such 6-month period, the date thereof).

(c) Election must decrease gross estate and estate tax.—No election may be made under this section with respect to an estate unless such election will decrease—

(1) the value of the gross estate, and

(2) the sum of the tax imposed by this chapter and the tax imposed by chapter 13 with respect to property includible in the decedent's gross estate (reduced by credits allowable against such taxes).

(d) Election.—

(1) In general.—The election provided for in this section shall be made by the executor on the return of the tax imposed by this chapter. Such election, once made, shall be irrevocable.

(2) Exception.—No election may be made under this section if such return is filed more than 1 year after the time prescribed by law (including extensions) for filing such return.

§ 2032A.   Valuation of certain farm, etc., real property

(a) Value based on use under which property qualifies.—

(1) General rule.—If—

(A) the decedent was (at the time of his death) a citizen or resident of the United States, and

(B) the executor elects the application of this section and files the agreement referred to in subsection (d)(2),

then, for purposes of this chapter, the value of qualified real property shall be its value for the use under which it qualifies, under subsection (b), as qualified real property.

(2) Limit on aggregate reduction in fair market value.—The aggregate decrease in the value of qualified real property taken into account for purposes of this chapter which results from the application of paragraph (1) with respect to any decedent shall not exceed the applicable limit set forth in the following table:

In the case of decedents dying in:	The applicable limit is:
1981	$600,000
1982	700,000
1983 or thereafter	750,000

(b) Qualified real property.—

(1) In general.—For purposes of this section, the term "qualified real property" means real property located in the United States which was acquired from or passed from the decedent to a qualified heir of the decedent and which, on the date of the decedent's death, was being used for a qualified use by the decedent or a member of the decedent's family, but only if—

(A) 50 percent or more of the adjusted value of the gross estate consists of the adjusted value of real or personal property which—

(i) on the date of the decedent's death, was being used for a qualified use by the decedent or a member of the decedent's family, and

(ii) was acquired from or passed from the decedent to a qualified heir of the decedent.

(B) 25 percent or more of the adjusted value of the gross estate consists of the adjusted value of real property which meets the requirements of subparagraphs (A)(ii) and (C),

(C) during the 8-year period ending on the date of the decedent's death there have been periods aggregating 5 years or more during which—

(i) such real property was owned by the decedent or a member of the decedent's family and used for a qualified use by the decedent or a member of the decedent's family, and

(ii) there was material participation by the decedent or a member of the decedent's family in the operation of the farm or other business, and

(D) such real property is designated in the agreement referred to in subsection (d)(2).

(2) Qualified use.—For purposes of this section, the term "qualified use" means the devotion of the property to any of the following:

(A) use as a farm for farming purposes, or

(B) use in a trade or business other than the trade or business of farming.

(3) Adjusted value.—For purposes of paragraph (1), the term "adjusted value" means—

(A) in the case of the gross estate, the value of the gross estate for purposes of this chapter (determined without regard to this section), reduced by any amounts allowable as a deduction under paragraph (4) of section 2053(a), or

(B) in the case of any real or personal property, the value of such property for purposes of this chapter (determined without regard to this section), reduced by any amounts allowable as a deduction in respect of such property under paragraph (4) of section 2053(a).

(4) Decedents who are retired or disabled.—

(A) **In general.**—If, on the date of the decedent's death, the requirements of paragraph (1)(C)(ii) with respect to the decedent for any property are not met, and the decedent—

(i) was receiving old-age benefits under title II of the Social Security Act for a continuous period ending on such date, or

(ii) was disabled for a continuous period ending on such date,

then paragraph (1)(C)(ii) shall be applied with respect to such property by substituting "the date on which the longer of such continuous periods began" for "the date of the decedent's death" in paragraph (1)(C).

(B) **Disabled defined.**—For purposes of subparagraph (A), an individual shall be disabled if such individual has a mental or physical impairment which renders him unable to materially participate in the operation of the farm or other business.

(C) **Coordination with recapture.**—For purposes of subsection (c)(6)(B)(i), if the requirements of paragraph (1)(C)(ii) are met with respect to any decedent by reason of subparagraph (A), the period ending on the date on which the continuous period taken into account under subparagraph (A) began shall be treated as the period immediately before the decedent's death.

(5) Special rules for surviving spouses.—

(A) **In general.**—If property is qualified real property with respect to a decedent (hereinafter in this paragraph referred to as the "first decedent") and such property was acquired from or passed from the first decedent to the surviving spouse of the first decedent, for purposes of applying this subsection and subsection (c) in the case of the estate of such surviving spouse, active management of the farm or other business by the surviving spouse shall be treated as material participation by such surviving spouse in the operation of such farm or business.

(B) **Special rule.**—For the purposes of subparagraph (A), the determination of whether property is qualified real property with respect to the first decedent shall be made without regard to subparagraph (D) of paragraph (1) and without regard to whether an election under this section was made.

(C) **Coordination with paragraph (4).**—In any case in which to do so will enable the requirements of paragraph (1)(C)(ii) to be met with respect to the surviving spouse, this subsection and subsection (c) shall be applied by taking into account any application of paragraph (4).

(c) **Tax treatment of dispositions and failures to use for qualified use.**—

(1) **Imposition of additional estate tax.**—If, within 10 years after the decedent's death and before the death of the qualified heir—

(A) the qualified heir disposes of any interest in the qualified real property (other than by a disposition to a member of his family), or

(B) the qualified heir ceases to use for the qualified use the qualified real property which was acquired (or passed) from the decedent,

then, there is hereby imposed an additional estate tax.

(2) **Amount of additional tax.**—

(A) **In general.**—The amount of the additional tax imposed by paragraph (1) with respect to any interest shall be the amount equal to the lesser of—

(i) the adjusted tax difference attributable to such interest, or

(ii) the excess of the amount realized with respect to the interest (or, in any case other than a sale or exchange at arm's length, the fair market value of the interest) over the value of the interest determined under subsection (a).

(B) **Adjusted tax difference attributable to interest.**—For purposes of subparagraph (A), the adjusted tax difference attributable to an interest is the amount which bears the same ratio to the adjusted tax difference with respect to the estate (determined under subparagraph (C)) as—

(i) the excess of the value of such interest for purposes of this chapter (determined without regard to subsection (a)) over the value of such interest determined under subsection (a), bears to

(ii) a similar excess determined for all qualified real property.

(C) **Adjusted tax difference with respect to the estate.**—For purposes of subparagraph (B), the term "adjusted tax difference with respect to the estate" means the excess of what would have been the estate tax liability but for subsection (a) over the estate tax liability. For purposes of this subparagraph, the term "estate tax liability" means the tax imposed by section 2001 reduced by the credits allowable against such tax.

(D) **Partial dispositions.**—For purposes of this paragraph, where the qualified heir disposes of a portion of the interest acquired by (or passing to) such heir (or a predecessor qualified heir) or there is a cessation of use of such a portion—

(i) the value determined under subsection (a) taken into account under subparagraph (A)(ii) with respect to such portion shall be its pro rata share of such value of such interest, and

(ii) the adjusted tax difference attributable to the interest taken into account with respect to the transaction involving the second or any succeeding portion shall be reduced by the amount of the tax imposed by this subsection with respect to all prior transactions involving portions of such interest.

(E) Special rule for disposition of timber.—In the case of qualified woodland to which an election under subsection (e)(13)(A) applies, if the qualified heir disposes of (or severs) any standing timber on such qualified woodland—

(i) such disposition (or severance) shall be treated as a disposition of a portion of the interest of the qualified heir in such property, and

(ii) the amount of the additional tax imposed by paragraph (1) with respect to such disposition shall be an amount equal to the lesser of—

(I) the amount realized on such disposition (or, in any case other than a sale or exchange at arm's length, the fair market value of the portion of the interest disposed or severed), or

(II) the amount of additional tax determined under this paragraph (without regard to this subparagraph) if the entire interest of the qualified heir in the qualified woodland had been disposed of, less the sum of the amount of the additional tax imposed with respect to all prior transactions involving such woodland to which this subparagraph applied.

For purposes of the preceding sentence, the disposition of a right to sever shall be treated as the disposition of the standing timber. The amount of additional tax imposed under paragraph (1) in any case in which a qualified heir disposes of his entire interest in the qualified woodland shall be reduced by any amount determined under this subparagraph with respect to such woodland.

(3) Only 1 additional tax imposed with respect to any 1 portion.—In the case of an interest acquired from (or passing from) any decedent, if subparagraph (A) or (B) of paragraph (1) applies to any portion of an interest, subparagraph (B) or (A), as the case may be, of paragraph (1) shall not apply with respect to the same portion of such interest.

(4) Due date.—The additional tax imposed by this subsection shall become due and payable on the day which is 6 months after the date of the disposition or cessation referred to in paragraph (1).

(5) Liability for tax; furnishing of bond.—The qualified heir shall be personally liable for the additional tax imposed by this subsection with respect to his interest unless the heir has furnished bond which meets the requirements of subsection (e)(11).

(6) Cessation of qualified use.—For purposes of paragraph (1)(B), real property shall cease to be used for the qualified use if—

(A) such property ceases to be used for the qualified use set forth in subparagraph (A) or (B) of subsection (b)(2) under which the property qualified under subsection (b), or

(B) during any period of 8 years ending after the date of the decedent's death and before the date of the death of the qualified heir, there had been periods aggregating more than 3 years during which—

(i) in the case of periods during which the property was held by the decedent, there was no material participation by the decedent or any member of his family in the operation of the farm or other business, and

(ii) in the case of periods during which the property was held by any qualified heir, there was no material participation by such qualified heir or any member of his family in the operation of the farm or other business.

(7) Special rules.—

703

(A) **No tax if use begins within 2 years.**—If the date on which the qualified heir begins to use the qualified real property (hereinafter in this subparagraph referred to as the commencement date) is before the date 2 years after the decedent's death—

(i) no tax shall be imposed under paragraph (1) by reason of the failure by the qualified heir to so use such property before the commencement date, and

(ii) the 10-year period under paragraph (1) shall be extended by the period after the decedent's death and before the commencement date.

(B) **Active management by eligible qualified heir treated as material participation.**—For purposes of paragraph (6)(B)(ii), the active management of a farm or other business by—

(i) an eligible qualified heir, or

(ii) a fiduciary of an eligible qualified heir described in clause (ii) or (iii) of subparagraph (C),

shall be treated as material participation by such eligible qualified heir in the operation of such farm or business. In the case of an eligible qualified heir described in clause (ii), (iii), or (iv) of subparagraph (C), the preceding sentence shall apply only during periods during which such heir meets the requirements of such clause.

(C) **Eligible qualified heir.**—For purposes of this paragraph, the term "eligible qualified heir" means a qualified heir who—

(i) is the surviving spouse of the decedent,

(ii) has not attained the age of 21,

(iii) is disabled (within the meaning of subsection (b)(4)(B)), or

(iv) is a student.

(D) **Student.**—For purposes of subparagraph (C), an individual shall be treated as a student with respect to periods during any calendar year if (and only if) such individual is a student (within the meaning of section 151(c)(4)) for such calendar year.

(d) Election; agreement.—

(1) **Election.**—The election under this section shall be made on the return of the tax imposed by section 2001. Such election shall be made in such manner as the Secretary shall by regulations prescribe. Such an election, once made, shall be irrevocable.

(2) **Agreement.**—The agreement referred to in this paragraph is a written agreement signed by each person in being who has an interest (whether or not in possession) in any property designated in such agreement consenting to the application of subsection (c) with respect to such property.

(3) **Modification of election and agreement to be permitted.**—The Secretary shall prescribe procedures which provide that in any case in which—

(A) the executor makes an election under paragraph (1) within the time prescribed for filing such election, and

(B) substantially complies with the regulations prescribed by the Secretary with respect to such election, but—

(i) the notice of election, as filed, does not contain all required information, or

(ii) signatures of 1 or more persons required to enter into the agreement described in paragraph (2) are not included on the agreement as filed, or the agreement does not contain all required information,

the executor will have a reasonable period of time (not exceeding 90 days) after notification of such failures to provide such information or agreements.

(e) Definitions; special rules.—For purposes of this section—

(1) Qualified heir.—The term "qualified heir" means, with respect to any property, a member of the decedent's family who acquired such property (or to whom such property passed) from the decedent. If a qualified heir disposes of any interest in qualified real property to any member of his family, such member shall thereafter be treated as the qualified heir with respect to such interest.

(2) Member of family.—The term "member of the family" means, with respect to any individual, only—

(A) an ancestor of such individual,

(B) the spouse of such individual,

(C) a lineal descendant of such individual, of such individual's spouse, or of a parent of such individual, or

(D) the spouse of any lineal descendant described in subparagraph (C).

For purposes of the preceding sentence, a legally adopted child of an individual shall be treated as the child of such individual by blood.

(3) Certain real property included.—In the case of real property which meets the requirements of subparagraph (C) of subsection (b)(1), residential buildings and related improvements on such real property occupied on a regular basis by the owner or lessee of such real property or by persons employed by such owner or lessee for the purpose of operating or maintaining such real property, and roads, buildings, and other structures and improvements functionally related to the qualified use shall be treated as real property devoted to the qualified use.

(4) Farm.—The term "farm" includes stock, dairy, poultry, fruit, furbearing animal, and truck farms, plantations, ranches, nurseries, ranges, greenhouses or other similar structures used primarily for the raising of agricultural or horticultural commodities, and orchards and woodlands.

(5) Farming purposes.—The term "farming purposes" means—

(A) cultivating the soil or raising or harvesting any agricultural or horticultural commodity (including the raising, shearing, feeding, caring for, training, and management of animals) on a farm;

(B) handling, drying, packing, grading, or storing on a farm any agricultural or horticultural commodity in its unmanufactured state, but only if the owner, tenant, or operator of the farm regularly produces more than one-half of the commodity so treated; and

(C)(i) the planting, cultivating, caring for, or cutting of trees, or

(ii) the preparation (other than milling) of trees for market.

(6) Material participation.—Material participation shall be determined in a manner similar to the manner used for purposes of paragraph (1) of section 1402(a) (relating to net earnings from self-employment).

(7) Method of valuing farms.—

(A) In general.—Except as provided in subparagraph (B), the value of a farm for farming purposes shall be determined by dividing—

705

(i) the excess of the average annual gross cash rental for comparable land used for farming purposes and located in the locality of such farm over the average annual State and local real estate taxes for such comparable land, by

(ii) the average annual effective interest rate for all new Federal Land Bank loans.

For purposes of the preceding sentence, each average annual computation shall be made on the basis of the 5 most recent calendar years ending before the date of the decedent's death.

(B) Value based on net share rental in certain cases.—

(i) In general.—If there is no comparable land from which the average annual gross cash rental may be determined but there is comparable land from which the average net share rental may be determined, subparagraph (A)(i) shall be applied by substituting "average annual net share rental" for "average annual gross cash rental".

(ii) Net share rental.—For purposes of this paragraph, the term "net share rental" means the excess of—

(I) the value of the produce received by the lessor of the land on which such produce is grown, over

(II) the cash operating expenses of growing such produce which, under the lease, are paid by the lessor.

(C) Exception.—The formula provided by subparagraph (A) shall not be used—

(i) where it is established that there is no comparable land from which the average annual gross cash rental may be determined and that there is no comparable land from which the average net share rental may be determined, or

(ii) where the executor elects to have the value of the farm for farming purposes determined under paragraph (8).

(8) Method of valuing closely held business interests, etc.—In any case to which paragraph (7)(A) does not apply, the following factors shall apply in determining the value of any qualified real property:

(A) The capitalization of income which the property can be expected to yield for farming or closely held business purposes over a reasonable period of time under prudent management using traditional cropping patterns for the area, taking into account soil capacity, terrain configuration, and similar factors,

(B) The capitalization of the fair rental value of the land for farmland or closely held business purposes,

(C) Assessed land values in a State which provides a differential or use value assessment law for farmland or closely held business,

(D) Comparable sales of other farm or closely held business land in the same geographical area far enough removed from a metropolitan or resort area so that nonagricultural use is not a significant factor in the sales price, and

(E) Any other factor which fairly values the farm or closely held business value of the property.

(9) Property acquired from decedent.—Property shall be considered to have been acquired from or to have passed from the decedent if—

(A) such property is so considered under section 1014(b) (relating to basis of property acquired from a decedent),

(B) such property is acquired by any person from the estate, or

(C) such property is acquired by any person from a trust (to the extent such property is includible in the gross estate of the decedent).

(10) Community property.— If the decedent and his surviving spouse at any time held qualified real property as community property, the interest of the surviving spouse in such property shall be taken into account under this section to the extent necessary to provide a result under this section with respect to such property which is consistent with the result which would have obtained under this section if such property had not been community property.

(11) Bond in lieu of personal liability.—If the qualified heir makes written application to the Secretary for determination of the maximum amount of the additional tax which may be imposed by subsection (c) with respect to the qualified heir's interest, the Secretary (as soon as possible, and in any event within 1 year after the making of such application) shall notify the heir of such maximum amount. The qualified heir, on furnishing a bond in such amount and for such period as may be required, shall be discharged from personal liability for any additional tax imposed by subsection (c) and shall be entitled to a receipt or writing showing such discharge.

(12) Active management.—The term "active management" means the making of the management decisions of a business (other than the daily operating decisions).

* * *

(f) Statute of limitations.—If qualified real property is disposed of or ceases to be used for a qualified use, then—

(1) the statutory period for the assessment of any additional tax under subsection (c) attributable to such disposition or cessation shall not expire before the expiration of 3 years from the date the Secretary is notified (in such manner as the Secretary may by regulations prescribe) of such disposition or cessation (or if later in the case of an involuntary conversion or exchange to which subsection (h) or (i) applies, 3 years from the date the Secretary is notified of the replacement of the converted property or of an intention not to replace or of the exchange of property), and

(2) such additional tax may be assessed before the expiration of such 3-year period notwithstanding the provisions of any other law or rule of law which would otherwise prevent such assessment.

(g) Application of this section and section 6324B to interests in partnerships, corporations, and trusts.—The Secretary shall prescribe regulations setting forth the application of this section and section 6324B in the case of an interest in a partnership, corporation, or trust which, with respect to the decedent, is an interest in a closely held business (within the meaning of paragraph (1) of section 6166(b)). For purposes of the preceding sentence, an interest in a discretionary trust all the beneficiaries of which are qualified heirs shall be treated as a present interest.

* * *

§ 2033. Property in which the decedent had an interest

The value of the gross estate shall include the value of all property to the extent of the interest therein of the decedent at the time of his death.

§ 2034.   Dower or curtesy interests

The value of the gross estate shall include the value of all property to the extent of any interest therein of the surviving spouse, existing at the time of the decedent's death as dower or curtesy, or by virtue of a statute creating an estate in lieu of dower or curtesy.

§ 2035.   Adjustments for gifts made within 3 years of decedent's death

(a) **Inclusion of gifts made by decedent.**—Except as provided in subsection (b), the value of the gross estate shall include the value of all property to the extent of any interest therein of which the decedent has at any time made a transfer, by trust or otherwise, during the 3-year period ending on the date of the decedent's death.

(b) **Exceptions.**—Subsection (a) shall not apply—

(1) to any bona fide sale for an adequate and full consideration in money or money's worth, and

(2) to any gift to a donee made during a calendar year if the decedent was not required by section 6019 (other than by reason of section 6019(2)) to file any gift tax return for such year with respect to gifts to such donee.

Paragraph (2) shall not apply to any transfer with respect to a life insurance policy.

(c) **Inclusion of gift tax on certain gifts made during 3 years before decedent's death.**—The amount of the gross estate (determined without regard to this subsection) shall be increased by the amount of any tax paid under chapter 12 by the decedent or his estate on any gift made by the decedent or his spouse after December 31, 1976, and during the 3-year period ending on the date of the decedent's death.

(d) **Decedents dying after 1981.**—

(1) **In general.**—Except as otherwise provided in this subsection, subsection (a) shall not apply to the estate of a decedent dying after December 31, 1981.

(2) **Exceptions for certain transfers.**—Paragraph (1) of this subsection and paragraph (2) of subsection (b) shall not apply to a transfer of an interest in property which is included in the value of the gross estate under section 2036, 2037, 2038, or 2042 or would have been included under any of such sections if such interest had been retained by the decedent.

(3) **3-year rule retained for certain purposes.**—Paragraph (1) shall not apply for purposes of—

(A) section 303(b) (relating to distributions in redemption of stock to pay death taxes),

(B) section 2032A (relating to special valuation of certain farm, etc., real property), and

(C) subchapter C of chapter 64 (relating to lien for taxes).

(4) **Coordination of 3-year rule with section 6166(a)(1).**—An estate shall be treated as meeting the 35-percent of adjusted gross estate requirement of section 6166(a)(1) only if the estate meets such requirement both with and without the application of paragraph (1).

§ 2036.   Transfers with retained life estate

(a) **General rule.**—The value of the gross estate shall include the value of all property to the extent of any interest therein of which the decedent has at any time

708

made a transfer (except in case of a bona fide sale for an adequate and full
consideration in money or money's worth), by trust or otherwise, under which he has
retained for his life or for any period not ascertainable without reference to his death
or for any period which does not in fact end before his death—

(1) the possession or enjoyment of, or the right to the income from, the property,
or

(2) the right, either alone or in conjunction with any person, to designate the
persons who shall possess or enjoy the property or the income therefrom.

(b) Voting rights.—

(1) In general.—For purposes of subsection (a) (1), the retention of the right to
vote (directly or indirectly) shares of stock of a controlled corporation shall be
considered to be a retention of the enjoyment of transferred property.

(2) Controlled corporation.—For purposes of paragraph (1), a corporation shall
be treated as a controlled corporation if, at any time after the transfer of the
property and during the 3-year period ending on the date of the decedent's death,
the decedent owned (with the application of section 318), or had the right (either
alone or in conjunction with any person) to vote, stock possessing at least 20
percent of the total combined voting power of all classes of stock.

(3) Coordination with section 2035.—For purposes of applying section 2035
with respect to paragraph (1), the relinquishment or cessation of voting rights shall
be treated as a transfer of property made by the decedent.

* * *

§ 2037. Transfers taking effect at death

(a) General rule.—The value of the gross estate shall include the value of all
property to the extent of any interest therein of which the decedent has at any time
after September 7, 1916, made a transfer (except in case of a bona fide sale for an
adequate and full consideration in money or money's worth), by trust or otherwise,
if—

(1) possession or enjoyment of the property can, through ownership of such
interest, be obtained only by surviving the decedent, and

(2) the decedent has retained a reversionary interest in the property (but in the
case of a transfer made before October 8, 1949, only if such reversionary interest
arose by the express terms of the instrument of transfer), and the value of such
reversionary interest immediately before the death of the decedent exceeds 5
percent of the value of such property.

(b) Special rules.—For purposes of this section, the term "reversionary interest"
includes a possibility that property transferred by the decedent—

(1) may return to him or his estate, or

(2) may be subject to a power of disposition by him,

but such term does not include a possibility that the income alone from such property
may return to him or become subject to a power of disposition by him. The value of
a reversionary interest immediately before the death of the decedent shall be
determined (without regard to the fact of the decedent's death) by usual methods of
valuation, including the use of tables of mortality and actuarial principles, under
regulations prescribed by the Secretary. In determining the value of a possibility
that property may be subject to a power of disposition by the decedent, such
possibility shall be valued as if it were a possibility that such property may return to
the decedent or his estate. Notwithstanding the foregoing, an interest so transferred

shall not be included in the decedent's gross estate under this section if possession or enjoyment of the property could have been obtained by any beneficiary during the decedent's life through the exercise of a general power of appointment (as defined in section 2041) which in fact was exercisable immediately before the decedent's death.

§ 2038. Revocable transfers

(a) In general.—The value of the gross estate shall include the value of all property—

(1) Transfers after June 22, 1936.—To the extent of any interest therein of which the decedent has at any time made a transfer (except in case of a bona fide sale for an adequate and full consideration in money or money's worth), by trust or otherwise, where the enjoyment thereof was subject at the date of his death to any change through the exercise of a power (in whatever capacity exercisable) by the decedent alone or by the decedent in conjunction with any other person (without regard to when or from what source the decedent acquired such power), to alter, amend, revoke, or terminate, or where any such power is relinquished during the 3-year period ending on the date of the decedent's death.

(2) Transfers on or before June 22, 1936.—To the extent of any interest therein of which the decedent has at any time made a transfer (except in case of a bona fide sale for an adequate and full consideration in money or money's worth), by trust or otherwise, where the enjoyment thereof was subject at the date of his death to any change through the exercise of a power, either by the decedent alone or in conjunction with any person, to alter, amend, or revoke, or where the decedent relinquished any such power during the 3-year period ending on the date of the decedent's death. Except in the case of transfers made after June 22, 1936, no interest of the decedent of which he has made a transfer shall be included in the gross estate under paragraph (1) unless it is includible under this paragraph.

(b) Date of existence of power.—For purposes of this section, the power to alter, amend, revoke, or terminate shall be considered to exist on the date of the decedent's death even though the exercise of the power is subject to a precedent giving of notice or even though the alteration, amendment, revocation, or termination takes effect only on the expiration of a stated period after the exercise of the power, whether or not on or before the date of the decedent's death notice has been given or the power has been exercised. In such cases proper adjustment shall be made representing the interests which would have been excluded from the power if the decedent had lived, and for such purpose, if the notice has not been given or the power has not been exercised on or before the date of his death, such notice shall be considered to have been given, or the power exercised, on the date of his death.

§ 2039. Annuities

(a) General.—The gross estate shall include the value of an annuity or other payment receivable by any beneficiary by reason of surviving the decedent under any form of contract or agreement entered into after March 3, 1931 (other than as insurance under policies on the life of the decedent), if, under such contract or agreement, an annuity or other payment was payable to the decedent, or the decedent possessed the right to receive such annuity or payment, either alone or in conjunction with another for his life or for any period not ascertainable without reference to his death or for any period which does not in fact end before his death.

(b) Amount includible.—Subsection (a) shall apply to only such part of the value of the annuity or other payment receivable under such contract or agreement as is proportionate to that part of the purchase price therefor contributed by the decedent.

For purposes of this section, any contribution by the decedent's employer or former employer to the purchase price of such contract or agreement (whether or not to an employee's trust or fund forming part of a pension, annuity, retirement, bonus or profit sharing plan) shall be considered to be contributed by the decedent if made by reason of his employment.

§ 2040. Joint interests

(a) **General rule.**—The value of the gross estate shall include the value of all property to the extent of the interest therein held as joint tenants with right of survivorship by the decedent and any other person, or as tenants by the entirety by the decedent and spouse, or deposited, with any person carrying on the banking business, in their joint names and payable to either or the survivor, except such part thereof as may be shown to have originally belonged to such other person and never to have been received or acquired by the latter from the decedent for less than an adequate and full consideration in money or money's worth: *Provided,* That where such property or any part thereof, or part of the consideration with which such property was acquired, is shown to have been at any time acquired by such other person from the decedent for less than an adequate and full consideration in money or money's worth, there shall be excepted only such part of the value of such property as is proportionate to the consideration furnished by such other person: *Provided further,* That where any property has been acquired by gift, bequest, devise, or inheritance, as a tenancy by the entirety by the decedent and spouse, then to the extent of one-half of the value thereof, or, where so acquired by the decedent and any other person as joint tenants with right of survivorship and their interests are not otherwise specified or fixed by law, then to the extent of the value of a fractional part to be determined by dividing the value of the property by the number of joint tenants with right of survivorship.

(b) **Certain joint interests of husband and wife.**—

(1) **Interests of spouse excluded from gross estate.**—Notwithstanding subsection (a), in the case of any qualified joint interest, the value included in the gross estate with respect to such interest by reason of this section is one-half of the value of such qualified joint interest.

(2) **Qualified joint interest defined.**—For purposes of paragraph (1), the term "qualified joint interest" means any interest in property held by the decedent and the decedent's spouse as—

(A) tenants by the entirety, or

(B) joint tenants with right of survivorship, but only if the decedent and the spouse of the decedent are the only joint tenants.

§ 2041. Powers of appointment

(a) **In general.**—The value of the gross estate shall include the value of all property—

(1) **Powers of appointment created on or before October 21, 1942.**—To the extent of any property with respect to which a general power of appointment created on or before October 21, 1942, is exercised by the decedent—

(A) by will, or

(B) by a disposition which is of such nature that if it were a transfer of property owned by the decedent, such property would be includible in the decedent's gross estate under sections 2035 to 2038, inclusive;

but the failure to exercise such a power or the complete release of such a power shall not be deemed an exercise thereof. If a general power of appointment created on or before October 21, 1942, has been partially released so that it is no longer a general power of appointment, the exercise of such power shall not be deemed to be the exercise of a general power of appointment if—

    (i) such partial release occurred before November 1, 1951, or

    (ii) the donee of such power was under a legal disability to release such power on October 21, 1942, and such partial release occurred not later than 6 months after the termination of such legal disability.

(2) Powers created after October 21, 1942.—To the extent of any property with respect to which the decedent has at the time of his death a general power of appointment created after October 21, 1942, or with respect to which the decedent has at any time exercised or released such a power of appointment by a disposition which is of such nature that if it were a transfer of property owned by the decedent, such property would be includible in the decedent's gross estate under sections 2035 to 2038, inclusive. For purposes of this paragraph (2), the power of appointment shall be considered to exist on the date of the decedent's death even though the exercise of the power is subject to a precedent giving of notice or even though the exercise of the power takes effect only on the expiration of a stated period after its exercise, whether or not on or before the date of the decedent's death notice has been given or the power has been exercised.

(3) Creation of another power in certain cases.—To the extent of any property with respect to which the decedent—

    (A) by will, or

    (B) by a disposition which is of such nature that if it were a transfer of property owned by the decedent such property would be includible in the decedent's gross estate under section 2035, 2036, or 2037,

exercises a power of appointment created after October 21, 1942, by creating another power of appointment which under the applicable local law can be validly exercised so as to postpone the vesting of any estate or interest in such property, or suspend the absolute ownership or power of alienation of such property, for a period ascertainable without regard to the date of the creation of the first power.

(b) Definitions.—For purposes of subsection (a)—

(1) General power of appointment.—The term "general power of appointment" means a power which is exercisable in favor of the decedent, his estate, his creditors, or the creditors of his estate; except that—

    (A) A power to consume, invade, or appropriate property for the benefit of the decedent which is limited by an ascertainable standard relating to the health, education, support, or maintenance of the decedent shall not be deemed a general power of appointment.

    (B) A power of appointment created on or before October 21, 1942, which is exercisable by the decedent only in conjunction with another person shall not be deemed a general power of appointment.

    (C) In the case of a power of appointment created after October 21, 1942, which is exercisable by the decedent only in conjunction with another person—

        (i) If the power is not exercisable by the decedent except in conjunction with the creator of the power—such power shall not be deemed a general power of appointment.

(ii) If the power is not exercisable by the decedent except in conjunction with a person having a substantial interest in the property, subject to the power, which is adverse to exercise of the power in favor of the decedent—such power shall not be deemed a general power of appointment. For the purposes of this clause a person who, after the death of the decedent, may be possessed of a power of appointment (with respect to the property subject to the decedent's power) which he may exercise in his own favor shall be deemed as having an interest in the property and such interest shall be deemed adverse to such exercise of the decedent's power.

(iii) If (after the application of clauses (i) and (ii)) the power is a general power of appointment and is exercisable in favor of such other person—such power shall be deemed a general power of appointment only in respect of a fractional part of the property subject to such power, such part to be determined by dividing the value of such property by the number of such persons (including the decedent) in favor of whom such power is exercisable.

For purposes of clauses (ii) and (iii), a power shall be deemed to be exercisable in favor of a person if it is exercisable in favor of such person, his estate, his creditors, or the creditors of his estate.

(2) Lapse of power.—The lapse of a power of appointment created after October 21, 1942, during the life of the individual possessing the power shall be considered a release of such power. The preceding sentence shall apply with respect to the lapse of powers during any calendar year only to the extent that the property, which could have been appointed by exercise of such lapsed powers, exceeded in value, at the time of such lapse, the greater of the following amounts:

(A) $5,000, or

(B) 5 percent of the aggregate value, at the time of such lapse, of the assets out of which, or the proceeds of which, the exercise of the lapsed powers could have been satisfied.

* * *

§ 2042. Proceeds of life insurance

The value of the gross estate shall include the value of all property—

(1) Receivable by the executor.—To the extent of the amount receivable by the executor as insurance under policies on the life of the decedent.

(2) Receivable by other beneficiaries.—To the extent of the amount receivable by all other beneficiaries as insurance under policies on the life of the decedent with respect to which the decedent possessed at his death any of the incidents of ownership, exercisable either alone or in conjunction with any other person. For purposes of the preceding sentence, the term "incident of ownership" includes a reversionary interest (whether arising by the express terms of the policy or other instrument or by operation of law) only if the value of such reversionary interest exceeded 5 percent of the value of the policy immediately before the death of the decedent. As used in this paragraph, the term "reversionary interest" includes a possibility that the policy, or the proceeds of the policy, may return to the decedent or his estate, or may be subject to a power of disposition by him. The value of a reversionary interest at any time shall be determined (without regard to the fact of the decedent's death) by usual methods of valuation, including the use of tables of mortality and actuarial principles, pursuant to regulations prescribed by the Secretary. In determining the value of a possibility that the policy or proceeds thereof may be subject to a power of disposition by the decedent, such possibility shall be valued as if it were a possibility that such policy or proceeds may return to the decedent or his estate.

§ 2043. Transfers for insufficient consideration

(a) In general.—If any one of the transfers, trusts, interests, rights, or powers enumerated and described in sections 2035 to 2038, inclusive, and section 2041 is made, created, exercised, or relinquished for a consideration in money or money's worth, but is not a bona fide sale for an adequate and full consideration in money or money's worth, there shall be included in the gross estate only the excess of the fair market value at the time of death of the property otherwise to be included on account of such transaction, over the value of the consideration received therefor by the decedent.

(b) Marital rights not treated as consideration.—

(1) In general.—For purposes of this chapter, a relinquishment or promised relinquishment of dower or curtesy, or of a statutory estate created in lieu of dower or curtesy, or of other marital rights in the decedent's property or estate, shall not be considered to any extent a consideration "in money or money's worth".

(2) Exception.—For purposes of section 2053 (relating to expenses, indebtedness, and taxes), a transfer of property which satisfies the requirements of paragraph (1) of section 2516 (relating to certain property settlements) shall be considered to be made for an adequate and full consideration in money or money's worth.

§ 2044. Certain property for which marital deduction was previously allowed

(a) General rule.—The value of the gross estate shall include the value of any property to which this section applies in which the decedent had a qualifying income interest for life.

(b) Property to which this section applies.—This section applies to any property if—

(1) a deduction was allowed with respect to the transfer of such property to the decedent—

(A) under section 2056 by reason of subsection (b)(7) thereof, or

(B) under section 2523 by reason of subsection (f) thereof, and

(2) section 2519 (relating to dispositions of certain life estates) did not apply with respect to a disposition by the decedent of part or all of such property.

(c) Property treated as having passed from decedent.—For purposes of this chapter and chapter 13, property includible in the gross estate of the decedent under subsection (a) shall be treated as property passing from the decedent.

§ 2045. Prior interests

Except as otherwise specifically provided by law, sections 2034 to 2042, inclusive, shall apply to the transfers, trusts, estates, interests, rights, powers, and relinquishment of powers, as severally enumerated and described therein, whenever made, created, arising, existing, exercised, or relinquished.

§ 2046. Disclaimers

For provisions relating to the effect of a qualified disclaimer for purposes of this chapter, see section 2518.

PART IV—TAXABLE ESTATE

§ 2051.   Definition of taxable estate

For purposes of the tax imposed by section 2001, the value of the taxable estate shall be determined by deducting from the value of the gross estate the deductions provided for in this part.

§ 2053.   Expenses, indebtedness, and taxes

(a) **General rule.**—For purposes of the tax imposed by section 2001, the value of the taxable estate shall be determined by deducting from the value of the gross estate such amounts—

(1) for funeral expenses,

(2) for administration expenses,

(3) for claims against the estate, and

(4) for unpaid mortgages on, or any indebtedness in respect of, property where the value of the decedent's interest therein, undiminished by such mortgage or indebtedness, is included in the value of the gross estate,

as are allowable by the laws of the jurisdiction, whether within or without the United States, under which the estate is being administered.

(b) **Other administration expenses.**—Subject to the limitations in paragraph (1) of subsection (c), there shall be deducted in determining the taxable estate amounts representing expenses incurred in administering property not subject to claims which is included in the gross estate to the same extent such amounts would be allowable as a deduction under subsection (a) if such property were subject to claims, and such amounts are paid before the expiration of the period of limitation for assessment provided in section 6501.

(c) **Limitations.**—

(1) **Limitations applicable to subsections (a) and (b).**—

(A) **Consideration for claims.**—The deduction allowed by this section in the case of claims against the estate, unpaid mortgages, or any indebtedness shall, when founded on a promise or agreement, be limited to the extent that they were contracted bona fide and for an adequate and full consideration in money or money's worth; except that in any case in which any such claim is founded on a promise or agreement of the decedent to make a contribution or gift to or for the use of any donee described in section 2055 for the purposes specified therein, the deduction for such claims shall not be so limited, but shall be limited to the extent that it would be allowable as a deduction under section 2055 if such promise or agreement constituted a bequest.

(B) **Certain taxes.**—Any income taxes on income received after the death of the decedent, or property taxes not accrued before his death, or any estate, succession, legacy, or inheritance taxes, shall not be deductible under this section.

(C) **Certain claims by remaindermen.**—No deduction shall be allowed under this section for a claim against the estate by a remainderman relating to any property described in section 2044.

(2) **Limitations applicable only to subsection (a).**—In the case of the amounts described in subsection (a), there shall be disallowed the amount by which the

deductions specified therein exceed the value, at the time of the decedent's death, of property subject to claims, except to the extent that such deductions represent amounts paid before the date prescribed for the filing of the estate tax return. For purposes of this section, the term "property subject to claims" means property includible in the gross estate of the decedent which, or the avails of which, would under the applicable law, bear the burden of the payment of such deductions in the final adjustment and settlement of the estate, except that the value of the property shall be reduced by the amount of the deduction under section 2054 attributable to such property.

(d) Certain state and foreign death taxes.—

    (1) General rule.—Notwithstanding the provisions of subsection (c) (1) (B) of this section, for purposes of the tax imposed by section 2001 the value of the taxable estate may be determined, if the executor so elects before the expiration of the period of limitation for assessment provided in section 6501, by deducting from the value of the gross estate the amount (as determined in accordance with regulations prescribed by the Secretary) of—

        (A) any estate, succession, legacy, or inheritance tax imposed by a State or the District of Columbia upon a transfer by the decedent for public, charitable, or religious uses described in section 2055 or 2106(a) (2), and

        (B) any estate, succession, legacy, or inheritance tax imposed by and actually paid to any foreign country, in respect of any property situated within such foreign country and included in the gross estate of a citizen or resident of the United States, upon a transfer by the decedent for public, charitable, or religious uses described in section 2055.

The determination under subparagraph (B) of the country within which property is situated shall be made in accordance with the rules applicable under subchapter B (sec. 2101 and following) in determining whether property is situated within or without the United States. Any election under this paragraph shall be exercised in accordance with regulations prescribed by the Secretary.

    (2) Condition for allowance of deduction.—No deduction shall be allowed under paragraph (1) for a State death tax or a foreign death tax specified therein unless the decrease in the tax imposed by section 2001 which results from the deduction provided in paragraph (1) will inure solely for the benefit of the public, charitable, or religious transferees described in section 2055 or section 2106(a) (2). In any case where the tax imposed by section 2001 is equitably apportioned among all the transferees of property included in the gross estate, including those described in sections 2055 and 2106(a) (2) (taking into account any exemptions, credits, or deductions allowed by this chapter), in determining such decrease, there shall be disregarded any decrease in the Federal estate tax which any transferees other than those described in sections 2055 and 2106(a) (2) are required to pay.

    (3) Effect on credits for state and foreign death taxes of deduction under this subsection.—

        (A) Election.—An election under this subsection shall be deemed a waiver of the right to claim a credit, against the Federal estate tax, under a death tax convention with any foreign country for any tax or portion thereof in respect of which a deduction is taken under this subsection.

        (B) Cross references.—

See section 2011(e) for the effect of a deduction taken under this subsection on the credit for State death taxes, and see section 2014(f) for the effect of a deduction taken under this subsection on the credit for foreign death taxes.

(e) Marital rights.—

For provisions treating certain relinquishments of marital rights as consideration in money or money's worth, see section 2043(b)(2).

§ 2054. Losses

For purposes of the tax imposed by section 2001, the value of the taxable estate shall be determined by deducting from the value of the gross estate losses incurred during the settlement of estates arising from fires, storms, shipwrecks, or other casualties, or from theft, when such losses are not compensated for by insurance or otherwise.

§ 2055. Transfers for public, charitable, and religious uses

(a) In general.—For purposes of the tax imposed by section 2001, the value of the taxable estate shall be determined by deducting from the value of the gross estate the amount of all bequests, legacies, devises, or transfers—

(1) to or for the use of the United States, any State, any political subdivision thereof, or the District of Columbia, for exclusively public purposes;

(2) to or for the use of any corporation organized and operated exclusively for religious, charitable, scientific, literary, or educational purposes, including the encouragement of art, or to foster national or international amateur sports competition (but only if no part of its activities involve the provision of athletic facilities or equipment), and the prevention of cruelty to children or animals, no part of the net earnings of which inures to the benefit of any private stockholder or individual, which is not disqualified for tax exemption under section 501(c)(3) by reason of attempting to influence legislation, and which does not participate in, or intervene in (including the publishing or distributing of statements), any political campaign on behalf of any candidate for public office;

(3) to a trustee or trustees, or a fraternal society, order, or association operating under the lodge system, but only if such contributions or gifts are to be used by such trustee or trustees, or by such fraternal society, order, or association, exclusively for religious, charitable, scientific, literary, or educational purposes, or for the prevention of cruelty to children or animals, such trust, fraternal society, order, or association would not be disqualified for tax exemption under section 501(c)(3) by reason of attempting to influence legislation, and such trustee or trustees, or such fraternal society, order, or association, does not participate in, or intervene in (including the publishing or distributing of statements), any political campaign on behalf of any candidate for public office; or

(4) to or for the use of any veterans' organization incorporated by Act of Congress, or of its departments or local chapters or posts, no part of the net earnings of which inures to the benefit of any private shareholder or individual.

For purposes of this subsection, the complete termination before the date prescribed for the filing of the estate tax return of a power to consume, invade, or appropriate property for the benefit of an individual before such power has been exercised by reason of the death of such individual or for any other reason shall be considered and deemed to be a qualified disclaimer with the same full force and effect as though he had filed such qualified disclaimer. Rules similar to the rules of section 501(j) shall apply for purposes of paragraph (2).

(b) Powers of appointment.—Property includible in the decedent's gross estate under section 2041 (relating to powers of appointment) received by a donee described in this section shall, for purposes of this section, be considered a bequest of such decedent.

(c) **Death taxes payable out of bequests.**—If the tax imposed by section 2001, or any estate, succession, legacy, or inheritance taxes, are, either by the terms of the will, by the law of the jurisdiction under which the estate is administered, or by the law of the jurisdiction imposing the particular tax, payable in whole or in part out of the bequests, legacies, or devises otherwise deductible under this section, then the amount deductible under this section shall be the amount of such bequests, legacies, or devises reduced by the amount of such taxes.

(d) **Limitation on deduction.**—The amount of the deduction under this section for any transfer shall not exceed the value of the transferred property required to be included in the gross estate.

(e) **Disallowance of deductions in certain cases.**—

* * *

(2) Where an interest in property (other than an interest described in section 170(f) (3) (B)) passes or has passed from the decedent to a person, or for a use, described in subsection (a), and an interest (other than an interest which is extinguished upon the decedent's death) in the same property passes or has passed (for less than an adequate and full consideration in money or money's worth) from the decedent to a person, or for a use, not described in subsection (a), no deduction shall be allowed under this section for the interest which passes or has passed to the person, or for the use, described in subsection (a) unless—

(A) in the case of a remainder interest, such interest is in a trust which is a charitable remainder annuity trust or a charitable remainder unitrust (described in section 664) or a pooled income fund (described in section 642(c) (5)), or

(B) in the case of any other interest, such interest is in the form of a guaranteed annuity or is a fixed percentage distributed yearly of the fair market value of the property (to be determined yearly).

(3) **Reformations to comply with paragraph (2).**—

(A) **In general.**—A deduction shall be allowed under subsection (a) in respect of any qualified reformation.

(B) **Qualified reformation.**—For purposes of this paragraph, the term "qualified reformation" means a change of a governing instrument by reformation, amendment, construction, or otherwise which changes a reformable interest into a qualified interest but only if—

(i) any difference between—

(I) the actuarial value (determined as of the date of the decedent's death) of the qualified interest, and

(II) the actuarial value (as so determined) of the reformable interest,

does not exceed 5 percent of the actuarial value (as so determined) of the reformable interest,

(ii) in the case of—

(I) a charitable remainder interest, the nonremainder interest (before and after the qualified reformation) terminated at the same time, or

(II) any other interest, the reformable interest and the qualified interest are for the same period, and

(iii) such change is effective as of the date of the decedent's death.

A nonremainder interest (before reformation) for a term of years in excess of 20 years shall be treated as satisfying subclause (I) of clause (ii) if such interest (after reformation) is for a term of 20 years.

(C) **Reformable interest.**—For purposes of this paragraph—

(i) **In general.**—The term "reformable interest" means any interest for which a deduction would be allowable under subsection (a) at the time of the decedent's death but for paragraph (2).

(ii) **Beneficiary's interest must be fixed.**—The term "reformable interest" does not include any interest unless, before the remainder vests in possession, all payments to persons other than an organization described in subsection (a) are expressed either in specified dollar amounts or a fixed percentage of the fair market value of the property. For purposes of determining whether all such payments are expressed as a fixed percentage of the fair market value of the property, section 664(d)(3) shall be taken into account.

(iii) **Special rule where timely commencement of reformation.**—Clause (ii) shall not apply to any interest if a judicial proceeding is commenced to change such interest into a qualified interest not later than the 90th day after—

(I) if an estate tax return is required to be filed, the last date (including extensions) for filing such return, or

(II) if no estate tax return is required to be filed, the last date (including extensions) for filing the income tax return for the 1st taxable year for which such a return is required to be filed by the trust.

(iv) **Special rule for will executed before January 1, 1979, etc.**—In the case of any interest passing under a will executed before January 1, 1979, or under a trust created before such date, clause (ii) shall not apply.

(D) **Qualified interest.**—For purposes of this paragraph, the term "qualified interest" means an interest for which a deduction is allowable under subsection (a).

(E) **Limitation.**—The deduction referred to in subparagraph (A) shall not exceed the amount of the deduction which would have been allowable for the reformable interest but for paragraph (2).

(F) **Special rule where income beneficiary dies.**—If (by reason of the death of any individual, or by termination or distribution of a trust in accordance with the terms of the trust instrument) by the due date for filing the estate tax return (including any extension thereof) a reformable interest is in a wholly charitable trust or passes directly to a person or for a use described in subsection (a), a deduction shall be allowed for such reformable interest as if it had met the requirements of paragraph (2) on the date of the decedent's death. For purposes of the preceding sentence, the term "wholly charitable trust" means a charitable trust which, upon the allowance of a deduction, would be described in section 4947(a)(1).

(G) **Statute of limitations.**—The period for assessing any deficiency of any tax attributable to the application of this paragraph shall not expire before the date 1 year after the date on which the Secretary is notified that such reformation has occurred.

(H) **Regulations.**—The Secretary shall prescribe such regulations as may be necessary to carry out the purposes of this paragraph, including regulations providing such adjustments in the application of the provisions of section 508 (relating to special rules relating to section 501(c)(3) organizations), subchapter J (relating to estates, trusts, beneficiaries, and decedents), and chapter 42 (relating to private foundations) as may be necessary by reason of the qualified reformation.

(I) **Reformations permitted in case of remainder interests in residence or farm, pooled income funds, etc.**—The Secretary shall prescribe regulations (consistent with the provisions of this paragraph) permitting reformations in the case of any failure—

(i) to meet the requirements of section 170(f)(3)(B) (relating to remainder interests in personal residence or farm, etc.), or

(ii) to meet the requirements of section 642(c)(5).

(4) Works of art and their copyrights treated as separate properties in certain cases.—

(A) **In general.**—In the case of a qualified contribution of a work of art, the work of art and the copyright on such work of art shall be treated as separate properties for purposes of paragraph (2).

(B) **Work of art defined.**—For purposes of this paragraph, the term "work of art" means any tangible personal property with respect to which there is a copyright under Federal law.

(C) **Qualified contribution defined.**—For purposes of this paragraph, the term "qualified contribution" means any transfer of property to a qualified organization if the use of the property by the organization is related to the purpose or function constituting the basis for its exemption under section 501.

(D) **Qualified organization defined.**—For purposes of this paragraph, the term "qualified organization" means any organization described in section 501(c)(3) other than a private foundation (as defined in section 509). For purposes of the preceding sentence, a private operating foundation (as defined in section 4942(j)(3)) shall not be treated as a private foundation.

(f) Special rule for irrevocable transfers of easements in real property.—A deduction shall be allowed under subsection (a) in respect of any transfer of a qualified real property interest (as defined in section 170(h)(2)(C)) which meets the requirements of section 170(h) (without regard to paragraph (4)(A) thereof).

(g) Cross references.—

(1) **For option as to time for valuation for purpose of deduction under this section, see section 2032.**

(2) **For treatment of certain organizations providing child care, see section 501(k).**

* * *

§ 2056.   Bequests, etc., to surviving spouse

(a) Allowance of marital deduction.—For purposes of the tax imposed by section 2001, the value of the taxable estate shall, except as limited by subsection (b), be determined by deducting from the value of the gross estate an amount equal to the value of any interest in property which passes or has passed from the decedent to his surviving spouse, but only to the extent that such interest is included in determining the value of the gross estate.

(b) Limitation in the case of life estate or other terminable interest.—

(1) **General rule.**—Where, on the lapse of time, on the occurrence of an event or contingency, or on the failure of an event or contingency to occur, an interest passing to the surviving spouse will terminate or fail, no deduction shall be allowed under this section with respect to such interest—

(A) if an interest in such property passes or has passed (for less than an adequate and full consideration in money or money's worth) from the decedent to any person other than such surviving spouse (or the estate of such spouse); and

(B) if by reason of such passing such person (or his heirs or assigns) may possess or enjoy any part of such property after such termination or failure of the interest so passing to the surviving spouse;

and no deduction shall be allowed with respect to such interest (even if such deduction is not disallowed under subparagraphs (A) and (B))—

(C) if such interest is to be acquired for the surviving spouse, pursuant to directions of the decedent, by his executor or by the trustee of a trust.

For purposes of this paragraph, an interest shall not be considered as an interest which will terminate or fail merely because it is the ownership of a bond, note, or similar contractual obligation, the discharge of which would not have the effect of an annuity for life or for a term.

(2) **Interest in unidentified assets.**—Where the assets (included in the decedent's gross estate) out of which, or the proceeds of which, an interest passing to the surviving spouse may be satisfied include a particular asset or assets with respect to which no deduction would be allowed if such asset or assets passed from the decedent to such spouse, then the value of such interest passing to such spouse shall, for purposes of subsection (a), be reduced by the aggregate value of such particular assets.

(3) **Interest of spouse conditional on survival for limited period.**—For purposes of this subsection, an interest passing to the surviving spouse shall not be considered as an interest which will terminate or fail on the death of such spouse if—

(A) such death will cause a termination or failure of such interest only if it occurs within a period not exceeding 6 months after the decedent's death, or only if it occurs as a result of a common disaster resulting in the death of the decedent and the surviving spouse, or only if it occurs in the case of either such event; and

(B) such termination or failure does not in fact occur.

(4) **Valuation of interest passing to surviving spouse.**—In determining for purposes of subsection (a) the value of any interest in property passing to the surviving spouse for which a deduction is allowed by this section—

(A) there shall be taken into account the effect which the tax imposed by section 2001, or any estate, succession, legacy, or inheritance tax, has on the net value to the surviving spouse of such interest; and

(B) where such interest or property is encumbered in any manner, or where the surviving spouse incurs any obligation imposed by the decedent with respect to the passing of such interest, such encumbrance or obligation shall be taken into account in the same manner as if the amount of a gift to such spouse of such interest were being determined.

(5) **Life estate with power of appointment in surviving spouse.**—In the case of an interest in property passing from the decedent, if his surviving spouse is entitled for life to all the income from the entire interest, or all the income from a specific portion thereof, payable annually or at more frequent intervals, with power in the surviving spouse to appoint the entire interest, or such specific portion (exercisable in favor of such surviving spouse, or of the estate of such surviving spouse, or in favor of either, whether or not in each case the power is exercisable in

favor of others), and with no power in any other person to appoint any part of the interest, or such specific portion, to any person other than the surviving spouse—

(A) the interest or such portion thereof so passing shall, for purposes of subsection (a), be considered as passing to the surviving spouse, and

(B) no part of the interest so passing shall, for purposes of paragraph (1) (A), be considered as passing to any person other than the surviving spouse.

This paragraph shall apply only if such power in the surviving spouse to appoint the entire interest, or such specific portion thereof, whether exercisable by will or during life, is exercisable by such spouse alone and in all events.

(6) Life insurance or annuity payments with power of appointment in surviving spouse.—In the case of an interest in property passing from the decedent consisting of proceeds under a life insurance, endowment, or annuity contract, if under the terms of the contract such proceeds are payable in installments or are held by the insurer subject to an agreement to pay interest thereon (whether the proceeds, on the termination of any interest payments, are payable in a lump sum or in annual or more frequent installments), and such installment or interest payments are payable annually or at more frequent intervals, commencing not later than 13 months after the decedent's death, and all amounts, or a specific portion of all such amounts, payable during the life of the surviving spouse are payable only to such spouse, and such spouse has the power to appoint all amounts, or such specific portion, payable under such contract (exercisable in favor of such surviving spouse, or of the estate of such surviving spouse, or in favor of either, whether or not in each case the power is exercisable in favor of others), with no power in any other person to appoint such amounts to any person other than the surviving spouse—

(A) such amounts shall, for purposes of subsection (a), be considered as passing to the surviving spouse, and

(B) no part of such amounts shall, for purposes of paragraph (1) (A), be considered as passing to any person other than the surviving spouse.

This paragraph shall apply only if, under the terms of the contract, such power in the surviving spouse to appoint such amounts, whether exercisable by will or during life, is exercisable by such spouse alone and in all events.

(7) Election with respect to life estate for surviving spouse.—

(A) In general.—In the case of qualified terminable interest property—

(i) for purposes of subsection (a), such property shall be treated as passing to the surviving spouse, and

(ii) for purposes of paragraph (1)(A), no part of such property shall be treated as passing to any person other than the surviving spouse.

(B) Qualified terminable interest property defined.—For purposes of this paragraph—

(i) In general.—The term "qualified terminable interest property" means property—

(I) which passes from the decedent,

(II) in which the surviving spouse has a qualifying income interest for life, and

(III) to which an election under this paragraph applies.

(ii) Qualifying income interest for life.—The surviving spouse has a qualifying income interest for life if—

(I) the surviving spouse is entitled to all the income from the property, payable annually or at more frequent intervals, or has a usufruct interest for life in the property, and

(II) no person has a power to appoint any part of the property to any person other than the surviving spouse.

Subclause (II) shall not apply to a power exercisable only at or after the death of the surviving spouse. To the extent provided in regulations, an annuity shall be treated in a manner similar to an income interest in property (regardless of whether the property from which the annuity is payable can be separately identified).

(iii) **Property includes interest therein.**—The term "property" includes an interest in property.

(iv) **Specific portion treated as separate property.**—A specific portion of property shall be treated as separate property.

(v) **Election.**—An election under this paragraph with respect to any property shall be made by the executor on the return of tax imposed by section 2001. Such an election, once made, shall be irrevocable.

(8) Special rule for charitable remainder trusts.—

(A) **In general.**—If the surviving spouse of the decedent is the only noncharitable beneficiary of a qualified charitable remainder trust, paragraph (1) shall not apply to any interest in such trust which passes or has passed from the decedent to such surviving spouse.

(B) **Definitions.**—For purposes of subparagraph (A)—

(i) **Noncharitable beneficiary.**—The term "noncharitable beneficiary" means any beneficiary of the qualified charitable remainder trust other than an organization described in section 170(c).

(ii) **Qualified charitable remainder trust.**—The term "qualified charitable remainder trust" means a charitable remainder annuity trust or charitable remainder unitrust (described in section 664).

(9) Denial of double deduction.—Nothing in this section or any other provision of this chapter shall allow the value of any interest in property to be deducted under this chapter more than once with respect to the same decedent.

(c) Definition.—For purposes of this section, an interest in property shall be considered as passing from the decedent to any person if and only if—

(1) such interest is bequeathed or devised to such person by the decedent;

(2) such interest is inherited by such person from the decedent;

(3) such interest is the dower or curtesy interest (or statutory interest in lieu thereof) of such person as surviving spouse of the decedent;

(4) such interest has been transferred to such person by the decedent at any time;

(5) such interest was, at the time of the decedent's death, held by such person and the decedent (or by them and any other person) in joint ownership with right of survivorship;

(6) the decedent had a power (either alone or in conjunction with any person) to appoint such interest and if he appoints or has appointed such interest to such person, or if such person takes such interest in default on the release or nonexercise of such power; or

(7) such interest consists of proceeds of insurance on the life of the decedent receivable by such person.

Except as provided in paragraph (5) or (6) of subsection (b), where at the time of the decedent's death it is not possible to ascertain the particular person or persons to whom an interest in property may pass from the decedent, such interest shall, for purposes of subparagraphs (A) and (B) of subsection (b) (1), be considered as passing from the decedent to a person other than the surviving spouse.

SUBCHAPTER C—MISCELLANEOUS

§ 2203. Definition of executor

The term "executor" wherever it is used in this title in connection with the estate tax imposed by this chapter means the executor or administrator of the decedent, or, if there is no executor or administrator appointed, qualified, and acting within the United States, then any person in actual or constructive possession of any property of the decedent.

§ 2204. Discharge of fiduciary from personal liability

(a) **General rule.**—If the executor makes written application to the Secretary for determination of the amount of the tax and discharge from personal liability therefor, the Secretary (as soon as possible, and in any event within 9 months after the making of such application, or, if the application is made before the return is filed, then within 9 months after the return is filed, but not after the expiration of the period prescribed for the assessment of the tax in section 6501) shall notify the executor of the amount of the tax. The executor, on payment of the amount of which he is notified (other than any amount the time for payment of which is extended under section 6161, 6163, or 6166), and on furnishing any bond which may be required for any amount for which the time for payment is extended, shall be discharged from personal liability for any deficiency in tax thereafter found to be due and shall be entitled to a receipt or writing showing such discharge.

(b) **Fiduciary other than the executor.**—If a fiduciary (not including a fiduciary in respect of the estate of a nonresident decedent) other than the executor makes written application to the Secretary for determination of the amount of any estate tax for which the fiduciary may be personally liable, and for discharge from personal liability therefor, the Secretary upon the discharge of the executor from personal liability under subsection (a), or upon the expiration of 6 months after the making of such application by the fiduciary, if later, shall notify the fiduciary (1) of the amount of such tax for which it has been determined the fiduciary is liable, or (2) that it has been determined that the fiduciary is not liable for any such tax. Such application shall be accompanied by a copy of the instrument, if any, under which such fiduciary is acting, a description of the property held by the fiduciary, and such other information for purposes of carrying out the provisions of this section as the Secretary may require by regulations. On payment of the amount of such tax for which it has been determined the fiduciary is liable (other than any amount the time for payment of which has been extended under section 6161, 6163, or 6166), and on furnishing any bond which may be required for any amount for which the time for payment has been extended, or on receipt by him of notification of a determination that he is not liable for any such tax, the fiduciary shall be discharged from personal liability for any deficiency in such tax thereafter found to be due and shall be entitled to a receipt or writing evidencing such discharge.

(c) **Special lien under section 6324A.**—For purposes of the second sentence of subsection (a) and the last sentence of subsection (b), an agreement which meets the requirements of section 6324A (relating to special lien for estate tax deferred under section 6166), shall be treated as the furnishing of bond with respect to the amount for which the time for payment has been extended under section 6166.

(d) **Good faith reliance on gift tax returns.**—If the executor in good faith relies on gift tax returns furnished under section 6103(e) (3) for determining the decedent's adjusted taxable gifts, the executor shall be discharged from personal liability with respect to any deficiency of the tax imposed by this chapter which is attributable to adjusted taxable gifts which—

(1) are made more than 3 years before the date of the decedent's death, and

(2) are not shown on such returns.

§ 2205. Reimbursement out of estate

If the tax or any part thereof is paid by, or collected out of, that part of the estate passing to or in the possession of any person other than the executor in his capacity as such, such person shall be entitled to reimbursement out of any part of the estate still undistributed or by a just and equitable contribution by the persons whose interest in the estate of the decedent would have been reduced if the tax had been paid before the distribution of the estate or whose interest is subject to equal or prior liability for the payment of taxes, debts, or other charges against the estate, it being the purpose and intent of this chapter that so far as is practicable and unless otherwise directed by the will of the decedent the tax shall be paid out of the estate before its distribution.

§ 2206. Liability of life insurance beneficiaries

Unless the decedent directs otherwise in his will, if any part of the gross estate on which tax has been paid consists of proceeds of policies of insurance on the life of the decedent receivable by a beneficiary other than the executor, the executor shall be entitled to recover from such beneficiary such portion of the total tax paid as the proceeds of such policies bear to the taxable estate. If there is more than one such beneficiary, the executor shall be entitled to recover from such beneficiaries in the same ratio. In the case of such proceeds receivable by the surviving spouse of the decedent for which a deduction is allowed under section 2056 (relating to marital deduction), this section shall not apply to such proceeds except as to the amount thereof in excess of the aggregate amount of the marital deductions allowed under such section.

§ 2207. Liability of recipient of property over which decedent had power of appointment

Unless the decedent directs otherwise in his will, if any part of the gross estate on which the tax has been paid consists of the value of property included in the gross estate under section 2041, the executor shall be entitled to recover from the person receiving such property by reason of the exercise, nonexercise, or release of a power of appointment such portion of the total tax paid as the value of such property bears to the taxable estate. If there is more than one such person, the executor shall be entitled to recover from such persons in the same ratio. In the case of such property received by the surviving spouse of the decedent for which a deduction is allowed under section 2056 (relating to marital deduction), this section shall not apply to such property except as to the value thereof reduced by an amount equal to the excess of the aggregate amount of the marital deductions allowed under section 2056 over the amount of proceeds of insurance upon the life of the decedent receivable by the surviving spouse for which proceeds a marital deduction is allowed under such section.

§ 2207A. Right of recovery in the case of certain marital deduction property

(a) Recovery with respect to estate tax.—

(1) In general.—If any part of the gross estate consists of property the value of which is includible in the gross estate by reason of section 2044 (relating to certain property for which marital deduction was previously allowed), the decedent's estate shall be entitled to recover from the person receiving the property the amount by which—

(A) the total tax under this chapter which has been paid, exceeds

(B) the total tax under this chapter which would have been payable if the value of such property had not been included in the gross estate.

(2) Decedent may otherwise direct by will.—Paragraph (1) shall not apply if the decedent otherwise directs by will.

(b) Recovery with respect to gift tax.—If for any calendar year tax is paid under chapter 12 with respect to any person by reason of property treated as transferred by such person under section 2519, such person shall be entitled to recover from the person receiving the property the amount by which—

(1) the total tax for such year under chapter 12, exceeds

(2) the total tax which would have been payable under such chapter for such year if the value of such property had not been taken into account for purposes of chapter 12.

(c) More than one recipient of property.—For purposes of this section, if there is more than one person receiving the property, the right of recovery shall be against each such person.

(d) Taxes and interest.—In the case of penalties and interest attributable to additional taxes described in subsections (a) and (b), rules similar to subsections (a), (b), and (c) shall apply.

CHAPTER 12—GIFT TAX

Subchapter
  A. Determination of tax liability.
  B. Transfers.
  C. Deductions.

SUBCHAPTER A—DETERMINATION OF TAX LIABILITY

§ 2501. Imposition of tax

(a) Taxable transfers.—

(1) General rule.—A tax, computed as provided in section 2502, is hereby imposed for each calendar year on the transfer of property by gift during such calendar year by any individual, resident or nonresident.

* * *

(5) Transfers to political organizations.—Paragraph (1) shall not apply to the transfer of money or other property to a political organization (within the meaning of section 527(e) (1)) for the use of such organization.

* * *

(d) Cross references.—

(1) For increase in basis of property acquired by gift for gift tax paid, see section 1015(d).

* * *

§ 2502.　Rate of tax

(a) **Computation of tax.**—The tax imposed by section 2501 for each calendar year shall be an amount equal to the excess of—

(1) a tentative tax, computed in accordance with the rate schedule set forth in section 2001(c), on the aggregate sum of the taxable gifts for such calendar year and for each of the preceding calendar periods, over

(2) a tentative tax, computed in accordance with such rate schedule, on the aggregate sum of the taxable gifts for each of the preceding calendar periods.

(b) **Preceding calendar period.**—Whenever used in this title in "connection with the gift" tax imposed by this chapter, the term preceding calendar period means—

(1) calendar years 1932 and 1970 and all calendar years intervening between calendar year 1932 and calendar year 1970,

(2) the first calendar quarter of calendar year 1971 and all calendar quarters intervening between such calendar quarter and the first calendar quarter of calendar year 1982, and

(3) all calendar years after 1981 and before the calendar year for which the tax is being computed.

For purposes of paragraph (1), the term "calendar year 1932" includes only that portion of such year after June 6, 1932.

(c) **Tax to be paid by donor.**—The tax imposed by section 2501 shall be paid by the donor.

§ 2503.　Taxable gifts

(a) **General definition.**—The term "taxable gifts" means the total amount of gifts made during the calendar year, less the deductions provided in subchapter C (section 2522 and following).

(b) **Exclusion from gifts.**—In the case of gifts (other than gifts of future interests in property) made to any person by the donor during the calendar year, the first $10,000 of such gifts to such person shall not, for purposes of subsection (a), be included in the total amount of gifts made during such year. Where there has been a transfer to any person of a present interest in property, the possibility that such interest may be diminished by the exercise of a power shall be disregarded in applying this subsection, if no part of such interest will at any time pass to any other person.

(c) **Transfer for the benefit of minor.**—No part of a gift to an individual who has not attained the age of 21 years on the date of such transfer shall be considered a gift of a future interest in property for purposes of subsection (b) if the property and the income therefrom—

(1) may be expended by, or for the benefit of, the donee before his attaining the age of 21 years, and

(2) will to the extent not so expended—

(A) pass to the donee on his attaining the age of 21 years, and

(B) in the event the donee dies before attaining the age of 21 years, be payable to the estate of the donee or as he may appoint under a general power of appointment as defined in section 2514(c).

[(d) Repealed.]

(e) Exclusion for certain transfers for educational expenses or medical expenses.—

(1) In general.—Any qualified transfer shall not be treated as a transfer of property by gift for purposes of this chapter.

(2) Qualified transfer.—For purposes of this subsection, the term "qualified transfer" means any amount paid on behalf of an individual—

(A) as tuition to an educational organization described in section 170(b)(1)(A)(ii) for the education or training of such individual, or

(B) to any person who provides medical care (as defined in section 213(e)) with respect to such individual as payment for such medical care.

(f) Waiver of certain pension rights.—If any individual waives, before the death of a participant, any survivor benefit, or right to such benefit, under section 401(a)(11) or 417, such waiver shall not be treated as a transfer of property by gift for purposes of this chapter.

§ 2504. Taxable gifts for preceding calendar periods

(a) In general.—In computing taxable gifts for preceding calendar periods for purposes of computing the tax for any calendar year—

(1) there shall be treated as gifts such transfers as were considered to be gifts under the gift tax laws applicable to the calendar period in which the transfers were made,

(2) there shall be allowed such deductions as were provided for under such laws, and

(3) the specific exemption in the amount (if any) allowable under section 2521 (as in effect before its repeal by the Tax Reform Act of 1976) shall be applied in all computations in respect of preceding calendar periods ending before January 1, 1977, for purposes of computing the tax for any calendar year.

(b) Exclusions from gifts for preceding calendar periods.—In the case of gifts made to any person by the donor during preceding calendar periods, the amount excluded, if any, by the provisions of gift tax laws applicable to the periods in which the gifts were made shall not, for purposes of subsection (a), be included in the total amount of the gifts made during such preceding calendar periods.

(c) Valuation of certain gifts for preceding calendar periods.—If the time has expired within which a tax may be assessed under this chapter or under corresponding provisions of prior laws on the transfer of property by gift made during a preceding calendar period, as defined in section 2502(b), and if a tax under this chapter or under corresponding provisions of prior laws has been assessed or paid for such preceding calendar period, the value of such gift made in such preceding calendar period shall, for purposes of computing the tax under this chapter for any calendar year, be the value of such gift which was used in computing the tax for the last preceding calendar period for which a tax under this chapter or under corresponding provisions of prior laws was assessed or paid.

(d) **Net gifts.**—The term "net gifts" as used in corresponding provisions of prior laws shall be read as "taxable gifts" for purposes of this chapter.

§ 2505. Unified credit against gift tax

(a) **General rule.**—In the case of a citizen or resident of the United States, there shall be allowed as a credit against the tax imposed by section 2501 for each calendar year an amount equal to—

(1) $192,800, reduced by

(2) the sum of the amounts allowable as a credit to the individual under this section for all preceding calendar periods.

(b) **Phase-in of credit.**—

In the case of gifts made in:	Subsection (a)(1) shall be applied by substituting for "$192,800" the following amount:
1982	62,800
1983	79,300
1984	96,300
1985	121,800
1986	155,800

(c) **Adjustment to credit for certain gifts made before 1977.**—The amount allowable under subsection (a) shall be reduced by an amount equal to 20 percent of the aggregate amount allowed as a specific exemption under section 2521 (as in effect before its repeal by the Tax Reform Act of 1976) with respect to gifts made by the individual after September 8, 1976.

(d) **Limitation based on amount of tax.**—The amount of the credit allowed under subsection (a) for any calendar year shall not exceed the amount of the tax imposed by section 2501 for such calendar year.

SUBCHAPTER B—TRANSFERS

§ 2511. Transfers in general

(a) **Scope.**—Subject to the limitations contained in this chapter, the tax imposed by section 2501 shall apply whether the transfer is in trust or otherwise, whether the gift is direct or indirect, and whether the property is real or personal, tangible or intangible; but in the case of a nonresident not a citizen of the United States, shall apply to a transfer only if the property is situated within the United States.

* * *

§ 2512. Valuation of gifts

(a) If the gift is made in property, the value thereof at the date of the gift shall be considered the amount of the gift.

(b) Where property is transferred for less than an adequate and full consideration in money or money's worth, then the amount by which the value of the property exceeded the value of the consideration shall be deemed a gift, and shall be included in computing the amount of gifts made during the calendar year.

(c) Cross reference.—

For individual's right to be furnished on request a statement regarding any valuation made by the Secretary of a gift by that individual, see section 7517.

§ 2513.   Gift by husband or wife to third party

(a) Considered as made one-half by each.—

(1) In general.—A gift made by one spouse to any person other than his spouse shall, for the purposes of this chapter, be considered as made one-half by him and one-half by his spouse, but only if at the time of the gift each spouse is a citizen or resident of the United States. This paragraph shall not apply with respect to a gift by a spouse of an interest in property if he creates in his spouse a general power of appointment, as defined in section 2514(c), over such interest. For purposes of this section, an individual shall be considered as the spouse of another individual only if he is married to such individual at the time of the gift and does not remarry during the remainder of the calendar year.

(2) Consent of both spouses.—Paragraph (1) shall apply only if both spouses have signified (under the regulations provided for in subsection (b)) their consent to the application of paragraph (1) in the case of all such gifts made during the calendar year by either while married to the other.

(b) Manner and time of signifying consent.—

(1) Manner.—A consent under this section shall be signified in such manner as is provided under regulations prescribed by the Secretary.

(2) Time.—Such consent may be so signified at any time after the close of the calendar year in which the gift was made, subject to the following limitations—

(A) The consent may not be signified after the 15th day of April following the close of such year, unless before such 15th day no return has been filed for such year by either spouse, in which case the consent may not be signified after a return for such year is filed by either spouse.

(B) The consent may not be signified after a notice of deficiency with respect to the tax for such year has been sent to either spouse in accordance with section 6212(a).

(c) Revocation of consent.—Revocation of a consent previously signified shall be made in such manner as is provided under regulations prescribed by the Secretary, but the right to revoke a consent previously signified with respect to a calendar year—

(1) shall not exist after the 15th day of April following the close of such year if the consent was signified on or before such 15th day; and

(2) shall not exist if the consent was not signified until after such 15th day.

(d) Joint and several liability for tax.—If the consent required by subsection (a) (2) is signified with respect to a gift made in any calendar year, the liability with respect to the entire tax imposed by this chapter of each spouse for such year shall be joint and several.

§ 2514.   Powers of appointment

(a) Powers created on or before October 21, 1942.—An exercise of a general power of appointment created on or before October 21, 1942, shall be deemed a transfer of property by the individual possessing such power; but the failure to exercise such a power or the complete release of such a power shall not be deemed an exercise thereof. If a general power of appointment created on or before October 21,

1942, has been partially released so that it is no longer a general power of appointment, the subsequent exercise of such power shall not be deemed to be the exercise of a general power of appointment if—

(1) such partial release occurred before November 1, 1951, or

(2) the donee of such power was under a legal disability to release such power on October 21, 1942, and such partial release occurred not later than six months after the termination of such legal disability.

(b) **Powers created after October 21, 1942.**—The exercise or release of a general power of appointment created after October 21, 1942, shall be deemed a transfer of property by the individual possessing such power.

(c) **Definition of general power of appointment.**—For purposes of this section, the term "general power of appointment" means a power which is exercisable in favor of the individual possessing the power (hereafter in this subsection referred to as the "possessor"), his estate, his creditors, or the creditors of his estate; except that—

(1) A power to consume, invade, or appropriate property for the benefit of the possessor which is limited by an ascertainable standard relating to the health, education, support, or maintenance of the possessor shall not be deemed a general power of appointment.

(2) A power of appointment created on or before October 21, 1942, which is exercisable by the possessor only in conjunction with another person shall not be deemed a general power of appointment.

(3) In the case of a power of appointment created after October 21, 1942, which is exercisable by the possessor only in conjunction with another person—

(A) if the power is not exercisable by the possessor except in conjunction with the creator of the power—such power shall not be deemed a general power of appointment;

(B) if the power is not exercisable by the possessor except in conjunction with a person having a substantial interest, in the property subject to the power, which is adverse to exercise of the power in favor of the possessor—such power shall not be deemed a general power of appointment. For the purposes of this subparagraph a person who, after the death of the possessor, may be possessed of a power of appointment (with respect to the property subject to the possessor's power) which he may exercise in his own favor shall be deemed as having an interest in the property and such interest shall be deemed adverse to such exercise of the possessor's power;

(C) if (after the application of subparagraphs (A) and (B)) the power is a general power of appointment and is exercisable in favor of such other person— such power shall be deemed a general power of appointment only in respect of a fractional part of the property subject to such power, such part to be determined by dividing the value of such property by the number of such persons (including the possessor) in favor of whom such power is exercisable.

For purposes of subparagraphs (B) and (C), a power shall be deemed to be exercisable in favor of a person if it is exercisable in favor of such person, his estate, his creditors, or the creditors of his estate.

(d) **Creation of another power in certain cases.**—If a power of appointment created after October 21, 1942, is exercised by creating another power of appointment which, under the applicable local law, can be validly exercised so as to postpone the vesting of any estate or interest in the property which was subject to the first power, or suspend the absolute ownership or power of alienation of such property, for a period ascertainable without regard to the date of the creation of the first power, such exercise of the first power shall, to the extent of the property subject to the second power, be deemed a transfer of property by the individual possessing such power.

(e) Lapse of power.—The lapse of a power of appointment created after October 21, 1942, during the life of the individual possessing the power shall be considered a release of such power. The rule of the preceding sentence shall apply with respect to the lapse of powers during any calendar year only to the extent that the property which could have been appointed by exercise of such lapsed powers exceeds in value the greater of the following amounts:

    (1) $5,000, or

    (2) 5 percent of the aggregate value of the assets out of which, or the proceeds of which, the exercise of the lapsed powers could be satisfied.

* * *

§ 2515. Treatment of generation-skipping transfer tax

In the case of any taxable gift which is a direct skip (within the meaning of chapter 13), the amount of such gift shall be increased by the amount of any tax imposed on the transferor under chapter 13 with respect to such gift.

(Added Pub.L. 99–514, Title XIV, § 1432(d)(1), Oct. 22, 1986, 100 Stat. ——.)

§ 2516. Certain property settlements

Where husband and wife enter into a written agreement relative to their marital and property rights and divorce occurs within the 3-year period beginning on the date 1 year before such agreement is entered into (whether or not such agreement is approved by the divorce decree), any transfers of property or interests in property made pursuant to such agreement—

    (1) to either spouse in settlement of his or her marital or property rights, or

    (2) to provide a reasonable allowance for the support of issue of the marriage during minority,

shall be deemed to be transfers made for a full and adequate consideration in money or money's worth.

§ 2517. Certain annuities under qualified plans [Repealed.]

§ 2518. Disclaimers

(a) General rule.—For purposes of this subtitle, if a person makes a qualified disclaimer with respect to any interest in property, this subtitle shall apply with respect to such interest as if the interest had never been transferred to such person.

(b) Qualified disclaimer defined.—For purposes of subsection (a), the term "qualified disclaimer" means an irrevocable and unqualified refusal by a person to accept an interest in property but only if—

    (1) such refusal is in writing,

    (2) such writing is received by the transferor of the interest, his legal representative, or the holder of the legal title to the property to which the interest relates not later than the date which is 9 months after the later of—

(A) the day on which the transfer creating the interest in such person is made, or

(B) the day on which such person attains age 21,

(3) such person has not accepted the interest or any of its benefits, and

(4) as a result of such refusal, the interest passes without any direction on the part of the person making the disclaimer and passes either—

(A) to the spouse of the decedent, or

(B) to a person other than the person making the disclaimer.

(c) Other rules.—For purposes of subsection (a)—

(1) Disclaimer of undivided portion of interest.—A disclaimer with respect to an undivided portion of an interest which meets the requirements of the preceding sentence shall be treated as a qualified disclaimer of such portion of the interest.

(2) Powers.—A power with respect to property shall be treated as an interest in such property.

(3) Certain transfers treated as disclaimers.—A written transfer of the transferor's entire interest in the property—

(A) which meets requirements similar to the requirements of paragraphs (2) and (3) of subsection (b), and

(B) which is to a person or persons who would have received the property had the transferor made a qualified disclaimer (within the meaning of subsection (b)),

shall be treated as a qualified disclaimer.

§ 2519. Dispositions of certain life estates

(a) General rule.—For purposes of this chapter and chapter 11, any disposition of all or part of a qualifying income interest for life in any property to which this section applies shall be treated as a transfer of all interests in such property other than the qualifying income interest.

(b) Property to which this subsection applies.—This section applies to any property if a deduction was allowed with respect to the transfer of such property to the donor—

(1) under section 2056 by reason of subsection (b)(7) thereof, or

(2) under section 2523 by reason of subsection (f) thereof.

(c) Cross reference.—

For right of recovery for gift tax in the case of property treated as transferred under this section, see section 2207A(b).

SUBCHAPTER C—DEDUCTIONS

§ 2522. Charitable and similar gifts

(a) Citizens or residents.—In computing taxable gifts for the calendar year, there shall be allowed as a deduction in the case of a citizen or resident the amount of all gifts made during such year to or for the use of—

(1) the United States, any State, or any political subdivision thereof, or the District of Columbia, for exclusively public purposes;

(2) a corporation, or trust, or community chest, fund, or foundation, organized and operated exclusively for religious, charitable, scientific, literary, or educational

purposes, or to foster national or international amateur sports competition (but only if no part of its activities involve the provision of athletic facilities or equipment), including the encouragement of art and the prevention of cruelty to children or animals, no part of the net earnings of which inures to the benefit of any private shareholder or individual, which is not disqualified for tax exemption under section 501(c) (3) by reason of attempting to influence legislation, and which does not participate in, or intervene in (including the publishing or distributing of statements), any political campaign on behalf of any candidate for public office;

(3) a fraternal society, order, or association, operating under the lodge system, but only if such gifts are to be used exclusively for religious, charitable, scientific, literary, or educational purposes, including the encouragement of art and the prevention of cruelty to children or animals;

(4) posts or organizations of war veterans, or auxiliary units or societies of any such posts or organizations, if such posts, organizations, units, or societies are organized in the United States or any of its possessions, and if no part of their net earnings inures to the benefit of any private shareholder or individual.

* * *

(c) **Disallowance of deductions in certain cases.**—

* * *

(2) Where a donor transfers an interest in property (other than an interest described in section 170(f) (3) (B)) to a person, or for a use, described in subsection (a) or (b) and an interest in the same property is retained by the donor, or is transferred or has been transferred (for less than an adequate and full consideration in money or money's worth) from the donor to a person, or for a use, not described in subsection (a) or (b), no deduction shall be allowed under this section for the interest which is, or has been transferred to the person, or for the use, described in subsection (a) or (b), unless—

(A) in the case of a remainder interest, such interest is in a trust which is a charitable remainder annuity trust or a charitable remainder unitrust (described in section 664) or a pooled income fund (described in section 642(c) (5)), or

(B) in the case of any other interest, such interest is in the form of a guaranteed annuity or is a fixed percentage distributed yearly of the fair market value of the property (to be determined yearly).

(3) Rules similar to the rules of section 2055(e)(4) shall apply for purposes of paragraph (2).

* * *

§ 2523. Gift to spouse

(a) **Allowance of deduction.**—Where a donor who is a citizen or resident transfers during the calendar year by gift an interest in property to a donee who at the time of the gift is the donor's spouse, there shall be allowed as a deduction in computing taxable gifts for the calendar year an amount with respect to such interest equal to its value.

(b) **Life estate or other terminable interest.**—Where, on the lapse of time, on the occurrence of an event or contingency, or on the failure of an event or contingency to occur, such interest transferred to the spouse will terminate or fail, no deduction shall be allowed with respect to such interest—

(1) if the donor retains in himself, or transfers or has transferred (for less than an adequate and full consideration in money or money's worth) to any person other

than such donee spouse (or the estate of such spouse), an interest in such property, and if by reason of such retention or transfer the donor (or his heirs or assigns) or such person (or his heirs or assigns) may possess or enjoy any part of such property after such termination or failure of the interest transferred to the donee spouse; or

(2) if the donor immediately after the transfer to the donee spouse has a power to appoint an interest in such property which he can exercise (either alone or in conjunction with any person) in such manner that the appointee may possess or enjoy any part of such property after such termination or failure of the interest transferred to the donee spouse. For purposes of this paragraph, the donor shall be considered as having immediately after the transfer to the donee spouse such power to appoint even though such power cannot be exercised until after the lapse of time, upon the occurrence of an event or contingency, or on the failure of an event or contingency to occur.

An exercise or release at any time by the donor, either alone or in conjunction with any person, of a power to appoint an interest in property, even though not otherwise a transfer, shall, for purposes of paragraph (1), be considered as a transfer by him. Except as provided in subsection (e), where at the time of the transfer it is impossible to ascertain the particular person or persons who may receive from the donor an interest in property so transferred by him, such interest shall, for purposes of paragraph (1), be considered as transferred to a person other than the donee spouse.

(c) Interest in unidentified assets.—Where the assets out of which, or the proceeds of which, the interest transferred to the donee spouse may be satisfied include a particular asset or assets with respect to which no deduction would be allowed if such asset or assets were transferred from the donor to such spouse, then the value of the interest transferred to such spouse shall, for purposes of subsection (a), be reduced by the aggregate value of such particular assets.

(d) Joint interests.—If the interest is transferred to the donee spouse as sole joint tenant with the donor or as tenant by the entirety, the interest of the donor in the property which exists solely by reason of the possibility that the donor may survive the donee spouse, or that there may occur a severance of the tenancy, shall not be considered for purposes of subsection (b) as an interest retained by the donor in himself.

(e) Life estate with power of appointment in donee spouse.—Where the donor transfers an interest in property, if by such transfer his spouse is entitled for life to all of the income from the entire interest, or all the income from a specific portion thereof, payable annually or at more frequent intervals, with power in the donee spouse to appoint the entire interest, or such specific portion (exercisable in favor of such donee spouse, or of the estate of such donee spouse, or in favor of either, whether or not in each case the power is exercisable in favor of others), and with no power in any other person to appoint any part of such interest, or such portion, to any person other than the donee spouse—

(1) the interest, or such portion, so transferred shall, for purposes of subsection (a) be considered as transferred to the donee spouse, and

(2) no part of the interest, or such portion, so transferred shall, for purposes of subsection (b) (1), be considered as retained in the donor or transferred to any person other than the donee spouse.

This subsection shall apply only if, by such transfer, such power in the donee spouse to appoint the interest, or such portion, whether exercisable by will or during life, is exercisable by such spouse alone and in all events.

(f) Election with respect to life estate for donee spouse.—

(1) In general.—In the case of qualified terminable interest property—

    (A) for purposes of subsection (a), such property shall be treated as transferred to the donee spouse, and

    (B) for purposes of subsection (b)(1), no part of such property shall be considered as retained in the donor or transferred to any person other than the donee spouse.

(2) Qualified terminable interest property.—For purposes of this subsection, the term "qualified terminable interest property" means any property—

    (A) which is transferred by the donor spouse,

    (B) in which the donee spouse has a qualifying income interest for life, and

    (C) to which an election under this subsection applies.

(3) Certain rules made applicable.—For purposes of this subsection, rules similar to the rules of clauses (ii), (iii), and (iv) of section 2056(b)(7)(B) shall apply.

(4) Election.—

    (A) Time and manner.—An election under this subsection with respect to any property shall be made on or before the date prescribed by section 6075(b) for filing a gift tax return with respect to the transfer (determined without regard to section 6019(2)) and shall be made in such manner as the Secretary shall by regulations prescribe.

    (B) Election irrevocable.—An election under this subsection, once made, shall be irrevocable.

(5) Treatment of interest retained by donor spouse.—

    (A) In general.—In the case of any qualified terminable interest property—

        (i) such property shall not be includible in the gross estate of the donor spouse, and

        (ii) any subsequent transfer by the donor spouse of an interest in such property shall not be treated as a transfer for purposes of this chapter.

    (B) Subparagraph (A) not to apply after transfer by donee spouse.—Subparagraph (A) shall not apply with respect to any property after the donee spouse is treated as having transferred such property under section 2519, or such property is includible in the donee spouse's gross estate under section 2044.

(g) Special rule for charitable remainder trusts.—

(1) In general.—If, after the transfer, the donee spouse is the only noncharitable beneficiary (other than the donor) of a qualified remainder trust, subsection (b) shall not apply to the interest in such trust which is transferred to the donee spouse.

(2) Definitions.—For purposes of paragraph (1), the term [1] "noncharitable beneficiary" and "qualified charitable remainder trust" have the meanings given to such terms by section 2056(b)(8)(B).

(h) Denial of double deduction.—Nothing in this section or any other provision of this chapter shall allow the value of any interest in property to be deducted under this chapter more than once with respect to the same donor.

§ 2524. Extent of deductions

The deductions provided in sections 2522 and 2523 shall be allowed only to the extent that the gifts therein specified are included in the amount of gifts against which such deductions are applied.

CHAPTER 13—TAX ON GENERATION–SKIPPING TRANSFERS

Subchapter
- A. Tax imposed.
- B. Generation-skipping transfers.
- C. Taxable amount.
- D. GST exemption.
- E. Applicable rate; inclusion ratio.
- F. Other definitions and special rules.
- G. Administration.

SUBCHAPTER A—TAX IMPOSED

§ 2601. Tax imposed

A tax is hereby imposed on every generation-skipping transfer (within the meaning of subchapter B).

(Added Pub.L. 99–514, Title XIV, § 1431(a), Oct. 22, 1986, 100 Stat. ___.)

§ 2602. Amount of tax

The amount of the tax imposed by section 2601 is—

(1) the taxable amount (determined under subchapter C), multiplied by

(2) the applicable rate (determined under subchapter E).

(Added Pub.L. 99–514, Title XIV, § 1431(a), Oct. 22, 1986, 100 Stat. ___.)

§ 2603. Liability for tax

(a) **Personal liability.—**

(1) **Taxable distributions.—**In the case of a taxable distribution, the tax imposed by section 2601 shall be paid by the transferee.

(2) **Taxable termination.—**In the case of a taxable termination or a direct skip from a trust, the tax shall be paid by the trustee.

(3) **Direct skip.—**In the case of a direct skip (other than a direct skip from a trust), the tax shall be paid by the transferor.

(b) **Source of tax.—**Unless otherwise directed pursuant to the governing instrument by specific reference to the tax imposed by this chapter, the tax imposed by this chapter on a generation-skipping transfer shall be charged to the property constituting such transfer.

(c) Cross reference.—

For provisions making estate and gift tax provisions with respect to transferee liability, liens, and related matters applicable to the tax imposed by section 2601, see section 2661.

(Added Pub.L. 99–514, Title XIV, § 1431(a), Oct. 22, 1986, 100 Stat. ___.)

§ 2604.   Credit for certain state taxes

(a) General rule.—If a generation-skipping transfer (other than a direct skip) occurs at the same time as and as a result of the death of an individual, a credit against the tax imposed by section 2601 shall be allowed in an amount equal to the generation-skipping transfer tax actually paid to any State in respect to any property included in the generation-skipping transfer.

(b) Limitation.—The aggregate amount allowed as a credit under this section with respect to any transfer shall not exceed 5 percent of the amount of the tax imposed by section 2601 on such transfer.

(Added Pub.L. 99–514, Title XIV, § 1431(a), Oct. 22, 1986, 100 Stat. ———.)

SUBCHAPTER B—GENERATION–SKIPPING TRANSFERS

§ 2611.   Generation-skipping transfer defined

(a) In general.—For purposes of this chapter, the term "generation-skipping transfers" mean—

    (1) a taxable distribution,

    (2) a taxable termination, and

    (3) a direct skip.

(b) Certain transfers excluded.—The term "generation-skipping transfer" does not include—

    (1) any transfer (other than a direct skip) from a trust, to the extent such transfer is subject to a tax imposed by chapter 11 or 12 with respect to a person in the 1st generation below that of the grantor, and

    (2) any transfer which, if made inter vivos by an individual, would not be treated as a taxable gift by reason of section 2503(e) (relating to exclusion of certain transfers for educational or medical expenses), and

    (3) any transfer to the extent—

        (A) the property transferred was subject to a prior tax imposed under this chapter,

        (B) the transferee in the prior transfer was assigned to the same generation as (or a lower generation than) the generation assignment of the transferee in this transfer, and

        (C) such transfers do not have the effect of avoiding tax under this chapter with respect to any transfer.

(Added Pub.L. 99–514, Title XIV, § 1431(a), Oct. 22, 1986, 100 Stat. ___.)

§ 2612.   Taxable termination; taxable distribution; direct skip

(a) Taxable termination.—

(1) General rule.—For purposes of this chapter, the term "taxable termination" means the termination (by death, lapse of time, release of power, or otherwise) of an interest in property held in a trust unless—

(A) immediately after such termination, a non-skip person has an interest in such property, or

(B) at no time after such termination may a distribution (including distributions on termination) be made from such trust to a skip person.

(2) Certain partial terminations treated as taxable.—If, upon the termination of an interest in property held in a trust, a specified portion of the trust assets are distributed to skip persons who are lineal descendants of the holder of such interest (or to 1 or more trusts for the exclusive benefit of such persons), such termination shall constitute a taxable termination with respect to such portion of the trust property.

(b) Taxable distribution.—For purposes of this chapter, the term "taxable distribution" means any distribution from a trust to a skip person (other than a taxable termination or a direct skip). ·

(c) Direct skip.—For purposes of this chapter—

(1) In general.—The term "direct skip" means a transfer subject to a tax imposed by chapter 11 or 12 of an interest in property to a skip person.

(2) Special rule for transfers to grandchildren.—For purposes of determining whether any transfer is a direct skip, if—

(A) an individual is a grandchild of the transferor (or the transferor's spouse or former spouse), and

(B) as of the time of the transfer, the parent of such individual who is a lineal descendant of the transferor (or the transferor's spouse or former spouse) is dead,

such individual shall be treated as if such individual were a child of the transferor and all of that grandchild's children shall be treated as if they were grandchildren of the transferor. In the case of lineal descendants below a grandchild, the preceding sentence may be reapplied.

(Added Pub.L. 99–514, Title XIV, § 1431(a), Oct. 22, 1986, 100 Stat. ____.)

§ 2613.   Skip person and non-skip person defined

(a) Skip person.—For purposes of this chapter, the term "skip person" means—

(1) a person assigned to a generation which is 2 or more generations below the generation assignment of the transferor, or

(2) a trust—

(A) if all interests in such trust are held by skip persons, or

(B) if—

(i) there is no person holding an interest in such trust, and

(ii) at no time after such transfer may a distribution (including distributions on termination) be made from such trust to a nonskip person.

(b) Non-skip person.—For purposes of this chapter, the term "non-skip person" means any person who is not a skip person.

(Added Pub.L. 99–514, Title XIV, § 1431(a), Oct. 22, 1986, 100 Stat. ____.)

SUBCHAPTER C—TAXABLE AMOUNT

§ 2621. Taxable amount in case of taxable distribution

(a) **In general.**—For purposes of this chapter, the taxable amount in the case of any taxable distribution shall be—

(1) the value of the property received by the transferee, reduced by

(2) any expense incurred by the transferee in connection with the determination, collection, or refund of the tax imposed by this chapter with respect to such distribution.

(b) **Payment of GST tax treated as taxable distribution.**—For purposes of this chapter, if any of the tax imposed by this chapter with respect to any taxable distribution is paid out of the trust, an amount equal to the portion so paid shall be treated as a taxable distribution.

(Added Pub.L. 99–514, Title XIV, § 1431(a), Oct. 22, 1986, 100 Stat. ___.)

§ 2622. Taxable amount in case of taxable termination

(a) **In general.**—For purposes of this chapter, the taxable amount in the case of a taxable termination shall be—

(1) the value of all property with respect to which the taxable termination has occurred, reduced by

(2) any deduction allowed under subsection (b).

(b) **Deduction for certain expenses.**—For purposes of subsection (a), there shall be allowed a deduction similar to the deduction allowed by section 2053 (relating to expenses, indebtedness, and taxes) for amounts attributable to the property with respect to which the taxable termination has occurred.

(Added Pub.L. 99–514, Title XIV, § 1431(a), Oct. 22, 1986, 100 Stat. ___.)

§ 2623. Taxable amount in case of direct skip

For purposes of this chapter, the taxable amount in the case of a direct skip shall be the value of the property received by the transferee.

(Added Pub.L. 99–514, Title XIV, § 1431(a), Oct. 22, 1986, 100 Stat. ___.)

§ 2624. Valuation

(a) **General rule.**—Except as otherwise provided in this chapter, property shall be valued as of the time of the generation-skipping transfer.

(b) **Alternate valuation and special use valuation elections apply to certain direct skips.**—In the case of any direct skip of property which is included in the transferor's gross estate, the value of such property for purposes of this chapter shall be the same as its value for purposes of chapter 11 (determined with regard to sections 2032 and 2032A).

(c) **Alternate valuation election permitted in the case of taxable terminations occurring at death.**—If 1 or more taxable terminations with respect to the same trust occur at the same time as and as a result of the death of an individual, an election may be made to value all of the property included in such terminations in accordance with section 2032.

(d) Reduction for consideration provided by transferee.—For purposes of this chapter, the value of the property transferred shall be reduced by the amount of any consideration provided by the transferee.

(Added Pub.L. 99–514, Title XIV, § 1431(a), Oct. 22, 1986, 100 Stat. ——.)

SUBCHAPTER D—GST EXEMPTION

§ 2631. GST exemption

(a) General rule.—For purposes of determining the inclusion ratio, every individual shall be allowed a GST exemption of $1,000,000 which may be allocated by such individual (or his executor) to any property with respect to which such individual is the transferor.

(b) Allocations irrevocable.—Any allocation under subsection (a), once made, shall be irrevocable.

(Added Pub.L. 99–514, Title XIV, § 1431(a), Oct. 22, 1986, 100 Stat. ——.)

§ 2632. Special rules for allocation of GST exemption

(a) Time and manner of allocation.—

(1) Time.—Any allocation by an individual of his GST exemption under section 2631(a) may be made at any time on or before the date prescribed for filing the estate tax return for such individual's estate (determined with regard to extensions), regardless of whether such a return is required to be filed.

(2) Manner.—The Secretary shall prescribe by forms or regulations the manner in which any allocation referred to in paragraph (1) is to be made.

(b) Deemed allocation to certain lifetime direct skips.—

(1) In general.—If any individual makes a direct skip during his lifetime, any unused portion of such individual's GST exemption shall be allocated to the property transferred to the extent necessary to make the inclusion ratio for such property zero. If the amount of the direct skip exceeds such unused portion, the entire unused portion shall be allocated to the property transferred.

(2) Unused portion.—For purposes of paragraph (1), the unused portion of an individual's GST exemption is that portion of such exemption which has not previously been allocated by such individual (or treated as allocated under paragraph (1)) with respect to a prior direct skip.

(3) Subsection not to apply in certain cases.—An individual may elect to have this subsection not apply to a transfer.

(c) Allocation of unused GST exemption.—

(1) In general.—Any portion of an individual's GST exemption which has not been allocated within the time prescribed by subsection (a) shall be deemed to be allocated as follows—

(A) first, to property which is the subject of a direct skip occurring at such individual's death, and

(B) second, to trusts with respect to which such individual is the transferor and from which a taxable distribution or a taxable termination might occur at or after such individual's death.

(2) Allocation within categories.—

741

(A) **In general.**—The allocation under paragraph (1) shall be made among the properties described in subparagraph (A) thereof and the trusts described in subparagraph (B) thereof, as the case may be, in proportion to the respective amounts (at the time of allocation) of the nonexempt portions of such properties or trusts.

(B) **Nonexempt portion.**—For purposes of subparagraph (A), the term "nonexempt portion" means the value (at the time of allocation) of the property or trust, multiplied by the inclusion ratio with respect to such property or trust.

(Added Pub.L. 99–514, Title XIV, § 1431(a), Oct. 22, 1986, 100 Stat. ——.)

SUBCHAPTER E—APPLICABLE RATE; INCLUSION RATIO

§ 2641. Applicable rate

(a) **General rule.**—For purposes of this chapter, the term "applicable rate" means, with respect to any generation-skipping transfer, the product of—

(1) the maximum Federal estate tax rate, and

(2) the inclusion ratio with respect to the transfer.

(b) **Maximum federal estate tax rate.**—For purposes of subsection (a), the term "maximum Federal estate tax rate" means the maximum rate imposed by section 2001 on the estates of decedents dying at the time of the taxable distribution, taxable termination, or direct skip, as the case may be.

(Added Pub.L. 99–514, Title XIV, § 1431(a), Oct. 22, 1986, 100 Stat. ——.)

§ 2642. Inclusion ratio

(a) **Inclusion ratio defined.**—For purposes of this chapter—

(1) **In general.**—Except as otherwise provided in this section, the inclusion ratio with respect to any property transferred in a generation-skipping transfer shall be the excess (if any) of 1 over—

(A) except as provided in subparagraph (B), the applicable fraction determined for the trust from which such transfer is made, or

(B) in the case of a direct skip, the applicable fraction determined for such skip.

(2) **Applicable fraction.**—For purposes of paragraph (1), the applicable fraction is a fraction—

(A) the numerator of which is the amount of the GST exemption allocated to the trust (or in the case of a direct skip, allocated to the property transferred in such skip), and

(B) the denominator of which is—

(i) the value of the property transferred to the trust (or involved in the direct skip), reduced by

(ii) the sum of—

(I) any Federal estate tax or State death tax actually recovered from the trust attributable to such property, and

(II) any charitable deduction allowed under section 2055 or 2522 with respect to such property.

742

Except as provided in paragraphs (3) and (4) of subsection (b), the value determined under subparagraph (B)(i) shall be of the property as of the time of the transfer to the trust (or the direct skip).

(b) Valuation rules, etc.—

(1) Gifts for which gift tax return filed or deemed allocation made.—If the allocation of the GST exemption to any property is made on a timely filed gift tax return required by section 6019 or is deemed to be made under section 2632(b)(1)—

(A) the value of such property for purposes of subsection (a) shall be its value for purposes of chapter 12, and

(B) such allocation shall be effective on and after the date of such transfer.

(2) Transfers and allocations at or after death.—

(A) Transfers at death.—If property is transferred as a result of the death of the transferor, the value of such property for purposes of subsection (a) shall be its value for purposes of chapter 11.

(B) Allocations at or after death of transferor.—Any allocation at or after the death of the transferor shall be effective on and after the date of the death of the transferor.

(3) Inter vivos allocations not made on timely filed gift tax return.—If any allocation of the GST exemption to any property is made during the life of the transferor but is not made on a timely filed gift tax return required by section 6019 and is not deemed to be made under section 2632(b)(1)—

(A) the value of such property for purposes of subsection (a) shall be determined as of the time such allocation is filed with the Secretary, and

(B) such allocation shall be effective on and after the date on which such allocation is filed with the Secretary.

(4) QTIP trusts.—If the value of property is included in the estate of a spouse by virtue of section 2044, and if such spouse is treated as the transferor of such property under section 2652(a), the value of such property for purposes of subsection (a) shall be its value for purposes of chapter 11 in the estate of such spouse.

(c) Treatment of certain nontaxable gifts.—

(1) Direct skips.—In the case of any direct skip which is a nontaxable gift, the inclusion ratio shall be zero.

(2) Treatment of nontaxable gifts made to trusts.—

(A) In general.—Except as provided in subparagraph (B), any nontaxable gift which is not a direct skip and which is made to a trust shall not be taken into account under subsection (a)(2)(B).

(B) Determination of 1st transfer to trust.—In the case of any nontaxable gift referred to in subparagraph (A) which is the 1st transfer to the trust, the inclusion ratio for such trust shall be zero.

(3) Nontaxable gift.—For purposes of this section, the term "nontaxable gift" means any transfer of property to the extent such transfer is not treated as a taxable gift by reason of—

(A) section 2503(b) (taking into account the application of section 2513), or

(B) section 2503(e).

(d) Special rules where more than 1 transfer made to trust.—

(1) **In general.**—If a transfer of property (other than a non-taxable gift) is made to a trust in existence before such transfer, the applicable fraction for such trust shall be recomputed as of the time of such transfer in the manner provided in paragraph (2).

(2) **Applicable fraction.**—In the case of any such transfer, the recomputed applicable fraction is a fraction—

(A) the numerator of which is the sum of—

(i) the amount of the GST exemption allocated to property involved in such transfer, plus

(ii) the nontax portion of such trust immediately before such transfer, and

(B) the denominator of which is the sum of—

(i) the value of the property involved in such transfer, reduced by any charitable deduction allowed under section 2055 or 2522 with respect to such property, and

(ii) the value of all of the property in the trust (immediately before such transfer).

(3) **Nontax portion.**—For purposes of paragraph (2), the term "nontax portion" means the product of—

(A) the value of all of the property in the trust, and

(B) the applicable fraction in effect for such trust.

(4) **Similar recomputation in case of certain late allocations.**—If—

(A) any allocation of the GST exemption to property transferred to a trust is not made on a timely filed gift tax return required by section 6019, and

(B) there was a previous allocation with respect to property transferred to such trust,

the applicable fraction for such trust shall be recomputed as of the time of such allocation under rules similar to the rules of paragraph (2).

(Added Pub.L. 99–514, Title XIV, § 1431(a), Oct. 22, 1986, 100 Stat. ——.)

SUBCHAPTER F—OTHER DEFINITIONS AND SPECIAL RULES

§ 2651. Generation assignment

(a) **In general.**—For purposes of this chapter, the generation to which any person (other than the transferor) belongs shall be determined in accordance with the rules set forth in this section.

(b) **Lineal descendants.**—

(1) **In general.**—An individual who is a lineal descendant of a grandparent of the transferor shall be assigned to that generation which results from comparing the number of generations between the grandparent and such individual with the number of generations between the grandparent and the transferor.

(2) **On spouse's side.**—An individual who is a lineal descendant of a grandparent of a spouse of the transferor (other than such spouse) shall be assigned to that generation which results from comparing the number of generations between such grandparent and such individual with the number of generations between such grandparent and such spouse.

(3) **Treatment of legal adoptions, etc.**—For purposes of this subsection—

(A) Legal adoptions.—A relationship by legal adoption shall be treated as a relationship by blood.

(B) Relationships by half-blood.—A relationship by the half-blood shall be treated as a relationship of the whole-blood.

(c) Marital relationship.—

(1) Marriage to transferor.—An individual who has been married at any time to the transferor shall be assigned to the transferor's generation.

(2) Marriage to other lineal descendants.—An individual who has been married at any time to an individual described in subsection (b) shall be assigned to the generation of the individual so described.

(d) Persons who are not lineal descendants.—An individual who is not assigned to a generation by reason of the foregoing provisions of this section shall be assigned to a generation on the basis of the date of such individual's birth with—

(1) an individual born not more than 12½ years after the date of the birth of the transferor assigned to the transferor's generation,

(2) an individual born more than 12½ years but not more than 37½ years after the date of the birth of the transferor assigned to the first generation younger than the transferor, and

(3) similar rules for a new generation every 25 years.

(e) Other special rules.—

(1) Individuals assigned to more than 1 generation.—Except as provided in regulations, an individual who, but for this subsection, would be assigned to more than 1 generation shall be assigned to the youngest such generation.

(2) Interests through entities.—Except as provided in paragraph (3), if an estate, trust, partnership, corporation, or other entity has an interest in property, each individual having a beneficial interest in such entity shall be treated as having an interest in such property and shall be assigned to a generation under the foregoing provisions of this subsection.

(3) Treatment of certain charitable organizations.—Any organization described in section 511(a)(2) and any charitable trust described in section 511(b)(2) shall be assigned to the transferor's generation.

(Added Pub.L. 99–514, Title XIV, § 1431(a), Oct. 22, 1986, 100 Stat. ——.)

§ 2652. Other definitions

(a) Transferor.—For purposes of this chapter—

(1) In general.—Except as provided in this subsection or section 2653(a), the term "transferor" means—

(A) in the case of a transfer of a kind subject to the tax imposed by chapter 11, the decedent, and

(B) in the case of a transfer of a kind subject to the tax imposed by chapter 12, the donor.

(2) Gift-splitting by married couples.—If, under section 2513, one-half of a gift is treated as made by an individual and one-half of such gift is treated as made by the spouse of such individual, such gift shall be so treated for purposes of this chapter.

(3) Special election for qualified terminable interest property.—In the case of—

(A) any property with respect to which a deduction is allowed to the decedent under section 2056 by reason of subsection (b)(7) thereof, and

(B) any property with respect to which a deduction to the donor spouse is allowed under section 2523 by reason of subsection (f) thereof,

the estate of the decedent or the donor spouse, as the case may be, may elect to treat such property for purposes of this chapter as if the election to be treated as qualified terminable interest property had not been made.

(b) Trust and trustee.—

(1) Trust.—The term "trust" includes any arrangement (other than an estate) which, although not a trust, has substantially the same effect as a trust.

(2) Trustee.—In the case of an arrangement which is not a trust but which is treated as a trust under this subsection, the term "trustee" shall mean the person in actual or constructive possession of the property subject to such arrangement.

(3) Examples.—Arrangements to which this subsection applies include arrangements involving life estates and remainders, estates for years, and insurance and annuity contracts.

(c) Interest.—

(1) In general.—A person has an interest in property held in trust if (at the time the determination is made) such person—

(A) has a right (other than a future right) to receive income or corpus from the trust,

(B) is a permissible current recipient of income or corpus from the trust and is not described in section 2055(a), or

(C) is described in section 2055(a) and the trust is—

(i) a charitable remainder annuity trust,

(ii) a charitable remainder unitrust within the meaning of section 664, or

(iii) a pooled income fund within the meaning of section 642(c)(5).

(2) Certain nominal interests disregarded.—For purposes of paragraph (1), an interest which is used primarily to postpone or avoid the tax imposed by this chapter shall be disregarded.

(Added Pub.L. 99–514, Title XIV, § 1431(a), Oct. 22, 1986, 100 Stat. ——.)

§ 2653. Taxation of multiple skips

(a) General rule.—For purposes of this chapter, if—

(1) there is a generation-skipping transfer of any property, and

(2) immediately after such transfer such property is held in trust,

for purposes of applying this chapter (other than section 2651) to subsequent transfers from the portion of such trust attributable to such property, the trust will be treated as if the transferor of such property were assigned to the first generation above the highest generation of any person who has an interest in such trust immediately after the transfer.

(b) Trust retains inclusion ratio.—

(1) In general.—Except as provided in paragraph (2), the provisions of subsection (a) shall not affect the inclusion ratio determined with respect to any trust. Under regulations prescribed by the Secretary, notwithstanding the preceding sentence, proper adjustment shall be made to the inclusion ratio with respect to such trust to take into account any tax under this chapter borne by such trust which is imposed by this chapter on the transfer described in subsection (a).

(2) Special rule for pour-over trust.—

(A) In general.—If the generation-skipping transfer referred to in subsection (a) involves the transfer of property from 1 trust to another trust (hereinafter in this paragraph referred to as the "pour-over trust"), the inclusion ratio for the pour-over trust shall be determined by treating the nontax portion of such distribution as if it were a part of a GST exemption allocated to such trust.

(B) Nontax portion.—For purposes of subparagraph (A), the nontax portion of any distribution is the amount of such distribution multiplied by the applicable fraction which applies to such distribution.

(Added Pub.L. 99–514, Title XIV, § 1431(a), Oct. 22, 1986, 100 Stat. ——.)

§ 2654. Special rules

(a) Basis adjustment.—

(1) In general.—Except as provided in paragraph (2), if property is transferred in a generation-skipping transfer, the basis of such property shall be increased (but not above the fair market value of such property) by an amount equal to that portion of the tax imposed by section 2601 (computed without regard to section 2604) with respect to the transfer which is attributable to the excess of the fair market value of such property over its adjusted basis immediately before the transfer.

(2) Certain transfers at death.—If property is transferred in a taxable termination which occurs at the same time as and as a result of the death of an individual, the basis of such property shall be adjusted in a manner similar to the manner provided under section 1014(a); except that, if the inclusion ratio with respect to such property is less than 1, any increase in basis shall be limited by multiplying such increase by the inclusion ratio.

(b) Separate shares treated as separate trusts.—Substantially separate and independent shares of different beneficiaries in a trust shall be treated as separate trusts.

(c) Disclaimers.—

For provisions relating to the effect of a qualified disclaimer for purposes of this chapter, see section 2518.

(d) Limitation on personal liability of trustee.—A trustee shall not be personally liable for any increase in the tax imposed by section 2601 which is attributable to the fact that—

(1) section 2642(c) (relating to exemption of certain nontaxable gifts) does not apply to a transfer to the trust which was made during the life of the transferor and for which a gift tax return was not filed, or

(2) the inclusion ratio with respect to the trust is greater than the amount of such ratio as computed on the basis of the return on which was made (or was deemed made) an allocation of the GST exemption to property transferred to such trust.

The preceding sentence shall not apply if the trustee has knowledge of facts sufficient reasonably to conclude that a gift tax return was required to be filed or that the inclusion ratio was erroneous.

(Added Pub.L. 99–514, Title XIV, § 1431(a), Oct. 22, 1986, 100 Stat. ——.)

SUBCHAPTER G—ADMINISTRATION

§ 2661. Administration

Insofar as applicable and not inconsistent with the provisions of this chapter—

(1) except as provided in paragraph (2), all provisions of subtitle F (including penalties) applicable to the gift tax, to chapter 12, or to section 2501, are hereby made applicable in respect of the generation-skipping transfer tax, this chapter, or section 2601, as the case may be, and

(2) in the case of a generation-skipping transfer occurring at the same time as and as a result of the death of an individual, all provisions of subtitle F (including penalties) applicable to the estate tax, to chapter 11, or to section 2001 are hereby made applicable in respect of the generation-skipping transfer tax, this chapter, or section 2601 (as the case may be).

(Added Pub.L. 99–514, Title XIV, § 1431(a), Oct. 22, 1986, 100 Stat. ——.)

§ 2662. Return requirements

(a) **In general.**—The Secretary shall prescribe by regulations the person who is required to make the return with respect to the tax imposed by this chapter and the time by which any such return must be filed. To the extent practicable, such regulations shall provide that—

(1) the person who is required to make such return shall be the person liable under section 2603(a) for payment of such tax, and

(2) the return shall be filed—

(A) in the case of a direct skip (other than from a trust), on or before the date on which an estate or gift tax return is required to be filed with respect to the transfer, and

(B) in all other cases, on or before the 15th day of the 4th month after the close of the taxable year of the person required to make such return in which such transfer occurs.

(b) **Information returns.**—The Secretary may by regulations require a return to be filed containing such information as he determines to be necessary for purposes of this chapter.

(Added Pub.L. 99–514, Title XIV, § 1431(a), Oct. 22, 1986, 100 Stat. ——.)

§ 2663. Regulations

The Secretary shall prescribe such regulations as may be necessary or appropriate to carry out the purposes of this chapter, including—

(1) such regulations as may be necessary to coordinate the provisions of this chapter with the recapture tax imposed under section 2032A(c), and

(2) regulations (consistent with the principles of chapters 11 and 12) providing for the application of this chapter in the case of transferors who are nonresidents not citizens of the United States.

(Added Pub.L. 99–514, Title XIV, § 1431(a), Oct. 22, 1986, 100 Stat. ——.)

SUBTITLE F—PROCEDURE AND ADMINISTRATION

CHAPTER 61—INFORMATION AND RETURNS

SUBCHAPTER A—RETURNS AND RECORDS

PART II—TAX RETURNS OR STATEMENTS

* Omitted entirely.

749

Subpart B—Income Tax Returns

§ 6012.   Persons required to make returns of income

(a) General Rule.—Returns with respect to income taxes under subtitle A shall be made by the following:

(1)(A) Every individual having for the taxable year gross income which equals or exceeds the exemption amount, except that a return shall not be required of an individual—

(i) who is not married (determined by applying section 7703), is not a surviving spouse (as defined in section 2(a)), is not a head of a household (as defined in section 2(b)), and for the taxable year has gross income of less than the sum of the exemption amount plus the basic standard deduction applicable to such an individual,

(ii) who is a head of a household (as so defined) and for the taxable year has gross income of less than the sum of the exemption amount plus the basic standard deduction applicable to such an individual,

(iii) who is a surviving spouse (as so defined) and for the taxable year has gross income of less than the sum of the exemption amount plus the basic standard deduction applicable to such an individual, or

(iv) who is entitled to make a joint return and whose gross income, when combined with the gross income of his spouse, is, for the taxable year, less than the sum of twice the exemption amount plus the basic standard deduction applicable to a joint return, but only if such individual and his spouse, at the close of the taxable year, had the same household as their home.

Clause (iv) shall not apply if for the taxable year such spouse makes a separate return or any other taxpayer is entitled to an exemption for such spouse under section 151(c).

(B) The amount specified in clause (i), (ii), or (iii) of subparagraph (A) shall be increased by the amount of 1 additional standard deduction (within the meaning of section 63(c)(3)) in the case of an individual entitled to such deduction by reason of section 63(f)(1)(A) (relating to individuals age 65 or more), and the amount specified in clause (iv) of subparagraph (A) shall be increased by the amount of the additional standard deduction for each additional standard deduction to which the individual or his spouse is entitled by reason of section 63(f)(1).

(C) The exception under subparagraph (A) shall not apply to any individual—

(i) who is described in section 63(c)(5) and who has—

(I) income (other than earned income) in excess of the amount in effect under section 63(c)(5)(A) (relating to limitation on standard deduction in the case of certain dependents), or

(II) total gross income in excess of the standard deduction, or

(ii) for whom the standard deduction is zero under section 63(c)(6).

(D) For purposes of this subsection—

(i) The terms "standard deduction", "basic standard deduction" and "additional standard deduction" have the respective meanings given such terms by section 63(c).

(ii) The term "exemption amount" has the meaning given such term by section 151(d). In the case of an individual described in section 151(d)(2), the exemption amount shall be zero.

(2) Every corporation subject to taxation under subtitle A;

(3) Every estate the gross income of which for the taxable year is $600 or more;

(4) Every trust having for the taxable year any taxable income, or having gross income of $600 or over, regardless of the amount of taxable income;

(5) Every estate or trust of which any beneficiary is a nonresident alien;

(6) Every political organization (within the meaning of section 527(e)(1)), and every fund treated under section 527(g) as if it constituted a political organization, which has political organization taxable income (within the meaning of section 527(c)(1)) for the taxable year; and

(7) Every homeowners association (within the meaning of section 528(c)(1)) which has homeowners association taxable income (within the meaning of section 528(d) for the taxable year.

(8) Every individual who receives payments during the calendar year in which the taxable year begins under section 3507 (relating to advance payment of earned income credit).

(9) Every estate of an individual under chapter 7 or 11 of title 11 of the United States Code (relating to bankruptcy) the gross income of which for the taxable year is not less than the sum of the exemption amount plus the basic standard deduction under section 63(c)(2)(D).

except that subject to such conditions, limitations, and exceptions and under such regulations as may be prescribed by the Secretary, nonresident alien individuals subject to the tax imposed by section 871 and foreign corporations subject to the tax imposed by section 881 may be exempted from the requirement of making returns under this section.

(b) Returns Made by Fiduciaries and Receivers.—

(1) Returns of decedents.—If an individual is deceased, the return of such individual required under subsection (a) shall be made by his executor, administrator, or other person charged with the property of such decedent.

(2) Persons under a disability.—If an individual is unable to make a return required under subsection (a), the return of such individual shall be made by a duly authorized agent, his committee, guardian, fiduciary or other person charged with the care of the person or property of such individual. The preceding sentence shall not apply in the case of a receiver appointed by authority of law in possession of only a part of the property of an individual.

(3) Receivers, trustees and assignees for corporation.—In a case where a receiver, trustee in a case under title 11 of the United States Code, or assignee, by order of a court of competent jurisdiction, by operation of law or otherwise, has possession of or holds title to all or substantially all the property or business of a corporation, whether or not such property or business is being operated, such receiver, trustee, or assignee shall make the return of income for such corporation in the same manner and form as corporations are required to make such returns.

(4) Returns of estates and trusts.—Returns of an estate, a trust, or an estate of an individual under chapter 7 or 11 of title 11 of the United States Code shall be made by the fiduciary thereof.

(5) Joint fiduciaries.—Under such regulations as the Secretary may prescribe, a return made by one of two or more joint fiduciaries shall be sufficient compliance with the requirements of this section. A return made pursuant to this paragraph shall contain a statement that the fiduciary has sufficient knowledge of the affairs of the person for whom the return is made to enable him to make the return, and that the return is, to the best of his knowledge and belief, true and correct.

(c) Certain Income Earned Abroad or From Sale of Residence.—For purposes of this section, gross income shall be computed without regard to the exclusion provided for in section 121 (relating to one-time exclusion of gain from sale of principal residence by individual who has attained age 55) and without regard to the exclusion provided for in section 911 (relating to citizens or residents of the United States living abroad).

(d) Tax-exempt interest required to be shown on return.—Every person required to file a return under this section for the taxable year shall include on such return the amount of interest received or accrued during the taxable year which is exempt from the tax imposed by chapter 1.

(e) Consolidated Returns.—

For provisions relating to consolidated returns by affiliated corporations, see chapter 6.

§ 6013. Joint returns of income tax by husband and wife

(a) Joint returns.—A husband and wife may make a single return jointly of income taxes under subtitle A, even though one of the spouses has neither gross income nor deductions, except as provided below:

* * *

(2) no joint return shall be made if the husband and wife have different taxable years; except that if such taxable years begin on the same day and end on different days because of the death of either or both, then the joint return may be made with respect to the taxable year of each. The above exception shall not apply if the surviving spouse remarries before the close of his taxable year, nor if the taxable year of either spouse is a fractional part of a year under section 443(a) (1);

(3) in the case of death of one spouse or both spouses the joint return with respect to the decedent may be made only by his executor or administrator; except that in the case of the death of one spouse the joint return may be made by the surviving spouse with respect to both himself and the decedent if no return for the taxable year has been made by the decedent, no executor or administrator has been appointed, and no executor or administrator is appointed before the last day prescribed by law for filing the return of the surviving spouse. If an executor or administrator of the decedent is appointed after the making of the joint return by the surviving spouse, the executor or administrator may disaffirm such joint return by making, within 1 year after the last day prescribed by law for filing the return of the surviving spouse, a separate return for the taxable year of the decedent with respect to which the joint return was made, in which case the return made by the survivor shall constitute his separate return.

* * *

(c) Treatment of joint return after death of either spouse.—For purposes of sections 15, 443, and 7851(a)(1)(A), where the husband and wife have different taxable years because of the death of either spouse, the joint return shall be treated as if the taxable years of both spouses ended on the date of the closing of the surviving spouse's taxable year.

(d) Special rules.—For purposes of this section—

(1) the status as husband and wife of two individuals having taxable years beginning on the same day shall be determined—

(A) if both have the same taxable year—as of the close of such year; or

(B) if one dies before the close of the taxable year of the other—as of the time of such death;

(2) an individual who is legally separated from his spouse under a decree of divorce or of separate maintenance shall not be considered as married; and

(3) if a joint return is made, the tax shall be computed on the aggregate income and the liability with respect to the tax shall be joint and several.

(e) Spouse relieved of liability in certain cases.—

(1) In general.—Under regulations prescribed by the Secretary, if—

(A) a joint return has been made under this section for a taxable year,

(B) on such return there is a substantial understatement of tax attributable to grossly erroneous items of one spouse,

(C) the other spouse establishes that in signing the return he or she did not know, and had no reason to know, that there was such substantial understatement, and

(D) taking into account all the facts and circumstances, it is inequitable to hold the other spouse liable for the deficiency in tax for such taxable year attributable to such substantial understatement,

then the other spouse shall be relieved of liability for tax (including interest, penalties, and other amounts) for such taxable year to the extent such liability is attributable to such substantial understatement.

(2) Grossly erroneous items.—For purposes of this subsection, the term "grossly erroneous items" means, with respect to any spouse—

(A) any item of gross income attributable to such spouse which is omitted from gross income, and

(B) any claim of a deduction, credit, or basis by such spouse in an amount for which there is no basis in fact or law.

(3) Substantial understatement.—For purposes of this subsection, the term "substantial understatement" means any understatement (as defined in section 6661(b)(2)(A)) which exceeds $500.

(4) Understatement must exceed specified percentage of spouse's income.—

(A) **Adjusted gross income of $20,000 or less.**—If the spouse's adjusted gross income for the preadjustment year is $20,000 or less, this subsection shall apply only if the liability described in paragraph (1) is greater than 10 percent of such adjusted gross income.

(B) **Adjusted gross income of more than $20,000.**—If the spouse's adjusted gross income for the preadjustment year is more than $20,000, subparagraph (A) shall be applied by substituting "25 percent" for "10 percent".

(C) **Preadjustment year.**—For purposes of this paragraph, the term "preadjustment year" means the most recent taxable year of the spouse ending before the date the deficiency notice is mailed.

(D) **Computation of spouse's adjusted gross income.**—If the spouse is married to another spouse at the close of the preadjustment year, the spouse's adjusted gross income shall include the income of the new spouse (whether or not they file a joint return).

(E) Exception for omissions from gross income.—This paragraph shall not apply to any liability attributable to the omission of an item from gross income.

(5) Special rule for community property income.—For purposes of this subsection, the determination of the spouse to whom items of gross income (other than gross income from property) are attributable shall be made without regard to community property laws.

* * *

Subpart C—Estate and Gift Tax Returns

§ 6018.   Estate tax returns

(a) Returns by executor.—

(1) Citizens or residents.—In all cases where the gross estate at the death of a citizen or resident exceeds $600,000, the executor shall make a return with respect to the estate tax imposed by subtitle B.

* * *

(3) Phase-in of filing requirement amount.—

In the case of decedents dying in:	Paragraph (1) shall be applied by substituting for "$600,000" the following amount:
1982	$225,000
1983	275,000
1984	325,000
1985	400,000
1986	500,000

(4) Adjustment for certain gifts.—The amount applicable under paragraph (1) and the amount set forth in paragraph (2) shall each be reduced (but not below zero) by the sum of—

(A) the amount of the adjusted taxable gifts (within the meaning of section 2001(b)) made by the decedent after December 31, 1976, plus

(B) the aggregate amount allowed as a specific exemption under section 2521 (as in effect before its repeal by the Tax Reform Act of 1976) with respect to gifts made by the decedent after September 8, 1976.

(b) Returns by beneficiaries.—If the executor is unable to make a complete return as to any part of the gross estate of the decedent, he shall include in his return a description of such part and the name of every person holding a legal or beneficial interest therein. Upon notice from the Secretary such person shall in like manner make a return as to such part of the gross estate.

* * *

§ 6019.   Gift tax returns

Any individual who in any calendar year makes any transfer by gift other than—

(1) a transfer which under subsection (b) or (e) of section 2503 is not to be included in the total amount of gifts for such year, or

(2) a transfer of an interest with respect to which a deduction is allowed under section 2523,

shall make a return for such year with respect to the gift tax imposed by subtitle B.

PART III—INFORMATION RETURNS

Subpart
 A. Information concerning persons subject to special provisions.
 B. Information concerning transactions with other persons.
 C. Information regarding wages paid employees.*
 [D. Repealed]
 E. Registration of and information concerning pension, etc., plans.*
 F. Information concerning income tax return preparers.*

Subpart A—Information Concerning Persons Subject to Special Provisions

§ 6031. Return of partnership income

(a) General rule.—Every partnership (as defined in section 761(a)) shall make a return for each taxable year, stating specifically the items of its gross income and the deductions allowable by subtitle A, and such other information for the purpose of carrying out the provisions of subtitle A as the Secretary may by forms and regulations prescribe, and shall include in the return the names and addresses of the individuals who would be entitled to share in the taxable income if distributed and the amount of the distributive share of each individual.

(b) Copies to partners.—Each partnership required to file a return under subsection (a) for any partnership taxable year shall (on or before the day on which the return for such taxable year was required to be filed) furnish to each person who is a partner or who holds an interest in such partnership as a nominee for another person at any time during such taxable year a copy of such information required to be shown on such return as may be required by regulations.

(c) Nominee reporting.—Any person who holds an interest in a partnership as a nominee for another person—

(1) shall furnish to the partnership, in the manner prescribed by the Secretary, the name and address of such other person, and any other information for such taxable year as the Secretary may by form and regulation prescribe, and

(2) shall furnish in the manner prescribed by the Secretary such other person the information provided by such partnership under subsection (b).

§ 6036. Notice of qualification as executor or receiver

Every receiver, trustee in a case under title 11 of the United States Code, assignee for benefit of creditors, or other like fiduciary, and every executor (as defined in section 2203), shall give notice of his qualification as such to the Secretary in such manner and at such time as may be required by regulations of the Secretary. The Secretary may by regulation provide such exemptions from the requirements of this section as the Secretary deems proper.

§ 6037. Return of S corporation

(a) In general.—Every S corporation shall make a return for each taxable year, stating specifically the items of its gross income and the deductions allowable by

* Omitted entirely.

subtitle A, the names and addresses of all persons owning stock in the corporation at any time during the taxable year, the number of shares of stock owned by each shareholder at all times during the taxable year, the amount of money and other property distributed by the corporation during the taxable year to each shareholder, the date of each such distribution, each shareholder's pro rata share of each item of the corporation for the taxable year, and such other information, for the purpose of carrying out the provisions of subchapter S of chapter 1, as the Secretary may by forms and regulations prescribe. Any return filed pursuant to this section shall, for purposes of chapter 66 (relating to limitations), be treated as a return filed by the corporation under section 6012.

(b) Copies to shareholders.—Each S corporation required to file a return under subsection (a) for any taxable year shall (on or before the day on which the return for such taxable year was filed) furnish to each person who is a shareholder at any time during such taxable year a copy of such information shown on such return as may be required by regulations.

Subpart B—Information Concerning Transactions With Other Persons

§ 6042. Returns regarding payments of dividends and corporate earnings and profits

(a) Requirement of reporting.—

(1) In general.—Every person—

(A) who makes payments of dividends aggregating $10 or more to any other person during any calendar year, or

(B) who receives payments of dividends as a nominee and who makes payments aggregating $10 or more during any calendar year to any other person with respect to the dividends so received,

shall make a return according to the forms or regulations prescribed by the Secretary, setting forth the aggregate amount of such payments and the name and address of the person to whom paid.

(2) Returns required by the Secretary.—Every person who makes payments of dividends aggregating less than $10 to any other person during any calendar year shall, when required by the Secretary, make a return setting forth the aggregate amount of such payments, and the name and address of the person to whom paid.

(b) Dividend defined.—

(1) General rule.—For purposes of this section, the term "dividend" means—

(A) any distribution by a corporation which is a dividend (as defined in section 316); and

(B) any payment made by a stockbroker to any person as a substitute for a dividend (as so defined).

* * *

(c) Statements to be furnished to persons with respect to whom information is required.—Every person required to make a return under subsection (a) shall furnish to each person whose name is required to be set forth in such return a written statement showing—

(1) the name and address of the person required to make such return, and

(2) the aggregate amount of payments to the person required to be shown on the return.

The written statement required under the preceding sentence shall be furnished (either in person or in a statement mailing by first-class mail which includes adequate notice that the statement is enclosed) to the person on or before January 31 of the year following the calendar year for which the return under subsection (a) was required to be made and shall be in such form as the Secretary may prescribe by regulations.

(d) Statements to be furnished by corporations to Secretary.—Every corporation shall, when required by the Secretary—

(1) furnish to the Secretary a statement stating the name and address of each shareholder, and the number of shares owned by each shareholder;

(2) furnish to the Secretary a statement of such facts as will enable him to determine the portion of the earnings and profits of the corporation (including gains, profits, and income not taxed) accumulated during such periods as the Secretary may specify, which have been distributed or ordered to be distributed, respectively, to its shareholders during such taxable years as the Secretary may specify; and

(3) furnish to the Secretary a statement of its accumulated earnings and profits and the names and addresses of the individuals or shareholders who would be entitled to such accumulated earnings and profits if divided or distributed, and of the amounts that would be payable to each.

§ 6043. Returns regarding liquidation, dissolution, termination, or contraction

(a) Corporations.—Every corporation shall—

(1) Within 30 days after the adoption by the corporation of a resolution or plan for the dissolution of the corporation or for the liquidation of the whole or any part of its capital stock, make a return setting forth the terms of such resolution or plan and such other information as the Secretary shall by forms or regulations prescribe; and

(2) When required by the Secretary, make a return regarding its distributions in liquidation, stating the name and address of, the number and class of shares owned by, and the amount paid to, each shareholder, or, if the distribution is in property other than money, the fair market value (as of the date the distribution is made) of the property distributed to each shareholder.

* * *

§ 6045. Returns of brokers

(a) General rule.—Every person doing business as a broker shall, when required by the Secretary, make a return, in accordance with such regulations as the Secretary may prescribe, showing the name and address of each customer, with such details regarding gross proceeds and such other information as the Secretary may by forms or regulations require with respect to such business.

(b) Statements to be furnished to customers.—Every person required to make a return under subsection (a) shall furnish to each customer whose name is required to be set forth in such return a written statement showing—

(1) the name and address of the person required to make such return, and

(2) the information required to be shown on such return with respect to such customer.

The written statement required under the preceding sentence shall be furnished to the customer on or before January 31 of the year following the calendar year for which the return under subsection (a) was required to be made.

(c) **Definitions.**—For purposes of this section—

(1) **Broker.**—The term "broker" includes—

(A) a dealer,

(B) a barter exchange, and

(C) any other person who (for a consideration) regularly acts as a middleman with respect to property or services.

(2) **Customer.**—The term "customer" means any person for whom the broker has transacted any business.

(3) **Barter exchange.**—The term "barter exchange" means any organization of members providing property or services who jointly contract to trade or barter such property or services.

(4) **Person.**—The term "person" includes any governmental unit and any agency or instrumentality thereof.

(d) **Statements required in case of certain substitute payments.**—If any broker—

(1) transfers securities of a customer for use in a short sale or similar transaction, and

(2) receives (on behalf of the customer) a payment in lieu of—

(A) a dividend,

(B) tax-exempt interest, or

(C) such other items as the Secretary may prescribe by regulations,

during the period such short sale or similar transaction is open, the broker shall furnish such customer a written statement (at such time and in the manner as the Secretary shall prescribe by regulations) identifying such payment as being in lieu of the dividend, tax-exempt interest, or such other item. The Secretary may prescribe regulations which require the broker to make a return which includes the information contained in such written statement.

(e) **Return required in the case of real estate transactions.**—

(1) **In general.**—In the case of a real estate transaction, the real estate broker shall file a return under subsection (a) and a statement under subsection (b) with respect to such transaction.

(2) **Real estate broker.**—For purposes of this subsection, the term "real estate broker" means any of the following persons involved in a real estate transaction in the following order:

(A) the person (including any attorney or title company) responsible for closing the transaction,

(B) the mortgage lender,

(C) the seller's broker,

(D) the buyer's broker, or

(E) such other person designated in regulations prescribed by the Secretary.

Any person treated as a real estate broker under the preceding sentence shall be treated as a broker for purposes of subsection (c)(1).

§ 6050K. Returns relating to exchanges of certain partnership interests

(a) In general.—Except as provided in regulations prescribed by the Secretary, if there is an exchange described in section 751(a) of any interest in a partnership during any calendar year, such partnership shall make a return for such calendar year stating—

(1) the name and address of the transferee and transferor in such exchange, and

(2) such other information as the Secretary may by regulations prescribe.

Such return shall be made at such time and in such manner as the Secretary may require by regulations.

(b) Statements to be furnished to transferor and transferee.—Every partnership required to make a return under subsection (a) shall furnish to each person whose name is required to be set forth in such return a written statement showing—

(1) the name and address of the partnership required to make such return, and

(2) the information required to be shown on the return with respect to such person.

The written statement required under the preceding sentence shall be furnished to the person on or before January 31 of the year following the calendar year for which the return under subsection (a) was required to be made.

(c) Requirement that transferor notify partnership.—

(1) **In general.**—In the case of any exchange described in subsection (a), the transferor of the partnership interest shall promptly notify the partnership of such exchange.

(2) **Partnership not required to make return until notice.**—A partnership shall not be required to make a return under this section with respect to any exchange until the partnership is notified of such exchange.

§ 6050L. Returns relating to certain dispositions of donated property

(a) General rule.—If the donee of any charitable deduction property sells, exchanges, or otherwise disposes of such property within 2 years after its receipt, the donee shall make a return (in accordance with forms and regulations prescribed by the Secretary) showing—

(1) the name, address, and TIN of the donor,

(2) a description of the property,

(3) the date of the contribution,

(4) the amount received on the disposition, and

(5) the date of such disposition.

(b) Charitable deduction property.—For purposes of this section, the term "charitable deduction property" means any property (other than publicly traded securities) contributed in a contribution for which a deduction was claimed under section 170 if the claimed value of such property (plus the claimed value of all similar items of property donated by the donor to 1 or more donees) exceeds $5,000.

(c) Statement to be furnished to donors.—Every person making a return under subsection (a) shall furnish a copy of such return to the donor at such time and in such manner as the Secretary may by regulations prescribe.

(d) Definition of publicly traded securities.—The term "publicly traded securities" means securities for which (as of the date of the contribution) market quotations are readily available on an established securities market.

PART V—TIME FOR FILING RETURNS AND OTHER DOCUMENTS

§ 6072. Time for filing income tax returns

(a) General rule.—In the case of returns under section 6012, 6013, 6017, or 6031 (relating to income tax under subtitle A), returns made on the basis of the calendar year shall be filed on or before the 15th day of April following the close of the calendar year and returns made on the basis of a fiscal year shall be filed on or before the 15th day of the fourth month following the close of the fiscal year, except as otherwise provided in the following subsections of this section.

(b) Returns of corporations.—Returns of corporations under section 6012 made on the basis of the calendar year shall be filed on or before the 15th day of March following the close of the calendar year, and such returns made on the basis of a fiscal year shall be filed on or before the 15th day of the third month following the close of the fiscal year. Returns required for a taxable year by section 6011(e) (2) (relating to returns of a DISC) shall be filed on or before the fifteenth day of the ninth month following the close of the taxable year.

* * *

§ 6075. Time for filing estate and gift tax returns

(a) Estate tax returns.—Returns made under section 6018(a) (relating to estate taxes) shall be filed within 9 months after the date of the decedent's death.

(b) Gift tax returns.—

(1) **General rule.**—Returns made under section 6019 (relating to gift taxes) shall be filed on or before the 15th day of April following the close of the calendar year.

(2) **Extension where taxpayer granted extension for filing income tax return.**—Any extension of time granted the taxpayer for filing the return of income taxes imposed by subtitle A for any taxable year which is a calendar year shall be deemed to be also an extension of time granted the taxpayer for filing the return under section 6019 for such calendar year.

(3) **Coordination with due date for estate tax return.**—Notwithstanding paragraphs (1) and (2), the time for filing the return made under section 6019 for the calendar year which includes the date of death of the donor shall not be later than the time (including extensions) for filing the return made under section 6018 (relating to estate tax returns) with respect to such donor.

SUBCHAPTER B—MISCELLANEOUS PROVISIONS

§ 6111. Registration of tax shelters

(a) Registration.—

(1) **In general.**—Any tax shelter organizer shall register the tax shelter with the Secretary (in such form and in such manner as the Secretary may prescribe) not later than the day on which the first offering for sale of interests in such tax shelter occurs.

(2) **Information included in registration.**—Any registration under paragraph (1) shall include—

(A) information identifying and describing the tax shelter,

(B) information describing the tax benefits of the tax shelter represented (or to be represented) to investors, and

(C) such other information as the Secretary may prescribe.

(b) Furnishing of tax shelter identification number; inclusion on return.—

(1) Sellers, etc.—Any person who sells (or otherwise transfers) an interest in a tax shelter shall (at such times and in such manner as the Secretary shall prescribe) furnish to each investor who purchases (or otherwise acquires) an interest in such tax shelter from such person the identification number assigned by the Secretary to such tax shelter.

(2) Inclusion of number on return.—Any person claiming any deduction, credit, or other tax benefit by reason of a tax shelter shall include (in such manner as the Secretary may prescribe) on the return of tax on which such deduction, credit, or other benefit is claimed the identification number assigned by the Secretary to such tax shelter.

(c) Tax shelter.—For purposes of this section—

(1) In general.—The term "tax shelter" means any investment—

(A) with respect to which any person could reasonably infer from the representations made, or to be made, in connection with the offering for sale of interests in the investment that the tax shelter ratio for any investor as of the close of any of the first 5 years ending after the date on which such investment is offered for sale may be greater than 2 to 1, and

(B) which is—

(i) required to be registered under a Federal or State law regulating securities,

(ii) sold pursuant to an exemption from registration requiring the filing of a notice with a Federal or State agency regulating the offering or sale of securities, or

(iii) a substantial investment.

(2) Tax shelter ratio defined.—For purposes of this subsection, the term "tax shelter ratio" means, with respect to any year, the ratio which—

(A) the aggregate amount of the deductions and 350 percent of the credits which are represented to be potentially allowable to any investor under subtitle A for all periods up to (and including) the close of such year, bears to

(B) the investment base as of the close of such year.

(3) Investment base.—

(A) In general.—Except as provided in this paragraph, the term "investment base" means, with respect to any year, the amount of money and the adjusted basis of other property (reduced by any liability to which such other property is subject) contributed by the investor as of the close of such year.

(B) Certain borrowed amounts excluded.—For purposes of subparagraph (A), there shall not be taken into account any amount borrowed from any person—

(i) who participated in the organization, sale, or management of the investment, or

(ii) who is a related person (as defined in section 456(b)(3)(C)) to any person described in clause (i), unless such amount is unconditionally required to be repaid by the investor before the close of the year for which the determination is being made.

(C) Certain other amounts included or excluded.—

(i) Amounts held in cash equivalents, etc.—No amount shall be taken into account under subparagraph (A) which is to be held in cash equivalent or marketable securities.

(ii) Amounts included or excluded by secretary.—The Secretary may by regulation—

(I) exclude from the investment base any amount described in subparagraph (A), or

(II) include in the investment base any amount not described in subparagraph (A),

if the Secretary determines that such exclusion or inclusion is necessary to carry out the purposes of this section.

(4) Substantial investment.—An investment is a substantial investment if—

(A) the aggregate amount which may be offered for sale exceeds $250,000, and

(B) there are expected to be 5 or more investors.

(d) Other definitions.—For purposes of this section—

(1) Tax shelter organizer.—The term "tax shelter organizer" means—

(A) the person principally responsible for organizing the tax shelter,

(B) if the requirements of subsection (a) are not met by a person described in subparagraph (A) at the time prescribed therefor, any other person who participated in the organization of the tax shelter, and

(C) if the requirements of subsection (a) are not met by a person described in subparagraph (A) or (B) at the time prescribed therefor, any person participating in the sale or management of the investment at a time when the tax shelter was not registered under subsection (a).

(2) Year.—The term "year" means—

(A) the taxable year of the tax shelter, or

(B) if the tax shelter has no taxable year, the calendar year.

(e) Regulations.—The Secretary may prescribe regulations which provide—

(1) rules for the aggregation of similar investments offered by the same person or persons for purposes of applying subsection (c)(4),

(2) that only 1 person shall be required to meet the requirements of subsection (a) in cases in which 2 or more persons would otherwise be required to meet such requirements,

(3) exemptions from the requirements of this section, and

(4) such rules as may be necessary or appropriate to carry out the purposes of this section in the case of foreign tax shelters.

CHAPTER 62—TIME AND PLACE FOR PAYING TAX

Subchapter
A. Place and due date for payment of tax.*
B. Extensions of time for payment.

SUBCHAPTER B—EXTENSIONS OF TIME FOR PAYMENT

§ 6163. Extension of time for payment of estate tax on value of reversionary or remainder interest in property

(a) **Extension permitted.**—If the value of a reversionary or remainder interest in property is included under chapter 11 in the value of the gross estate, the payment of the part of the tax under chapter 11 attributable to such interest may, at the election of the executor, be postponed until 6 months after the termination of the precedent interest or interests in the property, under such regulations as the Secretary may prescribe.

(b) **Extension for reasonable cause.**—At the expiration of the period of postponement provided for in subsection (a), the Secretary may, for reasonable cause, extend the time for payment for a reasonable period or periods not in excess of 3 years from the expiration of the period of postponement provided in subsection (a).

(c) **Cross reference.**—

For authority of the Secretary to require security in the case of an extension under this section, see section 6165.

§ 6164. Extension of time for payment of taxes by corporations expecting carrybacks

(a) **In general.**—If a corporation, in any taxable year, files with the Secretary a statement, as provided in subsection (b), with respect to an expected net operating loss carryback from such taxable year, the time for payment of all or part of any tax imposed by subtitle A for the taxable year immediately preceding such taxable year shall be extended, to the extent and subject to the conditions and limitations hereinafter provided in this section.

* * *

§ 6166. Extension of time for payment of estate tax where estate consists largely of interest in closely held business

(a) **5-year deferral; 10-year installment payment.**—

(1) **In general.**—If the value of an interest in a closely held business which is included in determining the gross estate of a decedent who was (at the date of his death) a citizen or resident of the United States exceeds 35 percent of the adjusted gross estate, the executor may elect to pay part or all of the tax imposed by section 2001 in 2 or more (but not exceeding 10) equal installments.

(2) **Limitation.**—The maximum amount of tax which may be paid in installments under this subsection shall be an amount which bears the same ratio to the tax imposed by section 2001 (reduced by the credits against such tax) as—

* Omitted entirely.

(A) the closely held business amount, bears to

(B) the amount of the adjusted gross estate.

(3) Date for payment of installments.—If an election is made under paragraph (1), the first installment shall be paid on or before the date selected by the executor which is not more than 5 years after the date prescribed by section 6151(a) for payment of the tax, and each succeeding installment shall be paid on or before the date which is 1 year after the date prescribed by this paragraph for payment of the preceding installment.

(b) Definitions and special rules.—

(1) Interest in closely held business.—For purposes of this section, the term "interest in a closely held business" means—

(A) an interest as a proprietor in a trade or business carried on as a proprietorship;

(B) an interest as a partner in a partnership carrying on a trade or business, if—

(i) 20 percent or more of the total capital interest in such partnership is included in determining the gross estate of the decedent, or

(ii) such partnership had 15 or fewer partners; or

(C) stock in a corporation carrying on a trade or business if—

(i) 20 percent or more in value of the voting stock of such corporation is included in determining the gross estate of the decedent, or

(ii) such corporation had 15 or fewer shareholders.

(2) Rules for applying paragraph (1).—For purposes of paragraph (1)—

(A) Time for testing.—Determinations shall be made as of the time immediately before the decedent's death.

(B) Certain interests held by husband and wife.—Stock or a partnership interest which—

(i) is community property of a husband and wife (or the income from which is community income) under the applicable community property law of a State, or

(ii) is held by a husband and wife as joint tenants, tenants by the entirety, or tenants in common,

shall be treated as owned by one shareholder or one partner, as the case may be.

(C) Indirect ownership.—Property owned, directly or indirectly, by or for a corporation, partnership, estate, or trust shall be considered as being owned proportionately by or for its shareholders, partners, or beneficiaries. For purposes of the preceding sentence, a person shall be treated as a beneficiary of any trust only if such person has a present interest in the trust.

(D) Certain interests held by members of decedent's family.—All stock and all partnership interests held by the decedent or by any member of his family (within the meaning of section 267(c)(4)) shall be treated as owned by the decedent.

(3) Farmhouses and certain other structures taken into account.—For purposes of the 35-percent requirement of subsection (a)(1), an interest in a closely held business which is the business of farming includes an interest in residential buildings and related improvements on the farm which are occupied on a regular basis by the owner or lessee of the farm or by persons employed by such owner or lessee for purposes of operating or maintaining the farm.

(4) **Value.**—For purposes of this section, value shall be value determined for purposes of chapter 11 (relating to estate tax).

(5) **Closely held business amount.**—For purposes of this section, the term "closely held business amount" means the value of the interest in a closely held business which qualifies under subsection (a)(1).

(6) **Adjusted gross estate.**—For purposes of this section, the term, "adjusted gross estate" means the value of the gross estate reduced by the sum of the amounts allowable as a deduction under section 2053 or 2054. Such sum shall be determined on the basis of the facts and circumstances in existence on the date (including extensions) for filing the return of tax imposed by section 2001 (or, if earlier, the date on which such return is filed).

(7) **Partnership interests and stock which is not readily tradable.**—

(A) **In general.**—If the executor elects the benefits of this paragraph (at such time and in such manner as the Secretary shall by regulations prescribe), then—

(i) for purposes of paragraph (1)(B)(i) or (1)(C)(i) (whichever is appropriate) and for purposes of subsection (c), any capital interest in a partnership and any non-readily-tradable stock which (after the application of paragraph (2)) is treated as owned by the decedent shall be treated as included in determining the value of the decedent's gross estate,

(ii) the executor shall be treated as having selected under subsection (a)(3) the date prescribed by section 6151(a), and

(iii) section 6601(j) (relating to 4-percent rate of interest) shall not apply.

(B) **Non-readily-tradable stock defined.**—For purposes of this paragraph, the term "non-readily-tradable stock" means stock for which, at the time of the decedent's death, there was no market on a stock exchange or in an over-the-counter market.

(8) **Stock in holding company treated as business company stock in certain cases.**—

(A) **In general.**—If the executor elects the benefits of this paragraph, then—

(i) **Holding company stock treated as business company stock.**—For purposes of this section, the portion of the stock of any holding company which represents direct ownership (or indirect ownership through 1 or more other holding companies) by such company in a business company shall be deemed to be stock in such business company.

(ii) **5-year deferral for principal not to apply.**—The executor shall be treated as having selected under subsection (a)(3) the date prescribed by section 6151(a).

(iii) **4-percent interest rate not to apply.**—Section 6601(j) (relating to 4-percent rate of interest) shall not apply.

(B) **All stock must be non-readily-tradable stock.**—No stock shall be taken into account for purposes of applying this paragraph unless it is non-readily-tradable stock (within the meaning of paragraph (7)(B)).

(C) **Application of voting stock requirement of paragraph (1)(C)(i).**—For purposes of clause (i) of paragraph (1)(C), the deemed stock resulting from the application of subparagraph (A) shall be treated as voting stock to the extent that voting stock in the holding company owns directly (or through the voting stock of 1 or more other holding companies) voting stock in the business company.

(D) Definitions.—For purposes of this paragraph—

(i) Holding company.—The term "holding company" means any corporation holding stock in another corporation.

(ii) Business company.—The term "business company" means any corporation carrying on a trade or business.

(9) Deferral not available for passive assets.—

(A) In general.—For purposes of subsection (a)(1) and determining the closely held business amount (but not for purposes of subsection (g)), the value of any interest in a closely held business shall not include the value of that portion of such interest which is attributable to passive assets held by the business.

(B) Passive asset defined.—For purposes of this paragraph—

(i) In general.—The term "passive asset" means any asset other than an asset used in carrying on a trade or business.

(ii) Stock treated as passive asset.—The term "passive asset" includes any stock in another corporation unless—

(I) such stock is treated as held by the decedent by reason of an election under paragraph (8), and

(II) such stock qualified under subsection (a)(1).

(iii) Exception for active corporations.—If—

(I) a corporation owns 20 percent or more in value of the voting stock of another corporation, or such other corporation has 15 or fewer shareholders, and

(II) 80 percent or more of the value of the assets of each such corporation is attributable to assets used in carrying on a trade or business,

then such corporations shall be treated as 1 corporation for purposes of clause (ii). For purposes of applying subclause (II) to the corporation holding the stock of the other corporation, such stock shall not be taken into account.

(c) Special rule for interests in 2 or more closely held businesses.—For purposes of this section, interests in 2 or more closely held businesses, with respect to each of which there is included in determining the value of the decedent's gross estate 20 percent or more of the total value of each such business, shall be treated as an interest in a single closely held business. For purposes of the 20-percent requirement of the preceding sentence, an interest in a closely held business which represents the surviving spouse's interest in property held by the decedent and the surviving spouse as community property or as joint tenants, tenants by the entirety, or tenants in common shall be treated as having been included in determining the value of the decedent's gross estate.

(d) Election.—Any election under subsection (a) shall be made not later than the time prescribed by section 6075(a) for filing the return of tax imposed by section 2001 (including extensions thereof), and shall be made in such manner as the Secretary shall by regulations prescribe. If an election under subsection (a) is made, the provisions of this subtitle shall apply as though the Secretary were extending the time for payment of the tax.

(e) Proration of deficiency to installments.—If an election is made under subsection (a) to pay any part of the tax imposed by section 2001 in installments and a deficiency has been assessed, the deficiency shall (subject to the limitation provided by subsection (a)(2)) be prorated to the installments payable under subsection (a). The part of the deficiency so prorated to any installment the date for payment of which has not arrived shall be collected at the same time as, and as a part of, such installment. The part of the deficiency so prorated to any installment the date for payment of which has arrived shall be paid upon notice and demand from the Secretary. This subsection shall not apply if the deficiency is due to negligence, to intentional disregard of rules and regulations, or to fraud with intent to evade tax.

(f) Time for payment of interest.—If the time for payment of any amount of tax has been extended under this section—

(1) Interest for first 5 years.—Interest payable under section 6601 of any unpaid portion of such amount attributable to the first 5 years after the date prescribed by section 6151(a) for payment of the tax shall be paid annually.

(2) Interest for periods after first 5 years.—Interest payable under section 6601 on any unpaid portion of such amount attributable to any period after the 5-year period referred to in paragraph (1) shall be paid annually at the same time as, and as a part of, each installment payment of the tax.

(3) Interest in the case of certain deficiencies.—In the case of a deficiency to which subsection (e) applies which is assessed after the close of the 5-year period referred to in paragraph (1), interest attributable to such 5-year period, and interest assigned under paragraph (2) to any installment the date for payment of which has arrived on or before the date of the assessment of the deficiency, shall be paid upon notice and demand from the Secretary.

(4) Selection of shorter period.—If the executor has selected a period shorter than 5 years under subsection (a)(3), such shorter period shall be substituted for 5 years in paragraphs (1), (2), and (3) of this subsection.

(g) Acceleration of payment.—

(1) Disposition of interest; withdrawal of funds from business.—

(A) If—

(i)(I) any portion of an interest in a closely held business which qualifies under subsection (a)(1) is distributed, sold, exchanged, or otherwise disposed of, or

(II) money and other property attributable to such an interest is withdrawn from such trade or business, and

(ii) the aggregate of such distributions, sales, exchanges, or other dispositions and withdrawals equals or exceeds 50 percent of the value of such interest,

then the extension of time for payment of tax provided in subsection (a) shall cease to apply, and the unpaid portion of the tax payable in installments shall be paid upon notice and demand from the Secretary.

(B) In the case of a distribution in redemption of stock to which section 303 (or so much of section 304 as relates to section 303) applies—

(i) the redemption of such stock, and the withdrawal of money and other property distributed in such redemption, shall not be treated as a distribution or withdrawal for purposes of subparagraph (A), and

(ii) for purposes of subparagraph (A), the value of the interest in the closely held business shall be considered to be such value reduced by the value of the stock redeemed.

This subparagraph shall apply only if, on or before the date prescribed by subsection (a)(3) for the payment of the first installment which becomes due after the date of the distribution (or, if earlier, on or before the day which is 1 year after the date of the distribution), there is paid an amount of the tax imposed by section 2001 not less than the amount of money and other property distributed.

(C) Subparagraph (A)(i) does not apply to an exchange of stock pursuant to a plan of reorganization described in subparagraph (D), (E), or (F) of section 368(a)(1) nor to an exchange to which section 355 (or so much of section 356 as relates to section 355) applies; but any stock received in such an exchange shall be treated for purposes of subparagraph (A)(i) as an interest qualifying under subsection (a)(1).

(D) Subparagraph (A)(i) does not apply to a transfer of property of the decedent to a person entitled by reason of the decedent's death to receive such property under the decedent's will, the applicable law of descent and distribution, or a trust created by the decedent. A similar rule shall apply in the case of a series of subsequent transfers of the property by reason of death so long as each transfer is to a member of the family (within the meaning of section 267(c)(4)) of the transferor in such transfer.

(E) Changes in interest in holding company.—If any stock in a holding company is treated as stock in a business company by reason of subsection (b)(8)(A)—

    (i) any disposition of any interest in such stock in such holding company which was included in determining the gross estate of the decedent, or

    (ii) any withdrawal of any money or other property from such holding company attributable to any interest included in determining the gross estate of the decedent,

shall be treated for purposes of subparagraph (a) as a disposition of (or a withdrawal with respect to) the stock qualifying under subsection (a)(1).

(F) Changes in interest in business company.—If any stock in a holding company is treated as stock in a business company by reason of subsection (b)(8)(A)—

    (i) any disposition of any interest in such stock in the business company by such holding company, or

    (ii) any withdrawal of any money or other property from such business company attributable to such stock by such holding company owning such stock,

shall be treated for purposes of subparagraph (a) as a disposition of (or a withdrawal with respect to) the stock qualifying under subsection (a)(1).

(2) Undistributed income of estate.—

(A) If an election is made under this section and the estate has undistributed net income for any taxable year ending on or after the due date for the first installment, the executor shall, on or before the date prescribed by law for filing the income tax return for such taxable year (including extensions thereof), pay an amount equal to such undistributed net income in liquidation of the unpaid portion of the tax payable in installments.

(B) For purposes of subparagraph (A), the undistributed net income of the estate for any taxable year is the amount by which the distributable net income of the estate for such taxable year (as defined in section 643) exceeds the sum of—

(i) the amounts for such taxable year specified in paragraphs (1) and (2) of section 661(a) (relating to deductions for distributions, etc.);

(ii) the amount of tax imposed for the taxable year on the estate under chapter 1; and

(iii) the amount of the tax imposed by section 2001 (including interest) paid by the executor during the taxable year (other than any amount paid pursuant to this paragraph).

(C) For purposes of this paragraph, if any stock in a corporation is treated as stock in another corporation by reason of subsection (b)(8)(A), any dividends paid by such other corporation to the corporation shall be treated as paid to the estate of the decedent to the extent attributable to the stock qualifying under subsection (a)(1).

(3) Failure to make payment of principal or interest.—

(A) In general.—Except as provided in subparagraph (B), if any payment of principal or interest under this section is not paid on or before the date fixed for its payment by this section (including any extension of time), the unpaid portion of the tax payable in installments shall be paid upon notice and demand from the Secretary.

(B) Payment within 6 months.—If any payment of principal or interest under this section is not paid on or before the date determined under subparagraph (A) but is paid within 6 months of such date—

(i) the provisions of subparagraph (A) shall not apply with respect to such payment,

(ii) the provisions of section 6601(j) shall not apply with respect to the determination of interest on such payment, and

(iii) there is imposed a penalty in an amount equal to the product of—

(I) 5 percent of the amount of such payment, multiplied by

(II) the number of months (or fractions thereof) after such date and before payment is made.

The penalty imposed under clause (iii) shall be treated in the same manner as a penalty imposed under subchapter B of chapter 68.

(h) Election in case of certain deficiencies.—

(1) In general.—If—

(A) a deficiency in the tax imposed by section 2001 is assessed,

(B) the estate qualifies under subsection (a)(1), and

(C) the executor has not made an election under subsection (a),

the executor may elect to pay the deficiency in installments. This subsection shall not apply if the deficiency is due to negligence, to intentional disregard of rules and regulations, or to fraud with intent to evade tax.

(2) Time of election.—An election under this subsection shall be made not later than 60 days after issuance of notice and demand by the Secretary for the payment of the deficiency, and shall be made in such manner as the Secretary shall by regulations prescribe.

(3) Effect of election on payment.—If an election is made under this subsection, the deficiency shall (subject to the limitation provided by subsection (a)(2)) be prorated to the installments which would have been due if an election had been timely made under subsection (a) at the time the estate tax return was filed. The part of the deficiency so prorated to any installment the date for payment of which would have arrived shall be paid at the time of the making of the election under this subsection. The portion of the deficiency so prorated to installments the date for payment of which would not have so arrived shall be paid at the time such installments would have been due if such an election had been made.

(i) Special rule for certain direct skips.—To the extent that an interest in a closely held business is the subject of a direct skip (within the meaning of section 2612(c)) occurring at the same time as and as a result of the decedent's death, then for purposes of this section any tax imposed by section 2601 on the transfer of such interest shall be treated as if it were additional tax imposed by section 2001.

(j) Regulations.—The Secretary shall prescribe such regulations as may be necessary to the application of this section.

* * *

CHAPTER 63—ASSESSMENT

Subchapter
- A. In general.
- B. Deficiency procedures in the case of income, estate, gift, and certain excise taxes.
- C. Tax treatment of partnership items.
- D. Tax treatment of subchapter S items.

SUBCHAPTER A—IN GENERAL

§ 6201. Assessment authority

(a) Authority of Secretary.—The Secretary is authorized and required to make the inquiries, determinations, and assessments of all taxes (including interest, additional amounts, additions to the tax, and assessable penalties) imposed by this title, or accruing under any former internal revenue law, which have not been duly paid by stamp at the time and in the manner provided by law. Such authority shall extend to and include the following:

(1) Taxes shown on return.—The Secretary shall assess all taxes determined by the taxpayer or by the Secretary as to which returns or lists are made under this title.

* * *

(c) Compensation of child.—Any income tax under chapter 1 assessed against a child, to the extent attributable to amounts includible in the gross income of the child, and not of the parent, solely by reason of section 73(a), shall, if not paid by the child, for all purposes be considered as having also been properly assessed against the parent.

* * *

SUBCHAPTER B—DEFICIENCY PROCEDURES IN THE CASE OF INCOME, ESTATE, GIFT, AND CERTAIN EXCISE TAXES

§ 6211. Definition of a deficiency

(a) In general.—For purposes of this title in the case of income, estate, and gift taxes imposed by subtitles A and B and excise taxes imposed by chapters 41, 42, 43,

44, and 45 the term "deficiency" means the amount by which the tax imposed by subtitle A or B, or chapter 41, 42, 43, 44, or 45 exceeds the excess of—

(1) the sum of

(A) the amount shown as the tax by the taxpayer upon his return, if a return was made by the taxpayer and an amount was shown as the tax by the taxpayer thereon, plus

(B) the amounts previously assessed (or collected without assessment) as a deficiency, over—

(2) the amount of rebates, as defined in subsection (b) (2), made.

(b) Rules for application of subsection (a).—For purposes of this section—

(1) The tax imposed by subtitle A and the tax shown on the return shall both be determined without regard to payments on account of estimated tax, without regard to the credit under section 31, without regard to the credit under section 33, and without regard to any credits resulting from the collection of amounts assessed under section 6851 (relating to termination assessments).

(2) The term "rebate" means so much of an abatement, credit, refund, or other repayment, as was made on the ground that the tax imposed by subtitle A or B or chapter 41, 42, 43, 44, or 45 was less than the excess of the amount specified in subsection (a) (1) over the rebates previously made.

* * *

§ 6212. Notice of deficiency

(a) In general.—If the Secretary determines that there is a deficiency in respect of any tax imposed by subtitles A or B or chapter 41, 42, 43, 44, or 45, he is authorized to send notice of such deficiency to the taxpayer by certified mail or registered mail.

(b) Address for notice of deficiency.—

(1) Income and gift taxes and certain excise taxes.—In the absence of notice to the Secretary under section 6903 of the existence of a fiduciary relationship, notice of a deficiency in respect of a tax imposed by subtitle A, chapter 12, chapter 41, chapter 42, chapter 43, chapter 44, or chapter 45, if mailed to the taxpayer at his last known address, shall be sufficient for purposes of subtitle A, chapter 12, chapter 41, chapter 42, chapter 43, chapter 44, chapter 45, and this chapter even if such taxpayer is deceased, or is under a legal disability, or, in the case of a corporation, has terminated its existence.

(2) Joint income tax return.—In the case of a joint income tax return filed by husband and wife, such notice of deficiency may be a single joint notice, except that if the Secretary has been notified by either spouse that separate residences have been established, then, in lieu of the single joint notice, a duplicate original of the joint notice shall be sent by certified mail or registered mail to each spouse at his last known address.

(3) Estate tax.—In the absence of notice to the Secretary under section 6903 of the existence of a fiduciary relationship, notice of a deficiency in respect of a tax imposed by chapter 11, if addressed in the name of the decedent or other person subject to liability and mailed to his last known address, shall be sufficient for purposes of chapter 11 and of this chapter.

(c) Further deficiency letters restricted.—

(1) General rule.—If the Secretary has mailed to the taxpayer a notice of deficiency as provided in subsection (a), and the taxpayer files a petition with the

Tax Court within the time prescribed in section 6213(a), the Secretary shall have no right to determine any additional deficiency of income tax for the same taxable year, of gift tax for the same calendar year, of estate tax in respect of the taxable estate of the same decedent, of chapter 41 tax for the same taxable year, of chapter 43 tax for the same taxable year, of chapter 44 tax for the same taxable year, of section 4940 tax for the same taxable year, or of chapter 42 tax (other than under section 4940) with respect to any act (or failure to act) to which such petition relates, or of chapter 45 tax for the same taxable period, except in the case of fraud, and except as provided in section 6214(a) (relating to assertion of greater deficiencies before the Tax Court), in section 6213(b)(1) (relating to mathematical or clerical errors), in section 6851 (relating to termination assessments), or in section 6861(c) (relating to the making of jeopardy assessments).

* * *

§ 6213. Restrictions applicable to deficiencies; petition to Tax Court

(a) Time for filing petition and restriction on assessment.—Within 90 days, or 150 days if the notice is addressed to a person outside the United States, after the notice of deficiency authorized in section 6212 is mailed (not counting Saturday, Sunday, or a legal holiday in the District of Columbia as the last day), the taxpayer may file a petition with the Tax Court for a redetermination of the deficiency. Except as otherwise provided in section 6851 or section 6861 no assessment of a deficiency in respect of any tax imposed by subtitle A, or B, chapter 41, 42, 43, 44, or 45 and no levy or proceeding in court for its collection shall be made, begun, or prosecuted until such notice has been mailed to the taxpayer, nor until the expiration of such 90-day or 150-day period, as the case may be, nor, if a petition has been filed with the Tax Court, until the decision of the Tax Court has become final. Notwithstanding the provisions of section 7421(a), the making of such assessment or the beginning of such proceeding or levy during the time such prohibition is in force may be enjoined by a proceeding in the proper court.

(b) Exceptions to restrictions on assessment.—

(1) Assessments arising out of mathematical or clerical errors.—If the taxpayer is notified that, on account of a mathematical or clerical error appearing on the return, an amount of tax in excess of that shown on the return is due, and that an assessment of the tax has been or will be made on the basis of what would have been the correct amount of tax but for the mathematical or clerical error, such notice shall not be considered as a notice of deficiency for the purposes of subsection (a) (prohibiting assessment and collection until notice of the deficiency has been mailed), or of section 6212(c) (1) (restricting further deficiency letters), or of section 6512(a) (prohibiting credits or refunds after petition to the Tax Court), and the taxpayer shall have no right to file a petition with the Tax Court based on such notice, nor shall such assessment or collection be prohibited by the provisions of subsection (a) of this section. Each notice under this paragraph shall set forth the error alleged and an explanation thereof.

(2) Abatement of assessment of mathematical or clerical errors.—

(A) Request for abatement.—Notwithstanding section 6404(b), a taxpayer may file with the Secretary within 60 days after notice is sent under paragraph (1) a request for an abatement of any assessment specified in such notice, and upon receipt of such request, the Secretary shall abate the assessment. Any reassessment of the tax with respect to which an abatement is made under this subparagraph shall be subject to the deficiency procedures prescribed by this subchapter.

(B) Stay of collection.—In the case of any assessment referred to in paragraph (1), notwithstanding paragraph (1), no levy or proceeding in court for the collection of such assessment shall be made, begun, or prosecuted during the period in which such assessment may be abated under this paragraph.

(3) Assessments arising out of tentative carryback or refund adjustments. —If the Secretary determines that the amount applied, credited, or refunded under section 6411 is in excess of the overassessment attributable to the carryback or the amount described in section 1341(b) (1) with respect to which such amount was applied, credited, or refunded, he may assess without regard to the provisions of paragraph (2) the amount of the excess as a deficiency as if it were due to a mathematical or clerical error appearing on the return.

(4) Assessment of amount paid.—Any amount paid as a tax or in respect of a tax may be assessed upon the receipt of such payment notwithstanding the provisions of subsection (a). In any case where such amount is paid after the mailing of a notice of deficiency under section 6212, such payment shall not deprive the Tax Court of jurisdiction over such deficiency determined under section 6211 without regard to such assessment.

(c) Failure to file petition.—If the taxpayer does not file a petition with the Tax Court within the time prescribed in subsection (a), the deficiency, notice of which has been mailed to the taxpayer, shall be assessed, and shall be paid upon notice and demand from the Secretary.

(d) Waiver of restrictions.—The taxpayer shall at any time (whether or not a notice of deficiency has been issued) have the right, by a signed notice in writing filed with the Secretary, to waive the restrictions provided in subsection (a) on the assessment and collection of the whole or any part of the deficiency.

* * *

§ 6214. Determinations by Tax Court

(a) Jurisdiction as to increase of deficiency, additional amounts, or additions to the tax.—Except as provided by section 7463, the Tax Court shall have jurisdiction to redetermine the correct amount of the deficiency even if the amount so redetermined is greater than the amount of the deficiency, notice of which has been mailed to the taxpayer, and to determine whether any additional amount, or any addition to the tax should be assessed, if claim therefor is asserted by the Secretary at or before the hearing or a rehearing.

(b) Jurisdiction over other years and quarters.—The Tax Court in redetermining a deficiency of income tax for any taxable year or of gift tax for any calendar year or calendar quarter shall consider such facts with relation to the taxes for other years or calendar quarters as may be necessary correctly to redetermine the amount of such deficiency, but in so doing shall have no jurisdiction to determine whether or not the tax for any other year or calendar quarter has been overpaid or underpaid.

* * *

§ 6215. Assessment of deficiency found by Tax Court

(a) General rule.—If the taxpayer files a petition with the Tax Court, the entire amount redetermined as the deficiency by the decision of the Tax Court which has become final shall be assessed and shall be paid upon notice and demand from the Secretary. No part of the amount determined as a deficiency by the Secretary but disallowed as such by the decision of the Tax Court which has become final shall be assessed or be collected by levy or by proceeding in court with or without assessment.

* * *

SUBCHAPTER C—TAX TREATMENT OF PARTNERSHIP ITEMS

§ 6221.　Tax treatment determined at partnership level

Except as otherwise provided in this subchapter, the tax treatment of any partnership item shall be determined at the partnership level.

§ 6222.　Partner's return must be consistent with partnership return or secretary notified of inconsistency

(a) In general.—A partner shall, on the partner's return, treat a partnership item in a manner which is consistent with the treatment of such partnership item on the partnership return.

* * *

§ 6223.　Notice to partners of proceedings

(a) Secretary must give partners notice of beginning and completion of administrative proceedings.—The Secretary shall mail to each partner whose name and address is furnished to the Secretary notice of—

(1) the beginning of an administrative proceeding at the partnership level with respect to a partnership item, and

(2) the final partnership administrative adjustment resulting from any such proceeding.

A partner shall not be entitled to any notice under this subsection unless the Secretary has received (at least 30 days before it is mailed to the tax matters partner) sufficient information to enable the Secretary to determine that such partner is entitled to such notice and to provide such notice to such partner.

* * *

§ 6224.　Participation in administrative proceedings; waivers; agreements

(a) Participation in administrative proceedings.—Any partner has the right to participate in any administrative proceeding relating to the determination of partnership items at the partnership level.

(b) Partner may waive rights.—

(1) In general.—A partner may at any time waive—

(A) any right such partner has under this subchapter, and

(B) any restriction under this subchapter on action by the Secretary.

(2) Form.—Any waiver under paragraph (1) shall be made by a signed notice in writing filed with the Secretary.

* * *

§ 6225. Assessments made only after partnership level proceedings are completed

(a) Restriction on assessment and collection.—Except as otherwise provided in this subchapter, no assessment of a deficiency attributable to any partnership item may be made (and no levy or proceeding in any court for the collection of any such deficiency may be made, begun, or prosecuted) before—

(1) the close of the 150th day after the day on which a notice of a final partnership administrative adjustment was mailed to the tax matters partner, and

(2) if a proceeding is begun in the Tax Court under section 6226 during such 150-day period, the decision of the court in such proceeding has become final.

(b) Premature action may be enjoined.—Notwithstanding section 7421(a), any action which violates subsection (a) may be enjoined in the proper court.

* * *

§ 6226. Judicial review of final partnership administrative adjustments

(a) Petition by tax matters partner.—Within 90 days after the day on which a notice of a final partnership administrative adjustment is mailed to the tax matters partner, the tax matters partner may file a petition for a readjustment of the partnership items for such taxable year with—

(1) the Tax Court,

(2) the district court of the United States for the district in which the partnership's principal place of business is located, or

(3) the Claims Court.

(b) Petition by partner other than tax matters partner.—

(1) In general.—If the tax matters partner does not file a readjustment petition under subsection (a) with respect to any final partnership administrative adjustment, any notice partner (and any 5-percent group) may, within 60 days after the close of the 90-day period set forth in subsection (a), file a petition for a readjustment of the partnership items for the taxable year involved with any of the courts described in subsection (a).

(2) Priority of the Tax Court action.—If more than 1 action is brought under paragraph (1) with respect to any partnership for any partnership taxable year, the first such action brought in the Tax Court shall go forward.

(3) Priority outside the Tax Court.—If more than 1 action is brought under paragraph (1) with respect to any partnership for any taxable year but no such action is brought in the Tax Court, the first such action brought shall go forward.

(4) Dismissal of other actions.—If an action is brought under paragraph (1) in addition to the action which goes forward under paragraph (2) or (3), such action shall be dismissed.

(5) Tax matters partner may intervene.—The tax matters partner may intervene in any action brought under this subsection.

(c) Partners treated as parties.—If an action is brought under subsection (a) or (b) with respect to a partnership for any partnership taxable year—

(1) each person who was a partner in such partnership at any time during such year shall be treated as a party to such action, and

(2) the court having jurisdiction of such action shall allow each such person to participate in the action.

* * *

§ 6229. Period of limitations for making assessments

(a) General rule.—Except as otherwise provided in this section, the period for assessing any tax imposed by subtitle A with respect to any person which is attributable to any partnership item (or affected item) for a partnership taxable year shall not expire before the date which is 3 years after the later of—

(1) the date on which the partnership return for such taxable year was filed, or

(2) the last day for filing such return for such year (determined without regard to extensions).

(b) Extension by agreement.—

(1) **In general.**—The period described in subsection (a) (including an extension period under this subsection) may be extended—

(A) with respect to any partner, by an agreement entered into by the Secretary and such partner, and

(B) with respect to all partners, by an agreement entered into by the Secretary and the tax matters partner (or any other person authorized by the partnership in writing to enter into such an agreement),

before the expiration of such period.

(2) **Coordination with section 6501(c)(4).**—Any agreement under section 6501(c)(4) shall apply with respect to the period described in subsection (a) only if the agreement expressly provides that such agreement applies to tax attributable to partnership items.

(c) Special rule in case of fraud, etc.—

(1) **False return.**—If any partner has, with the intent to evade tax, signed or participated directly or indirectly in the preparation of a partnership return which includes a false or fraudulent item—

(A) in the case of partners so signing or participating in the preparation of the return, any tax imposed by subtitle A which is attributable to any partnership item (or affected item) for the partnership taxable year to which the return relates may be assessed at any time, and

(B) in the case of all other partners, subsection (a) shall be applied with respect to such return by substituting "6 years" for "3 years".

(2) **Substantial omission of income.**—If any partnership omits from gross income an amount properly includible therein which is in excess of 25 percent of the amount of gross income stated in its return, subsection (a) shall be applied by substituting "6 years" for "3 years".

(3) **No return.**—In the case of a failure by a partnership to file a return for any taxable year, any tax attributable to a partnership item (or affected item) arising in such year may be assessed at any time.

(4) **Return filed by secretary.**—For purposes of this section, a return executed by the Secretary under subsection (b) of section 6020 on behalf of the partnership shall not be treated as a return of the partnership.

(d) Suspension when Secretary makes administrative adjustment.—If notice of a final partnership administrative adjustment with respect to any taxable year is mailed to the tax matters partner, the running of the period specified in subsection (a) (as modified by other provisions of this section) shall be suspended—

(1) for the period during which an action may be brought under section 6226 (and, if an action with respect to such administrative adjustment is brought during such period, until the decision of the court in such action becomes final), and

(2) for 1 year thereafter.

(e) Unidentified partner.—If—

(1) the name, address, and taxpayer identification number of a partner are not furnished on the partnership return for a partnership taxable year, and

(2)(A) the Secretary, before the expiration of the period otherwise provided under this section with respect to such partner, mails to the tax matters partner the notice specified in paragraph (2) of section 6223(a) with respect to such taxable year, or

(B) the partner has failed to comply with subsection (b) of section 6222 (relating to notification of inconsistent treatment) with respect to any partnership item for such taxable year,

the period for assessing any tax imposed by subtitle A which is attributable to any partnership item (or affected item) for such taxable year shall not expire with respect to such partner before the date which is 1 year after the date on which the name, address, and taxpayer identification number of such partner are furnished to the Secretary.

(f) Items becoming nonpartnership items.—If, before the expiration of the period otherwise provided in this section for assessing any tax imposed by subtitle A with respect to the partnership items of a partner for the partnership taxable year, such items become nonpartnership items by reason of 1 or more of the events described in subsection (b) of section 6231, the period for assessing any tax imposed by subtitle A which is attributable to such items (or any item affected by such items) shall not expire before the date which is 1 year after the date on which the items become nonpartnership items.

(g) Period of limitations for penalties.—The provisions of this section shall apply also in the case of any addition to tax or an additional amount imposed under subchapter A of chapter 68 which arises with respect to any tax imposed under subtitle A in the same manner as if such addition or additional amount were a tax imposed by subtitle A.

§ 6231. Definitions and special rules

(a) Definitions.—For purposes of this subchapter—

(1) Partnership.—

(A) In general.—Except as provided in subparagraph (B), the term "partnership" means any partnership required to file a return under section 6031(a).

(B) Exception for small partnerships.—

(i) **In general.**—The term "partnership" shall not include any partnership if—

(I) such partnership has 10 or fewer partners each of whom is a natural person (other than a nonresident alien) or an estate, and

(II) each partner's share of each partnership item is the same as his share of every other item.

For purposes of the preceding sentence, a husband and wife (and their estates) shall be treated as 1 partner.

(ii) **Election to have subchapter apply.**—A partnership (within the meaning of subparagraph (A)) may for any taxable year elect to have clause (i) not apply. Such election shall apply for such taxable year and all subsequent taxable years unless revoked with the consent of the Secretary.

(2) **Partner.**—The term "partner" means—

(A) a partner in the partnership, and

(B) any other person whose income tax liability under subtitle A is determined in whole or in part by taking into account directly or indirectly partnership items of the partnership.

(3) **Partnership item.**—The term "partnership item" means, with respect to a partnership, any item required to be taken into account for the partnership's taxable year under any provision of subtitle A to the extent regulations prescribed by the Secretary provide that, for purposes of this subtitle, such item is more appropriately determined at the partnership level than at the partner level.

* * *

(7) **Tax matters partner.**—The tax matters partner of any partnership is—

(A) the general partner designated as the tax matters partner as provided in regulations, or

(B) if there is no general partner who has been so designated, the general partner having the largest profits interest in the partnership at the close of the taxable year involved (or, where there is more than 1 such partner, the 1 of such partners whose name would appear first in an alphabetical listing).

If there is no general partner designated under subparagraph (A) and the Secretary determines that it is impracticable to apply subparagraph (B), the partner selected by the Secretary shall be treated as the tax matters partner.

* * *

SUBCHAPTER D—TAX TREATMENT OF SUBCHAPTER S ITEMS

§ 6241. Tax treatment determined at corporate level

Except as otherwise provided in regulations prescribed by the Secretary, the tax treatment of any subchapter S item shall be determined at the corporate level.

§ 6242. Shareholder's return must be consistent with corporate return or secretary notified of inconsistency

A shareholder of an S corporation shall, on such shareholder's return, treat a subchapter S item in a manner which is consistent with the treatment of such item on the corporate return unless the shareholder notifies the Secretary (at the time and in the manner prescribed by regulations) of the inconsistency.

§ 6243. All shareholders to be notified of proceedings and given opportunity to participate

In the manner and at the time prescribed in regulations, each shareholder in a corporation shall be given notice of, and the right to participate in, any administrative or judicial proceeding for the determination at the corporate level of any subchapter S item.

§ 6244. Certain partnership provisions made applicable

The provisions of—

(1) subchapter C which relate to—

(A) assessing deficiencies, and filing claims for credit or refund, with respect to partnership items, and

(B) judicial determination of partnership items, and

(2) so much of the other provisions of this subtitle as relate to partnership items,

are (except to the extent modified or made inapplicable in regulations) hereby extended to and made applicable to subchapter S items.

§ 6245. Subchapter S item defined

For purposes of this subchapter, the term "subchapter S item" means any item of an S corporation to the extent regulations prescribed by the Secretary provide that, for purposes of this subtitle, such item is more appropriately determined at the corporate level than at the shareholder level.

CHAPTER 64—COLLECTION

Subchapter
A. General provisions.*
B. Receipt of payment.
C. Lien for taxes.
D. Seizure of property for collection of taxes.
E. Collection of State individual income taxes.*

SUBCHAPTER B—RECEIPT OF PAYMENT

§ 6315. Payments of estimated income tax

Payment of the estimated income tax, or any installment thereof, shall be considered payment on account of the income taxes imposed by subtitle A for the taxable year.

SUBCHAPTER C—LIEN FOR TAXES

§ 6321. Lien for taxes

If any person liable to pay any tax neglects or refuses to pay the same after demand, the amount (including any interest, additional amount, addition to tax, or assessable penalty, together with any costs that may accrue in addition thereto) shall be a lien in favor of the United States upon all property and rights to property, whether real or personal, belonging to such person.

§ 6324. Special liens for estate and gift taxes

(a) Liens for estate tax.—Except as otherwise provided in subsection (c)—

* Omitted entirely.

(1) **Upon gross estate.**—Unless the estate tax imposed by chapter 11 is sooner paid in full, or becomes unenforceable by reason of lapse of time, it shall be a lien upon the gross estate of the decedent for 10 years from the date of death, except that such part of the gross estate as is used for the payment of charges against the estate and expenses of its administration, allowed by any court having jurisdiction thereof, shall be divested of such lien.

(2) **Liability of transferees and others.**—If the estate tax imposed by chapter 11 is not paid when due, then the spouse, transferee, trustee (except the trustee of an employees' trust which meets the requirements of section 401(a)), surviving tenant, person in possession of the property by reason of the exercise, nonexercise, or release of a power of appointment, or beneficiary, who receives, or has on the date of the decedent's death, property included in the gross estate under sections 2034 to 2042, inclusive, to the extent of the value, at the time of the decedent's death, of such property, shall be personally liable for such tax. Any part of such property transferred by (or transferred by a transferee of) such spouse, transferee, trustee, surviving tenant, person in possession, or beneficiary, to a purchaser or holder of a security interest shall be divested of the lien provided in paragraph (1) and a like lien shall then attach to all the property of such spouse, transferee, trustee, surviving tenant, person in possession, or beneficiary, or transferee of any such person, except any part transferred to a purchaser or a holder of a security interest.

(3) **Continuance after discharge of fiduciary.**—The provisions of section 2204 (relating to discharge of fiduciary from personal liability) shall not operate as a release of any part of the gross estate from the lien for any deficiency that may thereafter be determined to be due, unless such part of the gross estate (or any interest therein) has been transferred to a purchaser or a holder of a security interest, in which case such part (or such interest) shall not be subject to a lien or to any claim or demand for any such deficiency, but the lien shall attach to the consideration received from such purchaser or holder of a security interest, by the heirs, legatees, devisees, or distributees.

(b) Lien for gift tax.—Except as otherwise provided in subsection (c), unless the gift tax imposed by chapter 12 is sooner paid in full or becomes unenforceable by reason of lapse of time, such tax shall be a lien upon all gifts made during the period for which the return was filed, for 10 years from the date the gifts are made. If the tax is not paid when due, the donee of any gift shall be personally liable for such tax to the extent of the value of such gift. Any part of the property comprised in the gift transferred by the donee (or by a transferee of the donee) to a purchaser or holder of a security interest shall be divested of the lien imposed by this subsection and such lien, to the extent of the value of such gift, shall attach to all the property (including after-acquired property) of the donee (or the transferee) except any part transferred to a purchaser or holder of a security interest.

(c) Exceptions.—

(1) The lien imposed by subsection (a) or (b) shall not be valid as against a mechanic's lienor and, subject to the conditions provided by section 6323(b) (relating to protection for certain interests even though noticed filed), shall not be valid with respect to any lien or interest described in section 6323(b).

(2) If a lien imposed by subsection (a) or (b) is not valid as against a lien or security interest, the priority of such lien or security interest shall extend to any item described in section 6323(e) (relating to priority of interest and expenses) to the extent that, under local law, such item has the same priority as the lien or security interest to which it relates.

SUBCHAPTER D—SEIZURE OF PROPERTY FOR COLLECTION OF TAXES

§ 6331. Levy and distraint

(a) **Authority of Secretary.**—If any person liable to pay any tax neglects or refuses to pay the same within 10 days after notice and demand, it shall be lawful for the Secretary to collect such tax (and such further sum as shall be sufficient to cover the expenses of the levy) by levy upon all property and rights to property (except such property as is exempt under section 6334) belonging to such person or on which there is a lien provided in this chapter for the payment of such tax. Levy may be made upon the accrued salary or wages of any officer, employee, or elected official, of the United States, the District of Columbia, or any agency or instrumentality of the United States or the District of Columbia, by serving a notice of levy on the employer (as defined in section 3401(d)) of such officer, employee, or elected official. If the Secretary makes a finding that the collection of such tax is in jeopardy, notice and demand for immediate payment of such tax may be made by the Secretary and, upon failure or refusal to pay such tax, collection thereof by levy shall be lawful without regard to the 10-day period provided in this section.

(b) **Seizure and sale of property.**—The term "levy" as used in this title includes the power of distraint and seizure by any means. Except as otherwise provided in subsection (e), a levy shall extend only to property possessed and obligations existing at the time thereof. In any case in which the Secretary may levy upon property or rights to property, he may seize and sell such property or rights to property (whether real or personal, tangible or intangible).

(c) **Successive seizures.**—Whenever any property or right to property upon which levy has been made by virtue of subsection (a) is not sufficient to satisfy the claim of the United States for which levy is made, the Secretary may, thereafter, and as often as may be necessary, proceed to levy in like manner upon any other property liable to levy of the person against whom such claim exists, until the amount due from him, together with all expenses, is fully paid.

(d) **Requirement of notice before levy.**—

(1) **In general.**—Levy may be made under subsection (a) upon the salary or wages or other property of any person with respect to any unpaid tax only after the Secretary has notified such person in writing of his intention to make such levy.

(2) **10-day requirement.**—The notice required under paragraph (1) shall be—

(A) given in person,

(B) left at the dwelling or usual place of business of such person, or

(C) sent by certified or registered mail to such person's last known address,

no less than 10 days before the day of the levy.

(3) **Jeopardy.**—Paragraph (1) shall not apply to a levy if the Secretary has made a finding under the last sentence of subsection (a) that the collection of tax is in jeopardy.

(e) **Continuing levy on salary and wages.**—

(1) **Effect of levy.**—The effect of a levy on salary or wages payable to or received by a taxpayer shall be continuous from the date such levy is first made until the liability out of which such levy arose is satisfied or becomes unenforceable by reason of lapse of time.

(2) Release and notice of release.—With respect to a levy described in paragraph (1), the Secretary shall promptly release the levy when the liability out of which such levy arose is satisfied or becomes unenforceable by reason of lapse of time, and shall promptly notify the person upon whom such levy was made that such levy has been released.

* * *

CHAPTER 65—ABATEMENTS, CREDITS, AND REFUNDS

SUBCHAPTER A—PROCEDURE IN GENERAL

§ 6402.   Authority to make credits or refunds

(a) General rule.—In the case of any overpayment, the Secretary or his delegate, within the applicable period of limitations, may credit the amount of such overpayment, including any interest allowed thereon, against any liability in respect of an internal revenue tax on the part of the person who made the overpayment and shall, subject to subsection (c), refund any balance to such person.

(b) Credits against estimated tax.—The Secretary is authorized to prescribe regulations providing for the crediting against the estimated income tax for any taxable year of the amount determined by the taxpayer or the Secretary to be an overpayment of the income tax for a preceding taxable year.

(c) Offset of past-due support against overpayments.—The amount of any overpayment to be refunded to the person making the overpayment shall be reduced by the amount of any past-due support (as defined in section 464(c) of the Social Security Act) owed by that person of which the Secretary has been notified by a State in accordance with section 464 of the Social Security Act. The Secretary shall remit the amount by which the overpayment is so reduced to the State to which such support has been assigned and notify the person making the overpayment that so much of the overpayment as was necessary to satisfy his obligation for past-due support has been paid to the State. This subsection shall be applied to an overpayment prior to its being credited to a person's future liability for an internal revenue tax.

* * *

CHAPTER 66—LIMITATIONS

* Omitted entirely.

SUBCHAPTER A—LIMITATIONS ON ASSESSMENT AND COLLECTION

§ 6501. Limitations on assessment and collection

(a) **General rule.**—Except as otherwise provided in this section, the amount of any tax imposed by this title shall be assessed within 3 years after the return was filed (whether or not such return was filed on or after the date prescribed) or, if the tax is payable by stamp, at any time after such tax became due and before the expiration of 3 years after the date on which any part of such tax was paid, and no proceeding in court without assessment for the collection of such tax shall be begun after the expiration of such period.

(b) **Time return deemed filed.**—

(1) **Early return.**—For purposes of this section, a return of tax imposed by this title, except tax imposed by chapter 3, 21, or 24, filed before the last day prescribed by law or by regulations promulgated pursuant to law for the filing thereof, shall be considered as filed on such last day.

* * *

(c) **Exceptions.**—

(1) **False return.**—In the case of a false or fraudulent return with the intent to evade tax, the tax may be assessed, or a proceeding in court for collection of such tax may be begun without assessment, at any time.

(2) **Willful attempt to evade tax.**—In case of a willful attempt in any manner to defeat or evade tax imposed by this title (other than tax imposed by subtitle A or B), the tax may be assessed, or a proceeding in court for the collection of such tax may be begun without assessment, at any time.

(3) **No return.**—In the case of failure to file a return, the tax may be assessed, or a proceeding in court for the collection of such tax may be begun without assessment, at any time.

(4) **Extension by agreement.**—Where, before the expiration of the time prescribed in this section for the assessment of any tax imposed by this title, except the estate tax provided in chapter 11, both the Secretary and the taxpayer have consented in writing to its assessment after such time, the tax may be assessed at any time prior to the expiration of the period agreed upon. The period so agreed upon may be extended by subsequent agreements in writing made before the expiration of the period previously agreed upon.

* * *

(d) **Request for prompt assessment.**—Except as otherwise provided in subsection (c), (e), or (f), in the case of any tax (other than the tax imposed by chapter 11 of subtitle B, relating to estate taxes) for which return is required in the case of a decedent, or by his estate during the period of administration, or by a corporation, the tax shall be assessed, and any proceeding in court without assessment for the collection of such tax shall be begun, within 18 months after written request therefor (filed after the return is made and filed in such manner and such form as may be prescribed by regulations of the Secretary) by the executor, administrator, or other fiduciary representing the estate of such decedent, or by the corporation, but not after the expiration of 3 years after the return was filed. This subsection shall not apply in the case of a corporation unless—

(1) (A) such written request notifies the Secretary that the corporation contemplates dissolution at or before the expiration of such 18-month period, (B) the dissolution is in good faith begun before the expiration of such 18-month period, and (C) the dissolution is completed;

(2) (A) such written request notifies the Secretary that a dissolution has in good faith been begun, and (B) the dissolution is completed; or

(3) a dissolution has been completed at the time such written request is made.

(e) **Substantial omission of items.**—Except as otherwise provided in subsection (c)—

(1) **Income taxes.**—In the case of any tax imposed by subtitle A—

(A) **General rule.**—If the taxpayer omits from gross income an amount properly includible therein which is in excess of 25 percent of the amount of gross income stated in the return, the tax may be assessed, or a proceeding in court for the collection of such tax may be begun without assessment, at any time within 6 years after the return was filed. For purposes of this subparagraph—

(i) In the case of a trade or business, the term "gross income" means the total of the amounts received or accrued from the sale of goods or services (if such amounts are required to be shown on the return) prior to diminution by the cost of such sales or services; and

(ii) In determining the amount omitted from gross income, there shall not be taken into account any amount which is omitted from gross income stated in the return if such amount is disclosed in the return, or in a statement attached to the return, in a manner adequate to apprise the Secretary of the nature and amount of such item.

* * *

(2) **Estate and gift taxes.**—In the case of a return of estate tax under chapter 11 or a return of gift tax under chapter 12, if the taxpayer omits from the gross estate or from the total amount of the gifts made during the period for which the return was filed items includible in such gross estate or such total gifts, as the case may be, as exceed in amount 25 percent of the gross estate stated in the return or the total amount of gifts stated in the return, the tax may be assessed, or a proceeding in court for the collection of such tax may be begun without assessment, at any time within 6 years after the return was filed. In determining the items omitted from the gross estate or the total gifts, there shall not be taken into account any item which is omitted from the gross estate or from the total gifts stated in the return if such item is disclosed in the return, or in a statement attached to the return, in a manner adequate to apprise the Secretary of the nature and amount of such item.

* * *

(f) **Personal holding company tax.**—If a corporation which is a personal holding company for any taxable year fails to file with its return under chapter 1 for such year a schedule setting forth—

(1) the items of gross income and adjusted ordinary gross income, described in section 543, received by the corporation during such year, and

(2) the names and addresses of the individuals who owned, within the meaning of section 544 (relating to rules for determining stock ownership), at any time during the last half of such year more than 50 percent in value of the outstanding capital stock of the corporation,

the personal holding company tax for such year may be assessed, or a proceeding in court for the collection of such tax may be begun without assessment, at any time within 6 years after the return for such year was filed.

(g) **Certain income tax returns of corporations.**—

(1) **Trusts or partnerships.**—If a taxpayer determines in good faith that it is a trust or partnership and files a return as such under subtitle A, and if such taxpayer is thereafter held to be a corporation for the taxable year for which the return is filed, such return shall be deemed the return of the corporation for purposes of this section.

* * *

(h) **Net operating loss or capital loss carrybacks.**—In the case of a deficiency attributable to the application to the taxpayer of a net operating loss carryback or a capital loss carryback (including deficiencies which may be assessed pursuant to the provisions of section 6213(b) (3)), such deficiency may be assessed at any time before the expiration of the period within which a deficiency for the taxable year of the net operating loss or net capital loss which results in such carryback may be assessed.

* * *

§ 6502. Collection after assessment

(a) **Length of period.**—Where the assessment of any tax imposed by this title has been made within the period of limitation properly applicable thereto, such tax may be collected by levy or by a proceeding in court, but only if the levy is made or the proceeding begun—

(1) within 6 years after the assessment of the tax, or

(2) prior to the expiration of any period for collection agreed upon in writing by the Secretary and the taxpayer before the expiration of such 6-year period (or, if there is a release of levy under section 6343 after such 6-year period, then before such release).

The period so agreed upon may be extended by subsequent agreements in writing made before the expiration of the period previously agreed upon. The period provided by this subsection during which a tax may be collected by levy shall not be extended or curtailed by reason of a judgment against the taxpayer.

(b) **Date when levy is considered made.**—The date on which a levy on property or rights to property is made shall be the date on which the notice of seizure provided in section 6335(a) is given.

§ 6503. Suspension of running of period of limitation

(a) **Issuance of statutory notice of deficiency.**—

(1) **General rule.**—The running of the period of limitations provided in section 6501 or 6502 (or section 6229, but only with respect to a deficiency described in section 6230(a)(2)(A)) on the making of assessments or the collection by levy or a proceeding in court, in respect of any deficiency as defined in section 6211 (relating to income, estate, gift and certain excise taxes), shall (after the mailing of a notice under section 6212(a)) be suspended for the period during which the Secretary is prohibited from making the assessment or from collecting by levy or a proceeding in court (and in any event, if a proceeding in respect of the deficiency is placed on the docket of the Tax Court, until the decision of the Tax Court becomes final), and for 60 days thereafter.

(2) **Corporation joining in consolidated income tax return.**—If a notice under section 6212(a) in respect of a deficiency in tax imposed by subtitle A for any taxable year is mailed to a corporation, the suspension of the running of the period of limitations provided in paragraph (1) of this subsection shall apply in the case of

corporations with which such corporation made a consolidated income tax return for such taxable year.

(b) Assets of taxpayer in control or custody of court.—The period of limitations on collection after assessment prescribed in section 6502 shall be suspended for the period the assets of the taxpayer are in the control or custody of the court in any proceeding before any court of the United States or of any State or of the District of Columbia, and for 6 months thereafter.

(c) Taxpayer outside United States.—The running of the period of limitations on collection after assessment prescribed in section 6502 shall be suspended for the period during which the taxpayer is outside the United States if such period of absence is for a continuous period of at least 6 months. If the preceding sentence applies and at the time of the taxpayer's return to the United States the period of limitations on collection after assessment prescribed in section 6502 would expire before the expiration of 6 months from the date of his return, such period shall not expire before the expiration of such 6 months.

(d) Extensions of time for payment of estate tax.—The running of the period of limitations for collection of any tax imposed by chapter 11 shall be suspended for the period of any extension of time for payment granted under the provisions of section 6161(a) (2) or (b) (2) or under the provisions of section 6163 or 6166.

* * *

SUBCHAPTER B—LIMITATIONS ON CREDIT OR REFUND

§ 6511.   Limitations on credit or refund

(a) Period of limitation on filing claim.—Claim for credit or refund of an overpayment of any tax imposed by this title in respect of which tax the taxpayer is required to file a return shall be filed by the taxpayer within 3 years from the time the return was filed or 2 years from the time the tax was paid, whichever of such periods expires the later, or if no return was filed by the taxpayer, within 2 years from the time the tax was paid. Claim for credit or refund of an overpayment of any tax imposed by this title which is required to be paid by means of a stamp shall be filed by the taxpayer within 3 years from the time the tax was paid.

(b) Limitation on allowance of credits and refunds.—

(1) Filing of claim within prescribed period.—No credit or refund shall be allowed or made after the expiration of the period of limitation prescribed in subsection (a) for the filing of a claim for credit or refund, unless a claim for credit or refund is filed by the taxpayer within such period.

(2) Limit on amount of credit or refund.—

(A) Limit where claim filed within 3-year period.—If the claim was filed by the taxpayer during the 3-year period prescribed in subsection (a), the amount of the credit or refund shall not exceed the portion of the tax paid within the period, immediately preceding the filing of the claim, equal to 3 years plus the period of any extension of time for filing the return. If the tax was required to be paid by means of a stamp, the amount of the credit or refund shall not exceed the portion of the tax paid within the 3 years immediately preceding the filing of the claim.

(B) Limit where claim not filed within 3-year period.—If the claim was not filed within such 3-year period, the amount of the credit or refund shall not exceed the portion of the tax paid during the 2 years immediately preceding the filing of the claim.

(C) Limit if no claim filed.—If no claim was filed, the credit or refund shall not exceed the amount which would be allowable under subparagraph (A) or (B), as the case may be, if claim was filed on the date the credit or refund is allowed.

(c) Special rules applicable in case of extension of time by agreement.—If an agreement under the provisions of section 6501(c) (4) extending the period for assessment of a tax imposed by this title is made within the period prescribed in subsection (a) for the filing of a claim for credit or refund—

(1) Time for filing claim.—The period for filing claim for credit or refund or for making credit or refund if no claim is filed, provided in subsections (a) and (b) (1), shall not expire prior to 6 months after the expiration of the period within which an assessment may be made pursuant to the agreement or any extension thereof under section 6501(c) (4).

(2) Limit on amount.—If a claim is filed, or a credit or refund is allowed when no claim was filed, after the execution of the agreement and within 6 months after the expiration of the period within which an assessment may be made pursuant to the agreement or any extension thereof, the amount of the credit or refund shall not exceed the portion of the tax paid after the execution of the agreement and before the filing of the claim or the making of the credit or refund, as the case may be, plus the portion of the tax paid within the period which would be applicable under subsection (b) (2) if a claim had been filed on the date the agreement was executed.

(3) Claims not subject to special rule.—This subsection shall not apply in the case of a claim filed, or credit or refund allowed if no claim is filed, either—

(A) prior to the execution of the agreement or

(B) more than 6 months after the expiration of the period within which an assessment may be made pursuant to the agreement or any extension thereof.

(d) Special rules applicable to income taxes.—

(1) Seven-year period of limitation with respect to bad debts and worthless securities.—If the claim for credit or refund relates to an overpayment of tax imposed by subtitle A on account of—

(A) The deductibility by the taxpayer, under section 166 or section 832(c), of a debt as a debt which became worthless, or, under section 165(g), of a loss from worthlessness of a security, or

(B) The effect that the deductibility of a debt or loss described in subparagraph (A) has on the application to the taxpayer of a carryover,

in lieu of the 3-year period of limitation prescribed in subsection (a), the period shall be 7 years from the date prescribed by law for filing the return for the year with respect to which the claim is made. If the claim for credit or refund relates to an overpayment on account of the effect that the deductibility of such a debt or loss has on the application to the taxpayer of a carryback, the period shall be either 7 years from the date prescribed by law for filing the return for the year of the net operating loss which results in such carryback or the period prescribed in paragraph (2) of this subsection, whichever expires the later. In the case of a claim described in this paragraph the amount of the credit or refund may exceed the portion of the tax paid within the period prescribed in subsection (b) (2) or (c), whichever is applicable, to the extent of the amount of the overpayment attributable to the deductibility of items described in this paragraph.

(2) Special period of limitation with respect to net operating loss or capital loss carrybacks.—

(A) Period of limitation.—If the claim for credit or refund relates to an overpayment attributable to a net operating loss carryback or a capital loss carryback, in lieu of the 3-year period of limitation prescribed in subsection (a), the period shall be that period which ends 3 years after the time prescribed by law for filing the return (including extensions thereof) for the taxable year of the net operating loss or net capital loss which results in such carryback, or the period prescribed in subsection (c) in respect of such taxable year, whichever expires later; except that with respect to an overpayment attributable to the creation of, or an increase in a net operating loss carryback as a result of the elimination of excessive profits by a renegotiation (as defined in section 1481(a) (1) (A)), the period shall not expire before the expiration of the 12th month following the month in which the agreement or order for the elimination of such excessive profits becomes final. In the case of such a claim, the amount of the credit or refund may exceed the portion of the tax paid within the period provided in subsection (b) (2) or (c), whichever is applicable, to the extent of the amount of the overpayment attributable to such carryback.

(B) Applicable rules.—

(i) In general.—If the allowance of a credit or refund of an overpayment of tax attributable to a net operating loss carryback or a capital loss carryback is otherwise prevented by the operation of any law or rule of law other than section 7122 (relating to compromises), such credit or refund may be allowed or made, if claim therefor is filed within the period provided in subparagraph (A) of this paragraph.

(ii) Tentative carryback adjustments.—If the allowance of an application, credit, or refund of a decrease in tax determined under section 6411(b) is otherwise prevented by the operation of any law or rule of law other than section 7122, such application, credit, or refund may be allowed or made if application for a tentative carryback adjustment is made within the period provided in section 6411(a).

(iii) Determinations by courts to be conclusive.—In the case of any such claim for credit or refund or any such application for a tentative carryback adjustment, the determination by any court, including the Tax Court, in any proceeding in which the decision of the court has become final, shall be conclusive except with respect to—

(I) the net operating loss deduction and the effect of such deduction, and

(II) the determination of a short-term capital loss and the effect of such short-term capital loss, to the extent that such deduction or short-term capital loss is affected by a carryback which was not an issue in such proceeding.

* * *

§ 6512. Limitations in case of petition to Tax Court

(a) Effect of petition to Tax Court.—If the Secretary has mailed to the taxpayer a notice of deficiency under section 6212(a) (relating to deficiencies of income, estate, gift, and certain excise taxes) and if the taxpayer files a petition with the Tax Court within the time prescribed in section 6213(a), no credit or refund of income tax for the same taxable year, of gift tax for the same calendar year or calendar quarter, of estate tax in respect of the taxable estate of the same decedent, of tax imposed by chapter 41, 42, 43, or 44 with respect to any act (or failure to act) to which such petition relates, or of tax imposed by chapter 45 for the same taxable period, in respect of which the Secretary has determined the deficiency shall be allowed or made and no suit by the taxpayer for the recovery of any part of the tax shall be instituted in any court except—

(1) As to overpayments determined by a decision of the Tax Court which has become final;

(2) As to any amount collected in excess of an amount computed in accordance with the decision of the Tax Court which has become final;

(3) As to any amount collected after the period of limitation upon the making of levy or beginning a proceeding in court for collection has expired; but in any such claim for credit or refund or in any such suit for refund the decision of the Tax Court which has become final, as to whether such period has expired before the notice of deficiency was mailed, shall be conclusive, and

(4) As to overpayments attributable to partnership items, in accordance with subchapter C of chapter 63.

* * *

§ 6513. Time return deemed filed and tax considered paid

(a) **Early return or advance payment of tax.**—For purposes of section 6511, any return filed before the last day prescribed for the filing thereof shall be considered as filed on such last day. For purposes of section 6511(b) (2) and (c) and section 6512, payment of any portion of the tax made before the last day prescribed for the payment of the tax shall be considered made on such last day. For purposes of this subsection, the last day prescribed for filing the return or paying the tax shall be determined without regard to any extension of time granted the taxpayer and without regard to any election to pay the tax in installments.

(b) **Prepaid income tax.**—For purposes of section 6511 or 6512—

(1) Any tax actually deducted and withheld at the source during any calendar year under chapter 24 shall, in respect of the recipient of the income, be deemed to have been paid by him on the 15th day of the fourth month following the close of his taxable year with respect to which such tax is allowable as a credit under section 31.

(2) Any amount paid as estimated income tax for any taxable year shall be deemed to have been paid on the last day prescribed for filing the return under section 6012 for such taxable year (determined without regard to any extension of time for filing such return).

(3) Any tax withheld at the source under chapter 3 shall, in respect of the recipient of the income, be deemed to have been paid by such recipient on the last day prescribed for filing the return under section 6012 for the taxable year (determined without regard to any extension of time for filing) with respect to which such tax is allowable as a credit under section 1462. For this purpose, any exemption granted under section 6012 from the requirement of filing a return shall be disregarded.

* * *

SUBCHAPTER D—PERIODS OF LIMITATION IN JUDICIAL PROCEEDINGS

§ 6531. Periods of limitation on criminal prosecutions

No person shall be prosecuted, tried, or punished for any of the various offenses arising under the internal revenue laws unless the indictment is found or the information instituted within 3 years next after the commission of the offense, **except that the period of limitation shall be 6 years—**

(1) for offenses involving the defrauding or attempting to defraud the United States or any agency thereof, whether by conspiracy or not, and in any manner;

(2) for the offense of willfully attempting in any manner to evade or defeat any tax or the payment thereof;

(3) for the offense of willfully aiding or assisting in, or procuring, counseling, or advising, the preparation or presentation under, or in connection with any matter arising under, the internal revenue laws, of a false or fraudulent return, affidavit, claim, or document (whether or not such falsity or fraud is with the knowledge or consent of the person authorized or required to present such return, affidavit, claim, or document);

(4) for the offense of willfully failing to pay any tax, or make any return (other than a return required under authority of part III of subchapter A of chapter 61) at the time or times required by law or regulations;

(5) for offenses described in sections 7206(1) and 7207 (relating to false statements and fraudulent documents);

* * *

§ 6532. Periods of limitation on suits

(a) Suits by taxpayers for refund.—

(1) General rule.—No suit or proceeding under section 7422(a) for the recovery of any internal revenue tax, penalty, or other sum, shall be begun before the expiration of 6 months from the date of filing the claim required under such section unless the Secretary renders a decision thereon within that time, nor after the expiration of 2 years from the date of mailing by certified mail or registered mail by the Secretary to the taxpayer of a notice of the disallowance of the part of the claim to which the suit or proceeding relates.

(2) Extension of time.—The 2-year period prescribed in paragraph (1) shall be extended for such period as may be agreed upon in writing between the taxpayer and the Secretary.

(3) Waiver of notice of disallowance.—If any person files a written waiver of the requirement that he be mailed a notice of disallowance, the 2-year period prescribed in paragraph (1) shall begin on the date such waiver is filed.

(4) Reconsideration after mailing of notice.—Any consideration, reconsideration, or action by the Secretary with respect to such claim following the mailing of a notice by certified mail or registered mail of disallowance shall not operate to extend the period within which suit may be begun.

* * *

CHAPTER 67—INTEREST

Subchapter
  A. Interest on underpayments.
  B. Interest on overpayments.
  C. Determination of interest rate; compounding of interest.

SUBCHAPTER A—INTEREST ON UNDERPAYMENTS

§ 6601. Interest on underpayment, nonpayment, or extensions of time for payment, of tax

(a) General rule.—If any amount of tax imposed by this title (whether required to be shown on a return, or to be paid by stamp or by some other method) is not paid on or before the last date prescribed for payment, interest on such amount at the underpayment rate established under section 6621 shall be paid for the period from such last date to the date paid.

(b) Last date prescribed for payment.—For purposes of this section, the last date prescribed for payment of the tax shall be determined under chapter 62 with the application of the following rules:

    (1) Extensions of time disregarded.—The last date prescribed for payment shall be determined without regard to any extension of time for payment.

    (2) Installment payments.—In the case of an election under section 6156(a) or 6158(a) to pay the tax in installments—

        (A) The date prescribed for payment of each installment of the tax shown on the return shall be determined under section 6156(b) or 6158(a), and

        (B) The last date prescribed for payment of the first installment shall be deemed the last date prescribed for payment of any portion of the tax not shown on the return.

For purposes of subparagraph (A), section 6158(a) shall be treated as providing that the date prescribed for payment of each installment shall not be later than the date prescribed for payment of the 1985 installment.

* * *

    (4) Accumulated earnings tax.—In the case of the tax imposed by section 531 for any taxable year, the last date prescribed for payment shall be deemed to be the due date (without regard to extensions) for the return of tax imposed by subtitle A for such taxable year.

(c) Suspension of interest in certain income, estate, gift, and certain excise tax cases.—In the case of a deficiency as defined in section 6211 (relating to income, estate, gift, and certain excise taxes), if a waiver of restrictions under section 6213(d) on the assessment of such deficiency has been filed, and if notice and demand by the Secretary for payment of such deficiency is not made within 30 days after the filing of such waiver, interest shall not be imposed on such deficiency for the period beginning immediately after such 30th day and ending with the date of notice and demand and interest shall not be imposed during such period on any interest with respect to such deficiency for any prior period.

(d) Income tax reduced by carryback or adjustment for certain unused deductions.—

    (1) Net operating loss or capital loss carryback.—If the amount of any tax imposed by subtitle A is reduced by reason of a carryback of a net operating loss or net capital loss, such reduction in tax shall not affect the computation of interest under this section for the period ending with the filing date for the taxable year in which the net operating loss or net capital loss arises.

* * *

(e) Applicable rules.—Except as otherwise provided in this title—

(1) **Interest treated as tax.**—Interest prescribed under this section on any tax shall be paid upon notice and demand, and shall be assessed, collected, and paid in the same manner as taxes. Any reference in this title (except subchapter B of chapter 63, relating to deficiency procedures) to any tax imposed by this title shall be deemed also to refer to interest imposed by this section on such tax.

(2) **Interest on penalties, additional amounts, or additions to the tax.**—

(A) **In general.**—Interest shall be imposed under subsection (a) in respect of any assessable penalty, additional amount, or addition to the tax (other than an addition to tax imposed under section 6651(a)(1), 6659, 6660, or 6661) only if such assessable penalty, additional amount, or addition to the tax is not paid within 10 days from the date of notice and demand therefor, and in such case interest shall be imposed only for the period from the date of the notice and demand to the date of payment.

(B) **Interest on certain additions to tax.**—Interest shall be imposed under this section with respect to any addition to tax imposed by section 6651(a)(1), 6659, 6660, or 6661 for the period which—

(i) begins on the date on which the return of the tax with respect to which such addition to tax is imposed is required to be filed (including any extensions), and

(ii) ends on the date of payment of such addition to tax.

(3) **Payments made within 10 days after notice and demand.**—If notice and demand is made for payment of any amount, and if such amount is paid within 10 days after the date of such notice and demand, interest under this section on the amount so paid shall not be imposed for the period after the date of such notice and demand.

* * *

(j) **4-percent rate on certain portion of estate tax extended under section 6166.**—

(1) **In general.**—If the time for payment of an amount of tax imposed by chapter 11 is extended as provided in section 6166, interest on the 4-percent portion of such amount shall (in lieu of the annual rate provided by subsection (a)) be paid at the rate of 4 percent. For purposes of this subsection, the amount of any deficiency which is prorated to installments payable under section 6166 shall be treated as an amount of tax payable in installments under such section.

(2) **4-percent portion.**—For purposes of this subsection, the term "4-percent portion" means the lesser of—

(A) $345,800 reduced by the amount of the credit allowable under section 2010(a); or

(B) the amount of the tax imposed by chapter 11 which is extended as provided in section 6166.

(3) **Treatment of payments.**—If the amount of tax imposed by chapter 11 which is extended as provided in section 6166 exceeds the 4-percent portion, any payment of a portion of such amount shall, for purposes of computing interest for periods after such payment, be treated as reducing the 4-percent portion by an amount which bears the same ratio to the amount of such payment as the amount of the 4-percent portion (determined without regard to this paragraph) bears to the amount of the tax which is extended as provided in section 6166.

* * *

SUBCHAPTER B—INTEREST ON OVERPAYMENTS

§ 6611.   Interest on overpayments

(a) Rate.—Interest shall be allowed and paid upon any overpayment in respect of any internal revenue tax at the overpayment rate established under section 6621.

(b) Period.—Such interest shall be allowed and paid as follows:

(1) Credits.—In the case of a credit, from the date of the overpayment to the due date of the amount against which the credit is taken.

(2) Refunds.—In the case of a refund, from the date of the overpayment to a date (to be determined by the Secretary) preceding the date of the refund check by not more than 30 days, whether or not such refund check is accepted by the taxpayer after tender of such check to the taxpayer. The acceptance of such check shall be without prejudice to any right of the taxpayer to claim any additional overpayment and interest thereon.

(3) Late returns.—Notwithstanding paragraph (1) or (2) in the case of a return of tax which is filed after the last date prescribed for filing such return (determined with regard to extensions), no interest shall be allowed or paid for any day before the date on which the return is filed.

* * *

(d) Advance payment of tax, payment of estimated tax, and credit for income tax withholding.—The provisions of section 6513 (except the provisions of subsection (c) thereof), applicable in determining the date of payment of tax for purposes of determining the period of limitation on credit or refund, shall be applicable in determining the date of payment for purposes of subsection (a).

(e) Income tax refund within 45 days after return is filed.—If any overpayment of tax imposed by subtitle A is refunded within 45 days after the last date prescribed for filing the return of such tax (determined without regard to any extension of time for filing the return) or, in case the return is filed after such last date, is refunded within 45 days after the date the return is filed, no interest shall be allowed under subsection (a) on such overpayment.

(f) Refund of income tax caused by carryback or adjustment for certain unused deductions.—

(1) Net operating loss or capital loss carryback.—For purposes of subsection (a), if any overpayment of tax imposed by subtitle A results from a carryback of a net operating loss or net capital loss, such overpayment shall be deemed not to have been made prior to the filing date for the taxable year in which such net operating loss or net capital loss arises.

* * *

SUBCHAPTER C—DETERMINATION OF INTEREST RATE; COMPOUNDING OF INTEREST

§ 6621.   Determination of rate of interest

(a) General Rule.—

(1) Overpayment rate.—The overpayment rate established under this section shall be the sum of—

(A) the short-term Federal rate determined under subsection (b), plus

(B) 2 percentage points.

(2) Underpayment rate.—The underpayment rate established under this section shall be the sum of—

(A) the short-term Federal rate determined under subsection (b), plus

(B) 3 percentage points.

(b) Short-term federal rate.—For purposes of this section—

(1) General rule.—The Secretary shall determine the short-term Federal rate for the first month in each calendar quarter.

(2) Period during which rate applies.—

(A) In general.—Except as provided in subparagraph (B), the Federal short-term rate determined under paragraph (1) for any month shall apply during the first calendar quarter beginning after such month.

(B) Special rule for individual estimated tax.—In determining the addition to tax under section 6654 for failure to pay estimated tax for any taxable year, the Federal short-term rate which applies during the 3rd month following such taxable year shall also apply during the first 15 days of the 4th month following such taxable year.

(3) Federal short-term rate.—The Federal short-term rate for any month shall be the Federal short-term rate determined during such month by the Secretary in accordance with section 1274(d). Any such rate shall be rounded to the nearest full percent (or, if a multiple of ½ of 1 percent such rate shall be increased to the next highest full percent).

(c) Interest on substantial underpayments attributable to tax motivated transactions.—

(1) In general.—In the case of interest payable under section 6601 with respect to any substantial underpayment attributable to tax motivated transactions, the rate of interest established under this section shall be 120 percent of the underpayment rate established under this section.

(2) Substantial underpayment attributable to tax motivated transactions. —For purposes of this subsection, the term "substantial underpayment attributable to tax motivated transactions" means any underpayment of taxes imposed by subtitle A for any taxable year which is attributable to 1 or more tax motivated transactions if the amount of the underpayment for such year so attributable exceeds $1,000.

(3) Tax motivated transactions.—

(A) In general.—For purposes of this subsection, the term "tax motivated transaction" means—

(i) any valuation overstatement (within the meaning of section 6659(c)),

(ii) any loss disallowed by reason of section 465(a) and any credit disallowed under section 46(c)(8),

(iii) any straddle (as defined in section 1092(c) without regard to subsections (d) and (e) of section 1092),

(iv) any use of an accounting method specified in regulations prescribed by the Secretary as a use which may result in a substantial distortion of income for any period, and

(v) any sham or fraudulent transaction.

(B) Regulatory authority.—The Secretary may by regulations specify other types of transactions which will be treated as tax motivated for purposes of this subsection and may by regulations provide that specified transactions being treated as tax motivated will no longer be so treated. In prescribing regulations under the preceding sentence, the Secretary shall take into account—

(i) the ratio of tax benefits to cash invested,

(ii) the methods of promoting the use of this type of transaction, and

(iii) other relevant considerations.

(C) Effective date for regulations.—Any regulations prescribed under subparagraph (A)(iv) or (B) shall apply only to interest accruing after a date (specified in such regulations) which is after the date on which such regulations are prescribed.

(4) Jurisdiction of tax court.—In the case of any proceeding in the Tax Court for a redetermination of a deficiency, the Tax Court shall also have jurisdiction to determine the portion (if any) of such deficiency which is a substantial underpayment attributable to tax motivated transactions.

* * *

§ 6622. Interest compounded daily

(a) General rule.—In computing the amount of any interest required to be paid under this title or sections 1961(c)(1) or 2411 of title 28, United States Code, by the Secretary or by the taxpayer, or any other amount determined by reference to such amount of interest, such interest and such amount shall be compounded daily.

(b) Exception for penalty for failure to file estimated tax.—Subsection (a) shall not apply for purposes of computing the amount of any addition to tax under section 6654 or 6655.

CHAPTER 68—ADDITIONS TO THE TAX, ADDITIONAL AMOUNTS, AND ASSESSABLE PENALTIES

Subchapter
A. Additions to the tax and additional amounts.
B. Assessable penalties.

SUBCHAPTER A—ADDITIONS TO THE TAX AND ADDITIONAL AMOUNTS

§ 6651. Failure to file tax return or to pay tax

(a) Addition to the tax.—In case of failure—

(1) to file any return required under authority of subchapter A of chapter 61 (other than part III thereof), subchapter A of chapter 51 (relating to distilled spirits, wines, and beer), or of subchapter A of chapter 52 (relating to tobacco, cigars, cigarettes, and cigarette papers and tubes), or of subchapter A of chapter 53 (relating to machine guns and certain other firearms), on the date prescribed therefor (determined with regard to any extension of time for filing), unless it is shown that such failure is due to reasonable cause and not due to willful neglect,

there shall be added to the amount required to be shown as tax on such return 5 percent of the amount of such tax if the failure is for not more than 1 month, with an additional 5 percent for each additional month or fraction thereof during which such failure continues, not exceeding 25 percent in the aggregate;

(2) to pay the amount shown as tax on any return specified in paragraph (1) on or before the date prescribed for payment of such tax (determined with regard to any extension of time for payment), unless it is shown that such failure is due to reasonable cause and not due to willful neglect, there shall be added to the amount shown as tax on such return 0.5 percent of the amount of such tax if the failure is for not more than 1 month, with an additional 0.5 percent for each additional month or fraction thereof during which such failure continues, not exceeding 25 percent in the aggregate; or

(3) to pay any amount in respect of any tax required to be shown on a return specified in paragraph (1) which is not so shown (including an assessment made pursuant to section 6213(b)) within 10 days of the date of the notice and demand therefor, unless it is shown that such failure is due to reasonable cause and not due to willful neglect, there shall be added to the amount of tax stated in such notice and demand 0.5 percent of the amount of such tax if the failure is for not more than 1 month, with an additional 0.5 percent for each additional month or fraction thereof during which such failure continues, not exceeding 25 percent in the aggregate.

In the case of a failure to file a return of tax imposed by chapter 1 within 60 days of the date prescribed for filing of such return (determined with regard to any extensions of time for filing), unless it is shown that such failure is due to reasonable cause and not due to willful neglect, the addition to tax under paragraph (1) shall not be less than the lesser of $100 or 100 percent of the amount required to be shown as tax on such return.

* * *

§ 6653.   Additions to tax for negligence and fraud

(a) **Negligence.—**

(1) **In general.—**If any part of any underpayment (as defined in subsection (c)) is due to negligence or disregard of rules or regulations, there shall be added to the tax an amount equal to the sum of—

(A) 5 percent of the underpayment, and

(B) an amount equal to 50 percent of the interest payable under section 6601 with respect to the portion of such underpayment which is attributable to negligence for the period beginning on the last date prescribed by law for payment of such underpayment (determined without regard to any extension) and ending on the date of the assessment of the tax (or, if earlier, the date of the payment of the tax).

(2) **Underpayment taken into account reduced by portion attributable to fraud.—**There shall not be taken into account under this subsection any portion of an underpayment attributable to fraud with respect to which a penalty is imposed under subsection (b).

(3) **Negligence.—**For purposes of this subsection, the term "negligence" includes any failure to make a reasonable attempt to comply with the provisions of this title, and the term "disregard" includes any careless, reckless, or intentional disregard.

(b) **Fraud.—**

(1) In general.—If any part of any underpayment (as defined in subsection (c)) of tax required to be shown on a return is due to fraud, there shall be added to the tax an amount equal to the sum of—

    (A) 75 percent of the portion of the underpayment which is attributable to fraud, and

    (B) an amount equal to 50 percent of the interest payable under section 6601 with respect to such portion for the period beginning on the last day prescribed by law for payment of such underpayment (determined without regard to any extension) and ending on the date of the assessment of the tax or, if earlier, the date of the payment of the tax.

(2) Determination of portion attributable to fraud.—If the Secretary establishes that any portion of an underpayment is attributable to fraud, the entire underpayment shall be treated as attributable to fraud except with respect to any portion of the underpayment which the taxpayer establishes is not attributable to fraud.

(3) Special rule for joint returns.—In the case of a joint return, this subsection shall not apply with respect to a spouse unless some part of the underpayment is due to the fraud of such spouse.

§ **6654.** Failure by individual to pay estimated income tax

(a) Addition to the tax.—Except as otherwise provided in this section, in the case of any underpayment of estimated tax by an individual, there shall be added to the tax under chapter 1 and the tax under chapter 2 for the taxable year an amount determined by applying—

    (1) the underpayment rate established under section 6621,

    (2) to the amount of the underpayment,

    (3) for the period of the underpayment.

(b) Amount of underpayment; period of underpayment.—For purposes of subsection (a)—

    (1) Amount.—The amount of the underpayment shall be the excess of—

        (A) the required installment, over

        (B) the amount (if any) of the installment paid on or before the due date for the installment.

    (2) Period of underpayment.—The period of the underpayment shall run from the due date for the installment to whichever of the following dates is the earlier—

        (A) the 15th day of the 4th month following the close of the taxable year, or

        (B) with respect to any portion of the underpayment, the date on which such portion is paid.

    (3) Order of crediting payments.—For purposes of paragraph (2)(B), a payment of estimated tax shall be credited against unpaid required installments in the order in which such installments are required to be paid.

(c) Number of required installments; due dates.—For purposes of this section—

    (1) Payable in 4 installments.—There shall be 4 required installments for each taxable year.

    (2) Time for payment of installments.—

In the case of the following required installments:	The due date is:
1st	April 15
2nd	June 15

In the case of the following required installments:	The due date is:
3rd	September 15
4th	January 15 of the following taxable year

(d) Amount of required installments.—For purposes of this section—

(1) Amount.—

(A) In general.—Except as provided in paragraph (2), the amount of any required installment shall be 25 percent of the required annual payment.

(B) Required annual payment.—For purposes of subparagraph (A), the term "required annual payment" means the lesser of—

(i) 90 percent of the tax shown on the return for the taxable year (or, if no return is filed, 90 percent of the tax for such year), or

(ii) 100 percent of the tax shown on the return of the individual for the preceding taxable year.

Clause (ii) shall not apply if the preceding taxable year was not a taxable year of 12 months or if the individual did not file a return for such preceding taxable year.

(2) Lower required installment where annualized income installment is less than amount determined under paragraph (1).—

(A) In general.—In the case of any required installment, if the individual establishes that the annualized income installment is less than the amount determined under paragraph (1)—

(i) the amount of such required installment shall be the annualized income installment, and

(ii) any reduction in a required installment resulting from the application of this subparagraph shall be recaptured by increasing the amount of the next required installment determined under paragraph (1) by the amount of such reduction (and by increasing subsequent required installments to the extent that the reduction has not previously been recaptured under this clause).

(B) Determination of annualized income installment.—In the case of any required installment, the annualized income installment is the excess (if any) of—

(i) an amount equal to the applicable percentage of the tax for the taxable year computed by placing on an annualized basis the taxable income, alternative minimum taxable income, and adjusted self-employment income for months in the taxable year ending before the due date for the installment, over

(ii) the aggregate amount of any prior required installments for the taxable year.

(C) Special rules.—For purposes of this paragraph—

(i) Annualization.—The taxable income, alternative minimum taxable income, and adjusted self-employment income shall be placed on an annualized basis under regulations prescribed by the Secretary.

(ii) Applicable percentage.—

In the case of the following required installments:	The applicable percentage is:
1st	22.5
2nd	45

In the case of the following required installments:	The applicable percentage is:
3rd	67.5
4th	90

(iii) **Adjusted self-employment income.**—The term "adjusted self-employment income" means self-employment income (as defined in section 1402(b)); except that section 1402(b) shall be applied by placing wages (within the meaning of section 1402(b)) for months in the taxable year ending before the due date for the installment on an annualized basis consistent with clause (i).

(e) **Exceptions.**—

(1) **Where tax is small amount.**—No addition to tax shall be imposed under subsection (a) for any taxable year if the tax shown on the return for such taxable year (or, if no return is filed, the tax), reduced by the credit allowable under section 31, is less than $500.

(2) **Where no tax liability for preceding taxable year.**—No addition to tax shall be imposed under subsection (a) for any taxable year if—

(A) the preceding taxable year was a taxable year of 12 months,

(B) the individual did not have any liability for tax for the preceding taxable year, and

(C) the individual was a citizen or resident of the United States throughout the preceding taxable year.

(3) **Waiver in certain cases.**—

(A) **In general.**—No addition to tax shall be imposed under subsection (a) with respect to any underpayment to the extent the Secretary determines that by reason of casualty, disaster, or other unusual circumstances the imposition of such addition to tax would be against equity and good conscience.

(B) **Newly retired or disabled individuals.**—No addition to tax shall be imposed under subsection (a) with respect to any underpayment if the Secretary determines that—

(i) the taxpayer—

(I) retired after having attained age 62, or

(II) became disabled,

in the taxable year for which estimated payments were required to be made or in the taxable year preceding such taxable year, and

(ii) such underpayment was due to reasonable cause and not to willful neglect.

(f) **Tax computed after application of credits against tax.**—For purposes of this section, the term "tax" means—

(1) the tax imposed by chapter 1, plus

(2) the tax imposed by chapter 2, minus

(3) the sum of—

(A) the credits against tax allowed by part IV of subchapter A of chapter 1, other than the credit against tax provided by section 31 (relating to tax withheld on wages), plus

(B) to the extent allowed under regulations prescribed by the Secretary, any overpayment of the tax imposed by section 4986 (determined without regard to section 4995(a)(4)(B)).

(g) **Application of section in case of tax withheld on wages.**—

(1) **In general.**—For purposes of applying this section, the amount of the credit allowed under section 31 for the taxable year shall be deemed a payment of estimated tax, and an equal part of such amount shall be deemed paid on each due date for such taxable year, unless the taxpayer establishes the dates on which all amounts were actually withheld, in which case the amounts so withheld shall be deemed payments of estimated tax on the dates on which such amounts were actually withheld.

(2) **Separate application.**—The taxpayer may apply paragraph (1) separately with respect to—

(A) wage withholding, and

(B) all other amounts withheld for which credit is allowed under section 31.

(h) **Special rule where return filed on or before January 31.**—If, on or before January 31 of the following taxable year, the taxpayer files a return for the taxable year and pays in full the amount computed on the return as payable, then no addition to tax shall be imposed under subsection (a) with respect to any underpayment of the 4th required installment for the taxable year.

(i) **Special rules for farmers and fishermen.**—For purposes of this section—

(1) **In general.**—If an individual is a farmer or fisherman for any taxable year—

(A) there shall be only 1 required installment for the taxable year,

(B) the due date for such installment shall be January 15 of the following taxable year,

(C) the amount of such installment shall be equal to the required annual payment (determined under subsection (d)(1)(B) by substituting "66⅔ percent" for "90 percent", and

(D) subsection (h) shall be applied—

(I) by substituting "March 1" for "January 31", and

(II) by treating the required installment described in subparagraph (A) of this paragraph as the 4th required installment.

(2) **Farmer or fisherman defined.**—An individual is a farmer or fisherman for any taxable year if—

(A) the individual's gross income from farming or fishing (including oyster farming) for the taxable year is at least 66⅔ percent of the total gross income from all sources for the taxable year, or

(B) such individual's gross income from farming or fishing (including oyster farming) shown on the return of the individual for the preceding taxable year is at least 66⅔ percent of the total gross income from all sources shown on such return.

* * *

(k) **Fiscal years and short years.**—

(1) **Fiscal years.**—In applying this section to a taxable year beginning on any date other than January 1, there shall be substituted, for the months specified in this section, the months which correspond thereto.

(2) **Short taxable year.**—This section shall be applied to taxable years of less than 12 months in accordance with regulations prescribed by the Secretary.

(*l*) **Trusts and certain estates.**—This section shall apply to—

(1) any trust, and

(2) any estate with respect to any taxable year ending 2 or more years after the date of the death of the decedent's death.

(m) **Regulations.**—The Secretary shall prescribe such regulations as may be necessary to carry out the purposes of this section.

§ 6655. Failure by corporation to pay estimated income tax

(a) **Addition to tax.**—Except as provided in subsections (d) and (e), in the case of any underpayment of tax by a corporation—

(1) **In general.**—There shall be added to the tax under chapter 1 for the taxable year an amount determined at the underpayment rate established under section 6621 on the amount of the underpayment for the period of the underpayment.

(2) **Special rule where corporation paid 80 percent or more of tax.**—In any case in which there would be no underpayment if subsection (b) were applied by substituting "80 percent" for "90 percent" each place it appears, the addition to tax under paragraph (1) shall be equal to 75 percent of the amount otherwise determined under paragraph (1).

(b) **Amount of underpayment.**—For purposes of subsection (a), the amount of the underpayment shall be the excess of—

(1) The amount of the installment which would be required to be paid if the estimated tax were equal to 90 percent of the tax shown on the return for the taxable year or, if no return was filed, 90 percent of the tax for such year, over

(2) The amount, if any, of the installment paid on or before the last date prescribed for payment.

(c) **Period of underpayment.**—The period of the underpayment shall run from the date the installment was required to be paid to whichever of the following dates is the earlier—

(1) The 15th day of the third month following the close of the taxable year.

(2) With respect to any portion of the underpayment, the date on which such portion is paid. For purposes of this paragraph, a payment of estimated tax on any installment date shall be considered a payment of any previous underpayment only to the extent such payment exceeds the amount of the installment determined under subsection (b)(1) for such installment date.

(d) **Exception.**—Notwithstanding the provisions of the preceding subsections, the addition to the tax with respect to any underpayment of any installment shall not be imposed if the total amount of all payments of estimated tax made on or before the last date prescribed for the payment of such installment equals or exceeds the amount which would have been required to be paid on or before such date if the estimated tax were whichever of the following is the lesser—

(1) The tax shown on the return of the corporation for the preceding taxable year, if a return showing a liability for tax was filed by the corporation for the preceding taxable year and such preceding year was a taxable year of 12 months.

(2) An amount equal to the tax computed at the rates applicable to the taxable year but otherwise on the basis of the facts shown on the return of the corporation for, and the law applicable to, the preceding taxable year.

(3)(A) An amount equal to 90 percent of the tax for the taxable year computed by placing on an annualized basis the taxable income:

(i) for the first 3 months of the taxable year, in the case of the installment required to be paid in the 4th month,

(ii) for the first 3 months or for the first 5 months of the taxable year, in the case of the installment required to be paid in the 6th month,

(iii) for the first 6 months or for the first 8 months of the taxable year in the case of the installment required to be paid in the 9th month, and

(iv) for the first 9 months or for the first 11 months of the taxable year, in the case of the installment required to be paid in the 12th month of the taxable year.

(B) For purposes of this paragraph, the taxable income shall be placed on an annualized basis by—

(i) multiplying by 12 the taxable income referred to in subparagraph (A), and

(ii) dividing the resulting amount by the number of months in the taxable year (3, 5, 6, 8, 9, or 11, as the case may be) referred to in subparagraph (A).

(e) Additional exception for recurring seasonal income.—

(1) In general.—Notwithstanding the preceding subsections, the addition to the tax with respect to any underpayment of any installment shall not be imposed if the total amount of all payments of estimated tax made on or before the last date prescribed for the payment of such installment equals or exceeds 90 percent of the amount determined under paragraph (2).

(2) Determination of amount.—The amount determined under this paragraph for any installment shall be determined in the following manner—

(A) take the taxable income for all months during the taxable year preceding the filing month,

(B) divide such amount by the base period percentage for all months during the taxable year preceding the filing month,

(C) determine the tax on the amount determined under subparagraph (B), and

(D) multiply the tax computed under subparagraph (C) by the base period percentage for the filing month and all months during the taxable year preceding the filing month.

(3) Definitions and special rules.—For purposes of this subsection—

(A) Base period percentage.—The base period percentage for any period of months shall be the average percent which the taxable income for the corresponding months in each of the 3 preceding taxable years bears to the taxable income for the 3 preceding taxable years.

(B) Filing month.—The term "filing month" means the month in which the installment is required to be paid.

(C) Limitation on application of subsection.—This subsection shall only apply if the base period percentage for any 6 consecutive months of the taxable year equals or exceeds 70 percent.

(D) Reorganizations, etc.—The Secretary may by regulations provide for the determination of the base period percentage in the case of reorganizations, new corporations, and other similar circumstances.

(f) Definition of tax.—For purposes of subsections (b), (d), (e), and (i), the term "tax" means the excess of—

(1) the sum of—

(A) the tax imposed by section 11 or 1201(a), or subchapter L of chapter 1, whichever is applicable,

802

(B) the tax imposed by section 55, plus

(C) the tax imposed by section 59A, over

(2) the sum of—

(A) the credits against tax provided by part IV of subchapter A of chapter 1, plus

(B) to the extent allowed under regulations prescribed by the Secretary, any overpayment of the tax imposed by section 4986 (determined without regard to section 4995(a)(4)(B)).

(g) Short taxable year.—The application of this section to taxable years of less than 12 months shall be in accordance with regulations prescribed by the Secretary.

* * *

(i) Large corporations required to pay minimum percentage of current year tax.—

(1) Minimum percentage.—

(A) In general.—Except as provided in subparagraph (B), in the case of a large corporation, paragraphs (1) and (2) of subsection (d) shall not apply.

(B) Transition rule.—For taxable years beginning before 1984, in the case of a large corporation, the amount treated as the estimated tax for the taxable year under paragraphs (1) and (2) of subsection (d) shall in no event be less than the applicable percentage of—

(i) the tax shown on the return for the taxable year, or

(ii) if no return was filed, the tax for such year.

(C) Applicable percentage.—For purposes of subparagraph (B), the applicable percentage shall be determined in accordance with the following table:

If the taxable year begins in:	The applicable percentage is:
1982	65
1983	75

(2) Large corporation.—For purposes of this subsection, the term "large corporation" means any corporation if such corporation (or any predecessor corporation) had taxable income of $1,000,000 or more for any taxable year during the testing period.

(3) Rules for applying paragraph (2).—

(A) Testing period.—For purposes of this subsection, the term "testing period" means the 3 taxable years immediately preceding the taxable year involved.

(B) Members of controlled groups.—For purposes of applying paragraph (2) to any taxable year in the testing period with respect to corporations which are component members of a controlled group of corporations for such taxable year, the $1,000,000 amount specified in paragraph (2) shall be divided among such members under rules similar to the rules of section 1561.

§ 6659. Addition to tax in the case of valuation overstatements for purposes of the income tax

(a) Addition to the tax.—If—

(1) an individual, or

(2) a closely held corporation or a personal service corporation, has an underpayment of the tax imposed by chapter 1 for the taxable year which is attributable to a valuation overstatement, then there shall be added to the tax an amount equal to the applicable percentage of the underpayment so attributable.

(b) Applicable percentage defined.—For purposes of subsection (a), the applicable percentage shall be determined under the following table:

If the valuation claimed is the following percent of the correct valuation—	The applicable percentage is:
150 percent or more but not more than 200 percent	10
More than 200 percent but not more than 250 percent	20
More than 250 percent	30

(c) Valuation overstatement defined.—For purposes of this section, there is a valuation overstatement if the value of any property, or the adjusted basis of any property, claimed on any return is 150 percent or more of the amount determined to be the correct amount of such valuation or adjusted basis (as the case may be).

(d) Underpayment must be at least $1,000.—This section shall not apply if the underpayment for the taxable year attributable to valuation overstatements is less than $1,000.

(e) Authority to waive.—The Secretary may waive all or any part of the addition to the tax provided by this section on a showing by the taxpayer that there was a reasonable basis for the valuation or adjusted basis claimed on the return and that such claim was made in good faith.

(f) Special rules for overstatement of charitable deduction.—

(1) Amount of applicable percentage.—In the case of any underpayment attributable to a valuation overstatement with respect to charitable deduction property, the applicable percentage for purposes of subsection (a) shall be 30 percent.

(2) Limitation on authority to waive.—In the case of any underpayment attributable to a valuation overstatement with respect to charitable deduction property, the Secretary may not waive any portion of the addition to tax provided by this section unless the Secretary determines that—

(A) the claimed value of the property was based on a qualified appraisal made by a qualified appraiser, and

(B) in addition to obtaining such appraisal, the taxpayer made a good faith investigation of the value of the contributed property.

(3) Definitions.—For purposes of this subsection—

(A) Charitable deduction property.—The term "charitable deduction property" means any property contributed by the taxpayer in a contribution for which a deduction was claimed under section 170. For purposes of paragraph (2), such term shall not include any securities for which (as of the date of the contribution) market quotations are readily available on an established securities market.

(B) Qualified appraiser.—The term "qualified appraiser" means any appraiser meeting the requirements of the regulations prescribed under section 170(a)(1).

(C) Qualified appraisal.—The term "qualified appraisal" means any appraisal meeting the requirements of the regulations prescribed under section 170(a)(1).

(g) Other definitions.—For purposes of this section—

(1) **Underpayment.**—The term "underpayment" has the meaning given to such term by section 6653(c) (1).

(2) **Closely held corporation.**—The term "closely held corporation" means any corporation described in section 465(a) (1) (B).

(3) **Personal service corporation.**—The term "personal service corporation" means any corporation which is a service organization (within the meaning of section 414(m) (3)).

§ 6660. Addition to tax in the case of valuation understatement for purposes of estate or gift taxes

(a) **Addition to the tax.**—In the case of any underpayment of a tax imposed by subtitle B (relating to estate and gift taxes) which is attributable to a valuation understatement, there shall be added to the tax an amount equal to the applicable percentage of the underpayment so attributed.

(b) **Applicable percentage.**—For purposes of subsection (a), the applicable percentage shall be determined under the following table:

If the valuation claimed is the following percent of the correct valuation—	The applicable percentage is:
50 percent or more but not more than 66⅔ percent	10
40 percent or more but less than 50 percent	20
Less than 40 percent	30.

(c) **Valuation understatement defined.**—For purposes of this section, there is a valuation understatement if the value of any property claimed on any return is 66⅔ percent or less of the amount determined to be the correct amount of such valuation.

(d) **Underpayment must be at least $1,000.**—This section shall not apply if the underpayment is less than $1,000 for any taxable period (or, in the case of the tax imposed by chapter 11, with respect to the estate of the decedent).

(e) **Authority to waive.**—The Secretary may waive all or any part of the addition to the tax provided by this section on a showing by the taxpayer that there was a reasonable basis for the valuation claimed on the return and that such claim was made in good faith.

(f) **Underpayment defined.**—For purposes of this section, the term "underpayment" has the meaning given to such term by section 6653(c)(1).

§ 6661. Substantial understatement of liability

(a) **Addition to tax.**—If there is a substantial understatement of income tax for any taxable year, there shall be added to the tax an amount equal to 25 percent of the amount of any underpayment attributable to such understatement.

(b) **Definition and special rule.**—

(1) **Substantial understatement.**—

(A) **In general.**—For purposes of this section, there is a substantial understatement of income tax for any taxable year if the amount of the understatement for the taxable year exceeds the greater of—

(i) 10 percent of the tax required to be shown on the return for the taxable year, or

(ii) $5,000.

(B) Special rule for corporations.—In the case of a corporation other than an S corporation or a personal holding company (as defined in section 542), paragraph (1) shall be applied by substituting "$10,000" for "$5,000".

(2) Understatement.—

(A) In general.—For purposes of paragraph (1), the term "understatement" means the excess of—

(i) the amount of the tax required to be shown on the return for the taxable year, over

(ii) the amount of the tax imposed which is shown on the return, reduced by any rebate (within the meaning of section 6211(b)(2)).

(B) Reduction for understatement due to position of taxpayer or disclosed item.—The amount of the understatement under subparagraph (A) shall be reduced by that portion of the understatement which is attributable to—

(i) the tax treatment of any item by the taxpayer if there is or was substantial authority for such treatment, or

(ii) any item with respect to which the relevant facts affecting the item's tax treatment are adequately disclosed in the return or in a statement attached to the return.

(C) Special rules in cases involving tax shelters.—

(i) In general.—In the case of any item attributable to a tax shelter—

(I) subparagraph (B)(ii) shall not apply, and

(II) subparagraph (B)(i) shall not apply unless (in addition to meeting the requirements of such subparagraph) the taxpayer reasonably believed that the tax treatment of such item by the taxpayer was more likely than not the proper treatment.

(ii) Tax shelter.—For purposes of clause (i), the term "tax shelter" means—

(I) a partnership or other entity,

(II) any investment plan or arrangement, or

(III) any other plan or arrangement,

if the principal purpose of such partnership, entity, plan, or arrangement is the avoidance or evasion of Federal income tax.

(3) Coordination with penalty imposed by section 6659.—For purposes of determining the amount of the addition to tax assessed under subsection (a), there shall not be taken into account that portion of the substantial understatement on which a penalty is imposed under section 6659 (relating to addition to tax in the case of valuation overstatements).

(c) Authority to waive.—The Secretary may waive all or any part of the addition to tax provided by this section on a showing by the taxpayer that there was reasonable cause for the understatement (or part thereof) and that the taxpayer acted in good faith.

SUBCHAPTER B—ASSESSABLE PENALTIES

§ 6671. Rules for application of assessable penalties

(a) Penalty assessed as tax.—The penalties and liabilities provided by this subchapter shall be paid upon notice and demand by the Secretary, and shall be assessed and collected in the same manner as taxes. Except as otherwise provided, any reference in this title to "tax" imposed by this title shall be deemed also to refer to the penalties and liabilities provided by this subchapter.

(b) Person defined.—The term "person", as used in this subchapter, includes an officer or employee of a corporation, or a member or employee of a partnership, who as such officer, employee, or member is under a duty to perform the act in respect of which the violation occurs.

§ **6672.** Failure to collect and pay over tax, or attempt to evade or defeat tax

(a) General rule.—Any person required to collect, truthfully account for, and pay over any tax imposed by this title who willfully fails to collect such tax, or truthfully account for and pay over such tax, or willfully attempts in any manner to evade or defeat any such tax or the payment thereof, shall, in addition to other penalties provided by law, be liable to a penalty equal to the total amount of the tax evaded, or not collected, or not accounted for and paid over. No penalty shall be imposed under section 6653 for any offense to which this section is applicable.

* * *

§ **6673.** Damages assessable for instituting proceedings before the Tax Court primarily for delay, etc.

Whenever it appears to the Tax Court that proceedings before it have been instituted or maintained by the taxpayer primarily for delay, that the taxpayer's position in such proceeding is frivolous or groundless, or that the taxpayer unreasonably failed to pursue available administrative remedies, damages in an amount not in excess of $5,000 shall be awarded to the United States by the Tax Court in its decision. Damages so awarded shall be assessed at the same time as the deficiency and shall be paid upon notice and demand from the Secretary and shall be collected as a part of the tax.

* * *

§ **6682.** False information with respect to withholding

(a) Civil penalty.—In addition to any criminal penalty provided by law, if—

(1) any individual makes a statement under section 3402 or section 3406 which results in a decrease in the amounts deducted and withheld under chapter 24, and

(2) as of the time such statement was made, there was no reasonable basis for such statement,

such individual shall pay a penalty of $500 for such statement.

* * *

§ **6698.** Failure to file partnership return

(a) General rule.—In addition to the penalty imposed by section 7203 (relating to willful failure to file return, supply information, or pay tax), if any partnership required to file a return under section 6031 for any taxable year—

(1) fails to file such return at the time prescribed therefor (determined with regard to any extension of time for filing), or

(2) files a return which fails to show the information required under section 6031,

such partnership shall be liable for a penalty determined under subsection (b) for each month (or fraction thereof) during which such failure continues (but not to exceed 5 months), unless it is shown that such failure is due to reasonable cause.

(b) Amount per month.—For purposes of subsection (a), the amount determined under this subsection for any month is the product of—

(1) $50, multiplied by

(2) the number of persons who were partners in the partnership during any part of the taxable year.

(c) Assessment of penalty.—The penalty imposed by subsection (a) shall be assessed against the partnership.

(d) Deficiency procedures not to apply.—Subchapter B of chapter 63 (relating to deficiency procedures for income, estate, gift, and certain excise taxes) shall not apply in respect of the assessment or collection of any penalty imposed by subsection (a).

§ 6700. Promoting abusive tax shelters, etc.

(a) Imposition of penalty.—Any person who—

(1)(A) organizes (or assists in the organization of)—

(i) a partnership or other entity,

(ii) any investment plan or arrangement, or

(iii) any other plan or arrangement, or

(B) participates in the sale of any interest in an entity or plan or arrangement referred to in subparagraph (A), and

(2) makes or furnishes (in connection with such organization or sale)—

(A) a statement with respect to the allowability of any deduction or credit, the excludability of any income, or the securing of any other tax benefit by reason of holding an interest in the entity or participating in the plan or arrangement which the person knows or has reason to know is false or fraudulent as to any material matter, or

(B) a gross valuation overstatement as to any material matter,

shall pay a penalty equal to the greater of $1,000 or 20 percent of the gross income derived or to be derived by such person from such activity.

(b) Rules relating to penalty for gross valuation overstatements.—

(1) **Gross valuation overstatement defined.**—For purposes of this section, the term "gross valuation overstatement" means any statement as to the value of any property or services if—

(A) the value so stated exceeds 200 percent of the amount determined to be the correct valuation, and

(B) the value of such property or services is directly related to the amount of any deduction or credit allowable under chapter 1 to any participant.

(2) **Authority to waive.**—The Secretary may waive all or any part of the penalty provided by subsection (a) with respect to any gross valuation overstatement on a showing that there was a reasonable basis for the valuation and that such valuation was made in good faith.

(c) Penalty in addition to other penalties.—The penalty imposed by this section shall be in addition to any other penalty provided by law.

§ 6701. Penalties for aiding and abetting understatement of tax liability

(a) Imposition of penalty.—Any person—

(1) who aids or assists in, procures, or advises with respect to, the preparation or presentation of any portion of a return, affidavit, claim, or other document in connection with any matter arising under the internal revenue laws,

(2) who knows that such portion will be used in connection with any material matter arising under the internal revenue laws, and

(3) who knows that such portion (if so used) will result in an understatement of the liability for tax of another person,

shall pay a penalty with respect to each such document in the amount determined under subsection (b).

(b) Amount of penalty.—

(1) **In general.**—Except as provided in paragraph (2), the amount of the penalty imposed by subsection (a) shall be $1,000.

(2) **Corporations.**—If the return, affidavit, claim, or other document relates to the tax liability of a corporation, the amount of the penalty imposed by subsection (a) shall be $10,000.

(3) **Only 1 penalty per person per period.**—If any person is subject to a penalty under subsection (a) with respect to any document relating to any taxpayer for any taxable period (or where there is no taxable period, any taxable event), such person shall not be subject to a penalty under subsection (a) with respect to any other document relating to such taxpayer for such taxable period (or event).

(c) Activities of subordinates.—

(1) **In general.**—For purposes of subsection (a), the term "procures" includes—

(A) ordering (or otherwise causing) a subordinate to do an act, and

(B) knowing of, and not attempting to prevent, participation by a subordinate in an act.

(2) **Subordinate.**—For purposes of paragraph (1), the term "subordinate" means any other person (whether or not a director, officer, employee, or agent of the taxpayer involved) over whose activities the person has direction, supervision, or control.

(d) Taxpayer not required to have knowledge.—Subsection (a) shall apply whether or not the understatement is with the knowledge or consent of the persons authorized or required to present the return, affidavit, claim or other document.

(e) Certain actions not treated as aid or assistance.—For purposes of subsection (a)(1), a person furnishing typing, reproducing, or other mechanical assistance with respect to a document shall not be treated as having aided or assisted in the preparation of such document by reason of such assistance.

(f) Penalty in addition to other penalties.—

(1) **In general.**—Except as provided by paragraph (2), the penalty imposed by this section shall be in addition to any other penalty provided by law.

(2) **Coordination with return preparer penalties.**—No penalty shall be assessed under subsection (a) or (b) of section 6694 on any person with respect to any document for which a penalty is assessed on such person under subsection (a).

§ 6702.   Frivolous income tax return

(a) Civil penalty.—If—

(1) any individual files what purports to be a return of the tax imposed by subtitle A but which—

(A) does not contain information on which the substantial correctness of the self-assessment may be judged, or

(B) contains information that on its face indicates that the self-assessment is substantially incorrect; and

(2) the conduct referred to in paragraph (1) is due to—

(A) a position which is frivolous, or

(B) a desire (which appears on the purported return) to delay or impede the administration of Federal income tax laws,

then such individual shall pay a penalty of $500.

(b) Penalty in addition to other penalties.—The penalty imposed by subsection (a) shall be in addition to any other penalty provided by law.

§ 6706.   Original issue discount information requirements

(a) Failure to show information on debt instrument.—In the case of a failure to set forth on a debt instrument the information required to be set forth on such instrument under section 1275(c)(1), unless it is shown that such failure is due to reasonable cause and not to willful neglect, the issuer shall pay a penalty of $50 for each instrument with respect to which such a failure exists.

(b) Failure to furnish information to secretary.—Any issuer who fails to furnish information required under section 1275(c)(2) with respect to any issue of debt instruments on the date prescribed therefor (determined with regard to any extension of time for filing) shall pay a penalty equal to 1 percent of the aggregate issue price of such issue, unless it is shown that such failure is due to reasonable cause and not willful neglect. The amount of the penalty imposed under the preceding sentence with respect to any issue of debt instruments shall not exceed $50,000 for such issue.

(c) Deficiency procedures not to apply.—Subchapter B of chapter 63 (relating to deficiency procedures for income, estate, gift, and certain excise taxes) shall not apply in respect of the assessment or collection of any penalty imposed by this section.

§ 6707.   Failure to furnish information regarding tax shelters

(a) Failure to register tax shelter.—

(1) Imposition of penalty.—If a person who is required to register a tax shelter under section 6111(a)—

(A) fails to register such tax shelter on or before the date described in section 6111(a)(1), or

(B) files false or incomplete information with the Secretary with respect to such registration,

such person shall pay a penalty with respect to such registration in the amount determined under paragraph (2). No penalty shall be imposed under the preceding sentence with respect to any failure which is due to reasonable cause.

(2) Amount of penalty.—The penalty imposed under paragraph (1) with respect to any tax shelter shall be an amount equal to the greater of—

(A) 1 percent of the aggregate amount invested in such tax shelter, or

(B) $500.

(b) Failure to furnish tax shelter identification number.—

(1) Sellers, etc.—Any person who fails to furnish the identification number of a tax shelter which such person is required to furnish under section 6111(b)(1) shall pay a penalty of $100 for each such failure.

(2) Failure to include number on return.—Any person who fails to include an identification number on a return on which such number is required to be included under section 6111(b)(2) shall pay a penalty of $250 for each such failure, unless such failure is due to reasonable cause.

§ 6721. Failure to file certain information returns

(a) General rule.—In the case of each failure to file an information return with the Secretary on the date prescribed therefor (determined with regard to any extension of time for filing), the person failing to so file such return shall pay $50 for each such failure, but the total amount imposed on such person for all such failures during any calendar year shall not exceed $100,000.

(b) Penalty in case of intentional disregard.—If 1 or more failures to which subsection (a) applies are due to intentional disregard of the filing requirement, then, with respect to each such failure—

(1) the penalty imposed under subsection (a) shall be $100, or, if greater—

(A) in the case of a return other than a return required under section 6045(a), 6041A(b), 6050H, 6050J, 6050K, or 6050L, 10 percent of the aggregate amount of the items required to be reported, or

(B) in the case of a return required to be filed by section 6045(a), 6050K, or 6050L, 5 percent of the aggregate amount of the items required to be reported, and

(2) in the case of any penalty determined under paragraph (1)—

(A) the $100,000 limitation under subsection (a) shall not apply, and

(B) such penalty shall not be taken into account in applying the $100,000 limitation to penalties not determined under paragraph (1).

(Added Pub.L. 99–514, Title XV, § 1501(a), Oct. 22, 1986, 100 Stat. ——.)

§ 6722. Failure to furnish certain payee statements

(a) General rule.—In the case of each failure to furnish a payee statement on the date prescribed therefor to the person to whom such statement is required to be furnished, the person failing to so furnish such statement shall pay $50 for each such failure, but the total amount imposed on such person for all such failures during any calendar year shall not exceed $100,000.

(b) Failure to notify partnership of exchange of partnership interest.—In the case of any person who fails to furnish the notice required by section 6050K(c)(1) on the date prescribed therefor, such person shall pay a penalty of $50 for each such failure.

(Added Pub.L. 99–514, Title XV, § 1501(a), Oct. 22, 1986, 100 Stat. ——.)

§ 6723. Failure to include correct information

(a) General rule.—If—

(1) any person files an information return or furnishes a payee statement, and

(2) such person does not include all of the information required to be shown on such return or statement or includes incorrect information,

such person shall pay $5 for each return or statement with respect to which such failure occurs, but the total amount imposed on such person for all such failures during any calendar year shall not exceed $20,000.

(b) Penalty in case of intentional disregard.—If 1 or more failures to which subsection (a) applies are due to intentional disregard of the correct information reporting requirement, then, with respect to each such failure—

(1) the penalty imposed under subsection (a) shall be $100, or, if greater—

(A) in the case of a return other than a return required under section 6045(a), 6041A(b), 6050H, 6050J, 6050K, or 6050L, 10 percent of the aggregate amount of the items required to be reported correctly, or

(B) in the case of a return required to be filed by section 6045(a), 6050K, or 6050L, 5 percent of the aggregate amount of the items required to be reported correctly, and

(2) in the case of any penalty determined under paragraph (1)—

(A) the $20,000 limitation under subsection (a) shall not apply, and

(B) such penalty shall not be taken into account in applying the $20,000 limitation to penalties not determined under paragraph (1).

(c) Coordination with section 6676.—No penalty shall be imposed under subsection (a) or (b) with respect to any return or statement if a penalty is imposed under section 6676 (relating to failure to supply identifying number) with respect to such return or statement.

(Added Pub.L. 99–514, Title XV, § 1501(a), Oct. 22, 1986, 100 Stat. ——.)

§ 6724. Waiver; definitions and special rules

(a) Reasonable cause waiver.—No penalty shall be imposed under this part with respect to any failure if it is shown that such failure is due to reasonable cause and not to willful neglect.

(b) Payment of penalty.—Any penalty imposed by this part shall be paid on notice and demand by the Secretary and in the same manner as tax.

(c) Special rules for failure to file interest and dividend returns or statements.—

(1) **Higher standards for waiver.**—In the case of any interest or dividend return or statement—

(A) subsection (a) shall not apply, but

(B) no penalty shall be imposed under this part if it is shown that the person otherwise liable for such penalty exercised due diligence in attempting to satisfy the requirement with respect to such return or statement.

(2) **Limitations not to apply.**—In the case of any interest or dividend return or statement—

(A) the $100,000 limitations of sections 6721(a) and 6722(a) and the $20,000 limitation of section 6723(a) shall not apply (and any penalty imposed on any failure involving such a return or statement shall not be taken into account in applying such limitations to other penalties), and

(B) penalties imposed with respect to such returns or statements shall not be taken into account for purposes of applying such limitations with respect to other returns or statements.

(3) Self assessment.—Any penalty imposed under this part on any person with respect to an interest or dividend return or statement—

(A) shall be assessed and collected in the same manner as an excise tax imposed by subtitle D, and

(B) shall be due and payable on April 1 of the calendar year following the calendar year for which such return or statement is required.

(4) Deficiency procedures not to apply.—Subchapter B of chapter 63 (relating to deficiency procedures for income, estate, gift, and certain excise taxes) shall not apply in respect of the assessment or collection of any penalty imposed under this part with respect to an interest or dividend return or statement.

(5) Interest or dividend return or statement.—For purposes of this subsection, the term "interest or dividend return or statement" means—

(A) any return required by section 6042(a)(1), 6044(a)(1), or 6049(a), and

(B) any statement required under section 6042(c), 6044(e), or 6049(c).

(d) Definitions.—For purposes of this part—

(1) Information return.—The term "information return" means—

(A) any statement of the amount of payments to another person required by—

(i) section 6041(a) or (b) (relating to certain information at source),

(ii) section 6042(a)(1) (relating to payments of dividends),

(iii) section 6044(a)(1) (relating to payments of patronage dividends),

(iv) section 6049(a) (relating to payments of interest),

(v) section 6050A(a) (relating to reporting requirements of certain fishing boat operators),

(vi) section 6050N(a) (relating to payments of royalties), or

(vii) section 6051(d) (relating to information returns with respect to income tax withheld), and

(B) any return required by—

(i) section 4997(a) (relating to information with respect to windfall profit tax on crude oil),

(ii) section 6041A(a) or (b) (relating to returns of direct sellers),

(iii) section 6045(a) or (d) (relating to returns of brokers),

(iv) section 6050H(a) (relating to mortgage interest received in trade or business from individuals),

(v) section 6050I(a) (relating to cash received in trade or business),

(vi) section 6050J(a) (relating to foreclosures and abandonments of security),

(vii) section 6050K(a) (relating to exchanges of certain partnership interests),

(viii) section 6050L(a) (relating to returns relating to certain dispositions of donated property),

(ix) section 6052(a) (relating to reporting payment of wages in the form of group-term life insurance), or

(x) section 6053(c)(1) (relating to reporting with respect to certain tips).

(2) **Payee statement.**—The term "payee statement" means any statement required to be furnished under—

(A) section 4997(a) (relating to records and information; regulations),

(B) section 6031(b), 6034A, or 6037(b) (relating to statements furnished by certain pass-thru entities),

(C) section 6039(a) (relating to information required in connection with certain options),

(D) section 6041(d) (relating to information at source),

(E) section 6041A(e) (relating to returns regarding payments of remuneration for services and direct sales),

(F) section 6042(c) (relating to returns regarding payments of dividends and corporate earnings and profits),

(G) section 6044(e) (relating to returns regarding payments of patronage dividends),

(H) section 6045(b) or (d) (relating to returns of brokers),

(I) section 6049(c) (relating to returns regarding payments of interest),

(J) section 6050A(b) (relating to reporting requirements of certain fishing boat operators),

(K) section 6050C (relating to information regarding windfall profit tax on domestic crude oil),

(L) section 6050H(d) (relating to returns relating to mortgage interest received in trade or business from individuals),

(M) section 6050I(e) (relating to returns relating to cash received in trade or business),

(N) section 6050J(e) (relating to returns relating to foreclosures and abandonments of security),

(O) section 6050K(b) (relating to returns relating to exchanges of certain partnership interests),

(P) section 6050L(c) (relating to returns relating to certain dispositions of donated property),

(Q) section 6050N(b) (relating to returns regarding payments of royalties),

(R) section 6051 (relating to receipts for employees),

(S) section 6052(b) (relating to returns regarding payment of wages in the form of group-term life insurance), or

(T) section 6053(b) or (c) (relating to reports of tips).

(Added Pub.L. 99–514, Title XV, § 1501(a), Oct. 22, 1986, 100 Stat. ——.)

CHAPTER 70—JEOPARDY, BANKRUPTCY AND RECEIVERSHIPS

Subchapter
A. Jeopardy.

Part
  B. Receiverships, etc.*

PART II—JEOPARDY ASSESSMENTS

§ 6861. Jeopardy assessments of income, estate, gift, and certain excise taxes

(a) Authority for making.—If the Secretary believes that the assessment or collection of a deficiency, as defined in section 6211, will be jeopardized by delay, he shall, notwithstanding the provisions of section 6213(a), immediately assess such deficiency (together with all interest, additional amounts, and additions to the tax provided for by law), and notice and demand shall be made by the Secretary for the payment thereof.

(b) Deficiency letters.—If the jeopardy assessment is made before any notice in respect of the tax to which the jeopardy assessment relates has been mailed under section 6212(a), then the Secretary shall mail a notice under such subsection within 60 days after the making of the assessment.

* * *

CHAPTER 71—TRANSFEREES AND FIDUCIARIES

§ 6901. Transferred assets

(a) Method of collection.—The amounts of the following liabilities shall, except as hereinafter in this section provided, be assessed, paid, and collected in the same manner and subject to the same provisions and limitations as in the case of the taxes with respect to which the liabilities were incurred:

(1) Income, estate, and gift taxes.—

(A) Transferees.—The liability, at law or in equity, of a transferee of property—

(i) of a taxpayer in the case of a tax imposed by subtitle A (relating to income taxes),

(ii) of a decedent in the case of a tax imposed by chapter 11 (relating to estate taxes), or

(iii) of a donor in the case of a tax imposed by chapter 12 (relating to gift taxes),

in respect of the tax imposed by subtitle A or B.

(B) Fiduciaries.—The liability of a fiduciary under section 3713(b) of title 31, United States Code in respect of the payment of any tax described in subpara-

* Omitted entirely.

815

graph (A) from the estate of the taxpayer, the decedent, or the donor, as the case may be.

(2) Other taxes.—The liability, at law or in equity of a transferee of property of any person liable in respect of any tax imposed by this title (other than a tax imposed by subtitle A or B), but only if such liability arises on the liquidation of a partnership or corporation, or on a reorganization within the meaning of section 368(a).

(b) Liability.—Any liability referred to in subsection (a) may be either as to the amount of tax shown on a return or as to any deficiency or underpayment of any tax.

(c) Period of limitations.—The period of limitations for assessment of any such liability of a transferee or a fiduciary shall be as follows:

(1) Initial transferee.—In the case of the liability of an initial transferee, within 1 year after the expiration of the period of limitation for assessment against the transferor;

(2) Transferee of transferee.—In the case of the liability of a transferee of a transferee, within 1 year after the expiration of the period of limitation for assessment against the preceding transferee, but not more than 3 years after the expiration of the period of limitation for assessment against the initial transferor;

except that if, before the expiration of the period of limitation for the assessment of the liability of the transferee, a court proceeding for the collection of the tax or liability in respect thereof has been begun against the initial transferor or the last preceding transferee, respectively, then the period of limitation for assessment of the liability of the transferee shall expire 1 year after the return of execution in the court proceeding.

(3) Fiduciary.—In the case of the liability of a fiduciary, not later than 1 year after the liability arises or not later than the expiration of the period for collection of the tax in respect of which such liability arises, whichever is the later.

(d) Extension by agreement.—

(1) Extension of time for assessment.—If before the expiration of the time prescribed in subsection (c) for the assessment of the liability, the Secretary and the transferee or fiduciary have both consented in writing to its assessment after such time, the liability may be assessed at any time prior to the expiration of the period agreed upon. The period so agreed upon may be extended by subsequent agreements in writing made before the expiration of the period previously agreed upon. For the purpose of determining the period of limitation on credit or refund to the transferee or fiduciary of overpayments of tax made by such transferee or fiduciary or overpayments of tax made by the transferor of which the transferee or fiduciary is legally entitled to credit or refund, such agreement and any extension thereof shall be deemed an agreement and extension thereof referred to in section 6511(c).

(2) Extension of time for credit or refund.—If the agreement is executed after the expiration of the period of limitation for assessment against the taxpayer with reference to whom the liability of such transferee or fiduciary rises, then in applying the limitations under section 6511(c) on the amount of the credit or refund, the periods specified in section 6511(b) (2) shall be increased by the period from the date of such expiration to the date of the agreement.

(e) Period for assessment against transferor.—For purposes of this section, if any person is deceased, or is a corporation which has terminated its existence, the period of limitation for assessment against such person shall be the period that would be in effect had death or termination of existence not occurred.

(f) Suspension of running of period of limitations.—The running of the period of limitations upon the assessment of the liability of a transferee or fiduciary shall, after the mailing to the transferee or fiduciary of the notice provided for in section 6212 (relating to income, estate, and gift taxes), be suspended for the period during which the Secretary is prohibited from making the assessment in respect of the liability of the transferee or fiduciary (and in any event, if a proceeding in respect of the liability is placed on the docket of the Tax Court, until the decision of the Tax Court becomes final), and for 60 days thereafter.

(g) Address for notice of liability.—In the absence of notice to the Secretary under section 6903 of the existence of a fiduciary relationship, any notice of liability enforceable under this section required to be mailed to such person, shall, if mailed to the person subject to the liability at his last known address, be sufficient for purposes of this title, even if such person is deceased, or is under a legal disability, or, in the case of a corporation, has terminated its existence.

(h) Definition of transferee.—As used in this section, the term "transferee" includes donee, heir, legatee, devisee, and distributee, and with respect to estate taxes, also includes any person who, under section 6324(a) (2), is personally liable for any part of such tax.

* * *

§ 6902. Provisions of special application to transferees

(a) Burden of proof.—In proceedings before the Tax Court the burden of proof shall be upon the Secretary to show that a petitioner is liable as a transferee of property of a taxpayer, but not to show that the taxpayer was liable for the tax.

(b) Evidence.—Upon application to the Tax Court, a transferee of property of a taxpayer shall be entitled, under rules prescribed by the Tax Court, to a preliminary examination of books, papers, documents, correspondence, and other evidence of the taxpayer or a preceding transferee of the taxpayer's property, if the transferee making the application is a petitioner before the Tax Court for the redetermination of his liability in respect of the tax (including interest, additional amounts, and additions to the tax provided by law) imposed upon the taxpayer. Upon such application, the Tax Court may require by subpoena, ordered by the Tax Court or any division thereof and signed by a judge, the production of all such books, papers, documents, correspondence, and other evidence within the United States the production of which, in the opinion of the Tax Court or division thereof, is necessary to enable the transferee to ascertain the liability of the taxpayer or preceding transferee and will not result in undue hardship to the taxpayer or preceding transferee. Such examination shall be had at such time and place as may be designated in the subpoena.

§ 6903. Notice of fiduciary relationship

(a) Rights and obligations of fiduciary.—Upon notice to the Secretary that any person is acting for another person in a fiduciary capacity, such fiduciary shall assume the powers, rights, duties, and privileges of such other person in respect of a tax imposed by this title (except as otherwise specifically provided and except that the tax shall be collected from the estate of such other person), until notice is given that the fiduciary capacity has terminated.

(b) Manner of notice.—Notice under this section shall be given in accordance with regulations prescribed by the Secretary.

§ 6905. Discharge of executor from personal liability for decedent's income and gift taxes

(a) Discharge of liability.—In the case of liability of a decedent for taxes imposed by subtitle A or by chapter 12, if the executor makes written application (filed after the return with respect to such taxes is made and filed in such manner and such form as may be prescribed by regulations of the Secretary) for release from personal liability for such taxes, the Secretary may notify the executor of the amount of such taxes. The executor, upon payment of the amount of which he is notified, or 9 months after receipt of the application if no notification is made by the Secretary before such date, shall be discharged from personal liability for any deficiency in such tax thereafter found to be due and shall be entitled to a receipt or writing showing such discharge.

(b) Definition of executor.—For purposes of this section, the term "executor" means the executor or administrator of the decedent appointed, qualified, and acting within the United States.

* * *

CHAPTER 74—CLOSING AGREEMENTS AND COMPROMISES

§ 7121. Closing agreements

(a) Authorization.—The Secretary is authorized to enter into an agreement in writing with any person relating to the liability of such person (or of the person or estate for whom he acts) in respect of any internal revenue tax for any taxable period.

(b) Finality.—If such agreement is approved by the Secretary (within such time as may be stated in such agreement, or later agreed to) such agreement shall be final and conclusive, and, except upon a showing of fraud or malfeasance, or misrepresentation of a material fact—

(1) the case shall not be reopened as to the matters agreed upon or the agreement modified by any officer, employee, or agent of the United States, and

(2) in any suit, action, or proceeding, such agreement, or any determination, assessment, collection, payment, abatement, refund, or credit made in accordance therewith, shall not be annulled, modified, set aside, or disregarded.

§ 7122. Compromises

(a) Authorization.—The Secretary may compromise any civil or criminal case arising under the internal revenue laws prior to reference to the Department of Justice for prosecution or defense; and the Attorney General or his delegate may compromise any such case after reference to the Department of Justice for prosecution or defense.

(b) Record.—Whenever a compromise is made by the Secretary in any case, there shall be placed on file in the office of the Secretary the opinion of the General Counsel for the Department of the Treasury or his delegate, with his reasons therefor, with a statement of—

(1) The amount of tax assessed,

(2) The amount of interest, additional amount, addition to the tax, or assessable penalty, imposed by law on the person against whom the tax is assessed, and

(3) The amount actually paid in accordance with the terms of the compromise.

Notwithstanding the foregoing provisions of this subsection, no such opinion shall be required with respect to the compromise of any civil case in which the unpaid amount of tax assessed (including any interest, additional amount, addition to the tax, or assessable penalty) is less than $500.

CHAPTER 75—CRIMES, OTHER OFFENSES, AND FORFEITURES

Subchapter
- A. Crimes.
- B. Other offenses.*
- C. Forfeitures.*
- D. Miscellaneous penalty and forfeiture provisions.*

SUBCHAPTER A—CRIMES

Part
- I. General provisions.
- II. Penalties applicable to certain taxes.*

PART I—GENERAL PROVISIONS

§ 7201. Attempt to evade or defeat tax

Any person who willfully attempts in any manner to evade or defeat any tax imposed by this title or the payment thereof shall, in addition to other penalties provided by law, be guilty of a felony and, upon conviction thereof, shall be fined not more than $100,000 ($500,000 in the case of a corporation), or imprisoned not more than 5 years, or both, together with the costs of prosecution.

§ 7202. Willful failure to collect or pay over tax

Any person required under this title to collect, account for, and pay over any tax imposed by this title who willfully fails to collect or truthfully account for and pay over such tax shall, in addition to other penalties provided by law, be guilty of a felony and, upon conviction thereof, shall be fined not more than $10,000, or imprisoned not more than 5 years, or both, together with the costs of prosecution.

§ 7203. Willful failure to file return, supply information, or pay tax

Any person required under this title to pay any estimated tax or tax, or required by this title or by regulations made under authority thereof to make a return, keep any records, or supply any information, who willfully fails to pay such estimated tax or tax, make such return, keep such records, or supply such information, at the time or times required by law or regulations, shall, in addition to other penalties provided by law, be guilty of a misdemeanor and, upon conviction thereof, shall be fined not more than $25,000 ($100,000 in the case of a corporation), or imprisoned not more than 1 year, or both, together with the costs of prosecution. In the case of any person

* Omitted entirely.

with respect to whom there is a failure to pay any estimated tax, this section shall not apply to such person with respect to such failure if there is no addition to tax under section 6654 or 6655 with respect to such failure.

§ 7206.   Fraud and false statements

Any person who—

    (1) **Declaration under penalties of perjury.**—Willfully makes and subscribes any return, statement, or other document, which contains or is verified by a written declaration that it is made under the penalties of perjury, and which he does not believe to be true and correct as to every material matter; or

    (2) **Aid or assistance.**—Willfully aids or assists in, or procures, counsels, or advises the preparation or presentation under, or in connection with any matter arising under, the internal revenue laws, of a return, affidavit, claim, or other document, which is fraudulent or is false as to any material matter, whether or not such falsity or fraud is with the knowledge or consent of the person authorized or required to present such return, affidavit, claim, or document; or

    (3) **Fraudulent bonds, permits, and entries.**—Simulates or falsely or fraudulently executes or signs any bond, permit, entry, or other document required by the provisions of the internal revenue laws, or by any regulation made in pursuance thereof, or procures the same to be falsely or fraudulently executed, or advises, aids in, or connives at such execution thereof; or

    (4) **Removal or concealment with intent to defraud.**—Removes, deposits, or conceals, or is concerned in removing, depositing, or concealing, any goods or commodities for or in respect whereof any tax is or shall be imposed, or any property upon which levy is authorized by section 6331, with intent to evade or defeat the assessment or collection of any tax imposed by this title; or

    (5) **Compromises and closing agreements.**—In connection with any compromise under section 7122, or offer of such compromise, or in connection with any closing agreement under section 7121, or offer to enter into any such agreement, willfully—

        (A) **Concealment of property.**—Conceals from any officer or employee of the United States any property belonging to the estate of a taxpayer or other person liable in respect of the tax, or

        (B) **Withholding, falsifying, and destroying records.**—Receives, withholds, destroys, mutilates, or falsifies any book, document, or record, or makes any false statement, relating to the estate or financial condition of the taxpayer or other person liable in respect of the tax;

shall be guilty of a felony and, upon conviction thereof, shall be fined not more than $100,000 ($500,000 in the case of a corporation), or imprisoned not more than 3 years, or both, together with the costs of prosecution.

§ 7207.   Fraudulent returns, statements, or other documents

Any person who willfully delivers or discloses to the Secretary any list, return, account, statement, or other document, known by him to be fraudulent or to be false as to any material matter, shall be fined not more than $10,000 ($50,000 in the case of a corporation), or imprisoned not more than 1 year, or both. Any person required pursuant to subsection (b) of section 6047 or pursuant to subsection (d) of section 6104 to furnish any information to the Secretary or any other person who willfully furnishes to the Secretary or such other person any information known by him to be fraudulent or to be false as to any material matter shall be fined not more than

$10,000 ($50,000 in the case of a corporation), or imprisoned not more than 1 year, or both.

CHAPTER 76—JUDICIAL PROCEEDINGS

Subchapter
A. Civil actions by the United States.
B. Proceedings by taxpayers and third parties.
C. The Tax Court.
D. Court review of Tax Court decisions.

SUBCHAPTER A—CIVIL ACTIONS BY THE UNITED STATES

§ 7408. Action to enjoin promoters of abusive tax shelters, etc.

(a) Authority to seek injunction.—A civil action in the name of the United States to enjoin any person from further engaging in conduct subject to penalty under section 6700 (relating to penalty for promoting abusive tax shelters, etc.) or section 6701 (relating to penalties for aiding and abetting understatement of tax liability) may be commenced at the request of the Secretary. Any action under this section shall be brought in the district court of the United States for the district in which such person resides, has his principal place of business, or has engaged in conduct subject to penalty under section 6700 or section 6701. The court may exercise its jurisdiction over such action (as provided in section 7402(a)) separate and apart from any other action brought by the United States against such person.

(b) Adjudication and decree.—In any action under subsection (a), if the court finds—

(1) that the person has engaged in any conduct subject to penalty under section 6700 (relating to penalty for promoting abusive tax shelters, etc.), or section 6701 (relating to penalties for aiding and abetting understatement of tax liability), and

(2) that injunctive relief is appropriate to prevent recurrence of such conduct,

the court may enjoin such person from engaging in such conduct or in any other activity subject to penalty under section 6700 or section 6701.

* * *

SUBCHAPTER B—PROCEEDINGS BY TAXPAYERS AND THIRD PARTIES

§ 7421. Prohibition of suits to restrain assessment or collection

(a) Tax.—Except as provided in sections 6212(a) and (c), 6213(a), 6672(b), 6694(c), 7426(a) and (b) (1), and 7429(b), no suit for the purpose of restraining the assessment or collection of any tax shall be maintained in any court by any person, whether or not such person is the person against whom such tax was assessed.

(b) Liability of transferee or fiduciary.—No suit shall be maintained in any court for the purpose of restraining the assessment or collection (pursuant to the provisions of chapter 71) of—

(1) the amount of the liability, at law or in equity, of a transferee of property of a taxpayer in respect of any internal revenue tax, or

(2) the amount of the liability of a fiduciary under section 3713(b) of title 31, United States Code in respect of any such tax.

§ 7422. Civil actions for refund

(a) **No suit prior to filing claim for refund.**—No suit or proceeding shall be maintained in any court for the recovery of any internal revenue tax alleged to have been erroneously or illegally assessed or collected, or of any penalty claimed to have been collected without authority, or of any sum alleged to have been excessive or in any manner wrongfully collected, until a claim for refund or credit has been duly filed with the Secretary, according to the provisions of law in that regard, and the regulations of the Secretary established in pursuance thereof.

(b) **Protest or duress.**—Such suit or proceeding may be maintained whether or not such tax, penalty or sum has been paid under protest or duress.

* * *

(e) **Stay of proceedings.**—If the Secretary prior to the hearing of a suit brought by a taxpayer in a district court or the United States Claims Court for the recovery of any income tax, estate tax, gift tax, or tax imposed by chapter 41, 42, 43, 44, or 45 (or any penalty relating to such taxes) mails to the taxpayer a notice that a deficiency has been determined in respect of the tax which is the subject matter of taxpayer's suit, the proceedings in taxpayer's suit shall be stayed during the period of time in which the taxpayer may file a petition with the Tax Court for a redetermination of the asserted deficiency, and for 60 days thereafter. If the taxpayer files a petition with the Tax Court, the district court or the United States Claims Court, as the case may be, shall lose jurisdiction of taxpayer's suit to whatever extent jurisdiction is acquired by the Tax Court of the subject matter of taxpayer's suit for refund. If the taxpayer does not file a petition with the Tax Court for a redetermination of the asserted deficiency, the United States may counterclaim in the taxpayer's suit, or intervene in the event of a suit as described in subsection (c) (relating to suits against officers or employees of the United States), within the period of the stay of proceedings notwithstanding that the time for such pleading may have otherwise expired. The taxpayer shall have the burden of proof with respect to the issues raised by such counterclaim or intervention of the United States except as to the issue of whether the taxpayer has been guilty of fraud with intent to evade tax. This subsection shall not apply to a suit by a taxpayer which, prior to the date of enactment of this title, is commenced, instituted, or pending in a district court or the United States Claims Court for the recovery of any income tax, estate tax, or gift tax (or any penalty relating to such taxes).

(f) **Limitation on right of action for refund.**—

(1) **General rule.**—A suit or proceeding referred to in subsection (a) may be maintained only against the United States and not against any officer or employee of the United States (or former officer or employee) or his personal representative. Such suit or proceeding may be maintained against the United States notwithstanding the provisions of section 2502 of title 28 of the United States Code (relating to aliens' privilege to sue) and notwithstanding the provisions of section 1502 of such title 28 (relating to certain treaty cases).

(2) **Misjoinder and change of venue.**—If a suit or proceeding brought in a United States district court against an officer or employee of the United States (or former officer or employee) or his personal representative is improperly brought solely by virtue of paragraph (1), the court shall order, upon such terms as are just, that the pleadings be amended to substitute the United States as a party for such officer or employee as of the time such action commenced, upon proper service of

process on the United States. Such suit or proceeding shall upon request by the United States be transferred to the district or division where it should have been brought if such action initially had been brought against the United States.

* * *

SUBCHAPTER C—THE TAX COURT

Part
I. Organization and jurisdiction.
II. Procedure.
III. Miscellaneous provisions.*
IV. Declaratory judgments.*

PART I—ORGANIZATION AND JURISDICTION

§ 7441. Status

There is hereby established, under article I of the Constitution of the United States, a court of record to be known as the United States Tax Court. The members of the Tax Court shall be the chief judge and the judges of the Tax Court.

§ 7443. Membership

(a) **Number.**—The Tax Court shall be composed of 19 members.

(b) **Appointment.**—Judges of the Tax Court shall be appointed by the President, by and with the advice and consent of the Senate, solely on the grounds of fitness to perform the duties of the office.

PART II—PROCEDURE

§ 7463. Disputes involving $10,000 or less

(a) **In general.**—In the case of any petition filed with the Tax Court for a redetermination of a deficiency where neither the amount of the deficiency placed in dispute, nor the amount of any claimed overpayment, exceeds—

(1) $10,000 for any one taxable year, in the case of the taxes imposed by subtitle A,

(2) $10,000, in the case of the tax imposed by chapter 11,

(3) $10,000 for any one calendar year, in the case of the tax imposed by chapter 12, or

(4) $10,000 for any 1 taxable period (or, if there is no taxable period, taxable event) in the case of any tax imposed by subtitle D which is described in section 6212(a) (relating to a notice of deficiency),

at the option of the taxpayer concurred in by the Tax Court or a division thereof before the hearing of the case, proceedings in the case shall be conducted under this section. Notwithstanding the provisions of section 7453, such proceedings shall be conducted in accordance with such rules of evidence, practice, and procedure as the Tax Court may prescribe. A decision, together with a brief summary of the reasons therefor, in any such case shall satisfy the requirements of sections 7459(b) and 7460.

* Omitted entirely.

(b) Finality of decisions.—A decision entered in any case in which the proceedings are conducted under this section shall not be reviewed in any other court and shall not be treated as a precedent for any other case.

(c) Limitation of jurisdiction.—In any case in which the proceedings are conducted under this section, notwithstanding the provisions of sections 6214(a) and 6512(b), no decision shall be entered redetermining the amount of a deficiency, or determining an overpayment, except with respect to amounts placed in dispute within the limits described in subsection (a) and with respect to amounts conceded by the parties.

* * *

SUBCHAPTER D—COURT REVIEW OF TAX COURT DECISIONS

§ 7482. Courts of review

(a) Jurisdiction.—

(1) In general.—The United States Courts of Appeals (other than the United States Court of Appeals for the Federal Circuit) shall have exclusive jurisdiction to review the decisions of the Tax Court, except as provided in section 1254 of Title 28 of the United States Code, in the same manner and to the same extent as decisions of the district courts in civil actions tried without a jury; and the judgment of any such court shall be final, except that it shall be subject to review by the Supreme Court of the United States upon certiorari, in the manner provided in section 1254 of Title 28 of the United States Code.

* * *

(b) Venue.—

(1) In general.—Except as otherwise provided in paragraphs (2) and (3), such decisions may be reviewed by the United States court of appeals for the circuit in which is located—

(A) in the case of a petitioner seeking redetermination of tax liability other than a corporation, the legal residence of the petitioner,

(B) in the case of a corporation seeking redetermination of tax liability, the principal place of business or principal office or agency of the corporation, or, if it has no principal place of business or principal office or agency in any judicial circuit, then the office to which was made the return of the tax in respect of which the liability arises,

* * *

If for any reason no subparagraph of the preceding sentence applies, then such decisions may be reviewed by the Court of Appeals for the District of Columbia. For purposes of this paragraph, the legal residence, principal place of business, or principal office or agency referred to herein shall be determined as of the time the petition seeking redetermination of tax liability was filed with the Tax Court or as of the time the petition seeking a declaratory decision under section 7428 or 7476, or the petition under section 6226 or 6228(a), was filed with the Tax Court.

(2) By agreement.—Notwithstanding the provisions of paragraph (1), such decisions may be reviewed by any United States Court of Appeals which may be designated by the Secretary and the taxpayer by stipulation in writing.

* * *

(c) Powers.—

(1) To affirm, modify, or reverse.—Upon such review, such courts shall have power to affirm or, if the decision of the Tax Court is not in accordance with law, to modify or to reverse the decision of the Tax Court, with or without remanding the case for a rehearing, as justice may require.

(2) To make rules.—Rules for review of decisions of the Tax Court shall be those prescribed by the Supreme Court under section 2072 of title 28 of the United States Code.

(3) To require additional security.—Nothing in section 7483 shall be construed as relieving the petitioner from making or filing such undertakings as the court may require as a condition of or in connection with the review.

(4) To impose damages.—The United States Court of Appeals and the Supreme Court shall have power to impose damages in any case where the decision of the Tax Court is affirmed and it appears that the notice of appeal was filed merely for delay.

CHAPTER 77—MISCELLANEOUS PROVISIONS

§ 7502. Timely mailing treated as timely filing and paying

(a) General rule.—

(1) Date of delivery.—If any return, claim, statement, or other document required to be filed, or any payment required to be made, within a prescribed period or on or before a prescribed date under authority of any provision of the internal revenue laws is, after such period or such date, delivered by United States mail to the agency, officer, or office with which such return, claim, statement, or other document is required to be filed, or to which such payment is required to be made, the date of the United States postmark stamped on the cover in which such return, claim, statement, or other document, or payment, is mailed shall be deemed to be the date of delivery or the date of payment, as the case may be.

(2) Mailing requirements.—This subsection shall apply only if—

(A) the postmark date falls within the prescribed period or on or before the prescribed date—

(i) for the filing (including any extension granted for such filing) of the return, claim, statement, or other document, or

(ii) for making the payment (including any extension granted for making such payment), and

(B) the return, claim, statement, or other document, or payment was, within the time prescribed in subparagraph (A), deposited in the mail in the United States in an envelope or other appropriate wrapper, postage prepaid, properly addressed to the agency, officer, or office with which the return, claim, statement, or other document is required to be filed, or to which such payment is required to be made.

(b) Postmarks.—This section shall apply in the case of postmarks not made by the United States Postal Service only if and to the extent provided by regulations prescribed by the Secretary.

(c) Registered and certified mailing.—

(1) Registered mail.—For purposes of this section, if any such return, claim, statement, or other document, or payment, is sent by United States registered mail—

(A) such registration shall be prima facie evidence that the return, claim, statement, or other document was delivered to the agency, officer, or office to which addressed, and

(B) the date of registration shall be deemed the postmark date.

(2) Certified mail.—The Secretary is authorized to provide by regulations the extent to which the provisions of paragraph (1) of this subsection with respect to prima facie evidence of delivery and the postmark date shall apply to certified mail.

(d) Exceptions.—This section shall not apply with respect to—

(1) the filing of a document in, or the making of a payment to, any court other than the Tax Court,

(2) currency or other medium of payment unless actually received and accounted for, or

(3) returns, claims, statements, or other documents, or payments, which are required under any provision of the internal revenue laws or the regulations thereunder to be delivered by any method other than by mailing.

*   *   *

§ 7517. Furnishing on request of statement explaining estate or gift valuation

(a) General rule.—If the Secretary makes a determination or a proposed determination of the value of an item of property for purposes of the tax imposed under chapter 11, 12, or 13, he shall furnish, on the written request of the executor, donor, or the person required to make the return of the tax imposed by chapter 13 (as the case may be), to such executor, donor, or person a written statement containing the material required by subsection (b). Such statement shall be furnished not later than 45 days after the later of the date of such request or the date of such determination or proposed determination.

(b) Contents of statement.—A statement required to be furnished under subsection (a) with respect to the value of an item of property shall—

(1) explain the basis on which the valuation was determined or proposed,

(2) set forth any computation used in arriving at such value, and

(3) contain a copy of any expert appraisal made by or for the Secretary.

(c) Effect of statement.—Except to the extent otherwise provided by law, the value determined or proposed by the Secretary with respect to which a statement is furnished under this section, and the method used in arriving at such value, shall not be binding on the Secretary.

CHAPTER 79—DEFINITIONS

§ 7701. Definitions

(a) When used in this title, where not otherwise distinctly expressed or manifestly incompatible with the intent thereof—

(1) Person.—The term "person" shall be construed to mean and include an individual, a trust, estate, partnership, association, company or corporation.

(2) Partnership and partner.—The term "partnership" includes a syndicate, group, pool, joint venture, or other unincorporated organization, through or by means of which any business, financial operation, or venture is carried on, and which is not, within the meaning of this title, a trust or estate or a corporation; and the term "partner" includes a member in such a syndicate, group, pool, joint venture, or organization.

(3) Corporation.—The term "corporation" includes associations, joint-stock companies, and insurance companies.

(4) Domestic.—The term "domestic" when applied to a corporation or partnership means created or organized in the United States or under the law of the United States or of any State.

(5) Foreign.—The term "foreign" when applied to a corporation or partnership means a corporation or partnership which is not domestic.

(6) Fiduciary.—The term "fiduciary" means a guardian, trustee, executor, administrator, receiver, conservator, or any person acting in any fiduciary capacity for any person.

(7) Stock.—The term "stock" includes shares in an association, joint-stock company, or insurance company.

(8) Shareholder.—The term "shareholder" includes a member in an association, joint-stock company, or insurance company.

* * *

(14) Taxpayer.—The term "taxpayer" means any person subject to any internal revenue tax.

* * *

(17) Husband and wife.—As used in sections 152(b)(4), 682, and 2516 if the husband and wife therein referred to are divorced, wherever appropriate to the meaning of such sections, the term "wife" shall be read "former wife" and the term "husband" shall be read "former husband"; and, if the payments described in such sections are made by or on behalf of the wife or former wife to the husband or former husband instead of vice versa, wherever appropriate to the meaning of such sections, the term "husband" shall be read "wife" and the term "wife" shall be read "husband."

* * *

(24) Fiscal year.—The term "fiscal year" means an accounting period of 12 months ending on the last day of any month other than December.

(25) Paid or incurred, paid or accrued.—The terms "paid or incurred" and "paid or accrued" shall be construed according to the method of accounting upon the basis of which the taxable income is computed under subtitle A.

(26) Trade or business.—The term "trade or business" includes the performance of the functions of a public office.

* * *

(41) TIN.—The term "TIN" means the identifying number assigned to a person under section 6109.

(42) Substituted basis property.—The term "substituted basis property" means property which is—

  (A) transferred basis property, or

  (B) exchanged basis property.

(43) Transferred basis property.—The term "transferred basis property" means property having a basis determined under any provision of subtitle A (or under any corresponding provision of prior income tax law) providing that the basis shall be determined in whole or in part by reference to the basis in the hands of the donor, grantor, or other transferor.

(44) **Exchanged basis property.**—The term "exchanged basis property" means property having a basis determined under any provision of subtitle A (or under any corresponding provision of prior income tax law) providing that the basis shall be determined in whole or in part by reference to other property held at any time by the person for whom the basis is to be determined.

(45) **Nonrecognition transaction.**—The term "nonrecognition transaction" means any disposition of property in a transaction in which gain or loss is not recognized in whole or in part for purposes of subtitle A.

* * *

(c) **Includes and including.**—The terms "includes" and "including" when used in a definition contained in this title shall not be deemed to exclude other things otherwise within the meaning of the term defined.

* * *

(g) **Clarification of fair market value in the case of nonrecourse indebtedness.**—For purposes of subtitle A, in determining the amount of gain or loss (or deemed gain or loss) with respect to any property, the fair market value of such property shall be treated as being not less than the amount of any nonrecourse indebtedness to which such property is subject.

(h) **Motor vehicle operating leases.**—

(1) **In general.**—For purposes of this title, in the case of a qualified motor vehicle operating agreement which contains a terminal rental adjustment clause—

(A) such agreement shall be treated as a lease if (but for such terminal rental adjustment clause) such agreement would be treated as a lease under this title, and

(B) the lessee shall not be treated as the owner of the property subject to an agreement during any period such agreement is in effect.

(2) **Qualified motor vehicle operating agreement defined.**—For purposes of this subsection—

(A) **In general.**—The term "qualified motor vehicle operating agreement" means any agreement with respect to a motor vehicle (including a trailer) which meets the requirements of subparagraphs (B), (C), and (D) of this paragraph.

(B) **Minimum liability of lessor.**—An agreement meets the requirements of this subparagraph if under such agreement the sum of—

(i) the amount the lessor is personally liable to repay, and

(ii) the net fair market value of the lessor's interest in any property pledged as security for property subject to the agreement,

equals or exceeds all amounts borrowed to finance the acquisition of property subject to the agreement. There shall not be taken into account under clause (ii) any property pledged which is property subject to the agreement or property directly or indirectly financed by indebtedness secured by property subject to the agreement.

(C) **Certification by lessee; notice of tax ownership.**—An agreement meets the requirements of this subparagraph if such agreement contains a separate written statement separately signed by the lessee—

(i) under which the lessee certifies, under penalty of perjury, that it intends that more than 50 percent of the use of the property subject to such agreement is to be in a trade or business of the lessee, and

(ii) which clearly and legibly states that the lessee has been advised that it will not be treated as the owner of the property subject to the agreement for Federal income tax purposes.

(D) Lessor must have no knowledge that certification is false.—An agreement meets the requirements of this subparagraph if the lessor does not know that the certification described in subparagraph (C)(i) is false.

(3) Terminal rental adjustment clause defined.—

(A) In general.—For purposes of this subsection, the term "terminal rental adjustment clause" means a provision of an agreement which permits or requires the rental price to be adjusted upward or downward by reference to the amount realized by the lessor under the agreement upon sale or other disposition of such property.

(B) Special rule for lessee dealers.—The term "terminal rental adjustment clause" also includes a provision of an agreement which requires a lessee who is a dealer in motor vehicles to purchase the motor vehicle for a predetermined price and then resell such vehicle where such provision achieves substantially the same results as a provision described in subparagraph (A).

* * *

(k) Cross references.—

(1) Other definitions.—

For other definitions, see the following sections of Title 1 of the United States Code:

(1) Singular as including plural, section 1.

(2) Plural as including singular, section 1.

(3) Masculine as including feminine, section 1.

* * *

(2) Effect of cross references.—

For effect of cross references in this title, see section 7806(a).

§ 7703. Determination of marital status

(a) General Rule.—For purposes of part V of subchapter B of chapter 1 and those provisions of this title which refer to this subsection—

(1) the determination of whether an individual is married shall be made as of the close of his taxable year; except that if his spouse dies during his taxable year such determination shall be made as of the time of such death; and

(2) an individual legally separated from his spouse under a decree of divorce or of separate maintenance shall not be considered as married.

(b) Certain married individuals living apart.—For purposes of these provisions of this title which refer to this subsection, if—

(1) an individual who is married (within the meaning of subsection (a)) and who files a separate return maintains as his home a household which constitutes for more than one-half of the taxable year the principal place of abode of a child (within the meaning of section 151(e)(3)) with respect to whom such individual is entitled to a deduction for the taxable year under section 151 (or would be so entitled but for paragraph (2) or (4) of section 152(e)),

(2) such individual furnishes over one-half of the cost of maintaining such household during the taxable year, and

(3) during the last 6 months of the taxable year, such individual's spouse is not a member of such household,

such individual shall not be considered as married.

(Added Pub.L. 99–514, Title XIII, § 1301(j)(2)(A), Oct. 22, 1986, 100 Stat. ——.)

CHAPTER 80—GENERAL RULES

Subchapter
  A.   Application of internal revenue laws.
  B.   Effective date and related provisions.*
  C.   Provisions affecting more than one subtitle.

SUBCHAPTER A—APPLICATION OF INTERNAL REVENUE LAWS

§ 7805.   Rules and regulations

(a) Authorization.—Except where such authority is expressly given by this title to any person other than an officer or employee of the Treasury Department, the Secretary shall prescribe all needful rules and regulations for the enforcement of this title, including all rules and regulations as may be necessary by reason of any alteration of law in relation to internal revenue.

(b) Retroactivity of regulations or rulings.—The Secretary may prescribe the extent, if any, to which any ruling or regulation, relating to the internal revenue laws, shall be applied without retroactive effect.

* * *

§ 7806.   Construction of title

(a) Cross references.—The cross references in this title to other portions of the title, or other provisions of law, where the word "see" is used, are made only for convenience, and shall be given no legal effect.

(b) Arrangement and classification.—No inference, implication, or presumption of legislative construction shall be drawn or made by reason of the location or grouping of any particular section or provision or portion of this title, nor shall any table of contents, table of cross references, or similar outline, analysis, or descriptive matter relating to the contents of this title be given any legal effect. The preceding sentence also applies to the sidenotes and ancillary tables contained in the various prints of this Act before its enactment into law.

SUBCHAPTER C—PROVISIONS AFFECTING MORE THAN ONE SUBTITLE

§ 7872.   Treatment of loans with below-market interest rates

(a) Treatment of gift loans and demand loans.—

(1) **In general.**—For purposes of this title, in the case of any below-market loan to which this section applies and which is a gift loan or a demand loan, the foregone interest shall be treated as—

* Omitted entirely.

(A) transferred from the lender to the borrower, and

(B) retransferred by the borrower to the lender as interest.

(2) Time when transfers made.—Except as otherwise provided in regulations prescribed by the Secretary, any foregone interest attributable to periods during any calendar year shall be treated as transferred (and retransferred) under paragraph (1) on the last day of such calendar year.

(b) Treatment of other below-market loans.—

(1) In general.—For purposes of this title, in the case of any below-market loan to which this section applies and to which subsection (a)(1) does not apply, the lender shall be treated as having transferred on the date the loan was made (or, if later, on the first day on which this section applies to such loan), and the borrower shall be treated as having received on such date, cash in an amount equal to the excess of—

(A) the amount loaned, over

(B) the present value of all payments which are required to be made under the terms of the loan.

(2) Obligation treated as having original issue discount.—For purposes of this title—

(A) In general.—Any below-market loan to which paragraph (1) applies shall be treated as having original issue discount in an amount equal to the excess described in paragraph (1).

(B) Amount in addition to other original issue discount.—Any original issue discount which a loan is treated as having by reason of subparagraph (A) shall be in addition to any other original issue discount on such loan (determined without regard to subparagraph (A)).

(c) Below-market loans to which section applies.—

(1) In general.—Except as otherwise provided in this subsection and subsection (g), this section shall apply to—

(A) Gifts.—Any below-market loan which is a gift loan.

(B) Compensation-related loans.—Any below-market loan directly or indirectly between—

(i) an employer and an employee, or

(ii) an independent contractor and a person for whom such independent contractor provides services.

(C) Corporation-shareholder loans.—Any below-market loan directly or indirectly between a corporation and any shareholder of such corporation.

(D) Tax avoidance loans.—Any below-market loan 1 of the principal purposes of the interest arrangements of which is the avoidance of any Federal tax.

(E) Other below-market loans.—To the extent provided in regulations, any below-market loan which is not described in subparagraph (A), (B), (C), or (F) if the interest arrangements of such loan have a significant effect on any Federal tax liability of the lender or the borrower.

(F) Loans to qualified continuing care facilities.—Any loan to any qualified continuing care facility pursuant to a continuing care contract.

(2) $10,000 de minimis exception for gift loans between individuals.—

831

(A) In general.—In the case of any gift loan directly between individuals, this section shall not apply to any day on which the aggregate outstanding amount of loans between such individuals does not exceed $10,000.

(B) De minimis exception not to apply to loans attributable to acquisition of income-producing assets.—Subparagraph (A) shall not apply to any gift loan directly attributable to the purchase or carrying of income-producing assets.

(C) Cross reference.—

For limitation on amount treated as interest where loans do not exceed $100,000, see subsection (d)(1).

(3) $10,000 de minimis exception for compensation-related and corporate-shareholder loans.—

(A) In general.—In the case of any loan described in subparagraph (B) or (C) of paragraph (1), this section shall not apply to any day on which the aggregate outstanding amount of loans between the borrower and lender does not exceed $10,000.

(B) Exception not to apply where 1 of principal purposes is tax avoidance.—Subparagraph (A) shall not apply to any loan the interest arrangements of which have as 1 of their principal purposes the avoidance of any Federal tax.

(d) Special rules for gift loans.—

(1) Limitation on interest accrual for purposes of income taxes where loans do not exceed $100,000.—

(A) In general.—For purposes of subtitle A, in the case of a gift loan directly between individuals, the amount treated as retransferred by the borrower to the lender as of the close of any year shall not exceed the borrower's net investment income for such year.

(B) Limitation not to apply where 1 of principal purposes is tax avoidance.—Subparagraph (A) shall not apply to any loan the interest arrangements of which have as 1 of their principal purposes the avoidance of any Federal tax.

(C) Special rule where more than 1 gift loan outstanding.—For purposes of subparagraph (A), in any case in which a borrower has outstanding more than 1 gift loan, the net investment income of such borrower shall be allocated among such loans in proportion to the respective amounts which would be treated as retransferred by the borrower without regard to this paragraph.

(D) Limitation not to apply where aggregate amount of loans exceed $100,000.—This paragraph shall not apply to any loan made by a lender to a borrower for any day on which the aggregate outstanding amount of loans between the borrower and lender exceeds $100,000.

(E) Net investment income.—For purposes of this paragraph—

(i) In general.—The term "net investment income" has the meaning given such term by section 163(d)(4).

(ii) De minimis rule.—If the net investment income of any borrower for any year does not exceed $1,000, the net investment income of such borrower for such year shall be treated as zero.

(iii) Additional amounts treated as interest.—In determining the net investment income of a person for any year, any amount which would be included in the gross income of such person for such year by reason of section 1272 if such section applied to all deferred payment obligations shall be treated as interest received by such person for such year.

(iv) **Deferred payment obligations.**—The term "deferred payment obligation" includes any market discount bond, short-term obligation, United States savings bond, annuity, or similar obligation.

(2) **Special rule for gift tax.**—In the case of any gift loan which is a term loan, subsection (b)(1) (and not subsection (a)) shall apply for purposes of chapter 12.

(e) **Definitions of below-market loan and foregone interest.**—For purposes of this section—

(1) **Below-market loan.**—The term "below-market loan" means any loan if—

(A) in the case of a demand loan, interest is payable on the loan at a rate less than the applicable Federal rate, or

(B) in the case of a term loan, the amount loaned exceeds the present value of all payments due under the loan.

(2) **Foregone interest.**—The term "foregone interest" means, with respect to any period during which the loan is outstanding, the excess of—

(A) the amount of interest which would have been payable on the loan for the period if interest accrued on the loan at the applicable Federal rate and were payable annually on the day referred to in subsection (a)(2), over

(B) any interest payable on the loan properly allocable to such period.

(f) **Other definitions and special rules.**—For purposes of this section—

(1) **Present value.**—The present value of any payment shall be determined in the manner provided by regulations prescribed by the Secretary—

(A) as of the date of the loan, and

(B) by using a discount rate equal to the applicable Federal rate.

(2) **Applicable federal rate.**—

(A) **Term loans.**—In the case of any term loan, the applicable Federal rate shall be the applicable Federal rate in effect under section 1274(d) (as of the day on which the loan was made), compounded semiannually.

(B) **Demand loans.**—In the case of a demand loan, the applicable Federal rate shall be the Federal short-term rate in effect under section 1274(d) for the period for which the amount of foregone interest is being determined, compounded semiannually.

(3) **Gift loan.**—The term "gift loan" means any below-market loan where the foregoing of interest is in the nature of a gift.

(4) **Amount loaned.**—The term "amount loaned" means the amount received by the borrower.

(5) **Demand loan.**—The term "demand loan" means any loan which is payable in full at any time on the demand of the lender. Such term also includes (for purposes other than determining the applicable Federal rate under paragraph (2)) any loan if the benefits of the interest arrangements of such loan are not transferable and are conditioned on the future performance of substantial services by an individual. To the extent provided in regulations, such term also includes any loan with an indefinite maturity.

(6) **Term loan.**—The term "term loan" means any loan which is not a demand loan.

(7) **Husband and wife treated as 1 person.**—A husband and wife shall be treated as 1 person.

(8) Loans to which section 483 or 1274 applies.—This section shall not apply to any loan to which section 483 or 1274 applies.

(9) No withholding.—No amount shall be withheld under chapter 24 with respect to—

(A) any amount treated as transferred or retransferred under subsection (a), and

(B) any amount treated as received under subsection (b).

(10) Special rule for term loans.—If this section applies to any term loan on any day, this section shall continue to apply to such loan notwithstanding paragraphs (2) and (3) of subsection (c). In the case of a gift loan, the preceding sentence shall only apply for purposes of chapter 12.

(11) Special rule for certain employer security loans.—This section shall not apply to any loan between a corporation (or any member of the controlled group of corporations which includes such corporation) and an employee stock ownership **plan described** in section 4975(e)(7) to the extent that the interest rate on such loan is equal to the interest rate paid on a related securities acquisition loan (as described in section 133(b)) to such corporation.

(g) Exception for certain loans to qualified continuing care facilities.—

(1) In general.—This section shall not apply for any calendar year to any below-market loan made by a lender to a qualified continuing care facility pursuant to a continuing care contract if the lender (or the lender's spouse) attains age 65 before the close of such year.

(2) $90,000 limit.—Paragraph (1) shall apply only to the extent that the aggregate outstanding amount of any loan to which such paragraph applies (determined without regard to this paragraph), when added to the aggregate outstanding amount of all other previous loans between the lender (or the lender's spouse) and any qualified continuing care facility to which paragraph (1) applies, does not exceed $90,000.

(3) Continuing care contract.—For purposes of this section, the term "continuing care contract" means a written contract between an individual and a qualified continuing care facility under which—

(A) the individual or individual's spouse may use a qualified continuing care facility for their life or lives,

(B) the individual or individual's spouse—

(i) will first—

(I) reside in a separate, independent living unit with additional facilities outside such unit for the providing of meals and other personal care, and

(II) not require long-term nursing care, and

(ii) then will be provided long-term and skilled nursing care as the health of such individual or individual's spouse requires, and

(C) no additional substantial payment is required if such individual or individual's spouse requires increased personal care services or long-term and skilled nursing care.

(4) Qualified continuing care facility.—

(A) In general.—For purposes of this section, the term "qualified continuing care facility" means 1 or more facilities—

(i) which are designed to provide services under continuing care contracts, and

(ii) substantially all of the residents of which are covered by continuing care contracts.

(B) Substantially all facilities must be owned or operated by borrower.—A facility shall not be treated as a qualified continuing care facility unless substantially all facilities which are used to provide services which are required to be provided under a continuing care contract are owned or operated by the borrower.

(C) Nursing homes excluded.—The term "qualified continuing care facility" shall not include any facility which is of a type which is traditionally considered a nursing home.

(5) Adjustment of limit for inflation.—

(A) In general.—In the case of any loan made during any calendar year after 1986 to which paragraph (1) applies, the dollar amount in paragraph (2) shall be increased by the inflation adjustment for such calendar year. Any increase under the preceding sentence shall be rounded to the nearest multiple of $100 (or, if such increase is a multiple of $50, such increase shall be increased to the nearest multiple of $100).

(B) Inflation adjustment.—For purposes of subparagraph (A), the inflation adjustment for any calendar year is the percentage (if any) by which—

(i) the CPI for the preceding calendar year exceeds

(ii) the CPI for calendar year 1985.

For purposes of the preceding sentence, the CPI for any calendar year is the average of the Consumer Price Index as of the close of the 12-month period ending on September 30 of such calendar year.

(h) Regulations.—

(1) In general.—The Secretary shall prescribe such regulations as may be necessary or appropriate to carry out the purposes of this section, including—

(A) regulations providing that where, by reason of varying rates of interest, conditional interest payments, waivers of interest, disposition of the lender's or borrower's interest in the loan, or other circumstances, the provisions of this section do not carry out the purposes of this section, adjustments to the provisions of this section will be made to the extent necessary to carry out the purposes of this section,

(B) regulations for the purpose of assuring that the positions of the borrower and lender are consistent as to the application (or nonapplication) of this section, and

(C) regulations exempting from the application of this section any class of transactions the interest arrangements of which have no significant effect on any Federal tax liability of the lender or the borrower.

(2) Estate tax coordination.—Under regulations prescribed by the Secretary, any loan which is made with donative intent and which is a term loan shall be taken into account for purposes of chapter 11 in a manner consistent with the provisions of subsection (b).

*

TREASURY REGULATIONS

PART 1—INCOME TAX

NORMAL TAXES AND SURTAXES

DETERMINATION OF TAX LIABILITY

Credits Against Tax

Rules for Computing Credit for Investment in Certain Depreciable Property

COMPUTATION OF TAXABLE INCOME

Definition of Gross Income, Adjusted Gross Income, and Taxable Income

Items Specifically Included in Gross Income

Items Specifically Excluded From Gross Income

CORPORATE DISTRIBUTIONS AND ADJUSTMENTS

Distributions by Corporations

Effects on Recipients

Effects on Corporation

Definitions; Constructive Ownership of Stock

Corporate Liquidations

Effects on Recipients

PARTNERS AND PARTNERSHIPS

Determination of Tax Liability

Contributions, Distributions and Transfers

Contributions to a Partnership

Distributions by a Partnership

Transfers of Interests in a Partnership

Provisions Common to Part II, Subchapter K, Chapter 1 of the Code

Definitions

GAIN OR LOSS ON DISPOSITION OF PROPERTY

Determination of Amount and Recognition of Gain or Loss

ELECTION OF CERTAIN SMALL BUSINESS CORPORATIONS AS TO TAXABLE STATUS

Credits Against Tax

Rules for Computing Credit for Investment in Certain Depreciable Property

§ 1.47–3 Exceptions to the application of § 1.47–1.

* * *

(f) Mere change in form of conducting a trade or business—(1) General rule. (i) Notwithstanding the provisions of § 1.47–2, relating to "disposition" and "cessation", paragraph (a) of § 1.47–1 shall not apply to section 38 property which is disposed of, or otherwise ceases to be section 38 property with respect to the taxpayer, before the close of the estimated useful life which was taken into account in computing the taxpayer's qualified investment by reason of a mere change in the form of conducting the trade or business in which such section 38 property is used provided that the conditions set forth in subdivision (ii) of this subparagraph are satisfied.

(ii) The conditions referred to in subdivision (i) of this subparagraph are as follows:

(a) The section 38 property described in subdivision (i) of this subparagraph is retained as section 38 property in the same trade or business,

(b) The transferor (or in a case where the transferor is a partnership, estate, trust, or electing small business corporation, the partner, beneficiary, or shareholder) of such section 38 property retains a substantial interest in such trade or business,

(c) Substantially all the assets (whether or not section 38 property) necessary to operate such trade or business are transferred to the transferee to whom such section 38 property is transferred, and

(d) The basis of such section 38 property in the hands of the transferee is determined in whole or in part by reference to the basis of such section 38 property in the hands of the transferor. This subparagraph shall not apply to the transfer of section 38 property if paragraph (e) of this section, relating to transactions to which section 381 applies, applies with respect to such transfer.

(2) **Substantial interest.** For purposes of this paragraph, a transferor (or in a case where the transferor is a partnership, estate, trust, or electing small business corporation, the partner, beneficiary, or shareholder) shall be considered as having retained a substantial interest in the trade or business only if, after the change in form, his interest in such trade or business—

(i) Is substantial in relation to the total interest of all persons, or

(ii) Is equal to or greater than his interest prior to the change in form.

Thus, where a taxpayer owns a 5-percent interest in a partnership, and, after the incorporation of that partnership, the taxpayer retains at least a 5-percent interest in the corporation, the taxpayer will be considered as having retained a substantial interest in the trade or business as of the date of the change in form.

(3) **Property held for the production of income.** Subparagraph (1)(i) of this paragraph applies to section 38 property held for the production of income (within the meaning of section 167(a)(2)) as well as to section 38 property used in a trade or business.

(4) **Leased property.** In a case where a lessor of new section 38 property made a valid election, under § 1.48–4, to treat the lessee as having purchased such property for purposes of the credit allowed by section 38, in determining whether sub-

paragraph (1)(i) of this paragraph applies to an assignment of the lease and transfer of possession of such property, the condition contained in subparagraph (1)(ii)(d) of this paragraph is not applicable.

(5) Disposition or cessation. (i) If section 38 property described in subparagraph (1)(i) of this paragraph is disposed of by the transferee, or otherwise ceases to be section 38 property with respect to the transferee, before the close of the estimated useful life which was taken into account in computing the qualified investment of the transferor (or in a case where the transferor is a partnership, estate, trust, or electing small business corporation, the qualified investment of the partners, beneficiaries, or shareholders) then under paragraph (a) of § 1.47-1 such property ceases to be section 38 property with respect to the transferor (or such partners, beneficiaries, or shareholders), and a recapture determination shall be made with respect to such property. For purposes of recomputing qualified investment with respect to such property, the actual useful life shall be the period beginning with the date on which it was placed in service by the transferor and ending with the date of the disposition by, or cessation with respect to, the transferee.

(ii) If in any taxable year the transferor (or in a case where the transferor is a partnership, estate, trust, or electing small business corporation, the partner, beneficiary, or shareholder) of the section 38 property described in subparagraph (1)(i) of this paragraph does not retain a substantial interest in the trade or business directly or indirectly (through ownership in other entities provided that such other entities' bases in such interest are determined in whole or in part by reference to the basis of such interest in the hands of the transferor) then, under paragraph (a) of § 1.47-1, such property ceases to be section 38 property with respect to the transferor and he (or the partner, beneficiary, or shareholder) shall make a recapture determination. For purposes of recomputing qualified investment with respect to property described in this subdivision, its actual useful life shall be the period beginning with the date on which it was placed in service by the transferor and ending with the first date on which the transferor (or the partner, beneficiary, or shareholder) does not retain a substantial interest in the trade or business. Any taxpayer who seeks to establish his interest in a trade or business under the rule of this subdivision shall maintain adequate records to demonstrate his

indirect interest in such trade or business after any such transfer or transfers.

(iii) In making a recapture determination under this subparagraph there shall be taken into account any prior recapture determinations with respect to the transferor in connection with the same property.

(iv) Notwithstanding subparagraph (1) of this paragraph and subdivision (ii) of this subparagraph in the case of a mere change in the form of a trade or business, if the interest of a taxpayer in the trade or business is reduced but such taxpayer has retained a substantial interest in such trade or business, paragraph (a)(2) of § 1.47-4 (relating to electing small business corporations), paragraph (a)(2) of § 1.47-5 (relating to estates or trusts) or paragraph (a)(2) of § 1.47-6 (relating to partnerships) shall apply, as the case may be.

* * *

[T.D. 6931, 32 FR 14033, Oct. 10, 1967, as amended by T.D. 7126, 36 FR 11192, June 10, 1971; T.D. 7203, 37 FR 17128, Aug. 25, 1972]

§ 1.47-6 Partnerships.

(a) In general—(1) Disposition or cessation in hands of partnership. If a partnership disposes of any partnership section 38 property (or if any partnership section 38 property otherwise ceases to be section 38 property in the hands of the partnership) before the close of the estimated useful life which was taken into account in computing qualified investment with respect to such property, a recapture determination shall be made with respect to each partner who is treated, under paragraph (f) of § 1.46-3, as a taxpayer with respect to such property. Each such recapture determination shall be made with respect to the share of the basis (or cost) of such property taken into account by such partner in computing his qualified investment. For purposes of each such recapture determination the actual useful life of such property shall be the period beginning with the date on which it was placed in service by the partnership and ending with the date of the disposition or cessation. In making a recapture determination under this subparagraph there shall be taken into account any prior recapture determinations made with respect to the partner in connection with the same property. For definition of "recapture determination" see paragraph (a)(1) of § 1.47-1.

(2) Disposition of partner's interest. (i) If—

(a) The basis (or cost) of partnership section 38 property is taken into account by a partner in computing his qualified investment, and

(b) After the date on which such partnership section 38 property was placed in service by the partnership and before the close of the estimated useful life of the property, such partner's proportionate interest in the general profits of the partnership (or in the particular item of property) is reduced (for example, by a sale, by a change in the partnership agreement, or by the admission of a new partner) below the percentage specified in subdivision (ii) of this subparagraph, then, on the date of such reduction such partnership section 38 property ceases to be section 38 property with respect to such partner to the extent of the actual reduction in such partner's proportionate interest in the general profits of the partnership (or in the particular item of property). (For example, if $100 of the basis of section 38 property was taken into account by a partner and if his proportionate interest in the general profits of the partnership is reduced from 60 percent to 30 percent (that is, 50 percent of his original interest), then such property shall be treated as having ceased to be section 38 property to the extent of $50.) Accordingly, a recapture determination shall be made with respect to such partner. For purposes of such recapture determination the actual useful life of such property shall be the period beginning with the date on which it was placed in service by the partnership and ending with the date on which it is treated as having ceased to be section 38 property with respect to the partner. In making a recapture determination under this subparagraph there shall be taken into account any prior recapture determination made with respect to the partner in connection with the same property.

(ii) The percentage referred to in subdivision (i)(b) of this subparagraph is 66⅔ percent of the partner's proportionate interest in the general profits of the partnership (or in the particular item of property) for the year in which such property was placed in service. However, once property has been treated under this subparagraph as having ceased to be section 38 property to any extent the percentage referred to shall be 33⅓ percent of the partner's proportionate interest in the general profits of the partnership (or in the particular item of property) for the year in which such property was placed in service.

(iii) In determining a partner's proportionate interest in the general profits of a partnership for

purposes of this subparagraph, the partner shall be considered to own any interest in such a partnership which he owns directly or indirectly (through ownership in other entities provided the other entities' bases in such interest are determined in whole or in part by reference to the basis of such interest in the hands of the partner). For example, if A, whose proportionate interest in the general profits of partnership X is 20 percent, transfers all of such interest to corporation Y in exchange for all of the stock of Y in a transaction to which section 351 applies, then, for purposes of subdivision (i) of this subparagraph, A shall be considered to own a 20-percent interest in partnership X. Any taxpayer who seeks to establish his interest in a partnership under the rule of this subdivision shall maintain adequate records to demonstrate his indirect interest in the partnership after any such transfer or transfers.

* * *

[T.D. 6931, 32 FR 14039, Oct. 10, 1967]

§ 1.48-1 Definition of section 38 property.

* * *

(c) Definition of tangible personal property. If property is tangible personal property it may qualify as section 38 property irrespective of whether it is used as an integral part of an activity (or constitutes a research or storage facility used in connection with such activity) specified in paragraph (a) of this section. Local law shall not be controlling for purposes of determining whether property is or is not "tangible" or "personal". Thus, the fact that under local law property is held to be personal property or tangible property shall not be controlling. Conversely, property may be personal property for purposes of the investment credit even though under local law the property is considered to be a fixture and therefore real property. For purposes of this section, the term "tangible personal property" means any tangible property except land and improvements thereto, such as buildings or other inherently permanent structures (including items which are structural components of such buildings or structures). Thus, buildings, swimming pools, paved parking areas, wharves and docks, bridges, and fences are not tangible personal property. Tangible personal property includes all property (other than structural components) which is contained in or attached to a building. Thus, such property as production machinery, printing presses, transportation and office equipment, refrigerators, grocery counters, testing equipment, display racks and shelves, and neon and other signs, which is contained in or attached to a building constitutes tangible personal property for purposes of the credit allowed by section 38. Further, all property which is in the nature of machinery (other than structural components of a building or other inherently permanent structure) shall be considered tangible personal property even though located outside a building. Thus, for example, a gasoline pump, hydraulic car lift, or automatic vending machine, although annexed to the ground, shall be considered tangible personal property.

* * *

[T.D. 6731, 29 FR 6073, May 8, 1964, as amended by T.D. 6838, 30 FR 9060, July 20, 1965; T.D. 6958, 33 FR 9171, June 21, 1968; T.D. 6971, 33 FR 12899, Sept. 12, 1968; T.D. 7203, 37 FR 17129, Aug. 25, 1972; T.D. 7229, 37 FR 28142, Dec. 21, 1972; T.D. 7927, 48 FR 55849, Dec. 16, 1983; T.D. 8031, 50 FR 26697, June 28, 1985]

COMPUTATION OF TAXABLE INCOME

Definition of Gross Income, Adjusted Gross Income, and Taxable Income

§ 1.61–1   Gross income.

(a) **General definition.** Gross income means all income from whatever source derived, unless excluded by law. Gross income includes income realized in any form, whether in money, property, or services. Income may be realized, therefore, in the form of services, meals, accommodations, stock, or other property, as well as in cash. Section 61 lists the more common items of gross income for purposes of illustration. For purposes of further illustration, § 1.61–14 mentions several miscellaneous items of gross income not listed specifically in section 61. Gross income, however, is not limited to the items so enumerated.

* * *

§ 1.61–2   Compensation for services, including fees, commissions, and similar items.

(a) **In general.** (1) Wages, salaries, commissions paid salesmen, compensation for services on the basis of a percentage of profits, commissions on insurance premiums, tips, bonuses (including Christmas bonuses), termination or severance pay, rewards, jury fees, marriage fees and other contributions received by a clergyman for services, pay of persons in the military or naval forces of the United States, retired pay of employees, pensions, and retirement allowances are income to the recipients unless excluded by law. Several special rules apply to members of the Armed Forces, Coast and Geodetic Survey, and Public Health Service of the United States; see paragraph (b) of this section.

* * *

(c) **Payment to charitable, etc., organization on behalf of person rendering services.** The value of services is not includible in gross income when such services are rendered directly and gratuitously to an organization described in section 170(c). Where, however, pursuant to an agreement or understanding, services are rendered to a person for the benefit of an organization described in section 170(c) and an amount for such services is paid to such organization by the person to whom the services are rendered, the amount so paid constitutes income to the person performing the services.

(d) **Compensation paid other than in cash—** (1) **In general.** Except as otherwise provided in paragraph (d)(6)(i) of this section (relating to certain property transferred after June 30, 1969), if services are paid for in property, the fair market value of the property taken in payment must be included in income as compensation. If services are paid for in exchange for other services, the fair market value of such other services taken in payment must be included in income as compensation. If the services are rendered at a stipulated price, such price will be presumed to be the fair market value of the compensation received in the absence of evidence to the contrary. For special rules relating to certain options received as compensation, see §§ 1.61–15, 1.83–7, and section 421 and the regulations thereunder. For special rules relating to premiums paid by an employer for an annuity contract which is not subject to section 403(a), see section 403(c) and the regulations thereunder and § 1.83–8(a). For special rules relating to contributions made to an employees' trust which is not exempt under section 501, see section 402(b) and the regulations thereunder and § 1.83–8(a).

(2) Property transferred to employee or independent contractor. (i) Except as otherwise provided in section 421 and the regulations thereunder and § 1.61–15 (relating to stock options), and paragraph (d)(6)(i) of this section, if property is transferred by an employer to an employee or if property is transferred to an independent contractor, as compensation for services, for an amount less than its fair market value, then regardless of whether the transfer is in the form of a sale or exchange, the difference between the amount paid for the property and the amount of its fair market value at the time of the transfer is compensation and shall be included in the gross income of the employee or independent contractor. In computing the gain or loss from the subsequent sale of such property, its basis shall be the amount paid for the property increased by the amount of such difference included in gross income.

(ii) (a) Cost of life insurance on the life of the employee. Generally, life insurance premiums paid by an employer on the life of his employee where the proceeds of such insurance are payable to the beneficiary of such employee are part of the gross income of the employee. However, the amount includible in the employee's gross income is determined with regard to the provisions of section 403 and the regulations thereunder in the case of an individual contract issued after December 31, 1962, or a group contract, which provides incidental life insurance protection and which satisfies the requirements of section 401(g) and § 1.401–9, relating to the nontransferability of annuity contracts. For the special rules relating to the includibility in an employee's gross income of an amount equal to the cost of certain group term life insurance on the employee's life which is carried directly or indirectly by his employer, see section 79 and the regulations thereunder. For special rules relating to the exclusion of contributions by an employer to accident and health plans for the employee, see section 106 and the regulations thereunder.

(b) Cost of group-term life insurance on life of spouse or children of an employee. Generally, the cost (determined under paragraph (d)(2) of § 1.79–3) of group-term life insurance on the life of the spouse or children of an employee paid by the employee's employer is part of the gross income of the employee. However, such cost is not required to be included in the employee's gross income if it is merely incidental. Such cost shall be considered incidental if the amount of such insurance payable upon the death of a spouse or of a child does not exceed $2,000.

(3) Meals and living quarters. The value of living quarters or meals which an employee receives in addition to his salary constitutes gross income unless they are furnished for the convenience of the employer and meet the conditions specified in section 119 and the regulations thereunder. For the treatment of rental value of parsonages or rental allowance paid to ministers, see section 107 and the regulations thereunder; for the treatment of statutory subsistence allowances received by police, see section 120 and the regulations thereunder.

(4) Stock and notes transferred to employee or independent contractor. Except as otherwise provided by section 421 and the regulations thereunder and § 1.61–15 (relating to stock options), and paragraph (d)(6)(i) of this section, if a corporation transfers its own stock to an employee or independent contractor as compensation for services, the fair market value of the stock at the time of transfer shall be included in the gross income of the employee or independent contractor. Notes or other evidences of indebtedness received in payment for services constitute income in the amount of their fair market value at the time of the transfer. A taxpayer receiving as compensation a note regarded as good for its face value at maturity, but not bearing interest, shall treat as income as of the time of receipt its fair discounted value computed at the prevailing rate. As payments are received on such a note, there shall be included in income that portion of each payment which represents the proportionate part of the discount originally taken on the entire note.

* * *

(6) Certain property transferred, premiums paid, and contributions made in connection with the performance of services after June 30, 1969—(i) Exception. Paragraph (d)(1), (2), (4), and (5) of this section and § 1.61–15 do not apply to the transfer of property (as defined in § 1.83–3(e)) after June 30, 1969, unless § 1.83–8 (relating to the applicability of section 83 and transitional rules) applies. If section 83 applies to a transfer of property, and the property is not subject to a restriction that has a significant effect on the fair market value of such property, then the rules contained in paragraph (d)(1), (2), and (4) of this section and § 1.61–15 shall also apply to such transfer to the extent such rules are not inconsistent with section 83.

* * *

[T.D. 6500, 25 FR 11402, Nov. 26, 1960, as amended by T.D. 6696, 28 FR 13450, Dec. 12, 1963; T.D. 6856, 30 FR 13316, Oct. 20, 1965; T.D. 6888, 31 FR 9200, July 6, 1966; T.D. 7544, 43 FR 31913, July 24, 1978; T.D. 7623, 44 FR 28800, May 17, 1979]

§ 1.61–2T   Taxation of fringe benefits.

(a) **Fringe benefits—(1) In general.** Section 61(a)(1) provides that, except as otherwise provided in subtitle A, gross income includes compensation for services, including fees, commissions, fringe benefits, and similar items. Examples of fringe benefits include: an employer-provided automobile, a flight on an employer-provided aircraft, an employer-provided free or discounted commercial airline flight an employer-provided vacation and employer-provided discount on property or services, and employer-provided membership in a country club or other social club, and an employer-provided ticket to an entertainment or sporting event.

(2) **Fringe benefits excluded from income.** To the extent that a particular fringe benefit is specifically excluded from gross income pursuant to another section of subtitle A, that section shall govern the treatment of the fringe benefit. Thus, if the requirements of the governing section are satisfied, the fringe benefits may be excludable from gross income. Examples of excludable fringe benefits are qualified tuition reductions provided to an employee (section 117(d)); meals and lodging furnished to an employee for the convenience of the employer (section 119); and benefits provided under a dependent care assistance program (section 129). Similarly, the value of the use by an employee of an employer-provided vehicle or a flight provided to an employee on an employer-provided aircraft may be excludable from income under section 105 (because, for example, the transportation is provided for medical reasons) if and to the extent that the requirements of that section are satisfied. Section 61 and the regulations thereunder shall apply, however, to the extent that they are not inconsistent with such other section. For example, many fringe benefits specifically addressed in other sections of subtitle A are excluded from gross income only to the extent that they do not exceed specific dollar or percentage limits, or only if certain other requirements are met. If the limits are exceeded or the requirements are not met, some or all of the fringe benefit may be includible in gross income. See paragraph (b)(3) of this section.

(3) **Compensation for services.** A fringe benefit provided in connection with the performance of services shall be considered to have been provided as compensation for services. Refraining from the performance of services (such as pursuant to a covenant not to compete) is deemed to be the performance of services for purposes of this section.

(4) **Recipient of a fringe benefit—(i) Definition.** A fringe benefit is included in the income of the "recipient" of the fringe benefit. The recipient of a fringe benefit is the person performing the services in connection with which the fringe benefit is provided. Thus, a person may be considered to be a recipient, even though that person did not actually receive the fringe benefit. For example, a fringe benefit provided to any person in connection with the performance of services by another person is considered to have been provided to the person who performs the services and not the person who receives the fringe benefit. In addition, if a fringe benefit is provided to a person, but taxable to a second person as the recipient, such benefit is referred to as provided to the second person and use by the first person is considered use by the second person. For example, provision of an automobile to an employee's spouse by the employer is taxable to the employee as the recipient. The automobile is referred to as available to the employee and use by the employee's spouse is considered use by the employee.

(ii) **Recipient may be other than an employee.** The recipient of a fringe benefit need not be an employee of the provider of the fringe benefit, but may be a partner, director, or an independent contractor. For convenience, the term "employee" includes a reference to any recipient of a fringe benefit, unless otherwise specifically provided in this section.

(5) **Provider of a fringe benefit.** The "provider" of a fringe benefit is that person for whom the services are performed, regardless of whether that person actually provides the fringe benefit to the recipient. The provider of a fringe benefit need not be the employer of the recipient of the fringe benefit, but may be, for example, a client or customer of an independent contractor. For convenience, the term "employer" includes a reference to any provider of a fringe benefit, unless otherwise specifically provided in this section.

(6) Effective date. This section is effective as of January 1, 1985. No inference may be drawn from the promulgation or terms of this section concerning the application of law in effect prior to January 1, 1985.

(b) Valuation of fringe benefits—(1) In general. An employee must include in gross income the amount by which the fair market value of the fringe benefit exceeds the sum of (i) the amount, if any, paid for the benefit, and (ii) the amount, if any specifically excluded from gross income by some other section of subtitle A. Therefore, for example, if the employee pays fair market value for what is received, no amount is includible in the gross income of the employee.

(2) Fair market value. In general, fair market value is determined on the basis of all the facts and circumstances. Specifically, the fair market value of a fringe benefit is that amount a (hypothetical person would have to pay a hypothetical third party to obtain (i.e., purchase or lease) the particular fringe benefit. Thus, for example, the effect of any special relationship that may exist between the employer and the employee must be disregarded. This also means that an employee's subjective perception of the value of a fringe benefit is not relevant to the determination of a fringe benefit's fair market value. In addition, the cost incurred by the employer is not determinative of the fair market value of the fringe benefit. For special rules relating to the valuation of certain fringe benefits, see paragraph (c) of this section.

(3) Exclusion from income based on cost. If a statutory exclusion phrased in terms of cost applies to the provision of a fringe benefit, section 61 does not require the inclusion in the recipient's gross income of the difference between the fair market value and the excludable cost of that fringe benefit. For example, section 129 provides an exclusion from an employee's gross income for amounts paid or incurred by an employer to provide dependent care assistance to employees. Even if the fair market value of the dependent care assistance exceeds the employer's cost, the excess is not subject to inclusion under section 61 and this section. If the statutory cost exclusion is a limited amount, however, then the fair market value of the fringe benefit attributable to any excess cost is subject to inclusion.

(4) Fair market value of the availability of an employer-provided vehicle. If the vehicle special valuation rules of paragraph (d), (e), or (f) of this section are not used by a taxpayer entitled to use such rules, the value of the availability of an employer-provided vehicle is determined under the general valuation principles set forth in this section. In general, such valuation must be determined by reference to the cost to a hypothetical person of leasing from a hypothetical third party the same or comparable vehicle on the same or comparable terms in the geographic area in which the vehicle is available for use. Unless the employee can substantiate that the same or comparable vehicle could have been leased on a cents-per-mile basis, the value of the availability of the vehicle cannot be determined by reference to a cents-per-mile rate applied to the number of miles the vehicle is driven. An example of a comparable lease term is the amount of time that the vehicle is available to the employee for use, e.g., a one-year period.

(5) Fair market value of a flight on an employer-provided aircraft. If the noncommercial flight special valuation rule of paragraph (g) of this section is not used (or is not properly used) by a taxpayer entitled to use such rule, the value of a flight on an employer-provided aircraft is determined under the general valuation principles set forth in this section. An example of how the general valuation principles would apply is that if an employee whose flight is primarily personal controls the use of an aircraft with respect to such flight, such flight is valued by reference to how much it would cost a hypothetical person to charter the same or comparable aircraft for the same or comparable flight. The cost to charter the aircraft must be allocated among all employees on board the aircraft based on all the facts and circumstances, including which employees controlled the use of the aircraft. Notwithstanding the allocation required by the preceding sentence, no additional amount shall be included in the income of any employee whose flight is properly valued under the special valuation rule of paragraph (g) of this section.

* * *

[T.D. 8004, 50 FR 749, Jan. 7, 1985, as amended by T.D. 8009, 50 FR 7041, Feb. 20, 1985; 50 FR 9614, March 11, 1985; T.D. 8063, 50 FR 52285, Dec. 23, 1985]

§ 1.61–3 Gross income derived from business.

(a) In general. In a manufacturing, merchandising, or mining business, "gross income" means the total sales, less the cost of goods sold, plus any income from investments and from incidental or outside operations or sources. Gross income is determined without subtraction of depletion allowances based on a percentage of income to the extent that it exceeds cost depletion which may be required to be included in the amount of inventoriable costs as provided in § 1.471–11 and without subtraction of selling expenses, losses or other items not ordinarily used in computing costs of goods sold or amounts which are of a type for which a deduction would be disallowed under section 162(c), (f), or (g) in the case of a business expense. The cost of goods sold should be determined in accordance with the method of accounting consistently used by the taxpayer.

* * *

[T.D. 6500, 25 FR 11402, Nov. 26, 1960; 25 FR 14021, Dec. 31, 1960, as amended by T.D. 7207, 37 FR 20767, Oct. 5, 1972; T.D. 7285, 38 FR 26184, Sept. 19, 1973]

§ 1.61–4 Gross income of farmers.

(a) **Farmers using the cash method of accounting.** A farmer using the cash receipts and disbursements method of accounting shall include in his gross income for the taxable year—

(1) The amount of cash and the value of merchandise or other property received during the taxable year from the sale of livestock and produce which he raised,

(2) The profits from the sale of any livestock or other items which were purchased,

(3) All amounts received from breeding fees, fees from rent of teams, machinery, or land, and other incidental farm income,

(4) All subsidy and conservation payments received which must be considered as income, and

(5) Gross income from all other sources.

The profit from the sale of livestock or other items which were purchased is to be ascertained by deducting the cost from the sales price in the year in which the sale occurs, except that in the case of the sale of purchased animals held for draft, breeding, or dairy purposes, the profits shall be the amount of any excess of the sales price over the amount representing the difference between the cost and the depreciation allowed or allowable (determined in accordance with the rules applicable under sec-

tion 1016(a) and the regulations thereunder). * *

(b) **Farmers using an accrual method of accounting.** A farmer using an accrual method of accounting must use inventories to determine his gross income. His gross income on an accrual method is determined by adding the total of the items described in subparagraphs (1) through (5) of this paragraph and subtracting therefrom the total of the items described in subparagraphs (6) and (7) of this paragraph. These items are as follows:

(1) The sales price of all livestock and other products held for sale and sold during the year;

(2) The inventory value of livestock and products on hand and not sold at the end of the year;

(3) All miscellaneous items of income, such as breeding fees, fees from the rent of teams, machinery, or land, or other incidental farm income;

(4) Any subsidy or conservation payments which must be considered as income;

(5) Gross income from all other sources;

(6) The inventory value of the livestock and products on hand and not sold at the beginning of the year; and

(7) The cost of any livestock or products purchased during the year (except livestock held for draft, dairy, or breeding purposes, unless included in inventory).

All livestock raised or purchased for sale shall be added in the inventory at their proper valuation determined in accordance with the method authorized and adopted for the purpose. Livestock acquired for draft, breeding, or dairy purposes and not for sale may be included in the inventory (see subparagraphs (2), (6), and (7) of this paragraph) instead of being treated as capital assets subject to depreciation, provided such practice is followed consistently from year to year by the taxpayer. When any livestock included in an inventory are sold, their cost must not be taken as an additional deduction in computing taxable income, because such deduction is reflected in the inventory. See the regulations under section 471. * * *

(c) **Special rules for certain receipts.** In the case of the sale of machinery, farm equipment, or any other property (except stock in trade of the taxpayer, or property of a kind which would properly be included in the inventory of the taxpayer if on hand at the close of the taxable year, or property held by the taxpayer primarily for sale to customers in the ordinary course of his trade or business), any excess of the proceeds of the sale over the adjusted basis of such property shall be included in the taxpayer's gross income for the taxable year in which such sale is made. See, however, section 453 and the regulations thereunder for special rules relating to certain installment sales. If farm produce is exchanged for merchandise, groceries, or the like, the market value of the article received in exchange is to be included in gross income. * * *

* * *

[T.D. 6500, 25 FR 11402, Nov. 26, 1960; 25 FR 14021, Dec. 31, 1960, as amended by T.D. 7198, 37 FR 13679, July 13, 1972]

§ 1.61–6 Gains derived from dealings in property.

(a) **In general.** Gain realized on the sale or exchange of property is included in gross income, unless excluded by law. For this purpose property includes tangible items, such as a building, and intangible items, such as goodwill. Generally, the gain is the excess of the amount realized over the unrecovered cost or other basis for the property sold or exchanged. The specific rules for computing the amount of gain or loss are contained in section 1001 and the regulations thereunder. When a part of a larger property is sold, the cost or other basis of the entire property shall be equitably apportioned among the several parts, and the gain realized or loss sustained on the part of the entire property sold is the difference between the selling price and the cost or other basis allocated to such part. The sale of each part is treated as a separate transaction and gain or loss shall be computed separately on each part. Thus, gain or loss shall be determined at the time of sale of each part and not deferred until the entire property has been disposed of. This rule may be illustrated by the following examples:

Example (1). A, a dealer in real estate, acquires a 10-acre tract for $10,000, which he divides into 20 lots. The $10,000 cost must be equitably apportioned among the lots so that on the sale of each lot A can determine his taxable gain or deductible loss.

Example (2). B purchases for $25,000 property consisting of a used car lot and adjoining filling station. At the time, the fair market value of the filling station is $15,000 and the fair market value of the used car lot is $10,000. Five years later B sells the filling station for $20,000 at a time when $2,000 has been properly allowed as depreciation thereon. B's gain on this sale is $7,000, since $7,000 is the amount by which the selling price of

the filling station exceeds the portion of the cost equitably allocable to the filling station at the time of purchase reduced by the depreciation properly allowed.

(b) **Nontaxable exchanges.** Certain realized gains or losses on the sale or exchange of property are not "recognized", that is, are not included in or deducted from gross income at the time the transaction occurs. Gain or loss from such sales or exchanges is generally recognized at some later time. Examples of such sales or exchanges are the following:

(1) Certain formations, reorganizations, and liquidations of corporations, see sections 331, 333, 337, 351, 354, 355, and 361;

(2) Certain formations and distributions of partnerships, see sections 721 and 731;

(3) Exchange of certain property held for productive use or investment for property of like kind, see section 1031;

(4) A corporation's exchange of its stock for property, see section 1032;

(5) Certain involuntary conversions of property if replaced, see section 1033;

(6) Sale or exchange of residence if replaced, see section 1034;

(7) Certain exchanges of insurance policies and annuity contracts, see section 1035; and

(8) Certain exchanges of stock for stock in the same corporation, see section 1036.

(c) **Character of recognized gain.** Under subchapter P, chapter 1 of the Code, relating to capital gains and losses, certain gains derived from dealings in property are treated specially, and under certain circumstances the maximum rate of tax on such gains is 25 percent, as provided in section 1201. Generally, the property subject to this treatment is a "capital asset", or treated as a "capital asset". For definition of such assets, see sections 1221 and 1231, and the regulations thereunder. For some of the rules either granting or denying this special treatment, see the following sections and the regulations thereunder:

(1) Transactions between partner and partnership, section 707;

(2) Sale or exchange of property used in the trade or business and involuntary conversions, section 1231;

(3) Payment of bonds and other evidences of indebtedness, section 1232;

(4) Gains and losses from short sales, section 1233;

(5) Options to buy or sell, section 1234;

(6) Sale or exchange of patents, section 1235;

(7) Securities sold by dealers in securities, section 1236;

(8) Real property subdivided for sale, section 1237;

(9) Amortization in excess of depreciation, section 1238;

(10) Gain from sale of certain property between spouses or between an individual and a controlled corporation, section 1239;

* * *

§ 1.61–8   Rents and royalties.

(a) **In general.** Gross income includes rentals received or accrued for the occupancy of real estate or the use of personal property. For the inclusion of rents in income for the purpose of the retirement income credit, see section 37 and the regulations thereunder. Gross income includes royalties. Royalties may be received from books, stories, plays, copyrights, trademarks, formulas, patents, and from the exploitation of natural resources, such as coal, gas, oil, copper, or timber. Payments received as a result of the transfer of patent rights may under some circumstances constitute capital gain instead of ordinary income. See section 1235 and the regulations thereunder. For special rules for certain income from natural resources, see subchapter I (section 611 and following), chapter 1 of the Code, and the regulations thereunder.

(b) **Advance rentals; cancellation payments.** Gross income includes advance rentals, which must be included in income for the year of receipt regardless of the period covered or the method of accounting employed by the taxpayer. An amount received by a lessor from a lessee for cancelling a lease constitutes gross income for the year in which it is received, since it is essentially a substitute for rental payments. As to amounts received by a lessee for the cancellation of a lease, see section 1241 and the regulations thereunder.

(c) **Expenditures by lessee.** As a general rule, if a lessee pays any of the expenses of his lessor such payments are additional rental income of the lessor. If a lessee places improvements on real estate which constitute, in whole or in part, a substitute for rent, such improvements constitute

rental income to the lessor. Whether or not improvements made by a lessee result in rental income to the lessor in a particular case depends upon the intention of the parties, which may be indicated either by the terms of the lease or by the surrounding circumstances. For the exclusion from gross income of income (other than rent) derived by a lessor of real property on the termination of a lease, representing the value of such property attributable to buildings erected or other improvements made by a lessee, see section 109 and the regulations thereunder. For the exclusion from gross income of a lessor corporation of certain of its income taxes on rental income paid by a lessee corporation under a lease entered into before January 1, 1954, see section 110 and the regulations thereunder.

[T.D. 6500, 25 FR 11402, Nov. 26, 1960]

§ 1.61–9   Dividends.

(a) **In general.** Except as otherwise specifically provided, dividends are included in gross income under sections 61 and 301. For the principal rules with respect to dividends includible in gross income, see section 316 and the regulations thereunder. * * *

(b) **Dividends in kind; stock dividends; stock redemptions.** Gross income includes dividends in property other than cash, as well as cash dividends. For amounts to be included in gross income when distributions of property are made, see section 301 and the regulations thereunder. A distribution of stock, or rights to acquire stock, in the corporation making the distribution is not a dividend except under the circumstances described in section 305(b). However, the term "dividend" includes a distribution of stock, or rights to acquire stock, in a corporation other than the corporation making the distribution. For determining when distributions in complete liquidation shall be treated as dividends, see section 333 and the regulations thereunder. For rules determining when amounts received in exchanges under section 354 or exchanges and distributions under section 355 shall be treated as dividends, see section 356 and the regulations thereunder.

(c) **Dividends on stock sold.** When stock is sold, and a dividend is both declared and paid after the sale, such dividend is not gross income to the seller. When stock is sold after the declaration of a dividend and after the date as of which the seller becomes entitled to the dividend, the dividend ordinarily is income to the seller. When stock is sold between the time of declaration and the time of payment of the dividend, and the sale takes place at such time that the purchaser becomes entitled to the dividend, the dividend ordinarily is income to him. The fact that the purchaser may have included the amount of the dividend in his purchase price in contemplation of receiving the dividend does not exempt him from tax. Nor can the purchaser deduct the added amount he advanced to the seller in anticipation of the dividend. That added amount is merely part of the purchase price of the stock. In some cases, however, the purchaser may be considered to be the recipient of the dividend even though he has not received the legal title to the stock itself and does not himself receive the dividend. For example, if the seller retains the legal title to the stock as trustee solely for the purpose of securing the payment of the purchase price, with the understanding that he is to apply the dividends received from time to time in reduction of the purchase price, the dividends are considered to be income to the purchaser.

[T.D. 6500, 25 FR 11402, Nov. 26, 1960, as amended by T.D. 6777, 29 FR 17807, Dec. 16, 1964]

§ 1.61–11 Pensions.

(a) **In general.** Pensions and retirement allowances paid either by the Government or by private persons constitute gross income unless excluded by law. Usually, where the taxpayer did not contribute to the cost of a pension and was not taxable on his employer's contributions, the full amount of the pension is to be included in his gross income. But see sections 72, 402, and 403, and the regulations thereunder. When amounts are received from other types of pensions, a portion of the payment may be excluded from gross income. Under some circumstances, amounts distributed from a pension plan in excess of the employee's contributions may constitute long-term capital gain, rather than ordinary income.

* * *

[T.D. 6500, 25 FR 11402, Nov. 26, 1960, as amended by T.D. 6856, 30 FR 13316, Oct. 20. 1965]

§ 1.61–12 Income from discharge of indebtedness.

(a) **In general.** The discharge of indebtedness, in whole or in part, may result in the realization of income. If, for example, an individual performs services for a creditor, who in consideration thereof cancels the debt, the debtor realizes income in the amount of the debt as compensation for his services. A taxpayer may realize income by the payment or purchase of his obligations at less than their face value. In general, if a shareholder in a corporation which is indebted to him gratuitously forgives the debt, the transaction amounts to a contribution to the capital of the corporation to the extent of the principal of the debt.

* * *

[T.D. 6500, 25 FR 11402, Nov. 26, 1960, as amended by T.D. 6984, 33 FR 19174, Dec. 24, 1968; T.D. 7741, 45 FR 81745, Dec. 12, 1980]

§ 1.61–13 Distributive share of partnership gross income; income in respect of a decedent; income from an interest in an estate or trust.

(a) **In general.** A partner's distributive share of partnership gross income (under section 702(c)) constitutes gross income to him. Income in respect of a decedent (under section 691) constitutes gross income to the recipient. Income from an interest in an estate or trust constitutes gross income under the detailed rules of part I (section 641 and following), subchapter J, chapter 1 of the Code. In many cases, these sections also determine who is to include in his gross income the income from an estate or trust.

(b) **Creation of sinking fund by corporation.** If a corporation, for the sole purpose of securing the payment of its bonds or other indebtedness, places property in trust or sets aside certain amounts in a sinking fund under the control of a trustee who may be authorized to invest and reinvest such sums from time to time, the property or fund thus set aside by the corporation and held by the trustee is an asset of the corporation, and any gain arising therefrom is income of the corporation and shall be included as such in its gross income.

[T.D. 6500, 25 FR 11402, Nov. 26, 1960]

§ 1.61–14 Miscellaneous items of gross income.

(a) **In general.** In addition to the items enumerated in section 61(a), there are many other kinds of gross income. For example, punitive damages such as treble damages under the antitrust laws and exemplary damages for fraud are gross income. Another person's payment of the taxpayer's income taxes constitutes gross income to the taxpayer unless excluded by law. Illegal gains constitute gross income. Treasure trove, to the extent of its value in United States currency, constitutes gross income for the taxable year in which it is reduced to undisputed possession.

* * *

[T.D. 6500, 25 FR 11402, Nov. 26, 1960, as amended by T.D. 6856, 30 FR 13316, Oct. 20, 1965]

§ 1.62–1 Adjusted gross income.

(a) The term "adjusted gross income" means the gross income computed under section 61 minus such of the deductions allowed by chapter 1 of the Code as are specified in section 62. Adjusted gross income is used as the basis for the determination of the following:

(1) The optional tax if adjusted gross income is less than $5,000 (under section 3);

(2) The amount of the standard deduction (under section 141);

(3) The limitation on the amount of the deduction for charitable contributions (under section 170(b)(1));

(4) The limitation on the amount of the deduction for medical and dental expenses (under section 213); and

(5) In certain cases, the limitation on the deduction for expenses of care of certain dependents (under section 214).

(b) Section 62 merely specifies which of the deductions provided in Chapter 1 of the Code shall be allowed in computing adjusted gross income. It does not create any new deductions. The fact that a particular item may be specified in more than one of the paragraphs under section 62 does not permit the item to be twice deducted in computing either adjusted gross income or taxable income.

(c) The deductions specified in section 62 for the purpose of computing adjusted gross income are:

(1) Deductions allowable under Chapter 1 of the Code (other than by Part VII (section 211 and following), Subchapter B of such chapter) which are attributable to a trade or business carried on by the taxpayer not consisting of services performed as an employee;

(2) Deductions allowable under Part VI (section 161 and following), Subchapter B, Chapter 1 of the Code, which consist of expenses paid or incurred in connection with the performance of services by the

taxpayer as an employee under a reimbursement or other expense-allowance arrangement with his employer;

(3) Deductions allowable under Part VI which constitute expenses of travel, meals, and lodging while away from home, paid or incurred by the taxpayer in connection with the performance by him of services as an employee;

(4) Transportation expenses (as defined in paragraph (g) of this section) paid or incurred by the taxpayer in connection with the performance by him of services as an employee, allowable as a deduction under Part VI;

(5) Deductions allowable by Part VI which are attributable to a trade or business carried on by the taxpayer, if such trade or business consists of the performance of services by the taxpayer as an employee and if such trade or business is to solicit, away from the employer's place of business, business for the employer;

(6) The deduction for long-term capital gains allowed by section 1202;

(7) Deductions which are allowable under Part VI as losses from the sale or exchange of property;

(8) Deductions allowable under Part VI, section 212, and section 611 which are attributable to property held for the production of rents or royalties;

(9) Deductions for depreciation and depletion allowable under sections 167 and 611 to a life tenant of property or to an income beneficiary of property held in trust or to an heir, legatee, or devisee of an estate;

* * *

(11) The deduction for moving expenses allowed by section 217;

* * *

(13) The deduction allowed by section 219 for contributions to an individual retirement account described in section 408(a), for an individual retirement annuity described in section 408(b), or for a retirement bond described in section 409;

(14) The deduction allowed by section 402(e)(3) for the ordinary income portion of a lump sum distribution;

(15) For taxable years beginning after December 31, 1972, the deduction allowed by section 165 for losses incurred in any transaction entered into for profit though not connected with a trade or busi-

ness, to the extent that such losses include amounts forfeited to a bank, mutual savings bank, savings and loan association, building and loan association, cooperative bank or homestead association as a penalty for premature withdrawal of funds from a time savings account, certificate of deposit or similar class of deposit;

(16) For taxable years beginning after December 31, 1976, the deduction for alimony and separate maintenance payments allowed by section 215;

* * *

(d) For the purpose of the deductions specified in section 62, the performance of personal services as an employee does not constitute the carrying on of a trade or business, except as otherwise expressly provided. The practice of a profession, not as an employee, is considered the conduct of a trade or business within the meaning of such section. To be deductible for the purposes of determining adjusted gross income, expenses must be those directly, and not those merely remotely, connected with the conduct of a trade or business. For example, taxes are deductible in arriving at adjusted gross income only if they constitute expenditures directly attributable to a trade or business or to property from which rents or royalties are derived. Thus, property taxes paid or incurred on real property used in a trade or business are deductible, but State taxes on net income are not deductible even though the taxpayer's income is derived from the conduct of a trade or business.

(e) Traveling expenses paid or incurred by an employee in connection with his employment while away from home which are deductible from gross income under Part VI in computing taxable income may be deducted from gross income in computing adjusted gross income. Among the items included in traveling expenses are charges for transportation of persons or baggage, expenditures for meals and lodging, and payments for the use of sample rooms for the display of goods. See section 162 and the regulations thereunder.

(f)(1) Expenses paid or incurred by an employee which are deductible from gross income under Part VI in computing taxable income and for which he is reimbursed by the employer under an express agreement for reimbursement or pursuant to an expense allowance arrangement may be deducted from gross income in computing adjusted gross income. Where an employee is reimbursed by his employer in an amount less than his total expense, and the reimbursement is intended to cover all

types of deductible expenses, expenses other than those described in section 62(2)(B), (C), and (D) are taken into account in computing adjusted gross income in an amount which bears the same ratio to the amount of the reimbursement as the total amount of deductible expenses computed without those described in section 62(2)(B), (C), and (D) bears to the total amount of deductible expenses, including those described in section 62(2)(B), (C), and (D).

(2) The application of subparagraph (1) of this paragraph may be illustrated by the following example:

Example: S, who is not a full-time outside salesman, received a salary of $20,000 and an expense allowance of $1,200 for the calendar year 1954. He expended $800 for travel, meals, and lodging while away from home, $500 for local transportation expenses and $300 for the entertainment of customers. His adjusted gross income is computed as follows:

Salary	$20,000	
Expense allowance	1,200	
Gross income		$21,200
Less:		
Travel, meals and lodging while away from home	800	
Transportation expense	500	
Reimbursed expenses [1]	225	
		1,525
Adjusted gross income......................		$19,675

[1] The amount of the reimbursement allocable to entertainment expenses is determined as follows:

Travel, meals, and lodging while away from home	$800
Transportation expense	500
Expenses deductible in arriving at adjusted gross income (whether or not reimbursed)	1,300
Entertainment expense....................	300
Total expenses	1,600
Deductible for adjusted gross income: 300/1,600 × $1,200 (expense allowance) ..	225

(g) Transportation expenses paid or incurred by an employee in connection with performance by him of services for his employer are deductible from gross income under Part VI in computing adjusted gross income. "Transportation", as used in section 62(2)(C), is a narrower concept than "travel", as used in section 62(2)(B), and does not include meals and lodging. The term "transportation expense" includes only the cost of transporting the employee from one place to another in the course of his employment, while he is not away from home in a travel status. Thus, transportation costs may include cab fares, bus fares, and the like, and also a pro rata share of the employee's expenses of operating his automobile, including gas, oil, and depreciation. All transportation expenses must be allowable expenses under Part VI (section 161 and following), Subchapter B, Chapter 1 of the Code, as ordinary and necessary expenses incurred during the taxable year in carrying on a trade or business as an employee. Transportation expenses do not include the cost of commuting to and from work; this cost constitutes a personal, living, or family expense and is not deductible. (See section 262.)

(h) The expenses of an employee attributable to the trade or business carried on as an outside salesman which are allowed by Part VI are deductible from gross income in computing adjusted gross income. An outside salesman is an individual who solicits business as a full-time salesman for his employer away from his employer's place of business. The term "outside salesman" does not include a taxpayer whose principal activities consist of service and delivery. For example, a bread driver-salesman or a milk driver-salesman would not be included within the definition. However, an outside salesman may perform incidental inside activities at his employer's place of business, such as writing up and transmitting orders and spending short periods at the employer's place of business to make and receive telephone calls, without losing his classification as an outside salesman.

[T.D. 6500, 25 FR 11402, Nov. 26, 1960, as amended by T.D. 6722, 29 FR 5069, April 14, 1964; T.D. 6796, 30 FR 1037, Feb. 2, 1965; T.D. 7399, 41 FR 5099, Feb. 4, 1976; T.D. 7512, 42 FR 54947, Oct. 12, 1977; T.D. 7927, 48 FR 55849, Dec. 16, 1983]

Items Specifically Included in Gross Income

§ 1.71–1T Alimony and separate maintenance payments.

(a) In general.

Q–1. What is the income tax treatment of alimony or separate maintenance payments?

A–1. Alimony or separate maintenance payments are, under section 71, included in the gross income of the payee spouse and, under section 215, allowed as a deduction from the gross income of the payor spouse.

Q–2. What is an alimony or separate maintenance payment?

A–2. An alimony or separate maintenance payment is any payment received by or on behalf of a spouse (which for this purpose includes a former spouse) of the payor under a divorce or separation instrument that meets all of the following requirements:

(a) The payment is in cash (see A–5).

(b) The payment is not designated as a payment which is excludible from the gross income of the payee and nondeductible by the payor (see A–8).

(c) In the case of spouses legally separated under a decree of divorce or separate maintenance, the spouses are not members of the same household at the time the payment is made (see A–9).

(d) The payor has no liability to continue to make any payment after the death of the payee (or to make any payment as a substitute for such payment) and the divorce or separation instrument states that there is no such liability (see A–10).

(e) The payment is not treated as child support (see A–15).

(f) To the extent that one or more annual payments exceed $10,000 during any of the 6-post-separation years, the payor is obligated to make annual payments in each of the 6-post-separation years (see A–19).

Q–3. In order to be treated as alimony or separate maintenance payments, must the payments be "periodic" as that term was defined prior to enactment of the Tax Reform Act of 1984 or be made in discharge of a legal obligation of the payor to support the payee arising out of a marital or family relationship?

A–3. No. The Tax Reform Act of 1984 replaces the old requirements with the requirements described in A–2 above. Thus, the requirements that alimony or separate maintenance payments be "periodic" and be made in discharge of a legal obligation to support arising out of a marital or family relationship have been eliminated.

Q–4. Are the instruments described in section 71(a) of prior law the same as divorce or separation instruments described in section 71, as amended by the Tax Reform Act of 1984?

A–4. Yes.

(b) Specific requirements.

Q–5. May alimony or separate maintenance payments be made in a form other than cash?

A–5. No. Only cash payments (including checks and money orders payable on demand) qualify as alimony or separate maintenance payments. Transfers of services or property (including a debt instrument of a third party or an annuity contract), execution of a debt instrument by the payor, or the use of property of the payor do not qualify as alimony or separate maintenance payments.

Q–6. May payments of cash to a third party on behalf of a spouse qualify as alimony or separate maintenance payments if the payments are pursuant to the terms of a divorce or separation instrument?

A–6. Yes. Assuming all other requirements are satisfied, a payment of cash by the payor spouse to a third party under the terms of the divorce or separation instrument will qualify as a payment of cash which is received "on behalf of a spouse". For example, cash payments of rent, mortgage, tax, or tuition liabilities of the payee spouse made under the terms of the divorce or separation instrument will qualify as alimony or separate maintenance payments. Any payments to maintain property owned by the payor spouse and used by the payee spouse (including mortgage payments, real estate taxes and insurance premiums) are not payments on behalf of a spouse even if those payments are made pursuant to the terms of the divorce or separation instrument. Premiums paid by the payor spouse for term or whole life insurance on the payor's life made under the terms of the divorce or separation instrument will qualify as payments on behalf of the payee spouse to the extent that the payee spouse is the owner of the policy.

Q–7. May payments of cash to a third party on behalf of a spouse qualify as alimony or separate maintenance payments if the payments are made to the third party at the written request of the payee spouse?

A–7. Yes. For example, instead of making an alimony or separate maintenance payment directly to the payee, the payor spouse may make a cash payment to a charitable organization if such payment is pursuant to the written request, consent or ratification of the payee spouse. Such request, consent or ratification must state that the parties intend the payment to be treated as an alimony or separate maintenance payment to the payee spouse subject to the rules of section 71, and must be received by the payor spouse prior to the date of filing of the payor's first return of tax for the taxable year in which the payment was made.

Q–8. How may spouses designate that payments otherwise qualifying as alimony or separate maintenance payments shall be excludible from the gross income of the payee and nondeductible by the payor?

A–8. The spouses may designate that payments otherwise qualifying as alimony or separate maintenance payments shall be nondeductible by the payor and excludible from gross income by the payee by so providing in a divorce or separation instrument (as defined in section 71(b)(2)). If the spouses have executed a written separation agreement (as described in section 71(b)(2)(B)), any writing signed by both spouses which designates otherwise qualifying alimony or separate maintenance payments as nondeductible and excludible and which refers to the written separation agreement will be treated as a written separation agreement (and thus a divorce or separation instrument) for purposes of the preceding sentence. If the spouses are subject to temporary support orders (as described in section 71(b)(2)(C), the designation of otherwise qualifying alimony or separate payments as nondeductible and excludible must be made in the original or a subsequent temporary support order. A copy of the instrument containing the designation of payments as not alimony or separate maintenance payments must be attached to the payee's first filed return of tax (Form 1040) for each year in which the designation applies.

Q–9. What are the consequences if, at the time a payment is made, the payor and payee spouses are members of the same household?

A–9. Generally, a payment made at the time when the payor and payee spouses are members of the same household cannot qualify as an alimony or separate maintenance payment if the spouses are legally separated under a decree of divorce or of separate maintenance. For purposes of the preceding sentence, a dwelling unit formerly shared by both spouses shall not be considered two separate households even if the spouses physically separate themselves within the dwelling unit. The spouses will not be treated as members of the same household if one spouse is preparing to depart from the household of the other spouse, and does depart not more than one month after the date the payment is made. If the spouses are not legally separated under a decree of divorce or separate maintenance, a payment under a written separation agreement or a decree described in section 71(b)(2)(C) may qualify as an alimony or separate maintenance payment notwithstanding that the payor and payee are members of the same household at the time the payment is made.

Q–10. Assuming all other requirements relating to the qualification of certain payments as alimony or separate maintenance payments are met, what are the consequences if the payor spouse is required to continue to make the payments after the death of the payee spouse?

A–10. None of the payments before (or after) the death of the payee spouse qualify as alimony or separate maintenance payments.

Q–11. What are the consequences if the divorce or separation instrument fails to state that there is no liability for any period after the death of the payee spouse to continue to make any payments which would otherwise qualify as alimony or separate maintenance payments?

A–11. If the instrument fails to include such a statement, none of the payments, whether made before or after the death of the payee spouse, will qualify as alimony or separate maintenance payments.

Example (1). A is to pay B $10,000 in cash each year for a period of 10 years under a divorce or separation instrument which does not state that the payments will terminate upon the death of B. None of the payments will qualify as alimony or separate maintenance payments.

Example (2). A is to pay B $10,000 in cash each year for a period of 10 years under a divorce or separation instrument which states that the payments will terminate upon the death of B. In addition, under the instrument, A is to pay B or B's estate $20,000 in cash each year for a period of 10 years. Because the $20,000 annual payments will not terminate upon the death of B, these payments will not qualify as alimony or separate maintenance payments. However, the separate $10,000 annual payments will qualify as alimony or separate maintenance payments.

Q–12. Will a divorce or separation instrument be treated as stating that there is no liability to make payments after the death of the payee spouse if the liability to make such payments terminates pursuant to applicable local law or oral agreement?

A–12. No. Termination of the liability to make payments must be stated in the terms of the divorce or separation instrument.

Q–13. What are the consequences if the payor spouse is required to make one or more payments (in cash or property) after the death of the payee spouse as a substitute for the continuation of predeath payments which would otherwise qualify as alimony or separate maintenance payments?

A–13. If the payor spouse is required to make any such substitute payments, none of the otherwise qualifying payments will qualify as alimony or separate maintenance payments. The divorce or separation instrument need not state, however, that there is no liability to make any such substitute payment.

Q–14. Under what circumstances will one or more payments (in cash or property) which are to occur after the death of the payee spouse be treated as a substitute for the continuation of payments which would otherwise qualify as alimony or separate maintenance payments?

A–14. To the extent that one or more payments are to begin to be made, increase in amount, or become accelerated in time as a result of the death of the payee spouse, such payments may be treated as a substitute for the continuation of payments terminating on the death of the payee spouse which would otherwise qualify as alimony or separate maintenance payments. The determination of whether or not such payments are a substitute for the continuation of payments which would otherwise qualify as alimony or separate maintenance payments, and of the amount of the otherwise qualifying alimony or separate maintenance payments for which any such payments are a substitute, will depend on all of the facts and circumstances.

Example (1). Under the terms of a divorce decree, A is obligated to make annual alimony payments to B of $30,000, terminating on the earlier of the expiration of 6 years or the death of B. B maintains custody of the minor children of A and B. The decree provides that at the death of B, if there are minor children of A and B remaining, A will be obligated to make annual payments of $10,000 to a trust, the income and corpus of which are to be used for the benefit of the children until the youngest child attains the age of majority. These facts indicate that A's liability to make annual $10,000 payments in trust for the benefit of his minor children upon the death of B is a substitute for $10,000 of the $30,000 annual payments to B. Accordingly, $10,000 of each of the $30,000 annual payments to B will not qualify as alimony or separate maintenance payments.

Example (2). Under the terms of a divorce decree, A is obligated to make annual alimony payments to B of $30,000, terminating on the earlier of the expiration of 15 years or the death of B. The divorce decree provides that if B dies before the expiration of the 15 year period, A will pay to B's estate the difference between the total amount that A would have paid had B survived, minus the amount actually paid. For example, if B dies at the end of the 10th year in which payments are made, A will pay to B's estate $150,000 ($450,000–$300,000). These facts indicate that A's liability to make a lump sum payment to B's estate upon the death of B is a substitute for the full amount of each of the annual $30,000 payments to B. Accordingly, none of the annual $30,000 payments to B will qualify as alimony or separate maintenance payments. The result would be the same if the lump sum payable at B's death were discounted by an appropriate interest factor to account for the prepayment.

(c) Child support payments.

Q–15. What are the consequences of a payment which the terms of the divorce or separation instrument fix as payable for the support of a child of the payor spouse?

A–15. A payment which under the terms of the divorce or separation instrument is fixed (or treated as fixed) as payable for the support of a child of the payor spouse does not qualify as an alimony or separate maintenance payment. Thus, such a payment is not deductible by the payor spouse or includible in the income of the payee spouse.

Q–16. When is a payment fixed (or treated as fixed) as payable for the support of a child of the payor spouse?

A–16. A payment is fixed as payable for the support of a child of the payor spouse if the divorce or separation instrument specifically designates some sum or portion (which sum or portion may fluctuate) as payable for the support of a child of the payor spouse. A payment will be treated as fixed as payable for the support of a child of the payor spouse if the payment is reduced (a) on the happening of a contingency relating to a child of the payor, or (b) at a time which can clearly be associated with such a contingency. A payment may be treated as fixed as payable for the support of a child of the payor spouse even if other separate payments specifically are designated as payable for the support of a child of the payor spouse.

Q–17. When does a contingency relate to a child of the payor?

A–17. For this purpose, a contingency relates to a child of the payor if it depends on any event relating to that child, regardless of whether such event is certain or likely to occur. Events that relate to a child of the payor include the following: the child's attaining a specified age or income level, dying, marrying, leaving school, leaving the spouse's household, or gaining employment.

Q–18. When will a payment be treated as to be reduced at a time which can clearly be associated with the happening of a contingency relating to a child of the payor?

A–18. There are two situations, described below, in which payments which would otherwise qualify as alimony or separate maintenance payments will be presumed to be reduced at a time clearly associated with the happening of a contingency relating to a child of the payor. In all other situations, reductions in payments will not be treated as clearly associated with the happening of a contingency relating to a child of the payor.

The first situation referred to above is where the payments are to be reduced not more than 6 months before or after the date the child is to attain the age of 18, 21, or local age of majority. The second situation is where the payments are to be reduced on two or more occasions which occur not more than one year before or after a different child of the payor spouse attains a certain age between the ages of 18 and 24, inclusive. The certain age referred to in the preceding sentence must be the same for each such child, but need not be a whole number of years.

The presumption in the two situations described above that payments are to be reduced at a time clearly associated with the happening of a contingency relating to a child of the payor may be rebutted (either by the Service or by taxpayers) by showing that the time at which the payments are to be reduced was determined independently of any contingencies relating to the children of the payor. The presumption in the first situation will be rebutted conclusively if the reduction is a complete cessation of alimony or separate maintenance payments during the sixth post-separation year (described in A–21) or upon the expiration of a 72-month period. The presumption may also be rebutted in other circumstances, for example, by showing that alimony payments are to be made for a period customarily provided in the local jurisdiction, such as a period equal to one-half the duration of the marriage.

Example: A and B are divorced on July 1, 1985, when their children, C (born July 15, 1970) and D (born September 23, 1972), are 14 and 12, respectively. Under the divorce decree, A is to make alimony payments to B of $2,000 per month. Such payments are to be reduced to $1,500 per month on January 1, 1991 and to $1,000 per month on January 1, 1995. On January 1, 1991, the date of the first reduction in payments, C will be 20 years 5 months and 17 days old. On January 1, 1995, the date of the second reduction in payments, D will be 22 years 3 months and 9 days old. Each of the reductions in payments is to occur not more than one year before or after a different child of A attains the age of 21 years and 4 months. (Actually, the reductions are to occur not more than one year before or after C and D attain any of the ages 21 years 3 months and 9 days through 21 years 5 months and 17 days). Accordingly, the reductions will be presumed to clearly be associated with the happening of a contingency relating to C and D. Unless this presumption is rebutted, payments under the divorce decree equal to the sum of the reduction ($1,000 per month) will be treated as fixed for the support of the children of A and therefore will not qualify as alimony or separate maintenance payments.

(d) Excess front-loading rules.

Q–19. What are the excess front-loading rules?

A–19. The excess front-loading rules are two special rules which may apply to the extent that payments in any calendar year exceed $10,000. The first rule is a minimum term rule, which must be met in order for any annual payment, to the extent in excess of $10,000, to qualify as an alimony or separate maintenance payment (see A–2(f)). This rule requires that alimony or separate maintenance payments be called for, at a minimum, during the 6 "post-separation years". The second rule is a recapture rule which characterizes payments retrospectively by requiring a recalculation and inclusion in income by the payor and deduction by the payee of previously paid alimony or separate maintenance payment to the extent that the amount of such payments during any of the 6 "post-separation years" falls short of the amount of payments during a prior year by more than $10,-000.

Q–20. Do the excess front-loading rules apply to payments to the extent that annual payments never exceed $10,000?

A–20. No. For example, A is to make a single $10,000 payment to B. Provided that the other requirements of section 71 are met, the payment will qualify as an alimony or separate maintenance payment. If A were to make a single $15,000 payment to B, $10,000 of the payment would qualify as an alimony or separate maintenance payment and $5,000 of the payment would be disqualified under the minimum term rule because payments were not to be made for the minimum period.

Q–21. Do the excess front-loading rules apply to payments received under a decree described in section 71(b)(2)(C)?

A–21. No. Payments under decrees described in section 71(b)(2)(C) are to be disregarded entirely for purposes of applying the excess front-loading rules.

Q–22. Both the minimum term rule and the recapture rule refer to 6 "post-separation years". What are the 6 "post-separation years"?

A–22. The 6 "post-separation years" are the 6 consecutive calendar years beginning with the first calendar year in which the payor pays to the payee an alimony or separate maintenance payment (except a payment made under a decree described in section 71(b)(2)(C)). Each year within this period is referred to as a "post-separation year". The 6-year period need not commence with the year in which the spouses separate or divorce, or with the year in which payments under the divorce or separation instrument are made, if no payments during such year qualify as alimony or separate maintenance payments. For example, a decree for the divorce of A and B is entered in October, 1985. The decree requires A to make monthly payments to B commencing November 1, 1985, but A and B are members of the same household until February 15, 1986 (and as a result, the payments prior to January 16, 1986, do not qualify as alimony payments). For purposes of applying the excess front-loading rules to payments from A to B, the 6 calendar years 1986 through 1991 are post-separation years. If a spouse has been making payments pursuant to a divorce or separation instrument described in section 71(b)(2)(A) or (B), a modification of the instrument or the substitution of a new instrument (for example, the substitution of a divorce decree for a written separation agreement) will not result in the creation of additional post-separation years. However, if a spouse has been making payments pursuant to a divorce or separation instrument described in section 71(b)(2)(C), the 6-year period does not begin until the first calendar year in which alimony or separate maintenance payments are made under a divorce or separation instrument described in section 71(b)(2)(A) or (B).

Q–23. How does the minimum term rule operate?

A–23. The minimum term rule operates in the following manner. To the extent payments are made in excess of $10,000, a payment will qualify as an alimony or separate maintenance payment only if alimony or separate maintenance payments are to be made in each of the 6 post-separation years. For example, pursuant to a divorce decree, A is to make alimony payments to B of $20,000 in each of the 5 calendar years 1985 through 1989. A is to make no payment in 1990. Under the minimum term rule, only $10,000 will qualify as an alimony payment in each of the calendar years 1985 through 1989. If the divorce decree also required A to make a $1 payment in 1990, the minimum term rule would be satisfied and $20,000 would be treated as an alimony payment in each of the calendar years 1985 through 1989. The recapture rule would, however, apply for 1990. For purposes of determining whether alimony or separate maintenance payments are to be made in any year, the possible termination of such payments upon the happening of a contingency (other than the passage of time) which has not yet occurred is ignored (unless such contingency may cause all or a portion of the payment to be treated as a child support payment).

Q–24. How does the recapture rule operate?

A–24. The recapture rule operates in the following manner. If the amount of alimony or separate maintenance payments paid in any post-separation year (referred to as the "computation year") falls short of the amount of alimony or separate maintenance payments paid in any prior post-separation year by more than $10,000, the payor must compute an "excess amount" for the computation year. The excess amount for any computation year is the sum of excess amounts determined with respect to each prior post-separation year. The excess amount determined with respect to a prior post-separation year is the excess of (1) the amount of alimony or separate maintenance payments paid by the payor spouse during such prior post-separation year, over (2) the amount of the alimony or separate maintenance payments paid by the payor

spouse during the computation year plus $10,000. For purposes of this calculation, the amount of alimony or separate maintenance payments made by the payor spouse during any post-separation year preceding the computation year is reduced by any excess amount previously determined with respect to such year. The rules set forth above may be illustrated by the following example. A makes alimony payments to B of $25,000 in 1985 and $12,000 in 1986. The excess amount with respect to 1985 that is recaptured in 1986 is $3,000 ($25,000–($12,000+$10,000)). For purposes of subsequent computation years, the amount deemed paid in 1985 is $22,000. If A makes alimony payments to B of $1,000 in 1987, the excess amount that is recaptured in 1987 will be $12,000. This is the sum of an $11,000 excess amount with respect to 1985 ($22,000–($1,000+$10,000)) and a $1,000 excess amount with respect to 1986 ($12,000–($1,000+$10,000)). If, prior to the end of 1990, payments decline further, additional recapture will occur. The payor spouse must include the excess amount in gross income for his/her taxable year beginning with or in the computation year. The payee spouse is allowed a deduction for the excess amount in computing adjusted gross income for his/her taxable year beginning with or in the computation year. However, the payee spouse must compute the excess amount by reference to the date when payments were made and not when payments were received.

Q–25. What are the exceptions to the recapture rule?

A–25. Apart from the $10,000 threshold for application of the recapture rule, there are three exceptions to the recapture rule. The first exception is for payments received under temporary support orders described in section 71(b)(2)(C) (see A–21). The second exception is for any payment made pursuant to a continuing liability over the period of the post-separation years to pay a fixed portion of the payor's income from a business or property or from compensation for employment or self-employment. The third exception is where the alimony or separate maintenance payments in any post-separation year cease by reason of the death of the payor or payee or the remarriage (as defined under applicable local law) of the payee before the close of the computation year. For example, pursuant to a divorce decree, A is to make cash payments to B of $30,000 in each of the calendar years 1985 through 1990. A makes cash payments of

$30,000 in 1985 and $15,000 in 1986, in which year B remarries and A's alimony payments cease. The recapture rule does not apply for 1986 or any subsequent year. If alimony or separate maintenance payments made by A decline or cease during a post-separation year for any other reason (including a failure by the payor to make timely payments, a modification of the divorce or separation instrument, a reduction in the support needs of the payee, or a reduction in the ability of the payor to provide support) excess amounts with respect to prior post-separation years will be subject to recapture.

(e) Effective dates.

Q–26. When does section 71, as amended by the Tax Reform Act of 1984, become effective?

A–26. Generally, section 71, as amended, is effective with respect to divorce or separation instruments (as defined in section 71(b)(2)) executed after December 31, 1984. If a decree of divorce or separate maintenance executed after December 31, 1984, incorporates or adopts without change the terms of the alimony or separate maintenance payments under a divorce or separation instrument executed before January 1, 1985, such decree will be treated as executed before January 1, 1985. A change in the amount of alimony or separate maintenance payments or the time period over which such payments are to continue, or the addition or deletion of any contingencies or conditions relating to such payments is a change in the terms of the alimony or separate maintenance payments. For example, in November 1984, A and B executed a written separation agreement. In February 1985, a decree of divorce is entered in substitution for the written separation agreement. The decree of divorce does not change the terms of the alimony A pays to B. The decree of divorce will be treated as executed before January 1, 1985 and hence alimony payments under the decree will be subject to the rules of section 71 prior to amendment by the Tax Reform Act of 1984. If the amount or time period of the alimony or separate maintenance payments are not specified in the pre-1985 separation agreement or if the decree of divorce changes the amount or term of such payments, the decree of divorce will not be treated as executed before January 1, 1985, and alimony payments under the decree will be subject to the rules of section 71, as amended by the Tax Reform Act of 1984.

Section 71, as amended, also applies to any divorce or separation instrument executed (or treated as executed) before January 1, 1985 that has been modified on or after January 1, 1985, if such modification expressly provides that section 71, as amended by the Tax Reform Act of 1984, shall apply to the instrument as modified. In this case, section 71, as amended, is effective with respect to payments made after the date the instrument is modified.

[T.D. 7973, 49 FR 34455, Aug. 31, 1984; 49 FR 36645, Sept. 19, 1984]

§ 1.72–1 Introduction.

(a) General principle. Section 72 prescribes rules relating to the inclusion in gross income of amounts received under a life insurance, endowment, or annuity contract unless such amounts are specifically excluded from gross income under other provisions of chapter 1 of the Code. In general, these rules provide that amounts subject to the provisions of section 72 are includible in the gross income of the recipient except to the extent that they are considered to represent a reduction or return of premiums or other consideration paid.

(b) Amounts to be considered as a return of premiums. For the purpose of determining the extent to which amounts received represent a reduction or return of premiums or other consideration paid, the provisions of section 72 distinguish between "amounts received as an annuity" and "amounts not received as an annuity". In general, "amounts received as an annuity" are amounts which are payable at regular intervals over a period of more than one full year from the date on which they are deemed to begin, provided the total of the amounts so payable or the period for which they are to be paid can be determined as of that date. See paragraph (b)(2) and (3) of § 1.72–2. Any other amounts to which the provisions of section 72 apply are considered to be "amounts not received as an annuity". See § 1.72–11.

(c) "Amounts received as an annuity." (1) In the case of "amounts received as an annuity" (other than certain employees' annuities described in section 72(d) and in § 1.72–13), a proportionate part of each amount so received is considered to represent a return of premiums or other consideration paid. The proportionate part of each annuity payment which is thus excludable from gross income is determined by the ratio which the investment in the contract as of the date on which the annuity is deemed to begin bears to the expected return under the contract as of that date. See § 1.72–4.

* * *

(d) "Amounts not received as an annuity". In the case of "amounts not received as an annuity", if such amounts are received after an annuity has begun and during its continuance, amounts so received are generally includible in the gross income of the recipient. Amounts not received as an annuity which are received at any other time are generally includible in the gross income of the recipient only to the extent that such amounts, when added to all amounts previously received under the contract which were excludable from the gross income of the recipient under the income tax law applicable at the time of receipt, exceed the premiums or other consideration paid (see § 1.72–11). However, if the aggregate of premiums or other consideration paid for the contract includes amounts for which a deduction was allowed under section 404 as contributions on behalf of an owner-employee, the amounts received under the circumstances of the preceding sentence shall be includible in gross income until the amount so included equals the amount for which the deduction was so allowed. * * *

(e) Classification of recipients. For the purpose of the regulations under section 72, a recipient shall be considered an "annuitant" if he receives amounts under an annuity contract during the period that the annuity payments are to continue, whether for a term certain or during the continuing life or lives of the person or persons whose lives measure the duration of such annuity. However, a recipient shall be considered a "beneficiary" rather than an "annuitant" if the amounts he receives under a contract are received after the term of the annuity for a life or lives has expired and such amounts are paid by reason of the fact that the contract guarantees that payments of some minimum amount or for some minimum period shall be made. * * *

[T.D. 6500, 25 FR 11402, Nov. 26, 1960, as amended by T.D. 6676, 28 FR 10134, Sept. 17, 1963]

§ 1.72–2 Applicability of section.

(a) Contracts. (1) The contracts under which amounts paid will be subject to the provisions of section 72 include contracts which are considered to be life insurance, endowment, and annuity contracts in accordance with the customary practice of life insurance companies. For the purposes of section 72, however, it is immaterial whether such contracts are entered into with an insurance company. The term "endowment contract" also includes the "face-amount certificates" described in section 72(1).

* * *

(b) Amounts. (1)(i) In general, the amounts to which section 72 applies are any amounts received under the contracts described in paragraph (a)(1) of this section. However, if such amounts are specifically excluded from gross income under other provisions of chapter 1 of the Code, section 72 shall not apply for the purpose of including such amounts in gross income. For example, section 72 does not apply to amounts received under a life insurance contract if such amounts are paid by reason of the death of the insured and are excludable from gross income under section 101(a). See also sections 101(d), relating to proceeds of life insurance paid at a date later than death, and 104(a)(4), relating to compensation for injuries or sickness.

(ii) Section 72 does not exclude from gross income any amounts received under an agreement to hold an amount and pay interest thereon. See paragraph (a) of § 1.72–14. However, section 72 does apply to amounts received by a surviving annuitant under a joint and survivor annuity contract since such amounts are not considered to be paid by reason of the death of an insured. For a special deduction for the estate tax attributable to the inclusion of the value of the interest of a surviving annuitant under a joint and survivor annuity contract in the estate of the deceased primary annuitant, see section 691(d) and the regulations thereunder.

(2) Amounts subject to section 72 in accordance with subparagraph (1) of this paragraph are considered "amounts received as an annuity" only in the event that all of the following tests are met:

(i) They must be received on or after the "annuity starting date" as that term is defined in paragraph (b) of § 1.72–4;

(ii) They must be payable in periodic installments at regular intervals (whether annually, semiannually, quarterly, monthly, weekly, or otherwise) over a period of more than one full year from the annuity starting date; and

(iii) Except as indicated in subparagraph (3) of this paragraph, the total of the amounts payable must be determinable at the annuity starting date either directly from the terms of the contract or indirectly by the use of either mortality tables or compound interest computations, or both, in conjunction with such terms and in accordance with sound actuarial theory.

For the purpose of determining whether amounts subject to section 72(d) and § 1.72–13 are "amounts received as an annuity", however, the provisions of subdivision (i) of this subparagraph shall be disregarded. In addition, the term "amounts received as an annuity" does not include amounts received to which the provisions of paragraph (b) or (c) of § 1.72–11 apply, relating to dividends and certain amounts received by a beneficiary in the nature of a refund. If an amount is to be paid periodically until a fund plus interest at a fixed rate is exhausted, but further payments may be made thereafter because of earnings at a higher interest rate, the requirements of subdivision (iii) of this subparagraph are met with respect to the payments determinable at the outset by means of computations involving the fixed interest rate, but any payments received after the expiration of the period determinable by such computations shall be taxable as dividends received after the annuity starting date in accordance with paragraph (b)(2) of § 1.72–11.

* * *

[T.D. 6500, 25 FR 11402, Nov. 26, 1960, as amended by T.D. 6497, 25 FR 10019, Oct. 20, 1960; T.D. 6885, 31 FR 7798, June 2, 1966]

§ 1.72–4   Exclusion ratio.

(a) **General rule.** (1)(i) To determine the proportionate part of the total amount received each year as an annuity which is excludable from the gross income of a recipient in the taxable year of receipt (other than amounts received under (a) certain employee annuities described in section 72(d) and § 1.72–13, or (b) certain annuities described in section 72(o) and § 1.122–1), an exclusion ratio is to be determined for each contract. In general, this ratio is determined by dividing the investment in the contract as found under § 1.72–6 by the expected return under such contract as found under § 1.72–5. Where a single consideration is given for a particular contract which provides for two or more annuity elements, an exclusion ratio shall be determined for the contract as a whole by dividing the investment in such contract by the aggregate of the expected returns under all the annuity elements provided thereunder. * * *

(ii) The exclusion ratio for the particular contract is then applied to the total amount received as an annuity during the taxable year by each recipient. See, however, paragraph (e)(3) of § 1.72–5. Any excess of the total amount received as an annuity during the taxable year over the amount determined by the application of the exclusion ratio to such total amount shall be included in the gross income of the recipient for the taxable year of receipt.

(2) The principles of subparagraph (1) may be illustrated by the following example:

Example. Taxpayer A purchased an annuity contract providing for payments of $100 per month for a consideration of $12,650. Assuming that the expected return under this contract is $16,000, the exclusion ratio to be used by A is $12,650÷$16,000; or 79.1 percent (79.06 rounded to the nearest tenth). If 12 such monthly payments are received by A during his taxable year, the total amount he may exclude from his gross income in such year is $949.20 ($1,200×79.1 percent). The balance of $250.80 ($1,200 less $949.20) is the amount to be included in gross income. If A instead received only five such payments during the year, he should exclude $395.50 ($500×79.1 percent) of the total amounts received. * * *

(3) The exclusion ratio shall be applied only to amounts received as an annuity within the meaning of that term under paragraph (b)(2) and (3) of § 1.72–2. Where the periodic payments increase in amount after the annuity starting date in a manner not provided by the terms of the contract at such date, the portion of such payments representing the increase is not an amount received as an annuity. For the treatment of amounts not received as an annuity, see section 72(e) and § 1.72–11. For special rules where paragraph (b)(3) of § 1.72–2 applies to amounts received, see paragraph (d)(3) of this section.

(4) After an exclusion ratio has been determined for a particular contract, it shall be applied to any amounts received as an annuity thereunder unless or until one of the following occurs:

(i) The contract is assigned or transferred for a valuable consideration (see section 72(g) and paragraph (a) of § 1.72–10;

(ii) The contract matures or is surrendered, redeemed, or discharged in accordance with the provisions of paragraph (c) or (d) of § 1.72–11;

(iii) The contract is exchanged (or is considered to have been exchanged) in a manner described in paragraph (e) of § 1.72–11.

(b) **Annuity starting date.** (1) Except as provided in subparagraph (2) of this paragraph, the annuity starting date is the first day of the first period for which an amount is received as an annuity, except that if such date was before January 1, 1954, then the annuity starting date is January 1, 1954. The first day of the first period for which an amount is received as an annuity shall be whichever of the following is the later:

(i) The date upon which the obligations under the contract became fixed, or

(ii) The first day of the period (year, half-year, quarter, month, or otherwise, depending on whether payments are to be made annually, semiannually, quarterly, monthly, or otherwise) which ends on the date of the first annuity payment.

(2) Notwithstanding the provisions of paragraph (b)(1) of this section, the annuity starting date shall be determined in accordance with whichever of the following provisions is appropriate:

(i) In the case of a joint and survivor annuity contract described in section 72(i) and paragraph (b)(3) of § 1.72–5, the annuity starting date is January 1, 1954, or the first day of the first period for which an amount is received as an annuity by the surviving annuitant, whichever is the later;

* * *

(d) **Exceptions to the general rule.** (1) Where the provisions of section 72 would otherwise require an exclusion ratio to be determined, but the investment in the contract (determined under § 1.72–6) is an amount of zero or less, no exclusion ratio shall be determined and all amounts received under such a contract shall be includible in the gross income of the recipient for the purposes of section 72.

(2) Where the investment in the contract is equal to or greater than the total expected return under such contract found under § 1.72–5, the exclusion ratio shall be considered to be 100 percent and all amounts received as an annuity under such contract shall be excludable from the recipient's gross income. * * *

(3)(i) If a contract provides for payments to be made to a taxpayer in the manner described in paragraph (b)(3) of § 1.72–2, the investment in the contract shall be considered to be equal to the expected return under such contract and the resulting exclusion ratio (100%) shall be applied to all amounts received as an annuity under such contract. For any taxable year, payments received under such a contract shall be considered to be amounts received as an annuity only to the extent

that they do not exceed the portion of the investment in the contract which is properly allocable to that year and hence excludable from gross income as a return of premiums or other consideration paid for the contract. The portion of the investment in the contract which is properly allocable to any taxable year shall be determined by dividing the investment in the contract (adjusted for any refund feature in the manner described in paragraph (d) of § 1.72–7) by the applicable multiple (whether for a term certain, life, or lives) which would otherwise be used in determining the expected return for such a contract under § 1.72–5. The multiple shall be adjusted in accordance with the provisions of the table in paragraph (a)(2) of § 1.72–5, if any adjustment is necessary, before making the above computation. If payments are to be made more frequently than annually and the number of payments to be made in the taxable year in which the annuity begins are less than the number of payments to be made each year thereafter, the amounts considered received as an annuity (as otherwise determined under this subdivision) shall not exceed, for such taxable year (including a short taxable year), an amount which bears the same ratio to the portion of the investment in the contract considered allocable to each taxable year as the number of payments to be made in the first year bears to the number of payments to be made in each succeeding year. Thus, if payments are to be made monthly, only seven payments will be made in the first taxable year, and the portion of the investment in the contract allocable to a full year of payments is $600, the amounts considered received as an annuity in the first taxable year cannot exceed $350 ($600 × 7/12). See subdivision (iii) of this subparagraph for an example illustrating the determination of the portion of the investment in the contract allocable to one taxable year of the taxpayer.

(ii) If subdivision (i) of this subparagraph applies to amounts received by a taxpayer and the total amount of payments he receives in a taxable year is less than the total amount excludable for such year under subdivision (i) of this subparagraph, the taxpayer may elect, in a succeeding taxable year in which he receives another payment, to redetermine the amounts to be received as an annuity during the current and succeeding taxable years. This shall be computed in accordance with the provisions of subdivision (i) of this subparagraph except that:

(a) The difference between the portion of the investment in the contract allocable to a taxable year, as found in accordance with subdivision (i) of this subparagraph, and the total payments actually received in the taxable year prior to the election shall be divided by the life expectancy of the annuitant (or annuitants), found in accordance with the appropriate table in § 1.72–9 (and adjusted in accordance with paragraph (a)(2) of § 1.72–5), or by the remaining term of a term certain annuity, computed as of the first day of the first period for which an amount is received as an annuity in the taxable year of the election; and

(b) The amount determined under (a) of this subdivision shall be added to the portion of the investment in the contract allocable to each taxable year (as otherwise found). To the extent that the total periodic payments received under the contract in the taxable year of the election or any succeeding taxable year does not equal this total sum, such payments shall be excludable from the gross income of the recipient. To the extent such payments exceed the sum so found, they shall be fully includable in recipient's gross income.

See subdivision (iii) of this subparagraph for an example illustrating the redetermination of amounts to be received as an annuity and subdivision (iv) of this subparagraph for the method of making the election provided by this subdivision.

(iii) The application of the principles of this subparagraph may be illustrated by the following example:

Example. Taxpayer A, a 64 year old male, files his return on a calendar year basis and has a life expectancy of 15.6 years on June 30, 1954, the annuity starting date of a contract to which § 1.72–2(b)(3) applies and which he purchased for $20,000. The contract provides for variable annual payments for his life. He receives a payment of $1,000 on June 30, 1955, but receives no other payment until June 30, 1957. He excludes the $1,000 payment from his gross income for the year 1955 since this amount is less than $1,324.50, the amount determined by dividing his investment in the contract ($20,000) by his life expectancy adjusted for annual payments, 15.1 (15.6–0.5), as of the original annuity starting date. Taxpayer A may elect, in his return for the taxable year 1957, to redetermine amounts to be received as an annuity under his contract as of June 30, 1956. For the purpose of determining the extent to which amounts received in 1957 or thereafter shall be considered amounts received as an annuity (to which a 100 percent exclusion ratio shall apply) he shall add $118.63 to the $1,324.50 originally determined to be receivable as an annuity under the contract, making a total of $1,443.13. This is determined by dividing the difference between what was excludable in 1955 and 1956, $2,649 (2×$1,324.50) and what he actually received in those years ($1,000) by his life expect-

ancy adjusted for annual payments, 13.9 (14.4–0.5), as of his age at his nearest birthday (66) on the first day of the first period for which he received an amount as an annuity in the taxable year of election (June 30, 1956). The result, $1,443.13, is excludable in that year and each year thereafter as an amount received as an annuity to which the 100% exclusion ratio applies. It will be noted that in this example the taxpayer received amounts less than the excludable amounts in two successive years and deferred making his election until the third year, and thus was able to accumulate the portion of the investment in the contract allocable to each taxable year to the extent he failed to receive such portion in both years. Assuming that he received $1,500 in the taxable year of his election, he would include $56.87 in his gross income and exclude $1,443.13 therefrom for that year.

(iv) If the taxpayer chooses to make the election described in subdivision (ii) of this subparagraph he shall file with his return a statement that he elects to make a redetermination of the amounts excludable from gross income under his annuity contract in accordance with the provisions of paragraph (d)(3) of § 1.72–4. This statement shall also contain the following information:

(a) The original annuity starting date and his age on that date,

(b) The date of the first day of the first period for which he received an amount in the current taxable year,

(c) The investment in the contract originally determined (as adjusted for any refund feature), and

(d) The aggregate of all amounts received under the contract between the date indicated in (a) of this subdivision and the day after the date indicated in (b) of this subdivision to the extent such amounts were excludable from gross income.

He shall include in gross income any amounts received during the taxable year for which the return is made in accordance with the redetermination made under this subparagraph.

* * *

[T.D. 6500, 25 FR 11402, Nov. 26, 1960, as amended by T.D. 7043, 35 FR 8477, June 2, 1970; T.D. 7352, 40 FR 16663, April 14, 1975]

§ 1.72–5   Expected return.

(a) **Expected return for but one life.** (1) If a contract to which section 72 applies provides that one annuitant is to receive a fixed monthly income for life, the expected return is determined by multiplying the total of the annuity payments to be received annually by the multiple shown in Table I of § 1.72–9 under the age (as of annuity starting date) and sex of the measuring life (usually the annuitant's). Thus, where a male purchases a contract providing for an immediate annuity of $100 per month for his life and, as of the annuity starting date (in this case the date of purchase), the annuitant's age at his nearest birthday is 66, the expected return is computed as follows:

Monthly payment of $100 × 12 months
equals annual payment of $1,200
Multiple shown in Table I, male, age 66..... 14.4
Expected return ($1,200 × 14.4) 17,280

(2)(i) If payments are to be made quarterly, semiannually, or annually, an adjustment of the applicable multiple shown in Table I may be required. A further adjustment may be required where the interval between the annuity starting date and the date of the first payment is less than the interval between future payments. Neither adjustment shall be made, however, if the payments are to be made more frequently than quarterly. The amount of the adjustment, if any, is to be found in accordance with the following table:

If the number of whole months from the annuity starting date to the first payment date is—	0–1	2	3	4	5	6	7	8	9	10	11	12
And payments under the contract are to be made:												
Annually....................	+ 0.5	+ 0.4	+ 0.3	+ 0.2	+ 0.1	0	0	− 0.1	− 0.2	− 0.3	− 0.4	− 0.5
Semiannually	+ .2	+ .1	0	0	− .1	− .2	.....	.....	.....	.....	.....	.....
Quarterly	+ .1	0	− .1	.....	.....	.....	.....	.....	.....	.....	.....	.....

Thus, for a male, age 66, the multiple found in Table I adjusted for quarterly payments the first of which is to be made one full month after the annuity starting date, is 14.5 (14.4+0.1); for semi-annual payments the first of which is to be made six full months from the annuity starting date, the adjusted multiple is 14.2 (14.4−0.2); for annual payments the first of which is to be made one full month from the annuity starting date, the adjusted multiple is 14.9 (14.4+0.5). If the annuitant in the example shown in subparagraph (1) of this paragraph were to receive an annual payment of $1,200 commencing 12 full months after his annuity starting date, the amount of the expected return would be $16,680 ($1,200×13.9 [14.4−0.5]).

* * *

(4) If the contract provides for payments to be made to an annuitant for his lifetime, but the amount of the annual payments is to be decreased after the expiration of a specified limited period, the expected return is computed by considering the contract as a combination of a whole life annuity for the smaller amount plus a temporary life annuity for an amount equal to the difference between the larger and the smaller amount. For example, if a male annuitant, age 60, is to receive $150 per month for five years or until his earlier death, and is to receive $90 per month for the remainder of his lifetime after such five years, the expected return is computed as if the annuitant's contract consisted of a whole life annuity for $90 per month plus a five year temporary life annuity of $60 per

month. In such circumstances, the expected return is computed as follows:

Monthly payments of $90 × 12 months
equals annual payment of $1,080
Multiple shown in Table I for male, age 60 .. 18.2
Expected return for whole life annuity of
$1,080 per year $19,656
Expected return for 5-year temporary life
annuity of $720 per year (as found in
subparagraph (3)) of this paragraph $3,456
Total expected return $23,112

If payments are to be made quarterly, semiannually, or annually, an appropriate adjustment of the multiple found in Table I for the whole life annuity should be made in accordance with subparagraph (2) of this paragraph.

(5) If the contract described in subparagraph (4) of this paragraph provided that the amount of the annual payments to the annuitant were to be increased (instead of decreased) after the expiration of a specified limited period, the expected return would be computed as if the annuitant's contract consisted of a whole life annuity for the larger amount minus a temporary life annuity for an amount equal to the difference between the larger and smaller amount. Thus, if the annuitant described in subparagraph (4) of this paragraph were to receive $90 per month for five years or until his earlier death, and to receive $150 per month for the remainder of his lifetime after such five years, the expected return would be computed by subtracting the expected return under a five year temporary life annuity of $60 per month from the

expected return under a whole life annuity of $150 per month. In such circumstances, the expected return is computed as follows:

Monthly payments of $150 × 12 months equals annual payment of	$1,800
Multiple shown in Table I (male, age 60)	18.2
Expected return for annuity for whole life of $1,800 per year	$32,760
Less expected return for 5-year temporary life annuity of $720 per year (as found in subparagraph (3))	$3,456
Net expected return...................	$29,304

If payments are to be made quarterly, semiannually, or annually, an appropriate adjustment of the multiple found in Table I for the whole life annuity should be made in accordance with subparagraph (2) of this paragraph.

(b) Expected return under joint and survivor and joint annuities. (1) In the case of a joint and survivor annuity contract involving two annuitants which provides the first annuitant with a fixed monthly income for life and, after the death of the first annuitant, provides an identical monthly income for life to a second annuitant, the expected return shall be determined by multiplying the total amount of the payments to be received annually by the multiple obtained from Table II of § 1.72–9 under the ages (as of the annuity starting date) and sexes of the living annuitants. For example, a husband purchases a joint and survivor annuity contract providing for payments of $100 per month for life, and after his death, for the same amount to his wife for the remainder of her life. As of the annuity starting date his age at his nearest birthday is 70 and that of his wife at her nearest birthday is 67. The expected return is computed as follows:

Monthly payments of $100 × 12 months equals annual payment of	$1,200
Multiple shown in Table II (male, age 70; female, age 67)........................	19.7
Expected return ($1,200 × 19.7)	$23,640

If payments are to be made quarterly, semiannually, or annually, an appropriate adjustment of the multiple found in Table II should be made in accordance with paragraph (a)(2) of this section.

(2) If a contract of the type described in subparagraph (1) of this paragraph provides that a different (rather than an identical) monthly income is payable to the second annuitant, the expected return is computed in the following manner. The applicable multiple in Table II is first found as in the example in subparagraph (1) of this paragraph. The multiple applicable to the first annuitant is

then found in Table I as though the contract were for a single life annuity. The multiple from Table I is then subtracted from the multiple obtained from Table II and the resulting multiple is applied to the total payments to be received annually under the contract by the second annuitant. The result is the expected return with respect to the second annuitant. The portion of the expected return with respect to payments to be made during the first annuitant's life is then computed by applying the multiple found in Table I to the total annual payments to be received by such annuitant under the contract. The expected returns with respect to each of the annuitants separately are then aggregated to obtain the expected return under the entire contract.

Example. A husband purchases a joint and survivor annuity providing for payments of $100 per month for his life and, after his death, payments to his wife of $50 per month for her life. As of the annuity starting date his age at his nearest birthday is 70 and that of his wife at her nearest birthday is 67.

Multiple from Table II (male, age 70; female, age 67)	19.7
Multiple from Table I (male, age 70)	12.1
Difference (multiple applicable to second annuitant)	7.6
Portion of expected return, second annuitant ($600 × 7.6)	$4,560
Portion of expected return, first annuitant ($1,200 × 12.1)........................	$14,520
Expected return under the contract	$19,080

The expected return thus found, $19,080, is to be used in computing the amount to be excluded from gross income. Thus, if the investment in the contract in this example is $14,310, the exclusion ratio is $14,310÷$19,080; or 75 percent. The amount excludable from each monthly payment made to the husband is 75 percent of $100, or $75, and the remaining $25 of each payment received by him shall be included in his gross income. After the husband's death, the amount excludable by the second annuitant (the surviving wife) would be 75 percent of each monthly payment of $50, or $37.50, and the remaining $12.50 of each payment shall be included in her gross income.

The same method is used if the payments are to be increased after the death of the first annuitant. Thus, if the payments to be made until the husband's death were $50 per month and his widow were to receive $100 per month thereafter until her death, the 7.6 multiple in the above example would be applied to the $100 payments, yielding an expected return with respect to this portion of the annuity contract of $9,120 ($1,200 × 7.6). An expected return of $7,260 ($600 × 12.1) would be obtained with respect to the payments to be made the husband, yielding a total expected return under the contract of $16,380 ($9,120 plus $7,260). If payments are to be made quarterly, semiannually, or annually, an appropriate adjustment of the multiples found in Tables I and II should be made in accordance with paragraph (a)(2) of this section.

* * *

(c) **Expected return for term certain.** In the case of a contract providing for specific periodic payments which are to be paid for a term certain such as a fixed number of months or years, without regard to life expectancy, the expected return is determined by multiplying the fixed number of years or months for which payments are to be made on or after the annuity starting date by the amount of the payment provided in the contract for each such period.

* * *

[T.D. 6500, 25 FR 11402, Nov. 26, 1960]

§ 1.72–9   Tables.

The following tables are to be used in connection with computations under section 72 and the regulations thereunder:

TABLE I—ORDINARY LIFE ANNUITIES—ONE LIFE—EXPECTED RETURN MULTIPLES

Ages		Multiples
Male	Female	
* * *		
35	40	38.2
36	41	37.3
37	42	36.5
38	43	35.6
39	44	34.7
40	45	33.8
41	46	33.0
42	47	32.1
43	48	31.2
44	49	30.4
45	50	29.6
46	51	28.7
47	52	27.9
48	53	27.1
49	54	26.3
50	55	25.5
51	56	24.7
52	57	24.0
53	58	23.2
54	59	22.4
55	60	21.7
56	61	21.0
57	62	20.3
58	63	19.6
59	64	18.9
60	65	18.2
61	66	17.5
62	67	16.9
63	68	16.2
64	69	15.6
65	70	15.0
66	71	14.4
67	72	13.8
68	73	13.2
69	74	12.6
70	75	12.1
71	76	11.6
72	77	11.0
73	78	10.5
74	79	10.1
75	80	9.6
76	81	9.1
77	82	8.7
78	83	8.3
79	84	7.8
80	85	7.5
81	86	7.1
82	87	6.7
83	88	6.3
84	89	6.0
* * *		

TABLE II—ORDINARY JOINT LIFE AND LAST SURVIVOR ANNUITIES—TWO LIVES—EXPECTED RETURN MULTIPLES

Male	Female	Ages												
		Male 35	36	37	38	39	40	41	42	43	44	45	46	47
		Female 40	41	42	43	44	45	46	47	48	49	50	51	52
35	40	46.2	45.7	45.3	44.8	44.4	44.0	43.6	43.3	43.0	42.6	42.3	42.0	41.8
36	41	45.7	45.2	44.8	44.3	43.9	43.5	43.1	42.7	42.3	42.0	41.7	41.4	41.1
37	42	45.3	44.8	44.3	43.8	43.4	42.9	42.5	42.1	41.8	41.4	41.1	40.7	40.4
38	43	44.8	44.3	43.8	43.3	42.9	42.4	42.0	41.6	41.2	40.8	40.5	40.1	39.8
39	44	44.4	43.9	43.4	42.9	42.4	41.9	41.5	41.0	40.6	40.2	39.9	39.5	39.2
40	45	44.0	43.5	42.9	42.4	41.9	41.4	41.0	40.5	40.1	39.7	39.3	38.9	38.6
41	46	43.6	43.1	42.5	42.0	41.5	41.0	40.5	40.0	39.6	39.2	38.8	38.4	38.0
42	47	43.3	42.7	42.1	41.6	41.0	40.5	40.0	39.6	39.1	38.7	38.2	37.8	37.5
43	48	43.0	42.3	41.8	41.2	40.6	40.1	39.6	39.1	38.6	38.2	37.7	37.3	36.9
44	49	42.6	42.0	41.4	40.8	40.2	39.7	39.2	38.7	38.2	37.7	37.2	36.8	36.4
45	50	42.3	41.7	41.1	40.5	39.9	39.3	38.8	38.2	37.7	37.2	36.8	36.3	35.9
46	51	42.0	41.4	40.7	40.1	39.5	38.9	38.4	37.8	37.3	36.8	36.3	35.9	35.4
47	52	41.8	41.1	40.4	39.8	39.2	38.6	38.0	37.5	36.9	36.4	35.9	35.4	35.0

Male	Female	Ages												
		Male 48	49	50	51	52	53	54	55	56	57	58	59	60
		Female 53	54	55	56	57	58	59	60	61	62	63	64	65
35	40	41.5	41.3	41.0	40.8	40.6	40.4	40.3	40.1	40.0	39.8	39.7	39.6	39.5
36	41	40.8	40.6	40.3	40.1	39.9	39.7	39.5	39.3	39.2	39.0	38.9	38.8	38.6
37	42	40.2	39.9	39.6	39.4	39.2	39.0	38.8	38.6	38.4	38.3	38.1	38.0	37.9
38	43	39.5	39.2	39.0	38.7	38.5	38.3	38.1	37.9	37.7	37.5	37.3	37.2	37.1
39	44	38.9	38.6	38.3	38.0	37.8	37.6	37.3	37.1	36.9	36.8	36.6	36.4	36.3
40	45	38.3	38.0	37.7	37.4	37.1	36.9	36.6	36.4	36.2	36.0	35.9	35.7	35.5
41	46	37.7	37.3	37.0	36.7	36.5	36.2	36.0	35.7	35.5	35.3	35.1	35.0	34.8
42	47	37.1	36.8	36.4	36.1	35.8	35.6	35.3	35.1	34.8	34.6	34.4	34.2	34.1
43	48	36.5	36.2	35.8	35.5	35.2	34.9	34.7	34.4	34.2	33.9	33.7	33.5	33.3
44	49	36.0	35.6	35.3	34.9	34.6	34.3	34.0	33.8	33.5	33.3	33.0	32.8	32.6
45	50	35.5	35.1	34.7	34.4	34.0	33.7	33.4	33.1	32.9	32.6	32.4	32.2	31.9
46	51	35.0	34.6	34.2	33.8	33.5	33.1	32.8	32.5	32.2	32.0	31.7	31.5	31.3
47	52	34.5	34.1	33.7	33.3	32.9	32.6	32.2	31.9	31.6	31.4	31.1	30.9	30.6
48	53	34.0	33.6	33.2	32.8	32.4	32.0	31.7	31.4	31.1	30.8	30.5	30.2	30.0
49	54	33.6	33.1	32.7	32.3	31.9	31.5	31.2	30.8	30.5	30.2	29.9	29.6	29.4
50	55	33.2	32.7	32.3	31.8	31.4	31.0	30.6	30.3	29.9	29.6	29.3	29.0	28.8
51	56	32.8	32.3	31.8	31.4	30.9	30.5	30.1	29.8	29.4	29.1	28.8	28.5	28.2
52	57	32.4	31.9	31.4	30.9	30.5	30.1	29.7	29.3	28.9	28.6	28.2	27.9	27.6
53	58	32.0	31.5	31.0	30.5	30.1	29.6	29.2	28.8	28.4	28.1	27.7	27.4	27.1
54	59	31.7	31.2	30.6	30.1	29.7	29.2	28.8	28.3	27.9	27.6	27.2	26.9	26.5
55	60	31.4	30.8	30.3	29.8	29.3	28.8	28.3	27.9	27.5	27.1	26.7	26.4	26.0
56	61	3.1	30.5	29.9	29.4	28.9	28.4	27.9	27.5	27.1	26.7	26.3	25.9	25.5
57	62	30.8	30.2	29.6	29.1	28.6	28.1	27.6	27.1	26.7	26.2	25.8	25.4	25.1
58	63	30.5	29.9	29.3	28.8	28.2	27.7	27.2	26.7	26.3	25.8	25.4	25.0	24.6
59	64	30.2	29.6	29.0	28.5	27.9	27.4	26.9	26.4	25.9	25.4	25.0	24.6	24.2
60	65	30.0	29.4	28.8	28.2	27.6	27.1	26.5	26.0	25.5	25.1	24.6	24.2	23.8

TABLE II—ORDINARY JOINT LIFE AND LAST SURVIVOR ANNUITIES—TWO LIVES—EXPECTED RETURN MULTIPLES

Male	Female	Male 61 / Female 66	62 / 67	63 / 68	64 / 69	65 / 70	66 / 71	67 / 72	68 / 73	69 / 74	70 / 75	71 / 76	72 / 77	73 / 78
35	40	39.4	39.3	39.2	39.1	39.0	38.9	38.9	38.8	38.8	38.7	38.7	38.6	38.6
36	41	38.5	38.4	38.3	38.2	38.2	38.1	38.0	38.0	37.9	37.9	37.8	37.8	37.7
37	42	37.7	37.6	37.5	37.4	37.3	37.3	37.2	37.1	37.1	37.0	36.9	36.9	36.9
38	43	36.9	36.8	36.7	36.6	36.5	36.4	36.4	36.3	36.2	36.2	36.1	36.0	36.0
39	44	36.2	36.0	35.9	35.8	35.7	35.6	35.5	35.5	35.4	35.3	35.3	35.2	35.2
40	45	35.4	35.3	35.1	35.0	34.9	34.8	34.7	34.6	34.6	34.5	34.4	34.4	34.3
41	46	34.6	34.5	34.4	34.2	34.1	34.0	33.9	33.8	33.8	33.7	33.6	33.5	33.5
42	47	33.9	33.7	33.6	33.5	33.4	33.2	33.1	33.0	33.0	32.9	32.8	32.7	32.7
43	48	33.2	33.0	32.9	32.7	32.6	32.5	32.4	32.3	32.2	32.1	32.0	31.9	31.9
44	49	32.5	32.3	32.1	32.0	31.8	31.7	31.6	31.5	31.4	31.3	31.2	31.1	31.1
45	50	31.8	31.6	31.4	31.3	31.1	31.0	30.8	30.7	30.6	30.5	30.4	30.4	30.3
46	51	31.1	30.9	30.7	30.5	30.4	30.2	30.1	30.0	29.9	29.8	29.7	29.6	29.5
47	52	30.4	30.2	30.0	29.8	29.7	29.5	29.4	29.3	29.1	29.0	28.9	28.8	28.7
48	53	29.8	29.5	29.3	29.2	29.0	28.8	28.7	28.5	28.4	28.3	28.2	28.1	28.0
49	54	29.1	28.9	28.7	28.5	28.3	28.1	28.0	27.8	27.7	27.6	27.5	27.4	27.3
50	55	28.5	28.3	28.1	27.8	27.6	27.5	27.3	27.1	27.0	26.9	26.7	26.6	26.5
51	56	27.9	27.7	27.4	27.2	27.0	26.8	26.6	26.5	26.3	26.2	26.0	25.9	25.8
52	57	27.3	27.1	26.8	26.6	26.4	26.2	26.0	25.8	25.7	25.5	25.4	25.2	25.1
53	58	26.8	26.5	26.2	26.0	25.8	25.6	25.4	25.2	25.0	24.8	24.7	24.6	24.4
54	59	26.2	25.9	25.7	25.4	25.2	25.0	24.7	24.6	24.4	24.2	24.0	23.9	23.8
55	60	25.7	25.4	25.1	24.9	24.6	24.4	24.1	23.9	23.8	23.6	23.4	23.3	23.1
56	61	25.2	24.9	24.6	24.3	24.1	23.8	23.6	23.4	23.2	23.0	22.8	22.6	22.5
57	62	24.7	24.4	24.1	23.8	23.5	23.3	23.0	22.8	22.6	22.4	22.2	22.0	21.9
58	63	24.3	23.9	23.6	23.3	23.0	22.7	22.5	22.2	22.0	21.8	21.6	21.4	21.3
59	64	23.8	23.5	23.1	22.8	22.5	22.2	21.9	21.7	21.5	21.2	21.0	20.9	20.7
60	65	23.4	23.0	22.7	22.3	22.0	21.7	21.4	21.2	20.9	20.7	20.5	20.3	20.1
61	66	23.0	22.6	22.2	21.9	21.6	21.3	21.0	20.7	20.4	20.2	20.0	19.8	19.6
62	67	22.6	22.2	21.8	21.5	21.1	20.8	20.5	20.2	19.9	19.7	19.5	19.2	19.0
63	68	22.2	21.8	21.4	21.1	20.7	20.4	20.1	19.8	19.5	19.2	19.0	18.7	18.5
64	69	21.9	21.5	21.1	20.7	20.3	20.0	19.6	19.3	19.0	18.7	18.5	18.2	18.0
65	70	21.6	21.1	20.7	20.3	19.9	19.6	19.2	18.9	18.6	18.3	18.0	17.8	17.5
66	71	21.3	20.8	20.4	20.0	19.6	19.2	18.8	18.5	18.2	17.9	17.6	17.3	17.1
67	72	21.0	20.5	20.1	19.6	19.2	18.8	18.5	18.1	17.8	17.5	17.2	16.9	16.7
68	73	20.7	20.2	19.8	19.3	18.9	18.5	18.1	17.8	17.4	17.1	16.8	16.5	16.2
69	74	20.4	19.9	19.5	19.0	18.6	18.2	17.8	17.4	17.1	16.7	16.4	16.1	15.8
70	75	20.2	19.7	19.2	18.7	18.3	17.9	17.5	17.1	16.7	16.4	16.1	15.8	15.5
71	76	20.0	19.5	19.0	18.5	18.0	17.6	17.2	16.8	16.4	16.1	15.7	15.4	15.1
72	77	19.8	19.2	18.7	18.2	17.8	17.3	16.9	16.5	16.1	15.8	15.4	15.1	14.8
73	78	19.6	19.0	18.5	18.0	17.5	17.1	16.7	16.2	15.8	15.5	15.1	14.8	14.4

* * *

[T.D. 6500, 25 FR 11402, Nov. 26, 1960]

§ 1.72–11 Amounts not received as annuity payments.

* * *

(d) **Amounts received upon the surrender, redemption, or maturity of a contract.** (1) Any amount received upon the surrender, redemption, or maturity of a contract to which section 72 applies, which is not received as an annuity under the regulations of paragraph (b) of § 1.72–2, shall be included in the gross income of the recipient to the extent that it, when added to amounts previously received under the contract and which were excludable from the gross income of the recipient under the law applicable at the time of receipt, exceeds the aggregate of premiums or other consideration paid. See section 72(e)(2)(B). If amounts are to be received as an annuity, whether in lieu of or in addition to amounts described in the preceding sentence, such amounts shall be included in the gross income of the recipient in accordance with the provisions of paragraph (e) or (f) of this section, whichever is applicable. The rule stated in the first sentence of this paragraph shall not apply to payments received as an annuity or otherwise after the date of the first receipt of an amount as an annuity subsequent to the maturity, redemption, or surrender of the original contract. If amounts are so received and are other than amounts received as an annuity, they are includible in the gross income of the recipient. See section 72(e)(1)(A) and paragraph (b)(2) of this section.

(2) For the purpose of applying the rule contained in subparagraph (1) of this paragraph, it is

immaterial whether the recipient of the amount received upon the surrender, redemption, or maturity of the contract is the same as the recipient of amounts previously received under the contract which were excludable from gross income, except in the case of a contract transferred for a valuable consideration, with respect to which see paragraph (a) of § 1.72–10. For the limit on the amount of tax, for taxable years beginning before January 1, 1964, attributable to the receipt of certain lump sums to which this paragraph applies, see paragraph (g) of this section.

* * *

[T.D. 6500, 25 FR 11402, Nov. 26, 1960, as amended by T.D. 6885, 31 FR 7798, June 2, 1966]

§ 1.72–15 Applicability of section 72 to accident or health plans.

* * *

(g) **Payments to or on behalf of a self-employed individual.** A self-employed individual is not considered an employee for purposes of section 105, relating to amounts received by employees under accident and health plans, nor for purposes of excluding under section 104(a)(3) amounts received by him under an accident and health plan as referred to in section 105(e). See section 105(g) and paragraph (a) of § 1.105–1. Therefore, the other paragraphs of this section are not applicable to amounts received by or on behalf of a self-employed individual. Except where accident or health benefits are provided through an insurance contract or an arrangement having the effect of insurance, all amounts received by or on behalf of a self-employed individual from a plan described in section 401(a) and exempt under section 501(a) or a plan described in section 403(a) shall be taxed as otherwise provided in section 72, 402, or 403. If the accident or health benefits are paid under an insurance contract or under an arrangement having the effect of insurance, section 104(a)(3) shall apply. Section 72 shall not apply to any amounts received under such circumstances. For the treatment of the amounts paid for such accident or health benefits, see section 404(e)(3) and paragraph (f) of § 1.404(e)–1.

* * *

[T.D. 6500, 25 FR 11402, Nov. 26, 1960, as amended by T.D. 6676, 28 FR 10135, Sept. 17, 1963; T.D. 6722, 29 FR 5069, April 14, 1964; T.D. 6770, 29 FR 15366, Nov. 17, 1964; T.D. 7352, 40 FR 16664, April 14, 1975]

§ 1.73–1 Services of child.

(a) Compensation for personal services of a child shall, regardless of the provisions of State law relating to who is entitled to the earnings of the child, and regardless of whether the income is in fact received by the child, be deemed to be the gross income of the child and not the gross income of the parent of the child. Such compensation, therefore, shall be included in the gross income of the child and shall be reflected in the return rendered by or for such child. The income of a minor child is not required to be included in the gross income of the parent for income tax purposes. For requirements for making the return by such child, or for such child by his guardian, or other person charged with the care of his person or property, see section 6012.

(b) In the determination of taxable income or adjusted gross income, as the case may be, all expenditures made by the parent or the child attributable to amounts which are includible in the gross income of the child and not of the parent solely by reason of section 73 are deemed to have been paid or incurred by the child. In such determination, the child is entitled to take deductions not only for expenditures made on his behalf by his parent which would be commonly considered as business expenses, but also for other expenditures such as charitable contributions made by the parent in the name of the child and out of the child's earnings.

* * *

[T.D. 6500, 25 FR 11402, Nov. 26, 1960]

§ 1.74–1 Prizes and awards.

(a) **Inclusion in gross income.** (1) Section 74(a) requires the inclusion in gross income of all amounts received as prizes and awards, unless such prizes or awards qualify as an exclusion from gross income under subsection (b), or unless such prize or award is a scholarship or fellowship grant excluded from gross income by section 117. Prizes and awards which are includible in gross income include (but are not limited to) amounts received from radio and television giveaway shows, door prizes, and awards in contests of all types, as well as any prizes and awards from an employer to an employee in recognition of some achievement in connection with his employment.

(2) If the prize or award is not made in money but is made in goods or services, the fair market value of the goods or services is the amount to be included in income.

(b) Exclusion from gross income. Section 74(b) provides an exclusion from gross income of any amount received as a prize or award, if (1) such prize or award was made primarily in recognition of past achievements of the recipient in religious, charitable, scientific, educational, artistic, literary, or civic fields; (2) the recipient was selected without any action on his part to enter the contest or proceedings; and (3) the recipient is not required to render substantial future services as a condition to receiving the prize or award. Thus, such awards as the Nobel prize and the Pulitzer prize would qualify for the exclusion. Section 74(b) does not exclude prizes or awards from an employer to an employee in recognition of some achievement in connection with his employment.

(c) Scholarships and fellowship grants. See section 117 and the regulations thereunder for provisions relating to scholarships and fellowship grants.

[T.D. 6500, 25 FR 11402, Nov. 26, 1960]

§ 1.79-1 Group-term life insurance—general rules.

(a) What is group-term life insurance? Life insurance is not group-term life insurance for purposes of section 79 unless it meets the following conditions: (1) It provides a general death benefit that is excludable from gross income under section 101(a).

(2) It is provided to a group of employees.

(3) It is provided under a policy carried directly or indirectly by the employer.

(4) The amount of insurance provided to each employee is computed under a formula that precludes individual selection. This formula must be based on factors such as age, years of service, compensation, or position. This condition may be satisfied even if the amount of insurance provided is determined under a limited number of alternative schedules that are based on the amount each employee elects to contribute. However, the amount of insurance provided under each schedule must be computed under a formula that precludes individual selection.

(b) May group-term life insurance be combined with other benefits? No part of the life insurance provided under a policy that provides a permanent benefit is group-term life insurance unless—

(1) The policy or the employer designates in writing the part of the death benefit provided to each employee that is group-term life insurance; and

(2) The part of the death benefit that is provided to an employee and designated as the group-term life insurance benefit for any policy year is not less than the difference between the total death benefit provided under the policy and the employee's deemed death benefit (DDB) at the end of the policy year determined under paragraph (d)(3) of this section.

(c) May a group include fewer than 10 employees? (1) As a general rule, life insurance provided to a group of employees cannot qualify as group-term life insurance for purposes of section 79 unless, at some time during the calendar year, it is provided to at least 10 full-time employees who are members of the group of employees. For purposes of this rule, all life insurance provided under policies carried directly or indirectly by the employer is taken into account in determining the number of employees to whom life insurance is provided.

(2) The general rule of paragraph (c)(1) of this section does not apply if the following conditions are met:

(i) The insurance is provided to all full-time employees of the employer or, if evidence of insurability affects eligibility, to all full-time employees who provide evidence of insurability satisfactory to the insurer.

(ii) The amount of insurance provided is computed either as a uniform percentage of compensation or on the basis of coverage brackets established by the insurer. However, the amount computed under either method may be reduced in the case of employees who do not provide evidence of insurability satisfactory to the insurer. In general, no bracket may exceed 2½ times the next lower bracket and the lowest bracket must be at least 10 percent of the highest bracket. However, the insurer may establish a separate schedule of coverage brackets for employees who are over age 65, but no bracket in the over-65 schedule may exceed 2½ times the next lower bracket and the lowest bracket in the over-65 schedule must be at least 10 percent of the highest bracket in the basic schedule.

(iii) Evidence of insurability affecting employee's eligibility for insurance or the amount of insurance provided to that employee is limited to a medical questionnaire completed by the employee that does not require a physical examination.

(3) The general rule of paragraph (c)(1) of this section does not apply if the following conditions are met:

(i) The insurance is provided under a common plan to the employees of two or more unrelated employers.

(ii) The insurance is restricted to, but mandatory for, all employees of the employer who belong to or are represented by an organization (such as a union) that carries on substantial activities in addition to obtaining insurance.

(iii) Evidence of insurability does not affect an employee's eligibility for insurance or the amount of insurance provided to that employee.

(4) For purposes of paragraph (c)(2) and (3) of this section, employees are not taken into account if they are denied insurance for the following reasons:

(i) They are not eligible for insurance under the terms of the policy because they have not been employed for a waiting period, specified in the policy, which does not exceed six months.

(ii) They are part-time employees. Employees whose customary employment is for not more than 20 hours in any week, or 5 months in any calendar year, are presumed to be part-time employees.

(iii) They have reached the age of 65.

(5) For purposes of paragraph (c)(1) and (2) of this section, insurance is considered to be provided to an employee who elects not to receive insurance unless, in order to receive the insurance, the employee is required to contribute to the cost of benefits other than term life insurance. Thus, if an employee could receive term life insurance by contributing to its cost, the employee is taken into account in determining whether the insurance is provided to 10 or more employees even if such employee elects not to receive the insurance. However, an employee who must contribute to the cost of permanent benefits to obtain term life insurance is not taken into account in determining whether the term life insurance is provided to 10 or more employees unless the term life insurance is actually provided to such employee.

* * *

[T.D. 6888, 31 FR 9201, July 6, 1966, as amended by T.D. 6999, 34 FR 995.5011, Jan. 23, 1969; T.D. 7132, 36 FR 13091, July 14, 1971; T.D. 7236, 37 FR 28624, 38 FR 2417, Dec. 28, 1972; T.D. 7623, 44 FR 28798, May 17, 1979; T.D. 7623, 44 FR 28797, May 17, 1979; T.D. 7917, 48 FR 45761, Oct. 7, 1983; T.D. 7924, 48 FR 54594, Dec. 6, 1983]

§ 1.79–3 Determination of amount equal to cost of group-term life insurance.

* * *

(d) The cost of the portion of the group-term life insurance on an employee's life.

* * *

(2) The following table sets forth the cost of $1,000 of group-term life insurance provided after December 31, 1982, for 1 month computed on the basis of 5-year age brackets. See 26 CFR 1.79–3(d)(2) (revised as of April 1, 1983) for a table setting forth the cost of group-term life insurance provided before January 1, 1983. For purposes of Table 1, the age of the employee is his attained age on the last day of his taxable year. However, if an employee has attained an age greater than age 64, he shall be treated as if he were in the 5-year age bracket 60 to 64.

TABLE 1—UNIFORM PREMIUMS FOR $1,000 OF GROUP-TERM LIFE INSURANCE PROTECTION

5-year age bracket	Cost per $1,000 of protection for 1-month period
Under 30	$0.08
30 to 34	.09
35 to 39	.11
40 to 44	.17
45 to 49	.29
50 to 54	.48
55 to 59	.75
60 to 64	1.17

* * *

(f) Effect of provision of other benefits—

* * *

(2) Dependent coverage. An amount equal to the cost of group-term life insurance on the life of the spouse or other family member of the employee which is provided under a policy of group-term life insurance carried directly or indirectly by his employer is not subject to the provisions of section 79 since it is not on the life of the employee. See paragraph (d)(2)(ii)(b) of § 1.61–2 for rules regarding the tax treatment of such insurance.

* * *

[T.D. 6888, 31 FR 9203, July 6, 1966, as amended by T.D. 7623, 44 FR 28800, May 17, 1979; T.D. 7924, 48 FR 54595, Dec. 6, 1983]

§ 1.82–1 Payments for or reimbursements of expenses of moving from one residence to another residence attributable to employment or self-employment.

(a) Reimbursements in gross income—(1) In general. Any amount received or accrued, directly or indirectly, by an individual as a payment for or reimbursement of expenses of moving from one residence to another residence attributable to employment or self-employment is includible in gross income under section 82 as compensation for services in the taxable year received or accrued. For rules relating to the year a deduction may be allowed for expenses of moving from one residence to another residence, see section 217 and the regulations thereunder.

(2) Amounts received or accrued as reimbursement or payment. For purposes of this section, amounts are considered as being received or accrued by an individual as reimbursement or payment whether received in the form of money, property, or services. A cash basis taxpayer will include amounts in gross income under section 82 when they are received or treated as received by him. Thus, for example, if an employer moves an employee's household goods and personal effects from the employee's old resident to his new residence using the employer's facilities, the employee is considered as having received a payment in the amount of the fair market value of the services furnished at the time the services are furnished by the employer. If the employer pays a mover for moving the employee's household goods and personal effects, the employee is considered as having received the payment at the time the employer

pays the mover, rather than at the time the mover moves the employee's household goods and personal effects. Where an employee receives a loan or advance from an employer to enable him to pay his moving expenses, the employee will not be deemed to have received a reimbursement of moving expenses until such time as he accounts to his employer if he is not required to repay such loan or advance and if he makes such accounting within a reasonable time. Such loan or advance will be deemed to be a reimbursement of moving expenses at the time of such accounting to the extent used by the employee for such moving expenses.

(3) Direct or indirect payments or reimbursements. For purposes of this section amounts are considered as being received or accrued whether received directly (paid or provided to an individual by an employer, a client, a customer, or similar person) or indirectly (paid to a third party on behalf of an individual by an employer, a client, a customer, or similar person). Thus, if an employer pays a mover for the expenses of moving an employee's household goods and personal effects from one residence to another residence, the employee has indirectly received a payment which is includible in his gross income under section 82.

(4) Expenses of moving from one residence to another residence. An expense of moving from one residence to another residence is any expenditure, cost, loss, or similar item paid or incurred in connection with a move from one residence to another residence. Moving expenses include (but are not limited to) any expenditure, cost, loss, or similar item directly or indirectly resulting from the acquisition, sale, or exchange of property, the transportation of goods or property, or travel (by the taxpayer or any other person) in connection with a change in residence. Such expenses include items described in section 217(b) (relating to the definition of moving expenses), irrespective of the dollar limitations contained in section 217(b)(3) and the conditions contained in section 217(c), as well as items not described in section 217(b), such as a loss sustained on the sale or exchange of personal property, storage charges, taxes, or expenses of refitting rugs or draperies.

(5) Attributable to employment or self-employment. Any amount received or accrued from an employer, a client, a customer, or similar person in connection with the performance of services for such employer, client, customer, or similar person, is attributable to employment or self-employment. Thus, for example, if an employer reimburses an employee for a loss incurred on the sale of the employee's house, reimbursement is attributable to the performance of services if made because of the employer-employee relationship. Similarly, if an employer in order to prevent an employee's sustaining a loss on a sale of a house acquires the property from the employee at a price in excess of fair market value, the employee is considered to have received a payment attributable to employment to the extent that such payment exceeds the fair market value of the property.

* * *

[T.D. 7195, 37 FR 13533, July 11, 1972, as amended by T.D. 7578, 43 FR 59355, Dec. 20. 1978]

§ 1.83–1 Property transferred in connection with the performance of services.

(a) Inclusion in gross income—(1) General rule. Section 83 provides rules for the taxation of property transferred to an employee or independent contractor (or beneficiary thereof) in connection with the performance of services by such employee or independent contractor. In general, such property is not taxable under section 83(a) until it has been transferred (as defined in § 1.83–3(a)) to such person and become substantially vested (as defined in § 1.83–3(b)) in such person. In that case, the excess of—

(i) The fair market value of such property (determined without regard to any lapse restriction, as defined in § 1.83–3(i)) at the time that the property becomes substantially vested, over

(ii) The amount (if any) paid for such property,

shall be included as compensation in the gross income of such employee or independent contractor for the taxable year in which the property becomes substantially vested. Until such property becomes substantially vested, the transferor shall be regarded as the owner of such property, and any income from such property received by the employee or independent contractor (or beneficiary thereof) or the right to the use of such property by the employee or independent contractor constitutes additional compensation and shall be included in the gross income of such employee or independent contractor for the taxable year in which such income is received or such use is made available. This paragraph applies to a transfer of property in connection with the performance of services even though the transferor is not the person for whom such services are performed.

(2) Life insurance. The cost of life insurance protection under a life insurance contract, retirement income contract, endowment contract, or other contract providing life insurance protection is taxable generally under section 61 and the regulations thereunder during the period such contract remains substantially nonvested (as defined in § 1.83–3(b)). The cost of such life insurance protection is the reasonable net premium cost, as determined by the Commissioner, of the current life insurance protection (as defined in § 1.72–16(b)(3)) provided by such contract.

* * *

(b) Subsequent sale, forfeiture, or other disposition of nonvested property. (1) If substantially nonvested property (that has been transferred in connection with the performance of services) is subsequently sold or otherwise disposed of to a third party in an arm's length transaction while still substantially nonvested, the person who performed such services shall realize compensation in an amount equal to the excess of—

(i) The amount realized on such sale or other disposition, over

(ii) The amount (if any) paid for such property.

Such amount of compensation is includible in his gross income in accordance with his method of accounting. Two preceding sentences also apply when the person disposing of the property has received it in a non-arm's length transaction described in paragraph (c) of this section. In addition, section 83(a) and paragraph (a) of this section shall thereafter cease to apply with respect to such property.

(2) If substantially nonvested property that has been transferred in connection with the performance of services to the person performing such services is forfeited while still substantially nonvested and held by such person, the difference between the amount paid (if any) and the amount received upon forfeiture (if any) shall be treated as an ordinary gain or loss. This paragraph (b)(2) does not apply to property to which § 1.83–2(a) applies.

(3) This paragraph (b) shall not apply to, and no gain shall be recognized on, any sale, forfeiture, or other disposition described in this paragraph to the extent that any property received in exchange therefor is substantially nonvested. Instead, section 83 and this section shall apply with respect to such property received (as if it were substituted for the property disposed of).

(c) Dispositions of nonvested property not at arm's length. If substantially nonvested property (that has been transferred in connection with the performance of services) is disposed of in a transaction which is not at arm's length and the property remains substantially nonvested, the person who performed such services realizes compensation equal in amount to the sum of any money and the fair market value of any substantially vested property received in such disposition. Such amount of compensation is includible in his gross income in accordance with his method of accounting. However, such amount of compensation shall not exceed the fair market value of the property disposed of at the time of disposition (determined without regard to any lapse restriction), reduced by the amount paid for such property. In addition, section 83 and these regulations shall continue to apply with respect to such property, except that any amount previously includible in gross income under this paragraph (c) shall thereafter be treated as an amount paid for such property. For example, if in 1971 an employee pays $50 for a share of stock which has a fair market value of $100 and is substantially nonvested at that time and later in 1971 (at a time when the property still has a fair market value of $100 and is still substantially nonvested) the employee disposes of, in a transaction not at arm's length, the share of stock to his wife for $10, the employee realizes compensation of $10 in 1971. If in 1972, when the share of stock has a fair market value of $120, it becomes substantially vested, the employee realizes additional compensation in 1972 in the amount of $60 (the $120 fair market value of the stock less both the $50 price paid for the stock and the $10 taxed as compensation in 1971). For purposes of this paragraph, if substantially nonvested property has been transferred to a person other than the person who performed the services, and the transferee dies holding the property while the property is still substantially nonvested and while the person who performed the services is alive, the transfer which results by reason of the death of such transferee is a transfer not at arm's length.

* * *

(e) Forfeiture after substantial vesting. If a person is taxable under section 83(a) when the property transferred becomes substantially vested and thereafter the person's beneficial interest in such property is nevertheless forfeited pursuant to

a lapse restriction, any loss incurred by such person (but not by a beneficiary of such person) upon such forfeiture shall be an ordinary loss to the extent the basis in such property has been increased as a result of the recognition of income by such person under section 83(a) with respect to such property.

(f) Examples. The provisions of this section may be illustrated by the following examples:

Example (1). On November 1, 1978, X corporation sells to E, an employee, 100 shares of X corporation stock at $10 per share. At the time of such sale the fair market value of the X corporation stock is $100 per share. Under the terms of the sale each share of stock is subject to a substantial risk of forfeiture which will not lapse until November 1, 1988. Evidence of this restriction is stamped on the face of E's stock certificates, which are therefore nontransferable (within the meaning of § 1.83–3(d)). Since in 1978 E's stock is substantially nonvested, E does not include any of such amount in his gross income as compensation in 1978. On November 1, 1988, the fair market value of the X corporation stock is $250 per share. Since the X corporation stock becomes substantially vested in 1988, E must include $24,000 (100 shares of X corporation stock × $250 fair market value per share less $10 price paid by E for each share) as compensation for 1988. Dividends paid by X to E on E's stock after it was transferred to E on November 1, 1973, are taxable to E as additional compensation during the period E's stock is substantially nonvested and are deductible as such by X.

Example (2). Assume the facts are the same as in example (1), except that on November 1, 1985, each share of stock of X corporation in E's hands could as a matter of law be transferred to a bona fide purchaser who would not be required to forfeit the stock if the risk of forfeiture materialized. In the event, however, that the risk materializes, E would be liable in damages to X. On November 1, 1985, the fair market value of the X corporation stock is $230 per share. Since E's stock is transferable within the meaning of § 1.83–3(d) in 1985, the stock is substantially vested and E must include $22,000 (100 shares of X corporation stock × $230 fair market value per share less $10 price paid by E for each share) as compensation for 1985.

Example (3). Assume the facts are the same as in example (1) except that, in 1984 E sells his 100 shares of X corporation stock in an arm's length sale to I, an investment company, for $120 per share. At the time of this sale each share of X corporation's stock has a fair market value of $200. Under paragraph (b) of this section, E must include $11,000 (100 shares of X corporation stock × $120 amount realized per share less $10 price paid by E per share) as compensation for 1984 notwithstanding that the stock remains nontransferable and is still subject to a substantial risk of forfeiture at the time of such sale. Under § 1.83–4(b)(2), I's basis in the X corporation stock is $120 per share.

[T.D. 7554, 43 FR 31913, July 24, 1978]

§ 1.83–2 Election to include in gross income in year of transfer.

(a) In general. If property is transferred (within the meaning of § 1.83–3(a)) in connection with the performance of services, the person performing such services may elect to include in gross income under section 83(b) the excess (if any) of the fair market value of the property at the time of transfer (determined without regard to any lapse restriction, as defined in § 1.83–3(i)) over the amount (if any) paid for such property, as compensation for services. The fact that the transferee has paid full value for the property transferred, realizing no bargain element in the transaction, does not preclude the use of the election as provided for in this section. If this election is made, the substantial vesting rules of section 83(a) and the regulations thereunder do not apply with respect to such property, and except as otherwise provided in section 83(d)(2) and the regulations thereunder (relating to the cancellation of a nonlapse restriction), any subsequent appreciation in the value of the property is not taxable as compensation to the person who performed the services. Thus, property with respect to which this election is made shall be includible in gross income as of the time of transfer, even though such property is substantially nonvested (as defined in § 1.83–3(b)) at the time of transfer, and no compensation will be includible in gross income when such property becomes substantially vested (as defined in § 1.83–3(b)). In computing the gain or loss from the subsequent sale or exchange of such property, its basis shall be the amount paid for the property increased by the amount included in gross income under section 83(b). If property for which a section 83(b) election is in effect is forfeited while substantially nonvested, such forfeiture shall be treated as a sale or exchange upon which there is realized a loss equal to the excess (if any) of—

(1) The amount paid (if any) for such property, over,

(2) The amount realized (if any) upon such forfeiture.

If such property is a capital asset in the hands of the taxpayer, such loss shall be a capital loss. A sale or other disposition of the property that is in substance a forfeiture, or is made in contemplation of a forfeiture, shall be treated as a forfeiture under the two immediately preceding sentences.

(b) Time for making election. Except as provided in the following sentence, the election referred to in paragraph (a) of this section shall be filed not later than 30 days after the date the property was transferred (or, if later, January 29, 1970) and may be filed prior to the date of transfer. Any statement filed before February 15, 1970, which was amended not later than February 16, 1970, in order to make it conform to the requirements of paragraph (e) of this section, shall be deemed a proper election under section 83(b).

(c) Manner of making election. The election referred to in paragraph (a) of this section is made by filing one copy of a written statement with the internal revenue office with whom the person who performed the services files his return. In addition, one copy of such statement shall be submitted with this income tax return for the taxable year in which such property was transferred.

* * *

(f) Revocability of election. An election under section 83(b) may not be revoked except with the consent of the Commissioner. Consent will be granted only in the case where the transferee is under a mistake of fact as to the underlying transaction and must be requested within 60 days of the date on which the mistake of fact first became known to the person who made the election. In any event, a mistake as to the value, or decline in the value, of the property with respect to which an election under section 83(b) has been made or a failure to perform an act contemplated at the time of transfer of such property does not constitute a mistake of fact.

[T.D. 7554, 43 FR 31915, July 24, 1978]

§ 1.83–3 Meaning and use of certain terms.

(a) Transfer—(1) In general. For purposes of section 83 and the regulations thereunder, a transfer of property occurs when a person acquires a beneficial ownership interest in such property (disregarding any lapse restriction, as defined in § 1.83–3(i)).

(2) Option. The grant of an option to purchase certain property does not constitute a transfer of such property. However, see § 1.83–7 for the extent to which the grant of the option itself is subject to section 83. In addition, if the amount paid for the transfer of property is an indebtedness secured by the transferred property, on which there is no personal liability to pay all or a substantial part of such indebtedness, such transaction may be in substance the same as the grant of an option. The determination of the substance of the transaction shall be based upon all the facts and circumstances. The factors to be taken into account include the type of property involved, the extent to which the risk that the property will decline in value has been transferred, and the likelihood that the purchase price will, in fact, be paid. See also § 1.83–4(c) for the treatment of forgiveness of indebtedness that has constituted an amount paid.

(3) Requirement that property be returned. Similarly, no transfer may have occurred where property is transferred under conditions that require its return upon the happening of an event that is certain to occur, such as the termination of employment. In such a case, whether there is, in fact, a transfer depends upon all the facts and circumstances. Factors which indicate that no transfer has occurred are described in paragraph (a)(4), (5), and (6) of this section.

(4) Similarity to option. An indication that no transfer has occurred is the extent to which the conditions relating to a transfer are similar to an option.

(5) Relationship to fair market value. An indication that no transfer has occurred is the extent to which the consideration to be paid the transferee upon surrendering the property does not approach the fair market value of the property at the time of surrender. For purposes of paragraph (a)(5) and (6) of this section, fair market value includes fair market value determined under the rules of § 1.83–5(a)(1), relating to the valuation of property subject to nonlapse restrictions. Therefore, the existence of a nonlapse restriction referred to in § 1.83–5(a)(1) is not a factor indicating no transfer has occurred.

(6) Risk of loss. An indication that no transfer has occurred is the extent to which the transferee does not incur the risk of a beneficial owner that the value of the property at the time of transfer will decline substantially. Therefore, for purposes of this (6), risk of decline in property value is not limited to the risk that any amount paid for the property may be lost.

(7) Examples. The provisions of this paragraph may be illustrated by the following examples:

Example (1). On January 3, 1971, X corporation sells for $500 to S, a salesman of X, 10 shares of stock in X corporation with a fair market value of $1,000. The stock is nontransferable and subject to return to the corporation (for $500) if S's sales do not reach a certain level by December 31, 1971. Disregarding the restriction concerning S's sales (since the restrictions is a lapse restriction), S's interest in the stock is that of a beneficial owner and therefore a transfer occurs on January 3, 1971.

Example (2). On November 17, 1972, W sells to E 100 shares of stock in W corporation with a fair market value of $10,000 in exchange for a $10,000 note without personal liability. The note requires E to make yearly payments of $2,000 commencing in 1973. E collects the dividends, votes the stock and pays the interest on the note. However, he makes no payments toward the face amount of the note. Because E has no personal liability on the note, and since E is making no payments towards the face amount of the note, the likelihood of E paying the full purchase price is in substantial doubt. As a result E has not incurred the risks of a beneficial owner that the value of the stock will decline. Therefore, no transfer of the stock has occurred on November 17, 1972, but an option to purchase the stock has been granted to E.

Example (3). On January 3, 1971, X corporation purports to transfer to E, an employee, 100 shares of stock in X corporation. The X stock is subject to the sole restriction that E must sell such stock to X on termination of employment for any reason for an amount which is equal to the excess (if any) of the book value of the X stock at termination of employment over book value on January 3, 1971. The stock is not transferable by E and the restrictions on transfer are stamped on the certificate. Under these facts and circumstances, there is no transfer of the X stock within the meeting of section 83.

Example (4). Assume the same facts as in example (3) except that E paid $3,000 for the stock and that the restriction required E upon termination of employment to sell the stock to M for the total amount of dividends that have been declared on the stock since September 2, 1971, or $3,000 whichever is higher. Again, under the facts and circumstances, no transfer of the X stock has occurred.

Example (5). On July 4, 1971, X corporation purports to transfer to G, an employee, 100 shares of X stock. The stock is subject to the sole restriction that upon termination of employment G must sell the stock to X for the greater of its fair market value at such time or $100, the amount G paid for the stock. On July 4, 1971 the X stock has a fair market value of $100. Therefore, G does not incur the risk of a beneficial owner that the value of the stock at the time of transfer ($100) will decline substantially. Under these facts and circumstances, no transfer has occurred.

(b) Substantially vested and substantially nonvested property. For purposes of section 83 and the regulations thereunder, property is substantially nonvested when it is subject to a substantial risk of forfeiture, within the meaning of paragraph (c) of this section, and is nontransferable, within the meaning of paragraph (d) of this section. Property is substantially vested for such purposes when it is either transferable or not subject to a substantial risk of forfeiture.

(c) Substantial risk of forfeiture—(1) In general. For purposes of section 83 and the regulations thereunder, whether a risk of forfeiture is substantial or not depends upon the facts and circumstances. A substantial risk of forfeiture exists where rights in property that are transferred are conditioned, directly or indirectly, upon the future performance (or refraining from performance) of substantial services by any person, or the occurrence of a condition related to a purpose of the transfer, and the possibility of forfeiture is substantial if such condition is not satisfied.

Property is not transferred subject to a substantial risk of forfeiture to the extent that the employer is required to pay the fair market value of a portion of such property to the employee upon the return of such property. The risk that the value of property will decline during a certain period of time does not constitute a substantial risk of forfeiture. A nonlapse restriction, standing by itself, will not result in a substantial risk of forfeiture.

(2) Illustrations of substantial risks of forfeiture. The regularity of the performance of services and the time spent in performing such services tend to indicate whether services required by a condition are substantial. The fact that the person performing services has the right to decline to perform such services without forfeiture may tend to establish that services are insubstantial. Where stock is transferred to an underwriter prior to a public offering and the full enjoyment of such stock is expressly or impliedly conditioned upon the successful completion of the underwriting, the stock is subject to a substantial risk of forfeiture. Where an employee receives property from an employer subject to a requirement that it be returned if the total earnings of the employer do not increase, such property is subject to a substantial risk of forfeiture. On the other hand, requirements that the property be returned to the employer if the employee is discharged for cause or for committing a crime will not be considered to result in a substantial risk of forfeiture. An enforceable requirement that the property be returned to the employer if the employee accepts a job with a competing firm will not ordinarily be considered to result in a substantial risk of forfeiture unless the particular facts and circumstances indicate to the contrary. Factors which may be taken into account in determining whether a covenant not to compete constitutes a substantial risk of forfeiture are the age of the employee, the availability of alternative employment opportunities, the likelihood of the employee's obtaining such other employment, the degree of skill possessed by the employee, the employee's health, and the practice (if any) of the employer to enforce such covenants. Similarly, rights in property transferred to a retiring employee subject to the sole requirement that it be returned unless he renders consulting services upon the request of his former employer will not be considered subject to a substantial risk of forfeiture unless he is in fact expected to perform substantial services.

(3) Enforcement of forfeiture condition. In determining whether the possibility of forfeiture is substantial in the case of rights in property transferred to an employee of a corporation who owns a significant amount of the total combined voting power or value of all classes of stock of the employer corporation or of its parent corporation, there will be taken into account (i) the employee's relationship to other stockholders and the extent of their control, potential control and possible loss of control of the corporation, (ii) the position of the employee in the corporation and the extent to which he is subordinate to other employees, (iii) the employee's relationship to the officers and directors of the corporation, (iv) the person or persons who must approve the employee's discharge, and (v) past actions of the employer in enforcing the provisions of the restrictions. For example, if an employee would be considered as having received rights in property subject to a substantial risk of forfeiture, but for the fact that the employee owns 20 percent of the single class of stock in the transferor corporation, and if the remaining 80 percent of the class of stock is owned by an unrelated individual (or members of such an individual's family) so that the possibility of the corporation enforcing a restriction on such rights is substantial, then such rights are subject to a substantial risk of forfeiture. On the other hand, if 4 percent of the voting power of all the stock of a corporation is owned by the president of such corporation and the remaining stock is so diversely held by the public that the president, in effect, controls the corporation, then the possibility of the corporation enforcing a restriction on rights in property transferred to the president is not substantial, and such rights are not subject to a substantial risk of forfeiture.

(4) Examples. The rules contained in paragraph (c)(1) of this section may be illustrated by the following examples. In each example it is assumed that, if the conditions on transfer are not satisfied, the forfeiture provision will be enforced.

Example (1). On November 1, 1971, corporation X transfers in connection with the performance of services to E, an employee, 100 shares of corporation X stock for $90 per share. Under the terms of the transfer, E will be subject to a binding commitment to resell the stock to corporation X at $90 per share if he leaves the employment of corporation X for any reason prior to the expiration of a 2-year period from the date of such transfer. Since E must perform substantial services for corporation X and will not be paid more than $90 for the stock, regardless of its value, if he fails to perform such services during such 2-year period, E's rights in the stock are subject to a substantial risk of forfeiture during such period.

Example (2). On November 10, 1971, corporation X transfers in connection with the performance of services to a trust for the benefit of employees, $100x. Under the terms of the trust any child of an employee who is an enrolled full-time student at an accredited educational institution as a candidate for a degree will receive an annual grant of cash for each academic year the student completes as a student in good standing, up to a maximum of four years. E, an employee, has a child who is enrolled as a full-time student at an accredited college as a candidate for a degree. Therefore, E has a beneficial interest in the assets of the trust equalling the value of four cash grants. Since E's child must complete one year of college in order to receive a cash grant, E's interest in the trust assets are subject to a substantial risk of forfeiture to the extent E's child has not become entitled to any grants.

Example (3). On November 25, 1971, corporation X gives to E, an employee, in connection with his performance of services to corporation X, a bonus of 100 shares of corporation X stock. Under the terms of the bonus arrangement E is obligated to return the corporation X stock to corporation X if he terminates his employment for any reason. However, for each year occurring after November 25, 1971, during which E remains employed with corporation X, E ceases to be obligated to return 10 shares of the corporation X stock. Since in each year occurring after November 25, 1971, for which E remains employed he is not required to return 10 shares of corporation X's stock, E's rights in 10 shares each year for 10 years cease to be subject to a substantial risk of forfeiture for each year he remains so employed.

Example (4). (a) Assume the same facts as in example (3) except that for each year occurring after November 25, 1971, for which E remains employed with corporation X, X agrees to pay, in redemption of the bonus shares given to E if he terminates employment for any reason, 10 percent of the fair market value of each share of stock on the date of such termination of employment. Since corporation X will pay E 10 percent of the value of his bonus stock for each of the 10 years after November 25, 1971, in which he remains employed by X, and the risk of a decline in value is not a substantial risk of forfeiture, E's interest in 10 percent of such bonus stock becomes substantially vested in each of those years.

(b) The following chart illustrates the fair market value of the bonus stock and the fair market value of the portion of bonus stock that becomes substantially vested on November 25, for the following years:

Year	Fair market value of All stock	Portion of stock that becomes vested
1972	$200	$20
1973	300	30
1974	150	15
1975	150	15
1976	100	10

If E terminates his employment on July 1, 1977, when the fair market value of the bonus stock is $100, E must return the bonus stock to X, and X must pay, in redemption of the bonus stock, $50 (50 percent of the value of the bonus stock on the date of termination of employment). E has recognized income under section 83(a) and § 1.83–1(a) with respect to 50 percent of the bonus stock, and E's basis in that portion of the stock equals the amount of income recognized, $90. Under § 1.83–1(e), the $40 loss E incurred upon forfeiture ($90 basis less $50 redemption payment) is an ordinary loss.

Example (5). On January 7, 1971, corporation X, a computer service company, transfers to E, 100 shares of corporation X stock for $50. E is a highly compensated salesman who sold X's products in a three-state area since 1960. At the time of transfer each share of X stock has a fair market value of $100. The stock is transferred to E in connection with his termination of employment with X. Each share of X stock is subject to the sole condition that E can keep such share only if he does not engage in competition with X for a 5-year period in the three-state area where E had previously sold X's products. E, who is 45 years old, has no intention of retiring from the work force. In order to earn a salary comparable to his current compensation, while preventing the risk of forfeiture from arising, E will have to expend a substantial amount of time and effort in another industry or market to establish the necessary business contacts. Thus, under these facts and circumstances E's rights in the stock are subject to a substantial risk of forfeiture.

(d) Transferability of property. For purposes of section 83 and the regulations thereunder, the rights of a person in property are transferable if such person can transfer any interest in the property to any person other than the transferor of the property, but only if the rights in such property of such transferee are not subject to a substantial risk of forfeiture. Accordingly, property is transferable if the person performing the services or receiving the property can sell, assign, or pledge (as collateral for a loan, or as security for the performance of an obligation, or for any other purpose) his interest in the property to any person other than the transferor of such property and if the transferee is not required to give up the property or its value in the event the substantial risk of forfeiture materializes. On the other hand, property is not considered to be transferable merely because the person performing the services or receiving the property may designate a beneficiary to receive the property in the event of his death.

(e) **Property.** For purposes of section 83 and the regulations thereunder, the term "property" includes real and personal property other than either money or an unfunded and unsecured promise to pay money or property in the future. The term also includes a beneficial interest in assets (including money) which are transferred or set aside from the claims of creditors of the transferor, for example, in a trust or escrow account. See, however, § 1.83–8(a) with respect to employee trusts and annuity plans subject to section 402(b) and section 403(c). In the case of a transfer of a life insurance contract, retirement income contract, endowment contract, or other contract providing life insurance protection, only the cash surrender value of the contract is considered to be property. Where rights in a contract providing life insurance protection are substantially nonvested, see § 1.83–1(a)(2) for rules relating to taxation of the cost of life insurance protection.

(f) **Property transferred in connection with the performance of services.** Property transferred to an employee or an independent contractor (or beneficiary thereof) in recognition of the performance of, or the refraining from performance of, services is considered transferred in connection with the performance of services within the meaning of section 83. The existence of other persons entitled to buy stock on the same terms and conditions as an employee, whether pursuant to a public or private offering may, however, indicate that in such circumstances a transfer to the employee is not in recognition of the performance of, or the refraining from performance of, services. The transfer of property is subject to section 83 whether such transfer is in respect of past, present, or future services.

(g) **Amount paid.** For purposes of section 83 and the regulations thereunder, the term "amount paid" refers to the value of any money or property paid for the transfer of property to which section 83 applies, and does not refer to any amount paid for the right to use such property or to receive the income therefrom. Such value does not include any stated or unstated interest payments. For rules regarding the calculation of the amount of unstated interest payments, see § 1.483–1(c). When section 83 applies to the transfer of property pursuant to the exercise of an option, the term "amount paid" refers to any amount paid for the grant of the option plus any amount paid as the exercise price of the option. For rules regarding the forgiveness of indebtedness treated as an amount paid, see § 1.83–4(c).

(h) **Nonlapse restriction.** For purposes of section 83 and the regulations thereunder, a restriction which by its terms will never lapse (also referred to as a "nonlapse restriction") is a permanent limitation on the transferability of property—

(1) Which will require the transferee of the property to sell, or offer to sell, such property at a price determined under a formula, and

(2) Which will continue to apply to and be enforced against the transferee or any subsequent holder (other than the transferor).

A limitation subjecting the property to a permanent right of first refusal in a particular person at a price determined under a formula is a permanent nonlapse restriction. Limitations imposed by registration requirements of State or Federal security laws or similar laws imposed with respect to sales or other dispositions of stock or securities are not nonlapse restrictions. An obligation to resell or to offer to sell property transferred in connection with the performance of services to a specific person or persons at its fair market value at the time of such sale is not a nonlapse restriction. See § 1.83–5(c) for examples of nonlapse restrictions.

(i) **Lapse restriction.** For purposes of section 83 and the regulations thereunder, the term "lapse restriction" means a restriction other than a nonlapse restriction as defined in paragraph (h) of this section, and includes (but is not limited to) a restriction that carries a substantial risk of forfeiture.

(j) **Sales which may give rise to suit under section 16(b) of the Securities Exchange Act of 1934—(1) In general.** For purposes of section 83 and the regulations thereunder if the sale of property at a profit within six months after the purchase of the property could subject a person to suit under section 16(b) of the Securities Exchange Act of 1934, the person's rights in the property are treated as subject to a substantial risk of forfeiture and as not transferable until the earlier of (i) the expiration of such six-month period, or (ii) the first day on which the sale of such property at a profit will not subject the person to suit under section 16(b) of the Securities Exchange Act of 1934. However, whether an option is "transferable by the optionee" for purposes of § 1.83–7(b)(2)(i) is determined without regard to section 83(c)(3) and this paragraph (j).

(2) Examples. The provisions of this paragraph may be illustrated by the following examples:

Example (1). On January 1, 1983, X corporation sells to P, a beneficial owner of 12% of X corporation stock in connection with P's performance of services, 100 shares of X corporation stock at $10 per share. At the time of the sale the fair market value of the X corporation stock is $100 per share. P, as a beneficial owner of more 10% of X corporation stock, is liable to suit under section 16(b) of the Securities Exchange Act of 1934 for recovery of any profit from any sale and purchase or purchase and sale of X corporation stock within a six-month period, but no other restrictions apply to the stock. Because the section 16(b) restriction is applicable to P, P's rights in the 100 shares of stock purchased on January 1, 1983, are treated as subject to a substantial risk of forfeiture and as not transferable through June 29, 1983. P chooses not to make an election under section 83(b) and therefore does not include any amount with respect to the stock purchase in gross income as compensation on the date of purchase. On June 30, 1983, the fair market value of X corporation stock is $250 per share. P must include $24,000 (100 shares of X corporation stock * * $240 ($250 fair market value per share less $10 price paid by P for each share)) in gross income as compensation on June 30, 1983. If, in this example, restrictions other than section 16(b) applied to the stock, such other restrictions (but not section 16(b)) would be taken into account in determining whether the stock is subject to a substantial risk of forfeiture and is nontransferable for periods after June 29, 1983.

Example (2). Assume the same facts as in example (1) except that P is not an insider on or after May 1, 1983, and the section 16(b) restriction does not apply beginning on that date. On May 1, 1983, P must include in gross income as compensation the difference between the fair market value of the stock on that date and the amount paid for the stock.

Example (3). Assume the same facts as in example (1) except that on June 1, 1983, X corporation sells to P an additional 100 shares of X corporation stock at $20 per share. At the time of the sale the fair market value of the X corporation stock is $150 per share. On June 30, 1983, P must include $24,000 in gross income as compensation with respect to the January 1, 1983 purchase. On November 30, 1983, the fair market value of X corporation stock is $200 per share. Accordingly, on that date P must include $18,000 (100 shares of X corporation stock * * * * * $180 ($200 fair market value per share less $20 price paid by P for each share)) in gross income as compensation with respect to the June 1, 1983 purchase.

(3) Effective date. This paragraph applies property transferred after December 31, 1981.

(k) Special rule for certain accounting rules. (1) For purposes of section 83 and the regulations thereunder, property is subject to substantial risk of forfeiture and is not transferable so long as the property is subject to a restriction on transfer to

comply with the "Pooling-of-Interests Accounting" rules set forth in Accounting Series Release Numbered 130 ((10/5/72) 37 FR 20937; 17 CFR 211.130) and Accounting Series Release Numbered 135 ((1/18/73) 38 FR 1734; 17 CFR 211.135).

(2) Effective date. This paragraph applies to property transferred after December 31, 1981.

[T.D.7554, 43 FR 31916, July 24, 1978; as amended by T.D. 8042, 50 FR 31713, Aug. 6, 1985; 50 FR 39664, Sept. 30, 1985]

* * *

§ 1.83–4 Special rules.

(a) Holding period. Under section 83(f), the holding period of transferred property to which section 83(a) applies shall begin just after such property is substantially vested. However, if the person who has performed the services in connection with which property is transferred has made an election under section 83(b), the holding period of such property shall begin just after the date such property is transferred. If property to which section 83 and the regulations thereunder apply is transferred at arm's length, the holding period of such property in the hands of the transferee shall be determined in accordance with the rules provided in section 1223.

(b) Basis. (1) Except as provided in paragraph (b)(2) of this section, if property to which section 83 and the regulations thereunder apply is acquired by any person (including a person who acquires such property in a subsequent transfer which is not at arm's length), while such property is still substantially nonvested, such person's basis for the property shall reflect any amount paid for such property and any amount includible in the gross income of the person who performed the services (including any amount so includible as a result of a disposition by the person who acquired such property.) Such basis shall also reflect any adjustments to basis provided under sections 1015 and 1016.

(2) If property to which § 1.83–1 applies is transferred at arm's length, the basis of the property in the hands of the transferee shall be determined under section 1012 and the regulations thereunder.

(c) Forgiveness of indebtedness treated as an amount paid. If an indebtedness that has been treated as an amount paid under § 1.83–1(a)(1)(ii) is subsequently cancelled, forgiven or satisfied for an amount less than the amount of such indebtedness, the amount that is not, in fact, paid shall be includible in the gross income of the service provider in the taxable year in which such cancellation, forgiveness or satisfaction occurs.

[T.D. 7554, 43 FR 31918, July 24, 1978]

§ 1.83–5 Restrictions that will never lapse.

(a) **Valuation.** For purposes of section 83 and the regulations thereunder, in the case of property subject to a nonlapse restriction (as defined in § 1.83–3(h)), the price determined under the formula price will be considered to be the fair market value of the property unless established to the contrary by the Commissioner, and the burden of proof shall be on the commissioner with respect to such value. If stock in a corporation is subject to a nonlapse restriction which requires the transferee to sell such stock only at a formula price based on book value, a reasonable multiple of earnings or a reasonable combination thereof, the price so determined will ordinarily be regarded as determinative of the fair market value of such property for purposes of section 83. However, in certain circumstances the formula price will not be considered to be the fair market value of property subject to such a formula price restriction, even though the formula price restriction is a substantial factor in determining such value. For example, where the formula price is the current book value of stock, the book value of the stock at some time in the future may be a more accurate measure of the value of the stock than the current book value of the stock for purposes of determining the fair market value of the stock at the time the stock becomes substantially vested.

(b) **Cancellation—(1) In general.** Under section 83(d)(2), if a nonlapse restriction imposed on property that is subject to section 83 is cancelled, then, unless the taxpayer establishes—

(i) That such cancellation was not compensatory, and

(ii) That the person who would be allowed a deduction, if any, if the cancellation were treated as compensatory, will treat the transaction as not compensatory, as provided in paragraph (c)(2) of this section,

the excess of the fair market value of such property (computed without regard to such restriction) at the time of cancellation, over the sum of—

(iii) The fair market value of such property (computed by taking the restriction into account) immediately before the cancellation, and

(iv) The amount, if any, paid for the cancellation,

shall be treated as compensation for the taxable year in which such cancellation occurs. Whether there has been a noncompensatory cancellation of a nonlapse restriction under section 83(d)(2) depends upon the particular facts and circumstances. Ordinarily the fact that the employee or independent contractor is required to perform additional services or that the salary or payment of such a person is adjusted to take the cancellation into account indicates that such cancellation has a compensatory purpose. On the other hand, the fact that the original purpose of a restriction no longer exists may indicate that the purpose of such cancellation is noncompensatory. Thus, for example, if a so-called "buy-sell" restriction was imposed on a corporation's stock to limit ownership of such stock and is being cancelled in connection with a public offering of the stock, such cancellation will generally be regarded as noncompensatory. However, the mere fact that the employer is willing to forego a deduction under section 83(h) is insufficient evidence to establish a noncompensatory cancellation of a nonlapse restriction. The refusal by a corporation or shareholder to repurchase stock of the corporation which is subject to a permanent right of first refusal will generally be treated as a cancellation of a nonlapse restriction. The preceding sentence shall not apply where there is no nonlapse restriction, for example, where the price to be paid for the stock subject to the right of first refusal is the fair market value of the stock. Section 83(d)(2) and this (1) do not apply where immediately after the cancellation of a nonlapse restriction the property is still substantially nonvested and no section 83(b) election has been made with respect to such property. In such a case the rules of section 83(a) and § 1.83–1 shall apply to such property.

(2) **Evidence of noncompensatory cancellation.** In addition to the information necessary to establish the factors described in paragraph (b)(1) of this section, the taxpayer shall request the employer to furnish the taxpayer with a written statement indicating that the employer will not treat the cancellation of the nonlapse restriction as a compensatory event, and that no deduction will be taken with respect to such cancellation. The taxpayer shall file such written statement with his

income tax return for the taxable year in which or with which such cancellation occurs.

(c) **Examples.** The provisions of this section may be illustrated by the following examples:

Example (1). On November 1, 1971, X corporation whose shares are closely held and not regularly traded, transfers to E, an employee, 100 shares of X corporation stock subject to the condition that, if he desires to dispose of such stock during the period of his employment, he must resell the stock to his employer at its then existing book value. In addition, E or E's estate is obligated to offer to sell the stock at his retirement or death to his employer at its then existing book value. Under these facts and circumstances, the restriction to which the shares of X corporation stock are subject is a nonlapse restriction. Consequently, the fair market value of the X stock is includible in E's gross income as compensation for taxable year 1971. However, in determining the fair market value of the X stock, the book value formula price will ordinarily be regarded as being determinative of such value.

Example (2). Assume the facts are the same as in example (1), except that the X stock is subject to the condition that if E desires to dispose of the stock during the period of his employment he must resell the stock to his employer at a multiple of earnings per share that is in this case a reasonable approximation of value at the time of transfer to E. In addition, E or E's estate is obligated to offer to sell the stock at his retirement or death to his employer at the same multiple of earnings. Under these facts and circumstances, the restriction to which the X corporation stock is subject is a nonlapse restriction. Consequently, the fair market value of the X stock is includible in E's gross income for taxable year 1971. However, in determining the fair market value of the X stock, the multiple-of-earnings formula price will ordinarily be regarded as determinative of such value.

Example (3). On January 4, 1971, X corporation transfers to E, an employee, 100 shares of stock in X corporation. Each such share of stock is subject to an agreement between X and E whereby E agrees that such shares are to be held solely for investment purposes and not for resale (a so-called investment letter restriction). E's rights in such stock are substantially vested upon transfer, causing the fair market value of each share of X corporation stock to be includible in E's gross income as compensation for taxable year 1971. Since such an investment letter restriction does not constitute a nonlapse restriction, in determining the fair market value of each share, the investment letter restriction is disregarded.

Example (4). On September 1, 1971, X corporation transfers to B, an independent contractor, 500 shares of common stock in X corporation in exchange for B's agreement to provide services in the construction of an office building on property owned by X corporation. X corporation has 100 shares of preferred stock outstanding and an additional 500 shares of common stock outstanding. The preferred stock has a liquidation value of $1,000x, which is equal to the value of all assets owned by X. Therefore, the book value of the common stock in X corporation is $0. Under the terms of the transfer, if B wishes to dispose of the stock, B must offer to sell the stock to X for 150 percent of the then existing book value of B's common stock. The stock is also subject to a substantial risk of forfeiture until B performs the agreed-upon services. B makes a timely election under section 83(b) to include the value of the stock in gross income in 1971. Under these facts and circumstances, the restriction to which the shares of X corporation common stock are subject is a nonlapse restriction. In determining the fair market value of the X common stock at the time of transfer, the book value formula price would ordinarily be regarded as determinative of such value. However, the fair market value of X common stock at the time of transfer, subject to the book value restriction, is greater than $0 since B was willing to agree to provide valuable personal services in exchange for the stock. In determining the fair market value of the stock, the expected book value after construction of the office building would be given great weight. The likelihood of completion of construction would be a factor in determining the expected book value after completion of construction.

[T.D. 7554, 43 FR 31918, July 24, 1978]

§ 1.83–6 Deduction by employer.

(a) **Allowance of deduction—(1) General rule.** In the case of a transfer of property in connection with the performance of services, or a compensatory cancellation of a nonlapse restriction described in section 83(d) and § 1.83–5, a deduction is allowable under sections 162 or 212, to the person for whom such services were performed. The amount of the deduction is equal to the amount includible as compensation in the gross income of the service provider, under section 83(a), (b), or (d)(2), but only to the extent such amount meets the requirements of sections 162 or 212 and the regulations thereunder. Such deduction shall be allowed only for the taxable year of such person in which or with which ends the taxable year of the service provider in which such amount is includible as compensation. For purposes of this paragraph, any amount excluded from gross income under section 79 or section 101(b) or subchapter N shall be considered to have been includible in gross income.

(2) **Special rule.** If the service provider is an employee of the person for whom services were performed, such deduction is allowed for the taxable year of the employer in which or with which ends the taxable year of the employee in which such amount is includible as compensation, but only if the employer deducts and withholds upon such amount in accordance with section 3402. A deduction will not be disallowed under the preceding sentence if the employer does not withhold and deduct upon amounts excluded from gross income, such as amounts excluded under section 79, section 101(b), or subchapter N. * * *

(3) Exceptions. Where property is substantially vested upon transfer, the deduction shall be allowed to such person in accordance with his method of accounting (in conformity with sections 446 and 461). In the case of a transfer to an employee benefit plan described in § 1.162–10(a) or a transfer to an employees' trust or annuity plan described in section 404(a)(5) and the regulations thereunder, section 83(h) and this section do not apply.

(4) Capital expenditure, etc. No deduction is allowed under section 83(h) to the extent that the transfer of property constitutes a capital expenditure, an item of deferred expense, or an amount properly includible in the value of inventory items. In the case of a capital expenditure, for example, the basis of the property to which such capital expenditure relates shall be increased at the same time and to the same extent as any amount includible in the employee's gross income in respect of such transfer. Thus, for example, no deduction is allowed to a corporation in respect of a transfer of its stock to a promoter upon its organization, notwithstanding that such promoter must include the value of such stock in his gross income in accordance with the rules under section 83.

(b) Recognition of gain or loss. Except as provided in section 1032, at the time of a transfer of property in connection with the performance of services the transferor recognizes gain to the extent that the transferor receives an amount that exceeds the transferor's basis in the property. In addition, at the time a deduction is allowed under section 83(h) and paragraph (a) of this section, gain or loss is recognized to the extent of the difference between (i) the sum of the amount paid plus the amount allowed as a deduction under section 83(h), and (ii) the sum of the taxpayer's basis in the property plus any amount recognized pursuant to the previous sentence.

(c) Forfeitures. If, under section 83(h) and paragraph (a) of this section, a deduction, an increase in basis, or a reduction of gross income was allowable (disregarding the reasonableness of the amount of compensation) in respect of a transfer of property and such property is subsequently forfeited, the amount of such deduction, increase in basis or reduction of gross income shall be includible in the gross income of the person to whom it was allowable for the taxable year of forfeiture. The basis of such property in the hands of the person to whom it is forfeited shall include any such amount includible in the gross income of such person, as well as any amount such person pays upon forfeiture.

(d) Special rules for transfers by shareholders—(1) Transfers. If a shareholder of a corporation transfers property to an employee of such corporation or to an independent contractor (or to a beneficiary thereof), in consideration of services performed for the corporation, the transaction shall be considered to be a contribution of such property to the capital of such corporation by the shareholder, and immediately thereafter a transfer of such property by the corporation to the employee or independent contractor under paragraphs (a) and (b) of this section. For purposes of this (1), such a transfer will be considered to be in consideration for services performed for the corporation if either the property transferred is substantially nonvested at the time of transfer or an amount is includible in the gross income of the employee or independent contractor at the time of transfer under § 1.83–1(a)(1) or § 1.83–2(a). In the case of such a transfer, any money or other property paid to the shareholder for such stock shall be considered to be paid to the corporation and transferred immediately thereafter by the corporation to the shareholder as a distribution to which section 302 applies.

(2) Forfeiture. If, following a transaction described in paragraph (d)(1) of this section, the transferred property is forfeited to the shareholder, paragraph (c) of this section shall apply both with respect to the shareholder and with respect to the corporation. In addition, the corporation shall in the taxable year of forfeiture be allowed a loss (or realize a gain) to offset any gain (or loss) realized under paragraph (b) of this section. For example, if a shareholder transfers property to an employee of the corporation as compensation, and as a result the shareholder's basis of $200x in such property is allocated to his stock in such corporation and such corporation recognizes a short-term capital gain of $800x, and is allowed a deduction of $1,000x on such transfer, upon a subsequent forfeiture of the property to the shareholder, the shareholder shall take $200x into gross income, and the corporation shall take $1,000x into gross income and be allowed a short-term capital loss of $800x.

* * *

[T.D. 7554, 43 FR 31919, July 24, 1978]

§ 1.83–7 Taxation of nonqualified stock options.

(a) **In general.** If there is granted to an employee or independent contractor (or beneficiary thereof) in connection with the performance of services, an option to which section 421 (relating generally to certain qualified and other options) does not apply, section 83(a) shall apply to such grant if the option has a readily ascertainable fair market value (determined in accordance with paragraph (b) of this section) at the time the option is granted. The person who performed such services realizes compensation upon such grant at the time and in the amount determined under section 83(a). If section 83(a) does not apply to the grant of such an option because the option does not have a readily ascertainable fair market value at the time of grant, sections 83(a) and 83(b) shall apply at the time the option is exercised or otherwise disposed of, even though the fair market value of such option may have become readily ascertainable before such time. If the option is exercised, sections 83(a) and 83(b) apply to the transfer of property pursuant to such exercise, and the employee or independent contractor realizes compensation upon such transfer at the time and in the amount determined under section 83(a) or 83(b). If the option is sold or otherwise disposed of in an arm's length transaction, sections 83(a) and 83(b) apply to the transfer of money or other property received in the same manner as sections 83(a) and 83(b) would have applied to the transfer of property pursuant to an exercise of the option.

(b) **Readily ascertainable defined—(1) Actively traded on an established market.** Options have a value at the time they are granted, but that value is ordinarily not readily ascertainable unless the option is actively traded on an established market. If an option is actively traded on an established market, the fair market value of such option is readily ascertainable for purposes of this section by applying the rules of valuation set forth in § 20.2031–2.

(2) **Not actively traded on an established market.** When an option is not actively traded on an established market, it does not have a readily ascertainable fair market value unless its fair market value can otherwise be measured with reasonable accuracy. For purposes of this section, if an option is not actively traded on an established market, the option does not have a readily ascertainable fair market value when granted unless

the taxpayer can show that all of the following conditions exist:

(i) The option is transferable by the optionee;

(ii) The option is exercisable immediately in full by the optionee;

(iii) The option or the property subject to the option is not subject to any restriction or condition (other than a lien or other condition to secure the payment of the purchase price) which has a significant effect upon the fair market value of the option; and

(iv) The fair market value of the option privilege is readily ascertainable in accordance with paragraph (b)(3) of this section.

(3) **Option privilege.** The option privilege in the case of an option to buy is the opportunity to benefit during the option's exercise period from any increase in the value of property subject to the option during such period, without risking any capital. Similarly, the option privilege in the case of an option to sell is the opportunity to benefit during the exercise period from a decrease in the value of property subject to the option. For example, if at some time during the exercise period of an option to buy, the fair market value of the property subject to the option is greater than the option's exercise price, a profit may be realized by exercising the option and immediately selling the property so acquired for its higher fair market value. Irrespective of whether any such gain may be realized immediately at the time an option is granted, the fair market value of an option to buy includes the value of the right to benefit from any future increase in the value of the property subject to the option (relative to the option exercise price), without risking any capital. Therefore, the fair market value of an option is not merely the difference that may exist at a particular time between the option's exercise price and the value of the property subject to the option, but also includes the value of the option privilege for the remainder of the exercise period. Accordingly, for purposes of this section, in determining whether the fair market value of an option is readily ascertainable, it is necessary to consider whether the value of the entire option privilege can be measured with reasonable accuracy. In determining whether the value of the option privilege is readily ascertainable, and in determining the amount of such value when such value is readily ascertainable, it is necessary to consider—

(i) Whether the value of the property subject to the option can be ascertained;

(ii) The probability of any ascertainable value of such property increasing or decreasing; and

(iii) The length of the period during which the option can be exercised.

* * *

[T.D. 7554, 43 FR 31920, July 24, 1978]

Items Specifically Excluded From Gross Income

§ 1.101–1 Exclusion from gross income of proceeds of life insurance contracts payable by reason of death.

(a)(1) In general. Section 101(a)(1) states the general rule that the proceeds of life insurance policies, if paid by reason of the death of the insured, are excluded from the gross income of the recipient. Death benefit payments having the characteristics of life insurance proceeds payable by reason of death under contracts, such as workmen's compensation insurance contracts, endowment contracts, or accident and health insurance contracts, are covered by this provision. For provisions relating to death benefits paid by or on behalf of employers, see section 101(b) and § 1.101–2. The exclusion from gross income allowed by section 101(a) applies whether payment is made to the estate of the insured or to any beneficiary (individual, corporation, or partnership) and whether it is made directly or in trust. The extent to which this exclusion applies in cases where life insurance policies have been transferred for a valuable consideration is stated in section 101(a)(2) and in paragraph (b) of this section. In cases where the proceeds of a life insurance policy, payable by reason of the death of the insured, are paid other than in a single sum at the time of such death, the amounts to be excluded from gross income may be affected by the provisions of section 101(c) (relating to amounts held under agreements to pay interest) or section 101(d) (relating to amounts payable at a date later than death). See §§ 1.101–3 and 1.101–4. However, neither section 101(c) nor section 101(d) applies to a single sum payment which does not exceed the amount payable at the time of death even though such amount is actually paid at a date later than death.

* * *

(b) Transfers of life insurance policies. **(1)** In the case of a transfer, by assignment or otherwise, of a life insurance policy or any interest therein for a valuable consideration, the amount of the proceeds attributable to such policy or interest which is excludable from the transferee's gross income is generally limited to the sum of (i) the actual value of the consideration for such transfer, and (ii) the premiums and other amounts subsequently paid by the transferee (see section 101(a)(2) and example (1) of subparagraph (5) of this paragraph). However, this limitation on the amount excludable from the transferee's gross income does not apply (except in certain special cases involving a series of transfers), where the basis of the policy or interest transferred, for the purpose of determining gain or loss with respect to the transferee, is determinable, in whole or in part, by reference to the basis of such policy or interest in the hands of the transferor (see section 101(a)(2)(A) and examples (2) and (4) of subparagraph (5) of this paragraph). Neither does the limitation apply where the policy or interest therein is transferred to the insured, to a partner of the insured, to a partnership in which the insured is a partner, or to a corporation in which the insured is a shareholder or officer (see section 101(a)(2)(B)). For rules relating to gratuitous transfers, see subparagraph (2) of this paragraph. For special rules with respect to certain cases where a series of transfers is involved, see subparagraph (3) of this paragraph.

(2) In the case of a gratuitous transfer, by assignment or otherwise, of a life insurance policy or any interest therein, as a general rule the amount of the proceeds attributable to such policy or interest which is excludable from the transferee's gross income under section 101(a) is limited to the sum of (i) the amount which would have been excludable by the transferor (in accordance with this section) if no such transfer had taken place, and (ii) any premiums and other amounts subsequently paid by the transferee. See example (6) of subparagraph (5) of this paragraph. However, where the gratuitous transfer in question is made by or to the insured, a partner of the insured, a partnership in which the insured is a partner, or a corporation in which the insured is a shareholder or officer, the entire amount of the proceeds attributable to the policy or interest transferred shall be excludable from the transferee's gross income (see section

101(a)(2)(B) and example (7) of subparagraph (5) of this paragraph).

(3) In the case of a series of transfers, if the last transfer of a life insurance policy or an interest therein is for a valuable consideration—

(i) The general rule is that the final transferee shall exclude from gross income, with respect to the proceeds of such policy or interest therein, only the sum of—

(a) The actual value of the consideration paid by him, and

(b) The premiums and other amounts subsequently paid by him;

(ii) If the final transfer is to the insured, to a partner of the insured, to a partnership in which the insured is a partner, or to a corporation in which the insured is a shareholder or officer, the final transferee shall exclude the entire amount of the proceeds from gross income;

(iii) Except where subdivision (ii) of this subparagraph applies, if the basis of the policy or interest transferred, for the purpose of determining gain or loss with respect to the final transferee, is determinable, in whole or in part, by reference to the basis of such policy or interest therein in the hands of the transferor, the amount of the proceeds which is excludable by the final transferee is limited to the sum of—

(a) The amount which would have been excludable by his transferor if no such transfer had taken place, and

(b) Any premiums and other amounts subsequently paid by the final transferee himself.

(4) For the purposes of section 101(a)(2) and subparagraphs (1) and (3) of this paragraph, a "transfer for a valuable consideration" is any absolute transfer for value of a right to receive all or a part of the proceeds of a life insurance policy. Thus, the creation, for value, of an enforceable contractual right to receive all or a part of the proceeds of a policy may constitute a transfer for a valuable consideration of the policy or an interest therein. On the other hand, the pledging or assignment of a policy as collateral security is not a transfer for a valuable consideration of such policy or an interest therein, and section 101 is inapplicable to any amounts received by the pledgee or assignee.

(5) The application of this paragraph may be illustrated by the following examples:

Example (1). A pays premiums of $500 for an insurance policy in the face amount of $1,000 upon the life of B, and subsequently transfers the policy to C for $600. C receives the proceeds of $1,000 upon the death of B. The amount which C can exclude from his gross income is limited to $600 plus any premiums paid by C subsequent to the transfer.

Example (2). The X Corporation purchases for a single premium of $500 an insurance policy in the face amount of $1,000 upon the life of A, one of its employees, naming the X Corporation as beneficiary. The X Corporation transfers the policy to the Y Corporation in a tax-free reorganization (the policy having a basis for determining gain or loss in the hands of the Y Corporation determined by reference to its basis in the hands of the X Corporation). The Y Corporation receives the proceeds of $1,000 upon the death of A. The entire $1,000 is to be excluded from the gross income of the Y Corporation.

Example (3). The facts are the same as in example (2) except that, prior to the death of A, the Y Corporation transfers the policy to the Z Corporation for $600. The Z Corporation receives the proceeds of $1,000 upon the death of A. The amount which the Z Corporation can exclude from its gross income is limited to $600 plus any premiums paid by the Z Corporation subsequent to the transfer of the policy to it.

Example (4). The facts are the same as in example (3) except that, prior to the death of A, the Z Corporation transfers the policy to the M Corporation in a tax-free reorganization (the policy having a basis for determining gain or loss in the hands of the M Corporation determined by reference to its basis in the hands of the Z Corporation). The M Corporation receives the proceeds of $1,000 upon the death of A. The amount which the M Corporation can exclude from its gross income is limited to $600 plus any premiums paid by the Z Corporation and the M Corporation subsequent to the transfer of the policy to the Z Corporation.

Example (5). The facts are the same as in example (3) except that, prior to the death of A, the Z Corporation transfers the policy to the N Corporation, in which A is a shareholder. The N Corporation receives the proceeds of $1,000 upon the death of A. The entire $1,000 is to be excluded from the gross income of the N Corporation.

Example (6). A pays premiums of $500 for an insurance policy in the face amount of $1,000 upon his own life, and subsequently transfers the policy to his wife B for $600. B later transfers the policy without consideration to C, who is the son of A and B. C receives the proceeds of $1,000 upon the death of A. The amount which C can exclude from his gross income is limited to $600 plus any premiums paid by B and C subsequent to the transfer of the policy to B.

Example (7). The facts are the same as in example (6) except that, prior to the death of A, C transfers the policy without consideration to A, the insured. A's estate receives the proceeds of $1,000 upon the death of A. The entire $1,000 is to be excluded from the gross income of A's estate.

[T.D. 6500, 25 FR 11402, Nov. 26, 1960, as amended by T.D. 6783, 29 FR 18356, Dec. 24, 1964; T.D. 7836, 47 FR 42337, Sept. 27, 1982]

§ 1.101–2 Employees' death benefits.

(a) In general. (1) Section 101(b) states the general rule that amounts up to $5,000 which are paid to the beneficiaries or the estate of an employee, or former employee, by or on behalf of an employer and by reason of the death of the employee shall be excluded from the gross income of the recipient. This exclusion from gross income applies whether payment is made to the estate of the employee or to any beneficiary (individual, corporation, or partnership), whether it is made directly or in trust, and whether or not it is made pursuant to a contractual obligation of the employer. The exclusion applies whether payment is made in a single sum or otherwise, subject to the provisions of section 101(c), relating to amounts held under an agreement to pay interest thereon (see § 1.101–3). The exclusion from gross income also applies to any amount not actually paid which is otherwise taxable to a beneficiary of an employee because it was made available as a distribution from an employee's trust.

(2) The exclusion does not apply to amounts constituting income payable to the employee during his life as compensation for his services, such as bonuses or payments for unused leave or uncollected salary, nor to certain other amounts with respect to which the deceased employee possessed, immediately before his death, a nonforfeitable right to receive the amounts while living (see section 101(b)(2)(B) and paragraph (d) of this section). Further, the exclusion does not apply to amounts received as an annuity under a joint and survivor annuity obligation where the employee was the primary annuitant and the annuity starting date occurred before the death of the employee (see section 101(b)(2)(C) and paragraph (e)(1)(ii) of this section). In the case of amounts received by a beneficiary as an annuity (but not as a survivor under a joint and survivor annuity with respect to which the employee was the primary annuitant), the exclusion is applied indirectly by means of the provisions of section 72 and the regulations thereunder (see section 101(b)(2)(D) and paragraph (e)(1)(iii) and (iv) of this section). Thus, for example, the exclusion applies to amounts which are received by a survivor of an employee retired on disability under the provisions of the Civil Service retirement law (5 U.S.C. 8301 or any former corresponding provisions of law) or the Retired Serviceman's Family Protection Plan or Survivor Benefit Plan (10 U.S.C. 1431 et seq.), provided such employ-

ee dies before attaining mandatory retirement age (as defined in § 1.105–4(a)(3)(i)(B)).

(3) The total amount excludable with respect to any employee may not exceed $5,000, regardless of the number of employers or the number of beneficiaries. For allocation of the exclusion among beneficiaries, see paragraph (c) of this section. For rules governing the taxability of benefits payable on the death of an employee under pension, profit-sharing, or stock bonus plans described in section 401(a) and exempt under section 501(a), under annuity plans described in section 403(a), or under annuity contracts to which paragraph (a) or (b) of § 1.403(b)–1 applies, see sections 72(m)(3), 402(a), and 403 and the regulations thereunder.

(b) Payments under certain employee benefit plans—(1) In general. Where a payment is made by reason of the death of an employee by an employer-provided welfare fund or a trust, including a stock bonus, pension, or profitsharing trust described in section 401(a), or by an insurance company (if such payment does not constitute "life insurance" within the purview of section 101(a)), the payment shall be considered to have been made by or on behalf of the employer to the extent that it exceeds amounts contributed by, or deemed contributed by, the deceased employee.

* * *

(c) Allocation of the exclusion. (1) Where the aggregate payments by or on behalf of an employer or employers as death benefits to the beneficiaries or the estate of a deceased employee exceed $5,000, the $5,000 exclusion shall be apportioned among them in the same proportion as the amount received by or the present value of the amount payable to each bears to the total death benefits paid or payable by or on behalf of the employer or employers.

(2) The application of the rule in subparagraph (1) of this paragraph may be illustrated by the following example:

Example. The M Corporation, the employer of A, a deceased employee who died November 30, 1954, makes payments in 1955 to the beneficiaries of A as follows: $5,000 to W, A's widow, $2,000 to B, the son of A, and $3,000 to C, the daughter of A. No other amounts are paid by any other employer of A to his estate or beneficiaries. By application of the apportionment rule stated above, W, the widow, will exclude $2,500 ($5,000/$10,000, or one-half, of $5,000); B, the son, will exclude $1,000 ($2,000/$10,000, or one-fifth, of $5,000); and C, the daughter, will exclude $1,500 ($3,000/$10,000, or three-tenths, of $5,000).

(d) Nonforfeitable rights. (1) Except as provided in subparagraphs (3) and (4) of this paragraph, the exclusion provided by section 101(b) does not apply to amounts with respect to which the deceased employee possessed, immediately before his death, a nonforfeitable right to receive the amounts while living. Section 101(b)(2)(B). For the purpose of section 101(b) and this paragraph, an employee shall be considered to have had a nonforfeitable right with respect to—

(i) Any amount to which he would have been entitled—

(a) If he had made an appropriate election or demand, or

(b) Upon termination of his employment (see examples (5) and (6) of subparagraph (2) of this paragraph); or

(ii) The present value (immediately before his death) of—

(a) Amounts payable as an annuity (as defined in paragraph (b) of § 1.72–2, whether immediate or deferred) by or on behalf of the employer (see example (1) of subparagraph (2) of this paragraph), or

(b) Amounts which would have been so payable if the employee had terminated his employment and continued to live; or

(iii) Any amount to the extent it is paid in lieu of amounts described in either subdivision (i) or (ii) of this subparagraph. See examples (2), (3), and (4) of subparagraph (2) of this paragraph.

For purposes of subdivision (iii) of this subparagraph, any amount paid in discharge of an obligation which arose solely because of the existence of a particular fact or circumstance subsequent to the employee's death shall not be considered an amount paid in lieu of amounts described in subdivision (i) or (ii) of this subparagraph. Subdivision (iii) of this subparagraph shall apply, however, to the extent indicated therein, to amounts payable without regard to any such contingency (to the extent that such amounts are equal to or less than those described in subdivision (i) and (ii) of this subparagraph which are not paid). See paragraph (e)(1)(iii)(b) of this section for rules with respect to finding the present value of an annuity immediately before the employee's death.

(2) The application of paragraph (d)(1) of this section may be illustrated by the following examples, in which it is assumed that the plans are not "qualified plans" and that no employer is an organization referred to in section 170(b)(1)(A)(ii) or (vi) or a religious organization (other than a trust) which is exempt from tax under section 501(a):

Example (1). A, who was a participant under the X Company pension plan, retired on December 31, 1953. He had made no contributions to the plan. Upon his retirement, he became entitled to monthly payments of $100 payable for life, or 120 months certain. A died on October 31, 1954, having received 10 monthly payments of $100 each. After his death, the monthly payments became payable to his estate for the remaining 110 months certain. No exclusion from gross income is allowed to A's estate (or any beneficiary who receives the right to such payments from the estate), since the employee's right to the monthly payments was nonforfeitable at the date of his death. It will be noted that in this example it is unnecessary to consider the present value of the annuity to A just before his death since the payments to be made include only those certain to be made in any event under the plan whether or not A continued to live.

Example (2). C, a participant under the Y Company pension plan, died on December 15, 1954, while actively in the employment of the company, survived by a widow and minor children. Because of his years of service, he would have been entitled to an annuity for life, his own contributions to the plan and interest thereon being guaranteed, if he had retired or terminated his employment at a time immediately before his death. The plan further provides that—(a) if, but only if, an employee is survived by a widow and minor children, his widow is to receive an annuity for her life without regard to whether or not the employee had begun his annuity; (b) any payments made with respect to his widow's annuity are to reduce the guaranteed amount to an equal extent; and (c) if the employee is not so survived, the guaranteed amount is payable to his beneficiary or estate, but no amount is payable to anyone with respect to what would have been the widow's annuity. In view of these provisions, that portion of the present value of the annuity payable to C's widow which exceeds the guaranteed amount shall be considered paid neither as an amount, nor in lieu of an amount, which C had a nonforfeitable right to receive while living. The reason for this result is that the payment of such excess is contingent upon C's being survived by a widow and minor children, a circumstance existing subsequent to his death. Conversely, to the extent that the present value of the annuity payable to C's widow does not exceed the guaranteed amount, annuity payments attributable to such present value shall be considered paid in lieu of an amount which C had a nonforfeitable right to receive while living.

Example (3). D, a participant under the Y Company pension plan, died on January 1, 1955, while actively in the employment of the company. The Y Company plan provides that where an employee dies in service, the present value of the accumulated credits which he could have obtained at that time if he had instead separated from the service shall be paid in a single sum to his surviving spouse or to his estate if no widow survives him. The present value of D's accumulated credits, at the time of his death, was $10,000. However, the plan also provides that a surviving spouse may elect to take, in lieu of a single sum, an annuity the present value of which exceeds such sum by $2,500. D's widow elects to receive an annuity (the present value of which is $12,-500). Therefore, $2,500 is an amount to which the exclusion of section 101(b) and this section shall apply.

Example (4). A, an employee of the X Company, continues to work after reaching the normal retirement age of 60 years, although he could have retired at that age and obtained an annuity of $3,000 per year for his life. A is not entitled to any part of the annuity while he is employed and receiving compensation. A dies at the age of 67 while still in active employment. Since he had passed normal retirement age, his additional years of service did not entitle him to a larger annuity at age 67 than that which he could have obtained at age 60. However, the plan of the X Company provides that in the event of an employee's death prior to separation from the service, his widow is to be paid an annuity for her life in the same amount per year as that which the employee could have obtained if he had instead retired; but if no widow survives him, the present value of the annuity which the employee could have obtained at a time just before his death is to be paid to a named beneficiary or the estate of the employee. Assuming that the present value of the annuity to A's widow, whose age is 61, is $36,000 and the present value of the annuity which would have been payable to A at age 67 if he had then retired is $23,500, the present value of the widow's annuity, to the extent of $23,500, is an amount which is payable in lieu of amounts which the employee had a nonforfeitable right to receive while living because it does not exceed the value of his nonforfeitable rights and is not otherwise paid. On the other hand, the $12,500 excess of the value of the widow's annuity ($36,000) over the value of the employee's annuity ($23,500) is an amount to which section 101(b) applies since the employee had no right to any part of it. If no other death benefits are payable, a $5,000 exclusion is available (see section 101(b)(2)(D) and paragraph (e) of this section).

Example (5). The trustee of the X Corporation noncontributory profit-sharing plan is required under the provisions of the plan to pay to the beneficiary of B, an employee of the X Corporation who died on July 1, 1955, the benefit due on account of the death of B. The provisions of the profit-sharing plan give each participating employee in case of termination of employment a 10-percent vested interest in the amount accumulated in his account for each year of participation in the plan. In case of death, the entire credit in the participant's account is to be paid to his beneficiary. At the time of B's death, he had been a participant for three years and the accumulation in his account was $8,000. After his death this amount is paid to his beneficiary. At the time of B's death, the amount distributable to him on account of termination of employment would have been $2,400 (30 percent of $8,000). The difference of $5,600 ($8,000 minus $2,400), payable to the beneficiary of B, is an amount payable solely by reason of B's death. Accordingly, $5,000 of the $5,600 may be excluded from the gross income of the beneficiary receiving such payment (assuming no other death benefits are involved). However, if it is assumed that the facts are the same as above, except that at the time of his death B has been a participant for 6 years, the amount distributable to him on account of termination of employment would have been $4,800 (60 percent of $8,000). The difference of $3,200 (8,000 minus

$4,888), payable to B's beneficiary, is an amount payable solely by reason of B's death. Accordingly, only $3,200 may be excluded from the gross income of the beneficiary receiving such payment (assuming no other death benefits are involved).

Example (6). The X Corporation instituted a trust, forming part of a pension plan, for its employees, the cost thereof being borne entirely by the corporation. The plan provides, in part, that after 10 or more years of service and attaining the age of 55, an employee can elect to retire and receive benefits before the normal retirement date contingent upon the employer's approval. If he retires without the employer's consent, or voluntarily leaves the company, no benefits are or will be payable. The plan further provides that if the employee is involuntarily separated or dies before retirement, he or his beneficiary, respectively, will receive a percentage of the reserve provided for the employee in the trust fund on the following basis: 10 to 15 years of service, 25 percent; 15 to 20 years of service, 50 percent; 20 to 25 years of service, 75 percent; 25 or more years of service, 100 percent. A, an employee of the X Corporation for 17 years, died at the age of 56 while in the employ of the corporation. At the time of his death, $15,000 was the reserve provided for him in the trust. His beneficiary receives $7,500, an amount equal to 50 percent of the reserve provided for A's retirement; accordingly, $5,000 of the $7,500 may be excluded from the gross income of the beneficiary receiving such payment (assuming no other death benefits are involved) since A, prior to his death, had only a forfeitable right to receive $7,500.

* * *

[T.D. 6500, 25 FR 11402, Nov. 26, 1960, as amended by T.D. 6722, 29 FR 5070, April 14, 1964; T.D. 6783, 29 FR 18357, Dec. 24, 1964; T.D. 7352, 40 FR 16666, April 14, 1975; T.D. 7428, 41 FR 34619, Aug. 16, 1976; T.D. 7836, 47 FR 42337, Sept. 27, 1982; T.D. 7955, 49 FR 19975, May 11, 1984]

§ 1.101–3 Interest payments.

(a) **Applicability of section 101(c).** Section 101(c) provides that if any amount excluded from gross income by section 101(a) (relating to life insurance proceeds) or section 101(b) (relating to employees' death benefits) is held under an agreement to pay interest thereon, the interest payments shall be included in gross income. This provision applies to payments made (either by an insurer or by or on behalf of an employer) of interest earned on any amount so excluded from gross income which is held without substantial diminution of the principal amount during the period when such interest payments are being made or credited to the beneficiaries or estate of the insured or the employee. For example, if a monthly payment is $100, of which $99 represents interest and $1 represents diminution of the principal amount, the principal amount shall be considered held under an agreement to pay interest thereon and the interest payment shall be included in the gross income of the recipient. Section 101(c) applies whether the election to have an amount held under an agreement to pay interest thereon is made by the insured or employee or by his beneficiaries or estate, and whether or not an interest rate is explicitly stated in the agreement. Section 101(d), relating to the payment of life insurance proceeds at a date later than death, shall not apply to any amount to which section 101(c) applies. See section 101(d)(4). However, both section 101(c) and section 101(d) may apply to payments received under a single life insurance contract. For provisions relating to the application of this rule to payments received under a permanent life insurance policy with a family income rider attached, see paragraph (h) of § 1.101–4.

(b) Determination of "present value". For the purpose of determining whether section 101(c) or section 101(d) applies, the present value (at the time of the insured's death) of any amount which is to be paid at a date later than death shall be determined by the use of the interest rate and mortality tables used by the insurer in determining the size of the payments to be made.

[T.D. 6500, 25 FR 11402, Nov. 26, 1960, as amended by T.D. 6577, 26 FR 10127, Oct. 28, 1961]

§ 1.101–4　Payment of life insurance proceeds at a date later than death.

(a) In general. (1)(i) Section 101(d) states the provisions governing the exclusion from gross income of amounts (other than those to which section 101(c) applies) received under a life insurance contract and paid by reason of the death of the insured which are paid to a beneficiary on a date or dates later than the death of the insured. However, if the amounts payable as proceeds of life insurance to which section 101(a)(1) applies cannot in any event exceed the amount payable at the time of the insured's death, such amounts are fully excludable from the gross income of the recipient (or recipients) without regard to the actual time of payment and no further determination need be made under this section. Section 101(d)(1)(A) provides an exclusion from gross income of any amount determined by a proration, under applicable regulations, of "an amount held by an insurer with respect to any beneficiary". The quoted phrase is defined in section 101(d)(2). For the regulations governing the method of computation of this proration, see paragraphs (c) through (f) of

this section. The prorated amounts are to be excluded from the gross income of the beneficiary regardless of the taxable year in which they are actually received (see example (2) of subparagraph (2) of this paragraph).

(ii) Section 101(d)(1)(B) provides an additional exclusion where life insurance proceeds are paid to the surviving spouse of an insured. For purposes of this exclusion, the term "surviving spouse" means the spouse of the insured as of the date of death, including a spouse legally separated, but not under a decree of absolute divorce (section 101(d)(3)). To the extent that the total payments, under one or more agreements, made in excess of the amounts determined by proration under section 101(d)(1)(A) do not exceed $1,000 in the taxable year of receipt, they shall be excluded from the gross income of the surviving spouse (whether or not payment of any part of such amounts is guaranteed by the insurer). Amounts excludable under section 101(d)(1)(B) are not "prorated" amounts.

(2) The principles of this paragraph may be illustrated by the following examples:

Example (1). A surviving spouse elects to receive all of the life insurance proceeds with respect to one insured, amounting to $150,000, in ten annual installments of $16,500 each, based on a certain guaranteed interest rate. The prorated amount is $15,000 ($150,000÷10). As the second payment, the insurer pays $17,850, which exceeds the guaranteed payment by $1,350 as the result of earnings of the insurer in excess of those required to pay the guaranteed installments. The surviving spouse shall include $1,850 in gross income and exclude $16,000—determined in the following manner:

Fixed payment (including guaranteed interest)	$16,500
Excess interest	1,350
Total payment	17,850
Prorated amount	15,000
Excess over prorated amount	2,850
Annual excess over prorated amount excludable under section 101(d)(1)(B)	1,000
Amount includible in gross income	1,850

Example (2). Assume the same facts as in example (1), except that the third and fourth annual installments, totalling $33,000 (2×$16,500), are received in a single subsequent taxable year of the surviving spouse. The prorated amount of $15,000 of each annual installment, totalling $30,000, shall be excluded even though the spouse receives more than one annual installment in the single subsequent taxable year. However, the surviving spouse is entitled to only one exclusion of $1,000 under section 101(d)(1)(B) for each taxable year of receipt. The surviving spouse shall include $2,000 in her gross income for the taxable year with respect to the above installment payments ($33,000 less the sum of $30,000 plus $1,000).

* * *

(b) Amount held by an insurer. (1) For the purpose of the proration referred to in section 101(d)(1), an "amount held by an insurer with respect to any beneficiary" means an amount equal to the present value to such beneficiary (as of the date of death of the insured) of an agreement by the insurer under a life insurance policy (whether as an option or otherwise) to pay such beneficiary an amount or amounts at a date or dates later than the death of the insured (section 101(d)(2)). The present value of such agreement is to be computed as if the agreement under the life insurance policy had been entered into on the date of death of the insured, except that such value shall be determined by the use of the mortality table and interest rate used by the insurer in calculating payments to be made to the beneficiary under such agreement. Where an insurance policy provides an option for the payment of a specific amount upon the death of the insured in full discharge of the contract, such lump sum is the amount held by the insurer with respect to all beneficiaries (or their beneficiaries) under the contract. See, however, paragraph (e) of this section.

(2) In the case of two or more beneficiaries, the "amount held by the insurer" with respect to each beneficiary depends on the relationship of the different benefits payable to such beneficiaries. Where the amounts payable to two or more beneficiaries are independent of each other, the "amount held by the insurer with respect to each beneficiary" shall be determined and prorated over the periods involved independently. Thus, if a certain amount per month is to be paid to A for his life, and, concurrently, another amount per month is to be paid to B for his life, the "amount held by the insurer" shall be determined and prorated for both A and B independently, but the aggregate shall not exceed the total present value of such payments to both. On the other hand, if the obligation to pay B was contingent on his surviving A, the "amount held by the insurer" shall be considered an amount held with respect to both beneficiaries simultaneously. Furthermore, it is immaterial whether B is a named beneficiary or merely the ultimate recipient of payments for a term of years. For the special rules governing the computation of the proration of the "amount held by an insurer" in determining amounts excludable under the provisions of section 101(d), see paragraphs (c) to (f), inclusive, of this section.

(3) Notwithstanding any other provision of this section, if the policy was transferred for a valuable consideration, the total "amount held by an insurer" cannot exceed the sum of the consideration paid plus any premiums or other consideration paid subsequent to the transfer if the provisions of section 101(a)(2) and paragraph (b) of § 1.101–1 limit the excludability of the proceeds to such total.

(c) Treatment of payments for life to a sole beneficiary. If the contract provides for the payment of a specified lump sum, but, pursuant to an agreement between the beneficiary and the insurer, payments are to be made during the life of the beneficiary in lieu of such lump sum, the lump sum shall be divided by the life expectancy of the beneficiary determined in accordance with the mortality table used by the insurer in determining the benefits to be paid. However, if payments are to be made to the estate or beneficiary of the primary beneficiary in the event that the primary beneficiary dies before receiving a certain number of payments or a specified total amount, such lump sum shall be reduced by the present value (at the time of the insured's death) of amounts which may be paid by reason of the guarantee, in accordance with the provisions of paragraph (e) of this section, before making this calculation. To the extent that payments received in each taxable year do not exceed the amount found from the above calculation, they are "prorated amounts" of the "amount held by an insurer" and are excludable from the gross income of the beneficiary without regard to whether he lives beyond the life expectancy used in making the calculation. If the contract in question does not provide for the payment of a specific lump sum upon the death of the insured as one of the alternative methods of payment, the present value (at the time of the death of the insured) of the payments to be made the beneficiary, determined in accordance with the interest rate and mortality table used by the insurer in determining the benefits to be paid, shall be used in the above calculation in lieu of a lump sum.

* * *

(h) Applicability of both section 101(c) and 101(d) to payments under a single life insurance contract—(1) In general. Section 101(d) shall not apply to interest payments on any amount held by an insurer under an agreement to pay interest thereon (see sections 101(c) and 101(d)(4) and § 1.101–3). On the other hand, both section 101(c) and section 101(d) may be applicable to payments received under a single life insurance contract, if such payments consist both of interest on an amount held by an insurer under an agreement to pay interest thereon and of amounts held by the insurer and paid on a date or dates later than the death of the insured. One instance when both section 101(c) and section 101(d) may be applicable to payments received under a single life insurance contract is in the case of a permanent life insurance policy with a family income rider attached. A typical family income rider is one which provides additional term insurance coverage for a specified number of years from the register date of the basic policy. Under the policy with such a rider, if the insured dies at any time during the term period, the beneficiary is entitled to receive (i) monthly payments of a specified amount commencing as of the date of death and continuing for the balance of the term period, and (ii) a lump sum payment of the proceeds under the basic policy to be paid at the end of the term period. If the insured dies after the expiration of the term period, the beneficiary receives only the proceeds under the basic policy. If the insured dies before the expiration of the term period, part of each monthly payment received by the beneficiary during the term period consists of interest on the proceeds of the basic policy (such proceeds being retained by the insurer until the end of the term period). The remaining part consists of an installment (principal plus interest) of the proceeds of the terms insurance purchased under the family income rider. The amount of term insurance which is provided under the family income rider is, therefore, that amount which, at the date of the insured's death, will provide proceeds sufficient to fund such remaining part of each monthly payment. Since the proceeds under the basic policy are held by the insurer until the end of the term period, that portion of each monthly payment which consists of interest on such proceeds is interest on an amount held by an insurer under an agreement to pay interest thereon and is includible in gross income under section 101(c). On the other hand, since the remaining portion of each monthly payment consists of an installment payment (principal plus interest) of the proceeds of the term insurance, it is a payment of an amount held by the insurer and paid on a date later than the death of the insured to which section 101(d) and this section applies (including the $1,000 exclusion allowed the surviving spouse under section 101(d)(1)(B)). The proceeds of the basic policy, when received in a lump sum at the end of the term period, are excludable from gross income under section 101(a).

* * *

[T.D. 6500, 25 FR 11402, Nov. 26, 1960, as amended by T.D. 6577, 26 FR 10127, Oct. 28, 1961; 26 FR 10275, Nov. 2, 1961]

§ 1.102–1 Gifts and inheritances.

(a) **General rule.** Property received as a gift, or received under a will or under statutes of descent and distribution, is not includible in gross income, although the income from such property is includible in gross income. An amount of principal paid under a marriage settlement is a gift. However, see section 71 and the regulations thereunder for rules relating to alimony or allowances paid upon divorce or separation. Section 102 does not apply to prizes and awards (see section 74 and § 1.74–1) nor to scholarships and fellowship grants (see section 117 and the regulations thereunder).

(b) **Income from gifts and inheritances.** The income from any property received as a gift, or under a will or statute of descent and distribution shall not be excluded from gross income under paragraph (a) of this section.

(c) **Gifts and inheritances of income.** If the gift, bequest, devise, or inheritance is of income from property, it shall not be excluded from gross income under paragraph (a) of this section. Section 102 provides a special rule for the treatment of certain gifts, bequests, devises, or inheritances which by their terms are to be paid, credited, or distributed at intervals. Except as provided in section 663(a)(1) and paragraph (d) of this section, to the extent any such gift, bequest, devise, or inheritance is paid, credited, or to be distributed out of income from property, it shall be considered a gift, bequest, devise, or inheritance of income from property. Section 102 provides the same treatment for amounts of income from property which is paid, credited, or to be distributed under a gift or bequest whether the gift or bequest is in terms of a right to payments at intervals (regardless of income) or is in terms of a right to income. To the extent the amounts in either case are paid, credited, or to be distributed at intervals out of income, they are not to be excluded under section 102 from the taxpayer's gross income.

(d) **Effect of subchapter J.** Any amount required to be included in the gross income of a beneficiary under sections 652, 662, or 668 shall be treated for purposes of this section as a gift, bequest, devise, or inheritance of income from property. On the other hand, any amount excluded from the gross income of a beneficiary under section 663(a)(1) shall be treated for purposes of this section as property acquired by gift, bequest, devise, or inheritance.

(e) Income taxed to grantor or assignor. Section 102 is not intended to tax a donee upon the same income which is taxed to the grantor of a trust or assignor of income under section 61 or sections 671 through 677, inclusive.

[T.D. 6500, 25 FR 11402, Nov. 26, 1960]

§ 1.103–1 Interest upon obligations of a State, territory, etc.

(a) Interest upon obligations of a State, territory, a possession of the United States, the District of Columbia, or any political subdivision thereof (hereinafter collectively or individually referred to as "State or local governmental unit") is not includable in gross income, except as provided under section 103(c) and (d) and the regulations thereunder.

(b) Obligations issued by or on behalf of any State or local governmental unit by constituted authorities empowered to issue such obligations are the obligations of such a unit. However, section 103(a)(1) and this section do not apply to industrial development bonds except as otherwise provided in section 103(c). See section 103(c) and §§ 1.103–7 through 1.103–12 for the rules concerning interest paid on industrial development bonds. See section 103(d) for rules concerning interest paid on arbitrage bonds. Certificates issued by a political subdivision for public improvements (such as sewers, sidewalks, streets, etc.) which are evidence of special assessments against specific property, which assessments become a lien against such property and which the political subdivision is required to enforce, are, for purposes of this section, obligations of the political subdivision even though the obligations are to be satisfied out of special funds and not out of general funds or taxes. The term "political subdivision", for purposes of this section denotes any division of any State or local governmental unit which is a municipal corporation or which has been delegated the right to exercise part of the sovereign power of the unit. As thus defined, a political subdivision of any State or local governmental unit may or may not, for purposes of this section, include special assessment districts so created, such as road, water, sewer, gas, light, reclamation, drainage, irrigation, levee,

school, harbor, port improvement, and similar districts and divisions of any such unit.

[T.D. 6500, 25 FR 11402, Nov. 26, 1960, as amended by T.D. 7199, 37 FR 15486, Aug. 3, 1972]

§ 1.104–1 Compensation for injuries or sickness.

(a) In general. Section 104(a) provides an exclusion from gross income with respect to certain amounts described in paragraphs (b), (c), (d) and (e) of this section, which are received for personal injuries or sickness, except to the extent that such amounts are attributable to (but not in excess of) deductions allowed under section 213 (relating to medical, etc., expenses) for any prior taxable year. See section 213 and the regulations thereunder.

(b) Amounts received under workmen's compensation acts. Section 104(a)(1) excludes from gross income amounts which are received by an employee under a workmen's compensation act (such as the Longshoremen's and Harbor Workers' Compensation Act, 33 U.S.C., c. 18), or under a statute in the nature of a workmen's compensation act which provides compensation to employees for personal injuries or sickness incurred in the course of employment. Section 104(a)(1) also applies to compensation which is paid under a workmen's compensation act to the survivor or survivors of a deceased employee. However, section 104(a)(1) does not apply to a retirement pension or annuity to the extent that it is determined by reference to the employee's age or length of service, or the employee's prior contributions, even though the employee's retirement is occasioned by an occupational injury or sickness. Section 104(a)(1) also does not apply to amounts which are received as compensation for a nonoccupational injury or sickness nor to amounts received as compensation for an occupational injury or sickness to the extent that they are in excess of the amount provided in the applicable workmen's compensation act or acts.
* * *

(c) Damages received on account of personal injuries or sickness. Section 104(a)(2) excludes from gross income the amount of any damages received (whether by suit or agreement) on account of personal injuries or sickness. The term "damages received (whether by suit or agreement)" means an amount received (other than workmen's compensation) through prosecution of a legal suit or action based upon tort or tort type rights, or through a settlement agreement entered into in lieu of such prosecution.

(d) Accident or health insurance. Section 104(a)(3) excludes from gross income amounts received through accident or health insurance for personal injuries or sickness (other than amounts received by an employee, to the extent that such amounts (1) are attributable to contributions of the employer which were not includible in the gross income of the employee, or (2) are paid by the employer). Similar treatment is also accorded to amounts received under accident or health plans and amounts received from sickness or disability funds. See section 105(e) and § 1.105–5. If, therefore, an individual purchases a policy accident or health insurance out of his own funds, amounts received thereunder for personal injuries or sickness are excludable from his gross income under section 104(a)(3). See, however, section 213 and the regulations thereunder as to the inclusion in gross income of amounts attributable to deductions allowed under section 213 for any prior taxable year. Section 104(a)(3) also applies to amounts received by an employee for personal injuries or sickness from a fund which is maintained exclusively by employee contributions. Conversely, if an employer is either the sole contributor to such a fund, or is the sole purchaser of a policy of accident or health insurance for his employees (on either a group or individual basis), the exclusion provided under section 104(a)(3) does not apply to any amounts received by his employees through such fund or insurance. If the employer and his employees contribute to a fund or purchase insurance which pays accident or health benefits to employees, section 104(a)(3) does not apply to amounts received thereunder by employees to the extent that such amounts are attributable to the employer's contributions. See § 1.105–1 for rules relating to the determination of the amount attributable to employer contributions. * * *

* * *

[T.D. 6500, 25 FR 11402, Nov. 26, 1960, as amended by T.D. 6722, 29 FR 5070, April 14, 1964; T.D. 7043, 35 FR 8477, June 2, 1970]

§ 1.105–1 Amounts attributable to employer contributions.

(a) In general. Under section 105(a), amounts received by an employee through accident or health insurance for personal injuries or sickness must be included in his gross income to the extent that such amounts (1) are attributable to contributions of the employer which were not includible in the gross income of the employee, or (2) are paid by the employer, unless such amounts are excluded therefrom under section 105(b), (c), or (d). For purposes of this section, the term "amounts received by an employee through an accident or health plan" refers to any amounts received through accident or health insurance, and also to any amounts which, under section 105(e), are treated as being so received. See § 1.105–5. In determining the extent to which amounts received for personal injuries or sickness by an employee through an accident or health plan are subject to the provisions of section 105(a), rather than section 104(a)(3), the provisions of paragraphs (b), (c), (d), and (e) of this section shall apply. A self-employed individual is not an employee for purposes of section 105 and §§ 1.105–1 through 1.105–5. See paragraph (g) of § 1.72–15. Thus, such an individual will not be treated as an employee with respect to benefits described in section 105 received from a plan in which he participates as an employee within the meaning of section 401(c)(1) at the time he, his spouse, or any of his dependents becomes entitled to receive such benefits.

* * *

[T.D. 6500, 25 FR 11402, Nov. 26, 1960, as amended by T.D. 6722, 29 FR 5071, April 14, 1964]

§ 1.105–2 Amounts expended for medical care.

Section 105(b) provides an exclusion from gross income with respect to the amounts referred to in section 105(a) (see § 1.105–1) which are paid, directly or indirectly, to the taxpayer to reimburse him for expenses incurred for the medical care (as defined in section 213(e)) of the taxpayer, his spouse, and his dependents (as defined in section 152). However, the exclusion does not apply to amounts which are attributable to (and not in excess of) deductions allowed under section 213 (relating to medical, etc., expenses) for any prior taxable year. See section 213 and the regulations thereunder. Section 105(b) applies only to amounts which are paid specifically to reimburse the taxpayer for expenses incurred by him for the prescribed medical care. Thus, section 105(b) does not apply to amounts which the taxpayer would be entitled to receive irrespective of whether or not he incurs expenses for medical care. For example, if under a wage continuation plan the taxpayer is entitled to regular wages during a period of absence from work due to sickness or injury, amounts received under such plan are not excludable from his gross income under section 105(b) even though the taxpayer may have incurred medical expenses during the period of illness. * * * If the amounts are paid to the taxpayer solely to reimburse him for expenses which he incurred for the prescribed medical care, section 105(b) is applicable even though such amounts are paid without proof of the amount of the actual expenses incurred by the taxpayer, but section 105(b) is not applicable to the extent that such amounts exceed the amount of the actual expenses for such medical care. If the taxpayer incurs an obligation for medical care, payment to the obligee in discharge of such obligation shall constitute indirect payment to the taxpayer as reimbursement for medical care. Similarly, payment to or on behalf of the taxpayer's spouse or dependents shall constitute indirect payment to the taxpayer.

[T.D. 6500, 25 FR 11402, Nov. 26, 1960]

§ 1.105–3 Payments unrelated to absence from work.

Section 105(c) provides an exclusion from gross income with respect to the amounts referred to in section 105(a) to the extent that such amounts (a) constitute payments for the permanent loss or permanent loss of use of a member or function of the body, or the permanent disfigurement, of the taxpayer, his spouse, or a dependent (as defined in section 152), and (b) are computed with reference to the nature of the injury without regard to the period the employee is absent from work. Loss of use or disfigurement shall be considered permanent when it may reasonably be expected to continue for the life of the individual. For purposes of section 105(c), loss or loss of use of a member or function of the body includes the loss or loss of use of an appendage of the body, the loss of an eye, the loss of substantially all of the vision of an eye, and the loss of substantially all of the hearing in one or both ears. The term "disfigurement" shall be given a reasonable interpretation in the light of all the particular facts and circumstances. Section 105(c) does not apply if the amount of the benefits is determined by reference to the period the employee is absent from work. For example, if an employee is absent from work as a result of the loss of an arm, and under the accident and health plan established by his employer, he is to receive $125 a week so long as he is absent from work for a period not in excess of 52 weeks, section 105(c) is not applicable to such payments. See, however,

section 105(d) and § 1.105–4. However, for purposes of section 105(c), it is immaterial whether an amount is paid in a lump sum or in installments. Section 105(c) does not apply to amounts which are treated as workmen's compensation under paragraph (b) of § 1.104–1, or to amounts paid by reason of the death of the employee (see section 101).

[T.D. 6500, 25 FR 11402, Nov. 26, 1960]

§ 1.105–5 Accident and health plans.

(a) In general. Sections 104(a)(3) and 105(b), (c), and (d) exclude from gross income certain amounts received through accident or health insurance. Section 105(e) provides that for purposes of sections 104 and 105 amounts received through an accident or health plan for employees, and amounts received from a sickness and disability fund for employees maintained under the law of a State, a Territory, or the District of Columbia, shall be treated as amounts received through accident or health insurance. In general, an accident or health plan is an arrangement for the payment of amounts to employees in the event of personal injuries or sickness. A plan may cover one or more employees, and there may be different plans for different employees or classes of employees. An accident or health plan may be either insured or noninsured, and it is not necessary that the plan be in writing or that the employee's rights to benefits under the plan be enforceable. However, if the employee's rights are not enforceable, an amount will be deemed to be received under a plan only if, on the date the employee became sick or injured, the employee was covered by a plan (or a program, policy, or custom having the effect of a plan) providing for the payment of amounts to the employee in the event of personal injuries or sickness, and notice or knowledge of such plan was reasonably available to the employee. It is immaterial who makes payment of the benefits provided by the plan. For example, payment may be made by the employer, a welfare fund, a State sickness or disability benefits fund, an association of employers or employees, or by an insurance company.

(b) Self-employed individuals. Under section 105(g), a self-employed individual is not treated as an employee for purposes of section 105. Therefore, for example, benefits paid under an accident or health plan as referred to in section 105(e) to or on behalf of an individual who is self-employed in the business with respect to which the plan is established will not be treated as received through accident and health insurance for purposes of sections 104(a)(3) and 105.

[T.D. 6722, 29 FR 5071, April 14, 1964]

§ 1.105–11 Self-insured medical reimbursement plan.

(a) **In general.** Under section 105(a), amounts received by an employee through a self-insured medical reimbursement plan which are attributable to contributions of the employer, or are paid by the employer, are included in the employee's gross income unless such amounts are excludable under section 105(b). For amounts reimbursed to a highly compensated individual to be fully excludable from such individual's gross income under section 105(b), the plan must satisfy the requirements of section 105(h) and this section. Section 105(h) is not satisfied if the plan discriminates in favor of highly compensated individuals as to eligibility to participate or benefits. All or a portion of the reimbursements or payments on behalf of such individuals under a discriminatory plan are not excludable from gross income under section 105(b). However, benefits paid to participants who are not highly compensated individuals may be excluded from gross income if the requirements of section 105(b) are satisfied, even if the plan is discriminatory.

* * *

[T.D. 7754, 46 FR 3505, Jan. 15, 1981]

§ 1.106–1 Contributions by employer to accident and health plans.

The gross income of an employee does not include contributions which his employer makes to an accident or health plan for compensation (through insurance or otherwise) to the employee for personal injuries or sickness incurred by him, his spouse, or his dependents, as defined in section 152. The employer may contribute to an accident or health plan either by paying the premium (or a portion of the premium) on a policy of accident or health insurance covering one or more of his employees, or by contributing to a separate trust or fund (including a fund referred to in section 105(e)) which provides accident or health benefits directly or through insurance to one or more of his employees. However, if such insurance policy, trust, or fund provides other benefits in addition to accident or health benefits, section 106 applies only to the portion of the employer's contribution which is

allocable to accident or health benefits. See paragraph (d) of § 1.104–1 and §§ 1.105–1 through 1.105–5, inclusive, for regulations relating to exclusion from an employee's gross income of amounts received through accident or health insurance and through accident or health plans.

[T.D. 6500, 25 FR 11402, Nov. 26, 1960]

§ 1.107–1 Rental value of parsonages.

(a) In the case of a minister of the gospel, gross income does not include (1) the rental value of a home, including utilities, furnished to him as a part of his compensation, or (2) the rental allowance paid to him as part of his compensation to the extent such allowance is used by him to rent or otherwise provide a home. In order to qualify for the exclusion, the home or rental allowance must be provided as remuneration for services which are ordinarily the duties of a minister of the gospel. In general, the rules provided in § 1.1402(c)–5 will be applicable to such determination. Examples of specific services the performance of which will be considered duties of a minister for purposes of section 107 include the performance of sacerdotal functions, the conduct of religious worship, the administration and maintenance of religious organizations and their integral agencies, and the performance of teaching and administrative duties at theological seminaries. Also, the service performed by a qualified minister as an employee of the United States (other than as a chaplain in the Armed Forces, whose service is considered to be that of a commissioned officer in his capacity as such, and not as a minister in the exercise of his ministry), or a State, Territory, or possession of the United States, or a political subdivision of any of the foregoing, or the District of Columbia, is in the exercise of his ministry provided the service performed includes such services as are ordinarily the duties of a minister.

(b) For purposes of section 107, the term "home" means a dwelling place (including furnishings) and the appurtenances thereto, such as a garage. The term "rental allowance" means an amount paid to a minister to rent or otherwise provide a home if such amount is designated as rental allowance pursuant to official action taken prior to January 1, 1958, by the employing church or other qualified organization, or if such amount is designated as rental allowance pursuant to official action taken in advance of such payment by the employing church or other qualified organization when paid after December 31, 1957. The designation of an amount as rental allowance may be evidenced in an employment contract, in minutes of or in a resolution by a church or other qualified organization or in its budget, or in any other appropriate instrument evidencing such official action. The designation referred to in this paragraph is a sufficient designation if it permits a payment or a part thereof to be identified as a payment of rental allowance as distinguished from salary or other remuneration.

(c) A rental allowance must be included in the minister's gross income in the taxable year in which it is received, to the extent that such allowance is not used by him during such taxable year to rent or otherwise provide a home. Circumstances under which a rental allowance will be deemed to have been used to rent or provide a home will include cases in which the allowance is expended (1) for rent of a home, (2) for purchase of a home, and (3) for expenses directly related to providing a home. Expenses for food and servants are not considered for this purpose to be directly related to providing a home. Where the minister rents, purchases, or owns a farm or other business property in addition to a home, the portion of the rental allowance expended in connection with the farm or business property shall not be excluded from his gross income.

[T.D. 6500, 25 FR 11402, Nov. 26, 1960, as amended by T.D. 6691, 28 FR 12817, Dec. 3, 1963]

§ 1.109–1 Exclusion from gross income of lessor of real property of value of improvements erected by lessee.

(a) Income derived by a lessor of real property upon the termination, through forfeiture or otherwise, of the lease of such property and attributable to buildings erected or other improvements made by the lessee upon the leased property is excluded from gross income. However, where the facts disclose that such buildings or improvements represent in whole or in part a liquidation in kind of lease rentals, the exclusion from gross income shall not apply to the extent that such buildings or improvements represent such liquidation. The exclusion applies only with respect to the income realized by the lessor upon the termination of the lease and has no application to income, if any, in the form of rent, which may be derived by a lessor during the period of the lease and attributable to buildings erected or other improvements made by the lessee. It has no application to income which

may be realized by the lessor upon the termination of the lease but not attributable to the value of such buildings or improvements. Neither does it apply to income derived by the lessor subsequent to the termination of the lease incident to the ownership of such buildings or improvements.

(b) The provisions of this section may be illustrated by the following example:

Example. The A Corporation leased in 1945 for a period of 50 years unimproved real property to the B Corporation under a lease providing that the B Corporation erect on the leased premises an office building costing $500,000, in addition to paying the A Corporation a lease rental of $10,000 per annum beginning on the date of completion of the improvements, the sum of $100,000 being placed in escrow for the payment of the rental. The building was completed on January 1, 1950. The lease provided that all improvements made by the lessee on the leased property would become the absolute property of the A Corporation on the termination of the lease by forfeiture or otherwise and that the lessor would become entitled on such termination to the remainder of the sum, if any, remaining in the escrow fund. The B Corporation forfeited its lease on January 1, 1955, when the improvements had a value of $100,000. Under the provisions of section 109, the $100,000 is excluded from gross income. The amount of $50,000 representing the remainder in the escrow fund is forfeited to the A Corporation and is included in the gross income of that taxpayer. As to the basis of the property in the hands of the A Corporation, see § 1.1019–1.

[T.D. 6500, 25 FR 11402, Nov. 26, 1960]

§ 1.117–1 Exclusion of amounts received as a scholarship or fellowship grant.

(a) **In general.** Any amount received by an individual as a scholarship at an educational institution or as a fellowship grant, including the value of contributed services and accommodations, shall be excluded from the gross income of the recipient, subject to the limitations set forth in section 117(b) and § 1.117–2. The exclusion from gross income of an amount which is a scholarship or fellowship grant is controlled solely by section 117. Accordingly, to the extent that a scholarship or a fellowship grant exceeds the limitations of section 117(b) and § 1.117–2, it is includible in the gross income of the recipient notwithstanding the provisions of section 102 relating to exclusion from gross income of gifts, or section 74(b) relating to exclusion from gross income of certain prizes and awards. For definitions, see § 1.117–3.

(b) **Exclusion of amounts received to cover expenses.** (1) Subject to the limitations provided in subparagraph (2) of this paragraph, any amount received by an individual to cover expenses for travel (including meals and lodging while traveling and an allowance for travel of the individual's family), research, clerical help, or equipment is excludable from gross income provided that such expenses are incident to a scholarship or fellowship grant which is excludable from gross income under section 117(a)(1). If, however, only a portion of a scholarship or fellowship grant is excludable from gross income under section 117(a)(1) because of the part-time employment limitation contained in section 117(b)(1) or because of the expiration of the 36-month period described in section 117(b)(2)(B), only the amount received to cover expenses incident to such excludable portion is excludable from gross income. The requirement that these expenses be incident to the scholarship or the fellowship grant means that the expenses of travel, research, clerical help, or equipment must be incurred by the individual in order to effectuate the purpose for which the scholarship or the fellowship grant was awarded.

(2)(i) In the case of a scholarship or fellowship grant which is awarded after July 28, 1956, the exclusion provided under subparagraph (1) of this paragraph is not applicable unless the amount received by the individual is specifically designated to cover expenses for travel, research, clerical help, or equipment.

* * *

(iii) The exclusion provided under subparagraph (1) of this paragraph is applicable only to the extent that the amount received for travel, research, clerical help, or equipment is actually expended for such expenses by the recipient during the term of the scholarship or fellowship grant and within a reasonable time before and after such term.

(3) The portion of any amount received to cover the expenses described in subparagraph (1) of this paragraph which is not actually expended for such expenses within the exclusion period described in subparagraph (2) of this paragraph shall, if not returned to the grantor within this period, be included in the gross income of the recipient for the taxable year in which such exclusion period expires.

[T.D. 6500, 25 FR 11402, Nov. 26, 1960]

§ 1.117-2 Limitations.

(a) Individuals who are candidates for degrees—(1) In general. Under the limitations provided by section 117(b)(1) in the case of an individual who is a candidate for a degree at an educational institution, the exclusion from gross income shall not apply (except as otherwise provided in subparagraph (2) of this paragraph) to that portion of any amount received as payment for teaching, research, or other services in the nature of part-time employment required as a condition to receiving the scholarship or fellowship grant. Payments for such part-time employment shall be included in the gross income of the recipient in an amount determined by reference to the rate of compensation ordinarily paid for similar services performed by an individual who is not the recipient of a scholarship or a fellowship grant. A typical example of employment under this subparagraph is the case of an individual who is required, as a condition to receiving the scholarship or the fellowship grant, to perform part-time teaching services. A requirement that the individual shall furnish periodic reports to the grantor of the scholarship or the fellowship grant for the purpose of keeping the grantor informed as to the general progress of the individual shall not be deemed to constitute the performance of services in the nature of part-time employment.

(2) Exception. If teaching, research, or other services are required of all candidates (whether or not recipients of scholarships or fellowship grants) for a particular degree as a condition to receiving the degree, such teaching, research, or other services on the part of the recipient of a scholarship or fellowship grant who is a candidate for such degree shall not be regarded as part-time employment within the meaning of this paragraph. Thus, if all candidates for a particular education degree are required, as part of their regular course of study or curriculum, to perform part-time practice teaching services, such services are not to be regarded as part-time employment within the meaning of this paragraph.

(b) Individuals who are not candidates for degrees—(1) Conditions for exclusion. In the case of an individual who is not a candidate for a degree at an educational institution, the exclusion from gross income of an amount received as a scholarship or a fellowship grant shall apply (to the extent provided in subparagraph (2) of this paragraph) only if the grantor of the scholarship or fellowship grant is—

(i) An organization described in section 501(c)(3) which is exempt from tax under section 501(a),

(ii) The United States or an instrumentality or agency thereof, or a State, a territory, or a possession of the United States, or any political subdivision thereof, or the District of Columbia, or

(iii) For taxable years beginning after December 31, 1961, a foreign government, an international organization, or a binational or multinational educational and cultural foundation or commission created or continued pursuant to section 103 of the Mutual Educational and Cultural Exchange Act of 1961 (22 U.S.C. 2453).

(2) Extent of exclusion. **(i)** In the case of an individual who is not a candidate for a degree, the amount received as a scholarship or a fellowship grant which is excludable from gross income under section 117(a)(1) shall not exceed an amount equal to $300 times the number of months for which the recipient received amounts under the scholarship or fellowship grant during the taxable year. In determining the number of months during the period for which the recipient received amounts under a scholarship or fellowship grant, computation shall be made on the basis of whole calendar months. A whole calendar month means a period of time terminating with the day of the succeeding month numerically corresponding to the day of the month of its beginning, less one, except that if there be no corresponding day of the succeeding month the period terminates with the last day of the succeeding month. For purposes of this computation a fractional part of a calendar month consisting of a period of time including 15 days or more shall be considered to be a whole calendar month and a fractional part of a calendar month consisting of a period of time including 14 days or less shall be disregarded. For example, if an individual receives a fellowship grant on September 13 which is to expire on June 12 of the following year, the grant shall be considered to have extended for a period of 9 months. If in the preceding example the grant expired on June 27, instead of June 12, the grant shall be considered to have extended for a period of 10 months.

(ii) No exclusion shall be allowed under section 117(a)(1) to an individual who is not a candidate for a degree after the recipient has, as an individual who is not a candidate for a degree, been entitled to an exclusion under that section for a period of 36 months. This limitation applies if the individual has received any amount which was either excluded or excludable from his gross income under section 117(a)(1) for any prior 36 months, whether or not consecutive. For example, if the individual

received a fellowship grant of $7,200 for 3 years (which he elected to receive in 36 monthly installments of $200), his exclusion period would be exhausted even though he did not in any of the 36 months make use of the maximum exclusion. Accordingly, such individual would be entitled to no further exclusion from gross income with respect to any additional grants which he may receive as an individual who is not a candidate for a degree.

(iii) If an individual who is not a candidate for a degree receives amounts from more than one scholarship or fellowship grant during the taxable year, the total amounts received in the taxable year shall be aggregated for the purpose of computing the amount which may be excludable from gross income for such taxable year. If amounts are received from more than one scholarship or fellowship grant during the same month or months within the taxable year, such month or months shall be counted only once for the purpose of determining the number of months for which the individual received such amounts under the scholarships or fellowship grants during the taxable year. For example, if an individual receives a fellowship grant from one source for the months of January to June of the taxable year and also receives a fellowship grant from another source for the months of March through December of the same taxable year, he shall be considered to have received amounts for 12 months of the taxable year. See example (4) in subparagraph (3) of this paragraph for further illustration.

(3) Examples. The application of this paragraph may be further illustrated by the following examples, it being assumed that in each example the grantor is a grantor who is described in section 117(b)(2)(A) and subparagraph (1) of this paragraph:

Example (1). B, an individual who files his return on the calendar year basis, is awarded a post-doctorate fellowship grant in March 1955. The grant is to commence on September 1, 1955, and is to end on May 31, 1956, so that it will extend over a period of 9 months. The amount of the fellowship grant is $4,500 and B receives this amount in monthly installments of $500 on the first day of each month commencing September 1, 1955. During the taxable year 1955, B receives a total of $2,000 with respect to the 4-month period September through December, inclusive. He may exclude $1,200 from gross income in the taxable year 1955 ($300×4) and must include the remaining $800 in gross income for that year. For the year 1956, he will exclude $1,500 ($300×5) from gross income with respect to the $2,500 which he receives in that year and must include in gross income $1,000.

Example (2). Assume the same facts as in example (1) except that B receives the full amount of the grant ($4,500) on September 1, 1955. Since the amount received in the taxable year 1955 is for the full term of the fellowship grant (9 months), B may exclude $2,700 ($300×9) from gross income for the taxable year 1955. The remaining $1,800 must be included in gross income for that year.

Example (3). C, an individual who files his return on the calendar year basis, is awarded a post-doctorate fellowship grant in March 1955. The amount of the grant is $4,500 for a period commencing on September 1, 1955, and ending 24 months thereafter. C receives the full amount of the grant on September 1, 1955. C may exclude from gross income for the taxable year 1955, the full amount of the grant ($4,500) since this amount does not exceed an amount equal to $300 times the number of months (24) for which he received the amount of the grant during that taxable year.

* * *

[T.D. 6500, 25 FR 11402, Nov. 26, 1960, as amended by T.D. 6782, 29 FR 18355, Dec. 24, 1964]

§ 1.117-3 Definitions.

(a) Scholarship. A scholarship generally means an amount paid or allowed to, or for the benefit of, a student, whether an undergraduate or a graduate, to aid such individual in pursuing his studies. The term includes the value of contributed services and accommodations (see paragraph (d) of this section) and the amount of tuition, matriculation, and other fees which are furnished or remitted to a student to aid him in pursuing his studies. The term also includes any amount received in the nature of a family allowance as a part of a scholarship. However, the term does not include any amount provided by an individual to aid a relative, friend, or other individual in pursuing his studies where the grantor is motivated by family or philanthropic considerations. If an educational institution maintains or participates in a plan whereby the tuition of a child of a faculty member of such institution is remitted by any other participating educational institution attended by such child, the amount of the tuition so remitted shall be considered to be an amount received as a scholarship.

(b) Educational organization. For definition of "educational organization" paragraphs (a) and (b) of section 117 adopt the definition of that term which is prescribed in section 151(e)(4). Accordingly, for purposes of section 117 the term "educational organization" means only an educational organization which normally maintains a regular faculty and curriculum and normally has a regularly organized body of students in attendance at the

place where its educational activities are carried on. See section 151(e)(4) and regulations thereunder.

(c) Fellowship grant. A fellowship grant generally means an amount paid or allowed to, or for the benefit of, an individual to aid him in the pursuit of study or research. The term includes the value of contributed services and accommodations (see paragraph (d) of this section) and the amount of tuition, matriculation, and other fees which are furnished or remitted to an individual to aid him in the pursuit of study or research. The term also includes any amount received in the nature of a family allowance as a part of a fellowship grant. However, the term does not include any amount provided by an individual to aid a relative, friend, or other individual in the pursuit of study or research where the grantor is motivated by family or philanthropic considerations.

(d) Contributed services and accommodations. The term "contributed services and accommodations" means such services and accommodations as room, board, laundry service, and similar services or accommodations which are received by an individual as a part of a scholarship or fellowship grant.

(e) Candidate for a degree. The term "candidate for a degree" means an individual, whether an undergraduate or a graduate, who is pursuing studies or conducting research to meet the requirements for an academic or professional degree conferred by colleges or universities. It is not essential that such study or research be pursued or conducted at an educational institution which confers such degrees if the purpose thereof is to meet the requirements for a degree of a college or university which does confer such degrees. A student who receives a scholarship for study at a secondary school or other educational institution is considered to be a "candidate for a degree."

[T.D. 6500, 25 FR 11402, Nov. 26, 1960, as amended by T.D. 8032, 50 FR 27232, July 2, 1985]

§ 1.117-4 Items not considered as scholarships or fellowship grants.

The following payments or allowances shall not be considered to be amounts received as a scholarship or a fellowship grant for the purpose of section 117:

* * *

(c) Amounts paid as compensation for services or primarily for the benefit of the grantor. (1) Except as provided in paragraph (a) of § 1.117–2 and § 1.117–5, any amount paid or allowed to, or on behalf of, an individual to enable him to pursue studies or research, if such amount represents either compensation for past, present, or future employment services or represents payment for services which are subject to the direction or supervision of the grantor.

(2) Any amount paid or allowed to, or on behalf of, an individual to enable him to pursue studies or research primarily for the benefit of the grantor.

However, amounts paid or allowed to, or on behalf of, an individual to enable him to pursue studies or research are considered to be amounts received as a scholarship or fellowship grant for the purpose of section 117 if the primary purpose of the studies or research is to further the education and training of the recipient in his individual capacity and the amount provided by the grantor for such purpose does not represent compensation or payment for the services described in subparagraph (1) of this paragraph. Neither the fact that the recipient is required to furnish reports of his progress to the grantor, nor the fact that the results of his studies or research may be of some incidental benefits to the grantor shall, of itself, be considered to destroy the essential character of such amount as a scholarship or fellowship grant.

[T.D. 6500, 25 FR 11402, Nov. 26, 1960, as amended by T.D. 8032, 50 FR 27232, July 2, 1985]

§ 1.118–1 Contributions to the capital of a corporation.

In the case of a corporation, section 118 provides an exclusion from gross income with respect to any contribution of money or property to the capital of the taxpayer. Thus, if a corporation requires additional funds for conducting its business and obtains such funds through voluntary pro rata payments by its shareholders, the amounts so received being credited to its surplus account or to a special account, such amounts do not constitute income, although there is no increase in the outstanding shares of stock of the corporation. In such a case the payments are in the nature of assessments upon, and represent an additional price paid for, the shares of stock held by the individual shareholders, and will be treated as an addition to and as a part of the operating capital of the company. Section 118 also applies to contributions to capital made by persons other than shareholders. For example, the exclusion applies to the value of land or other property contributed to a corporation by a governmental unit or by a civic group for the purpose of inducing the corporation to locate its business in a particular community, or for the purpose of enabling the corporation to expand its operating facilities. However, the exclusion does not apply to any money or property transferred to the corporation in consideration for goods or services rendered, or to subsidies paid for the purpose of inducing the taxpayer to limit production. See section 362 for the basis of property acquired by a corporation through a contribution to its capital by its stockholders or by nonstockholders.

[T.D. 6500, 25 FR 11402, Nov. 26, 1960]

§ 1.119–1 Meals and lodging furnished for the convenience of the employer.

(a) Meals—(1) In general. The value of meals furnished to an employee by his employer shall be excluded from the employee's gross income if two tests are met: (i) The meals are furnished on the business premises of the employer, and (ii) the meals are furnished for the convenience of the employer. The question of whether meals are furnished for the convenience of the employer is one of fact to be determined by analysis of all the facts and circumstances in each case. If the tests described in subdivisions (i) and (ii) of this subparagraph are met, the exclusion shall apply irrespective of whether under an employment contract or a statute fixing the terms of employment such meals are furnished as compensation.

(2) Meals furnished without a charge. (i) Meals furnished by an employer without charge to the employee will be regarded as furnished for the convenience of the employer if such meals are furnished for a substantial noncompensatory business reason of the employer. If an employer furnishes meals as a means of providing additional compensation to his employee (and not for a substantial noncompensatory business reason of the employer), the meals so furnished will not be regarded as furnished for the convenience of the employer. Conversely, if the employer furnishes meals to his employee for a substantial noncompensatory business reason, the meals so furnished will be regarded as furnished for the convenience of the employer, even though such meals are also furnished for a compensatory reason. In determining the reason of an employer for furnishing meals, the mere declaration that meals are furnished for a noncompensatory business reason is not sufficient to prove that meals are furnished for the convenience of the employer, but such determination will be based upon an examination of all the surrounding facts and circumstances. In subdivision (ii) of this subparagraph, there are set forth some of the substantial noncompensatory business reasons which occur frequently and which justify the conclusion that meals furnished for such a reason are furnished for the convenience of the employer. In subdivision (iii) of this subparagraph, there are set forth some of the business reasons which are considered to be compensatory and which, in the absence of a substantial noncompensatory business reason, justify the conclusion that meals furnished for such a reason are not furnished for the convenience of the employer. Generally, meals furnished before or after the working hours of the employee will not be regarded as furnished for the convenience of the employer, but see subdivision (ii)(d) and (f) of this subparagraph for some exceptions to this general rule. Meals furnished on nonworking days do not qualify for the exclusion under section 119. If the employee is required to occupy living quarters on the business premises of his employer as a condition of his employment (as defined in paragraph (b) of this section), the exclusion applies to the value of any meal furnished without charge to the employee on such premises.

(ii)(a) Meals will be regarded as furnished for a substantial noncompensatory business reason of the employer when the meals are furnished to the employee during his working hours to have the employee available for emergency call during his meal period. In order to demonstrate that meals are furnished to the employee to have the employee available for emergency call during the meal period, it must be shown that emergencies have actually occurred, or can reasonably be expected to occur, in the employer's business which have resulted, or will result, in the employer calling on the employee to perform his job during his meal period.

(b) Meals will be regarded as furnished for a substantial noncompensatory business reason of the employer when the meals are furnished to the employee during his working hours because the employer's business is such that the employee must be restricted to a short meal period, such as 30 or 45 minutes, and because the employee could not be expected to eat elsewhere in such a short

meal period. For example, meals may qualify under this subdivision when the employer is engaged in a business in which the peak work load occurs during the normal lunch hours. However, meals cannot qualify under this subdivision (b) when the reason for restricting the time of the meal period is so that the employee can be let off earlier in the day.

(c) Meals will be regarded as furnished for a substantial noncompensatory business reason of the employer when the meals are furnished to the employee during his working hours because the employee could not otherwise secure proper meals within a reasonable meal period. For example, meals may qualify under this subdivision (c) when there are insufficient eating facilities in the vicinity of the employer's premises.

(d) A meal furnished to a restaurant employee or other food service employee for each meal period in which the employee works will be regarded as furnished for a substantial noncompensatory business reason of the employer, irrespective of whether the meal is furnished during, immediately before, or immediately after the working hours of the employee.

(e) If the employer furnishes meals to employees at a place of business and the reason for furnishing the meals to each of substantially all of the employees who are furnished the meals is a substantial noncompensatory business reason of the employer, the meals furnished to each other employee will also be regarded as furnished for a substantial noncompensatory business reason of the employer.

(f) If an employer would have furnished a meal to an employee during his working hours for a substantial noncompensatory business reason, a meal furnished to such an employee immediately after his working hours because his duties prevented him from obtaining a meal during his working hours will be regarded as furnished for a substantial noncompensatory business reason.

(iii) Meals will be regarded as furnished for a compensatory business reason of the employer when the meals are furnished to the employee to promote the morale or goodwill of the employee, or to attract prospective employees.

* * *

(b) **Lodging.** The value of lodging furnished to an employee by the employer shall be excluded from the employee's gross income if three tests are met:

(1) The lodging is furnished on the business premises of the employer,

(2) The lodging is furnished for the convenience of the employer, and

(3) The employee is required to accept such lodging as a condition of his employment.

The requirement of subparagraph (3) of this paragraph that the employee is required to accept such lodging as a condition of his employment means that he be required to accept the lodging in order to enable him properly to perform the duties of his employment. Lodging will be regarded as furnished to enable the employee properly to perform the duties of his employment when, for example, the lodging is furnished because the employee is required to be available for duty at all times or because the employee could not perform the services required of him unless he is furnished such lodging. If the tests described in subparagraphs (1), (2), and (3) of this paragraph are met, the exclusion shall apply irrespective of whether a charge is made, or whether, under an employment contract or statute fixing the terms of employment, such lodging is furnished as compensation. If the employer furnishes the employee lodging for which the employee is charged an unvarying amount irrespective of whether he accepts the lodging, the amount of the charge made by the employer for such lodging is not, as such, part of the compensation includible in the gross income of the employee; whether the value of the lodging is excludable from gross income under section 119 is determined by applying the other rules of this paragraph. If the tests described in subparagraph (1), (2), and (3) of this paragraph are not met, the employee shall include in gross income the value of the lodging regardless of whether it exceeds or is less than the amount charged. In the absence of evidence to the contrary, the value of the lodging may be deemed to be equal to the amount charged.

(c) **Business premises of the employer.**—(1) **In general.** For purposes of this section, the term "business premises of the employer" generally means the place of employment of the employee. For example, meals and lodging furnished in the employer's home to a domestic servant would constitute meals and lodging furnished on the business premises of the employer. Similarly, meals furnished to cowhands while herding their employer's cattle on leased land would be regarded as furnished on the business premises of the employer.

* * *

(e) **Rules.** The exclusion provided by section 119 applies only to meals and lodging furnished in kind by an employer to his employee. If the employee has an option to receive additional compensation in lieu of meals or lodging in kind, the value of such meals and lodging is not excluded from gross income. However, the mere fact that an employee, at his option, may decline to accept meals tendered in kind will not of itself require inclusion of the value thereof in gross income. Cash allowances for meals or lodging received by an employee are includible in gross income to the extent that such allowances constitute compensation.

(f) **Examples.** The provisions of section 119 may be illustrated by the following examples:

Example (1). A waitress who works from 7 a.m. to 4 p.m. is furnished without charge two meals a work day. The employer encourages the waitress to have her breakfast on his business premises before starting work, but does not require her to have breakfast there. She is required, however, to have her lunch on such premises. Since the waitress is a food service employee and works during the normal breakfast and lunch periods, the waitress is permitted to exclude from her gross income both the value of the breakfast and the value of the lunch.

Example (2). The waitress in example (1) is allowed to have meals on the employer's premises without charge on her days off. The waitress is not permitted to exclude the value of such meals from her gross income.

Example (3). A bank teller who works from 9 a.m. to 5 p.m. is furnished his lunch without charge in a cafeteria which the bank maintains on its premises. The bank furnishes the teller such meals in order to limit his lunch period to 30 minutes since the bank's peak work load occurs during the normal lunch period. If the teller had to obtain his lunch elsewhere, it would take him considerably longer than 30 minutes for lunch, and the bank strictly enforces the 30-minute time limit. The bank teller may exclude from his gross income the value of such meals obtained in the bank cafeteria.

Example (4). Assume the same facts as in example (3), except that the bank charges the bank teller an unvarying rate per meal regardless of whether he eats in the cafeteria. The bank teller is not required to include in gross income such flat amount charged as part of his compensation, and he is entitled to exclude from his gross income the value of the meals he receives for such flat charge.

Example (5). A Civil Service employee of a State is employed at an institution and is required by his employer to be available for duty at all times. The employer furnishes the employee with meals and lodging at the institution without charge. Under the applicable State statute, his meals and lodging are regarded as part of the employee's compensation. The employee would nevertheless be entitled to exclude the value of such meals and lodging from his gross income.

Example (6). An employee of an institution is given the choice of residing at the institution free of charge, or of residing elsewhere and receiving a cash allowance in addition to his regular salary. If he elects to reside at the institution, the value to the employee of the lodging furnished by the employer will be includible in the employee's gross income because his residence at the institution is not required in order for him to perform properly the duties of his employment.

Example (7). A construction worker is employed at a construction project at a remote job site in Alaska. Due to the inaccessibility of facilities for the employees who are working at the job site to obtain food and lodging and the prevailing weather conditions, the employer is required to furnish meals and lodging to the employee at the camp site in order to carry on the construction project. The employee is required to pay $40 a week for the meals and lodging. The weekly charge of $40 is not, as such, part of the compensation includible in the gross income of the employee, and under paragraphs (a) and (b) of this section the value of the meals and lodging is excludable from his gross income.

Example (8). A manufacturing company provides a cafeteria on its premises at which its employees can purchase their lunch. There is no other eating facility located near the company's premises, but the employee can furnish his own meal by bringing his lunch. The amount of compensation which any employee is required to include in gross income is not reduced by the amount charged for the meals, and the meals are not considered to be furnished for the convenience of the employer.

Example (9). A hospital maintains a cafeteria on its premises where all of its 230 employees may obtain a meal during their working hours. No charge is made for these meals. The hospital furnishes such meals in order to have each of 210 of the employees available for any emergencies that may occur, and it is shown that each such employee is at times called upon to perform services during his meal period. Although the hospital does not require such employees to remain on the premises during meal periods, they rarely leave the hospital during their meal period. Since the hospital furnishes meals to each of substantially all of its employees in order to have each of them available for emergency call during his meal period, all of the hospital employees who obtain their meals in the hospital cafeteria may exclude from their gross income the value of such meals.

[T.D. 6500, 25 FR 11402, Nov. 26, 1960; T.D. 6745, 29 FR 9380, July 9, 1964; T.D. 8006, 50 FR 2964, Jan. 23, 1985]

§ 1.121-1 Gain from sale or exchange of residence of individual who has attained age 55.

(a) General rule. Section 121(a) provides that a taxpayer may, under certain circumstances, elect to exclude from gross income gain realized on the sale or exchange of property which was the taxpayer's principal residence. Subject to the other provisions of section 121 and the regulations thereunder, the election may be made only if—

(1) The taxpayer attained the age of 55 before the date of the sale or exchange of the taxpayer's principal residence, and

(2) Except as provided in paragraph (b) of this section, during the 5-year period ending on the date of the sale or exchange of the property the taxpayer owned and used the property as the taxpayer's principal residence for periods aggregating 3 years or more.

* * *

(c) Ownership and use. The requirements of ownership and use for periods aggregating 3 years or more may be satisfied by establishing ownership and use for 36 full months (or 60 full months if the transitional rule is elected) or for 1,095 days (365×3) (or 1,825 days if the transitional rule is elected). In establishing whether a taxpayer has satisfied the requirement of three years of use, short temporary absences such as for vacation or other seasonal absence (although accompanied with rental of the residence) are counted as periods of use.

(d) Examples. The provisions of paragraph (a) are illustrated by the following examples:

Example (1). Taxpayer A owned and used his house as his principal residence since 1966. On January 1, 1980, when he is over 55, A retires and moves to another state with his wife. A leases his house from then until September 30, 1981, when he sells it. A may make an election under section 121(a) with respect to any gain on such sale since he has owned and used the house as his principal residence for 3 years out of the 5 years preceding the sale.

Example (2). Taxpayer B purchased his house in 1971 when he was 65 and lived there with his wife. On July 1, 1977, he moved out and leased the house to a tenant. On September 15, 1979, he sold the house. Although he does not meet the use requirements of section 1.121–1(a), he may elect to use the transitional rule in section 1.121–1(b), since the sale was made before July 26, 1981. Because he owned and used the house as his principal residence for 5 out of the 8 years preceding the sale, under the transitional rule he may elect the section 121 exclusion.

Example (3). Taxpayer C lived with his son and daughter-in-law in a house owned by his son from 1973 through 1979. On January 1, 1980, he purchased this house and on July 31, 1982, he sold it. Although B used the property as his principal residence for more than 3 years, he is not entitled to make an election under section 121(a) in respect of such sale since he did not own the residence for a period aggregating 3 years during the 5 year period ending on the date of the sale.

Example (4). Taxpayer D, a college professor, purchased and moved into a house on January 1, 1980. He used the house as his principal residence continuously to February 1, 1982, on which date he went abroad for a 1-year sabbatical leave. During a portion of the period of leave the property was unoccupied and it was leased during the balance of the period. On March 1, 1983, 1 month after returning from such leave, he sold the house. Since his leave is not considered to be a short temporary absence for purposes of section 121(a), the period of such leave may not be included in determining whether D used the house as his principal residence for periods aggregating 3 years during the 5 year period ending on the date of the sale. Thus, D is not entitled to make an election under section 121(a) since he did not use the residence for the requisite period.

Example (5). Assume the same facts as in example (1) except that during the three summers from 1977 through 1979, A left his residence for a 2-month vacation each year. Although, in the 5 year period preceding the date of sale, the total time spent away from his residence on such vacations (6 months) plus the time spent away from such residence from January 1, 1980, to September 30, 1981 (21 months) exceeds 2 years, he may make an election under section 121(a) since the 2-month vacations are counted as periods of use in determining whether A used the residence for the requisite period.

[T.D. 6856, 30 FR 13316, Oct. 20, 1965, as amended by T.D. 7614, 44 FR 24839, April 27, 1979]

§ 1.121–2 Limitations.

* * *

(b) Application to only one sale or exchange. (1) Except as provided in paragraph (c), a taxpayer may not make an election to exclude from gross income gain from the sale or exchange of a principal residence if there is in effect at the time the taxpayer wishes to make such election—

(i) An election made by the taxpayer, under section 121(a), in respect of any other sale or exchange of a residence, or

(ii) An election made by the taxpayer's spouse (such marital status to be determined at the time of the sale or exchange by the taxpayer, see paragraph (f) of § 1.121–5) under the provisions of section 121(a) in respect of any other sale or exchange of a residence (without regard to whether at the time of such sale or exchange such spouse was married to the taxpayer).

If the taxpayer and his spouse, before their marriage each owned and used a separate residence and if (after their marriage) both residences are sold, whether or not in a single transaction, an election under section 121(a) may be made with respect to a sale of either residence (but not with respect to both residences) if, at the time of sale, the age, ownership, and use requirements are met.

(2) The provisions of this paragraph are illustrated by the following examples:

Example (1). While A and B are married, A sells his separately owned residence and makes an election under section 121(a) in respect of such sale. Pursuant to the requirement of section 121(c), B joins in such election. Subsequently, A and B are divorced and B married C. While B and C are married, C sells his residence. C is not entitled to make an election under section 121(a) since an election by B, his spouse, is in effect. It does not matter that B obtained no personal benefit from her election.

* * *

[T.D. 6856, 30 FR 13317, Oct. 20, 1965, as amended by T.D. 7614, 44 FR 24840, April 27, 1979]

§ 1.121–3 Definitions.

(a) Principal residence. The term "principal residence" has the same meaning as in section 1034 (relating to sale or exchange of residence) and the regulations thereunder (see paragraph (c)(3) of § 1.1034–1).

(b) Sale or exchange. A "sale or exchange" of a residence includes the destruction, theft, seizure, requisition, or condemnation of such residence.

(c) Gain realized. The term "gain realized" has the same meaning as in paragraph (b)(5) of § 1.1034–1 (determined without regard to section 121(d)(7) and paragraph (g) of § 1.121–5).

[T.D. 6856, 30 FR 13317, Oct. 20, 1965, as amended by T.D. 7614, 44 FR 24840, April 27, 1979]

§ 1.121–4 Election.

(a) General rule. A taxpayer may make an election under section 121(a) in respect of a particular sale (or may revoke any such election) at any time before the expiration of the period for making a claim for credit or refund of Federal income tax for the taxable year in which the sale or exchange occurred. A taxpayer who is married at the time of the sale or exchange—

(1) May not make an election under section 121(a) unless his spouse (at the time of the sale or exchange) joins him in such election, and

(2) May not revoke an election previously made by him unless his spouse (at the time of the sale or exchange) joins him in the revocation.

If the taxpayer's spouse dies after the sale or exchange but before the expiration of the time for making an election under this section (and an election was not made by the husband and wife), the deceased spouse's personal representative (administrator or executor, etc.) must join with the taxpayer in making an election. For purposes of making an election under section 121(a), if no personal representative of the deceased spouse has been appointed at or before the time of making the election, then the surviving spouse shall be considered the personal representative of such deceased spouse. Any election previously made by the taxpayer may be revoked only if the personal representative of the taxpayer's deceased spouse joins in such revocation.

(b) Manner of making election. The election under section 121(a) shall be made in a statement signed by the taxpayer and (where required) by his spouse and attached to the taxpayer's income tax return, when filed, for the taxable year during which the sale or exchange of his residence occurs. (See Form 2119 and the accompanying instructions). The statement shall indicate that the taxpayer elects to exclude from his gross income for such year so much of the gain realized on such sale or exchange as may be excluded under section 121. The statement shall also show—

(1) The adjusted basis of the residence as of the date of disposition;

(2) The date of its acquisition;

(3) The date of its disposition;

(4) The names and social security numbers of the owners of the residence as of the date of sale, the form of such ownership, and the age and marital status (as determined under paragraph (f) of § 1.121–5) of such owner or owners at the time of the sale;

(5) The duration of any absences (other than vacation or other seasonal absence) by such owner or owners during the 5 years (8 years under the transitional rule) preceding the sale; and

(6) Whether any such owner or owners have previously made an election under section 121(a), the date of such election, the taxable year with respect to which such election was made, the district director with whom such election was filed, and, if such election has been revoked, the date of such revocation.

* * *

[T.D. 6856, 30 FR 13318, Oct. 20, 1965, as amended by T.D. 7614, 44 FR 24840, April 27, 1979; T.D. 7927, 48 FR 55849, Dec. 16, 1983]

§ 1.123–1   Exclusion of insurance proceeds for reimbursement of certain living expenses.

(a) In general. (1) Gross income does not include insurance proceeds received by an individual on or after January 1, 1969, pursuant to the terms of an insurance contract for indemnification of the temporary increase in living expenses resulting from the loss of use or occupancy of his principal residence, or a part thereof, due to damage or destruction by fire, storm, or other casualty. The term "other casualty" has the same meaning assigned to such term under section 165(c)(3). The exclusion also applies in the case of an individual who is denied access to his principal residence by governmental authorities because of the occurrence (or threat of occurrence) of such a casualty. The amount excludable under this section is subject to the limitation set forth in paragraph (b) of this section.

(2) This exclusion applies to amounts received as reimbursement or compensation for the reasonable and necessary increase in living expenses incurred by the insured and members of his household to maintain their customary standard of living during the loss period.

(3) This exclusion does not apply to an insurance recovery for the loss of rental income. Nor does the exclusion apply to any insurance recovery which compensates for the loss of, or damage to, real or personal property. See section 165(c)(3) relating to casualty losses; section 1231 relating to gain on an involuntary conversion of a capital asset held for more than 1 year (6 months for taxable years beginning before 1977; 9 months for taxable years beginning in 1977); and section 1033 relating to recognition of gain on an involuntary conversion. In the case of property used by an insured partially as a principal residence and partially for other purposes, the exclusion does not apply to the amount of insurance proceeds which compensates for the portion of increased expenses attributable to the nonresidential use of temporary replacement property during the loss period. In the case of denial of access to a principal residence by governmental authority, the exclusion provided by this section does not apply to an insurance recovery received by an individual as reimbursement for living expenses incurred by reason of a governmental condemnation or order not related to a casualty or the threat of a casualty.

(4)(i) Subject to the limitation set forth in paragraph (b), the amount excludable is the amount which is identified by the insurer as being paid exclusively for increased living expenses resulting from the loss of use or occupancy of the principal residence and pursuant to the terms of the insurance contract.

(ii) When a lump-sum insurance settlement includes, but does not specifically identify, compensation for property damage, loss of rental income, and increased living expenses, the amount of such settlement allocable to living expenses shall, in the case of uncontested claims, be that portion of the settlement which bears the same ratio to the total recovery as the amount of claimed increased living expense bears to the total amount of claimed losses and expenses, to the extent not in excess of the coverage limitations specified in the contract for such losses and expenses.

(iii) In the case of a lump-sum settlement involving contested claims, the insured shall establish the amount reasonably allocable to increased living expenses, consistent with the terms of the contract and other facts of the particular case.

(iv) In no event may the amount of a lump-sum settlement which is allocable to increased living expenses exceed the coverage limitation specified in the contract for increased living expenses. Where, however, a coverage limitation is applicable to the total amount payable for increased living expenses and, for example, loss of rental income, the amount of an unitized settlement which is allocable to increased living expenses may not exceed the portion of the applicable coverage limitation which bears the same ratio to such limitation as the amount of increased living expenses bears to the sum of the amount of such increased living expenses and the amount, if any, of lost rental income.

(5) The portion of any insurance recovery for increased living expenses which exceeds the limitation set forth in paragraph (b) shall be included in gross income under section 61 of the Code.

(b) Limitation—(1) Amount excludable. The amount excludable under this section is limited to amounts received which are not in excess of the amount by which (i) total actual living expenses incurred by the insured and members of his household which result from the loss of use or occupancy of their residence exceed (ii) the total normal living expenses which would have been incurred during the loss period but are not incurred as a result of the loss of use or occupancy of the principal residence. Generally, the excludable amount represents such excess expenses actually incurred by reason of a casualty, or threat thereof, for renting suitable housing and for extraordinary expenses for transportation, food, utilities, and miscellaneous services during the period of repair or replacement of the damaged principal residence or denial of access by governmental authority.

(2) Actual living expenses. For purposes of this section, actual living expenses are the reasonable and necessary expenses incurred as a result of the loss of use or occupancy of the principal residence to maintain the insured and members of his household in accordance with their customary standard of living. Actual living expenses must be of such a nature as to qualify as a reimbursable expense under the terms of the applicable insurance contract without regard to monetary limitations upon coverage. Generally, actual living expenses include the cost during the loss period of temporary housing, utilities furnished at the place of temporary housing, meals obtained at restaurants which customarily would have been prepared in the residence, transportation, and other miscellaneous services. To the extent that the loss of use or occupancy of the principal residence results merely in an increase in the amount expended for items of living expenses normally incurred, such as food and transportation, only the increase in such costs shall be considered as actual living expenses in computing the limitation.

(3) Normal living expenses not incurred. Normal living expenses consist of the same categories of expenses comprising actual living expenses which would have been incurred but are not incurred as a result of the casualty or threat thereof. If the loss of use of the residence results in a decrease in the amount normally expended for a living expense item during the loss period, the item of normal living expense is considered not to have been incurred to the extent of the decrease for purposes of computing the limitation.

* * *

[T.D. 7118, 36 FR 10729, June 2, 1971, as amended by T.D. 7728, 45 FR 72650, Nov. 3, 1980]

§ 1.132–1T Exclusion from gross income of certain fringe benefits.

(a) In general. Gross income does not include fringe benefit which qualifies as a—

(1) No-additional-cost service,

(2) Qualified employee discount,

(3) Working condition fringe, or

(4) De minimis fringe.

Special rules apply with respect to certain on-premises gyms and other athletic facilities (§ 1.132–1T(e)), demonstration use of employer-provided automobiles by full-time automobile salesmen (§ 1.132–1T(n)), parking provided to an employee on or near the business premises of the employer (§ 1.132–5T(o)), and on-premises eating facilities (§ 1.132–7T).

(b) Definition of employee—(1) No-additional-cost services and qualified employee discounts. For purposes of section 132(a)(1) (relating to no-additional-cost services) and section 132 (a)(2) (relating to qualified employee discounts), the term "employee" (with respect to a line of business of an employer) means—

(i) Any individual who is currently employed by the employer in the line of business,

(ii) Any individual who was formerly employed by the employer in the line of business and who separated from service with the employer in the line of business by reason of retirement or disability, and

(iii) Any widow or widower of an individual who died while employed by the employer in the line of business or who separated from service with the employer in the line of business by reason of retirement or disability.

For purposes of this paragraph (b)(1), any partner who performs services for a partnership is considered employed by the partnership. In addition, any use by the spouse or dependent child (as defined in this paragraph (b)) of the employee will be treated as use by the employee.

(2) Working condition fringes. For purposes of section 132(a)(2) (relating to working condition fringes), the term "employee" means—

(i) Any individual who is currently employed by the employer,

(ii) Any partner who performs services for the partnership,

(iii) Any director of the employer, and

(iv) Any independent contractor who performs services for the employer. Notwithstanding anything in this paragraph (b)(2) to the contrary, any independent contractor who performs services for the employer cannot exclude the value of parking or the use of consumer goods provided pursuant to a product testing program under § 1.132–5T(n); in addition, any director of the employer cannot exclude the value of the use of consumer goods provided pursuant to a product testing program under § 1.132–5T(n).

(3) De minimis fringe. For purpose of section 132(a)(4) (relating to de minimis fringes), the term "employee" means any recipient of a fringe benefit.

(4) Dependent child. For purposes of this paragraph (b), the term "dependent child" means any son, stepson, daughter or stepdaughter of the employee who is a dependent of the employee, or both of whose parents are deceased. Any child to whom section 152(e) applies will be treated as the dependent of both parents.

(c) Special rules for employers—Effect of section 414. All employees treated as employed by a single employer under section 414(b), (c) or (m) will be treated as employed by a single employer for purposes of this section. Thus, employees of one corporation that is part of a controlled group of corporations may under certain circumstances be eligible to receive section 132 benefits from the other corporations that comprise the controlled group. However, the aggregation of employers described in this paragraph (c) does not change the other requirements for an exclusion, such as the line of business requirement. Thus, for example, if a controlled group of corporations consists of two corporations that operate in different lines of business, the corporations are not treated as operating in the same line of business even though the corporations are treated as one employer.

(d) Customers not to include employees. For purposes of section 132 and the regulations thereunder, the term "customer" means customers who are not employees. However, the preceding sentence does not apply to section 132(c)(2) (relating to the gross profit percentage for determining a qualified employee discount). Thus, an employer that provides employee discounts cannot exclude sales made to employees in determining the aggregate sales to customers.

(e) Treatment of on-premises athletic facilities—(1) In general. Gross income does not include the value of any on-premises athletic facility provided by the employer to its employees. For purposes of section 132 and this paragraph (e), the term "on-premises athletic facility" means any gym or other athletic facility (such as a pool, tennis court, or golf course)—

(i) Which is located on the premises of the employer,

(ii) Which is operated by the employer, and

(iii) Where substantially all of the use of which is, during the calendar year, by employees of the employer, their spouses, and their dependent children.

For purposes of this paragraph (e)(1)(iii), the term "dependent children" has the same meaning as the plural of the term "dependent child" in paragraph (b)(4) of this section. The exclusion of this paragraph (e) does not apply to any athletic facility if access to the facility is made available to the general public through the sale of memberships, the rental of the facility, etc.

(2) **Premises of the employer.** The athletic facility need not be located on the employer's business premises. However, the athletic facility must be located on premises of the employer. The exclusion provided in this paragraph (e) applies whether the premises are owned or leased by the employer; in addition, the exclusion is available even if the employer is not a named lessee on the lease so long as the employer pays reasonable rent. The exclusion provided in this paragraph (e) does not apply to any athletic facility that is a facility for residential use. Thus, for example, a resort with accompanying athletic facilities (such as tennis courts, pool, and gym) would not qualify for the exclusion provided in this paragraph (e).

(3) **Application of rules to membership in an athletic facility.** The exclusion provided in this paragraph (e) does not apply to any membership in an athletic facility (including health clubs or country clubs) unless the facility is owned (or leased) and operated by the employer and substantially all the use of the facility is by employees of the employer, their spouses, and their dependent children. Therefore, membership in health club or country club not meeting the rules provided in this paragraph (e) would not qualify for the exclusion.

(4) **Operation by the employer.** An employer is considered to operate the athletic facility if the employer itself operates the facility through its own employees, or if the employer contracts out to another to operate the athletic facility. For example, if an employer hires an independent contractor to operate the athletic facility for the employer's

employees, the facility is considered to be operated by the employer. In addition, if an athletic facility is operated by more than one employer, it is considered to be operated by each employer. For purposes of paragraph (e)(1)(iii) of this section, substantially all the use of a facility operated by more than one employer must be by employees of all of the employers, their spouses, and their dependent children. Where the facility is operated by more than one employer, an employer that either pays rent directly to the owner of the premises or pays rent to a named lessor of the premises is eligible for the exclusion.

(5) **Nonapplicability of nondiscrimination rules.** The nondiscrimination rules of section 132 and § 1.132–8T do not apply to on-premises athletic facilities.

(f) **Nonapplicability of section 132.** If the tax treatment of a particular fringe benefit is expressly provided for in another section of Chapter 1, section 132 and the applicable regulations (except for section 132(e) and the regulations thereunder) do not apply to such fringe benefits. For example, since section 129 provides an exclusion from gross income for amounts paid or incurred by the employer for dependent care assistance for an employee, the exclusions under section 132 and this section do not apply to the provision by an employer to an employee of dependent care assistance.

[T.D. 8004, 50 FR 753, Jan. 7, 1985, as amended by T.D. 8009, 50 FR 7042, Feb. 20, 1985, T.D. 8063, 50 FR 52297, Dec. 23, 1985]

§ 1.132–2T No-additional-cost service.

(a) **In general—(1) Definition.** Gross income does not include the value of a no-additional-cost service. The term "no-additional-cost service" means any service provided by an employer to an employee for the employee's personal use if—

(i) The service is offered for sale to customers in the ordinary course of the line of business of the employer in which the employee performs substantial services, and

(ii) The employer incurs no substantial additional cost in providing the service to the employee (including forgone revenue and excluding any amount paid by or on behalf of the employee for the service).

For rules relating to the line of business limitation, see § 1.132–4T.

(2) **Examples.** Services that are eligible for treatment as no-additional-cost services are excess capacity services such as hotel accommodations; transportation by aircraft, train, bus, subway, or cruise line; and telephone services. Services that are not eligible for treatment as no-additional-cost services are non-excess capacity services such as the facilitation by a stock brokerage firm of the purchase of stock. Employees who receive non-excess capacity services may, however, be eligible for a qualified employee discount of up to 20 percent of the value of the service provided. See § 1.132–3T.

(3) **Cash rebates.** The exclusion for a no-additional-cost service applies whether the service is provided at no charge or at a reduced price. The exclusion also applies if the benefit is provided through a partial or total cash rebate of an amount paid for the service.

(4) **Applicability of nondiscrimination rules.** The exclusion for a no-additional-cost service applies to officers, owners, and highly compensated employees only if the service is available on substantially the same terms to each member of a group of employees that is defined under a reasonable classification set up by the employer that does not discriminate in favor of officers, owners, or highly compensated employees. See § 1.132–8T.

(5) **No substantial additional cost—(i) In general.** The exclusion for a non-additional-cost service applies only if the employer does not incur substantial additional cost in providing the service to the employee. For purposes of the preceding sentence, the term "cost" includes revenue that is forgone because the service is provided to an employee rather than a nonemployee. (For purposes of determining whether any revenue is forgone, it is assumed that the employee would not have purchased the service unless it were available to the employee at the actual price charged to the employee.) Whether an employer incurs substantial additional cost must be determined without regard to any amount paid by the employee for the service. Thus, any reimbursement by the employee for the cost of providing the service does not affect the determination of whether the employer incurs substantial additional cost.

(ii) **Labor intensive services.** An employer must include the cost of labor incurred in providing services to employees when determining whether the employer has incurred substantial additional cost. An employer incurs substantial additional cost, whether or not non-labor costs are incurred, if a substantial amount of time is spent by the employer or its employees in providing the service to employees. This would be the result whether or not the time spent by the employer or its employees in providing the services would have been "idle", or if the services were provided outside normal business hours. An employer generally incurs no substantial additional cost, however, if the employee services provided are merely incidental to the primary service being provided by the employer. For example, the in-flight services of a flight attendant provided to airline employees traveling on a space-available basis are merely incidental to the primary service being provided (i.e., air transportation). In addition, the cost of in-flight meals provided to airline employees is not considered substantial in relation to the air transportation being provided.

(b) **Reciprocal agreements.** For purposes of the exclusion for a no-additional-cost service, any service provided by an employer to an employee of another employer shall be treated as provided by the employer of such employee if all of the following requirements are satisfied:

(1) The service is provided pursuant to a written reciprocal agreement between the employers under which a group of employees of each employer, all of whom perform substantial services in the same line of business, may receive no-additional-cost services from the other employer;

(2) The service provided pursuant to the agreement to the employees of both employers is the same type of service provided by the employers to customers both in the line of business in which the employees perform substantial services and the line of business in which the service is provided to customers; and

(3) Neither employer incurs substantial additional cost (including forgone revenue) in providing the service to the employees of the other employer or pursuant to the agreement. If one employer receives a substantial payment from the other employer with respect to the reciprocal agreement, the paying employer will be considered to have incurred a substantial additional cost pursuant to the agreement.

[T.D. 8063, 50 FR 52298, Dec. 23, 1985]

§ 1.132–3T **Qualified employee discount.**

(a) **In general—(1) Definition.** Gross income does not include the value of a qualified employee discount. The term "qualified employee discount" means any employee discount with respect to qualified property or services provided by an employer to an employee for the employee's personal use to the extent the discount does not exceed—

(i) The gross profit percentage of the price at which the property is offered to customers, for discounts on property, or

(ii) 20 percent of the price at which the services are offered to customers, for discounts on services.

(2) **Qualified property or services—(i) In general.** The term "qualified property or services" means any property or services that are offered for sale to customers in the ordinary course of the line of business of the employer in which the employee performs substantial services. For rules relating to the line of business limitation, see § 1.132–4T.

(ii) **Exception for certain property.** The term "qualified property" does not include real property and it does not include personal property (whether tangible or intangible) of a kind commonly held for investment. Thus, an employee may not exclude from gross income the amount of an employee discount provided on the purchase of either residential or commercial real estate, securities, commodities, or currency, whether or not the particular purchase is made for investment purposes.

(iii) **Property and services not offered in ordinary course of business.** The term "qualified property or services" does not include any property or services of a kind that is not offered for sale to customers in the ordinary course of the line of business of the employer. For example, employee discounts provided on property or services that are offered for sale only to employees and their families (such as merchandise sold at an employee store or through an employer-provided catalog service) may not be excluded from gross income.

(3) **No reciprocal agreement exception.** The exclusion for a qualified employee discount does not apply to property or services provided by another employer pursuant to a written reciprocal agreement that exists between employers to provide discounts on property and services to employees of the other employer.

(4) **Cash or third-party rebates—(i)Property or services provided without charge or at a reduced price.** The exclusion for a qualified employee discount applies whether the property or service is provided at no charge (in which case only part of the discount may be excludable as a qualified employee discount) or at a reduced price. The exclusion also applies if the benefit is provided through a partial or total cash rebate of an amount paid for the property or service.

(ii) **Property or services provided directly by the employer or indirectly through a third party.** A qualified employee discount may be provided either directly by the employer or indirectly through a third party. For example, an employee of an appliance manufacturer may receive a qualified employee discount on the manufacturer's appliances purchased at a retail store that offers such appliances for sale to customers. The employee may exclude the amount of the qualified employee discount whether the employee is provided the appliance at no charge or purchases it at a reduced price, or whether the employee receives a partial or total cash rebate from either the employer-manufacturer or the retailer. If an employee receives additional rights associated with the property that are not provided by the employee's employer to customers in the ordinary course of the line of business in which the employee performs substantial services (such as the right to return or exchange the property or special warranty rights), the employee may only receive a qualified employee discount with respect to the property and not the additional rights. Receipt of such additional rights may occur, for example, when an employee of a manufacturer purchases property manufactured by the employee's employer at a retail outlet.

(5) **Applicability of nondiscrimination rules.** The exclusion for a qualified employee discount applies to officers, owners, and highly compensated employees only if the discount is available on substantially the same terms to each member of a group of employees that is defined under a reasonable classification set up by the employer that does not discriminate in favor of officers, owners, or highly compensated employees. See § 1.132–8T.

(b) **Employee discount—(1) Definition.** The term "employee discount" means the excess of—

(i) The price at which the property or service is being offered by the employer for sale to customers, over

(ii) The price at which the property or service is provided by the employer to an employee for use by the employee. A transfer of property by an employee without consideration is considered use by the employee for purposes of this section. Thus, for example, if an employee receives a discount on property offered for sale by his employer to customers and the employee makes a gift of the property to his parent, the property will be considered to be provided for use by the employee, thus enabling the discount to be eligible for exclusion as a qualified employee discount.

(2) Price to customers—(i) Determined at time of sale. In determining the amount of an employee discount, the price at which the property or service is being offered to customers at the time of the employee's purchase is controlling. For example, assume that an employer offers a product to customers for $20 during the first six months of a calendar year but at the time the employee purchases the product at a discount, the price at which the product is being offered to customers is $25. In this case, the price from which the employee discount is measured is $25.

(ii) Quantity discount not reflected. The price referred to in paragraph (b)(2)(i) of this section cannot reflect any quantity discount unless the employee actually purchases the requisite quantity of the property or service.

(iii) Customers of employee's employer controls. In determining the amount of an employee discount, the price at which the property or service is offered to customers of the employee's employer is controlling. Thus, the price at which the property is sold to the wholesale customers of a manufacturer will generally be lower than the price at which the same property is sold to the customers of a retailer. However, see paragraph (a)(4)(ii) of this section regarding the effect of a wholesaler providing to its employees additional rights not provided to customers of the wholesaler in the ordinary course of its business.

(iv) Discounts to discrete customer or consumer groups. In determining the amount of an employee discount, if an employer offers for sale property or services at one or more discounted prices to discrete customer or consumer groups, and sales at all such discounted prices comprise at least 35 percent of the employer's gross sales for a representative period, then the price at which property or service is being offered to customers is a discounted price. The applicable discounted price is the current undiscounted price, reduced by the percentage discount at which the greatest percentage of the employer's gross sales are made for such representative period. If sales at different percentage discounts equal the same percentage of the employer's gross sales, the price at which the property or service is being provided to customers may be reduced by the average of the two group discounts. For purposes of this section, a repre-

sentative period is the taxable year of the employer immediately preceding the taxable year in which the property or service is provided to the employee at a discount. If more than one employer would be aggregated under section 414(b), (c), or (m), and all of the employers do not have the same taxable year, the employers required to be aggregated must designate the 12–month period to be used in determining gross sales for a representative period.

(v) Examples. The rules provided in this paragraph (b)(2) are illustrated by the following examples:

Example (1). Assume that a wholesale employer offers property for sale to two discrete customer groups at differing prices. Assume further that during the prior taxable year of the employer, 70 percent of the employer's gross sales are made at a 15-percent discount and 30 percent at no discount. The current undiscounted price at which the property or service is being offered by the employer for sale to customers may be reduced by the 15-percent discount.

Example (2). Assume that a retail employer offers a 20 percent discount to members of the American Bar Association, a 15 percent discount to members of the American Medical Association, and a ten percent discount to employees of the Federal Government. Assume further that during the prior taxable year of the employer, sales to American Bar Association members equal 15 percent of the employer's gross sales, sales to American Medical Association members equal 20 percent of the employer's gross sales, and sales to Federal Government employees equal 25 percent of the employer's gross sales. The current undiscounted price at which the property or service is being offered by the employer for sale to customers may be reduced by the ten percent Federal Government discount.

(3) Damaged, distressed, or returned goods. If an employee pays at least fair market value for damaged, distressed, or returned property, such employee will not have income attributable to such purchase.

(c) Gross profit percentage—(1) In general—(i) General rule. An exclusion from gross income for an employee discount on qualified property is limited to the price at which the property is being offered to customers in the ordinary course of the employer's line of business, multiplied by the employer's gross profit percentage. The term "gross profit percentage" means the excess of the aggregate sales price of the property sold by the employer to customers (including employees) over the employer's aggregate cost of the property, then divided by the aggregate sales price.

(ii) Calculation of gross profit percentage. The gross profit percentage must be calculated separately for each line of business based on the aggregate sales price and aggregate cost of property in that line of business for a representative period. For purposes of this section, a representative period is the taxable year of the employer immediately preceding the taxable year in which the discount is available. For example, if the aggregate sales of property in an employer's line of business for the prior taxable year were $800,000, and the aggregate cost of the property for the year were $600,000, the gross profit percentage would be 25 percent ($800,000 minus $600,000, then divided by $800,000). If more than one employer would be aggregated under section 414(b), (c), or (m), and all of the employers do not have the same taxable year, the employers required to be aggregated must designate the 12-month period to be used in determining the gross profit percentage. If an employee performs substantial services in more than one line of business, the gross profit percentage of the line of business in which the property is sold determines the amount of the excludable employee discount.

(iii) **Special rule for employers in their first year of existence.** An employer in its first year of existence may estimate the gross profit percentage of a line of business based on its mark-up from the cost. Alternatively, an employer in its first year of existence may determine the gross profit percentage by reference to an appropriate industry average.

(iv) **Redetermination of gross profit percentage.** If substantial changes in an employer's business indicate at any time that it is inappropriate for the prior years' gross profit percentage to be used for the current year, the employer must, within a reasonable period, redetermine the gross profit percentage for the remaining portion of the current year as if such portion of the year were the first year of the employer's existence.

(2) **Line of business.** In general, an employer must determine the gross profit percentage on the basis of all property offered to customers (including employees) in each separate line of business. An employer may instead select a classification of property that is narrower than the applicable line of business. However, such classification must be reasonable. For example, if an employer computes gross profit percentage according to the department in which products are sold, such classification is reasonable. Similarly, it is reasonable to compute gross profit percentage on the basis of the type of merchandise sold (such as high mark-up

and low mark-up classifications). It is not reasonable, however, for an employer to classify certain low mark-up products preferred by certain employees (such as officers, owners, and highly compensated employees) with high mark-up products or to classify certain high mark-up products preferred by other employees with low mark-up products.

(3) **Generally accepted accounting principles.** In general, the aggregate sales price of property must be determined in accordance with generally accepted accounting principles. An employer must compute the aggregate cost of property in the same manner in which it is computed for the employer's Federal income tax liability, pursuant to the inventory rules in section 471 and the regulations thereunder.

* * *

(e) **Excess discounts.** Unless excludable under a statutory provision excludable under a statutory provision other than section 132(a)(2), an employee discount provided on property is excludable to the extent of the gross profit percentage multiplied by the price at which the property is being offered for sale to customers. If an employee discount exceeds the gross profit percentage, the excess discount is includible in the employee's income. For example, if the discount on property is 30 percent and the employer's gross profit percentage for the period in the relevant line of business is 25 percent, then 5 percent of the price at which the property is being offered for sale to customers is includible in the employee's income. With respect to services, an employee discount of up to 20 percent may be excludable. If an employee discount exceeds 20 percent, the excess discount is includible in the employee's income.

[T.D. 8063, 50 FR 52299, Dec. 23, 1985]

§ 1.132–4T **Line of business limitation.**

(a) **In general—(1) Applicability—(i) General rule.** A no-additional-cost service or qualified employee discount provided to an employee must be for property or services that are offered for sale to customers in the ordinary course of the same line of business in which the employee receiving the property or service performs substantial services. Thus, an employee who does not perform substantial services in a particular line of business of the employer may not exclude the value of services or employee discounts received on property or services in that line of business.

(ii) Property and services sold to employees rather than customers. Since the property or services must be offered for sale to customers in the ordinary course of the same line of business in which the employee performs substantial services, the line of business limitation is not satisfied if the employer's products or services are sold to employees of the employer, rather than to customers. Thus, for example, an employer in the banking line of business is not considered in the variety store line of business if the employer establishes an employee store that offers variety store items for sale to the employer's employees.

(iii) Performance of substantial services in more than one line of business. An employee who performs services in more than one of the employer's lines of business may only exclude no-additional-cost services and qualified employee discounts in the lines of business in which the employee performs substantial services.

(iv) Performance of services that directly benefit more than one line of business—(A) In general. An employee who performs substantial services that directly benefit more than one line of business of an employer is treated as performing substantial services in all such lines of business. For example, an employee who maintains accounting records for an employer's three lines of business may receive qualified employee discounts in all three lines of business.

(B) Significantly interrelated minor line of business. The employees of a minor line of business of an employer that is significantly interrelated with a major line of business of the employer who perform substantial services that directly benefit both the major and the minor lines of business are treated as employees of both the major and the minor lines of business. Employees of the minor line of business who do not perform substantial services which directly benefit the major line of business are not treated as employees of the major line of business. A minor line of business is significantly interrelated with a major line of business when, for example, the activity of the minor line of business is directly related to but is a minor part of the major line of business (such as laundry services provided at a hospital).

(C) Examples. The rules provided in this paragraph are illustrated in the following examples:

Example (1). Assume that employees of units of an employer provide repair or financing services, or sell by catalog, with respect to retail merchandise sold by the employer. Such employees may be considered as employees of the retail merchandise line of business under this paragraph (a)(1)(iv).

Example (2). Assume that an employer operates a hospital and a laundry service. Assume further that some of the gross receipts of the laundry service line of business are from laundry services sold to customers other than the hospital employer. Only the employees of the laundry service who perform substantial services which directly benefit the hospital line of business (through the provision of laundry services to the hospital) will be treated as employees of the hospital line of business. Other employees of the laundry service line of business will not be treated as employees of the hospital line of business.

Example (3). Assume the same facts as in example (2), except that the minor line of business also operates a chain of dry cleaning stores. Employees who perform substantial services which directly benefit the dry cleaning stores but who do not perform substantial services that directly benefit the hospital line of business will not be treated as employees of the hospital line of business.

* * *

[T.D. 8063, 50 FR 52301, Dec. 23, 1985]

§ 1.132–5T Working condition fringe.

(a) In general—(1) Definition. Gross income does not include the value of a working condition fringe. The term "working condition fringe" means any property or service provided to an employee of an employer to the extent that, if the employee paid for the property or service, the amount paid would be allowable as a deduction under section 162 or 167. If, under section 274 or any other section, certain substantiation requirements must be met in order for a deduction under section 162 or 167 to be allowable, those substantiation requirements apply to the determination of a working condition fringe. An amount that would be deductible by the employee under, for example, section 212 is not a working condition fringe.

(2) Trade or business of the employee. If the hypothetical payment for the property or service would be allowable as a deduction with respect to a trade or business of the employee other than the employee's trade or business of being an employee of the employer, it cannot be taken into account for purposes of determining the amount, if any, of the working condition fringe. For example, assume that, unrelated to company X's trade or business and unrelated to company X's employee's trade or business of being an employee of company X, the employee is a member of the board of directors of company Y. Assume further that company X provides the employee with air transportation to a company Y board of director's meeting. The employee may not exclude the value of the air transportation to the meeting as a working condition fringe. The employee may, however, deduct such amount under section 162 if the section 162 requirements are satisfied. The result would be the same whether the air transportation was provided in the form of a flight on a commercial airline or a seat on a company X airplane.

(b) **Vehicle allocation rules—(1) In general—(i) General rule.** In general, with respect to an employer-provided vehicle, the amount excludable as a working condition fringe is the amount that would be allowable as a deduction under section 162 or 167 if the employee paid for the availability of the vehicle. For example, assume that the value of the availability of an employer-provided vehicle for a full year is $2,000, without regard to any working condition fringe (i.e., assuming all personal use). Assume further that the employee drives the vehicle 6,000 miles for his employer's business and 2,000 miles for reasons other than the employer's business. In this situation, the value of the working condition fringe is $2,000 multiplied by a fraction, the numerator of which is the business-use mileage (6,000 miles) and the denominator of which is the total mileage (8,000 miles). Thus, the value of the working condition fringe is $1,500. The total amount includable in the employee's gross income on account of the availability of the vehicle is $500. For purposes of this section, the term "vehicle" has the same meaning given the term in § 1.61–2T(e)(2). Generally, when determining the amount of an employee's working condition fringe, miles accumulated on the vehicle by all employees of the employer during the period in which the vehicle is available to the employee must be considered. For example, assume that an employee of the employer is provided the availability of an automobile for one year. Assume further that during the year, the automobile is regularly used in the employer's business by other employees. All miles accumulated on the automobile by all employees of the employer during the year must be considered. If, however, substantially all the use of the automobile by other employees in the employer's business is permitted during a certain period, such as the last three months of the year, the miles driven by the other employees during that period would not be considered when determining the employee's working condition fringe exclusion.

(ii) **Use by an individual other than the employee.** For purposes of this section, if the availability of a vehicle to an individual would be taxed to an employee, use of the vehicle by the individual is included in references to use by the employee.

(iii) **Provision of an expensive vehicle for personal use.** Assume an employer provides an employee with an expensive vehicle that an employee may use in part for personal purposes. Even though the decision to provide an expensive rather than an inexpensive vehicle is made by the employer for bona fide noncompensatory business reasons, there is no working condition fringe exclusion with respect to the personal miles driven by the employee. If the employee paid for the availability of the vehicle, he would not be entitled to deduct any part of the payment attributable to personal miles.

(2) **Use of different employer-provided automobiles.** The working condition fringe exclusion must be applied on an automobile by automobile basis. For example, assume that automobile Y is available to employee D for 3 days in January and for 5 days in March, and automobile Z is available to D for a week in July. Assume further that the Daily Lease Value, as defined in § 1.61–2T, of each automobile is $50. For the eight days of availability of Y in January and March, D uses Y 90 percent for business (by mileage). During July, D uses Z 60 percent for business (by mileage). The value of the working condition fringe is determined separately for each automobile. Therefore, the working condition fringe for Y is $360 ($400 x .90) leaving an income inclusion of $40. The working condition fringe for Z is $210 ($350 x .60) leaving an income inclusion of $140. If the value of the availability of an automobile is determined under the Annual Lease Value rule for one period and Daily Lease Value rule for a second period (see § 1.61–2T), the working condition fringe exclusion must be calculated separately for the two periods.

(c) **Applicability of sections 162 and 274(d)—(1) In general.** The value of property or services provided to an employee may not be excluded from the employee's gross income as a working condition fringe, by either the employer or the employee, unless the applicable substantiation requirements of either section 274(d) or section 162 (whichever is applicable) and the regulations thereunder are satisfied. With respect to listed property, the substantiation requirements of section 274(d) and the regulations thereunder do not apply to the determination of an employee's working condition fringe exclusion prior to the date that those requirements apply to the first taxable year of the employer beginning after December 31, 1985. For example, if an employer's first taxable year beginning after December 31, 1985, begins on July 1, 1986, with respect to listed property, the substantiation requirements of section 274(d) apply as of that date. The substantiation requirements of section 274(d) apply to an employee even if the requirements of section 274 do not apply to the employee's employer for deduction purposes (such as when the employer is a tax-exempt organization or a governmental unit); in these cases, the requirements of section 274(d) apply to the employee as of January 1, 1986.

(2) **Section 274(d) requirements.** The substantiation requirements of section 274(d) are satisfied by "adequate records or sufficient evidence corroborating the [employee's] own statement". Therefore, such records or evidence provided by the employee, and relied upon the employer to the extent permitted by the regulations promulgated under section 274(d), will be sufficient to substantiate a working condition fringe exclusion.

* * *

(p) **Parking—(1) In general.** The value of parking provided to an employee on or near the business premises of the employer is excludable from gross income as a working condition fringe. The working condition fringe exclusion applies whether the employer owns or rents the parking facility or parking space.

(2) **Reimbursement of parking expenses.** Any reimbursement to the employee of the ordinary and necessary expenses of renting a parking space on or near the business premises of the employer is excludable as a working condition fringe. The preceding sentence does not apply, however, to cash payments that are not actually used for renting a parking space. Thus, that part of a general transportation allowance that is not used for parking is not excludable as a working condition fringe under this paragraph (p).

(3) **Parking on residential property.** With respect to an employee, this paragraph (p) does not apply to any parking facility or space located on property owned or leased for residential purposes by the employee.

(q) **Nonapplicability of nondiscrimination rules.** Except to the extent provided in paragraph (n)(3) of this section, the nondiscrimination rules of section 132(h)(1) and § 1.132–8T do not apply in

determining the amount, if any, of a working condition fringe.

[T.D. 8063, 50 FR 52303, Dec. 23, 1985]

§ 1.132–6T   De minimis fringe.

(a) **In general.** Gross income does not include the value of a de minimis fringe provided to an employee. The term "de minimis fringe" means any property or service the value of which is (after taking into account the frequency with which similar fringes are provided by the employer to the employer's employees) so small as to make accounting for it unreasonable or administratively impracticable.

(b) **Frequency.** Generally, the frequency with which similar fringes are provided by the employer to the employer's employees is determined by reference to the frequency with which the employer provides the fringe to each individual employee. For example, if an employer provides a free meal to one employee on a daily basis, but not to any other employee, the value of the meals is not de minimis with respect to that one employee even though with respect to the employer's entire workforce the meals are provided "infrequently." However, where it would be administratively difficult to determine frequency with respect to individual employees, the frequency with which similar fringes are provided by the employer to the employer's employees is determined by reference to the frequency with which the employer provides the fringes to the employees and not the frequency with which individual employees receive them. In these cases, if an employer occasionally provides a fringe benefit of de minimis value to the employer's employees, the de minimis fringe exclusion may apply even though a particular employee receives the benefit frequently. For example, if an employer exercises sufficient control and imposes significant restrictions on the personal use of a company copying machine so that at least 85 percent of the use of the machine is for business purposes, any personal use of the copying machine by particular employees is considered to be a de minimis fringe.

(c) **Administrability.** Unless excluded by a statutory provision other than section 132(a)(4), the value of any fringe benefit that would not be unreasonable or administratively impracticable to account for must be included in the employee's gross income. Thus, except as otherwise provided in this section, the provision of any cash fringe benefit (or any fringe benefit provided to an employee through the use of a charge or credit card) is not excludable as a de minimis fringe. For example, the provision of cash to an employee for personal entertainment is not excludable as a de minimis fringe.

(d) Special rules—(1) Transit passes. A transit pass provided to an employee at a discount not exceeding $15 per month may be excluded as a de minimis fringe. The exclusion provided in this paragraph (d) also applies to the provision of $15 in tokens or fare cards that enable an individual to travel on the transit system. The exclusion provided in this paragraph (d) does not apply to any provision of cash or other benefit to defray transit expenses incurred for personal travel.

(2) Occasional meal money or local transportation fare. Occasional meal money or local transportation fare provided to an employee because overtime work necessitates an extension of the employee's normal workday is excluded as a de minimis fringe.

(3) Use of special rules to establish a general rule. The special rules provided in this paragraph (d) may not be used to establish any general rule. For example, the fact that $180 ($15 per month for 12 months) worth of transit passes can be excluded in a year does not mean that any fringe benefit with a value equal to or less than $180 may be excluded as a de minimis fringe.

(4) Benefits exceeding value and frequency limitations. If the benefit provided to an employee is not de minimis because either the value or frequency exceeds a limit provided in this paragraph (d), no amount of the benefit is considered to be de minimis. For example, if an employer provides a $20 monthly transit pass, the entire $20 must be included in income, not just the excess value over $15.

(e) Nonapplicability of nondiscrimination rules. Except to the extent provided in §1.132–7T, the nondiscrimination rules of section 132(h)(1) and §1.132–8T do not apply. Thus, for example, a fringe benefit may be a de minimis fringe even if the benefit is provided exclusively to officers of the employer.

(f) Examples—(1) Benefits excludable from income. Examples of de minimis fringe benefits are occasional typing of personal letters by a company secretary; occasional personal use of an employer's copying machine, provided that the employer exercises sufficient control and imposes significant restrictions on the personal use of the machine so that at least 85 percent of the use of the machine is for business purposes; occasional cocktail parties or picnics for employees and their guests; traditional holiday gifts of property (not cash) with a low fair market value; occasional theatre or sporting event tickets; and coffee and doughnuts.

(2) Benefits not excludable as de minimis fringes. Examples of fringe benefits that are not excludable from income as de minimis fringes are: season tickets to sporting or theatrical events; the commuting use of an employer-provided automobile or other vehicle more than once a month; membership in a private country club or athletic facility, regardless of the frequency with which the employee uses the facility; and use of employer-owned or leased facilities (such as an apartment, hunting lodge, boat, etc.) for a weekend. Some amount of the value of these fringe benefits may be excluded under other statutory provisions, such as the exclusion for working condition fringes. See §1.132–5T.

[T.D. 8063, 50 FR 52308, Dec. 23, 1985]

§1.132–7T Treatment of employer-operated eating facilities.

(a) In general—(1) General rule. The value of meals provided to employees at an employer-operated eating facility for employees is excludable from gross income as a de minimis fringe only if—

(i) On an annual basis, the revenue from the facility equals or exceeds the direct operating costs of the facility, and

(ii) With respect to any officer, owner or highly compensated employee, access to the facility is available on substantially the same terms to each member of a group of employees that is defined under a reasonable classification set up by the employer that does not discriminate in favor of officers, owners, and highly compensated employees. See §1.132–8T.

(2) Employer-operated eating facility for employees. An employer-operated eating facility for employees is a facility that meets all of the following conditions—

(i) The facility is owned or leased by the employer,

(ii) The facility is operated by the employer,

(iii) The facility is located on or near the business premises of the employer,

(iv) Substantially all of the use of the facility is by employees of the employer operating the facility, and

(v) The meals furnished at the facility are provided during, or immediately before or after, the employee's workday.

For purposes of this section, the term "meals" means food, beverages, and related services provided at the facility. If an employer can determine the number of employees who receive meals that are excludable from income under section 119, the employer may, in determining whether the requirement of paragraph (a)(1)(i) of this section is satisfied, disregard all costs and revenues attributable to such meals provided to such employees. For purposes of this section, each dining room or cafeteria in which meals are served is treated as a separate eating facility, regardless of whether each such dining room or cafeteria has its own kitchen or other food-preparation area.

(3) Operation by the employer. If an employer contracts with another to operate an eating facility for its employees, the facility is considered to be operated by the employer for purposes of this section. If an eating facility is operated by more than one employer, it is considered to be operated by each employer.

(b) Direct operating costs. The direct operating costs test must be applied separately for each dining room or cafeteria. For purposes of this section, the direct operating costs of eating facilities are: (1) the cost of food and beverages and (2) the cost of labor for personnel whose services relating to the facility are performed primarily on the premises of the eating facility. Direct operating costs do not include the cost of labor for personnel whose services relating to the facility are not performed primarily on the premises of the eating facility. Thus, for example, the labor cost for cooks, waiters and waitresses is included in direct operating costs, but the labor costs for a manager of an eating facility whose services relating to the facility are not primarily performed on the premises of the eating facility is not included in direct operating costs. If an employee performs services both on and off the premises of the eating facility, only the applicable percentage of the total labor cost of the employee that bears the same proportion as time spent on the premises bears to total time is included in direct operating costs. For example, assume that 60 percent of the services of the cooks in the above example are not related to the eating facility. Only 40 percent of the total labor costs of the cooks is includible in direct operating costs. For purposes of this section, labor costs include all compensation required to be reported on a Form W–2 for income tax purposes and related employment taxes paid by the employer.

(c) Valuation of non-excluded meals provided at an employer-operated eating facility for employees. If the exclusion for meals provided at an employer-operated eating facility for employees is not available, the recipient of meals provided at such facility must include in income the amount by which the fair market value of the meals provided exceeds the sum of: (1) The amount, if any, paid for the meals, and (2) the amount, if any, specifically excluded by another section of the Code. For special valuation rules relating to such meals see § 1.61–2T(j).

[T.D. 8063, 50 FR 52308, Dec. 23, 1985]

§ 1.132–8T Nondiscrimination rules.

(a) Application of nondiscrimination rules— (1) General rule. To qualify under section 132 for the exclusions for non-additional-cost services, qualified employee discounts, or meals provided at employer-operated eating facilities for employees, the fringe benefit must be available on substantially the same terms to each member of a group of employees which is defined under a reasonable classification set up by the employer that does not discriminate in favor of officers, owners, or highly compensated employees (the "prohibited group employees").

(2) Consequences of discrimination. If the availability of or the provision of the fringe benefit does not satisfy the nondiscrimination rules provided in this section, the exclusion applies only to those employees (if any) who receive the benefit and who are not prohibited group employees. For example, if an employer offers a 20 percent discount (which otherwise satisfies the requirements for a qualified employee discount) to all nonprohibited group employees and a 35 percent discount to all prohibited group employees, the entire value of the 35 percent discount (not just the excess over 20 percent) is includible in the gross income and wages of the prohibited group employees who make purchases at a discount.

(3) Scope of the nondiscrimination rules provided in this section. The nondiscrimination rules provided in this section apply only to fringe benefits provided pursuant to section 132(a)(1), (a)(2), and (e)(2). These rules have no application to any other employee benefit that may be subject to nondiscrimination requirements under any other section of the Code.

(b) Coverage requirement—(1) Section 132(a)(1) and (2). For purposes of the exclusions for no-additional-cost services and qualified employee discounts, the nondiscrimination rules of this section are applied by aggregating the employees of all related employers (as defined in § 1.132–1T(c)), but without aggregating employees in different lines of business (as defined in § 1.132–4T). Employees in different lines of business will be aggregated, however, if the line of business limitation has been relaxed pursuant to either section 1.132–4T(b) or (c). Except as provided in paragraph (e) of this section, the nondiscrimination rules of this section are generally applied separately to each fringe benefit program of an employer.

(2) Section 132(e)(2). For purposes of the exclusion for meals provided at employer-operated eating facilities for employees, the nondiscrimination rules of this section are applied by aggregating the employees of all related employers, without regard to different lines of business, who regularly work at or near the premises on which the eating facility is located. The nondiscrimination rules of this section are applied separately to each eating facility. Each dining room or cafeteria in which meals are served is treated as a separate eating facility, regardless of whether each such dining room or cafeteria has its own kitchen or other food-preparation area.

(3) Classes of employees who may be excluded. Except as otherwise provided in this section, for purposes of applying the nondiscrimination rules of this section to a particular fringe benefit program, there may be excluded from consideration the following classes of employees provided that, with respect to each class (other than the class described in paragraph (b)(3)(iii) of this section), all employees in the class are excluded from participating in the particular fringe benefit program—

(i) All part-time or seasonal employees who are (or who are reasonably expected to be) credited with less than 1,000 hours (or such lesser number required for the program) of service during a calendar year;

(ii) All employees who are included in a unit of employees covered by an agreement with the Secretary of Labor finds to be a collective bargaining agreement between employee representatives and one or more employers, if there is evidence that the particular fringe benefit program was the subject of good faith bargaining between such employee representatives and such employer or employers (and if, after March 31, 1984, the additional condition of section 7701(a)(46) is satisfied);

(iii) All employees who are nonresident aliens and who receive no earned income (within the meaning of section 911(d)(2)) from the employer which constitutes income from services within the United States (within the meaning of section 861(a)(3));

(iv) All employees who have not completed at least one year (or such lesser period required for the program) of service with the employer;

(v) All employees who have separated from the service of the employer in a year prior to the current year (regardless of the reason for the separation);

(vi) All employees who have separated from the service of the employer in a year prior to the current year except for retired and/or disabled employees (either with or without a time limit based on a set number of years since separation from the service of the employer); and

(vii) All employees of a leased section of a department store.

(c) Classification requirement—(1) General rule. The determination of whether a particular classification established by an employer discriminates in favor of the prohibited group will depend on the facts and circumstances involved, based on principles similar to those applied in the qualified plan area (see section 410(b)(1)(B) and the regulations thereunder). In general, except as otherwise provided in this section, a classification that would be determined to be nondiscriminatory pursuant to the application of the nondiscrimination standards that are applied in the qualified plan area shall be deemed to be nondiscriminatory for purposes of section 132.

(2) Classifications that are per se discriminatory. A classification that, on its face, makes fringe benefits available only to prohibited group employees is per se discriminatory, and no exclusion from gross income is available to any prohibited group employee under section 132. In addition, a classification that is based on either an amount or rate of compensation is per se discriminatory if it favors those with the higher amount or rate of compensation. On the other hand, a classification that is based on factors such as seniority, full-time vs. part-time employment, or job description is not per se discriminatory but may be discriminatory as applied to the workforce of a particular employer.

(3) **Former employees.** When determining whether a classification is discriminatory, former employees shall not be considered together with other employees of the employer. Therefore, a classification is not discriminatory if the employer does not make the fringe benefits available to any former employee. Whether a classification of former employees discriminates in favor of prohibited group employees will depend on the facts and circumstances. The rules of this section shall apply separately to the former employee classification.

(4) **Employer-operated eating facilities for employees—(i) General rule.** If access to an employer-operated eating facility for employees is available to a classification of employees that discriminates in favor of highly compensated employees, the classification will not be treated as discriminating in favor of the prohibited group employees unless the facility is used, more than a de minimis amount, by any executive group employee.

(ii) **Executive group employees.** For purposes of this paragraph (c)(4), the term "executive group employees" has the same meaning as the term "prohibited group employees" (as defined in paragraph (g) of this section), except that for purposes of identifying highly compensated employees—

(A) The exception provided in paragraph (g)(1)(i)(A) of this section does not apply, and

(B) The phrase "highest-paid one percent of all employees of an employer" is substituted for the phrase "highest-paid ten percent of all employees of an employer" in paragraph (g)(1)(ii)(A) of this section.

(d) **Substantially-the-same-terms requirement—(1) General rule.** Fringe benefits available to a particular classification of employees must be available to each employee in the classification on substantially the same terms. The determination of whether this requirement is met shall depend on the facts and circumstances involved. For example, if a department store provides a 20 percent qualified employee discount to its employees on all merchandise, the substantially-the-same-

terms requirement will be satisfied. Similarly, if the discount provided to all employees is 30 percent on certain merchandise (such as apparel), and 20 percent on all other merchandise, the substantially-the-same-terms requirement will be satisfied. However, if the discount provided is 20 percent on all merchandise for hourly employees and 30 percent on all merchandise for salaried employees, the substantially-the-same-terms requirement will not be satisfied. In addition, if the percentage discount varies depending on either an employee's amount or rate of compensation, or volume of purchases, the substantially-the-same-terms requirement will not be satisfied. In order to determine whether such a discount program satisfies the nondiscrimination requirements of section 132, each group of employees that does receive fringe benefits on substantially the same terms must be treated as a separate classification. However, subject to the rules of paragraph (e)(2) of this section, an employer may divide a fringe benefit program into two programs for purposes of aggregating groups of employees. See Example (1) of paragraph (d)(3) of this section.

(2) **Terms relating to priority.** Certain fringe benefits made available to employees are available only in limited quantities that may be insufficient to meet employee demand. This may occur either because of employer policy (such as where an employer determines that only a certain number of units of a specific product will be made available to employees each year) or because of the nature of the fringe benefit (such as where an employer provides a no-additional-cost transportation service that is limited to the number of seats available just before departure). Under these circumstances, an employer may find it necessary to establish some method of allocating the limited fringe benefits among the employees eligible to receive the fringe benefits. An allocation among employees on a "first-come, first-served" basis will not violate the substantially-the-same-terms requirement provided that such an allocation is not discriminatory in practice. In addition, an allocation among employees on a lottery basis will not violate the substantially-the-same-terms requirement provided that such an allocation is nondiscriminatory in practice. For example, assume that an employer has a limited number of a particular benefit to offer to its employees. Assume further that the employees interested in receiving the benefit submit their names to the employer who then selects a number of names, at random, equal to the number of fringe

benefits available. This lottery system would not violate the substantially-the-same-terms requirement. An allocation among employees on other than a "first-come, first-served", lottery, or similar basis will violate the substantially-the-same-terms requirement. Therefore, an allocation based on seniority, full-time vs. part-time employment, or job description will violate the substantially-the-same-terms requirement. In order to determine whether such a fringe benefit program satisfies the nondiscrimination requirements of section 132, each group of employees that does receive fringe benefits on substantially the same terms must be treated as a separate classification. For purposes of this rule, the last two sentences of paragraph (d)(1) of this section apply.

(3) **Examples.** The following examples illustrate the provisions of this paragraph (d):

Example 1. Assume that with respect to a benefit available in limited quantities an employer provides priority to employees based on seniority. Assume further that all non-prohibited group employees have ten years of seniority and all prohibited group employees have nine years seniority. If each of these groups were tested separately, the benefits offered to prohibited group employees would be discriminatory under this section. In this case, the employer could divide the fringe benefit program provided to non-prohibited group employees into two parts: one relating to nine years of seniority and one relating to an additional year of seniority. As restructured in this manner, all employees receive the benefit relating to nine years seniority and only non-prohibited group employees receive the benefit relating to an additional year of seniority. Both groups (all employees and all non-prohibited group employees) are nondiscriminatory groups.

Example 2. Assume that prices charged to prohibited group employees at an employer-operated eating facility for employees are lower than prices charged to non-prohibited group employees. The substantially-the-same-terms requirement is not satisfied.

(4) **Disproportionate use of eating facility.** If access to an employer-operated eating facility for employees is technically available on substantially-the-same-terms to (i) all employees who regularly work at or near the premises on which the eating facility is located (the employee group), or (ii) a nondiscriminatory classification of the employee group, but in practice a highly disproportionate number of the prohibited group employees in the employee group, compared to the non-prohibited group employees in the employee group, use the facility, the substantially-the-same-terms requirement will not be satisfied unless no member of the executive group eats there more than a de minimis amount.

(e) **Aggregation of separate fringe benefit programs—(1) General rule.** If an employer maintains more than one fringe benefit program, i.e., two or more classifications of employees providing either identical or different fringe benefits, the nondiscrimination requirements of section 132 will generally be applied separately to each such program. Thus, a determination that one fringe benefit program discriminates in favor of prohibited group employees generally will not cause other fringe benefit programs covering the same prohibited group employees to be treated as discriminatory.

(2) **Exception—(i) Related fringe benefit programs.** If one of a group of fringe benefit programs discriminates in favor of prohibited group employees, no related fringe benefit provided to such prohibited group employees under any other fringe benefit program may be excluded from the gross income of such prohibited group employees. For example, assume a department store provides a 20 percent merchandise discount to all employees under one fringe benefit program. Assume further that under a second fringe benefit program, the department store provides an additional 15 percent merchandise discount to a group of employees defined under a classification which discriminates in favor of the prohibited group. Because the second fringe benefit program is discriminatory, the 15 percent merchandise discount provided to the prohibited group employees is not a qualified employee discount. In addition, because the 20 percent merchandise discount provided under the first fringe benefit program is related to the fringe benefit provided under the second fringe benefit program, the 20 percent merchandise discount provided the prohibited group employees is not a qualified employee discount. Thus, the entire 35 percent merchandise discount provided to the prohibited group employees is includible in such employees' gross incomes.

(ii) **Employer-operated eating facilities for employees.** For purposes of paragraph (e)(2)(i) of this section, meals at different employer-operated eating facilities for employees are not related fringe benefits, so that a prohibited group employee may exclude the value of a meal at a nondiscriminatory facility even though any meals provided to him or her at the discriminatory facility cannot be excluded.

(f) **Cash bonuses or rebates.** A cash bonus or rebate provided to an employee by an employer that is determined pursuant to the value of employer-provided property or services purchased by the employee, is treated as an equivalent employee discount. For example, assume a department store provides a 20 percent merchandise discount to all employees under a fringe benefit program. In addition, assume that the department store provides cash bonuses to a group of employees defined under a classification which discriminates in favor of the prohibited group. Assume further that such cash bonuses equal 15 percent of the value of merchandise purchased by each employee. This arrangement is substantively identical to the example described in paragraph (e)(2) of this section. Thus, both the 20 percent merchandise discount and the 15 percent cash bonus provided to the prohibited group employees are includible in such employees' gross incomes.

(g) **Prohibited group employees—(1) Highly compensated—(i) General rule.** Except as otherwise provided in this paragraph (g)(1)(i), any employee of an employer who has (or is reasonably expected to have) compensation during a calendar year equal to or greater than the employer's base compensation amount is highly compensated. There are two exceptions to this rule:

(A) Any employee who has (or is reasonably expected to have) compensation during a calendar year equal to or greater than $50,000 is highly compensated, regardless of whether such compensation is in excess of the base compensation amount, and

(B) Any employee who is reasonably expected to have compensation during a calendar year equal to or less than $20,000 is not highly compensated, unless no employee of the employer is reasonably expected to have compensation equal to or greater than $35,000.

The determination of whether an employee is a highly compensated employee will be determined based on the entire employee workforce of all employers aggregated pursuant to the rules of section 414(b), (c), or (m) without regard to the regular workplace of the employees.

(ii) **Base compensation amount—(A) General rule.** The term "base compensation amount" is defined as that amount corresponding to the lowest annual compensation amount received by the highest-paid ten percent of all employees of an employer (the number of employees in the top ten percent will be increased to the next highest integer if necessary), determined on the basis of the preceding calendar year. For purposes of this paragraph

(g)(1)(ii), the term "employer" includes all entities that would be aggregated pursuant to the rules of section 414(b), (c), or (m).

(B) **Employees that are excluded.** For purposes of determining the base compensation amount with respect to a fringe benefit program, employees described in paragraph (b)(3) of this section are excluded whether or not they are covered under the fringe benefit program, except that: (1) Employees described in paragraph (b)(3)(ii) of this section are taken into account with respect to the program even if they are excluded under paragraph (b)(3), and (2) employees described in paragraph (b)(3)(i) and (iv) of this section are taken into account with respect to the program unless they are excluded under paragraph (b)(3).

(C) **Exception to preceding calendar year rule.** In the case of an employer's first year of operation, or where an employer's business has changed significantly from the prior calendar year (e.g., due to an acquisition or merger), the employer must make a good faith attempt to either determine or adjust the base compensation amount for the current year based on reasonable estimates of current year compensation.

(iii) **Compensation.** The term "compensation" is defined as the amount reportable on a Form W–2 as income. Amounts that would be excluded from income but for section 132(h)(1) are not included in compensation for purposes of this paragraph (g)(1). Compensation includes amounts received from all entities which would be treated as a single employer under section 414(b), (c), or (m) and is not restricted to amounts received with respect to any one line of business.

(iv) **Employee.** Generally, for purposes of determining whether an employee is highly compensated under this paragraph (g)(1), the term "employee" does not include any individual who does not perform services for the employer as an employee during the calendar year. For example, if an employer has active employees, retired or disabled employees, and widows or widowers who are "employees" under section 132(f)(1)(B), the general rule (described in paragraph (g)(1)(i) of this section) applies only to the active employees.

(2) **Owner—(i) General rule.** For purposes of this section, the term "owner" means any employee who owns a one percent or greater interest in either the employer or in any entity that would be aggregated with the employer pursuant to the rules of section 414(b), (c), or (m). In addition, such

an employee shall be treated as an owner of all entities that would be aggregated with the employer pursuant to the rules of section 414(b), (c), or (m).

(ii) **Determining ownership.** Ownership in a corporation shall be determined pursuant to the rules of section 318(a). For purposes of determining ownership in an entity other than a corporation, the rules of section 318(a) shall apply in a manner similar to the way in which they apply for purposes of determining ownership in a corporation. For non-corporate interests, capital or profits interest must be substituted for stock.

(3) **Officer—(i) Non-government.** For purposes of this section, an officer of a non-government employer is any employee who is appointed, confirmed, or elected by the Board or shareholders of the employer. An employee who is an officer of an employer shall be treated as an officer of all entities treated as a single employer pursuant to section 414(b), (c), or (m). The number of officers is not to exceed one-percent of the total number of employees of all entities treated as a single employer pursuant to section 414(b), (c), or (m) (increased to the next highest integer, if necessary). If the number of officers exceeds one-percent of all employees, then the limitation is to be applied to employees in descending order of compensation (as defined in paragraph (g)(1)(iii) of this section). Thus, if an employer with 1,000 employees has 11 board-appointed officers, the employee with the least compensation of those officers would not be an officer under this paragraph (g)(3)(i). In deter-

mining the total number of employees with respect to a fringe benefit program, employees described in paragraph (b)(3) of this section are excluded whether or not they are covered under the fringe benefit program, except that (A) employees described in paragraph (b)(3)(ii) of this section are taken into account with respect to the program even if they are excluded under paragraph (b)(3), and (B) employees described in paragraph (b)(3)(i) and (iv) of this section are taken into account with respect to the program unless they are excluded under paragraph (b)(3).

(ii) **Government.** For purposes of this section, an officer of a government employer is any—

(A) Elected official,

(B) Federal employee appointed by the President and confirmed by the Senate. However, in the case of any commissioned officer of the United States Armed Forces, an officer is any employee with the rank of brigadier general or rear admiral (lower half) or above, and

(C) State or local executive officer comparable to individuals described in paragraphs (g)(3)(ii)(A) and (B) of this section.

For purposes of this paragraph (g)(3)(ii), the term "government" includes any Federal, state, or local governmental unit, and any agency or instrumentality thereof.

(4) **Former employees.** [Reserved]

[T.D. 8063, 50 FR 52309, Dec. 23, 1985]

Deductions for Personal Exemptions

§ 1.151-1 Deductions for personal exemptions.

(a) **In general.** (1) In computing taxable income, an individual is allowed a deduction for the exemptions specified in section 151. Such exemptions are: (i) The exemptions for an individual taxpayer and spouse (the so-called personal exemptions); (ii) the additional exemptions for a taxpayer attaining the age of 65 years and spouse attaining the age of 65 years (the so-called old-age exemptions); (iii) the additional exemptions for a blind taxpayer and a blind spouse; and (iv) the exemptions for dependents of the taxpayer.

* * *

(b) **Exemptions for individual taxpayer and spouse (so-called personal exemptions).** Sec-

tion 151(b) allows an exemption for the taxpayer and an additional exemption for the spouse of the taxpayer if a joint return is not made by the taxpayer and his spouse, and if the spouse, for the calendar year in which the taxable year of the taxpayer begins, has no gross income and is not the dependent of another taxpayer. Thus, a husband is not entitled to an exemption for his wife on his separate return for the taxable year beginning in a calendar year during which she has any gross income (though insufficient to require her to file a return). Since, in the case of a joint return, there are two taxpayers (although under section 6013 there is only one income for the two taxpayers on such return, i.e., their aggregate income), two exemptions are allowed on such return, one for each taxpayer spouse. If in any case a joint return is made by the taxpayer and his spouse, no other person is allowed an exemption for such spouse even though such other person would have been entitled to claim an exemption for such spouse as a dependent if such joint return had not been made.

(c) Exemptions for taxpayer attaining the age of 65 and spouse attaining the age of 65 (so-called old-age exemptions). (1) Section 151(c) provides an additional exemption for the taxpayer if he has attained the age of 65 before the close of his taxable year. An additional exemption is also allowed to the taxpayer for his spouse if a joint return is not made by the taxpayer and his spouse and if the spouse has attained the age of 65 before the close of the taxable year of the taxpayer and, for the calendar year in which the taxable year of the taxpayer begins, the spouse has no gross income and is not the dependent of another taxpayer. If a husband and wife make a joint return, an old-age exemption will be allowed as to each taxpayer spouse who has attained the age of 65 before the close of the taxable year for which the joint return is made. The exemptions under section 151(c) are in addition to the exemptions for the taxpayer and spouse under section 151(b).

(2) In determining the age of an individual for the purposes of the exemption for old age, the last day of the taxable year of the taxpayer is the controlling date. Thus, in the event of a separate return by a husband, no additional exemption for old age may be claimed for his spouse unless such spouse has attained the age of 65 on or before the close of the taxable year of the husband. In no event shall the additional exemption for old age be allowed with respect to a spouse who dies before attaining the age of 65 even though such spouse would have attained the age of 65 before the close of the taxable year of the taxpayer. For the purposes of the old-age exemption, an individual attains the age of 65 on the first moment of the day preceding his sixty-fifth birthday. Accordingly, an individual whose sixty-fifth birthday falls on January 1 in a given year attains the age of 65 on the last day of the calendar year immediately preceding.

(d) Exemptions for the blind. (1) Section 151(d) provides an additional exemption for the taxpayer if he is blind at the close of his taxable year. An additional exemption is also allowed to the taxpayer for his spouse if the spouse is blind and, for the calendar year in which the taxable year of the taxpayer begins, has no gross income

and is not the dependent of another taxpayer. The determination of whether the spouse is blind shall be made as of the close of the taxable year of the taxpayer, unless the spouse dies during such taxable year, in which case such determination shall be made as of the time of such death.

(2) The exemptions for the blind are in addition to the exemptions for the taxpayer and spouse under section 151(b) and are also in addition to the exemptions under section 151(c) for taxpayers and spouses attaining the age of 65 years. Thus, a single individual who has attained the age of 65 before the close of his taxable year and who is blind at the close of his taxable year is entitled, in addition to the so-called personal exemption, to two further exemptions, one by reason of his age and the other by reason of his blindness. If a husband and wife make a joint return, an exemption for the blind will be allowed as to each taxpayer spouse who is blind at the close of the taxable year for which the joint return is made.

(3) A taxpayer claiming an exemption allowed by section 151(d) for a blind taxpayer and a blind spouse shall, if the individual for whom the exemption is claimed is not totally blind as of the last day of the taxable year of the taxpayer (or, in the case of a spouse who dies during such taxable year, as of the time of such death), attach to his return a certificate from a physician skilled in the diseases of the eye or a registered optometrist stating that as of the applicable status determination date in the opinion of such physician or optometrist (i) the central visual acuity of the individual for whom the exemption is claimed did not exceed 20/200 in the better eye with correcting lenses or (ii) such individual's visual acuity was accompanied by a limitation in the fields of vision such that the widest diameter of the visual field subtends an angle no greater than 20 degrees. If such individual is totally blind as of the status determination date there shall be attached to the return a statement by the person or persons making the return setting forth such fact.

(4) Notwithstanding subparagraph (3) of this paragraph, this subparagraph may be applied where the individual for whom an exemption under section 151(d) is claimed is not totally blind, and in the certified opinion of an examining physician skilled in the diseases of the eye there is no reasonable probability that the individual's visual acuity will ever improve beyond the minimum standards described in subparagraph (3) of this paragraph. In this event, if the examination occurs during a taxable year for which the exemption is claimed, and the examining physician certifies that, in his opinion, the condition is irreversible, and a copy of this certification is filed with the return for that taxable year, then a statement described in subparagraph (3) of this paragraph need not be attached to such individual's return for subsequent taxable years so long as the condition remains irreversible. The taxpayer shall retain a copy of the certified opinion in his records, and a statement referring to such opinion shall be attached to future returns claiming the section 151(d) exemption.

[T.D. 6500, 25 FR 11402, Nov. 26, 1960, as amended by T.D. 7114, 36 FR 9018, May 18, 1971; T.D. 7230, 37 FR 28288, Dec. 22, 1972]

§ 1.152–1 General definition of a dependent.

(a)(1) For purposes of the income taxes imposed on individuals by chapter 1 of the Code, the term "dependent" means any individual described in paragraphs (1) through (10) of section 152(a) over half of whose support, for the calendar year in which the taxable year of the taxpayer begins, was received from the taxpayer.

(2)(i) For purposes of determining whether or not an individual received, for a given calendar year, over half of his support from the taxpayer, there shall be taken into account the amount of support received from the taxpayer as compared to the entire amount of support which the individual received from all sources, including support which the individual himself supplied. The term "support" includes food, shelter, clothing, medical and dental care, education, and the like. Generally, the amount of an item of support will be the amount of expense incurred by the one furnishing such item. If the item of support furnished an individual is in the form of property or lodging, it will be necessary to measure the amount of such item of support in terms of its fair market value.

(ii) In computing the amount which is contributed for the support of an individual, there must be included any amount which is contributed by such individual for his own support, including income which is ordinarily excludable from gross income, such as benefits received under the Social Security Act (42 U.S.C. ch. 7). For example, a father receives $800 social security benefits, $400 interest, and $1,000 from his son during 1955, all of which sums represent his sole support during that year. The fact that the social security benefits of $800

are not includible in the father's gross income does not prevent such amount from entering into the computation of the total amount contributed for the father's support. Consequently, since the son's contribution of $1,000 was less than one-half of the father's support ($2,200) he may not claim his father as a dependent.

(iii)(a) For purposes of determining the amount of support furnished for a child (or children) by a taxpayer for a given calendar year, an arrearage payment made in a year subsequent to a calendar year for which there is an unpaid liability shall not be treated as paid either during that calendar year or in the year of payment, but no amount shall be treated as an arrearage payment to the extent that there is an unpaid liability (determined without regard to such payment) with respect to the support of a child for the taxable year of payment; and

(b) Similarly, payments made prior to any calendar year (whether or not made in the form of a lump sum payment in settlement of the parent's liability for support) shall not be treated as made during such calendar year, but payments made during any calendar year from amounts set aside in trust by a parent in a prior year, shall be treated as made during the calendar year in which paid.

(b) Section 152(a)(9) applies to any individual (other than an individual who at any time during the taxable year was the spouse, determined without regard to section 153, of the taxpayer) who lives with the taxpayer and is a member of the taxpayer's household during the entire taxable year of the taxpayer. An individual is not a member of the taxpayer's household if at any time during the taxable year of the taxpayer the relationship between such individual and the taxpayer is in violation of local law. It is not necessary under section 152(a)(9) that the dependent be related to the taxpayer. For example, foster children may qualify as dependents. It is necessary, however, that the taxpayer both maintain and occupy the household. The taxpayer and dependent will be considered as occupying the household for such entire taxable year notwithstanding temporary absences from the household due to special circumstances. A nonpermanent failure to occupy the common abode by reason of illness, education, business, vacation, military service, or a custody agreement under which the dependent is absent for less than six months in the taxable year of the taxpayer, shall be considered temporary absence due to special circumstances. The fact that the dependent dies during the year shall not deprive the taxpayer of the deduction if the dependent lived in the household for the entire part of the year preceding his death. Likewise, the period during the taxable year preceding the birth of an individual shall not prevent such individual from qualifying as a dependent under section 152(a)(9). Moreover, a child who actually becomes a member of the taxpayer's household during the taxable year shall not be prevented from being considered a member of such household for the entire taxable year, if the child is required to remain in a hospital for a period following its birth, and if such child would otherwise have been a member of the taxpayer's household during such period.

(c) In the case of a child of the taxpayer who is under 19 or who is a student, the taxpayer may claim the dependency exemption for such child provided he has furnished more than one-half of the support of such child for the calendar year in which the taxable year of the taxpayer begins, even though the income of the child for such calendar year may be equal to or in excess of the amount determined pursuant to § 1.151–2 applicable to such calendar year. In such a case, there may be two exemptions claimed for the child: One on the parent's (or stepparent's) return, and one on the child's return. In determining whether the taxpayer does in fact furnish more than one-half of the support of an individual who is a child, as defined in paragraph (a) of § 1.151–3, of the taxpayer and who is a student, as defined in paragraph (b) of § 1.151–3, a special rule regarding scholarships applies. Amounts received as scholarships, as defined in paragraph (a) of § 1.117–3, for study at an educational institution shall not be considered in determining whether the taxpayer furnishes more than one-half the support of such individual. For example, A has a child who receives a $1,000 scholarship to the X college for 1 year. A contributes $500, which constitutes the balance of the child's support for that year. A may claim the child as a dependent, as the $1,000 scholarship is not counted in determining the support of the child. For purposes of this paragraph, amounts received for tuition payments and allowances by a veteran under the provisions of the Servicemen's Readjustment Act of 1944 (58 Stat. 284) or the Veterans' Readjustment Assistance Act of 1952 (38 U.S.C. ch. 38) are not amounts received as scholarships. See also § 1.117–4. For definition of the terms "child", "student", and "edu-

cational institution", as used in this paragraph, see § 1.151–3.

[T.D. 6500, 25 FR 11402, Nov. 26, 1960, as amended by T.D. 6603, 28 FR 7094, July 11, 1963; T.D. 7099, 36 FR 5337, March 20, 1971; T.D. 7114, 36 FR 9019, May 18, 1971]

§ 1.152–4T Dependency exemption in the case of a child of divorced parent, etc.

(a) In general.

Q–1. Which parent may claim the dependency exemption in the case of a child of divorced or separated parents?

A–1. Provided the parents together would have been entitled to the dependency exemption had they been married and filing a joint return, the parent having custody of a child for the greater portion of the year (the custodial parent) will generally be entitled to the dependency exemption. This rule applies to parents not living together during the last 6 months of the calendar year, as well as those divorced or separated under a separation agreement.

Q–2. Are there any exceptions to the general rule in A–1?

A–2. Yes, there are three exceptions. The general rule does not apply (i) if a multiple support agreement is in effect (see section 152(c)), (ii) if a decree or agreement executed prior to January 1, 1985 provides that the custodial parent has agreed to release his or her claim to the dependency exemption to the noncustodial parent and the noncustodial parent provides at least $600 of support to the child (see section 152(e)(4)), or (iii) if the custodial parent relinquishes the exemption in the manner described in A–3.

Q–3. How may the exemption for a dependent child be claimed by a noncustodial parent?

A–3. A noncustodial parent may claim the exemption for a dependent child only if the noncustodial parent attaches to his/her income tax return for the year of the exemption a written declaration from the custodial parent stating that he/she will not claim the child as a dependent for the taxable year beginning in such calendar year. The written declaration may be made on a form to be provided by the Service for this purpose. Once the Service has released the form, any declaration made other than on the official form shall conform to the substance of such form.

Q–4. For what period may a custodial parent release to the noncustodial parent a claim to the exemption for a dependent child?

A–4. The exemption may be released for a single year, for a number of specified years (for example, alternate years), or for all future years, as specified in the declaration. If the exemption is released for more than one year, the original release must be attached to the return of the noncustodial spouse and a copy of such release must be attached to his/her return for each succeeding taxable year for which he/she claims the dependency exemption.

Q–5. May only the custodial parent claim a deduction under section 213(d) for medical expenses paid by the parent or an income exclusion under section 105(b) for medical expenses paid by an employer for a dependent child?

A–5. No. Under the new rules, if a child receives over half of his support during the calendar year from his parents who are divorced or legally separated under a decree of divorce or separate maintenance, or who are separated under a written separation agreement, that child will be treated as a dependent of both parents for purposes of sections 105(b) and 213(d). Thus, a parent can deduct medical expenses paid by that parent for a child even though a dependency exemption for the child is claimed by the other parent. The special rule of sections 105(b) and 213(d) does not apply where over half of the support of a child is treated as having been received from a person under the provisions of section 152(c) (relating to multiple support agreements).

Q–6. When does section 152(e), as amended by the Tax Reform Act of 1984, become effective?

A–6. Section 152(e), as amended, is effective with respect to dependency exemptions for taxable years beginning after December 31, 1984.

[T.D. 7973, 49 FR 34459, Aug. 31, 1984]

Itemized Deductions for Individuals and Corporations

§ 1.161–1 Allowance of deductions.

Section 161 provides for the allowance as deductions, in computing taxable income under section 63(a), of the items specified in part VI (section 161 and following), subchapter B, chapter 1 of the Code, subject to the exceptions provided in part IX (section 261 and following), of such subchapter B, relating to items not deductible. Double deductions are not permitted. Amounts deducted under one provision of the Internal Revenue Code of 1954 cannot again be deducted under any other provision thereof. See also section 7852(c), relating to the taking into account, both in computing a tax under subtitle A of the Internal Revenue Code of 1954 and a tax under chapter 1 or 2 of the Internal Revenue Code of 1939, of the same item of deduction.

[T.D. 6500, 25 FR 11402, Nov. 26, 1960]

§ 1.162–1 Business expenses.

(a) In general. Business expenses deductible from gross income include the ordinary and necessary expenditures directly connected with or pertaining to the taxpayer's trade or business, except items which are used as the basis for a deduction or a credit under provisions of law other than section 162. The cost of goods purchased for resale, with proper adjustment for opening and closing inventories, is deducted from gross sales in computing gross income. See paragraph (a) of § 1.161–3. Among the items included in business expenses are management expenses, commissions (but see section 263 and the regulations thereunder), labor, supplies, incidental repairs, operating expenses of automobiles used in the trade or business, traveling expenses while away from home solely in the pursuit of a trade or business (see § 1.162–2), advertising and other selling expenses, together with insurance premiums against fire, storm, theft, accident, or other similar losses in the case of a business, and rental for the use of business property. No such item shall be included in business expenses, however, to the extent that it is used by the taxpayer in computing the cost of property included in its inventory or used in determining the gain or loss basis of its plant, equipment, or other property. See section 1054 and the regulations thereunder. A deduction for an expense paid or incurred after December 30, 1969, which would otherwise be allowable under section 162 shall not be denied on the grounds that allowance of such deduction would frustrate a sharply defined public policy. See section 162(c), (f), and (g) and the regulations thereunder. The full amount of the allowable deduction for ordinary and necessary expenses in carrying on a business is deductible, even though such expenses exceed the gross income derived during the taxable year from such business. * * *

* * *

[T.D. 6500, 25 FR 11402, Nov. 26, 1960, as amended by T.D. 6690, 28 FR 12253, Nov. 19, 1963; T.D. 6996, 34 FR 835, Jan. 18, 1969; T.D. 7315, 39 FR 20203, June 7, 1974; T.D. 7345, 40 FR 7437, Feb. 20, 1975]

§ 1.162–2 Traveling expenses.

(a) Traveling expenses include travel fares, meals and lodging, and expenses incident to travel such as expenses for sample rooms, telephone and telegraph, public stenographers, etc. Only such traveling expenses as are reasonable and necessary in the conduct of the taxpayer's business and directly attributable to it may be deducted. If the trip is undertaken for other than business purposes, the travel fares and expenses incident to travel are personal expenses and the meals and lodging are living expenses. If the trip is solely on business, the reasonable and necessary traveling expenses, including travel fares, meals and lodging, and expenses incident to travel, are business expenses. For the allowance of traveling expenses as deductions in determining adjusted gross income, see section 62(2)(B) and the regulations thereunder.

(b)(1) If a taxpayer travels to a destination and while at such destination engages in both business and personal activities, traveling expenses to and from such destination are deductible only if the trip is related primarily to the taxpayer's trade or business. If the trip is primarily personal in nature, the traveling expenses to and from the destination are not deductible even though the taxpayer engages in business activities while at such destination. However, expenses while at the destination which are properly allocable to the taxpayer's trade or business are deductible even though the traveling expenses to and from the destination are not deductible.

(2) Whether a trip is related primarily to the taxpayer's trade or business or is primarily personal in nature depends on the facts and circumstances in each case. The amount of time during the period of the trip which is spent on personal activity compared to the amount of time spent on activi-

ties directly relating to the taxpayer's trade or business is an important factor in determining whether the trip is primarily personal. If, for example, a taxpayer spends one week while at a destination on activities which are directly related to his trade or business and subsequently spends an additional five weeks for vacation or other personal activities, the trip will be considered primarily personal in nature in the absence of a clear showing to the contrary.

(c) Where a taxpayer's wife accompanies him on a business trip, expenses attributable to her travel are not deductible unless it can be adequately shown that the wife's presence on the trip has a bona fide business purpose. The wife's performance of some incidental service does not cause her expenses to qualify as deductible business expenses. The same rules apply to any other members of the taxpayer's family who accompany him on such a trip.

(d) Expenses paid or incurred by a taxpayer in attending a convention or other meeting may constitute an ordinary and necessary business expense under section 162 depending upon the facts and circumstances of each case. No distinction will be made between self-employed persons and employees. The fact that an employee uses vacation or leave time or that his attendance at the convention is voluntary will not necessarily prohibit the allowance of the deduction. The allowance of deductions for such expenses will depend upon whether there is a sufficient relationship between the taxpayer's trade of business and his attendance at the convention or other meeting so that he is benefiting or advancing the interests of his trade or business by such attendance. If the convention is for political, social or other purposes unrelated to the taxpayer's trade or business, the expenses are not deductible.

(e) Commuters' fares are not considered as business expenses and are not deductible.

* * *

[T.D. 6500, 25 FR 11402, Nov. 26, 1960]

§ 1.162–3 Cost of materials.

Taxpayers carrying materials and supplies on hand should include in expenses the charges for materials and supplies only in the amount that they are actually consumed and used in operation during the taxable year for which the return is made, provided that the costs of such materials and supplies have not been deducted in determining the net income or loss or taxable income for any previous year. If a taxpayer carries incidental materials or supplies on hand for which no record of consumption is kept or of which physical inventories at the beginning and end of the year are not taken, it will be permissible for the taxpayer to include in his expenses and to deduct from gross income the total cost of such supplies and materials as were purchased during the taxable year for which the return is made, provided the taxable income is clearly reflected by this method.

[T.D. 6500, 25 FR 11402, Nov. 26, 1960]

§ 1.162–4 Repairs.

The cost of incidental repairs which neither materially add to the value of the property nor appreciably prolong its life, but keep it in an ordinarily efficient operating condition, may be deducted as an expense, provided the cost of acquisition or production or the gain or loss basis of the taxpayer's plant, equipment, or other property, as the case may be, is not increased by the amount of such expenditures. Repairs in the nature of replacements, to the extent that they arrest deterioration and appreciably prolong the life of the property, shall either be capitalized and depreciated in accordance with section 167 or charged against the depreciation reserve if such an account is kept.

[T.D. 6500, 25 FR 11402, Nov. 26, 1960]

§ 1.162–5 Expenses for education.

(a) **General rule.** Expenditures made by an individual for education (including research undertaken as part of his educational program) which are not expenditures of a type described in paragraph (b)(2) or (3) of this section are deductible as ordinary and necessary business expenses (even though the education may lead to a degree) if the education—

(1) Maintains or improves skills required by the individual in his employment or other trade or business, or

(2) Meets the express requirements of the individual's employer, or the requirements of applicable law or regulations, imposed as a condition to the retention by the individual of an established employment relationship, status, or rate of compensation.

(b) **Nondeductible educational expenditures** —(1) **In general.** Educational expenditures described in subparagraphs (2) and (3) of this paragraph are personal expenditures or constitute an inseparable aggregate of personal and capital expenditures and, therefore, are not deductible as ordinary and necessary business expenses even though the education may maintain or improve skills required by the individual in his employment or other trade or business or may meet the express requirements of the individual's employer or of applicable law or regulations.

(2) **Minimum educational requirements.** (i) The first category of nondeductible educational expenses within the scope of subparagraph (1) of this paragraph are expenditures made by an individual for education which is required of him in order to meet the minimum educational requirements for qualification in his employment or other trade or business. The minimum education necessary to qualify for a position or other trade or business must be determined from a consideration of such factors as the requirements of the employer, the applicable law and regulations, and the standards of the profession, trade, or business involved. The fact that an individual is already performing service in an employment status does not establish that he has met the minimum educational requirements for qualification in that employment. Once an individual has met the minimum educational requirements for qualification in his employment or other trade or business (as in effect when he enters the employment or trade or business), he shall be treated as continuing to meet those requirements even though they are changed.

(ii) The minimum educational requirements for qualification of a particular individual in a position in an educational institution is the minimum level of education (in terms of aggregate college hours or degree) which under the applicable laws or regulations, in effect at the time this individual is first employed in such position, is normally required of an individual initially being employed in such a position. If there are no normal requirements as to the minimum level of education required for a position in an educational institution, then an individual in such a position shall be considered to have met the minimum educational requirements for qualification in that position when he becomes a member of the faculty of the educational institution. The determination of whether an individual is a member of the faculty of an educational institution must be made on the basis of the particular practices of the institution. However, an individual will ordinarily be considered to be a member of the faculty of an institution if (a) he has tenure or his years of service are being counted toward obtaining tenure; (b) the institution is making contributions to a retirement plan (other than Social Security or a similar program) in respect of his employment; or (c) he has a vote in faculty affairs.

(iii) The application of this subparagraph may be illustrated by the following examples:

Example (1). General facts: State X requires a bachelor's degree for beginning secondary school teachers which must include 30 credit hours of professional educational courses. In addition, in order to retain his position, a secondary school teacher must complete a fifth year of preparation within 10 years after beginning his employment. If an employing school official certifies to the State Department of Education that applicants having a bachelor's degree and the required courses in professional education cannot be found, he may hire individuals as secondary school teachers if they have completed a minimum of 90 semester hours of college work. However, to be retained in his position, such an individual must obtain his bachelor's degree and complete the required professional educational courses within 3 years after his employment commences. Under these facts, a bachelor's degree, without regard to whether it includes 30 credit hours of professional educational courses, is considered to be the minimum educational requirement for qualification as a secondary school teacher in State X. This is the case notwithstanding the number of teachers who are actually hired without such a degree. The following are examples of the application of these facts in particular situations:

Situation 1. A, at the time he is employed as a secondary school teacher in State X, has a bachelor's degree including 30 credit hours of professional educational courses. After his employment, A completes a fifth college year of education and, as a result, is issued a standard certificate. The fifth college year of education undertaken by A is not education required to meet the minimum educational requirements for qualification as a secondary school teacher. Accordingly, the expenditures for such education are deductible unless the expenditures are for education which is part of a program of study being pursued by A which will lead to qualifying him in a new trade or business.

Situation 2. Because of a shortage of applicants meeting the stated requirements, B, who has a bachelor's degree, is employed as a secondary school teacher in State X even though he has only 20 credit hours of professional educational courses. After his employment, B takes an additional 10 credit hours of professional educational courses. Since these courses do not constitute education required to meet the minimum educational requirements for qualification as a secondary school teacher which is a bachelor's degree and will not lead to qualifying B in a new trade or business, the expenditures for such courses are deductible.

Situation 3. Because of a shortage of applicants meeting the stated requirements, C is employed as a secondary school teacher in State X although he has only 90 semester hours of college work toward his bachelor's degree. After his employment, C undertakes courses leading to a bachelor's degree. These courses (including any courses in professional education) constitute education required to meet the minimum educational requirements for qualification as a secondary school teacher. Accordingly, the expenditures for such education are not deductible.

Situation 4. Subsequent to the employment of A, B, and C, but before they have completed a fifth college year of education, State X changes its requirements affecting secondary school teachers to provide that beginning teachers must have completed 5 college years of preparation. In the cases of A, B, and C, a fifth college year of education is not considered to be education undertaken to meet the minimum educational requirements for qualifications as a secondary school teacher. Accordingly, expenditures for a fifth year of college will be deductible unless the expenditures are for education which is part of a program being pursued by A, B, or C which will lead to qualifying him in a new trade or business.

Example (2). D, who holds a bachelor's degree, obtains temporary employment as an instructor at University Y and undertakes graduate courses as a candidate for a graduate degree. D may become a faculty member only if he obtains a graduate degree and may continue to hold a position as instructor only so long as he shows satisfactory progress towards obtaining this graduate degree. The graduate courses taken by D constitute education required to meet the minimum educational requirements for qualification in D's trade or business and, thus, the expenditures for such courses are not deductible.

Example (3). E, who has completed 2 years of a normal 3-year law school course leading to a bachelor of laws degree (LL.B.), is hired by a law firm to do legal research and perform other functions on a full-time basis. As a condition to continued employment, E is required to obtain an LL.B. and pass the State bar examination. E completes his law school education by attending night law school, and he takes a bar review course in order to prepare for the State bar examination. The law courses and bar review course constitute education required to meet the minimum educational requirements for qualification in E's trade or business and, thus, the expenditures for such courses are not deductible.

(3) Qualification for new trade or business. (i) The second category of nondeductible educational expenses within the scope of subparagraph (1) of this paragraph are expenditures made by an individual for education which is part of a program of study being pursued by him which will lead to qualifying him in a new trade or business. In the case of an employee, a change of duties does not constitute a new trade or business if the new duties involve the same general type of work as is involved in the individual's present employment. For this purpose, all teaching and related duties shall be considered to involve the same general type of work. The following are examples of changes in duties which do not constitute new trades or businesses:

(a) Elementary to secondary school classroom teacher.

(b) Classroom teacher in one subject (such as mathematics) to classroom teacher in another subject (such as science).

(c) Classroom teacher to guidance counselor.

(d) Classroom teacher to principal.

(ii) The application of this subparagraph to individuals other than teachers may be illustrated by the following examples:

Example (1). A, a self-employed individual practicing a profession other than law, for example, engineering, accounting, etc., attends law school at night and after completing his law school studies receives a bachelor of laws degree. The expenditures made by A in attending law school are nondeductible because this course of study qualifies him for a new trade or business.

Example (2). Assume the same facts as in example (1) except that A has the status of an employee rather than a self-employed individual, and that his employer requires him to obtain a bachelor of laws degree. A intends to continue practicing his nonlegal profession as an employee of such employer. Nevertheless, the expenditures made by A in attending law school are not deductible since this course of study qualifies him for a new trade or business.

Example (3). B, a general practitioner of medicine, takes a 2-week course reviewing new developments in several specialized fields of medicine. B's expenses for the course are deductible because the course maintains or improves skills required by him in his trade or business and does not qualify him for a new trade or business.

Example (4). C, while engaged in the private practice of psychiatry, undertakes a program of study and training at an accredited psychoanalytic institute which will lead to qualifying him to practice psychoanalysis. C's expenditures for such study and training are deductible because the study and training maintains or improves skills required by him in his trade or business and does not qualify him for a new trade or business.

(c) Deductible educational expenditures—(1) Maintaining or improving skills. The deduction under the category of expenditures for education which maintains or improves skills required by the individual in his employment or other trade or business includes refresher courses or courses dealing with current developments as well as academic or vocational courses provided the expenditures for the courses are not within either category of nondeductible expenditures described in paragraph (b)(2) or (3) of this section.

(2) Meeting requirements of employer. An individual is considered to have undertaken education in order to meet the express requirements of his employer, or the requirements of applicable law or regulations, imposed as a condition to the reten-

tion by the taxpayer of his established employment relationship, status, or rate of compensation only if such requirements are imposed for a bona fide business purpose of the individual's employer. Only the minimum education necessary to the retention by the individual of his established employment relationship, status, or rate of compensation may be considered as undertaken to meet the express requirements of the taxpayer's employer. However, education in excess of such minimum education may qualify as education undertaken in order to maintain or improve the skills required by the taxpayer in his employment or other trade or business (see subparagraph (1) of this paragraph). In no event, however, is a deduction allowable for expenditures for education which, even though for education required by the employer or applicable law or regulations, are within one of the categories of nondeductible expenditures described in paragraph (b)(2) and (3) of this section.

(d) Travel as a form of education. Subject to the provisions of paragraph (b) and (e) of this section, expenditures for travel (including travel while on sabbatical leave) as a form of education are deductible only to the extent such expenditures are attributable to a period of travel that is directly related to the duties of the individual in his employment or other trade or business. For this purpose, a period of travel shall be considered directly related to the duties of an individual in his employment or other trade or business only if the major portion of the activities during such period is of a nature which directly maintains or improves skills required by the individual in such employment or other trade or business. The approval of a travel program by an employer or the fact that travel is accepted by an employer in the fulfillment of its requirements for retention of rate of compensation, status or employment, is not determinative that the required relationship exists between the travel involved and the duties of the individual in his particular position.

(e) Travel away from home. (1) If an individual travels away from home primarily to obtain education the expenses of which are deductible under this section, his expenditures for travel, meals, and lodging while away from home are deductible. However, if as an incident of such trip the individual engages in some personal activity such as sightseeing, social visiting, or entertaining, or other recreation, the portion of the expenses attributable to such personal activity constitutes nondeductible personal or living expenses and is not allowable as a deduction. If the individual's travel away from home is primarily personal, the individual's expenditures for travel, meals and lodging (other than meals and lodging during the time spent in participating in deductible education pursuits) are not deductible. Whether a particular trip is primarily personal or primarily to obtain education the expenses of which are deductible under this section depends upon all the facts and circumstances of each case. An important factor to be taken into consideration in making the determination is the relative amount of time devoted to personal activity as compared with the time devoted to educational pursuits. The rules set forth in this paragraph are subject to the provisions of section 162(a)(2), relating to deductibility of certain traveling expenses, and section 274(c) and (d), relating to allocation of certain foreign travel expenses and substantiation required, respectively, and the regulations thereunder.

(2) **Examples.** The application of this subsection may be illustrated by the following examples:

Example (1). A, a self-employed tax practitioner, decides to take a 1-week course in new developments in taxation, which is offered in City X, 500 miles away from his home. His primary purpose in going to X is to take the course, but he also takes a side trip to City Y (50 miles from X) for 1 day, takes a sightseeing trip while in X, and entertains some personal friends. A's transportation expenses to City X and return to his home are deductible but his transportation expenses to City Y are not deductible. A's expenses for meals and lodging while away from home will be allocated between his educational pursuits and his personal activities. Those expenses which are entirely personal, such as sightseeing and entertaining friends, are not deductible to any extent.

Example (2). The facts are the same as in example (1) except that A's primary purpose in going to City X is to take a vacation. This purpose is indicated by several factors, one of which is the fact that he spends only 1 week attending the tax course and devotes 5 weeks entirely to personal activities. None of A's transportation expenses are deductible and his expenses for meals and lodging while away from home are not deductible to the extent attributable to personal activities. His expenses for meals and lodging allocable to the week attending the tax course are, however, deductible.

Example (3). B, a high school mathematics teacher in New York City, in the summertime travels to a university in California in order to take a mathematics course the expense of which is deductible under this section. B pursues only one-fourth of a full course of study and the remainder of her time is devoted to personal activities the expense of which is not deductible. Absent a showing by B of a substantial nonpersonal reason for taking the course in the university in California, the trip is considered taken primarily for personal reasons and the cost of traveling from New York City to California and return would not be deductible. However, one-fourth of the cost of B's meals and lodging while attending the university in California may be considered properly allocable to deductible educational pursuits and, therefore, is deductible.

[T.D. 6500, 25 FR 11402, Nov. 26, 1960, as amended by T.D. 6918, 32 FR 6679, May 2, 1967]

§ **1.162–6   Professional expenses.**

A professional man may claim as deductions the cost of supplies used by him in the practice of his profession, expenses paid or accrued in the operation and repair of an automobile used in making professional calls, dues to professional societies and subscriptions to professional journals, the rent paid or accrued for office rooms, the cost of the fuel, light, water, telephone, etc., used in such offices, and the hire of office assistance. Amounts currently paid or accrued for books, furniture, and professional instruments and equipment, the useful life of which is short, may be deducted.

[T.D. 6500, 25 FR 11402, Nov. 26, 1960]

§ **1.162–7   Compensation for personal services.**

(a) There may be included among the ordinary and necessary expenses paid or incurred in carrying on any trade or business a reasonable allowance for salaries or other compensation for personal services actually rendered. The test of deductibility in the case of compensation payments is whether they are reasonable and are in fact payments purely for services.

(b) The test set forth in paragraph (a) of this section and its practical application may be further stated and illustrated as follows:

(1) Any amount paid in the form of compensation, but not in fact as the purchase price of services, is not deductible. An ostensible salary paid by a corporation may be a distribution of a dividend on stock. This is likely to occur in the case of a corporation having few shareholders, practically all of whom draw salaries. If in such a case the salaries are in excess of those ordinarily paid for similar services and the excessive payments correspond or bear a close relationship to the stockholdings of the officers or employees, it would seem likely that the salaries are not paid wholly for services rendered, but that the excessive payments are a distribution of earnings upon the stock. An ostensible salary may be in part payment for property. This may occur, for example, where a partnership sells out to a corporation, the former partners agreeing to continue in the service

of the corporation. In such a case it may be found that the salaries of the former partners are not merely for services, but in part constitute payment for the transfer of their business.

(2) The form or method of fixing compensation is not decisive as to deductibility. While any form of contingent compensation invites scrutiny as a possible distribution of earnings of the enterprise, it does not follow that payments on a contingent basis are to be treated fundamentally on any basis different from that applying to compensation at a flat rate. Generally speaking, if contingent compensation is paid pursuant to a free bargain between the employer and the individual made before the services are rendered, not influenced by any consideration on the part of the employer other than that of securing on fair and advantageous terms the services of the individual, it should be allowed as a deduction even though in the actual working out of the contract it may prove to be greater than the amount which would ordinarily be paid.

(3) In any event the allowance for the compensation paid may not exceed what is reasonable under all the circumstances. It is, in general, just to assume that reasonable and true compensation is only such amount as would ordinarily be paid for like services by like enterprises under like circumstances. The circumstances to be taken into consideration are those existing at the date when the contract for services was made, not those existing at the date when the contract is questioned.

* * *

[T.D. 6500, 25 FR 11402, Nov. 26, 1960]

§ 1.162–8 Treatment of excessive compensation.

The income tax liability of the recipient in respect of an amount ostensibly paid to him as compensation, but not allowed to be deducted as such by the payor, will depend upon the circumstances of each case. Thus, in the case of excessive payments by corporations, if such payments correspond or bear a close relationship to stockholdings, and are found to be a distribution of earnings or profits, the excessive payments will be treated as a dividend. If such payments constitute payment for property, they should be treated by the payor as a capital expenditure and by the recipient as part of the purchase price. In the absence of evidence to justify other treatment, excessive payments for salaries or other compensation for personal services will be included in gross income of the recipient.

[T.D. 6500, 25 FR 11402, Nov. 26, 1960]

§ 1.162–9 Bonuses to employees.

Bonuses to employees will constitute allowable deductions from gross income when such payments are made in good faith and as additional compensation for the services actually rendered by the employees, provided such payments, when added to the stipulated salaries, do not exceed a reasonable compensation for the services rendered. It is immaterial whether such bonuses are paid in cash or in kind or partly in cash and partly in kind. Donations made to employees and others, which do not have in them the element of compensation or which are in excess of reasonable compensation for services, are not deductible from gross income.

[T.D. 6500, 25 FR 11402, Nov. 26, 1960]

§ 1.162–10 Certain employee benefits.

(a) **In general.** Amounts paid or accrued by a taxpayer on account of injuries received by employees and lump sum amounts paid or accrued as compensation for injuries, are proper deductions as ordinary and necessary expenses. Such deductions are limited to the amount not compensated for by insurance or otherwise. Amounts paid or accrued within the taxable year for dismissal wages, unemployment benefits, guaranteed annual wages, vacations, or a sickness, accident, hospitalization, medical expense, recreational, welfare, or similar benefit plan, are deductible under section 162(a) if they are ordinary and necessary expenses of the trade or business. However, except as provided in paragraph (b) of this section, such amounts shall not be deductible under section 162(a) if, under any circumstances, they may be used to provide benefits under a stock bonus, pension, annuity, profit-sharing, or other deferred compensation plan of the type referred to in section 404(a). In such an event, the extent to which these amounts are deductible from gross income shall be governed by the provisions of section 404 and the regulations issued thereunder.

* * *

(c) **Other plans providing deferred compensation.** For rules relating to the deduction of amounts paid to or under a stock bonus, pension, annuity, or profit-sharing plan or amounts paid or accrued under any other plan deferring the receipt of compensation, see section 404 and the regulations thereunder.

[T.D. 6500, 25 FR 11402, Nov. 26, 1960]

§ 1.162–11 Rentals.

(a) **Acquisition of a leasehold.** If a leasehold is acquired for business purposes for a specified sum, the purchaser may take as a deduction in his return an aliquot part of such sum each year, based on the number of years the lease has to run. Taxes paid by a tenant to or for a landlord for business property are additional rent and constitute a deductible item to the tenant and taxable income to the landlord, the amount of the tax being deductible by the latter. For disallowance of deduction for income taxes paid by a lessee corporation pursuant to a lease arrangement with the lessor corporation, see section 110 and the regulations thereunder. See section 178 and the regulations thereunder for rules governing the effect to be given renewal options in amortizing the costs incurred after July 28, 1958 of acquiring a lease.

(b) **Improvements by lessee on lessor's property.** (1) The cost to a lessee of erecting buildings or making permanent improvements on property of which he is the lessee is a capital investment, and is not deductible as a business expense. If the estimated useful life in the hands of the taxpayer of the building erected or of the improvements made, determined without regard to the terms of the lease, is longer than the remaining period of the lease, an annual deduction may be made from gross income of an amount equal to the total cost of such improvements divided by the number of years remaining in the term of the lease, and such deduction shall be in lieu of a deduction for depreciation. If, on the other hand, the useful life of such buildings or improvements in the hands of the taxpayer is equal to or shorter than the remaining period of the lease, this deduction shall be computed under the provisions of section 167 (relating to depreciation).

(2) If the lessee began improvements on leased property before July 28, 1958, or if the lessee was on such date and at all times thereafter under a binding legal obligation to make such improvements, the matter of spreading the cost of erecting buildings or making permanent improvements over the term of the original lease, together with the renewal period or periods depends upon the facts in the particular case, including the presence or absence of an obligation of renewal and the relationship between the parties. As a general rule, unless the lease has been renewed or the facts show with reasonable certainty that the lease will be renewed, the cost or other basis of the lease, or the cost of improvements shall be spread only over the number of years the lease has to run without taking into account any right of renewal. The provisions of this subparagraph may be illustrated by the following examples:

Example (1). A subsidiary corporation leases land from its parent at a fair rental for a 25-year period. The subsidiary erects on the land valuable factory buildings having an estimated useful life of 50 years. These facts show with reasonable certainty that the lease will be renewed, even though the lease contains no option of renewal. Therefore, the cost of the buildings shall be depreciated over the estimated useful life of the buildings in accordance with section 167 and the regulations thereunder.

Example (2). A retail merchandising corporation leases land at a fair rental from an unrelated lessor for the longest period that the lessor is willing to lease the land (30 years). The lessee erects on the land a department store having an estimated useful life of 40 years. These facts do not show with reasonable certainty that the lease will be renewed. Therefore, the cost of the building shall be spread over the remaining term of the lease. An annual deduction may be made of an amount equal to the cost of the building divided by the number of years remaining in the term of the lease, and such deduction shall be in lieu of a deduction for depreciation.

* * *

[T.D. 6500, 25 FR 11402, Nov. 26, 1960, as amended by T.D. 6520, 25 FR 13692, Dec. 24, 1960]

§ 1.162–12 Expenses of farmers.

(a) **Farms engaged in for profit.** A farmer who operates a farm for profit is entitled to deduct from gross income as necessary expenses all amounts actually expended in the carrying on of the business of farming. The cost of ordinary tools of short life or small cost, such as hand tools, including shovels, rakes, etc., may be deducted. The purchase of feed and other costs connected with raising livestock may be treated as expense deductions insofar as such costs represent actual outlay, but not including the value of farm produce grown upon the farm or the labor of the taxpayer. For taxable years beginning after July 12, 1972, where a farmer is engaged in producing crops and the process of gathering and disposal of such crops is not completed within the taxable year in which such crops were planted, expenses deducted may, with the consent of the Commissioner (see section 446 and the regulations thereunder), be determined upon the crop method, and such deductions must be taken in the taxable year in which the gross income from the crop has been realized. For taxable years beginning on or before July 12, 1972, where a farmer is engaged in producing crops which take more than a year from the time of planting to the process of gathering and disposal, expenses deducted may, with the consent of the Commissioner (see section 446 and the regulations thereunder), be determined upon the crop method, and such deductions must be taken in the taxable year in which the gross income from the crop has been realized. If a farmer does not compute income upon the crop method, the cost of seeds and young plants which are purchased for further development and cultivation prior to sale in later years may be deducted as an expense for the year of purchase, provided the farmer follows a consistent practice of deducting such costs as an expense from year to year. The preceding sentence does not apply to the cost of seeds and young plants connected with the planting of timber (see section 611 and the regulations thereunder). For provisions relating to citrus and almond groves, see section 278 and the regulations thereunder. The cost of farm machinery, equipment, and farm buildings represents a capital investment and is not an allowable deduction as an item of expense. Amounts expended in the development of farms, orchards, and ranches prior to the time when the productive state is reached may, at the election of the taxpayer, be regarded as investments of capital. For the treatment of soil and water conservation expenditures as expenses which are not chargeable to capital account, see section 175 and the regulations thereunder. For taxable years beginning after December 31, 1959, in the case of expenditures paid or incurred by farmers for fertilizer, lime, etc., see section 180 and the regulations thereunder. Amounts expended in purchasing work, breeding, dairy, or sporting animals are regarded as investments of capital, and shall be depreciated unless such animals are included in an inventory in accordance with § 1.61–4. The purchase price of an automobile, even when wholly used in carrying on farming operations, is not deductible, but is regarded as an investment of capital. The cost of gasoline, repairs, and upkeep of an automobile if used wholly in the business of farming is deductible as an expense; if used partly for business purposes and partly for the pleasure or convenience of the taxpayer or his family, such cost may be apportioned according to the extent of the use for purposes of business and pleasure or convenience, and only the proportion of such cost justly attributable to business purposes is deductible as a necessary expense.

* * *

[T.D. 6500, 25 FR 11402, Nov. 26, 1960, as amended by T.D. 6548, 26 FR 1486, Feb. 22, 1961; T.D. 7198, 37 FR 13679, July 13, 1972]

§ 1.162–15 Contributions, dues, etc.

(a) **Contributions to organizations described in section 170—(1) In general.** No deduction is allowable under section 162(a) for a contribution or gift by an individual or a corporation if any part thereof is deductible under section 170. For example, if a taxpayer makes a contribution of $5,000 and only $4,000 of this amount is deductible under section 170(a) (whether because of the percentage limitation under either section 170(b)(1) or (2), the requirement as to time of payment, or both) no deduction is allowable under section 162(a) for the remaining $1,000.

(2) **Scope of limitations.** The limitations provided in section 162(b) and this paragraph apply only to payments which are in fact contributions or gifts to organizations described in section 170. For example, payments by a transit company to a local hospital (which is a charitable organization within the meaning of section 170) in consideration of a binding obligation on the part of the hospital to provide hospital services and facilities for the company's employees are not contributions or gifts within the meaning of section 170 and may be deductible under section 162(a) if the requirements of section 162(a) are otherwise satisfied.

(b) **Other contributions.** Donations to organizations other than those described in section 170 which bear a direct relationship to the taxpayer's business and are made with a reasonable expectation of a financial return commensurate with the amount of the donation may constitute allowable deductions as business expenses, provided the donation is not made for a purpose for which a deduction is not allowable by reason of the provisions of paragraph (b)(1)(i) or (c) of § 1.162–20. For example, a transit company may donate a sum of money to an organization (of a class not referred to in section 170) intending to hold a convention in the city in which it operates, with a reasonable expectation that the holding of such convention will augment its income through a greater number of people using its transportation facilities.

941

(c) Dues. Dues and other payments to an organization, such as a labor union or a trade association, which otherwise meet the requirements of the regulations under section 162, are deductible in full. For limitations on the deductibility of dues and other payments, see paragraph (b) and (c) of § 1.162–20.

* * *

[T.D. 6500, 25 FR 11402, Nov. 26, 1960, as amended by T.D. 6819, 30 FR 5580, April 20, 1965]

§ 1.162–17　Reporting and substantiation of certain business expenses of employees.

(a) Introductory. The purpose of the regulations in this section is to provide rules for the reporting of information on income tax returns by taxpayers who pay or incur ordinary and necessary business expenses in connection with the performance of services as an employee and to furnish guidance as to the type of records which will be useful in compiling such information and in its substantiation, if required. The rules prescribed in this section do not apply to expenses paid or incurred for incidentals, such as office supplies for the employer or local transportation in connection with an errand. Employees incurring such incidental expenses are not required to provide substantiation for such amounts. The term "ordinary and necessary business expenses" means only those expenses which are ordinary and necessary in the conduct of the taxpayer's business and are directly attributable to such business. The term does not include nondeductible personal, living or family expenses.

(b) Expenses for which the employee is required to account to his employer—(1) Reimbursements equal to expenses. The employee need not report on his tax return (either itemized or in total amount) expenses for travel, transportation, entertainment, and similar purposes paid or incurred by him solely for the benefit of his employer for which he is required to account and does account to his employer and which are charged directly or indirectly to the employer (for example, through credit cards) or for which the employee is paid through advances, reimbursements, or otherwise, provided the total amount of such advances, reimbursements, and charges is equal to such expenses. In such a case the taxpayer need only state in his return that the total of amounts charged directly or indirectly to his employer through credit cards or otherwise and received

from the employer as advances or reimbursements did not exceed the ordinary and necessary business expenses paid or incurred by the employee.

(2) Reimbursements in excess of expenses. In case the total of amounts charged directly or indirectly to the employer and received from the employer as advances, reimbursements, or otherwise, exceeds the ordinary and necessary business expenses paid or incurred by the employee and the employee is required to and does account to his employer for such expenses, the taxpayer must include such excess in income and state on his return that he has done so.

(3) Expenses in excess of reimbursements. If the employee's ordinary and necessary business expenses exceed the total of the amounts charged directly or indirectly to the employer and received from the employer as advances, reimbursements, or otherwise, and the employee is required to and does account to his employer for such expenses, the taxpayer may make the statement in his return required by subparagraph (1) of this paragraph unless he wishes to claim a deduction for such excess. If, however, he wishes to secure a deduction for such excess, he must submit a statement showing the following information as part of his tax return:

(i) The total of any charges paid or borne by the employer and of any other amounts received from the employer for payment of expenses whether by means of advances, reimbursements or otherwise; and

(ii) The nature of his occupation, the number of days away from home on business, and the total amount of ordinary and necessary business expenses paid or incurred by him (including those charged directly or indirectly to the employer through credit cards or otherwise) broken down into such broad categories as transportation, meals and lodging while away from home overnight, entertainment expenses, and other business expenses.

(4) To "account" to his employer as used in this section means to submit an expense account or other required written statement to the employer showing the business nature and the amount of all the employee's expenses (including those charged directly or indirectly to the employer through credit cards or otherwise) broken down into such broad categories as transportation, meals and lodging while away from home overnight, entertainment expenses, and other business expenses. For this purpose, the Commissioner in his discretion may approve reasonable business practices under which mileage, per diem in lieu of subsistence, and similar allowances providing for ordinary and necessary business expenses in accordance with a fixed scale may be regarded as equivalent to an accounting to the employer.

(c) Expenses for which the employee is not required to account to his employer. If the employee is not required to account to his employer for his ordinary and necessary business expenses, e.g., travel, transportation, entertainment, and similar items, or, though required, fails to account for such expenses, he must submit, as a part of his tax return, a statement showing the following information:

(1) The total of all amounts received as advances or reimbursements from his employer in connection with the ordinary and necessary business expenses of the employee, including amounts charged directly or indirectly to the employer through credit cards or otherwise; and

(2) The nature of his occupation, the number of days away from home on business, and the total amount of ordinary and necessary business expenses paid or incurred by him (including those charged directly or indirectly to the employer through credit cards or otherwise) broken down into such broad categories as transportation, meals and lodging while away from home overnight, entertainment expenses, and other business expenses.

(d) Substantiation of items of expense. **(1)** Although the Commissioner may require any taxpayer to substantiate such information concerning expense accounts as may appear to be pertinent in determining tax liability, taxpayers ordinarily will not be called upon to substantiate expense account information except those in the following categories:

(i) A taxpayer who is not required to account to his employer, or who does not account;

(ii) A taxpayer whose expenses exceed the total of amounts charged to his employer and amounts received through advances, reimbursements or otherwise and who claims a deduction on his return for such excess;

(iii) A taxpayer who is related to his employer within the meaning of section 267(b); and

(iv) Other taxpayers in cases where it is determined that the accounting procedures used by the employer for the reporting and substantiation of expenses by employees are not adequate.

(2) The Code contemplates that taxpayers keep such records as will be sufficient to enable the Commissioner to correctly determine income tax liability. Accordingly, it is to the advantage of taxpayers who may be called upon to substantiate expense account information to maintain as adequate and detailed records of travel, transportation, entertainment, and similar business expenses as practical since the burden of proof is upon the taxpayer to show that such expenses were not only paid or incurred but also that they constitute ordinary and necessary business expenses. One method for substantiating expenses incurred by an employee in connection with his employment is through the preparation of a daily diary or record of expenditures, maintained in sufficient detail to enable him to readily identify the amount and nature of any expenditure, and the preservation of supporting documents, especially in connection with large or exceptional expenditures. Nevertheless, it is recognized that by reason of the nature of certain expenses or the circumstances under which they are incurred, it is often difficult for an employee to maintain detailed records or to preserve supporting documents for all his expenses. Detailed records of small expenditures incurred in traveling or for transportation, as for example, tips, will not be required.

(3) Where records are incomplete or documentary proof is unavailable, it may be possible to establish the amount of the expenditures by approximations based upon reliable secondary sources of information and collateral evidence. For example, in connection with an item of traveling expense a taxpayer might establish that he was in a travel status a certain number of days but that it was impracticable for him to establish the details of all his various items of travel expense. In such a case rail fares or plane fares can usually be ascertained with exactness and automobile costs approximated on the basis of mileage covered. A reasonable approximation of meals and lodging might be based upon receipted hotel bills or upon average daily rates for such accommodations and meals prevailing in the particular community for comparable accommodations. Since detailed records of incidental items are not required, deductions for these items may be based upon a reasonable approximation. In cases where a taxpayer is called upon to substantiate expense account information, the burden is on the taxpayer to establish that the amounts claimed as a deduction are reasonably accurate and constitute ordinary and necessary business expenses paid or incurred by him in connection with his trade or business. In connection with the determination of factual matters of this type, due consideration will be given to the reasonableness of the stated expenditures for the claimed purposes in relation to the taxpayer's circumstances (such as his income and the nature of his occupation), to the reliability and accuracy of records in connection with other items more readily lending themselves to detailed recordkeeping, and to all of the facts and circumstances in the particular case.

* * *

[T.D. 6500, 25 FR 11402, Nov. 26, 1960, as amended by T.D. 6630, 27 FR 12935, Dec. 29, 1962]

§ 1.162–18 Illegal bribes and kickbacks.

(a) **Illegal payments to government officials or employees—(1) In general.** No deduction shall be allowed under section 162(a) for any amount paid or incurred, directly or indirectly, to an official or employee of any government, or of any agency or other instrumentality of any government, if—

(i) In the case of a payment made to an official or employee of a government other than a foreign government described in subparagraph (3)(ii) or (iii) of this paragraph, the payment constitutes an illegal bribe or kickback, or

(ii) In the case of a payment made to an official or employee of a foreign government described in subparagraph (3)(ii) or (iii) of this paragraph, the making of the payment would be unlawful under the laws of the United States (if such laws were applicable to the payment and to the official or employee at the time the expenses were paid or incurred).

No deduction shall be allowed for an accrued expense if the eventual payment thereof would fall within the prohibition of this section. The place where the expenses are paid or incurred is immaterial. For purposes of subdivision (ii) of this subparagraph, lawfulness, or unlawfulness of the payment under the laws of the foreign country is immaterial.

(2) **Indirect payment.** For purposes of this paragraph, an indirect payment to an individual shall include any payment which inures to his benefit or promotes his interests, regardless of the medium in which the payment is made and regardless of the identity of the immediate recipient or payor. Thus, for example, payment made to an

agent, relative, or independent contractor of an official or employee, or even directly into the general treasury of a foreign country of which the beneficiary is an official or employee, may be treated as an indirect payment to the official or employee, if in fact such payment inures or will inure to his benefit or promotes or will promote his financial or other interests. A payment made by an agent or independent contractor of the taxpayer which benefits the taxpayer shall be treated as an indirect payment by the taxpayer to the official or employee.

(3) **Official or employee of a government.** Any individual officially connected with—

(i) The Government of the United States, a State, a territory or possession of the United States, the District of Columbia, or the Commonwealth of Puerto Rico,

(ii) The government of a foreign country, or

(iii) A political subdivision of, or a corporation or other entity serving as an agency or instrumentality of, any of the above,

in whatever capacity, whether on a permanent or temporary basis, and whether or not serving for compensation, shall be included within the term "official or employee of a government", regardless of the place of residence or post of duty of such individual. An independent contractor would not ordinarily be considered to be an official or employee. For purposes of section 162(c) and this paragraph, the term "foreign country" shall include any foreign nation, whether or not such nation has been accorded diplomatic recognition by the United States. Individuals who purport to act on behalf of or as the government of a foreign nation, or an agency or instrumentality thereof, shall be treated under this section as officials or employees of a foreign government, whether or not such individuals in fact control such foreign nation, agency, or instrumentality, and whether or not such individuals are accorded diplomatic recognition. Accordingly, a group in rebellion against an established government shall be treated as officials or employees of a foreign government, as shall officials or employees of the government against which the group is in rebellion.

(4) **Laws of the United States.** The term "laws of the United States", to which reference is made in paragraph (a)(1)(ii) of this section, shall be deemed to include only Federal statutes, including State laws which are assimilated into Federal law

by Federal statute, and legislative and interpretative regulations thereunder. The term shall also be limited to statutes which prohibit some act or acts, for the violation of which there is a civil or criminal penalty.

(5) **Burden of proof.** In any proceeding involving the issue of whether, for purposes of section 162(c)(1), a payment made to a government official or employee constitutes an illegal bribe or kickback (or would be unlawful under the laws of the United States) the burden of proof in respect of such issue shall be upon the Commissioner to the same extent as he bears the burden of proof in civil fraud cases under section 7454 (i.e., he must prove the illegality of the payment by clear and convincing evidence).

(6) **Example.** The application of this paragraph may be illustrated by the following example:

Example. X Corp. is in the business of selling hospital equipment in State Y. During 1970, X Corp. employed A who at the time was employed full time by State Y as Superintendent of Hospitals. The purpose of A's employment by X Corp. was to procure for it an improper advantage over other concerns in the making of sales to hospitals in respect of which A, as Superintendent, had authority. X Corp. paid A $5,000 during 1970. The making of this payment was illegal under the laws of State Y. Under section 162(c)(1), X Corp. is precluded from deducting as a trade or business expense the $5,000 paid to A.

(b) **Other illegal payments—(1) In general.** No deduction shall be allowed under section 162(a) for any payment (other than a payment described in paragraph (a) of this section) made, directly or indirectly, to any person, if the payment constitutes an illegal bribe, illegal kickback, or other illegal payment under the laws of the United States (as defined in paragraph (a)(4) of this section), or under any State law (but only if such State law is generally enforced), which subjects the payor to a criminal penalty or the loss (including a suspension) of license or privilege to engage in a trade or business (whether or not such penalty or loss is actually imposed upon the taxpayer). For purposes of this paragraph, a kickback includes a payment in consideration of the referral of a client, patient, or customer. This paragraph applies only to payments made after December 30, 1969.

(2) **State law.** For purposes of this paragraph, State law means a statute of a State or the District of Columbia.

(3) **Generally enforced.** For purposes of this paragraph, a State law shall be considered to be generally enforced unless it is never enforced or

the only persons normally charged with violations thereof in the State (or the District of Columbia) enacting the law are infamous or those whose violations are extraordinarily flagrant. For example, a criminal statute of a State shall be considered to be generally enforced unless violations of the statute which are brought to the attention of appropriate enforcement authorities do not result in any enforcement action in the absence of unusual circumstances.

(4) **Burden of proof.** In any proceeding involving the issue of whether, for purposes of section 162(c)(2), a payment constitutes an illegal bribe, illegal kickback, or other illegal payment the burden of proof in respect of such issue shall be upon the Commissioner to the same extent as he bears the burden of proof in civil fraud cases under section 7454 (i.e., he must prove the illegality of the payment by clear and convincing evidence).

(5) **Example.** The application of this paragraph may be illustrated by the following example:

Example. X Corp., a calendar-year taxpayer, is engaged in the ship repair business in State Y. During 1970, repairs on foreign ships accounted for a substantial part of its total business. It was X Corp.'s practice to kick back approximately 10 percent of the repair bill to the captain and chief engineer of all foreign-owned vessels, which kickbacks are illegal under a law of State Y (which is generally enforced) and potentially subject X Corp. to fines. During 1970, X Corp. paid $50,000 in such kickbacks. On X Corp.'s return for 1970, a deduction under section 162 was taken for the $50,000. The deduction of the $50,000 of illegal kickbacks during 1970 is disallowed under section 162(c)(2), whether or not X Corp. is prosecuted with respect to the kickbacks.

(c) **Kickbacks, rebates, and bribes under medicare and medicaid.** No deduction shall be allowed under section 162(a) for any kickback, rebate, or bribe (whether or not illegal) made on or after December 10, 1971, by any provider of services, supplier, physician, or other person who furnishes items or services for which payment is or may be made under the Social Security Act, as amended, or in whole or in part out of Federal funds under a State plan approved under such Act, if such kickback, rebate, or bribe is made in connection with the furnishing of such items or services or the making or receipt of such payments. For purposes of this paragraph, a kickback includes a payment in consideration of the referral of a client, patient, or customer.

[T.D. 6500, 25 FR 11402, Nov. 26, 1960, as amended by T.D. 7345, 40 FR 7437, Feb. 20, 1975; 40 FR 8948, March 4, 1975]

§ 1.162–20 Expenditures attributable to lobbying, political campaigns, attempts to influence legislation, etc., and certain advertising.

(a) **In general**—(1) **Scope of section.** This section contains rules governing the deductibility or nondeductibility of expenditures for lobbying purposes, for the promotion or defeat of legislation, for political campaign purposes (including the support of or opposition to any candidate for public office) or for carrying on propaganda (including advertising) related to any of the foregoing purposes. * *

(2) **Institutional or "good will" advertising.** Expenditures for institutional or "good will" advertising which keeps the taxpayer's name before the public are generally deductible as ordinary and necessary business expenses provided the expenditures are related to the patronage the taxpayer might reasonably expect in the future. For example, a deduction will ordinarily be allowed for the cost of advertising which keeps the taxpayer's name before the public in connection with encouraging contributions to such organizations as the Red Cross, the purchase of United States Savings Bonds, or participation in similar causes. In like fashion, expenditures for advertising which presents views on economic, financial, social, or other subjects of a general nature, but which does not involve any of the activities specified in paragraph (b) or (c) of this section for which a deduction is not allowable, are deductible if they otherwise meet the requirements of the regulations under section 162.

(b) **Taxable years beginning before January 1, 1963**—* * *

* * *

(c) **Taxable years beginning after December 31, 1962**—(1) **In general.** For taxable years beginning after December 31, 1962, certain types of expenses incurred with respect to legislative matters are deductible under section 162(a) if they otherwise meet the requirements of the regulations under section 162. These deductible expenses are described in subparagraph (2) of this paragraph. All other expenditures for lobbying purposes, for the promotion or defeat of legislation * * * for political campaign purposes (including the support of or opposition to any candidate for public office), or for carrying on propaganda (including advertising) relating to any of the foregoing purposes are not deductible from gross income for such taxable years. * * *

(2) **Appearances, etc., with respect to legislation**—(i) **General rule.** Pursuant to the provisions of section 162(e), expenses incurred with respect to legislative matters which may be deductible are those ordinary and necessary expenses (including, but not limited to, traveling expenses described in section 162(a)(2) and the cost of preparing testimony) paid or incurred by the taxpayer during a taxable year beginning after December 31, 1962, in carrying on any trade or business which are in direct connection with—

(a) Appearances before, submission of statements to, or sending communications to, the committees, or individual members of Congress or of any legislative body of a State, a possession of the United States, or a political subdivision of any of the foregoing with respect to legislation or proposed legislation of direct interest to the taxpayer, or

(b) Communication of information between the taxpayer and an organization of which he is a member with respect to legislation or proposed legislation of direct interest to the taxpayer and to such organization.

For provisions relating to dues paid or incurred with respect to an organization of which the taxpayer is a member, see subparagraph (3) of this paragraph.

(ii) **Legislation or proposed legislation of direct interest to the taxpayer**—(a) Legislation or proposed legislation. The term "legislation or proposed legislation" includes bills and resolutions introduced by a member of Congress or other legislative body referred to in subdivision (i)(a) of this subparagraph for consideration by such body as well as oral or written proposals for legislative action submitted to the legislative body or to a committee or member of such body.

(b) Direct interest—(1) In general. (i) Legislation or proposed legislation is of direct interest to a taxpayer if the legislation or proposed legislation is of such a nature that it will, or may reasonably be expected to, affect the trade or business of the taxpayer. It is immaterial whether the effect, or expected effect, on the trade or business will be beneficial or detrimental to the trade or business or whether it will be immediate. If legislation or proposed legislation has such a relationship to a trade or business that the expenses of any appearance or communication in connection with the legislation meets the ordinary and necessary test of section 162(a), then such legislation ordinarily meets the direct interest test of section 162(e). However, if the nature of the legislation or proposed legislation is such that the likelihood of its having an effect on the trade or business of the taxpayer is remote or speculative, the legislation or proposed legislation is not of direct interest to the taxpayer. Legislation or proposed legislation which will not affect the trade or business of the taxpayer is not of direct interest to the taxpayer even though such legislation will affect the personal, living, or family activities or expenses of the taxpayer. Legislation or proposed legislation is not of direct interest to a taxpayer merely because it may affect business in general; however, if the legislation or proposed legislation will, or may reasonably be expected to, affect the taxpayer's trade or business it will be of direct interest to the taxpayer even though it also will affect the trade or business of other taxpayers or business in general. To meet the direct interest test, it is not necessary that all provisions of the legislation or proposed legislation have an effect, or expected effect, on the taxpayer's trade or business. The test will be met if one of the provisions of the legislation has the specified effect. Legislation or proposed legislation will be considered to be of direct interest to a membership organization if it is of direct interest to the organization, as such, or if it is of direct interest to one or more of its members.

(ii) Legislation which would increase or decrease the taxes applicable to the trade or business, increase or decrease the operating costs or earnings of the trade or business, or increase or decrease the administrative burdens connected with the trade or business meets the direct interest test. Legislation which would increase the social security benefits or liberalize the right to such benefits meets the direct interest test because such changes in the social security benefits may reasonably be expected to affect the retirement benefits which the employer will be asked to provide his employees or to increase his taxes. Legislation which would impose a retailer's sales tax is of direct interest to a retailer because, although the tax may be passed on to his customers, collection of the tax will impose additional burdens on the retailer, and because the increased cost of his products to the consumer may reduce the demand for them. Legislation which would provide an income tax credit or exclusion for shareholders is of direct interest to a corporation, because those tax benefits may in-

crease the sources of capital available to the corporation. Legislation which would favorably or adversely affect the business of a competitor so as to affect the taxpayer's competitive position is of direct interest to the taxpayer. Legislation which would improve the school system of a community is of direct interest to a membership organization comprised of employers in the community because the improved school system is likely to make the community more attractive to prospective employees of such employers. On the other hand, proposed legislation relating to Presidential succession in the event of the death of the President has only a remote and speculative effect on any trade or business and therefore does not meet the direct interest test. Similarly, if a corporation is represented before a congressional committee to oppose an appropriation bill merely because of a desire to bring increased Government economy with the hope that such economy will eventually cause a reduction in the Federal income tax, the legislation does not meet the direct interest test because any effect it may have upon the corporation's trade or business is highly speculative.

* * *

(3) **Deductibility of dues and other payments to an organization.** If a substantial part of the activities of an organization, such as a labor union or a trade association, consists of one or more of the activities to which this paragraph relates (legislative matters, political campaigns, etc.), exclusive of any activity constituting an appearance or communication with respect to legislation or proposed legislation of direct interest to the organization (see subparagraph (2)(ii)(b)(1)), a deduction will be allowed only for such portion of the dues or other payments to the organization as the taxpayer can clearly establish is attributable to activities to which this paragraph does not relate and to any activity constituting an appearance or communication with respect to legislation or proposed legislation of direct interest to the organization. The determination of whether a substantial part of an organization's activities consists of one or more of the activities to which this paragraph relates (exclusive of appearances or communications with respect to legislation or proposed legislation of direct interest to the organization) shall be based on all the facts and circumstances. In no event shall a deduction be allowed for that portion of a special assessment or similar payment (including an increase in dues) made to any organization for any activity to which this paragraph relates if the

activity does not constitute an appearance or communication with respect to legislation or proposed legislation of direct interest to the organization. If an organization pays or incurs expenses allocable to legislative activities which meet the tests of subdivisions (i) and (ii) of subparagraph (2) of this paragraph (appearances or communications with respect to legislation or proposed legislation of direct interest to the organization), on behalf of its members, the dues paid by a taxpayer are deductible to the extent used for such activities. Dues paid by a taxpayer will be considered to be used for such an activity, and thus deductible, although the legislation or proposed legislation involved is not of direct interest to the taxpayer, if, pursuant to the provisions of subparagraph (2)(ii)(b)(1) of this paragraph, the legislation or proposed legislation is of direct interest to the organization, as such, or is of direct interest to one or more members of the organization. For other provisions relating to the deductibility of dues and other payments to an organization, such as a labor union or a trade association, see paragraph (c) of § 1.162-15.

(4) **Limitations.** No deduction shall be allowed under section 162(a) for any amount paid or incurred (whether by way of contribution, gift, or otherwise) in connection with any attempt to influence the general public, or segments thereof, with respect to legislative matters, elections, or referendums. For example, no deduction shall be allowed for any expenses incurred in connection with "grassroot" campaigns or any other attempts to urge or encourage the public to contact members of a legislative body for the purpose of proposing, supporting, or opposing legislation.

[T.D. 6819, 30 FR 5581, April 20, 1965, as amended by T.D. 6996, 34 FR 835, Jan. 18, 1969]

§ 1.162-21 **Fines and penalties.**

(a) **In general.** No deduction shall be allowed under section 162(a) for any fine or similar penalty paid to—

(1) The government of the United States, a State, a territory or possession of the United States, the District of Columbia, or the Commonwealth of Puerto Rico;

(2) The government of a foreign country; or

(3) A political subdivision of, or corporation or other entity serving as an agency or instrumentality of, any of the above.

(b) **Definition.** (1) For purposes of this section a fine or similar penalty includes an amount—

(i) Paid pursuant to conviction or a plea of guilty or *nolo contendere* for a crime (felony or misdemeanor) in a criminal proceeding;

(ii) Paid as a civil penalty imposed by Federal, State, or local law, including additions to tax and additional amounts and assessable penalties imposed by chapter 68 of the Internal Revenue Code of 1954;

(iii) Paid in settlement of the taxpayer's actual or potential liability for a fine or penalty (civil or criminal); or

(iv) Forfeited as collateral posted in connection with a proceeding which could result in imposition of such a fine or penalty.

(2) The amount of a fine or penalty does not include legal fees and related expenses paid or incurred in the defense of a prosecution or civil action arising from a violation of the law imposing the fine or civil penalty, nor court costs assessed against the taxpayer, or stenographic and printing charges. Compensatory damages (including damages under section 4A of the Clayton Act (15 U.S.C. 15a), as amended) paid to a government do not constitute a fine or penalty.

(c) **Examples.** The application of this section may be illustrated by the following examples:

Example (1). M Corp. was indicted under section 1 of the Sherman Anti-Trust Act (15 U.S.C. 1) for fixing and maintaining prices of certain electrical products. M Corp. was convicted and was fined $50,000. The United States sued M Corp. under section 4A of the Clayton Act (15 U.S.C. 15a) for $100,000, the amount of the actual damages resulting from the price fixing of which M Corp. was convicted. Pursuant to a final judgment entered in the civil action M Corp. paid the United States $100,000 in damages. Section 162(f) precludes M Corp. from deducting the fine of $50,000 as a trade or business expense. Section 162(f) does not preclude it from deducting the $100,000 paid to the United States as actual damages.

Example (2). N Corp. was found to have violated 33 U.S.C. 1321(b)(3) when a vessel it operated discharged oil in harmful quantities into the navigable waters of the United States. A civil penalty under 33 U.S.C. 1321(b)(6) of $5,000 was assessed against N Corp. with respect to the discharge. N Corp. paid $5,000 to the Coast Guard in payment of the civil penalty. Section 162(f) precludes N Corp. from deducting the $5,000 penalty.

Example (3). O Corp., a manufacturer of motor vehicles, was found to have violated 42 U.S.C. 1857f-2(a)(1) by selling a new motor vehicle which was not covered by the required certificate of conformity. Pursuant to 42 U.S.C. 1857f-4, O Corp. was required to pay, and did pay, a civil penalty of $10,000. In addition, pursuant to 42 U.S.C. 1857f-5a(c)(1), O Corp. was required to expend, and did expend, $500 in order to remedy the nonconformity of that motor vehicle. Section 162(f) precludes O Corp. from deducting the $10,000 penalty as a trade or business expense, but does not preclude it from deducting the $500 which it expended to remedy the nonconformity.

Example (4). P Corp. was the operator of a coal mine in which occurred a violation of a mandatory safety standard prescribed by the Federal Coal Mine Health and Safety Act of 1969 (30 U.S.C. 801 et seq.). Pursuant to 30 U.S.C. 819(a), a civil penalty of $10,000 was assessed against P Corp., and P Corp. paid the penalty. Section 162(f) precludes P Corp. from deducting the $10,000 penalty.

Example (5). Q Corp., a common carrier engaged in interstate commerce by railroad, hauled a railroad car which was not equipped with efficient hand brakes, in violation of 45 U.S.C. 11. Q Corp. was found to be liable for a penalty of $250 pursuant to 45 U.S.C. 13. Q Corp. paid that penalty. Section 162(f) precludes Q Corp. from deducting the $250 penalty.

Example (6). R Corp. owned and operated on the highways of State X a truck weighing in excess of the amount permitted under the law of State X. R Corp. was found to have violated the law and was assessed a fine of $85 which it paid to State X. Section 162(f) precludes R Corp. from deducting the amount so paid.

Example (7). S Corp. was found to have violated a law of State Y which prohibited the emission into the air of particulate matter in excess of a limit set forth in a regulation promulgated under that law. The Environmental Quality Hearing Board of State Y assessed a fine of $500 against S Corp. The fine was payable to State Y, and S Corp. paid it. Section 162(f) precludes S Corp. from deducting the $500 fine.

Example (8). T Corp. was found by a magistrate of City Z to be operating in such city an apartment building which did not conform to a provision of the city housing code requiring operable fire escapes on apartment buildings of that type. Upon the basis of the magistrate's finding, T Corp. was required to pay, and did pay, a fine of $200 to City Z. Section 162(f) precludes T Corp. from deducting the $200 fine.

[T.D. 7345, 40 FR 7437, Feb. 20, 1975; 40 FR 8948, March 4, 1975, as amended by T.D. 7366, 40 FR 29290, July 11, 1975]

§ 1.162–25T Deductions with respect to non-cash fringe benefits.

(a) Employer. If an employer includes the value of a noncash fringe benefit in an employee's gross income, the employer may not deduct this amount as compensation for services, but rather may deduct only the costs incurred by the employer in providing the benefit to the employee. The employer may be allowed a cost recovery deduction under section 168 or a deduction under section 179 for an expense not chargeable to capital account, or, if the noncash fringe benefit is property leased by the employer, a deduction for the ordinary and necessary business expense of leasing the property.

(b) Employee. If an employer provides the use of a vehicle (as defined in § 1.61–2T(e)(2)) to an employee as a noncash fringe benefit and includes the entire value of the benefit in an employee's gross income without taking into account any exclusion for a working condition fringe allowable under section 132 and the regulations thereunder, the employee may deduct, for purposes of determining adjusted gross income, that value multiplied by the percentage of the total use of the vehicle that is in connection with the employer's trade or business. If the employer determines the value of the noncash fringe benefit under a special accounting rule that allows the employer to treat the value of benefits provided during the last two months of the calendar year or any shorter period as paid during the subsequent calendar year, then the employee must determine the deduction allowable under this paragraph (b) without regard to any use of the benefit during those last two months or any shorter period. The employee may not use a cents-per-mile valuation method to determine the deduction allowable under this paragraph (b).

(c) Examples. The following examples illustrate the provisions of this section.

Example (1). On January 1, 1986, X Company owns and provides the use of an automobile with a fair market value of $20,000 to E, an employee, for the entire calendar year. Both X and E compute taxable income on the basis of the calendar year. Seventy percent of the use of the automobile by E is in connection with X's trade or business. If X uses the special rule provided in § 1.61–2T for valuing the availability of the automobile and takes into account the amount excludable as a working condition fringe, X would include $1,680 ($5,600, the Annual Lease Value, less 70 percent of $5,600) in E's gross income for 1986. X may not deduct the amount included in E's income as compensation for services. X may, however, determine a cost recovery deduction under section 168, subject to the limitations under section 280F, for taxable year 1986.

Example (2). The facts are the same as in example (1), except that X includes $5,600 in E's gross income, the value of the noncash fringe benefit without taking into account the amount excludable as a working condition fringe. X may not deduct that amount as compensation for services, but may determine a cost recovery deduction under section 168, subject to the limitations under section 280F. For purposes of determining adjusted gross income, E may deduct $3,920 ($5,600 multiplied by the percent of business use).

[T.D. 8004, 50 FR 755, Jan. 7, 1985; T.D. 8061, 50 FR 46013, Nov. 6, 1985; T.D. 8063, 50 FR 52312, Dec. 23, 1985]

§ 1.163–1   Interest deduction in general.

(a) Except as otherwise provided in sections 264 to 267, inclusive, interest paid or accrued within the taxable year on indebtedness shall be allowed as a deduction in computing taxable income. For rules relating to interest on certain deferred payments, see section 483 and the regulations thereunder.

(b) Interest paid by the taxpayer on a mortgage upon real estate of which he is the legal or equitable owner, even though the taxpayer is not directly liable upon the bond or note secured by such mortgage, may be deducted as interest on his indebtedness. Pursuant to the provisions of section 163(c), any annual or periodic rental payment made by a taxpayer on or after January 1, 1962, under a redeemable ground rent, as defined in section 1055(c) and paragraph (b) of § 1.1055–1, is required to be treated as interest on an indebtedness secured by a mortgage and, accordingly, may be deducted by the taxpayer as interest on his indebtedness. * * *

* * *

[T.D. 6500, 25 FR 11402, Nov. 26, 1960, as amended by T.D. 6821, 30 FR 6216, May 4, 1965; T.D. 6873, 31 FR 941, Jan. 25, 1966; T.D. 7408, 41 FR 9547, March 5, 1976]

§ 1.164–1   Deduction for taxes.

(a) **In general.** Only the following taxes shall be allowed as a deduction under this section for the taxable year within which paid or accrued, according to the method of accounting used in computing taxable income:

(1) State and local, and foreign, real property taxes.

(2) State and local personal property taxes.

(3) State and local, and foreign, income, war profits, and excess profits taxes.

(4) State and local general sales taxes.

(5) State and local taxes on the sale of gasoline, diesel fuel, and other motor fuels.

In addition, there shall be allowed as a deduction under this section State and local and foreign taxes not described in subparagraphs (1) through (5) of this paragraph which are paid or accrued within the taxable year in carrying on a trade or business or an activity described in section 212 (relating to expenses for production of income). For example,

dealers or investors in securities and dealers or investors in real estate may deduct State stock transfer and real estate transfer taxes, respectively, under section 164, to the extent they are expenses incurred in carrying on a trade or business or an activity for the production of income. In general, taxes are deductible only by the person upon whom they are imposed. However, see § 1.164–5 in the case of certain taxes paid by the consumer. Also, in the case of a qualified State individual income tax (as defined in section 6362 and the regulations thereunder) which is determined by reference to a percentage of the Federal income tax (pursuant to section 6362(c)), an accrual method taxpayer shall use the cash receipts and disbursements method to compute the amount of his deduction therefor. Thus, the deduction under section 164 is in the amount actually paid with respect to the qualified tax, rather than the amount accrued with respect thereto, during the taxable year even though the taxpayer uses the accrual method of accounting for other purposes. * * *

* * *

[T.D. 6500, 25 FR 11402, Nov. 26, 1960, as amended by T.D. 6780, 29 FR 18145, Dec. 22, 1964; T.D. 7577, 43 FR 59357, Dec. 20, 1978]

§ 1.164–2   Deduction denied in case of certain taxes.

This section and § 1.275 describe certain taxes for which no deduction is allowed. In the case of taxable years beginning before January 1, 1964, the denial is provided for by section 164(b) (prior to being amended by section 207 of the Revenue Act of 1964 (78 Stat. 40)). In the case of taxable years beginning after December 31, 1963, the denial is governed by sections 164 and 275. No deduction is allowed for the following taxes:

(a) **Federal income taxes.** Federal income taxes, including the taxes imposed by section 3101, relating to the tax on employees under the Federal Insurance Contributions Act (chapter 21 of the Code); sections 3201 and 3211, relating to the taxes on railroad employees and railroad employee representatives; section 3402, relating to the tax withheld at source on wages; and by corresponding provisions of prior internal revenue laws.

(b) **Federal war profits and excess profits taxes.** Federal war profits and excess profits taxes including those imposed by Title II of the Revenue

Act of 1917 (39 Stat. 1000), Title III of the Revenue Act of 1918 (40 Stat. 1088), Title III of the Revenue Act of 1921 (42 Stat. 271), section 216 of the National Industrial Recovery Act (48 Stat. 208), section 702 of the Revenue Act of 1934 (48 Stat. 770), subchapter D, chapter 1 of the Internal Revenue Code of 1939, and subchapter E, chapter 2 of the Internal Revenue Code of 1939.

(c) **Estate and gift taxes.** Estate, inheritance, legacy, succession, and gift taxes.

(d) **Foreign income, war profits, and excess profits taxes.** Income, war profits, and excess profits taxes imposed by the authority of any foreign country or possession of the United States, if the taxpayer chooses to take to any extent the benefits of section 901, relating to the credit for taxes of foreign countries and possessions of the United States.

(e) **Real property taxes.** Taxes on real property, to the extent that section 164(d) and § 1.164–6 require such taxes to be treated as imposed on another taxpayer.

(f) **Federal duties and excise taxes.** Federal import or tariff duties, business, license, privilege, excise, and stamp taxes (not described in paragraphs (a), (b), (c) or (h) of this section, or § 1.164–4) paid or accrued within the taxable year. The fact that any such tax is not deductible as a tax under section 164 does not prevent (1) its deduction under section 162 or section 212, provided it represents an ordinary and necessary expense paid or incurred during the taxable year by a corporation or an individual in the conduct of any trade or business or, in the case of an individual for the production or collection of income, for the management, conservation, or maintenance of property held for the production of income, or in connection with the determination, collection, or refund of any tax, or (2) its being taken into account during the taxable year by a corporation or an individual as a part of the cost of acquiring or producing property in the trade or business or, in the case of an individual, as a part of the cost of property held for the production of income with respect to which it relates.

(g) **Taxes for local benefits.** Except as provided in § 1.164–4, taxes assessed against local benefits of a kind tending to increase the value of the property assessed.

* * *

[T.D. 6500, 25 FR 11402, Nov. 26, 1960, as amended by T.D. 6780, 29 FR 18145, Dec. 22, 1964; T.D. 7767, 46 FR 11263, Feb. 6, 1981]

§ 1.164–3 **Definitions and special rules.**

For purposes of section 164 and § 1.164–1 to § 1.164–8, inclusive—

(a) **State or local taxes.** A State or local tax includes only a tax imposed by a State, a possession of the United States, or a political subdivision of any of the foregoing, or by the District of Columbia.

(b) **Real property taxes.** The term "real property taxes" means taxes imposed on interests in real property and levied for the general public welfare, but it does not include taxes assessed against local benefits. See § 1.164–4.

(c) **Personal property taxes.** The term "personal property tax" means an ad valorem tax which is imposed on an annual basis in respect of personal property. To qualify as a personal property tax, a tax must meet the following three tests:

(1) The tax must be ad valorem—that is, substantially in proportion to the value of the personal property. A tax which is based on criteria other than value does not qualify as ad valorem. For example, a motor vehicle tax based on weight, model year, and horsepower, or any of these characteristics is not an ad valorem tax. However, a tax which is partly based on value and partly based on other criteria may qualify in part. For example, in the case of a motor vehicle tax of 1 percent of value plus 40 cents per hundredweight, the part of the tax equal to 1 percent of value qualifies as an ad valorem tax and the balance does not qualify.

(2) The tax must be imposed on an annual basis, even if collected more frequently or less frequently.

(3) The tax must be imposed in respect of personal property. A tax may be considered to be imposed in respect of personal property even if in form it is imposed on the exercise of a privilege. Thus, for taxable years beginning after December 31, 1963, State and local taxes on the registration or licensing of highway motor vehicles are not deductible as personal property taxes unless and to the extent that the tests prescribed in this subparagraph are met. For example, an annual ad valorem tax qualifies as a personal property tax although it is denominated a registration fee imposed for the privilege of registering motor vehicles or of using them on the highways.

(d) Foreign taxes. The term "foreign tax" includes only a tax imposed by the authority of a foreign country. A tax imposed by a political subdivision of a foreign country is considered to be imposed by the authority of that foreign country.

(e) Sales tax. (1) The term "sales tax" means a tax imposed upon persons engaged in selling tangible personal property, or upon the consumers of such property, including persons selling gasoline or other motor vehicle fuels at wholesale or retail, which is a stated sum per unit of property sold or which is measured by the gross sales price or the gross receipts from the sale. The term also includes a tax imposed upon persons engaged in furnishing services which is measured by the gross receipts for furnishing such services.

(2) In general, the term "consumer" means the ultimate user or purchaser; it does not include a purchaser such as a retailer, who acquires the property for resale.

(f) General sales tax. A "general sales tax" is a sales tax which is imposed at one rate in respect of the sale at retail of a broad range of classes of items. No foreign sales tax is deductible under section 164(a) and paragraph (a)(4) of § 1.164–1. To qualify as a general sales tax, a tax must meet the following two tests:

(1) The tax must be a tax in respect of sales at retail. This may include a tax imposed on persons engaged in selling property at retail or furnishing services at retail, for example, if the tax is measured by gross sales price or by gross receipts from sales or services. Rentals qualify as sales at retail if so treated under applicable State sales tax laws.

(2) The tax must be general—that is, it must be imposed at one rate in respect of the retail sales of a broad range of classes of items. A sales tax is considered to be general although imposed on sales of various classes of items at more than one rate provided that one rate applies to the retail sales of a broad range of classes of items. The term "items" includes both commodities and services.

(g) Special rules relating to general sales taxes. (1) A sales tax which is general is usually imposed at one rate in respect of the retail sales of all tangible personal property (with exceptions and additions). However, a sales tax which is selective—that is, a tax which applies at one rate with respect to retail sales of specified classes of items also qualifies as general if the specified classes represent a broad range of classes of items. A selective sales tax which does not apply at one rate

to the retail sales of a broad range of classes of items is not general. For example, a tax which applies only to sales of alcoholic beverages, tobacco, admissions, luxury items, and a few other items is not general. Similarly, a tax imposed solely on services is not general. However, a selective sales tax may be deemed to be part of the general sales tax and hence may be deductible, even if imposed by a separate Title, etc., of the State or local law, if imposed at the same rate as the general rate of tax (as defined in subparagraph (4) of this paragraph) which qualifies a tax in the taxing jurisdiction as a general sales tax. For example, if a State has a 5 percent general sales tax and a separate selective sales tax of 5 percent on transient accommodations, the tax on transient accommodations is deductible.

(2) A tax is imposed at one rate only if it is imposed at that rate on generally the same base for all items subject to tax. For example, a sales tax imposed at a 3 percent rate on 100 percent of the sales price of some classes of items and at a 3 percent rate on 50 percent of the sales price of other classes of items would not be imposed at one rate with respect to all such classes. However, a tax is considered to be imposed at one rate although it allows dollar exemptions, if the exemptions are designed to exclude all sales under a certain dollar amount. For example, a tax may be imposed at one rate although it applies to all sales of tangible personal property but applies only to sales amounting to more than 10 cents.

(3) The fact that a sales tax exempts food, clothing, medical supplies, and motor vehicles, or any of them, shall not be taken into account in determining whether the tax applies to a broad range of classes of items. The fact that a sales tax applies to food, clothing, medical supplies, and motor vehicles, or any of them, at a rate which is lower than the general rate of tax (as defined in subparagraph (4) of this paragraph) is not taken into account in determining whether the tax is imposed at one rate on the retail sales of a broad range of classes of items. For purposes of this section, the term "food" means food for human consumption off the premises where sold, and the term "medical supplies" includes drugs, medicines, and medical devices.

(4) Except in the case of a lower rate of tax applicable in respect of food, clothing, medical supplies, and motor vehicles, or any of them, no deduction is allowed for a general sales tax in respect of

any item if the tax is imposed on such item at a rate other than the general rate of tax. The general rate of tax is the one rate which qualifies a tax in a taxing jurisdiction as a general sales tax because the tax is imposed at such one rate on a broad range of classes of items. There can be only one general rate of tax in any one taxing jurisdiction. However, a general sales tax imposed at a lower rate or rates on food, clothing, motor vehicles, and medical supplies, or any of them, may nonetheless be deductible with respect to such items. For example, a sales tax which is imposed at 1 percent with respect to food, imposed at 3 percent with respect to a broad range of classes of tangible personal property, and imposed at 4 percent with respect to transient accommodations would qualify as a general sales tax. Taxes paid at the 1 percent and the 3 percent rates are deductible, but tax paid at the 4 percent rate is not deductible. The fact that a sales tax provides for the adjustment of the general rate of tax to reflect the sales tax rate in another taxing jurisdiction shall not be taken into account in determining whether the tax is imposed at one rate on the retail sales of a broad range of classes of items. Moreover, a general sales tax imposed at a lower rate with respect to an item in order to reflect the tax rate in another jurisdiction is also deductible at such lower rate. For example, State E imposes a general sales tax whose general rate is 3 percent. The State E sales tax law provides that in areas bordering on States with general sales taxes, selective sales taxes, or special excise taxes, the rate applied in the adjoining State will be used if such rate is under 3 percent. State F imposes a 2 percent sales tax. The 2 percent sales tax paid by residents of State E in areas bordering on State F is deductible.

(h) Compensating use taxes. A compensating use tax in respect of any item is treated as a general sales tax. The term "compensating use tax" means, in respect of any item, a tax which is imposed on the use, storage, or consumption of such item and which is complementary to a general sales tax which is deductible with respect to sales of similar items.

(i) Special rules relating to compensating use taxes. (1) In general, a use tax on an item is complementary to a general sales tax on similar items if the use tax is imposed on an item which was not subject to such general sales tax but which would have been subject to such general sales tax if the sale of the item had taken place within the jurisdiction imposing the use tax. For example, a tax imposed by State A on the use of a motor vehicle purchased in State B is complementary to the general sales tax of State A on similar items, if the latter tax applies to motor vehicles sold in State A.

(2) Since a compensating use tax is treated as a general sales tax, it is subject to the rule of subparagraph (C) of section 164(b)(2) and paragraph (g)(4) of this section that no deduction is allowed for a general sales tax imposed in respect of an item at a rate other than the general rate of tax (except in the case of lower rates on the sale of food, clothing, medical supplies, and motor vehicles). The fact that a compensating use tax in respect of any item provides for an adjustment in the rate of the compensating use tax or the amount of such tax to be paid on account of a sales tax on such item imposed by another taxing jurisdiction is not taken into account in determining whether the compensating use tax is imposed in respect of the item at a rate other than the general rate of tax. For example, a compensating use tax imposed by State C on the use of an item purchased in State D is considered to be imposed at the general rate of tax even though the tax imposed by State C allows a credit for any sales tax paid on such item in State D, or the rate of such compensating use tax is adjusted to reflect the rate of sales tax imposed by State D.

[T.D. 6500, 25 FR 11402, Nov. 26, 1960, as amended by T.D. 6780, 29 FR 18146, Dec. 22, 1964]

§ 1.164–4 Taxes for local benefits.

(a) So-called taxes for local benefits referred to in paragraph (g) of § 1.164–2, more properly assessments, paid for local benefits such as street, sidewalk, and other like improvements, imposed because of and measured by some benefit inuring directly to the property against which the assessment is levied are not deductible as taxes. A tax is considered assessed against local benefits when the property subject to the tax is limited to property benefited. Special assessments are not deductible, even though an incidental benefit may inure to the public welfare. The real property taxes deductible are those levied for the general public welfare by the proper taxing authorities at a like rate against all property in the territory over which such authorities have jurisdiction. Assessments under the statutes of California relating to irrigation, and of Iowa relating to drainage, and under certain statutes of Tennessee relating to levees, are limited to property benefited, and if the assessments are so limited, the amounts paid thereunder are not deductible as taxes. For treatment of assessments for local benefits as adjustments to the basis of property, see section 1016(a)(1) and the regulations thereunder.

(b)(1) Insofar as assessments against local benefits are made for the purpose of maintenance or repair or for the purpose of meeting interest charges with respect to such benefits, they are deductible. In such cases, the burden is on the taxpayer to show the allocation of the amounts assessed to the different purposes. If the allocation cannot be made, none of the amount so paid is deductible.

* * *

[T.D. 6500, 25 FR 11402, Nov. 26, 1960, as amended by T.D. 6780, 29 FR 18147, Dec. 22, 1964]

§ 1.165–1   Losses.

(a) **Allowance of deduction.** Section 165(a) provides that, in computing taxable income under section 63, any loss actually sustained during the taxable year and not made good by insurance or some other form of compensation shall be allowed as a deduction subject to any provision of the internal revenue laws which prohibits or limits the amount of the deduction. This deduction for losses sustained shall be taken in accordance with section 165 and the regulations thereunder. For the disallowance of deductions for worthless securities issued by a political party, see § 1.271–1.

(b) **Nature of loss allowable.** To be allowable as a deduction under section 165(a), a loss must be evidenced by closed and completed transactions, fixed by identifiable events, and, except as otherwise provided in section 165(h) and § 1.165–11, relating to disaster losses, actually sustained during the taxable year. Only a bona fide loss is allowable. Substance and not mere form shall govern in determining a deductible loss.

(c) **Amount deductible.** (1) The amount of loss allowable as a deduction under section 165(a) shall not exceed the amount prescribed by § 1.1011–1 as the adjusted basis for determining the loss from the sale or other disposition of the property involved. In the case of each such deduction claimed, therefore, the basis of the property must be properly adjusted as prescribed by § 1.1011–1 for such items as expenditures, receipts, or losses, properly chargeable to capital account, and for such items as depreciation, obsolescence, amortiza-

tion, and depletion, in order to determine the amount of loss allowable as a deduction. * * *

(2) The amount of loss recognized upon the sale or exchange of property shall be determined for purposes of section 165(a) in accordance with § 1.1002–1.

(3) A loss from the sale or exchange of a capital asset shall be allowed as a deduction under section 165(a) but only to the extent allowed in section 1211 (relating to limitation on capital losses) and section 1212 (relating to capital loss carrybacks and carryovers), and in the regulations under those sections.

(4) In determining the amount of loss actually sustained for purposes of section 165(a), proper adjustment shall be made for any salvage value and for any insurance or other compensation received.

(d) **Year of deduction.** (1) A loss shall be allowed as a deduction under section 165(a) only for the taxable year in which the loss is sustained. For this purpose, a loss shall be treated as sustained during the taxable year in which the loss occurs as evidenced by closed and completed transactions and as fixed by identifiable events occurring in such taxable year. For provisions relating to situations where a loss attributable to a disaster will be treated as sustained in the taxable year immediately preceding the taxable year in which the disaster actually occurred, see section 165(h) and § 1.165–11.

(2)(i) If a casualty or other event occurs which may result in a loss and, in the year of such casualty or event, there exists a claim for reimbursement with respect to which there is a reasonable prospect of recovery, no portion of the loss with respect to which reimbursement may be received is sustained, for purposes of section 165, until it can be ascertained with reasonable certainty whether or not such reimbursement will be received. Whether a reasonable prospect of recovery exists with respect to a claim for reimbursement of a loss is a question of fact to be determined upon an examination of all facts and circumstances. Whether or not such reimbursement will be received may be ascertained with reasonable certainty, for example, by a settlement of the claim, by an adjudication of the claim, or by an abandonment of the claim. When a taxpayer claims that the taxable year in which a loss is sustained is fixed by his abandonment of the claim for reimbursement, he must be able to produce objective evidence of his having abandoned the claim, such as the execution of a release.

(ii) If in the year of the casualty or other event a portion of the loss is not covered by a claim for reimbursement with respect to which there is a reasonable prospect of recovery, then such portion of the loss is sustained during the taxable year in which the casualty or other event occurs. For example, if property having an adjusted basis of $10,000 is completely destroyed by fire in 1961, and if the taxpayer's only claim for reimbursement consists of an insurance claim for $8,000 which is settled in 1962, the taxpayer sustains a loss of $2,000 in 1961. However, if the taxpayer's automobile is completely destroyed in 1961 as a result of the negligence of another person and there exists a reasonable prospect of recovery on a claim for the full value of the automobile against such person, the taxpayer does not sustain any loss until the taxable year in which the claim is adjudicated or otherwise settled. If the automobile had an adjusted basis of $5,000 and the taxpayer secures a judgment of $4,000 in 1962, $1,000 is deductible for the taxable year 1962. If in 1963 it becomes reasonably certain that only $3,500 can ever be collected on such judgment, $500 is deductible for the taxable year 1963.

(iii) If the taxpayer deducted a loss in accordance with the provisions of this paragraph and in a subsequent taxable year receives reimbursement for such loss, he does not recompute the tax for the taxable year in which the deduction was taken but includes the amount of such reimbursement in his gross income for the taxable year in which received, subject to the provisions of section 111, relating to recovery of amounts previously deducted.

(3) Any loss arising from theft shall be treated as sustained during the taxable year in which the taxpayer discovers the loss (see § 1.165-8, relating to theft losses). However, if in the year of discovery there exists a claim for reimbursement with respect to which there is a reasonable prospect of recovery, no portion of the loss with respect to which reimbursement may be received is sustained, for purposes of section 165, until the taxable year in which it can be ascertained with reasonable certainty whether or not such reimbursement will be received.

* * *

(e) **Limitation on losses of individuals.** In the case of an individual, the deduction for losses granted by section 165(a) shall, subject to the provisions of section 165(c) and paragraph (a) of this section, be limited to:

(1) Losses incurred in a trade or business;

(2) Losses incurred in any transaction entered into for profit, though not connected with a trade or business; and

(3) Losses of property not connected with a trade or business and not incurred in any transaction entered into for profit, if such losses arise from fire, storm, shipwreck, or other casualty, or from theft, and if the loss involved has not been allowed for estate tax purposes in the estate tax return. For additional provisions pertaining to the allowance of casualty and theft losses, see §§ 1.165-7 and 1.165-8, respectively.

* * *

[T.D. 6500, 25 FR 11402, Nov. 26, 1960, as amended by T.D. 6735, 29 FR 6493, May 19, 1964; T.D. 6996, 34 FR 835, Jan. 18, 1969; T.D. 7301, 39 FR 963, Jan. 4, 1974; T.D. 7522, 42 FR 63411, Dec. 16, 1977]

§ 1.165-4 Decline in value of stock.

(a) **Deduction disallowed.** No deduction shall be allowed under section 165(a) solely on account of a decline in the value of stock owned by the taxpayer when the decline is due to a fluctuation in the market price of the stock or to other similar cause. A mere shrinkage in the value of stock owned by the taxpayer, even though extensive, does not give rise to a deduction under section 165(a) if the stock has any recognizable value on the date claimed as the date of loss. No loss for a decline in the value of stock owned by the taxpayer shall be allowed as a deduction under section 165(a) except insofar as the loss is recognized under § 1.1002-1 upon the sale or exchange of the stock and except as otherwise provided in § 1.165-5 with respect to stock which becomes worthless during the taxable year.

* * *

(d) **Definition.** As used in this section, the term "stock" means a share of stock in a corporation or a right to subscribe for, or to receive, a share of stock in a corporation.

§ 1.165–5 Worthless securities.

(a) Definition of security. As used in section 165(g) and this section, the term "security" means:

(1) A share of stock in a corporation;

(2) A right to subscribe for, or to receive, a share of stock in a corporation; or

(3) A bond, debenture, note, or certificate, or other evidence of indebtedness to pay a fixed or determinable sum of money, which has been issued with interest coupons or in registered form by a domestic or foreign corporation or by any government or political subdivision thereof.

(b) Ordinary loss. If any security which is not a capital asset becomes wholly worthless during the taxable year, the loss resulting therefrom may be deducted under section 165(a) as an ordinary loss.

(c) Capital loss. If any security which is a capital asset becomes wholly worthless at any time during the taxable year, the loss resulting therefrom may be deducted under section 165(a) but only as though it were a loss from a sale or exchange, on the last day of the taxable year, of a capital asset. See section 165(g)(1). The amount so allowed as a deduction shall be subject to the limitations upon capital losses described in paragraph (c)(3) of § 1.165–1.

(d) Loss on worthless securities of an affiliated corporation—(1) Deductible as an ordinary loss. If a taxpayer which is a domestic corporation owns any security of a domestic or foreign corporation which is affiliated with the taxpayer within the meaning of subparagraph (2) of this paragraph and such security becomes wholly worthless during the taxable year, the loss resulting therefrom may be deducted under section 165(a) as an ordinary loss in accordance with paragraph (b) of this section. The fact that the security is in fact a capital asset of the taxpayer is immaterial for this purpose, since section 165(g)(3) provides that such security shall be treated as though it were not a capital asset for the purposes of section 165(g)(1). A debt which becomes wholly worthless during the taxable year shall be as an ordinary loss in accordance with the provisions of this subparagraph, to the extent that such debt is a security within the meaning of paragraph (a)(3) of this section.

(2) Affiliated corporation defined. For purposes of this paragraph, a corporation shall be treated as affiliated with the taxpayer owning the security if—

(i)(a) In the case of a taxable year beginning on or after January 1, 1970, the taxpayer owns directly—

(1) Stock possessing at least 80 percent of the voting power of all classes of such corporation's stock, and

(2) At least 80 percent of each class of such corporation's nonvoting stock excluding for purposes of this subdivision (i)(a) nonvoting stock which is limited and preferred as to dividends (see section 1504(a)), or

(b) In the case of a taxable year beginning before January 1, 1970, the taxpayer owns directly at least 95 percent of each class of the stock of such corporation;

(ii) None of the stock of such corporation was acquired by the taxpayer solely for the purpose of converting a capital loss sustained by reason of the worthlessness of any such stock into an ordinary loss under section 165(g)(3), and

(iii) More than 90 percent of the aggregate of the gross receipts of such corporation for all the taxable years during which it has been in existence has been from sources other than royalties, rents (except rents derived from rental of properties to employees of such corporation in the ordinary course of its operating business), dividends, interest (except interest received on the deferred purchase price of operating assets sold), annuities, and gains from sales or exchanges of stocks and securities. For this purpose, the term "gross receipts" means total receipts determined without any deduction for cost of goods sold, and gross receipts from sales or exchanges of stocks and securities shall be taken into account only to the extent of gains from such sales or exchanges.

* * *

[T.D. 6500, 25 FR 11402, Nov. 26, 1960; 25 FR 14021, Dec. 31, 1960, as amended by T.D. 7224, 37 FR 25928, Dec. 6, 1972]

§ 1.165–6 Farming losses.

(a) Allowance of losses. (1) Except as otherwise provided in this section, any loss incurred in the operation of a farm as a trade or business shall be allowed as a deduction under section 165(a) or as a net operating loss deduction in accordance with the provisions of section 172. See § 1.172–1.

(2) If the taxpayer owns and operates a farm for profit in addition to being engaged in another trade or business, but sustains a loss from the operation of the farming business, then the amount of loss sustained in the operation of the farm may be deducted from gross income, if any, from all other sources.

(3) Loss incurred in the operation of a farm for recreation or pleasure shall not be allowed as a deduction from gross income. See § 1.162–12.

(b) **Loss from shrinkage.** If, in the course of the business of farming, farm products are held for a favorable market, no deduction shall be allowed under section 165(a) in respect of such products merely because of shrinkage in weight, decline in value, or deterioration in storage.

(c) **Loss of prospective crop.** The total loss by frost, storm, flood, or fire of a prospective crop being grown in the business of farming shall not be allowed as a deduction under section 165(a).

(d) **Loss of livestock—(1) Raised stock.** A taxpayer engaged in the business of raising and selling livestock, such as cattle, sheep, or horses, may not deduct as a loss under section 165(a) the value of animals that perish from among those which were raised on the farm.

(2) **Purchased stock.** The loss sustained upon the death by disease, exposure, or injury of any livestock purchased and used in the trade or business of farming shall be allowed as a deduction under section 165(a). See, also, paragraph (e) of this section.

(e) **Loss due to compliance with orders of governmental authority.** The loss sustained upon the destruction by order of the United States, a State, or any other governmental authority, of any livestock, or other property, purchased and used in the trade or business of farming shall be allowed as a deduction under section 165(a).

(f) **Amount deductible—(1) Expenses of operation.** The cost of any feed, pasture, or care which is allowed under section 162 as an expense of operating a farm for profit shall not be included as a part of the cost of livestock for purposes of determining the amount of loss deductible under section 165(a) and this section. For the deduction of farming expenses, see § 1.162–12.

(2) **Losses reflected in inventories.** If inventories are taken into account in determining the income from the trade or business of farming, no deduction shall be allowed under this section for losses sustained during the taxable year upon livestock or other products, whether purchased for resale or produced on the farm, to the extent such losses are reflected in the inventory on hand at the close of the taxable year. Nothing in this section shall be construed to disallow the deduction of any loss reflected in the inventories of the taxpayer. For provisions relating to inventories of farmers, see section 471 and the regulations thereunder.

* * *

§ 1.165–7 Casualty losses.

(a) **In general—(1) Allowance of deduction.** Except as otherwise provided in paragraphs (b)(4) and (c) of this section, any loss arising from fire, storm, shipwreck, or other casualty is allowable as a deduction under section 165(a) for the taxable year in which the loss is sustained. * * * The manner of determining the amount of a casualty loss allowable as a deduction in computing taxable income under section 63 is the same whether the loss has been incurred in a trade or business or in any transaction entered into for profit, or whether it has been a loss of property not connected with a trade or business and not incurred in any transaction entered into for profit. The amount of a casualty loss shall be determined in accordance with paragraph (b) of this section. For other rules relating to the treatment of deductible casualty losses, see § 1.1231–1, relating to the involuntary conversion of property.

(2) **Method of valuation.** (i) In determining the amount of loss deductible under this section, the fair market value of the property immediately before and immediately after the casualty shall generally be ascertained by competent appraisal. This appraisal must recognize the effects of any general market decline affecting undamaged as well as damaged property which may occur simultaneously with the casualty, in order that any deduction under this section shall be limited to the actual loss resulting from damage to the property.

(ii) The cost of repairs to the property damaged is acceptable as evidence of the loss of value if the taxpayer shows that (a) the repairs are necessary to restore the property to its condition immediately before the casualty, (b) the amount spent for such repairs is not excessive, (c) the repairs do not care for more than the damage suffered, and (d) the value of the property after the repairs does not as a result of the repairs exceed the value of the property immediately before the casualty.

(3) Damage to automobiles. An automobile owned by the taxpayer, whether used for business purposes or maintained for recreation or pleasure, may be the subject of a casualty loss, including those losses specifically referred to in subparagraph (1) of this paragraph. In addition, a casualty loss occurs when an automobile owned by the taxpayer is damaged and when:

(i) The damage results from the faulty driving of the taxpayer or other person operating the automobile but is not due to the willful act or willful negligence of the taxpayer or of one acting in his behalf or

(ii) The damage results from the faulty driving of the operator of the vehicle with which the automobile of the taxpayer collides.

* * *

(5) Property converted from personal use. In the case of property which originally was not used in the trade or business or for income-producing purposes and which is thereafter converted to either of such uses, the fair market value of the property on the date of conversion, if less than the adjusted basis of the property at such time, shall be used, after making proper adjustments in respect of basis, as the basis for determining the amount of loss under paragraph (b)(1) of this section. See paragraph (b) of § 1.165–9, and § 1.167(g)–1.

(6) Theft losses. A loss which arises from theft is not considered a casualty loss for purposes of this section. See § 1.165–8, relating to theft losses.

(b) Amount deductible—(1) General rule. In the case of any casualty loss whether or not incurred in a trade or business or in any transaction entered into for profit, the amount of loss to be taken into account for purposes of section 165(a) shall be the lesser of either—

(i) The amount which is equal to the fair market value of the property immediately before the casualty reduced by the fair market value of the property immediately after the casualty; or

(ii) The amount of the adjusted basis prescribed in § 1.1011–1 for determining the loss from the sale or other disposition of the property involved.

However, if property used in a trade or business or held for the production of income is totally destroyed by casualty, and if the fair market value of such property immediately before the casualty is less than the adjusted basis of such property, the amount of the adjusted basis of such property shall

be treated as the amount of the loss for purposes of section 165(a).

(2) Aggregation of property for computing loss. **(i)** A loss incurred in a trade or business or in any transaction entered into for profit shall be determined under subparagraph (1) of this paragraph by reference to the single, identifiable property damaged or destroyed. Thus, for example, in determining the fair market value of the property before and after the casualty in a case where damage by casualty has occurred to a building and ornamental or fruit trees used in a trade or business, the decrease in value shall be measured by taking the building and trees into account separately, and not together as an integral part of the realty, and separate losses shall be determined for such building and trees.

(ii) In determining a casualty loss involving real property and improvements thereon not used in a trade or business or in any transaction entered into for profit, the improvements (such as buildings and ornamental trees and shrubbery) to the property damaged or destroyed shall be considered an integral part of the property, for purposes of subparagraph (1) of this paragraph, and no separate basis need be apportioned to such improvements.

(3) Examples. The application of this paragraph may be illustrated by the following examples:

* * *

Example (2). In 1958 A purchases land containing an office building for the lump sum of $90,000. The purchase price is allocated between the land ($18,000) and the building ($72,000) for purposes of determining basis. After the purchase A planted trees and ornamental shrubs on the grounds surrounding the building. In 1961 the land, building, trees, and shrubs are damaged by hurricane. At the time of the casualty the adjusted basis of the land is $18,000 and the adjusted basis of the building is $66,000. At that time the trees and shrubs have an adjusted basis of $1,200. The fair market value of the land and building immediately before the casualty is $18,000 and $70,000, respectively, and immediately after the casualty is $18,000 and $52,000, respectively. The fair market value of the trees and shrubs immediately before the casualty is $2,000 and immediately after the casualty is $400. In 1961 insurance of $5,000 is received to cover the loss to the building. A has no other gains or losses in 1961 subject to section 1231 and § 1.1231–1. The amount of the deduction allowable under section 165(a) with respect to the building for the taxable year 1961 is $13,000, computed as follows:

Value of property immediately before casualty $70,000

Less: Value of **property** immediately after casualty	$52,000
Value of property actually **destroyed**	18,000
Less: Insurance received	5,000
Loss to be taken into account for purposes of section 165(a): **Lesser** amount of property actually destroyed ($18,000) or adjusted basis of property ($66,000)	18,000
Less: Insurance received	5,000
Deduction allowable	13,000

The amount of the deduction allowable under section 165(a) with respect to the trees and shrubs for the taxable year 1961 is $1,200, computed as follows:

Value of property immediately before casualty	$2,000
Less: Value of property immediately after casualty	$400
Value of property actually destroyed	1,600
Loss to be taken into account for purposes of section 165(a): Lesser amount of property actually destroyed ($1,600) or adjusted basis of property ($1,200)	1,200

Example (3). Assume the same facts as in example (2) except that A purchases land containing a house instead of an office building. The house is used as his private residence. Since the property is used for personal purposes, no allocation of the purchase price is necessary for the land and house. Likewise, no individual determination of the fair market values of the land, house, trees, and shrubs is necessary. The amount of the deduction allowable under section 165(a) with respect to the land, house, trees, and shrubs for the taxable year 1961 is $14,600, computed as follows:

Value of property immediately before casualty	$90,000
Less: Value of property immediately after casualty	70,400
Value of property actually destroyed	19,600
Loss to be taken into account for purposes of section 165(a): Lesser amount of property actually destroyed ($19,600) or adjusted basis of property ($91,200)	19,600
Less: Insurance received	5,000
Deduction allowable	14,600

* * *

(c) Loss sustained by an estate. A casualty loss of property not connected with a trade or business and not incurred in any transaction entered into for profit which is sustained during the settlement of an estate shall be allowed as a deduction under sections 165(a) and 641(b) in computing the taxable income of the estate if the loss has not been allowed under section 2054 in computing the taxable estate of the decedent and if the statement has been filed in accordance with § 1.642(g)–1. See section 165(c)(3).

* * *

[T.D. 6500, 25 FR 11402, Nov. 26, 1960, as amended by T.D. 6712, 29 FR 3652, March 24, 1964; T.D. 6735, 29 FR 6493, May 19, 1964; T.D. 6786, 29 FR 18501, Dec. 29, 1964; T.D. 7522, 42 FR 63411, Dec. 16, 1977]

§ 1.165–8 Theft losses.

(a) Allowance of deduction. (1) Except as otherwise provided in paragraphs (b) and (c) of this section, any loss arising from theft is allowable as a deduction under section 165(a) for the taxable year in which the loss is sustained. See section 165(c)(3).

(2) A loss arising from theft shall be treated under section 165(a) as sustained during the taxable year in which the taxpayer discovers the loss. See section 165(e). Thus, a theft loss is not deductible under section 165(a) for the taxable year in which the theft actually occurs unless that is also the year in which the taxpayer discovers the loss. However, if in the year of discovery there exists a claim for reimbursement with respect to which there is a reasonable prospect of recovery, see paragraph (d) of § 1.165–1.

* * *

(c) Amount deductible. The amount deductible under this section in respect of a theft loss shall be determined consistently with the manner prescribed in § 1.165–7 for determining the amount of casualty loss allowable as a deduction under section 165(a). In applying the provisions of paragraph (b) of § 1.165–7 for this purpose, the fair market value of the property immediately after the theft shall be considered to be zero. * * *

(d) Definition. For purposes of this section the term "theft" shall be deemed to include, but shall not necessarily be limited to, larceny, embezzlement, and robbery.

* * *

[T.D. 6500, 25 FR 11402, Nov. 26, 1960, as amended by T.D. 6786, 29 FR 18502, Dec. 29, 1964]

§ 1.165–9 Sale of residential property.

(a) Losses not allowed. A loss sustained on the sale of residential property purchased or constructed by the taxpayer for use as his personal residence and so used by him up to the time of the sale is not deductible under section 165(a).

(b) **Property converted from personal use.**
(1) If property purchased or constructed by the taxpayer for use as his personal residence is, prior to its sale, rented or otherwise appropriated to income-producing purposes and is used for such purposes up to the time of its sale, a loss sustained on the sale of the property shall be allowed as a deduction under section 165(a).

(2) The loss allowed under this paragraph upon the sale of the property shall be the excess of the adjusted basis prescribed in § 1.1011-1 for determining loss over the amount realized from the sale. For this purpose, the adjusted basis for determining loss shall be the lesser of either of the following amounts, adjusted as prescribed in § 1.1011-1 for the period subsequent to the conversion of the property to income-producing purposes:

(i) The fair market value of the property at the time of conversion, or

(ii) The adjusted basis for loss, at the time of conversion, determined under § 1.1011-1 but without reference to the fair market value.

* * *

(c) **Examples.** The application of paragraph (b) of this section may be illustrated by the following examples:

Example (1). Residential property is purchased by the taxpayer in 1943 for use as his personal residence at a cost of $25,000, of which $15,000 is allocable to the building. The taxpayer uses the property as his personal residence until January 1, 1952, at which time its fair market value is $22,000, of which $12,000 is allocable to the building. The taxpayer rents the property from January 1, 1952, until January 1, 1955, at which time it is sold for $16,000. On January 1, 1952, the building has an estimated useful life of 20 years. It is assumed that the building has no estimated salvage value and that there are no adjustments in respect of basis other than depreciation, which is computed on the straight-line method. The loss to be taken into account for purposes of section 165(a) for the taxable year 1955 is $4,200, computed as follows:

Basis of property at time of conversion for purposes of this section (that is, the lesser of $25,000 cost or $22,000 fair market value)	$22,000
Less: Depreciation allowable from January 1, 1952, to January 1, 1955 (3 years at 5 percent based on $12,000, the value of the building at time of conversion, as prescribed by § 1.167(g)-1)	1,800
Adjusted basis prescribed in § 1.1011-1 for determining loss on sale of the property	20,200
Less: Amount realized on sale	16,000
Loss to be taken into account for purposes of section 165(a)	4,200

In this example the value of the building at the time of conversion is used as the basis for computing depreciation. See example (2) of this paragraph wherein the adjusted basis of the building is required to be used for such purpose.

Example (2). Residential property is purchased by the taxpayer in 1940 for use as his personal residence at a cost of $23,000, of which $10,000 is allocable to the building. The taxpayer uses the property as his personal residence until January 1, 1953, at which time its fair market value is $20,000, of which $12,000 is allocable to the building. The taxpayer rents the property from January 1, 1953, until January 1, 1957, at which time it is sold for $17,000. On January 1, 1953, the building has an estimated useful life of 20 years. It is assumed that the building has no estimated salvage value and that there are no adjustments in respect of basis other than depreciation, which is computed on the straight-line method. The loss to be taken into account for purposes of section 165(a) for the taxable year 1957 is $1,000, computed as follows:

Basis of property at time of conversion for purposes of this section (that is, the lesser of $23,000 cost or $20,000 fair market value)	$20,000
Less: Depreciation allowable from January 1, 1953, to January 1, 1957 (4 years at 5 percent based on $10,000, the cost of the building, as prescribed by § 1.167(g)-1)	2,000
Adjusted basis prescribed in § 1.1011-1 for determining loss on sale of the property	18,000
Less: Amount realized on sale	17,000
Loss to be taken into account for purposes of section 165(a)	1,000

[T.D. 6500, 25 FR 11402, Nov. 26, 1960, as amended by T.D. 6712, 29 FR 3652, March 24, 1964]

§ 1.166-1   Bad debts.

(a) **Allowance of deduction.** Section 166 provides that, in computing taxable income under section 63, a deduction shall be allowed in respect of bad debts owed to the taxpayer. For this purpose, bad debts shall, subject to the provisions of section 166 and the regulations thereunder, be taken into account either as—

(1) A deduction in respect of debts which become worthless in whole or in part; or as

(2) A deduction for a reasonable addition to a reserve for bad debts.

(b) **Manner of selecting method.** (1) A taxpayer filing a return of income for the first taxable year for which he is entitled to a bad debt deduction may select either of the two methods prescribed by paragraph (a) of this section for treating bad debts, but such selection is subject to the approval of the district director upon examination of the return. If the method so selected is approved, it shall be used in returns for all subsequent taxable years unless the Commissioner grants permission to use the other method. A statement of facts substantiating any deduction claimed under section 166 on account of bad debts shall accompany each return of income.

* * *

(4) Notwithstanding paragraphs (b)(1), (2), and (3) of this section, a dealer in property currently employing the accrual method of accounting and currently maintaining a reserve for bad debts under section 166(c) (which may have included guaranteed debt obligations described in section 166(f)(1)(A)) may establish a reserve for section 166(f)(1)(A) guaranteed debt obligations for a taxable year ending after October 21, 1965 under section 166(f) and § 1.166–10 by filing on or before April 17, 1986 an amended return indicating that such a reserve has been established. The establishment of such a reserve will not be considered a change in method of accounting for purposes of section 446(e). However, an election by a taxpayer to establish a reserve for bad debts under section 166(c) shall be treated as a change in method of accounting. See also § 1.166–4, relating to reserve for bad debts, and § 1.166–10, relating to reserve for guaranteed debt obligations.

(c) **Bona fide debt required.** Only a bona fide debt qualifies for purposes of section 166. A bona fide debt is a debt which arises from a debtor-creditor relationship based upon a valid and enforceable obligation to pay a fixed or determinable sum of money. A debt arising out of the receivables of an accrual method taxpayer is deemed to be an enforceable obligation for purposes of the preceding sentence to the extent that the income such debt represents have been included in the return of income for the year for which the deduction as a bad debt is claimed or for a prior taxable year. For example, a debt arising out of gambling receivables that are unenforceable under state or local law, which an accrual method taxpayer includes in income under section 61, is an enforceable obligation for purposes of this paragraph. A gift or contribution to capital shall not be considered a debt for purposes of section 166. The fact that a bad debt is not due at the time of deduction shall not of itself prevent its allowance under section 166. For the disallowance of deductions for bad debts owed by a political party, see § 1.271–1.

(d) **Amount deductible—(1) General rule.** Except in the case of a deduction for a reasonable addition to a reserve for bad debts, the basis for determining the amount of deduction under section 166 in respect of a bad debt shall be the same as the adjusted basis prescribed by § 1.1011–1 for determining the loss from the sale or other disposition of property. * * *

(2) **Specific cases.** Subject to any provision of section 166 and the regulations thereunder which provides to the contrary, the following amounts are deductible as bad debts:

(i) **Notes or accounts receivable.** (a) If, in computing taxable income, a taxpayer values his notes or accounts receivable at their fair market value when received, the amount deductible as a bad debt under section 166 in respect of such receivables shall be limited to such fair market value even though it is less than their face value.

(b) A purchaser of accounts receivable which become worthless during the taxable year shall be entitled under section 166 to a deduction which is based upon the price he paid for such receivables but not upon their face value.

(ii) **Bankruptcy claim.** Only the difference between the amount received in distribution of the assets of a bankrupt and the amount of the claim may be deducted under section 166 as a bad debt.

(iii) **Claim against decedent's estate.** The excess of the amount of the claim over the amount received by a creditor of a decedent in distribution of the assets of the decedent's estate may be considered a worthless debt under section 166.

(e) **Prior inclusion in income required.** Worthless debts arising from unpaid wages, salaries, fees, rents, and similar items of taxable income shall not be allowed as a deduction under section 166 unless the income such items represent has been included in the return of income for the year for which the deduction as a bad debt is claimed or for a prior taxable year.

(f) **Recovery of bad debts.** Any amount attributable to the recovery during the taxable year of a bad debt, or of a part of a bad debt, which was allowed as a deduction from gross income in a prior taxable year shall be included in gross income for the taxable year of recovery, except to the extent that the recovery is excluded from gross income under the provisions of § 1.111–1, relating to the recovery of certain items previously deducted or credited. This paragraph shall not apply, however, to a bad debt which was previously charged against a reserve by a taxpayer on the reserve method of treating bad debts.

(g) Worthless securities. (1) Section 166 and the regulations thereunder do not apply to a debt which is evidenced by a bond, debenture, note, or certificate, or other evidence of indebtedness, issued by a corporation or by a government or political subdivision thereof, with interest coupons or in registered form. See section 166(e). For provisions allowing the deduction of a loss resulting from the worthlessness of such a debt, see § 1.165-5.

* * *

[T.D. 6500, 25 FR 11402, Nov. 26, 1960, as amended by T.D. 6996, 34 FR 835, Jan. 18, 1969; T.D. 7902, 48 FR 33260, July 21, 1983; T.D. 8071, 51 FR 2479, Jan. 17, 1986]

§ 1.166-2   Evidence of worthlessness.

(a) General rule. In determining whether a debt is worthless in whole or in part the district director will consider all pertinent evidence, including the value of the collateral, if any, securing the debt and the financial condition of the debtor.

(b) Legal action not required. Where the surrounding circumstances indicate that a debt is worthless and uncollectible and that legal action to enforce payment would in all probability not result in the satisfaction of execution on a judgment, a showing of these facts will be sufficient evidence of the worthlessness of the debt for purposes of the deduction under section 166.

(c) Bankruptcy—(1) General rule. Bankruptcy is generally an indication of the worthlessness of at least a part of an unsecured and unpreferred debt.

(2) Year of deduction. In bankruptcy cases a debt may become worthless before settlement in some instances; and in others, only when a settlement in bankruptcy has been reached. In either case, the mere fact that bankruptcy proceedings instituted against the debtor are terminated in a later year, thereby confirming the conclusion that the debt is worthless, shall not authorize the shifting of the deduction under section 166 to such later year.

* * *

[T.D. 6500, 25 FR 11402, Nov. 26, 1960; 25 FR 14021, Dec. 31, 1960, as amended by T.D. 7254, 38 FR 2418, Jan. 26, 1973]

§ 1.166-3   Partial or total worthlessness.

(a) Partial worthlessness—(1) Applicable to specific debts only. A deduction under section 166(a)(2) on account of partially worthless debts shall be allowed with respect to specific debts only.

(2) Charge-off required. (i) If, from all the surrounding and attending circumstances, the district director is satisfied that a debt is partially worthless, the amount which has become worthless shall be allowed as a deduction under section 166(a)(2) but only to the extent charged off during the taxable year.

(ii) If a taxpayer claims a deduction for a part of a debt for the taxable year within which that part of the debt is charged off and the deduction is disallowed for that taxable year, then, in a case where the debt becomes partially worthless after the close of that taxable year, a deduction under section 166(a)(2) shall be allowed for a subsequent taxable year but not in excess of the amount charged off in the prior taxable year plus any amount charged off in the subsequent taxable year. In such instance, the charge-off in the prior taxable year shall, if consistently maintained as such, be sufficient to that extent to meet the charge-off requirement of section 166(a)(2) with respect to the subsequent taxable year.

(iii) Before a taxpayer may deduct a debt in part, he must be able to demonstrate to the satisfaction of the district director the amount thereof which is worthless and the part thereof which has been charged off.

(b) Total worthlessness. If a debt becomes wholly worthless during the taxable year, the amount thereof which has not been allowed as a deduction from gross income for any prior taxable year shall be allowed as a deduction for the current taxable year.

[T.D. 6500, 25 FR 11402, Nov. 26, 1960]

§ 1.166-4   Reserve for bad debts.

(a) Allowance of deduction. A taxpayer who has established the reserve method of treating bad debts and has maintained proper reserve accounts for bad debts or who, in accordance with paragraph (b) of § 1.166-1, adopts the reserve method of treating bad debts may deduct from gross income a reasonable addition to a reserve for bad debts in lieu of deducting specific bad debt items. This paragraph applies both to bad debts owed to the taxpayer and to bad debts arising out of section 166(f)(1)(A) guaranteed debt obligations. If a reserve is maintained for bad debts arising out of section 166(f)(1)(A) guaranteed debt obligations, then a separate reserve must also be maintained for all other debt obligations of the taxpayer in the same trade or business, if any. A taxpayer may not maintain a reserve for bad debts arising out of section 166(f)(1)(A) guaranteed debt obligations if with respect to direct debt obligations in the same trade or business the taxpayer takes deductions when the debts become worthless in whole or in part rather than maintaining a reserve for such obligations. See § 1.166–10 for rules concerning section 166(f)(1)(A) guaranteed debt obligations.

(b) **Reasonableness of addition to reserve—** (1) **Relevant factors.** What constitutes a reasonable addition to a reserve for bad debts shall be determined in the light of the facts existing at the close of the taxable year of the proposed addition. The reasonableness of the addition will vary as between classes of business and with conditions of business prosperity. It will depend primarily upon the total amount of debts outstanding as of the close of the taxable year, including those arising currently as well as those arising in prior taxable years, and the total amount of the existing reserve.

(2) **Correction of errors in prior estimates.** In the event that subsequent realizations upon outstanding debts prove to be more or less than estimated at the time of the creation of the existing reserve, the amount of the excess or inadequacy in the existing reserve shall be reflected in the determination of the reasonable addition necessary in the current taxable year.

(c) **Statement required.** A taxpayer using the reserve method shall file with his return a statement showing—

(1) The volume of his charge sales or other business transactions for the taxable year and the percentage of the reserve to such amount;

(2) The total amount of notes and accounts receivable at the beginning and close of the taxable year;

(3) The amount of the debts which have become wholly or partially worthless and have been charged against the reserve account; and

(4) The computation of the addition to the reserve for bad debts.

* * *

[T.D. 6500, 25 FR 11402, Nov. 26, 1960, as amended by T.D. 6728, 29 FR 5855, May 5, 1964; T.D. 7444, 41 FR 53481, Dec. 7, 1976; T.D. 8071, 51 FR 2479, Jan. 17, 1986]

§ **1.166–5   Nonbusiness debts.**

(a) **Allowance of deduction as capital loss.** (1) The loss resulting from any nonbusiness debt's becoming partially or wholly worthless within the taxable year shall not be allowed as a deduction under either section 166(a) or section 166(c) in determining the taxable income of a taxpayer other than a corporation. See section 166(d)(1)(A).

(2) If, in the case of a taxpayer other than a corporation, a nonbusiness debt becomes wholly worthless within the taxable year, the loss resulting therefrom shall be treated as a loss from the sale or exchange, during the taxable year, of a capital asset held for not more than 1 year (6 months for taxable years beginning before 1977; 9 months for taxable years beginning in 1977). Such a loss is subject to the limitations provided in section 1211, relating to the limitation on capital losses, and section 1212, relating to the capital loss carryover, and in the regulations under those sections. A loss on a nonbusiness debt shall be treated as sustained only if and when the debt has become totally worthless, and no deduction shall be allowed for a nonbusiness debt which is recoverable in part during the taxable year.

(b) **Nonbusiness debt defined.** For purposes of section 166 and this section, a nonbusiness debt is any debt other than—

(1) A debt which is created, or acquired, in the course of a trade or business of the taxpayer, determined without regard to the relationship of the debt to a trade or business of the taxpayer at the time when the debt becomes worthless; or

(2) A debt the loss from the worthlessness of which is incurred in the taxpayer's trade or business.

The question whether a debt is a nonbusiness debt is a question of fact in each particular case. The determination of whether the loss on a debt's becoming worthless has been incurred in a trade or business of the taxpayer shall, for this purpose, be made in substantially the same manner for determining whether a loss has been incurred in a trade or business for purposes of section 165(c)(1). For purposes of subparagraph (2) of this paragraph, the character of the debt is to be determined by the relation which the loss resulting from the debt's becoming worthless bears to the trade or business of the taxpayer. If that relation is a proximate one in the conduct of the trade or business in which the taxpayer is engaged at the time the debt becomes worthless, the debt comes within the exception provided by that subparagraph. The use to which the borrowed funds are put by the debtor is of no consequence in making a determination under this paragraph. For purposes of section 166 and this section, a nonbusiness debt does not include a debt described in section 165(g)(2)(C). See § 1.165–5, relating to losses on worthless securities.

* * *

(d) **Examples.** The application of this section may be illustrated by the following examples involving a case where A, an individual who is engaged in the grocery business and who makes his return on the basis of the calendar year, extends credit to B in 1955 on an open account:

Example (1). In 1956 A sells the business but retains the claim against B. The claim becomes worthless in A's hands in 1957. A's loss is not controlled by the nonbusiness debt provisions, since the original consideration has been advanced by A in his trade or business.

Example (2). In 1956 A sells the business to C but sells the claim against B to the taxpayer, D. The claim becomes worthless in D's hands in 1957. During 1956 and 1957, D is not engaged in any trade or business. D's loss is controlled by the nonbusiness debt provisions even though the original consideration has been advanced by A in his trade or business, since the debt has not been created or acquired in connection with a trade or business of D and since in 1957 D is not engaged in a trade or business incident to the conduct of which a loss from the worthlessness of such claim is a proximate result.

Example (3). In 1956 A dies, leaving the business, including the accounts receivable, to his son, C, the taxpayer. The claim against B becomes worthless in C's hands in 1957. C's loss is not controlled by the nonbusiness debt provisions. While C does not advance any consideration for the claim, or create or acquire it in connection with his trade or business, the loss is sustained as a proximate incident to the conduct of the trade or business in which he is engaged at the time the debt becomes worthless.

Example (4). In 1956 A dies, leaving the business to his son, C, but leaving the claim against B to his son, D, the taxpayer. The claim against B becomes worthless in D's hands in 1957. During 1956 and 1957, D is not engaged in any trade or business. D's loss is controlled by the nonbusiness debt provisions even though the original consideration has been advanced by A in his trade or business, since the debt has not been created or acquired in connection with a trade or business of D and since in 1957 D is not engaged in a trade or business incident to

the conduct of which a loss from the worthlessness of such claim is a proximate result.

Example (5). In 1956 A dies; and, while his executor, C, is carrying on the business, the claim against B becomes worthless in 1957. The loss sustained by A's estate is not controlled by the nonbusiness debt provisions. While C does not advance any consideration for the claim on behalf of the estate, or create or acquire it in connection with a trade or business in which the estate is engaged, the loss is sustained as a proximate incident to the conduct of the trade or business in which the estate is engaged at the time the debt becomes worthless.

* * *

[T.D. 6500, 25 FR 11402, Nov. 26, 1960, as amended by T.D. 7657, 44 FR 68464, Nov. 29, 1979; T.D. 7728, 45 FR 72650, Nov. 3, 1980]

§ 1.167(a)–1 Depreciation in general.

(a) **Reasonable allowance.** Section 167(a) provides that a reasonable allowance for the exhaustion, wear and tear, and obsolescence of property used in the trade or business or of property held by the taxpayer for the production of income shall be allowed as a depreciation deduction. The allowance is that amount which should be set aside for the taxable year in accordance with a reasonably consistent plan (not necessarily at a uniform rate), so that the aggregate of the amounts set aside, plus the salvage value, will, at the end of the estimated useful life of the depreciable property, equal the cost or other basis of the property as provided in section 167(g) and § 1.167(g)–1. An asset shall not be depreciated below a reasonable salvage value under any method of computing depreciation. However, see section 167(f) and § 1.167(f)–1 for rules which permit a reduction in the amount of salvage value to be taken into account for certain personal property acquired after October 16, 1962. See also paragraph (c) of this section for definition of salvage. The allowance shall not reflect amounts representing a mere reduction in market value. * * *

(b) **Useful life.** For the purpose of section 167 the estimated useful life of an asset is not necessarily the useful life inherent in the asset but is the period over which the asset may reasonably be expected to be useful to the taxpayer in his trade or business or in the production of his income. This period shall be determined by reference to his experience with similar property taking into account present conditions and probable future developments. Some of the factors to be considered in determining this period are (1) wear and tear and decay or decline from natural causes, (2) the normal progress of the art, economic changes, inventions, and current developments within the industry and the taxpayer's trade or business, (3) the climatic and other local conditions peculiar to the taxpayer's trade or business, and (4) the taxpayer's policy as to repairs, renewals, and replacements. Salvage value is not a factor for the purpose of determining useful life. If the taxpayer's experience is inadequate, the general experience in the industry may be used until such time as the taxpayer's own experience forms an adequate basis for making the determination. The estimated remaining useful life may be subject to modification by reason of conditions known to exist at the end of the taxable year and shall be redetermined when necessary regardless of the method of computing depreciation. However, estimated remaining useful life shall be redetermined only when the change in the useful life is significant and there is a clear and convincing basis for the redetermination. * * *

(c) **Salvage.** (1) Salvage value is the amount (determined at the time of acquisition) which is estimated will be realizable upon sale or other disposition of an asset when it is no longer useful in the taxpayer's trade or business or in the production of his income and is to be retired from service by the taxpayer. Salvage value shall not be changed at any time after the determination made at the time of acquisition merely because of changes in price levels. However, if there is a redetermination of useful life under the rules of paragraph (b) of this section, salvage value may be redetermined based upon facts known at the time of such redetermination of useful life. Salvage, when reduced by the cost of removal, is referred to as net salvage. The time at which an asset is retired from service may vary according to the policy of the taxpayer. If the taxpayer's policy is to dispose of assets which are still in good operating condition, the salvage value may represent a relatively large proportion of the original basis of the asset. However, if the taxpayer customarily uses an asset until its inherent useful life has been substantially exhausted, salvage value may represent no more than junk value. Salvage value must be taken into account in determining the depreciation deduction either by a reduction of the amount subject to depreciation or by a reduction in the rate of depreciation, but in no event shall an asset (or an account) be depreciated below a reasonable salvage value. See, however, paragraph (a) of § 1.167(b)–2 for the treatment of salvage under the declining balance method, and § 1.179–1 for the

treatment of salvage in computing the additional first-year depreciation allowance. The taxpayer may use either salvage or net salvage in determining depreciation allowances but such practice must be consistently followed and the treatment of the costs of removal must be consistent with the practice adopted. For specific treatment of salvage value, see §§ 1.167(b)–1, 1.167(b)–2, and 1.167(b)–3. When an asset is retired or disposed of, appropriate adjustments shall be made in the asset and depreciation reserve accounts. For example, the amount of the salvage adjusted for the costs of removal may be credited to the depreciation reserve.

* * *

[T.D. 6500, 25 FR 11402, Nov. 26, 1960, as amended by T.D. 6712, 29 FR 3653, March 24, 1964; T.D. 7203, 37 FR 17133, Aug. 25, 1972]

§ 1.167(a)–2 Tangible property.

The depreciation allowance in the case of tangible property applies only to that part of the property which is subject to wear and tear, to decay or decline from natural causes, to exhaustion, and to obsolescence. The allowance does not apply to inventories or stock in trade, or to land apart from the improvements or physical development added to it. The allowance does not apply to natural resources which are subject to the allowance for depletion provided in section 611. No deduction for depreciation shall be allowed on automobiles or other vehicles used solely for pleasure, on a building used by the taxpayer solely as his residence, or on furniture or furnishings therein, personal effects, or clothing; but properties and costumes used exclusively in a business, such as a theatrical business, may be depreciated.

[T.D. 6500, 25 FR 11402, Nov. 26, 1960]

§ 1.167(a)–3 Intangibles.

If an intangible asset is known from experience or other factors to be of use in the business or in the production of income for only a limited period, the length of which can be estimated with reasonable accuracy, such an intangible asset may be the subject of a depreciation allowance. Examples are patents and copyrights. An intangible asset, the useful life of which is not limited, is not subject to the allowance for depreciation. No allowance will be permitted merely because, in the unsupported opinion of the taxpayer, the intangible asset has a limited useful life. No deduction for depreciation is allowable with respect to goodwill. For rules with respect to organizational expenditures, see section 248 and the regulations thereunder. For rules with respect to trademark and trade name expenditures, see section 177 and the regulations thereunder.

[T.D. 6500, 25 FR 11402, Nov. 26, 1960]

§ 1.167(a)–8 Retirements.

(a) **Gains and losses on retirements.** * * *

* * *

(4) Where an asset is retired by actual physical abandonment (as, for example, in the case of a building condemned as unfit for further occupancy or other use), loss will be recognized measured by the amount of the adjusted basis of the asset abandoned at the time of such abandonment. In order to qualify for the recognition of loss from physical abandonment, the intent of the taxpayer must be irrevocably to discard the asset so that it will neither be used again by him nor retrieved by him for sale, exchange, or other disposition.

Experience with assets which have attained an exceptional or unusual age shall, with respect to similar assets, be disregarded in determining the maximum expected useful life of the longest lived asset in a multiple asset account. For example, if a manufacturer establishes a proper multiple asset account for 50 assets which are expected to have an average life of 30 years but which will remain useful to him for varying periods between 20 and 40 years, the maximum expected useful life will be 40 years, even though an occasional asset of this kind may last 60 years.

* * *

[T.D. 6500, 25 FR 11402, Nov. 26, 1960]

§ 1.167(a)–10 When depreciation deduction is allowable.

(a) A taxpayer should deduct the proper depreciation allowance each year and may not increase his depreciation allowances in later years by reason of his failure to deduct any depreciation allowance or of his action in deducting an allowance plainly inadequate under the known facts in prior years. The inadequacy of the depreciation allowance for property in prior years shall be determined on the basis of the allowable method of depreciation used by the taxpayer for such property or under the straight line method if no allowance has ever been claimed for such property. The preceding sentence shall not be construed as precluding application of any method provided in section 167(b) if taxpayer's failure to claim any allowance for depreciation was due solely to erroneously treating as a deductible expense an item properly chargeable to capital account. For rules relating to adjustments to basis, see section 1016 and the regulations thereunder.

(b) The period for depreciation of an asset shall begin when the asset is placed in service and shall end when the asset is retired from service. A proportionate part of one year's depreciation is allowable for that part of the first and last year during which the asset was in service. However, in the case of a multiple asset account, the amount of depreciation may be determined by using what is commonly described as an "averaging convention", that is, by using an assumed timing of additions and retirements. For example, it might be assumed that all additions and retirements to the asset account occur uniformly throughout the taxable year, in which case depreciation is computed on the average of the beginning and ending balances of the asset account for the taxable year. See example (3) under paragraph (b) of § 1.167(b)–1. Among still other averaging conventions which may be used is the one under which it is assumed that all additions and retirements during the first half of a given year were made on the first day of that year and that all additions and retirements during the second half of the year were made on the first day of the following year. Thus, a full year's depreciation would be taken on additions in the first half of the year and no depreciation would be taken on additions in the second half. Moreover, under this convention, no depreciation would be taken on retirements in the first half of the year and a full year's depreciation would be taken on the retirements in the second half. An averaging convention, if used, must be consistently followed as to the account or accounts for which it is adopted, and must be applied to both additions and retirements. In any year in which an averaging convention substantially distorts the depreciation allowance for the taxable year, it may not be used.

§ 1.167(b)–0 Methods of computing depreciation.

(a) **In general.** Any reasonable and consistently applied method of computing depreciation may be used or continued in use under section 167.

Regardless of the method used in computing depreciation, deductions for depreciation shall not exceed such amounts as may be necessary to recover the unrecovered cost or other basis less salvage during the remaining useful life of the property. The reasonableness of any claim for depreciation shall be determined upon the basis of conditions known to exist at the end of the period for which the return is made. It is the responsibility of the taxpayer to establish the reasonableness of the deduction for depreciation claimed. Generally, depreciation deductions so claimed will be changed only where there is a clear and convincing basis for a change.

* * *

[T.D. 6500, 26 FR 11402, Nov. 26, 1960]

§ 1.167(b)–1 Straight line method.

(a) In general. Under the straight line method the cost or other basis of the property less its estimated salvage value is deductible in equal annual amounts over the period of the estimated useful life of the property. The allowance for depreciation for the taxable year is determined by dividing the adjusted basis of the property at the beginning of the taxable year, less salvage value, by the remaining useful life of the property at such time. For convenience, the allowance so determined may be reduced to a percentage or fraction. The straight line method may be used in determining a reasonable allowance for depreciation for any property which is subject to depreciation under section 167 and it shall be used in all cases where the taxpayer has not adopted a different acceptable method with respect to such property.

(b) Illustrations. The straight line method is illustrated by the following examples:

Example (1). Under the straight line method items may be depreciated separately:

Year and item	Cost or other basis less salaries	Useful life (years)	Depreciation allowable		
			1954	1955	1956
1954:					
Asset A ...	$1,600	4	[1]$200	$400	$400
Asset B ...	12,000	40	[1]150	300	300

[1] In this example it is assumed that the assets were placed in service on July 1, 1954.

Example (2). In group, classified, or composite accounting, a number of assets with the same or different

useful lives may be combined into one account, and a single rate of depreciation, i.e., the group, classified, or composite rate used for the entire account. In the case of group accounts, i.e., accounts containing assets which are similar in kind and which have approximately the same estimated useful lives, the group rate is determined from the average of the useful lives of the assets. In the case of classified or composite accounts, the classified or composite rate is generally computed by determining the amount of one year's depreciation for each item or each group of similar items, and by dividing the total depreciation thus obtained by the total cost or other basis of the assets. The average rate so obtained is to be used as long as subsequent additions, retirements, or replacements do not substantially alter the relative proportions of different types of assets in the account. An example of the computation of a classified or composite rate follows:

Cost or other basis	Estimated useful life (years)	Annual depreciation
$10,000	5	$2,000
10,000	15	667
20,000		2,667

Average rate is 13.33 percent ($2,667 ÷ $20,000) unadjusted for salvage. Assuming the estimated salvage value is 10 percent of the cost or other basis, the rate adjusted for salvage will be 13.33 percent minus 10 percent of 13.33 percent (13.33%–1.33%), or 12 percent.

* * *

[T.D. 6500, 25 FR 11402, Nov. 26, 1960]

§ 1.167(b)–2 Declining balance method.

(a) Application of method. Under the declining balance method a uniform rate is applied each year to the unrecovered cost or other basis of the property. The unrecovered cost or other basis is the basis provided by section 167(g), adjusted for depreciation previously allowed or allowable, and for all other adjustments provided by section 1016 and other applicable provisions of law. The declining balance rate may be determined without resort to formula. Such rate determined under section 167(b)(2) shall not exceed twice the appropriate straight line rate computed without adjustment for salvage. While salvage is not taken into account in determining the annual allowances under this method, in no event shall an asset (or an account) be depreciated below a reasonable salvage value. However, see section 167(f) and § 1.167(f)–1 for rules which permit a reduction in the amount of salvage value to be taken into account for certain personal property acquired after October 16, 1962. Also, see section 167(c) and § 1.167(c)–1 for restrictions on the use of the declining balance method.

(b) Illustrations. The declining balance method is illustrated by the following examples:

Example (1). A new asset having an estimated useful life of 20 years was purchased on January 1, 1954, for $1,000. The normal straight line rate (without adjustment for salvage) is 5 percent, and the declining balance rate at twice the normal straight line rate is 10 percent. The annual depreciation allowances for 1954, 1955, and 1956 are as follows:

Year	Basis	Declining balance rate (percent)	Depreciation allowance
1954	$1,000	10	$100
1955	900	10	90
1956	810	10	81

* * *

(c) Change in estimated useful life. In the declining balance method when a change is justified in the useful life estimated for an account, subsequent computations shall be made as though the revised useful life had been originally estimated. For example, assume that an account has an estimated useful life of ten years and that a declining balance rate of 20 percent is applicable. If, at the end of the sixth year, it is determined that the remaining useful life of the account is six years, computations shall be made as though the estimated useful life was originally determined as twelve years. Accordingly, the applicable depreciation rate will be 16⅔ percent. This rate is thereafter applied to the unrecovered cost or other basis.

[T.D. 6500, 25 FR 11402, Nov. 26, 1960, as amended by T.D. 6712, 29 FR 3653, March 24, 1964]

§ 1.167(b)-3 Sum of the years-digits method.

(a) Applied to a single asset—(1) General rule. Under the sum of the years-digits method annual allowances for depreciation are computed by applying changing fractions to the cost or other basis of the property reduced by estimated salvage. The numerator of the fraction changes each year to a number which corresponds to the remaining useful life of the asset (including the year for which the allowance is being computed), and the denominator which remains constant is the sum of all the years digits corresponding to the estimated useful life of the asset. See section 167(c) and § 1.167(c)-1 for restrictions on the use of the sum of the years-digits method.

(i) Illustrations. Computation of depreciation allowances on a single asset under the sum of the years-digits method is illustrated by the following examples:

Example (1). A new asset having an estimated useful life of five years was acquired on January 1, 1954, for $1,750. The estimated salvage is $250. For a taxpayer filing his returns on a calendar year basis, the annual depreciation allowances are as follows:

Year	Cost or other basis less salvage	Fraction[1]	Allowable depreciation	Depreciation reserve
1954	$1,500	5/15	$500	$500
1955	1,500	4/15	400	900
1956	1,500	3/15	300	1,200
1957	1,500	2/15	200	1,400
1958	1,500	1/15	100	1,500
Unrecovered value (salvage)				$250

[1] The denominator of the fraction is the sum of the digits representing the years of useful life, i.e., 5, 4, 3, 2, and 1, or 15.

* * *

(ii) Change in useful life. Where in the case of a single asset, a change is justified in the useful life, subsequent computations shall be made as though the remaining useful life at the beginning of the taxable year of change were the useful life of a new asset acquired at such time and with a basis equal to the unrecovered cost or other basis of the asset at that time. For example, assume that a new asset with an estimated useful life of ten years is purchased in 1954. At the time of making out his return for 1959, the taxpayer finds that the asset has a remaining useful life of seven years from January 1, 1959. Depreciation for 1959 should then be computed as though 1959 were the first year of the life of an asset estimated to have a useful life of seven years, and the allowance for 1959 would be 7/28 of the unrecovered cost or other basis of the asset after adjustment for salvage.

(2) Remaining life—(i) Application. Under the sum of the years-digits method, annual allowances for depreciation may also be computed by applying changing fractions to the unrecovered cost or other basis of the asset reduced by estimated salvage. The numerator of the fraction changes each year to a number which corresponds to the remaining useful life of the asset (including the year for which the allowance is being computed), and the denominator changes each year to a number which represents the sum of the digits corresponding to the years of estimated remaining useful life of the asset.

* * *

[T.D. 6500, 25 FR 11402, Nov. 26, 1960]

§ 1.167(g)–1 Basis for depreciation.

The basis upon which the allowance for depreciation is to be computed with respect to any property shall be the adjusted basis provided in section 1011 for the purpose of determining gain on the sale or other disposition of such property. In the case of property which has not been used in the trade or business or held for the production of income and which is thereafter converted to such use, the fair market value on the date of such conversion, if less than the adjusted basis of the property at that time, is the basis for computing depreciation.

[T.D. 6500, 25 FR 11402, Nov. 26, 1960. Redesignated by T.D. 6712, 29 FR 3653, March 24, 1964]

§ 1.167(h)–1 Life tenants and beneficiaries of trusts and estates.

(a) **Life tenants.** In the case of property held by one person for life with remainder to another person, the deduction for depreciation shall be computed as if the life tenant were the absolute owner of the property so that he will be entitled to the deduction during his life, and thereafter the deduction, if any, shall be allowed to the remainderman.

(b) **Trusts.** If property is held in trust, the allowable deduction is to be apportioned between the income beneficiaries and the trustee on the basis of the trust income allocable to each, unless the governing instrument (or local law) requires or permits the trustee to maintain a reserve for depreciation in any amount. In the latter case, the deduction is first allocated to the trustee to the extent that income is set aside for a depreciation reserve, and any part of the deduction in excess of the income set aside for the reserve shall be apportioned between the income beneficiaries and the trustee on the basis of the trust income (in excess of the income set aside for the reserve) allocable to each. For example:

(1) If under the trust instrument or local law the income of a trust computed without regard to depreciation is to be distributed to a named beneficiary, the beneficiary is entitled to the deduction to the exclusion of the trustee.

(2) If under the trust instrument or local law the income of a trust is to be distributed to a named beneficiary, but the trustee is directed to maintain a reserve for depreciation in any amount, the deduction is allowed to the trustee (except to the extent that income set aside for the reserve is less than the allowable deduction). The same result would follow if the trustee sets aside income for a depreciation reserve pursuant to discretionary authority to do so in the governing instrument.

No effect shall be given to any allocation of the depreciation deduction which gives any beneficiary or the trustee a share of such deduction greater than his pro rata share of the trust income, irrespective of any provisions in the trust instrument except as otherwise provided in this paragraph when the trust instrument or local law requires or permits the trustee to maintain a reserve for depreciation.

(c) **Estates.** In the case of an estate the allowable deduction shall be apportioned between the estate and the heirs legatees, and devisees on the basis of income of the estate which is allocable to each.

[T.D. 6500, 25 FR 11402, Nov. 26, 1960. Redesignated by T.D. 6712, 29 FR 3653, March 24, 1964]

§ 1.170A–1 Charitable, etc., contributions and gifts; allowance of deduction.

* * *

(b) **Time of making contribution.** Ordinarily, a contribution is made at the time delivery is effected. The unconditional delivery or mailing of a check which subsequently clears in due course will constitute an effective contribution on the date of delivery or mailing. If a taxpayer unconditionally delivers or mails a properly endorsed stock certificate to a charitable donee or the donee's agent, the gift is completed on the date of delivery or, if such certificate is received in the ordinary course of the mails, on the date of mailing. If the donor delivers the stock certificate to his bank or broker as the donor's agent, or to the issuing corporation or its agent, for transfer into the name of the donee, the gift is completed on the date the stock is transferred on the books of the corporation. For rules relating to the date of payment of a contribution consisting of a future interest in tangible personal property, see section 170(a)(3) and § 1.170A–5.

(c) **Value of a contribution in property.** (1) If a charitable contribution is made in property other than money, the amount of the contribution is the fair market value of the property at the time of the contribution reduced as provided in section 170(e)(1) * * *.

(2) The fair market value is the price at which the property would change hands between a willing buyer and a willing seller, neither being under any compulsion to buy or sell and both having reasonable knowledge of relevant facts. If the contribution is made in property of a type which the taxpayer sells in the course of his business, the fair market value is the price which the taxpayer would have received if he had sold the contributed property in the usual market in which he customarily sells, at the time and place of the contribution and, in the case of a contribution of goods in quantity, in the quantity contributed. The usual market of a manufacturer or other producer consists of the wholesalers or other distributors to or through whom he customarily sells, but if he sells only at retail the usual market consists of his retail customers.

(3) If a donor makes a charitable contribution of property, such as stock in trade, at a time when he could not reasonably have been expected to realize its usual selling price, the value of the gift is not the usual selling price but is the amount for which the quantity of property contributed would have been sold by the donor at the time of the contribution.

(4) Any costs and expenses pertaining to the contributed property which were incurred in taxable years preceding the year of contribution and are properly reflected in the opening inventory for the year of contribution must be removed from inventory and are not a part of the cost of goods sold for purposes of determining gross income for the year of contribution. Any costs and expenses pertaining to the contributed property which are incurred in the year of contribution and would, under the method of accounting used, be properly reflected in the cost of goods sold for such year are to be treated as part of the costs of goods sold for such year. If costs and expenses incurred in producing or acquiring the contributed property are, under the method of accounting used, properly deducted under section 162 or other section of the Code, such costs and expenses will be allowed as deductions for the taxable year in which they are paid or incurred whether or not such year is the year of the contribution. Any such costs and expenses which are treated as part of the cost of goods sold for the year of contribution, and any such costs and expenses which are properly deducted under section 162 or other section of the Code,

are not to be treated under any section of the Code as resulting in any basis for the contributed property. Thus, for example, the contributed property has no basis for purposes of determining under section 170(e)(1)(A) and paragraph (a) of § 1.170A–4 the amount of gain which would have been recognized if such property had been sold by the donor at its fair market value at the time of its contribution. The amount of any charitable contribution for the taxable year is not to be reduced by the amount of any costs or expenses pertaining to the contributed property which was properly deducted under section 162 or other section of the Code for any taxable year preceding the year of contribution. This subparagraph applies only to property which was held by the taxpayer for sale in the course of a trade or business. * * *

* * *

(5) Transfers of property to an organization described in section 170(c) which bear a direct relationship to the taxpayer's trade or business and which are made with a reasonable expectation of financial return commensurate with the amount of the transfer may constitute allowable deductions as trade or business expenses rather than as charitable contributions. See section 162 and the regulations thereunder.

* * *

(e) **Transfers subject to a condition or power.** If as of the date of a gift a transfer for charitable purposes is dependent upon the performance of some act or the happening of a precedent event in order that it might become effective, no deduction is allowable unless the possibility that the charitable transfer will not become effective is so remote as to be negligible. If an interest in property passes to, or is vested in, charity on the date of the gift and the interest would be defeated by the subsequent performance of some act or the happening of some event, the possibility of occurrence of which appears on the date of the gift to be so remote as to be negligible, the deduction is allowable. For example, A transfers land to a city government for as long as the land is used by the city for a public park. If on the date of the gift the city does plan to use the land for a park and the possibility that the city will not use the land for a public park is so remote as to be negligible, A is entitled to a deduction under section 170 for his charitable contribution.

* * *

(g) Contributions of services. No deduction is allowable under section 170 for a contribution of services. However, unreimbursed expenditures made incident to the rendition of services to an organization contributions to which are deductible may constitute a deductible contribution. For example, the cost of a uniform without general utility which is required to be worn in performing donated services is deductible. Similarly, out-of-pocket transportation expenses necessarily incurred in performing donated services are deductible. Reasonable expenditures for meals and lodging necessarily incurred while away from home in the course of performing donated services also are deductible. For the purposes of this paragraph, the phrase "while away from home" has the same meaning as that phrase is used for purposes of section 162 and the regulations thereunder.

* * *

[T.D. 7207, 37 FR 20771, Oct. 4, 1972, as amended by T.D. 7340, 40 FR 1238, Jan. 7, 1975; T.D. 7807, 47 FR 4508, Feb. 1, 1982; T.D. 8002, 49 FR 50666, Dec. 31, 1984]

§ 1.170A–4 Reduction in amount of charitable contributions of certain appreciated property.

(a) Amount of reduction. Section 170(e)(1) requires that the amount of the charitable contribution which would be taken into account under section 170(a) without regard to section 170(e) shall be reduced before applying the percentage limitations under section 170(b)—

(1) In the case of a contribution by an individual or by a corporation of ordinary income property, as defined in paragraph (b)(1) of this section, by the amount of gain (hereinafter in this section referred to as ordinary income) which would have been recognized as gain which is not long-term capital gain if the property had been sold by the donor at its fair market value at the time of its contribution to the charitable organization,

(2) In the case of a contribution by an individual of section 170(e) capital gain property, as defined in paragraph (b)(2) of this section, by 50 percent of the amount of gain (hereinafter in this section referred to as long-term capital gain) which would have been recognized as long-term capital gain if the property had been sold by the donor at its fair market value at the time of its contribution to the charitable organization, and

(3) In the case of a contribution by a corporation of section 170(e) capital gain property, as defined in paragraph (b)(2) of this section, by 62½ percent of the amount of gain (hereinafter in this section referred to as long-term capital gain) which would have been recognized as long-term capital gain if the property had been sold by the donor at its fair market value at the time of its contribution to the charitable organization.

Section 170(e)(1) and this paragraph do not apply to reduce the amount of the charitable contribution where, by reason of the transfer of the contributed property, ordinary income or capital gain is recognized by the donor in the same taxable year in which the contribution is made. Thus, where income or gain is recognized under section 453(d) upon the transfer of an installment obligation to a charitable organization, or under section 454(b) upon the transfer of an obligation issued at a discount to such an organization, or upon the assignment of income to such an organization, section 170(e)(1) and this paragraph do not apply if recognition of the income or gain occurs in the same taxable year in which the contribution is made. Section 170(e)(1) and this paragraph apply to a charitable contribution of an interest in ordinary income property or section 170(e) capital gain property which is described in paragraph (b) of § 1.170A–6, or paragraph (b) of § 1.170A–7. For purposes of applying section 170(e)(1) and this paragraph it is immaterial whether the charitable contribution is made "to" the charitable organization or whether it is made "for the use of" the charitable organization. See § 1.170A–8(a)(2).

(b) Definitions and other rules. For purposes of this section—

(1) **Ordinary income property.** The term "ordinary income property" means property any portion of the gain on which would not have been long term capital gain if the property had been sold by the donor at its fair market value at the time of its contribution to the charitable organization. Such term includes, for example, property held by the donor primarily for sale to customers in the ordinary course of his trade or business, a work of art created by the donor, a manuscript prepared by the donor, letters and memorandums prepared by or for the donor, a capital asset held by the donor for not more than 1 year (6 months for taxable years beginning before 1977; 9 months for taxable years beginning in 1977), and stock described in section 306(a), 341(a), or 1248(a) to the extent that, after applying such section, gain on its disposition would

not have been long-term capital gain. The term does not include an income interest in respect of which a deduction is allowed under section 170(f)(2)(B) and paragraph (c) of § 1.170A–6.

(2) Section 170(e) capital gain property. The term "section 170(e) capital gain property" means property any portion of the gain on which would have been treated as long-term capital gain if the property had been sold by the donor at its fair market value at the time of its contribution to the charitable organization and which—

(i) Is contributed to or for the use of a private foundation, as defined in section 509(a) and the regulations thereunder, other than a private foundation described in section 170(b)(1)(E),

(ii) Constitutes tangible personal property contributed to or for the use of a charitable organization, other than a private foundation to which subdivision (i) of this subparagraph applies, which is put to an unrelated use by the charitable organization within the meaning of subparagraph (3) of this paragraph, or

(iii) Constitutes property not described in subdivision (i) or (ii) of this subparagraph which is 30-percent capital gain property to which an election under paragraph (d)(2) of § 1.170A–8 applies.

For purposes of this subparagraph a fixture which is intended to be severed from real property shall be treated as tangible personal property.

(3) Unrelated use—(i) In general. The term "unrelated use" means a use which is unrelated to the purpose or function constituting the basis of the charitable organization's exemption under section 501 or, in the case of a contribution of property to a governmental unit, the use of such property by such unit for other than exclusively public purposes. For example, if a painting contributed to an educational institution is used by that organization for educational purposes by being placed in its library for display and study by art students, the use is not an unrelated use; but if the painting is sold and the proceeds used by the organization for educational purposes, the use of the property is an unrelated use. If furnishings contributed to a charitable organization are used by it in its offices and buildings in the course of carrying out its functions, the use of the property is not an unrelated use. If a set or collection of items of tangible personal property is contributed to a charitable organization or governmental unit, the use of the set or collection is not an unrelated use if the donee sells or otherwise disposes of only an insubstantial portion of the set or collection. The use by a trust of tangible personal property contributed to it for the benefit of a charitable organization is an unrelated use if the use by the trust is one which would have been unrelated if made by the charitable organization.

(ii) Proof of use. For purposes of applying subparagraph (2)(ii) of this paragraph, a taxpayer who makes a charitable contribution of tangible personal property to or for the use of a charitable organization or governmental unit may treat such property as not being put to an unrelated use by the donee if—

(a) He establishes that the property is not in fact put to an unrelated use by the donee, or

(b) At the time of the contribution or at the time the contribution is treated as made, it is reasonable to anticipate that the property will not be put to an unrelated use by the donee. In the case of a contribution of tangible personal property to or for the use of a museum, if the object donated is of a general type normally retained by such museum or other museums for museum purposes, it will be reasonable for the donor to anticipate, unless he has actual knowledge to the contrary, that the object will not be put to an unrelated use by the donee, whether or not the object is later sold or exchanged by the donee.

(4) Property used in trade or business. For purposes of applying subparagraphs (1) and (2) of this paragraph, property which is used in the trade or business, as defined in section 1231(b), shall be treated as a capital asset, except that any gain in respect of such property which would have been recognized if the property had been sold by the donor at its fair market value at the time of its contribution to the charitable organization shall be treated as ordinary income to the extent that such gain would have constituted ordinary income by reason of the application of section 617(d)(1), 1245(a), 1250(a), 1251(c), 1252(a), or 1254(a), * * *.

* * *

(c) Allocation of basis and gain—(1) In general. Except as provided in subparagraph (2) of this paragraph—

(i) If a taxpayer makes a charitable contribution of less than his entire interest in appreciated property, whether or not the transfer is made in trust, as, for example, in the case of a transfer of appreciated property to a pooled income fund described in section 642(c)(5) and § 1.642(c)–5, and is allowed a deduction under section 170 for a portion of the fair market value of such property, then for purposes of applying the reduction rules of section 170(e)(1) and this section to the contributed portion of the property the taxpayer's adjusted basis in such property at the time of the contribution shall be allocated under section 170(e)(2) between the contributed portion of the property and the noncontributed portion.

(ii) The adjusted basis of the contributed portion of the property shall be that portion of the adjusted basis of the entire property which bears the same ratio to the total adjusted basis as the fair market value of the contributed portion of the property bears to the fair market value of the entire property.

(iii) The ordinary income and the long-term capital gain which shall be taken into account in applying section 170(e)(1) and paragraph (a) of this section to the contributed portion of the property shall be the amount of gain which would have been recognized as ordinary income and long-term capital gain if such contributed portion had been sold by the donor at its fair market value at the time of its contribution to the charitable organization.

(2) **Bargain sale.** (i) If there is a bargain sale of property to the charitable organization and if section 1011(b) and § 1.1011–2 apply, then for purposes of applying the reduction rules of section 170(e)(1) and this section to the contributed portion of the property there shall be allocated under section 1011(b) to the contributed portion of the property the portion of the adjusted basis which is not allocated under section 1011(b) to the noncontributed portion of the property for purposes of determining gain from the bargain sale. The portion of the adjusted basis which is so allocated to the contributed portion of the property shall be that portion of the adjusted basis of the entire property which bears the same ratio to the total adjusted basis as the fair market value of the contributed portion of the property bears to the fair market value of the entire property. For purposes of applying section 170(e)(1) and paragraph (a) of this section to the contributed portion of the property in such a case, there shall be allocated to the contributed portion the amount of gain which is not recognized on the bargain sale but which would have been recognized as ordinary income or long-term capital gain if such contributed portion had been sold by the donor at its fair market value at

the time of its contribution to the charitable organization.

(ii) If there is a bargain sale of property to the charitable organization and if section 1011(b) and § 1.1011–2 do not apply, the taxpayer's adjusted basis of the entire property shall be allocated to the noncontributed portion of the property in accordance with paragraph (e) of § 1.1001–1 for purposes of determining gain from the sale. In such case, no portion of the adjusted basis shall be allocated to the contributed portion of the property.

(iii) The term "bargain sale", as used in this subparagraph, means a transfer of property which is in part a sale or exchange of the property and in part a charitable contribution, as defined in section 170(c), of the property.

(3) **Ratio of ordinary income and capital gain.** For purposes of applying subparagraphs (1)(iii) and (2)(i) of this paragraph, the amount of ordinary income (or long-term capital gain) which would have been recognized if the contributed portion of the property had been sold by the donor at its fair market value at the time of its contribution shall be that amount which bears the same ratio to the ordinary income (or long-term capital gain) which would have been recognized if the entire property had been sold by the donor at its fair market value at the time of its contribution as (i) the fair market value of the contributed portion at such time bears to (ii) the fair market value of the entire property at such time. In the case of a bargain sale, the fair market value of the contributed portion for purposes of subdivision (i) is the amount determined by subtracting from the fair market value of the entire property the amount realized on the sale.

* * *

[T.D. 7207, 37 FR 20776, Oct. 4, 1972; 37 FR 22982, Oct. 27, 1972, as amended by T.D. 7728, 45 FR 72650, Nov. 3, 1980; T.D. 7807, 47 FR 4510, Feb. 1, 1982]

§ 1.170A–5   **Future interests in tangible personal property.**

(a) **In general.** (1) A contribution consisting of a transfer of a future interest in tangible personal property shall be treated as made only when all intervening interests in, and rights to the actual possession or enjoyment of, the property—

(i) Have expired, or

(ii) Are held by persons other than the taxpayer or those standing in a relationship to the taxpayer described in section 267(b) and the regulations thereunder, relating to losses, expenses, and interest with respect to transactions between related taxpayers.

(2) Section 170(a)(3) and this section have no application in respect of a transfer of an undivided present interest in property. For example, a contribution of an undivided one-quarter interest in a painting with respect to which the donee is entitled to possession during 3 months of each year shall be treated as made upon the receipt by the donee of a formally executed and acknowledged deed of gift. However, the period of initial possession by the donee may not be deferred in time for more than 1 year.

(3) Section 170(a)(3) and this section have no application in respect of a transfer of a future interest in intangible personal property or in real property. However, a fixture which is intended to be severed from real property shall be treated as tangible personal property. For example, a contribution of a future interest in a chandelier which is attached to a building is considered a contribution which consists of a future interest in tangible personal property if the transferor intends that it be detached from the building at or prior to the time when the charitable organization's right to possession or enjoyment of the chandelier is to commence.

(4) For purposes of section 170(a)(3) and this section, the term "future interest" has generally the same meaning as it has when used in section 2503 and § 25.2503–3 of this chapter (Gift Tax Regulations); it includes reversions, remainders, and other interests or estates, whether vested or contingent, and whether or not supported by a particular interest or estate, which are limited to commence in use, possession, or enjoyment at some future date or time. The term "future interest" includes situations in which a donor purports to give tangible personal property to a charitable organization, but has an understanding, arrangement, agreement, etc., whether written or oral, with the charitable organization which has the effect of reserving to, or retaining in, such donor a right to the use, possession, or enjoyment of the property.

(5) In the case of a charitable contribution of a future interest to which section 170(a)(3) and this section apply the other provisions of section 170 and the regulations thereunder are inapplicable to the contribution until such time as the contribution is treated as made under section 170(a)(3).

(b) **Illustrations.** The application of this section may be illustrated by the following examples:

Example (1). On December 31, 1970, A, an individual who reports his income on the calendar year basis, conveys by deed of gift to a museum title to a painting, but reserves to himself the right to the use, possession, and enjoyment of the painting during his lifetime. It is assumed that there was no intention to avoid the application of section 170(f)(3)(A) by the conveyance. At the time of the gift the value of the painting is $90,000. Since the contribution consists of a future interest in tangible personal property in which the donor has retained an intervening interest, no contribution is considered to have been made in 1970.

Example (2). Assume the same facts as in example (1) except that on December 31, 1971, A relinquishes all of his right to the use, possession, and enjoyment of the painting and delivers the painting to the museum. Assuming that the value of the painting has increased to $95,000, A is treated as having made a charitable contribution of $95,000 in 1971 for which a deduction is allowable without regard to section 170(f)(3)(A).

Example (3). Assume the same facts as in example (1) except A dies without relinquishing his right to the use, possession, and enjoyment of the painting. Since A did not relinquish his right to the use, possession, and enjoyment of the property during his life, A is treated as not having made a charitable contribution of the painting for income tax purposes.

* * *

[T.D. 7207, 37 FR 20779, Oct. 4, 1972]

§ 1.170A–6   **Charitable contributions in trust.**

(a) **In general.** (1) No deduction is allowed under section 170 for the fair market value of a charitable contribution of any interest in property which is less than the donor's entire interest in the property and which is transferred in trust unless the transfer meets the requirements of paragraph (b) or (c) of this section. If the donor's entire interest in the property is transferred in trust and is contributed to a charitable organization described in section 170(c), a deduction is allowed under section 170. Thus, if on July 1, 1972, property is transferred in trust with the requirement that the income of the trust be paid for a term of 20 years to a church and thereafter the remainder be paid to an educational organization described in section 170(b)(1)(A), a deduction is allowed for the value of such property. See section 170(f)(2) and (3)(B), and paragraph (b)(1) of § 1.170A–7.

(2) A deduction is allowed without regard to this section for a contribution of a partial interest in

property if such interest is the taxpayer's entire interest in the property, such as an income interest or a remainder interest. If, however, the property in which such partial interest exists was divided in order to create such interest and thus avoid section 170(f)(2), the deduction will not be allowed. Thus, for example, assume that a taxpayer desires to contribute to a charitable organization the reversionary interest in certain stocks and bonds which he owns. If the taxpayer transfers such property in trust with the requirement that the income of the trust be paid to his son for life and that the reversionary interest be paid to himself and immediately after creating the trust contributes the reversionary interest to a charitable organization, no deduction will be allowed under section 170 for the contribution of the taxpayer's entire interest consisting of the reversionary interest in the trust.

(b) Charitable contribution of a remainder interest in trust—(1) In general. No deduction is allowed under section 170 for the fair market value of a charitable contribution of a remainder interest in property which is less than the donor's entire interest in the property and which the donor transfers in trust unless the trust is—

(i) A pooled income fund described in section 642(c)(5) and § 1.642(c)–5,

(ii) A charitable remainder annuity trust described in section 664(d)(1) and § 1.664–2, or

(iii) A charitable remainder unitrust described in section 664(d)(2) and § 1.664–3.

(2) Value of a remainder interest. The fair market value of a remainder interest in a pooled income fund shall be computed under § 1.642(c)–6. The fair market value of a remainder interest in a charitable remainder annuity trust shall be computed under § 1.664–2. The fair market value of a remainder interest in a charitable remainder unitrust shall be computed under § 1.664–4. However, in some cases a reduction in the amount of a charitable contribution of the remainder interest may be required. See section 170(e) and § 1.170A–4.

(c) Charitable contribution of an income interest in trust—(1) In general. No deduction is allowed under section 170 for the fair market value of a charitable contribution of an income interest in property which is less than the donor's entire interest in the property and which the donor transfers in trust unless the income interest is either a guaranteed annuity interest or a unitrust interest, as defined in paragraph (c)(2) of this section, and

the grantor is treated as the owner of such interest for purposes of applying section 671, relating to grantors and others treated as substantial owners. See section 4947(a)(2) for the application to such income interests in trust of the provisions relating to private foundations and section 508(e) for rules relating to provisions required in the governing instruments.

(2) Definitions. For purposes of this paragraph—

(i) Guaranteed annuity interest. (A) An income interest is a "guaranteed annuity interest", only if it is an irrevocable right pursuant to the governing instrument of the trust to receive a guaranteed annuity. A guaranteed annuity is an arrangement under which a determinable amount is paid periodically, but not less often than annually, for a specified term or for the life or lives of an individual or individuals, each of whom must be living at the date of transfer and can be ascertained at such date. For example, the annuity may be paid for the life of A plus a term of years. An amount is determinable if the exact amount which must be paid under the conditions specified in the governing instrument of the trust can be ascertained as of the date of transfer. For example, the amount to be paid may be a stated sum for a term, or for the life of an individual, at the expiration of which it may be changed by a specified amount, but it may not be redetermined by reference to a fluctuating index such as the cost of living index. In further illustration, the amount to be paid may be expressed in terms of a fraction or percentage of the cost of living index on the date of transfer.

(B) An income interest is a guaranteed annuity interest only if it is a guaranteed annuity interest in every respect. For example, if the income interest is the right to receive from a trust each year a payment equal to the lesser of a sum certain or a fixed percentage of the net fair market value of the trust assets, determined annually, such interest is not a guaranteed annuity interest.

(C) Where a charitable interest is in the form of a guaranteed annuity interest, the governing instrument of the trust may provide that income of the trust which is in excess of the amount required to pay the guaranteed annuity interest shall be paid to or for the use of a charitable organization. Nevertheless, the amount of the deduction under section 170(f)(2)(B) shall be limited to the fair market value of the guaranteed annuity interest as determined under paragraph (c)(3) of this section. For a rule relating to treatment by the grantor of any contribution made by the trust in excess of the amount required to pay the guaranteed annuity interest, see paragraph (d)(2)(ii) of this section.

(D) If the present value on the date of transfer of all the income interests for a charitable purpose exceeds 60 percent of the aggregate fair market value of all amounts in the trust (after the payment of liabilities), the income interest will not be considered a guaranteed annuity interest unless the governing instrument of the trust prohibits both the acquisition and the retention of assets which would give rise to a tax under section 4944 if the trustee had acquired such assets. The requirement in this subdivision (D) for a prohibition in the governing instrument against the retention of assets which would give rise to a tax under section 4944 if the trustee had acquired the assets shall not apply to a transfer in trust made on or before May 21, 1972.

(E) An income interest consisting of an annuity transferred in trust after May 21, 1972, will not be considered a guaranteed annuity interest if any amount other than an amount in payment of a guaranteed annuity interest may be paid by the trust for a private purpose before the expiration of all the income interests for a charitable purpose, unless such amount for a private purpose is paid from a group of assets which, pursuant to the governing instrument of the trust, are devoted exclusively to private purposes and to which section 4947(a)(2) is inapplicable by reason of section 4947(a)(2)(B). The exception in the immediately preceding sentence with respect to any guaranteed annuity for a private purpose shall apply only if the obligation to pay the annuity for a charitable purpose begins as of the date of creation of the trust and the obligation to pay the guaranteed annuity for a private purpose does not precede in point of time the obligation to pay the annuity for a charitable purpose and only if the governing instrument of the trust does not provide for any preference or priority in respect of any payment of the guaranteed annuity for a private purpose as opposed to any payment of any annuity for a charitable purpose. For purposes of this subdivision (E), an amount is not paid for a private purpose if it is paid for an adequate and full consideration in money or money's worth. See § 53.4947–1(c) of this chapter (Foundation Excise Tax Regulations) for rules relating to the inapplicability of

section 4947(a)(2) to segregated amounts in a split-interest trust.

Example. In 1975, E transfers $75,000 in trust with the requirement that an annuity of $5,000 a year, payable annually at the end of each year, be paid to B, an individual, for a period of 5 years and thereafter an annuity of $5,000 a year, payable annually at the end of each year, be paid to M Charity for a period of 5 years. The remainder is to be paid to C, an individual. No deduction is allowed under subparagraph (1) of this paragraph with respect to the charitable annuity because it is not a "guaranteed annuity interest" within the meaning of this subdivision.

* * *

(ii) **Unitrust interest.** (A) An income interest is a "unitrust interest" only if it is an irrevocable right pursuant to the governing instrument of the trust to receive payment, not less often than annually of a fixed percentage of the net fair market value of the trust assets, determined annually. In computing the net fair market value of the trust assets, all assets and liabilities shall be taken into account without regard to whether particular items are taken into account in determining the income of the trust. The net fair market value of the trust assets may be determined on any one date during the year or by taking the average of valuations made on more than one date during the year, provided that the same valuation date or dates and valuation methods are used each year. Where the governing instrument of the trust does not specify the valuation date or dates, the trustee shall select such date or dates and shall indicate his selection on the first return on Form 1041 which the trust is required to file. Payments under a unitrust interest may be paid for a specified term or for the life or lives of an individual or individuals, each of whom must be living at the date of transfer and can be ascertained at such date. For example, the unitrust interest may be paid for the life of A plus a term of years.

(B) An income interest is a unitrust interest only if it is a unitrust interest in every respect. For example, if the income interest is the right to receive from a trust each year a payment equal to the lesser of a sum certain or a fixed percentage of the net fair market value of the trust assets, determined annually, such interest is not a unitrust interest.

(C) Where a charitable interest is in the form of a unitrust interest, the governing instrument of the trust may provide that income of the trust which is in excess of the amount required to pay the unitrust interest shall be paid to or for the use of a charitable organization. Nevertheless, the amount of the deduction under section 170(f)(2)(B) shall be limited to the fair market value of the unitrust interest as determined under paragraph (c)(3) of this section. For a rule relating to treatment by the grantor of any contribution made by the trust in excess of the amount required to pay the unitrust interest, see paragraph (d)(2)(ii) of this section.

(D) An income interest in the form of a unitrust interest will not be considered a unitrust interest if any amount other than an amount in payment of a unitrust interest may be paid by the trust for a private purpose before the expiration of all the income interests for a charitable purpose, unless such amount for a private purpose is paid from a group of assets which, pursuant to the governing instrument of the trust, are devoted exclusively to private purposes and to which section 4947(a)(2) is inapplicable by reason of section 4947(a)(2)(B). The exception in the immediately preceding sentence with respect to any unitrust interest for a private purpose shall apply only if the obligation to pay the unitrust interest for a charitable purpose begins as of the date of creation of the trust and the obligation to pay the unitrust interest for a private purpose does not precede in point of time the obligation to pay the unitrust interest for a charitable purpose and only if the governing instrument of the trust does not provide for any preference or priority in respect of any payment of the unitrust interest for a private purpose as opposed to any payments of any unitrust interest for a charitable purpose. For purposes of this subdivision (D), an amount is not paid for a private purpose if it is paid for an adequate and full consideration in money or money's worth. See § 53.4947–1(c) of this chapter (Foundation Excise Tax Regulations) for rules relating to the inapplicability of section 4947(a)(2) to segregated amounts in a split-interest trust.

* * *

(3) **Valuation of income interest.** (i) The deduction allowed by section 170(f)(2)(B) for a charitable contribution of a guaranteed annuity interest is limited to the fair market value of such interest on the date of contribution, as computed under § 20.2031–7 or § 20.2031–10, whichever is appropriate, of this chapter (Estate Tax Regulations).

(ii) The deduction allowed under section 170(f)(2)(B) for a charitable contribution of a unitrust interest is limited to the fair market value of

the unitrust interest on the date of contribution. The fair market value of the unitrust interest shall be determined by subtracting the present value of all interests in the transferred property other than the unitrust interest from the fair market value of the transferred property.

(iii) If by reason of all the conditions and circumstances surrounding a transfer of an income interest in property in trust it appears that the charity may not receive the beneficial enjoyment of the interest, a deduction will be allowed under paragraph (c)(1) of this section only for the minimum amount it is evident the charity will receive. The application of this subdivision may be illustrated by the following examples:

Example (1). In 1972, B transfers $20,000 in trust with the requirement that M Church be paid a guaranteed annuity interest (as defined in subparagraph (2)(i) of this paragraph) of $4,000, payable annually at the end of each year for 9 years, and that the residue revert to himself. Since the fair market value of an annuity of $4,000 a year for a period of 9 years, as determined under Table B in § 20.2031–10(f) of this chapter, is $27,206.80 ($4,000 × 6.8017), it appears that M will not receive the beneficial enjoyment of the income interest. Accordingly, even though B is treated as the owner of the trust under section 673, he is allowed a deduction under subparagraph (1) of this paragraph for only $20,000, which is the minimum amount it is evident M will receive.

Example (2). In 1975, C transfers $40,000 in trust with the requirement that D, an individual, and X Charity be paid simultaneously guaranteed annuity interests (as defined in subparagraph (2)(i) of this paragraph) of $5,000 a year each, payable annually at the end of each year, for a period of 5 years and that the remainder be paid to C's children. The fair market value of two annuities of $5,000 each a year for a period of 5 years is $42,124 ([$5,000 × 4.2124] × 2), as determined under Table B in § 20.2031–10(f) of this chapter. The trust instrument provides that in the event the trust fund is insufficient to pay both annuities in a given year, the trust fund will be evenly divided between the charitable and private annuitants. The deduction under subparagraph (1) of this paragraph with respect to the charitable annuity will be limited to $20,000, which is the minimum amount it is evident X will receive.

* * *

(4) **Recapture upon termination of treatment as owner.** If for any reason the donor of an income interest in property ceases at any time before the termination of such interest to be treated as the owner of such interest for purposes of applying section 671, as for example, where he dies before the termination of such interest, he shall for purposes of this chapter be considered as having received, on the date he ceases to be so treated, an amount of income equal to (i) the amount of any deduction he was allowed under section 170 for the

contribution of such interest reduced by (ii) the discounted value of all amounts which were required to be, and actually were, paid with respect to such interest under the terms of trust to the charitable organization before the time at which he ceases to be treated as the owner of the interest. The discounted value of the amounts described in subdivision (ii) of this subparagraph shall be computed by treating each such amount as a contribution of a remainder interest after a term of years and valuing such amount as of the date of contribution of the income interest by the donor, such value to be determined under § 20.2031–1 or § 20.2031–10, whichever is appropriate, of this chapter consistently with the manner in which the fair market value of the income interest was determined pursuant to subparagraph (3)(i) of this paragraph. The application of this subparagraph will not be construed to disallow a deduction to the trust for amounts paid by the trust to the charitable organization after the time at which the donor ceased to be treated as the owner of the trust.

* * *

(d) **Denial of deduction for certain contributions by a trust.** (1) If by reason of section 170(f)(2)(B) and paragraph (c) of this section a charitable contributions deduction is allowed under section 170 for the fair market value of an income interest transferred in trust, neither the grantor of the income interest, the trust, nor any other person shall be allowed a deduction under section 170 or any other section for the amount of any charitable contribution made by the trust with respect to, or in fulfillment of, such income interest.

(2) Section 170(f)(2)(C) and subparagraph (1) of this paragraph shall not be construed, however, to—

(i) Disallow a deduction to the trust, pursuant to section 642(c)(1) and the regulations thereunder, for amounts paid by the trust after the grantor ceases to be treated as the owner of the income interest for purposes of applying section 671 and which are not taken into account in determining the amount of recapture under paragraph (c)(4) of this section, or

(ii) Disallow a deduction to the grantor under section 671 and § 1.671–2(c) for a charitable contribution made by the trust in excess of the contribution required to be made by the trust under the terms of the trust instrument with respect to, or in fulfillment of, the income interest.

* * *

[T.D. 7207, 37 FR 20780, Oct. 5, 1972; 37 FR 22982, Oct. 27, 1972, as amended by T.D. 7340, 40 FR 1238, Jan. 7, 1975; T.D. 7955, 49 FR 19975, May 11, 1984]

§ 1.172–1   Net operating loss deduction.

(a) **Allowance of deduction.** Section 172(a) allows as a deduction in computing taxable income for any taxable year subject to the Code the aggregate of the net operating loss carryovers and net operating loss carrybacks to such taxable year. This deduction is referred to as the net operating loss deduction. The net operating loss is the basis for the computation of the net operating loss carryovers and net operating loss carrybacks and ultimately for the net operating loss deduction itself. The net operating loss deduction shall not be disallowed for any taxable year merely because the taxpayer has no income from a trade or business for the taxable year.

(b) **Steps in computation of net operating loss deduction.** The three steps to be taken in the ascertainment of the net operating loss deduction for any taxable year subject to the Code are as follows:

(1) Compute the net operating loss for any preceding or succeeding taxable year from which a net operating loss may be carried over or carried back to such taxable year.

(2) Compute the net operating loss carryovers to such taxable year from such preceding taxable years and the net operating loss carrybacks to such taxable year from such succeeding taxable years.

(3) Add such net operating loss carryovers and carrybacks in order to determine the net operating loss deduction for such taxable year.

(c) **Statement with tax return.** Every taxpayer claiming a net operating loss deduction for any taxable year shall file with his return for such year a concise statement setting forth the amount of the net operating loss deduction claimed and all material and pertinent facts relative thereto, including a detailed schedule showing the computation of the net operating loss deduction.

(d) **Ascertainment of deduction dependent upon net operating loss carryback.** If the taxpayer is entitled in computing his net operating loss deduction to a carryback which he is not able to ascertain at the time his return is due, he shall compute the net operating loss deduction on his return without regard to such net operating loss carryback. When the taxpayer ascertains the net operating loss carryback, he may within the applicable period of limitations file a claim for credit or refund of the overpayment, if any, resulting from the failure to compute the net operating loss deduction for the taxable year with the inclusion of such carryback; or he may file an application under the provisions of section 6411 for a tentative carryback adjustment.

* * *

[T.D. 6500, 25 FR 11402, Nov. 26, 1960]

§ 1.172–2 Net operating loss in case of a corporation.

(a) **Modification of deductions.** A net operating loss is sustained by a corporation in any taxable year beginning after December 31, 1953, if and to the extent that, for such year, there is an excess of deductions allowed by chapter 1 of the Internal Revenue Code of 1954 over gross income computed thereunder; this rule shall apply even though the loss year is otherwise subject to the Internal Revenue Code of 1939. In determining the excess of deductions over gross income for such purpose—

(1) **Items not deductible.** No deduction shall be allowed under—

(i) Section 172 for the net operating loss deduction,

* * *

(2) **Dividends received.** The 85-percent limitation provided by section 246 (b) shall not apply to the deductions otherwise allowed under—

(i) Section 243(a) in respect of dividends received from domestic corporations,

* * *

[T.D. 6500, 25 FR 11402, Nov. 26, 1960, as amended by T.D. 7767, 46 FR 11263, Feb. 6, 1981]

§ 1.172–3 Net operating loss in case of a taxpayer other than a corporation.

(a) **Modification of deductions.** A net operating loss is sustained by a taxpayer other than a corporation in any taxable year beginning after December 31, 1953, if and to the extent that, for such year there is an excess of deductions allowed by chapter 1 of the Internal Revenue Code of 1954 over gross income computed thereunder; this rule shall apply even though the loss year is otherwise subject to the Internal Revenue Code of 1939. In determining the excess of deductions over gross income for such purpose—

(1) **Items not deductible.** No deduction shall be allowed under—

(i) Section 151 for the personal exemptions or under any other section which grants a deduction in lieu of the deductions allowed by section 151,

(ii) Section 172 for the net operating loss deduction, and

(iii) Section 1202 in respect of the net long-term capital gain.

(2) **Capital losses.** (i) The amount deductible on account of business capital losses shall not exceed the sum of the amount includible on account of business capital gains and that portion of nonbusiness capital gains which is computed in accordance with paragraph (c) of this section.

(ii) The amount deductible on account of nonbusiness capital losses shall not exceed the amount includible on account of nonbusiness capital gains.

(3) **Nonbusiness deductions—(i) Ordinary deductions.** Ordinary nonbusiness deductions shall be taken into account without regard to the amount of business deductions and shall be allowed in full to the extent, but not in excess, of that amount which is the sum of the ordinary nonbusiness gross income and the excess of nonbusiness capital gains over nonbusiness capital losses. See paragraph (c) of this section. For purposes of section 172, nonbusiness deductions and income are those deductions and that income which are not attributable to, or derived from, a taxpayer's trade or business. Wages and salary constitute income attributable to the taxpayer's trade or business for such purposes.

(ii) **Sale of business property.** Any gain or loss on the sale or other disposition of property which is used in the taxpayer's trade or business and which is of a character that is subject to the allowance for depreciation provided in section 167, or of real property used in the taxpayer's trade or business, shall be considered, for purposes of section 172(d)(4), as attributable to, or derived from, the taxpayer's trade or business. Such gains and losses are to be taken into account fully in computing a net operating loss without regard to the limitation on nonbusiness deductions. Thus, a farmer who sells at a loss land used in the business of farming may, in computing a net operating loss, include in full the deduction otherwise allowable with respect to such loss, without regard to the amount of his nonbusiness income and without regard to whether he is engaged in the trade or business of selling farms. Similarly, an individual who sells at a loss machinery which is used in his trade or business and which is of a character that is subject to the allowance for depreciation may, in computing the net operating loss, include in full the deduction otherwise allowable with respect to such loss.

(iii) Casualty losses. Any deduction allowable under section 165(c)(3) for losses of property not connected with a trade or business shall not be considered, for purposes of section 172(d)(4), to be a nonbusiness deduction but shall be treated as a deduction attributable to the taxpayer's trade or business.

(iv) Self-employed retirement plans. Any deduction allowed under section 404, relating to contributions of an employer to an employees' trust or annuity plan, or under section 405(c), relating to contributions to a bond purchase plan, to the extent attributable to contributions made on behalf of an individual while he is an employee within the meaning of section 401(c)(1), shall not be treated, for purposes of section 172(d)(4), as attributable to, or derived from, the taxpayer's trade or business, but shall be treated as a nonbusiness deduction.

(v) Limitation. The provisions of this subparagraph shall not be construed to permit the deduction of items disallowed by subparagraph (1) of this paragraph.

* * *

[T.D. 6500, 25 FR 11402, Nov. 26, 1960, as amended by T.D. 6828, 30 FR 7805, June 17, 1965; T.D. 6862, 30 FR 14427, Nov. 18, 1965]

§ 1.174–1 Research and experimental expenditures; in general.

Section 174 provides two methods for treating research or experimental expenditures paid or incurred by the taxpayer in connection with his trade or business. These expenditures may be treated as expenses not chargeable to capital account and deducted in the year in which they are paid or incurred (see § 1.174–3), or they may be deferred and amortized (see § 1.174–4). Research or experimental expenditures which are neither treated as expenses nor deferred and amortized under section 174 must be charged to capital ac-

count. The expenditures to which section 174 applies may relate either to a general research program or to a particular project. See § 1.174–2 for the definition of research and experimental expenditures. The term "paid or incurred", as used in section 174 and in §§ 1.174–1 to 1.174–4, inclusive, is to be construed according to the method of accounting used by the taxpayer in computing taxable income. See section 7701(a)(25).

[T.D. 6500, 25 FR 11402, Nov. 26, 1960]

§ 1.174–2 Definition of research and experimental expenditures.

(a) In general. (1) The term "research or experimental expenditures", as used in section 174, means expenditures incurred in connection with the taxpayer's trade or business which represent research and development costs in the experimental or laboratory sense. The term includes generally all such costs incident to the development of an experimental or pilot model, a plant process, a product, a formula, an invention, or similar property, and the improvement of already existing property of the type mentioned. The term does not include expenditures such as those for the ordinary testing or inspection of materials or products for quality control or those for efficiency surveys, management studies, consumer surveys, advertising, or promotions. However, the term includes the costs of obtaining a patent, such as attorneys' fees expended in making and perfecting a patent application. On the other hand, the term does not include the costs of acquiring another's patent, model, production or process, nor does it include expenditures paid or incurred for research in connection with literary, historical, or similar projects.

(2) The provisions of this section apply not only to costs paid or incurred by the taxpayer for research or experimentation undertaken directly by him but also to expenditures paid or incurred for research or experimentation carried on in his behalf by another person or organization (such as a research institute, foundation, engineering company, or similar contractor). However, any expenditures for research or experimentation carried on in the taxpayer's behalf by another person are not expenditures to which section 174 relates, to the extent that they represent expenditures for the acquisition or improvement of land or depreciable property, used in connection with the research or experimentation, to which the taxpayer acquires rights of ownership.

* * *

[T.D. 6500, 25 FR 11402, Nov. 26, 1960]

§ 1.183-1 Activities not engaged in for profit.

(a) **In general.** Section 183 provides rules relating to the allowance of deductions in the case of activities (whether active or passive in character) not engaged in for profit by individuals and electing small business corporations, creates a presumption that an activity is engaged in for profit if certain requirements are met, and permits the taxpayer to elect to postpone determination of whether such presumption applies until he has engaged in the activity for at least 5 taxable years, or, in certain cases, 7 taxable years. Whether an activity is engaged in for profit is determined under section 162 and section 212(1) and (2) except insofar as section 183(d) creates a presumption that the activity is engaged in for profit. If deductions are not allowable under sections 162 and 212(1) and (2), the deduction allowance rules of section 183(b) and this section apply. Pursuant to section 641(b), the taxable income of an estate or trust is computed in the same manner as in the case of an individual, with certain exceptions not here relevant. Accordingly, where an estate or trust engages in an activity or activities which are not for profit, the rules of section 183 and this section apply in computing the allowable deductions of such trust or estate. No inference is to be drawn from the provisions of section 183 and the regulations thereunder that any activity of a corporation (other than an electing small business corporation) is or is not a business or engaged in for profit. For rules relating to the deductions that may be taken into account by taxable membership organizations which are operated primarily to furnish services, facilities, or goods to members, see section 277 and the regulations thereunder. For the definition of an activity not engaged in for profit, see § 1.183-2. For rules relating to the election contained in section 183(e), see § 1.183-3.

(b) **Deductions allowable—(1) Manner and extent.** If an activity is not engaged in for profit, deductions are allowable under section 183(b) in the following order and only to the following extent:

(i) Amounts allowable as deductions during the taxable year under chapter 1 of the Code without regard to whether the activity giving rise to such amounts was engaged in for profit are allowable to the full extent allowed by the relevant sections of the Code, determined after taking into account any limitations or exceptions with respect to the allowability of such amounts. For example, the allowability-of-interest expenses incurred with respect to activities not engaged in for profit is limited by the rules contained in section 163(d).

(ii) Amounts otherwise allowable as deductions during the taxable year under chapter 1 of the Code, but only if such allowance does not result in an adjustment to the basis of property, determined as if the activity giving rise to such amounts was engaged in for profit, are allowed only to the extent the gross income attributable to such activity exceeds the deductions allowed or allowable under subdivision (i) of this subparagraph.

(iii) Amounts otherwise allowable as deductions for the taxable year under chapter 1 of the Code which result in (or if otherwise allowed would have resulted in) an adjustment to the basis of property, determined as if the activity giving rise to such deductions was engaged in for profit, are allowed only to the extent the gross income attributable to such activity exceeds the deductions allowed or allowable under subdivisions (i) and (ii) of this subparagraph. Deductions falling within this subdivision include such items as depreciation, partial losses with respect to property, partially worthless debts, amortization, and amortizable bond premium.

* * *

(c) **Presumption that activity is engaged in for profit—(1) In general.** If for—

(i) Any 2 of 7 consecutive taxable years, in the case of an activity which consists in major part of the breeding, training, showing, or racing of horses, or

(ii) Any 2 of 5 consecutive taxable years, in the case of any other activity, the gross income derived from an activity exceeds the deductions attributable to such activity which would be allowed or allowable if the activity were engaged in for profit, such activity is presumed, unless the Commissioner establishes to the contrary, to be engaged in for profit. For purposes of this determination the deduction permitted by section 1202 shall not be taken into account. Such presumption applies with respect to the second profit year and all years subsequent to the second profit year within the 5- or 7-year period beginning with the first profit year. This presumption arises only if the activity is substantially the same activity for each of the relevant taxable years, including the taxable year in question. If the taxpayer does not meet the requirements of section 183(d) and this paragraph, no inference that the activity is not engaged in for profit shall arise by reason of the provisions of section 183. For purposes of this paragraph, a net operating loss deduction is not taken into account as a deduction. For purposes of this subparagraph a short taxable year constitutes a taxable year.

* * *

(3) **Activity which consists in major part of the breeding, training, showing, or racing of horses.** For purposes of this paragraph an activity consists in major part of the breeding, training, showing, or racing of horses for the taxable year if the average of the portion of expenditures attributable to breeding, training, showing, and racing of horses for the 3 taxable years preceding the taxable year (or, in the case of an activity which has not been conducted by the taxpayer for 3 years, for so long as it has been carried on by him) was at least 50 percent of the total expenditures attributable to the activity for such prior taxable years.

* * *

(d) **Activity defined—(1) Ascertainment of activity.** In order to determine whether, and to what extent, section 183 and the regulations thereunder apply, the activity or activities of the taxpayer must be ascertained. For instance, where the taxpayer is engaged in several undertakings, each of these may be a separate activity, or several undertakings may constitute one activity. In ascertaining the activity or activities of the taxpayer, all the facts and circumstances of the case must be taken into account. Generally, the most significant facts and circumstances in making this determination are the degree of organizational and economic interrelationship of various undertakings, the business purpose which is (or might be) served by carrying on the various undertakings separately or together in a trade or business or in an investment setting, and the similarity of various undertakings. Generally, the Commissioner will accept the characterization by the taxpayer of several undertakings either as a single activity or as separate activities. The taxpayer's characterization will not be accepted, however, when it appears that his characterization is artificial and cannot be reasonably supported under the facts and circumstances of the case. If the taxpayer engages in two or more separate activities, deductions and income from each separate activity are not aggregated

either in determining whether a particular activity is engaged in for profit or in applying section 183. Where land is purchased or held primarily with the intent to profit from increase in its value, and the taxpayer also engages in farming on such land, the farming and the holding of the land will ordinarily be considered a single activity only if the farming activity reduces the net cost of carrying the land for its appreciation in value. Thus, the farming and holding of the land will be considered a single activity only if the income derived from farming exceeds the deductions attributable to the farming activity which are not directly attributable to the holding of the land (that is, deductions other than those directly attributable to the holding of the land such as interest on a mortgage secured by the land, annual property taxes attributable to the land and improvements, and depreciation of improvements to the land).

(2) **Rules for allocation of expenses.** If the taxpayer is engaged in more than one activity, an item of deduction or income may be allocated between two or more of these activities. Where property is used in several activities, and one or more of such activities is determined not to be engaged in for profit, deductions relating to such property must be allocated between the various activities on a reasonable and consistently applied basis.

(3) **Example.** The provisions of this paragraph may be illustrated by the following example:

Example. (i) A, an individual, owns a small house located near the beach in a resort community. Visitors come to the area for recreational purposes during only 3 months of the year. During the remaining 9 months of the year houses such as A's are not rented. Customarily, A arranges that the house will be leased for 2 months of 3-month recreational season to vacationers and reserves the house for his own vacation during the remaining month of the recreational season. In 1971, A leases the house for 2 months for $1,000 per month and actually uses the house for his own vacation during the other month of the recreational season. For 1971, the expenses attributable to the house are $1,200 interest, $600 real estate taxes, $600 maintenance, $300 utilities, and $1,200 which would have been allowed as depreciation had the activity been engaged in for profit. Under these facts and circumstances, A is engaged in a single activity, holding the beach house primarily for personal purposes, which is an "activity not engaged in for profit" within the meaning of section 183(c). See paragraph (b)(9) of § 1.183–2.

(ii) Since the $1,200 of interest and the $600 of real estate taxes are specifically allowable as deductions under sections 163 and 164(a) without regard to whether the beach house activity is engaged in for profit, no allocation of these expenses between the uses of the beach house is necessary. However, since section 262 specifically disallows personal, living, and family expenses as deductions, the maintenance and utilities expenses and the depreciation from the activity must be allocated between the rental use and the personal use of the beach house. Under the particular facts and circumstances, $\frac{2}{3}$ (2 months of rental use over 3 months of total use) of each of these expenses are allocated to the rental use, and $\frac{1}{3}$ (1 month of personal use over 3 months of total use) of each of these expenses are allocated to the personal use as follows:

	Rental use $\frac{2}{3}$ —expenses allocable to section 183(b)(2)	Personal use $\frac{1}{3}$ —expenses allocable to section 262
Maintenance expense $600	$400	$200
Utilities expense $300	200	100
Depreciation $1,200	800	400
Total..................	1,400	700

The $700 of expenses and depreciation allocated to the personal use of the beach house are disallowed as a deduction under section 262. In addition, the allowability of each of the expenses and the depreciation allocated to section 183(b)(2) is determined under paragraph (b)(1)(ii) and (iii) of this section. Thus, the maximum amount allowable as a deduction under section 183(b)(2) is $200 ($2,000 gross income from activity, less $1,800 deductions under section 183(b)(1)). Since the amounts described in section 183(b)(2) ($1,400) exceed the maximum amount allowable ($200), and since the amounts described in paragraph (b)(1)(ii) of this section ($600) exceed such maximum amount allowable ($200), none of the depreciation (an amount described in paragraph (b)(1)(iii) of this section) is allowable as a deduction.

(e) Gross income from activity not engaged in for profit defined. For purposes of section 183 and the regulations thereunder, gross income derived from an activity not engaged in for profit includes the total of all gains from the sale, exchange, or other disposition of property, and all other gross receipts derived from such activity. Such gross income shall include, for instance, capital gains, and rents received for the use of property which is held in connection with the activity. The taxpayer may determine gross income from any activity by subtracting the cost of goods sold from the gross receipts so long as he consistently does so and follows generally accepted methods of accounting in determining such gross income.

* * *

[T.D. 7198, 37 FR 13680, July 13, 1972]

§ 1.183-2 **Activity not engaged in for profit defined.**

(a) In general. For purposes of section 183 and the regulations thereunder, the term "activity not engaged in for profit" means any activity other than one with respect to which deductions are allowable for the taxable year under section 162 or under paragraph (1) or (2) of section 212. Deductions are allowable under section 162 for expenses of carrying on activities which constitute a trade or business of the taxpayer and under section 212 for expenses incurred in connection with activities engaged in for the production or collection of income or for the management, conservation, or maintenance of property held for the production of income. Except as provided in section 183 and § 1.183-1, no deductions are allowable for expenses incurred in connection with activities which are not engaged in for profit. Thus, for example, deductions are not allowable under section 162 or 212 for activities which are carried on primarily as a sport, hobby, or for recreation. The determination whether an activity is engaged in for profit is to be made by reference to objective standards, taking into account all of the facts and circumstances of each case. Although a reasonable expectation of profit is not required, the facts and circumstances must indicate that the taxpayer entered into the activity, or continued the activity, with the objective of making a profit. In determining whether such an objective exists, it may be sufficient that there is a small chance of making a large profit. Thus it may be found that an investor in a wildcat oil well who incurs very substantial expenditures is in the venture for profit even though the expectation of a profit might be considered unreasonable. In determining whether an activity is engaged in for profit, greater weight is given to objective facts than to the taxpayer's mere statement of his intent.

(b) Relevant factors. In determining whether an activity is engaged in for profit, all facts and circumstances with respect to the activity are to be taken into account. No one factor is determinative in making this determination. In addition, it is not intended that only the factors described in this paragraph are to be taken into account in making the determination, or that a determination is to be made on the basis that the number of factors (whether or not listed in this paragraph) indicating a lack of profit objective exceeds the number of factors indicating a profit objective, or vice versa. Among the factors which should normally be taken into account are the following:

(1) Manner in which the taxpayer carries on the activity. The fact that the taxpayer carries on the activity in a businesslike manner and maintains complete and accurate books and records may indicate that the activity is engaged in for profit. Similarly, where an activity is carried on in a manner substantially similar to other activities of the same nature which are profitable, a profit motive may be indicated. A change of operating methods, adoption of new techniques or abandonment of unprofitable methods in a manner consistent with an intent to improve profitability may also indicate a profit motive.

(2) **The expertise of the taxpayer or his advisors.** Preparation for the activity by extensive study of its accepted business, economic, and scientific practices, or consultation with those who are expert therein, may indicate that the taxpayer has a profit motive where the taxpayer carries on the activity in accordance with such practices. Where a taxpayer has such preparation or procures such expert advice, but does not carry on the activity in accordance with such practices, a lack of intent to derive profit may be indicated unless it appears that the taxpayer is attempting to develop new or superior techniques which may result in profits from the activity.

(3) **The time and effort expended by the taxpayer in carrying on the activity.** The fact that the taxpayer devotes much of his personal time and effort to carrying on an activity, particularly if the activity does not have substantial personal or recreational aspects, may indicate an intention to derive a profit. A taxpayer's withdrawal from another occupation to devote most of his energies to the activity may also be evidence that the activity is engaged in for profit. The fact that the taxpayer devotes a limited amount of time to an activity does not necessarily indicate a lack of profit motive where the taxpayer employs competent and qualified persons to carry on such activity.

(4) **Expectation that assets used in activity may appreciate in value.** The term "profit" encompasses appreciation in the value of assets, such as land, used in the activity. Thus, the taxpayer may intend to derive a profit from the operation of the activity, and may also intend that, even if no profit from current operations is derived, an overall profit will result when appreciation in the value of land used in the activity is realized since income from the activity together with the appreciation of land will exceed expenses of operation. See, however, paragraph (d) of § 1.183-1 for definition of an activity in this connection.

(5) **The success of the taxpayer in carrying on other similar or dissimilar activities.** The fact that the taxpayer has engaged in similar activities in the past and converted them from unprofitable to profitable enterprises may indicate that he is engaged in the present activity for profit, even though the activity is presently unprofitable.

(6) **The taxpayer's history of income or losses with respect to the activity.** A series of losses during the initial or start-up stage of an activity may not necessarily be an indication that the activity is not engaged in for profit. However, where losses continue to be sustained beyond the period which customarily is necessary to bring the operation to profitable status such continued losses, if not explainable, as due to customary business risks or reverses, may be indicative that the activity is not being engaged in for profit. If losses are sustained because of unforeseen or fortuitous circumstances which are beyond the control of the taxpayer, such as drought, disease, fire, theft, weather damages, other involuntary conversions, or depressed market conditions, such losses would not be an indication that the activity is not engaged in for profit. A series of years in which net income was realized would of course be strong evidence that the activity is engaged in for profit.

(7) **The amount of occasional profits, if any, which are earned.** The amount of profits in relation to the amount of losses incurred, and in relation to the amount of the taxpayer's investment and the value of the assets used in the activity, may provide useful criteria in determining the taxpayer's intent. An occasional small profit from an activity generating large losses, or from an activity in which the taxpayer has made a large investment, would not generally be determinative that the activity is engaged in for profit. However, substantial profit, though only occasional, would generally be indicative that an activity is engaged in for profit, where the investment or losses are comparatively small. Moreover, an opportunity to earn a substantial ultimate profit in a highly speculative venture is ordinarily sufficient to indicate that the activity is engaged in for profit even though losses or only occasional small profits are actually generated.

(8) **The financial status of the taxpayer.** The fact that the taxpayer does not have substantial income or capital from sources other than the activity may indicate that an activity is engaged in for profit. Substantial income from sources other

than the activity (particularly if the losses from the activity generate substantial tax benefits) may indicate that the activity is not engaged in for profit especially if there are personal or recreational elements involved.

(9) **Elements of personal pleasure or recreation.** The presence of personal motives in carrying on of an activity may indicate that the activity is not engaged in for profit, especially where there are recreational or personal elements involved. On the other hand, a profit motivation may be indicated where an activity lacks any appeal other than profit. It is not, however, necessary that an activity be engaged in with the exclusive intention of deriving a profit or with the intention of maximizing profits. For example, the availability of other investments which would yield a higher return, or which would be more likely to be profitable, is not evidence that an activity is not engaged in for profit. An activity will not be treated as not engaged in for profit merely because the taxpayer has purposes or motivations other than solely to make a profit. Also, the fact that the taxpayer derives personal pleasure from engaging in the activity is not sufficient to cause the activity to be classified as not engaged in for profit if the activity is in fact engaged in for profit as evidenced by other factors whether or not listed in this paragraph.

(c) **Examples.** The provisions of this section may be illustrated by the following examples:

Example (1). The taxpayer inherited a farm from her husband in an area which was becoming largely residential, and is now nearly all so. The farm had never made a profit before the taxpayer inherited it, and the farm has since had substantial losses in each year. The decedent from whom the taxpayer inherited the farm was a stockbroker, and he also left the taxpayer substantial stock holdings which yield large income from dividends. The taxpayer lives on an area of the farm which is set aside exclusively for living purposes. A farm manager is employed to operate the farm, but modern methods are not used in operating the farm. The taxpayer was born and raised on a farm, and expresses a strong preference for living on a farm. The taxpayer's activity of farming, based on all the facts and circumstances, could be found not to be engaged in for profit.

Example (2). The taxpayer is a wealthy individual who is greatly interested in philosophy. During the past 30 years he has written and published at his own expense several pamphlets, and he has engaged in extensive lecturing activity, advocating and disseminating his ideas. He has made a profit from these activities in only occasional years, and the profits in those years were small in relation to the amounts of the losses in all other years. The taxpayer has very sizable income from securities (dividends and capital gains) which constitutes the princi-

pal source of his livelihood. The activity of lecturing, publishing pamphlets, and disseminating his ideas is not an activity engaged in by the taxpayer for profit.

Example (3). The taxpayer, very successful in the business of retailing soft drinks, raises dogs and horses. He began raising a particular breed of dogs many years ago in the belief that the breed was in danger of declining, and he has raised and sold the dogs in each year since. The taxpayer recently began raising and racing thoroughbred horses. The losses from the taxpayer's dog and horse activities have increased in magnitude over the years, and he has not made a profit on these operations during any of the last 15 years. The taxpayer generally sells the dogs only to friends, does not advertise the dogs for sale, and shows the dogs only infrequently. The taxpayer races his horses only at the "prestige" tracks at which he combines his racing activities with social and recreational activities. The horse and dog operations are conducted at a large residential property on which the taxpayer also lives, which includes substantial living quarters and attractive recreational facilities for the taxpayer and his family. Since (i) the activity of raising dogs and horses and racing the horses is of a sporting and recreational nature, (ii) the taxpayer has substantial income from his business activities of retailing soft drinks, (iii) the horse and dog operations are not conducted in a businesslike manner, and (iv) such operations have a continuous record of losses, it could be determined that the horse and dog activities of the taxpayer are not engaged in for profit.

Example (4). The taxpayer inherited a farm of 65 acres from his parents when they died 6 years ago. The taxpayer moved to the farm from his house in a small nearby town, and he operates it in the same manner as his parents operated the farm before they died. The taxpayer is employed as a skilled machine operator in a nearby factory, for which he is paid approximately $8,500 per year. The farm has not been profitable for the past 15 years because of rising costs of operating farms in general, and because of the decline in the price of the produce of this farm in particular. The taxpayer consults the local agent of the State agricultural service from time to time, and the suggestions of the agent have generally been followed. The manner in which the farm is operated by the taxpayer is substantially similar to the manner in which farms of similar size, and which grow similar crops in the area, are operated. Many of these other farms do not make profits. The taxpayer does much of the required labor around the farm himself, such as fixing fences, planting crops, etc. The activity of farming could be found, based on all the facts and circumstances, to be engaged in by the taxpayer for profit.

Example (5). A, an independent oil and gas operator, frequently engages in the activity of searching for oil on undeveloped and unexplored land which is not near proven fields. He does so in a manner substantially similar to that of others who engage in the same activity. The chances, based on the experience of A and others who engaged in this activity, are strong that A will not find a commercially profitable oil deposit when he drills on land not established geologically to be proven oil bearing land. However, on the rare occasions that these activities do result in discovering a well, the operator generally realizes a very large return from such activity. Thus, there is a small chance that A will make a large profit from his soil exploration activity. Under these circumstances, A is engaged in the activity of oil drilling for profit.

* * *

[T.D. 7198, 37 FR 13683, July 13, 1972]

Additional Itemized Deductions for Individuals

§ 1.212-1   Nontrade or nonbusiness expenses.

(a) An expense may be deducted under section 212 only if—

(1) It has been paid or incurred by the taxpayer during the taxable year (i) for the production or collection of income which, if and when realized, will be required to be included in income for Federal income tax purposes, or (ii) for the management, conservation, or maintenance of property held for the production of such income, or (iii) in connection with the determination, collection, or refund of any tax; and

(2) It is an ordinary and necessary expense for any of the purposes stated in subparagraph (1) of this paragraph.

(b) The term "income" for the purpose of section 212 includes not merely income of the taxable year but also income which the taxpayer has realized in a prior taxable year or may realize in subsequent taxable years; and is not confined to recurring income but applies as well to gains from the disposition of property. For example, if defaulted bonds, the interest from which if received would be includible in income, are purchased with the expectation of realizing capital gain on their resale, even though no current yield thereon is anticipated, ordinary and necessary expenses thereafter paid or incurred in connection with such bonds are deductible. Similarly, ordinary and necessary expenses paid or incurred in the management, conservation, or maintenance of a building devoted to rental purposes are deductible notwithstanding that there is actually no income therefrom in the taxable year, and regardless of the manner in which or the purpose for which the property in question was acquired. Expenses paid or incurred in managing, conserving, or maintaining property held for investment may be deductible under section 212 even though the property is not currently productive and there is no likelihood that the property will be sold at a profit or will otherwise be productive of income and even though the property is held merely to minimize a loss with respect thereto.

* * *

(d) Expenses, to be deductible under section 212, must be "ordinary and necessary". Thus, such expenses must be reasonable in amount and must bear a reasonable and proximate relation to the production or collection of taxable income or to the management, conservation, or maintenance of property held for the production of income.

(e) A deduction under section 212 is subject to the restrictions and limitations in part IX (section 261 and following), subchapter B, chapter 1 of the Code, relating to items not deductible. Thus, no deduction is allowable under section 212 for any amount allocable to the production or collection of one or more classes of income which are not includible in gross income, or for any amount allocable to the management, conservation, or maintenance of property held for the production of income which is not included in gross income. See section 265. Nor does section 212 allow the deduction of any expenses which are disallowed by any of the provisions of subtitle A of the Code, even though such expenses may be paid or incurred for one of the purposes specified in section 212.

(f) Among expenditures not allowable as deductions under section 212 are the following: Commuter's expenses; expenses of taking special courses or training; expenses for improving personal appearance; the cost of rental of a safe-deposit box for storing jewelry and other personal effects; expenses such as those paid or incurred in seeking employment or in placing oneself in a position to begin rendering personal services for compensation, campaign expenses of a candidate for public office, bar examination fees and other expenses paid or incurred in securing admission to the bar, and corresponding fees and expenses paid or incurred by physicians, dentists, accountants, and other taxpayers for securing the right to practice their respective professions. See, however, section 162 and the regulations thereunder.

(g) Fees for services of investment counsel, custodial fees, clerical help, office rent, and similar expenses paid or incurred by a taxpayer in connection with investments held by him are deductible under section 212 only if (1) they are paid or incurred by the taxpayer for the production or collection of income or for the management, conservation, or maintenance of investments held by him for the production of income; and (2) they are ordinary and necessary under all the circumstances, having regard to the type of investment and to the relation of the taxpayer to such investment.

(h) Ordinary and necessary expenses paid or incurred in connection with the management, conservation, or maintenance of property held for use as a residence by the taxpayer are not deductible. However, ordinary and necessary expenses paid or incurred in connection with the management, conservation, or maintenance of property held by the taxpayer as rental property are deductible even though such property was formerly held by the taxpayer for use as a home.

(i) Reasonable amounts paid or incurred by the fiduciary of an estate or trust on account of administration expenses, including fiduciaries' fees and expenses of litigation, which are ordinary and necessary in connection with the performance of the duties of administration are deductible under section 212, notwithstanding that the estate or trust is not engaged in a trade or business, except to the extent that such expenses are allocable to the production or collection of tax-exempt income. But see section 642 (g) and the regulations thereunder for disallowance of such deductions to an estate where such items are allowed as a deduction under section 2053 or 2054 in computing the net estate subject to the estate tax.

(j) Reasonable amounts paid or incurred for the services of a guardian or committee for a ward or minor, and other expenses of guardians and committees which are ordinary and necessary, in connection with the production or collection of income inuring to the ward or minor, or in connection with the management, conservation, or maintenance of property, held for the production of income, belonging to the ward or minor, are deductible.

(k) Expenses paid or incurred in defending or perfecting title to property, in recovering property (other than investment property and amounts of income which, if and when recovered, must be included in gross income), or in developing or improving property, constitute a part of the cost of the property and are not deductible expenses. Attorneys' fees paid in a suit to quiet title to lands are not deductible; but if the suit is also to collect accrued rents thereon, that portion of such fees is deductible which is properly allocable to the services rendered in collecting such rents. Expenses paid or incurred in protecting or asserting one's right to property of a decedent as heir or legatee,

or as beneficiary under a testamentary trust, are not deductible.

(l) Expenses paid or incurred by an individual in connection with the determination, collection, or refund of any tax, whether the taxing authority be Federal, State, or municipal, and whether the tax be income, estate, gift, property, or any other tax, are deductible. Thus, expenses paid or incurred by a taxpayer for tax counsel or expenses paid or incurred in connection with the preparation of his tax returns or in connection with any proceedings involved in determining the extent of his tax liability or in contesting his tax liability are deductible.

(m) An expense (not otherwise deductible) paid or incurred by an individual in determining or contesting a liability asserted against him does not become deductible by reason of the fact that property held by him for the production of income may be required to be used or sold for the purpose of satisfying such liability.

(n) Capital expenditures are not allowable as nontrade or nonbusiness expenses. The deduction of an item otherwise allowable under section 212 will not be disallowed simply because the taxpayer was entitled under subtitle A of the Code to treat such item as a capital expenditure, rather than to deduct it as an expense. For example, see section 266. Where, however, the item may properly be treated only as a capital expenditure or where it was properly so treated under an option granted in subtitle A of the Code, no deduction is allowable under section 212; and this is true regardless of whether any basis adjustment is allowed under any other provision of the Code.

(o) The provisions of section 212 are not intended in any way to disallow expenses which would otherwise be allowable under section 162 and the regulations thereunder. Double deductions are not permitted. Amounts deducted under one provision of the Internal Revenue Code of 1954 cannot again be deducted under any other provision thereof.

(p) **Frustration of public policy.** The deduction of a payment will be disallowed under section 212 if the payment is of a type for which a deduction would be disallowed under section 162(c), (f), or (g) and the regulations thereunder in the case of a business expense.

[T.D. 6500, 25 FR 11402, Nov. 26, 1960; 25 FR 14021, Dec. 12, 1960, as amended by T.D. 7198, 37 FR 13685, July 13, 1972; T.D. 7345, 40 FR 7439, Feb. 20, 1975]

§ 1.213–1 Medical, dental, etc., expenses.

(a) **Allowance of deduction.** (1) Section 213 permits a deduction of payments for certain medical expenses (including expenses for medicine and drugs). Except as provided in paragraph (d) of this section (relating to special rule for decedents) a deduction is allowable only to individuals and only with respect to medical expenses actually paid during the taxable year, regardless of when the incident or event which occasioned the expenses occurred and regardless of the method of accounting employed by the taxpayer in making his income tax return. Thus, if the medical expenses are incurred but not paid during the taxable year, no deduction for such expenses shall be allowed for such year.

* * *

(e) **Definitions—(1) General.** (i) The term "medical care" includes the diagnosis, cure, mitigation, treatment, or prevention of disease. Expenses paid for "medical care" shall include those paid for the purpose of affecting any structure or function of the body or for transportation primarily for and essential to medical care. See subparagraph (4) of this paragraph for provisions relating to medical insurance.

(ii) Amounts paid for operations or treatments affecting any portion of the body, including obstetrical expenses and expenses of therapy or X-ray treatments, are deemed to be for the purpose of affecting any structure or function of the body and are therefore paid for medical care. Amounts expended for illegal operations or treatments are not deductible. Deductions for expenditures for medical care allowable under section 213 will be confined strictly to expenses incurred primarily for the prevention or alleviation of a physical or mental defect or illness. Thus, payments for the following are payments for medical care: hospital services, nursing services (including nurses' board where paid by the taxpayer), medical, laboratory, surgical, dental and other diagnostic and healing services, X-rays, medicine and drugs (as defined in subparagraph (2) of this paragraph, subject to the 1-percent limitation in paragraph (b) of this section), artificial teeth or limbs, and ambulance hire. However, an expenditure which is merely beneficial to the general health of an individual, such as an expenditure for a vacation, is not an expenditure for medical care.

(iii) Capital expenditures are generally not deductible for Federal income tax purposes. See section 263 and the regulations thereunder. However, an expenditure which otherwise qualifies as a medical expense under section 213 shall not be disqualified merely because it is a capital expenditure. For purposes of section 213 and this paragraph, a capital expenditure made by the taxpayer may qualify as a medical expense, if it has as its primary purpose the medical care (as defined in subdivisions (i) and (ii) of this subparagraph) of the taxpayer, his spouse, or his dependent. Thus, a capital expenditure which is related only to the sick person and is not related to permanent improvement or betterment of property, if it otherwise qualifies as an expenditure for medical care, shall be deductible; for example, an expenditure for eye glasses, a seeing eye dog, artificial teeth and limbs, a wheel chair, crutches, an inclinator or an air conditioner which is detachable from the property and purchased only for the use of a sick person, etc. Moreover, a capital expenditure for permanent improvement or betterment of property which would not ordinarily be for the purpose of medical care (within the meaning of this paragraph) may, nevertheless, qualify as a medical expense to the extent that the expenditure exceeds the increase in the value of the related property, if the particular expenditure is related directly to medical care. Such a situation could arise, for example, where a taxpayer is advised by a physician to install an elevator in his residence so that the taxpayer's wife who is afflicted with heart disease will not be required to climb stairs. If the cost of installing the elevator is $1,000 and the increase in the value of the residence is determined to be only $700, the difference of $300, which is the amount in excess of the value enhancement, is deductible as a medical expense. If, however, by reason of this expenditure, it is determined that the value of the residence has not been increased, the entire cost of installing the elevator would qualify as a medical expense. Expenditures made for the operation or maintenance of a capital asset are likewise deductible medical expenses if they have as their primary purpose the medical care (as defined in subdivisions (i) and (ii) of this subparagraph) of the taxpayer, his spouse, or his dependent. Normally, if a capital expenditure qualifies as a medical expense, expenditures for the operation or maintenance of the capital asset would also qualify provided that the medical reason for the capital expenditure still exists. The entire amount of such operation and maintenance expenditures qualifies, even if none or only a portion of the original cost of the capital asset itself qualified.

(iv) Expenses paid for transportation primarily for and essential to the rendition of the medical care are expenses paid for medical care. However, an amount allowable as a deduction for "transportation primarily for and essential to medical care" shall not include the cost of any meals and lodging while away from home receiving medical treatment. For example, if a doctor prescribes that a taxpayer go to a warm climate in order to alleviate a specific chronic ailment, the cost of meals and lodging while there would not be deductible. On the other hand, if the travel is undertaken merely for the general improvement of a taxpayer's health, neither the cost of transportation nor the cost of meals and lodging would be deductible. If a doctor prescribes an operation or other medical care, and the taxpayer chooses for purely personal considerations to travel to another locality (such as a resort area) for the operation or the other medical care, neither the cost of transportation nor the cost of meals and lodging (except where paid as part of a hospital bill) is deductible.

(v) The cost of in-patient hospital care (including the cost of meals and lodging therein) is an expenditure for medical care. The extent to which expenses for care in an institution other than a hospital shall constitute medical care is primarily a question of fact which depends upon the condition of the individual and the nature of the services he receives (rather than the nature of the institution). A private establishment which is regularly engaged in providing the types of care or services outlined in this subdivision shall be considered an institution for purposes of the rules provided herein. In general, the following rules will be applied:

(a) Where an individual is in an institution because his condition is such that the availability of medical care (as defined in subdivisions (i) and (ii) of this subparagraph) in such institution is a principal reason for his presence there, and meals and lodging are furnished as a necessary incident to such care, the entire cost of medical care and meals and lodging at the institution, which are furnished while the individual requires continual medical care, shall constitute an expense for medical care. For example, medical care includes the entire cost of institutional care for a person who is mentally ill and unsafe when left alone. While ordinary education is not medical care, the cost of medical care includes the cost of attending a special school for a mentally or physically handicapped individual, if his condition is such that the

resources of the institution for alleviating such mental or physical handicap are a principal reason for his presence there. In such a case, the cost of attending such a special school will include the cost of meals and lodging, if supplied, and the cost of ordinary education furnished which is incidental to the special services furnished by the school. Thus, the cost of medical care includes the cost of attending a special school designed to compensate for or overcome a physical handicap, in order to qualify the individual for future normal education or for normal living, such as a school for the teaching of braille or lip reading. Similarly, the cost of care and supervision, or of treatment and training, of a mentally retarded or physically handicapped individual at an institution is within the meaning of the term "medical care".

(b) Where an individual is in an institution, and his condition is such that the availability of medical care in such institution is not a principal reason for his presence there, only that part of the cost of care in the institution as is attributable to medical care (as defined in subdivisions (i) and (ii) of this subparagraph) shall be considered as a cost of medical care; meals and lodging at the institution in such a case are not considered a cost of medical care for purposes of this section. For example, an individual is in a home for the aged for personal or family considerations and not because he requires medical or nursing attention. In such case, medical care consists only of that part of the cost for care in the home which is attributable to medical care or nursing attention furnished to him; his meals and lodging at the home are not considered a cost of medical care.

(c) It is immaterial for purposes of this subdivision whether the medical care is furnished in a Federal or State institution or in a private institution.

(vi) See section 262 and the regulations thereunder for disallowance of deduction for personal living, and family expenses not falling within the definition of medical care.

* * *

(3) Status as spouse or dependent. In the case of medical expenses for the care of a person who is the taxpayer's spouse or dependent, the deduction under section 213 is allowable if the status of such person as "spouse" or "dependent" of the taxpayer exists either at the time the medical services were rendered or at the time the expenses were paid. In determining whether such status as "spouse" exists, a taxpayer who is legally separated from his spouse under a decree of separate maintenance is not considered as married. Thus, payments made in June 1956 by A, for medical services rendered in 1955 to B, his wife, may be deducted by A for 1956 even though, before the payments were made, B may have died or in 1956 secured a divorce. Payments made in July 1956 by C, for medical services rendered to D in 1955 may be deducted by C for 1956 even though C and D were not married until June 1956.

* * *

(g) **Reimbursement for expenses paid in prior years.** (1) Where reimbursement, from insurance or otherwise, for medical expenses is received in a taxable year subsequent to a year in which a deduction was claimed on account of such expenses, the reimbursement must be included in gross income in such subsequent year to the extent attributable to (and not in excess of) deductions allowed under section 213 for any prior taxable year. See section 104, relating to compensation for injuries or sickness, and section 105(b), relating to amounts expended for medical care, and the regulations thereunder, with regard to amounts in excess of or not attributable to deductions allowed.

(2) If no medical expense deduction was taken in an earlier year, for example, if the standard deduction under section 141 was taken for the earlier year, the reimbursement received in the taxable year for the medical expense of the earlier year is not includible in gross income.

* * *

[T.D. 6500, 25 FR 11402, Nov. 26, 1960, as amended by T.D. 6604, 27 FR 6972, July 24, 1962; T.D. 6661, 28 FR 6629, June 27, 1963; T.D. 6761, 29 FR 13423, Sept. 29, 1964; T.D. 6946, 33 FR 2893, Feb. 13, 1968; T.D. 6985, 33 FR 19812, Dec. 27, 1968; 34 FR 254, Jan. 8, 1969; T.D. 7114, 36 FR 9020, May 18, 1971; T.D. 7317, 39 FR 23995, June 28, 1974; T.D. 7643, 44 FR 50337, Aug. 28, 1979]

§ 1.217–2 **Deduction for moving expenses paid or incurred in taxable years beginning after December 31, 1969.**

(a) **Allowance of deduction—(1) In general.** Section 217(a) allows a deduction from gross income for moving expenses paid or incurred by the taxpayer during the taxable year in connection with his commencement of work as an employee or as a self-employed individual at a new principal place of work. For purposes of this section, amounts are considered as being paid or incurred by an individual whether goods or services are furnished to the taxpayer directly (by an employer, a client, a customer, or similar person) or indirectly (paid to a third party on behalf of the taxpayer by an employer, a client, a customer, or similar person). A cash basis taxpayer will treat moving expenses as being paid for purposes of section 217 and this section in the year in which the taxpayer is considered to have received such payment under section 82 and § 1.82–1. No deduction is allowable under section 162 for any expenses incurred by the taxpayer in connection with moving from one residence to another residence unless such expenses are deductible under section 162 without regard to such change in residence. To qualify for the deduction under section 217 the expenses must meet the definition of the term "moving expenses" provided in section 217(b) and the taxpayer must meet the conditions set forth in section 217(c). The term "employee" as used in this section has the same meaning as in § 31.3401(c)–1 of this chapter (Employment Tax Regulations). The term "self-employed individual" as used in this section is defined in paragraph (f)(1) of this section.

(2) **Expenses paid in a taxable year other than the taxable year in which reimbursement representing such expenses is received.** In general, moving expenses are deductible in the year paid or incurred. If a taxpayer who uses the cash receipts and disbursements method of accounting receives reimbursement for a moving expense in a taxable year other than the taxable year the taxpayer pays such expense, he may elect to deduct such expense in the taxable year that he receives such reimbursement, rather than the taxable year when he paid such expense in any case where—

(i) The expense is paid in a taxable year prior to the taxable year in which the reimbursement is received, or

(ii) The expense is paid in the taxable year immediately following the taxable year in which the reimbursement is received, provided that such expense is paid on or before the due date prescribed for filing the return (determined with regard to any extension of time for such filing) for the taxable year in which the reimbursement is received.

An election to deduct moving expenses in the taxable year that the reimbursement is received shall be made by claiming the deduction on the return, amended return, or claim for refund for the taxable year in which the reimbursement is received.

(3) Commencement of work. (i) To be deductible the moving expenses must be paid or incurred by the taxpayer in connection with his commencement of work at a new principal place of work (see paragraph (c)(3) of this section for a discussion of the term "principal place of work"). Except for those expenses described in section 217(b)(1)(C) and (D) it is not necessary for the taxpayer to have made arrangements to work prior to his moving to a new location; however, a deduction is not allowable unless employment or self-employment actually does occur. The term "commencement" includes (a) the beginning of work by a taxpayer as an employee or as a self-employed individual for the first time or after a substantial period of unemployment or part-time employment, (b) the beginning of work by a taxpayer for a different employer or in the case of a self-employed individual in a new trade or business, or (c) the beginning of work by a taxpayer for the same employer or in the case of a self-employed individual in the same trade or business at a new location. To qualify as being in connection with the commencement of work, the move must bear a reasonable proximity both in time and place to such commencement at the new principal place of work. In general, moving expenses incurred within 1 year of the date of the commencement of work are considered to be reasonably proximate in time to such commencement. Moving expenses incurred after the 1-year period may be considered reasonably proximate in time if it can be shown that circumstances existed which prevented the taxpayer from incurring the expenses of moving within the 1-year period allowed. Whether circumstances existed which prevented the taxpayer from incurring the expenses of moving within the period allowed is dependent upon the facts and circumstances of each case. The length of the delay and the fact that the taxpayer may have incurred part of the expenses of the move within the 1-year period allowed shall be taken into account in determining whether expenses incurred after such period are allowable. In general, a move is not considered to be reasonably proximate in place to the commencement of work at the new principal place of work where the distance between the taxpayer's new residence and his new principal place of work exceeds the distance between his former residence and his new principal place of work. A move to a new residence which does not satisfy this test may, however, be considered reasonably proximate in place

to the commencement of work if the taxpayer can demonstrate, for example, that he is required to live at such residence as a condition of employment or that living at such residence will result in an actual decrease in commuting time or expense. For example, assume that in 1977 A is transferred by his employer to a new principal place of work and the distance between his former residence and his new principal place of work is 35 miles greater than was the distance between his former residence and his former principal place of work. However, the distance between his new residence and his new principal place of work is 10 miles greater than was the distance between his former residence and his new principal place of work. Although the minimum distance requirement of section 217(c)(1) is met the expenses of moving to the new residence are not considered as incurred in connection with A's commencement of work at his new principal place of work since the new residence is not proximate in place to the new place of work. If, however, A can demonstrate, for example, that he is required to live at such new residence as a condition of employment or if living at such new residence will result in an actual decrease in commuting time or expense, the expenses of the move may be considered as incurred in connection with A's commencement of work at his new principal place of work.

(ii) The provisions of subdivision (i) of this subparagraph may be illustrated by the following examples:

Example (1). Assume that A is transferred by his employer from Boston, Mass., to Washington, D.C. A moves to a new residence in Washington, D.C., and commences work on February 1, 1971. A's wife and his two children remain in Boston until June 1972 in order to allow A's children to complete their grade school education in Boston. On June 1, 1972, A sells his home in Boston and his wife and children move to the new residence in Washington, D.C. The expenses incurred on June 1, 1972, in selling the old residence and in moving A's family, their household goods, and personal effects to the new residence in Washington are allowable as a deduction although they were incurred 16 months after the date of the commencement of work by A since A has moved to and established a new residence in Washington, D.C., and thus incurred part of the total expenses of the move prior to the expiration of the 1-year period.

Example (2). Assume that A is transferred by his employer from Washington, D.C., to Baltimore, Md. A commences work on January 1, 1971, in Baltimore. A commutes from his residence in Washington to his new principal place of work in Baltimore for a period of 18 months. On July 1, 1972, A decides to move to and establish a new residence in Baltimore. None of the moving expenses otherwise allowable under section 217 may be deducted since A neither incurred the expenses within 1 year nor has shown circumstances under which he was prevented from moving within such period.

(b) Definition of moving expenses—(1) In general. Section 217(b) defines the term "moving expenses" to mean only the reasonable expenses (i) of moving household goods and personal effects from the taxpayer's former residence to his new residence, (ii) of traveling (including meals and lodging) from the taxpayer's former residence to his new place of residence, (iii) of traveling (including meals and lodging), after obtaining employment, from the taxpayer's former residence to the general location of his new principal place of work and return, for the principal purpose of searching for a new residence, (iv) of meals and lodging while occupying temporary quarters in the general location of the new principal place of work during any period of 30 consecutive days after obtaining employment, or (v) of a nature constituting qualified residence sale, purchase, or lease expenses. Thus, the test of deductibility is whether the expenses are reasonable and are incurred for the items set forth in subdivisions (i) through (v) of this subparagraph.

(2) Reasonable expenses. (i) The term "moving expenses" includes only those expenses which are reasonable under the circumstances of the particular move. Expenses paid or incurred in excess of a reasonable amount are not deductible. Generally, expenses paid or incurred for movement of household goods and personal effects or for travel (including meals and lodging) are reasonable only to the extent that they are paid or incurred for such movement or travel by the shortest and most direct route available from the former residence to the new residence by the conventional mode or modes of transportation actually used and in the shortest period of time commonly required to travel the distance involved by such mode. Thus, if moving or travel arrangements are made to provide a circuitous route for scenic, stopover, or other similar reasons, additional expenses resulting therefrom are not deductible since they are not reasonable nor related to the commencement of work at the new principal place of work. In addition, expenses paid or incurred for meals and lodging while traveling from the former residence to the new place of residence or to the general location of the new principal place of work and return or occupying temporary quarters in the general location of the new principal place of work are reasonable only if under the facts and circumstanc-

es involved such expenses are not lavish or extravagant.

(ii) The application of this subparagraph may be illustrated by the following example:

Example. A, an employee of the M Company works and maintains his residence in Boston, Mass. Upon receiving orders from his employer that he is to be transferred to M's Los Angeles, Calif., office, A motors to Los Angeles with his family with stopovers at various cities between Boston and Los Angeles to visit friends and relatives. In addition, A detours into Mexico for sightseeing. Because of the stopovers and tour into Mexico, A's travel time and distance are increased over what they would have been had he proceeded directly to Los Angeles. To the extent that A's route of travel between Boston and Los Angeles is in a generally southwesterly direction it may be said that he is traveling by the shortest and most direct route available by motor vehicle. Since A's excursion into Mexico is away from the usual Boston-Los Angeles route, the portion of the expenses paid or incurred attributable to such excursion is not deductible. Likewise, that portion of the expenses attributable to A's delay en route in visiting personal friends and sightseeing are not deductible.

(3) Expense of moving household goods and personal effects. Expenses of moving household goods and personal effects include expenses of transporting such goods and effects from the taxpayer's former residence to his new residence, and expenses of packing, crating, and in-transit storage and insurance for such goods and effects. Such expenses also include any costs of connecting or disconnecting utilities required because of the moving of household goods, appliances, or personal effects. Expenses of storing and insuring household goods and personal effects constitute in-transit expenses if incurred within any consecutive 30-day period after the day such goods and effects are moved from the taxpayer's former residence and prior to delivery at the taxpayer's new residence. Expenses paid or incurred in moving household goods and personal effects to the taxpayer's new residence from a place other than his former residence are allowable, but only to the extent that such expenses do not exceed the amount which would be allowable had such goods and effects been moved from the taxpayer's former residence. Expenses of moving household goods and personal effects do not include, for example, storage charges (other than in-transit), costs incurred in the acquisition of property, costs incurred and losses sustained in the disposition of property, penalties for breaking leases, mortgage penalties, expenses of refitting rugs or draperies, losses sustained on the disposal of memberships in clubs, tuition fees, and similar items. The above expenses may, however, be described in other provisions of section 217(b) and if so a deduction may be allowed for them subject to the allowable dollar limitations.

(4) Expenses of traveling from the former residence to the new place of residence. Expenses of traveling from the former residence to the new place of residence include the cost of transportation and of meals and lodging en route (including the date of arrival) from the taxpayer's former residence to his new place of residence. Expenses of meals and lodging incurred in the general location of the former residence within 1 day after the former residence is no longer suitable for occupancy because of the removal of household goods and personal effects shall be considered as expenses of traveling for purposes of this subparagraph. The date of arrival is the day the taxpayer secures lodging at the new place of residence, even if on a temporary basis. Expenses of traveling from the taxpayer's former residence to his new place of residence do not include, for example, living or other expenses following the date of arrival at the new place of residence and while waiting to enter the new residence or waiting for household goods to arrive, expenses in connection with house or apartment hunting, living expenses preceding date of departure for the new place of residence (other than expenses of meals and lodging incurred within 1 day after the former residence is no longer suitable for occupancy), expenses of trips for purposes of selling property, expenses of trips to the former residence by the taxpayer pending the move by his family to the new place of residence, or any allowance for depreciation. The above expenses may, however, be described in other provisions of section 217(b) and if so a deduction may be allowed for them subject to the allowable dollar limitations. The deduction for traveling expenses from the former residence to the new place of residence is allowable for only one trip made by the taxpayer and members of his household; however, it is not necessary that the taxpayer and all members of his household travel together or at the same time.

(5) Expenses of traveling for the principal purpose of looking for a new residence. Expenses of traveling, after obtaining employment, from the former residence to the general location of the new principal place of work and return, for the principal purpose of searching for a new residence include the cost of transportation and meals and lodging during such travel and while at the general location of the new place of work for the principal purpose of searching for a new residence. However, such expenses do not include, for example, expenses of meals and lodging of the taxpayer and members of his household before departing for the new principal place of work, expenses for trips for purposes of selling property, expenses of trips to the former residence by the taxpayer pending the move by his family to the place of residence, or any allowance for depreciation. The above expenses may, however, be described in other provisions of section 217(b) and if so a deduction may be allowed for them. The deduction for expenses of traveling for the principal purpose of looking for a new residence is not limited to any number of trips by the taxpayer and by members of his household. In addition, the taxpayer and all members of his household need not travel together or at the same time. Moreover, a trip need not result in acquisition of a lease of property or purchase of property. An employee is considered to have obtained employment in the general location of the new principal place of work after he has obtained a contract or agreement of employment. A self-employed individual is considered to have obtained employment when he has made substantial arrangements to commence work at the new principal place of work (see paragraph (f)(2) of this section for a discussion of the term "made substantial arrangements to commence to work").

(6) Expenses of occupying temporary quarters. Expenses of occupying temporary quarters include only the cost of meals and lodging while occupying temporary quarters in the general location of the new principal place of work during any period of 30 consecutive days after the taxpayer has obtained employment in such general location. Thus, expenses of occupying temporary quarters do not include, for example, the cost of entertainment, laundry, transportation, or other personal, living family expenses, or expenses of occupying temporary quarters in the general location of the former place of work. The 30 consecutive day period is any one period of 30 consecutive days which can begin, at the option of the taxpayer, on any day after the day the taxpayer obtains employment in the general location of the new principal place of work.

(7) Qualified residence sale, purchase, or lease expenses. Qualified residence sale, purchase, or lease expenses (hereinafter "qualified real estate expenses") are only reasonable amounts paid or incurred for any of the following purposes:

(i) Expenses incident to the sale or exchange by the taxpayer or his spouse of the taxpayer's former residence which, but for section 217(b) and (e), would be taken into account in determining the amount realized on the sale or exchange of the residence. These expenses include real estate commissions, attorneys' fees, title fees, escrow fees, so called "points" or loan placement charges which the seller is required to pay, State transfer taxes and similar expenses paid or incurred in connection with the sale or exchange. No deduction, however, is permitted under section 217 and this section for the cost of physical improvements intended to enhance salability by improving the condition or appearance of the residence.

(ii) Expenses incident to the purchase by the taxpayer or his spouse of a new residence in the general location of the new principal place of work which, but for section 217(b) and (e), would be taken into account in determining either the adjusted basis of the new residence or the cost of a loan. These expenses include attorney's fees, escrow fees, appraisal fees, title costs, so-called "points" or loan placement charges not representing payments or prepayments of interest, and similar expenses paid or incurred in connection with the purchase of the new residence. No deduction, however, is permitted under section 217 and this section for any portion of real estate taxes or insurance, so-called "points" or loan placement charges which are, in essence, prepayments of interest, or the purchase price of the residence.

(iii) Expenses incident to the settlement of an unexpired lease held by the taxpayer or his spouse on property used by the taxpayer as his former residence. These expenses include consideration paid to a lessor to obtain a release from a lease, attorneys' fees, real estate commissions, or similar expenses incident to obtaining a release from a lease or to obtaining an assignee or a sublessee such as the difference between rent paid under a primary lease and rent received under a sublease. No deduction, however, is permitted under section 217 and this section for the cost of physical improvement intended to enhance marketability of the leasehold by improving the condition or appearance of the residence.

(iv) Expenses incident to the acquisition of a lease by the taxpayer or his spouse. These expenses include the cost of fees or commissions for obtaining a lease, a sublease, or an assignment of an interest in property used by the taxpayer as his new residence in the general location of the new

principal place of work. No deduction, however, is permitted under section 217 and this section for payments or prepayments of rent or payments representing the cost of a security or other similar deposit.

Qualified real estate expenses do not include losses sustained on the disposition of property or mortgage penalties, to the extent that such penalties are otherwise deductible as interest.

(8) **Residence.** The term "former residence" refers to the taxpayer's principal residence before his departure for his new principal place of work. The term "new residence" refers to the taxpayer's principal residence within the general location of his new principal place of work. Thus, neither term includes other residences owned or maintained by the taxpayer or members of his family or seasonal residences such as a summer beach cottage. Whether or not property is used by the taxpayer as his principal residence depends upon all the facts and circumstances in each case. Property used by the taxpayer as his principal residence may include a houseboat, a housetrailer, or similar dwelling. The term "new place of residence" generally includes the area within which the taxpayer might reasonably be expected to commute to his new principal place of work.

* * *

(c) **Conditions for allowance—(1) In general.** Section 217(c) provides two conditions which must be satisfied in order for a deduction of moving expenses to be allowed under section 217(a). The first is a minimum distance condition prescribed by section 217(c)(1), and the second is a minimum period of employment condition prescribed by section 217(c)(2).

* * *

(3) **Principal place of work.** (i) A taxpayer's "principal place of work" usually is the place where he spends most of his working time. The principal place of work of a taxpayer who performs services as an employee is his employer's plant, office, shop, store, or other property. The principal place of work of a taxpayer who is self-employed is the plant, office, shop, store, or other property which serves as the center of his business activities. However, a taxpayer may have a principal place of work even if there is no one place where he spends a substantial portion of his working time. In such case, the taxpayer's principal place of work is the place where his business activities

are centered—for example, because he reports there for work, or is required either by his employer or the nature of his employment to "base" his employment there. Thus, while a member of a railroad crew may spend most of his working time aboard a train, his principal place of work is his home terminal, station, or other such central point where he reports in, checks out, or receives instructions. The principal place of work of a taxpayer who is employed by a number of employers on a relatively short-term basis, and secures employment by means of a union hall system (such as a construction or building trades worker) would be the union hall.

(ii) Where a taxpayer has more than one employment (*i.e.*, the taxpayer is employed by more than one employer, or is self-employed in more than one trade or business, or is an employee and is self-employed at any particular time) his principal place of work is determined with reference to his principal employment. The location of a taxpayer's principal place of work is a question of fact determined on the basis of the particular circumstances in each case. The more important factors to be considered in making this determination are (a) the total time ordinarily spent by the taxpayer at each place, (b) the degree of the taxpayer's business activity at each place, and (c) the relative significance of the financial return to the taxpayer from each place.

(iii) Where a taxpayer maintains inconsistent positions by claiming a deduction for expenses of meals and lodging while away from home (incurred in the general location of the new principal place of work) under section 162 (relating to trade or business expenses) and by claiming a deduction under this section for moving expenses incurred in connection with the commencement of work at such place of work, it will be a question of facts and circumstances as to whether such new place of work will be considered a principal place of work, and accordingly, which category of deductions he will be allowed.

* * *

(d) **Rules for application of section 217(c)(2)—** (1) **Inapplicability of minimum period of employment condition in certain cases.** Section 217(d)(1) provides that the minimum period of employment condition of section 217(c)(2) does not apply in the case of a taxpayer who is unable to meet such condition by reason of—

(i) Death or disability, or

(ii) Involuntary separation (other than for willful misconduct) from the service of an employer or separation by reason of transfer for the benefit of an employer after obtaining full-time employment in which the taxpayer could reasonably have been expected to satisfy such condition.

For purposes of subdivision (i) of this paragraph disability shall be determined according to the rules in section 72(m)(7) and § 1.72-17(f). Subdivision (ii) of this subparagraph applies only where the taxpayer has obtained full-time employment in which he could reasonably have been expected to satisfy the minimum period of employment condition. A taxpayer could reasonably have been expected to satisfy the minimum period of employment condition if at the time he commences work at the new principal place of work he could have been expected, based upon the facts known to him at such time, to satisfy such condition. Thus, for example, if the taxpayer at the time of transfer was not advised by his employer that he planned to transfer him within 6 months to another principal place of work, the taxpayer could, in the absence of other factors, reasonably have been expected to satisfy the minimum employment period condition at the time of the first transfer. On the other hand, a taxpayer could not reasonably have been expected to satisfy the minimum employment condition if at the time of the commencement of the move he knew that his employer's retirement age policy would prevent his satisfying the minimum employment period condition.

(2) **Election of deduction before minimum period of employment condition is satisfied.** (i) Paragraph (2) of section 217(d) provides a rule which applies where a taxpayer paid or incurred, in a taxable year, moving expenses which would be deductible in that taxable year except that the minimum period of employment condition of section 217(c)(2) has not been satisfied before the time prescribed by law for filing the return for such taxable year. The rule provides that where a taxpayer has paid or incurred moving expenses and as of the date prescribed by section 6072 for filing his return for such taxable year (determined with regard to extensions of time for filing) there remains unexpired a sufficient portion of the 12-month or the 24-month period so that it is still possible for the taxpayer to satisfy the applicable period of employment condition, the taxpayer may elect to claim a deduction for such moving expenses on the return for such taxable year. The

election is exercised by taking the deduction on the return.

(ii) Where a taxpayer does not elect to claim a deduction for moving expenses on the return for the taxable year in which such expenses were paid or incurred in accordance with subdivision (i) of this subparagraph and the applicable minimum period of employment condition of section 217(c)(2) (as well as all other requirements of section 217) is subsequently satisfied, the taxpayer may file an amended return or a claim for refund for the taxable year such moving expenses were paid or incurred on which he may claim a deduction under section 217.

(iii) The application of this subparagraph may be illustrated by the following examples:

Example (1). A is transferred by his employer from Boston, Massachusetts, to Cleveland, Ohio. He begins working there on November 1, 1970. Moving expenses are paid by A in 1970 in connection with this move. On April 15, 1971, when he files his income tax return for the year 1970, A has been a full-time employee in Cleveland for approximately 24 weeks. Although he has not satisfied the 39-week employment condition at this time, A may elect to claim his 1970 moving expenses on his 1970 income tax return as there is still sufficient time remaining before November 1, 1971, to satisfy such condition.

Example (2). Assume the same facts as in example (1), except that on April 15, 1971, A has voluntarily left his employer and is looking for other employment in Cleveland. A may not be sure he will be able to meet the 39-week employment condition by November 1, 1971. Thus, he may if he wishes wait until such condition is met and file an amended return claiming as a deduction the expenses paid in 1970. Instead of filing an amended return A may file a claim for refund based on a deduction for such expenses. If A fails to meet the 39-week employment condition on or before November 1, 1971, no deduction is allowable for such expenses.

Example (3). B is a self-employed accountant. He moves from Rochester, N.Y., to New York, N.Y., and begins to work there on December 1, 1970. Moving expenses are paid by B in 1970 and 1971 in connection

with this move. On April 15, 1971, when he files his income tax return for the year 1970, B has been performing services as a self-employed individual on a full-time basis in New York City for approximately 20 weeks. Although he has not satisfied the 78-week employment condition at this time, A may elect to claim his 1970 moving expenses on his 1970 income tax return as there is still sufficient time remaining before December 1, 1972, to satisfy such condition. On April 15, 1972, when he files his income tax return for the year 1971, B has been performing services as a self-employed individual on a full-time basis in New York City for approximately 72 weeks. Although he has not met the 78-week employment condition at this time, B may elect to claim his 1971 moving expenses on his 1971 income tax return as there is still sufficient time remaining before December 1, 1972, to satisfy such requirement.

(3) **Recapture of deduction.** Paragraph (3) of section 217(d) provides a rule which applies where a taxpayer has deducted moving expenses under the election provided in section 217(d)(2) prior to satisfying the applicable minimum period of employment condition and such condition cannot be satisfied at the close of a subsequent taxable year. In such cases an amount equal to the expenses deducted must be included in the taxpayer's gross income for the taxable year in which the taxpayer is no longer able to satisfy such minimum period of employment condition. Where the taxpayer has deducted moving expenses under the election provided in section 217(d)(2) for the taxable year and subsequently files an amended return for such year on which he does not claim the deduction, such expenses are not treated as having been deducted for purposes of the recapture rule of the preceding sentence.

* * *

[T.D. 7195, 37 FR 13535, July 11, 1972; 37 FR 14230, July 18, 1972, as amended by T.D. 7578, 43 FR 59355, Dec. 20, 1978; T.D. 7605, 44 FR 18970, March 30, 1979; T.D. 7689, 45 FR 20796, March 31, 1980; T.D. 7810, 47 FR 6002, Feb. 10, 1982]

Special Deductions for Corporations

§ 1.248–1 Election to amortize organizational expenditures.

(a) **In general.** (1) Section 248(a) provides that a corporation may elect for any taxable year beginning after December 31, 1953, to treat its organizational expenditures, as defined in subsection (b) of section 248 and in paragraph (b) of this section, as deferred expenses. A corporation which exercises such election must, at the time it makes the elec-

tion, select a period of not less than 60 months, beginning with the month in which it began business, over which it will amortize its organizational expenditures. The period selected by the corporation may be equal to or greater, but not less, than 60 months, but in any event it must begin with the month in which the corporation began business. The organizational expenditures of the corporation which are treated as deferred expenses under the provisions of section 248 and this section shall then be allowed as a deduction in computing taxable income ratably over the period selected by the taxpayer. The period selected by the taxpayer in making its election may not be subsequently changed but shall be adhered to in computing taxable income for the taxable year for which the election is made and all subsequent taxable years.

(2) If a corporation exercises the election provided in section 248(a), such election shall apply to all of its expenditures which are organizational expenditures within the meaning of subsection (b) of section 248 and paragraph (b) of this section. The election shall apply, however, only with respect to expenditures incurred before the end of the taxable year in which the corporation begins business (without regard to whether the corporation files its returns on the accrual or cash method of accounting or whether the expenditures are paid in the taxable year in which they are incurred), if such expenditures are paid or incurred on or after August 16, 1954 (the date of enactment of the Internal Revenue Code of 1954).

(3) The deduction allowed under section 248 must be spread over a period beginning with the month in which the corporation begins business. The determination of the date the corporation begins business presents a question of fact which must be determined in each case in light of all the circumstances of the particular case. The words "begins business," however, do not have the same meaning as "in existence." Ordinarily, a corporation begins business when it starts the business operations for which it was organized; a corporation comes into existence on the date of its incorporation. Mere organizational activities, such as the obtaining of the corporate charter, are not alone sufficient to show the beginning of business. If the activities of the corporation have advanced to the extent necessary to establish the nature of its business operations, however, it will be deemed to have begun business. For example, the acquisition of operating assets which are necessary to the type of business contemplated may constitute the beginning of business.

(b) **Organizational expenditures defined.** (1) Section 248(b) defines the term "organizational expenditures." Such expenditures, for purposes of section 248 and this section, are those expenditures which are directly incident to the creation of the corporation. An expenditure, in order to qualify as an organizational expenditure, must be (i) incident to the creation of the corporation, (ii) charge-

able to the capital account of the corporation, and (iii) of a character which, if expended incident to the creation of a corporation having a limited life, would be amortizable over such life. An expenditure which fails to meet each of these three tests may not be considered an organizational expenditure for purposes of section 248 and this section.

(2) The following are examples of organizational expenditures within the meaning of section 248 and this section: legal services incident to the organization of the corporation, such as drafting the corporate charter, bylaws, minutes of organizational meetings, terms of original stock certificates, and the like; necessary accounting services; expenses of temporary directors and of organizational meetings of directors or stockholders; and fees paid to the State of incorporation.

(3) The following expenditures are not organizational expenditures within the meaning of section 248 and this section:

(i) Expenditures connected with issuing or selling shares of stock or other securities, such as commissions, professional fees, and printing costs. This is so even where the particular issue of stock to which the expenditures relate is for a fixed term of years;

(ii) Expenditures connected with the transfer of assets to a corporation.

(4) Expenditures connected with the reorganization of a corporation, unless directly incident to the creation of a corporation, are not organizational expenditures within the meaning of section 248 and this section.

(c) **Time and manner of making election.** The election provided by section 248(a) and paragraph (a) of this section shall be made in a statement attached to the taxpayer's return for the taxable year in which it begins business. Such taxable year must be one which begins after December 31, 1953. The return and statement must be filed not later than the date prescribed by law for filing the return (including any extensions of time) for the taxable year in which the taxpayer begins business. The statement shall set forth the description and amount of the expenditures involved, the date such expenditures were incurred, the month in which the corporation began business, and the number of months (not less than 60 and beginning with the month in which the taxpayer began business) over which such expenditures are to be deducted ratably.

[T.D. 6500, 25 FR 11402, Nov. 26, 1960]

Items Not Deductible

§ 1.262-1 Personal, living, and family expenses.

(a) In general. In computing taxable income, no deduction shall be allowed, except as otherwise expressly provided in chapter 1 of the Code, for personal, living, and family expenses.

(b) Examples of personal, living, and family expenses. Personal, living, and family expenses are illustrated in the following examples:

(1) Premiums paid for life insurance by the insured are not deductible. See also section 264 and the regulations thereunder.

(2) The cost of insuring a dwelling owned and occupied by the taxpayer as a personal residence is not deductible.

(3) Expenses of maintaining a household, including amounts paid for rent, water, utilities, domestic service, and the like, are not deductible. A taxpayer who rents a property for residential purposes, but incidentally conducts business there (his place of business being elsewhere) shall not deduct any part of the rent. If, however, he uses part of the house as his place of business, such portion of the rent and other similar expenses as is properly attributable to such place of business is deductible as a business expense.

(4) Losses sustained by the taxpayer upon the sale or other disposition of property held for personal, living, and family purposes are not deductible. But see section 165 and the regulations thereunder for deduction of losses sustained to such property by reason of casualty, etc.

(5) Expenses incurred in traveling away from home (which include transportation expenses, meals, and lodging) and any other transportation expenses are not deductible unless they qualify as expenses deductible under section 162, § 1.162-2, and paragraph (d) of § 1.162-5 (relating to trade or business expenses), section 170 and paragraph (a)(2) of § 1.170-2 or paragraph (g) of § 1.170A-1 (relating to charitable contributions), section 212 and § 1.212-1 (relating to expenses for production of income), section 213(e) and paragraph (e) of § 1.213-1 (relating to medical expenses) or section

217(a) and paragraph (a) of § 1.217-1 (relating to moving expenses). The taxpayer's costs of commuting to his place of business or employment are personal expenses and do not qualify as deductible expenses. The costs of the taxpayer's lodging not incurred in traveling away from home are personal expenses and are not deductible unless they qualify as deductible expenses under section 217. Except as permitted under section 162, 212, or 217, the costs of the taxpayer's meals not incurred in traveling away from home are personal expenses.

(6) Amounts paid as damages for breach of promise to marry, and attorney's fees and other costs of suit to recover such damages, are not deductible.

(7) Generally, attorney's fees and other costs paid in connection with a divorce, separation, or decree for support are not deductible by either the husband or the wife. However, the part of an attorney's fee and the part of the other costs paid in connection with a divorce, legal separation, written separation agreement, or a decree for support, which are properly attributable to the production or collection of amounts includible in gross income under section 71 are deductible by the wife under section 212.

(8) The cost of equipment of a member of the armed services is deductible only to the extent that it exceeds nontaxable allowances received for such equipment and to the extent that such equipment is especially required by his profession and does not merely take the place of articles required in civilian life. For example, the cost of a sword is an allowable deduction in computing taxable income, but the cost of a uniform is not. However, amounts expended by a reservist for the purchase and maintenance of uniforms which may be worn only when on active duty for training for temporary periods, when attending service school courses, or when attending training assemblies are deductible except to the extent that nontaxable allowances are received for such amounts.

(9) Expenditures made by a taxpayer in obtaining an education or in furthering his education are not deductible unless they qualify under section 162 and § 1.162-5 (relating to trade or business expenses).

* * *

[T.D. 6500, 25 FR 11402, Nov. 26, 1960, as amended by T.D. 6796, 30 FR 1041, Feb. 2, 1965; T.D. 6918, 32 FR 6681, May 2, 1967; T.D. 7207, 37 FR 20795, Oct. 4, 1972]

§ 1.263(a)-1 Capital expenditures; in general.

(a) Except as otherwise provided in chapter 1 of the Code, no deduction shall be allowed for—

(1) Any amount paid out for new buildings or for permanent improvements or betterments made to increase the value of any property or estate, or

(2) Any amount expended in restoring property or in making good the exhaustion thereof for which an allowance is or has been made in the form of a deduction for depreciation, amortization, or depletion.

(b) In general, the amounts referred to in paragraph (a) of this section include amounts paid or incurred (1) to add to the value, or substantially prolong the useful life, of property owned by the taxpayer, such as plant or equipment, or (2) to adapt property to a new or different use. Amounts paid or incurred for incidental repairs and maintenance of property are not capital expenditures within the meaning of subparagraphs (1) and (2) of this paragraph. See section 162 and § 1.162-4.

* * *

[T.D. 6500, 25 FR 11402, Nov. 26, 1960, as amended by T.D. 6794, 30 FR 792, Jan. 26, 1965]

§ 1.263(a)-2 Examples of capital expenditures.

The following paragraphs of this section include examples of capital expenditures:

(a) The cost of acquisition, construction, or erection of buildings, machinery and equipment, furniture and fixtures, and similar property having a useful life substantially beyond the taxable year.

(b) Amounts expended for securing a copyright and plates, which remain the property of the person making the payments.

(c) The cost of defending or perfecting title to property.

(d) The amount expended for architect's services.

(e) Commissions paid in purchasing securities. Commissions paid in selling securities are an offset against the selling price, except that in the case of dealers in securities such commissions may be treated as an ordinary and necessary business expense.

(f) Amounts assessed and paid under an agreement between bondholders or shareholders of a corporation to be used in a reorganization of the corporation or voluntary contributions by shareholders to the capital of the corporation for any corporate purpose. Such amounts are capital investments and are not deductible. See section 118 and § 1.118-1.

(g) A holding company which guarantees dividends at a specified rate on the stock of a subsidiary corporation for the purpose of securing new capital for the subsidiary and increasing the value of its stockholdings in the subsidiary shall not deduct amounts paid in carrying out this guaranty in computing its taxable income, but such payments are capital expenditures to be added to the cost of its stock in the subsidiary.

(h) The cost of good will in connection with the acquisition of the assets of a going concern is a capital expenditure.

[T.D. 6500, 25 FR 11402, Nov. 26, 1960]

§ 1.263(a)-3 Election to deduct or capitalize certain expenditures.

(a) Under certain provisions of the Code, taxpayers may elect to treat capital expenditures as deductible expenses or as deferred expenses, or to treat deductible expenses as capital expenditures.

(b) The sections referred to in paragraph (a) of this section include:

(1) Section 173 (circulation expenditures).

(2) Section 174 (research and experimental expenditures).

(3) Section 175 (soil and water conservation expenditures).

(4) Section 177 (trademark and trade name expenditures).

(5) Section 180 (expenditures by farmers for fertilizer, lime, etc.).

(6) Section 182 (expenditures by farmers for clearing land).

(7) Section 248 (organizational expenditures of a corporation).

(8) Section 266 (carrying charges).

(9) Section 615 (exploration expenditures).

(10) Section 616 (development expenditures).

[T.D. 6500, 25 FR 11402, Nov. 26, 1960, as amended by T.D. 6794, 30 FR 792, Jan. 26, 1965]

§ 1.264–1 Premiums on life insurance taken out in a trade or business.

(a) When premiums are not deductible. Premiums paid by a taxpayer on a life insurance policy are not deductible from the taxpayer's gross income, even though they would otherwise be deductible as trade or business expenses, if they are paid on a life insurance policy covering the life of any officer or employee of the taxpayer, or any person (including the taxpayer) who is financially interested in any trade or business carried on by the taxpayer, when the taxpayer is directly or indirectly a beneficiary of the policy. For additional provisions relating to the nondeductibility of premiums paid on life insurance policies (whether under section 162 or any other section of the Code), see section 262, relating to personal, living, and family expenses, and section 265, relating to expenses allocable to tax-exempt income.

(b) When taxpayer is a beneficiary. If a taxpayer takes out a policy for the purpose of protecting himself from loss in the event of the death of the insured, the taxpayer is considered a beneficiary directly or indirectly under the policy. However, if the taxpayer is not a beneficiary under the policy, the premiums so paid will not be disallowed as deductions merely because the taxpayer may derive a benefit from the increased efficiency of the officer or employee insured. See section 162 and the regulations thereunder. A taxpayer is considered a beneficiary under a policy where, for example, he, as a principal member of a partnership, takes out an insurance policy on his own life irrevocably designating his partner as the sole beneficiary in order to induce his partner to retain his investment in the partnership. Whether or not the taxpayer is a beneficiary under a policy, the proceeds of the policy paid by reason of the death of the insured may be excluded from gross income whether the beneficiary is an individual or a corporation, except in the case of (1) certain transferees, as provided in section 101(a)(2); (2) portions of amounts of life insurance proceeds received at a date later than death under the provisions of section 101(d); and (3) life insurance policy proceeds which are includible in the gross income of a husband or wife under section 71 (relating to alimony) or section 682 (relating to income of an estate or trust in case of divorce, etc.). (See section

101(e).) For further reference, see, generally, section 101 and the regulations thereunder.

[T.D. 6500, 25 FR 11402, Nov. 26, 1960]

§ 1.265–1 Expenses relating to tax-exempt income.

(a) Nondeductibility of expenses allocable to exempt income. (1) No amount shall be allowed as a deduction under any provision of the Code for any expense or amount which is otherwise allowable as a deduction and which is allocable to a class or classes of exempt income other than a class or classes of exempt interest income.

(2) No amount shall be allowed as a deduction under section 212 (relating to expenses for production of income) for any expense or amount which is otherwise allowable as a deduction and which is allocable to a class or classes of exempt interest income.

(b) Exempt income and nonexempt income. (1) As used in this section, the term "class of exempt income" means any class of income (whether or not any amount of income of such class is received or accrued) wholly exempt from the taxes imposed by subtitle A of the Code. For purposes of this section, a class of income which is considered as wholly exempt from the taxes imposed by subtitle A includes any class of income which is—

(i) Wholly excluded from gross income under any provision of subtitle A, or

(ii) Wholly exempt from the taxes imposed by subtitle A under the provisions of any other law.

(2) As used in this section the term "nonexempt income" means any income which is required to be included in gross income.

(c) Allocation of expenses to a class or classes of exempt income. Expenses and amounts otherwise allowable which are directly allocable to any class or classes of exempt income shall be allocated thereto; and expenses and amounts directly allocable to any class or classes of nonexempt income shall be allocated thereto. If an expense or amount otherwise allowable is indirectly allocable to both a class of nonexempt income and a class of exempt income, a reasonable proportion thereof determined in the light of all the facts and circumstances in each case shall be allocated to each.

(d) Statement of classes of exempt income; records. (1) A taxpayer receiving any class of exempt income or holding any property or engaging in any activity the income from which is exempt shall submit with his return as a part thereof an itemized statement, in detail, showing (i) the amount of each class of exempt income, and (ii) the amount of expenses and amounts otherwise allowable allocated to each such class (the amount allocated by apportionment being shown separately) as required by paragraph (c) of this section. If an item is apportioned between a class of exempt income and a class of nonexempt income, the statement shall show the basis of the apportionment. Such statement shall also recite that each deduction claimed in the return is not in any way attributable to a class of exempt income.

(2) The taxpayer shall keep such records as will enable him to make the allocations required by this section. See section 6001 and the regulations thereunder.

[T.D. 6500, 25 FR 11402, Nov. 26, 1960]

§ 1.266–1 **Taxes and carrying charges chargeable to capital account and treated as capital items.**

(a) **In general.** In accordance with section 266, items enumerated in paragraph (b)(1) of this section may be capitalized at the election of the taxpayer. Thus, taxes and carrying charges with respect to property of the type described in this section are chargeable to capital account at the election of the taxpayer, notwithstanding that they are otherwise expressly deductible under provisions of subtitle A of the Code. No deduction is allowable for any items so treated.

(b) **Taxes and carrying charges.** (1) The taxpayer may elect, as provided in paragraph (c) of this section, to treat the items enumerated in this subparagraph which are otherwise expressly deductible under the provisions of subtitle A of the Code as chargeable to capital account either as a component of original cost or other basis, for the purposes of section 1012, or as an adjustment to basis, for the purposes of section 1016(a)(1). The items thus chargeable to capital account are—

(i) In the case of unimproved and unproductive real property: Annual taxes, interest on a mortgage, and other carrying charges.

(ii) In the case of real property, whether improved or unimproved and whether productive or unproductive:

(a) Interest on a loan (but not theoretical interest of a taxpayer using his own funds),

(b) Taxes of the owner of such real property measured by compensation paid to his employees,

(c) Taxes of such owner imposed on the purchase of materials, or on the storage, use, or other consumption of materials, and

(d) Other necessary expenditures,

paid or incurred for the development of the real property or for the construction of an improvement or additional improvement to such real property, up to the time the development or construction work has been completed. The development or construction work with respect to which such items are incurred may relate to unimproved and unproductive real estate whether the construction work will make the property productive of income subject to tax (as in the case of a factory) or not (as in the case of a personal residence), or may relate to property already improved or productive (as in the case of a plant addition or improvement, such as the construction of another floor on a factory or the installation of insulation therein).

(iii) In the case of personal property:

(a) Taxes of an employer measured by compensation for services rendered in transporting machinery or other fixed assets to the plant or installing them therein,

(b) Interest on a loan to purchase such property or to pay for transporting or installing the same, and

(c) Taxes of the owner thereof imposed on the purchase of such property or on the storage, use, or other consumption of such property,

paid or incurred up to the date of installation or the date when such property is first put into use by the taxpayer, whichever date is later.

(iv) Any other taxes and carrying charges with respect to property, otherwise deductible, which in the opinion of the Commissioner are, under sound accounting principles, chargeable to capital account.

(2) The sole effect of section 266 is to permit the items enumerated in subparagraph (1) of this paragraph to be chargeable to capital account notwithstanding that such items are otherwise expressly deductible under the provisions of subtitle A of the Code. An item not otherwise deductible may not be capitalized under section 266.

(3) In the absence of a provision in this section for treating a given item as a capital item, this section has no effect on the treatment otherwise accorded such item. Thus, items which are otherwise deductible are deductible notwithstanding the provisions of this section, and items which are otherwise treated as capital items are to be so treated. Similarly, an item not otherwise deductible is not made deductible by this section. Nor is the absence of a provision in this section for treating a given item as a capital item to be construed as withdrawing or modifying the right now given to the taxpayer under any other provisions of subtitle A of the Code, or of the regulations thereunder, to elect to capitalize or to deduct a given item.

(c) **Election to charge taxes and carrying charges to capital account.** **(1)** If for any taxable year there are two or more items of the type described in paragraph (b)(1) of this section, which relate to the same project to which the election is applicable, the taxpayer may elect to capitalize any one or more of such items even though he does not elect to capitalize the remaining items or to capitalize items of the same type relating to other projects. However, if expenditures for several items of the same type are incurred with respect to a single project, the election to capitalize must, if exercised, be exercised as to all items of that type. For purposes of this section, a "project" means, in the case of items described in paragraph (b)(1)(ii) of this section, a particular development of, or construction of an improvement to, real property, and in the case of items described in paragraph (b)(1)(iii) of this section, the transportation and installation of machinery or other fixed assets.

(2)(i) An election with respect to an item described in paragraph (b)(1)(i) of this section is effective only for the year for which it is made.

(ii) An election with respect to an item described in—

(a) Paragraph (b)(1)(ii) of this section is effective until the development or construction work described in that subdivision has been completed;

(b) Paragraph (b)(1)(iii) of this section is effective until the later of either the date of installation of the property described in that subdivision, or the date when such property is first put into use by the taxpayer;

(c) Paragraph (b)(1)(iv) of this section is effective as determined by the Commissioner.

Thus, an item chargeable to capital account under this section must continue to be capitalized for the entire period described in this subdivision applicable to such election although such period may consist of more than one taxable year.

(3) If the taxpayer elects to capitalize an item or items under this section, such election shall be exercised by filing with the original return for the year for which the election is made a statement indicating the item or items (whether with respect to the same project or to different projects) which the taxpayer elects to treat as chargeable to capital account. Elections filed for taxable years beginning before January 1, 1954, and for taxable years ending before August 17, 1954, under section 24(a)(7) of the Internal Revenue Code of 1939, and the regulations thereunder, shall have the same effect as if they were filed under this section. See section 7807(b)(2).

(d) The following examples are illustrative of the application of the provisions of this section:

Example (1). In 1956 and 1957 A pays annual taxes and interest on a mortgage on a piece of real property. During 1956, the property is vacant and unproductive, but throughout 1957 A operates the property as a parking lot. A may capitalize the taxes and mortgage interest paid in 1956, but not the taxes and mortgage interest paid in 1957.

Example (2). In February 1957, B began the erection of an office building for himself. B in 1957, in connection with the erection of the building, paid $6,000 social security taxes, which in his 1957 return he elected to capitalize. B must continue to capitalize the social security taxes paid in connection with the erection of the building until its completion.

Example (3). Assume the same facts as in example (2) except that in November 1957, B also begins to build a hotel. In 1957 B pays $3,000 social security taxes in connection with the erection of the hotel. B's election to capitalize the social security taxes paid in erecting the office building started in February 1957 does not bind him to capitalize the social security taxes paid in erecting the hotel; he may deduct the $3,000 social security taxes paid in erecting the hotel.

Example (4). In 1957, M Corporation began the erection of a building for itself, which will take three years to complete. M Corporation in 1957 paid $4,000 social security taxes and $8,000 interest on a building loan in connection with this building. M Corporation may elect to capitalize the social security taxes although it deducts the interest charges.

Example (5). C purchases machinery in 1957 for use in his factory. He pays social security taxes on the labor for transportation and installation of the machinery, as well as interest on a loan to obtain funds to pay for the machinery and for transportation and installation costs. C may capitalize either the social security taxes or the interest, or both, up to the date of installation or until the machinery is first put into use by him, whichever date is later.

(e) **Allocation.** If any tax or carrying charge with respect to property is in part a type of item described in paragraph (b) of this section and in part a type of item or items with respect to which no election to treat as a capital item is given, a reasonable proportion of such tax or carrying charge, determined in the light of all the facts and circumstances in each case, shall be allocated to each item. The rule of this paragraph may be illustrated by the following example:

Example. N Corporation, the owner of a factory in New York on which a new addition is under construction, in 1957 pays its general manager, B, a salary of $10,000 and also pays a New York State unemployment insurance tax of $81 on B's salary. B spends nine-tenths of his time in the general business of the firm and the remaining one-tenth in supervising the construction work. N Corporation treats as expenses $9,000 of B's salary, and charges the remaining $1,000 to capital account. N Corporation may elect to capitalize $8.10 of the $81 New York State unemployment insurance tax paid in 1957 since such tax is deductible under section 164.

[T.D. 6500, 25 FR 11402, Nov. 26, 1960]

§ 1.267(a)-1 Deductions disallowed.

(a) **Losses.** Except in cases of distributions in corporate liquidations, no deduction shall be allowed for losses arising from direct or indirect sales or exchanges of property between persons who, on the date of the sale or exchange, are within any one of the relationships specified in section 267(b). See § 1.267(b)-1.

* * *

(c) **Scope of section.** Section 267(a) requires that deductions for losses or unpaid expenses or interest described therein be disallowed even though the transaction in which such losses, expenses, or interest were incurred was a bona fide transaction. However, section 267 is not exclusive. No deduction for losses or unpaid expenses or interest arising in a transaction which is not bona fide will be allowed even though section 267 does not apply to the transaction.

[T.D. 6500, 25 FR 11402, Nov. 26, 1960]

§ 1.267(d)-1 Amount of gain where loss previously disallowed.

(a) **General rule.** (1) If a taxpayer acquires property by purchase or exchange from a transferor who, on the transaction, sustained a loss not allowable as a deduction by reason of section 267(a)(1) (or by reason of section 24(b) of the Internal Revenue Code of 1939), then any gain realized by the taxpayer on a sale or other disposition of the property after December 31, 1953, shall be recognized only to the extent that the gain exceeds the amount of such loss as is properly allocable to the property sold or otherwise disposed of by the taxpayer.

(2) The general rule is also applicable to a sale or other disposition of property by a taxpayer when the basis of such property in the taxpayer's hands is determined directly or indirectly by reference to other property acquired by the taxpayer from a transferor through a sale or exchange in which a loss sustained by the transferor was not allowable. Therefore, section 267(d) applies to a sale or other disposition of property after a series of transactions if the basis of the property acquired in each transaction is determined by reference to the basis of the property transferred, and if the original property was acquired in a transaction in which a loss to a transferor was not allowable by reason of section 267(a)(1) (or by reason of section 24(b) of the Internal Revenue Code of 1939).

(3) The benefit of the general rule is available only to the original transferee but does not apply to any original transferee (*e.g.*, a donee) who acquired the property in any manner other than by purchase or exchange.

(4) The application of the provisions of this paragraph may be illustrated by the following examples:

Example (1). H sells to his wife, W, for $500, certain corporate stock with an adjusted basis for determining loss to him of $800. The loss of $300 is not allowable to H by reason of section 267(a)(1) and paragraph (a) of § 1.267(a)-1. W later sells this stock for $1,000. Although W's realized gain is $500 ($1,000 minus $500, her basis), her recognized gain under section 267(d) is only $200, the excess of the realized gain of $500 over the loss of $300 not allowable to H. In determining capital gain or loss W's holding period commences on the date of the sale from H to W.

Example (2). Assume the same facts as in example (1) except that W later sells her stock for $300 instead of $1,000. Her recognized loss is $200 and not $500 since section 267(d) applies only to the nonrecognition of gain and does not affect basis.

Example (3). Assume the same facts as in example (1) except that W transfers her stock as a gift to X. The basis of the stock in the hands of X for the purpose of determining gain, under the provisions of section 1015, is the same as W's, or $500. If X later sells the stock for $1,000 the entire $500 gain is taxed to him.

Example (4). H sells to his wife, W, for $5,500, farmland, with an adjusted basis for determining loss to him of $8,000. The loss of $2,500 is not allowable to H by reason of section 267(a)(1) and paragraph (a) of § 1.267(a)–1. W exchanges the farmland, held for investment purposes, with S, an unrelated individual, for two city lots, also held for investment purposes. The basis of the city lots in the hands of W ($5,500) is a substituted basis determined under section 1031(d) by reference to the basis of the farmland. Later W sells the city lots for $10,000. Although W's realized gain is $4,500 ($10,000 minus $5,500), her recognized gain under section 267(d) is only $2,000, the excess of the realized gain of $4,500 over the loss of $2,500 not allowable to H.

(b) Determination of basis and gain with respect to divisible property—(1) Taxpayer's basis. When the taxpayer acquires divisible property or property that consists of several items or classes of items by a purchase or exchange on which loss is not allowable to the transferor, the basis in the taxpayer's hands of a particular part, item, or class of such property shall be determined (if the taxpayer's basis for that part is not known) by allocating to the particular part, item, or class a portion of the taxpayer's basis for the entire property in the proportion that the fair market value of the particular part, item, or class bears to the fair market value of the entire property at the time of the taxpayer's acquisition of the property.

(2) Taxpayer's recognized gain. Gain realized by the taxpayer on sales or other dispositions after December 31, 1953, of a part, item, or class of the property shall be recognized only to the extent that such gain exceeds the amount of loss attributable to such part, item, or class of property not allowable to the taxpayer's transferor on the latter's sale or exchange of such property to the taxpayer.

(3) Transferor's loss not allowable. (i) The transferor's loss on the sale or exchange of a part, item, or class of the property to the taxpayer shall be the excess of the transferor's adjusted basis for determining loss on the part, item, or class of the property over the amount realized by the transferor on the sale or exchange of the part, item, or class. The amount realized by the transferor on the part, item, or class shall be determined (if such amount is not known) in the same manner that the taxpayer's basis for such part, item, or class is determined. See subparagraph (1) of this paragraph.

(ii) If the transferor's basis for determining loss on the part, item, or class cannot be determined, the transferor's loss on the particular part, item, or class transferred to the taxpayer shall be determined by allocating to the part, item, or class a

portion of his loss on the entire property in the proportion that the fair market value of such part, item, or class bears to the fair market value of the entire property on the date of the taxpayer's acquisition of the entire property.

(4) Examples. The application of the provisions of this paragraph may be illustrated by the following examples:

Example (1). During 1953, H sold class A stock which had cost him $1,100, and common stock which had cost him $2,000, to his wife W for a lump sum of $1,500. Under section 24(b)(1)(A) of the 1939 Code, the loss of $1,600 on the transaction was not allowable to H. At the time the stocks were purchased by W, the fair market value of class A stock was $900 and the fair market value of common stock was $600. In 1954, W sold the class A stock for $2,500. W's recognized gain is determined as follows:

Amount realized by W on sale of class A stock....................................		$2,500
Less: Basis allocated to class A stock—$900/$1,500 × $1,500		900
Realized gain on transaction		1,600
Less: Loss sustained by H on sale of class A stock to W not allowable as a deduction:		
Basis to H of class A stock	$1,100	
Amount realized by H on class A stock—$900/$1,500 × $1,500	900	
Unallowable loss to H on sale of class A stock		200
Recognized gain on sale of class A stock by W		1,400

Example (2). Assume the same facts as those stated in example (1) of this subparagraph except that H originally purchased both classes of stock for a lump sum of $3,100. The unallowable loss to H on the sale of all the stock to W is $1,600 ($3,100 minus $1,500). An exact determination of the unallowable loss sustained by H on sale to W of class A stock cannot be made because H's basis for class A stock cannot be determined. Therefore, a determination of the unallowable loss is made by allocating to class A stock a portion of H's loss on the entire property transferred to W in the proportion that the fair market value of class A stock at the time acquired by W ($900) bears to the fair market value of both classes of stock at that time ($1,500). The allocated portion is $900/$1,500 × $1,600, or $960. W's recognized gain is, therefore, $640 (W's realized gain of $1,600 minus $960).

(c) Special rules. (1) Section 267(d) does not affect the basis of property for determining gain. Depreciation and other items which depend on such basis are also not affected.

(2) The provisions of section 267(d) shall not apply if the loss sustained by the transferor is not allowable to the transferor as a deduction by reason of section 1091, or section 118 of the Internal

Revenue Code of 1939, which relate to losses from wash sales of stock or securities.

(3) In determining the holding period in the hands of the transferee of property received in an exchange with a transferor with respect to whom a loss on the exchange is not allowable by reason of section 267, section 1223(2) does not apply to include the period during which the property was held by the transferor. In determining such holding period, however, section 1223(1) may apply to include the period during which the transferee held the property which he exchanged where, for example, he exchanged a capital asset in a transaction which, as to him, was nontaxable under section 1031 and the property received in the exchange has the same basis as the property exchanged.

[T.D. 6500, 25 FR 11402, Nov. 26, 1960]

§ 1.269–1   Meaning and use of terms.

As used in section 269 and §§ 1.269–2 through 1.269–6—

(a) **Allowance.** The term "allowance" refers to anything in the internal revenue laws which has the effect of diminishing tax liability. The term includes, among other things, a deduction, a credit, an adjustment, an exemption, or an exclusion.

(b) **Evasion or avoidance.** The phrase "evasion or avoidance" is not limited to cases involving criminal penalties, or civil penalties for fraud.

(c) **Control.** The term "control" means the ownership of stock possessing at least 50 percent of the total combined voting power of all classes of stock entitled to vote, or at least 50 percent of the total value of shares of all classes of stock of the corporation. For control to be "acquired on or after October 8, 1940", it is not necessary that all of such stock be acquired on or after October 8, 1940. Thus, if A, on October 7, 1940, and at all times thereafter, owns 40 percent of the stock of X Corporation and acquires on October 8, 1940, an additional 10 percent of such stock, an acquisition within the meaning of such phrase is made by A on October 8, 1940. Similarly, if B, on October 7, 1940, owns certain assets and transfers on October 8, 1940, such assets to a newly organized Y Corporation in exchange for all the stock of Y Corporation, an acquisition within the meaning of such phrase is made by B on October 8, 1940. If, under the facts stated in the preceding sentence, B is a corporation, all of whose stock is owned by Z Cor-

poration, then an acquisition within the meaning of such phrase is also made by Z Corporation on October 8, 1940, as well as by the shareholders of Z Corporation taken as a group on such date, and by any of such shareholders if such shareholders as a group own 50 percent of the stock of Z on such date.

(d) **Person.** The term "person" includes an individual, a trust, an estate, a partnership, an association, a company or a corporation.

[T.D. 6595, 27 FR 3596, April 14, 1962]

§ 1.269–2   Purpose and scope of section 269.

(a) **General.** Section 269 is designed to prevent in the instances specified therein the use of the sections of the Internal Revenue Code providing deductions, credits, or allowances in evading or avoiding Federal income tax. See § 1.269–3.

(b) **Disallowance of deduction, credit, or other allowance.** Under the Code, an amount otherwise constituting a deduction, credit, or other allowance becomes unavailable as such under certain circumstances. Characteristic of such circumstances are those in which the effect of the deduction, credit, or other allowance would be to distort the liability of the particular taxpayer when the essential nature of the transaction or situation is examined in the light of the basic purpose or plan which the deduction, credit, or other allowance was designed by the Congress to effectuate. The distortion may be evidenced, for example, by the fact that the transaction was not undertaken for reasons germane to the conduct of the business of the taxpayer, by the unreal nature of the transaction such as its sham character, or by the unreal or unreasonable relation which the deduction, credit, or other allowance bears to the transaction. The principle of law making an amount unavailable as a deduction, credit, or other allowance in cases in which the effect of making an amount so available would be to distort the liability of the taxpayer, has been judicially recognized and applied in several cases. Included in these cases are Gregory v. Helvering (1935) (293 U.S. 465; Ct. D. 911, C.B. XIV–1, 193); Griffiths v. Helvering (1939) (308 U.S. 355; Ct. D. 1431, C.B. 1940–1, 136); Higgins v. Smith (1940) (308 U.S. 473; Ct. D. 1434, C.B. 1940–1, 127); and J. D. & A. B. Spreckles Co. v. Commissioner (1940) (41 B.T.A. 370). In order to give effect to such principle, but not in limitation thereof, several provisions of the Code, for example, section 267 and section 270, specify with some particularity instances in which disallowance of the deduction, credit, or other allowance is required. Section 269 is also included in such provisions of the Code. The principle of law and the particular sections of the Code are not mutually exclusive and in appropriate circumstances they may operate together or they may operate separately. See, for example, § 1.269-6.

[T.D. 6595, 27 FR 3596, April 14, 1962]

§ 1.269-3 Instances in which section 269(a) disallows a deduction, credit, or other allowance.

(a) **Instances of disallowance.** Section 269 specifies two instances in which a deduction, credit, or other allowance is to be disallowed. These instances, described in paragraphs (1) and (2) of section 269(a), are those in which—

(1) Any person or persons acquire, or acquired on or after October 8, 1940, directly or indirectly, control of a corporation, or

(2) Any corporation acquires, or acquired on or after October 8, 1940, directly or indirectly, property of another corporation (not controlled, directly or indirectly, immediately before such acquisition by such acquiring corporation or its stockholders), the basis of which property in the hands of the acquiring corporation is determined by reference to the basis in the hands of the transferor corporation.

In either instance the principal purpose for which the acquisition was made must have been the evasion or avoidance of Federal income tax by securing the benefit of a deduction, credit, or other allowance which such person, or persons, or corporation, would not otherwise enjoy. If this requirement is satisfied, it is immaterial by what method or by what conjunction of events the benefit was sought. Thus, an acquiring person or corporation can secure the benefit of a deduction, credit, or other allowance within the meaning of section 269 even though it is the acquired corporation that is entitled to such deduction, credit, or other allowance in the determination of its tax. If the purpose to evade or avoid Federal income tax exceeds in importance any other purpose, it is the principal purpose. This does not mean that only those acquisitions fall within the provisions of section 269 which would not have been made if the evasion or avoidance purpose was not present. The determination of the purpose for which an acquisition was made requires a scrutiny of the entire circumstanc-

es in which the transaction or course of conduct occurred, in connection with the tax result claimed to arise therefrom. * * *

(b) **Acquisition of control; transactions indicative of purpose to evade or avoid tax.** If the requisite acquisition of control within the meaning of paragraph (1) of section 269(a) exists, the transactions set forth in the following subparagraphs are among those which, in the absence of additional evidence to the contrary, ordinarily are indicative that the principal purpose for acquiring control was evasion or avoidance of Federal income tax:

(1) A corporation or other business enterprise (or the interest controlling such corporation or enterprise) with large profits acquires control of a corporation with current, past, or prospective credits, deductions, net operating losses, or other allowances and the acquisition is followed by such transfers or other action as is necessary to bring the deduction, credit, or other allowance into conjunction with the income (see further § 1.269-6). This subparagraph may be illustrated by the following example:

Example. Individual A acquires all of the stock of L Corporation which has been engaged in the business of operating retail drug stores. At the time of the acquisition, L Corporation has net operating loss carryovers aggregating $100,000 and its net worth is $100,000. After the acquisition, L Corporation continues to engage in the business of operating retail drug stores but the profits attributable to such business after the acquisition are not sufficient to absorb any substantial portion of the net operating loss carryovers. Shortly after the acquisition, individual A causes to be transferred to L Corporation the assets of a hardware business previously controlled by A which business produces profits sufficient to absorb a substantial portion of L Corporation's net operating loss carryovers. The transfer of the profitable business, which has the effect of using net operating loss carryovers to offset gains of a business unrelated to that which produced the losses, indicates that the principal purpose for which the acquisition of control was made is evasion or avoidance of Federal income tax.

(2) A person or persons organize two or more corporations instead of a single corporation in order to secure the benefit of multiple surtax exemptions (see section 11(c)) or multiple minimum accumulated earnings credits (see section 535(c)(2) and (3)).

(3) A person or persons with high earning assets transfer them to a newly organized controlled corporation retaining assets producing net operating losses which are utilized in an attempt to secure refunds.

(c) Acquisition of property; transactions indicative of purpose to evade or avoid tax. If the requisite acquisition of property within the meaning of paragraph (2) of section 269(a) exists, the transactions set forth in the following subparagraphs are among those which, in the absence of additional evidence to the contrary, ordinarily are indicative that the principal purpose for acquiring such property was evasion or avoidance of Federal income tax:

(1) A corporation acquires property having in its hands an aggregate carryover basis which is materially greater than its aggregate fair market value at the time of such acquisition and utilizes the property to create tax-reducing losses or deductions.

(2) A subsidiary corporation, which has sustained large net operating losses in the operation of business X and which has filed separate returns for the taxable years in which the losses were sustained, acquires high earning assets, comprising business Y, from its parent corporation. The acquisition occurs at a time when the parent would not succeed to the net operating loss carryovers of the subsidiary if the subsidiary were liquidated, and the profits of business Y are sufficient to offset a substantial portion of the net operating loss carryovers attributable to business X (see further example (3) of § 1.269–6).

[T.D. 6595, 27 FR 3596, April 14, 1962]

§ 1.274–1 Disallowance of certain entertainment, gift and travel expenses.

Section 274 disallows in whole, or in part, certain expenditures for entertainment, gifts and travel which would otherwise be allowable under chapter 1 of the Code. The requirements imposed by section 274 are in addition to the requirements for deductibility imposed by other provisions of the Code. If a deduction is claimed for an expenditure for entertainment, gifts, or travel, the taxpayer must first establish that it is otherwise allowable as a deduction under chapter 1 of the Code before the provisions of section 274 become applicable. An expenditure for entertainment, to the extent it is lavish or extravagant, shall not be allowable as a deduction. The taxpayer should then substantiate such an expenditure in accordance with the rules under section 274(d). See § 1.274–5. Section 274 is a disallowance provision exclusively, and does not make deductible any expense which is disallowed under any other provision of the Code. Sim-

ilarly, section 274 does not affect the includibility of an item in, or the excludability of an item from, the gross income of any taxpayer. * * *

[T.D. 6659, 28 FR 6499, June 25, 1963]

§ 1.274–2 Disallowance of deductions for certain expenses for entertainment, amusement, or recreation.

(a) General rules—(1) Entertainment activity. Except as provided in this section, no deduction otherwise allowable under chapter 1 of the Code shall be allowed for any expenditure with respect to entertainment unless the taxpayer establishes—

(i) That the expenditure was directly related to the active conduct of the taxpayer's trade or business, or

(ii) In the case of an expenditure directly preceding or following a substantial and bona fide business discussion (including business meetings at a convention or otherwise), that the expenditure was associated with the active conduct of the taxpayer's trade or business.

* * *

(b) Definitions—(1) Entertainment defined— (i) In general. For purposes of this section, the term "entertainment" means any activity which is of a type generally considered to constitute entertainment, amusement, or recreation, such as entertaining at night clubs, cocktail lounges, theaters, country clubs, golf and athletic clubs, sporting events, and on hunting, fishing, vacation and similar trips, including such activity relating solely to the taxpayer or the taxpayer's family. The term "entertainment" may include an activity, the cost of which is claimed as a business expense by the taxpayer, which satisfies the personal, living, or family needs of any individual, such as providing food and beverages, a hotel suite, or an automobile to a business customer or his family. The term "entertainment" does not include activities which, although satisfying personal, living, or family needs of an individual, are clearly not regarded as constituting entertainment, such as (a) supper money provided by an employer to his employee working overtime, (b) a hotel room maintained by an employer for lodging of his employees while in business travel status, or (c) an automobile used in the active conduct of trade or business even though used for routine personal purposes such as commuting to and from work. On the other hand, the providing of a hotel room or an automobile by an employer to his employee who is on vacation would constitute entertainment of the employee.

(ii) Objective test. An objective test shall be used to determine whether an activity is of a type generally considered to constitute entertainment. Thus, if an activity is generally considered to be entertainment, it will constitute entertainment for purposes of this section and section 274(a) regardless of whether the expenditure can also be described otherwise, and even though the expenditure relates to the taxpayer alone. This objective test precludes arguments such as that "entertainment" means only entertainment of others or that an expenditure for entertainment should be characterized as an expenditure for advertising or public relations. However, in applying this test the taxpayer's trade or business shall be considered. Thus, although attending a theatrical performance would generally be considered entertainment, it would not be so considered in the case of a professional theater critic, attending in his professional capacity. Similarly, if a manufacturer of dresses conducts a fashion show to introduce his products to a group of store buyers, the show would not be generally considered to constitute entertainment. However, if an appliance distributor conducts a fashion show for the wives of his retailers, the fashion show would be generally considered to constitute entertainment.

(iii) Special definitional rules—(a) In general. Except as otherwise provided in (b) or (c) of this subdivision, any expenditure which might generally be considered either for a gift or entertainment, or considered either for travel or entertainment, shall be considered an expenditure for entertainment rather than for a gift or travel.

(b) Expenditures deemed gifts. An expenditure described in (a) of this subdivision shall be deemed for a gift to which this section does not apply if it is:

(1) An expenditure for packaged food or beverages transferred directly or indirectly to another person intended for consumption at a later time.

(2) An expenditure for tickets of admission to a place of entertainment transferred to another person if the taxpayer does not accompany the recipient to the entertainment unless the taxpayer treats the expenditure as entertainment. The taxpayer may change his treatment of such an expenditure as either a gift or entertainment at any time within the period prescribed for assessment of

tax as provided in section 6501 of the Code and the regulations thereunder.

(3) Such other specific classes of expenditure generally considered to be for a gift as the Commissioner, in his discretion, may prescribe.

(c) Expenditures deemed travel. An expenditure described in (a) of this subdivision shall be deemed for travel to which this section does not apply if it is:

(1) With respect to a transportation type facility (such as an automobile or an airplane), even though used on other occasions in connection with an activity of a type generally considered to constitute entertainment, to the extent the facility is used in pursuit of a trade or business for purposes of transportation not in connection with entertainment. See also paragraph (e)(3)(iii)(b) of this section for provisions covering nonentertainment expenditures with respect to such facilities.

(2) Such other specific classes of expenditure generally considered to be for travel as the Commissioner, in his discretion, may prescribe.

(2) Other definitions—(i) Expenditure. The term "expenditure" as used in this section shall include expenses paid or incurred for goods, services, facilities, and items (including items such as losses and depreciation).

(ii) Expenses for production of income. For purposes of this section, any reference to "trade or business" shall include any activity described in section 212.

(iii) Business associate. The term "business associate" as used in this section means a person with whom the taxpayer could reasonably expect to engage or deal in the active conduct of the taxpayer's trade or business such as the taxpayer's customer, client, supplier, employee, agent, partner, or professional adviser, whether established or prospective.

(c) Directly related entertainment—(1) In general. Except as otherwise provided in paragraph (d) of this section (relating to associated entertainment) or under paragraph (f) of this section (relating to business meals and other specific exceptions), no deduction shall be allowed for any expenditure for entertainment unless the taxpayer establishes that the expenditure was directly related to the active conduct of his trade or business within the meaning of this paragraph.

(2) Directly related entertainment defined. Any expenditure for entertainment, if it is otherwise allowable as a deduction under chapter 1 of the Code, shall be considered directly related to the active conduct of the taxpayer's trade or business if it meets the requirements of any one of subparagraphs (3), (4), (5), or (6) of this paragraph.

(3) **Directly related in general.** Except as provided in subparagraph (7) of this paragraph, an expenditure for entertainment shall be considered directly related to the active conduct of the taxpayer's trade or business if it is established that it meets all of the requirements of subdivisions (i), (ii), (iii) and (iv) of this subparagraph.

(i) At the time the taxpayer made the entertainment expenditure (or committed himself to make the expenditure), the taxpayer had more than a general expectation of deriving some income or other specific trade or business benefit (other than the goodwill of the person or persons entertained) at some indefinite future time from the making of the expenditure. A taxpayer, however, shall not be required to show that income or other business benefit actually resulted from each and every expenditure for which a deduction is claimed.

(ii) During the entertainment period to which the expenditure related, the taxpayer actively engaged in a business meeting, negotiation, discussion, or other bona fide business transaction, other than entertainment, for the purpose of obtaining such income or other specific trade or business benefit (or, at the time the taxpayer made the expenditure or committed himself to the expenditure, it was reasonable for the taxpayer to expect that he would have done so, although such was not the case solely for reasons beyond the taxpayer's control).

(iii) In light of all the facts and circumstances of the case, the principal character or aspect of the combined business and entertainment to which the expenditure related was the active conduct of the taxpayer's trade or business (or at the time the taxpayer made the expenditure or committed himself to the expenditure, it was reasonable for the taxpayer to expect that the active conduct of trade or business would have been the principal character or aspect of the entertainment, although such was not the case solely for reasons beyond the taxpayer's control). It is not necessary that more time be devoted to business than to entertainment to meet this requirement. The active conduct of trade or business is considered not to be the principal character or aspect of combined business and entertainment activity on hunting or fishing trips

or on yachts and other pleasure boats unless the taxpayer clearly establishes to the contrary.

(iv) The expenditure was allocable to the taxpayer and a person or persons with whom the taxpayer engaged in the active conduct of trade or business during the entertainment or with whom the taxpayer establishes he would have engaged in such active conduct of trade or business if it were not for circumstances beyond the taxpayer's control. For expenditures closely connected with directly related entertainment, see paragraph (d)(4) of this section.

(4) **Expenditures in clear business setting.** An expenditure for entertainment shall be considered directly related to the active conduct of the taxpayer's trade or business if it is established that the expenditure was for entertainment occurring in a clear business setting directly in furtherance of the taxpayer's trade or business. Generally, entertainment shall not be considered to have occurred in a clear business setting unless the taxpayer clearly establishes that any recipient of the entertainment would have reasonably known that the taxpayer had no significant motive, in incurring the expenditure, other than directly furthering his trade or business. Objective rather than subjective standards will be determinative. Thus, entertainment which occurred under any circumstances described in subparagraph (7)(ii) of this paragraph ordinarily will not be considered as occurring in a clear business setting. Such entertainment will generally be considered to be socially rather than commercially motivated. Expenditures made for the furtherance of a taxpayer's trade or business in providing a "hospitality room" at a convention (described in paragraph (d)(3)(i)(b) of this section) at which goodwill is created through display or discussion of the taxpayer's products, will, however, be treated as directly related. In addition, entertainment of a clear business nature which occurred under circumstances where there was no meaningful personal or social relationship between the taxpayer and the recipients of the entertainment may be considered to have occurred in a clear business setting. For example, entertainment of business representatives and civic leaders at the opening of a new hotel or theatrical production, where the clear purpose of the taxpayer is to obtain business publicity rather than to create or maintain the goodwill of the recipients of the entertainment, would generally be considered to be in a clear business setting. Also, entertainment which has the principal effect of a price

rebate in connection with the sale of the taxpayer's products generally will be considered to have occurred in a clear business setting. Such would be the case, for example, if a taxpayer owning a hotel were to provide occasional free dinners at the hotel for a customer who patronized the hotel.

(5) **Expenditures for services performed.** An expenditure shall be considered directly related to the active conduct of the taxpayer's trade or business if it is established that the expenditure was made directly or indirectly by the taxpayer for the benefit of an individual (other than an employee), and if such expenditure was in the nature of compensation for services rendered or was paid as a prize or award which is required to be included in gross income under section 74 and the regulations thereunder. For example, if a manufacturer of products provides a vacation trip for retailers of his products who exceed sales quotas as a prize or award which is includible in gross income, the expenditure will be considered directly related to the active conduct of the taxpayer's trade or business.

(6) **Club dues, etc., allocable to business meals.** An expenditure shall be considered directly related to the active conduct of the taxpayer's trade or business if it is established that the expenditure was with respect to a facility (as described in paragraph (e) of this section) used by the taxpayer for the furnishing of food or beverages under circumstances described in paragraph (f)(2)(i) of this section (relating to business meals and similar expenditures), to the extent allocable to the furnishing of such food or beverages.

(7) **Expenditures generally considered not directly related.** Expenditures for entertainment, even if connected with the taxpayer's trade or business, will generally be considered not directly related to the active conduct of the taxpayer's trade or business, if the entertainment occurred under circumstances where there was little or no possibility of engaging in the active conduct of trade or business. The following circumstances will generally be considered circumstances where there was little or no possibility of engaging in the active conduct of a trade or business:

(i) The taxpayer was not present;

(ii) The distractions were substantial, such as—

(a) A meeting or discussion at night clubs, theaters, and sporting events, or during essentially social gatherings such as cocktail parties, or

(b) A meeting or discussion, if the taxpayer meets with a group which includes persons other than business associates, at places such as cocktail lounges, country clubs, golf and athletic clubs, or at vacation resorts.

An expenditure for entertainment in any such case is considered not to be directly related to the active conduct of the taxpayer's trade or business unless the taxpayer clearly establishes to the contrary.

(d) **Associated entertainment—(1) In general.** Except as provided in paragraph (f) of this section (relating to business meals and other specific exceptions) and subparagraph (4) of this paragraph (relating to expenditures closely connected with directly related entertainment), any expenditure for entertainment which is not directly related to the active conduct of the taxpayer's trade or business will not be allowable as a deduction unless—

(i) It was associated with the active conduct of trade or business as defined in subparagraph (2) of this paragraph, and

(ii) The entertainment directly preceded or followed a substantial and bona fide business discussion as defined in subparagraph (3) of this paragraph.

(2) **Associated entertainment defined.** Generally, any expenditure for entertainment, if it is otherwise allowable under chapter 1 of the Code, shall be considered associated with the active conduct of the taxpayer's trade or business if the taxpayer establishes that he had a clear business purpose in making the expenditure, such as to obtain new business or to encourage the continuation of an existing business relationship. However, any portion of an expenditure allocable to a person who was not closely connected with a person who engaged in the substantial and bona fide business discussion (as defined in subparagraph (3)(i) of this paragraph) shall not be considered associated with the active conduct of the taxpayer's trade or business. The portion of an expenditure allocable to the spouse of a person who engaged in the discussion will, if it is otherwise allowable under chapter 1 of the Code, be considered associated with the active conduct of the taxpayer's trade or business.

(3) **Directly preceding or following a substantial and bona fide business discussion defined—(i) Substantial and bona fide business discussion—(a) In general.** Whether any meeting, negotiation or discussion constitutes a "substantial and bona fide business discussion" within the meaning of this section depends upon the facts

and circumstances of each case. It must be established, however, that the taxpayer actively engaged in a business meeting, negotiation, discussion, or other bona fide business transaction, other than entertainment, for the purpose of obtaining income or other specific trade or business benefit. In addition, it must be established that such a business meeting, negotiation, discussion, or transaction was substantial in relation to the entertainment. This requirement will be satisfied if the principal character or aspect of the combined entertainment and business activity was the active conduct of business. However, it is not necessary that more time be devoted to business than to entertainment to meet this requirement.

(b) **Meetings at conventions, etc.** Any meeting officially scheduled in connection with a program at a convention or similar general assembly, or at a bona fide trade or business meeting sponsored and conducted by business or professional organizations, shall be considered to constitute a substantial and bona fide business discussion within the meaning of this section provided—

(1) **Expenses necessary to taxpayer's attendance.** The expenses necessary to the attendance of the taxpayer at the convention, general assembly, or trade or business meeting, were ordinary and necessary within the meaning of section 162 or 212;

(2) **Convention program.** The organization which sponsored the convention, or trade or business meeting had scheduled a program of business activities (including committee meetings or presentation of lectures, panel discussions, display of products, or other similar activities), and that such program was the principal activity of the convention, general assembly, or trade or business meeting.

(ii) **Directly preceding or following.** Entertainment which occurs on the same day as a substantial and bona fide business discussion (as defined in subdivision (i) of this subparagraph) will be considered to directly precede or follow such discussion. If the entertainment and the business discussion do not occur on the same day, the facts and circumstances of each case are to be considered, including the place, date and duration of the business discussion, whether the taxpayer or his business associates are from out of town, and, if so, the date of arrival and departure, and the reasons the entertainment did not take place on the day of the business discussion. For example, if a group of business associates comes from out of town to the taxpayer's place of business to hold a substantial business discussion, the entertainment of such business guests and their wives on the evening prior to, or on the evening of the day following, the business discussion would generally be regarded as directly preceding or following such discussion.

(4) **Expenses closely connected with directly related entertainment.** If any portion of an expenditure meets the requirements of paragraph (c)(3) of this section (relating to directly related entertainment in general), the remaining portion of the expenditure, if it is otherwise allowable under chapter 1 of the Code, shall be considered associated with the active conduct of the taxpayer's trade or business to the extent allocable to a person or persons closely connected with a person referred to in paragraph (c)(3)(iv) of this section. The spouse of a person referred to in paragraph(c)(3)(iv) of this section will be considered closely connected to such a person for purposes of this subparagraph. Thus, if a taxpayer and his wife entertain a business customer and the customer's wife under circumstances where the entertainment of the customer is considered directly related to the active conduct of the taxpayer's trade or business (within the meaning of paragraph (c)(3) of this section) the portion of the expenditure allocable to both wives will be considered associated with the active conduct of the taxpayer's trade or business under this subparagraph.

(e) **Expenditures paid or incurred before January 1, 1979, with respect to entertainment facilities or any time with respect to clubs—(1) In general.** Any expenditure paid or incurred before January 1, 1979, with respect to a facility, or paid or incurred at any time with respect to a club, used in connection with entertainment shall not be allowed as a deduction except to the extent it meets the requirements of paragraph (a)(2)(ii) of this section.

(2) **Facilities used in connection with entertainment—(i) In general.** Any item of personal or real property owned, rented, or used by a taxpayer shall (unless otherwise provided under the rules of subdivision (ii) of this subparagraph) be considered to constitute a facility used in connection with entertainment if it is used during the taxable year for, or in connection with, entertainment (as defined in paragraph (b)(1) of this section). Examples of facilities which might be used for, or in connection with, entertainment include yachts,

hunting lodges, fishing camps, swimming pools, tennis courts, bowling alleys, automobiles, airplanes, apartments, hotel suites, and homes in vacation resorts.

(ii) **Facilities used incidentally for entertainment.** A facility used only incidentally during a taxable year in connection with entertainment, if such use is insubstantial, will not be considered a "facility used in connection with entertainment" for purposes of this section or for purposes of the recordkeeping requirements of section 274(d). See § 1.274–5(c)(6)(iii).

(3) **Expenditures with respect to a facility used in connection with entertainment—(i) In general.** The phrase "expenditures with respect to a facility used in connection with entertainment" includes depreciation and operating costs, such as rent and utility charges (for example, water or electricity), expenses for the maintenance, preservation or protection of a facility (for example, repairs, painting, insurance charges), and salaries or expenses for subsistence paid to caretakers or watchmen. In addition, the phrase includes losses realized on the sale or other disposition of a facility.

(ii) **Club dues.** Dues or fees paid to any social, athletic, or sporting club or organization are considered expenditures with respect to a facility used in connection with entertainment. The purposes and activities of a club or organization, and not its name, determine its character. Generally, the phrase "social, athletic, or sporting club or organization" has the same meaning for purposes of this section as it has in part II of chapter 33 of the Code, and the regulations thereunder, relating to tax on club dues. However, for purposes of this section only, clubs operated solely to provide lunches under circumstances of a type generally considered to be conducive to business discussion, within the meaning of paragraph (f)(2)(i) of this section, will not be considered social clubs.

(iii) **Expenditures not with respect to a facility.** The following expenditures shall not be considered to constitute expenditures with respect to a facility used in connection with entertainment—

(a) **Out of pocket expenditures.** Expenses (exclusive of operating costs and other expenses referred to in subdivision (i) of this subparagraph) incurred at the time of an entertainment activity, even though in connection with the use of facility for entertainment purposes, such as expenses for food and beverages, or expenses for catering, or expenses for gasoline and fishing bait consumed on a fishing trip;

(b) **Non-entertainment expenditures.** Expenses or items attributable to the use of a facility for other than entertainment purposes such as expenses for an automobile when not used for entertainment; and

(c) **Expenditures otherwise deductible.** Expenses allowable as a deduction without regard to their connection with a taxpayer's trade or business such as taxes, interest, and casualty losses. The provisions of this subdivision shall be applied in the case of a taxpayer which is not an individual as if it were an individual. See also § 1.274–6.

(iv) **Cross reference.** For other rules with respect to treatment of certain expenditures for entertainment-type facilities, see § 1.274–7.

(4) **Determination of primary use—(i) In general.** A facility used in connection with entertainment shall be considered as used primarily for the furtherance of the taxpayer's trade or business only if it is established that the primary use of the facility during the taxable year was for purposes considered ordinary and necessary within the meaning of sections 162 and 212 and the regulations thereunder. All of the facts and circumstances of each case shall be considered in determining the primary use of a facility. Generally, it is the actual use of the facility which establishes the deductibility of expenditures with respect to the facility; not its availability for use and not the taxpayer's principal purpose in acquiring the facility. Objective rather than subjective standards will be determinative. If membership entitles the member's entire family to use of a facility, such as a country club, their use will be considered in determining whether business use of the facility exceeds personal use. The factors to be considered include the nature of each use, the frequency and duration of use for business purposes as compared with other purposes, and the amount of expenditures incurred during use for business compared with amount of expenditures incurred during use for other purposes. No single standard of comparison, or quantitative measurement, as to the significance of any such factor, however, is necessarily appropriate for all classes or types of facilities. For example, an appropriate standard for determining the primary use of a country club during a taxable year will not necessarily be appropriate for determining the primary use of an airplane. However, a taxpayer shall be deemed to have estab-

lished that a facility was used primarily for the furtherance of his trade or business if he establishes such primary use in accordance with subdivision (ii) or (iii) of this subparagraph. Subdivision (ii) and (iii) of this subparagraph shall not preclude a taxpayer from otherwise establishing the primary use of a facility under the general provisions of this subdivision.

(ii) Certain transportation facilities. A taxpayer shall be deemed to have established that a facility of a type described in this subdivision was used primarily for the furtherance of his trade or business if—

(a) Automobiles. In the case of an automobile, the taxpayer establishes that more than 50 percent of mileage driven during the taxable year was in connection with travel considered to be ordinary and necessary within the meaning of section 162 or 212 and the regulations thereunder.

(b) Airplanes. In the case of an airplane, the taxpayer establishes that more than 50 percent of hours flown during the taxable year was in connection with travel considered to be ordinary and necessary within the meaning of section 162 or 212 and the regulations thereunder.

(iii) Entertainment facilities in general. A taxpayer shall be deemed to have established that—

(a) A facility used in connection with entertainment, such as a yacht or other pleasure boat, hunting lodge, fishing camp, summer home or vacation cottage, hotel suite, country club, golf club or similar social, athletic, or sporting club or organization, bowling alley, tennis court, or swimming pool, or,

(b) A facility for employees not falling within the scope of section 274(e)(2) or (5)

was used primarily for the furtherance of his trade or business if he establishes that more than 50 percent of the total calendar days of use of the facility by, or under authority of, the taxpayer during the taxable year were days of business use. Any use of a facility (of a type described in this subdivision) during one calendar day shall be considered to constitute a "day of business use" if the primary use of the facility on such day was ordinary and necessary within the meaning of section 162 or 212 and the regulations thereunder. For the purposes of this subdivision, a facility shall be deemed to have been primarily used for such purposes on any one calendar day if the facility was

used for the conduct of a substantial and bona fide business discussion (as defined in paragraph (d)(3)(i) of this section) notwithstanding that the facility may also have been used on the same day for personal or family use by the taxpayer or any member of the taxpayer's family not involving entertainment of others by, or under the authority of, the taxpayer.

(f) Specific exceptions to application of this section—(1) In general. The provisions of paragraphs (a) through (e) of this section (imposing limitations on deductions for entertainment expenses) are not applicable in the case of expenditures set forth in subparagraph (2) of this paragraph. Such expenditures are deductible to the extent allowable under chapter 1 of the Code. This paragraph shall not be construed to affect the allowability or nonallowability of a deduction under section 162 or 212 and the regulations thereunder. The fact that an expenditure is not covered by a specific exception provided for in this paragraph shall not be determinative of the allowability or nonallowability of the expenditure under paragraphs (a) through (e) of this section. Expenditures described in subparagraph (2) of this paragraph are subject to the substantiation requirements of section 274(d) to the extent provided in § 1.274–5.

(2) Exceptions. The expenditures referred to in subparagraph (1) of this paragraph are set forth in subdivision (i) through (ix) of this subparagraph.

(i) Business meals and similar expenditures —(a) In general. Any expenditure for food or beverages furnished to an individual under circumstances of a type generally considered conducive to business discussion (taking into account the surroundings in which furnished, the taxpayer's trade, business, or income-producing activity, and the relationship to such trade, business or activity of the persons to whom the food or beverages are furnished) is not subject to the limitations on allowability of deductions provided for in paragraphs (a) through (e) of this section. There is no requirement that business actually be discussed for this exception to apply.

(b) Surroundings. The surroundings in which the food or beverages are furnished must be such as would provide an atmosphere where there are no substantial distractions to discussion. This exception applies primarily to expenditures for meals and beverages served during the course of a breakfast, lunch or dinner meeting of the taxpayer and his business associates at a restaurant, hotel dining room, eating club or similar place not involving distracting influences such as a floor show. This exception also applies to expenditures for beverages served apart from meals if the expenditure is incurred in surroundings similarly conducive to business discussion, such as an expenditure for beverages served during the meeting of the taxpayer and his business associates at a cocktail lounge or hotel bar not involving distracting influences such as a floor show. This exception may also apply to expenditures for meals or beverages served in the taxpayer's residence on a clear showing that the expenditure was commercially rather than socially motivated. However, this exception, generally, is not applicable to any expenditure for meals or beverages furnished in circumstances where there are major distractions not conducive to business discussion, such as at night clubs, sporting events, large cocktail parties, sizeable social gatherings, or other major distracting influences.

(c) **Taxpayer's trade or business and relationship of persons entertained.** The taxpayer's trade, business, or income-producing activity and the relationship of the persons to whom the food or beverages are served to such trade, business or activity must be such as will reasonably indicate that the food or beverages were furnished for the primary purpose of furthering the taxpayer's trade or business and did not primarily serve a social or personal purpose. Such a business purpose would be indicated, for example, if a salesman employed by a manufacturing supply company meets for lunch during a normal business day with a purchasing agent for a manufacturer which is a prospective customer. Such a purpose would also be indicated if a life insurance agent meets for lunch during a normal business day with a client.

(d) **Business programs.** Expenditures for business luncheons or dinners which are part of a business program, or banquets officially sponsored by business or professional associations, will be regarded as expenditures to which the exception of this subdivision (i) applies. In the case of such a business luncheon or dinner it is not always necessary that the taxpayer attend the luncheon or dinner himself. For example, if a dental equipment supplier purchased a table at a dental association banquet for dentists who are actual or prospective customers for his equipment, the cost of the table would not be disallowed under this section. See also paragraph (c)(4) of this section relating to expenditures made in a clear business setting.

(ii) **Food and beverages for employees.** Any expenditure by a taxpayer for food and beverages (or for use of a facility in connection therewith) furnished on the taxpayer's business premises primarily for his employees is not subject to the limitations on allowability of deductions provided for in paragraphs (a) through (e) of this section. This exception applies not only to expenditures for food or beverages furnished in a typical company cafeteria or an executive dining room, but also to expenditures with respect to the operation of such facilities. This exception applies even though guests are occasionally served in the cafeteria or dining room.

(iii) **Certain entertainment expenses treated as compensation.** Any expenditure by a taxpayer for entertainment (or for use of a facility in connection therewith), if an employee is the recipient of the entertainment, is not subject to the limitations on allowability of deductions provided for in paragraphs (a) through (e) of this section to the extent that such expenditure is treated by the taxpayer—

(a) On his income tax return as originally filed, as compensation paid to the employee, and

(b) As wages to the employee for purposes of withholding under chapter 24 (relating to collection of income tax at source on wages).

For example, if an employer rewards the employee (and the employee's wife) with an expense paid vacation trip, such an expense is deductible by the employer (if allowable under section 162 and the regulations thereunder) to the extent the employer so treats the expenses as compensation and as wages. On the other hand, if a taxpayer owns a yacht which he uses for the entertainment of business customers, the portion of salary paid to employee members of the crew which is allocable to use of the yacht for entertainment purposes (even though treated on the taxpayer's tax return as compensation and treated as wages for withholding tax purposes) would not come within this exception since the members of the crew were not recipients of the entertainment. If an expenditure of a type described in this subdivision properly constitutes a dividend paid to a shareholder or if it constitutes unreasonable compensation paid to an employee, nothing in this exception prevents disallowance of the expenditure to the taxpayer under other provisions of the Code.

(iv) Reimbursed entertainment expenses—(a) Introductory. In the case of any expenditure for entertainment paid or incurred by one person in connection with the performance by him of services for another person (whether or not such other person is an employer) under a reimbursement or other expense allowance arrangement, the limitations on allowability of deductions provided for in paragraphs (a) through (e) of this section shall be applied only once, either (1) to the person who makes the expenditure or (2) to the person who actually bears the expense, but not to both. For purposes of this subdivision (iv), the term "reimbursement or other expense allowance arrangement" has the same meaning as it has in section 62(2)(A), but without regard to whether the taxpayer is the employee of a person for whom services are performed. If an expenditure of a type described in this subdivision properly constitutes a dividend paid to a shareholder, unreasonable compensation paid to an employee, or a personal, living or family expense, nothing in this exception prevents disallowance of the expenditure to the taxpayer under other provisions of the Code.

(b) Reimbursement arrangements between employee and employer. In the case of an expenditure for entertainment paid or incurred by an employee under a reimbursement or other expense allowance arrangement with his employer, the limitations on deductions provided for in paragraphs (a) through (e) of this section shall not apply—

(1) Employees. To the employee except to the extent his employer has treated the expenditure on the employer's income tax return as originally filed as compensation paid to the employee and as wages to such employee for purposes of withholding under chapter 24 (relating to collection of income tax at source on wages).

(2) Employers. To the employer to the extent he has treated the expenditure as compensation and wages paid to an employee in the manner provided in (b)(1) of this subdivision.

(c) Reimbursement arrangements between independent contractors and clients or customers. In the case of an expenditure for entertainment paid or incurred by one person (hereinafter termed "independent contractor") under a reimbursement or other expense allowance arrangement with another person other than an employer (hereinafter termed "client or customer"), the limitations on deductions provided for in paragraphs (a) through (e) of this section shall not apply—

(1) Independent contractors. To the independent contractor to the extent he accounts to his client or customer within the meaning of section 274(d) and the regulations thereunder. See § 1.274–5.

(2) Clients or customers. To the client or customer if the expenditure is disallowed to the independent contractor under paragraphs (a) through (e) of this section.

(v) Recreational expenses for employees generally. Any expenditure by a taxpayer for a recreational, social, or similar activity (or for use of a facility in connection therewith), primarily for the benefit of his employees generally, is not subject to the limitations on allowability of deductions provided for in paragraphs (a) through (e) of this section. This exception applies only to expenditures made primarily for the benefit of employees of the taxpayer other than employees who are officers, shareholders or other owners who own a 10-percent or greater interest in the business, or other highly compensated employees. For purposes of the preceding sentence, an employee shall be treated as owning any interest owned by a member of his family (within the meaning of section 267(c)(4) and the regulations thereunder). Ordinarily, this exception applies to usual employee benefit programs such as expenses of a taxpayer (a) in holding Christmas parties, annual picnics, or summer outings, for his employees generally, or (b) of maintaining a swimming pool, baseball diamond, bowling alley, or golf course available to his employees generally. Any expenditure for an activity which is made under circumstances which discriminate in favor of employees who are officers, shareholders or other owners, or highly compensated employees shall not be considered made primarily for the benefit of employees generally. On the other hand, an expenditure for an activity will not be considered outside of this exception merely because, due to the large number of employees involved, the activity is intended to benefit only a limited number of such employees at one time, provided the activity does not discriminate in favor of officers, shareholders, other owners, or highly compensated employees.

(vi) Employee, stockholder, etc., business meetings. Any expenditure by a taxpayer for entertainment which is directly related to bona fide business meetings of the taxpayer's employees, stockholders, agents, or directors held principally for discussion of trade or business is not subject to the limitations on allowability of deductions provided for in paragraphs (a) through (e) of this section. For purposes of this exception, a partnership is to be considered a taxpayer and a member of a partnership is to be considered an agent. For example, an expenditure by a taxpayer to furnish refreshments to his employees at a bona fide meeting, sponsored by the taxpayer for the principal purpose of instructing them with respect to a new procedure for conducting his business, would be within provisions of this exemption. A similar expenditure made at a bona fide meeting of stockholders of the taxpayer for the election of directors and discussion of corporate affairs would also be within the provisions of this exception. While this exception will apply to bona fide business meetings even though some social activities are provided, it will not apply to meetings which are primarily for social or nonbusiness purposes rather than for the transaction of the taxpayer's business. A meeting under circumstances where there was little or no possibility of engaging in the active conduct of trade or business (as described in paragraph (c)(7) of this section) generally will not be considered a business meeting for purposes of this subdivision. This exception will not apply to a meeting or convention of employees or agents, or similar meeting for directors, partners or others for the principal purpose of rewarding them for their services to the taxpayer. However, such a meeting or convention of employees might come within the scope of subdivisions (iii) or (v) of this subparagraph.

(vii) Meetings of business leagues, etc. Any expenditure for entertainment directly related and necessary to attendance at bona fide business meetings or conventions of organizations exempt from taxation under section 501(c)(6) of the Code, such as business leagues, chambers of commerce, real estate boards, boards of trade, and certain professional associations, is not subject to the limitations on allowability of deductions provided in paragraphs (a) through (e) of this section.

(viii) Items available to the public. Any expenditure by a taxpayer for entertainment (or for a facility in connection therewith) to the extent the entertainment is made available to the general public is not subject to the limitations on allowability of deductions provided for in paragraphs (a) through (e) of this section. Expenditures for entertainment of the general public by means of television, radio, newspapers and the like, will come within this exception, as will expenditures for distributing samples to the general public. Similarly,

expenditures for maintaining private parks, golf courses and similar facilities, to the extent that they are available for public use, will come within this exception. For example, if a corporation maintains a swimming pool which it makes available for a period of time each week to children participating in a local public recreational program, the portion of the expense relating to such public use of the pool will come within this exception.

(ix) Entertainment sold to customers. Any expenditure by a taxpayer for entertainment (or for use of a facility in connection therewith) to the extent the entertainment is sold to customers in a bona fide transaction for an adequate and full consideration in money or money's worth is not subject to the limitations on allowability of deductions provided for in paragraphs (a) through (e) of this section. Thus, the cost of producing night club entertainment (such as salaries paid to employees of night clubs and amounts paid to performers) for sale to customers or the cost of operating a pleasure cruise ship as a business will come within this exception.

[T.D. 6659, 28 FR 6499, June 25, 1963, as amended by T.D. 6996, 34 FR 835, Jan. 13, 1969; T.D. 8051, 50 FR 36576, Sept. 9, 1985]

§ 1.274–3   Disallowance of deduction for gifts.

(a) In general. No deduction shall be allowed under section 162 or 212 for any expense for a gift made directly or indirectly by a taxpayer to any individual to the extent that such expense, when added to prior expenses of the taxpayer for gifts made to such individual during the taxpayer's taxable year, exceeds $25.

(b) Gift defined—(1) In general. Except as provided in subparagraph (2) of this paragraph the term "gift", for purposes of this section, means any item excludable from the gross income of the recipient under section 102 which is not excludable from his gross income under any other provision of chapter 1 of the Code. Thus, a payment by an employer to a deceased employee's widow is not a gift, for purposes of this section, to the extent the payment constitutes an employee's death benefit excludable by the recipient under section 101(b). Similarly, a scholarship which is excludable from a recipient's gross income under section 117, and a prize or award which is excludable from a recipient's gross income under section 74(b), are not subject to the provisions of this section.

(2) Items not treated as gifts. The term "gift", for purposes of this section, does not include the following:

(i) An item having a cost to the taxpayer not in excess of $4.00 on which the name of the taxpayer is clearly and permanently imprinted and which is one of a number of identical items distributed generally by such a taxpayer.

(ii) A sign, display rack, or other promotional material to be used on the business premises of the recipient, or

(iii) An item of tangible personal property having a cost to the taxpayer not in excess of $100 which is awarded to an employee by reason of length of service or for safety achievement.

The deductibility of the expense of any of the items described in this subparagraph is not governed by this section and the taxpayer need not take such items into account in determining whether the $25 limitation on gifts to any individual has been exceeded. The fact that such items are excepted from the applicability of this section has no effect in determining whether the value of such items is includible in the gross income of the recipient.

(c) Expense for a gift. For purposes of this section, the term "expense for a gift" means the cost of the gift to the taxpayer, other than incidental costs such as for customary engraving on jewelry, or for packaging, insurance, and mailing or other delivery. A related cost will be considered "incidental" only if it does not add substantial value to the gift. Although the cost of customary gift wrapping will be considered an incidental cost, the purchase of an ornamental basket for packaging fruit will not be considered an incidental cost of packaging if the basket has a value which is substantial in relation to the value of the fruit.

* * *

[T.D. 6659, 28 FR 6505, June 25, 1963]

§ 1.274–4 Disallowance of certain foreign travel expenses.

(a) Introductory. Section 274(c) and this section impose certain restrictions on the deductibility of travel expenses incurred in the case of an individual who, while traveling outside the United States away from home in the pursuit of trade or business (hereinafter termed "business activity"), engages in substantial personal activity not attributable to such trade or business (hereinafter termed "nonbusiness activity"). Section 274(c) and this section are limited in their application to individuals (whether or not an employee or other person traveling under a reimbursement or other expense allowance arrangement) who engage in nonbusiness activity while traveling outside the United States away from home, and do not impose restrictions on the deductibility of travel expenses incurred by an employer or client under an advance, reimbursement, or other arrangement with the individual who engages in nonbusiness activity. For purposes of this section, the term "United States" includes only the States and the District of Columbia, and any reference to "trade or business" or "business activity" includes any activity described in section 212. For rules governing the determination of travel outside the United States away from home, see paragraph (e) of this section. For rules governing the disallowance of travel expense to which this section applies, see paragraph (f) of this section.

(b) Limitations on application of section. The restrictions on deductibility of travel expenses contained in paragraph (f) of this section are applicable only if—

(1) The travel expense is otherwise deductible under section 162 or 212 and the regulations thereunder,

(2) The travel expense is for travel outside the United States away from home which exceeds 1 week (as determined under paragraph (c) of this section), and

(3) The time outside the United States away from home attributable to nonbusiness activity (as determined under paragraph (d) of this section) constitutes 25 percent or more of the total time on such travel.

(c) Travel in excess of 1 week. This section does not apply to an expense of travel unless the expense is for travel outside the United States away from home which exceeds 1 week. For purposes of this section, 1 week means 7 consecutive days. The day in which travel outside the United States away from home begins shall not be considered, but the day in which such travel ends shall be considered, in determining whether a taxpayer is outside the United States away from home for more than 7 consecutive days. For example, if a taxpayer departs on travel outside the United States away from home on a Wednesday morning and ends such travel the following Wednesday evening, he shall be considered as being outside the

United States away from home only 7 consecutive days. In such a case, this section would not apply because the taxpayer was not outside the United States away from home for more than 7 consecutive days. However, if the taxpayer travels outside the United States away from home for more than 7 consecutive days, both the day such travel begins and the day such travel ends shall be considered a "business day" or a "nonbusiness day", as the case may be, for purposes of determining whether nonbusiness activity constituted 25 percent or more of travel time under paragraph (d) of this section and for purposes of allocating expenses under paragraph (f) of this section. For purposes of determining whether travel is outside the United States away from home, see paragraph (e) of this section.

(d) Nonbusiness activity constituting 25 percent or more of travel time—(1) In general. This section does not apply to any expense of travel outside the United States away from home unless the portion of time outside the United States away from home attributable to nonbusiness activity constitutes 25 percent or more of the total time on such travel.

(2) Allocation on per day basis. The total time traveling outside the United States away from home will be allocated on a day-by-day basis to (i) days of business activity or (ii) days of nonbusiness activity (hereinafter termed "business days" or "nonbusiness days" respectively) unless the taxpayer establishes that a different method of allocation more clearly reflects the portion of time outside the United States away from home which is attributable to nonbusiness activity. For purposes of this section, a day spent outside the United States away from home shall be deemed entirely a business day even though spent only in part on business activity if the taxpayer establishes—

(i) Transportation days. That on such day the taxpayer was traveling to or returning from a destination outside the United States away from home in the pursuit of trade or business. However, if for purposes of engaging in nonbusiness activity, the taxpayer while traveling outside the United States away from home does not travel by a reasonably direct route, only that number of days shall be considered business days as would be required for the taxpayer, using the same mode of transportation, to travel to or return from the same destination by a reasonably direct route. Also, if, while so traveling, the taxpayer interrupts the normal course of travel by engaging in substantial diversions for nonbusiness reasons of his own

choosing, only that number of days shall be considered business days as equals the number of days required for the taxpayer, using the same mode of transportation, to travel to or return from the same destination without engaging in such diversion. For example, if a taxpayer residing in New York departs on an evening on a direct flight to Quebec for a business meeting to be held in Quebec the next morning, for purposes of determining whether nonbusiness activity constituted 25 percent or more of his travel time, the entire day of his departure shall be considered a business day. On the other hand, if a taxpayer travels by automobile from New York to Quebec to attend a business meeting and while en route spends 2 days in Ottawa and 1 day in Montreal on nonbusiness activities of his personal choice, only that number of days outside the United States shall be considered business days as would have been required for the taxpayer to drive by a reasonably direct route to Quebec, taking into account normal periods for rest and meals.

(ii) Presence required. That on such day his presence outside the United States away from home was required at a particular place for a specific and bona fide business purpose. For example, if a taxpayer is instructed by his employer to attend a specific business meeting, the day of the meeting shall be considered a business day even though, because of the scheduled length of the meeting, the taxpayer spends more time during normal working hours of the day on nonbusiness activity than on business activity.

(iii) Days primarily business. That during hours normally considered to be appropriate for business activity, his principal activity on such day was the pursuit of trade or business.

(iv) Circumstances beyond control. That on such day he was prevented from engaging in the conduct of trade or business as his principal activity due to circumstances beyond his control.

(v) Weekends, holidays, etc. That such day was a Saturday, Sunday, legal holiday, or other reasonably necessary standby day which intervened during that course of the taxpayer's trade or business while outside the United States away from home which the taxpayer endeavored to conduct with reasonable dispatch. For example, if a taxpayer travels from New York to London to take part in business negotiations beginning on a Wednesday and concluding on the following Tuesday, the intervening Saturday and Sunday shall be considered business days whether or not business is conducted on either of such days. Similarly, if in the above case the meetings which concluded on Tuesday evening were followed by business meetings with another business group in London on the immediately succeeding Thursday and Friday, the intervening Wednesday will be deemed a business day. However, if at the conclusion of the business meetings on Friday, the taxpayer stays in London for an additional week for personal purposes, the Saturday and Sunday following the conclusion of the business meeting will not be considered business days.

(e) **Domestic travel excluded—(1) In general.** For purposes of this section, travel outside the United States away from home does not include any travel from one point in the United States to another point in the United States. However, travel which is not from one point in the United States to another point in the United States shall be considered travel outside the United States. If a taxpayer travels from a place within the United States to a place outside the United States, the portion, if any, of such travel which is from one point in the United States to another point in the United States is to be disregarded for purposes of determining—

(i) Whether the taxpayer's travel outside the United States away from home exceeds 1 week (see paragraph (c) of this section),

(ii) Whether the time outside the United States away from home attributable to nonbusiness activity constitutes 25 percent or more of the total time on such travel (see paragraph (d) of this section), or

(iii) The amount of travel expense subject to the allocation rules of this section (see paragraph (f) of this section).

(2) **Determination of travel from one point in the United States to another point in the United States.** In the case of the following means of transportation, travel from one point in the United States to another point in the United States shall be determined as follows—

(i) **Travel by public transportation.** In the case of travel by public transportation, any place in the United States at which the vehicle makes a scheduled stop for the purpose of adding or discharging passengers shall be considered a point in the United States.

(ii) **Travel by private automobile.** In the case of travel by private automobile, any such travel which is within the United States shall be considered travel from one point in the United States to another point in the United States.

(iii) **Travel by private airplane.** In the case of travel by private airplane, any flight, whether or not constituting the entire trip, where both the takeoff and the landing are within the United States shall be considered travel from one point in the United States to another point in the United States.

(3) **Examples.** The provisions of subparagraph (2) may be illustrated by the following examples:

Example (1). Taxpayer A flies from Los Angeles to Puerto Rico with a brief scheduled stopover in Miami for the purpose of adding and discharging passengers and A returns by airplane nonstop to Los Angeles. The travel from Los Angeles to Miami is considered travel from one point in the United States to another point in the United States. The travel from Miami to Puerto Rico and from Puerto Rico to Los Angeles is not considered travel from one point in the United States to another point in the United States and, thus, is considered to be travel outside the United States away from home.

Example (2). Taxpayer B travels by train from New York to Montreal. The travel from New York to the last place in the United States where the train is stopped for the purpose of adding or discharging passengers is considered to be travel from one point in the United States to another point in the United States.

Example (3). Taxpayer C travels by automobile from Tulsa to Mexico City and back. All travel in the United States is considered to be travel from one point in the United States to another point in the United States.

Example (4). Taxpayer D flies nonstop from Seattle to Juneau. Although the flight passes over Canada, the trip is considered to be travel from one point in the United States to another point in the United States.

Example (5). If in example (4) above, the airplane makes a scheduled landing in Vancouver, the time spent in traveling from Seattle to Juneau is considered to be travel outside the United States away from home. However, the time spent in Juneau is not considered to be travel outside the United States away from home.

(f) **Application of disallowance rules—(1) In general.** In the case of expense for travel outside the United States away from home by an individual to which this section applies, except as otherwise provided in subparagraph (4) or (5) of this paragraph, no deduction shall be allowed for that amount of travel expense specified in subparagraph (2) or (3) of this paragraph (whichever is applicable) which is obtained by multiplying the total of such travel expense by a fraction—

(i) The numerator of which is the number of nonbusiness days during such travel, and

(ii) The denominator of which is the total number of business days and nonbusiness days during such travel.

For determination of "business days" and "nonbusiness days", see paragraph (d)(2) of this section.

(2) **Nonbusiness activity at, near, or beyond business destination.** If the place at which the individual engages in nonbusiness activity (hereinafter termed "nonbusiness destination") is at, near, or beyond the place to which he travels in the pursuit of a trade or business (hereinafter termed "business destination"), the amount of travel expense referred to in subparagraph (1) of this paragraph shall be the amount of travel expense, otherwise allowable as a deduction under section 162 or section 212, which would have been incurred in traveling from the place where travel outside the United States away from home begins to the business destination, and returning. Thus, if the individual travels from New York to London on business, and then takes a vacation in Paris before returning to New York, the amount of the travel expense subject to allocation is the expense which would have been incurred in traveling from New York to London and returning.

(3) **Nonbusiness activity on the route to or from business destination.** If the nonbusiness destination is on the route to or from the business destination, the amount of the travel expense referred to in subparagraph (1) of this paragraph shall be the amount of travel expense, otherwise allowable as the deduction under section 162 or 212, which would have been incurred in traveling from the place where travel outside the United States away from home begins to the nonbusiness destination and returning. Thus, if the individual travels on business from Chicago to Rio de Janeiro, Brazil with a scheduled stop in New York for the purpose of adding and discharging passengers, and while en route stops in Caracas, Venezuela for a vacation and returns to Chicago from Rio de Janeiro with another scheduled stop in New York for the purpose of adding and discharging passengers, the amount of travel expense subject to allocation is the expense which would have been incurred in traveling from New York to Caracas and returning.

(4) **Other allocation method.** If a taxpayer establishes that a method other than allocation on a day-by-day basis (as determined under paragraph (d)(2) of this section) more clearly reflects the portion of time outside the United States away from home which is attributable to nonbusiness activity, the amount of travel expense for which no deduction shall be allowed shall be determined by such other method.

(5) **Travel expense deemed entirely allocable to business activity.** Expenses of travel shall be considered allocable in full to business activity, and no portion of such expense shall be subject to disallowance under this section, if incurred under circumstances provided for in subdivision (i) or (ii) of this subparagraph.

(i) **Lack of control over travel.** Expenses of travel otherwise deductible under section 162 or 212 shall be considered fully allocable to business activity if, considering all the facts and circumstances, the individual incurring such expenses did not have substantial control over the arranging of the business trip. A person who is required to travel to a business destination will not be considered to have substantial control over the arranging of the business trip merely because he has control over the timing of the trip. Any individual who travels on behalf of his employer under a reimbursement or other expense allowance arrangement shall be considered not to have had substantial control over the arranging of his business trip, provided the employee is not—

(a) A managing executive of the employer for whom he is traveling (and for this purpose the term "managing executive" includes only an employee who, by reason of his authority and responsibility, is authorized, without effective veto procedures, to decide upon the necessity for his business trip), or

(b) Related to his employer within the meaning of section 267(b) but for this purpose the percentage referred to in section 267(b)(2) shall be 10 percent.

(ii) **Lack of major consideration to obtain a vacation.** Any expense of travel, which qualifies for deduction under section 162 or 212, shall be considered fully allocable to business activity if the individual incurring such expenses can establish that, considering all the facts and circumstances, he did not have a major consideration, in determining to make the trip, of obtaining a personal vacation or holiday. If such a major consideration were present, the provisions of subparagraphs (1) through (4) of this paragraph shall apply. However, if the trip were primarily personal in nature, the traveling expenses to and from the destination are not deductible even though the taxpayer engages in business activities while at such destination. See paragraph (b) of § 1.162–2.

(g) Examples. The application of this section may be illustrated by the following examples:

Example (1). Individual A flew from New York to Paris where he conducted business for 1 day. He spent the next 2 days sightseeing in Paris and then flew back to New York. The entire trip, including 2 days for travel en route, took 5 days. Since the time outside the United States, away from home during the trip did not exceed 1 week, the disallowance rules of this section do not apply.

Example (2). Individual B flew from Tampa to Honolulu (from one point in the United States to another point in the United States) for a business meeting which lasted 3 days and for personal matters which took 10 days. He then flew to Melbourne, Australia where he conducted business for 2 days and went sightseeing for 1 day. Immediately thereafter he flew back to Tampa, with a scheduled landing in Honolulu for the purpose of adding and discharging passengers. Although the trip exceeded 1 week, the time spent outside the United States away from home, including 2 days for traveling from Honolulu to Melbourne and return, was 5 days. Since the time outside the United States away from home during the trip did not exceed 1 week, the disallowance rules of this section do not apply.

Example (3). Individual C flew from Los Angeles to New York where he spent 5 days. He then flew to Brussels where he spent 14 days on business and 5 days on personal matters. He then flew back to Los Angeles by way of New York. The entire trip, including 4 days for travel en route, took 28 days. However, the 2 days spent traveling from Los Angeles to New York and return, and the 5 days spent in New York are not considered travel outside the United States away from home and, thus, are disregarded for purposes of this section. Although the time spent outside the United States away from home exceeded 1 week, the time outside the United States away from home attributable to nonbusiness activities (5 days out of 21) was less than 25 percent of the total time outside the United States away from home during the trip. Therefore, the disallowance rules of this section do not apply.

Example (4). D, an employee of Y Company, who is neither a managing executive of, nor related to, Y Company within the meaning of paragraph (f)(5)(i) of this section, traveled outside the United States away from home on behalf of his employer and was reimbursed by Y for his traveling expense to and from the business destination. The trip took more than a week and D took advantage of the opportunity to enjoy a personal vacation which exceeded 25 percent of the total time on the trip. Since D, traveling under a reimbursement arrangement, is not a managing executive of, or related to, Y Company, he is not considered to have substantial control over the arranging of the business trip, and the travel expenses shall be considered fully allocable to business activity.

Example (5). E, a managing executive and principal shareholder of X Company, travels from New York to Stockholm, Sweden, to attend a series of business meetings. At the conclusion of the series of meetings, which last 1 week, E spends 1 week on a personal vacation in Stockholm. If E establishes either that he did not have substantial control over the arranging of the trip or that a major consideration in his determining to make the trip was not to provide an opportunity for taking a personal vacation, the entire travel expense to and from Stockholm shall be considered fully allocable to business activity.

Example (6). F, a self-employed professional man, flew from New York to Copenhagen, Denmark, to attend a convention sponsored by a professional society. The trip lasted 3 weeks, of which 2 weeks were spent on vacation in Europe. F generally would be regarded as having substantial control over arranging this business trip. Unless F can establish that obtaining a vacation was not a major consideration in determining to make the trip, the disallowance rules of this section apply.

Example (7). Taxpayer G flew from Chicago to New York where he spent 6 days on business. He then flew to London where he conducted business for 2 days. G then flew to Paris for a 5 day vacation after which he flew back to Chicago, with a scheduled landing in New York for the purpose of adding and discharging passengers. G would not have made the trip except for the business he had to conduct in London. The travel outside the United States away from home, including 2 days for travel en route, exceeded a week and the time devoted to nonbusiness activities was not less than 25 percent of the total time on such travel. The 2 days spent traveling from Chicago to New York and return, and the 6 days spent in New York are disregarded for purposes of determining whether the travel outside the United States away from home exceeded a week and whether the time devoted to nonbusiness activities was less than 25 percent of the total time outside the United States away from home. If G is unable to establish either that he did not have substantial control over the arranging of the business trip or that an opportunity for taking a personal vacation was not a major consideration in his determining to make the trip, ⁵⁄₉ths (5 days devoted to nonbusiness activities out of a total 9 days outside the United States away from home on the trip) of the expenses attributable to transportation and food from New York to London and from London to New York will be disallowed (unless G establishes that a different method of allocation more clearly reflects the portion of time outside the United States away from home which is attributable to nonbusiness activity).

(h) Cross reference. For rules with respect to whether an expense is travel or entertainment, see paragraph (b)(1)(iii) of § 1.274–2.

[T.D. 6659, 28 FR 6505, June 24, 1963, as amended by T.D. 6758, 29 FR 12768, Sept. 10, 1964]

§ 1.274–5T Substantiation requirements.

(a) In general. For taxable years beginning on or after January 1, 1986, no deduction or credit shall be allowed with respect to—

(1) Traveling away from home (including meals and lodging),

(2) Any activity which is of a type generally considered to constitute entertainment, amusement, or recreation, or with respect to a facility used in connection with such an activity, including the items specified in section 274(e),

(3) Gifts defined in section 274(b), or

(4) Any listed property (as defined in section 280F(d)(4) and § 1.280F–6T(b)), unless the taxpayer substantiates each element of the expenditure or use (as described in paragraph (b) of this section) in the manner provided in paragraph (c) of this section. This limitation supersedes the doctrine founded in Cohan v. Commissioner, 39 F.2d 540 (2d Cir. 1930). The decision held that, where the evidence indicated a taxpayer incurred deductible travel or entertainment expenses but the exact amount could not be determined, the court should make a close approximation and not disallow the deduction entirely. Section 274(d) contemplates that no deduction or credit shall be allowed a taxpayer on the basis of such approximations or unsupported testimony of the taxpayer. For purposes of this section, the term "entertainment" means entertainment, amusement, or recreation, and use of a facility therefor; and the term "expenditure" includes expenses and items (including items such as losses and depreciation).

(b) **Elements of an expenditure or use—(1) In general.** Section 274(d) and this section contemplate that no deduction or credit shall be allowed for travel, entertainment, a gift, or with respect to listed property unless the taxpayer substantiates the requisite elements of each expenditure or use as set forth in this paragraph (b).

(2) **Travel away from home.** The elements to be proved with respect to an expenditure for travel away from home are—

(i) **Amount.** Amount of each separate expenditure for traveling away from home, such as cost of transportation or lodging, except that the daily cost of the traveler's own breakfast, lunch, and dinner and of expenditures incidental to such travel may be aggregated, if set forth in reasonable categories, such as for meals, for gasoline and oil, and for taxi fares;

(ii) **Time.** Dates of departure and return for each trip away from home, and number of days away from home spent on business;

(iii) **Place.** Destinations or locality of travel, described by name of city or town or other similar designation; and

(iv) **Business purpose.** Business reason for travel or nature of the business benefit derived or expected to be derived as a result of travel.

(3) **Entertainment in general.** The elements to be proved with respect to an expenditure for entertainment are—

(i) **Amount.** Amount of each separate expenditure for entertainment, except that such incidental items as taxi fares or telephone calls may be aggregated on a daily basis;

(ii) **Time.** Date of entertainment;

(iii) **Place.** Name, if any, address or location, and designation of type of entertainment, such as dinner or theater, if such information is not apparent from the designation of the place;

(iv) **Business purpose.** Business reason for the entertainment or nature of business benefit derived or expected to be derived as a result of the entertainment and, except in the case of business meals described in section 274(e)(1), the nature of any business discussion or activity;

(v) **Business relationship.** Occupation or other information relating to the person or persons entertained, including name, title, or other designation, sufficient to establish business relationship to the taxpayer.

(4) **Entertainment directly preceding or following a substantial and bona fide business discussion.** If a taxpayer claims a deduction for entertainment directly preceding or following a substantial and bona fide business discussion on the ground that such entertainment was associated with the active conduct of the taxpayer's trade or business, the elements to be proved with respect to such expenditure, in addition to those enumerated in paragraph (b)(3)(i), (ii), (iii), and (v) of this section are—

(i) **Time.** Date and duration of business discussion;

(ii) **Place.** Place of business discussion;

(iii) **Business purpose.** Nature of business discussion, and business reason for the entertainment or nature of business benefit derived or expected to be derived as the result of the entertainment;

(iv) **Business relationship.** Identification of those persons entertained who participated in the business discussion.

(5) **Gifts.** The elements to be proved with respect to an expenditure for a gift are—

(i) Amount. Cost of the gift to the taxpayer;

(ii) Time. Date of the gift;

(iii) Description. Description of the gift;

(iv) Business purpose. Business reason for the gift or nature of business benefit derived or expected to be derived as a result of the gift; and

(v) Business relationship. Occupation or other information relating to the recipient of the gift, including name, title, or other designation, sufficient to establish business relationship to the taxpayer.

(6) Listed property. The elements to be proved with respect to any listed property are—

(i) Amount—(A) Expenditures. The amount of each separate expenditure with respect to an item of listed property, such as the cost of acquisition, the cost of capital improvements, lease payments, the cost of maintenance and repairs, or other expenditures, and

(B) Uses. The amount of each business/investment use (as defined in § 1.280F–6T(d)(3) and (e)), based on the appropriate measure (i.e., mileage for automobiles and other means of transportation and time for other listed property, unless the Commissioner approves an alternative method), and the total use of the listed property for the taxable period.

(ii) Time. Date of the expenditure or use with respect to listed property, and

(iii) Business or investment purpose. The business purpose for an expenditure or use with respect to any listed property (see § 1.274–5T(c)(6)(i)(B) and (C) for special rules for the aggregation of expenditures and business use and § 1.280F–6T(d)(2) for the distinction between qualified business use and business/investment use).

See also § 1.274–5T(e) relating to the substantiation of business use of employer-provided listed property and § 1.274–6T for special rules for substantiating the business/investment use of certain types of listed property.

(c) Rules of substantiation—(1) In general. Except as otherwise provided in this section and § 1.274–6T, a taxpayer must substantiate each element of an expenditure or use (described in paragraph (b) of this section) by adequate records or by sufficient evidence corroborating his own statement. Section 274(d) contemplates that a taxpayer will maintain and produce such substantiation as will constitute proof of each expenditure or use

referred to in section 274. Written evidence has considerably more probative value than oral evidence alone. In addition, the probative value of written evidence is greater the closer in time it relates to the expenditure or use. A contemporaneous log is not required, but a record of the elements of an expenditure or of a business use of listed property made at or near the time of the expenditure or use, supported by sufficient documentary evidence, has a high degree of credibility not present with respect to a statement prepared subsequent thereto when generally there is a lack of accurate recall. Thus, the corroborative evidence required to support a statement not made at or near the time of the expenditure or use must have a high degree of probative value to elevate such statement and evidence to the level of credibility reflected by a record made at or near the time of the expenditure or use supported by sufficient documentary evidence. The substantiation requirements of section 274(d) are designed to encourage taxpayers to maintain the records, together with documentary evidence, as provided in paragraph (c)(2) of this section.

(2) Substantiation by adequate records—(i) In general. To meet the "adequate records" requirements of section 274(d), a taxpayer shall maintain an account book, diary, log, statement of expense, trip sheets, or similar record (as provided in paragraph (c)(2)(ii) of this section), and documentary evidence (as provided in paragraph (c)(2)(iii) of this section) which, in combination, are sufficient to establish each element of an expenditure or use specified in paragraph (b) of this section. It is not necessary to record information in an account book, diary, log, statement of expense, trip sheet, or similar record which duplicates information reflected on a receipt so long as the account book, etc., and receipt complement each other in an orderly manner.

(ii) Account book, diary, etc. An account book, diary, log, statement of expense, trip sheet, or similar record must be prepared or maintained in such manner that each recording of an element of an expenditure or use is made at or near the time of the expenditure or use.

(A) Made at or near the time of the expenditure or use. For purposes of this section, the phrase "made at or near the time of the expenditure or use" means the elements of an expenditure or use are recorded at a time when, in relation to the use or making of an expenditure, the taxpayer has full present knowledge of each element of the expenditure or use, such as the amount, time, place, and business purpose of the expenditure and business relationship. An expense account statement which is a transcription of an account book, diary, log, or similar record prepared or maintained in accordance with the provisions of this paragraph (c)(2)(ii) shall be considered a record prepared or maintained in the manner prescribed in the preceding sentence if such expense account statement is submitted by an employee to his employer or by an independent contractor to his client or customer in the regular course of good business practice. For example, a log maintained on a weekly basis, which accounts for use during the week, shall be considered a record made at or near the time of such use.

(B) Substantiation of business purpose. In order to constitute an adequate record of business purpose within the meaning of section 274(d) and this paragraph (c)(2), a written statement of business purpose generally is required. However, the degree of substantiation necessary to establish business purpose will vary depending upon the facts and circumstances of each case. Where the business purpose is evident from the surrounding facts and circumstances, a written explanation of such business purpose will not be required. For example, in the case of a salesman calling on customers on an established sales route, a written explanation of the business purpose of such travel ordinarily will not be required. Similarly, in the case of a business meal described in section 274(e)(1), if the business purpose of such meal is evident from the business relationship to the taxpayer of the persons entertained and other surrounding circumstances, a written explanation of such business purpose will not be required.

(C) Substantiation of business use of listed property—(1) Degree of substantiation. In order to constitute an adequate record (within the meaning of section 274(d) and this paragraph (c)(2)(ii)), which substantiates business/investment use of listed property (as defined in § 1.280F–6T(d)(3)), the record must contain sufficient information as to each element of every business/investment use. However, the level of detail required in an adequate record to substantiate business/investment use may vary depending upon the facts and circumstances. For example, a taxpayer who uses a truck for both business and personal purposes and whose only business use of a truck is to make deliveries to customers on an established route

may satisfy the adequate record requirement by recording the total number miles driven during the taxable year, the length of the delivery route once, and the date of each trip at or near the time of the trips. Alternatively, the taxpayer may establish the date of each trip with a receipt, record of delivery, or other documentary evidence.

(2) Written record. Generally, an adequate record must be written. However, a record of the business use of listed property, such as a computer or automobile, prepared in a computer memory device with the aid of a logging program will constitute an adequate record.

(D) Confidential information. If any information relating to the elements of an expenditure or use, such as place, business purpose, or business relationship, is of a confidential nature, such information need not be set forth in the account book, diary, log, statement of expense, trip sheet, or similar record, provided such information is recorded at or near the time of the expenditure or use and is elsewhere available to the district director to substantiate such element of the expenditure or use.

(iii) **Documentary evidence.** Documentary evidence, such as receipts, paid bills, or similar evidence sufficient to support an expenditure shall be required for—

(A) Any expenditure for lodging while traveling away from home, and

(B) Any other expenditure of $25 or more, except, for transportation charges, documentary evidence will not be required if not readily available,

provided, however that the Commissioner, in his discretion, may prescribe rules waiving such requirements in circumstances where he determines it is impracticable for such documentary evidence to be required. Ordinarily, documentary evidence will be considered adequate to support an expenditure if it includes sufficient information to establish the amount, date, place, and the essential character of the expenditure. For example, a hotel receipt is sufficient to support expenditures for business travel if it contains the following: name, location, date, and separate amounts for charges such as for lodging, meals, and telephone. Similarly a restaurant receipt is sufficient to support an expenditure for a business meal if it contains the following: name and location of the restaurant, the date and amount of the expenditure, the number of people served, and, if a charge is made for an item other than meals and beverages, an indication that such is the case. A document may be indicative of only one (or part of one) element of an expenditure. Thus, a cancelled check together with a bill from the payee, ordinarily would establish the element of cost. In contrast, a cancelled check drawn payable to a named payee would not by itself support a business expenditure without other evidence showing that the check was used for a certain business purpose.

(iv) Retention of written evidence. The Commissioner may, in his discretion, prescribe rules under which an employer may dispose of the adequate records and documentary evidence submitted to him by employees who are required to, and do, make an adequate accounting to the employer (within the meaning of paragraph (f)(4) of this section) if the employer maintains adequate accounting procedures with respect to such employees (within the meaning of paragraph (f)(5) of this section).

(v) Substantial compliance. If a taxpayer has not fully substantiated a particular element of an expenditure or use, but the taxpayer establishes to the satisfaction of the district director that he has substantially complied with the "adequate records" requirements of this paragraph (c)(2) with respect to the expenditure or use, the taxpayer may be permitted to establish such element by evidence which the district director shall deem adequate.

(3) Substantiation by other sufficient evidence—(i) In general. If a taxpayer fails to establish to the satisfaction of the district director that he has substantially complied with the "adequate records" requirements of paragraph (c)(2) of this section with respect to an element of an expenditure or use, then, except as otherwise provided in this paragraph, the taxpayer must establish such element—

(A) By his own statement, whether written or oral, containing specific information in detail as to such element; and

(B) By other corroborative evidence sufficient to establish such element.

If such element is the description of a gift, or the cost or amount, time, place, or date of an expenditure or use, the corroborative evidence shall be direct evidence, such as a statement in writing or the oral testimony of persons entertained or other witnesses setting forth detailed information about such element, or the documentary evidence described in paragraph (c)(2) of this section. If such

element is either the business relationship to the taxpayer of persons entertained, or the business purpose of an expenditure, the corroborative evidence may be circumstantial evidence.

(ii) Sampling—(A) In general. Except as provided in paragraph (c)(3)(ii)(B) of this section, a taxpayer may maintain an adequate record for portions of a taxable year and use that record to substantiate the business/investment use of listed property for all or a portion of the taxable year if the taxpayer can demonstrate by other evidence that the periods for which an adequate record is maintained are representative of the use for the taxable year or a portion thereof.

(B) Exception for pooled vehicles. The sampling method of paragraph (c)(3)(ii)(A) of this section may not be used to substantiate the business/investment use of an automobile or other vehicle of an employer that is made available for use by more than one employee for all or a portion of a taxable year.

(C) Examples. The following examples illustrate this paragraph (c)(3)(ii).

Example (1). A, a sole proprietor and calendar year taxpayer, operates an interior decorating business out of her home. A uses an automobile for local business travel to visit the homes or offices of clients, to meet with suppliers and other subcontractors, and to pick up and deliver certain items to clients when feasible. There is no other business use of the automobile but A and other members of her family also use the automobile for personal purposes. A maintains adequate records for the first three months of 1986 that indicate that 75 percent of the use of the automobile was in A's business. Invoices from subcontractors and paid bills indicate that A's business continued at approximately the same rate for the remainder of 1986. If other circumstances do not change (e.g., A does not obtain a second car for exclusive use in her business), the determination that the business/investment use of the automobile for the taxable year is 75 percent is based on sufficient corroborative evidence.

Example (2). The facts are the same as in example (1), except that A maintains adequate records during the first week of every month, which indicate that 75 percent of the use of the automobile is in A's business. The invoices from A's business indicate that A's business continued at the same rate during the subsequent weeks of each month so that A's weekly records are representative of each month's business use of the automobile. Thus, the determination that the business/investment use of the automobile for the taxable year is 75 percent is based on sufficient corroborative evidence.

Example (3). B, a sole proprietor and calendar year taxpayer, is a salesman in a large metropolitan area for a company that manufactures household products. For the first three weeks of each month, B uses his own automobile occasionally to travel within the metropolitan area on business. During these three weeks, B's use of the automobile for business purposes does not follow a consistent pattern from day to day or week to week. During the fourth week of each month, B delivers to his customers all the orders taken during the previous month. B's use of his automobile for business purposes, as substantiated by adequate records, is 70 percent of the total use during that fourth week. In this example, a determination based on the records maintained during that fourth week that the business/investment use of the automobile for the taxable year is 70 percent is not based on sufficient corroborative evidence because use during this week is not representative of use during other periods.

(iii) Special rules. See § 1.274–6T for special rules for substantiation by sufficient corroborating evidence with respect to certain listed property.

(4) Substantiation in exceptional circumstances. If a taxpayer establishes that, by reason of the inherent nature of the situation—

(i) He was unable to obtain evidence with respect to an element of the expenditure or use which conforms fully to the "adequate records" requirements of paragraph (c)(2) of this section,

(ii) He is unable to obtain evidence with respect to such element which conforms fully to the "other sufficient evidence" requirements of paragraph (c)(3) of this section, and

(iii) He has presented other evidence, with respect to such element, which possesses the highest degree of probative value possible under the circumstances, such other evidence shall be considered to satisfy the substantiation requirements of section 274(d) and this paragraph.

(5) Loss of records due to circumstances beyond control of the taxpayer. Where the taxpayer establishes that the failure to produce adequate records is due to the loss of such records through circumstances beyond the taxpayer's control, such as destruction by fire, flood, earthquake, or other casualty, the taxpayer shall have a right to substantiate a deduction by reasonable reconstruction of his expenditures or use.

(6) Special rules—(i) Separate expenditure or use—(A) In general. For the purposes of this section, each separate payment or use by the taxpayer shall ordinarily be considered to constitute a separate expenditure. However, concurrent or repetitious expenses or uses may be substantiated as a single item. To illustrate the above rules, where a taxpayer entertains a business guest at dinner and thereafter at the theater, the payment for dinner shall be considered to constitute one expenditure and the payment for the tickets for the theater shall be considered to constitute a separate expenditure. Similarly, if during a day of business travel a taxpayer makes separate payments for breakfast, lunch, and dinner, he shall be considered to have made three separate expenditures. However, if during entertainment at a cocktail lounge the taxpayer pays separately for each serving of refreshments, the total amount expended for the refreshments will be treated as a single expenditure. A tip may be treated as a separate expenditure.

(B) Aggregation of expenditures. Except as otherwise provided in this section, the account book, diary, log, statement of expense, trip sheet, or similar record required by paragraph (c)(2)(ii) of this section shall be maintained with respect to each separate expenditure and not with respect to aggregate amounts for two or more expenditures. Thus, each expenditure for such items as lodging and air or rail travel shall be recorded as a separate item and not aggregated. However, at the option of the taxpayer, amounts expended for breakfast, lunch, or dinner, may be aggregated. A tip or gratuity which is related to an underlying expense may be aggregated with such expense. In addition, amounts expended in connection with the use of listed property during a taxable year, such as for gasoline or repairs for an automobile, may be aggregated. If these expenses are aggregated, the taxpayer must establish the date and amount, but need not prove the business purpose of each expenditure. Instead, the taxpayer may prorate the expenses based on the total business use of the listed property. For other provisions permitting recording of aggregate amounts in an account book, diary, log, statement of expense, trip sheet, or similar record, see paragraphs (b)(2)(i) and (b)(3) of this section (relating to incidental costs of travel and entertainment).

(C) Aggregation of business use. Uses which may be considered part of a single use, for example, a round trip or uninterrupted business use, may be accounted for by a single record. For example, use of a truck to make deliveries at several different locations which begins and ends at the business premises and which may include a stop at the business premises in between two deliveries may be accounted for by a single record of miles driven. In addition, use of a passenger automobile by a salesman for a business trip away from home over a period of time may be accounted for by a single record of miles traveled. De minimis personal use (such as a stop for lunch on the way between two business stops) is not an interruption of business use.

(ii) Allocation of expenditure. For purposes of this section, if a taxpayer has established the amount of an expenditure, but is unable to establish the portion of such amount which is attributable to each person participating in the event giving rise to the expenditure, such amount shall ordinarily be allocated to each participant on a pro rata basis, if such determination is material. Accordingly, the total number of persons for whom a travel or entertainment expenditure is incurred must be established in order to compute the portion of the expenditure allocable to each such person.

(iii) Primary use of a facility. Section 274(a)(1)(B) and (2)(C) deny a deduction for any expenditure paid or incurred before January 1, 1979, with respect to a facility, or paid or incurred at any time with respect to a club, used in connection with an entertainment activity unless the taxpayer establishes that the facility (including a club) was used primarily for the furtherance of the taxpayer's trade or business. A determination whether a facility before January 1, 1979, or a club at any time, was used primarily for the furtherance of the taxpayer's trade or business will depend upon the facts and circumstances of each case. In order to establish that a facility was used primarily for the furtherance of his trade or business, the taxpayer shall maintain records of the use of the facility, the cost of using the facility, mileage or its equivalent (if appropriate), and such other information as shall tend to establish such primary use. Such records of use shall contain—

(A) For each use of the facility claimed to be in furtherance of the taxpayer's trade or business, the elements of an expenditure specified in paragraph (b)(3) of this section, and

(B) For each use of the facility not in furtherance of the taxpayer's trade or business, an appropriate description of such use, including cost, date, number of persons entertained, nature of entertainment and, if applicable, information such as mileage or its equivalent. A notation such as "personal use" or "family use" would, in the case of such use, be sufficient to describe the nature of entertainment.

If a taxpayer fails to maintain adequate records concerning a facility which is likely to serve the personal purposes of the taxpayer, it shall be presumed that the use of such facility was primarily personal.

(iv) Additional information. In a case where it is necessary to obtain additional information, either—

(A) To clarify information contained in records, statements, testimony, or documentary evidence submitted by a taxpayer under the provisions of paragraph (c)(2) or (c)(3) of this section, or

(B) To establish the reliability or accuracy of such records, statements, testimony, or documentary evidence,

the district director may, notwithstanding any other provision of this section, obtain such additional information by personal interview or otherwise as he determines necessary to implement properly the provisions of section 274 and the regulations thereunder.

(7) Specific exceptions. Except as otherwise prescribed by the Commissioner, substantiation otherwise required by this paragraph is not required for—

(i) Expenses described in section 274(e)(2) relating to food and beverages for employees, section 274(e)(3) relating to expenses treated as compensation, section 274(e)(8) relating to items available to the public, and section 274(e)(9) relating to entertainment sold to customers, and

(ii) Expenses described in section 274(e)(5) relating to recreational, etc., expenses for employees, except that a taxpayer shall keep such records or other evidence as shall establish that such expenses were for activities (or facilities used in connection therewith) primarily for the benefit of employees other than employees who are officers, shareholders or other owners (as defined in section 274(e)(5)), or highly compensated employees.

* * *

[T.D.7986, 49 FR 42704, Oct. 24, 1984, as amended by T.D 8009, 50 FR 7043, Feb. 20, 1985; T.D. 8061, 50 FR 46014, Nov. 6, 1985; T.D. 8063, 50 FR 52312, Dec. 23, 1985]

CORPORATE DISTRIBUTIONS AND ADJUSTMENTS

Distributions by Corporations

Effects on Recipients

§ 1.301–1 Rules applicable with respect to distributions of money and other property.

(a) General. Section 301 provides the general rule for treatment of distributions on or after June 22, 1954, of property by a corporation to a shareholder with respect to its stock. The term "property" is defined in section 317(a). Such distributions, except as otherwise provided in this chapter, shall be treated as provided in section 301(c). Under section 301(c), distributions may be included in gross income, applied against and reduce the adjusted basis of the stock, treated as gain from the sale or exchange of property, or (in the case of certain distributions out of increase in value accrued before March 1, 1913) may be exempt from tax. The amount of the distributions to which section 301 applies is determined in accordance with the provisions of section 301(b). The basis of property received in a distribution to which section 301 applies is determined in accordance with the provisions of section 301(d). Accordingly, except as otherwise provided in this chapter, a distribution on or after June 22, 1954, of property by a corporation to a shareholder with respect to its stock shall be included in gross income to the extent the amount distributed is considered a dividend under section 316. For examples of distributions treated otherwise, see sections 116, 301(c)(2), 301(c)(3)(B), 301(e), 302(b), 303, and 305. See also part II (relating to distributions in partial or complete liquidation), part III (relating to corporate organizations and reorganizations), and part IV (relating to insolvency reorganizations), subchapter C, chapter 1 of the Code.

(b) Time of inclusion in gross income and of determination of fair market value. A distribution made by a corporation to its shareholders shall be included in the gross income of the distributees when the cash or other property is unqualifiedly made subject to their demands. However, if such distribution is a distribution other than in cash, the fair market value of the property shall be determined as of the date of distribution without regard to whether such date is the same as that on which the distribution is includible in gross income. For example, if a corporation distributes a taxable dividend in property (the adjusted basis of

which exceeds its fair market value on December 31, 1955) on December 31, 1955, which is received by, or unqualifiedly made subject to the demand of, its shareholders on January 2, 1956, the amount to be included in the gross income of the shareholders will be the fair market value of such property on December 31, 1955, although such amount will not be includible in the gross income of the shareholders until January 2, 1956.

(c) Application of section to shareholders. Section 301 is not applicable to an amount paid by a corporation to a shareholder unless the amount is paid to the shareholder in his capacity as such.

(d) Distributions to corporate shareholders. (1) If the shareholder is a corporation, the amount of any distribution to be taken into account under section 301(c) shall be:

(i) The amount of money distributed,

(ii) An amount equal to the fair market value of any property distributed which consists of any obligations of the distributing corporation, stock of the distributing corporation treated as property under section 305(b), or rights to acquire such stock treated as property under section 305(b), plus

(iii) In the case of a distribution not described in subdivision (iv) of this subparagraph, an amount equal to (a) the fair market value of any other property distributed or, if lesser, (b) the adjusted basis of such other property in the hands of the distributing corporation (determined immediately before the distribution and increased for any gain recognized to the distributing corporation under section 311(b), (c), or (d), or under section 341(f), 617(d), 1245(a), 1250(a), 1251(c), or 1252(a)), or

(iv) In the case of a distribution made after November 8, 1971, to a shareholder which is a foreign corporation, an amount equal to the fair market value of any other property distributed, but only if the distribution received by such shareholder is not effectively connected for the taxable year with the conduct of a trade or business in the United States by such shareholder.

(2) In the case of a distribution the amount of which is determined by reference to the adjusted

basis described in subparagraph (1)(iii)(b) of this paragraph:

(i) That portion of the distribution which is a dividend under section 301(c)(1) may not exceed such adjusted basis, or

(ii) If the distribution is not out of earnings and profits, the amount of the reduction in basis of the shareholder's stock, and the amount of any gain resulting from such distribution, are to be determined by reference to such adjusted basis of the property which is distributed.

* * *

(e) Adjusted basis. In determining the adjusted basis of property distributed in the hands of the distributing corporation immediately before the distribution for purposes of section 301(b)(1)(B)(ii), (b)(1)(C)(i), and (d)(2)(B), the basis to be used shall be the basis for determining gain upon a sale or exchange.

(f) Examples. The application of this section (except paragraph (n)) may be illustrated by the following examples:

Example (1). On January 1, 1955, A, an individual owned all of the stock of Corporation M with an adjusted basis of $2,000. During 1955, A received distributions from Corporation M totaling $30,000, consisting of $10,-000 in cash and listed securities having a basis in the hands of Corporation M and a fair market value on the date distributed of $20,000. Corporation M's taxable year is the calendar year. As of December 31, 1954, Corporation M had earnings and profits accumulated after February 28, 1913, in the amount of $26,000, and it had no earnings and profits and no deficit for 1955. Of the $30,000 received by A, $26,000 will be treated as an ordinary dividend; the remaining $4,000 will be applied against the adjusted basis of his stock; the $2,000 in excess of the adjusted basis of his stock will either be treated as gain from the sale or exchange of property (under section 301(c)(3)(A)) or, if out of increase in value accrued before March 1, 1913, will (under section 301(c)(3)(B)) be exempt from tax. If A subsequently sells his stock in Corporation M, the basis for determining gain or loss on the sale will be zero.

Example (2). The facts are the same as in Example 1 with the exceptions that the shareholder of Corporation M is Corporation W and that the securities which were distributed had an adjusted basis to Corporation M of $15,000. The distribution received by Corporation W totals $25,000 consisting of $10,000 in cash and securities with an adjusted basis of $15,000. The total $25,000 will be treated as a dividend to Corporation W since the earnings and profits of Corporation M ($26,000) are in excess of the amount of the distribution.

Example (3). Corporation X owns timber land which it acquired prior to March 1, 1913, at a cost of $50,000 with $5,000 allocated as the separate cost of the land. On March 1, 1913, this property had a fair market value

of $150,000 of which $135,000 was attributable to the timber and $15,000 to the land. All of the timber was cut prior to 1955 and the full appreciation in the value thereof, $90,000 ($135,000–$45,000), realized through depletion allowances based on March 1, 1913, value. None of this surplus from realized appreciation had been distributed. In 1955, Corporation X sold the land for $20,-000 thereby realizing a gain of $15,000. Of this gain, $10,000 is due to realized appreciation in value which accrued before March 1, 1913 ($15,000–$5,000). Of the gain of $15,000, $5,000 is taxable. Therefore, at December 31, 1955, Corporation X had a surplus from realized appreciation in the amount of $100,000. It had no accumulated earnings and profits and no deficit at January 1, 1955. The net earnings for 1955 (including the $5,000 gain on the sale of the land) were $20,000. During 1955, Corporation X distributed $75,000 to its stockholders. Of this amount, $20,000 will be treated as a dividend. The remaining $55,000, which is a distribution of realized appreciation, will be applied against and reduce the adjusted basis of the shareholders' stock. If any part of the $55,000 is in excess of the adjusted basis of a shareholder's stock, such part will be exempt from tax.

(g) Reduction for liabilities. For the purpose of section 301(a), the amount of any distribution shall be reduced by—

(1) The amount of any liability of the corporation assumed by the shareholder in connection with the distribution, and

(2) The amount of any liability to which the property received by the shareholder is subject immediately before and immediately after the distribution.

Such reduction, however, shall not cause the amount of the distribution to be reduced below zero.

(h) Basis. The basis of property received in the distribution to which section 301 applies shall be—

(1) If the shareholder is not a corporation, the fair market value of such property;

(2) If the shareholder is a corporation—

(i) In the case of a distribution of the obligations of the distributing corporation or of the stock of such corporation or rights to acquire such stock (if such stock or rights are treated as property under section 305(b)), the fair market value of such obligations, stock, or rights;

(ii) In the case of the distribution of any other property, except as provided in subdivision (iii) (relating to certain distributions by a foreign corporation) or subdivision (iv) (relating to certain distributions to foreign corporate distributees) of this subparagraph, whichever of the following is the lesser—

(a) The fair market value of such property; or

(b) The adjusted basis (in the hands of the distributing corporation immediately before the distribution) of such property increased in the amount of gain to the distributing corporation which is recognized under section 311(b) (relating to distributions of LIFO inventory), section 311(c) (relating to distributions of property subject to liabilities in excess of basis), section 311(d) (relating to appreciated property used to redeem stock), section 341(f) (relating to certain sales of stock of consenting corporations), section 617(d) (relating to gain from dispositions of certain mining property), section 1245(a) or 1250(a) (relating to gain from dispositions of certain depreciable property), section 1251(c) (relating to gain from disposition of farm recapture property), or section 1252(a) (relating to gain from disposition of farm land);

(iii) In the case of the distribution by a foreign corporation of any other property after December 31, 1962, in a distribution not described in subdivision (iv) of this subparagraph, the amount determined under paragraph (n) of this section;

* * *

(i) [Reserved]

(j) **Transfers for less than fair market value.** If property is transferred by a corporation to a shareholder which is not a corporation for an amount less than its fair market value in a sale or exchange, such shareholder shall be treated as having received a distribution to which section 301 applies. In such case, the amount of the distribution shall be the difference between the amount paid for the property and its fair market value. If property is transferred in a sale or exchange by a corporation to a shareholder which is a corporation, for an amount less than its fair market value and also less than its adjusted basis, such shareholder shall be treated as having received a distribution to which section 301 applies, and—

(1) Where the fair market value of the property equals or exceeds its adjusted basis in the hands of the distributing corporation the amount of the distribution shall be the excess of the adjusted basis (increased by the amount of gain recognized under section 311(b), (c), or (d), or under section 341(f), 617(d), 1245(a), 1250(a), 1251(c), or 1252(a) to the distributing corporation) over the amount paid for the property;

(2) Where the fair market value of the property is less than its adjusted basis in the hands of the

distributing corporation, the amount of the distribution shall be the excess of such fair market value over the amount paid for the property. If property is transferred in a sale or exchange after December 31, 1962, by a foreign corporation to a shareholder which is a corporation for an amount less than the amount which would have been computed under paragraph (n) of this section if such property had been received in a distribution to which section 301 applied, such shareholder shall be treated as having received a distribution to which section 301 applies, and the amount of the distribution shall be the excess of the amount which would have been computed under paragraph (n) of this section with respect to such property over the amount paid for the property. In all cases, the earnings and profits of the distributing corporation shall be decreased by the excess of the basis of the property in the hands of the distributing corporation over the amount received therefor. In computing gain or loss from the subsequent sale of such property, its basis shall be the amount paid for the property increased by the amount of the distribution.

If property is transferred in a sale or exchange after December 31, 1962, by a foreign corporation to a shareholder which is a corporation for an amount less than the amount which would have been computed under paragraph (n) of this section if such property had been received in a distribution to which section 301 applied, such shareholder shall be treated as having received a distribution to which section 301 applies, and the amount of the distribution shall be the excess of the amount which would have been computed under paragraph (n) of this section with respect to such property over the amount paid for the property. Notwithstanding the preceding provisions of this paragraph, if property is transferred in a sale or exchange after November 8, 1971, by a corporation to a shareholder which is a foreign corporation, for an amount less than its fair market value, and if paragraph (d)(1)(iv) of this section would apply if such property were received in a distribution to which section 301 applies, such shareholder shall be treated as having received a distribution to which section 301 applies and the amount of the distribution shall be the difference between the amount paid for the property and its fair market value. In all cases, the earnings and profits of the distributing corporation shall be decreased by the excess of the basis of the property in the hands of the distributing corporation over the amount received therefor. In computing gain or loss from the subsequent sale of such property, its basis shall be the amount paid for the property increased by the amount of the distribution.

(k) Application of rule respecting transfers for less than fair market value. The application of paragraph (j) of this section may be illustrated by the following examples:

Example (1). On January 1, 1955, A, an individual shareholder of corporation X, purchased property from that corporation for $20. The fair market value of such property was $100, and its basis in the hands of corporation X was $25. The amount of the distribution determined under section 301(b) is $80. If A were a corporation, the amount of the distribution would be $5 (assuming that sections 311(b) and (c), 1245(a), and 1250(a) do not apply), the excess of the basis of the property in the hands of corporation X over the amount received therefor. The basis of such property to corporation A would be $25. If the basis of the property in the hands of corporation X were $10, the corporate shareholder, A, would not receive a distribution. The basis of such property to corporation A would be $20. Whether or not A is a corporation, the excess of the amount paid over the basis of the property in the hands of corporation X ($20 over $10) would be a taxable gain to corporation X.

Example (2). On January 1, 1963, corporation A, which is a shareholder of corporation B (a foreign corporation engaged in business within the United States), purchased one share of corporation X stock from B for $20. The fair market value of the share was $100, and its adjusted basis in the hands of B was $25. Assume that if the share of corporation X stock had been received by A in a distribution to which section 301 applied, the amount of the distribution under paragraph (n) of this section would have been $55. The amount of the distribution under section 301 is $35, i.e., $55 (amount computed under paragraph (n) of this section) minus $20 (amount paid for the property). The basis of such property to A is $55.

(*l*) Transactions treated as distributions. A distribution to shareholders with respect to their stock is within the terms of section 301 although it takes place at the same time as another transaction if the distribution is in substance a separate transaction whether or not connected in a formal sense. This is most likely to occur in the case of a recapitalization, a reincorporation, or a merger of a corporation with a newly organized corporation having substantially no property. For example, if a corporation having only common stock outstanding, exchanges one share of newly issued common stock and one bond in the principal amount of $10 for each share of outstanding common stock, the distribution of the bonds will be a distribution of property (to the extent of their fair market value) to which section 301 applies, even though the exchange of common stock for common stock may be pursuant to a plan of reorganization under the terms of section 368(a)(1)(E) (recapitalization) and even though the exchange of common stock for common stock may be tax free by virtue of section 354.

(m) Cancellation of indebtedness. The cancellation of indebtedness of a shareholder by a corporation shall be treated as a distribution of property.

* * *

[T.D. 6500, 25 FR 11607, Nov. 26, 1960, as amended by T.D. 6752, 29 FR 12701, Sept. 9, 1964; T.D. 7084, 36 FR 267, Jan. 8, 1971; T.D. 7209, 37 FR 20800, Oct. 5, 1972; T.D. 7238, 38 FR 20824, Aug. 3, 1973; T.D. 7293, 38 FR 32794, Nov. 28, 1973; T.D. 7556, 44 FR 1376, Jan. 5, 1979]

§ 1.302-1 General.

(a) Under section 302(d), unless otherwise provided in subchapter C, chapter 1 of the Code, a distribution in redemption of stock shall be treated as a distribution of property to which section 301 applies if the distribution is not within any of the provisions of section 302(b). A distribution in redemption of stock shall be considered a distribution in part or full payment in exchange for the stock under section 302(a) provided paragraph (1), (2), (3), or (4) of section 302(b) applies. Section 318(a) (relating to constructive ownership of stock) applies to all redemptions under section 302 except that in the termination of a shareholder's interest certain limitations are placed on the application of section 318(a)(1) by section 302(c)(2). The term "redemption of stock" is defined in section 317(b). * * *

* * *

[T.D. 6500, 25 FR 11402, Nov. 26, 1960]

§ 1.302-2 Redemptions not taxable as dividends.

(a) The fact that a redemption fails to meet the requirements of paragraph (2), (3) or (4) of section 302(b) shall not be taken into account in determining whether the redemption is not essentially equivalent to a dividend under section 302(b)(1). See, however, paragraph (b) of this section. For example, if a shareholder owns only nonvoting stock of a corporation which is not section 306 stock and which is limited and preferred as to dividends and in liquidation, and one-half of such stock is redeemed, the distribution will ordinarily meet the requirements of paragraph (1) of section 302(b) but will not meet the requirements of paragraph (2), (3) or (4) of such section. The determination of whether or not a distribution is within the phrase "essentially equivalent to a dividend" (that is, having the same effect as a distribution without any redemption of stock) shall be made without regard to the earnings and profits of the corporation at the time of the distribution. For example, if A owns all the stock of a corporation and the corporation redeems part of his stock at a time when it has no earnings and profits, the distribution shall be treated as a distribution under section 301 pursuant to section 302(d).

(b) The question whether a distribution in redemption of stock of a shareholder is not essentially equivalent to a dividend under section 302(b)(1) depends upon the facts and circumstances of each case. One of the facts to be considered in making this determination is the constructive stock ownership of such shareholder under section 318(a). All distributions in pro rata redemptions of a part of the stock of a corporation generally will be treated as distributions under section 301 if the corporation has only one class of stock outstanding. * * * The redemption of all of one class of stock (except section 306 stock) either at one time or in a series of redemptions generally will be considered as a distribution under section 301 if all classes of stock outstanding at the time of the redemption are held in the same proportion. Distribution in redemption of stock may be treated as distributions under section 301 regardless of the provisions of the stock certificate and regardless of whether all stock being redeemed was acquired by the stockholders from whom the stock was redeemed by purchase or otherwise. In every case in which a shareholder transfers stock to the corporation which issued such stock in exchange for property, the facts and circumstances shall be reported on his return except as provided in paragraph (d) of § 1.331–1. See sections 346(a) and 6043 for requirements relating to returns by corporations.

(c) In any case in which an amount received in redemption of stock is treated as a distribution of a dividend, proper adjustment of the basis of the remaining stock will be made with respect to the stock redeemed. The following examples illustrate the application of this rule:

Example (1). A, an individual, purchased all of the stock of Corporation X for $100,000. In 1955 the corporation redeems half of the stock for $150,000, and it is determined that this amount constitutes a dividend. The remaining stock of Corporation X held by A has a basis of $100,000.

Example (2). H and W, husband and wife, each own half of the stock of Corporation X. All of the stock was purchased by H for $100,000 cash. In 1950 H gave one-half of the stock to W, the stock transferred having a value in excess of $50,000. In 1955 all of the stock of H is redeemed for $150,000, and it is determined that the distribution to H in redemption of his shares constitutes the distribution of a dividend. Immediately after the transaction, W holds the remaining stock of Corporation X with a basis of $100,000.

Example (3). The facts are the same as in Example (2) with the additional facts that the outstanding stock of Corporation X consists of 1,000 shares and all but 10 shares of the stock of H is redeemed. Immediately after the transaction, H holds 10 shares of the stock of Corporation X with a basis of $50,000, and W holds 500 shares with a basis of $50,000.

[T.D. 6500, 25 FR 11607, Nov. 26, 1960]

§ 1.302–3 Substantially disproportionate redemption.

(a) Section 302(b)(2) provides for the treatment of an amount received in redemption of stock as an amount received in exchange for such stock if—

(1) Immediately after the redemption the shareholder owns less than 50 percent of the total combined voting power of all classes of stock as provided in section 302(b)(2)(B),

(2) The redemption is a substantially disproportionate redemption within the meaning of section 302(b)(2)(C), and

(3) The redemption is not pursuant to a plan described in section 302(b)(2)(D).

Section 318(a) (relating to constructive ownership of stock) shall apply both in making the disproportionate redemption test and in determining the percentage of stock ownership after the redemption. The requirements under section 302(b)(2) shall be applied to each shareholder separately and shall be applied only with respect to stock which is issued and outstanding in the hands of the shareholders. Section 302(b)(2) only applies to a redemption of voting stock or to a redemption of both voting stock and other stock. Section 302(b)(2) does not apply to the redemption solely of nonvoting stock (common or preferred). However, if a redemption is treated as an exchange to a particular shareholder under the terms of section 302(b)(2), such section will apply to the simultaneous redemption of nonvoting preferred stock (which is not section 306 stock) owned by such shareholder and such redemption will also be treated as an exchange. Generally, for purposes of this section, stock which does not have voting rights until the happening of an event, such as a default in the payment of dividends on preferred stock, is not voting stock until the happening of the specified event. Subsection 302(b)(2)(D) provides that a redemption will not be treated as substantially disproportionate if made pursuant to a plan the purpose or effect of which is a series of redemptions which result in the aggregate in a distribution which is not substantially disproportionate. Whether or not such a plan exists will be determined from all the facts and circumstances.

(b) The application of paragraph (a) of this section is illustrated by the following example:

Example. Corporation M has outstanding 400 shares of common stock of which A, B, C and D each own 100 shares or 25 percent. No stock is considered constructively owned by A, B, C or D under section 318. Corporation M redeems 55 shares from A, 25 shares from B, and 20 shares from C. For the redemption to be disproportionate as to any shareholder, such shareholder must own after the redemptions less than 20 percent (80 percent of 25 percent) of the 300 shares of stock then outstanding. After the redemptions, A owns 45 shares (15 percent), B owns 75 shares (25 percent), and C owns 80 shares (26⅔ percent). The distribution is disproportionate only with respect to A.

[T.D. 6500, 25 FR 11607, Nov. 26, 1960]

§ 1.302–4 Termination of shareholder's interest.

Section 302(b)(3) provides that a distribution in redemption of all of the stock of the corporation owned by a shareholder shall be treated as a distribution in part or full payment in exchange for the stock of such shareholder. In determining whether all of the stock of the shareholder has been redeemed, the general rule of section 302(c)(1) requires that the rules of constructive ownership provided in section 318(a) shall apply. Section 302(c)(2), however, provides that section 318(a)(1) (relating to constructive ownership of stock owned by members of a family) shall not apply where the specific requirements of section 302(c)(2) are met. The following rules shall be applicable in determining whether the specific requirements of section 302(c)(2) are met:

(a)(1) The agreement specified in section 302(c)(2)(A)(iii) shall be in the form of a separate statement in duplicate signed by the distributee and attached to the first return filed by the distributee for the taxable year in which the distribution described in section 302(b)(3) occurs. The agreement shall recite that the distributee has not acquired, other than by bequest or inheritance, any interest in the corporation (as described in section 302(c)(2)(A)(i)) since the distribution and that the distributee agrees to notify the district director for the internal revenue district in which the distributee resides of any acquisition, other than by bequest or inheritance, of such an interest in the corporation within 30 days after the acquisition, if the acquisition occurs within 10 years from the date of the distribution.

(2) If the distributee fails to file the agreement specified in section 302(c)(2)(A)(iii) at the time provided in paragraph (a)(1) of this section, then the district director for the internal revenue district in which the distributee resided at the time of filing the first return for the taxable year in which the distribution occurred shall grant a reasonable extension of time for filing such agreement, provided (i) it is established to the satisfaction of the district director that there was reasonable cause for failure to file the agreement within the prescribed time and (ii) a request for such extension is filed within such time as the district director considers reasonable under the circumstances.

(b) The distributee who files an agreement under section 302(c)(2)(A)(iii) shall retain copies of income tax returns and any other records indicating fully the amount of tax which would have been payable had the redemption been treated as a distribution subject to section 301.

(c) If stock of a parent corporation is redeemed, section 302(c)(2)(A), relating to acquisition of an interest in the corporation within 10 years after termination shall be applied with reference to an interest both in the parent corporation and any subsidiary of such parent corporation. If stock of a parent corporation is sold to a subsidiary in a transaction described in section 304, section 302(c)(2)(A) shall be applicable to the acquisition of an interest in such subsidiary corporation or in the parent corporation. If stock of a subsidiary corporation is redeemed, section 302(c)(2)(A) shall be applied with reference to an interest both in such subsidiary corporation and its parent. Section 302(c)(2)(A) shall also be applied with respect to an interest in a corporation which is a successor corporation to the corporation the interest in which has been terminated.

(d) For the purpose of section 302(c)(2)(A)(i), a person will be considered to be a creditor only if the rights of such person with respect to the corporation are not greater or broader in scope than necessary for the enforcement of his claim. Such claim must not in any sense be proprietary and must not be subordinate to the claims of general creditors. An obligation in the form of a debt may thus constitute a proprietary interest. For example, if under the terms of the instrument the corporation may discharge the principal amount of its obligation to a person by payments, the amount or certainty of which are dependent upon the earnings of the corporation, such a person is not a creditor of the corporation. Furthermore, if under the terms of the instrument the rate of purported interest is dependent upon earnings, the holder of such instrument may not, in some cases, be a creditor.

(e) In the case of a distributee to whom section 302(b)(3) is applicable, who is a creditor after such transaction, the acquisition of the assets of the corporation in the enforcement of the rights of such creditor shall not be considered an acquisition of an interest in the corporation for purposes of section 302(c)(2) unless stock of the corporation, its parent corporation, or, in the case of a redemption of stock of a parent corporation, of a subsidiary of such corporation is acquired.

(f) In determining whether an entire interest in the corporation has been terminated under section 302(b)(3), under all circumstances paragraphs (2), (3), (4), and (5) of section 318(a) (relating to constructive ownership of stock) shall be applicable.

(g) Section 302(c)(2)(B) provides that section 302(c)(2)(A) shall not apply—

(1) If any portion of the stock redeemed was acquired directly or indirectly within the 10-year period ending on the date of the distribution by the distributee from a person, the ownership of whose stock would (at the time of distribution) be attributable to the distributee under section 318(a), or

(2) If any person owns (at the time of the distribution) stock, the ownership of which is attributable to the distributee under section 318(a), such person acquired any stock in the corporation directly or indirectly from the distributee within the 10-year period ending on the date of the distribution, and such stock so acquired from the distributee is not redeemed in the same transaction, unless the acquisition (described in subparagraph (1) of this paragraph) or the disposition by the distributee (described in subparagraph (2) of this paragraph) did not have as one of its principal purposes the avoidance of Federal income tax. A transfer of stock by the transferor, within the 10-year period ending on the date of the distribution, to a person whose stock would be attributable to the transferor shall not be deemed to have as one of its principal purposes the avoidance of Federal income tax merely because the transferee is in a lower income tax bracket than the transferor.

[T.D. 6500, 25 FR 11607, Nov. 26, 1960, as amended by T.D. 6969, 33 FR 11997, Aug. 23, 1968; T.D. 7535, 43 FR 10686, March 15, 1978]

§ 1.303–1   General.

Section 303 provides that in certain cases a distribution in redemption of stock, the value of which is included in determining the value of the gross estate of a decedent, shall be treated as a distribution in full payment in exchange for the stock so redeemed.

[T.D. 6500, 25 FR 11607, Nov. 26, 1960]

§ 1.303–2   Requirements.

(a) Section 303 applies only where the distribution is with respect to stock of a corporation the value of whose stock in the gross estate of the decedent for Federal estate tax purposes is an amount in excess of (1) 35 percent of the value of the gross estate of such decedent, or (2) 50 percent of the taxable estate of such decedent. For the purposes of such 35 percent and 50 percent requirements, stock of two or more corporations shall be treated as the stock of a single corporation if more than 75 percent in value of the outstanding stock of each such corporation is included in determining the value of the decedent's gross estate. For the purpose of the 75 percent requirement, stock which, at the decedent's death, represents the surviving spouse's interest in community property shall be considered as having been included in determining the value of the decedent's gross estate.

(b) For the purpose of section 303(b)(2)(A)(i), the term "gross estate" means the gross estate as computed in accordance with section 2031 (or, in the case of the estate of a decedent nonresident not a citizen of the United States, in accordance with section 2103). For the purpose of section 303(b)(2)(A)(ii), the term "taxable estate" means the taxable estate as computed in accordance with section 2051 (or, in the case of the estate of a decedent nonresident not a citizen of the United States, in accordance with section 2106). In case the value of an estate is determined for Federal estate tax purposes under section 2032 (relating to alternate valuation), then, for purposes of section

303(b)(2), the value of the gross estate, the taxable estate, and the stock shall each be determined on the applicable date prescribed in section 2032.

(c)(1) In determining whether the estate of the decedent is comprised of stock of a corporation of sufficient value to satisfy the percentage requirements of section 303(b)(2)(A) and section 303(b)(2)(B), the total value, in the aggregate, of all classes of stock of the corporation includible in determining the value of the gross estate is taken into account. A distribution under section 303(a) may be in redemption of the stock of the corporation includible in determining the value of the gross estate, without regard to the class of such stock.

(2) The above may be illustrated by the following example:

Example. The gross estate of the decedent has a value of $1,000,000, the taxable estate is $700,000, and the sum of the death taxes and funeral and administration expenses is $275,000. Included in determining the gross estate of the decedent is stock of three corporations which, for Federal estate tax purposes, is valued as follows:

Corporation A:
Common stock $100,000
Preferred stock 100,000
Corporation B:
Common stock 50,000
Preferred stock 350,000
Corporation C: Common stock 200,000

The stock of Corporation A and Corporation C included in the estate of the decedent constitutes all of the outstanding stock of both corporations. The stock of Corporation A and the stock of Corporation C, treated as the stock of a single corporation under section 303(b)(2)(B), has a value in excess of $350,000 (35 percent of the gross estate or 50 percent of the taxable estate). Likewise, the stock of Corporation B has a value in excess of $350,000. The distribution by one or more of the above corporations, within the period prescribed in section 303(b)(1), of amounts not exceeding, in the aggregate, $275,000, in redemption of preferred stock or common stock of such corporation or corporations, will be treated as in full payment in exchange for the stock so redeemed.

(d) If stock includible in determining the value of the gross estate of a decedent is exchanged for new stock, the basis of which is determined by reference to the basis of the old stock, the redemption of the new stock will be treated the same under section 303 as the redemption of the old stock would have been. Thus section 303 shall apply with respect to a distribution in redemption of stock received by the estate of a decedent (1) in connection with a reorganization under section 368, (2) in a distribution or exchange under section 355 (or so much of section 356 as relates to section

355), (3) in an exchange under section 1036 or (4) in a distribution to which section 305(a) applies. Similarly, a distribution in redemption of stock will qualify under section 303, notwithstanding the fact that the stock redeemed is section 306 stock to the extent that the conditions of section 303 are met.

(e) Section 303 applies to distributions made after the death of the decedent and (1) before the expiration of the 3-year period of limitations for the assessment of estate tax provided in section 6501(a) (determined without the application of any provisions of law extending or suspending the running of such period of limitations), or within 90 days after the expiration of such period, or (2) if a petition for redetermination of a deficiency in such estate tax has been filed with the Tax Court within the time prescribed in section 6213, at any time before the expiration of 60 days after the decision of the Tax Court becomes final. The extension of the period of distribution provided in section 303(b)(1)(B) has reference solely to bona fide contests in the Tax Court and will not apply in the case of a petition for redetermination of a deficiency which is initiated solely for the purpose of extending the period within which section 303 would otherwise be applicable.

(f) While section 303 will most frequently have application in the case where stock is redeemed from the executor or administrator of an estate, the section is also applicable to distributions in redemption of stock included in the decedent's gross estate and held at the time of the redemption by any person who acquired the stock by any of the means comprehended by part III, subchapter A, chapter 11 of the Code, including the heir, legatee, or donee of the decedent, a surviving joint tenant, surviving spouse, appointee, or taker in default of appointment, or a trustee of a trust created by the decedent. Thus section 303 may apply with respect to a distribution in redemption of stock from a donee to whom the decedent has transferred stock in contemplation of death where the value of such stock is included in the decedent's gross estate under section 2035. Similarly, section 303 may apply to the redemption of stock from a beneficiary of the estate to whom an executor has distributed the stock pursuant to the terms of the will of the decedent. However, section 303 is not applicable to the case where stock is redeemed from a stockholder who has acquired the stock by gift or purchase from any person to whom such stock has passed from the decedent. Nor is section 303 applicable to the case where stock is redeemed from a stockholder who has acquired the stock from the executor in satisfaction of a specific monetary bequest.

(g)(1) The total amount of the distributions to which section 303 may apply with respect to redemptions of stock included in the gross estate of a decedent may not exceed the sum of the estate, inheritance, legacy, and succession taxes (including any interest collected as a part of such taxes) imposed because of the decedent's death and the amount of funeral and administration expenses allowable as deductions to the estate. Where there is more than one distribution in redemption of stock described in section 303(b)(2) during the period of time prescribed in section 303(b)(1), the distributions shall be applied against the total amount which qualifies for treatment under section 303 in the order in which the distributions are made. For this purpose, all distributions in redemption of such stock shall be taken into account, including distributions which under another provision of the Code are treated as in part or full payment in exchange for the stock redeemed.

(2) Subparagraph (1) of this paragraph may be illustrated by the following example:

Example. (i) The gross estate of the decedent has a value of $800,000, the taxable estate is $500,000, and the sum of the death taxes and funeral and administrative expenses is $225,000. Included in determining the gross estate of the decedent is the stock of a corporation which for Federal estate tax purposes is valued at $450,000. During the first year of administration, one-third of such stock is distributed to a legatee and shortly thereafter this stock is redeemed by the corporation for $150,000. During the second year of administration, another one-third of such stock includible in the estate is redeemed for $150,000.

(ii) The first distribution of $150,000 is applied against the $225,000 amount that qualifies for treatment under section 303, regardless of whether the first distribution was treated as in payment in exchange for stock under section 302(a). Thus, only $75,000 of the second distribution may be treated as in full payment in exchange for stock under section 303. The tax treatment of the remaining $75,000 would be determined under other provisions of the Code.

(h) For the purpose of section 303, the estate tax or any other estate, inheritance, legacy, or succession tax shall be ascertained after the allowance of any credit, relief, discount, refund, remission or reduction of tax.

[T.D. 6500, 25 FR 11607, Nov. 26, 1969, as amended by T.D. 6724, 29 FR 5343, April 21, 1964; T.D. 7346, 40 FR 10669, March 7, 1975]

§ 1.303–3 Application of other sections.

(a) The sole effect of section 303 is to exempt from tax as a dividend a distribution to which such section is applicable when made in redemption of stock includible in a decedent's gross estate. Such section does not, however, in any other manner affect the principles set forth in sections 302 and 306. Thus, if stock of a corporation is owned equally by A, B, and the C Estate, and the corporation redeems one-half of the stock of each shareholder, the determination of whether the distributions to A and B are essentially equivalent to dividends shall be made without regard to the effect which section 303 may have upon the taxability of the distribution to the C Estate.

(b) See section 304 relative to redemption of stock through the use of related corporations.

[T.D. 6500, 25 FR 11607, Nov. 26, 1960]

§ 1.304–2 Acquisition by related corporation (other than subsidiary).

(a) If a corporation, in return for property, acquires stock of another corporation from one or more persons, and the person or persons from whom the stock was acquired were in control of both such corporations before the acquisition, then such property shall be treated as received in redemption of stock of the acquiring corporation. The stock received by the acquiring corporation shall be treated as a contribution to the capital of such corporation. See section 362(a) for determination of the basis of such stock. The transferor's basis for his stock in the acquiring corporation shall be increased by the basis of the stock surrendered by him. (But see below in this paragraph for subsequent reductions of basis in certain cases.) As to each person transferring stock, the amount received shall be treated as a distribution of property under section 302(d), unless as to such person such amount is to be treated as received in exchange for the stock under the terms of section 302(a) or section 303. In applying section 302(b), reference shall be had to the shareholder's ownership of stock in the issuing corporation and not to his ownership of stock in the acquiring corporation (except for purposes of applying section 318(a)). In determining control and applying section 302(b), section 318(a) (relating to the constructive ownership of stock) shall be applied without regard to the 50-percent limitation contained in section 318(a)(2)(C) and (3)(C). A series of redemptions referred to in section 302(b)(2)(D) shall include acquisitions by either of the corporations of stock of the other and stock redemptions by both corporations. If section 302(d) applies to the surrender of stock by a shareholder, his basis for his stock in the acquiring corporation after the transaction (increased as stated above in this paragraph) shall not be decreased except as provided in section 301. If section 302(d) does not apply, the property received shall be treated as received in a distribution in payment in exchange for stock of the acquiring corporation under section 302(a), which stock has a basis equal to the amount by which the shareholder's basis for his stock in the acquiring corporation was increased on account of the contribution to capital as provided for above in this paragraph. Accordingly, such amount shall be applied in reduction of the shareholder's basis for his stock in the acquiring corporation. Thus, the basis of each share of the shareholder's stock in the acquiring corporation will be the same as the basis of such share before the entire transaction. The holding period of the stock which is considered to have been redeemed shall be the same as the holding period of the stock actually surrendered.

(b) In any case in which two or more persons, in the aggregate, control two corporations, section 304(a)(1) will apply to sales by such persons of stock in either corporation to the other (whether or not made simultaneously) provided the sales by each of such persons are related to each other. The determination of whether the sales are related to each other shall be dependent upon the facts and circumstances surrounding all of the sales. For this purpose, the fact that the sales may occur during a period of one or more years (such as in the case of a series of sales by persons who together control each of such corporations immediately prior to the first of such sales and immediately subsequent to the last of such sales) shall be disregarded, provided the other facts and circumstances indicate related transactions.

(c) The application of section 304(a)(1) may be illustrated by the following examples:

Example (1). Corporation X and corporation Y each have outstanding 200 shares of common stock. One-half of the stock of each corporation is owned by an individual, A, and one-half by another individual, B, who is unrelated to A. On or after August 31, 1964, A sells 30 shares of corporation X stock to corporation Y for $50,-000, such stock having an adjusted basis of $10,000 to A. After the sale, A is considered as owning corporation X stock as follows: (i) 70 shares directly, and (ii) 15 shares constructively, since by virtue of his 50-percent ownership of Y he constructively owns 50 percent of the 30

shares owned directly by Y. Since A's percentage of ownership of X's voting stock after the sale (85 out of 200 shares, or 42.5%) is not less than 80 percent of his percentage of ownership of X's voting stock before the sale (100 out of 200 shares, or 50%), the transfer is not "substantially disproportionate" as to him as provided in section 302(b)(2). Under these facts, and assuming that section 302(b)(1) is not applicable, the entire $50,000 is treated as a dividend to A to the extent of the earnings and profits of corporation Y. The basis of the corporation X stock to corporation Y is $10,000, its adjusted basis to A. The amount of $10,000 is added to the basis of the stock of corporation Y in the hands of A.

* * *

Example (3). Corporation X and corporation Y each have outstanding 100 shares of common stock. A, an individual, owns one-half the stock of corporation X, and C owns one-half the stock of corporation Y. A, B, and C are unrelated. A sells 30 shares of the stock of corporation X to corporation Y for $50,000, such stock having an adjusted basis of $10,000 to him. After the sale, A is considered as owning 35 shares of the stock of corporation X (20 shares directly and 15 constructively because one-half of the 30 shares owned by corporation Y are attributed to him). Since before the sale he owned 50 percent of the stock of corporation X and after the sale he owned directly and constructively only 35 percent of such stock, the redemption is substantially disproportionate as to him pursuant to the provisions of section 302(b)(2). He, therefore, realizes a gain of $40,000 ($50,000 minus $10,000). If the stock surrendered is a capital asset, such gain is long-term or short-term capital gain depending on the period of time that such stock was held. The basis to A for the stock of corporation Y is not changed as a result of the entire transaction. The basis to corporation Y for the stock of corporation X is $50,000, i.e., the basis of the transferor ($10,000), increased in the amount of gain recognized to the transferor ($40,000) on the transfer.

Example (4). Corporation X and corporation Y each have outstanding 100 shares of common stock. H, an individual, W, his wife, S, his son, and G, his grandson, each own 25 shares of stock of each corporation. H sells all of his 25 shares of stock of corporation X to corporation Y. Since both before and after the transaction H owned directly and constructively 100 percent of the stock of corporation X, and assuming that section 302(b)(1) is not applicable, the amount received by him for his stock of corporation X is treated as a dividend to him to the extent of the earnings and profits of corporation Y.

[T.D. 6500, 25 FR 11607, Nov. 26, 1960, as amended by T.D. 6533, 26 FR 401, Jan. 19, 1961; T.D. 6969, 33 FR 11997, Aug. 23, 1968]

§ 1.304–3 Acquisition by a subsidiary.

(a) If a subsidiary acquires stock of its parent corporation from a shareholder of the parent corporation, the acquisition of such stock shall be treated as though the parent corporation had redeemed its own stock. For the purpose of this section, a corporation is a parent corporation if it meets the 50 percent ownership requirements of section 304(c). The determination whether the amount received shall be treated as an amount received in payment in exchange for the stock shall be made by applying section 303, or by applying section 302(b) with reference to the stock of the issuing parent corporation. If such distribution would have been treated as a distribution of property (pursuant to section 302(d)) under section 301, the entire amount of the selling price of the stock shall be treated as a dividend to the seller to the extent of the earnings and profits of the parent corporation determined as if the distribution had been made to it of the property that the subsidiary exchanged for the stock. In such cases, the transferor's basis for his remaining stock in the parent corporation will be determined by including the amount of the basis of the stock of the parent corporation sold to the subsidiary.

(b) Section 304(a)(2) may be illustrated by the following example:

Example. Corporation M has outstanding 100 shares of common stock which are owned as follows: B, 75 shares, C, son of B, 20 shares, and D, daughter of B, 5 shares. Corporation M owns the stock of Corporation X. B sells his 75 shares of Corporation M stock to Corporation X. Under section 302(b)(3) this is a termination of B's entire interest in Corporation M and the full amount received from the sale of his stock will be treated as payment in exchange for this stock, provided he fulfills the requirements of section 302(c)(2) (relating to an acquisition of an interest in the corporations).

[T.D. 6500, 25 FR 11607, Nov. 26, 1960]

§ 1.305–1 Stock dividends.

(a) **In general.** Under section 305, a distribution made by a corporation to its shareholders in its stock or in rights to acquire its stock is not included in gross income except as provided in section 305(b) and the regulations promulgated under the authority of section 305(c). A distribution made by a corporation to its shareholders in its stock or rights to acquire its stock which would not otherwise be included in gross income by reason of section 305 shall not be so included merely because such distribution was made out of Treasury stock or consisted of rights to acquire Treasury stock. See section 307 for rules as to basis of stock and stock rights acquired in a distribution.

(b) **Amount of distribution.** (1) In general, where a distribution of stock or rights to acquire stock of a corporation is treated as a distribution of property to which section 301 applies by reason of

section 305(b), the amount of the distribution, in accordance with section 301(b) and § 1.301–1, is the fair market value of such stock or rights on the date of distribution. See example (1) of § 1.305–2(b).

(2) Where a corporation which regularly distributes its earnings and profits, such as a regulated investment company, declares a dividend pursuant to which the shareholders may elect to receive either money or stock of the distributing corporation of equivalent value, the amount of the distribution of the stock received by any shareholder electing to receive stock will be considered to equal the amount of the money which could have been received instead. See example (2) of § 1.305–2(b).

* * *

(c) **Adjustment in purchase price.** A transfer of stock (or rights to acquire stock) or an increase or decrease in the conversion ratio or redemption price of stock which represents an adjustment of the price to be paid by the distributing corporation in acquiring property (within the meaning of section 317(a)) is not within the purview of section 305 because it is not a distribution with respect to its stock. For example, assume that on January 1, 1970, pursuant to a reorganization, corporation X acquires all the stock of corporation Y solely in exchange for its convertible preferred class B stock. Under the terms of the class B stock, its conversion ratio is to be adjusted in 1976 under a formula based upon the earnings of corporation Y over the 6-year period ending on December 31, 1975. Such an adjustment in 1976 is not covered by section 305.

* * *

[T.D. 7281, 38 FR 18532, July 12, 1973; 38 FR 19910, July 25, 1973]

§ 1.305–2 Distributions in lieu of money.

(a) **In general.** Under section 305(b)(1), if any shareholder has the right to an election or option with respect to whether a distribution shall be made either in money or any other property, or in stock or rights to acquire stock of the distributing corporation, then, with respect to all shareholders, the distribution of stock or rights to acquire stock is treated as a distribution of property to which section 301 applies regardless of—

(1) Whether the distribution is actually made in whole or in part in stock or in stock rights;

(2) Whether the election or option is exercised or exercisable before or after the declaration of the distribution;

(3) Whether the declaration of the distribution provides that the distribution will be made in one medium unless the shareholder specifically requests payment in the other;

(4) Whether the election governing the nature of the distribution is provided in the declaration of the distribution or in the corporate charter or arises from the circumstances of the distribution; or

(5) Whether all or part of the shareholders have the election.

(b) Examples. The application of section 305(b)(1) may be illustrated by the following examples:

Example (1). (i) Corporation X declared a dividend payable in additional shares of its common stock to the holders of its outstanding common stock on the basis of two additional shares for each share held on the record date but with the provision that, at the election of any shareholder made within a specified period prior to the distribution date, he may receive one additional share for each share held on the record date plus $12 principal amount of securities of corporation Y owned by corporation X. The fair market value of the stock of corporation X on the distribution date was $10 per share. The fair market value of $12 principal amount of securities of corporation Y on the distribution date was $11 but such securities had a cost basis to corporation X of $9.

(ii) The distribution to all shareholders of one additional share of stock of corporation X (with respect to which no election applies) for each share outstanding is not a distribution to which section 301 applies.

(iii) The distribution of the second share of stock of corporation X to those shareholders who do not elect to receive securities of corporation Y is a distribution of property to which section 301 applies, whether such shareholders are individuals or corporations. The amount of the distribution to which section 301 applies is $10 per share of stock of corporation X held on the record date (the fair market value of the stock of corporation X on the distribution date).

(iv) The distribution of securities of corporation Y in lieu of the second share of stock of corporation X to the shareholders of corporation X whether individuals or corporations, who elect to receive such securities, is also a distribution of property to which section 301 applies.

(v) In the case of the individual shareholders of corporation X who elects to receive such securities, the amount of the distribution to which section 301 applies is $11 per share of stock of corporation X held on the record date (the fair market value of the $12 principal amount of securities of corporation Y on the distribution date).

(vi) In the case of the corporate shareholders of corporation X electing to receive such securities, the amount of the distribution to which section 301 applies is $9 per share of stock of corporation X held on the record date (the basis of the securities of corporation Y in the hands of corporation X).

Example (2). On January 10, 1970, corporation X, a regulated investment company, declared a dividend of $1 per share on its common stock payable on February 11, 1970, in cash or in stock of corporation X of equivalent value determined as of January 22, 1970, at the election of the shareholder made on or before January 22, 1970. The amount of the distribution to which section 301 applies is $1 per share whether the shareholder elects to take cash or stock and whether the shareholder is an individual or a corporation. Such amount will also be used in determining the dividend paid deduction of corporation X and the reduction in earnings and profits of corporation X.

[T.D. 7281, 38 FR 18532, July 12, 1973]

§ 1.305-3 Disproportionate distributions.

(a) In general. Under section 305(b)(2), a distribution (including a deemed distribution) by a corporation of its stock or rights to acquire its stock is treated as a distribution of property to which section 301 applies if the distribution (or a series of distributions of which such distribution is one) has the result of (1) the receipt of money or other property by some shareholders, and (2) an increase in the proportionate interests of other shareholders in the assets or earnings and profits of the corporation. Thus, if a corporation has two classes of common stock outstanding and cash dividends are paid on one class and stock dividends are paid on the other class, the stock dividends are treated as distributions to which section 301 applies.

(b) Special rules. (1) As used in section 305(b)(2), the term "a series of distributions" encompasses all distributions of stock made or deemed made by a corporation which have the result of the receipt of cash or property by some shareholders and an increase in the proportionate interests of other shareholders.

(2) In order for a distribution of stock to be considered as one of a series of distributions it is not necessary that such distribution be pursuant to a plan to distribute cash or property to some shareholders and to increase the proportionate interests of other shareholders. It is sufficient if there is an actual or deemed distribution of stock (of which such distribution is one) and as a result of such distribution or distributions some shareholders receive cash or property and other shareholders increase their proportionate interests. For example, if a corporation pays quarterly stock dividends to one class of common shareholders and annual cash

dividends to another class of common shareholders the quarterly stock dividends constitute a series of distributions of stock having the result of the receipt of cash or property by some shareholders and an increase in the proportionate interests of other shareholders. This is so whether or not the stock distributions and the cash distributions are steps in an overall plan or are independent and unrelated. Accordingly, all the quarterly stock dividends are distributions to which section 301 applies.

(3) There is no requirement that both elements of section 305(b)(2) (*i.e.,* receipt of cash or property by some shareholders and an increase in proportionate interests of other shareholders) occur in the form of a distribution or series of distributions as long as the result of a distribution or distributions of stock is that some shareholders' proportionate interests increase and other shareholders in fact receive cash or property. Thus, there is no requirement that the shareholders receiving cash or property acquire the cash or property by way of a corporate distribution with respect to their shares, so long as they receive such cash or property in their capacity as shareholders, if there is a stock distribution which results in a change in the proportionate interests of some shareholders and other shareholders receive cash or property. However, in order for a distribution of property to meet the requirement of section 305(b)(2), such distribution must be made to a shareholder in his capacity as a shareholder, and must be a distribution to which section 301, 356(a)(2), 871(a)(1)(A), 881(a)(1), 852(b), or 857(b) applies. (Under section 305(d)(2), the payment of interest to a holder of a convertible debenture is treated as a distribution of property to a shareholder for purposes of section 305(b)(2).) For example if a corporation makes a stock distribution to its shareholders and, pursuant to a prearranged plan with such corporation, a related corporation purchases such stock from those shareholders who want cash, in a transaction to which section 301 applies by virtue of section 304, the requirements of section 305(b)(2) are satisfied. In addition, a distribution of property incident to an isolated redemption of stock (for example, pursuant to a tender offer) will not cause section 305(b)(2) to apply even though the redemption distribution is treated as a distribution of property to which section 301, 871(a)(1)(A), 881(a)(1), or 356(a)(2) applies.

(4) Where the receipt of cash or property occurs more than 36 months following a distribution or series of distributions of stock, or where a distribution or series of distributions of stock is made more than 36 months following the receipt of cash or property, such distribution or distributions will be presumed not to result in the receipt of cash or property by some shareholders and an increase in the proportionate interest of other shareholders, unless the receipt of cash or property and the distribution or series of distributions of stock are made pursuant to a plan. For example, if, pursuant to a plan, a corporation pays cash dividends to some shareholders on January 1, 1971 and increases the proportionate interests of other shareholders on March 1, 1974, such increases in proportionate interests are distributions to which section 301 applies.

(5) In determining whether a distribution or a series of distributions has the result of a disproportionate distribution, there shall be treated as outstanding stock of the distributing corporation (i) any right to acquire such stock (whether or not exercisable during the taxable year), and (ii) any security convertible into stock of the distributing corporation (whether or not convertible during the taxable year).

(6) In cases where there is more than one class of stock outstanding, each class of stock is to be considered separately in determining whether a shareholder has increased his proportionate interest in the assets or earnings and profits of a corporation. The individual shareholders of a class of stock will be deemed to have an increased interest if the class of stock as a whole has an increased interest in the corporation.

(c) **Distributions of cash in lieu of fractional shares.** (1) Section 305(b)(2) will not apply if—

(i) A corporation declares a dividend payable in stock of the corporation and distributes cash in lieu of fractional shares to which shareholders would otherwise be entitled, or

(ii) Upon a conversion of convertible stock or securities a corporation distributes cash in lieu of fractional shares to which shareholders would otherwise be entitled.

Provided the purpose of the distribution of cash is to save the corporation the trouble, expense, and inconvenience of issuing and transferring fractional shares (or scrip representing fractional shares), or issuing full shares representing the sum of fractional shares, and not to give any particular group of shareholders an increased interest in the assets or earnings and profits of the corporation. For purposes of paragraph (c)(1)(i) of this section, if the total amount of cash distributed in lieu of fractional shares is 5 percent or less of the total fair market value of the stock distributed (determined as of the date of declaration), the distribution shall be considered to be for such valid purpose.

(2) In a case to which subparagraph (1) of this paragraph applies, the transaction will be treated as though the fractional shares were distributed as part of the stock distribution and then were redeemed by the corporation. The treatment of the cash received by a shareholder will be determined under section 302.

(d) **Adjustment in conversion ratio.** (1)(i) Except as provided in subparagraph (2) of this paragraph, if a corporation has convertible stock or convertible securities outstanding (upon which it pays or is deemed to pay dividends or interest in money or other property) and distributes a stock dividend (or rights to acquire such stock) with respect to the stock into which the convertible stock or securities are convertible, an increase in proportionate interest in the assets or earnings and profits of the corporation by reason of such stock dividend shall be considered to have occurred unless a full adjustment in the conversion ratio or conversion price to reflect such stock dividend is made. Under certain circumstances, however, the application of an adjustment formula which in effect provides for a "credit" where stock is issued for consideration in excess of the conversion price may not satisfy the requirement for a "full adjustment." Thus, if under a "conversion price" antidilution formula the formula provides for a "credit" where stock is issued for consideration in excess of the conversion price (in effect as an offset against any decrease in the conversion price which would otherwise be required when stock is subsequently issued for consideration below the conversion price) there may still be an increase in proportionate interest by reason of a stock dividend after application of the formula, since any downward adjustment of the conversion price that would otherwise be required to reflect the stock dividend may be offset, in whole or in part, by the effect of prior sales made at prices above the conversion price. On the other hand, if there were no prior sales of stock above the conversion price then a full adjustment would occur upon the application of such an adjustment formula and there would be no change in proportionate interest. Similarly, if consideration is to be received in connection with the issuance of stock, such as in the case of a rights offering or a distribution of warrants, the fact that

such consideration is taken into account in making the antidilution adjustment will not preclude a full adjustment. See paragraph (b) of the example in this subparagraph for a case where the application of an adjustment formula with a cumulative feature does not result in a full adjustment and where a change in proportionate interest therefore occurs. See paragraph (c) for a case where the application of an adjustment formula with a cumulative feature does result in a full adjustment and where no change in proportionate interest therefore occurs. See paragraph (d) for an application of an antidilution formula in the case of a rights offering. See paragraph (e) for a case where the application of a noncumulative type adjustment formula will in all cases prevent a change in proportionate interest from occurring in the case of a stock dividend, because of the omission of the cumulative feature.

(ii) The principles of this subparagraph may be illustrated by the following example.

Example. (a) Corporation S has two classes of securities outstanding, convertible debentures and common stock. At the time of issuance of the debentures the corporation had 100 shares of common stock outstanding. Each debenture is interest-paying and is convertible into common stock at a conversion price of $2. The debenture's conversion price is subject to reduction pursuant to the following formula:

(Number of common shares outstanding at date of issue of debentures times initial conversion price) *plus* (Consideration received upon issuance of additional common shares) *divided by* (Number of common shares outstanding at date of issue of debentures) *plus* (Number of additional common shares issued)

Under the formula, common stock dividends are treated as an issue of common stock for zero consideration. If the computation results in a figure which is less than the existing conversion price the conversion price is reduced. However, under the formula, the existing conversion price is never increased. The formula works upon a cumulative basis since the numerator includes the consideration received upon the issuance of all common shares subsequent to the issuance of the debentures, and the reduction effected by the formula because of a sale or issuance of common stock below the existing conversion price is thus limited by any prior sales made above the existing conversion price.

(b) In 1972 corporation S sells 100 common shares at $3 per share. In 1973 the corporation declares a stock dividend of 20 shares to all holders of common stock. Under the antidilution formula no adjustment will be made to the conversion price of the debentures to reflect the stock dividend to common stockholders since the prior sale of common stock in excess of the conversion price in 1972 offsets the reduction in the conversion price which would otherwise result, as follows:

$$100 \times \$2 + \$300 \div 100 + 120 = \$500 \div 220 = \$2.27$$

Since $2.27 is greater than the existing conversion price of $2 no adjustment is required. As a result, there is an increase in proportionate interest of the common stockholders by reason of the stock dividend and the additional shares of common stock will be treated, pursuant to section 305(b)(2), as a distribution of property to which section 301 applies.

(c) Assume the same facts as above, but instead of selling 100 common shares at $3 per share in 1972, assume corporation S sold no shares. Application of the antidilution formula would give rise to an adjustment in the conversion price as follows:

$$100 \times \$2 + \$0 \div 100 + 20 = \$200 \div 120 = \$1.67$$

The conversion price, being reduced from $2 to $1.67, fully reflects the stock dividend distributed to the common stockholders. Hence, the distribution of common stock is not treated under section 305(b)(2) as one to which section 301 applies because the distribution does not increase the proportionate interests of the common shareholders as a class.

(d) Corporation S distributes to its shareholders rights entitling the shareholders to purchase a total of 20 shares at $1 per share. Application of the antidilution formula would produce an adjustment in the conversion price as follows:

$$100 \times \$2 + 20 \times \$1 \div 100 + 20 = \$220 \div 120 = \$1.83$$

The conversion price, being reduced from $2 to $1.83, fully reflects the distribution of rights to purchase stock at a price lower than the conversion price. Hence, the distribution of the rights is not treated under section 305(b)(2) as one to which section 301 applies because the distribution does not increase the proportionate interests of the common shareholders as a class.

(e) Assume the same facts as in (b) above, but instead of using a "conversion price" antidilution formula which operates on a cumulative basis, assume corporation S has employed a formula which operates as follows with respect to all stock dividends: The conversion price in effect at the opening of business on the day following the dividend record date is reduced by multiplying such conversion price by a fraction the numerator of which is the number of shares of common stock outstanding at the close of business on the record date and the denominator of which is the sum of such shares so outstanding and the number of shares constituting the stock dividend. Under such a formula the following adjustment would be made to the conversion price upon the declaration of a stock dividend of 20 shares in 1973:

$$200 \div 200 + 20 = 200 \div 220 \times \$2 = \$1.82$$

The conversion price, being reduced from $2 to $1.82, fully reflects the stock dividend distributed to the common stockholders. Hence, the distribution of common stock is not treated under section 305(b)(2) as one to which section 301 applies because the distribution does not increase the proportionate interests of the common shareholders as a class.

(2)(i) A distributing corporation either must make the adjustment required by subparagraph (1) of this paragraph as of the date of the distribution of the stock dividend, or must elect (in the manner provided in subdivision (iii) of this subparagraph) to make such adjustment within the time provided in subdivision (ii) of this subparagraph.

(ii) If the distributing corporation elects to make such adjustment, such adjustment must be made no later than the earlier of (a) 3 years after the date of the stock dividend, or (b) that date as of which the aggregate stock dividends for which adjustment of the conversion ratio has not previously been made total at least 3 percent of the issued and outstanding stock with respect to which such stock dividends were distributed.

(iii) The election provided by subdivision (ii) of this subparagraph shall be made by filing with the income tax return for the taxable year during which the stock dividend is distributed—

(a) A statement that an adjustment will be made as provided by that subdivision, and

(b) A description of the antidilution provisions under which the adjustment will be made.

* * *

(e) **Examples.** The application of section 305(b)(2) to distributions of stock and section 305(c) to deemed distributions of stock may be illustrated by the following examples:

Example (1). Corporation X is organized with two classes of common stock, class A and class B. Each share of stock is entitled to share equally in the assets and earnings and profits of the corporation. Dividends may be paid in stock or in cash on either class of stock without regard to the medium of payment of dividends on the other class. A dividend is declared on the class A stock payable in additional shares of class A stock and a dividend is declared on class B stock payable in cash. Since the class A shareholders as a class will have increased their proportionate interests in the assets and earnings and profits of the corporation and the class B shareholders will have received cash, the additional shares of class A stock are distributions of property to which section 301 applies. This is true even with respect to those shareholders who may own class A stock and class B stock in the same proportion.

Example (2). Corporation Y is organized with two classes of stock, class A common, and class B, which is nonconvertible and limited and preferred as to dividends. A dividend is declared upon the class A stock payable in additional shares of class A stock and a dividend is declared on the class B stock payable in cash. The distribution of class A stock is not one to which section 301 applies because the distribution does not increase the proportionate interests of the class A shareholders as a class.

Example (3). Corporation K is organized with two classes of stock, class A common, and class B, which is nonconvertible preferred stock. A dividend is declared upon the class A stock payable in shares of class B stock and a dividend is declared on the class B stock payable in cash. Since the class A shareholders as a class have an increased interest in the assets and earnings and profits of the corporation, the stock distribution is treated as a distribution to which section 301 applies. If, however, a dividend were declared upon the class A stock payable in a new class of preferred stock that is subordinated in all respects to the class B stock, the distribution would not increase the proportionate interests of the class A shareholders in the assets or earnings and profits of the corporation and would not be treated as a distribution to which section 301 applies.

Example (4). (i) Corporation W has one class of stock outstanding, class A common. The corporation also has outstanding interest paying securities convertible into class A common stock which have a fixed conversion ratio that is not subject to full adjustment in the event stock dividends or rights are distributed to the class A shareholders. Corporation W distributes to the class A shareholders rights to acquire additional shares of class A stock. During the year, interest is paid on the convertible securities.

(ii) The stock rights and convertible securities are considered to be outstanding stock of the corporation and the distribution increases the proportionate interests of the class A shareholders in the assets and earnings and profits of the corporation. Therefore, the distribution is treated as a distribution to which section 301 applies. The same result would follow if, instead of convertible securities, the corporation had outstanding convertible stock. If, however, the conversion ratio of the securities or stock were fully adjusted to reflect the distribution of rights to the class A shareholders, the rights to acquire class A stock would not increase the proportionate interests of the class A shareholders in the assets and earnings and profits of the corporation and would not be treated as a distribution to which section 301 applies.

Example (5). (i) Corporation S is organized with two classes of stock, class A common and class B convertible preferred. The class B is fully protected against dilution in the event of a stock dividend or stock split with respect to the class A stock; however, no adjustment in the conversion ratio is required to be made until the stock dividends equal 3 percent of the common stock issued and outstanding on the date of the first such stock dividend except that such adjustment must be made no later than 3 years after the date of the stock dividend. Cash dividends are paid annually on the class B stock.

(ii) Corporation S pays a 1 percent stock dividend on the class A stock in 1970. In 1971, another 1 percent stock dividend is paid and in 1972 another 1 percent stock dividend is paid. The conversion ratio of the class B stock is increased in 1972 to reflect the three stock dividends paid on the class A stock. The distributions of class A stock are not distributions to which section 301 applies because they do not increase the proportionate interests of the class A shareholders in the assets and earnings and profits of the corporation.

Example (6). (i) Corporation M is organized with two classes of stock outstanding, class A and class B. Each class B share may be converted, at the option of the holder, into class A shares. During the first year, the conversion ratio is one share of class A stock for each

share of class B stock. At the beginning of each subsequent year, the conversion ratio is increased by 0.05 share of class A stock for each share of class B stock. Thus, during the second year, the conversion ratio would be 1.05 shares of class A stock for each share of class B stock, during the third year, the ratio would be 1.10 shares, etc.

(ii) M pays an annual cash dividend on the class A stock. At the beginning of the second year, when the conversion ratio is increased to 1.05 shares of class A stock for each share of class B stock, a distribution of 0.05 shares of class A stock is deemed made under section 305(c) with respect to each share of class B stock, since the proportionate interests of the class B shareholders in the assets or earnings and profits of M are increased and the transaction has the effect described in section 305(b)(2). Accordingly, sections 305(b)(2) and 301 apply to the transaction.

Example (7). (i) Corporation N has two classes of stock outstanding, class A and class B. Each class B share is convertible into class A stock. However, in accordance with a specified formula, the conversion ratio is decreased each time a cash dividend is paid on the class B stock to reflect the amount of the cash dividend. The conversion ratio is also adjusted in the event that cash dividends are paid on the class A stock to increase the number of class A shares into which the class B shares are convertible to compensate the class B shareholders for the cash dividend paid on the class A stock.

(ii) In 1972, a $1 cash dividend per share is declared and paid on the class B stock. On the date of payment, the conversion ratio of the class B stock is decreased. A distribution of stock is deemed made under section 305(c) to the class A shareholders, since the proportionate interest of the class A shareholders in the assets or earnings and profits of the corporation is increased and the transaction has the effect described in section 305(b)(2). Accordingly, sections 305(b)(2) and 301 apply to the transaction.

(iii) In the following year a cash dividend is paid on the class A stock and none is paid on the class B stock. The increase in conversion rights of the class B shares is deemed to be a distribution under section 305(c) to the class B shareholders since their proportionate interest in the assets or earnings and profits of the corporation is increased and since the transaction has the effect described in section 305(b)(2). Accordingly, sections 305(b)(2) and 301 apply to the transaction.

Example (8). Corporation T has 1,000 shares of stock outstanding. C owns 100 shares. Nine other shareholders each owns 100 shares. Pursuant to a plan for periodic redemptions, T redeems up to 5 percent of each shareholder's stock each year. During the year, each of the nine other shareholders has 5 shares of his stock redeemed for cash. Thus, C's proportionate interest in the assets and earnings and profits of T is increased. Assuming that the cash received by the nine other shareholders is taxable under section 301, C is deemed under section 305(c) to have received a distribution under section 305(b)(2) of 5.25 shares of T stock to which section 301 applies. The amount of C's distribution is measured by the fair market value of the number of shares which would have been distributed to C had the corporation sought to increase his interest by 0.47 percentage points (C owned 10 percent of the T stock immediately before the redemption and 10.47 percent immediately thereafter) and the other shareholders continued to hold 900 shares (*i.e.,*)

(a) $100 \div 955 = 10.47\%$ (percent of C's ownership after redemption)

(b) $100 + x \div 1000 + x = 10.47\%$; $x = 5.25$ (additional shares considered to be distributed to C).

Since in computing the amount of additional shares deemed to be distributed to C the redemption of shares is disregarded, the redemption of shares will be similarly disregarded in determining the value of the stock of the corporation which is deemed to be distributed. Thus, in the example, 1,005.25 shares of stock are considered as outstanding after the redemption. The value of each share deemed to be distributed to C is then determined by dividing the 1,005.25 shares into the aggregate fair market value of the actual shares outstanding (955) after the redemption.

Example (9). (i) Corporation O has a stock redemption program under which, instead of paying out earnings and profits to its shareholders in the form of dividends, it redeems the stock of its shareholders up to a stated amount which is determined by the earnings and profits of the corporation. If the stock tendered for redemption exceeds the stated amount, the corporation redeems the stock on a pro rata basis up to the stated amount.

(ii) During the year corporation O offers to distribute $10,000 in redemption of its stock. At the time of the offering, corporation O has 1,000 shares outstanding of which E and F each owns 150 shares and G and H each owns 350 shares. The corporation redeems 15 shares from E and 35 shares from G. F and H continue to hold all of their stock.

(iii) F and H have increased their proportionate interests in the assets and earnings and profits of the corporation. Assuming that the cash E and G receive is taxable under section 301, F will be deemed under section 305(c) to have received a distribution under section 305(b)(2) of 16.66 shares of stock to which section 301 applies and H will be deemed under section 305(c) to have received a distribution under section 305(b)(2) of 38.86 shares of stock to which section 301 applies. The amount of the distribution to F and H is measured by the number of shares which would have been distributed to F and H had the corporation sought to increase the interest of F by 0.79 percentage points (F owned 15 percent of the stock immediately before the redemption and 15.79 percent immediately thereafter) and the interest of H by 1.84 percentage points (H owned 35 percent of the stock immediately before the redemption and 36.84 percent immediately thereafter) and E and G had continued to hold 150 shares and 350 shares, respectively (*i.e.,*)

(a) $150 \div 950 + 350 \div 950 = 52.63\%$ (percent of F and H's ownership after redemption)

(b) $500 + y \div 1000 + y = 52.63\%$; $y = 55.52$ (additional shares considered to be distributed to F and H)

(c)(1) $150 \div 500 \times 55.52 = 16.66$ (shares considered to be distributed to F)

(2) $350 \div 500 \times 55.52 = 38.86$ (shares considered to be distributed to H).

Since in computing the amount of additional shares deemed to be distributed to F and H the redemption of shares is disregarded, the redemption of shares will be similarly disregarded in determining the value of the stock of the corporation which is deemed to be distributed. Thus, in the example, 1,055.52 shares of stock are considered as outstanding after the redemption. The value of each share deemed to be distributed to F and H is then determined by dividing the 1,055.52 shares into the aggregate fair market value of the actual shares outstanding (950) after the redemption.

Example (10). Corporation P has 1,000 shares of stock outstanding. T owns 700 shares of the P stock and G owns 300 shares of the P stock. In a single and isolated redemption to which section 301 applies, the corporation redeems 150 shares of T's stock. Since this is an isolated redemption and is not a part of a periodic redemption plan, G is not treated as having received a deemed distribution under section 305(c) to which sections 305(b)(2) and 301 apply even though he has an increased proportionate interest in the assets and earnings and profits of the corporation.

Example (11). Corporation Q is a large corporation whose sole class of stock is widely held. However, the four largest shareholders are officers of the corporation and each owns 8 percent of the outstanding stock. In 1974, in a distribution to which section 301 applies, the corporation redeems 1.5 percent of the stock from each of the four largest shareholders in preparation for their retirement. From 1970 through 1974, the corporation distributes annual stock dividends to its shareholders. No other distributions were made to these shareholders. Since the 1974 redemptions are isolated and are not part of a plan for periodically redeeming the stock of the corporation, the shareholders receiving stock dividends will not be treated as having received a distribution under section 305(b)(2) even though they have an increased proportionate interest in the assets and earnings and profits of the corporation and whether or not the redemptions are treated as distributions to which section 301 applies.

Example (12). Corporation R has 2,000 shares of class A stock outstanding. Five shareholders own 300 shares each and five shareholders own 100 shares each. In preparation for the retirement of the five major shareholders, corporation R, in a single and isolated transaction, has a recapitalization in which each share of class A stock may be exchanged either for five shares of new class B nonconvertible preferred stock plus 0.4 share of new class C common stock, or for two shares of new class C common stock. As a result of the exchanges, each of the five major shareholders receives 1,500 shares of class B nonconvertible preferred stock and 120 shares of class C common stock. The remaining shareholders each receives 200 shares of class C common stock. None of the exchanges are within the purview of section 305.

* * *

[T.D. 7281, 38 FR 18532, July 12, 1973; 38 FR 19910, 19911, July 25, 1973, as amended by T.D. 7329, 39 FR 36860, Oct. 15, 1974]

§ 1.305–4   Distributions of common and preferred stock.

(a) **In general.** Under section 305(b)(3), a distribution (or a series of distributions) by a corporation which results in the receipt of preferred stock (whether or not convertible into common stock) by some common shareholders and the receipt of common stock by other common shareholders is treated as a distribution of property to which section 301 applies. For the meaning of the term "a series of distribution," see subparagraphs (1) through (6) of § 1.305–3(b).

(b) **Examples.** The application of section 305(b)(3) may be illustrated by the following examples:

Example (1). Corporation X is organized with two classes of common stock, class A and class B. Dividends may be paid in stock or in cash on either class of stock without regard to the medium of payment of dividends on the other class. A dividend is declared on the class A stock payable in additional shares of class A stock and a dividend is declared on class B stock payable in newly authorized class C stock which is nonconvertible and limited and preferred as to dividends. Both the distribution of class A shares and the distribution of new class C shares are distributions to which section 301 applies.

Example (2). Corporation Y is organized with one class of stock, class A common. During the year the corporation declares a dividend on the class A stock payable in newly authorized class B preferred stock which is convertible into class A stock no later than 6 months from the date of distribution at a price that is only slightly higher than the market price of class A stock on the date of distribution. Taking into account the dividend rate, redemption provisions, the marketability of the convertible stock, and the conversion price, it is reasonable to anticipate that within a relatively short period of time some shareholders will exercise their conversion rights and some will not. Since the distribution can reasonably be expected to result in the receipt of preferred stock by some common shareholders and the receipt of common stock by other common shareholders, the distribution is a distribution of property to which section 301 applies.

[T.D. 7281, 38 FR 18536, July 12, 1973]

§ 1.305–5   Distributions on preferred stock.

(a) **In general.** Under section 305(b)(4), a distribution by a corporation of its stock (or rights to acquire its stock) made (or deemed made under section 305(c)) with respect to its preferred stock is treated as a distribution of property to which section 301 applies unless the distribution is made with respect to convertible preferred stock to take into account a stock dividend, stock split, or any similar event (such as the sale of stock at less than the fair market value pursuant to a rights offering) which would otherwise result in the dilution of the conversion right. For purposes of the preceding sentence, an adjustment in the conversion ratio of convertible preferred stock made solely to take into account the distribution by a closed end regulated investment company of a capital gain dividend with respect to the stock into which such stock is convertible shall not be considered a "similar event." The term "preferred stock" generally refers to stock which, in relation to other classes of stock outstanding, enjoys certain limited rights and privileges (generally associated with specified dividend and liquidation priorities) but does not participate in corporate growth to any significant extent. The distinguishing feature of "preferred stock" for the purposes of section 305(b)(4) is not its privileged position as such, but that such privileged position is limited, and that such stock does not participate in corporate growth to any significant extent. However, a right to participate which lacks substance will not prevent a class of stock from being treated as preferred stock. Thus, stock which enjoys a priority as to dividends and on liquidation but which is entitled to participate, over and above such priority, with another less privileged class of stock in earnings and profits and upon liquidation, may nevertheless be treated as preferred stock for purposes of section 305 if, taking into account all the facts and circumstances, it is reasonable to anticipate at the time a distribution is made (or is deemed to have been made) with respect to such stock that there is little or no likelihood of such stock actually participating in current and anticipated earnings and upon liquidation beyond its preferred interest. Among the facts and circumstances to be considered are the prior and anticipated earnings per share, the cash dividends per share, the book value per share, the extent of preference and of participation of each class, both absolutely and relative to each other, and any other facts which indicate whether or not the stock has a real and meaningful probability of actually participating in the earnings and growth of the corporation. The determination of whether stock is preferred for purposes of section 305 shall be made without regard to any right to convert such stock into another class of stock of the corporation. The term "preferred stock", however, does not include convertible debentures.

(b) **Redemption premium.** (1) If a corporation issues preferred stock which may be redeemed after a specified period of time at a price higher than the issue price, the difference will be considered under the authority of section 305(c) to be a distribution of additional stock on preferred stock which is constructively received by the shareholder over the period of time during which the preferred stock cannot be called for redemption.

(2) Subparagraph (1) of this paragraph shall not apply to the extent that the difference between issue price and redemption price is a reasonable redemption premium. A redemption premium will be considered reasonable if it is in the nature of a penalty for a premature redemption of the preferred stock and if such premium does not exceed the amount the corporation would be required to pay for the right to make such premature redemption under market conditions existing at the time of issuance. Such an amount can be established by comparing call premium rates on comparable stock paying comparable dividends. However, for purposes of this subparagraph, a redemption premium not in excess of 10 percent of the issue price on stock which is not redeemable for 5 years from the date of issue shall be considered reasonable.

* * *

(d) **Examples.** The application of sections 305(b)(4) and 305(c) may be illustrated by the following examples:

Example (1). (i) Corporation T has outstanding 1,000 shares of $100 par 5-percent cumulative preferred stock and 10,000 shares of no-par common stock. The corporation is 4 years in arrears on dividends to the preferred shareholders. The issue price of the preferred stock is $100 per share. Pursuant to a recapitalization under section 368(a)(1)(E), the preferred shareholders exchange their preferred stock, including the right to dividend arrearages, on the basis of one old preferred share for 1.20 newly authorized class A preferred shares. Immediately following the recapitalization, the new class A shares are traded at $100 per share. The class A shares are entitled to a liquidation preference of $100. The preferred shareholders have increased their proportionate interest in the assets or earnings and profits of corporation T since the fair market value of 1.20 shares of class A preferred stock ($120) exceeds the issue price of the old preferred stock ($100). Accordingly, the preferred shareholders are deemed under section 305(c) to receive a distribution in the amount of $20 on each share of old preferred stock and the distribution is one to which sections 305(b)(4) and 301 apply.

(ii) The same result would occur if the fair market value of the common stock immediately following the recapitalization were $20 per share and each share of preferred stock were exchanged for one share of the new class A preferred stock and one share of common stock.

Example (2). Corporation A, a publicly held company whose stock is traded on a securities exchange (or in the over-the-counter market) has two classes of stock outstanding, common and cumulative preferred. Each share

of preferred stock is convertible into .75 shares of common stock. There are no dividend arrearages. At the time of issue of the preferred stock, there was no plan or prearrangement by which it was to be exchanged for common stock. The issue price of the preferred stock is $100 per share. In order to retire the preferred stock, corporation A recapitalizes in a transaction to which section 368(a)(1)(E) applies and each share of preferred stock is exchanged for one share of common stock. Immediately after the recapitalization the common stock has a fair market value of $110 per share. Notwithstanding the fact that the fair market value of the common stock received in the exchange (determined immediately following the recapitalization) exceeds the issue price of the preferred stock surrendered, the recapitalization is not deemed under section 305(c) to result in a distribution to which sections 305(b)(4) and 301 apply since the recapitalization is not pursuant to a plan to periodically increase a shareholder's proportionate interest in the assets or earnings and profits and does not involve dividend arrearages.

Example (3). Corporation V is organized with two classes of stock, 1,000 shares of class A common and 1,000 shares of class B convertible preferred. Each share of class B stock may be converted into two shares of class A stock. Pursuant to a recapitalization under section 368(a)(1)(E), the 1,000 shares of class A stock are surrendered in exchange for 500 shares of new class A common and 500 shares of newly authorized class C common. The conversion right of class B stock is changed to one share of class A stock and one share of class C stock for each share of class B stock. The change in the conversion right is not deemed under section 305(c) to be a distribution on preferred stock to which sections 305(b)(4) and 301 apply.

Example (4). Corporation X issues preferred stock for $100 per share. The stock is redeemable in 5 years or any time thereafter for $110. The redemption price at no time exceeds 10 percent of the issue price. The difference between redemption price and issue price is not deemed under section 305(c) to be a distribution on preferred stock to which sections 305(b)(4) and 301 supply.

Example (5). Corporation W issues preferred stock for $100 per share. The stock pays no dividends but is redeemable at the end of 5 years for $185 with yearly increases thereafter of $15. There are no facts to indicate that a call premium in excess of $10 is reasonable. Since the difference between redemption price and issue price exceeds the reasonable call premium to the extent of $75 that amount is considered to be a distribution of additional stock on preferred stock which is constructively received over the 5-year period. Therefore, the shareholder is deemed under section 305(c) to receive on the last day of each year during the 5-year period a distribution on his preferred stock in an amount equal to 15 percent of the issue price. Each $15 increase in the redemption price thereafter is considered to be a distribution on the preferred stock at the time each such increase becomes effective.

Example (6). Corporation A, a publicly held company whose stock is traded on a securities exchange (or in the over-the-counter market) has two classes of stock outstanding, common and preferred. The preferred stock is nonvoting and nonconvertible, limited and preferred as to dividends, and has a fixed liquidation preference. There are no dividend arrearages. At the time of issue of the preferred stock, there was no plan or prearrangement by which it was to be exchanged for common stock. In order to retire the preferred stock, corporation A recapitalizes in a transaction to which section 368(a)(1)(E) applies and the preferred stock is exchanged for common stock. The transaction is not deemed to be a distribution under section 305(c) and sections 305(b) and 301 do not apply to the transaction. The same result would follow if the preferred stock was exchanged in any reorganization described in section 368(a)(1) for a new preferred stock having substantially the same market value and having no greater call price or liquidation preference than the old preferred stock, whether the new preferred stock has voting rights or is convertible into common stock of corporation A at a fixed ratio subject to change solely to take account of stock dividends, stock splits, or similar transactions with respect to the stock into which the preferred stock is convertible.

Example (7). Corporation R has only common stock outstanding. Corporation R distributes to the common shareholders on a pro rata basis, newly authorized 2-percent preferred stock. Such stock has a par value of $100 per share and is redeemable at the end of 5 years for $105 per share. At the time of the distribution, the fair market value of the preferred stock is $50 per share. There are no facts to indicate that a call premium in excess of $5 is reasonable. Since the difference between redemption price and issue price (*i.e.,* the fair market value of the preferred stock immediately following its distribution as a stock dividend) exceeds the reasonable call premium to the extent of $50, that amount is considered to be a distribution of additional stock on preferred stock which is constructively received over the 5-year period. Therefore, each shareholder is deemed under section 305(c) to receive each year during the 5-year period a distribution in the amount of $10 on his preferred stock to which sections 305(b)(4) and 301 apply.

Example (8). Corporation Q is organized with 10,000 shares of class A stock and 1,000 shares of class B stock. The terms of the class B stock require that the class B have a preference of $5 per share with respect to dividends and $100 per share with respect to liquidation. In addition, upon a distribution of $10 per share to the class A stock, class B participates equally in any additional dividends. The terms also provide that upon liquidation the class B stock participates equally after the class A stock receives $100 per share. Corporation Q has no accumulated earnings and profits. In 1971 it earned $10,000, the highest earnings in its history. The corporation is in an industry in which it is reasonable to anticipate a growth in earnings of 5 percent per year. In 1971 the book value of corporation Q's assets totalled $100,000. In that year the corporation paid a dividend of $5 per share to the class B stock and $.50 per share to the class A. In 1972 the corporation had no earnings and in lieu of a $5 dividend distributed one share of class B stock for each outstanding share of class B. No distribution was made to the class A stock. Since, in 1972, it was not reasonable to anticipate that the class B stock would participate in the current and anticipated earnings and growth of the corporation beyond its preferred interest, the class B stock is preferred stock and the distribution of

class B shares to the class B shareholders is a distribution to which sections 305(b)(4) and 301 apply.

Example (9). Corporation P is organized with 10,000 shares of class A stock and 1,000 shares of class B stock. The terms of the class B stock require that the class B have a preference of $5 per share with respect to dividends and $100 per share with respect to liquidation. In addition, upon a distribution of $5 per share to the class A stock, class B participates equally in any additional dividends. The terms also provide that upon liquidation the class B stock participates equally after the class A receives $100 per share. Corporation P has accumulated earnings and profits of $100,000. In 1971 it earned $75,000. The corporation is in an industry in which it is reasonable to anticipate a growth in earnings of 10 percent per year. In 1971 the book value of corporation P's assets totalled $5 million. In that year the corporation paid a dividend of $5 per share to the class B stock, $5 per share to the class A stock, and it distributed an additional $1 per share to both class A and class B stock. In 1972 the corporation had earnings of $82,500. In that year it paid a dividend of $5 per share to the class B stock and $5 per share to the class A stock. In addition, the corporation declared stock dividends of one share of class B stock for every 10 outstanding shares of class B and one share of class A stock for every 10 outstanding shares of class A. Since, in 1972, it was reasonable to anticipate that both the class B stock and the class A stock would participate in the current and anticipated earnings and growth of the corporation beyond their preferred interests, neither class is preferred stock and the stock dividends are not distributions to which section 305(b)(4) applies.

[T.D. 7281, 38 FR 18536, July 12, 1973, as amended by T.D. 7329, 39 FR 36860, Oct. 15, 1974]

§ 1.305-6 Distributions of convertible preferred.

(a) **In general.** (1) Under section 305(b)(5), a distribution by a corporation of its convertible preferred stock or rights to acquire such stock made or considered as made with respect to its stock is treated as a distribution of property to which section 301 applies unless the corporation establishes that such distribution will not result in a disproportionate distribution as described in § 1.305-3.

(2) The distribution of convertible preferred stock is likely to result in a disproportionate distribution when both of the following conditions exist: (i) The conversion right must be exercised within a relatively short period of time after the date of distribution of the stock; and (ii) taking into account such factors as the dividend rate, the redemption provisions, the marketability of the convertible stock, and the conversion price, it may be anticipated that some shareholders will exercise their conversion rights and some will not. On the other hand, where the conversion right may be

exercised over a period of many years and the dividend rate is consistent with market conditions at the time of distribution of the stock, there is no basis for predicting at what time and the extent to which the stock will be converted and it is unlikely that a disproportionate distribution will result.

(b) **Examples.** The application of section 305(b)(5) may be illustrated by the following examples:

Example (1). Corporation Z is organized with one class of stock, class A common. During the year the corporation declares a dividend on the class A stock payable in newly authorized class B preferred stock which is convertible into class A stock for a period of 20 years from the date of issuance. Assuming dividend rates are normal in light of existing conditions so that there is no basis for predicting the extent to which the stock will be converted, the circumstances will ordinarily be sufficient to establish that a disproportionate distribution will not result since it is impossible to predict the extent to which the class B stock will be converted into class A stock. Accordingly, the distribution of class B stock is not one to which section 301 applies.

Example (2). Corporation X is organized with one class of stock, class A common. During the year the corporation declares a dividend on the class A stock payable in newly authorized redeemable class C preferred stock which is convertible into class A common stock no later than 4 months from the date of distribution at a price slightly higher than the market price of class A stock on the date of distribution. By prearrangement with corporation X, corporation Y, an insurance company, agrees to purchase class C stock from any shareholder who does not wish to convert. By reason of this prearrangement, it is anticipated that the shareholders will either sell the class C stock to the insurance company (which expects to retain the shares for investment purposes) or will convert. As a result, some of the shareholders exercise their conversion privilege and receive additional shares of class A stock, while other shareholders sell their class C stock to corporation Y and receive cash. The distribution is a distribution to which section 301 applies since it results in the receipt of property by some shareholders and an increase in the proportionate interests of other shareholders.

[T.D. 7281, 38 FR 18538, July 12, 1973]

§ 1.305–7 Certain transactions treated as distributions.

(a) **In general.** Under section 305(c), a change in conversion ratio, a change in redemption price, a difference between redemption price and issue price, a redemption which is treated as a distribution to which section 301 applies, or any transaction (including a recapitalization) having a similar effect on the interest of any shareholder may be treated as a distribution with respect to any shareholder whose proportionate interest in the earnings and profits or assets of the corporation is increased by such change, difference, redemption, or similar transaction. In general, such change, difference, redemption, or similar transaction will be treated as a distribution to which sections 305(b) and 301 apply where—

(1) The proportionate interest of any shareholder in the earnings and profits or assets of the corporation deemed to have made such distribution is increased by such change, difference, redemption, or similar transaction; and

(2) Such distribution has the result described in paragraph (2), (3), (4), or (5) of section 305(b).

Where such change, difference, redemption, or similar transaction is treated as a distribution under the provisions of this section, such distribution will be deemed made with respect to any shareholder whose interest in the earnings and profits or assets of the distributing corporation is increased thereby. Such distribution will be deemed to be a distribution of the stock of such corporation made by the corporation to such shareholder with respect to his stock. Depending upon the facts presented, the distribution may be deemed to be made in common or preferred stock. For example, where a redemption price in excess of a reasonable call premium exists with respect to a class of preferred stock and the other requirements of this section are also met, the distribution will be deemed made with respect to such preferred stock, in stock of the same class. Accordingly, the preferred shareholders are considered under sections 305(b)(4) and 305(c) to have received a distribution of preferred stock to which section 301 applies. See the examples in §§ 1.305–3(e) and 1.305–5(d) for further illustrations of the application of section 305(c).

(b) **Antidilution provisions.** (1) For purposes of applying section 305(c) in conjunction with section 305(b), a change in the conversion ratio or conversion price of convertible preferred stock (or securities), or in the exercise price of rights or warrants, made pursuant to a bona fide, reasonable, adjustment formula (including, but not limited to, either the so-called "market price" or "conversion price" type of formulas) which has the effect of preventing dilution of the interest of the holders of such stock (or securities) will not be considered to result in a deemed distribution of stock. An adjustment in the conversion ratio or price to compensate for cash or property distributions to other shareholders that are taxable under section 301, 356(a)(2), 871(a)(1)(A), 881(a)(1), 852(b), or 857(b) will not be considered as made pursuant to a bona fide adjustment formula.

(2) The principles of this paragraph may be illustrated by the following example:

Example. (i) Corporation U has two classes of stock outstanding, class A and class B. Each class B share is convertible into class A stock. In accordance with a bona fide, reasonable, antidilution provision, the conversion price is adjusted if the corporation transfers class A stock to anyone for a consideration that is below the conversion price.

(ii) The corporation sells class A stock to the public at the current market price but below the conversion price. Pursuant to the antidilution provision, the conversion price is adjusted downward. Such a change in conversion price will not be deemed to be a distribution under section 305(c) for the purposes of section 305(b).

(c) Recapitalizations. (1) A recapitalization (whether or not an isolated transaction) will be deemed to result in a distribution to which section 305(c) and this section apply if—

(i) It is pursuant to a plan to periodically increase a shareholder's proportionate interest in the assets or earnings and profits of the corporation, or

(ii) A shareholder owning preferred stock with dividends in arrears exchanges his stock for other stock and, as a result, increases his proportionate interest in the assets or earnings and profits of the corporation. An increase in a preferred shareholder's proportionate interest occurs in any case where the fair market value or the liquidation preference, whichever is greater, of the stock received in the exchange (determined immediately following the recapitalization), exceeds the issue price of the preferred stock surrendered.

(2) In a case to which subparagraph (1)(ii) of this paragraph applies, the amount of the distribution deemed under section 305(c) to result from the recapitalization is the lesser of (i) the amount by which the fair market value or the liquidation preference, whichever is greater, of the stock received in the exchange (determined immediately following the recapitalization) exceeds the issue price of the preferred stock surrendered, or (ii) the amount of the dividends in arrears.

(3) For purposes of applying subparagraphs (1) and (2) of this paragraph with respect to stock issued before July 12, 1973, the term "issue price of the preferred stock surrendered" shall mean the greater of the issue price or the liquidation preference (not including dividends in arrears) of the stock surrendered.

* * *

[T.D. 7281, 38 FR 18538, July 12, 1973]

§ 1.306–1 General.

(a) Section 306 provides, in general, that the proceeds from the sale or redemption of certain stock (referred to as "section 306 stock") shall be treated either as ordinary income or as a distribution of property to which section 301 applies. Section 306 stock is defined in section 306(c) and is usually preferred stock received either as a nontaxable dividend or in a transaction in which no gain or loss is recognized. Section 306(b) lists certain circumstances in which the special rules of section 306(a) shall not apply.

(b)(1) If a shareholder sells or otherwise disposes of section 306 stock (other than by redemption or within the exceptions listed in section 306(b)), the entire proceeds received from such disposition shall be treated as ordinary income to the extent that the fair market value of the stock sold, on the date distributed to the shareholder, would have been a dividend to such shareholder had the distributing corporation distributed cash in lieu of stock. Any excess of the amount received over the sum of the amount treated as ordinary income plus the adjusted basis of the stock disposed of, shall be treated as gain from the sale of a capital asset or noncapital asset as the case may be. No loss shall be recognized. No reduction of earnings and profits results from any disposition of stock other than a redemption. The term "disposition" under section 306(a)(1) includes, among other things, pledges of stock under certain circumstances, particularly where the pledgee can look only to the stock itself as its security.

(2) Section 306(a)(1) may be illustrated by the following examples:

Example (1). On December 15, 1954, A and B owned equally all of the stock of Corporation X which files its income tax return on a calendar year basis. On that date Corporation X distributed pro rata 100 shares of preferred stock as a dividend on its outstanding common stock. On December 15, 1954, the preferred stock had a fair market value of $10,000. On December 31, 1954, the earnings and profits of Corporation X were $20,000. The 50 shares of preferred stock so distributed to A had an allocated basis to him of $10 per share or a total of $500 for the 50 shares. Such shares had a fair market value of $5,000 when issued. A sold the 50 shares of preferred stock on July 1, 1955, for $6,000. Of this amount $5,000 will be treated as ordinary income; $500 ($6,000 minus $5,500) will be treated as gain from the sale of a capital or noncapital asset as the case may be.

Example (2). The facts are the same as in Example 1 except that A sold his 50 shares of preferred stock for $5,100. Of this amount $5,000 will be treated as ordinary income. No loss will be allowed. There will be added back to the basis of the common stock of Corporation X with respect to which the preferred stock was distributed, $400, the allocated basis of $500 reduced by the $100 received.

Example (3). The facts are the same as in example 1 except that A sold 25 of his shares of preferred stock for $2,600. Of this amount $2,500 will be treated as ordinary income. No loss will be allowed. There will be added back to the basis of the common stock of Corporation X with respect to which the preferred stock was distributed, $150, the allocated basis of $250 reduced by the $100 received.

(c) The entire amount received by a shareholder from the redemption of section 306 stock shall be treated as a distribution of property under section 301. See also section 303 (relating to distribution in redemption of stock to pay death taxes).

[T.D. 6500, 25 FR 11607, Nov. 26, 1960, as amended by T.D. 7556, 43 FR 34128, Aug. 3, 1978]

§ 1.306–2   Exception.

(a) If a shareholder terminates his entire stock interest in a corporation—

(1) By a sale or other disposition within the requirements of section 306(b)(1)(A), or

(2) By redemption under section 302(b)(3) (through the application of section 306(b)(1)(B)),

the amount received from such disposition shall be treated as an amount received in part or full payment for the stock sold or redeemed. In the case of a sale, only the stock interest need be terminated. In determining whether an entire stock interest has been terminated under section 306(b)(1)(A), all of the provisions of section 318(a) (relating to constructive ownership of stock) shall be applicable. In determining whether a shareholder has terminated his entire interest in a corporation by a redemption of his stock under section 302(b)(3), all of the provisions of section 318(a) shall be applicable unless the shareholder meets the requirements of section 302(c)(2) (relating to termination of all interest in the corporation). If the requirements of section 302(c)(2) are met, section 318(a)(1) (relating to members of a family) shall be inapplicable. Under all circumstances paragraphs (2), (3), (4), and (5) of section 318(a) shall be applicable.

(b) Section 306(a) does not apply to—

(1) Redemptions of section 306 stock pursuant to a partial or complete liquidation of a corporation to which part II (section 331 and following), subchapter C, chapter 1 of the Code applies,

(2) Exchanges of section 306 stock solely for stock in connection with a reorganization or in an exchange under section 351, 355, or section 1036 (relating to exchanges of stock for stock in the same corporation) to the extent that gain or loss is not recognized to the shareholder as the result of the exchange of the stock (see paragraph (d) of § 1.306–3 relative to the receipt of other property), and

(3) A disposition or redemption, if it is established to the satisfaction of the Commissioner that the distribution, and the disposition or redemption, was not in pursuance of a plan having as one of its principal purposes the avoidance of Federal income tax. However, in the case of a prior or simultaneous disposition (or redemption) of the stock with respect to which the section 306 stock disposed of (or redeemed) was issued, it is not necessary to establish that the distribution was not in pursuance of such a plan. For example, in the absence of such a plan and of any other facts the first sentence of this subparagraph would be applicable to the case of dividends and isolated dispositions of section 306 stock by minority shareholders. Similarly, in the absence of such a plan and of any other facts, if a shareholder received a distribution of 100 shares of section 306 stock on his holdings of 100 shares of voting common stock in a corporation and sells his voting common stock before he disposes of his section 306 stock, the subsequent disposition of his section 306 stock would not ordinarily be considered a disposition one of the principal purposes of which is the avoidance of Federal income tax.

[T.D. 6500, 25 FR 11607, Nov. 26, 1960, as amended by T.D. 6969, 33 FR 11998, Aug. 23, 1968]

§ 1.306–3   Section 306 stock defined.

(a) For the purpose of subchapter C, chapter 1 of the Code, the term "section 306 stock" means stock which meets the requirements of section 306(c)(1). Any class of stock distributed to a shareholder in a transaction in which no amount is includible in the income of the shareholder or no gain or loss is recognized may be section 306 stock, if a distribution of money by the distributing corporation in lieu of such stock would have been a dividend in whole or in part. However, except as provided in section 306(g), if no part of a distribution of money by the distributing corporation in lieu of such stock would have been a dividend, the stock distributed will not constitute section 306 stock.

(b) For the purpose of section 306, rights to acquire stock shall be treated as stock. Such rights shall not be section 306 stock if no part of the distribution would have been a dividend if money had been distributed in lieu of the rights. When stock is acquired by the exercise of rights which are treated at section 306 stock, the stock acquired is section 306 stock. Upon the disposition of such stock (other than by redemption or within the exceptions listed in section 306(b)), the proceeds received from the disposition shall be treated as ordinary income to the extent that the fair market value of the stock rights, on the date distributed to the shareholder, would have been a dividend to the shareholder had the distributing corporation distributed cash in lieu of stock rights. Any excess of the amount realized over the sum of the amount treated as ordinary income plus the adjusted basis of the stock, shall be treated as gain from the sale of the stock.

(c) Section 306(c)(1)(A) provides that section 306 stock is any stock (other than common issued with respect to common) distributed to the shareholder selling or otherwise disposing thereof if, under section 305(a) (relating to distributions of stock and stock rights) any part of the distribution was not included in the gross income of the distributee.

(d) Section 306(c)(1)(B) includes in the definition of section 306 stock any stock except common stock, which is received by a shareholder in connection with a reorganization under section 368 or in a distribution or exchange under section 355 (or so much of section 356 as relates to section 355) provided the effect of the transaction is substantially the same as the receipt of a stock dividend, or the stock is received in exchange for section 306 stock. If, in a transaction to which section 356 is applicable, a shareholder exchanges section 306 stock for stock and money or other property, the entire amount of such money and of the fair market value of the other property (not limited to the gain recognized) shall be treated as a distribution of property to which section 301 applies. Common stock received in exchange for section 306 stock in a recapitalization shall not be considered section 306 stock. Ordinarily, section 306 stock includes stock which is not common stock received in pursuance of a plan of reorganization (within the meaning of section 368(a)) or received in a distribu-

tion or exchange to which section 355 (or so much of section 356 as relates to section 355) applies if cash received in lieu of such stock would have been treated as a dividend under section 356(a)(2) or would have been treated as a distribution to which section 301 applies by virtue of section 356(b) or section 302(d). The application of the preceding sentence is illustrated by the following examples:

Example (1). Corporation A, having only common stock outstanding, is merged in a statutory merger (qualifying as a reorganization under section 368(a)) with Corporation B. Pursuant to such merger, the shareholders of Corporation A received both common and preferred stock in Corporation B. The preferred stock received by such shareholders is section 306 stock.

Example (2). X and Y each own one-half of the 2,000 outstanding shares of preferred stock and one-half of the 2,000 outstanding shares of common stock of Corporation C. Pursuant to a reorganization within the meaning of section 368(a)(1)(E) (recapitalization) each shareholder exchanges his preferred stock for preferred stock of a new issue which is not substantially different from the preferred stock previously held. Unless the preferred stock exchanged was itself section 306 stock the preferred stock received is not section 306 stock.

(e) Section 306(c)(1)(C) includes in the definition of section 306 stock any stock (except as provided in section 306(c)(1)(B)) the basis of which in the hands of the person disposing of such stock, is determined by reference to section 306 stock held by such shareholder or any other person. Under this paragraph common stock can be section 306 stock. Thus, if a person owning section 306 stock in Corporation A transfers it to Corporation B which is controlled by him in exchange for common stock of Corporation B in a transaction to which section 351 is applicable, the common stock so received by him would be section 306 stock and subject to the provisions of section 306(a) on its disposition. In addition, the section 306 stock transferred is section 306 stock in the hands of Corporation B, the transferee. Section 306 stock transferred by gift remains section 306 stock in the hands of the donee. Stock received in exchange for section 306 stock under section 1036(a) (relating to exchange of stock for stock in the same corporation) or under so much of section 1031(b) as relates to section 1036(a) becomes section 306 stock and acquires, for purposes of section 306, the characteristics of the section 306 stock exchanged. The entire amount of the fair market value of the other property received in such transaction shall be considered as received upon a disposition (other than a redemption) to which section 306(a) applies. Section 306 stock ceases to be so classified if the basis of such stock is determined by reference to its fair market value on the date of the decedent-stockholder's death or the optional valuation date under section 1014.

(f) If section 306 stock which was distributed with respect to common stock is exchanged for common stock in the same corporation (whether or not such exchange is pursuant to a conversion privilege contained in section 306 stock), such common stock shall not be section 306 stock. This paragraph applies to exchanges not coming within the purview of section 306(c)(1)(B). Common stock which is convertible into stock other than common stock or into property, shall not be considered common stock. It is immaterial whether the conversion privilege is contained in the stock or in some type of collateral agreement.

(g) If there is a substantial change in the terms and conditions of any stock, then, for the purpose of this section—

(1) The fair market value of such stock shall be the fair market value at the time of distribution or the fair market value at the time of such change, whichever is higher;

(2) Such stock's ratable share of the amount which would have been a dividend if money had been distributed in lieu of stock shall be determined by reference to the time of distribution or by reference to the time of such change, whichever ratable share is higher; and

(3) Section 306(c)(2) shall be inapplicable if there would have been a dividend to any extent if money had been distributed in lieu of the stock either at the time of the distribution or at the time of such change.

* * *

[T.D. 6500, 25 FR 11607, Nov. 26, 1960, as amended by T.D. 7281, 38 FR 18540, July 12, 1973; T.D. 7556, 43 FR 34128, Aug. 3, 1978]

§ 1.307–1 General.

(a) If a shareholder receives stock or stock rights as a distribution on stock previously held and under section 305 such distribution is not includible in gross income then, except as provided in section 307(b) and § 1.307–2, the basis of the stock with respect to which the distribution was made shall be allocated between the old and new stocks or rights in proportion to the fair market values of each on the date of distribution. If a shareholder receives stock or stock rights as a distribution on stock previously held and pursuant to section 305 part of

the distribution is not includible in gross income, then (except as provided in section 307(b) and § 1.307–2) the basis of the stock with respect to which the distribution is made shall be allocated between (1) the old stock and (2) that part of the new stock or rights which is not includible in gross income, in proportion to the fair market values of each on the date of distribution. The date of distribution in each case shall be the date the stock or the rights are distributed to the stockholder and not the record date. The general rule will apply with respect to stock rights only if such rights are exercised or sold.

(b) The application of paragraph (a) of this section is illustrated by the following example:

Example. A taxpayer in 1947 purchased 100 shares of common stock at $100 per share and in 1954 by reason of the ownership of such stock acquired 100 rights entitling him to subscribe to 100 additional shares of such stock at $90 a share. Immediately after the issuance of the rights, each of the shares of stock in respect of which the rights were acquired had a fair market value, ex-rights, of $110 and the rights had a fair market value of $19 each. The basis of the rights and the common stock for the purpose of determining the basis for gain or loss on a subsequent sale or exercise of the rights or a sale of the old stock is computed as follows:

100 (shares)×$100=$10,000, cost of old stock (stock in respect of which the rights were acquired).

100 (shares)×$110=$11,000, market value of old stock.

100 (rights)×$19=$1,900, market value of rights.

11,000/12,900 of $10,000=$8,527.13, cost of old stock apportioned to such stock.

1,900/12,900 of $10,000=$1,472.87, cost of old stock apportioned to rights.

If the rights are sold, the basis for determining gain or loss will be $14.7287 per right. If the rights are exercised, the basis of the new stock acquired will be the subscription price paid therefor ($90) plus the basis of the rights exercised ($14.7287 each) or $104.7287 per share. The remaining basis of the old stock for the purpose of determining gain or loss on a subsequent sale will be $85.2713 per share.

[T.D. 6500, 25 FR 11607, Nov. 26, 1960]

§ 1.307–2 Exception.

The basis of rights to buy stock which are excluded from gross income under section 305(a), shall be zero if the fair market value of such rights on the date of distribution is less than 15 percent of the fair market value of the old stock on that date, unless the shareholder elects to allocate part of the basis of the old stock to the rights as provided in paragraph (a) of § 1.307–1. The election shall be made by a shareholder with respect to all the rights received by him in a particular distribution in respect of all the stock of the same class owned by him in the issuing corporation at the time of such distribution. Such election to allocate basis to rights shall be in the form of a statement attached to the shareholder's return for the year in which the rights are received. This election, once made, shall be irrevocable with respect to the rights for which the election was made. Any shareholder making such an election shall retain a copy of the election and of the tax return with which it was filed, in order to substantiate the use of an allocated basis upon a subsequent disposition of the stock acquired by exercise.

[T.D. 6500, 25 FR 11607, Nov. 26, 1960]

Effects on Corporation

§ 1.311–1 General.

(a) Except as provided in subsections (b), (c), and (d) of section 311, section 453(d) (relating to installment obligations) and such other provisions of the Code as sections 341(f), 617(d), 1245(a), 1250(a), 1251(c), and 1252(a), no gain or loss is recognized to a corporation on the distribution, with respect to its stock, of stock, or rights to acquire its stock, or property (regardless of the fact that such property may have appreciated or depreciated in value since its acquisition by the corporation). However, the proceeds of the sale of property in form made by a shareholder receiving such property in kind from the corporation may be imputed to the corporation if, in substance the corporation made the sale. Moreover, where property is distributed by a corporation, which distribution is in effect an anticipatory assignment of income, such income may be taxable to the corporation. The term "distributions with respect to its stock" includes distributions made in redemption of stock (other than distributions in complete or partial liquidations). See, however, paragraph (e) of this section for distributions to which section 311 does not apply. For the rule respecting the taxation of a corporation making a distribution of property in partial or complete liquidation, see section 336.

(b) In any case in which a corporation distributes with respect to its stock assets which have been part of an inventory, the value of which has been computed for income tax purposes under the method provided in section 472 (relating to last-in, first-out inventories), such corporation shall—

(1) Compute the amount of its inventory under the method provided in section 472 immediately prior to the distribution and immediately after such distribution;

(2) Compute the difference between the two amounts described in subparagraph (1) of this paragraph;

(3) Compute the amount of its inventory under the method authorized by section 471 (relating to general rule for inventories) immediately prior to the distribution and immediately after such distribution;

(4) Compute the difference between the two amounts determined under subparagraph (3) of this paragraph.

If the amount computed under subparagraph (4) of this paragraph is in excess of the amount computed under subparagraph (2) of this paragraph, then such excess shall, under section 311(b), be included in the income of the corporation for the year in which such distribution occurs. In any case in which a corporation distributes assets which have been a part of an inventory whose value has been computed for income tax purposes under the method provided in section 472, such corporation shall on the date of distribution record a specific statement of the amount of its inventory under each of the applicable methods for use in the determination of the amount of income includible under section 311. Section 311(b) and this paragraph do not apply to any distribution which is governed by section 311(d)(1).

(c) The following example illustrates the application of section 311(b):

Example. Corporation R, a manufacturing corporation inventorying goods under the method provided in section 472, distributes 200 units of its inventory assets to its shareholders on November 15, 1955. Immediately before the distribution, the corporation held 300 identical inventory units at the following basis determined by reference to the value computed by using the LIFO method and the value computed by using the FIFO method, in the order of acquisition:

	No. of units	Basis LIFO
a.	100	$1,000
b.	100	2,000
c.	50	1,000
d.	50	2,000

No. of units	Basis LIFO
100	$4,000
50	2,500
50	2,500
100	6,000

The amount includible in income pursuant to section 311(b) is $4,000 computed as follows:

(1) Inventory before distribution under FIFO method (a, b, c, and d)	$15,000
(2) Inventory under FIFO method immediately after distribution (d)	6,000
(3) Difference (FIFO basis of inventory distributed)	$9,000
(4) Inventory before distribution under LIFO method (a, b, c and d)	$6,000
(5) Inventory under LIFO method immediately after distribution (a)	1,000
(6) Difference (LIFO basis of inventory distributed)	5,000
(7) Amount includible in income under section 311(b)	4,000

(d) Section 311(c) provides in general for the inclusion in the income of a corporation, on a distribution of property by such corporation to its shareholders, of an amount equal to the excess of a liability over the basis of the property distributed. Thus, section 311(c) applies where the property distributed is subject to a liability or where the shareholder assumes a liability of the corporation in connection with the distribution. For example, if property which is a capital asset having an adjusted basis to the distributing corporation of $100 and a fair market value of $1,000 (but subject to a liability of $900) is distributed to a shareholder, such distribution is taxable (as long-term or short-term gain, as the case may be) to the corporation to the extent of the excess of the liability ($900) over the adjusted basis ($100) or $800. However, if in the preceding example the fair market value of the property distributed were $800, the amount taxable to the corporation is limited to the excess of the fair market value of the property ($800) over its adjusted basis ($100) or $700. If the property subject to a liability were not a capital asset in the hands of the distributing corporation, the gain would be taxable as gain from the sale of a noncapital asset. The holding period of assets so distributed shall be determined as if such property were sold on the date of the distribution. Section

311(c) and this paragraph do not apply to any distribution which is governed by section 311(d)(1).

(e)(1) Section 311 is limited to distributions which are made by reason of the corporation-stockholder relationship. Section 311 does not apply to transactions between a corporation and a shareholder in his capacity as debtor, creditor, employee, or vendee, where the fact that such debtor, creditor, employee, or vendee is a shareholder is incidental to the transaction. Thus, if the corporation receives its own stock as consideration upon the sale of property by it, or in satisfaction of indebtedness to it, the gain or loss resulting is to be computed in the same manner as though the payment had been made in any other property.

(2) The following examples illustrate the application of subparagraph (1) of this paragraph:

Example (1). Corporation A has a claim against Corporation B for damages for loss of profits due to patent infringement. Corporation B satisfies such claim by surrendering shares of the stock of Corporation A to Corporation A. The fair market value of such stock is includible in the gross income of Corporation A.

Example (2). Corporation C, a corporation engaged in the manufacture and sale of automobiles, sells an automobile to individual X, and receives in payment therefor shares of the stock of Corporation C. The transaction will be treated in the same manner as if an amount of cash equal to the fair market value of such stock had been received by Corporation C.

[T.D. 6500, 25 FR 11607, Nov. 26, 1960, as amended by T.D. 7209, 37 FR 20801, Oct. 5, 1972; 37 FR 22375, Oct. 19, 1972]

§ 1.312–1 Adjustment to earnings and profits reflecting distributions by corporations.

(a) In general, on the distribution of property by a corporation with respect to its stock, its earnings, and profits (to the extent thereof) shall be decreased by—

(1) The amount of money,

(2) The principal amount of the obligations of such corporation issued in such distribution, and

(3) The adjusted basis of other property.

For special rule with respect to distributions to which section 312(e) applies, see § 1.312–5.

(b) The adjustment provided in section 312(a)(3) and paragraph (a)(3) of this section with respect to a distribution of property (other than money or its own obligations) shall be made notwithstanding the fact that such property has appreciated or depreciated in value since acquisition.

(c) The application of paragraphs (a) and (b) of this section may be illustrated by the following examples:

Example (1). Corporation A distributes to its sole shareholder property with a value of $10,000 and a basis of $5,000. It has $12,500 in earnings and profits. The reduction in earnings and profits by reason of such distribution is $5,000. Such is the reduction even though the amount of $10,000 is includible in the income of the shareholder (other than a corporation) as a dividend.

Example (2). The facts are the same as in example (1) above except that the property has a basis of $15,000 and the earnings and profits of the corporation are $20,000. The reduction in earnings and profits is $15,000. Such is the reduction even though only the amount of $10,000 is includible in the income of the shareholder as a dividend.

(d) In the case of a distribution of stock or rights to acquire stock a portion of which is includible in income by reason of section 305(b), the earnings and profits shall be reduced by the fair market value of such portion. No reduction shall be made if a distribution of stock or rights to acquire stock is not includible in income under the provisions of section 305.

(e) No adjustment shall be made in the amount of the earnings and profits of the issuing corporation upon a disposition of section 306 stock unless such disposition is a redemption.

§ 1.312–2 Distribution of inventory assets.

Section 312(b) provides for the increase and the decrease of the earnings and profits of a corporation which distributes, with respect to its stock, inventory assets as defined in section 312(b)(2), where the fair market value of such assets exceeds their adjusted basis. The rules provided in section 312(b) (relating to distributions of certain inventory assets) shall be applicable without regard to the method used in computing inventories for the purpose of the computation of taxable income. Section 312(b) does not apply to distributions described in section 312(e).

[T.D. 6500, 25 FR 11607, Nov. 26, 1960]

§ 1.312–3 Liabilities.

The amount of any reductions in earnings and profits described in section 312(a) or (b) shall be (a) reduced by the amount of any liability to which the property distributed was subject and by the amount of any other liability of the corporation assumed by the shareholder in connection with such distribution, and (b) increased by the amount of gain recognized to the corporation * * *.

[T.D. 6500, 25 FR 11607, Nov. 26, 1960, as amended by T.D. 6832, 30 FR 8574, July 7, 1965; T.D. 7084, 36 FR 267, Jan. 8, 1971; T.D. 7209, 37 FR 20804, Oct. 5, 1972]

§ 1.312–4 Examples of adjustments provided in section 312(c).

The adjustments provided in section 312(c) may be illustrated by the following examples:

Example (1). On December 2, 1954, Corporation X distributed to its sole shareholder, A, an individual, as a dividend in kind a vacant lot which was not an inventory asset. On that date, the lot had a fair market value of $5,000 and was subject to a mortgage of $2,000. The adjusted basis of the lot was $3,100. The amount of the earnings and profits was $10,000. The amount of the dividend received by A is $3,000 ($5,000, the fair market value, less $2,000, the amount of the mortgage) and the reduction in the earnings and profits of Corporation X is $1,100 ($3,100, the basis, less $2,000, the amount of mortgage).

Example (2). The facts are the same as in example (1) above with the exception that the amount of the mortgage to which the property was subject was $4,000. The amount of the dividend received by A is $1,000, and there is no reduction in the earnings and profits of the corporation as a result of the distribution (disregarding such reduction as may result from an increase in tax to Corporation X because, of gain resulting from the distribution). There is a gain of $900 recognized to Corporation X, the difference between the basis of the property ($3,100) and the amount of the mortgage ($4,000), under section 311(c) and an increase in earnings and profits of $900.

Example (3). Corporation A, having accumulated earnings and profits of $100,000, distributed in kind to its shareholders, not in liquidation, inventory assets which had a basis to it on the "Lifo" method (section 472) of $46,000 and on the basis of cost or market (section 471) of $50,000. The inventory had a fair market value of $55,000 and was subject to a liability of $35,000. This distribution results in a net decrease in earnings and profits of Corporation A of $11,000, (without regard to any tax on Corporation A) computed as follows:

"FIFO" basis of inventory	$50,000	
Less: "LIFO" basis of inventory	46,000	
Gain recognized—addition to earnings and profits (section 311(b))		$ 4,000
Adjustment to earnings and profits required by section 312(b)(1)(A):		
Fair market value of inventory....................	$55,000	
Less: "LIFO" basis plus adjustment under section 311(b)	50,000	5,000
Total increase in earnings and profits		9,000

Decrease in earnings and profits—under section 312(b)(1)(B)(i) $55,000
Less: Liability assumed 35,000

Net amount of distribution (decrease in earnings) 20,000

Net decrease in earnings and profits.. 11,000

[T.D. 6500, 25 FR 11607, Nov. 26, 1960]

§ 1.312–5 Special rule for partial liquidations and certain redemptions.

The part of the distribution properly chargeable to capital account within the provisions of section 312(e) shall not be considered a distribution of earnings and profits within the meaning of section 301 for the purpose of determining taxability of subsequent distributions by the corporation.

[T.D. 6500, 25 FR 11607, Nov. 26, 1960]

§ 1.312–6 Earnings and profits.

(a) In determining the amount of earnings and profits (whether of the taxable year, or accumulated since February 28, 1913, or accumulated before March 1, 1913) due consideration must be given to the facts, and, while mere bookkeeping entries increasing or decreasing surplus will not be conclusive, the amount of the earnings and profits in any case will be dependent upon the method of accounting properly employed in computing taxable income (or net income, as the case may be). For instance, a corporation keeping its books and filing its income tax returns under subchapter E, chapter 1 of the Code, on the cash receipts and disbursements basis may not use the accrual basis in determining earnings and profits; a corporation computing income on the installment basis as provided in section 453 shall, with respect to the installment transactions, compute earnings and profits on such basis; and an insurance company subject to taxation under section 831 shall exclude from earnings and profits that portion of any premium which is unearned under the provisions of section 832(b)(4) and which is segregated accordingly in the unearned premium reserve.

(b) Among the items entering into the computation of corporate earnings and profits for a particular period are all income exempted by statute, income not taxable by the Federal Government under the Constitution, as well as all items includible in gross income under section 61 or corresponding provisions of prior revenue acts. Gains and losses within the purview of section 1002 or corresponding provisions of prior revenue acts are brought into the earnings and profits at the time and to the extent such gains and losses are recognized under that section. Interest on State bonds and certain other obligations, although not taxable when received by a corporation, is taxable to the same extent as other dividends when distributed to shareholders in the form of dividends.

(c)(1) In the case of a corporation in which depletion or depreciation is a factor in the determination of income, the only depletion or depreciation deductions to be considered in the computation of the total earnings and profits are those based on cost or other basis without regard to March 1, 1913, value. In computing the earnings and profits for any period beginning after February 28, 1913, the only depletion or depreciation deductions to be considered are those based on (i) cost or other basis, if the depletable or depreciable asset was acquired subsequent to February 28, 1913, or (ii) adjusted cost or March 1, 1913, value, whichever is higher, if acquired before March 1, 1913. Thus, discovery or percentage depletion under all revenue acts for mines and oil and gas wells is not to be taken into consideration in computing the earnings and profits of a corporation. Similarly, where the basis of property in the hands of a corporation is a substituted basis, such basis, and not the fair market value of the property at the time of the acquisition by the corporation, is the basis for computing depletion and depreciation for the purpose of determining earnings and profits of the corporation.

(2) The application of subparagraph (1) of this paragraph may be illustrated by the following example:

Example. Oil producing property which A had acquired in 1949 at a cost of $28,000 was transferred to Corporation Y in December 1951, in exchange for all of its capital stock. The fair market value of the stock and of the property as of the date of the transfer was $247,000. Corporation Y, after four years' operation, effected in 1955 a cash distribution to A in the amount of $165,000. In determining the extent to which the earnings and profits of Corporation Y available for dividend distributions have been increased as the result of production and sale of oil, the depletion to be taken into account is to be computed upon the basis of $28,000 established in the nontaxable exchange in 1951 regardless of the fair market value of the property or of the stock issued in exchange therefor.

(d) A loss sustained for a year before the taxable year does not affect the earnings and profits of the taxable year. However, in determining the earnings and profits accumulated since February 28, 1913, the excess of a loss sustained for a year subsequent to February 28, 1913, over the undistributed earnings and profits accumulated since February 28, 1913, and before the year for which the loss was sustained, reduces surplus as of March 1, 1913, to the extent of such excess. If the surplus as of March 1, 1913, was sufficient to absorb such excess, distributions to shareholders after the year of the loss are out of earnings and profits accumulated since the year of the loss to the extent of such earnings.

* * *

[T.D. 6500, 25 FR 11607, Nov. 26, 1960]

§ 1.312-7 Effect on earnings and profits of gain or loss realized after February 28, 1913.

(a) In order to determine the effect on earnings and profits of gain or loss realized from the sale or other disposition (after February 28, 1913) of property by a corporation, section 312(f)(1) prescribed certain rules for—

(1) The computation of the total earnings and profits of the corporation of most frequent application in determining invested capital; and

(2) The computation of earnings and profits of the corporation for any period beginning after February 28, 1913, of most frequent application in determining the source of dividend distributions.

Such rules are applicable whenever under any provision of subtitle A of the Code it is necessary to compute either the total earnings and profits of the corporation or the earnings and profits for any period beginning after February 28, 1913. For example, since the earnings and profits accumulated after February 28, 1913, or the earnings and profits of the taxable year, are earnings and profits for a period beginning after February 28, 1913, the determination of either must be in accordance with the regulations prescribed by this section for the ascertainment of earnings and profits for any period beginning after February 28, 1913. Under subparagraph (1) of this paragraph, such gain or loss is determined by using the adjusted basis (under the law applicable to the year in which the sale or other disposition was made) for determining gain, but disregarding value as of March 1, 1913. Under subparagraph (2) of this paragraph, there is used such adjusted basis for determining gain, giving effect to the value as of March 1, 1913, whenever applicable. In both cases the rules are the same as those governing depreciation and depletion in computing earnings and profits (see § 1.312-6). Under

both subparagraphs (1) and (2) of this paragraph, the adjusted basis is subject to the limitations of the third sentence of section 312(f)(1) requiring the use of adjustments proper in determining earnings and profits. The proper adjustments may differ under section 312(f)(1)(A) and (B) depending upon the basis to which the adjustments are to be made. If the application of section 312(f)(1)(B) results in a loss and if the application of section 312(f)(1)(A) to the same transaction reaches a different result, then the loss under section 312(f)(1)(B) will be subject to the adjustment thereto required by section 312(g)(2). * * *

(b)(1) The gain or loss so realized increases or decreases the earnings and profits to, but not beyond, the extent to which such gain or loss was recognized in computing taxable income (or net income, as the case may be) under the law applicable to the year in which such sale or disposition was made. As used in this paragraph, the term "recognized" has reference to that kind of realized gain or loss which is recognized for income tax purposes by the statute applicable to the year in which the gain or loss was realized. For example, see section 356. A loss (other than a wash sale loss with respect to which a deduction is disallowed under the provisions of section 1091 or corresponding provisions of prior revenue laws) may be recognized though not allowed as a deduction (by reason, for example, of the operation of sections 267 and 1211 and corresponding provisions of prior revenue laws) but the mere fact that it is not allowed does not prevent decrease in earnings and profits by the amount of such disallowed loss. Wash sale losses, however, disallowed under section 1091 and corresponding provisions of prior revenue laws, are deemed nonrecognized losses and do not reduce earnings or profits. The "recognized" gain or loss for the purpose of computing earnings and profits is determined by applying the recognition provisions to the realized gain or loss computed under the provisions of section 312(f)(1) as distinguished from the realized gain or loss used in computing taxable income (or net income, as the case may be).

(2) The application of subparagraph (1) of this paragraph may be illustrated by the following examples:

Example (1). Corporation X on January 1, 1952, owned stock in Corporation Y which it had acquired from Corporation Y in December 1951, in an exchange transaction in which no gain or loss was recognized. The adjusted basis to Corporation X of the property exchanged by it for the stock in Corporation Y was $30,000. The fair market value of the stock in Corporation Y when received by Corporation X was $930,000. On April 9, 1955, Corporation X made a cash distribution of $900,000 and, except for the possible effect of the transaction in 1951, had no earnings or profits accumulated after February 28, 1913, and had no earnings or profits for the taxable year. The amount of $900,000 representing the excess of the fair market value of the stock of Corporation Y over the adjusted basis of the property exchanged therefor was not recognized gain to Corporation X under the provisions of section 112 of the Internal Revenue Code of 1939. Accordingly, the earnings and profits of Corporation X are not increased by $900,000, the amount of the gain realized but not recognized in the exchange, and the distribution was not a taxable dividend. The basis in the hands of Corporation Y of the property acquired by it from Corporation X is $30,000. If such property is thereafter sold by Corporation Y, gain or loss will be computed on such basis of $30,000, and earnings and profits will be increased or decreased accordingly.

* * *

(c)(1) The third sentence of section 312(f)(1) provides for cases in which the adjustments, prescribed in section 1016, to the basis indicated in section 312(f)(1)(A) or (B), as the case may be, differ from the adjustments to such basis proper for the purpose of determining earnings or profits. The adjustments provided by such third sentence reflect the treatment provided by §§ 1.312–6 and 1.312–15 relative to cases where the deductions for depletion and depreciation in computing taxable income (or net income, as the case may be) differ from the deductions proper for the purpose of computing earnings and profits.

(2) The effect of the third sentence of section 312(f)(1) may be illustrated by the following examples:

Example (1). Corporation X purchased on January 2, 1931, an oil lease at a cost of $10,000. The lease was operated only for the years 1931 and 1932. The deduction for depletion in each of the years 1931 and 1932 amounted to $2,750, of which amount $1,750 represented percentage depletion in excess of depletion based on cost. The lease was sold in 1955 for $15,000. Under section 1016(a)(2), in determining the gain or loss from the sale of the property, the basis must be adjusted for cost depletion of $1,000 in 1931 and percentage depletion of $2,750 in 1932. However, the adjustment of such basis, proper for the determination of earnings and profits, is $1,000 for each year, or $2,000. Hence, the cost is to be adjusted only to the extent of $2,000, leaving an adjusted basis of $8,000 and the earnings and profits will be increased by $7,000, and not by $8,750. The difference of $1,750 is equal to the amount by which the percentage depletion for the year 1932 ($2,750) exceeds the depletion on cost for that year ($1,000) and has already been applied in the computation of earnings and profits for the year 1932 by taking into account only $1,000 instead of $2,750 for depletion in the computation of such earnings and profits. (See § 1.316–1.)

Example (2). If, in example (1), above, the property, instead of being sold, is exchanged in a transaction described in section 1031 for like property having a fair market value of $7,750 and cash of $7,250, then the increase in earnings and profits amounts to $7,000, that is, $15,000 ($7,750 plus $7,250) minus the basis of $8,000. However, in computing taxable income of Corporation X, the gain is $8,750, that is, $15,000 minus $6,250 ($10,000 less depletion of $3,750), of which only $7,250 is recognized because the recognized gain cannot exceed the sum of money received in the transaction. See section 1031(b) and the corresponding provisions of prior revenue laws. If, however, the cash received was only $2,250 and the value of the property received was $12,750, then the increase in earnings and profits would be $2,250, that amount being the gain recognized under section 1031.

Example (3). On January 1, 1973, corporation X purchased for $10,000 a depreciable asset with an estimated useful life of 20 years and no salvage value. In computing depreciation on the asset, corporation X used the declining balance method with a rate twice the straight line rate. On December 31, 1976, the asset was sold for $9,000. Under section 1016(a)(2), the basis of the asset is adjusted for depreciation allowed for the years 1973 through 1976, or a total of $3,439. Thus, X realizes a gain of $2,439 (the excess of the amount realized, $9,000, over the adjusted basis, $6,561). However, the proper adjustment to basis for the purpose of determining earnings and profits is only $2,000, i.e., the total amount which, under § 1.312–15, was applied in the computation of earnings and profits for the years 1973–76. Hence, upon sale of the asset, earnings and profits are increased by only $1,000, i.e., the excess of the amount realized, $9,000, over the adjusted basis for earnings and profits purposes, $8,000.

(d) For adjustment and allocation of the earnings and profits of the transferor as between the transferor and the transferee in cases where the transfer of property by one corporation to another corporation results in the nonrecognition in whole or in part of gain or loss, see § 1.312–10; and see section 381 for earnings and profits of successor corporations in certain transactions.

[T.D. 6500, 25 FR 11607, Nov. 26, 1960, as amended by T.D. 7221, 37 FR 24746, Nov. 21, 1972]

§ 1.312–10　Allocation of earnings in certain corporate separations.

(a) If one corporation transfers part of its assets constituting an active trade or business to another corporation in a transaction to which section 368(a)(1)(D) applies and immediately thereafter the stock and securities of the controlled corporation are distributed in a distribution or exchange to which section 355 (or so much of section 356 as relates to section 355) applies, the earnings and profits of the distributing corporation immediately before the transaction shall be allocated between the distributing corporation and the controlled corporation. In the case of a newly created controlled corporation, such allocation generally shall be made in proportion to the fair market value of the business or businesses (and interests in any other properties) retained by the distributing corporation and the business or businesses (and interests in any other properties) of the controlled corporation immediately after the transaction. In a proper case, allocation shall be made between the distributing corporation and the controlled corporation in proportion to the net basis of the assets transferred and of the assets retained or by such other method as may be appropriate under the facts and circumstances of the case. The term "net basis" means the basis of the assets less liabilities assumed or liabilities to which such assets are subject. The part of the earnings and profits of the taxable year of the distributing corporation in which the transaction occurs allocable to the controlled corporation shall be included in the computation of the earnings and profits of the first taxable year of the controlled corporation ending after the date of the transaction.

(b) If a distribution or exchange to which section 355 applies (or so much of section 356 as relates to section 355) is not in pursuance of a plan meeting the requirements of a reorganization as defined in section 368(a)(1)(D), the earnings and profits of the distributing corporation shall be decreased by the lesser of the following amounts:

(1) The amount by which the earnings and profits of the distributing corporation would have been decreased if it had transferred the stock of the controlled corporation to a new corporation in a reorganization to which section 368(a)(1)(D) applied and immediately thereafter distributed the stock of such new corporation or,

(2) The net worth of the controlled corporation. (For this purpose the term "net worth" means the sum of the basis of all of the properties plus cash minus all liabilities.)

If the earnings and profits of the controlled corporation immediately before the transaction are less than the amount of the decrease in earnings and profits of the distributing corporation (including a case in which the controlled corporation has a deficit) the earnings and profits of the controlled corporation, after the transaction, shall be equal to the amount of such decrease. If the earnings and profits of the controlled corporation immediately before the transaction are more than the amount of the decrease in the earnings and profits of the

distributing corporation, they shall remain unchanged.

(c) In no case shall any part of a deficit of a distributing corporation within the meaning of section 355 be allocated to a controlled corporation.

[T.D. 6500, 25 FR 11607, Nov. 26, 1960]

§ 1.312–11 Effect on earnings and profits of certain other tax-free exchanges, tax-free distributions, and tax-free transfers from one corporation to another.

(a) If property is transferred by one corporation to another, and, under the law applicable to the year in which the transfer was made, no gain or loss was recognized (or was recognized only to the extent of the property received other than that permitted by such law to be received without the recognition of gain), then proper adjustment and allocation of the earnings and profits of the transferor shall be made as between the transferor and the transferee. Transfers to which the preceding sentence applies include contributions to capital, transfers under section 351, transfers in connection with reorganizations under section 368, transfers in liquidations under section 332 and intercompany transfers during a period of affiliation. However, if, for example, property is transferred from one corporation to another in a transaction under section 351 or as a contribution to capital and the transfer is not followed or preceded by a reorganization, a transaction under section 302(a) involving a substantial part of the transferor's stock, or a total or partial liquidation, then ordinarily no allocation of the earnings and profits of the transferor shall be made. For specific rules as to allocation of earnings and profits in certain reorganizations under section 368 and in certain liquidations under section 332 see section 381 and the regulations thereunder. For allocation of earnings and profits in certain corporate separations see section 312(i) and § 1.312–10.

* * *

[T.D. 6500, 25 FR 11607, Nov. 26, 1960]

§ 1.312–15 Effect of depreciation on earnings and profits.

(a) **Depreciation for taxable years beginning after June 30, 1972—(1) In general.** Except as provided in subparagraph (2) of this paragraph and paragraph (c) of this section, for purposes of computing the earnings and profits of a corporation (including a real estate investment trust as defined in section 856) for any taxable year beginning after June 30, 1972, the allowance for depreciation (and amortization, if any) shall be deemed to be the amount which would be allowable for such year if the straight line method of depreciation had been used for all property for which depreciation is allowable for each taxable year beginning after June 30, 1972. Thus, for taxable years beginning after June 30, 1972, in determining the earnings and profits of a corporation, depreciation must be computed under the straight line method, notwithstanding that in determining taxable income the corporation uses an accelerated method of depreciation described in subparagraph (A), (B), or (C) of section 312(m)(2) or elects to amortize the basis of property under section 169, 184, 187, or 188, or any similar provision.

(2) **Exception.** (i) If, for any taxable year beginning after June 30, 1972, a method of depreciation is used by a corporation in computing taxable income which the Secretary or his delegate has determined results in a reasonable allowance under section 167(a) and which is not a declining balance method of depreciation (described in § 1.167(b)–2), the sum of the years-digits method (described in § 1.167(b)–3), or any other method allowed solely by reason of the application of subsection (b)(4) or (j)(1)(C) of section 167, then the adjustment to earnings and profits for depreciation for such year shall be determined under the method so used (in lieu of the straight line method).

(ii) The Commissioner has determined that the "unit of production" (see § 1.167(b)–0(b)), and the "machine hour" methods of depreciation, when properly used under appropriate circumstances, meet the requirements of subdivision (i) of this subparagraph. Thus, the adjustment to earnings and profits for depreciation (for the taxable year for which either of such methods is properly used under appropriate circumstances) shall be determined under whichever of such methods is used to compute taxable income.

(3) **Determinations under straight line method.** (i) In the case of property with respect to which an allowance for depreciation is claimed in computing taxable income, the determination of the amount which would be allowable under the straight line method shall be based on the manner in which the corporation computes depreciation in

determining taxable income. Thus, if an election under § 1.167(a)–11 is in effect with respect to the property, the amount of depreciation which would be allowable under the straight line method shall be determined under § 1.167(a)–11(g)(3). On the other hand, if property is not depreciated under the provisions of § 1.167(a)–11, the amount of depreciation which would be allowable under the straight line method shall be determined under § 1.167(b)–1. Any election made under section 167(f), with respect to reducing the amount of salvage value taken into account in computing the depreciation allowance for certain property, or any convention adopted under § 1.167(a)–10(b) or § 1.167(a)–11(c)(2), with respect to additions and retirements from multiple asset accounts, which is used in computing depreciation for taxable income shall be used in computing depreciation for earnings and profits purposes.

(ii) In the case of property with respect to which an election to amortize is in effect under section 169, 184, 187, or 188, or any similar provision, the amount which would be allowable under the straight line method of depreciation shall be determined under the provisions of § 1.167(b)–1. Thus, the cost or other basis of the property, less its estimated salvage value, is to be deducted in equal annual amounts over the period of the estimated useful life of the property. In computing the amount of depreciation for earnings and profits purposes, a taxpayer may utilize the provisions of section 167(f) (relating to the reduction in the amount of salvage value taken into account in computing the depreciation allowance for certain property) and any convention which could have been adopted for such property under § 1.167(a)–10(b) (relating to additions and retirements from multiple asset accounts).

* * *

(d) **Books and records.** Wherever different methods of depreciation are used for taxable income and earnings and profits purposes, records shall be maintained which show the depreciation taken for earnings and profits purposes each year and which will allow computation of the adjusted basis of the property in each account using the depreciation taken for earnings and profits purposes.

[T.D. 7221, 37 FR 24746, Nov. 21, 1972]

Definitions; Constructive Ownership of Stock

§ 1.316-1 Dividends.

(a)(1) The term "dividend" for the purpose of subtitle A of the Code (except when used in subchapter L, chapter 1 of the Code, in any case where the reference is to dividends and similar distributions of insurance companies paid to policyholders as such) comprises any distribution of property as defined in section 317 in the ordinary course of business, even though extraordinary in amount, made by a domestic or foreign corporation to its shareholders out of either—

(i) Earnings and profits accumulated since February 28, 1913, or

(ii) Earnings and profits of the taxable year computed without regard to the amount of the earnings and profits (whether of such year or accumulated since February 28, 1913) at the time the distribution was made.

The earnings and profits of the taxable year shall be computed as of the close of such year, without diminution by reason of any distributions made during the taxable year. For the purpose of determining whether a distribution constitutes a dividend, it is unnecessary to ascertain the amount of the earnings and profits accumulated since February 28, 1913, if the earnings and profits of the taxable year are equal to or in excess of the total amount of the distributions made within such year.

(2) Where a corporation distributes property to its shareholders on or after June 22, 1954, the amount of the distribution which is a dividend to them may not exceed the earnings and profits of the distributing corporation.

(3) The rule of (2) above may be illustrated by the following example:

Example. X and Y, individuals, each own one-half of the stock of Corporation A which has earnings and profits of $10,000. Corporation A distributes property having a basis of $6,000 and a fair market value of $16,000 to its shareholders, each shareholder receiving property with a basis of $3,000 and with a fair market value of $8,000 in a distribution to which section 301 applies. The amount taxable to each shareholder as a dividend under section 301(c) is $5,000.

(b)(1) In the case of a corporation which, under the law applicable to the taxable year in which a distribution is made, is a personal holding company or which, for the taxable year in respect of which a distribution is made under section 563 (relating to dividends paid within 2½ months after the close of the taxable year), or section 547 (relating to deficiency dividends), or corresponding provisions of a prior income tax law, was under the applicable law a personal holding company, the term "dividend", in addition to the meaning set forth in the first sentence of section 316, also means a distribution to its shareholders as follows: A distribution within a taxable year of the corporation, or of a shareholder, is a dividend to the extent of the corporation's undistributed personal holding company income (determined under section 545 without regard to distributions under section 316(b)(2)) for the taxable year in which, or, in the case of a distribution under section 563 or section 547, the taxable year in respect of which, the distribution was made. This subparagraph does not apply to distributions in partial or complete liquidation of a personal holding company. In the case of certain complete liquidations of a personal holding company see subparagraph (2) of this paragraph.

(2) In the case of a corporation which, under the law applicable to the taxable year in which a distribution is made, is a personal holding company or which, for the taxable year in respect of which a distribution is made under section 563, or section 547, or corresponding provisions of a prior income tax law, was under the applicable law a personal holding company, the term "dividend", in addition to the meaning set forth in the first sentence of section 316, also means, in the case of a complete liquidation occurring within 24 months after the adoption of a plan of liquidation, a distribution of property to its shareholders within such period, but—

(i) Only to the extent of the amounts distributed to distributees other than corporate shareholders, and

(ii) Only to the extent that the corporation designates such amounts as a dividend distribution and duly notifies such distributees in accordance with subparagraph (5) of this paragraph, but

(iii) Not in excess of the sum of such distributees' allocable share of the undistributed personal holding company income for such year (determined under section 545 without regard to sections 562(b) and 316(b)(2)(B)).

Section 316(b)(2)(B) and this subparagraph apply only to distributions made in any taxable year of the distributing corporation beginning after December 31, 1963. The amount designated with respect to a noncorporate distributee may not exceed the amount actually distributed to such distributee. For purposes of determining a noncorporate distributee's gain or loss on liquidation, amounts distributed in complete liquidation to such distributee during a taxable year are reduced by the amounts designated as a dividend with respect to such distributee for such year. For purposes of section 333(e)(1), a shareholder's ratable share of the earnings and profits of the corporation accumulated after February 28, 1913, shall be reduced by the amounts designated as a dividend with respect to such shareholder (even though such designated amounts are distributed during the 1-month period referred to in section 333).

(3) For purposes of subparagraph (2)(iii) of this paragraph—

(i) Except as provided in subdivision (ii) of this subparagraph, the sum of the noncorporate distributees' allocable share of undistributed personal holding company income for the taxable year in which, or in respect of which, the distribution was made (computed without regard to sections 562(b) and 316(b)(2)(B)) shall be determined by multiplying such undistributed personal holding company income by the ratio which the aggregate value of the stock held by all noncorporate shareholders immediately before the record date of the last liquidating distribution in such year bears to the total value of all stock outstanding on such date. For rules applicable in a case where the distributing corporation has more than one class of stock, see subdivision (iii) of this subparagraph.

(ii) If more than one liquidating distribution was made during the year, and if, after the record date of the first distribution but before the record date of the last distribution, there was a change in the relative shareholdings as between noncorporate shareholders and corporate shareholders, then the sum of the noncorporate distributees' allocable share of undistributed personal holding company income for the taxable year in which, or in respect of which, the distributions were made (computed without regard to sections 562(b) and 316(b)(2)(B)) shall be determined as follows:

(a) First, allocate the corporation's undistributed personal holding company income among the distributions made during the taxable year by reference to the ratio which the aggregate amount of each distribution bears to the total amount of all distributions during such year;

(b) Second, determine the noncorporate distributees' allocable share of the corporation's undistributed personal holding company income for each distribution by multiplying the amount determined under (a) of this subdivision (ii) for each distribu-

tion by the ratio which the aggregate value of the stock held by all noncorporate shareholders immediately before the record date of such distribution bears to the total value of all stock outstanding on such date; and

(c) Last, determine the sum of the noncorporate distributees' allocable share of the corporation's undistributed personal holding company income for all such distributions.

For rules applicable in a case where the distributing corporation has more than one class of stock, see subdivision (iii) of this subparagraph.

(iii) Where the distributing corporation has more than one class of stock—

(a) The undistributed personal holding company income for the taxable year in which, or in respect of which, the distribution was made shall be treated as a fund from which dividends may properly be paid and shall be allocated between or among the classes of stock in a manner consistent with the dividend rights of such classes under local law and the pertinent governing instruments, such as, for example, the distributing corporation's articles or certificate of incorporation and bylaws;

(b) The noncorporate distributees' allocable share of the undistributed personal holding company income for each class of stock shall be determined separately in accordance with the rules set forth in subdivisions (i) or (ii) of this subparagraph, as if each class of stock were the only class of stock outstanding; and

(c) The sum of the noncorporate distributees' allocable share of the undistributed personal holding company income for the taxable year in which, or in respect of which, the distribution was made shall be the sum of the noncorporate distributees' allocable share of the undistributed personal holding company income for all classes of stock.

(iv) For purposes of this subparagraph, in any case where the record date of a liquidating distribution cannot be ascertained, the record date of the distribution shall be the date on which the liquidating distribution was actually made.

(4) The amount designated as a dividend to a noncorporate distributee for any taxable year of the distributing corporation may not exceed an amount equal to the sum of the noncorporate distributees' allocable share of undistributed personal holding company income (as determined under subparagraph (3) of this paragraph) for such year multiplied by the ratio which the aggregate value

of the stock held by such distributee immediately before the record date of the liquidating distribution or, if the record date cannot be ascertained, immediately before the date on which the liquidating distribution was actually made, bears to the aggregate value of stock outstanding held by all noncorporate distributees on such date. In any case where more than one liquidating distribution is made during the taxable year, the aggregate amount which may be designated as a dividend to a noncorporate distributee for such year may not exceed the aggregate of the amounts determined by applying the principle of the preceding sentence to the amounts determined under subparagraph (3)(ii)(a) and (b) of this paragraph for each distribution. Where the distributing corporation has more than one class of stock, the limitation on the amount which may be designated as a dividend to a noncorporate distributee for any taxable year shall be determined by applying the rules of this subparagraph separately with respect to the noncorporate distributees' allocable share of the undistributed personal holding company income for each class of stock (as determined under subparagraph (3)(iii)(a) and (b) of this paragraph).

(5) A corporation may designate as a dividend to a shareholder all or part of a distribution in complete liquidation described in section 316(b)(2)(B) of this paragraph by:

(i) Claiming a dividends paid deduction for such amount in its return for the year in which, or in respect of which, the distribution is made,

(ii) Including such amount as a dividend in Form 1099 filed in respect of such shareholder pursuant to section 6042(a) and the regulations thereunder and in a written statement of dividend payments furnished to such shareholder pursuant to section 6042(c) and § 1.6042–4, and

(iii) Indicating on the written statement of dividend payments furnished to such shareholder the amount included in such statement which is designated as a dividend under section 316(b)(2)(B) and this paragraph.

If a corporation complies with the procedure prescribed in the preceding sentence, it satisfies both the designation and notification requirements of section 316(b)(2)(B)(ii) and paragraph (b)(2)(ii) of this section. An amount designated as a dividend shall not be included as a distribution in liquidation on Form 1099L filed pursuant to § 1.6043–2 (relating to returns of information respecting distributions in liquidation). If a corporation desig-

nates a dividend in accordance with this subparagraph, it shall attach to the return in which it claims a deduction for such designated dividend a schedule indicating all facts necessary to determine the sum of the noncorporate distributees' allocable share of undistributed personal holding company income (determined in accordance with subparagraph (3) of this paragraph) for the year in which, or in respect of which, the distribution is made.

* * *

(e) The application of section 316 may be illustrated by the following examples:

Example (1). At the beginning of the calendar year 1955, Corporation M had an operating deficit of $200,000 and the earnings and profits for the year amounted to $100,000. Beginning on March 16, 1955, the corporation made quarterly distributions of $25,000 during the taxable year to its shareholders. Each distribution is a taxable dividend in full, irrespective of the actual or the pro rata amount of the earnings and profits on hand at any of the dates of distribution, since the total distributions made during the year ($100,000) did not exceed the total earnings and profits of the year ($100,000).

* * *

[T.D. 6500, 25 FR 11607, Nov. 26, 1960, as amended by T.D. 6625, 27 FR 12541, Dec. 19, 1962; T.D. 6949, 33 FR 5519, April 9, 1968; T.D. 7767, 46 FR 11264, Feb. 6, 1981; T.D. 7936, 49 FR 2105, Jan. 18, 1984]

§ 1.316–2 Sources of distribution in general.

(a) For the purpose of income taxation every distribution made by a corporation is made out of earnings and profits to the extent thereof and from the most recently accumulated earnings and profits. In determining the source of a distribution, consideration should be given first, to the earnings and profits of the taxable year; second, to the earnings and profits accumulated since February 28, 1913, only in the case where, and to the extent that, the distributions made during the taxable year are not regarded as out of the earnings and profits of that year; third, to the earnings and profits accumulated before March 1, 1913, only after all the earnings and profits of the taxable year and all the earnings and profits accumulated since February 28, 1913, have been distributed; and, fourth, to sources other than earnings and profits only after the earnings and profits have been distributed.

(b) If the earnings and profits of the taxable year (computed as of the close of the year without diminution by reason of any distributions made during the year and without regard to the amount of earnings and profits at the time of the distribution) are sufficient in amount to cover all the distributions made during that year, then each distribution is a taxable dividend. See § 1.316–1. If the distributions made during the taxable year consist only of money and exceed the earnings and profits of such year, then that proportion of each distribution which the total of the earnings and profits of the year bears to the total distributions made during the year shall be regarded as out of the earnings and profits of that year. The portion of each such distribution which is not regarded as out of earnings and profits of the taxable year shall be considered a taxable dividend to the extent of the earnings and profits accumulated since February 28, 1913, and available on the date of the distribution. In any case in which it is necessary to determine the amount of earnings and profits accumulated since February 28, 1913, and the actual earnings and profits to the date of a distribution within any taxable year (whether beginning before January 1, 1936, or, in the case of an operating deficit, on or after that date) cannot be shown, the earnings and profits for the year (or accounting period, if less than a year) in which the distribution was made shall be prorated to the date of the distribution not counting the date on which the distribution was made.

(c) The provisions of the section may be illustrated by the following example:

Example. At the beginning of the calendar year 1955, Corporation M had $12,000 in earnings and profits accumulated since February 28, 1913. Its earnings and profits for 1955 amounted to $30,000. During the year it made quarterly cash distributions of $15,000 each. Of each of the four distributions made, $7,500 (that portion of $15,000 which the amount of $30,000, the total earnings and profits of the taxable year, bears to $60,000, the total distributions made during the year) was paid out of the earnings and profits of the taxable year; and of the first and second distributions, $7,500 and $4,500, respectively, were paid out of the earnings and profits accumulated after February 28, 1913, and before the taxable year, as follows:

Distributions during 1955				
Date	Amount	Portion out of earnings and profits of the taxable year	Portion out of earnings accumulated since Feb. 28, 1913, and before the taxable year	Taxable amt. of each distribution
March 10	$15,000	$7,500	$7,500	$15,000
June 10	15,000	7,500	4,500	12,000
September 10	15,000	7,500	......	7,500
December 10	15,000	7,500	......	7,500
Total amount taxable as dividends	......	......	......	42,000

* * *

[T.D. 6500, 25 FR 11607, Nov. 26, 1960]

§ 1.317–1 Property defined.

The term "property", for purposes of part 1, subchapter C, chapter 1 of the Code, means any property (including money, securities, and indebtedness to the corporation) other than stock, or rights to acquire stock, in the corporation making the distribution.

[T.D. 6500, 25 FR 11607, Nov. 26, 1960]

§ 1.318–1 Constructive ownership of stock; introduction.

(a) For the purposes of certain provisions of chapter 1 of the Code, section 318(a) provides that stock owned by a taxpayer includes stock constructively owned by such taxpayer under the rules set forth in such section. An individual is considered to own the stock owned, directly or indirectly, by or for his spouse (other than a spouse who is legally separated from the individual under a decree of divorce or separate maintenance), and by or for his children, grandchildren, and parents. Under section 318(a)(2) and (3), constructive ownership rules are established for partnerships and partners, estates and beneficiaries, trusts and beneficiaries, and corporations and stockholders. If any person has an option to acquire stock, such stock is considered as owned by such person. The term "option" includes an option to acquire such an option and each of a series of such options.

(b) In applying section 318(a) to determine the stock ownership of any person for any one purpose—

(1) A corporation shall not be considered to own its own stock by reason of section 318(a)(3)(C);

(2) In any case in which an amount of stock owned by any person may be included in the computation more than one time, such stock shall be included only once, in the manner in which it will impute to the person concerned the largest total stock ownership; and

(3) In determining the 50-percent requirement of section 318(a)(2)(C) and (3)(C), all of the stock owned actually and constructively by the person concerned shall be aggregated.

[T.D. 6500, 25 FR 11607, Nov. 26, 1960, as amended by T.D. 6598, 27 FR 4092, April 28, 1962; T.D. 6621, 27 FR 11877, Dec. 1, 1962; T.D. 6969, 33 FR 11999, Aug. 23, 1968]

§ 1.318–2 Application of general rules.

(a) The application of paragraph (b) of § 1.318–1 may be illustrated by the following examples:

Example (1). H, an individual, owns all of the stock of corporation A. Corporation A is not considered to own the stock owned by H in corporation A.

Example (2). H, an individual, his wife, W, and his son, S, each own one-third of the stock of the Green Corporation. For purposes of determining the amount of stock owned by H, W, or S for purposes of section 318(a)(2)(C) and (3)(C), the amount of stock held by the other members of the family shall be added pursuant to paragraph (b)(3) of § 1.318–1 in applying the 50-percent requirement of such section. H, W, or S, as the case may be, is for this purpose deemed to own 100 percent of the stock of the Green Corporation.

(b) The application of section 318(a)(1), relating to members of a family, may be illustrated by the following example:

Example. An individual, H, his wife, W, his son, S, and his grandson (S's son), G, own the 100 outstanding shares of stock of a corporation, each owning 25 shares. H, W, and S are each considered as owning 100 shares. G is considered as owning only 50 shares, that is, his own and his father's.

(c) The application of section 318(a)(2) and (3), relating to partnerships, trusts and corporations, may be illustrated by the following examples:

Example (1). A, an individual, has a 50 percent interest in a partnership. The partnership owns 50 of the 100 outstanding shares of stock of a corporation, the remaining 50 shares being owned by A. The partnership is considered as owning 100 shares. A is considered as owning 75 shares.

Example (2). A testamentary trust owns 25 of the outstanding 100 shares of stock of a corporation. A, an individual, who holds a vested remainder in the trust having a value, computed actuarially equal to 4 percent

of the value of the trust property, owns the remaining 75 shares. Since the interest of A in the trust is a vested interest rather than a contingent interest (whether or not remote), the trust is considered as owning 100 shares. A is considered as owning 76 shares.

Example (3). The facts are the same as in (2), above, except that A's interest in the trust is a contingent remainder. A is considered as owning 76 shares. However, since A's interest in the trust is a remote contingent interest, the trust is not considered as owning any of the shares owned by A.

Example (4). A and B, unrelated individuals, own 70 percent and 30 percent, respectively, in value of the stock of Corporation M. Corporation M owns 50 of the 100 outstanding shares of stock of Corporation O, the remaining 50 shares being owned by A. Corporation M is considered as owning 100 shares of Corporation O, and A is considered as owning 85 shares.

Example (5). A and B, unrelated individuals, own 70 percent and 30 percent, respectively, of the stock of corporation M. A, B, and corporation M all own stock of corporation O. Since B owns less than 50 percent in value of the stock of corporation M, neither B nor corporation M constructively owns the stock of corporation O owned by the other. However, for purposes of certain sections of the Code, such as sections 304 and 856(d), the 50-percent limitation of section 318(a)(2)(C) and (3)(C) is disregarded or is reduced to less than 30 percent. For such purposes, B constructively owns his proportionate share of the stock of corporation O owned directly by corporation M, and corporation M constructively owns the stock of corporation O owned by B.

[T.D. 6500, 25 FR 11607, Nov. 26, 1960, as amended by T.D. 6969, 33 FR 11999, Aug. 23, 1968]

§ 1.318–3 Estates, trusts, and options.

(a) For the purpose of applying section 318(a), relating to estates, property of a decedent shall be considered as owned by his estate if such property is subject to administration by the executor or administrator for the purpose of paying claims against the estate and expenses of administration notwithstanding that, under local law, legal title to such property vests in the decedent's heirs, legatees or devisees immediately upon death. The term "beneficiary" includes any person entitled to receive property of a decedent pursuant to a will or pursuant to laws of descent and distribution. A person shall no longer be considered a beneficiary of an estate when all the property to which he is entitled has been received by him, when he no longer has a claim against the estate arising out of having been a beneficiary, and when there is only a remote possibility that it will be necessary for the estate to seek the return of property or to seek payment from him by contribution or otherwise to satisfy claims against the estate or expenses of administration. When, pursuant to the preceding sentence, a person ceases to be a beneficiary, stock owned by him shall not thereafter be considered owned by the estate, and stock owned by the estate shall not thereafter be considered owned by him. The application of section 318(a) relating to estates may be illustrated by the following examples:

Example (1). (a) A decedent's estate owns 50 of the 100 outstanding shares of stock of corporation X. The remaining shares are owned by three unrelated individuals, A, B, and C, who together own the entire interest in the estate. A owns 12 shares of stock of corporation X directly and is entitled to 50 percent of the estate. B owns 18 shares directly and has a life estate in the remaining 50 percent of the estate. C owns 20 shares directly and also owns the remainder interest after B's life estate.

(b) If section 318(a)(5)(C) applies (see paragraph (c)(3) of § 1.318–4), the stock of corporation X is considered to be owned as follows: the estate is considered as owning 80 shares, 50 shares directly, 12 shares constructively through A, and 18 shares constructively through B; A is considered as owning 37 shares, 12 shares directly, and 25 shares constructively (50 percent of the 50 shares owned directly by the estate); B is considered as owning 43 shares, 18 shares directly and 25 shares constructively (50 percent of the 50 shares owned directly by the estate); C is considered as owning 20 shares directly and no shares constructively. C is not considered a beneficiary of the estate under section 318(a) since he has no direct present interest in the property held by the estate nor in the income produced by such property.

(c) If section 318(a)(5)(C) does not apply, A is considered as owning nine additional shares (50 percent of the 18 shares owned constructively by the estate through B), and B is considered as owning six additional shares (50 percent of the 12 shares owned constructively by the estate through A).

Example (2). Under the will of A, Blackacre is left to B for life, remainder to C, an unrelated individual. The residue of the estate consisting of stock of a corporation is left to D. B and D are beneficiaries of the estate under section 318(a). C is not considered a beneficiary since he has no direct present interest in Blackacre nor in the income produced by such property. The stock owned by the estate is considered as owned proportionately by B and D.

(b) For the purpose of section 318(a)(2)(B) stock owned by a trust will be considered as being owned by its beneficiaries only to the extent of the interest of such beneficiaries in the trust. Accordingly, the interest of income beneficiaries, remainder beneficiaries, and other beneficiaries will be computed on an actuarial basis. Thus, if a trust owns 100 percent of the stock of Corporation A, and if, on an actuarial basis, W's life interest in the trust is 15 percent, Y's life interest is 25 percent, and Z's remainder interest is 60 percent, under this provision W will be considered to be the owner of 15 percent of the stock of Corporation A, Y will be considered to be the owner of 25 percent of such stock, and Z will be considered to be the owner of 60 percent of such stock. The factors and methods prescribed in § 20.2031–7 of this chapter (Estate Tax Regulations) for use in ascertaining the value of an interest in property for estate tax purposes shall be used in determining a beneficiary's actuarial interest in a trust for purposes of this section. See § 20.2031–7 of this chapter (Estate Tax Regulations) for examples illustrating the use of these factors and methods.

(c) The application of section 318(a) relating to options may be illustrated by the following example:

Example. A and B, unrelated individuals, own all of the 100 outstanding shares of stock of a corporation, each owning 50 shares. A has an option to acquire 25 of B's shares and has an option to acquire a further option to acquire the remaining 25 of B's shares. A is considered as owning the entire 100 shares of stock of the corporation.

[T.D. 6500, 25 FR 11607, Nov. 26, 1960, as amended by T.D. 6969, 33 FR 11999, Aug. 23, 1968]

§ 1.318–4 Constructive ownership as actual ownership; exceptions.

(a) In general. Section 318(a)(5)(A) provides that, except as provided in section 318(a)(5)(B) and (C), stock constructively owned by a person by reason of the application of section 318(a)(1), (2), (3), or (4) shall be considered as actually owned by such person for purposes of applying section 318(a)(1), (2), (3), and (4). For example, if a trust owns 50 percent of the stock of corporation X, stock of corporation Y owned by corporation X which is attributed to the trust may be further attributed to the beneficiaries of the trust.

(b) Constructive family ownership. Section 318(a)(5)(B) provides that stock constructively owned by an individual by reason of ownership by a member of his family shall not be considered as owned by him for purposes of making another family member the constructive owner of such stock under section 318(a)(1). For example, if F and his two sons, A and B, each own one-third of the stock of a corporation, under section 318(a)(1), A is treated as owning constructively the stock owned by his father but is not treated as owning the stock owned by B. Section 318(a)(5)(B) prevents the attribution of the stock of one brother through the father to the other brother, an attribution beyond the scope of section 318(a)(1) directly.

(c) Reattribution. (1) Section 318(a)(5)(C) provides that stock constructively owned by a partnership, estate, trust, or corporation by reason of the application of section 318(a)(3) shall not be considered as owned by it for purposes of applying section 318(a)(2) in order to make another the constructive owner of such stock. For example, if two unrelated individuals are beneficiaries of the same trust, stock held by one which is attributed to the trust under section 318(a)(3) is not reattributed from the trust to the other beneficiary. However, stock constructively owned by reason of section 318(a)(2) may be reattributed under section 318(a)(3). Thus, for example, if all the stock of corporations X and Y is owned by A, stock of corporation Z held by X is attributed to Y through A.

(2) Section 318(a)(5)(C) does not prevent reattribution under section 318(a)(2) of stock constructively owned by an entity under section 318(a)(3) if the stock is also constructively owned by the entity under section 318(a)(4). For example, if individuals A and B are beneficiaries of a trust and the trust has an option to buy stock from A, B is considered under section 318(a)(2)(B) as owning a proportionate part of such stock.

* * *

[T.D. 6500, 25 FR 11607, Nov. 26, 1960, as amended by T.D. 6969, 33 FR 11999, Aug. 23, 1968]

Corporate Liquidations

Effects on Recipients

§ 1.331–1 Corporate liquidations.

(a) Section 331 contains rules governing the extent to which gain or loss is recognized to a shareholder receiving a distribution in complete or partial liquidation of a corporation. Under section 331(a)(1), it is provided that amounts distributed in complete liquidation of a corporation shall be treated as in full payment in exchange for the stock. Under section 331(a)(2), it is provided that amounts distributed in partial liquidation of a corporation shall be treated as in full or part payment in exchange for the stock. For this purpose, the term "partial liquidation" shall have the meaning ascribed in section 346. If section 331 is applicable to the distribution of property by a corporation, section 301 (relating to the effects on a shareholder of distributions of property) has no application other than to a distribution in complete liquidation to which section 316(b)(2)(B) applies. See paragraph (b)(2) of § 1.316–1.

(b) The gain or loss to a shareholder from a distribution in partial or complete liquidation is to be determined under section 1001 by comparing the amount of the distribution with the cost or other basis of the stock. The gain or loss will be recognized to the extent provided in section 1002 and will be subject to the provisions of parts I, II, and III (section 1201 and following), subchapter P, chapter 1 of the Code.

(c) A liquidation which is followed by a transfer to another corporation of all or part of the assets of the liquidating corporation or which is preceded by such a transfer may, however, have the effect of the distribution of a dividend or of a transaction in which no loss is recognized and gain is recognized only to the extent of "other property." See sections 301 and 356.

(d) In every case in which a shareholder transfers stock in exchange for property to the corporation which issued such stock, the facts and circumstances shall be reported on his return unless the property is part of a distribution made pursuant to a corporate resolution reciting that the distribution is made in liquidation of the corporation and the corporation is completely liquidated and dissolved within one year after the distribution. See section 6043 for requirements relating to returns by corporations.

(e) The provisions of this section may be illustrated by the following example:

Example. A, an individual who makes his income tax returns on the calendar year basis, owns 20 shares of stock of the P Corporation, a domestic corporation, 10 shares of which were acquired in 1951 at a cost of $1,500 and the remainder of 10 shares in December 1954 at a cost of $2,900. He receives in April 1955 a distribution of $250 per share in complete liquidation, or $2,500 on the 10 shares acquired in 1951, and $2,500 on the 10 shares acquired in December 1954. The gain of $1,000 on the shares acquired in 1951 is a long-term capital gain to be treated as provided in parts I, II, and III (section 1201 and following), subchapter P, chapter 1 of the Code. The loss of $400 on the shares acquired in 1954 is a short-term capital loss to be treated as provided in parts I, II, and III (section 1201 and following), subchapter P, chapter 1 of the Code.

[T.D. 6500, 25 FR 11607, Nov. 26, 1960, as amended by T.D. 6949, 33 FR 5521, April 9, 1968]

§ 1.332-1   Distributions in liquidation of subsidiary corporation; general.

Under the general rule prescribed by section 331 for the treatment of distributions in liquidation of a corporation, amounts received by one corporation in complete liquidation of another corporation are treated as in full payment in exchange for stock in such other corporation, and gain or loss from the receipt of such amounts is to be determined as provided in section 1001. Section 332 excepts from the general rule property received, under certain specifically described circumstances, by one corporation as a distribution in complete liquidation of the stock of another corporation and provides for the nonrecognition of gain or loss in those cases which meet the statutory requirements. Section 367 places a limitation on the application of section 332 in the case of foreign corporations. See section 334(b) for the basis for determining gain or loss from the subsequent sale of property received upon complete liquidations such as described in this section. * * *

[T.D. 6500, 25 FR 11607, Nov. 26, 1960]

§ 1.332-2   Requirements for nonrecognition of gain or loss.

(a) The nonrecognition of gain or loss is limited to the receipt of such property by a corporation which is the actual owner of stock (in the liquidating corporation) possessing at least 80 percent of the total combined voting power of all classes of stock entitled to vote and the owner of at least 80 percent of the total number of shares of all other classes of stock (except nonvoting stock which is limited and preferred as to dividends). The recipient corporation must have been the owner of the specified amount of such stock on the date of the adoption of the plan of liquidation and have continued so to be at all times until the receipt of the property. If the recipient corporation does not continue qualified with respect to the ownership of stock of the liquidating corporation and if the failure to continue qualified occurs at any time prior to the completion of the transfer of all the property, the provisions for the nonrecognition of gain or loss do not apply to any distribution received under the plan.

(b) Section 332 applies only to those cases in which the recipient corporation receives at least partial payment for the stock which it owns in the liquidating corporation. If section 332 is not appli-

cable, see section 165(g) relative to allowance of losses on worthless securities.

(c) To constitute a distribution in complete liquidation within the meaning of section 332, the distribution must be (1) made by the liquidating corporation in complete cancellation or redemption of all of its stock in accordance with a plan of liquidation, or (2) one of a series of distributions in complete cancellation or redemption of all its stock in accordance with a plan of liquidation. Where there is more than one distribution, it is essential that a status of liquidation exist at the time the first distribution is made under the plan and that such status continue until the liquidation is completed. Liquidation is completed when the liquidating corporation and the receiver or trustees in liquidation are finally divested of all the property (both tangible and intangible). A status of liquidation exists when the corporation ceases to be a going concern and its activities are merely for the purpose of winding up its affairs, paying its debts, and distributing any remaining balance to its shareholders. A liquidation may be completed prior to the actual dissolution of the liquidating corporation. However, legal dissolution of the corporation is not required. Nor will the mere retention of a nominal amount of assets for the sole purpose of preserving the corporation's legal existence disqualify the transaction. * * *

(d) If a transaction constitutes a distribution in complete liquidation within the meaning of the Internal Revenue Code of 1954 and satisfies the requirements of section 332, it is not material that it is otherwise described under the local law. If a liquidating corporation distributes all of its property in complete liquidation and if pursuant to the plan for such complete liquidation a corporation owning the specified amount of stock in the liquidating corporation receives property constituting amounts distributed in complete liquidation within the meaning of the Code and also receives other property attributable to shares not owned by it, the transfer of the property to the recipient corporation shall not be treated, by reason of the receipt of such other property, as not being a distribution (or one of a series of distributions) in complete cancellation or redemption of all of the stock of the liquidating corporation within the meaning of section 332, even though for purposes of those provisions relating to corporate reorganizations the amount received by the recipient corporation in excess of its ratable share is regarded as acquired upon the issuance of its stock or securities in a tax-free exchange as described in section 361 and the cancellation or redemption of the stock not owned by the recipient corporation is treated as occurring as a result of a taxfree exchange described in section 354.

(e) The application of these rules may be illustrated by the following example:

Example. On September 1, 1954, the M Corporation had outstanding capital stock consisting of 3,000 shares of common stock, par value $100 a share, and 1,000 shares of preferred stock, par value $100 a share, which preferred stock was limited and preferred as to dividends and had no voting rights. On that date, and thereafter until the date of dissolution of the M Corporation, the O Corporation owned 2,500 shares of common stock of the M Corporation. By statutory merger consummated on October 1, 1954, pursuant to a plan of liquidation adopted on September 1, 1954, the M Corporation was merged into the O Corporation, the O Corporation under the plan issuing stock which was received by the other holders of the stock of the M Corporation. The receipt by the O Corporation of the properties of the M Corporation is a distribution received by the O Corporation in complete liquidation of the M Corporation within the meaning of section 332, and no gain or loss is recognized as the result of the receipt of such properties.

[T.D. 6500, 25 FR 11607, Nov. 26, 1960]

§ 1.332–3 Liquidations completed within one taxable year.

If in a liquidation completed within one taxable year pursuant to a plan of complete liquidation, distributions in complete liquidation are received by a corporation which owns the specified amount of stock in the liquidating corporation and which continues qualified with respect to the ownership of such stock until the transfer of all the property within such year is completed (see paragraph (a) of § 1.332–2), then no gain or loss shall be recognized with respect to the distributions received by the recipient corporation. In such case no waiver or bond is required of the recipient corporation under section 332.

[T.D. 6500, 25 FR 11607, Nov. 26, 1960]

§ 1.332–4 Liquidations covering more than one taxable year.

(a) If the plan of liquidation is consummated by a series of distributions extending over a period of more than one taxable year, the nonrecognition of gain or loss with respect to the distributions in liquidation shall, in addition to the requirements of § 1.332–2, be subject to the following requirements:

(1) In order for the distribution in liquidation to be brought within the exception provided in section 332 to the general rule for computing gain or loss with respect to amounts received in liquidation of a corporation, the entire property of the corporation shall be transferred in accordance with a plan of liquidation, which plan shall include a statement showing the period within which the transfer of the property of the liquidating corporation to the recipient corporation is to be completed. The transfer of all the property under the liquidation must be completed within three years from the close of the taxable year during which is made the first of the series of distributions under the plan.

(2) For each of the taxable years which falls wholly or partly within the period of liquidation, the recipient corporation shall, at the time of filing its return, file with the district director of internal revenue a waiver of the statute of limitations on assessment. The waiver shall be executed on such form as may be prescribed by the Commissioner and shall extend the period of assessment of all income and profits taxes for each such year to a date not earlier than one year after the last date of the period for assessment of such taxes for the last taxable year in which the transfer of the property of such liquidating corporation to the controlling corporation may be completed in accordance with section 332. Such waiver shall also contain such other terms with respect to assessment as may be considered by the Commissioner to be necessary to insure the assessment and collection of the correct tax liability for each year within the period of liquidation.

(3) For each of the taxable years which falls wholly or partly within the period of liquidation, the recipient corporation may be required to file a bond, the amount of which shall be fixed by the district director. The bond shall contain all terms specified by the Commissioner, including provisions unequivocally assuring prompt payment of the excess of income and profits taxes (plus penalty, if any, and interest) as computed by the district director without regard to the provisions of sections 332 and 334(b) over such taxes computed with regard to such provisions, regardless of whether such excess may or may not be made the subject of a notice of deficiency under section 6212 and regardless of whether it may or may not be assessed. Any bond required under section 332 shall have such surety or sureties as the Commissioner may require. However, see 6 U.S.C. 15, providing that where a bond is required by law or regulations, in

lieu of surety or sureties there may be deposited bonds or notes of the United States. Only surety companies holding certificates of authority from the Secretary as acceptable sureties on Federal bonds will be approved as sureties. The bonds shall be executed in triplicate so that the Commissioner, the taxpayer, and the surety or the depositary may each have a copy. On and after September 1, 1953, the functions of the Commissioner with respect to such bonds shall be performed by the district director for the internal revenue district in which the return was filed and any bond filed on or after such date shall be filed with such district director.

(b) Pending the completion of the liquidation, if there is a compliance with paragraph (a)(1), (2), and (3) of this section and § 1.332–2 with respect to the nonrecognition of gain or loss, the income and profits tax liability of the recipient corporation for each of the years covered in whole or in part by the liquidation shall be determined without the recognition of any gain or loss on account of the receipt of the distributions in liquidation. In such determination, the basis of the property or properties received by the recipient corporation shall be determined in accordance with section 334(b). However, if the transfer of the property is not completed within the three-year period allowed by section 332 or if the recipient corporation does not continue qualified with respect to the ownership of stock of the liquidating corporation as required by that section, gain or loss shall be recognized with respect to each distribution and the tax liability for each of the years covered in whole or in part by the liquidation shall be recomputed without regard to the provisions of section 332 or section 334(b) and the amount of any additional tax due upon such recomputation shall be promptly paid.

[T.D. 6500, 25 FR 11607, Nov. 26, 1960]

§ 1.332–5   Distribution in liquidation as affecting minority interests.

Upon the liquidation of a corporation in pursuance of a plan of complete liquidation, the gain or loss of minority shareholders shall be determined without regard to section 332, since it does not apply to that part of distributions in liquidation received by minority shareholders.

[T.D. 6500, 25 FR 11607, Nov. 26, 1960]

§ 1.332–6   Records to be kept and information to be filed with return.

(a) Permanent records in substantial form shall be kept by every corporation receiving distributions in complete liquidation within the exception provided in section 332 showing the information required by this section to be submitted with its return. The plan of liquidation must be adopted by each of the corporations parties thereto; and the adoption must be shown by the acts of its duly constituted responsible officers, and appear upon the official records of each such corporation.

(b) For the taxable year in which the liquidation occurs, or, if the plan of liquidation provides for a series of distributions over a period of more than one year, for each taxable year in which a distribution is received under the plan the recipient must file with its return a complete statement of all facts pertinent to the nonrecognition of gain or loss, including:

(1) A certified copy of the plan for complete liquidation, and of the resolutions under which the plan was adopted and the liquidation was authorized, together with a statement under oath showing in detail all transactions incident to, or pursuant to, the plan.

(2) A list of all the properties received upon the distribution, showing the cost or other basis of such properties to the liquidating corporation at the date of distribution and the fair market value of such properties on the date distributed.

(3) A statement of any indebtedness of the liquidating corporation to the recipient corporation on the date the plan of liquidation was adopted and on the date of the first liquidating distribution. If any such indebtedness was acquired at less than face value, the cost thereof to the recipient corporation must also be shown.

(4) A statement as to its ownership of all classes of stock of the liquidating corporation (showing as to each class the number of shares and percentage owned and the voting power of each share) as of the date of the adoption of the plan of liquidation, and at all times since, to and including the date of the distribution in liquidation. The cost or other basis of such stock and the date or dates on which purchased must also be shown.

[T.D. 6500, 25 FR 11607, Nov. 26, 1960]

§ 1.332-7 Indebtedness of subsidiary to parent.

If section 332(a) is applicable to the receipt of the subsidiary's property in complete liquidation, then no gain or loss shall be recognized to the subsidiary upon the transfer of such properties even though some of the properties are transferred in satisfaction of the subsidiary's indebtedness to its parent. However, any gain or loss realized by the parent corporation on such satisfaction of indebtedness, shall be recognized to the parent corporation at the time of the liquidation. For example, if the parent corporation purchased its subsidiary's bonds at a discount and upon liquidation of the subsidiary the parent corporation receives payment for the face amount of such bonds, gain shall be recognized to the parent corporation. Such gain shall be measured by the difference between the cost or other basis of the bonds to the parent and the amount received in payment of the bonds.

[T.D. 6500, 25 FR 11607, Nov. 26, 1960]

§ 1.333-1 Corporate liquidations in some one calendar month.

(a) **In general.** Section 333 provides a special rule, in the case of certain specifically described complete liquidations of domestic corporations occurring within some one calendar month, for the treatment of gain on the shares of stock owned by qualified electing shareholders at the time of the adoption of the plan of liquidation. The effect of such section is in general to postpone the recognition of that portion of a qualified electing shareholder's gain on the liquidation which would otherwise be recognized and which is attributable to appreciation in the value of certain corporate assets unrealized by the corporation at the time such assets are distributed in complete liquidation. Only qualified electing shareholders are entitled to the benefits of section 333. The determination of who is a qualified electing shareholder is to be made under section 333(c). * * * For the basis of property received on such liquidations, see section 334(c). Section 333 has no application to gain in respect of stock of a collapsible corporation to which section 341(a) applies.

(b) **Type of liquidation.** (1) The liquidation must be in pursuance of a plan of liquidation adopted on or after June 22, 1954. The plan must be adopted before the first distribution under the liquidation occurs. The 1954 Code requires that the transfer of all the property, both tangible and intangible, of the corporation to its shareholders shall occur entirely within some one calendar month. This requirement will be considered to have been complied with if cash is set aside under arrangements for the payment, after the close of such month, of unascertained or contingent liabilities and expenses, and such arrangements are made in good faith and the amount set aside is reasonable. It is not necessary that the month in which the transfer occurs must fall within the taxable or calendar year in which the plan of liquidation is adopted. Though it is not necessary that the corporation dissolve in the month of liquidation, it is essential that a status of liquidation exist at the time the first distribution is made under the plan and that such status continue to the date of dissolution of the corporation. A status of liquidation exists when the corporation ceases to be a going concern and its activities are merely for the purpose of winding up its affairs, paying its debts, and distributing any remaining balance to its shareholders.

(2) If a transaction constitutes a distribution in complete liquidation within the meaning of the Code and satisfies the requirements of section 333, it is immaterial that it is otherwise described under the local law.

[T.D. 6500, 25 FR 11607, Nov. 26, 1960, as amended by T.D. 6809, 25 FR 2805, March 5, 1965; T.D. 6949, 33 FR 5521, April 9, 1968]

§ 1.333-2 Qualified electing shareholder.

(a) No corporate shareholder may be a qualified electing shareholder if at any time between January 1, 1954, and the date of the adoption of the plan of liquidation, both dates inclusive, it is the owner of stock of the liquidating corporation possessing 50 percent or more of the total combined voting power of all classes of stock entitled to vote upon the adoption of the plan of liquidation. All other shareholders are divided into two groups for the purpose of determining whether they are qualified electing shareholders: (1) shareholders other than corporations, and (2) corporate shareholders.

(b) Any shareholder of either of such two groups, whether or not the stock he owns is entitled to vote on the adoption of the plan of liquidation, is a qualified electing shareholder if:

(1) His written election to be governed by the provisions of section 333, which cannot be withdrawn or revoked * * *, has been made and filed as prescribed in § 1.333-3; and

(2) Like elections have been made and filed by owners of stock possessing at least 80 percent of the total combined voting power of all classes of stock owned by shareholders of the same group at the time of, and entitled to vote upon, the adoption of the plan of liquidation, whether or not the shareholders making such elections actually realize gain upon the cancellation or redemption of such stock upon the liquidation.

(c) The application of this section may be illustrated by the following example:

Example. The R Corporation has outstanding 20 shares of common stock on July 1, 1954, at the time of the adoption of a plan of liquidation within the provisions of section 333, each entitled to one vote upon the adoption of such plan of liquidation. At that time ten of such shares are owned by the S Corporation, two each by the X Corporation and the Y Corporation, one by the Z Corporation, and one each by A, B, C, D, and E, individuals. There are also outstanding at such time two shares of preferred stock, not entitled to vote on liquidation, one share being owned by F, an individual, and one share by the P Corporation. The S Corporation, being a corporate shareholder and the owner of 50 percent of the voting stock, may not be a qualified electing shareholder under any circumstances. In order for any other corporate shareholder to be a qualified electing shareholder, it is necessary that the X Corporation and the Y Corporation file their written elections to be governed by section 333. If this is done, the P Corporation will also be a qualified electing shareholder if it has filed a like election. Similarly, in the case of the individual shareholders, some combination of four of the individual holders of the common stock must have filed their written elections, before any individual shareholder may be considered a qualified electing shareholder, but if this is done, F will also be a qualified electing shareholder if he has filed a like election.

(d) An election to be governed by the provisions of section 333 relates to the treatment of gain realized upon the cancellation or redemption of stock upon liquidation. Such election, therefore, can be made only by or on behalf of the person by whom gains, if any, will be realized. Thus, the shareholder who may make such election must be the actual owner of stock and not a mere record holder, such as a nominee.

(e) A shareholder is entitled to make an election relative to the gain only on stock owned by him at the time of the adoption of the plan of liquidation. The election is personal to the shareholder making it and does not follow such stock into the hands of a transferee.

[T.D. 6500, 25 FR 11607, Nov. 26, 1960, as amended by T.D. 6949, 33 FR 5521, April 9, 1968]

§ 1.333–3 Making and filing of written elections.

An election to be governed by section 333 shall be made on Form 964 (revised) in accordance with the instructions printed thereon and with this section. The original and one copy shall be filed by the shareholder with the district director with whom the final income tax return of the corporation will be filed. The elections must be filed within 30 days after the adoption of the plan of liquidation.

Under no circumstances shall section 333 be applicable to any shareholders who fail to file their elections within the 30-day period prescribed. An election shall be considered as timely filed if it is placed in the mail on or before midnight of the 30th day after the adoption of the plan of liquidation, as shown by the postmark on the envelope containing the written election or as shown by other available evidence of the mailing date. Another copy of the election shall be attached to and made a part of the shareholder's income tax return for his taxable year in which the transfer of all the property under the liquidation occurs.

[T.D. 6500, 25 FR 11607, Nov. 26, 1960]

§ 1.333–4 Treatment of gain.

(a) Computation of gain. As in the case of shareholders generally, amounts received by qualified electing shareholders are treated as in full payment in exchange for their stock, as provided in section 331 and gain from the receipt of such amounts is determined as provided in section 1001. Gain or loss must be computed separately on each share of stock owned by a qualified electing shareholder at the time of the adoption of the plan of liquidation. The limited recognition and special treatment accorded by section 333 applies only to the gain on such shares of stock upon which gain was realized and not to net gain computed by setting off losses realized on some shares against gain on others. Since section 333 applies only to gain recognized, losses realized on the liquidation will be allowable only in the year of liquidation even though Forms 964 (revised) have been filed by those shareholders who realize only losses. Such filings may be necessary to fulfill the 80 percent requirement (under section 333(c)) so that those shareholders who realize gain may qualify under this section.

(b) Recognition of gain. Pursuant to section 333 only so much of the gain on each share of stock owned by a qualified electing shareholder at the time of the adoption of the plan of liquidation is recognized as does not exceed the greater of the following:

(1) Such share's ratable share of the earnings and profits of the corporation accumulated after February 28, 1913, computed as of the last day of the month of liquidation, without diminution by reason of distributions made during such month, and including in such computation all items of income and expense accrued up to the date on which the transfer of all the property under the liquidation is completed; or

(2) Such share's ratable share of the sum of the amount of money received by such shareholder on shares of the same class and the fair market value of all the stock or securities so received which were acquired by the liquidating corporation after December 31, 1953. The mere replacement after December 31, 1953 of lost or destroyed certificates or instruments acquired on or before December 31, 1953, or the mere conversion of certificates or instruments into certificates or instruments of larger or smaller denominations will not constitute an acquisition within the meaning of the phrase "acquired after December 31, 1953." Nor will such an acquisition result from the issuance after December 31, 1953 of certificates of stock in connection with a subscription made and accepted on or before December 31, 1953.

(c) Treatment of recognized gain. **(1)** In the case of a qualified electing shareholder other than a corporation, that part of the recognized gain on a share of stock owned at the time of the adoption of the plan of liquidation which is not in excess of his ratable share of the earnings and profits of the liquidating corporation accumulated after February 28, 1913, determined as provided in section 333(e)(1), is treated as a dividend. It retains its character as a dividend for all tax purposes. The remainder of the gain which is recognized is treated as a short-term or long-term capital gain, as the case may be. In the case of a qualified electing shareholder which is a corporation, the entire amount of the gain which is recognized is treated as a short-term or long-term capital gain, as the case may be.

(2) The application of subparagraph (1) of this paragraph may be illustrated by the following example:

Example. (i) X Corporation has only one class of stock outstanding, owned in equal amounts by three shareholders. The basis of the stock owned by each shareholder is $50, each having bought his stock in a single block prior to the date of the adoption of a plan of liquidation conforming to the requirements of section 333. One of the shareholders is an individual; two are corporations. All are "qualified electing shareholders".

(ii) X Corporation has earnings and profits accumulated after February 28, 1913, of $60 (computed as provided in section 333). Its assets consist of (a) cash of $75, (b) stock and securities acquired after December 31, 1953, having a fair market value of $90, and (c) other property having a fair market value of $240. In October 1954, all of these assets are distributed to the shareholders pro rata in complete liquidation of the corporation, as provided in section 333. Each shareholder thus receives $135 in cash and property, and has $85 gain.

(iii) Each shareholder's gain is recognized to the extent of $55 since such amount represents the sum of (a) the cash received by him and (b) the fair market value of the stock and securities received by him which were acquired by the X Corporation after December 31, 1953, and is greater than his ratable share of the earnings and profits ($20). The remainder of each shareholder's gain ($30) is not recognized.

(iv) In the case of the corporate shareholders the entire amount of the recognized gain ($55) is treated as capital gain. In the case of the individual shareholder, $20, being the amount of the shareholder's ratable share of the earnings and profits, is recognized and treated as a dividend, and $35, being the difference between the shareholder's ratable share of the earnings and profits and the sum of the cash and stock and securities received by him, is treated as a short-term or long-term capital gain, as the case may be.

(v) If the basis of each shareholder's stock had been $100, instead of $50, each of the corporate shareholders would be taxed on only $35 as capital gain and the individual shareholder would be taxed on $20 as a dividend and on only $15 as capital gain, since the total amount taxed is limited to the amount of gain realized by the shareholder upon the cancellation or redemption of his stock.

[T.D. 6500, 25 FR 11607, Nov. 26, 1960]

§ 1.333–6 Records to be kept and information to be filed with return.

(a) Permanent records in substantial form shall be kept by every qualified electing shareholder receiving distributions in complete liquidation of a domestic corporation. Such shareholder must file with his income tax return for his taxable year in which the liquidation occurs a statement of all facts pertinent to the recognition and treatment of the gain realized by him upon the shares of stock owned by him at the time of the adoption of the plan of liquidation including:

(1) A statement of his stock ownership in the liquidating corporation as of the record date of the distribution, showing the number of shares of each class owned on such date, the cost or other basis of each such share, and the date of acquisition of each such share;

(2) A list of all the property, including money, received upon the distribution, showing the fair market value of each item of such property other than money on the date distributed and stating what items, if any, consist of stock or securities acquired by the liquidating corporation after December 31, 1953, or after December 31, 1962, whichever date is applicable;

(3) A statement of his ratable share of the earnings and profits of the liquidating corporation accumulated after February 28, 1913, computed without diminution by reason of distributions made during the month of liquidation (other than designated dividends under section 316(b)(2)(B));

* * *

(5) A copy of such shareholder's written election to be governed by the provisions of section 333. See § 1.333–3.

(b) For information to be filed by the liquidating corporation, see section 6043.

[T.D. 6949, 33 FR 5524, April 9, 1968]

§ 1.334–2 Property received in liquidation under section 333.

The basis of assets (other than money) acquired by stockholders in a liquidation upon which the amount of gain recognized was limited under section 333 shall be the same as the basis of the shares of stock redeemed or cancelled, decreased in the amount of any money received and increased in the amount of gain recognized and the amount of the unsecured liabilities assumed by the stockholders. The amount thus arrived at should be allocated to the various assets received on the basis of their net fair market values (the net fair market value of an asset is its fair market value less any specific mortgage or pledge to which it is subject).

To that portion of the basis thus determined, for each property against which there is a lien, should be added the amount of such lien. Where more than one property is covered by the same lien, the amount of the lien should be divided among the properties, allocating to each that portion of the lien that the fair market value of such property bears to the total market value of the properties covered by the same lien. Whether the mortgage indebtedness is assumed by the shareholders or the property is taken subject to the mortgage is immaterial. The application of this section may be illustrated by the following example:

Example. The X corporation distributed all its property in complete liquidation during the month of October 1954 pursuant to the provisions of section 333. A, an individual, and a qualifying electing shareholder, received, in cancellation or redemption of 100 shares of stock owned by him at the time of the adoption of the plan of liquidation, $1,000 in cash, property (other than stock or securities acquired by the corporation after December 31, 1953) with a fair market value of $22,000 subject to a lien of $1,000, and stock acquired by the liquidating corporation after December 31, 1953 with a fair market value of $4,000. A, also assumed a $2,000 liability of the liquidating corporation. The basis of the shares owned by A was $120 per share or $12,000. A's ratable share of the earnings and profits of the X corporation accumulated after February 28, 1913 (computed as provided in section 333) was $2,500. His gain is $12,000, but under section 333 only $5,000 of this gain is recognized, $2,500 thereof being taxed as a dividend. The basis of all the property other than money received by A is $19,000, computed as follows:

Adjusted basis of stock cancelled or redeemed	$12,000
Less: money received	1,000
Remainder	11,000
Liability assumed	2,000
Specific lien against property (other than stock)	1,000
Gain recognized	5,000
Basis of property acquired	19,000

The basis, excluding the specific lien attached to the property, ($19,000 less $1,000, $18,000) will be apportioned among the classes of property other than money received as follows: $21,000/$25,000 of $18,000 or $15,120 to the property other than stock; $4,000/$25,000 of $18,000 or $2,880 to the stock. The basis of the property other than stock, $15,120, must be increased by the amount of the specific lien attached thereto, $1,000, making a total basis for such property of $16,120.

[T.D. 6500, 25 FR 11607, Nov. 26, 1960]

Effects on Corporation

§ 1.336–1 General rule on liquidation of corporation.

Except as provided in section 453(d), no gain or loss is recognized to a corporation on the distribution by it of property in kind in partial or complete liquidation (regardless of the fact that such property may have appreciated or depreciated in value since its acquisition by the corporation). However, gain or loss is recognized to a corporation on all sales by it, whether directly or indirectly (as through trustees or a receiver), except as provided in section 337 (relating to sales or exchanges in connection with certain liquidations). * * *

[T.D. 6500, 25 FR 11607, Nov. 26, 1960]

§ 1.337–1 General.

Except as provided in section 337(c) and * * *, if a corporation distributes all of its assets in complete liquidation within 12 months * * * no gain or loss shall be recognized from the sale of property (as defined in section 337(b)) during such 12-month period. For this purpose such sales may be made before the adoption of the plan of liquidation if made on the same day such plan is adopted. All assets (less assets retained to meet claims), both tangible and intangible, must be distributed within the 12-month period. Any assets retained after the expiration of the 12-month period for the payment of claims (including unascertained or contingent liabilities or expenses) must be specifically set apart for that purpose and must be reasonable in amount in relation to the items involved. The 12-month period shall begin on the date of adoption of the plan determined as provided in paragraph (b) of § 1.337–2 and no extension of such period can be granted. * * * Except to the extent provided in section 341(e)(4), sales or exchanges made by a collapsible corporation (as defined in section 341(b)) are excluded from the operation of section 337 by section 337(c). Accordingly, except as provided in section 341(e)(4), section 337 does not apply to any sale or exchange of property whenever the distribution of such property in partial or complete liquidation to the shareholders in lieu of such sale or exchange would have resulted in the taxation of the gain from such distribution in the manner provided in section 341(a) as to any shareholder or would have resulted in the taxation of the gain in such manner, but for the application of section 341(d). Likewise, section 337 does not apply to sales or exchanges made by a corporation if such corporation is liquidated in a transaction to which section 333 is applicable, or in a transaction to which section 332 applies (except to the extent provided in section 337(c)(2)(B)). * * *

[T.D. 6500, 25 FR 11607, Nov. 26, 1960, as amended by T.D. 6806, 30 FR 2850, March 5, 1965]

§ 1.337–2 Sales or exchanges within the scope of section 337.

(a) Provided the other conditions of section 337 are met, sales or exchanges which occur on or after the date on which the plan of complete liquidation is adopted and within the 12-month period thereafter are subject to the provisions of such section. The date on which a sale occurs depends primarily upon the intent of the parties to be gathered from the terms of the contract and the surrounding circumstances. In ascertaining whether a sale or exchange occurs on or after the date on which the plan of complete liquidation is adopted, the fact that negotiations for sale may have been commenced, either by the corporation or its shareholders, or both shall be disregarded. Moreover, an executory contract to sell is to be distinguished from a contract of sale. Ordinarily, a sale has not occurred when a contract to sell has been entered into but title and possession of the property have not been transferred and the obligation of the seller to sell or the buyer to buy is conditional.

(b) Ordinarily the date of the adoption of a plan of complete liquidation by a corporation is the date of adoption by the shareholders of the resolution authorizing the distribution of all the assets of the corporation (other than those retained to meet claims) in redemption of all of its stock. Where the corporation sells substantially all of its property of the type defined in section 337(b) prior to the date of adoption by the shareholders of such resolution, then the date of the adoption of the plan of complete liquidation by such corporation is the date of the adoption by the shareholders of such resolution and gain or loss will be recognized with respect to such sales. Where no substantial part of the property of the type defined in section 337(b) has been sold by the corporation prior to the date of adoption by the shareholders of such resolution, the date of the adoption of the plan of complete liquidation by such corporation is the date of adoption by the shareholders of such resolution and no gain or loss will be recognized on sales of such property on or after such date, if all the corporate assets (other than those retained to meet claims) are distributed in liquidation to the shareholders within 12 months after the date of the adoption of such resolution. In all other cases the date of the adoption of the plan of liquidation shall be determined from all the facts and circumstances. Section 337 shall not apply in any case in which all of the corporate assets (other than those retained to meet claims) are not distributed to the shareholders within 12 months after the date of the adoption of a resolution by the shareholders authorizing the distribution of all the corporate assets in redemption of all the corporate stock. A corporation will be considered to have distributed all of its property other than assets retained to meet claims even though it has retained an amount of cash equal to its known liabilities and liquidating expenses plus an amount of cash set aside under arrangements for the payment after the close of the 12-month period of unascertained or contingent liabilities and contingent expenses. Such arrangements for payment must be made in good faith, the amount set aside must be reasonable, and no amount may be set aside to meet claims of shareholders with respect to their stock. If it is established to the satisfaction of the Commissioner that there are shareholders who cannot be located, a distribution in liquidation includes a transfer to a State official, trustee, or other person authorized by law to receive distributions for the benefit of such shareholders. For the purposes of this paragraph "property of the type defined in section 337(b)" means property upon the sale of which section 337(a) may provide for the nonrecognition of gain or loss upon sale or exchange during a 12-month period, including property described in subparagraph (A) of section 337(b)(1) if sold or exchanged at any time under the conditions set forth in section 337(b)(2) and including installment obligations acquired in respect of such sale or exchange.

[T.D. 6500, 25 FR 11607, Nov. 26, 1960]

§ 1.337-3 Property defined.

(a) Except as provided in section 337(b)(2) and this section, the term "property" as used in section 337(a) and § 1.337-1 does not include, (1) stock in trade of the corporation, or other property of a kind which would properly be included in the inventory of the corporation if on hand at the close of

the taxable year and property held by the corporation primarily for sale to customers in the ordinary course of its trade or business (hereinafter for purposes of section 337 referred to as "inventory"), (2) installment obligations acquired at any time from the sale or exchange of inventory, or (3) installment obligations acquired from the sale or exchange of property (other than inventory) prior to the adoption of the plan of liquidation. With the exceptions listed in this paragraph, the term "property" includes all assets owned by a corporation.

(b) Except as provided in paragraph (c) of this section, if substantially all of the inventory is sold or exchanged to one person in one transaction, then for the purpose of section 337(a) the term "property" shall include:

(1) The inventory so sold or exchanged, and

(2) Installment obligations acquired in such sale or exchange.

For this purpose, the term "substantially all" means substantially all of the inventory at the time of the sale and includes inventory subject to liabilities, specific or otherwise. Section 337(b)(2) shall be inapplicable if the inventory so sold is replaced by like inventory, or by a new kind of inventory.

(c) The term "property" in the case of a corporation which is engaged in two or more distinct businesses shall include the inventory of any one of such trades or businesses if substantially all of the inventory attributable to such trade or business is sold or exchanged to one person in one transaction. If installment obligations are received upon such a sale, such obligations are also included within the meaning of the term "property".

(d) This section may be illustrated by the following examples:

Example (1). Corporation A operates a grocery store at one location and a hardware store at another. Neither store handles items similar to those handled by the other. Both stores are served by a common warehouse. Pursuant to a plan of liquidation adopted by the corporation, the grocery store and all of its inventory, including that part of its inventory held in the warehouse, are sold to one person in one transaction. Thereafter, and within 12 months after the adoption of the plan of liquidation, all of the assets of the corporation are distributed to the shareholders. No gain or loss will be recognized upon the sale of all of the assets attributable to the grocery business, including the inventory items.

Example (2). Corporation B operates two department stores, one in the downtown business district and the other in a suburban shopping center. Both handle the same items and are served by a common warehouse which contains an amount of inventory items equal to the total of that in both stores. The part of the inventory in the warehouse which is attributable to each store cannot be clearly determined. Pursuant to a plan of liquidation adopted by the corporation, the assets of the suburban store, including the inventory held in such store, but not including any portion of the inventory held in the warehouse, are sold to one person in one transaction. Thereafter, and within 12 months after the adoption of the plan of liquidation, all of the assets of the corporation are distributed to the shareholders. No gain or loss will be recognized with respect to the sale of the property other than the inventory, but gain or loss will be recognized upon the sale of the inventory.

Example (3). The facts are the same as in example (2) except that the part oh the inventory in the warehouse which is attributable to the suburban store can be clearly determined and both the inventory held in the store and that part of the inventory in the warehouse attributable to such store are sold. No gain or loss will be recognized upon the sale of the inventory.

[T.D. 6500, 25 FR 11607, Nov. 26, 1960]

§ 1.337-4 Limitation of gain.

(a) Section 337(c)(2)(B) provides a limitation upon the amount of gain not recognized where a corporation sells or exchanges property pursuant to a plan of complete liquidation (and such property, if distributed, would take the basis of the stock held by the distributee pursuant to the provisions of section 334(b)(2) (relating to plans of liquidation adopted within 2 years after purchase of the stock)). The amount of gain not recognized shall not be greater than the excess of (1) that portion of the adjusted basis (further adjusted as provided in the second sentence of section 334(b)(2) and in paragraph (c) of § 1.334-1) of the stock of the liquidating corporation in the hands of its parent corporation allocable to the property sold or exchanged over (2) the adjusted basis of such property in the hands of the liquidating corporation.

(b) Paragraph (a) of this section may be illustrated by the following example:

Example. Corporation A owns more than 80 percent of the stock of Corporation B, which it purchased for $10,000. All of the assets of Corporation B, having a total basis of $4,000 are sold for $12,000. The portion of the realized gain of $8,000 which is not recognized is $6,000, computed as follows:

Basis of stock allocable to property sold.....	$10,000
Basis of property sold....................	4,000
Excess (not recognized).............	6,000

In general, where section 337(c)(2)(B) is applicable and where the gain realized from the sale of property is greater than the excess of the selling price

of the property over the basis of the stock allocable to the property sold, the amount of gain to be recognized from such sale is equal to such excess. In the above example, the $2,000 gain representing the excess of the selling price of $12,000 over the basis of the stock allocable to the property sold ($10,000) would be recognized to the liquidating corporation.

(c) For the purpose of this section only, the basis (adjusted as described in paragraph (a) of this section) of the liquidating corporation's stock in the hands of its parent corporation on the date of the first sale of property, shall be allocated to the assets of the liquidating corporation (unreduced by any amount applicable to minority interests) on the basis of the fair market value of such assets (see paragraph (c) of § 1.334-1), both tangible and intangible, on the date the first property is sold by the liquidating corporation. The allocation then made shall remain unchanged for the purpose of determining recognized gain upon subsequent sales of property by the liquidating corporation unless the stock ownership of the parent corporation changes. In the event of such a change, a new allocation shall be made at the time of the next sale of property thereafter. The new allocation shall be made on the basis of the fair market value of the liquidating corporation's assets on the date of such sale.

[T.D. 6500, 25 FR 11607, Nov. 26, 1960]

§ 1.337-5 Special rule for certain minority shareholders.

(a) General. If, with respect to a plan of complete liquidation adopted on or after January 1, 1958, the liquidating corporation fails to qualify for the treatment prescribed by section 337(a) solely by reason of the application of section 337(c)(2)(A), then, for the first taxable year of any shareholder (other than a corporation which meets the 80-percent stock ownership requirement specified in section 332(b)(1)) in which he receives a distribution in complete liquidation, the treatment prescribed by section 337(d) and this section shall be applicable to such shareholder. Since section 337(d) applies only with respect to distributions in complete liquidation under section 331, it does not apply with respect to a distribution which is treated as part of an exchange to which section 354 or 356 applies.

(b) Treatment of minority shareholders. (1) In cases to which section 337(d) and paragraph (a) of this section apply—

(i) The amount realized by the shareholder on the distribution shall be increased by his proportionate share of the amount by which the tax imposed by subtitle A of the Code (income taxes) on the liquidating corporation would have been reduced if section 337(c)(2)(A) had not been applicable (see paragraph (c) of this section for determination of the proportionate share of each shareholder), and

(ii) For purposes of the Code, the shareholder shall be deemed to have paid on the last day prescribed by section 6151 for the payment of the tax (the last day prescribed by section 6072 for the filing of his income tax return) for the taxable year in which he receives the first distribution in complete liquidation (whether the return is filed before, on, or after such last day), an amount of income tax equal to the amount of the increase described in subdivision (i) of this subparagraph.

* * *

(c) **Determination of each minority shareholder's increase in amount realized.** (1) Under section 337(d) and paragraph (b) of this section, the amount realized by each minority shareholder of the liquidating corporation shall be increased by his proportionate share of the amount by which the tax imposed by subtitle A of the Code on the liquidating corporation would have been reduced if section 337(c)(2)(A) had not been applicable. Where the corporation has only the one class of stock outstanding, the increase in the amount realized by each minority shareholder shall be determined by multiplying the reduction in the corporation's tax that would be applicable if section 337(c)(2)(A) did not apply by a fraction, the numerator of which is equal to the sum of all liquidating distributions received by such shareholder and the denominator of which is equal to the sum of all liquidating distributions received by all shareholders. Where the corporation has outstanding preferred stock which is limited to a specified amount on liquidation, as well as common stock, if the holders of the preferred stock receive the entire amount to which they are entitled, the fraction described in the preceding sentence shall be applied to determine the increase in the amount realized by the holders of common stock on the liquidation without taking the preferred stock into account. In all other cases, in determining the increase in the amount realized by each minority shareholder, consideration must be given to the extent to which different classes of stock are entitled to participate in the assets of the corporation on liquidation.

(2) If two or more minority shareholders receive distributions in liquidation with respect to the same stock (e.g., if a minority shareholder sells his stock after receiving one of a series of distributions in complete liquidation), the increase in the amount realized by the minority shareholder who surrenders the stock in liquidation shall be determined as though he received all the distributions in liquidation with respect to such stock and shall then be divided between himself and the shareholder who has already received distributions in liquidation with respect to the same stock. This division must be in proportion to the amount each minority shareholder received in liquidation with respect to such stock.

* * *

(e) **Illustrations.** The application of this section may be illustrated by the following examples:

Example (1). (i) Assume that corporation S, having only common stock outstanding, is owned 90 percent by corporation P (which has owned the S stock for 3 years) and 10 percent by individual A (a calendar year taxpayer), and that the sole assets of corporation S are two buildings, each having a fair market value of $100,000 and a basis to the corporation of $50,000. Assume further that A's basis for his stock is $10,000. On August 1, 1958, corporation S adopts a plan of complete liquidation. On September 1, 1958, corporation S sells building No. 1 for $100,000 and, during October 1958, the corporation makes a pro rata distribution of building No. 2 and the proceeds of the sale of building No. 1 (less $12,500 retained to pay the tax on such sale at the rate of 25 percent).

(ii) Under section 337(d) and this section, the amount realized by A on the distribution is increased by $1,250, A's proportionate share (10 percent) of the amount by which the tax imposed on corporation S upon such sale would have been reduced ($12,500) if section 337(a) had been applicable. Thus, the tax imposed on A with respect to the complete liquidation is computed as follows: The amount realized by A is $18,750 ($10,000 for A's one-tenth interest in building No. 2, plus $8,750 representing A's proportionate share of the $100,000 received by corporation S on the sale of building No. 1 less the tax imposed on corporation S upon such sale plus $1,250 (the increase in the amount realized), or $20,000. Since A's basis for his stock is $10,000, the tax imposed on A with respect to the complete liquidation (assuming A's gain is taxed at a rate of 25 percent) is $2,500. Under section 337(d) and this section, A shall be deemed to have paid $1,250 in tax. Accordingly, A will be left with $17,500 in property and money ($18,750 minus $1,250).

Example (2). (i) Assume all the facts set forth in example (1) and the following additional facts: Corporation S has outstanding 1,000 shares of $100 par value preferred stock, the holders of which are entitled to receive full par value on liquidation, after which the common shareholders receive the balance of the assets. Individual A owns 10 percent of the preferred stock, with a basis to him of $10,000, as well as 10 percent of the common stock. Corporation S has, in addition to its two buildings, $100,000 in cash which it distributes in full payment in exchange for the outstanding preferred stock.

(ii) Individual A receives $10,000 in exchange for his preferred stock and recognizes no gain or loss on this portion of the liquidation. Under section 337(d) and this section, A is accorded the same treatment described in example (1) with respect to his common stock as though it were the only stock outstanding. Thus, with respect to his common stock the amount realized by A on the distribution is increased by $1,250, and the tax deemed paid by him is $1,250. Accordingly, after credit, A will be left with $27,500 in property and money ($10,000 on his preferred stock and $17,500 on his common stock).

Example (3). (i) Assume the same facts as in example (1) except that on August 2, 1958, corporation S makes a pro rata distribution of building No. 2 as a first distribution in complete liquidation. Assume further that on August 15, 1958, individual A sells his stock to B, and that on October 1, 1958, building No. 1 is sold and final distribution in liquidation is made of $87,500 ($100,000 sales proceeds less $12,500 retained to pay tax, assuming a 25-percent rate).

(ii) Under section 337(d) and this section, the increase in the amount realized by B shall first be determined as though he had received all the distributions in liquidation with respect to such stock. Then the increase in the amount realized ($1,250) is divided between A and B in proportion to the amount each shareholder received in liquidation with respect to such stock. Thus, A's share of the increase in the amount realized is $666.67 ($1,250×10,000/18,750) and B's share is $583.33 ($1,250×8,750/18,750). A is deemed to have paid tax in the amount of $666.67 and B is deemed to have paid tax in the amount of $583.33.

* * *

[T.D. 6500, 25 FR 11607, Nov. 26, 1960, as amended by T.D. 6533, 26 FR 402, Jan. 19, 1961, T.D. 7332, 39 FR 44216, Dec. 23, 1974; T.D. 7410, 41 FR 11020, March 16, 1976]

§ 1.337–6 Information to be filed.

(a) **Cases to which section 337(a) applies.** In cases to which section 337(a) applies, there must be attached to the return of the liquidating corporation the following information:

(1) A copy of the minutes of the stockholders' meeting at which the plan of liquidation was formally adopted, including a copy of the plan of liquidation.

(2) A statement of the assets sold after the adoption of the plan of liquidation, including the dates of such sales. If section 337(c)(2)(B), relating to limited nonrecognition of gain on sales by subsidiaries, is applicable, this statement must include a computation of the total gain and of the gain not recognized under section 337.

(3) Information as to the date of the final liquidating distribution.

(4) A statement of the assets, if any, retained to pay liabilities and the nature of the liabilities.

* * *

[T.D. 6533, 26 FR 404, Jan. 19, 1961, as amended by T.D. 7410, 41 FR 11020, March 16, 1976; T.D. 7722, 45 FR 64907, Oct. 1, 1980]

Elections and Miscellaneous Matters

§ 1.338–4T Questions and answers relating to miscellaneous issues under section 338.

(a) **Introduction—(1) Effective date.** Except as otherwise provided in this section, this section applies to stock acquisitions for which the acquisition date (determined without section 224(d)(5) of TEFRA) occurs after August 31, 1982.

(2) **Scope of regulations.** This section provides guidance on a broad range of issues under section 338. This section deals principally with domestic aspects of section 338. For guidance on international aspects of section 338 and on the extent to which the provisions of this section apply in that context, see § 1.338–5T.

* * *

(b) **Nomenclature and definitions.** For purposes of this section (and except as otherwise provided in this section)—

(1) **Nomenclature—(i)** P is a domestic corporation that directly purchases all of the outstanding stock in a second domestic corporation.

(ii) T is the domestic corporation the stock of which is purchased by P. T has only one class of stock outstanding. Except as otherwise provided in this section, T is an original target if a qualified stock purchase is made of its stock.

(iii) P1, P2, etc., are domestic corporations that are members of the P group.

(iv) The P group is an affiliated group (as defined in section 338(h)(5)) that includes one or more P corporations as members.

(v) T1, T2, etc., are domestic corporations that are target affiliates of T. Those corporations (T1, T2, etc.) have only one class of stock outstanding, and also may be targets. None of the stock of those corporations is owned by T.

(vi) S is a domestic corporation (unrelated to P and B) that owns all of the outstanding stock of T prior to the purchase of T stock by P. (S is referred to in cases in which it is appropriate to consider the effects of having all of the outstanding stock of T owned by a domestic corporation.)

(vii) A is an individual (unrelated to P and B) who is a U.S. resident or citizen and who owns all of the outstanding stock of T prior to the purchase of T stock by P. (A is referred to in cases in which it is appropriate to consider the effects of having all of the outstanding stock of T owned by an individual who is a U.S. resident or citizen. Ownership of the stock of T by A and ownership of the stock of T by S are mutually exclusive circumstances.)

(viii) B is an individual (unrelated to T, S, and A) who is a U.S. resident or citizen and who owns all of the outstanding stock of P.

(2) Definitions in section 338(h) and § 1.338–1T. The definitions in section 338 and § 1.338–1T also apply to this section.

(3) Affected target. A corporation is an "affected target" if a deemed election would occur for that corporation in the event of a section 338 election for T.

(4) Original target. A corporation ("X") is an "original target" if there exists no previously acquired target as to which a section 338 election would cause a deemed election under section 338(f)(1) for X. If two corporations are acquired at the same time, either corporation (but not both) may be considered by the purchasing corporation as the original target.

(5) Consistency period. The "consistency period" is the period described in section 338(h)(4)(A) unless extended pursuant to paragraph (g)(1) Answer 1 of this section.

(6) Domestic corporation. A "domestic corporation" is a corporation (i) that is created or organized in the United States or under the law of the United States or of any State and (ii) that is not a DISC, a corporation described in section 934(b) or 1248(e), or a corporation to which an election under section 936 applies.

(7) Section 338 election. A "section 338 election" is an election to apply section 338(a) to a target. A section 338 election is either an express election or a deemed election.

(8) Express election. An "express election" is a section 338 election made for the original target by filing a statement of section 338 election (Form 8023) pursuant to § 1.338–1T(c).

(9) Deemed election. A "deemed election" is a section 338 election that is not an express election. A deemed election is made under the authority of section 338(e), (f), or (i) or under the authority of more than one of those provisions. If an express election for the original target causes a section 338 election by reason of section 338(f)(1) for another target, that other target is considered subject to a deemed election. A statement of section 338 election (Form 8023) need not be filed for that other target, but that other target may be required to be included in a schedule attached to the statement of section 338 election filed for the original target. See § 1.338–1T(c) and (e).

(10) Related persons. Two persons are related to each other if stock in a corporation owned by one such person would be attributed under section 318(a) (other than paragraph (4) thereof) to the other, or vice versa.

(c) Qualified stock purchase and miscellaneous related rules—(1) Purchase requirement of section 338(h)(3). The purpose of this paragraph (c)(1) is to provide guidance on whether particular stock acquisitions qualify as purchases under section 338(h)(3). It is assumed in each question and answer that no exception to the purchase requirement is potentially applicable other than the exception discussed in the particular question and answer.

Question 1: If P acquires T stock from S solely for cash in a transaction with respect to which S does not recognize gain or loss pursuant to section 337, has P acquired that T stock by purchase?

Answer 1: Yes. Such an acquisition of stock is not excepted from the definition of purchase under the regulatory authority in section 338(h)(3)(A)(ii).

Question 2: If P acquires T stock from S solely for cash in a transaction with respect to which S recognizes its income under the installment method, has P acquired that T stock by purchase?

Answer 2: Yes. Such an acquisition of stock is not excepted from the definition of purchase under the regulatory authority in section 338(h)(3)(A)(ii).

Question 3: If P acquires T stock from S solely for cash and if S is a foreign person that is not required to pay United States income tax on the disposition of the T stock, has P acquired that T stock by purchase?

Answer 3: Yes. Such an acquisition of stock is not excepted from the definition of purchase under the regulatory authority in section 338(h)(3)(A)(ii).

Question 4: Assume that P owns less than 50 percent in value of the stock of S and that S owns 100 percent of the only class of T stock. If P acquires all of the T stock from S in a distribution with respect to P's S stock or in a redemption of P's S stock, has P acquired that T stock by purchase?

Answer 4: (i) Distribution with respect to which section 311(d)(1) applies. If P acquires the T stock in a distribution with respect to which S recognizes gain under section 311(d)(1), then P has acquired that T stock by purchase.

(ii) Distributions with respect to which section 311(d)(1) does not apply—(A) Fair market value of T stock does not exceed its adjusted basis in the hands of S. If P acquires the T stock in a distribution to which sections 301–307 apply and if the fair market value of the T stock does not exceed its adjusted basis in the hands of S (so that section 311(d)(1) does not apply to the distribution), then P has acquired that T stock by purchase. This result applies even though S realizes but does not recognize a loss, since such an acquisition of stock is not excepted from the definition of purchase under the regulatory authority in section 338(h)(3)(A)(ii).

(B) Fair market value of T stock exceeds its adjusted basis in the hands of S. Under the authority of section 338(h)(3)(A)(ii), if (1) P acquires the T stock in a distribution to which sections 301–307 apply, (2) the fair market value of the T stock exceeds its adjusted basis in the hands of S, and (3) section 311(d)(1) does not apply to the distribution, then P has not acquired that T stock by purchase.

Example (1). P owns less than 50 percent in value of the stock of S, and S owns all of the stock of T. The stock of T has a fair market value of $1,000, and S's basis in that stock is $400. On November 1, 1986, S distributes all of the stock of T to P in a redemption qualifying under section 302(a) of the S stock held by P. S recognizes a

gain of $600 on the distribution pursuant to section 311(d)(1). Accordingly, P has acquired the T stock by purchase under section 338(h)(3).

Example (2). Assume the same facts as in Example (1), except that S's basis in the T stock is $1,400. The result is the same.

Example (3). Assume the same facts as in Example (1), except that the distribution is a dividend distribution rather than a distribution in redemption of S stock. S recognizes a gain of $600 on the distribution pursuant to section 311(d)(1). Accordingly, P has acquired the T stock by purchase under section 338(h)(3).

Example (4). Assume the same facts as in Example (3), except that the distribution occurs on January 1, 1984. S does not recognize a gain on the distribution under section 311(d)(1). P has not acquired the T stock by purchase under section 338(h)(3).

* * *

(e) **Application of the stock consistency rules of section 338(f).** This paragraph (e) provides general guidance on the operation of section 338(f). For special consistency rules issued under the authority of section 338(e)(3), (h)(4)(B), and (i), see paragraph (g) of this section.

Question 1: Assume that S owns directly all of the stock of T and T1, that P makes a qualified stock purchase of T stock, and that, after the acquisition date of T but within T's consistency period, P makes a qualified stock purchase of T1 stock. If no section 338 election has been made for T so that T1 is not already subject to a deemed election under section 338(f)(1), may P make an express election for T1?

Answer 1: No. Under section 338(f)(2), the express election must be made for T, the original target. An express election made for T will cause a deemed election under section 338(f)(1) for T1. If P makes qualified stock purchases of the stock of T and T1 at the same time, the express election may be made for either target (but not both), and that election will cause a deemed election under section 338(f)(1) for the other target. For guidance on making the express election and complying with related requirements (e.g., inclusion of schedule of corporations subject to the express election by reason of section 338(f)(1), attachments to T returns, etc.), see § 1.338–1T.

Question 2: If P makes qualified stock purchases of the stock of T and T1 on January 1, 1985, and November 1, 1986, respectively, will T1 be affected by a section 338 election for T (or by the absence of such an election for T)?

Answer 2: No. The acquisition date of T1 must occur during T's consistency period in order for T1 to be subject to section 338(f)(1) and (2) by reason of the status of T. Under section 338(h)(4)(A)(iii), T's consistency period normally will end at the close of the one-year period beginning on January 2, 1985 (the day after the acquisition date of T). It is irrelevant that the beginning of T1's consistency period overlaps with the end of T's consistency period. Thus, assuming that T's consistency period is not extended, the section 338 election for T will not cause a deemed election under section 338(f)(1) for T1, and the absence of a section 338 election for T will not bar an express election for T1 by reason of section 338(f)(2).

Question 3: Would the answer to Question 2 of this paragraph (e) be different if (i) P also makes a qualified stock purchase of T2 stock on December 15, 1985, (ii) T2 is a target affiliate of T, and (iii) T1 is a target affiliate of T2?

Answer 3: Yes. T1 will be affected by a section 338 election for T (or by the absence of such an election for T). This result follows because T2 is a target affiliate of T and is acquired by P during T's consistency period. Similarly, T1 is a target affiliate of T2 and is acquired by P during T2's consistency period. Thus, a section 338 election for T causes a deemed election under section 338(f)(1) for T2, which in turn causes a deemed election under section 338(f)(1) for T1. Similarly, under section 338(f)(2), the absence of a section 338 election for T bars an express election for T2, which in turn bars an express election for T1.

Question 4: Assume that P makes a qualified stock purchase of all of the stock of T from S and thereafter, within one year, also makes a qualified stock purchase of all of the stock of X from Y. Assume further that S and Y are and always have been unrelated corporations that respectively have held all of the stock of T and X since those corporations were organized. If P makes a valid section 338 election for T, is a deemed election under section 338(f)(1) made for X?

Answer 4: No. A deemed election is made for X only if X is a target affiliate of T. Under section 338(h)(6)(A), X is a target affiliate of T only if, at any time during so much of T's consistency period as ends on the acquisition date of T, X and T were members of an affiliated group that had the same common parent. Even though X and T are both members of the P group after the acquisition date

of X, X is not a target affiliate of T because X was not a member of the P group during so much of T's consistency period as ends on the acquisition date of T. Even if the acquisition date of X were the same as the acquisition date of T, X would not be a target affiliate of T and T would not be a target affiliate of X under these facts.

(f) Application of the asset consistency rule of section 338(e)—(1) Introduction and general operating rules—(i) Introduction. This paragraph (f) provides general guidance on the operation of section 338(e). For special consistency rules issued under the authority of section 338(e)(3), (h)(4)(B), and (i), see paragraph (g) of this section.

(ii) General operating rules.

Question 1: Under what circumstances will a deemed election under section 338(e)(1) be made by P with respect to its qualified stock purchase of T stock?

Answer 1: Under the authority of section 338(e)(2)(D) and (i), a deemed election under section 338(e)(1) will be made by P with respect to its qualified stock purchase of T stock *only* if the District Director determines, in connection with the examination of a return that would be affected by a deemed election for T, that—

(i) P (or another member of the P group) has acquired an asset of T (or a target affiliate of T) during T's consistency period in an acquisition that is described in section 338(e)(1) and that is not subject to an exception (other than the carryover basis election exception of paragraph (f)(6) of this section) to section 338(e)(1).

(ii) Neither a section 338 election nor a protective carryover election under paragraph (f)(6)(ii) Answer 1 of this section is made by P with respect to T, and

(iii) A deemed election for T, in lieu of the affirmative action carryover election for T under paragraph (f)(6)(ii) Answer 3 of this section, is appropriate to carry out the purposes of the consistency rules of section 338(e), (f), or (i) (see paragraph (f)(6)(i)(A) and (ii) Answer 3 Example (1)).

Question 2: Will section 338(f)(2) apply to bar the District Director's determination of a deemed election under section 338(e)(1) for T1 if—

(i) P makes a qualified stock purchase of T stock,

(ii) After the acquisition date of T but within T's consistency period, P makes a qualified stock purchase of the stock of T1, a target affiliate of T,

(iii) No section 338 election has been made for T so that T1 is not already subject to a deemed election under section 338(f)(1), and

(iv) P acquires an asset from T1 during T1's consistency period but after the close of T's consistency period in an acquisition that is described in section 338(e)(1) and that is not subject to an exception (other than the carryover basis election exception of paragraph (f)(6) of this section) to section 338(e)(1)?

Answer 2: No. Section 338(f)(2) will not bar the District Director's determination of a deemed election under section 338(e)(1) for T1.

Question 3: Will the District Director's determination of a deemed election under section 338(e)(1) for T1 under the facts described in Question 2 of this paragraph (f)(1)(ii) cause a deemed election for T?

Answer 3: Yes. Under the authority of section 338(f)(1) and (i), T will be subject to a deemed election whenever the District Director determines that a deemed election under section 338(e)(1) is made for a later-acquired target (i.e., a target acquired by the P group subsequent to the P group's acquisition of T), provided that a deemed election under section 338(f)(1) would be considered made for the later-acquired target if a section 338 election were made for T. It is irrelevant, for purposes of this Answer 3, whether the asset acquisition occurs before or after the period within which to make an express election for T or before or after the close of T's consistency period.

(2) Asset acquisition by P (or another member of the P group) from T or T's target affiliate.

Question 1: Is an asset acquisition by a future or a former member of the P group considered an asset acquisition by a member of the P group for purposes of section 338(e)(1)?

Answer 1: No, provided that the acquisition is not treated as made by a member of the P group under paragraph (g)(2) of this section.

Question 2: Is an asset acquisition by T after the acquisition date of T and while T is a member of the P group considered an asset acquisition by a member of the P group for purposes of section 338(e)(1)?

Answer 2: Yes. For purposes of determining whether an asset acquisition is made by a P group member, T is treated like any other P group member once it joins that group.

(3) Exception of section 338(e)(2)(A) for acquisitions in ordinary course of trade or business.

Question: Under what circumstances will an asset sale by T (or a target affiliate of T) ("selling corporation") to P (or another member of the P group) be subject to the exception to section 338(e)(1) provided by section 338(e)(2)(A) (relating to sales in the ordinary course of the selling corporation's trade or business)?

Answer: (i) General rule. An asset sale will be subject to the exception of section 338(e)(2)(A) if the sale is either customary for the selling corporation or a normal incident to the conduct of the trade or business in which that selling corporation is engaged. For purposes of applying this exception, all sales made by a selling corporation to members of the P group during T's consistency period will be aggregated and treated as a single sale by that selling corporation if, on the basis of all of the facts and circumstances, it appears that such sales were separated for the purpose of satisfying the ordinary course of trade or business exception. In addition, all sales by all of the selling corporations to members of the P group during the consistency period will be aggregated and treated as a single sale by each selling corporation for purposes of applying the ordinary course of trade or business exception to each such selling corporation if, on the basis of all of the facts and circumstances, it appears that some or all of the assets sold were dispersed among T and its target affiliates for the purpose of satisfying the ordinary course of trade or business exception.

(ii) Customary for selling corporation. The determination whether the sale is customary for the selling corporation is based on all of the facts and circumstances of the particular sale in light of the selling corporation's customary practice. Factors that must be considered in determining customary practice include the frequency and magnitude (both in terms of quantity and value) of prior sales of such property as well as the circumstances under which such prior sales occurred.

(iii) **Normal incident to trade or business.** In general, a sale is considered a normal incident to the conduct of the trade or business in which the selling corporation is engaged if, taking into consideration all of the facts and circumstances of the particular sale, it is one that reasonably would occur in the context of the ongoing business operations of a similarly situated company engaged in the same trade or business as the selling corporation.

Example (1). On January 1, 1985, P acquires all of the stock of T in a qualified stock purchase. T is a corporation engaged in the manufacture and sale of steel products. On April 1, 1985, P purchases steel girders from T for use in P's construction business. P makes no additional purchases from T (or from a target affiliate of T) during T's consistency period. T customarily sells girders in its business, and the magnitude of P's purchase is not unusual. The ordinary course of trade or business exception applies.

Example (2). (i) Assume the same facts as in Example (1). Assume in addition that T owns several tractor-trailers used to deliver its steel products. T has owned and operated these vehicles for four years. It is a general practice in T's industry to replace such vehicles after three or four years. T sells the tractor-trailers to P1 pursuant to T's standard procedure for disposing of and replacing used equipment. T promptly purchases new tractor-trailers and continues in the business of delivering steel products. In terms of both the sales price of the used equipment and the quantity, the sale to P1 is unexceptional.

(ii) While T may not be engaged in the business of selling tractor-trailers, the sale of the tractor-trailers to P1 is customary in its business. Accordingly, the ordinary course of trade or business exception applies.

Example (3). Assume the same facts as in Example (1). Assume in addition that a fire at one of T's plants destroys uninsured machinery used in T's business, and that T sells the machinery to P as scrap for cash in an amount that exceeds T's adjusted basis in the machinery. Such a sale reasonably would occur in T's industry in the context of ongoing business operations in the event of a fire. Accordingly, the ordinary course of trade or business exception applies.

* * *

(h) **Determination of section 338(a)(1) deemed sale price—(1) Introduction.** The price at which old T is treated as selling its assets in the section 338(a)(1) deemed sale must be determined in order to measure the gain or loss recognized by T in the deemed sale. The questions and answers in this paragraph (h) provide guidance on the determination of the aggregate deemed sale price. For purposes of applying this paragraph (h), T stock is considered purchased or held by P if it is purchased or held by any member of the P group. See section 338(h)(8). This paragraph (h) does not ap-

ply if an election under section 338(h)(10) is made. For the effect of old T's tax liabilities, as determined under this paragraph (h), on the basis of new T's assets, see paragraph (j) of this section. See § 1.338(b)–3T(h) and (j) for certain rules and examples relating to any change in the aggregate deemed sale price of old target's assets.

(2) **Definitions—(i) ADSP.** The "ADSP" is the aggregate deemed sale price, *i.e.*, the price at which T is deemed to have sold all of its assets in the deemed sale under section 338(a)(1). In the absence of a subscript, "ADSP" refers to ADSP for Class III assets only. See § 1.338(b)–2T(b).

(ii) **Elective ADSP formula.** The "elective ADSP formula" is an elective formula prescribed under the authority of section 338(h)(11) for determining the ADSP.

(iii) **Allocable ADSP amount.** The "allocable ADSP amount" is the portion of the ADSP as calculated under the elective ADSP formula that is allocable to a particular T asset. Except as provided in section 7701(g) (relating to fair market value in the case of nonrecourse indebtedness), and unless a transitional allocation election under § 1.338(b)–4T is made, the ADSP is allocated among T assets for this purpose in accordance with the rules in § 1.338(b)–2T (without regard to § 1.338(b)–2T(c)(2)). If a transitional allocation election under § 1.338(b)–4T is made, the ADSP is allocated among T assets for this purpose in accordance with the rules in § 1.338(b)–4T(e). Recapture gain on a T asset under the elective ADSP formula is computed by reference to the allocable ADSP amount for that asset.

(iv) **Recapture gain.** "Recapture gain" is gain that is recognized in the section 338(a)(1) deemed sale notwithstanding the application of section 337 to the deemed sale. Examples of recapture gain include depreciation and LIFO recapture, section 338(c)(1) amounts, and tax benefit items.

(v) **Section 338(c)(1) percentage.** The "section 338(c)(1) percentage" is 100 percent minus the maximum percentage specified in section 338(c)(1). Items of gain or loss that are realized in the deemed sale but that would not be recognized in an actual sale under section 337 are multiplied by the section 338(c)(1) percentage to arrive at the section 338(c)(1) gain (or loss) recognized in the deemed sale.

(vi) **Classes of assets.** The four classes of assets are defined in § 1.338(b)–2T(b). Examples of each class are: Class I, cash; Class II, marketable securities; Class III, assets other than Classes I, II, and IV; and Class IV, goodwill and going concern value.

(3) Determination of ADSP

Question 1: How is the ADSP determined?

Answer 1: (i) General rule. The ADSP is the aggregate of the fair market values of all of old T's assets at the close of the acquisition date. Section 338(a)(1). Except as provided in section 7701(g) (relating to fair market value in the case of nonrecourse indebtedness), for assets other than Class IV assets (i.e., goodwill and going concern value), the same fair market values shall be used for purposes of this paragraph (h) (old T's aggregate deemed sale price) and for purposes of § 1.338(b)–2T(b) and (c)(1) or (c)(3) (allocating new T's adjusted grossed-up basis to its assets). If the elective ADSP formula is not used, a proper appraisal of Class IV assets will be considered evidence of their fair market value.

(ii) Elective ADSP formula for determining ADSP—(A) General rule. Under the authority of section 338(h)(11), the ADSP may be determined under the elective ADSP formula, which takes into account liabilities and other relevant items.

(B) Procedure for electing elective ADSP formula and for revoking election. The election to apply the elective ADSP formula ("formula election") is made by attaching to the final return of old T (including an amended final return) a statement containing the following declaration (or a substantially similar declaration): "THIS RETURN REFLECTS A FORMULA ELECTION FOR T UNDER SECTION 338 AND § 1.338–4T(h)(3)." The formula election is revoked by attaching to an amended final return of old T a statement containing the following declaration (or a substantially similar declaration): "THIS RETURN DOES NOT REFLECT A FORMULA ELECTION FOR T UNDER SECTION 338 AND § 1.338–4T(h)(3)." In addition, a formula election may be made or revoked in connection with the examination of the final return of old T. A formula election made for T also applies to all affected targets, as does the revocation of a formula election for T. A formula election may not be made or revoked if the period within which to make an assessment of tax has expired for any return that would be affected by the election or the revocation. For this purpose, a return would be affected by the election (or revocation) if the election (or revocation) would have the effect, directly or indirectly, of increasing the tax liability reported in that return.

Question 2: How is the ADSP determined under the elective ADSP formula?

Answer 2: (i) Introduction. The ADSP under the elective ADSP formula is the sum of (A) the grossed-up basis of P's recently purchased T stock (as defined in section 338(b)(6)(A)), (B) the liabilities of T (including any tax liability resulting from the deemed sale), and (C) other relevant items. If T is acquired in a true bargain purchase (i.e., if the cost of the stock acquisition to P is less than the aggregate fair market value of the assets of T), the ADSP as determined under the elective ADSP formula will reflect that bargain element. This result follows because the elective ADSP formula takes into account the actual price paid by P for T stock. If the elective ADSP formula is not used in such a case, recapture gain items measured by reference to the ADSP will be disproportionately high as compared to the price P actually paid for the T stock and the basis of new T's assets.

(ii) Grossed-up basis of P's recently purchased T stock. The grossed-up basis of P's recently purchased T stock is an amount equal to P's basis in recently purchased T stock, divided by the percentage of T stock (by value) attributable to that recently purchased T stock. If T has a single class of outstanding stock, the grossed-up basis of P's recently purchased T stock for purposes of the elective ADSP formula reflects the total price P would have paid for all outstanding T stock had it purchased all such stock for a price per share equal to the average price per share that it paid for the recently purchased T stock.

(iii) Tax liability resulting from the deemed sale. The elective ADSP formula takes into account both tax credit recapture liability arising by reason of the deemed sale and the tax liability on recapture gain. The elective ADSP formula reflects that fact that recapture gain both increases the ADSP (by creating a tax liability) and is computed by reference to the ADSP.

(iv) Calculation of recapture gain with respect to certain property. Section 1245 depreciation recapture gain on a T asset under the elective ADSP formula is the amount by which (A) the lesser of the recomputed basis of that asset or the allocable ADSP amount for that asset exceeds (B) the adjusted basis of that asset. Proper use of recomputed basis for items of section 1245 property results in the lowest ADSP. When a large number of items subject to section 1245 depreciation recapture must be included in the elective ADSP formula, the determination as to which of those assets should be measured by reference to recomputed basis to arrive at the lowest ADSP requires a very large number of trial and error computations. Similar rules apply to other classes of property with respect to which recapture gain is properly determined by reference to the lesser of the allocable ADSP amount or some other amount.

(v) *Other applicable rules apply in elective ADSP formula.* The elective ADSP formula may not be applied in such a way as to contravene other applicable rules. Thus, for example, a capital loss under section 338(c)(1) cannot be applied in the elective ADSP formula to reduce ordinary income recapture gain.

(vi) *Sample elective ADSP formula.* The sample ADSP formula shown below takes into account the existence of recapture gain arising under sections 1245 and 338(c)(1). For illustrative purposes, Examples (1) through (3) of this subdivision (vi) assume that the target has only Class III assets (e.g., property other than certain cash items, certain securities, and goodwill, etc.). For examples illustrating the effect on the elective ADSP formula of Class I, II, or IV assets, see Examples (4) through (9) of this subdivision (vi). In Examples (1) through (9) of this subdivision (vi) it is assumed that a transitional allocation election under § 1.338(b)–4T is not made. Other items of recapture gain may be added to the elective ADSP formula as appropriate.

The sample formula is as follows:

$$ADSP = G + L = t_R \times [\,(\text{Lesser of } R \text{ or } (ADSP \times F)) - B\,] + C \times t_R \times [\,(ADSP \times F) - Cb\,]$$

For purposes of this sample formula—

(A) "G" is the grossed-up basis of P's recently purchased T stock (as determined under subdivision (ii) of this Answer 2).

(B) "L" is the sum of T's liabilities other than T's tax liability for recapture gain amounts determined by reference to the ADSP. (Investment tax credit recapture under section 47 that results from the deemed sale of T's assets is included in L, for example, since that liability is not determined by reference to the ADSP.)

(C) "t_R" is the tax rate applicable to the recapture gain item represented by the bracketed material immediately following this symbol. In the sample formula, the bracketed material following the first use of the "t_R" symbol represents section 1245 depreciation recapture gain on an asset. (If there is more than one asset subject to section 1245 depreciation recapture, the recapture gain for each asset is separately computed in the elective ADSP formula.) The bracketed material following the second use of the "t_R" symbol in the sample formula represents section 338(c)(1) gain on an asset.

(D) "R" is the recomputed basis (as defined in section 1245(a)(2)) of an item of section 1245 property.

(E) "F" is a fraction the numerator of which is the fair market value of a T asset on T's acquisition date and the denominator of which is the aggregate fair market value of all T assets on T's acquisition date. This fraction is multiplied by the ADSP to arrive at the allocable ADSP amount for a T asset.

(F) [Reserved]

(G) "B" is the adjusted basis of a T asset on the acquisition date.

(H) "C" is the section 338(c)(1) percentage (as defined in paragraph (h)(2)(v) of this section).

(I) "Cb" is the basis of an asset for purposes of determining the section 338(c)(1) gain or loss on that asset. An item of section 1245 property, for example, is taken into account for purposes of determining section 338(c)(1) gain only if the recomputed basis of that item (rather than the allocable ADSP amount for that item) is the measure of section 1245 depreciation recapture gain on that asset, since only in that case is there realized gain on the item that, absent section 338(c)(1), would not be recognized by reason of section 337. In such a case, the recomputed basis is the "Cb" amount.

Example (1). (i) T is a calendar year taxpayer that files separate returns and that has no loss or tax credit carryovers to 1985. As of July 1, 1985, T's only asset, which T has held for more than one year, is an item of section 1245 property with an adjusted basis to T of $50,400, a recomputed basis of $80,000, and a fair market value of $100,000. On July 1, 1985, P purchases all of the stock of T for $75,000 and makes an express election for T. Assume that T has no liabilities other than a tax liability resulting from the deemed sale of assets. Assume in addition that T's marginal tax rate for any ordinary income resulting from the deemed sale of assets is 46 percent.

(ii) Section 1245 depreciation recapture gain on the item of section 1245 property is determined under the elective ADSP formula by reference to the lesser of the recomputed basis of that item ($80,000) or the allocable ADSP amount for that item. Since the ADSP for T ($88,616) does not exceed the fair market value of T's one asset ($100,000), a Class III asset, its entire ADSP is allocated to that asset. See § 1.338(b)–2T(c)(1) (relating to fair market value limitation). The elective ADSP formula as applied to these facts is as follows:

$$ADSP = G + L + t_R \times [\,(\text{Lesser of R or ADSP}) - B\,]$$

$$ADSP = (\$75,000/1) + \$0 + .46 \times [\,(\text{Lesser of } \$80,000 \text{ or } ADSP) - \$50,400\,]$$

ADSP—Recomputed basis measurement:

$$ADSP = \$75,000 + .46 \times (\$80,000 - \$50,400)$$

$$ADSP = \$88,616$$

ADSP—ADSP measurement:

$$ADSP = \$75,000 + .46 \times (ADSP - \$50,400)$$

$$ADSP = \$75,000 + (.46 \times ADSP) - 23,184$$

$$ADSP = \$51,816 + .46 ADSP$$

$$ADSP - .46 ADSP = \$51,816$$

$$.54 ADSP/.54 = \$51,816/.54$$

$$ADSP = \$95,955.56$$

Accordingly, the ADSP of T is $88,616, *i.e.*, the recomputed basis measurement ($88,616), which is less than the ADSP measurement ($95,955.56).

* * *

(j) Determination of basis of target assets after section 338 election—(1) Introduction. The questions and answers in this paragraph (j) provide guidance under section 338(b) on the determination of the total sum ("adjusted grossed-up basis") to be allocated as basis to the assets of new T. These questions and answers do not specifically deal with the manner in which the adjusted grossed-up basis is allocated among T's assets. Rules relating to allocation of adjusted grossed-up basis among T's assets are provided in §§ 1.338(b)–2T and 1.338(b)–3T. For purposes of applying this paragraph (j), T stock is considered purchased or held by P if it is purchased or held by any member of the P group. See section 338(h)(8).

(2) Determination of adjusted grossed-up basis.

Question 1: How is the adjusted grossed-up basis determined?

Answer 1: (i) General rule. The adjusted grossed-up basis is the sum of (A) P's grossed-up basis in recently purchased T stock, (B) P's basis in nonrecently purchased T stock, (C) the liabilities of T (including tax liabilities computed under para-

graph (h) of this section), and (D) other relevant items.

(ii) P's grossed-up basis in recently purchased T stock. P's grossed-up basis in recently purchased T stock is the product of P's basis in recently purchased T stock (as defined in section 338(b)(6)(A)), multiplied by the fraction described in section 338(b)(4). If T has a single class of outstanding stock, P's grossed-up basis in recently purchased T stock reflects the total price P would have paid for all outstanding T stock (other than P's nonrecently purchased T stock, as defined in section 338(b)(6)(B)) had P purchased all such stock (other than such nonrecently purchased T stock) for a price per share equal to the average price per share that P paid for the recently purchased T stock. Note that P's grossed-up basis in recently purchased T stock as calculated for purposes of the adjusted grossed-up basis differs from the "grossed-up basis of P's recently purchased T stock" as calculated in the elective ADSP formula. The elective ADSP formula treats P's nonrecently purchased T stock in the same manner as T stock not held by P. See Answer 2 (ii) of paragraph (h)(3) of this section.

(iii) P's basis in nonrecently purchased T stock. In the absence of an election under section 338(b)(3) ("gain recognition election"), P's basis in nonrecently purchased T stock is P's historic basis in that stock.

Question 2: What is the effect of a gain recognition election under section 338(b)(3)?

Answer 2: If P makes a gain recognition election, then, for all purposes of the Code and regulations, (i) P is treated as if it sold on the acquisition date the nonrecently purchased T stock for the basis amount determined under section 338(b)(3)(B), and (ii) P's basis on the acquisition date in nonrecently purchased T stock is the basis amount. If T has a single class of outstanding stock, P's basis in each share of nonrecently purchased T stock after the gain recognition election is equal to the average price per share of P's recently purchased T stock. In such a case, the sum of P's grossed-up basis in recently purchased T stock and P's basis in nonrecently purchased T stock will be equal to the "grossed-up basis of P's recently purchased T stock" as calculated in the elective ADSP formula. See Answer 2(ii) of paragraph (h)(3) of this section. Absent a gain recognition election, the adjusted grossed-up basis will differ from the

ADSP as calculated under the elective ADSP formula whenever P holds nonrecently purchased T stock at a basis that differs from P's basis in recently purchased T stock.

Question 3: May losses on nonrecently purchased T stock be recognized in the deemed sale of such stock under section 338(b)(3)?

Answer 3: No. Only gains (unreduced by losses) on the nonrecently purchased T stock are recognized.

Question 4: If P makes a gain recognition election for T, what stock held by P is subject to that election?

Answer 4: All T stock held by P (or other members of the P group) on T's acquisition date that is not recently purchased T stock is subject to the election. In addition, stock in an affected target held by P group members on the affected target's acquisition date also is subject to the gain recognition election for T if such stock is not recently purchased affected target stock.

* * *

[T.D. 8021, 50 FR 16405, April 25, 1985; T.D. 8068, 51 FR 749, Jan. 8, 1986; T.D. 8072, 51 FR 3587, Jan. 29, 1986; T.D. 8074, 51 FR 5193, Feb. 12, 1986; 51 FR 6219, Feb. 21, 1986; 51 FR 10621, March 28, 1986; T.D. 8092, 51 FR 23741, July 1, 1986]

Collapsible Corporations

§ 1.341–1 Collapsible corporations; in general.

Subject to the limitations contained in § 1.341–4 and the exceptions contained in § 1.341–6 and § 1.341–7(a), the entire gain from the actual sale or exchange of stock of a collapsible corporation, (b) amounts distributed in complete or partial liquidation of a collapsible corporation which are treated, under section 331, as payment in exchange for stock, and (c) a distribution made by a collapsible corporation which, under section 301(c)(3), is treated, to the extent it exceeds the basis of the stock, in the same manner as a gain from the sale or exchange of property, shall be considered as ordinary income.

[T.D. 6500, 25 FR 11607, Nov. 26, 1960, as amended by T.D. 6806, 30 FR 2850, March 5, 1965; T.D. 7655, 44 FR 68459, Nov. 29, 1979]

§ 1.341–2 Definitions.

(a) Determination of collapsible corporation. (1) A collapsible corporation is defined by section 341(b)(1) to be a corporation formed or availed of principally (i) for the manufacture, construction, or production of property, (ii) for the purchase of property which (in the hands of the corporation) is property described in section 341(b)(3), or (iii) for the holding of stock in a corporation so formed or availed of, with a view to (a) the sale or exchange of stock by its shareholders (whether in liquidation or otherwise), or a distribution to its shareholders, prior to the realization by the corporation manufacturing, constructing, producing, or purchasing

the property of a substantial part of the taxable income to be derived from such property, and (b) the realization by such shareholders of gain attributable to such property. See § 1.341–5 for a description of the facts which will ordinarily be considered sufficient to establish whether or not a corporation is a collapsible corporation under the rules of this section. See paragraph (d) of § 1.341–5 for examples of the application of section 341.

(2) Under section 341(b)(1) the corporation must be formed or availed of with a view to the action therein described, that is, the sale or exchange of its stock by its shareholders, or a distribution to them prior to the realization by the corporation manufacturing, constructing, producing, or purchasing the property of a substantial part of the taxable income to be derived from such property, and the realization by the shareholders of gain attributable to such property. This requirement is satisfied in any case in which such action was contemplated by those persons in a position to determine the policies of the corporation, whether by reason of their owning a majority of the voting stock of the corporation or otherwise. The requirement is satisfied whether such action was contemplated, unconditionally, conditionally, or as a recognized possibility. If the corporation was so formed or availed of, it is immaterial that a particular shareholder was not a shareholder at the time of the manufacture, construction, production, or purchase of the property, or if a shareholder at such time, did not share in such view. Any gain of such a shareholder on his stock in the corporation

shall be treated in the same manner as gain of a shareholder who did share in such view. The existence of a bona fide business reason for doing business in the corporate form does not, by itself, negate the fact that the corporation may also have been formed or availed of with a view to the action described in section 341(b).

(3) A corporation is formed or availed of with a view to the action described in section 341(b) if the requisite view existed at any time during the manufacture, production, construction, or purchase referred to in that section. Thus, if the sale, exchange, or distribution is attributable solely to circumstances which arose after the manufacture, construction, production, or purchase (other than circumstances which reasonably could be anticipated at the time of such manufacture, construction, production, or purchase), the corporation shall, in the absence of compelling facts to the contrary, be considered not to have been so formed or availed of. However, if the sale, exchange or distribution is attributable to circumstances present at the time of the manufacture, construction, production, or purchase, the corporation shall, in the absence of compelling facts to the contrary, be considered to have been so formed or availed of.

(4) The property referred to in section 341(b) is that property or the aggregate of those properties with respect to which the requisite view existed. In order to ascertain the property or properties as to which the requisite view existed, reference shall be made to each property as to which, at the time of the sale, exchange, or distribution referred to in section 341(b) there has not been a realization by the corporation manufacturing, constructing, producing, or purchasing the property of a substantial part of the taxable income to be derived from such property. However, where any such property is a unit of an integrated project involving several properties similar in kind, the determination whether the requisite view existed shall be made only if a substantial part of the taxable income to be derived from the project has not been realized at the time of the sale, exchange, or distribution, and in such case the determination shall be made by reference to the aggregate of the properties constituting the single project.

(5) A corporation shall be deemed to have manufactured, constructed, produced, or purchased property if it (i) engaged in the manufacture, construction, or production of property to any extent, or (ii) holds property having a basis determined, in whole or in part, by reference to the cost of such property

in the hands of a person who manufactured, constructed, produced, or purchased the property, or (iii) holds property having a basis determined, in whole or in part, by reference to the cost of property manufactured, constructed, produced, or purchased by the corporation. Thus, under subdivision (i) of this subparagraph, for example, a corporation need not have originated nor have completed the manufacture, construction, or production of the property. Under subdivision (ii) of this subparagraph, for example, if an individual were to transfer property constructed by him to a corporation in exchange for all of the capital stock of such corporation, and such transfer qualifies under section 351, then the corporation would be deemed to have constructed the property, since the basis of the property in the hands of the corporation would, under section 362 be determined by reference to the basis of the property in the hands of the individual. Under subdivision (iii) of this subparagraph, for example, if a corporation were to exchange property constructed by it for property of like kind constructed by another person, and such exchange qualifies under section 1031(a), then the corporation would be deemed to have constructed the property received by it in the exchange, since the basis of the property received by it in the exchange would, under section 1031(d), be determined by reference to the basis of the property constructed by the corporation.

(6) In determining whether a corporation is a collapsible corporation by reason of the purchase of property, it is immaterial whether the property is purchased from the shareholders of the corporation or from persons other than such shareholders. The property, however, must be property which, in the hands of the corporation, is property of a kind described in section 341(b)(3). The determination whether property is of a kind described in section 341(b)(3) shall be made without regard to the fact that the corporation is formed or availed of with a view to the action described in section 341(b)(1).

(7) Section 341 is applicable whether the shareholder is an individual, a trust, an estate, a partnership, a company, or a corporation.

(b) **Section 341 assets.** For the purposes of this section, the term "section 341 assets" means the following listed property if held for less than 3 years:

(1) Stock in trade of the corporation, or other property of a kind which would properly be includ-

ed in the inventory of the corporation if on hand at the close of the taxable year.

(2) Property held primarily for sale to customers in the ordinary course of a trade or business.

(3) Property used in a trade or business as defined in section 1231(b) and held for less than 3 years, except property that is or has been used in connection with the manufacture, construction, production or sale of property described in subparagraphs (1) and (2) of this paragraph.

(4) Unrealized receivables or fees pertaining to property listed in this paragraph. The term "unrealized receivables or fees" means any rights (contractual or otherwise) to payment for property listed in subparagraphs (1), (2), and (3) of this paragraph which has been delivered or is to be delivered and rights to payments for services rendered or to be rendered, to the extent such rights have not been included in the income of the corporation under the method of accounting used by it. In determining whether the assets referred to in this paragraph have been held for 3 years, the time such assets were held by a transferor shall be taken into consideration (section 1223). However, no such period shall begin before the date the manufacture, construction, production, or purchase of such assets is completed.

[T.D. 6500, 25 FR 11607, Nov. 26, 1960]

§ 1.341–3 Presumptions.

(a) Unless shown to the contrary a corporation shall be considered to be a collapsible corporation if at the time of the transactions described in § 1.341–1 the fair market value of the section 341 assets held by it constitutes 50 percent or more of the fair market value of its total assets and the fair market value of the section 341 assets is 120 percent or more of the adjusted basis of such assets. In determining the fair market value of the total assets, cash, obligations which are capital assets in the hands of the corporation, governmental obligations, and stock in any other corporation shall not be taken into consideration. The failure of a corporation to meet the requirements of this paragraph, shall not give rise to the presumption that the corporation was not a collapsible corporation.

(b) The following example will illustrate the application of this section:

Example. A corporation, filing its income tax returns on the accrual basis, on July 31, 1955, owned assets with the following fair market values: Cash, $175,000; note receivable held for investment, $130,000; stocks of other corporations, $545,000; rents receivable, $15,000; and a building constructed by the corporation in 1953 and held thereafter as rental property, $750,000. The adjusted basis of the building on that date was $600,000. The only debt outstanding was a $500,000 mortgage on the building. On July 31, 1955, the corporation liquidated and distributed all of its assets to its shareholders. In computing whether the fair market value of the section 341 assets (only the building) is 50 percent or more of the fair market value of the total assets, the cash, note receivable, and stocks of other corporations are not taken into account in determining the value of the total assets, with the result that the fair market value of the total assets was $765,000 ($750,000 (building) plus $15,000 rents receivable). Therefore, the value of the building is 98 percent of the total assets ($750,000 ÷ $765,000). The value of the building is also 125 percent of the adjusted basis of the building ($750,000 ÷ $600,000). In view of the above facts, there arises a presumption that the corporation is a collapsible corporation.

[T.D. 6500, 25 FR 11607, Nov. 26, 1960]

§ 1.341–4 Limitations on application of section.

(a) **General.** This section shall apply only to the extent that the recognized gain of a shareholder upon his stock in a collapsible corporation would be considered, but for the provisions of this section, as gain from the sale or exchange of a capital asset held for more than 1 year (6 months for taxable years beginning before 1977; 9 months for taxable years beginning in 1977). Thus, if a taxpayer sells at a gain stock of a collapsible corporation which he had held for six months or less, this section would not, in any event, apply to such gain. Also, if it is determined, under provisions of law other than section 341, that a sale or exchange at a gain of stock of a collapsible corporation which has been held for more than 1 year (6 months for taxable years beginning before 1977; 9 months for taxable years beginning in 1977) results in ordinary income rather than long-term capital gain, then this section (including the limitations contained herein) has no application whatsoever to such gain.

(b) **Stock ownership rules.** (1) This section shall apply in the case of gain realized by a shareholder upon his stock in a collapsible corporation only if the shareholder, at any time after the actual commencement of the manufacture, construction, or production of the property, or at the time of the purchase of the property described in section 341(b)(3) or at any time thereafter, (i) owned, or was considered as owning, more than 5 percent in value of the outstanding stock of the corporation, or (ii) owned stock which was considered as owned at such time by another shareholder who then owned, or was considered as owning, more than 5 percent in value of the outstanding stock of the corporation.

(2) The ownership of stock shall be determined in accordance with the rules prescribed by section 544(a)(1), (2), (3), (5), and (6), except that, in addition to the persons prescribed by section 544(a)(2), the family of an individual shall include the spouses of that individual's brothers and sisters, whether such brothers and sisters are by the whole or the half blood, and the spouses of that individual's lineal descendants.

(3) For the purpose of this limitation, treasury stock shall not be considered as outstanding stock.

(4) It is possible, under this limitation, that a shareholder in a collapsible corporation may have gain upon his stock in that corporation treated differently from the gain of another shareholder in the same collapsible corporation.

(c) **Seventy-percent rule.** (1) This section shall apply to the gain recognized during a taxable year upon the stock in a collapsible corporation only if more than 70 percent of such gain is attributable to the property referred to in section 341(b)(1). If more than 70 percent of such gain is so attributable, then all of such gain is subject to this section, and, if 70 percent or less of such gain is so attributable, then none of such gain is subject to this section.

(2) For the purpose of this limitation, the gain attributable to the property referred to in section 341(b)(1) is the excess of the recognized gain of the shareholder during the taxable year upon his stock in the collapsible corporation over the recognized gain which the shareholder would have if the property had not been manufactured, constructed, produced, or purchased. In the case of gain on a distribution in partial liquidation or a distribution described in section 301(c)(3)(A), the gain attributable to the property shall not be less than an amount which bears the same ratio to the gain on such distribution as the gain which would be attributable to the property if there had been a complete liquidation at the time of such distribution bears to the total gain which would have resulted from such complete liquidation.

(3) Gain may be attributable to the property referred to in section 341(b)(1) even though such gain is represented by an appreciation in the value of property other than that manufactured, constructed, produced, or purchased. Where, for example, a corporation owns a tract of land and the development of one-half of the tract increases the value of the other half, the gain attributable to the developed half of the tract includes the increase in the value of the other half.

(4) The following example will illustrate the application of the 70 percent rule:

Example: On January 2, 1954, A formed the Z Corporation and contributed $1,000,000 cash in exchange for all of the stock thereof. The Z Corporation invested $400,000 in one project for the purpose of building and selling residential houses. As of December 31, 1954, the residential houses in this project were all sold, resulting in a profit of $100,000 (after taxes). Simultaneously with the development of the first project and in connection with a second and separate project the Z Corporation invested $600,000 in land for the purpose of subdividing such land into lots suitable for sale as home sites and distributing such lots in liquidation before the realization by the corporation of a substantial part of the taxable income to be realized from this second project. As of December 31, 1954, Corporation Z had derived $60,000 in profits (after taxes) from the sale of some of the lots. On January 2, 1955, the Z Corporation made a distribution in complete liquidation to shareholder A who received:

(i) $560,000 in cash and notes, and

(ii) Lots having a fair market value of $940,000.

The gain recognized to shareholder A upon the liquidation is $500,000 ($1,500,000 minus $1,000,000). The gain which would have been recognized to A if the second project had not been undertaken is $100,000 ($1,100,000 minus $1,000,000). Therefore, the gain attributable to the second project which is property referred to in section 341(b)(1), is $400,000 ($500,000 minus $100,000). Since this gain ($400,000) is more than 70 percent of the entire gain ($500,000) recognized to A on the liquidation, the entire gain so recognized is gain subject to section 341(a).

(d) **Three-year rule.** This section shall not apply to that portion of the gain of a shareholder that is realized more than three years after the actual completion of the manufacture, construction, production, or purchase of the property referred to in section 341(b)(1) to which such portion is attributable. However, if the actual completion of the manufacture, construction, production, or purchase of all of such property occurred more than 3 years before the date on which the gain is realized, this section shall not apply to any part of the gain realized.

[T.D. 6500, 25 FR 11607, Nov. 26, 1960, as amended by T.D. 6738, 29 FR 7671, June 16, 1964; T.D. 7728, 45 FR 72650, Nov. 3, 1980]

§ 1.341-5 **Application of section.**

(a) Whether or not a corporation is a collapsible corporation shall be determined under the regulations of §§ 1.341-2 and 1.341-3 on the basis of all the facts and circumstances in each particular case. The following paragraphs of this section set forth those facts which will ordinarily be considered sufficient to establish that a corporation is or is not a collapsible corporation. The facts set forth in the following paragraphs of this section are not exclusive of other facts which may be controlling in any particular case. For example, if the facts in paragraph (b) of this section, but not the facts in paragraph (c) of this section, are present, the corporation may nevertheless not be a collapsible corporation if there are other facts which clearly establish that the regulations of §§ 1.341-2 and 1.341-3 are not satisfied. Similarly, if the facts in paragraph (c) of this section are present, the corporation may nevertheless be a collapsible corporation if there are other facts which clearly establish that the corporation was formed or availed of in the manner described in §§ 1.341-2 and 1.341-3 or if the facts in paragraph (c) of this section are not significant by reason of other facts, such as the fact that the corporation is subject to the control of persons other than those who were in control immediately prior to the manufacture, construction, production, or purchase of the property. See § 1.341-4 for provisions which make section 341 inapplicable to certain shareholders of collapsible corporations.

(b) The following facts will ordinarily be considered sufficient (except as otherwise provided in paragraph (a) of this section and paragraph (c) of this section) to establish that a corporation is a collapsible corporation:

(1) A shareholder of the corporation sells or exchanges his stock, or receives a liquidating distribution, or a distribution described in section 301(c)(3)(A),

(2) Upon such sale, exchange, or distribution, such shareholder realizes gain attributable to the property described in subparagraphs (4) and (5) of this paragraph, and

(3) At the time of the manufacture, construction, production, or purchase of the property described in subparagraphs (4) and (5) of this paragraph, such activity was substantial in relation to the other activities of the corporation which manufactured, constructed, produced, or purchased such property.

The property referred to in subparagraphs (2) and (3) of this paragraph is that property or the aggregate of those properties which meet the following two requirements:

(4) The property is manufactured, constructed, or produced by the corporation or by another corporation stock of which is held by the corporation, or is property purchased by the corporation or by such other corporation which (in the hands of the corporation holding such property) is property described in section 341(b)(3), and

(5) At the time of the sale, exchange, or distribution described in subparagraph (1) of this paragraph, the corporation which manufactured, constructed, produced, or purchased such property has not realized a substantial part of the taxable income to be derived from such property.

In the case of property which is a unit of an integrated project involving several properties similar in kind, the rules of this subparagraph shall be applied to the aggregate of the properties constituting the single project rather than separately to such unit. Under the rules of this subparagraph, a corporation shall be considered a collapsible corporation by reason of holding stock in other corporations which manufactured, constructed, produced, or purchased the property only if the activity of the corporation in holding stock in such other corporations is substantial in relation to the other activities of the corporation.

(c) The absence of any of the facts set forth in paragraph (b) of this section or the presence of the following facts will ordinarily be considered sufficient (except as otherwise provided in paragraph (a) of this section) to establish that a corporation is not a collapsible corporation:

(1) In the case of a corporation subject to paragraph (b) of this section only by reason of the manufacture, construction, production, or purchase (either by the corporation or by another corporation the stock of which is held by the corporation) of property which is property described in section 341(b)(3)(A) and (B), the amount (both in quantity and value) of such property is not in excess of the amount which is normal—

(i) For the purpose of the business activities of the corporation which manufactured, constructed, produced, or purchased the property if such corporation has a substantial prior business history involving the use of such property and continues in business, or

(ii) For the purpose of an orderly liquidation of the business if the corporation which manufactured, constructed, produced, or purchased such property has a substantial prior business history involving the use of such property and is in the process of liquidation.

(2) In the case of a corporation subject to paragraph (b) of this section with respect to the manufacture, construction, or production (either by the corporation or by another corporation the stock of which is held by the corporation) of property, the amount of the unrealized taxable income from such property is not substantial in relation to the amount of the taxable income realized (after the completion of a material part of such manufacture, construction, or production, and prior to the sale, exchange, or distribution referred to in paragraph (b)(1) of this section) from such property and from other property manufactured, constructed, or produced by the corporation.

(d) The following examples will illustrate the application of this section:

Example (1). (i) On January 2, 1954, A formed the W Corporation and contributed $50,000 cash in exchange for all of the stock thereof. The W Corporation borrowed $900,000 from a bank and used $800,000 of such sum in the construction of an apartment house on land which it purchased for $50,000. The apartment house was completed on December 31, 1954. On December 31, 1954, the corporation, having determined that the fair market value of the apartment house, separate and apart from the land, was $900,000, made a distribution (permitted under the applicable State law) to A of $100,000. At this time, the fair market value of the land was $50,000. As of December 31, 1954, the corporation has not realized any earnings and profits. In 1955, the corporation began the operation of the apartment house and received rentals therefrom. The corporation has since continued to own and operate the building. The corporation reported on the basis of the calendar year and cash receipts and disbursements.

(ii) Since A received a distribution and realized a gain attributable to the building constructed by the corporation, since, at the time of such distribution, the corporation has not realized a substantial part of the taxable income to be derived from such building, and since the construction of the building was a substantial activity of the corporation, the W Corporation is considered a collapsible corporation under paragraph (b) of § 1.341-5. The

provisions of section 341(d) do not prohibit the application of section 341(a). Therefore, the distribution, if and to the extent that it may be considered long-term capital gain rather than ordinary income without regard to section 341, will be considered ordinary income under section 341(a).

(iii) In the event of the existence of additional facts and circumstances in the above case, the corporation, notwithstanding the above facts, might not be considered a collapsible corporation. See § 1.342-2 and paragraph (a) of § 1.341-5.

Example (2). (i) On January 2, 1954, B formed X Corporation and became its sole shareholder. In August 1954, the corporation completed construction of an office building. It immediately sold this building at a gain of $50,000, included this entire gain in its return for 1954, and distributed this entire gain (less taxes) to B. In June 1955, the corporation completed construction of a second office building. In August 1955, B sold the entire stock of X Corporation at a gain of $12,000, which gain is attributable to the second building.

(ii) X Corporation is a collapsible corporation under section 341(b) for the following reasons: The gain realized through the sale of the stock of X Corporation was attributable to the second office building; the construction of that building was a substantial activity of X Corporation during the time of construction and, at the time of sale, the corporation had not realized a substantial part of the taxable income to be derived from such building. Since the provisions of section 341(d) do not prohibit the application of section 341(a) to B, the gain of $12,000 to B is, accordingly, considered ordinary income.

Example (3). The facts are the same as in example (2), except that the following facts are shown: B was the president of the X Corporation and active in the conduct of its business. The second building was constructed as the first step in a project of the X Corporation for the development for rental purposes of a large suburban center involving the construction of several buildings by the corporation. The sale of the stock by B was caused by his retiring from all business activity as a result of illness arising after the second building was constructed. Under these additional facts, the corporation is not considered a collapsible corporation. See § 1.341-2 and paragraph (a) of § 1.341-5.

* * *

[T.D. 6500, 25 FR 11607, Nov. 26, 1960]

Definition

§ 1.346-1 Partial liquidation.

(a) General. This section defines a partial liquidation. If amounts are distributed in partial liquidation such amounts are treated under section 331(a)(2) as received in part or full payment in exchange for the stock. A distribution is treated as in partial liquidation of a corporation if:

(1) The distribution is one of a series of distributions in redemption of all of the stock of the corporation pursuant to a plan of complete liquidation, or

(2) The distribution:

(i) Is not essentially equivalent to a dividend,

(ii) Is in redemption of a part of the stock of the corporation pursuant to a plan, and

(iii) Occurs within the taxable year in which the plan is adopted or within the succeeding taxable year.

An example of a distribution which will qualify as a partial liquidation under subparagraph (2) of this paragraph and section 346(a) is a distribution resulting from a genuine contraction of the corporate business such as the distribution of unused insurance proceeds recovered as a result of a fire which destroyed part of the business causing a cessation of a part of its activities. On the other hand, the distribution of funds attributable to a reserve for an expansion program which has been abandoned does not qualify as a partial liquidation within the meaning of section 346(a). A distribution to which section 355 applies (or so much of section 356 as relates to section 355) is not a distribution in partial liquidation within the meaning of section 346(a).

(b) **Special requirements on termination of business.** A distribution which occurs within the taxable year in which the plan is adopted or within the succeeding taxable year and which meets the requirements of subsection (b) of section 346 falls within paragraph (a)(2) of this section and within section 346(a)(2). The requirements which a distribution must meet to fall within subsection (b) of section 346 are:

(1) Such distribution is attributable to the corporation's ceasing to conduct, or consists of assets of, a trade or business which has been actively conducted throughout the five-year period immediately before the distribution, which trade or business was not acquired by the corporation within such period in a transaction in which gain or loss was recognized in whole or in part, and

(2) Immediately after such distribution by the corporation it is actively engaged in the conduct of a trade or business, which trade or business was actively conducted throughout the five-year period ending on the date of such distribution and was not acquired by the corporation within such period in a transaction in which gain or loss was recognized in whole or in part.

A distribution shall be treated as having been made in partial liquidation pursuant to section 346(b) if it consists of the proceeds of the sale of the assets of a trade or business which has been actively conducted for the five-year period and has been terminated, or if it is a distribution in kind of the assets of such a business, or if it is a distribution in kind of some of the assets of such a business and of the proceeds of the sale of the remainder of the assets of such a business. In general, a distribution which will qualify under section 346(b) may consist of, but is not limited to:

(i) Assets (other than inventory or property described in subdivision (ii) of this subparagraph) used in the trade or business throughout the five-year period immediately before the distribution (for this purpose an asset shall be considered used in the trade or business during the period of time the asset which it replaced was so used), or

(ii) Proceeds from the sale of assets described in subdivision (i) of this subparagraph, and, in addition,

(iii) The inventory of such trade or business or property held primarily for sale to customers in the ordinary course of business, if:

(a) The items constituting such inventory or such property were substantially similar to the items constituting such inventory or property during the five-year period immediately before the distribution, and

(b) The quantity of such items on the date of distribution was not substantially in excess of the quantity of similar items regularly on hand in the conduct of such business during such five-year period, or

(iv) Proceeds from the sale of inventory or property described in subdivision (iii) of this subparagraph, if such inventory or property is sold in bulk in the course of termination of such trade or business and if with respect to such inventory the conditions of subdivision (iii)(a) and (b) of this subparagraph would have been met had such inventory or property been distributed on the date of such sale.

(c) **Active conduct of a trade or business.** For the purpose of section 346(b)(1), a corporation shall be deemed to have actively conducted a trade or business immediately before the distribution, if:

(1) In the case of a business the assets of which have been distributed in kind, the business was operated by such corporation until the date of distribution, or

(2) In the case of a business the proceeds of the sale of the assets of which are distributed, such business was actively conducted until the date of sale and the proceeds of such sale were distributed as soon thereafter as reasonably possible.

The term "active conduct of a trade or business" shall have the same meaning in this section as in paragraph (c) of § 1.355–1.

[T.D. 6500, 25 FR 11607, Nov. 26, 1960]

§ 1.346–2 Treatment of certain redemptions.

If a distribution in a redemption of stock qualifies as a distribution in part or full payment in exchange for the stock under both section 302(a) and this section, then only this section shall be applicable. None of the limitations of section 302 shall be applicable to such redemption.

[T.D. 6500, 25 FR 11607, Nov. 26, 1960]

§ 1.346–3 Effect of certain sales.

The determination of whether assets sold in connection with a partial liquidation are sold by the distributing corporation or by the shareholder is a question of fact to be determined under the facts and circumstances of each case.

[T.D. 6500, 25 FR 11607, Nov. 26, 1960]

Corporate Organizations and Reorganizations

Corporate Organizations

§ 1.351–1 Transfer to corporation controlled by transferor.

(a)(1) Section 351(a) provides, in general, for the nonrecognition of gain or loss upon the transfer by one or more persons of property to a corporation solely in exchange for stock or securities in such corporation, if immediately after the exchange, such person or persons are in control of the corporation to which the property was transferred. As used in section 351, the phrase "one or more persons" includes individuals, trusts, estates, partnerships, associations, companies, or corporations (see section 7701(a)(1)). To be in control of the transferee corporation, such person or persons must own immediately after the transfer stock possessing at least 80 percent of the total combined voting power of all classes of stock entitled to vote and at least 80 percent of the total number of shares of all other classes of stock of such corporation (see section 368(c)). In determining control under this section, the fact that any corporate transferor distributes part or all of the stock which it receives in the exchange to its shareholders shall not be taken into account. The phrase "immediately after the exchange" does not necessarily require simultaneous exchanges by two or more persons, but comprehends a situation where the rights of the parties have been previously defined and the execution of the agreement proceeds with an expedition consistent with orderly procedure. For purposes of this section—

(i) Stock or securities issued for services rendered or to be rendered to or for the benefit of the issuing corporation will not be treated as having been issued in return for property, and

(ii) Stock or securities issued for property which is of relatively small value in comparison to the value of the stock and securities already owned (or to be received for services) by the person who transferred such property, shall not be treated as having been issued in return for property if the primary purpose of the transfer is to qualify under this section the exchanges of property by other persons transferring property.

For the purpose of section 351, stock rights or stock warrants are not included in the term "stock or securities."

(2) The application of section 351(a) is illustrated by the following examples:

Example (1). C owns a patent right worth $25,000 and D owns a manufacturing plant worth $75,000. C and D organize the R Corporation with an authorized capital stock of $100,000. C transfers his patent right to the R Corporation for $25,000 of its stock and D transfers his plant to the new corporation for $75,000 of its stock. No gain or loss to C or D is recognized.

Example (2). B owns certain real estate which cost him $50,000 in 1930, but which has a fair market value of $200,000 in 1955. He transfers the property to the N Corporation in 1955 for 78 percent of each class of stock of the corporation having a fair market value of $200,000, the remaining 22 percent of the stock of the corporation having been issued by the corporation in 1940 to other persons for cash. B realized a taxable gain of $150,000 on this transaction.

Example (3). E, an individual, owns property with a basis of $10,000 but which has a fair market value of $18,000. E also had rendered services valued at $2,000 to Corporation F. Corporation F has outstanding 100 shares of common stock all of which are held by G. Corporation F issues 400 shares of its common stock (having a fair market value of $20,000) to E in exchange for his property worth $18,000 and in compensation for the services he has rendered worth $2,000. Since immediately after the transaction, E owns 80 percent of the outstanding stock of Corporation F, no gain is recognized upon the exchange of the property for the stock. However, E realized $2,000 of ordinary income as compensation for services rendered to Corporation F.

(b)(1) Where property is transferred to a corporation by two or more persons in exchange for stock or securities, as described in paragraph (a) of this section, it is not required that the stock and securities received by each be substantially in proportion to his interest in the property immediately prior to the transfer. However, where the stock and securities received are received in disproportion to such interest, the entire transaction will be given tax effect in accordance with its true nature, and in appropriate cases the transaction may be treated as if the stock and securities had first been received in proportion and then some of such stock and securities had been used to make gifts (section 2501 and following), to pay compensation (section 61(a)(1)), or to satisfy obligations of the transferor of any kind.

(2) The application of paragraph (b)(1) of this section may be illustrated as follows:

Example (1). Individuals A and B, father and son, organize a corporation with 100 shares of common stock to which A transfers property worth $8,000 in exchange for 20 shares of stock, and B transfers property worth $2,000 in exchange for 80 shares of stock. No gain or loss will be recognized under section 351. However, if it is determined that A in fact made a gift to B, such gift will be subject to tax under section 2501 and following. Similarly, if B had rendered services to A (such services having no relation to the assets transferred or to the business of the corporation) and the disproportion in the amount of stock received constituted the payment of compensation by A to B, B will be taxable upon the fair market value of the 60 shares of stock received as compensation for services rendered, and A will realize gain or loss upon the difference between the basis to him of the 60 shares and their fair market value at the time of the exchange.

Example (2). Individuals C and D each transferred, to a newly organized corporation, property having a fair market value of $4,500 in exchange for the issuance by the corporation of 45 shares of its capital stock to each transferor. At the same time, the corporation issued to E, an individual, 10 shares of its capital stock in payment for organizational and promotional services rendered by E for the benefit of the corporation. E transferred no property to the corporation. C and D were under no obligation to pay for E's services. No gain or loss is recognized to C or D. E received compensation taxable as ordinary income to the extent of the fair market value of the 10 shares of stock received by him.

(c)(1) The general rule of section 351 does not apply, and consequently gain or loss will be recognized, where property is transferred to an investment company after June 30, 1967. A transfer of property after June 30, 1967, will be considered to be a transfer to an investment company if—

(i) The transfer results, directly or indirectly, in diversification of the transferors' interests, and

(ii) The transferee is (a) a regulated investment company, (b) a real estate investment trust, or (c) a corporation more than 80 percent of the value of whose assets (excluding cash and nonconvertible debt obligations from consideration) are held for investment and are readily marketable stocks or securities, or interests in regulated investment companies or real estate investment trusts.

(2) The determination of whether a corporation is an investment company shall ordinarily be made by reference to the circumstances in existence immediately after the transfer in question. However, where circumstances change thereafter pursuant to a plan in existence at the time of the transfer, this determination shall be made by reference to the later circumstances.

(3) Stocks and securities will be considered readily marketable if (and only if) they are part of a class of stock or securities which is traded on a securities exchange or traded or quoted regularly in the over-the-counter market. For purposes of subparagraph (1)(ii)(c) of this paragraph, the term "readily marketable stocks or securities" includes convertible debentures, convertible preferred stock, warrants, and other stock rights if the stock for which they may be converted or exchanged is readily marketable. Stocks and securities will be considered to be held for investment unless they are (i) held primarily for sale to customers in the ordinary course of business, or (ii) used in the trade or business of banking, insurance, brokerage, or a similar trade or business.

(4) In making the determination required under subparagraph (1)(ii)(c) of this paragraph, stock and securities in subsidiary corporations shall be disregarded and the parent corporation shall be deemed to own its ratable share of its subsidiaries' assets. A corporation shall be considered a subsidiary if the parent owns 50 percent or more of (i) the combined voting power of all classes of stock entitled to vote, or (ii) the total value of shares of all classes of stock outstanding.

(5) A transfer ordinarily results in the diversification of the transferors' interests if two or more persons transfer nonidentical assets to a corporation in the exchange. For this purpose, if any transaction involves one or more transfers of nonidentical assets which, taken in the aggregate, con-

stitute an insignificant portion of the total value of assets transferred, such transfers shall be disregarded in determining whether diversification has occurred. If there is only one transferor (or two or more transferors of identical assets) to a newly organized corporation, the transfer will generally be treated as not resulting in diversification. If a transfer is part of a plan to achieve diversification without recognition of gain, such as a plan which contemplates a subsequent transfer, however delayed, of the corporate assets (or of the stock or securities received in the earlier exchange) to an investment company in a transaction purporting to qualify for nonrecognition treatment, the original transfer will be treated as resulting in diversification.

(6) The application of subparagraph (5) of this paragraph may be illustrated as follows:

Example (1). Individuals A, B, and C organize a corporation with 101 shares of common stock. A and B each transfers to it $10,000 worth of the only class of stock of corporation X, listed on the New York Stock Exchange, in exchange for 50 shares of stock. C transfers $200 worth of readily marketable securities in corporation Y for one share of stock. In determining whether or not diversification has occurred, C's participation in the transaction will be disregarded. There is, therefore, no diversification, and gain or loss will not be recognized.

Example (2). A, together with 50 other transferors, organizes a corporation with 100 shares of stock. A transfers $10,000 worth of stock in corporation X, listed on the New York Stock Exchange, in exchange for 50 shares of stock. Each of the other 50 transferors transfers $200 worth of readily marketable securities in corporations other than X in exchange for one share of stock. In determining whether or not diversification has occurred, all transfers will be taken into account. Therefore, diversification is present, and gain or loss will be recognized.

[T.D. 6500, 25 FR 11607, Nov. 26, 1960, as amended by T.D. 6942, 32 FR 20977, Dec. 29, 1967]

§ 1.351–2 Receipt of property.

(a) If an exchange would be within the provisions of section 351(a) if it were not for the fact that the property received in exchange consists not only of property permitted by such subsection to be received without the recognition of gain, but also of other property or money, then the gain, if any, to the recipient shall be recognized, but in an amount not in excess of the sum of such money and the fair market value of such other property. No loss to the recipient shall be recognized.

(b) See section 357 and the regulations pertaining to that section for applicable rules as to the treatment of liabilities as "other property" in cases subject to section 351, where another party to the exchange assumes a liability, or acquires property subject to a liability.

(c) See sections 358 and 362 and the regulations pertaining to those sections for applicable rules with respect to the determination of the basis of stock, securities, or other property received in exchanges subject to section 351.

(d) See part I (section 301 and following), subchapter C, chapter 1 of the Code, and the regulations thereunder for applicable rules with respect to the taxation of dividends where a distribution by a corporation of its stock or securities in connection with an exchange subject to section 351(a) has the effect of the distribution of a taxable dividend.

[T.D. 6500, 25 FR 11607, Nov. 26, 1960]

§ 1.351–3 Records to be kept and information to be filed.

(a) Every person who received the stock or securities of a controlled corporation, or other property as part of the consideration, in exchange for property under section 351, shall file with his income tax return for the taxable year in which the exchange is consummated a complete statement of all facts pertinent to such exchange, including—

(1) A description of the property transferred, or of his interest in such property, together with a statement of the cost or other basis thereof, adjusted to the date of transfer.

(2) With respect to stock of the controlled corporation received in the exchange, a statement of—

(i) The kind of stock and preferences, if any;

(ii) The number of shares of each class received; and

(iii) The fair market value per share of each class at the date of the exchange.

(3) With respect to securities of the controlled corporation received in the exchange, a statement of—

(i) The principal amount and terms; and

(ii) The fair market value at the date of exchange.

(4) The amount of money received, if any.

(5) With respect to other property received—

(i) A complete description of each separate item;

(ii) The fair market value of each separate item at the date of exchanges; and

(iii) In the case of a corporate shareholder, the adjusted basis of the other property in the hands of the controlled corporation immediately before the distribution of such other property to the corporate shareholder in connection with the exchange.

(6) With respect to liabilities of the transferors assumed by the controlled corporation, a statement of—

(i) The nature of the liabilities;

(ii) When and under what circumstances created;

(iii) The corporate business reason for assumption by the controlled corporation; and

(iv) Whether such assumption eliminates the transferor's primary liability.

(b) Every such controlled corporation shall file with its income tax return for the taxable year in which the exchange is consummated—

(1) A complete description of all the property received from the transferors.

(2) A statement of the cost or other basis thereof in the hands of the transferors adjusted to the date of transfer.

(3) The following information with respect to the capital stock of the controlled corporation—

(i) The total issued and outstanding capital stock immediately prior to and immediately after the exchange, with a complete description of each class of stock;

(ii) The classes of stock and number of shares issued to each transferor in the exchange, and the number of shares of each class of stock owned by each transferor immediately prior to and immediately after the exchange, and

(iii) The fair market value of the capital stock as of the date of exchange which was issued to each transferor.

(4) The following information with respect to securities of the controlled corporation—

(i) The principal amount and terms of all securities outstanding immediately prior to and immediately after the exchange,

(ii) The principal amount and terms of securities issued to each transferor in the exchange, with a statement showing each transferor's holdings of securities of the controlled corporation immediately prior to and immediately after the exchange,

(iii) The fair market value of the securities issued to the transferors on the date of the exchange, and

(iv) A statement as to whether the securities issued in the exchange are subordinated in any way to other claims against the controlled corporation.

(5) The amount of money, if any, which passed to each of the transferors in connection with the transaction.

(6) With respect to other property which passed to each transferor—

(i) A complete description of each separate item;

(ii) The fair market value of each separate item at the date of exchange, and

(iii) In the case of a corporate transferor, the adjusted basis of each separate item in the hands of the controlled corporation immediately before the distribution of such other property to the corporate transferor in connection with the exchange.

(7) The following information as to the transferor's liabilities assumed by the controlled corporation in the exchange—

(i) The amount and a description thereof,

(ii) When and under what circumstances created, and

(iii) The corporate business reason or reasons for assumption by the controlled corporation.

(c) Permanent records in substantial form shall be kept by every taxpayer who participates in the type of exchange described in section 351, showing the information listed above, in order to facilitate the determination of gain or loss from a subsequent disposition of stock or securities and other property, if any, received in the exchange.

[T.D. 6500, 25 FR 11607, Nov. 26, 1960]

Effects on Shareholders and Security Holders

§ 1.354-1 Exchanges of stock and securities in certain reorganizations.

(a) Section 354 provides that under certain circumstances no gain or loss is recognized to a shareholder who surrenders his stock in exchange for other stock or to a security holder who surrenders his securities in exchange for stock. Section 354 also provides that under certain circumstances a security holder may surrender securities and receive securities in the same principal amount or in a lesser principal amount without the recognition of gain or loss to him. The exchanges to which section 354 applies must be pursuant to a plan of reorganization as provided in section 368(a) and the stock and securities surrendered as well as the stock and securities received must be those of a corporation which is a party to the reorganization. Section 354 does not apply to exchanges pursuant to a reorganization described in section 368(a)(1)(D) unless the transferor corporation—

(1) Transfers all or substantially all of its assets to a single corporation, and

(2) Distributes all of its remaining properties (if any) and the stock, securities and other properties received in the exchange to its shareholders or security holders in pursuance of the plan of reorganization. The fact that properties retained by the transferor corporation, or received in exchange for the properties transferred in the reorganization, are used to satisfy existing liabilities not represented by securities and which were incurred in the ordinary course of business before the reorganization does not prevent the application of section 354 to an exchange pursuant to a plan of reorganization defined in section 368(a)(1)(D).

(b) Except as provided in section 354(c) and (d), section 354 is not applicable to an exchange of stock or securities if a greater principal amount of securities is received than the principal amount of securities the recipient surrenders, or if securities are received and the recipient surrenders no securities. See, however, section 356 and regulations pertaining to such section. See also section 306 with respect to the receipt of preferred stock in a transaction to which section 354 is applicable.

* * *

(d) The rules of section 354 may be illustrated by the following examples:

Example (1). Pursuant to a reorganization under section 368(a) to which Corporations T and W are parties, A, a shareholder in Corporation T, surrenders all his common stock in Corporation T in exchange for common stock of Corporation W. No gain or loss is recognized to A.

Example (2). Pursuant to a reorganization under section 368(a) to which Corporations X and Y (which are not railroad corporations) are parties, B, a shareholder in Corporation X, surrenders all his stock in X for stock and securities in Y. Section 354 does not apply to this exchange. See, however, section 356.

Example (3). C, a shareholder in Corporation Z (which is not a railroad corporation), surrenders all his stock in Corporation Z in exchange for securities in Corporation Z. Whether or not this exchange is in connection with a recapitalization under section 368(a)(1)(E), section 354 does not apply. See, however, section 302.

(e) For the purpose of section 354, stock rights or stock warrants are not included in the term "stock or securities".

[T.D. 6500, 25 FR 11607, Nov. 26, 1960, as amended by T.D. 7616, 44 FR 26869, May 8, 1979]

§ 1.355-1 Distribution of stock and securities of controlled corporation.

(a) Application of section. Section 355 provides for the separation, without recognition of gain or loss to the shareholders and security holders, of two or more existing businesses formerly operated, directly or indirectly, by a single corporation. It applies only to the separation of existing businesses which have been in active operation for at least five years, and which, in general, have been owned for at least five years by the corporation making the distribution of stock or of stock and securities. Section 355 does not apply to the division of a single business. For the purpose of section 355, stock rights or stock warrants are not included in the term "stock and securities".

(b) Types of separations. Section 355 is concerned with two general types of separations of businesses. The first is the distribution of the stock of an existing corporation. The second is the distribution of the stock of a new corporation which stock was received in exchange for the assets of a business previously operated by the distributing corporation. In both cases, this section contemplates the continued operation of the businesses existing prior to the separation.

(c) Active business. Section 355 is not applicable unless the controlled corporation and the distributing corporation are each engaged in the active conduct of a trade or business. For specific rules in this connection see section 355(b)(1) and (2). Without regard to such rules, for purposes of section 355, a trade or business consists of a specific existing group of activities being carried on for the purpose of earning income or profit from only such group of activities, and the activities included in such group must include every operation which forms a part of, or a step in, the process of earning income or profit from such group. Such group of activities ordinarily must include the collection of income and the payment of expenses. It does not include—

(1) The holding for investment purposes of stock, securities, land or other property, including casual sales thereof (whether or not the proceeds of such sales are reinvested),

(2) The ownership and operation of land or buildings all or substantially all of which are used and occupied by the owner in the operation of a trade or business, or

(3) A group of activities which, while a part of a business operated for profit, are not themselves independently producing income even though such activities would produce income with the addition of other activities or with large increases in activities previously incidental or insubstantial.

(d) Examples. The following examples illustrate the application of the rules described in paragraph (c) of this section:

Example (1). Corporation A is engaged in the manufacture and sale of soap and detergents and owns investment securities. It proposes to place the investment securities in a new corporation and distribute the stock of such new corporation to its shareholders. The holding of investment securities does not constitute a trade or business.

Example (2). Corporation B is engaged in the business of manufacturing and selling hats in its own factory building. It proposes to transfer the factory building to a new corporation and distribute the stock of such new corporation to its shareholders. The activities in connection with the manufacturing of hats constitute a trade or business; but the operation of the factory building does not.

Example (3). Corporation C, a bank, owns an eleven-story downtown office building, the ground floor of which is occupied by it in the conduct of its banking business and the remaining ten floors of which it rents to various tenants. The ten floors are rented, managed and maintained by the real estate department of the bank. It is proposed to transfer the building to a new corporation and distribute the stock of such new corporation to the

bank's shareholders. The activities in connection with banking constitute a trade or business as do also the activities in connection with the rental of the building.

Example (4). Corporation D, a bank, owns a two-story building in a suburban area, the ground floor and approximately one-half of the second floor of which is occupied by it in the conduct of its banking business. The remainder of the second floor is rented as storage space to a neighboring retail merchant. It is proposed to transfer the building to a new corporation and distribute the stock of such new corporation to the bank's shareholders. With respect to the rental of part of the second floor of its building, the bank is not engaged in the active conduct of a trade or business, such activity being only incidental to its banking business.

Example (5). Corporation E is engaged in the manufacture and sale of wood products. In connection with such manufacturing, it maintains a research department for its own use. It proposes to transfer the research department to a new corporation after which it will engage the services of the new corporation on a contract basis. The activities of the research department do not constitute a trade or business.

Example (6). Corporation F owns and rents an office building and owns vacant land. It proposes to transfer the vacant land to a new corporation and distribute the stock of such new corporation to its shareholders. The holding of the vacant land does not constitute a trade or business.

Example (7). Corporation G owns land on which it engages in the ranching business. Oil has been discovered in the area and it is apparent that oil may be found under the land on which the ranching activities are maintained. Corporation G has engaged in no activities in connection with the mineral rights. It proposes to transfer the mineral rights to a new corporation and distribute the stock of such new corporation to shareholders. Corporation G is not engaged in an active trade or business with respect to the mineral rights.

Example (8). Corporation H manufactures and sells ice cream at a plant in State X and at a plant in State Y. Corporation H proposes to transfer the plant and related activities in State Y to a new corporation and distribute the stock of such new corporation to its shareholders. The activities in each State constitute a trade or business.

Example (9). Corporation I manufactures and sells ice cream in State X. It purchases land and constructs a new plant in State Y. After manufacturing and selling operations have commenced at the new plant, it proposes to transfer it to a new corporation and distribute the stock of such new corporation to its shareholders. The activities at the new plant constitute a trade or business which, however, has been in existence only since such activities began.

Example (10). Corporation J has owned and operated a men's retail clothing store in the downtown area of the City of R for seven years and has also owned and operated a men's retail clothing store in the suburban area of the City of R for nine years. The manager of each store directs its operations and makes the necessary purchases. No common warehouse is maintained. Corporation J proposes to transfer the store building, fixtures, and inventory of the suburban store to a new corporation and distribute the stock of such new corporation to the shareholders of Corporation J. The activities of each store constitute a trade or business which has been in existence for more than five years.

Example (11). Corporation K processes and sells meat products. It is proposed to separate the selling from the manufacturing activities by forming a separate corporation, L, to handle sales. Corporation K will transfer to Corporation L certain physical assets pertaining to the sales function plus cash for working capital in exchange for the capital stock of Corporation L which will be distributed to the shareholders of Corporation K. Since the manufacturing and selling operations constitute only one integrated business, neither Corporation K nor Corporation L will be continuing the active conduct of a trade or business formerly conducted by Corporation K.

Example (12). Corporation M is engaged in the manufacture and sale of steel and steel products. In addition, Corporation M owns and operates a coal mine for the sole purpose of supplying its coal requirements in the manufacture of steel. It is proposed to transfer the coal mine to a new corporation and distribute the stock of such new corporation to the shareholders of Corporation M. The activities of Corporation M in connection with the operation of the coal mine do not constitute a trade or business, since such activities are not themselves independently producing income although a part of the business operated for profit.

Example (13). Corporation N manufactures steel containers for oil and oil products at a plant in State X and at a plant in State Y. Pursuant to a sales contract with Corporation O, Corporation N sells its entire product to Corporation O. Corporation N proposes to transfer the plant and related activities in State Y, together with that portion of the sales contract with Corporation O applicable to the sales of that plant to a new corporation and distribute the stock of such new corporation to its shareholders. The activities in each State constitute a trade or business before and after the transfer to the new corporation.

Example (14). Corporation P manufactures and sells steel containers for oil and oil products at a plant in State X and at a plant in State Y. Corporation P makes all of its sales through its wholly-owned subsidiary pursuant to a sales contract, by virtue of which the subsidiary acts either as principal or sales agent for Corporation P. Corporation P proposes to transfer the plant and related activities in State Y, together with that portion of the sales contract applicable to the sales of that plant to a new corporation and distribute the stock of such new corporation to its shareholders. The activities in each State constitute a trade or business before and after the transfer to the new corporation.

Example (15). Corporation Q manufactures electrical products at a plant in State X and at a plant in State Y. The sales of the electrical products produced by each plant are made by the corporation's sales office located at the plant in State X. Corporation Q proposes to transfer the plant and related activities in State Y, together with that portion of the facilities and personnel of the sales office allocable to the sales of the plant in State Y to a new corporation and distribute the stock of such new corporation to its shareholders. The activities in each

state constitute a trade or business before and after the transfer to the new corporation.

Example (16). Corporation R manufactures and sells automobiles and operates an executive dining room primarily for the convenience of its executives. The dining room is managed and operated as a separate unit and the executives are charged for their meals. Corporation R derives a profit from the operation of the dining room. The activities connected with the executive dining room do not constitute a trade or business.

(e) Businesses operated by one corporation. For further examples of businesses operated by one corporation, see paragraph (d) of § 1.337–3.

[T.D. 6500, 25 FR 11607, Nov. 26, 1960]

§ 1.355–1 *(Proposed, published 1–13–77.)* **Distribution of stock and securities of a controlled corporation.**

(a) Application of section. Section 355 provides for the separation, without recognition of gain or loss to the shareholders and security holders, of one or more existing businesses formerly operated, directly or indirectly, by a single corporation. It applies only to the separation of existing businesses which have been in active operation for at least 5 years (or a business which has been in active operation for at least 5 years into separate businesses), and which, in general, have been owned, directly or indirectly, for at least 5 years by the corporation making the distribution of stock or of stock and securities. For the purpose of section 355, stock rights or stock warrants are not included in the term "stock and securities".

(b) Type of separations. Section 355 is concerned with two general types of separations. The first is the distribution of the stock of an existing corporation. The second is the distribution of the stock of a corporation holding assets of a business previously operated by the distributing corporation. In both cases, section 355 contemplates the continued operation of the business or businesses existing prior to the separation.

§ 1.355–2 Limitations.

(a) Property distributed. The property distributed must consist solely of stock or stock and securities of a controlled corporation. If additional property (including an excess principal amount of securities received over securities surrendered) is received, see section 356.

(b) Distribution of earnings and profits. (1) The transaction must not have been used principally as a device for the distribution of the earnings and profits of the distributing corporation or of the controlled corporation or of both. If, pursuant to an arrangement negotiated or agreed upon prior to the distribution of stock or securities of the controlled corporation, part or all of the stock or securities of either corporation are sold or exchanged after the distribution, such sale or exchange will be evidence that the transaction was used principally as a device for the distribution of the earnings and profits of the distributing corporation or of the controlled corporation, or both. However, if the rules respecting continuity of interest contained in paragraph (c) of this section are not met, section 355 will not apply. If a sale of such stock or securities is made after the distribution and is not pursuant to an arrangement negotiated or agreed upon prior to the distribution, the mere fact of such sale is not determinative that the transaction was used principally as a device for the distribution of earnings and profits, but such fact will be evidence that the transaction was used principally as such a device.

(2) A sale is pursuant to an arrangement agreed upon prior to the distribution when enforcible rights to buy or to sell exist before such distribution. In any case in which a sale or exchange was discussed by the buyer and the seller before the distribution, but enforcible rights to buy or to sell did not exist before such distribution, the question whether an arrangement was negotiated within the meaning of section 355(a)(1)(B) shall be determined from all the facts and circumstances.

(3) In determining whether a transaction was used principally as a device for the distribution of the earnings and profits of the distributing corporation or of the controlled corporation or both, consideration will be given to all of the facts and circumstances of the transaction. In particular, consideration will be given to the nature, kind and amount of the assets of both corporations (and corporations controlled by them) immediately after the transaction. The fact that at the time of the transaction substantially all of the assets of each of the corporations involved are and have been used in the active conduct of trades or businesses which meet the requirements of section 355(b) will be considered evidence that the transaction was not used principally as such a device.

(c) **Business purpose.** The distribution by a corporation of stock or securities of a controlled corporation to its shareholders with respect to its own stock or to its security holders in exchange for

its own securities will not qualify under section 355 where carried out for purposes not germane to the business of the corporation. The principal reason for this requirement is to limit the application of section 355 to certain specified distributions or exchanges with respect to the stock or securities of controlled corporations incident to such readjustment of corporate structures as is required by business exigencies and which, in general, effect only a readjustment of continuing interests in property under modified corporate forms. Section 355 contemplates a continuity of the entire business enterprise under modified corporate forms and a continuity of interest in all or part of such business enterprise on the part of those persons who, directly or indirectly, were the owners of the enterprise prior to the distribution or exchange. All the requisites of business and corporate purposes described under § 1.368 must be met to exempt a transaction from the recognition of gain or loss under this section.

(d) **Stock and securities distributed.** The distributing corporation must distribute:

(1) All of the stock and securities of the controlled corporation which it owns, or

(2) At least an amount of the stock which constitutes control as defined in section 368(c). In such case all, or any part, of the securities of the controlled corporation may be distributed.

Where a part of either the stock or securities is retained under subparagraph (2) of this paragraph, it must be established to the satisfaction of the Commissioner that such retention was not in pursuance of a plan having as one of its principal purposes the avoidance of Federal income tax. Ordinarily, the business reasons (as distinguished from the desire to make a distribution of the earnings and profits) which support a distribution of stock and securities of a controlled corporation under paragraph (c) of this section will require the distribution of all of the stock and securities. If the distribution of all of the stock and securities of a controlled corporation would be treated to any extent as a distribution of "other property" under section 356, this fact does not tend to establish that the retention of any of such stock and securities is not in pursuance of a plan having as one of its principal purposes the avoidance of Federal income tax.

(e) **Principal amount of securities.** (1) Section 355(a)(1) is not applicable if the principal amount of securities received exceeds the principal amount of securities surrendered or if securities are received and no securities are surrendered. In such cases, see section 356.

(2) If only stock is received in a transaction to which section 355 is applicable, the principal amount of securities surrendered, if any, and the par or stated value of stock is not relevant to the application of such section. For example: All of the stock of Corporation A is owned by X, an individual, and securities in the principal amount of $100,000 which were issued by Corporation A are owned by Y, an individual. Corporation A distributes all of the stock of a controlled corporation to Y in exchange for his securities. The par or stated value of the stock of the controlled corporation is $150,000. No gain or loss is recognized to Y upon the receipt of the stock of the controlled corporation.

(f) **Period of ownership.** (1) For the purposes of determining whether gain or loss will be recognized upon a distribution, stock of a controlled corporation acquired (in a transaction in which gain or loss is recognized, in whole or in part) within five years of the date of the distribution of such stock is treated as "other property." Section 355 does not apply to a transaction which includes a distribution of such stock. See section 356. The stock so acquired is "stock" however, for the purpose of the requirements respecting the distribution of stock of such controlled corporation provided in section 355(a)(1)(D).

(2) Subparagraph (1) of this paragraph may be illustrated by the following example:

Example. Corporation A has held 85 of the 100 outstanding shares of the stock of Corporation B for more than five years on the date of distribution. Six months before such date, it purchased 10 shares of such stock. If all of the stock of the controlled corporation owned by Corporation A is distributed, section 355 is not applicable to such distribution since the 10 shares would represent "other property." See, however, section 356. If however, for proper business reasons it is decided to retain some of the stock of Corporation B, then the determination of the amount of such stock which must be distributed under section 355(a)(1)(D) in order to constitute a distribution to which section 355 is applicable must be made by reference to all of the stock of the controlled corporation including the 10 shares acquired six months before such date and the 5 shares owned by others, similarly, if, by the use of any agency, the distributing corporation acquires stock of the controlled corporation within five years of the date of distribution, for example, where another subsidiary purchases such stock, such stock will be treated as "other property." If Corporation A had held only 75 of the 100 outstanding shares of stock of Corporation B for more than five years on the date of

distribution and had purchased the remaining 25 shares six months before such date, neither section 355 nor section 356 would be applicable.

(g) **Active businesses.** The rules of section 355(b) and § 1.355–4, relating to active businesses, must be satisfied.

[T.D. 6500, 25 FR 11607, Nov. 26, 1960]

§ 1.355–2 *(Proposed, published 1–13–77.)* **Limitations.**

(a) **Property distributed.** In order for section 355 to apply, the property distributed must consist solely of stock, or stock and securities, of a controlled corporation. If additional property (including an excess principal amount of securities received over securities surrendered) is received, see section 356.

(b) **Business purpose and continuity of interest.** (1) **In general.** A distribution by a corporation of stock or securities of a controlled corporation to its shareholders with respect to its own stock or to its security holders in exchange for its own securities will qualify under section 355 only if carried out for real and substantial nontax reasons germane to the business of the corporations. The principal reason for this requirement is to provide nonrecognition treatment only to those distributions or exchanges of stock or securities of the controlled corporation which are incident to such readjustment of corporate structures as is required by business exigencies and which effect only a readjustment of continuing interests in property under modified corporate forms. Depending upon the facts of a particular case, a shareholder purpose for a transaction may be so nearly coextensive with a corporate business purpose as to preclude any distinction between them. In such a case, the transaction is carried out for purposes germane to the business of the corporations. On the other hand, if a transaction is motivated solely by the personal reasons of a shareholder, for example, if a transaction is undertaken solely for the purpose of fulfilling the personal planning purposes of a shareholder, the distribution will not qualify under section 355 since it is not carried out for purposes germane to the business of the corporations. Section 355 contemplates a continuity of interest in all or part of the business enterprise on the part of those persons who, directly or indirectly, were the owners of the enterprise prior to the distribution or exchange. For rules with respect to the requirement of a business purpose for a transfer of assets to a controlled corporation in connection with a reorganization described in section 368(a)(1)(D), see § 1.368–1(b).

(2) Examples. The provisions of paragraph (b)(1) of this section may be illustrated by the following examples:

Example (1). Corporation P is engaged in the production, transportation, and refining of petroleum products. In 1962, P acquired all of the properties of corporation S, which was also engaged in the production, transportation, and refining of petroleum products. In 1968, as a result of anti-trust litigation, P was ordered to divest itself of all properties acquired from S. P proposes to transfer the assets acquired from S to a new corporation and to distribute the stock of such new corporation to its shareholders. In view of the divestiture order, the distribution of the stock of the new corporation to the shareholders of P will be considered to have been carried out for a real and substantial nontax reason germane to the business of the corporations.

Example (2). Corporation R owns and operates two men's retail clothing stores. The outstanding stock of R is owned equally by two brothers, A and B, and F, their father, who does not take an active part in the retail clothing business. A and B no longer can agree on major decisions affecting the operation of the corporation. Corporation R proposes to transfer one store to a new corporation and distribute 66.7 percent of the stock of such new corporation to one brother in exchange for all of his R stock. The other 33.3 percent of the stock of such new corporation will be exchanged for one-half of F's stock of corporation R. In view of the disagreement between managing shareholders, the distribution of the stock of the new corporation will be considered to have been carried out for a real and substantial nontax reason germane to the business of the corporations.

Example (3). Corporation T is engaged in the manufacture and sale of children's novelty toys. It also manufactures and sells candy and candy products. The shareholders wish to separate the candy business from the risks and vicissitudes of the novelty toy business. It is proposed that the assets and activities associated with the toy business be transferred to a new corporation, the stock of which would then be distributed to T's shareholders. The purpose of protecting the candy business from the risks of the novelty toy business, which is fulfilled when the novelty toy assets and activities are transferred to the new corporation, does not satisfy the requirement there be a substantial nontax reason, germane to the business of the corporation, for the distribution of the stock of the new corporation to the shareholders.

Example (4). The facts are the same as in example (3) except that T also requires outside financing in order to substantially expand its candy business. As a condition of the loan, in order to prevent the potential diversion of funds to the toy business, the lender requires the separation of the candy business and the novelty toy business and the distribution of the stock of the novelty toy corporation to the shareholders. The lender's requirements are based upon customary business practice. In this case, the distribution of the stock of the novelty toy corporation to the shareholders will be considered to have been carried out for a real and substantial nontax reason germane to the business of the corporations.

(c) Device for distribution of earnings and profits—(1) In general. Section 355 does not apply to a transaction which has been used principally as a device for the distribution of the earnings and profits of the distributing corporation, of the controlled corporation, or of both. The Code recognizes that a tax-free distribution of the stock of a controlled corporation presents an extraordinary potential for tax avoidance by placing the shareholders of the distributing corporation in a position whereby, as a consequence of the subsequent sale of stock or the liquidation of either the distributing corporation or the controlled corporation, they can avoid the dividend provisions of the Code. A distribution which is pro rata or substantially pro rata among the shareholders of the distributing corporation presents the greatest potential for the withdrawal of earnings and profits and is more likely to be undertaken principally as a device for the distribution of earnings and profits. Whether a transaction which has the potential for the distribution of earnings and profits was used principally as such a device shall be determined from all the facts and circumstances. Among the factors to be considered are those factors described in paragraph (c)(2) and (3) of this section. However, in any case in which a distribution with respect to each distributee would be treated as a redemption to which section 302(a) would apply if it were taxable, the transaction is ordinarily not considered to be a device for the distribution of earnings and profits. For purposes of the preceding sentence, section 302(c)(2)(A) shall be applied without regard to clauses (ii) and (iii). Further, if on the date of the distribution, no part of a distribution of money by the distributing corporation, the controlled corporation, or any corporation controlled, directly or indirectly, by either of such corporations could have been taxable as a dividend as defined in section 316 because of the absence of earnings and profits, the transaction is ordinarily not considered to be such a device.

(2) Subsequent sales of stock. If, pursuant to an arrangement negotiated or agreed upon before the distribution, 20 percent or more of the stock of either the distributing corporation or the controlled corporation is to be sold or exchanged after the distribution, the distribution will be considered to have been used principally as a device for the distribution of earnings and profits of the distributing corporation, the controlled corporation, or both. If, pursuant to such an arrangement, part or all of the securities or less than 20 percent of the stock of either corporation is to be sold or exchanged after the distribution, this fact will be considered as substantial evidence that the transaction was used principally as such a device. For purposes of this subparagraph, the term "exchange" does not include an exchange of stock or securities pursuant to a plan of reorganization if no gain or loss is recognized on the exchange or an insubstantial amount of gain is recognized on the exchange. A sale is always pursuant to an arrangement negotiated or agreed upon before the distribution when enforceable rights to buy or sell exist before such distribution. If a sale was discussed by the buyer and the seller before the distribution and was reasonably to be anticipated by both parties, such sale shall ordinarily be considered as made pursuant to an arrangement negotiated or agreed upon before the distribution.

Whether or not a sale is negotiated or agreed upon prior to the distribution, the fact of any sale of stock or securities shall be taken into account with other evidence in determining whether a transaction was used principally as a device for the distribution of earnings and profits.

(3) **Nature and use of assets—(i) General.** In determining whether a transaction was used principally as a device for the distribution of earnings and profits of the distributing corporation, the controlled corporation, or both, consideration will be given to the nature, kind, and amount of the assets of both corporations (and corporations controlled by them) immediately after the transactions and to the use of such assets by such corporations.

(ii) **New trade or business.** If a substantial portion of the assets of any post-distribution corporation consists of a trade or business acquired within the 5-year period ending on the date of the distribution in a transaction in which the basis of such assets was not determined in whole or in part by reference to the transferor's basis, this will be considered as evidence that the transaction was used principally as a device for the distribution of earnings and profits.

(iii) **Liquid assets.** The transfer or retention of cash or liquid assets (for example, securities and accounts receivable) which is not related to the reasonable needs of the business of the transferee or retaining corporation will be considered as evidence that the transaction was used principally as a device for the distribution of earnings and profits.

(iv) **Related function.** In certain cases the relationship between the nature and use of the assets of the distributing corporation and the controlled corporation will be considered as evidence that a transaction was used principally as a device for the distribution of earnings and profits. For example, where the principal function of one corporation before the transaction is to perform services for or supply technical or research data to the other corporation, and after the transaction that corporation continues to function on the same basis, this would be considered as evidence that the transaction was used principally as such a device. Thus, in example (9) of § 1.355–3(c), involving a controlled corporation operating a coal mine for the sole purpose of satisfying the requirements of the parent steel corporation before the transaction, if the coal mining business continued to operate on the same basis after the transaction, this fact would be considered as evidence that the distribution of the stock of the coal mining corporation in example (9) is principally a device for the distribution of earnings and profits. Similarly, in a transaction which separates the manufacturing and sales operations, as in example (8) of § 1.355–3(c), if the sales corporation merely functions as the exclusive agent for the manufacturing corporation after the transaction, this fact would be considered as evidence that the transaction was principally a device for the distribution of earnings and profits.

(4) **Examples.** The provisions of this paragraph (c) may be illustrated by the following examples:

Example (1). Corporation W has engaged in the commercial banking business in state N for 20 years. The stock of W is owned equally by individuals A, B, and C. Six years ago, W organized corporation X as a wholly-owned subsidiary to offer computerized bookkeeping services to the public. W and X have substantial accumulated earnings and profits. State N has recently amended its banking laws to provide that commercial banks operating in N may not offer computerized bookkeeping services directly or through a subsidiary. D, an individual, has offered to purchase the stock of X. At a stockholders' meeting the offer was rejected and it was decided to distribute the stock of X pro rata to A, B, and C. After the meeting and before the distribution, A, B, and C agreed to sell D one-half of X stock they were to receive in the distribution. Notwithstanding the existence of a corporate business reason for the distribution of the stock of X, the distribution will be considered to have been used principally as a device for the distribution of earnings and profits of W.

Example (2). Assume the same facts as in example (1) except that A, B, and C did not agree to sell any of the X stock they were to receive to D. At the shareholders' meeting it was decided to transfer cash to X before making the pro rata distribution. The amount of cash transferred substantially exceeded the reasonable business needs of X. After the distribution A and B agreed to sell to E, an individual, one-half of their X stock. Notwithstanding the existence of a real and substantial non-tax reason for the distribution, the transaction will be considered to have been used principally as a device for the distribution of earnings and profits because of the transfer of cash to X and the subsequent sale of X stock by A and B.

* * *

§ 1.355–3　Non pro rata distributions, etc.

(a) The rule of section 355(a)(1) prescribing that gain or loss will not be recognized applies whether or not the distribution is pro rata with respect to the interests of all the shareholders in the distributing corporation provided all other requirements of section 355 are satisfied. For example, if two individuals, A and B, own all of the stock of Corporation X which operates two active businesses, one business may be transferred to a new corporation in exchange for all of its stock and such stock distributed to either A or B in exchange for all of his stock of Corporation X. Similarly, if, in the above example, only a part of the stock of the new corporation is transferred to one of the shareholders in exchange for all of his stock of Corporation X and the balance of such stock is distributed to the other shareholder (whether or not such other shareholder surrenders stock in Corporation X), no gain or loss will be recognized. The same rule will be applicable if the stock of an existing controlled corporation is distributed to the shareholders even though such distribution is not pursuant to a plan of reorganization. Section 355 does not apply, however, if the substance of the transaction is merely an exchange between shareholders or security holders of stock or securities in one corporation for stock or securities in another corporation. For example, if two individuals, C and D, each own directly fifty percent of the stock of Corporation M and fifty percent of the stock of Corporation N, section 355 would not apply to a transaction in which C and D transfer all of their stock in Corporation M and Corporation N to a new corporation, P, for all of the stock of Corporation P, and Corporation P then distributes the stock of Corporation M to C and the stock of Corporation N to D.

(b) The stock of the controlled corporation which is distributed may consist of either common or preferred stock. See, however, section 306 with respect to the receipt of preferred stock in a transaction to which section 355 is applicable.

(c) The rule of section 355(a)(1) prescribing that gain or loss will not be recognized applies whether or not the shareholder surrenders stock in the distributing corporation and whether or not the distribution is in pursuance of a plan of reorganization (within the meaning of section 368(a)(1)(D)).

[T.D. 6500, 25 FR 11607, Nov. 26, 1960]

§ 1.355–3　(Proposed, published 1–13–77.) Active conduct of a trade or business.

(a) Requirements as to active business—(1) In general—(i) Application of section 355. Under section 355(b)(1), a distribution of stock or securities of a controlled corporation is subject to section 355(a) only if—

(A) The distributing corporation and the controlled corporation are each engaged in the active conduct of a trade or business immediately after the distribution of stock or securities of the controlled corporation (section 355(b)(1)(A)), or

(B) Immediately before the distribution the distributing corporation had no assets other than stock or securities in the controlled corporations and each of the controlled corporations is engaged in the active conduct of a trade or business immediately after the distribution (section 355(b)(1)(B)). In connection with the requirement of "no assets" a de minimis rule is applicable.

(ii) Examples. Paragraph (a)(1)(i) of this section may be illustrated by the following examples:

Example (1). Corporation A, prior to the distribution, is engaged in the active conduct of a trade or business and owns all of the stock of corporation B which also is engaged in the active conduct of a business. A distributes all of the stock of B to its shareholders, and each corporation continues the active conduct of its business. The active business requirement of section 355(b)(1)(A) is satisfied.

Example (2). The facts are the same as in example (1), except that A transfers all of its assets except the stock of B to a new corporation in exchange for all of the new corporation's stock and transfers the stock of both controlled corporations to its shareholders. The active business requirement of section 355(b)(1)(B) is satisfied.

(b) Active conduct of a trade or business defined—(1) In general. Section 355(b)(2) provides rules for determining whether any corporation is treated as engaged in the active conduct of a trade or business for purposes of ascertaining whether the distributing corporation and the controlled corporation meet the requirements of section 355(b)(1). Under section 355(b)(2)(A), a corporation is treated as engaged in the active conduct of a trade or business if it is itself engaged in such a trade or business or if substantially all of its assets consist of the stock and securities of a corporation or corporations controlled by it (immediately after the distribution) each of which is engaged in the active conduct of a trade or business.

(2) **Active conduct of trade or business immediately after distribution—(i) General.** For purposes of section 355(b), a corporation shall be treated as engaged in the "active conduct of a trade or business" immediately after a distribution if the assets and activities of such corporation meet the tests and limitations described in paragraph (b)(2)(ii), (iii), and (iv) of this section.

(ii) **Trade or business.** A corporation shall be treated as engaged in a trade or business immediately after a distribution of stock if a specific group of activities are being carried on by such corporation for the purpose of earning income or profit from such group of activities, and the activities included in such group include every operation which forms a part of, or a step in, the process of earning income or profit from such group. Such group of activities ordinarily must include the collection of income and the payment of expenses.

(iii) **Active conduct.** For purposes of section 355, the determination of whether a trade or business is actively conducted is a question of fact to be determined under all the facts and circumstances. In general, the corporation must perform active and substantial management and operational functions.

(iv) **Limitations.** The active conduct of a trade or business does not include—

(A) The holding for investment purposes of stock, securities, land, or other property, or

(B) The ownership and operation (including leasing) of real or personal property used in a trade or business, unless the owner performs significant services with respect to the operation and management of the property.

(3) **Active conduct for 5-year period preceding distribution.** Under section 355(b)(2)(B), a trade or business must have been actively conducted for the 5-year period ending on the date of distribution of the stock and securities of the controlled corporation. For this purpose, activities which constitute a trade or business under the tests described in paragraph (b)(2) of this section, shall be treated as meeting the test contained in the preceding sentence if such activities were actively conducted throughout such 5-year period.

For the purpose of determining whether such trade or business has been actively conducted throughout the 5-year period described in section 355(b)(2), the fact that during such 5-year period such trade or business underwent change (for example, by the addition of new or the dropping of old products, changes in production capacity, and the like) shall be disregarded provided the changes are not of such a character as to constitute the acquisition of a new or different business.

(4) **Special rules for acquisition of a trade or business—(i) General.** For purposes of section 355(b), a trade or business which is relied upon to meet the requirements of such section must not have been acquired by the distributing corporation, the controlled corporation, or another member of the affiliated group during the 5-year period ending on the date of distribution of the stock and securities of the controlled corporation unless it was acquired in a transaction in which no gain or loss was recognized (section 355(b)(2)(C)). For purposes of this subparagraph (4), the term "affiliated group" means an affiliated group as defined in section 1504(a) (without regard to section 1504(b)) except that the term "stock" includes nonvoting stock which is limited and preferred as to dividends. In addition, under section 355(b)(2)(D), such trade or business must not have been indirectly acquired during such 5-year period in a transaction in which gain or loss was recognized in whole or in part by means of the acquisition of control of the corporation that was engaged in such trade or business or by means of an indirect acquisition of control of such corporation through another corporation or any of its predecessors in interest. A business acquired, directly or indirectly, within the 5-year period ending on the date of the distribution in a transaction in which the basis of the assets acquired is not determined in whole or in part by reference to the transferor's basis for such assets will not qualify under section 355(b)(2), even though no gain or loss was recognized by the transferor (for example, by reason of section 337).

(ii) **Gain or loss recognized in certain transactions.** The rules of section 355(b)(2)(C) and (D) are intended to prevent the direct or indirect acquisition of a trade or business by a corporation as a temporary investment of liquid assets in anticipation of a distribution by such corporation of such trade or business in a transaction to which section 355 would otherwise apply. A direct or indirect acquisition of a trade or business by one member of an affiliated group from another member of such group is not the type of transaction to which section 355(b)(2)(C) and (D) is intended to apply. Therefore, in applying section 355(b)(2)(C) or (D), such an acquisition, even though taxable, shall be disregarded.

(iii) Example. Paragraph (b)(4)(i) may be illustrated by the following example:

Example: In 1956m corporation B, having cash and other liquid assets, purchased all of the stock of corporation A which was engaged in an active business. Later, in the same year, B in a "downstream" statutory merger merges into A. In 1958, A places the assets formerly owned by B in a new subsidiary, corporation X. A's distribution of the stock of X to the stockholders of A is not within the terms of section 355, since the active business of A had, in effect, been purchased less than 5 years prior to the distribution.

(c) Examples. The following examples illustrate the application of the rules provided in section 355(b)(2)(A) and (B). However, a transaction which satisfies the active conduct of a trade or business requirement in these examples will qualify under section 355(a) only if the other requirements of that section are met.

Example (1). Corporation A is engaged in the manufacture and sale of soap and detergents and owns investment securities. It proposes to place the investment securities in a new corporation and distribute the stock of such new corporation to its shareholders. The new corporation's holding of investment securities does not qualify as the active conduct of a trade or business immediately after the distribution.

Example (2). Corporation B owns, manages, and derives rental income from an office building and also owns vacant land. It proposes to transfer the vacant land to a new corporation and distribute the stock of such new corporation to its shareholders. The new corporation's holding of the vacant land does not qualify as the active conduct of a trade or business immediately after the distribution.

Example (3). Corporation C owns land on which it engages in the ranching business. Oil has been discovered in the area and it is apparent that oil may be found under the land on which the ranching activities are conducted. Corporation C has engaged in no significant activities in connection with the mineral rights. It proposes to transfer the mineral rights to a new corporation and distribute the stock of the new corporation to its shareholders. The new corporation's holding of mineral rights does not qualify as the active conduct of a trade or business immediately after the distribution.

Example (4). Corporation D, a bank, has for the past 7 years owned an 11-story downtown office building, the ground floor of which has been occupied by it in the conduct of its banking business. The remaining 10 floors are rented to various tenants and the building is managed and maintained by employees of the bank. Corporation D proposes to transfer the building to a new corporation and to distribute the stock of such new corpo-

ration to the bank's shareholders. The new corporation will manage the building, negotiate leases, seek new tenants, and will repair and maintain the building. Immediately after the distribution the activities in connection with banking will constitute the active conduct of a trade or business, as will the activities in connection with the rental of the building.

Example (5). Corporation E, a bank, has for the past 9 years owned a 2-story building in a suburban area, the ground floor and one-half of the second floor of which are occupied by it in the conduct of its banking business. The other one-half of the second floor is rented as storage space to a neighboring retail merchant. Corporation E proposes to transfer the building to a new corporation and distribute the stock of the new corporation to its shareholders. Corporation E will lease the space formerly occupied by it in the bank building from the new corporation and, under the lease, will repair and maintain its portion of the building and pay property taxes and insurance. The new corporation will not be engaged in the active conduct of a trade or business immediately after the distribution.

Example (6). Corporation F is engaged in the retail grocery business and owns all of the stock of corporation G. Corporation G has for the past 10 years derived all of its gross income from the rental of its land and building to F, under a lease in which G's principal activity consists of the collection of rent from the building. Corporation F proposes to distribute the G stock to its shareholders. Corporation G will not be engaged in the active conduct of a trade or business immediately after the distribution, since it has not actively conducted a trade or business throughout the 5-year period ending on the date of the distribution.

Example (7). Corporation H has owned and operated a men's retail clothing store in the downtown area of the City of R for 7 years and has also owned and operated a men's retail clothing store in the suburban area of the City of R for 9 years. Corporation H proposes to transfer the store building, fixtures, inventory, and other assets related to suburban store's activity to a new corporation. However, the warehouses which formerly served both the downtown and suburban stores will be retained by H, and the new corporation will lease warehouse space from an unrelated public warehouse company. Moreover, the delivery trucks and employees which formerly served both stores will be transferred to the new corporation for its exclusive use, and corporation H will contract with a local public delivery organization to effect its deliveries. Corporation H proposes to distribute the stock of the new corporation to its shareholders. Immediately after the distribution the activities in connection with the downtown store will constitute the active conduct of a trade or business, as will the activities in connection with the suburban store.

Example (8). Corporation I has processed and sold meat products for 8 years. It has no other income. Corporation I proposes to separate the selling from the processing activities by forming a separate corporation, J, to purchase for resale the meats processed by I. Corporation I will transfer to J certain physical assets pertaining to the sales function, plus cash for working capital, in exchange for the capital stock of J which will be distributed to the shareholders of I. Immediately after the distribution corporation I will be engaged in the active conduct of a meat products processing business and corporation J will be engaged in the active conduct of a meat distribution business. The business of each corporation is deemed to have been actively conducted from the date corporation I began its meat processing and sales business.

Example (9). For 8 years corporation K has been engaged in the manufacture and sale of steel and steel products. For 6 years K's wholly-owned subsidiary, corporation L, has owned and operated a coal mine for the sole purpose of supplying K's coal requirements in the manufacture of steel. It is proposed that the stock of L be distributed to the shareholders of K. Immediately after the distribution, the activities of L in connection with the operation of the coal mine constitute the active conduct of a trade or business. The activities of K in connection with the manufacture and sale of steel products immediately after the distribution also constitute the active conduct of a trade or business.

Example (10). Corporation M has for more than 5 years been engaged in the single business of constructing sewage disposal plants and other facilities. Corporation M proposes to transfer one-half of its assets to corporation N. These assets will include a contract for the construction of a sewage disposal plant in State X, construction equipment, cash, and other tangible assets. Corporation M will retain a contract for the construction of a sewage disposal plant in State Y, construction equipment, cash and other intangible assets. The N stock is then to be distributed to one of the M shareholders in exchange for all of his M stock. Both corporations will be engaged in the active conduct of the construction business immediately after the distribution.

Example (11). Corporation O has for the past 6 years owned three factories devoted to the production of edible pork skins. The entire output of two of the factories is sold to one customer. The third factory's output is sold to a number of different customers. Corporation O proposes to transfer the two factories which produce pork skins for the single customer, together with their related activities, to a new corporation and to distribute the stock of such new corporation to its shareholders. Immediately after the distribution the activities in connection with the production and sale of edible pork skins to the one customer will constitute the active conduct of a trade or business, as well the activities in connection with the production and sale of pork skins to the other customers.

Example (12). Corporation P has owned and operated a department store in the City of W for 9 years. Three years ago P acquired a parcel of land and constructed a branch store in a suburban area of the City of W. The two stores are operated as a single unit and have common advertising, bank accounts, billing, purchasing, and management. Corporation P proposes to transfer the suburban store, together with its related activities, to a new corporation and to distribute the stock of such new corporation to its shareholders. Each store will have its own manager and will be operated independently of the other store. Immediately after the distribution the activities in connection with each of the department stores constitute the active conduct of a trade or business since

each store was an integrated part of the single department store business conducted by P for 9 years.

Example (13). Corporation Q is engaged in the business of manufacturing hats in its own factory building. It proposes to transfer the factory building to corporation R and distribute the stock of R to its shareholders. After the transfer, Q will lease the factory building under a long-term lease and will operate and maintain the building and the machinery in the building. The activities of R in connection with the leased factory building immediately after the distribution will not constitute the active conduct of a trade or business.

Example (14). Corporation S has been engaged in the manufacture and sale of household products for 8 years. Throughout this period, in connection with such manufacturing, it has maintained a research department for its own use. The research department has 30 employees actively engaged in the development of new products. Corporation S proposes to transfer the research department to a new corporation and to distribute the stock of the new corporation to its shareholders. After the distribution the new corporation will continue its research operations on a contractual basis with several corporations including S. Immediately after the distribution the activities of the new corporation in connection with research will constitute the active conduct of a trade or business, as will the activities of S in connection with manufacturing.

§ 1.355–4 Active conduct of a trade or business.

(a) A distribution of stock or securities of a controlled corporation is subject to section 355(a) only, if:

(1) The distributing corporation and the controlled corporation are each engaged in the active conduct of a trade or business immediately after the distribution of stock or securities of the controlled corporation; or

(2) Immediately before the distribution the distributing corporation had no assets other than stock or securities in the controlled corporations and each of the controlled corporations is engaged in the active conduct of a trade or business immediately after the distribution. In connection with the requirement of "no assets" a de minimis rule is applicable.

(3) These rules are illustrated by the following examples:

Example (1). Corporation A, prior to the distribution, operates an active business and owns all of the stock of Corporation B which also is engaged in the active conduct of a business. Corporation A distributes all of the stock of Corporation B to its shareholders, and both continue the operations of their separate businesses. The active business requirement of section 355(b)(1)(A) is satisfied.

Example (2). The facts are the same as in example 1, except that Corporation A transfers all of its assets except the stock of Corporation B to a new corporation in exchange for all of its stock and transfers the stock of both controlled corporations to its shareholders. The active business requirement of section 355(b)(1)(B) is satisfied.

(b)(1) Section 355(b)(2) provides rules for determining whether any corporation is treated as engaged in the active conduct of a trade or business for purposes of ascertaining whether the distributing corporation and the controlled corporation meet the requirements of section 355(b)(1). Under section 355(b)(2)(A), a corporation is treated as engaged in the active conduct of a trade or business if it is itself engaged in such a trade or business or if substantially all of its assets consist of the stock and securities of a corporation or corporations controlled by it (immediately after the distribution) each of which is engaged in the active conduct of a trade or business. Regardless of whether the determination is based upon a corporation's own conduct of a trade or business or on the basis of its ownership of the stock of a corporation or corporations which conduct a trade or business, such trade or business must have been actively conducted for the five-year period ending on the date of distribution of the stock and securities of the controlled corporation the stock of which was distributed as provided in section 355(b)(2)(B). Furthermore, such trade or business must not have been acquired by either corporation during such five-year period unless it was acquired in a transaction in which gain or loss was not recognized (section 355(b)(2)(C)). In addition, under section 355(b)(2)(D), such business must not have been indirectly acquired during such five-year period by means of the acquisition of control of another corporation in a transaction in which gain or loss was recognized. Thus, section 355(b)(2)(D) requires that during the five-year period during which the trade or business must be actively conducted, such business cannot have been acquired, directly or indirectly, through another corporation by such other corporation or any of its predecessors in interest in a transaction in which gain or loss was recognized in whole or in part.

(2) Subparagraph (1) of this paragraph may be illustrated by the following example:

Example. In 1956, Corporation B, having cash and other liquid assets and engaged in only one active business purchases all of the stock of Corporation A, also engaged in a single active business. Later in the same year, Corporation B in a "downstairs" statutory merger merges into Corporation A. In 1958, Corporation A

places the assets of the active business formerly operated by Corporation B in a new subsidiary X. A distribution of the stock of Corporation X to the stockholders of Corporation A is not within the terms of section 355, since one of the active businesses had, in effect, been purchased less than five years prior to the distribution.

(3) For the purpose of determining whether such trade or business has been actively conducted throughout the five-year period described in section 355(b)(2), the fact that during such five-year period such trade or business underwent change (for example, by the addition of new or the dropping of old products, changes in production capacity, and the like) shall be disregarded provided the changes are not of such a character as to constitute the acquisition of a new or different business.

[T.D. 6500, 25 FR 11607, Nov. 26, 1960]

§ 1.355-5   Records to be kept and information to be filed.

(a) Every corporation that makes a distribution of stock or securities of a controlled corporation, as described in section 355, shall attach to its return for the year of the distribution a detailed statement setting forth such data as may be appropriate in order to show compliance with the provisions of such section.

(b) Every taxpayer who receives a distribution of stock or securities of a corporation that was controlled by a corporation in which he holds stock or securities shall attach to his return for the year in which such distribution is received a detailed statement setting forth such data as may be appropriate in order to show the applicability of section 355. Such statement shall include, but shall not be limited to, a description of the stock and securities surrendered (if any) and received, and the names and addresses of all of the corporations involved in the transaction.

[T.D. 6500, 25 FR 11607, Nov. 26, 1960]

§ 1.356-1   Receipt of additional consideration in connection with an exchange.

(a) If in any exchange to which the provisions of section 354 or section 355 would apply except for the fact that there is received by the shareholders or the security holders other property (in addition to property permitted to be received without recognition of gain by such sections) or money, then—

(1) The gain, if any, to the taxpayer shall be recognized in an amount not in excess of the sum

of the money and the fair market value of the other property, but,

(2) The loss, if any, to the taxpayer from the exchange or distribution shall not be recognized to any extent.

(b) If the distribution of such other property or money by or on behalf of a corporation has the effect of the distribution of a dividend, then there shall be chargeable to each distributee (either an individual or a corporation)—

(1) As a dividend, such an amount of the gain recognized as is not in excess of the distributee's ratable share of the undistributed earnings and profits of the corporation accumulated after February 28, 1913, and

(2) As a gain from the exchange of property, the remainder of the gain so recognized.

(c) This section may be illustrated by the following examples:

Example (1). In an exchange to which the provisions of section 356 apply and to which section 354 would apply but for the receipt of property not permitted to be received without the recognition of gain or loss, A (either an individual or a corporation), received the following in exchange for a share of stock having an adjusted basis to him of $85:

One share of stock worth	$100
Cash	25
Other property (basis $25) fair market value	50
Total fair market value of consideration received	175
Adjusted basis of stock surrendered in exchange	85
Total gain	90
Gain to be recognized, limited to cash and other property received..................	75
A's pro rata share of earnings and profits accumulated after February 28, 1913 (taxable dividend)	30
Remainder to be treated as a gain from the exchange of property	45

Example (2). If, in example (1), A's stock had an adjusted basis to him of $200, he would have realized a loss of $25 on the exchange, which loss would not be recognized.

(d) Section 301(b)(1)(B) and section 301(d)(2) do not apply to a distribution of "other property" to a corporate shareholder if such distribution is within the provisions of section 356.

(e) See paragraph (1) of § 1.301–1 for certain transactions which are not within the scope of section 356.

[T.D. 6500, 25 FR 11607, Nov. 26, 1960]

§ 1.356–2 Receipt of additional consideration not in connection with an exchange.

(a) If, in a transaction to which section 355 would apply except for the fact that a shareholder (individual or corporate) receives property permitted by section 355 to be received without the recognition of gain, together with other property or money, without the surrender of any stock or securities of the distributing corporation, then the sum of the money and the fair market value of the other property as of the date of the distribution shall be treated as a distribution of property to which the rules of section 301 (other than section 301(b) and section 301(d)) apply. See section 358 for determination of basis of such other property.

(b) Paragraph (a) of this section may be illustrated by the following examples:

Example (1). Individuals A and B each own 50 of the 100 outstanding shares of common stock of Corporation X. Corporation X owns all of the stock of Corporation Y, 100 shares. Corporation X distributes to each shareholder 50 shares of the stock of Corporation Y plus $100 cash without requiring the surrender of any shares of its own stock. The $100 cash received by each is treated as a distribution of property to which the rules of section 301 apply.

Example (2). If, in the above example, Corporation X distributes 50 shares of stock of Corporation Y to A and 30 shares of such stock plus $100 cash to B without requiring the surrender of any of its own stock, the amount of cash received by B is treated as a distribution of property to which the rules of section 301 apply.

[T.D. 6500, 25 FR 11607, Nov. 26, 1960]

§ 1.356–3 Rules for treatment of securities as "other property".

(a) As a general rule, for purposes of section 356, the term "other property" includes securities. However, it does not include securities permitted under section 354 or section 355 to be received tax free. Thus, when securities are surrendered in a transaction to which section 354 or section 355 is applicable, the characterization of the securities received as "other property" does not include securities received where the principal amount of such securities does not exceed the principal amount of securities surrendered in the transaction. If a greater principal amount of securities is received in an exchange described in section 354 (other than subsection (c) or (d) thereof) or section 355 over the principal amount of securities surrendered, the term "other property" includes the fair market value of such excess principal amount as of the date of the exchange. If no securities are surrendered in exchange, the term "other property" includes the fair market value, as of the date of receipt, of the entire principal amount of the securities received.

(b) The following examples illustrate the application of the above regulations:

Example (1). A, an individual, exchanged 100 shares of stock for 100 shares of stock and a security in the principal amount of $1,000 with a fair market value of $990. The amount of $990 is treated as "other property."

Example (2). B, an individual, exchanged 100 shares of stock and a security in the principal amount of $1,000 for 300 shares of stock and a security in the principal amount of $1,500. The security had a fair market value on the date of receipt of $1,575. The fair market value of the excess principal amount, or $525, is treated as "other property."

Example (3). C, an individual, exchanged a security in the principal amount of $1,000 for 100 shares of stock and a security in the principal amount of $900. No part of the security received is treated as "other property."

Example (4). D, an individual, exchanged a security in the principal amount of $1,000 for 100 shares of stock and a security in the principal amount of $1,200 with a fair market value of $1,100. The fair market value of the excess principal amount, or $183.33, is treated as "other property."

Example (5). E, an individual, exchanged a security in the principal amount of $1,000 for another security in the principal amount of $1,200 with a fair market value of $1,080. The fair market value of the excess principal amount, or $180, is treated as "other property."

Example (6). F, an individual, exchanged a security in the principal amount of $1,000 for two different securities each in the principal amount of $750. One of the securities had a fair market value of $750, the other had a fair market value of $600. One-third of the fair market value of each security ($250 and $200) is treated as "other property."

[T.D. 6500, 25 FR 11607, Nov. 26, 1960, as amended by T.D. 7616, 44 FR 26869, May 8, 1979]

§ 1.356–4   Exchanges for section 306 stock.

If, in a transaction to which section 356 is applicable, other property or money is received in exchange for section 306 stock, an amount equal to the fair market value of the property plus the money, if any, shall be treated as a distribution of property to which section 301 is applicable. The determination of whether section 306 stock is surrendered for other property (including money) is a question of fact to be decided under all of the circumstances of each case. Ordinarily, the other property (including money) received will first be treated as received in exchange for any section 306 stock owned by a shareholder prior to such transaction. For example, if a shareholder who owns a share of common stock (having a basis to him of $100) and a share of preferred stock which is section 306 stock (having a basis to him of $100) surrenders both shares in a transaction to which section 356 is applicable for one share of common stock having a fair market value of $80 and one $100 bond having a fair market value of $100, the bond will be deemed received in exchange for the section 306 stock and it will be treated as a distribution to which section 301 is applicable to the extent of its entire fair market value ($100).

[T.D. 6500, 25 FR 11607, Nov. 26, 1960]

§ 1.356–5   Transactions involving gift or compensation.

With respect to transactions described in sections 354, 355, or 356, but which—

(a) Result in a gift, see section 2501 and following, and the regulations pertaining thereto, or

(b) Have the effect of the payment of compensation, see section 61(a)(1), and the regulations pertaining thereto.

§ 1.357–1   Assumption of liability.

(a) General rule. Section 357(a) does not affect the rule that liabilities assumed are to be taken into account for the purpose of computing the amount of gain or loss realized under section 1001 upon an exchange. Section 357(a) provides, subject to the exceptions and limitations specified in section 357(b) and (c), that—

(1) Liabilities assumed are not to be treated as "other property or money" for the purpose of determining the amount of realized gain which is to be recognized under section 351, 361, 371, or 374, if the transactions would, but for the receipt of "other property or money" have been exchanges of the type described in any one of such sections; and

(2) If the only type of consideration received by the transferor in addition to that permitted to be received by section 351, 361, 371, or 374, consists of an assumption of liabilities, the transaction, if otherwise qualified, will be deemed to be within the provisions of section 351, 361, 371, or 374.

(b) Application of general rule. The application of paragraph (a) of this section may be illustrated by the following example:

Example. A, an individual, transfers to a controlled corporation property with an adjusted basis of $10,000 in exchange for stock of the corporation with a fair market value of $8,000, $3,000 cash, and the assumption by the corporation of indebtedness of A amounting to $4,000. A's gain is $5,000, computed as follows:

Stock received, fair market value	$8,000
Cash received............................	3,000
Liability assumed by transferee	4,000
Total consideration received	15,000
Less: Adjusted basis of property transferred	10,000
Gain realized	5,000

Assuming that the exchange falls within section 351 as a transaction in which the gain to be recognized is limited to "other property or money" received, the gain recognized to A will be limited to the $3,000 cash received, since, under the general rule of section 357(a), the assumption of the $4,000 liability does not constitute "other property."

(c) Tax avoidance purpose. The benefits of section 357(a) do not extend to any exchange involving an assumption of liabilities where it appears that the principal purpose of the taxpayer with respect to such assumption was to avoid Federal income tax on the exchange, or, if not such purpose, was not a bona fide business purpose. In such cases, the total amount of liabilities assumed or acquired pursuant to such exchange (and not merely a particular liability with respect to which the tax avoidance purpose existed) shall, for the purpose of determining the amount of gain to be recognized upon the exchange in which the liabilities are assumed or acquired, be treated as money received by the taxpayer upon the exchange. Thus, if in the example set forth in paragraph (b) of this section, the principal purpose of the assumption of the $4,000 liability was to avoid tax on the exchange, or was not a bona fide business purpose, then the amount of gain recognized would be $5,000. In any suit or proceeding where the burden is on the taxpayer to prove that an assumption of liabilities is not to be treated as "other property or money" under section 357, which is the case if the Commissioner determines that the taxpayer's purpose with respect thereto was a purpose to avoid Federal income tax on the exchange or was not a bona fide business purpose, and the taxpayer contests such determination by litigation, the taxpayer must sustain such burden by the clear preponderance of the evidence. Thus, the taxpayer must prove his case by such a clear preponderance of all the evidence that the absence of a purpose to avoid Federal income tax on the exchange, or the presence of a bona fide business purpose, is unmistakable.

[T.D. 6500, 25 FR 11607, Nov. 26, 1960, as amended by T.D. 6528, 26 FR 399, Jan. 19, 1961]

§ 1.357-2 Liabilities in excess of basis.

(a) Section 357(c) provides in general that in an exchange to which section 351 (relating to a transfer to a corporation controlled by the transferor) is applicable, or to which section 361 (relating to the nonrecognition of gain or loss to corporations) is applicable by reason of a section 368(a)(1)(D) reorganization, if the sum of the amount of liabilities assumed plus the amount of liabilities to which the property is subject exceeds the total of the adjusted basis of the property transferred pursuant to such exchange, then such excess shall be considered as a gain from the sale or exchange of a capital asset or of property which is not a capital asset as the case may be. Thus, if an individual transfers, under section 351, properties having a total basis in his hands of $20,000, one of which has a basis of $10,000 but is subject to a mortgage of $30,000, to a corporation controlled by him, such individual will be subject to tax with respect to $10,000, the excess of the amount of the liability over the total adjusted basis of all the properties in his hands. The same result will follow whether or not the liability is assumed by the transferee. The determination of whether a gain resulting from the transfer of capital assets is long-term or short-term capital gain shall be made by reference to the holding period to the transferor of the assets transferred. An exception to the general rule of section 357(c) is made (1) for any exchange as to which under section 357(b) (relating to assumption of liabilities for tax-avoidance purposes) the entire amount of the liabilities is treated as money received * * *.

(b) The application of paragraph (a) of this section may be illustrated by the following examples:

Example (1). If all such assets transferred are capital assets and if half the assets (ascertained by reference to their fair market value at the time of the transfer) have been held for less than 1 year (6 months for taxable years beginning before 1977; 9 months for taxable years beginning in 1977), and the remaining half for more than 1 year (6 months for taxable years beginning before 1977; 9 months for taxable years beginning in 1977), half the excess of the amount of the liability over the total of the adjusted basis of the property transferred pursuant to the exchange shall be treated as short-term capital gain, and the remaining half shall be treated as long-term capital gain.

Example (2). If half of the assets (ascertained by reference to their fair market value at the time of the transfer) transferred are capital assets and half are assets other than capital assets, then half of the excess of the amount of the liability over the total of the adjusted basis of the property transferred pursuant to the exchange shall be treated as capital gain, and the remaining half shall be treated as gain from the sale or exchange of assets other than capital assets.

[T.D. 6500, 25 FR 11607, Nov. 26, 1960, as amended by T.D. 6528, 26 FR 399, Jan. 19, 1961; T.D. 7728, 45 FR 72650, Nov. 3, 1980]

§ 1.358–1   Basis to distributees.

(a) In the case of an exchange or distribution to which section 354, 355, or 371(b) applies in which, under the law applicable to the year in which the exchange is made, only nonrecognition property is received, the sum of the basis of all of the stock and securities in the corporation whose stock and securities are exchanged or with respect to which the distribution is made, held immediately after the transaction, plus the basis of all stock and securities received in the transaction shall be the same as the basis of all the stock and securities in such corporation held immediately before the transaction allocated in the manner described in § 1.358–2. In the case of an exchange to which section 351, 361, or 374 applies in which, under the law applicable to the year in which the exchange was made, only nonrecognition property is received, the basis of all the stock and securities received in the exchange shall be the same as the basis of all property exchange therefor. If in an exchange or distribution to which section 351, 356, 361, 371(b), or 374 applies both nonrecognition property and "other property" are received, the basis of all the property except "other property" held after the transaction shall be determined as described in the preceding two sentences decreased by the sum of the money and the fair market value of the "other property" (as of the date of the transaction) and increased by the sum of the amount treated as a dividend (if any) and the amount of the gain recognized on the exchange, but the term "gain" as here used does not include any portion of the recognized gain that was treated as a dividend. In any case in which a taxpayer transfers property with respect to which loss is recognized, such loss shall be reflected in determining the basis of the property received in the exchange. The basis of the "other property" is its fair market value as of the date of the transaction.

(b) The application of paragraph (a) of this section may be illustrated by the following example:

Example. A purchased a share of stock in Corporation X in 1935 for $150. Since that date he has received distributions out of other than earnings and profits (as defined in section 316) totalling $60, so that his adjusted basis for the stock is $90. In a transaction qualifying under section 356, A exchanged this share for one share in Corporation Y, worth $100, cash in the amount of $10, and other property with a fair market value of $30. The exchanging had the effect of the distribution of a dividend. A's ratable share of the earnings and profits of Corporation X accumulated after February 28, 1913, was $5. A realized a gain of $50 on the exchange, but the amount recognized is limited to $40, the sum of the cash received and the fair market value of the other property. Of the gain recognized, $5 is taxable as a dividend, and $35 as a gain from the exchange of property. The basis to A of the one share of stock of Corporation Y is $90, that is, the adjusted basis of the one share of stock Corporation X ($90), decreased by the sum of the cash received ($10) and the fair market value of the other property received ($30) and increased by the sum of the amount treated as a dividend ($5) and the amount treated as a gain from the exchange of property ($35). The basis of the other property received is $30.

[T.D. 6500, 25 FR 11607, Nov. 26, 1960, as amended by T.D. 6533, 26 FR 404, Jan. 19, 1965; T.D. 7616, 44 FR 26869, May 8, 1979]

§ 1.358–2   Allocation of basis among nonrecognition property.

(a)(1) As used in this paragraph the term "stock" means stock which is not "other property" under section 356 or 371(b), stock with respect to which a distribution is made, and, in the case of a surrender of part of the stock of a particular class, the retained part of such stock. The term "securities" means securities (including, where appropriate, fractional parts of securities) which are not "other property" under section 356 or 371(b) and in the case of a surrender of part of the securities of a particular class, the retained part of such securities. Stock, or securities, as the case may be, which differ either because they are in different corporations or because the rights attributable to them differ (although they are in the same corporation) are considered different classes of stock or securities, as the case may be, for purposes of this section.

(2) If as the result of an exchange or distribution under the terms of section 354, 355, 356 or 371(b) a shareholder who owned stock of only one class before the transaction owns stock of two or more classes after the transaction, then the basis of all the stock held before the transaction (as adjusted under § 1.358–1) shall be allocated among the stock of all classes (whether or not such stock was received in the transaction) held immediately after

the transaction in proportion to the fair market values of the stock of each class.

(3) If as the result of an exchange under the terms of section 354, 355, 356 or 371(b) a security holder who owned only securities, all of one class, before the transaction, owns securities or stock of more than one class, or owns both stock and securities, then the basis of all the securities held before the transaction (as adjusted under § 1.358–1) shall be allocated among all the stock and securities (whether or not received in the transaction) held immediately after the transaction in proportion to the fair market values of the stock of each class and the securities of each class.

(4) In every case in which, before the transactions, a person owned stock of more than one class or securities of more than one class or owned both stock and securities, a determination must be made, upon the basis of all the facts, of the stock or securities received with respect to stock and securities of each class held (whether or not surrendered). The allocation described in subparagraph (2) of this paragraph shall be separately made as to the stock of each class with respect to which there is an exchange or distribution and the allocation described in subparagraph (3) of this paragraph shall be separately made with respect to the securities of each class, part or all of which are surrendered in the exchange.

(5) Notwithstanding the provisions of subparagraphs (2), (3), and (4) of this paragraph, in any case in which a plan of recapitalization under section 368(a)(1)(E) provides that each holder of stock or securities of a particular class shall have an option to surrender some or none of such stock or securities in exchange for stock or securities, and a shareholder or security holder exchanges an identifiable part of his stock or securities, the basis of the part of the stock or securities retained shall remain unchanged and shall not be taken into account in determining the basis of the stock or securities received.

(b)(1) As used in this paragraph the term "stock" refers only to stock which is not "other property" under section 351, 361, or 374 and the term "securities" refers only to securities which are not "other property" under section 351, 361, or 374.

(2) If in an exchange to which section 351 or 361 applies property is transferred to a corporation and the transferor receives stock or securities of more than one class or receives both stock and securities,

then the basis of the property transferred (as adjusted under § 1.358–1) shall be allocated among all of the stock and securities received in proportion to the fair market values of the stock of each class and the securities of each class.

(c) The application of paragraphs (a) and (b) of this section may be illustrated by the following examples:

Example (1). A, an individual, owns stock in Corporation X with an adjusted basis of $1,000. In a transaction qualifying under section 356 (so far as such section relates to section 354), he exchanged this stock for 20 shares of stock of Corporation Y worth $1,200 and securities of Corporation Y worth $400. A realizes a gain of $600 of which $400 is recognized. The adjusted basis in A's hands of each share of the stock of Corporation Y is $50 determined by allocating the basis of the stock of Corporation X ratably to the stock of Corporation Y received in the exchange. The securities of Corporation Y have a basis in the hands of A of $400.

Example (2). B, an individual, owns a security in the principal amount of $10,000 with a basis of $5,000. In a transaction to which section 354 is applicable, he exchanges this security for four securities in the principal amount of $750 each, worth $800 each, four securities in the principal amount of $750 each, worth $600 each, class A common stock worth $1,000, and class B common stock worth $400. B realizes a gain of $2,000 none of which is recognized. The basis of his original security, $5,000, will be allocated $32/70$ths to the four securities worth $800, $24/70$ths to the four securities worth $600, $10/70$ths to the class A common stock, and $4/70$ths to the class B common stock.

Example (3). C, an individual, owns stock of Corporation Y with a basis of $5,000 and owns a security issued by Corporation Y in the principal amount of $5,000 with a basis of $5,000. In a transaction to which section 354 is applicable, he exchanges the stock of Corporation Y for stock of Corporation Z with a value of $6,000, and he exchanges the security of Corporation Y for stock of Corporation Z worth $1,500 and a security of Corporation Z in the principal amount of $4,500 worth $4,500. No gain is recognized to C on either exchange. The basis of the stock of Corporation Z received for the stock of Corporation Y is $5,000. The bases of the stock and security of Corporation Z received in exchange for the security of Corporation Y are $1,250 and $3,750, respectively.

Example (4). D, an individual, owns stock in Corporation M with a basis of $15,000, worth $40,000, and owns a security issued by Corporation M in the principal amount of $5,000 with a basis of $4,000. In a transaction qualifying under section 356 (so far as such section relates to section 355), he exchanges the security of Corporation M for a security of Corporation O (a controlled corporation) in the principal amount of $5,000, worth $5,000, and exchanges one-half of his stock of Corporation M for stock of Corporation O worth $15,000 and a security of Corporation O in the principal amount of $5,000, worth $5,000. All of the stock and securities of Corporation O are distributed pursuant to the transaction. D realizes a gain of $12,500 on the exchange of the stock of Corporation M for the stock and security of Corporation O of which $5,000 is recognized. D also realizes a gain of $1,000 on the exchange of a security of Corporation M for a security of Corporation O, none of which is recognized. The basis of his stock of Corporation M held before the transaction is allocated ²⁰/₃₅ths to the stock of Corporation M held after the transaction and ¹⁵/₃₅ths to the stock of Corporation O. The basis of the security of Corporation O received in exchange for his security of Corporation M is $4,000, the basis of the security of Corporation M exchanged. The basis of the security of Corporation O received with respect to D's stock of Corporation M is $5,000, its fair market value.

* * *

[T.D. 6500, 25 FR 11607, Nov. 26, 1960, as amended by T.D. 7616, 44 FR 26869, May 8, 1979]

§ 1.358-3 Treatment of assumption of liabilities.

(a) For purposes of section 358, where a party to the exchange assumes a liability of a distributee or acquires from him property subject to a liability, the amount of such liability is to be treated as money received by the distributee upon the exchange, whether or not the assumption of liabilities resulted in a recognition of gain or loss to the taxpayer under the law applicable to the year in which the exchange was made.

(b) The application of paragraph (a) of this section may be illustrated by the following examples:

Example (1). A, an individual, owns property with an adjusted basis of $100,000 on which there is a purchase money mortgage of $25,000. On December 1, 1945, A organizes Corporation X to which he transfers the property in exchange for all the stock of Corporation X and the assumption by Corporation X of the mortgage. The capital stock of the Corporation X has a fair market value of $150,000. Under sections 351 and 357, no gain or loss is recognized to A. The basis in A's hands of the stock of Corporation X is $75,000, computed as follows:

Adjusted basis of property transferred	$100,000
Less: Amount of money received (amount of liabilities assumed)......................	− 25,000
Basis of Corporation X stock to A	75,000

Example (2). A, an individual, owns property with an adjusted basis of $25,000 on which there is a mortgage of $50,000. On December 1, 1954, A organizes Corporation X to which he transfers the property in exchange for all the stock of Corporation X and the assumption by Corporation X of the mortgage. The stock of Corporation X has a fair market value of $50,000. Under sections 351 and 357, gain is recognized to A in the amount of $25,000. The basis in A's hands of the stock of Corporation X is zero, computed as follows:

Adjusted basis of property transferred	$25,000
Less: Amount of money received (amount of liabilities)	− 50,000
Plus: Amount of gain recognized to taxpayer	25,000
Basis of Corporation X stock to A	0

* * *

[T.D. 6500, 25 FR 11607, Nov. 26, 1960]

Effects on Corporation

§ 1.361-1 Nonrecognition of gain or loss to corporations.

Section 361 provides the general rule that no gain or loss shall be recognized if a corporation, a party to a reorganization, exchanges property in pursuance of the plan of reorganization solely for stock or securities in another corporation, a party to the reorganization. This provision includes only stock and securities received in connection with a reorganization defined in section 368(a). It also includes nonvoting stock and securities in a corporation, a party to a reorganization, received in a transaction to which section 368(a)(1)(C) is applicable only by reason of section 368(a)(2)(B).

[T.D. 6500, 25 FR 11607, Nov. 26, 1960]

§ 1.362-1 Basis to corporations.

(a) **In general.** Section 362 provides, as a general rule, that if property was acquired on or after June 22, 1954, by a corporation (1) in connection with a transaction to which section 351 (relating to transfer of property to corporation controlled by transferor) applies, (2) as paid-in surplus or as a contribution to capital, or (3) in connection with a reorganization to which Part III, subchapter C, Chapter 1 of the Code applies, then the basis shall be the same as it would be in the hands of the transferor, increased in the amount of gain recognized to the transferor on such transfer. (See also § 1.362-2.)

(b) **Exceptions.** (1) In the case of a plan of reorganization adopted after October 22, 1968, section 362 does not apply if the property acquired in connection with such reorganization consists of stock or securities in a corporation a party to the reorganization, unless acquired by the exchange of stock or securities of the transferee (or of a corporation which is in control of the transferee) as consideration in whole or in part for the transfer.

(2) In the case of a plan of reorganization adopted before October 23, 1968, section 362 does

not apply if the property acquired in connection with such reorganization consists of stock or securities in a corporation a party to the reorganization, unless acquired by the issuance of stock or securities of the transferee (or, in the case of transactions occurring after December 31, 1963, of a corporation which is in control of the transferee) as the consideration in whole or in part for the transfer. The term "issuance of stock or securities" includes any transfer of stock or securities, including stock or securities which were purchased or were acquired as a contribution to capital.

[T.D. 6500, 25 FR 11607, Nov. 26, 1960, as amended by T.D. 7422, 41 FR 26569, June 28, 1976]

§ 1.362-2 Certain contributions to capital.

The following regulations shall be used in the application of section 362(c):

(a) Property deemed to be acquired with contributed money shall be that property, if any, the acquisition of which was the purpose motivating the contribution;

(b) In the case of an excess of the amount of money contributed over the cost of the property deemed to be acquired with such money (as defined in paragraph (a) of this section) such excess shall be applied to the reduction of the basis (but not below zero) of other properties held by the corporation, on the last day of the 12-month period beginning on the day the contribution is received, in the following order—

(1) All property of a character subject to an allowance for depreciation (not including any properties as to which a deduction for amortization is allowable),

(2) Property with respect to which a deduction for amortization is allowable,

(3) Property with respect to which a deduction for depletion is allowable under section 611 but not under section 613, and

(4) All other remaining properties.

The reduction of the basis of each of the properties within each of the above categories shall be made in proportion to the relative bases of such properties.

(c) With the consent of the Commissioner, the taxpayer may, however, have the basis of the various units of property within a particular category adjusted in a manner different from the general rule set forth in paragraph (b) of this section. Variations from such rule may, for example, involve adjusting the basis of only certain units of the taxpayer's property within a given category. A request for variations from the general rule should be filed by the taxpayer with its return for the taxable year for which the transfer of the property has occurred.

[T.D. 6500, 25 FR 11607, Nov. 26, 1960]

Special Rule; Definitions

§ 1.368-1 Purpose and scope of exception of reorganization exchanges.

(a) Reorganizations. As used in the regulations under parts I, II, and III (section 301 and following), subchapter C, chapter 1 of the Code, the terms "reorganization" and "party to a reorganization" mean only a reorganization or a party to a reorganization as defined in subsections (a) and (b) of section 368. * * *

(b) Purpose. Under the general rule, upon the exchange of property, gain or loss must be accounted for if the new property differs in a material particular, either in kind or in extent, from the old property. The purpose of the reorganization provisions of the Code is to except from the general rule certain specifically described exchanges incident to such readjustments of corporate structures made in one of the particular ways specified in the Code, as are required by business exigencies and which effect only a readjustment of continuing interest in property under modified corporate forms. Requisite to a reorganization under the Code are a continuity of the business enterprise under the modified corporate form, and (except as provided in section 368(a)(1)(D)) a continuity of interest therein on the part of those persons who, directly or indirectly, were the owners of the enterprise prior to the reorganization. The continuity of business enterprise requirement is described in paragraph (d) of this section. The Code recognizes as a reorganization the amalgamation (occurring in a specified way) of two corporate enterprises under a single corporate structure if there exists among the holders of the stock and securities of either of the old corporations the requisite continuity of interest in the new corporation, but there is not a reorganization if the holders of the stock and securities of the old corporation are merely the holders of short-term notes in the new corporation. In order to exclude transactions not intended to be included, the specifications of the reorganization provisions of the law are precise. Both the terms of the specifications and their underlying assumptions and purposes must be satisfied in order to entitle the taxpayer to the benefit of the exception from the general rule. Accordingly, under the Code, a short-term purchase money note is not a security of a party to a reorganization, an ordinary dividend is to be treated as an ordinary dividend, and a sale is nevertheless to be treated as a sale even though the mechanics of a reorganization have been set up.

(c) **Scope.** The nonrecognition of gain or loss is prescribed for two specifically described types of exchanges, viz: The exchange that is provided for in section 354(a)(1) in which stock or securities in a corporation, a party to a reorganization, are, in pursuance of a plan of reorganization, exchanged for the stock or securities in a corporation, a party to the same reorganization; and the exchange that is provided for in section 361(a) in which a corporation, a party to a reorganization, exchanges property, in pursuance of a plan of reorganization, for stock or securities in another corporation, a party to the same reorganization. Section 368(a)(1) limits the definition of the term "reorganization" to six kinds of transactions and excludes all others. From its context, the term "a party to a reorganization" can only mean a party to a transaction specifically defined as a reorganization by section 368(a). Certain rules respecting boot received in either of the two types of exchanges provided for in section 354(a)(1) and section 361(a) are prescribed in sections 356, 357, and 361(b). A special rule respecting a transfer of property with a liability in excess of its basis is prescribed in section 357(c). Under section 367 a limitation is placed on all these provisions by providing that except under specified conditions foreign corporations shall not be deemed within their scope. The provisions of the Code referred to in this paragraph are inapplicable unless there is a plan of reorganization. A plan of reorganization must contemplate the bona fide execution of one of the transactions specifically described as a reorganization in section 368(a) and for the bona fide consummation of each of the requisite acts under which nonrecognition of gain is claimed. Such transaction and such acts must be an ordinary and necessary incident of the conduct of the enterprise and must provide for a continuation of the enterprise. A scheme, which involves an abrupt departure from normal reorganization procedure in connection with a transaction on which the imposition of tax is imminent, such as a mere device that puts on the form of a corporate reorganization as a disguise for concealing its real character, and the object and accomplishment of which is the consummation of a preconceived plan having no business or corporate purpose, is not a plan of reorganization.

(d) **Continuity of business enterprise—(1) Effective date.** (i) This paragraph (d) applies to acquisitions occurring after January 30, 1981.

(ii) For an asset acquisition, the date of acquisition is the date of transfer. To determine the date of transfer, see § 1.381(b)–1(b).

(iii) For a stock acquisition, the date of acquisition is the date on which the exchange of stock occurs. If all stock is not exchanged on the same date, the date of exchange is the date the exchange of all stock under the plan of reorganization is complete.

(2) **General rule.** Continuity of business enterprise requires that the acquiring corporation (P) either (i) continue the acquired corporation's (T's) historic business or (ii) use a significant portion of T's historic business assets in a business. The application of this general rule to certain transactions, such as mergers of holding companies, will depend on all facts and circumstances. The policy underlying this general rule, which is to ensure that reorganizations are limited to readjustments of continuing interests in property under modified corporate form, provides the guidance necessary to make these facts and circumstances determinations.

(3) **Business continuity.** (i) The continuity of business enterprise requirement is satisfied if P continues T's historic business. The fact P is in the same line of business as T tends to establish the requisite continuity, but is not alone sufficient.

(ii) If T has more than one line of business, continuity of business enterprise requires only that P continue a significant line of business.

(iii) In general, a corporation's historic business is the business it has conducted most recently. However, a corporation's historic business is not one the corporation enters into as part of a plan of reorganization.

(iv) All facts and circumstances are considered in determining the time when the plan comes into existence and in determining whether a line of business is "significant".

(4) Asset continuity. (i) The continuity of business enterprise requirement is satisfied if P uses a significant portion of T's historic business assets in a business.

(ii) A corporation's historic business assets are the assets used in its historic business. Business assets may include stock and securities and intangible operating assets such as good will, patents, and trademarks, whether or not they have a tax basis.

(iii) In general, the determination of the portion of a corporation's assets considered "significant" is based on the relative importance of the assets to operation of the business. However, all other facts and circumstances, such as the net fair market value of those assets, will be considered.

(5) Examples. The following examples illustrate this paragraph (d).

Example (1). T conducts three lines of business: manufacture of synthetic resins, manufacture of chemicals for the textile industry, and distribution of chemicals. The three lines of business are approximately equal in value. On July 1, 1981, T sells the synthetic resin and chemicals distribution businesses to a third party for cash and marketable securities. On December 31, 1981, T transfers all of its assets to P solely for P voting stock. P continues the chemical manufacturing business without interruption. The continuity of business enterprise requirement is met. Continuity of business enterprise requires only that P continue one of T's three significant lines of business.

Example (2). P manufactures computers and T manufactures components for computers. T sells all of its output to P. On January 1, 1981, P decides to buy imported components only. On March 1, 1981, T merges into P. P continues buying imported components but retains T's equipment as a backup source of supply. The use of the equipment as a backup source of supply constitutes use of significant portion of T's historic business assets, thus establishing continuity of business enterprise. P is not required to continue T's business.

Example (3). T is a manufacturer of boys' and men's trousers. On January 1, 1978, as part of a plan of reorganization, T sold all of its assets to a third party for cash and purchased a highly diversified portfolio of stocks and bonds. As part of the plan T operates an investment business until July 1, 1981. On that date, the plan of reorganization culminates in a transfer by T of all its assets to P, a regulated investment company, solely in exchange for P voting stock. The continuity of business enterprise requirement is not met. T's investment activity is not its historic business, and the stocks and bonds are not T's historic business assets.

Example (4). T manufactures children's toys and P distributes steel and allied products. On January 1, 1981, T sells all of its assets to a third party for $100,000

cash and $900,000 in notes. On March 1, 1981, T merges into P. Continuity of business enterprise is lacking. The use of the sales proceeds in P's business is not sufficient.

Example (5). T manufactures farm machinery and P operates a lumber mill. T merges into P. P disposes of T's assets immediately after the merger as part of the plan of reorganization. P does not continue T's farm machinery manufacturing business. Continuity of business enterprise is lacking.

[T.D. 6500, 25 FR 11607, Nov. 26, 1960, as amended by T.D. 7745, 45 FR 86437, Dec. 31, 1980]

§ 1.368–2 Definition of terms.

(a) The application of the term "reorganization" is to be strictly limited to the specific transactions set forth in section 368(a). The term does not embrace the mere purchase by one corporation of the properties of another corporation, for it imports a continuity of interest on the part of the transferor or its shareholders in the properties transferred. If the properties are transferred for cash and deferred payment obligations of the transferee evidenced by short-term notes, the transaction is a sale and not an exchange in which gain or loss is not recognized.

(b)(1) In order to qualify as a reorganization under section 368(a)(1)(A) the transaction must be a merger or consolidation effected pursuant to the corporation laws of the United States or a State or territory, or the District of Columbia.

(2) In order for the transaction to qualify under section 368(a)(1)(A) by reason of the application of section 368(a)(2)(D), one corporation (the acquiring corporation) must acquire substantially all of the properties of another corporation (the acquired corporation) partly or entirely in exchange for stock of a corporation which is in control of the acquiring corporation (the controlling corporation), provided that (i) the transaction would have qualified under section 368(a)(1)(A) if the merger had been into the controlling corporation, and (ii) no stock of the acquiring corporation is used in the transaction. The foregoing test of whether the transaction would have qualified under section 368(a)(1)(A) if the merger had been into the controlling corporation means that the general requirements of a reorganization under section 368(a)(1)(A) (such as a business purpose, continuity of business enterprise, and continuity of interest) must be met in addition to the special requirements of section 368(a)2)(D). Under this test, it is not relevant whether the merger into the controlling corporation could have been effected pursuant to State or Federal corpora-

tion law. The term "substantially all" has the same meaning as it has in section 368(a)(1)C). Although no stock of the acquiring corporation can be used in the transaction, there is no prohibition (other than the continuity of interest requirement) against using other property, such as cash or securities, of either the acquiring corporation or the parent or both. In addition, the controlling corporation may assume liabilities of the acquired corporation without disqualifying the transaction under section 368(a)(2)(D), and for purposes of section 357(a) the controlling corporation is considered a party to the exchange. For example, if the controlling corporation agrees to substitute its stock for stock of the acquired corporation under an outstanding employee stock option agreement, this assumption of liability will not prevent the transaction from qualifying as a reorganization under section 368(a)(2)(D) and the assumption of liability is not treated as money or other property for purposes of section 361(b). Section 368(a)(2)(D) applies whether or not the controlling corporation (or the acquiring corporation) is formed immediately before the merger, in anticipation of the merger, or after preliminary steps have been taken to merge directly into the controlling corporation. Section 368(a)(2)(D) applies only to statutory mergers occurring after October 22, 1968.

(3) For regulations under section 368(a)(2)(E), see paragraph (j) of this section.

(c) In order to qualify as a "reorganization" under section 368(a)(1)(B), the acquisition by the acquiring corporation of stock of another corporation must be in exchange solely for all or a part of the voting stock of the acquiring corporation (or, in the case of transactions occurring after December 31, 1963, solely for all or a part of the voting stock of a corporation which is in control of the acquiring corporation), and the acquiring corporation must be in control of the other corporation immediately after the transaction. If, for example, Corporation X in one transaction exchanges nonvoting preferred stock or bonds in addition to all or a part of its voting stock in the acquisition of stock of Corporation Y, the transaction is not a reorganization under section 368(a)(1)(B). Nor is a transaction a reorganization described in section 368(a)(1)(B) if stock is acquired in exchange for voting stock both of the acquiring corporation and of a corporation which is in control of the acquiring corporation. The acquisition of stock of another corporation by the acquiring corporation solely for its voting stock (or solely for voting stock of a corporation which is

in control of the acquiring corporation) is permitted tax-free even though the acquiring corporation already owns some of the stock of the other corporation. Such an acquisition is permitted taxfree in a single transaction or in a series of transactions taking place over a relatively short period of time such as 12 months. For example, Corporation A purchased 30 percent of the common stock of Corporation W (the only class of stock outstanding) for cash in 1939. On March 1, 1955, Corporation A offers to exchange its own voting stock for all the stock of Corporation W tendered within 6 months from the date of the offer. Within the 6-months' period Corporation A acquires an additional 60 percent of stock of Corporation W solely for its own voting stock, so that it owns 90 percent of the stock of Corporation W. No gain or loss is recognized with respect to the exchanges of stock of Corporation A for stock of Corporation W. For this purpose, it is immaterial whether such exchanges occurred before Corporation A acquired control (80 percent) of Corporation W or after such control was acquired. If Corporation A had acquired 80 percent of the stock of Corporation W for cash in 1939, it could likewise acquire some or all of the remainder of such stock solely in exchange for its own voting stock without recognition of gain or loss.

(d) In order to qualify as a reorganization under section 368(a)(1)(C), the transaction must be one described in subparagraph (1) or (2) of this paragraph:

(1) One corporation must acquire substantially all the properties of another corporation solely in exchange for all or a part of its own voting stock, or solely in exchange for all or a part of the voting stock of a corporation which is in control of the acquiring corporation. For example, Corporation P owns all the stock of Corporation A. All the properties of Corporation W are transferred to Corporation A either solely in exchange for voting stock of Corporation P or solely in exchange for less than 80 percent of the voting stock of Corporation A. Either of such transactions constitutes a reorganization under section 368(a)(1)(C). However, if the properties of Corporation W are acquired in exchange for voting stock of both Corporation P and Corporation A, the transaction will not constitute a reorganization under section 368(a)(1)(C). In determining whether the exchange meets the requirement of "solely for voting stock", the assumption by the acquiring corporation of liabilities of the transferor corporation, or the fact that property acquired from the transferor corpo-

ration is subject to a liability, shall be disregarded. Though such an assumption does not prevent an exchange from being solely for voting stock for the purposes of the definition of a reorganization contained in section 368(a)(1)(C), it may in some cases, however, so alter the character of the transaction as to place the transaction outside the purposes and assumptions of the reorganization provisions. Section 368(a)(1)(C) does not prevent consideration of the effect of an assumption of liabilities on the general character of the transaction but merely provides that the requirement that the exchange be solely for voting stock is satisfied if the only additional consideration is an assumption of liabilities.

(2) One corporation:

(i) Must acquire substantially all of the properties of another corporation in such manner that the acquisition would qualify under (1) above, but for the fact that the acquiring corporation exchanges money, or other property in addition to such voting stock, and

(ii) Must acquire solely for voting stock (either of the acquiring corporation or of a corporation which is in control of the acquiring corporation) properties of the other corporation having a fair market value which is at least 80 percent of the fair market value of all the properties of the other corporation.

(3) For the purposes of subparagraph (2)(ii) only, a liability assumed or to which the properties are subject is considered money paid for the properties. For example, Corporation A has properties with a fair market value of $100,000 and liabilities of $10,000. In exchange for these properties, Corporation Y transfers its own voting stock, assumes the $10,000 liabilities, and pays $8,000 in cash. The transaction is a reorganization even though a part of the properties of Corporation A is acquired for cash. On the other hand, if the properties of Corporation A worth $100,000, were subject to $50,000 in liabilities, an acquisition of all the properties, subject to the liabilities, for any consideration other than solely voting stock would not qualify as a reorganization under this section since the liabilities alone are in excess of 20 percent of the fair market value of the properties. If the transaction would qualify under either subparagraph (1) or (2) of this paragraph and also under section 368(a)(1)(D), such transaction shall not be treated as a reorganization under section 368(a)(1)(C).

(e) A "recapitalization", and therefore a reorganization, takes place if, for example:

(1) A corporation with $200,000 par value of bonds outstanding, instead of paying them off in cash, discharges them by issuing preferred shares to the bondholders;

(2) There is surrendered to a corporation for cancellation 25 percent of its preferred stock in exchange for no par value common stock;

(3) A corporation issues preferred stock, previously authorized but unissued, for outstanding common stock;

(4) An exchange is made of a corporation's outstanding preferred stock, having certain priorities with reference to the amount and time of payment of dividends and the distribution of the corporate assets upon liquidation, for a new issue of such corporation's common stock having no such rights;

(5) An exchange is made of an amount of a corporation's outstanding preferred stock with dividends in arrears for other stock of the corporation. However, if pursuant to such an exchange there is an increase in the proportionate interest of the preferred shareholders in the assets or earnings and profits of the corporation, then under § 1.305–7(c)(2), an amount equal to the lesser of (i) the amount by which the fair market value or liquidation preference, whichever is greater, of the stock received in the exchange (determined immediately following the recapitalization) exceeds the issue price of the preferred stock surrendered, or (ii) the amount of the dividends in arrears, shall be treated under section 305(c) as a deemed distribution to which sections 305(b)(4) and 301 apply.

(f) The term "a party to a reorganization" includes a corporation resulting from a reorganization, and both corporations, in a transaction qualifying as a reorganization where one corporation acquires stock or properties of another corporation. A corporation remains a party to the reorganization although it transfers all or part of the assets acquired to a controlled subsidiary. A corporation controlling an acquiring corporation is a party to the reorganization when the stock of such controlling corporation is used in the acquisition of properties. Both corporations are parties to the reorganization if, under statutory authority, Corporation A is merged into Corporation B. All three of the corporations are parties to the reorganization if, pursuant to statutory authority, Corporation C and Corporation D are consolidated into Corporation E. Both corporations are parties to the reorganization if Corporation F transfers substantially all its assets to Corporation G in exchange for all or a part of the voting stock of Corporation G. All three corporations are parties to the reorganization if Corporation H transfers substantially all its assets to Corporation K in exchange for all or a part of the voting stock of Corporation L, which is in control of Corporation K. Both corporations are parties to the reorganization if Corporation M transfers all or part of its assets to Corporation N in exchange for all or a part of the stock and securities of Corporation N, but only if (1) immediately after such transfer, Corporation M, or one or more of its shareholders (including persons who were shareholders immediately before such transfer), or any combination thereof, is in control of Corporation N, and (2) in pursuance of the plan, the stock and securities of Corporation N are transferred or distributed by Corporation M in a transaction in which gain or loss is not recognized under section 354 or 355, or is recognized only to the extent provided in section 356. Both Corporation O and Corporation P, but not Corporation S, are parties to the reorganization if Corporation O acquires stock of Corporation P from Corporation S in exchange solely for a part of the voting stock of Corporation O, if (1) the stock of Corporation P does not constitute substantially all of the assets of Corporation S, (2) Corporation S is not in control of Corporation O immediately after the acquisition, and (3) Corporation O is in control of Corporation P immediately after the acquisition.

(g) The term "plan of reorganization" has reference to a consummated transaction specifically defined as a reorganization under section 368(a). The term is not to be construed as broadening the definition of "reorganization" as set forth in section 368(a), but is to be taken as limiting the nonrecognition of gain or loss to such exchanges or distributions as are directly a part of the transaction specifically described as a reorganization in section 368(a). Moreover, the transaction, or series of transactions, embraced in a plan of reorganization must not only come within the specific language of section 368(a), but the readjustments involved in the exchanges or distributions effected in the consummation thereof must be undertaken for reasons germane to the continuance of the business of a corporation a party to the reorganization. Section 368(a) contemplates genuine corporate reorganizations which are designed to effect a readjustment of continuing interests under modified corporate forms.

(h) As used in section 368, as well as in other provisions of the Internal Revenue Code, if the context so requires, the conjunction "or" denotes both the conjunctive and the disjunctive, and the singular includes the plural. For example, the provisions of the statute are complied with if "stock and securities" are received in exchange as well as if "stock or securities" are received.

(i) [Reserved]

(j)(1) This paragraph (j) prescribes rules relating to the application of section 368(a)(2)(E). Section 368(a)(2)(E) applies to statutory mergers occurring after December 31, 1970.

(2) Section 368(a)(2)(E) does not apply to a consolidation.

(3) A transaction otherwise qualifying under section 368(a)(1)(A) is not disqualified by reason of the fact that stock of a corporation (the controlling corporation) which before the merger was in control of the merged corporation is used in the transaction, if the conditions of section 368(a)(2)(E) are satisfied. Those conditions are as follows:

(i) In the transaction, shareholders of the surviving corporation must surrender stock in exchange for voting stock of the controlling corporation. Further, the stock so surrendered must constitute control of the surviving corporation. Control is defined in section 368(c). The amount of stock constituting control is measured immediately before the transaction. For purposes of this subdivision (i), stock in the surviving corporation which is surrendered in the transaction (by any shareholder except the controlling corporation) in exchange for consideration furnished by the surviving corporation (and not by the controlling corporation of the merged corporation) is considered not to be outstanding immediately before the transaction. For effect on "substantially all" test of consideration furnished by the surviving corporation, see paragraph (j)(3)(iii) of this section.

(ii) Except as provided in paragraph (j)(4) of this section, the controlling corporation must control the surviving corporation immediately after the transaction.

(iii) After the transaction, except as provided in paragraph (j)(4) of this section, the surviving corporation must hold substantially all of its own properties and substantially all of the properties of the merged corporation (other than stock of the controlling corporation distributed in the transaction). The term "substantially all" has the same meaning as in section 368(a)(1)(C). The "substantially all" test applies separately to the merged corporation and to the surviving corporation. In applying the "substantially all" test to the surviving corporation, consideration furnished in the transaction by the surviving corporation in exchange for its stock is property of the surviving corporation which it does not hold after the transaction. In applying the "substantially all" test to the merged corporation, assets transferred from the controlling corporation to the merged corporation in pursuance of the plan of reorganization are not taken into account. Thus, for example, money transferred from the controlling corporation to the merged corporation to be used for the following purposes is not taken into account for purposes of the "substantially all" test:

(A) To pay additional consideration to shareholders of the surviving corporation;

(B) To pay dissenting shareholders of the surviving corporation;

(C) To pay creditors of the surviving corporation;

(D) To pay reorganization expenses; or

(E) To enable the merged corporation to satisfy state minimum capitalization requirements (where the money is returned to the controlling corporation as part of the transaction).

(4) A transaction qualifying under section 368(a)(1)(A) by reason of the application of section 368(a)(2)(E) is not disqualified merely because part or all of the stock of the surviving corporation is transferred to a corporation controlled by the controlling corporation, or because part or all of the assets of the surviving corporation or the merged corporation are transferred to a corporation controlled by the surviving corporation. See section 368(a)(2)(C).

(5) The controlling corporation may assume liabilities of the surviving corporation without disqualifying the transaction under section 368(a)(2)(E). An assumption of liabilities of the surviving corporation by the controlling corporation is a contribution to capital by the controlling corporation to the surviving corporation. If, in pursuance of the plan of reorganization, securities of the surviving corporation are exchanged for securities of the controlling corporation, or for other securities of the surviving corporation, see sections 354 and 356.

(6) In applying section 368(a)(2)(E), it makes no difference if the merged corporation is an existing corporation, or is formed immediately before the merger, in anticipation of the merger, or after preliminary steps have been taken to otherwise acquire control of the surviving corporation.

(7) The following examples illustrate the application of this paragraph (j). In each of the examples, Corporation P owns all of the stock of Corporation S and, except as otherwise stated, Corporation T has outstanding 1,000 shares of common stock and no shares of any other class. In each of the examples, it is also assumed that the transaction qualifies under section 368(a)(1)(A) if the conditions of section 368(a)(2)(E) are satisfied.

Example (1). P owns no T stock. On January 1, 1981, S merges into T. In the merger, T's shareholders surrender 950 shares of common stock in exchange for P voting stock. The holders of the other 50 shares (who dissent from the merger) are paid in cash with funds supplied by P. After the transaction, T holds all of its own assets and all of S's assets. Based on these facts, the transaction qualifies under section 368(a)(1)(A) by reason of the application of section 368(a)(2)(E). In the transaction, former shareholders of T surrender, in exchange for P voting stock, an amount of T stock (950/1,000 shares or 95 percent) which constitutes control of T.

Example (2). The facts are the same as in example (1) except that holders of 100 shares in corporation T, who dissented from the merger, are paid in cash with funds supplied by T (and not by P or S) and in the merger. T's remaining shareholders surrender 720 shares of common stock in exchange for P voting stock and 180 shares of common stock for cash supplied by P. The requirements of section 368(a)(2)(E)(ii) are satisfied since, in the transaction, former shareholders of T surrender, in exchange for P voting stock, an amount of T stock (720/900 shares or 80 percent) which constitutes control of T. The T stock surrendered in exchange for consideration furnished by T is not considered outstanding for purposes of determining whether the amount of T stock surrendered by T shareholders for P stock constitutes control of T.

Example (3). T has outstanding 1,000 shares of common stock, 100 shares of nonvoting preferred stock, and no shares of any other class. On January 1, 1981, S merges into T. Prior to the merger, as part of the transaction, T distributes its own cash in redemption of the 100 shares of preferred stock. In the transaction, T's remaining shareholders surrender their 1,000 shares of common stock in exchange for P voting stock. The requirements of section 368(a)(2)(E)(ii) are satisfied since, in the transaction, former shareholders of T surrender, in exchange for P voting stock, an amount of T stock (1,000/1,000 shares or 100 percent) which constitutes control of T. The preferred stock surrendered in exchange for consideration furnished by T is not considered outstanding for purposes of determining whether the amount of T stock surrendered by T shareholders for P stock constitutes control of T. However, the consideration furnished by T for its stock is property of T which T does not hold after the transaction for purposes of the substantially all test in paragraph (j)(3)(iii) of this section.

Example (4). On January 1, 1971, P purchased 201 shares of T's stock. On January 1, 1981, S merges into T. In the merger, T's shareholders (other than P) surrender 799 shares of T stock in exchange for P voting stock. Based on these facts, in the transaction, former shareholders of T do not surrender, in exchange for P voting stock, an amount of T stock which constitutes control of T (799/1,000 shares being less than 80 percent). Therefore, the transaction does not qualify under section 368(a)(1)(A). However, if S is a transitory corporation, formed solely for purposes of effectuating the transaction, the transaction may qualify as a reorganization described in section 368(a)(1)(B) provided all of the applicable requirements are satisfied.

Example (5). On January 1, 1971, P purchased 200 shares of T's stock. On January 1, 1981, S merges into T. Prior to the merger, as part of the transaction, T distributes its own cash in redemption of 1 share of T stock from a T shareholder other than P. In the merger, T's remaining shareholders (other than P) surrender 799 shares of T stock in exchange for P voting stock. Based on these facts, in the transaction, former shareholders of T do not surrender, in exchange for P voting stock, an amount of T stock which constitutes control of T (799/999 shares being less than 80 percent). Therefore, the transaction does not qualify under section 368(a)(1)(A). However, if S is a transitory corporation, formed for purposes of effectuating the transaction, the transaction may qualify as a reorganization described in section 368(a)(1)(B) provided all of the applicable requirements are satisfied.

Example (6). The stock of S has a value of $25,000. The stock of T has a value of $75,000. On January 1, 1984, S merges into T. In the merger, T's shareholders surrender all of their T stock in exchange for P voting stock. After the transaction, T holds all of its own assets and all of S's assets. Based on these facts, the transaction qualifies under section 368(a)(1)(A) by reason of the application of section 368(a)(2)(E). In the transaction, former shareholders of T surrender, in exchange for P voting stock, an amount of T stock (1,000/1,000 shares or 100 percent) which constitutes control of T. The stock of T received by P in exchange for P's prior interest in S is not taken into account for purposes of section 368(a)(2)(E)(ii) since the amount of T stock constituting control of T is measured before the transaction.

Example (7). The stock of T has a value of $75,000. On January 1, 1984, S merges into T. In the merger, T's shareholders surrender all of their T stock in exchange for P voting stock. As part of the transaction, P contributes $25,000 to T in exchange for new shares of T stock. None of the cash received by T is distributed or otherwise paid out to former T shareholders. After the transaction, T holds all of its own assets and all of S's assets. Based on these facts, the transaction qualifies under section 368(a)(1)(A) by reason of the application of section 368(a)(2)(E). In the transaction, former shareholders of T surrender, in exchange for P voting stock, an amount of T stock (1,000/1,000 shares or 100 percent) which constitutes control of T. The T stock received by P in exchange for its contribution to T is not taken into account for purposes of section 368(a)(2)(E)(ii) since the amount of T stock constituting control of T is measured before the transaction.

Example (8). The facts are the same as in example (7) except that, as part of the transaction, corporation R, instead of P, contributes $25,000 to T in exchange for T stock. Based on these facts, the transaction does not qualify under section 368(a)(1)(A) by reason of section 368(a)(2)(E) since P does not control T immediately after the transaction.

Example (9). T stock has a value of $75,000. P owns 500 shares (½) of that stock with a value of $37,500. The stock of S has a value of $125,000. On January 1, 1984, S merges into T. In the merger, T's shareholders (other than P) surrender their T stock in exchange for P voting stock. Based on these facts, in the transaction, former shareholders of T do not surrender, in exchange for P voting stock, an amount of T stock which constitutes control of T (500/1,000 shares being less than 80 percent). Therefore, the transaction does not qualify under section 368(a)(1)(A). The stock of T received by P in exchange for P's prior interest in S does not contribute to satisfaction of the requirement of section 368(a)(2)(E)(ii).

[T.D. 6500, 25 FR 11607, Nov. 26, 1960, as amended by T.D. 7281, 38 FR 18540, July 12, 1973; T.D. 7422, 41 FR 26570, June 28, 1976; T.D. 8059, 50 FR 42689, Oct. 22, 1985; 51 FR 6400, Feb. 24, 1986]

§ 1.368–3 Records to be kept and information to be filed with returns.

(a) The plan of reorganization must be adopted by each of the corporations parties thereto; and the adoption must be shown by the acts of its duly constituted responsible officers, and appear upon the official records of the corporation. Each corporation, a party to a reorganization, shall file as a part of its return for its taxable year within which the reorganization occurred a complete statement of all facts pertinent to the nonrecognition of gain or loss in connection with the reorganization, including:

(1) A copy of the plan of reorganization, together with a statement, executed under the penalties of perjury, showing in full the purposes thereof and in detail all transactions incident to, or pursuant to, the plan.

(2) A complete statement of the cost or other basis of all property, including all stock or securities, transferred incident to the plan.

(3) A statement of the amount of stock or securities and other property or money received from the exchange, including a statement of all distributions or other disposition made thereof. The amount of each kind of stock or securities and other property received shall be stated on the basis of the fair market value thereof at the date of the exchange.

(4) A statement of the amount and nature of any liabilities assumed upon the exchange, and the

amount and nature of any liabilities to which any of the property acquired in the exchange is subject.

(b) Every taxpayer, other than a corporation a party to the reorganization, who receives stock or securities and other property or money upon a tax-free exchange in connection with a corporate reorganization shall incorporate in his income tax return for the taxable year in which the exchange takes place a complete statement of all facts pertinent to the nonrecognition of gain or loss upon such exchange including:

(1) A statement of the cost or other basis of the stock or securities transferred in the exchange, and

(2) A statement in full of the amount of stock or securities and other property or money received from the exchange, including any liabilities assumed upon the exchange, and any liabilities to which property received is subject. The amount of each kind of stock or securities and other property (other than liabilities assumed upon the exchange) received shall be set forth upon the basis of the fair market value thereof at the date of the exchange.

(c) Permanent records in substantial form shall be kept by every taxpayer who participates in a tax-free exchange in connection with a corporate reorganization showing the cost or other basis of the transferred property and the amount of stock or securities and other property or money received (including any liabilities assumed on the exchange, or any liabilities to which any of the properties received were subject), in order to facilitate the determination of gain or loss from a subsequent disposition of such stock or securities and other property received from the exchange.

[T.D. 6500, 25 FR 11607, Nov. 26, 1960, as amended by T.D. 6622, 27 FR 11918, Dec. 4, 1962]

DEFERRED COMPENSATION, ETC.

Pension, Profit-Sharing, Stock Bonus Plans, Etc.

§ 1.401–1 Qualified pension, profit-sharing, and stock bonus plans.

(a) Introduction. (1) Sections 401 through 405 relate to pension, profit-sharing, stock bonus, and annuity plans, compensation paid under a deferred-payment plan, and bond purchase plans. Section 401(a) prescribes the requirements which must be met for qualification of a trust forming part of a pension, profit-sharing, or stock bonus plan.

(2) A qualified pension, profit-sharing, or stock bonus plan is a definite written program and arrangement which is communicated to the employees and which is established and maintained by an employer—

(i) In the case of a pension plan, to provide for the livelihood of the employees or their beneficiaries after the retirement of such employees through the payment of benefits determined without regard to profits (see paragraph (b)(1)(i) of this section);

(ii) In the case of a profit-sharing plan, to enable employees or their beneficiaries to participate in the profits of the employer's trade or business, or in the profits of an affiliated employer who is entitled to deduct his contributions to the plan under section 404(a)(3)(B), pursuant to a definite formula for allocating the contributions and for distributing the funds accumulated under the plan (see paragraph (b)(1)(ii) of this section); and

(iii) In the case of a stock bonus plan, to provide employees or their beneficiaries benefits similar to those of profit-sharing plans, except that such benefits are distributable in stock of the employer, and that the contributions by the employer are not necessarily dependent upon profits. If the employer's contributions are dependent upon profits, the plan may enable employees or their beneficiaries to participate not only in the profits of the employer, but also in the profits of an affiliated employer who is entitled to deduct his contributions to the plan under section 404(a)(3)(B) (see paragraph (b)(1)(iii) of this section).

(3) In order for a trust forming part of a pension, profit-sharing, or stock bonus plan to constitute a qualified trust under section 401(a), the following tests must be met:

(i) It must be created or organized in the United States, as defined in section 7701(a)(9), and it must be maintained at all times as a domestic trust in the United States;

(ii) It must be part of a pension, profit-sharing, or stock bonus plan established by an employer for the exclusive benefit of his employees or their beneficiaries (see paragraph (b)(2) through (5) of this section);

(iii) It must be formed or availed of for the purpose of distributing to the employees or their beneficiaries the corpus and income of the fund accumulated by the trust in accordance with the plan, and, in the case of a plan which covers (as defined in paragraph (a)(2) of § 1.401–10) any self-employed individual, the time and method of such distribution must satisfy the requirements of section 401(a)(9) with respect to each employee covered by the plan (see paragraph (e) of § 1.401–11);

(iv) It must be impossible under the trust instrument at any time before the satisfaction of all liabilities with respect to employees and their beneficiaries under the trust, for any part of the corpus or income to be used for, or diverted to, purposes other than for the exclusive benefit of the employees or their beneficiaries (see § 1.401–2);

(v) It must be part of a plan which benefits prescribed percentages of the employees, or which benefits such employees as qualify under a classification set up by the employer and found by the Commissioner not to be discriminatory in favor of certain specified classes of employees (see § 1.401–3 and, in addition, see § 1.401–12 for special rules as to plans covering owner-employees);

(vi) It must be part of a plan under which contributions or benefits do not discriminate in favor of certain specified classes of employees (see § 1.401–4);

(vii) It must be part of a plan which provides the nonforfeitable rights described in section 401(a)(7) (see § 1.401–6);

(viii) If the trust forms part of a pension plan, the plan must provide that forfeitures must not be applied to increase the benefits any employee would receive under such plan (see § 1.401–7);

(b) General rules. (1)(i) A pension plan within the meaning of section 401(a) is a plan established and maintained by an employer primarily to provide systematically for the payment of definitely determinable benefits to his employees over a period of years, usually for life, after retirement. Retirement benefits generally are measured by, and based on, such factors as years of service and compensation received by the employees. The determination of the amount of retirement benefits and the contributions to provide such benefits are not dependent upon profits. Benefits are not definitely determinable if funds arising from forfeitures on termination of service, or other reason,

may be used to provide increased benefits for the remaining participants (see § 1.401–7, relating to the treatment of forfeitures under a qualified pension plan). A plan designed to provide benefits for employees or their beneficiaries to be paid upon retirement or over a period of years after retirement will, for the purposes of section 401(a), be considered a pension plan if the employer contributions under the plan can be determined actuarially on the basis of definitely determinable benefits, or, as in the case of money purchase pension plans, such contributions are fixed without being geared to profits. A pension plan may provide for the payment of a pension due to disability and may also provide for the payment of incidental death benefits through insurance or otherwise. However, a plan is not a pension plan if it provides for the payment of benefits not customarily included in a pension plan such as layoff benefits or benefits for sickness, accident, hospitalization, or medical expenses (except medical benefits described in section 401(h) as defined in paragraph (a) of § 1.401–14).

(ii) A profit-sharing plan is a plan established and maintained by an employer to provide for the participation in his profits by his employees or their beneficiaries. The plan must provide a definite predetermined formula for allocating the contributions made to the plan among the participants and for distributing the funds accumulated under the plan after a fixed number of years, the attainment of a stated age, or upon the prior occurrence of some event such as layoff, illness, disability, retirement, death, or severance of employment. A formula for allocating the contributions among the participants is definite if, for example, it provides for an allocation in proportion to the basic compensation of each participant. A plan (whether or not it contains a definite predetermined formula for determining the profits to be shared with the employees) does not qualify under section 401(a) if the contributions to the plan are made at such times or in such amounts that the plan in operation discriminates in favor of officers, shareholders, persons whose principal duties consist in supervising the work of other employees, or highly compensated employees. For the rules with respect to discrimination, see §§ 1.401–3 and 1.401–4. A profit-sharing plan within the meaning of section 401 is primarily a plan of deferred compensation, but the amounts allocated to the account of a participant may be used to provide for him or his family incidental life or accident or health insurance.

(iii) A stock bonus plan is a plan established and maintained by an employer to provide benefits similar to those of a profit-sharing plan, except that the contributions by the employer are not necessarily dependent upon profits and the benefits are distributable in stock of the employer company. For the purpose of allocating and distributing the stock of the employer which is to be shared among his employees or their beneficiaries, such a plan is subject to the same requirements as a profit-sharing plan.

* * *

(2) The term "plan" implies a permanent as distinguished from a temporary program. Thus, although the employer may reserve the right to change or terminate the plan, and to discontinue contributions thereunder, the abandonment of the plan for any reason other than business necessity within a few years after it has taken effect will be evidence that the plan from its inception was not a bona fide program for the exclusive benefit of employees in general. Especially will this be true if, for example, a pension plan is abandoned soon after pensions have been fully funded for persons in favor of whom discrimination is prohibited under section 401(a). The permanency of the plan will be indicated by all of the surrounding facts and circumstances, including the likelihood of the employer's ability to continue contributions as provided under the plan. In the case of a profit-sharing plan, other than a profit-sharing plan which covers employees and owner-employees (see section 401(d)(2)(B)), it is not necessary that the employer contribute every year or that he contribute the same amount or contribute in accordance with the same ratio every year. However, merely making a single or occasional contribution out of profits for employees does not establish a plan of profit-sharing. To be a profit-sharing plan, there must be recurring and substantial contributions out of profits for the employees. In the event a plan is abandoned, the employer should promptly notify the district director, stating the circumstances which led to the discontinuance of the plan.

(3) If the plan is so designed as to amount to a subterfuge for the distribution of profits to shareholders, it will not qualify as a plan for the exclusive benefit of employees even though other employees who are not shareholders are also included under the plan. The plan must benefit the employees in general, although it need not provide benefits for all of the employees. Among the employees to be benefited may be persons who are officers and shareholders. However, a plan is not for the exclusive benefit of employees in general if, by any device whatever, it discriminates either in eligibility requirements, contributions, or benefits in favor of employees who are officers, shareholders, persons whose principal duties consist in supervising the work of other employees, or the highly compensated employees. See section 401(a)(3), (4), and (5). Similarly, a stock bonus or profit-sharing plan is not a plan for the exclusive benefit of employees in general if the funds therein may be used to relieve the employer from contributing to a pension plan operating concurrently and covering the same employees. All of the surrounding and attendant circumstances and the details of the plan will be indicative of whether it is a bona fide stock bonus, pension, or profit-sharing plan for the exclusive benefit of employees in general. The law is concerned not only with the form of a plan but also with its effects in operation. For example, section 401(a)(5) specifies certain provisions which of themselves are not discriminatory. However, this does not mean that a plan containing these provisions may not be discriminatory in actual operation.

(4) A plan is for the exclusive benefit of employees or their beneficiaries even though it may cover former employees as well as present employees and employees who are temporarily on leave, as, for example, in the Armed Forces of the United States. A plan covering only former employees may qualify under section 401(a) if it complies with the provisions of section 401(a)(3)(B), with respect to coverage, and section 401(a)(4), with respect to contributions and benefits, as applied to all of the former employees. The term "beneficiaries" of an employee within the meaning of section 401 includes the estate of the employee, dependents of the employee, persons who are the natural objects of the employee's bounty, and any persons designated by the employee to share in the benefits of the plan after the death of the employee.

(5)(i) No specific limitations are provided in section 401(a) with respect to investments which may be made by the trustees of a trust qualifying under section 401(a). Generally, the contributions may be used by the trustees to purchase any investments permitted by the trust agreement to the extent allowed by local law. However, such a trust will be subject to tax under section 511 with respect to any "unrelated business taxable income" (as defined in section 512) realized by it from its investments.

* * *

[T.D. 6500, 25 FR 11670, Nov. 26, 1960, as amended by T.D. 6675, 28 FR 10118, Sept. 17, 1963; T.D. 6722, 29 FR 5071, April 14, 1964; T.D. 7168, 37 FR 5024, March 9, 1972; T.D. 7428, 41 FR 34619, Aug. 16, 1976]

§ 1.401(a)-1 Post-ERISA qualified plans and qualified trusts; in general.

* * *

(b) Requirements for pension plans—(1) Definitely determinable benefits. (i) In order for a pension plan to be a qualified plan under section 401(a), the plan must be established and maintained by an employer primarily to provide systematically for the payment of definitely determinable benefits to its employees over a period of years, usually for life, after retirement.

* * *

[T.D. 7748, 46 FR 1695, Jan. 7, 1981]

ACCOUNTING PERIODS AND METHODS OF ACCOUNTING

Accounting Periods

§ 1.441-1 Period for computation of taxable income.

(a) Computation of taxable income. Taxable income shall be computed and a return shall be made for a period known as the "taxable year." For rules relating to methods of accounting, the taxable year for which items of gross income are included and deductions are taken, inventories, and adjustments, see parts II and III (section 446 and following), subchapter E, chapter 1 of the Code, and the regulations thereunder.

(b) Taxable year. (1) The term "taxable year" means—

(i) The taxpayer's annual accounting period, if it is a calendar year or a fiscal year;

(ii) The calendar year, if section 441(g) (relating to taxpayers who keep no books or have no accounting period) applies; or

(iii) The period for which the return is made, if the return is made under section 443 for a period of less than 12 months, referred to as a "short period."

(2) A taxable year may not cover a period of more than 12 calendar months except in the case of a 52–53-week taxable year. See § 1.441–2.

(3) A new taxpayer in his first return may adopt any taxable year which meets the requirements of section 441 and this section without obtaining prior approval. The first taxable year of a new taxpayer must be adopted on or before the time prescribed by law (not including extensions) for the filing of the return for such taxable year. However, for rules applicable to the adoption of a taxable year by a partnership, see paragraph (b)(2)

of § 1.442–1, section 706(b), and paragraph (b) of § 1.706–1. * * *

(4) After a taxpayer has adopted a calendar or a fiscal year, he must use it in computing his taxable income and making his returns for all subsequent years unless prior approval is obtained from the Commissioner to make a change or unless a change is otherwise permitted under the internal revenue laws or regulations. See section 442 and § 1.442–1. For rules applicable to changes in taxable years of partners and partnerships, see also section 706(b) and paragraph (b) of § 1.706–1.

(c) Annual accounting period. The term "annual accounting period" means the annual period (calendar year or fiscal year) on the basis of which the taxpayer regularly computes his income in keeping his books.

(d) Calendar year. The term "calendar year" means a period of 12 months ending on December 31. A taxpayer who has not established a fiscal year must make his return on the basis of a calendar year.

(e) Fiscal year. (1) The term "fiscal year" means—

(i) A period of 12 months ending on the last day of any month other than December, or

(ii) The 52–53-week annual accounting period, if such period has been elected by the taxpayer.

(2) A fiscal year will be recognized only if it is established as the annual accounting period of the taxpayer and only if the books of the taxpayer are kept in accordance with such fiscal year.

* * *

(g) No books kept; no accounting period. Except in the case of a short period under section 443, the taxpayer's taxable year shall be the calendar year if—

(1) The taxpayer keeps no books;

(2) The taxpayer does not have an annual accounting period (as defined in section 441(c) and paragraph (c) of this section); or

(3) The taxpayer has an annual accounting period, but such period does not qualify as a fiscal year (as defined in section 441(e) and paragraph (e) of this section).

For the purposes of subparagraph (1) of this paragraph, the keeping of books does not require that records be bound. Records which are sufficient to reflect income adequately and clearly on the basis of an annual accounting period will be regarded as the keeping of books. A taxpayer whose taxable year is required to be a calendar year under section 441(g) and this paragraph may not adopt a fiscal year without obtaining prior approval from the Commissioner since such adoption is treated as a change of annual accounting period. See section 442 and paragraph (a)(2) of § 1.442–1.

[T.D. 6500, 25 FR 11701, Nov. 26, 1960, as amended by T.D. 7244, 37 FR 28897, Dec. 30, 1972; T.D. 7767, 46 FR 11264, Feb. 6, 1981; T.D. 7936, 49 FR 2104, Jan. 18, 1984]

§ 1.442–1 Change of annual accounting period.

(a) Manner of effecting such change—(1) In general. If a taxpayer wishes to change his annual accounting period (as defined in section 441(c)) and adopt a new taxable year (as defined in section 441(b)), he must obtain prior approval from the Commissioner by application, as provided in paragraph (b) of this section, or the change must be authorized under the Income Tax Regulations. A new taxpayer who adopts an annual accounting period as provided in section 441 and §§ 1.441–1 or 1.441–2 need not secure the permission of the Commissioner under section 442 and this section. However, see subparagraph (2) of this paragraph. For adoption of and changes to or from a 52–53-week taxable year, see section 441(f) and § 1.441–2; for adoption of and changes in the taxable years of partners and partnerships, see paragraph (b)(2) of this section, section 706(b) and paragraph (b) of § 1.706–1; for special rules relating to certain corporations, subsidiary corporations, and newly mar-

ried couples, see paragraphs (c), (d), and (e), respectively, of this section. * * *

(2) Taxpayers to whom section 441(g) applies. Section 441(g) provides that if a taxpayer keeps no books, does not have an annual accounting period, or has an accounting period which does not meet the requirements for a fiscal year, his taxable year shall be the calendar year. If section 441(g) applies to a taxpayer, the adoption of a fiscal year will be treated as a change in his annual accounting period under section 442. Therefore, such fiscal year can become the taxpayer's taxable year only with the approval of the Commissioner. Approval of any such change will be denied unless the taxpayer agrees in his application to establish and maintain accurate records of his taxable income for the short period involved in the change and for the fiscal year proposed. The keeping of records which adequately and clearly reflect income for the taxable year constitutes the keeping of books within the meaning of section 441(g) and paragraph (g) of § 1.441–1.

(b) Prior approval of the Commissioner—(1) In general. In order to secure prior approval of a change of a taxpayer's annual accounting period, the taxpayer must file an application on Form 1128 with the Commissioner of Internal Revenue, Washington, D. C. 20224, to effect the change of accounting period. If the short period involved in the change ends after December 31, 1973, such form shall be filed on or before the 15th day of the second calendar month following the close of such short period; if such short period ends before January 1, 1974, such form shall be filed on or before the last day of the first calendar month following the close of such short period. Approval will not be granted unless the taxpayer and the Commissioner agree to the terms, conditions, and adjustments under which the change will be effected. In general, a change of annual accounting period will be approved where the taxpayer established a substantial business purpose for making the change. In determining whether a taxpayer has established a substantial business purpose for making the change, consideration will be given to all the facts and circumstances relating to the change, including the tax consequences resulting therefrom. Among the nontax factors that will be considered in determining whether a substantial business purpose has been established is the effect of the change on the taxpayer's annual cycle of business activity. The agreement between the taxpayer and the Commissioner under which the change will be effected shall, in appropriate cases, provide terms, conditions, and adjustments necessary to prevent a substantial distortion of income which otherwise would result from the change. The following are examples of effects of the change which would substantially distort income: (i) Deferral of a substantial portion of the taxpayer's income, or shifting of a substantial portion of deductions, from one year to another so as to reduce substantially the taxpayer's tax liability; (ii) causing a similar deferral or shifting in the case of any other person, such as a partner, a beneficiary, or a shareholder in an electing small business corporation as defined in section 1371(b); or (iii) creating a short period in which there is either (a) a substantial net operating loss, or (b) in the case of an electing small business corporation, a substantial portion of amounts treated as long-term capital gain. Even though a substantial business purpose is not established, the Commissioner in appropriate cases may permit a husband or wife to change his or her taxable year in order to secure the benefits of section 1(a) (relating to tax in case of a joint return). * * *

(2) **Partnerships and partners.** (i) A newly-formed partnership may adopt a taxable year which is the same as the taxable year of all its principal partners (or is the same taxable year to which its principal partners who do not have such taxable year concurrently change) without securing prior approval from the Commissioner. If all its principal partners are not on the same taxable year, a newly-formed partnership may adopt a calendar year without securing prior approval from the Commissioner. If a newly-formed partnership wishes to adopt a taxable year that does not qualify under the preceding two sentences, the adoption of such year requires the prior approval of the Commissioner in accordance with section 706(b)(1) and paragraph (b) of § 1.706–1. An existing partnership may change its taxable year without securing prior approval from the Commissioner if all its principal partners have the same taxable year to which the partnership changes, or if all its principal partners who do not have such a taxable year concurrently change to such taxable year. In any other case, an existing partnership may not change its taxable year unless it secures the prior approval of the Commissioner in accordance with paragraph (b)(1) of this section and section 706(b)(1) and paragraph (b) of § 1.706–1.

(ii) A partner may change his taxable year only if he secures the prior approval of the Commissioner in accordance with paragraph (b)(1) of this section.

* * *

[T.D. 6500, 25 FR 11703, Nov. 26, 1960, as amended by T.D. 6614, 27 FR 10098, Oct. 13, 1962; T.D. 7235, 37 FR 28624, Dec. 28, 1972; T.D. 7244, 37 FR 28897, Dec. 30, 1972; T.D. 7286, 38 FR 26911, Sept. 27, 1973; T.D. 7323, 39 FR 34409, Sept. 25, 1974; T.D. 7470, 42 FR 12178, March 3, 1977; T.D. 7767, 45 FR 11265, Feb. 6, 1981; T.D. 7936, 49 FR 2106, Jan. 18, 1984]

Methods of Accounting

§ 1.446–1 General rule for methods of accounting.

(a) **General rule.** (1) Section 446(a) provides that taxable income shall be computed under the method of accounting on the basis of which a taxpayer regularly computes his income in keeping his books. The term "method of accounting" includes not only the overall method of accounting of the taxpayer but also the accounting treatment of any item. Examples of such over all methods are the cash receipts and disbursements method, an accrual method, combinations of such methods, and combinations of the foregoing with various methods provided for the accounting treatment of special items. These methods of accounting for special items include the accounting treatment prescribed for research and experimental expenditures, soil and water conservation expenditures, depreciation, net operating losses, etc. Except for deviations permitted or required by such special accounting treatment, taxable income shall be computed under the method of accounting on the basis of which the taxpayer regularly computes his income in keeping his books. For requirement respecting the adoption or change of accounting method, see section 446(e) and paragraph (e) of this section.

(2) It is recognized that no uniform method of accounting can be prescribed for all taxpayers. Each taxpayer shall adopt such forms and systems as are, in his judgment, best suited to his needs. However, no method of accounting is acceptable unless, in the opinion of the Commissioner, it clearly reflects income. A method of accounting which

reflects the consistent application of generally accepted accounting principles in a particular trade or business in accordance with accepted conditions or practices in that trade or business will ordinarily be regarded as clearly reflecting income, provided all items of gross income and expense are treated consistently from year to year.

(3) Items of gross income and expenditures which are elements in the computation of taxable income need not be in the form of cash. It is sufficient that such items can be valued in terms of money. For general rules relating to the taxable year for inclusion of income and for taking deductions, see sections 451 and 461, and the regulations thereunder.

(4) Each taxpayer is required to make a return of his taxable income for each taxable year and must maintain such accounting records as will enable him to file a correct return. See section 6001 and the regulations thereunder. Accounting records include the taxpayer's regular books of account and such other records and data as may be necessary to support the entries on his books of account and on his return, as for example, a reconciliation of any differences between such books and his return. The following are among the essential features that must be considered in maintaining such records:

(i) In all cases in which the production, purchase, or sale of merchandise of any kind is an income-producing factor, merchandise on hand (including finished goods, work in process, raw materials, and supplies) at the beginning and end of the year shall be taken into account in computing the taxable income of the year. (For rules relating to computation of inventories, see sections 471 and 472, and the regulations thereunder.)

(ii) Expenditures made during the year shall be properly classified as between capital and expense. For example, expenditures for such items as plant and equipment, which have a useful life extending substantially beyond the taxable year, shall be charged to a capital account and not to an expense account.

(iii) In any case in which there is allowable with respect to an asset a deduction for depreciation, amortization, or depletion, any expenditures (other than ordinary repairs) made to restore the asset or prolong its useful life shall be added to the asset account or charged against the appropriate reserve.

(b) **Exceptions.** (1) If the taxpayer does not regularly employ a method of accounting which clearly reflects his income, the computation of taxable income shall be made in a manner which, in the opinion of the Commissioner, does clearly reflect income.

(2) A taxpayer whose sole source of income is wages need not keep formal books in order to have an accounting method. Tax returns, copies thereof, or other records may be sufficient to establish the use of the method of accounting used in the preparation of the taxpayer's income tax returns.

(c) **Permissible methods—(1) In general.** Subject to the provisions of paragraphs (a) and (b) of this section, a taxpayer may compute his taxable income under any of the following methods of accounting:

(i) **Cash receipts and disbursements method.** Generally, under the cash receipts and disbursements method in the computation of taxable income, all items which constitute gross income (whether in the form of cash, property, or services) are to be included for the taxable year in which actually or constructively received. Expenditures are to be deducted for the taxable year in which actually made. For rules relating to constructive receipt, see § 1.451-2. For treatment of an expenditure attributable to more than one taxable year, see section 461(a) and paragraph (a)(1) of § 1.461-1.

(ii) **Accrual method.** Generally, under an accrual method, income is to be included for the taxable year when all the events have occurred which fix the right to receive such income and the amount thereof can be determined with reasonable accuracy. Under such a method, deductions are allowable for the taxable year in which all the events have occurred which establish the fact of the liability giving rise to such deduction and the amount thereof can be determined with reasonable accuracy. The method used by the taxpayer in determining when income is to be accounted for will be acceptable if it accords with generally accepted accounting principles, is consistently used by the taxpayer from year to year, and is consistent with the Income Tax Regulations. For example, under an accrual method, a taxpayer engaged in manufacturing may account for the sale of an item when the item is shipped, when the item is delivered, when the item is accepted, or when title to the item passes to the purchaser, whether or not billed, depending upon the method regularly employed in keeping the taxpayer's books; however, see § 1.451-5 relating to advance payments. The determination of when an item is shipped, delivered or accepted, or when title passes, does not depend upon when any other item in the contract is shipped, delivered or accepted, or when title passes.

(iii) **Other permissible methods.** Special methods of accounting are described elsewhere in chapter 1 of the Code and the regulations thereunder. For example, see the following sections and the regulations thereunder: Sections 61 and 162, relating to the crop method of accounting; section 453, relating to the installment method; section 451, relating to the long-term contract methods. In addition, special methods of accounting for particular items of income and expense are provided under other sections of chapter 1. For example, see section 174, relating to research and experimental expenditures, and section 175, relating to soil and water conservation expenditures.

(iv) **Combinations of the foregoing methods.** (a) In accordance with the following rules, any combination of the foregoing methods of accounting will be permitted in connection with a trade or business if such combination clearly reflects income and is consistently used. Where a combination of methods of accounting includes any special methods, such as those referred to in subdivision (iii) of this subparagraph, the taxpayer must comply with the requirements relating to such special methods. A taxpayer using an accrual method of accounting with respect to purchases and sales may use the cash method in computing all other items of income and expense. However, a taxpayer who uses the cash method of accounting in computing gross income from his trade or business shall use the cash method in computing expenses of such trade or business. Similarly, a taxpayer who uses an accrual method of accounting in computing business expenses shall use an accrual method in computing items affecting gross income from his trade or business.

(b) A taxpayer using one method of accounting in computing items of income and deductions of his trade or business may compute other items of income and deductions not connected with his trade or business under a different method of accounting.

(2) **Special rules.** (i) In any case in which it is necessary to use an inventory the accrual method of accounting must be used with regard to purchases and sales unless otherwise authorized under subdivision (ii) of this subparagraph.

(ii) No method of accounting will be regarded as clearly reflecting income unless all items of gross profit and deductions are treated with consistency from year to year. The Commissioner may authorize a taxpayer to adopt or change to a method of accounting permitted by this chapter although the method is not specifically described in the regulations in this part if, in the opinion of the Commissioner, income is clearly reflected by the use of such method. Further, the Commissioner may authorize a taxpayer to continue the use of a method of accounting consistently used by the taxpayer, even though not specifically authorized by the regulations in this part, if, in the opinion of the Commissioner, income is clearly reflected by the use of such method. See section 446(a) and paragraph (a) of this section, which require that taxable income shall be computed under the method of accounting on the basis of which the taxpayer regularly computes his income in keeping his books, and section 446(e) and paragraph (e) of this section, which require the prior approval of the Commissioner in the case of changes in accounting method.

(d) **Taxpayer engaged in more than one business.** (1) Where a taxpayer has two or more separate and distinct trades or businesses, a different method of accounting may be used for each trade or business, provided the method used for each trade or business clearly reflects the income of that particular trade or business. For example, a taxpayer may account for the operations of a personal service business on the cash receipts and disbursements method and of a manufacturing business on an accrual method, provided such businesses are separate and distinct and the methods used for each clearly reflect income. The method first used in accounting for business income and deductions in connection with each trade or business, as evidenced in the taxpayer's income tax return in which such income or deductions are first reported, must be consistently followed thereafter.

(2) No trade or business will be considered separate and distinct for purposes of this paragraph unless a complete and separable set of books and records is kept for such trade or business.

(3) If, by reason of maintaining different methods of accounting, there is a creation or shifting of profits or losses between the trades or businesses of the taxpayer (for example, through inventory adjustments, sales, purchases, or expenses) so that income of the taxpayer is not clearly reflected, the

trades or businesses of the taxpayer will not be considered to be separate and distinct.

(e) Requirement respecting the adoption or change of accounting method. (1) A taxpayer filing his first return may adopt any permissible method of accounting in computing taxable income for the taxable year covered by such return. See section 446(c) and paragraph (c) of this section for permissible methods. Moreover, a taxpayer may adopt any permissible method of accounting in connection with each separate and distinct trade or business, the income from which is reported for the first time. See section 446(d) and paragraph (d) of this section. See also section 446(a) and paragraph (a) of this section.

(2)(i) Except as otherwise expressly provided in chapter 1 of the Code and the regulations thereunder, a taxpayer who changes the method of accounting employed in keeping his books shall, before computing his income upon such new method for purposes of taxation, secure the consent of the Commissioner. Consent must be secured whether or not such method is proper or is permitted under the Internal Revenue Code or the regulations thereunder.

(ii)(a) A change in the method of accounting includes a change in the overall plan of accounting for gross income or deductions or a change in the treatment of any material item used in such overall plan. Although a method of accounting may exist under this definition without the necessity of a pattern of consistent treatment of an item, in most instances a method of accounting is not established for an item without such consistent treatment. A material item is any item which involves the proper time for the inclusion of the item in income or the taking of a deduction. Changes in method of accounting include a change from the cash receipts and disbursement method to an accrual method, or vice versa, a change involving the method or basis used in the valuation of inventories (see sections 471 and 472 and the regulations thereunder), a change from the cash or accrual method to a long-term contract method, or vice versa (see § 1.451-3), a change involving the adoption, use or discontinuance of any other specialized method of computing taxable income, such as the crop method, and a change where the Internal Revenue Code and regulations thereunder specifically require that the consent of the Commissioner must be obtained before adopting such a change.

(b) A change in method of accounting does not include correction of mathematical or posting er-

rors, or errors in the computation of tax liability (such as errors in computation of the foreign tax credit, net operating loss, percentage depletion or investment credit). Also, a change in method of accounting does not include adjustment of any item of income or deduction which does not involve the proper time for the inclusion of the item of income or the taking of a deduction. For example, corrections of items that are deducted as interest or salary, but which are in fact payments of dividends, and of items that are deducted as business expenses, but which are in fact personal expenses, are not changes in method of accounting. In addition, a change in the method of accounting does not include an adjustment with respect to the addition to a reserve for bad debts or an adjustment in the useful life of a depreciable asset. Although such adjustments may involve the question of the proper time for the taking of a deduction, such items are traditionally corrected by adjustments in the current and future years. For the treatment of the adjustment of the addition to a bad debt reserve, see the regulations under section 166 of the Code; for the treatment of a change in the useful life of a depreciable asset, see the regulations under section 167(b) of the Code. A change in the method of accounting also does not include a change in treatment resulting from a change in underlying facts. On the other hand, for example, a correction to require depreciation in lieu of a deduction for the cost of a class of depreciable assets which has been consistently treated as an expense in the year of purchase involves the question of the proper timing of an item, and is to be treated as a change in method of accounting.

(c) A change in an overall plan or system of identifying or valuing items in inventory is a change in method of accounting. Also a change in the treatment of any material item used in the overall plan for identifying or valuing items in inventory is a change in method of accounting.

(iii) A change in the method of accounting may be illustrated by the following examples:

Example (1). Although the sale of merchandise is an income producing factor, and therefore inventories are required, a taxpayer in the retail jewelry business reports his income on the cash receipts and disbursements method of accounting. A change from the cash receipts and disbursements method of accounting to the accrual method of accounting is a change in the overall plan of accounting and thus is a change in method of accounting.

Example (2). A taxpayer in the wholesale dry goods business computes its income and expenses on the accrual method of accounting and files its Federal income tax returns on such basis except for real estate taxes which have been reported on the cash receipts and disbursements method of accounting. A change in the treatment of real estate taxes from the cash receipts and disbursements method to the accrual method is a change in method of accounting because such change is a change in the treatment of a material item within his overall accounting practice.

* * *

Example (5). A taxpayer values inventories at cost. A change in the basis for valuation of inventories from cost to the lower of cost or market is a change in an overall practice of valuing items in inventory. The change, therefore, is a change of method of accounting for inventories.

* * *

(3)(i) Except as otherwise provided under the authority of subdivision (ii) of this subparagraph, in order to secure the Commissioner's consent to a change of a taxpayer's method of accounting, the taxpayer must file an application on Form 3115 with the Commissioner of Internal Revenue, Washington, D.C. 20224, within 180 days after the beginning of the taxable year in which it is desired to make the change. The taxpayer shall, to the extent applicable, furnish (a) all information requested on such form, disclosing in detail all classes of items which would be treated differently under the new method of accounting and showing all amounts which would be duplicated or omitted as a result of the proposed change and (b) the taxpayer's computation of the adjustments to take into account such duplications or omissions. The Commissioner may require such other information as may be necessary in order to determine whether the proposed change will be permitted. Permission to change a taxpayer's method of accounting will not be granted unless the taxpayer and the Commissioner agree to the terms, conditions, and adjustments under which the change will be effected. See section 481 and the regulations thereunder, relating to certain adjustments required by such changes, section 472 and the regulations thereunder, relating to changes to and from the last-in, first-out method of inventorying goods, and section 453 and the regulations thereunder, relating to certain adjustments required by a change from an accrual method to the installment method.

(ii) Notwithstanding the provisions of subdivision (i) of this subparagraph, the Commissioner may prescribe administrative procedures, subject to such limitations, terms, and conditions as he deems necessary to obtain his consent, to permit taxpayers to change their accounting practices or methods to an acceptable treatment consistent with applicable regulations. Limitations, terms, and conditions, as may be prescribed in such administrative procedures by the Commissioner, shall include those necessary to prevent the omission or duplication of items includible in gross income or deductions.

[T.D. 6500, 25 FR 11708, Nov. 26, 1960, as amended by T.D. 7073, 35 FR 17710, Nov. 18, 1970; T.D. 7285, 38 FR 26184, Sept. 19, 1973; T.D. 8067, 51 FR 378, Jan. 6, 1986]

Taxable Year for Which Items Of Gross Income Included

§ 1.451-1 General rule for taxable year of inclusion.

(a) **General rule.** Gains, profits, and income are to be included in gross income for the taxable year in which they are actually or constructively received by the taxpayer unless includible for a different year in accordance with the taxpayer's method of accounting. Under an accrual method of accounting, income is includible in gross income when all the events have occurred which fix the right to receive such income and the amount thereof can be determined with reasonable accuracy. Therefore, under such a method of accounting if, in the case of compensation for services, no determination can be made as to the right to such compensation or the amount thereof until the services are completed, the amount of compensation is ordinarily income for the taxable year in which the determination can be made. Under the cash receipts and disbursements method of accounting, such an amount is includible in gross income when actually or constructively received. Where an amount of income is properly accrued on the basis of a reasonable estimate and the exact amount is subsequently determined, the difference, if any, shall be taken into account for the taxable year in which such determination is made. To the extent that income is attributable to the recovery of bad debts for accounts charged off in prior years, it is includible in the year of recovery in accordance with the taxpayer's method of accounting, regardless of the date when the amounts were charged off. For treatment of bad debts and bad debt recoveries, see sections 166 and 111 and the regulations thereunder. For rules relating to the treatment of amounts received in crop shares, see section 61 and the regulations thereunder. For the year in which a partner must include his distributive share of partnership income, see section 706(a) and paragraph (a) of § 1.706–1. If a taxpayer ascertains that an item should have been included in gross income in a prior taxable year, he should, if within the period of limitation, file an amended return and pay any additional tax due. Similarly, if a taxpayer ascertains that an item was improperly included in gross income in a prior taxable year, he should, if within the period of limitation, file claim for credit or refund of any overpayment of tax arising therefrom.

(b) Special rule in case of death. (1) A taxpayer's taxable year ends on the date of his death. See section 443(a)(2) and paragraph (a)(2) of § 1.443–1. In computing taxable income for such year, there shall be included only amounts properly includible under the method of accounting used by the taxpayer. However, if the taxpayer used an accrual method of accounting, amounts accrued only by reason of his death shall not be included in computing taxable income for such year. If the taxpayer uses no regular accounting method, only amounts actually or constructively received during such year shall be included. (For rules relating to the inclusion of partnership income in the return of a decedent partner, see subchapter K, chapter 1 of the Code, and the regulations thereunder.)

(2) If the decedent owned an installment obligation the income from which was taxable to him under section 453, no income is required to be reported in the return of the decedent by reason of the transmission at death of such obligation. See section 453(d)(3). For the treatment of installment obligations acquired by the decedent's estate or by any person by bequest, devise, or inheritance from the decedent, see section 691(a)(4) and the regulations thereunder.

* * *

[T.D. 6500, 25 FR 11709, Nov. 26, 1960, as amended by T.D. 7001, 34 FR 997, Jan. 23, 1969; T.D. 7154, 36 FR 24996, Dec. 28, 1971; T.D. 7577, 43 FR 59357, Dec. 20, 1978]

§ 1.451–2 Constructive receipt of income.

(a) General rule. Income although not actually reduced to a taxpayer's possession is constructively received by him in the taxable year during which it is credited to his account, set apart for him, or otherwise made available so that he may draw

upon it at any time, or so that he could have drawn upon it during the taxable year if notice of intention to withdraw had been given. However, income is not constructively received if the taxpayer's control of its receipt is subject to substantial limitations or restrictions. Thus, if a corporation credits its employees with bonus stock, but the stock is not available to such employees until some future date, the mere crediting on the books of the corporation does not constitute receipt. In the case of interest, dividends, or other earnings (whether or not credited) payable in respect of any deposit or account in a bank, building and loan association, savings and loan association, or similar institution, the following are not substantial limitations or restrictions on the taxpayer's control over the receipt of such earnings:

(1) A requirement that the deposit or account, and the earnings thereon, must be withdrawn in multiples of even amounts;

(2) The fact that the taxpayer would, by withdrawing the earnings during the taxable year, receive earnings that are not substantially less in comparison with the earnings for the corresponding period to which the taxpayer would be entitled had he left the account on deposit until a later date (for example, if an amount equal to three months' interest must be forfeited upon withdrawal or redemption before maturity of a one year or less certificate of deposit, time deposit, bonus plan, or other deposit arrangement then the earnings payable on premature withdrawal or redemption would be substantially less when compared with the earnings available at maturity);

(3) A requirement that the earnings may be withdrawn only upon a withdrawal of all or part of the deposit or account. However, the mere fact that such institutions may pay earnings on withdrawals, total or partial, made during the last three business days of any calendar month ending a regular quarterly or semiannual earnings period at the applicable rate calculated to the end of such calendar month shall not constitute constructive receipt of income by any depositor or account holder in any such institution who has not made a withdrawal during such period;

(4) A requirement that a notice of intention to withdraw must be given in advance of the withdrawal. In any case when the rate of earnings payable in respect of such a deposit or account depends on the amount of notice of intention to withdraw that is given, earnings at the maximum rate are constructively received during the taxable year regardless of how long the deposit or account was held during the year or whether, in fact, any notice of intention to withdraw is given during the year. However, if in the taxable year of withdrawal the depositor or account holder receives a lower rate of earnings because he failed to give the required notice of intention to withdraw, he shall be allowed an ordinary loss in such taxable year in an amount equal to the difference between the amount of earnings previously included in gross income and the amount of earnings actually received. See section 165 and the regulations thereunder.

(b) Examples of constructive receipt. Amounts payable with respect to interest coupons which have matured and are payable but which have not been cashed are constructively received in the taxable year during which the coupons mature, unless it can be shown that there are no funds available for payment of the interest during such year. Dividends on corporate stock are constructively received when unqualifiedly made subject to the demand of the shareholder. However, if a dividend is declared payable on December 31 and the corporation followed its usual practice of paying the dividends by checks mailed so that the shareholders would not receive them until January of the following year, such dividends are not considered to have been constructively received in December. Generally, the amount of dividends or interest credited on savings bank deposits or to shareholders of organizations such as building and loan associations or cooperative banks is income to the depositors or shareholders for the taxable year when credited. However, if any portion of such dividends or interest is not subject to withdrawal at the time credited, such portion is not constructively received and does not constitute income to the depositor or shareholder until the taxable year in which the portion first may be withdrawn. Accordingly, if, under a bonus or forfeiture plan, a portion of the dividends or interest is accumulated and may not be withdrawn until the maturity of the plan, the crediting of such portion to the account of the shareholder or depositor does not constitute constructive receipt. In this case, such credited portion is income to the depositor or shareholder in the year in which the plan matures. However, in the case of certain deposits made after December 31, 1970, in banks, domestic building and loan associations, and similar financial institutions, the ratable inclusion rules of section 1232(a)(3) apply. See § 1.1232-3A. Accrued interest on unwithdrawn insurance policy dividends is gross income to the taxpayer for the first taxable year during which such interest may be withdrawn by him.

[T.D. 6500, 25 FR 11709, Nov. 26, 1960, as amended by T.D. 6723, 29 FR 5342, April 21, 1964; T.D. 7154, 36 FR 24997, Dec. 28, 1971; T.D. 7663, 44 FR 76782, Dec. 28, 1979]

§ 1.451-5 Advance payments for goods and long-term contracts.

(a) Advance payment defined. (1) For purposes of this section, the term "advance payment" means any amount which is received in a taxable year by a taxpayer using an accrual method of accounting for purchases and sales or a long-term contract method of accounting (described in § 1.451-3), pursuant to, and to be applied against, an agreement:

(i) For the sale or other disposition in a future taxable year of goods held by the taxpayer primarily for sale to customers in the ordinary course of his trade or business, or

(ii) For the building, installing, constructing or manufacturing by the taxpayer of items where the agreement is not completed within such taxable year.

(2) For purposes of subparagraph (1) of this paragraph:

(i) The term "agreement" includes (a) a gift certificate that can be redeemed for goods, and (b) an agreement which obligates a taxpayer to perform activities described in subparagraph (1)(i) or (ii) of this paragraph and which also contains an obligation to perform services that are to be performed as an integral part of such activities; and

(ii) Amounts due and payable are considered "received".

(3) If a taxpayer (described in subparagraph (1) of this paragraph) receives an amount pursuant to, and to be applied against, an agreement that not only obligates the taxpayer to perform the activities described in subparagraph (1)(i) and (ii) of this paragraph, but also obligates the taxpayer to perform services that are not to be performed as an integral part of such activities, such amount will be treated as an "advance payment" (as defined in subparagraph (1) of this paragraph) only to the extent such amount is properly allocable to the obligation to perform the activities described in subparagraph (1)(i) and (ii) of this paragraph. The portion of the amount not so allocable will not be considered an "advance payment" to which this section applies. If, however, the amount not so allocable is less than 5 percent of the total contract price, such amount will be treated as so allocable except that such treatment cannot result in delaying the time at which the taxpayer would otherwise accrue the amounts attributable to the activities described in subparagraph (1)(i) and (ii) of this paragraph.

(b) **Taxable year of inclusion.** (1)**In general.** Advance payments must be included in income either—

(i) In the taxable year of receipt; or

(ii) Except as provided in paragraph (c) of this section,

(a) In the taxable year in which properly accruable under the taxpayer's method of accounting for tax purposes if such method results in including advance payments in gross receipts no later than the time such advance payments are included in gross receipts for purposes of all of his reports (including consolidated financial statements) to shareholders, partners, beneficiaries, other proprietors, and for credit purposes, or

(b) If the taxpayer's method of accounting for purposes of such reports results in advance payments (or any portion of such payments) being included in gross receipts earlier than for tax purposes, in the taxable year in which includible in gross receipts pursuant to his method of accounting for purposes of such reports.

(2) **Examples.** This paragraph may be illustrated by the following examples:

Example (1). S, a retailer who uses for tax purposes and for purposes of the reports referred to in subparagraph (1)(ii)(a) of this paragraph, an accrual method of accounting under which it accounts for its sales of goods when the goods are shipped, receives advance payments for such goods. Such advance payments must be included in gross receipts for tax purposes either in the taxable year the payments are received or in the taxable year such goods are shipped (except as provided in paragraph (c) of this section).

Example (2). T, a manufacturer of household furniture, is a calendar year taxpayer who uses an accrual method of accounting pursuant to which income is accrued when furniture is shipped for purposes of its financial reports (referred to in subparagraph (1)(ii)(a) of this paragraph) and an accrual method of accounting pursuant to which the income is accrued when furniture is delivered and accepted for tax purposes. See, § 1.446-1(c)(1)(ii). In 1974, T receives an advance payment of $8,000 from X with respect to an order of furniture to be manufactured for X for a total price of $20,000. The furniture is shipped to X in December 1974, but it is not delivered to and accepted by X until January 1975. As a result of this contract, T must include the entire advance payment in its gross income for tax purposes in 1974 pursuant to subparagraph (1)(ii)(b) of this paragraph. T must include the remaining $12,000 of the gross contract price in its gross income in 1975 for tax purposes.

* * *

[T.D. 7103, 36 FR 5495, 5977, Mar. 24, 1971, as amended by T.D. 7397, 41 FR 2641, Jan. 19, 1976; T.D. 8067, 51 FR 393, Jan. 6, 1986]

§ 1.453-1 Installment method of reporting income.

* * *

(b) **Income to be reported.** (1) Persons permitted to use the installment method of accounting prescribed in section 453 may return as income from installment sales in any taxable year that proportion of the installment payments actually received in that year which the gross profit realized or to be realized when the property is paid for bears to the total contract price. In the case of dealers in personal property, for this purpose, gross profit means sales less cost of goods sold. See § 1.453-2 for rules applicable to the computation of income of dealers in personal property reporting on the installment method. In the case of sales of real estate and casual sales of personal property, gross profit means the selling price less the adjusted basis as defined in section 1011 and the regulations thereunder. Gross profit, in the case of a sale of real estate by a person other than a dealer and a casual sale of personal property, is reduced by commissions and other selling expenses for purposes of determining the proportion of installment payments returnable as income. For rules applicable in determining "selling price" and the use of certain other terms, see also paragraph (c) of § 1.453-4.

(2) For purposes of section 453, any total unstated interest (as defined in section 483(b)) under a contract for the sale or exchange of property, payments on account of which are subject to the application of section 483, shall not be included as a part of the selling price or the total contract price.
* * *

* * *

[T.D. 6500, 25 FR 11714, Nov. 26, 1960, as amended by T.D. 6682, 28 FR 11173, Oct. 18, 1963; T.D. 6873, 31 FR 941, Jan. 25, 1966; T.D. 7154, 36 FR 24997, Dec. 28, 1971; T.D. 7197, 37 FR 13531, July 11, 1972]

§ 1.453–4 Sale of real property involving deferred periodic payments.

* * *

(c) **Determination of "selling price".** In the sale of mortgaged property the amount of the mortgage, whether the property is merely taken subject to the mortgage or whether the mortgage is assumed by the purchaser, shall, for the purpose of determining whether a sale is on the installment plan, be included as a part of the "selling price"; and for the purpose of determining the payments and the total contract price as those terms are used in section 453, and §§ 1.453–1 through 1.453–7, the amount of such mortgage shall be included only to the extent that it exceeds the basis of the property. The term "payments" does not include amounts received by the vendor in the year of sale from the disposition to a third person of notes given by the vendee as part of the purchase price which are due and payable in subsequent years. Commissions and other selling expenses paid or incurred by the vendor shall not reduce the amount of the payments, the total contract price, or the selling price.

[T.D. 6500, 25 FR 11715, Nov. 26, 1960]

§ 1.453–6 Deferred payment sale of real property not on installment method.

(a) **Value of obligations.** (1) In transactions included in paragraph (b)(2) of § 1.453–4, that is, sales of real property involving deferred payments in which the payments received during the year of sale exceed 30 percent of the selling price, the obligations of the purchaser received by the vendor are to be considered as an amount realized to the extent of their fair market value in ascertaining the profit or loss from the transaction. Such obligations, however, are not considered in determining whether the payments during the year of sale exceed 30 percent of the selling price.

(2) If the obligations received by the vendor have no fair market value, the payments in cash or other property having a fair market value shall be applied against and reduce the basis of the property sold and, if in excess of such basis, shall be taxable to the extent of the excess. Gain or loss is realized when the obligations are disposed of or satisfied, the amount thereof being the difference between the reduced basis as provided in the preceding sentence and the amount realized therefor. Only in rare and extraordinary cases does property have no fair market value.

* * *

[T.D. 6500, 25 FR 11716, Nov. 26, 1960, as amended by T.D. 6916, 32 FR 5923, April 13, 1967]

§ 1.453–9 Gain or loss on disposition of installment obligations.

(a) **In general.** Subject to the exceptions contained in section 453(d)(4) and paragraph (c) of this section, the entire amount of gain or loss resulting from any disposition or satisfaction of installment obligations, computed in accordance with section 453(d), is recognized in the taxable year of such disposition or satisfaction and shall be considered as resulting from the sale or exchange of the property in respect of which the installment obligation was received by the taxpayer.

(b) **Computation of gain or loss.** (1) The amount of gain or loss resulting under paragraph (a) of this section is the difference between the basis of the obligation and (i) the amount realized, in the case of satisfaction at other than face value or in the case of a sale or exchange, or (ii) the fair market value of the obligation at the time of disposition, if such disposition is other than by sale or exchange.

(2) The basis of an installment obligation shall be the excess of the face value of the obligation over an amount equal to the income which would be returnable were the obligation satisfied in full.

(3) The application of subparagraphs (1) and (2) of this paragraph may be illustrated by the following examples:

Example (1). In 1960 the M Corporation sold a piece of unimproved real estate to B for $20,000. The company acquired the property in 1948 at a cost of $10,000. During 1960 the company received $5,000 cash and vendee's notes for the remainder of the selling price, or $15,000, payable in subsequent years. In 1962, before the vendee made any further payments, the company sold the notes for $13,000 in cash. The corporation makes its returns on the calendar year basis. The income to be reported for 1962 is $5,500, computed as follows:

Proceeds of sale of notes		$13,000
Selling price of property	$20,000	
Cost of property	10,000	
Total profit	10,000	
Total contract price	20,000	

Percent of profit, or proportion of each payment returnable as income, $10,000 divided by $20,000, 50 percent.

Face value of notes	15,000

Amount of income returnable were the notes satisfied in full, 50 percent of $15,000 ... $7,500

Basis of obligation—excess of face value of notes over amount of income returnable were the notes satisfied in full   7,500

Taxable income to be reported for 1962   5,500

Example (2). Suppose in example (1) the M Corporation, instead of selling the notes, distributed them in 1962 to its shareholders as a dividend, and at the time of such distribution, the fair market value of the notes was $14,000. The income to be reported for 1962 is $6,500, computed as follows:

Fair market value of notes $14,000

Basis of obligation—excess of face value of notes over amount of income returnable were the notes satisfied in full (computed as in example (1))   7,500

Taxable income to be reported for 1962   6,500

(c) Disposition from which no gain or loss is recognized. (1)(i) Under section 453(d)(4)(A), no gain or loss shall be recognized to a distributing corporation with respect to the distribution made after November 13, 1966, of installment obligations if (a) the distribution is made pursuant to a plan for the complete liquidation of a subsidiary under section 332, and (b) the basis of such obligations in the hands of the distributee is determined under section 334(b)(1).

(ii) Under section 453(d)(4)(B), no gain or loss shall be recognized to a distributing corporation with respect to the distribution of installment obligations if the distribution is made, pursuant to a plan for the complete liquidation of a corporation which meets the requirements of section 337, under conditions whereby no gain or loss would have been recognized to the corporation had such installment obligations been sold or exchanged on the day of the distribution. The preceding sentence shall not apply to the extent that under section 453(d)(1) gain to the distributing corporation would be considered as gain to which section 341(f)(2), 617(d)(1), 1245(a)(1), 1250(a)(1), 1251(c)(1), or 1252(a)(1) applies, computed under the principles of the regulations under such provisions. See paragraph (d) of § 1.1245–6, paragraph (c)(6) of § 1.1250–1, paragraph (e)(6) of § 1.1251–1, and paragraph (d)(3) of § 1.1252–1.

(2) Where the Code provides for exceptions to the recognition of gain or loss in the case of certain dispositions, no gain or loss shall result under section 453(d) in the case of a disposition of an installment obligation. Such exceptions include: Certain transfers to corporations under sections 351 and 361; contributions of property to a partnership by a partner under section 721; and distributions by a partnership to a partner under section 731 (except as provided by section 736 and section 751).

(3) Any amount received by a person in payment or settlement of an installment obligation acquired in a transaction described in subparagraphs (1) or (2) of this paragraph (other than an amount received by a stockholder with respect to an installment obligation distributed to him pursuant to section 337) shall be considered to have the character it would have had in the hands of the person from whom such installment obligation was acquired.

* * *

[T.D. 6500, 25 FR 11718, Nov. 26, 1960, as amended by T.D. 6590, 27 FR 1319, Feb. 13, 1962; T.D. 6832, 30 FR 8574, July 7, 1965; T.D. 7084, 36 FR 267, Jan. 8, 1971; T.D. 7418, 41 FR 18812, May 7, 1976]

§ 15a.453–0 Taxable years affected.

(a) In general. Except as otherwise provided, the provisions of § 15a.453–1(a) through (e) generally apply to installment method reporting for sales of real property and casual sales of personal property occurring after October 19, 1980. See 26 CFR § 1.453–1 (rev. as of April 1, 1980) for the provisions relating to installment method reporting for sales of real property and casual sales before October 20, 1980 (except as provided in paragraph (b) of this section) and for provisions relating to installment sales by dealers in personal property occurring before October 20, 1980.

(b) Certain limitations. The provisions of prior law (section 453(b) of the Internal Revenue Code of 1954, in effect as of October 18, 1980) which required that the buyer receive no more than 30 percent of the selling price in the taxable year of the installment sale and that at least two payments be received shall not apply to reporting for casual installment sales of personal property and installment sales of real property occurring in a taxable year ending after October 19, 1980.

[T.D. 7768, 46 FR 10709, Feb. 4, 1981; 46 FR 43036, Aug. 26, 1981]

§ 15a.453–1 Installment method reporting for sales of real property and casual sales of personal property.

(a) In general. Unless the taxpayer otherwise elects in the manner prescribed in paragraph (d)(3) of this section, income from a sale of real property or a casual sale of personal property, where any payment is to be received in a taxable year after the year of sale, is to be reported on the installment method.

(b) Installment sale defined—(1) In general. The term "installment sale" means a disposition of property (except as provided in paragraph (b)(4) of this section) where at least one payment is to be received after the close of the taxable year in which the disposition occurs. The term "installment sale" includes dispositions from which payment is to be received in a lump sum in a taxable year subsequent to the year of sale. For purposes of this paragraph, the taxable year in which payments are to be received is to be determined without regard to section 453(e) (relating to related party sales), section (f)(3) (relating to the definition of a "payment") and section (g) (relating to sales of depreciable property to a spouse or 80-percent-owned entity).

(2) Installment method defined—(i) In general. Under the installment method, the amount of any payment which is income to the taxpayer is that portion of the installment payment received in that year which the gross profit realized or to be realized bears to the total contract price (the "gross profit ratio"). See paragraph (c) of this section for rules describing installment method reporting of contingent payment sales.

(ii) Selling price defined. The term "selling price" means the gross selling price without reduction to reflect any existing mortgage or other encumbrance on the property (whether assumed or taken subject to by the buyer) and, for installment sales in taxable years ending after October 19, 1980, without reduction to reflect any selling expenses. Neither interest, whether stated or unstated, nor original issue discount is considered to be a part of the selling price. See paragraph (c) of this section for rules describing installment method reporting of contingent payment sales.

(iii) Contract price defined. The term "contract price" means the total contract price equal to selling price reduced by that portion of any qualifying indebtedness (as defined in paragraph (b)(2)(iv) of this section), assumed or taken subject to by the buyer, which does not exceed the seller's basis in the property (adjusted, for installment sales in taxable years ending after October 19, 1980, to reflect commissions and other selling expenses as provided in paragraph (b)(2)(v) of this section). See paragraph (c) of this section for rules describing installment method reporting of contingent payment sales.

(iv) Qualifying indebtedness. The term "qualifying indebtedness" means a mortgage or other indebtedness encumbering the property and indebtedness, not secured by the property but incurred or assumed by the purchaser incident to the purchaser's acquisition, holding, or operation in the ordinary course of business or investment, of the property. The term "qualifying indebtedness" does not include an obligation of the taxpayer incurred incident to the disposition of the property (e.g., legal fees relating to the taxpayer's sale of the property) or an obligation functionally unrelated to the acquisition, holding, or operating of the property (e.g., the taxpayer's medical bill). Any obligation created subsequent to the taxpayer's acquisition of the property and incurred or assumed by the taxpayer or placed as an encumbrance on the property in contemplation of disposition of the property is not qualifying indebtedness if the arrangement results in accelerating recovery of the taxpayer's basis in the installment sale.

(v) Gross profit defined. The term "gross profit" means the selling price less the adjusted basis as defined in section 1011 and the regulations thereunder. For sales in taxable years ending after October 19, 1980, in the case of sales of real property by a person other than a dealer and casual sales of personal property, commissions and other selling expenses shall be added to basis for purposes of determining the proportion of payments which is gross profit attributable to the disposition. Such additions to basis will not be deemed to affect the taxpayer's holding period in the transferred property.

(3) Payment—(i) In general. Except as provided in paragraph (e) of this section (relating to purchaser evidences of indebtedness payable on demand or readily tradable), the term "payment" does not include the receipt of evidences of indebtedness of the person acquiring the property ("installment obligation"), whether or not payment of such indebtedness is guaranteed by a third party (including a government agency). A standby letter of credit (as defined in paragraph (b)(3)(iii) of this section) shall be treated as a third party guarantee.

Payments include amounts actually or constructively received in the taxable year under an installment obligation. Receipt of an evidence of indebtedness which is secured directly or indirectly by cash or a cash equivalent, such as a bank certificate of deposit or a treasury note, will be treated as the receipt of payment. Payment may be received in cash or other property, including foreign currency, marketable securities, and evidences of indebtedness which are payable on demand or readily tradable. However, for special rules relating to the receipt of certain property with respect to which gain is not recognized, see paragraph (f) of this section (relating to transactions described in sections 351, 356(a) and 1031). Except as provided in § 15a.453-2 of these regulations (relating to distributions of installment obligations in corporate liquidations described in section 337), payment includes receipt of an evidence of indebtedness of a person other than the person acquiring the property from the taxpayer. For purposes of determining the amount of payment received in the taxable year, the amount of qualifying indebtedness (as defined in paragraph (b)(2)(iv) of this section) assumed or taken subject to by the person acquiring the property shall be included only to the extent that it exceeds the basis of the property (determined after adjustment to reflect selling expenses). For purposes of the preceding sentence, an arrangement under which the taxpayer's liability on qualifying indebtedness is eliminated incident to the disposition (e.g., a novation) shall be treated as an assumption of the qualifying indebtedness. If the taxpayer sells property to a creditor of the taxpayer and indebtedness of the taxpayer is cancelled in consideration of the sale, such cancellation shall be treated as payment. To the extent that cancellation is not in consideration of the sale, see §§ 1.61–12(b)(1) and 1.1001–2(a)(2) relating to discharges of indebtedness. If the taxpayer sells property which is encumbered by a mortgage or other indebtedness on which the taxpayer is not personally liable, and the person acquiring the property is the obligee, the taxpayer shall be treated as having received payment in the amount of such indebtedness.

(ii) **Wrap-around mortgage.** This paragraph (b)(3)(ii) shall apply generally to any installment sale after March 4, 1981 unless the installment sale was completed before June 1, 1981 pursuant to a written obligation binding on the seller that was executed on or before March 4, 1981. A "wrap-around mortgage" means an agreement in which the buyer initially does not assume and purportedly does not take subject to part or all of the mortgage or other indebtedness encumbering the property ("wrapped indebtedness") and, instead, the buyer issues to the seller an installment obligation the principal amount of which reflects such wrapped indebtedness. Ordinarily, the seller will use payments received on the installment obligation to service the wrapped indebtedness. The wrapped indebtedness shall be deemed to have been taken subject to even though title to the property has not passed in the year of sale and even though the seller remains liable for payments on the wrapped indebtedness. In the hands of the seller, the wrap-around installment obligation shall have a basis equal to the seller's basis in the property which was the subject of the installment sale, increased by the amount of gain recognized in the year of sale, and decreased by the amount of cash and the fair market value of other nonqualifying property received in the year of sale. For purposes of this paragraph (b)(3)(ii), the amount of any indebtedness assumed or taken subject to by the buyer (other than wrapped indebtedness) is to be treated as cash received by the seller in the year of sale. Therefore, except as otherwise required by section 483 or 1232, the gross profit ratio with respect to the wrap-around installment obligation is a fraction, the numerator of which is the face value of the obligation less the taxpayer's basis in the obligation and the denominator of which is the face value of the obligation.

(iii) **Standby letter of credit.** The term "standby letter of credit" means a non-negotiable, nontransferable (except together with the evidence of indebtedness which it secures) letter of credit, issued by a bank or other financial institution, which serves as a guarantee of the evidence of indebtedness which is secured by the letter of credit. Whether or not the letter of credit explicitly states it is non-negotiable and nontransferable, it will be treated as non-negotiable and nontransferable if applicable local law so provides. The mere right of the secured party (under applicable local law) to transfer the proceeds of a letter of credit shall be disregarded in determining whether the instrument qualifies as a standby letter of credit. A letter of credit is not a standby letter of credit if it may be drawn upon in the absence of default in payment of the underlying evidence of indebtedness.

(4) **Exceptions.** The term "installment sale" does not include, and the provisions of section 453 do not apply to, dispositions of personal property

on the installment plan by a person who regularly sells or otherwise disposes of personal property on the installment plan, or to dispositions of personal property of a kind which is required to be included in the inventory of the taxpayer if on hand at the close of the taxable year. See section 453A and the regulations thereunder for rules relating to installment sales by dealers in personal property. A dealer in real property or a farmer who is not required under his method of accounting to maintain inventories may report the gain on the installment method under section 453.

(5) Examples. The following examples illustrate installment method reporting under this section:

Example (1). In 1980, A, a calendar year taxpayer, sells Blackacre, an unencumbered capital asset in A's hands, to B for $100,000: $10,000 down and the remainder payable in equal annual installments over the next 9 years, together with adequate stated interest. A's basis in Blackacre, exclusive of selling expenses, is $38,000. Selling expenses paid by A are $2,000. Therefore, the gross profit is $60,000 ($100,000 selling price—$40,000 basis inclusive of selling expenses). The gross profit ratio is $3/5$ (gross profit of $60,000 divided by $100,000 contract price). Accordingly, $6,000 ($3/5$ of $10,000) of each $10,000 payment received is gain attributable to the sale and $4,000 ($10,000–$6,000) is recovery of basis. The interest received in addition to principal is ordinary income to A.

Example (2). C sells Whiteacre to D for a selling price of $160,000. Whiteacre is encumbered by a longstanding mortgage in the principal amount of $60,000. D will assume or take subject to the $60,000 mortgage and pay the remaining $100,000 in 10 equal annual installments together with adequate stated interest. C's basis in Whiteacre is $90,000. There are no selling expenses. The contract price is $100,000, the $160,000 selling price reduced by the mortgage of $60,000 assumed or taken subject to. Gross profit is $70,000 ($160,000 selling price less C's basis of $90,000). C's gross profit ratio is $7/10$ (gross profit of $70,000 divided by $100,000 contract price). Thus, $7,000 ($7/10$ of $10,000) of each $10,000 annual payment is gain attributable to the sale, and $3,000 ($10,000–$7,000) is recovery of basis.

Example (3). The facts are the same as in example (2), except that C's basis in the land is $40,000. In the year of the sale C is deemed to have received payment of $20,000 ($60,000–$40,000, the amount by which the mortgage D assumed or took subject to exceeds C's basis). Since basis is fully recovered in the year of sale, the gross profit ratio is 1 ($120,000/$120,000) and C will report 100% of the $20,000 deemed payment in the year of sale and each $10,000 annual payment as gain attributable to the sale.

Example (4). E sells Blackacre, an unencumbered capital gain property in E's hands, to F on January 2, 1981. F makes a cash down payment of $500,000 and issues a note to E obliging F to pay an additional $500,000 on the fifth anniversary date. The note does not require a payment of interest. In determining selling price, section 483 will apply to recharacterize as interest a portion of the $500,000 future payment. Assume that under section 483 and the applicable regulations $193,045 is treated as total unstated interest, and the selling price is $806,955 ($1 million less unstated interest). Assuming E's basis (including selling expenses) in Blackacre is $200,000, gross profit is $606,955 ($806,955–$200,000) and the gross profit ratio is 75.21547%. Accordingly, of the $500,000 cash down payment received by E in 1981, $376,077 (75.21547% of $500,000) is gain attributable to the sale and $123,923 is recovery of basis ($500,000–$376,077).

* * *

(c) Contingent payment sales—(1) In general. Unless the taxpayer otherwise elects in the manner prescribed in paragraph (d)(3) of this section, contingent payment sales are to be reported on the installment method. As used in this section, the term "contingent payment sale" means a sale or other disposition of property in which the aggregate selling price cannot be determined by the close of the taxable year in which such sale or other disposition occurs.

The term "contingent payment sale" does not include transactions with respect to which the installment obligation represents, under applicable principles of tax law, a retained interest in the property which is the subject of the transaction, an interest in a joint venture or a partnership, an equity interest in a corporation or similar transactions, regardless of the existence of a stated maximum selling price or a fixed payment term. * * *

This paragraph prescribes the rules to be applied in allocating the taxpayer's basis (including selling expenses except for selling expenses of dealers in real estate) to payments received and to be received in a contingent payment sale. The rules are designed appropriately to distinguish contingent payment sales for which a maximum selling price is determinable, sales for which a maximum selling price is not determinable but the time over which payments will be received is determinable, and sales for which neither a maximum selling price nor a definite payment term is determinable. In addition, rules are prescribed under which, in appropriate circumstances, the taxpayer will be permitted to recover basis under an income forecast computation.

(2) Stated maximum selling price—(i) In general. (A) Contingent payment sale will be treated as having a stated maximum selling price if, under the terms of the agreement, the maximum amount of sale proceeds that may be received by the taxpayer can be determined as of the end of the taxable year in which the sale or other disposition occurs. The stated maximum selling price shall be determined by assuming that all of the contingencies contemplated by the agreement are met or otherwise resolved in a manner that will maximize the selling price and accelerate payments to the earliest date or dates permitted under the agreement. Except as provided in paragraph (c)(2)(ii) and (7) of this section (relating to certain payment recomputations), the taxpayer's basis shall be allocated to payments received and to be received under a stated maximum selling price agreement by treating the stated maximum selling price as the selling price for purposes of paragraph (b) of this section. The stated maximum selling price, as initially determined, shall thereafter be treated as the selling price unless and until that maximum amount is reduced, whether pursuant to the terms of the original agreement, by subsequent amendment, by application of the payment recharacterization rule (described in paragraph (c)(2)(ii) of this section), or by a subsequent supervening event such as bankruptcy of the obligor. When the maximum amount is subsequently reduced, the gross profit ratio will be recomputed with respect to payments received in or after the taxable year in which an event requiring reduction occurs. If, however, application of the foregoing rules in a particular case would substantially and inappropriately accelerate or defer recovery of the taxpayer's basis, a special rule will apply. See paragraph (c)(7) of this section.

(B) The following examples illustrate the provisions of paragraph (e)(2)(i) of this section. In each example, it is assumed that application of the rules illustrated will not substantially and inappropriately defer or accelerate recovery of the taxpayer's basis.

Example (1). A sells all of the stock of X corporation to B for $100,000 payable at closing plus an amount equal to 5% of the net profits of X for each of the next nine years, the contingent payments to be made annually together with adequate stated interest. The agreement provides that the maximum amount A may receive, inclusive of the $100,000 down payment but exclusive of interest, shall be $2,000,000. A's basis in the stock of X inclusive of selling expenses, is $200,000. Selling price and contract price are considered to be $2,000,000. Gross profit is $1,800,000, and the gross profit ratio is $9/10$ ($1,800,000/$2,000,000). Accordingly, of the $100,000 received by A in the year of sale, $90,000 is reportable as gain attributable to the sale and $10,000 is recovery of basis.

Example (2). C owns Blackacre which is encumbered by a long-standing mortgage of $100,000. On January 15, 1981, C sells Blackacre to D under the following payment arrangement: $100,000 in cash on closing; nine equal annual installment payments of $100,000 commencing January 15, 1982; and nine annual payments (the first to be made on March 30, 1982) equal to 5% of the gross annual rental receipts from Blackacre generated during the preceding calendar year. The agreement provides that each deferred payment shall be accompanied by a payment of interest calculated at the rate of 12% per annum and that the maximum amount payable to C under the agreement (exclusive of interest) shall be $2,100,000. The agreement also specifies that D will assume the long-standing mortgage. C's basis (inclusive of selling expenses) in Blackacre is $300,000. Accordingly, selling price is $2,100,000 and contract price is $2,000,000 (selling price of $2,100,000 less the $100,000 mortgage). The gross profit ratio is $9/10$ (gross profit of $1,800,000 divided by $2,000,000 contract price). Of the $100,000 cash payment received by C in 1981, $90,000 is gain attributable to the sale of Blackacre and $10,000 is recovery of basis.

(ii) Certain interest recomputations. When interest is stated in the contingent price sale agreement at a rate equal to or greater than the applicable prescribed test rate referred to in § 1.483–1(d)(1)(ii) and such stated interest is payable in addition to the amounts otherwise payable under the agreement, such stated interest is not considered a part of the selling price. In other circumstances (i.e., section 483 is applicable because no interest is stated or interest is stated below the applicable test rate, or interest is stated under a payment recharacterization provision of the sale agreement), the special rule set forth in this (ii) shall be applied in the initial computation and subsequent recomputations of selling price, contract price, and gross profit ratio. The special rule is referred to in this section as the "price-interest recomputation rule." As used in this section, the term "payment recharacterization" refers to a contractual arrangement under which a computed amount otherwise payable as part of the selling price is denominated an interest payment. The amount of unstated interest determined under section 483 or (if section 483 is inapplicable in the particular case) the amount of interest determined under a payment recharacterization arrangement is collectively referred to in this section as "internal interest" amounts. The price-interest recomputation rule is applicable to any stated maximum selling price agreement which contemplates receipt of internal interest by the taxpayer. Under the rule, stated maximum selling price will be determined as of the end of the taxpayer's taxable year in which the sale or other disposition occurs, taking into account all events which have occurred and are subject to prompt subsequent calculation and verification and assuming that all amounts that may become payable under the agreement will be paid on the earliest date or dates permitted under the agreement. With respect to the year of sale, the amount (if any) of internal interest then shall be determined taking account of the respective components of that calculation. The maximum amount initially calculated, minus the internal interest so determined, is the initial stated maximum selling price under the price-interest recomputation rule. For each subsequent taxable year, stated maximum selling price (and thus selling price, contract price, and gross profit ratio) shall be recomputed, taking into account all events which have occurred and are subject to prompt subsequent calculation and verification and assuming that all amounts that may become payable under the agreement will be paid on the earliest date or dates permitted under the agreement. The redetermined gross profit ratio, adjusted to reflect payments received and gain recognized in prior taxable years, shall be applied to payments received in that taxable year.

* * *

(3) Fixed period—(i) In general. When a stated maximum selling price cannot be determined as of the close of the taxable year in which the sale or other disposition occurs, but the maximum period over which payments may be received under the contingent sale price agreement is fixed, the taxpayer's basis (inclusive of selling expenses) shall be allocated to the taxable years in which payment may be received under the agreement in equal annual increments. In making the allocation it is not relevant whether the buyer is required to pay adequate stated interest. However, if the terms of the agreement incorporate an arithmetic component that is not identical for all taxable years, basis shall be allocated among the taxable years to accord with that component unless, taking into account all of the payment terms of the agreement, it is inappropriate to presume that payments under the contract are likely to accord with the variable component. If in any taxable year no payment is received or the amount of payment received (exclusive of interest) is less than the basis allocated to that taxable year, no loss shall be allowed unless the taxable year is the final payment year under the agreement or unless it is otherwise determined in accordance with the rules generally applicable to worthless debts that the future payment obligation under the agreement has become worthless. When no loss is allowed, the unrecovered portion of basis allocated to the

taxable year shall be carried forward to the next succeeding taxable year. If application of the foregoing rules to a particular case would substantially and inappropriately defer or accelerate recovery of the taxpayer's basis, a special rule will apply. See paragraph (c)(7) of this section.

(ii) Examples. The following examples illustrate the rules for recovery of basis in a contingent payment sale in which stated maximum selling price cannot be determined but the period over which payments are to be received under the agreement is fixed. In each case, it is assumed that application of the described rules will not substantially and inappropriately defer or accelerate recovery of the taxpayer's basis.

Example (1). A sells Blackacre to B for 10 percent of Blackacre's gross yield for each of the next 5 years. A's basis in Blackacre is $5 million. Since the sales price is indefinite and the maximum selling price is not ascertainable from the terms of the contract, basis is recovered ratably over the period during which payment may be received under the contract. Thus, assuming A receives the payments (exclusive of interest) listed in the following table, A will report the following:

Year	Payment	Basis Recovered	Gain Attributable to the Sale
1	$1,300,000	$1,000,000	$ 300,000
2	$1,500,000	$1,000,000	$ 500,000
3	$1,400,000	$1,000,000	$ 400,000
4	$1,800,000	$1,000,000	$ 800,000
5	$2,100,000	$1,000,000	$1,100,000

Example (2). The facts are the same as in example (1), except that the payment in year 1 is only $900,000. Since the installment payment is less than the amount of basis allocated to that year, the unrecovered basis, $100,000, is carried forward to year 2.

Year	Payment	Basis Recovered	Gain Attributable to the Sale
1	$ 900,000	$ 900,000	–0–
2	$1,500,000	$1,100,000	$ 400,000
3	$1,400,000	$1,000,000	$ 400,000
4	$1,800,000	$1,000,000	$ 800,000
5	$2,100,000	$1,000,000	$1,100,000

Example (3). C owns all of the stock of X corporation with a basis of $100,000 (inclusive of selling expenses). D purchases the X stock from C and agrees to make four payments computed in accordance with the following formula: 40% of net profits of X in year 1, 30% in year 2, 20% in year 3, and 10% in year 4. Accordingly, C's basis is allocated as follows: $40,000 to year 1, $30,000 to year 2, $20,000 to year 3, and $10,000 to year 4.

Example (4). The facts are the same as in example (3), but the agreement also requires that D make fixed installment payments in accordance with the following schedule: no payment in year 1, $100,000 in year 2, $200,000 in year 3, $300,000 in year 4, and $400,000 in year 5. Thus, while it is reasonable to project that the contingent component of the payments will decrease each year, the fixed component of the payments will increase each year. Accordingly, C is required to allocate $20,000 of basis to each of the taxable years 1 through 5.

(4) Neither stated maximum selling price nor fixed period. If the agreement neither specifies a maximum selling price nor limits payments to a fixed period, a question arises whether a sale realistically has occurred or whether, in economic effect, payments received under the agreement are in the nature of rent or royalty income. Arrangements of this sort will be closely scrutinized. If, taking into account all of the pertinent facts, including the nature of the property, the arrangement is determined to qualify as a sale, the taxpayer's basis (including selling expenses) shall be recovered in equal annual increments over a period of 15 years commencing with the date of sale. However, if in any taxable year no payment is received or the amount of payment received (exclusive of interest) is less than basis allocated to the year, no loss shall be allowed unless it is otherwise determined in accordance with the timing rules generally applicable to worthless debts that the future payment obligation under the agreement has become worthless; instead the excess basis shall be reallocated in level amounts over the balance of the 15 year term. Any basis not recovered at the end of the 15th year shall be carried forward to the next succeeding year, and to the extent unrecovered thereafter shall be carried forward from year to year until all basis has been recovered or the future payment obligation is determined to be worthless. The general rule requiring initial level allocation of basis over 15 years shall not apply if the taxpayer can establish to the satisfaction of the Internal Revenue Service that application of the general rule would substantially and inappropriately defer recovery of the taxpayer's basis. See paragraph (c)(7) of this section. If the Service determines that initially allocating basis in level amounts over the first 15 years will substantially and inappropriately accelerate recovery of the taxpayer's basis in early years of that 15-year term, the Service may require that basis be reallocated within the 15-year term but the Service will not require that basis initially be allocated over more than 15 years. See paragraph (c)(7) of this section.

* * *

(d) Election not to report an installment sale on the installment method—(1) In general. An installment sale is to be reported on the install-

ment method unless the taxpayer elects otherwise in accordance with the rules set forth in paragraph (d)(3) of this section.

(2) Treatment of an installment sale when a taxpayer elects not to report on the installment method—(i) In general. A taxpayer who elects not to report an installment sale on the installment method must recognize gain on the sale in accordance with the taxpayer's method of accounting. The fair market value of an installment obligation shall be determined in accordance with paragraph (d)(2)(ii) and (iii) of this section. In making such determination, any provision of contract or local law restricting the transferability of the installment obligation shall be disregarded. Receipt of an installment obligation shall be treated as a receipt of property, in an amount equal to the fair market value of the installment obligation, whether or not such obligation is the equivalent of cash. An installment obligation is considered to be property and is subject to valuation, as provided in paragraph (d)(2)(ii) and (iii) of this section, without regard to whether the obligation is embodied in a note, an executory contract, or any other instrument, or is an oral promise enforceable under local law.

(ii) Fixed amount obligations. (A) A fixed amount obligation means an installment obligation the amount payable under which is fixed. Solely for the purpose of determining whether the amount payable under an installment obligation is fixed, the provisions of section 483 and any "payment recharacterization" arrangement (as defined in paragraph (c)(2)(ii) of this section) shall be disregarded. If the fixed amount payable is stated in identified, fungible units of property the value of which will or may vary over time in relation to the United States dollar (e.g., foreign currency, ounces of gold, or bushels of wheat), such units shall be converted to United States dollars at the rate of exchange or dollar value on the date the installment sale is made. A taxpayer using the cash receipts and disbursements methods of accounting shall treat as an amount realized in the year of sale the fair market value of the installment obligation. In no event will the fair market value of the installment obligation be considered to be less than the fair market value of the property sold (minus any other consideration received by the taxpayer on the sale). A taxpayer using the accrual method of accounting shall treat as an amount realized in the year of sale the total amount payable under the installment obligation. For this purpose, neither interest (whether stated or unstated) nor original issue discount is considered to be part of the amount payable. If the amount payable is otherwise fixed, but because the time over which payments may be made is contingent, a portion of the fixed amount will or may be treated as internal interest (as defined in paragraph (c)(2)(ii) of this section), the amount payable shall be determined by applying the price interest recomputation rule (described in paragraph (c)(2)(ii) of this section). Under no circumstances will an installment sale for a fixed amount obligation be considered an "open" transaction. For purposes of this (ii), remote or incidental contingencies are not to be taken into account.

(B) The following examples illustrate the provisions of paragraph (d)(2) of this section.

Example (1). A, an accrual method taxpayer, owns all of the stock of X corporation with a basis of $20 million. On July 1, 1981, A sells the stock of X corporation to B for $60 million payable on June 15, 1992. The agreement also provides that, against this fixed amount, B shall make annual prepayments (on June 15) equal to 5% of the net profits of X earned in the immediately preceding fiscal year beginning with the fiscal year ending March 31, 1982. Thus the first prepayment will be made on June 15, 1982. No stated interest is payable under the agreement and thus the unstated interest provisions of section 483 are applicable. Under section 483, no part of any payment made on June 15, 1982 (which is within one year following the July 1, 1981 sale date), will be treated as unstated interest. Under the price interest recomputation rule, it is presumed that the entire $60 million fixed amount will be paid on June 15, 1982. Accordingly, if A elects not to report the transaction on the installment method, in 1981 A must report $60 million as the amount realized on the sale and must report $40 million as gain on the sale in that year.

Example (2). The facts are the same as in example (1) except that A uses the cash receipts and disbursements method of accounting. In 1981 A must report as an amount realized on the sale the fair market value of the installment obligation and must report as gain on the sale in 1981 the excess of that amount realized over A's basis of $20 million. In no event will the fair market value of the installment obligation be considered to be less than the fair market value of the stock of X. In determining the fair market value of the installment obligation, any contractual or legal restrictions on the transferability of the installment obligation, and any remote or incidental contingencies otherwise affecting the amount payable or time of payments under the installment obligation, shall be disregarded.

(iii) Contingent payment obligations. Any installment obligation which is not a fixed amount obligation (as defined in paragraph (d)(2)(ii) of this section) is a contingent payment obligation. If an installment obligation contains both a fixed amount component and a contingent payment component, the fixed amount component shall be treated under the rules of paragraph (d)(2)(ii) of this section and the contingent amount component shall be treated under the rules of this (iii). The fair market value of a contingent payment obligation shall be determined by disregarding any restrictions on transfer imposed by agreement or under local law. The fair market value of a contingent payment obligation may be ascertained from, and in no event shall be considered to be less than, the fair market value of the property sold (less the amount of any other consideration received in the sale). Only in those rare and extraordinary cases involving sales for a contingent payment obligation in which the fair market value of the obligation (determinable under the preceding sentences) cannot reasonably be ascertained will the taxpayer be entitled to assert that the transaction is "open." Any such transaction will be carefully scrutinized to determine whether a sale in fact has taken place. A taxpayer using the cash receipts and disbursements method of accounting must report as an amount realized in the year of sale the fair market value of the contingent payment obligation. A taxpayer using the accrual method of accounting must report an amount realized in the year of sale determined in accordance with that method of accounting, but in no event less than the fair market value of the contingent payment obligation.

(3) Time and manner for making election—(i) In general. An election under paragraph (d)(1) of this section must be made on or before the due date prescribed by law (including extensions) for filing the taxpayer's return for the taxable year in which the installment sale occurs. The election must be made in the manner prescribed by the appropriate forms for the taxpayer's return for the taxable year of the sale. A taxpayer who reports an amount realized equal to the selling price including the full face amount of any installment obligation on the tax return filed for the taxable year in which the installment sale occurs will be considered to have made an effective election under paragraph (d)(1) of this section. A cash method taxpayer receiving an obligation the fair market value of which is less than the face value must make the election in the manner prescribed by appropriate instructions for the return filed for the taxable year of the sale.

(ii) Election made after the due date. Elections after the time specified in paragraph (d)(3)(i) of this section will be permitted only in those rare circumstances when the Internal Revenue Service concludes that the taxpayer had good cause for failing to make a timely election. A recharacterization of a transaction as a sale in a taxable year subsequent to the taxable year in which the transaction occurred (e.g., a transaction initially reported as a lease later is determined to have been an installment sale) will not justify a late election. No conditional elections will be permitted. * * *

(4) Revoking an election. Generally, an election made under paragraph (d)(1) is irrevocable. An election may be revoked only with the consent of the Internal Revenue Service. A revocation is retroactive. A revocation will not be permitted when one of its purposes is the avoidance of federal income taxes, or when the taxable year in which any payment was received has closed. * * *

* * *

[T.D. 7768, 46 FR 10708, Feb. 4, 1981; 46 FR 13688, Feb. 24, 1981; 46 FR 43036, Aug. 26, 1981, as amended by T.D. 7788, 46 FR 48920, Oct. 5, 1981]

§ 1.455-1 Treatment of prepaid subscription income.

Effective with respect to taxable years beginning after December 31, 1957, section 455 permits certain taxpayers to elect with respect to a trade or business in connection with which prepaid subscription income is received, to include such income in gross income for the taxable years during which a liability exists to furnish or deliver a newspaper, magazine, or other periodical. If a taxpayer does not elect to treat prepaid subscription income under the provisions of section 455, such income is includible in gross income for the taxable year in which received by the taxpayer, unless under the method or practice of accounting used in computing taxable income such amount is to be properly accounted for as of a different period.

[T.D. 6591, 27 FR 1798, Feb. 27, 1962]

Taxable Year for Which Deductions Taken

§ 1.461-1 General rule for taxable year of deduction.

(a) General rule—(1) Taxpayer using cash receipts and disbursements method. Under the cash receipts and disbursements method of accounting, amounts representing allowable deductions shall, as a general rule, be taken into account for the taxable year in which paid. Further, a taxpayer using this method may also be entitled to certain deductions in the computation of taxable income which do not involve cash disbursements during the taxable year, such as the deductions for depreciation, depletion, and losses under sections 167, 611, and 165, respectively. If an expenditure results in the creation of an asset having a useful life which extends substantially beyond the close of the taxable year, such an expenditure may not be deductible, or may be deductible only in part, for the taxable year in which made. An example is an expenditure for the construction of improvements by the lessee on leased property where the estimated life of the improvements is in excess of the remaining period of the lease. In such a case, in lieu of the allowance for depreciation provided by section 167, the basis shall be amortized ratably over the remaining period of the lease. See section 178 and the regulations thereunder for rules governing the effect to be given renewal options in

determining whether the useful life of the improvements exceeds the remaining term of the lease where a lessee begins improvements on leased property after July 28, 1958, other than improvements which on such date and at all times thereafter, the lessee was under a binding legal obligation to make. See section 263 and the regulations thereunder for rules relating to capital expenditures.

(2) Taxpayer using an accrual method. Under an accrual method of accounting, an expense is deductible for the taxable year in which all the events have occurred which determine the fact of the liability and the amount thereof can be determined with reasonable accuracy. However, any expenditure which results in the creation of an asset having a useful life which extends substantially beyond the close of the taxable year may not be deductible, or may be deductible only in part, for the taxable year in which incurred. While no accrual shall be made in any case in which all of the events have not occurred which fix the liability, the fact that the exact amount of the liability which has been incurred cannot be determined will not prevent the accrual within the taxable year of such part thereof as can be computed with reasonable accuracy. For example, A renders services to

B during the taxable year for which A claims $10,000. B admits the liability to A for $5,000 but contests the remainder. B may accrue only $5,000 as an expense for the taxable year in which the services were rendered. In the case of certain contested liabilities in respect of which a taxpayer transfers money or other property to provide for the satisfaction of the contested liability, see § 1.461-2. Where a deduction is properly accrued on the basis of a computation made with reasonable accuracy and the exact amount is subsequently determined in a later taxable year, the difference, if any, between such amounts shall be taken into account for the later taxable year in which such determination is made.

(3) **Other factors which determine when deductions may be taken.** (i) Each year's return should be complete in itself, and taxpayers shall ascertain the facts necessary to make a correct return. The expenses, liabilities, or loss of one year cannot be used to reduce the income of a subsequent year. A taxpayer may not take advantage in a return for a subsequent year of his failure to claim deductions in a prior taxable year in which such deductions should have been properly taken under his method of accounting. If a taxpayer ascertains that a deduction should have been claimed in a prior taxable year, he should, if within the period of limitation, file a claim for credit or refund of any overpayment of tax arising therefrom. Similarly, if a taxpayer ascertains that a deduction was improperly claimed in a prior taxable year, he should, if within the period of limitation, file an amended return and pay any additional tax due. However, in a going business there are certain overlapping deductions. If these overlapping items do not materially distort income, they may be included in the years in which the taxpayer consistently takes them into account.

(ii) Where there is a dispute and the entire liability is contested, judgments on account of damages for patent infringement, personal injuries or other causes, or other binding adjudications, including decisions of referees and boards of review under workmen's compensation laws, are deductions from gross income when the claim is finally adjudicated or is paid, depending upon the taxpayer's method of accounting. However, see subparagraph (2) of this paragraph.

(iii) For special rules relating to certain deductions, see the following sections and the regulations thereunder: Section 1481, relating to accounting for amounts repaid in connection with renegotia-

tion of a government contract; section 1341, relating to the computation of tax where the taxpayer repays a substantial amount received under a claim of right in a prior taxable year; section 165(e), relating to losses resulting from theft; and section 165(h), relating to an election of the year of deduction of disaster losses.

* * *

(b) **Special rule in case of death.** A taxpayer's taxable year ends on the date of his death. See section 443(a)(2) and paragraph (a)(2) of § 1.443-1. In computing taxable income for such year, there shall be deducted only amounts properly deductible under the method of accounting used by the taxpayer. However, if the taxpayer used an accrual method of accounting, no deduction shall be allowed for amounts accrued only by reason of his death. For rules relating to the inclusion of items of partnership deduction, loss, or credit in the return of a decedent partner, see subchapter K, chapter 1 of the Code, and the regulations thereunder.

* * *

[T.D. 6500, 25 FR 11720, Nov. 26, 1960, as amended by T.D. 6520, 25 FR 13692, Dec. 24, 1960; T.D. 6710, 29 FR 3473, March 18, 1964; T.D. 6735, 29 FR 6494, May 19, 1964; T.D. 6772, 29 FR 15753, Nov. 24, 1964; T.D. 6917, 32 FR 6682, May 2, 1967]

§ 1.461-2 **Timing of deductions in certain cases where asserted liabilities are contested.**

(a) **General rule—(1) Taxable year of deduction.** If—

(i) The taxpayer contests an asserted liability,

(ii) The taxpayer transfers money or other property to provide for the satisfaction of the asserted liability,

(iii) The contest with respect to the asserted liability exists after the time of the transfer, and

(iv) But for the fact that the asserted liability is contested, a deduction would be allowed for the taxable year of the transfer (or, in the case of an accrual method taxpayer, for an earlier taxable year for which such amount would be accruable),

then the deduction with respect to the contested amount shall be allowed for the taxable year of the transfer.

(2) Exception. Subparagraph (1) of this paragraph shall not apply in respect of the deduction for income, war profits, and excess profits taxes imposed by the authority of any foreign country or possession of the United States, including a tax paid in lieu of a tax on income, war profits, or excess profits otherwise generally imposed by any foreign country or by any possession of the United States.

(3) Refunds includible in gross income. If any portion of the contested amount which is deducted under subparagraph (1) of this paragraph for the taxable year of transfer is refunded when the contest is settled, such portion is includible in gross income except as provided in § 1.111-1, relating to recovery of certain items previously deducted or credited. Such refunded amount is includible in gross income for the taxable year of receipt, or for an earlier taxable year if properly accruable for such earlier year.

(4) Examples. The provisions of this paragraph are illustrated by the following examples:

Example (1). X Corporation, which uses an accrual method of accounting, in 1964 contests $20 of a $100 asserted real property tax liability but pays the entire $100 to the taxing authority. In 1968, the contest is settled and X receives a refund of $5. X deducts $100 for the taxable year 1964, and includes $5 in gross income for the taxable year 1968 (assuming § 1.111-1 does not apply to such amount). If in 1964 X pays only $80 to the taxing authority, X deducts only $80 for 1964. The result would be the same if X Corporation used the cash method of accounting.

Example (2). Y Corporation makes its return on the basis of a calendar year and uses an accrual method of accounting. Y's real property taxes are assessed and become a lien on December 1, but are not payable until March 1 of the following year. On December 10, 1964, Y contests $20 of the $100 asserted real property tax which was assessed and became a lien on December 1, 1964. On March 1, 1965, Y pays the entire $100 to the taxing authority. In 1968, the contest is settled and Y receives a refund of $5. Y deducts $80 for the taxable year 1964, deducts $20 for the taxable year 1965, and includes $5 in gross income for the taxable year 1968 (assuming § 1.111-1 does not apply to such amount).

(b) Contest of asserted liability—(1) Asserted liability. For purposes of paragraph (a)(1) of this section, the term "asserted liability" means an item with respect to which, but for the existence of any contest in respect of such item, a deduction would be allowable under an accrual method of accounting. For example, a notice of a local real estate tax assessment and a bill received for services may represent asserted liabilities.

(2) Definition of the term "contest". Any contest which would prevent accrual of a liability under section 461(a) shall be considered to be a contest in determining whether the taxpayer satisfies paragraph (a)(1)(i) of this section. A contest arises when there is a bona fide dispute as to the proper evaluation of the law or the facts necessary to determine the existence or correctness of the amount of an asserted liability. It is not necessary to institute suit in a court of law in order to contest an asserted liability. An affirmative act denying the validity or accuracy, or both, of an asserted liability to the person who is asserting such liability, such as including a written protest with payment of the asserted liability, is sufficient to commence a contest. Thus, lodging a protest in accordance with local law is sufficient to contest an asserted liability for taxes. It is not necessary that the affirmative act denying the validity or accuracy, or both, of an asserted liability be in writing if, upon examination of all the facts and circumstances, it can be established to the satisfaction of the Commissioner that a liability has been asserted and contested.

(3) Example. The provisions of this paragraph are illustrated by the following example:

Example. O Corporation makes its return on the basis of a calendar year and uses an accrual method of accounting. O receives a large shipment of typewriter ribbons from S Company on January 30, 1964, which O pays for in full on February 10, 1964. Subsequent to their receipt, several of the ribbons prove defective because of inferior materials used by the manufacturer. On August 9, 1964, O orally notifies S and demands refund of the full purchase price of the ribbons. After negotiations prove futile and a written demand is rejected by S, O institutes an action for the full purchase price. For purposes of paragraph (a)(1)(i) of this section, S has asserted a liability against O which O contests on August 9, 1964. O deducts the contested amount for 1964.

(c) Transfer to provide for the satisfaction of an asserted liability—(1) In general. A taxpayer may provide for the satisfaction of an asserted liability by transferring money or other property beyond his control (i) to the person who is asserting the liability, (ii) to an escrowee or trustee pursuant to a written agreement (among the escrowee or trustee, the taxpayer, and the person who is asserting the liability) that the money or other property be delivered in accordance with the settlement of the contest, or (iii) to an escrowee or trustee pursuant to an order of the United States, any State or political subdivision thereof, or any agency or instrumentality of the foregoing, or a court that the money or other property be delivered in accordance with the settlement of the contest. A taxpayer may also provide for the satisfaction of an asserted liability by transferring money or other property beyond his control to a court with jurisdiction over the contest. Purchasing a bond to guarantee payment of the asserted liability, an entry on the taxpayer's books of account, and a transfer to an account which is within the control of the taxpayer are not transfers to provide for the satisfaction of an asserted liability. In order for money or other property to be beyond the control of a taxpayer, the taxpayer must relinquish all authority over such money or other property.

(2) **Examples.** The provisions of this paragraph are illustrated by the following examples:

Example (1). M Corporation contests a $5,000 liability asserted against it by L Company for services rendered. To provide for the contingency that it might have to pay the liability, M establishes a separate bank account in its own name. M then transfers $5,000 from its general account to such separate account. Such transfer does not qualify as a transfer to provide for the satisfaction of an asserted liability because M has not transferred the money beyond its control.

Example (2). M Corporation contests a $5,000 liability asserted against it by L Company for services rendered. To provide for the contingency that it might have to pay the liability, M transfers $5,000 to an irrevocable trust pursuant to a written agreement among the trustee, M (the taxpayer), and L (the person who is asserting the liability) that the money shall be held until the contest is settled and then disbursed in accordance with the settlement. Such transfer qualifies as a transfer to provide for the satisfaction of an asserted liability.

(d) **Contest exists after transfer.** In order for a contest with respect to an asserted liability to exist after the time of transfer, such contest must be pursued subsequent to such time. Thus, the contest must have been neither settled nor abandoned at the time of the transfer. A contest may be settled by a decision, judgment, decree, or other order of any court of competent jurisdiction which has become final, or by written or oral agreement between the parties. For example, Z Corporation, which uses an accrual method of accounting, in 1964 contests a $100 asserted liability. In 1967 the contested liability is settled as being $80 which Z accrues and deducts for such year. In 1968 Z pays the $80. Section 461(f) does not apply to Z with respect to the transfer because a contest did not exist after the time of such transfer.

(e) **Deduction otherwise allowed—(1) In general.** The existence of the contest with respect to an asserted liability must prevent (without regard to section 461(f)) and be the only factor preventing a deduction for the taxable year of the transfer (or, in the case of an accrual method taxpayer, for an earlier taxable year for which such amount would be accruable) to provide for the satisfaction of such liability. Nothing in section 461(f) or this section shall be construed to give rise to a deduction since section 461(f) and this section relate only to the timing of deductions which are otherwise allowable under the Code.

(2) **Example.** The provisions of this paragraph are illustrated by the following example:

Example. A, an individual, makes a gift of certain property to B, an individual. A pays the entire amount of gift tax assessed against him but contests his liability for such tax. Section 275(a)(3) provides that gift taxes are not deductible. A does not satisfy the requirement of paragraph (a)(1)(iv) of this section since a deduction would not be allowed for the taxable year of the transfer even if A did not contest his liability for such tax.

* * *

[T.D. 6772, 29 FR 15753, Nov. 24, 1964]

Inventories

§ 1.471–1 Need for inventories.

In order to reflect taxable income correctly, inventories at the beginning and end of each taxable year are necessary in every case in which the production, purchase, or sale of merchandise is an income-producing factor. The inventory should include all finished or partly finished goods and, in the case of raw materials and supplies, only those which have been acquired for sale or which will physically become a part of merchandise intended for sale, in which class fall containers, such as kegs, bottles, and cases, whether returnable or not, if title thereto will pass to the purchaser of the product to be sold therein. Merchandise should be included in the inventory only if title thereto is vested in the taxpayer. Accordingly, the seller should include in his inventory goods under contract for sale but not yet segregated and applied to the contract and goods out upon consignment, but should exclude from inventory goods sold (including containers), title to which has passed to the purchaser. A purchaser should include in inventory merchandise purchased (including containers), title to which has passed to him, although such merchandise is in transit or for other reasons has not been reduced to physical possession, but should not include **goods** ordered for future delivery, transfer of title to which has not yet been effected. (But see § 1.472–1.)

[T.D. 6500, 25 FR 11724, Nov. 26, 1960]

§ 1.471–2 Valuation of inventories.

(a) Section 471 provides two tests to which each inventory must conform:

(1) It must conform as nearly as may be to the best accounting practice in the trade or business, and

(2) It must clearly reflect the income.

(b) It follows, therefore, that inventory rules cannot be uniform but must give effect to trade customs which come within the scope of the best accounting practice in the particular trade or business. In order to clearly reflect income, the inventory practice of a taxpayer should be consistent from year to year, and greater weight is to be given to consistency than to any particular method of inventorying or basis of valuation so long as the method or basis used is in accord with §§ 1.471–1 through 1.471–11.

(c) The bases of valuation most commonly used by business concerns and which meet the requirements of section 471 are (1) cost and (2) cost or market, whichever is lower. (For inventories by dealers in securities, see § 1.471–5.) Any goods in an inventory which are unsalable at normal prices or unusable in the normal way because of damage, imperfections, shop wear, changes of style, odd or broken lots, or other similar causes, including second-hand goods taken in exchange, should be valued at bona fide selling prices less direct cost of disposition, whether subparagraph (1) or (2) of this paragraph is used, or if such goods consist of raw materials or partly finished goods held for use or consumption, they shall be valued upon a reasonable basis, taking into consideration the usability and the condition of the goods, but in no case shall such value be less than the scrap value. Bona fide selling price means actual offering of goods during a period ending not later than 30 days after inventory date. The burden of proof will rest upon the taxpayer to show that such exceptional goods as are valued upon such selling basis come within the classifications indicated above, and he shall maintain such records of the disposition of the goods as will enable a verification of the inventory to be made.

* * *

(f) The following methods, among others, are sometimes used in taking or valuing inventories, but are not in accord with the regulations in this part:

(1) Deducting from the inventory a reserve for price changes, or an estimated depreciation in the value thereof.

(2) Taking work in process, or other parts of the inventory, at a nominal price or at less than its proper value.

(3) Omitting portions of the stock on hand.

(4) Using a constant price or nominal value for so-called normal quantity of materials or goods in stock.

(5) Including stock in transit, shipped either to or from the taxpayer, the title to which is not vested in the taxpayer.

* * *

[T.D. 6500, 25 FR 11724, Nov. 26, 1960, as amended by T.D. 7285, 38 FR 26185, Sept. 19, 1973]

§ 1.471–3 Inventories at cost.

Cost means:

(a) In the case of merchandise on hand at the beginning of the taxable year, the inventory price of such goods.

(b) In the case of merchandise purchased since the beginning of the taxable year, the invoice price less trade or other discounts, except strictly cash discounts approximating a fair interest rate, which may be deducted or not at the option of the taxpayer, provided a consistent course is followed. To this net invoice price should be added transportation or other necessary charges incurred in acquiring possession of the goods.

(c) In the case of merchandise produced by the taxpayer since the beginning of the taxable year, (1) the cost of raw materials and supplies entering into or consumed in connection with the product, (2) expenditures for direct labor, and (3) indirect production costs incident to and necessary for the production of the particular article, including in such indirect production costs an appropriate portion of management expenses, but not including any cost of selling or return on capital, whether by way of interest or profit. See § 1.471–11 for more specific rules regarding the treatment of indirect production costs.

(d) In any industry in which the usual rules for computation of cost of production are inapplicable, costs may be approximated upon such basis as may be reasonable and in conformity with established trade practice in the particular industry. Among such cases are: (1) Farmers and raisers of livestock (see § 1.471–6); (2) miners and manufacturers who by a single process or uniform series of processes derive a product of two or more kinds, sizes, or grades, the unit cost of which is substantially alike (see § 1.471–7); and (3) retail merchants who use what is known as the "retail method" in ascertaining approximate cost (see § 1.471–8). Notwithstanding the other rules of this section, cost shall not include an amount which is of a type for which a deduction would be disallowed under section 162(c), (f), or (g) and the regulations thereunder in the case of a business expense.

[T.D. 6500, 25 FR 11725, Nov. 26, 1960, as amended by T.D. 7285, 38 FR 26185, Sept. 19, 1973; T.D. 7345, 40 FR 7439, Feb. 20, 1975]

§ 1.471–4 Inventories at cost or market, whichever is lower.

(a) Under ordinary circumstances and for normal goods in an inventory, "market" means the current bid price prevailing at the date of the inventory for the particular merchandise in the volume in which usually purchased by the taxpayer, and is applicable in the cases—

(1) Of goods purchased and on hand, and

(2) Of basic elements of cost (materials, labor, and burden) in goods in process of manufacture and in finished goods on hand; exclusive, however, of goods on hand or in process of manufacture for delivery upon firm sales contracts (*i.e.*, those not legally subject to cancellation by either party) at fixed prices entered into before the date of the inventory, under which the taxpayer is protected against actual loss, which goods must be inventoried at cost.

(b) Where no open market exists or where quotations are nominal, due to inactive market conditions, the taxpayer must use such evidence of a fair market price at the date or dates nearest the inventory as may be available, such as specific purchases or sales by the taxpayer or others in reasonable volume and made in good faith, or compensation paid for cancellation of contracts for purchase commitments. Where the taxpayer in the regular course of business has offered for sale such merchandise at prices lower than the current price as above defined, the inventory may be valued at such prices less direct cost of disposition, and the correctness of such prices will be determined by reference to the actual sales of the taxpayer for a reasonable period before and after the date of the inventory. Prices which vary materially from the actual prices so ascertained will not be accepted as reflecting the market.

(c) Where the inventory is valued upon the basis of cost or market, whichever is lower, the market value of each article on hand at the inventory date shall be compared with the cost of the article, and the lower of such values shall be taken as the inventory value of the article.

[T.D. 6500, 25 FR 11725, Nov. 26, 1960]

§ 1.471–5 Inventories by dealers in securities.

A dealer in securities who in his books of account regularly inventories unsold securities on hand either—

(a) At cost,

(b) At cost or market, whichever is lower, or

(c) At market value,

may make his return upon the basis upon which his accounts are kept, provided that a description of the method employed is included in or attached to the return, that all the securities are inventoried by the same method, and that such method is adhered to in subsequent years, unless another method is authorized by the Commissioner pursuant to a written application therefor filed as provided in paragraph (e) of § 1.446–1. A dealer in securities in whose books of account separate computations of the gain or loss from the sale of the various lots of securities sold are made on the basis of the cost of each lot shall be regarded, for the purposes of this section, as regularly inventorying his securities at cost. For the purposes of this section, a dealer in securities is a merchant of securities, whether an individual, partnership, or corporation, with an established place of business, regularly engaged in the purchase of securities and their resale to customers; that is, one who as a merchant buys securities and sells them to customers with a view to the gains and profits that may be derived therefrom. If such business is simply a branch of the activities carried on by such person, the securities inventoried as provided in this section may include only those held for purposes of resale and not for investment. Taxpayers who buy and sell or hold securities for investment or speculation, irrespective of whether such buying or selling constitutes the carrying on of a trade or business, and officers of corporations and members of partnerships who in their individual capacities buy and sell securities, are not dealers in securities within the meaning of this section.

[T.D. 6500, 25 FR 11725, Nov. 26, 1960]

§ 1.471–11 Inventories of manufacturers.

(a) **Use of full absorption method of inventory costing.** In order to conform as nearly as may be possible to the best accounting practices and to clearly reflect income (as required by section 471 of the Code), both direct and indirect production costs must be taken into account in the computation of inventoriable costs in accordance with the "full absorption" method of inventory costing. Under the full absorption method of inventory costing production costs must be allocated to goods produced during the taxable year, whether sold during the taxable year or in inventory at the close of the taxable year determined in accordance with the taxpayer's method of identifying goods in inventory. Thus, the taxpayer must include as inventoriable costs all direct production costs and, to the extent provided by paragraphs (c) and (d) of this section, all indirect production costs. For purposes of this section, the term "financial reports" means financial reports (including consolidated financial statements) to shareholders, partners, beneficiaries or other proprietors and for credit purposes.

(b) **Production costs—(1) In general.** Costs are considered to be production costs to the extent that they are incident to and necessary for production or manufacturing operations or processes. Production costs include direct production costs and fixed and variable indirect production costs.

(2) **Direct production costs.** (i) Costs classified as "direct production costs" are generally those costs which are incident to and necessary for production or manufacturing operations or processes and are components of the cost of either direct material or direct labor. Direct material costs include the cost of those materials which become an integral part of the specific product and those materials which are consumed in the ordinary course of manufacturing and can be identified or associated with particular units or groups of units of that product. See § 1.471–3 for the elements of direct material costs. Direct labor costs include the cost of labor which can be identified or associated with particular units or groups of units of a

specific product. The elements of direct labor costs include such items as basic compensation, overtime pay, vacation and holiday pay, sick leave pay (other than payments pursuant to a wage continuation plan under section 105(d)), shift differential, payroll taxes and payments to a supplemental unemployment benefit plan paid or incurred on behalf of employees engaged in direct labor. For the treatment of rework labor, scrap, spoilage costs, and any other costs not specifically described as direct production costs see § 1.471–11(c)(2).

(ii) Under the full absorption method, a taxpayer must take into account all items of direct production cost in his inventoriable costs. Nevertheless, a taxpayer will not be treated as using an incorrect method of inventory costing if he treats any direct production costs as indirect production costs, provided such costs are allocated to the taxpayer's ending inventory to the extent provided by paragraph (d) of this section. Thus, for example, a taxpayer may treat direct labor costs as part of indirect production costs (for example, by use of the conversion cost method), provided all such costs are allocated to ending inventory to the extent provided by paragraph (d) of this section.

(3) **Indirect production costs—(i) In general.** The term "indirect production costs" includes all costs which are incident to and necessary for production or manufacturing operations or processes other than direct production costs (as defined in subparagraph (2) of this paragraph). Indirect production costs may be classified as to kind or type in accordance with acceptable accounting principles so as to enable convenient identification with various production or manufacturing activities or functions and to facilitate reasonable groupings of such costs for purposes of determining unit product costs.

(ii) **Fixed and variable classifications.** For purposes of this section, fixed indirect production costs are generally those costs which do not vary significantly with changes in the amount of goods produced at any given level of production capacity. These fixed costs may include, among other costs, rent and property taxes on buildings and machinery incident to and necessary for manufacturing operations or processes. On the other hand, variable indirect production costs are generally those costs which do vary significantly with changes in the amount of goods produced at any given level of production capacity. These variable costs may include, among other costs, indirect materials, factory janitorial supplies, and utilities. Where a particular cost contains both fixed and variable elements, these elements should be segregated into fixed and variable classifications to the extent necessary under the taxpayer's method of allocation, such as for the application of the practical capacity concept (as described in paragraph (d)(4) of this section).

* * *

[T.D. 7285, 38 FR 26185, Sept. 19, 1973; T.D. 8067, 51 FR 393, Jan. 6, 1986]

§ 1.472–1   Last-in, first-out inventories.

(a) Any taxpayer permitted or required to take inventories pursuant to the provisions of section 471, and pursuant to the provisions of §§ 1.471–1 to 1.471–9, inclusive, may elect with respect to those goods specified in his application and properly subject to inventory to compute his opening and closing inventories in accordance with the method provided by section 472, this section, and § 1.472–2. Under this last-in, first-out (LIFO) inventory method, the taxpayer is permitted to treat those goods remaining on hand at the close of the taxable year as being:

(1) Those included in the opening inventory of the taxable year, in the order of acquisition and to the extent thereof, and

(2) Those acquired during the taxable year.

The LIFO inventory method is not dependent upon the character of the business in which the taxpayer is engaged, or upon the identity or want of identity through commingling of any of the goods on hand, and may be adopted by the taxpayer as of the close of any taxable year.

(b) If the LIFO inventory method is used by a taxpayer who regularly and consistently, in a manner similar to hedging on a futures market, matches purchases with sales, then firm purchases and sales contracts (*i.e.*, those not legally subject to cancellation by either party) entered into at fixed prices on or before the date of the inventory may be included in purchases or sales, as the case may be, for the purpose of determining the cost of goods sold and the resulting profit or loss, provided that this practice is regularly and consistently adhered to by the taxpayer and provided that, in the opinion of the Commissioner, income is clearly reflected thereby.

(c) A manufacturer or processor who has adopted the LIFO inventory method as to a class of goods may elect to have such method apply to the raw materials only (including those included in goods in process and in finished goods) expressed in terms of appropriate units. If such method is adopted, the adjustments are confined to costs of the raw material in the inventory and the cost of the raw material in goods in process and in finished goods produced by such manufacturer or processor and reflected in the inventory. The provisions of this paragraph may be illustrated by the following examples:

Example (1). Assume that the opening inventory had 10 units of raw material, 10 units of goods in process, and 10 units of finished goods, and that the raw material cost was 6 cents a unit, the processing cost 2 cents a unit, and overhead cost 1 cent a unit. For the purposes of this example, it is assumed that the entire amount of goods in process was 50 percent processed.

Opening Inventory

	Raw material	Goods in process	Finished goods
Raw material	$0.60	$0.60	$0.60
Processing cost	.....	.10	.20
Overhead	.....	.05	.10

In the closing inventory there are 20 units of raw material, 6 units of goods in process, and 8 units of finished goods and the costs were: Raw material 10 cents, processing cost 4 cents, and overhead 1 cent.

Closing Inventory

[Based on cost and prior to adjustment]

	Raw material	Goods in process	Finished goods
Raw material	$2.00	$0.60	$0.80
Processing costs	.....	.12	.32
Overhead	.....	.03	.08
Total	2.00	.75	1.20

There were 30 units of raw material in the opening inventory and 34 units in the closing inventory. The adjustment to the closing inventory would be as follows:

Closing Inventory As Adjusted

	Raw material	Goods in process	Finished goods
Raw material:			
20 at 6 cents	$1.20	.....	.....
6 at 6 cents	.....	$0.36	.....
4 at 6 cents	.....	.....	$0.24
4 at 10 cents [1]	.....	.....	.40
Processing costs	.....	.12	.32
Overhead	.....	.03	.08
Total	1.20	.51	1.04

[1] This excess is subject to determination of price under section 472(b)(1) and § 1.472–2. If the excess falls in goods in process, the same adjustment is applicable.

The only adjustment to the closing inventory is the cost of the raw material; the processing costs and overhead cost are not changed.

Example (2). Assume that the opening inventory had 5 units of raw material, 10 units of goods in process, and 20 units of finished goods, with the same prices as in example (1), and that the closing inventory had 20 units of raw material, 20 units of goods in process, and 10 units of finished goods, with raw material costs as in the closing inventory in example (1). The adjusted closing inventory would be as follows in so far as the raw material is concerned:

Raw material, 20 at 6 cents	$1.20
Goods in process:	
15 at 6 cents	.90
5 at 10 cents [1]	.50
Finished goods:	
None at 6 cents	0.00
10 at 10 cents [1]	1.00

[1] This excess is subject to determination of price under section 472(b)(1) and § 1.472–2.

The 20 units of raw material in the raw state plus 15 units of raw material in goods in process make up the 35 units of raw material that were contained in the opening inventory.

(d) For the purposes of this section, raw material in the opening inventory must be compared with similar raw material in the closing inventory. There may be several types of raw materials, depending upon the character, quality, or price, and each type of raw material in the opening inventory must be compared with a similar type in the closing inventory.

* * *

[T.D. 6500, 25 FR 11727, Nov. 26, 1960, as amended by T.D. 6539, 26 FR 518, Jan. 20. 1961]

§ 1.472–2 Requirements incident to adoption and use of LIFO inventory method.

* * *

(e) LIFO conformity requirement—(1) In general. The taxpayer must establish to the satisfaction of the Commissioner that the taxpayer, in ascertaining the income, profit, or loss for the taxable year for which the LIFO inventory method is first used, or for any subsequent taxable year, for credit purposes or for purposes of reports to shareholders, partners, or other proprietors, or to beneficiaries, has not used any inventory method other than that referred to in § 1.472–1 or at variance with the requirement referred to in § 1.472–2(c). See paragraph (e)(2) of this section for rules relating to the meaning of the term "taxable year" as used in this paragraph. The following are not considered at variance with the requirement of this paragraph:

(i) The taxpayer's use of an inventory method other than LIFO for purposes of ascertaining information reported as a supplement to or explanation of the taxpayer's primary presentation of the taxpayer's income, profit, or loss for a taxable year in credit statements or financial reports (including preliminary and unaudited financial reports). See paragraph (e)(3) of this section for rules relating to the reporting of supplemental and explanatory information ascertained by the use of an inventory method other than LIFO.

(ii) The taxpayer's use of an inventory method other than LIFO to ascertain the value of the taxpayer's inventory of goods on hand for purposes of reporting the value of such inventories as assets. See paragraph (e)(4) of this section for rules relating to such disclosures.

(iii) The taxpayer's use of an inventory method other than LIFO for purposes of ascertaining information reported in internal management reports. See paragraph (e)(5) of this section for rules relating to such reports.

(iv) The taxpayer's use of an inventory method other than LIFO for purposes of issuing reports or credit statements covering a period of operations that is less than the whole of a taxable year for which the LIFO method is used for Federal income tax purposes. See paragraph (e)(6) of this section for rules relating to series of interim reports.

(v) The taxpayer's use of the lower of LIFO cost or market method to value LIFO inventories for purposes of financial reports and credit statements. However, except as provided in paragraph (e)(7) of this section, a taxpayer may not use market value in lieu of cost to value inventories for purposes of financial reports or credit statements.

(vi) The taxpayer's use of a costing method or accounting method to ascertain income, profit, or loss for credit purposes or for purposes of financial reports if such costing method or accounting method is neither inconsistent with the inventory method referred to in § 1.472–1 nor at variance with the requirement referred to in § 1.472–2(c), regardless of whether such costing method or accounting method is used by the taxpayer for Federal income tax purposes. See paragraph (e)(8) of this section for examples of such costing methods and accounting methods.

(vii) For credit purposes or for purposes of financial reports, the taxpayer's treatment of inventories, after such inventories have been acquired in a transaction to which section 351 applies from a transferor that used the LIFO method with respect to such inventories, as if such inventories had the same acquisition dates and costs as in the hands of the transferor.

(viii) For credit purposes or for purposes of financial reports relating to a taxable year, the taxpayer's determination of income, profit, or loss for the taxable year by valuing inventories in accordance with the procedures described in section 472(b)(1) and (3), notwithstanding that such valuation differs from the valuation of inventories for Federal income tax purposes because the taxpayer either—

(A) Adopted such procedures for credit or financial reporting purposes beginning with an accounting period other than the taxable year for which the LIFO method was first used by the taxpayer for Federal income tax purposes, or

(B) With respect to such inventories treated a business combination for credit or financial reporting purposes in a manner different from the treatment of the business combination for Federal income tax purposes.

* * *

[T.D. 6500, 25 FR 11728, Nov. 26, 1960, as amended by T.D. 6539, 26 FR 518, Jan. 20, 1961; T.D. 7756, 46 FR 6920, Jan. 22, 1981; T.D. 7760, 46 FR 15685, March 9, 1981]

§ 1.472–3 Time and manner of making election.

(a) The LIFO inventory method may be adopted and used only if the taxpayer files with his income tax return for the taxable year as of the close of which the method is first to be used a statement of his election to use such inventory method. The statement shall be made on Form 970 pursuant to the instructions printed with respect thereto and to the requirements of this section, or in such other manner as may be acceptable to the Commissioner. Such statement shall be accompanied by an analysis of all inventories of the taxpayer as of the beginning and as of the end of the taxable year for which the LIFO inventory method is proposed first to be used, and also as of the beginning of the prior taxable year. In the case of a manufacturer, this analysis shall show in detail the manner in which

costs are computed with respect to raw materials, goods in process, and finished goods, segregating the products (whether in process or finished goods) into natural groups on the basis of either (1) similarity in factory processes through which they pass, or (2) similarity of raw materials used, or (3) similarity in style, shape, or use of finished products. Each group of products shall be clearly described.

(b) The taxpayer shall submit for the consideration of the Commissioner in connection with the taxpayer's adoption or use of the LIFO inventory method such other detailed information with respect to his business or accounting system as may be at any time requested by the Commissioner.

(c) As a condition to the taxpayer's use of the LIFO inventory method, the Commissioner may require that the method be used with respect to goods other than those specified in the taxpayer's statement of election if, in the opinion of the Commissioner, the use of such method with respect to such other goods is essential to a clear reflection of income.

(d) Whether or not the taxpayer's application for the adoption and use of the LIFO inventory method should be approved, and whether or not such method, once adopted, may be continued, and the propriety of all computations incidental to the use of such method, will be determined by the Commissioner in connection with the examination of the taxpayer's income tax returns.

[T.D. 6500, 25 FR 11729, Nov. 26, 1960, as amended by T.D. 7295, 38 FR 34203, Dec. 12, 1973]

§ 1.472–4 Adjustments to be made by taxpayer.

A taxpayer may not change to the LIFO method of taking inventories unless, at the time he files his application for the adoption of such method, he agrees to such adjustments incident to the change to or from such method, or incident to the use of such method, in the inventories of prior taxable years or otherwise, as the district director upon the examination of the taxpayer's returns may deem necessary in order that the true income of the taxpayer will be clearly reflected for the years involved.

[T.D. 6500, 25 FR 11730, Nov. 26, 1960]

Adjustments

§ 1.481–1 Adjustments in general.

(a)(1) Section 481 prescribes the rules to be followed in computing taxable income in cases where the taxable income of the taxpayer is computed under a method of accounting different from that under which the taxable income was previously computed. A change in method of accounting to which section 481 applies includes a change in the over-all method of accounting for gross income or deductions, or a change in the treatment of a material item. For rules relating to changes in methods of accounting, see section 446(e) and paragraph (e) of § 1.446–1. In computing taxable income for the taxable year of the change, there shall be taken into account those adjustments which are determined to be necessary solely by reason of such change in order to prevent amounts from being duplicated or omitted. The "year of the change" is the taxable year for which the taxable income of the taxpayer is computed under a method of accounting different from that used for the preceding taxable year.

(2) Unless the adjustments are attributable to a change in method of accounting initiated by the taxpayer, no part of the adjustments required by subparagraph (1) of this paragraph shall be based on amounts which were taken into account in computing income (or which should have been taken into account had the new method of accounting been used) for taxable years beginning before January 1, 1954, or ending before August 17, 1954.

(b) The adjustments specified in section 481(a) and this section shall take into account inventories, accounts receivable, accounts payable, and any other item determined to be necessary in order to prevent amounts from being duplicated or omitted.

(c)(1) The term "adjustments", as used in section 481, has reference to the net amount of the adjustments required by section 481(a) and paragraph (b) of this section. In the case of a change in the over-all method of accounting, such as from the cash receipts and disbursements method to an accrual method, the term "net amount of the adjustments" means the consolidation of adjustments (whether the amounts thereof represent increases or decreases in items of income or deductions) arising with respect to balances in various accounts, such as inventory, accounts receivable, and accounts payable, at the beginning of the taxable

year of the change in method of accounting. With respect to the portion of the adjustments attributable to pre-1954 Code years, it is immaterial that the same items or class of items with respect to which adjustments would have to be made (for the first taxable year to which section 481 applies) do not exist at the time the actual change in method of accounting occurs. For purposes of section 481, only the net dollar balance is to be taken into account. In the case of a change in the treatment of a single material item, the amount of the adjustment shall be determined with reference only to the net dollar balances in that particular account.

(2)(i) If the change in method of accounting is voluntary (that is, initiated by the taxpayer), the entire amount of the adjustments required by section 481(a) is to be taken into account in computing taxable income for the taxable year of the change, except as otherwise provided by section 481(b)(4) and (5). However, in such a case, if the portion of the adjustments which is attributable to taxable years subject to the Internal Revenue Code of 1954 increases taxable income by more than $3,000, the limitations on tax provided in section 481(b)(1) or (2) apply.

(ii) The portion of the adjustments arising from a voluntary change in method of accounting and attributable to taxable years not subject to the 1954 Code is determined in accordance with section 481(b)(4)(A) and paragraph (a) of § 1.481–4. If such portion increases taxable income by more than $3,000 for the first taxable year to which section 481 applies, such portion may be taken into account over the period prescribed in section 481(b)(4)(B). If the total increase in taxable income arising from the adjustments required by section 481(a) is more than $3,000 for the taxable year of the change, but the portion of such adjustments attributable by $3,000 or less for the first taxable year to which section 481 applies, then the limitations provided in section 481(b)(1) or (2) apply to the total adjustments. On the other hand, if the portion of such adjustments attributable to pre-1954 Code years under section 481(b)(4)(A) increases taxable income taxable year to which section 481 applies, and the portion attributable to 1954 Code years increases taxable income by $3,000 or less for the taxable year of the change, then the portion of the adjustments attributable to pre-1954

Code years may be taken into account over the period prescribed in section 481(b)(4)(B), and the portion of the adjustments attributable to 1954 Code years is to be taken into account in the taxable year of the change.

(3) If the change in method of accounting is not voluntary (that is, not initiated by the taxpayer), then only the adjustments required by section 481(a) which are attributable to taxable years subject to the Internal Revenue Code of 1954 are taken into account in computing taxable income for the taxable year of the change. If the amount of such adjustments increases taxable income by more than $3,000 for the taxable year of the change, the limitations on tax provided in section 481(b)(1) or (2) apply.

(4) If the adjustments required by section 481(a) as a result of a change in method of accounting decrease taxable income for the taxable year of the change, such decrease is taken into account for that year and the provisions of section 481(b) do not apply. In the case of an involuntary change in method of accounting, no adjustments attributable to pre-1954 Code years are taken into account, whether or not such adjustments would decrease taxable income.

(5) A change in the method of accounting initiated by the taxpayer includes not only a change which he originates by securing the consent of the Commissioner, but also a change from one method of accounting to another made without the advance approval of the Commissioner. A change in the taxpayer's method of accounting required as a result of an examination of the taxpayer's income tax return will not be considered as initiated by the taxpayer. On the other hand, a taxpayer who, on his own initiative, changes his method of accounting in order to conform to the requirements of any Federal income tax regulation or ruling shall not, merely because of such fact, be considered to have made an involuntary change.

(6) Where the total adjustments required by section 481(a) include both—

(i) An amount attributable to 1954 Code years to which the limitations on tax provided by section 481(b)(1) or (2) apply, and

(ii) An amount attributable to pre-1954 Code years of which all or a pro rata portion thereof is to be taken into account under section 481(b)(4)(A) or (B),

two separate computations of tax must be made for the taxable year of the change. The tax for such year must first be computed under section 481(b)(1) or (2) in respect of the portion of the adjustments attributable to 1954 Code years, without regard to amounts taken into account under section 481(b)(4)(A) or (B). Then the tax for such year must be computed in respect of the portion of the adjustments attributable to pre-1954 Code years, taking into account the portion of the adjustments attributable to 1954 Code years. The total tax for the taxable year of the change will be the aggregate of the tax computed under section 481(b)(1) or (2) and the increase in tax attributable to taking into account the portion of the adjustments attributable to pre-1954 Code years under section 481(b)(4)(A) or (B).

(7) For rules relating to the limitations on tax provided by section 481(b)(1) and (2), see § 1.481-2. For rules relating to the adjustments attributable to taxable years beginning before January 1, 1954, or ending before August 17, 1954, see §§ 1.481-3 and 1.481-4.

(d) In determining the amount of any item of gain, loss, deduction, or credit which depends upon gross income, adjusted gross income, or taxable income for the taxable year of the change, the full amount of the adjustments required under section 481(a) shall be taken into account for such year if such adjustments increase taxable income by $3,000 or less, or decrease taxable income. However, if the amount of the adjustments increase taxable income by more than $3,000, the provisions of section 481(b) apply. Since section 481(b)(1) and (2) merely provide for limitations on the tax for the taxable year of the change, the entire amount of the adjustments which is subject to section 481(b)(1) and (2) is taken into account in such year. See § 1.481-2. Where section 481(b)(4) applies and the taxpayer does not elect to have the 10-year period begin with the first taxable year beginning after December 31, 1957, the pro rata portion of the adjustments attributable to pre-1954 Code years is also taken into account in the taxable year of the change. See § 1.481-4.

(e) The provisions of section 481 shall not apply in the case of a change from an accrual method to the installment method of accounting. In such case the rules provided in section 453 shall apply. However, section 481 does apply in the case of a change from the installment method of accounting to any other method.

[T.D. 6500, 25 FR 11731, Nov. 26, 1960]

§ 1.481–5 Adjustments taken into account with consent.

(a) In addition to the methods of allocation described in section 481(b), the adjustments required by section 481(a) may be taken into account in computing the tax under chapter 1 of the Code for such taxable years, in such manner and subject to such conditions as may be agreed upon between the Commissioner and the taxpayer. See section 481(c). Requests for approval of a method of allocation differing from those described in section 481(b) shall be addressed to the Commissioner of Internal Revenue, Attention: T:R, Washington, D.C. 20224, and shall set forth in detail the facts and circumstances upon which the taxpayer bases his request. Permission will be granted only if the taxpayer and the Commissioner agree to the terms and conditions under which the allocation is to be effected.

(b) The agreement shall be in writing and shall be signed by the Commissioner and the taxpayer. It shall set forth the items to be adjusted, the amount of the adjustments, the taxable year or years for which the adjustments are to be taken into account, and the amount of the adjustments allocable to each such year. The agreement shall be binding on the parties except upon a showing of fraud, malfeasance, or misrepresentation of a material fact.

[T.D. 6500, 25 FR 11737, Nov. 26, 1960]

§ 1.482–1 Allocation of income and deductions among taxpayers.

(a) **Definitions.** When used in this section and in § 1.482–2—

(1) The term "organization" includes any organization of any kind, whether it be a sole proprietorship, a partnership, a trust, an estate, an association, or a corporation (as each is defined or understood in the Internal Revenue Code or the regulations thereunder), irrespective of the place where organized, where operated, or where its trade or business is conducted, and regardless of whether domestic or foreign, whether exempt, whether affiliated, or whether a party to a consolidated return.

(2) The term "trade" or "business" includes any trade or business activity of any kind, regardless of whether or where organized, whether owned individually or otherwise, and regardless of the place where carried on.

(3) The term "controlled" includes any kind of control, direct or indirect, whether legally enforceable, and however exercisable or exercised. It is the reality of the control which is decisive, not its form or the mode of its exercise. A presumption of control arises if income or deductions have been arbitrarily shifted.

(4) The term "controlled taxpayer" means any one of two or more organizations, trades, or businesses owned or controlled directly or indirectly by the same interests.

(5) The terms "group" and "group of controlled taxpayers" mean the organizations, trades, or businesses owned or controlled by the same interests.

(6) The term "true taxable income" means, in the case of a controlled taxpayer, the taxable income (or, as the case may be, any item or element affecting taxable income) which would have resulted to the controlled taxpayer, had it in the conduct of its affairs (or, as the case may be, in the particular contract, transaction, arrangement, or other act) dealt with the other member or members of the group at arm's length. It does not mean the income, the deductions, the credits, the allowances, or the item or element of income, deductions, credits, or allowances, resulting to the controlled taxpayer by reason of the particular contract, transaction, or arrangement, the controlled taxpayer, or the interests controlling it, chose to make (even though such contract, transaction, or arrangement be legally binding upon the parties thereto).

(b) **Scope and purpose.** (1) The purpose of section 482 is to place a controlled taxpayer on a tax parity with an uncontrolled taxpayer, by determining, according to the standard of an uncontrolled taxpayer, the true taxable income from the property and business of a controlled taxpayer. The interests controlling a group of controlled taxpayers are assumed to have complete power to cause each controlled taxpayer so to conduct its affairs that its transactions and accounting records truly reflect the taxable income from the property and business of each of the controlled taxpayers. If, however, this has not been done, and the taxable incomes are thereby understated, the district director shall intervene, and, by making such distributions, apportionments, or allocations as he may deem necessary of gross income, deductions, credits, or allowances, or of any item or element affecting taxable income, between or among the controlled taxpayers constituting the group, shall determine the true taxable income of each controlled taxpayer. The standard to be applied in every case is that of an uncontrolled taxpayer dealing at arm's length with another uncontrolled taxpayer.

(2) Section 482 and this section apply to the case of any controlled taxpayer, whether such taxpayer makes a separate or a consolidated return. If a controlled taxpayer makes a separate return, the determination is of its true separate taxable income. If a controlled taxpayer is a party to a consolidated return, the true consolidated taxable income of the affiliated group and the true separate taxable income of the controlled taxpayer are determined consistently with the principles of a consolidated return.

(3) Section 482 grants no right to a controlled taxpayer to apply its provisions at will, nor does it grant any right to compel the district director to apply such provisions. It is not intended (except in the case of the computation of consolidated taxable income under a consolidated return) to effect in any case such a distribution, apportionment, or allocation of gross income, deductions, credits, or allowances, or any item of gross income, deductions, credits, or allowances, as would produce a result equivalent to a computation of consolidated taxable income under subchapter A, chapter 6 of the Code.

(c) **Application.** Transactions between one controlled taxpayer and another will be subjected to special scrutiny to ascertain whether the common control is being used to reduce, avoid, or escape taxes. In determining the true taxable income of a controlled taxpayer, the district director is not restricted to the case of improper accounting, to the case of a fraudulent, colorable, or sham transaction, or to the case of a device designed to reduce or avoid tax by shifting or distorting income, deductions, credits, or allowances. The authority to determine true taxable income extends to any case in which either by inadvertence or design the taxable income, in whole or in part, of a controlled taxpayer, is other than it would have been had the taxpayer in the conduct of his affairs been an uncontrolled taxpayer dealing at arm's length with another uncontrolled taxpayer.

(d) **Method of allocation.** (1) The method of allocating, apportioning, or distributing income, deductions, credits, and allowances to be used by the district director in any case, including the form of the adjustments and the character and source of amounts allocated, shall be determined with reference to the substance of the particular transactions or arrangements which result in the avoidance of

taxes or the failure to clearly reflect income. The appropriate adjustments may take the form of an increase or decrease in gross income, increase or decrease in deductions (including depreciation), increase or decrease in basis of assets (including inventory), or any other adjustment which may be appropriate under the circumstances. See § 1.482-2 for specific rules relating to methods of allocation in the case of several types of business transactions.

(2) Whenever the district director makes adjustments to the income of one member of a group of controlled taxpayers (such adjustments being referred to in this paragraph as "primary" adjustments) he shall also make appropriate correlative adjustments to the income of any other member of the group involved in the allocation. The correlative adjustment shall actually be made if the U.S. income tax liability of the other member would be affected for any pending taxable year. Thus, if the district director makes an allocation of income, he shall not only increase the income of one member of the group, but shall decrease the income of the other member if such adjustment would have an effect on the U.S. income tax liability of the other member for any pending taxable year. For the purposes of this subparagraph, a "pending taxable year" is any taxable year with respect to which the U.S. income tax return of the other member has been filed by the time the allocation is made, and with respect to which a credit or refund is not barred by the operation of any law or rule of law. If a correlative adjustment is not actually made because it would have no effect on the U.S. income tax liability of the other member involved in the allocation for any pending taxable year, such adjustment shall nevertheless be deemed to have been made for the purpose of determining the U.S. income tax liability of such member for a later taxable year, or for the purposes of determining the U.S. income tax liability of any person for any taxable year. The district director shall furnish to the taxpayer with respect to which the primary adjustment is made a written statement of the amount and nature of the correlative adjustment which is deemed to have been made. For purposes of this subparagraph, a primary adjustment shall not be considered to have been made (and therefore a correlative adjustment is not required to be made) until the first occurring of the following events with respect to the primary adjustment:

(i) The date of assessment of the tax following execution by the taxpayer of a Form 870 (Waiver of

Restrictions on Assessment and Collection of Deficiency in Tax and Acceptance of Overassessment) with respect to such adjustment,

(ii) Acceptance of a Form 870–AD (Offer of Waiver of Restriction on Assessment and Collection Deficiency in Tax and Acceptance of Overassessment),

(iii) Payment of the deficiency,

(iv) Stipulation in the Tax Court of the United States, or

(v) Final determination of tax liability by offer-in-compromise, closing agreement, or court action.

The principles of this subparagraph may be illustrated by the following examples in each of which it is assumed that X and Y are members of the same group of controlled entities and that they regularly compute their incomes on the basis of a calendar year:

Example (1). Assume that in 1968 the district director proposes to adjust X's income for 1966 to reflect an arm's length rental charge for Y's use of X's tangible property in 1966; that X consents to an assessment reflecting such adjustment by executing a Waiver, Form 870; and that an assessment of the tax with respect to such adjustment is made in 1968. The primary adjustment is therefore considered to have been made in 1968. Assume further that both X and Y are United States corporations and that Y had net operating losses in 1963, 1964, 1965, 1966, and 1967. Although a correlative adjustment would not have an effect on Y's U.S. income tax liability for any pending taxable year, an adjustment increasing Y's net operating loss for 1966 shall be deemed to have been made for the purposes of determining Y's U.S. income tax liability for 1968 or a later taxable year to which the increased operating loss may be carried. The district director shall notify X in writing of the amount and nature of the adjustment which is deemed to have been made to Y.

Example (2). Assume that X and Y are United States corporations; that X is in the business of rendering engineering services; that in 1968 the district director proposes to adjust X's income for 1966 to reflect an arm's length fee for the rendition of engineering services by X in 1966 relating to the construction of Y's factory; that X consents to an assessment reflecting such adjustment by executing a Waiver, Form 870; and that an assessment of the tax with respect to such adjustment is made in 1968. Assume further that fees for such services would properly constitute a capital expenditure by Y, and that Y does not place the factory in service until 1969. Although a correlative adjustment (increase in basis) would not have an effect on Y's U.S. income tax liability for a pending taxable year, an adjustment increasing the basis of Y's assets for 1966 shall be deemed to have been made in 1968 for the purpose of computing allowable depreciation or gain or loss on disposition for 1969 and any future taxable year. The district director shall notify X in

writing of the amount and nature of the adjustment which is deemed to have been made to Y.

* * *

(3) In making distributions, apportionments, or allocations between two members of a group of controlled entities with respect to particular transactions, the district director shall consider the effect upon such members of an arrangement between them for reimbursement within a reasonable period before or after the taxable year if the taxpayer can establish that such an arrangement in fact existed during the taxable year under consideration. The district director shall also consider the effect of any other nonarm's length transaction between them in the taxable year which, if taken into account, would result in a setoff against any allocation which would otherwise be made, provided the taxpayer is able to establish with reasonable specificity that the transaction was not at arm's length and the amount of the appropriate arm's length charge. For purposes of the preceding sentence, the term arm's length refers to the amount which was charged or would have been charged in independent transactions with unrelated parties under the same or similar circumstances considering all the relevant facts and without regard to the rules found in § 1.482–2 by which certain charges are deemed to be equal to arm's length. For example, assume that one member of a group performs services which benefit a second member, which would in itself require an allocation to reflect an arm's length charge for the performance of such services. Assume further that the first member can establish that during the same taxable year the second member engages in other nonarm's length transactions which benefit the first member, such as by selling products to the first member at a discount, or purchasing products from the first member at a premium, or paying royalties to the first member in an excessive amount. In such case, the value of the benefits received by the first member as a result of the other activities will be set-off against the allocation which would otherwise be made. If the effect of the set-off is to change the characterization or source of the income or deductions, or otherwise distort taxable income, in such a manner as to affect the United States tax liability of any member, allocations will be made to reflect the correct amount of each category of income or deductions. In order to establish that a set-off to the adjustments proposed by the district director is appropriate, the taxpayer must notify the district director of the basis of any claimed set-off at any time before the expiration of the period ending 30 days after the date of a letter by which the district director transmits an examination report notifying the taxpayer of proposed adjustments or before July 16, 1968, whichever is later. The principles of this subparagraph may be illustrated by the following examples, in each of which it is assumed that P and S are calendar year corporations and are both members of the same group of controlled entities:

Example (1). P performs services in 1966 for the benefit of S in connection with S's manufacture and sale of a product. S does not pay P for such services in 1966, but in consideration for such services, agrees in 1966 to pay P a percentage of the amount of sales of the product in 1966 through 1970. In 1966 it appeared this agreement would provide adequate consideration for the services. No allocation will be made with respect to the services performed by P.

Example (2). P renders services to S in connection with the construction of S's factory. An arm's length charge for such services, determined under paragraph (b) of § 1.482-2, would be $100,000. During the same taxable year P makes available to S a machine to be used in such construction. P bills S $125,000 for the services, but does not bill for the use of the machine. No allocation will be made with respect to the excessive charge for services or the undercharge for the machine if P can establish that the excessive charge for services was equal to an arm's length charge for the use of the machine, and if the taxable income and income tax liabilities of P and S are not distorted.

Example (3). Assume the same facts as in example (2), except that, if P had reported $25,000 as rental income and $25,000 less service income, it would have been subject to the tax on personal holding companies. Allocations will be made to reflect the correct amounts of rental income and service income.

(4) If the members of a group of controlled taxpayers engage in transactions with one another, the district director may distribute, apportion, or allocate income, deductions, credits, or allowances to reflect the true taxable income of the individual members under the standards set forth in this section and in § 1.482-2 notwithstanding the fact that the ultimate income anticipated from a series of transactions may not be realized or is realized during a later period. For example, if one member of a controlled group sells a product at less than an arm's length price to a second member of the group in one taxable year and the second member resells the product to an unrelated party in the next taxable year, the district director may make an appropriate allocation to reflect an arm's length price for the sale of the product in the first taxable year, notwithstanding that the second member of the group had not realized any gross income from the resale of the product in the first year. Similarly, if one member of a group lends money to a second member of the group in a taxable year, the district director may make an appropriate allocation to reflect an arm's length charge for interest during such taxable year even if the second member does not realize income during such year. The provisions of this subparagraph apply even if the gross income contemplated from a series of transactions is never, in fact, realized by the other members.

(5) Section 482 may, when necessary to prevent the avoidance of taxes or to clearly reflect income, be applied in circumstances described in sections of the Code (such as section 351) providing for nonrecognition of gain or loss. See, for example, National Securities Corporation v. Commissioner of Internal Revenue, 137 F.2d 600 (3d Cir. 1943), cert. denied 320 U.S. 794 (1943).

(6) If payment or reimbursement for the sale, exchange, or use of property, the rendition of services, or the advance of other consideration among members of a group of controlled entities was prevented, or would have been prevented, at the time of the transaction because of currency or other restrictions imposed under the laws of any foreign country, any distributions, apportionments, or allocations which may be made under section 482 with respect to such transactions may be treated as deferrable income or deductions, providing the taxpayer has, for the year to which the distributions, apportionments, or allocations relate, elected to use a method of accounting in which the reporting of deferrable income is deferred until the income ceases to be deferrable income. Under such method of accounting, referred to in this section as the deferred income method of accounting, any payments or reimbursements which were prevented or would have been prevented, and any deductions attributable directly or indirectly to such payments or reimbursements, shall be deferred until they cease to be deferrable under such method of accounting. If such method of accounting has not been elected with respect to the taxable year to which the allocations under section 482 relate, the taxpayer may elect such method with respect to such allocations (but not with respect to other deferrable income) at any time before the first occurring of the following events with respect to the allocations:

(i) Execution by the taxpayer of Form 870 (Waiver of Restrictions on Assessment and Collection of Deficiency in Tax and Acceptance of Overassessment);

(ii) Expiration of the period ending 30 days after the date of a letter by which the district director transmits an examination report notifying the taxpayer of proposed adjustments reflecting such allocations or before July 16, 1968, whichever is later; or

(iii) Execution of a closing agreement or offer-in-compromise.

The principles of this subparagraph may be illustrated by the following example in which it is assumed that X, a domestic corporation, and Y, a foreign corporation, are members of the same group of controlled entities:

Example. X, which is in the business of rendering a certain type of service to unrelated parties, renders such services for the benefit of Y in 1965. The direct and indirect costs allocable to such services are $60,000, and an arm's length charge for such services is $100,000. Assume that the district director proposes to increase X's income by $100,000, but that the country in which Y is located would have blocked payment in 1965 for such services. If, prior to the first occurring of the events described in subdivisions (i), (ii), or (iii) of this subparagraph, X elects to use the deferred income method of accounting with respect to such allocation, the $100,000 allocation and the $60,000 of costs are deferrable until such amounts cease to be deferrable under X's method of accounting.

[T.D. 6595, 27 FR 3598, April 14, 1962, as amended by T.D. 6952, 33 FR 5848, April 16, 1968]

§ 1.482–2 Determination of taxable income in specific situations.

(a) Loans or advances—(1) In general. Where one member of a group of controlled entities makes a loan or advance directly or indirectly to, or otherwise becomes a creditor of, another member of such group, and charges no interest, or charges interest at a rate which is not equal to an arm's length rate as defined in subparagraph (2) of this paragraph, the district director may make appropriate allocations to reflect an arm's length interest rate for the use of such loan or advance.

(2) Arm's length interest rate—(i) In general. For the purposes of this paragraph, the arm's length interest rate shall be the rate of interest which was charged, or would have been charged at the time the indebtedness arose, in independent transactions with or between unrelated parties under similar circumstances. All relevant factors will be considered, including the amount and duration of the loan, the security involved, the credit standing of the borrower, and the interest rate prevailing at the situs of the lender or creditor for comparable loans.

* * *

(iii) Safe haven rule for certain loans and advances. (A) Paragraph (a)(2)(iii) of this section applies to interest paid or accrued—

(1) Pursuant to a loan or advance (other than a loan or advance entered into pursuant to a binding contract entered into prior to August 29, 1980), which was entered into on or after July 1, 1981, and

(2) On or after July 1, 1981, pursuant to a demand loan or advance.

(B) If a creditor was not regularly engaged in the business of making loans or advances of the same general type as the loan or advance in question to unrelated parties, the arm's length rate of interest to which paragraph (a)(2)(iii) of this section applies shall be for purposes of this paragraph—

(1) The rate of interest actually charged if at least 11, but not in excess of 13, percent per annum simple interest, or

(2) 12 percent per annum simple interest if no interest was charged or if the rate of interest charged was less than 11, or in excess of 13 percent per annum simple interest, unless the taxpayer establishes a more appropriate rate under the standards set forth in paragraph (a)(2)(i) of this section. For purposes of the preceding sentence, if the rate actually charged is greater than 13 percent per annum simple interest and less than the rate determined under the standards set forth in paragraph (a)(2)(i) of this section, or if the rate actually charged is less than 11 percent per annum simple interest and greater than the rate determined under the standards set forth in paragraph (a)(2)(i) of the section, then the rate actually charged shall be deemed to be a more appropriate rate under the standards set forth in paragraph (a)(2)(i) of this section.

* * *

(3) Loans or advances to which subparagraph (1) applies. Subparagraph (1) of this paragraph applies to all forms of bona fide indebtedness and includes:

(i) Loans or advances of money or other consideration (whether or not evidenced by a written instrument), and

(ii) Indebtedness arising in the ordinary course of business out of sales, leases, or the rendition of services by or between members of the group, or any other similar extension of credit.

Subparagraph (1) of this paragraph does not apply to alleged indebtedness which was in fact a contribution of capital or a distribution by a corporation with respect to its shares. The interest period shall commence at the date the indebtedness arises, except that with respect to indebtedness described in subdivision (ii) of this subparagraph that is not evidenced by a written instrument requiring payment of interest, the interest period shall not commence until a date 6 months after the date the indebtedness arises, or until a later date if the taxpayer is able to demonstrate that either it or others in its industry, as a regular trade practice, permit comparable balances in the case of similar transactions with unrelated parties to remain outstanding for a longer period without charging interest. For the purpose of determining the period of time for which a balance is outstanding, payments or credits shall be applied against the earliest balance outstanding, unless the taxpayer applies such payments or credits in some other order on its books in accordance with an agreement or understanding of the parties if the taxpayer can demonstrate that either it or others in its industry, as a regular trade practice, enter into such agreements or understandings.

* * *

(b) **Performance of services for another—(1) General rule.** Where one member of a group of controlled entities performs marketing, managerial, administrative, technical, or other services for the benefit of, or on behalf of another member of the group without charge, or at a charge which is not equal to an arm's length charge as defined in subparagraph (3) of this paragraph, the district director may make appropriate allocations to reflect an arm's length charge for such services.

(2) **Benefit test.** (i) Allocations may be made to reflect arm's length charges with respect to services undertaken for the joint benefit of the members of a group of controlled entities, as well as with respect to services performed by one member of the group exclusively for the benefit of another member of the group. Any allocations made shall be consistent with the relative benefits intended from the services, based upon the facts known at the time the services were rendered, and shall be made even if the potential benefits anticipated are not realized. No allocations shall be made if the probable benefits to the other members were so indirect or remote that unrelated parties would not have charged for such services. In general, allocations may be made if the service, at the time it was performed, related to the carrying on of an activity by another member or was intended to benefit another member, either in the member's overall operations or in its day-to-day activities. The principles of this subdivision may be illustrated by the following examples in each of which it is assumed that X and Y are corporate members of the same group of controlled entities:

Example (1). X's International Division engages in a wide range of sales promotion activities. Although most of these activities are undertaken exclusively for the benefit of X's international operations, some are intended to jointly benefit both X and Y and others are undertaken exclusively for the benefit of Y. The district director may make an allocation to reflect an arm's length charge with respect to the activities undertaken for the joint benefit of X and Y consistent with the relative benefits intended as well as with respect to the services performed exclusively for the benefit of Y.

Example (2). X operates an international airline, and Y owns and operates hotels in several cities which are serviced by X. X, in conjunction with its advertising of the airline, often pictures Y's hotels and mentions Y's name. Although such advertising was primarily intended to benefit X's airline operations, it was reasonable to anticipate that there would be substantial benefits to Y resulting from patronage by travelers who responded to X's advertising. Since an unrelated hotel operator would have been charged for such advertising, the district director may make an appropriate allocation to reflect an arm's length charge consistent with the relative benefits intended.

Example (3). Assume the same facts as in Example (2) except that X's advertising neither mentions nor pictures Y's hotels. Although it is reasonable to anticipate that increased air travel attributable to X's advertising will result in some benefit to Y due to increased patronage by air travelers, the district director will not make an allocation with respect to such advertising since the probable benefit to Y was so indirect and remote that an unrelated hotel operator would not have been charged for such advertising.

(ii) Allocations will generally not be made if the service is merely a duplication of a service which the related party has independently performed or is performing for itself. In this connection, the ability to independently perform the service (in terms of qualification and availability of personnel) shall be taken into account. The principles of this subdivision may be illustrated by the following examples, in each of which it is assumed that X and Y are corporate members of the same group of controlled entities:

Example (1). At the request of Y, the financial staff of X makes an analysis to determine the amount and source of the borrowing needs of Y. Y does not have personnel qualified to make the analysis, and it does not undertake the same analysis. The district director may make an appropriate allocation to reflect an arm's length charge for such analysis.

Example (2). Y, which has a qualified financial staff, makes an analysis to determine the amount and source of its borrowing needs. Its report, recommending a loan from a bank, is submitted to X. X's financial staff reviews the analysis to determine whether X should advise Y to reconsider its plan. No allocation should be made with respect to X's review.

(3) Arm's length charge. For the purpose of this paragraph an arm's length charge for services rendered shall be the amount which was charged or would have been charged for the same or similar services in independent transactions with or between unrelated parties under similar circumstances considering all relevant facts. However, except in the case of services which are an integral part of the business activity of either the member rendering the services or the member receiving the benefit of the services (as described in subparagraph (7) of this paragraph), the arm's length charge shall be deemed equal to the costs or deductions incurred with respect to such services by the member or members rendering such services unless the taxpayer establishes a more appropriate charge under the standards set forth in the first sentence of this subparagraph. Where costs or deductions are a factor in applying the provisions of this paragraph adequate books and records must be maintained by taxpayers to permit verification of such costs or deductions by the Internal Revenue Service.

* * *

(c) Use of tangible property—(1) General rule. Where possession, use, or occupancy of tangible property owned or leased by one member of a group of controlled entities (referred to in this paragraph as the owner) is transferred by lease or other arrangement to another member of such group (referred to in this paragraph as the user) without charge or at a charge which is not equal to an arm's length rental charge (as defined in subdivision (i) of subparagraph (2) of this paragraph), the district director may make appropriate allocations to properly reflect such arm's length charge. Where possession, use, or occupancy of only a portion of such property is transferred, the determination of the arm's length charge and the allocation shall be made with reference to the portion transferred.

(2) Arm's length charge. (i) For the purposes of this paragraph, an arm's length rental charge shall be the amount of rent which was charged, or would have been charged for the use of the same or similar property, during the time it was in use, in independent transactions with or between unrelated parties under similar circumstances considering the period and location of the use, the owner's investment in the property or rent paid for the property, expenses of maintaining the property, the type of property involved, its condition, and all other relevant facts. If neither the owner nor the user was engaged in the trade or business of renting property, the arm's length rental charge for the taxable year shall be deemed to be equal to the amount specified in subdivision (ii) or (iii) of this subparagraph, whichever is appropriate, unless the taxpayer establishes a more appropriate charge under the standards set forth in the first sentence of this subdivision. For purposes of this subdivision, an owner or user shall be considered to be in the trade or business of renting property if it engages in the trade or business of renting property of the same general type as the property in question to unrelated parties. An owner or user will not be considered to be engaged in the trade or business of renting property of the same general type solely on the basis of casual or infrequent rentals of property which is predominantly used in its trade or business.

* * *

(d) Transfer or use of intangible property—(1) In general. (i) Except as otherwise provided in subparagraph (4) of this paragraph, where intangible property or an interest therein is transferred, sold, assigned, loaned, or otherwise made available in any manner by one member of a group of controlled entities (referred to in this paragraph as the transferor) to another member of the group (referred to in this paragraph as the transferee) for other than an arm's length consideration, the district director may make appropriate allocations to reflect an arm's length consideration for such property or its use. Subparagraph (2) of this paragraph provides rules for determining the form an amount of an appropriate allocation, subparagraph (3) of this paragraph provides a definition of "intangible property", and subparagraph (4) of this paragraph provides rules with respect to certain cost-sharing arrangements in connection with the development of intangible property. For purposes of this paragraph, an interest in intangible property may take the form of the right to use such property.

* * *

(e) Sales of tangible property—(1) In general. (i) Where one member of a group of controlled entities (referred to in this paragraph as the "seller") sells or otherwise disposes of tangible property to another member of such group (referred to in this paragraph as the "buyer") at other than an arm's length price (such a sale being referred to in this paragraph as a "controlled sale"), the district director may make appropriate allocations between the seller and the buyer to reflect an arm's length price for such sale or disposition. An arm's length price is the price that an unrelated party would have paid under the same circumstances for the property involved in the controlled sale. Since unrelated parties normally sell products at a profit, an arm's length price normally involves a profit to the seller.

* * *

[T.D. 6952, 33 FR 5849, April 16, 1968; 33 FR 6290, April 25, 1968, as amended by T.D. 6964, 33 FR 10569, July 25, 1968; T.D. 6998, 84 FR 933, Jan. 22, 1969; 34 FR 1380, Jan. 29, 1969; T.D. 7170, 37 FR 5373, March 15, 1972; T.D. 7394, 41 FR 1280, Jan. 7, 1976; T.D. 7747, 46 FR 86459, Dec. 31, 1980; T.D. 7781, 46 FR 34569, July 2, 1981; T.D. 7920, 48 FR 50711, Nov. 3, 1983]

CORPORATIONS USED TO AVOID INCOME TAX ON SHAREHOLDERS

Corporations Improperly Accumulating Surplus

§ 1.531–1 Imposition of tax.

Section 531 imposes (in addition to the other taxes imposed upon corporations by chapter 1 of the Code) a graduated tax on the accumulated taxable income of every corporation described in section 532 and § 1.532–1. In the case of an affiliated group which makes or is required to make a consolidated return see § 1.1502–43. All of the taxes on corporations under chapter 1 of the Code are treated as one tax for purposes of assessment, collection, payment, period of limitations, etc. See section 535 and §§ 1.535–1, 1.535–2, and 1.535–3 for the definition and determination of accumulated taxable income.

[T.D. 6500, 25 FR 11737, Nov. 26, 1960, as amended by T.D. 7244, 37 FR 28897, Dec. 30, 1972; T.D. 7937, 49 FR 3462, Jan. 27, 1984]

§ 1.532–1 Corporations subject to accumulated earnings tax.

(a) General rule. (1) The tax imposed by section 531 applies to any domestic or foreign corporation (not specifically excepted under section 532(b) and paragraph (b) of this section) formed or availed of to avoid or prevent the imposition of the individual income tax on its shareholders, or on the shareholders of any other corporation, by permitting earnings and profits to accumulate instead of dividing or distributing them. See section 533 and § 1.533–1, relating to evidence of purpose to avoid income tax with respect to shareholders.

(2) The tax imposed by section 531 may apply if the avoidance is accomplished through the formation or use of one corporation or a chain of corporations. For example, if the capital stock of the M Corporation is held by the N Corporation, the earnings and profits of the M Corporation would not be returned as income subject to the individual income tax until such earnings and profits of the M Corporation were distributed to the N Corporation and distributed in turn by the N Corporation to its shareholders. If either the M Corporation or the N Corporation was formed or is availed of for the purpose of avoiding or preventing the imposition of the individual income tax upon the shareholders of the N Corporation, the accumulated taxable income of the corporation so formed or availed of (M or N, as the case may be) is subject to the tax imposed by section 531.

(b) Exceptions. The accumulated earnings tax imposed by section 531 does not apply to a personal holding company (as defined in section 542), to a foreign personal holding company (as defined in section 552), or to a corporation exempt from tax under subchapter F, chapter 1 of the Code.

* * *

§ 1.533–1 Evidence of purpose to avoid income tax.

(a) In general. (1) The Commissioner's determination that a corporation was formed or availed of for the purpose of avoiding income tax with respect to shareholders is subject to disproof by competent evidence. Section 533(a) provides that the fact that earnings and profits of a corporation are permitted to accumulate beyond the reasonable needs of the business shall be determinative of the purpose to avoid the income tax with respect to shareholders unless the corporation, by the preponderance of the evidence, shall prove to the contrary. The burden of proving that earnings and profits have been permitted to accumulate beyond the reasonable needs of the business may be shifted to the Commissioner under section 534. See §§ 1.534-1 through 1.534-4. Section 533(b) provides that the fact that the taxpayer is a mere holding or investment company shall be prima facie evidence of the purpose to avoid income tax with respect to shareholders.

(2) The existence or nonexistence of the purpose to avoid income tax with respect to shareholders may be indicated by circumstances other than the conditions specified in section 533. Whether or not such purpose was present depends upon the particular circumstances of each case. All circumstances which might be construed as evidence of the purpose to avoid income tax with respect to shareholders cannot be outlined, but among other things, the following will be considered:

(i) Dealings between the corporation and its shareholders, such as withdrawals by the shareholders as personal loans or the expenditure of funds by the corporation for the personal benefit of the shareholders,

(ii) The investment by the corporation of undistributed earnings in assets having no reasonable connection with the business of the corporation (see § 1.537-3), and

(iii) The extent to which the corporation has distributed its earnings and profits.

The fact that a corporation is a mere holding or investment company or has an accumulation of earnings and profits in excess of the reasonable needs of the business is not absolutely conclusive against it if the taxpayer satisfies the Commissioner that the corporation was neither formed nor availed of for the purpose of avoiding income tax with respect to shareholders.

(b) **General burden of proof and statutory presumptions.** The Commissioner may determine that the taxpayer was formed or availed of to avoid income tax with respect to shareholders through the medium of permitting earnings and profits to accumulate. In the case of litigation involving any such determination (except where the burden of proof is on the Commissioner under section 534), the burden of proving such determination wrong by a preponderance of the evidence, together with the corresponding burden of first going forward with the evidence, is on the taxpayer under principles applicable to income tax cases generally. For the burden of proof in a proceeding before the Tax Court with respect to the allegation that earnings and profits have been permitted to accumulate beyond the reasonable needs of the business, see section 534 and §§ 1.534-2 through 1.534-4. For a definition of a holding or investment company, see paragraph (c) of this section. For determination of the reasonable needs of the business, see section 537 and §§ 1.537-1 through 1.537-3. If the taxpayer is a mere holding or investment company, and the Commissioner therefore determines that the corporation was formed or availed of for the purpose of avoiding income tax with respect to shareholders, then section 533(b) gives further weight to the presumption of correctness already arising from the Commissioner's determination by expressly providing an additional presumption of the existence of a purpose to avoid income tax with respect to shareholders. Further, if it is established (after complying with section 534 where applicable) that earnings and profits were permitted to accumulate beyond the reasonable needs of the business and the Commissioner has therefore determined that the corporation was formed or availed of for the purpose of avoiding income tax with respect to shareholders, then section 533(a) adds still more weight to the Commissioner's determination. Under such circumstances, the existence of such an accumulation is made determinative of the purpose to avoid income tax with respect to shareholders unless the taxpayer proves to the contrary by the preponderance of the evidence.

(c) **Holding or investment company.** A corporation having practically no activities except holding property and collecting the income therefrom or investing therein shall be considered a holding company within the meaning of section 533(b). If the activities further include, or consist substantially of, buying and selling stocks, securities, real estate, or other investment property (whether upon an outright or marginal basis) so that the income is derived not only from the investment yield but also from profits upon market fluctuations, the corporation shall be considered an investment company within the meaning of section 533(b).

* * *

[T.D. 6500, 25 FR 11737, Nov. 26, 1960, as amended by T.D. 6652, 28 FR 4786, May 14, 1963]

§ 1.533–2   Statement required.

The corporation may be required to furnish a statement of its accumulated earnings and profits, the payment of dividends, the name and address of, and number of shares held by, each of its shareholders, the amounts that would be payable to each of the shareholders if the income of the corporation were distributed and other information required under section 6042.

[T.D. 6500, 25 FR 11737, Nov. 26, 1960]

§ 1.534–1   Burden of proof as to unreasonable accumulations generally.

For purposes of applying the presumption provided for in section 533(a) and in determining the extent of the accumulated earnings credit under section 535(c)(1), the burden of proof with respect to an allegation by the Commissioner that all or any part of the earnings and profits of the corporation have been permitted to accumulate beyond the reasonable needs of the business may vary under section 534 as between litigation in the Tax Court and that in any other court. In case of a proceeding in a court other than the Tax Court, see paragraph (b) of § 1.533–1.

[T.D. 6500, 25 FR 11737, Nov. 26, 1960]

§ 1.534–2   Burden of proof as to unreasonable accumulations in cases before the Tax Court.

(a) **Burden of proof on Commissioner.** Under the general rule provided in section 534(a), in any proceeding before the Tax Court involving a notice of deficiency based in whole or in part on the allegation that all or any part of the earnings and profits have been permitted to accumulate beyond the reasonable needs of the business, the burden of proof with respect to such allegation is upon the Commissioner if—

(1) A notification, as provided for in section 534(b) and paragraph (c) of this section, has not been sent to the taxpayer; or

(2) A notification, as provided for in section 534(b) and paragraph (c) of this section, has been sent to the taxpayer and, in response to such notification, the taxpayer has submitted a statement, as provided in section 534(c) and paragraph (d) of this section, setting forth the ground or grounds (together with facts sufficient to show the basis thereof) on which it relies to establish that all or any part of its earnings and profits have not

been permitted to accumulate beyond the reasonable needs of the business. However, the burden of proof in the latter case is upon the Commissioner only with respect to the relevant ground or grounds set forth in the statement submitted by the taxpayer, and only if such ground or grounds are supported by facts (contained in the statement) sufficient to show the basis thereof.

(b) **Burden of proof on the taxpayer.** The burden of proof in a Tax Court proceeding with respect to an allegation that all or any part of the earnings and profits have been permitted to accumulate beyond the reasonable needs of the business is upon the taxpayer if—

(1) A notification, as provided for in section 534(b) and paragraph (c) of this section, has been sent to the taxpayer and the taxpayer has not submitted a statement, in response to such notification, as provided in section 534(c) and paragraph (d) of this section; or

(2) A statement has been submitted by the taxpayer in response to such notification, but the ground or grounds on which the taxpayer relies are not relevant to the allegation or, if relevant, the statement does not contain facts sufficient to show the basis thereof.

* * *

(d) **Statement by taxpayer.** (1) A taxpayer who has received a notification, as provided in section 534(b) and paragraph (c) of this section, that the proposed notice of deficiency includes an amount with respect to the accumulated earnings tax imposed by section 531, may, under section 534(c), submit a statement that all or any part of the earnings and profits of the corporation have not been permitted to accumulate beyond the reasonable needs of the business. Such statement shall set forth the ground or grounds (together with facts sufficient to show the basis thereof) on which the taxpayer relies to establish that there has been no accumulation of earnings and profits beyond the reasonable needs of the business. See paragraphs (a) and (b) of this section for rules concerning the effect of the statement with respect to burden of proof. See §§ 1.537–1 to 1.537–3, inclusive, relating to reasonable needs of the business.

(2) The taxpayer's statement, under section 534(c) and this paragraph, must be submitted to the Internal Revenue office which issued the notification (referred to in section 534(b) and paragraph

(c) of this section) within 60 days after the mailing of such notification. If the taxpayer is unable, for good cause, to submit the statement within such 60-day period, an additional period not exceeding 30 days may be granted upon receipt in the Internal Revenue office concerned (before the expiration of the 60-day period provided herein) of a request from the taxpayer, setting forth the reasons for such request. See section 534(d) and § 1.534–3 with respect to a statement in the case of a jeopardy assessment.

[T.D. 6500, 25 FR 11737, Nov. 26, 1960]

§ 1.535–1 Definition.

(a) The accumulated earnings tax is imposed by section 531 on the accumulated taxable income. Accumulated taxable income is the taxable income of the corporation with the adjustments prescribed by section 535(b) and § 1.535–2, minus the sum of the dividends paid deduction and the accumulated earnings credit. See section 561 and the regulations thereunder, relating to the definition of the deduction for dividends paid, and section 535(c) and § 1.535–3, relating to the accumulated earnings credit.

* * *

[T.D. 6500, 25 FR 11737, Nov. 26, 1960, as amended by T.D. 7244, 37 FR 28897, Dec. 30, 1972]

§ 1.535–2 Adjustments to taxable income.

(a) Taxes—(1) United States taxes. In computing accumulated taxable income for any taxable year, there shall be allowed as a deduction the amount by which Federal income and excess profits taxes accrued during the taxable year exceed the credit provided by section 33 (relating to taxes of foreign countries and possessions of the United States), except that no deduction shall be allowed for (i) the accumulated earnings tax imposed by section 531 (or a corresponding section of a prior law), (ii) the personal holding company tax imposed by section 541 (or a corresponding section of a prior law), and (iii) the excess profits tax imposed by subchapter E, chapter 2 of the Internal Revenue Code of 1939, for taxable years beginning after December 31, 1940. The deduction is for taxes accrued during the taxable year, regardless of whether the corporation uses an accrual method of accounting, the cash receipts and disbursements method, or any other allowable method of accounting. In computing the amount of taxes accrued, an

unpaid tax which is being contested is not considered accrued until the contest is resolved.

* * *

[T.D. 6500, 25 FR 11737, Nov. 26, 1960, as amended by T.D. 6805, 30 FR 3209, March 9, 1965; T.D. 6841, 30 FR 9305, July 27, 1965; T.D. 7301, 39 FR 964, Jan. 4, 1974; T.D. 7649, 44 FR 60086, Oct. 18, 1979]

§ 1.535–3 Accumulated earnings credit.

(a) In general. As provided in section 535(a) and § 1.535–1, the accumulated earnings credit, provided by section 535(c), reduces taxable income in computing accumulated taxable income. In the case of a corporation, not a mere holding or investment company, the accumulated earnings credit is determined as provided in paragraph (b) of this section and, in the case of a holding or investment company, as provided in paragraph (c) of this section.

(b) Corporation which is not a mere holding or investment company—(1) General rule. (i) In the case of a corporation, not a mere holding or investment company, the accumulated earnings credit is the amount equal to such part of the earnings and profits of the taxable year which is retained for the reasonable needs of the business, minus the deduction allowed by section 535(b)(6) (see paragraph (f) of § 1.535–2, relating to the deduction for long-term capital gains). In no event shall the accumulated earnings credit be less than the minimum credit provided for in section 535(c)(2) and subparagraph (2) of this paragraph. The amount of the earnings and profits for the taxable year retained is the amount by which the earnings and profits for the taxable year exceed the dividends paid deduction for such taxable year. See section 561 and §§ 1.561–1 and 1.561–2, relating to the deduction for dividends paid.

(ii) In determining whether any amount of the earnings and profits of the taxable year has been retained for the reasonable needs of the business, the accumulated earnings and profits of prior years will be taken into consideration. Thus, for example, if such accumulated earnings and profits of prior years are sufficient for the reasonable needs of the business, then any earnings and profits of the current taxable year which are retained will not be considered to be retained for the reasonable needs of the business. See section 537 and §§ 1.537–1 and 1.537–2.

* * *

[T.D. 6500, 25 FR 11737, Nov. 26, 1960, as amended by T.D. 6992, 34 FR 826, Jan. 18, 1969; T.D. 7181, 37 FR 8066, April 25, 1972; T.D. 7244, 37 FR 28897, Dec. 30, 1972; T.D. 7376, 40 FR 42744, Sept. 16, 1975; T.D. 7528, 42 FR 64694, Dec. 28, 1977]

§ 1.537–1   Reasonable needs of the business.

(a) **In general.** The term "reasonable needs of the business" includes (1) the reasonable anticipated needs of the business (including product liability loss reserves, as defined in paragraph (f) of this section), (2) the section 303 redemption needs of the business, as defined in paragraph (c) of this section, and (3) the excess business holdings redemption needs of the business as described in paragraph (d) of this section. See paragraph (e) of this section for additional rules relating to the section 303 redemption needs and the excess business holdings redemption needs of the business. An accumulation of the earnings and profits (including the undistributed earnings and profits of prior years) is in excess of the reasonable needs of the business if it exceeds the amount that a prudent businessman would consider appropriate for the present business purposes and for the reasonably anticipated future needs of the business. The need to retain earnings and profits must be directly connected with the needs of the corporation itself and must be for bona fide business purposes. For purposes of this paragraph the section 303 redemption needs of the business and the excess business holdings redemption needs of the business are deemed to be directly connected with the needs of the business and for a bona fide business purpose. See § 1.537–3 for a discussion of what constitutes the business of the corporation. The extent to which earnings and profits have been distributed by the corporation may be taken into account in determining whether or not retained earnings and profits exceed the reasonable needs of the business. See § 1.537–2, relating to grounds for accumulation of earnings and profits.

(b) **Reasonable anticipated needs.** (1) In order for a corporation to justify an accumulation of earnings and profits for reasonably anticipated future needs, there must be an indication that the future needs of the business require such accumulation, and the corporation must have specific, definite, and feasible plans for the use of such accumulation. Such an accumulation need not be used immediately, nor must the plans for its use be consummated within a short period after the close

of the taxable year, provided that such accumulation will be used within a reasonable time depending upon all the facts and circumstances relating to the future needs of the business. Where the future needs of the business are uncertain or vague, where the plans for the future use of an accumulation are not specific, definite, and feasible, or where the execution of such a plan is postponed indefinitely, an accumulation cannot be justified on the grounds of reasonably anticipated needs of the business.

(2) Consideration shall be given to reasonably anticipated needs as they exist on the basis of the facts at the close of the taxable year. Thus, subsequent events shall not be used for the purpose of showing that the retention of earnings or profits was unreasonable at the close of the taxable year if all the elements of reasonable anticipation are present at the close of such taxable year. However, subsequent events may be considered to determine whether the taxpayer actually intended to consummate or has actually consummated the plans for which the earnings and profits were accumulated. In this connection, projected expansion or investment plans shall be reviewed in the light of the facts during each year and as they exist as of the close of the taxable year. If a corporation has justified an accumulation for future needs by plans never consummated, the amount of such an accumulation shall be taken into account in determining the reasonableness of subsequent accumulations.

(c) **Section 303 redemption needs of the business.** (1) The term "section 303 redemption needs" means, with respect to the taxable year of the corporation in which a shareholder of the corporation died or any taxable year thereafter, the amount needed (or reasonably anticipated to be needed) to redeem stock included in the gross estate of such shareholder but not in excess of the amount necessary to effect a distribution to which section 303 applies. For purposes of this paragraph, the term "shareholder" includes an individual in whose gross estate stock of the corporation is includable upon his death for Federal estate tax purposes.

(2) This paragraph applies to a corporation to which section 303(c) would apply if a distribution described therein were made.

(3) If stock included in the gross estate of a decedent is stock of two or more corporations described in section 303(b)(2)(B), the amount needed

by each such corporation for section 303 redemption purposes under this section shall, unless the particular facts and circumstances indicate otherwise, be that amount which bears the same ratio to the amount described in section 303(a) as the fair market value of such corporation's stock included in the gross estate of such decedent bears to the fair market value of all of the stock of such corporations included in the gross estate. For example, facts and circumstances indicating that the allocation prescribed by this subparagraph is not required would include notice given to the corporations by the executor or administrator of the decedent's estate that he intends to request the redemption of stock of only one of such corporations or the redemption of stock of such corporations in a ratio which is unrelated to the respective fair market values of the stock of the corporations included in the decedent's gross estate.

* * *

(f) **Product liability loss reserves.** (1) The term "product liability loss reserve" means, with respect to taxable years beginning after September 30, 1979, reasonable amounts accumulated for the payment of reasonably anticipated product liability losses, as defined in section 172(j) and § 1.172–13(b)(1).

(2) For purposes of this paragraph, whether an accumulation for anticipated product liability losses is reasonable in amount and whether such anticipated product liability losses are likely to occur shall be determined in light of all facts and circumstances of the taxpayer making such accumulation. Some of the factors to be considered in determining the reasonableness of the accumulation include the taxpayer's previous product liability experience, the extent of the taxpayer's coverage by commercial product liability insurance, the income tax consequences of the taxpayer's ability to deduct product liability losses and related expenses, and the taxpayer's potential future liability to defective products in light of the taxpayer's plans to expand the production of products currently being manufactured, provided such plans are specific, definite and feasible. Additionally, a factor to be considered in determining whether the accumulation is reasonable in amount is whether the taxpayer, in accounting for its potential future liability, took into account the reasonably estimated present value of the potential future liability.

(3) Only those accumulations made with respect to products that have been manufactured, leased, or sold shall be considered as accumulations made under this paragraph. Thus, for example, accumulations with respect to a product which has not progressed beyond the development stage are not reasonable accumulations under this paragraph.

[T.D. 6500, 25 FR 11737, Nov. 26, 1960, as amended by T.D. 7165, 37 FR 5022, March 9, 1972, 37 FR 5703, March 18, 1972; T.D. 7678, 44 FR 12416, Feb. 26, 1980; T.D. 8096, 51 FR 30483, Aug. 27, 1986]

§ 1.537–2 Grounds for accumulation of earnings and profits.

(a) **In general.** Whether a particular ground or grounds for the accumulation of earnings and profits indicate that the earnings and profits have been accumulated for the reasonable needs of the business or beyond such needs is dependent upon the particular circumstances of the case. Listed below in paragraphs (b) and (c) of this section are some of the grounds which may be used as guides under ordinary circumstances.

(b) **Reasonable accumulation of earnings and profits.** Although the following grounds are not exclusive, one or more of such grounds, if supported by sufficient facts, may indicate that the earnings and profits of a corporation are being accumulated for the reasonable needs of the business provided the general requirements under §§ 1.537–1 and 1.537–3 are satisfied:

(1) To provide for bona fide expansion of business or replacement of plant;

(2) To acquire a business enterprise through purchasing stock or assets;

(3) To provide for the retirement of bona fide indebtedness created in connection with the trade or business, such as the establishment of a sinking fund for the purpose of retiring bonds issued by the corporation in accordance with contract obligations incurred on issue;

(4) To provide necessary working capital for the business, such as, for the procurement of inventories;

(5) To provide for investments or loans to suppliers or customers if necessary in order to maintain the business of the corporation; or

(6) To provide for the payment of reasonably anticipated product liability losses, as defined in section 172(j), § 1.172–13(b)(1), and § 1.537–1(f).

(c) **Unreasonable accumulations of earnings and profits.** Although the following purposes are not exclusive, accumulations of earnings and profits to meet any one of such objectives may indicate that the earnings and profits of a corporation are being accumulated beyond the reasonable needs of the business:

(1) Loans to shareholders, or the expenditure of funds of the corporation for the personal benefit of the shareholders;

(2) Loans having no reasonable relation to the conduct of the business made to relatives or friends of shareholders, or to other persons;

(3) Loans to another corporation, the business of which is not that of the taxpayer corporation, if the capital stock of such other corporation is owned, directly or indirectly, by the shareholder or shareholders of the taxpayer corporation and such shareholder or shareholders are in control of both corporations;

(4) Investments in properties, or securities which are unrelated to the activities of the business of the taxpayer corporation; or

(5) Retention of earnings and profits to provide against unrealistic hazards.

[T.D. 6500, 25 FR 11737, Nov. 26, 1960; T.D. 8096, 51 FR 30484, Aug. 27, 1986]

§ 1.537-3 Business of the corporation.

(a) The business of a corporation is not merely that which it has previously carried on but includes, in general, any line of business which it may undertake.

(b) If one corporation owns the stock of another corporation and, in effect, operates the other corporation, the business of the latter corporation may be considered in substance, although not in legal form, the business of the first corporation. However, investment by a corporation of its earnings and profits in stock and securities of another corporation is not, of itself, to be regarded as employment of the earnings and profits in its business. Earnings and profits of the first corporation put into the second corporation through the purchase of stock or securities or otherwise, may, if a subsidiary relationship is established, constitute employment of the earnings and profits in its own business. Thus, the business of one corporation may be regarded as including the business of another corporation if such other corporation is a mere instrumentality of the first corporation; that may be established by showing that the first corporation owns at least 80 percent of the voting stock of the second corporation. If the taxpayer's ownership of stock is less than 80 percent in the other corporation, the determination of whether the funds are employed in a business operated by the taxpayer will depend upon the particular circumstances of the case. Moreover, the business of one corporation does not include the business of another corporation if such other corporation is a personal holding company, an investment company, or a corporation not engaged in the active conduct of a trade or business.

[T.D. 6500, 25 FR 11737, Nov. 26, 1960]

Personal Holding Companies

§ 1.541-1 Imposition of tax.

(a) Section 541 imposes a graduated tax upon corporations classified as personal holding companies under section 542. This tax, if applicable, is in addition to the tax imposed upon corporations generally under section 11. Unless specifically excepted under section 542(c) the tax applies to domestic and foreign corporations and, to the extent provided by section 542(b), to an affiliated group of corporations filing a consolidated return. Corporations classified as personal holding companies are exempt from the accumulated earnings tax imposed under section 531 but are not exempt from other income taxes imposed upon corporations, generally, under any other provisions of the Code. Unlike the accumulated earnings tax imposed under section 531, the personal holding company tax imposed by section 541 applies to all personal holding companies as defined in section 542, whether or not they were formed or availed of to avoid income tax upon shareholders. See section 6501(f) and § 301.6501(f)-1 of this chapter (Regulations on Procedure and Administration) with respect to the period of limitation on assessment of personal holding company tax upon failure to file a schedule of personal holding company income.

* * *

[T.D. 6500, 25 FR 11737, Nov. 26, 1960]

§ 1.542-2 Gross income requirement.

To meet the gross income requirement it is necessary that at least 80 percent of the total gross income of the corporation for the taxable year be personal holding company income as defined in section 543 and §§ 1.543–1 and 1.543–2. For the definition of "gross income" see section 61 and §§ 1.61–1 through 1.61–14. Under such provisions gross income is not necessarily synonymous with gross receipts. Further, in the case of transactions in stocks and securities and in commodities transactions, gross income for personal holding company tax purposes shall include only the excess of gains over losses from such transactions. See section 543(b), paragraph (b)(5) and (6) of § 1.543–1 and § 1.543–2. For determining the character of the amount includible in gross income under section 951(a), see paragraph (a) of § 1.951–1.

* * *

[T.D. 6500, 25 FR 11737, Nov. 26, 1960, as amended by T.D. 6795, 30 FR 934, Jan. 29, 1965]

§ 1.543–1 Personal holding company income.

(a) **General rule.** The term "personal holding company income" means the portion of the gross income which consists of the classes of gross income described in paragraph (b) of this section. See section 543(b) and § 1.543–2 for special limitations on gross income and personal holding company income in cases of gains from stocks', securities', and commodities' transactions.

(b) **Definitions—(1) Dividends.** The term "dividends" includes dividends as defined in section 316 and amounts required to be included in gross income under section 551 and §§ 1.551–1—1.551–2 (relating to foreign personal holding company income taxed to United States shareholders).

(2) **Interest.** The term "interest" means any amounts, includible in gross income, received for the use of money loaned. However, (i) interest which constitutes "rent" shall not be classified as interest but shall be classified as "rents" (see subparagraph (10) of this paragraph) * * * shall not be included in personal holding company income.

(3) **Royalties (other than mineral, oil, or gas royalties or certain copyright royalties).** The term "royalties" (other than mineral, oil, or gas royalties or certain copyright royalties) includes amounts received for the privilege of using patents, copyrights, secret processes and formulas, good will, trade marks, trade brands, franchises, and other like property. It does not, however, include rents. * * *

(4) **Annuities.** The term "annuities" includes annuities only to the extent includible in the computation of gross income. See section 72 and §§ 1.72–1—1.72–14 for rules relating to the inclusion of annuities in gross income.

(5) **Gains from the sale or exchange of stock or securities.** (i) Except in the case of regular dealers in stock or securities as provided in subdivision (ii) of this subparagraph, gross income and personal holding company income include the amount by which the gains exceed the losses from the sale or exchange of stock or securities. See section 543(b)(1) and § 1.543–2 for provisions relating to this limitation. For this purpose, there shall be taken into account all those gains includible in gross income (including gains from liquidating dividends and other distributions from capital) and all those losses deductible from gross income which are considered under chapter 1 of the Code to be gains or losses from the sale or exchange of stock or securities. The term "stock or securities" as used in section 543(a)(2) and this subparagraph includes shares or certificates of stock, stock rights or warrants, or interest in any corporation (including any joint stock company, insurance company, association, or other organization classified as a corporation by the Code), certificates of interest or participation in any profit-sharing agreement, or in any oil, gas, or other mineral property, or lease, collateral trust certificates, voting trust certificates, bonds, debentures, certificates of indebtedness, notes, car trust certificates, bills of exchange, obligations issued by or on behalf of a State, Territory, or political subdivision thereof.

(ii) In the case of "regular dealers in stock or securities" there shall not be included gains or losses derived from the sale or exchange of stock or securities made in the normal course of business. The term "regular dealer in stock or securities" means a corporation with an established place of business regularly engaged in the purchase of stock or securities and their resale to customers. However, such corporations shall not be considered as regular dealers with respect to stock or securities which are held for investment. See section 1236 and § 1.1236–1.

(6) **Gains from futures transactions in commodities.** Gross income and personal holding company income include the amount by which the gains exceed the losses from futures transactions in any commodity on or subject to the rules of a board of trade or commodity exchange. See § 1.543–2 for provisions relating to this limitation.

In general, for the purpose of determining such excess, there are included all gains and losses on futures contracts which are speculative. However, for the purpose of determining such excess, there shall not be included gains or losses from cash transactions, or gains or losses by a producer, processor, merchant, or handler of the commodity, which arise out of bona fide hedging transactions reasonably necessary to the conduct of its business in the manner in which such business is customarily and usually conducted by others. See section 1233 and § 1.1233–1.

(7) Estates and trusts. Under section 543(a)(4) personal holding company income includes amounts includible in computing the taxable income of the corporation under part I, subchapter J, chapter 1 of the Code (relating to estates, trusts, and beneficiaries); and any gain derived by the corporation from the sale or other disposition of any interest in an estate or trust.

(8) Personal service contracts. (i) Under section 543(a)(5) amounts received under a contract under which the corporation is to furnish personal services, as well as amounts received from the sale or other disposition of such contract, shall be included as personal holding company income if—

(a) Some person other than the corporation has the right to designate (by name or by description) the individual who is to perform the services, or if the individual who is to perform the services is designated (by name or by description) in the contract; and

(b) At any time during the taxable year 25 percent or more in value of the outstanding stock of the corporation is owned, directly or indirectly, by or for the individual who has performed, is to perform, or may be designated (by name or by description) as the one to perform, such services. For this purpose, the amount of stock outstanding and its value shall be determined in accordance with the rules set forth in the last two sentences of paragraph (b) and in paragraph (c) of § 1.542–3. It should be noted that the stock ownership requirement of section 543(a)(5) and this subparagraph relates to the stock ownership at any time during the taxable year. For rules relating to the determination of stock ownership, see section 544 and §§ 1.544–1 through 1.544–7.

(ii) If the contract, in addition to requiring the performance of services by a 25-percent stockholder who is designated or who could be designated (as specified in section 543(a)(5) and subdivision (i) of this subparagraph), requires the performance of services by other persons which are important and essential, then only that portion of the amount received under such contract which is attributable to the personal services of the 25-percent stockholder shall constitute personal holding company income. Incidental personal services of other persons employed by the corporation to facilitate the performance of the services by the 25-percent stockholder, however, shall not constitute important or essential services. Under section 482 gross income, deductions, credits, or allowances between or among organizations, trades, or businesses may be allocated if it is determined that allocation is necessary in order to prevent evasion of taxes or clearly to reflect the income of any such organizations, trades, or businesses.

(iii) The application of section 543(a)(5) and this subparagraph may be illustrated by the following examples:

Example (1). A, whose profession is that of an actor, owns all of the outstanding capital stock of the M Corporation. The M Corporation entered into a contract with A under which A was to perform personal services for the person or persons whom the M Corporation might designate, in consideration of which A was to receive $10,000 a year from the M Corporation. The M Corporation entered into a contract with the O Corporation in which A was designated to perform personal services for the O Corporation in consideration of which the O Corporation was to pay the M Corporation $500,000 a year. The $500,000 received by the M Corporation from the O Corporation constitutes personal holding company income.

Example (2). Assume the same facts as in example (1), except that, in addition to A's contract with the M Corporation, B, whose profession is that of a dancer and C, whose profession is that of a singer, were also under contract to the M Corporation to perform personal services for the person or persons whom the M Corporation might designate, in consideration of which they were each to receive $25,000 a year from the M Corporation. Neither B nor C were stockholders of the M Corporation. The contract entered into by the M Corporation with the O Corporation, in addition to designating that A was to perform personal services for the O Corporation, designated that B and C were also to perform personal services for the O Corporation. Although the O Corporation particularly desired the services of A for an entertainment program it planned, it also desired the services of B and C, who were prominent in their fields, to provide a good supporting cast for the program. The services of B and C required under the contract are determined to be important and essential; therefore, only that portion of the $500,000 received by the M Corporation which is attributable to the personal services of A constitutes personal holding company income. The same result would obtain although the dancer and the singer required by the contract were not designated by name but the contract gave the M Corporation discretion to select and provide the services of a singer and a dancer for the program and such services were provided.

Example (3). The N Corporation is engaged in engineering. Its entire outstanding capital stock is owned by four individuals. The N Corporation entered into a contract with the R Corporation to perform engineering services in consideration of which the R Corporation was to pay the N Corporation $50,000. The individual who was to perform the services was not designated (by name or by description) in the contract and no one but the N Corporation had the right to designate (by name or by description) such individual. The $50,000 received by the N Corporation from the R Corporation does not constitute personal holding company income.

(9) Compensation for use of property. Under section 543(a)(6) amounts received as compensation for the use of, or right to use, property of the corporation shall be included as personal holding company income if, at any time during the taxable year, 25 percent or more in value of the outstanding stock of the corporation is owned, directly or indirectly, by or for an individual entitled to the use of the property. Thus, if a shareholder who meets the stock ownership requirement of section 543(a)(6) and this subparagraph uses, or has the right to use, a yacht, residence, or other property owned by the corporation, the compensation to the corporation for such use, or right to use, the property constitutes personal holding company income. This is true even though the shareholder may acquire the use of, or the right to use, the property by means of a sublease or under any other arrangement involving parties other than the corporation and the shareholder. However, if the personal holding company income of the corporation (after excluding any such income described in section 543(a)(6) and this subparagraph, relating to compensation for use of property, and after excluding any such income described in section 543(a)(7) and subparagraph (10) of this paragraph, relating to rents) is not more than 10 percent of its gross income, compensation for the use of property shall not constitute personal holding company income. For purposes of the preceding sentence, in determining whether personal holding company income is more than 10 percent of gross income, copyright royalties constitute personal holding company income, regardless of whether such copyright royalties are excluded from personal holding company income under section 543(a)(9) and subparagraph (12)(ii) of this paragraph. For purposes of applying section 543(a)(6) and this subparagraph, the amount of stock outstanding and its value shall be determined in accordance with the rules set forth in the last two sentences of paragraph (b) and in paragraph (c) of § 1.542–3. It should be noted that

the stock ownership requirement of section 543(a)(6) and this subparagraph relates to the stock outstanding at any time during the entire taxable year. For rules relating to the determination of stock ownership, see section 544 and §§ 1.544–1 through 1.544–7.

(10) Rents (including interest constituting rents). Rents which are to be included as personal holding company income consist of compensation (however designated) for the use, or right to use, property of the corporation. The term "rents" does not include amounts includible in personal holding company income under section 543(a)(6) and subparagraph (9) of this paragraph. The amounts considered as rents include charter fees, etc., for the use of, or the right to use, property, as well as interest on debts owed to the corporation (to the extent such debts represent the price for which real property held primarily for sale to customers in the ordinary course of the corporation's trade or business was sold or exchanged by the corporation). However, if the amount of the rents includible under section 543(a)(7) and this subparagraph constitutes 50 percent or more of the gross income of the corporation, such rents shall not be considered to be personal holding company income.

(11) Mineral, oil, or gas royalties. (i) The income from mineral, oil, or gas royalties is to be included as personal holding company income, unless (a) the aggregate amount of such royalties constitutes 50 percent or more of the gross income of the corporation for the taxable year and (b) the aggregate amount of deductions allowable under section 162 (other than compensation for personal services rendered by the shareholders of the corporation) equals 15 percent or more of the gross income of the corporation for the taxable year.

(ii) The term "mineral, oil, or gas royalties" means all royalties, including overriding royalties and, to the extent not treated as loans under section 636, mineral production payments, received from any interest in mineral, oil, or gas properties. The term "mineral" includes those minerals which are included within the meaning of the term "minerals" in the regulations under section 611.

(iii) The first sentence of subdivision (ii) of this subparagraph shall apply to overriding royalties received from the sublessee by the operating company which originally leased and developed the natural resource property in respect of which such overriding royalties are paid, and to mineral, oil, or gas production payments, only with respect to amounts received after September 30, 1958.

(12) Copyright royalties—(i) In general. The income from copyright royalties constitutes, generally, personal holding company income. However, for taxable years beginning after December 31, 1959, those copyright royalties which come within the definition of "copyright royalties" in section 543(a)(9) and subdivision (iv) of this subparagraph shall be excluded from personal holding company income only if the conditions set forth in subdivision (ii) of this subparagraph are satisfied.

(ii) Exclusion from personal holding company income. For taxable years beginning after December 31, 1959, copyright royalties (as defined in section 543(a)(9) and subdivision (iv) of this subparagraph) shall be excluded from personal holding company income only if the conditions set forth in (a), (b), and (c) of this subdivision are met.

(a) Such copyright royalties for the taxable year must constitute 50 percent or more of the corporation's gross income. For this purpose, copyright royalties shall be computed by excluding royalties received for the use of, or the right to use, copyrights or interests in copyrights in works created, in whole or in part, by any person who, at any time during the corporation's taxable year, is a shareholder.

(b) Personal holding company income for the taxable year must be 10 percent or less of the corporation's gross income. For this purpose, personal holding company income shall be computed by excluding (1) copyright royalties (except that there shall be included royalties received for the use of, or the right to use, copyrights or interests in copyrights in works created, in whole or in part, by any shareholder owning, at any time during the corporation's taxable year, more than 10 percent in value of the outstanding stock of the corporation), and (2) dividends from any corporation in which the taxpayer owns, on the date the taxpayer becomes entitled to the dividends, at least 50 percent of all classes of stock entitled to vote and at least 50 percent of the total value of all classes of stock, provided the corporation which pays the dividends meets the requirements of subparagraphs (A), (B), and (C) of section 543(a)(9).

(c) The aggregate amount of the deductions allowable under section 162 must constitute 50 percent or more of the corporation's gross income for the taxable year. For this purpose, the deductions allowable under section 162 shall be computed by

excluding deductions for compensation for personal services rendered by, and deductions for copyright and other royalties to, shareholders of the corporation.

(iii) Determination of stock value and stock ownership. For purposes of section 543(a)(9) and this subparagraph, the following rules shall apply:

(a) The amount and value of the outstanding stock of a corporation shall be determined in accordance with the rules set forth in the last two sentences of paragraph (b) and in paragraph (c) of § 1.542–3.

(b) The ownership of stock shall be determined in accordance with the rules set forth in section 544 and §§ 1.544–1 through 1.544–7.

(c) Any person who is considered to own stock within the meaning of section 544 and §§ 1.544–1 through 1.544–7 shall be a shareholder.

(iv) Copyright royalties defined. For purposes of section 543(a)(9) and this subparagraph, the term "copyright royalties" means compensation, however designated, for the use of, or the right to use, copyrights in works protected by copyright issued under Title 17 of the United States Code (other than by reason of section 2 or 6 thereof), and to which copyright protection is also extended by the laws of any foreign country as a result of any international treaty, convention, or agreement to which the United States is a signatory. Thus, "copyright royalties" includes not only royalties from sources within the United States under protection of United States laws relating to statutory copyrights but also royalties from sources within a foreign country with respect to United States statutory copyrights protected in such foreign country by any international treaty, convention, or agreement to which the United States is a signatory. The term "copyright royalties" includes compensation for the use of, or right to use, an interest in any such copyrighted works as well as payments from any person for performing rights in any such copyrighted works.

(v) Compensation which is rent. Section 543(a)(9) and subdivisions (i) through (iv) of this subparagraph shall not apply to compensation which is "rent" within the meaning of the second sentence of section 543(a)(7).

[T.D. 6500, 25 FR 11737, Nov. 26, 1960, as amended by T.D. 6739, 29 FR 7713, June 17, 1964; T.D. 7261, 38 FR 5467, March 1, 1973]

§ 1.545–2 Adjustments to taxable income.

(a) Taxes—(1) General rule. (i) In computing undistributed personal holding company income for any taxable year, there shall be allowed as a deduction the amount by which Federal income and excess profits taxes accrued during the taxable year exceed the credit provided by section 33 (relating to taxes of foreign countries and possessions of the United States), and the income, war profits, and excess profits taxes of foreign countries and possessions of the United States accrued during the taxable year (to the extent provided by subparagraph (3) of this paragraph), except that no deduction shall be allowed for (a) the accumulated earnings tax imposed by section 531 (or a corresponding section of a prior law), (b) the personal holding company tax imposed by section 541 (or a corresponding section of a prior law), and (c) the excess profits tax imposed by subchapter E, chapter 2 of the Internal Revenue Code of 1939, for taxable years beginning after December 31, 1940. The deduction is for taxes for the taxable year, determined under the accrual method of accounting, regardless of whether the corporation uses an accrual method of accounting, the cash receipts and disbursement method, or any other allowable method of accounting. In computing the amount of taxes accrued, an unpaid tax which is being contested is not considered accrued until the contest is resolved.

* * *

(b) Charitable contributions—(1) Taxable years beginning before January 1, 1970. * * *

* * *

(2) Taxable years beginning after December 31, 1969. (i) Section 545(b)(2) provides that, in computing the deduction allowable for charitable contributions for purposes of determining undistributed personal holding company income of a corporation for taxable years beginning after December 31, 1969, the limitations in section 170(b)(1)(A), (B), and (D)(i) (relating to charitable contributions by individuals) shall apply, and section 170(b)(1)(D)(ii) (relating to excess charitable contributions by individuals of certain capital gain property, section 170(b)(2) (relating to the 5-percent limitation on charitable contributions by corporations), and section 170(d)(relating to carryovers of excess contributions of individuals and corporations) shall not apply.

(ii) Although the limitations of section 170(b)(1)(A), (B), and (D)(i) are 50, 20, and 30 per-cent, respectively, of an individual's contribution base, these limitations are applied for purposes of section 545(b)(2) by using 50, 20, and 30 percent, respectively, of the corporation's taxable income as adjusted for purposes of section 170(b)(2), that is, the same amount of taxable income to which the 5-percent limitation applies. Thus, the term "contribution base" when used in section 170(b)(1) means the corporation's taxable income computed with the adjustments, other than the 5-percent limitation, provided in section 170(b)(2). However, a further adjustment for this purpose is that the taxable income shall also be computed without the deduction of the amount disallowed under section 545(b)(8), relating to expenses and depreciation applicable to property of the taxpayer. The carryover of charitable contributions made in a prior year, otherwise allowable as a deduction in computing taxable income to the extent provided in section 170(b)(1)(D)(ii) and (d), shall not be allowed as a deduction in computing undistributed personal holding company income for any taxable year.

(iii) See § 1.170A–8 for the rules with respect to the charitable contributions to which the 50-, 20-, and 30-percent limitations apply.

* * *

(d) Net operating loss. The net operating loss deduction provided in section 172 is not allowed for purposes of the computation of undistributed personal holding company income. For purposes of such a computation, however, there is allowed as a deduction the amount of the net operating loss (as defined in section 172(c)) for the preceding taxable year, except that, in computing undistributed personal holding company income for a taxable year beginning after December 31, 1957, the amount of such net operating loss shall be computed without the deductions provided in part VIII (section 241 and following, except section 248), subchapter B, chapter 1 of the Code.

(e) Long-term capital gains. (1) There is allowed as a deduction the excess of the net long-term capital gain for the taxable year over the net short-term capital loss for such year, minus the taxes attributable to such excess, as provided in section 545(b)(5).

(2) Section 631(c) (relating to gain or loss in the case of disposal of coal or domestic iron ore) shall have no application.

* * *

(h) Expenses and depreciation applicable to property of the taxpayer. (1) In computing undistributed personal holding company income in the case of a personal holding company which owns or operates property, section 545(b)(8) provides a specific limitation with respect to the allowance of deductions for trade or business expenses and depreciation allocable to the operation or maintenance of such property. Under this limitation, these deductions shall not be allowed in an amount in excess of the aggregate amount of the rent or other compensation received for the use of, or the right to use, the property, unless it is established to the satisfaction of the Commissioner—

(i) That the rent or other compensation received was the highest obtainable, or if none was received, that none was obtainable;

(ii) That the property was held in the course of a business carried on bona fide for profit; and

(iii) Either that there was reasonable expectation that the operation of the property would result in a profit, or that the property was necessary to the conduct of the business.

(2) The burden of proof will rest upon the taxpayer to sustain the deduction claimed. If, in computing undistributed personal holding company income, a personal holding company claims deductions for expenses and depreciation allocable to the operation and maintenance of property owned or operated by the company, in an aggregate amount in excess of the rent or other compensation received for the use of, or the right to use, the property, it shall attach to its income tax return a statement setting forth its claim for allowance of the additional deductions, together with a complete statement of the facts and circumstances pertinent to its claim and the arguments on which it relies. Such statement shall set forth:

(i) A description of the property;

(ii) The cost or other basis to the corporation and the nature and value of the consideration paid for the property;

(iii) The name and address of the person from whom the property was acquired and the date the property was acquired;

(iv) The name and address of the person to whom the property is leased or rented, or the person permitted to use the property, and the number of shares of stock, if any, held by such person and the members of his family;

(v) The nature and gross amount of the rent or other compensation received for the use of, or the right to use, the property during the taxable year and for each of the five preceding years and the amount of the expenses incurred with respect to, and the depreciation sustained on, the property for such years;

(vi) Evidence that the rent or other compensation was the highest obtainable or, if none was received, a statement of the reasons therefore;

(vii) A copy of the contract, lease or rental agreement;

(viii) The purpose for which the property was used;

(ix) The business, carried on by the corporation, with respect to which the property was held and the gross income, expenses, and taxable income derived from the conduct of such business for the taxable year and for each of the five preceding years;

(x) A statement of any reasons which existed for expectation that the operation of the property would be profitable, or a statement of the necessity for the use of the property in the business of the corporation, and the reasons why the property was acquired; and

(xi) Any other information pertinent to the taxpayer's claim.

* * *

[T.D. 6500, 25 FR 11737, Nov. 26, 1960, as amended by T.D. 6805, 30 FR 3209, March 9, 1965; T.D. 6841, 30 FR 9305, July 27, 1965; T.D. 6900, 31 FR 14643, Nov. 17, 1966; T.D. 6949, 33 FR 5526, April 9, 1968; T.D. 7207, 37 FR 20796, Oct. 5, 1972; T.D. 7429, 41 FR 35492, Aug. 23, 1976; T.D. 7649, 44 FR 60086, Oct. 18, 1979]

§ 1.547–1 General rule.

Section 547 provides a method under which, by virtue of dividend distributions, a corporation may be relieved from the payment of a deficiency in the personal holding company tax imposed by section 541 (or by a corresponding provision of a prior income tax law), or may be entitled to a credit or refund of a part or all of any such deficiency which has been paid. The method provided by section 547 is to allow an additional deduction for a dividend distribution (which meets the requirements of this section) in computing undistributed personal holding company income for the taxable year for which a deficiency in personal holding company tax is determined. The additional deduction for deficiency dividends will not, however, be allowed for the purpose of determining interest, additional amounts, or assessable penalties, computed with respect to the personal holding company tax prior to the allowance of the additional deduction for deficiency dividends. Such amounts remain payable as if section 547 had not been enacted. [T.D. 6500, 25 FR 11737, Nov. 26, 1960]

§1.547-2 Requirements for deficiency dividends.

(a) In general. There are certain requirements which must be fulfilled before a deduction is allowed for a deficiency dividend under section 547 and this section. These are—

(1) The taxpayer's liability for personal holding company tax shall be determined only in the manner provided in section 547(c) and paragraph (b)(1) of this section.

(2) The deficiency dividend shall be paid by the corporation on, or within 90 days after, the date of such determination and prior to the filing of a claim under section 547(e) and paragraph (b)(2) of this section for deduction for deficiency dividends. This claim must be filed within 120 days after such determination.

(3) The deficiency dividend must be of such a nature as would have permitted its inclusion in the computation of a deduction for dividends paid under section 561 for the taxable year with respect to which the liability for personal holding company tax exists, if it had been distributed during such year. See section 562 and §§ 1.562-1 through 1.562-3. In this connection, it should be noted that under section 316(b)(2), the term "dividend" means (in addition to the usual meaning under section 316(a)) any distribution of property (whether or not a dividend as defined in section 316(a)) made by a corporation to its shareholders, to the extent of its undistributed personal holding company income (determined under section 545 and §§ 1.545-1 and 1.545-2 without regard to section 316(b)(2)) for the taxable year in respect of which the distribution is made.

(b) Special rules—(1) Nature and details of determination. (i) A determination of a taxpayer's liability for personal holding company tax shall, for the purposes of section 547, be established in the manner specified in section 547(c) and this subparagraph.

(ii) The date of determination by a decision of the Tax Court of the United States is the date upon which such decision becomes final, as prescribed in section 7481.

(iii) The slate upon which a judgment of a court becomes final, which is the date of the determination in such cases, must be determined upon the basis of the facts in the particular case. Ordinarily, a judgment of a United States district court becomes final upon the expiration of the time allowed for taking an appeal, if no such appeal is duly taken within such time; and a judgment of the United States Court of Claims becomes final upon the expiration of the time allowed for filing a petition for certiorari if no such petition is duly filed within such time.

(iv) The date of determination by a closing agreement, made under section 7121, is the date such agreement is approved by the Commissioner.

(v) A determination under section 547(c)(3) may be made by an agreement signed by the district director or such other official to whom authority to sign the agreement is delegated, and by or on behalf of the taxpayer. The agreement shall set forth the total amount of the liability for personal holding company tax for the taxable year or years. An agreement under this subdivision which is signed by the district director (or such other official to whom authority to sign the agreement is delegated) on or after July 15, 1963, shall be sent to the taxpayer at his last known address by either registered or certified mail. If registered mail is used for such purpose, the date of registration shall be treated as the date of determination; if certified mail is used for such purpose, the date of the postmark on the sender's receipt for such mail shall be treated as the date of determination. However, if a dividend is paid by the corporation before such registration or postmark date but on or after the date such agreement is signed by the district director or such other official to whom authority to sign the agreement is delegated, the date of determination shall be such date of signing. The date of determination with respect to an agreement which is signed by the district director (or such other official to whom authority to sign the agreement is delegated) before July 15, 1963, shall be the date of the postmark on the cover envelope in which such agreement is sent by ordinary mail, except that if a dividend is paid by the corporation before such postmark date but on or after the date such agreement is signed by the district director or such other official to whom authority to sign the agreement is delegated, the date of determination shall be such date of signing.

(2) **Claim for deduction—(i) Contents of claim.** A claim for deduction for a deficiency dividend shall be made with the requisite declaration, on Form 976 and shall contain the following information:

(a) The name and address of the corporation;

(b) The place and date of incorporation;

(c) The amount of the deficiency determined with respect to the tax imposed by section 541 (or a corresponding provision of a prior income tax law) and the taxable year or years involved; the amount of the unpaid deficiency or, if the deficiency has been paid in whole or in part, the date of payment and the amount thereof; a statement as to how the deficiency was established, if unpaid; or if paid in whole or in part, how it was established that any portion of the amount paid was a deficiency at the time when paid and, in either case whether it was by an agreement under section 547(c)(3), by a closing agreement under section 7121, or by a decision of the Tax Court or court judgment and the date thereof; if established by a final judgment in a suit against the United States for refund, the date of payment of the deficiency, the date the claim for refund was filed, and the date the suit was brought; if established by a Tax Court decision or court judgment, a copy thereof

shall be attached, together with an explanation of how the decision became final; if established by an agreement under section 547(c)(3), a copy of such agreement shall be attached;

(d) The amount and date of payment of the dividend with respect to which the claim for the deduction for deficiency dividends is filed;

(e) A statement setting forth the various classes of stock outstanding, the name and address of each shareholder, the class and number of shares held by each on the date of payment of the dividend with respect to which the claim is filed, and the amount of such dividend paid to each shareholder;

(f) The amount claimed as a deduction for deficiency dividends; and

(g) Such other information as may be required by the claim form.

(ii) **Filing of claim and corporate resolution.** The claim together with a certified copy of the resolution of the board of directors or other authority, authorizing the payment of the dividend with respect to which the claim is filed, shall be filed with the district director for the internal revenue district in which the return is filed.

* * *

[T.D. 6500, 25 FR 11737, Nov. 26, 1960, as amended by T.D. 6657, 28 FR 5720, June 12, 1963; T.D. 7604, 44 FR 18661, March 29, 1979]

Deduction for Dividends Paid

§ 1.561–1 Deduction for dividends paid.

(a) The deduction for dividends paid is applicable in determining accumulated taxable income under section 535, undistributed personal holding company income under section 545, undistributed foreign personal holding company income under section 556, investment company taxable income under section 852, and real estate investment trust taxable income under section 857. The deduction for dividends paid includes—

(1) The dividends paid during the taxable year;

(2) The consent dividends for the taxable year, determined as provided in section 565; and

(3) In the case of a personal holding company, the dividend carryover computed as provided in section 564.

(b) For dividends for which the dividends paid deduction is allowable, see section 562 and § 1.562–1. As to when dividends are considered paid, see § 1.561–2.

[T.D. 6500, 25 FR 11737, Nov. 26, 1960, as amended by T.D. 6598, 27 FR 4093, April 28, 1962]

§ 1.561–2 When dividends are considered paid.

(a) **In general.** (1) A dividend will be considered as paid when it is received by the shareholder. A deduction for dividends paid during the taxable year will not be permitted unless the shareholder receives the dividend during the taxable year for which the deduction is claimed. See section 563 for special rule with respect to dividends paid after the close of the taxable year.

(2) If a dividend is paid by check and the check bearing a date within the taxable year is deposited in the mails, in a cover properly stamped and addressed to the shareholder at his last known address, at such time that in the ordinary handling of the mails the check would be received by the shareholder within the taxable year, a presumption arises that the dividend was paid to the shareholder in such year.

(3) The payment of a dividend during the taxable year to the authorized agent of the shareholder will be deemed payment of the dividend to the shareholder during such year.

(4) If a corporation, instead of paying the dividend directly to the shareholder, credits the account of the shareholder on the books of the corporation with the amount of the dividend, the deduction for a dividend paid will not be permitted unless it be shown to the satisfaction of the Commissioner that such crediting constituted payment of the dividend to the shareholder within the taxable year.

(5) A deduction will not be permitted for the amount of a dividend credited during the taxable year upon an obligation of the shareholder to the corporation unless it is shown to the satisfaction of the Commissioner that such crediting constituted payment of the dividend to the shareholder within the taxable year.

(6) If the dividend is payable in obligations of the corporation, they should be entered or registered in the taxable year on the books of the corporation, in the name of the shareholder (or his nominee or transferee), and, in the case of obligations payable to bearer, should be received in the taxable year by the shareholder (or his nominee or transferee) to constitute payment of the dividend within the taxable year.

(7) In the case of a dividend from which the tax has been deducted and withheld as required by chapter 3 (section 1441 and following), of the Code the dividend is considered as paid when such deducting and withholding occur.

(b) **Methods of accounting.** The determination of whether a dividend has been paid to the shareholder by the corporation during its taxable year is in no way dependent upon the method of accounting regularly employed by the corporation in keeping its books or upon the method of accounting upon the basis of which the taxable income of the corporation is computed.

(c) **Records.** Every corporation claiming a deduction for dividends paid shall keep such permanent records as are necessary (1) to establish that the dividends with respect to which such deduction is claimed were actually paid during the taxable year and (2) to supply the information required to be filed with the income tax return of the corporation. Such corporation shall file with its return (i) a copy of the dividend resolution; and (ii) a concise statement of the pertinent facts relating to the payment of the dividend, clearly specifying (a) the medium of payment and (b) if not paid in money, the fair market value and adjusted basis (or face value, if paid in its own obligations) on the date of distribution of the property distributed and the manner in which such fair market value and adjusted basis were determined. Canceled dividend checks and receipts obtained from shareholders acknowledging payment of dividends paid otherwise than by check need not be filed with the return but shall be kept by the corporation as a part of its records.

[T.D. 6500, 25 FR 11737, Nov. 26, 1960]

§1.562-1 Dividends for which the dividends paid deduction is allowable.

(a) **General rule.** Except as otherwise provided in section 562 (b) and (d), the term "dividend", for purposes of determining dividends eligible for the dividends paid deduction, refers only to a dividend described in section 316 (relating to definition of dividends for purposes of corporate distributions). No distribution, however, which is preferential within the meaning of section 562(c) and §1.562-2 shall be eligible for the dividends paid deduction. Moreover, when computing the dividends paid deduction with respect to a U.S. person (as defined in section 957(d)), no distribution which is excluded from the gross income of a foreign corporation under section 959(b) with respect to such person or from gross income of such person under section 959(a) shall be eligible for such deduction. Further, for purposes of the dividends paid deduction, the term "dividend" does not include a distribution in liquidation unless the distribution is treated as a dividend under section 316(b)(2) and paragraph (b)(2) of §1.316-1, or under section 333(e)(1) and paragraph (c) of §1.333-4 or paragraph (c)(2), (d)(1)(ii), or (d)(2) of §1.333-5, or qualifies under section 562(b) and paragraph (b) of this section. If a dividend is paid in property (other than money) the amount of the dividends paid deduction with respect to such property shall be the adjusted basis of the property in the hands of the distributing corporation at the time of the distribution. See paragraph (b)(2) of this section for special rules with respect to liquidating distributions by personal holding companies occurring during a taxable year of the distributing corporation beginning after December 31, 1963. Also see section 563 for special rules with respect to dividends paid after the close of the taxable year.

* * *

[T.D. 6500, 25 FR 11737, Nov. 26, 1960, as amended by T.D. 6949, 33 FR 5529, April 9, 1968; T.D. 7767, 46 FR 11265, Feb. 6, 1981]

§ 1.562–2 Preferential dividends.

(a) Section 562(c) imposes a limitation upon the general rule that a corporation is entitled to a deduction for dividends paid with respect to all dividends which it actually pays during the taxable year. Before a corporation may be entitled to any such deduction with respect to a distribution regardless of the medium in which the distribution is made, every shareholder of the class of stock with respect to which the distribution is made must be treated the same as every other shareholder of that class, and no class of stock may be treated otherwise than in accordance with its dividend rights as a class. The limitation imposed by section 562(c) is unqualified, except in the case of an actual distribution made in connection with a consent distribution (see section 565), if the entire distribution composed of such actual distribution and consent distribution is not preferential. The existence of a preference is sufficient to prohibit the deduction regardless of the fact (1) that such preference is authorized by all the shareholders of the corporation or (2) that the part of the distribution received by the shareholder benefited by the preference is taxable to him as a dividend. A corporation will not be entitled to a deduction for dividends paid with respect to any distribution upon a class of stock if there is distributed to any shareholder of such class (in proportion to the number of shares held by him) more or less than his pro rata part of the distribution as compared with the distribution made to any other shareholder of the same class. Nor will a corporation be entitled to a deduction for dividends paid in the case of any distribution upon a class of stock if there is distributed upon such class of stock more or less than the amount to which it is entitled as compared with any other class of stock. A preference exists if any rights to preference inherent in any class of stock are violat-

ed. The disallowance, where any preference in fact exists, extends to the entire amount of the distribution and not merely to a part of such distribution. As used in this section, the term "distribution" includes a dividend as defined in subchapter C, chapter 1 of the Code, and a distribution in liquidation referred to in section 562(b).

(b) The application of the provisions of section 562(c) may be illustrated by the following examples:

Example (1). A, B, C, and D are the owners of all the shares of class A common stock in the M Corporation, which makes its income tax returns on a calendar year basis. With the consent of all the shareholders, the M Corporation on July 15, 1954, declared a dividend of $5 a share payable in cash on August 1, 1954, to A. On September 15, 1954, it declared a dividend of $5 a share payable in cash on October 1, 1954, to B, C, and D. No allowance for dividends paid for the taxable year 1954 is permitted to the M Corporation with respect to any part of the dividends paid on August 1, 1954, and October 1, 1954.

Example (2). The N Corporation, which makes its income tax returns on the calendar year basis, has a capital of $100,000 (consisting of 1,000 shares of common stock of a par value of $100) and earnings or profits accumulated after February 28, 1913, in the amount of $50,000. In the year 1954, the N Corporation distributes $7,500 in cancellation of 50 shares of the stock owned by three of the four shareholders of the corporation. No deduction for dividends paid is permissible under section 562(c) and paragraph (a) of this section with respect to such distribution.

Example (3). The P Corporation has two classes of stock outstanding, 10 shares of cumulative preferred, owned by E, entitled to $5 per share and on which no dividends have been paid for two years, and 10 shares of common, owned by F. On December 31, 1954, the corporation distributes a dividend of $125, $50 to E, and $75 to F. The corporation is entitled to no deduction for any part of such dividend paid, since there has been a preference to F. If, however, the corporation had distributed $100 to E and $25 to F, it would have been entitled to include $125 as a dividend paid deduction.

[T.D. 6500, 25 FR 11737, Nov. 26, 1960]

§ 1.563–1 Accumulated earnings tax.

In the determination of the dividends paid deduction for purposes of the accumulated earnings tax imposed by section 531, a dividend paid after the close of any taxable year and on or before the 15th day of the third month following the close of such taxable year shall be considered as paid during such taxable year, and shall not be included in the computation of the dividends paid deduction for the year of payment. However, the rule provided in section 563(a) is not applicable to dividends paid during the first two and one-half months of the first taxable year of the corporation subject to tax under chapter 1 of the Internal Revenue Code of 1954.

[T.D. 6500, 25 FR 11737, Nov. 26, 1960]

§ 1.565–1 General rule.

(a) Consent dividends. The dividends paid deduction, as defined in section 561, includes the consent dividends for the taxable year. A consent dividend is a hypothetical distribution (as distinguished from an actual distribution) which any person, who owns consent stock on the last day of the taxable year of the corporation, agrees to treat as a dividend subject to the limitations in section 565(b) and § 1.565–2. The amount of the distribution must be specified by such person in a consent (or consents) filed at the time and in the manner specified in paragraph (b) of this section.

(b) Making and filing of consents. (1) A consent shall be made on Form 972 in accordance with this section and the instructions on the form issued therewith. It may be made only by or on behalf of a person who was the actual owner on the last day of the corporation's taxable year of any class of consent stock, that is, the person who would have been required to include in gross income any dividends on such stock actually distributed on the last day of such year. Form 972 shall contain or be verified by a written declaration that it is made under the penalties of perjury. In the consent such person must agree to include in his gross income for his taxable year in which or with which the taxable year of the corporation ends a specific amount as a taxable dividend.

(2) See § 1.565–2 for rules as to when all or a portion of the amount so specified will be disregarded for tax purposes.

(3) A consent may be filed at any time not later than the due date of the corporation's income tax return for the taxable year for which the dividends paid deduction is claimed. With such return, and not later than the due date thereof, the corporation must file Form 972 duly executed by each consenting shareholder, and a return on Form 973 showing by classes the stock outstanding on the first and last days of the taxable year, the dividend rights of such stock, distributions made during the taxable year to shareholders, and giving all the other information required by the form. Form 973 shall contain or be verified by a written declaration that it is made under the penalties of perjury.

(c) Taxability of amounts specified in consents. (1) Once a shareholder's consent is filed, the full amount specified therein shall be included in his gross income as a taxable dividend, except as otherwise provided in section 565(b) and § 1.565–2. Where the shareholder is taxable on a dividend only if received from sources within the United States, the amount specified in the consent of such shareholder shall be treated as a dividend from such sources in the same manner as if the dividend had been paid in money to the shareholder on the last day of the corporation's taxable year. See paragraph (b) of this section, relating to the making and filing of consents, and section 565(e) and § 1.565–5, with respect to the payment requirements in the case of nonresident aliens and foreign corporations.

(2) Except as provided in section 565(b) and § 1.565–2, the ground upon which a consent dividends deduction is denied the corporation does not affect the taxability of a shareholder whose consent has been filed for the amount specified in his consent. Thus, he is taxable on the full amount so specified even though a consent dividends deduction may be denied the corporation or may be of less value to it because, for example, (i) it is determined that it is not a corporation subject to part I, II, or III, subchapter G, chapter 1 of the Code, (ii) although subject to part II, subchapter G, chapter 1 of the Code, its taxable income (as adjusted under section 545(b) and § 1.545–2) is less than the total of the consent dividends, or (iii) in the case of nonresident aliens or foreign corporations, payment has not been made as required by section 565(e) and § 1.565–5.

[T.D. 6500, 25 FR 11737, Nov. 26, 1960]

§ 1.565–2 Limitations.

(a) Amounts specified in consents are not treated as consent dividends to the extent that they would constitute a preferential dividend, or would not constitute a dividend (as defined in section 316), if distributed in money to shareholders on the last day of the taxable year of the corporation. If any portion of an amount specified in a consent is not treated as a consent dividend under section 565(b) and this section, it is disregarded for all tax purposes. For example, it is not taxable to the consenting shareholder, and paragraph (c) of § 1.565–1 is not applicable to such portion of the amount specified in the consent.

(b)(1) A preferential distribution is an actual distribution, or a consent distribution, or a combination of the two, which involves a preference to one or more shares of stock as compared with other shares of the same class or to one class of stock as compared with any other class of stock. See section 562(c) and § 1.562-2.

(2) The application of section 565(b)(1) may be illustrated by the following examples:

Example (1). The X Corporation, which makes its income tax returns on the calendar year basis, has 200 shares of stock outstanding, owned by A and B in equal amounts. On December 15, 1954, the corporation distributes $600 to B and $100 to A. As a part of the same distribution A executes a consent to include $500 in his gross income as a taxable dividend though such amount is not distributed to him. The X Corporation, assuming the other requirements of section 565 have been complied with, is entitled to a consent dividends deduction of $500. Although the consent dividend is deemed to have been paid on December 31, 1954, the last day of the taxable year of the corporation, they constitute a single nonpreferential distribution of $1,200.

Example (2). The Y Corporation, which makes its income tax returns on the calendar year basis, has one class of consent stock outstanding, owned in equal amounts by A, B, and C. On December 15, 1954, the corporation makes a distribution in cash of $5,000 each to A and B, and $3,000 to C. The distribution is preferential. If A and B each receive a distribution in cash of $5,000 and C consents to include $3,000 in gross income as a taxable dividend, the combined actual and consent distribution is preferential. Similarly, if no one receives a distribution in cash, but A and B each consents to include $5,000 as a taxable dividend in gross income and C agrees to include only $3,000, the consent distribution is preferential.

Example (3). The Z Corporation, which makes its income tax returns on the calendar year basis, has only two classes of stock outstanding, each class being consent stock and consisting of 500 shares. Class A, with a par value of $40 per share, is entitled to two-thirds of any distribution of earnings and profits. Class B, with a par value of $20 per share, is entitled to one-third of any distribution of earnings and profits. On December 15, 1954, there is distributed on the class B stock $2 per share, or $1,000, and shareholders of the class A stock consent to include in gross income amounts equal to $2 per share, or $1,000. The distribution is preferential, inasmuch as the class B stock has received more than its pro rata share of the combined amounts of the actual distributions and the consent distributions.

(c)(1) An additional limitation under section 565(b) is that the amounts specified in consents which may be treated as consent dividends cannot exceed the amounts which would constitute a dividend (as defined in section 316) if the corporation had distributed the total specified amounts in money to shareholders on the last day of the taxable year of the corporation. If only a portion of such total would constitute a dividend, then only a corresponding portion of each specified amount is treated as a consent dividend.

(2) The application of section 565(b)(2) may be illustrated by the following example:

Example. The X Corporation, which makes its income tax returns on the calendar year basis, has only one class of stock outstanding, owned in equal amounts by A and B. It makes no distributions during the taxable year 1954. Its earnings and profits for the calendar year 1954 amount to $8,000, there being at the beginning of such year no accumulated earnings or profits. A and B execute proper consents to include $5,000 each in their gross income as a dividend received by them on December 31, 1954. The sum of the amount specified in the consents executed by A and B is $10,000, but if $10,000 had actually been distributed by the X Corporation on December 31, 1954, only $8,000 would have constituted a dividend under section 316(a). The amount which could be considered as consent dividends in computing the dividends paid deduction for purposes of the accumulated earnings tax is limited to $8,000, or $4,000 of the $5,000 specified in each consent. The remaining $1,000 in each consent is disregarded for all tax purposes. In the case of a personal holding company, the amount which could be considered as consent dividends in computing the dividends paid deduction for purposes of the personal holding company tax is $10,000 (assuming that the undistributed personal holding company income, determined without regard to distributions under section 316(b)(2), is equal to at least that amount). In that event, A and B would each include $5,000 in gross income as a dividend received on December 31, 1954.

[T.D. 6500, 25 FR 11737, Nov. 26, 1960]

§ 1.565-3 Effect of consent.

(a) The amount of the consent dividend shall be considered, for all purposes of the Code, as if it were distributed in money by the corporation to the shareholder on the last day of the taxable year of the corporation, received by the shareholder on such day, and immediately contributed by the shareholder as paid-in capital to the corporation on such day. Thus, the amount of the consent dividend will be treated by the shareholder as a dividend. The shareholder will be entitled to the dividends received credit under section 34 (for dividends received on or before December 31, 1964) and the exclusion under section 116, or to the dividends received deduction under section 243, with respect to such consent dividend. The basis of the shareholder's consent stock in a corporation will be increased by the amount thus treated in his hands as a dividend which he is considered as having contributed to the corporation as paid-in capital. The amount of the consent dividend will also be treated as a dividend received from sources within the United States in the same manner as if the dividend had been paid in money to the shareholders. Among other effects of the consent dividend, the earnings and profits of the corporation will be decreased by the amount of the consent dividends. Moreover, if the shareholder is a corporation, its accumulated earnings and profits will be increased by the amount of the consent dividend with respect to which it makes a consent.

* * *

[T.D. 6500, 25 FR 11737, Nov. 26, 1960, as amended by T.D. 6777, 29 FR 17808, Dec. 16, 1964]

§ 1.565-6 Definitions.

(a) **Consent stock.** (1) The term "consent stock" includes what is generally known as common stock. It also includes participating preferred stock, the participation rights of which are unlimited.

(2) The definition of consent stock may be illustrated by the following example:

Example. If in the case of the X Corporation there is only one class of stock outstanding, it would all be consent stock. If, on the other hand, there were two classes of stock, class A and class B, and class A was entitled to 6 percent before any distribution could be made on class B, but class B was entitled to everything distributed after class A had received its 6 percent, only class B stock would be consent stock. Similarly, if class A, after receiving its 6 percent, was to participate equally or in some fixed proportion with class B until it had received a second 6 percent, after which class B alone was entitled to any further distributions, only class B stock would be consent stock. The same result would follow if the order of preferences were class A 6 percent, then class B 6 percent, then class A a second 6 percent, either alone or in conjunction with class B, then class B the remainder. If, however, class A stock is entitled to ultimate participation without limit as to amount, then it, too, may be consent stock. For example, if class A is to receive 3 percent and then share equally or in some fixed proportion with class B in the remainder of the earnings or profits distributed, both class A stock and class B stock are consent stock.

* * *

[T.D. 6500, 25 FR 11737, Nov. 26, 1960]

ESTATES, TRUSTS, BENEFICIARIES, AND DECEDENTS

Estates, Trusts, and Beneficiaries

General Rule for Taxation of Estates and Trusts

§ 1.641(a)-0 Scope of Subchapter J.

(a) **In general.** Subchapter J (sections 641 and following), Chapter 1 of the Code, deals with the taxation of income of estates and trusts and their beneficiaries, and of income in respect of decedents. Part I of Subchapter J contains general rules for taxation of estates and trusts (Subpart A), specific rules relating to trusts which distribute current income only (Subpart B), estates and trusts which may accumulate income or which distribute corpus (Subpart C), treatment of excess distributions by trusts (Subpart D), grantors and other persons treated as substantial owners (Subpart E), and miscellaneous provisions relating to limitations on charitable deductions, income of an estate or trust in case of divorce, and taxable years to which the provisions of Subchapter J are applicable (Subpart F). Part I has no application to any organization which is not to be classified for tax purposes as a trust under the classification rules of §§ 301.7701-2, 301.7701-3, and 301.7701-4 of this chapter (Regulations on Procedure and Administration). Part II of Subchapter J relates to the treatment of income in respect of decedents. However, the provisions of Subchapter J do not apply to employee trusts subject to Subchapters D and F, Chapter 1 of the Code, and common trust funds subject to Subchapter H, Chapter 1 of the Code.

(b) **Scope of subparts A, B, C, and D.** Subparts A, B, C, and D (section 641 and following), part I, subchapter J, chapter 1 of the Code, relate to the taxation of estates and trusts and their beneficiaries. These subparts have no application to any portion of the corpus or income of a trust which is to be regarded, within the meaning of the Code, as that of the grantor or others treated as its substantial owners. See subpart E (section 671 and following), part I, subchapter J, chapter 1 of the Code, and the regulations thereunder for rules for the treatment of any portion of a trust where the grantor (or another person) is treated as the substantial owner. So-called alimony trusts are treated under subparts A, B, C, and D, except to the extent otherwise provided in section 71 or section 682. These subparts have no application to beneficiaries of nonexempt employees' trusts. See section 402(b) and the regulations thereunder.

(c) Multiple trusts. Multiple trusts that have—

(1) No substantially independent purposes (such as independent dispositive purposes),

(2) The same grantor and substantially the same beneficiary, and

(3) The avoidance or mitigation of (a) the progressive rates of tax (including mitigation as a result of deferral of tax) or (b) the minimum tax for tax preferences imposed by section 56 as their principal purpose,

shall be consolidated and treated as one trust for the purposes of subchapter J.

[T.D. 6500, 25 FR 11814, Nov. 26, 1960, as amended by T.D. 6989, 34 FR 731, Jan. 17, 1969; T.D. 7204, 37 FR 17158, Aug. 25, 1972]

§ 1.641(a)–1 Imposition of tax; application of tax.

For taxable years beginning after December 31, 1970, section 641 prescribes that the taxes imposed by section 1(d), as amended by the Tax Reform Act of 1969, shall apply to the income of estates or of any kind of property held in trust. For taxable years ending before January 1, 1971, section 641 prescribes that the taxes imposed upon individuals by chapter 1 of the Code apply to the income of estates or of any kind of property held in trust. The rates of tax, the statutory provisions respecting gross income, and, with certain exceptions, the deductions and credits allowed to individuals apply also to estates and trust.

[T.D. 6500, 25 FR 11814, Nov. 26, 1960, as amended by T.D. 7117, 36 FR 9421, May 25, 1971]

§ 1.641(b)–1 Computation and payment of tax; deductions and credits of estates and trusts.

Generally, the deductions and credits allowed to individuals are also allowed to estates and trusts. However, there are special rules for the computation of certain deductions and for the allocation between the estate or trust and the beneficiaries of certain credits and deductions. See section 642 and the regulations thereunder. In addition, an estate or trust is allowed to deduct, in computing its taxable income, the deductions provided by sections 651 and 661 and regulations thereunder, relating to distributions to beneficiaries.

[T.D. 6500, 25 FR 11814, Nov. 26, 1960]

§ 1.641(b)–2 Filing of returns and payment of the tax.

(a) The fiduciary is required to make and file the return and pay the tax on the taxable income of an estate or of a trust. Liability for the payment of the tax on the taxable income of an estate attaches to the person of the executor or administrator up to and after his discharge if, prior to distribution and discharge, he had notice of his tax obligations or failed to exercise due diligence in ascertaining whether or not such obligations existed. For the extent of such liability, see section 3467 of the Revised Statutes, as amended by section 518 of the Revenue Act of 1934 (31 U.S.C. 192). Liability for the tax also follows the assets of the estate distributed to heirs, devisees, legatees, and distributees, who may be required to discharge the amount of the tax due and unpaid to the extent of the distributive shares received by them. See section 6901. The same considerations apply to trusts.

(b) The estate of an infant, incompetent, or other person under a disability, or, in general, of an individual or corporation in receivership or a corporation in bankruptcy is not a taxable entity separate from the person for whom the fiduciary is acting, in that respect differing from the estate of a deceased person or of a trust. See section 6012(b)(2) and (3) for provisions relating to the obligation of the fiduciary with respect to returns of such persons.

[T.D. 6500, 25 FR 11814, Nov. 26, 1960, as amended by T.D. 6580, 26 FR 11486, Dec. 5, 1961]

§ 1.641(b)–3 Termination of estates and trusts.

(a) The income of an estate of a deceased person is that which is received by the estate during the period of administration or settlement. The period of administration or settlement is the period actually required by the administrator or executor to perform the ordinary duties of administration, such as the collection of assets and the payment of debts, taxes, legacies, and bequests, whether the period required is longer or shorter than the period specified under the applicable local law for the settlement of estates. For example, where an executor who is also named as trustee under a will fails to obtain his discharge as executor, the period of administration continues only until the duties of administration are complete and he actually assumes his duties as trustee, whether or not pursuant to a court order. However, the period of administration of an estate cannot be unduly prolonged. If the administration of an estate is unreasonably prolonged, the estate is considered terminated for Federal income tax purposes after the expiration of a reasonable period for the performance by the executor of all the duties of administration. Further, an estate will be considered as terminated when all the assets have been distributed except for a reasonable amount which is set aside in good faith for the payment of unascertained or contingent liabilities and expenses (not including a claim by a beneficiary in the capacity of beneficiary).

(b) Generally, the determination of whether a trust has terminated depends upon whether the property held in trust has been distributed to the persons entitled to succeed to the property upon termination of the trust rather than upon the technicality of whether or not the trustee has rendered his final accounting. A trust does not automatically terminate upon the happening of the event by which the duration of the trust is measured. A reasonable time is permitted after such event for the trustee to perform the duties necessary to complete the administration of the trust. Thus, if under the terms of the governing instrument, the trust is to terminate upon the death of the life beneficiary and the corpus is to be distributed to the remainderman, the trust continues after the death of the life beneficiary for a period reasonably necessary to a proper winding up of the affairs of the trust. However, the winding up of a trust cannot be unduly postponed and if the distribution of the trust corpus is unreasonably delayed, the trust is considered terminated for Federal income tax purposes after the expiration of a reasonable period for the trustee to complete the administration of the trust. Further, a trust will be considered as terminated when all the assets have been distributed except for a reasonable amount which is set aside in good faith for the payment of unascertained or contingent liabilities and expenses (not including a claim by a beneficiary in the capacity of beneficiary).

(c)(1) Except as provided in subparagraph (2) of this paragraph, during the period between the occurrence of an event which causes a trust to terminate and the time when the trust is considered as terminated under this section, whether or not the income and the excess of capital gains over capital losses of the trust are to be considered as amounts required to be distributed currently to the ultimate distributee for the year in which they are received

depends upon the principles stated in § 1.651(a)–2. See § 1.663–1 et seq. for application of the separate share rule.

(2)(i) Except in cases to which the last sentence of this subdivision applies, for taxable years of a trust ending before September 1, 1957, subparagraph (1) of this paragraph shall not apply and the rule of subdivision (ii) of this subparagraph shall apply unless the trustee elects to have subparagraph (1) of this paragraph apply. Such election shall be made by the trustee in a statement filed on or before April 15, 1959, with the district director with whom such trust's return for any such taxable year was filed. The election provided by this subdivision shall not be available if the treatment given the income and the excess of capital gains over capital losses for taxable years for which returns have been filed was consistent with the provisions of subparagraph (1) of this paragraph.

(ii) The rule referred to in subdivision (i) of this subparagraph is as follows: During the period between the occurrence of an event which causes a trust to terminate and the time when a trust is considered as terminated under this section, the income and the excess of capital gains over capital losses of the trust are in general considered as amounts required to be distributed for the year in which they are received. For example, a trust instrument provides for the payment of income to A during her life, and upon her death for the payment of the corpus to B. The trust reports on the basis of the calendar year. A dies on November 1, 1955, but no distribution is made to B until January 15, 1956. The income of the trust and the excess of capital gains over capital losses for the entire year 1955, to the extent not paid, credited, or required to be distributed to A or A's estate, are treated under sections 661 and 662 as amounts required to be distributed to B for the year 1955.

(d) If a trust or the administration or settlement of an estate is considered terminated under this section for Federal income tax purposes (as for instance, because administration has been unduly prolonged), the gross income, deductions, and credits of the estate or trust are, subsequent to the termination, considered the gross income, deductions, and credits of the person or persons succeeding to the property of the estate or trust.

[T.D. 6500, 25 FR 11814, Nov. 26, 1960]

§ 1.642(c)–1 Unlimited deduction for amounts paid for a charitable purpose.

(a) **In general.** (1) Any part of the gross income of an estate, or trust which, pursuant to the terms of the governing instrument is paid (or treated under paragraph (b) of this section as paid) during the taxable year for a purpose specified in section 170(c) shall be allowed as a deduction to such estate or trust in lieu of the limited charitable contributions deduction authorized by section 170(a). In applying this paragraph without reference to paragraph (b) of this section, a deduction shall be allowed for an amount paid during the taxable year in respect of gross income received in a previous taxable year, but only if no deduction was allowed for any previous taxable year for the amount so paid.

(2) In determining whether an amount is paid for a purpose specified in section 170(c)(2) the provisions of section 170(c)(2)(A) shall not be taken into account. Thus, an amount paid to a corporation, trust, or community chest, fund, or foundation otherwise described in section 170(c)(2) shall be considered paid for a purpose specified in section 170(c) even though the corporation, trust, or community chest, fund, or foundation is not created or organized in the United States, any State, the District of Columbia, or any possession of the United States.

(3) See section 642(c)(6) and § 1.642(c)–4 for disallowance of a deduction under this section to a trust which is, or is treated under section 4947(a)(1) as though it were a private foundation (as defined in section 509(a) and the regulations thereunder) and not exempt from taxation under section 501(a).

(b) **Election to treat contributions as paid in preceding taxable year**—(1) **In general.** For purposes of determining the deduction allowed under paragraph (a) of this section, the fiduciary (as defined in section 7701(a)(6)) of an estate or trust may elect under section 642(c)(1) to treat as paid during the taxable year (whether or not such year begins before January 1, 1970) any amount of gross income received during such taxable year or any preceding taxable year which is otherwise deductible under such paragraph and which is paid after the close of such taxable year but on or before the last day of the next succeeding taxable year of the estate or trust. The preceding sentence applies only in the case of payments actually made in a taxable year which is a taxable year beginning after December 31, 1969. No election shall be

made, however, in respect of any amount which was deducted for any previous taxable year or which is deducted for the taxable year in which such amount is paid.

(2) **Time for making election.** The election under subparagraph (1) of this paragraph shall be made not later than the time, including extensions thereof, prescribed by law for filing the income tax return for the succeeding taxable year. Such election shall, except as provided in subparagraph (4) of this paragraph, become irrevocable after the last day prescribed for making it. Having made the election for any taxable year, the fiduciary may, within the time prescribed for making it, revoke the election without the consent of the Commissioner.

(3) **Manner of making the election.** The election shall be made by filing with the income tax return (or an amended return) for the taxable year in which the contribution is treated as paid a statement which—

(i) States the name and address of the fiduciary,

(ii) Identifies the estate or trust for which the fiduciary is acting,

(iii) Indicates that the fiduciary is making an election under section 642(c)(1) in respect of contributions treated as paid during such taxable year,

(iv) Gives the name and address of each organization to which any such contribution is paid, and

(v) States the amount of each contribution and date of actual payment or, if applicable, the total amount of contributions paid to each organization during the succeeding taxable year, to be treated as paid in the preceding taxable year.

(4) **Revocation of certain elections with consent.** An application to revoke with the consent of the Commissioner any election made on or before June 8, 1970, must be in writing and must be filed not later than September 2, 1975.

No consent will be granted to revoke an election for any taxable year for which the assessment of a deficiency is prevented by the operation of any law or rule of law. If consent to revoke the election is granted, the fiduciary must attach a copy of the consent to the return (or amended return) for each taxable year affected by the revocation. The application must be addressed to the Commissioner of Internal Revenue, Washington, D.C. 20224, and must indicate—

(i) The name and address of the fiduciary and the estate or trust for which he was acting,

(ii) The taxable year for which the election was made,

(iii) The office of the district director, or the service center, where the return (or amended return) for the year of election was filed, and

(iv) The reason for revoking the election.

[T.D. 6500, 25 FR 11814, Nov. 26, 1960, as amended by T.D. 7357, 40 FR 23739, June 2, 1975; 40 FR 24361, June 6, 1975]

§ 1.642(c)-2 Unlimited deduction for amounts permanently set aside for a charitable purpose.

(a) Estates. Any part of the gross income of an estate which pursuant to the terms of the will—

(1) Is permanently set aside during the taxable year for a purpose specified in section 170(c), or

(2) Is to be used (within or without the United States or any of its possessions) exclusively for religious, charitable, scientific, literary, or educational purposes, or for the prevention of cruelty to children or animals, or for the establishment, acquisition, maintenance, or operation of a public cemetery not operated for profit,

shall be allowed as a deduction to the estate in lieu of the limited charitable contributions deduction authorized by section 170(a).

(b) Certain trusts—(1) In general. Any part of the gross income of a trust to which either subparagraph (3) or (4) of this paragraph applies, that by the terms of the governing instrument—

(i) Is permanently set aside during the taxable year for a purpose specified in section 170(c), or

(ii) Is to be used (within or without the United States or any of its possessions) exclusively for religious, charitable, scientific, literary, or educational purposes, or for the prevention of cruelty to children or animals, or for the establishment, acquisition, maintenance, or operation of a public cemetery not operated for profit,

shall be allowed, subject to the limitation provided in subparagraph (2) of this paragraph, as a deduction to the trust in lieu of the limited charitable contributions deduction authorized by section 170(a). The preceding sentence applied only to a trust which is required by the terms of its governing instrument to set amounts aside. See section

642(c)(6) and § 1.642(c)-4 for disallowance of a deduction under this section to a trust which is, or is treated under section 4947(a)(1) as though it were, a private foundation (as defined in section 509(a) and the regulations thereunder) that is not exempt from taxation under section 501(a).

(2) Limitation of deduction. Subparagraph (1) of this paragraph applies only to the gross income earned by a trust with respect to amounts transferred to the trust under a will executed on or before October 9, 1969, and satisfying the requirements of subparagraph (4) of this paragraph or transferred to the trust on or before October 9, 1969. For such purposes, any income, gains, or losses, which are derived at any time from the amounts so transferred to the trust shall also be taken into account in applying subparagraph (1) of this paragraph. If any such amount so transferred to the trust is invested or reinvested at any time, any asset received by the trust upon such investment or reinvestment shall also be treated as an amount which was so transferred to the trust. In the case of a trust to which this paragraph applies which contains (i) amounts transferred pursuant to transfers described in the first sentence of this subparagraph and (ii) amounts transferred pursuant to transfers not so described, subparagraph (1) of this paragraph shall apply only if the amounts described in subdivision (i) of this subparagraph, together with all income, gains, and losses derived therefrom, are separately accounted for from the amounts described in subdivision (ii) of this subparagraph, together with all income, gains, and losses derived therefrom. Such separate accounting shall be carried out consistently with the principles of paragraph (c)(4) of § 53.4947-1 of this chapter (Foundation Excise Tax Regulations), relating to accounting for segregated amounts of split-interest trusts.

(3) Trusts created on or before October 9, 1969. A trust to which this subparagraph applies is a trust, testamentary or otherwise, which was created on or before October 9, 1969, and which qualifies under either subdivision (i) or (ii) of this subparagraph.

(i) Transfer of irrevocable remainder interest to charity. To qualify under this subdivision the trust must have been created under the terms of an instrument granting an irrevocable remainder interest in such trust to or for the use of an organization described in section 170(c). If the instrument granted a revocable remainder interest but the power to revoke such interest terminated on or before October 9, 1969, without the remainder interest having been revoked, the remainder interest will be treated as irrevocable for purposes of the preceding sentence.

(ii) Grantor under a mental disability to change terms of trust. (A) To qualify under this subdivision (ii) the trust must have been created by a grantor who was at all times after October 9, 1969, under a mental disability to change the terms of the trust. The term "mental disability" for this purpose means mental incompetence to change the terms of the trust, whether or not there has been an adjudication of mental incompetence and whether or not there has been an appointment of a committee, guardian, fiduciary, or other person charged with the care of the person or property of the grantor.

(B) If the grantor has not been adjudged mentally incompetent, the trustee must obtain from a qualified physician a certificate stating that the grantor of the trust has been mentally incompetent at all times after October 9, 1969, and that there is no reasonable probability that the grantor's mental capacity will ever improve to the extent that he will be mentally competent to change the terms of the trust. A copy of this certification must be filed with the first return on which a deduction is claimed by reason of this subdivision (ii) and subparagraph (1) of this paragraph. Thereafter, a statement referring to such medical opinion must be attached to any return for a taxable year for which such a deduction is claimed and during which the grantor's mental incompetence continues. The original certificate must be retained by the trustee of the trust.

(C) If the grantor has been adjudged mentally incompetent, a copy of the judgment or decree, and any modification thereof, must be filed with the first return on which a deduction is claimed by reason of this subdivision (ii) and subparagraph (1) of this paragraph. Thereafter, a statement referring to such judgment or decree must be attached to any return for a taxable year for which such a deduction is claimed and during which the grantor's mental incompetence continues. A copy of such judgment or decree must also be retained by the trustee of the trust.

(D) This subdivision (ii) applies even though a person charged with the care of the person or property of the grantor has the power to change the terms of the trust.

* * *

(c) Pooled income funds. Any part of the gross income of a pooled income fund to which § 1.642(c)–5 applies for the taxable year that is attributable to net long-term capital gain (as defined in section 1222(7)) which, pursuant to the terms of the governing instrument, is permanently set aside during the taxable year for a purpose specified in section 170(c) shall be allowed as a deduction to the fund in lieu of the limited charitable contributions deduction authorized by section 170(a). No deduction shall be allowed under this paragraph for any portion of the gross income of such fund which is (1) attributable to income other than net long-term capital gain (2) earned with respect to amounts transferred to such fund before August 1, 1969. However, see paragraph (b) of this section for a deduction (subject to the limitations of such paragraph) for amounts permanently set aside by a pooled income fund which meets the requirements of that paragraph. The principles of paragraph (b) or (2) of this section with respect to investment, reinvestment, and separate accounting shall apply under this paragraph in the case of amounts transferred to the fund after July 31, 1969.

(d) Disallowance of deduction for certain amounts not deemed to be permanently set aside for charitable purposes. No amount will be considered to be permanently set aside, or to be used, for a purpose described in paragraph (a) or (b)(1) of this section unless under the terms of the governing instrument and the circumstances of the particular case the possibility that the amount set aside, or to be used, will not be devoted to such purpose or use is so remote as to be negligible. Thus, for example, where there is possibility of the invasion of the corpus of a charitable remainder trust, as defined in § 1.664–1(a)(1)(ii), in order to make payment of the annuity amount or unitrust amount, no deduction will be allowed under paragraph (a) of this section in respect of any amount set aside by an estate for distribution to such a charitable remainder trust.

For treatment of distributions by an estate to a charitable remainder trust, see paragraph (a)(5)(iii) of § 1.664–1.

[T.D. 6500, 25 FR 11814, Nov. 26, 1960, as amended by T.D. 7357, 40 FR 23740, June 2, 1975; 40 FR 24361, June 6, 1975]

§ 1.642(c)–3 Adjustments and other special rules for determining unlimited charitable contributions deduction.

(a) Income in respect of a decedent. For purposes of §§ 1.642(c)–1 and 1.642(c)–2, an amount received by an estate or trust which is includible in its gross income under section 691(a)(1) as income in respect of a decedent shall be included in the gross income of the estate or trust.

(b) Reduction of charitable contributions deduction by amounts not included in gross income. (1) If an estate, pooled income fund, or other trust pays, permanently sets aside, or uses any amount of its income for a purpose specified in section 642(c)(1), (2) or (3) and that amount includes any items of estate or trust income not entering into the gross income of the estate or trust, the deduction allowable under § 1.642(c)–1 or § 1.642(c)–2 is limited to the gross income so paid, permanently set aside, or used. In the case of a pooled income fund for which a deduction is allowable under paragraph (c) of § 1.642(c)–2 for amounts permanently set aside, only the gross income of the fund which is attributable to net long-term capital gain (as defined in section 1222(7)) shall be taken into account.

(2) In determining whether the amounts of income so paid, permanently set aside, or used for a purpose specified in section 642(c)(1), (2), or (3) include particular items of income of an estate or trust not included in gross income, the specific provision controls if the governing instrument specifically provides as to the source out of which amounts are to be paid, permanently set aside, or used for such a purpose.

In the absence of specific provisions in the governing instrument, an amount to which section 642(c)(1), (2) or (3) applies is deemed to consist of the same proportion of each class of the items of income of the estate or trust as the total of each class bears to the total of all classes. See paragraph (b) of § 1.643(a)–5 for the method of determining the allocable portion of exempt income and foreign income.

(3) For examples showing the determination of the character of an amount deductible under § 1.642(c)–1 or § 1.642(c)–2, see examples (1) and (2) in § 1.662(b)–2 and paragraph (e) of the example in § 1.662(c)–4.

(4) For the purpose of this paragraph, the provisions of section 116 are not to be taken into account.

(c) Capital gains included in charitable contribution. Where any amount of the income paid, permanently set aside, or used for a purpose specified in section 642(c)(1), (2), or (3), is attributable to net long-term capital gain (as defined in section

1222(7)), the amount of the deduction otherwise allowable under § 1.642(c)–1 or § 1.642(c)–2, must be adjusted for any deduction provided in section 1202 of 50 percent of the excess, if any, of the net long-term capital gain over the net short-term capital loss. For determination of the extent to which the contribution to which § 1.642(c)–1 or § 1.642(c)–2 applies is deemed to consist of net long-term capital gains, see paragraph (b) of this section. The application of this paragraph may be illustrated by the following examples:

Example (1). Under the terms of the trust instrument, the income of a trust described in § 1.642(c)–2(b)(3)(i) is currently distributable to A during his life and capital gains are allocable to corpus. No provision is made in the trust instrument for the invasion of corpus for the benefit of A. Upon A's death the corpus of the trust is to be distributed to M University, an organization described in section 501(c)(3) which is exempt from taxation under section 501(a). During the taxable year ending December 31, 1970, the trust has long-term capital gains of $100,000 from property transferred to it on or before October 9, 1969, which are permanently set aside for charitable purposes. The trust includes $100,000 in gross income but is allowed a deduction of $50,000 under section 1202 for the long-term capital gains and a charitable contributions deduction of $50,000 under section 642(c)(2) ($100,000 permanently set aside for charitable purposes less $50,000 allowed as a deduction under section 1202 with respect to such $100,000).

Example (2). Under the terms of the will, $200,000 of the income (including $100,000 capital gains) for the taxable year 1972 of an estate is distributed, one-quarter to each of two individual beneficiaries and one-half to N University, an organization described in section 501(c)(3) which is exempt from taxation under section 501(a). During 1972 the estate has ordinary income of $200,000, long-term capital gains of $100,000, and no capital losses. It is assumed that for 1972 the estate has no other items of income or any deductions other than those discussed herein. The entire capital gains of $100,000 are included in the gross income of the estate for 1972, and N University receives $100,000 from the estate in such year. However, the amount allowable to the estate under section 642(c)(1) is subject to appropriate adjustment for the deduction allowable under section 1202. In view of the distributions of $25,000 of capital gains to each of the individual beneficiaries, the deduction allowable to the estate under section 1202 is limited by such section to $25,000 [($100,000 capital gains less $50,000 capital gains includible in income of individual beneficiaries under section 662) × 50%]. Since the whole of this $25,000 deduction under section 1202 is attributable to the distribution of $50,000 of capital gains to N University, the deduction allowable to the estate in 1972 under section 642(c)(1) is $75,000 [$100,000 (distributed to N) less $25,000 (proper adjustment for section 1202 deduction)].

Example (3). Under the terms of the trust instrument, 30 percent of the gross income (exclusive of capital gains) of a trust described in § 1.642(c)–2(b)(3)(i) is currently distributed to B, the sole income beneficiary. Net capital gains (capital gain net income for taxable years beginning after December 31, 1976) and undistributed ordinary income are allocable to corpus. No provision is made in the trust instrument for the invasion of corpus for the benefit of B. Upon B's death the remainder of the trust is to be distributed to M Church. During the taxable year 1972, the trust has ordinary income of $100,000, long-term capital gains of $15,000, short-term capital gains of $1,000, long-term capital losses of $5,000, and short-term capital losses of $2,500. It is assumed that the trust has no other items of income or any deductions other than those discussed herein. All the ordinary income and capital gains and losses are attributable to amounts transferred to the trust before October 9, 1969. The trust includes in gross income for 1972 the total amount of $116,000 [$100,000 (ordinary income)+$16,000 (total capital gains determined without regard to capital losses)]. Pursuant to the terms of the governing instrument the trust distributes to B in 1972 the amount of $30,000 ($100,000×30%). The balance of $78,500 [($116,000 less $7,500 capital losses)–$30,000 distribution] is available for the set-aside for charitable purposes. In determining taxable income for 1972 the capital losses of $7,500 ($5,000+$2,500) are allowable in full under section 1211(b)(1). The net capital gain (capital gain net income for taxable years beginning after December 31, 1976) of $8,500 ($16,000 less $7,500) is the excess of the net long-term capital gain of $10,000 ($15,000 less $5,000) over the net short-term capital loss of $1,500 ($2,500 less $1,000). The deduction under section 1202 is $4,250 ($8,500×50%), all of which is attributable to the set-aside for charitable purposes. Accordingly, for 1972 the deduction allowable to the trust under section 642(c)(2) is $74,250 [$78,500 (set-aside for M) less $4,250 (proper adjustment for section 1202 deduction)].

Example (4). During the taxable year a pooled income fund, as defined in § 1.642(c)–5, has in addition to ordinary income long-term capital gains of $150,000, short-term capital gains of $15,000, long-term capital losses of $100,000, and short-term capital losses of $10,000. Under the Declaration of Trust and pursuant to State law net long-term capital gain is allocable to corpus and net short-term capital gain is to be distributed to the income beneficiaries of the fund. All the capital gains and losses are attributable to amounts transferred to the fund after July 31, 1969. In view of the distribution of the net short-term capital gain of $5,000 ($15,000 less $10,000) to the income beneficiaries, the deduction allowed to the fund under section 1202 is limited by such section to $25,000 [($150,000 (long-term capital gains) less $100,000 (long-term capital losses) ×50%]. Since the whole of this deduction under section 1202 is attributable to the set-aside for charitable purposes, the deduction of $50,000 ($150,000 less $100,000) otherwise allowable under section 642(c)(3) is subject to appropriate adjustment under section 642(c)(4) for the deduction allowable under section 1202. Accordingly, the amount of the set-aside deduction is $25,000 [$50,000 (set-aside for public charity) less $25,000 (proper adjustment for section 1202 deduction)].

Example (5). The facts are the same as in example (4) except that under the Declaration of Trust and pursuant to State law all the net capital gain (capital gain net income for taxable years beginning after December 31, 1976) for the taxable year is allocable to corpus of the fund. The fund would thus include in gross income total

capital gains of $165,000 ($150,000+$15,000). In determining taxable income for the taxable year the capital losses of $110,000 ($100,000+$10,000) are allowable in full under section 1211(b)(1). The net capital gain of $55,000 ($165,000 less $110,000) is available for the set-aside for charitable purposes under section 642(c)(3) only in the amount of the net long-term capital gain of $50,000 ($150,000 long-term gains less $100,000 long-term losses). The deduction under section 1202 is $25,000 ($50,000×50%), all of which is attributable to the set-aside for charitable purposes. Accordingly, the deduction allowable to the fund under section 642(c)(3) is $25,000 [$50,000 (set-aside for public charity) less $25,000 (proper adjustment for section 1202 deduction)]. The $5,000 balance of net capital gain (capital gain net income for taxable years beginning after December 31, 1976) is taken into account in determining taxable income of the pooled income fund for the taxable year.

* * *

[T.D. 6500, 25 FR 11814, Nov. 26, 1960, as amended by T.D. 7357, 40 FR 23741, June 2, 1975; 40 FR 24361, June 6, 1975; T.D. 7728, 45 FR 72650, Nov. 3, 1980]

§ 1.642(d)–1   Net operating loss deduction.

The net operating loss deduction allowed by section 172 is available to estates and trusts generally, with the following exceptions and limitations:

(a) In computing gross income and deductions for the purposes of section 172, a trust shall exclude that portion of the income and deductions attributable to the grantor or another person under sections 671 through 678 (relating to grantors and others treated as substantial owners).

(b) An estate or trust shall not, for the purposes of section 172, avail itself of the deductions allowed by section 642(c)(relating to charitable contributions deductions) and sections 651 and 661 (relating to deductions for distributions).

[T.D. 6500, 25 FR 11814, Nov. 26, 1960]

§ 1.642(e)–1   Depreciation and depletion.

An estate or trust is allowed the deductions for depreciation and depletion, but only to the extent the deductions are not apportioned to beneficiaries under sections 167(h) and 611(b). For purposes of sections 167(h) and 611(b), the term "beneficiaries" includes charitable beneficiaries. See the regulations under those sections.

[T.D. 6500, 25 FR 11814, Nov. 26, 1960, as amended by T.D. 6712, 29 FR 3655, March 24, 1964]

§ 1.642(g)–1 Disallowance of double deductions; in general.

Amounts allowable under section 2053(a)(2) (relating to administration expenses) or under section 2054 (relating to losses during administration) as deductions in computing the taxable estate of a decedent are not allowed as deductions in computing the taxable income of the estate unless there is filed a statement, in duplicate, to the effect that the items have not been allowed as deductions from the gross estate of the decedent under section 2053 or 2054 and that all rights to have such items allowed at any time as deductions under section 2053 or 2054 are waived. The statement should be filed with the return for the year for which the items are claimed as deductions or with the district director for the internal revenue district in which the return was filed, for association with the return. The statement may be filed at any time before the expiration of the statutory period of limitation applicable to the taxable year for which the deduction is sought. Allowance of a deduction in computing an estate's taxable income is not precluded by claiming a deduction in the estate tax return, so long as the estate tax deduction is not finally allowed and the statement is filed. However, after a statement is filed under section 642(g) with respect to a particular item or portion of an item, the item cannot thereafter be allowed as a deduction for estate tax purposes since the waiver operates as a relinquishment of the right to have the deduction allowed at any time under section 2053 or 2054.

[T.D. 6500, 25 FR 11814, Nov. 26, 1960]

§ 1.642(g)–2 Deductions included.

It is not required that the total deductions, or the total amount of any deduction, to which section 642(g) is applicable be treated in the same way. One deduction or portion of a deduction may be allowed for income tax purposes if the appropriate statement is filed, while another deduction or portion is allowed for estate tax purposes. Section 642(g) has no application to deductions for taxes, interest, business expenses, and other items accrued at the date of a decedent's death so that they are allowable as a deduction under section 2053(a)(3) for estate tax purposes as claims against the estate, and are also allowable under section 691(b) as deductions in respect of a decedent for income tax purposes. However, section 642(g) is applicable to deductions for interest, business expenses, and other items not accrued at the date of

the decedent's death so that they are allowable as deductions for estate tax purposes only as administration expenses under section 2053(a)(2). Although deductible under section 2053(a)(3) in determining the value of the taxable estate of a decedent, medical, dental, etc., expenses of a decedent which are paid by the estate of the decedent are not deductible in computing the taxable income of the estate. See section 213(d) and the regulations thereunder for rules relating to the deductibility of such expenses in computing the taxable income of the decedent.

[T.D. 6500, 25 FR 11814, Nov. 26, 1960]

§ 1.642(h)–1 Unused loss carryovers on termination of an estate or trust.

(a) If, on the final termination of an estate or trust, a net operating loss carryover under section 172 or a capital loss carryover under section 1212 would be allowable to the estate or trust in a taxable year subsequent to the taxable year of termination but for the termination, the carryover or carryovers are allowed under section 642(h)(1) to the beneficiaries succeeding to the property of the estate or trust. See § 1.641(b)–3 for the determination of when an estate or trust terminates.

(b) The net operating loss carryover and the capital loss carryover are the same in the hands of a beneficiary as in the estate or trust, except that the capital loss carryover in the hands of a beneficiary which is a corporation is a short-term loss irrespective of whether it would have been a long-term or short-term capital loss in the hands of the estate or trust. The net operating loss carryover and the capital loss carryover are taken into account in computing taxable income, adjusted gross income, and the tax imposed by section 56 (relating to the minimum tax for tax preferences). The first taxable year of the beneficiary to which the loss shall be carried over is the taxable year of the beneficiary in which or with which the estate or trust terminates. However, for purposes of determining the number of years to which a net operating loss, or a capital loss under paragraph (a) of § 1.1212–1, may be carried over by a beneficiary, the last taxable year of the estate or trust (whether or not a short taxable year) and the first taxable year of the beneficiary to which a loss is carried over each constitute a taxable year, and, in the case of a beneficiary of an estate or trust that is a corporation, capital losses carried over by the estate or trust to any taxable year of the estate or trust beginning after December 31, 1963, shall be treated as if they were incurred in the last taxable year of the estate or trust (whether or not a short taxable year). For the treatment of the net operating loss carryover when the last taxable year of the estate or trust is the last taxable year to which such loss can be carried over, see § 1.642(h)–2.

(c) The application of this section may be illustrated by the following examples:

Example (1). A trust distributes all of its assets to A, the sole remainderman, and terminates on December 31, 1954, when it has a capital loss carryover of $10,000 attributable to transactions during the taxable year 1952. A, who reports on the calendar year basis, otherwise has ordinary income of $10,000 and capital gains of $4,000 for the taxable year 1954. A would offset his capital gains of $4,000 against the capital loss of the trust and, in addition, deduct under section 1211(b) $1,000 on his return for the taxable year 1954. The balance of the capital loss carryover of $5,000 may be carried over only to the years 1955 and 1956, in accordance with paragraph (a) of § 1.1212–1 and the rules of this section.

Example (2). A trust distributes all of its assets, one-half to A, an individual, and one-half to X, a corporation, who are the sole remaindermen, and terminates on December 31, 1966, when it has a short-term capital loss carryover of $20,000 attributable to short-term transactions during the taxable years 1964, 1965, and 1966, and a long-term capital loss carryover of $12,000 attributable to long-term transactions during such years. A, who reports on the calendar year basis, otherwise has ordinary income of $15,000, short-term capital gains of $4,000 and long-term capital gains of $6,000, for the taxable year 1966. A would offset his short-term capital gains of $4,000 against his share of the short-term capital loss carryover of the trust, $10,000 (one-half of $20,000), and, in addition deduct under section 1211(b) $1,000 (treated as a short-term gain for purposes of computing capital loss carryovers) on his return for the taxable year 1966. A would also offset his long-term capital gains of $6,000 against his share of the long-term capital loss carryover of the trust, $6,000 (one-half of $12,000). The balance of A's share of the short-term capital loss carryover, $5,000, may be carried over as a short-term capital loss carryover to the succeeding taxable year and treated as a short-term capital loss incurred in such succeeding taxable year in accordance with paragraph (b) of § 1.1212–1. X, which also reports on the calendar year basis, otherwise has capital gains of $4,000 for the taxable year 1966. X would offset its capital gains of $4,000 against its share of the capital loss carryovers of the trust, $16,000 (the sum of one-half of each the short-term carryover and the long-term carryover of the trust), on its return for the taxable year 1966. The balance of X's share, $12,000, may be carried over as a short-term capital loss only to the years 1967, 1968, 1969, and 1970, in accordance with paragraph (a) of § 1.1212–1 and the rules of this section.

[T.D. 6500, 25 FR 11814, Nov. 26, 1960, as amended by T.D. 6828, 30 FR 7805, June 17, 1965; T.D. 7564, 43 FR 40495, Sept. 12, 1978]

§ 1.642(h)–2   Excess deductions on termination of an estate or trust.

(a) If, on the termination of an estate or trust, the estate or trust has for its last taxable year deductions (other than the deductions allowed under section 642(b) (relating to personal exemption) or section 642(c) (relating to charitable contributions)) in excess of gross income, the excess is allowed under section 642(h)(2) as a deduction to the beneficiaries succeeding to the property of the estate or trust. The deduction is allowed only in computing taxable income and must be taken into account in computing the items of tax preference of the beneficiary; it is not allowed in computing adjusted gross income. The deduction is allowable only in the taxable year of the beneficiary in which or with which the estate or trust terminates, whether the year of termination of the estate or trust is of normal duration or is a short taxable year. For example: Assume that a trust distributes all of its assets to B and terminates on December 31, 1954. As of that date it has excess deductions, for example, because of corpus commissions on termination, of $18,000. B, who reported on the calendar year basis, could claim the $18,000 as a deduction for the taxable year 1954. However, if the deduction (when added to his other deductions) exceeds his gross income, the excess may not be carried over to the year 1955 or subsequent years.

(b) A deduction based upon a net operating loss carryover will never be allowed to beneficiaries under both paragraphs (1) and (2) of section 642(h). Accordingly, a net operating loss deduction which is allowable to beneficiaries succeeding to the property of the estate or trust under the provisions of paragraph (1) of section 642(h) cannot also be considered a deduction for purposes of paragraph (2) of section 642(h) and paragraph (a) of this section. However, if the last taxable year of the estate or trust is the last year in which a deduction on account of a net operating loss may be taken, the deduction, to the extent not absorbed in that taxable year by the estate or trust, is considered an "excess deduction" under section 642(h)(2) and paragraph (a) of this section.

(c) Any item of income or deduction, or any part thereof, which is taken into account in determining the net operating loss or capital loss carryover of the estate or trust for its last taxable year shall not be taken into account again in determining excess deductions on termination of the trust or estate within the meaning of section 642(h)(2) and paragraph (a) of this section (see example in § 1.642(h)–5).

[T.D. 6500, 25 FR 11814, Nov. 26, 1960, as amended by T.D. 7564, 43 FR 40495, Sept. 12, 1978]

§ 1.642(h)–3 Meaning of "beneficiaries succeeding to the property of the estate or trust".

(a) The phrase "beneficiaries succeeding to the property of the estate or trust" means those beneficiaries upon termination of the estate or trust who bear the burden of any loss for which a carryover is allowed, or of any excess of deductions over gross income for which a deduction is allowed, under section 642(h).

(b) With reference to an intestate estate, the phrase means the heirs and next of kin to whom the estate is distributed, or if the estate is insolvent, to whom it would have been distributed if it had not been insolvent. If a decedent's spouse is entitled to a specified dollar amount of property before any distribution to other heirs and next of kin, and if the estate is less than that amount, the spouse is the beneficiary succeeding to the property of the estate or trust to the extent of the deficiency in amount.

(c) In the case of a testate estate, the phrase normally means the residuary beneficiaries (including a residuary trust), and not specific legatees or devisees, pecuniary legatees, or other nonresiduary beneficiaries. However, the phrase does not include the recipient of a specific sum of money even though it is payable out of the residue, except to the extent that it is not payable in full. On the other hand, the phrase includes a beneficiary (including a trust) who is not strictly a residuary beneficiary but whose devise or bequest is determined by the value of the decedent's estate as reduced by the loss or deductions in question. Thus the phrase includes:

(1) A beneficiary of a fraction of a decedent's net estate after payment of debts, expenses, etc.;

(2) A nonresiduary legatee or devisee, to the extent of any deficiency in his legacy or devise resulting from the insufficiency of the estate to satisfy it in full;

(3) A surviving spouse receiving a fractional share of an estate in fee under a statutory right of election, to the extent that the loss or deductions are taken into account in determining the share. However, the phrase does not include a recipient of

dower or curtesy, or any income beneficiary of the estate or trust from which the loss or excess deduction is carried over.

(d) The principles discussed in paragraph (c) of this section are equally applicable to trust beneficiaries. A remainderman who receives all or a fractional share of the property of a trust as a result of the final termination of the trust is a beneficiary succeeding to the property of the trust. For example, if property is transferred to pay the income to A for life and then to pay $10,000 to B and distribute the balance of the trust corpus to C, C and not B is considered to be the succeeding beneficiary except to the extent that the trust corpus is insufficient to pay B $10,000.

[T.D. 6500, 25 FR 11814, Nov. 26, 1960]

§ 1.642(h)–4 Allocation.

The carryovers and excess deductions to which section 642(h) applies are allocated among the beneficiaries succeeding to the property of an estate or trust (see § 1.642(h)–3) proportionately according to the share of each in the burden of the loss or deductions. A person who qualified as a beneficiary succeeding to the property of an estate or trust with respect to one amount and does not qualify with respect to another amount is a beneficiary succeeding to the property of the estate or trust as to the amount with respect to which he qualifies. The application of this section may be illustrated by the following example:

Example. A decedent's will leaves $100,000 to A, and the residue of his estate equally to B and C. His estate is sufficient to pay only $90,000 to A, and nothing to B and C. There is an excess of deductions over gross income for the last taxable year of the estate or trust of $5,000, and a capital loss carryover of $15,000, to both of which section 642(h) applies. A is a beneficiary succeeding to the property of the estate to the extent of $10,000, and since the total of the excess of deductions and the loss carryover is $20,000, A is entitled to the benefit of one half of each item, and the remaining half is divided equally between B and C.

[T.D. 6500, 25 FR 11814, Nov. 26, 1960]

§ 1.643(a)–0 Distributable net income; deduction for distributions; in general.

The term "distributable net income" has no application except in the taxation of estates and trusts and their beneficiaries. It limits the deductions allowable to estates and trusts for amounts paid, credited, or required to be distributed to beneficiaries and is used to determine how much of an amount paid, credited, or required to be distributed to a beneficiary will be includible in his gross income. It is also used to determine the character of distributions to the beneficiaries. Distributable net income means for any taxable year, the taxable income (as defined in section 63) of the estate or trust, computed with the modifications set forth in §§ 1.643(a)–1 through 1.643(a)–7.

[T.D. 6500, 25 FR 11814, Nov. 26, 1960]

§ 1.643(a)–1 Deduction for distributions.

The deduction allowable to a trust under section 651 and to an estate or trust under section 661 for amounts paid, credited, or required to be distributed to beneficiaries is not allowed in the computation of distributable net income.

[T.D. 6500, 25 FR 11814, Nov. 26, 1960]

§ 1.643(a)–2 Deduction for personal exemption.

The deduction for personal exemption under section 642(b) is not allowed in the computation of distributable net income.

[T.D. 6500, 25 FR 11814, Nov. 26, 1960]

§ 1.643(a)–3 Capital gains and losses.

(a) Except as provided in § 1.643(a)–6, gains from the sale or exchange of capital assets are ordinarily excluded from distributable net income, and are not ordinarily considered as paid, credited, or required to be distributed to any beneficiary unless they are:

(1) Allocated to income under the terms of the governing instrument or local law by the fiduciary on its books or by notice to the beneficiary,

(2) Allocated to corpus and actually distributed to beneficiaries during the taxable year, or

(3) Utilized (pursuant to the terms of the governing instrument or the practice followed by the fiduciary) in determining the amount which is distributed or required to be distributed.

However, if capital gains are paid, permanently set aside, or to be used for the purposes specified in section 642(c), so that a charitable deduction is allowed under that section in respect of the gains, they must be included in the computation of distributable net income.

(b) Losses from the sale or exchange of capital assets are excluded in computing distributable net income except to the extent that they enter into the determination of any capital gains that are paid, credited, or required to be distributed to any beneficiary during the taxable year (but see § 1.642(h)–1 with respect to capital loss carryovers in the year of final termination of an estate or trust).

* * *

(d) The application of this section may be illustrated by the following examples:

Example (1). A trust is created to pay the income to A for life, with a discretionary power in the trustee to invade principal for A's benefit. In the taxable year, $10,000 is realized from the sale of securities at a profit, and $10,000 in excess of income is distributed to A. The capital gain is not allocated to A by the trustee. During the taxable year the trustee received and paid out $5,000 of dividends. No other cash was received or on hand during the taxable year. The capital gain will not ordinarily be included in distributable net income. However, if the trustee follows a regular practice of distributing the exact net proceeds of the sale of trust property, capital gains will be included in distributable net income.

Example (2). The result in example (1) would have been the same if the trustee had been directed to pay an annuity of $15,000 a year to A (instead of being directed to pay the income to A with a discretionary power to distribute principal).

Example (3). The trustee of a trust containing Blackacre and other property is directed to hold Blackacre for ten years, and then sell it and distribute its proceeds to A. Any capital gain realized from the sale of Blackacre will be included in distributable net income.

Example (4). A trust instrument directs that the income shall be paid to A, and that the principal shall be distributed to A when he reaches age 35. All capital gains realized in the year of termination will be included in distributable net income. (See § 1.641(b)–3 for the determination of the year of final termination and the taxability of capital gains realized after the terminating event and before final distribution.)

Example (5). If in example (4) the trustee had been directed to distribute half of the principal to A when he reached 35, the capital gain would be included in distributable net income (and in the distribution to A) to the extent the capital gain is allocable to A under the governing instrument and local law. Thus, if the trust assets consisted entirely of 100 shares of corporation M stock and the trustee sold half the shares and distributed the proceeds to A, the entire capital gain would normally be considered as allocated to A. On the other hand, if the trustee sold all the shares and distributed half the proceeds to A, half the capital gain would be considered as allocable to A.

Example (6). If in example (4) the trustee had been directed to pay $10,000 to B before making distribution to A, no portion of the capital gains would be allocable to B since the distribution to B is a gift of a specific sum of money within the meaning of section 663(a)(1).

[T.D. 6500, 25 FR 11814, Nov. 26, 1960, as amended by T.D. 6989, 34 FR 731, Jan. 17, 1969; T.D. 7357, 40 FR 23742, June 2, 1975]

§ 1.643(a)–5 Tax-exempt interest.

(a) There is included in distributable net income any tax-exempt interest excluded from gross income under section 103, reduced by disbursements allocable to such interest which would have been deductible under section 212 but for the provisions of section 265 (relating to disallowance of deductions allocable to tax-exempt income).

(b) If the estate or trust is allowed a charitable contributions deduction under section 642(c), the amounts specified in paragraph (a) of this section and § 1.643(a)–6 are reduced by the portion deemed to be included in income paid, permanently set aside, or to be used for the purposes specified in section 642(c). If the governing instrument specifically provides as to the source out of which amounts are paid, permanently set aside, or to be used for such charitable purposes, the specific provisions control. In the absence of specific provisions in the governing instrument, an amount to which section 642(c) applies is deemed to consist of the same proportion of each class of the items of income of the estate or trust as the total of each class bears to the total of all classes. * * *

* * *

[T.D. 6500, 25 FR 11814, Nov. 26, 1960]

§ 1.643(b)–1 Definition of "income".

For purposes of subparts A through D, part I, subchapter J, chapter 1 of the Code, the term "income" when not preceded by the words "taxable", "distributable net", "undistributed net", or "gross", means the amount of income of an estate or trust for the taxable year determined under the terms of its governing instrument and applicable local law. Trust provisions which depart fundamentally from concepts of local law in the determination of what constitutes income are not recognized for this purpose. For example, if a trust instrument directs that all the trust income shall be paid to A, but defines ordinary dividends and interest as corpus, the trust will not be considered one which under its governing instrument is required to distribute all its income currently for purposes of section 642(b) (relating to the personal

exemption) and section 651 (relating to "simple" trusts).

[T.D. 6500, 25 FR 11814, Nov. 26, 1960]

§ 1.643(b)–2 Dividends allocated to corpus.

Extraordinary dividends or taxable stock dividends which the fiduciary, acting in good faith, determines to be allocable to corpus under the terms of the governing instrument and applicable local law are not considered "income" for purposes of Subpart A, B, C, or D, Part I, Subchapter J, Chapter 1 of the Code. * * *

[T.D. 6500, 25 FR 11814, Nov. 26, 1960, as amended by T.D. 6989, 34 FR 741, Jan. 17, 1969; T.D. 7204, 37 FR 17134, Aug. 25, 1972]

§ 1.643(c)–1 Definition of "beneficiary".

An heir, legatee, or devisee (including an estate or trust) is a beneficiary. A trust created under a decedent's will is a beneficiary of the decedent's estate. The following persons are treated as beneficiaries:

(a) Any person with respect to an amount used to discharge or satisfy that person's legal obligation as that term is used in § 1.662(a)–4.

(b) The grantor of a trust with respect to an amount applied or distributed for the support of a dependent under the circumstances specified in section 677(b) out of corpus or out of other than income for the taxable year of the trust.

(c) The trustee or cotrustee of a trust with respect to an amount applied or distributed for the support of a dependent under the circumstances specified in section 678(c) out of corpus or out of other than income for the taxable year of the trust.

[T.D. 6500, 25 FR 11814, Nov. 26, 1960]

§ 1.643(d)–2 Illustration of the provisions of section 643.

(a) The provisions of section 643 may be illustrated by the following example:

Example. (1) Under the terms of the trust instrument, the income of a trust is required to be currently distributed to W during her life. Capital gains are allocable to corpus and all expenses are charges against corpus. During the taxable year the trust has the following items of income and expenses:

Dividends from domestic corporations	$30,000
Extraordinary dividends allocated to corpus by the trustee in good faith	20,000
Taxable interest	10,000

Tax-exempt interest	$10,000
Long-term capital gains	10,000
Trustee's commissions and miscellaneous expenses allocable to corpus	5,000

(2) The "income" of the trust determined under section 643(b) which is currently distributable to W is $50,000, consisting of dividends of $30,000, taxable interest of $10,000, and tax-exempt interest of $10,000. The trustee's commissions and miscellaneous expenses allocable to tax-exempt interest amount to $1,000 (10,000/50,000 × $5,000).

(3) The "distributable net income" determined under section 643(a) amounts to $45,000, computed as follows:

Dividends from domestic corporations		$30,000
Taxable interest		10,000
Nontaxable interest	$10,000	
Less: Expenses allocable thereto	1,000	
		9,000
Total		49,000

Less: Expenses ($5,000 less $1,000 allocable to tax-exempt interest)	$4,000
Distributable net income	45,000

In determining the distributable net income of $45,000, the taxable income of the trust is computed with the following modifications: No deductions are allowed for distributions to W and for personal exemption of the trust (section 643(a)(1) and (2)); capital gains allocable to corpus are excluded and the deduction allowable under section 1202 is not taken into account (section 643(a)(3)): the extraordinary dividends allocated to corpus by the trustee in good faith are excluded (sections 643(a)(4)); and the tax-exempt interest (as adjusted for expenses) and the dividend exclusion of $50 are included (section 643(a)(5) and (7)).

(b) See paragraph (c) of the example in § 1.661(c)–2 for the computation of distributable net income where there is a charitable contributions deduction.

[T.D. 6500, 25 FR 11814, Nov. 26, 1960. Redesignated by T.D. 6989, 34 FR 732, Jan. 1, 1969]

Trusts Which Distribute Current Income Only

§ 1.651(a)–1 Simple trusts; deduction for distributions; in general.

Section 651 is applicable only to a trust the governing instruments of which:

(a) Requires that the trust distribute all of its income currently for the taxable year, and

(b) Does not provide that any amounts may be paid, permanently set aside, or used in the taxable year for the charitable, etc., purposes specified in section 642(c),

and does not make any distribution other than of current income. A trust to which section 651 applies is referred to in this part as a "simple" trust. Trusts subject to section 661 are referred to as "complex" trusts. A trust may be a simple trust for one year and a complex trust for another year. It should be noted that under section 651 a trust qualifies as a simple trust in a taxable year in which it is required to distribute all its income currently and makes no other distributions, whether or not distributions of current income are in fact made. On the other hand a trust is not a complex trust by reason of distributions of amounts other than income unless such distributions are in fact made during the taxable year, whether or not they are required in that year.

[T.D. 6500, 25 FR 11814, Nov. 26, 1960]

§ 1.651(a)–2 Income required to be distributed currently.

(a) The determination of whether trust income is required to be distributed currently depends upon the terms of the trust instrument and the applicable local law. For this purpose, if the trust instrument provides that the trustee in determining the distributable income shall first retain a reserve for depreciation or otherwise make due allowance for keeping the trust corpus intact by retaining a reasonable amount of the current income for that purpose, the retention of current income for that purpose will not disqualify the trust from being a "simple" trust. The fiduciary must be under a duty to distribute the income currently even if, as a matter of practical necessity, the income is not distributed until after the close of the trust's taxable year. For example: Under the terms of the trust instrument, all of the income is currently distributable to A. The trust reports on the calendar year basis and as a matter of practical necessity makes distribution to A of each quarter's income on the fifteenth day of the month following the close of the quarter. The distribution made by the trust on January 15, 1955, of the income for the fourth quarter of 1954 does not disqualify the trust from treatment in 1955 under section 651, since the income is required to be distributed currently. However, if the terms of a trust require that none of the income be distributed until after the year of its receipt by the trust, the income of the trust is not required to be distributed currently and the trust is not a simple trust. For definition of the term "income" see section 643(b) and § 1.643(b)-1.

(b) It is immaterial, for purposes of determining whether all the income is required to be distributed currently, that the amount of income allocated to a particular beneficiary is not specified in the instrument. For example, if the fiduciary is required to distribute all the income currently, but has discretion to "sprinkle" the income among a class of beneficiaries, or among named beneficiaries, in such amount as he may see fit, all the income is required to be distributed currently, even though the amount distributable to a particular beneficiary is unknown until the fiduciary has exercised his discretion.

(c) If in one taxable year of a trust its income for that year is required or permitted to be accumulated, and in another taxable year its income for the year is required to be distributed currently (and no other amounts are distributed), the trust is a simple trust for the latter year. For example, a trust under which income may be accumulated until a beneficiary is 21 years old, and thereafter must be distributed currently, is a simple trust for taxable years beginning after the beneficiary reaches the age of 21 years in which no other amounts are distributed.

[T.D. 6500, 25 FR 11814, Nov. 26, 1960]

§ 1.651(a)-3 Distribution of amounts other than income.

(a) A trust does not qualify for treatment under section 651 for any taxable year in which it actually distributes corpus. For example, a trust which is required to distribute all of its income currently would not qualify as a simple trust under section 651 in the year of its termination since in that year actual distributions of corpus would be made.

(b) A trust, otherwise qualifying under section 651, which may make a distribution of corpus in the discretion of the trustee, or which is required under the terms of its governing instrument to make a distribution of corpus upon the happening of a specified event, will be disqualified for treatment under section 651 only for the taxable year in which an actual distribution of corpus is made. For example: Under the terms of a trust, which is required to distribute all of its income currently, half of the corpus is to be distributed to beneficiary A when he becomes 30 years of age. The trust

reports on the calendar year basis. On December 28, 1954, A becomes 30 years of age and the trustee distributes half of the corpus of the trust to him on January 3, 1955. The trust will be disqualified for treatment under section 651 only for the taxable year 1955, the year in which an actual distribution of corpus is made.

(c) See section 661 and the regulations thereunder for the treatment of trusts which distribute corpus or claim the charitable contributions deduction provided by section 642(c).

[T.D. 6500, 25 FR 11814, Nov. 26, 1960]

§ 1.651(a)-4 Charitable purposes.

A trust is not considered to be a trust which may pay, permanently set aside, or use any amount for charitable, etc., purposes for any taxable year for which it is not allowed a charitable, etc., deduction under section 642(c). Therefore, a trust with a remainder to a charitable organization is not disqualified for treatment as a simple trust if either (a) the remainder is subject to a contingency, so that no deduction would be allowed for capital gains or other amounts added to corpus as amounts permanently set aside for a charitable, etc., purpose under section 642 (c), or (b) the trust receives no capital gains or other income added to corpus for the taxable year for which such a deduction would be allowed.

[T.D. 6500, 25 FR 11814, Nov. 26, 1960]

§ 1.651(b)-1 Deduction for distributions to beneficiaries.

In computing its taxable income, a simple trust is allowed a deduction for the amount of income which is required under the terms of the trust instrument to be distributed currently to beneficiaries. If the amount of income required to be distributed currently exceeds the distributable net income, the deduction allowable to the trust is limited to the amount of the distributable net income. For this purpose the amount of income required to be distributed currently, or distributable net income, whichever is applicable, does not include items of trust income (adjusted for deductions allocable thereto) which are not included in the gross income of the trust. For determination of the character of the income required to be distributed currently, see § 1.652(b)-2. Accordingly, for the purposes of determining the deduction allowable to the trust under section 651, distributable net income is computed without the modifications specified in paragraphs (5), (6), and (7) of section 643(a), relating to tax-exempt interest, foreign income, and excluded dividends. For example: Assume that the distributable net income of a trust as computed under section 643(a) amounts to $99,000 but includes nontaxable income of $9,000. Then distributable net income for the purpose of determining the deduction allowable under section 651 is $90,000 ($99,000 less $9,000 nontaxable income).

[T.D. 6500, 25 FR 11814, Nov. 26, 1960]

§ 1.652(a)–1   Simple trusts; inclusion of amounts in income of beneficiaries.

Subject to the rules in §§ 1.652(a)–2 and 1.652(b)–1, a beneficiary of a simple trust includes in his gross income for the taxable year the amounts of income required to be distributed to him for such year, whether or not distributed. Thus, the income of a simple trust is includible in the beneficiary's gross income for the taxable year in which the income is required to be distributed currently even though, as a matter of practical necessity, the income is not distributed until after the close of the taxable year of the trust. See § 1.642(a)(3)–2 with respect to time of receipt of dividends. See § 1.652(c)–1 for treatment of amounts required to be distributed where a beneficiary and the trust have different taxable years. The term "income required to be distributed currently" includes income required to be distributed currently which is in fact used to discharge or satisfy any person's legal obligation as that term is used in § 1.662(a)–4.

[T.D. 6500, 25 FR 11814, Nov. 26, 1960]

§ 1.652(a)–2   Distributions in excess of distributable net income.

If the amount of income required to be distributed currently to beneficiaries exceeds the distributable net income of the trust (as defined in section 643(a)), each beneficiary includes in his gross income an amount equivalent to his proportionate share of such distributable net income. Thus, if beneficiary A is to receive two-thirds of the trust income and B is to receive one-third, and the income required to be distributed currently is $99,000, A will receive $66,000 and B, $33,000. However, if the distributable net income, as determined under section 643(a) is only $90,000, A will include two-thirds ($60,000) of that sum in his gross in-

come, and B will include one-third ($30,000) in his gross income. See §§ 1.652(b)–1 and 1.652(b)–2, however, for amounts which are not includible in the gross income of a beneficiary because of their tax-exempt character.

[T.D. 6500, 25 FR 11814, Nov. 26, 1960]

§ 1.652(b)–1   Character of amounts.

In determining the gross income of a beneficiary, the amounts includible under § 1.652(a)–1 have the same character in the hands of the beneficiary as in the hands of the trust. For example, to the extent that the amounts specified in § 1.652(a)–1 consist of income exempt from tax under section 103, such amounts are not included in the beneficiary's gross income. Similarly, dividends distributed to a beneficiary retain their original character in the beneficiary's hands for purposes of determining the availability to the beneficiary of the dividends received credit under section 34 (for dividends received on or before December 31, 1964) and the dividend exclusion under section 116. Also, to the extent that the amounts specified in § 1.652(a)–1 consist of "earned income" in the hands of the trust under the provisions of section 1348 such amount shall be treated under section 1348 as "earned income" in the hands of the beneficiary. Similarly, to the extent such amounts consist of an amount received as a part of a lump sum distribution from a qualified plan and to which the provisions of section 72(n) would apply in the hands of the trust, such amount shall be treated as subject to such section in the hands of the beneficiary except where such amount is deemed under section 666(a) to have been distributed in a preceding taxable year of the trust and the partial tax described in section 668(a)(2) is determined under section 668(b)(1)(B). The tax treatment of amounts determined under § 1.652(a)–1 depends upon the beneficiary's status with respect to them not upon the status of the trust. Thus, if a beneficiary is deemed to have received foreign income of a foreign trust, the includibility of such income in his gross income depends upon his taxable status with respect to that income.

[T.D. 6500, 25 FR 11814, Nov. 26, 1960, as amended by T.D. 6777, 29 FR 17809, Dec. 16, 1964; T.D. 7204, 37 FR 17134, Aug. 25, 1972]

§ 1.652(b)–2   Allocation of income items.

(a) The amounts specified in § 1.652(a)–1 which are required to be included in the gross income of a beneficiary are treated as consisting of the same proportion of each class of items entering into distributable net income of the trust (as defined in section 643(a)) as the total of each class bears to such distributable net income, unless the terms of the trust specifically allocate different classes of income to different beneficiaries, or unless local law requires such an allocation. For example: Assume that under the terms of the governing instrument, beneficiary A is to receive currently one-half of the trust income and beneficiaries B and C are each to receive currently one-quarter, and the distributable net income of the trust (after allocation of expenses) consists of dividends of $10,000, taxable interest of $10,000, and tax-exempt interest of $4,000. A will be deemed to have received $5,000 of dividends, $5,000 of taxable interest, and $2,000 of tax-exempt interest; B and C will each be deemed to have received $2,500 of dividends, $2,500 of taxable interest, and $1,000 of tax-exempt interest. However, if the terms of the trust specifically allocate different classes of income to different beneficiaries, entirely or in part, or if local law requires such an allocation, each beneficiary will be deemed to have received those items of income specifically allocated to him.

(b) The terms of the trust are considered specifically to allocate different classes of income to different beneficiaries only to the extent that the allocation is required in the trust instrument, and only to the extent that it has an economic effect independent of the income tax consequences of the allocation. For example:

(1) Allocation pursuant to a provision in a trust instrument granting the trustee discretion to allocate different classes of income to different beneficiaries is not a specific allocation by the terms of the trust.

(2) Allocation pursuant to a provision directing the trustee to pay all of one income to A, or $10,000 out of the income to A, and the balance of the income to B, but directing the trustee first to allocate a specific class of income to A's share (to the extent there is income of that class and to the extent it does not exceed A's share) is not a specific allocation by the terms of the trust.

(3) Allocation pursuant to a provision directing the trustee to pay half the class of income (whatever it may be) to A, and the balance of the income to B, is a specific allocation by the terms of the trust.

[T.D. 6500, 25 FR 11814, Nov. 26, 1960]

§ 1.652(b)–3 Allocation of deductions.

Items of deduction of a trust that enter into the computation of distributable net income are to be allocated among the items of income in accordance with the following principles:

(a) All deductible items directly attributable to one class of income (except dividends excluded under section 116) are allocated thereto. For example, repairs to, taxes on, and other expenses directly attributable to the maintenance of rental property or the collection of rental income are allocated to rental income. See § 1.642(e)–1 for treatment of depreciation of rental property. Similarly, all expenditures directly attributable to a business carried on by a trust are allocated to the income from such business. If the deductions directly attributable to a particular class of income exceed that income, the excess is applied against other classes of income in the manner provided in paragraph (d) of this section.

(b) The deductions which are not directly attributable to a specific class of income may be allocated to any item of income (including capital gains) included in computing distributable net income, but a portion must be allocated to nontaxable income (except dividends excluded under section 116) pursuant to section 265 and the regulations thereunder. For example, if the income of a trust is $30,000 (after direct expenses), consisting equally of $10,000 of dividends, tax-exempt interest, and rents, and income commissions amount to $3,000, one-third ($1,000) of such commissions should be allocated to tax-exempt interest, but the balance of $2,000 may be allocated to the rents or dividends in such proportions as the trustee may elect. The fact that the governing instrument or applicable local law treats certain items of deduction as attributable to corpus or to income not included in distributable net income does not affect allocation under this paragraph. For instance, if in the example set forth in this paragraph the trust also had capital gains which are allocable to corpus under the terms of the trust instrument, no part of the deductions would be allocable thereto since the capital gains are excluded from the computation of distributable net income under section 643(a)(3).

(c) Examples of expenses which are considered as not directly attributable to a specific class of income are trustee's commissions, the rental of safe deposit boxes, and State income and personal property taxes.

(d) To the extent that any items of deduction which are directly attributable to a class of income exceed that class of income, they may be allocated to any other class of income (including capital gains) included in distributable net income in the manner provided in paragraph (b) of this section, except that any excess deductions attributable to tax-exempt income (other than dividends excluded under section 116) may not be offset against any other class of income. See section 265 and the regulations thereunder. Thus, if the trust has rents, taxable interest, dividends, and tax-exempt interest, and the deductions directly attributable to the rents exceed the rental income, the excess may be allocated to the taxable interest or dividends in such proportions as the fiduciary may elect. However, if the excess deductions are attributable to the tax-exempt interest, they may not be allocated to either the rents, taxable interest, or dividends.

[T.D. 6500, 25 FR 11814, Nov. 26, 1960]

§ 1.652(c)-1 Different taxable years.

If a beneficiary has a different taxable year (as defined in section 441 or 442) from the taxable year of the trust, the amount he is required to include in gross income in accordance with section 652(a) and (b) is based on the income of the trust for any taxable year or years ending with or within his taxable year. This rule applies to taxable years of normal duration as well as to so-called short taxable years. Income of the trust for its taxable year or years is determined in accordance with its method of accounting and without regard to that of the beneficiary.

[T.D. 6500, 25 FR 11814, Nov. 26, 1960]

§ 1.652(c)-2 Death of individual beneficiaries.

If income is required to be distributed currently to a beneficiary, by a trust for a taxable year which does not end with or within the last taxable year of a beneficiary (because of the beneficiary's death), the extent to which the income is included in the gross income of the beneficiary for his last taxable year or in the gross income of his estate is determined by the computations under section 652 for the taxable year of the trust in which his last taxable year ends. Thus, the distributable net income of the taxable year of the trust determines the extent to which the income required to be distributed currently to the beneficiary is included in his gross income for his last taxable year or in the gross income of his estate. (Section 652(c) does not apply to such amounts.) The gross income for the last taxable year of a beneficiary on the cash basis includes only income actually distributed to the beneficiary before his death. Income required to be distributed, but in fact distributed to his estate, is included in the gross income of the estate as income in respect of a decedent under section 691. See paragraph (e) of § 1.663(c)-3 with respect to separate share treatment for the periods before and after the decedent's death. If the trust does not qualify as a simple trust for the taxable year of the trust in which the last taxable year of the beneficiary ends, see section 662(c) and § 1.662(c)-2.

[T.D. 6500, 25 FR 11814, Nov. 26, 1960]

§ 1.652(c)-3 Termination of existence of other beneficiaries.

If the existence of a beneficiary which is not an individual terminates, the amount to be included under section 652(a) in its gross income for its last taxable year is computed with reference to §§ 1.652(c)-1 and 1.652(c)-2 as if the beneficiary were a deceased individual, except that income required to be distributed prior to the termination but actually distributed to the beneficiary's successor in interest is included in the beneficiary's income for its last taxable year.

[T.D. 6500, 25 FR 11814, Nov. 26, 1960]

§ 1.652(c)-4 Illustration of the provisions of sections 651 and 652.

The rules applicable to a trust required to distribute all of its income currently to its beneficiaries may be illustrated by the following example:

Example. (a) Under the terms of a simple trust all of the income is to be distributed equally to beneficiaries A and B and capital gains are to be allocated to corpus. The trust and both beneficiaries file returns on the calendar year basis. No provision is made in the governing instrument with respect to depreciation. During the taxable year 1955, the trust had the following items of income and expense:

Rents	$25,000
Dividends of domestic corporations	50,000
Tax-exempt interest on municipal bonds	25,000
Long-term capital gains	15,000
Taxes and expenses directly attributable to rents	5,000
Trustee's commissions allocable to income account	2,600

Trustee's commissions allocable to principal
    account $1,300
Depreciation............................ 5,000

(b) The income of the trust for fiduciary accounting purposes is $92,400, computed as follows:

Rents $25,000
Dividends 50,000
Tax-exempt interest...................... 25,000
    Total............................. 100,000
Deductions:
  Expenses directly attributa-
    ble to rental income $5,000
  Trustee's commissions alloca-
    ble to income account 2,600
                        7,600
    Income computed under section 643(b) 92,400

One-half ($46,200) of the income of $92,400 is currently distributable to each beneficiary.

(c) The distributable net income of the trust computed under section 643(a) is $91,100, determined as follows (cents are disregarded in the computation):

Rents $25,000
Dividends 50,000
Tax-exempt interest........... $25,000
Less: Expenses allocable there-
to (25,000/100,000 × $3,900) 975
                             24,025
    Total........................... 99,025
Deductions:
  Expenses directly attributa-
    ble to rental income $5,000
  Trustee's commissions
    ($3,900 less $975 alloca-
    ble to tax-exempt inter-
    est) 2,925
                         7,925
    Distributable net income 91,100

In computing the distributable net income of $91,100, the taxable income of the trust was computed with the following modifications: No deductions were allowed for distributions to the beneficiaries and for personal exemption of the trust (section 643(a)(1) and (2)); capital gains were excluded and no deduction under section 1202 (relating to the 50-percent deduction for long-term capital gains) was taken into account (section 643(a)(3)); the tax-exempt interest (as adjusted for expenses) and the dividend exclusion of $50 were included (section 643(a)(5) and (7)). Since all of the income of the trust is required

to be currently distributed, no deduction is allowable for depreciation in the absence of specific provisions in the governing instrument providing for the keeping of the trust corpus intact. See section 167(h) and the regulations thereunder.

(d) The deduction allowable to the trust under section 651(a) for distributions to the beneficiaries is $67,025, computed as follows:

Distributable net income computed under
  section 643(a) (see paragraph (c)) $91,100
Less:
  Tax-exempt interest as ad-
    justed $24,025
  Dividend exclusion 50
                             24,075
  Distributable net income as determined
    under section 651(b) 67,025

Since the amount of the income ($92,400) required to be distributed currently by the trust exceeds the distributable net income ($67,025) as computed under section 651(b), the deduction allowable under section 651(a) is limited to the distributable net income of $67,025.

(e) The taxable income of the trust is $7,200 computed as follows:

Rents $25,000
Dividends ($50,000 less $50 exclusion) 49,950
Long-term capital gains 15,000
    Gross income 89,950
Deductions:
  Rental expenses $5,000
  Trustee's commissions....... 2,925
  Capital gain deduction 7,500
  Distributions to beneficiaries 67,025
  Personal exemption 300
                             82,750
    Taxable income 7,200

The trust is not allowed a deduction for the portion ($975) of the trustee's commissions allocable to tax-exempt interest in computing its taxable income.

(f) In determining the character of the amounts includible in the gross income of A and B, it is assumed that the trustee elects to allocate to rents the expenses not directly attributable to a specific item of income other than the portion ($975) of such expenses allocated to tax-exempt interest. The allocation of expenses among the items of income is shown below:

	Rents	Dividends	Tax-exempt interest	Total
Income for trust accounting purposes	$25,000	$50,000	$25,000	$100,000
Less:				
Rental expenses	5,000	....	....	5,000
Trustee's commissions...........................	2,925	....	975	3,900
Total deductions	7,925	0	975	8,900
Character of amounts in the hands of the beneficiaries	17,075	50,000	24,025	[1]91,100

[1] Distributable net income.

Inasmuch as the income of the trust is to be distributed equally to A and B, each is deemed to have received one-half of each item of income; that is, rents of $8,537.50, dividends of $25,000, and tax-exempt interest of $12,012.50. The dividends of $25,000 allocated to each beneficiary are to be aggregated with his other dividends (if any) for purposes of the dividend exclusion provided by section 116 and the dividend received credit allowed under section 34. Also, each beneficiary is allowed a deduction of $2,500 for depreciation of rental property attributable to the portion (one-half) of the income of the trust distributed to him.

[T.D. 6500, 25 FR 11814, Nov. 26, 1960, as amended by T.D. 6712, 29 FR 3655, March 24, 1964]

Estates and Trusts Which May Accumulate Income or Which Distribute Corpus

§ 1.661(a)–1 Estates and trusts accumulating income or distributing corpus; general.

Subpart C, part I, subchapter J, chapter 1 of the Code, is applicable to all decedents' estates and their beneficiaries, and to trusts and their beneficiaries other than trusts subject to the provisions of subpart B of such part I (relating to trusts which distribute current income only, or "simple" trusts). A trust which is required to distribute amounts other than income during the taxable year may be subject to subpart B, and not subpart C, in the absence of an actual distribution of amounts other than income during the taxable year. See §§ 1.651(a)–1 and 1.651(a)–3. A trust to which subpart C is applicable is referred to as a "complex" trust in this part. Section 661 has no application to amounts excluded under section 663(a).

[T.D. 6500, 25 FR 11814, Nov. 26, 1960]

§ 1.661(a)–2 Deduction for distributions to beneficiaries.

(a) In computing the taxable income of an estate or trust there is allowed under section 661(a) as a deduction for distributions to beneficiaries the sum of:

(1) The amount of income for the taxable year which is required to be distributed currently, and

(2) Any other amounts properly paid or credited or required to be distributed for such taxable year.

However, the total amount deductible under section 661(a) cannot exceed the distributable net income as computed under section 643(a) and as modified by section 661(c). See § 1.661(c)–1.

(b) The term "income required to be distributed currently" includes any amount required to be distributed which may be paid out of income or corpus (such as an annuity), to the extent it is paid out of income for the taxable year. See § 1.651(a)–2 which sets forth additional rules which are applicable in determining whether income of an estate or trust is required to be distributed currently.

(c) The term "any other amounts properly paid, credited, or required to be distributed" includes all amounts properly paid, credited, or required to be distributed by an estate or trust during the taxable year other than income required to be distributed currently. Thus, the term includes the payment of an annuity to the extent it is not paid out of income for the taxable year, and a distribution of property in kind (see paragraph (f) of this section). However, see section 663(a) and regulations thereunder for distributions which are not included. Where the income of an estate or trust may be accumulated or distributed in the discretion of the fiduciary, or where the fiduciary has a power to distribute corpus to a beneficiary, any such discretionary distribution would qualify under section 661(a)(2). The term also includes an amount applied or distributed for the support of a dependent of a grantor or of a trustee or cotrustee under the circumstances described in section 677(b) or section 678(c) out of corpus or out of other than income for the taxable year.

(d) The terms "income required to be distributed currently" and "any other amounts properly paid or credited or required to be distributed" also include any amount used to discharge or satisfy any person's legal obligation as that term is used in § 1.662(a)–4.

(e) The terms "income required to be distributed currently" and "any other amounts properly paid or credited or required to be distributed" include amounts paid, or required to be paid, during the taxable year pursuant to a court order or decree or under local law, by a decedent's estate as an allowance or award for the support of the decedent's widow or other dependent for a limited period during the administration of the estate. The term "any other amounts properly paid or credited or required to be distributed" does not include the value of any interest in real estate owned by a decedent, title to which under local law passes directly from the decedent to his heirs or devisees.

(f) If property is paid, credited, or required to be distributed in kind:

(1) No gain or loss is realized by the trust or estate (or the other beneficiaries) by reason of the distribution, unless the distribution is in satisfaction of a right to receive a distribution in a specific dollar amount or in specific property other than that distributed.

(2) In determining the amount deductible by the trust or estate and includible in the gross income of the beneficiary the property distributed in kind is taken into account at its fair market value at the time it was distributed, credited, or required to be distributed.

(3) The basis of the property in the hands of the beneficiary is its fair market value at the time it was paid, credited, or required to be distributed, to the extent such value is included in the gross income of the beneficiary. To the extent that the value of property distributed in kind is not included in the gross income of the beneficiary, its basis in the hands of the beneficiary is governed by the rules in sections 1014 and 1015 and the regulations thereunder. For this purpose, if the total value of cash and property distributed, credited, or required to be distributed in kind to a beneficiary in any taxable year exceeds the amount includible in his gross income for that year, the value of the property other than cash is normally considered as includible in his gross income only to the extent that the amount includible exceeds the cash paid, credited, or required to be distributed to the beneficiary in that year. Further, to the extent that the value of different items of property other than cash is includible in the gross income of a beneficiary in accordance with the preceding sentence, a pro rata portion of the total value of each item of property distributed, credited, or required to be distributed is normally considered as includible in the beneficiary's gross income.

[T.D. 6500, 25 FR 11814, Nov. 26, 1960; 25 FR 14021, Dec. 31, 1960, as amended by T.D. 7287, 38 FR 26912, Sept. 27, 1973]

§ 1.661(b)–1 Character of amounts distributed; in general.

In the absence of specific provisions in the governing instrument for the allocation of different classes of income, or unless local law requires such an allocation, the amount deductible for distributions to beneficiaries under section 661(a) is treated as consisting of the same proportion of each class of items entering into the computation of distributable net income as the total of each class bears to the total distributable net income. For example, if a trust has distributable net income of $20,000, consisting of $10,000 each of taxable interest and royalties and distributes $10,000 to beneficiary A, the deduction of $10,000 allowable under section 661(a) is deemed to consist of $5,000 each of taxable interest and royalties, unless the trust instrument specifically provides for the distribution or accumulation of different classes of income or unless local law requires such an allocation. See also § 1.661(c)–1.

[T.D. 6500, 25 FR 11814, Nov. 26, 1960]

§ 1.661(c)–2 Illustration of the provisions of section 661.

The provisions of section 661 may be illustrated by the following example:

Example. (a) Under the terms of a trust, which reports on the calendar year basis, $10,000 a year is required to be paid out of income to a designated charity. The balance of the income may, in the trustee's discretion, be accumulated or distributed to beneficiary A. Expenses are allocable against income and the trust instrument requires a reserve for depreciation. During the taxable year 1955 the trustee contributes $10,000 to charity and in his discretion distributes $15,000 of income to A. The trust has the following items of income and expense for the taxable year 1955:

Dividends	$10,000
Partially tax-exempt interest	10,000
Fully tax-exempt interest	10,000
Rents	20,000
Rental expenses	2,000
Depreciation of rental property	3,000
Trustee's commissions	5,000

(b) The income of the trust for fiduciary accounting purposes is $40,000, computed as follows:

Dividends		$10,000
Partially tax-exempt interest		10,000
Fully tax-exempt interest		10,000
Rents		20,000
Total		50,000
Less:		
Rental expenses	$ 2,000	
Depreciation	3,000	
Trustee's commissions	5,000	
		10,000
Income as computed under section 643(b)		40,000

(c) The distributable net income of the trust as computed under section 643(a) is $30,000, determined as follows:

Rents	$20,000
Dividends	10,000
Partially tax-exempt interest	10,000

Fully tax-exempt interest	$10,000		
Less:			
Expenses allocable thereto (10,000/50,000 × $5,000).	$1,000		
Charitable contributions allocable thereto (10,000/50,000 × $10,000). . . .	2,000		
		3,000	
			7,000
Total.			47,000
Deductions:			
Rental expenses	$ 2,000		
Depreciation of rental property.	3,000		

Trustee's commissions ($5,000 less $1,000 allocated to tax-exempt interest).	4,000	
Charitable contributions ($10,000 less $2,000 allocated to tax-exempt interests).	8,000	
		17,000
Distributable net income (section 643(a)).		30,000

(d) The character of the amounts distributed under section 661(a), determined in accordance with the rules prescribed in §§ 1.661(b)–1 and 1.661(b)–2 is shown by the following table (for the purpose of this allocation, it is assumed that the trustee elected to allocate the trustee's commissions to rental income except for the amount required to be allocated to tax-exempt interest):

	Rental income	Taxable dividends	Excluded dividends	Partially Tax-exempt interest	Tax-exempt interest	Total
Trust income	$20,000	$9,950	$50	$10,000	$10,000	$50,000
Less:						
Charitable contributions.	4,000	2,000	. . . .	2,000	2,000	10,000
Rental expenses	2,000	. . . .	. . . .	. . . .	. . . .	2,000
Depreciation.	3,000	. . . .	. . . .	. . . .	. . . .	3,000
Trustee's commissions	4,000	. . . .	. . . .	. . . .	1,000	5,000
Total deductions	13,000	2,000	0	2,000	3,000	20,000
Distributable net income	7,000	7,950	50	8,000	7,000	30,000
Amounts deemed distributed under section 661(a) before applying the limitation of section 661(c)	3,500	3,975	25	4,000	3,500	15,000

In the absence of specific provisions in the trust instrument for the allocation of different classes of income, the charitable contribution is deemed to consist of a pro rata portion of the gross amount of each items of income of the trust (except dividends excluded under section 116) and the trust is deemed to have distributed to A a pro rata portion (one-half) of each item of income included in distributable net income.

(e) The taxable income of the trust is $11,375 computed as follows:

Rental income		$20,000
Dividends ($10,000 less $50 exclusion)		9,950
Partially tax-exempt interest		10,000
Gross income		39,950
Deductions:		
Rental expenses	$2,000	
Depreciation of rental property.	3,000	
Trustee's commissions	4,000	
Charitable contributions	8,000	
Distributions to A	11,475	
Personal exemption	100	
		28,575
Taxable income		11,375

In computing the taxable income of the trust no deduction is allowable for the portions of the charitable contri-

butions deduction ($2,000) and trustee's commissions ($1,000) which are treated under section 661(b) as attributable to the tax-exempt interest excludable from gross income. Also, of the dividends of $4,000 deemed to have been distributed to A under section 661(a), $25 (^{25}/50ths of $50) is deemed to have been distributed from the excluded dividends and is not an allowable deduction to the trust. Accordingly, the deduction allowable under section 661 is deemed to be composed of $3,500 rental income, $3,975 of dividends, and $4,000 partially tax-exempt interest. No deduction is allowable for the portion of tax-exempt interest or for the portion of the excluded dividends deemed to have been distributed to the beneficiary.

(f) The trust is entitled to the credit allowed by section 34 with respect to dividends of $5,975 ($9,950 less $3,975 distributed to A) included in gross income. Also, the trust is allowed the credit provided by section 35 with respect to partially tax-exempt interest of $6,000 ($10,000 less $4,000 deemed distributed to A) included in gross income.

(g) Dividends of $4,000 allocable to A are to be aggregated with his other dividends (if any) for purposes of the dividend exclusion under section 116 and the dividend received credit under section 84.

[T.D. 6500, 25 FR 11814, Nov. 26, 1960]

§ 1.662(a)–1 Inclusion of amounts in gross income of beneficiaries of estates and complex trusts; general.

There is included in the gross income of a beneficiary of an estate or complex trust the sum of:

(1) Amounts of income required to be distributed currently to him, and

(2) All other amounts properly paid, credited, or required to be distributed to him

by the estate or trust. The preceding sentence is subject to the rules contained in § 1.662(a)–2 (relating to currently distributable income), § 1.662(a)–3 (relating to other amounts distributed), and §§ 1.662(b)–1 and 1.662(b)–2 (relating to character of amounts). Section 662 has no application to amounts excluded under section 663(a).

[T.D. 6500, 25 FR 11814, Nov. 26, 1960]

§ 1.662(a)–2 Currently distributable income.

(a) There is first included in the gross income of each beneficiary under section 662(a)(1) the amount of income for the taxable year of the estate or trust required to be distributed currently to him, subject to the provisions of paragraph (b) of this section. Such amount is included in the beneficiary's gross income whether or not it is actually distributed.

(b) If the amount of income required to be distributed currently to all beneficiaries exceeds the distributable net income (as defined in section 643(a) but computed without taking into account the payment, crediting, or setting aside of an amount for which a charitable contributions deduction is allowable under section 642(c)) of the estate or trust, then there is included in the gross income of each beneficiary an amount which bears the same ratio to distributable net income (as so computed) as the amount of income required to be distributed currently to the beneficiary bears to the amount required to be distributed currently to all beneficiaries.

(c) The phrase "the amount of income for the taxable year required to be distributed currently" includes any amount required to be paid out of income or corpus to the extent the amount is satisfied out of income for the taxable year. Thus, an annuity required to be paid in all events (either out of income or corpus) would qualify as income required to be distributed currently to the extent there is income (as defined in section 643(b)) not paid, credited, or required to be distributed to other beneficiaries for the taxable year. If an annuity or a portion of an annuity is deemed under this paragraph to be income required to be distributed currently, it is treated in all respects in the same manner as an amount of income actually required to be distributed currently. The phrase "the amount of income for the taxable year required to be distributed currently" also includes any amount required to be paid during the taxable year in all events (either out of income or corpus) pursuant to a court order or decree or under local law, by a decedent's estate as an allowance or award for the support of the decedent's widow or other dependent for a limited period during the administration of the estate to the extent there is income (as defined in section 643(b)) of the estate for the taxable year not paid, credited, or required to be distributed to other beneficiaries.

(d) If an annuity is paid, credited, or required to be distributed tax free, that is, under a provision whereby the executor or trustee will pay the income tax of the annuitant resulting from the receipt of the annuity, the payment of or for the tax by the executor or trustee will be treated as income paid, credited, or required to be distributed currently to the extent it is made out of income.

(e) The application of the rules stated in this section may be illustrated by the following examples:

Example (1). (1) Assume that under the terms of the trust instrument $5,000 is to be paid to X charity out of income each year; that $20,000 of income is currently distributable to A; and that an annuity of $12,000 is to be paid to B out of income or corpus. All expenses are charges against income and capital gains are allocable to corpus. During the taxable year the trust had income of $30,000 (after the payment of expenses) derived from taxable interest and made the payments to X charity and distributions to A and B as required by the governing instrument.

(2) The amounts treated as distributed currently under section 662(a)(1) total $25,000 ($20,000 to A and $5,000 to B). Since the charitable contribution is out of income the amount of income available for B's annuity is only $5,000. The distributable net income of the trust computed under section 643(a) without taking into consideration the charitable contributions deduction of $5,000 as provided by section 661(a)(1), is $30,000. Since the amounts treated as distributed currently of $25,000 do not exceed the distributable net income (as modified) of $30,000, A is required to include $20,000 in his gross income and B is required to include $5,000 in his gross income under section 662(a)(1).

Example (2). Assume the same facts as in paragraph (1) of example (1), except that the trust has, in addition, $10,000 of administration expenses, commissions, etc., chargeable to corpus. The amounts treated as distributed currently under section 662(a)(1) total $25,000 ($20,000 to A and $5,000 to B), since trust income under section 643(b) remains the same as in example (1). Distributable net income of the trust computed under section 643(a) but without taking into account the charitable contributions deduction of $5,000 as provided by section 662(a)(1) is only $20,000. Since the amounts treated as distributed currently of $25,000 exceed the distributable net income (as so computed) of $20,000, A is required to include $16,000 (20,000/25,000 of $20,000) in his gross income and B is required to include $4,000 (5,000/25,000 of $20,000) in his gross income under section 662(a)(1). Because A and B are beneficiaries of amounts of income required to be distributed currently, they do not benefit from the reduction of distributable net income by the charitable contributions deduction.

[T.D. 6500, 25 FR 11814, Nov. 26, 1960; 25 FR 14021, Dec. 31, 1960, as amended by T.D. 7287, 38 FR 26912, Sept. 27, 1973]

§ 1.662(a)–3 Other amounts distributed.

(a) There is included in the gross income of a beneficiary under section 662(a)(2) any amount properly paid, credited, or required to be distributed to the beneficiary for the taxable year, other than (1) income required to be distributed currently, as determined under § 1.662(a)–2, (2) amounts excluded under section 663(a) and the regulations thereunder, and (3) amounts in excess of distributable net income (see paragraph (c) of this section). An amount which is credited or required to be distributed is included in the gross income of a beneficiary whether or not it is actually distributed.

(b) Some of the payments to be included under paragraph (a) of this section are: (1) A distribution made to a beneficiary in the discretion of the fiduciary; (2) a distribution required by the terms of the governing instrument upon the happening of a specified event; (3) an annuity which is required to be paid in all events but which is payable only out of corpus; (4) a distribution of property in kind (see paragraph (f) of § 1.661(a)–2); (5) an amount applied or distributed for the support of a dependent of a grantor or a trustee or cotrustee under the circumstances specified in section 677(b) or section 678(c) out of corpus or out of other than income for the taxable year; and (6) an amount required to be paid during the taxable year pursuant to a court order or decree or under local law, by a decedent's estate as an allowance or award for the support of the decedent's widow or other dependent for a limited period during the administration of the estate which is payable only out of corpus of the estate under the order or decree or local law.

(c) If the sum of the amounts of income required to be distributed currently (as determined under § 1.662(a)–2) and other amounts properly paid, credited, or required to be distributed (as determined under paragraph (a) of this section) exceeds distributable net income (as defined in section 643(a)), then such other amounts properly paid, credited, or required to be distributed are included in gross income of the beneficiary but only to the extent of the excess of such distributable net income over the amounts of income required to be distributed currently. If the other amounts are paid, credited, or required to be distributed to more than one beneficiary, each beneficiary includes in gross income his proportionate share of the amount includible in gross income pursuant to the preceding sentence. The proportionate share is an amount which bears the same ratio to distributable net income (reduced by amounts of income required to be distributed currently) as the other amounts (as determined under paragraphs (a) and (d) of this section) distributed to the beneficiary bear to the other amounts distributed to all beneficiaries. For treatment of excess distributions by trusts, see sections 665 to 668, inclusive, and the regulations thereunder.

(d) The application of the rules stated in this section may be illustrated by the following example:

Example. The terms of a trust require the distribution annually of $10,000 of income to A. If any income remains, it may be accumulated or distributed to B, C, and D in amounts in the trustee's discretion. He may also invade corpus for the benefit of A, B, C, or D. In the taxable year, the trust has $20,000 of income after the deduction of all expenses. Distributable net income is $20,000. The trustee distributes $10,000 of income to A. Of the remaining $10,000 of income, he distributes $3,000 each to B, C, and D, and also distributes an additional $5,000 to A. A includes $10,000 in income under section 662(a)(1). The "other amounts distributed" amount of $14,000, includible in the income of the recipients to the extent of $10,000, distributable net income less the income currently distributable to A. A will include an additional $3,571 (5,000/14,000 × $10,000) in income under this section, and B, C, and D will each include $2,143 (3,000/14,000 × $10,000).

[T.D. 6500, 25 FR 11814, Nov. 26, 1960; 25 FR 14021, Dec. 31, 1960, as amended by T.D. 7287, 38 FR 26913, Sept. 27, 1973]

§ 1.662(a)–4 Amounts used in discharge of a legal obligation.

Any amount which, pursuant to the terms of a will or trust instrument, is used in full or partial discharge or satisfaction of a legal obligation of any person is included in the gross income of such person under section 662(a)(1) or (2), whichever is applicable, as though directly distributed to him as a beneficiary, except in cases to which section 71 (relating to alimony payments) or section 682 (relating to income of a trust in case of divorce, etc.) applies. The term "legal obligation" includes a legal obligation to support another person if, and only if, the obligation is not affected by the adequacy of the dependent's own resources. For example, a parent has a "legal obligation" within the meaning of the preceding sentence to support his minor child if under local law property or income from property owned by the child cannot be used for his support so long as his parent is able to support him. On the other hand, if under local law a mother may use the resources of a child for the child's support in lieu of supporting him herself, no obligation of support exists within the meaning of this paragraph, whether or not income is actually used for support. Similarly, since under local law a child ordinarily is obligated to support his parent only if the parent's earnings and resources are insufficient for the purpose, no obligation exists whether or not the parent's earnings and resources are sufficient. In any event the amount of trust income which is included in the gross income of a person obligated to support a dependent is limited by the extent of his legal obligation under local law. In the case of a parent's obligation to support his child, to the extent that the parent's legal obligation of support, including education, is determined under local law by the family's station in life and by the means of the parent, it is to be determined without consideration of the trust income in question.

[T.D. 6500, 25 FR 11814, Nov. 26, 1960]

§ 1.662(b)–1 Character of amounts; when no charitable contributions are made.

In determining the amount includible in the gross income of a beneficiary, the amounts which are determined under section 662(a) and §§ 1.662(a)–1 through 1.662(a)–4 shall have the same character in the hands of the beneficiary as in the hands of the estate or trust. The amounts are treated as consisting of the same proportion of each class of items entering into the computation of distributable net income as the total of each class bears to the total distributable net income of the estate or trust unless the terms of the governing instrument specifically allocate different classes of income to different beneficiaries, or unless local law requires such an allocation. For this purpose, the principles contained in § 1.652(b)–1 shall apply.

[T.D. 6500, 25 FR 11814, Nov. 26, 1960]

§ 1.662(c)–4 Illustration of the provisions of sections 661 and 662.

The provisions of sections 661 and 662 may be illustrated in general by the following example:

Example. (a) Under the terms of a testamentary trust one-half of the trust income is to be distributed currently to W, the decedent's wife, for her life. The remaining trust income may, in the trustee's discretion, either be paid to D, the grantor's daughter, paid to designated charities, or accumulated. The trust is to terminate at the death of W and the principal will then be payable to D. No provision is made in the trust instrument with respect to depreciation of rental property. Capital gains are allocable to the principal account under the applicable local law. The trust and both beneficiaries file returns on the calendar year basis. The records of the fiduciary show the following items of income and deduction for the taxable year 1955:

Rents	$50,000
Dividends of domestic corporations	50,000
Tax-exempt interest	20,000
Partially tax-exempt interest	10,000
Capital gains (long term)	20,000
Depreciation of rental property	10,000
Expenses attributable to rental income	15,400
Trustee's commissions allocable to income account	2,800
Trustee's commissions allocable to principal account	1,100

(b) The income for trust accounting purposes is $111,800, and the trustee distributes one-half ($55,900) to W and in his discretion makes a contribution of one-quarter ($27,950) to charity X and distributes the remaining one-quarter ($27,950) to D. The total of the distributions to beneficiaries is $83,850, consisting of (1) income required to be distributed currently to W of $55,900 and (2) other amounts properly paid or credited to D of $27,950. The income for trust accounting purposes of $111,800 is determined as follows:

Rents		$50,000
Dividends		50,000
Tax-exempt interest		20,000
Partially tax-exempt interest		10,000
Total		130,000
Less:		
Rental expenses	$15,400	
Trustee's commissions allocable to income account	2,800	
		18,200
Income as computed under section 643(b)		111,800

(c) The distributable net income of the trust as computed under section 643(a) is $82,750, determined as follows:

Rents		$50,000
Dividends		50,000
Partially tax-exempt interest		10,000
Tax-exempt interest	$20,000	
Less:		
Trustee's commissions allocable thereto (20,000/130,000 of $3,900)	$600	
Charitable contributions allocable thereto (20,000/130,000 of $27,950)	4,300	
		4,900
		15,100
Total		125,100
Deductions:		
Rental expenses	15,400	
Trustee's commissions ($3,900 less $600 allocated to tax-exempt interest)	3,300	
Charitable deduction ($27,950 less $4,300 attributable to tax-exempt interest)	23,650	
		42,350
Distributable net income		82,750

In computing the distributable net income of $82,750, the taxable income of the trust was computed with the following modifications: No deductions were allowed for distributions to beneficiaries and for personal exemption of the trust (section 643(a)(1) and (2)); capital gains were excluded and no deduction under section 1202 (relating to the 50 percent deduction for long-term capital gains) was taken into account (section 643(a)(3)); and the tax-exempt interest (as adjusted for expenses and charitable contributions) and the dividend exclusion of $50 were included (section 643(a)(5) and (7)).

(d) Inasmuch as the distributable net income of $82,750 as determined under section 643(a) is less than the sum of the amounts distributed to W and D of $83,850, the deduction allowable to the trust under section 661(a) is such distributable net income as modified under section 661(c) to exclude therefrom the items of income not included in the gross income of the trust, as follows:

Distributable net income		$82,750
Less:		
Tax-exempt interest (as adjusted for expenses and the charitable contributions)	$15,100	
Dividend exclusion allowable under section 116	50	
		15,150
Deduction allowable under section 661(a)		67,600

(e) For the purpose of determining the character of the amounts deductible under section 642(c) and section 661(a), the trustee elected to offset the trustee's commissions (other than the portion required to be allocated to tax-exempt interest) against the rental income. The following table shows the determination of the character of the amounts deemed distributed to beneficiaries and contributed to charity.

	Rents	Taxable dividends	Excluded dividends	Tax exempt interest	Partially tax exempt interest	Total
Trust income	$50,000	$49,950	$50	$20,000	$10,000	$130,000
Less:						
Charitable contribution	10,750	10,750	....	4,300	2,150	27,950
Rental expenses	15,400	....	....	....	....	15,400
Trustee's commissions	3,300	....	....	600	....	3,900
Total deductions	29,450	10,750	0	4,900	2,150	47,250
Amounts distributable to beneficiaries	20,550	39,200	50	15,100	7,850	82,750

The character of the charitable contribution is determined by multiplying the total charitable contribution ($27,950) by a fraction consisting of each item of trust income, respectively, over the total trust income, except that no part of the dividends excluded from gross income are deemed included in the charitable contribution. For example, the charitable contribution is deemed to consist of rents of $10,750 (50,000/130,000×$27,950).

(f) The taxable income of the trust is $9,900 determined as follows:

Rental income	$50,000
Dividends ($50,000 less $50 exclusion)	49,950
Partially tax-exempt interest	10,000
Capital gains	20,000
Gross income	129,950

Deductions:	
Rental expenses	$15,400
Trustee's commissions	3,300
Charitable contributions	23,650
Capital gain deductions	10,000
Distributions to beneficiaries	67,600
Personal exemption	100
	120,050
Taxable income	9,900

(g) In computing the amount includible in W's gross income under section 662(a)(1), the $55,900 distribution to her is deemed to be composed of the following proportions of the items of income deemed to have been distributed to the beneficiaries by the trust (see paragraph (e) of this example):

Rents (20,550/82,750 × $55,900) $13,882

Dividends (39,250/82,750 × $55,900)........ 26,515

Partially tax-exempt interest (7,850/82,750 × $55,900) 5,303

Tax-exempt interest (15,100/82,750 × $55,-900)................................... 10,200

Total............................. 55,900

Accordingly, W will exclude $10,200 of tax-exempt interest from gross income and will receive the credits and exclusion for dividends received and for partially tax-exempt interest provided in sections 34, 116, and 35, respectively, with respect to the dividends and partially tax-exempt interest deemed to have been distributed to her, her share of the dividends being aggregated with other dividends received by her for purposes of the dividend credit and exclusion. In addition, she may deduct a share of the depreciation deduction proportionate to the trust income allocable to her; that is, one-half of the total depreciation deduction, or $5,000.

(h) Inasmuch as the sum of the amount of income required to be distributed currently to W ($55,900) and the other amounts properly paid, credited, or required to be distributed to D ($27,950) exceeds the distributable net income ($82,750) of the trust as determined under section 643(a), D is deemed to have received $26,850 ($82,750 less $55,900) for income tax purposes. The character of the amounts deemed distributed to her is determined as follows:

Rents (20,550/82,750 × $26,850) $6,668

Dividends (39,250/82,750 × $26,850)........ 12,735

Partially tax-exempt interest (7,850/82,750 × $26,850) 2,547

Tax-exempt interest (15,100/82,750 × $26,-850)................................... 4,900

Total............................. 26,850

Accordingly, D will exclude $4,900 of tax-exempt interest from gross income and will receive the credits and exclusion for dividends received and for partially tax-exempt interest provided in sections 34, 116, and 35, respectively, with respect to the dividends and partially tax-exempt interest deemed to have been distributed to her, her share of the dividends being aggregated with other dividends received by her for purposes of the dividend credit and exclusion. In addition, she may deduct a share of the depreciation deduction proportionate to the trust income allocable to her; that is, one-fourth of the total depreciation deduction, or $2,500.

(i) [Reserved]

(j) The remaining $2,500 of the depreciation deduction is allocated to the amount distributed to charity X and is hence nondeductible by the trust, W, or D. (See § 1.642(e)–1.)

[T.D. 6500, 25 FR 11814, Nov. 26, 1960]

§ 1.663(a)–1 Special rules applicable to sections 661 and 662; exclusions; gifts, bequests, etc.

(a) **In general.** A gift or bequest of a specific sum of money or of specific property, which is required by the specific terms of the will or trust instrument and is properly paid or credited to a beneficiary, is not allowed as a deduction to an estate or trust under section 661 and is not included in the gross income of a beneficiary under section 662, unless under the terms of the will or trust instrument the gift or bequest is to be paid or credited to the recipient in more than three installments. Thus, in order for a gift or bequest to be excludable from the gross income of the recipient, (1) it must qualify as a gift or bequest of a specific sum of money or of specific property (see paragraph (b) of this section), and (2) the terms of the governing instrument must not provide for its payment in more than three installments (see paragraph (c) of this section). The date when the estate came into existence or the date when the trust was created is immaterial.

(b) **Definition of a gift or bequest of a specific sum of money or of specific property.** (1) In order to qualify as a gift or bequest of a specific sum of money or of specific property under section 663(a), the amount of money or the identity of the specific property must be ascertainable under the terms of a testator's will as of the date of his death, or under the terms of an inter vivos trust instrument as of the date of the inception of the trust. For example, bequests to a decedent's son of the decedent's interest in a partnership and to his daughter of a sum of money equal to the value of the partnership interest are bequests of specific property and of a specific sum of money, respectively. On the other hand, a bequest to the decedent's spouse of money or property, to be selected by the decedent's executor, equal in value to a fraction of the decedent's "adjusted gross estate" is neither a bequest of a specific sum of money or of specific property. The identity of the property and the amount of money specified in the preceding sentence are dependent both on the exercise of the executor's discretion and on the payment of administration expenses and other charges, neither of which are facts existing on the date of the decedent's death. It is immaterial that the value of the bequest is determinable after the decedent's death before the bequest is satisfied (so that gain or loss may be realized by the estate in the transfer of property in satisfaction of it).

(2) The following amounts are not considered as gifts or bequests of a sum of money or of specific property within the meaning of this paragraph:

(i) An amount which can be paid or credited only from the income of an estate or trust, whether from the income for the year of payment or crediting, or from the income accumulated from a prior year;

(ii) An annuity, or periodic gifts of specific property in lieu of or having the effect of an annuity;

(iii) A residuary estate or the corpus of a trust; or

(iv) A gift or bequest paid in a lump sum or in not more than three installments, if the gift or bequest is required to be paid in more than three installments under the terms of the governing instrument.

(3) The provisions of subparagraphs (1) and (2) of this paragraph may be illustrated by the following examples, in which it is assumed that the gift or bequest is not required to be made in more than three installments (see paragraph (c)):

Example (1). Under the terms of a will, a legacy of $5,000 was left to A, 1,000 shares of X company stock was left to W, and the balance of the estate was to be divided equally between W and X. No provision was made in the will for the disposition of income of the estate during the period of administration. The estate had income of $25,000 during the taxable year 1954, which was accumulated and added to corpus for estate accounting purposes. During the taxable year, the executor paid the legacy of $5,000 in a lump sum to A and transferred the X company stock to W. No other distributions to beneficiaries were made during the taxable year. The distributions to A and W qualify as exclusions within the meaning of section 663(a)(1).

Example (2). Under the terms of a will, the testator's estate was to be divided equally between A and B. No provision was made in the will for the disposition of income of the estate during the period of administration. The estate had income of $50,000 for the taxable year 1954. In accordance with an agreement among the beneficiaries that part of the assets of the estate would be distributed in kind to the beneficiaries, stock in corporation X was distributed to A during 1954. The fair market value of the stock was $40,000 on the date of distribution. No other distribution was made during the year. The distribution does not qualify as an exclusion within the meaning of section 663(a)(1), since it is not a specific gift to A required by the terms of the will. Accordingly, the fair market value of the property ($40,000) represents a distribution within the meaning of section 661(a) and section 662(a) (see paragraph (c) of § 1.661(a)–2).

Example (3). Under the terms of a trust instrument, income is to be accumulated during the minority of A. Upon A's reaching the age of 21, $10,000 is to be distributed to B out of income or corpus. Also at that time, $10,000 is to be distributed to C out of the accumulated income and the remainder of the accumulations are to be paid to A. A is then to receive all the income until he is 25, when the trust is to terminate. Only the distribution to B would qualify for exclusion under section 663(a)(1).

(4) A gift or bequest of a specific sum of money or of specific property is not disqualified under this paragraph solely because its payment is subject to a condition. For example, provision for a payment by a trust to beneficiary A of $10,000 when he reaches age 25, and $10,000 when he reaches age 30, with payment over to B of any amount not paid to A because of his death, is a gift to A of a specific sum of money payable in two installments, within the meaning of this paragraph, even though the exact amount payable to A cannot be ascertained with certainty under the terms of the trust instrument.

(c) **Installment payments.** **(1)** In determining whether a gift or bequest of a specific sum of money or of specific property, as defined in paragraph (b) of this section, is required to be paid or credited to a particular beneficiary in more than three installments—

(i) Gifts or bequests of articles for personal use (such as personal and household effects, automobiles, and the like) are disregarded.

(ii) Specifically devised real property, the title to which passes directly from the decedent to the devisee under local law, is not taken into account, since it would not constitute an amount paid, credited, or required to be distributed under section 661 (see paragraph (e) of § 1.661(a)–2).

(iii) All gifts and bequests under a decedent's will (which are not disregarded pursuant to subdivisions (i) and (ii) of this subparagraph) for which no time of payment or crediting is specified, and which are to be paid or credited in the ordinary course of administration of the decedent's estate, are considered as required to be paid or credited in a single installment.

(iv) All gifts and bequests (which are not disregarded pursuant to subdivisions (i) and (ii) of this subparagraph) payable at any one specified time under the terms of the governing instrument are taken into account as a single installment.

For purposes of determining the number of installments paid or credited to a particular beneficiary, a decedent's estate and a testamentary trust shall each be treated as a separate entity.

(2) The application of the rules stated in subparagraph (1) of this paragraph may be illustrated by the following examples:

Example (1). (i) Under the terms of a decedent's will, $10,000 in cash, household furniture, a watch, an automobile, 100 shares of X company stock, 1,000 bushels of grain, 500 head of cattle, and a farm (title to which passed directly to A under local law) are bequeathed or devised outright to A. The will also provides for the creation of a trust for the benefit of A, under the terms of which there are required to be distributed to A, $10,000 in cash and 100 shares of Y company stock when he reaches 25 years of age, $25,000 in cash and 200 shares of Y company stock when he reaches 30 years of age, and $50,000 in cash and 300 shares of Y company stock when he reaches 35 years of age.

(ii) The furniture, watch, automobile, and the farm are excluded in determining whether any gift or bequest is required to be paid or credited to A in more than three installments. These items qualify for the exclusion under section 663(a)(1) regardless of the treatment of the other items of property bequeathed to A.

(iii) The $10,000 in cash, the shares of X company stock, the grain, the cattle and the assets required to create the trust, to be paid or credited by the estate to A and the trust are considered as required to be paid or credited in a single installment to each, regardless of the manner of payment or distribution by the executor, since no time of payment or crediting is specified in the will. The $10,000 in cash and shares of Y company stock required to be distributed by the trust to A when he is 25 years old are considered as required to be paid or distributed as one installment under the trust. Likewise, the distributions to be made by the trust to A when he is 30 and 35 years old are each considered as one installment under the trust. Since the total number of installments to be made by the estate does not exceed three, all of the items of money and property distributed by the estate qualify for the exclusion under section 663(a)(1). Similarly, the three distributions by the trust qualify.

Example (2). Assume the same facts as in example (1), except that another distribution of a specified sum of money is required to be made by the trust to A when he becomes 40 years old. This distribution would also qualify as an installment, thus making four installments in all under the trust. None of the gifts to A under the trust would qualify for the exclusion under section 663(a)(1). The situation as to the estate, however, would not be changed.

Example (3). A trust instrument provides that A and B are each to receive $75,000 in installments of $25,000, to be paid in alternate years. The trustee distributes $25,000 to A in 1954, 1956, and 1958, and to B in 1955, 1957, and 1959. The gifts to A and B qualify for exclusion under section 663(a)(1), although a total of six payments is made. The gifts of $75,000 to each beneficiary are to be separately treated.

[T.D. 6500, 25 FR 11814, Nov. 26, 1960]

§ 1.663(c)–1 Separate shares treated as separate trusts; in general.

(a) If a single trust has more than one beneficiary, and if different beneficiaries have substantially separate and independent shares, their shares are treated as separate trusts for the sole purpose of determining the amount of distributable net income allocable to the respective beneficiaries under sections 661 and 662. Application of this rule will be significant in, for example, situations in which income is accumulated for beneficiary A but a distribution is made to beneficiary B of both income and corpus in an amount exceeding the share of income that would be distributable to B had there been separate trusts. In the absence of a separate share rule B would be taxed on income which is accumulated for A. The division of distributable net income into separate shares will limit the tax liability of B. Section 663(c) does not affect the principles of applicable law in situations in which a single trust instrument creates not one but several separate trusts, as opposed to separate shares in the same trust within the meaning of this section.

(b) The separate share rule does not permit the treatment of separate shares as separate trusts for any purpose other than the application of distributable net income. It does not, for instance, permit the treatment of separate shares as separate trusts for purposes of:

(1) The filing of returns and payment of tax,

(2) The exclusion of dividends under section 116,

(3) The deduction of personal exemption under section 642(b), and

(4) The allowance to beneficiaries succeeding to the trust property of excess deductions and unused net operating loss and capital loss carryovers on termination of the trust under section 642(h).

(c) The separate share rule may be applicable even though separate and independent accounts are not maintained and are not required to be maintained for each share on the books of account of the trust, and even though no physical segregation of assets is made or required.

(d) Separate share treatment is not elective. Thus, if a trust is properly treated as having separate and independent shares, such treatment must prevail in all taxable years of the trust unless an event occurs as a result of which the terms of the trust instrument and the requirements of proper administration require different treatment.

[T.D. 6500, 25 FR 11814, Nov. 26, 1960]

§ 1.663(c)–2 Computation of distributable net income.

The amount of distributable net income for any share under section 663(c) is computed for each share as if each share constituted a separate trust.

Accordingly, any deduction or any loss which is applicable solely to one separate share of the trust is not available to any other share of the same trust.

[T.D. 6500, 25 FR 11814, Nov. 26, 1960]

§ 1.663(c)–3 Applicability of separate share rule.

(a) The applicability of the separate share rule provided by section 663(c) will generally depend upon whether distributions of the trust are to be made in substantially the same manner as if separate trusts had been created. Thus, if an instrument directs a trustee to divide the testator's residuary estate into separate shares (which under applicable law do not constitute separate trusts) for each of the testator's children and the trustee is given discretion, with respect to each share, to distribute or accumulate income or to distribute principal or accumulated income, or to do both, separate shares will exist under section 663(c). In determining whether separate shares exist, it is immaterial whether the principal and any accumulated income of each share is ultimately distributable to the beneficiary of such share, to his descendants, to his appointees under a general or special power of appointment, or to any other beneficiaries (including a charitable organization) designated to receive his share of the trust and accumulated income upon termination of the beneficiary's interest in the share. Thus, a separate share may exist if the instrument provides that upon the death of the beneficiary of the share, the share will be added to the shares of the other beneficiaries of the trust.

(b) Separate share treatment will not be applied to a trust or portion of a trust subject to a power to:

(1) Distribute, apportion, or accumulate income, or

(2) Distribute corpus

to or for one or more beneficiaries within a group or class of beneficiaries, unless payment of income, accumulated income, or corpus of a share of one beneficiary cannot affect the proportionate share of income, accumulated income, or corpus of any shares of the other beneficiaries, or unless substantially proper adjustment must thereafter be made (under the governing instrument) so that substantially separate and independent shares exist.

(c) A share may be considered as separate even though more than one beneficiary has an interest in it. For example, two beneficiaries may have equal, disproportionate, or indeterminate interests in one share which is separate and independent from another share in which one or more beneficiaries have an interest. Likewise, the same person may be a beneficiary of more than one separate share.

(d) Separate share treatment may be given to a trust or portion of a trust otherwise qualifying under this section if the trust or portion of a trust is subject to a power to pay out to a beneficiary of a share (of such trust or portion) an amount of corpus in excess of his proportionate share of the corpus of the trust if the possibility of exercise of the power is remote. For example, if the trust is subject to a power to invade the entire corpus for the health, education, support, or maintenance of A, separate share treatment is applied if exercise of the power requires consideration of A's other income which is so substantial as to make the possibility of exercise of the power remote. If instead it appears that A and B have separate shares in a trust, subject to a power to invade the entire corpus for the comfort, pleasure, desire, or happiness of A, separate share treatment shall not be applied.

(e) For taxable years ending before December 31, 1978, the separate share rule may also be applicable to successive interests in point of time, as for instance in the case of a trust providing for a life estate to A and a second life estate or outright remainder to B. In such a case, in the taxable year of a trust in which a beneficiary dies items of income and deduction properly allocable under trust accounting principles to the period before a beneficiary's death are attributed to one share, and those allocable to the period after the beneficiary's death are attributed to the other share. Separate share treatment is not available to a succeeding interest, however, with respect to distributions which would otherwise be deemed distributed in a taxable year of the earlier interest under the throwback provisions of subpart D (section 665 and following), part 1, subchapter J, chapter 1 of the Code. The application of this paragraph may be illustrated by the following example:

Example. A trust instrument directs that the income of a trust is to be paid to A for her life. After her death income may be distributed to B or accumulated. A dies on June 1, 1956. The trust keeps its books on the basis of the calendar year. The trust instrument permits invasions of corpus for the benefit of A and B, and an invasion of corpus was in fact made for A's benefit in 1956. In determining the distributable net income of the trust for the purpose of determining the amounts includible in A's income, income and deductions properly allocable to the period before A's death are treated as income and deductions of a separate share; and for that purpose no account is taken of income and deductions allocable to the period after A's death.

(f) Separate share treatment is not applicable to an estate.

[T.D. 6500, 25 FR 11814, Nov. 26, 1960; 25 FR 14021, Dec. 31, 1960, as amended by T.D. 7633, 44 FR 57926, Oct. 9, 1979]

§ 1.663(c)–4 Example.

Section 663(c) may be illustrated by the following example:

Example. (a) A single trust was created in 1940 for the benefit of A, B, and C, who were aged 6, 4, and 2, respectively. Under the terms of the instrument, the trust income is required to be divided into three equal shares. Each beneficiary's share of the income is to be accumulated until he becomes 21 years of age. When a beneficiary reaches the age of 21, his share of the income may thereafter be either accumulated or distributed to him in the discretion of the trustee. The trustee also has discretion to invade corpus for the benefit of any beneficiary to the extent of his share of the trust estate, and the trust instrument requires that the beneficiary's right to future income and corpus will be proportionately reduced. When each beneficiary reaches 35 years of age, his share of the trust estate shall be paid over to him. The interest in the trust estate of any beneficiary dying without issue and before he has attained the age of 35 is to be equally divided between the other beneficiaries of the trust. All expenses of the trust are allocable to income under the terms of the trust instrument.

(b) No distributions of income or corpus were made by the trustee prior to 1955, although A became 21 years of age on June 30, 1954. During the taxable year of 1955, the trust has income from royalties of $20,000 and expenses of $5,000. The trustee in his discretion distributes $12,000 to A. Both A and the trust report on the calendar year basis.

(c) The trust qualifies for the separate share treatment under section 663(c) and the distributable net income must be divided into three parts for the purpose of determining the amount deductible by the trust under section 661 and the amount includible in A's gross income under section 662.

(d) The distributable net income of each share of the trust is $5,000 ($6,667 less $1,667). Since the amount ($12,000) distributed to A during 1955 exceeds the distributable net income of $5,000 allocated to his share, the trust is deemed to have distributed to him $5,000 of 1955 income and $7,000 of amounts other than 1955 income. Accordingly, the trust is allowed a deduction of $5,000 under section 661. The taxable income of the trust for 1955 is $9,900, computed as follows:

Royalties $20,000

Deductions:

Expenses	$5,000	
Distribution to A	5,000	
Personal exemption	100	
		10,100
Taxable income		9,900

(e) In accordance with section 662, A must include in his gross income for 1955 an amount equal to the portion ($5,000) of the distributable net income of the trust allocated to his share. Also, the excess distribution of $7,000 made by the trust is subject to the throwback provisions of subpart D (section 665 and following), part I, subchapter J, chapter 1 of the Code, and the regulations thereunder.

[T.D. 6500, 25 FR 11814, Nov. 26, 1960]

§ 1.664–1 Charitable remainder trusts.

(a) In general—(1) Introduction—(i) General description of a charitable remainder trust. Generally, a charitable remainder trust is a trust which provides for a specified distribution, at least annually, to one or more beneficiaries, at least one of which is not a charity, for life or for a term of years, with an irrevocable remainder interest to be held for the benefit of, or paid over to, charity. The specified distribution to be paid at least annually must be a sum certain which is not less than 5 percent of the initial net fair market value of all property placed in trust (in the case of a charitable remainder annuity trust) or a fixed percentage which is not less than 5 percent of the net fair market value of the trust assets, valued annually (in the case of a charitable remainder unitrust). A trust created after July 31, 1969, which is a charitable remainder trust is exempt from all of the taxes imposed by subtitle A of the Code for any taxable year of the trust except a taxable year in which it has unrelated business taxable income.

* * *

(2) Requirement that the trust must be either a charitable remainder annuity trust or a charitable remainder unitrust. A trust is a charitable remainder trust only if it is either a charitable remainder annuity trust in every respect or a charitable remainder unitrust in every respect. For example, a trust which provides for the payment each year to a noncharitable beneficiary of the greater of a sum certain or a fixed percentage of the annual value of the trust assets is not a charitable remainder trust inasmuch as the trust is neither a charitable remainder annuity trust (for the reason that the payment for the year may be a fixed percentage of the annual value of the trust assets which is not a "sum certain") nor a charitable remainder unitrust (for the reason that the payment for the year may be a sum certain which is not a "fixed percentage" of the annual value of the trust assets).

(3) Restrictions on investments. A trust is not a charitable remainder trust if the provisions of the trust include a provision which restricts the trustee from investing the trust assets in a manner which could result in the annual realization of a reasonable amount of income or gain from the sale or disposition of trust assets. In the case of transactions with, or for the benefit of, a disqualified person, see section 4941(d) and the regulations thereunder for rules relating to the definition of self-dealing.

(4) Requirement that trust must meet definition of and function exclusively as a charitable remainder trust from its creation. In order for a trust to be a charitable remainder trust, it must meet the definition of and function exclusively as a charitable remainder trust from the creation of the trust. Solely for the purposes of section 664 and the regulations thereunder, the trust will be deemed to be created at the earliest time that neither the grantor nor any other person is treated as the owner of the entire trust under subpart E, part 1, subchapter J, chapter 1, subtitle A of the Code (relating to grantors and others treated as substantial owners), but in no event prior to the time property is first transferred to the trust. For purposes of the preceding sentence, neither the grantor nor his spouse shall be treated as the owner of the trust under such subpart E merely because the grantor or his spouse is named as a recipient.

* * *

[T.D. 7202, 37 FR 16913, Aug. 23, 1972; 37 FR 28288, Dec. 22, 1972; T.D. 7955, 49 FR 19983, May 11, 1984]

§ 1.664–2 Charitable remainder annuity trust.

(a) Description. A charitable remainder annuity trust is a trust which complies with the applicable provisions of § 1.664–1 and meets all of the following requirements:

(1) Required payment of annuity amount—(i) Payment of sum certain at least annually. The governing instrument provides that the trust shall pay a sum certain not less often than annually to a person or persons described in subparagraph (3) of this paragraph for each taxable year of the period specified in subparagraph (5) of this paragraph. The trust will not be deemed to have engaged in an act of self-dealing (within the meaning of section 4941), to have unrelated debt-financed income (within the meaning of section 514), to have received an additional contribution (within the meaning of § 1.664–2(b)), or to have failed to function exclusively as a charitable remainder trust (within the meaning of § 1.664–4(a)(4)) merely because payment of the annuity amount is made after the close of the taxable year: Provided, That such payment is made within a reasonable time after the close of such taxable year. For purposes of the preceding sentence, a reasonable time will not ordinarily extend beyond the date by which the trustee is required to file Form 1041–B (including extensions) for such year.

(ii) Definition of sum certain. A sum certain is a stated dollar amount which is the same either as to each recipient or as to the total amount payable for each year of such period. For example, a provision for an amount which is the same every year to A until his death and concurrently an amount which is the same every year to B until his death, with the amount to each recipient to terminate at his death, would satisfy the above rule. Similarly, provisions for an amount to A and B for their joint lives and then to the survivor would satisfy the above rule. In the case of a distribution to an organization described in section 170(c) at the death of a recipient or the expiration of a term of years, the governing instrument may provide for a reduction of the stated amount payable after such a distribution provided that:

(a) The reduced amount payable is the same either as to each recipient or as to the total amount payable for each year of the balance of such period, and

(b) The requirements of subparagraph (2)(ii) of this paragraph are met.

(iii) Sum certain stated as a fraction or percentage. The stated dollar amount may be expressed as a fraction or a percentage of the initial net fair market value of the property irrevocably passing in trust as finally determined for Federal tax purposes. If the stated dollar amount is so expressed and such market value is incorrectly determined by the fiduciary, the requirement of this subparagraph will be satisfied if the governing instrument provides that in such event the trust shall pay to the recipient (in the case of an undervaluation) or be repaid by the recipient (in the case of an overvaluation) an amount equal to the difference between the amount which the trust should have paid the recipient if the correct value were used and the amount which the trust actually paid the recipient. Such payments or repayments must be made within a reasonable period after the final determination of such value. Any payment due to a recipient by reason of such incorrect valuation shall be considered to be a payment required to be distributed at the time of such final determination for purposes of paragraph (d)(4)(ii) of § 1.664–1. See paragraph (d)(4) of § 1.664–1 for rules relating to the year of inclusion of such payments and the allowance of a deduction for such repayments. See paragraph (b) of this section for rules relating to future contributions. For rules relating to required adjustments for underpayments or overpayments of the amount described in this paragraph in respect of payments made during a reasonable period of administration, see paragraph (a)(5) of § 1.664–1. The application of the rule permitting the stated dollar amount to be expressed as a fraction or a percentage of the initial net fair market value of the property irrevocably passing in trust as finally determined for Federal tax purposes may be illustrated by the following example:

Example. The will of X provides for the transfer of one-half of his residuary estate to a charitable remainder annuity trust which is required to pay to W for life an annuity equal to 5 percent of the initial net fair market value of the interest passing in trust as finally determined for Federal tax purposes. The annuity is to be paid on December 31 of each year computed from the date of X's death. The will also provides that if such initial net fair market value is incorrectly determined, the trust shall pay to W, in the case of an undervaluation, or be repaid by W, in the case of an overvaluation, an amount equal to the difference between the amount which the trust should have paid if the correct value were used and the amount which the trust actually paid. X dies on March 1, 1971. The executor files an estate tax return showing the value of the residuary estate as $250,000 before reduction for taxes and expenses of $50,-000. The executor paid to W $4,192 ([$250,000–$50,-000]×½×5 percent×306/365) on December 31, 1971. On January 1, 1972, the executor transfers one-half of the residue of the estate to the trust. The trust adopts the calendar year as its taxable year. The value of the residuary estate is finally determined for Federal tax purposes to be $240,000 ($290,000–$50,000). Accordingly, the amount which the executor should have paid to W is $5,030 ([$290,000–$50,000]×½×5 percent×306/365). Consequently, an additional amount of $838 ($5,030–$4,-192) must be paid to W within a reasonable period after the final determination of value for Federal tax purposes.

* * *

(2) Minimum annuity amount—(i) General rule. The total amount payable under subparagraph (1) of this paragraph is not less than 5 percent of the initial net fair market value of the property placed in trust as finally determined for Federal tax purposes.

(ii) Reduction of annuity amount in certain cases. A trust will not fail to meet the requirements of this subparagraph by reason of the fact that it provides for a reduction of the stated amount payable upon the death of a recipient or the expiration of a term of years provided that:

(a) A distribution is made to an organization described in section 170(c) at the death of such recipient or the expiration of such term of years, and

(b) The total amounts payable each year under subparagraph (1) of this paragraph after such distribution are not less than a stated dollar amount which bears the same ratio to 5 percent of the initial net fair market value of the trust assets as the net fair market value of the trust assets immediately after such distribution bears to the net fair market value of the trust assets immediately before such distribution.

(iii) Rule applicable to inter vivos trust which does not provide for payment of minimum annuity amount. In the case where the grantor of an inter vivos trust underestimates in good faith the initial net fair market value of the property placed in trust as finally determined for Federal tax purposes and specifies a fixed dollar amount for the annuity which is less than 5 percent of the initial net fair market value of the property placed in trust as finally determined for Federal tax purposes, the trust will be deemed to have met the 5 percent requirement if the grantor or his representative consents, by appropriate agreement with the District Director, to accept an amount equal to 20 times the annuity as the fair market value of the property placed in trust for purposes of determining the appropriate charitable contributions deduction.

(3) Permissible recipients—(i) General rule. The amount described in subparagraph (1) of this paragraph is payable to or for the use of a named person or persons, at least one of which is not an organization described in section 170(c). If the amount described in subparagraph (1) of this paragraph is to be paid to an individual or individuals, all such individuals must be living at the time of the creation of the trust. A named person or persons may include members of a named class provided that, in the case of a class which includes any individual, all such individuals must be alive and ascertainable at the time of the creation of the trust unless the period for which the annuity amount is to be paid to such class consists solely of a term of years. For example, in the case of a testamentary trust, the testator's will may provide that an amount shall be paid to his children living at his death.

(ii) **Power to alter amount paid to recipients.** A trust is not a charitable remainder annuity trust if any person has the power to alter the amount to be paid to any named person other than an organization described in section 170(c) if such power would cause any person to be treated as the owner of the trust, or any portion thereof, if subpart E, Part 1, subchapter J, chapter 1, Subtitle A of the Code were applicable to such trust. See paragraph (a)(4) of this section for a rule permitting the retention by a grantor of a testamentary power to revoke or terminate the interest of any recipient other than an organization described in section 170(c). For example, the governing instrument may not grant the trustee the power to allocate the annuity among members of a class unless such power falls within one of the exceptions to section 674(a).

(4) **Other payments.** No amount other than the amount described in subparagraph (1) of this paragraph may be paid to or for the use of any person other than an organization described in section 170(c). An amount is not paid to or for the use of any person other than an organization described in section 170(c) if the amount is transferred for full and adequate consideration. The trust may not be subject to a power to invade, alter, amend, or revoke for the beneficial use of a person other than an organization described in section 170(c). Notwithstanding the preceding sentence, the grantor may retain the power exercisable only by will to revoke or terminate the interest of any recipient other than an organization described in section 170(c). The governing instrument may provide that any amount other than the amount described in subparagraph (1) of this paragraph shall be paid (or may be paid in the discretion of the trustee) to an organization described in section 170(c) provided that in the case of distributions in kind, the adjusted basis of the property distributed is fairly representative of the adjusted basis of the property available for payment on the date of payment. For example, the governing instrument

may provide that a portion of the trust assets may be distributed currently, or upon the death of one or more recipients, to an organization described in section 170(c).

(5) **Period of payment of annuity amount—(i) General rules.** The period for which an amount described in subparagraph (1) of this paragraph is payable begins with the first year of the charitable remainder trust and continues either for the life or lives of a named individual or individuals or for a term of years not to exceed 20 years. Only an individual or an organization described in section 170(c) may receive an amount for the life of an individual. If an individual receives an amount for life, it must be solely for his life. Payment of the amount described in subparagraph (1) of this paragraph may terminate with the regular payment next preceding the termination of the period described in this subparagraph. The fact that the recipient may not receive such last payment shall not be taken into account for purposes of determining the present value of the remainder interest. In the case of an amount payable for a term of years, the length of the term of years shall be ascertainable with certainty at the time of the creation of the trust, except that the term may be terminated by the death of the recipient or by the grantor's exercise by will of a retained power to revoke or terminate the interest of any recipient other than an organization described in section 170(c). In any event, the period may not extend beyond either the life or lives of a named individual or individuals or a term of years not to exceed 20 years. For example, the governing instrument may not provide for the payment of an annuity amount to A for his life and then to B for a term of years because it is possible for the period to last longer than either the lives of recipients in being at the creation of the trust or a term of years not to exceed 20 years. On the other hand, the governing instrument may provide for the payment of an annuity amount to A for his life and then to B for his life or a term of years (not to exceed 20 years), whichever is shorter (but not longer), if both A and B are in being at the creation of the trust because it is not possible for the period to last longer than the lives of recipients in being at the creation of the trust.

(ii) **Relationship to 5 percent requirement.** The 5 percent requirement provided in subparagraph (2) of this paragraph must be met until the termination of all of the payments described in subparagraph (1) of this paragraph. For example, the following provisions would satisfy the above rules:

(a) An amount equal to at least 5 percent of the initial net fair market value of the property placed in trust to A and B for their joint lives and then to the survivor for his life;

(b) An amount equal to at least 5 percent of the initial net fair market value of the property placed in trust to A for life or for a term of years not longer than 20 years, whichever is longer (or shorter);

(c) An amount equal to at least 5 percent of the initial net fair market value of the property placed in trust to A for a term of years not longer than 20 years and then to B for life (provided B was living at the date of creation of the trust);

(d) An amount to A for his life and concurrently an amount to B for his life (the amount to each recipient to terminate at his death) if the amount given to each individual is not less than 5 percent of the initial net fair market value of the property placed in trust; or

(e) An amount to A for his life and concurrently an equal amount to B for his life, and at the death of the first to die, the trust to distribute one-half of the then value of its assets to an organization described in section 170(c), if the total of the amounts given to A and B is not less than 5 percent of the initial net fair market value of the property placed in trust.

(6) **Permissible remaindermen—(i) General rule.** At the end of the period specified in subparagraph (5) of this paragraph the entire corpus of the trust is required to be irrevocably transferred, in whole or in part, to or for the use of one or more organizations described in section 170(c) or retained, in whole or in part, for such use.

(ii) **Treatment of trust.** If all of the trust corpus is to be retained for such use, the taxable year of the trust shall terminate at the end of the period specified in subparagraph (5) of this paragraph and the trust shall cease to be treated as a charitable remainder trust for all purposes. If all or any portion of the trust corpus is to be transferred to or for the use of such organization or organizations, the trustee shall have a reasonable time after the period specified in subparagraph (5) of this paragraph to complete the settlement of the trust. During such time, the trust shall continue to be treated as a charitable remainder trust for all purposes, such as sections 664, 4947(a)(2), and 4947(b)(3)(B). Upon the expiration of such period,

the taxable year of the trust shall terminate and the trust shall cease to be treated as a charitable remainder trust for all purposes. If the trust continues in existence, it will be subject to the provisions of section 4947(a)(1) unless the trust is exempt from taxation under section 501(a). For purposes of determining whether the trust is exempt under section 501(a) as an organization described in section 501(c)(3), the trust shall be deemed to have been created at the time it ceases to be treated as a charitable remainder trust.

(iii) **Concurrent or successive remaindermen.** Where interests in the corpus of the trust are given to more than one organization described in section 170(c) such interests may be enjoyed by them either concurrently or successively.

(iv) **Alternative remaindermen.** The governing instrument shall provide that if an organization to or for the use of which the trust corpus is to be transferred or for the use of which the trust corpus is to be retained is not an organization described in section 170(c) at the time any amount is to be irrevocably transferred to or for the use of such organization, such amount shall be transferred to or for the use of one or more alternative organizations which are described in section 170(c) at such time or retained for such use. Such alternative organization or organizations may be selected in any manner provided by the terms of the governing instrument.

(b) **Additional contributions.** A trust is not a charitable remainder annuity trust unless its governing instrument provides that no additional contributions may be made to the charitable remainder annuity trust after the initial contribution. For purposes of this section, all property passing to a charitable remainder annuity trust by reason of death of the grantor shall be considered one contribution.

(c) **Calculation of the fair market value of the remainder interest of a charitable remainder annuity trust.** For purposes of sections 170, 2055, 2106, and 2522, the fair market value of the remainder interest of a charitable remainder annuity trust (as described in this section) is the net fair market value (as of the appropriate valuation date) of the property placed in trust less the present value of the annuity. For purposes of this section, the term "appropriate valuation date" means the date on which the property is transferred to the trust by the donor except that, for purposes of section 2055 or 2106, it means the date of death unless the alternate valuation date is elected in accordance with section 2032 and the regulations thereunder in which event it means the alternate valuation date. The present value of an annuity is computed under § 20.2031–7 or 20.2031–10, whichever is appropriate, of the Estate Tax Regulations regardless of when the trust was created.

(d) Deduction for transfers to a charitable remainder annuity trust. For rules relating to a deduction for transfers to a charitable remainder annuity trust, see sections 170, 2055, 2106, or 2522 and the regulations thereunder. Any claim for deduction on any return for the value of a remainder interest in a charitable remainder annuity trust must be supported by a full statement attached to the return showing the computation of the present value of such interest. The deduction allowed by section 170 is limited to the fair market value of the remainder interest of a charitable remainder annuity trust regardless of whether an organization described in section 170(c) also receives a portion of the annuity. For a special rule relating to the reduction of the amount of a charitable contribution deduction with respect to a contribution of certain ordinary income property or capital gain property, see sections 170(e)(1)(A) or 170(e)(1)(B)(i) and the regulations thereunder. For rules for postponing the time for deduction of a charitable contribution of a future interest in tangible personal property, see section 170(a)(3) and the regulations thereunder.

[T.D. 7202, 37 FR 16918, Aug. 23, 1972, as amended by T.D. 7955, 49 FR 19983, May 11, 1984]

§ 1.664–3   Charitable remainder unitrust.

(a) Description. A charitable remainder unitrust is a trust which complies with the applicable provisions of § 1.664–1 and meets all of the following requirements:

(1) Required payment of unitrust amount—(i) Payment of fixed percentage at least annually —(a) General rule. The governing instrument provides that the trust shall pay not less often than annually a fixed percentage of the net fair market value of the trust assets determined annually to a person or persons described in subparagraph (3) of this paragraph for each taxable year of the period specified in subparagraph (5) of this paragraph. The trust will not be deemed to have engaged in an act of self-dealing (within the meaning of section 4941), to have unrelated debt-financed income (within the meaning of section 4941), to have re-

ceived an additional contribution (within the meaning of § 1.664–3(b)), or to have failed to function exclusively as a charitable remainder trust (within the meaning of § 1.664–1(a)(4)) merely because payment of the unitrust amount is made after the close of the taxable year: Provided, That such payment is made within a reasonable time after the close of such taxable year. For purposes of the preceding sentence, a reasonable time will not ordinarily extend beyond the date by which the trustee is required to file Form 1041–B (including extensions) for such year.

(b) Income exception. Instead of the amount described in (a) of this subdivision (i), the governing instrument may provide that the trust shall pay for any year either the amount described in (1) or the total of the amounts described in (1) and (2) of this subdivision (b).

(1) The amount of trust income (as defined in section 643(b) and the regulations thereunder), for a taxable year to the extent that such amount is not more than the amount required to be distributed under (a) of this subdivision (i).

(2) An amount of trust income for a taxable year which is in excess of the amount required to be distributed under (a) of this subdivision (i) for such year, to the extent that (by reason of (1)) the aggregate of the amounts paid in prior years was less than the aggregate of such required amounts.

(ii) Definition of fixed percentage. The fixed percentage may be expressed either as a fraction or as a percentage and must be payable each year in the period specified in subparagraph (5) of this paragraph. A percentage is fixed if the percentage is the same either as to each recipient or as to the total percentage payable each year of such period. For example, provision for a fixed percentage which is the same every year to A until his death and concurrently a fixed percentage which is the same every year to B until his death, the fixed percentage to each recipient to terminate at his death, would satisfy the rule. Similarly, provision for a fixed percentage to A and B for their joint lives and then to the survivor would satisfy the rule. In the case of a distribution to an organization described in section 170(c) at the death of a recipient or the expiration of a term of years, the governing instrument may provide for a reduction of the fixed percentage payable after such distribution provided that:

(a) The reduced fixed percentage is the same either as to each recipient or as to the total amount payable for each year of the balance of such period, and

(b) The requirements of subparagraph (2)(ii) of this paragraph are met.

* * *

[T.D. 7202, 37 FR 16920, Aug. 23, 1972]

Treatment of Excess Distributions By Trusts

§ 1.665(a)–1A Undistributed net income.

(a) **Domestic trusts.** The term "undistributed net income", in the case of a trust (other than a foreign trust created by a U.S. person) means, for any taxable year beginning after December 31, 1968, the distributable net income of the trust for that year (as determined under section 643(a)), less:

(1) The amount of income required to be distributed currently and any other amounts properly paid or credited or required to be distributed to beneficiaries in the taxable year as specified in section 661(a), and

(2) The amount of taxes imposed on the trust attributable to such distributable net income, as defined in § 1.665(d)–1A. The application of the rule in this paragraph to a taxable year of a trust in which income is accumulated may be illustrated by the following example:

Example. Under the terms of the trust, $10,000 of income is required to be distributed currently to A and the trustee has discretion to make additional distributions to A. During the taxable year 1971 the trust had distributable net income of $30,100 derived from royalties and the trustee made distributions of $20,000 to A. The taxable income of the trust is $10,000 on which a tax of $2,190 is paid. The undistributed net income of the trust for the taxable year 1971 is $7,910, computed as follows:

Distributable net income		$30,100
Less:		
Income currently distributable to A	$10,000	
Other amounts distributed to A	10,000	
Taxes imposed on the trust attributable to the undistributed net income (see § 1.665(d)–1A)	2,190	
Total		22,190
Undistributed net income		7,910

* * *

[T.D. 7204, 37 FR 17136, Aug. 25, 1972]

§ 1.665(b)–1A Accumulation distributions.

(a) **In General.** (1) For any taxable year of a trust the term "accumulation distribution" means an amount by which the amounts properly paid, credited, or required to be distributed within the meaning of section 661(a)(2) (*i.e.*, all amounts properly paid, credited, or required to be distributed to the beneficiary other than income required to be distributed currently within the meaning of section 661(a)(1)) for that year exceed the distributable net income (determined under section 643(a)) of the trust, reduced (but not below zero) by the amount of income required to be distributed currently. To the extent provided in section 663(b) and the regulations thereunder, distributions made within the first 65 days following a taxable year may be treated as having been distributed on the last day of such taxable year.

(2) An accumulation distribution also includes, for a taxable year of the trust, any amount to which section 661(a)(2) and the preceding paragraph are inapplicable and which is paid, credited, or required to be distributed during the taxable year of the trust by reason of the exercise of a power to appoint, distribute, consume, or withdraw corpus of the trust or income of the trust accumulated in a preceding taxable year. No accumulation distribution is deemed to be made solely because the grantor or any other person is treated as owner of a portion of the trust by reason of an unexercised power to appoint, distributed, consume, or withdraw corpus or accumulated income of the trust. Nor will an accumulation distribution be deemed to have been made by reason of the exercise of a power that may affect only taxable income previously attributed to the holders of such power under subpart E (section 671 and following). See example 4 of paragraph (d) of this section for an example of an accumulation distribution occurring as a result of the exercise of a power of withdrawal.

(3) Although amounts properly paid or credited under section 661(a) do not exceed the income of the trust during the taxable year, an accumulation distribution may result if the amounts properly paid or credited under section 661(a)(2) exceed distributable net income reduced (but not below zero) by the amount required to be distributed currently under section 661(a)(1). This may occur, for example, when expenses, interest, taxes, or other items

allocable to corpus are taken into account in determining taxable income and hence causing distributable net income to be less than the trust's income.

(b) Payments that are accumulation distributions. The following are some instances in which an accumulation distribution may arise:

(1) One trust to another. A distribution from one trust to another trust is generally an accumulation distribution. See § 1.643(c)–1. This general rule will apply regardless of whether the distribution is to an existing trust or to a newly created trust and regardless of whether the trust to which the distribution is made was created by the same person who created the trust from which the distribution is made or a different person. However, a distribution made from one trust to a second trust will be deemed an accumulation distribution by the first trust to an ultimate beneficiary of the second trust if the primary purpose of the distribution to the second trust is to avoid the capital gain distribution provisions (see section 669 and the regulations thereunder). An amount passing from one separate share of a trust to another separate share of the same trust is not an accumulation distribution. See § 1.665(g)–2A. For rules relating to the computation of the beneficiary's tax under section 668 by reason of an accumulation distribution from the second trust, see paragraphs (b)(1) and (c)(1)(i) of § 1.668(b)–1A and paragraphs (b)(1) and (c)(1)(i) of § 1.669(b)–1A.

(2) Income accumulated during minority. A distribution of income accumulated during the minority of the beneficiary is generally an accumulation distribution. For example, if a trust accumulates income until the beneficiary's 21st birthday, and then distributes the income to the beneficiary, such a distribution is an accumulation distribution. However, see § 1.665(b)–2A for rules governing income accumulated in taxable years beginning before January 1, 1969.

(3) Amounts paid for support. To the extent that amounts forming all or part of an accumulation distribution are applied or distributed for the support of a dependent under the circumstances specified in section 677(b) or section 678(c) or are used to discharge or satisfy any person's legal obligation as that term is used in § 1.662(a)–4, such amounts will be considered as having been distributed directly to the person whose obligation is being satisfied.

(c) Payments that are not accumulation distributions—(1) Gifts, bequests, etc., described in section 663(a)(1). A gift or bequest of a specific sum of money or of specific property described in section 663(a)(1) is not an accumulation distribution.

(2) Charitable payments. Any amount paid, permanently set aside, or used for the purposes specified in section 642(c) is not an accumulation distribution, even though no charitable deduction is allowed under such section with respect to such payment.

(3) Income required to be distributed currently. No accumulation distribution will arise by reason of a payment of income required to be distributed currently even though such income exceeds the distributable net income of the trust because the payment is an amount specified in section 661(a)(1).

(d) Examples. The provisions of this section may be illustrated by the following examples:

Example (1). A trustee properly makes a distribution to a beneficiary of $20,000 during the taxable year 1976, of which $10,000 is income required to be distributed currently to the beneficiary. The distributable net income of the trust is $15,000. There is an accumulation distribution of $5,000 computed as follows:

Total distribution		$20,000
Less: Income required to be distributed currently (section 661(a)(1))		10,000
Other amounts distributed (section 661(a)(2))		10,000
Distributable net income	$15,000	
Less: Income required to be distributed currently	10,000	
Balance of distributable net income		5,000
Accumulation distribution		5,000

Example (2). Under the terms of the trust instrument, an annuity of $15,000 is required to be paid to A out of income each year and the trustee may in his discretion make distributions out of income or corpus to B. During the taxable year the trust had income of $18,000, as defined in section 643(b), and expenses allocable to corpus of $5,000. Distributable net income amounted to $13,000. The trustee distributed $15,000 of income to A and, in the exercise of his discretion, paid $5,000 to B. There is an accumulation distribution of $5,000 computed as follows:

Total distribution		$20,000
Less: Income required to be distributed currently to A (section 661(a)(1))		15,000
Other amounts distributed (section 661(a)(2))		5,000
Distributable net income	$13,000	
Less: Income required to be distributed currently to A	15,000	
Balance of distributable net income		0
Accumulation distribution to B		5,000

Example (3). Under the terms of a trust instrument, the trustee may either accumulate the trust income or make distributions to A and B. The trustee may also invade corpus for the benefit of A and B. During the taxable year, the trust had income as defined in section 643(b) of $22,000 and expenses of $5,000 allocable to corpus. Distributable net income amounts to $17,000. The trustee distributed $10,00 each to A and B during the taxable year. There is an accumulation distribution of $3,000 computed as follows:

Total distribution		$20,000
Less: Income required to be distributed currently		0
Other amounts distributed (section 661(a)(2))		20,000
Distributable net income	$17,000	
Less: Income required to be distributed currently	0	
Balance of distributable net income		17,000
Accumulation distribution		3,000

Example (4). A dies in 1974 and bequeaths one-half the residue of his estate in trust. His widow, W, is given a power, exercisable solely by her, to require the trustee to pay her each year of the trust $5,000 from corpus. W's right to exercise such power was exercisable at any time during the year but was not cumulative, so that, upon her failure to exercise it before the end of any taxable year of the trust, her right as to that year lapsed. The trust's taxable year is the calendar year. During the calendar years 1975 and 1976, W did not exercise her right and it lapsed as to those years. In the calendar years 1977 and 1978, in which years the trust had no distributable net income, she exercised her right and withdrew $4,000 in 1977 and $5,000 in 1978. No accumulation distribution was made by the trust in the calendar years 1975 and 1976. An accumulation distribution of $4,000 was made in 1977 and an accumulation distribution of $5,000 was made in 1978. The accumulation distribution for the years 1977 and 1978 is not reduced by any amount of income of the trust attributable to her under section 678 by reason of her power of withdrawal.

[T.D. 7204, 37 FR 17137, Aug. 25, 1972]

§ 1.665(d)–1A Taxes imposed on the trust.

(a) In general. (1) For purposes of subpart D, the term "taxes imposed on the trust" means the amount of Federal income taxes properly imposed for any taxable year on the trust that are attributable to the undistributed portions of distributable net income and gains in excess of losses from the sales or exchanges of capital assets. Except as provided in paragraph (c)(2) of this section, the minimum tax for tax preferences imposed by section 56 is not a tax attributable to the undistributed portions of distributable net income and gains in excess of losses from the sales or exchanges of capital assets. See section 56 and the regulations thereunder.

(2) In the case of a trust that has received an accumulation distribution from another trust, the term "taxes imposed on the trust" also includes the amount of taxes deemed distributed under §§ 1.666(b)–1A, 1.666(c)–1A, 1.669(d)–1A, and 1.669(e)–1A (whichever are applicable) as a result of such accumulation distribution, to the extent that they were taken into account under paragraphs (b)(2) or (c)(1)(vi) of § 1.668(b)–1A and (b)(2) or (c)(1)(vi) of § 1.669(b)–1A in computing the partial tax on such accumulation distribution. For example, assume that trust A, a calendar year trust, makes an accumulation distribution in 1975 to trust B, also on the calendar year basis, in connection with which $500 of taxes are deemed under § 1.666(b)–1A to be distributed to trust B. The partial tax on the accumulation distribution is computed under paragraph (b) of § 1.668(b)–1A (the exact method) to be $600 and all of the $500 is used under paragraph (b)(2) of § 1.668(b)–1A to reduce the partial tax to $100. The taxes imposed on trust B for 1975 will, in addition to the $100 partial tax, also include the $500 used to reduce the partial tax.

(b) Taxes imposed on the trust attributable to undistributed net income. (1) For the purpose of subpart D, the term "taxes imposed on the trust attributable to the undistributed net income" means the amount of Federal income taxes for the taxable year properly allocable to the undistributed portion of the distributable net income for such taxable year. This amount is (i) an amount that bears the same relationship to the total taxes of the trust for the year (other than the minimum tax for tax preferences imposed by section 56), computed after the allowance of credits under section 642(a), as (a) the taxable income of the trust, other than the capital gains not included in distributable net income less their share of section 1202 deduction, bears to (b) the total taxable income of the trust for such year or, (ii) if the alternative tax computation under section 1201(b) is used and there are no net short-term gains, an amount equal to such total taxes less the amount of the alternative tax imposed on the trust and attributable to the capital gain. Thus, for the purposes of subpart D, in determining the amount of taxes imposed on the trust attributable to the undistributed net income, that portion of the taxes paid by the trust attributable to capital gain allocable to corpus is excluded. The rule stated in this subparagraph may be illustrated by the following example, which assumes that the alternative tax computation is not used:

Example. (1) Under the terms of a trust, which reports on the calendar year basis, the income may be accumulated or distributed to A in the discretion of the trustee and capital gains are allocable to corpus. During the taxable year 1974, the trust had income of $20,000 from royalties, long-term capital gains of $10,000, and expenses of $2,000. The trustee in his discretion made a distribution of $10,000 to A. The taxes imposed on the trust for such year attributable to the undistributed net income are $2,319, determined as shown below.

(2) The distributable net income of the trust computed under section 643(a) is $18,000 (royalties of $20,000 less expenses of $2,000). The total taxes paid by the trust are $3,787, computed as follows:

Royalties		$20,000
Capital gain allocable to corpus		10,000
Gross income		30,000
Deductions:		
Expenses	$2,000	
Distributions to A	10,000	
Capital gain deduction	5,000	
Personal exemption	100	
		17,100
Taxable income		12,900
Total income taxes		3,787

(3) Taxable income other than capital gains less the section 1202 deduction is $7,900 ($12,900–($10,000–$5,000)). Therefore, the amount of taxes imposed on the trust attributable to the undistributed net income is $2,319, computed as follows:

$3,787 (total taxes) × $7,900 (taxable income other than capital gains not included in d.n.i. less the 1202 deduction) divided by $12,900 (taxable income) $2,319

* * *

[T.D. 7204, 37 FR 17139, Aug. 25, 1972, as amended by T.D. 7728, 45 FR 72650, Nov. 3, 1980]

§ 1.665(e)–1A Preceding taxable year.

* * *

(b) **Simple trusts.** A taxable year of a trust during which the trust was a simple trust (that is, was subject to subpart B) for the entire year shall not be considered a "preceding taxable year" unless during such year the trust received "outside income" or unless the trustee did not distribute all of the income of the trust that was required to be distributed currently for such year. In such event, undistributed net income for such year shall not exceed the greater of the "outside income" or income not distributed during such year. For purposes of this paragraph, the term "outside income" means amounts that are included in distributable net income of the trust for the year but that are not "income" of the trust as that term is defined in

§ 1.643(b)–1. Some examples of "outside income" are:

(1) Income taxable to the trust under section 691;

(2) Unrealized accounts receivable that were assigned to the trust; and

(3) Distributions from another trust that include distributable net income or undistributed net income of such other trust.

The term "outside income," however, does not include amounts received as distributions from an estate, other than income specified in (1) and (2), for which the estate was allowed a deduction under section 661(a). The application of this paragraph may be illustrated by the following examples:

Example (1). By his will D creates a trust for his widow W. The terms of the trust require that the income be distributed currently (*i.e.*, it is a simple trust), and authorize the trustee to make discretionary payments of corpus to W. Upon W's death the trust corpus is to be distributed to D's then living issue. The executor of D's will makes a $10,000 distribution of corpus to the trust that carries out estate income consisting of dividends and interest to the trust under section 662(a)(2). The trust reports this income as its only income on its income tax return for its taxable year in which ends the taxable year of the estate in which the $10,000 distribution was made, and pays a tax thereon of $2,106. Thus, the trust has undistributed net income of $7,894 ($10,000–$2,106). Several years later the trustee makes a discretionary corpus payment of $15,000 to W. This payment is an accumulation distribution under section 665(b). However, since the trust had no "outside income" in the year of the estate distribution, such year is not a preceding taxable year. Thus, W is not treated as receiving undistributed net income of $7,894 and taxes thereon of $2,106 for the purpose of including the same in her gross income under section 668. The result would be the same if the invasion power were not exercised and the accumulation distribution occurred as a result of the distribution of the corpus to D's issue upon the death of W.

Example (2). Trust A, a simple trust on the calendar year basis, received in 1972 extraordinary dividends or taxable stock dividends that the trustee in good faith allocated to corpus, but that are determined in 1974 to have been currently distributable to the beneficiary. See section 643(a)(4) and § 1.643(a)–4. Trust A would qualify for treatment under subpart C for 1974, the year of distribution of the extraordinary dividends or taxable stock dividends, because the distribution is not out of income of the current taxable year and is treated as another amount properly paid or credited or required to be distributed for such taxable year within the meaning of section 661(a)(2). Also, the distribution in 1974 qualifies as an accumulation distribution for the purposes of subpart D. For purposes only of such subpart D, trust A would be treated as subject to the provisions of such subpart C for 1972, the preceding taxable year in which the extraordinary or taxable stock dividends were received, and, in computing undistributed net income for

1972, the extraordinary or taxable stock dividends would be included in distributable net income under section 643(a). The rule stated in the preceding sentence would also apply if the distribution in 1974 was made out of corpus without regard to a determination that the extraordinary dividends or taxable stock dividends in question were currently distributable to the beneficiary.

[T.D. 7204, 37 FR 17141, Aug. 25, 1972]

§ 1.666(a)–1A Amount allocated.

(a) **In general.** In the case of a trust that is subject to subpart C of part I of subchapter J of chapter 1 of the Code (relating to estates and trusts that may accumulate income or that distribute corpus), section 666(a) prescribes rules for determining the taxable years from which an accumulation distribution will be deemed to have been made and the extent to which the accumulation distribution is considered to consist of undistributed net income. * * *

(b) **Distributions by domestic trusts—(1) Taxable years beginning after December 31, 1973.** An accumulation distribution made by a trust (other than a foreign trust created by a U.S. person) in any taxable year beginning after December 31, 1973, is allocated to the preceding taxable years of the trust (defined in § 1.665(e)–1A(a)(1)(ii) as those beginning after December 31, 1968) according to the amount of undistributed net income of the trust for such years. For this purpose, an accumulation distribution is first to be allocated to the earliest such preceding taxable year in which there is undistributed net income and shall then be allocated, beginning with the next earliest, to any remaining preceding taxable years of the trust. The portion of the accumulation distribution allocated to the earliest preceding taxable year is the amount of the undistributed net income for that preceding taxable year. The portion of the accumulation distribution allocated to any preceding taxable year subsequent to the earliest such preceding taxable year is the excess of the accumulation distribution over the aggregate of the undistributed net income for all earlier preceding taxable years. See paragraph (d) of this section for adjustments to undistributed net income for prior distributions. The provisions of this subparagraph may be illustrated by the following example:

Example. In 1977, a domestic trust reporting on the calendar year basis makes an accumulation distribution of $33,000. Therefore, years before 1969 are ignored. In 1969, the trust had $6,000 of undistributed net income; in 1970, $4,000; in 1971, none; in 1972, $7,000; in 1973, $5,000; in 1974, $8,000; in 1975, $6,000; and $4,000 in 1976. The accumulation distribution is deemed distribut-

ed $6,000 in 1969, $4,000 in 1970, none in 1971, $7,000 in 1972, $5,000 in 1973, $8,000 in 1974, and $3,000 in 1975.

* * *

[T.D. 7204, 37 FR 17143, Aug. 25, 1972]

§ 1.666(b)–1A Total taxes deemed distributed.

(a) If an accumulation distribution is deemed under § 1.666(a)–1A to be distributed on the last day of a preceding taxable year and the amount is not less than the undistributed net income for such preceding taxable year, then an additional amount equal to the "taxes imposed on the trust attributable to the undistributed net income" (as defined in § 1.665(d)–1A(b)) for such preceding taxable year is also deemed distributed under section 661(a)(2). For example, a trust has undistributed net income of $8,000 for the taxable year 1974. The taxes imposed on the trust attributable to the undistributed net income are $3,032. During the taxable year 1977, an accumulation distribution of $8,000 is made to the beneficiary, which is deemed under § 1.666(a)–1A to have been distributed on the last day of 1974. The 1977 accumulation distribution is not less than the 1974 undistributed net income. Accordingly, the taxes of $3,032 imposed on the trust attributable to the undistributed net income for 1974 are also deemed to have been distributed on the last day of 1974. Thus, a total of $11,032 will be deemed to have been distributed on the last day of 1974.

(b) For the purpose of paragraph (a) of this section, the undistributed net income of any preceding taxable year and the taxes imposed on the trust for such preceding taxable year attributable to such undistributed net income are computed after taking into account any accumulation distributions of taxable years intervening between such preceding taxable year and the taxable year. See paragraph (d) of § 1.666(a)–1A.

[T.D. 7204, 37 FR 17145, Aug. 25, 1972]

§ 1.666(c)–1A Pro rata portion of taxes deemed distributed.

(a) If an accumulation distribution is deemed under § 1.666(a)–1A to be distributed on the last day of a preceding taxable year and the amount is less than the undistributed net income for such preceding taxable year, then an additional amount is also deemed distributed under section 661(a)(2). The additional amount is equal to the "taxes imposed on the trust attributable to the undistributed net income" (as defined in § 1.665(a)–1A(b)) for such preceding taxable year, multiplied by a fraction, the numerator of which is the amount of the accumulation distribution allocated to such preceding taxable year and the denominator of which is the undistributed net income for such preceding taxable year. * * *

(b) For the purpose of paragraph (a) of this section, the undistributed net income of any preceding taxable year and the taxes imposed on the trust for such preceding taxable year attributable to such undistributed net income are computed after taking into account any accumulation distributions of any taxable years intervening between such preceding taxable year and the taxable year. * * *

* * *

[T.D. 7204, 37 FR 17145, Aug. 25, 1972]

Grantors and Others Treated as Substantial Owners

§ 1.671–1 Grantors and others treated as substantial owners; scope.

(a) Subpart E (section 671 and following), part I, subchapter J, chapter 1 of the Code, contains provisions taxing income of a trust to the grantor or another person under certain circumstances even though he is not treated as a beneficiary under subparts A through D (section 641 and following) of such part I. Sections 671 and 672 contain general provisions relating to the entire subpart. Sections 673 through 677 define the circumstances under which income of a trust is taxed to a grantor. These circumstances are in general as follows:

(1) If the grantor has retained a reversionary interest in the trust, within specified time limits (section 673);

(2) If the grantor or a nonadverse party has certain powers over the beneficial interests under the trust (section 674);

(3) If certain administrative powers over the trust exist under which the grantor can or does benefit (section 675).

(4) If the grantor or a nonadverse party has a power to revoke the trust or return the corpus to the grantor (section 676); or

(5) If the grantor or a nonadverse party has the power to distribute income to or for the benefit of the grantor or the grantor's spouse (section 677).

Under section 678, income of a trust is taxed to a person other than the grantor to the extent that he has the sole power to vest corpus or income in himself.

(b) Sections 671 through 677 do not apply if the income of a trust is taxable to a grantor's spouse under section 71 or 682 (relating respectively to alimony and separate maintenance payments, and the income of an estate or trust in the case of divorce, etc.).

(c) Except as provided in such subpart E, income of a trust is not included in computing the taxable income and credits of a grantor or another person solely on the grounds of his dominion and control over the trust. However, the provisions of subpart E do not apply in situations involving an assignment of future income, whether or not the assignment is to a trust. Thus, for example, a person who assigns his right to future income under an employment contract may be taxed on that income even though the assignment is to a trust over which the assignor has retained none of the controls specified in sections 671 through 677. Similarly, a bondholder who assigns his right to interest may be taxed on interest payments even though the assignment is to an uncontrolled trust. Nor are the rules as to family partnerships affected by the provisions of subpart E, even though a partnership interest is held in trust. Likewise, these sections have no application in determining the right of a grantor to deductions for payments to a trust under a transfer and leaseback arrangement. In addition, the limitation of the last sentence of section 671 does not prevent any person from being taxed on the income of a trust when it is used to discharge his legal obligation. See § 1.662(a)–4. He is then treated as a beneficiary under subparts A through D or treated as an owner under section 677 because the income is distributed for his benefit, and not because of his dominion or control over the trust.

* * *

[T.D. 6500, 25 FR 11814, Nov. 26, 1960, as amended by T.D. 7148, 36 FR 20749, Oct. 29, 1971; T.D. 7741, 45 FR 81745, Dec. 12, 1980]

§ 1.671–2 Applicable principles.

(a) Under section 671 a grantor or another person includes in computing his taxable income and credits those items of income, deduction, and credit against tax which are attributable to or included in any portion of a trust of which he is treated as the owner. Sections 673 through 678 set forth the rules for determining when the grantor or another person is treated as the owner of any portion of a trust. The rules for determining the items of income, deduction, and credit against tax that are attributable to or included in a portion of the trust are set forth in § 1.671–3.

(b) Since the principle underlying subpart E (section 671 and following), part I, subchapter J, chapter 1 of the Code, is in general that income of a trust over which the grantor or another person has retained substantial dominion or control should be taxed to the grantor or other person rather than to the trust which receives the income or to the beneficiary to whom the income may be distributed, it is ordinarily immaterial whether the income involved constitutes income or corpus for trust accounting purposes. Accordingly, when it is stated in the regulations under subpart E that "income" is attributed to the grantor or another person, the reference, unless specifically limited, is to income determined for tax purposes and not to income for trust accounting purposes. When it is intended to emphasize that income for trust accounting purposes (determined in accordance with the provisions set forth in § 1.643(b)–1 is meant, the phrase "ordinary income" is used.

(c) An item of income, deduction, or credit included in computing the taxable income and credits of a grantor or another person under section 671 is treated as if it had been received or paid directly by the grantor or other person (whether or not an individual). For example, a charitable contribution made by a trust which is attributed to the grantor (an individual) under sections 671 through 677 will be aggregated with his other charitable contributions to determine their deductibility under the limitations of section 170(b)(1). Likewise, dividends received by a trust from sources in a particular foreign country which are attributed to a grantor or another person under subpart E will be aggregated with his other income from sources within that country to determine whether the taxpayer is subject to the limitations of section 904 with respect to credit for the tax paid to that country.

(d) Items of income, deduction, and credit not attributed to or included in any portion of a trust of which the grantor or another person is treated as the owner under subpart E are subject to the provisions of subparts A through D (section 641 and following), of such part I.

(e) The term "grantor" as used in the regulations under subpart E includes a corporation.

[T.D. 6500, 25 FR 11814, Nov. 26, 1960]

§ 1.671–3 Attribution or inclusion of income, deductions, and credits against tax.

(a) When a grantor or another person is treated under subpart E (section 671 and following) as the owner of any portion of a trust, there are included in computing his tax liability those items of income, deduction, and credit against tax attributable to or included in that portion. For example:

(1) If a grantor or another person is treated as the owner of an entire trust (corpus as well as ordinary income), he takes into account in computing his income tax liability all items of income, deduction, and credit (including capital gains and losses) to which he would have been entitled had the trust not been in existence during the period he is treated as owner.

(2) If the portion treated as owned consists of specific trust property and its income, all items directly related to that property are attributable to the portion. Items directly related to trust property not included in the portion treated as owned by the grantor or other person are governed by the provisions of subparts A through D (section 641 and following), part I, subchapter J, chapter 1 of the Code. Items that relate both to the portion treated as owned by the grantor and to the balance of the trust must be apportioned in a manner that is reasonable in the light of all the circumstances of each case, including the terms of the governing instrument, local law, and the practice of the trustee if it is reasonable and consistent.

(3) If the portion of a trust treated as owned by a grantor or another person consists of an undivided fractional interest in the trust, or of an interest represented by a dollar amount, a pro rata share of each item of income, deduction, and credit is normally allocated to the portion. Thus, where the portion owned consists of an interest in or a right to an amount of corpus only, a fraction of each item (including items allocated to corpus, such as capital gains) is attributed to the portion. The numerator of this fraction is the amount which is subject to the control of the grantor or other person and the denominator is normally the fair market value of the trust corpus at the beginning of

the taxable year in question. The share not treated as owned by the grantor or other person is governed by the provisions of subparts A through D. See the last three sentences of paragraph (c) of this section for the principles applicable if the portion treated as owned consists of an interest in part of the ordinary income in contrast to an interest in corpus alone.

(b) If a grantor or another person is treated as the owner of a portion of a trust, that portion may or may not include both ordinary income and other income allocable to corpus. For example—

(1) Only ordinary income is included by reason of an interest in or a power over ordinary income alone. Thus, if a grantor is treated under section 673 as an owner by reason of a reversionary interest in ordinary income only, items of income allocable to corpus will not be included in the portion he is treated as owning. Similarly, if a grantor or another person is treated under sections 674–678 as an owner of a portion by reason of a power over ordinary income only, items of income allocable to corpus are not included in that portion. (See paragraph (c) of this section to determine the treatment of deductions and credits when only ordinary income is included in the portion.)

(2) Only income allocable to corpus is included by reason of an interest in or a power over corpus alone, if satisfaction of the interest or an exercise of the power will not result in an interest in or the exercise of a power over ordinary income which would itself cause that income to be included. For example, if a grantor has a reversionary interest in a trust which is not such as to require that he be treated as an owner under section 673, he may nevertheless be treated as an owner under section 677(a)(2) since any income allocable to corpus is accumulated for future distribution to him, but items of income included in determining ordinary income are not included in the portion he is treated as owning. Similarly, he may have a power over corpus which is such that he is treated as an owner under section 674 or 676(a), but ordinary income will not be included in the portion he owns, if his power can only affect income received after a period of time such that he would not be treated as an owner of the income if the power were a reversionary interest. (See paragraph (c) of this section to determine the treatment of deductions and credits when only income allocated to corpus is included in the portion.)

(3) Both ordinary income and other income allocable to corpus are included by reason of an interest in or a power over both ordinary income and corpus, or an interest in or a power over corpus alone which does not come within the provisions of subparagraph (2) of this paragraph. For example, if a grantor is treated under section 673 as the owner of a portion of a trust by reason of a reversionary interest in corpus, both ordinary income and other income allocable to corpus are included in the portion. Further, a grantor includes both ordinary income and other income allocable to corpus in the portion he is treated as owning if he is treated under section 674 or 676 as an owner because of a power over corpus which can affect income received within a period such that he would be treated as an owner under section 673 if the power were a reversionary interest. Similarly, a grantor or another person includes both ordinary income and other income allocable to corpus in the portion he is treated as owning if he is treated as an owner under section 675 or 678 because of a power over corpus.

(c) If only income allocable to corpus is included in computing a grantor's tax liability, he will take into account in that computation only those items of income, deductions, and credit which would not be included under subparts A through D in the computation of the tax liability of the current income beneficiaries if all distributable net income had actually been distributed to those beneficiaries. On the other hand, if the grantor or another person is treated as an owner solely because of his interest in or power over ordinary income alone, he will take into account in computing his tax liability those items which would be included in computing the tax liability of a current income beneficiary, including expenses allocable to corpus which enter into the computation of distributable net income. If the grantor or other person is treated as an owner because of his power over or right to a dollar amount of ordinary income, he will first take into account a portion of those items of income and expense entering into the computation of ordinary income under the trust instrument or local law sufficient to produce income of the dollar amount required. There will then be attributable to him a pro rata portion of other items entering into the computation of distributable net income under subparts A through D, such as expenses allocable to corpus, and a pro rata portion of credits of the trust. For examples of computations under this paragraph, see paragraph (g) of § 1.677(a)–1.

[T.D. 6500, 25 FR 11814, Nov. 26, 1960, as amended by T.D. 6989, 34 FR 742, Jan. 17, 1969]

§ 1.672(a)-1 Definition of adverse party.

(a) Under section 672(a) an adverse party is defined as any person having a substantial beneficial interest in a trust which would be adversely affected by the exercise or nonexercise of a power which he possesses respecting the trust. A trustee is not an adverse party merely because of his interest as trustee. A person having a general power of appointment over the trust property is deemed to have a beneficial interest in the trust. An interest is a substantial interest if its value in relation to the total value of the property subject to the power is not insignificant.

(b) Ordinarily, a beneficiary will be an adverse party, but if his right to share in the income or corpus of a trust is limited to only a part, he may be an adverse party only as to that part. Thus, if A, B, C, and D are equal income beneficiaries of a trust and the grantor can revoke with A's consent, the grantor is treated as the owner of a portion which represents three-fourths of the trust; and items of income, deduction, and credit attributable to that portion are included in determining the tax of the grantor.

(c) The interest of an ordinary income beneficiary of a trust may or may not be adverse with respect to the exercise of a power over corpus. Thus, if the income of a trust is payable to A for life, with a power (which is not a general power of appointment) in A to appoint the corpus to the grantor either during his life or by will, A's interest is adverse to the return of the corpus to the grantor during A's life, but is not adverse to a return of the corpus after A's death. In other words, A's interest is adverse as to ordinary income but is not adverse as to income allocable to corpus. Therefore, assuming no other relevant facts exist, the grantor would not be taxable on the ordinary income of the trust under section 674, 676, or 677, but would be taxable under section 677 on income allocable to corpus (such as capital gains), since it may in the discretion of a nonadverse party be accumulated for future distribution to the grantor. Similarly, the interest of a contingent income beneficiary is adverse to a return of corpus to the grantor before the termination of his interest but not to a return of corpus after the termination of his interest.

(d) The interest of a remainderman is adverse to the exercise of any power over the corpus of a trust, but not to the exercise of a power over any income interest preceding his remainder. For ex-

ample, if the grantor creates a trust which provides for income to be distributed to A for 10 years and then for the corpus to go to X if he is then living, a power exercisable by X to revest corpus in the grantor is a power exercisable by an adverse party; however, a power exercisable by X to distribute part or all of the ordinary income to the grantor may be a power exercisable by a nonadverse party (which would cause the ordinary income to be taxed to the grantor).

[T.D. 6500, 25 FR 11814, Nov. 26, 1960]

§ 1.672(c)-1 Related or subordinate party.

Section 672(c) defines the term "related or subordinate party". The term, as used in sections 674(c) and 675(3), means any nonadverse party who is the grantor's spouse if living with the grantor; the grantor's father, mother, issue, brother or sister; an employee of the grantor; a corporation or any employee of a corporation in which the stock holdings of the grantor and the trust are significant from the viewpoint of voting control; or a subordinate employee of a corporation in which the grantor is an executive. For purposes of sections 674(c) and 675(3), these persons are presumed to be subservient to the grantor in respect of the exercise or nonexercise of the powers conferred on them unless shown not to be subservient by a preponderance of the evidence.

[T.D. 6500, 25 FR 11814, Nov. 26, 1960]

§ 1.672(d)-1 Power subject to condition precedent.

Section 672(d) provides that a person is considered to have a power described in subpart E (section 671 and following), part I, subchapter J, chapter 1 of the Code, even though the exercise of the power is subject to a precedent giving of notice or takes effect only after the expiration of a certain period of time. However, although a person may be considered to have such a power, the grantor will nevertheless not be treated as an owner by reason of the power if its exercise can only affect beneficial enjoyment of income received after the expiration of a period of time such that, if the power were a reversionary interest, he would not be treated as an owner under section 673. See sections 674(b)(2), 676(b), and the last sentence of section 677(a). Thus, for example, if a grantor creates a trust for the benefit of his son and retains a power to revoke which takes effect only after the expiration of 2 years from the date of exercise, he is treated as an owner from the inception of the trust. However, if the grantor retains a power to revoke, exercisable at any time, which can only affect the beneficial enjoyment of the ordinary income of a trust received after the expiration of 10 years commencing with the date of the transfer in trust, or after the death of the income beneficiary, the power does not cause him to be treated as an owner with respect to ordinary income during the first 10 years of the trust or during the income beneficiary's life, as the case may be. See section 676(b).

[T.D. 6500, 25 FR 11814, Nov. 26, 1960]

§ 1.673(a)–1 Reversionary interests; income payable to beneficiaries other than certain charitable organizations; general rule.

(a) Under section 673(a), a grantor, in general, is treated as the owner of any portion of a trust in which he has a reversionary interest in either the corpus or income if, as of the inception of that portion of the trust, the grantor's interest will or may reasonably be expected to take effect in possession or enjoyment within 10 years commencing with the date of transfer of that portion of the trust. However, the following types of reversionary interests are excepted from the general rule of the preceding sentence:

(1) A reversionary interest after the death of the income beneficiary of a trust (see paragraph (b) of this section); and

* * *

Even though the duration of the trust may be such that the grantor is not treated as its owner under section 673, and therefore is not taxed on the ordinary income, he may nevertheless be treated as an owner under section 677(a)(2) if he has a reversionary interest in the corpus. In the latter case, items of income, deduction, and credit allocable to corpus, such as capital gains and losses, will be included in the portion he owns. See § 1.671–3 and the regulations under section 677. See § 1.673(d)–1 with respect to a postponement of the date specified for reacquisition of a reversionary interest.

(b) Section 673(c) provides that a grantor is not treated as the owner of any portion of a trust by reason of section 673 if his reversionary interest in the portion is not to take effect in possession or enjoyment until the death of the person or persons to whom the income of the portion is regardless of

the life expectancies of the income beneficiaries. If his reversionary interest is to take effect on or after the death of an income beneficiary or upon the expiration of a specific term of years, whichever is earlier, the grantor is treated as the owner if the specific term of years is less than 10 years (but not if the term is 10 years or longer).

(c) Where the grantor's reversionary interest in a portion of a trust is to take effect in possession or enjoyment by reason of some event other than the expiration of a specific term of years or the death of the income beneficiary, the grantor is treated as the owner of the portion if the event may reasonably be expected to occur within 10 years from the date of transfer of that portion, but he is not treated as the owner under section 673 if the event may not reasonably be expected to occur within 10 years from that date. For example, if the reversionary interest in any portion of a trust is to take effect on or after the death of the grantor (or any person other than the person to whom the income is payable) the grantor is treated under section 673 as the owner of the portion if the life expectancy of the grantor (or other person) is less than 10 years on the date of transfer of the portion, but not if the life expectancy is 10 years or longer. If the reversionary interest in any portion is to take effect on or after the death of the grantor (or any person other than the person to whom the income is payable) or upon the expiration of a specific term of years, whichever is earlier, the grantor is treated as the owner of the portion if on the date of transfer of the portion either the life expectancy of the grantor (or other person) or the specific term is less than 10 years; however, if both the life expectancy and the specific term are 10 years or longer the grantor is not treated as the owner of the portion under section 673. Similarly, if the grantor has a reversionary interest in any portion which will take effect at the death of the income beneficiary or the grantor, whichever is earlier, the grantor is not treated as an owner of the portion unless his life expectancy is less than 10 years.

(d) It is immaterial that a reversionary interest in corpus or income is subject to a contingency if the reversionary interest may, taking the contingency into consideration, reasonably be expected to take effect in possession or enjoyment within 10 years. For example, the grantor is taxable where the trust income is to be paid to the grantor's son for 3 years, and the corpus is then to be returned to the grantor if he survives that period, or to be paid to the grantor's son if he is already deceased.

(e) See section 671 and §§ 1.671–2 and 1.671–3 for rules for treatment of items of income, deduction, and credit when a person is treated as the owner of all or only a portion of a trust.

[T.D. 6500, 25 FR 11814, Nov. 26, 1960, as amended by T.D. 7357, 40 FR 23742, June 2, 1975]

§ 1.673(d)–1 Postponement of date specified for reacquisition.

Any postponement of the date specified for the reacquisition of possession or enjoyment of any reversionary interest is considered a new transfer in trust commencing with the date on which the postponement is effected and terminating with the date prescribed by the postponement. However, the grantor will not be treated as the owner of any portion of a trust for any taxable year by reason of the foregoing sentence if he would not be so treated in the absence of any postponement. The rules contained in this section may be illustrated by the following example:

Example. G places property in trust for the benefit of his son B. Upon the expiration of 12 years or the earlier death of B the property is to be paid over to G or his estate. After the expiration of 9 years G extends the term of the trust for an additional 2 years. G is considered to have made a new transfer in trust for a term of 5 years (the remaining 3 years of the original transfer plus the 2-year extension). However, he is not treated as the owner of the trust under section 673 for the first 3 years of the new term because he would not be so treated if the term of the trust had not been extended. G is treated as the owner of the trust, however, for the remaining 2 years.

[T.D. 6500, 25 FR 11814, Nov. 26, 1960]

§ 1.674(a)–1 Power to control beneficial enjoyment; scope of section 674.

(a) Under section 674, the grantor is treated as the owner of a portion of trust if the grantor or a nonadverse party has a power, beyond specified limits, to dispose of the beneficial enjoyment of the income or corpus, whether the power is a fiduciary power, a power of appointment, or any other power. Section 674(a) states in general terms that the grantor is treated as the owner in every case in which he or a nonadverse party can affect the beneficial enjoyment of a portion of a trust, the limitations being set forth as exceptions in subsections (b), (c), and (d) of section 674. These exceptions are discussed in detail in §§ 1.674(b)–1 through 1.674(d)–1. Certain limitations applicable to section 674(b), (c), and (d) are set forth in § 1.674(d)–2. Section 674(b) describes powers

which are excepted regardless of who holds them. Section 674(c) describes additional powers of trustees which are excepted if at least half the trustees are independent, and if the grantor is not a trustee. Section 674(d) describes a further power which is excepted if it is held by trustees other than the grantor or his spouse (if living with the grantor).

(b) In general terms the grantor is treated as the owner of a portion of a trust if he or a nonadverse party or both has a power to dispose of the beneficial enjoyment of the corpus or income unless the power is one of the following:

(1) **Miscellaneous powers over either ordinary income or corpus.** (i) A power that can only affect the beneficial enjoyment of income (including capital gains) received after a period of time such that the grantor would not be treated as an owner under section 673 if the power were a reversionary interest (section 674(b)(2));

(ii) A testamentary power held by anyone (other than a testamentary power held by the grantor over accumulated income) (section 674(b)(3));

(iii) A power to choose between charitable beneficiaries or to affect the manner of their enjoyment of a beneficial interest (section 674(b)(4));

(iv) A power to allocate receipts and disbursements between income and corpus (section 674(b)(8)).

(2) **Powers of distribution primarily affecting only one beneficiary.** (i) A power to distribute corpus to or for a current income beneficiary, if the distribution must be charged against the share of corpus from which the beneficiary may receive income (section 674(b)(5)(B));

(ii) A power to distribute income to or for a current income beneficiary or to accumulate it either (a) if accumulated income must either be payable to the beneficiary from whom it was withheld or as described in paragraph (b)(6) of § 1.674(b)–1 (section 674(b)(6)); (b) if the power is to apply income to the support of a dependent of the grantor, and the income is not so applied (section 674(b)(1)); or (c) if the beneficiary is under 21 or under a legal disability and accumulated income is added to corpus (section 674(b)(7)).

(3) **Powers of distribution affecting more than one beneficiary.** A power to distribute corpus or income to or among one or more beneficiaries or to accumulate income, either (i) if the power is held by a trustee or trustees other than the grantor, at least half of whom are independent

(section 674(c)), or (ii) if the power is limited by a reasonably definite standard in the trust instrument, and in the case of a power over income, if in addition the power is held by a trustee or trustees other than the grantor and the grantor's spouse living with the grantor (section 674(b)(5)(A) and (d)). (These powers include both powers to "sprinkle" income or corpus among current beneficiaries, and powers to shift income or corpus between current beneficiaries and remaindermen; however, certain of the powers described under subparagraph (2) of this paragraph can have the latter effect incidentally.)

(c) See section 671 and §§ 1.671–2 and 1.671–3 for rules for the treatment of income, deductions, and credits when a person is treated as the owner of all or only a portion of a trust.

[T.D. 6500, 25 FR 11814, Nov. 26, 1960]

§ 1.674(b)–1 Excepted powers exercisable by any person.

(a) Paragraph (b)(1) through (8) of this section sets forth a number of powers which may be exercisable by any person without causing the grantor to be treated as an owner of a trust under section 674(a). Further, with the exception of powers described in paragraph (b)(1) of this section, it is immaterial whether these powers are held in the capacity of trustee. It makes no difference under section 674(b) that the person holding the power is the grantor, or a related or subordinate party (with the qualifications noted in paragraph (b)(1) and (3) of this section).

(b) The exceptions referred to in paragraph (a) of this section are as follows (see, however, the limitations set forth in § 1.674(d)–2):

(1) **Powers to apply income to support of a dependent.** Section 674(b)(1) provides, in effect, that regardless of the general rule of section 674(a), the income of a trust will not be considered as taxable to the grantor merely because in the discretion of any person (other than a grantor who is not acting as a trustee or cotrustee) it may be used for the support of a beneficiary whom the grantor is legally obligated to support, except to the extent that it is in fact used for that purpose. See section 677(b) and the regulations thereunder.

(2) **Powers affecting beneficial enjoyment only after a period.** Section 674(b)(2) provides an exception to section 674(a) if the exercise of a power can only affect the beneficial enjoyment of the income of a trust received after a period of time which is such that a grantor would not be treated as an owner under section 673 if the power were a reversionary interest. See §§ 1.673(a)–1 and 1.673(b)–1. For example, if a trust created on January 1, 1955, provides for the payment of income to the grantor's son, and the grantor reserves the power to substitute other beneficiaries of income or corpus in lieu of his son on or after January 1, 1965, the grantor is not treated under section 674 as the owner of the trust with respect to ordinary income received before January 1, 1965. But the grantor will be treated as an owner on and after that date unless the power is relinquished. If the beginning of the period during which the grantor may substitute beneficiaries is postponed, the rules set forth in § 1.673(d)–1 are applicable in order to determine whether the grantor should be treated as an owner during the period following the postponement.

(3) **Testamentary powers.** Under paragraph (3) of section 674(b) a power in any person to control beneficial enjoyment exercisable only by will does not cause a grantor to be treated as an owner under section 674(a). However, this exception does not apply to income accumulated for testamentary disposition by the grantor or to income which may be accumulated for such distribution in the discretion of the grantor or a nonadverse party, or both, without the approval or consent of any adverse party. For example, if a trust instrument provides that the income is to be accumulated during the grantor's life and that the grantor may appoint the accumulated income by will, the grantor is treated as the owner of the trust. Moreover, if a trust instrument provides that the income is payable to another person for his life, but the grantor has a testamentary power of appointment over the remainder, and under the trust instrument and local law capital gains are added to corpus, the grantor is treated as the owner of a portion of the trust and capital gains and losses are included in that portion. (See § 1.671–3.)

* * *

(5) **Powers to distribute corpus.** Paragraph (5) of section 674(b) provides an exception to section 674(a) for powers to distribute corpus, subject to certain limitations, as follows:

(i) If the power is limited by a reasonably definite standard which is set forth in the trust instrument, it may extend to corpus distributions to any beneficiary or beneficiaries or class of beneficiaries (whether income beneficiaries or remaindermen) without causing the grantor to be treated as an owner under section 674. See section 674(b)(5)(A). It is not required that the standard consist of the needs and circumstances of the beneficiary. A clearly measurable standard under which the holder of a power is legally accountable is deemed a reasonably definite standard for this purpose. For instance, a power to distribute corpus for the education, support, maintenance, or health of the beneficiary; for his reasonable support and comfort; or to enable him to maintain his accustomed standard of living; or to meet an emergency, would be limited by a reasonably definite standard. However, a power to distribute corpus for the pleasure, desire, or happiness of a beneficiary is not limited by a reasonably definite standard. The entire context of a provision of a trust instrument granting a power must be considered in determining whether the power is limited by a reasonably definite standard. For example, if a trust instrument provides that the determination of the trustee shall be conclusive with respect to the exercise or nonexercise of a power, the power is not limited by a reasonably definite standard. However, the fact that the governing instrument is phrased in discretionary terms is not in itself an indication that no reasonably definite standard exists.

(ii) If the power is not limited by a reasonably definite standard set forth in the trust instrument, the exception applies only if distributions of corpus may be made solely in favor of current income beneficiaries, and any corpus distribution to the current income beneficiary must be chargeable against the proportionate part of corpus held in trust for payment of income to that beneficiary as if it constituted a separate trust (whether or not physically segregated). See section 674(b)(5)(B).

(iii) This subparagraph may be illustrated by the following examples:

Example (1). A trust instrument provides for payment of the income to the grantor's two brothers for life, and for payment of the corpus to the grantor's nephews in equal shares. The grantor reserves the power to distribute corpus to pay medical expenses that may be incurred by his brothers or nephews. The grantor is not treated as an owner by reason of this power because section 674(b)(5)(A) excepts a power, exercisable by any person, to invade corpus for any beneficiary, including a remainderman, if the power is limited by a reasonably definite standard which is set forth in the trust instrument. However, if the power were also exercisable in favor of a person (for example, a sister) who was not otherwise a beneficiary of the trust, section 674(b)(5)(A) would not be applicable.

Example (2). The facts are the same as in example (1) except that the grantor reserves the power to distribute any part of the corpus to his brothers or to his nephews for their happiness. The grantor is treated as the owner of the trust. Paragraph (5)(A) of section 674(b) is inapplicable because the power is not limited by a reasonably definite standard. Paragraph (5)(B) is inapplicable because the power to distribute corpus permits a distribution of corpus to persons other than current income beneficiaries.

Example (3). A trust instrument provides for payment of the income to the grantor's two adult sons in equal shares for 10 years, after which the corpus is to be distributed to his grandchildren in equal shares. The grantor reserves the power to pay over to each son up to one-half of the corpus during the 10-year period, but any such payment shall proportionately reduce subsequent income and corpus payments made to the son receiving the corpus. Thus, if one-half of the corpus is paid to one son, all the income from the remaining half is thereafter payable to the other son. The grantor is not treated as an owner under section 674(a) by reason of this power because it qualifies under the exception of section 674(b)(5)(B).

(6) Powers to withhold income temporarily. (i) Section 674(b)(6) excepts a power which, in general, enables the holder merely to effect a postponement in the time when the ordinary income is enjoyed by a current income beneficiary. Specifically, there is excepted a power to distribute or apply ordinary income to or for a current income beneficiary or to accumulate the income, if the accumulated income must ultimately be payable either:

(a) To the beneficiary from whom it was withheld, his estate, or his appointees (or persons designated by name, as a class, or otherwise as alternate takers in default of appointment) under a power of appointment held by the beneficiary which does not exclude from the class of possible appointees any person other than the beneficiary, his estate, his creditors, or the creditors of his estate (section 674(b)(6)(A));

(b) To the beneficiary from whom it was withheld, or if he does not survive a date of distribution which could reasonably be expected to occur within his lifetime, to his appointees (or alternate takers in default of appointment) under any power of appointment, general or special, or if he has no power of appointment to one or more designated alternate takers (other than the grantor of the grantor's estate) whose shares have been irrevocably specified in the trust instrument (section 674(b)(6)(A) and the flush material following); or

(c) On termination of the trust, or in conjunction with a distribution of corpus which is augmented by the accumulated income, to the current income beneficiaries in shares which have been irrevocably specified in the trust instrument, or if any beneficiary does not survive a date of distribution which would reasonably be expected to occur within his lifetime, to his appointees (or alternate takers in default of appointment) under any power of appointment, general or special, or if he has no power of appointment to one or more designated alternate takers (other than the grantor or the grantor's estate) whose shares have been irrevocably specified in the trust instrument (section 674(b)(6)(B) and the flush material following).

(In the application of (a) of this subdivision, if the accumulated income of a trust is ultimately payable to the estate of the current income beneficiary or is ultimately payable to his appointees or takers in default of appointment, under a power of the type described in (a) of this subdivision, it need not be payable to the beneficiary from whom it was withheld under any circumstances. Furthermore, if a trust otherwise qualifies for the exception in (a) of this subdivision the trust income will not be considered to be taxable to the grantor under section 677 by reason of the existence of the power of appointment referred to in (a) of this subdivision.) In general, the exception in section 674(b)(6) is not applicable if the power is in substance one to shift ordinary income from one beneficiary to another. Thus, a power will not qualify for this exception if ordinary income may be distributed to beneficiary A, or may be added to corpus which is ultimately payable to beneficiary B, a remainderman who is not a current income beneficiary. However, section 674(b)(6)(B), and (c) of this subdivision, permit a limited power to shift ordinary income among current income beneficiaries, as illustrated in example (1) of this subparagraph.

(ii) The application of section 674(b)(6) may be illustrated by the following examples:

Example (1). A trust instrument provides that the income shall be paid in equal shares to the grantor's two adult daughters but the grantor reserves the power to withhold from either beneficiary any part of that beneficiary's share of income and to add it to the corpus of the trust until the younger daughter reaches the age of 30 years. When the younger daughter reaches the age of 30, the trust is to terminate and the corpus is to be divided equally between the two daughters or their estates. Although exercise of this power may permit the shifting of accumulated income from one beneficiary to the other (since the corpus with the accumulations is to be divided equally) the power is excepted under section 674(b)(6)(B) and subdivision (i)(c) of this subparagraph.

Example (2). The facts are the same as in example (1), except that the grantor of the trust reserves the power to distribute accumulated income to the beneficiaries in such shares as he chooses. The combined powers are not excepted by section 674(b)(6)(B) since income accumulated pursuant to the first power is neither required to be payable only in conjunction with a corpus distribution nor required to be payable in shares specified in the trust instrument. See, however, section 674(c) and § 1.674(c)–1 for the effect of such a power if it is exercisable only by independent trustees.

Example (3). A trust provides for payment of income to the grantor's adult son with the grantor retaining the power to accumulate the income until the grantor's death, when all accumulations are to be paid to the son. If the son predeceases the grantor, all accumulations are, at the death of the grantor, to be paid to his daughter, or if she is not living, to alternate takers (which do not include the grantor's estate) in specified shares. The power is excepted under section 674(b)(6)(A) since the date of distribution (the date of the grantor's death) may, in the usual case, reasonably be expected to occur during the beneficiary's (the son's) lifetime. It is not necessary that the accumulations be payable to the son's estate or his appointees if he should predecease the grantor for this exception to apply.

(7) Power to withhold income during disability. Section 674(b)(7) provides an exception for a power which, in general, will permit ordinary income to be withheld during the legal disability of an income beneficiary or while he is under 21. Specifically, there is excepted a power, exercisable only during the existence of a legal disability of any current income beneficiary or the period during which any income beneficiary is under the age of 21 years, to distribute or apply ordinary income to or for that beneficiary or to accumulate the income and add it to corpus. To qualify under this exception it is not necessary that the income ultimately be payable to the income beneficiary from whom it was withheld, his estate, or his appointees; that is, the accumulated income may be added to corpus and ultimately distributed to others. For example, the grantor is not treated as an owner under section 674 if the income of a trust is payable to his son for life, remainder to his grandchildren, although he reserves the power to accumulate income and add it to corpus while his son is under 21.

(8) Powers to allocate between corpus and income. Paragraph (8) of section 674(b) provides that a power to allocate receipts and disbursements between corpus and income, even though expressed in broad language, will not cause the grantor to be treated as an owner under the general rule of section 674(a).

[T.D. 6500, 25 FR 11814, Nov. 26, 1960]

§ 1.674(c)-1 Excepted powers exercisable only by independent trustees.

Section 674(c) provides an exception to the general rule of section 674(a) for certain powers that are exercisable by independent trustees. This exception is in addition to those provided for under section 674(b) which may be held by any person including an independent trustee. The powers to which section 674(c) apply are powers (a) to distribute, apportion, or accumulate income to or for a beneficiary or beneficiaries, or to, for, or within a class of beneficiaries, or (b) to pay out corpus to or for a beneficiary or beneficiaries or to or for a class of beneficiaries (whether or not income beneficiaries). In order for such a power to fall within the exception of section 674(c) it must be exercisable solely (without the approval or consent of any other person) by a trustee or trustees none of whom is the grantor and no more than half of whom are related or subordinate parties who are subservient to the wishes of the grantor. (See section 672(c) for definitions of these terms.) An example of the application of section 674(c) is a trust whose income is payable to the grantor's three adult sons with power in an independent trustee to allocate without restriction the amounts of income to be paid to each son each year. Such a power does not cause the grantor to be treated as the owner of the trust. See however, the limitations set forth in § 1.674(d)-2.

[T.D. 6500, 25 FR 11814, Nov. 26, 1960]

§ 1.674(d)-1 Excepted powers exercisable by any trustee other than grantor or spouse.

Section 674(d) provides an additional exception to the general rule of section 674(a) for a power to distribute, apportion, or accumulate income to or for a beneficiary or beneficiaries or to, for, or within a class of beneficiaries, whether or not the conditions of section 674(b)(6) or (7) are satisfied, if the power is solely exercisable (without the approval or consent of any other person) by a trustee or trustees none of whom is the grantor or spouse living with the grantor, and if the power is limited by a reasonably definite external standard set forth in the trust instrument (see paragraph (b)(5) of § 1.674(b)-1 with respect to what constitutes a reasonably definite standard). See, however, the limitations set forth in § 1.674(d)-2.

[T.D. 6500, 25 FR 11814, Nov. 26, 1960]

§ 1.674(d)-2 Limitations on exceptions in section 674(b), (c), and (d).

(a) **Power to remove trustee.** A power in the grantor to remove, substitute, or add trustees (other than a power exercisable only upon limited conditions which do not exist during the taxable year, such as the death or resignation of, or breach of fiduciary duty by, an existing trustee) may prevent a trust from qualifying under section 674(c) or (d). For example, if a grantor has an unrestricted power to remove an independent trustee and substitute any person including himself as trustee, the trust will not qualify under section 674(c) or (d). On the other hand if the grantor's power to remove, substitute, or add trustees is limited so that its exercise could not alter the trust in a manner that would disqualify it under section 674(c) or (d), as the case may be, the power itself does not disqualify the trust. Thus, for example, a power in the grantor to remove or discharge an independent trustee on the condition that he substitute another independent trustee will not prevent a trust from qualifying under section 674(c).

(b) **Power to add beneficiaries.** The exceptions described in section 674(b)(5), (6), and (7), (c), and (d), are not applicable if any person has a power to add to the beneficiary or beneficiaries or to a class of beneficiaries designated to receive the income or corpus, except where the action is to provide for after-born or after-adopted children. This limitation does not apply to a power held by a beneficiary to substitute other beneficiaries to succeed to his interest in the trust (so that he would be an adverse party as to the exercise or nonexercise of that power). For example, the limitation does not apply to a power in a beneficiary of a nonspendthrift trust to assign his interest. Nor does the limitation apply to a power held by any person which would qualify as an exception under section 674(b)(3) (relating to testamentary powers).

[T.D. 6500, 25 FR 11814, Nov. 26, 1960]

§ 1.675-1 Administrative powers.

(a) **General rule.** Section 675 provides in effect that the grantor is treated as the owner of any portion of a trust if under the terms of the trust instrument or circumstances attendant on its operation administrative control is exercisable primarily for the benefit of the grantor rather than the beneficiaries of the trust. If a grantor retains a power to amend the administrative provisions of a trust instrument which is broad enough to permit an amendment causing the grantor to be treated as the owner of a portion of the trust under section 675, he will be treated as the owner of the portion from its inception. See section 671 and §§ 1.671–2 and 1.671–3 for rules for treatment of items of income, deduction, and credit when a person is treated as the owner of all or only a portion of a trust.

(b) **Prohibited controls.** The circumstances which cause administrative controls to be considered exercisable primarily for the benefit of the grantor are specifically described in paragraphs (1) through (4) of section 675 as follows:

(1) The existence of a power, exercisable by the grantor or a nonadverse party, or both, without the approval or consent of any adverse party, which enables the grantor or any other person to purchase, exchange, or otherwise deal with or dispose of the corpus or the income of the trust for less than adequate consideration in money or money's worth. Whether the existence of the power itself will constitute the holder an adverse party will depend on the particular circumstances.

(2) The existence of a power exercisable by the grantor or a nonadverse party, or both, which enables the grantor to borrow the corpus or income of the trust, directly or indirectly, without adequate interest or adequate security. However, this paragraph does not apply where a trustee (other than the grantor acting alone) is authorized under a general lending power to make loans to any person without regard to interest or security. A general lending power in the grantor, acting alone as trustee, under which he has power to determine interest rates and the adequacy of security is not in itself an indication that the grantor has power to borrow the corpus or income without adequate interest or security.

(3) The circumstance that the grantor has directly or indirectly borrowed the corpus or income of the trust and has not completely repaid the loan, including any interest, before the beginning of the taxable year. The preceding sentence does not apply to a loan which provides for adequate interest and adequate security, if it is made by a trustee other than the grantor or a related or subordinate trustee subservient to the grantor. See section 672(c) for definition of "a related or subordinate party".

(4) The existence of certain powers of administration exercisable in a nonfiduciary capacity by any nonadverse party without the approval or consent of any person in a fiduciary capacity. The term "powers of administration" means one or more of the following powers:

(i) A power to vote or direct the voting of stock or other securities of a corporation in which the holdings of the grantor and the trust are significant from the viewpoint of voting control;

(ii) A power to control the investment of the trust funds either by directing investments or reinvestments, or by vetoing proposed investments or reinvestments, to the extent that the trust funds consist of stocks or securities of corporations in which the holdings of the grantor and the trust are significant from the viewpoint of voting control; or

(iii) A power to reacquire the trust corpus by substituting other property of an equivalent value.

If a power is exercisable by a person as trustee, it is presumed that the power is exercisable in a fiduciary capacity primarily in the interests of the beneficiaries. This presumption may be rebutted only by clear and convincing proof that the power is not exercisable primarily in the interests of the beneficiaries. If a power is not exercisable by a person as trustee, the determination of whether the power is exercisable in a fiduciary or a nonfiduciary capacity depends on all the terms of the trust and the circumstances surrounding its creation and administration.

(c) **Authority of trustee.** The mere fact that a power exercisable by a trustee is described in broad language does not indicate that the trustee is authorized to purchase, exchange, or otherwise deal with or dispose of the trust property or income for less than an adequate and full consideration in money or money's worth, or is authorized to lend the trust property or income to the grantor without adequate interest. On the other hand, such authority may be indicated by the actual administration of the trust.

[T.D. 6500, 25 FR 11814, Nov. 26, 1960]

§ 1.676(a)–1 Power to revest title to portion of trust property in grantor; general rule.

If a power to revest in the grantor title to any portion of a trust is exercisable by the grantor or a nonadverse party, or both, without the approval or consent of an adverse party, the grantor is treated as the owner of that portion, except as provided in section 676(b) (relating to powers affecting beneficial enjoyment of income only after the expiration of certain periods of time). If the title to a portion of the trust will revest in the grantor upon the exercise of a power by the grantor or a nonadverse party, or both, the grantor is treated as the owner of that portion regardless of whether the power is a power to revoke, to terminate, to alter or amend, or to appoint. See section 671 and §§ 1.671–2 and 1.671–3 for rules for treatment of items of income, deduction, and credit when a person is treated as the owner of all or only a portion of a trust.

[T.D. 6500, 25 FR 11814, Nov. 26, 1960]

§ 1.676(b)–1 Powers exercisable only after a period of time.

Section 676(b) provides an exception to the general rule of section 676(a) when the exercise of a power can only affect the beneficial enjoyment of the income of a trust received after the expiration of a period of time which is such that a grantor would not be treated as the owner of that portion, except as power were a reversionary interest. See §§ 1.673(a)–1 and 1.673(b)–1. Thus, for example, a grantor is excepted from the general rule of section 676(a) with respect to ordinary income if exercise of a power to revest corpus in him cannot affect the beneficial enjoyment of the income received within 10 years after the date of transfer of that portion of the trust. It is immaterial for this purpose that the power is vested at the time of the transfer. However, the grantor is subject to the general rule of section 676(a) after the expiration of the period unless the power is relinquished. Thus, in the above example, the grantor may be treated as the owner and be taxed on all income in the eleventh and succeeding years if exercise of the power can affect beneficial enjoyment of income received in those years. If the beginning of the period during which the grantor may revest is postponed, the rules set forth in § 1.673(d)–1 are applicable to determine whether the grantor should be treated as an owner during the period following the postponement.

[T.D. 6500, 25 FR 11814, Nov. 26, 1960]

§ 1.677(a)–1 Income for benefit of grantor; general rule.

(a)(1) Scope. Section 677 deals with the treatment of the grantor of a trust as the owner of a portion of the trust because he has retained an interest in the income from that portion. For convenience, "grantor" and "spouse" are generally referred to in the masculine and feminine genders, respectively, but if the grantor is a woman the

reference to "grantor" is to her and the reference to "spouse" is to her husband. Section 677 also deals with the treatment of the grantor of a trust as the owner of a portion of the trust because the income from property transferred in trust after October 9, 1969, is, or may be, distributed to his spouse or applied to the payment of premiums on policies of insurance on the life of his spouse. However, section 677 does not apply when the income of a trust is taxable to a grantor's spouse under section 71 (relating to alimony and separate maintenance payments) or section 682 (relating to income of an estate or trust in case of divorce, etc.). See section 671–1(b).

* * *

(b) Income for benefit of grantor or his spouse; general rule—(1) Property transferred in trust prior to October 10, 1969. * * *

(2) Property transferred in trust after October 9, 1969. With respect to property transferred in trust after October 9, 1969, the grantor is treated, under section 677, in any taxable year as the owner (whether or not he is treated as an owner under section 674) of a portion of a trust of which the income for the taxable year or for a period not within the exception described in paragraph (e) of this section is, or in the discretion of the grantor, or his spouse, or a nonadverse party, or any combination thereof (without the approval or consent of any adverse party other than the grantor's spouse) may be:

(i) Distributed to the grantor or the grantor's spouse;

(ii) Held or accumulated for future distribution to the grantor or the grantor's spouse; or

(iii) Applied to the payment of premiums on policies of insurance on the life of the grantor or the grantor's spouse, except policies of insurance irrevocably payable for a charitable purpose specified in section 170(c).

With respect to the treatment of a grantor as the owner of a portion of a trust solely because its income is, or may be, distributed or held or accumulated for future distribution to a beneficiary who is his spouse or applied to the payment of premiums for insurance on the spouse's life, section 677(a) applies to the income of a trust solely during the period of the marriage of the grantor to a beneficiary. In the case of divorce or separation, see sections 71 and 682 and the regulations thereunder.

(c) Constructive distribution; cessation of interest. Under section 677 the grantor is treated as the owner of a portion of a trust if he has retained any interest which might, without the approval or consent of an adverse party, enable him to have the income from that portion distributed to him at some time either actually or constructively (subject to the exception described in paragraph (e) of this section). In the case of a transfer in trust after October 9, 1969, the grantor is also treated as the owner of a portion of a trust if he has granted or retained any interest which might, without the approval or consent of an adverse party (other than the grantor's spouse), enable his spouse to have the income from the portion at some time, whether or not within the grantor's lifetime, distributed to the spouse either actually or constructively. See paragraph (b)(2) of this section for additional rules relating to the income of a trust prior to the grantor's marriage to a beneficiary. Constructive distribution to the grantor or to his spouse includes payment on behalf of the grantor or his spouse to another in obedience to his or her direction and payment of premiums upon policies of insurance on the grantor's, or his spouse's, life (other than policies of insurance irrevocably payable for charitable purposes specified in section 170(c)). If the grantor (in the case of property transferred prior to Oct. 10, 1969) or the grantor and his spouse (in the case of property transferred after Oct. 9, 1969) are divested permanently and completely of every interest described in this paragraph, the grantor is not treated as an owner under section 677 after that divesting. The word "interest" as used in this paragraph does not include the possibility that the grantor or his spouse might receive back from a beneficiary an interest in a trust by inheritance. Further, with respect to transfers in trust prior to October 10, 1969, the word "interest" does not include the possibility that the grantor might receive back from a beneficiary an interest in a trust as a surviving spouse under a statutory right of election or a similar right.

(d) Discharge of legal obligation of grantor or his spouse. Under section 677 a grantor is, in general, treated as the owner of a portion of a trust whose income is, or in the discretion of the grantor or a nonadverse party, or both, may be applied in discharge of a legal obligation of the grantor (or his spouse in the case of property transferred in trust by the grantor after October 9, 1969). However, see § 1.677(b)–1 for special rules for trusts whose income may not be applied for the discharge of any legal obligation of the grantor or the grantor's spouse other than the support or maintenance of a beneficiary (other than the grantor's spouse) whom the grantor or grantor's spouse is legally obligated to support.

(e) Exception for certain discretionary rights affecting income. The last sentence of section 677(a) provides that a grantor shall not be treated as the owner when a discretionary right can only affect the beneficial enjoyment of the income of a trust received after a period of time during which a grantor would not be treated as an owner under section 673 if the power were a reversionary interest. See §§ 1.673(a)–1 and 1.673(b)–1. For example, if the ordinary income of a trust is payable to B for 10 years and then in the grantor's discretion income or corpus may be paid to B or to the grantor (or his spouse in the case of property transferred in trust by the grantor after October 9, 1969), the grantor is not treated as an owner with respect to the ordinary income under section 677 during the first 10 years. He will be treated as an owner under section 677 after the expiration of the 10-year period unless the power is relinquished. If the beginning of the period during which the grantor may substitute beneficiaries is postponed, the rules set forth in § 1.673(d)–1 are applicable in determining whether the grantor should be treated as an owner during the period following the postponement.

(f) Accumulation of income. If income is accumulated in any taxable year for future distribution to the grantor (or his spouse in the case of property transferred in trust by the grantor after Oct. 9, 1969), section 677(a)(2) treats the grantor as an owner for that taxable year. The exception set forth in the last sentence of section 677(a) does not apply merely because the grantor (or his spouse in the case of property transferred in trust by the grantor after Oct. 9, 1969) must await the expiration of a period of time before he or she can receive or exercise discretion over previously accumulated income of the trust, even though the period is such that the grantor would not be treated as an owner under section 673 if a reversionary interest were involved. Thus, if income (including capital gains) of a trust is to be accumulated for 10 years and then will be, or at the discretion of the grantor, or his spouse in the case of property transferred in trust after October 9, 1969, or a nonadverse party, may be, distributed to the grantor (or his spouse in the case of property transferred in trust after Oct. 9, 1969), the grantor is treated as the owner of the trust from its inception. If income attributable to transfers after October 9, 1969 is accumulated in any taxable year during the grantor's lifetime for future distribution to his spouse, section 677(a)(2) treats the grantor as an owner for that taxable year even though his spouse may not receive or exercise discretion over such income prior to the grantor's death.

(g) Examples. The application of section 677(a) may be illustrated by the following examples:

Example (1). G creates an irrevocable trust which provides that the ordinary income is to be payable to him for life and that on his death the corpus shall be distributed to B, an unrelated person. Except for the right to receive income, G retains no right or power which would cause him to be treated as an owner under sections 671 through 677. Under the applicable local law capital gains must be applied to corpus. During the taxable year 1970 the trust has the following items of gross income and deductions:

Dividends	$5,000
Capital gain	1,000
Expenses allocable to income	200
Expenses allocable to corpus	100

Since G has a right to receive income he is treated as an owner of a portion of the trust under section 677. Accordingly, he should include the $5,000 of dividends, $200 income expense, and $100 corpus expense in the computation of his taxable income for 1970. He should not include the $1,000 capital gain since that is not attributable to the portion of the trust that he owns. See § 1.671-3(b). The tax consequences of the capital gain are governed by the provisions of subparts A, B, C, and D (section 641 and following), part I, subchapter J, chapter 1 of the Code. Had the trust sustained a capital loss in any amount the loss would likewise not be included in the computation of G's taxable income, but would also be governed by the provisions of such subparts.

Example (2). G creates a trust which provides that the ordinary income is payable to his adult son. Ten years and one day from the date of transfer or on the death of his son, whichever is earlier, corpus is to revert to G. In addition, G retains a discretionary right to receive $5,000 of ordinary income each year. (Absent the exercise of this right all the ordinary income is to be distributed to his son.) G retained no other right or power which would cause him to be treated as an owner under subpart E (section 671 and following). Under the terms of the trust instrument and applicable local law capital gains must be applied to corpus. During the taxable year 1970 the trust had the following items of income and deductions:

Dividends	$10,000
Capital gain	2,000
Expenses allocable to income	400
Expenses allocable to corpus	200

Since the capital gain is held or accumulated for future distributions to G, he is treated under section 677(a)(2) as an owner of a portion of the trust to which the gain is attributable. See § 1.671-3(b).

Therefore, he must include the capital gain in the computation of his taxable income. (Had the trust sustained a capital loss in any amount, G would likewise include that loss in the computation of his taxable income.) In addition, because of G's discretionary right (whether exercised or not) he is treated as the owner of a portion of the trust which will permit a distribution of income to him of $5,000. Accordingly, G includes dividends of $5,208.33 and income expenses of $208.33 in computing his taxable income, determined in the following manner:

Total dividends	$10,000.00
Less: Expenses allocable to income	400.00
Distributable income of the trust	9,600.00
Portion of dividends attributable to G (5,000 /9,600 × $10,000)	5,208.33
Portion of income expenses attributable to G (5,000/9,600 × $400)	208.33
Amount of income subject to discretionary right	5,000.00

In accordance with § 1.671-3(c), G also takes into account $104.17 (5,000/9,600 × $200) of corpus expenses in computing his tax liability. The portion of the dividends and expenses of the trust not attributable to G are governed by the provisions of Subparts A through D.

[T.D. 6500, 25 FR 11814, Nov. 26, 1960, as amended by T.D. 7148, 36 FR 20750, Oct. 29, 1971]

§ 1.677(b)-1 Trusts for support.

(a) Section 677(b) provides that a grantor is not treated as the owner of a trust merely because its income may in the discretion of any person other than the grantor (except when he is acting as trustee or cotrustee) be applied or distributed for the support or maintenance of a beneficiary (other than the grantor's spouse in the case of income from property transferred in trust after October 9, 1969), such as the child of the grantor, whom the grantor or his spouse is legally obligated to support. If income of the current year of the trust is actually so applied or distributed the grantor may be treated as the owner of any portion of the trust under section 677 to that extent, even though it might have been applied or distributed for other purposes. In the case of property transferred to a trust before October 10, 1969, for the benefit of the grantor's spouse, the grantor may be treated as the owner to the extent income of the current year is actually applied for the support or maintenance of his spouse.

(b) If any amount applied or distributed for the support of a beneficiary, including the grantor's spouse in the case of property transferred in trust before October 10, 1969, whom the grantor is legally obligated to support is paid out of corpus or out of income other than income of the current year, the grantor is treated as a beneficiary of the trust, and the amount applied or distributed is considered to be an amount paid within the meaning of section 661(a)(2), taxable to the grantor under section 662. Thus, he is subject to the other relevant portions of subparts A through D (section 641 and following), part I, subchapter J, chapter 1 of the Code. Accordingly, the grantor may be taxed on an accumulation distribution or a capital gain distribution under subpart D (section 665 and following) of such part I. Those provisions are applied on the basis that the grantor is the beneficiary.

(c) For the purpose of determining the items of income, deduction, and credit of a trust to be included under this section in computing the grantor's tax liability, the income of the trust for the taxable year of distribution will be deemed to have been first distributed. For example, in the case of a trust reporting on the calendar year basis, a distribution made on January 1, 1956, will be deemed to have been made out of ordinary income of the trust for the calendar year 1956 to the extent of the income for that year even though the trust had received no income as of January 1, 1956. Thus, if a distribution of $10,000 is made on January 1, 1956, for the support of the grantor's dependent, the grantor will be treated as the owner of the trust for 1956 to that extent. If the trust received dividends of $5,000 and incurred expenses of $1,000 during that year but subsequent to January 1, he will take into account dividends of $5,000 and expenses of $1,000 in computing his tax liability for 1956. In addition, the grantor will be treated as a beneficiary of the trust with respect to the $6,000 ($10,000 less distributable income of $4,000 (dividends of $5,000 less expenses of $1,000)) paid out of corpus or out of other than income of the current year. See paragraph (b) of this section.

(d) The exception provided in section 677(b) relates solely to the satisfaction of the grantor's legal obligation to support or maintain a beneficiary. Consequently, the general rule of section 677(a) is applicable when in the discretion of the grantor or nonadverse parties income of a trust may be applied in discharge of a grantor's obligations other than his obligation of support or maintenance falling within section 677(b). Thus, if the grantor creates a trust the income of which may in the discretion of a nonadverse party be applied in the payment of the grantor's debts, such as the payment of his rent or other household expenses, he is treated as an owner of the trust regardless of whether the income is actually so applied.

(e) The general rule of section 677(a), and not section 677(b), is applicable if discretion to apply or distribute income of a trust rests solely in the grantor, or in the grantor in conjunction with other persons, unless in either case the grantor has such discretion as trustee or cotrustee.

(f) The general rule of section 677(a), and not section 677(b), is applicable to the extent that income is required, without any discretionary determination, to be applied to the support of a beneficiary whom the grantor is legally obligated to support.

[T.D. 6500, 25 FR 11814, Nov. 26, 1960, as amended by T.D. 7148, 36 FR 20750, Oct. 29, 1971]

§ 1.678(a)–1 Person other than grantor treated as substantial owner; general rule.

(a) Where a person other than the grantor of a trust has a power exercisable solely by himself to vest the corpus or the income of any portion of a testamentary or inter vivos trust in himself, he is treated under section 678(a) as the owner of that portion, except as provided in section 678(b) (involving taxation of the grantor) and section 678(c) (involving an obligation of support). The holder of such a power also is treated as an owner of the trust even though he has partially released or otherwise modified the power so that he can no longer vest the corpus or income in himself, if he has retained such control of the trust as would, if retained by a grantor, subject the grantor to treatment as the owner under sections 671 to 677, inclusive. See section 671 and §§ 1.671–2 and 1.671–3 for rules for treatment of items of income, deduction, and credit where a person is treated as the owner of all or only a portion of a trust.

(b) Section 678(a) treats a person as an owner of a trust if he has a power exercisable solely by himself to apply the income or corpus for the satisfaction of his legal obligations, other than an obligation to support a dependent (see § 1.678(c)–1 subject to the limitation of section 678(b)). Section 678 does not apply if the power is not exercisable solely by himself. However, see § 1.662(a)–4 for principles applicable to income of a trust which, pursuant to the terms of the trust instrument, is used to satisfy the obligations of a person other than the grantor.

[T.D. 6500, 25 FR 11814, Nov. 26, 1960]

§ 1.678(b)–1 If grantor is treated as the owner.

Section 678(a) does not apply with respect to a power over income, as originally granted or thereafter modified, if the grantor of the trust is treated as the owner under sections 671 to 677, inclusive.

[T.D. 6500, 25 FR 11814, Nov. 26, 1960]

§ 1.678(c)–1 Trusts for support.

(a) Section 678(a) does not apply to a power which enables the holder, in the capacity of trustee or cotrustee, to apply the income of the trust to the support or maintenance of a person whom the holder is obligated to support, except to the extent the income is so applied. See paragraphs (a), (b), and (c) of § 1.677(b)–1 for applicable principles where any amount is applied for the support or maintenance of a person whom the holder is obligated to support.

(b) The general rule in section 678(a) (and not the exception in section 678(c)) is applicable in any case in which the holder of a power exercisable solely by himself is able, in any capacity other than that of trustee or cotrustee, to apply the income in discharge of his obligation of support or maintenance.

(c) Section 678(c) is concerned with the taxability of income subject to a power described in section 678(a). It has no application to the taxability of income which is either required to be applied pursuant to the terms of the trust instrument or is applied pursuant to a power which is not described in section 678(a), the taxability of such income being governed by other provisions of the Code. See § 1.662(a)–4.

[T.D. 6500, 25 FR 11814, Nov. 26, 1960]

Income in Respect of Decedents

§ 1.691(a)–1 Income in respect of a decedent.

(a) **Scope of section 691.** In general, the regulations under section 691 cover: (1) The provisions requiring that amounts which are not includible in gross income for the decedent's last taxable year or for a prior taxable year be included in the gross income of the estate or persons receiving such income to the extent that such amounts constitute "income in respect of a decedent"; (2) the taxable effect of a transfer of the right to such income; (3) the treatment of certain deductions and credit in respect of a decedent which are not allowable to the decedent for the taxable period ending with his death or for a prior taxable year; (4) the allowance to a recipient of income in respect of a decedent of a deduction for estate taxes attributable to the inclusion of the value of the right to such income in the decedent's estate; (5) special provisions with respect to installment obligations acquired from a decedent and with respect to the allowance of a deduction for estate taxes to a surviving annuitant under a joint and survivor annuity contract; and (6) special provisions relating to installment obligations transmitted at death when prior law applied to the transmission.

(b) **General definition.** In general, the term "income in respect of a decedent" refers to those amounts to which a decedent was entitled as gross income but which were not properly includible in computing his taxable income for the taxable year ending with the date of his death or for a previous

taxable year under the method of accounting employed by the decedent. See the regulations under section 451. Thus, the term includes—

(1) All accrued income of a decedent who reported his income by use of the cash receipts and disbursements method;

(2) Income accrued solely by reason of the decedent's death in case of a decedent who reports his income by use of an accrual method of accounting; and

(3) Income to which the decedent had a contingent claim at the time of his death.

See sections 736 and 753 and the regulations thereunder for "income in respect of a decedent" in the case of a deceased partner.

(c) **Prior decedent.** The term "income in respect of a decedent" also includes the amount of all items of gross income in respect of a prior decedent, if (1) the right to receive such amount was acquired by the decedent by reason of the death of the prior decedent or by bequest, devise, or inheritance from the prior decedent and if (2) the amount of gross income in respect of the prior decedent was not properly includible in computing the decedent's taxable income for the taxable year ending with the date of his death or for a previous taxable year. See example (2) of paragraph (b) of § 1.691(a)–2.

(d) Items excluded from gross income. Section 691 applies only to the amount of items of gross income in respect of a decedent, and items which are excluded from gross income under subtitle A of the Code are not within the provisions of section 691.

* * *

[T.D. 6500, 25 FR 11814, Nov. 26, 1960, as amended by T.D. 6808, 30 FR 3435, March 16, 1965]

§ 1.691(a)-2　Inclusion in gross income by recipients.

(a) Under section 691(a)(1), income in respect of a decedent shall be included in the gross income, for the taxable year when received, of—

(1) The estate of the decedent, if the right to receive the amount is acquired by the decedent's estate from the decedent;

(2) The person who, by reason of the death of the decedent, acquires the right to receive the amount, if the right to receive the amount is not acquired by the decedent's estate from the decedent; or

(3) The person who acquires from the decedent the right to receive the amount by bequest, devise, or inheritance, if the amount is received after a distribution by the decedent's estate of such right.

These amounts are included in the income of the estate or of such persons when received by them whether or not they report income by use of the cash receipts and disbursements methods.

(b) The application of paragraph (a) of this section may be illustrated by the following examples, in each of which it is assumed that the decedent kept his books by use of the cash receipts and disbursements method.

Example (1). The decedent was entitled at the date of his death to a large salary payment to be made in equal annual installments over five years. His estate, after collecting two installments, distributed the right to the remaining installment payments to the residuary legatee of the estate. The estate must include in its gross income the two installments received by it, and the legatee must include in his gross income each of the three installments received by him.

Example (2). A widow acquired, by bequest from her husband, the right to receive renewal commissions on life insurance sold by him in his lifetime, which commissions were payable over a period of years. The widow died before having received all of such commissions, and her son inherited the right to receive the rest of the commissions. The commissions received by the widow were includible in her gross income. The commissions received by the son were not includible in the widow's gross income but must be included in the gross income of the son.

Example (3). The decedent owned a Series E United States savings bond, with his wife as co-owner or beneficiary, but died before the payment of such bond. The entire amount of interest accruing on the bond and not includible in income by the decedent, not just the amount accruing after the death of the decedent, would be treated as income to his wife when the bond is paid.

Example (4). A, prior to his death, acquired 10,000 shares of the capital stock of the X Corporation at a cost of $100 per share. During his lifetime, A had entered into an agreement with X Corporation whereby X Corporation agreed to purchase and the decedent agreed that his executor would sell the 10,000 shares of X Corporation stock owned by him at the book value of the stock at the date of A's death. Upon A's death, the shares are sold by A's executor for $500 a share pursuant to the agreement. Since the sale of stock is consummated after A's death, there is no income in respect of a decedent with respect to the appreciation in value of A's stock to the date of his death. If, in this example, A had in fact sold the stock during his lifetime but payment had not been received before his death, any gain on the sale would constitute income in respect of a decedent when the proceeds were received.

* * *

[T.D. 6500, 25 FR 11814, Nov. 26, 1960]

§ 1.691(a)-3　Character of gross income.

(a) The right to receive an amount of income in respect of a decedent shall be treated in the hands of the estate, or by the person entitled to receive such amount by bequest, devise, or inheritance from the decedent or by reason of his death, as if it had been acquired in the transaction by which the decedent (or a prior decedent) acquired such right, and shall be considered as having the same character it would have had if the decedent (or a prior decedent) had lived and received such amount. The provisions of section 1014(a), relating to the basis of property acquired from a decedent, do not apply to these amounts in the hands of the estate and such persons. See section 1014(c).

* * *

[T.D. 6500, 25 FR 11814, Nov. 26, 1960, as amended by T.D. 6885, 31 FR 7803, June 2, 1966; T.D. 7728, 45 FR 72650, Nov. 3, 1980]

§ 1.691(a)-4　Transfer of right to income in respect of a decedent.

(a) Section 691(a)(2) provides the rules governing the treatment of income in respect of a decedent (or a prior decedent) in the event a right to receive such income is transferred by the estate or person entitled thereto by bequest, devise, or inheritance, or by reason of the death of the decedent. In general, the transferor must include in his gross income for the taxable period in which the transfer occurs the amount of the consideration, if any, received for the right or the fair market value of the right at the time of the transfer, whichever is greater. Thus, upon a sale of such right by the estate or person entitled to receive it, the fair market value of the right or the amount received upon the sale, whichever is greater, is included in the gross income of the vendor. Similarly, if such right is disposed of by gift, the fair market value of the right at the time of the gift must be included in the gross income of the donor. In the case of a satisfaction of an installment obligation at other than face value, which is likewise considered a transfer under section 691(a)(2), see § 1.691(a)–5.

(b) If the estate of a decedent or any person transmits the right to income in respect of a decedent to another who would be required by section 691(a)(1) to include such income when received in his gross income, only the transferee will include such income when received in his gross income. In this situation, a transfer within the meaning of section 691(a)(2) has not occurred. This paragraph may be illustrated by the following:

(1) If a person entitled to income in respect of a decedent dies before receiving such income, only his estate or other person entitled to such income by bequest, devise, or inheritance from the latter decedent, or by reason of the death of the latter decedent, must include such amount in gross income when received.

(2) If a right to income in respect of a decedent is transferred by an estate to a specific or residuary legatee, only the specific or residuary legatee must include such income in gross income when received.

(3) If a trust to which is bequeathed a right of a decedent to certain payments of income terminates and transfers the right to a beneficiary, only the beneficiary must include such income in gross income when received.

If the transferee described in subparagraphs (1), (2), and (3) of this paragraph transfers his right to receive the amounts in the manner described in paragraph (a) of this section, the principles contained in paragraph (a) are applied to such transfer. On the other hand, if the transferee transmits his right in the manner described in this para-

graph, the principles of this paragraph are again applied to such transfer.

[T.D. 6500, 25 FR 11814, Nov. 26, 1960]

§ 1.691(b)–1 Allowance of deductions and credit in respect to decedents.

(a) Under section 691(b) the expenses, interest, and taxes described in sections 162, 163, 164, and 212 for which the decedent (or a prior decedent) was liable, which were not properly allowable as a deduction in his last taxable year or any prior taxable year, are allowed when paid—

(1) As a deduction by the estate; or

(2) If the estate was not liable to pay such obligation, as a deduction by the person who by bequest, devise, or inheritance from the decedent or by reason of the death of the decedent acquires, subject to such obligation, an interest in property of the decedent (or the prior decedent).

Similar treatment is given to the foreign tax credit provided by section 33. For the purposes of subparagraph (2) of this paragraph, the right to receive an amount of gross income in respect of a decedent is considered property of the decedent; on the other hand, it is not necessary for a person, otherwise within the provisions of subparagraph (2) of this paragraph, to receive the right to any income in respect of a decedent. Thus, an heir who receives a right to income in respect of a decedent (by reason of the death of the decedent) subject to any income tax imposed by a foreign country during the decedent's life, which tax must be satisfied out of such income, is entitled to the credit provided by section 33 when he pays the tax. If a decedent who reported income by use of the cash receipts and disbursements method owned real property on which accrued taxes had become a lien, and if such property passed directly to the heir of the decedent in a jurisdiction in which real property does not become a part of a decedent's estate, the heir, upon paying such taxes, may take the same deduction under section 164 that would be allowed to the decedent if, while alive, he had made such payment.

(b) The deduction for percentage depletion is allowable only to the person (described in section 691(a)(1)) who receives the income in respect of the decedent to which the deduction relates, whether or not such person receives the property from which such income is derived. Thus, an heir who (by reason of the decedent's death) receives income derived from sales of units of mineral by the decedent (who reported income by use of the cash receipts and disbursements method) shall be allowed the deduction for percentage depletion, computed on the gross income from such number of units as if the heir had the same economic interest in the property as the decedent. Such heir need not also receive any interest in the mineral property other than such income. If the decedent did not compute his deduction for depletion on the basis of percentage depletion, any deduction for depletion to which the decedent was entitled at the date of his death would be allowable in computing his taxable income for his last taxable year, and there can be no deduction in respect of the decedent by any other person for such depletion.

[T.D. 6500, 25 FR 11814, Nov. 26, 1960]

* * *

PARTNERS AND PARTNERSHIPS

Determination of Tax Liability

§ 1.701–1 Partners, not partnership, subject to tax.

Partners are liable for income tax only in their separate capacities. Partnerships as such are not subject to the income tax imposed by subtitle A but are required to make returns of income under the provisions of section 6031 and the regulations thereunder. For definition of the terms "partner" and "partnership", see sections 761 and 7701(a)(2), and the regulations thereunder. For provisions relating to the election of certain partnerships to be taxed as domestic corporations, see section 1361 and the regulations thereunder.

[T.D. 6500, 25 FR 11814, Nov. 26, 1960]

§ 1.702–1 Income and credits of partner.

(a) **General rule.** Each partner is required to take into account separately in his return his distributive share, whether or not distributed, of each class or item of partnership income, gain, loss, deduction, or credit described in subparagraphs (1) through (9) of this paragraph. (For the taxable year in which a partner includes his distributive share of partnership taxable income, see section 706(a) and § 1.706–1(a). Such distributive share shall be determined as provided in section 704 and § 1.704–1.) Accordingly, in determining his income tax:

(1) Each partner shall take into account, as part of his gains and losses from sales or exchanges of capital assets held for not more than 1 year (6 months for taxable years beginning before 1977; 9 months for taxable years beginning in 1977), his distributive share of the combined net amount of such gains and losses of the partnership.

(2) Each partner shall take into account, as part of his gains and losses from sales or exchanges of capital assets held for more than 1 year (6 months for taxable years beginning before 1977; 9 months for taxable years beginning in 1977), his distributive share of the combined net amount of such gains and losses of the partnership.

(3) Each partner shall take into account, as part of his gains and losses from sales or exchanges of property described in section 1231 (relating to property used in the trade or business and involuntary conversions), his distributive share of the combined net amount of such gains and losses of the partnership. The partnership shall not combine such items with items set forth in subparagraph (1) or (2) of this paragraph.

(4) Each partner shall take into account, as part of the charitable contributions paid by him, his distributive share of each class of charitable contributions paid by the partnership within the partnership's taxable year. Section 170 determines the extent to which such amount may be allowed as a deduction to the partner. For the definition of the term "charitable contribution", see section 170(c).

(5) Each partner shall take into account, as part of the dividends received by him from domestic corporations, his distributive share of dividends received by the partnership, with respect to which the partner is entitled to a credit under section 34 (for dividends received on or before December 31, 1964), an exclusion under section 116, or a deduction under part VIII, subchapter B, chapter 1 of the Code.

* * *

(8)(i) Each partner shall take into account separately, as part of any class of income, gain, loss, deduction, or credit, his distributive share of the following items: Recoveries of bad debts, prior taxes, and delinquency amounts (section 111); gains and losses from wagering transactions (section 165(d)); soil and water conservation expenditures (section 175); nonbusiness expenses as described in section 212; medical, dental, etc., expenses (section 213); expenses for care of certain dependents (section 214); alimony, etc., payments (section 215); amounts representing taxes and interest paid to cooperative housing corporations (section 216); intangible drilling and developments costs (section 263(c)); pre-1970 exploration expenditures (section 615); certain mining exploration expenditures (section 617); income, gain, or loss to the partnership under section 751(b); and any items of income, gain, loss, deduction, or credit subject to a special allocation under the partnership agreement which differs from the allocation of partnership taxable income or loss generally.

(ii) Each partner must also take into account separately his distributive share of any partnership item which if separately taken into account by any partner would result in an income tax liability for that partner different from that which would result if that partner did not take the item into account separately. Thus, if any partner would qualify for the retirement income credit under section 37 if the partnership pensions and annuities, interest, rents, dividends, and earned income were separately stated, such items must be separately stated for all partners. Under section 911(a), if any partner is a bona fide resident of a foreign country who may exclude from his gross income the part of his distributive share which qualifies as earned income as defined in section 911(b), the earned income of the partnership for all partners must be separately stated. Similarly, all relevant items of income or deduction of the partnership must be separately stated for all partners in determining the applicability of section 270 (relating to "hobby losses") and the recomputation of tax thereunder for any partner.

(iii) Each partner shall aggregate the amount of his separate deductions or exclusions and his distributive share of partnership deductions or exclusions separately stated in determining the amount allowable to him of any deduction or exclusion under subtitle A of the Code as to which a limitation is imposed. For example, partner A has individual domestic exploration expenditures of $300,000. He is also a member of the AB partnership which in 1971 in its first year of operation has foreign exploration expenditures of $400,000. A's distributable share of this item is $200,000. How-

ever, the total amount of his distributable share that A can deduct as exploration expenditures under section 617(a) is limited to $100,000 in view of the limitation provided in section 617(h). Therefore, the excess of $100,000 ($200,000 minus $100,000) is not deductible by A.

(9) Each partner shall also take into account separately his distributive share of the taxable income or loss of the partnership, exclusive of items requiring separate computations under subparagraphs (1) through (8) of this paragraph. For limitation on allowance of a partner's distributive share of partnership losses, see section 704(d) and paragraph (d) of § 1.704-1.

(b) **Character of items constituting distributive share.** The character in the hands of a partner of any item of income, gain, loss, deduction, or credit described in section 702(a)(1) through (8) shall be determined as if such item were realized directly from the source from which realized by the partnership or incurred in the same manner as incurred by the partnership. For example, a partner's distributive share of gain from the sale of depreciable property used in the trade or business of the partnership shall be considered as gain from the sale of such depreciable property in the hands of the partner. Similarly, a partner's distributive share of partnership "hobby losses" (section 270) or his distributive share of partnership charitable contributions to organizations qualifying under section 170(b)(1)(A) retains such character in the hands of the partner.

(c) **Gross income of a partner.** (1) Where it is necessary to determine the amount or character of the gross income of a partner, his gross income shall include the partner's distributive share of the gross income of the partnership, that is, the amount of gross income of the partnership from which was derived the partner's distributive share of partnership taxable income or loss (including items described in section 702(a)(1) through (8)). For example, a partner is required to include his distributive share of partnership gross income:

(i) In computing his gross income for the purpose of determining the necessity of filing a return (section 6012 (a));

(ii) In determining the application of the provisions permitting the spreading of income for services rendered over a 36-month period (section 1301, as in effect for taxable years beginning before January 1, 1964);

(iii) In computing the amount of gross income received from sources within possessions of the United States (section 931); and

(iv) In determining a partner's "gross income from farming" (sections 175 and 6073).

(2) In determining the applicability of the 6-year period of limitation on assessment and collection provided in section 6501(e) (relating to omission of more than 25 percent of gross income), a partner's gross income includes his distributive share of partnership gross income (as described in section 6501(e)(1)(A)(i)). In this respect, the amount of partnership gross income from which was derived the partner's distributive share of any item of partnership income, gain, loss, deduction, or credit (as included or disclosed in the partner's return) is considered as an amount of gross income stated in the partner's return for the purposes of section 6501(e). For example, A, who is entitled to one-fourth of the profits of the ABCD partnership, which has $10,000 gross income and $2,000 taxable income, reports only $300 as his distributive share of partnership profits. A should have shown $500 as his distributive share of profits, which amount was derived from $2,500 of partnership gross income. However, since A included only $300 on his return without explaining in the return the difference of $200, he is regarded as having stated in his return only $1,500 ($300/$500 of $2,500) as gross income from the partnership.

(d) **Partners in community property States.** If separate returns are made by a husband and wife domiciled in a community property State, and only one spouse is a member of the partnership, the part of his or her distributive share of any item or items listed in paragraph (a)(1) through (9) of this section which is community property, or which is derived from community property, should be reported by the husband and wife in equal proportions.

* * *

[T.D. 6500, 25 FR 11814, Nov. 26, 1960, as amended by T.D. 6605, 27 FR 8097, Aug. 15, 1962; T.D. 6777, 29 FR 17809, Dec. 16, 1964; T.D. 6885, 31 FR 7803, June 2, 1966; T.D. 7192, 37 FR 12949, June 30, 1972; T.D. 7564, 43 FR 40496, Sept. 12, 1978; T.D. 7728, 45 FR 72650, Nov. 3, 1980]

§ 1.702-2 Net operating loss deduction of partner.

For the purpose of determining a net operating loss deduction under section 172, a partner shall

take into account his distributive share of items of income, gain, loss, deduction, or credit of the partnership. The character of any such item shall be determined as if such item were realized directly from the source from which realized by the partnership, or incurred in the same manner as incurred by the partnership. See section 702(b) and paragraph (b) of § 1.702-1. To the extent necessary to determine the allowance under section 172(d)(4) of the nonbusiness deductions of a partner (arising from both partnership and nonpartnership sources), the partner shall separately take into account his distributive share of the deductions of the partnership which are not attributable to a trade or business and combine such amount with his nonbusiness deductions from nonpartnership sources. Such partner shall also separately take into account his distributive share of the gross income of the partnership not derived from a trade or business and combine such amount with his nonbusiness income from nonpartnership sources. See section 172 and the regulations thereunder.

[T.D. 6500, 25 FR 11814, Nov. 26, 1960]

§ 1.703-1 Partnership computations.

(a) **Income and deductions.** (1) The taxable income of a partnership shall be computed in the same manner as the taxable income of an individual, except as otherwise provided in this section. A partnership is required to state separately in its return the items described in section 702(a)(1) through (7) and, in addition, to attach to its return a statement setting forth separately those items described in section 702(a)(8) which the partner is required to take into account separately in determining his income tax. See paragraph (a)(8) of § 1.702-1. The partnership is further required to compute and to state separately in its return:

(i) As taxable income under section 702(a)(9), the total of all other items of gross income (not separately stated) over the total of all other allowable deductions (not separately stated), or

(ii) As loss under section 702(a)(9), the total of all other allowable deductions (not separately stated) over the total of all other items of gross income (not separately stated).

The taxable income or loss so computed shall be accounted for by the partners in accordance with their partnership agreement.

(2) The partnership is not allowed the following deductions:

(i) The standard deduction provided in section 141.

(ii) The deduction for personal exemptions provided in section 151.

(iii) The deduction provided in section 164(a) for taxes, described in section 901, paid or accrued to foreign countries or possessions of the United States. Each partner's distributive share of such taxes shall be accounted for separately by him as provided in section 702(a)(6).

(iv) The deduction for charitable contributions provided in section 170. Each partner is considered as having paid within his taxable year his distributive share of any contribution or gift, payment of which was actually made by the partnership within its taxable year ending within or with the partner's taxable year. This item shall be accounted for separately by the partners as provided in section 702(a)(4). See also paragraph (b) of § 1.702–1.

(v) The net operating loss deduction provided in section 172. See § 1.702–2.

(vi) The additional itemized deductions for individuals provided in part VII, subchapter B, chapter 1 of the Code, as follows: Expenses for production of income (section 212); medical, dental, etc., expenses (section 213); expenses for care of certain dependents (section 214); alimony, etc., payments (section 215); and amounts representing taxes and interest paid to cooperative housing corporation (section 216). However, see paragraph (a)(8) of § 1.702–1.

(vii) The deduction for capital gains provided by section 1202 and the deduction for capital loss carryover provided by section 1212.

(b) **Elections of the partnership—(1) General rule.** Any elections (other than those described in subparagraph (2) of this paragraph) affecting the computation of income derived from a partnership shall be made by the partnership. For example, elections of methods of accounting, of computing depreciation, of treating soil and water conservation expenditures, and the option to deduct as expenses intangible drilling and development costs, shall be made by the partnership and not by the partners separately. All partnership elections are applicable to all partners equally, but any election made by a partnership shall not apply to any partner's nonpartnership interests.

* * *

[T.D. 6500, 25 FR 11814, Nov. 26, 1960, as amended by T.D. 7192, 37 FR 12949, June 30, 1972; T.D. 7332, 39 FR 44232, Dec. 23, 1974]

§ 1.704–1 Partner's distributive share.

(a) **Effect of partnership agreement.** A partner's distributive share of any item or class of items of income, gain, loss, deduction, or credit of the partnership shall be determined by the partnership agreement, unless otherwise provided by section 704 and paragraphs (b) through (e) of this section. For definition of partnership agreement see section 761(c).

(b) **Determination of partner's distributive share—(0) Cross-references.**

Heading	Section
Cross-references	1.704–1(b)(0)
In general	1.704–1(b)(1)
Basic principles	1.704–1(b)(1)(i)
Effective dates	1.704–1(b)(1)(ii)
Effect of other sections	1.704–1(b)(1)(iii)
Other possible tax consequences	1.704–1(b)(1)(iv)
Purported allocations	1.704–1(b)(1)(v)
Section 704(c) determinations	1.704–1(b)(1)(vi)
Bottom line allocations	1.704–1(b)(1)(vii)
Substantial economic effect	1.704–1(b)(2)
Two-part analysis	1.704–1(b)(2)(i)
Economic effect	1.704–1(b)(2)(ii)
Fundamental principles	1.704–1(b)(2)(ii)(a)
Three requirements	1.704–1(b)(2)(ii)(b)
Obligation to restore deficit	1.704–1(b)(2)(ii)(c)
Alternate test for economic effect	1.704–1(b)(2)(ii)(d)
Partial economic effect	1.704–1(b)(2)(ii)(e)
Reduction of obligation to restore	1.704–1(b)(2)(ii)(f)
Liquidation defined	1.704–1(b)(2)(ii)(g)
Partnership agreement defined	1.704–1(b)(2)(ii)(h)
Economic effect equivalence	1.704–1(b)(2)(ii)(i)
Substantiality	1.704–1(b)(2)(iii)
General rules	1.704–1(b)(2)(iii)(a)
Shifting tax consequences	1.704–1(b)(2)(iii)(b)
Transitory allocations	1.704–1(b)(2)(iii)(c)
Maintenance of capital accounts	1.704–1(b)(2)(iv)
In general	1.704–1(b)(2)(iv)(a)
Basic rules	1.704–1(b)(2)(iv)(b)
Treatment of liabilities	1.704–1(b)(2)(iv)(c)
Contributed property	1.704–1(b)(2)(iv)(d)
In general	1.704–1(b)(2)(iv)(d)(1)
Contribution of promissory notes	1.704–1(b)(2)(iv)(d)(2)
Section 704(c) considerations	1.704–1(b)(2)(iv)(d)(3)
Distributed property	1.704–1(b)(2)(iv)(e)
In general	1.704–1(b)(2)(iv)(e)(1)
Distribution of promissory notes	1.704–1(b)(2)(iv)(e)(2)

(1) In general—(i) Basic principles. Under section 704(b) if a partnership agreement does not provide for the allocation of income, gain, loss, deduction, or credit (or item thereof) to a partner, or if the partnership agreement provides for the allocation of income, gain, loss, deduction, or credit (or item thereof) to a partner but such allocation does not have substantial economic effect, then the partner's distributive share of such income, gain, loss, deduction, or credit (or item thereof) shall be determined in accordance with such partner's interest in the partnership (taking into account all facts and circumstances). If the partnership agreement provides for the allocation of income, gain, loss, deduction, or credit (or item thereof) to a partner, there are three ways in which such allocation will be respected under section 704(b) and this paragraph. First, the allocation can have substantial economic effect in accordance with paragraph (b)(2) of this section. Second, taking into account all facts and circumstances, the allocation can be in accordance with the partner's interest in the partnership. See paragraph (b)(3) of this section. Third, the allocation can be deemed to be in accordance with the partner's interest in the partnership pursuant to one of the special rules contained in paragraph (b)(4) of this section. To the extent an allocation under the partnership agreement of income, gain, loss, deduction, or credit (or item thereof) to a partner does not have substantial economic effect, is not in accordance with the partner's interest in the partnership, and is not deemed to be in accordance with the partner's interest in the partnership, such income, gain, loss, deduction, or credit (or item thereof) will be reallocated in accordance with the partner's interest in the partnership (determined under paragraph (b)(3) of this section).

(ii) Effective dates. The provisions of this paragraph are effective for partnership taxable years beginning after December 31, 1975. However, for partnership taxable years beginning after December 31, 1975, but before May 1, 1986, (January 1, 1987, in the case of allocations of nonrecourse deductions as defined in paragraph (b)(4)(iv)(a) of this section) an allocation of income, gain, loss, deduction, or credit (or item thereof) to a partner that is not respected under this paragraph nevertheless will be respected under section 704(b) if such allocation has substantial economic effect or is in accordance with the partners' interests in the partnership as those terms have been interpreted under the relevant case law, the legislative history of section 210(d) of the Tax Reform Act of 1976, and the provisions of this paragraph in effect for partnership taxable years beginning before May 1, 1986.

(iii) **Effect of other sections.** The determination of a partner's distributive share of income, gain, loss, deduction, or credit (or item thereof) under section 704(b) and this paragraph is not conclusive as to the tax treatment of a partner with respect to such distributive share. For example, an allocation of loss or deduction to a partner that is respected under section 704(b) and this paragraph may not be deductible by such partner if the partner lacks the requisite motive for economic gain (see, *e.g.*, *Goldstein v. Commissioner*, 364 F.2d 734 (2d Cir.1966)), or may be disallowed for that taxable year (and held in suspense) if the limitations of section 465 or section 704(d) are applicable. Similarly, an allocation that is respected under section 704(b) and this paragraph nevertheless may be reallocated under other provisions, such as section 482, section 704(e)(2), section 706(d) (and related assignment of income principles), and paragraph (b)(2)(ii) of § 1.751-1. If a partnership has a section 754 election in effect, a partner's distributive share of partnership income, gain, loss, or deduction may be affected as provided in § 1.743-1 (see paragraph (b)(2)(iv)(m)(2) of this section). A deduction that appears to be a nonrecourse deduction deemed to be in accordance with the partners' interests in the partnership may not be such because purported nonrecourse liabilities of the partnership in fact constitute equity rather than debt. The examples in paragraph (b)(5) of this section concern the validity of allocations under section 704(b) and this paragraph and, except as noted, do not address the effect of other sections or limitations on such allocations.

(iv) **Other possible tax consequences.** Allocations that are respected under section 704(b) and this paragraph may give rise to other tax consequences, such as those resulting from the application of section 61, section 83, section 751, section 2501, paragraph (f) of § 1.46-3, § 1.47-6, para-

graph (b)(1) of § 1.721-1 (and related principles), and paragraph (e) of § 1.752-1. The examples in paragraph (b)(5) of this section concern the validity of allocations under section 704(b) and this paragraph and, except as noted, do not address other tax consequences that may result from such allocations.

(v) **Purported allocations.** Section 704(b) and this paragraph do not apply to a purported allocation if it is made to a person who is not a partner of the partnership (see section 7701(a)(2) and paragraph (d) of § 301.7701-3) or to a person who is not receiving the purported allocation in his capacity as a partner (see section 707(a) and paragraph (a) of § 1.707-1).

(vi) **Section 704(c) determinations.** Under section 704(c) if property is contributed by a partner to a partnership, the partners' distributive shares of income, gain, loss, and deduction, as computed for tax purposes, with respect to such property are determined so as to take account of the variation between the adjusted tax basis and fair market value of such property. Although section 704(b) does not directly determine the partners' distributive shares of tax items governed by section 704(c), the partners' distributive shares of tax items are determined under section 704(c) with reference to the partners' distributive shares of the corresponding book items, as determined under section 704(b) and this paragraph. (See paragraphs (b)(2)(iv)(d) and (b)(4)(i) of this section.) Section 704(c), as cited in this paragraph, refers to such section as in effect for property contributed to a partnership after March 31, 1984. See example (13)(i) of paragraph (b)(5) of this section.

(vii) **Bottom line allocations.** Section 704(b) and this paragraph are applicable to allocations of income, gain, loss, deduction, and credit, allocations of specific items of income, gain, loss, deduction, and credit, and allocations of partnership net or "bottom line" taxable income and loss. An allocation to a partner of a share of partnership net or "bottom line" taxable income or loss shall be treated as an allocation to such partner of the same share of each item of income, gain, loss, and deduction that is taken into account in computing such net or "bottom line" taxable income or loss. See example (15)(i) of paragraph (b)(5) of this section.

(2) **Substantial economic effect—(i) Two-part analysis.** The determination of whether an allocation of income, gain, loss, or deduction (or item thereof) to a partner has substantial economic ef-

fect involves a two-part analysis that is made as of the end of the partnership taxable year to which the allocation relates. First, the allocation must have economic effect (within the meaning of paragraph (b)(2)(ii) of this section). Second, the economic effect of the allocation must be substantial (within the meaning of paragraph (b)(2)(iii) of this section).

(ii) **Economic effect—(a) Fundamental principles.** In order for an allocation to have economic effect, it must be consistent with the underlying economic arrangement of the partners. This means that in the event there is an economic benefit or economic burden that corresponds to an allocation, the partner to whom the allocation is made must receive such economic benefit or bear such economic burden.

(b) **Three requirements.** Based on the principles contained in paragraph (b)(2)(ii)(a) of this section, and except as otherwise provided in this paragraph, an allocation of income, gain, loss, or deduction (or item thereof) to a partner will have economic effect if, and only if, throughout the full term of the partnership, the partnership agreement provides—

(1) For the determination and maintenance of the partners' capital accounts in accordance with the rules of paragraph (b)(2)(iv) of this section.

(2) Upon liquidation of the partnership (or any partner's interest in the partnership), liquidating distributions are required in all cases to be made in accordance with the positive capital account balances of the partners, as determined after taking into account all capital account adjustments for the partnership taxable year during which such liquidation occurs (other than those made pursuant to this requirement (2) and requirement (3) of this paragraph (b)(2)(ii)(b)), by the end of such taxable year (or, if later, within 90 days after the date of such liquidation), and

(3) If such partner has a deficit balance in his capital account following the liquidation of his interest in the partnership, as determined after taking into account all capital account adjustments for the partnership taxable year during which such liquidation occurs (other than those made pursuant to this requirement (3)), he is unconditionally obligated to restore the amount of such deficit balance to the partnership by the end of such taxable year (or, if later, within 90 days after the date of such liquidation), which amount shall, upon liquidation of the partnership, be paid to creditors of the

partnership or distributed to other partners in accordance with their positive capital account balances (in accordance with requirement (2) of this paragraph (b)(2)(ii)(b)).

For purposes of the preceding sentence, a partnership taxable year shall be determined without regard to section 706(c)(2)(A). Requirements (2) and (3) of this paragraph (b)(2)(ii)(b) are not violated if all or part of the partnership interest of one or more partners is purchased (other than in connection with the liquidation of the partnership) by the partnership or by one or more partners (or one or more persons related, within the meaning of section 267(b) (without modification by section 267(e)(1)) or section 707(b)(1), to a partner) pursuant to an agreement negotiated at arm's length by persons who at the time such agreement is entered into have materially adverse interests and if a principal purpose of such purchase and sale is not to avoid the principles of the second sentence of paragraph (b)(2)(ii)(a) of this section. In addition, requirement (2) of this paragraph (b)(2)(ii)(b) is not violated if, upon the liquidation of the partnership, the capital accounts of the partners are increased or decreased pursuant to paragraph (b)(2)(iv)(f) of this section as of the date of such liquidation and the partnership makes liquidating distributions within the time set out in that requirement (2) in the ratios of the partners' positive capital accounts, except that it does not distribute reserves reasonably required to provide for liabilities (contingent or otherwise) of the partnership and installment obligations owed to the partnership, so long as such withheld amounts are distributed as soon as practicable and in the ratios of the partners' positive capital account balances. See examples (1)(i) and (ii), (4)(i), (8)(i), and (16)(i) of paragraph (b)(5) of this section.

(c) **Obligation to restore deficit.** If a partner is not expressly obligated to restore the deficit balance in his capital account, such partner nevertheless will be treated as obligated to restore the deficit balance in his capital account (in accordance with requirement (3) of paragraph (b)(2)(ii)(b) of this section) to the extent of—

(1) The outstanding principal balance of any promissory note (of which such partner is the maker) contributed to the partnership by such partner (other than a promissory note that is readily tradable on an established securities market), and

(2) The amount of any unconditional obligation of such partner (whether imposed by the partnership agreement or by State or local law) to make

subsequent contributions to the partnership (other than pursuant to a promissory note of which such partner is the maker),

provided that such note or obligation is required to be satisfied at a time no later than the end of the partnership taxable year in which such partner's interest is liquidated (or, if later, within 90 days after the date of such liquidation). If a promissory note referred to in the previous sentence is negotiable, a partner will be considered required to satisfy such note within the time period specified in such sentence if the partnership agreement provides that, in lieu of actual satisfaction, the partnership will retain such note and such partner will contribute to the partnership the excess, if any, of the outstanding principal balance of such note over its fair market value at the time of liquidation. See paragraph (b)(2)(iv)(d)(2) of this section. See examples (1)(ix) and (x) of paragraph (b)(5) of this section. A partner in no event will be considered obligated to restore the deficit balance in his capital account to the partnership (in accordance with requirement (3) of paragraph (b)(2)(ii)(b) of this section) to the extent such partner's obligation is not legally enforceable, or the facts and circumstances otherwise indicate a plan to avoid or circumvent such obligation. See paragraphs (b)(2)(ii)(f), (b)(2)(ii)(h), and (b)(4)(vi) of this section for other rules regarding such obligation.

(d) **Alternate test for economic effect.** If—

(1) Requirements (1) and (2) of paragraph (b)(2)(ii)(b) of this section are satisfied, and

(2) The partner to whom an allocation is made is not obligated to restore the deficit balance in his capital account to the partnership (in accordance with requirement (3) of paragraph (b)(2)(ii)(b) of this section), or is obligated to restore only a limited dollar amount of such deficit balance, and

(3) The partnership agreement contains a "qualified income offset," such allocation will be considered to have economic effect under this paragraph (b)(2)(ii)(d) to the extent such allocation does not cause or increase a deficit balance in such partner's capital account (in excess of any limited dollar amount of such deficit balance that such partner is obligated to restore) as of the end of the partnership taxable year to which such allocation relates. In determining the extent to which the previous sentence is satisfied, such partner's capital account also shall be reduced for—

(4) Adjustments that, as of the end of such year, reasonably are expected to be made to such part-

ner's capital account under paragraph (b)(2)(iv)(k) of this section for depletion allowances with respect to oil and gas properties of the partnership, and

(5) Allocations of loss and deduction that, as of the end of such year, reasonably are expected to be made to such partner pursuant to section 704(e)(2), section 706(d), and paragraph (b)(2)(ii) of § 751–1, and

(6) Distributions that, as of the end of such year, reasonably are expected to be made to such partner to the extent they exceed offsetting increases to such partner's capital account that reasonably are expected to occur during (or prior to) the partnership taxable years in which such distributions reasonably are expected to be made (other than increases pursuant to a minimum gain chargebook under paragraph (b)(4)(iv)(e) of this section.)

For purposes of determining the amount of expected distributions and expected capital account increases described in (6) above, the rule set out in paragraph (b)(2)(iii)(c) of this section concerning the presumed value of partnership property shall apply. The partnership agreement contains a "qualified income offset" if, and only if, it provides that a partner who unexpectedly receives an adjustment, allocation, or distribution described in (4), (5), or (6) above, will be allocated items of income and gain (consisting of a pro rata portion of each item of partnership income, including gross income, and gain for such year) in an amount and manner sufficient to eliminate such deficit balance as quickly as possible. Allocations of items of income and gain made pursuant to the immediately preceding sentence shall be deemed to be made in accordance with the partners' interests in the partnership if requirements (1) and (2) of paragraph (b)(2)(ii)(b) of this section are satisfied. See examples (1)(iii), (iv), (v), (vi), (viii), (ix), and (x), (15), and (16)(ii) of paragraph (b)(5) of this section.

(e) **Partial economic effect.** If only a portion of an allocation made to a partner with respect to a partnership taxable year has economic effect, both the portion that has economic effect and the portion that is reallocated shall consist of a proportionate share of all items that made up the allocation to such partner for such year. See examples (15)(ii) and (iii) of paragraph (b)(5) of this section.

(f) **Reduction of obligation to restore.** If requirements (1) and (2) of paragraph (b)(2)(ii)(b) of this section are satisfied, a partner's obligation to restore the deficit balance in his capital account (or any limited dollar amount thereof) to the partnership may be eliminated or reduced as of the end of a partnership taxable year without affecting the validity of prior allocations (see paragraph (b)(4)(vi) of this section) to the extent the deficit balance (if any) in such partner's capital account, after reduction for the items described in (4), (5), and (6) of paragraph (b)(2)(ii)(d) of this section, will not exceed the partner's remaining obligation (if any) to restore the deficit balance in his capital account. See example (1)(viii) of paragraph (b)(5) of this section.

(g) Liquidation defined. For purposes of this paragraph, a liquidation of a partner's interest in the partnership occurs upon the earlier of (1) the date upon which there is a liquidation of the partnership, or (2) the date upon which there is a liquidation of the partner's interest in the partnership under paragraph (d) of § 1.761–1. For purposes of this paragraph, the liquidation of a partnership occurs upon the earlier of (3) the date upon which the partnership is terminated under section 708(b)(1), or (4) the date upon which the partnership ceases to be a going concern (even though it may continue in existence for the purpose of winding up its affairs, paying its debts, and distributing any remaining balance to its partners). Requirements (2) and (3) of paragraph (b)(2)(ii)(b) of this section will be considered unsatisfied if the liquidation of a partner's interest in the partnership is delayed after its primary business activities have been terminated (for example, by continuing to engage in a relatively minor amount of business activity, if such actions themselves do not cause the partnership to terminate pursuant to section 708(b)(1)) for a principal purpose of deferring any distribution pursuant to requirement (2) of paragraph (b)(2)(ii)(b) of this section or deferring any partner's obligations under requirement (3) of paragraph (b)(2)(ii)(b) of this section.

(h) Partnership agreement defined. For purposes of this paragraph, the partnership agreement includes all agreements among the partners, or between one or more partners and the partnership, concerning affairs of the partnership and responsibilities of partners, whether oral or written, and whether or not embodied in a document referred to by the partners as the partnership agreement. Thus, in determining whether distributions are required in all cases to be made in accordance with the partners' positive capital account balances (requirement (2) of paragraph (b)(2)(ii)(b) of this section), and in determining the extent to which a

partner is obligated to restore a deficit balance in his capital account (requirement (3) of paragraph (b)(2)(ii)(b) of this section), all arrangements among partners, or between one or more partners and the partnership relating to the partnership, direct and indirect, including puts, options, and other buy-sell agreements, and any other "stop-loss" arrangement, are considered to be part of the partnership agreement. (Thus, for example, if one partner who assumes a liability of the partnership is indemnified by another partner for a portion of such liability, the indemnifying partner (depending upon the particular facts) may be viewed as in effect having a partial deficit makeup obligation as a result of such indemnity agreement.) In addition, the partnership agreement includes provisions of Federal, State, or local law that govern the affairs of the partnership or are considered under such law to be a part of the partnership agreement (see the last sentence of paragraph (c) of § 1.761–1). For purposes of this paragraph (b)(2)(ii)(h), an agreement with a partner or a partnership shall include an agreement with a person related, within the meaning of section 267(b) (without modification by section 267(e)(1)) or section 707(b)(1), to such partner or partnership.

(i) Economic effect equivalence. Allocations made to a partner that do not otherwise have economic effect under this paragraph (b)(2)(ii) shall nevertheless be deemed to have economic effect, provided that as of the end of each partnership taxable year a liquidation of the partnership at the end of such year or at the end of any future year would produce the same economic results to the partners as would occur if requirements (1), (2), and (3) of paragraph (b)(2)(ii)(b) of this section had been satisfied, regardless of the economic performance of the partnership. See examples (4)(ii) and (iii) of paragraph (b)(5) of this section.

(iii) Substantiality—(a) General rules. Except as otherwise provided in this paragraph (b)(2)(iii), the economic effect of an allocation (or allocations) is substantial if there is a reasonable possibility that the allocation (or allocations) will affect substantially the dollar amounts to be received by the partners from the partnership, independent of tax consequences. Notwithstanding the preceding sentence, the economic effect of an allocation (or allocations) is not substantial if, at the time the allocation becomes part of the partnership agreement, (1) the after-tax economic consequences of at least one partner may, in present value terms, be enhanced compared to such consequences if the allocation (or allocations) were not contained in the partnership agreement, and (2) there is a strong likelihood that the after-tax economic consequences of no partner will, in present value terms, be substantially diminished compared to such consequences if the allocation (or allocations) were not contained in the partnership agreement. In determining the after-tax economic benefit or detriment to a partner, tax consequences that result from the interaction of the allocation with such partner's tax attributes that are unrelated to the partnership will be taken into account. See examples (5) and (9) of paragraph (b)(5) of this section. The economic effect of an allocation is not substantial in the two situations described in paragraphs (b)(2)(iii)(b) and (c) of this section. However, even if an allocation is not described therein, its economic effect may be insubstantial under the general rules stated in this paragraph (b)(2)(iii)(a). References in this paragraph (b)(2)(iii) to allocations include capital account adjustments made pursuant to paragraph (b)(2)(iv)(k) of this section.

(b) Shifting tax consequences. The economic effect of an allocation (or allocations) in a partnership taxable year is not substantial if, at the time the allocation (or allocations) becomes part of the partnership agreement, there is a strong likelihood that—

(1) The net increases and decreases that will be recorded in the partners' respective capital accounts for such taxable year will not differ substantially from the net increases and decreases that would be recorded in such partners' respective capital accounts for such year if the allocations were not contained in the partnership agreement, and

(2) The total tax liability of the partners (for their respective taxable years in which the allocations will be taken into account) will be less than if the allocations were not contained in the partnership agreement (taking into account tax consequences that result from the interaction of the allocation (or allocations) with partner tax attributes that are unrelated to the partnership).

If, at the end of a partnership taxable year to which an allocation (or allocations) relates, the net increases and decreases that are recorded in the partners' respective capital accounts do not differ substantially from the net increases and decreases that would have been recorded in such partners' respective capital accounts had the allocation (or allocations) not been contained in the partnership agreement, and the total tax liability of the part-

ners is (as described in (2) above) less than it would have been had the allocation (or allocations) not been contained in the partnership agreement, it will be presumed that, at the time the allocation (or allocations) became part of such partnership agreement, there was a strong likelihood that these results would occur. This presumption may be overcome by a showing of facts and circumstances that prove otherwise. See examples (6), (7)(ii) and (iii), and (10)(ii) of paragraph (b)(5) of this section.

(c) Transitory allocations. If a partnership agreement provides for the possibility that one or more allocations (the "original allocation(s)") will be largely offset by one or more other allocations (the "offsetting allocation(s)"), and, at the time the allocations become part of the partnership agreement, there is a strong likelihood that—

(1) The net increases and decreases that will be recorded in the partners' respective capital accounts for the taxable years to which the allocations relate will not differ substantially from the net increases and decreases that would be recorded in such partners' respective capital accounts for such years if the original allocation(s) and offsetting allocation(s) were not contained in the partnership agreement, and

(2) The total tax liability of the partners (for their respective taxable years in which the allocations will be taken into account) will be less than if the allocations were not contained in the partnership agreement (taking into account tax consequences that result from the interaction of the allocation (or allocations) with partner tax attributes that are unrelated to the partnership) the economic effect of the original allocation(s) and offsetting allocation(s) will not be substantial. If, at the end of a partnership taxable year to which an offsetting allocation(s) relates, the net increases and decreases recorded in the partners' respective capital accounts do not differ substantially from the net increases and decreases that would have been recorded in such partners' respective capital accounts had the original allocation(s) and the offsetting allocation(s) not been contained in the partnership agreement, and the total tax liability of the partners is (as described in (2) above) less than it would have been had such allocations not been contained in the partnership agreement, it will be presumed that, at the time the allocations became part of the partnership agreement, there was a strong likelihood that these results would occur.

This presumption may be overcome by a showing of facts and circumstances that prove otherwise. See examples (1)(xi), (2), (3), (7), (8)(ii), and (17) of paragraph (b)(5) of this section. Notwithstanding the foregoing, the original allocation(s) and the offsetting allocation(s) will not be insubstantial (under this paragraph (b)(2)(iii)(c)) and, for purposes of paragraph (b)(2)(iii)(a), it will be presumed that there is a reasonable possibility that the allocations will affect substantially the dollar amounts to be received by the partners from the partnership if, at the time the allocations become part of the partnership agreement, there is a strong likelihood that the offsetting allocation(s) will not, in large part, be made within five years after the original allocation(s) is made (determined on a first-in, first-out basis). See example (2) of paragraph (b)(5) of this section. For purposes of applying the provisions of this paragraph (b)(2)(iii) (and paragraphs (b)(2)(ii)(d)(6) and (b)(3)(iii) of this section), the adjusted tax basis of partnership property (or, if partnership property is properly reflected on the books of the partnership at a book value that differs from its adjusted tax basis, the book value of such property) will be presumed to be the fair market value of such property, and adjustments to the adjusted tax basis (or book value) of such property will be presumed to be matched by corresponding changes in such property's fair market value. Thus, there cannot be a strong likelihood that the economic effect of an allocation (or allocations) will be largely offset by an allocation (or allocations) of gain or loss from the disposition of partnership property. See examples (1)(vi) and (xi) of paragraph (b)(5) of this section.

(iv) **Maintenance of capital accounts—(a) In general.** The economic effect test described in paragraph (b)(2)(ii) of this section requires an examination of the capital accounts of the partners of a partnership, as maintained under the partnership agreement. Except as otherwise provided in paragraph (b)(2)(ii)(i) of this section, an allocation of income, gain, loss, or deduction will not have economic effect under paragraph (b)(2)(ii) of this section, and will not be deemed to be in accordance with a partner's interest in the partnership under paragraph (b)(4) of this section, unless the capital accounts of the partners are determined and maintained throughout the full term of the partnership in accordance with the capital accounting rules of this paragraph (b)(2)(iv).

(b) **Basic rules.** Except as otherwise provided in this paragraph (b)(2)(iv), the partners' capital accounts will be considered to be determined and maintained in accordance with the rules of this paragraph (b)(2)(iv) if, and only if, each partner's capital account is increased by (1) the amount of money contributed by him to the partnership, (2) the fair market value of property contributed by him to the partnership (net of liabilities secured by such contributed property that the partnership is considered to assume or take subject to under section 752), and (3) allocations to him of partnership income and gain (or items thereof), including income and gain exempt from tax and income and gain described in paragraph (b)(2)(iv)(g) of this section, but excluding income and gain described in paragraph (b)(4)(i) of this section; and is decreased by (4) the amount of money distributed to him by the partnership, (5) the fair market value of property distributed to him by the partnership (net of liabilities secured by such distributed property that such partner is considered to assume or take subject to under section 752), (6) allocations to him of expenditures of the partnership described in section 705(a)(2)(B), and (7) allocations of partnership loss and deduction (or item thereof), including loss and deduction described in paragraph (b)(2)(iv)(g) of this section, but excluding items described in (6) above and loss or deduction described in paragraphs (b)(4)(i) or (b)(4)(iii) of this section; and is otherwise adjusted in accordance with the additional rules set forth in this paragraph (b)(2)(iv). For purposes of this paragraph, a partner who has more than one interest in a partnership shall have a single capital account that reflects all such interests, regardless of the class of interest owned by such partner (e.g., general or limited) and regardless of the time or manner in which such interests were acquired.

(c) **Treatment of liabilities.** For purposes of this paragraph (b)(2)(iv), (1) money contributed by a partner to a partnership includes the amount of any partnership liabilities that are assumed by such partner (other than liabilities described in paragraph (b)(2)(iv)(b)(5) of this section that are assumed by a distributee partner) but does not include increases in such partner's share of partnership liabilities (see section 752(a)), and (2) money distributed to a partner by a partnership includes the amount of such partner's individual liabilities that are assumed by the partnership (other than liabilities described in paragraph (b)(2)(iv)(b)(2) of this section that are assumed by the partnership) but does not include decreases in such partner's share of partnership liabilities (see section 752(b)). For purposes of this paragraph (b)(2)(iv)(c), liabilities are considered assumed only to the extent the assuming party is thereby subjected to personal liability with respect to such obligation, the obligee is aware of the assumption and can directly enforce the assuming party's obligation, and, as between the assuming party and the party from whom the liability is assumed, the assuming party is ultimately liable.

(d) Contributed property—(1) In general. The basic capital accounting rules contained in paragraph (b)(2)(iv)(b) of this section require that a partner's capital account be increased by the fair market value of property contributed to the partnership by such partner on the date of contribution. See examples (13)(i) and (v) of paragraph (b)(5) of this section. Consistent with section 752(c), section 7701(g) does not apply in determining such fair market value.

(2) Contribution of promissory notes. Notwithstanding the general rule of paragraph (b)(2)(iv)(b)(2) of this section, except as provided in this paragraph (b)(2)(iv)(d)(2), if a promissory note is contributed to a partnership by a partner who is the maker of such note, such partner's capital account will be increased with respect to such note only when there is a taxable disposition of such note by the partnership or when the partner makes principal payments on such note. See example (1)(ix) of paragraph (b)(5) of this section. The first sentence of this paragraph (b)(2)(iv)(d)(2) shall not apply if the note referred to therein is readily tradable on an established securities market. See also paragraph (b)(2)(ii)(c) of this section. Furthermore, a partner whose interest is liquidated will be considered as satisfying his obligation to restore the deficit balance in his capital account to the extent of (i) the fair market value, at the time of contribution, of any negotiable promissory note (of which such partner is the maker) that such partner contributes to the partnership on or after the date his interest is liquidated and within the time specified in paragraph (b)(2)(ii)(b)(3) of this section, and (ii) the fair market value, at the time of liquidation, of the unsatisfied portion of any negotiable promissory note (of which such partner is the maker) that such partner previously contributed to the partnership. For purposes of the preceding sentence, the fair market value of a note will be no less than the outstanding principal balance of such note, provided that such note bears interest at a rate no less than the applicable federal rate at the time of valuation.

(3) Section 704(c) considerations. Section 704(c) governs the determination of the partner's distributive shares of income, gain, loss, and deduction, as computed for tax purposes, with respect to property contributed to a partnership (see paragraph (b)(1)(vi) of this section). In cases where section 704(c) applies to partnership property, the capital accounts of the partners will not be considered to be determined and maintained in accordance with the rules of this paragraph (b)(2)(iv) unless the partnership agreement requires that the partners' capital accounts be adjusted in accordance with paragraph (b)(2)(iv)(g) of this section for allocation to them of depreciation, depletion, amortization, and gain and loss, as computed for book purposes, with respect to such property. See example (13)(i) of paragraph (b)(5) of this section.

(e) Distributed property—(1) In general. The basic capital accounting rules contained in paragraph (b)(2)(iv)(b) of this section require that a partner's capital account be decreased by the fair market value of property distributed by the partnership (without regard to section 7701(g)) to such partner (whether in connection with a liquidation or otherwise). To satisfy this requirement, the capital accounts of the partners first must be adjusted to reflect the manner in which the unrealized income, gain, loss, and deduction inherent in such property (that has not been reflected in the capital accounts previously) would be allocated among the partners if there were a taxable disposition of such property for the fair market value of such property (taking section 7701(g) into account) on the date of distribution. See example (14)(v) of paragraph (b)(5) of this section.

(2) Distribution of promissory notes. Notwithstanding the general rule of paragraph (b)(2)(iv)(b)(5), except as provided in this paragraph (b)(2)(iv)(e)(2), if a promissory note is distributed to a partner by a partnership that is the maker of such note, such partner's capital account will be decreased with respect to such note only when there is a taxable disposition of such note by the partner or when the partnership makes principal payments on the note. The previous sentence shall not apply if a note distributed to a partner by a partnership who is the maker of such note is readily tradable on an established securities market. Furthermore, the capital account of a partner whose interest in a partnership is liquidated will be reduced to the extent of (i) the fair market value, at the time of distribution, of any negotiable promissory note (of which such partnership is the maker) that such partnership distributes to the partner on or after the date such partner's interest is liquidated and within the time specified in paragraph (b)(2)(ii)(b)(2) of this section, and (ii) the fair market value, at the time of liquidation, of the unsatisfied portion of any negotiable promissory note (of which such partnership is the maker) that such partnership previously distributed to the partner. For purposes of the preceding sentence, the fair market value of a note will be no less than the outstanding principal balance of such note, provided that such note bears interest at a rate no less than the applicable federal rate at time of valuation.

(f) Revaluations of property. A partnership agreement may, upon the occurrence of certain events, increase or decrease the capital accounts of the partners to reflect a revaluation of partnership property (including intangible assests such as goodwill) on the partnership's books. Capital accounts so adjusted will not be considered to be determined and maintained in accordance with the rules of this paragraph (b)(2)(iv) unless—

(1) The adjustments are based on the fair market value of partnership property (taking section 7701(g) into account) on the date of adjustment, and

(2) The adjustments reflect the manner in which the unrealized income, gain, loss, or deduction inherent in such property (that has not been reflected in the capital accounts previously) would be allocated among the partners if there were a taxable disposition of such property for such fair market value on that date, and

(3) The partnership agreement requires that the partners' capital accounts be adjusted in accordance with paragraph (b)(2)(iv)(g) of this section for allocations to them of depreciation, depletion, amortization, and gain or loss, as computed for book purposes, with respect to such property, and

(4) The partnership agreement requires that the partners' distributive shares of depreciation, depletion, amortization, and gain or loss, as computed for tax purposes, with respect to such property be determined so as to take account of the variation between the adjusted tax basis and book value of such property in the same manner as under section 704(c) (see paragraph (b)(4)(i) of this section), and

(5) The adjustments are made principally for a substantial non-tax business purpose—

(i) In connection with a contribution of money or other property (other than a de minimis amount)

to the partnership by a new or existing partner as consideration for an interest in the partnership, or

(ii) In connection with the liquidation of the partnership or a distribution of money or other property (other than a de minimis amount) by the partnership to a retiring or continuing partner as consideration for an interest in the partnership, or

(iii) Under generally accepted industry accounting practices, provided substantially all of the partnership's property (excluding money) consists of stock, securities, commodities, options, warrants, futures, or similar instruments that are readily tradable on an established securities market.

See example (14) and (18) of paragraph (b)(5) of this section. If the capital accounts of the partners are not adjusted to reflect the fair market value of partnership property when an interest in the partnership is acquired from or relinquished to the partnership, paragraphs (b)(1)(iii) and (b)(1)(iv) of this section should be consulted regarding the potential tax consequences that may arise if the principles of section 704(c) are not applied to determine the partners' distributive shares of depreciation, depletion, amortization, and gain or loss as computed for tax purposes, with respect to such property.

(g) Adjustments to reflect book value—(1) In general. Under paragraphs (b)(2)(iv)(d) and (b)(2)(iv)(f) of this section, property may be properly reflected on the books of the partnership at a book value that differs from the adjusted tax basis of such property. In these circumstances, paragraphs (b)(2)(iv)(d)(3) and (b)(2)(iv)(f)(3) of this section provide that the capital accounts of the partners will not be considered to be determined and maintained in accordance with the rules of this paragraph (b)(2)(iv) unless the partnership agreement requires the partners' capital accounts to be adjusted in accordance with this paragraph (b)(2)(iv)(g) for allocations to them of depreciation, depletion, amortization, and gain or loss, as computed for book purposes, with respect to such property. In determining whether the economic effect of an allocation of book items is substantial, consideration will be given to the effect of such allocation on the determination of the partners' distributive shares of corresponding tax items under section 704(c) and paragraph (b)(4)(i) of this section. See example (17) of paragraph (b)(5) of this section. If an allocation of book items under the partnership agreement does not have substantial economic effect (as determined under paragraphs (b)(2)(ii) and (b)(2)(iii) of this section), or is not otherwise respected under this paragraph, such items will be reallocated in accordance with the partners' interests in the partnership, and such reallocation will be the basis upon which the partners' distributive shares of the corresponding tax items are determined under section 704(c) and paragraph (b)(4)(i) of this section. See examples (13), (14), and (18) of paragraph (b)(5) of this section.

(2) Payables and receivables. References in this paragraph (b)(2)(iv) and paragraph (b)(4)(i) of this section to book and tax depreciation, depletion, amortization, and gain or loss with respect to property that has an adjusted tax basis that differs from book value include, under analogous rules and principles, the unrealized income or deduction with respect to accounts receivable, accounts payable, and other accrued but unpaid items.

(3) Determining amount of book items. The partners' capital accounts will not be considered adjusted in accordance with this paragraph (b)(2)(iv)(g) unless the amount of book depreciation, depletion, or amortization for a period with respect to an item of partnership property is the amount that bears the same relationship to the book value of such property as the depreciation (or cost recovery deduction), depletion, or amortization computed for tax purposes with respect to such property for such period bears to the adjusted tax basis of such property. If such property has a zero adjusted tax basis, the book depreciation, depletion, or amortization may be determined under any reasonable method selected by the partnership.

(h) Determinations of fair market value. For purposes of this paragraph (b)(2)(iv), the fair market value assigned to property contributed to a partnership, property distributed by a partnership, or property otherwise revalued by a partnership, will be regarded as correct, provided that (1) such value is reasonably agreed to among the partners in arm's-length negotiations, and (2) the partners have sufficiently adverse interests. If, however, these conditions are not satisfied and the value assigned to such property is overstated or understated (by more than an insignificant amount), the capital accounts of the partners will not be considered to be determined and maintained in accordance with the rules of this paragraph (b)(2)(iv). Valuation of property contributed to the partnership, distributed by the partnership, or otherwise revalued by the partnership shall be on a property-by-property basis, except to the extent the regulations under section 704(c) permit otherwise.

(i) Section 705(a)(2)(B) expenditures—(1) In general. The basic capital accounting rules contained in paragraph (b)(2)(iv)(b) of this section require that a partner's capital account be decreased by allocations made to such partner of expenditures described in section 705(a)(2)(B). See example (11) of paragraph (b)(5) of this section. If an allocation of these expenditures under the partnership agreement does not have substantial economic effect (as determined under paragraphs (b)(2)(ii) and (b)(2)(iii) of this section), or is not otherwise respected under this paragraph, such expenditures will be reallocated in accordance with the partners' interest in the partnership.

(2) Expenses described in section 709. Except for amounts with respect to which an election is properly made under section 709(b), amounts paid or incurred to organize a partnership or to promote the sale of (or to sell) an interest in such a partnership shall, solely for purposes of this paragraph, be treated as section 705(a)(2)(B) expenditures, and upon liquidation of the partnership no further capital account adjustments will be made in respect thereof.

(3) Disallowed losses. If a deduction for a loss incurred in connection with the sale or exchange of partnership property is disallowed to the partnership under section 267(a)(1) or section 707(b), that deduction shall, solely for purposes of this paragraph, be treated as a section 705(a)(2)(B) expenditure.

(j) Basis adjustments to section 38 property. The capital accounts of the partners will not be considered to be determined and maintained in accordance with the rules of this paragraph (b)(2)(iv) unless such capital accounts are adjusted by the partners' shares of any upward or downward basis adjustments allocated to them under this paragraph (b)(2)(iv)(j). When there is a reduction in the adjusted tax basis of partnership section 38 property under section 48(q)(1) or section 48(q)(3), section 48(q)(6) provides for an equivalent downward adjustment to the aggregate basis of partnership interests (and no additional adjustment is made under section 705(a)(2)(B)). These downward basis adjustments shall be shared among the partners in the same proportion as the adjusted tax basis or cost of (or the qualified investment in) such section 38 property is allocated among the partners under paragraph (f) of § 1.46–3 (or paragraph (a)(4)(iv) of § 1.48–8). Conversely, when there is an increase in the adjusted tax basis of partnership section 38 property under section 48(q)(2), section 48(q)(6) provides for an equivalent upward adjustment to the aggregate basis of partnership interests. These upward adjustments shall be allocated among the partners in the same proportion as the investment tax credit from such property is recaptured by the partners under § 1.47–6.

(k) Depletion of oil and gas properties—(1) In general. The capital accounts of the partners will not be considered to be determined and maintained in accordance with the rules of this paragraph (b)(2)(iv) unless such capital accounts are adjusted for depletion and gain or loss with respect to the oil or gas properties of the partnership in accordance with this paragraph (b)(2)(iv)(k).

(2) Simulated depletion. Except as provided in paragraph (b)(2)(iv)(k)(3) of this section, a partnership shall, solely for purposes of maintaining capital accounts under this paragraph, compute simulated depletion allowances with respect to its oil and gas properties at the partnership level. These allowances shall be computed on each depletable oil or gas property of the partnership by using either the cost depletion method or the percentage depletion method (computed in accordance with section 613 at the rates specified in section 613A(c)(5) without regard to the limitations of section 613A, which theoretically could apply to any partner) for each partnership taxable year that the property is owned by the partnership and subject to depletion. The choice between the simulated cost depletion method and the simulated percentage depletion method shall be made on a property-by-property basis in the first partnership taxable year beginning after April 30, 1986, for which it is relevant for the property, and shall be binding for all partnership taxable years during which the oil or gas property is held by the partnership. The partnership shall make downward adjustments to the capital accounts of the partners for the simulated depletion allowance with respect to each oil or gas property of the partnership, in the same proportion as such partners (or their predecessors in interest) were properly allocated the adjusted tax basis of each such property. The aggregate capital account adjustments for simulated percentage depletion allowances with respect to an oil or gas property of the partnership shall not exceed the aggregate adjusted tax basis allocated to the partners with respect to such property. Upon the taxable disposition of an oil or gas property by a partnership, such partnership's simulated gain or loss shall be determined by subtracting its simulated adjusted basis in such property from the amount realized upon such disposition. (The partnership's simulated adjusted basis in an oil or gas property is determined in the same manner as adjusted tax basis except that simulated depletion allowances are taken into account instead of actual depletion allowances.) The capital accounts of the partners shall be adjusted upward by the amount of any simulated gain in proportion to such partners' allocable shares of the portion of the total amount realized from the disposition of such property that exceeds the partnership's simulated adjusted basis in such property. The capital accounts of such partners shall be adjusted downward by the amount of any simulated loss in proportion to such partners' allocable shares of the total amount realized from the disposition of such property that represents recovery of the partnership's simulated adjusted basis in such property. See section 613A(c)(7)(D) and the regulations thereunder and paragraph (b)(4)(v) of this section. See example (19)(iv) of paragraph (b)(5) of this section.

(3) Actual depletion. Pursuant to section 613A(c)(7)(D) and the regulations thereunder, the depletion allowance under section 611 with respect to the oil and gas properties of a partnership is computed separately by the partners. Accordingly, in lieu of adjusting the partner's capital accounts as provided in paragraph (b)(2)(iv)(k)(2) of this section, the partnership may make downward adjustments to the capital account of each partner equal to such partner's depletion allowance with respect to each oil or gas property of the partnership (for the partner's taxable year that ends with or within the partnership's taxable year). The aggregate adjustments to the capital account of a partner for depletion allowances with respect to an oil or gas property of the partnership shall not exceed the adjusted tax basis allocated to such partner with respect to such property. Upon the taxable disposition of an oil or gas property by a partnership, the capital account of each partner shall be adjusted upward by the amount of any excess of such partner's allocable share of the total amount realized from the disposition of such property over such partner's remaining adjusted tax basis in such property. If there is no such excess, the capital account of such partner shall be adjusted downward by the amount of any excess of such partner's remaining adjusted tax basis in such property over such partner's allocable share of the total amount realized from the disposition thereof.

See section 613A(c)(7)(4)(D) and the regulations thereunder and paragraph (b)(4)(v) of this section.

(4) Effect of book values. If an oil or gas property of the partnership is, under paragraphs (b)(2)(iv)(d) or (b)(2)(iv)(f) of this section, properly reflected on the books of the partnership at a book value that differs from the adjusted tax basis of such property, the rules contained in this paragraph (b)(2)(iv)(k) and paragraph (b)(4)(v) of this section shall be applied with reference to such book value. A revaluation of a partnership oil or gas property under paragraph (b)(2)(iv)(f) of this section may give rise to a reallocation of the adjusted tax basis of such property, or a change in the partners' relative shares of simulated depletion from such property, only to the extent permitted by section 613A(c)(7)(D) and the regulations thereunder.

(*l*) **Transfers of partnership interests.** The capital accounts of the partners will not be considered to be determined and maintained in accordance with the rules of this paragraph (b)(2)(iv) unless, upon the transfer of all or a part of an interest in the partnership, the capital account of the transferor that is attributable to the transferred interest carries over to the transferee partner. (See paragraph (b)(2)(iv)(m) of this section for rules concerning the effect of a section 754 election on the capital accounts of the partners.) However, if the transfer of an interest in a partnership causes a termination of the partnership under section 708(b)(1)(B), the capital account that carriers over to the transferee partner will be adjusted in accordance with paragraph (b)(2)(iv)(e) of this section in connection with the constructive liquidation of the partnership under paragraph (b)(1)(iv) of § 1.708–1. Moreover, the constructive reformation of such partnership will, for purposes of this paragraph, be treated as the formation of a new partnership, and the capital accounts of the partners of such new partnership will be determined and maintained accordingly. See example (13) of paragraph (b)(5) of this section.

(m) Section 754 elections—(1) In general. The capital accounts of the partners will not be considered to be determined and maintained in accordance with the rules of this paragraph (b)(2)(iv) unless, upon adjustment to the adjusted tax basis of partnership property under section 732, 734, or 743, the capital accounts of the partners are adjusted as provided in this paragraph (b)(2)(iv)(m).

(2) Section 743 adjustments. In the case of a transfer of all or a part of an interest in a partnership that has a section 754 election in effect for the partnership taxable year in which such transfer occurs, adjustments to the adjusted tax basis of partnership property under section 743 shall not be reflected in the capital account of the transferee partner or on the books of the partnership, and subsequent capital account adjustments for distributions (see paragraph (b)(2)(iv)(e)(1) of this section) and for depreciation, depletion, amortization, and gain or loss with respect to such property will disregard the effect of such basis adjustment. The preceding sentence shall not apply to the extent such basis adjustment is allocated to the common basis of partnership property under paragraph (b)(1) of § 1.734–2; in these cases, such basis adjustment shall, except as provided in paragraph (b)(2)(iv)(m)(5) of this section, give rise to adjustments to the capital accounts of the partners in accordance with their interests in the partnership under paragraph (b)(3) of this section. See examples (13)(iii) and (iv) of paragraph (b)(5) of this section.

(3) Section 732 adjustments. In the case of a transfer of all or a part of an interest in a partnership that does not have a section 754 election in effect for the partnership taxable year in which such transfer occurs, adjustments to the adjusted tax basis of partnership property under section 732(d) will be treated in the capital accounts of the partners in the same manner as section 743 basis adjustments are treated under paragraph (b)(2)(iv)(m)(2) of this section.

(4) Section 734 adjustments. Except as provided in paragraph (b)(2)(iv)(m)(5) of this section, in the case of a distribution of property in liquidation of a partner's interest in the partnership by a partnership that has a section 754 election in effect for the partnership taxable year in which the distribution occurs, the partner who receives the distribution that gives rise to the adjustment to the adjusted tax basis of partnership property under section 734 shall have a corresponding adjustment made to his capital account. If such distribution is made other than in liquidation of a partner's interest in the partnership, however, except as provided in paragraph (b)(2)(iv)(m)(5) of this section, the capital accounts of the partners shall be adjusted by the amount of the adjustment to the adjusted tax basis of partnership property under section 734, and such capital account adjustment shall be shared among the partners in the manner in which the unrealized income and gain that is displaced by such adjustment would have been shared if the property whose basis is adjusted were sold immediately prior to such adjustment for its recomputed adjusted tax basis.

(5) **Limitations on adjustments.** Adjustments may be made to the capital account of a partner (or his successor in interest) in respect of basis adjustments to partnership property under sections 732, 734, and 743 only to the extent that such basis adjustments (i) are permitted to be made to one or more items of partnership property under section 755, and (ii) result in an increase or a decrease in the amount at which such property is carried on the partnership's balance sheet, as computed for book purposes. For example, if the book value of partnership property exceeds the adjusted tax basis of such property, a basis adjustment to such property may be reflected in a partner's capital account only to the extent such adjustment exceeds the difference between the book value of such property and the adjusted tax basis of such property prior to such adjustment.

(n) **Partnership level characterization.** Except as otherwise provided in paragraph (b)(2)(iv)(k) of this section, the capital accounts of the partners will not be considered to be determined and maintained in accordance with the rules of this paragraph (b)(2)(iv) unless adjustments to such capital accounts in respect of partnership income, gain, loss, deduction, and section 705(a)(2)(B) expenditures (or item thereof) are made with reference to the Federal tax treatment of such items (and in the case of book items, with reference to the Federal tax treatment of the corresponding tax items) at the partnership level, without regard to any requisite or elective tax treatment of such items at the partner level (for example, under section 58(i)). However, a partnership that incurs mining exploration expenditures will determine the Federal tax treatment of income, gain, loss, and deduction with respect to the property to which such expenditures relate at the partnership level only after first taking into account the elections made by its partners under section 617 and section 703(b)(4).

(*o*) **Guaranteed payments.** Guaranteed payments to a partner under section 707(c) cause the capital account of the recipient partner to be adjusted only to the extent of such partner's distributive share of any partnership deduction, loss, or other downward capital account adjustment resulting from such payment.

(p) **Minor discrepancies.** Discrepancies between the balances in the respective capital accounts of the partners and the balances that would be in such respective capital accounts if they had been determined and maintained in accordance with this paragraph (b)(2)(iv) will not adversely affect the validity of an allocation, provided that such discrepancies are minor and are attributable to good faith error by the partnership.

(q) **Adjustments where guidance is lacking.** If the rules of this paragraph (b)(2)(iv) fail to provide guidance on how adjustments to the capital accounts of the partners should be made to reflect particular adjustments to partnership capital on the books of the partnership, such capital accounts will not be considered to be determined and maintained in accordance with those rules unless such capital account adjustments are made in a manner that (1) maintains equality between the aggregate governing capital accounts of the partners and the amount of partnership capital reflected on the partnership's balance sheet, as computed for book purposes, (2) is consistent with the underlying economic arrangement of the partners, and (3) is based, wherever practicable, on Federal tax accounting principles.

(r) **Restatement of capital accounts.** With respect to partnerships that began operating in a taxable year beginning before May 1, 1986, the capital accounts of the partners of which have not been determined and maintained in accordance with the rules of this paragraph (b)(2)(iv) since inception, such capital accounts shall not be considered to be determined and maintained in accordance with the rules of this paragraph (b)(2)(iv) for taxable years beginning after April 30, 1986, unless either—

(1) such capital accounts are adjusted, effective for the first partnership taxable year beginning after April 30, 1986, to reflect the fair market value of partnership property as of the first day of such taxable year, and in connection with such adjustment, the rules contained in paragraph (b)(2)(iv)(f)(2), (3), and (4) of this section are satisfied, or

(2) the differences between the balance in each partner's capital account and the balance that would be in such partner's capital account if capital accounts had been determined and maintained in accordance with this paragraph (b)(2)(iv) throughout the full term of the partnership are not significant (for example, such differences are solely attributable to a failure to provide for treatment of section 709 expenses in accordance with the rules of paragraph (b)(2)(iv)(i)(2) of this section or to a

failure to follow the rules in paragraph (b)(2)(iv)(m) of this section), and capital accounts are adjusted to bring them into conformity with the rules of this paragraph (b)(2)(iv) no later than the end of the first partnership taxable year beginning after April 30, 1986.

However, compliance with the previous sentence will have no bearing on the validity of allocations that relate to partnership taxable years beginning before May 1, 1986.

(3) **Partner's interest in the partnership—(i) In general.** References in section 704(b) and this paragraph to a partner's interest in the partnership, or to the partner's interests in the partnership, signify the manner in which the partners have agreed to share the economic benefit or burden (if any) corresponding to the income, gain, loss, deduction, or credit (or item thereof) that is allocated. Except with respect to partnership items that cannot have economic effect (such as nonrecourse deductions of the partnership), this sharing arrangement may or may not correspond to the overall economic arrangement of the partners. Thus, a partner who has a 50 percent overall interest in the partnership may have a 90 percent interest in a particular item of income or deduction. (For example, in the case of an unexpected downward adjustment to the capital account of a partner who does not have a deficit make-up obligation that causes such partner to have a negative capital account, it may be necessary to allocate a disproportionate amount of gross income of the partnership to such partner for such year so as to bring that partner's capital account back up to zero.) The determination of a partner's interest in a partnership shall be made by taking into account all facts and circumstances relating to the economic arrangement of the partners. All partners' interests in the partnership are presumed to be equal (determined on a per capita basis). However, this presumption may be rebutted by the taxpayer of the Internal Revenue Service by establishing facts and circumstances that show that the partners' interests in the partnership are otherwise.

(ii) **Factors considered.** In determining a partner's interest in the partnership, the following factors are among those that will be considered:

(a) The partners' relative contributions to the partnership,

(b) The interests of the partners in economic profits and losses (if different than that in taxable income or loss),

(c) The interests of the partners in cash flow and other non-liquidating distributions, and

(d) The rights of the partners to distributions of capital upon liquidation.

The provisions of this subparagraph (b)(3) are illustrated by examples (1)(i) and (ii), (4)(i), (5)(i) and (ii), (6), (7), (8), (10)(ii), (16)(i), and (19)(iii) of paragraph (b)(5) of this section. See paragraph (b)(4)(i) of this section concerning rules for determining the partners' interests in the partnership, with respect to certain tax items.

(iii) **Certain determinations.** If—

(a) Requirements (1) and (2) of paragraph (b)(2)(ii)(b) of this section are satisfied, and

(b) All or a portion of an allocation of income, gain, loss, or deduction made to a partner for a partnership taxable year does not have economic effect under paragraph (b)(2)(ii) of this section, the partners' interests in the partnership with respect to the portion of the allocation that lacks economic effect will be determined by comparing the manner in which distributions (and contributions) would be made if all partnership property were sold at book value and the partnership were liquidated immediately following the end of the taxable year to which the allocation relates with the manner in which distributions (and contributions) would be made if all partnership property were sold at book value and the partnership were liquidated immediately following the end of the prior taxable year, and adjusting the result for the items described in (4), (5), and (6) of paragraph (b)(2)(ii)(d) of this section. A determination made under this paragraph (b)(3)(iii) will have no force if the economic effect of valid allocations made in the same manner is insubstantial under paragraph (b)(2)(iii) of this section. See examples (1)(iv), (v), and (vi), and (15)(ii) and (iii) of paragraph (b)(5) of this section.

(4) **Special rules—(i) Allocations to reflect revaluations.** If partnership property is, under paragraphs (b)(2)(iv)(d) or (b)(2)(iv)(f) of this section, properly reflected in the capital accounts of the partners and on the books of the partnership at a book value that differs from the adjusted tax basis of such property, then depreciation, depletion, amortization, and gain or loss, as computed for book purposes, with respect to such property will be greater or less than the depreciation, depletion, amortization, and gain or loss, as computed for tax purposes, with respect to such property. In these cases the capital accounts of the partners are re-

quired to be adjusted solely for allocations of the book items to such partners (see paragraph (b)(2)(iv)(g) of this section), and the partners' shares of the corresponding tax items are not independently reflected by further adjustments to the partners' capital accounts. Thus, separate allocations of these tax items cannot have economic effect under paragraph (b)(2)(ii)(b)(1) of this section, and the partners' distributive shares of such tax items must (unless governed by section 704(c)) be determined in accordance with the partners' interest in the partnership. These tax items must be shared among the partners in a manner that takes account of the variations between the adjusted tax basis of such property and its book value in the same manner as variation between the adjusted tax basis and fair market value of property contributed to the partnership are taken into account in determining the partners' shares of tax items under section 704(c). See examples (14) and (18) of paragraph (b)(5) of this section.

(ii) **Credits.** Allocations of tax credits and tax credit recapture are not reflected by adjustments to the partners' capital accounts (except to the extent that adjustments to the adjusted tax basis of partnership section 38 property in respect of tax credits and tax credit recapture give rise to capital account adjustments under paragraph (b)(2)(iv)(j) of this section). Thus, such allocations cannot have economic effect under paragraph (b)(2)(ii)(b)(1) of this section, and the tax credits and tax credit recapture must be allocated in accordance with the partners' interests in the partnership as of the time the tax credit or credit recapture arises. With respect to the investment tax credit provided by section 38, allocations of cost or qualified investment made in accordance with paragraph (f) of § 1.46–3 and paragraph (a)(4)(iv) of § 1.48–8 shall be deemed to be made in accordance with the partners' interests in the partnership. With respect to other tax credits, if a partnership expenditure (whether or not deductible) that gives rise to a tax credit in a partnership taxable year also gives rise to valid allocations of partnership loss or deduction (or other downward capital account adjustments) for such year, then the partners' interests in the partnership with respect to such credit (or the cost giving rise thereto) shall be in the same proportion as such partners' respective distributive shares of such loss or deduction (and adjustments). See example (11) of paragraph (b)(5) of this section. Identical principles shall apply in determining the partners' interests in the partnership with respect

to tax credits that arise from receipts of the partnership (whether or not taxable).

(iii) **Excess percentage depletion.** To the extent the percentage depletion in respect of an item of depletable property of the partnership exceeds the adjusted tax basis of such property, allocations of such excess percentage depletion are not reflected by adjustments to the partners' capital accounts. Thus, such allocations cannot have economic effect under paragraph (b)(2)(ii)(b)(1) of this section, and such excess percentage depletion must be allocated in accordance with the partners' interests in the partnership. The partners' interests in the partnership for a partnership taxable year with respect to such excess percentage depletion shall be in the same proportion as such partners' respective distributive shares of gross income from the depletable property (as determined under section 613(c)) for such year. See example (12) of paragraph (b)(5) of this section. See paragraphs (b)(2)(iv)(k) and (b)(4)(v) of this section for special rules concerning oil and gas properties of the partnership.

(iv) **Nonrecourse deductions—(a) Allocation of nonrecourse deductions.** An allocation of loss, deduction, or section 705(a)(2)(B) expenditure (or item thereof) attributable to nonrecourse liabilities of the partnership ("nonrecourse deductions") cannot have economic effect because, in the event there is an economic burden that corresponds to such an allocation, the creditor alone bears that burden. Thus, nonrecourse deductions must be allocated in accordance with the partners' interests in the partnership. Paragraph (b)(4)(iv)(d) of this section, however, provides a test under which certain allocations of nonrecourse deductions will be deemed to be in accordance with the partners' interests in the partnership. If that test is not satisfied, the partners' distributive shares of nonrecourse deductions will be determined, under paragraph (b)(3) of this section, according to the partners' overall economic interests in the partnership.

(b) **Determination of nonrecourse deductions.** The amount of nonrecourse deductions for a partnership taxable year equals the net increase, if any, in the amount of partnership minimum gain during that taxable year. See examples (20)(i), (21), and (22) of paragraph (b)(5) of this section. In determining such net increase for any partnership taxable year in which the capital accounts of the partners are increased pursuant to paragraph (b)(2)(iv)(f) of this section to reflect a revaluation of partnership property subject to one or more nonrecourse liabilities of the partnership, any decrease in partnership minimum gain attributable to each such revaluation shall be added back to the net decrease or increase otherwise determined. See example (22)(iii) of paragraph (b)(5) of this section. The nonrecourse deductions for a partnership taxable year shall consist first of depreciation or cost recovery deductions with respect to items of partnership property subject to one or more nonrecourse liabilities of the partnership to the extent of the increase in minimum gain attributable to the nonrecourse liabilities to which each such item of property is subject, with the remainder of such nonrecourse deductions, if any, made up of a pro rata portion of the partnership's other items of deduction, loss, and section 705(a)(2)(B) expenditure for that year. If, however, such depreciation or cost recovery deductions exceed the net increase in partnership minimum gain, a proportional share of each such deduction shall constitute a nonrecourse deduction. See example (23) of paragraph (b)(5) of this section. In addition, if the net increase in partnership minimum gain during a partnership taxable year exceeds the total amount of items of partnership loss, deduction, and section 705(a)(2)(B) expenditure for such year, then an amount of partnership loss, deduction, and section 705(a)(2)(B) expenditure for the partnership's next succeeding taxable year (or years) equal to such excess shall constitute nonrecourse deductions, as if there had been a net increase in partnership minimum gain during such succeeding year (or years) in the amount of such excess.

(c) **Partnership minimum gain.** The amount of partnership minimum gain is determined by computing, with respect to each nonrecourse liability of the partnership, the amount of gain (of whatever character), if any, that would be realized by the partnership if it disposed of (in a taxable transaction) the partnership property subject to such liability in full satisfaction thereof, and by then aggregating the amounts so computed. See examples (20)(i) and (iv), (21), and (22) of paragraph (b)(5) of this section. For the purpose of determining the amount of such gain, (1) the adjusted basis of partnership property subject to two or more liabilities of equal priority shall be allocated among such liabilities in proportion to the respective outstanding balances of such liabilities, and (2) the adjusted basis of partnership property subject to two or more liabilities of unequal priority shall be allocated to the liabilities of an inferior priority (in accordance with (1) above) only to the extent of

the excess, if any, of the adjusted tax basis of such property over the aggregate outstanding balance of the liabilities of superior priority. Only the portion of the property's adjusted basis allocated to nonrecourse liabilities of the partnership shall be used in computing minimum gain. See example (20)(v) and (vi) of paragraph (b)(5) of this section. If partnership property subject to one or more nonrecourse liabilities of the partnership is, under paragraph (b)(2)(iv)(d) or (b)(2)(iv)(f) of this section, properly reflected on the books of the partnership at a book value that differs from the adjusted tax basis of such property, the determinations under this paragraph (b)(4)(iv) shall be made with reference to such book value. See example (22) of paragraph (b)(5) of this section.

(d) **Requirements to be satisfied.** Allocations of nonrecourse deductions shall be deemed to be made in accordance with the partners' interests in the partnership if, and only if—

(1) Throughout the full term of the partnership, requirements (1) and (2) of paragraph (b)(2)(ii)(b) of this section are satisfied,

(2) Beginning in the first taxable year in which there are nonrecourse deductions and thereafter throughout the full term of the partnership, the partnership agreement provides for allocations of nonrecourse deductions among the partners in a manner that is reasonably consistent with allocations, which have substantial economic effect, of some other significant partnership item attributable to the property securing nonrecourse liabilities of the partnership (other than minimum gain recognized by the partnership),

(3) Beginning in the first taxable year of the partnership in which the partnership has nonrecourse deductions and thereafter throughout the full term of the partnership, (i) requirement (3) of paragraph (b)(2)(ii)(b) of this section is satisfied, or (ii) the partnership agreement contains a "minimum gain chargeback" (as defined in paragraph (b)(4)(iv)(e) of this section), and

(4) All other material allocations and capital account adjustments under the partnership agreement are recognized under this paragraph (b) (without regard to whether allocations of adjusted tax basis and amount realized under section 613A(c)(7)(D) are recognized under paragraph (b)(4)(v) of this section).

(e) **Minimum gain chargeback.** A partnership agreement contains a "minimum gain chargeback" if, and only if, it provides that, if there is a net decrease in partnership minimum gain during a partnership taxable year, all partners with a deficit capital account balance at the end of such year (excluding from each partner's deficit capital account balance any amount that such partner is obligated to restore under paragraph (b)(2)(ii)(c) of this section, as well as any addition thereto pursuant to the next to last sentence of paragraph (b)(4)(iv)(f) of this section computed with respect to the amount of partnership minimum gain after such net decrease) will be allocated, before any other allocation is made under section 704(b) of partnership items for such taxable year, items of income and gain for such year (and, if necessary, subsequent years) in the amount and in the proportions needed to eliminate such deficits as quickly as possible. For purposes of the preceding sentence, partners' capital accounts shall be reduced for the items described in paragraphs (b)(2)(ii)(d)(4), (5), and (6) of this section. Allocations of items of income and gain made pursuant to a minimum gain chargeback shall be deemed to be made in accordance with the partners' interests in the partnership if requirements (1) and (2) of paragraph (b)(2)(ii)(b) of this section are satisfied. The minimum gain chargeback allocated in any taxable year shall consist first of gains recognized from the disposition of items of partnership property subject to one or more nonrecourse liabilities of the partnership to the extent of the decrease in minimum gain attributable to the disposition of such items of property, with the remainder of such minimum gain chargeback, if any, made up of a pro rata portion of the partnership's other items of income and gain for that year. If, however, such gains exceed the amount of the minimum gain chargeback, a proportional share of each such gain shall constitute a part of the minimum gain chargeback. For purposes of paragraph (b)(2)(ii)(d)(6) of this section, offsetting increases to a partner's capital account taken into account under that paragraph shall not include income and gain that is expected to be allocated to such partner pursuant to a minimum gain chargeback.

(f) Partner's share of partnership minimum gain. A partner's share of partnership minimum gain at the end of any partnership taxable year equals the aggregate nonrecourse deductions allocated to such partner (and such partner's predecessors in interest) up to that time, less such partner's (and such predecessors') aggregate share of the net decreases in partnership minimum gain up to that time. A partner's share of the net decrease in partnership minimum gain during a partnership taxable year equals an amount that bears the same relation to the net decrease in partnership minimum gain during such year as such partner's share of partnership minimum gain at the end of the prior taxable year of the partnership (or, if later, at the time immediately following the last time that the capital accounts of the partners are increased pursuant to paragraph (b)(2)(iv)(f) of this section to reflect a revaluation of partnership property subject to one or more nonrecourse liabilities of the partnership) bears to the amount of partnership minimum gain at the end of such prior taxable year (or such later date). See examples (20)(i) and (iv) and (21) of paragraph (b)(5) of this section. In addition, if there is a decrease in partnership minimum gain in a taxable year of the partnership (whether or not there is a net decrease in partnership minimum gain during such year) attributable to the revaluation of partnership property subject to one or more nonrecourse liabilities of the partnership, each partner's share of partnership minimum gain as of the time of such revaluation shall be reduced by the amount of the increase in such partner's capital account attributable to such revaluation to the extent of the reduction in minimum gain caused by such revaluation. See example (22)(ii) of paragraph (b)(5) of this section. For purposes of paragraph (b)(2)(ii)(d) of this section, the amount of a partner's share of minimum gain shall be added to the limited dollar amount, if any, of the deficit balance in such partner's capital account that such partner is obligated to restore. See examples (20)(i) and (22)(i) of paragraph (b)(5) of this section.

(g) Nonrecourse liabilities of the partnership where a partner has economic risk of loss. The rationale for the special rule contained in this paragraph (b)(4)(iv) is that, in the event there is an economic burden that corresponds to the nonrecourse deductions, none of the partners will bear that burden. Accordingly, for purposes of this paragraph, a nonrecourse liability of the partnership is a liability of the partnership (or portion thereof) with respect to which none of the partners has any economic risk of loss (other than through their interests as partners in the partnership assets subject to the liability). Therefore, to the extent a partner may bear the burden of an economic loss corresponding to a loss, deduction, or section 705(a)(2)(B) expenditure attributable to a partnership liability that would be considered nonrecourse for purposes of § 1.1001-2 (e.g., a purported nonrecourse loan made by such partner to the partnership or guaranteed by such partner), allocations of such loss, deduction, or section 705(a)(2)(B) expenditure are not governed by this paragraph (b)(4)(iv). Instead, allocations of such loss or deduction shall be made in accordance with the partners' interests in the partnership under paragraph (b)(3) of this section. This will require allocations of such loss or deduction to be made to the partner or partners who bear the burden of an economic loss corresponding to such loss or deduction. See examples (20)(vii) and (viii) of paragraph (b)(5) of this section.

(h) Nonrecourse liabilities of the partnership where a person related to a partner has economic risk of loss. [Reserved]

(v) Allocations under section 613A(c)(7)(D). Allocations of the adjusted tax basis of a partnership oil or gas property are controlled by section 613A(c)(7)(D) and the regulations thereunder. However, if the partnership agreement provides for an allocation of the adjusted tax basis of an oil or gas property among the partners, and such allocation is not otherwise governed under section 704(c) (or related principles under paragraph (b)(4)(i) of this section), that allocation will be recognized as being in accordance with the partners' interests in partnership capital under section 613A(c)(7)(D), provided (a) such allocation does not give rise to capital account adjustments under paragraph (b)(2)(iv)(k) of this section the economic effect of which is insubstantial (as determined under paragraph (b)(2)(iii) of this section), and (b) all other material allocations and capital account adjustments under the partnership agreement are recognized under this paragraph (b). Otherwise, such adjusted tax basis must be allocated among the partners pursuant to section 613A(c)(7)(D) in accordance with the partners' actual interests in partnership capital or income. For purposes of section 613A(c)(7)(D) the partners' allocable shares of the amount realized upon the partnership's taxable disposition of an oil or gas property will, except to the extent governed by section 704(c) (or related principles under paragraph (b)(4)(i) of this section), be determined under this paragraph (b)(4)(v). If, pursuant to paragraph (b)(2)(iv)(k)(2) of this section, the partners' capital accounts are adjusted to reflect the simulated depletion of an oil or gas property of the partnership, the portion of the total amount realized by the partnership upon the taxable disposition of such property that represents recovery of its simulated adjusted tax basis

therein will be allocated to the partners in the same proportion as the aggregate adjusted tax basis of such property was allocated to such partners (or their predecessors in interest). If, pursuant to paragraph (b)(2)(iv)(k)(3) of this section, the partners' capital accounts are adjusted to reflect the actual depletion of an oil or gas property of the partnership, the portion of the total amount realized by the partnership upon the taxable disposition of such property that equals the partners' aggregate remaining adjusted basis therein will be allocated to the partners in proportion to their respective remaining adjusted tax bases in such property. An allocation provided by the partnership agreement of the portion of the total amount realized by the partnership on its taxable disposition of an oil or gas property that exceeds the portion of the total amount realized allocated under either of the previous two sentences (whichever is applicable) shall be deemed to be made in accordance with the partners' allocable shares of such amount realized, provided (c) such allocation does not give rise to capital account adjustments under paragraph (b)(2)(iv)(k) of this section the economic effect of which is insubstantial (as determined under paragraph (b)(2)(ii) of this section), and (d) all other allocations and capital account adjustments under the partnership agreement are recognized under this paragraph. Otherwise, the partners' allocable shares of the total amount realized by the partnership on its taxable disposition of an oil or gas property shall be determined in accordance with the partners' interests in the partnership under paragraph (b)(3) of this section. See example (19) of paragraph (b)(5) of this section. (See paragraph (b)(2)(iv)(k) of this section for the determination of appropriate adjustments to the partners' capital accounts relating to section 613A(c)(7)(D).)

(vi) Amendments to partnership agreement. If an allocation has substantial economic effect under paragraph (b)(2) of this section or is deemed to be made in accordance with the partners' interests in the partnership under paragraph (b)(4) of this section under the partnership agreement that is effective for the taxable year to which such allocation relates, and such partnership agreement thereafter is modified, both the tax consequences of the modification and the facts and circumstances surrounding the modification will be closely scrutinized to determine whether the purported modification was part of the original agreement. If it is determined that the purported modification was part of the original agreement, prior allocations may be reallocated in a manner consistent with the modified terms of the agreement, and subsequent allocations may be reallocated to take account of such modified terms. For example, if a partner is obligated by the partnership agreement to restore the deficit balance in his capital account (or any limited dollar amount thereof) in accordance with requirement (3) of paragraph (b)(2)(ii)(b) of this section and, thereafter, such obligation is eliminated or reduced (other than as provided in paragraph (b)(2)(ii)(f) of this section), or is not complied with in a timely manner, such elimination, reduction, or noncompliance may be treated as if it always were part of the partnership agreement for purposes of making any reallocations and determining the appropriate limitations period.

(vii) **Recapture.** For special rules applicable to the allocation of recapture income or credit, see paragraph (e) of § 1.1245-1, paragraph (f) of § 1.1250-1, paragraph (c) of § 1.1254-1, and paragraph (a) of § 1.47-6.

(5) **Examples.** The operation of the rules in this paragraph is illustrated by the following examples:

Example (1). (i) A and B form a general partnership with cash contributions of $40,000 each, which cash is used to purchase depreciable personal property at a cost of $80,000. The partnership elects under section 48(q)(4) to reduce the amount of investment tax credit in lieu of adjusting the tax basis of such property. The partnership agreement provides that A and B will have equal shares of taxable income and loss (computed without regard to cost recovery deductions) and cash flow and that all cost recovery deductions on the property will be allocated to A. The agreement further provides that the partners' capital accounts will be determined and maintained in accordance with paragraph (b)(2)(iv) of the section, but that upon liquidation of the partnership, distributions will be made equally between the partners (regardless of capital account balances) and no partner will be required to restore the deficit balance in his capital account for distribution to partners with positive capital accounts balances. In the partnership's first taxable year, it recognizes operating income equal to its operating expenses and has an additional $20,000 cost recovery deduction, which is allocated entirely to A. That A and B will be entitled to equal distributions on liquidation, even though A is allocated the entire $20,000 cost recovery deduction, indicates A will not bear the full risk of the economic loss corresponding to such deduction if such loss occurs. Under paragraph (b)(2)(ii) of this section, the allocation lacks economic effect and will be disregarded. The partners made equal contributions to the partnership, share equally in other taxable income and loss and in cash flow, and will share equally in liquidation proceeds, indicating that their actual economic arrangement is to bear the risk imposed by the potential decrease in the value of the property equally. Thus, under paragraph (b)(3) of this section the partners' interests in the

partnership are equal, and the cost recovery deduction will be reallocated equally between A and B.

(ii) Assume the same facts as in (i) except that the partnership agreement provides that liquidation proceeds will be distributed in accordance with capital account balances if the partnership is liquidated during the first five years of its existence but that liquidation proceeds will be distributed equally if the partnership is liquidated thereafter. Since the partnership agreement does not provide for the requirement contained in paragraph (b)(2)(ii)(b)(2) of this section to be satisfied throughout the term of the partnership, the partnership allocations do not have economic effect. Even if the partnership agreement provided for the requirement contained in paragraph (b)(2)(ii)(b)(2) to be satisfied throughout the term of the partnership, such allocations would not have economic effect unless the requirement contained in paragraph (b)(2)(ii)(b)(3) of this section or the alternate economic effect test contained in paragraph(b)(2)(ii)(d) of this section were satisfied.

(iii) Assume the same facts as in (i) except that distributions in liquidation of the partnership (or any partner's interest) are to be made in accordance with the partners' positive capital account balances throughout the term of the partnership (as set forth in paragraph (b)(2)(ii)(b)(2) of this section). Assume further that the partnership agreement contains a qualified income offset (as defined in paragraph (b)(2)(ii)(d) of this section) and that, as of the end of each partnership taxable year, the items described in paragraphs (b)(2)(ii)(d)(4), (5), and (6) of this section are not reasonably expected to cause or increase a deficit balance in A's capital account.

	A	B
Capital account upon formation	$40,000	$40,000
Less: year 1 cost recovery deduction	(20,000)	0
Capital account at end of year 1	$20,000	$40,000

Under the alternate economic effect test contained in paragraph (b)(2)(ii)(d) of this section, the allocation of the $20,000 cost recovery deduction to A has economic effect.

(iv) Assume the same facts as in (iii) and that in the partnership's second taxable year it recognizes operating income equal to its operating expenses and has a $25,000 cost recovery deduction which, under the partnership agreement, is allocated entirely to A.

	A	B
Capital account at beginning of year 2	$20,000	$40,000
Less: year 2 cost recovery deduction	(25,000)	0
Capital account at end of year 2	($5,000)	$40,000

The allocation of the $25,000 cost recovery deduction to A satisfies that alternate economic effect test contained in paragraph (b)(2)(ii)(d) of this section only to the extent of $20,000. Therefore, only $20,000 of such allocation has economic effect, and the remaining $5,000 must be reallocated in accordance with the partners' interests in the partnership. Under the partnership agreement, if the property were sold immediately following the end of the partnership's second taxable year for $35,000 (its adjusted tax basis), the $35,000 would be distributed to B. Thus, B, and not A, bears the economic burden corresponding to $5,000 of the $25,000 cost recovery deduction allocated to A. Under paragraph (b)(3)(iii) of this section, $5,000 of such cost recovery deduction will be reallocated to B.

(v) Assume the same facts as in (iv) except that the cost recovery deduction for the partnership's second taxable year is $20,000 instead of $25,000. The allocation of such cost recovery deduction to A has economic effect under the alternate economic effect test contained in paragraph (b)(2)(ii)(d) of this section. Assume further that the property is sold for $35,000 immediately following the end of the partnership's second taxable year, resulting in a $5,000 taxable loss ($40,000 adjusted tax basis less $35,000 sales price), and the partnership is liquidated.

	A	B
Capital account at beginning of year 2	$20,000	$40,000
Less: year 2 cost recovery deduction	(20,000)	0
Capital account at end of year 2	0	$40,000
Less: loss on sale	(2,500)	(2,500)
Capital account before liquidation	($2,500)	$37,500

Under the partnership agreement the $35,000 sales proceeds are distributed to B. Since B bears the entire economic burden corresponding to the $5,000 taxable loss from the sale of the property, the allocation of $2,500 of such loss to A does not have economic effect and must be reallocated in accordance with the partners' interests in the partnership. Under paragraph (b)(3)(iii) of this section, such $2,500 loss will be reallocated to B.

(vi) Assume the same facts as in (iv) except that the cost recovery deduction for the partnership's second taxable year is $20,000 instead of $25,000, and that as of the end of the partnership's second taxable year it is reasonably expected that during its third taxable year the partnership will (1) have operating income equal to its operating expenses (but will have no cost recovery deductions), (2) borrow $10,000 (recourse) and distribute such amount $5,000 to A and $5,000 to B, and (3) thereafter sell the partnership property, repay the $10,000 liability, and liquidate. In determining the extent to which the alternate economic effect test contained in paragraph (b)(2)(ii)(d) of this section is satisfied as of the end of the partnership's second taxable year, the fair market value of partnership property is presumed to be equal to its adjusted tax basis (in accordance with paragraph (b)(2)(iii)(c) of this section). Thus, it is presumed that the selling price of such property during the partnership's third taxable year will be its $40,000 adjusted tax basis. Accordingly, there can be no reasonable expectation that there will be increases to A's capital account in the partnership's third taxable year that will offset the expected $5,000 distribution to A. Therefore, the distribution of the loan proceeds must be taken into account in determining to what extent the alternate economic effect test contained in paragraph (b)(2)(ii)(d) is satisfied.

	A	B
Capital account at beginning of year 2	$20,000	$40,000
Less: expected future distribution	(5,000)	(5,000)
Less: year 2 cost recovery deduction	(20,000)	(0)
Hypothetical capital account at end of year 2	($5,000)	$35,000

Upon sale of the partnership property, the $40,000 presumed sales proceeds would be used to repay the $10,000 liability, and the remaining $30,000 would be distributed to B. Under these circumstances the allocation of the $20,000 cost recovery deduction to A in the partnership's second taxable year satisfies the alternate economic effect test contained in paragraph (b)(2)(ii)(d) of this section only to the extent of $15,000. Under paragraph (b)(3)(iii) of this section, the remaining $5,000 of such deduction will be reallocated to B. The results in this example would be the same even if the partnership agreement also provided that any gain (whether ordinary income or capital gain) upon the sale of the property would be allocated to A to the extent of the prior allocations of cost recovery deductions to him, and, at end of the partnership's second taxable year, the partners were confident that the gain on the sale of the property in the partnership's third taxable year would be sufficient to offset the expected $5,000 distribution to A.

(vii) Assume the same facts as in (iv) except that the partnership agreement also provides that any partner with a deficit balance in his capital account following the liquidation of his interest must restore that deficit to the partnership (as set forth in paragraph (b)(2)(ii)(b)(3) of this section). Thus, if the property were sold for $35,000 immediately after the end of the partnership's second taxable year, the $35,000 would be distributed to B, A would contribute $5,000 (the deficit balance in his capital account) to the partnership, and that $5,000 would be distributed to B. The allocation of the entire $25,000 cost recovery deduction to A in the partnership's second taxable year has economic effect.

(viii) Assume the same facts as in (vii) except that A's obligation to restore the deficit balance in his capital account is limited to a maximum of $5,000. The allocation of the $25,000 cost recovery deduction to A in the partnership's second taxable year has economic effect under alternate economic effect test contained in paragraph (b)(2)(ii)(d) of this section. At the end of such year, A makes an additional $5,000 contribution to the partnership (thereby eliminating the $5,000 deficit balance in his capital account). Under paragraph (b)(2)(ii)(f) of this section, A's obligation to restore up to $5,000 of the deficit balance in his capital account may be eliminated after he contributes the additional $5,000 without affecting the validity of prior allocations.

(ix) Assume the same facts as in (iv) except that upon formation of the partnership A also contributes to the partnership his promissory note with a $5,000 principal balance. The note unconditionally obligates A to pay an additional $5,000 to the partnership at the earlier of (a) the beginning of the partnership's fourth taxable year, or (b) the end of the partnership taxable year in which A's interest is liquidated. Under paragraph (b)(2)(ii)(c) of this section, A is considered obligated to restore up to $5,000 of the deficit balance in his capital account to the partnership. Accordingly, under the alternate economic effect test contained in paragraph (b)(2)(ii)(d) of this section, the allocation of the $25,000 cost recovery deduction to A in the partnership's second taxable year has economic effect. The results in this example would be the same if (1) the note A contributed to the partnership were payable only at the end of the partnership's fourth taxable year (so that A would not be required to satisfy the note upon liquidation of his interest in the partnership), and (2) the partnership agreement provided that upon liquidation of A's interest, the partnership would retain A's note, and A would contribute to the partnership the excess of the outstanding principal balance of the note over its then fair market value.

(x) Assume the same facts as in (ix) except that A's obligation to contribute an additional $5,000 to the partnership is not evidenced by a promissory note. Instead, the partnership agreement imposes upon A the obligation to make an additional $5,000 contribution to the partnership at the earlier of (a) the beginning of the partnership's fourth taxable year, or (b) the end of the partnership taxable year in which A's interest is liquidated. Under paragraph (b)(2)(ii)(c) of this section, as a result of A's deferred contribution requirement, A is considered obligated to restore up to $5,000 of the deficit balance in his capital account to the partnership. Accordingly, under the alternate economic effect test contained in paragraph (b)(2)(ii)(d) of this section, the allocation of the $25,000 cost recovery deduction to A in the partnership's second taxable year has economic effect.

(xi) Assume the same facts as in (vii) except that the partnership agreement also provides that any gain (whether ordinary income or capital gain) upon the sale of the property will be allocated to A to the extent of the prior allocations to A of cost recovery deductions from such property, and additional gain will be allocated equally between A and B. At the time the allocations of cost recovery deductions were made to A, the partners believed there would be gain on the sale of the property in an amount sufficient to offset the allocations of cost recovery deductions to A. Nevertheless, the existence of the gain chargeback provision will not cause the economic effect of the allocations to be insubstantial under paragraph (b)(2)(iii)(c) of this section, since in testing whether the economic effect of such allocations is substantial, the recovery property is presumed to decrease in value by the amount of such deductions.

Example (2). C and D form a general partnership solely to acquire and lease machinery that is 5-year recovery property under section 168. Each contributes $100,000 and the partnership obtains an $800,000 recourse loan to purchase the machinery. The partnership elects under section 48(q)(4) to reduce the amount of investment tax credit in lieu of adjusting the tax basis of such machinery. The partnership, C and D have calendar taxable years. The partnership agreement provides that the partners' capital accounts will be determined and maintained in accordance with paragraph (b)(2)(iv) of this section, distributions in liquidation of the partnership (or any partner's interest) will be made in accordance with the partners' positive capital account balances, and any partner with a deficit balance in his capital account following the liquidation of his interest must restore that deficit to the partnership (as set forth in

paragraphs (b)(2)(ii)(b)(2) and (3) of this section). The partnership agreement further provides that (a) partnership net taxable loss will be allocated 90 percent to C and 10 percent to D until such time as there is partnership net taxable income, and therefore C will be allocated 90 percent of such taxable income until he has been allocated partnership net taxable income equal to the partnership net taxable loss previously allocated to him, (b) all further partnership net taxable income or loss will be allocated equally between C and D, and (c) distributions of operating cash flow will be made equally between C and D. The partnership enters into a 12-year lease with a financially secure corporation under which the partnership expects to have a net taxable loss in each of its first 5 partnership taxable years due to cost recovery deductions with respect to the machinery and net taxable income in each of its following 7 partnership taxable years, in part due to the absence of such cost recovery deductions. There is a strong likelihood that the partnership's net taxable loss in partnership taxable years 1 through 5 will be $100,000, $90,000, $80,000, $70,000, and $60,000, respectively, and the partnership's net taxable income in partnership taxable years 6 through 12 will be $40,000, $50,000, $60,000, $70,000, $80,000, $90,000, and $100,000, respectively. Even though there is a strong likelihood that the allocations of net taxable loss in years 1 through 5 will be largely offset by other allocations in partnership taxable years 6 through 12, and even if it is assumed that the total tax liability of the partners in years 1 through 12 will be less than if the allocations had not been provided in the partnership agreement, the economic effect of the allocations will not be insubstantial under paragraph (b)(2)(iii)(c) of this section. This is because at the time such allocations became part of the partnership agreement, there was a strong likelihood that the allocations of net taxable loss in years 1 through 5 would not be largely offset by allocations of income within 5 years (determined on a first-in, first-out basis). The year 1 allocation will not be offset until years 6, 7, and 8, the year 2 allocation will not offset until years 8 and 9, the year 3 allocation will not be offset until years 9 and 10, the year 4 allocation will not be offset until years 10 and 11, and the year 5 allocation will not be offset until years 11 and 12.

Example (3). E and F enter into a partnership agreement to develop and market experimental electronic devices. E contributes $2,500 cash and agrees to devote his full-time services to the partnership. F contributes $100,000 cash and agrees to obtain a loan for the partnership for any additional capital needs. The partnership agreement provides that all deductions for research and experimental expenditures and interest on partnership loans are to be allocated to F. In addition, F will be allocated 90 percent, and E 10 percent, of partnership taxable income or loss, computed net of the deductions for such research and experimental expenditures and interest, until F has received allocations of such taxable income equal to the sum of such research and experimental expenditures, such interest expense, and his share of such taxable loss. Thereafter E and F will share all taxable income and loss equally. Operating cash flow will be distributed equally between E and F. The partnership agreement also provides that E's and F's capital accounts will be determined and maintained in accordance with paragraph (b)(2)(iv) of this section, distributions in liquidation of the partnership (or any partner's interest) will be made in accordance with the partners' positive capital account balances, and any partner with a deficit balance in his capital account following the liquidation of his interest must restore that deficit to the partnership (as set forth in paragraphs (b)(2)(ii)(b)(2) and (3) of this section). These allocations have economic effect. In addition, in view of the nature of the partnership's activities, there is not a strong likelihood at the time the allocations become part of the partnership agreement that the economic effect of the allocations to F of deductions for research and experimental expenditures and interest on partnership loans will be largely offset by allocations to F of partnership net taxable income. The economic effect of the allocations is substantial.

Example (4). (i) G and H contribute $75,000 and $25,000, respectively, in forming a general partnership. The partnership agreement provides that all income, gain, loss, and deduction will be allocated equally between the partners, that the partners' capital accounts will be determined and maintained in accordance with paragraph (b)(2)(iv) of this section, but that all partnership distributions will, regardless of capital account balances, be made 75 percent to G and 25 percent to H. Following the liquidation of the partnership, neither partner is required to restore the deficit balance in his capital account to the partnership for distribution to partners with positive capital account balances. The allocations in the partnership agreement do not have economic effect. Since contributions were made in a 75/25 ratio and the partnership agreement indicates that all economic profits and losses of the partnership are to be shared in a 75/25 ratio, under paragraph (b)(3) of this section, partnership income, gain, loss, and deduction will be reallocated 75 percent to G and 25 percent to H.

(ii) Assume the same facts as in (i) except that the partnership maintains no capital accounts and the partnership agreement provides that all income, gain, loss, deduction, and credit will be allocated 75 percent to G and 25 percent to H. G and H are ultimately liable (under a State law right of contribution) for 75 percent and 25 percent respectively, of any debts of the partnership. Although the allocations do not satisfy the requirements of paragraph (b)(2)(ii)(b) of this section, the allocations have economic effect under the economic effect equivalence test of paragraph (b)(2)(ii)(i) of this section.

(iii) Assume the same facts as in (i) except that the partnership agreement provides that any partner with a deficit balance in his capital account must restore that deficit to the partnership (as set forth in paragraph (b)(2)(ii)(b)(2) of this section). Although the allocations do not satisfy the requirements of paragraph (b)(2)(ii)(b) of this section, the allocations have economic effect under the economic effect equivalence test of paragraph (b)(2)(ii)(i) of this section.

Example (5). (i) Individuals I and J are the only partners of an investment partnership. The partnership owns corporate stocks, corporate debt instruments, and tax-exempt debt instruments. Over the next several years, I expects to be in the 50 percent marginal tax bracket, and J expects to be in the 15 percent marginal tax bracket. There is a strong likelihood that in each of the next several years the partnership will realize between $450 and $550 of tax-exempt interest and between

$450 and $550 of a combination of taxable interest and dividends from its investments. I and J made equal capital contributions to the partnership, and they have agreed to share equally in gains and losses from the sale of the partnership's investment securities. I and J agree, however, that rather than share interest and dividends of the partnership equally, they will allocate the partnership's tax-exempt interest 80 percent to I and 20 percent to J and will distribute cash derived from interest received on the tax-exempt bonds in the same percentages. In addition, they agree to allocate 100 percent of the partnership's taxable interest and dividends to J and to distribute cash derived from interest and dividends received on the corporate stocks and debt instruments 100 percent to J. The partnership agreement further provides that the partners' capital accounts will be determined and maintained in accordance with paragraph (b)(2)(iv) of this section, distributions in liquidation of the partnership (or any partner's interest) will be made in accordance with the partner's positive capital account balances, and any partner with a deficit balance in his capital account following the liquidation of his interest must restore that deficit to the partnership (as set forth in paragraphs (b)(2)(ii)(b)(2) and (3) of this section). The allocation of taxable interest and dividends and tax-exempt interest has economic effect, but that economic effect is not substantial under the general rules set forth in paragraph (b)(2)(iii) of this section. Without the allocation I would be allocated between $225 and $275 of tax-exempt interest and between $225 and $275 of a combination of taxable interest and dividends, which (net of Federal income taxes he would owe on such income) would give I between $337.50 and $412.50 after tax. With the allocation, however, I will be allocated between $360 and $440 of tax-exempt interest and no taxable interest and dividends, which (net of Federal income taxes) will give I between $360 and $440 after tax. Thus, at the time the allocations became part of the partnership agreement, I is expected to enhance his after-tax economic consequences as a result of the allocations. On the other hand, there is a strong likelihood that neither I nor J will substantially diminish his after-tax economic consequences as a result of the allocations. Under the combination of likely investment outcomes least favorable for J, the partnership would realize $550 of tax-exempt interest and $450 of taxable interest and dividends, giving J $492.50 after tax (which is more than the $466.25 after tax J would have received if each of such amounts had been allocated equally between the partners). Under the combination of likely investment outcomes least favorable for I, the partnership would realize $450 of tax-exempt interest and $550 of taxable interest and dividends, giving I $360 after tax (which is not substantially less than the $362.50 he would have received if each such amounts had been allocated equally between the partners). Accordingly, the allocations in the partnership agreement must be reallocated in accordance with the partners' interests in the partnership under paragraph (b)(3) of this section.

(ii) Assume the same facts as in (i). In addition, assume that in the first partnership taxable year in which the allocation arrangement described in (i) applies, the partnership realizes $450 of tax-exempt interest and $550 of taxable interest and dividends, so that, pursuant to the partnership agreement, I's capital account is credited with $360 (80 percent of the tax-exempt interest), and J's capital account is credited with $640 (20 percent of the tax-exempt interest and 100 percent of the taxable interest and dividends). The allocations of tax-exempt interest and taxable interest and dividends (which do not have substantial economic effect for the reasons stated in (i) will be disregarded and will be reallocated. Since under the partnership agreement I will receive 36 percent (360/1,000) and J will receive 64 percent (640/1,000) of the partnership's total investment income in such year, under paragraph (b)(3) of this section the partnership's tax-exempt interest and taxable interest and dividends each will be reallocated 36 percent to I and 64 percent to J.

Example (6). K and L are equal partners in a general partnership formed to acquire and operate property described in section 1231(b). The partnership, K, and L have calendar taxable years. The partnership agreement provides that the partners' capital accounts will be determined and maintained in accordance with paragraph (b)(2)(iv) of this section, that distributions in liquidation of the partnership (or any partner's interest) will be made in accordance with the partners' positive capital account balances, and that any partner with a deficit balance in his capital account following the liquidation of his interest must restore that deficit to the partnership (as set forth in paragraphs (b)(2)(ii)(b)(2) and (3) of this section). For a taxable year in which the partnership expects to incur a loss on the sale of a portion of such property, the partnership agreement is amended (at the beginning of the taxable year) to allocate such loss to K, who expects to have no gains from the sale of depreciable property described in section 1231(b) in that taxable year, and to allocate an equivalent amount of partnership loss and deduction for that year of a different character to L, who expects to have such gains. Any partnership loss and deduction in excess of these allocations will be allocated equally between K and L. The amendment is effective only for that taxable year. At the time the partnership agreement is amended, there is a strong likelihood that the partnership will incur deduction or loss in the taxable year other than loss from the sale of property described in section 1231(b) in an amount that will substantially equal or exceed the expected amount of the section 1231(b) loss. The allocations in such taxable year have economic effect. However, the economic effect of the allocations is insubstantial under the test described in paragraph (b)(2)(iii)(b) of this section because there is a strong likelihood, at the time the allocations become part of the partnership agreement, that the net increases and decreases to K's and L's capital accounts will be the same at the end of the taxable year to which they apply with such allocations in effect as they would have been in the absence of such allocations, and that the total taxes of K and L for such year will be reduced as a result of such allocations. If in fact the partnership incurs deduction or loss, other than loss from the sale of property described in section 1231(b), in an amount at least equal to the section 1231(b) loss, the loss and deduction in such taxable year will be reallocated equally between K and L under paragraph (b)(3) of this section. If not, the loss from the sale of property described in section 1231(b) and the items of deduction and other loss realized in such year will be reallocated between K and L in proportion to the net decreases in their capital accounts due to the allocation of such items under the partnership agreement.

Example (7). (i) M and N are partners in the MN general partnership, which is engaged in an active business. Income, gain, loss, and deduction from MN's business is allocated equally between M and N. The partnership, M, and N have calendar taxable years. Under the partnership agreement the partners' capital accounts will be determined and maintained in accordance with paragraph (b)(2)(iv) of this section, distributions in liquidation of the partnership (or any partner's interest) will be made in accordance with the partner's positive capital account balances, and any partner with a deficit balance in his capital account following the liquidation of his interest must restore that deficit to the partnership (as set forth in paragraphs (b)(2)(ii)(b)(2) and (3) of this section). In order to enhance the credit standing of the partnership, the partners contribute surplus funds to the partnership, which the partners agree to invest in equal dollar amounts of tax-exempt bonds and corporate stock for the partnership's first 3 taxable years. M is expected to be in a higher marginal tax bracket than N during those 3 years. At the time the decision to make these investments is made, it is agreed that, during the 3-year period of the investment, M will be allocated 90 percent and N 10 percent of the interest income from the tax-exempt bonds as well as any gain or loss from the sale thereof, and that M will be allocated 10 percent and N 90 percent of the dividend income from the corporate stock as well as any gain or loss from the sale thereof. At the time the allocations concerning the investments become part of the partnership agreement, there is not a strong likelihood that the gain or loss from the sale of the stock will be substantially equal to the gain or loss from the sale of the tax-exempt bonds, but there is a strong likelihood that the tax-exempt interest and the taxable dividends realized from these investments during the 3-year period will not differ substantially. These allocations have economic effect, and the economic effect of the allocations of the gain or loss on the sale of the tax-exempt bonds and corporate stock is substantial. The economic effect of the allocations of the tax-exempt interest and the taxable dividends, however, is not substantial under the test described in paragraph (b)(2)(iii)(c) of this section because there is a strong likelihood, at the time the allocations become part of the partnership agreement, that at the end of the 3-year period to which such allocations relate, the net increases and decreases to M's and N's capital accounts will be the same with such allocations as they would have been in the absence of such allocations, and that the total taxes of M and N for the taxable years to which such allocations relate will be reduced as a result of such allocations. If in fact the amounts of the tax-exempt interest and taxable dividends earned by the partnership during the 3-year period are equal, the tax-exempt interest and taxable dividends will be reallocated to the partners in equal shares under paragraph (b)(3) of this section. If not, the tax-exempt interest and taxable dividends will be reallocated between M and N in proportion to the net increases in their capital accounts during such 3-year period due to the allocation of such items under the partnership agreement.

(ii) Assume the same facts as in (i) except that gain or loss from the sale of the tax-exempt bonds and corporate stock will be allocated equally between M and N and the partnership agreement provides that the 90/10 allocation arrangement with respect to the investment income applies only to the first $10,000 of interest income from the tax-exempt bonds and the first $10,000 of dividend income from the corporate stock, and only to the first taxable year of the partnership. There is a strong likelihood at the time the 90/10 allocation of the investment income became part of the partnership agreement that in the first taxable year of the partnership, the partnership will earn more than $10,000 of tax-exempt interest and more than $10,000 of taxable dividends. The allocations of tax-exempt interest and taxable dividends provided in the partnership agreement have economic effect, but under the test contained in paragraph (b)(2)(iii)(b) of this section, such economic effect is not substantial for the same reasons stated in (i) (but applied to the 1 taxable year, rather than to a 3-year period). If in fact the partnership realizes at least $10,000 of tax-exempt interest and at least $10,000 of taxable dividends in such year, the allocations of such interest income and dividend income will be reallocated equally between M and N under paragraph (b)(3) of this section. If not, the tax-exempt interest and taxable dividends will be reallocated between M and N in proportion to the net increases in their capital accounts due to the allocations of such items under the partnership agreement.

(iii) Assume the same facts as in (ii) except that at the time the 90/10 allocation of investment income becomes part of the partnership agreement, there is not a strong likelihood that (1) the partnership will earn $10,000 or more of tax-exempt interest and $10,000 or more of taxable dividends in the partnership's first taxable year, and (2) the amount of tax-exempt interest and taxable dividends earned during such year will be substantially the same. Under these facts the economic effect of the allocations generally will be substantial. (Additional facts may exist in certain cases, however, so that the allocation is insubstantial under the second sentence of paragraph (b)(2)(iii). See example (5) above.)

Example (8). (i) O and P are equal partners in the OP general partnership. The partnership, O, and P have calendar taxable years. Partner O has a net operating loss carryover from another venture that is due to expire at the end of the partnership's second taxable year. Otherwise, both partners expect to be in the 50 percent marginal tax bracket in the next several taxable years. The partnership agreement provides that the partners' capital accounts will be determined and maintained in accordance with paragraph (b)(2)(iv) of this section, distributions in liquidation of the partnership (or any partner's interest) will be made in accordance with the partners' positive capital account balances, and any partner with a deficit balance in his capital account following the liquidation of his interest must restore that deficit to the partnership (as set forth in paragraphs (b)(2)(ii)(b)(2) and (3) of this section). The partnership agreement is amended (at the beginning of the partnership's second taxable year) to allocate all the partnership net taxable income for that year to O. Future partnership net taxable loss is to be allocated to O, and future partnership net taxable income to P, until the allocation of income to O in the partnership's second taxable year is offset. It is further agreed orally that in the event the partnership is liquidated prior to completion of such offset, O's capital account will be adjusted downward to the extent of one-half

of the allocations of income to O in the partnership's second taxable year that have not been offset by other allocations, P's capital account will be adjusted upward by a like amount, and liquidation proceeds will be distributed in accordance with the partners' adjusted capital account balances. As a result of this oral amendment, all allocations of partnership net taxable income and net taxable loss made pursuant to the amendment executed at the beginning of the partnership's second taxable year lack economic effect and will be disregarded. Under the partnership agreement other allocations are made equally to O and P, and O and P will share equally in liquidation proceeds, indicating that the partners' interests in the partnership are equal. Thus, the disregarded allocations will be reallocated equally between the partners under paragraph (b)(3) of this section.

(ii) Assume the same facts as in (i) except that there is no agreement that O's and P's capital accounts will be adjusted downward and upward, respectively, to the extent of one-half of the partnership net taxable income allocated to O in the partnership's second taxable year that is not offset subsequently by other allocations. The income of the partnership is generated primarily by fixed interest payments received with respect to highly rated corporate bonds, which are expected to produce sufficient net taxable income prior to the end of the partnership's seventh taxable year to offset in large part the net taxable income to be allocated to O in the partnership's second taxable year. Thus, at the time the allocations are made part of the partnership agreement, there is a strong likelihood that the allocation of net taxable income to be made to O in the second taxable year will be offset in large part within 5 taxable years thereafter. These allocations have economic effect. However, the economic effect of the allocation of partnership net taxable income to O in the partnership's second taxable year, as well as the offsetting allocations to P, is not substantial under the test contained in paragraph (b)(2)(iii)(c) of this section because there is a strong likelihood that the net increases or decreases in O's and P's capital accounts will be the same at the end of the partnership's seventh taxable year with such allocations as they would have been in the absence of such allocations, and the total taxes of O and P for the taxable years to which such allocations relate will be reduced as a result of such allocations. If in fact the partnership, in its taxable years 3 through 7, realizes sufficient net taxable income to offset the amount allocated to O in the second taxable year, the allocations provided in the partnership agreement will be reallocated equally between the partners under paragraph (b)(3) of this section.

Example (9). Q and R form a limited partnership with contributions of $20,000 and $180,000, respectively. Q, the limited partner, is a corporation that has $2,000,000 of net operating loss carryforwards that will not expire for 8 years. Q does not expect to have sufficient income (apart from the income of the partnership) to absorb any of such net operating loss carryforwards. R, the general partner, is a corporation that expects to be in the 46 percent marginal tax bracket for several years. The partnership agreement provides that the partners' capital accounts will be determined and maintained in accordance with paragraph (b)(2)(iv) of this section, distributions in liquidation of the partnership (or any partner's interest) will be made in accordance with the partners' positive capital account balances, and any partner with a deficit balance in his capital account following the liquidation of his interest must restore that deficit to the partnership (as set forth in paragraphs (b)(2)(ii)(b)(2) and (3) of this section). The partnership's cash, together with the proceeds of an $800,000 loan, are invested in assets that are expected to produce taxable income and cash flow (before debt service) of approximately $150,000 a year for the first 8 years of the partnership's operations. In addition, it is expected that the partnership's total taxable income in its first 8 taxable years will not exceed $2,000,000. The partnership's $150,000 of cash flow in each of its first 8 years will be used to retire the $800,000 loan. The partnership agreement provides that partnership net taxable income will be allocated 90 percent to Q and 10 percent to R in the first through eighth partnership taxable years, and 90 percent to R and 10 percent to Q in all subsequent partnership taxable years. Net taxable loss will be allocated 90 percent to R and 10 percent to Q in all partnership taxable years. All distributions of cash from the partnership to partners (other than the priority distributions to Q described below) will be made 90 percent to R and 10 percent to Q. At the end of the partnership's eighth taxable year, the amount of Q's capital account in excess of one-ninth of R's capital account on such date will be designated as Q's "excess capital account." Beginning in the ninth taxable year of the partnership, the undistributed portion of Q's excess capital account will begin to bear interest (which will be paid and deducted under section 707(c) at a rate of interest below the rate that the partnership can borrow from commercial lenders, and over the next several years (following the eighth year) the partnership will make priority cash distributions to Q in prearranged percentages of Q's excess capital account designed to amortize Q's excess capital account and the interest thereon over a prearranged period. In addition, the partnership's agreement prevents Q from causing his interest in the partnership from being liquidated (and thereby receiving the balance in his capital account) without R's consent until Q's excess capital account has been eliminated. The below market rate of interest and the period over which the amortization will take place are prescribed such that, as of the end of the partnership's eighth taxable year, the present value of Q's right to receive such priority distributions is approximately 46 percent of the amount of Q's excess capital account as of such date. However, because the partnership's income for its first 8 taxable years will be realized approximately ratably over that period, the present value of Q's right to receive the priority distributions with respect to its excess capital account is, as of the date the partnership agreement is entered into, less than the present value of the additional Federal income taxes for which R would be liable if, during the partnership's first 8 taxable years, all partnership income were to be allocated 90 percent to R and 10 to Q. The allocations of partnership taxable income to Q and R in the first through eighth partnership taxable years have economic effect. However, such economic effect is not substantial under the general rules set forth in paragraph (b)(2)(iii) of this section. This is true because R may enhance his after-tax economic consequences, on a present value basis, as a result of the allocations to Q of 90 percent of partnership's income during taxable years 1 through 8, and there is a strong likelihood that neither R

nor Q will substantially diminish its after-tax economic consequences, on a present value basis, as a result of such allocation. Accordingly, partnership taxable income for partnership taxable years 1 through 8 will be reallocated in accordance with the partners' interests in the partnership under paragraph (b)(3) of this section.

Example (10). (i) S and T form a general partnership to operate a travel agency. The partnership agreement provides that the partners' capital accounts will be determined and maintained in accordance with paragraph (b)(2)(iv) of this section, distributions in liquidation of the partnership (or any partner's interest) will be made in accordance with the partners' positive capital account balances, and any partner with a deficit balance in his capital account following the liquidation of his interest must restore that deficit to the partnership (as set forth in paragraphs (b)(2)(ii)(b)(2) and (3) of this section). The partnership agreement provides that T, a resident of a foreign country, will be allocated 90 percent, and S 10 percent, of the income, gain, loss, and deduction derived from operations conducted by T within his country, and all remaining income, gain, loss, and deduction will be allocated equally. The amount of such income, gain, loss, or deduction cannot be predicted with any reasonable certainty. The allocations provided by the partnership agreement have substantial economic effect.

(ii) Assume the same facts as in (i) except that the partnership agreement provides that all income, gain, loss, and deduction of the partnership will be shared equally, but that T will be allocated all income, gain, loss, and deduction derived from operations conducted by him within his equal share of partnership income, gain, loss, and deduction, upon [1] to the amount of such share. Assume the total tax liability of S and T for each year to which these allocations relate will be reduced as a result of such allocation. These allocations have economic effect. However, such economic effect is not substantial under the test stated in paragraph (b)(2)(iii)(b) of this section because, at the time the allocations became part of the partnership agreement, there is a strong likelihood that the net increases and decreases to S's and T's capital accounts will be the same at the end of each partnership taxable year with such allocations as they would have been in the absence of such allocations, and that the total tax liability of S and T for each year to which such allocations relate will be reduced as a result of such allocations. Thus, all items of partnership income, gain, loss, and income, gain, loss, and deduction will be reallocated equally between S and T under paragraph (b)(3) of this section.

Example (11). (i) U and V share equally all income, gain, loss, and deduction of the UV general partnership, as well as all non-liquidating distributions made by the partnership. The partnership agreement provides that the partners' capital accounts will be determined and maintained in accordance with paragraph (b)(2)(iv) of this section, distributions in liquidation of the partnership (or any partner's interest) will be made in accordance with the partners' positive capital account balances, and any partner with a deficit balance in his capital account following the liquidation of his interest must restore such deficit to the partnership (as set forth in paragraphs (b)(2)(ii)(b)(2) and (3) of this section). The agreement

[1] So in original.

further provides that the partners will be allocated equal shares of any section 705(a)(2)(B) expenditures of the partnership. In the partnership's first taxable year, it pays qualified first-year wages of $6,000 and is entitled to a $3,000 targeted jobs tax credit under sections 44B and 51 of the Code. Under section 280C the partnership must reduce its deduction for wages paid by the $3,000 credit claimed (which amount constitutes a section 705(a)(2)(B) expenditure). The partnership agreement allocates the credit to U. Although the allocations of wage deductions and section 705(a)(2)(B) expenditures have substantial economic effect, the allocation of tax credit cannot have economic effect since it cannot properly be reflected in the partners' capital accounts. Furthermore, the allocation is not in accordance with the special partners' interests in the partnership rule contained in paragraph (b)(4)(ii) of this section. Under that rule, since the expenses that gave rise to the credit are shared equally by the partners, the credit will be shared equally between U and V.

(ii) Assume the same facts as in (i) and that at the beginning of the partnership's second taxable year, the partnership agreement is amended to allocate to U all wage expenses incurred in that year (including wage expenses that constitute section 705(a)(2)(B) expenditures) whether or not such wages qualify for the credit. The partnership agreement contains no offsetting allocations. That taxable year the partnership pays $8,000 in total wages to its employees. Assume that the partnership has operating income equal to its operating expenses (exclusive of expenses for wages). Assume further that $6,000 of the $8,000 wage expense constitutes qualified first-year wages. U is allocated the $3,000 deduction and the $3,000 section 705(a)(2)(B) expenditure attributable to the $6,000 of qualified first-year wages, as well as the deduction for the other $2,000 in wage expenses. The allocations of wage deductions and section 705(a)(2)(B) expenditures have substantial economic effect. Furthermore, since the wage credit is allocated in the same proportion as the expenses that gave rise to the credit, and the allocation of those expenses has substantial economic effect, the allocation of such credit to U is in accordance with the special partners' interests in the partnership rule contained in paragraph (b)(4)(ii) of this section and is recognized thereunder.

Example (12). (i) W and X form a general partnership for the purpose of mining iron ore. W makes an initial contribution of $75,000, and X makes an initial contribution of $25,000. The partnership agreement provides that non-liquidating distributions will be made 75 percent to W and 25 percent to X, and that all items of income, gain, loss, and deduction will be allocated 75 percent to W and 25 percent to X, except that all percentage depletion deductions will be allocated to W. The agreement further provides that the partners' capital accounts will be determined and maintained in accordance with paragraphs (b)(2)(iv) of this section, distributions in liquidation of the partnership (or any partner's interest) will be made in accordance with the partners' positive capital account balances, and any partner with a deficit balance in his capital account following the liquidation of his interest must restore such deficit to the partnership (as set forth in paragraphs (b)(2)(ii)(b)(2) and (3) of this section). Assume that the adjusted tax basis of the partnership's only depletable iron ore property is $1,000 and that the per-

centage depletion deduction for the taxable year with respect to such property is $1,500. The allocation of partnership income, gain, loss, and deduction (excluding the percentage depletion deduction) as well as the allocation of $1,000 of the percentage depletion deduction have substantial economic effect. The allocation to W of the remaining $500 of the percentage depletion deduction, representing the excess of percentage depletion over adjusted tax basis of the iron ore property, cannot have economic effect since such amount cannot properly be reflected in the partners' capital accounts. Furthermore, the allocation to W of that $500 excess percentage depletion deduction is not in accordance with the special partners' interests in the partnership rule contained in paragraph (b)(4)(iii) of this section, under which such $500 excess depletion deduction (and all further percentage depletion deductions from the mine) will be reallocated 75 percent to W and 25 percent to X.

(ii) Assume the same facts as in (i) except that the partnership agreement provides that all percentage depletion deductions of the partnership will be allocated 75 percent to W and 25 percent to X. Once again, the allocation of partnership income, gain, loss, and deduction (excluding the percentage depletion deduction) as well as the allocation of $1,000 of the percentage depletion deduction have substantial economic effect. Furthermore, since the $500 portion of the percentage depletion deduction that exceeds the adjusted basis of such iron ore property is allocated in the same manner as valid allocations of the gross income from such property during the taxable year (i.e., 75 percent to W and 25 percent to X), the allocation of the $500 excess percentage depletion contained in the partnership agreement is in accordance with the special partners' interests in the partnership rule contained in paragraph (b)(4)(iii) of this section.

Example (13). (i) Y and Z form a brokerage general partnership for the purpose of investing and trading in marketable securities. Y contributes cash of $10,000, and Z contributes securities of P corporation, which have an adjusted basis of $3,000 and a fair market value of $10,000. The partnership would not be an investment company under section 351(e) if it were incorporated. The partnership agreement provides that the partners' capital accounts will be determined and maintained in accordance with paragraph (b)(2)(iv) of this section, distributions in liquidation of the partnership (or any partner's interest) will be made in accordance with the partners' positive capital account balances, and any partner with a deficit balance in his capital account following the liquidation of his interest must restore that deficit to the partnership (as set forth in paragraphs (b)(2)(ii)(b)(2) and (3) of this section). The partnership uses the interim closing of books method for purposes of section 706. The initial capital accounts of Y and Z are fixed at $10,000 each. The agreement further provides that all partnership distributions, income, gain, loss, deduction, and credit will be shared equally between Y and Z, except that the taxable gain attributable to the precontribution appreciation in the value of the securities of P corporation will be allocated to Z in accordance with section 704(c). During the partnership's first taxable year, it sells the securities of P corporation for $12,000, resulting in a $2,000 book gain ($12,000 less $10,000 book value) and a $9,000 taxable gain ($12,000 less $3,000 adjusted tax basis). The partnership has no other income, gain, loss, or deductions for the taxable year. The gain from the sale of the securities is allocated as follows:

	Y		Z	
	Tax	Book	Tax	Book
Capital account upon formation	$10,000	$10,000	$3,000	$10,000
Plus: gain	1,000	1,000	8,000	1,000
Capital account at end of year 1	$11,000	$11,000	$11,000	$11,000

The allocation of the $2,000 book gain, $1,000 each to Y and Z, has substantial economic effect. Furthermore, under section 704(c) the partners' distributive shares of the $9,000 taxable gain are $1,000 to Y and $8,000 to Z.

(ii) Assume the same facts as in (i) and that at the beginning of the partnership's second taxable year, it invests its $22,000 of cash in securities of G Corp. The G Corp. securities increase in value to $40,000, at which time Y sells 50 percent of his partnership interest (i.e., a 25 percent interest in the partnership) to LK for $10,000. The partnership does not have a section 754 election in effect for the partnership taxable year during which such sale occurs. In accordance with paragraph (b)(2)(iv)(l) of this section, the partnership agreement provides that LK inherits 50 percent of Y's $11,000 capital account balance. Thus, following the sale, LK and Y each have a capital account of $5,500, and Z's capital account remains at $11,000. Prior to the end of the partnership's second taxable year, the securities are sold for their $40,000 fair market value, resulting in an $18,000 taxable gain ($40,-000 less $22,000 adjusted tax basis). The partnership has no other income, gain, loss, or deduction in such taxable year. Under the partnership agreement the $18,000 taxable gain is allocated as follows:

	Y	Z	LK
Capital account before sale of securities	$5,500	$11,000	$5,500
Plus: gain	4,500	9,000	4,500
Capital account at end of year 2 ...	$10,000	$20,000	$10,000

The allocation of the $18,000 taxable gain has substantial economic effect.

(iii) Assume the same facts as in (ii) except that the partnership has a section 754 election in effect for the partnership taxable year during which Y sells 50 percent of his interest to LK. Accordingly, under § 1.743–1 there is a $4,500 basis increase to the G Corp. securities with respect to LK. Notwithstanding this basis adjustment, as a result of the sale of the G Corp. securities, LK's capital account is, as in (ii), increased by $4,500. The fact that LK recognizes no taxable gain from such sale (due to his $4,500 section 743 basis adjustment) is irrelevant for capital accounting purposes since, in accordance with paragraph (b)(2)(iv)(m)(2) of this section, that basis adjustment is disregarded in the maintenance and computation of the partners' capital accounts.

(iv) Assume the same facts as in (iii) except that immediately following Y's sale of 50 percent of this interest to LK, the G Corp. securities decrease in value to $32,000 and are sold. The $10,000 taxable gain ($32,000 less $22,000 adjusted tax basis) is allocated as follows:

	Y	Z	LK
Capital account before sale of securities	$5,500	$11,000	$5,500
Plus: gain	2,500	5,000	2,500
Capital account at end of year 2 ...	$8,000	$16,000	$8,000

The fact that LK recognizes a $2,000 taxable loss from the sale of the G Corp. securities (due to his $4,500 section 743 basis adjustment) is irrelevant for capital accounting purposes since, in accordance with paragraph (b)(2)(iv)(m)(2) of this section, that basis adjustment is disregarded in the maintenance and computation of the partners' capital accounts.

(v) Assume the same facts as in (ii) except that Y sells 100 percent of his partnership interest (i.e., a 50 percent interest in the partnership) to LK for $20,000. Under section 708(b)(1)(B) the partnership terminates. Under paragraph (b)(1)(iv) of § 1.708–1, there is a constructive liquidation of the partnership. Immediately preceding the constructive liquidation, the capital accounts of Z and LK equal $11,000 each (LK having inherited Y's $11,000 capital account). In accordance with paragraph (b)(2)(iv)(e) of this section, the partnership agreement provides that the partners' capital accounts are adjusted to reflect how unrealized taxable gain would have been allocated if the securities had been sold for their $40,000 fair market value. Accordingly, the $18,000 of unrealized gain ($40,000 less $22,000 adjusted tax basis is credited to the partners' capital accounts as follows:

	Z	LK
Capital account following sale ..	$11,000	$11,000
Deemed sale adjustment	9,000	9,000
Capital account before constructive liquidation	$20,000	$20,000

Constructive liquidating distributions of the securities are made with reference to their $40,000 fair market value. Under section 732(b) the adjusted tax basis of the G Corp. securities constructively distributed to Z is equal to the $11,000 adjusted tax basis of Z's partnership interest before the constructive liquidation, and the adjusted tax basis of the G Corp. securities constructively distributed to Z is equal to the $20,000 adjusted tax basis of LK's partnership interest before the constructive liquidation. Under paragraph (b)(1)(iv) of § 1.708–1, the partners then are treated as contributing to a new partnership the property constructively distributed to them in connection with the partnership's termination. In accordance with paragraph (b)(2)(iv)(d) of this section, the capital accounts of Z and LK in the reconstituted partnership are stated at $20,000 each (i.e., the fair market value of the property constructively contributed to the new partnership by each of the partners).

Example (14). (i) MC and RW form a general partnership to which each contributes $10,000. The $20,000 is invested in securities of Ventureco (which are not readily tradable on an established securities market). In each of the partnership's taxable years, it recognizes operating income equal to its operating deductions (excluding gain or loss from the sale of securities). The partnership agreement provides that the partners' capital accounts will be determined and maintained in accordance with paragraph (b)(2)(iv) of this section, distributions in liquidation of the partnership (or any partner's interest) will be made in accordance with the partners' positive capital account balances, and any partner with a deficit balance in his capital account following the liquidation of his interest must restore that deficit to the partnership (as set forth in paragraphs (b)(2)(ii)(b)(2) and (3) of this section). The partnership uses the interim closing of the books method for purposes of section 706. Assume that the Ventureco securities subsequently appreciate in value to $50,000. At that time SK makes a $25,000 cash contribution to the partnership (thereby acquiring a one-third interest in the partnership), and the $25,000 is placed in a bank account. Upon SK's admission to the partnership, the capital accounts of MC and RW (which were $10,000 each prior to SK's admission) are, in accordance with paragraph (b)(2)(iv)(f) of this section, adjusted upward (to $25,000 each) to reflect their shares of the unrealized appreciation in the Ventureco securities that occurred before SK was admitted to the partnership. Immediately after SK's admission to the partnership, the securities are sold for their $50,000 fair market value, resulting in taxable gain of $30,000 ($50,000 less $20,000 adjusted tax basis) and no book gain or loss. An allocation of the $30,000 taxable gain cannot have economic effect since it cannot properly be reflected in the partners' book capital accounts. Under paragraph (b)(2)(iv)(f) of this section and the special partners' interests in the partnership rule contained in paragraph (b)(4)(i) of this section, unless the partnership agreement provides that the $30,000 taxable gain will, in accordance with section 704(c) principles, be shared $15,000 to MC and $15,000 to RW, the partners' capital accounts will not be considered maintained in accordance with paragraph (b)(2)(iv) of this section.

	MC		RW		SK	
	Tax	Book	Tax	Book	Tax	Book
Capital account following SK's admission	$10,000	$25,000	$10,000	$25,000	$25,000	$25,000
Plus: gain	15,000	0	15,000	0	0	0
Capital account following sale	$25,000	$25,000	$25,000	$25,000	$25,000	$25,000

(ii) Assume the same facts as (i) except that after SK's admission to the partnership, the Ventureco securities appreciate in value to $74,000 and are sold, resulting in taxable gain of $54,000 ($74,000 less $20,000 adjusted tax basis) and book gain of $24,000 ($74,000 less $50,000 book value). Under the partnership agreement the $24,000 book gain (the appreciation in value occurring after SK became a partner) is allocated equally among MC, RW, and SK, and such allocations have substantial economic effect. An allocation of the $54,000 taxable gain cannot have economic effect since it cannot properly be reflected in the partners' book capital accounts. Under paragraph (b)(2)(iv)(f) of this section and the special partners' interests in the partnership rule contained in paragraph (b)(4)(i) of this section, unless the partnership agreement provides that the taxable gain will, in accordance with section 704(c) principles, be shared $23,000 to MC, $23,000 to RW, and $8,000 to SK, the partners' capital accounts will not be considered maintained in accordance with paragraph (b)(2)(iv) of this section.

	MC		RW		SK	
	Tax	Book	Tax	Book	Tax	Book
Capital account following SK's admission	$10,000	$25,000	$10,000	$25,000	$25,000	$25,000
Plus: gain	23,000	8,000	23,000	8,000	8,000	8,000
Capital account following sale	$33,000	$33,000	$33,000	$33,000	$33,000	$33,000

(iii) Assume the same facts as (i) except that after SK's admission to the partnership, the Ventureco securities depreciate in value to $44,000 and are sold, resulting in taxable gain of $24,000 ($44,000 less $20,000 adjusted tax basis) and a book loss of $6,000 ($50,000 book value less $44,000). Under the partnership agreement the $6,000 book loss is allocated equally among MC, RW, and SK, and such allocations have substantial economic effect. An allocation of the $24,000 taxable gain cannot have economic effect since it cannot properly be reflected in the partners' book capital accounts. Under paragraph (b)(2)(iv)(f) of this section and the special partners' interests in the partnership rule contained in paragraph (b)(4)(i) of this section, unless the partnership agreement provides that the $24,000 taxable gain will, in accordance with section 704(c) principles, be shared equally between MC and RW, the partners' capital accounts will not be considered maintained in accordance with paragraph (b)(2)(iv) of this section.

	MC		RW		SK	
	Tax	Book	Tax	Book	Tax	Book
Capital account following SK's admission	$10,000	$25,000	$10,000	$25,000	$25,000	$25,000
Plus: gain	12,000	0	12,000	0	0	0
Less: loss	0	(2,000)	0	(2,000)	0	(2,000)
Capital account following sale	$22,000	$23,000	$22,000	$23,000	$25,000	$25,000

That SK bears an economic loss of $2,000 without a corresponding taxable loss is attributable entirely to the "ceiling rule." See paragraph (c)(2) of § 1.704–1.

(iv) Assume the same facts as in (ii) except that upon the admission of SK the capital accounts of MC and RW are not each adjusted upward from $10,000 to $25,000 to reflect the appreciation in the partnership's securities that occurred before SK was admitted to the partnership. Rather, upon SK's admission to the partnership, the partnership agreement is amended to provide that the first $30,000 of taxable gain upon the sale of such securities will be allocated equally between MC and RW, and that all other income, gain, loss and deduction will be allocated equally between MC, RW, and SK. When the securities are sold for $74,000, the $54,000 of taxable gain is so allocated. These allocations of taxable gain have substantial economic effect. (If the agreement instead provides for all taxable gain (including the $30,000 taxable gain attributable to the appreciation in the securities prior to SK's admission to the partnership) to be allocated equally between MC, RW, and SK, the partners should consider whether, and to what extent, the provisions of paragraphs (b)(1)(iii) and (iv) of this section are applicable.)

(v) Assume the same facts as in (iv) except that instead of selling the securities, the partnership makes a distribution of the securities (which have a fair market value of $74,000). Assume the distribution does not give rise to a transaction described in section 707(a)(2)(B). In accordance with paragraph (b)(2)(iv)(e) of this section, the partners' capital accounts are adjusted immediately prior to the distribution to reflect how taxable gain ($54,000) would have been allocated had the securities been sold

for their $74,000 fair market value, and capital account adjustments in respect of the distribution of the securities are made with reference to the $74,000 "booked-up" fair market value.

	MC	RW	SK
Capital account before adjustment	$10,000	$10,000	$25,000
Deemed sale adjustment	23,000	23,000	8,000
Less: distribution	(24,667)	(24,667)	(24,667)
Capital account after distribution	$8,333	$8,333	$8,333

(vi) Assume the same facts as in (i) except that the partnership does not sell the Ventureco securities. During the next 3 years the fair market value of the Ventureco securities remains at $50,000, and the partnership engages in no other investment activities. Thus, at the end of that period the balance sheet of the partnership and the partners' capital accounts are the same as they were at the beginning of such period. At the end of the 3 years, MC's interest in the partnership is liquidated for the $25,000 cash held by the partnership. Assume the distribution does not give rise to a transaction described in section 707(a)(2)(B). Assume further that the partnership has a section 754 election in effect for the taxable year during which such liquidation occurs. Under sections 734(b) and 755 the partnership increases the basis of the Ventureco securities by the $15,000 basis adjustment (the excess of $25,000 over the $10,000 adjusted tax basis of MC's partnership interest).

	MC		RW		SK	
	Tax	Book	Tax	Book	Tax	Book
Capital account before distribution	$10,000	$25,000	$10,000	$25,000	$25,000	$25,000
Plus: basis adjustment	15,000	0	0	0	0	0
Less: distribution	(25,000)	(25,000)	0	0	0	0
Capital account after liquidation	0	0	$10,000	$25,000	$25,000	$25,000

(vii) Assume the same facts as in (vi) except that the partnership has no section 754 election in effect for the taxable year during which such liquidation occurs.

	MC		RW		SK	
	Tax	Book	Tax	Book	Tax	Book
Capital account before distribution	$10,000	$25,000	$10,000	$25,000	$25,000	$25,000
Less: distribution	(25,000)	(25,000)	0	0	0	0
Capital account after liquidation	($15,000)	0	$10,000	$25,000	$25,000	$25,000

Following the liquidation of MC's interest in the partnership, the Ventureco securities are sold for their $50,000 fair market value, resulting in no book gain or loss but a $30,000 taxable gain. An allocation of this $30,000 taxable gain cannot have economic effect since it cannot properly be reflected in the partners' book capital accounts. Under paragraph (b)(2)(iv)(f) of this section and

the special partners' interests in the partnership rule contained in paragraph (b)(4)(i) of this section, unless the partnership agreement provides that $15,000 of such taxable gain will, in accordance with section 704(c) principles, be included in RW's distributive share, the partners' capital accounts will not be considered maintained in accordance with paragraph (b)(2)(iv) of this section. The remaining $15,000 of such gain will, under paragraph (b)(3) of this section, be shared equally between RW and SK.

Example (15). (i) JB and DK form a limited partnership for the purpose of purchasing residential real estate to lease. JB, the limited partner, contributes $13,500, and DK, the general partner, contributes $1,500. The partnership, which uses the cash receipts and disbursements method of accounting, purchases a building for $100,000 (on leased land), incurring a recourse mortgage of $85,000 that requires the payment of interest only for a period of 3 years. The partnership agreement provides that partnership net taxable income and loss will be allocated 90 percent to JB and 10 percent to DK, the partners' capital accounts will be determined and maintained in accordance with paragraph (b)(2)(iv) of this section, distributions in liquidation of the partnership (or any partner's interest) will be made in accordance with the partners' positive capital account balances (as set forth in paragraph (b)(2)(ii)(b)(2) of this section), and JB is not required to restore any deficit balance in his capital account, but DK is so required. The partnership agreement contains a qualified income offset (as defined in paragraph (b)(2)(ii)(d) of this section). As of the end of each of the partnership's first 3 taxable years, the items described in paragraphs (b)(2)(ii)(d)(4), (5), and (6) of this section are not reasonably expected to cause or increase a deficit balance in JB's capital account. In the partnership's first taxable year, it has rental income of $10,000, operating expenses of $2,000, interest expense of $8,000, and cost recovery deductions of $12,000. Under the partnership agreement JB and DK are allocated $10,800 and $1,200, respectively, of the $12,000 net taxable loss incurred in the partnership's first taxable year.

	JB	DK
Capital account upon formation	$13,500	$1,500
Less: year 1 net loss	(10,800)	(1,200)
Capital account at end of year 1	$2,700	$300

The alternate economic effect test contained in paragraph (b)(2)(ii)(d) of this section is satisfied as of the end of the partnership's first taxable year. Thus, the allocation made in the partnership's first taxable year has economic effect.

(ii) Assume the same facts as in (i) and that in the partnership's second taxable year it again has rental income of $10,000, operating expenses of $2,000, interest expense of $8,000, and cost recovery deductions of $12,-000. Under the partnership agreement JB and DK are allocated $10,800 and $1,200, respectively, of the $12,000 net taxable loss incurred in the partnership's second taxable year.

	JB	JB
Capital account at beginning of year 1.....................	$2,700	$300
Less: year 2 net loss	(10,800)	(1,200)
Capital account at end of year 2..................	($8,100)	($900)

Only $2,700 of the $10,800 net taxable loss allocated to JB satisfies the alternate economic effect test contained in paragraph (b)(2)(ii)(d) of this section as of the end of the

partnership's second taxable year. The allocation of such $2,700 net taxable loss to JB (consisting of $2,250 of rental income, $450 of operating expenses, $1,800 of interest expense, and $2,700 of cost recovery deductions) has economic effect. The remaining $8,100 of net taxable loss allocated by the partnership agreement to JB must be reallocated in accordance with the partners' interests in the partnership. Under paragraph (b)(3)(iii) of this section, the determination of the partners' interests in the remaining $8,100 net taxable loss is made by comparing how distributions (and contributions) would be made if the partnership sold its property at its adjusted tax basis and liquidated immediately following the end of the partnership's first taxable year with the results of such a sale and liquidation immediately following the end of the partnership's second taxable year. If the partnership's real property were sold for its $88,000 adjusted tax basis and the partnership were liquidated immediately following the end of the partnership's first taxable year, the $88,000 sales proceeds would be used to repay the $85,000 note, and there would be $3,000 remaining in the partnership, which would be used to make liquidating distributions to DK and JB of $300 and $2,700, respectively. If such property were sold for its $76,000 adjusted tax basis and the partnership were liquidated immediately following the end of the partnership's second taxable year, DK would be required to contribute $9,000 to the partnership in order for the partnership to repay the $85,000 note, and there would be no assets remaining in the partnership to distribute. A comparison of these outcomes indicates that JB bore $2,700 and DK $9,300 of the economic burden that corresponds to the $12,000 net taxable loss. Thus, in addition to the $1,200 net taxable loss allocated to DK under the partnership agreement, $8,100 of net taxable loss will be reallocated to DK under paragraph (b)(3)(iii) of this section. Similarly, for subsequent taxable years, absent an increase in JB's capital account, all net taxable loss allocated to JB under the partnership agreement will be reallocated to DK.

(iii) Assume the same facts as in (ii) and that in the partnership's third taxable year there is rental income of $35,000, operating expenses of $2,000, interest expense of $8,000, and cost recovery deductions of $10,000. The capital accounts of the partners maintained on the books of the partnership do not take into account the reallocation to DK of the $8,100 net taxable loss in the partnership's second taxable year. Thus, an allocation of the $15,000 net taxable income, $13,500 to JB and $1,500 to DK (as dictated by the partnership agreement and as reflected in the capital accounts of the partners) does not have economic effect. The partners' interests in the partnership with respect to such $15,000 taxable gain again is made in the manner described in paragraph (b)(3)(iii) of this section. If the partnership's real property were sold for its $76,000 adjusted tax basis and the partnership were liquidated immediately following the end of the partnership's second taxable year, DK would be required to contribute $9,000 to the partnership in order for the partnership to repay the $85,000 note, and there would be no assets remaining to distribute. If such property were sold for its $66,000 adjusted tax basis and the partnership were liquidated immediately following the end of the partnership's third taxable year, the $91,-000 ($66,000 sales proceeds plus $25,000 cash on hand) would be used to repay the $85,000 note and there would be $6,000 remaining in the partnership, which would be used to make liquidating distributions to DK and JB of $600 and $5,400, respectively. Accordingly, under paragraph (b)(3)(iii) of this section the $15,000 net taxable income in the partnership's third taxable year will be reallocated $9,600 to DK (minus $9,000 at end of the second taxable year to positive $600 at end of the third taxable year) and $5,400 to JB (zero at end of the second taxable year to positive $5,400 at end of the third taxable year).

Example (16). (i) KG and WN form a limited partnership for the purpose of investing in improved real estate. KG, the general partner, contributes $10,000 to the partnership, and WN, the limited partner, contributes $990,000 to the partnership. The $1,000,000 is used to purchase an apartment building on leased land. The partnership agreement provides that (1) the partners' capital accounts will be determined and maintained in accordance with paragraph (b)(2)(iv) of this section; (2) cash will be distributed first to WN until such time as he has received the amount of his original capital contribution ($990,000), next to KG until such time as he has received the amount of his original capital contribution ($10,000), and thereafter equally between WN and KG; (3) partnership net taxable income will be allocated 99 percent to WN and 1 percent to KG until the cumulative net taxable income allocated for all taxable years is equal to the cumulative net taxable loss previously allocated to the partners, and thereafter equally between WN and KG; (4) partnership net taxable loss will be allocated 99 percent to WN and 1 percent to KG, unless net taxable income has previously been allocated equally between WN and KG, in which case such net taxable loss first will be allocated equally until the cumulative net taxable loss allocated for all taxable years is equal to the cumulative net taxable income previously allocated to the partners; and (5) upon liquidation, WN is not required to restore any deficit balance in his capital account, but KG is so required. Since distributions in liquidation are not required to be made in accordance with the partners' positive capital account balances, and since WN is not required, upon the liquidation of his interest, to restore the deficit balance in his capital account to the partnership, the allocations provided by the partnership agreement do not have economic effect and will be reallocated in accordance with the partners' interests in the partnership under paragraph (b)(3) of this section.

(ii) Assume the same facts as in (i) except that the partnership agreement further provides that distributions in liquidation of the partnership (or any partner's interest) are to be made in accordance with the partners' positive capital account balances (as set forth in paragraph (b)(2)(ii)(b)(2) of this section). Assume further that the partnership agreement contains a qualified income offset (as defined in paragraph (b)(2)(ii)(d) of this section) and that, as of the end of each partnership taxable year, the items described in paragraphs (b)(2)(iii)(d)(4), (5), and (6) of this section are not reasonably expected to cause or increase a deficit balance in WN's capital account. The allocations provided by the partnership agreement have economic effect.

Example (17). FG and RP form a partnership with FG contributing cash of $100 and RP contributing property, with 2 years of cost recovery deductions remaining, that has an adjusted tax basis of $80 and a fair market value

of $100. The partnership, FG, and RP have calendar taxable years. The partnership agreement provides that the partners' capital accounts will be determined and maintained in accordance with paragraph (b)(2)(iv) of this section, liquidation proceeds will be made in accordance with capital account balances, and each partner is liable to restore the deficit balance in his capital account to the partnership upon liquidation of his interest (as set forth in paragraphs (b)(2)(ii)(b)(2) and (3) of this section). FG expects to be in a substantially higher tax bracket than RP in the partnership's first taxable year. In the partnership's second taxable year, and in subsequent taxable years, it is expected that both will be in approximately equivalent tax brackets. The partnership agreement allocates all items equally except that all $50 of book depreciation is allocated to FG in the partnership's first taxable year and all $50 of book depreciation is allocated to RP in the partnership's second taxable year. If the allocation to FG of all book depreciation in the partnership's first taxable year is respected, FG would be entitled under section 704(c) to the entire cost recovery deduction ($40) for such year. Likewise, if the allocation to RP of all the book depreciation in the partnership's second taxable year is respected, RP would be entitled under section 704(c) to the entire cost recovery deduction ($40) for such year. The allocation of book depreciation to FG and RP in the partnership's first 2 taxable years has economic effect within the meaning of paragraph (b)(2)(ii) of this section. However, the economic effect of these allocations is not substantial under the test described in paragraph (b)(2)(iii)(c) of this section since there is a strong likelihood at the time such allocations became part of the partnership agreement that at the end of the 2-year period to which such allocations relate, the net increases and decreases to FG's and RP's capital accounts will be the same with such allocations as they would have been in the absence of such allocation, and the total tax liability of FG and RP for the taxable years to which the section 704(c) determinations relate would be reduced as a result of the allocations of book depreciation. As a result the allocations of book depreciation in the partnership agreement will be disregarded. FG and RP will be allocated such book depreciation in accordance with the partners' interests in the partnership under paragraph (b)(3) of this section. Under these facts the book depreciation deductions will be reallocated equally between the partners, and section 704(c) will be applied with reference to such reallocation of book depreciation.

Example (18). (i) WM and JL form a general partnership by each contributing $300,000 thereto. The partnership uses the $600,000 to purchase an item of tangible personal property, which it leases out. The partnership elects under section 48(q)(4) to reduce the amount of investment tax credit in lieu of adjusting the tax basis of such property. The partnership agreement provides that (1) the partners' capital account will be determined and maintained in accordance with paragraph (b)(2)(iv) of this section, (2) distributions in liquidation of the partnership (or any partner's interest) will be made in accordance with the partners' positive capital account balances (as set forth in paragraph (b)(2)(ii)(b)(2) of this section), (3) any partner with a deficit balance in his capital account following the liquidation of his interest must restore that deficit to the partnership (as set forth in paragraph (b)(2)(ii)(b)(3) of this section), (4) all income, gain, loss, and deduction of the partnership will be allocated equally between the partners, and (5) all non-liquidating distributions of the partnership will be made equally between the partners. Assume that in each of the partnership's taxable years, it recognizes operating income equal to its operating deductions (excluding cost recovery and depreciation deductions and gain or loss on the sale of its property). During its first 2 taxable years, the partnership has an additional $200,000 cost recovery deduction in each year. Pursuant to the partnership agreement these items are allocated equally between WM and JL.

	WM	JL
Capital account upon formation	$300,000	$300,000
Less: net loss for years 1 and 2	(200,000)	(200,000)
Capital account at end of year 2..................	$100,000	$100,000

The allocations made in the partnership's first 2 taxable years have substantial economic effect.

(ii) Assume the same facts as in (i) and that MK is admitted to the partnership at the beginning of the partnership's third taxable year. At the time of his admission, the fair market value of the partnership property is $600,000. MK contributes $300,000 to the partnership in exchange for an equal one-third interest in the partnership, and, as permitted under paragraph (b)(2)(iv)(g), the capital accounts of WM and JL are adjusted upward to $300,000 each to reflect the fair market value of partnership property. In addition, the partnership agreement is modified to provide that depreciation

and gain or loss, as computed for tax purposes, with respect to the partnership property that appreciated prior to MK's admission will be shared among the partners in a manner that takes account of the variation between such property's $200,000 adjusted tax basis and its $600,000 book value in accordance with paragraph (b)(2)(iv)(f) and the special rule contained in paragraph (b)(4)(i) of this section. Depreciation and gain or loss, as computed for book purposes, with respect to such property will be allocated equally among the partners and, in accordance with paragraph (b)(2)(iv)(g) of this section, will be reflected in the partner's capital accounts, as will all other partnership income, gain, loss, and deduction. Since the requirements of (b)(2)(iv)(g) of this section are satisfied, the capital accounts of the partners (as adjusted) continue to be maintained in accordance with paragraph (b)(2)(iv) of this section.

(iii) Assume the same facts as in (iii) and that immediately after MK's admission to the partnership, the partnership property is sold for $600,000, resulting in a taxable gain of $400,000 ($600,000 less $200,000 adjusted tax basis) and no book gain or loss, and the partnership is liquidated. An allocation of the $400,000 taxable gain cannot have economic effect because such gain cannot properly be reflected in the partners' book capital accounts. Consistent with the special partners' interests in the partnership rule contained in paragraph (b)(4)(i) of this section, the partnership agreement provides that the $400,000 taxable gain will, in accordance with section 704(c) principles, be shared equally between WM and JL.

	WM		JL		MK	
	Tax	Book	Tax	Book	Tax	Book
Capital account at beginning of year 3 ...	$100,000	$300,000	$100,000	$300,000	$300,000	$300,000
Plus: gain...........................	200,000	0	200,000	0	0	0
Capital account before liquidation ...	$300,000	$300,000	$300,000	$300,000	$300,000	$300,000

The $900,000 of partnership cash ($600,000 sales proceeds plus $300,000 contributed by MK) is distributed equally among WM, JL, and MK in accordance with their adjusted positive capital account balances, each of which is $300,000.

(iv) Assume the same facts as in (iii) except that prior to liquidation the property appreciates and is sold for

$900,000, resulting in a taxable gain of $700,000 ($900,000 less $200,000 adjusted tax basis) and a book gain of $300,000 ($900,000 less $600,000 book value). Under the partnership agreement the $300,000 of book gain is allocated equally among the partners, and such allocation has substantial economic effect.

	WM		JL		MK	
	Tax	Book	Tax	Book	Tax	Book
Capital account at beginning of year 3 ...	$100,000	$300,000	$100,000	$300,000	$300,000	$300,000
Plus: gain...........................	300,000	100,000	300,000	100,000	100,000	100,000
Capital account before liquidation ...	$400,000	$400,000	$400,000	$400,000	$400,000	$400,000

Consistent with the special partners' interests in the partnership rule contained in paragraph (b)(4)(i) of this section, the partnership agreement provides that the $700,000 taxable gain is, in accordance with section 704(c) principles, shared $300,000 to JL, $300,000 to WM, and $100,000 to MK. This ensures that (1) WM and JL share equally the $400,000 taxable gain that is attributable to appreciation in the property that occurred prior to MK's admission to the partnership in the same manner as it was reflected in their capital accounts upon MK's admis-

sion, and (2) WM, JL, and MK share equally the additional $300,000 taxable gain in the same manner as they shared the $300,000 book gain.

(v) Assume the same facts as in (ii) except that shortly after MK's admission the property depreciates and is sold for $450,000, resulting in a taxable gain of $250,000 ($450,000 less $200,000 adjusted tax basis) and a book loss of $150,000 ($450,000 less $600,000 book value). Under the partnership agreement these items are allocated as follows:

	WM		JL		MK	
	Tax	Book	Tax	Book	Tax	Book
Capital account at beginning of year 3 ...	$100,000	$300,000	$100,000	$300,000	$300,000	$300,000
Plus: gain	125,000	0	125,000	0	0	0
Less: loss	0	(50,000)	0	(50,000)	0	(50,000)
Capital account before liquidation ...	$225,000	$250,000	$225,000	$250,000	$300,000	$250,000

The $150,000 book loss is allocated equally among the partners, and such allocation has substantial economic effect. Consistent with the special partners' interests in the partnership rule contained in paragraph (b)(4)(i) of this section, the partnership agreement provides that the $250,000 taxable gain is, in accordance with section 704(c) principles, shared equally between WM and JL. The fact the MK bears an economic loss of $50,000 without a corresponding taxable loss is attributable entirely to the "ceiling rule." See paragraph (c)(2) of § 1.704–1.

(vi) Assume the same facts as in (ii) except that the property depreciates and is sold for $170,000, resulting in a $30,000 taxable loss ($200,000 adjusted tax basis less $170,000) and a book loss of $430,000 ($600,000 book value less $170,000). The book loss of $430,000 is allocated equally among the partners ($143,333 each) and has substantial economic effect. Consistent with the special partners' interests in the partnership rule contained in paragraph (b)(4)(i) of this section, the partnership agreement provides that the entire $30,000 taxable loss is, in accordance with section 704(c) principles, included in MK's distributive share.

	WM		JL		MK	
	Tax	Book	Tax	Book	Tax	Book
Capital account at beginning of year 3 ...	$100,000	$300,000	$100,000	$300,000	$300,000	$300,000
Less Loss	0	(143,333)	0	(143,333)	(30,000)	(143,333)
Capital account before liquidation	$100,000	$156,667	$100,000	$156,667	$270,000	$156,667

(vii) Assume the same facts as in (ii) and that during the partnership's third taxable year, the partnership has an additional $100,000 cost recovery deduction and $300,000 book depreciation deduction attributable to the property purchased by the partnership in its first taxable year. The $300,000 book depreciation deduction is allocated equally among the partners, and that allocation has substantial economic effect. Consistent with the special partners' interests in the partnership rule contained in paragraph (b)(4)(i) of this section, the partnership agreement provides that the $100,000 cost recovery deduction for the partnership's third taxable year is, in accordance with section 704(c) principles, included in MK's distributive share. This is because under these facts those principles require MK to include the cost recovery deduction for such property in his distributive share up to the amount of the book depreciation deduction for such property properly allocated to him.

	WM		JL		MK	
	Tax	Book	Tax	Book	Tax	Book
Capital account at beginning of year 3 ...	$100,000	$300,000	$100,000	$300,000	$300,000	$300,000
Less: recovery/depreciation deduction for year 3	0	(100,000)	0	(100,000)	(100,000)	(100,000)
Capital account at end of year 3	$100,000	$200,000	$100,000	$200,000	$200,000	$200,000

(viii) Assume the same facts as in (vii) except that upon MK's admission the partnership property has an adjusted tax basis of $220,000 (instead of $200,000), and thus the cost recovery deduction for the partnership's third taxable year is $110,000. Assume further that upon MK's admission WM and JL have adjusted capital account balances of $110,000 and $100,000, respectively. Consistent with the special partners' interests in the partnership rule contained in paragraph (b)(4)(i) of this section, the partnership agreement provides that the excess $10,000 cost recovery deduction ($110,000 less $100,000 included in MK's distributive share) is, in accordance with section 704(c) principles, shared equally between WM and JL and is so included in their respective distributive shares for the partnership's third taxable year.

(ix) Assume the same facts as in (vii) except that upon MK's admission the partnership agreement is amended to allocate the first $400,000 of book depreciation and loss on partnership property equally between WM and JL and the last $200,000 of such book depreciation and loss to MK. Assume such allocations have substantial economic effect. Pursuant to this amendment the $300,000 book depreciation deduction in the partnership's third taxable year is allocated equally between WM and JL. Consistent with the special partners' interests in the partnership rule contained in paragraph (b)(4)(i) of this section, the partnership agreement provides that the $100,000 cost recovery deduction is, in accordance with section 704(c) principles, shared equally between WM and JL. In the partnership's fourth taxable year, it has a $60,000 cost recovery deduction and a $180,000 book depreciation deduction. Under the amendment described above, the $180,000 book depreciation deduction is allocated $50,000 to WM, $50,000 to JL, and $80,000 to MK. Consistent with the special partners' interests in the partnership rule contained in paragraph (b)(4)(i) of this section, the partnership agreement provides that the $60,000 cost recovery deduction is, in accordance with section 704(c) principles, included entirely in MK's distributive share.

	WM		JL		MK	
	Tax	Book	Tax	Book	Tax	Book
Capital account at beginning of year 3 ...	$100,000	$300,000	$100,000	$300,000	$300,000	$300,000
Less:						
(a) recovery/depreciation deduction for year 3	(50,000)	(150,000)	(50,000)	(150,000)	0	0
(b) recovery/depreciation deduction for year 4	0	(50,000)	0	(50,000)	(60,000)	(80,000)
Capital account at end of year 4	$50,000	$100,000	$50,000	$100,000	$240,000	$220,000

(x) Assume the same facts as in (vii) and that at the beginning of the partnership's third taxable year, the partnership purchases a second item of tangible personal property for $300,000 and elects under section 48(q)(4) to reduce the amount of investment tax credit in lieu of adjusting the tax basis of such property. The partnership agreement is amended to allocate the first $150,000 of cost recovery deductions and loss from such property to WM and the next $150,000 of cost recovery deductions and loss from such property equally between JL and MK. Thus, in the partnership's third taxable year it has, in addition to the items specified in (vii), a cost recovery and book depreciation deduction of $100,000 attributable to the newly acquired property, which is allocated entirely to WM.

As in (vii), the allocation of the $300,000 book depreciation attributable to the property purchased in the partnership's first taxable year equally among the partners has substantial economic effect, and consistent with the special partners' interests in the partnership rule contained in paragraph (b)(4)(i) of this section, the partnership agreement properly provides for the entire $100,000 cost recovery deduction attributable to such property to be included in MK's distributive share. Furthermore, the allocation to WM of the $100,000 cost recovery deduction attributable to the property purchased in the partnership's third taxable year has substantial economic effect.

	WM		JL		MK	
	Tax	Book	Tax	Book	Tax	Book
Capital account at beginning of year 3 ...	$100,000	$300,000	$100,000	$300,000	$300,000	$300,000
Less:						
(a) recovery/depreciation deduction for property bought in year 1	0	(100,000)	0	(100,000)	(100,000)	(100,000)
(b) recovery/depreciation deduction for property bought in year 3	(100,000)	(100,000)	0	0	0	0
Capital account at end of year 3	0	$100,000	$100,000	$200,000	$200,000	$200,000

(xi) Assume the same facts as in (x) and that at the beginning of the partnership's fourth taxable year, the properties purchased in the partnership's first and third taxable years are disposed of for $90,000 and $180,000, respectively, and the partnership is liquidated. With respect to the property purchased in the first taxable year, there is a book loss of $210,000 ($300,000 book value less $90,000) and a taxable loss of $10,000 ($100,000 adjusted tax basis less $90,000). The book loss is allocated equally among the partners, and such allocation has substantial economic effect. Consistent with the special

partners' interests in the partnership rule contained in paragraph (b)(4)(i) of this section, the partnership agreement provides that the taxable loss of $10,000 will, in accordance with section 704(c) principles, be included entirely in MK's distributive share. With respect to the property purchased in the partnership's third taxable year, there is a book and taxable loss of $20,000. Pursuant to the partnership agreement this loss is allocated entirely to WM, and such allocation has substantial economic effect.

	WM		JL		MK	
	Tax	Book	Tax	Book	Tax	Book
Capital account at beginning of year 4 ...	0	$100,000	$100,000	$200,000	$200,000	$200,000
Less:						
(a) loss on property bought in year 1 ...	0	(70,000)	0	(70,000)	(10,000)	(70,000)
(b) loss on property bought in year 3 ...	(20,000)	(20,000)	0	0	0	0
Capital account before liquidation ...	($20,000)	$10,000	$100,000	$130,000	$190,000	$130,000

Partnership liquidation proceeds ($270,000) are properly distributed in accordance with the partners' adjusted positive book capital account balances ($10,000 to WM, $130,000 to JL and $130,000 to MK).

(xii) Assume the same facts as in (x) and that in the partnership's fourth taxable year it has a cost recovery deduction of $60,000 and book depreciation deduction of $180,000 attributable to the property purchased in the partnership's first taxable year, and a cost recovery and book depreciation deduction of $100,000 attributable to the property purchased in the partnership's third taxable year. The $180,000 book depreciation deduction attributable to the property purchased in the partnership's first taxable year is allocated equally among the partners, and such allocation has substantial economic effect. Consist-

ent with the special partners' interests in the partnership rule contained in paragraph (b)(4)(i) of this section, the partnership agreement provides that the $60,000 cost recovery deduction attributable to the property purchased in the first taxable year is, in accordance with section 704(c) principles, included entirely in MK's distributive share. Furthermore the $100,000 cost recovery deduction attributable to the property purchased in the third taxable year is allocated $50,000 to WM, $25,000 to JL, and $25,000 to MK, and such allocation has substantial economic effect.

	WM		JL		MK	
	Tax	Book	Tax	Book	Tax	Book
Capital account at beginning of year 4 ...	0	$100,000	$100,000	$200,000	$200,000	$200,000
Less:						
(a) recovery/depreciation deduction for property bought in year 1...........	0	(60,000)	0	(60,000)	(60,000)	(60,000)
(b) recovery/depreciation deduction for property bought in year 3...........	(50,000)	(50,000)	(25,000)	(25,000)	(25,000)	(25,000)
Capital account at end of year 4	($50,000)	($10,000)	$75,000	$115,000	$115,000	$115,000

At the end of the partnership's fourth taxable year the adjusted tax bases of the partnership properties acquired in its first and third taxable years are $40,000 and $100,000, respectively. If the properties are disposed of at the beginning of the partnership's fifth taxable year

for their adjusted tax bases, there would be no taxable gain or loss, a book loss of $80,000 on the property purchased in the partnership's first taxable year ($120,000 book value less $40,000), and cash available for distribution of $140,000.

	WM		JL		MK	
	Tax	Book	Tax	Book	Tax	Book
Capital account at beginning of year 5 ...	($50,000)	($10,000)	$75,000	$115,000	$115,000	$115,000
Less: loss	0	(26,667)	0	(26,667)	0	(26,667)
Capital account before liquidation ...	($50,000)	($36,667)	$75,000	$88,333	$115,000	$88,333

If the partnership is then liquidated, the $140,000 of cash on hand plus the $36,667 balance that WM would be required to contribute to the partnership (the deficit balance in his book capital account) would be distributed equally between JL and MK in accordance with their adjusted positive book capital account balances.

(xii) Assume the same facts as in (i). Any tax preferences under section 57(a)(12) attributable to the partnership's cost recovery deductions in the first 2 taxable years will be taken into account equally by WM and JL. If the partnership agreement instead provides that the partnership's cost recovery deductions in its first 2 taxable years are allocated 25 percent to WM and 75 percent to JL (and such allocations have substantial economic effect), the tax preferences attributable to such cost recovery deductions would be taken into account 25 percent by WM and 75 percent by JL. The conclusion in the previous sentence is unchanged even if the partnership's operating expenses (exclusive of cost recovery and depreciation deductions) exceed its operating income in each of the partnership's first 2 taxable years, the resulting net loss is allocated entirely to WM, and the cost recovery deductions are allocated 25 percent to WM and 75 percent to JL (provided such allocations have substantial economic effect). If the partnership agreement instead provides that all income, gain, loss, and deduction (including cost recovery and depreciations) are allocated equally between JL and WM, the tax preferences attributable to the cost recovery

deductions would be taken into account equally by JL and WM. In this case, if the partnership has a $100,000 cost recovery deduction in its first taxable year and an additional net loss of $100,000 in its first taxable year (i.e., its operating expenses exceed its operating income by $100,000) and purports to categorize JL's $100,000 distributive share of partnership loss as being attributable to the cost recovery deduction and WM's $100,000 distributive share of partnership loss as being attributable to the net loss, the economic effect of such allocations is not substantial, and each partner will be allocated one-half of all partnership income, gain, loss, and deduction and will take into account one-half of the tax preferences attributable to the cost recovery deductions.

Example (19). (i) DG and JC form a general partnership for the purpose of drilling oil wells. DG contributes an oil lease, which has a fair market value and adjusted tax basis of $100,000. JC contributes $100,000 in cash, which is used to finance the drilling operations. The partnership agreement provides that DG is credited with a capital account of $100,000, and JC is credited with a capital account of $100,000. The agreement further provides that the partners' capital accounts will be determined and maintained in accordance with paragraph (b)(2)(iv) of this section, distributions in liquidation of the partnership (or any partner's interest) will be made in accordance with the partners' positive capital account balances, and any partner with a deficit balance in his capital account following the liquidation of his interest must restore such deficit to the partnership (as set forth in paragraphs (b)(2)(ii)(b)(2) and (3) of this section). The partnership chooses to adjust capital accounts on a simulated cost depletion basis and elects under section 48(q)(4) to reduce the amount of investment tax credit in lieu of adjusting the basis of its section 38 property. The agreement further provides that (1) all additional cash requirements of the partnership will be borne equally by DG and JC, (2) the deductions attributable to the property (including money) contributed by each partner will be allocated to such partner, (3) all other income, gain, loss, and deductions (and item thereof) will be allocated equally between DG and JC, and (4) all cash from operations will be distributed equally between DG and JC. In the partnership's first taxable year $80,000 of partnership intangible drilling cost deductions and $20,000 of cost recovery deductions on partnership equipment are allocated to JC, and the $100,000 basis of the lease is, for purposes of the depletion allowance under sections 611 and 613A(c)(7)(D), allocated to DG. The allocations of income, gain, loss, and deduction provided in the partnership agreement have substantial economic effect. Furthermore, since the allocation of the entire basis of the lease to DG will not result in capital account adjustments (under paragraph (b)(2)(iv)(k) of this section) the economic effect of which is insubstantial, and since all other partnership allocations are recognized under this paragraph, the allocation of the $100,000 adjusted basis of the lease to DG is, under paragraph (b)(4)(v) of this section, recognized as being in accordance with the partners' interests in partnership capital for purposes of section 613A(c)(7)(D).

(ii) Assume the same facts as in (i) except that the partnership agreement provides that (1) all additional cash requirements of the partnership for additional expenses will be funded by additional contributions from JC, (2) all cash from operations will first be distributed to JC until the excess of such cash distributions over the amount of such additional expense equals his initial $100,000 contributions, (3) all deductions attributable to such additional operating expenses will be allocated to JC, and (4) all income will be allocated to JC until the aggregate amount of income allocated to him equals the amount of partnership operating expenses funded by his initial $100,000 contribution plus the amount of additional operating expenses paid from contributions made solely by him. The allocations of income, gain, loss, and deduction provided in partnership agreement have economic effect. In addition, the economic effect of the allocations provided in the agreement is substantial. Because the partnership's drilling activities are sufficiently speculative, there is not a strong likelihood at the time the disproportionate allocations of loss and deduction to JC are provided for by the partnership agreement that the economic effect of such allocations will be largely offset by allocations of income. In addition, since the allocation of the entire basis of the lease to DG will not result in capital account adjustments (under paragraph (b)(2)(iv)(k) of this section) the economic effect of which is insubstantial, and since all other partnership allocations are recognized under this paragraph, the allocation of the adjusted basis of the lease to DG is, under paragraph (b)(4)(v) of this section, recognized as being in accordance with the partners' interests in partnership capital under section 613A(c)(7)(D).

(iii) Assume the same facts as in (i) except that all distributions, including those made upon liquidation of the partnership, will be made equally between DG and JC, and no partner is obligated to restore the deficit balance in his capital account to the partnership following the liquidation of his interest for distribution to partners with positive capital account balances. Since liquidation proceeds will be distributed equally between DG and JC irrespective of their capital account balances, and since no partner is required to restore the deficit balance in his capital account to the partnership upon liquidation (in accordance with paragraph (b)(2)(ii)(b)(3) of this section), the allocations of income, gain, loss, and deduction provided in the partnership agreement do not have economic effect and must be reallocated in accordance with the partners' interests in the partnership under paragraph (b)(3) of this section. Under these facts all partnership income, gain, loss, and deduction (and item thereof) will be reallocated equally between JC and DG. Furthermore, the allocation of the $100,000 adjusted tax basis of the lease of DG is not, under paragraph (b)(4)(v) of this section, deemed to be in accordance with the partners' interests in partnership capital under section 613A(c)(7)(D), and such basis must be reallocated in accordance with the partners' interests in partnership capital or income as determined under section 613A(c)(7)(D). The results in this example would be the same if JC's initial cash contribution were $1,000,000 (instead of $100,000), but in such case the partners should consider whether, and to what extent, the provisions of paragraph (b)(1) of § 1.721–1, and principles related thereto, may be applicable.

(iv) Assume the same facts as in (i) and that for the partnership's first taxable year the simulated depletion deduction with respect to the lease is $10,000. Since DG properly was allocated the entire depletable basis of the lease (such allocation having been recognized as being in accordance with DG's interest in partnership capital with respect to such lease), under paragraph (b)(2)(iv)(k)(1) of this section the partnership's $10,000 simulated depletion deduction is allocated to DG and will reduce his capital account accordingly. If (prior to any additional simulated depletion deductions) the lease is sold for $100,000, paragraph (b)(4)(v) of this section requires that the first $90,000 (i.e., the partnership's simulated adjusted basis in the lease) out of the $100,000 amount realized on such sale be allocated to DG (but does not directly affect his capital account). The partnership agreement allocates the remaining $10,000 amount realized equally between JC and DG (but such allocation does not directly affect their capital accounts). This allocation of the $10,000 portion of amount realized that exceeds the partnership's simulated adjusted basis in the lease will be treated as being in accordance with the partners' allocable shares of such amount realized under section 613A(c)(7)(D) because such allocation will not result in capital account adjustments (under paragraph (b)(2)(iv)(k) of this section) the economic effect of which is insubstantial, and all other partnership allocations are recognized under this paragraph. Under paragraph (b)(2)(iv)(k) of this section, the partners' capital accounts are adjusted upward by the partnership's simulated gain of $10,000 ($100,000 sales price less $90,000 simulated adjusted basis) in proportion to such partners' allocable shares of the $10,000 portion of the total amount realized that exceeds the partnership's $90,000 simulated adjusted basis ($5,000 to JC and $5,000 to DG). If the lease is sold for $50,000, under paragraph (b)(4)(v) of this section the entire $50,000 amount realized on the sale of the lease will be allocated to DG (but will not directly affect his capital account). Under paragraph (b)(2)(iv)(k) of this section the partners' capital accounts will be adjusted downward by the partnership's $40,000 simulated loss ($50,000 sales price less $90,000 simulated adjusted basis) in proportion to the partners' allocable shares of the total amount realized from the property that represents recovery of the partnership's simulated adjusted basis therein. Accordingly, DG's capital account will be reduced by such $40,000.

Example (20). (i) RM and HB form a limited partnership to acquire and operate a commercial office building. RM, the limited partner, contributes $180,000, and HB, the general partner, contributes $20,000 to the partnership, which obtains an $800,000 nonrecourse loan and purchases the building (on leased land) for $1,000,000. The nonrecourse loan is secured only by the building, and no principal payments are due for 5 years. The partnership agreement provides that the partners' capital accounts will be determined and maintained in accordance with paragraph (b)(2)(iv) of this section, distributions in liquidation of the partnership (or any partner's interest) will be made in accordance with the partners' positive capital account balances (as set forth in paragraph (b)(2)(ii)(b)(2) of this section), HB will be required to restore any deficit balance in his capital account following the liquidation of his interest (as set forth in paragraph (b)(2)(ii)(b)(3) of this section), and RM will not be required to restore any deficit balance in his capital account following the liquidation of his interest. The partnership agreement contains a qualified income offset (as defined in paragraph (b)(2)(ii)(d) of this section), and, as of the end of each partnership taxable year discussed herein, the items described in paragraphs (b)(2)(ii)(d)(4), (5), and (6) of this section are not reasonably expected to cause or increase a deficit balance in RM's capital account. In addition, the agreement contains a minimum gain chargeback (in accordance with paragraph (b)(4)(iv)(e) of this section). The partnership agreement provides that, except as otherwise required by its qualified income offset and minimum gain chargeback provisions, (a) all partnership items will be allocated 90 percent to RM and 10 percent to HB until the first time when the partnership has recognized items of income and gain that exceed the items of loss and deduction it has recognized over its life, and (b) all further partnership items will be allocated equally between RM and HB. Finally, the partnership agreement provides that all distributions, other than distributions in liquidation of the partnership or of a partner's interest in the partnership, will be made 90 percent to RM and 10 percent to HB until a total of $200,000 has been distributed, and thereafter all such distributions will be made equally to RM and HB. In each of the partnership's first 2 taxable years, it generates rental income of $95,000, operating expenses (including land lease payments) of $10,000, interest expense of $80,000, and a cost recovery deduction of $90,000, resulting in a net taxable loss of $85,000 in each of those years. The allocations of these losses, 90 percent to RM and 10 percent to HB, have substantial economic effect.

	RM	HB
Capital account upon formation	$180,000	$20,000
Less: net loss in years 1 and 2	(153,000)	(17,000)
Capital account at end of year 2	$ 27,000	$ 3,000

In the partnership's third taxable year, it again generates rental income of $95,000, operating expenses of $10,-000, interest expense of $80,000, and a cost recovery deduction of $90,000, resulting in a net taxable loss of $85,000. If the partnership were to dispose of the building in full satisfaction of the nonrecourse liability at the end of that year, it would realize $70,000 of gain ($800,-000 amount realized less $730,000 adjusted tax basis). Since the amount of partnership minimum gain at the end of that year (and the net increase in partnership minimum gain during that year) is $70,000, the amount of partnership nonrecourse deductions for that year is $70,000, consisting of cost recovery deductions allowable with respect to the building of $70,000. Pursuant to the partnership agreement all partnership items comprising the net taxable loss of $85,000, including the $70,000 nonrecourse deduction, are allocated 90 percent to RM and 10 percent to HB. The allocation of these items, other than the nonrecourse deductions, has substantial economic effect.

	RM	HB
Capital account at end of year 2	$27,000	$3,000
Less: net loss in year 3 (without nonrecourse deduction)	(13,500)	(1,500)
Less: nonrecourse deduction in year 3	(63,000)	(7,000)
Capital account at end of year 3	($49,500)	($5,500)

This allocation of the $70,000 nonrecourse deduction, 90 percent, to RM and 10 percent to HB, satisfies requirement (2) of paragraph (b)(4)(iv)(d) of this section because the allocation is consistent with allocations, which have substantial economic effect, of other significant partnership items attributable to the building. Since the remaining requirements of paragraph (b)(4)(iv)(d) of this section are satisfied, the allocation of nonrecourse deductions is deemed to be made in accordance with the partners' interests in the partnership. At the end of the partnership's third taxable year, RM's and HB's shares of partnership minimum gain are $63,000 and $7,000, respectively. Therefore, pursuant to the next to last sentence in paragraph (b)(4)(iv)(f) of this section, RM is treated as obligated to restore a deficit balance in his capital account of $63,000, so that in the succeeding year RM could be allocated up to an additional $13,500 of partnership deductions, losses, and section 705(a)(2)(B) expenditures that are not nonrecourse deductions, and that allocation would be considered to have economic effect under the alternate economic effect test contained in paragraph (b)(2)(ii)(d) of this section even though such an allocation would increase a deficit capital account balance. If the partnership were to dispose of the building in full satisfaction of the nonrecourse liability at the beginning of the partnership's fourth taxable year (and had no other economic activity in that year), the partnership minimum gain would be decreased from $70,000 to zero. RM's and HB's shares of that net decrease would be $63,000 and $7,000, respectively. Upon such a disposition the minimum gain chargeback would require that RM be allocated an amount of that gain equal to $49,500 (the deficit balance in his capital account before any allocation is made to him under section 704(b) with respect to partnership items for the partnership's fourth taxable year).

(ii) Assume the same facts as originally stated in (i) except that the partnership agreement provides that all nonrecourse deductions of the partnership will be allocated equally between RM and HB. Furthermore, at the time the partnership agreement is entered into, there is a reasonable likelihood that over the partnership's life it will recognize amounts of income and gain significantly in excess of amounts of loss and deduction (other than nonrecourse deductions). The allocation of such excess equally between the partners pursuant to the partnership agreement will have substantial economic effect. The allocation of all items, other than the nonrecourse deductions, 90 percent to RM and 10 percent to HB, has substantial economic effect.

	RM	HB
Capital account upon formation	$180,000	$20,000
Less: net loss in years 1 and 2	(153,000)	(17,000)
Capital account at end of year 2	27,000	3,000
Less: net loss in year 3 (without nonrecourse deduction)	(13,500)	(1,500)
Less: nonrecourse deduction in year 3	(35,000)	(35,000)
Capital account at end of year 3	($21,500)	($33,500)

The allocation of the $70,000 nonrecourse deduction equally between RM and HB satisfies requirement (2) of paragraph (b)(4)(iv)(d) of this section because the allocation is consistent with allocations, which will have substantial economic effect, of other significant partnership items attributable to the building. Since the remaining requirements of paragraph (b)(4)(iv)(d) of this section are satisfied, the allocation of nonrecourse deductions is deemed to be made in accordance with the partners' interests in the partnership. The allocation of the nonrecourse deductions, 75 percent to RM and 25 percent to HB (or in any other ratio between 90 percent to RM/10 percent to HB and 50 percent to RM/50 percent to HB), also would satisfy requirement (2) of paragraph (b)(4)(iv)(d) of this section.

(iii) Assume the same facts as originally stated in (i) except that the partnership agreement provides that RM will be allocated 99 percent, and HB 1 percent, of all nonrecourse deductions of the partnership. This allocation of the $70,000 nonrecourse deduction does not satisfy requirement (2) of paragraph (b)(4)(iv)(d) because it is not reasonably consistent with allocations, which have substantial economic effect, of any other significant partnership item attributable to the building. Therefore, the allocation of nonrecourse deductions will be disregarded,

and the nonrecourse deductions of the partnership will be reallocated according to the partners' overall economic interests in the partnership, determined with reference to the factors set forth in paragraph (b)(3)(ii) of this section.

(iv) Assume the same facts as originally stated in (i) except that, at the beginning of the partnership's fourth taxable year, RM contributes $144,000 and HB contributes $16,000 of additional capital to the partnership, which the partnership uses to reduce the amount of its nonrecourse liability from $800,000 to $640,000. In addition, in the partnership's fourth taxable year, it again generates rental income of $95,000, operating expenses of $10,000, and a cost recovery deduction of $90,000, resulting in a net taxable loss of $85,000. If the partnership were to dispose of the building in full satisfaction of the nonrecourse liability at the end of that year, it would realize no gain ($640,000 amount realized less $640,000 adjusted tax basis). Therefore, the amount of partnership minimum gain at the end of the year is zero, which represents a net decrease in partnership minimum gain of $70,000 during the year. RM's and HB's shares of this net decrease are $63,000 and $7,000, respectively, so that at the end of the partnership's fourth taxable year, RM's and HB's shares of partnership minimum gain are zero. Therefore, pursuant to the next to last sentence in paragraph (b)(4)(iv)(f) of this section, RM is no longer treated as being obligated to restore any deficit balance in his capital account. Assuming the sum of the reductions to RM's capital account described in paragraph (b)(2)(ii)(d)(4), (5), and (6) of this section do not exceed $94,500, the minimum gain chargeback does not require that either RM or HB be allocated items of income and gain in the partnership's fourth taxable year even though there is a net decrease in partnership minimum gain during that year. This is true because at the end of the year, before any allocation is made under section 704(b) to RM with respect to partnership items for the fourth taxable year, RM's capital account balance is $94,500 (his capital account balance at the end of the partnership's third taxable year increased by his $144,000 capital contribution), and HB has a full deficit makeup obligation.

	RM	HB
Capital account at end of year 3	($49,500)	($5,500)
Plus: contribution	144,000	16,000
Less: net loss in year 4	(76,500)	(8,500)
Capital account at end of year 4	$18,000	$2,000

(v) Assume the same facts as originally stated in (i) except that the partnership incurred only a $700,000 nonrecourse loan and, in addition, incurred a $100,000 recourse loan, subordinate in priority to the nonrecourse loan, to which the partnership's building is also subject. Under paragraph (b)(4)(iv)(c) of this section, $700,000 of the adjusted basis of the building at the end of the partnership's third taxable year is allocated to the nonrecourse liability (with the remaining $30,000 allocated to the recourse liability) so that if the partnership disposed of the building in full satisfaction of the nonrecourse liability at the end of that year, it would realize no gain ($700,000 amount realized less $700,000 adjusted tax basis). Therefore, there is no minimum gain at the end of the partnership's third taxable year (and no increase in

1285

partnership minimum gain in such year). If, however, the $700,000 nonrecourse loan were subordinate in priority to the $100,000 recourse loan, under paragraph (b)(4)(iv)(c) of this section, only $630,000 of the adjusted basis of the building would be allocated to the $700,000 nonrecourse loan (the excess of the $730,000 adjusted tax basis of the building at the end of the partnership's third taxable year over the balance of the superior $100,000 recourse liability). In that case the balance of the $700,000 nonrecourse liability would exceed the adjusted tax basis of the building so allocated by $70,000 so that there would be $70,000 of minimum gain (and a $70,000 increase in partnership minimum gain) in the partnership's third taxable year.

(vi) Assume the same facts as originally stated in (i) except that RM and HB personally guarantee the "first" $100,000 of the $800,000 nonrecourse loan (i.e., only if the building is worth less than $100,000 will they be called upon to make up any deficiency). Under paragraph (b)(4)(iv)(c) of this section, only $630,000 of the adjusted tax basis of the building is allocated to the $700,000 nonrecourse portion of the loan because the collateral will be applied first to satisfy the $100,000 guaranteed portion, in effect making it superior in priority to the remainder of the loan. On the other hand, if RM and HB were to guarantee the "last" $100,000 (i.e., if the building is worth less than $800,000, they will be called upon to make up the deficiency up to $100,000), $700,000 of the adjusted tax basis of the building would be allocated to the $700,000 nonrecourse portion of the loan because the guaranteed portion in effect would be inferior in priority to it.

(vii) Assume the same facts as originally stated in (i) except that the $800,000 loan was made by HB, the general partner. Under paragraph (b)(4)(iv)(g) of this section, the $800,000 obligation does not constitute a nonrecourse liability of the partnership for purposes of this paragraph (b)(4)(iv). To the extent that such obligation constitutes a nonrecourse liability under § 1.1001-2, $70,000 of the $90,000 cost recovery deduction in the partnership's third taxable year must be allocated in accordance with the partners' interests in the partnership, under paragraph (b)(3) of this section. HB bears the burden of any economic loss corresponding to that $70,000 deduction. Therefore, HB must be allocated the entire amount of such deduction.

(viii) Assume the same facts as in (vii) except that the $800,000 loan from HB to the partnership is a purchase money loan that "wraps around" a $700,000 underlying nonrecourse note (also secured by the building) issued by HB to an unrelated person in connection with HB's acquisition of the building. Under these circumstances if the partnership were to convey the building to HB in satisfaction of the partnership's $800,000 liability, HB would bear the economic risk of loss with respect to only $100,000 of the liability. Therefore, for purposes of this paragraph (b)(4)(iv), the $800,000 liability will be treated as a $700,000 nonrecourse liability of the partnerships and a $100,000 liability (inferior in priority to the $700,000 liability) of the partnership to HB. Under paragraph (b)(4)(iv)(g) of this section, the $100,000 liability does not constitute a nonrecourse liability of the partnership for purposes of this paragraph (b)(4)(iv). To the extent that such obligation constitutes a nonrecourse liability under § 1.1001-2, $70,000 of the $90,000 cost recovery deduc-

tion realized in the partnership's third taxable year must be allocated to HB.

Example (21) (i) RD and PK form a general partnership to acquire and operate residential real properties. Each partner contributes $150,000 to the partnership. The partnership obtains a $1,500,000 nonrecourse loan and purchases 3 apartment buildings (on leased land) for $720,000 ("Property A"), $540,000 ("Property B"), and $540,000 ("Property C"), respectively. The nonrecourse loan is secured only by the 3 buildings, and no principal payments are due for 5 years. In each of the partnership's first 3 taxable years, it generates rental income of $225,000, operating expenses (including land lease payments) of $50,000, interest expense of $175,000, and cost recovery deductions on the 3 properties of $150,000 ($60,000 on Property A, $45,000 on Property B, and $45,000 on Property C), resulting in a net taxable loss of $150,000 in each of those years. If the partnership were to dispose of the 3 apartment buildings in full satisfaction of its nonrecourse liability at the end of its third taxable year, it would realize $150,000 of gain ($1,500,000 amount realized less $1,350,000 adjusted tax basis). Since the amount of partnership minimum gain at the end of that year (and the net increase in partnership minimum gain during that year) is $150,000, the amount of partnership nonrecourse deductions for that year is $150,000, consisting of cost recovery deductions allowable with respect to the 3 apartment buildings of $150,000. The result would be the same if the partnership obtained 3 separate nonrecourse loans that were "cross-collateralized" (i.e., if each separate loan were secured by all 3 of the apartment buildings).

(ii) Assume the same facts as originally stated in (i) and that at the beginning of the partnership's fourth taxable year, the partnership (with the permission of the nonrecourse lender) disposes of Property A for $835,000 and uses a portion of the proceeds to repay $600,000 of the nonrecourse liability, reducing the balance to $900,000. As a result of the disposition, the partnership recognizes gain of $295,000 ($835,000 amount realized less $540,000 adjusted tax basis). Also during the partnership's fourth taxable year it generates rental income of $135,000 and operating expenses of $30,000, interest expense of $105,000, and cost recovery deductions of $90,000 ($45,000 on each remaining building). If the partnership were to dispose of the remaining 2 buildings in full satisfaction of its nonrecourse liability at the end of the partnership's fourth taxable year, it would realize gain of $180,000 ($900,000 amount realized less $720,000 aggregate adjusted tax basis), which represents the amount of partnership minimum gain at the end of such year. Since the amount of partnership minimum gain increased from $150,000 to $180,000 during the partnership's fourth taxable year, the amount of partnership nonrecourse deductions for such year is $30,000, consisting of cost recovery deductions allowable with respect to the 2 remaining apartment buildings.

Example (22). (i) OC and DR form a limited partnership to acquire and lease machinery that is 5-year recovery property. OC, the limited partner, and DR, the general partner, contribute $100,000 each to the partnership, which obtains an $800,000 nonrecourse loan and purchases the equipment for $1,000,000. The partnership elects under section 48(q)(4) to reduce the amount of investment tax credit in lieu of adjusting the tax basis of such machinery. The nonrecourse loan is secured only by the machinery. The principal amount of the loan is to be repaid $50,000 per year during each of the partnership's first 5 taxable years, with the remaining $550,000 of unpaid principal due on the first day of the partnership's sixth taxable year. The partnership agreement provides that the partners' capital accounts will be determined and maintained in accordance with paragraph (b)(2)(iv) of this section, distributions in liquidation of the partnership (or any partner's interest) will be made in accordance with the partners' positive capital account balances (as set forth in paragraph (b)(2)(ii)(b)(2) of this section), DR will be required to restore any deficit balance in his capital account following the liquidation of his interest (as set forth in paragraph (b)(2)(ii)(b)(3) of this section), and OC will not be required to restore any deficit balance in his capital account following the liquidation of his interest. The partnership agreement contains a qualified income offset (as defined in paragraph (b)(2)(ii)(d) of this section), and, as of the end of each partnership taxable year discussed herein, the items described in paragraphs (b)(2)(ii)(d)(4), (5), and (6) of this section are not reasonably expected to cause or increase a deficit balance in RM's capital account. In addition, the agreement contains a minimum gain chargeback (in accordance with paragraph (b)(4)(iv)(e) of this section). The partnership agreement provides that, except as otherwise required by its qualified income offset and minimum gain chargeback provisions, all partnership items will be allocated equally between OC and DR. Finally, the partnership agreement provides that all distributions, other than distributions in liquidation of the partnership or of a partner's interest in the partnership, will be made equally between OC and DR. In the partnership's first taxable year, it generates rental income of $130,000, interest expense of $80,000, and a cost recovery deduction of $150,000, resulting in a net taxable loss of $100,000. In addition, the partnership repays $50,000 of the nonrecourse liability, reducing that liability to $750,000. Allocations of these losses equally between OC and DR have substantial economic effect.

	OC	DR
Capital account upon formation	$100,000	$100,000
Less: net loss in year 1	(50,000)	(50,000)
Capital account at end of year 1	$50,000	$50,000

In the partnership's second taxable year it generates rental income of $130,000, interest expense of $75,000, and a cost recovery deduction of $220,000, resulting in a net taxable loss of $165,000. In addition, the partnership repays $50,000 of the nonrecourse liability, reducing that liability to $700,000, and distributes $2,500 of cash to each partner. If the partnership were to dispose of the machinery in full satisfaction of the nonrecourse liability at the end of that year, it would realize $70,000 of gain ($700,000 amount realized less $630,000 adjusted tax basis). Therefore, the amount of partnership minimum gain at the end of that year (and the net increase in partnership minimum gain during that year) is $70,000, and the amount of partnership nonrecourse deductions for that year is $70,000, consisting of cost recovery deductions allowable with respect to the machinery of $70,000.

Pursuant to the partnership agreement all partnership items comprising the net taxable loss of $165,000, including the $70,000 nonrecourse deduction, are allocated equally between OC and DR. The allocation of these items, other than the nonrecourse deductions, has substantial economic effect.

	OC	DR
Capital account at end of year 1	$50,000	$50,000
Less: net loss in year 2 (without nonrecourse deduction)	(47,500)	(47,500)
Less: nonrecourse deduction in year 2	(35,000)	(35,000)
Less: distribution	(2,500)	(2,500)
Capital account at end of year 2	($35,000)	($35,000)

This allocation of the $70,000 nonrecourse deduction equally between OC and DR satisfies requirement (2) of paragraph (b)(4)(iv)(d) of this section because the allocation is consistent with allocations, which have substantial economic effect, of other significant partnership items attributable to the machinery. Since the remaining requirements of paragraph (b)(4)(iv)(d) of this section are satisfied, the allocation of nonrecourse deductions is deemed to be made in accordance with the partners' interests in the partnership. At the end of the partnership's second taxable year, OC's and DR's shares of partnership minimum gain are $35,000 each. Therefore, pursuant to the next to last sentence in paragraph (b)(4)(iv)(f) of this section, OC is treated as obligated to restore a deficit balance in his capital account of $35,000. If the partnership were to dispose of the machinery in full satisfaction of the nonrecourse liability at the beginning of the partnership's third taxable year (and had no other economic activity in that year), the partnership minimum gain would be decreased from $70,000 to zero. OC's and DR's shares of that net decrease would be $35,000 each. Upon such a disposition the minimum gain chargeback would require that OC be allocated an amount of that gain equal to $35,000 (the deficit balance in his capital account before any allocation is made to him under section 704(b) with respect to partnership items for the partnership's third taxable year). The minimum gain chargeback would not require that DR be allocated any amount of such gain, since he has a full deficit makeup obligation.

(ii) Assume the same facts as originally stated in (i) and that DT is admitted to the partnership at the beginning of the partnership's third taxable year. At the time of DT's admission, the fair market value of the machinery is $900,000. DT contributes $100,000 to the partnership (which amount the partnership invests in undeveloped land) in exchange for an interest in the partnership. Pursuant to paragraph (b)(2)(iv)(f) of this section, the capital accounts of OC and DR are adjusted upward to $100,000 each. This reflects the manner in which the partnership gain of $270,000 ($900,000 fair market value minus $630,000 adjusted basis) would be shared if the machinery were sold for its fair market value immediately prior to DT's admission to the partnership.

	OC	DR
Capital account before DT's admission	($35,000)	($35,000)
Deemed sale adjustment ...	135,000	135,000
Capital account adjusted for DT's admission	$100,000	$100,000

The partnership agreement is modified to provide that, except as otherwise required by its qualified income offset and minimum gain chargeback provisions, partnership income, gain, loss, and deduction, as computed for book purposes, will be allocated equally among the partners, and such allocations will be reflected in the partners' capital accounts. The partnership agreement also is modified to provide that depreciation and gain or loss, as computed for tax purposes, with respect to the machinery will be shared among the partners in a manner that takes account of the variation between such property's $630,000 adjusted tax basis and its $900,000 book value, in accordance with paragraph (b)(2)(iv)(f) of this section and the special rule contained in paragraph (b)(4)(i) of this section. Finally, the partnership agreement is modified to provide that DT will not be required to restore any deficit balance in his capital account following the liquidation of his interest. Since the requirements of paragraph (b)(2)(iv)(g) of this section are satisfied, the capital accounts of the partners (as adjusted) continue to be maintained in accordance with paragraph (b)(2)(iv) of this section. If the partnership were to dispose of the machinery in full satisfaction of the nonrecourse liability immediately following the revaluation of the machinery, it would realize no book gain ($700,000 amount realized less $900,000 book value). Thus, as a result of the revaluation of the machinery upward by $270,000, the partnership minimum gain is reduced from $70,000 immediately prior to such revaluation to zero. OC's and DR's shares of that decrease are $35,000 each.

(iii) Assume the same facts as in (ii) and that also during the partnership's third taxable year the partnership generates rental income of $130,000, interest expense of $70,000, a cost recovery deduction of $210,000, and a book depreciation deduction (attributable to the machinery) of $300,000. As a result the partnership has a net taxable loss of $150,000 and a net book loss of $240,000. In addition, the partnership repays $50,000 of the nonrecourse liability (after the date of DT's admission), reducing that liability to $650,000, and distributes $3,333 of cash to each partner. If the partnership were to dispose of the machinery in full satisfaction of the nonrecourse liability at the end of the year, $50,000 of book gain would result ($650,000 amount realized less $600,000 book value). Therefore, the amount of partnership minimum gain at the end of the year is $50,000, which represents a net decrease in partnership minimum gain of $20,000 during the year. (This is so even though there would be an increase in partnership minimum gain in the partnership's third taxable year if minimum gain were computed with reference to the adjusted tax basis of the machinery.) Nevertheless, pursuant to the second sentence of paragraph (b)(4)(iv)(b) of this section the amount of nonrecourse deductions of the partnership for its third taxable year is $50,000 (the net increase in partnership minimum gain during the year determined by adding back the $70,000 decrease in partnership minimum gain attributable to the revaluation of the machinery to the $20,000 net decrease in partnership minimum gain during the year). The $50,000 of partnership nonrecourse deductions for the year consist of book depreciation deductions allowable with respect to the machinery of $50,000. Pursuant to the partnership agreement all partnership items comprising the net book loss of $240,000, including the $50,000 nonrecourse deduction, are allocated equally among the partners. The allocation of these items, other than the nonrecourse deductions, has substantial economic effect. Consistent with the special partners' interests in the partnership rule contained in paragraph (b)(4)(i) of this section, the partnership agreement provides that the $210,000 cost recovery deduction for the partnership's third taxable year is, in accordance with section 704(c) principles, shared $55,000 to OC, $55,000 to DR, and $100,000 to DT.

	OC		DR		DT	
	Tax	Book	Tax	Book	Tax	Book
Capital account at end of year 2	($35,000)	$100,000	($35,000)	$100,000	$100,000	$100,000
Less: nonrecourse deduction	(9,166)	(16,666)	(9,166)	(16,666)	(16,666)	(16,666)
Plus: items other than nonrecourse deduction in year 3	(25,834)	(63,334)	(25,834)	(63,334)	(63,334)	(63,334)
Less: Distribution	(5,000)	(5,000)	(5,000)	(5,000)	(5,000)	(5,000)
Capital account at end of year 3	(75,000)	(15,000)	(75,000)	(15,000)	(15,000)	(15,000)

The allocation of the $50,000 nonrecourse deduction equally among OC, DR, and DT satisfies requirement (2) of paragraph (b)(4)(iv)(d) of this section because the allocation is consistent with allocations, which have substantial economic effect, of other significant partnership items attributable to the machinery. Since the remaining requirements of paragraph (b)(4)(iv)(d) of this section are satisfied, such allocation is deemed to be made in accordance with the partners' interest in the partnership. At the end of the partnership's third taxable year, OC's, DR's, and DT's shares of partnership minimum gain are $16,666 each.

(iv) Assume the same facts as in (iii) and that during the partnership's fourth taxable year the partnership generates rental income of $130,000, interest expense of $65,000, a cost recovery deduction of $210,000, and a book depreciation deduction (attributable to the machinery) of $300,000. As a result the partnership has a net taxable loss of $145,000 and a net book loss of $235,000. In addition, the partnership repays $50,000 of the nonrecourse liability, reducing that liability to $600,000, and distributes $5,000 of cash to each partner. If the partnership were to dispose of the machinery in full satisfaction of the nonrecourse liability at the end of the year, $300,000 of book gain would result ($600,000 amount realized less $300,000 book value). Therefore, the amount of partnership minimum gain as of the end of the year is

$300,000, which represents a net increase in partnership minimum gain during the year of $250,000. Thus, the amount of partnership nonrecourse deductions for that year equals $250,000, consisting of book depreciation deductions of $250,000. Pursuant to the partnership agreement all partnership items comprising the net book loss of $235,000, including the $250,000 nonrecourse deduction, are allocated equally among the partners. That

allocation of all items, other than the nonrecourse deductions, has substantial economic effect. Consistent with the special partners' interests in the partnership rule contained in paragraph (b)(4)(i) of this section, the partnership agreement provides that the $210,000 cost recovery deduction for the partnership's fourth taxable year is, in accordance with section 704(c) principles, shared $55,000 to OC, $55,000 to DR, and $100,000 to DT.

	OC		DR		DT	
	Tax	Book	Tax	Book	Tax	Book
Capital account at end of year 3	($75,000)	$15,000	($75,000)	$15,000	$15,000	$15,000
Less: nonrecourse deduction	(45,833)	(83,333)	(45,833)	(83,333)	(83,333)	(83,333)
Plus: items other than nonrecourse deduction in year 4	(12,449)	5,000	12,449	5,000	5,000	5,000
Less: Distribution	(5,000)	(5,000)	(5,000)	(5,000)	(5,000)	(5,000)
Capital account at end of year 4	(113,334)	(68,333)	(113,334)	(68,333)	(68,333)	(68,333)

The allocation of the $250,000 nonrecourse deduction equally among OC, DR, and DT satisfies requirement (2) of paragraph (b)(4)(iv)(d) of this section. Since the remaining requirements of paragraph (b)(4)(iv)(d) of this section are satisfied, such allocation is deemed to be made in accordance with the partners' interest in the partnership. At the end of the partnership's third taxable year, OC's, DR's, and DT's shares of partnership minimum gain are $100,000 each.

(v) Assume the same facts as (iv) and that at the beginning of the partnership's fifth taxable year it sells the machinery for $650,000 (using $600,000 of the proceeds to repay the nonrecourse liability), resulting in a taxable gain of $440,000 ($650,000 amount realized less $210,000 adjusted tax basis) and a book gain of $350,000 ($650,000 amount realized less $300,000 book basis). The partnership has no other items of income, gain, loss, or deduction for such year. As a result of the sale, partnership minimum gain is reduced from $300,000 to zero, reducing OC's, DR's and DT's shares of partnership mini-

mum gain to zero from $100,000 each. The minimum gain chargeback requires that OC and DT each be allocated an amount of that gain equal to $68,333 (the deficit balance in each of their capital accounts at the end of the partnership's fifth taxable year before any allocation is made to them under section 704(b) with respect to partnership items for that year). Thus, the allocation of the first $136,666 of book gain $68,333 to OC and $68,333 to DT is deemed to be made in accordance with the partners' interests in the partnership under paragraph (b)(4)(iv)(e) of this section. The allocation of the remaining $213,334 of book gain in a manner such that the total book gain is allocated equally among the partners has substantial economic effect. Consistent with the special partners' interests in the partnership rule contained in paragraph (b)(4)(i) of this section, the partnership agreement provides that the $440,000 taxable gain is, in accordance with section 704(c) principles, shared $161,667 to OC, $161,667 DR, and $116,666 to DT.

	OC		DR		DT	
	Tax	Book	Tax	Book	Tax	Book
Capital account at end of year 4	($113,334)	($68,333)	($113,334)	($68,333)	($68,333)	($68,333)
Plus: minimum gain chargeback	94,691	68,333	0	0	68,333	68,333
Plus: additional gain	66,976	48,333	161,667	116,666	48,333	48,333
Capital account before liquidation	48,333	48,333	48,333	48,333	48,333	48,333

Example 23. (i) A partnership owns 4 properties, each of which is subject to a nonrecourse liability of the partnership. During a taxable year of the partnership, the following events take place. First, the partnership generates a cost recovery deduction (for both book and tax purposes) with respect to Property W of $10,000 and repays $5,000 of the nonrecourse liability secured only by that property, resulting in an increase in minimum gain with respect to that liability of $5,000. Second, the partnership generates a cost recovery deduction (for both book and tax purposes) with respect to Property X of $10,000 and repays none of the nonrecourse liability secured by that property, resulting in an increase in minimum gain with respect to that liability of $10,000. Third, the partnership generates a cost recovery deduction (for both book and tax purposes) of $2,000 on Property Y and repays $11,000 of the nonrecourse liability

secured only by that property, resulting in a decrease in minimum gain with respect to that liability of $9,000 (although at the end of that year, there remains minimum gain with respect to that liability). Finally, the partnership borrows $5,000 on a nonrecourse basis, giving as the only security for that liability Property Z, which is a parcel of undeveloped land with an adjusted tax basis (and book value) of $2,000, resulting in a net increase in minimum gain with respect to that liability of $3,000. The net increase in partnership minimum gain during that year is $9,000, so that the amount of nonrecourse deductions of the partnership for that taxable year is $9,000. Those nonrecourse deductions consist of $3,000 of cost recovery deductions with respect to Property W and $6,000 of cost recovery deductions with respect to Property X. The amount of nonrecourse deductions consisting of cost recovery deductions is determined as follows. With respect to the nonrecourse liability secured by Property Z, with respect to which there is no cost recovery deduction, the amount of cost recovery deductions that constitutes nonrecourse deductions is zero. Similarly, with respect to the nonrecourse liability secured by Property Y, for which there is no increase in minimum gain, the amount of cost recovery deductions that constitutes nonrecourse deductions is zero. With respect to each of the nonrecourse liabilities secured by Properties W and X, which are (i) secured by property with respect to which there are cost recovery deductions and (ii) for which there is an increase in minimum gain, the amount of cost recovery deductions that constitutes nonrecourse deductions equals the product obtained by multiplying the net increase in partnership minimum gain ($9,000) times a fraction, the numerator of which is the total cost recovery deductions with respect to the partnership property securing that particular liability to the extent of the increase in minimum gain with respect to that liability and the denominator of which is the sum of the numerators for each such liability. Thus, for the liability secured by Property W, the amount is $9,000 times $5,000/$15,000. For the liability secured by Property X, the amount is $9,000 times $10,000/$15,000. (If one depreciable property secured 2 partnership nonrecourse liabilities, the amount of cost recovery or book depreciation with respect to that property would be allocated among such liabilities in accordance with the method by which adjusted basis is allocated under paragraph (b)(2)(iv)(b) of this section.

(ii) Assume the facts as in (i) except that the loan secured by Property Z is $15,000 (rather than $5,000), resulting in a net increase in minimum gain with respect to that liability of $13,000. Thus, the net increase in partnership minimum gain is $19,000, and the amount of nonrecourse deductions of the partnership for that taxable year is $19,000. Those nonrecourse deductions consist of $5,000 of cost recovery deductions with respect to Property W, $10,000 of cost recovery deductions with respect to Property X, and a pro rata portion of the partnership's other items of deduction, loss, and section 705(a)(2)(B) expenditure for that year. The method for computing the amounts of cost recovery deductions that constitute nonrecourse deductions is the same as in (i) for the liabilities secured by Properties Y and Z. With respect to each of the nonrecourse liabilities secured by Properties W and X, the amount of cost recovery deductions that constitutes nonrecourse deductions equals the total cost recovery deductions with respect to the partnership property securing that particular liability to the extent of the increase in minimum gain with respect to that liability.

(c) Contributed property—(1) In general. Where property has actually been contributed by a partner to a partnership (so as to become partnership property as among the partners and not merely property subject to the claims of partnership creditors), section 704(c) and this paragraph provide rules for determining a partner's distributive share of depreciation, depletion, or gain or loss with respect to such contributed property. These rules do not apply to property, only the use of which is permitted the partnership by the partner who owns it. Section 704(c) and this paragraph provide certain alternatives in determining the partners' distributive shares of such items in order to account for precontribution appreciation or diminution in value of the property contributed. When the partnership agreement is silent as to the treatment of such items with respect to contributed property (and if such property is not an undivided interest as described in section 704(c)(3)), depreciation, depletion, or gain or loss with respect to such property shall be treated in the same manner as though such items arose with respect to property purchased by the partnership. The application of this provision may be illustrated by the following examples:

Example (1). A and B form an equal partnership. A contributes $1,000 cash and B contributes inventory with an adjusted basis to him of $800 and a fair market value of $1,000. Under section 723, the basis of the inventory to the partnership is also $800. During the year, the inventory is sold for $1,100. There is no provision in the partnership agreement for treatment of items with respect to contributed property. Under section 704(c)(1), the $300 profit on the sale of the inventory is treated as if it were gain on property that had been purchased by the partnership and subsequently sold. Therefore, each partner's distributive share of such profit on the inventory is $150.

Example (2). C and D form an equal partnership. C contributes machinery worth $10,000 with an adjusted basis to him of $4,000. D contributes $10,000 cash. Under the provisions of section 722, the basis of C's partnership interest is $4,000 and the basis of D's interest is $10,000. There is no provision in the partnership agreement relating to contributed property. If the contributed property depreciates at an annual rate of 10 percent, the partnership will have an annual depreciation deduction of $400, which will result in a reduction of $200 in each partner's distributive share of partnership income. Thus, at the end of the first year, the adjusted basis of the contributed property will be $3,600. If the partnership has no other taxable income or loss for that year, each partner will have a deduction of $200, representing his distributive share of partnership loss for the year. C's adjusted basis for his interest will be $3,800 ($4,000, the original basis of his interest, reduced by $200); D's adjusted basis will be $9,800 ($10,000, reduced by $200).

Example (3). Assume that the property in example (2) of this subparagraph is sold at the beginning of the second year of partnership operation for $9,000. The partnership gain will be $5,400 ($9,000, the amount realized, less the adjusted basis of $3,600). Each partner's share of the $5,400 gain will be $2,700. If the partnership has no other taxable income or loss for that year, each partner will have a gain from the partnership of $2,700, representing his distributive share of gain from the sale of property used in the partnership business. C's adjusted basis for his interest will then be $6,500 (the basis of $3,800, increased by the gain of $2,700). D's adjusted basis will be $12,500 (the basis of $9,800, increased by the gain of $2,700). If the partnership is then terminated, and its assets consisting of $19,000 in cash are distributed to the partners pro rata in liquidation of their entire interests, C will have a capital gain of $3,000 ($9,500, the amount received, less $6,500, the adjusted basis of his interest). D will have a capital loss of $3,000 (D's adjusted basis, $12,500, reduced by the amount received $9,500).

(2) **Effect of partnership agreement.** (i) If the partners so provide in the partnership agreement, depreciation, depletion, or gain or loss with respect to contributed property may be allocated among the partners in a manner which takes into account all or any portion of the difference between the adjusted basis and the fair market value of contributed property at the time of contribution. The allocation may apply to all contributed property or to specific items. The appreciation or diminution in value represented by the difference between the adjusted basis and the fair market value of contributed property at the time of contribution may thus be attributed to the contributing partner upon a subsequent sale or exchange of the property by the partnership. Such appreciation or diminution also may be used in allocating the allowable depreciation or depletion with respect to such property among the contributing partner and the noncontributing partners. In any case, however, the total depreciation, depletion, or gain or loss allocated to the partners is limited to a "ceiling" which cannot exceed the amount of gain or loss realized by the partnership or the depreciation or depletion allowable to it. The application of this subdivision may be illustrated by the following examples:

Example (1). Assume that partners C and D, in examples (2) and (3) of subparagraph (1) of this paragraph, agree under section 704(c)(2) to attribute to C, the contributor of the machinery, the potential gain of $6,000 represented by the difference between its adjusted basis of $4,000 and its fair market value of $10,000. With his contribution of $10,000 cash, D has, in effect, purchased an undivided one-half interest in the property for $5,000. Since the property depreciates at an annual rate of 10 percent, D would have been entitled to a depreciation deduction of $500 per year. However, since under the "ceiling" approach the partnership is allowed only $400 per year (10 percent of $4,000), no more than $400 may be allocated between the partners, i.e., the partnership cannot allocate $500 of depreciation to D and thereby treat C as if C had received an additional $100 of income. Therefore, the partners allocate the $400 deduction for depreciation entirely to D and none to C, the contributor. At the end of the first year, the adjusted basis of the contributed property will be $3,600. Since the $400 deduction is allocated entirely to D, if the partnership has no other taxable income or loss, C will have no income or loss, and D will have a deduction of $400. C's basis for his interest will remain $4,000. D's adjusted basis for his

interest will be $9,600 ($10,000, the original basis of his interest, reduced by the deduction of $400).

Example (2). Assume that the partners in example (1) of this subdivision also agree under section 704(c)(2) that, upon a sale of the contributed property, the portion of the proceeds attributable to the excess of the fair market value of the property at date of contribution (less accumulated depreciation on such value) over its basis at date of contribution (less accumulated depreciation on such basis) shall result in gain to the contributing partner only. If the property is sold at the beginning of the second year of partnership operation for $9,000, the partnership gain of $5,400 ($9,000, the amount realized, less the adjusted basis of $3,600) must be allocated to the partners under the terms of the agreement. The fair market value of the property as depreciated is $9,000 ($10,000, the value on contribution, less $1,000, the accumulated depreciation on such value). Under section 704(c)(2) and the terms of the partnership agreement, the $5,400 difference between $9,000, the fair market value as depreciated, and $3,600, the adjusted basis of the property, represents the portion of the gain to be allocated to C. None of this gain is allocated to D. (If the property were sold for more than $9,000, the portion of the gain in excess of $5,400 would be allocated equally between the partners in accordance with their agreement for sharing gains. If the property were sold for less than $9,000, the entire gain would be allocated to C and nothing to D.) If the partnership and partners engaged in no other transactions that year, C will report a gain of $5,400, and D, no income or loss. C's adjusted basis for his interest will then be $9,400 ($4,000, his original basis, increased by the gain of $5,400). D's adjusted basis will be $9,600 ($10,000, his original basis, less $400 depreciation deduction in the first partnership year). If the partnership is then terminated, and its assets consisting of $19,000 in cash are distributed to the partners pro rata in liquidation of their interests, C will have a capital gain of $100 ($9,500, the amount received, less $9,400, the adjusted basis of his interest). D will have a capital loss of $100 (the excess of D's adjusted basis, $9,600, over the amount received, $9,500).

(ii) For the effect of an agreement under section 704(c)(2) on undivided interests in property contributed to the partnership where the partners' interests in the capital and profits of the partnership do not correspond with such undivided interests, see subparagraph (3)(ii) of this paragraph.

(3) **Undivided interests.** (i) Section 704(c)(3) provides a special rule for the allocation of depreciation, depletion, or gain or loss with respect to undivided interests in property contributed by the partners to a partnership where the partnership agreement does not provide otherwise. This provision applies only to property contributed to a partnership by all of its partners and only where the relative undivided interests of the partners in the property prior to the contribution are in the same ratio as their interests in the capital and in the profits of the partnership (except for depreciation, depletion, or gain or loss with respect to the con-

tributed undivided interest) after the contribution. Where these conditions are met, depreciation, depletion, or gain or loss with respect to the undivided interests in contributed property shall be determined in the same manner as though such undivided interests continued to be held by the partners outside the partnership. The rule stated in section 704(c)(3) applies only to the case where persons actually contribute undivided interests to a partnership. The provisions of this subdivision may be illustrated by the following examples:

Example (1). A and B are tenants in common owning undivided one-half interests in improved real estate consisting of land on which a factory is situated. They each contribute their respective undivided interests in the real estate to a partnership in which the profits are to be divided equally and, because the partners have equal shares in the capital, the assets will be divided equally on dissolution. A's basis for his undivided one-half interest is $4,000, of which $1,000 is allocable to the land and $3,000 to the factory. B's basis for his undivided one-half interest is $10,000, of which $3,000 is allocable to the land and $7,000 to the factory. The partnership agreement contains no provisions as to the allocation of depreciation or gain or loss on disposition of the property by the partnership. The factory depreciates at a rate of 5 percent a year. The annual partnership allowance for depreciation of $500 (5 percent of $10,000) will be allocated between the partners by allowing A a deduction of $150 (5 percent of $7.000, his basis for his undivided interest in the factory), and by allowing B a deduction of $350 (5 percent of $3,000, his basis for his undivided interest in the factory). At the end of the first year of partnership operation, A's adjusted basis for his undivided interest in the factory is $2,850 ($3,000 less $150), and B's adjusted basis is $6,650 ($7,000 less $350).

Example (2). If, in example (1) of this subdivision, the partnership at the end of the first year's operation sells the factory and land for $12,000, each partner's share of the gain or loss would be determined as follows: Since the undivided interests in the factory and the land are to be treated as though held by the partners outside the partnership, A's share of the proceeds of the sale is $6,000. His adjusted basis in the contributed property is $3,850 ($1,000 for the land and $2,850 for the factory). Therefore, his gain from the sale is $2,150. Since B's share of the proceeds is also $6,000, and his adjusted basis in the contributed property is $9,650 ($3,000 for the land and $6,650 for the factory), his loss is $3,650.

Example (3). Assume the same facts as in examples (1) and (2) of this subdivision, except that A and B do not enter into a partnership agreement. Assume further that they are found to be a partnership for income tax purposes because of their joint business activity, but that the factory and the land are not actually contributed by them to the partnership. Although A and B have permitted the partnership to use such properties, they continue to own the factory and the land in their individual capacities (as tenants in common), and the same tax consequences result as in examples (1) and (2) of this subdivision.

(ii) The allocation illustrated in subdivision (i) of this subparagraph will not be affected by the contribution, either at the time of the original contribution or subsequent thereto, of additional property not held as undivided interests if the partners' respective interests in the capital and in the profits of the partnership (except for depreciation, depletion, or gain or loss with respect to the contributed undivided interests) remain the same as their undivided interests in the property previously contributed to the partnership. If the partners' interests in the capital and profits of the partnership are changed from their undivided interests in the property previously contributed to the partnership, the method of allocation of depreciation, depletion, or gain or loss with respect to such property no longer applies. Such a change of the partner's interests in capital and profits may result from a modification of the agreement, or from a change in a partner's respective interest in capital either as a result of a further contribution or as a result of a distribution. (However, drawings made throughout the year against profits, and loans will be disregarded.) Where such a change takes place, the partners may agree under section 704(c)(2) that depreciation, depletion, or gain or loss with respect to the property formerly held as undivided interests shall continue to be allocated in the same manner as prior to the change. These provisions may be illustrated by the following examples:

Example (1). C and D are tenants in common, each owning an undivided one-half interest in certain unimproved land. Each contributes his respective undivided interest in the land to a partnership in which each has an equal interest in capital and profits. C's basis for his one-half interest is $4,000; D's basis is $10,000. The fair market value of the land is $20,000. Subsequently, C contributes $5,000 cash to his share of partnership capital. As a result of C's additional contribution, he now has a 60-percent interest in partnership capital and D, a 40-percent interest, although profits and losses still are to be shared equally. Since the interests of the partners in the capital and profits of the partnership no longer correspond to their undivided interests in the land, the method of allocation prescribed by section 704(c)(3) no longer applies. Therefore, if the land is sold for $12,000, the partnership will have a loss of $2,000 ($14,000 partnership basis minus $12,000). Since the partnership agreement contains no special allocation for gain or loss with respect to contributed property, the $2,000 loss is allocated as if such property had been purchased by the partnership, i.e., $1,000 to each partner.

Example (2). Assume in example (1) of this subdivision that the partners agree that, because of C's additional contribution of $5,000 cash, he is to have a 60-percent interest in partnership capital. Profits and losses still are to be shared equally, except that gain or loss with respect to the land is, under section 704(c)(2), to continue to be allocated in the same manner as it had been allocated under section 704(c)(3) prior to the additional contribution. The land is sold for $12,000. C's share of the proceeds is $6,000. His basis for the land is $4,000. Therefore, he has a $2,000 gain. D's loss is $4,000 ($10,000 basis less $6,000 proceeds).

(d) Limitation on allowance of losses. (1) A partner's distributive share of partnership loss will be allowed only to the extent of the adjusted basis (before reduction by current year's losses) of such partner's interest in the partnership at the end of the partnership taxable year in which such loss occurred. A partner's share of loss in excess of his adjusted basis at the end of the partnership taxable year will not be allowed for that year. However, any loss so disallowed shall be allowed as a deduction at the end of the first succeeding partnership taxable year, and subsequent partnership taxable years, to the extent that the partner's adjusted basis for his partnership interest at the end of any such year exceeds zero (before reduction by such loss for such year).

(2) In computing the adjusted basis of a partner's interest for the purpose of ascertaining the extent to which a partner's distributive share of partnership loss shall be allowed as a deduction for the taxable year, the basis shall first be increased under section 705(a)(1) and decreased under section 705(a)(2), except for losses of the taxable year and losses previously disallowed. If the partner's distributive share of the aggregate of items of loss specified in section 702(a)(1), (2), (3), (8), and (9) exceeds the basis of the partner's interest computed under the preceding sentence, the limitation on losses under section 704(d) must be allocated to his distributive share of each such loss. This allocation shall be determined by taking the proportion that each loss bears to the total of all such losses. For purposes of the preceding sentence, the total losses for the taxable year shall be the sum of his distributive share of losses for the current year and his losses disallowed and carried forward from prior years.

(3) For the treatment of certain liabilities of the partner or partnership, see section 752 and § 1.752-1.

(4) The provisions of this paragraph may be illustrated by the following examples:

Example (1). At the end of the partnership taxable year 1955, partnership AB has a loss of $20,000. Partner A's distributive share of this loss is $10,000. At the end of such year, A's adjusted basis for his interest in the partnership (not taking into account his distributive share of the loss) is $6,000. Under section 704(d), A's distributive share of partnership loss is allowed to him (in his taxable year within or with which the partnership taxable year ends) only to the extent of his adjusted basis of $6,000. The $6,000 loss allowed for 1955 decreases the adjusted basis of A's interest to zero. Assume that, at the end of partnership taxable year 1956, A's share of partnership income has increased the adjusted basis of A's interest in the partnership to $3,000 (not taking into account the $4,000 loss disallowed in 1955). Of the $4,000 loss disallowed for the partnership taxable year 1955, $3,000 is allowed A for the partnership taxable year 1956, thus again decreasing the adjusted basis of his interest to zero. If, at the end of partnership taxable year 1957, A has an adjusted basis of his interest of at least $1,000 (not taking into account the disallowed loss of $1,000), he will be allowed the $1,000 loss previously disallowed.

Example (2). At the end of partnership taxable year 1955, partnership CD has a loss of $20,000. Partner C's distributive share of this loss is $10,000. The adjusted basis of his interest in the partnership (not taking into account his distributive share of such loss) is $6,000. Therefore, $4,000 of the loss is disallowed. At the end of partnership taxable year 1956, the partnership has no taxable income or loss, but owes $8,000 to a bank for money borrowed. Since C's share of this liability is $4,000, the basis of his partnership interest is increased from zero to $4,000. (See sections 752 and 722, and §§ 1.752-1 and 1.722-1.) C is allowed the $4,000 loss, disallowed for the preceding year under section 704(d), for his taxable year within or with which partnership taxable year 1956 ends.

Example (3). At the end of partnership taxable year 1955, partner C has the following distributive share of partnership items described in section 702(a): Long-term capital loss, $4,000; short-term capital loss, $2,000; income as described in section 702(a)(9), $4,000. Partner C's adjusted basis for his partnership interest at the end of 1955, before adjustment for any of the above items, is $1,000. As adjusted under section 705(a)(1)(A), C's basis is increased from $1,000 to $5,000 at the end of the year. C's total distributive share of partnership loss is $6,000. Since without regard to losses, C has a basis of only $5,000, C is allowed only $5,000/$6,000 of each loss, that is, $3,333 of his long-term capital loss, and $1,667 of his short-term capital loss. C must carry forward to succeeding taxable years $667 as a long-term capital loss and $333 as a short-term capital loss.

(e) Family partnerships—(1) In general—(i) Introduction. The production of income by a partnership is attributable to the capital or services, or both, contributed by the partners. The provisions of subchapter K, chapter 1 of the Code, are to be read in the light of their relationship to section 61, which requires, inter alia, that income be taxed to the person who earns it through his own labor and skill and the utilization of his own capital.

(ii) Recognition of donee as partner. With respect to partnerships in which capital is a material income-producing factor, section 704(e)(1) provides that a person shall be recognized as a partner for income tax purposes if he owns a capital interest in such a partnership whether or not such interest is derived by purchase or gift from any other person. If a capital interest in a partnership in which capital is a material income-producing factor is created by gift, section 704(e)(2) provides that the distributive share of the donee under the partnership agreement shall be includible in his gross income, except to the extent that such distributive share is determined without allowance of reasonable compensation for services rendered to the partnership by the donor, and except to the extent that the portion of such distributive share attributable to donated capital is proportionately greater than the share of the donor attributable to the donor's capital. For rules of allocation in such cases, see subparagraph (3) of this paragraph.

(iii) **Requirement of complete transfer to donee.** A donee or purchaser of a capital interest in a partnership is not recognized as a partner under the principles of section 704(e)(1) unless such interest is acquired in a bona fide transaction, not a mere sham for tax avoidance or evasion purposes, and the donee or purchaser is the real owner of such interest. To be recognized, a transfer must vest dominion and control of the partnership interest in the transferee. The existence of such dominion and control in the donee is to be determined from all the facts and circumstances. A transfer is not recognized if the transferor retains such incidents of ownership that the transferee has not acquired full and complete ownership of the partnership interest. Transactions between members of a family will be closely scrutinized, and the circumstances, not only at the time of the purported transfer but also during the periods preceding and following it, will be taken into consideration in determining the bona fides or lack of bona fides of the purported gift or sale. A partnership may be recognized for income tax purposes as to some partners but not as to others.

(iv) **Capital as a material income-producing factor.** For purposes of section 704(e)(1), the determination as to whether capital is a material income-producing factor must be made by reference to all the facts of each case. Capital is a material income-producing factor if a substantial portion of the gross income of the business is attributable to the employment of capital in the business conducted by the partnership. In general, capital is not a material income-producing factor where the income of the business consists principally of fees,

commissions, or other compensation for personal services performed by members or employees of the partnership. On the other hand, capital is ordinarily a material income-producing factor if the operation of the business requires substantial inventories or a substantial investment in plant, machinery, or other equipment.

(v) **Capital interest in a partnership.** For purposes of section 704(e), a capital interest in a partnership means an interest in the assets of the partnership, which is distributable to the owner of the capital interest upon his withdrawal from the partnership or upon liquidation of the partnership. The mere right to participate in the earnings and profits of a partnership is not a capital interest in the partnership.

(2) **Basic tests as to ownership—(i) In general.** Whether an alleged partner who is a donee of a capital interest in a partnership is the real owner of such capital interest, and whether the donee has dominion and control over such interest, must be ascertained from all the facts and circumstances of the particular case. Isolated facts are not determinative; the reality of the donee's ownership is to be determined in the light of the transaction as a whole. The execution of legally sufficient and irrevocable deeds or other instruments of gift under State law is a factor to be taken into account but is not determinative of ownership by the donee for the purposes of section 704(e). The reality of the transfer and of the donee's ownership of the property attributed to him are to be ascertained from the conduct of the parties with respect to the alleged gift and not by any mechanical or formal test. Some of the more important factors to be considered in determining whether the donee has acquired ownership of the capital interest in a partnership are indicated in subdivisions (ii) to (x), inclusive, of this subparagraph.

(ii) **Retained controls.** The donor may have retained such controls of the interest which he has purported to transfer to the donee that the donor should be treated as remaining the substantial owner of the interest. Controls of particular significance include, for example, the following:

(a) Retention of control of the distribution of amounts of income or restrictions on the distributions of amounts of income (other than amounts retained in the partnership annually with the consent of the partners, including the donee partner, for the reasonable needs of the business). If there is a partnership agreement providing for a managing partner or partners, then amounts of income may be retained in the partnership without the acquiescence of all the partners if such amounts are retained for the reasonable needs of the business.

(b) Limitation of the right of the donee to liquidate or sell his interest in the partnership at his discretion without financial detriment.

(c) Retention of control of assets essential to the business (for example, through retention of assets leased to the alleged partnership).

(d) Retention of management powers inconsistent with normal relationships among partners. Retention by the donor of control of business management or of voting control, such as is common in ordinary business relationships, is not by itself to be considered as inconsistent with normal relationships among partners, provided the donee is free to liquidate his interest at his discretion without financial detriment. The donee shall not be considered free to liquidate his interest unless, considering all the facts, it is evident that the · donee is independent of the donor and has such maturity and understanding of his rights as to be capable of deciding to exercise, and capable of exercising, his right to withdraw his capital interest from the partnership.

The existence of some of the indicated controls, though amounting to less than substantial ownership retained by the donor, may be considered along with other facts and circumstances as tending to show the lack of reality of the partnership interest of the donee.

(iii) **Indirect controls.** Controls inconsistent with ownership by the donee may be exercised indirectly as well as directly, for example, through a separate business organization, estate, trust, individual, or other partnership. Where such indirect controls exist, the reality of the donee's interest will be determined as if such controls were exercisable directly.

(iv) **Participation in management.** Substantial participation by the donee in the control and management of the business (including participation in the major policy decisions affecting the business) is strong evidence of a donee partner's exercise of dominion and control over his interest. Such participation presupposes sufficient maturity and experience on the part of the donee to deal with the business problems of the partnership.

(v) **Income distributions.** The actual distribution to a donee partner of the entire amount or a major portion of his distributive share of the business income for the sole benefit and use of the donee is substantial evidence of the reality of the donee's interest, provided the donor has not retained controls inconsistent with real ownership by the donee. Amounts distributed are not considered to be used for the donee's sole benefit if, for example, they are deposited, loaned, or invested in such manner that the donor controls or can control the use or enjoyment of such funds.

(vi) **Conduct of partnership business.** In determining the reality of the donee's ownership of a capital interest in a partnership, consideration shall be given to whether the donee is actually treated as a partner in the operation of the business. Whether or not the donee has been held out publicly as a partner in the conduct of the business, in relations with customers, or with creditors or other sources of financing, is of primary significance. Other factors of significance in this connection include:

(a) Compliance with local partnership, fictitious names, and business registration statutes.

(b) Control of business bank accounts.

(c) Recognition of the donee's rights in distributions of partnership property and profits.

(d) Recognition of the donee's interest in insurance policies, leases, and other business contracts and in litigation affecting business.

(e) The existence of written agreements, records, or memoranda, contemporaneous with the taxable year or years concerned, establishing the nature of the partnership agreement and the rights and liabilities of the respective partners.

(f) Filing of partnership tax returns as required by law.

However, despite formal compliance with the above factors, other circumstances may indicate that the donor has retained substantial ownership of the interest purportedly transferred to the donee.

(vii) **Trustees as partners.** A trustee may be recognized as a partner for income tax purposes under the principles relating to family partnerships generally as applied to the particular facts of the trust-partnership arrangement. A trustee who is unrelated to and independent of the grantor, and who participates as a partner and receives distribution of the income distributable to the trust, will ordinarily be recognized as the legal owner of the partnership interest which he holds in trust unless the grantor has retained controls inconsistent with such ownership. However, if the grantor is the trustee, or if the trustee is amenable to the will of the grantor, the provisions of the trust instrument (particularly as to whether the trustee is subject to the responsibilities of a fiduciary), the provisions of the partnership agreement, and the conduct of the parties must all be taken into account in determining whether the trustee in a fiduciary capacity has become the real owner of the partnership interest. Where the grantor (or person amenable to his will) is the trustee, the trust may be recognized as a partner only if the grantor (or such other person) in his participation in the affairs of the partnership actively represents and protects the interests of the beneficiaries in accordance with the obligations of a fiduciary and does not subordinate such interests to the interests of the grantor. Furthermore, if the grantor (or person amenable to his will) is the trustee, the following factors will be given particular consideration:

(a) Whether the trust is recognized as a partner in business dealings with customers and creditors, and

(b) Whether, if any amount of the partnership income is not properly retained for the reasonable needs of the business, the trust's share of such amount is distributed to the trust annually and paid to the beneficiaries or reinvested with regard solely to the interests of the beneficiaries.

(viii) Interests (not held in trust) of minor children. Except where a minor child is shown to be competent to manage his own property and participate in the partnership activities in accordance with his interest in the property, a minor child generally will not be recognized as a member of a partnership unless control of the property is exercised by another person as fiduciary for the sole benefit of the child, and unless there is such judicial supervision of the conduct of the fiduciary as is required by law. The use of the child's property or income for support for which a parent is legally responsible will be considered a use for the parent's benefit. "Judicial supervision of the conduct of the fiduciary" includes filing of such accountings and reports as are required by law of the fiduciary who participates in the affairs of the partnership on behalf of the minor. A minor child will be considered as competent to manage his own property if he actually has sufficient maturity and experience to be treated by disinterested persons as competent to enter business dealings and otherwise

to conduct his affairs on a basis of equality with adult persons, notwithstanding legal disabilities of the minor under State law.

(ix) Donees as limited partners. The recognition of a donee's interest in a limited partnership will depend, as in the case of other donated interests, on whether the transfer of property is real and on whether the donee has acquired dominion and control over the interest purportedly transferred to him. To be recognized for Federal income tax purposes, a limited partnership must be organized and conducted in accordance with the requirements of the applicable State limited-partnership law. The absence of services and participation in management by a donee in a limited partnership is immaterial if the limited partnership meets all the other requirements prescribed in this paragraph. If the limited partner's right to transfer or liquidate his interest is subject to substantial restrictions (for example, where the interest of the limited partner is not assignable in a real sense or where such interest may be required to be left in the business for a long term of years), or if the general partner retains any other control which substantially limits any of the rights which would ordinarily be exercisable by unrelated limited partners in normal business relationships, such restrictions on the right to transfer or liquidate, or retention of other control, will be considered strong evidence as to the lack of reality of ownership by the donee.

(x) Motive. If the reality of the transfer of interest is satisfactorily established, the motives for the transaction are generally immaterial. However, the presence or absence of a tax-avoidance motive is one of many factors to be considered in determining the reality of the ownership of a capital interest acquired by gift.

(3) Allocation of family partnership income —(i) In general. (a) Where a capital interest in a partnership in which capital is a material income-producing factor is created by gift, the donee's distributive share shall be includible in his gross income, except to the extent that such share is determined without allowance of reasonable compensation for services rendered to the partnership by the donor, and except to the extent that the portion of such distributive share attributable to donated capital is proportionately greater than the distributive share attributable to the donor's capital. For the purpose of section 704, a capital interest in a partnership purchased by one member of a family from another shall be considered to be created by gift from the seller, and the fair market value of the purchased interest shall be considered to be donated capital. The "family" of any individual, for the purpose of the preceding sentence, shall include only his spouse, ancestors, and lineal descendants, and any trust for the primary benefit of such persons.

(b) To the extent that the partnership agreement does not allocate the partnership income in accordance with (a) of this subdivision, the distributive shares of the partnership income of the donor and donee shall be reallocated by making a reasonable allowance for the services of the donor and by attributing the balance of such income (other than a reasonable allowance for the services, if any, rendered by the donee) to the partnership capital of the donor and donee. The portion of income, if any, thus attributable to partnership capital for the taxable year shall be allocated between the donor and donee in accordance with their respective interests in partnership capital.

(c) In determining a reasonable allowance for services rendered by the partners, consideration shall be given to all the facts and circumstances of the business, including the fact that some of the partners may have greater managerial responsibility than others. There shall also be considered the amount that would ordinarily be paid in order to obtain comparable services from a person not having an interest in the partnership.

(d) The distributive share of partnership income, as determined under (b) of this subdivision, of a partner who rendered services to the partnership before entering the Armed Forces of the United States shall not be diminished because of absence due to military service. Such distributive share shall be adjusted to reflect increases or decreases in the capital interest of the absent partner. However, the partners may by agreement allocate a smaller share to the absent partner due to his absence.

(ii) **Special rules.** (a) The provisions of subdivision (i) of this subparagraph, relating to allocation of family partnership income, are applicable where the interest in the partnership is created by gift, indirectly or directly. Where the partnership interest is created indirectly, the term "donor" may include persons other than the nominal transferor. This rule may be illustrated by the following examples:

Example (1). A father gives property to his son who shortly thereafter conveys the property to a partnership consisting of the father and the son. The partnership interest of the son may be considered created by gift and the father may be considered the donor of the son's partnership interest.

Example (2). A father, the owner of a business conducted as a sole proprietorship, transfers the business to a partnership consisting of his wife and himself. The wife subsequently conveys her interest to their son. In such case, the father, as well as the mother, may be considered the donor of the son's partnership interest.

Example (3). A father makes a gift to his son of stock in the family corporation. The corporation is subsequently liquidated. The son later contributes the property received in the liquidation of the corporation to a partnership consisting of his father and himself. In such case, for purposes of section 704, the son's partnership interest may be considered created by gift and the father may be considered the donor of his son's partnership interest.

(b) The allocation rules set forth in section 704(e) and subdivision (i) of this subparagraph apply in any case in which the transfer or creation of the partnership interest has any of the substantial characteristics of a gift. Thus, allocation may be required where transfer of a partnership interest is made between members of a family (including collaterals) under a purported purchase agreement, if the characteristics of a gift are ascertained from the terms of the purchase agreement, the terms of any loan or credit arrangements made to finance the purchase, or from other relevant data.

(c) In the case of a limited partnership, for the purpose of the allocation provisions of subdivision (i) of this subparagraph, consideration shall be given to the fact that a general partner, unlike a limited partner, risks his credit in the partnership business.

(4) **Purchased interest**—(i) **In general.** If a purported purchase of a capital interest in a partnership does not meet the requirements of subdivision (ii) of this subparagraph, the ownership by the transferee of such capital interest will be recognized only if it qualifies under the requirements applicable to a transfer of a partnership interest by gifts. In a case not qualifying under subdivision (ii) of this subparagraph, if payment of any part of the purchase price is made out of partnership earnings, the transaction may be regarded in the same light as a purported gift subject to deferred enjoyment of income. Such a transaction may be lacking in reality either as a gift or as a *bona fide* purchase.

(ii) **Tests as to reality of purchased interests.** A purchase of a capital interest in a partnership, either directly or by means of a loan or credit extended by a member of the family, will be recognized as *bona fide* if:

(a) It can be shown that the purchase has the usual characteristics of an arm's-length transaction, considering all relevant factors, including the terms of the purchase agreement (as to price, due date of payment, rate of interest, and security, if any) and the terms of any loan or credit arrangement collateral to the purchase agreement; the credit standing of the purchaser (apart from relationship to the seller) and the capacity of the purchaser to incur a legally binding obligation; or

(b) It can be shown, in the absence of characteristics of an arm's-length transaction, that the purchase was genuinely intended to promote the success of the business by securing participation of the purchaser in the business or by adding his credit to that of the other participants.

However, if the alleged purchase price or loan has not been paid or the obligation otherwise discharged, the factors indicated in (a) and (b) of this subdivision shall be taken into account only as an aid in determining whether a *bona fide* purchase or loan obligation existed.

[T.D. 6500, 25 FR 11814, Nov. 26, 1960, as amended by T.D. 6771, 29 FR 15571, Nov. 20, 1964; T.D. 8365, 50 FR 53423, Dec. 31, 1985; T.D. 8065, 51 FR 10826, March 31, 1986; T.D. 8099, 51 FR 32062, Sept. 9, 1986]

§ 1.705–1 Determination of basis of partner's interest.

(a) **General rule.** (1) Section 705 and this section provide rules for determining the adjusted basis of a partner's interest in a partnership. A partner is required to determine the adjusted basis of his interest in a partnership only when necessary for the determination of his tax liability or that of any other person. The determination of the adjusted basis of a partnership interest is ordinarily made as of the end of a partnership taxable year. Thus, for example, such year-end determination is necessary in ascertaining the extent to which a partner's distributive share of partnership losses may be allowed. See section 704(d). However, where there has been a sale or exchange of all or a part of a partnership interest or a liquidation of a partner's entire interest in a partnership, the adjusted basis of the partner's interest should be determined as of the date of sale or exchange or liquidation. The adjusted basis of a partner's interest in a partnership is determined

without regard to any amount shown in the partnership books as the partner's "capital", "equity", or similar account. For example, A contributes property with an adjusted basis to him of $400 (and a value of $1,000) to a partnership. B contributes $1,000 cash. While under their agreement each may have a "capital account" in the partnership of $1,000, the adjusted basis of A's interest is only $400 and B's interest $1,000.

(2) The original basis of a partner's interest in a partnership shall be determined under section 722 (relating to contributions to a partnership) or section 742 (relating to transfers of partnership interests). Such basis shall be increased under section 722 by any further contributions to the partnership and by the sum of the partner's distributive share for the taxable year and prior taxable years of—

(i) Taxable income of the partnership as determined under section 703(a),

(ii) Tax-exempt receipts of the partnership, and

(iii) The excess of the deductions for depletion over the basis of the depletable property.

(3) The basis shall be decreased (but not below zero) by distributions from the partnership as provided in section 733 and by the sum of the partner's distributive share for the taxable year and prior taxable years of—

(i) Partnership losses (including capital losses), and

(ii) Partnership expenditures which are not deductible in computing partnership taxable income or loss and which are not capital expenditures.

(4) For the effect of liabilities in determining the amount of contributions made by a partner to a partnership or the amount of distributions made by a partnership to a partner, see section 752 and § 1.752–1, relating to the treatment of certain liabilities. In determining the basis of a partnership interest on the effective date of subchapter K, chapter 1 of the Code, or any of the sections thereof, the partner's share of partnership liabilities on that date shall be included.

(b) **Alternative rule.** In certain cases, the adjusted basis of a partner's interest in a partnership may be determined by reference to the partner's share of the adjusted basis of partnership property which would be distributable upon termination of the partnership. The alternative rule may be used to determine the adjusted basis of a partner's interest where circumstances are such that the partner cannot practicably apply the general rule set forth in section 705(a) and paragraph (a) of this section, or where, from a consideration of all the facts, it is, in the opinion of the Commissioner, reasonable to conclude that the result produced will not vary substantially from the result obtainable under the general rule. Where the alternative rule is used, adjustments may be necessary in determining the adjusted basis of a partner's interest in a partnership. Adjustments would be required, for example, in order to reflect in a partner's share of the adjusted basis of partnership property any significant discrepancies arising as a result of contributed property, transfers of partnership interests, or distributions of property to the partners. The operation of the alternative rules may be illustrated by the following examples:

Example (1). The ABC partnership, in which A, B, and C are equal partners, owns various properties with a total adjusted basis of $1,500 and has earned and retained an additional $1,500. The total adjusted basis of partnership property is thus $3,000. Each partner's share in the adjusted basis of partnership property is one-third of this amount, or $1,000. Under the alternative rule, this amount represents each partner's adjusted basis for his partnership interest.

Example (2). Assume that partner A in example (1) of this paragraph sells his partnership interest to D for $1,250 at a time when the partnership property with an adjusted basis of $1,500 had appreciated in value to $3,000, and when the partnership also had $750 in cash. The total adjusted basis of all partnership property is $2,250 and the value of such property is $3,750. D's basis for his partnership interest is his cost, $1,250. However, his one-third share of the adjusted basis of partnership property is only $750. Therefore, for the purposes of the alternative rule, D has an adjustment of $500 in determining the basis of his interest. This amount represents the difference between the cost of his partnership interest and his share of partnership basis at the time of his purchase. If the partnership subsequently earns and retains an additional $1,500, its property will have an adjusted basis of $3,750. D's adjusted basis for his interest under the alternative rule is $1,750, determined by adding $500, his basis adjustment to $1,250 (his one-third share of the $3,750 adjusted basis of partnership property). If the partnership distributes $250 to each partner in a current distribution, D's adjusted basis for his interest will be $1,500 ($1,000, his one-third share of the remaining basis of partnership property, $3,000, plus his basis adjustment of $500).

Example (3). Assume that BCD partnership in example (2) of this paragraph continues to operate. In 1960, D proposes to sell his partnership interest and wishes to evaluate the tax consequences of such sale. It is necessary, therefore, to determine the adjusted basis of his interest in the partnership. Assume further that D cannot determine the adjusted basis of his interest under the general rule. The balance sheet of the BCD partnership is as follows:

Assets	Adjusted basis per books	Market value
Cash	$3,000	$3,000
Receivables	4,000	4,000
Depreciable property	5,000	5,000
Land held for investment	18,000	30,000
Total	30,000	42,000

Liabilities and capital	Per books
Liabilities	$6,000
Capital accounts:	
B	4,500
C	4,500
D	15,000
Total	30,000

The $15,000 representing the amount of D's capital account does not reflect the $500 basis adjustment arising from D's purchase of his interest. See example (2) of this paragraph. The adjusted basis of D's partnership interest determined under the alternative rule is as follows:

D's share of the adjusted basis of partnership property (reduced by the amount of liabilities) at time of proposed sale	$15,000
D's share of partnership liabilities (under the partnership agreement liabilities are shared equally)	2,000
D's basis adjustment from example (2)	500
Adjusted basis of D's interest at the time of proposed sale, as determined under alternative rule	17,500

[T.D. 6500, 25 FR 11814, Nov. 26, 1960]

§ 1.706–1 Taxable years of partner and partnership.

(a) Year in which partnership income is includible. (1) In computing his taxable income for a taxable year, a partner is required to include his distributive share of partnership items set forth in section 702 for any partnership year ending within or with his taxable year. A partner shall also include in his taxable income for a taxable year "guaranteed payments" under section 707(c) which are made to him in a partnership taxable year ending within or with his taxable year. The provisions of this subparagraph may be illustrated by the following example:

Example. Partner A reports his income for a calendar year, while the partnership of which he is a member reports its income for a fiscal year ending May 31. During the partnership taxable year ending May 31, 1956, A received guaranteed payments of $1,200 for services and for the use of capital. Of this amount, $700 was received by A between June 1 and December 31, 1955, and the remaining $500 was received by him between January 1 and May 31, 1956. This entire $1,200 received by A is includible in his taxable income for the calendar year 1956 (together with his distributive share of partnership items set forth in section 702 for the partnership taxable year ending May 31, 1956).

(2) If a partner receives distributions under section 731 or sells or exchanges all or part of his partnership interest, any gain or loss arising therefrom does not constitute partnership income and is includible in the partner's gross income for his taxable year in which the payment is made. See sections 451 and 461.

(b) **Adoption or change in taxable year—(1) Partnership taxable year.** (i) The taxable year of a partnership shall be determined as though the partnership were a taxpayer.

(ii) A newly formed partnership may adopt a taxable year which is the same as the taxable year of all its principal partners (or the same as the taxable year to which all of its principal partners are concurrently changing) without securing prior approval from the Commissioner, or it may adopt a calendar year without securing prior approval from the Commissioner if all its principal partners are not on the same taxable year. In any other case, a newly formed partnership must secure prior approval from the Commissioner for the adoption of a taxable year.

(iii) An existing partnership may not change its taxable year without securing prior approval from the Commissioner, unless all its principal partners have the same taxable year to which the partnership changes, or unless all its principal partners concurrently change to such taxable year.

(2) **Partner's taxable year.** A partner may not change his taxable year without securing prior approval from the Commissioner. See section 442 and the regulations thereunder.

(3) **Principal partner.** For the purpose of this paragraph, a principal partner is a partner having an interest of 5 percent or more in partnership profits or capital.

(4) **Application for approval—(i) Change.** Application for a change in a taxable year shall be filed on Form 1128 with the Commissioner of Internal Revenue, Washington, D.C. 20224. If the short period involved in the change ends after December 31, 1973, such form shall be filed on or before the 15th day of the second calendar month following the close of such short period; if such short period ends before January 1, 1974, such form shall be filed on or before the last day of the first calendar month following the close of such short period.

(ii) **Adoption.** Where a newly formed partnership is required to secure prior approval from the Commissioner for the adoption of a taxable year, the partnership shall file an application on Form 1128 with the Commissioner on or before the last day of the month following the close of the taxable year to be adopted. The partnership shall modify Form 1128 to the extent necessary to indicate that it is an application for adoption of a taxable year.

(iii) **Business purpose.** Where prior approval is required under this paragraph, the applicant must establish a business purpose to the satisfaction of the Commissioner. For example, partnership AB, which is on a calendar year, is engaged in a business which has a natural business year (the annual accounting period encompassing all related income and expenses) ending on September 30th. The intention of the partnership to make its tax year coincide with such natural business year constitutes a sufficient business purpose.

(5) **Returns—(i) Partner.** A partner who changes his taxable year shall make his return for a short period in accordance with section 443, and shall attach to the return a copy of the letter from the Commissioner granting approval for the change of taxable year.

(ii) **Partnership.** (a) A partnership which changes its taxable year shall make its return for a short period in accordance with section 443, but shall not annualize the partnership taxable income. The partnership shall attach to the return either a copy of the letter from the Commissioner granting approval of the change of taxable year, or a statement indicating that the partnership is changing its taxable year to the same taxable year as that of all its principal partners or to the same taxable year as that to which all its principal partners are concurrently changing.

(b) Any newly formed partnership shall file with its first return either:

(1) A copy of the letter from the Commissioner approving the adoption of a partnership taxable year which is not the same as the taxable year of all its principal partners; or

(2) A statement indicating that the taxable year it has adopted is the same as the taxable year of all its principal partners, or that all its principal partners are concurrently changing to the taxable year it has adopted; or

(3) A statement that all its principal partners are not on the same taxable year and that it is adopting a calendar year without prior approval.

* * *

(c) **Closing of partnership year—(1) General rule.** Section 706(c) and this paragraph provide rules governing the closing of partnership years. The closing of a partnership taxable year or a termination of a partnership for Federal income tax purposes is not necessarily governed by the "dissolution", "liquidation", etc., of a partnership under State or local law. The taxable year of a partnership shall not close as the result of the death of a partner, the entry of a new partner, the liquidation of a partner's entire interest in the partnership (as defined in section 761(d)), or the sale or exchange of a partner's interest in the partnership, except in the case of a termination of a partnership and except as provided in subparagraph (2) of this paragraph. In the case of termination, the partnership taxable year closes for all partners as of the date of termination. See section 708(b) and paragraph (b) of § 1.708–1.

(2) **Partner who retires or sells interest in partnership—(i) Disposition of entire interest.** A partnership taxable year shall close with respect to a partner who sells or exchanges his entire interest in a partnership, and with respect to a partner whose entire interest is liquidated. However, a partnership taxable year with respect to a partner who dies shall not close prior to the end of such partnership taxable year, or the time when such partner's interest (held by his estate or other successor) is liquidated or sold or exchanged, whichever is earlier. See subparagraph (3) of this paragraph.

(ii) **Inclusions in taxable income.** In the case of a sale, exchange, or liquidation of a partner's entire interest in a partnership, the partner shall include in his taxable income for his taxable year within or with which his membership in the partnership ends, his distributive share of items described in section 702(a), and any guaranteed payments under section 707(c), for his partnership taxable year ending with the date of such sale, exchange, or liquidation. In order to avoid an interim closing of the partnership books, such partner's distributive share of items described in section 702(a) may, by agreement among the partners, be estimated by taking his *pro rata* part of the amount of such items he would have included in his taxable income had he remained a partner until the end of the partnership taxable year. The

proration may be based on the portion of the taxable year that has elapsed prior to the sale, exchange, or liquidation, or may be determined under any other method that is reasonable. Any partner who is the transferee of such partner's interest shall include in his taxable income, as his distributive share of items described in section 702(a) with respect to the acquired interest, the *pro rata* part (determined by the method used by the transferor partner) of the amount of such items he would have included had he been a partner from the beginning of the taxable year of the partnership. The application of this subdivision may be illustrated by the following example:

Example. Assume that a partner selling his partnership interest on June 30, 1955, has an adjusted basis for his interest of $5,000 on that date; that his *pro rata* share of partnership income up to June 30 is $15,000; and that he sells his interest for $20,000. Under the provisions of section 706(c)(2), the partnership year with respect to him closes at the time of the sale. The $15,000 is includible in his income as his distributive share and, under section 705, it increases the basis of his partnership interest to $20,000, which is also the selling price of his interest. Therefore, no gain is realized on the sale of his partnership interest. The purchaser of this partnership interest shall include in his income as his distributive share his *pro rata* part of partnership income for the remainder of the partnership taxable year.

(3) **Partner who dies.** (i) When a partner dies, the partnership taxable year shall not close with respect to such partner prior to the end of the partnership taxable year. The partnership taxable year shall continue both for the remaining partners and the decedent partner. Where the death of a partner results in the termination of the partnership, the partnership taxable year shall close for all partners on the date of such termination under section 708(b)(1)(A). See also paragraph (b)(1)(i)(b) of § 1.708–1 for the continuation of a 2-member partnership under certain circumstances after the death of a partner. However, if the decedent partner's estate or other successor sells or exchanges its entire interest in the partnership, or if its entire interest is liquidated, the partnership taxable year with respect to the estate or other successor in interest shall close on the date of such sale or exchange, or the date of completion of the liquidation.

(ii) The last return of a decedent partner shall include only his share of partnership taxable income for any partnership taxable year or years ending within or with the last taxable year for such decedent partner (*i.e.*, the year ending with the date of his death). The distributive share of partnership taxable income for a partnership taxable year ending after the decedent's last taxable year is includible in the return of his estate or other successor in interest. If the estate or other successor in interest of a partner continues to share in the profits or losses of the partnership business, the distributives share thereof is includible in the taxable year of the estate or other successor in interest within or with which the taxable year of the partnership ends. See also paragraph (a)(1)(ii) of § 1.736–1. Where the estate or other successor in interest receives distributions, any gain or loss on such distributions is includible in its gross income for its taxable year in which the distribution is made.

(iii) If a partner (or a retiring partner), in accordance with the terms of the partnership agreement, designates a person to succeed to his interest in the partnership after his death, such designated person shall be regarded as a successor in interest of the deceased for purposes of this chapter. Thus, where a partner designates his widow as the successor in interest, her distributive share of income for the taxable year of the partnership ending within or with her taxable year may be included in a joint return in accordance with the provisions of sections 2 and 6013(a)(2) and (3).

(iv) If, under the terms of an agreement existing at the date of death of a partner, a sale or exchange of the decedent partner's interest in the partnership occurs upon that date, then the taxable year of the partnership with respect to such decedent partner shall close upon the date of death. See section 706(c)(2)(A)(i). The sale or exchange of a partnership interest does not, for the purpose of this rule, include any transfer of a partnership interest which occurs at death as a result of inheritance or any testamentary disposition.

(v) To the extent that any part of a distributive share of partnership income of the estate or other successor in interest of a deceased partner is attributable to the decedent for the period ending with the date of his death, such part of the distributive share is income in respect of the decedent under section 691. See section 691 and the regulations thereunder.

(vi) The provisions of this subparagraph may be illustrated by the following examples:

Example (1). B has a taxable year ending December 31 and is a member of partnership ABC, the taxable year of which ends on June 30. B dies on October 31, 1955. His estate (which as a new taxpayer may, under section 441 and the regulations thereunder, adopt any taxable year) adopts a taxable year ending October 31. The return of the decedent for the period January 1 to October 31, 1955, will include only his distributive share of taxable income of the partnership for its taxable year ending June 30, 1955. The distributive share of taxable income of the partnership for its taxable year ending June 30, 1956, arising from the interest of the decedent, will be includible in the return of the estate for its taxable year ending October 31, 1956. That part of the distributive share attributable to the decedent for the period ending with the date of his death (July 1 through October 31, 1955) is income in respect of a decedent under section 691.

Example (2). Assume the same facts as in example (1) of this subdivision, except that, prior to B's death, B and D had agreed that, upon B's death, D would purchase B's interest for $10,000. When B dies on October 31, 1955, the partnership taxable year beginning July 1, 1955, closes with respect to him. Therefore, the return for B's last taxable year (January 1 to October 31, 1955) will include his distributive share of taxable income of the partnership for its taxable year ending June 30, 1955, plus his distributive share of partnership taxable income for the period July 1 to October 31, 1955. See subdivision (iv) of this subparagraph.

Example (3). H is a member of a partnership having a taxable year ending December 31. Both H and his wife W are on a calendar year and file joint returns. H dies on March 31, 1955. Administration of the estate is completed and the estate, including the partnership interest, is distributed to W as legatee on November 30, 1955. Such distribution by the estate is not a sale or exchange of H's partnership interest. No part of the taxable income of the partnership for the taxable year ending December 31, 1955, which is allocable to H, will be included in H's taxable income for his last taxable year (January 1 through March 31, 1955) or in the taxable income of H's estate for the taxable year April 1 through November 30, 1955. The distributive share of partnership taxable income for the full calendar year that is allocable to H will be includible in the taxable income of W for her taxable year ending December 31, 1955, and she may file a joint return under sections 2 and 6013(a)(3). That part of the distributive share attributable to the decedent for the period ending with the date of his death (January 1 through March 31, 1955) is income in respect of a decedent under section 691.

* * *

(4) **Disposition of less than entire interest.** If a partner sells or exchanges a part of his interest in a partnership, or if the interest of a partner is reduced, the partnership taxable year shall continue to its normal end. In such case, the partner's distributive share of items which he is required to include in his taxable income under the provisions of section 702(a) shall be determined by taking into account his varying interests in the partnership during the partnership taxable year in which such sale, exchange, or reduction of interest occurred.

(5) Transfer of interest by gift. The transfer of a partnership interest by gift does not close the partnership taxable year with respect to the donor. However, the income up to the date of gift attributable to the donor's interest shall be allocated to him under section 704(e)(2).

[T.D. 6500, 25 FR 11814, Nov. 26, 1960; 25 FR 14021, Dec. 31, 1960, as amended by 38 FR 26912, Sept. 27, 1973]

§ 1.707-1 Transactions between partner and partnership.

(a) Partner not acting in capacity as partner. A partner who engages in a transaction with a partnership other than in his capacity as a partner shall be treated as if he were not a member of the partnership with respect to such transaction. Such transactions include, for example, loans of money or property by the partnership to the partner or by the partner to the partnership, the sale of property by the partner to the partnership, the purchase of property by the partner from the partnership, and the rendering of services by the partnership to the partner or by the partner to the partnership. Where a partner retains the ownership of property but allows the partnership to use such separately owned property for partnership purposes (for example, to obtain credit or to secure firm creditors by guaranty, pledge, or other agreement) the transaction is treated as one between a partnership and a partner not acting in his capacity as a partner. However, transfers of money or property by a partner to a partnership as contributions, or transfers of money or property by a partnership to a partner as distributions, are not transactions included within the provisions of this section. In all cases, the substance of the transaction will govern rather than its form. See paragraph (c)(3) of § 1.731-1.

(b) Certain sales or exchanges of property with respect to controlled partnerships—(1) Losses disallowed. (i) No deduction shall be allowed for a loss on a sale or exchange of property (other than an interest in the partnership, directly or indirectly, between a partnership and a partner who owns, directly or indirectly, more than 50 percent of the capital interest or profits interest in such partnership. A loss on a sale or exchange of property, directly or indirectly, between two partnerships in which the same persons own, directly or indirectly, more than 50 percent of the capital interest or profits interest in each partnership shall not be allowed.

(ii) If a gain is realized upon the subsequent sale or exchange by a transferee of property with respect to which a loss was disallowed under the provisions of subdivision (i) of this subparagraph, section 267(d) (relating to amount of gain where loss previously disallowed) shall apply as though the loss were disallowed under section 267(a)(1).

(2) Gains treated as ordinary income. Any gain recognized upon the sale or exchange, directly or indirectly, of property which, in the hands of the transferee immediately after the transfer, is property other than a capital asset, as defined in section 1221, shall be ordinary income if the transaction is between a partnership and a partner who owns, directly or indirectly, more than 80 percent of the capital interest or profits interest in the partnership. This rule also applies where such a transaction is between partnerships in which the same persons own, directly or indirectly, more than 80 percent of the capital interest or profits interest in each partnership. The term "property other than a capital asset" includes (but is not limited to) trade accounts receivable, inventory, stock in trade, and depreciable or real property used in the trade or business.

(3) Ownership of a capital or profits interest. In determining the extent of the ownership by a partner, as defined in section 761(b), of his capital interest or profits interest in a partnership, the rules for constructive ownership of stock provided in section 267(c)(1), (2), (4), and (5) shall be applied for the purpose of section 707(b) and this paragraph. Under these rules, ownership of a capital or profits interest in a partnership may be attributed to a person who is not a partner as defined in section 761(b) in order that another partner may be considered the constructive owner of such interest under section 267(c). However, section 707(b)(1)(A) does not apply to a constructive owner of a partnership interest since he is not a partner as defined in section 761(b). For example, where trust T is a partner in the partnership ABT, and AW, A's wife, is the sole beneficiary of the trust, the ownership of a capital and profits interest in the partnership by T will be attributed to AW only for the purpose of further attributing the ownership of such interest to A. See section 267(c)(1) and (5). If A, B, and T are equal partners, then A will be considered as owning more than 50 percent of the capital and profits interest in the partnership, and losses on transactions between him and the partnership will be disallowed by section

707(b)(1)(A). However, a loss sustained by AW on a sale or exchange of property with the partnership would not be disallowed by section 707, but will be disallowed to the extent provided in paragraph (b) of § 1.267(b)–1. See section 267(a) and (b), and the regulations thereunder.

(c) **Guaranteed payments.** Payments made by a partnership to a partner for services or for the use of capital are considered as made to a person who is not a partner, to the extent such payments are determined without regard to the income of the partnership. However, a partner must include such payments as ordinary income for his taxable year within or with which ends the partnership taxable year in which the partnership deducted such payments as paid or accrued under its method of accounting. See section 706(a) and paragraph (a) of § 1.706–1. Guaranteed payments are considered as made to one who is not a member of the partnership only for the purposes of section 61(a) (relating to gross income) and section 162(a) (relating to trade or business expenses). For a guaranteed payment to be a partnership deduction, it must meet the same tests under section 162(a) as it would if the payment had been made to a person who is not a member of the partnership, and the rules of section 263 (relating to capital expenditures) must be taken into account. This rule does not affect the deductibility to the partnership of a payment described in section 736(a)(2) to a retiring partner or to a deceased partner's successor in interest. Guaranteed payments do not constitute an interest in partnership profits for purposes of sections 706(b)(3), 707(b), and 708(b). For the purposes of other provisions of the internal revenue laws, guaranteed payments are regarded as a partner's distributive share of ordinary income. Thus, a partner who receives guaranteed payments for a period during which he is absent from work because of personal injuries or sickness is not entitled to exclude such payments from his gross income under section 105(d). Similarly, a partner who receives guaranteed payments is not regarded as an employee of the partnership for the purposes of withholding of tax at source, deferred compensation plans, etc. The provisions of this paragraph may be illustrated by the following examples:

Example (1). Under the ABC partnership agreement, partner A is entitled to a fixed annual payment of $10,000 for services, without regard to the income of the partnership. His distributive share is 10 percent. After deducting the guaranteed payment, the partnership has $50,000 ordinary income. A must include $15,000 as ordinary income for his taxable year within or with which the partnership taxable year ends ($10,000 guaranteed payment plus $5,000 distributive share).

Example (2). Partner C in the CD partnership is to receive 30 percent of partnership income as determined before taking into account any guaranteed payments, but not less than $10,000. The income of the partnership is $60,000, and C is entitled to $18,000 (30 percent of $60,000) as his distributive share. No part of this amount is a guaranteed payment. However, if the partnership had income of $20,000 instead of $60,000, $6,000 (30 percent of $20,000) would be partner C's distributive share, and the remaining $4,000 payable to C would be a guaranteed payment.

Example (3). Partner X in the XY partnership is to receive a payment of $10,000 for services, plus 30 percent of the taxable income or loss of the partnership. After deducting the payment of $10,000 to partner X, the XY partnership has a loss of $9,000. Of this amount, $2,700 (30 percent of the loss) is X's distributive share of partnership loss and, subject to section 704(d), is to be taken into account by him in his return. In addition, he must report as ordinary income the guaranteed payment of $10,000 made to him by the partnership.

Example (4). Assume the same facts as in example (3) of this paragraph, except that, instead of a $9,000 loss, the partnership has $30,000 in capital gains and no other items of income or deduction except the $10,000 paid X as a guaranteed payment. Since the items of partnership income or loss must be segregated under section 702(a), the partnership has a $10,000 ordinary loss and $30,000 in capital gains. X's 30 percent distributive shares of these amounts are $3,000 ordinary loss and $9,000 capital gain. In addition, X has received a $10,000 guaranteed payment which is ordinary income to him.

[T.D. 6500, 25 FR 11814, Nov. 26, 1960; as amended by T.D. 7891, 48 FR 20049, May 4, 1983]

§ 1.708–1 Continuation of partnership.

(a) **General rule.** For purposes of subchapter K, chapter 1 of the Code, an existing partnership shall be considered as continuing if it is not terminated.

(b) **Termination—(1) General rule.** (i) A partnership shall terminate when the operations of the partnership are discontinued and no part of any business, financial operation, or venture of the partnership continues to be carried on by any of its partners in a partnership. For example, on November 20, 1956, A and B, each of whom is a 20-percent partner in partnership ABC, sell their interests to C, who is a 60-percent partner. Since the business is no longer carried on by any of its partners in a partnership, the ABC partnership is terminated as of November 20, 1956. However, where partners DEF agree on April 30, 1957, to dissolve their partnership, but carry on the business through a winding up period ending September 30, 1957, when all remaining assets, consisting only of cash, are distributed to the partners, the partnership does not terminate because of cessation of business until September 30, 1957.

(a) Upon the death of one partner in a 2-member partnership, the partnership shall not be considered as terminated if the estate or other successor in interest of the deceased partner continues to share in the profits or losses of the partnership business.

(b) For the continuation of a partnership where payments are being made under section 736 (relating to payments to a retiring partner or a deceased partner's successor in interest), see paragraph (a)(6) of § 1.736-1.

(ii) A partnership shall terminate when 50-percent or more of the total interest in partnership capital and profits is sold or exchanged within a period of 12 consecutive months. Such sale or exchange includes a sale or exchange to another member of the partnership. However, a disposition of a partnership interest by gift (including assignment to a successor in interest), bequest, or inheritance, or the liquidation of a partnership interest, is not a sale or exchange for purposes of this subparagraph. Furthermore, the contribution of property to a partnership does not constitute such a sale or exchange. See, however, paragraph (c)(3) of § 1.731-1. Fifty percent or more of the total interest in partnership capital and profits means 50 percent or more of the total interest in partnership capital plus 50-percent or more of the total interest in partnership profits. Thus, the sale of a 30-percent interest in partnership capital and a 60-percent interest in partnership profits is not the sale or exchange of 50 percent or more of the total interest in partnership capital and profits. If one or more partners sell or exchange interests aggregating 50-percent or more of the total interest in partnership capital and 50-percent or more of the total interest in partnership profits within a period of 12 consecutive months, such sale or exchange is considered as being within the provisions of this subparagraph. When interests are sold or exchanged on different dates, the percentages to be added are determined as of the date of each sale. For example, with respect to the ABC partnership, the sale by A on May 12, 1956, of a 30-percent interest in capital and profits to D, and the sale by B on March 27, 1957, of a 30-percent interest in capital and profits to E, is a sale of a 50-percent or more interest. Accordingly, the partnership is terminated as of March 27, 1957. However, if, on March 27, 1957, D instead of B, sold his 30-percent interest in capital and profits to E, there would be no termination since only one 30-percent interest would have been sold or exchanged within a 12-month period.

(iii) For purposes of subchapter K, chapter 1 of the Code, a partnership taxable year closes with respect to all partners on the date on which the partnership terminates. See section 706(c)(1) and paragraph (c)(1) of § 1.706-1. The date of termination is:

(a) For purposes of section 708(b)(1)(A), the date on which the winding up of the partnership affairs is completed.

(b) For purposes of section 708(b)(1)(B), the date of the sale or exchange of a partnership interest which, of itself or together with sales or exchanges in the preceding 12 months, transfers an interest of 50-percent or more in both partnership capital and profits.

(iv) If a partnership is terminated by a sale or exchange of an interest, the following is deemed to occur: The partnership distributes its properties to the purchaser and the other remaining partners in proportion to their respective interests in the partnership properties; and, immediately thereafter, the purchaser and the other remaining partners contribute the properties to a new partnership, either for the continuation of the business or for its dissolution and winding up. In the latter case, the new partnership terminates in accordance with subdivision (i) of this subparagraph. See sections 731 and 732 and §§ 1.731-1 and 1.732-1. For election of basis adjustments by the purchaser and other remaining partners, see sections 732(d) and 743(b) and paragraph (d) of § 1.732-1 and paragraph (b) of § 1.743-1.

(2) Special rules—(i) Merger or consolidation. If two or more partnerships merge or consolidate into one partnership, the resulting partnership shall be considered a continuation of the merging or consolidating partnership the members of which own an interest of more than 50 percent in the capital and profits of the resulting partnership. If the resulting partnership can, under the preceding sentence, be considered a continuation of more than one of the merging or consolidating partnerships, it shall, unless the Commissioner permits otherwise, be considered the continuation of that partnership which is credited with the contribution of the greatest dollar value of assets to the resulting partnership. Any other merging or consolidating partnerships shall be considered as terminated.

If the members of none of the merging or consolidating partnerships have an interest of more than 50 percent in the capital and profits of the resulting partnership, all of the merged or consolidated partnerships are terminated, and a new partnership results. The taxable years of such merging or consolidating partnerships which are considered terminated shall be closed in accordance with the provisions of section 706(c), and such partnerships shall file their returns for a taxable year ending upon the date of termination, *i.e.*, the date of merger or consolidation. The resulting partnership shall file a return for the taxable year of the merging or consolidating partnership that is considered as continuing. The return shall state that the resulting partnership is a continuation of such merging or consolidating partnership and shall include the names and addresses of the merged or consolidated partnerships. The respective distributive shares of the partners for the periods prior to and subsequent to the date of merger or consolidation shall be shown as a part of the return. The provisions of this subdivision may be illustrated by the following example:

Example. Partnership AB, in whose capital and profits A and B each own a 50-percent interest, and partnership CD, in whose capital and profits C and D each own a 50-percent interest, merge on September 30, 1955, and form partnership ABCD. Partners A, B, C, and D are on a calendar year; partnership AB is also on a calendar year; and partnership CD is on a fiscal year ending June 30th. After the merger, the partners have capital and profits interests as follows: A, 30 percent; B, 30 percent; C, 20 percent; and D, 20 percent. Since A and B together own an interest of more than 50 percent in the capital and profits of partnership ABCD, such partnership shall be considered a continuation of partnership AB and shall continue to file returns on a calendar year. Since C and D own an interest of less than 50 percent in the capital and profits of partnership ABCD, the taxable year of partnership CD closes as of September 30, 1955, the date of the merger, and CD partnership is terminated as of that date. Partnership ABCD is required to file a return for the taxable year January 1 to December 31, 1955, indicating thereon that, until September 30, 1955, it was partnership AB. Partnership CD is required to file a return for its final taxable year, July 1 through September 30, 1955.

(ii) Division of a partnership. Upon the division of a partnership into two or more partnerships, any resulting partnership or partnerships shall be considered a continuation of the prior partnership if its members had an interest of more than 50 percent in the capital and profits of the prior partnership. Any other resulting partnership will not be considered a continuation of the prior partnership but will be considered a new partnership. If the members of none of the result-

ing partnerships owned an interest of more than 50 percent in the capital and profits of the divided partnership, the divided partnership is terminated. Where members of a partnership which has been divided into two or more partnerships do not become members of a resulting partnership which is considered a continuation of the prior partnership, such partner's interests shall be considered liquidated as of the date of the division. The resulting partnership that is regarded as continuing shall file a return for the taxable year of the partnership that has been divided. The return shall state that the partnership is a continuation of the divided partnership and shall set forth separately the respective distributive shares of the partners for the periods prior to and subsequent to the date of division. The provisions of this subdivision may be illustrated by the following example:

Example. Partnership ABCD is in the real estate and insurance business. A owns a 40-percent interest, and B, C, and D each owns a 20-percent interest, in the capital and profits of the partnership. The partnership and the partners report their income on a calendar year. They agree to separate the real estate and insurance business as of November 1, 1955, and to form two partnerships; partnership AB to take over the real estate business, and partnership CD to take over the insurance business. Since members of resulting partnership AB owned more than a 50-percent interest in the capital and profits of partnership ABCD (A, 40 percent, and B, 20 percent), partnership AB shall be considered a continuation of partnership ABCD. Partnership AB is required to file a return for the taxable year January 1 to December 31, 1955, indicating thereon that until November 1, 1955, it was partnership ABCD. In forming partnership CD, partners C and D may contribute the property distributed to them in liquidation of their entire interests in divided partnership ABCD. Partnership CD will be required to file a return for the taxable year it adopts pursuant to section 706(b) and paragraph (b) of § 1.706-1(b).

[T.D. 6500, 25 FR 11814, Nov. 26, 1960]

§ 1.709-1 Treatment of organization and syndication costs.

(a) General rule. Except as provided in paragraph (b) of this section, no deduction shall be allowed under Chapter 1 of the Code to a partnership or to any partner for any amounts paid or incurred, directly or indirectly, in partnership taxable years beginning after December 31, 1975, to organize a partnership, or to promote the sale of, or to sell, an interest in the partnership.

(b) Amortization of organization expenses. (1) Under section 709(b) of the Code, a partnership may elect to treat its organizational expenses (as defined in section 709(b)(2) and in § 1.709-2(a)) paid or incurred in partnership taxable years beginning after December 31, 1976, as deferred expenses. If a partnership elects to amortize organizational expenses, it must select a period of not less than 60 months, over which the partnership will amortize all such expenses on a straight line basis. This period must begin with the month in which the partnership begins business (as determined under § 1.709-2(c)). However, in the case of a partnership on the cash receipts and disbursements method of accounting, no deduction shall be allowed for a taxable year with respect to any such expenses that have not been paid by the end of that taxable year. Portions of such expenses which would have been deductible under section 709(b) in a prior taxable year if the expenses had been paid are deductible in the year of payment. The election is irrevocable and the period selected by the partnership in making its election may not be subsequently changed.

(2) If there is a winding up and complete liquidation of the partnership prior to the end of the amortization period, the unamortized amount of organizational expenses is a partnership deduction in its final taxable year to the extent provided under section 165 (relating to losses). However, there is no partnership deduction with respect to its capitalized syndication expenses.

(c) **Time and manner of making election.** The election to amortize organizational expenses provided by section 709(b) shall be made by attaching a statement to the partnership's return of income for the taxable year in which the partnership begins business. The statement shall set forth a description of each organizational expense incurred (whether or not paid) with the amount of the expense, the date each expense was incurred, the month in which the partnership began business, and the number of months (not less than 60) over which the expenses are to be amortized. A taxpayer on the cash receipts and disbursements method of accounting shall also indicate the amount paid before the end of the taxable year with respect to each such expense. Expenses less than $10 need not be separately listed, provided the total amount of these expenses is listed with the dates on which the first and last of such expenses were incurred, and, in the case of a taxpayer on the cash receipts and disbursements method of accounting, the aggregate amount of such expenses that was paid by the end of the taxable year is stated. In the case of a partnership which begins business in a taxable year that ends after March 31, 1983, the original return and statement must be filed (and the election made) not later than the date prescribed by law for filing the return (including any extensions of time) for that taxable year. Once an election has been made, an amended return (or returns) and statement (or statements) may be filed to include any organizational expenses not included in the partnership's original return and statement.

[T.D. 7891, 48 FR 20048, May 4, 1983]

§ 1.709-2 **Definitions.**

(a) **Organizational expenses.** Section 709(b)(2) of the Internal Revenue Code defines organizational expenses as expenses which:

(1) Are incident to the creation of the partnership;

(2) Are chargeable to capital account; and

(3) Are of a character which, if expended incident to the creation of a partnership having an ascertainable life, would (but for section 709(a)) be amortized over such life.

An expenditure which fails to meet one or more of these three tests does not qualify as an organizational expense for purposes of section 709(b) and this section. To satisfy the statutory requirement described in paragraph (a)(1) of this section, the expense must be incurred during the period beginning at a point which is a reasonable time before the partnership begins business and ending with the date prescribed by law for filing the partnership return (determined without regard to any extensions of time) for the taxable year the partnership begins business. In addition, the expenses must be for creation of the partnership and not for operation or starting operation of the partnership trade or business. To satisfy the statutory requirement described in paragraph (a)(3) of this section, the expense must be for an item of a nature normally expected to benefit the partnership throughout the entire life of the partnership. The following are examples of organizational expenses within the meaning of section 709 and this section: Legal fees for services incident to the organization of the partnership, such as negotiation and preparation of a partnership agreement; accounting fees for services incident to the organization of the partnership; and filing fees. The following are examples of expenses that are not organizational expenses within the meaning of section 709 and this section (regardless of how the partnership characterizes them): Expenses connected with acquiring assets for the partnership or transferring assets to the partnership; expenses connected with the admission or removal of partners other than at the time the partnership is first organized; expenses connected with a contract relating to the operation of the partnership trade or business (even where the contract is between the partnership and one of its members); and syndication expenses.

(b) **Syndication expenses.** Syndication expenses are expenses connected with the issuing and marketing of interests in the partnership. Examples of syndication expenses are brokerage fees; registration fees; legal fees of the underwriter or placement agent and the issuer (the general partner or the partnership) for securities advice and for advice pertaining to the adequacy of tax disclosures in the prospectus or placement memorandum for securities law purposes; accounting fees for preparation of representations to be included in the offering materials; and printing costs of the prospectus, placement memorandum, and other selling and promotional material. These expenses

are not subject to the election under section 709(b) and must be capitalized.

(c) **Beginning business.** The determination of the date a partnership begins business for purposes of section 709 presents a question of fact that must be determined in each case in light of all the circumstances of the particular case. Ordinarily, a partnership begins business when it starts the business operations for which it was organized. The mere signing of a partnership agreement is not alone sufficient to show the beginning of business.

If the activities of the partnership have advanced to the extent necessary to establish the nature of its business operations, it will be deemed to have begun business. Accordingly, the acquisition of operating assets which are necessary to the type of business contemplated may constitute beginning business for these purposes. The term "operating assets", as used herein, means assets that are in a state of readiness to be placed in service within a reasonable period following their acquisition.

[T.D. 7891, 48 FR 20049, May 4, 1983]

Contributions, Distributions, and Transfers

Contributions to a Partnership

§ 1.721–1 Nonrecognition of gain or loss on contribution.

(a) No gain or loss shall be recognized either to the partnership or to any of its partners upon a contribution of property, including installment obligations, to the partnership in exchange for a partnership interest. This rule applies whether the contribution is made to a partnership in the process of formation or to a partnership which is already formed and operating. Section 721 shall not apply to a transaction between a partnership and a partner not acting in his capacity as a partner since such a transaction is governed by section 707. Rather than contributing property to a partnership, a partner may sell property to the partnership or may retain the ownership of property and allow the partnership to use it. In all cases, the substance of the transaction will govern, rather than its form. See paragraph (c)(3) of § 1.731–1. Thus, if the transfer of property by the partner to the partnership results in the receipt by the partner of money or other consideration, including a promissory obligation fixed in amount and time for payment, the transaction will be treated as a sale

or exchange under section 707 rather than as a contribution under section 721. For the rules governing the treatment of liabilities to which contributed property is subject, see section 752 and § 1.752–1.

(b)(1) Normally, under local law, each partner is entitled to be repaid his contributions of money or other property to the partnership (at the value placed upon such property by the partnership at the time of the contribution) whether made at the formation of the partnership or subsequent thereto. To the extent that any of the partners gives up any part of his right to be repaid his contributions (as distinguished from a share in partnership profits) in favor of another partner as compensation for services (or in satisfaction of an obligation), section 721 does not apply. The value of an interest in such partnership capital so transferred to a partner as compensation for services constitutes income to the partner under section 61. The amount of such income is the fair market value of the interest in capital so transferred, either at the time the transfer is made for past services, or at the time the services have been rendered where the transfer is conditioned on the completion of the transferee's future services. The time when such income is realized depends on all the facts and circumstances, including any substantial restrictions or conditions on the compensated partner's right to withdraw or otherwise dispose of such interest. To the extent that an interest in capital representing compensation for services rendered by the decedent prior to his death is transferred after his death to the decedent's successor in interest, the fair market value of such interest is income in respect of a decedent under section 691.

(2) To the extent that the value of such interest is: (i) Compensation for services rendered to the partnership, it is a guaranteed payment for services under section 707(c); (ii) compensation for services rendered to a partner, it is not deductible by the partnership, but is deductible only by such partner to the extent allowable under this chapter.

[T.D. 6500, 25 FR 11814, Nov. 26, 1960]

§ 1.722-1 Basis of contributing partner's interest.

The basis to a partner of a partnership interest acquired by a contribution of property, including money, to the partnership shall be the amount of money contributed plus the adjusted basis at the time of contribution of any property contributed. If the acquisition of an interest in partnership capital results in taxable income to a partner, such income shall constitute an addition to the basis of the partner's interest. See paragraph (b) of § 1.721-1. If the contributed property is subject to indebtedness or if liabilities of the partner are assumed by the partnership, the basis of the contributing partner's interest shall be reduced by the portion of the indebtedness assumed by the other partners, since the partnership's assumption of his indebtedness is treated as a distribution of money to the partner. Conversely, the assumption by the other partners of a portion of the contributor's indebtedness is treated as a contribution of money by them. See section 752 and § 1.752-1. The

provisions of this section may be illustrated by the following examples:

Example (1). A acquired a 20-percent interest in a partnership by contributing property. At the time of A's contribution, the property had a fair market value of $10,000, an adjusted basis to A of $4,000, and was subject to a mortgage of $2,000. Payment of the mortgage was assumed by the partnership. The basis of A's interest in the partnership is $2,400, computed as follows:

Adjusted basis to A of property contributed	$4,000
Less portion of mortgage assumed by other partners which must be treated as a distribution (80 percent of $2,000)	1,600
Basis of A's interest	2,400

Example (2). If, in example (1) of this section, the property contributed by A was subject to a mortgage of $6,000, the basis of A's interest would be zero, computed as follows:

Adjusted basis to A of property contributed	$4,000
Less portion of mortgage assumed by other partners which must be treated as a distribution (80 percent of $6,000)	4,800
	(800)

Since A's basis cannot be less than zero, the $800 in excess of basis, which is considered as a distribution of money under section 752(b), is treated as capital gain from the sale or exchange or a partnership interest. See section 731(a).

[T.D. 6500, 25 FR 11814, Nov. 26, 1960]

§ 1.723-1 Basis of property contributed to partnership.

The basis to the partnership of property contributed to it by a partner is the adjusted basis of such property to the contributing partner at the time of the contribution. Since such property has the same basis in the hands of the partnership as it had in the hands of the contributing partner, the holding period of such property for the partnership includes the period during which it was held by the partner. See section 1223(2). For elective adjustments to the basis of partnership property arising from distributions or transfers of partnership interests, see sections 732(d), 734(b), and 743(b).

[T.D. 6500, 25 FR 11814, Nov. 26, 1960]

Distributions by a Partnership

§ 1.731-1 Extent of recognition of gain or loss on distribution.

(a) **Recognition of gain or loss to partner—(1) Recognition of gain.** (i) Where money is distributed by a partnership to a partner, no gain shall be

recognized to the partner except to the extent that the amount of money distributed exceeds the adjusted basis of the partner's interest in the partnership immediately before the distribution. This rule is applicable both to current distributions (i.e., distributions other than in liquidation of an entire interest) and to distributions in liquidation of a partner's entire interest in a partnership. Thus, if a partner with a basis for his interest of $10,000 receives a distribution of cash of $8,000 and property with a fair market value of $3,000, no gain is recognized to him. If $11,000 cash were distributed, gain would be recognized to the extent of $1,000. No gain shall be recognized to a distributee partner with respect to a distribution of property (other than money) until he sells or otherwise disposes of such property, except to the extent otherwise provided by section 736 (relating to payments to a retiring partner or a deceased partner's successor in interest) and section 751 (relating to unrealized receivables and inventory items). See section 731(c) and paragraph (c) of this section.

(ii) For the purposes of sections 731 and 705, advances or drawings of money or property against a partner's distributive share of income shall be treated as current distributions made on the last day of the partnership taxable year with respect to such partner.

(2) **Recognition of loss.** Loss is recognized to a partner only upon liquidation of his entire interest in the partnership, and only if the property distributed to him consists solely of money, unrealized receivables (as defined in section 751(c)), and inventory items (as defined in section 751(d)(2)). The term "liquidation of a partner's interest", as defined in section 761(d), is the termination of the partner's entire interest in the partnership by means of a distribution or a series of distributions. Loss is recognized to the distributee partner in such cases to the extent of the excess of the adjusted basis of such partner's interest in the partnership at the time of the distribution over the sum of—

(i) Any money distributed to him, and

(ii) The basis to the distributee, as determined under section 732, of any unrealized receivables and inventory items that are distributed to him.

If the partner whose interest is liquidated receives any property other than money, unrealized receivables, or inventory items, then no loss will be recognized. * * *

* * *

(3) **Character of gain or loss.** Gain or loss recognized under section 731(a) on a distribution is considered gain or loss from the sale or exchange of the partnership interest of the distributee partner, that is, capital gain or loss.

(b) **Gain or loss recognized by partnership.** A distribution of property (including money) by a partnership to a partner does not result in recognized gain or loss to the partnership under section 731. However, recognized gain or loss may result to the partnership from certain distributions which, under section 751(b), must be treated as a sale or exchange of property between the distributee partner and the partnership.

(c) **Exceptions.** (1) Section 731 does not apply to the extent otherwise provided by—

(i) Section 736 (relating to payments to a retiring partner or to a deceased partner's successor in interest) and

(ii) Section 751 (relating to unrealized receivables and inventory items).

For example, payments under section 736(a), which are considered as a distributive share or guaranteed payment, are taxable as such under that section.

(2) The receipt by a partner from the partnership of money or property under an obligation to repay the amount of such money or to return such property does not constitute a distribution subject to section 731 but is a loan governed by section 707(a). To the extent that such an obligation is canceled, the obligor partner will be considered to have received a distribution of money or property at the time of cancellation.

(3) If there is a contribution of property to a partnership and within a short period:

(i) Before or after such contribution other property is distributed to the contributing partner and the contributed property is retained by the partnership, or

(ii) After such contribution the contributed property is distributed to another partner,

such distribution may not fall within the scope of section 731. Section 731 does not apply to a distribution of property, if, in fact, the distribution was made in order to effect an exchange of property between two or more of the partners or between the partnership and a partner. Such a transaction shall be treated as an exchange of property.

[T.D. 6500, 25 FR 11814, Nov. 26, 1960]

§ 1.732–1 Basis of distributed property other than money.

(a) Distributions other than in liquidation of a partner's interest. The basis of property (other than money) received by a partner in a distribution from a partnership, other than in liquidation of his entire interest, shall be its adjusted basis to the partnership immediately before such distribution. However, the basis of the property to the partner shall not exceed the adjusted basis of the partner's interest in the partnership, reduced by the amount of any money distributed to him in the same transaction. The provisions of this paragraph may be illustrated by the following examples:

Example (1). Partner A, with an adjusted basis of $15,000 for his partnership interest, receives in a current distribution property having an adjusted basis of $10,000 to the partnership immediately before distribution, and $2,000 cash. The basis of the property in A's hands will be $10,000. Under sections 733 and 705, the basis of A's partnership interest will be reduced by the distribution to $3,000 ($15,000 less $2,000 cash, less $10,000, the basis of the distributed property to A).

Example (2). Partner R has an adjusted basis of $10,000 for his partnership interest. He receives a current distribution of $4,000 cash and property with an adjusted basis to the partnership of $8,000. The basis of the distributed property to partner R is limited to $6,000 ($10,000, the adjusted basis of his interest, reduced by $4,000, the cash distributed).

(b) Distribution in liquidation. Where a partnership distributes property (other than money) in liquidation of a partner's entire interest in the partnership, the basis of such property to the partner shall be an amount equal to the adjusted basis of his interest in the partnership reduced by the amount of any money distributed to him in the same transaction. Application of this rule may be illustrated by the following example:

Example. Partner B, with a partnership interest having an adjusted basis to him of $12,000, retires from the partnership and receives cash of $2,000, and real property with an adjusted basis to the partnership of $6,000 and a fair market value of $14,000. The basis of the real property to B is $10,000 (B's basis for his partnership interest, $12,000, reduced by $2,000, the cash distributed).

(c) Allocation of basis among properties distributed to a partner. (1) Under section 732(a)(2) or (b), the basis to be allocated to properties distributed to a partner shall be allocated first to any unrealized receivables (as defined in section 751(c)) and inventory items (as defined in section 751(d)(2)) included in the distribution. However, such receivables or inventory items may not take a higher basis in the hands of the partner than their common adjusted basis to the partnership immediately

before the distribution, unless such distribution is treated as a sale or exchange under section 751(b), or unless the distributee partner has a special basis adjustment for the distributed property under sections 732(d) or 743(b). Any basis not allocated to unrealized receivable or inventory items shall be allocated to any other properties distributed to the partner in the same transaction, in proportion to the bases of such other properties in the hands of the partnership before distribution. The provisions of this subparagraph may be illustrated by the following example:

Example. Partner A, whose partnership interest in partnership ABC has an adjusted basis of $15,000, receives as a distribution in liquidation of his entire interest inventory items having a basis to the partnership of $6,000. In addition, he receives cash of $5,000, and two parcels of real property with adjusted bases to the partnership of $6,000 and $2,000, respectively. Basis in the amount of $10,000 ($15,000 basis, less $5,000 cash received) is allocated $6,000 to inventory items, and $3,000 $(6,000/8,000 \times \$4,000)$ and $1,000 $(2,000/8,000 \times \$4,000)$, respectively, to the two parcels of real property.

(2) If the adjusted basis to the partnership of the unrealized receivables and inventory items distributed to a partner is greater than the partner's adjusted basis of his interest (reduced by the amount of money distributed to him in the same transaction), the amount of the basis to be allocated to such unrealized receivables and inventory items shall be allocated in proportion to the adjusted bases of such properties in the hands of the partnership. If the basis of the partner's interest to be allocated upon a distribution in liquidation of his entire interest is in excess of the adjusted basis to the partnership of the unrealized receivables and inventory items distributed, and if there is no other property distributed to which such excess can be allocated, the distributee partner sustains a capital loss under section 731(a)(2) to the extent of the unallocated basis of his partnership interest.
* * *

* * *

(d) Special partnership basis to transferee under section 732(d). (1)(i) A transfer of a partnership interest occurs upon a sale or exchange of an interest or upon the death of a partner. Section 732(d) provides a special rule for the determination of the basis of property distributed to a transferee partner who acquired any part of his partnership interest in a transfer with respect to which the election under section 754 (relating to the optional adjustment to basis of partnership property) was not in effect.

(ii) Where an election under section 754 is in effect, see section 743(b) and paragraph (b) of § 1.743–1 and § 1.732–2.

(iii) If a transferee partner receives a distribution of property (other than money) from the partnership within 2 years after he acquired his interest or part thereof in the partnership by a transfer with respect to which the election under section 754 was not in effect, he may elect to treat as the adjusted partnership basis of such property the adjusted basis such property would have if the adjustment provided in section 743(b) were in effect.

(iv) If an election under section 732(d) is made upon a distribution of property to a transferee partner, the amount of the adjustment with respect to the transferee partner is not diminished by any depletion or depreciation of that portion of the basis of partnership property which arises from the special basis adjustment under section 732(d), since depletion or depreciation on such portion for the period prior to distribution is allowed or allowable only if the optional adjustment under section 743(b) is in effect.

(v) If property is distributed to a transferee partner who elects under section 732(d), and if such property is not the same property which would have had a special basis adjustment, then such special basis adjustment shall apply to any like property received in the distribution, provided that the transferee, in exchange for the property distributed, has relinquished his interest in the property with respect to which he would have had a special basis adjustment. This rule applies whether the property in which the transferee has relinquished his interest is retained or disposed or by the partnership. * * *

* * *

(2) A transferee partner who wishes to elect under section 732(d) shall make the election with his tax return—

(i) For the year of the distribution, if the distribution includes any property subject to the allowance for depreciation, depletion, or amortization, or

(ii) For any taxable year no later than the first taxable year in which the basis of any of the distributed property is pertinent in determining his income tax, if the distribution does not include any such property subject to the allowance for depreciation, depletion or amortization.

(3) A taxpayer making an election under section 732(d) shall submit with the return in which the election is made a schedule setting forth the following:

(i) That under section 732(d) he elects to adjust the basis of property received in a distribution; and

(ii) The computation of the special basis adjustment for the property distributed and the properties to which the adjustment has been allocated. For rules of allocation, see section 755.

(4) A partner who acquired any part of his partnership interest in a transfer to which the election provided in section 754 was not in effect, is required to apply the special basis rule contained in section 732(d) to a distribution to him, whether or not made within 2 years after the transfer, if at the time of his acquisition of the transferred interest—

(i) The fair market value of all partnership property (other than money) exceeded 110 percent of its adjusted basis to the partnership.

(ii) An allocation of basis under section 732(c) upon a liquidation of his interest immediately after the transfer of the interest would have resulted in a shift of basis from property not subject to an allowance for depreciation, depletion, or amortization, to property subject to such an allowance, and

(iii) A special basis adjustment under section 743(b) would change the basis to the transferee partner of the property actually distributed.

* * *

(e) Exception. When a partnership distributes unrealized receivables (as defined in section 751(c)) or substantially appreciated inventory items (as defined in section 751(d)) in exchange for any part of a partner's interest in other partnership property (including money), or, conversely, partnership property (including money) other than unrealized receivables or substantially appreciated inventory items in exchange for any part of a partner's interest in the partnership's unrealized receivables or substantially appreciated inventory items, the distribution will be treated as a sale or exchange of property under the provisions of section 751(b). In such case, section 732 (including subsection(d) thereof) applies in determining the partner's basis of the property which he is treated as having sold to or exchanged with the partnership (as constituted after the distribution). The partner is considered as having received such property in a current distribution and, immediately thereafter, as having sold or exchanged it. See section 751(b) and paragraph (b) of § 1.751–1. However, section 732 does not apply in determining the basis of that part of property actually distributed to a partner which is treated as received by him in a sale or exchange under section 751(b). Consequently, the basis of such property shall be its cost to the partner.

[T.D. 6500, 25 FR 11814, Nov. 26, 1960]

§ 1.732–2 Special partnership basis of distributed property.

(a) **Adjustments under section 734(b).** In the case of a distribution of property to a partner, the partnership bases of the distributed properties shall reflect any increases or decreases to the basis of partnership property which have been made previously under section 734(b) (relating to the optional adjustment to basis of undistributed partnership property) in connection with previous distributions.

(b) **Adjustments under section 743(b).** In the case of a distribution of property to a partner who acquired any part of his interest in a transfer as to which an election under section 754 was in effect, then, for the purposes of section 732 (other than subsection (d) thereof), the adjusted partnership bases of the distributed property shall take into account, in addition to any adjustments under section 734(b), the transferee's special basis adjustment for the distributed property under section 743(b). The application of this paragraph may be illustrated by the following example:

Example. Partner D acquired his interest in partnership ABD from a previous partner. Since the partnership had made an election under section 754, a special basis adjustment with respect to D is applicable to the basis of partnership property in accordance with section 743(b). One of the assets of the partnership at the time D acquired his interest was property X, which is later distributed to D in a current distribution. Property X has an adjusted basis to the partnership of $1,000 and with respect to D it has a special basis adjustment of $500. Therefore, for purposes of section 732(a)(1), the adjusted basis of such property to the partnership with respect to D immediately before its distribution is $1,500. However, if property X is distributed to partner A, a nontransferee partner, its adjusted basis to the partnership for purposes of section 732(a)(1) is only $1,000. In such case, D's $500 special basis adjustment may shift over to other property. See paragraph (b)(2)(ii) of § 1.743–1.

(c) **Adjustments to basis of distributed inventory and unrealized receivables.** Under section 732, the basis to be allocated to distributed proper-

ties shall be allocated first to any unrealized receivables and inventory items. If the distributee partner is a transferee of a partnership interest and has a special basis adjustment for unrealized receivables or inventory items under either section 743(b) or section 732(d), then the partnership adjusted basis immediately prior to distribution of any unrealized receivables or inventory items distributed to such partner shall be determined as follows: If the distributee partner receives his entire share of the fair market value of the inventory items or unrealized receivables of the partnership, the adjusted basis of such distributed property to the partnership, for the purposes of section 732, shall take into account the entire amount of any special basis adjustment which the distributee partner may have for such assets. If the distributee partner receives less than his entire share of the fair market value of partnership inventory items or unrealized receivables, then, for purposes of section 732, the adjusted basis of such distributed property to the partnership shall take into account the same proportion of the distributee's special basis adjustment for unrealized receivables or inventory items as the value of such items distributed to him bears to his entire share of the total value of all such items of the partnership. The provisions of this paragraph may be illustrated by the following example:

Example. Partner C acquired his 40-percent interest in partnership AC from a previous partner. Since the partnership had made an election under section 754, C has a special basis adjustment to partnership property under section 743(b). C retires from the partnership when the adjusted basis of his partnership interest is $3,000. He receives from the partnership in liquidation of his entire interest, $1,000 cash, certain capital assets, depreciable property, and certain inventory items and unrealized receivables. C has a special basis adjustment of $800 with respect to partnership inventory items and of $200 with respect to unrealized receivables. The common partnership basis for the inventory items distributed to him is $500 and for the unrealized receivables is zero. If the value of inventory items and the unrealized receivables distributed to C in his 40 percent share of the total value of all partnership inventory items and unrealized receivables, then, for purposes of section 732, the adjusted basis of such property in C's hands will be $1,300 for the inventory items ($500 plus $800) and $200 for the unrealized receivables (zero plus $200). The remaining basis of $500, which constitutes the basis of the capital assets and depreciable property distributed to C, is determined as follows: $3,000 (total basis) less $1,000 cash, or $2,000 (the amount to be allocated to the basis of all distributed property), less $1,500 ($800 and $200 special basis adjustments, plus $500 common partnership basis, the amount allocated to inventory items and unrealized receivables). However, if the value of the inventory items and unrealized receivables distributed to C consisted of only 20 percent of the total fair market value of such property (*i.e.,* only one-half of C's 40-percent share), then only one-half of C's special basis adjustment of $800 for partnership inventory items and $200 for unrealized receivables would be taken into account. In that case, the basis of the inventory items in C's hands would be $650 ($250, the common partnership basis for inventory items distributed to him, plus $400, one-half of C's special basis adjustment for inventory items). The basis of the unrealized receivables in C's hands would be $100 (zero plus $100, one-half of C's special basis adjustment for unrealized receivables).

[T.D. 6500, 25 FR 11814, Nov. 26, 1960]

§ 1.733–1 Basis of distributee partner's interest.

In the case of a distribution by a partnership to a partner other than in liquidation of a partner's entire interest, the adjusted basis to such partner of his interest in the partnership shall be reduced (but not below zero) by the amount of any money distributed to such partner and by the amount of the basis to him of distributed property other than money as determined under section 732 and §§ 1.732–1 and 1.732–2.

[T.D. 6500, 25 FR 11814, Nov. 26, 1960]

§ 1.734–1 Optional adjustment to basis of undistributed partnership property.

(a) General rule. A partnership shall not adjust the basis of partnership property as the result of a distribution of property to a partner, unless the election provided in section 754 (relating to optional adjustment to basis of partnership property) is in effect.

(b) Method of adjustment—(1) Increase in basis. Where an election under section 754 is in effect and a distribution of partnership property is made, whether or not in liquidation of the partner's entire interest in the partnership, the adjusted basis of the remaining partnership assets shall be increased by—

(i) The amount of any gain recognized under section 731(a)(1) to the distributee partner, or

(ii) The excess of the adjusted basis to the partnership immediately before the distribution of any property distributed (including adjustments under section 743(b) or section 732(d) when applied) over the basis under section 732 (including such special basis adjustments) of such property to the distributee partner.

The provisions of this subparagraph may be illustrated by the following examples:

Example (1). Partner A has a basis of $10,000 for his one-third interest in partnership ABC. The partnership has no liabilities and has assets consisting of cash of $11,000 and property with a partnership basis of $19,000 and a value of $22,000. A receives $11,000 in cash in liquidation of his entire interest in the partnership. He has a gain of $1,000 under section 731(a)(1). If the election under section 754 is in effect, the partnership basis for the property becomes $20,000 ($19,000 plus $1,000).

Example (2). Partner D has a basis of $10,000 for his one-third interest in partnership DEF. The partnership balance sheet before the distribution shows the following:

Assets

	Adjusted basis	Value
Cash	$4,000	$4,000
Property X	11,000	11,000
Property Y	15,000	18,000
Total	30,000	33,000

Liabilities and Capital

	Adjusted basis	Value
Liabilities	$0	$0
Capital:		
D	10,000	11,000
E	10,000	11,000
F	10,000	11,000
Total	30,000	33,000

In liquidation of his entire interest in the partnership, D received property X with a partnership basis of $11,000. D's basis for property X is $10,000 under section 732(b). Where the election under section 754 is in effect, the excess of $1,000 (the partnership basis before the distribution less D's basis for property X after distribution) is added to the basis of property Y. The basis of property Y becomes $16,000 ($15,000 plus $1,000). If the distribution is made to a transferee partner who elects under section 732(d), see § 1.734–2.

(2) Decrease in basis. Where the election provided in section 754 is in effect and a distribution is made in liquidation of a partner's entire interest, the partnership shall decrease the adjusted basis of the remaining partnership property by—

(i) The amount of loss, if any, recognized under section 731(a)(2) to the distributee partner, or

(ii) The excess of the basis of the distributed property to the distributee, as determined under section 732 (including adjustments under section 743(b) or section 732(d) when applied) over the adjusted basis of such property to the partnership (including such special basis adjustments) immediately before such distribution.

The provisions of this subparagraph may be illustrated by the following examples:

Example (1). Partner G has a basis of $11,000 for his one-third interest in partnership GHI. Partnership assets consist of cash of $10,000 and property with a basis of $23,000 and a value of $20,000. There are no partnership liabilities. In liquidation of his entire interest in the partnership, G receives $10,000 in cash. He has a loss of $1,000 under section 731(a)(2). If the election under section 754 is in effect, the partnership basis for the property becomes $22,000 ($23,000 less $1,000).

Example (2). Partner J has a basis of $11,000 for his one-third interest in partnership JKL. The partnership balance sheet before the distribution shows the following:

Assets

	Adjusted basis	Value
Cash	$5,000	$5,000
Property X	10,000	10,000
Property Y	18,000	15,000
Total	33,000	30,000

Liabilities and Capital

	Adjusted basis	Value
Liabilities	$0	$0
Capital:		
J	11,000	10,000
K	11,000	10,000
L	11,000	10,000
Total	33,000	30,000

In liquidation of his entire interest in the partnership, J receives property X with a partnership basis of $10,000. J's basis for property X under section 732(b) is $11,000. Where the election under section 754 is in effect, the excess of $1,000 ($11,000 basis of property X to J, the distributee, less its $10,000 adjusted basis to the partnership immediately before the distribution) decreases the basis of property Y in the partnership. Thus, the basis of property Y becomes $17,000 ($18,000 less $1,000). If the distribution is made to a transferee partner who elects under section 732(d), see § 1.734-2.

(c) Allocation of basis. For allocation among the partnership properties of basis adjustments under section 734(b) and paragraph (b) of this section, see section 755 and § 1.755-1.

(d) Returns. A partnership which must adjust the bases of partnership properties under section 734 shall attach a statement to the partnership return for the year of the distribution setting forth the computation of the adjustment and the partnership properties to which the adjustment has been allocated.

[T.D. 6500, 25 FR 11814, Nov. 26, 1960]

§ 1.734-2 Adjustment after distribution to transferee partner.

(a) In the case of a distribution of property by the partnership to a partner who has obtained all or part of his partnership interest by transfer, the adjustments to basis provided in section 743(b) and section 732(d) shall be taken into account in applying the rules under section 734(b). For determining the adjusted basis of distributed property to the partnership immediately before the distribution where there has been a prior transfer of a partnership interest with respect to which the election provided in section 754 or section 732(d) is in effect, see §§ 1.732-1 and 1.732-2.

(b)(1) If a transferee partner, in liquidation of his entire partnership interest, receives a distribution of property (including money) with respect to which he has no special basis adjustment, in exchange for his interest in property with respect to which he has a special basis adjustment, and does not utilize his entire special basis adjustment in determining the basis of the distributed property to him under section 732, the unused special basis adjustment of the distributee shall be applied as an adjustment to the partnership basis of the property retained by the partnership and as to which the distributee did not use his special basis adjustment. The provisions of this subparagraph may be illustrated by the following example:

Example. Upon the death of his father, partner S acquires by inheritance a half-interest in partnership ACS. Partners A and C each have a one-quarter interest. The assets of the partnership consist of $10,000 cash and land used in farming worth $10,000 with a basis of $1,000 to the partnership. Since the partnership had made the election under section 754 at the time of transfer, partner S had a special basis adjustment of $4,500 under section 743(b) with respect to his undivided half-interest in the real estate. The basis of S's partnership interest, in accordance with section 742, is $10,000. S retires from the partnership and receives $10,000 in cash in exchange for his entire interest. Since S has received no part of the real estate, his special basis adjustment of $4,500 will be allocated to the real estate, the remaining partnership property, and will increase its basis to the partnership to $5,500.

* * *

[T.D. 6500, 25 FR 11814, Nov. 26, 1960]

§ 1.735-1 Character of gain or loss on disposition of distributed property.

(a) Sale or exchange of distributed property —(1) Unrealized receivables. Any gain realized or loss sustained by a partner on a sale or exchange or other disposition of unrealized receivables (as defined in paragraph (c)(1) of § 1.751–1) received by him in a distribution from a partnership shall be considered gain or loss from the sale or exchange of property other than a capital asset.

(2) **Inventory items.** Any gain realized or loss sustained by a partner on a sale or exchange of inventory items (as defined in section 751(d)(2)) received in a distribution from a partnership shall be considered gain or loss from the sale or exchange of property other than a capital asset if such inventory items are sold or exchanged within 5 years from the date of the distribution by the partnership. The character of any gain or loss from a sale or exchange by the distributee partner of such inventory items after 5 years from the date of distribution shall be determined as of the date of such sale or exchange by reference to the character of the assets in his hands at that date (inventory items, capital assets, property used in a trade or business, etc.).

(b) **Holding period for distributed property.** A partner's holding period for property distributed to him by a partnership shall include the period such property was held by the partnership. The provisions of this paragraph do not apply for the purpose of determining the 5-year period described in section 735(a)(2) and paragraph (a)(2) of this section. If the property has been contributed to the partnership by a partner, then the period that the property was held by such partner shall also be included. See section 1223(2). For a partnership's holding period for contributed property, see § 1.723–1.

* * *

[T.D. 6500, 25 FR 11814, Nov. 26, 1960, as amended by T.D. 6832, 30 FR 8574, July 7, 1965]

§ 1.736–1 Payments to a retiring partner or a deceased partner's successor in interest.

(a) **Payments considered as distributive share or guaranteed payment.** (1)(i) Section 736 and this section apply only to payments made to a retiring partner or to a deceased partner's successor in interest in liquidation of such partner's entire interest in the partnership. See section 761(d). Section 736 and this section do not apply if the estate or other successor in interest of a deceased partner continues as a partner in its own right under local law. Section 736 and this section apply only to payments made by the partnership and not to transactions between the partners.

Thus, a sale by partner A to partner B of his entire one-fourth interest in partnership ABCD would not come within the scope of section 736.

(ii) A partner retires when he ceases to be a partner under local law. However, for the purposes of subchapter K, chapter 1 of the Code, a retired partner or a deceased partner's successor will be treated as a partner until his interest in the partnership has been completely liquidated.

(2) When payments (including assumption of liabilities treated as a distribution of money under section 752) are made to a withdrawing partner, that is, a retiring partner or the estate or other successor in interest of a deceased partner, the amounts paid may represent several items. In part, they may represent the fair market value at the time of his death or retirement of the withdrawing partner's interest in all the assets of the partnership (including inventory) unreduced by partnership liabilities. Also, part of such payments may be attributable to his interest in unrealized receivables and part to an arrangement among the partners in the nature of mutual insurance. When a partnership makes such payments, whether or not related to partnership income, to retire the withdrawing partner's entire interest in the partnership, the payments must be allocated between (i) payments for the value of his interest in assets, except unrealized receivables and, under some circumstances, good will (section 736(b)), and (ii) other payments (section 736(a)). The amounts paid for his interest in assets are treated in the same manner as a distribution in complete liquidation under sections 731, 732, and, where applicable, 751. See paragraph (b)(4)(ii) of § 1.751–1. The remaining partners are allowed no deduction for these payments since they represent either a distribution or a purchase of the withdrawing partner's capital interest by the partnership (composed of the remaining partners).

(3) Under section 736(a), the portion of the payments made to a withdrawing partner for his share of unrealized receivables, good will (in the absence of an agreement to the contrary), or otherwise not in exchange for his interest in assets under the rules contained in paragraph (b) of this section will be considered either—

(i) A distributive share of partnership income, if the amount of payment is determined with regard to income of the partnership; or

(ii) A guaranteed payment under section 707(c), if the amount of the payment is determined without regard to income of the partnership.

(4) Payments, to the extent considered as a distributive share of partnership income under section 736(a)(1), are taken into account under section 702 in the income of the withdrawing partner and thus reduce the amount of the distributive shares of the remaining partners. Payments, to the extent considered as guaranteed payments under section 736(a)(2), are deductible by the partnership under section 162(a) and are taxable as ordinary income to the recipient under section 61(a). See section 707(c).

(5) The amount of any payments under section 736(a) shall be included in the income of the recipient for his taxable year with or within which ends the partnership taxable year for which the payment is a distributive share, or in which the partnership is entitled to deduct such amount as a guaranteed payment. On the other hand, payments under section 736(b) shall be taken into account by the recipient for his taxable year in which such payments are made. See paragraph (b)(4) of this section.

(6) A retiring partner or a deceased partner's successor in interest receiving payments under section 736 is regarded as a partner until the entire interest of the retiring or deceased partner is liquidated. Therefore, if one of the members of a 2-man partnership retires under a plan whereby he is to receive payments under section 736, the partnership will not be considered terminated, nor will the partnership year close with respect to either partner, until the retiring partner's entire interest is liquidated, since the retiring partner continues to hold a partnership interest in the partnership until that time. Similarly, if a partner in a 2-man partnership dies, and his estate or other successor in interest receives payments under section 736, the partnership shall not be considered to have terminated upon the death of the partner but shall terminate as to both partners only when the entire interest of the decedent is liquidated. See section 708(b).

(b) **Payments for interest in partnership.** (1) Payments made in liquidation of the entire interest of a retiring partner or deceased partner shall, to the extent made in exchange for such partner's interest in partnership property (except for unrealized receivables and good will as provided in subparagraphs (2) and (3) of this paragraph), be con-

sidered as a distribution by the partnership (and not as a distributive share or guaranteed payment under section 736(a)). Generally, the valuation placed by the partners upon a partner's interest in partnership property in an arm's length agreement will be regarded as correct. If such valuation reflects only the partner's net interest in the property (i.e., total assets less liabilities), it must be adjusted so that both the value of the partner's interest in property and the basis for his interest take into account the partner's share of partnership liabilities. Gain or loss with respect to distributions under section 736(b) and this paragraph will be recognized to the distributee to the extent provided in section 731 and, where applicable, section 751.

(2) Payments made to a retiring partner or to the successor in interest of a deceased partner for his interest in unrealized receivables of the partnership in excess of their partnership basis, including any special basis adjustment for them to which such partner is entitled, shall not be considered as made in exchange for such partner's interest in partnership property. Such payments shall be treated as payments under section 736(a) and paragraph (a) of this section. For definition of unrealized receivables, see section 751(c).

(3) For the purposes of section 736(b) and this paragraph, payments made to a retiring partner or to a successor in interest of a deceased partner in exchange for the interest of such partner in partnership property shall not include any amount paid for the partner's share of good will of the partnership in excess of its partnership basis, including any special basis adjustments for it to which such partner is entitled, except to the extent that the partnership agreement provides for a reasonable payment with respect to such good will. Such payments shall be considered as payments under section 736(a). To the extent that the partnership agreement provides for a reasonable payment with respect to good will, such payments shall be treated under section 736(b) and this paragraph. Generally, the valuation placed upon good will by an arm's length agreement of the partners, whether specific in amount or determined by a formula, shall be regarded as correct.

(4) Payments made to a retiring partner or to a successor in interest of a deceased partner for his interest in inventory shall be considered as made

in exchange for such partner's interest in partnership property for the purposes of section 736(b) and this paragraph. However, payments for an interest in substantially appreciated inventory items, as defined in section 751(d), are subject to the rules provided in section 751(b) and paragraph (b) of § 1.751–1. The partnership basis in inventory items as to a deceased partner's successor in interest does not change because of the death of the partner unless the partnership has elected the optional basis adjustment under section 754. But see paragraph (b)(3)(iii) of § 1.751–1.

(5) Where payments made under section 736 are received during the taxable year, the recipient must segregate that portion of each such payment which is determined to be in exchange for the partner's interest in partnership property and treated as a distribution under section 736(b) from that portion treated as a distributive share or guaranteed payment under section 736(a). Such allocation shall be made as follows—

(i) If a fixed amount (whether or not supplemented by any additional amounts) is to be received over a fixed number of years, the portion of each payment to be treated as a distribution under section 736(b) for the taxable year shall bear the same ratio to the total fixed agreed payments for such year (as distinguished from the amount actually received) as the total fixed agreed payments under section 736(b) bear to the total fixed agreed payments under section 736 (a) and (b). The balance, if any, of such amount received in the same taxable year shall be treated as a distributive share or a guaranteed payment under section 736(a)(1) or (2). However, if the total amount received in any one year is less than the amount considered as a distribution under section 736(b) for that year, then any unapplied portion shall be added to the portion of the payments for the following year or years which are to be treated as a distribution under section 736(b). For example, retiring partner W who is entitled to an annual payment of $6,000 for 10 years for his interest in partnership property, receives only $3,500 in 1955. In 1956, he receives $10,000. Of this amount, $8,500 ($6,000 plus $2,500 from 1955) is treated as a distribution under section 736(b) for 1956; $1,500, as a payment under section 736(a).

(ii) If the retiring partner or deceased partner's successor in interest receives payments which are not fixed in amount, such payments shall first be treated as payments in exchange for his interest in partnership property under section 736(b) to the extent of the value of that interest and, thereafter, as payments under section 736(a).

(iii) In lieu of the rules provided in subdivisions (i) and (ii) of this subparagraph, the allocation of each annual payment between section 736(a) and (b) may be made in any manner to which all the remaining partners and the withdrawing partner or his successor in interest agree, provided that the total amount allocated to property under section 736(b) does not exceed the fair market value of such property at the date of death or retirement.

(6) Except to the extent section 751(b) applies, the amount of any gain or loss with respect to payments under section 736(b) for a retiring or deceased partner's interest in property for each year of payment shall be determined under section 731. However, where the total of section 736(b) payments is a fixed sum, a retiring partner or a deceased partner's successor in interest may elect (in his tax return for the first taxable year for which he receives such payments), to report and to measure the amount of any gain or loss by the difference between—

(i) The amount treated as a distribution under section 736(b) in that year, and

(ii) The portion of the adjusted basis of the partner for his partnership interest attributable to such distribution (i.e., the amount which bears the same proportion to the partner's total adjusted basis for his partnership interest as the amount distributed under section 736(b) in that year bears to the total amount to be distributed under section 736(b)).

A recipient who elects under this subparagraph shall attach a statement to his tax return for the first taxable year for which he receives such payments, indicating his election and showing the computation of the gain included in gross income.

* * *

[T.D. 6500, 25 FR 11814, Nov. 26, 1960, as amended by T.D. 6832, 30 FR 8574, July 7, 1965]

Transfers of Interests in a Partnership

§ 1.741–1 Recognition and character of gain or loss on sale or exchange.

(a) The sale or exchange of an interest in a partnership shall, except to the extent section 751(a) applies, be treated as the sale or exchange of a capital asset, resulting in capital gain or loss measured by the difference between the amount realized and the adjusted basis of the partnership interest, as determined under section 705. For treatment of selling partner's distributive share up to date of sale, see section 706(c)(2). Where the provisions of section 751 require the recognition of ordinary income or loss with respect to a portion of the amount realized from such sale or exchange, the amount realized shall be reduced by the amount attributable under section 751 to unrealized receivables and substantially appreciated inventory items, and the adjusted basis of the transferor partner's interest in the partnership shall be reduced by the portion of such basis attributable to such unrealized receivables and substantially appreciated inventory items. See section 751 and § 1.751–1.

(b) Section 741 shall apply whether the partnership interest is sold to one or more members of the partnership or to one or more persons who are not members of the partnership. Section 741 shall also apply even though the sale of the partnership interest results in a termination of the partnership under section 708(b). Thus, the provisions of section 741 shall be applicable (1) to the transferor partner in a 2-man partnership when he sells his interest to the other partner, and (2) to all the members of a partnership when they sell their interests to one or more persons outside the partnership.

(c) See section 351 for nonrecognition of gain or loss upon transfer of a partnership interest to a corporation controlled by the transferor.

(d) For rules relating to the treatment of liabilities on the sale or exchange of interests in a partnership see §§ 1.752–1 and 1.1001–2.

[T.D. 6500, 25 FR 11814, Nov. 26, 1960; 25 FR 14021, Dec. 31, 1960, as amended by T.D. 7741, 45 FR 81745, Dec. 12, 1980]

§ 1.742–1 Basis of transferee partner's interest.

The basis to a transferee partner of an interest in a partnership shall be determined under the general basis rules for property provided by part II (section 1011 and following), subchapter O, chapter 1 of the Code. Thus, the basis of a purchased interest will be its cost. The basis of a partnership interest acquired from a decedent is the fair market value of the interest at the date of his death or at the alternate valuation date, increased by his estate's or other successor's share of partnership liabilities, if any, on that date, and reduced to the extent that such value is attributable to items constituting income in respect of a decedent (see section 753 and paragraph (c)(3)(v) of § 1.706–1 and paragraph (b) of § 1.753–1) under section 691. See section 1014(c). For basis of contributing partner's interest, see section 722. The basis so determined is then subject to the adjustments provided in section 705.

[T.D. 6500, 25 FR 11814, Nov. 26, 1960]

§ 1.743–1 Optional adjustment to basis of partnership property.

(a) General rule. The basis of partnership property shall not be adjusted as the result of a transfer of an interest in a partnership, either by sale or exchange or as a result of the death of a partner, unless the election provided by section 754 (relating to optional adjustment to basis of partnership property) is in effect with respect to the partnership. However, whether or not the election provided in section 754 is in effect, the basis of partnership property shall not be adjusted as the result of a contribution of property, including money, to the partnership.

(b) Adjustment to basis of partnership property—(1) Determination of adjustment. In the case of a transfer of an interest in a partnership, either by sale or exchange or as a result of the death of a partner, a partnership as to which the election under section 754 is in effect shall:

(i) Increase the adjusted basis of partnership property by the excess of the transferee's basis for his partnership interest over his share of the adjusted basis to the partnership of all partnership property, or

(ii) Decrease the adjusted basis of partnership property by the excess of the transferee partner's share of the adjusted basis of all partnership property over his basis for his partnership interest.

The amount of the increase or decrease constitutes an adjustment affecting the basis of partnership property with respect to the transferee partner only. Thus, for purposes of depreciation, depletion, gain or loss, and distributions, the transferee partner will have a special basis for those partnership properties which are adjusted under section 743(b) and this paragraph. This special basis is his share of the common partnership basis (*i.e.*, the adjusted basis of such properties to the partnership without regard to any special basis adjustments of any transferee) plus or minus his special basis adjustments. A partner's share of the adjusted basis of partnership property is equal to the sum of his interest as a partner in partnership capital and surplus, plus his share of partnership liabilities. Where an agreement with respect to contributed property is in effect under section 704(c)(2), such agreement shall be taken into account in determining a partner's share of the adjusted basis of partnership property. Generally, if a partner's interest in partnership capital and profits is one-third, his share of the adjusted basis of partnership property will be one-third of such basis. The provisions of this paragraph may be illustrated by the following examples:

Example (1). A is a member of partnership ABC in which the partners have equal interests in capital and profits. The partnership has made the election under section 754, relating to the optional adjustment to the basis of partnership property. A sells his interest to P for $22,000. The balance sheet of the partnership at the date of sale shows the following:

Assets

	Adjusted basis per books	Market value
Cash	$5,000	$5,000
Accounts receivable	10,000	10,000
Inventory	20,000	21,000
Depreciable assets	20,000	40,000
Total	55,000	76,000

Liabilities and Capital

	Adjusted basis per books	Market value
Liabilities	$10,000	$10,000
Capital:		
A	15,000	22,000
B	15,000	22,000
C	15,000	22,000
Total	55,000	76,000

The amount of the adjustment under section 743(b) is the difference between the basis of the transferee's interest in the partnership and his share of the adjusted basis of

partnership property. Under section 742, the basis of P's interest is $25,333 (the cash paid for A's interest, $22,000, plus $3,333, P's share of partnership liabilities). P's share of the adjusted basis of partnership property is $18,333, *i.e.*, $15,000 plus $3,333. The amount to be added to the basis of partnership property is, therefore, $7,000, the difference between $25,333 and $18,333. This amount will be allocated to partnership properties in accordance with the rules set forth in section 755 and § 1.755–1.

Example (2). D is a member of partnership DEF in which the partners have equal interests in profits, but not in capital. The partnership has made the election under section 754. D dies and his interest passes to W, his widow. The balance sheet of the partnership at the date of D's death shows the following:

Assets

	Adjusted basis per books	Market value
Cash	$7,000	$7,000
Accounts receivable	10,000	10,000
Inventory	20,000	24,000
Depreciable assets	20,000	40,000
Total	57,000	81,000

Liabilities and Capital

	Adjusted basis per books	Value
Liabilities	$10,000	$10,000
Capital:		
D	18,000	26,000
E	15,000	23,000
F	14,000	22,000
Total	57,000	81,000

The amount of the adjustment under section 743(b) is the difference between the basis of the transferee's interest in the partnership and her share of the adjusted basis of partnership property. Under section 742, the basis of W's interest is $29,333 (the fair market value of D's interest at his death, $26,000, plus $3,333, his share of partnership liabilities). W's share of the adjusted basis of partnership property is $21,333 (*i.e.*, $18,000 plus $3,333, her share of partnership liabilities). The amount to be added to the basis of partnership property is, therefore, $8,000, the difference between $29,333 and $21,333. This amount will be allocated to partnership properties in accordance with the rules set forth in section 755 and § 1.755–1.

Note that in examples (1) and (2) of this subparagraph the amount of the adjustment does not depend upon the adjusted basis to the transferor for his interest in partnership capital.

(2) Determination of partner's share of adjusted basis of partnership property. (i) Under the provisions of section 743(b), a partner's share of the adjusted basis of partnership property shall be determined by taking into account the effect of any partnership agreement with respect to contributed property as described in section 704(c)(2), or the effect of the contribution of undivided interests under section 704(c)(3). This rule may be illustrated by the following examples:

Example (1). A, B, and C form partnership ABC, to which A contributes land worth $1,000 (property X) with an adjusted basis to him of $400, and B and C each contributes $1,000 cash. Each partner has $1,000 credited to him on the books of the partnership as his capital contribution. The partners share in profits equally. During the partnership's first taxable year, property X appreciates in value to $1,300. A sells his one-third interest in the partnership to D for $1,100, when the election under section 754 is in effect. No agreement under section 704(c)(2) is in effect. The adjusted basis of the partnership property is increased with respect to D by the excess of his basis for his partnership interest, $1,100, over his share of the adjusted basis of partnership property, $800 ($\frac{1}{3}$ of $2,400, the total adjusted basis of partnership property). The amount of the adjustment, therefore, is $300 ($1,100 minus $800), which is an increase in the basis of partnership property with respect to D only. This special basis adjustment will be allocated to property X. (See section 755 and § 1.755–1.) If property X is sold for $1,600, the gain to the partnership is $1,200 ($1,600 received, less the adjusted common partnership basis of $400 for property X). Thus, each partner's distributive share of the gain on the sale is $400. However, D's recognized gain is only $100 (his $400 distributive share of the gain, reduced by $300, his special basis adjustment with respect to property X). If D purchased his interest from B or C, the partners who contributed cash, D's adjustment under section 743(b) would also be $300, computed in exactly the same manner as in the case of a purchase from A.

Example (2). Assume that partnership ABC described in example (1) of this subdivision has an agreement under section 704(c)(2) with respect to property X, stating that upon the sale of that property any gain, to the extent attributable to the precontribution appreciation of $600 (the difference between its value, $1,000, and its basis, $400, at the time of the contribution) is to be allocated entirely to A, who contributed property X. Upon the purchase of A's interest by D for $1,100, the computation of D's special basis would differ from that indicated in example (1) of this subdivision as follows: Under the partnership agreement, A's share of the $2,400 adjusted basis of partnership property is only $400 (his basis for property X prior to its contribution to the partnership), and B's and C's share is $1,000 each (the amount of the cash investment of each). The amount of the increase to D in the adjusted basis of partnership property under section 743(b)(1) is $700 (the excess of $1,100, D's cost basis for his interest, over $400, A's share of the adjusted basis of partnership property to which D succeeds). This amount constitutes an adjustment to the basis of partnership property with respect to D only. If X is sold by the partnership for $1,600, the gain is $1,200 ($1,600 received less the adjusted common partnership basis of $400). Under the partnership agreement, $600 of this gain, which is attributable to precontribution appreciation in value, is allocable to D, who is A's successor. The re-

maining $600 gain is not subject to the agreement and is allocable to the partners equally, $200 each. D's distributive share of the partnership gain is thus $600 plus $200, or $800. However, D has a special basis adjustment of $700 under section 743(b)(1), which reduces his gain from $800 to $100. B and C each has a gain of $200, which is unaffected by the transfer of A's interest to D.

Example (3). Assume the same facts as in example (2) of this subdivision, except that D has purchased his interest from B instead of from A. His special basis adjustment for partnership property in this case differs from that where he had purchased his interest from A, because of the effect of the agreement under section 704(c)(2). In this case, D is a successor to B, whose share of the adjusted basis of partnership property is $1,000, instead of A, whose share is only $400. As a result, the adjustment under section 743(b)(1) is the excess of D's cost basis for his interest, $1,100, over his share of the adjusted basis of partnership property, $1,000, or $100. In this case, if property X is sold for $1,600, the partnership gain is $1,200 ($1,600 less the adjusted partnership basis of $400). Of this gain, $600, representing precontribution appreciation, is allocable to A under the partnership agreement. The remaining $600 is allocable in the amount of $200 to each partner. Since D as a transferee has a special basis adjustment of $100 under section 743(b)(1), his gain is reduced from $200 to $100.

(ii) If a partner receives a distribution of property with respect to which another partner has a special basis adjustment, the distributee shall not take into account the special basis adjustment of the other partner. However, the partner with the special basis adjustment will reallocate it under section 755 to remaining partnership property of a like kind or, if he receives a distribution of like property, to such distributed property. If a partner receives a distribution of property with respect to which he has a special basis adjustment, such basis adjustment will be taken into account when relevant under section 732. See paragraph (b) of § 1.732–2. If, at the time a partner receives property (whether or not he has a special basis adjustment with respect to such property), he relinquishes his interest in other property of a like kind with respect to which he has a special basis adjustment, the adjusted basis to the partnership of the distributed property shall include his special basis adjustment for the property in which he relinquished his interest. For the purposes of the preceding sentence, a partner will be considered as having relinquished his interest in any remaining partnership properties when his interest has been completely liquidated; however, when a partner receives a distribution not in liquidation, he will be considered as relinquishing his interest only in property distributed to other partners. For the purposes of this subdivision, like property means property of the same class, that is, stock in trade, property used in the trade or business, capital assets, etc. For certain adjustments to the basis of remaining partnership property after a distribution to a transferee partner, see paragraph (b) of § 1.734–2. The provisions of this subdivision may be illustrated by the following examples:

Example (1). C is a transferee partner in partnership BC. The partnership owns, among other assets, X, a depreciable asset with a common basis to the partnership of $1,000 and a special basis adjustment to C of $200, and Y, another depreciable asset with a common basis of $800 and a special basis adjustment to C of $300. B and C agree that B will receive a distribution of property Y, and C will receive a distribution of property X, with all other property to remain in the partnership. With respect to B, the partnership basis of property Y is $800, the common partnership basis. Y will, therefore, have a basis of $800 in B's hands under section 732(a) which provides for the use of a carryover basis in the case of current distributions. With respect to C, however, the partnership basis of property X is $1,500, the common partnership basis of $1,000, plus C's special basis adjustment of $200 for property X, plus C's additional special basis adjustment of $300 for property Y, in which he has relinquished his interest.

Example (2). (a) Partner D acquired his one-third interest in partnership BCD for $14,000 from a previous partner when an election under section 754 was in effect. Therefore, under section 743(b), D has a special basis adjustment for certain partnership property. Assume that at the time of the distribution in paragraph (b) of this example, the partnership assets consist of cash and rental property and that such assets and D's special basis adjustments under section 743(b) are as follows:

Item	Fair market value	Common partnership basis	D's share	D's special basis adjustment	Partnership basis to D
Cash	$12,000	$12,000	$4,000	......	$4,000
House:					
U	9,000	1,200	400	......	400
V	6,000	4,500	1,500	......	1,500
W	8,000	1,500	500	......	500
X	9,000	4,800	1,600	$2,000	3,600
Y	9,000	6,000	2,000	......	2,000
Z	7,000	3,000	1,000	1,000	2,000
Total	60,000	33,000	11,000	3,000	14,000

(b) Assume further that D receives $4,000 in cash and houses Y and Z in complete liquidation of his interest in partnership BCD. In determining the basis to D of houses Y and Z under section 732(b) and (c), D must allocate $10,000 basis ($14,000 basis for his interest, less $4,000 cash received) to houses Y and Z in proportion to their adjusted basis to the partnership. For purposes of section 732(c), the adjusted basis of house Y is $7,200 ($6,000 common partnership basis, plus $1,200, allocated share of D's special basis adjustment of $2,000 for house X, in which D relinquished his interest). The adjusted basis of house Z is $4,800 ($3,000 common partnership basis, plus $1,000, D's special basis for house Z, plus $800,

allocated share of D's special basis of $2,000 for house X, in which D relinquished his interest). Under the rule of this subdivision, 6,000/10,000 of the $2,000 special basis adjustment for X is allocated to Y and 4,000/10,000 of such amount to Z. Therefore, $6,000 basis (7,200/12,000 of $10,000) is allocated to house Y and $4,000 basis (4,800/12,000 of $10,000) to house Z.

(c) Since houses Y and Z had $12,000 basis to the partnership, as computed in paragraph (b) of this example, and only $10,000 basis to D, as determined under section 732, the partnership, under section 734(b)(1)(B), must increase the basis of remaining partnership property (houses U, V, W, and X) by $2,000 (excess of $12,000 over $10,000). For allocation of this amount, see section 755 and § 1.755–1.

(iii) Where an adjustment is made under section 743(b) to the basis of partnership property subject to depletion, any depletion allowable shall be determined separately for each partner, including the transferee partner, based on his interest in such property. See paragraph (a)(8) of § 1.702–1. This rule may be illustrated by the following example:

Example. A, B, and C each contributes $5,000 cash to form partnership ABC, which purchases oil property for $15,000. C subsequently sells his partnership interest to D for $100,000 when the election under section 754 is in effect. D has a special basis adjustment for the oil property of $95,000 (the difference between D's basis, $100,000, and his share of the basis of partnership property, $5,000). Assume that the depletion allowance computed under the percentage method would be $21,000 for the taxable year so that each partner would be entitled to $7,000 as his share of the deduction for depletion. However, under the cost depletion method, at an assumed rate of 10 percent, the allowance with respect to D's one-third interest which has a basis to him of $100,000 ($5,000, plus his special basis adjustment of $95,000) is $10,000, although the cost depletion allowance with respect to the one-third interest of A and B in the oil property, each of which has a basis of $5,000, is only $500. For partners A and B, the percentage depletion is greater than cost depletion and each will deduct $7,000 based on the percentage depletion method. However, as to D, the transferee partner, the cost depletion method results in a greater allowance and D will, therefore, deduct $10,000 based on cost depletion. See section 613(a).

(iv) Where there has been more than one transfer of partnership interests, the last transferee's special basis adjustment, if any, under section 743(b) shall be determined by reference to the partnership common basis for its property without regard to any prior transferee's special basis adjustment. For example, A, B, and C form a partnership. A and B each contributes $1,000 cash and C contributes land with a basis and value of $1,000. When the land has appreciated in value to $1,300, A sells his interest to D for $1,100 (⅓ of $3,300, the value of the partnership property).

The election under section 754 is in effect; therefore, D has a special basis adjustment of $100 with respect to the land under section 743(b). After the land has further appreciated in value to $1,600, D sells his interest to E for $1,200 (⅓ of $3,600, the value of the partnership property). Under section 743(b), E has a special basis adjustment of $200. This amount is determined without regard to any special basis adjustment that D may have had in the partnership assets.

(3) **Returns.** A transferee partner who has a special basis adjustment under section 743(b) shall attach a statement to his income tax return for the first taxable year in which the basis of any partnership property subject to the adjustment is pertinent in determining his income tax, showing the computation of the adjustment and the partnership properties to which the adjustment has been allocated.

(c) **Allocation of basis.** For the allocation of basis among partnership properties where section 743(b) applies, see section 755 and § 1.755-1.

[T.D. 6500, 25 FR 11814, Nov. 26, 1960]

Provisions Common to Part II, Subchapter K, Chapter 1 of the Code

§ 1.751-1 **Unrealized receivables and inventory items.**

(a) **Sale or exchange of interest in a partnership—(1) Character of amount realized.** To the extent that money or property received by a partner in exchange for all or part of his partnership interest is attributable to his share of the value of partnership unrealized receivables or substantially appreciated inventory items, the money or fair market value of the property received shall be considered as an amount realized from the sale or exchange of property other than a capital asset. The remainder of the total amount realized on the sale or exchange of the partnership interest is realized from the sale or exchange of a capital asset under section 741. For definition of "unrealized receivables" and "inventory items which have appreciated substantially in value", see section 751(c) and (d). Unrealized receivables and substantially appreciated inventory items are hereafter in this section referred to as "section 751 property". See paragraph (e) of this section.

(2) **Determination of gain or loss.** The income or loss realized by a partner upon the sale or exchange of his interest in section 751 property is the difference between (i) the portion of the total amount realized for the partnership interest allocated to section 751 property, and (ii) the portion of the selling partner's basis for his entire interest allocated to such property. Generally, the portion of the total amount realized which the seller and the purchaser allocate to section 751 property in an arm's length agreement will be regarded as correct. The portion of the partner's adjusted basis for his partnership interest to be allocated to section 751 property shall be an amount equal to the basis such property would have had under section 732 (including subsection (d) thereof) if the selling partner had received his share of such properties in a current distribution made immediately before the sale. See §§ 1.732-1 and 1.732-2. Such basis shall reflect the rules of section 704(c)(3), if applicable, or any agreement under section 704(c)(2). Any gain or loss recognized which is attributable to section 751 property will be ordinary gain or loss. The difference between the remainder, if any, of the partner's adjusted basis for his partnership interest and the balance, if any, of the amount realized is the transferor's capital gain or loss on the sale of his partnership interest.

(3) **Statement required.** A transferor partner selling or exchanging any part of his interest in a partnership which has any section 751 property at the time of sale or exchange shall submit with his income tax return for the taxable year in which the sale or exchange occurs a statement setting forth separately the following information:

(i) The date of the sale or exchange, the amount of the transferor partner's adjusted basis for his partnership interest, and the portion thereof attributable to section 751 property under section 732; and

(ii) The amount of any money and the fair market value of any other property received or to be received for the transferred interest in the partnership, and the portion thereof attributable to section 751 property.

(iii) If the transferor partner computes his adjusted basis for section 751 property under the provisions of section 732(d), he must also include in the statement the information required by paragraph (d)(3) of § 1.732-1.

(iv) If the transferor partner has a special basis adjustment under section 743(b), he must also include in the statement the computation of his special basis adjustment and the partnership properties to which the adjustment has been allocated.

(b) Certain distributions treated as sales or exchanges—(1) In general. (i) Certain distributions to which section 751(b) applies are treated in part as sales or exchanges of property between the partnership and the distributee partner, and not as distributions to which sections 731 through 736 apply. A distribution treated as a sale or exchange under section 751(b) is not subject to the provisions of section 707(b). Section 751(b) applies whether or not the distribution is in liquidation of the distributee partner's entire interest in the partnership. However, section 751(b) applies only to the extent that a partner either receives section 751 property in exchange for his relinquishing any part of his interest in other property, or receives other property in exchange for his relinquishing any part of his interest in section 751 property.

(ii) Section 751(b) does not apply to a distribution to a partner which is not in exchange for his interest in other partnership property. Thus, section 751(b) does not apply to the extent that a distribution consists of the distributee partner's share of section 751 property or his share of other property. Similarly, section 751(b) does not apply to current drawings or to advances against the partner's distributive share, or to a distribution which is, in fact, a gift or payment for services or for the use of capital. In determining whether a partner has received only his share of either section 751 property or of other property, his interest in such property remaining in the partnership immediately after a distribution must be taken into account. For example, the section 751 property in partnership ABC has a fair market value of $100,000 in which partner A has an interest of 30 percent, or $30,000. If A receives $20,000 of section 751 property in a distribution, and continues to have a 30-percent interest in the $80,000 of section 751 property remaining in the partnership after the distribution, only $6,000 ($30,000 minus $24,000 (30 percent of $80,000)) of the section 751 property received by him will be considered to be his share of such property. The remaining $14,000 ($20,000 minus $6,000) received is in excess of his share.

(iii) If a distribution is, in part, a distribution of the distributee partner's share of section 751 property, or of other property (including money) and, in part, a distribution in exchange of such properties, the distribution shall be divided for the purpose of applying section 751(b). The rules of section 751(b) shall first apply to the part of the distribution treated as a sale or exchange of such properties, and then the rules of sections 731 through 736 shall apply to the part of the distribution not treated as a sale or exchange. See paragraph (b)(4)(ii) of this section for treatment of payments under section 736(a).

(2) Distribution of section 751 property (unrealized receivables or substantially appreciated inventory items). (i) To the extent that a partner receives section 751 property in a distribution in exchange for any part of his interest in partnership property (including money) other than section 751 property, the transaction shall be treated as a sale or exchange of such properties between the distributee partner and the partnership (as constituted after the distribution).

(ii) At the time of the distribution, the partnership (as constituted after the distribution) realizes ordinary income or loss on the sale or exchange of the section 751 property. The amount of the income or loss to the partnership will be measured by the difference between the adjusted basis to the partnership of the section 751 property considered as sold to or exchanged with the partner, and the fair market value of the distributee partner's interest in other partnership property which he relinquished in the exchange. In computing the partners' distributive shares of such ordinary income or loss, the income or loss shall be allocated only to partners other than the distributee and separately taken into account under section 702(a)(8).

(iii) At the time of the distribution, the distributee partner realizes gain or loss measured by the difference between his adjusted basis for the property relinquished in the exchange (including any special basis adjustment which he may have) and the fair market value of the section 751 property received by him in exchange for his interest in other property which he has relinquished. The distributee's adjusted basis for the property relinquished is the basis such property would have had under section 732 (including subsection (d) thereof) if the distributee partner had received such property in a current distribution immediately before the actual distribution which is treated wholly or partly as a sale or exchange under section 751(b). The character of the gain or loss to the distributee partner shall be determined by the character of the property in which he relinquished his interest.

(3) Distribution of partnership property other than section 751 property. (i) To the extent that a partner receives a distribution of partnership property (including money) other than section 751 property in exchange for any part of his interest in section 751 property of the partnership, the distribution shall be treated as a sale or exchange of such properties between the distributee partner and the partnership (as constituted after the distribution).

(ii) At the time of the distribution, the partnership (as constituted after the distribution) realizes gain or loss on the sale or exchange of the property other than section 751 property. The amount of the gain to the partnership will be measured by the difference between the adjusted basis to the partnership of the distributed property considered as sold to or exchanged with the partner, and the fair market value of the distributee partner's interest in section 751 property which he relinquished in the exchange. The character of the gain or loss to the partnership is determined by the character of the distributed property treated as sold or exchanged by the partnership. In computing the partners' distributive shares of such gain or loss, the gain or loss shall be allocated only to partners other than the distributee and separately taken into account under section 702(a)(8).

(iii) At the time of the distribution, the distributee partner realizes ordinary income or loss on the sale or exchange of the section 751 property. The amount of the distributee partner's income or loss shall be measured by the difference between his adjusted basis for the section 751 property relinquished in the exchange (including any special basis adjustment which he may have), and the fair market value of other property (including money) received by him in exchange for his interest in the section 751 property which he has relinquished. The distributee partner's adjusted basis for the section 751 property relinquished is the basis such property would have had under section 732 (including subsection (d) thereof) if the distributee partner had received such property in a current distribution immediately before the actual distribution which is treated wholly or partly as a sale or exchange under section 751(b).

(4) Exceptions. (i) Section 751(b) does not apply to the distribution to a partner of property which the distributee partner contributed to the partnership. The distribution of such property is governed by the rules set forth in sections 731 through 736, relating to distributions by a partnership.

(ii) Section 751(b) does not apply to payments made to a retiring partner or to a deceased partner's successor in interest to the extent that, under section 736(a), such payments constitute a distributive share of partnership income or guaranteed payments. Payments to a retiring partner or to a deceased partner's successor in interest for his interest in unrealized receivables of the partnership in excess of their partnership basis, including any special basis adjustment for them to which such partner is entitled, constitute payments under section 736(a) and, therefore, are not subject to section 751(b). However, payments under section 736(b) which are considered as made in exchange for an interest in partnership property are subject to section 751(b) to the extent that they involve an exchange of substantially appreciated inventory items for other property. Thus, payments to a retiring partner or to a deceased partner's successor in interest under section 736 must first be divided between payments under section 736(a) and section 736(b). The section 736(b) payments must then be divided, if there is an exchange of substantially appreciated inventory items for other property, between the payments treated as a sale or exchange under section 751(b) and payments treated as a distribution under sections 731 through 736. See subparagraph (1)(iii) of this paragraph, and section 736 and § 1.736-1.

(5) Statement required. A partnership which distributes section 751 property to a partner in exchange for his interest in other partnership property, or which distributes other property in exchange for any part of the partner's interest in section 751 property, shall submit with its return for the year of the distribution a statement showing the computation of any income, gain, or loss to the partnership under the provisions of section 751(b) and this paragraph. The distributee partner shall submit with his return a statement showing the computation of any income, gain, or loss to him. Such statement shall contain information similar to that required under paragraph (a)(3) of this section.

(c) Unrealized receivables. (1) The term "unrealized receivables", as used in subchapter K, chapter 1 of the Code, means any rights (contractual or otherwise) to payment for—

(i) Goods delivered or to be delivered (to the extent that such payment would be treated as received for property other than a capital asset), or

(ii) Services rendered or to be rendered,

to the extent that income arising from such rights to payment was not previously includible in income under the method of accounting employed by the partnership. Such rights must have arisen under contracts or agreements in existence at the time of sale or distribution, although the partnership may not be able to enforce payment until a later time. For example, the term includes trade accounts receivable of a cash method taxpayer, and rights to payment for work or goods begun but incomplete at the time of the sale or distribution.

(2) The basis for such unrealized receivables shall include all costs or expenses attributable thereto paid or accrued but not previously taken into account under the partnership method of accounting.

(3) In determining the amount of the sale price attributable to such unrealized receivables, or their value in a distribution treated as a sale or exchange, any arm's length agreement between the buyer and the seller, or between the partnership and the distributee partner, will generally establish the amount or value. In the absence of such an agreement, full account shall be taken not only of the estimated cost of completing performance of the contract or agreement, but also of the time between the sale or distribution and the time of payment.

(4)(i) With respect to any taxable year of a partnership beginning after December 31, 1962, the term "unrealized receivables," for purposes of this section and sections 731, 736, 741, and 751, also includes "potential section 1245 income." With respect to each item of partnership section 1245 property (as defined in sec. 1245(a)(3)), "potential section 1245 income" is the amount which would be treated as gain to which section 1245(a)(1) would apply if (at the time of the transaction described in section 731, 736, 741, or 751, as the case may be) the item of section 1245 property were sold by the partnership at its fair market value. See paragraph (e)(1) of § 1.1245-1. For example, if a partnership would recognize under section 1245(a)(1) gain of $600 upon a sale of one item of section 1245 property and gain of $300 upon a sale of its only other item of such property, the potential section 1245 income of the partnership would be $900.

(ii) With respect to any taxable year of a partnership ending after December 31, 1963, the term "unrealized receivables," for purposes of this section and sections 731, 736, 741, and 751, also in-

cludes "potential section 1250 income." With respect to each item of partnership section 1250 property (as defined in section 1250(c)), "potential section 1250 income" is the amount which would be treated as gain to which section 1250(a) would apply if (at the time of the transaction described in section 731, 736, 741, or 751, as the case may be) the item of section 1250 property were sold by the partnership at its fair market value. See paragraph (f)(1) of § 1.1250-1.

(iii) For purposes of determining potential section 1245 income or potential section 1250 income, any arm's-length agreement between the buyer and seller, or between the partnership and distributee partner, will generally establish the fair market value of section 1245 property or section 1250 property (as the case may be).

(5) For purposes of subtitle A of the Code, the basis of potential section 1245 income and of potential section 1250 income is zero.

(6)(i) If (at the time of the transaction referred to in subparagraph (4) of this paragraph) a partnership holds section 1245 (or 1250) property and if (a) a partner had a special basis adjustment under section 743(b) in respect of the property, or (b) the basis under section 732 of the property if distributed to the partner would reflect a special basis adjustment under section 732(d), or (c) on the date a partner acquires his partnership interest by way of a sale or exchange (or upon death of another partner) the partnership owned the property and an election under section 754 was in effect with respect to the partnership, then the partner's share of the potential section 1245 (or 1250) income of the partnership in respect of the property shall be determined under subdivision (ii) of this subparagraph.

(ii) The partner's share of the potential section 1245 (or 1250) income of the partnership in respect of the property to which this subdivision applies shall be that amount of gain which the partner would recognize under paragraph (e)(3) of § 1.1245-1 (or paragraph (f) of § 1.1250-1) upon a sale of the property by the partnership, except that, for purposes of this subparagraph (a) the items which are allocated under (or in a manner consistent with the principles provided in) paragraph (e)(3)(ii) of § 1.1245-1 shall be allocated to the partner in the same manner as his share of partnership property is determined, and (b) the amount of a special basis adjustment under section

732(d) shall be treated as if it were the amount of a special basis adjustment under section 743(b).

(d) Inventory items which have substantially appreciated in value—(1) Substantial appreciation. Partnership inventory items shall be considered to have appreciated substantially in value if, at the time of the sale or distribution, the total fair market value of all the inventory items of the partnership exceeds 120 percent of the aggregate adjusted basis for such property in the hands of the partnership (without regard to any special basis adjustment of any partner) and, in addition, exceeds 10 percent of the fair market value of all partnership property other than money. The terms "inventory items which have appreciated substantially in value" or "substantially appreciated inventory items" refer to the aggregate of all partnership inventory items. These terms do not refer to specific partnership inventory items or to specific groups of such items. For example, any distribution of inventory items by a partnership the inventory items of which as a whole are substantially appreciated in value shall be a distribution of substantially appreciated inventory items for the purposes of section 751(b), even though the specific inventory items distributed may not be appreciated in value. Similarly, if the aggregate of partnership inventory items are not substantially appreciated in value, a distribution of specific inventory items, the value of which is more than 120 percent of their adjusted basis, will not constitute a distribution of substantially appreciated inventory items. For the purpose of this paragraph, the "fair market value" of inventory items has the same meaning as "market" value in the regulations under section 471, relating to general rule for inventories.

(2) Inventory items. The term "inventory items" as used in subchapter K, chapter 1 of the Code, includes the following types of property:

(i) Stock in trade of the partnership, or other property of a kind which would properly be included in the inventory of the partnership if on hand at the close of the taxable year, or property held by the partnership primarily for sale to customers in the ordinary course of its trade or business. See section 1221(1).

(ii) Any other property of the partnership which, on sale or exchange by the partnership, would be considered property other than a capital asset and other than property described in section 1231. Thus, accounts receivable acquired in the ordinary course of business for services or from the sale of

stock in trade constitute inventory items (see section 1221(4)), as do any unrealized receivables.

(iii) Any other property retained by the partnership which, if held by the partner selling his partnership interest or receiving a distribution described in section 751(b), would be considered property described in subdivision (i) or (ii) of this subparagraph. Property actually distributed to the partner does not come within the provisions of section 751(d)(2)(C) and this subdivision.

(e) Section 751 property and other property. For the purposes of this section, "section 751 property" means unrealized receivables or substantially appreciated inventory items, and "other property" means all property (including money) except section 751 property.

* * *

(g) Examples. Application of the provisions of section 751 may be illustrated by the following examples:

Example (1). C buys B's interest in personal service partnership AB for $15,000, when the balance sheet of the firm (reflecting a cash receipts and disbursements method of accounting) is as follows:

Assets

	Adjusted basis per books	Market value
Cash	$3,000	$3,000
Loans receivable	10,000	10,000
Other assets	7,000	7,000
Unrealized receivables	0	12,000
Total	20,000	32,000

Liabilities and Capital

	Per books	Value
Liabilities	$2,000	$2,000
Capital:		
A	9,000	15,000
B	9,000	15,000
Total	20,000	32,000

Section 751(a) applies to the sale. The total amount realized by B is $16,000, consisting of the cash received, $15,000, plus $1,000, B's share of the partnership liabilities assumed by C. See section 752. B's undivided half interest in the partnership property includes a half-interest in the partnership's unrealized receivables which are worth $12,000. Consequently, $6,000 of the $16,000 realized by B shall be considered received in exchange for B's interest in the partnership attributable to its unrealized receivables. The remaining $10,000 realized by B is in exchange for a capital asset. B's basis for his partnership interest is $10,000 ($9,000, plus $1,000, B's share of partnership liabilities). No portion of this basis is attributable to B's share of the unrealized receivables of the partnership since such property has a zero basis in the hands of the partnership; therefore, B has a basis of zero for the unrealized receivables because the partnership basis for such receivables would have carried over to him under section 732 had they been distributed to him. The difference between the zero basis and the $6,000 B realized for the unrealized receivables is ordinary income to him. The entire $10,000 of B's basis is the basis for his interest in partnership property other than unrealized receivables and is applied against the remaining $10,000 ($16,000 minus $6,000) received from the sale of his interest. Therefore, B has no capital gain or loss. (If B's basis for his interest in partnership property, other than unrealized receivables, were $9,000, he would realize capital gain of $1,000. If his basis were $11,000, he would sustain a capital loss of $1,000).

Example (2). **(a) Facts.** Partnership ABC makes a distribution to partner C in liquidation of his entire one-third interest in the partnership. At the time of the distribution, the balance sheet of the partnership, which uses the accrual method of accounting, is as follows:

Assets

	Adjusted basis per books	Market value
Cash	$15,000	$15,000
Accounts receivable	9,000	9,000
Inventory	21,000	30,000
Depreciable property	42,000	48,000
Land	9,000	9,000
Total	96,000	111,000

Liabilities and Capital

	Per books	Value
Current liabilities	$15,000	$15,000
Mortgage payable	21,000	21,000
Capital:		
A	20,000	25,000
B	20,000	25,000
C	20,000	25,000
Total	96,000	111,000

The distribution received by C consists of $10,000 cash and depreciable property with a fair market value of $15,000 and an adjusted basis to the partnership of $15,000.

(b) Presence of section 751 property. The partnership has no unrealized receivables, but the dual test provided in section 751(d)(1) must be applied to determine whether the inventory items of the partnership, in the aggregate, have appreciated substantially in value. The fair market value of all partnership inventory items, $39,000 (inventory $30,000, and accounts receivable $9,000), exceeds 120 percent of the $30,000 adjusted basis of such items to the partnership. The fair market value of the inventory items, $39,000, also exceeds 10 percent of the fair market value of all partnership property other than money (10 percent of $96,000 or $9,600). Therefore, the partnership inventory items have substantially appreciated in value.

(c) The properties exchanged. Since C's entire partnership interest is to be liquidated, the provisions of section 736 are applicable. No part of the payment, however, is considered as a distributive share or as a guaranteed payment under section 736(a) because the entire payment is made for C's interest in partnership property. Therefore, the entire payment is for an interest in partnership property under section 736(b), and, to the extent applicable, subject to the rules of section 751. In the distribution, C received his share of cash ($5,000) and $15,000 in depreciable property ($1,000 less than his $16,000 share). In addition, he received other partnership property ($5,000 cash and $12,000 liabilities assumed, treated as money distributed under section 752(b)) in exchange for his interest in accounts receivable ($3,000), inventory ($10,000), land ($3,000), and the balance of his interest in depreciable property ($1,000). Section 751(b) applies only to the extent of the exchange of other property for section 751 property (i.e., inventory items, which include trade accounts receivable). The section 751 property exchanged has a fair market value of $13,000 ($3,000 in accounts receivable and $10,000 in inventory). Thus, $13,000 of the total amount C received is considered as received for the sale of section 751 property.

(d) Distributee partner's tax consequences. C's tax consequences on the distribution are as follows:

(1) The section 751(b) sale or exchange. C's share of the inventory items is treated as if he received them in a current distribution, and his basis for such items is $10,000 ($7,000 for inventory and $3,000 for accounts receivable) as determined under paragraph (b)(3)(iii) of this section. Then C is considered as having sold his share of inventory items to the partnership for $13,000. Thus, on the sale of his share of inventory items, C realizes $3,000 of ordinary income.

(2) The part of the distribution not under section 751(b). Section 751(b) does not apply to the balance of the distribution. Before the distribution, C's basis for his partnership interest was $32,000 ($20,000 plus $12,000, his share of partnership liabilities). See section 752(a). This basis is reduced by $10,000, the basis attributed to the section 751 property treated as distributed to C and sold by him to the partnership. Thus, C has a basis of $22,000 for the remainder of his partnership interest. The total distribution to C was $37,000 ($22,000 in cash and liabilities assumed, and $15,000 in depreciable property). Since C received no more than his share of the depreciable property, none of the depreciable property constitutes proceeds of the sale under section 751(b). C did receive more than his share of money. Therefore, the sale proceeds, treated separately in subparagraph (1) of this paragraph of this example, must consist of money and therefore must be deducted from the money distribution. Consequently, in liquidation of the balance of C's interest, he receives depreciable property and $9,000 in money ($22,000 less $13,000). Therefore, no gain or loss is recognized to C on the distribution. Under section 732(b), C's basis for the depreciable property is $13,000 (the remaining basis of his partnership interest, $22,000, reduced by $9,000, the money received in the distribution).

(e) Partnership's tax consequences. The tax consequences to the partnership on the distribution are as follows:

(1) The section 751(b) sale or exchange. The partnership consisting of the remaining members has no ordinary income on the distribution since it did not give up any section 751 property in the exchange. Of the $22,000 money distributed (in cash and the assumption of C's share of liabilities), $13,000 was paid to acquire C's interest in inventory ($10,000 fair market value) and in accounts receivable ($3,000). Since under section 751(b) the partnership is treated as buying these properties, it has a new cost basis for the inventory and accounts receivable acquired from C. Its basis for C's share of inventory and accounts receivable is $13,000, the amount which the partnership is considered as having paid C in the exchange. Since the partnership is treated as having distributed C's share of inventory and accounts receivable to him, the partnership must decrease its basis for inventory and accounts receivable ($30,000) by $10,000, the basis of C's share treated as distributed to him, and then increase the basis for inventory and accounts receivable by $13,000 to reflect the purchase prices of the items acquired. Thus, the basis of the partnership inventory is increased from $21,000 to $24,000 in the transaction. (Note that the basis of property acquired in a section 751(b) exchange is determined under section 1012 without regard to any elections of the partnership. See paragraph (e) of § 1.732–1.) Further, the partnership realizes no capital gain or loss on the portion of the distribution treated as a sale under section 751(b) since, to acquire C's interest in the inventory and accounts receivable, it gave up money and assumed C's share of liabilities.

(2) The part of the distribution not under section 751(b). In the remainder of the distribution to C which was not in exchange for C's interest in section 751 property, C received only other property as follows: $15,000 in depreciable property (with a basis to the partnership of $15,000) and $9,000 in money ($22,000 less $13,000 treated under subparagraph (1) of this paragraph of this example). Since this part of the distribution is not an exchange of section 751 property for other property, section 751(b) does not apply. Instead, the provisions which apply are sections 731 through 736, relating to distributions by a partnership. No gain or loss is recognized to the partnership on the distribution. (See section 731(b).) Further, the partnership makes no adjustment to the basis of remaining depreciable property unless an election under section 754 is in effect. (See section 734(a).) Thus, the basis of the depreciable property before the distribution, $42,000, is reduced by the basis of the depreciable property distributed, $15,000, leaving a basis for the depreciable property in the partnership of $27,000. However, if an election under section 754 is in effect, the partnership must make the adjustment required under section 734(b) as follows: Since the adjusted basis of the distributed property to the partnership had been $15,000, and is only $13,000 in C's hands (see paragraph (d)(2) of this example), the partnership will increase the basis of the depreciable property remaining in the partnership by $2,000 (the excess of the adjusted basis to the partnership of the distributed depreciable property immediately before the distribution over its basis to the distributee). Whether or not an election under section 754 is in effect, the basis for each of the

remaining partner's partnership interests will be $38,000 ($20,000 original contribution, plus $12,000, each partner's original share of the liabilities, plus $6,000, the share of C's liabilities each assumed).

(f) Partnership trial balance. A trial balance of the AB partnership after the distribution in liquidation of C's entire interest would reflect the results set forth in the schedule below. Column I shows the amounts to be reflected in the records if an election is in effect under section 754 with respect to an optional adjustment under section 734(b) to the basis of undistributed partnership property. Column II shows the amounts to be reflected in the records where an election under section 754 is not in effect. Note that in column II, the total bases for the partnership assets do not equal the total of the bases for the partnership interests.

Example (3). **(a) Facts.** Assume that the distribution to partner C in example (2) of this paragraph in liquidation of his entire interest in partnership ABC consists of $5,000 in cash and $20,000 worth of partnership inventory with a basis of $14,000.

	I		II	
	Sec. 754, Election in effect		Sec. 754, Election not in effect	
	Basis	Fair market value	Basis	Fair market value
Cash	$5,000	$5,000	$5,000	$5,000
Accounts receivable ..	9,000	9,000	9,000	9,000
Inventory	24,000	30,000	24,000	30,000
Depreciable property ...	29,000	33,000	27,000	33,000
Land	9,000	9,000	9,000	9,000
	76,000	86,000	74,000	86,000
Current liabilities........	15,000	15,000	15,000	15,000
Mortgage.....	21,000	21,000	21,000	21,000
Capital:				
....	20,000	25,000	20,000	25,000
....	20,000	25,000	20,000	25,000
	76,000	86,000	76,000	86,000

(b) Presence of section 751 property. For the same reason as stated in paragraph (b) of example (2), the partnership inventory items have substantially appreciated in value.

(c) The properties exchanged. In the distribution, C received his share of cash ($5,000) and his share of appreciated inventory items ($13,000). In addition, he received appreciated inventory with a fair market value of $7,000 (and with an adjusted basis to the partnership of $4,900) and $12,000 in money (liabilities assumed). C has relinquished his interest in $16,000 of depreciable property and $3,000 of land. Although C relinquished his interest in $3,000 of accounts receivable, such accounts receivable are inventory items and, therefore, that exchange was not an exchange of section 751 property for other property. Section 751(b) applies only to the extent of the exchange of other property for section 751 property (i.e., depreciable property or land for inventory items). Assume that the partners agree that the $7,000 of inventory in excess of C's share was received by him in exchange for $7,000 of depreciable property.

(d) Distributee partner's tax consequences. C's tax consequence on the distributions are as follows:

(1) The section 751(b) sale or exchange. C is treated as if he had received his ⁷/₁₆ths share of the depreciable property in a current distribution. His basis for that share is $6,125 (42,000/48,000 of $7,000), as determined under paragraph (b)(2)(iii) of this section. Then C is considered as having sold his ⁷/₁₆ths share of depreciable property to the partnership for $7,000, realizing a gain of $875.

(2) The part of the distribution not under section 751(b). Section 751(b) does not apply to the balance of the distribution. Before the distribution, C's basis for his partnership interest was $32,000 ($20,000, plus $12,000, his share of partnership liabilities). See section 752(a). This basis is reduced by $6,125, the basis of property treated as distributed to C and sold by him to the partnership. Thus, C will have a basis of $25,875 for the remainder of his partnership interest. Of the $37,000 total distribution to C, $30,000 ($17,000 in money, including liabilities assumed, and $13,000 in inventory) is not within section 751(b). Under section 732(b), C's basis for the inventory with a fair market value of $13,000 (which had an adjusted basis to the partnership of $9,100) is limited to $8,875, the amount of the remaining basis for his partnership interest, $25,875, reduced by $17,000, the money received. Thus, C's total aggregate basis for the inventory received is $15,875 ($7,000 plus $8,875), and not its $14,000 basis in the hands of the partnership.

(e) Partnership's tax consequences. The tax consequences to the partnership on the distribution are as follows:

(1) The section 751(b) sale or exchange. The partnership consisting of the remaining members has $2,100 of ordinary income on the sale of the $7,000 of inventory which had a basis to the partnership of $4,900 (21,000/30,000 of $7,000). This $7,000 of inventory was paid to acquire ⁷/₁₆ths of C's interest in the depreciable property. Since, under section 751(b), the partnership is treated as buying this property from C, it has a new cost basis for such property. Its basis for the depreciable property is $42,875 ($42,000 less $6,125, the basis of the ⁷/₁₆ths share considered as distributed to C, plus $7,000, the partnership purchase price for this share).

(2) The part of the distribution not under section 751(b). In the remainder of the distribution to C which was not a sale or exchange of section 751 property for other property, the partnership realizes no gain or loss. See section 731(b). Further, under section 734(a), the partnership makes no adjustment to the basis of the accounts receivable or the ⁹/₁₆ths interest in depreciable property which C relinquished. However, if an election under section 754 is in effect, the partnership must make the adjustment required under section 734(b) since the adjusted basis to the partnership of the inventory distributed had been $9,100, and C's basis for such inventory after distribution is only $8,875. The basis of the inventory remaining in the partnership must be increased by $225. Whether or not an election under section 754 is in effect, the basis for each of the remaining partnership interests will be $39,050 ($20,000 original contribution,

plus $12,000, each partner's original share of the liabilities, plus $6,000, the share of C's liabilities now assumed, plus $1,050, each partner's share of ordinary income realized by the partnership upon that part of the distribution treated as a sale or exchange).

Example (4). (a) Facts. Assume the same facts as in example (3) of this paragraph, except that the partners did not identify the property which C relinquished in exchange for the $7,000 of inventory which he received in excess of his share.

(b) Presence of section 751 property. For the same reasons stated in paragraph (b) of example (2) of this paragraph, the partnership inventory items have substantially appreciated in value.

(c) The properties exchanged. The analysis stated in paragraph (c) of example (3) of this paragraph is the same in this example, except that, in the absence of a specific agreement among the partners as to the properties exchanged, C will be presumed to have sold to the partnership a proportionate amount of each property in which he relinquished an interest. Thus, in the absence of an agreement, C has received $7,000 of inventory in exchange for his release of ⁷/₁₉ths of the depreciable property and ⁷/₁₉ths of the land. ($7,000, fair market value of property released, over $19,000, the sum of the fair market values of C's interest in the land and C's interest in the depreciable property.)

(d) Distributee partner's tax consequences. C's tax consequences on the distribution are as follows:

(1) The section 751(b) sale or exchange. C is treated as if he had received his ⁷/₁₉ths shares of the depreciable property and land in a current distribution. His basis for those shares is $6,263 (51,000/57,000 of $7,000, their fair market value), as determined under paragraph (b)(2)(iii) of this section. Then C is considered as having sold his ⁷/₁₉ths shares of depreciable property and land to the partnership for $7,000, realizing a gain of $737.

(2) The part of the distribution not under section 751(b). Section 751(b) does not apply to the balance of the distribution. Before the distribution C's basis for his partnership interest was $32,000 ($20,000 plus $12,000, his share of partnership liabilities). See section 752(a). This basis is reduced by $6,263, the bases of C's shares of depreciable property and land treated as distributed to him and sold by him to the partnership. Thus, C will have a basis of $25,737 for the remainder of his partnership interest. Of the total $37,000 distributed to C, $30,000 ($17,000 in money, including liabilities assumed, and $13,000 in inventory) is not within section 751(b). Under section 732(b), C's basis for the inventory (with a fair market value of $13,000 and an adjusted basis to the partnership of $9,100) is limited to $8,737, the amount of the remaining basis for his partnership interest ($25,737 less $17,000), money received. Thus, C's total aggregate basis for the inventory he received is $15,737 ($7,000 plus $8,737), and not the $14,000 basis it had in the hands of the partnership.

(e) Partnership's tax consequences. The tax consequences to the partnership on the distribution are as follows:

(1) The section 751(b) sale or exchange. The partnership consisting of the remaining members has $2,100 of ordinary income on the sale of $7,000 of inventory which had a basis to the partnership of $4,900 (21,000/30,000 of $7,000). This $7,000 of inventory was paid to acquire $7/19$ths of C's interest in the depreciable property and land. Since, under section 751(b), the partnership is treated as buying this property from C, it has a new cost basis for such property. The bases of the depreciable property and land would be $42,737 and $9,000, respectively. The basis for the depreciable property is computed as follows: The common partnership basis of $42,000 is reduced by the $5,158 basis (42,000/48,000 of $5,895) for C's $7/19$ths interest constructively distributed and increased by $5,895 (16,000/19,000 of $7,000), the part of the purchase price allocated to the depreciable property. The basis of the land would be computed in the same way. The $9,000 original partnership basis is reduced by $1,105 basis (9,000/9,000 of $1,105) of land constructively distributed to C, and increased by $1,105 (3,000/19,000 of $7,000), the portion of the purchase price allocated to the land.

(2) **The part of the distribution not under section 751(b).** In the remainder of the distribution to C which was not a sale or exchange of section 751 property for other property, the partnership realizes no gain or loss. See section 731(b). Further, under section 734(a), the partnership makes no adjustment to the basis of the accounts receivable or the $12/19$ths interests in depreciable property and land which C relinquished. However, if an election under section 754 is in effect, the partnership must make the adjustment required under section 734(b) since the adjusted basis to the partnership of the inventory distributed had been $9,100 and C's basis for such inventory after the distribution is only $8,737. The basis of the inventory remaining in the partnership must be increased by the difference of $363. Whether or not an election under section 754 is in effect, the basis for each of the remaining partnership interests will be $39,050 ($20,000 original contribution plus $12,000, each partner's original share of the liabilities, plus $6,000, the share of C's liabilities assumed, plus $1,050, each partner's share of ordinary income realized by the partnership upon the part of the distribution treated as a sale or exchange).

Example (5). (a) **Facts.** Assume that partner C in example (2) of this paragraph agrees to reduce his interest in capital and profits from one-third to one-fifth for a current distribution consisting of $5,000 in cash, and $7,500 of accounts receivable with a basis to the partnership of $7,500. At the same time, the total liabilities of the partnership are not reduced. Therefore, after the distribution, C's share of the partnership liabilities has been reduced by $4,800 from $12,000 ($1/3$ of $36,000) to $7,200 ($1/5$ of $36,000).

(b) **Presence of section 751 property.** For the same reasons as stated in paragraph (b) of example (2) of this paragraph, the partnership inventory items have substantially appreciated in value.

(c) **The properties exchanged.** C's interest in the fair market value of the partnership properties before and after the distribution can be illustrated by the following table:

Item	C's interest Fair Market Value		C received		C relinquished
	One-third before	One-fifth after	Distribution of share	In excess of share	
Cash	$5,000	$2,000	$3,000	$2,000	....
Liabilities assumed	(12,000)	(7,200)	....	4,800	....
Inventory items:					
Accounts receivable	3,000	300	2,700	4,800	....
Inventory	10,000	6,000	....	....	$4,000
Depreciable property	16,000	9,600	....	....	6,400
Land	3,000	1,800	....	....	1,200
Total	25,000	12,500	5,700	11,600	11,600

Although C relinquished his interest in $4,000 of inventory and received $4,800 of accounts receivable, both items constitute section 751 property and C has received only $800 of accounts receivable for $800 worth of depreciable property or for an $800 undivided interest in land. In the absence of an agreement identifying the properties exchanged, it is presumed C received $800 for proportionate shares of his interests in both depreciable property and land. To the extent that inventory was exchanged for accounts receivable, or to the extent cash was distributed for the release of C's interest in the balance of the depreciable property and land, the transaction does not fall within section 751(b) and is a current distribution under section 732(a). Thus, the remaining $6,700 of accounts receivable are received in a current distribution.

(d) **Distributee partner's tax consequences.** C's tax consequences on the distribution are as follows:

(1) **The section 751(b) sale or exchange.** Assuming that the partners paid $800 worth of accounts receivable for $800 worth of depreciable property, C is treated as if he received the depreciable property in a current distribution, and his basis for the $800 worth of depreciable property is $700 (42,000/48,000 of $800, its fair market value), as determined under paragraph (b)(2)(iii) of this section. Then C is considered as having sold his $800 share of depreciable property to the partnership for $800. On the sale of the depreciable property, C realizes a gain of $100. If, on the other hand, the partners had agreed that C exchanged an $800 interest in the land for $800 worth of accounts receivable, C would realize no gain or loss, because under paragraph (b)(2)(iii) of this section his basis for the land sold would be $800. In the absence of an agreement, the basis for the depreciable property and land (which C is considered as having received in a current distribution and then sold back to the partnership) would be $716 (51,000/57,000 of $800). In that case,

on the sale of the balance of the $800 share of depreciable property and land, C would realize $84 of gain ($800 less $716).

(2) The part of the distribution not under section 751(b). Section 751(b) does not apply to the balance of the distribution. Under section 731, C does not realize either gain or loss on the balance of the distribution. The adjustments to the basis of C's interest are illustrated in the following table:

	If accounts receivable received for depreciable property	If accounts receivable received for land	If there is no agreement
Original basis for C's interest	$32,000	$32,000	$32,000
Less basis of property distributed prior to sec. 751(b) sale or exchange	–700	–800	–716
	31,300	31,200	31,284
Less money received in distribution	–9,800	–9,800	–9,800
	21,500	21,400	21,484
Less basis of property received in a current distribution under sec. 732	–6,700	–6,700	–6,700
Resulting basis for C's interest	14,800	14,700	14,784

C's basis for the $1,500 worth of accounts receivable which he received in the distribution will be $7,500, composed of $800 for the portion purchased in the section 751(b) exchange, plus $6,700, the basis carried over under section 732(a) for the portion received in the current distribution.

(e) Partnership's tax consequences. The tax consequences to the partnership on the distribution are as follows:

(1) The section 751(b) sale or exchange. The partnership realizes no gain or loss in the section 751 sale or exchange because it had a basis of $800 for the accounts receivable for which it received $800 worth of other property. If the partnership agreed to purchase $800 worth of depreciable property, the partnership basis of depreciable property becomes $42,100 ($42,000 less $700 basis of property constructively distributed to C, plus $800, price of property purchased). If the partnership purchased land with the accounts receivable, there would be no change in the basis of the land to the partnership because the basis of land distributed was equal to its purchase price. If there were no agreement, the basis of the depreciable property and land would be $51,084 (depreciable property, $42,084 and land $9,000). The basis for the depreciable property is computed as follows: The common partnership basis of $42,000 is reduced by the $590 basis (42,000/48,000 of $674) for C's $674 interest constructively distributed, and increased by $674 (6,400/7,600 of $800), the part of the purchase price allocated to the depreciable property. The basis of the land would be computed in the same way. The $9,000 original partnership basis is reduced by $126 basis (9,000/9,000 of $126) of the land constructively distributed to C, and increased by $126 (1,200/7,600 of $800), the portion of the purchase price allocated to the land.

(2) The part of the distribution not under section 751(b). The partnership will realize no gain or loss in the balance of the distribution under section 731. Since the property in C's hands after the distribution will have the same basis it had in the partnership, the basis of partnership property remaining in the partnership after the distribution will not be adjusted (whether or not an election under 754 is in effect).

Example (6). (a) Facts. Partnership ABC distributes to partner C, in liquidation of his entire one-third interest in the partnership, a machine which is section 1245 property with a recomputed basis (as defined in section 1245(a)(2)) of $18,000. At the time of the distribution, the balance sheet of the partnership is as follows:

Assets

	Adjusted basis per books	Market value
Cash	$3,000	$3,000
Machine (section 1245 property)	9,000	15,000
Land	18,000	27,000
Total	30,000	45,000

Liabilities and Capital

	Per books	Value
Liabilities	$0	$0
Capital:		
A	10,000	15,000
B	10,000	15,000
C	10,000	15,000
Total	30,000	45,000

(b) Presence of section 751 property. The section 1245 property is an unrealized receivable of the partnership to the extent of the potential section 1245 income in respect of the property. Since the fair market value of the property ($15,000) is lower than its recomputed basis ($18,000), the excess of the fair market value over its adjusted basis ($9,000), or $6,000, is the potential section 1245 income of the partnership in respect of the property. The partnership has no other section 751 property.

(c) The properties exchanged. In the distribution C received his share of section 751 property (potential section 1245 income of $2,000, *i.e.*, 1/3 of $6,000) and his share of section 1245 property (other than potential section 1245 income) with a fair market value of $3,000, *i.e.*, 1/3 of ($15,000 minus $6,000), and an adjusted basis of $3,000, *i.e.*, 1/3 of $9,000. In addition he received $4,000 of section

751 property (consisting of $4,000 ($6,000 minus $2,000) of potential section 1245 income) and section 1245 property (other than potential section 1245 income) with a fair market value of $6,000 ($9,000 minus $3,000) and an adjusted basis of $6,000 ($9,000 minus $3,000). C relinquished his interest in $1,000 of cash and $9,000 of land. Assume that the partners agree that the $4,000 of section 751 property in excess of C's share was received by him in exchange for $4,000 of land.

(d) Distributee partner's tax consequences. C's tax consequences on the distributions are as follows:

(1) The section 751(b) sale or exchange. C is treated as if he received in a current distribution ⁴⁄₉ths of his share of the land with a basis of $2,667 (18,000/27,000 × $4,000). Then C is considered as having sold his ⁴⁄₉ths share of the land to the partnership for $4,000, realizing a gain of $1,333. C's basis for the remainder of his partnership interest after the current distribution is $7,333, *i.e.*, the basis of his partnership interest before the current distribution ($10,000) minus the basis of the land treated as distributed to him ($2,667).

(2) The part of the distribution not under section 751(b). Of the $15,000 total distribution to C, $11,000 ($2,000 of potential section 1245 income and $9,000 section 1245 property other than potential section 1245 income) is not within section 751(b). Under section 732(b) and (c), C's basis for his share of potential section 1245 income is zero (see paragraph (c)(5) of this section) and his basis for $9,000 of section 1245 property (other than potential section 1245 income) is $7,333, *i.e.*, the amount of the remaining basis for his partnership interest ($7,333) reduced by the basis for his share of potential section 1245 income (zero). Thus C's total aggregate basis for the section 1245 property (fair market value of $15,000) distributed to him is $11,333 ($4,000 plus $7,333). For an illustration of the computation of his recomputed basis for the section 1245 property immediately after the distribution, see example (2) of paragraph (f)(3) of § 1.1245-4.

(e) Partnership's tax consequences. The tax consequences to the partnership on the distribution are as follows:

(1) The section 751(b) sale or exchange. Upon the sale of $4,000 potential section 1245 income, with a basis of zero, for ⁴⁄₉ths of C's interest in the land, the partnership consisting of the remaining members has $4,000 ordinary income under sections 751(b) and 1245(a)(1). See section 1245(b)(3) and (6)(A). The partnership's new basis for the land is $19,333, *i.e.*, $18,000, less the basis of the ⁴⁄₉ths share considered as distributed to C ($2,667), plus the partnership purchase price for this share ($4,000).

(2) The part of the distribution not under section 751(b). The analysis under this subparagraph should be made in accordance with the principles illustrated in paragraph (e)(2) of examples (3), (4), and (5) of this paragraph.

[T.D. 6500, 25 FR 11814, Nov. 26, 1960, as amended by T.D. 6832, 30 FR 8575, July 7, 1965; T.D. 7084, 36 FR 268, Jan. 8, 1971]

§ 1.752-1 Treatment of certain liabilities.

(a) Increase in partner's liabilities. (1) Where the liabilities of a partnership are increased, and each partner's share of such liabilities is thereby increased, the amount of each partner's increase shall be treated as a contribution of money by that partner to the partnership. For example, partnership AB borrows $1,000. If A and B are equal partners, the basis of the partnership interest of each is increased by $500 since each is considered under section 752(a) to have contributed that amount of money to the partnership.

(2) Any increase in a partner's individual liabilities because of the assumption by him of partnership liabilities shall also be considered as a contribution of money by him to the partnership. For example, equal partnership AB owns real property with an adjusted basis to the partnership of $1,000, a fair market value of $800, and which is subject to a mortgage of $400 which the partnership has not assumed. The mortgage is considered as a liability of the partnership under section 752(c). Since A and B each share one-half thereof, under section 752(a) the liability of each has been increased $200. Under section 722 such $200 increase is reflected in the basis of each partner for his interest. The real property is distributed by the partnership to A. Under the provisions of section 733(2), there is a net decrease of $800 in A's basis for his partnership interest. This amount is computed as follows: The basis of A's partnership interest is decreased in the distribution by $1,000 (the partnership basis for the distributed property) and further decreased under section 752(b) by $200 (the decrease in A's share of partnership liabilities) and increased under section 752(a) by $400 (the increase in A's individual liability by reason of section 752(c)). Conversely, the basis of B's partnership interest is decreased by $200 since the distribution of the real property to A resulted in a decrease in B's share of the partnership liability under section 752(b).

(b) Decrease in partner's liabilities. (1) Where the liabilities of a partnership are decreased, and each partner's share of such liabilities is thereby decreased, the amount of the decrease shall be treated as a distribution of money to the partner by the partnership. For example, partnership AB, in which A and B are equal partners, repays an obligation of $10,000. The repayment reduces each partner's share of partnership liabilities by $5,000 and is considered a distribution of money which reduces the basis of each partner's interest in the partnership by that amount. For the effect of a discharge of indebtedness on the basis of partnership property, see sections 108 and 1017.

(2) Where a partnership assumes the separate liabilities of a partner or a liability to which property owned by such partner is subject (see paragraph (c) of this section), the amount of the decrease in such partner's liabilities is treated as a distribution of money by the partnership to such partner. For example, partner A contributes property with a basis of $1,000 to partnership ABC in exchange for a one-third interest in the partnership. The property is subject to a mortgage of $150. (It is immaterial whether the mortgage is assumed by the partnership. See section 752(c).) The basis of A's partnership interest is $900, computed as follows: $1,000, A's basis for the contributed property, reduced by $100, two-thirds of A's original liability of $150 now attributable to partners B and C and reflected in their bases under the provisions of paragraph (a) of this section.

(c) **Liability to which property is subject.** Where property subject to a liability is contributed by a partner to a partnership, or distributed by a partnership to a partner, the amount of the liability, to an extent not exceeding the fair market value of the property at the time of the contribution or distribution, shall be considered as a liability assumed by the transferee. For example, A contributes property with a basis to him of $1,000 to equal partnership AB. The property is subject to a mortgage of $2,500 and its value exceeds $2,500. Under paragraph (b) of this section, A will be treated as receiving a distribution in money of $1,250, one-half of the liability of $2,500 assumed by the partnership. Since the basis of A's partnership interest is $1,000 (the basis of the property contributed by him), the distribution to him of $1,250 results in his realizing a capital gain of $250 under section 731(a). A's basis for his partnership interest is zero. Although as a partner A has a $1,250 share of the $2,500 partnership liability, this $1,250 is not added to the basis of A's partnership interest since it does not represent an increase in liabilities as to him.

(d) **Sale or exchange of a partnership interest.** Where there is a sale or exchange of an interest in a partnership, liabilities shall be treated in the same manner as liabilities in connection with the sale or exchange of property not associated with partnerships. For example, if a partner sells his interest in a partnership for $750 cash and at the same time transfers to the purchaser his share of partnership liabilities amounting to $250, the amount realized by the seller on the transaction is $1,000.

(e) **Partner's share of partnership liabilities.** A partner's share of partnership liabilities shall be determined in accordance with his ratio for sharing losses under the partnership agreement. In the case of a limited partnership, a limited partner's share of partnership liabilities shall not exceed the difference between his actual contribution credited to him by the partnership and the total contribution which he is obligated to make under the limited partnership agreement. However, where none of the partners have any personal liability with respect to a partnership liability (as in the case of a mortgage on real estate acquired by the partnership without the assumption by the partnership or any of the partners of any liability on the mortgage), then all partners, including limited partners, shall be considered as sharing such liability under section 752(c) in the same proportion as they share the profits. The provisions of this paragraph may be illustrated by the following example:

Example. G is a general partner and L is a limited partner in partnership GL. Each makes equal contributions of $20,000 cash to the partnership upon its formation. Under the terms of the partnership agreement, they are to share profits equally but L's liabilities are limited to the extent of his contribution. Subsequently, the partnership pays $10,000 for real property which is subject to a mortgage of $5,000. Neither the partnership nor any of the partners assume any liability on the mortgage. The basis of such property to the partnership is $15,000. The basis of G and L for their partnership interests is increased by $2,500 each, since each partner's share of the partnership liability (the $5,000 mortgage) has increased by that amount. However, if the partnership had assumed the mortgage so that G had become personally liable thereunder, G's basis for his interest would have been increased by $5,000 and L's basis would remain unchanged.

(f) **Limitation.** In determining the amount of liabilities for the purposes of section 752 and this section, the amount of an indebtedness is to be taken into account only once, even though a partner (in addition to his liability for such indebtedness as a partner) may be separately liable therefor in a capacity other than as a partner.

[T.D. 6500, 25 FR 11814, Nov. 26, 1960]

§ 1.753–1 **Partner receiving income in respect of decedent.**

(a) **Income in respect of a decedent under section 736(a).** All payments coming within the provisions of section 736(a) made by a partnership to the estate or other successor in interest of a deceased partner are considered income in respect of the decedent under section 691. The estate or other successor in interest of a deceased partner shall be considered to have received income in respect of a decedent to the extent that amounts are paid by a third person in exchange for rights to future payments from the partnership under section 736(a). When a partner who is receiving payments under section 736(a) dies, section 753 applies to any remaining payments under section 736(a) made to his estate or other successor in interest.

(b) Other income in respect of a decedent. When a partner dies, the entire portion of the distributive share which is attributable to the period ending with the date of his death and which is taxable to his estate or other successor constitutes income in respect of a decedent under section 691. This rule applies even though that part of the distributive share for the period before death which the decedent withdrew is not included in the value of the decedent's partnership interest for estate tax purposes. See paragraph (c)(3) of § 1.706–1.

* * *

[T.D. 6500, 25 FR 11814, Nov. 26, 1960]

§ 1.754–1 Time and manner of making election to adjust basis of partnership property.

(a) In general. A partnership may adjust the basis of partnership property under sections 734(b) and 743(b) if it files an election in accordance with the rules set forth in paragraph (b) of this section. An election may not be filed to make the adjustments provided in either section 734(b) or section 743(b) alone, but such an election must apply to both sections. An election made under the provisions of this section shall apply to all property distributions and transfers of partnership interests taking place in the partnership taxable year for which the election is made and in all subsequent partnership taxable years unless the election is revoked pursuant to paragraph (c) of this section.

(b) Time and method of making election. (1) An election under section 754 and this section to adjust the basis of partnership property under sections 734(b) and 743(b), with respect to a distribution of property to a partner or a transfer of an interest in a partnership, shall be made in a writ-

ten statement filed with the partnership return for the taxable year during which the distribution or transfer occurs. For the election to be valid, the return must be filed not later than the time prescribed by paragraph (e) of § 1.6031–1 (including extensions thereof) for filing the return for such taxable year (or before August 23, 1956, whichever is later). Notwithstanding the preceding two sentences, if a valid election has been made under section 754 and this section for a preceding taxable year and not revoked pursuant to paragraph (c) of this section, a new election is not required to be made. The statement required by this subparagraph shall (i) set forth the name and address of the partnership making the election, (ii) be signed by any one of the partners, and (iii) contain a declaration that the partnership elects under section 754 to apply the provisions of section 734(b) and section 743(b). For rules regarding extensions of time for filing elections, see § 1.9100–1.

(2) The principles of this paragraph may be illustrated by the following example:

Example. A, a U.S. citizen, is a member of partnership ABC, which has not previously made an election under section 754 to adjust the basis of partnership property. The partnership and the partners use the calendar year as the taxable year. A sells his interest in the partnership to D on January 1, 1971. The partnership may elect under section 754 and this section to adjust the basis of partnership property under sections 734(b) and 743(b). Unless an extension of time to make the election is obtained under the provisions of § 1.9100–1, the election must be made in a written statement filed with the partnership return for 1971 and must contain the information specified in subparagraph (1) of this paragraph. Such return must be filed by April 17, 1972 (unless an extension of time for filing the return is obtained). The election will apply to all distributions of property to a partner and transfers of an interest in the partnership occurring in 1971 and subsequent years, unless revoked pursuant to paragraph (c) of this section.

(c) Revocation of election. A partnership having an election in effect under this section may revoke such election with the approval of the district director for the internal revenue district in which the partnership return is required to be filed. A partnership which wishes to revoke such an election shall file with the district director for the internal revenue district in which the partnership return is required to be filed an application setting forth the grounds on which the revocation is desired. The application shall be filed not later than 30 days after the close of the partnership taxable year with respect to which revocation is intended to take effect and shall be signed by any one of the partners. Examples of situations which may be considered sufficient reason for approving an application for revocation include a change in the nature of the partnership business, a substantial increase in the assets of the partnership, a change in the character of partnership assets, or an increased frequency of retirements or shifts of partnership interests, so that an increased administrative burden would result to the partnership from the election. However, no application for revocation of an election shall be approved when the purpose of the revocation is primarily to avoid stepping down the basis of partnership assets upon a transfer or distribution.

[T.D. 6500, 25 FR 11814, Nov. 26, 1960, as amended by T.D. 7208, 37 FR 20686, Oct. 3, 1972]

§ 1.755–1   Rules for allocation of basis.

(a) **General rule.** (1)(i) A partnership which has elected under section 754 must adjust the basis of partnership property under the provisions of section 734(b) (relating to the optional adjustment to the basis of undistributed partnership property) and section 743(b) (relating to the optional adjustment to the basis of partnership property where a partnership interest is transferred). The amount of the increase or decrease (as determined in those sections) in the adjusted basis of the partnership property shall first be divided, under paragraph (b) of this section, between the two classes of property described in section 755(b). Then, the portion of the increase or decrease allocated to each class shall be further allocated to the bases of the properties within the class in a manner which will reduce the difference between the fair market value and the adjusted basis of partnership properties. In the alternative, any increase or decrease may be allocated in any other manner approved by the district director under subparagraph (2) of this paragraph.

(ii) If there is an increase in basis to be allocated to partnership assets, such increase must be allocated only to assets whose values exceed their bases and in proportion to the difference between the value and basis of each. No increase shall be made to the basis of any asset the adjusted basis of which equals or exceeds its fair market value.

(iii) If there is a decrease in basis to be allocated to partnership assets, such decrease must be allocated to assets whose bases exceed their value and in proportion to the difference between the basis and value of each. No decrease shall be made to the basis of any asset, the fair market value of which equals or exceeds its adjusted basis.

(iv) The application of the rules with respect to the allocation of an adjustment in basis under subdivisions (ii) and (iii) of this subparagraph requires that a portion of such adjustment be allocated to partnership good will, to the extent that good will exists and is reflected in the value of the property distributed, the price at which the partnership interest is sold, or the basis of the partnership interest determined under section 1014, in accordance with the difference between such value of the good will and its adjusted basis at the time of the transaction.

(2) If a partnership (or a partner electing under section 732(d)) desires to adjust the basis of assets under section 734(b) or 743(b) in a manner other than that prescribed in subparagraph (1) of this paragraph, it must file an application for permission to use such method with the district director no later than 30 days after the close of the partnership taxable year in which the proposed adjustment is to be made. The application must describe the proposed adjustments in detail and set forth the reasons for the desired use of the other method. Under section 755(a)(2), the district director may permit the partnership to increase the bases of some partnership properties and decrease the bases of other partnership properties under section 734(b) or 743(b). Each increase or decrease to the basis of an asset must reduce or eliminate the difference between such basis and the value of the asset. The net amount of all such adjustments must equal the amount of the adjustment under section 734(b) or 743(b). Adjustments that both increase and decrease the basis of partnership assets will be permitted by the district director only upon a satisfactory showing of the values for partnership assets used by the parties to determine the price at which a partnership interest was sold, the value of the decedent's partnership interest at date of death (or at the alternate valuation date, if used), or the amount of a distribution.

(b) **Special rules.** For the purposes of applying section 755, all partnership property shall be classified into two categories: Capital assets and property described in section 1231(b) (certain property used in the trade or business), or any other property of the partnership.

(1) **Distributions.** (i) Where there is a distribution of partnership property resulting in an adjustment to the basis of undistributed partnership property under section 734(b)(1)(B) or (b)(2)(B), such

adjustment must be allocated to remaining partnership property of a character similar to that of the distributed property with respect to which the adjustment arose. Thus, when the partnership adjusted basis of distributed capital assets and section 1231(b) property immediately prior to distribution exceeds the basis of such property to the distributee partner (as determined under section 732), the basis of the undistributed capital assets and section 1231(b) property remaining in the partnership shall be increased by an amount equal to such excess. Conversely, when the basis to the distributee partner (as determined under section 732) of distributed capital assets and section 1231(b) property exceeds the partnership adjusted basis of such property immediately prior to the distribution, the basis of the undistributed capital assets and section 1231(b) property remaining in the partnership shall be decreased by an amount equal to such excess. Similarly, where there is a distribution of partnership property other than capital assets and section 1231(b) property, and the basis of such other property to the distributee partner (as determined under section 732) is not the same as the partnership adjusted basis of such property immediately prior to distribution, the adjustment shall be made only to undistributed property of the same category remaining in the partnership.

(ii) Where there is a distribution resulting in an adjustment under section 734(b)(1)(A) or (b)(2)(A) to the basis of undistributed partnership property, such adjustment must be allocated only to capital assets or section 1231(b) property.

(2) **Transfers.** Where there is a basis adjustment under section 743(b) arising from a transfer of an interest in a partnership by sale or exchange or upon the death of a partner, the amount of the adjustment shall be allocated between the two classes of property described in section 755(b) and then the amount allocated to each class shall be further allocated under the rules of paragraph (a)(1) of this section. Thus, to the extent that an amount paid by a purchaser of a partnership interest (or the basis of the partnership interest to the estate or other successor in interest of a deceased partner) is attributable to the value of capital assets and section 1231(b) property, any difference between the amount so attributable and the transferee partner's share of the partnership basis of such property shall constitute a special basis adjustment with respect to partnership capital assets and section 1231 (b) property. Similarly, any such

difference attributable to any other property of the partnership shall constitute a special basis adjustment with respect to such property.

(3) **Limitation on decrease of basis.** Where a decrease in the basis of partnership assets is required under section 734(b)(2) and the amount of the decrease exceeds the adjusted basis to the partnership of property of the required character, the basis of such property shall be reduced to zero (but not below zero), and the balance of the decrease in basis shall be made when the partnership subsequently acquires property of a like character to which an adjustment can be made.

(4) **Carryover of adjustment.** Where, in the case of a distribution, an increase or decrease required under paragraph (a) of this section in the basis of undistributed partnership property cannot be made because the partnership owns no property of the character required to be adjusted, or because the adjustment has been limited under subparagraph (3) of this paragraph, the adjustment shall be made when the partnership subsequently acquires property of a like character to which an adjustment can be made.

(c) **Examples.** The provisions of this section may be illustrated by the following examples:

Example (1). Assume that partnership ABC has three assets: X, a capital asset with an adjusted basis of $1,000 and a value of $1,500; Y, a depreciable asset with an adjusted basis of $1,000 and a value of $900; and Z, inventory items with an adjusted basis of $700 and a value of $600. A sells his interest to D (when an election under 754 is in effect) for $1,000 (⅓ of $3,000, the total value of partnership assets). D's share of the adjusted basis of partnership property is $900 (⅓ of $2,700). Therefore, under section 743(b), D has a special basis adjustment of $100 ($1,000 minus $900). This adjustment must be allocated entirely to property X, since such allocation will have the effect of reducing the difference between the value and basis of such asset. Therefore, D has a special basis adjustment of $100 with respect to property X, which now has a special basis to him of $1,100. No part of the adjustment is made to depreciable property Y or inventory items Z, since any such adjustment would increase the difference between the basis and value of each such asset.

Example (2). Assume the same facts as in example (1) of this paragraph, except that capital asset X has a value of $1,500, depreciable property Y has a value of $1,100, and inventory items Z have a value of only $400. Therefore, under section 743(b), D has a special basis adjustment of $100, the excess of D's basis for his interest in the partnership ($1,000) over his share of the adjusted basis of partnership property ($900). This $100 adjustment must be allocated entirely to capital asset X and depreciable property Y in proportion to the difference between the value and basis of each since such allocation has the effect of reducing the difference between the value and basis of each such asset. Therefore, D has a special basis adjustment of $83 ($500/$600 of $100) with respect to capital asset X, which now has a special basis to him of $1,083, and of $17 ($100/$600 of $100) with respect to depreciable property Y, which now has a special basis to him of $1,017. No part of the adjustment is made to inventory items Z, since any such adjustment would increase the difference between the basis of such asset and its value.

Example (3). Assume that partnership EFG has three assets: X, a capital asset with an adjusted basis of $1,000 and a value of $1,500; Y, a depreciable asset with an adjusted basis of $1,000 and a value of $700; and Z, inventory items with an adjusted basis of $700 and a value of $800. E sells his interest to H (when an election under section 754 is in effect) for $1,000 (⅓ of $3,000, the total value of the partnership assets). H's share of the adjusted basis of partnership is $900 (⅓ of $2,700). Therefore, H has a special basis adjustment of $100 ($1,000 minus $900) under section 743(b). Since, of the total $300 difference between the value and the adjusted basis of all partnership property, $200 ($500, appreciation in value of X, minus $300, depreciation in value of Y) is attributable to the class of capital assets and depreciable property, and $100 (appreciation in value of inventory items Z) to the class of other property, H's special basis adjustment of $100 must be allocated ⅔ to capital assets and depreciable property and ⅓ to other property (inventory). The $67 increase (⅔ of $100) to be allocated to capital assets and depreciable property must further be allocated so as to reduce the difference between the value and basis of such assets. This can be done only by allocating the entire $67 increase to capital asset X (the basis of which is less than its value), and no part of the increase to depreciable property Y (the basis of which exceeds its value). Therefore, H has a special basis adjustment of $67 for capital asset X, which now has a special basis to him of $1,067; he has no special basis adjustment for depreciable property Y. H also has a special basis adjustment of $33 (⅓ of $100) for inventory items Z, the special basis of which is now $733.

[T.D. 6500, 25 FR 11814, Nov. 26, 1960]

Definitions

§ 1.761–1   Terms defined.

(a) **Partnership.** The term "partnership" includes a syndicate, group, pool, joint venture, or other unincorporated organization through or by means of which any business, financial operation, or venture is carried on, and which is not a corporation or a trust or estate within the meaning of the Code. The term "partnership" is broader in scope than the common law meaning of partnership, and may include groups not commonly called partnerships. See section 7701(a)(2). See regulations under section 7701(a)(1), (2), and (3) for the description of those unincorporated organizations taxable as corporations or trusts. A joint undertaking merely to share expenses is not a partnership. For example, if two or more persons jointly construct a ditch merely to drain surface water from their properties, they are not partners. Mere coownership of property which is maintained, kept in repair, and rented or leased does not constitute a partnership. For example, if an individual owner, or tenants in common, of farm property lease it to a farmer for a cash rental or a share of the crops, they do not necessarily create a partnership thereby. Tenants in common, however, may be partners if they actively carry on a trade, business, financial operation, or venture and divide the profits thereof. For example, a partnership exists if coowners of an apartment building lease space and in addition provide services to the occupants either directly or through an agent. For rules relating to the exclusion of certain partnerships from the application of all or part of subchapter K of chapter 1 of the Code, see § 1.761–2.

* * *

(c) **Partnership agreement.** For the purposes of subchapter K, a partnership agreement includes the original agreement and any modifications thereof agreed to by all the partners or adopted in any other manner provided by the partnership agreement. Such agreement or modifications can be oral or written. A partnership agreement may be modified with respect to a particular taxable year subsequent to the close of such taxable year, but not later than the date (not including any extension of time) prescribed by law for the filing of the partnership return. As to any matter on which the partnership agreement, or any modification thereof, is silent, the provisions of local law shall be considered to constitute a part of the agreement.

(d) **Liquidation of partner's interest.** The term "liquidation of a partner's interest" means the termination of a partner's entire interest in a partnership by means of a distribution, or a series of distributions, to the partner by the partnership. A series of distributions will come within the meaning of this term whether they are made in one year or in more than one year. Where a partner's interest is to be liquidated by a series of distributions, the interest will not be considered as liquidated until the final distribution has been made. For the basis of property distributed in one liquidating distribution, or in a series of distributions in liquidation, see section 732(b). A distribution which is not in liquidation of a partner's entire interest, as defined in this paragraph, is a current distribution. Current distributions, therefore, include distributions in partial liquidation of a partner's interest, and distributions of the part-

ner's distributive share. See paragraph (a)(1)(ii) of § 1.731–1.

[T.D. 6500, 25 FR 11814, Nov. 26, 1960, as amended by T.D. 7208, 37 FR 20686, Oct. 3, 1972]

* * *

GAIN OR LOSS ON DISPOSITION OF PROPERTY

Determination of Amount and Recognition of Gain or Loss

§ 1.1001–1 Computation of gain or loss.

(a) **General rule.** Except as otherwise provided in subtitle A of the Code, the gain or loss realized from the conversion of property into cash, or from the exchange of property for other property differing materially either in kind or in extent, is treated as income or as loss sustained. The amount realized from a sale or other disposition of property is the sum of any money received plus the fair market value of any property (other than money) received. The fair market value of property is a question of fact, but only in rare and extraordinary cases will property be considered to have no fair market value. The general method of computing such gain or loss is prescribed by section 1001(a) through (d) which contemplates that from the amount realized upon the sale or exchange there shall be withdrawn a sum sufficient to restore the adjusted basis prescribed by section 1011 and the regulations thereunder (*i.e.*, the cost or other basis adjusted for receipts, expenditures, losses, allowances, and other items chargeable against and applicable to such cost or other basis). The amount which remains after the adjusted basis has been restored to the taxpayer constitutes the realized gain. If the amount realized upon the sale or exchange is insufficient to restore to the taxpayer the adjusted basis of the property, a loss is sustained to the extent of the difference between such adjusted basis and the amount realized. The basis may be different depending upon whether gain or loss is being computed. For example, see section 1015(a) and the regulations thereunder. Section 1001(e) and paragraph (f) of this section prescribe the method of computing gain or loss upon the sale or other disposition of a term interest in property the adjusted basis (or a portion) of which is determined pursuant, or by reference, to section 1014 (relating to the basis of property acquired from a decedent) or section 1015 (relating to the basis of property acquired by gift or by a transfer in trust).

(b) **Real estate taxes as amounts received.** (1) Section 1001(b) and section 1012 state rules applicable in making an adjustment upon a sale of real property with respect to the real property taxes apportioned between seller and purchaser under section 164(d). Thus, if the seller pays (or agrees to pay) real property taxes attributable to the real property tax year in which the sale occurs, he shall not take into account, in determining the amount realized from the sale under section 1001(b), any amount received as reimbursement for taxes which are treated under section 164(d) as imposed upon the purchaser. Similarly, in computing the cost of the property under section 1012, the purchaser shall not take into account any amount paid to the seller as reimbursement for real property taxes which are treated under section 164(d) as imposed upon the purchaser. These rules apply whether or not the contract of sale calls for the purchaser to reimburse the seller for such real property taxes paid or to be paid by the seller.

(2) On the other hand, if the purchaser pays (or is to pay) an amount representing real property taxes which are treated under section 164(d) as imposed upon the seller, that amount shall be taken into account both in determining the amount realized from the sale under section 1001(b) and in computing the cost of the property under section 1012. It is immaterial whether or not the contract of sale specifies that the sale price has been reduced by, or is in any way intended to reflect, the taxes allocable to the seller. See also paragraph (b) of § 1.1012–1.

(3) Subparagraph (1) of this paragraph shall not apply to a seller who, in a taxable year prior to the taxable year of sale, pays an amount representing real property taxes which are treated under section 164(d) as imposed on the purchaser, if such seller has elected to capitalize such amount in accordance with section 266 and the regulations

thereunder (relating to election to capitalize certain carrying charges and taxes).

(4) The application of this paragraph may be illustrated by the following examples:

Example (1). Assume that the contract price on the sale of a parcel of real estate is $50,000 and that real property taxes thereon in the amount of $1,000 for the real property tax year in which occurred the date of sale were previously paid by the seller. Assume further that $750 of the taxes are treated under section 164(d) as imposed upon the purchaser and that he reimburses the seller in that amount in addition to the contract price. The amount realized by the seller is $50,000. Similarly, $50,000 is the purchaser's cost. If, in this example, the purchaser made no payment other than the contract price of $50,000, the amount realized by the seller would be $49,250, since the sales price would be deemed to include $750 paid to the seller in reimbursement for real property taxes imposed upon the purchaser. Similarly, $49,250 would be the purchaser's cost.

Example (2). Assume that the purchaser in example (1), above, paid all of the real property taxes. Assume further that $250 of the taxes are treated under section 164(d) as imposed upon the seller. The amount realized by the seller is $50,250. Similarly, $50,250 is the purchaser's cost, regardless of the taxable year in which the purchaser makes actual payment of the taxes.

* * *

(c) Other rules. (1) Even though property is not sold or otherwise disposed of, gain is realized if the sum of all the amounts received which are required by section 1016 and other applicable provisions of subtitle A of the Code to be applied against the basis of the property exceeds such basis. Except as otherwise provided in section 301(c)(3)(B) with respect to distributions out of increase in value of property accrued prior to March 1, 1913, such gain is includible in gross income under section 61 as "income from whatever source derived". On the other hand, a loss is not ordinarily sustained prior to the sale or other disposition of the property, for the reason that until such sale or other disposition occurs there remains the possibility that the taxpayer may recover or recoup the adjusted basis of the property. Until some identifiable event fixes the actual sustaining of a loss and the amount thereof, it is not taken into account.

(2) The provisions of subparagraph (1) of this paragraph may be illustrated by the following example:

Example. A, an individual on a calendar year basis, purchased certain shares of stock subsequent to February 28, 1913, for $10,000. On January 1, 1954, A's adjusted basis for the stock had been reduced to $1,000 by reason of receipts and distributions described in sections 1016(a)(1) and 1016(a)(4). He received in 1954 a further distribution of $5,000, being a distribution covered by section 1016(a)(4), other than a distribution out of increase of value of property accrued prior to March 1, 1913. This distribution applied against the adjusted basis as required by section 1016(a)(4) exceeds that basis by $4,000. The $4,000 excess is a gain realized by A in 1954 and is includible in gross income in his return for that calendar year. In computing gain from the stock, as in adjusting basis, no distinction is made between items of receipts or distributions described in section 1016. If A sells the stock in 1955 for $5,000, he realizes in 1955 a gain of $5,000, since the adjusted basis of the stock for the purpose of computing gain or loss from the sale is zero.

(d) Installment sales. In the case of property sold on the installment plan, special rules for the taxation of the gain are prescribed in section 453.

(e) Transfers in part a sale and in part a gift. (1) Where a transfer of property is in part a sale and in part a gift, the transferor has a gain to the extent that the amount realized by him exceeds his adjusted basis in the property. However, no loss is sustained on such a transfer if the amount realized is less than the adjusted basis. For the determination of basis of property in the hands of the transferee, see § 1.1015-4. For the allocation of the adjusted basis of property in the case of a bargain sale to a charitable organization, see § 1.1011-2.

(2) **Examples.** The provisions of subparagraph (1) may be illustrated by the following examples:

Example (1). A transfers property to his son for $60,000. Such property in the hands of A has an adjusted basis of $30,000 (and a fair market value of $90,000). A's gain is $30,000, the excess of $60,000, the amount realized, over the adjusted basis, $30,000. He has made a gift of $30,000, the excess of $90,000, the fair market value, over the amount realized, $60,000.

Example (2). A transfers property to his son for $30,000. Such property in the hands of A has an adjusted basis of $60,000 (and a fair market value of $90,000). A has no gain or loss, and has made a gift of $60,000, the excess of $90,000, the fair market value, over the amount realized, $30,000.

Example (3). A transfers property to his son for $30,000. Such property in A's hands has an adjusted basis of $30,000 (and a fair market value of $60,000). A has no gain and has made a gift of $30,000, the excess of $60,000, the fair market value, over the amount realized, $30,000.

Example (4). A transfers property to his son for $30,000. Such property in A's hands has an adjusted basis of $90,000 (and a fair market value of $60,000). A has sustained no loss, and has made a gift of $30,000, the excess of $60,000, the fair market value, over the amount realized, $30,000.

(f) Sale or other disposition of a term interest in property—(1) General rule. Except as otherwise provided in subparagraph (3) of this paragraph, for purposes of determining gain or loss from the sale or other disposition after October 9, 1969, of a term interest in property (as defined in subparagraph (2) of this paragraph) a taxpayer shall not take into account that portion of the adjusted basis of such interest which is determined pursuant, or by reference, to section 1014 (relating to the basis of property acquired from a decedent) or section 1015 (relating to the basis of property acquired by gift or by a transfer in trust) to the extent that such adjusted basis is a portion of the adjusted uniform basis of the entire property (as defined in § 1.1014–5). Where a term interest in property is transferred to a corporation in connection with a transaction to which section 351 applies and the adjusted basis of the term interest (i) is determined pursuant to section 1014 or 1015 and (ii) is also a portion of the adjusted uniform basis of the entire property, a subsequent sale or other disposition of such term interest by the corporation will be subject to the provisions of section 1001(e) and this paragraph to the extent that the basis of the term interest so sold or otherwise disposed of is determined by reference to its basis in the hands of the transferor as provided by section 362(a). See subparagraph (2) of this paragraph for rules relating to the characterization of stock received by the transferor of a term interest in property in connection with a transaction to which section 351 applies. That portion of the adjusted uniform basis of the entire property which is assignable to such interest at the time of its sale or other disposition shall be determined under the rules provided in § 1.1014–5. Thus, gain or loss realized from a sale or other disposition of a term interest in property shall be determined by comparing the amount of the proceeds of such sale with that part of the adjusted basis of such interest which is not a portion of the adjusted uniform basis of the entire property.

(2) **Term interest defined.** For purposes of section 1001(e) and this paragraph, a "term interest in property" means—

(i) A life interest in property,

(ii) An interest in property for a term of years, or

(iii) An income interest in a trust.

Generally, subdivisions (i), (ii), and (iii) refer to an interest, present or future, in the income from property or the right to use property which will terminate or fail on the lapse of time, on the occurrence of an event or contingency, or on the failure of an event or contingency to occur. Such divisions do not refer to remainder or reversionary interests in the property itself or other interests in the property which will ripen into ownership of the entire property upon termination or failure of a preceding term interest. A "term interest in property" also includes any property received upon a sale or other disposition of a life interest in property, an interest in property for a term of years, or an income interest in a trust by the original holder of such interest, but only to the extent that the adjusted basis of the property received is determined by reference to the adjusted basis of the term interest so transferred.

(3) **Exception.** Paragraph (1) of section 1001(e) and subparagraph (1) of this paragraph shall not apply to a sale or other disposition of a term interest in property as a part of a single transaction in which the entire interest in the property is transferred to a third person or to two or more other persons, including persons who acquire such entire interest as joint tenants, tenants by the entirety, or tenants in common. See § 1.1014–5 for computation of gain or loss upon such a sale or other disposition where the property has been acquired from a decedent or by gift or transfer in trust.

(4) **Illustrations.** For examples illustrating the application of this paragraph, see paragraph (c) of § 1.1014–5.

(g) **Certain exchanges involving original issue discount.** In the case of certain obligations or investment units exchanged for property, involving original issue discount under the provisions of section 1232(b), the amount realized will be determined in accordance with the rules of paragraph (b)(2)(iii)(b) of § 1.1232–3.

[T.D. 6500, 25 FR 11910, Nov. 26, 1960, as amended by T.D. 7142, 36 FR 18950, Sept. 24, 1971; T.D. 7207, 37 FR 20797, Oct. 5, 1972; T.D. 7213, 37 FR 21992, Oct. 18, 1972]

§ 1.1001–2 **Discharge of liabilities.**

(a) **Inclusion in amount realized—(1) In general.** Except as provided in paragraph (a)(2) and (3) of this section, the amount realized from a sale or other disposition of property includes the amount of liabilities from which the transferor is discharged as a result of the sale or disposition.

(2) **Discharge of indebtedness.** The amount realized on a sale or other disposition of property that secures a recourse liability does not include

amounts that are (or would be if realized and recognized) income from the discharge of indebtedness under section 61(a)(12). For situations where amounts arising from the discharge of indebtedness are not realized and recognized, see section 108 and § 1.61–12(b)(1).

(3) Liability incurred on acquisition. In the case of a liability incurred by reason of the acquisition of the property, this section does not apply to the extent that such liability was not taken into account in determining the transferor's basis for such property.

(4) Special rules. For purposes of this section—

(i) The sale or other disposition of property that secures a nonrecourse liability discharges the transferor from the liability;

(ii) The sale or other disposition of property that secures a recourse liability discharges the transferor from the liability if another person agrees to pay the liability (whether or not the transferor is in fact released from liability);

(iii) A disposition of property includes a gift of the property or a transfer of the property in satisfaction of liabilities to which it is subject;

(iv) Contributions and distributions of property between a partner and a partnership are not sales or other dispositions of property; and

(v) The liabilities from which a transferor is discharged as a result of the sale or disposition of a partnership interest include the transferor's share of the liabilities of the partnership.

(b) Effect of fair market value of security. The fair market value of the security at the time of sale or disposition is not relevant for purposes of determining under paragraph (a) of this section the amount of liabilities from which the taxpayer is discharged or treated as discharged. Thus, the fact that the fair market value of the property is less than the amount of the liabilities it secures does not prevent the full amount of those liabilities from being treated as money received from the sale or other disposition of the property. However, see paragraph (a)(2) of this section for a rule relating to certain income from discharge of indebtedness.

(c) Examples. The provisions of this section may be illustrated by the following examples. In each example assume the taxpayer uses the cash receipts and disbursements method of accounting, makes a return on the basis of the calendar year,

and sells or disposes of all property which is security for a given liability.

Example (1). In 1976 A purchases an asset for $10,000. A pays the seller $1,000 in cash and signs a note payable to the seller for $9,000. A is personally liable for repayment with the seller having full recourse in the event of default. In addition, the asset which was purchased is pledged as security. During the years 1976 and 1977 A takes depreciation deductions on the asset in the amount of $3,100. During this same time period A reduces the outstanding principal on the note to $7,600. At the beginning of 1978 A sells the asset. The buyer pays A $1,600 in cash and assumes personal liability for the $7,600 outstanding liability. A becomes secondarily liable for repayment of the liability. A's amount realized is $9,200 ($1,600 + $7,600). Since A's adjusted basis in the asset is $6,900 ($10,000 – $3,100) A realizes a gain of $2,300 ($9,200 – $6,900).

Example (2). Assume the same facts as in example (1) except that A is not personally liable on the $9,000 note given to the seller and in the event of default the seller's only recourse is to the asset. In addition, on the sale of the asset by A, the purchaser takes the asset subject to the liability. Nevertheless, A's amount realized is $9,200 and A's gain realized is $2,300 on the sale.

Example (3). In 1975 L becomes a limited partner in partnership GL. L contributes $10,000 in cash to GL and L's distributive share of partnership income and loss is 10 percent. L is not entitled to receive any guaranteed payments. In 1978 M purchases L's entire interest in partnership GL. At the time of the sale L's adjusted basis in the partnership interest is $20,000. At that time L's proportionate share of liabilities, of which no partner has assumed personal liability, is $15,000. M pays $10,000 in cash for L's interest in the partnership. Under section 752(d) and this section, L's share of partnership liabilities, $15,000, is treated as money received. Accordingly, L's amount realized on the sale of the partnership interest is $25,000 ($10,000 + $15,000). L's gain realized on the sale is $5,000 ($25,000–$20,000).

Example (4). In 1976 B becomes a limited partner in partnership BG. In 1978 B contributes B's entire interest in BG to a charitable organization described in section 170(c). At the time of the contribution all of the partnership liabilities are liabilities for which neither B nor G has assumed any personal liability and B's proportionate share of which is $9,000. The charitable organization does not pay any cash or other property to B, but takes the partnership interest subject to the $9,000 of liabilities. Assume that the contribution is treated as a bargain sale to a charitable organization and that under section 1011(b) $3,000 is determined to be the portion of B's basis in the partnership interest allocable to the sale. Under section 752(d) and this section, the $9,000 of liabilities is treated by B as money received, thereby making B's amount realized $9,000. B's gain realized is $6,000 ($9,000–$3,000).

Example (5). In 1975 C, an individual, creates T, an irrevocable trust. Due to certain powers expressly retained by C, T is a "grantor trust" for purposes of subpart E of part 1 of subchapter J of the Code and therefore C is treated as the owner of the entire trust. T purchases an interest in P, a partnership. C, as owner of T, deducts the distributive share of partnership losses attributable to the partnership interest held by T. In 1978, when the adjusted basis of the partnership interest held by T is $1,200, C renounces the powers previously and expressly retained that initially resulted in T being classified as a grantor trust. Consequently, T ceases to be a grantor trust and C is no longer considered to be the owner of the trust. At the time of the renunciation all of P's liabilities are liabilities on which none of the partners have assumed any personal liability and the proportionate share of which of the interest held by T is $11,000. Since prior to the renunciation C was the owner of the entire trust, C was considered the owner of all the trust property for Federal income tax purposes, including the partnership interest. Since C was considered to be the owner of the partnership interest, C not T, was considered to be the partner in P during the time T was a "grantor trust". However, at the time C renounced the powers that gave rise to T's classification as a grantor trust, T no longer qualified as a grantor trust with the result that C was no longer considered to be the owner of the trust and trust property for Federal income tax purposes. Consequently, at that time, C is considered to have transferred ownership of the interest in P to T, now a separate taxable entity, independent of its grantor C. On the transfer, C's share of partnership liabilities ($11,000) is treated as money received. Accordingly, C's amount realized is $11,000 and C's gain realized is $9,800 ($11,000–$1,200).

Example (6). In 1977 D purchases an asset for $7,500. D pays the seller $1,500 in cash and signs a note payable to the seller for $6,000. D is not personally liable for repayment but pledges as security the newly purchased asset. In the event of default, the seller's only recourse is to the asset. During the years 1977 and 1978 D takes depreciation deductions on the asset totaling $4,200 thereby reducing D's basis in the asset to $3,300 ($7,500–$4,200). In 1979 D transfers the asset to a trust which is not a "grantor trust" for purposes of subpart 1 of subchapter J of the Code. Therefore D is not treated as the owner of the trust. The trust takes the asset subject to the liability and in addition pays D $750 in cash. Prior to the transfer D had reduced the amount outstanding on the liability to $4,700. D's amount realized on the transfer is $5,450 ($4,700 + $750). Since D's adjusted basis is $3,300, D's gain realized is $2,150 ($5,450–$3,300).

Example (7). In 1974 E purchases a herd of cattle for breeding purposes. The purchase price is $20,000 consisting of $1,000 cash and a $19,000 note. E is not personally liable for repayment of the liability and the seller's only recourse in the event of default is to the herd of cattle. In 1977 E transfers the herd back to the original seller thereby satisfying the indebtedness pursuant to a provision in the original sales agreement. At the time of the transfer the fair market value of the herd is $15,000 and the remaining principal balance on the note is $19,000. At that time E's adjusted basis in the herd is $16,500 due to a deductible loss incurred when a portion of the herd died as a result of disease. As a result of the indebtedness being satisfied, E's amount realized is $19,000 notwithstanding the fact that the fair market value of the herd was less than $19,000. E's realized gain is 2,500 ($19,000–$16,500).

Example (8). In 1980, F transfers to a creditor an asset with a fair market value of $6,000 and the creditor discharges $7,500 of indebtedness for which F is personally liable. The amount realized on the disposition of the asset is its fair market value ($6,000). In addition, F has income from the discharge of indebtedness of $1,500 ($7,500–$6,000).

[T.D. 7741, 45 FR 81744, Dec. 12, 1980]

§ 1.1002–1 Sales or exchanges.

(a) **General rule.** The general rule with respect to gain or loss realized upon the sale or exchange of property as determined under section 1001 is that the entire amount of such gain or loss is recognized except in cases where specific provisions of subtitle A of the Code provide otherwise.

(b) **Strict construction of exceptions from general rule.** The exceptions from the general rule requiring the recognition of all gains and losses, like other exceptions from a rule of taxation of general and uniform application, are strictly construed and do not extend either beyond the words or the underlying assumptions and purposes of the exception. Nonrecognition is accorded by the Code only if the exchange is one which satisfies both (1) the specific description in the Code of an excepted exchange, and (2) the underlying purpose for which such exchange is excepted from the general rule. The exchange must be germane to, and a necessary incident of, the investment or enterprise in hand. The relationship of the exchange to the venture or enterprise is always material, and the surrounding facts and circumstances must be shown. As elsewhere, the taxpayer claiming the benefit of the exception must show himself within the exception.

(c) **Certain exceptions to general rule.** Exceptions to the general rule are made, for example, by sections 351(a), 354, 361(a), 371(a)(1), 371(b)(1), 721, 1031, 1035 and 1036. These sections describe certain specific exchanges of property in which at the time of the exchange particular differences exist between the property parted with and the property acquired, but such differences are more formal than substantial. As to these, the Code provides that such differences shall not be deemed controlling, and that gain or loss shall not be recognized at the time of the exchange. The underlying assumption of these exceptions is that the new property is substantially a continuation of the old investment still unliquidated; and, in the case of reorganizations, that the new enterprise, the new corporate structure, and the new property are substantially continuations of the old still unliquidated.

(d) Exchange. Ordinarily, to constitute an exchange, the transaction must be a reciprocal transfer of property, as distinguished from a transfer of property for a money consideration only.

[T.D. 6500, 25 FR 11910, Nov. 26, 1960]

Basis Rules of General Application

§ 1.1011–1　Adjusted basis.

The adjusted basis for determining the gain or loss from the sale or other disposition of property is the cost or other basis prescribed in section 1012 or other applicable provisions of subtitle A of the Code, adjusted to the extent provided in sections 1016, 1017, and 1018 or as otherwise specifically provided for under applicable provisions of internal revenue laws.

[T.D. 6500, 25 FR 11910, Nov. 26, 1960]

§ 1.1011–2　Bargain sale to a charitable organization.

(a) In general. (1) If for the taxable year a charitable contributions deduction is allowable under section 170 by reason of a sale or exchange of property, the taxpayer's adjusted basis of such property for purposes of determining gain from such sale or exchange must be computed as provided in section 1011(b) and paragraph (b) of this section. If after applying the provisions of section 170 for the taxable year, including the percentage limitations of section 170(b), no deduction is allowable under that section by reason of the sale or exchange of the property, section 1011(b) does not apply and the adjusted basis of the property is not required to be apportioned pursuant to paragraph (b) of this section. In such case the entire adjusted basis of the property is to be taken into account in determining gain from the sale or exchange, as provided in § 1.1001–1(e). In ascertaining whether or not a charitable contributions deduction is allowable under section 170 for the taxable year for such purposes, that section is to be applied without regard to this section and the amount by which the contributed portion of the property must be reduced under section 170(e)(1) is the amount determined by taking into account the amount of gain which would have been ordinary income or long-term capital gain if the entire property had been sold by the donor at its fair market value at the time of the sale or exchange.

(2) If in the taxable year there is a sale or exchange of property which gives rise to a charitable contribution which is carried over under section 170(b)(1)(D)(ii) or section 170(d) to a subsequent taxable year or is postponed under section 170(a)(3) to a subsequent taxable year, section 1011(b) and paragraph (b) of this section must be applied for purposes of apportioning the adjusted basis of the property for the year of the sale or exchange, whether or not such contribution is allowable as a deduction under section 170 in such subsequent year.

(3) If property is transferred subject to an indebtedness, the amount of the indebtedness must be treated as an amount realized for purposes of determining whether there is a sale or exchange to which section 1011(b) and this section apply, even though the transferee does not agree to assume or pay the indebtedness.

(4)(i) Section 1011(b) and this section apply where property is sold or exchanged in return for an obligation to pay an annuity and a charitable contributions deduction is allowable under section 170 by reason of such sale or exchange.

(ii) If in such case the annuity received in exchange for the property is nonassignable, or is assignable but only to the charitable organization to which the property is sold or exchanged, and if the transferor is the only annuitant or the transferor and a designated survivor annuitant or annuitants are the only annuitants, any gain on such exchange is to be reported as provided in example (8) in paragraph (c) of this section. In determining the period over which gain may be reported as provided in such example, the life expectancy of the survivor annuitant may not be taken into account. The fact that the transferor may retain the right to revoke the survivor's annuity or relinquish his own right to the annuity will not be considered, for purposes of this subdivision, to make the annuity assignable to someone other than the charitable organization. Gain on an exchange of the type described in this subdivision pursuant to an agreement which is entered into after December 19, 1969, and before May 3, 1971, may be reported as provided in example (8) in paragraph (c) of this section, even though the annuity is assignable.

(iii) In the case of an annuity to which subdivision (ii) of this subparagraph applies, the gain unreported by the transferor with respect to annuity payments not yet due when the following events occur is not required to be included in gross income of any person where—

(a) The transferor dies before the entire amount of gain has been reported and there is no surviving annuitant, or

(b) The transferor relinquishes the annuity to the charitable organization.

If the transferor dies before the entire amount of gain on a two-life annuity has been reported, the unreported gain is required to be reported by the surviving annuitant or annuitants with respect to the annuity payments received by them.

(b) **Apportionment of adjusted basis.** For purposes of determining gain on a sale or exchange to which this paragraph applies, the adjusted basis of the property which is sold or exchanged shall be that portion of the adjusted basis of the entire property which bears the same ratio to the adjusted basis as the amount realized bears to the fair market value of the entire property. The amount of such gain which shall be treated as ordinary income (or long-term capital gain) shall be that amount which bears the same ratio to the ordinary income (or long-term capital gain) which would have been recognized if the entire property had been sold by the donor at its fair market value at the time of the sale or exchange as the amount realized on the sale or exchange bears to the fair market value of the entire property at such time. The terms "ordinary income" and "long-term capital gain", as used in this section, have the same meaning as they have in paragraph (a) of § 1.170A–4. For determining the portion of the adjusted basis, ordinary income, and long-term capital gain allocated to the contributed portion of the property for purposes of applying section 170(e)(1) and paragraph (a) of § 1.170A–4 to the contributed portion of the property, and for determining the donee's basis in such contributed portion, see paragraph (c)(2) and (4) of § 1.170A–4. For determining the holding period of such contributed portion, see section 1223(2) and the regulations thereunder.

(c) **Illustrations.** The application of this section may be illustrated by the following examples, which are supplemented by other examples in paragraph (d) of § 1.170A–4:

Example (1). In 1970, A, a calendar-year individual taxpayer, sells to a church for $4,000 stock held for more than 6 months which has an adjusted basis of $4,000 and a fair market value of $10,000. A's contribution base for 1970, as defined in section 170(b)(1)(F), is $100,000, and during that year he makes no other charitable contributions. Thus, A makes a charitable contribution to the church of $6,000 ($10,000 value –$4,000 amount realized). Without regard to this section, A is allowed a deduction under section 170 of $6,000 for his charitable contribution to the church, since there is no reduction under section 170(e)(1) with respect to the long-term capital gain. Accordingly, under paragraph (b) of this section the adjusted basis for determining gain on the bargain sale is $1,600 ($4,000 adjusted basis × $4,000 amount realized/$10,000 value of property). A has recognized long-term capital gain of $2,400 ($4,000 amount realized –$1,600 adjusted basis) on the bargain sale.

Example (2). The facts are the same as in example (1) except that A also makes a charitable contribution in 1970 of $50,000 cash to the church. By reason of section 170(b)(1)(A), the deduction allowed under section 170 for 1970 is $50,000 for the amount of cash contributed to the church; however, the $6,000 contribution of property is carried over to 1971 under section 170(d). Under paragraphs (a)(2) and (b) of this section the adjusted basis for determining gain for 1970 on the bargain sale in that year is $1,600 ($4,000×$4,000/$10,000). A has a recognized long-term capital gain for 1970 of $2,400 ($4,000–$1,600) on the sale.

* * *

Example (7). In 1970, C, a calendar-year individual taxpayer, sells to a church for $4,000 tangible personal property used in his business for more than 6 months which has an adjusted basis of $4,000 and a fair market value of $10,000. Thus, C makes a charitable contribution to the church of $6,000 ($10,000 value –$4,000 amount realized). C's contribution base for 1970, as defined in section 170(b)(1)(F), is $100,000 and during such year he makes no other charitable contributions. If C had sold the property at its fair market value at the time of its contribution, it is assumed that under section 1245 $4,000 of the gain of $6,000 ($10,000 value –$4,000 adjusted basis) would have been treated as ordinary income. Thus, there would have been long-term capital gain of $2,000. It is also assumed that the church does not put the property to an unrelated use, as defined in paragraph (b)(3) of § 1.170A–4. Since without regard to this section C is allowed a deduction under section 170 of $2,000 ($6,000 gift –$4,000 ordinary income), under paragraph (b) of this section the adjusted basis for determining gain on the bargain sale is $1,600 ($4,000 adjusted basis × $4,000 amount realized/$10,000 value of property). Accordingly, C has a recognized gain of $2,400 ($4,000 amount realized –$1,600 adjusted basis) on the bargain sale, consisting of ordinary income of $1,600 ($4,000 ordinary income × $4,000 amount realized/$10,000 value of property) and of long-term capital gain of $800 ($2,000 long-term gain × $4,000 amount realized/$10,000 value of property). After applying section 1011(b) and paragraphs (a) and (c)(2)(i) of § 1.170A–4, C is allowed a charitable contributions deduction for 1970 of $3,600 ($6,000 gift –[$4,000 ordinary income × $6,000 value of gift/$10,000 value of property]).

Example (8). (a) On January 1, 1970, A, a male of age 65, transfers capital assets consisting of securities held for more than 6 months to a church in exchange for a promise by the church to pay A a nonassignable annuity of $5,000 per year for life. The annuity is payable monthly with the first payment to be made on February 1, 1970. A's contribution base for 1970, as defined in section 170(b)(1)(F), is $200,000, and during that year he makes no other charitable contributions. On the date of transfer the securities have a fair market value of $100,-000 and an adjusted basis to A of $20,000.

(b) The present value of the right of a male age 65 to receive a life annuity of $5,000 per annum, payable in equal installments at the end of each monthly period, is $59,755 ($5,000×[11.469+0.482]), determined in accordance with section 101(b) of the Code, paragraph (e)(1)(iii)(b)(2) of § 1.101–2, and section 3 of Rev. Rul. 62–216, C.B. 1962–2, 30. Thus, A makes a charitable contribution to the church of $40,245 ($100,000–$59,755). Without regard to this section, A is allowed a deduction under section 170 of $40,245 for his charitable contribution to the church, since the property contributed is not section 170(e) capital gain property within the meaning of paragraph (b)(3) of § 1.170A–4 and no reduction of the contribution is made under section 170(e)(1).

(c) Under paragraph (b) of this section, the adjusted basis for determining gain on the bargain sale is $11,951 ($20,000×$59,755/$100,000). Accordingly, A has a recognized long-term capital gain of $47,804 ($59,755–$11,951) on the bargain sale. Such gain is to be reported by A ratably over the period of years measured by the expected return multiple under the contract, but only from that portion of the annual payments which is a return of his investment in the contract under section 72 of the Code. For such purposes, the investment in the contract is $59,755, that is, the present value of the annuity.

(d) The computation and application of the exclusion ratio, the gain, and the ordinary annuity income are as follows, determined by using the expected return multiple of 15.0 applicable under Table I of § 1.72–9:

A's expected return (annual payments of $5,000 × 15)	$75,000.00
Exclusion ratio ($59,755 investment in contract divided by expected return of $75,-000)	79.7%
Annual exclusion (annual payments of $5,000 × 79.7%)	$3,985.00
Ordinary annuity income ($5,000–$3,985)	$1,015.00
Long-term capital gain per year ($47,804/15) with respect to the annual exclusion	$3,186.93

(e) The exclusion ratio of 79.7 percent applies throughout the life of the contract. During the first 15 years of the annuity, A is required to report ordinary income of $1,015 and long-term capital gain of $3,186.93 with respect to the annuity payments he receives. After the total long-term capital gain of $47,804 has been reported by A, he is required to report only ordinary income of $1,015.00 per annum with respect to the annuity payments he receives.

* * *

[T.D. 7207, 37 FR 20798, Oct. 5, 1972, as amended by T.D. 7741, 45 FR 81745, Dec. 12, 1980]

§ 1.1012–1   Basis of property.

(a) **General rule.** In general, the basis of property is the cost thereof. The cost is the amount paid for such property in cash or other property. This general rule is subject to exceptions stated in subchapter O (relating to gain or loss on the disposition of property), subchapter C (relating to corporate distributions and adjustments), subchapter K (relating to partners and partnerships), and subchapter P (relating to capital gains and losses), chapter 1 of the Code.

(b) **Real estate taxes as part of cost.** In computing the cost of real property, the purchaser shall not take into account any amount paid to the seller as reimbursement for real property taxes which are treated under section 164(d) as imposed upon the purchaser. This rule applies whether or not the contract of sale calls for the purchaser to reimburse the seller for such real estate taxes paid or to be paid by the seller. On the other hand, where the purchaser pays (or assumes liability for) real estate taxes which are treated under section 164(d) as imposed upon the seller, such taxes shall be considered part of the cost of the property. It is immaterial whether or not the contract of sale specifies that the sale price has been reduced by, or is in any way intended to reflect, real estate taxes allocable to the seller under section 164(d). For illustrations of the application of this paragraph, see paragraph (b) of § 1.1001–1.

(c) **Sale of stock—(1) In general.** If shares of stock in a corporation are sold or transferred by a taxpayer who purchased or acquired lots of stock on different dates or at different prices, and the lot from which the stock was sold or transferred cannot be adequately identified, the stock sold or transferred shall be charged against the earliest of such lots purchased or acquired in order to determine the cost or other basis of such stock and in order to determine the holding period of such stock for purposes of subchapter P, chapter 1 of the Code. If, on the other hand, the lot from which the stock is sold or transferred can be adequately identified, the rule stated in the preceding sentence is not applicable. As to what constitutes "adequate identification", see subparagraphs (2), (3), and (4) of this paragraph.

(2) **Identification of stock.** An adequate identification is made if it is shown that certificates representing shares of stock from a lot which was purchased or acquired on a certain date or for a certain price were delivered to the taxpayer's

transferee. Except as otherwise provided in subparagraph (3) or (4) of this paragraph, such stock certificates delivered to the transferee constitute the stock sold or transferred by the taxpayer. Thus, unless the requirements of subparagraph (3) or (4) of this paragraph are met, the stock sold or transferred is charged to the lot to which the certificates delivered to the transferee belong, whether or not the taxpayer intends, or instructs his broker or other agent, to sell or transfer stock from a lot purchased or acquired on a different date or for a different price.

(3) Identification on confirmation document. (i) Where the stock is left in the custody of a broker or other agent, an adequate identification is made if—

(a) At the time of the sale or transfer, the taxpayer specifies to such broker or other agent having custody of the stock the particular stock to be sold or transferred, and

(b) Within a reasonable time thereafter, confirmation of such specification is set forth in a written document from such broker or other agent.

Stock identified pursuant to this subdivision is the stock sold or transferred by the taxpayer, even though stock certificates from a different lot are delivered to the taxpayer's transferee.

(ii) Where a single stock certificate represents stock from different lots, where such certificate is held by the taxpayer rather than his broker or other agent, and where the taxpayer sells a part of the stock represented by such certificate through a broker or other agent, an adequate identification is made if—

(a) At the time of the delivery of the certificate to the broker or other agent, the taxpayer specifies to such broker or other agent the particular stock to be sold or transferred, and

(b) Within a reasonable time thereafter, confirmation of such specification is set forth in a written document from such broker or agent.

Where part of the stock represented by a single certificate is sold or transferred directly by the taxpayer to the purchaser or transferee instead of through a broker or other agent, an adequate identification is made if the taxpayer maintains a written record of the particular stock which he intended to sell or transfer.

* * *

[T.D. 6500, 25 FR 11910, Nov. 26, 1960, as amended by T.D. 6837, 30 FR 8787, July 13, 1965; T.D. 6887, 31 FR 8814, June 24, 1966; T.D. 6934, 32 FR 15671, 15676, Nov. 14, 1967; T.D. 6984, 33 FR 19176, Dec. 21, 1968; T.D. 7015, 34 FR 9672, June 20, 1969; T.D. 7081, 35 FR 19996, Dec. 31, 1970; T.D. 7129, 36 FR 12736, July 7, 1971; T.D. 7154, 36 FR 24997, Dec. 28, 1971; 36 FR 13208, July 16, 1971; 36 FR 24997, Dec. 28, 1971; T.D. 7213, 37 FR 21992, Oct. 18, 1972; T.D. 7568, 43 FR 47505, Oct. 16, 1978; T.D. 7728, 45 FR 72650, Nov. 3, 1980]

§ 1.1012–2 Transfers in part a sale and in part a gift.

For rules relating to basis of property acquired in a transfer which is in part a gift and in part a sale, see § 1.170A–4(c), § 1.1011–2(b), and § 1.105–4.

[T.D. 6500, 25 FR 11910, Nov. 26, 1960, as amended by T.D. 7207, 37 FR 20799, Oct. 5, 1972]

§ 1.1013–1 Property included in inventory.

The basis of property required to be included in inventory is the last inventory value of such property in the hands of the taxpayer. The requirements with respect to the valuation of an inventory are stated in subpart D (section 471 and following), part II, subchapter E, chapter 1 of the Code, and the regulations thereunder.

[T.D. 6500, 25 FR 11910, Nov. 26, 1960]

§ 1.1014–1 Basis of property acquired from a decedent.

(a) General rule. The purpose of section 1014 is, in general, to provide a basis for property acquired from a decedent which is equal to the value placed upon such property for purposes of the Federal estate tax. Accordingly, the general rule is that the basis of property acquired from a decedent is the fair market value of such property at the date of the decedent's death, or, if the decedent's executor so elects, at the alternate valuation date prescribed in section 2032, or in section 811(j) of the Internal Revenue Code of 1939. Property acquired from a decedent includes, principally, property acquired by bequest, devise, or inheritance, and, in the case of decedents dying after December 31, 1953, property required to be included in determining the value of the decedent's gross estate under any provision of the Internal Revenue

Code of 1954 or the Internal Revenue Code of 1939. The general rule governing basis of property acquired from a decedent, as well as other rules prescribed elsewhere in this section, shall have no application if the property is sold, exchanged, or otherwise disposed of before the decedent's death by the person who acquired the property from the decedent. * * *

* * *

[T.D. 6500, 25 FR 11910, Nov. 26, 1960, as amended by T.D. 6527, 26 FR 413, Jan. 19, 1961; T.D. 6887, 31 FR 8812, June 24, 1966; T.D. 7283, 38 FR 20825, Aug. 3, 1973]

§ 1.1014–2 Property acquired from a decedent.

(a) In general. The following property, except where otherwise indicated, is considered to have been acquired from a decedent and the basis thereof is determined in accordance with the general rule in § 1.1014–1:

(1) Without regard to the date of the decedent's death, property acquired by bequest, devise, or inheritance, or by the decedent's estate from the decedent, whether the property was acquired under the decedent's will or under the law governing the descent and distribution of the property of decedents. However, see paragraph (c)(1) of this section if the property was acquired by bequest or inheritance from a decedent dying after August 26, 1937, and if such property consists of stock or securities of a foreign personal holding company.

(2) Without regard to the date of the decedent's death, property transferred by the decedent during his lifetime in trust to pay the income for life to or on the order or direction of the decedent, with the right reserved to the decedent at all times before his death to revoke the trust.

(3) In the case of decedents dying after December 31, 1951, property transferred by the decedent during his lifetime in trust to pay the income for life to or on the order or direction of the decedent with the right reserved to the decedent at all times before his death to make any change in the enjoyment thereof through the exercise of a power to alter, amend, or terminate the trust.

(4) Without regard to the date of the decedent's death, property passing without full and adequate consideration under a general power of appointment exercised by the decedent by will. (See sec-

tion 2041(b) for definition of general power of appointment.)

(5) In the case of decedents dying after December 31, 1947, property which represents the surviving spouse's one-half share of community property held by the decedent and the surviving spouse under the community property laws of any State, Territory, or possession of the United States or any foreign country, if at least one-half of the whole of the community interest in that property was includible in determining the value of the decedent's gross estate under part III, chapter 11 of the Internal Revenue Code of 1954 (relating to the estate tax) or section 811 of the Internal Revenue Code of 1939. It is not necessary for the application of this subparagraph that an estate tax return be required to be filed for the estate of the decedent or that an estate tax be payable.

* * *

(b) Property acquired from a decedent dying after December 31, 1953—(1) In general. In addition to the property described in paragraph (a) of this section, and except as otherwise provided in subparagraph (3) of this paragraph, in the case of a decedent dying after December 31, 1953, property shall also be considered to have been acquired from the decedent to the extent that both of the following conditions are met: (i) The property was acquired from the decedent by reason of death, form of ownership, or other conditions (including property acquired through the exercise or non-exercise of a power of appointment), and (ii) the property is includible in the decedent's gross estate under the provisions of the Internal Revenue Code of 1954, or the Internal Revenue Code of 1939, because of such acquisition. The basis of such property in the hands of the person who acquired it from the decedent shall be determined in accordance with the general rule in § 1.1014–1. See, however, § 1.1014–6 for special adjustments if such property is acquired before the death of the decedent. See also subparagraph (3) of this paragraph for a description of property not within the scope of this paragraph.

(2) Rules for the application of subparagraph (1) of this paragraph. Except as provided in subparagraph (3) of this paragraph, this paragraph generally includes all property acquired from a decedent, which is includible in the gross estate of the decedent if the decedent died after December 31, 1953. It is not necessary for the application of this paragraph that an estate tax

return be required to be filed for the estate of the decedent or that an estate tax be payable. Property acquired prior to the death of a decedent which is includible in the decedent's gross estate, such as property transferred by a decedent in contemplation of death, and property held by a taxpayer and the decedent as joint tenants or as tenants by the entireties is within the scope of this paragraph. Also, this paragraph includes property acquired through the exercise or nonexercise of a power of appointment where such property is includible in the decedent's gross estate. It does not include property not includible in the decedent's gross estate such as property not situated in the United States acquired from a nonresident who is not a citizen of the United States.

(3) **Exceptions to application of this paragraph.** The rules in this paragraph are not applicable to the following property:

(i) Annuities described in section 72;

(ii) Stock or securities of a foreign personal holding company as described in section 1014(b)(5) (see paragraph (c)(1) of this section);

(iii) Property described in any paragraph other than paragraph (9) of section 1014(b). See paragraphs (a) and (c) of this section.

In illustration of subdivision (ii), assume that A acquired by gift stock of a character described in paragraph (c)(1) of this section from a donor and upon the death of the donor the stock was includible in the donor's estate as being a gift in contemplation of death. A's basis in the stock would not be determined by reference to its fair market value at the donor's death under the general rule in section 1014(a). Furthermore, the special basis rules prescribed in paragraph (c)(1) of this section are not applicable to such property acquired by gift in contemplation of death. It will be necessary to refer to the rules in section 1015(a) to determine the basis.

* * *

[T.D. 6500, 25 FR 11910, Nov. 26, 1960]

§ 1.1014-3 **Other basis rules.**

(a) **Fair market value.** For purposes of this section and § 1.1014-1, the value of property as of the date of the decedent's death as appraised for the purpose of the Federal estate tax or the alternate value as appraised for such purpose, whichever is applicable, shall be deemed to be its fair market value. If no estate tax return is required to be filed under section 6018 (or under section 821 or 864 of the Internal Revenue Code of 1939), the value of the property appraised as of the date of the decedent's death for the purpose of State inheritance or transmission taxes shall be deemed to be its fair market value and no alternate valuation date shall be applicable.

* * *

(c) **Reinvestments by a fiduciary.** The basis of property acquired after the death of the decedent by a fiduciary as an investment is the cost or other basis of such property to the fiduciary, and not the fair market value of such property at the death of the decedent. For example, the executor of an estate purchases stock of X company at a price of $100 per share with the proceeds of the sale of property acquired from a decedent. At the date of the decedent's death the fair market value of such stock was $98 per share. The basis of such stock to the executor or to a legatee, assuming the stock is distributed, is $100 per share.

(d) **Reinvestments of property transferred during life.** Where property is transferred by a decedent during life and the property is sold, exchanged, or otherwise disposed of before the decedent's death by the person who acquired the property from the decedent, the general rule stated in paragraph (a) of § 1.1014-1 shall not apply to such property. However, in such a case, the basis of any property acquired by such donee in exchange for the original property, or of any property acquired by the donee through reinvesting the proceeds of the sale of the original property, shall be the fair market value of the property thus acquired at the date of the decedent's death (or applicable alternate valuation date) if the property thus acquired is properly included in the decedent's gross estate for Federal estate tax purposes. These rules also apply to property acquired by the donee in any further exchanges or in further reinvestments. For example, on January 1, 1956, the decedent made a gift of real property to a trust for the benefit of his children, reserving to himself the power to revoke the trust at will. Prior to the decedent's death, the trustee sold the real property and invested the proceeds in stock of the Y Company at $50 per share. At the time of the decedent's death, the value of such stock was $75 per share. The corpus of the trust was required to be included in the decedent's gross estate owing to his reservation of the power of revocation. The basis of the Y company stock following the decedent's death is

$75 per share. Moreover, if the trustee sold the Y Company stock before the decedent's death for $65 a share and reinvested the proceeds in Z company stock which increased in value to $85 per share at the time of the decedent's death, the basis of the Z company stock following the decedent's death would be $85 per share.

* * *

[T.D. 6500, 25 FR 11910, Nov. 26, 1960]

§ 1.1014–4 Uniformity of basis; adjustment to basis.

(a) **In general.** (1) The basis of property acquired from a decedent, as determined under section 1014(a), is uniform in the hands of every person having possession or enjoyment of the property at any time under the will or other instrument or under the laws of descent and distribution. The principle of uniform basis means that the basis of the property (to which proper adjustments must, of course, be made) will be the same, or uniform, whether the property is possessed or enjoyed by the executor or administrator, the heir, the legatee or devisee, or the trustee or beneficiary of a trust created by a will or an inter vivos trust. In determining the amount allowed or allowable to a taxpayer in computing taxable income as deductions for depreciation or depletion under section 1016(a)(2), the uniform basis of the property shall at all times be used and adjusted. The sale, exchange, or other disposition by a life tenant or remainderman of his interest in property will, for purposes of this section, have no effect upon the uniform basis of the property in the hands of those who acquired it from the decedent. Thus, gain or loss on sale of trust assets by the trustee will be determined without regard to the prior sale of any interest in the property. Moreover, any adjustment for depreciation shall be made to the uniform basis of the property without regard to such prior sale, exchange, or other disposition.

(2) Under the law governing wills and the distribution of the property of decedents, all titles to property acquired by bequest, devise, or inheritance relate back to the death of the decedent, even though the interest of the person taking the title was, at the date of death of the decedent, legal, equitable, vested, contingent, general, specific, residual, conditional, executory, or otherwise. Accordingly, there is a common acquisition date for all titles to property acquired from a decedent within the meaning of section 1014, and, for this reason, a common or uniform basis for all such interests. For example, if distribution of personal property left by a decedent is not made until one year after his death, the basis of such property in the hands of the legatee is its fair market value at the time when the decedent died, and not when the legatee actually received the property. If the bequest is of the residue to trustees in trust, and the executors do not distribute the residue to such trustees until five years after the death of the decedent, the basis of each piece of property left by the decedent and thus received, in the hands of the trustees, is its fair market value at the time when the decedent dies. If the bequest is to trustees in trust to pay to A during his lifetime the income of the property bequeathed, and after his death to distribute such property to the survivors of a class, and upon A's death the property is distributed to the taxpayer as the sole survivor, the basis of such property, in the hands of the taxpayer, is its fair market value at the time when the decedent died. The purpose of the Code in prescribing a general uniform basis rule for property acquired from a decedent is, on the one hand, to tax the gain, in respect of such property, to him who realizes it (without regard to the circumstances that at the death of the decedent it may have been quite uncertain whether the taxpayer would take or gain anything); and, on the other hand, not to recognize as gain any element of value resulting solely from the circumstance that the possession or enjoyment of the taxpayer was postponed. Such postponement may be, for example, until the administration of the decedent's estate is completed, until the period of the possession or enjoyment of another has terminated, or until an uncertain event has happened. It is the increase or decrease in the value of property reflected in a sale or other disposition which is recognized as the measure of gain or loss.

(3) The principles stated in subparagraphs (1) and (2) of this paragraph do not apply to property transferred by an executor, administrator or trustee, to an heir, legatee, devisee or beneficiary under circumstances such that the transfer constitutes a sale or exchange. In such a case, gain or loss must be recognized by the transferor to the extent required by the revenue laws, and the transferee acquires a basis equal to the fair market value of the property on the date of the transfer. Thus, for example, if the trustee of a trust created by will transfers to a beneficiary, in satisfaction of a specific bequest of $10,000, securities which had a fair market value of $9,000 on the date of the dece-

dent's death (the applicable valuation date) and $10,000 on the date of the transfer, the trust realizes a taxable gain of $1,000 and the basis of the securities in the hands of the beneficiary would be $10,000. As a further example, if the executor of an estate transfers to a trust property worth $200,-000, which had a fair market value of $175,000 on the date of the decedent's death (the applicable valuation date), in satisfaction of the decedent's bequest in trust for the benefit of his wife of cash or securities to be selected by the executor in an amount sufficient to utilize the marital deduction to the maximum extent authorized by law (after taking into consideration any other property qualifying for the marital deduction), capital gain in the amount of $25,000 would be realized by the estate and the basis of the property in the hands of the trustees would be $200,000. If, on the other hand, the decedent bequeathed a fraction of his residuary estate to a trust for the benefit of his wife, which fraction will not change regardless of any fluctuations in value of property in the decedent's estate after his death, no gain or loss would be realized by the estate upon transfer of property to the trust, and the basis of the property in the hands of the trustee would be its fair market value on the date of the decedent's death or on the alternate valuation date.

(b) **Multiple interests.** Where more than one person has an interest in property acquired from a decedent, the basis of such property shall be determined and adjusted without regard to the multiple interests. The basis of computing gain or loss on the sale of any one of such multiple interests shall be determined under § 1.1014–5. Thus, the deductions for depreciation and for depletion allowed or allowable, under sections 167 and 611, to a legal life tenant as if the life tenant were the absolute owner of the property, constitute an adjustment to the basis of the property not only in the hands of the life tenant, but also in the hands of the remainderman and every other person to whom the same uniform basis is applicable. Similarly, the deductions allowed or allowable under sections 167 and 611, both to the trustee and to the trust beneficiaries, constitute an adjustment to the basis of the property not only in the hands of the trustee, but also in the hands of the trust beneficiaries and every other person to whom the uniform basis is applicable. See, however, section 262. Similarly, adjustments in respect of capital expenditures or losses, tax-free distributions, or other distributions applicable in reduction of basis, or other items for which the basis is adjustable are made without

regard to which one of the persons to whom the same uniform basis is applicable makes the capital expenditures or sustains the capital losses, or to whom the tax-free or other distributions are made, or to whom the deductions are allowed or allowable. See § 1.1014–6 for adjustments in respect of property acquired from a decedent prior to his death.

(c) **Records.** The executor or other legal representative of the decedent, the fiduciary of a trust under a will, the life tenant and every other person to whom a uniform basis under this section is applicable, shall maintain records showing in detail all deductions, distributions, or other items for which adjustment to basis is required to be made by sections 1016 and 1017, and shall furnish to the district director such information with respect to those adjustments as he may require.

[T.D. 6500, 25 FR 11910, Nov. 26, 1960]

§ 1.1014–5 **Gain or loss.**

(a) **Sale or other disposition of a life interest, remainder interest, or other interest in property acquired from a decedent.** (1) Except as provided in paragraph (b) of this section with respect to the sale or other disposition after October 9, 1969, of a term interest in property, gain or loss from a sale or other disposition of a life interest, remainder interest, or other interest in property acquired from a decedent is determined by comparing the amount of the proceeds with the amount of that part of the adjusted uniform basis which is assignable to the interest so transferred. The adjusted uniform basis is the uniform basis of the entire property adjusted to the date of sale or other disposition of any such interest as required by sections 1016 and 1017. The uniform basis is the unadjusted basis of the entire property determined immediately after the decedent's death under the applicable sections of part II of subchapter O of chapter 1 of the Code.

(2) Except as provided in paragraph (b) of this section, the proper measure of gain or loss resulting from a sale or other disposition of an interest in property acquired from a decedent is so much of the increase or decrease in the value of the entire property as is reflected in such sale or other disposition. Hence, in ascertaining the basis of a life interest, remainder interest, or other interest which has been so transferred, the uniform basis rule contemplates that proper adjustments will be

made to reflect the change in relative value of the interests on account of the passage of time.

(3) The factors set forth in the tables contained in § 20.2031–7 or § 20.2031–10, whichever is applicable, of Part 20 of this chapter (Estate Tax Regulations) shall be used in the manner provided therein in determining the basis of the life interest, the remainder interest, or the term certain interest in the property on the date such interest is sold. The basis of the life interest, the remainder interest, or the term certain interest is computed by multiplying the uniform basis (adjusted to the time of the sale) by the appropriate factor. In the case of the sale of a life interest or a remainder interest, the factor used is the factor (adjusted where appropriate) which appears in the life interest or the remainder interest column of the table opposite the age (on the date of the sale) of the person at whose death the life interest will terminate. In the case of the sale of a term certain interest, the factor used is the factor (adjusted where appropriate) which appears in the term certain column of the table opposite the number of years remaining (on the date of sale) before the term certain interest will terminate.

(b) Sale or other disposition of certain term interests. In determining gain or loss from the sale or other disposition after October 9, 1969, of a term interest in property (as defined in paragraph (f)(2) of § 1.1001–1) the adjusted basis of which is determined pursuant, or by reference, to section 1014 (relating to the basis of property acquired from a decedent) or section 1015 (relating to the basis of property acquired by gift or by a transfer in trust), that part of the adjusted uniform basis assignable under the rules of paragraph (a) of this section to the interest sold or otherwise disposed of shall be disregarded to the extent and in the manner provided by section 1001(e) and paragraph (f) of § 1.1001–1.

* * *

[T.D. 6500, 25 FR 11910, Nov. 26, 1960, as amended by T.D. 7142, 36 FR 18951, Sept. 24, 1971]

§ 1.1014–6 Special rule for adjustments to basis where property is acquired from a decedent prior to his death.

(a) In general. (1) The basis of property described in section 1014(b)(9) which is acquired from a decedent prior to his death shall be adjusted for depreciation, obsolescence, amortization, and depletion allowed the taxpayer on such property for the

period prior to the decedent's death. Thus, in general, the adjusted basis of such property will be its fair market value at the decedent's death, or the applicable alternate valuation date, less the amount allowed (determined with regard to section 1016(a)(2)(B)) to the taxpayer as deductions for exhaustion, wear and tear, obsolescence, amortization, and depletion for the period held by the taxpayer prior to the decedent's death. The deduction allowed for a taxable year in which the decedent dies shall be an amount properly allocable to that part of the year prior to his death. For a discussion of the basis adjustment required by section 1014(b)(9) where property is held in trust, see paragraph (c) of this section.

* * *

[T.D. 6500, 25 FR 11910, Nov. 26, 1960, as amended by T.D. 6712, 29 FR 3656, March 24, 1964; T.D. 7142, 36 FR 18952, Sept. 24, 1971]

§ 1.1015–1 Basis of property acquired by gift after December 31, 1920.

(a) General rule. (1) In the case of property acquired by gift after December 31, 1920 (whether by a transfer in trust or otherwise), the basis of the property for the purpose of determining gain is the same as it would be in the hands of the donor or the last preceding owner by whom it was not acquired by gift. The same rule applies in determining loss unless the basis (adjusted for the period prior to the date of gift in accordance with sections 1016 and 1017) is greater than the fair market value of the property at the time of the gift. In such case, the basis for determining loss is the fair market value at the time of the gift.

(2) The provisions of subparagraph (1) of this paragraph may be illustrated by the following example.

Example. A acquires by gift income-producing property which has an adjusted basis of $100,000 at the date of gift. The fair market value of the property at the date of gift is $90,000. A later sells the property for $95,000. In such case there is neither gain nor loss. The basis for determining loss is $90,000; therefore, there is no loss. Furthermore, there is no gain, since the basis for determining gain is $100,000.

* * *

(b) Uniform basis; proportionate parts of. Property acquired by gift has a single or uniform basis although more than one person may acquire an interest in such property. The uniform basis of the property remains fixed subject to proper adjustment for items under sections 1016 and 1017. However, the value of the proportionate parts of the uniform basis represented, for instance, by the respective interests of the life tenant and remainderman are adjustable to reflect the change in the relative values of such interest on account of the lapse of time. The portion of the basis attributable to an interest at the time of its sale or other disposition shall be determined under the rules provided in § 1.1014–5. In determining gain or loss from the sale or other disposition after October 9, 1969, of a term interest in property (as defined in § 1.1001–1(f)(2)) the adjusted basis of which is determined pursuant, or by reference, to section 1015, that part of the adjusted uniform basis assignable under the rules of § 1.1014–5(a) to the interest sold or otherwise disposed of shall be disregarded to the extent and in the manner provided by section 1001(e) and § 1.1001–1(f).

(c) **Time of acquisition.** The date that the donee acquires an interest in property by gift is when the donor relinquishes dominion over the property and not necessarily when title to the property is acquired by the donee. Thus, the date that the donee acquires an interest in property by gift where he is a successor in interest, such as in the case of a remainderman of a life estate or a beneficiary of the distribution of the corpus of a trust, is the date such interests are created by the donor and not the date the property is actually acquired.

(d) **Property acquired by gift from a decedent dying after December 31, 1953.** If an interest in property was acquired by the taxpayer by gift from a donor dying after December 31, 1953, under conditions which required the inclusion of the property in the donor's gross estate for estate tax purposes, and the property had not been sold, exchanged, or otherwise disposed of by the taxpayer before the donor's death, see the rules prescribed in section 1014 and the regulations thereunder.

(e) **Fair market value.** For the purposes of this section, the value of property as appraised for the purpose of the Federal gift tax, or, if the gift is not subject to such tax, its value as appraised for the purpose of a State gift tax, shall be deemed to be the fair market value of the property at the time of the gift.

* * *

(g) **Records.** To insure a fair and adequate determination of the proper basis under section 1015, persons making or receiving gifts of property should preserve and keep accessible a record of the facts necessary to determine the cost of the property and, if pertinent, its fair market value as of March 1, 1913, or its fair market value as of the date of the gift.

[T.D. 6500, 25 FR 11910, Nov. 26, 1960, as amended by T.D. 6693, 28 FR 12818, Dec. 3, 1963; T.D. 7142, 36 FR 18952, Sept. 24, 1971]

§ 1.1015–4 Transfers in part a gift and in part a sale.

(a) **General rule.** Where a transfer of property is in part a sale and in part a gift, the unadjusted basis of the property in the hands of the transferee is the sum of—

(1) Whichever of the following is the greater:

(i) The amount paid by the transferee for the property, or

(ii) The transferor's adjusted basis for the property at the time of the transfer, and

(2) The amount of increase, if any, in basis authorized by section 1015(d) for gift tax paid (see § 1.1015–5).

For determining loss, the unadjusted basis of the property in the hands of the transferee shall not be greater than the fair market value of the property at the time of such transfer. For determination of gain or loss of the transferor, see § 1.1001–1(e) and § 1.1011–2. For special rule where there has been a charitable contribution of less than a taxpayer's entire interest in property, see section 170(e)(2) and § 1.170A–4(c).

(b) **Examples.** The rule of paragraph (a) of this section is illustrated by the following examples:

Example (1). If A transfers property to his son for $30,000, and such property at the time of the transfer has an adjusted basis of $30,000 in A's hands (and a fair market value of $60,000), the unadjusted basis of the property in the hands of the son is $30,000.

Example (2). If A transfers property to his son for $60,000, and such property at the time of transfer has an adjusted basis of $30,000 in A's hands (and a fair market value of $90,000), the unadjusted basis of such property in the hands of the son is $60,000.

Example (3). If A transfers property to his son for $30,000, and such property at the time of transfer has an adjusted basis in A's hands of $60,000 (and a fair market value of $90,000), the unadjusted basis of such property in the hands of the son is $60,000.

Example (4). If A transfers property to his son for $30,000 and such property at the time of transfer has an adjusted basis of $90,000 in A's hands (and a fair market value of $60,000), the unadjusted basis of the property in the hands of the son is $90,000. However, since the adjusted basis of the property in A's hands at the time of the transfer was greater than the fair market value at that time, for the purpose of determining any loss on a later sale or other disposition of the property by the son its unadjusted basis in his hands is $60,000.

[T.D. 6500, 25 FR 11910, Nov. 26, 1960, as amended by T.D. 6693, 28 FR 12818, Dec. 3, 1963; T.D. 7207, 37 FR 20799, Oct. 5, 1972]

§ 1.1015–5 Increased basis for gift tax paid.

(a) General rule. (1)(i) Subject to the conditions and limitations provided in section 1015(d), as added by the Technical Amendments Act of 1958, the basis (as determined under section 1015(a) and paragraph (a) of § 1.1015–1) of property acquired by gift is increased by the amount of gift tax paid with respect to the gift of such property. Under section 1015(d)(1)(A), such increase in basis applies to property acquired by gift on or after September 2, 1958 (the date of enactment of the Technical Amendments Act of 1958). Under section 1015(d)(1)(B), such increase in basis applies to property acquired by gift before September 2, 1958, and not sold, exchanged, or otherwise disposed of before such date. If section 1015(d)(1)(A) applies, the basis of the property is increased as of the date of the gift regardless of the date of payment of the gift tax. For example, if the property was acquired by gift on September 8, 1958, and sold by the donee on October 15, 1958, the basis of the property would be increased (subject to the limitation of section 1015(d)) as of September 8, 1958 (the date of the gift), by the amount of gift tax applicable to such gift even though such tax was not paid until March 1, 1959. If section 1015(d)(1)(B) applies, any increase in the basis of the property due to gift tax paid (regardless of date of payment) with respect to the gift is made as of September 2, 1958. Any increase in basis under section 1015(d) can be no greater than the amount by which the fair market value of the property at the time of the gift exceeds the basis of such property in the hands of the donor at the time of the gift. See paragraph (b) of this section for rules for determining the amount of gift tax paid in respect of property transferred by gift.

(ii) With respect to property acquired by gift before September 2, 1958, the provisions of section 1015(d) and this section do not apply if, before such date, the donee has sold, exchanged, or otherwise disposed of such property. The phrase "sold, ex-

changed, or otherwise disposed of" includes the surrender of a stock certificate for corporate assets in complete or partial liquidation of a corporation pursuant to section 331. It also includes the exchange of property for property of a like kind such as the exchange of one apartment house for another. The phrase does not, however, extend to transactions which are mere changes in form. Thus, it does not include a transfer of assets to a corporation in exchange for its stock in a transaction with respect to which no gain or loss would be recognizable for income tax purposes under section 351. Nor does it include an exchange of stock or securities in a corporation for stock or securities in the same corporation or another corporation in a transaction such as a merger, recapitalization, reorganization, or other transaction described in section 368(a) or 355, with respect to which no gain or loss is recognizable for income tax purposes under section 354 or 355. If a binding contract for the sale, exchange, or other disposition of property is entered into, the property is considered as sold, exchanged, or otherwise disposed of on the effective date of the contract, unless the contract is not subsequently carried out substantially in accordance with its terms. The effective date of a contract is normally the date it is entered into (and not the date it is consummated, or the date legal title to the property passes) unless the contract specifies a different effective date. For purposes of this subdivision, in determining whether a transaction comes within the phrase "sold, exchanged, or otherwise disposed of", if a transaction would be treated as a mere change in the form of the property if it occurred in a taxable year subject to the Internal Revenue Code of 1954, it will be so treated if the transaction occurred in a taxable year subject to the Internal Revenue Code of 1939 or prior revenue law.

(2) Application of the provisions of subparagraph (1) of this paragraph may be illustrated by the following examples:

Example (1). In 1938, A purchased a business building at a cost of $120,000. On September 2, 1958, at which time the property had an adjusted basis in A's hands of $60,000, he gave the property to his nephew, B. At the time of the gift to B, the property had a fair market value of $65,000 with respect to which A paid a gift tax in the amount of $7,545. The basis of the property in B's hands at the time of the gift, as determined under section 1015(a) and § 1.1015–1, would be the same as the adjusted basis in A's hands at the time of the gift, or $60,000. Under section 1015(d) and this section, the basis of the building in B's hands as of the date of the gift would be increased by the amount of the gift tax paid with respect to such gift, limited to an amount by which the fair market value of the property at the time of the gift exceeded the basis of the property in the hands of A at the time of gift, or $5,000. Therefore, the basis of the property in B's hands immediately after the gift, both for determining gain or loss on the sale of the property, would be $65,000.

Example (2). C purchased property in 1938 at a cost of $100,000. On October 1, 1952, at which time the property had an adjusted basis of $72,000 in C's hands, he gave the property to his daughter, D. At the date of the gift to D, the property had a fair market value of $85,000 with respect to which C paid a gift tax in the amount of $11,745. On September 2, 1958, D still held the property which then had an adjusted basis in her hands of $65,000. Since the excess of the fair market value of the property at the time of the gift to D over the adjusted basis of the property in C's hands at such time is greater than the amount of gift tax paid, the basis of the property in D's hands would be increased as of September 2, 1958, by the amount of the gift tax paid, or $11,745. The adjusted basis of the property in D's hands, both for determining gain or loss on the sale of the property, would then be $76,745 ($65,000 plus $11,745).

Example (3). On December 31, 1951, E gave to his son, F, 500 shares of common stock of the X Corporation which shares had been purchased earlier by E at a cost of $100 per share, or a total cost of $50,000. The basis in E's hands was still $50,000 on the date of the gift to F. On the date of the gift, the fair market value of the 500 shares was $80,000 with respect to which E paid a gift tax in the amount of $10,695. In 1956, the 500 shares of X Corporation stock were exchanged for 500 shares of common stock of the Y Corporation in a reorganization with respect to which no gain or loss was recognized for income tax purposes under section 354. F still held the 500 shares of Y Corporation stock on September 2, 1958. Under such circumstances, the 500 shares of X Corporation stock would not, for purposes of section 1015(d) and this section, be considered as having been "sold, exchanged, or otherwise disposed of" by F before September 2, 1958. Therefore, the basis of the 500 shares of Y Corporation stock held by F as of such date would, by reason of section 1015(d) and this section, be increased by $10,695, the amount of gift tax paid with respect to the gift to F of the X Corporation stock.

Example (4). On November 15, 1953, G gave H property which had a fair market value of $53,000 and a basis in the hands of G of $20,000. G paid gift tax of $5,250 on the transfer. On November 16, 1956, H gave the property to J who still held it on September 2, 1958. The value of the property on the date of the gift to J was $63,000 and H paid gift tax of $7,125 on the transfer. Since the property was not sold, exchanged, or otherwise disposed of by J before September 2, 1958, and the gift tax paid on the transfer to J did not exceed $43,000 ($63,000, fair market value of property at time of gift to J, less $20,000, basis of property in H's hands at that time), the basis of property in his hands is increased on September 2, 1958, by $7,125, the amount of gift tax paid by H on the transfer. No increase in basis is allowed for the $5,250 gift tax paid by G on the transfer to H, since H had sold, exchanged, or otherwise disposed of the property before September 2, 1958.

[T.D. 6693, 28 FR 12818, Dec. 3, 1963, as amended by T.D. 7238, 37 FR 28715, Dec. 29, 1972; T.D. 7910, 48 FR 40372, Sept. 7, 1983]

* * *

§ 1.1016–2 Items properly chargeable to capital account.

(a) The cost or other basis shall be properly adjusted for any expenditure, receipt, loss, or other item, properly chargeable to capital account, including the cost of improvements and betterments made to the property. No adjustment shall be made in respect of any item which, under any applicable provision of law or regulation, is treated as an item not properly chargeable to capital account but is allowable as a deduction in computing net or taxable income for the taxable year. For example, in the case of oil and gas wells no adjustment may be made in respect of any intangible drilling and development expense allowable as a deduction in computing net or taxable income. See the regulations under section 263(c).

(b) The application of the foregoing provisions may be illustrated by the following example:

Example. A, who makes his returns on the calendar year basis, purchased property in 1941 for $10,000. He subsequently expended $6,000 for improvements. Disregarding, for the purpose of this example, the adjustments required for depreciation, the adjusted basis of the property is $16,000. If A sells the property in 1954 for $20,000, the amount of his gain will be $4,000.

* * *

[T.D. 6500, 25 FR 11910, Nov. 26, 1960]

§ 1.1016–3 Exhaustion, wear and tear, obsolescence, amortization, and depletion for periods since February 28, 1913.

(a) **In general—(1) Adjustment where deduction is claimed.** (i) For taxable periods beginning on or after January 1, 1952, the cost or other basis of property shall be decreased for exhaustion, wear and tear, obsolescence, amortization, and depletion by the greater of the following two amounts: (a) the amount allowed as deductions in computing taxable income, to the extent resulting in a reduction of the taxpayer's income taxes, or (b) the amount allowable for the years involved. See paragraph (b) of this section. Where the taxpayer makes an appropriate election the above rule is applicable for periods since February 28, 1913, and before January 1, 1952. See paragraph (d) of this section. For rule for such periods where no election is made, see paragraph (c) of this section.

(ii) The determination of the amount properly allowable for exhaustion, wear and tear, obsolescence, amortization, and depletion shall be made on the basis of facts reasonably known to exist at the end of the taxable year. A taxpayer is not permitted to take advantage in a later year of his prior failure to take any such allowance or his taking an allowance plainly inadequate under the known facts in prior years. In the case of depreciation, if in prior years the taxpayer has consistently taken proper deductions under one method, the amount allowable for such prior years shall not be increased even though a greater amount would have been allowable under another proper method. For rules governing losses on retirement of depreciable property, including rules for determining basis, see § 1.167(a)–8. This subdivision may be illustrated by the following example:

Example. An asset was purchased January 1, 1950, at a cost of $10,000. The useful life of the asset is 10 years. It has no salvage value. Depreciation was deducted and allowed for 1950 to 1954 as follows:

1950	$500
1951	.....
1952	1,000
1953	1,000
1954	1,000
Total amount allowed	3,500

The correct reserve as of December 31, 1954, is computed as follows:

Dec. 31:

1950 ($10,000 ÷ 10)	$1,000
1951 ($9,000 ÷ 9)	1,000
1952 ($8,000 ÷ 8)	1,000
1953 ($7,000 ÷ 7)	1,000
1954 ($6,000 ÷ 6)	1,000
Reserve Dec. 31, 1954	5,000

Depreciation for 1955 is computed as follows:

Cost	10,000
Reserve as of December 31, 1954	5,000
Unrecovered cost	5,000
Depreciation allowable for 1955 ($5,000 ÷ 5)	1,000

(2) Adjustment for amount allowable where no depreciation deduction claimed. (i) If the taxpayer has not taken a depreciation deduction either in the taxable year or for any prior taxable year, adjustments to basis of the property for depreciation allowable shall be determined by using the straight-line method of depreciation. (See § 1.1016–4 for adjustments in the case of persons exempt from income taxation.)

(ii) For taxable years beginning after December 31, 1953, and ending after August 16, 1954, if the

taxpayer with respect to any property has taken a deduction for depreciation properly under one of the methods provided in section 167(b) for one or more years but has omitted the deduction in other years, the adjustment to basis for the depreciation allowable in such a case will be the deduction under the method which was used by the taxpayer with respect to that property. Thus, if A acquired property in 1954 on which he properly computed his depreciation deduction under the method described in section 167(b)(2) (the declining-balance method) for the first year of its useful life but did not take a deduction in the second and third year of the asset's life, the adjustment to basis for depreciation allowable for the second and third year will be likewise computed under the declining-balance method.

* * *

(b) Adjustment for periods beginning on or after January 1, 1952. The decrease required by paragraph (a) of this section for deductions in respect of any period beginning on or after January 1, 1952, shall be whichever is the greater of the following amounts:

(1) The amount allowed as deductions in computing taxable income under subtitle A of the Code or prior income tax laws and resulting (by reason of the deductions so allowed) in a reduction for any taxable year of the taxpayer's taxes under subtitle A of the Code (other than chapter 2, relating to tax on self-employment income) or prior income, war-profits, or excess-profits tax laws; or

(2) The amount properly allowable as deductions in computing taxable income under subtitle A of the Code or prior income tax laws (whether or not the amount properly allowable would have caused a reduction for any taxable year of the taxpayer's taxes).

* * *

[T.D. 6500, 25 FR 11910, Nov. 26, 1960]

§ 1.1017–1 Adjusted basis; discharge of indebtedness; general rule.

(a) In addition to the adjustments provided in section 1016 and the regulations thereunder which are required to be made with respect to the cost or other basis of property, and except as otherwise provided in section 372(a), 373(b)(2), or 1018, a further adjustment shall be made in any case in which there shall have been an exclusion from gross income under section 108(a) on account of a discharge of indebtedness during the taxable year. Such further adjustments shall, except as otherwise provided in § 1.1017-2, be made in the following manner and order (but in the case of an individual, subparagraphs (1) to (4), inclusive, of this paragraph, shall apply only to property used in any trade or business of such individual):

(1) In the case of indebtedness incurred to purchase specific property (other than inventory or notes or accounts receivable), whether or not a lien is placed against such property securing the payment of all or part of such indebtedness, which indebtedness shall have been discharged, the cost or other basis of such property shall be decreased by an amount equal to the amount excluded from gross income under section 108(a) and attributable to the discharge of the indebtedness so incurred with respect to such property;

(2) In the case of specific property (other than inventory or notes or accounts receivable) against which, at the time of the discharge of the indebtedness, there is a lien (other than a lien securing indebtedness incurred to purchase such property), the cost or other basis of such property shall be decreased by an amount equal to the amount excluded from gross income under section 108(a) and attributable to the discharge of the indebtedness secured by such lien;

(3) Any excess of the total amount excluded from gross income under section 108(a) over the sum of the adjustments made under subparagraphs (1) and (2) of this paragraph shall next be applied to reduce the cost or other basis of all the property of the debtor (other than inventory and notes and accounts receivable) as follows: The cost or other basis of each unit of property shall be decreased in an amount equal to such proportion of such excess as the adjusted basis (without reference to this section) of each such unit of property bears to the sum of adjusted bases (without reference to this section) of all the property of the debtor other than inventory and notes and accounts receivable;

(4) Any excess of the total amount excluded from gross income under section 108(a) over the sum of the adjustments made under subparagraphs

(1), (2), and (3) of this paragraph shall next be applied to reduce the cost or other basis of inventory and notes and accounts receivable, as follows: The cost or other basis of inventory or notes or accounts receivable, as the case may be, shall be decreased in an amount equal to such proportion of such excess as the adjusted basis of inventory, notes receivable or accounts receivable, as the case may be, bears to the sum of the adjusted bases of such inventory and notes and accounts receivable;

(5) In the case of an individual, any excess of the total amount excluded from gross income under section 108(a) over the sum of the adjustments made under subparagraphs (1), (2), (3), and (4) of this paragraph shall next be applied to reduce the cost or other basis of his property held for the production of income, as follows: The cost or other basis of each unit of such property shall be decreased in an amount equal to such proportion of such excess as the adjusted basis (without reference to this section) of each such unit of property bears to the sum of the adjusted bases (without reference to this section) of all of such property of the debtor; and

(6) In the case of an individual, any excess of the total amount excluded from gross income under section 108(a) over the sum of the adjustments made under subparagraphs (1), (2), (3), (4), and (5) of this paragraph shall next be applied to reduce the cost or other basis of his property other than property used in any trade or business and property held for the production of income, as follows: The cost or other basis of each unit of such property shall be decreased in an amount equal to such proportion of such excess as the adjusted basis (without reference to this section) of each such unit of property bears to the sum of the adjusted bases (without reference to this section) of all of such property of the debtor.

In the application of subparagraphs (1), (2), (3), (4), (5) and (6) of this paragraph, no decrease in the cost or other basis of any property shall exceed the amount of adjusted basis of such property without reference to this section.

* * *

[T.D. 6500, 25 FR 11910, Nov. 26, 1960]

Common Nontaxable Exchanges

§ 1.1031(a)–1 Property held for productive use in trade or business or for investment.

(a) Section 1031(a) provides an exception from the general rule requiring the recognition of gain or loss upon the sale or exchange of property. * * Under section 1031(a), no gain or loss is recognized if property held for productive use in trade or business or for investment is exchanged solely for property of a like kind to be held either for productive use in trade or business or for investment. Under section 1031(a), property held for productive use in trade or business may be exchanged for property held for investment. Similarly, property held for investment may be exchanged for property held for productive use in trade or business. However, section 1031(a) provides that property held for productive use in trade or business or for investment does not include stock in trade or other property held primarily for sale, nor stocks, bonds, notes, choses in action, certificates of trust or beneficial interest, or other securities or evidences of indebtedness or interest. A transfer is not within the provisions of section 1031(a) if as part of the consideration the taxpayer receives money or property which does not meet the requirements of section 1031(a), but the transfer, if otherwise qualified, will be within the provisions of section 1031(b). Similarly, a transfer is not within the provisions of section 1031(a) if as part of the consideration the other party to the exchange assumes a liability of the taxpayer (or acquires property from the taxpayer that is subject to a liability), but the transfer, if otherwise qualified, will be within the provisions of section 1031(b). A transfer of property meeting the requirements of section 1031(a) may be within the provisions of section 1031(a) even though the taxpayer transfers in addition property not meeting the requirements of section 1031(a) or money. However, the nonrecognition treatment provided by section 1031(a) does not apply to the property transferred which does not meet the requirements of section 1031(a).

(b) As used in section 1031(a), the words "like kind" have reference to the nature or character of the property and not to its grade or quality. One kind or class of property may not, under that section, be exchanged for property of a different kind or class. The fact that any real estate involved is improved or unimproved is not material, for that fact relates only to the grade or quality of the property and not to its kind or class. Unpro-

ductive real estate held by one other than a dealer for future use or future realization of the increment in value is held for investment and not primarily for sale.

(c) No gain or loss is recognized if (1) a taxpayer exchanges property held for productive use in his trade or business, together with cash, for other property of like kind for the same use, such as a truck for a new truck or a passenger automobile for a new passenger automobile to be used for a like purpose; or (2) a taxpayer who is not a dealer in real estate exchanges city real estate for a ranch or farm, or exchanges a leasehold of a fee with 30 years or more to run for real estate, or exchanges improved real estate for unimproved real estate; or (3) a taxpayer exchanges investment property and cash for investment property of a like kind.

(d) Gain or loss is recognized if, for instance, a taxpayer exchanges (1) Treasury bonds maturing March 15, 1958, for Treasury bonds maturing December 15, 1968, unless section 1037(a)(or so much of section 1031 as relates to section 1037(a)) applies to such exchange, or (2) a real estate mortgage for consolidated farm loan bonds.

[T.D. 6500, 25 FR 11910, Nov. 26, 1960, as amended by T.D. 6935, 32 FR 15822, Nov. 17, 1967]

§ 1.1031(b)–1 Receipt of other property or money in tax-free exchange.

(a) If the taxpayer receives other property (in addition to property permitted to be received without recognition of gain) or money—

(1) In an exchange described in section 1031(a) of property held for investment or productive use in trade or business for property of like kind to be held either for productive use or for investment,

(2) In an exchange described in section 1035(a) of insurance policies or annuity contracts,

(3) In an exchange described in section 1036(a) of common stock for common stock, or preferred stock for preferred stock, in the same corporation and not in connection with a corporate reorganization, or

(4) In an exchange described in section 1037(a) of obligations of the United States, issued under the

Second Liberty Bond Act (31 U.S.C. 774(2)), solely for other obligations issued under such Act, the gain, if any, to the taxpayer will be recognized under section 1031(b) in an amount not in excess of the sum of the money and the fair market value of the other property, but the loss, if any, to the taxpayer from such an exchange will not be recognized under section 1031(c) to any extent.

(b) The application of this section may be illustrated by the following examples:

Example (1). A, who is not a dealer in real estate, in 1954 exchanges real estate held for investment, which he purchased in 1940 for $5,000, for other real estate (to be held for productive use in trade or business) which has a fair market value of $6,000, and $2,000 in cash. The gain from the transaction is $3,000, but is recognized only to the extent of the cash received of $2,000.

* * *

(c) Consideration received in the form of an assumption of liabilities (or a transfer subject to a liability) is to be treated as "other property or money" for the purposes of section 1031(b). Where, on an exchange described in section 1031(b), each party to the exchange either assumes a liability of the other party or acquires property subject to a liability, then, in determining the amount of "other property or money" for purposes of section 1031(b), consideration given in the form of an assumption of liabilities (or a receipt of property subject to a liability) shall be offset against consideration received in the form of an assumption of liabilities (or a transfer subject to a liability). See § 1.1031(d)–2, examples (1) and (2).

[T.D. 6500, 25 FR 11910, Nov. 26, 1960, as amended by T.D. 6935, 32 FR 15822, Nov. 17, 1967]

§ 1.1031(c)–1 Nonrecognition of loss.

Section 1031(c) provides that a loss shall not be recognized from an exchange of property described in section 1031(a), 1035(a), 1036(a), or 1037(a) where there is received in the exchange other property or money in addition to property permitted to be received without recognition of gain or loss. See example (4) of paragraph (a)(3) of § 1.1037–1 for an illustration of the application of this section in the case of an exchange of U.S. obligations described in section 1037(a).

[T.D. 6500, 25 FR 11910, Nov. 26, 1960, as amended by T.D. 6935, 32 FR 15822, Nov. 17, 1967]

§ 1.1031(d)–1 Property acquired upon a tax-free exchange.

(a) If, in an exchange of property solely of the type described in section 1031, section 1035(a), section 1036(a), or section 1037(a), no part of the gain or loss was recognized under the law applicable to the year in which the exchange was made, the basis of the property acquired is the same as the basis of the property transferred by the taxpayer with proper adjustments to the date of the exchange. If additional consideration is given by the taxpayer in the exchange, the basis of the property acquired shall be the same as the property transferred increased by the amount of additional consideration given (see section 1016 and the regulations thereunder).

(b) If, in an exchange of properties of the type indicated in section 1031, section 1035(a), section 1036(a), or section 1037(a), gain to the taxpayer was recognized under the provisions of section 1031(b) or a similar provision of a prior revenue law, on account of the receipt of money in the transaction, the basis of the property acquired is the basis of the property transferred (adjusted to the date of the exchange), decreased by the amount of money received and increased by the amount of gain recognized on the exchange. The application of this paragraph may be illustrated by the following example:

Example. A, an individual in the moving and storage business, in 1954 transfers one of his moving trucks with an adjusted basis in his hands of $2,500 to B in exchange for a truck (to be used in A's business) with a fair market value of $2,400 and $200 in cash. A realizes a gain of $100 upon the exchange, all of which is recognized under section 1031(b). The basis of the truck acquired by A is determined as follows:

Adjusted basis of A's former truck	$2,500
Less: Amount of money received	200
Difference	2,300
Plus: Amount of gain recognized	100
Basis of truck acquired by A	2,400

(c) If, upon an exchange of properties of the type described in section 1031, section 1035(a), section 1036(a), or section 1037(a), the taxpayer received other property (not permitted to be received without the recognition of gain) and gain from the transaction was recognized as required under section 1031(b), or a similar provision of a prior revenue law, the basis (adjusted to the date of the exchange) of the property transferred by the taxpayer, decreased by the amount of any money received and increased by the amount of gain recognized, must be allocated to and is the basis of the properties (other than money) received on the exchange. For the purpose of the allocation of the basis of the properties received, there must be assigned to such other property an amount equivalent to its fair market value at the date of the exchange. The application of this paragraph may be illustrated by the following example:

Example. A, who is not a dealer in real estate, in 1954 transfers real estate held for investment which he purchased in 1940 for $10,000 in exchange for other real estate (to be held for investment) which has a fair market value of $9,000, an automobile which has a fair market value of $2,000, and $1,500 in cash. A realizes a gain of $2,500, all of which is recognized under section 1031(b). The basis of the property received in exchange is the basis of the real estate A transfers ($10,000) decreased by the amount of money received ($1,500) and increased in the amount of gain that was recognized ($2,500), which results in a basis for the property received of $11,000. This basis of $11,000 is allocated between the automobile and the real estate received by A, the basis of the automobile being its fair market value at the date of the exchange, $2,000, and the basis of the real estate received being the remainder, $9,000.

(d) Section 1031(c) and, with respect to section 1031 and section 1036(a), similar provisions of prior revenue laws provide that no loss may be recognized on an exchange of properties of a type described in section 1031, section 1035(a), section 1036(a), or section 1037(a), although the taxpayer receives other property or money from the transaction. However, the basis of the property or properties (other than money) received by the taxpayer is the basis (adjusted to the date of the exchange) of the property transferred, decreased by the amount of money received. This basis must be allocated to the properties received, and for this purpose there must be allocated to such other property an amount of such basis equivalent to its fair market value at the date of the exchange.

(e) If, upon an exchange of properties of the type described in section 1031, section 1035(a), section 1036(a), or section 1037(a), the taxpayer also exchanged other property (not permitted to be transferred without the recognition of gain or loss) and gain or loss from the transaction is recognized under section 1002 or a similar provision of a prior revenue law, the basis of the property acquired is the total basis of the properties transferred (adjusted to the date of the exchange) increased by the amount of gain and decreased by the amount of loss recognized on the other property. For purposes of this rule, the taxpayer is deemed to have received in exchange for such other property an amount equal to its fair market value on the date

of the exchange. The application of this paragraph may be illustrated by the following example:

Example. A exchanges real estate held for investment plus stock for real estate to be held for investment. The real estate transferred has an adjusted basis of $10,000 and a fair market value of $11,000. The stock transferred has an adjusted basis of $4,000 and a fair market value of $2,000. The real estate acquired has a fair market value of $13,000. A is deemed to have received a $2,000 portion of the acquired real estate in exchange for the stock, since $2,000 is the fair market value of the stock at the time of the exchange. A $2,000 loss is recognized under section 1002 on the exchange of the stock for real estate. No gain or loss is recognized on the exchange of the real estate since the property received is of the type permitted to be received without recognition of gain or loss. The basis of the real estate acquired by A is determined as follows:

Adjusted basis of real estate transferred	$10,000
Adjusted basis of stock transferred	4,000
	14,000
Less: Loss recognized on transfer of stock ...	2,000
Basis of real estate acquired upon the exchange	12,000

[T.D. 6500, 25 FR 11910, Nov. 16, 1960, as amended by T.D. 6935, 32 FR 15823, Nov. 17, 1967]

§ 1.1031(d)–2   Treatment of assumption of liabilities.

For the purposes of section 1031(d), the amount of any liabilities of the taxpayer assumed by the other party to the exchange (or of any liabilities to which the property exchanged by the taxpayer is subject) is to be treated as money received by the taxpayer upon the exchange, whether or not the assumption resulted in a recognition of gain or loss to the taxpayer under the law applicable to the year in which the exchange was made. The application of this section may be illustrated by the following examples:

Example (1). B, an individual, owns an apartment house which has an adjusted basis in his hands of $500,000, but which is subject to a mortgage of $150,000. On September 1, 1954, he transfers the apartment house to C, receiving in exchange therefor $50,000 in cash and another apartment house with a fair market value on that date of $600,000. The transfer to C is made subject to the $150,000 mortgage. B realizes a gain of $300,000 on the exchange, computed as follows:

Value of property received	$600,000
Cash	50,000
Liabilities subject to which old property was transferred	150,000
Total consideration received	800,000
Less: Adjusted basis of property transferred	500,000
Gain realized	$300,000

Under section 1031(b), $200,000 of the $300,000 gain is recognized. The basis of the apartment house acquired by B upon the exchange is $500,000 computed as follows:

Adjusted basis of property transferred		500,000
Less: Amount of money received:		
Cash	$50,000	
Amount of liabilities subject to which property was transferred	150,000	
		200,000
Difference		300,000
Plus: Amount of gain recognized upon the exchange		200,000
Basis of property acquired upon the exchange		500,000

Example (2). (a) D, an individual, owns an apartment house. On December 1, 1955, the apartment house owned by D has an adjusted basis in his hands of $100,000, a fair market value of $80,000, but is subject to a mortgage of $80,000. E, an individual, also owns an apartment house. On December 1, 1955, the apartment house owned by E has an adjusted basis of $175,000, a fair market value of $250,000, but is subject to a mortgage of $150,000. On December 1, 1955, D transfers his apartment house to E, receiving in exchange therefore $40,000 in cash and the apartment house owned by E. Each apartment house is transferred subject to the mortgage on it.

(b) D realizes a gain of $120,000 on the exchange, computed as follows:

Value of property received		$250,000
Cash		40,000
Liabilities subject to which old property was transferred		80,000
Total consideration received		370,000
Less:		
Adjusted basis of property transferred	$100,000	
Liabilities to which new property is subject	$150,000	
		250,000
Gain realized		120,000

For purposes of section 1031(b), the amount of "other property or money" received by D is $40,000. (Consideration received by D in the form of a transfer subject to a liability of $80,000 is offset by consideration given in the form of a receipt of property subject to a $150,000 liability. Thus, only the consideration received in the form of cash, $40,000, is treated as "other property or money" for purposes of section 1031(b).) Accordingly, under section 1031(b), $40,000 of the $120,000 gain is recognized. The basis of the apartment house acquired by D is $170,000, computed as follows:

Adjusted basis of property transferred		$100,000
Liabilities to which new property is subject		150,000
Total...............................		250,000
Less: Amount of money received: Cash................	$40,000	
Amount of liabilities subject to which property was transferred	80,000	

		120,000
Difference		$130,000
Plus: Amount of gain recognized upon the exchange		40,000
Basis of property acquired upon the exchange		170,000

(c) E realizes a gain of $75,000 on the exchange, computed as follows:

Value of property received..................		$220,000
Liabilities subject to which old property was transferred		150,000
Total consideration received		370,000
Less:		
Adjusted basis of property transferred	$175,000	
Cash	40,000	
Liabilities to which new property is subject.............	80,000	
		295,000
Gain realized		75,000

For purposes of section 1031(b), the amount of "other property or money" received by E is $30,000. (Consideration received by E in the form of a transfer subject to a liability of $150,000 is offset by consideration given in the form of a receipt of property subject to an $80,000 liability and by the $40,000 cash paid by E. Although consideration received in the form of cash or other property is not offset by consideration given in the form of an assumption of liabilities or a receipt of property subject to a liability, consideration given in the form of cash or other property is offset against consideration received in the form of an assumption of liabilities or a transfer of property subject to a liability.) Accordingly, under section 1031(b), $30,000 of the $75,000 gain is recognized. The basis of the apartment house acquired by E is $175,000, computed as follows:

Adjusted basis of property transferred		$175,000
Cash		40,000
Liabilities to which new property is subject		80,000
Total................................		295,000
Less: Amount of money received: Amount of liabilities subject to which property was transferred	$150,000	
		150,000
Difference		145,000
Plus: Amount of gain recognized upon the exchange		30,000
Basis of property acquired upon the exchange		175,000

[T.D. 6500, 25 FR 11910, Nov. 26, 1960]

§ 1.1032–1 Disposition by a corporation of its own capital stock.

(a) The disposition by a corporation of shares of its own stock (including treasury stock) for money or other property does not give rise to taxable gain or deductible loss to the corporation regardless of the nature of the transaction or the facts and circumstances involved. For example, the receipt by a corporation of the subscription price of shares of its stock upon their original issuance gives rise to neither taxable gain nor deductible loss, whether the subscription or issue price be equal to, in excess of, or less than, the par or stated value of such stock. Also, the exchange or sale by a corporation of its own shares for money or other property does not result in taxable gain or deductible loss, even though the corporation deals in such shares as it might in the shares of another corporation. A transfer by a corporation of shares of its own stock (including treasury stock) as compensation for services is considered, for purposes of section 1032(a), as a disposition by the corporation of such shares for money or other property.

(b) Section 1032(a) does not apply to the acquisition by a corporation of shares of its own stock except where the corporation acquires such shares in exchange for shares of its own stock (including treasury stock). See paragraph (e) of § 1.311–1, relating to treatment of acquisitions of a corporation's own stock. Section 1032(a) also does not relate to the tax treatment of the recipient of a corporation's stock.

(c) Where a corporation acquires shares of its own stock in exchange for shares of its own stock (including treasury stock) the transaction may qualify not only under section 1032(a), but also under section 368(a)(1)(E) (recapitalization) or section 305(a) (distribution of stock and stock rights).

(d) For basis of property acquired by a corporation in connection with a transaction to which section 351 applies or in connection with a reorganization, see section 362. For basis of property acquired by a corporation in a transaction to which section 1032 applies but which does not qualify under any other nonrecognition provision, see section 1012.

[T.D. 6500, 25 FR 11910, Nov. 26, 1960]

§ 1.1033(a)–1　Involuntary conversions; nonrecognition of gain.

(a) In general. Section 1033 applies to cases where property is compulsorily or involuntarily converted. An "involuntary conversion" may be the result of the destruction of property in whole or in part, the theft of property, the seizure of property, the requisition or condemnation of property, or the threat or imminence of requisition or condemnation of property. An "involuntary conversion" may be a conversion into similar property or into money or into dissimilar property. Section 1033 provides that, under certain specified circumstances, any gain which is realized from an involuntary conversion shall not be recognized. In cases where property is converted into other property similar or related in service or use to the converted property, no gain shall be recognized regardless of when the disposition of the converted property occurred and regardless of whether or not the taxpayer elects to have the gain not recognized. In other types of involuntary conversion cases, however, the proceeds arising from the disposition of the converted property must (within the time limits specified) be reinvested in similar property in order to avoid recognition of any gain realized. Section 1033 applies only with respect to gains; losses from involuntary conversions are recognized or not recognized without regard to this section.

(b) Special rules. For rules relating to the application of section 1033 to involuntary conversions of a principal residence with respect to which an election has been made under section 121 (relating to gain from sale or exchange of residence of individual who has attained age 65), see paragraph (g) of § 1.121–5. For rules applicable to involuntary conversions of a principal residence occurring before January 1, 1951, see § 1.1033(a)–3. For rules applicable to involuntary conversions of a principal residence occurring after December 31, 1950, and before January 1, 1954, see paragraph (h)(1) of § 1.1034–1. For rules applicable to involuntary conversions of a personal residence occurring after December 31, 1953, see § 1.1033(a)–3. For special rules relating to the election to have section 1034 apply to certain involuntary conversions of a principal residence occurring after December 31, 1957, see paragraph (h)(2) of § 1.1034–1. For special rules relating to certain involuntary conversions of real property held either for productive use in trade or business or for investment and occurring after December 31, 1957, see § 1.1033(g)–1. See also special rules applicable to involuntary conversions of property sold pursuant to reclamation laws, livestock destroyed by disease, and livestock sold on account of drought provided in §§ 1.1033(c)–1, 1.1033(d)–1, and 1.1033(e)–1, respectively. For rules relating to basis of property acquired through involuntary conversions, see § 1.1033(b)–1. For determination of the period for which the taxpayer has held property acquired as a result of certain involuntary conversions, see section 1223 and regulations issued thereunder. For treatment of gains from involuntary conversions as capital gains in certain cases, see section 1231(a) and regulations issued thereunder. For portion of war loss recoveries treated as gain on involuntary conversion, see section 1332(b)(3) and regulations issued thereunder.

[T.D. 6500, 25 FR 11910, Nov. 26, 1960, as amended by T.D. 6856, 30 FR 13318, Oct. 20, 1965; T.D. 7625, 44 FR 31013, May 30, 1979; T.D. 7758, 46 FR 6925, Jan. 22, 1981]

§ 1.1033(a)–2 Involuntary conversion into similar property, into money or into dissimilar property.

(a) In general. The term "disposition of the converted property" means the destruction, theft, seizure, requisition, or condemnation of the converted property, or the sale or exchange of such property under threat or imminence of requisition or condemnation.

(b) Conversion into similar property. If property (as a result of its destruction in whole or in part, theft, seizure, or requisition or condemnation or threat or imminence thereof) is compulsorily or involuntarily converted only into property similar or related in service or use to the property so converted, no gain shall be recognized. Such nonrecognition of gain is mandatory.

(c) Conversion into money or into dissimilar property. (1) If property (as a result of its destruction in whole or in part, theft, seizure, or requisition or condemnation or threat or imminence thereof) is compulsorily or involuntarily converted into money or into property not similar or related in service or use to the converted property, the gain, if any, shall be recognized, at the election of the taxpayer, only to the extent that the amount realized upon such conversion exceeds the cost of other property purchased by the taxpayer which is similar or related in service or use to the property so converted, or the cost of stock of a corporation owning such other property which is purchased by the taxpayer in the acquisition of control of such corporation, if the taxpayer purchased such other property, or such stock, for the purpose of replacing the property so converted and during the period specified in subparagraph (3) of this paragraph. For the purposes of section 1033, the term "control" means the ownership of stock possessing at least 80 percent of the total combined voting power of all classes of stock entitled to vote and at least

80 percent of the total number of shares of all other classes of stock of the corporation.

(2) All of the details in connection with an involuntary conversion of property at a gain (including those relating to the replacement of the converted property, or a decision not to replace, or the expiration of the period for replacement) shall be reported in the return for the taxable year or years in which any of such gain is realized. An election to have such gain recognized only to the extent provided in subparagraph (1) of this paragraph shall be made by including such gain in gross income for such year or years only to such extent. If, at the time of filing such a return, the period within which the converted property must be replaced has expired, or if such an election is not desired, the gain should be included in gross income for such year or years in the regular manner. A failure to so include such gain in gross income in the regular manner shall be deemed to be an election by the taxpayer to have such gain recognized only to the extent provided in subparagraph (1) of this paragraph even though the details in connection with the conversion are not reported in such return. If, after having made an election under section 1033(a)(2), the converted property is not replaced within the required period of time, or replacement is made at a cost lower than was anticipated at the time of the election, or a decision is made not to replace, the tax liability for the year or years for which the election was made shall be recomputed. Such recomputation should be in the form of an "amended return". If a decision is made to make an election under section 1033(a)(2) after the filing of the return and the payment of the tax for the year or years in which any of the gain on an involuntary conversion is realized and before the expiration of the period within which the converted property must be replaced, a claim for credit or refund for such year or years should be filed. If the replacement of the converted property occurs in a year or years in which none of the gain on the conversion is realized, all of the details in connection with such replacement shall be reported in the return for such year or years.

(3) The period referred to in subparagraphs (1) and (2) of this paragraph is the period of time commencing with the date of the disposition of the converted property, or the date of the beginning of the threat or imminence of requisition or condemnation of the converted property, whichever is earlier, and ending 2 years (or, in the case of a disposition occurring before Dec. 31, 1969, 1 year)

after the close of the first taxable year in which any part of the gain upon the conversion is realized, or at the close of such later date as may be designated pursuant to an application of the taxpayer. Such application shall be made prior to the expiration of 2 years (or, in the case of a disposition occurring before Dec. 31, 1969, 1 year) after the close of the first taxable year in which any part of the gain from the conversion is realized, unless the taxpayer can show to the satisfaction of the district director—

(i) Reasonable cause for not having filed the application within the required period of time, and

(ii) The filing of such application was made within a reasonable time after the expiration of the required period of time. The application shall contain all of the details in connection with the involuntary conversion. Such application shall be made to the district director for the internal revenue district in which the return is filed for the first taxable year in which any of the gain from the involuntary conversion is realized. No extension of time shall be granted pursuant to such application unless the taxpayer can show reasonable cause for not being able to replace the converted property within the required period of time.

See section 1033(g)(4) and § 1.1033(g)-1 for the circumstances under which, in the case of the conversion of real property held either for productive use in trade or business or for investment, the 2-year period referred to in this paragraph (c)(3) shall be extended to 3 years.

(4) Property or stock purchased before the disposition of the converted property shall be considered to have been purchased for the purpose of replacing the converted property only if such property or stock is held by the taxpayer on the date of the disposition of the converted property. Property or stock shall be considered to have been purchased only if, but for the provisions of section 1033(b), the unadjusted basis of such property or stock would be its cost to the taxpayer within the meaning of section 1012. If the taxpayer's unadjusted basis of the replacement property would be determined, in the absence of section 1033(b), under any of the exceptions referred to in section 1012, the unadjusted basis of the property would not be its cost within the meaning of section 1012. For example, if property similar or related in service or use to the converted property is acquired by gift and its basis is determined under section 1015, such prop-

erty will not qualify as a replacement for the converted property.

(5) If a taxpayer makes an election under section 1033(a)(2), any deficiency, for any taxable year in which any part of the gain upon the conversion is realized, which is attributable to such gain may be assessed at any time before the expiration of three years from the date the district director with whom the return for such year has been filed is notified by the taxpayer of the replacement of the converted property or of an intention not to replace, or of a failure to replace, within the required period, notwithstanding the provisions of section 6212(c) or the provisions of any other law or rule of law which would otherwise prevent such assessment. If replacement has been made, such notification shall contain all of the details in connection with such replacement. Such notification should be made in the return for the taxable year or years in which the replacement occurs, or the intention not to replace is formed, or the period for replacement expires, if this return is filed with such district director. If this return is not filed with such district director, then such notification shall be made to such district director at the time of filing this return. If the taxpayer so desires, he may, in either event, also notify such district director before the filing of such return.

(6) If a taxpayer makes an election under section 1033(a)(2) and the replacement property or stock was purchased before the beginning of the last taxable year in which any part of the gain upon the conversion is realized, any deficiency, for any taxable year ending before such last taxable year, which is attributable to such election may be assessed at any time before the expiration of the period within which a deficiency for such last taxable year may be assessed, notwithstanding the provisions of section 6212(c) or 6501 or the provisions of any law or rule of law which would otherwise prevent such assessment.

(7) If the taxpayer makes an election under section 1033(a)(2), the gain upon the conversion shall be recognized to the extent that the amount realized upon such conversion exceeds the cost of the replacement property or stock, regardless of whether such amount is realized in one or more taxable years.

(8) The proceeds of a use and occupancy insurance contract, which by its terms insured against actual loss sustained of net profits in the business, are not proceeds of an involuntary conversion but are income in the same manner that the profits for which they are substituted would have been.

(9) There is no investment in property similar in character and devoted to a similar use if—

(i) The proceeds of unimproved real estate, taken upon condemnation proceedings, are invested in improved real estate.

(ii) The proceeds of conversion of real property are applied in reduction of indebtedness previously incurred in the purchase or a leasehold.

(iii) The owner of a requisitioned tug uses the proceeds to buy barges.

(10) If, in a condemnation proceeding, the Government retains out of the award sufficient funds to satisfy special assessments levied against the remaining portion of the plot or parcel of real estate affected for benefits accruing in connection with the condemnation, the amount so retained shall be deducted from the gross award in determining the amount of the net award.

(11) If, in a condemnation proceeding, the Government retains out of the award sufficient funds to satisfy liens (other than liens due to special assessments levied against the remaining portion of the plot or parcel of real estate affected for benefits accruing in connection with the condemnation) and mortgages against the property, and itself pays the same, the amount so retained shall not be deducted from the gross award in determining the amount of the net award. If, in a condemnation proceeding, the Government makes an award to a mortgagee to satisfy a mortgage on the condemned property, the amount of such award shall be considered as a part of the "amount realized" upon the conversion regardless of whether or not the taxpayer was personally liable for the mortgage debt. Thus, if a taxpayer has acquired property worth $100,000 subject to a $50,000 mortgage (regardless of whether or not he was personally liable for the mortgage debt) and, in a condemnation proceeding, the Government awards the taxpayer $60,000 and awards the mortgagee $50,000 in satisfaction of the mortgage, the entire $110,000 is considered to be the "amount realized" by the taxpayer.

(12) An amount expended for replacement of an asset, in excess of the recovery for loss, represents a capital expenditure and is not a deductible loss for income tax purposes.

[T.D. 6500, 25 FR 11910, Nov. 26, 1960, as amended by T.D. 6679, 28 FR 10515, Oct. 1, 1963; T.D. 7075, 35 FR 17996, Nov. 24, 1970; T.D. 7625, 44 FR 31013, May 30, 1979; T.D. 7758, 46 FR 6925, Jan. 22, 1981]

§ 1.1033(b)–1 Basis of property acquired as a result of an involuntary conversion.

* * *

(b) The provisions of the last sentence of section 1033(b) may be illustrated by the following example:

Example. A taxpayer realizes $22,000 from the involuntary conversion of his barn in 1955; the adjusted basis of the barn to him was $10,000, and he spent in the same year $20,000 for a new barn which resulted in the nonrecognition of $10,000 of the $12,000 gain on the conversion. The basis of the new barn to the taxpayer would be $10,000—the cost of the new barn ($20,000) less the amount of the gain not recognized on the conversion ($10,000). The basis of the new barn would not be a substituted basis in the hands of the taxpayer within the meaning of section 1016(b)(2). If the replacement of the converted barn had been made by the purchase of two smaller barns which, together, were similar or related in service or use to the converted barn and which cost $8,000 and $12,000, respectively, then the basis of the two barns would be $4,000 and $6,000, respectively, the total basis of the purchased property ($10,000) allocated in proportion to their respective costs (8,000/20,000 of $10,000 or $4,000; and 12,000/20,000 of $10,000, or $6,000).

[T.D. 6500, 25 FR 11910, Nov. 26, 1960; 25 FR 14021, Dec. 31, 1960. Redesignated and amended by T.D. 7625, 44 FR 31013, May 30, 1979]

§ 1.1033(g)–1 Condemnation of real property held for productive use in trade or business or for investment.

(a) Special rule in general. This section provides special rules for applying section 1033 with respect to certain dispositions, occurring after December 31, 1957, of real property held either for productive use in trade or business or for investment (not including stock in trade or other property held primarily for sale). For this purpose, disposition means the seizure, requisition, or condemnation (but not destruction) of the converted property, or the sale or exchange of such property under threat or imminence of seizure, requisition, or condemnation. In such cases, for purposes of applying section 1033, the replacement of such property with property of like kind to be held either for productive use in trade or business or for investment shall be treated as property similar or related in service or use to the property so converted. For principles in determining whether the replacement property is property of like kind, see paragraph (b) of § 1.1031(a)–1.

* * *

[T.D. 6500, 25 FR 11910, Nov. 26, 1960; 25 FR 14021, Dec. 31, 1960, § 1.1033(g)–1. Redesignated and amended by T.D. 7625, 44 FR 31013, May 30, 1979; 44 FR 38458, July 2, 1979; T.D. 7758, 46 FR 6925, Jan. 22, 1981]

§ 1.1034–1 Sale or exchange of residence.

(a) Nonrecognition of gain; general statement. Section 1034 provides rules for the nonrecognition of gain in certain cases where a taxpayer sells one residence after December 31, 1953, and buys or builds, and uses as his principal residence, another residence within specified time limits before or after such sale. In general, if the taxpayer invests in a new residence an amount at least as large as the adjusted sales price of his old residence, no gain is recognized on the sale of the old residence (see paragraph (b) of this section for definitions of "adjusted sales price", "new residence", and "old residence"). On the other hand, if the new residence costs the taxpayer less than the adjusted sales price of the old residence, gain is recognized to the extent of the difference. Thus, if an amount equal to or greater than the adjusted sales price of an old residence is invested in a new residence, according to the rules stated in section 1034, none of the gain (if any) realized from the sale shall be recognized. If an amount less than such adjusted sales price is so invested, gain shall be recognized, but only to the extent provided in section 1034. If there is no investment in a new residence, section 1034 is inapplicable and all of the gain shall be recognized. Whenever, as a result of the application of section 1034, any or all of the gain realized on the sale of an old residence is not recognized, a corresponding reduction must be made in the basis of the new residence. The provisions of section 1034 are mandatory, so that the taxpayer cannot elect to have gain recognized under circumstances where this section is applicable. Section 1034 applies only to gains; losses are recognized or not recognized without regard to the provisions of this section. Section 1034 affects only the amount of gain recognized, and not the amount of gain realized (see also section 1001 and the regulations issued thereunder). Any gain realized upon disposition of other property in exchange for the new residence is not affected by section 1034. * * *

(b) Definitions. The following definitions of frequently used terms are applicable for purposes of section 1034 (other definitions and detailed explanations appear in subsequent paragraphs of this regulation):

(1) "Old residence" means property used by the taxpayer as his principal residence which is the subject of a sale by him after December 31, 1953 (section 1034(a); for detailed explanation see paragraph (c)(3) of this section).

(2) "New residence" means property used by the taxpayer as his principal residence which is the subject of a purchase by him (section 1034(a); for detailed explanation and limitations see paragraph (c)(3) and (d)(1) of this section).

(3) "Adjusted sales price" means the amount realized reduced by the fixing-up expenses (section 1034(b)(1); for special rule applicable in some cases to husband and wife, see paragraph (f) of this section).

(4) "Amount realized" is to be computed by subtracting,

(i) The amount of the items which, in determining the gain from the sale of the old residence, are properly an offset against the consideration received upon the sale (such as commissions and expenses of advertising the property for sale, of preparing the deed, and of other legal services in connection with the sale); from

(ii) The amount of the consideration so received, determined (in accordance with section 1001(b) and regulations issued thereunder) by adding to the sum of any money so received, the fair market value of the property (other than money) so received. If, as part of the consideration for the sale, the purchaser either assumes a liability of the taxpayer or acquires the old residence subject to a liability (whether or not the taxpayer is personally liable on the debt), such assumption or acquisition, in the amount of the liability, shall be treated as money received by the taxpayer in computing the "amount realized."

(5) "Gain realized" is the excess (if any) of the amount realized over the adjusted basis of the old residence (see also section 1001(a) and regulations issued thereunder).

(6) "Fixing-up expenses" means the aggregate of the expenses for work performed (in any taxable year, whether beginning before, on, or after January 1, 1954) on the old residence in order to assist in its sale, provided that such expenses (i) are incurred for work performed during the 90-day period ending on the day on which the contract to

sell the old residence is entered into; and (ii) are paid on or before the 30th day after the date of the sale of the old residence; and (iii) are neither (a) allowable as deductions in computing taxable income under section 63(a), nor (b) taken into account in computing the amount realized from the sale of the old residence (section 1034(b)(2) and (3)). "Fixing-up expenses" does not include expenditures which are properly chargeable to capital account and which would, therefore, constitute adjustments to the basis of the old residence (see section 1016 and regulations issued thereunder).

(7) "Cost of purchasing the new residence" means the total of all amounts which are attributable to the acquisition, construction, reconstruction, and improvements constituting capital expenditures, * * *

* * *

(9) "Purchase" (of a residence) means a purchase or an acquisition (of a residence) on the exchange of property or the partial or total construction or reconstruction (of a residence) by the taxpayer (section 1034(c)(1) and (2)). However, the mere improvement of a residence, not amounting to reconstruction, does not constitute "purchase" of a residence.

(c) **Rules for application of section 1034—**

* * *

(3) **Property used by the taxpayer as his principal residence.** (i) Whether or not property is used by the taxpayer as his residence, and whether or not property is used by the taxpayer as his principal residence (in the case of a taxpayer using more than one property as a residence), depends upon all the facts and circumstances in each case, including the good faith of the taxpayer. The mere fact that property is, or has been, rented is not determinative that such property is not used by the taxpayer as his principal residence. For example, if the taxpayer purchases his new residence before he sells his old residence, the fact that he temporarily rents out the new residence during the period before he vacates the old residence may not, in the light of all the facts and circumstances in the case, prevent the new residence from being considered as property used by the taxpayer as his principal residence. Property used by the taxpayer as his principal residence may include a houseboat, a house trailer, or stock held by a tenant-stockholder in a cooperative housing corporation (as those terms are defined in section 216(b)(1) and (2)), if the dwelling which the taxpayer is entitled to occupy as such stockholder is used by him as his principal residence (section 1034(f)). Property used by the taxpayer as his principal residence does not include personal property such as a piece of furniture, a radio, etc., which, in accordance with the applicable local law, is not a fixture.

(ii) Where part of a property is used by the taxpayer as his principal residence and part is used for other purposes, an allocation must be made to determine the application of this section. If the old residence is used only partially for residential purposes, only that part of the gain allocable to the residential portion is not to be recognized under this section and only an amount allocable to the selling price of such portion need by invested in the new residence in order to have the gain allocable to such portion not recognized under this section. If the new residence is used only partially for residential purposes only so much of its cost as is allocable to the residential portion may be counted as the cost of purchasing the new residence.

(4) **Cost of purchasing new residence.** (i) The taxpayer's cost of purchasing the new residence includes not only cash but also any indebtedness to which the property purchased is subject at the time of purchase whether or not assumed by the taxpayer (including purchase-money mortgages, etc.) and the face amount of any liabilities of the taxpayer which are part of the consideration for the purchase. Commissions and other purchasing expenses paid or incurred by the taxpayer on the purchase of the new residence are to be included in determining such cost. In the case of an acquisition of a residence upon an exchange which is considered as a "purchase" under this section, the fair market value of the new residence on the date of the exchange shall be considered as the taxpayer's cost of purchasing the new residence. Where any part of the new residence is acquired by the taxpayer other than by "purchase", the value of such part is not to be included in determining the taxpayer's cost of the new residence (see paragraph (b)(9) of this section for definition of "purchase"). For example, if the taxpayer acquires a residence by gift or inheritance, and spends $20,000 in reconstructing such residence, only such $20,000 may be treated as his cost of purchasing the new residence.

* * *

[T.D. 6500, 25 FR 11910, Nov. 26, 1960, as amended by T.D. 6856, 30 FR 13319, Oct. 20, 1965; T.D. 6916, 32 FR 5924, April 13, 1967; 32 FR 6971, May 6, 1967; T.D. 7404, 41 FR 6758, Feb. 13, 1976; T.D. 7625, 44 FR 31013, May 30, 1979]

§ 1.1036–1 Stock for stock of the same corporation.

(a) Section 1036 permits the exchange, without the recognition of gain or loss, of common stock for common stock, or of preferred stock for preferred stock, in the same corporation. Section 1036 applies even though voting stock is exchanged for nonvoting stock or nonvoting stock is exchanged for voting stock. It is not limited to an exchange between two individual stockholders; it includes a transaction between a stockholder and the corporation. However, a transaction between a stockholder and the corporation may qualify not only under section 1036(a), but also under section 368(a)(1)(E) (recapitalization) or section 305(a) (distribution of stock and stock rights). The provisions of section 1036(a) do not apply if stock is exchanged for bonds, or preferred stock is exchanged for common stock, or common stock is exchanged for preferred stock, or common stock in one corporation is exchanged for common stock in another corporation. See paragraph (1) of § 1301–1 for certain transactions treated as distributions under section 301. See paragraph (e)(5) of § 1.368–2 for certain transactions which result in deemed distributions under section 305(c) to which sections 305(b)(4) and 301 apply.

* * *

[T.D. 6500, 25 FR 11910, Nov. 26, 1960, as amended by T.D. 7281, 38 FR 18540, July 12, 1973]

Transfers Between Spouses

§ 1.1041–1T Treatment of transfer of property between spouses or incident to divorce.

Q–1 How is the transfer of property between spouses treated under section 1041?

A–1 Generally, no gain or loss is recognized on a transfer of property from an individual to (or in trust for the benefit of) a spouse or, if the transfer is incident to a divorce, a former spouse. The following questions and answers describe more fully the scope, tax consequences and other rules which apply to transfers of property under section 1041.

(a) Scope of section 1041 in general.

Q–2 Does section 1041 apply only to transfers of property incident to divorce?

A–2 No. Section 1041 is not limited to transfers of property incident to divorce. Section 1041 applies to any transfer of property between spouses regardless of whether the transfer is a gift or is a sale or exchange between spouses acting at arm's length (including a transfer in exchange for the relinquishment of property or marital rights or an exchange otherwise governed by another nonrecognition provision of the Code). A divorce or legal separation need not be contemplated between the spouses at the time of the transfer nor must a divorce or legal separation ever occur.

Example (1). A and B are married and file a joint return. A is the sole owner of a condominium unit. A sale or gift of the condominium from A to B is a transfer which is subject to the rules of section 1041.

Example (2). A and B are married and file separate returns. A is the owner of an independent sole proprietorship, X Company. In the ordinary course of business, X Company makes a sale of property to B. This sale is a transfer of property between spouses and is subject to the rules of section 1041.

Example (3). Assume the same facts as in example (2), except that X Company is a corporation wholly owned by A. This sale is not a sale between spouses subject to the rules of section 1041. However, in appropriate circumstances, general tax principles, including the step-transaction doctrine, may be applicable in recharacterizing the transaction.

Q–3 Do the rules of section 1041 apply to a transfer between spouses if the transferee spouse is a nonresident alien?

A–3 No. Gain or loss (if any) is recognized (assuming no other nonrecognition provision applies) at the time of a transfer of property if the property is transferred to a spouse who is a nonresident alien.

Q–4 What kinds of transfers are governed by section 1041?

A–4 Only transfers of property (whether real or personal, tangible or intangible) are governed by section 1041. Transfers of services are not subject to the rules of section 1041.

Q–5 Must the property transferred to a former spouse have been owned by the transferor spouse during the marriage?

A–5 No. A transfer of property acquired after the marriage ceases may be governed by section 1041.

(b) Transfer incident to the divorce.

Q–6 When is a transfer of property "incident to the divorce"?

A–6 A transfer of property is "incident to the divorce" in either of the following 2 circumstances—

(1) The transfer occurs not more than one year after the date on which the marriage ceases, or

(2) The transfer is related to the cessation of the marriage.

Thus, a transfer of property occurring not more than one year after the date on which the marriage ceases need not be related to the cessation of the marriage to qualify for section 1041 treatment. (See A–7 for transfers occurring more than one year after the cessation of the marriage.)

Q–7 When is a transfer of property "related to the cessation of the marriage"?

A–7 A transfer of property is treated as related to the cessation of the marriage if the transfer is pursuant to a divorce or separation instrument, as defined in section 71(b)(2), and the transfer occurs not more than 6 years after the date on which the marriage ceases. A divorce or separation instrument includes a modification or amendment to such decree or instrument. Any transfer not pursuant to a divorce or separation instrument and any transfer occurring more than 6 years after the cessation of the marriage is presumed to be not related to the cessation of the marriage. This presumption may be rebutted only by showing that the transfer was made to effect the division of property owned by the former spouses at the time of the cessation of the marriage. For example, the presumption may be rebutted by showing that (a) the transfer was not made within the one- and six-year periods described above because of factors which hampered an earlier transfer of the property, such as legal or business impediments to transfer or disputes concerning the value of the property owned at the time of the cessation of the marriage, and (b) the transfer is effected promptly after the impediment to transfer is removed.

Q–8 Do annulments and the cessations of marriages that are void *ab initio* due to violations of state law constitute divorces for purposes of section 1041?

A–8 Yes.

(c) Transfers on behalf of a spouse.

Q–9 May transfers of property to third parties on behalf of a spouse (or former spouse) qualify under section 1041?

A–9 Yes. There are three situations in which a transfer of property to a third party on behalf of a spouse (or former spouse) will qualify under section 1041, provided all other requirements of the section are satisfied. The first situation is where the transfer to the third party is required by a divorce or separation instrument. The second situation is where the transfer to the third party is pursuant to the written request of the other spouse (or former spouse). The third situation is where the transferor receives from the other spouse (or former spouse) a written consent or ratification of the transfer to the third party. Such consent or ratification must state that the parties intend the transfer to be treated as a transfer to the nontransferring spouse (or former spouse) subject to the rules of section 1041 and must be received by the transferor prior to the date of filing of the transferor's first return of tax for the taxable year in which the transfer was made. In the three situations described above, the transfer of property will be treated as made directly to the nontransferring spouse (or former spouse) and the nontransferring spouse will be treated as immediately transferring the property to the third party. The deemed transfer from the nontransferring spouse (or former spouse) to the third party is not a transaction that qualifies for nonrecognition of gain under section 1041.

(d) Tax consequences of transfers subject to section 1041.

Q–10 How is the transferor of property under section 1041 treated for income tax purposes?

A–10 The transferor of property under section 1041 recognizes no gain or loss on the transfer even if the transfer was in exchange for the release of marital rights or other consideration. This rule applies regardless of whether the transfer is of property separately owned by the transferor or is a division (equal or unequal) of community property. Thus, the result under section 1041 differs from the result in *United States* v. Davis, 370 U.S. 65 (1962).

Q–11 How is the transferee of property under section 1041 treated for income tax purposes?

A–11 The transferee of property under section 1041 recognizes no gain or loss upon receipt of the transferred property. In all cases, the basis of the transferred property in the hands of the transferee is the adjusted basis of such property in the hands of the transferor immediately before the transfer. Even if the transfer is a bona fide sale, the transferee does not acquire a basis in the transferred property equal to the transferee's costs (the fair market value). This carryover basis rule applies whether the adjusted basis of the transferred property is less than, equal to, or greater than its fair market value at the time of transfer (or the value of any consideration provided by the transferee) and applies for purposes of determining loss as well as gain upon the subsequent disposition of the property by the transferee. Thus, this rule is different from the rule applied in section 1015(a) for determining the basis of property acquired by gift.

Q–12 Do the rules described in A–10 and A–11 apply even if the transferred property is subject to liabilities which exceed the adjusted basis of the property?

A–12 Yes. For example, assume A owns property having a fair market value of $10,000 and an adjusted basis of $1,000. In contemplation of making a transfer of this property incident to a divorce from B, A borrows $5,000 from a bank, using the property as security for the borrowing. A then transfers the property to B and B assumes, or takes the property subject to, the liability to pay the $5,000 debt. Under section 1041, A recognizes no gain or loss upon the transfer of the property, and the adjusted basis of the property in the hands of B is $1,000.

Q–13 Will a transfer under section 1041 result in a recapture of investment tax credits with respect to the property transferred?

A–13 In general, no. Property transferred under section 1041 will not be treated as being disposed of by, or ceasing to be section 38 property with respect to, the transferor. However, the transferee will be subject to investment tax credit recapture if, upon or after the transfer, the property is disposed of by, or ceases to be section 38 property with respect to, the transferee. For example, as part of a divorce property settlement, B receives a car from A that has been used in A's business for two years and for which an investment tax credit was taken by A. No part of A's business

is transferred to B and B's use of the car is solely personal. B is subject to recapture of the investment tax credit previously taken by A.

(e) Notice and recordkeeping requirement with respect to transactions under section 1041.

Q–14 Does the transferor of property in a transaction described in section 1041 have to supply, at the time of the transfer, the transferee with records sufficient to determine the adjusted basis and holding period of the property at the time of the transfer and (if applicable) with notice that the property transferred under section 1041 is potentially subject to recapture of the investment tax credit?

A–14 Yes. A transferor of property under section 1041 must, at the time of the transfer, supply the transferee with records sufficient to determine the adjusted basis and holding period of the property as of the date of the transfer. In addition, in the case of a transfer of property which carries with it a potential liability for investment tax credit recapture, the transferor must, at the time of the transfer, supply the transferee with records sufficient to determine the amount and period of such potential liability. Such records must be preserved and kept accessible by the transferee.

(f) Property settlements—effective dates, transitional periods and elections.

Q–15 When does section 1041 become effective?

A–15 Generally, section 1041 applies to all transfers after July 18, 1984. However, it does not apply to transfers after July 18, 1984 pursuant to instruments in effect on or before July 18, 1984. (See A–16 with respect to exceptions to the general rule.)

Q–16 Are there any exceptions to the general rule stated in A–15 above?

A–16 Yes. Two transitional rules provide exceptions to the general rule stated in A–15. First, section 1041 will apply to transfers after July 18, 1984 under instruments that were in effect on or before July 18, 1984 if both spouses (or former spouses) elect to have section 1041 apply to such transfers. Second, section 1041 will apply to all transfers after December 31, 1983 (including transfers under instruments in effect on or before July 18, 1984) if both spouses (or former spouses) elect to have section 1041 apply. (See A–18 relating to the time and manner of making the elections under the first or second transitional rule.)

Q–17 Can an election be made to have section 1041 apply to some, but not all, transfers made after December 31, 1983, or some but not all, transfers made after July 18, 1984 under instruments in effect on or before July 18, 1984?

A–17 No. Partial elections are not allowed. An election under either of the two elective transitional rules applies to all transfers governed by that election whether before or after the election is made, and is irrevocable.

(g) Property settlements—time and manner of making the elections under section 1041.

Q–18 How do spouses (or former spouses) elect to have section 1041 apply to transfers after December 31, 1983, or to transfers after July 18, 1984 under instruments in effect on or before July 18, 1984?

A–18 In order to make an election under section 1041 for property transfers after December 31, 1983, or property transfers under instruments that were in effect on or before July 18, 1984, both spouses (or former spouses) must elect the application of the rules of section 1041 by attaching to the transferor's first filed income tax return for the taxable year in which the first transfer occurs, a statement signed by both spouses (or former spouses) which includes each spouse's social security number and is in substantially the form set forth at the end of this answer.

In addition, the transferor must attach a copy of such statement to his or her return for each subsequent taxable year in which a transfer is made that is governed by the transitional election. A copy of the signed statement must be kept by both parties.

The election statements shall be in substantially the following form:

In the case of an election regarding transfers after 1983:

Section 1041 Election

The undersigned hereby elect to have the provisions of section 1041 of the Internal Revenue Code apply to all qualifying transfers of property after December 31, 1983. The undersigned understand that section 1041 applies to all property transferred between spouses, or former spouses incident to divorce. The parties further understand that the effects for Federal income tax purposes of having section 1041 apply are that (1) no gain or loss is recognized by the transferor spouse or former spouse as a result of this transfer; and (2) the basis of the transferred property in the hands of the transferee is the adjusted basis of the property in the hands of the transferor immediately before the transfer, whether or not the adjusted basis of the transferred property is less than, equal to, or greater than its fair market value at the time of the transfer. The undersigned understand that if the transferee spouse or former spouse disposes of the property in a transaction in which gain is recognized, the amount of gain which is taxable may be larger than it would have been if this election had not been made.

In the case of an election regarding preexisting decrees:

Section 1041 Election

The undersigned hereby elect to have the provisions of section 1041 of the Internal Revenue Code apply to all qualifying transfers of property after July 18, 1984 under any instrument in effect on or before July 18, 1984. The undersigned understand that section 1041 applies to all property transferred between spouses, or former spouses incident to the divorce. The parties further understand that the effects for Federal income tax purposes of having section 1041 apply are that (1) no gain or loss is recognized by the transferor spouse or former spouse as a result of this transfer; and (2) the basis of the transferred property in the hands of the transferee is the adjusted basis of the property in the hands of the transferor immediately before the transfer, whether or not the adjusted basis of the transferred property is less than, equal to, or greater than its fair market value at the time of the transfer. The undersigned understand that if the transferee spouse or former spouse disposes of the property in a transaction in which gain is recognized, the amount of gain which is taxable may be larger than it would have been if this election had not been made.

[T.D. 7973, 49 FR 34452, Aug. 31, 1984]

Wash Sales of Stock or Securities

§ 1.1091–1 Losses from wash sales of stock or securities.

(a) A taxpayer cannot deduct any loss claimed to have been sustained from the sale or other disposition of stock or securities if, within a period beginning 30 days before the date of such sale or disposition and ending 30 days after such date (referred to in this section as the 61-day period), he has acquired (by purchase or by an exchange upon which the entire amount of gain or loss was recognized by law), or has entered into a contract or option so to acquire, substantially identical stock or securities.

However, this prohibition does not apply (1) in the case of a taxpayer, not a corporation, if the sale or other disposition of stock or securities is made in connection with the taxpayer's trade or business, or (2) in the case of a corporation, a dealer in stock or securities, if the sale or other disposition of stock or securities is made in the ordinary course of its business as such dealer.

(b) Where more than one loss is claimed to have been sustained within the taxable year from the sale or other disposition of stock or securities, the provisions of this section shall be applied to the losses in the order in which the stock or securities the disposition of which resulted in the respective losses were disposed of (beginning with the earliest disposition). If the order of disposition of stock or securities disposed of at a loss on the same day cannot be determined, the stock or securities will be considered to have been disposed of in the order in which they were originally acquired (beginning with the earliest acquisition).

(c) Where the amount of stock or securities acquired within the 61-day period is less than the amount of stock or securities sold or otherwise disposed of, then the particular shares of stock or securities the loss from the sale or other disposition of which is not deductible shall be those with which the stock or securities acquired are matched in accordance with the following rule: The stock or securities acquired will be matched in accordance with the order of their acquisition (beginning with the earliest acquisition) with an equal number of the shares of stock or securities sold or otherwise disposed of.

(d) Where the amount of stock or securities acquired within the 61-day period is not less than the amount of stock or securities sold or otherwise disposed of, then the particular shares of stock or securities the acquisition of which resulted in the nondeductibility of the loss shall be those with which the stock or securities disposed of are matched in accordance with the following rule: The stock or securities sold or otherwise disposed of will be matched with an equal number of the shares of stock or securities acquired in accordance with the order of acquisition (beginning with the earliest acquisition) of the stock or securities acquired.

(e) The acquisition of any share of stock or any security which results in the nondeductibility of a loss under the provisions of this section shall be disregarded in determining the deductibility of any other loss.

(f) The word "acquired" as used in this section means acquired by purchase or by an exchange upon which the entire amount of gain or loss was recognized by law, and comprehends cases where the taxpayer has entered into a contract or option within the 61-day period to acquire by purchase or by such an exchange.

(g) For purposes of determining under this section the 61-day period applicable to a short sale of stock or securities, the principles of paragraph (a) of § 1.1233–1 for determining the consummation of a short sale shall generally apply except that the date of entering into the short sale shall be deemed to be the date of sale if, on the date of entering into the short sale, the taxpayer owns (or on or before such date has entered into a contract or option to acquire) stock or securities identical to those sold short and subsequently delivers such stock or securities to close the short sale.

(h) The following examples illustrate the application of this section:

Example (1). A, whose taxable year is the calendar year, on December 1, 1954, purchased 100 shares of common stock in the M Company for $10,000 and on December 15, 1954, purchased 100 additional shares for $9,000. On January 3, 1955, he sold the 100 shares purchased on December 1, 1954, for $9,000. Because of the provisions of section 1091, no loss from the sale is allowable as a deduction.

Example (2). A, whose taxable year is the calendar year, on September 21, 1954, purchased 100 shares of the common stock of the M Company for $5,000. On December 21, 1954, he purchased 50 shares of substantially identical stock for $2,750, and on December 27, 1954, he purchased 25 additional shares of such stock for $1,125. On January 3, 1955, he sold for $4,000 the 100 shares purchased on September 21, 1954. There is an indicated loss of $1,000 on the sale of the 100 shares. Since, within the 61-day period, A purchased 75 shares of substantially identical stock, the loss on the sale of 75 of the shares ($3,750–$3,000, or $750) is not allowable as a deduction because of the provisions of section 1091. The loss on the sale of the remaining 25 shares ($1,250–$1,000, or $250) is deductible subject to the limitations provided in sections 267 and 1211. The basis of the 50 shares purchased December 21, 1954, the acquisition of which resulted in the nondeductibility of the loss ($500) sustained on 50 of the 100 shares sold on January 3, 1955, is $2,500 (the cost of 50 of the shares sold on January 3, 1955) + $750 (the difference between the purchase price ($2,750) of the 50 shares acquired on December 21, 1954, and the selling price ($2,000) of 50 of the shares sold on January 3, 1955), or $3,250. Similarly, the basis of the 25 shares purchased on December 27, 1954, the acquisition of which resulted in the nondeductibility of the loss ($250) sustained on 25 of the shares sold on January 3, 1955, is $1,250+$125, or $1,375. See § 1.1091–2.

[T.D. 6500, 25 FR 11910, Nov. 26, 1960, as amended by T.D. 6926, 32 FR 11468, Aug. 9, 1967]

§ 1.1091-2 Basis of stock or securities acquired in "wash sales".

(a) **In general.** The application of section 1091(d) may be illustrated by the following examples:

Example (1). A purchased a share of common stock of the X Corporation for $100 in 1935, which he sold January 15, 1955, for $80. On February 1, 1955, he purchased a share of common stock of the same corporation for $90. No loss from the sale is recognized under section 1091. The basis of the new share is $110; that is, the basis of the old share ($100) increased by $10, the excess of the price at which the new share was acquired ($90) over the price at which the old share was sold ($80).

Example (2). A purchased a share of common stock of the Y Corporation for $100 in 1935, which he sold January 15, 1955, for $80. On February 1, 1955, he purchased a share of common stock of the same corporation for $70. No loss from the sale is recognized under section 1091. The basis of the new share is $90; that is, the basis of the old share ($100) decreased by $10, the excess of the price at which the old share was sold ($80) over the price at which the new share was acquired ($70).

* * *

[T.D. 6500, 25 FR 11910, Nov. 26, 1960, as amended by T.D. 7129, 36 FR 12738, July 7, 1971]

CAPITAL GAINS AND LOSSES

General Rules for Determining Capital Gains and Losses

§ 1.1221-1 Meaning of terms.

(a) The term "capital assets" includes all classes of property not specifically excluded by section 1221. In determining whether property is a "capital asset", the period for which held is immaterial.

(b) Property used in the trade or business of a taxpayer of a character which is subject to the allowance for depreciation provided in section 167 and real property used in the trade or business of a taxpayer is excluded from the term "capital assets". Gains and losses from the sale or exchange of such property are not treated as gains and losses from the sale or exchange of capital assets, except to the extent provided in section 1231. See § 1.1231-1. Property held for the production of income, but not used in a trade or business of the taxpayer, is not excluded from the term "capital assets" even though depreciation may have been allowed with respect to such property under section 23(*l*) of the Internal Revenue Code of 1939 before its amendment by section 121(c) of the Revenue Act of 1942 (56 Stat. 819). However, gain or loss upon the sale or exchange of land held by a taxpayer primarily for sale to customers in the ordinary course of his business, as in the case of a dealer in real estate, is not subject to the provisions of subchapter P (section 1201 and following), chapter 1 of the Code.

(c)(1) A copyright, a literary, musical, or artistic composition, and similar property are excluded from the term "capital assets" if held by a taxpayer whose personal efforts created such property, or if held by a taxpayer in whose hands the basis of such property is determined, for purposes of determining gain from a sale or exchange, in whole or in part by reference to the basis of such property in the hands of a taxpayer whose personal efforts created such property. For purposes of this subparagraph, the phrase "similar property" includes for example, such property as a theatrical production, a radio program, a newspaper cartoon strip, or any other property eligible for copyright protection (whether under statute or common law), but does not include a patent or an invention, or a design which may be protected only under the patent law and not under the copyright law.

(2) In the case of sales and other dispositions occurring after July 25, 1969, a letter, a memorandum, or similar property is excluded from the term "capital asset" if held by (i) a taxpayer whose personal efforts created such property, (ii) a taxpayer for whom such property was prepared or produced, or (iii) a taxpayer in whose hands the basis of such property is determined, for purposes of determining gain from a sale or exchange, in whole or in part by reference to the basis of such property in the hands of a taxpayer described in subdivision (i) or (ii) of this subparagraph. In the case of a collection of letters, memorandums, or similar property held by a person who is a taxpayer described in subdivision (i), (ii), or (iii) of this subparagraph as to some of such letters, memorandums, or similar property but not as to others, this subparagraph shall apply only to those letters, memorandums, or similar property as to which

such person is a taxpayer described in such subdivision. For purposes of this subparagraph, the phrase "similar property" includes, for example, such property as a draft of a speech, a manuscript, a research paper, an oral recording of any type, a transcript of an oral recording, a transcript of an oral interview or of dictation, a personal or business diary, a log or journal, a corporate archive, including a corporate charter, office correspondence, a financial record, a drawing, a photograph, or a dispatch. A letter, memorandum, or property similar to a letter or memorandum, addressed to a taxpayer shall be considered as prepared or produced for him. This subparagraph does not apply to property, such as a corporate archive, office correspondence, or a financial record, sold or disposed of as part of a going business if such property has no significant value separate and apart from its relation to and use in such business; it also does not apply to any property to which subparagraph (1) of this paragraph applies (i.e., property to which section 1221(3) applied before its amendment by section 514(a) of the Tax Reform Act of 1969 (83 Stat. 643)).

(3) For purposes of this paragraph, in general, property is created in whole or in part by the personal efforts of a taxpayer if such taxpayer performs literary, theatrical, musical, artistic, or other creative or productive work which affirmatively contributes to the creation of the property, or if such taxpayer directs and guides others in the performance of such work. A taxpayer, such as corporate executive, who merely has administrative control of writers, actors, artists, or personnel and who does not substantially engage in the direction and guidance of such persons in the performance of their work, does not create property by his personal efforts. However, for purposes of subparagraph (2) of this paragraph, a letter or memorandum, or property similar to a letter or memorandum, which is prepared by personnel who are under the administrative control of a taxpayer, such as a corporate executive, shall be deemed to have been prepared or produced for him whether or not such letter, memorandum, or similar property is reviewed by him.

(4) For the application of section 1231 to the sale or exchange of property to which this paragraph applies, see § 1.1231-1. For the application of section 170 to the charitable contribution of property to which this paragraph applies, see section 170(e) and the regulations thereunder.

(d) Section 1221(4) excludes from the definition of "capital asset" accounts or notes receivable acquired in the ordinary course of trade or business for services rendered or from the sale of stock in trade or inventory or property held for sale to customers in the ordinary course of trade or business. Thus, if a taxpayer acquires a note receivable for services rendered, reports the fair market value of the note as income, and later sells the note for less than the amount previously reported, the loss is an ordinary loss. On the other hand, if the taxpayer later sells the note for more than the amount originally reported, the excess is treated as ordinary income.

(e) Obligations of the United States or any of its possessions, or of a State or Territory, or any political subdivision thereof, or of the District of Columbia, issued on or after March 1, 1941, on a discount basis and payable without interest at a fixed maturity date not exceeding one year from the date of issue, are excluded from the term "capital assets." * * *

* * *

[T.D. 6500, 25 FR 12003, Nov. 26, 1960, as amended by T.D. 7369, 40 FR 29840, July 16, 1975]

§ 1.1223-1 Determination of period for which capital assets are held.

(a) The holding period of property received in an exchange by a taxpayer includes the period for which the property which he exchanged was held by him, if the property received has the same basis in whole or in part for determining gain or loss in the hands of the taxpayer as the property exchanged. However, this rule shall apply, in the case of exchanges after March 1, 1954, only if the property exchanged was at the time of the exchange a capital asset in the hands of the taxpayer or property used in his trade or business as defined in section 1231(b). For the purposes of this paragraph, the term "exchange" includes the following transactions: (1) An involuntary conversion described in section 1033, and (2) a distribution to which section 355 (or so much of section 356 as relates to section 355) applies. Thus, if property acquired as the result of a compulsory or involuntary conversion of other property of the taxpayer has under section 1033(c) the same basis in whole or in part in the hands of the taxpayer as the property so converted, its acquisition is treated as an exchange and the holding period of the newly acquired property shall include the period during which the converted property was held by the taxpayer. Thus, also, where stock of a controlled corporation is received by a taxpayer pursuant to a distribution to which section 355 (or so much of section 356 as relates to section 355) applies, the distribution is treated as an exchange and the period for which the taxpayer has held the stock of the controlled corporation shall include the period for which he held the stock of the distributing corporation with respect to which such distribution was made.

(b) The holding period of property in the hands of a taxpayer shall include the period during which the property was held by any other person, if such property has the same basis in whole or in part in the hands of the taxpayer for determining gain or loss from a sale or exchange as it would have in the hands of such other person. For example, the period for which property acquired by gift after December 31, 1920, was held by the donor must be included in determining the period for which the property was held by the taxpayer if, under the provisions of section 1015, such property has, for the purpose of determining gain or loss from the sale or exchange, the same basis in the hands of the taxpayer as it would have in the hands of the donor.

* * *

(d) If the acquisition of stock or securities resulted in the nondeductibility (under section 1091, relating to wash sales) of the loss from the sale or other disposition of substantially identical stock or securities, the holding period of the newly acquired securities shall include the period for which the taxpayer held the securities with respect to which the loss was not allowable.

(e) The period for which the taxpayer has held stock, or stock subscription rights, received on a distribution shall be determined as though the stock dividend, or stock right, as the case may be, were the stock in respect of which the dividend was issued if the basis for determining gain or loss upon the sale or other disposition of such stock dividend or stock right is determined under section 307. If the basis of stock received by a taxpayer pursuant to a spin-off is determined under so much of section 1052(c) as refers to section 113(a)(23) of the Internal Revenue Code of 1939, and such stock is sold or otherwise disposed of in a taxable year which is subject to the Internal Revenue Code of 1954, the period for which the taxpayer has held the stock received in such spin-off shall include the period for which he held the stock of the distributing corporation with respect to which such distribution was made.

(f) The period for which the taxpayer has held stock or securities issued to him by a corporation pursuant to the exercise by him of rights to acquire such stock or securities from the corporation will, in every case and whether or not the receipt of taxable gain was recognized in connection with the distribution of the rights, begin with and include the day upon which the rights to acquire such stock or securities were exercised. A taxpayer will be deemed to have exercised rights received from a corporation to acquire stock or securities therein where there is an expression of assent to the terms of such rights made by the taxpayer in the manner requested or authorized by the corporation.

(g) The period for which the taxpayer has held a residence, the acquisition of which resulted under the provisions of section 1034 in the nonrecognition of any part of the gain realized on the sale or exchange of another residence, shall include the period for which such other residence had been held as of the date of such sale or exchange. See § 1.1034-1. For purposes of this paragraph, the term "sale or exchange" includes an involuntary conversion occurring after December 31, 1950, and before January 1, 1954.

(h) If a taxpayer accepts delivery of a commodity in satisfaction of a commodity futures contract, the holding period of the commodity shall include the period for which the taxpayer held the commodity futures contract, if such futures contract was a capital asset in his hands.

(i) If shares of stock in a corporation are sold from lots purchased at different dates or at different prices and the identity of the lots cannot be determined, the rules prescribed by the regulations under section 1012 for determining the cost or other basis of such stocks so sold or transferred shall also apply for the purpose of determining the holding period of such stock.

* * *

[T.D. 6500, 25 FR 12005, Nov. 26, 1960, as amended by T.D. 7238, 37 FR 28717, Dec. 29, 1972; T.D. 7728, 45 FR 72650, Nov. 3, 1980]

Special Rules for Determining Capital Gains and Losses

§ 1.1233–1 Gains and losses from short sales.

(a) General. (1) For income tax purposes, a short sale is not deemed to be consummated until delivery of property to close the short sale. Whether the recognized gain or loss from a short sale is capital gain or loss or ordinary gain or loss depends upon whether the property so delivered constitutes a capital asset in the hands of the taxpayer.

(2) Thus, if a dealer in securities makes a short sale of X Corporation stock, ordinary gain or loss results on closing of the short sale if the stock used to close the short sale was stock which he held primarily for sale to customers in the ordinary course of his trade or business. If the stock used to close the short sale was a capital asset in his hands, or if the taxpayer in this example was not a dealer, a capital gain or loss would result.

(3) Generally, the period for which a taxpayer holds property delivered to close a short sale determines whether long-term or short-term capital gain or loss results.

(4) Thus, if a taxpayer makes a short sale of shares of stock and covers the short sale by purchasing and delivering shares which he held for not more than 1 year (6 months for taxable years beginning before 1977; 9 months for taxable years beginning in 1977), the recognized gain or loss would be considered short-term capital gain or loss. If the short sale is made through a broker and the broker borrows property to make a delivery, the short sale is not deemed to be consummated until the obligation of the seller created by the short sale is finally discharged by delivery of property to the broker to replace the property borrowed by the broker.

(5) For rules for determining the date of sale for purposes of applying under section 1091 the 61-day period applicable to a short sale of stock or securities at a loss, see paragraph (g) of § 1.1091–1.

(b) Hedging transactions. Under section 1233(g), the provisions of section 1233 and this section shall not apply to any bona fide hedging transaction in commodity futures entered into by flour millers, producers of cloth, operators of grain elevators, etc., for the purpose of their business. Gain or loss from a short sale of commodity futures which does not qualify as a hedging transaction shall be considered gain or loss from the sale or exchange of a capital asset if the commodity future used to close the short sale constitutes a capital asset in the hands of the taxpayer as explained in paragraph (a) of this section.

[T.D. 6500, 25 FR 12011, Nov. 26, 1960, as amended by T.D. 6494, 25 FR 9372, Sept. 30, 1960; T.D. 6926, 32 FR 11468, Aug. 9, 1967; T.D. 7728, 45 FR 72650, Nov. 3, 1980]

§ 1.1234–1 Options to buy or sell.

(a) Sale or exchange—(1) Capital assets. Gain or loss from the sale or exchange of an option (or privilege) to buy or sell property which is (or if acquired would be) a capital asset in the hands of the taxpayer holding the option is considered as gain or loss from the sale or exchange of a capital asset (unless, under the provisions of subparagraph (2) of this paragraph, the gain or loss is subject to the provisions of section 1231). The period for which the taxpayer has held the option determines whether the capital gain or loss is short-term or long-term.

(2) Section 1231 transactions. Gain or loss from the sale or exchange of an option to buy or sell property is considered a gain or loss subject to the provisions of section 1231 if, had the sale or exchange been of the property subject to the option, held by the taxpayer for the length of time he held the option, the sale or exchange would have been subject to the provisions of section 1231.

(3) Other property. Gain or loss from the sale or exchange of an option to buy or sell property which is not (or if acquired would not be) a capital asset in the hands of the taxpayer holding the option is considered ordinary income or loss (unless under the provisions of subparagraph (2) of this paragraph, the gain or loss is subject to the provisions of section 1231).

(b) Failure to exercise option. If the holder of an option to buy or sell property incurs a loss on failure to exercise the option, the option is deemed to have been sold or exchanged on the date that it expired. Any such loss to the holder of an option is treated under the general rule provided in paragraph (a) of this section. In general, any gain to the grantor of an option arising from the failure of the holder to exercise it, and any gain or loss realized by the grantor of an option as a result of a closing transaction, such as repurchasing the option from the holder, is considered ordinary income or loss. However, for the treatment of gain or loss from a closing transaction with respect to or gain on the lapse of an option granted in stock, securities, commodities or commodity futures, see section

1234(b) and § 1.1234–3. For special rules for grantors of straddles applicable to certain options granted on or before September 1, 1976, see § 1.1234–2.

(c) **Certain options to sell property at a fixed price.** Section 1234 does not apply to a loss on the failure to exercise an option to sell property at a fixed price which is acquired on the same day on which the property identified as intended to be used in exercising the option is acquired. Such a loss is not recognized, but the cost of the option is added to the basis of the property with which it is identified. See section 1233(c) and the regulations thereunder.

(d) **Dealers in options to buy or sell.** Any gain or loss realized by a dealer in options from the sale or exchange or an option to buy or sell property is considered ordinary income or loss under paragraph (a)(3) of this section. A dealer in options to buy or sell property is considered a dealer in the property subject to the option.

(e) **Other exceptions.** Section 1234 does not apply to gain resulting from the sale or exchange of an option:

(1) To the extent that the gain is in the nature of compensation (see sections 61 and 421, and the regulations thereunder, relating to employee stock options);

(2) If the option is treated as section 306 stock (see section 306 and the regulations thereunder, relating to dispositions of certain stock);

(3) To the extent that the gain is a distribution of earnings or profits taxable as a dividend (see section 301 and the regulations thereunder, relating to distributions of property); or

(4) Acquired by the taxpayer before March 1, 1954, if in the hands of the taxpayer such option is a capital asset (whether or not the property to which the option relates is, or would be if acquired by the taxpayer, a capital asset in the hands of the taxpayer).

(f) **Limitations on effect of section.** Losses to which section 1234 applies are subject to the limitations on losses under sections 165(c) and 1211 when applicable. Section 1234 does not permit the deduction of any loss which is disallowed under any other provision of law. In addition, section 1234 does not apply to an option to lease property, but does apply to an option to buy or sell a lease. Thus, an option to obtain all the right, title, and interest of a lessee in leased property is subject to

the provisions of section 1234, but an option to obtain a sublease from the lessee is not. Furthermore, if section 1234 applies to an option to buy or sell a lease, it is the character the lease itself, if acquired, would have in the hands of the taxpayer, and not the character of the property leased, which determines the treatment of gain or loss experienced by the taxpayer with respect to such an option.

(g) **Examples.** The rules set forth in this section may be illustrated by the following examples:

Example (1). A taxpayer is considering buying a new house for his residence and acquires an option to buy a certain house at a fixed price. Although the property goes up in value, the taxpayer decides he does not want the house for his residence and sells the option for more than he paid for it. The gain which taxpayer realized is a capital gain since the property, if acquired, would have been a capital asset in his hands.

Example (2). Assume the same facts as in example (1), except that the property goes down in value, and the taxpayer decides not to purchase the house. He sells the option at a loss. While this is a capital loss under section 1234, it is not a deductible loss because of the provisions of section 165(c).

Example (3). A dealer in industrial property acquires an option to buy an industrial site and fails to exercise the option. The loss is an ordinary loss since he would have held the property for sale to customers in the ordinary course of his trade or business if he had acquired it.

[T.D. 6500, 25 FR 12013, Nov. 26, 1960; T.D. 7652, 44 FR 62282, Oct. 30, 1979]

§ 1.1235–1 Sale or exchange of patents.

(a) **General rule.** Section 1235 provides that a transfer (other than by gift, inheritance, or devise) of all substantial rights to a patent, or of an undivided interest in all such rights to a patent, by a holder to a person other than a related person constitutes the sale or exchange of a capital asset held for more than 1 year (6 months for taxable years beginning before 1977; 9 months for taxable years beginning in 1977), whether or not payments therefor are:

(1) Payable periodically over a period generally coterminous with the transferee's use of the patent, or

(2) Contingent on the productivity, use, or disposition of the property transferred.

(b) **Scope of section 1235.** If a transfer is not one described in paragraph (a) of this section, section 1235 shall be disregarded in determining whether or not such transfer is the sale or exchange of a capital asset. For example, a transfer by a person other than a holder or a transfer by a holder to a related person is not governed by section 1235. The tax consequences of such transfers shall be determined under other provisions of the internal revenue laws.

(c) **Special rules—(1) Payments for infringement.** If section 1235 applies to the transfer of all substantial rights to a patent (or an undivided interest therein), amounts received in settlement of, or as the award of damages in, a suit for compensatory damages for infringement of the patent shall be considered payments attributable to a transfer to which section 1235 applies to the extent that such amounts relate to the interest transferred. * * *

(2) **Payments to an employee.** Payments received by an employee as compensation for services rendered as an employee under an employment contract requiring the employee to transfer to the employer the rights to any invention by such employee are not attributable to a transfer to which section 1235 applies. However, whether payments received by an employee from his employer (under an employment contract or otherwise) are attributable to the transfer by the employee of all substantial rights to a patent (or an undivided interest therein) or are compensation for services rendered the employer by the employee is a question of fact. In determining which is the case, consideration shall be given not only to all the facts and circumstances of the employment relationship but also to whether the amount of such payments depends upon the production, sale, or use by, or the value to, the employer of the patent rights transferred by the employee. If it is determined that payments are attributable to the transfer of patent rights, and all other requirements under section 1235 are met, such payments shall be treated as proceeds derived from the sale of a patent.

(3) **Successive transfers.** The applicability of section 1235 to transfers of undivided interest in patents, or to successive transfers of such rights, shall be determined separately with respect to each transfer. For example, X, who is a holder, and Y, who is not a holder, transfer their respective two-thirds and one-third undivided interests in a patent to Z. Assume the transfer by X qualifies under section 1235 and that X in a later transfer acquires all the rights with respect to Y's interest, including the rights to payments from Z. One-third of all the payments thereafter received by X from Z are

not attributable to a transfer to which section 1235 applies.

(d) **Payor's treatment of payments in a transfer under section 1235.** Payments made by the transferee of patent rights pursuant to a transfer satisfying the requirements of section 1235 are payments of the purchase price for the patent rights and are not the payment of royalties.

* * *

[T.D. 6500, 25 FR 12014, Nov. 26, 1960, as amended by T.D. 6885, 31 FR 7803, June 2, 1966; T.D. 7728, 45 FR 72650, Nov. 3, 1980]

§ 1.1235–2 Definition of terms.

For the purposes of section 1235 and § 1.1235–1:

(a) **Patent.** The term "patent" means a patent granted under the provisions of title 35 of the United States Code, or any foreign patent granting rights generally similar to those under a United States patent. It is not necessary that the patent or patent application for the invention be in existence if the requirements of section 1235 are otherwise met.

(b) **All substantial rights to a patent.** (1) The term "all substantial rights to a patent" means all rights (whether or not then held by the grantor) which are of value at the time the rights to the patent (or an undivided interest therein) are transferred. The term "all substantial rights to a patent" does not include a grant of rights to a patent:

(i) Which is limited geographically within the country of issuance;

(ii) Which is limited in duration by the terms of the agreement to a period less than the remaining life of the patent;

(iii) Which grants rights to the grantee, in fields of use within trades or industries, which are less than all the rights covered by the patent, which exist and have value at the time of the grant; or

(iv) Which grants to the grantee less than all the claims or inventions covered by the patent which exist and have value at the time of the grant.

The circumstances of the whole transaction, rather than the particular terminology used in the instrument of transfer, shall be considered in determining whether or not all substantial rights to a patent are transferred in a transaction.

(2) Rights which are not considered substantial for purposes of section 1235 may be retained by the holder. Examples of such rights are:

(i) The retention by the transferor of legal title for the purpose of securing performance or payment by the transferee in a transaction involving transfer of an exclusive license to manufacture, use, and sell for the life of the patent;

(ii) The retention by the transferor of rights in the property which are not inconsistent with the passage of ownership, such as the retention of a security interest (such as a vendor's lien), or a reservation in the nature of a condition subsequent (such as a provision for forfeiture on account of nonperformance).

(3) Examples of rights which may or may not be substantial, depending upon the circumstances of the whole transaction in which rights to a patent are transferred, are:

(i) The retention by the transferor of an absolute right to prohibit sublicensing or subassignment by the transferee;

(ii) The failure to convey to the transferee the right to use or to sell the patent property.

(4) The retention of a right to terminate the transfer at will is the retention of a substantial right for the purposes of section 1235.

(c) **Undivided interest.** A person owns an "undivided interest" in all substantial rights to a patent when he owns the same fractional share of each and every substantial right to the patent. It does not include, for example, a right to the income from a patent, or a license limited geographically, or a license which covers some, but not all, of the valuable claims or uses covered by the patent. A transfer limited in duration by the terms of the instrument to a period less than the remaining life of the patent is not a transfer of an undivided interest in all substantial rights to a patent.

(d) **Holder.** (1) The term "holder" means any individual:

(i) Whose efforts created the patent property and who would qualify as the "original and first" inventor, or joint inventor, within the meaning of title 35 of the United States Code, or

(ii) Who has acquired his interest in the patent property in exchange for a consideration paid to the inventor in money or money's worth prior to the actual reduction of the invention to practice (see paragraph (e) of this section), provided that such individual was neither the employer of the inventor nor related to him (see paragraph (f) of this section). The requirement that such individual is neither the employer of the inventor nor related to him must be satisfied at the time when the substantive rights as to the interest to be acquired are determined, and at the time when the consideration in money or money's worth to be paid is definitely fixed. For example, if prior to the actual reduction to practice of an invention an individual who is neither the employer of the inventor nor related to him agrees to pay the inventor a sum of money definitely fixed as to amount in return for an undivided one-half interest in rights to a patent and at a later date, when such individual has become the employer of the inventor, he pays the definitely fixed sum of money pursuant to the earlier agreement, such individual will not be denied the status of a holder because of such employment relationship.

(2) Although a partnership cannot be a holder, each member of a partnership who is an individual may qualify as a holder as to his share of a patent owned by the partnership. For example, if an inventor who is a member of a partnership composed solely of individuals uses partnership property in the development of his invention with the understanding that the patent when issued will become partnership property, each of the inventor's partners during this period would qualify as a holder. If, in this example, the partnership were not composed solely of individuals, nevertheless, each of the individual partners' distributive shares of income attributable to the transfer of all substantial rights to the patent or an undivided interest therein, would be considered proceeds from the sale or exchange of a capital asset held for more than 1 year (6 months for taxable years beginning before 1977; 9 months for taxable years beginning in 1977).

(3) An individual may qualify as a holder whether or not he is in the business of making inventions or in the business of buying and selling patents.

(e) **Actual reduction to practice.** For the purposes of determining whether an individual is a holder under paragraph (d) of this section, the term "actual reduction to practice" has the same meaning as it does under section 102(g) of title 35 of the United States Code. Generally, an invention is reduced to actual practice when it has been tested and operated successfully under operating conditions. This may occur either before or after application for a patent but cannot occur later than the earliest time that commercial exploitation of the invention occurs.

* * *

[T.D. 6500, 25 FR 12014, Nov. 26, 1960, as amended by T.D. 6852, 30 FR 12730, Oct. 6, 1965; T.D. 7728, 45 FR 72650, Nov. 3, 1980]

§ 1.1236-1 Dealers in securities.

(a) **Capital gains.** Section 1236(a) provides that gain realized by a dealer in securities from the sale or exchange of a security (as defined in paragraph (c) of this section) shall not be considered as gain from the sale or exchange of a capital asset unless:

(1) The security is, before the expiration of the thirtieth day after the date of its acquisition, clearly identified in the dealer's records as a security held for investment or, if acquired before October 20, 1951, was so identified before November 20, 1951; and

(2) The security is not held by the dealer primarily for sale to customers in the ordinary course of his trade or business at any time after the identification referred to in subparagraph (1) of this paragraph has been made.

Unless both of these requirements are met, the gain is considered as gain from the sale of assets held by the dealer primarily for sale to customers in the course of his business.

(b) **Ordinary losses.** Section 1236(b) provides that a loss sustained by a dealer in securities from the sale or exchange of a security shall not be considered a loss from the sale or exchange of property which is not a capital asset if at any time after November 19, 1951, the security has been clearly identified in the dealer's records as a security held for investment. Once a security has been identified after November 19, 1951, as being held by the dealer for investment, it shall retain that character for purposes of determining loss on its ultimate disposition, even though at the time of its disposition the dealer holds it primarily for sale to his customers in the ordinary course of his business. However, section 1236 has no application to the extent that section 582(c) applies to losses of banks.

(c) **Definitions—(1) Security.** For the purposes of this section, the term "security" means any share of stock in any corporation, any certificate of stock or interest in any corporation, any note, bond, debenture, or other evidence of indebtedness, or any evidence of any interest in, or right to subscribe to or purchase, any of the foregoing.

(2) **Dealer in securities.** For definition of a "dealer in securities", see the regulations under section 471.

(d) **Identification of security in dealer's records.** (1) A security is clearly identified in the dealer's records as a security held for investment when there is an accounting separation of the security from other securities, as by making appropriate entries in the dealer's books of account to distinguish the security from inventories and to designate it as an investment and by (i) indicating with such entries, to the extent feasible, the individual serial number of, or other characteristic symbol imprinted upon, the individual security, or (ii) adopting any other method of identification satisfactory to the Commissioner.

(2) In computing the 30-day period prescribed by section 1236(a), the first day of the period is the day following the date of acquisition. Thus, in the case of a security acquired on March 18, 1957, the 30-day period expires at midnight on April 17, 1957.

[T.D. 6500, 25 FR 12015, Nov. 26, 1960, as amended by T.D. 6726, 29 FR 5667, April 29, 1964]

§ 1.1237-1 Real property subdivided for sale.

(a) **General rule—(1) Introductory.** This section provides a special rule for determining whether the taxpayer holds real property primarily for sale to customers in the ordinary course of his business under section 1221(1). This rule is to permit taxpayers qualifying under it to sell real estate from a single tract held for investment without the income being treated as ordinary income merely because of subdividing the tract or of active efforts to sell it. The rule is not applicable to dealers in real estate or to corporations, except a corporation making such sales in a taxable year beginning after December 31, 1954, if such corporation qualifies under the provisions of paragraph (c)(5)(iv) of this section.

(2) **When subdividing and selling activities are to be disregarded.** When its conditions are met, section 1237 provides that if there is no other substantial evidence that a taxpayer holds real estate primarily for sale to customers in the ordinary course of his business, he shall not be considered a real estate dealer holding it primarily for sale merely because he has (i) subdivided the tract into lots (or parcels) and (ii) engaged in advertising,

promotion, selling activities or the use of sales agents in connection with the sale of lots in such subdivision. Such subdividing and selling activities shall be disregarded in determining the purpose for which the taxpayer held real property sold from a subdivision whenever it is the only substantial evidence indicating that the taxpayer has ever held the real property sold primarily for sale to customers in the ordinary course of his business.

(3) When subdividing and selling activities are to be taken into account. When other substantial evidence tends to show that the taxpayer held real property for sale to customers in the ordinary course of his business, his activities in connection with the subdivision and sale of the property sold shall be taken into account in determining the purpose for which the taxpayer held both the subdivided property and any other real property. For example, such other evidence may consist of the taxpayer's selling activities in connection with other property in prior years during which he was engaged in subdividing or selling activities with respect to the subdivided tract, his intention in prior years (or at the time of acquiring the property subdivided) to hold the tract primarily for sale in his business, his subdivision of other tracts in the same year, his holding other real property for sale to customers in the same year, or his construction of a permanent real estate office which he could use in selling other real property. On the other hand, if the only evidence of the taxpayer's purpose in holding real property consisted of not more than one of the following, in the year in question, such fact would not be considered substantial other evidence:

(i) Holding a real estate dealer's license;

(ii) Selling other real property which was clearly investment property;

(iii) Acting as a salesman for a real estate dealer, but without any financial interest in the business; or

(iv) Mere ownership of other vacant real property without engaging in any selling activity whatsoever with respect to it.

If more than one of the above exists, the circumstances may or may not constitute substantial evidence that the taxpayer held real property for sale in his business, depending upon the particular facts in each case.

(4) Section 1237 not exclusive. (i) The rule in section 1237 is not exclusive in its application.

Section 1237 has no application in determining whether or not real property is held by a taxpayer primarily for sale in his business if any requirement under the section is not met. Also, even though the conditions of section 1237 are met, the rules of section 1237 are not applicable if without regard to section 1237 the real property sold would not have been considered real property held primarily for sale to customers in the ordinary course of his business. Thus, the district director may at all times conclude from convincing evidence that the taxpayer held the real property solely as an investment. Furthermore, whether or not the conditions of section 1237 are met, the section has no application to losses realized upon the sale of realty from subdivided property.

(ii) If, owing solely to the application of section 1237, the real property sold is deemed not to have been held primarily for sale in the ordinary course of business, any gain realized upon such sale shall be treated as ordinary income to the extent provided in section 1237(b)(1) and (2) and paragraph (e) of this section. Any additional gain realized upon the sale shall be treated as gain arising from the sale of a capital asset or, if the circumstances so indicate, as gain arising from the sale of real property used in the trade or business as defined in section 1231(b)(1). For the relationship between sections 1237 and 1231, see paragraph (f) of this section.

(5) Principal conditions of qualification. Before section 1237 applies, the taxpayer must meet three basic conditions, more fully explained later: He cannot have held any part of the tract at any time previously for sale in the ordinary course of his business, nor in the year of sale held any other real estate for sale to customers; he cannot make substantial improvements on the tract which increase the value of the lot sold substantially; and he must have owned the property 5 years, unless he inherited it. However, the taxpayer may make certain improvements if they are necessary to make the property marketable if he elects neither to add their cost to the basis of the property, or of any other property, nor to deduct the cost as an expense, and he has held the property at least 10 years. If the requirements of section 1237 are met, gain (but not more than 5 percent of the selling price of each lot) shall be treated as ordinary income in and after the year in which the sixth lot or parcel is sold.

[T.D. 6500, 25 FR 12016, Nov. 26, 1960]

§ 1.1241-1 Cancellation of lease or distributor's agreement.

(a) In general. Section 1241 provides that proceeds received by lessees or distributors from the cancellation of leases or of certain distributorship agreements are considered as amounts received in exchange therefor. Section 1241 applies to leases of both real and personal property. Distributorship agreements to which section 1241 applies are described in paragraph (c) of this section. Section 1241 has no application in determining whether or not a cancellation not qualifying under that section is a sale or exchange. Further, section 1241 has no application in determining whether or not a lease or a distributorship agreement is a capital asset, even though its cancellation qualifies as an exchange under section 1241.

(b) Definition of "cancellation". The term "cancellation" of a lease or a distributor's agreement, as used in section 1241, means a termination of all the contractual rights of a lessee or distributor with respect to particular premises or a particular distributorship, other than by the expiration of the lease or agreement in accordance with its terms. A payment made in good faith for a partial cancellation of a lease or a distributorship agreement is recognized as an amount received for cancellation under section 1241 if the cancellation relates to a severable economic unit, such as a portion of the premises covered by a lease, a reduction in the unexpired term of a lease or distributorship agreement, or a distributorship in one of several areas or of one of several products. Payments made for other modifications of leases or distributorship agreements, however, are not recognized as amounts received for cancellation under section 1241.

(c) Amounts received upon cancellation of a distributorship agreement. Section 1241 applies to distributorship agreements only if they are for marketing or marketing and servicing of goods. It does not apply to agreements for selling intangible property or for rendering personal services as, for example, agreements establishing insurance agencies or agencies for the brokerage of securities. Further, it applies to a distributorship agreement only if the distributor has made a substantial investment of capital in the distributorship. The substantial capital investment must be reflected in physical assets such as inventories of tangible goods, equipment, machinery, storage facilities, or similar property. An investment is not considered substantial for purposes of section 1241 unless it consists of a significant fraction or more of the facilities for storing, transporting, processing, or otherwise dealing with the goods distributed, or consists of a substantial inventory of such goods. The investment required in the maintenance of an office merely for clerical operations is not considered substantial for purposes of this section. Furthermore, section 1241 shall not apply unless a substantial amount of the capital or assets needed for carrying on the operations of a distributorship are acquired by the distributor and actually used in carrying on the distributorship at some time before the cancellation of the distributorship agreement. It is immaterial for the purposes of section 1241 whether the distributor acquired the assets used in performing the functions of the distributorship before or after beginning his operations under the distributorship agreement. It is also immaterial whether the distributor is a retailer, wholesaler, jobber, or other type of distributor. The application of this paragraph may be illustrated by the following examples:

Example (1). Taxpayer is a distributor of various food products. He leases a warehouse including cold storage facilities and owns a number of motor trucks. In 1955 he obtains the exclusive rights to market certain frozen food products in his State. The marketing is accomplished by using the warehouse and trucks acquired before he entered into the agreement and entails no additional capital. Payments received upon the cancellation of the agreement are treated under section 1241 as though received upon the sale or exchange of the agreement.

Example (2). Assume that the taxpayer in example (1) entered into an exclusive distributorship agreement with the producer under which the taxpayer merely solicits orders through his staff of salesmen, the goods being shipped direct to the purchasers. Payments received upon the cancellation of the agreement would not be treated under section 1241 as though received upon the sale or exchange of the agreement.

Example (3). Taxpayer is an exclusive distributor for M city of certain frozen food products which he distributes to frozen-food freezer and locker customers. The terms of his distributorship do not make it necessary for him to have any substantial investment in inventory. Taxpayer rents a loading platform for a nominal amount, but has no warehouse space. Orders for goods from customers are consolidated by the taxpayer and forwarded to the producer from time to time. Upon receipt of these goods, taxpayer allocates them to the individual orders of customers and delivers them immediately by truck. Although it would require a fleet of fifteen or twenty trucks to carry out this operation, the distributor uses only one truck of his own and hires cartage companies to deliver the bulk of the merchandise to the customers. Payments received upon the cancellation of the distributorship agreement in such a case would not be considered received upon the sale or exchange of the agreement under section 1241 since the taxpayer does not have facilities for the physical handling of more than a small fraction of the goods involved in carrying on the distributorship and, therefore, does not have a substantial capital investment in the distributorship. On the other hand, if the taxpayer had acquired and used a substantial number of the trucks necessary for the deliveries to his customers, payments received upon the cancellation of the agreement would be considered received in exchange therefor under section 1241.

[T.D. 6500, 25 FR 12021, Nov. 26, 1960]

§ 1.1244(a)-1 Loss on small business stock treated as ordinary loss.

(a) **In general.** Subject to certain conditions and limitations, section 1244 provides that a loss on the sale or exchange (including a transaction treated as a sale or exchange, such as worthlessness) of "section 1244 stock" which would otherwise be treated as a loss from the sale or exchange of a capital asset shall be treated as a loss from the sale or exchange of an asset which is not a capital asset (referred to in this section and §§ 1.1244(b)-1 to 1.1244(e)-1, inclusive, as an "ordinary loss"). Such a loss shall be allowed as a deduction from gross income in arriving at adjusted gross income. The requirements that must be satisfied in order that stock may be considered section 1244 stock are described in §§ 1.1244(c)-1 and 1.1244(c)-2. These requirements relate to the stock itself and the corporation issuing such stock. In addition, the taxpayer who claims an ordinary loss deduction pursuant to section 1244 must satisfy the requirements of paragraph (b) of this section.

(b) **Taxpayers entitled to ordinary loss.** The allowance of an ordinary loss deduction for a loss of section 1244 stock is permitted only to the following two classes of taxpayers:

(1) An individual sustaining the loss to whom the stock was issued by a small business corporation, or

(2) An individual who is a partner in a partnership at the time the partnership acquired the stock in an issuance from a small business corporation and whose distributive share of partnership items reflects the loss sustained by the partnership. The ordinary loss deduction is limited to the lesser of the partner's distributive share at the time of the issuance of the stock or the partner's distributive share at the time the loss is sustained.

In order to claim a deduction under section 1244 the individual, or the partnership, sustaining the loss must have continuously held the stock from the date of issuance. A corporation, trust, or estate is not entitled to ordinary loss treatment under section 1244 regardless of how the stock was acquired. An individual who acquires stock from a shareholder by purchase, gift, devise, or in any other manner is not entitled to an ordinary loss under section 1244 with respect to this stock. Thus, ordinary loss treatment is not available to a partner to whom the stock is distributed by the partnership. Stock acquired through an investment banking firm, or other person, participating in the sale of an issue may qualify for ordinary loss treatment only if the stock is not first issued to the firm or person. Thus, for example, if the firm acts as a selling agent for the issuing corporation the stock may qualify. On the other hand, stock purchased by an investment firm and subsequently resold does not qualify as section 1244 stock in the hands of the person acquiring the stock from the firm.

(c) **Examples.** The provisions of paragraph (b) of this section may be illustrated by the following examples:

Example (1). A and B, both individuals, and C, a trust, are equal partners in a partnership to which a small business corporation issues section 1244 stock. The partnership sells the stock at a loss. A's and B's distributive share of the loss may be treated as an ordinary loss pursuant to section 1244, but C's distributive share of the loss may not be so treated.

Example (2). The facts are the same as in example (1) except that the section 1244 stock is distributed by the partnership to partner A and he subsequently sells the stock at a loss. Section 1244 is not applicable to the loss since A did not acquire the stock by issuance from the small business corporation.

[T.D. 6495, 25 FR 9675, Oct. 8, 1960, as amended by T.D. 7779, 46 FR 29467, June 18, 1981]

§ 1.1244(b)-1 Annual limitation.

(a) **In general.** Subsection (b) of section 1244 imposes a limitation on the aggregate amount of loss that for any taxable year may be treated as an ordinary loss by a taxpayer by reason of that section. In the case of a partnership, the limitation is determined separately as to each partner. Any amount of loss in excess of the applicable limitation is treated as loss from the sale or exchange of a capital asset.

(b) **Amount of loss—(1) Taxable years beginning after December 31, 1978.** For any taxable year beginning after December 31, 1978, the maximum amount that may be treated as an ordinary loss under section 1244 is:

(i) $50,000, or

(ii) $100,000, if a husband and wife file a joint return under section 6013. These limitations on the maximum amount of ordinary loss apply whether the loss or losses are sustained on pre-November 1978 stock (as defined in § 1.1244(c)–1(a)(1)), post-November 1978 stock (as defined in § 1.1244(c)–1(a)(2)), or on any combination of pre-November 1978 stock and post-November 1978 stock. The limitation referred to in (ii) applies to a joint return whether the loss or losses are sustained by one or both spouses.

* * *

[T.D. 6495, 25 FR 9676, Oct. 8, 1960, as amended by T.D. 7779, 46 FR 29467, June 18, 1981]

§ 1.1244(c)–1 Section 1244 stock defined.

(a) **In general.** For purposes of §§ 1.1244(a)–1 to 1.244(e)–1, inclusive:

(1) The term "pre-November 1978 stock" means stock issued after June 30, 1958, and on or before November 6, 1978.

(2) The term "post-November 1978 stock" means stock issued after November 6, 1978.

In order that stock may qualify as section 1244 stock, the requirements described in paragraphs (b) through (e) of this section must be satisfied. In addition, the requirements of paragraph (f) of this section must be satisfied in the case of pre-November 1978 stock. Whether these requirements have been met is determined at the time the stock is issued, except for the requirement in paragraph (e) of this section. Whether the requirement in paragraph (e) of this section, relating to gross receipts of the corporation, has been satisfied is determined at the time a loss is sustained. Therefore, at the time of issuance it cannot be said with certainty that stock will qualify for the benefits of section 1244.

* * *

(c) **Small business corporation.** At the time the stock is issued (or, in the case of pre-November 1978 stock, at the time of adoption of the plan described in paragraph (f)(1) of this section) the corporation must be a "small business corpora-

tion". See § 1.1244(c)–2 for the definition of a small business corporation.

(d) **Issued for money or other property.** (1) The stock must be issued to the taxpayer for money or other property transferred by the taxpayer to the corporation. However, stock issued in exchange for stock or securities, including stock or securities, of the issuing corporation, cannot qualify as section 1244 stock, except as provided in § 1.1244(d)–3, relating to certain cases where stock is issued in exchange for section 1244 stock. Stock issued for services rendered or to be rendered to, or for the benefit of, the issuing corporation does not qualify as section 1244 stock. Stock issued in consideration for cancellation of indebtedness of the corporation shall be considered issued in exchange for money or other property unless such indebtedness is evidenced by a security, or arises out of the performance of personal services.

(2) The following examples illustrate situations where stock fails to qualify as section 1244 stock as a result of the rules in subparagraph (1) of this paragraph:

Example (1). A taxpayer owns stock of Corporation X issued to him prior to July 1, 1958. Under a plan adopted in 1977, he exchanges his stock for a new issuance of stock of Corporation X. The stock received by the taxpayer in the exchange may not qualify as section 1244 stock even if the corporation has adopted a valid plan and is a small business corporation.

Example (2). A taxpayer owns stock in Corporation X. Corporation X merges into Corporation Y. In exchange for his stock, Corporation Y issues shares of its stock to the taxpayer. The stock in Corporation Y does not qualify as section 1244 stock even if the stock exchanged by the taxpayer did qualify.

Example (3). Corporation X transfers part of its business assets to Corporation Y, a new corporation, and all of the stock of Corporation Y is issued directly to the shareholders of Corporation X. Since the Corporation Y stock was not issued to the shareholders for a transfer by them of money or other property, none of the Corporation Y stock in the hands of the shareholders can qualify.

(e) **Gross receipts.** (1)(i)(a) Except as provided in subparagraph (2) of this paragraph, stock will not qualify under section 1244, if 50 percent or more of the gross receipts of the corporation, for the period consisting of the five most recent taxable years of the corporation ending before the date the loss on such stock is sustained by the shareholders, is derived from royalties, rents, dividends, interest, annuities, and sales or exchanges of stock or securities. If the corporation has not been in existence for five taxable years ending before such date, the percentage test referred to in the preceding sentence applies to the period of the taxable years ending before such date during which the corporation has been in existence; and if the loss is sustained during the first taxable year of the corporation such test applies to the period beginning with the first day of such taxable year and ending on the day before the loss is sustained. The test under this paragraph shall be made on the basis of total gross receipts, except that gross receipts from the sales or exchanges of stock or securities shall be taken into account only to the extent of gains therefrom. The term "gross receipts" as used in section 1244(c)(1)(C) is not synonymous with "gross income". Gross receipts means the total amount received or accrued under the method of accounting used by the corporation in computing its taxable income. Thus, the total amount of receipts is not reduced by returns and allowances, cost, or deductions. For example, gross receipts will include the total amount received or accrued during the corporation's taxable year from the sale or exchange (including a sale or exchange to which section 337 applies) of any kind of property, from investments, and for services rendered by the corporation. However, gross receipts does not include amounts received in nontaxable sales or exchanges (other than those to which section 337 applies), except to the extent that gain is recognized by the corporation, nor does that term include amounts received as a loan, as a repayment of a loan, as a contribution to capital, or on the issuance by the corporation of its own stock.

(b) The meaning of the term "gross receipts" as used in section 1244(c)(1)(C) may be further illustrated by the following examples:

Example (1). A corporation on the accrual method sells property (other than stock or securities) and receives payment partly in money and partly in the form of a note payable at a future time. The amount of the money and the face amount of the note would be considered gross receipts in the taxable year of the sale and would not be reduced by the adjusted basis of the property, the costs of sale, or any other amount.

Example (2). A corporation has a long-term contract as defined in paragraph (a) of § 1.451-3 with respect to which it reports income according to the percentage-of-completion method as described in paragraph (b)(1) of § 1.451-3. The portion of the gross contract price which corresponds to the percentage of the entire contract which has been completed during the taxable year shall be included in gross receipts for such year.

Example (3). A corporation which regularly sells personal property on the installment plan elects to report its taxable income from the sale of property (other than stock or securities) on the installment method in accordance with section 453. The installment payments actually received in a given taxable year of the corporation shall be included in gross receipts for such year.

(ii) The term "royalties" as used in subdivision (i) of this subparagraph means all royalties, including mineral, oil, and gas royalties (whether or not the aggregate amount of such royalties constitutes 50 percent or more of the gross income of the corporation for the taxable year), and amounts received for the privilege of using patents, copyrights, secret processes and formulas, good will, trademarks, trade brands, franchises, and other like property. The term "royalties" does not include amounts received upon the disposal of timber, coal, or domestic iron ore with a retained economic interest to which the special rules of section 631(b) and (c) apply or amounts received from the transfer of patent rights to which section 1235 applies. For the definition of "mineral, oil, or gas royalties", see paragraph (b)(11)(ii) and (iii) of § 1.543-1. For purposes of this subdivision, the gross amount of royalties shall not be reduced by any part of the cost of the rights under which they are received or by any amount allowable as a deduction in computing taxable income.

(iii) The term "rents" as used in subdivision (i) of this subparagraph means amounts received for the use of, or right to use, property (whether real or personal) of the corporation, whether or not such amounts constitute 50 percent or more of the gross income of the corporation for the taxable year. The term "rents" does not include payments for the use or occupancy of rooms or other space where significant services are also rendered to the occupant, such as for the use or occupancy of rooms or other quarters in hotels, boarding houses, or apartment houses furnishing hotel services, or in tourist homes, motor courts, or motels. Generally, services are considered rendered to the occupant if they are primarily for his convenience and are other than those usually or customarily rendered in connection with the rental of rooms or other space for occupancy only. The supplying of maid service, for example, constitutes such services; whereas the furnishing of heat and light, the cleaning of public entrances, exits, stairways, and lobbies, the collection of trash, etc., are not considered as services rendered to the occupant. Payments for the use or occupancy of entire private residences or living quarters in duplex or multiple housing units, of offices in an office building, etc., are generally "rents" under section 1244(c)(1)(C). Payments for the parking of automobiles ordinarily do not constitute rents. Payments for the warehousing of goods or for the use of personal property do not constitute rents if significant services are rendered in connection with such payments.

(iv) The term "dividends" as used in subdivision (i) of this subparagraph includes dividends as defined in section 316, amounts required to be included in gross income under section 551 (relating to foreign personal holding company income taxed to United States shareholders), and consent dividends determined as provided in section 565.

(v) The term "interest" as used in subdivision (i) of this subparagraph means any amounts received for the use of money (including tax-exempt interest).

(vi) The term "annuities" as used in subdivision (i) of this subparagraph means the entire amount received as an annuity under an annuity, endowment, or life insurance contract, regardless of whether only part of such amount would be includible in gross income under section 72.

(vii) For purposes of subdivision (i) of this subparagraph, gross receipts from the sales or exchanges of stock or securities are taken into account only to the extent of gains therefrom. Thus, the gross receipts from the sale of a particular share of stock will be the excess of the amount realized over the adjusted basis of such share. If the adjusted basis should equal or exceed the amount realized on the sale or exchange of a certain share of stock, bond, etc., there would be no gross receipts resulting from the sale of such security. Losses on sales or exchanges of stock or securities do not offset gains on the sales or exchanges of other stock or securities for purposes of computing gross receipts from such sales or exchanges. Gross receipts from the sale or exchange of stocks and securities include gains received from such sales or exchanges by a corporation even though such corporation is a regular dealer in stocks and securities. For the meaning of the term "stocks or securities", see paragraph (b)(5)(i) of § 1.543–1.

(2) The requirement of subparagraph (1) of this paragraph need not be satisfied if for the applicable period the aggregate amount of deductions allowed to the corporation exceeds the aggregate amount of its gross income. But for this purpose the deductions allowed by section 172, relating to the net operating loss deduction, and by sections 242, 243, 244, and 245, relating to certain special deductions for corporations, shall not be taken into account. Notwithstanding the provisions of this subparagraph and of subparagraph (1) of this paragraph, pursuant to the specific delegation of authority granted in section 1244(e) to prescribe such regulations as may be necessary to carry out the purposes of section 1244, ordinary loss treatment will not be available with respect to stock of a corporation which is not largely an operating company within the five most recent taxable years (or such lesser period as the corporation is in existence) ending before the date of the loss. Thus, for example, assume that a person who is not a dealer in real estate forms a corporation which issues stock to him which meets all the formal requirements of section 1244 stock. The corporation then acquires a piece of unimproved real estate which it holds as an investment. The property declines in value and the stockholder sells his stock at a loss. The loss does not qualify for ordinary loss treatment under section 1244 but must be treated as a capital loss.

(3) In applying subparagraphs (1) and (2) of this paragraph to a successor corporation in a reorganization described in section 368(a)(1)(F), such corporation shall be treated as the same corporation as its predecessor. See paragraph (d)(2) of § 1.1244(d)–3.

* * *

[T.D. 6495, 25 FR 9676, Oct. 8, 1960, as amended by T.D. 6508, 25 FR 12345, Dec. 2, 1960; T.D. 6637, 28 FR 1765, Feb. 26, 1963; T.D. 6841, 30 FR 9309, July 27, 1965; T.D. 7779, 46 FR 29465, June 18, 1981]

§ 1.1244(c)–2   Small business corporation defined.

(a) In general. A corporation is treated as a small business corporation if it is a domestic corporation that satisfies the requirements described in paragraph (b) or (c) of this section. The requirements of paragraph (b) of this section apply if a loss is sustained on post-November 1978 stock. The requirements of paragraph (c) of this section apply if a loss is sustained on pre-November 1978 stock. If losses are sustained on both pre-November 1978 stock and post-November 1978 stock in the same taxable year, the requirements of paragraph (b) of this section are applied to the corporation at the time of the issuance of the stock (as required by paragraph (b) in the case of a loss on post-November 1978 stock) in order to determine whether the loss on post-November 1978 stock qualifies as a section 1244 loss, and the requirements of paragraph (c) of this section are applied to the corporation at the time of the adoption of the plan (as required by paragraph (c) in the case of a loss on pre-November 1978 stock) in order to determine whether the loss on pre-November 1978 stock qualifies as a section 1244 loss. For definition of domestic corporation, see section 7701(a)(4) and the regulations under that section.

(b) Post-November 1978 stock—(1) Amount received by corporation for stock. Capital receipts of a small business corporation may not exceed $1,000,000. For purposes of this paragraph the term "capital receipts" means the aggregate dollar amount received by the corporation for its stock, as a contribution to capital, and as paid-in surplus. If the $1,000,000 limitation is exceeded, the rules of subparagraph (2) of this paragraph (b) apply. In making these determinations, (i) property is taken into account at its adjusted basis to the corporation (for determining gain) as of the date received by the corporation, and (ii) this aggregate amount is reduced by the amount of any liability to which the property was subject and by the amount of any liability assumed by the corporation at the time the property was received. Capital receipts are not reduced by distributions to shareholders, even though the distributions may be capital distributions.

(2) Requirement of designation in event $1,000,000 limitation exceeded. (i) If capital receipts exceed $1,000,000, the corporation shall designate as section 1244 stock certain shares of post-November 1978 common stock issued for money or other property in the transitional year. For purposes of this paragraph, the term "transitional year" means the first taxable year in which capital receipts exceed $1,000,000 and in which the corporation issues stock. This designation shall be made in accordance with the rules of subdivision (iii) of this paragraph (b)(2). The amount received for designated stock shall not exceed $1,000,000, less amounts received (i) in exchange for stock in years prior to the transitional year; (ii) as contributions to capital in years prior to the transitional year; and (iii) as paid-in surplus in years prior to the transitional year.

(ii) Post-November 1978 common stock issued for money or other property before the transitional year qualifies as section 1244 stock without affirmative designation by the corporation. Post-November 1978 common stock issued after the transitional year does not qualify as section 1244 stock.

(iii) The corporation shall make the designation required by subdivision (i), of this paragraph (b)(2) not later than the 15th day of the third month

following the close of the transitional year. However, in the case of post-November 1978 common stock issued on or before June 2, 1981 the corporation shall make the required designation by August 3, 1981 or by the 15th day of the 3rd month following the close of the transitional year, whichever is later. The designation shall be made by entering the numbers of the qualifying share certificates on the corporation's records. If the shares do not bear serial numbers or other identifying numbers or letters, or are not represented by share certificates, the corporation shall make an alternative designation in writing at the time of issuance, or, in the case of post-November 1978 common stock issued on or before June 2, 1981 by August 3, 1981. This alternative designation may be made in any manner sufficient to identify the shares qualifying for section 1244 treatment. If the corporation fails to make a designation by share certificate number or an alternative written designation as described, the rules of subparagraph (3) of this paragraph (b) apply.

* * *

[T.D. 6495, 25 FR 9678, Oct. 8, 1960, as amended by T.D. 7779, 46 FR 29470, June 2, 1981; T.D. 7837, 47 FR 42729, Sept. 29, 1982]

§ 1.1244(d)-1 Contributions of property having basis in excess of value.

(a) In general. (1) Section 1244(d)(1)(A) provides a special rule which limits the amount of loss on section 1244 stock that may be treated as an ordinary loss. This rule applies only when section 1244 stock is issued by a corporation in exchange for property that, immediately before the exchange, has an adjusted basis (for determining loss) in excess of its fair market value. If section 1244 stock is issued in exchange for such property and the basis of such stock in the hands of the taxpayer is determined by reference to the basis of such property, then for purposes of section 1244, the basis of such stock shall be reduced by an amount equal to the excess, at the time of the exchange, of the adjusted basis of the property over its fair market value.

(2) The provisions of section 1244(d)(1)(A) do not affect the basis of stock for purposes other than section 1244. Such provisions are to be used only in determining the portion of the total loss sustained that may be treated as an ordinary loss pursuant to section 1244.

(b) Transfer of more than one item. If a taxpayer exchanges several items of property for stock in a single transaction so that the basis of the property transferred is allocated evenly among the shares of stock received, the computation under this section should be made by reference to the aggregate fair market value and the aggregate basis of the property transferred.

(c) Examples. The provisions of this section may be illustrated by the following examples:

Example (1). B transfers property with an adjusted basis of $1,000 and a fair market value of $250 to a corporation for 10 shares of section 1244 stock in an exchange that qualifies under section 351. The basis of B's stock is $1,000 ($100 per share), but, solely for purposes of section 1244, the total basis of the stock must be reduced by $750, the excess of the adjusted basis of the property exchanged over its fair market value. Thus, the basis of such stock for purposes of section 1244 is $250 and the basis of each share for such purposes is $25. If B sells his 10 shares for $250, he will recognize a loss of $750, all of which must be treated as a capital loss. If he sells the 10 shares for $200, then $50 of his total loss of $800 will be treated as an ordinary loss under section 1244, assuming the various requirements of such section are satisfied, and the remaining $750 will be a capital loss.

Example (2). B owns property with a basis of $20,000. The fair market value of the property unencumbered is $15,000 but the property is subject to a $2,000 mortgage. B transfers the encumbered property to a corporation for 100 shares of section 1244 stock in an exchange that qualifies under section 351. The basis of the shares, determined in accordance with section 358, is $18,000 or $180 per share, but solely for purposes of section 1244 the basis is $13,000 ($130 per share), which is its basis for purposes other than section 1244, reduced by $5,000, the excess of the adjusted basis, immediately before the exchange, of the property transferred over its fair market value.

Example (3). C transfers business assets to a corporation for 100 shares of section 1244 stock in an exchange that qualifies under section 351. The assets transferred are as follows:

	Basis	Fair market value
Cash	$10,000	$10,000
Inventory	15,000	30,000
Depreciable property	50,000	20,000
Land	25,000	10,000
	100,000	70,000

The basis for the shares received by C is $100,000, which is applied $1,000 to each share. However, the basis of the shares for purposes of section 1244 is $70,000 ($700 per share), the basis for general purposes reduced by $30,000, the excess of the aggregate adjusted basis of the property transferred over the aggregate fair market value of such property.

[T.D. 6495, 25 FR 9679, Oct. 8, 1960]

§ 1.1244(d)-3 Stock dividends, recapitalizations, changes in name, etc.

(a) In general. Section 1244(c)(1) provides that stock may not qualify for the benefits of section 1244 unless it is issued to the taxpayer for money or other property not including stock or securities. However, section 1244(d)(2) authorizes exceptions to this rule. The exceptions may apply in three situations: (1) The receipt of a stock dividend; (2) the exchange of stock for stock pursuant to a reorganization described in section 368(a)(1)(E); and (3) the exchange of stock for stock pursuant to a reorganization described in section 368(a)(1)(F).

(b) Stock dividends. (1) If common stock is received by an individual or partnership in a nontaxable distribution under section 305(a) made solely with respect to stock owned by such individual or partnership which meets the requirements of section 1244 stock determinable at the time of the distribution, then the common stock so received will also be treated as meeting such requirements. For purposes of this paragraph and paragraphs (c) and (d) of this section, the requirements of section 1244 stock determinable at the time of the distribution or exchange are all of the requirements of section 1244(c)(1) other than the one described in subparagraph (C) thereof, relating to the gross receipts test.

(2) If, however, such stock dividend is received by such individual or partnership partly with respect to stock meeting the requirements of section 1244 stock determinable at the time of the distribution, and partly with respect to stock not meeting such requirements, then only part of the stock received as a stock dividend will be treated as meeting such requirements. Assuming all the shares with respect to which the dividend is received have equal rights to dividends, such part is the number of shares which bears the same ratio to the total number of shares received as the number of shares owned immediately before the stock dividend which meets such qualifications bears to the total number of shares with respect to which the stock dividend is received. In determining the basis of shares received in the stock dividend and of the shares held before the stock dividend, section 307 shall apply as if two separate nontaxable stock dividends were made, one with respect to the shares that meet the requirements and the other with respect to shares that do not meet the requirements.

(3) The provisions of subparagraphs (1) and (2) of this paragraph may be illustrated by the following examples:

Example (1). Corporation X issues 100 shares of its common stock to B for $1,000. Subsequently, in a nontaxable stock dividend B receives 5 more shares of common stock of Corporation X. If the 100 shares meet all the requirements of section 1244 stock determinable at the time of the distribution of the stock dividend, the 5 additional shares shall also be treated as meeting such requirements.

Example (2). In 1959, Corporation Y issues 100 shares of its common stock to C for $1,000 and these shares meet the requirements of section 1244 stock determinable at the time of the issuance. In 1960, C purchases an additional 200 shares of such stock from another shareholder for $3,000; however, these shares do not meet the requirements of section 1244 stock because they were not originally issued to C by the corporation. In 1961, C receives 15 shares of Corporation Y common stock as a stock dividend. Of the shares received, 5 shares, the number received with respect to the 100 shares of stock which met the requirements of section 1244 at the time of the distribution, i.e., $^{100}/_{300} \times 15$, shall also be treated as meeting such requirements. The remaining 10 shares do not meet such requirements as they are not received with respect to section 1244 stock. The basis of such 5 shares is determined by applying section 307 as if the 5 shares were received as a separate stock dividend made solely with respect to shares that meet the requirements of section 1244 stock at the time of the distribution. Thus, the basis of the 5 shares is $47.61 (5/105 of $1,000).

(c) **Recapitalizations.** (1) If, pursuant to a recapitalization described in section 368(a)(1)(E), common stock of a corporation is received by an individual or partnership in exchange for stock of such corporation meeting the requirements of section 1244 stock determinable at the time of the exchange, such common stock shall be treated as meeting such requirements.

(2) If common stock is received pursuant to such a recapitalization partly in exchange for stock meeting the requirements of section 1244 stock determinable at the time of the exchange and partly in exchange for stock not meeting such requirements, then only part of such common stock will be treated as meeting such requirements. Such part is the number of shares which bears the same ratio to the total number of shares of common stock so received as the basis of the shares transferred which meet such requirements bears to the basis of all the shares transferred for such common stock. The basis allocable, pursuant to section 358, to the common stock which is treated as meeting such requirements is limited to the basis of stock that meets such requirements transferred in the exchange.

(3) The provisions of subparagraphs (1) and (2) of this paragraph may be illustrated by the following examples:

Example (1). A owns 500 shares of voting common stock of Corporation X. Corporation X revises its capital structure to provide for two classes of common stock: Class A voting and Class B nonvoting. In a recapitalization described in subparagraph (E) of section 368(a)(1), A exchanges his 500 shares for 750 shares of Class B nonvoting stock. If the 500 shares meet all the requirements of section 1244 stock determinable at the time of the exchange, the 750 shares received in the exchange are treated as meeting such requirements.

Example (2). B owns 500 shares of common stock of Corporation X with a basis of $5,000, and 100 shares of preferred stock of that corporation with a basis of $2,500. Pursuant to a recapitalization described in section 368(a)(1)(E), B exchanges all of his shares for 900 shares of common stock of Corporation X. The 500 common shares meet the requirements of section 1244 stock determinable at the time of the exchange, but the 100 preferred shares do not meet such requirements since only common stock may qualify. Of the 900 common shares received, 600 shares ($5,000/$7,500% 2A 900 shares) are treated as meeting the requirements of section 1244 stock at the time of the exchange, because they are deemed to be received in exchange for the 500 common shares which met such requirements. The remaining 300 shares do not meet such requirements as they are not deemed to be received in exchange for section 1244 stock. The basis of the 600 shares is $5,000, the basis of the relinquished shares meeting the requirements of section 1244.

(d) **Change of name, etc.** (1) If, pursuant to a reorganization described in section 368(a)(1)(F), common stock of a successor corporation is received by an individual or partnership in exchange for stock of the predecessor corporation meeting the requirements of section 1244 stock determinable at the time of the exchange, such common stock shall be treated as meeting such requirements. If common stock is received pursuant to such a reorganization partly in exchange for stock meeting the requirements of section 1244 stock determinable at the time of the exchange and partly in exchange for stock not meeting such requirements, the principles of paragraph (c)(2) of this section apply in determining the number of shares received which are treated as meeting the requirements of section 1244 stock and the basis of those shares.

(2) For purposes of paragraphs (1)(C) and (3)(A) of section 1244(c), a successor corporation in a reorganization described in section 368(a)(1)(F) shall be treated as the same corporation as its predecessor.

[T.D. 6495, 25 FR 9680, Oct. 8, 1960, as amended by T.D. 7779, 46 FR 29472, June 2, 1981]

§ 1.1245-1 General rule for treatment of gain from dispositions of certain depreciable property.

(a) **General.** (1) In general, section 1245(a)(1) provides that, upon a disposition of an item of section 1245 property, the amount by which the lower of (i) the "recomputed basis" of the property, or (ii) the amount realized on a sale, exchange, or involuntary conversion (or the fair market value of the property on any other disposition), exceeds the adjusted basis of the property shall be treated as gain from the sale or exchange of property which is neither a capital asset nor property described in section 1231 (that is, shall be recognized as ordinary income). The amount of such gain shall be determined separately for each item of section 1245 property. In general, the term "recomputed basis" means the adjusted basis of property plus all adjustments reflected in such adjusted basis on account of depreciation allowed or allowable for all periods after December 31, 1961. See section 1245(a)(2) and § 1.1245-2. Generally, the ordinary income treatment applies even though in the absence of section 1245 no gain would be recognized under the Code. For example, if a corporation distributes section 1245 property as a dividend, gain may be recognized as ordinary income to the corporation even though, in the absence of section 1245, section 311(a) would preclude any recognition of gain to the corporation. For the definition of "section 1245 property", see section 1245(a)(3) and § 1.1245-3. For exceptions and limitations to the application of section 1245(a)(1), see section 1245(b) and § 1.1245-4.

(2) Section 1245(a)(1) applies to dispositions of section 1245 property in taxable years beginning after December 31, 1962, except that:

(i) In respect of section 1245 property which is an elevator or escalator, section 1245(a)(1) applies to dispositions after December 31, 1963, and

(ii) In respect of section 1245 property which is livestock (described in subparagraph (4) of § 1.1245-3(a)), section 1245(a)(1) applies to dispositions made in taxable years beginning after December 31, 1969, and (iii) [reserved].

(3) For purposes of this section and §§ 1.1245-2 through 1.1245-6, the term "disposition" includes a sale in a sale-and-leaseback transaction and a transfer upon the foreclosure of a security interest, but such term does not include a mere transfer of title to a creditor upon creation of a security interest or to a debtor upon termination of a security

interest. Thus, for example, a disposition occurs upon a sale of property pursuant to a conditional sales contract even though the seller retains legal title to the property for purposes of security but a disposition does not occur when the seller ultimately gives up his security interest following payment by the purchaser.

* * *

(5) In case of a sale, exchange, or involuntary conversion of section 1245 and non-section 1245 property in one transaction, the total amount realized upon the disposition shall be allocated between the section 1245 property and the non-section 1245 property in proportion to their respective fair market values. In general, if a buyer and seller have adverse interests as to the allocation of the amount realized between the section 1245 property and the non-section 1245 property, any arm's length agreement between the buyer and the seller will establish the allocation. In the absence of such an agreement, the allocation shall be made by taking into account the appropriate facts and circumstances. Some of the facts and circumstances which shall be taken into account to the extent appropriate include, but are not limited to, a comparison between the section 1245 property and all the property disposed of in such transaction of (i) the original cost and reproduction cost of construction, erection, or production, (ii) the remaining economic useful life, (iii) state of obsolescence, and (iv) anticipated expenditures to maintain, renovate, or to modernize.

(b) **Sale, exchange, or involuntary conversion.** (1) In the case of a sale, exchange, or involuntary conversion of section 1245 property, the gain to which section 1245(a)(1) applies is the amount by which (i) the lower of the amount realized upon the disposition of the property or the recomputed basis of the property, exceeds (ii) the adjusted basis of the property.

(2) The provisions of this paragraph may be illustrated by the following examples:

Example (1). On January 1, 1964, Brown purchases section 1245 property for use in his manufacturing business. The property has a basis for depreciation of $3,300. After taking depreciation deductions of $1,300 (the amount allowable), Brown realizes after selling expenses the amount of $2,900 upon sale of the property on January 1, 1969. Brown's gain is $900 ($2,900 amount realized minus $2,000 adjusted basis). Since the amount realized upon disposition of the property ($2,900) is lower than its recomputed basis ($3,300, i.e., $2,000 adjusted basis plus $1,300 in depreciation deductions), the entire gain is treated as ordinary income under section

1245(a)(1) and not as gain from the sale or exchange of property described in section 1231.

Example (2). Assume the same facts as in example (1) except that Brown exchanges the section 1245 property for land which has a fair market value of $3,700, thereby realizing a gain of $1,700 ($3,700 amount realized minus $2,000 adjusted basis). Since the recomputed basis of the property ($3,300) is lower than the amount realized upon its disposition ($3,700), the excess of recomputed basis over adjusted basis, or $1,300, is treated as ordinary income under section 1245(a)(1). The remaining $400 of the gain may be treated as gain from the sale or exchange of property described in section 1231.

(c) Other dispositions. (1) In the case of a disposition of section 1245 property other than by way of a sale, exchange, or involuntary conversion, the gain to which section 1245(a)(1) applies is the amount by which (i) the lower of the fair market value of the property on the date of disposition or the recomputed basis of the property, exceeds (ii) the adjusted basis of the property. If property is transferred by a corporation to a shareholder for an amount less than its fair market value in a sale or exchange, for purposes of applying section 1245 such transfer shall be treated as a disposition other than by way of a sale, exchange, or involuntary conversion.

(2) The provisions of this paragraph may be illustrated by the following examples:

Example (1). X Corporation distributes section 1245 property to its shareholders as a dividend. The property has an adjusted basis of $2,000 to the corporation, a recomputed basis of $3,300, and a fair market value of $3,100. Since the fair market value of the property ($3,100) is lower than its recomputed basis ($3,300), the excess of fair market value over adjusted basis, or $1,100, is treated under section 1245(a)(1) as ordinary income to the corporation even though, in the absence of section 1245, section 311(a) would preclude recognition of gain to the corporation.

Example (2). Assume the same facts as in example (1) except that X Corporation distributes the section 1245 property to its shareholders in complete liquidation of the corporation. Assume further that section 1245(b)(3) does not apply and that the fair market value of the property is $3,800 at the time of the distribution. Since the recomputed basis of the property ($3,300) is lower than its fair market value ($3,800), the excess of recomputed basis over adjusted basis, or $1,300, is treated under section 1245(a)(1) as ordinary income to the corporation even though, in the absence of section 1245, section 336 would preclude recognition of gain to the corporation.

(d) Losses. Section 1245(a)(1) does not apply to losses. Thus, section 1245(a)(1) does not apply if a loss is realized upon a sale, exchange, or involuntary conversion of property, all of which is considered section 1245 property, nor does the section apply to a disposition of such property other than

by way of sale, exchange, or involuntary conversion if at the time of the disposition the fair market value of such property is not greater than its adjusted basis.

* * *

[T.D. 6832, 30 FR 8576, July 7, 1965, as amended by T.D. 7084, 36 FR 268, Jan. 8, 1971; T.D. 7141, 36 FR 18793, Sept. 22, 1971]

§ 1.1245-2 Definition of recomputed basis.

(a) General rule—(1) Recomputed basis defined. The term "recomputed basis" means, with respect to any property, an amount equal to the sum of:

(i) The adjusted basis of the property, as defined in section 1011, plus

(ii) The amount of the adjustments reflected in the adjusted basis.

(2) **Definition of adjustments reflected in adjusted basis.** The term "adjustments reflected in the adjusted basis" means:

(i) With respect to any property other than property described in subdivision (ii), (iii), or (iv) of this subparagraph, the amount of the adjustments attributable to periods after December 31, 1961,

(ii) With respect to an elevator or escalator, the amount of the adjustments attributable to periods after June 30, 1963,

(iii) With respect to livestock (described in subparagraph (4) of § 1.1245–3(a)), the amount of the adjustments attributable to periods after December 31, 1969, or (iv) [reserved]

which are reflected in the adjusted basis of such property on account of deductions allowed or allowable for depreciation or amortization (within the meaning of subparagraph (3) of this paragraph). For cases where the taxpayer can establish that the amount allowed for any period was less than the amount allowable, see subparagraph (7) of this paragraph. * * *

(3) **Meaning of "depreciation or amortization."** (i) For purposes of subparagraph (2) of this paragraph, the term "depreciation or amortization" includes allowances (and amounts treated as allowances) for depreciation (or amortization in lieu thereof), and deductions for amortization of emergency facilities under section 168. Thus, for example, such term includes a reasonable allowance for exhaustion, wear and tear (including a

reasonable allowance for obsolescence) under section 167, an additional first-year depreciation allowance for small business under section 179, an expenditure treated as an amount allowed under section 167 by reason of the application of section 182(d)(2)(B) (relating to expenditures by farmers for clearing land), and a deduction for depreciation of improvements under section 611 (relating to depletion). For further examples, the term "depreciation or amortization" includes periodic deductions referred to in § 1.162–11 in respect of a specified sum paid for the acquisition of a leasehold and in respect of the cost to a lessee of improvements on property of which he is the lessee. However, such term does not include deductions for the periodic payment of rent.

(ii) The provisions of this subparagraph may be illustrated by the following example:

Example. On January 1, 1966, Smith purchases for $1,000, and places in service, an item of property described in section 1245(a)(3)(A). Smith deducts an additional first-year allowance for depreciation under section 179 of $200. Accordingly, the basis of the property for purposes of depreciation is $800 on January 1, 1966. Between that date and January 1, 1974, Smith deducts $640 in depreciation (the amount allowable) with respect to the property, thereby reducing its adjusted basis to $160. Since this adjusted basis reflects deductions for depreciation and amortization (within the meaning of this subparagraph) amounting to $840 ($200 plus $640), the recomputed basis of the property is $1,000 ($160 plus $840).

* * *

(7) Depreciation or amortization allowed or allowable. For purposes of determining recomputed basis, generally all adjustments (for periods after Dec. 31, 1961, or, in the case of property described in subparagraph (2)(ii), (iii), or (iv) of this paragraph, for periods after the applicable date) attributable to allowed or allowable depreciation or amortization must be taken into account. See section 1016(a)(2) and the regulations thereunder for the meaning of "allowed" and "allowable". However, if a taxpayer can establish by adequate records or other sufficient evidence that the amount allowed for depreciation or amortization for any period was less than the amount allowable for such period, the amount to be taken into account for such period shall be the amount allowed. No adjustment is to be made on account of the tax imposed by section 56 (relating to the minimum tax for tax preferences). See paragraph (b) of this section (relating to records to be kept and information to be filed). For example, assume that in the year 1967 it becomes necessary to determine the

recomputed basis of property, the $500 adjusted basis of which reflects adjustments of $1,000 with respect to depreciation deductions allowable for periods after December 31, 1961. If the taxpayer can establish by adequate records or other sufficient evidence that he had been allowed deductions amounting to only $800 for the period, then in determining recomputed basis the amount added to adjusted basis with respect to the $1,000 adjustments to basis for the period will be only $800.

* * *

(c) Adjustments reflected in adjusted basis immediately after certain acquisitions—(1) Zero. (i) If on the date a person acquires property his basis for the property is determined solely by reference to its cost (within the meaning of section 1012), then on such date the amount of the adjustments reflected in his adjusted basis for the property is zero.

(ii) If on the date a person acquires property his basis for the property is determined solely by reason of the application of section 301(d) (relating to basis of property received in corporate distribution) or section 334(a) (relating to basis of property received in a liquidation in which gain or loss is recognized), then on such date the amount of the adjustments reflected in his adjusted basis for the property is zero.

(iii) If on the date a person acquires property his basis for the property is determined solely under the rules of section 334(b)(2) or (c) relating to basis of property received in certain corporate liquidations), then on such date the amount of the adjustments reflected in his adjusted basis for the property is zero.

(iv) If as of the date a person acquires property from a decedent such person's basis is determined, by reason of the application of section 1014(a), solely by reference to the fair market value of the property on the date of the decedent's death or on the applicable date provided in section 2032 (relating to alternate valuation date), then on such date the amount of the adjustments reflected in his adjusted basis for the property is zero.

(2) Gifts and certain tax-free transactions. (i) If property is disposed of in a transaction described in subdivision (ii) of this subparagraph, then the amount of the adjustments reflected in the adjusted basis of the property in the hands of a transferee immediately after the disposition shall be an amount equal to:

(a) The amount of the adjustments reflected in the adjusted basis of the property in the hands of the transferor immediately before the disposition, minus

(b) The amount of any gain taken into account under section 1245(a)(1) by the transferor upon the disposition.

(ii) The transactions referred to in subdivision (i) of this subparagraph are:

(a) A disposition which is in part a sale or exchange and in part a gift (see paragraph (a)(3) of § 1.1245–4).

(b) A disposition (other than a disposition to which section 1245(b)(6)(A) applies) which is described in section 1245(b)(3) (relating to certain tax-free transactions), or

(c) An exchange described in paragraph (e)(2) of § 1.1245–4 (relating to transfers described in section 1081(d)(1)(A)).

(iii) The provisions of this subparagraph may be illustrated by the following example:

Example. Jones transfers section 1245 property to a corporation in exchange for stock of the corporation and $1,000 cash in a transaction which qualifies under section 351 (relating to transfer to a corporation controlled by transferor). Before the exchange the amount of the adjustments reflected in the adjusted basis of the property is $3,000. Upon the exchange $1,000 gain is recognized under section 1245(a)(1). Immediately after the exchange, the amount of the adjustments reflected in the adjusted basis of the property in the hands of the corporation is $2,000 (that is, $3,000 minus $1,000).

* * *

(4) **Property received in a like kind exchange, involuntary conversion, or F.C.C. transaction.** (i) If property is acquired in a transaction described in subdivision (ii) of this subparagraph then immediately after the acquisition (and before applying subparagraph (5) of this paragraph, if applicable) the amount of the adjustments reflected in the adjusted basis of the property acquired shall be an amount equal to:

(a) The amount of the adjustments reflected in the adjusted basis of the property disposed of immediately before the disposition, minus

(b) The sum of (1) the amount of any gain recognized under section 1245(a)(1) upon the disposition, plus (2) the amount of gain (if any) referred to in subparagraph (5)(ii) of this paragraph.

* * *

[T.D. 6832, 30 FR 8578, July 7, 1965, as amended by T.D. 7084, 36 FR 268, Jan. 8, 1971; T.D. 7141, 36 FR 18793, Sept. 22, 1971; 36 FR 19160, Sept. 30, 1971; T.D. 7564, 43 FR 40496, Sept. 12, 1978]

§ 1.1245–3 **Definition of section 1245 property.**

(a) **In general.** (1) The term "section 1245 property" means any property (other than livestock excluded by the effective date limitation in subparagraph (4) of this paragraph) which is or has been property of a character subject to the allowance for depreciation provided in section 167 and which is either:

(i) Personal property (within the meaning of paragraph (b) of this section),

(ii) Property described in section 1245(a)(3)(B) (see paragraph (c) of this section), or

(iii) An elevator or an escalator within the meaning of subparagraph (C) of section 48(a)(1) (relating to the definition of "section 38 property" for purposes of the investment credit), but without regard to the limitations in such subparagraph (C).

(2) If property is section 1245 property under a subdivision of subparagraph (1) of this paragraph, a leasehold of such property is also section 1245 property under such subdivision. Thus, for example, if A owns personal property which is section 1245 property under subparagraph (1)(i) of this paragraph, and if A leases the personal property to B, B's leasehold is also section 1245 property under such provision. For a further example, if C owns and leases to D for a single lump-sum payment of $100,000 property consisting of land and a fully equipped factory building thereon, and if 40 percent of the fair market value of such property is properly allocable to section 1245 property, then 40 percent of D's leasehold is also section 1245 property. A leasehold of land is not section 1245 property.

(3) Even though property may not be of a character subject to the allowance for depreciation in the hands of the taxpayer, such property may nevertheless be section 1245 property if the taxpayer's basis for the property is determined by reference to its basis in the hands of a prior owner of the property and such property was of a character subject to the allowance for depreciation in the hands of such prior owner, or if the taxpayer's basis for the property is determined by reference to the basis of other property which in the hands of

the taxpayer was property of a character subject to the allowance for depreciation. Thus, for example, if a father uses an automobile in his trade or business during a period after December 31, 1961, and then gives the automobile to his son as a gift for the son's personal use, the automobile is section 1245 property in the hands of the son.

(4) Section 1245 property includes livestock, but only with respect to taxable years beginning after December 31, 1969. For purposes of section 1245, the term "livestock" includes horses, cattle, hogs, sheep, goats, and mink and other furbearing animals, irrespective of the use to which they are put or the purpose for which they are held.

(b) **Personal property defined.** The term "personal property" means:

(1) Tangible personal property (as defined in paragraph (c) of § 1.48-1, relating to the definition of "section 38 property" for purposes of the investment credit), and

(2) Intangible personal property.

(c) **Property described in section 1245(a)(3)(B).** (1) The term "property described in section 1245(a)(3)(B)" means tangible property of the requisite depreciable character other than personal property (and other than a building and its structural components), but only if there are adjustments reflected in the adjusted basis of the property (within the meaning of paragraph (a)(2) of § 1.1245-2) for a period during which such property (or other property):

(i) Was used as an integral part of manufacturing, production, or extraction, or as an integral part of furnishing transportation, communications, electrical energy, gas, water, or sewage disposal services by a person engaged in a trade or business of furnishing any such service, or

(ii) Constituted a research or storage facility used in connection with any of the foregoing activities.

Thus, even though during the period immediately preceding its disposition the property is not used as an integral part of an activity specified in subdivision (i) of this subparagraph and does not constitute a facility specified in subdivision (ii) of this subparagraph, such property is nevertheless property described in section 1245(a)(3)(B) if, for example, there are adjustments reflected in the adjusted basis of the property for a period during which the property was used as an integral part of manufacturing by the taxpayer or another taxpayer, or for

a period during which other property (which was involuntarily converted into, or exchanged in a like kind exchange for, the property) was so used by the taxpayer or another taxpayer. For rules applicable to involuntary conversions and like kind exchanges, see paragraph (d)(3) of § 1.1245-4.

* * *

[T.D. 6832, 30 FR 8580, July 7, 1965, as amended by T.D. 7141, 36 FR 18794, Sept. 22, 1971]

§ **1.1245-4 Exceptions and limitations.**

(a) **Exception for gifts—(1) General rule.** Section 1245(b)(1) provides that no gain shall be recognized under section 1245(a)(1) upon a disposition by gift. For purposes of this paragraph, the term "gift" means, except to the extent that subparagraph (3) of this paragraph applies, a transfer of property which, in the hands of the transferee, has a basis determined under the provisions of section 1015(a) or (d) (relating to basis of property acquired by gifts). For reduction in amount of charitable contribution in case of a gift of section 1245 property, see section 170(e) and the regulations thereunder.

* * *

(3) **Disposition in part a sale or exchange and in part a gift.** Where a disposition of property is in part a sale or exchange and in part a gift, the gain to which section 1245(a)(1) applies is the amount by which (i) the lower of the amount realized upon the disposition of the property or the recomputed basis of the property, exceeds (ii) the adjusted basis of the property. For determination of the recomputed basis of the property in the hands of the transferee, see paragraph (c)(2) of § 1.1245-2.

(4) **Example.** The provisions of subparagraph (3) of this paragraph may be illustrated by the following example:

Example. (i) Smith transfers section 1245 property, which he has held in excess of 1 year (6 months for taxable years beginning before 1977; 9 months for taxable years beginning in 1977), to his son for $60,000. Immediately before the transfer the property in the hands of Smith has an adjusted basis of $30,000, a fair market value of $90,000, and a recomputed basis of $110,000. Since the amount realized upon disposition of the property ($60,000) is lower than its recomputed basis ($110,000), the excess of the amount realized over adjusted basis, or $30,000, is treated as ordinary income under section 1245(a)(1) and not as gain from the sale or exchange of property described in section 1231. Smith has made a gift of $30,000 ($90,000 fair market value minus

$60,000 amount realized) to which section 1245(a)(1) does not apply.

(ii) Immediately before the transfer, the amount of adjustments reflected in the adjusted basis of the property was $80,000. Under paragraph (c)(2) of § 1.1245-2, $50,000 of adjustments are reflected in the adjusted basis of the property immediately after the transfer, that is, $80,000 of such adjustments immediately before the transfer, minus $30,000 gain taken into account under section 1245(a)(1) upon the transfer. Thus, the recomputed basis of the property in the hands of the son is $110,000.

* * *

(c) Limitation for certain tax-free transactions—(1) Limitation on amount of gain. Section 1245(b)(3) provides that upon a transfer of property described in subparagraph (2) of this paragraph, the amount of gain taken into account by the transferor under section 1245(a)(1) shall not exceed the amount of gain recognized to the transferor on the transfer (determined without regard to section 1245). For purposes of this subparagraph, in case of a transfer of both section 1245 property and non-section 1245 property in one transaction, the amount realized from the disposition of the section 1245 property (as determined under paragraph (a)(5) of § 1.1245-1) shall be deemed to consist of that portion of the fair market value of each property acquired which bears the same ratio to the fair market value of such acquired property as the amount realized from the disposition of the section 1245 property bears to the total amount realized. The preceding sentence shall be applied solely for purposes of computing the portion of the total gain (determined without regard to section 1245) which shall be recognized as ordinary income under section 1245(a)(1). For determination of the recomputed basis of the section 1245 property in the hands of the transferee, see paragraph (c)(2) of § 1.1245-2. Section 1245(b)(3) does not apply to a disposition of property to an organization (other than a cooperative described in section 521) which is exempt from the tax imposed by chapter 1 of the Code.

(2) Transfers covered. The transfers referred to in subparagraph (1) of this paragraph are transfers of property in which the basis of the property in the hands of the transferee is determined by reference to its basis in the hands of the transferor by reason of the application of any of the following provisions:

(i) Section 332 (relating to distributions in complete liquidation of an 80-percent-or-more con-

trolled subsidiary corporation). See subparagraph (3) of this paragraph.

(ii) Section 351 (relating to transfer to a corporation controlled by transferor).

(iii) Section 361 (relating to exchanges pursuant to certain corporate reorganizations).

* * *

(vi) Section 721 (relating to transfers to a partnership in exchange for a partnership interest).

(vii) Section 731 (relating to distributions by a partnership to a partner). For special carryover basis rule, see section 1245(b)(6)(A) and paragraph (f)(1) of this section.

(3) Complete liquidation of subsidiary. In the case of a distribution in complete liquidation of an 80-percent-or-more controlled subsidiary to which section 332 applies, the limitation provided in section 1245(b)(3) is confined to instances in which the basis of the property in the hands of the transferee is determined, under section 334(b)(1), by reference to its basis in the hands of the transferor. Thus, for example, the limitation of section 1245(b)(3) may apply in respect of a liquidating distribution of section 1245 property by an 80-percent-or-more controlled corporation to the parent corporation, but does not apply in respect of a liquidating distribution of section 1245 property to a minority shareholder. Section 1245(b)(3) does not apply to a liquidating distribution of property by an 80-percent-or-more controlled subsidiary to its parent if the parent's basis for the property is determined, under section 334(b)(2), by reference to its basis for the stock of the subsidiary.

(4) Examples. The provisions of this paragraph may be illustrated by the following examples:

Example (1). Section 1245 property, which is owned by Smith, has a fair market value of $10,000, a recomputed basis of $8,000, and an adjusted basis of $4,000. Smith transfers the property to a corporation in exchange for stock in the corporation worth $9,000 plus $1,000 in cash in a transaction qualifying under section 351. Without regard to section 1245, Smith would recognize $1,000 gain under section 351(b), and the corporation's basis for the property would be determined under section 362(a) by reference to its basis in the hands of Smith. Since the recomputed basis of the property disposed of ($8,000) is lower than the amount realized ($10,000), the excess of recomputed basis over adjusted basis ($4,000), or $4,000, would be treated as ordinary income under section 1245(a)(1) if the provisions of section 1245(b)(3) did not apply. However, section 1245(b)(3) limits the gain taken into account by Smith under section 1245(a)(1) to $1,000. If, instead, Smith transferred the property to the corporation solely in exchange for stock of the corporation worth

$10,000, then, because of the application of section 1245(b)(3), Smith would not take any gain into account under section 1245(a)(1). If, however, Smith transferred the property to the corporation for stock worth $5,000 and $5,000 cash, only $4,000 of the $5,000 gain under section 351(b) would be treated as ordinary income under section 1245(a)(1).

Example (2). Assume the same facts as in example (1) except that Smith contributes the property to a new partnership in which he has a one-half interest. Since, without regard to section 1245, no gain would be recognized to Smith under section 721, and by reason of the application of section 721 the partnership's basis for the property would be determined under section 723 by reference to its basis in the hands of Smith, the application of section 1245(b)(3) results in no gain being taken into account by Smith under section 1245(a)(1).

* * *

[T.D. 6832, 30 FR 8581, July 7, 1965, as amended by T.D. 7084, 36 FR 268, Jan. 8, 1971; T.D. 7207, 37 FR 20799, Oct. 14, 1972; T.D. 7728, 45 FR 72650, Nov. 3, 1980; T.D. 7927, 48 FR 55847, Dec. 16, 1983]

§ 1.1245–6 Relation of section 1245 to other sections.

(a) **General.** The provisions of section 1245 apply notwithstanding any other provision of subtitle A of the Code. Thus, unless an exception or limitation under section 1245(b) applies, gain under section 1245(a)(1) is recognized notwithstanding any contrary nonrecognition provision or income characterizing provision. For example, since section 1245 overrides section 1231 (relating to property used in the trade or business), the gain recognized under section 1245(a)(1) upon a disposition will be treated as ordinary income and only the remaining gain, if any, from the disposition may be considered as gain from the sale or exchange of a capital asset if section 1231 is applicable. See example (2) of paragraph (b)(2) of § 1.1245–1. For effect of section 1245 on basis provisions of the Code, see § 1.1245–5.

(b) **Nonrecognition sections overridden.** The nonrecognition provisions of subtitle A of the Code which section 1245 overrides include, but are not limited to, sections 267(d), 311(a), 336, 337, 501(a), 512(b)(5), and 1039. See section 1245(b) for the extent to which section 1245(a)(1) overrides sections 332, 351, 361, 371(a), 374(a), 721, 731, 1031, 1033, 1071, and 1081(b)(1) and (d)(1)(A). * * *

* * *

(d) **Installment method.** (1) Gain from a disposition to which section 1245(a)(1) applies may be reported under the installment method if such method is otherwise available under section 453 of the Code. In such case, the income (other than interest) on each installment payment shall be deemed to consist of gain to which section 1245(a)(1) applies until all such gain has been reported, and the remaining portion (if any) of such income shall be deemed to consist of gain to which section 1245(a)(1) does not apply. For treatment of amounts as interest on certain deferred payments, see section 483.

(2) The provisions of this paragraph may be illustrated by the following example:

Example. Jones contracts to sell an item of section 1245 property for $10,000 to be paid in 10 equal payments of $1,000 each, plus a sufficient amount of interest so that section 483 does not apply. He properly elects under section 453 to report under the installment method gain of $2,000 to which section 1245(a)(1) applies and gain of $1,000 to which section 1231 applies. Accordingly, $300 of each of the first 6 installment payments and $200 of the seventh installment payment is ordinary income under section 1245(a)(1), and $100 of the seventh installment payment and $300 of each of the last 3 installment payments is gain under section 1231.

* * *

(f) **Treatment of gain not recognized under section 1245.** Section 1245 does not prevent gain which is not recognized under section 1245 from being considered as gain under another provision of the Code, such as, for example, section 311(c) (relating to liability in excess of basis), section 341(f) (relating to collapsible corporations), section 357(c) (relating to liabilities in excess of basis), section 1238 (relating to amortization in excess of depreciation), or section 1239 (relating to gain from sale of depreciable property between certain related persons). Thus, for example, if section 1245 property, which has an adjusted basis of $1,000 and a recomputed basis of $1,500, is sold for $1,750 in a transaction to which section 1239 applies, $500 of the gain would be recognized under section 1245(a)(1) and the remaining $250 of the gain would be treated as ordinary income under section 1239.

[T.D. 6832, 30 FR 8584, July 7, 1965, as amended by T.D. 7084, 36 FR 269, Jan. 8, 1971; T.D. 7400, 41 FR 5101, Feb. 4, 1976]

§ 1.1250–1 Gain from dispositions of certain depreciable realty.

(a) **Dispositions after December 31, 1969—(1) Ordinary income.** (i) In general, section 1250(a)(1) provides that, upon a disposition of an item of section 1250 property after December 31, 1969, the applicable percentage of the lower of:

(a) The additional depreciation (as defined in § 1.1250–2) attributable to periods after December 31, 1969 in respect of the property, or

(b) The excess of the amount realized on a sale, exchange, or involuntary conversion (or the fair market value of the property on any other disposition) over the adjusted basis of the property,

shall be treated as gain from the sale or exchange of property which is neither a capital asset nor property described in section 1231 (that is, shall be recognized as ordinary income). The amount of such gain shall be determined separately for each item (see subparagraph (2)(ii) of this paragraph) of section 1250 property. If the amount determined under (b) of this subdivision exceeds the amount determined under (a) of this subdivision, then such excess shall be treated as provided in subdivision (ii) of this subparagraph. For relation of section 1250 to other provisions, see paragraph (c) of this section.

(ii) If the amount determined under subdivision (i)(b) of this subparagraph exceeds the amount determined under subdivision (i)(a) of this subparagraph, then the applicable percentage of the lower of:

(a) The additional depreciation attributable to periods before January 1, 1970, or

(b) Such excess,

shall also be recognized as ordinary income.

(iii) If gain would be recognized upon a disposition of an item of section 1250 property under subdivisions (i) and (ii) of this subparagraph, and if section 1250(d) applies, then the gain recognized shall be considered as recognized first under subdivision (i) of this subparagraph. (See example (3)(i) of paragraph (c)(4) of § 1.1250–3.)

(2) **Meaning of terms.** (i) For purposes of section 1250, the term "disposition" shall have the same meaning as in paragraph (a)(3) of § 1.1245–1. "Section 1250 property" is, in general, depreciable real property other than section 1245 property. See paragraph (e) of this section. See paragraph (d)(1) of this section for meaning of the term "applicable percentage." If, however, the property is considered to have two or more elements with separate periods (for example, because units thereof are placed in service on different dates, improvements are made to the property, or because of the

application of paragraph (h) of § 1.1250–3), see the special rules of § 1.1250–5.

(ii) For purposes of applying section 1250, the facts and circumstances of each disposition shall be considered in determining what is the appropriate item of section 1250 property. In general, a building is an item of section 1250 property, but in an appropriate case more than one building may be treated as a single item. For example, if two or more buildings or structures on a single tract or parcel (or contiguous tracts or parcels) of land are operated as an integrated unit (as evidenced by their actual operation, management, financing, and accounting), they may be treated as a single item of section 1250 property. For the manner of determining whether an expenditure shall be treated as an addition to capital account of an item of section 1250 property or as a separate item of section 1250 property, see paragraph (d)(2)(iii) of § 1.1250–5.

(3) **Sale, exchange, or involuntary conversion after December 31, 1969.** (i) In the case of a disposition of section 1250 property by a sale, exchange, or involuntary conversion after December 31, 1969, the gain to which section 1250(a)(1) applies is the applicable percentage for the property (determined under paragraph (d)(1) of this section) multiplied by the lower of (a) the additional depreciation in respect of the property attributable to periods after December 31, 1969, or (b) the excess (referred to as "gain realized") of the amount realized over the adjusted basis of the property.

(ii) In addition to gain recognized under section 1250(a)(1) and subdivision (i) of this subparagraph, gain may also be recognized under section 1250(a)(2) and this subdivision if the gain realized exceeds the additional depreciation attributable to periods after December 31, 1969. In such a case, the amount of gain recognized under section 1250(a)(2) and this subdivision is the applicable percentage for the property (determined under paragraph (d)(2) of this section) multiplied by the lower of (a) the additional depreciation attributable to periods before January 1, 1970, or (b) the excess (referred to as "remaining gain") of the gain realized over the additional depreciation attributable to periods after December 31, 1969.

* * *

(4) **Other dispositions after December 31, 1969.** (i) In the case of a disposition of section 1250 property after December 31, 1969, other than by way of a sale, exchange, or involuntary conver-

sion, the gain to which section 1250(a)(1) applies is the applicable percentage for the property (determined under paragraph (d)(1) of this section) multiplied by the lower of (a) the additional depreciation in respect of the property attributable to periods after December 31, 1969, or (b) the excess (referred to as "potential gain") of the fair market value of the property over its adjusted basis. In addition, if the potential gain exceeds the additional depreciation attributable to periods after December 31, 1969, then the gain to which section 1250(a)(2) applies is the applicable percentage for the property (determined under paragraph (d)(2) of this section) multiplied by the lower of (c) the additional depreciation attributable to periods before January 1, 1970, or (d) the excess (referred to as "remaining potential gain") of the potential gain over the additional depreciation attributable to periods after December 31, 1969. If property is transferred by a corporation to a shareholder for an amount less than its fair market value in a sale or exchange, for purposes of applying section 1250 such transfer shall be treated as a disposition other than by way of a sale, exchange, or involuntary conversion.

(ii) The provisions of this subparagraph may be illustrated by the following examples:

Example (1). Section 1250 property having an adjusted basis of $500,000 and a fair market value of $550,000 is distributed by a corporation to a stockholder in complete liquidation of the corporation after December 31, 1969, and thus the potential gain is $50,000. At the time of the liquidation, the additional depreciation for the property attributable to periods after December 31, 1969, is $80,000 and the applicable percentage is 100 percent (paragraph (d)(1)(i)(e) of this section). Since the potential gain of $50,000 is lower than the additional depreciation attributable to periods after December 31, 1969 ($80,000), the amount of gain recognized as ordinary income under section 1250(a)(1) is $50,000 (that is, 100 percent of $50,000) even though in the absence of section 1250, section 336 would preclude recognition of gain to the corporation.

Example (2). The facts are the same as in example (1) except that the fair market value of the property is $650,000, and thus the potential gain is $150,000. Since the additional depreciation attributable to periods after December 31, 1969 ($80,000), is lower than the potential gain of $150,000, the amount of gain recognized as ordinary income under section 1250(a)(1) is $80,000 (that is, 100 percent of $80,000). In addition, section 1250(a)(2) applies since there is remaining potential gain of $70,000, that is, potential gain ($150,000) minus additional depreciation attributable to periods after December 31, 1969 ($80,000). The additional depreciation attributable to periods before January 1, 1970, is $90,000 and the applicable percentage under paragraph (d)(2) of this section is 50 percent. Since the remaining potential gain of $70,000 is lower than the additional depreciation attributable to periods before January 1, 1970 ($90,000), the amount of

gain recognized as ordinary income under section 1250(a)(2) is $35,000 (that is, 50 percent of $70,000). Thus under section 1250(a), $115,000 (that is, $80,000 under section 1250(a)(1), plus $35,000 under section 1250(a)(2)) is recognized as ordinary income, even though in the absence of section 1250, section 336 would preclude recognition of gain to the corporation.

(5) **Instances of nonapplication.** (i) Section 1250(a)(1) does not apply to losses. Thus, section 1250(a)(1) does not apply if a loss is realized upon a sale, exchange, or involuntary conversion of property, all of which is considered section 1250 property, nor does the section apply to a disposition of such property other than by way of sale, exchange, or involuntary conversion if at the time of the disposition the fair market value of such property is not greater than its adjusted basis.

(ii) In general, in the case of section 1250 property with a holding period under section 1223 of more than 1 year, section 1250(a)(1) does not apply if for periods after December 31, 1969, there are no "depreciation adjustments in excess of straight line" (as computed under section 1250(b) and paragraph (b) of § 1.1250–2).

(6) **Allocation rules.** (i) In the case of a sale, exchange, or involuntary conversion of section 1250 property and nonsection 1250 property in one transaction after December 31, 1969, the total amount realized upon the disposition shall be allocated between the section 1250 property and the other property in proportion to their respective fair market values. Such allocation shall be made in accordance with the principles set forth in paragraph (a)(5) of § 1.1245–1 (relating to allocation between section 1245 property and nonsection 1245 property).

(ii) If an item of section 1250 property has two (or more) applicable percentages because one subdivision of paragraph (d)(1)(i) of this section applies to one portion of the taxpayer's holding period (determined under § 1.1250–4) and another subdivision of such paragraph applies with respect to another such portion, then the gain realized on a sale, exchange, or involuntary conversion, or the potential gain in the case of any other disposition, shall be allocated to each such portion of the taxpayer's holding period after December 31, 1969, in the same proportion as the additional depreciation with respect to such item for such portion bears to the additional depreciation with respect to such item for the entire holding period after December 31, 1969.

* * *

(c) **Relation of section 1250 to other provisions—(1) General.** The provisions of section 1250 apply notwithstanding any other provision of subtitle A of the Code. See section 1250(i). Thus, unless an exception or limitation under section 1250(d) and § 1.1250–3 applies, gain under section 1250(a) is recognized notwithstanding any contrary nonrecognition provision or income characterizing provision. For example, since section 1250 overrides section 1231 (relating to property used in the trade or business), the gain recognized under section 1250(a) upon a disposition will be treated as ordinary income and only the remaining gain, if any, from the disposition may be considered as gain from the sale or exchange of a capital asset if section 1231 is applicable. See the example in paragraph (b)(3)(ii) of this section.

(2) **Nonrecognition sections overridden.** The nonrecognition provisions of subtitle A of the Code which section 1250 overrides include, but are not limited to, sections 267(d), 311(a), 336, 337, 501(a), and 512(b)(5). See section 1250(d) for the extent to which section 1250(a) overrides sections 332, 351, 361, 371(a), 374(a), 721, 731, 1031, 1033, 1039, 1071, and 1081 (b)(1) and (d)(1)(A). * * *

* * *

(4) **Treatment of gain not recognized under section 1250.** Section 1250 does not prevent gain which is not recognized under section 1250 from being considered as gain under another provision of the Code, such as, for example, section 1239 (relating to gain from sale of depreciable property between certain related persons). Thus, for example, if section 1250 property which has an adjusted basis of $10,000 is sold for $17,500 in a transaction to which section 1239 applies, and if $5,000 of the gain would be recognized under section 1250(a) then the remaining $2,500 of the gain would be treated as ordinary income under section 1239.

* * *

(6) **Installment method.** Gain from a disposition to which section 1250(a) applies may be reported under the installment method if such method is otherwise available under section 453 of the Code. In such case, the income (other than interest) on each installment payment shall be deemed to consist of gain to which section 1250(a) applies until all such gain has been reported, and the remaining portion (if any) of such income shall be deemed to consist of other gain. For treatment of amounts as interest on certain deferred payments, see section 483.

(d) **Applicable percentage—(1) Definition for purposes of section 1250(a)(1).** * * *

* * *

(4) **Full month.** For purposes of this paragraph, the term "full month" (or "full months") means the period beginning on a date in 1 month and terminating on the date before the corresponding date in the next succeeding month (or in another succeeding month), or, if a particular succeeding month does not have such a corresponding date, terminating on the last day of such particular succeeding month.

(5) **Examples.** The provisions of this paragraph may be illustrated by the following examples:

Example (1). Property is purchased on January 17, 1959. Under paragraph (b)(1) of § 1.1250–4, its holding period begins on January 18, 1959, and thus at any time during the period beginning on October 17, 1960, and ending on November 16, 1960, the property is considered held 21 full months and has an applicable percentage under section 1250(a)(2) of 99 percent. On and after January 17, 1969, the property has a holding period of at least 120 full months (10 years) and, therefore, the applicable percentage under section 1250(a)(2) for the property is zero. Accordingly, no gain would be recognized under section 1250(a)(2) upon disposition of the property. If, however, the property consists of two or more elements, see the special rules of § 1.1250–5.

Example (2). Property is purchased on January 31, 1968. Under paragraph (b)(1) of § 1.1250–4 its holding period begins on February 1, 1968, and thus at any time during the period beginning on February 29, 1968, and ending on March 30, 1968, the property is considered held 1 full month. At any time during the period beginning on March 31, 1970, and ending on April 29, 1970, the property is considered held 26 full months. At any time during the period beginning on April 30, 1970, and ending on May 30, 1970, the property is considered held 27 full months.

(e) **Section 1250 property—(1) Definition.** The term "section 1250 property" means any real property (other than section 1245 property, as defined in section 1245(a)(3) and § 1.1245–3) which is or has been property of a character subject to the allowance for depreciation provided in section 167. See section 1250(c).

(2) **Character of property.** For purposes of subparagraph (1) of this paragraph, the term "is or has been property of a character subject to the allowance for depreciation provided in section 167" shall have the same meaning as when used in paragraph (a)(1) and (3) of § 1.1245–3. Thus, if a father uses a house in his trade or business during a period after December 31, 1963, and then gives the house to his son as a gift for the son's personal

use, the house is section 1250 property in the hands of the son. For exception to the application of section 1250(a) upon disposition of a principal residence, see section 1250(d)(7).

(3) **Real property.** (i) For purposes of subparagraph (1) of this paragraph, the term "real property" means any property which is not personal property within the meaning of paragraph (b) of § 1.1245–3. The term section 1250 property includes three types of depreciable real property. The first type is intangible real property. For purposes of this paragraph, a leasehold of land or of section 1250 property is intangible real property, and accordingly such a leasehold is section 1250 property. However, a fee simple interest in land is not depreciable, and therefore is not section 1250 property. The second type is a building or its structural components within the meaning of paragraph (c) of § 1.1245–3. The third type is all other tangible real property except (a) "property described in section 1245(a)(3)(B)" as defined in paragraph (c)(1) of § 1.1245–3 (relating to property used as an integral part of a specified activity or as a specified facility), and (b) property described in section 1245(a)(3)(D). An elevator or escalator (within the meaning of section 1245(a)(3)(C)) is not section 1250 property.

(ii) The provisions of this subparagraph may be illustrated by the following example:

Example. A owns and leases to B for a single lump-sum payment of $100,000 property consisting of land and a fully equipped factory building thereon. If 30 percent of the fair market value of such property is properly allocable to the land, 25 percent to section 1250 property (the building and its structural components), and 45 percent to section 1245 property (the equipment), then 55 percent of B's leasehold is section 1250 property.

(4) **Coordination with definition of section 1245 property.** (i) Property may lose its character as section 1250 property and become section 1245 property. Thus, for example, if section 1250 property of the third type described in subparagraph (3)(i)(a) of this paragraph is converted to use as an integral part of manufacturing, the property would lose its character as section 1250 property and would become section 1245 property. However, once property in the hands of a taxpayer is section 1245 property, it can never become section 1250 property in the hands of such taxpayer. See also paragraph (a)(4) and (5) of § 1.1245–2.

* * *

[T.D. 7084, 36 FR 271, Jan. 8, 1971, as amended by T.D. 7193, 37 FR 12953, June 30, 1972]

§ 1.1250–2 Additional depreciation defined.

(a) **In general**—(1) **Definition for purposes of section 1250(b)(1).** Except as otherwise provided in paragraph (e) of this section, for purposes of section 1250(b)(1), the term "additional depreciation" means:

(i) In the case of property which at the time of disposition has a holding period under section 1223 of not more than 1 year, the "depreciation adjustments" (as defined in paragraph (d) of this section) in respect of such property for periods after December 31, 1963, and

(ii) In the case of property which at the time of disposition has a holding period under section 1223 of more than 1 year, the depreciation adjustments in excess of straight line for periods after December 31, 1963, computed under paragraph (b)(1) of this section.

* * *

(b) **Computation of depreciation adjustments in excess of straight line**—(1) **General rule.** For purposes of paragraph (a)(1) of this section, depreciation adjustments in excess of straight line shall be, in the case of any property, the excess of (i) the sum of the "depreciation adjustments" (as defined in paragraph (d) of this section) in respect of the property attributable to periods after December 31, 1963, over (ii) the sum such adjustments would have been for such periods if such adjustments had been determined for the entire period the property was held under the straight line method of depreciation (or, if applicable, under the lease-renewal-period provision in paragraph (c) of this section). Depreciation in excess of straight line may arise, for example, if the declining balance method, the sum of the years-digits method, or the units of production method is used, or for another example, if the cost of a leasehold improvement or of a leasehold is depreciated over a period which does not take into account certain renewal periods referred to in paragraph (c) of this section. For computations of depreciation adjustments in excess of straight line (or a deficit therein) both on an annual basis and on the basis of the entire period the property was held, see subparagraph (6) of this paragraph.

* * *

(3) **General rule for computing useful life and salvage value.** For purposes of computing

under subparagraph (1)(ii) of this paragraph the sum of the depreciation adjustments would have been under the straight line method, if a useful life (or salvage value) was used in determining the amount allowed as a depreciation adjustment for any taxable year, such life (or value) shall be used in determining the amount such depreciation adjustment would have been for such taxable year under the straight line method. If, however, for any taxable year a method of depreciation was used as to which a useful life was not taken into account such as, for example, the units of production method, or as to which salvage value was not taken into account in determining the annual allowances, such as, for example, the declining balance method or the amortization of a leasehold improvement over the term of a lease, then, for the purpose of determining the amount such depreciation adjustment would have been under the straight line method for such taxable year:

(i) There shall be used the useful life (or salvage value) which would have been proper if depreciation had actually been determined under the straight line method throughout the period the property was held, and

(ii) Such useful life (or such salvage value) shall be determined by taking into account for each taxable year the same facts and circumstances as would have been taken into account if the taxpayer had used such method throughout the period the property was held.

* * *

(c) Property held by lessee—(1) Amount depreciation would have been. For purposes of paragraph (b) of this section, in case of a leasehold which is section 1250 property, in determining the amount the depreciation adjustments would have been under the straight line method in respect of any building or other improvement (which is section 1250 property) erected or made on the leased property, or in respect of any cost of acquiring the lease, the lease period shall be treated as including all renewal periods. See section 1250(b)(2). For determination of the extent to which a leasehold is section 1250 property, see paragraph (e)(3) of § 1.1250–1.

(2) Renewal period. (i) For purposes of this paragraph, the term "renewal period" means any period for which the lease may be renewed, extended, or continued pursuant to an option or options exercisable by the lessee (whether or not specifically provided for in the lease) except that the inclu-

sion of one or more renewal periods shall not extend the period taken into account by more than two-thirds of the period on the basis of which the depreciation adjustments were allowed.

(ii) In respect of the cost of any building erected (or other improvement made) on the leased property by the lessee, or in respect of the portion of the cost of acquiring a leasehold which is attributable to an existing building (or other improvement) on the leasehold at the time the lessee acquires the leasehold, the inclusion of one or more renewal periods shall not extend the period taken into account to a period which exceeds the useful life remaining, at the time the leasehold is disposed of, of such building (or such other improvement). Determinations under this subdivision shall be made without regard to the proper period under section 167 or 178 for depreciating or amortizing a leasehold acquisition cost or improvement.

(iii) The provisions of this subparagraph may be illustrated by the following example:

Example. Assume that a leasehold improvement with a useful life of 30 years is properly amortized on the basis of a 10-year initial lease term. The lease is renewable for an additional 9 years. The period taken into account is 16⅔ years, that is, 10 years plus two-thirds of 10 years. If, however, the leasehold improvement were disposed of at the end of 12 years, and if its remaining useful life were only 3 years, then the period taken into account would be 15 years.

(d) Depreciation adjustments—(1) General. For purposes of this section, the term "depreciation adjustments" means, in respect of any property, all adjustments reflected in the adjusted basis of such property on account of deductions described in subparagraph (2) of this paragraph allowed or allowable (whether in respect of the same or other property) to the taxpayer or to any other person. For cases where the taxpayer can establish that the amount allowed for any period was less than the amount allowable, see subparagraph (4) of this paragraph. For determination of adjusted basis of property in a multiple asset account, see paragraph (c)(3) of § 1.167(a)–8. The term "depreciation adjustments" as used in this section does not have the same meaning as the term "adjustments reflected in the adjusted basis" as defined in paragraph (a)(2) of § 1.1245–2.

(2) Deductions. The deductions described in this subparagraph are allowances (and amounts treated as allowances) for depreciation or amortization (other than amortization under sections 168, 169 (as enacted by section 704(a), Tax Reform Act

of 1969 (83 Stat. 667)), or 185). Thus, for example, such deductions include a reasonable allowance for exhaustion, wear, and tear (including a reasonable allowance for obsolescence) under section 167, the periodic deductions referred to in § 1.162–11 in respect of a specified sum paid for the acquisition of a leasehold and in respect of the cost to a lessee of improvements on property of which he is the lessee. However, such deductions do not include deductions for the periodic payment of rent.

(3) Depreciation of other taxpayers or in respect of other property. (i) The depreciation adjustments (reflected in the adjusted basis) referred to in subparagraph (1) of this paragraph (a) are not limited to adjustments with respect to the property disposed of, nor to those allowed or allowable to the taxpayer disposing of such property, and (b) except as provided in subparagraph (4) of this paragraph, are taken into account, whether allowed or allowable in respect of the same or other property and whether to the taxpayer or to any other person. For manner of determining the amount of additional depreciation after certain dispositions, see paragraph (e) of this section.

(ii) The provisions of this subparagraph may be illustrated by the following example:

Example. On January 1, 1966, a calendar year taxpayer purchases for $100,000 a building for use in his trade or business. He takes depreciation deductions of $20,000 (the amount allowable), of which $3,000 is additional depreciation, and transfers the building to his son as a gift on January 1, 1968. Since the exception for gifts in section 1250(d)(1) applies, the taxpayer does not recognize gain under section 1250(a)(2). In the son's adjusted basis of $80,000 for the building there is reflected $3,000 of additional depreciation. On January 1, 1969, after taking a depreciation deduction of $10,000 (the amount allowable), of which $1,000 is additional depreciation, the son sells the building. At the time of the sale the additional depreciation is $4,000 ($3,000 allowed the father plus $1,000 allowed the son).

(4) Depreciation allowed or allowable. (i) For purposes of subparagraph (1) of this paragraph, generally all deductions (described in subparagraph (2) of this paragraph) allowed or allowable shall be taken into account. See section 1016(a)(2) and the regulations thereunder for the meaning of "allowed" and "allowable." However, if a taxpayer can establish by adequate records or other sufficient evidence that the amount allowed for any period was less than the amount allowable for such period, the amount to be taken into account for such period shall be the amount allowed. The preceding sentence shall not apply for purposes of computing under paragraph (b)(1)(ii) of this section

the amount such deductions would have been under the straight line method.

(ii) The provisions of subdivision (i) of this subparagraph may be illustrated by the following example:

Example. In the year 1969 it becomes necessary to determine the additional depreciation in respect of section 1250 property, the adjusted basis of which reflects a depreciation adjustment of $1,000 with respect to depreciation deductions allowable for the calendar year 1965 under the sum of the years-digits method. Under paragraph (b)(1)(ii) of this section, the depreciation which would have resulted under the straight line method for 1965 is $800. If the taxpayer can establish by adequate records or other sufficient evidence that he did not take, and was not allowed, any deduction for depreciation in respect of the property in 1965, then, for purposes of computing the depreciation adjustments in excess of straight line in respect of the property, the amount to be taken into account for 1965 as allowed or allowable is zero, and the amount to be taken into account in computing deductions which would have resulted under the straight line method in 1965 is $800. Thus, in effect, there is a deficit in additional depreciation for 1965 of $800.

* * *

(e) Additional depreciation immediately after certain acquisitions—(1) Zero. If on the date a person acquires property his basis for the property is determined solely (i) by reference to its cost (within the meaning of sec. 1012), (ii) by reason of the application of section 301(d) (relating to basis of property received in corporate distribution) or section 334(a) (relating to basis of property received in a liquidation in which gain or loss is recognized), or (iii) under the rules of section 334(b)(2) or (c) (relating to basis of property received in certain corporate liquidations), then on such date the additional depreciation for the property is zero.

(2) Transactions referred to in section 1250(d). In the case of property acquired in a disposition described in section 1250(d) (relating to exceptions and limitations to application of section 1250), additional depreciation shall be computed in accordance with the rules prescribed in § 1.1250–3.

* * *

[T.D. 7084, 36 FR 273, Jan. 8, 1971, as amended by T.D. 7193, 37 FR 12956, June 30, 1972]

§ 1.1250–3 Exceptions and limitations.

(a) Exception for gifts—(1) General rule. Section 1250(d)(1) provides that no gain shall be recognized under section 1250(a) upon a disposition by gift. For purposes of this paragraph, the term "gift" shall have the same meaning as in paragraph (a) of § 1.1245–4. For reduction in amount of charitable contribution in case of a gift of section 1250 property, see section 170(e) and paragraph (c)(3) of § 1.170–1.

(2) **Disposition in part a sale or exchange and in part a gift.** Where a disposition of property is in part a sale or exchange and in part a gift, the disposition shall be subject to the provisions of § 1.1250–1 and the gain to which section 1250(a) applies, shall be computed under that section.

(3) **Treatment of property in hands of transferee.** If property is disposed of in a transaction which is a gift:

(i) The additional depreciation for the property in the hands of the transferee immediately after the disposition shall be an amount equal to (a) the amount of the additional depreciation for the property in the hands of the transferor immediately before the disposition, minus (b) the amount of any gain (in case the disposition is in part a sale or exchange and in part a gift) which would have been taken into account under section 1250(a) by the transferor upon the disposition if the applicable percentage had been 100 percent.

(ii) For purposes of computing the applicable percentage, the holding period under section 1250(e)(2) of property received as a gift in the hands of the transferee includes the transferor's holding period,

* * *

(c) **Limitation for certain tax-free transactions—(1) General.** Section 1250(d)(3) provides that upon a transfer of property described in subparagraph (2) of this paragraph, the amount of gain taken into account by the transferor under section 1250(a) shall not exceed the amount of gain recognized to the transferor on the transfer (determined without regard to section 1250). For purposes of this subparagraph, in case of a transfer of both section 1250 property and nonsection 1250 property in one transaction, the amount realized from the disposition of the section 1250 property shall be deemed to consist of that portion of the fair market value of each property acquired which bears the same ratio to the fair market value of such acquired property as the amount realized from the disposition of the section 1250 property bears to the total amount realized. The preceding sentence shall be applied solely for purposes of computing the portion of the total gain (determined without regard to section 1250) which shall

be recognized as ordinary income under section 1250(a). Section 1250(d)(3) does not apply to a disposition of property to an organization (other than a cooperative described in section 521) which is exempt from the tax imposed by chapter 1 of the Code.

(2) **Transfers covered.** The transfers described in this subparagraph are transfers of property in which the basis of the property in the hands of the transferee is determined by reference to its basis in the hands of the transferor by reason of the application of any of the following provisions:

(i) Section 332 (relating to distributions in complete liquidation of an 80 percent or more controlled subsidiary corporation). For application of section 1250(d)(3) to such a complete liquidation, the principles of paragraph (c)(3) of § 1.1245–4 shall apply.

(ii) Section 351 (relating to transfer to a corporation controlled by transferor).

(iii) Section 361 (relating to exchanges pursuant to certain corporate reorganizations).

* * *

(vi) Section 721 (relating to transfers to a partnership in exchange for a partnership interest).

(vii) Section 731 (relating to distributions by a partnership to a partner). For special carryover basis rule, see section 1250(d)(6)(A) and paragraph (f)(1) of this section.

(3) **Treatment of property in hands of transferee.** In the case of a transfer described in subparagraph (2) (other than subdivision (vii) thereof) of this paragraph—

(i) The additional depreciation for the property in the hands of the transferee immediately after the disposition shall be an amount equal to (a) the amount of the additional depreciation for the property in the hands of the transferor immediately before the disposition, minus (b) the amount of additional depreciation necessary to produce an amount equal to the gain taken into account under section 1250(a) by the transferor upon the disposition (taking into account the applicable percentage for the property),

(ii) For purposes of computing applicable percentage, the holding period under section 1250(e)(2) of the property in the hands of the transferee includes the transferor's holding period,

(iii) If the adjusted basis of the property in the hands of the transferee exceeds its adjusted basis immediately before the transferee, the excess is an addition to capital account under paragraph (d)(2)(ii) of § 1.1250–5 (relating to property with 2 or more elements), and

(iv) If the property disposed of consists of 2 or more elements within the meaning of paragraph (c) of § 1.1250–5, see paragraph (e)(1) of § 1.1250–5 for the amount of additional depreciation and the holding period for each element in the hands of the transferee.

(4) Examples. The provisions of this paragraph may be illustrated by the following examples:

Example (1). (i) Green transfers section 1250 property on March 1, 1968, to a corporation, which is not exempt from taxation, in exchange for cash of $9,000 and stock in the corporation worth $91,000, in a transaction qualifying under section 351. Thus, the amount realized is $100,000 ($9,000 plus $91,000). The property has an applicable percentage under section 1250(a)(2) of 60 percent, an adjusted basis of $40,000, and additional depreciation of $20,000. The gain realized is $60,000, that is, amount realized ($100,000) minus adjusted basis ($40,000). Since the additional depreciation ($20,000) is lower than the gain realized ($60,000), the amount of gain which would be treated as ordinary income under section 1250(a)(2) would be $12,000 (60 percent of $20,000) if the limitation provided in section 1250(d)(3) did not apply. Since under section 351(b) gain in the amount of $9,000 would be recognized to the transferor without regard to section 1250, the limitation provided in section 1250(d)(3) limits the gain taken into account by the transferor under section 1250(a)(2) to $9,000.

(ii) The amount of additional depreciation for the property in the hands of the transferee immediately after the transfer is $5,000, that is, the amount of additional depreciation before the transfer ($20,000) minus the amount of additional depreciation necessary to produce an amount equal to the gain recognized under section 1250(a)(2) upon the transfer ($15,000, that is, $9,000 of gain recognized divided by 60 percent, the applicable percentage). (If the property is subsequently disposed of, and for the period after the initial transfer there is additional depreciation in respect of the property, then at the time of the subsequent disposition the additional depreciation will exceed $5,000. If, however, for the period after the initial transfer there was a deficit in additional depreciation, then at the time of the subsequent disposition the additional depreciation would be less than $5,000.)

Example (2). (i) Assume the same facts as in example (1) except that the additional depreciation is $10,000. Since additional depreciation ($10,000) is lower than the gain realized ($60,000), the amount of gain which would be treated as ordinary income under section 1250(a)(2) would be $6,000 (60 percent of $10,000) if the limitation provided in section 1250(d)(3) did not apply. Since under section 351(b) gain in the amount of $9,000 would be recognized to the transferor without regard to section 1250, the limitation under section 1250(d)(3) does not prevent treatment of the entire $6,000 as ordinary in-

come under section 1250(a)(2). The $3,000 remaining portion of the $9,000 gain may be treated as gain from the sale of property described in section 1231.

(ii) Immediately after the transfer, the amount of additional depreciation is zero, that is, the amount of additional depreciation before the transfer ($10,000) minus the amount of additional depreciation necessary to produce an amount equal to the gain taken into account under section 1250(a)(2) upon the transfer ($10,000) that is, $6,000 divided by 60 percent.

* * *

[T.D. 7084, 36 FR 275, Jan. 8, 1971, as amended by T.D. 7193, 37 FR 12957, June 30, 1972; T.D. 7400, 41 FR 5101, Feb. 4, 1976; 41 FR 7095, Feb. 17, 1976]

§ 1.1250–4 Holding period.

(a) General. In general, for purposes only of determining the applicable percentage (as defined in sec. 1250(1)(C) and (2)(B)) of section 1250 property, the holding period of the property shall be determined under the rules of section 1250(e) and this section and not under the rules of section 1223. If the property is treated as consisting of two or more elements (within the meaning of paragraph (c)(1) of § 1.1250–5), see paragraph (a)(2)(ii) of § 1.1250–5 for application of this section to determination of holding period of each element. Section 1250(e) does not affect the determination of the amount of additional depreciation in respect of section 1250 property.

(b) Beginning of holding period. (1) For the purpose of determining the applicable percentage, in the case of property acquired by the taxpayer (other than by means of a transaction referred to in paragraph (c) or (d) of this section), the holding period of the property shall begin on the day after the date of its acquisition. See section 1250(e)(1)(A). Thus, for example, if a taxpayer purchases section 1250 property on January 1, 1965, the holding period of the property begins on January 2, 1965. If he sells the property on October 1, 1966, the holding period on the day of the sale is 21 full months, and, accordingly, the applicable percentage is 99 percent. This result would not be changed even if the property initially had been used solely as the taxpayer's residence for a portion of the 21-month period. If, however, the property were sold on September 30, 1966, the holding period would be only 20 full months.

* * *

[T.D. 7084, 36 FR 281, Jan. 8, 1971, as amended by
T.D. 7400, 41 FR 5103, Feb. 4, 1976]

READJUSTMENT OF TAX BETWEEN YEARS AND SPECIAL LIMITATIONS

Claim of Right

§ 1.1341–1 Restoration of amounts received or accrued under claim of right.

(a) **In general.** (1) If, during the taxable year, the taxpayer is entitled under other provisions of chapter 1 of the Internal Revenue Code of 1954 to a deduction of more than $3,000 because of the restoration to another of an item which was included in the taxpayer's gross income for a prior taxable year (or years) under a claim of right, the tax imposed by chapter 1 of the Internal Revenue Code of 1954 for the taxable year shall be the tax provided in paragraph (b) of this section.

(2) For the purpose of this section "income included under a claim of right" means an item included in gross income because it appeared from all the facts available in the year of inclusion that the taxpayer had an unrestricted right to such item, and "restoration to another" means a restoration resulting because it was established after the close of such prior taxable year (or years) that the taxpayer did not have an unrestricted right to such item (or portion thereof).

(3) For purposes of determining whether the amount of a deduction described in section 1341(a)(2) exceeds $3,000 for the taxable year, there shall be taken into account the aggregate of all such deductions with respect to each item of income (described in section 1341(a)(1)) of the same class.

(b) **Determination of tax.** (1) Under the circumstances described in paragraph (a) of this section, the tax imposed by chapter 1 of the Internal Revenue Code of 1954 for the taxable year shall be the lesser of:

(i) The tax for the taxable year computed under section 1341(a)(4), that is, with the deduction taken into account, or

(ii) The tax for the taxable year computed under section 1341(a)(5), that is, without taking such deduction into account, minus the decrease in tax (net of any increase in tax imposed by section 56, relating to the minimum tax for tax preferences) (under chapter 1 of the Internal Revenue Code of 1954, under chapter 1 (other than subchapter E) and subchapter E of chapter 2 of the Internal Revenue Code of 1939, or under the corresponding provisions of prior revenue laws) for the prior taxable year (or years) which would result solely from the exclusion from gross income of all or that portion of the income included under a claim of right to which the deduction is attributable. For the purpose of this subdivision, the amount of the decrease in tax is not limited to the amount of the tax for the taxable year. See paragraph (i) of this section where the decrease in tax for the prior taxable year (or years) exceeds the tax for the taxable year.

* * *

(c) **Application to deductions which are capital in nature.** Section 1341 and this section shall also apply to a deduction which is capital in nature otherwise allowable in the taxable year. If the deduction otherwise allowable is capital in nature, the determination of whether the taxpayer is entitled to the benefits of section 1341 and this section shall be made without regard to the net capital loss limitation imposed by section 1211. For example, if a taxpayer restores $4,000 in the taxable year and such amount is a long-term capital loss, the taxpayer will, nevertheless, be considered to have met the $3,000 deduction requirement for purposes of applying this section, although the full amount of the loss might not be allowable as a deduction for the taxable year. However, if the tax for the taxable year is computed with the deduction taken into account, the deduction allowable will be subject to the limitation on capital losses provided in section 1211, and the capital loss carryover provided in section 1212.

* * *

(f) **Inventory items, stock in trade, and property held primarily for sale in the ordinary course of trade or business.** (1) Except for amounts specified in subparagraphs (2) and (3) of this paragraph, the provisions of section 1341 and this section do not apply to deductions attributable to items which were included in gross income by reason of the sale or other disposition of stock in trade of the taxpayer (or other property of a kind which would properly have been included in the inventory of the taxpayer if on hand at the close of the prior taxable year) or property held by the taxpayer primarily for sale to customers in the ordinary course of the taxpayer's trade or business. This section is, therefore, not applicable to sales returns and allowances and similar items.

* * *

(h) Legal fees and other expenses. Section 1341 and this section do not apply to legal fees or other expenses incurred by a taxpayer in contesting the restoration of an item previously included in income. This rule may be illustrated by the following example:

Example. A sold his personal residence to B in a prior taxable year and realized a capital gain on the sale. C claimed that under an agreement with A he was entitled to a 5-percent share of the purchase price since he brought the parties together and was instrumental in closing the sale. A rejected C's demand and included the entire amount of the capital gain in gross income for the year of sale. C instituted action and in the taxable year judgment is rendered against A who pays C the amount involved. In addition, A pays legal fees in the taxable year which were incurred in the defense of the action. Section 1341 applies to the payment of the 5-percent share of the purchase price to C. However, the payment of the legal fees, whether or not otherwise deductible, does not constitute an item restored for purposes of section 1341(a) and paragraph (a) of this section.

* * *

[T.D. 6500, 25 FR 12049, Nov. 26, 1960, as amended by T.D. 6617, 27 FR 10824, Nov. 7, 1962; T.D. 6747, 29 FR 9790, July 21, 1964; T.D. 7244, 37 FR 28897, Dec. 30, 1972; T.D. 7564, 43 FR 40496, Sept. 12, 1978]

ELECTION OF CERTAIN SMALL BUSINESS CORPORATIONS AS TO TAXABLE STATUS

§ 1.1361–0A　Effective date.

(a) Except as otherwise provided in the regulations, the provisions of §§ 1.1374–1A and 1.1375–1A apply to taxable years beginning after December 31, 1982.

(b) The provisions of §§ 1.1371–1 through 1.1378–3 apply to a qualified casualty insurance electing small business corporation and to a qualified oil corporation for taxable years beginning after December 31, 1982, and the provisions of §§ 1.1374–1A and 1.1375–1A shall not apply. See section 6(c)(2), (3), and (4) of the Subchapter S Revision Act of 1982.

[T.D. 8104, 51 FR 34201, Sept. 26, 1986]

§ 18.1362–1　Election to be an S corporation.

(a) **Manner of making election.** To make the election to be an S corporation, a small business corporation should file Form 2553, containing all the information required by that form. With respect to each shareholder who is required by paragraph (b) of § 18.1362–2 to consent to the election of the corporation, such shareholder shall make the consent in the manner provided in paragraph (a) of that section. The election form shall be signed by any person who is authorized to sign the return required to be filed under section 6037 and shall be filed with the service center designated in the instructions applicable to Form 2553.

(b) **Time of making election.** The election must be filed either at any time during the taxable year that immediately precedes the first taxable year for which the election is to be effective, or at any time during that portion of the first taxable year for which the election is to be effective which occurs before the 16th day of the third month of that year (or at any time during that year, if that year does not extend beyond the prescribed period of time). For example, if a corporation begins its first taxable year on January 5, 1983, an election will be effective beginning with the corporation's first taxable year only if the election is made within the period beginning after January 4, 1983, and ending before March 20, 1983. If a corporation makes an election for a taxable year that meets all the requirements provided in this section except that—

(1) The election is made at any time during that portion of that year which occurs after the 15th day of the third month of that year, or

(2) Any person who held stock at any time during that portion of that year which occurs before the time the election is made, and who does not hold stock at the time the election is made, does not consent to the election,

the election is treated as being made for the next taxable year. In addition, if a corporation makes an election for a taxable year that meets all the requirements provided in this section, but if the corporation does not meet all the requirements provided in section 1361(b) at any time during that portion of that year which occurs before the time the election is made, the election is treated as being made for the next taxable year provided that the corporation meets all the requirements provided in section 1361(b) at the time the election is made.

[T.D. 7872, 48 FR 3590, Jan. 26, 1983; 48 FR 33481, July 22, 1983, as amended by T.D. 7976, 49 FR 35492, Sept. 10, 1984; T.D. 7979, 49 FR 38920, Oct. 1, 1984]

§ 18.1362-2 Shareholders' consent.

(a) **Manner of making consent.** The consent of a shareholder to an election by a small business corporation must be made either on Form 2553 or on a separate statement signed by the shareholder in which the shareholder consents to the election of the corporation. The separate statement must also set forth the name, address, and taxpayer identification number of the corporation and of the shareholder, the number of shares of stock owned by the shareholder, and the date (or dates) on which the stock was acquired. When a shareholder's consent is made on a separate statement, that statement must be attached to the election of the corporation. The shareholder's consent is binding and may not be withdrawn after a valid election is made by the corporation. The election of the corporation is not valid if any consent required by paragraph (b) of this section is not timely filed. See paragraph (c) of this section for the rules relating to extension of time for filing consents.

(b) **Persons required to consent—(1) In general.** Each person who is a shareholder (including any person who is treated as a shareholder under section 1361(c)(2)(B)) at the time the election is made must consent to the election of the corporation. If the election is made within the corporation's first taxable year for which it is effective, each person who was a shareholder (including any person who was treated as a shareholder under section 1361(c)(2)(B)) at any time during that portion of that year which occurs before the time the election is made, and who is not a shareholder at the time the election is made, must also consent to the election of the corporation.

(2) **Special rules.** When stock of the corporation is owned by a husband and wife as community property (or the income from which is community property), or is owned by tenants in common, joint tenants, or tenants by the entirety, each person having a community interest in such stock and each tenant in common, joint tenant, and tenant by the entirety must consent to the election. The consent of a minor must be made by the minor or by the legal representative of the minor (or by a natural or an adopted parent of the minor if no legal representative has been appointed). The consent of an estate must be made by an executor or administrator thereof. Where stock of the corporation is held by a trust that is described in section 1361(c)(2)(A)(i) or that is treated as a trust described in that section, each deemed owner who is considered to be a shareholder for purposes of section 1361(b)(1) must consent to the election; in the case of stock that is held by a trust to which that stock was transferred pursuant to the terms of a will, the estate of the testator that is considered to be the shareholder for purposes of section 1361(b)(1) must consent to the election; in the case of stock that is held by a trust that is described in section 1361(c)(2)(A)(iii), each beneficiary who is considered to be a shareholder for purposes of section 1361(b)(1) must consent to the election.

(c) **Extension of time for filing consents.** An election that is timely filed for any taxable year, and that would be valid except for the failure of any shareholder to file a timely consent, is not invalid for such reason if—

(1) It is shown to the satisfaction of the district director or director of the service center with which the corporation files its income tax return that there was reasonable cause for the failure to file such consent and that the interests of the Government will not be jeopardized by treating such election as valid,

(2) Such shareholder files a proper consent to the election within such extended period of time as may be granted by the Internal Revenue Service, and

(3) New consents are filed within such extended period of time as may be granted by the Internal Revenue Service, by all persons who were shareholders of the corporation at any time during the taxable year with respect to which the failure to consent would (but for the provisions of this paragraph) cause the corporation's election to be invalid, and by all persons who were shareholders of the corporation within the period beginning after such taxable year and ending before the date on which an extension of time is granted in accordance with this paragraph.

[T.D. 7872, 48 FR 3590, Jan. 26, 1983]

§ 18.1362–3 Revocation of election.

An election made under section 1362(a) may be revoked by the corporation for any taxable year of the corporation. A revocation can be made only with the consent of shareholders who hold at the time the revocation is made more than one-half of the number of issued and outstanding shares of stock (including nonvoting stock) of the corporation. Such revocation shall be made by the corporation by filing a statement that the corporation revokes the election made under section 1362(a), which statement shall state the number of shares of stock (including nonvoting stock) that is issued and outstanding at the time the revocation is made and shall indicate the date on which the revocation shall be effective. The statement shall be signed by any person authorized to sign the return required to be filed under section 6037 and shall be filed with the service center with which the election was properly filed. In addition, there shall be attached to the statement of revocation a statement of consent, signed by each shareholder who consents to the revocation by the corporation of the election made under section 1362(a) and stating the number of issued and outstanding shares of stock (including nonvoting stock) that is held by each such shareholder at the time the revocation is made, in which each such shareholder consents to the revocation by the corporation of the election made under section 1362(a). For the rules relating to the effective date of a revocation, see section 1362(d)(1)(C) and (D).

[T.D. 7872, 48 FR 3590, Jan. 26, 1983]

§ 18.1362–4 Treatment of S termination year.

In the case of a taxable year of a corporation that is an S termination year (as defined in section 1362(e)(4)), the corporation may elect under section 1362(e)(3) to have the rules provided in section 1362(e)(2) (relating to pro rata allocation of items) not apply. The election can be made only with the consent of all persons who are or were shareholders in the corporation at any time during the S termination year. Such election shall be made by the corporation by filing a statement that the corporation elects under section 1362(e)(3) to have the rules provided in section 1362(e)(2) not apply, which statement shall set forth the cause of the termination and the date thereof. The statement shall be signed by any person authorized to sign the return required to be filed under section 6037 and shall be filed with the return for the short taxable year described in section 1362(e)(1)(B). In addition, there shall be attached to the statement of election a statement of consent, signed by each person who is or was a shareholder in the corporation at any time during the S termination year, in which each such shareholder consents to the corporation making the election under section 1362(e)(3).

[T.D. 7872, 48 FR 3590, Jan. 26, 1983, as amended by T.D. 7976, 49 FR 35492, Sept. 10, 1984]

§ 1.1371–1 Definition of small business corporation.

* * *

(d) Number of shareholders—(1) In general. A corporation does not qualify as a small business corporation if it has more than 10 shareholders. Ordinarily, the persons who would have to include in gross income dividends distributed with respect to the stock of the corporation are considered to be the shareholders of the corporation. For example, if stock is owned by tenants in common, joint tenants, or tenants by the entirety, each tenant in common, joint tenant, or tenant by the entirety is generally considered a shareholder, but see subparagraph (2) of this paragraph relating to stock owned by husband and wife. Persons for whom a stock in a corporation is held by a nominee, agent, guardian, or custodian will generally be considered shareholders of the corporation. If stock is owned by a trust which is subject to the provisions of subchapters D, F, H, or J, chapter 1 of the Code, or by a voting trust, the trust is considered the shareholder even though the dividends paid to the trust are includible directly in the income of the grantor or some other person. If stock is owned by a partnership, such partnership and not its partners is considered to be the shareholder.

(2) Stock owned by husband and wife. (i) Except as otherwise provided in this paragraph, in determining whether a corporation meets the 10-or-fewer-shareholders requirement of section 1371(a)(1), stock which:

(a) Is community property of a husband and wife (or the income from which is community income) under the applicable community-property law of a State, or

(b) Is held by a husband and wife as joint tenants, tenants by the entirety, or tenants in common,

shall be treated as owned by one shareholder. For this purpose, if a husband or wife owns stock in a corporation individually, and the husband and wife own other stock in the corporation jointly, the husband and wife will be considered one shareholder. However, if the husband and wife each owns stock in the corporation individually, they will be treated as two shareholders. This subdivision applies only in determining the number of shareholders for purposes of section 1371(a)(1) and does not apply for purposes of any other provisions of Subchapter S, chapter 1 of the Code. Thus, for example, the husband and wife will each be considered a shareholder for purposes of section 1372(a), relating to the requirement that all shareholders consent to the corporation's election, and section 1373(a), relating to the inclusion in the shareholder's gross income of the corporation's undistributed taxable income.

* * *

[T.D. 6500, 25 FR 12053, Nov. 26, 1960, as amended by T.D. 6667, 28 FR 7730, July 30, 1963; T.D. 6904, 31 FR 16527, Dec. 28, 1966; T.D. 6960, 33 FR 9289, June 25, 1968; T.D. 7747, 45 FR 86459, Dec. 31, 1980; T.D. 7920, 48 FR 50712, Nov. 3, 1983]

§ 1.1372–2 Manner and time for making election and filing shareholders' consent.

* * *

(b) Time of making election—(1) Taxable years beginning on or after September 3, 1958. For taxable years beginning on or after September 3, 1958, the election shall be filed either (i) during the first month of such taxable year, or (ii) during the month preceding such first month. In the case of a new corporation whose taxable year begins after the first day of a particular month, the term "month" means the period commencing with the beginning of the first day of the taxable year and ending with the close of the day preceding the numerically corresponding day of the succeeding calendar month or, if there is no such corresponding day, with the close of the last day of such succeeding calendar month. For purposes of this subparagraph, the first month of the taxable year of a new corporation does not begin until the corporation has shareholders or acquires assets or begins doing business, whichever is the first to occur.

* * *

[T.D. 6500, 25 FR 12055, Nov. 26, 1960, as amended by T.D. 7012, 34 FR 7688, May 15, 1969]

§ 1.1372–4   Termination of election.

* * *

(5) Passive investment income—(i) In general. (b) Methods of termination—Except as otherwise provided in subdivisions (ii) and (iii) of this subparagraph, an election under section 1372(a) shall terminate if for any taxable year of the corporation the corporation has gross receipts more than 20 percent of which is derived from royalties, rents, dividends, interest, annuities, and sales or exchanges of stock or securities (hereinafter referred to as "passive investment income"), as determined in accordance with the rules of this subparagraph.

* * *

(iv) Gross receipts. (a) The term "gross receipts" as used in section 1372(e) is not synonymous with "gross income". The test under section 1372(e)(4) and (5) shall be made on the basis of total gross receipts, except that, for purposes of section 1372(e)(5), gross receipts from the sales or exchanges of stock or securities shall be taken into account only to the extent of gains therefrom. The term "gross receipts" means the total amount received or accrued under the method of accounting used by the corporation in computing its taxable income. Thus, the total amount of receipts is not reduced by returns and allowances, cost, or deductions. For example, gross receipts will include the total amount received or accrued during the corporation's taxable year from the sale or exchange (including a sale or exchange to which section 337 applies) or any kind of property, from investments, and for services rendered by the corporation. However, gross receipts do not include (1) amounts received in nontaxable sales or exchanges (other than those to which section 337 applies), except to the extent that gain is recognized by the corporation, (2) amounts received as a loan, as a repayment of a loan, as a contribution to capital, or on the issuance by the corporation of its own stock, or (3) certain amounts which are treated under section 331 (relating to corporate liquidations) as payments in exchange for stock (see subdivision (xi) of this subparagraph).

(b) The meaning of the term "gross receipts" as used in section 1372(e)(4) and (5) may be further illustrated by the following examples:

Example (1). A corporation on the accrual method sells property (other than stock or securities) and receives payment partly in money and partly in the form of a note payable at a future time. The amount of the money and the face amount of the note would be considered gross receipts in the taxable year of the sale and would not be reduced by the adjusted basis of the property, the costs of sale, or any other amount.

Example (2). A corporation has a long-term contract as defined in paragraph (a) of § 1.451–3 with respect to which it reports income according to the percentage-of-completion method as described in paragraph (b)(1) of § 1.451–3. The portion of the gross contract price which corresponds to the percentage of the entire contract which has been completed during the taxable year shall be included in gross receipts for such year.

Example (3). A corporation which regularly sells personal property on the installment plan elects to report its taxable income from the sale of property (other than stock or securities) on the installment method in accordance with section 453. The installment payments actually received in a given taxable year of the corporation shall be included in gross receipts for such year.

(v) Royalties. The term "royalties" as used in section 1372(e)(5) means all royalties, including mineral, oil, and gas royalties, and amounts received for the privilege of using patents, copyrights, secret processes and formulas, good will, trademarks, trade brands, franchises, and other like property. The term "royalties" does not include amounts received upon disposal of timber, coal, or domestic iron ore with a retained economic interest with respect to which the special rules of section 631(b) and (c) apply. For the definition of "mineral, oil, or gas royalties," see paragraph 5(b)(11)(ii) and (iii) of § 1.543–1. For purposes of this subdivision, the gross amount of royalties shall not be reduced by any part of the cost of the rights under which they are received or by any amount allowable as a deduction in computing taxable income.

(vi) Rents. The term "rents" as used in section 1372(e)(5) means amounts received for the use of, or right to use, property (whether real or personal) of the corporation. The term "rents" does not include payments for the use or occupancy of rooms or other space where significant services are also rendered to the occupant, such as for the use or occupancy of rooms or other quarters in hotels, boarding houses, or apartment houses furnishing hotel services, or in tourist homes, motor courts, or motels. Generally, services are considered rendered to the occupant if they are primarily for his convenience and are other than those usually or customarily rendered in connection with the rental of rooms or other space for occupancy only. The supplying of maid service, for example, constitutes

such services; whereas the furnishing of heat and light, the cleaning of public entrances, exits, stairways and lobbies, the collection of trash, etc., are not considered as services rendered to the occupant. Payments for the use or occupancy of entire private residences or living quarters in duplex or multiple housing units, of offices in an office building, etc., are generally "rents" under section 1372(e)(5). Payments for the parking of automobiles ordinarily do not constitute rents. Payments for the warehousing of goods or for the use of personal property do not constitute rents if significant services are rendered in connection with such payments.

(vii) Dividends. The term "dividends" as used in section 1372(e)(5) includes dividends as defined in section 316, amounts required to be included in gross income under section 551 (relating to foreign personal holding company income taxed to U.S. shareholders), and consent dividends determined as provided in section 565.

(viii) Interest. The term "interest" as used in section 1372(e)(5) means any amounts received for the use of money (including tax-exempt interest and amounts treated as interest under section 483).

(ix) Annuities. The term "annuities" as used in section 1372(e)(5) means the entire amount received as an annuity under an annuity, endowment, or life insurance contract, regardless of whether only part of such amount would be includible in gross income under section 72.

(x) Gross receipts from the sale of stock or securities. For purposes of section 1372(e)(5), gross receipts from the sales or exchanges of stock or securities are taken into account only to the extent of gains therefrom. Thus, the gross receipts from the sale of a particular share of stock will be the excess of the amount realized over the adjusted basis of such share. If the adjusted basis should equal or exceed the amount realized on the sale or exchange of a certain share of stock, bond, etc., there would be no gross receipts resulting from the sale of such security. Losses on sales or exchanges of stock or securities do not offset gains on the sales or exchanges of other stock or securities for purposes of computing gross receipts from such sales or exchanges. Gross receipts from the sale or exchange of stock and securities include gains received from such sales or exchanges by a corporation even though such corporation is a regular dealer in stocks and securities. However, gross receipts do not include certain amounts which are treated under section 331 (relating to corporate liquidations) as payments in exchange for stock (see subdivision (xi) of this subparagraph). For the meaning of the term "stock or securities", see paragraph (b)(5)(i) of § 1.543–1.

* * *

[T.D. 6500, 25 FR 12056, Nov. 26, 1960, as amended by T.D. 6707, 29 FR 3197, Mar. 10, 1964; T.D. 6841, 30 FR 9304, July 27, 1965; T.D. 6960, 33 FR 9291, June 25, 1968; T.D. 7012, 34 FR 7689, May 15, 1969; T.D. 7414, 41 FR 13918, April 1, 1976]

§ 1.1374–1A Tax imposed on certain capital gains.

(a) General rule. Except as otherwise provided in paragraph (c) of this section, if for a taxable year beginning after 1982 of an S corporation—

(1) The net capital gain of such corporation exceeds $25,000, and

(2) The net capital gain of such corporation exceeds 50 percent of its taxable income (as defined in paragraph (d) of this section) for such year, and

(3) The taxable income of such corporation (as defined in paragraph (d) of this section) for such year exceeds $25,000,

section 1374 imposes a tax (computed under paragraph (b) of this section) on the income of such corporation. The tax is imposed on the S corporation and not on the shareholders.

(b) Amount of tax. The amount of tax shall be the lower of—

(1) An amount equal to the tax, determined as provided in section 1201(a)(2), on the amount by which the net capital gain of the corporation for the taxable year exceeds $25,000, or

(2) An amount equal to the tax which would be imposed by section 11 on the taxable income of the corporation (as defined in paragraph (d) of this section) for the taxable year were it not an S corporation.

No credit shall be allowable under Part IV of Subchapter A of Chapter 1 of the Internal Revenue Code of 1954 (other than under section 34) against the tax imposed by section 1374(a) and this section. See section 1375(c)(2) and § 1.1375–1A(c)(2) for a special rule that reduces the amount of the net capital gain of the corporation for purposes of this paragraph (b) in cases where a net capital gain is taxed as excess net passive income under section 1375. See section 1374(c)(3) and paragraph (c)(1)(ii) of this section for a special rule that limits the amount of tax on property with a substituted basis in certain cases.

(c) Exceptions to taxation—(1) New corporations and corporations with election in effect for 3 immediately preceding years—(i) In general. If an S corporation would be subject to the tax imposed by section 1374 for a taxable year pursuant to paragraph (a) of this section, the corporation shall, nevertheless, not be subject to such tax for such year, if:

(A) The election under section 1362(a) which is in effect with respect to such corporation for such year has been in effect for the corporation's three immediately preceding taxable years, or

(B) An election under section 1362(a) has been in effect with respect to such corporation for each of its taxable years for which it has been in existence, unless there is a net capital gain for the taxable year which is attributable to property with a substituted basis within the meaning of paragraph (c)(1)(iii) of this section.

(ii) Amount of tax on net capital gain attributable to property with a substituted basis. If for a taxable year of an S corporation either paragraph (c)(1)(i)(A) or (B) of this section is satisfied, but the S corporation has a net capital gain for such taxable year which is attributable to property with a substituted basis (within the meaning of paragraph (c)(1)(iii) of this section), then paragraph (a) of this section shall apply for the taxable year, but the amount of tax determined under paragraph (b) of this section shall not exceed a tax, determined as provided in section 1201 (a), on the net capital gain attributable to property with a substituted basis.

(iii) Property with substituted basis. For purposes of this section, the term "property with a substituted basis" means:

(A) Property acquired by a corporation ("the acquiring corporation") during the period beginning 36 months before the first day of the acquiring corporation's taxable year and ending on the last day of such year;

(B) The basis of such property in the hands of the acquiring corporation is determined in whole or in part by reference to the basis of any property in the hands of another corporation; and

(C) Such other corporation was not an S corporation throughout the period beginning the later of:

(1) 36 months before the first day of the acquiring corporation's taxable year, or

(2) The time such other corporation came into existence,

and ending on the date such other corporation transferred the property, the basis of which is used to determine, in whole or in part, the basis of the property in the hands of the acquiring corporation. An S corporation and any predecessor corporation shall not be treated as one corporation for purposes of this paragraph (c)(1).

(iv) **Existence of a corporation.** For purposes of this section, a corporation shall not be considered to be in existence for any month which precedes the first month in which such corporation has shareholders or acquires assets or begins business, whichever is first to occur.

(v) **References to prior law included.** For purposes of this paragraph (c), the term "S corporation" shall include an electing small business corporation under prior Subchapter S law, and the term "election under section 1362(a)" shall include an election under section 1372 of prior Subchapter S law.

(iv) **Examples.** The provisions of this paragraph may be illustrated by the following examples:

Example (1). M corporation was organized and began business in 1977. M subsequently made an election under section 1362(a) which was effective for its 1984 taxable year. If such election does not terminate under section 1362 for its taxable years 1984, 1985, and 1986, M is not subject to the tax imposed by section 1374 for its taxable year 1987, or for any subsequent year for which such election remains in effect, unless it has, for any such year, an excess of net long-term capital gain over net short-term capital loss attributable to property with a substituted basis. If there is such an excess for any such year, and the requirements of paragraph (a) of this section are met, M will be subject to the tax for such year. If there is no such excess for any year after 1986, M will not be subject to the tax for any such year even though the requirements of paragraph (a) of this section are met.

Example (2). N corporation was organized in 1983, and was an S corporation for its first taxable year, N is not subject to the tax imposed by section 1374 for 1983, or for any subsequent year for which its original election under section 1362(a) has not terminated under section 1362(d), unless, for any such year, it has an excess of net long-term capital gain over net short-term capital loss attributable to property with a substituted basis and the requirements of paragraph (a) of this section are met.

(2) **Treatment of certain gains of options and commodities dealers—(i) Exclusion of certain capital gains.** For purposes of this section, the net capital gain of any options dealer or commodities dealer shall be determined by not taking into account any gain or loss (in the normal course of the taxpayer's activity of dealing in or trading section 1256 contracts) from any section 1256 contract or property related to such a contract.

(ii) **Definitions.** For purposes of this paragraph (c)(2)—

(A) Options dealer. The term "options dealer" has the meaning given to such term by section 1256(g)(8).

(B) Commodities dealer. The term "commodities dealer" means a person who is actively engaged in trading section 1256 contracts and is registered with a domestic board of trade which is designated as a contract market by the Commodities Futures Trading Commission.

(C) Section 1256 contracts. The term "section 1256 contracts" has the meaning given to such term by section 1256(b).

(iii) **Effective dates—(A) In general.** Except as otherwise provided in this paragraph (c)(2)(iii), this paragraph (c)(2) shall apply to positions established after July 18, 1984, in taxable years ending after such date.

(B) Special rule for options on regulated futures contracts. In the case of any option with respect to a regulated futures contract (within the meaning of section 1256), this paragraph (c)(2) shall apply to positions established after October 31, 1983, in taxable years ending after such date.

(C) Elections with respect to property held on or before July 18, 1984. See §§ 1.1256(h)–1T and 1.1256(h)–2T for rules concerning an election to have this paragraph (c)(2) apply to certain property held on or before July 18, 1984.

(d) **Determination of taxable income—(1) General rule.** For purposes of this section, taxable income of the corporation shall be determined under section 63(a) as if the corporation were a C corporation rather than an S corporation, except that the following deductions shall not apply in the computation—

(i) The deduction allowed by section 172 (relating to net operating loss deduction), and

(ii) The deductions allowed by Part VIII of Subchapter B (other than the deduction allowed by section 248, relating to organization expenditures).

For any taxable year in which a tax under this section is imposed on an S corporation, the S corporation shall attach a Form 1120 completed in accordance with this paragraph (d) and instructions to Form 1120S to its tax return filed for such taxable year.

(2) Special rule for net capital gains taxed as excess net passive income under section 1375. See section 1375(c)(2) and § 1.1375–1A(c)(2) for a special rule that reduces the taxable income of the corporation for purposes of section 1374(b)(2) and § 1.1374–1A(b)(2) in cases where a net capital gain is taxed as excess net passive income under section 1375.

(e) Reduction in pass-thru for tax imposed on capital gain. See section 1366(f)(2) for a special rule reducing the S corporation's long-term capital gains and the corporation's gain from sales or exchanges of property described in section 1231 for purposes of section 1366(a) by an amount of tax imposed under section 1374 and this section.

(f) Examples. The following examples illustrate the principles of this section and assume that a tax will not be imposed under section 1375:

Example (1). Corporation M is an S corporation for its taxable year beginning January 1, 1983. For 1983, M has an excess of net long-term capital gain over net short-term capital loss in the amount of $30,000. However, its taxable income for the year is only $20,000 as a result of other deductions in excess of other income. Thus, although the excess of the net long-term capital gain over the net short-term capital loss exceeds $25,000 and also exceeds 50 percent of taxable income, M is not subject to the tax imposed by section 1374 for 1983 because its taxable income does not exceed $25,000.

Example (2). Corporation N is an S corporation for its 1983 taxable year. For 1983, N has an excess of net long-term capital gain over net short-term capital loss in the amount of $30,000 and taxable income of $65,000. Thus, although N's net capital gain ($30,000) exceeds $25,000, it does not exceed 50 percent of the corporation's taxable income for the year (50 percent of $65,000, or $32,500), and therefore N is not subject to the tax imposed by section 1374 for such year.

Example (3). Assume that Corporation O, an S corporation, is subject to the tax imposed by section 1374 for its taxable year 1983. For 1983, O has an excess of net long-term capital gain over net short-term capital loss in the amount of $73,000, and taxable income within the meaning of section 1374, which includes capital gains and losses, of $100,000. The amount of tax computed under paragraph (b)(1) of this section is 28 percent of $48.00 ($73,000—$25,000), or $13,440. Since this is lower than the amount computed under paragraph (b)(2) of this section, which is $25,750 ($3,750 + $4,500 + $7,500 + $10,000), $13,440 is the amount of tax imposed by section 1374.

Example (4). Assume that in example (3) the taxable income of O for 1983 is $35,000. This results from an excess of deductions over income with respect to items which were not included in determining the excess of the net long-term capital gain over the net short-term capital loss. In such case, the amount of tax, computed under paragraph (b)(2) of this section, is $5,550. Since this is lower than the amount computed under paragraph (b)(1) of this section, $5,550 is the amount of tax imposed by section 1374.

Example (5). Corporation P, an S corporation, for its taxable year 1983 has an excess of net long-term capital gain over net short-term capital loss in the amount of $65,000 and has taxable income of $80,000. P's election under section 1362 has been in effect for its three immediately preceding taxable years, but P, nevertheless, is subject to the tax imposed by section 1374 for 1983 since it has an excess of net long-term capital gain over net short-term capital loss (in the amount of $20,000) attributable to property with a substituted basis. The tax computed under paragraph (b)(1) of this section, $11,200 (28 percent of $40,000 ($65,000—$25,000)), is less than the tax computed under paragraph (b)(2) of this section, $17,750. However, under the limitation provided in paragraph (c) of this section which is applicable in this factual situation, the tax imposed by section 1374 for 1983 may not exceed $5,600 (28 percent of $20,000, the excess of net long-term capital gain over net short-term capital loss attributable to property with a substituted basis).

[T.D. 8104, 51 FR 34201, Sept. 26, 1986]

§ 1.1375–1 Special rules applicable to capital gains.

* * *

(d) Level for determining character of gain. Ordinarily, for purposes of determining whether gain on the sale or exchange of an asset by an electing small business corporation is capital gain, the character of the asset is determined at the corporate level. However, if an electing small business corporation is availed of by any shareholder or group of shareholders owning a substantial portion of the stock of such corporation for the purpose of selling property which in the hands of such shareholder or shareholders would not have been an asset, gain from the sale of which would be capital gain, then the gain on the sale of such property by the corporation shall not be treated as a capital gain. For this purpose, in determining the character of the asset in the hands of the shareholder, the activities of other electing small business corporations in which he is a shareholder shall be taken into consideration.

* * *

[T.D. 6500, 25 FR 12061, Nov. 26, 1960, as amended by T.D. 6960, 33 FR 9294, June 25, 1968; T.D. 7337, 39 FR 44978, Dec. 30, 1974; T.D. 7564, 43 FR 40497, Sept. 12, 1978; T.D. 7728, 45 FR 72650, Nov. 3, 1980]

§ 1.1375–1A Tax imposed when passive investment income of corporation having Subchapter C earnings and profits exceed 25 percent of gross receipts.

(a) General rule. For taxable years beginning after 1981, section 1375(a) imposes a tax on the income of certain S corporations that have passive investment income. In the case of a taxable year beginning during 1982, an electing small business corporation may elect to have the rules under this section not apply. See the regulations under section 1362 for rules on the election. For purposes of this section, the term "S corporation" shall include an electing small business corporation under prior law. This tax shall apply to an S corporation for a taxable year if the S corporation has—

(1) Subchapter C earnings and profits at the close of such taxable year, and

(2) Gross receipts more than 25 percent of which are passive investment income.

If the S corporation has no Subchapter C earnings and profits at the close of the taxable year (because, for example, such earnings and profits were distributed in accordance with section 1368), the tax shall not be imposed even though the S corporation has passive investment income for the taxable year. If the tax is imposed, the tax shall be computed by multiplying the excess net passive income (as defined in paragraph (b) of this section) by the highest rate of tax specified in section 11(b).

(b) Definitions—(1) Excess net passive income—(i) In general. The term "excess net passive income" is defined in section 1375(b)(1), and can be expressed by the following formula:

$$\text{ENPI} = \text{NPI} \times \frac{\text{PII} - (.25 \times \text{GR})}{\text{PII}}$$

Where:

ENPI=excess net passive income

NPI=net passive income

PII=passive investment income

GR=total gross receipts

(ii) Limitation. The amount of the excess net passive income for any taxable year shall not exceed the corporation's taxable income for the taxable year (determined in accordance with section 1374(d) and § 1.1374–1A(d)).

(2) Net passive income. The term "net passive income" means—

(i) Passive investment income, reduced by

(ii) The deductions allowable under Chapter 1 of the Internal Revenue Code of 1954 which are directly connected (within the meaning of paragraph (b)(3) of this section) with the production of such income (other than deductions allowable under section 172 and Part VIII of Subchapter B).

(3) Directly connected—(i) In general. For purposes of paragraph (b)(2)(ii) of this section to be directly connected with the production of income, an item of deduction must have proximate and primary relationship to/the income. Expenses, depreciation, and similar items attributable solely to such income qualify for deduction.

(ii) Allocation of deduction. If an item of deduction is attributable (within the meaning of paragraph (b)(3)(i) of this section) in part to passive investment income and in part to income other than passive investment income, the deduction shall be allocated between the two types of items on a reasonable basis. The portion of any deduction so allocated to passive investment income shall be treated as proximately and primarily related to such income.

(4) Other definitions. The terms "subchapter C earnings and profits," "passive investment income," and "gross receipts" shall have the same meaning given these terms in section 1362(d)(3) and the regulations thereunder.

(c) Special rules—(1) Disallowance of credits. No credit is allowed under Part IV of Subchapter A of Chapter 1 of the Code (other than section 34) against the tax imposed by section 1375(a) and this section.

(2) Coordination with section 1374. If any gain—

(i) is taken into account in determining passive income for purposes of this section, and

(ii) is taken into account under section 1374,

the amount of such gain taken into account under section 1374(b) and § 1.1374–1A(b)(1) and (2) in determining the amount of tax shall be reduced by the portion of the excess net passive income for the taxable year which is attributable (on a pro rata basis) to such gain. For purposes of the preceding sentence, the portion of excess net passive income for the taxable year which is attributable to such capital gain is equal to the amount determined by multiplying the excess net passive income by the following fraction:

$$\frac{NCG-E}{NPI}$$

Where:

NCG=net capital gain

NPI=net passive income

E=Expense attributable to net capital gain

(d) **Waiver of tax in certain cases—(1) In general.** If an S corporation establishes to the satisfaction of the Commissioner that—

(i) It determined in good faith that it had no Subchapter C earnings and profits at the close of the taxable year, and

(ii) During a reasonable period of time after it was determined that it did have Subchapter C earnings and profits at the close of such taxable year such earnings and profits were distributed,

the Commissioner may waive the tax imposed by section 1375 for such taxable year. The S corporation has the burden of establishing that under the relevant facts and circumstances the Commissioner should waive the tax. For example, if an S corporation establishes that in good faith and using due diligence it determined that it had no Subchapter C earnings and profits at the close of a taxable year, but it was later determined on audit that it did have Subchapter C earnings and profits at the close of such taxable year, and if the corporation establishes that it distributed such earnings and profits within a reasonable time after the audit, it may be appropriate for the Commissioner to waive the tax on passive income for such taxable year.

(2) **Corporation's request for a waiver.** A request for waiver of the tax imposed by section 1375 shall be made in writing to the district director request and shall contain all relevant facts to establish that the requirements of paragraph (d)(1) of this section are met. Such request shall contain a description of how and on what date the S corporation in good faith and using due diligence determined that it had no Subchapter C earnings and profits at the close of the taxable year, a description of how and on what date it was determined that the S corporation had Subchapter C earnings and profits at the close of the year and a description (including dates) of any steps taken to distribute such earnings and profits. If the earnings and profits have not yet been distributed, the request shall contain a timetable for distribution and an explanation of why such timetable is reasonable. On the date the waiver is to become effective, all Subchapter C earnings and profits must have been distributed.

(e) **Reduction in pass-thru for tax imposed on excess net passive income.** See section 1366(f)(3) for a special rule reducing each item of the corporation's passive investment income for purposes of section 1366(a) if a tax is imposed on the corporation under section 1375.

Examples. The following example illustrates the principles of this section:

Example (1). Assume Corporation M, an S corporation, has for its taxable year total gross receipts of $200,000, passive investment income of $100,000, $60,000 of which is interest income, and expenses directly connected with the production of such interest income in the amount of $10,000. Assume also that at the end of the taxable year Corporation M has Subchapter C earnings and profits. Since more than 25 percent of the Corporation M's total gross receipts are passive investment income, and since Corporation M has Subchapter C earnings and profits at the end of the taxable year, Corporation M will be subject to the tax imposed by section 1375. The amount of excess net passive investment income is $45,000 ($90,000+($50,000/$100,000)). Assume that the other $40,000 of passive investment income is attributable to net capital gain and that there are no expenses directly connected with such gain. Under these facts, $20,000 of the excess net passive income is attributable to the net capital gain ($45,000+($40,000/$90,000)). Accordingly, the amount of gain taken into account under section 1374(b)(1) and the taxable income of Corporation M under section 1374(b)(2) shall be reduced by $20,000.

Example (2). Assume an S corporation with Subchapter C earnings and profits has tax-exempt income of $400, its only passive income, gross receipts of $1,000 and taxable income of $250 and there are no expenses associated with the tax-exempt income. The corporation's excess net passive income for the taxable year would total $150 (400+((400-250)/400)). This amount is subject to the tax imposed by section 1375, notwithstanding that such amount is otherwise tax-exempt income.

[T.D. 8104, 51 FR 34203, Sept. 26, 1986]

§ 18.1377–1 Election to terminate year.

In the case of a taxable year of an S corporation during which any shareholder terminates his or her entire shareholder interest in the corporation, the corporation may elect under section 1377(a)(2) to have the rules provided in section 1377(a)(1) applied as if the taxable year consisted of two taxable years. The election can be made only with the consent of all persons who are or were shareholders in the corporation at any time during such taxable year. Such election shall be made by the corporation by filing a statement that the corporation elects under section 1377(a)(2) to have the rules provided in section 1377(a)(1) applied as if the taxable year consisted of two taxable years, which statement shall set forth the manner of the termination (e.g., the sale of a shareholder's entire shareholder interest) and the date thereof and shall be filed with the return for such taxable year. The statement to be filed with the return for such taxable year shall be signed by any person authorized to sign the return required to be filed under section 6037. In addition, there shall be attached to the statement of election a statement of consent, signed by each person who is or was a shareholder in the corporation at any time during the taxable year, in which each such shareholder consents to the corporation making the election under section 1377(a)(2).

[T.D. 7872, 48 FR 3590, Jan. 26, 1983]

PART 20—ESTATE TAX

Gross Estate

§ 20.2031–1 Definition of gross estate; valuation of property.

(a) **Definition of gross estate.** Except as otherwise provided in this paragraph the value of the gross estate of a decedent who was a citizen or resident of the United States at the time of his death is the total value of the interests described in sections 2033 through 2044. * * * Except as provided in paragraph (c) of this section (relating to the estates of decedents dying after October 16, 1962, and before July 1, 1964), in the case of a decedent dying after October 16, 1962, real property situated outside the United States which comes within the scope of sections 2033 through 2044 is included in the gross estate to the same extent as any other property coming within the scope of those sections. In arriving at the value of the gross estate the interests described in sections 2033 through 2044 are valued as described in this section, §§ 20.2031–2 through 20.2031–9 and § 20.-2032–1. The contents of sections 2033 through 2044 are, in general, as follows:

(1) Sections 2033 and 2034 are concerned mainly with interests in property passing through the decedent's probate estate. Section 2033 includes in the decedent's gross estate any interest that the decedent had in property at the time of his death. Section 2034 provides that any interest of the decedent's surviving spouse in the decedent's property, such as dower or curtesy, does not prevent the inclusion of such property in the decedent's gross estate.

(2) Sections 2035 through 2038 deal with interests in property transferred by the decedent during his life under such circumstances as to bring the interests within the decedent's gross estate. Section 2035 includes in the decedent's gross estate property transferred in contemplation of death, even though the decedent had not interest in, or control over, the property at the time of his death. Section 2036 provides for the inclusion of transferred property with respect to which the decedent retained the income or the power to designate who shall enjoy the income. Section 2037 includes in the decedent's gross estate certain transfers under which the beneficial enjoyment of the property could be obtained only by surviving the decedent. Section 2038 provides for the inclusion of transferred property if the decedent had at the time of his death the power to change the beneficial enjoyment of the property. It should be noted that

there is considerable overlap in the application of sections 2036 through 2038 with respect to reserved powers, so that transferred property may be includible in the decedent's gross estate in varying degrees under more than one of those sections.

(3) Sections 2039 through 2042 deal with special kinds of property and powers. Sections 2039 and 2040 concern annuities and jointly held property respectively. Section 2041 deals with powers held by the decedent over the beneficial enjoyment of property not originating with the decedent. Section 2042 concerns insurance under policies on the life of the decedent.

(4) Section 2043 concerns the sufficiency of consideration for transfers made by the decedent during his life. This has a bearing on the amount to be included in the decedent's gross estate under sections 2035 through 2038, and 2041. Section 2044 deals with retroactivity.

(b) **Valuation of property in general.** The value of every item of property includible in a decedent's gross estate under sections 2031 through 2044 is its fair market value at the time of the decedent's death, except that if the executor elects the alternate valuation method under section 2032, it is the fair market value thereof at the date, and with the adjustments, prescribed in that section. The fair market value is the price at which the property would change hands between a willing buyer and a willing seller, neither being under any compulsion to buy or to sell and both having reasonable knowledge of relevant facts. The fair market value of a particular item of property includible in the decedent's gross estate is not to be determined by a forced sale price. Nor is the fair market value of an item of property to be determined by the sale price of the item in a market other than that in which such item is most commonly sold to the public, taking into account the location of the item wherever appropriate. Thus, in the case of an item of property includible in the decedent's gross estate, which is generally obtained by the public in the retail market, the fair market value of such an item of property is the price at which the item or a comparable item would be sold at retail. For example, the fair market value of an automobile (an article generally obtained by the public in the retail market) includible in the decedent's gross estate is the price for which an automobile of the same or approximately the same description, make, model, age, condition, etc., could be purchased by a member of the general public and not the price for which the particular automobile of the decedent would be purchased by a dealer in used automobiles. Examples of items of property which are generally sold to the public at retail may be found in §§ 20.-2031-6 and 20.2031-8. The value is generally to be determined by ascertaining as a basis the fair market value as of the applicable valuation date of each unit of property. For example, in the case of shares of stock or bonds, such unit of property is generally a share of stock or a bond. Livestock, farm machinery, harvested and growing crops must generally be itemized and the value of each item separately returned. Property shall not be returned at the value at which it is assessed for local tax purposes unless that value represents the fair market value as of the applicable valuation date. All relevant facts and elements of value as of the applicable valuation date shall be considered in every case. The value of items of property which were held by the decedent for sale in the course of a business generally should be reflected in the value of the business. For valuation of interests in businesses, see § 20.2031-3. See § 20.2031-2 and §§ 20.2031-4 through 20.2031-8 for further information concerning the valuation of other particular kinds of property. For certain circumstances under which the sale of an item of property at a price below its fair market value may result in a deduction for the estate, see paragraph (d)(2) of § 20.2053-3.

* * *

[T.D. 6296, 23 FR 4529, June 24, 1958, as amended by T.D. 6684, 28 FR 11408, Oct. 24, 1963; T.D. 6826, 30 FR 7708, June 15, 1965]

§ 20.2031-2 Valuation of stocks and bonds.

(a) **In general.** The value of stocks and bonds is the fair market value per share or bond on the applicable valuation date.

(b) **Based on selling prices.** (1) In general, if there is a market for stocks or bonds, on a stock exchange, in an over-the-counter market, or otherwise, the mean between the highest and lowest quoted selling prices on the valuation date is the fair market value per share or bond. If there were no sales on the valuation date but there were sales on dates within a reasonable period both before and after the valuation date, the fair market value is determined by taking a weighted average of the means between the highest and lowest sales on the nearest date before and the nearest date after the valuation date. The average is to be weighted inversely by the respective numbers of trading days between the selling dates and the valuation date. If the stocks or bonds are listed on more than one exchange, the records of the exchange where the stocks or bonds are principally dealt in should be employed if such records are available in a generally available listing or publication of general circulation. In the event that such records are not so available and such stocks or bonds are listed on a composite listing of combined exchanges available in a generally available listing or publication of general circulation, the records of such combined exchanges should be employed. In valuing listed securities, the executor should be careful to consult accurate records to obtain values as of the applicable valuation date. If quotations of unlisted securities are obtained from brokers, or evidence as to their sale is obtained from officers of the issuing companies, copies of the letters furnishing such quotations or evidence of sale should be attached to the return.

(2) If it is established with respect to bonds for which there is a market on a stock exchange, that the highest and lowest selling prices are not available for the valuation date in a generally available listing or publication of general circulation but that closing selling prices are so available, the fair market value per bond is the mean between the quoted closing selling price on the valuation date and the quoted closing selling price on the trading day before the valuation date. If there were no sales on the trading day before the valuation date but there were sales on a date within a reasonable period before the valuation date, the fair market value is determined by taking a weighted average of the quoted closing selling price on the valuation date and the quoted closing selling price on the nearest date before the valuation date. The closing selling price for the valuation date is to be weighted by the number of trading days between the previous selling date and the valuation date. If there were no sales within a reasonable period before the valuation date but there were sales on the valuation date, the fair market value is the closing selling price on such valuation date. If there were no sales on the valuation date but there were sales on dates within a reasonable period both before and after the valuation date, the fair market value is determined by taking a weighted

average of the quoted closing selling prices on the nearest date before and the nearest date after the valuation date. The average is to be weighted inversely by the respective numbers of trading days between the selling dates and the valuation date. If the bonds are listed on more than one exchange, the records of the exchange where the bonds are principally dealt in should be employed. In valuing listed securities, the executor should be careful to consult accurate records to obtain values as of the applicable valuation date.

(3) The application of this paragraph may be illustrated by the following examples:

Example (1). Assume that sales of X Company common stock nearest the valuation date (Friday, June 15) occurred two trading days before (Wednesday, June 13) and three trading days after (Wednesday, June 20) and on these days the mean sale prices per share were $10 and $15, respectively. The price of $12 is taken as representing the fair market value of a share of X Company common stock as of the valuation date

$$[(3\times10)+(2\times15)]/5.$$

Example (2). Assume the same facts as in example (1) except that the mean sale prices per share on June 13, and June 20 were $15 and $10, respectively. The price of $13 is taken as representing the fair market value of a share of X Company common stock as of the valuation date

$$[(3\times5)+(2\times10)]/5.$$

Example (3). Assume the decedent died on Sunday, October 7, and that Saturday and Sunday were not trading days. If sales of X Company common stock occurred on Friday, October 5, at mean sale prices per share of $20 and on Monday, October 8, at mean sale prices per share of $23, the price of $21.50 is taken as representing the fair market value of a share of X Company common stock as of the valuation date

$$[(1\times20)+(23\times1)]/2.$$

Example (4). Assume that on the valuation date (Tuesday, April 3, 1973) the closing selling price of a listed bond was $25 per bond and that the highest and lowest selling prices are not available in a generally available listing or publication of general circulation for that date. Assume further, that the closing selling price of the same listed bond was $21 per bond on the day before the valuation date (Monday, April 2, 1973). Thus, under paragraph (b)(2) of this section the price of $23 is taken as representing the fair market value per bond as of the valuation date

$$(25+21)/2.$$

Example (5). Assume the same facts as in example (4) except that there were no sales on the day before the valuation date. Assume further, that there were sales on Thursday, March 29, 1973, and that the closing selling price on that day was $23. The price of $24.50 is taken as representing the fair market value per bond as of the valuation date

$$[(1\times23)+(3\times25)]/4.$$

Example (6). Assume that no bonds were traded on the valuation date (Friday, April 20). Assume further, that sales of bonds nearest the valuation date occurred two trading days before (Wednesday, April 18) and three trading days after (Wednesday, April 25) the valuation date and that on these two days the closing selling prices per bond were $29 and $22, respectively. The highest and lowest selling prices are not available for these dates in a generally available listing or publication of general circulation. Thus, under paragraph (b)(2) of this section, the price of $26.20 is taken as representing the fair market value of a bond as of the valuation date

$$[(3\times29)+(2\times22)]/5.$$

(c) Based on bid and asked prices. If the provisions of paragraph (b) of this section are inapplicable because actual sales are not available during a reasonable period beginning before and ending after the valuation date, the fair market value may be determined by taking the mean between the bona fide bid and asked prices on the valuation date, or if none, by taking a weighted average of the means between the bona fide bid and asked prices on the nearest trading date before and the nearest trading date after the valuation date, if both such nearest dates are within a reasonable period. The average is to be determined in the manner described in paragraph (b) of this section.

(d) Based on incomplete selling prices or bid and asked prices. If the provisions of paragraphs (b) and (c) of this section are inapplicable because no actual sale prices or bona fide bid and asked prices are available on a date within a reasonable period before the valuation date, but such prices are available on a date within a reasonable period after the valuation date, or vice versa, then the mean between the highest and lowest available sale prices or bid and asked prices may be taken as the value.

(e) Where selling prices or bid and asked prices do not reflect fair market value. If it is established that the value of any bond or share of stock determined on the basis of selling or bid and asked prices as provided under paragraphs (b), (c), and (d) of this section does not reflect the fair market value thereof, then some reasonable modification of that basis or other relevant facts and elements of value are considered in determining the fair market value. Where sales at or near the date of death are few or of a sporadic nature, such sales alone may not indicate fair market value. In certain exceptional cases, the size of the block of stock to be valued in relation to the number of shares changing hands in sales may be relevant in determining whether selling prices reflect the fair market value of the block of stock to be valued. If the executor can show that the block of stock to be valued is so large in relation to the actual sales on the existing market that it could not be liquidated in a reasonable time without depressing the market, the price at which the block could be sold as such outside the usual market, as through an underwriter, may be a more accurate indication of value than market quotations. Complete data in support of any allowance claimed due to the size of the block of stock being valued shall be submitted with the return. On the other hand, if the block of stock to be valued represents a controlling interest, either actual or effective, in a going business, the price at which other lots change hands may have little relation to its true value.

(f) Where selling prices or bid and asked prices are unavailable. If the provisions of paragraphs (b), (c), and (d) of this section are inapplicable because actual sale prices and bona fide bid and asked prices are lacking, then the fair market value is to be determined by taking the following factors into consideration:

(1) In the case of corporate or other bonds, the soundness of the security, the interest yield, the date of maturity, and other relevant factors; and

(2) In the case of shares of stock, the company's net worth, prospective earning power and dividend-paying capacity, and other relevant factors.

Some of the "other relevant factors" referred to in subparagraphs (1) and (2) of this paragraph are: The good will of the business; the economic outlook in the particular industry; the company's position in the industry and its management; the degree of control of the business represented by the block of stock to be valued; and the values of securities of corporations engaged in the same or similar lines of business which are listed on a stock exchange. However, the weight to be accorded such comparisons or any other evidentiary factors considered in the determination of a value depends upon the facts of each case. In addition to the relevant factors described above, consideration shall also be given to nonoperating assets, including proceeds of life insurance policies payable to or for the benefit of the company, to the extent such nonoperating assets have not been taken into account in the determination of net worth, prospective earning power and dividend-earning capacity. Complete financial and other data upon which the valuation is based should be submitted with the return, including copies of reports of any examinations of the company made by accountants, engineers, or any technical experts as of or near the applicable valuation date.

(g) Pledged securities. The full value of securities pledged to secure an indebtedness of the decedent is included in the gross estate. If the decedent had a trading account with a broker, all securities belonging to the decedent and held by the broker at the date of death must be included at their fair market value as of the applicable valuation date. Securities purchased on margin for the decedent's account and held by a broker must also be returned at their fair market value as of the applicable valuation date. The amount of the decedent's indebtedness to a broker or other person with whom securities were pledged is allowed as a deduction from the gross estate in accordance with the provisions of § 20.2053–1 or § 20.2106–1 (for estates of nonresidents not citizens).

(h) Securities subject to an option or contract to purchase. Another person may hold an option or a contract to purchase securities owned by a decedent at the time of his death. The effect, if any, that is given to the option or contract price in determining the value of the securities for estate tax purposes depends upon the circumstances of the particular case. Little weight will be accorded a price contained in an option or contract under which the decedent is free to dispose of the underlying securities at any price he chooses during his lifetime. Such is the effect, for example, of an agreement on the part of a shareholder to purchase whatever shares of stock the decedent may own at the time of his death. Even if the decedent is not free to dispose of the underlying securities at other than the option or contract price, such price will be disregarded in determining the value of the securities unless it is determined under the circumstances of the particular case that the agreement represents a bona fide business arrangement and not a device to pass the decedent's shares to the natural objects of his bounty for less than an adequate and full consideration in money or money's worth.

(i) Stock sold "ex-dividend." In any case where a dividend is declared on a share of stock before the decedent's death but payable to stock holders of record on a date after his death and the stock is selling "ex-dividend" on the date of the decedent's death, the amount of the dividend is added to the ex-dividend quotation in determining the fair market value of the stock as of the date of the decedent's death.

[T.D. 6296, 23 FR 4529, June 24, 1958; 25 FR 14021, Dec. 31, 1960, as amended by T.D. 7312, 39 FR 14948, April 29, 1974; T.D. 7327, 39 FR 35354, Oct. 1, 1974; T.D. 7432, 41 FR 38769, Sept. 13, 1976]

§ 20.2031–3   Valuation of interests in businesses.

The fair market value of any interest of a decedent in a business, whether a partnership or a proprietorship, is the net amount which a willing purchaser whether an individual or a corporation, would pay for the interest to a willing seller, neither being under any compulsion to buy or to sell and both having reasonable knowledge of relevant facts. The net value is determined on the basis of all relevant factors including—

(a) A fair appraisal as of the applicable valuation date of all the assets of the business, tangible and intangible, including good will;

(b) The demonstrated earning capacity of the business; and

(c) The other factors set forth in paragraphs (f) and (h) of § 20.2031–2 relating to the valuation of corporate stock, to the extent applicable.

Special attention should be given to determining an adequate value of the good will of the business in all cases in which the decedent has not agreed, for an adequate and full consideration in money or money's worth, that his interest passes at his death to, for example, his surviving partner or partners. Complete financial and other data upon which the valuation is based should be submitted with the return, including copies of reports of examinations of the business made by accountants, engineers, or any technical experts as of or near the applicable valuation date.

§ 20.2031–4   Valuation of notes.

The fair market value of notes, secured or unsecured, is presumed to be the amount of unpaid principal, plus interest accrued to the date of death, unless the executor establishes that the value is lower or that the notes are worthless. However, items of interest shall be separately stated on the estate tax return. If not returned at face value, plus accrued interest, satisfactory evidence must be submitted that the note is worth less than the unpaid amount (because of the interest rate, date of maturity, or other cause), or that the note is uncollectible, either in whole or in part (by reason of the insolvency of the party or parties liable, or for other cause), and that any property pledged or mortgaged as security is insufficient to satisfy the obligation.

§ 20.2031–5   Valuation of cash on hand or on deposit.

The amount of cash belonging to the decedent at the date of his death, whether in his possession or in the possession of another, or deposited with a bank, is included in the decedent's gross estate. If bank checks outstanding at the time of the decedent's death and given in discharge of bona fide legal obligations of the decedent incurred for an adequate and full consideration in money or money's worth are subsequently honored by the bank and charged to the decedent's account, the balance remaining in the account may be returned, but only if the obligations are not claimed as deductions from the gross estate.

§ 20.2031–6   Valuation of household and personal effects.

(a) General rule. The fair market value of the decedent's household and personal effects is the price which a willing buyer would pay to a willing seller, neither being under any compulsion to buy or to sell and both having reasonable knowledge of relevant facts. A room by room itemization of household and personal effects is desirable. All the articles should be named specifically, except that a number of articles contained in the same room, none of which has a value in excess of $100, may be grouped. A separate value should be given for each article named. In lieu of an itemized list, the executor may furnish a written statement, containing a declaration that it is made under penalties of perjury, setting forth the aggregate value as appraised by a competent appraiser or appraisers of recognized standing and ability, or by a dealer or dealers in the class of personalty involved.

(b) Special rule in cases involving a substantial amount of valuable articles. Notwithstanding the provisions of paragraph (a) of this section, if there are included among the household and personal effects articles having marked artistic or intrinsic value of a total value in excess of $3,000 (e.g., jewelry, furs, silverware, paintings, etchings, engravings, antiques, books, statuary, vases, oriental rugs, coin or stamp collections), the appraisal of an expert or experts, under oath, shall be filed with the return. The appraisal shall be accompanied by a written statement of the executor containing a declaration that it is made under the penalties of perjury as to the completeness of the itemized list of such property and as to the disinterested character and the qualifications of the appraiser or appraisers.

(c) **Disposition of household effects prior to investigation.** If it is desired to effect distribution or sale of any portion of the household or personal effects of the decedent in advance of an investigation by an officer of the Internal Revenue Service, information to that effect shall be given to the district director. The statement to the district director shall be accompanied by an appraisal of such property, under oath, and by a written statement of the executor, containing a declaration that it is made under the penalties of perjury, regarding the completeness of the list of such property and the qualifications of the appraiser, as heretofore described. If a personal inspection by an officer of the Internal Revenue Service is not deemed necessary, the executor will be so advised. This procedure is designed to facilitate disposition of such property and to obviate future expense and inconvenience to the estate by affording the district director an opportunity to make an investigation should one be deemed necessary prior to sale or distribution.

(d) **Additional rules if an appraisal involved.** If, pursuant to paragraphs (a), (b), and (c) of this section, expert appraisers are employed, care should be taken to see that they are reputable and of recognized competency to appraise the particular class of property involved. In the appraisal, books in sets by standard authors should be listed in separate groups. In listing paintings having artistic value, the size, subject, and artist's name should be stated. In the case of oriental rugs, the size, make, and general condition should be given. Sets of silverware should be listed in separate groups. Groups or individual pieces of silverware should be weighed and the weights given in troy ounces. In arriving at the value of silverware, the appraisers should take into consideration its antiquity, utility, desirability, condition, and obsolescence.

§ 20.2031-7 **Valuation of annuities, life estates, terms for years, remainders, and reversions for estates of decedents dying after November 30, 1983.**

(a) **In general.** (1) Except as otherwise provided in this paragraph (a)(1), for estates of decedents dying after November 30, 1983, the fair market value of annuities, life estates, terms for years, remainders, and reversions is their present value determined under this section. If a decedent dies after November 30, 1983, and before August 9, 1984, or if on December 1, 1983, a decedent was under a mental disability such that the disposition of the decedent's property could not be changed, and such decedent dies any time on or after December 1, 1983 without such decedent ever having regained competency to dispose of such decedent's property, or dies within 90 days of the date on which such decedent first regains competency, the fair market value of annuities, life estates, terms for years, remainders, and reversions included in the estate of such decedent is their present value determined under this section or § 20.2031-10, whichever is most beneficial to the taxpayer. The value of annuities issued by companies regularly engaged in their sale, and of insurance policies on the lives of persons other than the decedent is determined under § 20.2031-8. The fair market value of a remainder interest in a charitable remainder unitrust as defined in § 1.664-3 is its present value determined under § 1.664-4. The fair market value of a life interest or term for years in a charitable remainder unitrust is the fair market value of the property as of the date of valuation less the fair market value of the remainder interest on such date determined under § 1.664-4. The fair market value of interests in a pooled income fund, as defined in § 1.642(c)-5, is their value determined under § 1.642(c)-6. (See § 20.2031-10 with respect to the valuation of annuities, life estates, terms for years, remainders, and reversions includable in estates of decedents dying after December 31, 1970, and before December 1, 1983; § 20.2042-1 with respect to insurance policies on the decedent's life.) With respect to the valuation of annuities, life estates, terms for years, remainders and reversions includable in estates of decedents dying before January 1, 1971, see T.D. 6296, 23 FR 4529, June 24, 1958, as amended by T.D. 7077, 35 FR 18461, December 4, 1970.

(2) The present value of an annuity, life estate, remainder, or reversion determined under this section which is dependent on the continuation or termination of the life of one person is computed by the use of Table A in paragraph (f) of this section. The present value of an annuity, term for years, remainder, or reversion dependent on a

term certain is computed by the use of Table B in paragraph (f) of this section. If the interest to be valued is dependent upon more than one life or there is a term certain concurrent with one or more lives, see paragraph (e) of this section. For purposes of the computations described in this section, the age of a person is to be taken as the age of that person at his or her nearest birthday.

(3) In all examples set forth in this section, the decedent is assumed to have died on or after August 9, 1984, and to have been competent to change the disposition of the property on December 1, 1983.

(b) **Annuities.** (1) If an annuity is payable annually at the end of each year during the life of an individual (as for example if the first payment is due one year after the decedent's death), the amount payable annually is multiplied by the figure in column 2 of Table A opposite the number of years in column 1 nearest the age of the individual whose life measures the duration of the annuity. If the annuity is payable annually at the end of each year for a definite number of years, the amount payable annually is multiplied by the figure in column 2 of Table B opposite the number of years in column 1 representing the duration of the annuity. The application of this paragraph (b)(1) may be illustrated by the following examples:

Example (1). The decedent received, under the terms of the decedent's father's will an annuity of $10,000 a year payable annually for the life of the decedent's elder brother. At the time the decedent died, an annual payment had just been made. The brother at the decedent's death was 40 years eight months old. By reference to Table A, the figure in column 2 opposite 41 years, the number nearest to the brother's actual age, is found to be 9.1030. The present value of the annuity at the date of the decedent's death is, therefore, $91,030 ($10,000 × 9.1030).

Example (2). The decedent was entitled to receive an annuity of $10,000 a year payable annually throughout a term certain. At the time the decedent died, the annual payment had just been made and five more annual payments were still to be made. By reference to Table B, it is found that the figure in column 2 opposite five years is 3.7908. The present value of the annuity is, therefore, $37,908 ($10,000 × 3.7808).

(2) If an annuity is payable at the end of semiannual, quarterly, monthly, or weekly periods during the life of an individual (as for example if the first payment is due one month after the decedent's death), the aggregate amount to be paid within a year is first multiplied by the figure in column 2 of Table A opposite the number of years in column 1 nearest the age of the individual whose life measures the duration of the annuity. The product so

obtained is then multiplied by whichever of the following factors is appropriate:

1.0244 for semiannual payments,

1.0368 for quarterly payments,

1.0450 for monthly payments,

1.0482 for weekly payments.

If the annuity is payable at the end of semiannual, quarterly, monthly, or weekly periods for a definite number of years, the aggregate amount to be paid within a year is first multiplied by the figure in column 2 of Table B opposite the number of years in column 1 representing the duration of the annuity. The product so obtained is then multiplied by whichever of the above factors is appropriate. The application of this paragraph (b)(2) may be illustrated by the following example:

Example. The facts are the same as those contained in example (1) set forth in paragraph (b)(1) of this section, except that the annuity is payable semiannually. The aggregate annual amount, $10,000, is multiplied by the factor 9.1030 and the product multiplied by 1.0244. The present value of the annuity at the date of the decedent's death is, therefore, $93,251.13 ($10,000 × 9.1030 × 1.0244).

(3)(i) If the first payment of an annuity for the life of an individual is due at the beginning of the annual or other payment period rather than at the end (as for example if the first payment is to be made immediately after the decedent's death), the value of the annuity is the sum of (A) the first payment plus (B) the present value of a similar annuity, the first payment of which is not to be made until the end of the payment period, determined as provided in paragraphs (b)(1) or (2) of this section, the application of this paragraph (b)(3)(i) may be illustrated by the following example:

Example. The decedent was entitled to receive an annuity of $50 a month during the life of another person. The decedent died on the date the payment was due. At the date of the decedent's death, the person whose life measures the duration of the annuity was 50 years of age. The value of the annuity at the date of the decedent's death is $50 plus the product of $50 × 12 × 8.4743 (see Table A) × 1.0450 (See paragraph (b)(2) of this section). That is $50 plus $5,313.39, or $5,363.39.

(ii) If the first payment of an annuity for a definite number of years is due at the beginning of the annual or other payment period, the applicable factor is the product of the factor shown in Table B multiplied by whichever of the following factors is appropriate:

1.1000 for annual payments,

1.0744 for semiannual payments,

1.0618 for quarterly payments,

1.0534 for monthly payments,

1.0502 for weekly payments.

The application of this paragraph (b)(3)(ii) may be illustrated by the following example:

Example. The decedent was the beneficiary of an annuity of $50 a month. On the day a payment was due, the decedent died. There were 300 payments to be made, including the payment due. The value of the annuity as of the date of decedent's death is the product of $50 × 12 × 9.0770 (see Table B) × 1.0534, or $5,737.03.

(c) Life estates and terms for years. If the interest to be valued is the right of a person for his or her life, or for the life of another person, to receive the income of certain property or to use nonincome-producing property, the value of the interest is the value of the property multiplied by the figure in column 3 of Table A opposite the number of years nearest to the actual age of the measuring life. If the interest to be valued is the right to receive income of property or to use nonincome-producing property for a term of years, column 3 of Table B is used. The application of this paragraph (c) may be illustrated by the following example:

Example. The decedent or the decedent's estate was entitled to receive the income from a fund of $50,000 during the life of the decedent's elder brother. Upon the brother's death, the remainder is to go to B. The brother was 31 years, five months old at the time of decedent's death. By reference to Table A the figure in column 3 opposite 31 years is found to be 0.95254. The present value of the decedent's interest is, therefore, $47,627 ($50,000 × 0.95254).

(d) Remainders or reversionary interests. If a decedent had, at the time of the decedent's death, a remainder or a reversionary interest in property to take effect after an estate for the life of another, the present value of the decedent's interest is obtained by multiplying the value of the property by the figure in column 4 of Table A opposite the number of years nearest to the actual age of the person whose life measures the preceding estate. If the remainder or reversion is to take effect at the end of the term for years, column 4 of Table B is used. The application of this paragraph (d) may be illustrated by the following example:

Example. The decedent was entitled to receive certain property worth $50,000 upon the death of the decedent's elder sister, to whom the income was bequeathed for life. At the time of the decedent's death, the elder sister was 31 years five months old. By reference to Table A the figure in column 4 opposite 31 years is found to be .04746. The present value of the remainder interest at the date of the decedent's death is, therefore, $2,373 ($50,000 × .04746).

(e) Actuarial computations by the Internal Revenue Service. If the valuation of the interest involved is dependent upon the continuation or the termination of more than one life or upon a term certain concurrent with one or more lives a special factor must be used. The factor is to be computed on the basis of interest at the rate of 10 percent a year, compounded annually, and life contingencies determined, as to each person involved, from the values of lx that are set forth in column 2 of Table LN of paragraph (f). Table LN contains values of lx taken from the life table for the total population appearing as Table 1 of United States Life Tables: 1969–71, published by the Department of Health, Education, and Welfare, Public Health Service. A copy of the publication containing many such special factors, may be purchased from the Superintendent of Documents, United States Government Printing Office, Washington, D.C. 20404. However, if a special factor is required in the case of an actual decedent, the Commissioner will furnish the factor to the executor upon request. The request must be accompanied by a statement of the date of birth of each person, the duration of whose life may affect the value of the interest, and by copies of the relevant instruments. Special factors are not furnished for prospective transfers.

(f) Tables. The following tables shall be used in the application of the provisions of this section:

TABLE A.—SINGLE LIFE, UNISEX, 10 PERCENT SHOWING THE PRESENT WORTH OF AN ANNUITY, OF A LIFE INTEREST, AND OF A REMAINDER INTEREST

(1) Age	(2) Annuity	(3) Life estate	(4) Remainder
	* * *		
20	9.7365	.97365	.02635
21	9.7245	.97245	.02755
22	9.7120	.97120	.02880
23	9.6986	.96986	.03014
24	9.6841	.96841	.03159
25	9.6678	.96678	.03322
26	9.6495	.96495	.03505
27	9.6290	.96290	.03710
28	9.6062	.96062	.03938
29	9.5813	.95813	.04187
30	9.5543	.95543	.04457
31	9.5254	.95254	.04746
32	9.4942	.94942	.05058
33	9.4608	.94608	.05392
34	9.4250	.94250	.05750
35	9.3868	.93868	.06132
36	9.3460	.93460	.06540
37	9.3026	.93026	.06974
38	9.2567	.92567	.07433

(1) Age	(2) Annuity	(3) Life estate	(4) Remainder
39	9.2083	.92083	.07917
40	9.1571	.91571	.08429
41	9.1030	.91030	.08970
42	9.0457	.90457	.09543
43	8.9855	.89855	.10145
44	8.9221	.89221	.10779
45	8.8558	.88558	.11442
46	8.7863	.87863	.12137
47	8.7137	.87137	.12863
48	8.6374	.86374	.13626
49	8.5578	.85578	.14422
50	8.4743	.84743	.15257
51	8.3874	.83874	.16126
52	8.2969	.82969	.17031
53	8.2028	.82028	.17972
54	8.1054	.81054	.18946
55	8.0046	.80046	.19954
56	7.9006	.79006	.20994
57	7.7931	.77931	.22069
58	7.6822	.76822	.23178
59	7.5675	.75675	.24325
60	7.4491	.74491	.25509
61	7.3267	.73267	.26733
62	7.2002	.72002	.27998
63	7.0696	.70696	.29304
64	6.9352	.69352	.30648
65	6.7970	.67970	.32030
66	6.6551	.66551	.33449
67	6.5098	.65098	.343902
68	6.3610	.63610	.363690
69	6.2086	.62086	.37914
70	6.0522	.60522	.39478
71	5.8914	.58914	.41086
72	5.7261	.57261	.42739
73	5.5571	.55571	.44429
74	5.3862	.53862	.46138
75	5.2149	.52149	.47851
76	5.0441	.50441	.49559
77	4.8742	.48742	.51258
78	4.7049	.47049	.52951
79	4.5357	.45357	.54643
80	4.3659	.43659	.56341
81	4.1967	.41967	.58033
82	4.0295	.40295	.59705
83	3.8642	.38642	.61358
84	3.6998	.36998	.63002
85	3.5359	.35359	.64641

* * *

TABLE B.—TABLE SHOWING THE PRESENT WORTH AT 10 PERCENT OF AN ANNUITY FOR A TERM CERTAIN, OF AN INCOME INTEREST FOR A TERM CERTAIN AND OF A REMAINDER INTEREST POSTPONED FOR A TERM CERTAIN

(1) Number of years	(2) Annuity	(3) Term certain	(4) Remainder
1	.9091	.090909	.909091
2	1.7355	.173554	.826446

(1) Number of years	(2) Annuity	(3) Term certain	(4) Remainder
3	2.4869	.248685	.751315
4	3.1699	.316987	.683013
5	3.7908	.379079	.620921
6	4.3553	.435526	.564474
7	4.8684	.486842	.513158
8	5.3349	.533493	.466507
9	5.7590	.575902	.424098
10	6.1446	.614457	.385543
11	6.4951	.649506	.350494
12	6.8137	.681369	.318631
13	7.1034	.710336	.289664
14	7.3667	.736669	.263331
15	7.6061	.760608	.239392
16	7.8237	.782371	.217629
17	8.0216	.802155	.197845
18	8.2014	.820141	.179659
19	8.3649	.836492	.163508
20	8.5136	.851356	.146644
21	8.6487	.864869	.135131
22	8.7715	.877154	.122846
23	8.8832	.888322	.111678
24	8.9847	.898474	.101526
25	9.0770	.907704	.092296
26	9.1609	.916095	.083905
27	9.2372	.923722	.076278
28	9.3066	.930657	.069343
29	9.3696	.936961	.063039
30	9.4269	.942691	.057309
31	9.4790	.947901	.052099
32	9.5264	.952638	.047362
33	9.5694	.956943	.043057
34	9.6086	.960857	.039143
35	9.6442	.964416	.035584
36	9.6765	.967651	.032349
37	9.7059	.970592	.029408
38	9.7327	.973265	.026735
39	9.7570	.975696	.024304
40	9.7791	.977905	.022095
41	9.7991	.979914	.020086
42	9.8174	.981740	.018260
43	9.8340	.983400	.016600
44	9.8491	.984909	.015091
45	9.8628	.986281	.013719

* * *

* * *

[T.D. 6296, 23 FR 4529, June 24, 1958, as amended by T.D. 7077, 35 FR 18461, Dec. 4, 1970; T.D. 7955, 49 FR 19992, May 11, 1984]

§ 20.2031–8 Valuation of certain life insurance and annuity contracts; valuation of shares in an open-end investment company.

(a) Valuation of certain life insurance and annuity contracts. (1) The value of a contract for the payment of an annuity, or an insurance policy on the life of a person other than the decedent, issued by a company regularly engaged in the selling of contracts of that character is established through the sale by that company of comparable contracts. An annuity payable under a combination annuity contract and life insurance policy on the decedent's life (*e.g.*, a "retirement income" policy with death benefit) under which there was no insurance element at the time of the decedent's death (see paragraph (d) of § 20.2039–1) is treated like a contract for the payment of an annuity for purposes of this section.

(2) As valuation of an insurance policy through sale of comparable contracts is not readily ascertainable when, at the date of the decedent's death, the contract has been in force for some time and further premium payments are to be made, the value may be approximated by adding to the interpolated terminal reserve at the date of the decedent's death the proportionate part of the gross premium last paid before the date of the decedent's death which covers the period extending beyond that date. If, however, because of the unusual nature of the contract such an approximation is not reasonably close to the full value of the contract, this method may not be used.

(3) The application of this section may be illustrated by the following examples. In each case involving an insurance contract, it is assumed that there are no accrued dividends or outstanding indebtedness on the contract.

Example (1). X purchased from a life insurance company a joint and survivor annuity contract under the terms of which X was to receive payments of $1,200 annually for his life and, upon X's death, his wife was to receive payments of $1,200 annually for her life. Five years after such purchase, when his wife was 50 years of age, X died. The value of the annuity contract at the date of X's death is the amount which the company would charge for an annuity providing for the payment of $1,200 annually for the life of a female 50 years of age.

Example (2). Y died holding the incidents of ownership in a life insurance policy on the life of his wife. The policy was one on which no further payments were to be made to the company (*e.g.*, a single premium policy or a paid-up policy). The value of the insurance policy at the date of Y's death is the amount which the company would charge for a single premium contract of the same specified amount on the life of a person of the age of the insured.

Example (3). Z died holding the incidents of ownership in a life insurance policy on the life of his wife. The policy was an ordinary life policy issued nine years and four months prior to Z's death and at a time when Z's wife was 35 years of age. The gross annual premium is $2,811 and the decedent died four months after the last premium due date. The value of the insurance policy at the date of Z's death is computed as follows:

Terminal reserve at end of tenth year	$14,601.00
Terminal reserve at end of ninth year	12,965.00
Increase	1,636.00
One-third of such increase (Z having died four months following the last preceding premium date) is	545.33
Terminal reserve at end of ninth year	12,965.00
Interpolated terminal reserve at date of Z's death	13,510.33
Two-thirds of gross premium ($\frac{2}{3} \times \$2,811$) ..	1,874.00
Value of the insurance policy	15,384.33

(b) **Valuation of shares in an open-end investment company.** (1) The fair market value of a share in an open-end investment company (commonly known as a "mutual fund") is the public redemption price of a share. In the absence of an affirmative showing of the public redemption price in effect at the time of death, the last public redemption price quoted by the company for the date of death shall be presumed to be the applicable public redemption price. If the alternate valuation method under 2032 is elected, the last public redemption price quoted by the company for the alternate valuation date shall be the applicable redemption price. If there is no public redemption price quoted by the company for the applicable valuation date (*e.g.*, the valuation date is a Saturday, Sunday, or holiday), the fair market value of the mutual fund share is the last public redemption price quoted by the company for the first day preceding the applicable valuation date for which there is a quotation. In any case where a dividend is declared on a share in an open-end investment company before the decedent's death but payable to shareholders of record on a date after his death and the share is quoted "exdividend" on the date of the decedent's death, the amount of the dividend is added to the ex-dividend quotation in determining the fair market value of the share as of the date of the decedent's death. As used in this paragraph, the term "open-end investment company" includes only a company which on the applicable valuation date was engaged in offering its shares to the public in the capacity of an open-end investment company.

* * *

[T.D. 6680, 28 FR 10872, Oct. 10, 1963, as amended by T.D. 7319, 39 FR 26723, July 23, 1974]

§ 20.2031–10 **Valuation of annuities, life estates, terms for years, remainders, and reversions for estates of decedents dying after December 31, 1970 and before December 1, 1983.**

(a) **In general.** (1) Except as otherwise provided in this paragraph, for estates of decedents dying after December 31, 1970, and before December 1, 1983, the fair market value of annuities, life estates, terms for years, remainders, and reversions is their present value determined under this section. The value of annuities issued by companies regularly engaged in their sale, and of insurance policies on the lives of persons other than the decedent is determined under § 20.2031–8. The fair market value of a remainder interest in a charitable remainder unitrust as defined in § 1.664–3 is its present value determined under § 1.664–4. The fair market value of a life interest or term for years in a charitable remainder unitrust is the fair market value of the property as of the date of valuation less the fair market value of the remainder interest on such date determined under § 1.664–4. The fair market value of interests in a pooled income fund, as defined in § 1.642(c)–5, is their value determined under § 1.642(c)–6. * * *

(2) The present value of an annuity, life estate, remainder or reversion determined under this section which is dependent on the continuation or termination of the life of one person is computed by the use of Table A(1) or A(2) in paragraph (f) of this section. Table A(1) is to be used when the person upon whose life the interest is based is a male and Table A(2) is to be used when such person is a female. The present value of an annuity, term for years, remainder or reversion dependent on a term certain is computed by the use of Table B in paragraph (f) of this section. If the interest to be valued is dependent upon more than one life or there is a term certain concurrent with one or more lives, see paragraph (e) of this section. For purposes of the computations described in this section, the age of a person is to be taken as the age of that person at his nearest birthday.

(3) In all examples set forth in this section, the decedent is assumed to have died after December 31, 1970, and before December 1, 1983.

(b) Annuities—(1) Payable annually at end of year. If an annuity is payable annually at the end of each year during the life of an individual (as, for example, if the first payment is due 1 year after decedent's death), the amount payable annually is multiplied by the figure in column 2 of Table A(1) or A(2), whichever is appropriate, opposite the number of years in column 1 nearest the age of the individual whose life measures the duration of the annuity. If the annuity is payable annually at the end of each year for definite number of years, the amount payable annually is multiplied by the fig-

ure in column 2 of Table B opposite the number of years in column 1 representing the duration of the annuity. The application of this subparagraph may be illustrated by the following examples:

Example (1). The decedent received, under the terms of his father's will, an annuity of $10,000 a year payable annually for the life of his elder brother. At the time he died, an annual payment had just been made. The brother at the decedent's death was 40 years 8 months old. By reference to Table A(1) the figure in column 2 opposite 41 years, the number nearest to the brother's actual age, is found to be 12.9934. The present value of the annuity at the date of the decedent's death is, therefore, $129,934 ($10,000×12.9934).

Example (2). The decedent was entitled to receive an annuity of $10,000 a year payable annually throughout a term certain. At the time he died, an annual payment had just been made and five more annual payments were still to be made. By reference to Table B, it is found that the figure in column 2 opposite 5 years is 4.2124. The present value of the annuity is, therefore, $42,124 ($10,000×4.2124).

(2) Payable at the end of semiannual, quarterly, monthly, or weekly periods. If an annuity is payable at the end of semiannual, quarterly, monthly, or weekly periods during the life of an individual (as for example if the first payment is due 1 month after the decedent's death), the aggregate amount to be paid within a year is first multiplied by the figure in column 2 of Table A(1) or A(2), whichever is appropriate, opposite the number of years in column 1 nearest the age of the individual whose life measures the duration of the annuity. The product so obtained is then multiplied by whichever of the following factors is appropriate:

1.0148 for semiannual payments,

1.0222 for quarterly payments,

1.0272 for monthly payments,

1.0291 for weekly payments.

If the annuity is payable at the end of semiannual, quarterly, monthly, or weekly periods for a definite number of years, the aggregate amount to be paid within a year is first multiplied by the figure in column 2 of Table B opposite the number of years in column 1 representing the duration of the annuity. The product so obtained is then multiplied by whichever of the above factors is appropriate. The application of this subparagraph may be illustrated by the following example:

Example. The facts are the same as those contained in example (1) set forth in subparagraph (1) of this paragraph, except that the annuity is payable semiannually. The aggregate annual amount, $10,000, is multiplied by the factor 12.9934, and the product multiplied by

1.0148. The present value of the annuity at the date of the decedent's death is, therefore, $131,857.02 ($10,000×12.9934×1.0148).

(3) Payable at the beginning of annual, semiannual, quarterly, monthly, or weekly periods. (i) If the first payment of an annuity for the life of an individual is due at the beginning of the annual or other payment period rather than at the end (as, for example, if the first payment is to be made immediately after the decedent's death), the value of the annuity is the sum of (a) the first payment plus (b) the present value of a similar annuity, the first payment of which is not to be made until the end of the payment period, determined as provided in subparagraph (1) or (2) of this paragraph. The application of this subdivision may be illustrated by the following example:

Example. The decedent was entitled to receive an annuity of $50 a month during the life of another, a woman. The decedent died on the day a payment was due. At the date of the decedent's death, the person whose life measures the duration of the annuity is 50 years of age. The value of the annuity at the date of the decedent's death is $50 plus the product of $50×12×12.5793 (see Table A(2)) × 1.0272 (see subparagraph (2) of this paragraph). That is, $50 plus $7,752.87, or $7,802.87.

(ii) If the first payment of an annuity for a definite number of years is due at the beginning of the annual or other payment period, the applicable factor is the product of the factor shown in Table B multiplied by whichever of the following factors is appropriate:

1.0600 for annual payments,

1.0448 for semiannual payments,

1.0372 for quarterly payments,

1.0322 for monthly payments,

1.0303 for weekly payments.

The application of this subdivision may be illustrated by the following example:

Example. The decedent was the beneficiary of an annuity of $50 a month. On the day a payment was due, the decedent died. There were 300 payments to be made, including the payment due. The value of the annuity as of the date of decedent's death is the product of $50 × 12 × 12.7834 (see Table B) ×1.0322, or $7,917.02.

(c) Life estates and terms for years. If the interest to be valued is the right of a person for his life, or for the life of another person, to receive the income of certain property or to use nonincome-producing property, the value of the interest is the value of the property multiplied by the figure in column 3 of Table A(1) or A(2), whichever is appropriate, opposite the number of years nearest to the actual age of the measuring life. If the interest to be valued is the right to receive income of property or to use nonincome-producing property for a term of years, column 3 of Table B is used. The application of this paragraph may be illustrated by the following example:

Example. The decedent or his estate was entitled to receive the income from a fund of $50,000 during the life of his elder brother. Upon the brother's death, the remainder is to go to X. The brother was 31 years 5 months old at the time of decedent's death. By reference to Table A(1) the figure in column 3 opposite 31 years is found to be 0.86117. The present value of decedent's interest is therefore, $43,058.50 ($50,000×0.86117).

(d) Remainders or reversionary interests. If a decedent had, at the time of his death, a remainder or a reversionary interest in property to take effect after an estate for the life of another, the present value of his interest is obtained by multiplying the value of the property by the figure in column 4 of Table A(1) or A(2), whichever is appropriate, opposite the number of years nearest to the actual age of the person whose life measures the preceding estate. If the remainder or reversion is to take effect at the end of a term for years, column 4 of Table B is used. The application of this paragraph may be illustrated by the following example:

Example. The decedent was entitled to receive certain property worth $50,000 upon the death of his elder sister, to whom the income was bequeathed for life. At the time of the decedent's death, the elder sister was 31 years 5 months old. By reference to Table A(2), the figure in column 4 opposite 31 years is found to be 0.10227. The present value of the remainder interest at the date of decedent's death is, therefore, $5,113.50 ($50,000×0.10227).

(e) Actuarial computations by the Internal Revenue Service. If the valuation of the interest involved is dependent upon the continuation or the termination of more than one life or upon a term certain concurrent with one or more lives, a special factor must be used. The factor is to be computed on the basis of interest at the rate of 6 percent a year, compounded annually, and life contingencies determined, as to each male and female life involved, from the values of lx that are set forth in columns 2 and 3, respectively, of Table LN of paragraph (f). Table LN contains values of lx taken from the life table for total males and the life table for total females appearing as Tables 2 and 3, respectively, in United States Life Tables: 1959–61, published by the Department of Health, Education, and Welfare, Public Health Service, except that for technical reasons Table LN employs graduated data, furnished by that Department, to increase the number of significant figures shown at ages of male lives older than 86 and female lives older than 90. Many such special factors may be found in, or computed with the use of the tables contained in, the publications entitled "Actuarial Values I: Valuation of Last Survivor Charitable Remainders" and "Actuarial Values II: Factors at 6 Percent Involving One and Two Lives." These publications may be purchased from the Superintendent of Documents, U.S. Government Printing Office, Washington, DC 20402. However, if a special factor is required in the case of an actual decedent, the Commissioner will furnish the factor to the executor upon request. The request must be accompanied by a statement of the sex and date of birth of each person, the duration of whose life may affect the value of the interest, and by copies of the relevant instruments.

(f) The following tables shall be used in the application of the provisions of this section:

TABLE A(1)—SINGLE LIFE MALE, 6 PERCENT, SHOWING THE PRESENT WORTH OF AN ANNUITY, OF A LIFE INTEREST, AND OF A REMAINDER INTEREST

(1)—Age	(2)—Annuity	(3)—Life estate	(4)—Remainder
	* * *		
20	15.2339	.91403	.08597
21	15.1744	.91046	.08954
22	15.1130	.90678	.09328
23	15.0487	.90292	.09702
24	14.9807	.89884	.10116
25	14.9075	.89445	.10555
26	14.8287	.88972	.11028
27	14.7442	.88465	.11535
28	14.6542	.87925	.12075
29	14.5588	.87353	.12647
30	14.4584	.86750	.13250
31	14.3528	.86117	.13883
32	14.2418	.85451	.14549
33	14.1254	.84752	.15248
34	14.0034	.84020	.15980
35	13.8758	.83255	.16745
36	13.7425	.82455	.17545
37	13.6036	.81622	.18378
38	13.4591	.80755	.19245
39	13.3090	.79854	.20146
40	13.1538	.78923	.21077
41	12.9934	.77960	.22040
42	12.8279	.76967	.23033
43	12.6574	.75944	.24056
44	12.4819	.74891	.25109
45	12.3013	.73808	.26192
46	12.1158	.72695	.27305
47	11.9253	.71552	.28448
48	11.7308	.70385	.29615
49	11.5330	.69198	.30802
50	11.3329	.67997	.32003
51	11.1308	.66785	.33215

(1)—Age	(2)—Annuity	(3)—Life estate	(4)—Remainder
52	10.9267	.65560	.34440
53	10.7200	.64320	.35680
54	10.5100	.63060	.36940
55	10.2960	.61776	.38224
56	10.0777	.60466	.39534
57	9.8552	.59131	.40869
58	9.6297	.57778	.42222
59	9.4028	.56417	.43583
60	9.1753	.55052	.44948
61	8.9478	.53687	.46313
62	8.7202	.52321	.47679
63	8.4924	.50954	.49046
64	8.2642	.49585	.50415
65	8.0353	.48212	.51788
66	7.8060	.46836	.53164
67	7.5763	.45458	.54542
68	7.3462	.44077	.55923
69	7.1149	.42689	.57311
70	6.8823	.41294	.58706
71	6.6481	.39889	.60111
72	6.4123	.38474	.61526
73	6.1752	.37051	.62949
74	5.9373	.35624	.64376
75	5.6990	.34194	.65806
76	5.4602	.32761	.67239
77	5.2211	.31327	.68673
78	4.9825	.29895	.70105
79	4.7469	.28481	.71519
80	4.5164	.27098	.72902
81	4.2955	.25773	.74227
82	4.0879	.24527	.75473
83	3.8924	.23354	.76646
84	3.7029	.22217	.77783
85	3.5117	.21070	.78930

* * *

TABLE A(2)—SINGLE LIFE FEMALE, 6 PERCENT, SHOWING THE PRESENT WORTH OF AN ANNUITY, OF A LIFE INTEREST, AND OF A REMAINDER INTEREST

(1)—Age	(2)—Annuity	(3)—Life estate	(4)—Remainder
	* * *		
20	15.6701	.94021	.05979
21	15.6207	.93724	.06276
22	15.5687	.93412	.06588
23	15.5141	.93085	.06915
24	15.4565	.92739	.07261
25	15.3959	.92375	.07625
26	15.3322	.91993	.08007
27	15.2652	.91591	.08409
28	15.1946	.91168	.08832
29	15.1208	.90725	.09275
30	15.0432	.90259	.09741
31	14.9622	.89773	.10227
32	14.8775	.89265	.10735
33	14.7888	.88733	.11267
34	14.6960	.88176	.11824
35	14.5989	.87593	.12407
36	14.4975	.86985	.13015
37	14.3915	.86349	.13651
38	14.2811	.85687	.14313

(1)—Age	(2)— Annuity	(3)—Life estate	(4)— Remainder
39	14.1663	.84998	.15002
40	14.0468	.84281	.15719
41	13.9227	.83536	.16464
42	13.7940	.82764	.17236
43	13.6604	.81962	.18038
44	13.5219	.81131	.18869
45	13.3781	.80269	.19731
46	13.2290	.79374	.20626
47	13.0746	.78448	.21552
48	12.9147	.77488	.22512
49	12.7496	.76498	.23502
50	12.5793	.75476	.24524
51	12.4039	.74423	.25577
52	12.2232	.73339	.26661
53	12.0367	.72220	.27780
54	11.8436	.71062	.28938
55	11.6432	.69859	.30141
56	11.4353	.68612	.31388
57	11.2200	.67320	.32680
58	10.9980	.65988	.34012
59	10.7703	.64622	.35378
60	10.5376	.63226	.36774
61	10.3005	.61803	.38197
62	10.0587	.60352	.39648
63	9.8118	.58871	.41129
64	9.5592	.57355	.42645
65	9.3005	.55803	.44197
66	9.0352	.54211	.45789
67	8.7639	.52583	.47417
68	8.4874	.50924	.49076
69	8.2068	.49241	.50759
70	7.9234	.47540	.52460
71	7.6371	.45823	.54177
72	7.3480	.44088	.55912
73	7.0568	.42341	.57659
74	6.7645	.40587	.59413
75	6.4721	.38833	.61167
76	6.1788	.37073	.62927
77	5.8845	.35307	.64693
78	5.5910	.33546	.66454
79	5.3018	.31811	.68189
80	5.0195	.30117	.69883
81	4.7482	.28489	.71511
82	4.4892	.26935	.73065
83	4.2398	.25439	.74561
84	3.9927	.23956	.76044
85	3.7401	.22441	.77559

* * *

TABLE B—SHOWING THE PRESENT WORTH AT 6 PERCENT OF AN ANNUITY FOR A TERM CERTAIN, OF AN INCOME INTEREST FOR A TERM CERTAIN, AND OF A REMAINDER INTEREST POSTPONED FOR A TERM CERTAIN

(1)—Number of years	(2)— Annuity	(3)— Term certain	(4)— Remainder
1	0.9434	0.056604	0.943396
2	1.8334	.110004	.889996
3	2.6730	.160381	.839619
4	3.4651	.207906	.792094
5	4.2124	.252742	.747258
6	4.9173	.295039	.704961
7	5.5824	.334943	.665057
8	6.2098	.372588	.627412
9	6.8017	.408102	.591898
10	7.3601	.441605	.558395
11	7.8869	.473212	.526788
12	8.3838	.503031	.496969
13	8.8527	.531161	.468839
14	9.2950	.557699	.442301
15	9.7122	.582735	.417265
16	10.1059	.606354	.393646
17	10.4773	.628636	.371364
18	10.8276	.649656	.350344
19	11.1581	.669487	.330513
20	11.4699	.688195	.311805
21	11.7641	.705845	.294155
22	12.0416	.722495	.277505
23	12.3034	.738203	.261797
24	12.5504	.753021	.246979
25	12.7834	.767001	.232999
26	13.0032	.780190	.219810
27	13.2105	.792632	.207368
28	13.4062	.804370	.195630
29	13.5907	.815443	.184557
30	13.7648	.825890	.174110
31	13.9291	.835745	.164255
32	14.0840	.845043	.154957
33	14.2302	.853814	.146186
34	14.3681	.862088	.137912
35	14.4982	.869895	.130105
36	14.6210	.877259	.122741
37	14.7368	.884207	.115793
38	14.8460	.890761	.109239
39	14.9491	.896944	.103056
40	15.0463	.902778	.097222
41	15.1380	.908281	.091719
42	15.2245	.913473	.086527
43	15.3062	.918370	.081630
44	15.3832	.922991	.077009
45	15.4558	.927350	.072650

* * *

[T.D. 6296, 23 FR 4529, June 24, 1958, as amended by T.D. 7077, 35 FR 18461, Dec. 4, 1970; T.D. 7955, 49 FR 19995, May 11, 1984]

§ 20.2032–1 Alternate valuation.

(a) **In general.** In general, section 2032 provides for the valuation of a decedent's gross estate at a date other than the date of the decedent's death. More specifically, if an executor elects the alternate valuation method under section 2032, the property included in the decedent's gross estate on the date of his death is valued as of whichever of the following dates is applicable:

(1) Any property distributed, sold, exchanged, or otherwise disposed of within 6 months (1 year, if the decedent died on or before December 31, 1970) after the decedent's death is valued as of the date

on which it is first distributed, sold, exchanged, or otherwise disposed of;

(2) Any property not distributed, sold, exchanged, or otherwise disposed of within 6 months (1 year, if the decedent died on or before December 31, 1970) after the decedent's death is valued as of the date 6 months (1 year, if the decedent died on or before December 31, 1970) after the date of the decedent's death;

(3) Any property, interest, or estate which is affected by mere lapse of time is valued as of the date of the decedent's death, but adjusted for any difference in its value not due to mere lapse of time as of the date 6 months (1 year, if the decedent died on or before December 31, 1970) after the decedent's death, or as of the date of its distribution, sale, exchange, or other disposition, whichever date first occurs.

* * *

(c) Meaning of "distributed, sold, exchanged, or otherwise disposed of". (1) The phrase "distributed, sold, exchanged, or otherwise disposed of" comprehends all possible ways by which property ceases to form a part of the gross estate. For example, money on hand at the date of the decedent's death which is thereafter used in the payment of funeral expenses, or which is thereafter invested, falls within the term "otherwise disposed of." The term also includes the surrender of a stock certificate for corporate assets in complete or partial liquidation of a corporation pursuant to section 331. The term does not, however, extend to transactions which are mere changes in form. Thus, it does not include a transfer of assets to a corporation in exchange for its stock in a transaction with respect to which no gain or loss would be recognizable for income tax purposes under section 351. Nor does it include an exchange of stock or securities in a corporation for stock or securities in the same corporation or another corporation in a transaction, such as a merger, recapitalization, reorganization or other transaction described in section 368(a) or 355, with respect to which no gain or loss is recognizable for income tax purposes under section 354 or 355.

(2) Property may be "distributed" either by the executor, or by a trustee of property included in the gross estate under section 2035 through 2038, or section 2041. Property is considered as "distributed" upon the first to occur of the following:

(i) The entry of an order or decree of distribution, if the order or decree subsequently becomes final;

(ii) The segregation or separation of the property from the estate or trust so that it becomes unqualifiedly subject to the demand or disposition of the distributee; or

(iii) The actual paying over or delivery of the property to the distributee.

(3) Property may be "sold, exchanged, or otherwise disposed of" by: (i) The executor; (ii) a trustee or other donee to whom the decedent during his lifetime transferred property included in his gross estate under sections 2035 through 2038, or section 2041; (iii) an heir or devisee to whom title to property passes directly under local law; (iv) a surviving joint tenant or tenant by the entirety; or (v) any other person. If a binding contract for the sale, exchange, or other disposition of property is entered into, the property is considered as sold, exchanged, or otherwise disposed of on the effective date of the contract, unless the contract is not subsequently carried out substantially in accordance with its terms. The effective date of a contract is normally the date it is entered into (and not the date it is consummated, or the date legal title to the property passes) unless the contract specifies a different effective date.

(d) "Included property" and "excluded property". If the executor elects the alternate valuation method under section 2432, all property interests existing at the date of decedent's death which form a part of his gross estate as determined under sections 2033 through 2044 are valued in accordance with the provisions of this section. Such property interests are referred to in this section as "included property". Furthermore, such property interests remain "included property" for the purpose of valuing the gross estate under the alternate valuation method even though they change in form during the alternate valuation period by being actually received, or disposed of, in whole or in part, by the estate. On the other hand, property earned or accrued (whether received or not) after the date of the decedent's death and during the alternate valuation period with respect to any property interest existing at the date of the decedent's death, which does not represent a form of "included property" itself or the receipt of "included property" is excluded in valuing the gross estate under the alternate valuation method. Such property is referred to in this section as "excluded property". Illustrations of "included property" and "excluded property" are contained in the subparagraphs (1) to (4) of this paragraph:

(1) Interest-bearing obligations. Interest-bearing obligations, such as bonds or notes, may comprise two elements of "included property" at the date of the decedent's death, namely, (i) the principal of the obligation itself, and (ii) interest accrued to the date of death. Each of these elements is to be separately valued as of the applicable valuation date. Interest accrued after the date of death and before the subsequent valuation date constitutes "excluded property". However, any part payment or principal made between the date of death and the subsequent valuation date, or any advance payment of interest for a period after the subsequent valuation date made during the alternate valuation period which has the effect of reducing the value of the principal obligation as of the subsequent valuation date, will be included in the gross estate, and valued as of the date of such payment.

(2) Leased property. The principles set forth in subparagraph (1) of this paragraph with respect to interest-bearing obligations also apply to leased realty or personalty which is included in the gross estate and with respect to which an obligation to pay rent has been reserved. Both the realty or personalty itself and the rents accrued to the date of death constitute "included property", and each is to be separately valued as of the applicable valuation date. Any rent accrued after the date of death and before the subsequent valuation date is "excluded property". Similarly, the principle applicable with respect to interest paid in advance is equally applicable with respect to advance payments of rent.

(3) Noninterest-bearing obligations. In the case of noninterest-bearing obligations sold at a discount, such as savings bonds, the principal obligation and the discount amortized to the date of death are property interests existing at the date of death and constitute "included property". The obligation itself is to be valued at the subsequent valuation date without regard to any further increase in value due to amortized discount. The additional discount amortized after death and during the alternate valuation period is the equivalent of interest accruing during that period and is, therefore, not to be included in the gross estate under the alternate valuation method.

(4) Stock of a corporation. Shares of stock in a corporation and dividends declared to stockholders of record on or before the date of the decedent's death and not collected at the date of death constitute "included property" of the estate. On the other hand, ordinary dividends out of earnings and profits (whether in cash, shares of the corporation, or other property) declared to stockholders of record after the date of the decedent's death are "excluded property" and are not to be valued under the alternate valuation method. If, however, dividends are declared to stockholders of record after the date of the decedent's death with the effect that the shares of stock at the subsequent valuation date do not reasonably represent the same "included property" of the gross estate as existed at the date of the decedent's death, the dividends are "included property", except to the extent that they are out of earnings of the corporation after the date of the decedent's death. For example, if a corporation makes a distribution in partial liquidation to stockholders of record during the alternate valuation period which is not accompanied by a surrender of a stock certificate for cancellation, the amount of the distribution received on stock included in the gross estate is itself "included property", except to the extent that the distribution was out of earnings and profits since the date of the decedent's death. Similarly, if a corporation, in which the decedent owned a substantial interest and which possessed at the date of the decedent's death accumulated earnings and profits equal to its paid-in capital, distributed all of its accumulated earnings and profits as a cash dividend to shareholders of record during the alternate valuation period, the amount of the dividends received on stock includible in the gross estate will be included in the gross estate under the alternate valuation method. Likewise, a stock dividend distributed under such circumstances is "included property".

* * *

(f) Mere lapse of time. In order to eliminate changes in value due only to mere lapse of time, section 2032(a)(3) provides that any interest or estate "affected by mere lapse of time" is included in a decedent's gross estate under the alternate valuation method at its value as of the date of the decedent's death, but with adjustment for any difference in its value as of the subsequent valuation date not due to mere lapse of time. Properties, interests, or estates which are "affected by mere lapse of time" include patents, estates for the life of a person other than the decedent, remainders, reversions, and other like properties, interests, or estates. The phrase "affected by mere lapse of time" has no reference to obligations for the payment of money, whether or not interest-bearing, the value of which changes with the passing of time. However, such an obligation, like any other property, may become affected by lapse of time when made the subject of a bequest or transfer which itself is creative of an interest or estate so affected. The application of this paragraph is illustrated in subparagraphs (1) and (2) of this paragraph:

(1) **Life estates, remainders, and similar interests.** The values of life estates, remainders, and similar interests are to be obtained by applying the methods prescribed in § 20.2031–7, using (i) the age of each person, the duration of whose life may affect the value of the interest, as of the date of the decedent's death, and (ii) the value of the property as of the alternate date. For example, assume that the decedent or his estate was entitled to receive property upon the death of his elder brother who was entitled to receive the income therefrom for life. At the date of the decedent's death, the property was worth $50,000 and the elder brother was 31 years old. The value of the decedent's remainder interest at the date of the decedent's death would, as explained in paragraph (d) of § 20.2031–7, be $2,373 ($50,000 X .04746). If, because of economic conditions, the property declined in value and was worth only $40,000 6 months after the date of the decedent's death, the value of the remainder interest would be $1,898.40 ($40,000 X .04746), even though the elder brother may be 32 years old on the alternate date.

* * *

(g) **Effect of election on deductions.** If the executor elects the alternate valuation method under section 2032, any deduction for administration expenses under section 2053(b) (pertaining to property not subject to claims) or losses under section 2054 (or section 2106(a)(1), relating to estates of nonresidents not citizens) is allowed only to the extent that it is not otherwise in effect allowed in determining the value of the gross estate. Furthermore, the amount of any charitable deduction under section 2055 (or section 2106(a)(2), relating to the estates of nonresidents not citizens) or the amount of any marital deduction under section 2056 is determined by the value of the property with respect to which the deduction is allowed as of the date of the decedent's death, adjusted, however, for any difference in its value as of the date 6 months (1 year, if the decedent died on or before

December 31, 1970) after death, or as of the date of its distribution, sale, exchange, or other disposition, whichever first occurs. However, no such adjustment may take into account any difference in value due to lapse of time or to the occurrence or nonoccurrence of a contingency.

[T.D. 6296, 23 FR 4529, June 24, 1958, as amended by T.D. 7238, 37 FR 28718, Dec. 29, 1972; T.D. 7955, 49 FR 19995, May 11, 1984]

§ 20.2033–1   Property in which the decedent had an interest.

(a) **In general.** The gross estate of a decedent who was a citizen or resident of the United States at the time of his death includes under section 2033 the value of all property, whether real or personal, tangible or intangible, and wherever situated, beneficially owned by the decedent at the time of his death. (For certain exceptions in the case of real property situated outside the United States, see paragraphs (a) and (c) of § 20.2031–1.) Real property is included whether it came into the possession and control of the executor or administrator or passed directly to heirs or devisees. Various statutory provisions which exempt bonds, notes, bills, and certificates of indebtedness of the Federal Government or its agencies and the interest thereon from taxation are generally not applicable to the estate tax, since such tax is an excise tax on the transfer of property at death and is not a tax on the property transferred.

(b) **Miscellaneous examples.** A cemetery lot owned by the decedent is part of his gross estate, but its value is limited to the salable value of that part of the lot which is not designed for the interment of the decedent and the members of his family. Property subject to homestead or other exemptions under local law is included in the gross estate. Notes or other claims held by the decedent are likewise included even though they are cancelled by the decedent's will. Interest and rents accrued at the date of the decedent's death constitute a part of the gross estate. Similarly, dividends which are payable to the decedent or his estate by reason of the fact that on or before the date of the decedent's death he was a stockholder of record (but which have not been collected at death) constitute a part of the gross estate.

[T.D. 6296, 23 FR 4529, June 24, 1958, as amended by T.D. 6684, 28 FR 11409, Oct. 24, 1963]

§ 20.2034–1 Dower or curtesy interests.

A decedent's gross estate includes under section 2034 any interest in property of the decedent's surviving spouse existing at the time of the decedent's death as dower or curtesy, or any interest created by statute in lieu thereof (although such other interest may differ in character from dower or curtesy). Thus, the full value of property is included in the decedent's gross estate, without deduction of such an interest of the surviving husband or wife, and without regard to when the right to such an interest arose.

[T.D. 6296, 23 FR 4529, June 24, 1958]

§ 20.2035–1 Transactions in contemplation of death.

* * *

(b) **Application of other sections.** If a decedent transfers an interest in property or relinquishes a power in contemplation of death, the decedent's gross estate includes the property subject to the interest or power to the extent that it would be included under section 2036, 2037, or 2038 if the decedent had retained the interest or power until his death. If a decedent exercises or releases a general power of appointment in contemplation of death, the property subject to the power is included in the decedent's gross estate to the extent provided in section 2041 and the regulations thereunder.

* * *

(e) **Valuation.** The value of an interest in transferred property includible in a decedent's gross estate under this section is the value of the interest as of the applicable valuation date. In this connection, see sections 2031, 2032, and the regulations thereunder. However, if the transferee has made improvements or additions to the property, any resulting enhancement in the value of the property is not considered in ascertaining the value of the gross estate. Similarly, neither income received subsequent to the transfer nor property purchased with such income is considered.

[T.D. 6296, 23 FR 4529, June 24, 1958]

§ 20.2036–1 Transfers with retained life estate.

(a) **In general.** A decedent's gross estate includes under section 2036 the value of any interest in property transferred by the decedent after March 3, 1931, whether in trust or otherwise, except to the extent that the transfer was for an adequate and full consideration in money or money's worth (see § 20.2043–1), if the decedent retained or reserved (1) for his life, or (2) for any period not ascertainable without reference to his death (if the transfer was made after June 6, 1932), or (3) for any period which does not in fact end before his death:

(i) The use, possession, right to the income, or other enjoyment of the transferred property, or

(ii) The right, either alone or in conjunction with any other person or persons, to designate the person or persons who shall possess or enjoy the transferred property or its income (except that, if the transfer was made before June 7, 1932, the right to designate must be retained by or reserved to the decedent alone).

If the decedent retained or reserved an interest or right with respect to all of the property transferred by him, the amount to be included in his gross estate under section 2036 is the value of the entire property, less only the value of any outstanding income interest which is not subject to the decedent's interest or right and which is actually being enjoyed by another person at the time of the decedent's death. If the decedent retained or reserved an interest or right with respect to a part only of the property transferred by him, the amount to be included in his gross estate under section 2036 is only a corresponding proportion of the amount described in the preceding sentence. An interest or right is treated as having been retained or reserved if at the time of the transfer there was an understanding, express, or implied, that the interest or right would later be conferred.

(b) **Meaning of terms.** (1) A reservation by the decedent "for any period not ascertainable without reference to his death" may be illustrated by the following examples:

(i) A decedent reserved the right to receive the income from transferred property in quarterly payments, with the proviso that no part of the income between the last quarterly payment and the date of the decedent's death was to be received by the decedent or his estate; and

(ii) A decedent reserved the right to receive the income from transferred property after the death of another person who was in fact enjoying the income at the time of the decedent's death. In such a case, the amount to be included in the decedent's gross estate under this section does not include the value of the outstanding income interest of the other person. It may be noted that if the other person predeceased the decedent, the reservation by the decedent may be considered to be either for his life, or for a period which does not in fact end before his death.

(2) The "use, possession, right to the income, or other enjoyment of the transferred property" is considered as having been retained by or reserved to the decedent to the extent that the use, possession, right to the income, or other enjoyment is to be applied toward the discharge of a legal obligation of the decedent, or otherwise for his pecuniary benefit. The term "legal obligation" includes a legal obligation to support a dependent during the decedent's lifetime.

(3) The phrase "right * * * to designate the person or persons who shall possess or enjoy the transferred property or the income therefrom" includes a reserved power to designate the person or persons to receive the income from the transferred property, or to possess or enjoy nonincome-producing property, during the decedent's life or during any other period described in paragraph (a) of this section. With respect to such a power, it is immaterial (i) whether the power was exercisable alone or only in conjunction with another person or persons, whether or not having an adverse interest; (ii) in what capacity the power was exercisable by the decedent or by another person or persons in conjunction with the decedent; and (iii) whether the exercise of the power was subject to a contingency beyond the decedent's control which did not occur before his death (e.g., the death of another person during the decedent's lifetime). The phrase, however, does not include a power over the transferred property itself which does not affect the enjoyment of the income received or earned during the decedent's life. (See, however, section 2038 for the inclusion of property in the gross estate on account of such a power.) Nor does the phrase apply to a power held solely by a person other than the decedent. But, for example, if the decedent reserved the unrestricted power to remove or discharge a trustee at any time and appoint himself as trustee, the decedent is considered as having the powers of the trustee.

[T.D. 6296, 23 FR 4529, June 24, 1958, as amended by T.D. 6501, 25 FR 10869, Nov. 16, 1960]

§ 20.2037–1　Transfers taking effect at death.

(a) **In general.** A decedent's gross estate includes under section 2037 the value of any interest in property transferred by the decedent after September 7, 1916, whether in trust or otherwise, except to the extent that the transfer was for an adequate and full consideration in money or money's worth (see § 20.2043–1), if—

(1) Possession or enjoyment of the property could, through ownership of the interest, have been obtained only by surviving the decedent,

(2) The decedent had retained a possibility (referred to in this section as a "reversionary interest") that the property, other than the income alone, would return to the decedent or his estate or would be subject to a power of disposition by him, and

(3) The value of the reversionary interest immediately before the decedent's death exceeded 5 percent of the value of the entire property.

However, if the transfer was made before October 8, 1949, section 2037 is applicable only if the reversionary interest arose by the express terms of the instrument of transfer and not by operation of law (see paragraph (f) of this section). * * *

(b) **Condition of survivorship.** As indicated in paragraph (a) of this section, the value of an interest in transferred property is not included in a decedent's gross estate under section 2037 unless possession or enjoyment of the property could, through ownership of such interest, have been obtained only by surviving the decedent. Thus, property is not included in the decedent's gross estate if, immediately before the decedent's death, possession or enjoyment of the property could have been obtained by any beneficiary either by surviving the decedent or through the occurrence of some other event such as the expiration of a term of years. However, if a consideration of the terms and circumstances of the transfer as a whole indicates that the "other event" is unreal and if the death of the decedent does, in fact, occur before the "other event", the beneficiary will be considered able to possess or enjoy the property only by surviving the decedent. Notwithstanding the foregoing, an interest in transferred property is not includible in a decedent's gross estate under section 2037 if possession or enjoyment of the property could have been obtained by any beneficiary during the decedent's life through the exercise of a general power of appointment (as defined in section 2041) which in fact was exercisable immediately before the decedent's death. See examples (5) and (6) in paragraph (e) of this section.

(c) **Retention of reversionary interest.** (1) As indicated in paragraph (a) of this section, the value of an interest in transferred property is not included in a decedent's gross estate under section 2037 unless the decedent had retained a reversionary interest in the property, and the value of the reversionary interest immediately before the death of the decedent exceeded 5 percent of the value of the property.

(2) For purposes of section 2037, the term "reversionary interest" includes a possibility that property transferred by the decedent may return to him or his estate and a possibility that property transferred by the decedent may become subject to a power of disposition by him. The term is not used in a technical sense, but has reference to any reserved right under which the transferred property shall or may be returned to the grantor. Thus, it encompasses an interest arising either by the express terms of the instrument of transfer or by operation of law. (See, however, paragraph (f) of this section with respect to transfers made before October 8, 1949.) The term "reversionary interest" does not include rights to income only, such as the right to receive the income from a trust after the death of another person. (However, see section 2036 for the inclusion of property in the gross estate on account of such rights.) Nor does the term "reversionary interest" include the possibility that the decedent during his lifetime might have received back an interest in transferred property by inheritance through the estate of another person. Similarly, a statutory right of a spouse to receive a portion of whatever estate a decedent may leave at the time of his death is not a "reversionary interest".

(3) For purposes of this section, the value of the decedent's reversionary interest is computed as of the moment immediately before his death, without regard to whether or not the executor elects the alternate valuation method under section 2032 and without regard to the fact of the decedent's death. The value is ascertained in accordance with recognized valuation principles for determining the value for estate tax purposes of future or conditional interests in property. (See §§ 20.2031-1, 20.2031-7, and 20.2031-9). For example, if the decedent's reversionary interest was subject to an outstanding life estate in his wife, his interest is valued according to the actuarial rules set forth in § 20.2031-7.

On the other hand, if the decedent's reversionary interest was contingent on the death of his wife without issue surviving and if it cannot be shown that his wife is incapable of having issue (so that his interest is not subject to valuation according to the actuarial rules in § 20.2031-7), his interest is valued according to the general rules set forth in § 20.2031-1. A possibility that the decedent may be able to dispose of property under certain conditions is considered to have the same value as a right of the decedent to the return of the property under those same conditions.

(4) In order to determine whether or not the decedent retained a reversionary interest in transferred property of a value in excess of 5 percent, the value of the reversionary interest is compared with the value of the transferred property, including interests therein which are not dependent upon survivorship of the decedent. For example, assume that the decedent, A, transferred property in trust with the income payable to B for life and with the remainder payable to C if A predeceases B, but with the property to revert to A if B predeceases A. Assume further that A does, in fact, predecease B. The value of A's reversionary interest immediately before his death is compared with the value of the trust corpus, without deduction of the value of B's outstanding life estate. If, in the above example, A had retained a reversionary interest in one-half only of the trust corpus, the value of his reversionary interest would be compared with the value of one-half of the trust corpus, again without deduction of any part of the value of B's outstanding life estate.

(d) **Transfers partly taking effect at death.** If separate interests in property are transferred to one or more beneficiaries, paragraphs (a) to (c) of this section are to be separately applied with respect to each interest. For example, assume that the decedent transferred an interest in Blackacre to A which could be possessed or enjoyed only by surviving the decedent, and that the decedent transferred an interest in Blackacre to B which could be possessed or enjoyed only on the occurrence of some event unrelated to the decedent's death. Assume further that the decedent retained a reversionary interest in Blackacre of a value in excess of 5 percent. Only the value of the interest transferred to A is includible in the decedent's gross estate. Similar results would obtain if possession or enjoyment of the entire property could have been obtained only by surviving the decedent, but the decedent had retained a reversionary interest in a part only of such property.

(e) Examples. The provisions of paragraphs (a) to (d) of this section may be further illustrated by the following examples. It is assumed that the transfers were made on or after October 8, 1949; for the significance of this date, see paragraphs (f) and (g) of this section:

Example (1). The decedent transferred property in trust with the income payable to his wife for life and, at her death, remainder to the decedent's then surviving children, or if none, to the decedent or his estate. Since each beneficiary can possess or enjoy the property without surviving the decedent, no part of the property is includible in the decedent's gross estate under section 2037, regardless of the value of the decedent's reversionary interest. (However, see section 2033 for inclusion of the value of the reversionary interest in the decedent's gross estate.)

Example (2). The decedent transferred property in trust with the income to be accumulated for the decedent's life, and at his death, principal and accumulated income to be paid to the decedent's then surviving issue, or, if none, to A or A's estate. Since the decedent retained no reversionary interest in the property, no part of the property is includible in the decedent's gross estate, even though possession or enjoyment of the property could be obtained by the issue only by surviving the decedent.

Example (3). The decedent transferred property in trust with the income payable to his wife for life and with the remainder payable to the decedent or, if he is not living at his wife's death, to his daughter or her estate. The daughter cannot obtain possession or enjoyment of the property without surviving the decedent. Therefore, if the decedent's reversionary interest immediately before his death exceeded 5 percent of the value of the property, the value of the property, less the value of the wife's outstanding life estate, is includible in the decedent's gross estate.

Example (4). The decedent transferred property in trust with the income payable to his wife for life and with the remainder payable to his son or, if the son is not living at the wife's death, to the decedent or, if the decedent is not then living, to X or X's estate. Assume that the decedent was survived by his wife, his son, and X. Only X cannot obtain possession or enjoyment of the property without surviving the decedent. Therefore, if the decedent's reversionary interest immediately before his death exceeded 5 percent of the value of the property, the value of X's remainder interest (with reference to the time immediately after the decedent's death) is includible in the decedent's gross estate.

Example (5). The decedent transferred property in trust with the income to be accumulated for a period of 20 years or until the decedent's prior death, at which time the principal and accumulated income was to be paid to the decedent's son if then surviving. Assume that the decedent does, in fact, die before the expiration of the 20-year period. If, at the time of the transfer, the decedent was 30 years of age, in good health, etc., the son will be considered able to possess or enjoy the property without surviving the decedent. If, on the other hand, the decedent was 70 years of age at the time of the transfer, the son will not be considered able to possess or enjoy the property without surviving the decedent. In this latter case, if the value of the decedent's reversionary interest (arising by operation of law) immediately before his death exceeded 5 percent of the value of the property, the value of the property is includible in the decedent's gross estate.

Example (6). The decedent transferred property in trust with the income to be accumulated for his life and, at his death, the principal and accumulated income to be paid to the decedent's then surviving children. The decedent's wife was given the unrestricted power to alter, amend, or revoke the trust. Assume that the wife survived the decedent but did not, in fact, exercise her power during the decedent's lifetime. Since possession or enjoyment of the property could have been obtained by the wife during the decedent's lifetime under the exercise of a general power of appointment, which was, in fact, exercisable immediately before the decedent's death, no part of the property is includible in the decedent's gross estate.

* * *

[T.D. 6296, 23 FR 4529, June 24, 1958]

§ 20.2038-1   Revocable transfers.

(a) In general. A decedent's gross estate includes under section 2038 the value of any interest in property transferred by the decedent, whether in trust or otherwise, if the enjoyment of the interest was subject at the date of the decedent's death to any change through the exercise of a power by the decedent to alter, amend, revoke, or terminate, or if the decedent relinquished such a power in contemplation of death. However, section 2038 does not apply—

(1) To the extent that the transfer was for an adequate and full consideration in money or money's worth (see § 20.2043–1);

(2) If the decedent's power could be exercised only with the consent of all parties having an interest (vested or contingent) in the transferred property, and if the power adds nothing to the rights of the parties under local law; or

(3) To a power held solely by a person other than the decedent. But, for example, if the decedent had the unrestricted power to remove or discharge a trustee at any time and appoint himself trustee, the decedent is considered as having the powers of the trustee. However, this result would not follow if he only had the power to appoint himself trustee under limited conditions which did not exist at the time of his death. (See last two sentences of paragraph (b) of this section.)

Except as provided in this paragraph, it is immaterial in what capacity the power was exercisable by the decedent or by another person or persons in conjunction with the decedent; whether the power was exercisable alone or only in conjunction with another person or persons, whether or not having an adverse interest (unless the transfer was made before June 2, 1924; see paragraph (d) of this section); and at what time or from what source the decedent acquired his power (unless the transfer was made before June 23, 1936; see paragraph (c) of this section). Section 2038 is applicable to any power affecting the time or manner of enjoyment of property or its income, even though the identity of the beneficiary is not affected. For example, section 2038 is applicable to a power reserved by the grantor of a trust to accumulate income or distribute it to A, and to distribute corpus to A, even though the remainder is vested in A or his estate, and no other person has any beneficial interest in the trust. However, only the value of an interest in property subject to a power to which section 2038 applies is included in the decedent's gross estate under section 2038.

(b) **Date of existence of power.** A power to alter, amend, revoke, or terminate will be considered to have existed at the date of the decedent's death even though the exercise of the power was subject to a precedent giving of notice or even though the alteration, amendment, revocation, or termination would have taken effect only on the expiration of a stated period after the exercise of the power, whether or not on or before the date of the decedent's death notice had been given or the power had been exercised. In determining the value of the gross estate in such cases, the full value of the property transferred subject to the power is discounted for the period required to elapse between the date of the decedent's death and the date upon which the alteration, amendment, revocation, or termination could take effect. In this connection, see especially § 20.2031-7. However, section 2038 is not applicable to a power the exercise of which was subject to a contingency beyond the decedent's control which did not occur before his death (*e.g.*, the death of another person during the decedent's life). See, however, section 2036(a)(2) for the inclusion of property in the decedent's gross estate on account of such a power.

* * *

[T.D. 6296, 23 FR 4529, June 24, 1958, as amended by T.D. 6600, 27 FR 4985, May 29, 1962]

§ 20.2039-1 Annuities.

(a) **In general.** A decedent's gross estate includes under section 2039(a) and (b) the value of an annuity or other payment receivable by any beneficiary by reason of surviving the decedent under certain agreements or plans to the extent that the value of the annuity or other payment is attributable to contributions made by the decedent or his employer. Section 2039(a) and (b), however, has no application to an amount which constitutes the proceeds of insurance under a policy on the decedent's life. Paragraph (b) of this section describes the agreements or plans to which section 2039(a) and (b) applies; paragraph (c) of this section provides rules for determining the amount includible in the decedent's gross estate; and paragraph (d) of this section distinguishes proceeds of life insurance. The fact that an annuity or other payment is not includible in a decedent's gross estate under section 2039(a) and (b) does not mean that it is not includible under some other section of part III of subchapter A of chapter 11. However, see section 2039(c) and (d) and § 20.2039-2 for rules relating to the exclusion from a decedent's gross estate of annuities and other payments under certain "qualified plans".

(b) **Agreements or plans to which section 2039(a) and (b) applies.** (1) Section 2039(a) and (b) applies to the value of an annuity or other payment receivable by any beneficiary under any form of contract or agreement entered into after March 3, 1931, under which—

(i) An annuity or other payment was payable to the decedent, either alone or in conjunction with another person or persons, for his life or for any period not ascertainable without reference to his death or for any period which does not in fact end before his death, or

(ii) The decedent possessed, for his life or for any period not ascertainable without reference to his death or for any period which does not in fact end before his death, the right to receive such an annuity or other payment, either alone or in conjunction with another person or persons.

The term "annuity or other payment" as used with respect to both the decedent and the beneficiary has reference to one or more payments extending over any period of time. The payments may be equal or unequal, conditional or unconditional, periodic or sporadic. The term "contract or agreement" includes any arrangement, understanding or plan, or any combination of arrangements, understandings or plans arising by reason of the decedent's employment. An annuity or other payment "was payable" to the decedent if, at the time of his death, the decedent was in fact receiving an annuity or other payment, whether or not he had an enforceable right to have payments continued. The decedent "possessed the right to receive" an annuity or other payment if, immediately before his death, the decedent had an enforceable right to receive payments at some time in the future, whether or not, at the time of his death, he had a present right to receive payments. In connection with the preceding sentence, the decedent will be regarded as having had "an enforceable right to receive payments at some time in the future" so long as he had complied with his obligations under the contract or agreement up to the time of his death. For the meaning of the phrase "for his life or for any period not ascertainable without reference to his death or for any period which does not in fact end before his death", see section 2036 and § 20.2036–1.

(2) The application of this paragraph is illustrated and more fully explained in the following examples. In each example: (i) It is assumed that all transactions occurred after March 3, 1931, and (ii) the amount stated to be includible in the decedent's gross estate is determined in accordance with the provisions of paragraph (c) of this section.

Example (1). The decedent purchased an annuity contract under the terms of which the issuing company agreed to pay an annuity to the decedent for his life and, upon his death, to pay a specified lump sum to his designated beneficiary. The decedent was drawing his annuity at the time of his death. The amount of the lump sum payment to the beneficiary is includible in the decedent's gross estate under section 2039(a) and (b).

Example (2). Pursuant to a retirement plan, the employer made contributions to a fund which was to provide the employee, upon his retirement at age 60, with an annuity for life, and which was to provide the employee's wife, upon his death after retirement, with a similar annuity for life. The benefits under the plan were completely forfeitable during the employee's life, but upon his death after retirement, the benefits to the wife were forfeitable only upon her remarriage. The employee had no right to originally designate or to ever change the employer's designation of the surviving beneficiary. The retirement plan at no time met the requirements of section 401(a) (relating to qualified plans). Assume that the employee died at age 61 after the employer started payment of his annuity as described above. The value of the wife's annuity is includible in the decedent's gross estate under section 2039(a) and (b). Includibility in this case is based on the fact that the annuity to the decedent "was payable" at the time of his death. The fact that the decedent's annuity was forfeitable is of no consequence

since, at the time of his death, he was in fact receiving payments under the plan. Nor is it important that the decedent had no right to choose the surviving beneficiary. The element of forfeitability in the wife's annuity may be taken into account only with respect to the valuation of the annuity in the decedent's gross estate.

Example (3). Pursuant to a retirement plan, the employer made contributions to a fund which was to provide the employee, upon his retirement at age 60, with an annuity of $100 per month for life, and which was to provide his designated beneficiary, upon the employee's death after retirement, with a similar annuity for life. The plan also provided that (a) upon the employee's separation from service before retirement, he would have a nonforfeitable right to receive a reduced annuity starting at age 60, and (b) upon the employee's death before retirement, a lump sum payment representing the amount of the employer's contributions credited to the employee's account would be paid to the designated beneficiary. The plan at no time met the requirements of section 401(a) (relating to qualified plans). Assume that the employee died at age 49 and that the designated beneficiary was paid the specified lump sum payment. Such amount is includible in the decedent's gross estate under section 2039(a) and (b). Since immediately before his death, the employee had an enforceable right to receive an annuity commencing at age 60, he is considered to have "possessed the right to receive" an annuity as that term is used in section 2039(a). If, in this example, the employee would not be entitled to any benefits in the event of his separation from service before retirement for any reason other than death, the result would be the same so long as the decedent had complied with his obligations under the contract up to the time of his death. In such case, he is considered to have had, immediately before his death, an enforceable right to receive an annuity commencing at age 60.

Example (4). Pursuant to a retirement plan, the employee made contributions to a fund which was to provide the employee, upon his retirement at age 60, with an annuity for life, and which was to provide his designated beneficiary, upon the employee's death after retirement, with a similar annuity for life. The plan provided, however, that no benefits were payable in the event of the employee's death before retirement. The retirement plan at no time met the requirements of section 401(a) (relating to qualified plans). Assume that the employee died at age 59 but that the employer nevertheless started payment of an annuity in a slightly reduced amount to the designated beneficiary. The value of the annuity is not includible in the decedent's gross estate under section 2039(a) and (b). Since the employee died before reaching the retirement age, the employer was under no obligation to pay the annuity to the employee's designated beneficiary. Therefore, the annuity was not paid under a "contract or agreement" as that term is used in section 2039(a). If, however, it can be established that the employer has consistently paid an annuity under such circumstances, the annuity will be considered as having been paid under a "contract or agreement".

Example (5). The employer made contributions to a retirement fund which were credited to the employee's individual account. Under the plan, the employee was to receive one-half the amount credited to his account upon his retirement at age 60, and his designated beneficiary was to receive the other one-half upon the employee's death after retirement. If the employee should die before reaching the retirement age, the entire amount credited to his account at such time was to be paid to the designated beneficiary. The retirement plan at no time met the requirements of section 401(a) (relating to qualified plans). Assume that the employee received one-half the amount credited to his account upon reaching the retirement age and that he died shortly thereafter. Since the employee received all that he was entitled to receive under the plan before his death, no amount was payable to him for his life or for any period not ascertainable without reference to his death, or for any period which did not in fact end before his death. Thus, the amount of the payment to the designated beneficiary is not includible in the decedent's gross estate under section 2039(a) and (b). If, in this example, the employee died before reaching the retirement age, the amount of the payment to the designated beneficiary would be includible in the decedent's gross estate under section 2039(a) and (b). In this latter case, the decedent possessed the right to receive lump sum payment for a period which did not in fact end before his death.

Example (6). The employer made contributions to two different funds set up under two different plans. One plan was to provide the employee upon his retirement at age 60, with an annuity for life, and the other plan was to provide the employee's designated beneficiary, upon the employee's death, with a similar annuity for life. Each plan was established at a different time and each plan was administered separately in every respect. Neither plan at any time met the requirements of section 401(a) (relating to qualified plans). The value of the designated beneficiary's annuity is includible in the employee's gross estate. All rights and benefits accruing to an employee and to others by reason of the employment (except rights and benefits accruing under certain plans meeting the requirements of section 401(a) (see § 20.2039-2)) are considered together in determining whether or not section 2039(a) and (b) applies. The scope of section 2039(a) and (b) cannot be limited by indirection.

(c) Amount includible in the gross estate. The amount to be included in a decedent's gross estate under section 2039(a) and (b) is an amount which bears the same ratio to the value at the decedent's death of the annuity or other payment receivable by the beneficiary as the contribution made by the decedent, or made by his employer (or former employer) for any reason connected with his employment, to the cost of the contract or agreement bears to its total cost. In applying this ratio, the value at the decedent's death of the annuity or other payment is determined in accordance with the rules set forth in §§ 20.2031-1, 20.-2031-7, 20.2031-8, and 20.2031-9. The application of this paragraph may be illustrated by the following examples:

Example (1). On January 1, 1945, the decedent and his wife each contributed $15,000 to the purchase price of an annuity contract under the terms of which the issuing company agreed to pay an annuity to the decedent and his wife for their joint lives and to continue the annuity to the survivor for his life. Assume that the value of the survivor's annuity at the decedent's death (computed under § 20.2031-8) is $20,000. Since the decedent contributed one-half of the cost of the contract, the amount to be included in his gross estate under section 2039(a) and (b) is $10,000.

* * *

(d) Insurance under policies on the life of the decedent. If an annuity or other payment receivable by a beneficiary under a contract or agreement is in substance the proceeds of insurance under a policy on the life of the decedent, section 2039(a) and (b) does not apply. For the extent to which such an annuity or other payment is includable in a decedent's gross estate, see section 2042 and § 20.2042-1. A combination annuity contract and life insurance policy on the decedent's life (e.g., a "retirement income" policy with death benefits) which matured during the decedent's lifetime so that there was no longer an insurance element under the contract at the time of the decedent's death is subject to the provisions of section 2039(a) and (b). On the other hand, the treatment of a combination annuity contract and life insurance policy on the decedent's life which did not mature during the decedent's lifetime depends upon the nature of the contract at the time of the decedent's death. The nature of the contract is generally determined by the relation of the reserve value of the policy to the value of the death benefit at the time of the decedent's death. If the decedent dies before the reserve value equals the death benefit, there is still an insurance element under the contract. The contract is therefore considered, for estate tax purposes, to be an insurance policy subject to the provisions of section 2042. However, if the decedent dies after the reserve value equals the death benefit, there is no longer an insurance element under the contract. The contract is therefore considered to be a contract for an annuity or other payment subject to the provisions of section 2039(a) and (b) or some other section of part III of subchapter A of chapter 11. Notwithstanding the relation of the reserve value to the value of the death benefit, a contract under which the death benefit could never exceed the total premiums paid, plus interest, contains no insurance element.

Example. Pursuant to a retirement plan established January 1, 1945, the employer purchased a contract from an insurance company which was to provide the employee, upon his retirement at age 65, with an annuity of $100 per month for life, and which was to provide his designated beneficiary, upon the employee's death after retirement, with a similar annuity for life. The contract further provided that if the employee should die before reaching the retirement age, a lump sum payment of $20,000 would be paid to his designated beneficiary in lieu of the annuity described above. The plan at no time met the requirements of section 401(a) (relating to qualified plans). Assume that the reserve value of the contract at the retirement age would be $20,000. If the employee died after reaching the retirement age, the death benefit to the designated beneficiary would constitute an annuity, the value of which would be includable in the employee's gross estate under section 2039(a) and (b). If, on the other hand, the employee died before reaching his retirement age, the death benefit to the designated beneficiary would constitute insurance under a policy on the life of the decedent since the reserve value would be less than the death benefit. Accordingly, its includability would depend upon section 2042 and § 20.-2042–1.

[T.D. 6296, 23 FR 4529, June 24, 1958; 25 FR 14021, Dec. 31, 1960, as amended by T.D. 7416, 41 FR 14514, April 6, 1976]

§ 20.2040–1   Joint interests.

(a) **In general.** A decedent's gross estate includes under section 2040 the value of property held jointly at the time of the decedent's death by the decedent and another person or persons with right of survivorship, as follows:

(1) To the extent that the property was acquired by the decedent and the other joint owner or owners by gift, devise, bequest, or inheritance, the decedent's fractional share of the property is included.

(2) In all other cases, the entire value of the property is included except such part of the entire value as is attributable to the amount of the consideration in money or money's worth furnished by the other joint owner or owners. See § 20.2043–1 with respect to adequacy of consideration. Such part of the entire value is that portion of the entire value of the property at the decedent's death (or at the alternate valuation date described in section 2032 which the consideration in money or money's worth furnished by the other joint owner or owners bears to the total cost of acquisition and capital additions. In determining the consideration furnished by the other joint owner or owners, there is taken into account only that portion of such consideration which is shown not to be attributable to money or other property acquired by the other joint owner or owners from the decedent for less than a full and adequate consideration in money or money's worth.

The entire value of jointly held property is included in a decedent's gross estate unless the executor submits facts sufficient to show that property was not acquired entirely with consideration furnished by the decedent, or was acquired by the decedent and the other joint owner or owners by gift, bequest, devise, or inheritance.

(b) **Meaning of "property held jointly".** Section 2040 specifically covers property held jointly by the decedent and any other person (or persons), property held by the decedent and spouse as tenants by the entirety, and a deposit of money, or a bond or other instrument, in the name of the decedent and any other person and payable to either or the survivor. The section applies to all classes of property, whether real or personal, and regardless of when the joint interests were created. Furthermore, it makes no difference that the survivor takes the entire interest in the property by right of survivorship and that no interest therein forms a part of the decedent's estate for purposes of administration. The section has no application to property held by the decedent and any other person (or persons) as tenants in common.

(c) **Examples.** The application of this section may be explained in the following examples in each of which it is assumed that the other joint owner or owners survived the decedent:

(1) If the decedent furnished the entire purchase price of the jointly held property, the value of the entire property is included in his gross estate;

(2) If the decedent furnished a part only of the purchase price, only a corresponding portion of the value of the property is so included;

(3) If the decedent furnished no part of the purchase price, no part of the value of the property is so included;

(4) If the decedent, before the acquisition of the property by himself and the other joint owner, gave the latter a sum of money or other property which thereafter became the other joint owner's entire contribution to the purchase price, then the value of the entire property is so included, notwithstanding the fact that the other property may have appreciated in value due to market conditions between the time of the gift and the time of the acquisition of the jointly held property;

(5) If the decedent, before the acquisition of the property by himself and the other joint owner, transferred to the latter for less than an adequate and full consideration in money or money's worth

other income-producing property, the income from which belonged to and became the other joint owner's entire contribution to the purchase price, then the value of the jointly held property less that portion attributable to the income which the other joint owner did furnish is included in the decedent's gross estate;

(6) If the property originally belonged to the other joint owner and the decedent purchased his interest from the other joint owner, only that portion of the value of the property attributable to the consideration paid by the decedent is included;

(7) If the decedent and his spouse acquired the property by will or gift as tenants by the entirety, one-half of the value of the property is included in the decedent's gross estate; and

(8) If the decedent and his two brothers acquired the property by will or gift as joint tenants, one-third of the value of the property is so included.

§ 20.2041-1 Powers of appointment; in general.

(a) **Introduction.** A decedent's gross estate includes under section 2041 the value of property in respect of which the decedent possessed, exercised, or released certain powers of appointment. This section contains rules of general application; § 20.2041-2 contains rules specifically applicable to general powers of appointment created on or before October 21, 1942; and § 20.2041-3 sets forth specific rules applicable to powers of appointment created after October 21, 1942.

(b) **Definition of "power of appointment"**—(1) **In general.** The term "power of appointment" includes all powers which are in substance and effect powers of appointment regardless of the nomenclature used in creating the power and regardless of local property law connotations. For example, if a trust instrument provides that the beneficiary may appropriate or consume the principal of the trust, the power to consume or appropriate is a power of appointment. Similarly, a power given to a decedent to affect the beneficial enjoyment of trust property or its income by altering, amending, or revoking the trust instrument or terminating the trust is a power of appointment. If the community property laws of a State confer upon the wife a power of testamentary disposition over property in which she does not have a vested interest she is considered as having a power of appointment. A power in a donee to remove or discharge a trustee and appoint himself may be a power of

appointment. For example, if under the terms of a trust instrument, the trustee or his successor has the power to appoint the principal of the trust for the benefit of individuals including himself, and the decedent has the unrestricted power to remove or discharge the trustee at any time and appoint any other person including himself, the decedent is considered as having a power of appointment. However, the decedent is not considered to have a power of appointment if he only had the power to appoint a successor, including himself, under limited conditions which did not exist at the time of his death, without an accompanying unrestricted power of removal. Similarly, a power to amend only the administrative provisions of a trust instrument, which cannot substantially affect the beneficial enjoyment of the trust property or income, is not a power of appointment. The mere power of management, investment, custody of assets, or the power to allocate receipts and disbursements as between income and principal, exercisable in a fiduciary capacity, whereby the holder has no power to enlarge or shift any of the beneficial interests therein except as an incidental consequence of the discharge of such fiduciary duties is not a power of appointment. Further, the right in a beneficiary of a trust to assent to a periodic accounting, thereby relieving the trustee from further accountability, is not a power of appointment if the right of assent does not consist of any power or right to enlarge or shift the beneficial interest of any beneficiary therein.

(2) **Relation to other sections.** For purposes of §§ 20.2041-1 to 20.2041-3, the term "power of appointment" does not include powers reserved by the decedent to himself within the concept of sections 2036 through 2038. (See §§ 20.2036-1 to 20.2038-1.) No provision of section 2041 or of §§ 20.2041-1 to 20.2041-3 is to be construed as in any way limiting the application of any other section of the Internal Revenue Code or of these regulations. The power of the owner of a property interest already possessed by him to dispose of his interest, and nothing more, is not a power of appointment, and the interest is includable in his gross estate to the extent it would be includable under section 2033 or some other provision of part III of subchapter A of chapter 11. For example, if a trust created by S provides for payment of the income to A for life with power in A to appoint the remainder by will and, in default of such appointment for payment of the income to A's widow, W, for her life and for payment of the remainder to

A's estate, the value of A's interest in the remainder is includable in his gross estate under section 2033 regardless of its includability under section 2041.

(3) **Powers over a portion of property.** If a power of appointment exists as to part of an entire group of assets or only over a limited interest in property, section 2041 applies only to such part or interest. For example, if a trust created by S provides for the payment of income to A for life, then to W for life, with power in A to appoint the remainder by will and in default of appointment for payment of the remainder to B or his estate, and if A dies before W, section 2041 applies only to the value of the remainder interest excluding W's life estate. If A dies after W, section 2041 would apply to the value of the entire property. If the power were only over one-half the remainder interest, section 2041 would apply only to one-half the value of the amounts described above.

(c) **Definition of "general power of appointment"—(1) In general.** The term "general power of appointment" as defined in section 2041(b)(1) means any power of appointment exercisable in favor of the decedent, his estate, his creditors, or the creditors of his estate, except (i) joint powers, to the extent provided in §§ 20.2041–2 and 20.2041–3, and (ii) certain powers limited by an ascertainable standard, to the extent provided in subparagraph (2) of this paragraph. A power of appointment exercisable to meet the estate tax, or any other taxes, debts, or charges which are enforceable against the estate, is included within the meaning of a power of appointment exercisable in favor of the decedent's estate, his creditors, or the creditors of his estate. A power of appointment exercisable for the purpose of discharging a legal obligation of the decedent or for his pecuniary benefit is considered a power of appointment exercisable in favor of the decedent or his creditors. However, for purposes of §§ 20.2041–1 to 20.2041–3, a power of appointment not otherwise considered to be a general power of appointment is not treated as a general power of appointment merely by reason of the fact that an appointee may, in fact, be a creditor of the decedent or his estate. A power of appointment is not a general power if by its terms it is either—

(a) Exercisable only in favor of one or more designated persons or classes other than the decedent or his creditors, or the decedent's estate or the creditors of his estate, or

(b) Expressly not exercisable in favor of the decedent or his creditors, or the decedent's estate or the creditors of his estate.

A decedent may have two powers under the same instrument, one of which is a general power of appointment and the other of which is not. For example, a beneficiary may have a power to withdraw trust corpus during his life, and a testamentary power to appoint the corpus among his descendants. The testamentary power is not a general power of appointment.

(2) **Powers limited by an ascertainable standard.** A power to consume, invade, or appropriate income or corpus, or both, for the benefit of the decedent which is limited by an ascertainable standard relating to the health, education, support, or maintenance of the decedent is, by reason of section 2041(b)(1)(A), not a general power of appointment. A power is limited by such a standard if the extent of the holder's duty to exercise and not to exercise the power is reasonably measurable in terms of his needs for health, education, or support (or any combination of them). As used in this subparagraph, the words "support" and "maintenance" are synonymous and their meaning is not limited to the bare necessities of life. A power to use property for the comfort, welfare, or happiness of the holder of the power is not limited by the requisite standard. Examples of powers which are limited by the requisite standard are powers exercisable for the holder's "support," "support in reasonable comfort," "maintenance in health and reasonable comfort," "support in his accustomed manner of living," "education, including college and professional education," "health," and "medical, dental, hospital and nursing expenses and expenses of invalidism." In determining whether a power is limited by an ascertainable standard, it is immaterial whether the beneficiary is required to exhaust his other income before the power can be exercised.

* * *

(d) **Definition of "exercise".** Whether a power of appointment is in fact exercised may depend upon local law. For example, the residuary clause of a will may be considered under local law as an exercise of a testamentary power of appointment in the absence of evidence of a contrary intention drawn from the whole of the testator's will. However, regardless of local law, a power of appointment is considered as exercised for purposes of section 2041 even though the exercise is in favor of the taker in default of appointment, and irrespective of whether the appointed interest and the interest in default of appointment are identical or whether the appointee renounces any right to take under the appointment. A power of appointment is also considered as exercised even though the disposition cannot take effect until the occurrence of an event after the exercise takes place, if the exercise is irrevocable and, as of the time of the exercise, the condition was not impossible of occurrence. For example, if property is left in trust to A for life, with a power in B to appoint the remainder by will, and B dies before A, exercising his power by appointing the remainder to C if C survives A, B is considered to have exercised his power if C is living at B's death. On the other hand, a testamentary power of appointment is not considered as exercised if it is exercised subject to the occurrence during the decedent's life of an express or implied condition which did not in fact occur. Thus, if in the preceding example, C dies before B, B's power of appointment would not be considered to have been exercised. Similarly, if a trust provides for income to A for life, remainder as A appoints by will, and A appoints a life estate in the property to B and does not otherwise exercise his power, but B dies before A, A's power is not considered to have been exercised.

(e) **Time of creation of power.** A power of appointment created by will is, in general, considered as created on the date of the testator's death. However, section 2041(b)(3) provides that a power of appointment created by a will executed on or before October 21, 1942, is considered a power created on or before that date if the testator dies before July 1, 1949, without having republished the will, by codicil or otherwise, after October 21, 1942. A power of appointment created by an inter vivos instrument is considered as created on the date the instrument takes effect. Such a power is not considered as created at some future date merely because it is not exercisable on the date the instrument takes effect, or because it is revocable, or because the identity of its holders is not ascertainable until after the date the instrument takes effect. However, if the holder of a power exercises it by creating a second power, the second power is considered as created at the time of the exercise of the first. The application of this paragraph may be illustrated by the following examples:

Example (1). A created a revocable trust before October 22, 1942, providing for payment of income to B for life with remainder as B shall appoint by will. Even though A dies after October 21, 1942, without having exercised

his power of revocation, B's power of appointment is considered a power created before October 22, 1942.

Example (2). C created an irrevocable inter vivos trust before October 22, 1942, naming T as trustee and providing for payment of income to D for life with remainder to E. T was given the power to pay corpus to D and the power to appoint a successor trustee. If T resigns after October 21, 1942, and appoints D as successor trustee, D is considered to have a power of appointment created before October 22, 1942.

Example (3). F created an irrevocable inter vivos trust before October 22, 1942, providing for payment of income to G for life with remainder as G shall appoint by will, but in default of appointment income to H for life with remainder as H shall appoint by will. If G died after October 21, 1942, without having exercised his power of appointment, H's power of appointment is considered a power created before October 22, 1942, even though it was only a contingent interest until G's death.

Example (4). If in example (3) above G had exercised his power of appointment by creating a similar power in J, J's power of appointment would be considered a power created after October 21, 1942.

[T.D. 6296, 23 FR 4529, June 24, 1958, as amended by T.D. 6582, 26 FR 11861, Dec. 12, 1961]

§ 20.2041–3 Powers of appointment created after October 21, 1942.

(a) **In general.** (1) Property subject to a power of appointment created after October 21, 1942, is includable in the gross estate of the holder of the power under varying conditions depending on whether the power is (i) general in nature, (ii) possessed at death, or (iii) exercised or released. See paragraphs (b), (c), and (d) of § 20.2041–1 for the definition of various terms used in this section. See paragraph (c) of this section for the rules applicable to determine the extent to which joint powers created after October 21, 1942, are to be treated as general powers of appointment.

(2) If the power is a general power of appointment, the value of an interest in property subject to such a power is includable in a decedent's gross estate under section 2041(a)(2) if either—

(i) The decedent has the power at the time of his death (and the interest exists at the time of his death), or

(ii) The decedent exercised or released the power, or the power lapsed, under the circumstances and to the extent described in paragraph (d) of this section.

(3) If the power is not a general power of appointment, the value of property subject to the power is includable in the holder's gross estate

under section 2041(a)(3) only if it is exercised to create a further power under certain circumstances (see paragraph (e) of this section).

(b) Existence of power at death. For purposes of section 2041(a)(2), a power of appointment is considered to exist on the date of a decedent's death even though the exercise of the power is subject to the precedent giving of notice, or even though the exercise of the power takes effect only on the expiration of a stated period after its exercise, whether or not on or before the decedent's death notice has been given or the power has been exercised. However, a power which by its terms is exercisable only upon the occurrence during the decedent's lifetime of an event or a contingency which did not in fact take place or occur during such time is not a power in existence on the date of the decedent's death. For example, if a decedent was given a general power of appointment exercisable only after he reached a certain age, only if he survived another person, or only if he died without descendants, the power would not be in existence on the date of the decedent's death if the condition precedent to its exercise had not occurred.

(c) Joint powers created after October 21, 1942. The treatment of a power of appointment created after October 21, 1942, which is exercisable only in conjunction with another person is governed by section 2041(b)(1)(C), which provides as follows:

(1) Such a power is not considered a general power of appointment if it is not exercisable by the decedent except with the consent or joinder of the creator of the power.

(2) Such power is not considered a general power of appointment if it is not exercisable by the decedent except with the consent or joinder of a person having a substantial interest in the property subject to the power which is adverse to the exercise of the power in favor of the decedent, his estate, his creditors, or the creditors of his estate. An interest adverse to the exercise of a power is considered as substantial if its value in relation to the total value of the property subject to the power is not insignificant. For this purpose, the interest is to be valued in accordance with the actuarial principles set forth in § 20.2031–7 or, if it is not susceptible to valuation under those provisions, in accordance with the general principles set forth in § 20.2031–1. A taker in default of appointment under a power has an interest which is adverse to an exercise of the power. A coholder of the power has no adverse interest merely because of his joint

possession of the power nor merely because he is a permissible appointee under a power. However, a coholder of a power is considered as having an adverse interest where he may possess the power after the decedent's death and may exercise it at that time in favor of himself, his estate, his creditors, or the creditors of his estate. Thus, for example, if X, Y, and Z held a power jointly to appoint among a group of persons which includes themselves and if on the death of X the power will pass to Y and Z jointly, then Y and Z are considered to have interests adverse to the exercise of the power in favor of X. Similarly, if on Y's death the power will pass to Z, Z is considered to have an interest adverse to the exercise of the power in favor of Y. The application of this subparagraph may be further illustrated by the following additional examples in each of which it is assumed that the value of the interest in question is substantial:

Example (1). The decedent and R were trustees of a trust under the terms of which the income was to be paid to the decedent for life and then to M for life, and the remainder was to be paid to R. The trustees had power to distribute corpus to the decedent. Since R's interest was substantially adverse to an exercise of the power in favor of the decedent the latter did not have a general power of appointment. If M and the decedent were the trustees, M's interest would likewise have been adverse.

Example (2). The decedent and L were trustees of a trust under the terms of which the income was to be paid to L for life and then to M for life, and the remainder was to be paid to the decedent. The trustees had power to distribute corpus to the decedent during L's life. Since L's interest was adverse to an exercise of the power in favor of the decedent, the decedent did not have a general power of appointment. If the decedent and M were the trustees, M's interest would likewise have been adverse.

Example (3). The decedent and L were trustees of a trust under the terms of which the income was to be paid to L for life. The trustees could designate whether corpus was to be distributed to the decedent or to A after L's death. L's interest was not adverse to an exercise of the power in favor of the decedent, and the decedent therefore had a general power of appointment.

(3) A power which is exercisable only in conjunction with another person, and which after application of the rules set forth in subparagraphs (1) and (2) of this paragraph constitutes a general power of appointment, will be treated as though the holders of the power who are permissible appointees of the property were joint owners of property subject to the power. The decedent, under this rule, will be treated as possessed of a general power of appointment over an aliquot share of the property to be determined with reference to the number of joint holders, including the decedent, who (or whose estates or creditors) are permissible appointees. Thus, for example, if X, Y, and Z hold an unlimited power jointly to appoint among a group of persons, including themselves, but on the death of X the power does not pass to Y and Z jointly, then Y and Z are not considered to have interests adverse to the exercise of the power in favor of X. In this case X is considered to possess a general power of appointment as to one-third of the property subject to the power.

(d) Releases, lapses, and disclaimers of general powers of appointment. (1) Property subject to a general power of appointment created after October 21, 1942, is includable in the gross estate of a decedent under section 2041(a)(2) even though he does not have the power at the date of his death, if during his life he exercised or released the power under circumstances such that, if the property subject to the power had been owned and transferred by the decedent, the property would be includable in the decedent's gross estate under section 2035, 2036, 2037, or 2038. Further, section 2041(b)(2) provides that the lapse of a power of appointment is considered to be a release of the power to the extent set forth in subparagraph (3) of this paragraph. A release of a power of appointment need not be formal or express in character. The principles set forth in § 20.2041-2 for determining the application of the pertinent provisions of sections 2035 through 2038 to a particular exercise of a power of appointment are applicable for purposes of determining whether or not an exercise or release of a power of appointment created after October 21, 1942, causes the property to be included in a decedent's gross estate under section 2041(a)(2). If a general power of appointment created after October 21, 1942, is partially released, a subsequent exercise or release of the power under circumstances described in the first sentence of this subparagraph, or its possession at death will nevertheless cause the property subject to the power to be included in the gross estate of the holder of the power.

* * *

(3) The failure to exercise a power of appointment created after October 21, 1942, within a specified time, so that the power lapses, constitutes a release of the power. However, section 2041(b)(2) provides that such a lapse of a power of appointment during any calendar year during the decedent's life is treated as a release for purposes of inclusion of property in the gross estate under section 2041(a)(2) only to the extent that the property which could have been appointed by exercise of the lapsed power exceeds the greater of (i) $5,000 or (ii) 5 percent of the aggregate value, at the time of the lapse, of the assets out of which, or the proceeds of which, the exercise of the lapsed power could have been satisfied. For example, assume that A transferred $200,000 worth of securities in trust providing for payment of income to B for life with remainder to B's issue. Assume further that B was given a noncumulative right to withdraw $10,000 a year from the principal of the trust fund (which neither increased nor decreased in value prior to B's death). In such case, the failure of B to exercise his right of withdrawal will not result in estate tax with respect to the power to withdraw $10,000 which lapses each year before the year of B's death. At B's death there will be included in his gross estate the $10,000 which he was entitled to withdraw for the year in which his death occurs less any amount which he may have taken during that year. However, if in the above example B had possessed the right to withdraw $15,000 of the principal annually, the failure to exercise such power in any year will be considered a release of the power to the extent of the excess of the amount subject to withdrawal over 5 percent of the trust fund (in this example, $5,000, assuming that the trust fund is worth $200,000 at the time of the lapse). Since each lapse is treated as though B had exercised dominion over the trust property by making a transfer of principal reserving the income therefrom for his life, the value of the trust property (but only to the extent of the excess of the amount subject to withdrawal over 5 percent of the trust fund) is includable in B's gross estate (unless before B's death he has disposed of his right to the income under circumstances to which sections 2035 through 2038 would not be applicable). The extent to which the value of the trust property is included in the decedent's gross estate is determined as provided in subparagraph (4) of this paragraph.

(4) The purpose of section 2041(b)(2) is to provide a determination, as of the date of the lapse of the power, of the proportion of the property over which the power lapsed which is an exempt disposition for estate tax purposes and the proportion which, if the other requirements of sections 2035 through 2038 are satisfied, will be considered as a taxable disposition. Once the taxable proportion of any disposition at the date of lapse has been determined, the valuation of that proportion as of the date of the decedent's death (or, if the executor has elected the alternate valuation method under sec-

tion 2032, the value as of the date therein provided), is to be ascertained in accordance with the principles which are applicable to the valuation of transfers of property by the decedent under the corresponding provisions of sections 2035 through 2038. For example, if the life beneficiary of a trust had a right exercisable only during one calendar year to draw down $50,000 from the corpus of a trust, which he did not exercise, and if at the end of the year the corpus was worth $800,000, the taxable portion over which the power lapsed is $10,000 (the excess of $50,000 over 5 percent of the corpus), or 1/80 of the total value. On the decedent's death, if the total value of the corpus of the trust (excluding income accumulated after the lapse of the power) on the applicable valuation date was $1,200,000, $15,000 (1/80 of $1,200,000) would be includable in the decedent's gross estate. However, if the total value was then $600,000, only $7,500 (1/80 of $600,000) would be includable.

(5) If the failure to exercise a power, such as a right of withdrawal, occurs in more than a single year, the proportion of the property over which the power lapsed which is treated as a taxable disposition will be determined separately for each such year. The aggregate of the taxable proportions for all such years, valued in accordance with the above principles, will be includable in the gross estate by reason of the lapse. The includable amount, however, shall not exceed the aggregate value of the assets out of which, or the proceeds of which, the exercise of the power could have been satisfied, valued as of the date of the decedent's death (or, if the executor has elected the alternate valuation method under section 2032, the value as of the date therein provided).

(6)(i) A disclaimer or renunciation of a general power of appointment created in a taxable transfer after December 31, 1976, in the person disclaiming is not considered a release of the power if the disclaimer or renunciation is a qualified disclaimer as described in section 2518 and the corresponding regulations. If the disclaimer or renunciation is not a qualified disclaimer, it is considered a release of the power by the disclaimant.

(ii) The disclaimer or renunciation of a general power of appointment created in a taxable transfer before January 1, 1977, in the person disclaiming is not considered to be a release of the power. The disclaimer or renunciation must be unequivocal and effective under local law. A disclaimer is a complete and unqualified refusal to accept the rights to which one is entitled. There can be no

disclaimer or renunciation of a power after its acceptance. In the absence of facts to the contrary, the failure to renounce or disclaim within a reasonable time after learning of its existence will be presumed to constitute an acceptance of the power. In any case where a power is purported to be disclaimed or renounced as to only a portion of the property subject to the power, the determination as to whether or not there has been a complete and unqualified refusal to accept the rights to which one is entitled will depend on all the facts and circumstances of the particular case, taking into account the recognition and effectiveness of such a disclaimer under local law. Such rights refer to the incidents of the power and not to other interests of the decedent in the property. If effective under local law, the power may be disclaimed or renounced without disclaiming or renouncing such other interests.

(e) **Successive powers.** (1) Property subject to a power of appointment created after October 21, 1942, which is not a general power, is includable in the gross estate of the holder of the power under section 2041(a)(3) if the power is exercised, and if both of the following conditions are met:

(i) If the exercise is (a) by will, or (b) by a disposition which is of such nature that if it were a transfer of property owned by the decedent, the property would be includable in the decedent's gross estate under sections 2035 through 2037; and

(ii) If the power is exercised by creating another power of appointment which, under the terms of the instruments creating and exercising the first power and under applicable local law, can be validly exercised so as to (a) postpone the vesting of any estate or interest in the property for a period ascertainable without regard to the date of the creation of the first power, or (b) (if the applicable rule against perpetuities is stated in terms of suspension of ownership or of the power of alienation, rather than of vesting) suspend the absolute ownership or the power of alienation of the property for a period ascertainable without regard to the date of the creation of the first power.

(2) For purposes of the application of section 2041(a)(3), the value of the property subject to the second power of appointment is considered to be its value unreduced by any precedent or subsequent interest which is not subject to the second power. Thus, if a decedent has a power to appoint by will $100,000 to a group of persons consisting of his children and grandchildren and exercises the pow-

er by making an outright appointment of $75,000 and by giving one appointee a power to appoint $25,000, no more than $25,000 will be includable in the decedent's gross estate under section 2041(a)(3). If, however, the decedent appoints the income from the entire fund to a beneficiary for life with power in the beneficiary to appoint the remainder by will, the entire $100,000 will be includable in the decedent's gross estate under section 2041(a)(3) if the exercise of the second power can validly postpone the vesting of any estate or interest in the property or can suspend the absolute ownership or power of alienation of the property for a period ascertainable without regard to the date of the creation of the first power.

* * *

[T.D. 6296, 23 FR 4529, June 24, 1958; T.D. 8095, 51 FR 28367, Aug. 7, 1986]

§ 20.2042–1 Proceeds of life insurance.

(a) **In general.** (1) Section 2042 provides for the inclusion in a decedent's gross estate of the proceeds of insurance on the decedent's life (i) receivable by or for the benefit of the estate (see paragraph (b) of this section) and (ii) receivable by other beneficiaries (see paragraph (c) of this section). The term "insurance" refers to life insurance of every description, including death benefits paid by fraternal beneficial societies operating under the lodge system.

(2) Proceeds of life insurance which are not includable in the gross estate under section 2042 may, depending upon the facts of the particular case, be includable under some other section of part III of subchapter A of chapter 11. For example, if the decedent possessed incidents of ownership in an insurance policy on his life but gratuitously transferred all rights in the policy in contemplation of death, the proceeds would be includable under section 2035. Section 2042 has no application to the inclusion in the gross estate of the value of rights in an insurance policy on the life of a person other than the decedent, or the value of rights in a combination annuity contract and life insurance policy on the decedent's life (*i.e.*, a "retirement income" policy with death benefit or an "endowment" policy) under which there was no insurance element at the time of the decedent's death (see paragraph (d) of § 20.2039–1).

(3) Except as provided in paragraph (c)(6), the amount to be included in the gross estate under section 2042 is the full amount receivable under

the policy. If the proceeds of the policy are made payable to a beneficiary in the form of an annuity for life or for a term of years, the amount to be included in the gross estate is the one sum payable at death under an option which could have been exercised either by the insured or by the beneficiary, or if no option was granted, the sum used by the insurance company in determining the amount of the annuity.

(b) **Receivable by or for the benefit of the estate.** (1) Section 2042 requires the inclusion in the gross estate of the proceeds of insurance on the decedent's life receivable by the executor or administrator, or payable to the decedent's estate. It makes no difference whether or not the estate is specifically named as the beneficiary under the terms of the policy. Thus, if under the terms of an insurance policy the proceeds are receivable by another beneficiary but are subject to an obligation, legally binding upon the other beneficiary, to pay taxes, debts, or other charges enforceable against the estate, then the amount of such proceeds required for the payment in full (to the extent of the beneficiary's obligation) of such taxes, debts, or other charges is includable in the gross estate. Similarly, if the decedent purchased an insurance policy in favor of another person or a corporation as collateral security for a loan or other accommodation, its proceeds are considered to be receivable for the benefit of the estate. The amount of the loan outstanding at the date of the decedent's death, with interest accrued to that date, will be deductible in determining the taxable estate. See § 20.2053–4.

(2) If the proceeds of an insurance policy made payable to the decedent's estate are community assets under the local community property law and, as a result, one-half of the proceeds belongs to the decedent's spouse, then only one-half of the proceeds is considered to be receivable by or for the benefit of the decedent's estate.

(c) **Receivable by other beneficiaries.** (1) Section 2042 requires the inclusion in the gross estate of the proceeds of insurance on the decedent's life not receivable by or for the benefit of the estate if the decedent possessed at the date of his death any of the incidents of ownership in the policy, exercisable either alone or in conjunction with any other person. However, if the decedent did not possess any of such incidents of ownership at the time of his death nor transfer them in contemplation of death, no part of the proceeds would be includible in his gross estate under section 2042. Thus, if the decedent owned a policy of insurance on his life and, 4 years before his death, irrevocably assigned his entire interest in the policy to his wife retaining no reversionary interest therein (see subparagraph (3) of this paragraph), the proceeds of the policy would not be includible in his gross estate under section 2042.

(2) For purposes of this paragraph, the term "incidents of ownership" is not limited in its meaning to ownership of the policy in the technical legal sense. Generally speaking, the term has reference to the right of the insured or his estate to the economic benefits of the policy. Thus, it includes the power to change the beneficiary, to surrender or cancel the policy, to assign the policy, to revoke an assignment, to pledge the policy for a loan, or to obtain from the insurer a loan against the surrender value of the policy, etc. See subparagraph (6) of this paragraph for rules relating to the circumstances under which incidents of ownership held by a corporation are attributable to a decedent through his stock ownership.

(3) The term "incidents of ownership" also includes a reversionary interest in the policy or its proceeds, whether arising by the express terms of the policy or other instrument or by operation of law, but only if the value of the reversionary interest immediately before the death of the decedent exceeded 5 percent of the value of the policy.

As used in this subparagraph, the term "reversionary interest" includes a possibility that the policy or its proceeds may return to the decedent or his estate and a possibility that the policy or its proceeds may become subject to a power of disposition by him. In order to determine whether or not the value of a reversionary interest immediately before the death of the decedent exceeded 5 percent of the value of the policy, the principles contained in paragraph (c)(3) and (4) of § 20.2037–1, insofar as applicable, shall be followed under this subparagraph. In that connection, there must be specifically taken into consideration any incidents of ownership held by others immediately before the decedent's death which would affect the value of the reversionary interest. For example, the decedent would not be considered to have a reversionary interest in the policy of a value in excess of 5 percent if the power to obtain the cash surrender value existed in some other person immediately before the decedent's death and was exercisable by such other person alone and in all events. The terms "reversionary interest" and "incidents of

ownership" do not include the possibility that the decedent might receive a policy or its proceeds by inheritance through the estate of another person, or as a surviving spouse under a statutory right of election or a similar right.

(4) A decedent is considered to have an "incident of ownership" in an insurance policy on his life held in trust if, under the terms of the policy, the decedent (either alone or in conjunction with another person or persons) has the power (as trustee or otherwise) to change the beneficial ownership in the policy or its proceeds, or the time or manner of enjoyment thereof, even though the decedent has no beneficial interest in the trust. Moreover, assuming the decedent created the trust, such a power may result in the inclusion in the decedent's gross estate under section 2036 or 2038 of other property transferred by the decedent to the trust if, for example, the decedent has the power to surrender the insurance policy and if the income otherwise used to pay premiums on the policy would become currently payable to a beneficiary of the trust in the event that the policy were surrendered.

(5) As an additional step in determining whether or not a decedent possessed any incidents of ownership in a policy or any part of a policy, regard must be given to the effect of the State or other applicable law upon the terms of the policy. For example, assume that the decedent purchased a policy of insurance on his life with funds held by him and his surviving wife as community property, designating their son as beneficiary but retaining the right to surrender the policy. Under the local law, the proceeds upon surrender would have inured to the marital community. Assuming that the policy is not surrendered and that the son receives the proceeds on the decedent's death, the wife's transfer of her one-half interest in the policy was not considered absolute before the decedent's death. Upon the wife's prior death, one-half of the value of the policy would have been included in her gross estate. Under these circumstances, the power of surrender possessed by the decedent as agent for his wife with respect to one-half of the policy is not, for purposes of this section, an "incident of ownership", and the decedent is, therefore, deemed to possess an incident of ownership in only one-half of the policy.

(6) In the case of economic benefits of a life insurance policy on the decedent's life that are reserved to a corporation of which the decedent is

the sole or controlling stockholders, the corporations' incidents of ownership will not be attributed to the decedent through his stock ownership to the extent the proceeds of the policy are payable to the corporation. Any proceeds payable to a third party for a valid business purpose, such as in satisfaction of a business debt of the corporation, so that the net worth of the corporation is increased by the amount of such proceeds, shall be deemed to be payable to the corporation for purposes of the preceding sentence. See § 20.2031–2(f) for a rule providing that the proceeds of certain life insurance policies shall be considered in determining the value of the decedent's stock. Except as hereinafter provided with respect to a group-term life insurance policy, if any part of the proceeds of the policy are not payable to or for the benefit of the corporation, and thus are not taken into account in valuing the decedent's stock holdings in the corporation for purposes of section 2031, any incidents of ownership held by the corporation as to that part of the proceeds will be attributed to the decedent through his stock ownership where the decedent is the sole or controlling stockholder. Thus, for example, if the decedent is the controlling stockholder in a corporation, and the corporation owns a life insurance policy on his life, the proceeds of which are payable to the decedent's spouse, the incidents of ownership held by the corporation will be attributed to the decedent through his stock ownership and the proceeds will be included in his gross estate under section 2042. If in this example the policy proceeds had been payable 40 percent to decedent's spouse and 60 percent to the corporation, only 40 percent of the proceeds would be included in decedent's gross estate under section 2042. For purposes of this subparagraph, the decedent will not be deemed to be the controlling stockholder of a corporation unless, at the time of his death, he owned stock possessing more than 50 percent of the total combined voting power of the corporation. Solely for purposes of the preceding sentence, a decedent shall be considered to be the owner of only the stock with respect to which legal title was held, at the time of his death, by (i) the decedent (or his agent or nominee); (ii) the decedent and another person jointly (but only the proportionate number of shares which corresponds to the portion of the total consideration which is considered to be furnished by the decedent for purposes of section 2040 and the regulations thereunder); and (iii) by a trustee of a voting trust (to the extent of the decedent's beneficial interest

therein) or any other trust with respect to which the decedent was treated as an owner under subpart E, part I, subchapter J, chapter 1 of the Code immediately prior to his death. In the case of group-term life insurance, as defined in the regulations under section 79, the power to surrender or cancel a policy held by a corporation shall not be attributed to any decedent through his stock ownership.

[T.D. 6296, 23 FR 4529, June 24, 1958; 25 FR 14021, Dec. 31, 1960 as amended by T.D. 7312, 39 FR 14949, April 29, 1974; T.D. 7623, 44 FR 28800, May 17, 1979]

§ 20.2043–1 Transfers for insufficient consideration.

(a) **In general.** The transfers, trusts, interests, rights or powers enumerated and described in sections 2035 through 2038 and section 2041 are not subject to the Federal estate tax if made, created, exercised, or relinquished in a transaction which constituted a bona fide sale for an adequate and full consideration in money or money's worth. To constitute a bona fide sale for an adequate and full consideration in money or money's worth, the transfer must have been made in good faith, and the price must have been an adequate and full equivalent reducible to a money value. If the price was less than such a consideration, only the excess of the fair market value of the property (as of the applicable valuation date) over the price received by the decedent is included in ascertaining the value of his gross estate.

* * *

[T.D. 6296, 23 FR 4529, June 24, 1958]

§ 20.2046–1 Disclaimed property.

This section shall apply to the disclaimer or renunciation of a taxable transfer creating an interest in the person disclaiming made after December 31, 1976. If a qualified disclaimer is made with respect to such a transfer, the Federal estate tax provisions are to apply with respect to the property interest disclaimed as if the interest had never been transferred to the person making the disclaimer. See section 2518 and the corresponding regulations for rules relating to a qualified disclaimer.

[T.D. 8095, 51 FR 28368, Aug. 7, 1986]

§ 20.2053–1 Deductions for expenses, indebtedness, and taxes; in general.

(a) **General rule.** In determining the taxable estate of a decedent who was a citizen or resident of the United States at the time of his death, there are allowed as deductions under section 2053(a) and (b) amounts falling within the following two categories (subject to the limitations contained in this section and in §§ 20.2053–2 through 20.2053–9):

(1) **First category.** Amounts which are payable out of property subject to claims and which are allowable by the law of the jurisdiction, whether within or without the United States, under which the estate is being administered for—

(i) Funeral expenses;

(ii) Administration expenses;

(iii) Claims against the estate (including taxes to the extent set forth in § 20.2053–6 and charitable pledges to the extent set forth in § 20.2053–5); and

(iv) Unpaid mortgages on, or any indebtedness in respect of, property, the value of the decedent's interest in which is included in the value of the gross estate undiminished by the mortgage or indebtedness.

As used in this subparagraph, the phrase "allowable by the law of the jurisdiction" means allowable by the law governing the administration of decedents' estates. The phrase has no reference to amounts allowable as deductions under a law which imposes a State death tax. See further §§ 20.2053–2 through 20.2053–7.

(2) **Second category.** Amounts representing expenses incurred in administering property which is included in the gross estate but which is not subject to claims and which—

(i) Would be allowed as deductions in the first category if the property being administered were subject to claims; and

(ii) Were paid before the expiration of the period of limitation for assessment provided in section 6501.

See further § 20.2053–8.

(b) **Provisions applicable to both categories —(1) In general.** If the item is not one of those described in paragraph (a) of this section, it is not deductible merely because payment is allowed by the local law. If the amount which may be expended for the particular purpose is limited by the local law no deduction in excess of that limitation is permissible.

(2) **Effect of court decree.** The decision of a local court as to the amount and allowability under local law of a claim or administration expense will ordinarily be accepted if the court passes upon the facts upon which deductibility depends. If the court does not pass upon those facts, its decree will, of course, not be followed. For example, if the question before the court is whether a claim should be allowed, the decree allowing it will ordinarily be accepted as establishing the validity and amount of the claim. However, the decree will not necessarily be accepted even though it purports to decide the facts upon which deductibility depends. It must appear that the court actually passed upon the merits of the claim. This will be presumed in all cases of an active and genuine contest. If the result reached appears to be unreasonable, this is some evidence that there was not such a contest, but it may be rebutted by proof to the contrary. If the decree was rendered by consent, it will be accepted, provided the consent was a bona fide recognition of the validity of the claim (and not a mere cloak for a gift) and was accepted by the court as satisfactory evidence upon the merits. It will be presumed that the consent was of this character, and was so accepted, if given by all parties having an interest adverse to the claimant. The decree will not be accepted if it is at variance with the law of the State; as, for example, an allowance made to an executor in excess of that prescribed by statute. On the other hand, a deduction for the amount of a bona fide indebtedness of the decedent, or of a reasonable expense of administration, will not be denied because no court decree has been entered if the amount would be allowable under local law.

(3) **Estimated amounts.** An item may be entered on the return for deduction though its exact amount is not then known, provided it is ascertainable with reasonable certainty, and will be paid. No deduction may be taken upon the basis of a vague or uncertain estimate. If the amount of a liability was not ascertainable at the time of final audit of the return by the district director and, as a consequence, it was not allowed as a deduction in

the audit, and subsequently the amount of the liability is ascertained, relief may be sought by a petition to the Tax Court or a claim for refund as provided by sections 6213(a) and 6511, respectively.

(c) **Provision applicable to first category only.** Deductions of the first category (described in paragraph (a)(1) of this section) are limited under section 2053(a) to amounts which would be property allowable out of property subject to claims by the law of the jurisdiction under which the decedent's estate is being administered. Further, the total allowable amount of deductions of the first category is limited by section 2053(c)(2) to the sum of—

(1) The value of property included in the decedent's gross estate and subject to claims, plus

(2) Amounts paid, out of property not subject to claims against the decedent's estate, within 9 months (15 months in the case of the estate of a decedent dying before January 1, 1971) after the decedent's death (the period within which the estate tax return must be filed under section 6075), or within any extension of time for filing the return granted under section 6081.

The term "property subject to claims" is defined in section 2053(c)(2) as meaning the property includible in the gross estate which, or the avails of which, under the applicable law, would bear the burden of the payment of these deductions in the final adjustment and settlement of the decedent's estate. However, for the purposes of this definition, the value of property subject to claims is first reduced by the amount of any deduction allowed under section 2054 for any losses from casualty or theft incurred during the settlement of the estate attributable to such property. The application of this paragraph may be illustrated by the following examples:

Example (1). The only item in the gross estate is real property valued at $250,000 which the decedent and his surviving spouse held as tenants by the entirety. Under the local law this real property is not subject to claims. Funeral expenses of $1,200 and debts of the decedent in the amount of $1,500 are allowable under local law. Before the prescribed date for filing the estate tax return, the surviving spouse paid the funeral expenses and $1,000 of the debts. The remaining $500 of the debts was paid by her after the prescribed date for filing the return. The total amount allowable as deductions under section 2053 is limited to $2,200, the amount paid prior to the prescribed date for filing the return.

Example (2). The only two items in the gross estate were a bank deposit of $20,000 and insurance in the amount of $150,000. The insurance was payable to the

decedent's surviving spouse and under local law was not subject to claims. Funeral expenses of $1,000 and debts in the amount of $29,000 were allowable under local law. A son was executor of the estate and before the prescribed date for filing the estate tax return he paid the funeral expenses of $9,000 of the debts, using therefor $5,000 of the bank deposit and $5,000 supplied by the surviving spouse. After the prescribed date for filing the return, the executor paid the remaining $20,000 of the debts, using for that purpose the $15,000 left in the bank account plus an additional $5,000 supplied by the surviving spouse. The total amount allowable as deductions under section 2053 is limited to $25,000 ($20,000 of property subject to claims plus the $5,000 additional amount which, before the prescribed date for filing the return, was paid out of property not subject to claims).

(d) **Disallowance of double deductions.** See section 642(g) and § 1.642(g)–1 with respect to the disallowance for income tax purposes of certain deductions unless the right to take such deductions for estate tax purposes is waived.

[T.D. 6296, 23 FR 4529, June 24, 1958, as amended by T.D. 7238, 37 FR 28719, Dec. 29, 1972]

§ 20.2053–2 Deduction for funeral expenses.

Such amounts for funeral expenses are allowed as deductions from a decedent's gross estate as (a) are actually expended, (b) would be properly allowable out of property subject to claims under the laws of the local jurisdiction, and (c) satisfy the requirements of paragraph (c) of § 20.2053–1. A reasonable expenditure for a tombstone, monument, or mausoleum, or for a burial lot, either for the decedent or his family, including a reasonable expenditure for its future care, may be deducted under this heading, provided such an expenditure is allowable by the local law. Included in funeral expenses is the cost of transportation of the person bringing the body to the place of burial.

[T.D. 6296, 23 FR 4529, June 24, 1958]

§ 20.2053–3 Deduction for expenses of administering estate.

(a) **In general.** The amounts deductible from a decedent's gross estate as "administration expenses" of the first category (see paragraphs (a) and (c) of § 20.2053–1) are limited to such expenses as are actually and necessarily, incurred in the administration of the decedent's estate; that is, in the collection of assets, payment of debts, and distribution of property to the persons entitled to it. The expenses contemplated in the law are such only as attend the settlement of an estate and the transfer of the property of the estate to individual beneficiaries or to a trustee, whether the trustee is the executor or some other person. Expenditures not essential to the proper settlement of the estate, but incurred for the individual benefit of the heirs, legatees, or devisees, may not be taken as deductions. Administration expenses include (1) executor's commissions; (2) attorney's fees; and (3) miscellaneous expenses. Each of these classes is considered separately in paragraphs (b) through (d) of this section.

(b) **Executor's commissions.** (1) The executor or administrator, in filing the estate tax return, may deduct his commissions in such an amount as has actually been paid or in an amount which at the time of filing the estate tax return may reasonably be expected to be paid, but no deduction may be taken if no commissions are to be collected. If the amount of the commissions has not been fixed by decree of the proper court, the deduction will be allowed on the final audit of the return, to the extent that all three of the following conditions are satisfied:

(i) The district director is reasonably satisfied that the commissions claimed will be paid;

(ii) The amount claimed as a deduction is within the amount allowable by the laws of the jurisdiction in which the estate is being administered; and

(iii) It is in accordance with the usually accepted practice in the jurisdiction to allow such an amount in estates of similar size and character.

If the deduction is disallowed in whole or in part on final audit, the disallowance will be subject to modification as the facts may later require. If the deduction is allowed in advance of payment and payment is thereafter waived, it shall be the duty of the executor to notify the district director and to pay the resulting tax, together with interest.

(2) A bequest or devise to the executor in lieu of commissions is not deductible. If, however, the decedent fixed by his will the compensation payable to the executor for services to be rendered in the administration of the estate, deduction may be taken to the extent that the amount so fixed does not exceed the compensation allowable by the local law or practice.

(3) Except to the extent that a trustee is in fact performing services with respect to property subject to claims which would normally be performed by an executor, amounts paid as trustees' commissions do not constitute expenses of administration under the first category, and are only deductible as

expenses of the second category to the extent provided in § 20.2053–8.

(c) **Attorney's fees.** (1) The executor or administrator, in filing the estate tax return, may deduct such an amount of attorney's fees as has actually been paid, or an amount which at the time of filing may reasonably be expected to be paid. If on the final audit of a return the fees claimed have not been awarded by the proper court and paid, the deduction will, nevertheless, be allowed, if the district director is reasonably satisfied that the amount claimed will be paid and that it does not exceed a reasonable remuneration for the services rendered, taking into account the size and character of the estate and the local law and practice. If the deduction is disallowed in whole or in part on final audit, the disallowance will be subject to modification as the facts may later require.

(2) A deduction for attorneys' fees incurred in contesting an asserted deficiency or in prosecuting a claim for refund should be claimed at the time the deficiency is contested or the refund claim is prosecuted. A deduction for reasonable attorneys' fees actually paid in contesting an asserted deficiency or in prosecuting a claim for refund will be allowed even though the deduction, as such, was not claimed in the estate tax return or in the claim for refund. A deduction for these fees shall not be denied, and the sufficiency of a claim for refund shall not be questioned, solely by reason of the fact that the amount of the fees to be paid was not established at the time that the right to the deduction was claimed.

(3) Attorneys' fees incurred by beneficiaries incident to litigation as to their respective interests are not deductible if the litigation is not essential to the proper settlement of the estate within the meaning of paragraph (a) of this section. An attorney's fee not meeting this test is not deductible as an administration expense under section 2053 and this section, even if it is approved by a probate court as an expense payable or reimbursable by the estate.

(d) **Miscellaneous administration expenses.** (1) Miscellaneous administration expenses include such expenses as court costs, surrogates' fees, accountants' fees, appraisers' fees, clerk hire, etc. Expenses necessarily incurred in preserving and distributing the estate are deductible, including the cost of storing or maintaining property of the estate, if it is impossible to effect immediate distribution to the beneficiaries. Expenses for preserving and caring for the property may not include outlays for additions or improvements; nor will such expenses be allowed for a longer period than the executor is reasonably required to retain the property.

(2) Expenses for selling property of the estate are deductible if the sale is necessary in order to pay the decedent's debts, expenses of administration, or taxes, to preserve the estate, or to effect distribution. The phrase "expenses for selling property" includes brokerage fees and other expenses attending the sale, such as the fees of an auctioneer if it is reasonably necessary to employ one. Where an item included in the gross estate is disposed of in a bona fide sale (including a redemption) to a dealer in such items at a price below its fair market value, for purposes of this paragraph there shall be treated as an expense for selling the item whichever of the following amounts is the lesser: (i) The amount by which the fair market value of the property on the applicable valuation date exceeds the proceeds of the sale, or (ii) the amount by which the fair market value of the property on the date of the sale exceeds the proceeds of the sale. The principles used in determining the value at which an item of property is included in the gross estate shall be followed in arriving at the fair market value of the property for purposes of this paragraph. See §§ 20.2031–1 through 20.2031–9.

[T.D. 6296, 23 FR 4529, June 24, 1958, as amended by T.D. 6826, 30 FR 7708, June 15, 1965; 44 FR 23525, April 20, 1979]

§ 20.2053–4 Deduction for claims against the estate; in general.

The amounts that may be deducted as claims against a decedent's estate are such only as represent personal obligations of the decedent existing at the time of his death, whether or not then matured, and interest thereon which had accrued at the time of death. Only interest accrued at the date of the decedent's death is allowable even though the executor elects the alternate valuation method under section 2032. Only claims enforceable against the decedent's estate may be deducted. Except as otherwise provided in § 20.2053–5 with respect to pledges or subscriptions, section 2053(c)(1)(A) provides that the allowance of a deduction for a claim founded upon a promise or agreement is limited to the extent that the liability was contracted bona fide and for an adequate and full consideration in money or money's worth. See

§ 20.2043–1. Liabilities imposed by law or arising out of torts are deductible.

[T.D. 6296, 23 FR 4529, June 24, 1958]

§ 20.2053–7 Deduction for unpaid mortgages.

A deduction is allowed from a decedent's gross estate of the full unpaid amount of a mortgage upon, or of any other indebtedness in respect of, any property of the gross estate, including interest which had accrued thereon to the date of death, provided the value of the property, undiminished by the amount of the mortgage or indebtedness, is included in the value of the gross estate. If the decedent's estate is liable for the amount of the mortgage or indebtedness, the full value of the property subject to the mortgage or indebtedness must be included as part of the value of the gross estate; the amount of the mortgage or indebtedness being in such case allowed as a deduction. But if the decedent's estate is not so liable, only the value of the equity of redemption (or the value of the property, less the mortgage or indebtedness) need be returned as part of the value of the gross estate. In no case may the deduction on account of the mortgage or indebtedness exceed the liability therefor contracted bona fide and for an adequate and full consideration in money or money's worth. See § 20.2043–1. Only interest accrued to the date of the decedent's death is allowable even though the alternate valuation method under section 2032 is selected. In any case where real property situated outside the United States no deduction may be taken of any mortgage thereon or any other indebtedness does not form a part of the gross estate, in respect thereof.

[T.D. 6296, 23 FR 4529, June 24, 1958 as amended by T.D. 6684, 28 FR 11409, Oct. 24, 1963]

§ 20.2053–8 Deduction for expenses in administering property not subject to claims.

(a) Expenses incurred in administering property included in a decedent's gross estate but not subject to claims fall within the second category of deductions set forth in § 20.2053–1, and may be allowed as deductions if they—

(1) Would be allowed as deductions in the first category if the property being administered were subject to claims; and

(2) Were paid before the expiration of the period of limitation for assessment provided in section 6501.

Usually, these expenses are incurred in connection with the administration of a trust established by a decedent during his lifetime. They may also be incurred in connection with the collection of other assets or the transfer or clearance of title to other property included in a decedent's gross estate for estate tax purposes but not included in his probate estate.

(b) These expenses may be allowed as deductions only to the extent that they would be allowed as deductions under the first category if the property were subject to claims. See § 20.2053-3. The only expenses in administering property not subject to claims which are allowed as deductions are those occasioned by the decedent's death and incurred in settling the decedent's interest in the property or vesting good title to the property in the beneficiaries. Expenses not coming within the description in the preceding sentence but incurred on behalf of the transferees are not deductible.

(c) The principles set forth in paragraphs (b), (c), and (d) of § 20.2053-3 (relating to the allowance of executor's commissions, attorney's fees, and miscellaneous administration expenses of the first category) are applied in determining the extent to which trustee's commissions, attorney's and accountant's fees, and miscellaneous administration expenses are allowed in connection with the administration of property not subject to claims.

(d) The application of this section may be illustrated by the following examples:

Example (1). In 1940, the decedent made an irrevocable transfer of property to the X Trust Company, as trustee. The instrument of transfer provided that the trustee should pay the income from the property to the decedent for the duration of his life and upon his death, distribute the corpus of the trust among designated beneficiaries. The property was included in the decedent's gross estate under the provisions of section 2036. Three months after the date of death, the trustee distributed the trust corpus among the beneficiaries, except for $6,000 which it withheld. The amount withheld represented $5,000 which it retained as trustee's commissions in connection with the termination of the trust and $1,000 which it had paid to an attorney for representing it in connection with the termination. Both the trustee's commissions and the attorney's fees were allowable under the law of the jurisdiction in which the trust was being administered, were reasonable in amount, and were in accord with local custom. Under these circumstances, the estate is allowed a deduction of $6,000.

Example (2). In 1945, the decedent made an irrevocable transfer of property to Y Trust Company, as trustee. The instrument of transfer provided that the trustee should pay the income from the property to the decedent during his life. If the decedent's wife survived him, the trust was to continue for the duration of her life, with Y

Trust Company and the decedent's son as co-trustees, and with income payable to the decedent's wife for the duration of her life. Upon the death of both the decedent and his wife, the corpus is to be distributed among designated remaindermen. The decedent was survived by his wife. The property was included in the decedent's gross estate under the provisions of section 2036. In accordance with local custom, the trustee made an accounting to the court as of the date of the decedent's death. Following the death of the decedent, a controversy arose among the remaindermen as to their respective rights under the instrument of transfer, and a suit was brought in court to which the trustee was made a party. As part of the accounting, the court approved the following expenses which the trustee had paid within 3 years following the date of death: $10,000, trustee's commissions; $5,000, accountant's fees; $25,000, attorney's fees; and $2,500, representing fees paid to the guardian of a remainderman who was a minor. The trustee's commissions and accountant's fees were for services in connection with the usual issues involved in a trust accounting as also were one-half of the attorney's and guardian's fees. The remainder of the attorney's and guardian's fees were for services performed in connection with the suit brought by the remaindermen. The amount allowed as a deduction is the $28,750 ($10,000, trustee's commissions; $5,000, accountant's fees; $12,500, attorney's fees; and $1,250, guardian's fees) incurred as expenses in connection with the usual issues involved in a trust accounting. The remaining expenses are not allowed as deductions since they were incurred on behalf of the transferees.

* * *

[T.D. 6296, 23 FR 4529, June 24, 1958]

§ 20.2054-1 Deduction for losses from casualties or theft.

A deduction is allowed for losses incurred during the settlement of the estate arising from fires, storms, shipwrecks, or other casualties, or from theft, if the losses are not compensated for by insurance or otherwise. If the loss is partly compensated for, the excess of the loss over the compensation may be deducted. Losses which are not of the nature described are not deductible. In order to be deductible a loss must occur during the settlement of the estate. If a loss with respect to an asset occurs after its distribution to the distributee it may not be deducted. Notwithstanding the foregoing, no deduction is allowed under this section if the estate has waived its right to take such a deduction pursuant to the provisions of section 642(g) in order to permit its allowance for income tax purposes. * * *

[T.D. 6296, 23 FR 4529, June 24, 1958]

§ 20.2055-1 Deduction for transfers for public, charitable, and religious uses; in general.

(a) General rule. A deduction is allowed under section 2055(a) from the gross estate of a decedent who was a citizen or resident of the United States at the time of his death for the value of property included in the decedent's gross estate and transferred by the decedent during his lifetime or by will—

(1) To or for the use of the United States, any State, Territory, any political subdivision thereof, or the District of Columbia, for exclusively public purposes;

(2) To or for the use of any corporation or association organized and operated exclusively for religious, charitable, scientific, literary, or educational purposes (including the encouragement of art and the prevention of cruelty to children or animals), if no part of the net earnings of the corporation or association inures to the benefit of any private stockholder or individual (other than as a legitimate object of such purposes), if no substantial part of its activities is carrying on propaganda, or otherwise attempting, to influence legislation, and if, in the case of transfers made after December 31, 1969, it does not participate in, or intervene in (including the publishing or distributing of statements), any political campaign on behalf of any candidate for public office;

(3) To a trustee or trustees, or a fraternal society, order, or association operating under the lodge system, if the transferred property is to be used exclusively for religious, charitable, scientific, literary, or educational purposes (or for the prevention of cruelty to children or animals), if no substantial part of the activities of such transferee is carrying on propaganda, or otherwise attempting, to influence legislation, and if, in the case of transfers made after December 31, 1969, such transferee does not participate in, or intervene in (including the publishing or distributing of statements), any political campaign on behalf of any candidate for public office; or

(4) To or for the use of any veterans' organization incorporated by act of Congress, or of any of its departments, local chapters, or posts, no part of the net earnings of which inures to the benefit of any private shareholder or individual.

The deduction is not limited, in the case of estates of citizens or residents of the United States, to transfers to domestic corporations or associations, or to trustees for use within the United States. Nor is the deduction subject to percentage limitations such as are applicable to the charitable deduction under the income tax. An organization will not be considered to meet the requirements of

subparagraph (2) or (3) of this paragraph if such organization engages in any activity which would cause it to be classified as an "action" organization under paragraph (c)(3) of § 1.501(c)(3)–1 of this chapter (Income Tax Regulations). See §§ 20.-2055–4 and 20.2055–5 for rules relating to the disallowance of deductions to trusts and organizations which engage in certain prohibited transactions or whose governing instruments do not contain certain specified requirements.

* * *

(c) **Submission of evidence.** In establishing the right of the estate to the deduction authorized by section 2055, the executor should submit the following with the return:

(1) A copy of any instrument in writing by which the decedent made a transfer of property in his lifetime the value of which is required by statute to be included in his gross estate, for which a deduction under section 2055 is claimed. If the instrument is of record the copy should be certified, and if not of record, the copy should be verified.

(2) A written statement by the executor containing a declaration that it is made under penalties of perjury and stating whether any action has been instituted to construe or to contest the decedent's will or any provision thereof affecting the charitable deduction claimed and whether, according to his information and belief, any such action is designed or contemplated.

The executor shall also submit such other documents or evidence as may be requested by the district director.

* * *

[T.D. 6296, 23 FR 4529, June 24, 1958; 25 FR 14021, Dec. 31, 1960 as amended by T.D. 8318, 39 FR 25452, July 11, 1974]

§ 20.2055–2 Transfers not exclusively for charitable purposes.

* * *

(e) **Limitation applicable to decedents dying after December 31, 1969**—(1) **Disallowance of deduction**—(i) **In general.** In the case of decedents dying after December 31, 1969, where an interest in property passes or has passed from the decedent for charitable purposes and an interest (other than an interest which is extinguished upon the decedent's death) in the same property passes or has passed from the decedent for private purposes (for less than an adequate and full consideration in money or money's worth) after October 9, 1969, no deduction is allowed under section 2055 for the value of the interest which passes or has passed for charitable purposes unless the interest in property is a deductible interest described in subparagraph (2) of this paragraph. The principles of section 2056 and the regulations thereunder shall apply for purposes of determining under this paragraph (e)(1)(i) whether an interest in property passes or has passed from the decedent. If however, as of the date of a decedent's death, a transfer for a private purpose is dependent upon the performance of some act on the happening of a precedent event in order that it might become effective, an interest in property will be considered to pass for a private purpose unless the possibility of occurrence of such act or event is so remote as to be negligible. The application of this paragraph (e)(1)(i) may be illustrated by the following examples, in each of which it is assumed that the interest in property which passes for private purposes does not pass for an adequate and full consideration in money or money's worth:

Example (1). In 1973, H creates a trust which is to pay the income of the trust to W for her life, the reversionary interest in the trust being retained by H. H predeceases W in 1975. H's will provide that the residue of his estate (including the reversionary interest in the trust) is to be transferred to charity. For purposes of this paragraph (e)(1)(i), interests in the same property have passed from H for charitable purposes and for private purposes.

Example (2). In 1973, H creates a trust which is to pay the income of the trust to W for her life and upon termination of the life estate to transfer the remainder to S. S predeceases W in 1975. S's will provides that the residue of his estate (including the remainder interest in the trust) is to be transferred to charity. For purposes of this paragraph (e)(1)(i), interests in the same property have not passed from H or S for charitable purposes and for private purposes.

Example (3). H transfers Blackacre to A by gift, reserving the right to the rentals of Blackacre for a term of 20 years. H dies within the 20-year term, bequeathing the right to the remaining rentals to charity. For purposes of this paragraph (e)(1)(i), the term "property" refers to Blackacre, and the right to rentals from Blackacre consist of an interest in Blackacre. An interest in Blackacre has passed from H for charitable purposes and for private purposes.

Example (4). H bequeaths the residue of his estate in trust for the benefit of A and a charity. An annuity of $5,000 a year is to be paid to charity for 20 years. Upon termination of the 20-year term the corpus is to be distributed to A if living. However, if A should die

during the 20-year term, the corpus is to be distributed to charity upon termination of the term. An interest in the residue of the estate has passed from H for charitable purposes. In addition, an interest in the residue of the estate has passed from H for private purposes, unless the possibility that A will survive the 20-year term is so remote as to be negligible.

Example (5). H bequeaths the residue of his estate in trust. Under the terms of the trust an annuity of $5,000 a year is to be paid to charity for 20 years. Upon termination of the term, the corpus is to pass to such of A's children and their issue as A may appoint. However, if A should die during the 20-year term without exercising the power of appointment, the corpus is to be distributed to charity upon termination of the term. Since the possible appointees include private persons, an interest in the residue of the estate is considered to have passed from H for private purposes.

Example (6). H devises Blackacre to X Charity. Under applicable local law, W, H's widow, is entitled to elect a dower interest in Blackacre. W elects to take her dower interest in Blackacre. For purposes of this paragraph (e)(1)(i), interests in the same property have passed from H for charitable purposes and for private purposes. If, however, W does not elect to take her dower interest in Blackacre, then, for purposes of this paragraph (e)(1)(i), interests in the same property have not passed from H for charitable purposes and for private purposes.

* * *

(2) Deductible interests. A deductible interest for purposes of subparagraph (1) of this paragraph is a charitable interest in property where—

(i) Undivided portion of decedent's entire interest. The charitable interest is an undivided portion, not in trust, of the decedent's entire interest in property. An undivided portion of a decedent's entire interest in property must consist of a fraction or percentage of each and every substantial interest or right owned by the decedent in such property and must extend over the entire term of the decedent's interest in such property and in other property into which such property is converted. For example, if the decedent transferred a life estate in an office building to his wife for her life and retained a reversionary interest in the office building, the devise by the decedent of one-half of that reversionary interest to charity while his wife is still alive will not be considered the transfer of a deductible interest; because an interest in the same property has already passed from the decedent for private purposes, the reversionary interest will not be considered the decedent's entire interest in the property. If, on the other hand, the decedent had been given a life estate in Blackacre for the life of his wife and the decedent had no other interest in Blackacre at any time during his life, the devise by the decedent of one-half of that life estate to charity would be considered the transfer of a deductible interest; because the life estate would be considered the decedent's entire interest in the property, the devise would be of an undivided portion of such entire interest. An undivided portion of a decedent's entire interest in the property includes an interest in property whereby the charity is given the right, as a tenant in common with the decedent's devisee or legatee, to possession, dominion, and control of the property for a portion of each year appropriate to its interest in such property. However, except as provided in paragraphs (e)(2)(ii), (iii), and (iv) of this section, for purposes of this subdivision a charitable contribution of an interest in property not in trust where the decedent transfers some specific rights to one party and transfers other substantial rights to another party will not be considered a contribution of an undivided portion of the decedent's entire interest in property. A bequest to charity made on or before December 17, 1980, of an open space easement in gross in perpetuity shall be considered the transfer to charity of an undivided portion of the decedent's entire interest in the property. For the definition of an open space easement in gross in perpetuity, see § 1.170A-7(b)(1)(ii) of this chapter (Income Tax Regulations).

(ii) **Remainder interest in personal residence.** The charitable interest is a remainder interest, not in trust, in a personal residence. Thus, for example, if the decedent devises to charity a remainder interest in a personal residence and bequeaths to his surviving spouse a life estate in such property, the value of the remainder interest is deductible under section 2055. For purposes of this subdivision, the term "personal residence" means any property which was used by the decedent as his personal residence even though it was not used as his principal residence. For example, a decedent's vacation home may be a personal residence for purposes of this subdivision. The term "personal residence" also includes stock owned by the decedent as a tenant-stockholder in a cooperative housing corporation (as those terms are defined in section 216(b)(1) and (2)) if the dwelling which the decedent was entitled to occupy as such stockholder was used by him as his personal residence.

(iii) **Remainder interest in a farm.** The charitable interest is a remainder interest, not in trust, in a farm. Thus, for example, if the decedent devises to charity a remainder interest in a farm and bequeaths to his daughter a life estate in such property, the value of the remainder interest is deductible under section 2055. For purposes of this subdivision, the term "farm" means any land used by the decedent or his tenant for the production of crops, fruits, or other agricultural products or for the sustenance of livestock. The term "livestock" includes cattle, hogs, horses, mules, donkeys, sheep, goats, captive furbearing animals, chickens, turkeys, pigeons, and other poultry. A farm includes the improvements thereon.

(iv) **Qualified conservation contribution.** The charitable interest is a qualified conservation contribution. For the definition of a qualified conservation contribution, see § 1.170A-14.

(v) **Charitable remainder trusts and pooled income funds.** The charitable interest is a remainder interest in a trust which is a charitable remainder annuity trust, as defined in section 664(d)(1) and § 1.664-2 of this chapter; a charitable remainder unitrust, as defined in section 664(d)(2) and (3) and § 1.664-3 of this chapter; or a pooled income fund, as defined in section 642(c)(5) and § 1.642(c)-5 of this chapter. The charitable organization to or for the use of which the remainder interest passes must meet the requirements of both section 2055(a) and section 642(c)(5)(A), section 664(d)(1)(C), or section 664(d)(2)(C), whichever applies. For example, the charitable organization to which the remainder interest in a charitable remainder annuity trust passes may not be a foreign corporation.

(vi) **Guaranteed annuity interest.** (a) The charitable interest is a guaranteed annuity interest, whether or not such interest is in trust. For purposes of this subdivision (vi), the term "guaranteed annuity interest" means the right pursuant to the instrument of transfer to receive a guaranteed annuity. A guaranteed annuity is an arrangement under which a determinable amount is paid periodically, but not less often than annually, for a specified term or for the life or lives of an individual or individuals, each of whom must be living at the date of death of the decedent and can be ascertained at such date. For example, the annuity may be paid for the life of A plus a term of years. An amount is determinable if the exact amount which must be paid under the conditions specified in the instrument of transfer can be ascertained as of the appropriate valuation date. For example, the amount to be paid may be a stated sum for a term, or for the life of an individual, at the expiration of which it may be changed by a specified amount, but it may not be redetermined by reference to a fluctuating index such as the cost of living index. In further illustration, the amount to be paid may be expressed in terms of a fraction or a percentage of the net fair market value, as finally determined for Federal estate tax purposes, of the residue of the estate on the appropriate valuation date, or it may be expressed in terms of a fraction or percentage of the cost of living index on the appropriate valuation date.

(b) A charitable interest is a guaranteed annuity interest only if it is a guaranteed annuity interest in every respect. For example, if the charitable interest is the right to receive from a trust each year a payment equal to the lesser of a sum certain or a fixed percentage of the net fair market value of the trust assets, determined annually, such interest is not a guaranteed annuity interest.

(c) Where a charitable interest in the form of a guaranteed annuity interest is not in trust, the interest will be considered a guaranteed annuity interest only if it is to be paid by an insurance company or by an organization regularly engaged in issuing annuity contracts.

(d) Where a charitable interest in the form of a guaranteed annuity interest is in trust, the governing instrument of the trust may provide that income of the trust which is in excess of the amount required to pay the guaranteed annuity interest shall be paid to or for the use of a charity. Nevertheless, the amount of the deduction under section 2055 shall be limited to the fair market value of the guaranteed annuity interest as determined under paragraph (f)(2)(iv) of this section.

(e) Where a charitable interest in the form of a guaranteed annuity interest is in trust and the present value, on the appropriate valuation date, of all the income interests for a charitable purpose exceeds 60 percent of the aggregate fair market value of all amounts in such trust (after the payment of estate taxes and all other liabilities), the charitable interest will not be considered a guaranteed annuity interest unless the governing instrument of the trust prohibits both the acquisition and the retention of assets which would give rise to a tax under section 4944 if the trustee had acquired such assets.

* * *

(**vii**) **Unitrust interest.** (a) The charitable interest is a unitrust interest, whether or not such interest is in trust. For purposes of this subdivision (vii), the term "unitrust interest" means the right pursuant to the instrument of transfer to receive payment, not less often than annually, of a fixed percentage of the net fair market value, determined annually, of the property which funds the unitrust interest. In computing the net fair market value of the property which funds the unitrust interest, all assets and liabilities shall be taken into account without regard to whether particular items are taken into account in determining the income from the property. The net fair market value of the property which funds the unitrust interest may be determined on any one date during the year or by taking the average of valuations made on more than one date during the year, provided that the same valuation date or dates and valuation methods are used each year. Where the charitable interest is a unitrust interest to be paid by a trust and the governing instrument of the trust does not specify the valuation date or dates, the trustee shall select such date or dates and shall indicate his selection on the first return on Form 1041 which the trust is required to file. Payments under a unitrust interest may be paid for a specified term or for the life or lives of an individual or individuals, each of whom must be living at the date of death of the decedent and can be ascertained at such date. For example, the unitrust interest may be paid for the life of A plus a term of years.

(b) A charitable interest is a unitrust interest only if it is a unitrust interest in every respect. For example, if the charitable interest is the right to receive from a trust each year a payment equal to the lesser of a sum certain or a fixed percentage of the net fair market value of the trust assets, determined annually, such interest is not a unitrust interest.

(c) Where a charitable interest in the form of a unitrust interest is not in trust, the interest will be considered a unitrust interest only if it is to be paid by an insurance company or by an organization regularly engaged in issuing interests otherwise meeting the requirements of a unitrust interest.

(d) Where a charitable interest in the form of a unitrust interest is in trust, the governing instrument of the trust may provide that income of the trust which is in excess of the amount required to pay the unitrust interest shall be paid to or for the use of a charity. Nevertheless, the amount of the deduction under section 2055 shall be limited to the fair market value of the unitrust interest as determined under paragraph (f)(2)(v) of this section.

[T.D. 6296, 23 FR 4529, June 24, 1958, as amended by T.D. 7238, 37 FR 28719, Dec. 29, 1972; T.D. 7318, 39 FR 25453, July 11, 1974, 39 FR 26154, July 17, 1974; T.D. 7340, 40 FR 1240, Jan. 7, 1975; T.D. 7955, 49 FR 19996, May 11, 1984; T.D. 7957, 49 FR 20811, May 17, 1984; T.D. 8069, 51 FR 1507, Jan. 14, 1986; 51 FR 32071, Sept. 9, 1986]

§ 20.2056(a)–1 Marital deduction; in general.

(a) A deduction is allowed under section 2056 from the gross estate of a decedent who was a citizen or resident of the United States at the time of his death for the value of any property interest which passed from the decedent to his surviving spouse, if the interest is a "deductible interest" as defined in § 20.2056(a)–2, and if the total of such interests does not exceed the percentage limitation set forth in §§ 20.2056(c)–1 and 20.2056(c)–2. This deduction is referred to as the "marital deduction". The marital deduction is generally not available if the decedent's gross estate consists exclusively of property held by the decedent and his surviving spouse as community property under the law of any State, Territory, or possession of the United States, or any foreign country. See § 20.2056(c)–2. Except as otherwise provided by a death tax convention with a foreign country, the marital deduction is not allowed in the case of an estate of a nonresident who was not a citizen of the United States at the time of his death. However, if the decedent was a citizen or resident, his estate is not deprived of the right to the marital deduction by the reason of the fact that his surviving spouse was neither a resident nor a citizen. For convenience, the surviving spouse is generally referred to in the feminine gender, but if the decedent was a woman the reference is to her surviving husband. * * *

* * *

[T.D. 6296, 23 FR 4529, June 24, 1958]

§ 20.2056(a)–2 Marital deduction; "deductible interests" and "nondeductible interests".

(a) Property interests which passed from a decedent to his surviving spouse fall within two general categories: (1) Those with respect to which the marital deduction is authorized, and (2) those with respect to which the marital deduction is not authorized. These categories are referred to in this section and other sections of the regulations under section 2056 as "deductible interests" and "nondeductible interests", respectively (see paragraph (b) of this section). Subject to the percentage limitation set forth in §§ 20.2056(c)–1 and 20.2056(c)–2, the marital deduction is equal in amount to the aggregate value of the "deductible interests".

(b) An interest passing to a decedent's surviving spouse is a "deductible interest" if it does not fall within one of the following categories of "nondeductible interests";

(1) Any property interest which passed from the decedent to his surviving spouse is a "nondeductible interest" to the extent it is not included in the decedent's gross estate.

(2) If a deduction is allowed under section 2053 (relating to deductions for expenses and indebtedness) by reason of the passing of a property interest from the decedent to his surviving spouse, such interest is, to the extent of the deduction under section 2053, a "nondeductible interest." Thus, a property interest which passed from the decedent to his surviving spouse in satisfaction of a deductible claim of the spouse against the estate is, to the extent of the claim, a "nondeductible interest" (see § 20.2056(b)–4). Similarly, amounts deducted under section 2053(a)(2) for commissioners allowed to the surviving spouse as executor are "nondeductible interests". As to the valuation, for the purpose of the marital deduction, of any property interest which passed from the decedent to his surviving spouse subject to a mortgage or other encumbrance, see § 20.2056(b)–4.

(3) If during settlement of the estate a loss deductible under section 2054 occurs with respect to a property interest, then that interest is, to the extent of the deductible loss, a "nondeductible interest" for the purpose of the marital deduction.

(4) A property interest passing to a decedent's surviving spouse which is a "terminable interest", as defined in § 20.2056(b)–1, is a "nondeductible interest" to the extent specified in that section.

[T.D. 6296, 23 FR 4529, June 24, 1958]

§ 20.2056(b)–1 Marital deduction; limitation in case of life estate or other "terminable interest".

(a) In general. Section 2056(b) provides that no marital deduction is allowed with respect to certain property interests, referred to generally as "terminable interests", passing from a decedent to his surviving spouse. The phrase "terminable interest" is defined in paragraph (b) of this section. However, the fact that an interest in property passing to a decedent's surviving spouse is a "terminable interest" makes it nondeductible only (1) under the circumstances described in paragraph (c) of this section, and (2) if it does not come within one of the exceptions referred to in paragraph (d) of this section.

(b) **"Terminable interests".** A "terminable interest" in property is an interest which will terminate or fail on the lapse of time or on the occurrence or the failure to occur of some contingency. Life estates, terms for years, annuities, patents, and copyrights are therefore terminable interests. However, a bond, note, or similar contractual obligation, the discharge of which would not have the effect of an annuity or a term for years, is not a terminable interest.

(c) **Nondeductible terminable interests.** (1) A property interest which constitutes a terminable interest, as defined in paragraph (b) of this section, is nondeductible if—

(i) Another interest in the same property passed from the decedent to some other person for less than an adequate and full consideration in money or money's worth, and

(ii) By reason of its passing, the other person or his heirs or assigns may possess or enjoy any part of the property after the termination or failure of the spouse's interest.

(2) Even though a property interest which constitutes a terminable interest is not nondeductible by reason of the rules stated in subparagraph (1) of this paragraph, such an interest is nondeductible if—

(i) The decedent has directed his executor or a trustee to acquire such an interest for the decedent's surviving spouse (see further paragraph (f) of this section), or

(ii) Such an interest passing to the decedent's surviving spouse may be satisfied out of a group of assets which includes a nondeductible interest (see further § 20.2056(b)-2). In this case, however, full nondeductibility may not result.

(d) **Exceptions.** A property interest passing to a decedent's surviving spouse is deductible (if it is not otherwise disqualified under § 20.2056(a)-2) even though it is a terminable interest, and even though an interest therein passed from the decedent to another person, if it is a terminable interest only because—

(1) It is conditioned on the spouse's surviving for a limited period, in the manner described in § 20.2056(b)-3;

(2) It is a right to income for life with a general power of appointment, meeting the requirements set forth in § 20.2056(b)-5; or

(3) It consists of life insurance or annuity payments held by the insurer with a general power of appointment in the spouse, meeting the requirements set forth in § 20.2056(b)-6.

(e) **Miscellaneous principles.** (1) In determining whether an interest passed from the decedent to some other person, it is immaterial whether interests in the same property passed to the decedent's spouse and another person at the same time, or under the same instrument.

(2) In determining whether an interest in the same property passed from the decedent both to his surviving spouse and to some other person, a distinction is to be drawn between "property", as such term is used in section 2056, and an "interest in property". The term "property" refers to the underlying property in which various interests exist; each such interest is not for this purpose to be considered as "property".

(3) Whether or not an interest is nondeductible because it is a terminable interest is to be determined by reference to the property interests which actually passed from the decedent. Subsequent conversions of the property are immaterial for this purpose. Thus, where a decedent bequeathed his estate to his wife for life with remainder to his children, the interest which passed to his wife is a nondeductible interest, even though the wife agrees with the children to take a fractional share of the estate in fee in lieu of the life interest in the whole, or sells the life estate for cash, or acquires the remainder interest of the children either by purchase or gift.

(4) The terms "passed from the decedent", "passed from the decedent to his surviving spouse", and "passed from the decedent to a person other than his surviving spouse" are defined in §§ 20.-2056(e)-1 through 20.2056(e)-3.

(f) **Direction to acquire a terminable interest.** No marital deduction is allowed with respect to a property interest which a decedent directs his executor or a trustee to covert after his death into a terminable interest for his surviving spouse. The marital deduction is not allowed even though no interest in the property subject to the terminable interest passes to another person and even though the interest would otherwise come within the exceptions described in §§ 20.2056(b)-5 and 20.-2056(b)-6 (relating to life estates and life insurance and annuity payments with powers of appointment). However, a general investment power, authorizing investments in both terminable interests and other property, is not a direction to invest in a terminable interest.

(g) **Examples.** The application of this section may be illustrated by the following examples, in each of which it is assumed that the property interest which passed from the decedent to a person other than his surviving spouse did not pass for an adequate and full consideration in money or money's worth:

Example (1). H (the decedent) devised real property to W (his surviving wife) for life, with remainder to A and his heirs. The interest which passed from H to W is a nondeductible interest since it will terminate upon her death and A (or his heirs or assigns) will thereafter possess or enjoy the property.

Example (2). H bequeathed the residue of his estate in trust for the benefit of W and A. The trust income is to be paid to W for life, and upon her death the corpus is to be distributed to A or his issue. However, if A should die without issue, leaving W surviving, the corpus is then to be distributed to W. The interest which passed from H to W is a nondeductible interest since it will terminate in the event of her death if A or his issue survive, and A or his issue will thereafter possess or enjoy the property.

Example (3). H during his lifetime purchased an annuity contract providing for payments to himself for life and then to W for life if she should survive him. Upon the death of the survivor of H and W, the excess, if any, of the cost of the contract over the annuity payments theretofore made was to be refunded to A. The interest which passed from H to W is a nondeductible interest since A may possess or enjoy a part of the property following the termination of the interest of W. If, however, the contract provided for no refund upon the death of the survivor of H and W, or provided that any refund was to go to the estate of the survivor, then the interest which passed from H to W is (to the extent it is included in H's gross estate) a deductible interest.

Example (4). H, in contemplation of death, transferred a residence to A for life with remainder to W provided W survives A, but if W predeceases A, the property is to pass to B and his heirs. If it is assumed that H died during A's lifetime, and the value of the residence was included in determining the value of his gross estate, the interest which passed from H to W is a nondeductible interest since it will terminate if W predeceases A and the property will thereafter be possessed or enjoyed by B (or his heirs or assigns). This result is not affected by B's assignment of his interest during H's lifetime, whether made in favor of W or another person, since the term "assigns" (as used in section 2056(b)(1)(B)) includes such an assignee. However, if it is assumed that A predeceased H, the interest of B in the property was extinguished, and, viewed as of the time of the subsequent

death of H, the interest which passed from him to W is the entire interest in the property and, therefore, a deductible interest.

Example (5). H transferred real property to A by gift (reserving the right to the rentals) of the property for a term of 20 years. H died within the 20-year term, bequeathing the right to the remaining rentals to a trust for the benefit of W. The terms of the trust satisfy the five conditions stated in § 20.2056(b)-5, so that the property interest which passed in trust is considered to have passed from H to W. However, the interest is a nondeductible interest since it will terminate upon the expiration of the term and A will thereafter possess or enjoy the property.

Example (6). H bequeathed a patent to W and A as tenants in common. In this case, the interest of W will terminate upon the expiration of the term of the patent, but possession or enjoyment of the property by A must necessarily cease at the same time. Therefore, since A's possession or enjoyment cannot outlast the termination of W's interest, the latter is a deductible interest.

Example (7). A decedent bequeathed $100,000 to his wife, subject to a direction to his executor to use the bequest for the purchase of an annuity for the wife. The bequest is a nondeductible interest.

Example (8). Assume that pursuant to local law an allowance for support is payable to the decedent's surviving spouse during the period of the administration of the decedent's estate, but that upon her death or remarriage during such period her right to any further allowance will terminate. Assume further that the surviving spouse is sole beneficiary of the decedent's estate. Under such circumstances, the allowance constitutes a deductible interest since any part of the allowance not receivable by the surviving spouse during her lifetime will pass to her estate under the terms of the decedent's will. If, in this example, the decedent bequeathed only one-third of his residuary estate to his surviving spouse, then two-thirds of the allowance for support would constitute a nondeductible terminable interest.

[T.D. 6296, 23 FR 4529, June 24, 1958]

§ 20.2056(b)-2 Marital deduction; interest in unidentified assets.

(a) Section 2056(b)(2) provides that if an interest passing to a decedent's surviving spouse may be satisfied out of assets (or their proceeds) which include a particular asset that would be a nondeductible interest if it passed from the decedent to his spouse, the value of the interest passing to the spouse is reduced, for the purpose of the marital deduction, by the value of the particular asset.

(b) In order for section 2056(b)(2) to apply, two circumstances must coexist, as follows:

(1) The property interest which passed from the decedent to his surviving spouse must be payable out of a group of assets included in the gross estate. Examples of property interests payable out of a

group of assets are a general legacy, a bequest of the residue of the decedent's estate or of a proportion of the residue, and a right to a share of the corpus of a trust upon its termination.

(2) The group of assets out of which the property interest is payable must include one or more particular assets which, if passing specifically to the surviving spouse, would be nondeductible interests. Therefore, section 2056(b)(2) is not applicable merely because the group of assets includes a terminable interest, but would only be applicable if the terminable interest were nondeductible under the provisions of § 20.2056(b)–1.

(c) If both of the circumstances set forth in paragraph (b) of this section are present, the property interest payable out of the group of assets is (except as to any excess of its value over the aggregate value of the particular asset or assets which would not be deductible if passing specifically to the surviving spouse) a nondeductible interest.

(d) The application of this section may be illustrated by the following example:

Example. A decedent bequeathed one-third of the residue of his estate to his wife. The property passing under the decedent's will included a right to the rentals of an office building for a term of years, reserved by the decedent under a deed of the building by way of gift to his son. The decedent did not make a specific bequest of the right to such rentals. Such right, if passing specifically to the wife, would be a nondeductible interest (see example (5) of paragraph (g) of § 20.2056(b)–1). It is assumed that the value of the bequest of one-third of the residue of the estate to the wife was $85,000, and that the right to the rentals was included in the gross estate at a value of $60,000. If the decedent's executor had the right under the decedent's will or local law to assign the entire lease in satisfaction of the bequest, the bequest is a nondeductible interest to the extent of $60,000. If the executor could only assign a one-third interest in the lease in satisfaction of the bequest, the bequest is a nondeductible interest to the extent of $20,000. If the decedent's will provided that his wife's bequest could not be satisfied with a nondeductible interest, the entire bequest is a deductible interest. If, in this example, the asset in question had been foreign real estate not included in the decedent's gross estate, the results would be the same.

[T.D. 6296, 23 FR 4529, June 24, 1958]

§ 20.2056(b)–3 Marital deduction; interest of spouse conditioned on survival for limited period.

(a) **In general.** Generally, no marital deduction is allowable if the interest passing to the surviving spouse is a terminable interest as defined in paragraph (b) of § 20.2056(b)(1). However, section 2056(b)(3) provides an exception to this rule so as to allow a deduction if (1) the only condition under which it will terminate is the death of the surviving spouse within 6 months after the decedent's death, or her death as a result of a common disaster which also resulted in the decedent's death, and (2) the condition does not in fact occur.

(b) **Six months' survival.** If the only condition which will cause the interest taken by the surviving spouse to terminate is the death of the surviving spouse and the condition is of such nature that it can occur only within 6 months following the decedent's death, the exception provided by section 2056(b)(3) will apply, provided the condition does not in fact occur. However, if the condition (unless it relates to death as a result of a common disaster) is one which may occur either within the 6-month period or thereafter, the exception provided by section 2056(b)(3) will not apply.

(c) **Common disaster.** If a property interest passed from the decedent to his surviving spouse subject to the condition that she does not die as a result of a common disaster which also resulted in the decedent's death, the exception provided by section 2056(b)(3) will not be applied in the final audit of the return if there is still a possibility that the surviving spouse may be deprived of the property interest by operation of the common disaster provision as given effect by the local law.

(d) **Examples.** The application of this section may be illustrated by the following examples:

Example (1). A decedent bequeathed his entire estate to his spouse on condition that she survive him by 6 months. In the event his spouse failed to survive him by 6 months, his estate was to go to his niece and her heirs. The decedent was survived by his spouse. It will be observed that, as of the time of the decedent's death, it was possible that the niece would, by reason of the interest which passed to her from the decedent possess or enjoy the estate after the termination of the interest which passed to the spouse. Hence, under the general rule set forth in § 20.2056(b)–1, the interest which passed to the spouse would be regarded as a nondeductible interest. If the surviving spouse in fact died within 6 months after the decedent's death, that general rule is to be applied, and the interest which passed to the spouse is a nondeductible interest. However, if the spouse in fact survived the decedent by 6 months, thus extinguishing the interest of the niece, the case comes within the exception provided by section 2056(b)(3), and the interest which passed to the spouse is a deductible interest. (It is assumed for the purpose of this example that no other factor which would cause the interest to be nondeductible is present.)

Example (2). The facts are the same as in example (1) except that the will provided that the estate was to go to the niece either in case the decedent and his spouse should both die as a result of a common disaster, or in case the spouse should fail to survive the decedent by 3 months. It is assumed that the decedent was survived by his spouse. In this example, the interest which passed from the decedent to his surviving spouse is to be regarded as a nondeductible interest if the surviving spouse in fact died either within 3 months after the decedent's death or as a result of a common disaster which also resulted in the decedent's death. However, if the spouse in fact survived the decedent by 3 months, and did not thereafter die as a result of a common disaster which also resulted in the decedent's death, the exception provided under section 2056(b)(3) will apply and the interest will be deductible.

Example (3). The facts are the same as in example (1) except that the will provided that the estate was to go to the niece if the decedent and his spouse should both die as a result of a common disaster and if the spouse failed to survive the decedent by 3 months. If the spouse in fact survived the decedent by 3 months, the interest of the niece is extinguished, and the interest passing to the spouse is a deductible interest.

Example (4). A decedent devised and bequeathed his residuary estate to his wife if she was living on the date of distribution of his estate. The devise and bequest is a nondeductible interest even though distribution took place within 6 months after the decedent's death and the surviving spouse in fact survived the date of distribution.

[T.D. 6296, 23 FR 4529, June 24, 1958]

§ 20.2056(b)–4 Marital deduction; valuation of interest passing to surviving spouse.

(a) In general. The value, for the purpose of the marital deduction, of any deductible interest which passed from the decedent to his surviving spouse is to be determined as of the date of the decedent's death, except that if the executor elects the alternate valuation method under section 2032 the valuation is to be determined as of the date of the decedent's death but with the adjustment described in paragraph (a)(3) of § 20.2032–1. The marital deduction may be taken only with respect to the net value of any deductible interest which passed from the decedent to his surviving spouse, the same principles being applicable as if the amount of a gift to the spouse were being determined. In determining the value of the interest in property passing to the spouse account must be taken of the effect of any material limitations upon her right to income from the property. An example of a case in which this rule may be applied is a bequest of property in trust for the benefit of the decedent's spouse but the income from the property from the date of the decedent's death until distribution of the property to the trustee is to be used to pay expenses incurred in the administration of the estate.

(b) Property interest subject to an encumbrance or obligation. If a property interest passed from the decedent to his surviving spouse subject to a mortgage or other encumbrance, or if an obligation is imposed upon the surviving spouse by the decedent in connection with the passing of a property interest, the value of the property interest is to be reduced by the amount of the mortgage, other encumbrance, or obligation. However, if under the terms of the decedent's will or under local law the executor is required to discharge, out of other assets of the decedent's estate, a mortgage or other encumbrance on property passing from the decedent to his surviving spouse, or is required to reimburse the surviving spouse for the amount of the mortgage or other encumbrance, the payment or reimbursement constitutes an additional interest passing to the surviving spouse. The passing of a property interest subject to the imposition of an obligation by the decedent does not include a bequest, devise, or transfer in lieu of dower, curtesy, or of a statutory estate created in lieu of dower or curtesy, or of other marital rights in the decedent's property or estate. The passing of a property interest subject to the imposition of an obligation by the decedent does, however, include a bequest, etc., in lieu of the interest of his surviving spouse under community property laws unless such interest was, immediately prior to the decedent's death, a mere expectancy. (As to the circumstances under which the interest of the surviving spouse is regarded as a mere expectancy, see § 20.2056(c)–2.) The following examples are illustrative of property interests which passed from the decedent to his surviving spouse subject to the imposition of an obligation by the decedent:

Example (1). A decedent devised a residence valued at $25,000 to his wife, with a direction that she pay $5,000 to his sister. For the purpose of the marital deduction, the value of the property interest passing to the wife is only $20,000.

Example (2). A decedent devised real property to his wife in satisfaction of a debt owing to her. The debt is a deductible claim under section 2053. Since the wife is obligated to relinquish the claim as a condition to acceptance of the devise, the value of the devise is, for the purpose of the marital deduction, to be reduced by the amount of the claim.

Example (3). A decedent bequeathed certain securities to his wife in lieu of her interest in property held by them as community property under the law of the State of their residence. The wife elected to relinquish her community property interest and to take the bequest. For the purpose of the marital deduction, the value of the bequest is to be reduced by the value of the community property interest relinquished by the wife.

(c) **Effect of death taxes.** (1) In the determination of the value of any property interest which passed from the decedent to his surviving spouse, there must be taken into account the effect which the Federal estate tax, or any estate, succession, legacy, or inheritance tax, has upon the net value to the surviving spouse of the property interest.

(2) For example, assume that the only bequest to the surviving spouse is $100,000 and the spouse is required to pay a State inheritance tax in the amount of $1,500. If no other death taxes affect the net value of the bequest, the value, for the purpose of the marital deduction, is $98,500.

(3) As another example, assume that a decedent devised real property to his wife having a value for Federal estate tax purposes of $100,000 and also bequeathed to her a nondeductible interest for life under a trust. The State of residence valued the real property at $90,000 and the life interest at $30,000, and imposed an inheritance tax (at graduated rates) of $4,800 with respect to the two interests. If it is assumed that the inheritance tax on the devise is required to be paid by the wife, the amount of tax to be ascribed to the devise is:

$$(90{,}000 \div 120{,}000) \times \$4{,}800 = \$3{,}600.$$

Accordingly, if no other death taxes affect the net value of the bequest, the value, for the purpose of the marital deduction, is $100,000 less $3,600, or $96,400.

(4) If the decedent bequeaths his residuary estate, or a portion of it, to his surviving spouse, and his will contains a direction that all death taxes shall be payable out of the residuary estate, the value of the bequest, for the purpose of the marital deduction, is based upon the amount of the residue as reduced pursuant to such direction, if the residuary estate, or a portion of it, is bequeathed to the surviving spouse, and by the local law the Federal estate tax is payable out of the residuary estate, the value of the bequest, for the purpose of the marital deduction, may not exceed its value as reduced by the Federal estate tax. Methods of computing the deduction, under such circumstances, are set forth in supplemental instructions to the estate tax return.

(d) **Remainder interests.** If the income from property is made payable to another individual for life, or for a term of years, with remainder absolutely to the surviving spouse or to her estate, the marital deduction is based upon the present value of the remainder. * * *

[T.D. 6296, 23 FR 4529, June 24, 1958]

§ 20.2056(b)–5 **Marital deduction; life estate with power of appointment in surviving spouse.**

(a) **In general.** Section 2056(b)(5) provides that if an interest in property passes from the decedent to his surviving spouse (whether or not in trust) and the spouse is entitled for life to all the income from the entire interest or all the income from a specific portion of the entire interest, with a power in her to appoint the entire interest or the specific portion, the interest which passes to her is a deductible interest, to the extent that it satisfies all five of the conditions set forth below (see paragraph (b) of this section if one or more of the conditions is satisfied as to only a portion of the interest):

(1) The surviving spouse must be entitled for life to all of the income from the entire interest or a specific portion of the entire interest, or to a specific portion of all the income from the entire interest.

(2) The income payable to the surviving spouse must be payable annually or at more frequent intervals.

(3) The surviving spouse must have the power to appoint the entire interest or the specific portion to either herself or her estate.

(4) The power in the surviving spouse must be exercisable by her alone and (whether exercisable by will or during life) must be exercisable in all events.

(5) The entire interest or the specific portion must not be subject to a power in any other person to appoint any part to any person other than the surviving spouse.

(b) **Specific portion; deductible amount.** If either the right to income or the power of appointment passing to the surviving spouse pertains only to a specific portion of a property interest passing from the decedent, the marital deduction is allowed only to the extent that the rights in the surviving spouse meet all of the five conditions described in paragraph (a) of this section. While the rights over the income and the power must coexist as to the same interest in property, it is not necessary that the rights over the income or the power as to such interest be in the same proportion. However, if the rights over income meeting the required conditions set forth in paragraph (a)(1) and (2) of the section extend over a smaller share of the property interest than the share with respect to which the power of appointment requirements set forth in paragraph (a)(3) through (5) of this section are satisfied, the deductible interest is limited to the smaller share. Correspondingly, if a power of appointment meeting all the requirements extends to a smaller portion of the property interest than the portion over which the income rights pertain, the deductible interest cannot exceed the value of the portion to which such power of appointment applies. Thus, if the decedent leaves to his surviving spouse the right to receive annually all of the income from a particular property interest and a power of appointment meeting the specifications prescribed in paragraph (a)(3) through (5) of this section as to only one-half of the property interest, then only one-half of the property interest is treated as a deductible interest. Correspondingly, if the income interest of the spouse satisfying the requirements extends to only one-fourth of the property interest and a testamentary power of appointment satisfying the requirements extends to all of the property interest, then only one-fourth of the interest in the spouse qualifies as a deductible interest. Further, if the surviving spouse has no right to income from a specific portion of a property interest but a testamentary power of appointment which meets the necessary conditions over the entire interest, then none of the interest qualifies for the deduction. In addition, if, from the time of the decedent's death, the surviving spouse has a power of appointment meeting all of the required conditions over three-fourths of the entire property interest and the prescribed income rights over the entire interest, but with a power in another person to appoint one-half of the entire interest, the value of the interest in the surviving spouse over only one-half of the property interest will qualify as a deductible interest.

(c) **Definition of "specific portion".** A partial interest in property is not treated as a specific portion of the entire interest unless the rights of the surviving spouse in income and as to the power constitute a fractional or percentile share of a property interest so that such interest or share in the surviving spouse reflects its proportionate share of the increment or decline in the whole of the property interest to which the income rights and the power relate. Thus, if the right of the spouse to income and the power extend to one-half or a specified percentage of the property, or the equivalent, the interest is considered as a specific portion. On the other hand, if the annual income of the spouse is limited to a specific sum, or if she

has a power to appoint only a specific sum out of a larger fund, the interest is not a deductible interest. Even though the rights in the surviving spouse may not be expressed in terms of a definite fraction or percentage, a deduction may be allowable if it is shown that the effect of local law is to give the spouse rights which are identical to those she would have acquired if the size of the share had been expressed in terms of a definite fraction or percentage. The following examples illustrate the application of this and the preceding paragraphs of this section:

Example (1). The decedent transferred to a trustee 500 identical shares of X Company stock. He provided that during the lifetime of the surviving spouse the trustee should pay her annually one-half of the trust income or $6,000, whichever is the larger. The spouse was also given a general power of appointment, exercisable by her last will over the sum of $160,000 or over three-fourths of the trust corpus, whichever should be of larger value. Since there is no certainty that the trust income will not vary from year to year, for purposes of paragraphs (a) and (b) of this section, an annual payment of a specified sum, such as the $6,000 provided for in this case, is not considered as representing the income from a definite fraction or a specific portion of the entire interest if that were the extent of the spouse's interest. However, since the spouse is to receive annually at least one-half of the trust income, she will, for purposes of paragraphs (a) and (b) of this section, be considered as receiving all of the income from one-half of the entire interest in the stock. Inasmuch as there is no certainty that the value of the stock will be the same on the date of the surviving spouse's death as it was on the date of the decedent's death, for purposes of paragraphs (a) and (b) of this section, a specified sum such as the $160,000 provided for in this case, is not considered to be a definite fraction of the entire interest. However, since the surviving spouse has a general power of appointment over at least three-fourths of the trust corpus, she is considered as having a general power of appointment over three-fourths of the entire interest in the stock.

Example (2). The decedent bequeathed to a trustee an office building and 250 identical shares of Y Company stock. He provided that during the lifetime of the surviving spouse of the trustee should pay her annually three-fourths of the trust income. The spouse was given a general power of appointment, exercisable by will, over the office building and 100 shares of the stock. By the terms of the decedent's will the spouse is given all the income from a definite fraction of the entire interest in the office building and in the stock. She also has a general power of appointment over the entire interest in the office building. However, since the amount of property represented by a single share of stock would be altered if the corporation split its stock, issued stock dividends, made a distribution of capital, etc., a power to appoint 100 shares at the time of the surviving spouse's death is not the same necessarily as a power to appoint $100/250$ of the entire interest which the 250 shares represented on the date of the decedent's death. If it is shown in this case that the effect of local law is to give the spouse a general power to appoint not only the 100 shares designated by the decedent but also $^{100}/_{250}$ of any shares or amounts which are distributed by the corporation and included in the corpus, the requirements of this paragraph will be satisfied and the surviving spouse will be considered as having a general power to appoint $^{100}/_{250}$ of the entire interest in the 250 shares.

(d) **Definition of "entire interest".** Since a marital deduction is allowed for each qualifying separate interest in property passing from the decedent to his surviving spouse (subject to the percentage limitation contained in §§ 20.2056(c)–1 and 20.2056(c)–2 concerning the aggregate amount of the deductions), for purposes of paragraphs (a) and (b) of this section, each property interest with respect to which the surviving spouse received some rights is considered separately in determining whether her rights extend to the entire interest or to a specific portion of the entire interest. A property interest which consists of several identical units of property (such as a block of 250 shares of stock, whether the ownership is evidenced by one or several certificates) is considered one property interest, unless certain of the units are to be segregated and accorded different treatment, in which case each segregated group of items is considered a separate property interest. The bequest of a specified sum of money constitutes the bequest of a separate property interest if immediately following distribution by the executor and thenceforth it, and the investments made with it, must be so segregated or accounted for as to permit its identification as a separate item of property. The application of this paragraph may be illustrated by the following examples:

Example (1). The decedent transferred to a trustee three adjoining farms, Blackacre, Whiteacre, and Greenacre. His will provided that during the lifetime of the surviving spouse the trustee should pay her all of the income from the trust. Upon her death, all of Blackacre, a one-half interest in Whiteacre, and a one-third interest in Greenacre were to be distributed to the person or persons appointed by her in her will. The surviving spouse is considered as being entitled to all of the income from the entire interest in Blackacre, all of the income from the entire interest in Whiteacre, and all of the income from the entire interest in Greenacre. She also is considered as having a power of appointment over the entire interest in Blackacre, over one-half of the entire interest in Whiteacre, and over one-third of the entire interest in Greenacre.

Example (2). The decedent bequeathed $250,000 to C, as trustee. C is to invest the money and pay all of the income from the investments to W, the decedent's surviving spouse, annually. W was given a general power, exercisable by will, to appoint one-half of the corpus of the trust. Here, immediately following distribution by the executor, the $250,000 will be sufficiently segregated

to permit its identification as a separate item, and the $250,000 will constitute an entire property interest. Therefore, W has a right to income and a power of appointment such that one-half of the entire interest is a deductible interest.

Example (3). The decedent bequeathed 100 shares of Z corporation stock to D, as trustee. W, the decedent's surviving spouse, is to receive all of the income of the trust annually and is given a general power, exercisable by will, to appoint out of the trust corpus the sum of $25,000. In this case the $25,000 is not, immediately following distribution, sufficiently segregated to permit its identification as a separate item of property in which the surviving spouse has the entire interest. Therefore, the $25,000 does not constitute the entire interest in a property for the purpose of paragraphs (a) and (b) of this section.

(e) **Application of local law.** In determining whether or not the conditions set forth in paragraph (a)(1) through (5) of this section are satisfied by the instrument of transfer, regard is to be had to the applicable provisions of the law of the jurisdiction under which the interest passes and, if the transfer is in trust, the applicable provisions of the law governing the administration of the trust. For example, silence of a trust instrument as to the frequency of payment will not be regarded as a failure to satisfy the condition set forth in paragraph (a)(2) of this section that income must be payable to the surviving spouse annually or more frequently unless the applicable law permits payment to be made less frequently than annually. The principles outlined in this paragraph and paragraphs (f) and (g) of this section which are applied in determining whether transfers in trust meet such conditions are equally applicable in ascertaining whether, in the case of interests not in trust, the surviving spouse has the equivalent in rights over income and over the property.

(f) **Right to income.** (1) If an interest is transferred in trust, the surviving spouse is "entitled for life to all of the income from the entire interest or a specific portion of the entire interest", for the purpose of the condition set forth in paragraph (a)(1) of this section, if the effect of the trust is to give her substantially that degree of beneficial enjoyment of the trust property during her life which the principles of the law of trusts accord to a person who is unqualifiedly designated as the life beneficiary of a trust. Such degree of enjoyment is given only if it was the decedent's intention, as manifested by the terms of the trust instrument and the surrounding circumstances, that the trust should produce for the surviving spouse during her life such an income, or that the spouse should have such use of the trust property as is consistent with the value of the trust corpus and with its preservation. The designation of the spouse as sole income beneficiary for life of the entire interest or a specific portion of the entire interest will be sufficient to qualify the trust unless the terms of the trust and the surrounding circumstances considered as a whole evidence an intention to deprive the spouse of the requisite degree of enjoyment. In determining whether a trust evidences that intention, the treatment required or permitted with respect to individual items must be considered in relation to the entire system provided for the administration of the trust.

(2) If the over-all effect of a trust is to give to the surviving spouse such enforceable rights as will preserve to her the requisite degree of enjoyment, it is immaterial whether that result is effected by rules specifically stated in the trust instrument, or, in their absence, by the rules for the management of the trust property and the allocation of receipts and expenditures supplied by the State law. For example, a provision in the trust instrument for amortization of bond premium by appropriate periodic charges to interest will not disqualify the interest passing in trust even though there is no State law specifically authorizing amortization, or there is a State law denying amortization which is applicable only in the absence of such a provision in the trust instrument.

(3) In the case of a trust, the rules to be applied by the trustee in allocation of receipts and expenses between income and corpus must be considered in relation to the nature and expected productivity of the assets passing in trust, the nature and frequency of occurrence of the expected receipts, and any provisions as to change in the form of investments. If it is evident from the nature of the trust assets and the rules provided for management of the trust that the allocation to income of such receipts as rents, ordinary cash dividends, and interest will give to the spouse the substantial enjoyment during life required by the statute, provisions that such receipts as stock dividends and proceeds from the conversion of trust assets shall be treated as corpus will not disqualify the interest passing in trust. Similarly, provision for a depletion charge against income in the case of trust assets which are subject to depletion will not disqualify the interest passing in trust, unless the effect is to deprive the spouse of the requisite beneficial enjoyment. The same principle is applicable in the case of depreciation, trustees' commissions, and other charges.

(4) Provisions granting administrative powers to the trustee will not have the effect of disqualifying an interest passing in trust unless the grant of powers evidences the intention to deprive the surviving spouse of the beneficial enjoyment required by the statute. Such an intention will not be considered to exist if the entire terms of the instrument are such that the local courts will impose reasonable limitations upon the exercise of the powers. Among the powers which if subject to reasonable limitations will not disqualify the interest passing in trust are the power to determine the allocation or apportionment of receipts and disbursements between income and corpus, the power to apply the income or corpus for the benefit of the spouse, and the power to retain the assets passing to the trust. For example, a power to retain trust assets which consist substantially of unproductive property will not disqualify the interest if the applicable rules for the administration of the trust require, or permit the spouse to require, that the trustee either make the property productive or convert it within a reasonable time. Nor will such a power disqualify the interest if the applicable rules for administration of the trust require the trustee to use the degree of judgment and care in the exercise of the power which a prudent man would use if he were owner of the trust assets. Further, a power to retain a residence or other property for the personal use of the spouse will not disqualify the interest passing in trust.

(5) An interest passing in trust will not satisfy the condition set forth in paragraph (a)(1) of this section that the surviving spouse be entitled to all the income if the primary purpose of the trust is to safeguard property without providing the spouse with the required beneficial enjoyment. Such trusts include not only trusts which expressly provide for the accumulation of the income but also trusts which indirectly accomplish a similar purpose. For example, assume that the corpus of a trust consists substantially of property which is not likely to be income producing during the life of the surviving spouse and that the spouse cannot compel the trustee to convert or otherwise deal with the property as described in subparagraph (4) of this paragraph. An interest passing to such a trust will not qualify unless the applicable rules for the administration require, or permit the spouse to require, that the trustee provide the required beneficial enjoyment such as by payments to the spouse out of other assets of the trust.

(6) If a trust is created during the decedent's life, it is immaterial whether or not the interest passing in trust satisfied the conditions set forth in paragraph (a)(1) through (5) of this section prior to the decedent's death. If a trust may be terminated during the life of the surviving spouse, under her exercise of a power of appointment or by distribution of the corpus to her, the interest passing in trust satisfies the condition set forth in paragraph (a)(1) of this section (that the spouse be entitled to all the income) if she (i) is entitled to the income until the trust terminates, or (ii) has the right, exercisable in all events, to have the corpus distributed to her at any time during her life.

(7) An interest passing in trust fails to satisfy the condition set forth in paragraph (a)(1) of this section, that the spouse be entitled to all the income, to the extent that the income is required to be accumulated in whole or in part or may be accumulated in the discretion of any person other than the surviving spouse; to the extent that the consent of any person other than the surviving spouse is required as a condition precedent to distribution of the income; or to the extent that any person other than the surviving spouse has the power to alter the terms of the trust so as to deprive her of her right to the income. An interest passing in trust will not fail to satisfy the condition that the spouse be entitled to all the income merely because its terms provide that the right of the surviving spouse to the income shall not be subject to assignment, alienation, pledge, attachment or claims of creditors.

(8) In the case of an interest passing in trust, the terms "entitled for life" and "payable annually or at more frequent intervals," as used in the conditions set forth in paragraph (a)(1) and (2) of this section, require that under the terms of the trust the income referred to must be currently (at least annually; see paragraph (e) of this section) distributable to the spouse or that she must have such command over the income that it is virtually hers. Thus, the conditions in paragraph (a)(1) and (2) of this section are satisfied in this respect if, under the terms of the trust instrument, the spouse has the right exercisable annually (or more frequently) to require distribution to herself of the trust income, and otherwise the trust income is to be accumulated and added to corpus. Similarly, as respects the income for the period between the last distribution date and the date of the spouse's death, it is sufficient if that income is subject to the spouse's power to appoint. Thus, if the trust instrument provides that income accrued or undistributed on the date of the spouse's death is to be disposed of as if it had been received after her death, and if the spouse has a power of appointment over the trust corpus, the power necessarily extends to the undistributed income.

(9) An interest is not to be regarded as failing to satisfy the conditions set forth in paragraph (a)(1) and (2) of this section (that the spouse be entitled to all the income and that it be payable annually or more frequently) merely because the spouse is not entitled to the income from estate assets for the period before distribution of those assets by the executor, unless the executor is, by the decedent's will, authorized or directed to delay distribution beyond the period reasonably required for administration of the decedent's estate. As to the valuation of the property interest passing to the spouse in trust where the right to income is expressly postponed, see § 20.2056(b)–4.

(g) **Power of appointment in surviving spouse.** (1) The conditions set forth in paragraph (a)(3) and (4) of this section, that is, that the surviving spouse must have a power of appointment exercisable in favor of herself or her estate and exercisable alone and in all events are not met unless the power of the surviving spouse to appoint the entire interest or a specific portion of it falls within one of the following categories:

(i) A power so to appoint fully exercisable in her own favor at any time following the decedent's death (as, for example, an unlimited power to invade); or

(ii) A power so to appoint exercisable in favor of her estate. Such a power, if exercisable during life, must be fully exercisable at any time during life, or, if exercisable by will, must be fully exercisable irrespective of the time of her death (subject in either case to the provisions of § 20.2053(b)–3, relating to interests conditioned on survival for a limited period); or

(iii) A combination of the powers described under subdivisions (i) and (ii) of this subparagraph. For example, the surviving spouse may, until she attains the age of 50 years, have a power to appoint to herself and thereafter have a power to appoint to her estate. However, the condition that the spouse's power must be exercisable in all events is not satisfied unless irrespective of when the surviving spouse may die the entire interest or a specific portion of it will at the time of her death be subject to one power or the other (subject to the exception in § 20.2053(b)-3, relating to interests contingent on survival for a limited period).

(2) The power of the surviving spouse must be a power to appoint the entire interest or a specific portion of it as unqualified owner (and free of the trust if a trust is involved, or free of the joint tenancy if a joint tenancy is involved) or to appoint the entire interest or a specific portion of it as a part of her estate (and free of the trust if a trust is involved), that is, in effect, to dispose of it to whomsoever she pleases. Thus, if the decedent devised property to a son and the surviving spouse as joint tenants with right of survivorship and under local law the surviving spouse has a power of severance exercisable without consent of the other joint tenant, and by exercising this power could acquire a one-half interest in the property as a tenant in common, her power of severance will satisfy the conditions set forth in paragraph (a)(3) of this section that she have a power of appointment in favor of herself or her estate. However, if the surviving spouse entered into a binding agreement with the decedent to exercise the power only in favor of their issue, that condition is not met. An interest passing in trust will not be regarded as failing to satisfy the condition merely because takers in default of the surviving spouse's exercise of the power are designated by the decedent. The decedent may provide that, in default of exercise of the power, the trust shall continue for an additional period.

(3) A power is not considered to be a power exercisable by a surviving spouse alone and in all events as required by paragraph (a)(4) of this section if the exercise of the power in the surviving spouse to appoint the entire interest or a specific portion of it to herself or to her estate requires the joinder or consent of any other person. The power is not "exercisable in all events", if it can be terminated during the life of the surviving spouse by any event other than her complete exercise or release of it. Further, a power is not "exercisable in all events" if it may be exercised for a limited purpose only. For example, a power which is not exercisable in the event of the spouse's remarriage is not exercisable in all events. Likewise, if there are any restrictions, either by the terms of the instrument or under applicable local law, on the exercise of a power to consume property (whether or not held in trust) for the benefit of the spouse, the power is not exercisable in all events. Thus, if a power of invasion is exercisable only for the spouse's support, or only for her limited use, the

power is not exercisable in all events. In order for a power of invasion to be exercisable in all events, the surviving spouse must have the unrestricted power exercisable at any time during her life to use all or any part of the property subject to the power, and to dispose of it in any manner, including the power to dispose of it by gift (whether or not she has power to dispose of it by will).

(4) The power in the surviving spouse is exercisable in all events only if it exists immediately following the decedent's death. For example, if the power given to the surviving spouse is exercisable during life, but cannot be effectively exercised before distribution of the assets by the executor, the power is not exercisable in all events. Similarly, if the power is exercisable by will, but cannot be effectively exercised in the event the surviving spouse dies before distribution of the assets by the executor, the power is not exercisable in all events. However, an interest will not be disqualified by the mere fact that, in the event the power is exercised during administration of the estate, distribution of the property to the appointee will be delayed for the period of administration. If the power is in existence at all times following the decedent's death, limitations of a formal nature will not disqualify an interest. Examples of formal limitations on a power exercisable during life are requirements that an exercise must be in a particular form, that it must be filed with a trustee during the spouse's life, that reasonable notice must be given, or that reasonable intervals must elapse between successive partial exercises. Examples of formal limitations on a power exercisable by will are that it must be exercised by a will executed by the surviving spouse after the decedent's death or that exercise must be by specific reference to the power.

(5) If the surviving spouse has the requisite power to appoint to herself or her estate, it is immaterial that she also has one or more lesser powers. Thus, if she has a testamentary power to appoint to her estate, she may also have a limited power of withdrawal or of appointment during her life. Similarly, if she has an unlimited power of withdrawal, she may have a limited testamentary power.

(h) **Requirement of survival for a limited period.** A power of appointment in the surviving spouse will not be treated as failing to meet the requirements of paragraph (a)(3) of this section even though the power may terminate, if the only conditions which would cause the termination are those described in paragraph (a) of § 20.2056(b)–3, and if those conditions do not in fact occur. Thus, the entire interest or a specific portion of it will not be disqualified by reason of the fact that the exercise of the power in the spouse is subject to a condition of survivorship described in § 20.-2056(b)–3 if the terms of the condition, that is, the survivorship of the surviving spouse, or the failure to die in a common disaster, are fulfilled.

(i) [Reserved]

(j) Existence of a power in another. Paragraph (a)(5) of this section provides that a transfer described in paragraph (a) is nondeductible to the extent that the decedent created a power in the trustee or in any other person to appoint a part of the interest to any person other than the surviving spouse. However, only powers in other persons which are in opposition to that of the surviving spouse will cause a portion of the interest to fail to satisfy the condition set forth in paragraph (a)(5) of this section. Thus, a power in a trustee to distribute corpus to or for the benefit of a surviving spouse will not disqualify the trust. Similarly, a power to distribute corpus to the spouse for the support of minor children will not disqualify the trust if she is legally obligated to support such children. The application of this paragraph may be illustrated by the following examples:

Example (1). Assume that a decedent created a trust, designating his surviving spouse as income beneficiary for life with an unrestricted power in the spouse to appoint the corpus during her life. The decedent further provided that in the event the surviving spouse should die without having exercised the power, the trust should continue for the life of his son with a power in the son to appoint the corpus. Since the power in the son could become exercisable only after the death of the surviving spouse, the interest is not regarded as failing to satisfy the condition set forth in paragraph (a)(5) of this section.

Example (2). Assume that the decedent created a trust, designating his surviving spouse as income beneficiary for life and as donee of a power to appoint by will the entire corpus. The decedent further provided that the trustee could distribute 30 percent of the corpus to the decedent's son when he reached the age of 35 years. Since the trustee has a power to appoint 30 percent of the entire interest for the benefit of a person other than the surviving spouse, only 70 percent of the interest placed in trust satisfied the condition set forth in paragraph (a)(5) of this section. If, in this case, the surviving spouse had a power, exercisable by her will, to appoint only one-half of the corpus as it was constituted at the time of her death, it should be noted that only 35 percent of the interest placed in the trust would satisfy the condition set forth in paragraph (a)(3) of this section.

[T.D. 6296, 23 FR 4529, June 24, 1958]

§ 20.2056(b)–6 Marital deduction; life insurance or annuity payments with power of appointment in surviving spouse.

(a) In general. Section 2056(b)(6) provides that an interest in property passing from a decedent to his surviving spouse, which consists of proceeds held by an insurer under the terms of a life insurance, endowment, or annuity contract, is a "deductible interest" to the extent that is satisfied all five of the following conditions (see paragraph (b) of this section if one or more of the conditions is satisfied as to only a portion of the proceeds):

(1) The proceeds, or a specific portion of the proceeds, must be held by the insurer subject to an agreement either to pay the entire proceeds or a specific portion thereof in installments, or to pay interest thereon, and all or a specific portion of the installments or interest payable during the life of the surviving spouse must be payable only to her.

(2) The installments or interest payable to the surviving spouse must be payable annually, or more frequently, commencing not later than 13 months after the decedent's death.

(3) The surviving spouse must have the power to appoint all or a specific portion of the amounts so held by the insurer to either herself or her estate.

(4) The power in the surviving spouse must be exercisable by her alone and (whether exercisable by will or during life) must be exercisable in all events.

(5) The amounts or the specific portion of the amounts payable under such contract must not be subject to a power in any other person to appoint any part thereof to any person other than the surviving spouse.

(b) Specific portion; deductible interest. If the right to receive interest or installment payments or the power of appointment passing to the surviving spouse pertains only to a specific portion of the proceeds held by the insurer, the marital deduction is allowed only to the extent that the rights of the surviving spouse in the specific portion meet the five conditions described in paragraph (a) of this section. While the rights to interest, or to receive payment in installments, and the power must coexist as to the proceeds of the same contract, it is not necessary that the rights to each be in the same proportion. If the rights to interest meeting the required conditions set forth in paragraph (a)(1) and (2) of this section extend over a smaller share of the proceeds than the share with respect to which the power of appointment requirements set forth in paragraph (a)(3) through (5) of this section are satisfied, the deductible interest is limited to the smaller share. Similarly, if the portion of the proceeds payable in installments is a smaller portion of the proceeds than the portion to which the power of appointment meeting such requirements relates, the deduction is limited to the smaller portion. In addition, if a power of appointment meeting all the requirements extends to a smaller portion of the proceeds than the portion over which the interest or installment rights pertain, the deductible interest cannot exceed the value of the portion to which such power of appointment applies. Thus, if the contract provides that the insurer is to retain the entire proceeds and pay all of the interest thereon annually to the surviving spouse and if the surviving spouse has a power of appointment meeting the specifications prescribed in paragraph (a)(3) through (5) of this section, as to only one-half of the proceeds held, then only one-half of the proceeds may be treated as a deductible interest. Correspondingly, if the rights of the spouse to receive installment payments or interest satisfying the requirements extend to only one-fourth of the proceeds and a testamentary power of appointment satisfying the requirements of paragraph (a)(3) through (5) of this section extends to all of the proceeds, then only one-fourth of the proceeds qualifies as a deductible interest. Further, if the surviving spouse has no right to installment payments (or interest) over any portion of the proceeds but a testamentary power of appointment which meets the necessary conditions over the entire remaining proceeds, then none of the proceeds qualifies for the deduction. In addition, if, from the time of the decedent's death, the surviving spouse has a power of appointment meeting all of the required conditions over three-fourths of the proceeds and the right to receive interest from the entire proceeds, but with a power in another person to appoint one-half of the entire proceeds, the value of the interest in the surviving spouse over only one-half of the proceeds will qualify as a deductible interest.

(c) **Applicable principles.** (1) The principles set forth in paragraph (c) of § 20.2056(b)–5 for determining what constitutes a "specific portion of the entire interest" for the purpose of section 2056(b)(5) are applicable in determining what constitutes a "specific portion of all such amounts" for the purpose of section 2056(b)(6). However, the interest in the proceeds passing to the surviving spouse will not be disqualified by the fact that the

installment payments or interest to which the spouse is entitled or the amount of the proceeds over which the power of appointment is exercisable may be expressed in terms of a specific sum rather than a fraction or a percentage of the proceeds provided it is shown that such sums are a definite or fixed percentage or fraction of the total proceeds.

(2) The provisions of paragraph (a) of this section are applicable with respect to a property interest which passed from the decedent in the form of proceeds of a policy of insurance upon the decedent's life, a policy of insurance upon the life of a person who predeceased the decedent, a matured endowment policy, or an annuity contract, but only in case the proceeds are to be held by the insurer. With respect to proceeds under any such contract which are to be held by a trustee, with power of appointment in the surviving spouse, see § 20.-2056(b)–5. As to the treatment of proceeds not meeting the requirements of § 20.2056(b)–5 or of this section, see § 20.2056(a)–2.

(3) In the case of a contract under which payments by the insurer commenced during the decedent's life, it is immaterial whether or not the conditions in subparagraphs (1) through (5) of paragraph (a) of this section were satisfied prior to the decedent's death.

(d) **Payments of installments or interest.** The conditions in subparagraphs (1) and (2) of paragraph (a) of this section relative to the payments of installments or interest to the surviving spouse are satisfied if, under the terms of the contract, the spouse has the right exercisable annually (or more frequently) to require distribution to herself of installments of the proceeds or a specific portion thereof, as the case may be, and otherwise such proceeds or interest are to be accumulated and held by the insurer pursuant to the terms of the contract. A contract which otherwise requires the insurer to make annual or more frequent payments to the surviving spouse following the decedent's death, will not be disqualified merely because the surviving spouse must comply with certain formalities in order to obtain the first payment. For example, the contract may satisfy the conditions in subparagraphs (1) and (2) of paragraph (a) of this section even though it requires the surviving spouse to furnish proof of death before the first payment is made. The condition in paragraph (a)(1) of this section is satisfied where interest on the proceeds or a specific portion thereof is payable, annually or more frequently, for a term, or until the occurrence of a specified event, following which the proceeds or a specific portion thereof are to be paid in annual or more frequent installments.

(e) **Powers of appointment.** (1) In determining whether the terms of the contract satisfy the conditions in subparagraph (3), (4), or (5) of paragraph (a) of this section relating to a power of appointment in the surviving spouse or any other person, the principles stated in § 20.2056(b)–5 are applicable. As stated in § 20.2056(b)–5, the surviving spouse's power to appoint is "exercisable in all events" only if it is in existence immediately following the decedent's death, subject, however, to the operation of § 20.2056(b)–3 relating to interests conditioned on survival for a limited period.

(2) For examples of formal limitations on the power which will not disqualify the contract, see paragraph (g)(4) of § 20.2056(b)–5. If the power is exercisable from the moment of the decedent's death, the contract is not disqualified merely because the insurer may require proof of the decedent's death as a condition to making payment to the appointee. If the submission of proof of the decedent's death is a condition to the exercise of the power, the power will not be considered "exercisable in all events" unless in the event the surviving spouse had died immediately following the decedent, her power to appoint would have been considered to exist at the time of her death, within the meaning of section 2041(a)(2). See paragraph (b) of § 20.2041–3.

(3) It is sufficient for the purposes of the condition in paragraph (a)(3) of this section that the surviving spouse have the power to appoint amounts held by the insurer to herself or her estate if the surviving spouse has the unqualified power, exercisable in favor of herself or her estate, to appoint amounts held by the insurer which are payable after her death. Such power to appoint need not extend to installments or interest which will be paid to the spouse during her life. Further, the power to appoint need not be a power to require payment in a single sum. For example, if the proceeds of a policy are payable in installments, and if the surviving spouse has the power to direct that all installments payable after her death be paid to her estate, she has the requisite power.

(4) It is not necessary that the phrase "power to appoint" be used in the contract. For example, the condition in paragraph (a)(3) of this section that the surviving spouse have the power to appoint

amounts held by the insurer to herself or her estate is satisfied by terms of a contract which give the surviving spouse a right which is, in substance and effect, a power to appoint to herself or her estate, such as a right to withdraw the amount remaining in the fund held by the insurer, or a right to direct that any amount held by the insurer under the contract at her death shall be paid to her estate.

[T.D. 6296, 23 FR 4529, June 24, 1958]

§ 20.2056(b)–7 *(Proposed, published 5–21–84.)*
Election with respect to life estate for surviving spouse.

(a) **In general.** A marital deduction is allowed under section 2056(b)(7) with respect to estates of decedents dying after December 31, 1981, for "qualified terminable interest property." All of the property for which a deduction is allowed under this paragraph (a) shall be treated as passing to the surviving spouse (for purposes of § 20.2056(a)–1) and no part of such property shall be treated as passing to any person other than the surviving spouse (for purposes of § 20.2056(b)–1).

(b) **Qualified terminable interest property defined.** For purposes of this section, the term "qualified terminable interest property" means property—

(1) Which passes from the decedent,

(2) In which the surviving spouse has a "qualifying income interest for life" as defined in paragraph (c) of this section, and

(3) Which the executor elected to treat as qualified terminable interest property.

For purposes of this section, the term "property" generally means an "entire interest in property" (within the meaning of § 20.2056(b)–5(d)) or a "specific portion of the entire interest" (within the meaning of § 20.2056(b)–5(c)). The election may relate to all or any part of property that meets the requirements of paragraphs (b)(1) and (2) of this section, provided that any partial election shall relate to a fractional or percentile share of the property so that the elective part will reflect its proportionate share of the increment or decline in the whole of the property for purposes of applying section 2044 or 2519. Thus, if the interest of the surviving spouse in a trust meets the requirements of paragraphs (b)(1) and (2) of this section, the executor may make an election under paragraph (b)(3) with respect to a part of the trust only if the election relates to a defined fraction or percentage of the entire trust or specific portion thereof (within the meaning of § 20.2056(b)–5(c)). The fraction or percentage may be defined by means of a formula. If the interest of the surviving spouse in a trust meets the requirements of paragraphs (b)(1) and (2) of this section, the trust may be divided into separate trusts to reflect a partial election that has been made or is to be made. If a trust is severed, it must be clear, by virtue of the duties imposed on the fiduciary either by applicable state law or by the express or implied provisions of the instrument governing the trust, that the fiduciary must divide the trust according to the fair market value of the assets of the trust at the time of the division. To have a valid election under paragraph (b)(3) of this section, the election shall be made by the executor (defined in section 2203 and the regulations under that section) who is in possession of the qualified terminable interest property and shall be made by such executor on the return of tax imposed by section 2001. For purposes of this paragraph, the term "return of tax imposed by section 2001" means the last estate tax return filed by such executor on or before the due date of the return, or if a timely return is not filed by such executor, the first estate tax return filed by the executor after the due date. The election, once made, is irrevocable. If an executor appointed under state law has made an election with respect to one or more properties, then no subsequent election may be made with respect to other properties in the executor's possession.

(c) Qualifying income interest for life defined. (1) In general. For purposes of this section, the term "qualifying income interest for life" means—

(i) The surviving spouse is entitled for life to all the income from the property, payable annually or at more frequent intervals, and

(ii) No person (including the surviving spouse) has a power, other than a power the exercise of which takes effect only at or after the surviving spouse's death, to appoint any part of the property to any person other than the surviving spouse.

In general, the principles outlined in § 20.2056(b)–5(f), relating to whether the spouse is entitled for life to all of the income from the entire interest or a specific portion of the entire interest, are applicable in determining whether the surviving spouse is entitled for life to all the income from the property, regardless of whether the interest passing to the spouse is in trust. An income interest granted for a term of years, or a life estate subject to termination upon the occurrence of a specified event (*e.g.*, remarriage), is not a qualifying income interest for life. In addition, an income interest (or life estate) that is contingent upon the executor's election under paragraph (b)(3) of this section is not a qualifying income interest for life, regardless of whether the election is actually made. On the other hand, an income interest will not fail to constitute a qualifying income interest for life solely because income between the last distribution date and the date of the surviving spouse's death is not required to be distributed to the surviving spouse or the surviving spouse's estate. See § 20.2044–1 relating to the inclusion of such undistributed income in the surviving spouse's estate. An income interest in a trust will not fail to constitute a qualifying income interest for life solely because the trustee has a power to distribute corpus to or for the benefit of the surviving spouse. Also, the fact that property (*i.e.*, income or corpus) distributed to a surviving spouse may be transferred by the spouse to another person does not result in a failure to satisfy the requirement of paragraph (c)(1)(ii) of this section. However, if the governing instrument requires the surviving spouse to transfer the distributed property to another person without full and adequate consideration in money or money's worth, the requirement of paragraph (c)(1)(ii) of this section is not satisfied.

(2) Annuities. In general, a surviving spouse's lifetime annuity interest shall be treated as a qualifying income interest for life for purposes of section 2056(b)(7)(B)(ii). The deductible interest, for purposes of § 20.2056(a)–1(a), is the specific portion of the property (including an annuity contract) that, assuming the interest rate generally applicable for the valuation of annuities at the time of the decedent's death, would produce income equal to the minimum amount payable annually to the surviving spouse for life. In no case may the value of the deductible interest exceed the value of the property out of which the annuity is paid. If the annual payment may increase, the annuity interest will not be disqualified, but the increased amount shall not be taken into account in valuing the deductible interest. However, an annuity interest will not be treated as a qualifying income interest for life for purposes of section 2056(b)(7)(B)(ii), if any person other than the surviving spouse may receive, during the surviving spouse's lifetime, any distribution of the property or its income (including any distribution under an annuity contract) out of which the annuity is payable. To determine the applicable interest rate for valuing annuities, see section 2031 and regulations under that section. If, assuming such interest rate, the entire property from which the annuity may be satisfied is insufficient to produce income equal to the minimum annual payment, the value of the deductible interest is the entire value of such property.

(d) Application of local law. The provisions of local law shall be taken into account in determining whether or not the conditions of paragraphs (b) and (c) of this section are satisfied. For example, silence of a trust instrument as to the frequency of payment will not be regarded as a failure to satisfy the condition in paragraph (c) of this section that the income must be payable to the surviving spouse annually or more frequently, unless the applicable law permits payment to be made less frequently than annually.

(e) Examples. The following examples illustrate the application of paragraphs (a) through (c) of this section. In each example it is assumed that the decedent dies after 1981.

Example (1). A decedent at the time of death owns a personal residence valued at $250,000 for estate tax purposes. Under the decedent's will, which was executed after September 11, 1981, the exclusive and unrestricted right to use such property (including the right to continue to occupy the property as a personal residence or to rent such property and receive the income) passes to the decedent's surviving spouse, S, for life. After S's death the property passes to the decedent's children. If the executor elects to treat all of such property as qualified terminable interest property, the deductible interest is the value of such property for estate tax purposes, *i.e.,* $250,000.

Example (2). Assume that the facts are the same as in example (1) except that the property is a recently planted tree farm which is not expected to be income producing for 20 years after the decedent's death. In addition, assume that S is 70 years old at the time of the decedent's death, and that applicable local law does not require or permit S to require the conversion of the property into a productive asset within a reasonable time after the decedent's death. S does not have a qualifying income interest for life because the bequest does not give S that degree of beneficial enjoyment during S's life which the principles of the law of trusts accord to a person who is unqualifiedly designated as the life beneficiary of a trust. See § 20.2056(b)–5(f). Therefore, no deduction for the bequest is allowable under section 2056(b)(7).

Example (3). Pursuant to a will executed after September 11, 1981, the decedent establishes a trust that is funded with property valued a $500,000 for estate tax purposes. The assets used to fund the trust include both income producing assets and nonproductive assets. The

surviving spouse, S, is given the right exercisable annually to require distribution of all the trust income to himself or herself. There is no power to distribute trust property during S's lifetime to any person other than S. Applicable State law permits S to require that the trustee either make the trust property productive or sell the property and reinvest in productive property within a reasonable time. If the executor elects to treat all of the trust as qualified terminable interest property, the deductible interest is $500,000. If the executor elects to treat only 20 percent of the trust as qualified terminable interest property, the deductible interest is only $100,000, that is, $500,000 multiplied by 20 percent.

Example (4). Assume that the facts are the same as in example (3) except that S is given the right exercisable annually to require distribution to herself or himself of only 50 percent of the trust income for life. The other 50 percent of the trust income is to be distributed among S and the decedent's children in the trustee's discretion or accumulated. If the executor elects to treat the entire portion of the trust in which S has a qualifying income interest as qualified terminable interest property, the deductible interest is $250,000, which is the value of the trust for estate tax purposes ($500,000) multiplied by the spouse's percentile share of the trust income (50 percent). If the executor elects to treat only 20 percent of the portion of the trust in which S has a qualifying income interest as qualified terminable interest property, the deductible interest is only $50,000, that is, $250,000 multiplied by 20 percent.

Example (5). Assume that the facts are the same as in example (3) except that the trustee is given the power to use annually $5,000 from the trust for the maintenance and support of X. S does not have a qualifying income interest for life in any portion of the trust because the bequest fails to satisfy the condition set forth in § 20.-2056(b)–7(c)(2), which is the condition that no person have a power, other than a power the exercise of which takes effect only at or after S's death, to appoint any part of the property to any person other than S. The trust would also be nondeductible under section 2056(b)(7) if S were given the power, rather than the trustee, to appoint a portion of the corpus to X.

Example (6). Assume that the facts are the same as in example (3) except that, upon S's remarriage, S's interest in the trust will pass to X. The trust is not deductible under section 2056(b)(7). S's income interest is not a "qualifying income interest for life" because it is not for life, but rather is terminable upon S's remarriage.

Example (7). Assume that the facts are the same as in example (3) except that S is given the right to require distribution to S of only that percentage of the trust income which the executor elects to treat as qualified terminable interest property. S does not have a qualifying income interest for life in any portion of the trust because the income interest is contingent upon the executor's election. Accordingly, the executor cannot elect qualified terminable interest treatment for any portion of the trust. If the decedent's will gives the surviving spouse a qualifying income interest for life in a specific portion of the trust (such as the minimum portion of the trust that is necessary to reduce Federal estate tax to zero) and such interest is not contingent on the executor's election of qualified terminable interest treatment, the executor can elect qualified terminable interest treatment for the specified portion of the trust.

Example (8). Pursuant to a will executed after September 11, 1981, the decedent, D, establishes a trust funded with the residue of D's estate. Income of the trust is to be paid annually to D's surviving spouse, S, for S's life, and the principal is to be distributed to D's children upon S's death. S has the power to require that all the trust property be made productive. There is no power to distribute trust property during S's lifetime to any person other than S. D's executor elects to deduct under section 2056(b)(7) a fractional share of the residuary estate. The executor provides that the numerator of the fraction is the amount of deduction necessary to reduce the Federal estate taxes to zero (taking into account final estate tax values) and the denominator of the fraction is the final estate tax value of the residuary trust (after taking into account any specific bequests or liabilities of the estate paid out of the residuary estate). The formula election is of a fractional share. The value of such share qualifies for the marital deduction even though the executor's determinations to claim administration expenses as estate or income tax deductions and the final estate tax value will affect the amount of the fractional share.

Example (9). Assume that the facts are the same as in example (8) except that, rather than defining a fraction, the executor's formula states: "I elect that portion of the residuary trust, up to 100 percent, necessary to reduce the Federal estate taxes to zero, after taking into account the available unified credit, final estate tax values and any liabilities paid out of and specific bequests funded out of the residuary estate." The formula election is of a fractional share. The share is equivalent to the fractional share determined in example (8).

Example (10). Assume that the facts are the same as in example (8) except that S is also the life beneficiary of the sixteen remaining annual installments of D's individual retirement account for which the 19 original annual installments began being paid when D reached age 70½. Also assume that each installment is equal to all the income earned on the remaining principal in the account plus a share of the remaining principal equal to $1/19$ in the first year, $1/18$ in the second year, $1/17$ in the third year, etc. Any remaining payment after S's death passes to D's children. S's interest in the account is a qualifying income interest for life. If D's executor makes two separate elections, one as to 100 percent of the retirement account and a second as to the residuary trust in the same manner as example (8), each election qualifies the property subject to the election for the marital deduction.

Example (11). Assume that the facts are the same as in example (8) except that D's will directs the executor to elect qualified terminable interest treatment for the minimum amount of property necessary to reduce estate taxes on D's estate to zero, directs the executor to divide the residuary estate into two separate trusts to reflect the election and directs that any payments of principal to S shall be charged first to the marital deduction trust. S remains the sole life beneficiary of both trusts. The authorization and direction have no effect on the allowance of a marital deduction, and only the property remaining in the marital deduction trust, after payments of principal to S, will be subject to inclusion in S's gross

estate (by section 2044) or subject to gift tax (by section 2519). If rather than authorizing the executor to form two separate trusts, D's will directs the executor to form a single trust and reduce the marital deduction share of that trust by any invasions of principal for S, the executor's formula election will be valid. See §§ 20.2044-1(d) and 25.2519-1(d) for the effect of appointments of principal.

Example (12). Pursuant to a will executed after September 11, 1981, the decedent, D, establishes a trust funded with income producing property valued at $500,000 for estate tax purposes. The trustee is required by the trust instrument to pay $20,000 a year to D's surviving spouse, S, for life. The rest of the income from the trust is to be accumulated in the trust and may not be distributed during S's lifetime to any person other than S. S's lifetime annuity interest is treated as a qualifying income interest for life. If the executor elects to treat the entire portion of the trust in which S has a qualifying income interest as qualified terminable interest property, the value of the deductible interest is $200,000, since such amount would yield an income to S of $20,000 a year (assuming D died in March 1984 and a 10 percent interest rate applies in valuing annuities).

Example (13). Assume the same facts as in example (12) except that the trustee is required to pay S $70,000 a year for life. If the executor elects to treat the entire portion of the trust in which S has a qualifying income interest as qualified terminable interest property, the value of the deductible interest is $500,000, which is the lesser of the entire value of the property ($500,000), or the amount of property that (assuming a 10 percent interest rate) would yield an income to S of $70,000 a year ($70,000).

Example (14). Pursuant to a will executed after September 11, 1981, the decedent, D, provides that upon his death, the executor shall purchase a commercial annuity for his surviving spouse, S, that will pay S $100,000 a year for life. Based on S's life expectancy at the time of D's death, the cost of the annuity is $700,000. S's annuity interest is treated as a qualifying income interest for life. If the executor elects to treat the entire property in which S has a qualifying income interest for life as qualified terminable interest property, the deductible interest is the cost of the annuity, or $700,000.

Example (15). Pursuant to a will executed after September 11, 1981, the decedent transfers $200,000 to a pooled income fund, within the meaning of section 642(c)(5), designating his wife as the income beneficiary for her life. If the executor elects to treat the entire $200,000 as qualified terminable interest property, the deductible interest is $200,000, the deduction will not be denied under this section if the decedent's transfer to his wife is conditioned on the payment by the wife of state death taxes attributable to the pooled income fund.

§ 20.2056(d)-1 Marital deduction; effect of disclaimers of post-December 31, 1976 transfers.

(a) Disclaimer by a surviving spouse. If a surviving spouse disclaims an interest in property passing to such spouse from the decedent in a taxable transfer made after December 31, 1976, the efficacy of the disclaimer will be determined by section 2518 and the corresponding regulations. If a qualified disclaimer is determined to have been made by the surviving spouse, the property interest disclaimed is treated as if such interest had never been transferred to the surviving spouse.

(b) Disclaimer by a person other than a surviving spouse. If an interest in property passes to one other than the surviving spouse from a decedent in a taxable transfer made after December 31, 1976 and—

(1) The person other than the surviving spouse makes a qualified disclaimer with respect to such interest in property, and

(2) The surviving spouse is entitled to such interest in property as a result of such disclaimer.

the disclaimed interest is treated as passing directly from the decedent to the surviving spouse. If the disclaimer is not a qualified disclaimer, the interest in property is considered as passing from the decedent to the person who made the disclaimer as if the disclaimer had not been made. See section 2518 and the corresponding regulations for rules relating to a qualified disclaimer.

[T.D. 8095, 51 FR 28368, Aug. 7, 1986]

§ 20.2056(e)–1 Marital deduction; definition of "passed from the decedent".

(a) The following rules are applicable in determining the person to whom any property interest "passed from the decedent":

(1) Property interests devolving upon any person (or persons) as surviving coowner with the decedent under any form of joint ownership under which the right of survivorship existed are considered as having passed from the decedent to such person (or persons).

(2) Property interests at any time subject to the decedent's power to appoint (whether alone or in conjunction with any person) are considered as having passed from the decedent to the appointee under his exercise of the power, or, in case of the lapse, release or nonexercise of the power, as having passed from the decedent to the taker in default of exercise.

(3) The dower or curtesy interest (or statutory interest in lieu thereof) of the decedent's surviving spouse is considered as having passed from the decedent to his spouse.

(4) The proceeds of insurance upon the life of the decedent are considered as having passed from the decedent to the person who, at the time of the decedent's death, was entitled to receive the proceeds.

(5) Any property interest transferred during life, bequeathed or devised by the decedent, or inherited from the decedent, is considered as having passed to the person to whom he transferred, bequeathed, or devised the interest, or to the person who inherited the interest from him.

(6) The survivor's interest in an annuity or other payment described in section 2039 (see §§ 20.-2039–1 and 20.2039–2) is considered as having passed from the decedent to the survivor only to the extent that the value of such interest is included in the decedent's gross estate under that section. If only a portion of the entire annuity or other payment is included in the decedent's gross estate and the annuity or other payment is payable to more than one beneficiary, then the value of the interest considered to have passed to each beneficiary is that portion of the amount payable to each beneficiary that the amount of the annuity or other payment included in the decedent's gross estate bears to the total value of the annuity or other payment payable to all beneficiaries.

(b) If before the decedent's death the decedent's surviving spouse had merely an expectant interest in property held by her and the decedent under community property laws, that interest is considered as having passed from the decedent to the spouse. As to the circumstances under which the interest of the surviving spouse under community property laws is regarded as merely expectant, see paragraph (d) of § 20.2056(c)–2.

[T.D. 6296, 23 FR 4529, June 24, 1958]

§ 20.2056(e)–2 Marital deduction; definition of "passed from the decedent to his surviving spouse".

(a) **In general.** In general, the definition stated in § 20.2056(e)–1 is applicable in determining the property interests which "passed from the decedent to his surviving spouse". Special rules are provided, however, for the following:

(1) In the case of certain interests with income for life to the surviving spouse with power of appointment in her (see § 20.2056(b)–5);

(2) In the case of proceeds held by the insurer under a life insurance, endowment, or annuity

contract with power of appointment in the surviving spouse (see § 20.2056(b)–6);

(3) In case of the disclaimer of an interest by the surviving spouse or by any other person (see § 20.2056(d)–1);

(4) In case of an election by the surviving spouse (see paragraph (c) of this section); and

(5) In case of a controversy involving the decedent's will, see paragraph (d) of this section.

A property interest is considered as passing to the surviving spouse only if it passed to her as beneficial owner, except to the extent otherwise provided in §§ 20.2056(b)–5 and 20.2056(b)–6 in the case of certain life estates and insurance and annuity contracts with powers of appointment. For this purpose, where a property interest passed from the decedent in trust, such interest is considered to have passed from him to his surviving spouse to the extent of her beneficial interest therein. The deduction may not be taken with respect to a property interest which passed to such spouse merely as trustee, or subject to a binding agreement by the spouse to dispose of the interest in favor of a third person. An allowance or award paid to a surviving spouse pursuant to local law for her support during the administration of the decedent's estate constitutes a property interest passing from the decedent to his surviving spouse. In determining whether or not such an interest is deductible, however, see generally the terminable interest rules of § 20.2056(b)–1 and especially example (8) of paragraph (g) of that section.

(b) Examples. The following illustrate the provisions of paragraph (a) of this section:

(1) A property interest bequeathed in trust by H (the decedent) is considered as having passed from him to W (his surviving spouse)—

(i) If the trust income is payable to W for life and upon her death the corpus is distributable to her executors or administrators;

(ii) If W is entitled to the trust income for a term of years following which the corpus is to be paid to W or her estate;

(iii) If the trust income is to be accumulated for a term of years or for W's life and the augmented fund paid to W or her estate; or

(iv) If the terms of the transfer satisfy the requirements of § 20.2056(b)–5.

(2) If H devised property—

(i) To A for life with remainder absolutely to W or her estate, the remainder interest is considered to have passed from H to W;

(ii) To W for life with remainder to her estate, the entire property is considered as having passed from H to W; or

(iii) Under conditions which satisfy the provisions of § 20.2056(b)–5, the entire property is considered as having passed from H to W.

(3) Proceeds of insurance upon the life of H are considered as having passed from H to W if the terms of the contract—

(i) Meet the requirements of § 20.2056(b)–6;

(ii) Provide that the proceeds are payable to W in a lump sum;

(iii) Provide that the proceeds are payable in installments to W for life and after her death any remaining installments are payable to her estate;

(iv) Provide that interest on the proceeds is payable to W for life and upon her death the principal amount is payable to her estate; or

(v) Provide that the proceeds are payable to a trustee under an arrangement whereby the requirements of section 2056(b)(5) are satisfied.

(c) Effect of election by surviving spouse. This paragraph contains rules applicable if the surviving spouse may elect between a property interest offered to her under the decedent's will or other instrument and a property interest to which she is otherwise entitled (such as dower, a right in the decedent's estate, or her interest under community property laws) of which adverse disposition was attempted by the decedent under the will or other instrument. If the surviving spouse elects to take against the will or other instrument, then the property interests offered thereunder are not considered as having "passed from the decedent to his surviving spouse" and the dower or other property interest retained by her is considered as having so passed (if it otherwise so qualifies under this section). If the surviving spouse elects to take under the will or other instrument, then the dower or other property interest relinquished by her is not considered as having "passed from the decedent to his surviving spouse" (irrespective of whether it otherwise comes within the definition stated in paragraph (a) of this section) and the interest taken under the will or other instrument is considered as having so passed (if it otherwise so qualifies). As to the valuation of the property interest taken under the will or other instrument, see paragraph (b) of § 20.2056(b)–4.

(d) Will contests. (1) If as a result of a controversy involving the decedent's will, or involving any bequest or devise thereunder, his surviving spouse assigns or surrenders a property interest in settlement of the controversy, the interest so assigned or surrendered is not considered as having "passed from the decedent to his surviving spouse."

(2) If as a result of the controversy involving the decedent's will, or involving any bequest or devise thereunder, a property interest is assigned or surrendered to the surviving spouse, the interest so acquired will be regarded as having "passed from the decedent to his surviving spouse" only if the assignment or surrender as a bona fide recognition of enforceable rights of the surviving spouse in the decedent's estate. Such a bona fide recognition will be presumed where the assignment or surrender was pursuant to a decision of a local court upon the merits in an adversary proceeding following a genuine and active contest. However, such a decree will be accepted only to the extent that the court passed upon the facts upon which deductibility of the property interest depends. If the assignment or surrender was pursuant to a decree rendered by consent, or pursuant to an agreement not to contest the will or not to probate the will, it will not necessarily be accepted as a bona fide evaluation of the rights of the spouse.

(e) Survivorship. If the order of deaths of the decedent and his spouse cannot be established by proof, a presumption (whether supplied by local law, the decedent's will, or otherwise) that the decedent was survived by his spouse will be recognized as satisfying paragraph (b)(1) of § 20.2056(a)–1, but only to the extent that it has the effect of giving to the spouse an interest in property includible in her gross estate under part III of subchapter A of chapter 11. Under these circumstances, if an estate tax return is required to be filed for the estate of the decedent's spouse, the marital deduction will not be allowed in the final audit of the estate tax return of the decedent's estate with respect to any property interest which has not been finally determined to be includible in the gross estate of his spouse.

[T.D. 6296, 23 FR 4529, June 24, 1958]

§ 20.2056(e)–3 Marital deduction; definition of "passed from the decedent to a person other than his surviving spouse".

The expression "passed from the decedent to a person other than his surviving spouse" refers to any property interest which, under the definition stated in § 20.2056(e)–1 is considered as having "passed from the decedent" and which under the rules referred to in § 20.2056(e)–2 is not considered as having "passed from the decedent to his surviving spouse." Interests which passed to a person other than the surviving spouse include interests so passing under the decedent's exercise, release, or nonexercise of a nontaxable power to appoint. It is immaterial whether the property interest which passed from the decedent to a person other than his surviving spouse is included in the decedent's gross estate. The term "person other than his surviving spouse" includes the possible unascertained takers of a property interest, as, for example, the members of a class to be ascertained in the future. As another example, assume that the decedent created a power of appointment over a property interest, which does not come within the purview of § 20.2056(b)–5 or § 20.2056(b)–6. In such a case, the term "person other than his surviving spouse" refers to the possible appointees and possible takers in default (other than the spouse) of such property interest. Whether or not there is a possibility that the "person other than his surviving spouse" (or the heirs or assigns of such person) may possess or enjoy the property following termination or failure of the interest therein which passed from the decedent to his surviving spouse is to be determined as of the time of the decedent's death.

[T.D. 6296, 23 FR 4529, June 24, 1958]

§ 22.2056–1 Qualified terminable interest property elections.

(a) In general. This paragraph (a) applies to the election under section 2056(b)(7)(B)(v) to deduct the value of property in which the surviving spouse receives a qualifying income interest for life. The new election was added to the Code by section 403(d)(1) of the Economic Recovery Tax Act of 1981. The executor shall make this election on the estate tax return. This election is available with respect to estates of decedents dying after 1981. The election, once made, is irrevocable.

(b) Partial elections allowed. The election described in paragraph (a) of this section may be made for all or any part of a property that meets the requirements of section 2056(b)(7)(B)(i)(I) and (II), provided that any partial election shall relate to a fractional or percentile share of the property so that the elective part will reflect its proportionate share of the increment or decline in the whole of the property for purposes of applying sections 2044 or 2519. Thus, if the interest of the surviving spouse in a trust (or other property in which the spouse has a life estate) meets the requirements of section 2056(b)(7)(B)(i)(I) and (II), the executor may make an election under paragraph (a) with respect to a part of the trust (or other property) only if the election relates to a defined fraction or percentage of the entire trust (or other property). The fraction or percentage may be defined by means of a formula.

§ 20.2203-1 Definition of executor.

The term "executor" means the executor or administrator of the decedent's estate. However, if there is no executor or administrator appointed, qualified and acting within the United States, the term means any person in actual or constructive possession of any property of the decedent. The term "person in actual or constructive possession of any property of the decedent" includes, among others, the decedent's agents and representatives; safe-deposit companies, warehouse companies, and other custodians of property in this country; brokers holding, as collateral, securities belonging to the decedent; and debtors of the decedent in this country.

[T.D. 6296, 23 FR 4529, June 24, 1958]

PART 25—GIFT TAX

Determination of Tax Liability

§ 25.2502–1 Rate of tax.

(a) **Computation of tax.** The rate of tax is determined by the total of all gifts made by the donor during the calendar period and all the preceding calendar periods since June 6, 1932. See § 25.2502–1(c)(1) for the definition of "calendar period" and § 25.2502–1(c)(2) for the definition of "preceding calendar periods." The following six steps are to be followed in computing the tax:

(1) **First step.** Ascertain the amount of the "taxable gifts" (as defined in § 25.2503–1) for the calendar period for which the return is being prepared.

(2) **Second step.** Ascertain "the aggregate sum of the taxable gifts for each of the preceding calendar periods" (as defined in § 25.2504–1), considering only those gifts made after June 6, 1932.

(3) **Third step.** Ascertain the total amount of the taxable gifts which is the sum of the amounts determined in the first and second steps.

(4) **Fourth step.** Compute the tentative tax on the total amount of taxable gifts (as determined in the third step) using the rate schedule in effect at the time the gift (for which the return is being filed) is made.

(5) **Fifth step.** Compute the tentative tax on the aggregate sum of the taxable gifts for each of the preceding calendar periods (as determined in the second step), using the same rate schedule set forth in the fourth step of this paragraph (a).

(6) **Sixth step.** Subtract the amount determined in the fifth step from the amount determined in the fourth step. The amount remaining is the gift tax for the calendar period for which the return is being prepared.

(b) **Rate of tax.** The tax is computed in accordance with the rate schedule in effect at the time the gift was made as set forth in section 2001(c) or corresponding provisions of prior law.

(c) **Definitions.** (1) The term "calendar period" means:

(i) Each calendar year for the calendar years 1932 (but only that portion of such year after June 6, 1932) through 1970;

(ii) Each calendar quarter for the first calendar quarter of the calendar year 1971 through the last calendar quarter of calendar year 1981; or

(iii) Each calendar year for the calendar year 1982 and each succeeding calendar year.

(2) The term "preceding calendar periods" means all calendar periods ending prior to the calendar period for which the tax is being computed.

* * *

[T.D. 6334, 23 FR 8904, Nov. 15, 1958, as amended by T.D. 7238, 37 FR 28725, Dec. 29, 1972; T.D. 7910, 48 FR 40371, Sept. 7, 1983]

§ 25.2503–1 General definitions of "taxable gifts" and of "total amount of gifts."

The term "taxable gifts" means the "total amount of gifts" made by the donor during the "calendar period" (as defined in § 25.2502–1(c)(1)) less the deductions provided for in sections 2521 (as in effect before its repeal by the Tax Reform Act of 1976), 2522, and 2523 (specific exemption, charitable, etc., gifts and the marital deduction, respectively). The term "total amount of gifts" means the sum of the values of the gifts made during the calendar period less the amounts excludable under section 2503(b). See § 25.2503–2. The entire value of any gift of a future interest in property must be included in the total amount of gifts for the calendar period in which the gift is made. See § 25.2503–3.

[T.D. 7238, 37 FR 28727, Dec. 29, 1972, as amended by T.D. 7910, 48 FR 40371, Sept. 7, 1983]

§ 25.2503–3 Future interests in property.

(a) No part of the value of a gift of a future interest may be excluded in determining the total amount of gifts made during the "calendar period" (as defined in § 25.2502–1(c)(1)). "Future interest" is a legal term, and includes reversions, remainders, and other interests or estates, whether vested or contingent, and whether or not supported by a particular interest or estate, which are limited to commence in use, possession, or enjoyment at some future date or time. The term has no reference to such contractual rights as exist in a bond, note (though bearing no interest until maturity), or in a

policy of life insurance, the obligations of which are to be discharged by payments in the future. But a future interest or interests in such contractual obligations may be created by the limitations contained in a trust or other instrument of transfer used in effecting a gift.

(b) An unrestricted right to the immediate use, possession, or enjoyment of property or the income from property (such as a life estate or term certain) is a present interest in property. An exclusion is allowable with respect to a gift of such an interest (but not in excess of the value of the interest). If a donee has received a present interest in property, the possibility that such interest may be diminished by the transfer of a greater interest in the same property to the donee through the exercise of a power is disregarded in computing the value of the present interest, to the extent that no part of such interest will at any time pass to any other person (see example (4) of paragraph (c) of this section). For an exception to the rule disallowing an exclusion for gifts of future interests in the case of certain gifts to minors, see § 25.2503–4.

(c) The operation of this section may be illustrated by the following examples:

Example (1). Under the terms of a trust created by A the trustee is directed to pay the net income to B, so long as B shall live. The trustee is authorized in his discretion to withhold payments of income during any period he deems advisable and add such income to the trust corpus. Since B's right to receive the income payments is subject to the trustee's discretion, it is not a present interest and no exclusion is allowable with respect to the transfer in trust.

Example (2). C transfers certain insurance policies on his own life to a trust created for the benefit of D. Upon C's death the proceeds of the policies are to be invested and the net income therefrom paid to D during his lifetime. Since the income payments to D will not begin until after C's death the transfer in trust represents a gift of a future interest in property against which no exclusion is allowable.

Example (3). Under the terms of a trust created by E the net income is to be distributed to E's three children in such shares as the trustee, in his uncontrolled discretion deems advisable. While the terms of the trust provide that all of the net income is to be distributed, the amount of income any one of the three beneficiaries will receive rests entirely within the trustee's discretion and cannot be presently ascertained. Accordingly, no exclusions are allowable with respect to the transfers to the trust.

Example (4). Under the terms of a trust the net income is to be paid to F for life, with the remainder payable to G on F's death. The trustee has the uncontrolled power to pay over the corpus to F at any time. Although F's present right to receive the income may be terminated, no other person has the right to such income interest. Accordingly, the power in the trustee is disregarded in determining the value of F's present interest. The power would not be disregarded to the extent that the trustee during F's life could distribute corpus to persons other than F.

Example (5). The corpus of a trust created by J consists of certain real property, subject to a mortgage. The terms of the trust provide that the net income from the property is to be used to pay the mortgage. After the mortgage is paid in full the net income is to be paid to K during his lifetime. Since K's right to receive the income payments will not begin until after the mortgage is paid in full the transfer in trust represents a gift of a future interest in property against which no exclusion is allowable.

Example (6). L pays premiums on a policy of insurance on his life, all the incidents of ownership in the policy (including the right to surrender the policy) are vested in M. The payment of premiums by L constitutes a gift of a present interest in property.

[T.D. 6334, 23 FR 8904, Nov. 15, 1958, as amended by T.D. 7238, 37 FR 28727, Dec. 29, 1972; T.D. 7910, 48 FR 40371, Sept. 7, 1983]

§ 25.2503-4 Transfer for the benefit of a minor.

(a) Section 2503(c) provides that no part of a transfer for the benefit of a donee who has not attained the age of 21 years on the date of the gift will be considered a gift of a future interest in property if the terms of the transfer satisfy all of the following conditions:

(1) Both the property itself and its income may be expended by or for the benefit of the donee before he attains the age of 21 years;

(2) Any portion of the property and its income not disposed of under subparagraph (1) of this paragraph will pass to the donee when he attains the age of 21 years; and

(3) Any portion of the property and its income not disposed of under subparagraph (1) of this paragraph will be payable either to the estate of the donee or as he may appoint under a general power of appointment as defined in section 2514(c) if he dies before attaining the age of 21 years.

(b) Either a power of appointment exercisable by the donee by will or a power of appointment exercisable by the donee during his lifetime will satisfy the conditions set forth in paragraph (a)(3) of this section. However, if the transfer is to qualify for the exclusion under this section, there must be no restrictions of substance (as distinguished from formal restrictions of the type described in paragraph (g)(4) of § 25.2523(e)-1) by the terms of the instrument of transfer on the exercise of the power by the donee. However, if the minor is given a power of appointment exercisable during lifetime or is given a power of appointment exercisable by will, the fact that under the local law a minor is under a disability to exercise an *inter vivos* power or to execute a will does not cause the transfer to fail to satisfy the conditions of section 2503(c). Further, a transfer does not fail to satisfy the conditions of section 2503(c) by reason of the mere fact that—

(1) There is left to the discretion of a trustee the determination of the amounts, if any, of the income or property to be expended for the benefit of the minor and the purpose for which the expenditure is to be made, provided there are no substantial restrictions under the terms of the trust instrument on the exercise of such discretion;

(2) The donee, upon reaching age 21, has the right to extend the term of the trust; or

(3) The governing instrument contains a disposition of the property or income not expended during the donee's minority to persons other than the donee's estate in the event of the default of appointment by the donee.

(c) A gift to a minor which does not satisfy the requirements of section 2503(c) may be either a present or a future interest under the general rules of § 25.2503-3. Thus, for example, a transfer of property in trust with income required to be paid annually to a minor beneficiary and corpus to be distributed to him upon his attaining the age of 21 is a gift of a present interest with respect to the right to income but is a gift of a future interest with respect to the right to corpus.

[T.D. 6334, 23 FR 8904, Nov. 15, 1958]

§ 25.2503-6 Exclusion for certain qualified transfer for tuition or medical expenses.

(a) **In general.** Section 2503(e) provides that any qualified transfer after December 31, 1981, shall not be treated as a transfer of property by gift for purposes of chapter 12 of subtitle B of the Code. Thus, a qualified transfer on behalf of any individual is excluded in determining the total amount of gifts in calendar year 1982 and subsequent years. This exclusion is available in addition to the $10,000 annual gift tax exclusion. Furthermore, an exclusion for a qualified transfer is permitted without regard to the relationship between the donor and the donee.

(b) **Qualified transfers—(1) Definition.** For purposes of this paragraph, the term "qualified transfer" means any amount paid on behalf of an individual—

(i) As tuition to a qualifying educational organization for the education or training of that individual, or

(ii) To any person who provides medical care with respect to that individual as payment for the qualifying medical expenses arising from such medical care.

(2) **Tuition expenses.** For purposes of paragraph (b)(1)(i) of this section, a qualifying educational organization is one which normally maintains a regular faculty and curriculum and normally has a regularly enrolled body of pupils or students in attendance at the place where its educational activities are regularly carried on. See section 170(b)(1)(A)(ii) and the regulations thereunder. The unlimited exclusion is permitted for tuition expenses of full-time or part-time students paid directly to the qualifying educational organization providing the education. No unlimited exclusion is permitted for amounts paid for books, supplies, dormitory fees, board, or other similar expenses which do not constitute direct tuition costs.

(3) **Medical expenses.** For purposes of paragraph (b)(1)(ii) of this section, qualifying medical expenses are limited to those expenses defined in section 213(d) (section 213(e) prior to January 1, 1984) and include expenses incurred for the diagnosis, cure, mitigation, treatment or prevention of disease, or for the purpose of affecting any structure or function of the body or for transportation primarily for and essential to medical care. In addition, the unlimited exclusion from the gift tax includes amounts paid for medical insurance on behalf of any individual. The unlimited exclusion from the gift tax does not apply to amounts paid for medical care that are reimbursed by the donee's insurance. Thus, if payment for a medical expense is reimbursed by the donee's insurance

company, the donor's payment for that expense, to the extent of the reimbursed amount, is not eligible for the unlimited exclusion from the gift tax and the gift is treated as having been made on the date the reimbursement is received by the donee.

(c) **Examples.** The provisions of paragraph (b) of this section may be illustrated by the following examples.

Example (1). In 1982, A made a tuition payment directly to a foreign university on behalf of B. A had no legal obligation to make this payment. The foreign university is described in section 170(b)(1)(A)(ii) of the Code. A's tuition payment is exempt from the gift tax under section 2503(e) of the Code.

Example (2). A transfers $100,000 to a trust the provisions of which state that the funds are to be used for tuition expenses incurred by A's grandchildren. A's transfer to the trust is a completed gift for Federal gift tax purposes and is not a direct transfer to an educational organization as provided in paragraph (b)(2) of this section and does not qualify for the unlimited exclusion from gift tax under section 2503(e).

Example (3). C was seriously injured in an automobile accident in 1982. D, who is unrelated to C, paid C's various medical expenses by checks made payable to the physician. D also paid the hospital for C's hospital bills. These medical and hospital expenses were types described in section 213 of the Code and were not reimbursed by insurance or otherwise. Because the medical and hospital bills paid in 1982 for C were medical expenses within the meaning of section 213 of the Code, and since they were paid directly by D to the person rendering the medical care, they are not treated as transfers subject to the gift tax.

Example (4). Assume the same facts as in example (3) except that instead of making the payments directly to the medical service provided, D reimbursed C for the medical expenses which C had previously paid. The payments made by D to C do not qualify for the exclusion under section 2503(e) of the Code and are subject to the gift tax on the date the reimbursement is received by C to the extent the reimbursement and all other gifts from D to C during the year of the reimbursement exceed the $10,000 annual exclusion provided in section 2503(b).

[T.D. 7978, 49 FR 38541, Oct. 1, 1984; T.D. 1978, 49 FR 39843, Oct. 11, 1984]

Transfers

§ 25.2511–1　Transfers in general.

(a) The gift tax applies to a transfer by way of gift whether the transfer is in trust or otherwise, whether the gift is direct or indirect, and whether the property is real or personal, tangible or intangible. For example, a taxable transfer may be effected by the creation of a trust, the forgiving of

a debt, the assignment of a judgment, the assignment of the benefits of an insurance policy, or the transfer of cash, certificates of deposit, or Federal, State or municipal bonds. Statutory provisions which exempt bonds, notes, bills and certificates of indebtedness of the Federal Government or its agencies and the interest thereon from taxation are not applicable to the gift tax, since the gift tax is an excise tax on the transfer, and is not a tax on the subject of the gift.

* * *

(c)(1) The gift tax also applies to gifts indirectly made. Thus, any transaction in which an interest in property is gratuitously passed or conferred upon another, regardless of the means or device employed, constitutes a gift subject to tax. See further § 25.2512–8 relating to transfers for insufficient consideration. However, in the case of a taxable transfer creating an interest in the person disclaiming made after December 31, 1976, this paragraph (c)(1) shall not apply to the donee if, as a result of a qualified disclaimer by the donee, the property passes to a different donee. Nor shall it apply to a donor if, as a result of a qualified disclaimer by the donee, a completed transfer of an interest in property is not effected. See section 2518 and the corresponding regulations for rules relating to a qualified disclaimer.

(2) In the case of taxable transfers creating an interest in the person disclaiming made before January 1, 1977, where the law governing the administration of the decedent's estate gives a beneficiary, heir, or next-of-kin a right completely and unqualifiedly to refuse to accept ownership of property transferred from a decedent (whether the transfer is effected by the decedent's will or by the law of descent and distribution), a refusal to accept ownership does not constitute the making of a gift if the refusal is made within a reasonable time after knowledge of the existence of the transfer. The refusal must be unequivocal and effective under the local law. There can be no refusal of ownership of property after its acceptance. In the absence of the facts to the contrary, if a person fails to refuse to accept a transfer to him of ownership of a decedent's property within a reasonable time after learning of the existence of the transfer, he will be presumed to have accepted the property. Where the local law does not permit such a refusal, any disposition by the beneficiary, heir, or next-of-kin whereby ownership is transferred gratuitously to another constitutes the making of a gift by the beneficiary, heir, or next-of-kin. In any case where a refusal is purported to relate to only a part of the property, the determination of whether or not there has been a complete and unqualified refusal to accept ownership will depend on all of the facts and circumstances in each particular case, taking into account the recognition and effectiveness of such a purported refusal under the local law. In illustration, if Blackacre was devised to A under the decedent's will (which also provided that all lapsed legacies and devises shall go to B, the residuary beneficiary), and under the local law A could refuse to accept ownership in which case title would be considered as never having passed to A, A's refusal to accept Blackacre within a reasonable time of learning of the devise will not constitute the making of a gift by A to B. However, if a decedent who owned Greenacre died intestate with C and D as his only heirs, and under local law the heir of a decedent cannot, by refusal to accept, prevent himself from becoming an owner of intestate property, any gratuitous disposition by C (by whatever term it is known) whereby he gives up his ownership of a portion of Greenacre and D acquires the whole thereof constitutes the making of a gift by C to D.

(d) If a joint income tax return is filed by a husband and wife for a taxable year, the payment by one spouse of all or part of the income tax liability for such year is not treated as resulting in a transfer that is subject to gift tax. The same rule is applicable to the payment of gift tax for a "calendar period" (as defined in § 25.2502–1(c)(1)) in the case of a husband and wife who have consented to have the gifts made considered as made half by each of them in accordance with the provisions of section 2513.

(e) If a donor transfers by gift less than his entire interest in property, the gift tax is applicable to the interest transferred. The tax is applicable, for example, to the transfer of an undivided half interest in property, or to the transfer of a life estate when the grantor retains the remainder interest, or vice versa. However, if the donor's retained interest is not susceptible of measurement on the basis of generally accepted valuation principles, the gift tax is applicable to the entire value of the property subject to the gift. Thus if a donor, aged 65 years, transfers a life estate in property to A, aged 25 years, with remainder to A's issue, or in default of issue, with reversion to the donor, the gift tax will normally be applicable to the entire value of the property.

(f) If a donor is the owner of only a limited interest in property, and transfers his entire interest, the interest is in every case to be valued by the rules set forth in §§ 25.2512–1 through 25.2512–7. If the interest is a remainder or reversion or other future interest, it is to be valued on the basis of actuarial principles set forth in § 25.2512–5, or if it is not susceptible of valuation in that manner, in accordance with the principles set forth in § 25.-2512–1.

(g)(1) Donative intent on the part of the transferor is not an essential element in the application of the gift tax to the transfer. The application of the tax is based on the objective facts of the transfer and the circumstances under which it is made, rather than on the subjective motives of the donor. However, there are certain types of transfers to which the tax is not applicable. It is applicable only to a transfer of a beneficial interest in property. It is not applicable to a transfer of bare legal title to a trustee. A transfer by a trustee of trust property in which he has no beneficial interest does not constitute a gift by the trustee (but such a transfer may constitute a gift by the creator of the trust, if until the transfer he had the power to change the beneficiaries by amending or revoking the trust). The gift tax is not applicable to a transfer for a full and adequate consideration in money or money's worth, or to ordinary business transactions, described in § 25.2512–8.

(2) If a trustee has a beneficial interest in trust property, a transfer of the property by the trustee is not a taxable transfer if it is made pursuant to a fiduciary power the exercise or nonexercise of which is limited by a reasonably fixed or ascertainable standard which is set forth in the trust instrument. A clearly measurable standard under which the holder of a power is legally accountable is such a standard for this purpose. For instance, a power to distribute corpus for the education, support, maintenance, or health of the beneficiary; for his reasonable support and comfort; to enable him to maintain his accustomed standard of living; or to meet an emergency, would be such a standard. However, a power to distribute corpus for the pleasure, desire, or happiness of a beneficiary is not such a standard. The entire context of a provision of a trust instrument granting a power must be considered in determining whether the power is limited by a reasonably definite standard. For example, if a trust instrument provides that the determination of the trustee shall be conclusive with respect to the exercise or nonexercise of a power, the power is not limited by a reasonably definite standard. However, the fact that the governing instrument is phrased in discretionary terms is not in itself an indication that no such standard exists.

(h) The following are examples of transactions resulting in taxable gifts and in each case it is assumed that the transfers were not made for an adequate and full consideration in money or money's worth:

(1) A transfer of property by a corporation to B is a gift to B from the stockholders of the corporation. If B himself is a stockholder, the transfer is a gift to him from the other stockholders but only to the extent it exceeds B's own interest in such amount as a shareholder. A transfer of property by B to a corporation generally represents gifts by B to the other individual shareholders of the corporation to the extent of their proportionate interests in the corporation. However, there may be an exception to this rule, such as a transfer made by an individual to a charitable, public, political or similar organization which may constitute a gift to the organization as a single entity, depending upon the facts and circumstances in the particular case.

(2) The transfer of property to B if there is imposed upon B the obligation of paying a commensurate annuity to C is a gift to C.

(3) The payment of money or the transfer of property to B in consideration of B's promise to render a service to C is a gift to C, or to both B and C, depending on whether the service to be rendered to C is or is not an adequate and full consideration in money or money's worth for that which is received by B. See section 2512(b) and the regulations thereunder.

(4) If A creates a joint bank account for himself and B (or a similar type of ownership by which A can regain the entire fund without B's consent), there is a gift to B when B draws upon the account for his own benefit, to the extent of the amount drawn without any obligation to account for a part of the proceeds to A. Similarly, if A purchases a United States savings bond registered as payable to "A or B," there is a gift to B when B surrenders the bond for cash without any obligation to account for a part of the proceeds to A.

(5) If A with his own funds purchases property and has the title conveyed to himself and B as joint owners, with rights of survivorship (other than a joint ownership described in example (4) but which rights may be defeated by either party severing his interest, there is a gift to B in the amount of half the value of the property. However, see § 25.-2515–1 relative to the creation of a joint tenancy (or tenancy by the entirety) between husband and wife in real property with rights of survivorship which, unless the donor elects otherwise is not considered as a transfer includible for Federal gift tax purposes at the time of the creation of the joint

tenancy. See § 25.2515–2 with respect to determining the extent to which the creation of a tenancy by the entirety constitutes a taxable gift if the donor elects to have the creation of the tenancy so treated. See also § 25.2523(d)–1 with respect to the marital deduction allowed in the case of the creation of a joint tenancy or a tenancy by the entirety.

(6) If A is possessed of a vested remainder interest in property, subject to being divested only in the event he should fail to survive one or more individuals or the happening of some other event, an irrevocable assignment of all or any part of his interest would result in a transfer includible for Federal gift tax purposes. See especially paragraph (e) of § 25.2512–5 or paragraph (e) of § 25.2512–9, whichever is applicable, for the valuation of an interest of this type.

(7) If A, without retaining a power to revoke the trust or to change the beneficial interests therein, transfers property in trust whereby B is to receive the income for life and at his death the trust is to terminate and the corpus is to be returned to A, provided A survives, but if A predeceases B the corpus is to pass to C, A has made a gift equal to the total value of the property less the value of his retained interest. See paragraph (e) of § 25.-2512–5 or paragraph (e) of § 25.2512–9, whichever is applicable, for the valuation of the donor's retained interest.

(8) If the insured purchases a life insurance policy, or pays a premium on a previously issued policy, the proceeds of which are payable to a beneficiary or beneficiaries other than his estate, and with respect to which the insured retains no reversionary interest in himself or his estate and no power to revest the economic benefits in himself or his estate or to change the beneficiaries or their proportionate benefits (or if the insured relinquishes by assignment, by designation of a new beneficiary or otherwise, every such power that was retained in a previously issued policy), the insured has made a gift of the value of the policy, or to the extent of the premium paid, even though the right of the assignee or beneficiary to receive the benefits is conditioned upon his surviving the insured. For the valuation of life insurance policies see § 25.2512–6.

(9) Where property held by a husband and wife as community property is used to purchase insurance upon the husband's life and a third person is revocably designated as beneficiary and under the State law the husband's death is considered to make absolute the transfer by the wife, there is a gift by the wife at the time of the husband's death of half the amount of the proceeds of such insurance.

(10) If under a pension plan (pursuant to which he has an unqualified right to an annuity) an employee has an option to take either a retirement annuity for himself alone or a smaller annuity for himself with a survivorship annuity payable to his wife, an irrevocable election by the employee to take the reduced annuity in order that an annuity may be paid, after the employee's death, to his wife results in the making of a gift. However, see section 2517 and the regulations thereunder for the exemption from gift tax of amounts attributable to employers' contributions under qualified plans and certain other contracts.

[T.D. 6334, 23 FR 8904, Nov. 15, 1958, as amended by T.D. 6542, 26 FR 550, Jan. 20, 1961; T.D. 7150, 36 FR 22900, Dec. 2, 1971; T.D. 7238, 37 FR 28728, Dec. 29, 1972; T.D. 7296, 38 FR 34202, Dec. 12, 1973; T.D. 7910, 48 FR 40371, Sept. 7, 1983; T.D. 8095, 51 FR 28369, Aug. 7, 1986]

§ 25.2511–2 Cessation of donor's dominion and control.

(a) The gift tax is not imposed upon the receipt of the property by the donee, nor is it necessarily determined by the measure of enrichment resulting to the donee from the transfer, nor is it conditioned upon ability to identify the donee at the time of the transfer. On the contrary, the tax is a primary and personal liability of the donor, is an excise upon his act of making the transfer, is measured by the value of the property passing from the donor, and attaches regardless of the fact that the identity of the donee may not then be known or ascertainable.

(b) As to any property, or part thereof or interest therein, of which the donor has so parted with dominion and control as to leave in him no power to change its disposition, whether for his own benefit or for the benefit of another, the gift is complete. But if upon a transfer of property (whether in trust or otherwise) the donor reserves any power over its disposition, the gift may be wholly incomplete, or may be partially complete and partially incomplete, depending upon all the facts in the particular case. Accordingly, in every case of a transfer of property subject to a reserved power, the terms of the power must be examined and its scope determined. For example, if a donor transfers property to another in trust to pay the income to the donor or accumulate it in the discretion of the trustee, and the donor retains a testamentary power to appoint the remainder among his descendants, no portion of the transfer is a completed gift. On the other hand, if the donor had not retained the testamentary power of appointment, but instead provided that the remainder should go to X or his heirs, the entire transfer would be a completed gift. However, if the exercise of the trustee's power in favor of the grantor is limited by a fixed or ascertainable standard (see paragraph (g)(2) of § 25.2511–1), enforceable by or on behalf of the grantor, then the gift is incomplete to the extent of the ascertainable value of any rights thus retained by the grantor.

(c) A gift is incomplete in every instance in which a donor reserves the power to revest the beneficial title to the property in himself. A gift is also incomplete if and to the extent that a reserved power gives the donor the power to name new beneficiaries or to change the interests of the beneficiaries as between themselves unless the power is a fiduciary power limited by a fixed or ascertainable standard. Thus, if an estate for life is transferred but, by an exercise of a power, the estate may be terminated or cut down by the donor to one of less value, and without restriction upon the extent to which the estate may be so cut down, the transfer constitutes an incomplete gift. If in this example the power was confined to the right to cut down the estate for life to one for a term of five years, the certainty of an estate for not less than that term results in a gift to that extent complete.

(d) A gift is not considered incomplete, however, merely because the donor reserves the power to change the manner or time of enjoyment. Thus, the creation of a trust the income of which is to be paid annually to the donee for a period of years, the corpus being distributable to him at the end of the period, and the power reserved by the donor being limited to a right to require that, instead of the income being so payable, it should be accumulated and distributed with the corpus to the donee at the termination of the period, constitutes a completed gift.

(e) A donor is considered as himself having a power if it is exercisable by him in conjunction with any person not having a substantial adverse interest in the disposition of the transferred property or the income therefrom. A trustee, as such, is not a person having an adverse interest in the disposition of the trust property or its income.

(f) The relinquishment or termination of a power to change the beneficiaries of transferred property, occurring otherwise than by the death of the donor (the statute being confined to transfers by living donors), is regarded as the event that completes the gift and causes the tax to apply. For example, if A transfers property in trust for the benefit of B and C but reserves the power as trustee to change the proportionate interests of B and C, and if A thereafter has another person appointed trustee in place of himself, such later relinquishment of the power by A to the new trustee completes the gift of the transferred property, whether or not the new trustee has a substantial adverse interest. The receipt of income or of other enjoyment of the transferred property by the transferee or by the beneficiary (other than by the donor himself) during the interim between the making of the initial transfer and the relinquishment or termination of the power operates to free such income or other enjoyment from the power, and constitutes a gift of such income or of such other enjoyment taxable as of the "calendar period" (as defined in § 25.2502–1(c)(1)) of its receipt. If property is transferred in trust to pay the income to A for life with remainder to B, powers to distribute corpus to A, and to withhold income from A for future distribution to B, are powers to change the beneficiaries of the transferred property.

(g) If a donor transfers property to himself as trustee (or to himself and some other person, not possessing a substantial adverse interest, as trustees), and retains no beneficial interest in the trust property and no power over it except fiduciary powers, the exercise or nonexercise of which is limited by a fixed or ascertainable standard, to change the beneficiaries of the transferred property, the donor has made a completed gift and the entire value of the transferred property is subject to the gift tax.

(h) If a donor delivers a properly indorsed stock certificate to the donee or the donee's agent, the gift is completed for gift tax purposes on the date of delivery. If the donor delivers the certificate to his bank or broker as his agent, or to the issuing corporation or its transfer agent, for transfer into the name of the donee, the gift is completed on the date the stock is transferred on the books of the corporation.

(i) [Reserved]

(j) If the donor contends that a power is of such nature as to render the gift incomplete, and hence not subject to the tax as of the "calendar period" (as defined in § 25.2502–1(c)(1)) of the initial transfer, the transaction shall be disclosed in the return and evidence showing all relevant facts, including a copy of the instrument of transfer, should be submitted.

* * *

[T.D. 6334, 23 FR 8904, Nov. 15, 1958, as amended by T.D. 7238, 37 FR 28728, Dec. 29, 1972; T.D. 7910, 48 FR 40371, Sept. 7, 1983]

§ 25.2512–1 Valuation of property; in general.

Section 2512 provides that if a gift is made in property, its value at the date of the gift shall be considered the amount of the gift. The value of the property is the price at which such property would change hands between a willing buyer and a willing seller, neither being under any compulsion to buy or to sell, and both having reasonable knowledge of relevant facts. The value of a particular item of property is not the price that a forced sale of the property would produce. Nor is the fair market value of an item of property the sale price in a market other than that in which such item is most commonly sold to the public, taking into account the location of the item wherever appropriate. Thus, in the case of an item of property made the subject of a gift, which is generally obtained by the public in the retail market, the fair market value of such an item of property is the price at which the item or a comparable item would be sold at retail. For example, the value of an automobile (an article generally obtained by the public in the retail market) which is the subject of a gift, is the price for which an automobile of the same or approximately the same description, make, model, age, condition, etc., could be purchased by a member of the general public and not the price for which the particular automobile of the donor would be purchased by a dealer in used automobiles. Examples of items of property which are generally sold to the public at retail may be found in § 25.2512–6. The value is generally to be determined by ascertaining as a basis the fair market value at the time of the gift of each unit of the property. For example, in the case of shares of stocks or bonds, such unit of property is generally a share or a bond. Property shall not be returned at the value at which it is assessed for local tax purposes unless that value represents the fair market value thereof on the date of the gift. All relevant facts and elements of value as of the time of the gift shall be considered. Where the subject of a gift is an interest in a business, the value of items of property in the inventory of the business generally should be reflected in the value of the business. * * *

[T.D. 6334, 23 FR 8904, Nov. 15, 1958, as amended by T.D. 6826, 30 FR 7709, June 15, 1965]

§ 25.2512–2 Stocks and bonds.

(a) **In general.** The value of stocks and bonds is the fair market value per share or bond on the date of the gift.

(b) **Based on selling prices.** (1) In general, if there is a market for stocks or bonds, on a stock exchange, in an over-the-counter market or otherwise, the mean between the highest and lowest quoted selling prices on the date of the gift is the fair market value per share or bond. If there were no sales on the date of the gift but there were sales on dates within a reasonable period both before and after the date of the gift, the fair market value is determined by taking a weighted average of the means between the highest and lowest sales on the nearest date before and the nearest date after the date of the gift. The average is to be weighted inversely by the respective numbers of trading days between the selling dates and the date of the gift. If the stocks or bonds are listed on more than one exchange, the records of the exchange where the stocks or bonds are principally dealt in should be employed if such records are available in a generally available listing or publication of general circulation. In the event that such records are not so available and such stocks or bonds are listed on a composite listing of combined exchanges available in a generally available listing or publication of general circulation, the records of such combined exchanges should be employed. In valuing listed securities, the donor should be careful to consult accurate records to obtain values as of the date of the gift. If quotations of unlisted securities are obtained from brokers, or evidence as to their sale is obtained from the officers of the issuing companies, copies of letters furnishing such quotations or evidence of sale should be attached to the return.

(2) If it is established with respect to bonds for which there is a market on a stock exchange, that the highest and lowest selling prices are not available for the date of the gift in a generally available listing or publication of general circulation but

that closing prices are so available, the fair market value per bond is the mean between the quoted closing selling price on the date of the gift and the quoted closing selling price on the trading day before the date of the gift. If there were no sales on the trading day before the date of the gift but there were sales on dates within a reasonable period before the date of the gift, the fair market value is determined by taking a weighted average of the quoted closing selling prices on the date of the gift and the nearest date before the date of the gift. The closing selling price for the date of the gift is to be weighted by the respective number of trading days between the previous selling date and the date of the gift. If there were no sales within a reasonable period before the date of the gift but there were sales on the date of the gift, the fair market value is the closing selling price on the date of the gift. If there were no sales on the date of the gift but there were sales within a reasonable period both before and after the date of the gift, the fair market value is determined by taking a weighted average of the quoted closing selling prices on the nearest date before and the nearest date after the date of the gift. The average is to be weighed inversely by the respective numbers of trading days between the selling dates and the date of the gift. If the bonds are listed on more than one exchange, the records of the exchange where the bonds are principally dealt in should be employed. In valuing listed securities, the donor should be careful to consult accurate records to obtain values as of the date of the gift.

* * *

(c) Based on bid and asked prices. If the provisions of paragraph (b) of this section are inapplicable because actual sales are not available during reasonable period beginning before and ending after the date of the gift, the fair market value may be determined by taking the mean between the bona fide bid and asked prices on the date of the gift, or if none, by taking a weighted average of the means between the bona fide bid and asked prices on the nearest trading date before and the nearest trading date after the date of the gift, if both such nearest dates are within a reasonable period. The average is to be determined in the manner described in paragraph (b) of this section.

(d) Where selling prices and bid and asked prices are not available for dates both before and after the date of gift. If the provisions of paragraphs (b) and (c) of this section are inapplicable because no actual sale prices or quoted bona fide bid and asked prices are available on a date within a reasonable period before the date of the gift, but such prices are available on a date within a reasonable period after the date of the gift, or vice versa, then the mean between the highest and lowest available sale prices or bid and asked prices may be taken as the value.

(e) Where selling prices or bid and asked prices do not represent fair market value. In cases in which it is established that the value per bond or share of any security determined on the basis of the selling or bid and asked prices as provided under paragraphs (b), (c), and (d) of this section does not represent the fair market value thereof, then some reasonable modification of the value determined on that basis or other relevant facts and elements of value shall be considered in determining fair market value. Where sales at or near the date of the gift are few or of a sporadic nature, such sales alone may not indicate fair market value. In certain exceptional cases, the size of the block of securities made the subject of each separate gift in relation to the number of shares changing hands in sales may be relevant in determining whether selling prices reflect the fair market value of the block of stock to be valued. If the donor can show that the block of stock to be valued, with reference to each separate gift, is so large in relation to the actual sales on the existing market that it could not be liquidated in a reasonable time without depressing the market, the price at which the block could be sold as such outside the usual market, as through an underwriter, may be a more accurate indication of value than market quotations. Complete data in support of any allowance claimed due to the size of the block of stock being valued should be submitted with the return. On the other hand, if the block of stock to be valued represents a controlling interest, either actual or effective, in a going business, the price at which other lots change hands may have little relation to its true value.

(f) Where selling prices or bid and asked prices are unavailable. If the provisions of paragraphs (b), (c), and (d) of this section are inapplicable because actual sale prices and bona fide bid and asked prices are lacking, then the fair market value is to be determined by taking the following factors into consideration:

(1) In the case of corporate or other bonds, the soundness of the security, the interest yield, the date of maturity, and other relevant factors; and

(2) In the case of shares of stock, the company's net worth, prospective earning power and dividend-paying capacity, and other relevant factors.

Some of the "other relevant factors" referred to in subparagraphs (1) and (2) of this paragraph are: The goodwill of the business; the economic outlook in the particular industry; the company's position in the industry and its management; the degree of control of the business represented by the block of stock to be valued; and the values of securities of corporations engaged in the same or similar lines of business which are listed on a stock exchange. However, the weight to be accorded such comparisons or any other evidentiary factors considered in the determination of a value depends upon the facts of each case. Complete financial and other data upon which the valuation is based should be submitted with the return, including copies of reports of any examinations of the company made by accountants, engineers, or any technical experts as of or near the date of the gift.

[T.D. 6334, 23 FR 8904, Nov. 15, 1958; 25 FR 14021, Dec. 31, 1960, as amended by T.D. 7327, 39 FR 35355, Oct. 1, 1974; T.D. 7432, 41 FR 38769, Sept. 13, 1976]

§ 25.2512–3 Valuation of interest in businesses.

(a) Care should be taken to arrive at an accurate valuation of any interest in a business which the donor transfers without an adequate and full consideration in money or money's worth. The fair market value of any interest in a business, whether a partnership or a proprietorship, is the net amount which a willing purchaser, whether an individual or a corporation, would pay for the interest to a willing seller, neither being under any compulsion to buy or to sell and both having reasonable knowledge of the relevant facts. The net value is determined on the basis of all relevant factors including—

(1) A fair appraisal as of the date of the gift of all the assets of the business, tangible and intangible, including good will;

(2) The demonstrated earning capacity of the business; and

(3) The other factors set forth in paragraph (f) of § 25.2512–2 relating to the valuation of corporate stock, to the extent applicable.

Special attention should be given to determining an adequate value of the good will of the business.

Complete financial and other data upon which the valuation is based should be submitted with the return, including copies of reports of examinations of the business made by accountants, engineers, or any technical experts as of or near the date of the gift.

[T.D. 6334, 23 FR 8904, Nov. 15, 1958]

§ 25.2512–4 Valuation of notes.

The fair market value of notes, secured or unsecured, is presumed to be the amount of unpaid principal, plus accrued interest to the date of the gift, unless the donor establishes a lower value. Unless returned at face value, plus accrued interest, it must be shown by satisfactory evidence that the note is worth less than the unpaid amount (because of the interest rate, or date of maturity, or other cause), or that the note is uncollectible in part (by reason of the insolvency of the party or parties liable, or for other cause), and that the property, if any, pledged or mortgaged as security is insufficient to satisfy it.

[T.D. 6334, 23 FR 8904, Nov. 15, 1958]

§ 25.2512–5 Valuation of annuities, life estates, terms for years, remainders, and reversions transferred after November 30, 1983.

(a) In general. (1)(i) Except as otherwise provided in this paragraph (a)(1)(i), the fair market value of annuities, life estates, terms for years, remainders, and reversions transferred after November 30, 1983, is their present value determined under this section. The value of annuities issued by companies regularly engaged in their sale and of insurance policies issued by companies regularly engaged in their sale is determined under § 25.-2512–6. The fair market value of a remainder interest in a charitable remainder unitrust, as defined in § 1.664–3, is its present value determined under § 1.664–4. The fair market value of a life interest or term for years in a charitable remainder unitrust is the fair market value of the property as of the date of transfer less the fair market value of the remainder interest on such date determined under § 1.664–4. The fair market value of interests in a pooled income fund, as defined in § 1.642(c)–5, is their value determined under § 1.642(c)–6. Where the donor transfers property in trust or otherwise and retains an interest therein, the value of the gift is the value of the property

1493

transferred less the value of the donor's retained interest. If the donor assigns or relinquishes an annuity, life estate, remainder, or reversion which the donor holds by virtue of a transfer previously made by the donor or another, the value of the gift is the value of the interest transferred. See § 25.2512–9 with respect to the valuation of annuities, life estates, terms for years, remainders, and reversions transferred after December 31, 1970, and before December 1, 1983. With respect to the valuation of annuities, life estates, terms for years, remainders, and reversions transferred before January 1, 1971, see T.D. 6334, 23 FR 8904, November 15, 1958, as amended by T.D. 7077, 35 FR 18464, December 4, 1970.

(ii) If the donor transfers in December of 1983, either—

(A) A remainder or a reversion subject to a life interest or a term for years where the life interest or term for years was transferred by the donor after December 31, 1982, and before December 1, 1983, or

(B) A life interest or term for years, the remainder interest of which was transferred by the donor after December 31, 1982, and before December 1, 1983, the donor shall make an election. The donor may elect to value both interests transferred in 1983 under § 25.2512–9 as if such section applied to all transfers made before January 1, 1984, or the donor may elect to have both transfers valued under this section. The donor shall indicate the election being made in a statement attached to the donor's gift tax return for 1983.

(iii) If the donor transfers in calendar year 1984, either—

(A) A remainder on a reversion subject to a life interest or a term for years where the life interest or term for years was transferred by the donor in the first eleven months of 1983, or

(B) A life interest or term for years, the remainder interest of which was transferred by the donor in the first eleven months of 1983, the donor shall make an election. The donor may elect to value the interest transferred in 1984 under § 25.2512–9 as if such section applied to all transfers made before January 1, 1985, or the donor may elect to have the transfer valued under this section. If the donor elects to value the interest transferred in 1984 under § 25.2512–9, the donor shall indicate the election being made by a statement attached to the donor's gift tax return for 1984. If the donor elects to value the interest transferred in 1984

under this section the election shall not be effective unless the donor declares, in a statement attached to the donor's gift tax return for 1984, that the donor has filed an amended gift tax return for 1983, in which the donor has revalued the transfers made in the first eleven months of 1983 under this section as if this section applied to transfers made after December 31, 1982.

(2) The present value of an annuity, life estate, remainder, or reversion determined under this section which is dependent on the continuation or termination of the life of one person is computed by the use of Table A in paragraph (f) of this section. The present value of an annuity, term for years, remainder, or reversion dependent on a term certain is computed by the use of Table B in paragraph (f) of this section. If the interest to be valued is dependent upon more than one life or there is a term certain concurrent with one or more lives, see paragraph (e) of this section. For purposes of the computations described in this section, the age of the person is to be taken at his or her nearest birthday.

(3) In all examples set forth in this section, the interest is assumed to have been transferred after November 30, 1983.

(b) **Annuities.** (1) If an annuity is payable annually at the end of each year during the life of an individual (as for example if the first payment is due one year after the date of the gift), the amount payable annually is multiplied by the figure in column 2 of Table A opposite the number of years in column 1 nearest the age of the individual whose life measures the duration of the annuity. If the annuity is payable annually at the end of each year for a definite number of years, the amount payable annually is multiplied by the figure in column 2 of Table B opposite the number of years in column 1 representing the duration of the annuity. The application of this paragraph (b)(1) may be illustrated by the following examples:

Example (1). The donor assigns an annuity of $10,000 a year payable annually during the donor's life immediately after an annual payment has been made. The age of the donor on the date of assignment is 40 years and eight months. By reference to Table A, it is found that the figure in column 2 opposite 41 years is 9.1030. The value of the gift is, therefore, $91,030 ($10,000 multiplied by 9.1030).

Example (2). The donor was entitled to receive an annuity of $10,000 a year payable annually at the end of annual periods throughout a term of 20 years. The donor, when 15 years have elapsed, makes a gift thereof to the donor's son. By reference to Table B, it is found that the figure in column 2 opposite five years, the unexpired portion of the 20-year period, is 3.7908. The present value of the annuity is, therefore, $37,908 ($10,-000 multiplied by 3.7908).

(2) If an annuity is payable at the end of semiannual, quarterly, monthly, or weekly periods during the life of an individual (as for example if the first payment is due one month after the date of the gift), the aggregate amount to be paid within a year is first multiplied by the figure in column 2 of Table A opposite the number of years in column 1 nearest the age of the individual whose life measures the duration of the annuity. The product so obtained is then multiplied by whichever of the following factors is appropriate:

1.0244 for semiannual payments,

1.0368 for quarterly payments,

1.0450 for monthly payments,

1.0482 for weekly payments.

If the annuity is payable at the end of semiannual, quarterly, monthly, or weekly periods for a definite number of years the aggregate amount to be paid within a year is first multiplied by the figure in column 2 of Table B opposite the number of years in column 1 representing the duration of the annuity. The product so obtained is then multiplied by whichever of the above factors is appropriate. The application of this paragraph (b)(2) may be illustrated by the following example:

Example. The facts are the same as those contained in example (1) set forth in paragraph (b)(1) above, except that the annuity is payable semiannually. The aggregate annual amount, $10,000 is multiplied by the factor 9.1030, and the product multiplied by 1.0244. The value of the gift is, therefore, $93,251.13 ($10,000 × 9.1030 × 1.0244).

(3)(i) If the first payment of an annuity for the life of an individual is due at the beginning of the annual or other payment period rather than at the end (as for example if the first payment is to be made immediately after the date of the gift), the value of the annuity is the sum of (A) the first payment plus (B) the present value of a similar annuity, the first payment of which is not to be made until the end of the payment period, determined as provided in paragraphs (b)(1) or (2) of this section. The application of this paragraph (b)(3)(i) may be illustrated by the following example:

Example. The donee is made the beneficiary for life of an annuity of $50 a month from the income of a trust, subject to the right reserved by the donor to cause the annuity to be paid for the donor's own benefit or for the benefit of another. On the day a payment is due, the donor relinquishes the reserved power. The donee is then 50 years of age. The value of the gift is $50 plus the

product of $50 × 12 × 8.4743 (see Table A) × 1.0450. That is, $50 plus $5,313.39, or $5,363.39.

(ii) If the first payment of an annuity for a definite number of years is due at the beginning of the annual or other payment period, the applicable factor is the product of the factor shown in Table B multiplied by whichever of the following factors is appropriate:

1.1000 for annual payments,

1.0744 for semiannual payments,

1.0618 for quarterly payments,

1.0534 for monthly payments, or

1.0502 for weekly payments.

The application of this paragraph (b)(3)(ii) may be illustrated by the following example:

Example. The donee is the beneficiary of an annuity of $50 a month, subject to a reserved right in the donor to cause the annuity or the cash value thereof to be paid for the donor's own benefit or the benefit of another. On the day a payment is due, the donor relinquishes the power. There are 300 payments to be made covering a period of 25 years, including the payment due. The value of the gift is the product of $50 × 12 × 9.0770 (factor for 25 years Table B) × 1.0534, or $5,737.03.

(c) **Life estates and terms for years.** If the interest to be valued is the right of a person for his or her life, or for the life of another person, to receive the income of certain property or to use non-income-producing property, the value of the interest is the value of the property multiplied by the figure in column 3 of Table A opposite the number of years nearest to the actual age of the measuring life. If the interest to be valued is the right to receive income of property or to use non-income-producing property for a term of years, column 3 of Table B is used. The application of this paragraph (c) may be illustrated by the following example:

Example. The donor who during the donor's life is entitled to receive the income from property worth $50,-000, makes a gift of such interest. The donor is 31 years old on the date of the gift. The value of the gift is $47,627 ($50,000 × .95254).

(d) **Remainders or reversionary interests.** If the interest to be valued is a remainder or reversionary interest subject to a life estate, the value of the interest should be obtained by multiplying the value of the property at the date of the gift by the figure in column 4 of Table A opposite the number of years nearest the age of the life tenant. If the remainder or reversion is to take effect at the end of a term for years, column 4 of Table B should be used. The application of this paragraph (d) may be illustrated by the following example:

Example. The donor transfers by gift a remainder interest in property worth $50,000, subject to the donor's sister's right to receive the income therefrom for her life. The sister at the date of the gift is 31 years of age. By reference to Table A it is found that the figure in column 4 opposite age 31 is .04746. The value of the gift is, therefore, $2,373 ($50,000 × .04746).

(e) Actuarial computations by the Internal Revenue Service. If the interest to be valued is dependent upon the continuation or termination of more than one life, or there is a term certain concurrent with one or more lives, or if the retained interest of the donor is conditioned upon survivorship, a special factor is necessary. The factor is to be computed on the basis of interest at the rate of 10 percent a year, compounded annually, and life contingencies is determined, as to each person involved, from the values of lx that are set forth in column 2 of Table LN of paragraph (f) of § 20.2031–7. Table LN contains values of lx taken from the life table for the total population appearing as Table 1 in United States Life Tables: 1969–71, published by the Department of Health, Education, and Welfare, Public Health Service. A copy of the publication containing many such special factors, may be purchased from the Superintendent of Documents, United States Government Printing Office, Washington, D.C. 20402. However, if a special factor is required in the case of an actual gift, the Commissioner will furnish the factor to the donor upon request. The request must be accompanied by a statement of the date of birth of each person the duration of whose life may affect the value of the interest, and by copies of the relevant instruments. Special factors are not furnished for prospective transfers.

(f) Tables. The following tables shall be used in the application of the provisions of this section:

TABLE A.—SINGLE LIFE, UNISEX, 10 PERCENT SHOWING THE PRESENT WORTH OF AN ANNUITY, OF A LIFE INTEREST, AND OF A REMAINDER INTEREST

Age	Annuity	Life Estate	Remainder
(1)	(2)	(3)	(4)
	* * *		
20	9.7365	.97365	.02635
21	9.7245	.97245	.02755
22	9.7120	.97120	.02880
23	9.6986	.96986	.03014

Age	Annuity	Life Estate	Remainder
(1)	(2)	(3)	(4)
24	9.6841	.96841	.03159
25	9.6678	.96678	.03322
26	9.6495	.96495	.03505
27	9.6290	.96290	.03710
28	9.6062	.96062	.03938
29	9.5813	.95813	.04187
30	9.5543	.95543	.04457
31	9.5254	.95254	.04746
32	9.4942	.94942	.05058
33	9.4608	.94608	.05392
34	9.4250	.94250	.05750
35	9.3868	.93868	.06132
36	9.3460	.93460	.06540
37	9.3026	.93026	.06974
38	9.2567	.92567	.07433
39	9.2083	.92083	.07917
40	9.1571	.91571	.08429
41	9.1030	.91030	.08970
42	9.0457	.90457	.09543
43	8.9855	.89855	.10145
44	8.9221	.89221	.10779
45	8.8558	.88558	.11442
46	8.7863	.87863	.12137
47	8.7137	.87137	.12863
48	8.6374	.86374	.13626
49	8.5578	.85578	.14422
50	8.4743	.84743	.15257
51	8.3874	.83874	.16126
52	8.2969	.82969	.17031
53	8.2028	.82028	.17972
54	8.1054	.81054	.18946
55	8.0046	.80046	.19954
56	7.9006	.79006	.20994
57	7.7931	.77931	.22069
58	7.6822	.76822	.23178
59	7.5675	.75675	.24325
60	7.4491	.74491	.25509
61	7.3267	.73267	.26733
62	7.2002	.72002	.27998
63	7.0696	.70696	.29304
64	6.9352	.69352	.30648
65	6.7970	.67970	.32030
66	6.6551	.66551	.33449
67	6.5098	.65098	.34902
68	6.3610	.63610	.36390
69	6.2086	.62086	.37914
70	6.0522	.60522	.39478
71	5.8914	.58914	.41086
72	5.7261	.57261	.42739
73	5.5571	.55571	.44429
74	5.3862	.53862	.46138
75	5.2149	.52149	.47851
76	5.0441	.50441	.49559
77	4.8742	.48742	.51258
78	4.7049	.47049	.52951
79	4.5357	.45357	.54643
80	4.3659	.43659	.58341
81	4.1967	.41967	.58033
82	4.0295	.40295	.59705
83	3.8642	.38642	.61358
84	3.6998	.36998	.63002
85	3.5359	.35359	.64641
	* * *		

TABLE B.—TABLE SHOWING THE PRESENT WORTH AT 10 PERCENT OF AN ANNUITY FOR A TERM CERTAIN, OF AN INCOME INTEREST FOR A TERM CERTAIN AND OF A REMAINDER INTEREST POSTPONED FOR A TERM CERTAIN

Number of years	Annuity	Term certain	Remain-der
(1)	(2)	(3)	(4)
1	.9091	.090909	.909091
2	1.7355	.173554	.826446
3	2.4869	.248685	.751315
4	3.1699	.316987	.683013
5	3.7908	.379079	.620921
6	4.3553	.435526	.564474
7	4.8684	.486842	.513158
8	5.3349	.533493	.466507
9	5.7590	.575902	.424098
10	6.1446	.614457	.385543
11	6.4951	.649506	.350494
12	6.8137	.681369	.318831
13	7.1034	.710336	.289664
14	7.3667	.738669	.263331
15	7.6061	.760608	.239392
16	7.8237	.782371	.217629
17	8.0216	.802155	.197845
18	8.2014	.820141	.179859
19	8.3649	.836492	.163508
20	8.5136	.851356	.148644
21	8.6487	.864869	.135131
22	8.7715	.877154	.122846
23	8.8832	.888322	.111678
24	8.9847	.898474	.101526
25	9.0770	.907704	.092298
26	9.1609	.916095	.083905
27	9.2372	.923722	.076278
28	9.3066	.930657	.069343
29	9.3696	.936961	.063039
30	9.4269	.942691	.057309
31	9.4790	.947901	.052099
32	9.5264	.952638	.047362
33	9.5694	.956943	.043057
34	9.6086	.960857	.039143
35	9.6442	.964416	.035584
36	9.6765	.967651	.032349
37	9.7059	.970592	.029408
38	9.7327	.973265	.026735
39	9.7570	.975696	.024304
40	9.7791	.977905	.022095
41	9.7991	.979914	.020086
42	9.8174	.981740	.018260
43	9.8340	.983400	.016600
44	9.8491	.984909	.015091
45	9.8628	.986281	.013719

* * *

[T.D. 6334, 23 FR 8904, Nov. 15, 1958; 25 FR 14021, Dec. 31, 1960, as amended by T.D. 7077, 35 FR 18464, Dec. 4, 1970; 35 FR 18965, Dec. 15, 1970; T.D. 7955, 49 FR 19995, May 11, 1984]

§ 25.2512–6 Valuation of certain life insurance and annuity contracts; valuation of shares in an open-end investment company.

(a) Valuation of certain life insurance and annuity contracts. The value of a life insurance contract or of a contract for the payment of an annuity issued by a company regularly engaged in the selling of contracts of that character is established through the sale of the particular contract by the company, or through the sale by the company of comparable contracts. As valuation of an insurance policy through sale of comparable contracts is not readily ascertainable when the gift is of a contract which has been in force for some time and on which further premium payments are to be made, the value may be approximated by adding to the interpolated terminal reserve at the date of the gift the proportionate part of the gross premium last paid before the date of the gift which covers the period extending beyond that date. If, however, because of the unusual nature of the contract such approximation is not reasonably close to the full value, this method may not be used. * * *

* * *

(b) Valuation of shares in an open-end investment company. (1) The fair market value of a share in an open-end investment company (commonly known as a "mutual fund") is the public redemption price of a share. In the absence of an affirmative showing of the public redemption price in effect at the time of the gift, the last public redemption price quoted by the company for the date of the gift shall be presumed to be the applicable public redemption price. If there is no public redemption price quoted by the company for the date of the gift (e.g., the date of the gift is a Saturday, Sunday, or holiday), the fair market value of the mutual fund share is the last public redemption price quoted by the company for the first day preceding the date of the gift for which there is a quotation. As used in this paragraph the term "open-end investment company" includes only a company which on the date of the gift was engaged in offering its shares to the public in the capacity of an open-end investment company.

* * *

[T.D. 6334, 23 FR 8904, Nov. 15, 1958, as amended by T.D. 6542, 26 FR 549, Jan. 20, 1961; T.D. 6680, 28 FR 10872, Oct. 10, 1963; T.D. 7319, 39 FR 26723, July 23, 1974]

§ 25.2512–8 Transfers for insufficient consideration.

Transfers reached by the gift tax are not confined to those only which, being without a valuable consideration, accord with the common law concept of gifts, but embrace as well sales, exchanges, and other dispositions of property for a consideration to the extent that the value of the property transferred by the donor exceeds the value in money or money's worth of the consideration given therefor. However, a sale, exchange, or other transfer of property made in the ordinary course of business (a transaction which is bona fide, at arm's length, and free from any donative intent), will be considered as made for an adequate and full consideration in money or money's worth. A consideration not reducible to a value in money or money's worth, as love and affection, promise of marriage, etc., is to be wholly disregarded, and the entire value of the property transferred constitutes the amount of the gift. Similarly, a relinquishment or promised relinquishment of dower or curtesy, or of a statutory estate created in lieu of dower or curtesy, or of other marital rights in the spouse's property or estate, shall not be considered to any extent a consideration "in money or money's worth." See, however, section 2516 and the regulations thereunder with respect to certain transfers incident to a divorce.

[T.D. 6334, 23 FR 8904, Nov. 15, 1958]

§ 25.2512–9 Valuation of annuities, life estates, terms for years, remainders, and reversions transferred after December 31, 1970, and before December 1, 1983.

(a) In general. (1)(i) Except as otherwise provided in this subparagraph, the fair market value of annuities, life estates, terms for years, remainders, and reversions transferred after December 31, 1970 and before December 1, 1983, is their present value determined under this section. The value of annuities issued by companies regularly engaged in their sale and of insurance policies issued by companies regularly engaged in their sale is determined under § 25.2512–6. The fair market value of a remainder interest in a charitable remainder unitrust, as defined in § 1.664–3, is its present value determined under § 1.664–4. The fair market value of a life interest or term for years in a charitable remainder unitrust is the fair market value of the property as of the date of transfer less the fair market value of the remainder interest on such date determined under § 1.664–4. The fair market value of interests in a pooled income fund, as defined in § 1.642(c)–5, is their value determined under § 1.642(c)–6. Where the donor transfers property in trust or otherwise and retains an interest therein, the value of the gift is the value of the property transferred less the

value of the donor's retained interest. If the donor assigns or relinquishes an annuity, life estate, remainder, or reversion which he holds by virtue of a transfer previously made by himself or another, the value of the gift is the value of the interest transferred. (See § 25.2512–5 with respect to the valuation of annuities, life estates, terms for years, remainders, and reversions transferred after November 30, 1983.)

* * *

(2) The present value of an annuity, life estate, remainder or reversion determined under this section which is dependent on the continuation or termination of the life of one person is computed by the use of Table A(1) or A(2) in paragraph (f) of this section. Table A(1) is to be used when the person upon whose life the interest is based is a male and Table A(2) is to be used when such person is a female. The present value of an annuity, term for years, remainder or reversion dependent on a term certain is computed by the use of Table B in paragraph (f) of this section. If the interest to be valued is dependent upon more than one life or there is a term certain concurrent with one or more lives, see paragraph (e) of this section. For purposes of the computations described in this section, the age of a person is to be taken as the age of that person at his nearest birthday.

(3) In all examples set forth in this section, the interest is assumed to have been transferred after December 31, 1970, and before December 1, 1983.

(b) Annuities—(1) Payable annually at end of year. If an annuity is payable annually at the end of each year during the life of an individual (as for example if the first payment is due 1 year after the date of the gift), the amount payable annually is multiplied by the figure in column 2 of Table A(1) or A(2), whichever is appropriate, opposite the number of years in column 1 nearest the age of the individual whose life measures the duration of the annuity. If the annuity is payable annually at the end of each year for a definite number of years, the amount payable annually is multiplied by the figure in column 2 of Table B opposite the number of years in column 1 representing the duration of the annuity. The application of this subparagraph may be illustrated by the following examples:

Example (1). The donor, a male, assigns an annuity of $10,000 a year payable annually during his life immediately after an annual payment has been made. The age of the donor on the date of assignment is 40 years and 8 months. By reference to Table A(1), it is found that the figure in column 2 opposite 41 years is 12.9934. The value of the gift is, therefore, $129,934 ($10,000 multiplied by 12.9934).

Example (2). The donor was entitled to receive an annuity of $10,000 a year payable annually at the end of annual periods throughout a term of 20 years; the donor, when 15 years have elapsed, makes a gift thereof to his son. By reference to Table B, it is found that the figure in column 2 opposite 5 years, the unexpired portion of the 20-year period, is 4.2124. The present value of the annuity is, therefore, $42,124 ($10,000 multiplied by 4.2124).

* * *

(c) Life estates and terms for years. If the interest to be valued is the right of a person for his life, or for the life of another person, to receive the income of certain property or to use nonincome-producing property, the value of the interest is the value of the property multiplied by the figure in column 3 of Table A(1) or A(2), whichever is appropriate, opposite the number of years nearest to the actual age of the measuring life. If the interest to be valued is the right to receive income of property or to use nonincome-producing property for a term of years, column 3 of Table B is used. The application of this paragraph may be illustrated by the following example:

Example. The donor, a male, who during his life is entitled to receive the income from property worth $50,-000, makes a gift of such interest. The donor is 31 years old on the date of the gift. The value of the gift is $43,058.50 ($50,000×0.86117).

(d) Remainders or reversionary interests. If the interest to be valued is a remainder or reversionary interest subject to a life estate, the value of the interest should be obtained by multiplying the value of the property at the date of the gift by the figure in column 4 of Table A(1) or A(2), whichever is appropriate, opposite the number of years nearest the age of the life tenant. If the remainder or reversion is to take effect at the end of a term of years, column 4 of Table B should be used. The application of this paragraph may be illustrated by the following example:

Example. The donor transfers by gift a remainder interest in property worth $50,000, subject to his sister's right to receive the income therefrom for her life. The sister at the date of the gift is 31 years of age. By reference to Table A(2), it is found that the figure in column 4 opposite age 31 is 0.10227. The value of the gift is, therefore, $5,113.50 ($50,000×0.10227).

(e) Actuarial computations by the Internal Revenue Service. If the interest to be valued is dependent upon the continuation or termination of more than one life, or there is a term certain concurrent with one or more lives, or if the retained interest of the donor is conditioned upon survivorship, a special factor is necessary. The factor is to be computed on the basis of interest at the rate of 6 percent a year, compounded annually, and life contingencies determined, as to each male and female life involved, from the values of 1_x that are set forth in columns 2 and 3, respectively, of Table LN of paragraph (f) of § 20.2031–10. Table LN contains values of 1_x taken from the life table for total males and the life table for total females appearing as Tables 2 and 3, respectively, in United States Life Tables: 1959–61, published by the Department of Health, Education, and Welfare, Public Health Service, except that for technical reasons Table LN employs graduated data, furnished by that Department, to increase the number of significant figures shown at ages of male lives older than 86 and female lives older than 90. Many such special factors may be found in, or computed with the use of the tables contained in, the publications entitled "Actuarial Values I: Valuation of Last Survivor Charitable Remainders" and "Actuarial Values II: Factors at 6 percent Involving One and Two Lives." These publications may be purchased from the Superintendent of Documents, United States Government Printing Office, Washington, DC 20402. However, if a special factor is required in the case of an actual gift, the Commissioner will furnish the factor to the donor upon request. The request must be accompanied by a statement of the sex and date of birth of each person the duration of whose life may affect the value of the interest, and by copies of the relevant instruments.

(f) The following tables shall be used in the application of the provisions of this section:

Table A(1)—single life male, 6 percent, showing the present worth of an annuity, of a life interest, and of a remainder interest

(1)—Age	(2)—Annuity	(3)—Life estate	(4)—Remainder
	* * *		
40	13.1538	.78923	.21077
41	12.9934	.77960	.22040
42	12.8279	.76967	.23033
43	12.6574	.75944	.24056
44	12.4819	.74891	.25109
45	12.3013	.73808	.26192
46	12.1158	.72695	.27305
47	11.9253	.71552	.28448
48	11.7308	.70385	.29615
49	11.5330	.69198	.30802
50	11.3329	.67997	.32003
51	11.1308	.66785	.33215
52	10.9267	.65560	.34440
53	10.7200	.64320	.35680

(1)—Age	(2)—Annuity	(3)—Life estate	(4)—Remainder
54	10.5100	.63060	.36940
55	10.2960	.61776	.38224
56	10.0777	.60466	.39534
57	9.8552	.59131	.40869
58	9.6297	.57778	.42222
59	9.4028	.56417	.43583
60	9.1753	.55052	.44948
61	8.9478	.53687	.46313
62	8.7202	.52321	.47679
63	8.4924	.50954	.49046
64	8.2642	.49585	.50415
65	8.0353	.48212	.51788
66	7.8060	.46836	.53164
67	7.5763	.45458	.54542
68	7.3462	.44077	.55923
69	7.1149	.42689	.57311
70	6.8823	.41294	.58706

* * *

Table A(2)—single life female, 6 percent, showing the present worth of an annuity, of a life interest, and of a remainder interest

(1)—Age	(2)—Annuity	(3)—Life estate	(4)—Remainder
	* * *		
40	14.0468	.84281	.15719
41	13.9227	.83536	.16464
42	13.7940	.82764	.17236
43	13.6604	.81962	.18038
44	13.5219	.81131	.18869
45	13.3781	.80269	.19731
46	13.2290	.79374	.20626
47	13.0746	.78448	.21552
48	12.9147	.77488	.22512
49	12.7496	.76498	.23502
50	12.5793	.75476	.24524
51	12.4039	.74423	.25577
52	12.2232	.73339	.26661
53	12.0367	.72220	.27780
54	11.8436	.71062	.28938
55	11.6432	.69859	.30141
56	11.4353	.68612	.31388
57	11.2200	.67320	.32680
58	10.9980	.65988	.34012
59	10.7703	.64622	.35378
60	10.5376	.63226	.36774
61	10.3005	.61803	.38197
62	10.0587	.60352	.39648
63	9.8118	.58871	.41129
64	9.5592	.57355	.42645
65	9.3005	.55803	.44197
66	9.0352	.54211	.45789
67	8.7639	.52583	.47417
68	8.4874	.50924	.49076
69	8.2068	.49241	.50759
70	7.9234	.47540	.52460

* * *

Table B—showing the present worth at 6 percent of an annuity for a term certain, of an income interest for a term certain, and of a remainder interest postponed for a term certain

(1)—Number of years	(2)—Annuity	(3)—Term certain	(4)—Remainder
1	0.9434	0.056604	0.943396
2	1.8334	.110004	.889996
3	2.6730	.160381	.839619
4	3.4651	.207906	.792094
5	4.2124	.252742	.747258
6	4.9173	.295039	.704961
7	5.5824	.334943	.665057
8	6.2098	.372588	.627412
9	6.8017	.408102	.591898
10	7.3601	.441605	.558395
11	7.8869	.473212	.526788
12	8.3838	.503031	.496969
13	8.8527	.531161	.468839
14	9.2950	.557699	.442301
15	9.7122	.582735	.417265
16	10.1059	.606354	.393646
17	10.4773	.628636	.371364
18	10.8276	.649656	.350344
19	11.1581	.669487	.330513
20	11.4699	.688195	.311805
21	11.7641	.705845	.294155
22	12.0416	.722495	.277505
23	12.3034	.738203	.261797
24	12.5504	.753021	.246979
25	12.7834	.767001	.232999

* * *

[T.D. 7077, 35 FR 18464, Dec. 4, 1970; T.D. 7955, 49 FR 19998, May 11, 1984]

§ 25.2513–1 Gifts by husband or wife to third party considered as made one-half by each.

(a) A gift made by one spouse to a person other than his (or her) spouse may, for the purpose of the gift tax, be considered as made one-half by his spouse, but only if at the time of the gift each spouse was a citizen or resident of the United States. For purposes of this section, an individual is to be considered as the spouse of another individual only if he was married to such individual at the time of the gift and does not remarry during the remainder of the "calendar period" (as defined in § 25.2502–1(c)(1).

(b) The provisions of this section will apply to gifts made during a particular "calendar period" (as defined in § 25.2502–1(c)(1)) only if both spouses signify their consent to treat all gifts made to third parties during that calendar period by both spouses while married to each other as having been made one-half by each spouse. As to the manner and time for signifying consent, see § 25.2513-2. Such consent, if signified with respect to any calendar period, is effective with respect to all gifts made to third parties during such calendar period except as follows:

(1) If the consenting spouses were not married to each other during a portion of the calendar period, the consent is not effective with respect to any gifts made during such portion of the calendar period. Where the consent is signified by an executor or administrator of a deceased spouse, the consent is not effective with respect to gifts made by the surviving spouse during the portion of the calendar period that his spouse was deceased.

(2) If either spouse was a nonresident not a citizen of the United States during any portion of the calendar period, the consent is not effective with respect to any gift made during that portion of the calendar period.

(3) The consent is not effective with respect to a gift by one spouse of a property interest over which he created in his spouse a general power of appointment (as defined in section 2514(c)).

(4) If one spouse transferred property in part to his spouse and in part to third parties, the consent is effective with respect to the interest transferred to third parties only insofar as such interest is ascertainable at the time of the gift and hence severable from the interest transferred to his spouse. See § 25.2512-5 for the principles to be applied in the valuation of annuities, life estates, terms for years, remainders and reversions.

(5) The consent applies alike to gifts made by one spouse alone and to gifts made partly by each spouse, provided such gifts were to third parties and do not fall within any of the exceptions set forth in subparagraphs (1) through (4) of this paragraph. The consent may not be applied only to a portion of the property interest constituting such gifts. For example, a wife may not treat gifts made by her spouse from his separate property to third parties as having been made one-half by her if her spouse does not consent to treat gifts made by her to third parties during the same calendar period as having been made one-half by him. If the consent is effectively signified on either the husband's return or the wife's return, all gifts made by the spouses to third parties (except as described in subparagraphs (1) through (4) of this paragraph), during the calendar period will be treated as having been made one-half by each spouse.

(c) If a husband and wife consent to have the gifts made to third party donees considered as made one-half by each spouse, and only one spouse makes gifts during the "calendar period" (as defined in § 25.2502-1(c)(1)), the other spouse is not required to file a gift tax return provided: (1) The total value of the gifts made to each third party donee since the beginning of the calendar year is not in excess of $20,000 ($6,000 for calendar years prior to 1982), and (2) no portion of the property transferred constitutes a gift of a future interest. If a transfer made by either spouse during the calendar period to a third-party represents a gift of a future interest in property and the spouses consent to have the gifts considered as made one-half by each, a gift tax return for such calendar period must be filed by each spouse regardless of the value of the transfer. (See § 25.2503-3 for the definition of a future interest.)

* * *

[T.D. 6334, 23 FR 8904, Nov. 15, 1958, as amended by T.D. 7238, 37 FR 28729, Dec. 29, 1972; T.D. 7910, 48 FR 40371, Sept. 7, 1983]

§ 25.2513-2 Manner and time of signifying consent.

(a)(1) Consent to the application of the provisions of section 2513 with respect to a "calendar period" (as defined in § 25.2502-1(c)(1)) shall, in order to be effective, be signified by both spouses. If both spouses file gift tax returns within the time for signifying consent, it is sufficient if—

(i) The consent of the husband is signified on the wife's return, and the consent of the wife is signified on the husband's return;

(ii) The consent of each spouse is signified on his own return; or

(iii) The consent of both spouses is signified on one of the returns.

If only one spouse files a gift tax return within the time provided for signifying consent, the consent of both spouses shall be signified on that return. However, wherever possible, the notice of the consent is to be shown on both returns and it is preferred that the notice be executed in the manner described in subdivision (i) of this subparagraph. The consent may be revoked only as provided in § 25.2513-3. If one spouse files more than one gift tax return for a calendar period on or before the due date of the return, the last return so filed shall, for the purpose of determining whether a consent has been signified, be considered as the return. (See §§ 25.6075–1 and 25.6075–2 for the due date of a gift tax return.)

(2) For gifts made after December 31, 1970, and before January 1, 1982, subject to the limitations of paragraph (b) of this section, the consent signified on a return filed for a calendar quarter will be effective for a previous calendar quarter of the same calendar year for which no return was filed because the gifts made during such previous calendar quarter did not exceed the annual exclusion provided by section 2503(b), if the gifts in such previous calendar quarter are listed on that return. Thus, for example, if A gave $2,000 to his son in the first quarter of 1972 (and filed no return because of section 2503(b)) and gave a further $4,000 to such son in the last quarter of the year, A and his spouse could signify consent to the application of section 2513 on the return filed for the fourth quarter and have it apply to the first quarter as well, provided that the $2,000 gift is listed on such return.

* * *

(c) The executor or administrator of a deceased spouse, or the guardian or committee of a legally incompetent spouse, as the case may be, may signify the consent.

(d) If the donor and spouse consent to the application of section 2513, the return or returns for the "calendar period" (as defined in § 25.2502–1(c)(1)) must set forth, to the extent provided thereon, information relative to the transfers made by each spouse.

[T.D. 6334, 23 FR 8904, Nov. 15, 1958, as amended by T.D. 7238, 37 FR 28730, Dec. 29, 1972; T.D. 7910, 48 FR 40371, Sept. 7, 1983]

§ 25.2513–4   Joint and several liability for tax.

If consent to the application of the provisions of section 2513 is signified as provided in § 25.2513–2, and not revoked as provided in § 25.2513–3, the liability with respect to the entire gift tax of each spouse for such "calendar period" (as defined in § 25.2502–1(c)(1)) is joint and several. See paragraph (d) of § 25.2511–1.

[T.D. 6334, 23 FR 8904, Nov. 15, 1958, as amended by T.D. 7238, 37 FR 28730, Dec. 29, 1972; T.D. 7910, 48 FR 40371, Sept. 7, 1983]

§ 25.2514–1   Transfers under power of appointment.

(a) **Introductory.** (1) Section 2514 treats the exercise of a general power of appointment created on or before October 21, 1942, as a transfer of property for purposes of the gift tax. The section also treats as a transfer of property the exercise or complete release of a general power of appointment created after October 21, 1942, and under certain circumstances the exercise of a power of appointment (not a general power of appointment) created after October 21, 1942, by the creation of another power of appointment. See paragraph (d) of § 25.2514–3. Under certain circumstances, also, the failure to exercise a power of appointment created after October 21, 1942, within a specified time, so that the power lapses, constitutes a transfer of property. Paragraphs (b) through (e) of this section contain definitions of certain terms used in §§ 25.2514–2 and 25.2514–3. See § 25.2514–2 for specific rules applicable to certain powers created on or before October 21, 1942. See § 25.2514–3 for specific rules applicable to powers created after October 21, 1942.

(b) **Definition of "power of appointment"**—(1) **In general.** The term "power of appointment" includes all powers which are in substance and effect powers of appointment received by the donee of the power from another person, regardless of the nomenclature used in creating the power and regardless of local property law connotations. For example, if a trust instrument provides that the beneficiary may appropriate or consume the principal of the trust, the power to consume or appropriate is a power of appointment. Similarly, a power given to a donee to affect the beneficial enjoyment of a trust property or its income by altering, amending or revoking the trust instrument or terminating the trust is a power of appointment. A power in a donee to remove or discharge a trustee and appoint himself may be a power of appointment. For example, if under the terms of a trust instrument, the trustee or his successor has the power to appoint the principal of the trust for the benefit of individuals including himself, and A, another person, has the unrestricted power to remove or discharge the trustee at any time and appoint any other person, including himself, A is considered as having a power of appointment. However, he would not be considered to have a power of appointment if he only had the power to appoint a successor, including himself, under limited conditions which did not exist at the time of exercise, release or lapse of the trustee's power, without an accompanying unrestricted power of removal. Similarly, a power to amend only the administrative provisions of a trust instrument, which cannot substantially affect the beneficial enjoyment of the trust property or income, is not a power of appointment. The mere power of management, investment, custody of assets, or the power to allocate receipts and disbursements as between income and principal, exercisable in a fiduciary capacity, whereby the holder has no power to enlarge or shift any of the beneficial interests therein except as an incidental consequence of the discharge of such fiduciary duties is not a power of appointment. Further, the right in a beneficiary of a trust to assent to a periodic accounting, thereby relieving the trustee from further accountability, is not a power of appointment if the right of assent does not consist of any power or right to enlarge or shift the beneficial interest of any beneficiary therein.

(2) **Relation to other sections.** For purposes of §§ 25.2514–1 through 25.2514–3, the term "power of appointment" does not include powers reserved by a donor to himself. No provision of section 2514 or of §§ 25.2514–1 through 25.2514–3 is to be construed as in any way limiting the application of any other section of the Internal Revenue Code or of these regulations. The power of the owner of a property interest already possessed by him to dispose of his interest, and nothing more, is not a power of appointment, and the interest is includible in the amount of his gifts to the extent it would be includible under section 2511 or other provisions of the Internal Revenue Code. For example, if a trust created by S provides for payment of the income to A for life with power in A to appoint the entire trust property by deed during her lifetime to a class consisting of her children, and a further power to dispose of the entire corpus by will to anyone, including her estate, and A exercises the inter vivos power in favor of her children, she has necessarily made a transfer of her income interest which constitutes a taxable gift under section 2511(a), without regard to section 2514. This transfer also results in a relinquishment of her general power to appoint by will which constitutes a transfer under section 2514 if the power was created after October 21, 1942.

(3) **Powers over a portion of property.** If a power of appointment exists as to part of an entire group of assets or only over a limited interest in property, section 2514 applies only to such part or interest.

(c) **Definition of "general power of appointment"**—(1) **In general.** The term "general power of appointment" as defined in section 2514(c) means any power of appointment exercisable in favor of the person possessing the power (referred to as the "possessor"), his estate, his creditors, or the creditors of his estate, except (i) joint powers, to the extent provided in §§ 25.2514–2 and 25.2514–3 and (ii) certain powers limited by an ascertainable standard, to the extent provided in subparagraph (2) of this paragraph. A power of appointment exercisable to meet the estate tax, or any other taxes, debts, or charges which are enforceable against the possessor or his estate, is included within the meaning of a power of appointment exercisable in favor of the possessor, his estate, his creditors, or the creditors of his estate. A power of appointment exercisable for the purpose of discharging a legal obligation of the possessor or for his pecuniary benefit is considered a power of appointment exercisable in favor of the possessor or his creditors. However, for purposes of §§ 25.2514–1 through 25.2514–3, a power of appointment not otherwise considered to be a general power of appointment is not treated as a general power of appointment merely by reason of the fact that an appointee may, in fact, be a creditor of the possessor or his estate. A power of appointment is not a general power if by its terms it is either—

(a) Exercisable only in favor of one or more designated persons or classes other than the possessor or his creditors, or the possessor's estate, or the creditors of his estate, or

(b) Expressly not exercisable in favor of the possessor or his creditors, the possessor's estate, or the creditors of his estate.

A beneficiary may have two powers under the same instrument, one of which is a general power of appointment and the other of which is not. For example, a beneficiary may have a general power to withdraw a limited portion of trust corpus during his life, and a further power exercisable during his lifetime to appoint the corpus among his children. The latter power is not a general power of appointment (but its exercise may result in the exercise of the former power; see paragraph (d) of this section).

(2) **Powers limited by an ascertainable standard.** A power to consume, invade, or appropriate income or corpus, or both, for the benefit of the

possessor which is limited by an ascertainable standard relating to the health, education, support, or maintenance of the possessor is, by reason of section 2514(c)(1), not a general power of appointment. A power is limited by such a standard if the extent of the possessor's duty to exercise and not to exercise the power is reasonably measurable in terms of his needs for health, education, or support (or any combination of them). As used in this subparagraph, the words "support" and "maintenance" are synonymous and their meaning is not limited to the bare necessities of life. A power to use property for the comfort, welfare, or happiness of the holder of the power is not limited by the requisite standard. Examples of powers which are limited by the requisite standard are powers exercisable for the holder's "support," "support in reasonable comfort," "maintenance in health and reasonable comfort," "support in his accustomed manner of living," "education, including college and professional education," "health," and "medical, dental, hospital and nursing expenses and expenses of invalidism." In determining whether a power is limited by an ascertainable standard, it is immaterial whether the beneficiary is required to exhaust his other income before the power can be exercised.

* * *

(d) Definition of "exercise." Whether a power of appointment is in fact exercised may depend upon local law. However, regardless of local law, a power of appointment is considered as exercised for purposes of section 2514 even though the exercise is in favor of the taker in default of appointment, and irrespective of whether the appointed interest and the interest in default of appointment are identical or whether the appointee renounces any right to take under the appointment. A power of appointment is also considered as exercised even though the disposition cannot take effect until the occurrence of an event after the exercise takes place, if the exercise is irrevocable and, as of the time of the exercise, the condition was not impossible of occurrence. For example, if property is left in trust to A for life, with a power in A to appoint the remainder by an instrument filed with the trustee during his life, and A exercises his power by appointing the remainder to B in the event that B survives A, A is considered to have exercised his power if the exercise was irrevocable. Furthermore, if a person holds both a presently exercisable general power of appointment and a presently exercisable nongeneral power of appointment over the same property, the exercise of the nongeneral

power is considered the exercise of the general power only to the extent that immediately after the exercise of the nongeneral power the amount of money or property subject to being transferred by the exercise of the general power is decreased. For example, assume A has a noncumulative annual power to withdraw the greater of $5,000 or 5 percent of the value of a trust having a value of $300,000 and a lifetime nongeneral power to appoint all or a portion of the trust corpus to A's child or grandchildren. If A exercises the nongeneral power by appointing $150,000 to A's child, the exercise of the nongeneral power is treated as the exercise of the general power to the extent of $7,500 (maximum exercise of general power before the exercise of the nongeneral power, 5% of $300,000 or $15,000, less maximum exercise of the general power after the exercise of the nongeneral power, 5% of $150,000 or $7,500).

(e) Time of creation of power. A power of appointment created by will is, in general, considered as created on the date of the testator's death. However, section 2514(f) provides that a power of appointment created by a will executed on or before October 21, 1942, is considered a power created on or before that date if the testator dies before July 1, 1949, without having republished the will, by codicil or otherwise, after October 21, 1942. A power of appointment created by an inter vivos instrument is considered as created on the date the instrument takes effect. Such a power is not considered as created at some future date merely because it is not exercisable on the date the instrument takes effect, or because it is revocable, or because the identity of its holders is not ascertainable until after the date the instrument takes effect. However, if the holder of a power exercises it by creating a second power, the second power is considered as created at the time of the exercise of the first. The application of this paragraph may be illustrated by the following examples:

Example (1). A created a revocable trust before October 22, 1942, providing for payment of income to B for life with remainder as B shall appoint by deed or will. Even though A dies after October 21, 1942, without having exercised his power of revocation, B's power of appointment is considered a power created before October 22, 1942.

Example (2). C created an irrevocable inter vivos trust before October 22, 1942, naming T as trustee and providing for payment of income to D for life with remainder to E. T was given the power to pay corpus to D and the power to appoint a successor trustee. If T resigns after October 21, 1942, and appoints D as successor trustee, D is considered to have a power of appointment created before October 22, 1942.

Example (3). F created an irrevocable inter vivos trust before October 22, 1942, providing for payment of income to G for life with remainder as G shall appoint by deed or will, but in default of appointment income to H for life with remainder as H shall appoint by deed or will. If G died after October 21, 1942, without having exercised his power of appointment, H's power of appointments is considered a power created before October 22, 1942, even though it was only a contingent interest until G's death.

Example (4). If in example (3) above G had exercised by will his power of appointment, by creating a similar power in J, J's power of appointment would be considered a power created after October 21, 1942.

[T.D. 6334, 23 FR 8904, Nov. 15, 1958, as amended by T.D. 6582, 26 FR 11861, Dec. 12, 1961; T.D. 7757, 46 FR 6929, Jan. 22, 1981]

§ 25.2514-3 Powers of appointment created after October 21, 1942.

(a) In general. The exercise, release, or lapse (except as provided in paragraph (c) of this section) of a general power of appointment created after October 21, 1942, is deemed to be a transfer of property by the individual possessing the power. The exercise of a power of appointment that is not a general power is considered to be a transfer if it is exercised to create a further power under certain circumstances (see paragraph (d) of this section). See paragraph (c) of § 25.2514-1 for the definition of various terms used in this section. See paragraph (b) of this section for the rules applicable to determine the extent to which joint powers created after October 21, 1942, are to be treated as general powers of appointment.

(b) Joint powers created after October 21, 1942. The treatment of a power of appointment created after October 21, 1942, which is exercisable only in conjunction with another person is governed by section 2514(c)(3), which provides as follows:

(1) Such a power is not considered as a general power of appointment if it is not exercisable by the possessor except with the consent or joinder of the creator of the power.

(2) Such power is not considered as a general power of appointment if it is not exercisable by the possessor except with the consent or joinder of a person having a substantial interest in the property subject to the power which is adverse to the exercise of the power in favor of the possessor, his estate, his creditors, or the creditors of his estate. An interest adverse to the exercise of a power is

considered as substantial if its value in relation to the total value of the property subject to the power is not insignificant. For this purpose, the interest is to be valued in accordance with the actuarial principles set forth in § 25.2512-5 or, if it is not susceptible to valuation under those provisions, in accordance with the general principles set forth in § 25.2512-1. A taker in default of appointment under a power has an interest which is adverse to an exercise of the power. A coholder of the power has no adverse interest merely because of his joint possession of the power nor merely because he is a permissible appointee under a power. However, a coholder of a power is considered as having an adverse interest where he may possess the power after the possessor's death and may exercise it at that time in favor of himself, his estate, his creditors, or the creditors of his estate. Thus, for example, if X, Y, and Z held a power jointly to appoint among a group of persons which includes themselves and if on the death of X the power will pass to Y and Z jointly, then Y and Z are considered to have interests adverse to the exercise of the power in favor of X. Similarly, if on Y's death the power will pass to Z, Z is considered to have an interest adverse to the exercise of the power in favor of Y. The application of this subparagraph may be further illustrated by the following examples in each of which it is assumed that the value of the interest in question is substantial:

Example (1). The taxpayer and R are trustees of a trust under which the income is to be paid to the taxpayer for life and then to M for life, and R is remainderman. The trustees have power to distribute corpus to the taxpayer. Since R's interest is substantially adverse to an exercise of the power in favor of the taxpayer, the latter does not have a general power of appointment. If M and the taxpayer were trustees, M's interest would likewise be adverse.

Example (2). The taxpayer and L are trustees of a trust under which the income is to be paid to L for life and then to M for life, and the taxpayer is remainderman. The trustees have power to distribute corpus to the taxpayer during L's life. Since L's interest is adverse to an exercise of the power in favor of the taxpayer, the taxpayer does not have a general power of appointment. If the taxpayer and M were trustees, M's interest would likewise be adverse.

Example (3). The taxpayer and L are trustees of a trust under which the income is to be paid to L for life. The trustees can designate whether corpus is to be distributed to the taxpayer or to A after L's death. L's interest is not adverse to an exercise of the power in favor of the taxpayer, and the taxpayer therefore has a general power of appointment.

(3) A power which is exercisable only in conjunction with another person, and which after applica-

tion of the rules set forth in subparagraphs (1) and (2) of this paragraph, constitutes a general power of appointment, will be treated as though the holders of the power who are permissible appointees of the property were joint owners of property subject to the power. The possessor, under this rule, will be treated as possessed of a general power of appointment over an aliquot share of the property to be determined with reference to the number of joint holders, including the possessor, who (or whose estates or creditors) are permissible appointees. Thus, for example, if X, Y, and Z hold an unlimited power jointly to appoint among a group of persons, including themselves, but on the death of X the power does not pass to Y and Z jointly, then Y and Z are not considered to have interests adverse to the exercise of the power in favor of X. In this case, X is considered to possess a general power of appointment as to one-third of the property subject to the power.

(c) **Partial releases, lapses, and disclaimers of general powers of appointment created after October 21, 1942—(1) Partial release of power.** The general principles set forth in § 25.2511–2 for determining whether a donor of property (or of a property right or interest) has divested himself of all or any portion of his interest therein to the extent necessary to effect a completed gift are applicable in determining whether a partial release of a power of appointment constitutes a taxable gift. Thus, if a general power of appointment is partially released so that thereafter the donor may still appoint among a limited class of persons not including himself the partial release does not effect a complete gift, since the possessor of the power has retained the right to designate the ultimate beneficiaries of the property over which he holds the power and since it is only the termination of such control which completes a gift.

(2) **Power partially released before June 1, 1951.** If a general power of appointment created after October 21, 1942, was partially released prior to June 1, 1951, so that it no longer represented a general power of appointment, as defined in paragraph (c) of § 25.2514–1, the subsequent exercise, release, or lapse of the partially released power at any time thereafter will not constitute the exercise or release of a general power of appointment. For example, assume that A created a trust in 1943 under which B possessed a general power of appointment. By an instrument executed in 1948 such general power of appointment was reduced in scope by B to an excepted power. The inter vivos

exercise in 1955, or in any "calendar period" (as defined in § 25.2502–1(c)(1)) thereafter, of such excepted power is not considered an exercise or release of a general power of appointment for purposes of the gift tax.

(3) **Power partially released after May 31, 1951.** If a general power of appointment created after October 21, 1942, was partially released after May 31, 1951, the subsequent exercise, release or a lapse of the power at any time thereafter, will constitute the exercise or release of a general power of appointment for gift tax purposes.

(4) **Release or lapse of power.** A release of a power of appointment need not be formal or express in character. For example, the failure to exercise a general power of appointment created after October 21, 1942, within a specified time so that the power lapses, constitutes a release of the power. In any case where the possessor of a general power of appointment is incapable of validly exercising or releasing a power, by reason of minority, or otherwise, and the power may not be validly exercised or released on his behalf, the failure to exercise or release the power is not a lapse of the power. If a trustee has in his capacity as trustee a power which is considered as a general power of appointment, his resignation or removal as trustee will cause a lapse of his power. However, section 2514(e) provides that a lapse during any calendar year is considered as a release so as to be subject to the gift tax only to the extent that the property which could have been appointed by exercise of the lapsed power of appointment exceeds the greater of (i) $5,000, or (ii) 5 percent of the aggregate value, at the time of the lapse, of the assets out of which, or the proceeds of which, the exercise of the lapsed power could be satisfied. For example, if an individual has a noncumulative right to withdraw $10,000 a year from the principal of a trust fund, the failure to exercise this right of withdrawal in a particular year will not constitute a gift if the fund at the end of the year equals or exceeds $200,000. If, however, at the end of the particular year the fund should be worth only $100,000, the failure to exercise the power will be considered a gift to the extent of $5,000, the excess of $10,000 over 5 percent of a fund of $100,000. Where the failure to exercise a power, such as a right of withdrawal, occurs in more than a single year, the value of the taxable transfer will be determined separately for each year.

(5) **Disclaimer of power created after December 31, 1976.** A disclaimer or renunciation of a

general power of appointment created in a taxable transfer after December 31, 1976, in the person disclaiming is not considered a release of the power for gift tax purposes if the disclaimer or renunciation is a qualified disclaimer as described in section 2518 and the corresponding regulations. If the disclaimer or renunciation is not a qualified disclaimer, it is considered a release of the power.

(6) Disclaimer of power created before January 1, 1977. A disclaimer or renunciation of a general power of appointment created in a taxable transfer before January 1, 1977, in the person disclaiming is not considered a release of the power. The disclaimer or renunciation must be unequivocal and effective under local law. A disclaimer is a complete and unqualified refusal to accept the rights to which one is entitled. There can be no disclaimer or renunciation of a power after its acceptance. In the absence of facts to the contrary, the failure to renounce or disclaim within a reasonable time after learning of the existence of a power shall be presumed to constitute an acceptance of the power. In any case where a power is purported to be disclaimed or renounced as to only a portion of the property subject to the power, the determination as to whether there has been a complete and unqualified refusal to accept the rights to which one is entitled will depend on all the facts and circumstances of the particular case, taking into account the recognition and effectiveness of such a disclaimer under local law. Such rights refer to the incidents of the power and not to other interests of the possessor of the power in the property. If effective under local law, the power may be disclaimed or renounced without disclaiming or renouncing such other interests.

(d) Creation of another power in certain cases. Paragraph (d) of section 2514 provides that there is a transfer for purposes of the gift tax of the value of property (or of property rights or interests) with respect to which a power of appointment, which is not a general power of appointment, created after October 21, 1942, is exercised by creating another power of appointment which, under the terms of the instruments creating and exercising the first power and under applicable local law, can be validly exercised so as to (1) postpone the vesting of any estate or interest in the property for a period ascertainable without regard to the date of the creation of the first power, or (2) (if the applicable rule against perpetuities is stated in terms of suspensions of ownership or of the power of alienation, rather than of vest-

ing) suspend the absolute ownership or the power of alienation of the property for a period ascertainable without regard to the date of the creation of the first power. For the purpose of section 2514(d), the value of the property subject to the second power of appointment is considered to be its value unreduced by any precedent or subsequent interest which is not subject to the second power. Thus, if a donor has a power to appoint $100,000 among a group consisting of his children or grandchildren and during his lifetime exercises the power by making an outright appointment of $75,000 and by giving one appointee a power to appoint $25,000, no more than $25,000 will be considered a gift under section 2514(d). If, however, the donor appoints the income from the entire fund to a beneficiary for life with power in the beneficiary to appoint the remainder, the entire $100,000 will be considered a gift under section 2514(d), if the exercise of the second power can validly postpone the vesting of any estate or interest in the property or can suspend the absolute ownership or power of alienation of the property for a period ascertainable without regard to the date of the creation of the first power.

(e) Examples. The application of this section may be further illustrated by the following examples in each of which it is assumed, unless otherwise stated, that S has transferred property in trust after October 21, 1942, with the remainder payable to R at L's death, and that neither L nor R has any interest in or power over the enjoyment of the trust property except as is indicated separately in each example:

Example (1). The income is payable to L for life. L has the power to cause the income to be paid to R. The exercise of the right constitutes the making of a transfer of property under section 2511. L's power does not constitute a power of appointment since it is only a power to dispose of his income interest, a right otherwise possessed by him.

Example (2). The income is to be accumulated during L's life. L has the power to have the income distributed to himself. If L's power is limited by an ascertainable standard (relating to health, etc.) as defined in paragraph (c)(2) of § 25.2514-1, the lapse of such power will not constitute a transfer of property for gift tax purposes. If L's power is not so limited, its lapse or release during L's lifetime may constitute a transfer of property for gift tax purposes. See especially paragraph (c)(4) of § 25.2514-3.

Example (3). The income is to be paid to L for life. L has a power, exercisable at any time, to cause the corpus to be distributed to himself. L has a general power of appointment over the remainder interest, the release of which constitutes a transfer for gift tax purposes of the remainder interest. If in this example L had a power to cause the corpus to be distributed only to X, L would have a power of appointment which is not a general power of appointment, the exercise or release of which would not constitute a transfer of property for purposes of the gift tax. Although the exercise or release of the nongeneral power is not taxable under this section, see § 25.2514–1(b)(2) for the gift tax consequences of the transfer of the life income interest.

Example (4). The income is payable to L for life. R has the right to cause the corpus to be distributed to L at any time. R's power is not a power of appointment, but merely a right to dispose of his remainder interest, a right already possessed by him. In such a case, the exercise of the right constitutes the making of a transfer of property under section 2511 of the value, if any, of his remainder interest. See paragraph (e) of § 25.2511–1.

Example (5). The income is to be paid to L. R has the right to appoint the corpus to himself at any time. R's general power of appointment over the corpus includes a general power to dispose of L's income interest therein. The lapse or release of R's general power over the income interest during his life may constitute the making of a transfer of property. See especially paragraph (c)(4) of § 25.2514–3.

[T.D. 6334, 23 FR 8904, Nov. 15, 1958, as amended by T.D. 7238, 37 FR 28730, Dec. 29, 1972; T.D. 7776, 46 FR 27642, May 21, 1981; T.D. 7910, 48 FR 40371, Sept. 7, 1983; T.D. 8095, 51 FR 28370, Aug. 7, 1986]

§ 25.2518–1 Qualified disclaimers of property; In general.

(a) Applicability—(1) In general. The rules described in §§ 25.2518–1 through 25.2518–3 apply to the qualified disclaimer of an interest in property which is created in the person disclaiming by a taxable transfer made after December 31, 1976. In general, a qualified disclaimer is an irrevocable and unqualified refusal to accept the ownership of an interest in property. For rules relating to the determination of when a transfer occurs, see § 25.2518–2(c)(3) and (4).

(2) Example. The provisions of paragraph (a)(1) of this section may be illustrated by the following example:

Example. W creates an irrevocable trust on December 10, 1968, and retains the right to receive the income for life. Upon the death of W, which occurs after December 31, 1976, the trust property is distributable to W's surviving issue, per stirpes. The creation of the remainder interest in the trust was a taxable transfer. Therefore, section 2518 does not apply to the disclaimer of the remainder interest because the taxable transfer was made prior to January 1, 1977. If, however, W had also retained the power to designate the person or persons to receive the trust principal at her death, and as a result no taxable gift was made of the remainder interest at the time of the creation of the trust, section 2518 would apply

to any disclaimer made after W's death with respect to an interest in the trust property.

(b) Effect of a qualified disclaimer. If a person makes a qualified disclaimer as described in section 2518(b) and § 25.2518–2, for purposes of the Federal estate, gift, and generation-skipping transfer tax provisions, the disclaimed interest in property is treated as if it had never been transferred to the person making the qualified disclaimer. Instead, it is considered as passing directly from the transferor of the property to the person entitled to receive the property as a result of the disclaimer. Accordingly, a person making a qualified disclaimer is not treated as making a gift. Similarly, the value of a decedent's gross estate for purposes of the Federal estate tax does not include the value of property with respect to which the decedent, or the decedent's executor or administrator on behalf of the decedent, has made a qualified disclaimer. If the disclaimer is not a qualified disclaimer, for the purposes of the Federal estate, gift, and generation-skipping transfer tax provisions, the disclaimer is disregarded and the disclaimant is treated as having received the interest.

(c) Effect of local law—(1) In general—(i) Interests created before 1982. A disclaimer of an interest created in a taxable transfer before 1982 which otherwise meets the requirements of a qualified disclaimer under section 2518 and the corresponding regulations but which, by itself, is not effective under applicable local law to divest ownership of the disclaimed property from the disclaimant and vest it in another, is nevertheless treated as a qualified disclaimer under section 2518 if, under applicable local law, the disclaimed interest in property is transferred, as a result of attempting the disclaimer, to another person without any direction on the part of the disclaimant. An interest in property will not be considered to be transferred without any direction on the part of the disclaimant if, under applicable local law, the disclaimant has any discretion (whether or not such discretion is exercised) to determine who will receive such interest. Actions by the disclaimant which are required under local law merely to divest ownership of the property from the disclaimant and vest ownership in another person will not disqualify the disclaimer for purposes of section 2518(a). See § 25.2518–2(d)(1) for rules relating to the immediate vesting of title in the disclaimant.

(ii) Interests created after 1981. [Reserved].

(2) Creditor's claims. The fact that a disclaimer is voidable by the disclaimant's creditors has no effect on the determination of whether such disclaimer constitutes a qualified disclaimer. However, a disclaimer that is wholly void or that is voided by the disclaimant's creditors cannot be a qualified disclaimer.

(3) **Examples.** The provisions of paragraphs (c)(1) and (2) of this section may be illustrated by the following examples:

Example (1). F dies testate in State Y on June 17, 1978. G and H are beneficiaries under the will. The will provides that any disclaimed property is to pass to the residuary estate. H has no interest in the residuary estate. Under the applicable laws of State Y, a disclaimer must be made within 6 months of the death of the testator. Seven months after F's death, H disclaimed the real property H received under the will. The disclaimer statute of State Y has a provision stating that an untimely disclaimer will be treated as an assignment of the interest disclaimed to those persons who would have taken had the disclaimer been valid. Pursuant to this provision, the disclaimed property became part of the residuary estate. Assuming the remaining requirements of section 2518 are met, H has made a qualified disclaimer for purposes of section 2518(a).

Example (2). Assume the same facts as in example (1) except that the law of State Y does not treat an ineffective disclaimer as a transfer to alternative takers. H assigns the disclaimed interest by deed to those who would have taken had the disclaimer been valid. Under these circumstances, H has not made a qualified disclaimer for purposes of section 2518(a) because the disclaimant directed who would receive the property.

Example (3). Assume the same facts as in example (1) except that the law of State Y requires H to pay a transfer tax in order to effectuate the transfer under the ineffective disclaimer provision. H pays the transfer tax. H has made a qualified disclaimer for purposes of section 2518(a).

(d) **Cross-reference.** For rules relating to the effect of qualified disclaimers on the estate tax charitable and marital deductions, see §§ 20.2055-2(c) and 20.2056(d)-1 respectively. For rules relating to the effect of a qualified disclaimer of a general power of appointment, see § 20.2041-3(d).

[T.D. 8095, 51 FR 28370, Aug. 7, 1986]

§ 25.2518-2 Requirements for a qualified disclaimer.

(a) **In general.** For the purposes of section 2518(a), a disclaimer shall be a qualified disclaimer only if it satisfies the requirements of this section. In general, to be a qualified disclaimer—

(1) The disclaimer must be irrevocable and unqualified:

(2) The disclaimer must be in writing;

(3) The writing must be delivered to the person specified in paragraph (b)(2) of this section within the time limitations specified in paragraph (c)(1) of this section;

(4) The disclaimant must not have accepted the interest disclaimed or any of its benefits; and

(5) The interest disclaimed must pass either to the spouse of the decedent or to a person other than the disclaimant without any direction on the part of the person making the disclaimer.

(b) **Writing—(1) Requirements.** A disclaimer is a qualified disclaimer only if it is in writing. The writing must identify the interest in property disclaimed and be signed either by the disclaimant or by the disclaimant's legal representative.

(2) **Delivery.** The writing described in paragraph (b)(1) of this section must be delivered to the transferor of the interest, the transferor's legal representative, the holder of the legal title to the property to which the interest relates, or the person in possession of such property.

(c) **Time limit—(1) In general.** A disclaimer is a qualified disclaimer only if the writing described in paragraph (b)(1) of this section is delivered to the persons described in paragraph (b)(2) of this section no later than the date which is 9 months after the later of—

(i) The date on which the transfer creating the interest in the disclaimant is made, or

(ii) The day on which the disclaimant attains age 21.

(2) **A timely mailing of a disclaimer treated as a timely delivery.** Although section 7502 and the regulations under that section apply only to documents to be filed with the Service, a timely mailing of a disclaimer to the person described in paragraph (b)(2) of this section is treated as a timely delivery if the mailing requirements under paragraphs (c)(1), (c)(2) and (d) of § 301.7502-1 are met. Further, if the last day of the period specified in paragraph (c)(1) of this section falls on Saturday, Sunday or a legal holiday (as defined in paragraph (b) of § 301.7503-1), then the delivery of the writing described in paragraph (b)(1) of this section shall be considered timely if delivery is made on the first succeeding day which is not Saturday, Sunday or a legal holiday. See paragraph (d)(3) of this section for rules applicable to the exception for individuals under 21 years of age.

(3) **Transfer.** For purposes of the time limitation described in paragraph (c)(1)(i) of this section,

the 9-month period for making a disclaimer generally is to be determined with reference to the taxable transfer creating the interest in the disclaimant. With respect to inter vivos transfers, a taxable transfer occurs when there is a completed gift for Federal gift tax purposes regardless of whether a gift tax is imposed on the completed gift. Thus, gifts qualifying for the gift tax annual exclusion under section 2503(b) are regarded as taxable transfers for this purpose. With respect to transfers made by a decedent at death or transfers which become irrevocable at death, a taxable transfer occurs upon the date of the decedent's death. However, where there is a taxable transfer of an interest for Federal gift tax purposes and such interest is later included in the transferor's gross estate for Federal estate tax purposes, the 9-month period for making a qualified disclaimer is determined with reference to the earlier taxable transfer. In the case of a general power of appointment, the holder of the power has a 9-month period after the creation of the power in which to disclaim. A person to whom any interest in property passes by reason of the exercise or lapse of a general power may disclaim such interest within a 9-month period after the exercise or lapse. In the case of a nongeneral power of appointment, the holder of the power, permissible appointees, or takers in default of appointment must disclaim within a 9-month period after the original taxable transfer that created or authorized the creation of the power. If the transfer is for the life of an income beneficiary with succeeding interests to other persons, both the life tenant and the other remaindermen, whether their interests are vested or contingent, must disclaim no later than 9 months after the original taxable transfer. In the case of a remainder interest in property which an executor elects to treat as qualified terminable interest property under section 2056(b)(7), the remainderman must disclaim within 9 months of the transfer creating the interest, rather than 9 months from the date such interest is subject to tax under section 2044 or 2519. A person who receives an interest in property as the result of a qualified disclaimer of the interest must disclaim the previously disclaimed interest no later than 9 months after the date of the taxable transfer creating the interest in the preceding disclaimant. Thus, if A were to make a qualified disclaimer of a specific bequest and as a result of the qualified disclaimer the property passed as part of the residue, the beneficiary of the residue could make a qualified disclaimer no later than 9 months after

the date of the testator's death. See paragraph (d)(3) of this section for the time limitation rule with reference to recipients who are under 21 years of age.

(4) **Joint property—(i) In general.** Except as otherwise provided in paragraph (c)(4)(ii) of this section, a qualified disclaimer under section 2518(a) of an interest or any portion of an interest in a joint tenancy or a tenancy by the entirety must be made no later than 9 months after the transfer creating the tenancy. Thus, a surviving joint tenant cannot disclaim any part of the interest including the survivorship interest, if more than 9 months have passed since the transfer creating the joint tenancy. In addition, a joint tenant cannot make a qualified disclaimer of any portion of the joint interest attributable to consideration furnished by that tenant.

(ii) **Tenancies in real property between spouses created before 1982.** In the case of joint tenancies between spouses or a tenancy by the entirety in real property created after 1976 and before 1982 where no election was made under section 2515, the surviving spouse must make a qualified disclaimer no later than 9 months after the date of death of the first spouse to die. Such a qualified disclaimer will be effective for—

(A) The entire joint interest (except any portion attributable to consideration furnished by the surviving spouse) if the date of death of the deceased spouse is before 1982; or

(B) One-half the value of the joint interest if the date of death of the deceased spouse is after 1981. See examples (7) and (8) under paragraph (c)(5) of this section.

(5) **Examples.** The provisions of paragraphs (c)(1) through (c)(4) of this section may be illustrated by the following examples. For purposes of the following examples, assume that all beneficiaries are over 21 years of age.

Example (1). On May 13, 1978, in a transfer which constitutes a completed gift for Federal gift tax purposes, A creates a trust in which B is given a lifetime interest in the income from the trust. B is also given a nongeneral testamentary power of appointment over the corpus of the trust. The power of appointment may be exercised in favor of any of the issue of A and B. If there are no surviving issue at B's death or if the power is not exercised, the corpus is to pass to E. On May 13, 1978, A and B have two surviving children, C and D. If A, B, C or D wishes to make a qualified disclaimer, the disclaimer must be made no later than 9 months after May 13, 1978.

Example (2). Assume the same facts as in example (1) except that B is given a general power of appointment over the corpus of the trust. B exercises the general power of appointment in favor of C upon B's death on June 17, 1989. C may make a qualified disclaimer no later than 9 months after June 17, 1989. If B had died without exercising the general power of appointment, E could have made a qualified disclaimer no later than 9 months after June 17, 1989.

Example (3). F creates a trust on April 1, 1978, in which F's child G is to receive the income from the trust for life. Upon G's death, the corpus of the trust is to pass to G's child H. If either G or H wishes to make a qualified disclaimer, it must be made no later than 9 months after April 1, 1978.

Example (4). A creates a trust on February 15, 1978, in which B is named the income beneficiary for life. The trust further provides that upon B's death the proceeds of the trust are to pass to C, if then living. If C predeceases D, the proceeds shall pass to D or D's estate. To have timely disclaimers for purposes of section 2518, B, C, and D must disclaim their respective interests no later than 9 months after February 15, 1978.

Example (5). A, a resident of State Q, dies on January 10, 1979, devising certain real property to B. The disclaimer laws of State Q require that a disclaimer be made within a reasonable time after a transfer. B disclaims the entire interest in real property on November 10, 1979. Although B's disclaimer may be effective under State Q law, it is not a qualified disclaimer under section 2518 because the disclaimer was made later than 9 months after the taxable transfer to B.

Example (6). A creates a revocable trust on June 1, 1980, in which B and C are given the income interest for life. Upon the death of the last income beneficiary, the remainder interest is to pass to D. The creation of the trust is not a completed gift for Federal gift tax purposes, but each distribution of trust income to B and C is a completed gift at the date of distribution. B and C disclaim each income distribution no later than 9 months after the date of the particular distribution. In order to disclaim an income distribution in the form of a check, the recipient must return the check to the trustee uncashed along with a written disclaimer. A dies on September 1, 1982, causing the trust to become irrevocable, and the trust corpus is includible in A's gross estate for Federal estate tax purposes under section 2038. If B or C wishes to make a qualified disclaimer of his income interest, he must do so no later than 9 months after September 1, 1982. If D wishes to make a qualified disclaimer of his remainder interest, he must do so no later than 9 months after September 1, 1982.

Example (7). On March 1, 1977, H and W purchase a tract of vacant land which is conveyed to them as tenants by the entirety. The entire consideration is paid by H. H does not elect, under section 2515, to have the transaction treated as a transfer for purposes of Chapter 12. H dies on June 1, 1981. On October 1, 1981, W disclaims the property. Assuming the other requirements of section 2518(b) are satisfied, W has made a qualified disclaimer because the transfer which created W's interest is treated as not occurring until H's death since no election was made under section 2515. Had an election been made under section 2515, then W's disclaimer of any of W's interest in the property would not be a qualified disclaimer.

Example (8). Assume the same facts as in example (7) except that H dies on September 3, 1984. W has until 9 months after September 3, 1984 to make a qualified disclaimer, but she can only make a qualified disclaimer of one-half of the joint interest.

Example (9). On July 1, 1980, B transfers $10,000 to a bank account which is held jointly by B and C. Assume the transfer is not a completed gift for Federal gift tax purposes. The funds in the bank account may be withdrawn in full by either B or C at any time. C never receives funds from the bank account. B dies on August 15, 1989, and C disclaims the amount in the bank account on October 15, 1989. Assuming the remaining requirements of section 2518(b) are satisfied, C made a qualified disclaimer under section 2518(a) because it was made no later than 9 months after the taxable transfer that created an interest in C.

Example (10). H and W reside in State X, a community property state. On April 1, 1978, H and W purchase real property with community funds. The property is not held by H and W as jointly owned property with rights of survivorship. H and W hold the property until January 3, 1985, when H dies. H devises his portion of the property to W. On March 15, 1985, W disclaims the portion of the property devised to her by H. Assuming all the other requirements of section 2518(b) have been met, W has made a qualified disclaimer of the interest devised to her by H. However, W could not disclaim the interest in the property that she acquired on April 1, 1978.

(d) No acceptance of benefits—(1) Acceptance. A qualified disclaimer cannot be made with respect to an interest in property if the disclaimant has accepted the interest or any of its benefits, expressly or impliedly, prior to making the disclaimer. Acceptance is manifested by an affirmative act which is consistent with ownership of the interest in property. Acts indicative of acceptance include using the property or the interest in property; accepting dividends, interest, or rents from the property; and directing others to act with respect to the property or interest in property. However, merely taking delivery of an instrument of title, without more, does not constitute acceptance. Moreover, a disclaimant is not considered to have accepted property merely because under applicable local law title to the property vests immediately in the disclaimant upon the death of a decedent. The acceptance of one interest in property will not, by itself, constitute an acceptance of any other separate interests created by the transferor and held by the disclaimant in the same property. In the case of residential property, held in joint tenancy by some or all of the residents, a joint tenant will not be considered to have accepted the joint interest merely because the tenant resided on the property prior to disclaiming his interest in the property. The exercise of a power of appointment to any extent by the donee of the power is an acceptance of its benefits. In addition, the acceptance of any consideration in return for making the disclaimer is an acceptance of the benefits of the entire interest disclaimed.

(2) **Fiduciaries.** If a beneficiary who disclaims an interest in property is also a fiduciary, actions taken by such person in the exercise of fiduciary powers to preserve or maintain the disclaimed property shall not be treated as an acceptance of such property or any of its benefits. Under this rule, for example, an executor who is also a beneficiary may direct the harvesting of a crop or the general maintenance of a home. A fiduciary, however, cannot retain a wholly discretionary power to direct the enjoyment of the disclaimed interest. For example, a fiduciary's disclaimer of a beneficial interest does not meet the requirements of a qualified disclaimer if the fiduciary exercised or retains a discretionary power to allocate enjoyment of that interest among members of a designated class. See paragraph (e) of this section for rules relating to the effect of directing the redistribution of disclaimed property.

(3) **Under 21 years of age.** A beneficiary who is under 21 years of age has until 9 months after his twenty-first birthday in which to make a qualified disclaimer of his interest in property. Any actions taken with regard to an interest in property by a beneficiary or a custodian prior to the beneficiary's twenty-first birthday will not be an acceptance by the beneficiary of the interest.

(4) **Examples.** The provisions of paragraphs (d)(1), (2) and (3) of this section may be illustrated by the following examples:

Example (1). On April 9, 1977, A established a trust for the benefit of B, then age 22. Under the terms of the trust, the current income of the trust is to be paid quarterly to B. Additionally, one half the principal is to be distributed to B when B attains the age of 30 years. The balance of the principal is to be distributed to B when B attains the age of 40 years. Pursuant to the terms of the trust, B received a distribution of income on June 30, 1977. On August 1, 1977, B disclaimed B's right to receive both the income from the trust and the principal of the trust, B's disclaimer of the income interest is not a qualified disclaimer for purposes of section 2518(a) because B accepted income prior to making the disclaimer. B's disclaimer of the principal, however, does satisfy section 2518(b)(3). See also § 25.2518–3 for rules relating to the disclaimer of less than an entire interest in property.

Example (2). B is the recipient of certain property devised to B under the will of A. The will stated that any disclaimed property was to pass to C. B and C entered into negotiations in which it was declined that B would disclaim all interest in the real property that was devised to B. In exchange, C promised to let B live in the family home for life. B's disclaimer is not a qualified disclaimer for purposes of section 2518(a) because B accepted consideration for making the disclaimer.

Example (3). A received a gift of Blackacre on December 25, 1978. A never resided on Blackacre but when property taxes on Blackacre became due on July 1, 1979, A paid them out of personal funds. On August 15, 1979, A disclaimed the gift of Blackacre. Assuming all the requirements of section 2518 (b) have been met, A has made a qualified disclaimer of Blackacre. Merely paying the property taxes does not constitute an acceptance of Blackacre even though A's personal funds were used to pay the taxes.

Example (4). A died on February 15, 1978. Pursuant to A's will, B received a farm in State Z. B requested the executor to sell the farm and to give the proceeds to B. The executor then sold the farm pursuant to B's request. B then disclaimed $50,000 of the proceeds from the sale of the farm. B's disclaimer is not a qualified disclaimer. By requesting the executor to sell the farm B accepted the farm even though the executor may not have been legally obligated to comply with B's request. See also § 25.2518–3 for rules relating to the disclaimer of less than an entire interest in property.

Example (5). Assume the same facts as in example (4) except that instead of requesting the executor to sell the farm, B pledged the farm as security for a short-term loan which was paid off prior to distribution of the estate. B then disclaimed his interest in the farm. B's disclaimer is not a qualified disclaimer. By pledging the farm as security for the loan, B accepted the farm.

Example (6). A delivered 1,000 shares of stock in Corporation X to B as a gift on February 1, 1980. A had the shares registered in B's name on that date. On April 1, 1980, B disclaimed the interest in the 1,000 shares. Prior to making the disclaimer, B did not pledge the shares, accept any dividends or otherwise commit any acts indicative of acceptance. Assuming the remaining requirements of section 2518 are satisfied, B's disclaimer is a qualified disclaimer.

Example (7). On January 1, 1980, A created an irrevocable trust in which B was given a testamentary general power of appointment over the trust's corpus. B executed a will on June 1, 1980, in which B provided for the exercise of the power of appointment. On September 1, 1980, B disclaimed the testamentary power of appointment. Assuming the remaining requirements of section 2518(b) are satisfied, B's disclaimer of the testamentary power of appointment is a qualified disclaimer.

Example (8). H and W reside in X, a community property state. On January 1, 1981, H and W purchase a residence with community funds. They continue to reside in the house until H dies testate on February 1, 1990. Although H could devise his portion of the residence to any person, H devised his portion of the residence to W. On September 1, 1990, W disclaims the portion of the residence devised to her pursuant to H's will but continues to live in the residence. Assuming the remaining requirements of section 2518(b) are satisfied, W's disclaimer is a qualified disclaimer under section 2518(a). W's continued occupancy of the house prior to making the disclaimer will not by itself be treated as an acceptance of the benefits of the portion of the residence devised to her by H.

Example (9). In 1979, D established a trust for the benefit of D's minor children E and F. Under the terms of the trust, the trustee is given the power to make discretionary distributions of current income and corpus to both children. The corpus of the trust is to be distributed equally between E and F when E becomes 35 years of age. Prior to attaining the age of 21 years on April 8, 1982, E receives several distributions of income from the trust. E receives no distributions of income between April 8, 1982 and August 15, 1982, which is the date on which E disclaims all interest in the income from the trust. As a result of the disclaimer the income will be distributed to F. If the remaining requirements of section 2518 are met, E's disclaimer is a qualified disclaimer under section 2518(a). To have a qualified disclaimer of the interest in corpus, E must disclaim the interest no later than 9 months after April 8, 1982, E's 21st birthday.

Example (10). Assume the same facts as in example (9) except that E accepted a distribution of income on May 13, 1982. E's disclaimer is not a qualified disclaimer under section 2518 because by accepting an income distribution after attaining the age of 21, F accepted benefits from the income interest.

Example (11). F made a gift of 10 shares of stock to G as custodian for H under the State X Uniform Gifts to Minors Act. At the time of the gift, H was 15 years old. At age 18, the local age of majority, the 10 shares were delivered to and registered in the name of H. Between the receipt of the shares and H's 21st birthday, H received dividends from the shares. Within 9 months of attaining age 21, H disclaimed the 10 shares. Assuming H did not accept any dividends from the shares after attaining age 21, the disclaimer by H is a qualified disclaimer under section 2518.

(e) Passage without direction by the disclaimant of beneficial enjoyment of disclaimed interest—(1) In general. A disclaimer is not a qualified disclaimer unless the disclaimed interest passes without any direction on the part of the disclaimant to a person other than the disclaimant (except as provided in paragraph (e)(2) of this section). If there is an express or implied agreement that the disclaimed interest in property is to be given or bequeathed to a person specified by the disclaimant, the disclaimant shall be treated as directing the transfer of the property interest. The requirements of a qualified disclaimer under section 2518 are not satisfied if—

(i) The disclaimant, either alone or in conjunction with another, directs the redistribution or transfer of the property or interest in property to another person (or has the power to direct the redistribution or transfer of the property or interest in property to another person unless such power is limited by an ascertainable standard); or

(ii) The disclaimed property or interest in property passes to or for the benefit of the disclaimant as a result of the disclaimer (except as provided in paragraph (e)(2) of this section).

If a power of appointment is disclaimed, the requirements of this paragraph (e)(1) are satisfied so long as there is no direction on the part of the disclaimant with respect to the transfer of the interest subject to the power or with respect to the transfer of the power to another person. A person may make a qualified disclaimer of a beneficial interest in property even if after such disclaimer the disclaimant has a fiduciary power to distribute to designated beneficiaries, but only if the power is subject to an ascertainable standard. See examples (11) and (12) of paragraph (e)(5) of this section.

(2) Disclaimer by surviving spouse. In the case of a disclaimer made by a decedent's surviving spouse with respect to property transferred by the decedent, the disclaimer satisfies the requirements of this paragraph (e) if the interest passes as a result of the disclaimer without direction on the part of the surviving spouse either to the surviving spouse or to another person. If the surviving spouse, however, retains the right to direct the beneficial enjoyment of the disclaimed property in a transfer that is not subject to Federal estate and gift tax (whether as trustee or otherwise), such spouse will be treated as directing the beneficial enjoyment of the disclaimed property, unless such power is limited by an ascertainable standard. See examples (4), (5), and (6) in paragraph (e)(5) of this section.

(3) Partial failure of disclaimer. If a disclaimer made by a person other than the surviving spouse is not effective to pass completely an interest in property to a person other than the disclaimant because—

(i) The disclaimant also has a right to receive such property as an heir at law, residuary beneficiary, or by any other means; and

(ii) The disclaimant does not effectively disclaim these rights, the disclaimer is not a qualified disclaimer with respect to the portion of the disclaimed property which the disclaimant has a right to receive. If the portion of the disclaimed interest in property which the disclaimant has a right to receive is not severable property or an undivided portion of the property, then the disclaimer is not a qualified disclaimer with respect to any portion of the property. Thus, for example, if a disclaimant who is not a surviving spouse receives a specific bequest of a fee simple interest in property and as a result of the disclaimer of the entire interest, the property passes to a trust in which the disclaimant has a remainder interest, then the disclaimer will not be a qualified disclaimer unless the remainder interest in the property is also disclaimed. See § 25.2518–3(a)(1)(ii) for the definition of severable property.

(4) **Effect of precatory language.** Precatory language in a disclaimer naming takers of disclaimed property will not be considered as directing the redistribution or transfer of the property or interest in property to such persons if the applicable State law gives the language no legal effect.

(5) **Examples.** The provisions of this paragraph (e) may be illustrated by the following examples:

Example (1). A, a resident of State X, died on July 30, 1978. Pursuant to A's will, B, A's son and heir at law, received the family home. In addition, B and C each received 50 percent of A's residuary estate. B disclaimed the home. A's will made no provision for the distribution of property in the case of a beneficiary's disclaimer. Therefore, pursuant to the disclaimer laws of State X, the disclaimed property became part of the residuary estate. Because B's 50 percent share of the residuary estate will be increased by 50 percent of the value of the family home, the disclaimed property will not pass solely to another person. Consequently, B's disclaimer of the family home is a qualified disclaimer only with respect to the 50 percent portion that passes solely to C. Had B also disclaimed B's 50 percent interest in the residuary estate, the disclaimer would have been a qualified disclaimer under section 2518 of the entire interest in the home (assuming the remaining requirements of a qualified disclaimer were satisfied). Similarly, if under the laws of State X, the disclaimer has the effect of divesting B of all interest in the home, both as devisee and as a beneficiary of the residuary estate, including any property resulting from its sale, the disclaimer would be a qualified disclaimer of B's entire interest in the home.

Example (2). D, a resident of State Y, died testate on June 30, 1978. E, an heir at law of D, received specific bequests of certain severable personal property from D. E disclaimed the property transferred by D under the will. The will made no provision for the distribution of property in the case of a beneficiary's disclaimer. The disclaimer laws of State Y provide that such property shall pass to the decedent's heirs at law in the same manner as if the disclaiming beneficiary had died immediately before the testator's death. Because State Y's law treats E as predeceasing D, the property disclaimed by E does not pass to E as an heir at law or otherwise. Consequently, if the remaining requirements of section 2518(b) are satisfied, E's disclaimer is a qualified disclaimer under section 2518(a).

Example (3). Assume the same facts as in example (2) except that State Y has no provision treating the disclaimant as predeceasing the testator. E's disclaimer satisfies section 2518(b)(4) only to the extent that E does not have a right to receive the property as an heir at law.

Had E disclaimed both the share E received under D's will and E's intestate share, the requirement of section 2518(b)(4) would have been satisfied.

Example (4). B died testate on February 13, 1980. B's will established both a marital trust and a nonmarital trust. The decedent's surviving spouse, A, is an income beneficiary of the martial trust and has a testamentary general power of appointment over its assets. A is also an income beneficiary of the nonmarital trust, but has no power to appoint or invade the corpus. The provisions of the will specify that any portion of the marital trust disclaimed is to be added to the nonmarital trust. A disclaimed 30 percent of the marital trust. (See § 25.-2518–3(b) for rules relating to the disclaimer of an undivided portion of an interest in property.) Pursuant to the will, this portion of the marital trust property was transferred to the nonmarital trust without any direction on the part of A. This disclaimer by A satisfies section 2518(b)(4).

Example (5). Assume the same facts as in example (4) except that A, the surviving spouse, has both an income interest in the nonmarital trust and a testamentary nongeneral power to appoint among designated beneficiaries. This power is not limited by an ascertainable standard. The requirements of section 2518(b)(4) are not satisfied unless A also disclaims the nongeneral power to appoint the portion of the trust corpus that is attributable to the property that passed to the nonmarital trust as a result of A's disclaimer. Assuming that the fair market value of the disclaimed property on the date of the disclaimer is $250,000 and that the fair market value of the nonmarital trust (including the disclaimed property) immediately after the disclaimer is $750,000, A must disclaim the power to appoint one-third of the nonmarital trust's corpus. The result is the same regardless of whether the nongeneral power is testamentary or inter vivos.

Example (6). Assume the same facts as in example (4) except that A has both an income interest in the nonmarital trust and a power to invade corpus if needed for A's health or maintenance. In addition, an independent trustee has power to distribute to A any portion of the corpus which the trustee determines to be desirable for A's happiness. Assuming the other requirements of section 2518 are satisfied, A may make a qualified disclaimer of interests in the marital trust without disclaiming any of A's interests in the nonmarital trust.

Example (7). B died testate on June 1, 1980. B's will created both a marital trust and a nonmarital trust. The decedent's surviving spouse, C, is an income beneficiary of the marital trust and has a testamentary general power of appointment over its assets. C is an income beneficiary of the nonmarital trust, and additionally has the noncumulative right to withdraw yearly the greater of $5,000 or 5 percent of the aggregate value of the principal. The provisions of the will specify that any portion of the marital trust disclaimed is to be added to the nonmarital trust. C disclaims 50 percent of the marital trust corpus. Pursuant to the will, this amount is transferred to the nonmarital trust. Assuming the remaining requirements of section 2518(b) are satisfied, C's disclaimer is a qualified disclaimer.

Example (8). A, a resident of State X, died on July 19, 1979. A was survived by a spouse B, and three children,

C, D, and E. Pursuant to A's will, B received one-half of A's estate and the children received equal shares of the remaining one-half of the estate. B disclaimed the entire interest B had received. The will made no provisions for the distribution of property in the case of a beneficiary's disclaimer. The disclaimer laws of State X provide that under these circumstances disclaimed property passes to the decedent's heirs at law in the same manner as if the disclaiming beneficiary had died immediately before the testator's death. As a result, C, D, and E are A's only remaining heirs at law, and will divide the disclaimed property equally among themselves. B's disclaimer includes language stating that "it is my intention that C, D, and E will share equally in the division of this property as a result of my disclaimer." State X considers these to be precatory words and gives them no legal effect. B's disclaimer meets all other requirements imposed by State X on disclaimers, and is considered an effective disclaimer under which the property will vest solely in C, D, and E in equal shares without any further action required by B. Therefore, B is not treated as directing the redistribution or transfer of the property. If the remaining requirements of section 2518 are met, B's disclaimer is a qualified disclaimer.

Example (9). C died testate on January 1, 1979. According to C's will, D was to receive ⅓ of the residuary estate with any disclaimed property going to E. D was also to receive a second ⅓ of the residuary estate with any disclaimed property going to F. Finally, D was to receive a final ⅓ of the residuary estate with any disclaimed property going to G. D specifically states that he is disclaiming the interest in which the disclaimed property is designated to pass to E. D has effectively directed that the disclaimed property will pass to E and therefore D's disclaimer is not a qualified disclaimer under section 2518(a).

Example (10). Assume the same facts as in example (9) except that C's will also states that D was to receive Blackacre and Whiteacre. C's will further provides that if D disclaimed Blackacre then such property was to pass to E and that if D disclaimed Whiteacre then Whiteacre was to pass to F. D specifically disclaims Blackacre with the intention that it pass to E. Assuming the other requirements of section 2518 are met, D has made a qualified disclaimer of Blackacre. Alternatively, D could disclaim an undivided portion of both Blackacre and Whiteacre. Assuming the other requirements of section 2518 are met, this would also be a qualified disclaimer.

Example (11). G creates an irrevocable trust on February 16, 1983, naming H, I and J as the income beneficiaries for life and F as the remainderman. F is also named the trustee and as trustee has the discretionary power to invade the corpus and make discretionary distributions to H, I or J during their lives. F disclaims the remainder interest on August 8, 1983, but retains his discretionary power to invade the corpus. F has not made a qualified disclaimer because F retains the power to direct enjoyment of the corpus and the retained fiduciary power is not limited by an ascertainable standard.

Example (12). Assume the same facts as in example (11) except that F may only invade the corpus to make distributions for the health, maintenance or support of H, I or J during their lives. If the other requirements of section 2518(b) are met, F has made a qualified disclaim-

er of the remainder interest because the retained fiduciary power is limited by an ascertainable standard.

[T.D. 8095, 51 FR 28371, Aug. 7, 1986]

§25.2518–3 Disclaimer of less than an entire interest.

(a) Disclaimer of a partial interest—(1) In general—(i) Interest. If the requirements of this section are met, the disclaimer of all or an undivided portion of any separate interest in property may be a qualified disclaimer even if the disclaimant has another interest in the same property. In general, each interest in property that is separately created by the transferor is treated as a separate interest. For example, if an income interest in securities is bequeathed to A for life, then to B for life, with the remainder interest in such securities bequeathed to A's estate, and if the remaining requirements of section 2518(b) are met, A could make a qualified disclaimer of either the income interest or the remainder, or an undivided portion of either interest. A could not, however, make a qualified disclaimer of the income interest for a certain number of years. Further, where local law merges interests separately created by the transferor, a qualified disclaimer will be allowed only if there is a disclaimer of the entire merged interest or an undivided portion of such merged interest. See example (12) in paragraph (d) of this section. See §25.2518–3(b) for rules relating to the disclaimer of an undivided portion. Where the merger of separate interests would occur but for the creation by the transferor of a nominal interest (as defined in paragraph (a)(1)(iv) of this section), a qualified disclaimer will be allowed only if there is a disclaimer of all the separate interests, or an undivided portion of all such interests, which would have merged but for the nominal interest.

(ii) Severable property. A disclaimant shall be treated as making a qualified disclaimer of a separate interest in property if the disclaimer relates to severable property and the disclaimant makes a disclaimer which would be a qualified disclaimer if such property were the only property in which the disclaimant had an interest. If applicable local law does not recognize a purported disclaimer of severable property, the disclaimant must comply with the requirements of paragraph (c)(1) of §25.2518–1 in order to make a qualified disclaimer of the severable property. Severable property is property which can be divided into separate parts each of which, after severance, maintains a complete and independent existence.

For example, a legatee of shares of corporate stock may accept some shares of the stock and make a qualified disclaimer of the remaining shares.

(iii) **Powers of appointment.** A power of appointment with respect to property is treated as a separate interest in such property and such power of appointment with respect to all or an undivided portion of such property may be disclaimed independently from any other interests separately created by the transferor in the property if the requirements of section 2518(b) are met. See example (21) of paragraph (d) of this section. Further, a disclaimer of a power of appointment with respect to property is a qualified disclaimer only if any right to direct the beneficial enjoyment of the property which is retained by the disclaimant is limited by an ascertainable standard. See example (9) of paragraph (d) of this section.

(iv) **Nominal interest.** A nominal interest is an interest in property created by the transferor that—

(A) Has an actuarial value (as determined under § 20.2031–10) of less than 5 percent of the total value of the property at the time of the taxable transfer creating the interest,

(B) Prevents the merger under local law or two or more other interests created by the transferor, and

(C) Can be clearly shown from all the facts and circumstances to have been created primarily for the purpose of preventing the merger of such other interests.

Factors to be considered in determining whether an interest is created primarily for the purpose of preventing merger include (but are not limited to) the following: the relationship between the transferor and the interest holder; the age difference between the interest holder and the beneficiary whose interests would have merged; the interest holder's state of health at the time of the taxable transfer; and, in the case of a contingent remainder, any other factors which indicate that the possibility of the interest vesting as a fee simple is so remote as to be negligible.

(2) **In trust.** A disclaimer is not a qualified disclaimer under section 2518 if the beneficiary disclaims income derived from specific property transferred in trust while continuing to accept income derived from the remaining properties in the same trust unless the disclaimer results in such property being removed from the trust and

passing, without any direction on the part of the disclaimant, to persons other than the disclaimant or to the spouse of the decedent. Moreover, a disclaimer of both an income interest and a remainder interest in specific trust assets is not a qualified disclaimer if the beneficiary retains interests in other trust property unless, as a result of the disclaimer, such assets are removed from the trust and pass, without any direction on the part of the disclaimant, to persons other than the disclaimant or to the spouse of the decedent. The disclaimer of an undivided portion of an interest in a trust may be a qualified disclaimer. See also paragraph (b) of this section for rules relating to the disclaimer of an undivided portion of an interest in property.

(b) **Disclaimer of undivided portion.** A disclaimer of an undivided portion of a separate interest in property which meets the other requirements of a qualified disclaimer under section 2518(b) and the corresponding regulations is a qualified disclaimer. An undivided portion of a disclaimant's separate interest in property must consist of a fraction or percentage of each and every substantial interest or right owned by the disclaimant in such property and must extend over the entire term of the disclaimant's interest in such property and in other property into which such property is converted. A disclaimer of some specific rights while retaining other rights with respect to an interest in the property is not a qualified disclaimer of an undivided portion of the disclaimant's interest in property. Thus, for example, a disclaimer made by the devisee of a fee simple interest in Blackacre is not a qualified disclaimer if the disclaimant disclaims a remainder interest in Blackacre but retains a life estate.

(c) **Disclaimer of a pecuniary amount.** A disclaimer of a specific pecuniary amount out of a pecuniary or nonpecuniary bequest or gift which satisfies the other requirements of a qualified disclaimer under section 2518 (b) and the corresponding regulations is a qualified disclaimer provided that no income or other benefit of the disclaimed amount inures to the benefit of the disclaimant either prior to or subsequent to the disclaimer. Thus, following the disclaimer of a specific pecuniary amount from a bequest or gift, the amount disclaimed and any income attributable to such amount must be segregated from the portion of the gift or bequest that was not disclaimed. Such a segregation of assets making up the disclaimer of a pecuniary amount must be made on the basis of the fair market value of the assets on the date of the disclaimer or on a basis that is fairly representative of value changes that may have occurred between the date of transfer and the date of the disclaimer. A pecuniary amount distributed to the disclaimant from the bequest or gift prior to the disclaimer shall be treated as a distribution of corpus from the bequest or gift. However, the

acceptance of a distribution from the gift or bequest shall also be considered to be an acceptance of a proportionate amount of income earned by the bequest or gift. The proportionate share of income considered to be accepted by the disclaimant shall be determined at the time of the disclaimer according to the following formula:

$$\frac{\text{Total amount of distributions received by the disclaimant out of the gift or bequest}}{\text{Total value of the gift or bequest on the date of transfer}} \times \begin{array}{c}\text{Total amount of income earned by the} \\ \text{gift or bequest between date of transfer} \\ \text{and date of disclaimer.}\end{array}$$

See examples (17), (18), and (19) in § 25.2518–3(d) for illustrations of the rules set forth in this paragraph (c).

(d) Examples. The provisions of this section may be illustrated by the following examples:

Example (1). A, a resident of State Q, died on August 1, 1978. A's will included specific bequests of 100 shares of stock in X corporation; 200 shares of stock in Y corporation; 500 shares of stock in Z corporation; personal effects consisting of paintings, home furnishings, jewelry, and silver, and a 500 acre farm consisting of a residence, various outbuildings, and 500 head of cattle. The laws of State Q provide that a disclaimed interest passes in the same manner as if the disclaiming beneficiary had died immediately before the testator's death. Pursuant to A's will, B was to receive both the personal effects and the farm. C was to receive all the shares of stock in Corporation X and Y and D was to receive all the shares of stock in Corporation Z. B disclaimed 2 of the paintings and all the jewelry, C disclaimed 50 shares of Y corporation stock, and D disclaimed 100 shares of Z corporation stock. If the remaining requirements of section 2518(b) and the corresponding regulations are met, each of these disclaimers is a qualified disclaimer for purposes of section 2518(a).

Example (2). Assume the same facts as in example (1) except that D disclaimed the income interest in the shares of Z corporation stock while retaining the remainder interest in such shares. D's disclaimer is not a qualified disclaimer.

Example (3). Assume the same facts as in example (1) except that B disclaimed 300 identified acres of the 500 acres. Assuming that B's disclaimer meets the remaining requirements of section 2518(b), it is a qualified disclaimer.

Example (4). Assume the same facts as in example (1) except that A devised the income from the farm to B for life and the remainder interest to C. B disclaimed 40 percent of the income from the farm. Assuming that it meets the remaining requirements of section 2518(b), B's disclaimer of an undivided portion of the income is a qualified disclaimer.

Example (5). E died on September 13, 1978. Under the provisions of E's will, E's shares of stock in X, Y, and Z corporations were to be transferred to a trust. The trust provides that all income is to be distributed current-

ly to F and G in equal parts until F attains the age of 45 years. At that time the corpus of the trust is to be divided equally between F and G. F disclaimed the income arising from the shares of X stock. G disclaimed 20 percent of G's interest in the trust. F's disclaimer is not a qualified disclaimer because the X stock remains in the trust. If the remaining requirements of section 2518(b) are met, G's disclaimer is a qualified disclaimer.

Example (6). Assume the same facts as in example (5) except that F disclaimed both the income interest and the remainder interest in the shares of X stock. F's disclaimer results in the X stock being transferred out of the trust to G without any direction on F's part. F's disclaimer is a qualified disclaimer under section 2518(b).

Example (7). Assume the same facts as in example (5) except that F is only an income beneficiary of the trust. The X stock remains in the trust after F's disclaimer of the income arising from the shares of X stock. F's disclaimer is not a qualified disclaimer under section 2518.

Example (8). Assume the same facts as in example (5) except that F disclaimed the entire income interest in the trust while retaining the interest F has in corpus. Alternatively, assume that G disclaimed G's entire corpus interest while retaining G's interest in the income from the trust. If the remaining requirements of section 2518(b) are met, either disclaimer will be a qualified disclaimer.

Example (9). G creates an irrevocable trust on May 13, 1980, with H, I, and J as the income beneficiaries. In addition, H, who is the trustee, holds the power to invade corpus for H's health, maintenance, support and happiness and a testamentary power of appointment over the corpus. In the absence of the exercise of the power of appointment, the property passes to I and J in equal shares. H disclaimed the power to invade corpus for H's health, maintenance, support and happiness. Because H retained the testamentary power to appoint the property in the corpus, H's disclaimer is not a qualified disclaimer. If H also disclaimed the testamentary power of appointment, H's disclaimer would have been a qualified disclaimer.

Example (10). E creates an irrevocable trust on May 1, 1980, in which D is the income beneficiary for life. Subject to the trustee's discretion, E's children, A, B, and C, have the right to receive corpus during D's lifetime. The remainder passes to D if D survives A, B, C, and all their issue. D also holds an inter vivos power to appoint

1517

the trust corpus to A, B, and C. On September 1, 1980, D disclaimed the remainder interest. D's disclaimer is not a qualified disclaimer because D retained the power to direct the use and enjoyment of corpus during D's life.

Example (11). Under H's will, a trust is created from which W is to receive all of the income for life. The trustee has the power to invade the trust corpus for the support or maintenance of D during the life of W. The trust is to terminate at W's death, at which time the trust property is to be distributed to D. D makes a timely disclaimer of the right to corpus during W's lifetime, but does not disclaim the remainder interest. D's disclaimer is a qualified disclaimer assuming the remaining requirements of section 2518 are met.

Example (12). Under the provisions of G's will A received a life estate in a farm, and was the sole beneficiary of property in the residuary estate. The will also provided that the remainder interest in the farm pass to the residuary estate. Under local law A's interests merged to give A a fee simple in the farm. A made a timely disclaimer of the life estate. A's disclaimer of a partial interest is not a qualified disclaimer under section 2518(a). If A makes a disclaimer of the entire merged interest in the farm or an undivided portion of such merged interest then A would be making a qualified disclaimer assuming all the other requirements of section 2518(b) are met.

Example (13). A, a resident of State Z, dies on September 3, 1980. Under A's will, Blackacre is devised to C for life, then to D for 1 month, remainder to C. Had A not created D's interest, State Z law would have merged C's life estate and the remainder to C to create a fee simple interest in C. Assume that the actuarial value of D's interest is less than 5 percent of the total value of Blackacre on the date of A's death. Further assume that facts and circumstances (particularly the duration of D's interest) clearly indicate that D's interest was created primarily for the purpose of preventing the merger of C's two interests in Blackacre. D's interest in Blackacre is a nominal interest and C's two interests will, for purposes of making a qualified disclaimer, be considered to have merged. Thus, C cannot make a qualified disclaimer of his remainder while retaining the life estate. C can, however, make a qualified disclaimer of both of these interests entirely or an undivided portion of both

Example (14). A, a resident of State X, dies on October 12, 1978. Under A's will, Blackacre was devised to B for life, then to C for life if C survives B, remainder to B's estate. On the date of A's death, B and C are both 8 year old grandchildren of A. In addition, C is in good health. The actual value of C's interest is less than 5 percent of the total value of Blackacre on the date of A's death. No facts are present which would indicate that the possibility of C's contingent interest vesting is so remote as to be negligible. Had C's contingent life estate not been created, B's life estate and remainder interest would have merged under local law to give B a fee simple interest in Blackacre. Although C's interest prevents the merger of B's two interests and has an actual value of less than 5 percent, C's interest is not a nominal interest within the meaning of § 25.2518–3(a)(1)(iv) because the facts and circumstances do not clearly indicate that the interest was created primarily for the purpose of preventing the merger of other interests in the property. Assuming all

the other requirements of section 2518(b) are met, B can make a qualified disclaimer of the remainder while retaining his life estate.

Example (15). In 1981, A transfers $60,000 to a trust created for the benefit of B who was given the income interest for life and who also has a testamentary nongeneral power of appointment over the corpus. A transfers an additional $25,000 to the trust on June 1, 1984. At that time the trust corpus (exclusive of the $25,000 transfer) has a fair market value of $75,000. On January 1, 1985, B disclaims the right to receive income attributable to 25 percent of the corpus.

$$\left(\frac{\$25,000 \ (1984 \ \text{transfer})}{\begin{array}{c}\$100,000 \ (\text{fair market value of corpus}\\ \text{immediately after the 1984 transfer})\end{array}} = 25\%. \right)$$

Assuming that no distributions were made to B attributable to the $25,000, B's disclaimer is a qualified disclaimer for purposes of section 2518(a) if all the remaining requirements of section 2518(b) are met.

Example (16). Under the provisions of B's will, A is left an outright cash legacy of $50,000 and has no other interest in B's estate. A timely disclaimer by A of any stated dollar amount is a qualified disclaimer under section 2518(a).

Example (17). D bequeaths his brokerage account to E. The account consists of stocks and bonds and a cash amount earning interest. The total value of the cash and assets in the account on the date of D's death is $100,000. Four months after D's death, E makes a withdrawal of cash from the account for personal use amounting to $40,000. Eight months after D's death, E disclaims $60,000 of the account without specifying any particular assets or cash. The cumulative fair market value of the stocks and bonds in the account on the date of the disclaimer is equal to the value of such stocks and bonds on the date of D's death. The income earned by the account between the date of D's death and the date of E's disclaimer was $20,000. The amount of income earned by the account that E accepted by withdrawing $40,000 from the account prior to the disclaimer is determined by applying the formula set forth in § 25.2518–3(c) as follows:

$$\frac{\$40,000}{\$100,000} \times \$20,000 = \$8,000$$

E is considered to have accepted $8,000 of the income earned by the account. If (i) the $60,000 disclaimed by E and the $12,000 of income earned prior to the disclaimer which is attributable to that amount are segregated from the $8,000 of income E is considered to have accepted, (ii) E does not accept any benefits of the $72,000 so segregated, and (iii) the other requirements of section 2518(b) are met, then E's disclaimer of $60,000 from the account is a qualified disclaimer.

Example (18). A bequeathed his residuary estate to B. The residuary estate had a value of $1 million on the date of A's death. Six months later, B disclaimed $200,000 out of this bequest. B received distributions of all the income from the entire estate during the period of administration. When the estate was distributed, B received the entire residuary estate except for $200,000 in cash. B did not make a qualified disclaimer since he accepted the benefits of the $200,000 during the period of estate administration.

Example (19). Assume the same facts as in example (18) except that no income was paid to B and the value of the residuary estate on the date of the disclaimer (including interest earned from date of death) was $1.5 million. In addition, as soon as B's disclaimer was made, the executor of A's estate set aside assets worth $300,000.

$$\left(\frac{\$200,000}{\$1,000,000} \times \$1,500,000 \right)$$

and the interest earned after the disclaimer on that amount in a separate fund so that none of the income was paid to B. B's disclaimer is a qualified disclaimer under section 2518(a).

Example (20). A bequeathed his residuary estate to B. B disclaims a fractional share of the residuary estate. Any disclaimed property will pass to A's surviving spouse, W. The numerator of the fraction disclaimed is the smallest amount which will allow A's estate to pass free of Federal estate tax and the denominator is the value of the residuary estate. B's disclaimer is a qualified disclaimer.

Example (21). A created a trust on July 1, 1979. The trust provides that all current income is to be distributed equally between B and C for the life of B. B also is given a testamentary general power of appointment over the corpus. If the power is not exercised, the corpus passes to C or C's heirs. B disclaimed the testamentary power to appoint an undivided one-half of the trust corpus. Assuming the remaining requirements of section 2518(b) are satisfied, B's disclaimer is a qualified disclaimer under section 2518(a).

[T.D. 8095, 51 FR 28375, Aug. 7, 1986]

Deductions

§ 25.2523(b)–1 Life estate or other terminable interest.

(a) In general. (1) The provisions of section 2523(b) generally prevent the allowance of the marital deduction with respect to certain property interests (referred to generally as "terminable interests," defined in subparagraph (3) of this paragraph), transferred to the donee spouse under the circumstances described in subparagraph (2) of this paragraph, unless the transfer comes within one of the exceptions set forth in § 25.2523(d)–1, relating to certain joint interests, or § 25.2523(e)–1, relating to certain life estates with powers of appointment.

(2) If a donor transfers a terminable interest in property to the donee spouse, the marital deduction is disallowed with respect to the transfer if the donor spouse also—

(i) Transferred an interest in the same property to another donee (see paragraph (b) of this section), or

(ii) Retained an interest in the same property in himself (see paragraph (c) of this section), or

(iii) Retained a power to appoint an interest in the same property (see paragraph (d) of this section).

Notwithstanding the preceding sentence, the marital deduction is disallowed under these circumstances only if the other donee, the donor, or the possible appointee, may, by reason of the transfer or retention, possess or enjoy any part of the property after the termination or failure of the interest therein transferred to the donee spouse.

(3) For purposes of this section, a distinction is to be drawn between "property," as such term is used in section 2523, and an "interest in property." The "property" referred to is the underlying property in which various interests exist; each such interest is not, for this purpose, to be considered as "property." A "terminable interest" in property is an interest which will terminate or fail on the lapse of time or on the occurrence or failure to occur of some contingency. Life estates, terms for years, annuities, patents, and copyrights are therefore terminable interests. However, a bond, note, or similar contractual obligation, the discharge of which would not have the effect of an annuity or term for years, is not a terminable interest.

(b) Interest in property which another donee may possess or enjoy. (1) Section 2523(b) provides that no marital deduction shall be allowed with respect to the transfer to the donee spouse of a "terminable interest" in property, in case—

(i) The donor transferred (for less than an adequate and full consideration in money or money's worth) an interest in the same property to any person other than the donee spouse (or the estate of such spouse), and

(ii) By reason of such transfer, such person (or his heirs or assigns) may possess or enjoy any part of such property after the termination or failure of the interest therein transferred to the donee spouse.

(2) In determining whether the donor transferred an interest in property to any person other than the donee spouse, it is immaterial whether the transfer to the person other than the donee

spouse was made at the same time as the transfer to such spouse, or at any earlier time.

(3) Except as provided in § 25.2523(e)–1, if at the time of the transfer it is impossible to ascertain the particular person or persons who may receive a property interest transferred by the donor, such interest is considered as transferred to a person other than the donee spouse for the purpose of section 2523(b). This rule is particularly applicable in the case of the transfer of a property interest by the donor subject to a reserved power. See § 25.2511–2. Under this rule, any property interest over which the donor reserved a power to revest the beneficial title in himself, or over which the donor reserved the power to name new beneficiaries or to change the interests of the beneficiaries as between themselves, is for the purpose of section 2523(b), considered as transferred to a "person other than the donee spouse." The following examples illustrate the application of the provisions of this subparagraph:

Example (1). If a donor transferred property in trust naming his wife as the irrevocable income beneficiary for 10 years, and providing that, upon the expiration of that term, the corpus should be distributed among his wife and children in such proportions as the trustee should determine, the right to the corpus, for the purpose of the marital deduction, is considered as transferred to a "person other than the donee spouse."

Example (2). If, in the above example, the donor had provided that, upon the expiration of the 10-year term, the corpus was to be paid to his wife, but also reserved the power to revest such corpus in himself, the right to corpus, for the purpose of the marital deduction, is considered as transferred to a "person other than the donee spouse."

(4) The term "person other than the donee spouse" includes the possible unascertained takers of a property interest, as, for example, the members of a class to be ascertained in the future. As another example, assume that the donor created a power of appointment over a property interest, which does not come within the purview of § 25.-2523(e)–1. In such a case, the term "person other than the donee spouse" refers to the possible appointees and takers in default (other than the spouse) of such property interest.

(5) An exercise or release at any time by the donor (either alone or in conjunction with any person) of a power to appoint an interest in property, even though not otherwise a transfer by him is considered as a transfer by him in determining, for the purpose of section 2523(b), whether he transferred an interest in such property to a person other than the donee spouse.

(6) The following examples illustrate the application of this paragraph. In each example it is assumed that the property interest which the donor transferred to a person other than the donee spouse was not transferred for an adequate and full consideration in money or money's worth:

Example (1). H (the donor) transferred real property to W (his wife) for life, with remainder to A and his heirs. No marital deduction may be taken with respect to the interest transferred to W, since it will terminate upon her death and A (or his heirs or assigns) will thereafter possess or enjoy the property.

Example (2). H transferred property for the benefit of W and A. The income was payable to W for life and upon her death the principal was to be distributed to A or his issue. However, if A should die without issue, leaving W surviving, the principal was then to be distributed to W. No marital deduction may be taken with respect to the interest transferred to W, since it will terminate in the event of his issue will thereafter possess or enjoy the property.

Example (3). H purchased for $100,000 a life annuity for W. If the annuity payments made during the life of W should be less than $100,000, further payments were to be made to A. No marital deduction may be taken with respect to the interest transferred to W; since A may possess or enjoy a part of the property following the termination of W's interest. If, however, the contract provided for no continuation of payments, and provided for no refund upon the death of W, or provided that any refund was to go to the estate of W, then a marital deduction may be taken with respect to the gift.

Example (4). H transferred property to A for life with remainder to W provided W survives A, but if W predeceases A, the property is to pass to B and his heirs. No marital deduction may be taken with respect to the interest transferred to W.

Example (5). H transferred real property to A, reserving the right to the rentals of the property for a term of 20 years. H later transferred the right to the remaining rentals to W. No marital deduction may be taken with respect to the interest since it will terminate upon the expiration of the balance of the 20-year term and A will thereafter possess or enjoy the property.

Example (6). H transferred a patent to W and A as tenants in common. In this case, the interest of W will terminate upon the expiration of the term of the patent, but possession and enjoyment of the property by A must necessarily cease at the same time. Therefore, since A's possession or enjoyment cannot outlast the termination of W's interest, the provisions of section 2523(b) do not disallow the marital deduction with respect to the interest.

(c) **Interest in property which the donor may possess or enjoy.** (1) Section 2523(b) provides that no marital deduction is allowed with respect to the transfer to the donee spouse of a "terminable interest" in property, if—

(i) The donor retained in himself an interest in the same property, and

(ii) By reason of such retention, the donor (or his heirs or assigns) may possess or enjoy any part of the property after the termination or failure of the interest transferred to the donee spouse. * * *

(2) In general, the principles illustrated by the examples under paragraph (b) of this section are applicable in determining whether the marital deduction may be taken with respect to a property interest transferred to the donee spouse subject to the retention by the donor of an interest in the same property. The application of this paragraph may be further illustrated by the following example:

Example. The donor purchased three annuity contracts for the benefit of his wife and himself. The first contract provided for payments to the wife for life, with refund to the donor in case the aggregate payments made to the wife were less than the cost of the contract. The second contract provided for payments to the donor for life, and then to the wife for life if she survived the donor. The third contract provided for payments to the donor and his wife for their joint lives and then to the survivor of them for life. No marital deduction may be taken with respect to the gifts resulting from the purchases of the contracts since, in the case of each contract, the donor may possess or enjoy a part of the property after the termination or failure of the interest transferred to the wife.

(d) Interest in property over which the donor retained a power to appoint. (1) Section 2523(b) provides that no marital deduction is allowed with respect to the transfer to the donee spouse of a terminable interest" in property if—

(i) The donor had, immediately after the transfer, a power to appoint an interest in the same property, and

(ii) The donor's power was exercisable (either alone or in conjunction with any person) in such manner that the appointee may possess or enjoy any part of the property after the termination or failure of the interest transferred to the donee spouse.

(2) For the purposes of section 2523(b), the donor is to be considered as having, immediately after the transfer to the donee spouse, such a power to appoint even though the power cannot be exercised until after the lapse of time, upon the occurrence of an event or contingency, or upon the failure of an event or contingency to occur. It is immaterial whether the power retained by the donor was a taxable power of appointment under section 2514.

(3) The principles illustrated by the examples under paragraph (b) of this section are generally applicable in determining whether the marital deduction may be taken with respect to a property interest transferred to the donee spouse subject to retention by the donor of a power to appoint an interest in the same property. The application of this paragraph may be further illustrated by the following example:

Example. The donor, having a power of appointment over certain property, appointed a life estate to his spouse. No marital deduction may be taken with respect to such transfer, since, if the retained power to appoint the remainder interest is exercised, the appointee thereunder may possess or enjoy the property after the termination or failure of the interest taken by the donee spouse.

[T.D. 6334, 23 FR 8904, Nov. 15, 1958]

§ 25.2523(c)–1 Interest in unidentified assets.

(a) Section 2523(c) provides that if an interest passing to a donee spouse may be satisfied out of a group of assets (or their proceeds) which include a particular asset that would be a nondeductible interest if it passed from the donor to his spouse, the value of the interest passing to the spouse is reduced, for the purpose of the marital deduction, by the value of the particular asset.

(b) In order for this section to apply, two circumstances must coexist, as follows:

(1) The property interest transferred to the donee spouse must be payable out of a group of assets. An example of a property interest payable out of a group of assets is a right to a share of the corpus of a trust upon its termination.

(2) The group of assets out of which the property interest is payable must include one or more particular assets which, if transferred by the donor to the donee spouse, would not qualify for the marital deduction. Therefore, section 2523(c) is not applicable merely because a group of assets includes a terminable interest, but would only be applicable if the terminable interest were nondeductible under the provisions of § 25.2523(b)–1.

(c) If the circumstances in the preceding paragraph are both present, the marital deduction with respect to such property interest may not exceed one-half of the excess, if any, of its value over the aggregate value of the particular asset or assets which, if transferred to the donee spouse, would not qualify for the marital deduction. The application of this section may be illustrated by the following example:

Example. H was absolute owner of a rental property and on July 1, 1950, transferred it to A by gift, reserving the income for a period of 20 years. On July 1, 1955, he created a trust to last for a period of 10 years. H was to receive the income from the trust and at the termination of the trust the trustee is to turn over to H's wife, W, property having a value of $100,000. The trustee has absolute discretion in deciding which properties in the corpus he shall turn over to W in satisfaction of the gift to her. The trustee received two items of property from H. Item (1) consisted of shares of corporate stock. Item (2) consisted of the right to receive the income from the rental property during the unexpired portion of the 20-year term. Assume that at the termination of the trust on July 1, 1965, the value of the right to the rental income for the then unexpired term of 5 years (item (2)) will be $30,000. Since item (2) is a nondeductible interest and the trustee can turn it over to W in partial satisfaction of her gift, only $70,000 of the $100,000 receivable by her on July 1, 1965, will be considered as property with respect to which a marital deduction is allowable. The present value on July 1, 1955, of the right to receive $70,000 at the end of 10 years is $49,624.33 ($70,000×0.708919, as found in Table II of § 25.2512–5). The value of the property qualifying for the marital deduction, therefore, is $49,624.33 and a marital deduction is allowed for one-half of that amount, or $24,812.17.

[T.D. 6334, 23 FR 8904, Nov. 15, 1958]

§ 25.2524–1 Extent of deductions.

Under the provisions of section 2524, the charitable deduction provided for in section 2522 and the marital deduction provided for in section 2523 are allowable only to the extent that the gifts, with respect to which those deductions are authorized,

are included in the "total amount of gifts" made during the "calendar period" (as defined in § 25.2502–1(c)(1)), computed as provided in section 2503 and § 25.2503–1 (*i.e.*, the total gifts less exclusions). The following examples (in both of which it is assumed that the donor has previously utilized his entire $30,000 specific exemption provided by section 2521, which was in effect at the time) illustrate the application of the provisions of this section:

Example (1). A donor made transfers by gift to his spouse of $5,000 cash on January 1, 1971, and $1,000 cash on April 5, 1971. The donor made no other transfers during 1971. The first $3,000 of such gifts for the calendar year is excluded under the provisions of section 2503(b) in determining the "total amount of gifts" made during the first calendar quarter of 1971. The marital deduction for the first calendar quarter of $2,500 (one-half of $5,000) otherwise allowable is limited by section 2524 to $2,000. The amount of taxable gifts is zero ($5,000–$3,000 (annual exclusion)–$2,000 (marital deduction)). For the second calendar quarter of 1971, the marital deduction is $500 (one-half of $1,000); the amount excluded under section 2503(b) is zero because the entire $3,000 annual exclusion was applied against the gift in the first calendar quarter of 1971; and the amount of taxable gifts is $500 ($1,000–$500 (marital deduction)).

* * *

[T.D. 6334, 23 FR 8904, Nov. 15, 1958, as amended by T.D. 7238, 37 FR 28734, Dec. 29, 1972; T.D. 7905, 48 FR 36807, Aug. 15, 1983]

PART 301—PROCEDURE AND ADMINISTRATION

DEFINITIONS

§ 301.7701-1 Classification of organizations for tax purposes.

(a) **Person.** The term "person" includes an individual, a corporation, a partnership, a trust or estate, a joint-stock company, an association, or a syndicate, group, pool, joint venture, or other unincorporated organization or group. Such term also includes a guardian, committee, trustee, executor, administrator, trustee in bankruptcy, receiver, assignee for the benefit of creditors, conservator, or any person acting in a fiduciary capacity.

(b) **Standards.** The Internal Revenue Code prescribes certain categories, or classes, into which various organizations fall for purposes of taxation. These categories, or classes, include associations (which are taxable as corporations), partnerships, and trusts. The tests, or standards, which are to be applied in determining the classification in which an organization belongs (whether it is an association, a partnership, a trust, or other taxable entity) are determined under the Internal Revenue Code. Sections 301.7701-2 to 301.7701-4 set forth these tests, or standards, which are to be applied in determining whether an organization is (1) an association (see § 301.7701-2), (2) a partnership (see § 301.7701-3), or (3) a trust (see § 301.7701-4).

(c) **Effect of local law.** As indicated in paragraph (b) of this section, the classes into which organizations are to be placed for purposes of taxation are determined under the Internal Revenue Code. Thus, a particular organization might be classified as a trust under the law of one State and a corporation under the law of another State. However, for purposes of the Internal Revenue Code, this organization would be uniformly classed as a trust, an association (and therefore, taxable as a corporation), or some other entity, depending upon its nature under the classification standards of the Internal Revenue Code. Similarly, the term "partnership" is not limited to the common-law meaning of partnership, but is broader in its scope and includes groups not commonly called partnerships. See § 1.761-1 of this chapter (Income Tax Regulations) and § 301.7701-3. The term "corporation" is not limited to the artificial entity usually known as a corporation, but includes also an association, a trust classed as an association because of its nature or its activities, a joint-stock company, and an insurance company. Although it is the Internal Revenue Code rather than local law which establishes the tests or standards which will be applied in determining the classification in which an organization belongs, local law governs in determining whether the legal relationships which have been established in the formation of an organization are such that the standards are met. Thus, it is local law which must be applied in determining such matters as the legal relationships of the members of the organization among themselves and with the public at large, and the interests of the members of the organization in its assets.

[32 FR 15241, Nov. 3, 1967, as amended by T.D. 7515, 42 FR 55612, Oct. 18, 1977]

§ 301.7701-2 Associations.

(a) **Characteristics of corporations.** (1) The term "association" refers to an organization whose characteristics require it to be classified for purposes of taxation as a corporation rather than as another type of organization such as a partnership or a trust. There are a number of major characteristics ordinarily found in a pure corporation which, taken together, distinguish it from other organizations. These are: (i) Associates, (ii) an objective to carry on business and divided the gains therefrom, (iii) continuity of life, (iv) centralization of management, (v) liability for corporate debts

1523

limited to corporate property, and (vi) free transferability of interests. Whether a particular organization is to be classified as an association must be determined by taking into account the presence or absence of each of these corporate characteristics. The presence or absence of these characteristics will depend upon the facts in each individual case. In addition to the major characteristics set forth in this subparagraph other factors may be found in some cases which may be significant in classifying an organization as an association, a partnership, or a trust. An organization will be treated as an association if the corporate characteristics are such that the organization more nearly resembles a corporation than a partnership or trust. See *Morrissey et al. v. Commissioner* (1935) 296 U.S. 344.

(2) Since associates and an objective to carry on business for joint profit are essential characteristics of all organizations engaged in business for profit (other than the so-called one-man corporation and the sole proprietorship), the absence of either of these essential characteristics will cause an arrangement among co-owners of property for the development of such property for the separate profit of each not to be classified as an association. Some of the major characteristics of a corporation are common to trusts and corporations, and others are common to partnerships and corporations. Characteristics common to trusts and corporations are not material in attempting to distinguish between a trust and an association, and characteristics common to partnerships and corporations are not material in attempting to distinguish between an association and a partnership. For example, since centralization of management, continuity of life, free transferability of interests, and limited liability are generally common to trusts and corporations, the determination of whether a trust which has such characteristics is to be treated for tax purposes as a trust or as an association depends on whether there are associates and an objective to carry on business and divide the gains therefrom. On the other hand, since associates and an objective to carry on business and divide the gains therefrom are generally common to both corporations and partnerships, the determination of whether an organization which has such characteristics is to be treated for tax purposes as a partnership or as an association depends on whether there exists centralization of management, continuity of life, free transferability of interests, and limited liability.

(3) An unincorporated organization shall not be classified as an association unless such organization has more corporate characteristics than noncorporate characteristics. In determining whether an organization has more corporate characteristics than noncorporate characteristics, all characteristics common to both types of organizations shall not be considered. For example, if a limited partnership has centralized management and free transferability of interests but lacks continuity of life and limited liability, and if the limited partnership has no other characteristics which are significant in determining its classification, such limited partnership is not classified as an association. Although the limited partnership also has associates and an objective to carry on business and divide the gains therefrom, these characteristics are not considered because they are common to both corporations and partnerships.

* * *

(5) All references in this section to the Uniform Limited Partnership Act shall be deemed to refer both to the original Uniform Limited Partnership Act (adopted in 1916) and to the revised Uniform Limited Partnership Act (adopted by the National Conference of Commissioners on Uniform State Laws in 1976).

(b) **Continuity of life.** (1) An organization has continuity of life if the death, insanity, bankruptcy, retirement, resignation, or expulsion of any member will not cause a dissolution of the organization. On the other hand, if the death, insanity, bankruptcy, retirement, resignation, or expulsion of any member will cause a dissolution of the organization, continuity of life does not exist. If the retirement, death, or insanity of a general partner of a limited partnership causes a dissolution of the partnership, unless the remaining general partners agree to continue the partnership or unless all remaining members agree to continue the partnership, continuity of life does not exist. See *Glensder Textile Company* (1942) 46 B.T.A. 176 (A., C.B. 1942–1, 8).

(2) For purposes of this paragraph, dissolution of an organization means an alteration of the identity of an organization by reason of a change in the relationship between its members as determined under local law. For example, since the resignation of a partner from a general partnership destroys the mutual agency which exists between such partner and his copartners and thereby alters the personal relation between the partners which

constitutes the identity of the partnership itself, the resignation of a partner dissolves the partnership. A corporation, however, has a continuing identity which is detached from the relationship between its stockholders. The death, insanity, or bankruptcy of a shareholder or the sale of a shareholder's interest has no effect upon the identity of the corporation and, therefore, does not work a dissolution of the organization. An agreement by which an organization is established may provide that the business will be continued by the remaining members in the event of the death or withdrawal of any member, but such agreement does not establish continuity of life if under local law the death or withdrawal of any member causes a dissolution of the organization. Thus, there may be a dissolution of the organization and no continuity of life although the business is continued by the remaining members.

(3) An agreement establishing an organization may provide that the organization is to continue for a stated period or until the completion of a stated undertaking or such agreement may provide for the termination of the organization at will or otherwise. In determining whether any member has the power of dissolution, it will be necessary to examine the agreement and to ascertain the effect of such agreement under local law. For example, if the agreement expressly provides that the organization can be terminated by the will of any member, it is clear that the organization lacks continuity of life. However, if the agreement provides that the organization is to continue for a stated period or until the completion of a stated transaction, the organization has continuity of life if the effect of the agreement is that no member has the power to dissolve the organization in contravention of the agreement. Nevertheless, if, notwithstanding such agreement, any member has the power under local law to dissolve the organization, the organization lacks continuity of life. Accordingly, a general partnership subject to a statute corresponding to the Uniform Partnership Act and a limited partnership subject to a statute corresponding to the Uniform Limited Partnership Act both lack continuity of life.

(c) **Centralization of management.** (1) An organization has centralized management if any person (or any group of persons which does not include all the members) has continuing exclusive authority to make the management decisions necessary to the conduct of the business for which the organization was formed. Thus, the persons who are vested with such management authority resemble in powers and functions the directors of a statutory corporation. The effective operation of a business organization composed of many members generally depends upon the centralization in the hands of a few of exclusive authority to make management decisions for the organization, and therefore, centralized management is more likely to be found in such an organization than in a smaller organization.

(2) The persons who have such authority may, or may not, be members of the organization and may hold office as a result of a selection by the members from time to time, or may be self-perpetuating in office. See *Morrissey et al. v. Commissioner* (1935) 296 U.S. 344. Centralized management can be accomplished by election to office, by proxy appointment, or by any other means which has the effect of concentrating in a management group continuing exclusive authority to make management decisions.

(3) Centralized management means a concentration of continuing exclusive authority to make independent business decisions on behalf of the organization which do not require ratification by members of such organization. Thus, there is not centralized management when the centralized authority is merely to perform ministerial acts as an agent at the direction of a principal.

(4) There is no centralization of continuing exclusive authority to make management decisions, unless the managers have sole authority to make such decisions. For example, in the case of a corporation or a trust, the concentration of management powers in a board of directors or trustees effectively prevents a stockholder or a trust beneficiary, simply because he is a stockholder or beneficiary, from binding the corporation or the trust by his acts. However, because of the mutual agency relationship between members of a general partnership subject to a statute corresponding to the Uniform Partnership Act, such a general partnership cannot achieve effective concentration of management powers and, therefore, centralized management. Usually, the act of any partner within the scope of the partnership business binds all the partners; and even if the partners agree among themselves that the powers of management shall be exclusively in a selected few, this agreement will be ineffective as against an outsider who had no notice of it. In addition, limited partnerships subject to a statute corresponding to the Uniform Limited Partnership Act,

generally do not have centralized management, but centralized management ordinarily does exist in such a limited partnership if substantially all the interests in the partnership are owned by the limited partners. Furthermore, if all or a specified group of the limited partners may remove a general partner, all the facts and circumstances must be taken into account in determining whether the partnership possesses centralized management. A substantially restricted right of the limited partners to remove the general partner (e.g., in the event of the general partner's gross negligence, self-dealing, or embezzlement) will not itself cause the partnership to possess centralized management.

(d) **Limited liability.** (1) An organization has the corporate characteristic of limited liability if under local law there is no member who is personally liable for the debts of or claims against the organization. Personal liability means that a creditor of an organization may seek personal satisfaction from a member of the organization to the extent that the assets of such organization are insufficient to satisfy the creditor's claim. A member of the organization who is personally liable for the obligations of the organization may make an agreement under which another person, whether or not a member of the organization, assumes such liability or agrees to indemnify such member for any such liability. However, if under local law the member remains liable to such creditors notwithstanding such agreement, there exists personal liability with respect to such member. In the case of a general partnership subject to a statute corresponding to the Uniform Partnership Act, personal liability exists with respect to each general partner. Similarly, in the case of a limited partnership subject to a statute corresponding to the Uniform Limited Partnership Act, personal liability exists with respect to each general partner, except as provided in subparagraph (2) of this paragraph (d).

(2) In the case of an organization formed as a limited partnership, personal liability does not exist, for purposes of this paragraph, with respect to a general partner when he has no substantial assets (other than his interest in the partnership) which could be reached by a creditor of the organization and when he is merely a "dummy" acting as the agent of the limited partners. Notwithstanding the formation of the organization as a limited partnership, when the limited partners act as the principals of such general partner, personal liability will exist with respect to such limited partners. Also, if a corporation is a general partner, personal liability exists with respect to such general partner when the corporation has substantial assets (other than its interest in the partnership) which could be reached by a creditor of the limited partnership. A general partner may contribute his services, but no capital, to the organization, but if such general partner has substantial assets (other than his interest in the partnership), there exists personal liability. Furthermore, if the organization is engaged in financial transactions which involve large sums of money, and if the general partners have substantial assets (other than their interests in the partnership), there exists personal liability although the assets of such general partners would be insufficient to satisfy any substantial portion of the obligations of the organization. In addition, although the general partner has no substantial assets (other than his interest in the partnership), personal liability exists with respect to such general partner when he is not merely a "dummy" acting as the agent of the limited partners. If the limited partnership agreement provides that a general partner is not personally liable to creditors for the debts of the partnership (other than debts for which another general partner is personally liable), it shall be presumed that personal liability does not exist with respect to that partner unless it is established that the provision is ineffective under local law.

(e) **Free transferability of interests.** (1) An organization has the corporate characteristic of free transferability of interests if each of its members or those members owning substantially all of the interests in the organization have the power, without the consent of other members, to substitute for themselves in the same organization a person who is not a member of the organization. In order for this power of substitution to exist in the corporate sense, the member must be able, without the consent of other members, to confer upon his substitute all the attributes of his interest in the organization. Thus, the characteristic of free transferability of interests does not exist in a case in which each member can, without the consent of other members, assign only his right to share in profits but cannot so assign his rights to participate in the management of the organization. Furthermore, although the agreement provides for the transfer of a member's interest, there is no power of substitution and no free transferability of interest if under local law a transfer of a member's interest results in the dissolution of the old organization and the formation of a new organization.

(2) If each member of an organization can transfer his interest to a person who is not a member of the organization only after having offered such interest to the other members at its fair market value, it will be recognized that a modified form of free transferability of interests exists. In determining the classification of an organization, the presence of this modified corporate characteristic will be accorded less significance than if such characteristic were present in an unmodified form.

* * *

(g) **Examples.** The application of the rules described in this section may be illustrated by the following examples:

Example (1). [Deleted]

Example (2). A group of seven doctors forms a clinic for the purpose of furnishing, for profit, medical and surgical services to the public. They each transfer assets to the clinic, and their agreement provides that except upon complete liquidation of the organization on the vote of three-fourths of its members, no member has any individual interest in its assets. Their agreement also provides that neither the death, insanity, bankruptcy, retirement, resignation, nor expulsion of a member shall cause the dissolution of the organization. However, under the applicable local law, a member who withdraws does have the power to dissolve the organization. While the agreement provides that the management of the clinic is to be vested exclusively in an executive committee of four members elected by all the members, this provision is ineffective as against outsiders who had no notice of it; and, therefore, the act of any member within the scope of the organization's business binds the organization insofar as such outsiders are concerned. While the agreement declares that each individual doctor alone is liable for acts of malpractice, members of the clinic are, nevertheless, personally liable for all debts of the clinic including claims based on malpractice. No member has the right, without the consent of all the other members, to transfer his interest to a doctor who is not a member of the clinic. The organization has associates and an objective to carry on business and divide the gains therefrom. However, it does not have the corporate characteristics of continuity of life, centralized management, limited liability, and free transferability of interests. The organization will be classified as a partnership for all purposes of the Internal Revenue Code.

Example (3). A group of 25 lawyers forms an organization for the purpose of furnishing, for profit, legal services to the public. Their agreement provides that the organization will dissolve upon the death, insanity, bankruptcy, retirement, or expulsion of a member. While their agreement provides that the management of the organization is to be vested exclusively in an executive committee of five members elected by all the members, this provision is ineffective as against outsiders who had no notice of it; and, therefore, the act of any member within the scope of the organization's business binds the organization insofar as such outsiders are concerned. Members of the organization are personally liable for all

debts, or claims against, the organization. No member has the right, without the consent of all the other members, to transfer his interest to a lawyer who is not a member of the organization. The organization has associates and an objective to carry on business and divide the gains therefrom. However, the four corporate characteristics of limited liability, centralized management, free transferability of interests, and continuity of life are absent in this case. The organization will be classified as a partnership for all purposes of the Internal Revenue Code.

Example (4). A group of 25 persons forms an organization for the purpose of engaging in real estate investment activities. Each member has the power to dissolve the organization at any time. The management of the organization is vested exclusively in an executive committee of five members elected by all the members, and under the applicable local law, no one acting without the authority of this committee has the power to bind the organization by his acts. Under the applicable local law, each member is personally liable for the obligations of the organization. Every member has the right to transfer his interest to a person who is not a member of the organization, but he must first advise the organization of the proposed transfer and give it the opportunity on a vote of the majority to purchase the interest at its fair market value. The organization has associates and an objective to carry on business and divide the gains therefrom. While the organization does have the characteristics of centralized management and a modified form of free transferability of interests, it does not have the corporate characteristics of continuity of life and limited liability. Under the circumstances presented, the organization will be classified as a partnership for all purposes of the Internal Revenue Code.

Example (5). A group of 25 persons forms an organization for the purpose of engaging in real estate investment activities. Under their agreement, the organization is to have a life of 20 years, and under the applicable local law, no member has the power to dissolve the organization prior to the expiration of that period. The management of the organization is vested exclusively in an executive committee of five members elected by all the members, and under the applicable local law, no one acting without the authority of this committee has the power to bind the organization by his acts. Under the applicable local law, each member is personally liable for the obligations of the organization. Every member has the right to transfer his interest to a person who is not a member of the organization, but he must first advise the organization of the proposed transfer and give it the opportunity on a vote of the majority to purchase the interest at its fair market value. The organization has associates and an objective to carry on business and divide the gains therefrom. While the organization does not have the corporate characteristics of limited liability, it does have continuity of life, centralized management, and a modified form of free transferability of interests. The organization will be classified as an association for all purposes of the Internal Revenue Code.

Example (6). A group of 25 persons forms an organization for purposes of engaging in real estate investment activities. Each member has the power to dissolve the organization at any time. The management of the organization is vested exclusively in an executive committee of five members elected by all the members, and under the applicable local law, no one acting without the authority of this committee has the power to bind the organization by his acts. Under the applicable local law, the liability of each member for the obligations of the organization is limited to paid and subscribed capital. Every member has the right to transfer his interest to a person who is not a member of the organization, but he must first advise the organization of the proposed transfer and give it the opportunity on a vote of the majority to purchase the interest at its fair market value. The organization has associates and an objective to carry on business and divide the gains therefrom. While the organization does not have the characteristic of continuity of life, it does have limited liability, centralized management, and a modified form of free transferability of interests. The organization will be classified as an association for all purposes of the Internal Revenue Code.

Example (7). A group of 25 persons forms an organization for the purpose of investing in securities so as to educate the members in principles and techniques of investment practices and to share the income from such investments. While the agreement states that the organization will operate until terminated by a three-fourths vote of the total membership and will not terminate upon the withdrawal or death of any member, under the applicable local law, a member has the power to dissolve the organization at any time. The business of the organization is carried on by the members at regular monthly meetings and buy or sell action may be taken only when voted by a majority of the organization's membership present. Elected officers perform only ministerial functions such as presiding at meetings and carrying out the directions of the members. Members of the organization are personally liable for all debts of, or claims against, the organization. No member may transfer his membership. The organization has associates and an objective to carry on business and divide the gains therefrom. However, the organization does not have the corporate characteristics of limited liability, free transferability of interests, continuity of life, and centralized management. The organization will be treated as a partnership for all purposes of the Internal Revenue Code.

[32 FR 15241, Nov. 3, 1967, as amended by T.D. 7515, 42 FR 55612, Oct. 18, 1977; T.D. 7889, 48 FR 18804, April 26, 1983]

§ 301.7701–3 Partnerships.

(a) In general. The term "partnership" is broader in scope than the common law meaning of partnership and may include groups not commonly called partnerships. Thus, the term "partnership" includes a syndicate, group, pool, joint venture, or other unincorporated organization through or by means of which any business, financial operation, or venture is carried on, and which is not a corporation or a trust or estate within the meaning of the Internal Revenue Code of 1954. A joint undertaking merely to share expenses is not a partnership. For example, if two or more persons jointly construct a ditch merely to drain surface water from their properties, they are not partners. Mere co-ownership of property which is maintained, kept in repair, and rented or leased does not constitute a partnership. For example, if an individual owner, or tenants in common, of farm property lease it to a farmer for a cash rental or a share of the crops, they do not necessarily create a partnership thereby. Tenants in common, however, may be partners if they actively carry on a trade, business, financial operation, or venture and divide the profits thereof. For example, a partnership exists if co-owners of an apartment building lease space and in addition provide services to the occupants either directly or through an agent.

(b) Limited partnerships—(1) In general. An organization which qualifies as a limited partnership under State law may be classified for purposes of the Internal Revenue Code as an ordinary partnership or as an association. Such a limited partnership will be treated as an association if, applying the principles set forth in § 301.7701–2, the organization more nearly resembles a corporation than an ordinary partnership or other business entity.

(2) Examples. The principles of this paragraph may be illustrated by the following examples:

Example (1). Three individuals form an organization which qualifies as a limited partnership under the laws of the State in which the organization was formed. The purpose of the organization is to acquire and operate various pieces of commercial and other investment property for profit. Each of the three individuals who are general partners invests $100,000 in the enterprise. Five million dollars of additional capital is raised through contributions of $100,000 or more by each of 30 limited partners. The three general partners are personally capable of assuming a substantial part of the obligations to be incurred by the organization. While a limited partner may assign his right to receive a share of the profits and a return of his contribution, his assignee does not become a substituted limited partner except with the unanimous consent of the general partners. The life of the organization as stated in the certificate is 20 years, but the death, insanity, or retirement of a general partner prior to the expiration of the 20-year period will dissolve the organization. The general partners have exclusive authority to manage the affairs of the organization but can act only upon the unanimous consent of all of them. The organization has associates and an objective to carry on business and divide the gains therefrom, which characterize both partnerships and corporations. While the organization has the corporate characteristic of centralized management, since substantially all of the interests in the organization are owned by the limited partners, it does not have the characteristics of continuity of life, free transferability of interests, or limited liability. The organization will be classified as a partnership for all purposes of the Internal Revenue Code.

Example (2). Three individuals form an organization which qualifies as a limited partnership under the laws of the State in which the organization was formed. The purpose of the organization is to acquire and operate various pieces of commercial and other investment property for profit. The certificate provides that the life of the organization is to be 40 years, unless a general partner dies, becomes insane, or retires during such period. On the occurrence of such death, insanity, or retirement, the remaining general partners may continue the business of the partnership for the balance of the 40-year period under a right so to do stated in the certificate. Each of the three individuals who is a general partner invests $50,000 in the enterprise and has means to satisfy the business obligations of the organization to a substantial extent. Five million dollars of additional capital is raised through the sale of freely transferable interests in amounts of $10,000 or less to limited partners. Nine hundred such interests are sold. The interests of the 900 limited partners are fully transferable, that is, a transferee acquires all the attributes of the transferor's interest in the organization. The general partners have exclusive control over management of the business, their interests are not transferable, and their liability for debts of the organization is not limited to their capital contributions. The organization has associates and an objective to carry on business and divide the gains therefrom. It does not have the corporate characteristics of limited liability and continuity of life. It has centralized management, however, since the three general partners exercise exclusive control over the management of the business, and since substantially all of the interests in the organization are owned by the limited partners. While the interests of the general partners are not transferable, the transferability test of an association is met since substantially all of the interests in the organization are represented by transferable interests. The organization will be classified as a partnership for all purposes of the Internal Revenue Code.

(c) Partnership associations. The laws of a number of States provide for the formation of organizations commonly known as partnership associations. Such a partnership association will be treated as an association if, applying the principles set forth in § 301.7701–2, the organization more nearly resembles a corporation than the other types of business entities.

* * *

[32 FR 15241, Nov. 3, 1967]

§ 301.7701–4 Trusts.

(a) Ordinary trusts. In general, the term "trust" as used in the Internal Revenue Code refers to an arrangement created either by a will or by an inter vivos declaration whereby trustees take title to property for the purpose of protecting or conserving it for the beneficiaries under the ordinary rules applied in chancery or probate courts. Usually the beneficiaries of such a trust do no more than accept the benefits thereof and are not the voluntary planners or creators of the trust arrangement. However, the beneficiaries of such a trust may be the persons who create it and it will be recognized as a trust under the Internal Revenue Code if it was created for the purpose of protecting or conserving the trust property for beneficiaries who stand in the same relation to the trust as they would if the trust had been created by others for them. Generally speaking, an arrangement will be treated as a trust under the Internal Revenue Code if it can be shown that the purpose of the arrangement is to vest in trustees responsibility for the protection and conservation of property for beneficiaries who cannot share in the discharge of this responsibility and, therefore, are not associates in a joint enterprise for the conduct of business for profit.

(b) Business trusts. There are other arrangements which are known as trusts because the legal title to property is conveyed to trustees for the benefit of beneficiaries, but which are not classified as trusts for purposes of the Internal Revenue Code because they are not simply arrangements to protect or conserve the property for the beneficiaries. These trusts, which are often known as business or commercial trusts, generally are created by the beneficiaries simply as a device to carry on a profit-making business which normally would have been carried on through business organizations that are classified as corporations or partnerships under the Internal Revenue Code. However, the fact that the corpus of the trust is not supplied by the beneficiaries is not sufficient reason in itself for classifying the arrangement as an ordinary trust rather than as an association or partnership. The fact that any organization is technically cast in the trust form, by conveying title to property to trustees for the benefit of persons designated as beneficiaries, will not change the real character of the organization if, applying the principles set forth in §§ 301.7701–2 and 301.7701–3, the organization more nearly resembles an association or a partnership than a trust.

(c) Certain investment trusts—(1) An "investment" trust will not be classified as a trust if there is a power under the trust agreement to vary the investment of the certificate holders. See Commissioner v. North American Bond Trust, 122 F.2d 545 (2d Cir.1941), cert. denied, 314 U.S. 701 (1942). An investment trust with a single class of ownership interests, representing undivided beneficial interests in the assets of the trust, will be classified as a trust if there is no power under the trust agreement to vary the investment of the certificate holders. An investment trust with multiple classes of ownership interests will ordinarily be classified as an association or a partnership under § 301.7701–2; however, an investment trust with multiple classes of ownership interests, in which there is no power under the trust agreement to vary the investment of the certificate holders, will be classified as a trust if the trust is formed to facilitate direct investment in the assets of the trust and the existence of multiple classes of ownership interests is incidental to that purpose.

(2) The provisions of paragraph (c)(1) of this section may be illustrated by the following examples:

Example (1) A corporation purchases a portfolio of residential mortgages and transfers the mortgages to a bank under a trust agreement. At the same time, the bank as trustee delivers to the corporation certificates evidencing rights to payments from the pooled mortgages; the corporation sells the certificates to the public. The trustee holds legal title to the mortgages in the pool for the benefit of the certificate holders but has no power to reinvest proceeds attributable to the mortgages in the pool or to vary investments in the pool in any other manner. There are two classes of certificates. Holders of class A certificates are entitled to all payments of mortgage principal, both scheduled and prepaid, until their certificates are retired; holders of class B certificates receive payments of principal only after all class A certificates have been retired. The different rights of the class A and class B certificates serve to shift to the holders of the class A certificates, in addition to the earlier scheduled payments of principal, the risk that mortgages in the pool will be prepaid so that the holders of the class B certificates will have "call protection" (freedom from premature termination of their interests on account of prepayments). The trust thus serves to create investment interests with respect to the mortgages held by the trust that differ significantly from direct investment in the mortgages. As a consequence, the existence of multiple classes of trust ownership is not incidental to any purpose of the trust facilitate direct investment, and accordingly, the trust is classified as an association or a partnership under § 301.7701–2.

Example (2): Corporation M is the originator of a portfolio of residential mortgages and transfers the mortgages to a bank under a trust agreement. At the same time, the bank as trustee delivers to M certificates evidencing rights to payments from the pooled mortgages. The trustee holds legal title to the mortgages in the pool for the benefit of the certificate holders, but has no power to reinvest proceeds attributable to the mortgages in the pool or to vary investments in the pool in any other manner. There are two classes of certificates. Holders of class C certificates are entitled to receive 90 percent of the payments of principal and interest on the mortgages; class D certificate holders are entitled to receive the other ten percent. The two classes of certificates are identical except that, in the event of a default on the underlying mortgages, the payment rights of class D certificate holders are subordinated to the rights of class C certificate holders. M sells the class C certificates to investors and retains the class D certificates. The trust has multiple classes of ownership interests, given the greater security provided to holders of class C certificates. The interests of certificate holders, however, are substantially equivalent to undivided interests in the pool of mortgages, coupled with a limited recourse guarantee running from M to the holders of class C certificates. In such circumstances, the existence of multiple classes of ownership interests is incidental to the trust's purpose of facilitating direct investment in the assets of the trust. Accordingly, the trust is classified as a trust.

Example (3): A promoter forms a trust in which shareholders of a publicly traded corporation can deposit their stock. For each share of stock deposited with the trust, the participant receives two certificates that are initially attached, but may be separated and traded independently of each other. One certificate represents the right to dividends and the value of the underlying stock up to a specified amount; the other certificate represents the right to appreciation in the stock's value above the specified amount. The separate certificates represent two different classes of ownership interest in the trust, which effectively separate dividend rights on the stock held by the trust from a portion of the right to appreciation in the value of such stock. The multiple classes of ownership interests are designed to permit investors, by transferring one of the certificates and retaining the other, to fulfill their varying investment objectives of seeking primarily either dividend income or capital appreciation from the stock held by the trust. Given that the trust serves to create investment interests with respect to the stock held by the trust that differ significantly from direct investment in such stock, the trust is not formed to facilitate direct investment in the assets of the trust. Accordingly, the trust is classified as an association or a partnership under § 301.7701–2.

Example (4): Corporation N purchases a portfolio of bonds and transfers the bonds to a bank under a trust agreement. At the same time, the trustee delivers to N certificates evidencing interests in the bonds. These certificates are sold to public investors. Each certificate represents the right to receive a particular payment with respect to a specific bond. Under section 1286, stripped coupons and stripped bonds are treated as separate bonds for federal income tax purposes. Although the interest of each certificate holder is different from that of each other certificate holder, and the trust thus has multiple classes of ownership, the multiple classes simply provide each certificate holder with a direct interest in what is treated under section 1286 as a separate bond. Given the similarity of the interests acquired by the certificate holders to the interests that could be acquired by direct investment, the multiple classes of trust interests merely facilitate direct investment in the assets held by the trust. Accordingly, the trust is classified as a trust.

(d) Liquidating trusts. Certain organizations which are commonly known as liquidating trusts are treated as trusts for purposes of the Internal Revenue Code. An organization will be considered a liquidating trust if it is organized for the primary purpose of liquidating and distributing the assets transferred to it, and if its activities are all reasonably necessary to, and consistent with, the accomplishment of that purpose. A liquidating trust is treated as a trust for purposes of the Internal Revenue Code because it is formed with the objective of liquidating particular assets and not as an organization having as its purpose the carrying on of a profit-making business which normally would be conducted through business organizations classified as corporations or partnerships. However, if the liquidation is unreasonably prolonged or if the liquidation purpose becomes so obscured by business activities that the declared purpose of liquidation can be said to be lost or abandoned, the status of the organization will no longer be that of a liquidating trust. Bondholders' protective committees, voting trusts, and other agencies formed to protect the interests of security holders during insolvency, bankruptcy, or corporate reorganization proceedings are analogous to liquidating trusts

but if subsequently utilized to further the control or profitable operation of a going business on a permanent continuing basis, they will lose their classification as trusts for purposes of the Internal Revenue Code.

[32 FR 15241, Nov. 3, 1967; T.D. 8080, 51 FR 9952, March 24, 1986]

§ 301.7701–6 Fiduciary.

"Fiduciary" is a term which applies to persons who occupy positions of peculiar confidence toward others, such as trustees, executors, and administrators. A fiduciary is a person who holds in trust an estate to which another has the beneficial title or in which another has a beneficial interest, or receives and controls income of another, as in the case of receivers. A committee or guardian of the property of an incompetent person is a fiduciary.

[32 FR 15241, Nov. 3, 1967]

GENERAL RULES

Loans With Below-Market Interest Rates

§ 1.7872–5T Exempted loans.

(a) **In general—(1) General rule.** Except as provided in paragraph (a)(2) of this section, notwithstanding any other provision of section 7872 and the regulations thereunder, section 7872 does not apply to the loans listed in paragraph (b) of this section because the interest arrangements do not have a significant effect on the Federal tax liability of the borrower or the lender.

(2) **No exemption for tax avoidance loans.** If a taxpayer structures a transaction to be a loan described in paragraph (b) of this section and one of the principal purposes of so structuring the transaction is the avoidance of Federal tax, then the transaction will be recharacterized as a tax avoidance loan as defined in section 7872(c)(1)(D).

(b) **List of exemptions.** Except as provided in paragraph (a) of this section, the following transactions are exempt from section 7872:

(1) Loans which are made available by the lender to the general public on the same terms and conditions and which are consistent with the lender's customary business practice;

(2) Accounts or withdrawable shares with a bank (as defined in section 581), or an institution to

which section 591 applies, or a credit union, made in the ordinary course of its business;

(3) Acquisitions of publicly traded debt obligations for an amount equal to the public trading price at the time of acquisition;

(4) Loans made by a life insurance company (as defined in section 816(a)), in the ordinary course of its business, to an insured, under a loan right contained in a life insurance policy and in which the cash surrender values are used as collateral for the loans;

(5) Loans subsidized by the Federal, State (including the District of Columbia), or Municipal government (or any agency or instrumentality thereof), and which are made available under a program of general application to the public;

(6) Employee-relocation loans that meet the requirements of paragraph (c)(1) of this section;

(7) Obligations the interest on which is excluded from gross income under section 103;

(8) Obligations of the United States government;

(9) Gift loans to a charitable organization (described in section 170(c)), but only if at no time during the taxable year will the aggregate out-

standing amount of loans by the lender to that organization exceed $250,000. Charitable organizations which are effectively controlled, within the meaning of section 1.482–1(a)(1), by the same person or persons shall be considered one charitable organization for purposes of this limitation.

(10) Loans made to or from a foreign person that meet the requirements of paragraph (c)(2) of this section;

(11) Loans made by a private foundation or other organization described in section 170(c), the primary purpose of which is to accomplish one or more of the purposes described in section 170(c)(2)(B);

(12) Any loan expected from the application of section 482 for the period referred to in § 1.482–2(a)(3).

(13) All money, securities, and property—

(i) Received by a futures commission merchant or registered broker/dealer or by a clearing organization (A) to margin, guarantee or secure contracts for future delivery on or subject to the rules of a qualified board or exchange (as defined in section 1256(g)(7)), or (B) to purchase, margin, guarantee or secure options contracts traded on or subject to the rules of a qualified board or exchange, so long as the amounts so received to purchase, margin, guarantee or secure such contracts for future delivery or such options contracts are reasonably necessary for such purposes and so long as any commissions received by the futures commission merchant, registered broker-dealer, or clearing organization are not reduced for those making deposits of money, and all money accruing to account holders as the result of such futures and options contacts or

(ii) Received by a clearing organization from a member thereof as a required deposit to a clearing fund, guaranty fund, or similar fund maintained by the clearing organization to protect it against defaults by members.

(14) Loans the interest arrangements of which the taxpayer is able to show have no significant effect on any Federal tax liability of the lender or the borrower, as described in paragraph (c)(3) of this section; and

(15) Loans, described in revenue rulings or revenue procedures issued under section 7872(g)(1)(C), if the Commissioner finds that the factors justifying an exemption for such loans are sufficiently similar to the factors justifying the exemptions contained in this section.

(c) **Special rules—(1) Employee-relocation loans—(i) Mortgage loans.** In the case of a compensation-related loan to an employee, where such loan is secured by a mortgage on the new principal residence (within the meaning of section 217 and the regulations thereunder) of the employee, acquired in connection with the transfer of that employee to a new principal place of work (which meets the requirements in section 217(c) and the regulations thereunder), the loan will be exempt from section 7872 if the following conditions are satisfied:

(A) The loan is a demand loan or is a term loan the benefits of the interest arrangements of which are not transferable by the employee and are conditioned on the future performance of substantial services by the employee;

(B) The employee certifies to the employer that the employee reasonably expects to be entitled to and will itemize deductions for each year the loan is outstanding; and

(C) The loan agreement requires that the loan proceeds be used only to purchase the new principal residence of the employee.

(ii) **Bridge loans.** In the case of a compensation-related loan to an employee which is not described in paragraph (c)(1)(i) of this section, and which is used to purchase a new principal residence (within the meaning of section 217 and the regulations thereunder) of the employee acquired in connection with the transfer of that employee to a new principal place of work (which meets the requirements in section 217(c) and the regulations thereunder), the loan will be exempt from section 7872 if the following conditions are satisfied:

(A) The conditions contained in paragraphs (c)(1)(i)(A), (B), and (C) of this section;

(B) The loan agreement provides that the loan is payable in full within 15 days after the date of the sale of the employee's immediately former principal residence;

(C) The aggregate principal amount of all outstanding loans described in this paragraph (c)(1)(ii) to an employee is no greater than the employer's reasonable estimate of the amount of the equity of the employee and the employee's spouse in the employee's immediately former principal residence, and

(D) The employee's immediately former principal residence is not converted to business or investment use.

* * *

(3) **Loans without significant tax effect.** Whether a loan will be considered to be a loan the interest arrangements of which have a significant effect on any Federal tax liability of the lender or the borrower will be determined according to all of the facts and circumstances. Among the factors to be considered are—

(i) Whether items of income and deduction generated by the loan offset each other;

(ii) the amount of such items;

(iii) the cost to the taxpayer of complying with the provisions of section 7872 if such section were applied; and

(iv) any non-tax reasons for deciding to structure the transaction as a below-market loan rather than a loan with interest at a rate equal to or greater than the applicable Federal rate and a payment by the lender to the borrower.

[T.D. 8045, 50 FR 33520, Aug. 20, 1985; T.D. 8093, 51 FR 25032, July 10, 1986; 51 FR 28553, Aug. 8, 1986]

*

APPENDIX

Rev.Proc. 85-55 Cost-of-Living Adjustment

Section 1. Purpose

The purpose of this revenue procedure is to provide the income tax cost-of-living adjustment (indexing) factor as determined pursuant to section 1(f)(3) of the Internal Revenue Code for taxable years beginning in 1986. It also sets forth the application of the factor to the tax tables, the zero bracket amount, the personal exemption amount, and the tax return exemption amount.

Sec. 2. Background

Section 104 of the Economic Recovery Tax Act of 1981, 1981-2 C.B. 256, 267-68, instituted, for taxable years beginning after December 31, 1984, adjustments to prevent inflation-caused income tax increases. It provides that the tax tables, the zero bracket amount, the personal exemption amount, and the tax return exemption amount are to be adjusted (indexed) each calendar year by a cost-of-living factor determined under a prescribed method. Rev.Proc. 84-79, 1984-2 C.B. 755, sets forth the adjustments for taxable years beginning in 1985.

Sec. 3. Cost-of-living adjustment factor

Based on the method prescribed in section 1(f) of the Code, the cost-of-living adjustment factor for taxable years beginning in 1986 has been determined to be 7.9112588 percent, the percentage by which the average CPI for the 12 months ending in September 1985 (319.4083333) exceeds the average CPI for the 12 months ending in September 1983 (295.9916667). The adjustment factor is applied to the amounts that were in effect for taxable years beginning in 1984.

Sec. 4. Application of factor to sections 1, 63, 151, 6012, and 6013 of the Code

.01 The following adjusted tax tables are prescribed in lieu of the tables contained in paragraph (3) of subsections (a), (b), (c), (d), and (e) of section 1 of the Code with respect to taxable years beginning in 1986:

TABLE 1—Section 1(a)(3).—Married Individuals Filing Joint Returns and Surviving Spouses:

If taxable income is:	The tax is:
Not over 3,670	No tax.
Over $ 3,670 but not over $ 5,940	11% of the excess over $ 3,670
Over $ 5,940 but not over $ 8,200	$ 249.70 plus 12% of the excess over $ 5,940
Over $ 8,200 but not over $ 12,840	$ 520.90 plus 14% of the excess over $ 8,200
Over $ 12,840 but not over $ 17,270	$ 1,170.50 plus 16% of the excess over $ 12,840
Over $ 17,270 but not over $ 21,800	$ 1,879.30 plus 18% of the excess over $ 17,270
Over $ 21,800 but not over $ 26,550	$ 2,694.70 plus 22% of the excess over $ 21,800
Over $ 26,550 but not over $ 32,270	$ 3,739.70 plus 25% of the excess over $ 26,550
Over $ 32,270 but not over $ 37,980	$ 5,169.70 plus 28% of the excess over $ 32,270
Over $ 37,980 but not over $ 49,420	$ 6,768.50 plus 33% of the excess over $ 37,980
Over $ 49,420 but not over $ 64,750	$10,543.70 plus 38% of the excess over $ 49,420
Over $ 64,750 but not over $ 92,370	$16,369.10 plus 42% of the excess over $ 64,750
Over $ 92,370 but not over $118,050	$27,969.50 plus 45% of the excess over $ 92,370
Over $118,050 but not over $175,250	$39,525.50 plus 49% of the excess over $118,050
Over $175,250	$67,553.50 plus 50% of the excess over $175,250

TABLE 2—Section 1(b)(3).—Heads of Households.—

If taxable income is:	The tax is:
Not over $2,480	No tax.

APPENDIX

If taxable income is:	The tax is:
Over $ 2,480 but not over $ 4,750	11% of the excess over $ 2,480
Over $ 4,750 but not over $ 7,010	$ 249.70 plus 12% of the excess over $ 4,750
Over $ 7,010 but not over $ 9,390	$ 520.90 plus 14% of the excess over $ 7,010
Over $ 9,390 but not over $ 12,730	$ 854.10 plus 17% of the excess over $ 9,390
Over $ 12,730 but not over $ 16,190	$ 1,421.90 plus 18% of the excess over $ 12,730
Over $ 16,190 but not over $ 19,640	$ 2,044.70 plus 20% of the excess over $ 16,190
Over $ 19,640 but not over $ 25,360	$ 2,734.70 plus 24% of the excess over $ 19,640
Over $ 25,360 but not over $ 31,080	$ 4,107.50 plus 28% of the excess over $ 25,360
Over $ 31,080 but not over $ 36,800	$ 5,709.10 plus 32% of the excess over $ 31,080
Over $ 36,800 but not over $ 48,240	$ 7,539.50 plus 35% of the excess over $ 36,800
Over $ 48,240 but not over $ 65,390	$11,543.50 plus 42% of the excess over $ 48,240
Over $ 65,390 but not over $ 88,270	$18,746.50 plus 45% of the excess over $ 65,390
Over $ 88,270 but not over $116,870	$29,042.50 plus 48% of the excess over $ 88,270
Over $116,870	$42,770.50 plus 50% of the excess over $116,870

TABLE 3—Section 1(c)(3).—Unmarried Individuals (Other Than Surviving Spouses and Heads of Households).—

If taxable income is:	The tax is:
Not over $ 2,480	No tax.
Over $ 2,480 but not over $ 3,670	11% of the excess over $ 2,480
Over $ 3,670 but not over $ 4,750	$ 130.90 plus 12% of the excess over $ 3,670
Over $ 4,750 but not over $ 7,010	$ 260.50 plus 14% of the excess over $ 4,750
Over $ 7,010 but not over $ 9,170	$ 576.90 plus 15% of the excess over $ 7,010
Over $ 9,170 but not over $11,650	$ 900.90 plus 16% of the excess over $ 9,170
Over $11,650 but not over $13,920	$ 1,297.70 plus 18% of the excess over $11,650
Over $13,920 but not over $16,190	$ 1,706.30 plus 20% of the excess over $13,920
Over $16,190 but not over $19,640	$ 2,160.30 plus 23% of the excess over $16,190
Over $19,640 but not over $25,360	$ 2,953.80 plus 26% of the excess over $19,640
Over $25,360 but not over $31,080	$ 4,441.00 plus 30% of the excess over $25,360
Over $31,080 but not over $36,800	$ 6,157.00 plus 34% of the excess over $31,080
Over $36,800 but not over $44,780	$ 8,101.80 plus 38% of the excess over $36,800
Over $44,780 but not over $59,670	$11,134.20 plus 42% of the excess over $44,780
Over $59,670 but not over $88,270	$17,388.00 plus 48% of the excess over $59,670
Over $88,270	$31,116.00 plus 50% of the excess over $88,270

TABLE 4—Section 1(d)(3).—Married Individuals Filing Separate Returns.—

If taxable income is:	The tax is:
Not over $ 1,835	No tax.
Over $ 1,835 but not over $ 2,970	11% of the excess over $ 1,835
Over $ 2,970 but not over $ 4,100	$ 124.85 plus 12% of the excess over $ 2,970
Over $ 4,100 but not over $ 6,420	$ 260.45 plus 14% of the excess over $ 4,100
Over $ 6,420 but not over $ 8,635	$ 585.25 plus 16% of the excess over $ 6,420
Over $ 8,635 but not over $10,900	$ 939.65 plus 18% of the excess over $ 8,635
Over $10,900 but not over $13,275	$ 1,347.35 plus 22% of the excess over $10,900
Over $13,275 but not over $16,135	$ 1,869.85 plus 25% of the excess over $13,275
Over $16,135 but not over $18,990	$ 2,584.85 plus 28% of the excess over $16,135
Over $18,990 but not over $24,710	$ 3,384.25 plus 33% of the excess over $18,990
Over $24,710 but not over $32,375	$ 5,271.85 plus 38% of the excess over $24,710
Over $32,375 but not over $46,185	$ 8,184.75 plus 42% of the excess over $32,375
Over $46,185 but not over $59,025	$13,984.75 plus 45% of the excess over $46,185
Over $59,025 but not over $87,625	$19,762.75 plus 49% of the excess over $59,025
Over $87,625	$33,776.75 plus 50% of the excess over $87,625

TABLE 5—Section 1(e)(3).—Estates and Trusts.—

If taxable income is:	The tax is:
Not over $ 1,135	11% of taxable income.
Over $ 1,135 but not over $ 2,265	$ 124.85 plus 12% of the excess over $ 1,135
Over $ 2,265 but not over $ 4,585	$ 260.45 plus 14% of the excess over $ 2,265
Over $ 4,585 but not over $ 6,800	$ 585.25 plus 16% of the excess over $ 4,585
Over $ 6,800 but not over $ 9,065	$ 939.65 plus 18% of the excess over $ 6,800
Over $ 9,065 but not over $11,440	$ 1,347.35 plus 22% of the excess over $ 9,065

1536

If taxable income is:	The tax is:
Over $11,440 but not over $14,300	$ 1,869.85 plus 25% of the excess over $11,440
Over $14,300 but not over $17,160	$ 2,584.85 plus 28% of the excess over $14,300
Over $17,160 but not over $22,875	$ 3,385.65 plus 33% of the excess over $17,160
Over $22,875 but not over $30,540	$ 5,271.60 plus 38% of the excess over $22,875
Over $30,540 but not over $44,350	$ 8,184.30 plus 42% of the excess over $30,540
Over $44,350 but not over $57,195	$13,984.50 plus 45% of the excess over $44,350
Over $57,195 but not over $85,790	$19,764.75 plus 49% of the excess over $57,195
Over $85,790	$33,776.30 plus 50% of the excess over $85,790

.02 The following adjusted "zero bracket amounts" are set forth for purposes of section 63(d)(1) of the Code:

If the applicable tax table is:	The amount is:
Table 1	$3,670
Table 2	$2,480
Table 3	$2,480
Table 4	$1,835

.03 For purposes of the personal "exemption amount" under section 151(f) of the Code, the adjusted amount is $1,080.

.04 The following adjusted amounts are set forth for purposes of section 6012 of the Code:

1. The section 6012(a)(1)(D)(i) "zero bracket amount" is $2,480 for section 6012(a)(1)(A)(i) and $3,670 for sections 6012(a)(1)(A)(ii) and (iii).

2. The section 6012(a)(1)(D)(ii) "exemption amount" is $1,080.

3. The section 6012(a)(1)(A)(i) "sum of the exemption amount plus the zero bracket amount" is $3,560 ($1,080 + $2,480).

4. The section 6012(a)(1)(A)(ii) "sum of the exemption amount plus the zero bracket amount" is $4,750 ($1,080 + $3,670).

5. The section 6012(a)(1)(A)(iii) "sum of twice the exemption amount plus the zero bracket amount" is $5,830 ((2 × $1,080) + $3,670).

.05 For purposes of section 6013(b)(3) of the Code, the adjusted "exemption amount" is $1,080.

Sec. 5. Effective date

This revenue procedure is effective January 1, 1986, for any taxable year beginning in 1986.

[Published in 1985–46 IRB 43, Nov. 18, 1985]

LR–19–80 Unisex Annuity Tables

* * *

SUMMARY: This document contains proposed regulations relating to the annuity tables used to compute the portion of the amount received as an annuity that is includible in gross income. Questions have arisen concerning the gender distinction in the existing tables and the outdated mortality experience upon which those tables are based. These regulations would affect taxpayers receiving amounts as annuities under annuity, endowment, or life insurance contracts for which they have paid premiums or other consideration and provide them with the guidance needed to determine the amount includible in gross income with respect to such contracts. This document also contains proposed regulations relating to the computations necessary to determine the amount excludable from an employee's gross income by allocation of contributions when the actual employer contributions are not known. This document also proposes to remove certain regulations relating to defined benefit plans that provided benefits for employees who were either self-employed or a shareholder-employee.

DATES: Written comments and requests for a public hearing must be delivered or mailed by May 8, 1986. The amendments to §§ 1.72–4, 1.72–5, 1.72–6, 1.72–7, 1.72–9, and 1.72–11 are proposed to be effective on July 1, 1986, and to apply to amounts received as an annuity after June 30, 1986. In addition, the proposed amendments to § 1.72–6 include transitional rules applicable to amounts received under contracts in which an amount is invested before July 1, 1986. The amendments to § 1.403(b)–1(d)(4)(iv) are proposed to be effective for taxable years beginning after July 1, 1986. The removal of §§ 1.401(a)–18 and 1.401(j)–1 through –6 is proposed to be effective for plan years beginning after December 31, 1983.

* * *

SUPPLEMENTARY INFORMATION:

Background

This document contains proposed amendments to the Income Tax Regulations (26 CFR Part 1) and the Table of OMB Control Numbers (26 CFR Part 602). The proposed amendments would update and gender-neutralize the annuity tables used to determine the exclusion ratio applicable to amounts received as annuities under annuity, endowment, or life insurance contracts. Section 72 permits a taxpayer to exclude from gross income that part of any amount received as an annuity which bears the same ratio to such amount as the investment in the contract as of the annuity starting date bears to the expected return under the contract as of such date. If the expected return depends in whole or in part on the life expectancy of one or more individuals, the statute requires that the expected return be computed with reference to actuarial tables prescribed by the Secretary of the Treasury. Soon after section 72 was enacted in 1954, the Secretary published regulations containing tables based on 1937 individual annuitant mortality and distinguished by gender. The effect of this gender distinction is that women are not entitled to exclude from gross income as high a proportion of the amount received as an annuity as men of the same age.

Revised Annuity Tables

These proposed amendments provide new tables that eliminate the gender distinction and are based on more recent mortality experience. The proposed tables are based, as are the tables currently in effect, on individual annuitant mortality. The 1983 experience table used to produce the annuity tables proposed in this document was developed by the Society of Actuaries and reflects application of improvement factors to a 1973 individual-annuitant experience table. See Report of the Committee to Recommend a New Mortality Basis for Individual Annuity Valuation (Derivation of the 1983 Table a) Vol. XXXIII, Transactions of the Society of Actuaries 675, 708 (1981). In addition, the proposed unisex tables assume that the population

mix of males and females at each age is the same as that of individual annuitants. The individual-annuitant gender mix reflected in the proposed tables is based on the same Society of Actuaries study.

The Service and Treasury would appreciate any comments on these proposed amendments that focus on whether the assumptions used to develop the tables are appropriate for determining life expectancies of taxpayers receiving amounts taxable under section 72, especially those taxpayers who can be expected to use the section 72 annuity tables (rather than, for example, the three-year recovery rule of section 72(d)) to compute an exclusion ratio under sections 72(b) and 72(c). In particular, the Service and Treasury would be interested in data, undifferentiated by gender, on the mortality experience of taxpayers receiving amounts to which section 72 applies.

Section 72 Transitional Rule

The exclusion ratio with respect to amounts received as an annuity after June 30, 1986, would generally be computed using the updated annuity tables proposed in this document. Two transitional rules are provided, however. The first applies to amounts received under a contract in which no amount was invested after June 30, 1986, and provides that the tables in the existing regulations would apply. The second transitional rule applies to contracts in which amounts were invested both before July 1, 1986, and after June 30, 1986. The second transitional rule is optional and would allow a taxpayer either to compute one exclusion ratio using the updated annuity tables, or to compute separate exclusion ratios with respect to the amounts invested in the contract before July 1, 1986, and the amounts invested after June 30, 1986. If the separate computation option were chosen, the tables in the existing regulations would be used to compute the exclusion ratio with respect to portions of the payments under the contract attributable to amounts invested in the contract before July 1, 1986, and the updated tables would be used to compute the exclusion ratio with respect to portions of payments under the contract attributable to amounts invested after June 30, 1986. The amount excludable from gross income would be the sum of the amounts determined by applying the two exclusion ratios to the amount received as an annuity.

The regulations provide that the transitional rules do not apply to an annuity contract with an annuity starting date occurring after June 30, 1986, if the contract provides, at the option of the annuitant or of any other person, for any form of payment or settlement that permits receipt of amounts under the contract in a form other than a life annuity. The transitional rules may not be used, for example, if the contract permits the taxpayer to withdraw the investment in the contract before the annuity starting date, to receive a lump sum in full discharge of the obligation under the contract, or to receive an annuity for a period certain (without regard to life expectancy) or its substantial equivalent. In effect, a contract that provides for these options is treated for purposes of the transitional rules as if the entire investment in the contract were made on the annuity starting date. Thus, the taxpayer must apply the updated, gender-neutral annuity tables proposed in this document to the entire investment in such a contract if the annuity starting date occurs after June 30, 1986.

* * *

Proposed Amendments to the Regulations

The proposed amendments to 26 CFR Part 1 is as follows:

Par. 2. Section 1.72–4 is amended by revising paragraphs (a), (d), and (e) to read as follows:

§ 1.72–4 Exclusion ratio.

(a) General rule. (1)(i) To determine the proportionate part of the total amount received each year as an annuity which is excludable from the gross income of a recipient in the taxable year of receipt (other than amounts received under (a) certain employee annuities described in section 72(d) and § 1.72–13, or (b) certain annuities described in section 72(*o*) and § 1.122–1), an exclusion ratio is to be determined for each contract. In general, this ratio is determined by dividing the investment in the contract as found under § 1.72–6 by the expected return under such contract as found under § 1.72–5. Where a single consideration is given for a particular contract which provides for two or more annuity elements, an exclusion ratio shall be determined for the contract as a whole by dividing the investment in such contract by the aggregate of the expected returns under all the annuity elements provided thereunder. However, where the provisions of paragraph (b)(3) of

§ 1.72–2 apply to payments received under such a contract, see paragraph (b)(3) of § 1.72–6. In the case of a contract to which § 1.72–6(d) (relating to contracts in which amounts were invested both before July 1, 1986, and after June 30, 1986) applies, the exclusion ratio for purposes of this paragraph (a) is determined in accordance with § 1.72–6(d) and, in particular, § 1.72–6(d)(5)(i).

(ii) The exclusion ratio for the particular contract is then applied to the total amount received as an annuity during the taxable year by each recipient. See, however, paragraph (e)(3) of § 1.72–5. Any excess of the total amount received as an annuity during the taxable year over the amount determined by the application of the exclusion ratio to such total amount shall be included in the gross income of the recipient for the taxable year of receipt.

(2) The principles of subparagraph (1) may be illustrated by the following example:

Example. Taxpayer A purchased an annuity contract providing for payments of $100 per month for a consideration of $12,650. Assuming that the expected return under this contract is $16,000 the exclusion ratio to be used by A is $12,650÷16,000; or 79.1 percent (79.06 rounded to the nearest tenth). If 12 such monthly payments are received by A during his taxable year, the total amount he may exclude from his gross income in such year is $949.20 ($1,200×79.1 percent). The balance of $250.80 ($1,200 less $949.20) is the amount to be included in gross income. If A instead received only five such payments during the year, he should exclude $395.50 (500×79.1 percent) of the total amounts received.

For an example of the computation of the exclusion ratio in cases where two annuity elements are acquired for a single consideration, see paragraph (b)(1) of § 1.72–6.

(3) The exclusion ratio shall be applied only to amounts received as an annuity within the meaning of that term under paragraph (b)(2) and (3) of § 1.72–2. Where the periodic payments increase in amount after the annuity starting date in a manner not provided by the terms of the contract at such date, the portion of such payments representing the increase is not an amount received as an annuity. For the treatment of amounts not received as an annuity, see section 72(e) and § 1.72–11. For special rules where paragraph (b)(3) of § 1.72–2 applies to amounts received, see paragraph (d)(3) of this section.

(4) After an exclusion ratio has been determined for a particular contract, it shall be applied to any amounts received as an annuity thereunder unless or until one of the following occurs:

(i) The contract is assigned or transferred for a valuable consideration (see section 72(g) and paragraph (a) of § 1.72–10);

(ii) The contract matures or is surrendered, redeemed, or discharged in accordance with the provisions of paragraph (c) or (d) of § 1.72–11;

(iii) The contract is exchanged (or is considered to have been exchanged) in a manner described in paragraph (e) of § 1.72–11.

* * *

(d) **Exceptions to the general rule.** (1) Where the provisions of section 72 would otherwise require an exclusion ratio to be determined, but the investment in the contract (determined under § 1.72–6) is an amount zero or less, no exclusion ratio shall be determined and all amounts received under such a contract shall be includible in the gross income of the recipient for the purposes of section 72.

(2) Where the investment in the contract is equal to or greater than the total expected return under such contract found under § 1.72–5, the exclusion ratio shall be considered to be 100 percent and all amounts received as an annuity under such contract shall be excludable from the recipient's gross income. See, for example, paragraph (f)(1) of § 1.72–5. In the case of a contract to which § 1.72–6(d) (relating to contracts in which amounts were invested both before July 1, 1986, and after June 30, 1986) applies, this paragraph (d)(2) is applied in the manner prescribed in § 1.72–6(d) and, in particular, § 1.72–6(d)(5)(ii).

(3)(i) If a contract provides for payments to be made to a taxpayer in the manner described in paragraph (b)(3) of § 1.72–2, the investment in the contract shall be considered to be equal to the expected return under such contract and the resulting exclusion ratio (100%) shall be applied to all amounts received as an annuity under such contract. For any taxable year, payments received under such a contract shall be considered to be amounts received as an annuity only to the extent that they do not exceed the portion of the investment in the contract which is properly allocable to that year and hence excludable from gross income as a return of premiums or other consideration paid for the contract. The portion of the investment in the contract which is properly allocable to any taxable year shall be determined by dividing

the investment in the contract (adjusted for any refund feature in the manner described in paragraph (d) of § 1.72–7) by the applicable multiple (whether for a term certain, life, or lives) which would otherwise be used in determining the expected return for such a contract under § 1.72–5. The multiple shall be adjusted in accordance with the provisions of the table in paragraph (a)(2) of § 1.72–5, if any adjustment is necessary, before making the above computation. If payments are to be made more frequently than annually and the number of payments to be made in the taxable year in which the annuity begins are less than the number of payments to be made each year thereafter, the amounts considered received as an annuity (as otherwise determined under this subdivision) shall not exceed, for such taxable year (including a short taxable year), an amount which bears the same ratio to the portion of the investment in the contract considered allocable to each taxable year as the number of payments to be made in the first year bears to the number of payments to be made in each succeeding year. Thus, if payments are to be made monthly, only seven payments will be made in the first taxable year, and the portion of the investment in the contract allocable to a full year of payments is $600, the amounts considered received as an annuity in the first taxable year cannot exceed $350 ($600 × $7/12$). See subdivision (iii) of this subparagraph for an example illustrating the determination of the portion of the investment in the contract allocable to one taxable year of the taxpayer.

(ii) If subdivision (i) of this subparagraph applies to amounts received by a taxpayer and the total amount of payments he receives in a taxable year is less than the total amount excludable for such year under subdivision (i) of this subparagraph, the taxpayer may elect, in a succeeding taxable year in which he receives another payment, to redetermine the amounts to be received as an annuity during the current and succeeding taxable years. This shall be computed in accordance with the provisions of subdivision (i) of this subparagraph except that:

(a) The difference between the portion of the investment in the contract allocable to a taxable year, as found in accordance with subdivision (i) of this subparagraph, and the total payments actually received in the taxable year prior to the election shall be divided by the applicable life expectancy of the annuitant (or annuitants), found in accordance with the appropriate table in § 1.72–9 (and adjusted in accordance with paragraph (a)(2) of § 1.72–5), or by the remaining term of a term certain annuity, computed as of the first day of the first period for which an amount is received as an annuity in the taxable year of the election; and

(b) The amount determined under (a) of this subdivision shall be added to the portion of the investment in the contract allocable to each taxable year (as otherwise found). To the extent that the total periodic payments received under the contract in the taxable year of the election or any succeeding taxable year does not equal this total sum, such payments shall be excludable from the gross income of the recipient. To the extent such payments exceed the sum so found, they shall be fully includable in the recipient's gross income.

See subdivision (iii) of this subparagraph for an example illustrating the redetermination of amounts to be received as an annuity and subdivision (iv) of this subparagraph for the method of making the election provided by this subdivision.

(iii) The application of the principles of paragraph (d)(3)(i) and (ii) of this section may be illustrated by the following example:

Example. Taxpayer A, a 64 year old male, files his return on a calendar year basis and has a life expectancy of 15.6 years on June 30, 1954, the annuity starting date of a contract to which § 1.72–2(b)(3) applies and which he purchased for $20,000. The contract provides for variable annual payments for his life. He receives a payment of $1,000 on June 30, 1955, but receives no other payment until June 30, 1957. He excludes the $1,000 payment from his gross income for the year 1955 since this amount is less than $1,324.50, the amount determined by dividing his investment in the contract ($20,000) by his life expectancy adjusted for annual payments, 15.1 (15.6–0.5), as of the original annuity starting date. Taxpayer A may elect, in his return for the taxable year 1957, to redetermine amounts to be received as an annuity under his contract as of June 30, 1956. For the purpose of determining the extent to which amounts received in 1957 or thereafter shall be considered amounts received as an annuity (to which a 100 percent exclusion ratio shall apply) he shall add $118.63 to the $1,324.50 originally determined to be receivable as an annuity under the contract, making a total of $1,443.13. This is determined by dividing the difference between what was excludable in 1955 and 1956, $2,649 (2 × $1,324.50) and what he actually received in those years ($1,000) by his life expectancy adjusted for annual payments, 13.9 (14.4–0.5), as of his age at his nearest birthday (66) on the first day of the first period for which he received an amount as an annuity in the taxable year of election (June 30, 1956). The result, $1,443.13, is excludable in that year and each year thereafter as a amount received as an annuity to which the 100% exclusion ratio applies. It will be noted that in this example the taxpayer received amounts less than the excludable amounts in two successive years and

deferred making his election until the third year, and thus was able to accumulate the portion of the investment in the contract allocable to each taxable year to the extent he failed to receive such portion in both years. Assuming that he received $1,500 in the taxable year of his election, he would include $56.87 in his gross income and exclude $1,443.13 therefrom for that year.

(iv) If the taxpayer chooses to make the election described in subdivision (ii) of this subparagraph, he shall file with his return a statement that he elects to make a redetermination of the amounts excludable from gross income under his annuity contract in accordance with the provisions of paragraph (d)(3) of § 1.72–4. This statement shall also contain the following information:

(a) The original annuity starting date and his age on that date,

(b) The date of the first day of the first period for which he received an amount in the current taxable year

(c) The investment in the contract originally determined (as adjusted for any refund feature), and

(d) The aggregate of all amounts received under the contract between the date indicated in *(a)* of this subdivision and the day after the date indicated in *(b)* of this subdivision to the extent such amounts were excludable from gross income.

He shall include in gross income any amounts received during the taxable year for which the return is made in accordance with the redetermination made under this subparagraph.

(v) In the case of a contract to which § 1.72–6(d) (relating to contracts in which amounts were invested both before July 1, 1986, and after June 30, 1986) applies, this paragraph (d)(3) is applied in the manner prescribed in § 1.72–6(d) and, in particular, § 1.72–6(d)(5)(iii). This application may be illustrated by the following example:

Example. B, a male calendar year taxpayer, purchases a contract which provides for variable annual payments for life and to which § 1.72–2(b)(3) applies. The annuity starting date of the contract is June 30, 1990, when B is 64 years old. B receives a payment of $1,000 on June 30, 1991, but receives no other payment until June 30, 1993. B's total investment in the contract is $25,000. B's pre-July 1986 investment in the contract is $12,000. If B makes the election described in § 1.72–6(d)(6), separate computations are required to determine the amounts received as an annuity and excludable from gross income with respect to the pre-July 1986 investment in the contract and the post-June 1986 investment in the contract. In the separate computations, B first determines the applicable portions of the total payment received which are allocable to the pre-July 1986 investment in the contract and the post-June 1986 investment in the contract. The portion of the payment received allocable to the pre-July 1986 investment in the contract is $480 ($12,000/$25,000 × $1,000). The portion of the payment received allocable to the post-June 1986 investment in the contract is $520 ($13,000/$25,000 × $1,000).

Second, B determines the pre-July 1986 investment in the contract and the post-June 1986 investment in the contract allocable to the taxable year by dividing the pre-July 1986 and post-June 1986 investments in the contract by the applicable life expectancy multiple. The life expectancy multiple applicable to pre-July 1986 investment in the contract is B's life expectancy as of the original annuity starting date adjusted for annual payments and is determined under Table I of § 1.72–9 (15.-1(15.6–0.05)). The life expectancy multiple applicable to post-June 1986 investment in the contract is determined under Table V of § 1.72–9 (20.3(20.8–0.5)). Thus, the pre-July 1986 investment in the contract allocable to each taxable year is $794.70 ($12,000 – 15.1), and the post-June 1986 investment in the contract so allocable is $640.39 ($13,000 – 20.3). Because the applicable portions of the total payment received in 1991 under the contract ($480 allocable to the pre-July 1986 investment in the contract and $520 allocable to the post-June 1986 investment in the contract) are treated as amounts received as an annuity and are excludable from gross income to the extent they do not exceed the portion of the corresponding investment in the contract allocable to 1991 ($794.70 pre-July 1986 investment in the contract and $640.39 post-June 1986 investment in the contract), the entire amount of each applicable portion of the total payment is excludable from gross income. B may elect, in the return filed for taxable year 1993, to redetermine amounts to be received as an annuity under the contract as of June 30, 1992. The extent to which the amounts received in 1993 or thereafter shall be considered amounts received as an annuity is determined as follows:

Pre-July 1986 investment in the contract allocable to taxable years 1991 and 1992 ($794.70 × 2)	$1,589.40
Less: Portion of total payments allocable to pre-July 1986 investment in the contract actually received as an annuity in taxable years 1991 and 1992	480.00
	1,109.40
Divided by: Life expectancy multiple applicable to pre-July 1986 investment in the contract for B, age 66 (14.4–0.5)	13.9
	79.81
Plus: Amount originally determined with respect to pre-July 1986 investment in the contract	794.70
Pre-July 1986 amount	874.51
Post-June 1986 investment in the contract allocable to taxable years 1991 and 1992 ($640.39 × 2)	$1,280.78
Less: Portion of total payments allocable to post-June 1986 investment in the contract actually received as an annuity in taxable years 1991 and 1992	520.00
	760.78

Divided by: Life expectancy multiple applicable to post-June 1986 investment in the contract for B, age 66 (19.2–0.5)	18.7
	40.68
Plus: Amount originally determined with respect to post-June 1986 investment in the contract	640.39
Post-June 1986 amount	681.07

(vi) The method of making an election to perform the separate computations illustrated in paragraph (d)(3)(v) of this section is described in § 1.72–6(d)(6).

* * *

Par. 3. Section 1.72–5 is amended by revising paragraphs (a), (b), and (e), and adding a new paragraph (g) to read as follows:

§ 1.72–5 Expected return.

(a) Expected return for but one life. (1) If a contract to which section 72 applies provides that one annuitant is to receive a fixed monthly income for life, the expected return is determined by multiplying the total of the annuity payments to be received annually by the multiple shown in Table I or V (whichever is applicable) of § 1.72–9 under the age (as of annuity starting date) and, if applicable, sex of the measuring life (usually the annuitant's). Thus, where a male purchases a contract before July 1, 1986, providing for an immediate annuity of $100 per month for his life and, as of the annuity starting date (in this case the date of purchase), the annuitant's age at his nearest birthday is 66, the expected return is computed as follows:

Monthly payment of $100×12 months equals annual payment of	$1,200
Multiple shown in Table 1, male, age 66	14.4
Expected return (1,200×14.4)	17,280

If, however, the taxpayer had purchased the contract after June 30, 1986, the expected return would be $23,040, determined by multiplying 19.2 (multiple shown in Table V, age 66) by $1,200.

(2)(i) If payments are to be made quarterly, semiannually, or annually, an adjustment of the applicable multiple shown in Table 1 or V (whichever is applicable) may be required. A further adjustment may be required where the interval between the annuity starting date and the date of the first payment is less than the interval between future payments. Neither adjustment shall be made, however, if the payments are to be made more frequently than quarterly. The amount of the adjustment, if any, is to be found in accordance with the following table:

If the number of whole months from the annuity starting date to the first payment date is—	0–1	2	3	4	5	6	7	8	9	10	11	12
And the payments under the contract are to be made:												
Annually..................	+ 0.5	+ 0.4	+ 0.3	+ 0.2	+ 0.1	0	0	−0.1	−0.2	−0.3	−0.4	−0.5
Semiannually	+ .2	+ .1	0	0	− .1	− .2	....	....	....	....	....	....
Quarterly	+ .1	0	− .1	....	....	....	....	....	....	....	....	....

Thus, for a male, age 66, the multiple found in Table I, adjusted for quarterly payments the first of which is to be made one full month after the annuity starting date, is 14.5 (14.4 + 0.1); for semiannual payments the first of which is to be made six full months from the annuity starting date, the adjusted multiple is 14.2 (14.4 − 0.2); for annual payments the first of which is to be made one full month from the annuity starting date, the adjusted multiple is 14.9 (14.4 + 0.5). If the annuitant in the example shown in subparagraph (1) of this paragraph were to receive an annual payment of $1,200 commencing 12 full months after his annuity starting date, the amount of the expected return would be $16,680 ($1,200 × 13.9 [14.4 − 0.5]). Similarly, for an annuitant, age 50, the multiple found in Table V, adjusted for quarterly payments the first of which is to be made one full month after the annuity starting date, is 33.2 (33.1 + 0.1); for semi-annual payments the first of which is to be made six full months from the annuity starting date, the adjusted multiple is 32.9 (33.1 − 0.2); for annual payments the first of which is to be made one full month from the annuity starting date, the adjusted multiple is 33.6 (33.1 + 0.5).

(ii) Notwithstanding the table in subdivision (i) of this subparagraph, adjustments of multiples for early or other than monthly payments determined prior to February 19, 1956, under the table prescribed in paragraph 1(b)(4) of T.D. 6118 (19 FR 9897, C.B. 1955–1,699), approved December 30, 1954, need not be redetermined.

(3) If the contract provides for fixed payments to be made to an annuitant until death or until the expiration of a specified limited period, whichever occurs earlier, the expected return of such temporary life annuity is determined by multiplying the total of the annuity payments to be received annually by the multiple shown in Table IV or VIII (whichever is applicable) of § 1.72–9 for the age (as of the annuity starting date) and, if applicable, sex of the annuitant and the nearest whole number of years in the specified period. For example, if a male annuitant, age 60 (at his nearest birthday), is to receive $60 per month for five years or until he dies, whichever is earlier, and there is no post-June 1986, investment in the contract, the expected return under such a contract is $3,456, computed as follows:

Monthly payments of $60 × 12 months equals annual payment of	$720
Multiple shown in Table IV for male, age 60, for term of 5 years	4.8
Expected return for 5 year temporary life annuity of $720 per year ($720 × 4.8).....	$3,456

If the annuitant purchased the same contract after June 30, 1986, the expected return under the contract would be $3,528, computed as follows:

Monthly payments of $60 × 12 months equals annual payment of	$720.00
Multiple shown in Table VIII for annuitant, age 60, for term of 5 years	4.9
Expected return for 5-year temporary life annuity of $720 per year ($720 × 4.9).....	$3,528.00

The adjustment provided by subparagraph (2) of this paragraph shall not be made with respect to the multiple found in Table IV or VIII (whichever is applicable).

(4) If the contract provides for payments to be made to an annuitant for the annuitant's lifetime, but the amount of the annual payments is to be decreased after the expiration of a specified limited period, the expected return is computed by considering the contract as a combination of a whole life annuity for the smaller amount plus a temporary life annuity for an amount equal to the difference between the larger and the smaller amount. For example, if a male annuitant, age 60, is to receive $150 per month for five years or until his earlier death, and is to receive $90 per month for the remainder of his lifetime after such five years, the expected return is computed as if the annuitant's contract consisted of a whole life annuity for $90 per month plus a five year temporary life annuity

of $60 per month. In such circumstances, the expected return if there is no post-June 1986 investment in the contract is computed as follows:

Monthly payments of $90 × 12 months equals annual payment of	$1,080
Multiple shown in Table I for male, age 60 ..	18.2
Expected return for whole life annuity of $1,080 per year	$19,656
Expected return for 5-year temporary life annuity of $720 per year (as found in subparagraph (3) of this paragraph (a)) ...	$3,456
Total expected return	$23,112

If the annuitant purchased the same contract after June 30, 1986, the expected return would be $29,664, computed as follows:

Monthly payments of $90 × 12 months equals annual payment of	$1,080
Multiple shown in Table V for annuitant, age 60...................................	24.2
Expected return for whole life annuity of $1,080 per year	$26,136
Plus: Expected return for 5-year temporary life annuity of $720 per year (as found in subparagraph (3) of this paragraph (a)) ...	$3,528
Total expected return	$29,664

If payments are to be made quarterly, semiannually, or annually, an appropriate adjustment of the multiple found in Table I or V (whichever is applicable) for the whole life annuity should be made in accordance with subparagraph (2) of this paragraph.

(5) If the contract described in subparagraph (4) of this paragraph provided that the amount of the annual payments to the annuitant were to be increased (instead of decreased) after the expiration of a specified limited period, the expected return would be computed as if the annuitant's contract consisted of a whole life annuity for the larger amount minus a temporary life annuity for an amount equal to the difference between the larger and smaller amount. Thus, if the annuitant described in subparagraph (4) of this paragraph were to receive $90 per month for five years or until his earlier death, and to receive $150 per month for the remainder of his lifetime after such five years, the expected return would be computed by subtracting the expected return under a five year temporary life annuity of $60 per month from the expected return under a whole life annuity of $150 per month. In such circumstances, the expected return if there is no post-June 1986 investment in the contract is computed as follows:

Monthly payments of $150 × 12 months equals annual payment of	$1,800
Multiple shown in Table I (male, age 60)	18.2
Expected return for annuity for whole life of $1,800 per year	$32,760
Less expected return for 5-year temporary life annuity of $720 per year (as found in subparagraph (3))	$3,456
Net expected return	$29,304

If the annuitant purchased the same contract after June 30, 1986, the expected return would be $40,032, computed as follows:

Monthly payments of $150 × 12 months equals annual payments of	$1,800
Multiple shown in Table V (age 60)	24.2
Expected return for annuity for whole life of $1,800 per year	$43,560
Less expected return for 5-year temporary life annuity of $720 per year (as found in subparagraph (3) of this paragraph (a)) ...	$3,528
Net expected return	$40,032

If payments are to be made quarterly, semiannually, or annually, an appropriate adjustment of the multiple found in Table I or V (whichever is applicable) for the whole life annuity should be made in accordance with subparagraph (2) of this paragraph.

(b) Expected return under joint and survivor and joint annuities. (1) In the case of a joint and survivor annuity contract involving two annuitants which provides the first annuitant with a fixed monthly income for life and, after the death of the first annuitant, provides an identical monthly income for life to a second annuitant, the expected return shall be determined by multiplying the total amount of the payments to be received annually by the multiple obtained from Table II or VI (whichever is applicable) of § 1.72–9 under the ages (as of the annuity starting date) and, if applicable, sexes of the living annuitants. For example, a husband purchases a joint and survivor annuity contract providing for payments of $100 per month for life and, after his death, for the same amount to his wife for the remainder of her life. As of the annuity starting date his age at his nearest birthday is 70 and that of his wife at her nearest birthday is 67. If there is no post-June 1986 investment in the contract, the expected return is computed as follows:

Monthly payments of $100 × 12 months equals annual payment of	$1,200
Multiple shown in Table II (male, age 70, female, age 67).........................	19.7
Expected return ($1,200 × 19.7)...........	$23,640

If the annuitants purchased the same contract after June 30, 1986, the expected return would be $26,400, computed as follows:

Monthly payments of $100 × 12 equals annual payment of	$1,200
Multiple shown in Table VI (ages 70, 67)	22.0
Expected return ($1,200 × 22.0)	$26,400

If payments are to be made quarterly, semiannually, or annually, an appropriate adjustment of the multiple found in Table II or VI (whichever is applicable) should be made in accordance with paragraph (a)(2) of this section.

(2) If a contract of the type described in subparagraph (1) of this paragraph provides that a different (rather than an identical) monthly income is payable to the second annuitant, the expected return is computed in the following manner. The applicable multiple in Table II or VI (whichever is applicable) is first found as in the example in subparagraph (1) of this paragraph. The multiple applicable to the first annuitant is then found in Table I or V (whichever is applicable) as though the contract were for a single life annuity. The multiple from Table I or V is then subtracted from the multiple obtained from Table II or VI and the resulting multiple is applied to the total payments to be received annually under the contract by the second annuitant. The result is the expected return with respect to the second annuitant. The portion of the expected return with respect to payments to be made during the first annuitant's life is then computed by applying the multiple found in Table I or V to the total annual payments to be received by such annuitant under the contract. The expected returns with respect to each of the annuitants separately are then aggregated to obtain the expected return under the entire contract.

Example (1). A husband purchases a joint and survivor annuity providing for payments of $100 per month for his life and, after his death, payments to his wife of $50 per month for her life. As of the annuity starting date his age at his nearest birthday is 70 and that of his wife at her nearest birthday is 67. There is no post-June 1986 investment in the contract.

Multiple from Table II (male, age 70, female, age 67)	19.7
Multiple from Table I (male, age 70)	12.1
Difference (multiple applicable to second annuitant)	7.6
Portion of expected return, second annuitant ($600 × 7.6)	$4,560
Portion of expected return, first annuitant ($1,200 × 12.1)	$14,520
Expected return under the contract	$19,080

The expected return thus found, $19,080, is to be used in computing the amount to be excluded from gross income. Thus, if the investment in the contract in this example is $14,310, the exclusion ratio is $14,310 ÷ $19,080; or 75 percent. The amount excludable from each monthly payment made to the husband is 75 percent of $100, or $75, and the remaining $25 of each payment received by him shall be included in his gross income. After the husband's death, the amount excludable by the second annuitant (the surviving wife) would be 75 percent of each monthly payment of $50, or $37.50, and the remaining $12.50 of each payment shall be included in her gross income.

Example (2). If the same contract were purchased after June 30, 1986, the expected return would be $22,800, computed as follows:

Multiple from Table VI (ages 70, 67)	22.0
Multiple from Table V (age 70)	16.0
Difference (multiple applicable to second annuitant)	6.0
Portion of expected return, second annuitant ($600 × 6.0)	$3,600
Plus: Portion of expected return, first annuitant ($1,200 × 16.0)	$19,200
Expected return under the contract	$22,800

If the investment in the contract is $14,310, the exclusion ratio is $14,310 ÷ $22,800, or 62.8 percent. Thus, the husband would exclude $62.80 of each $100 payment received by him. After his death, his wife would exclude 62.8 percent, or $31.40 of each $50 monthly payment.

Example (3). If amounts were invested in the same contract both before July 1, 1986, and after June 30, 1986, and the election described in § 1.72–6(d)(6) were made, two exclusion ratios would be determined pursuant to § 1.72–6(d). Assume that the husband's total investment in the contract is $14,310 and that $7,310 is the pre-July 1986 investment in the contract. The pre-July 1986 exclusion ratio would be $7,310 ÷ $19.080, or 38.3 percent. The post-June 1986 exclusion ratio would be $7,000 ÷ $22,800, or 30.7 percent. The husband would exclude $69.00 ($38.30 + $30.70) of the $100 monthly payment received by him. The remaining $31.00 would be included in his gross income. After the husband's death, the amount excludable by his wife would be $34.50 (38.3 percent of $50 plus 30.7 percent of $50). The remaining $15.50 would be included in gross income.

The same method is used if the payments are to be increased after the death of the first annuitant. Thus, if the payments to be made until the husband's death were $50 per month and his widow were to receive $100 per month thereafter until her death, the 7.6 multiple in example (1) above would be applied to the $100 payments, yielding an expected return with respect to this portion of the annuity contract of $9,120 ($1,200 × 7.6). An expected return of $7,260 ($600 × 12.1) would be obtained with respect to the payments to be made to the husband, yielding a total expected return under the contract of $16,380 ($9,120 plus $7,260). If payments are to be made quarterly, semiannually, or annually, an appropriate adjustment of the multiples found in Tables I and II or Tables V and VI (whichever are applicable) should be made in accordance with paragraph (a)(2) of this section.

(3) In the case of a joint and survivor annuity contract in respect of which the first annuitant died in 1951, 1952, or 1953, and the basis of the surviving annuitant's interest in the contract was determinable under section 113(a)(5) of the Internal Revenue Code of 1938, such basis shall be considered the "aggregate of premiums or other consideration paid" by the surviving annuitant for the contract. (For rules governing this determination, see 26 CFR (1939) 39.22(b)(2)–2 and 39.-113(a)(5)–1 (Regulation 118).) In determining such an annuitant's investment in the contract, such aggregate shall be reduced by any amounts received under the contract by the surviving annuitant before the annuity starting date, to the extent such amounts were excludable from his gross income at the time of receipt. The expected return of the surviving annuitant in such cases shall be determined in the manner prescribed in paragraph (a) of this section, as though the surviving annuitant alone were involved. For this purpose, the appropriate multiple for the survivor shall be obtained from Table I as of the annuity starting date determined in accordance with paragraph (b)(2)(i) of § 1.72–4.

(4) If a contract involving two annuitants provides for fixed monthly payments to be made as a joint life annuity until the death of the first annuitant to die (in other words, only as long as both remain alive), the expected return under such contract shall be determined by multiplying the total of the annuity payments to be received annually under the contract by the multiple obtained from Table IIA or VIA (whichever is applicable) of § 1.72–9 under the ages (as of the annuity starting date) and, if applicable, sexes of the annuitants. If, however, payments are to be made under the contract quarterly, semiannually, or annually, an appropriate adjustment of the multiple found in Table IIA or VIA shall be made in accordance with paragraph (a)(2) of this section.

(5) If a joint and survivor annuity contract involving two annuitants provides that a specified amount shall be paid during their joint lives and a different specified amount shall be paid to the survivor upon the death of whichever of the annuitants is the first to die, the following preliminary computation shall be made in all cases preparatory to determining the expected return under the contract:

(i) From Table II or VI (whichever is applicable), obtain the multiple under both of the annuitants' ages (as of the annuity starting date) and, if applicable, their appropriate sexes;

(ii) From Table IIA or VIA (whichever is applicable), obtain the multiple applicable to both annuitants' ages (as of the annuity starting date) and, if applicable, their appropriate sexes;

(iii) Apply the multiple found in subdivision (i) of this subparagraph to the total of the amounts to be received annually after the death of the first to die; and

(iv) Apply the multiple found in subdivision (ii) of this subparagraph to the difference between the total of the amounts to be received annually before and the total of the amounts to be received annually after the death of the first to die.

If the original annual payment is in excess of the annual payment to be made after the death of the first to die, the expected return is the sum of the amounts determined under subdivisions (iii) and (iv) of this subparagraph. This may be illustrated by the following examples:

Example (1). A husband purchases a joint and survivor annuity providing for payments of $100 a month for as long as both he and his wife live, and, after the death of the first to die, payments to the survivor of $75 a month for life. As of the annuity starting date, his age at his nearest birthday is 70 and that of his wife at her nearest birthday is 67. If there is no post–June 1986 investment in the contract, the expected return under the contract is computed as follows:

Multiple from Table II (male age 70, female age 67)	19.7
Multiple from Table IIA (male age 70, female age 67)	9.3
Portion of expected return ($900 × 19.7—sum per year after first death)	$17,730
Portion of expected return ($300 × 9.3—amount of change in sum at first death) ..	$2,790
Expected return under the contract ..	$20,520

The total expected return in this example, $20,520, is to be used in computing the amount to be excluded from gross income.

Thus, if the investment in the contract is $17,887, the exclusion ratio is $17,887–$20,520, or 87.2 percent. The amount excludable from each monthly payment made while both are alive is 87.2 percent of $100 or $87.20, and the remaining $12.80 of each payment shall be included in gross income. After the death of the first to die, the amount excludable by the survivor shall be 87.2 percent of each monthly payment of $75, or $65.40, and the remaining $960 of each payment shall be included in gross income.

Example (2). Assume the same facts as in example (1), except that the contract is purchased after June 30, 1986.

The expected return under the contract is computed as follows:

Multiple from Table VI (ages 70, 67)	22.0
Multiple from Table VIA (ages 70, 67)	12.4
Portion of expected return ($900 × 22.0—sum per year after first death)	$19,800
Plus: Portion of expected return ($300 × 12.4—amount of change in sum at first death)	$3,720
Expected return under the contract . .	$23,520

Thus, if the investment in the contract is $17,887, the exclusion ratio is $17,887 ÷ $23,520, or 76.1 percent. The amount excludable from each monthly payment made while both are alive would be 76.1 percent of $100, or $76.10, and the remaining $23.90 of each payment would be included in gross income. After the death of the first to die, the amount excludable by the survivor would be 76.1 percent of each monthly payment of $75, or $57.08, and the remaining $17.92 of each payment would be included in gross income.

Example (3). Assume the same facts as in examples (1) and (2), except that the total investment in the contract is $17,887, and that the pre–July 1986 investment in the contract is $8,000. Assume also that one of the annuitants makes the election described in § 1.72–6(d)(6). Separate computations shall be performed pursuant to § 1.72–6(d) to determine the amount excludable from gross income. The pre–July 1986 exclusion ratio would be $8,000 ÷ $23,520, or 34 percent. The post–June 1986 exclusion ratio would be $9,887 ÷ $23,520, or 42 percent. The amount excludable from each monthly payment made while both are alive would be $76 ((.34 × 100) + (.42 × 100)), and the remaining $24 of each $100 payment would be included in gross income. After the death of the first to die, the amount excludable by the survivor would be $57.00 of each monthly payment of $75((.34 × 75) + (.42 × 75)), and the remaining $18.00 of each payment would be included in gross income.

If the original annual payment is less than the annual payment to be made after the death of the first to die, the expected return is the difference between the amounts determined under subdivisions (iii) and (iv) of this subparagraph. If, however, payments are to be made quarterly, semiannually, or annually under the contract, the multiples obtained from both Tables II and IIA or Tables VI and VIA (whichever are applicable) shall first

be adjusted in a manner prescribed in paragraph (a)(2) of this section.

(6) If a contract provides for the payment of life annuities to two persons during their respective lives and, after the death of one (without regard to which one dies first), provides that the survivor shall receive for life both his own annuity payments and the payments made formerly to the deceased person, the expected return shall be determined in accordance with paragraph (e)(4) of this section.

(7) If paragraph (b)(3) of § 1.72–2 applies to payments provided under a contract and this paragraph applies to such payments, the principles of this paragraph shall be used in making the computations described in paragraph (d)(3) of § 1.72–4. This may be illustrated by the following examples, examples (1) through (3) of which assume that there is no post–June 1986 investment in the contract:

Example (1). Taxpayer A, a male age 63, pays $24,000 for a contract which provides that the proceeds (both income and return of capital) from eight units of an investment fund shall be paid monthly to him for his life and that after his death the proceeds from six such units shall be paid monthly to B, a female age 55, for her life. The portion of the investment in the contract allocable to each taxable year of A is $955.20 and that allocable to each taxable year of B is $715.40. This is determined in the following manner:

Multiple from Table II (male, age 63, and female, age 55)	26.1
Number of units to be paid, in effect, as a joint and survivor annuity	×6
Number of total annual unit payments anticipatable with respect to the joint and survivor annuity element	168.6
Multiple from Table I (male, age 63)	16.2
Number of units to be paid, in effect, as a single life annuity	×2
Number of total annual unit payments anticipatable with respect to A alone	32.4
Total number of unit payments anticipatable	201
Portion of investment in the contract allocable to unit payments ($24,000 ÷ 201) on an annual basis	$119.40
Number of units to A while he continues to live	×8
Portion of the investment in the contract allocable to each taxable year of A	$955.20
Portion of investment in the contract allocable to unit payments ($24.000 ÷ 201) on an annual basis	$119.40
Number of units payable to B for her life after A's death	×6
Portion of the investment in the contract allocable to each taxable year of B	$716.40

For the purpose of the above computation it is immaterial whether or not A lives to or beyond the life expectancy shown for him in Table I.

Example (2). Assume that Taxpayer A in example (1) receives payments for five years which are at least as large as the portion of the investment in the contract allocable to such years, but in the sixth year he receives a total of only $626.40 rather than the $955.20 allocable to such year. A is 69 and B is 61 at the beginning of the first monthly period for which an amount is payable in the seventh taxable year. A makes the election in that year provided under paragraph (d)(3) of § 1.72–4. The difference between the portion of the investment in the contract allocable to the sixth year and the amount actually received in that year is $328.80 ($955.20 less $626.40). In this case, 139.2 unit payments are anticipatable (on an annual basis), since the appropriate multiple from Table II of § 1.72–9, 23.2, multiplied by the number of units payable, in effect, as a joint and survivor annuity yields this result (6×23.2). A's appropriate multiple from Table I of § 1.72–9 for the two units which will cease to be paid at his death is 12.6, and the total number of unit payments anticipatable (on an annual basis) is, therefore, 164.4 (2×12.6 plus 139.2). Dividing the difference previously found ($328.80) by the total number of unit payments thus determined (164.4) indicates that A will have an additional allocation of the investment in the contract of $16 to the seventh and every succeeding full taxable year (8 units×$2), and B will have an additional allocation of the investment in the contract of $12 (6 units×$2) to each taxable year in which she receives 12 monthly payments subsequent to the death of A. The total allocable to each taxable year of A is, therefore, $971.20, and that allocable to each taxable year of B will be $728.40.

Example (3). If, in example (2), A had died at the end of the fifth year, in the sixth year B would have received a payment of $469.80 (that portion of the $626.40 that A would have received which is in the same ratio that 6 units bear to 8 units) and would thus have received $246.60 less than the portion of the investment in the contract originally determined to be allocable to each of her taxable years. In these circumstances, B would be entitled to elect to redetermine the portion of the investment in the contract allocable to the taxable year of election and all subsequent years. The new amount allocable thereto would be found by dividing the $246.60 difference by her life expectancy as of the first day of the first period for which she received an amount as an annuity in the seventh year of the annuity contract, and adding the result to her originally determined allocation of $716.40.

Example (4). On July 1, 1986, Taxpayer C, age 60, pays $28,000 for a contract which provides that the proceeds (both income and return of capital) from 10 units of an investment fund shall be paid monthly to C for C's life and that after C's death the proceeds from 4 such units shall be paid monthly to D, age 57, for D's life. The portion of the investment in the contract allocable to each taxable year of C is $1,037.00 and that allocable to each taxable year of D is $414.80. This is determined as follows:

Multiple from Table VI (ages 60, 57)	31.2
Number of units to be paid, in effect, as a joint and survivor annuity	×4
Number of total annual unit payments anticipatable with respect to the joint and survivor annuity element	124.8
Multiple from Table V (age 60)	24.2
Number of units to be paid, in effect, as a single life annuity	×6
Number of total annual unit payments anticipatable with respect to C alone	145.2
Total number of unit payments anticipatable	270
Portion of investment in the contracts allocable to unit payments ($28,000÷270) on an annual basis	103.70
Number of units payable to C while C continues to live	×10
Portion of the investment in the contract allocable to each taxable year of C	$1,037.00
Portion of investment in the contract allocable to unit payments ($28,000÷270) on an annual basis	$103.70
Number of units payable to D for D's life after C's death	×4
Portion of the investment in the contract allocable to each taxable year of D	$414.80

For purposes of the above computation it is immaterial whether or not C lives to or beyond the life expectancy shown in Table V.

* * *

Par. 6. Section 1.72–9 is amended by revising the introductory text preceding the tables and the concluding text following the tables and adding new Tables V, VI, VIA, VII, and VIII to read as follows:

§ 1.72–9 Tables.

The following tables are to be used in connection with computations under section 72 and the regulations thereunder. Tables I, II, IIA, III, and IV are to be used if the investment in the contract does not include a post-June 1986 investment in the contract (as defined in § 1.72–6(d)(3)). Tables V, VI, VIA, VII, and VIII are to be used if the investment in the contract includes a post-June 1986 investment in the contract (as defined in § 1.72–6(d)(3)). See § 1.72–6(d)(3) for rules treating the entire investment in a contract as post-June 1986 investment in a contract if the annuity starting date of the contract is after June 30, 1986, and the contract provides for a disqualifying form of payment of settlement, such as an option to receive a lump sum in full discharge of the obligation under the contract. In addition, see § 1.72–6(d) for special rules concerning the tables to be used and

APPENDIX

the separate computations required if the investment in the contract includes both a pre-July 1986 investment in the contract and a post-June 1986 investment in the contract and the election described in § 1.72–6(d)(6) is made with respect to the contract.

* * *

APPENDIX

TABLE V—ORDINARY LIFE ANNUITIES
ONE LIFE—EXPECTED RETURN MULTIPLES

AGE	MULTIPLE	AGE	MULTIPLE	AGE	MULTIPLE
5	76.6	42	40.6	79	10.0
6	75.6	43	39.6	80	9.5
7	74.7	44	38.7	81	8.9
8	73.7	45	37.7	82	8.4
9	72.7	46	36.8	83	7.9
10	71.7	47	35.9	84	7.4
11	70.7	48	34.9	85	6.9
12	69.7	49	34.0	86	6.5
13	68.8	50	33.1	87	6.1
14	67.8	51	32.2	88	5.7
15	66.8	52	31.3	89	5.3
16	65.8	53	30.4	90	5.0
17	64.8	54	29.5	91	4.7
18	63.9	55	28.6	92	4.4
19	62.9	56	27.7	93	4.1
20	61.9	57	26.8	94	3.9
21	60.9	58	25.9	95	3.7
22	59.9	59	25.0	96	3.4
23	59.0	60	24.2	97	3.2
24	58.0	61	23.3	98	3.0
25	57.0	62	22.5	99	2.8
26	56.0	63	21.6	100	2.7
27	55.1	64	20.8	101	2.5
28	54.1	65	20.0	102	2.3
29	53.1	66	19.2	103	2.1
30	52.2	67	18.4	104	1.9
31	51.2	68	17.6	105	1.8
32	50.2	69	16.8	106	1.6
33	49.3	70	16.0	107	1.4
34	48.3	71	15.3	108	1.3
35	47.3	72	14.6	109	1.1
36	46.4	73	13.9	110	1.0
37	45.4	74	13.2	111	.9
38	44.4	75	12.5	112	.8
39	43.5	76	11.9	113	.7
40	42.5	77	11.2	114	.6
41	41.5	78	10.6	115	.5

* * *

TABLE VI—ORDINARY JOINT LIFE AND LAST SURVIVOR ANNUITIES
TWO LIVES—EXPECTED RETURN MULTIPLES

AGES	45	46	47	48	49	50	51	52	53	54
45	44.0	43.6	43.1	42.6	42.3	41.9	41.6	41.3	41.0	40.7
46	43.6	43.1	42.7	42.1	41.7	41.4	41.0	40.7	40.3	40.0
47	43.1	42.7	42.2	41.6	41.2	40.8	40.4	40.1	39.7	39.4
48	42.6	42.1	41.6	41.1	40.6	40.2	39.8	39.4	39.0	38.7
49	42.3	41.7	41.2	40.6	40.1	39.7	39.3	38.8	38.5	38.1
50	41.9	41.4	40.8	40.2	39.7	39.2	38.8	38.3	37.9	37.5
51	41.6	41.0	40.4	39.8	39.3	38.8	38.3	37.8	37.4	37.0
52	41.3	40.7	40.1	39.4	38.8	38.3	37.8	37.3	36.9	36.4
53	41.0	40.3	39.7	39.0	38.5	37.9	37.4	36.9	36.4	35.9
54	40.7	40.0	39.4	38.7	38.1	37.5	37.0	36.4	35.9	35.4
55	40.4	39.7	39.1	38.4	37.7	37.1	36.6	36.0	35.5	34.9
56	40.2	39.5	38.8	38.0	37.4	36.8	36.2	35.6	35.0	34.5
57	39.9	39.2	38.5	37.7	37.1	36.4	35.8	35.2	34.6	34.1
58	39.7	39.0	38.3	37.5	36.8	36.1	35.5	34.8	34.2	33.7
59	39.5	38.7	38.0	37.2	36.5	35.8	35.1	34.5	33.9	33.3
60	39.4	38.6	37.9	37.0	36.3	35.6	34.9	34.3	33.6	33.0
61	39.2	38.4	37.6	36.8	36.1	35.3	34.6	34.0	33.3	32.6
62	39.1	38.3	37.5	36.7	35.9	35.2	34.5	33.8	33.1	32.4
63	38.9	38.1	37.3	36.4	35.7	34.9	34.2	33.5	32.8	32.1
64	38.8	38.0	37.2	36.3	35.5	34.8	34.0	33.3	32.6	31.8
65	38.7	37.9	37.1	36.2	35.4	34.6	33.9	33.1	32.4	31.6
66	38.6	37.8	37.0	36.1	35.3	34.5	33.7	32.9	32.2	31.4
67	38.5	37.7	36.9	36.0	35.1	34.3	33.5	32.8	32.0	31.2
68	38.4	37.6	36.8	35.8	35.0	34.2	33.4	32.6	31.8	31.0
69	38.3	37.5	36.6	35.7	34.9	34.1	33.2	32.4	31.6	30.9
70	38.2	37.4	36.5	35.6	34.7	33.9	33.1	32.3	31.5	30.7
71	38.2	37.3	36.5	35.5	34.7	33.9	33.0	32.2	31.4	30.6
72	38.2	37.3	36.4	35.5	34.6	33.8	33.0	32.1	31.3	30.5
73	38.1	37.2	36.4	35.4	34.6	33.7	32.9	32.0	31.2	30.4
74	38.1	37.2	36.3	35.4	34.5	33.6	32.8	31.9	31.1	30.3
75	38.0	37.1	36.2	35.3	34.4	33.5	32.7	31.8	31.0	30.1

* * *

1550

APPENDIX

AGES	55	56	57	58	59	60	61	62	63	64
55	34.5	34.0	33.5	33.1	32.7	32.4	32.0	31.7	31.4	31.1
56	34.0	33.5	33.0	32.5	32.1	31.8	31.4	31.1	30.7	30.5
57	33.5	33.0	32.5	32.0	31.5	31.2	30.8	30.5	30.1	29.8
58	33.1	32.5	32.0	31.5	31.0	30.6	30.2	29.9	29.5	29.2
59	32.7	32.1	31.5	31.0	30.5	30.1	29.6	29.3	28.9	28.5
60	32.4	31.8	31.2	30.6	30.1	29.7	29.2	28.8	28.4	28.0
61	32.0	31.4	30.8	30.2	29.6	29.2	28.7	28.3	27.8	27.4
62	31.7	31.1	30.5	29.9	29.3	28.8	28.3	27.9	27.3	27.0
63	31.4	30.7	30.1	29.5	28.9	28.4	27.8	27.3	26.8	26.4
64	31.1	30.5	29.8	29.2	28.5	28.0	27.4	27.0	26.4	26.0
65	30.9	30.2	29.5	28.9	28.2	27.7	27.1	26.6	26.0	25.5
66	30.7	30.0	29.3	28.6	27.9	27.4	26.7	26.2	25.6	25.1
67	30.5	29.8	29.0	28.3	27.6	27.1	26.4	25.9	25.3	24.7
68	30.3	29.5	28.8	28.1	27.4	26.8	26.1	25.5	24.9	24.4
69	30.1	29.3	28.6	27.8	27.1	26.5	25.8	25.2	24.5	24.0
70	29.9	29.1	28.3	27.6	26.8	26.2	25.5	24.9	24.2	23.6
71	29.8	29.0	28.2	27.4	26.7	26.0	25.3	24.7	24.0	23.4
72	29.7	28.9	28.1	27.3	26.5	25.9	25.1	24.5	23.8	23.1
73	29.5	28.7	27.9	27.1	26.4	25.7	24.9	24.3	23.5	22.9
74	29.4	28.6	27.8	27.0	26.2	25.5	24.7	24.1	23.3	22.7
75	29.3	28.5	27.6	26.8	26.0	25.3	24.5	23.9	23.1	22.4
76	29.3	28.4	27.6	26.8	26.0	25.2	24.4	23.8	23.0	22.3
77	29.1	28.3	27.4	26.6	25.8	25.1	24.2	23.5	22.8	22.1
78	29.1	28.2	27.4	26.5	25.7	25.0	24.1	23.4	22.6	21.9
79	29.0	28.1	27.3	26.4	25.6	24.9	24.0	23.3	22.5	21.8
80	29.0	28.2	27.3	26.4	25.6	24.8	24.0	23.3	22.4	21.7
81	28.9	28.1	27.2	26.3	25.5	24.7	23.9	23.1	22.3	21.6
82	28.9	28.0	27.2	26.3	25.4	24.7	23.8	23.1	22.2	21.5
83	28.9	28.0	27.1	26.3	25.4	24.6	23.8	23.0	22.2	21.4
84	28.8	28.0	27.1	26.2	25.3	24.6	23.7	22.9	22.1	21.3
85	28.8	27.9	27.0	26.1	25.3	24.5	23.6	22.9	22.0	21.2

* * *

AGES	65	66	67	68	69	70	71	72	73	74
65	25.1	24.7	24.3	23.9	23.5	23.1	22.8	22.6	22.3	22.0
66	24.7	24.2	23.8	23.4	22.9	22.6	22.3	22.0	21.7	21.4
67	24.3	23.8	23.3	22.9	22.4	22.0	21.7	21.4	21.1	20.8
68	23.9	23.4	22.9	22.4	21.9	21.5	21.2	20.8	20.5	20.2
69	23.5	22.9	22.4	21.9	21.5	21.0	20.7	20.3	20.0	19.6
70	23.1	22.6	22.0	21.5	21.0	20.5	20.1	19.8	19.4	19.1
71	22.8	22.3	21.7	21.2	20.7	20.1	19.7	19.4	19.0	18.6
72	22.6	22.0	21.4	20.8	20.3	19.8	19.4	19.0	18.6	18.2
73	22.3	21.7	21.1	20.5	20.0	19.4	19.0	18.6	18.1	17.7
74	22.0	21.4	20.8	20.2	19.6	19.1	18.6	18.2	17.7	17.3
75	21.8	21.2	20.5	19.9	19.3	18.7	18.3	17.8	17.3	16.9
76	21.6	21.0	20.4	19.7	19.1	18.5	18.0	17.5	17.0	16.6
77	21.4	20.7	20.1	19.4	18.8	18.2	17.7	17.2	16.7	16.2
78	21.2	20.6	19.9	19.2	18.6	17.9	17.4	16.9	16.4	15.9
79	21.1	20.4	19.7	19.0	18.4	17.7	17.2	16.6	16.1	15.6
80	21.0	20.3	19.6	18.9	18.3	17.6	17.0	16.5	15.9	15.4
81	20.9	20.1	19.4	18.7	18.0	17.4	16.8	16.2	15.7	15.1
82	20.8	20.1	19.3	18.6	17.9	17.2	16.6	16.1	15.5	14.9
83	20.7	20.0	19.2	18.5	17.8	17.1	16.5	15.9	15.3	14.7
84	20.6	19.9	19.1	18.4	17.7	17.0	16.3	15.7	15.1	14.6
85	20.5	19.7	19.0	18.3	17.5	16.8	16.2	15.6	15.0	14.4
86	20.5	19.7	19.0	18.2	17.5	16.7	16.1	15.5	14.9	14.3
87	20.4	19.7	18.9	18.1	17.4	16.7	16.0	15.4	14.8	14.1
88	20.4	19.6	18.8	18.1	17.3	16.6	15.9	15.3	14.6	14.0
89	20.3	19.5	18.7	18.0	17.2	16.5	15.8	15.2	14.5	13.9
90	20.3	19.5	18.7	18.0	17.2	16.4	15.8	15.1	14.5	13.8

* * *

APPENDIX

TABLE VIA—ANNUITIES FOR JOINT LIFE ONLY
TWO LIVES—EXPECTED RETURN MULTIPLES

AGES	55	56	57	58	59	60	61	62	63	64
55	22.7	22.3	21.9	21.4	20.9	20.4	19.9	19.4	18.8	18.3
56	22.3	21.9	21.5	21.1	20.6	20.1	19.6	19.1	18.6	18.0
57	21.9	21.5	21.1	20.7	20.3	19.8	19.3	18.8	18.3	17.8
58	21.4	21.1	20.7	20.3	19.9	19.5	19.0	18.5	18.0	17.5
59	20.9	20.6	20.3	19.9	19.5	19.1	18.7	18.2	17.7	17.3
60	20.4	20.1	19.8	19.5	19.1	18.7	18.3	17.9	17.4	17.0
61	19.9	19.6	19.3	19.0	18.7	18.3	17.9	17.5	17.1	16.7
62	19.4	19.1	18.8	18.5	18.2	17.9	17.5	17.1	16.8	16.3
63	18.8	18.6	18.3	18.0	17.7	17.4	17.1	16.8	16.4	16.0
64	18.3	18.0	17.8	17.5	17.3	17.0	16.7	16.3	16.0	15.6
65	17.7	17.5	17.3	17.0	16.8	16.5	16.2	15.9	15.6	15.3
66	17.1	16.9	16.7	16.5	16.3	16.0	15.8	15.5	15.2	14.9
67	16.5	16.3	16.2	16.0	15.8	15.5	15.3	15.0	14.7	14.5
68	15.9	15.8	15.6	15.4	15.2	15.0	14.8	14.6	14.3	14.0
69	15.3	15.2	15.0	14.9	14.7	14.5	14.3	14.1	13.9	13.6
70	14.7	14.6	14.5	14.3	14.2	14.0	13.8	13.6	13.4	13.2
71	14.1	14.0	13.9	13.8	13.6	13.5	13.3	13.1	12.9	12.7
72	13.5	13.4	13.3	13.2	13.1	12.9	12.8	12.6	12.4	12.3
73	13.0	12.9	12.8	12.7	12.5	12.4	12.3	12.1	12.0	11.8
74	12.4	12.3	12.2	12.1	12.0	11.9	11.8	11.6	11.5	11.3
75	11.8	11.7	11.7	11.6	11.5	11.4	11.3	11.1	11.0	10.9
76	11.2	11.2	11.1	11.0	10.9	10.9	10.8	10.6	10.5	10.4
77	10.7	10.6	10.6	10.5	10.4	10.3	10.3	10.2	10.0	9.9
78	10.1	10.1	10.0	10.0	9.9	9.8	9.8	9.7	9.6	9.5
79	9.6	9.6	9.5	9.5	9.4	9.3	9.3	9.2	9.1	9.0
80	9.1	9.0	9.0	9.0	8.9	8.9	8.8	8.7	8.7	8.6
81	8.6	8.5	8.5	8.5	8.4	8.4	8.3	8.3	8.2	8.1
82	8.1	8.1	8.0	8.0	8.0	7.9	7.9	7.8	7.8	7.7
83	7.6	7.6	7.6	7.5	7.5	7.5	7.4	7.4	7.3	7.3
84	7.2	7.1	7.1	7.1	7.1	7.0	7.0	7.0	6.9	6.9
85	6.7	6.7	6.7	6.7	6.6	6.6	6.6	6.5	6.5	6.5

* * *

TABLE VIA—ANNUITIES FOR JOINT LIFE ONLY
TWO LIVES—EXPECTED RETURN MULTIPLES

AGES	65	66	67	68	69	70	71	72	73	74
65	14.9	14.5	14.1	13.7	13.3	12.9	12.5	12.0	11.6	11.2
66	14.5	14.2	13.8	13.4	13.1	12.6	12.2	11.8	11.4	11.0
67	14.1	13.8	13.5	13.1	12.8	12.4	12.0	11.6	11.2	10.8
68	13.7	13.4	13.1	12.8	12.5	12.1	11.7	11.4	11.0	10.6
69	13.3	13.1	12.8	12.5	12.1	11.8	11.4	11.1	10.7	10.4
70	12.9	12.6	12.4	12.1	11.8	11.5	11.2	10.8	10.5	10.1
71	12.5	12.2	12.0	11.7	11.4	11.2	10.9	10.5	10.2	9.9
72	12.0	11.8	11.6	11.4	11.1	10.8	10.5	10.2	9.9	9.6
73	11.6	11.4	11.2	11.0	10.7	10.5	10.2	9.9	9.7	9.4
74	11.2	11.0	10.8	10.6	10.4	10.1	9.9	9.6	9.4	9.1
75	10.7	10.5	10.4	10.2	10.0	9.8	9.5	9.3	9.1	8.8
76	10.3	10.1	9.9	9.8	9.6	9.4	9.2	9.0	8.8	8.5
77	9.8	9.7	9.5	9.4	9.2	9.0	8.8	8.6	8.4	8.2
78	9.4	9.2	9.1	9.0	8.8	8.7	8.5	8.3	8.1	7.9
79	8.9	8.8	8.7	8.6	8.4	8.3	8.1	8.0	7.8	7.6
80	8.5	8.4	8.3	8.2	8.0	7.9	7.8	7.6	7.5	7.3
81	8.0	8.0	7.9	7.8	7.7	7.5	7.4	7.3	7.1	7.0
82	7.6	7.5	7.5	7.4	7.3	7.2	7.1	6.9	6.8	6.7
83	7.2	7.1	7.1	7.0	6.9	6.8	6.7	6.6	6.5	6.4
84	6.8	6.7	6.7	6.6	6.5	6.4	6.4	6.3	6.2	6.0
85	6.4	6.4	6.3	6.2	6.2	6.1	6.0	5.9	5.8	5.7
86	6.0	6.0	5.9	5.9	5.8	5.8	5.7	5.6	5.5	5.4
87	5.7	5.6	5.6	5.6	5.5	5.4	5.4	5.3	5.2	5.2
88	5.3	5.3	5.3	5.2	5.2	5.1	5.1	5.0	5.0	4.9
89	5.0	5.0	5.0	4.9	4.9	4.8	4.8	4.7	4.7	4.6
90	4.7	4.7	4.7	4.6	4.6	4.6	4.5	4.5	4.4	4.4

* * *

[Published in 51 FR 9978, March 24, 1986]

Tax Reform Act of 1986, Public Law 99–514, October 22nd, 1986

Sec. 631. Recognition of Gain and Loss on Distributions of Property in Liquidation

(a) General rule. Subpart B of part II of subchapter C (relating to effects on corporation) is amended by striking out sections 336 and 337 and inserting in lieu thereof the following:

"Sec. 336. Gain or Loss Recognized on Property Distributed in Complete Liquidation

"(a) General rule.—Except as otherwise provided in this section or section 337, gain or loss shall be recognized to a liquidating corporation on the distribution of property in complete liquidation as if such property were sold to the distributee at its fair market value.

"(b) Treatment of liabilities in excess of basis.—If any property distributed in the liquidation is subject to a liability or the shareholder assumes a liability of the liquidating corporation in connection with the distribution, for purposes of subsection (a) and section 337, the fair market value of such property shall be treated as not less than the amount of such liability.

"(c) Exception for certain liquidations to which part III applies.—This section shall not apply with respect to any distribution of property to the extent there is nonrecognition of gain or loss with respect to such property to the recipient under part III.

"(d) Limitations on recognition of loss.—

"(1) No loss recognized in certain distributions to related persons.—

"(A) In general.—No loss shall be recognized to a liquidating corporation on the distribution of any property to a related person (within the meaning of section 267) if—

"(i) such distribution is not pro rate, or

"(ii) such property is disqualified property.

"(B) Disqualified property.—For purposes of subparagraph (A), the term 'disqualified property' means any property which is acquired by the liquidating corporation in a transaction to which section 351 applied, or as a contribution to capital, during the 5-year period ending on the date of the distribution. Such term includes any property if the adjusted basis of such property is determined (in whole or in part) by reference to the adjusted basis of property described in the preceding sentence.

"(2) Special rule for certain property acquired in certain carryover basis transactions.—

"(A) In general.—For purposes of determining the amount of loss recognized by any liquidating corporation on any sale, exchange, or distribution of property described in subparagraph (B), the adjusted basis of such property shall be reduced (but not below zero) by the excess (if any) of—

"(i) the adjusted basis of such property immediately after its acquisition by such corporation, over

"(ii) the fair market value of such property as of such time.

"(B) Description of property.—

"(i) In general.—For purposes of subparagraph (A), property is described in this subparagraph if—

"(I) such property is acquired by the liquidating corporation in a transaction to which section 351 applied or as a contribution to capital, and

"(II) the acquisition of such property by the liquidating corporation was part of a plan a principal purpose of which was to recognize loss by the liquidating corporation with respect to such property in connection with the liquidation.

Other property shall be treated as so described if the adjusted basis of such other property is determined (in whole or in part) by reference to the adjusted basis of property described in the preceding sentence.

"(ii) Certain acquisitions treated as part of plan.—For purposes of clause (i), any property described in clause (i)(I) acquired by the liquidating corporation during the 2-year period ending on the date of the adoption of the plan of complete liquidation shall, except as provided in regulations, be treated as part of a plan described in clause (i)(II).

"(C) Recapture in lieu of disallowance.—The Secretary may prescribe regulations under which, in lieu of disallowing a loss under subparagraph (A) for a prior taxable year, the gross income of the liquidating corporation for the taxable year in which the plan of complete liquidation is adopted shall be increased by the amount of the disallowed loss.

"(3) **Special rule in case of liquidation to which section 332 applies.**—In the case of any liquidation to which section 332 applies, no loss shall be recognized to the liquidating corporation on any distribution in such liquidation.

"(e) Certain stock sales and distributions may be treated as asset transfers.—**Under regulations prescribed by the Secretary, if—**

"(1) a corporation owns stock in another corporation meeting the requirements of section 1504(a)(2), and

"(2) such corporation sells, exchanges, or distributes all of such stock,

such corporation may elect to treat such sale, exchange, or distribution as a disposition of all of the assets of such other corporation, and no gain or loss shall be recognized on the sale, exchange, or distribution of such stock.

"Sec. 337. Nonrecognition For Property Distributed to Parent in Complete Liquidation of Subsidiary

"(a) **In general.**—No gain or loss shall be recognized to the liquidating corporation on the distribution to the 80-percent distributee of any property in a complete liquidation to which section 332 applies.

"(b) **Treatment of indebtedness of subsidiary, etc.—**

"(1) **Indebtedness of subsidiary to parent.**—If—

"(A) a corporation is liquidated in a liquidation to which section 332 applies, and

"(B) on the date of the adoption of the plan of liquidation, such corporation was indebted to the 80-percent distributee,

for purposes of this section and section 336, any transfer of property to the 80-percent distributee in satisfaction of such indebtedness shall be treated as a distribution to such distributee in such liquidation.

"(2) **Treatment of tax-exempt distributee.—**

"(A) **In general.**—Except as provided in subparagraph (B), paragraph (1) and subsection (a) shall not apply where the 80-percent distributee is an organization (other than a cooperative described in section 521) which is exempt from the tax imposed by this chapter.

"(B) **Exception where property will be used in unrelated business.—**

"(i) **In general.**—Subparagraph (A) shall not apply to any distribution of property to an organization described in section 511(a)(2) or 511(b)(2) if, immediately after such distribution, such organization uses such property in an unrelated trade or business (as defined in section 513).

"(ii) **Later disposition or change in use.**—If any property to which clause (i) applied is disposed of by the organization acquiring such property, notwithstanding any other provision of law, any gain (not in excess of the amount not recognized by reason of clause (i) shall be included in such organization's unrelated business taxable income. For purposes of the preceding sentence, if such property ceases to be used in an unrelated trade or business of such organization, such organization shall be treated as having disposed of such property on the date of such cessation.

"(c) **80-percent distributee.**—For purposes of this section, the term '80-percent distributee' means only the corporation which meets the 80-percent stock ownership requirements specified in section 332(b).

"(d) **Regulations.**—The Secretary shall prescribe such regulations as may be necessary or appropriate to carry out the purposes of the amendments made to this subpart by the Tax Reform Act of 1986, including—

"(1) regulations to ensure that such purposes may not be circumvented through the use of any provision of law or regulations (including the consolidated return regulations and part III of this subchapter), and

"(2) regulations providing for appropriate coordination of the provisions of this section with the provisions of this title relating to taxation of foreign corporations and their shareholders."

* * *

(c) **Treatment of distributions of appreciated property.**—Section 311 is amended to read as follows:

"Sec. 311. Taxability of Corporation on Distribution

"(a) **General rule.**—Except as provided in subsection (b), no gain or loss shall be recognized to a corporation on the distribution, with respect to its stock, of—

"(1) its stock (or rights to acquire its stock), or

"(2) property.

"(b) Distributions of appreciated property.—

"(1) In general.—If—

"(A) a corporation distributes property (other than an obligation of such corporation) to a shareholder in a distribution to which subpart A applies, and

"(B) the fair market value of such property exceeds its adjusted basis (in the hands of the distributing corporation),

then gain shall be recognized to the distributing corporation as if such property were sold to the distributee at its fair market value.

"(2) Treatment of liabilities in excess of basis.—Rules similar to the rules of section 336(b) shall apply for purposes of this subsection."

* * *

(e) Technical and conforming amendments.—

* * *

(2) Subsection (c) of section 332 is hereby repealed.

(3) Section 333 is hereby repealed.

(4)(A) Subsection (a) of section 334 is amended by striking out "(other than a distribution to which section 333 applies)".

(B) Subsection (c) of section 334 is hereby repealed.

* * *

Sec. 633. Effective Dates

(a) General rule. Except as otherwise provided in this section, the amendments made by this subtitle shall apply to—

(1) any distribution in complete liquidation, and any sale or exchange, made by a corporation after July 31, 1986, unless such corporation is completely liquidated before January 1, 1987,

(2) any transaction described in section 338 of the Internal Revenue Code of 1986 for which the acquisition date occurs after December 31, 1986, and

(3) any distribution (not in complete liquidation) made after December 31, 1986.

* * *

(c) Exception for certain plans of liquidation and binding contracts.—

(1) In general.—The amendments made by this subtitle shall not apply to—

(A) any distribution or sale or exchange made pursuant to a plan of liquidation adopted before August 1, 1986, if the liquidating corporation is completely liquidated before January 1, 1988,

(B) any distribution or sale or exchange made by any corporation if 50 percent or more of the voting stock by value of such corporation is acquired on or after August 1, 1986, pursuant to a written binding contract in effect before such date and if such corporation is completely liquidated before January 1, 1988,

(C) any distribution or sale or exchange made by any corporation if substantially all of the assets of such corporation are sold on or after August 1, 1986, pursuant to 1 or more written binding contracts in effect before such date and if such corporation is completely liquidated before January 1, 1988, or

(D) any transaction described in section 338 of the Internal Revenue Code of 1986 with respect to any target corporation if a qualified stock purchase of such target corporation is made on or after August 1, 1986, pursuant to a written binding contract in effect before such date and the acquisition date (within the meaning of such section 338) is before January 1, 1988.

* * *

(d) Transitional rule for certain small corporations.—

(1) In general.—In the case of the complete liquidation before January 1, 1989, of a qualified corporation, the amendments made by this section shall not apply to the applicable percentage of each gain or loss which (but for this paragraph) would be recognized by reason of the amendments made by this subtitle.

(2) Paragraph (1) not to apply to certain items.—Paragraph (1) shall not apply to—

(A) any gain or loss which is an ordinary gain or loss (determined without regard to section 1239 of the Internal Revenue Code of 1986),

(B) any gain or loss on a capital asset held for not more than 6 months, and

(C) any gain to the extent section 453B of such Code applies.

(3) Applicable percentage.—For purposes of this subsection, the term "applicable percentage" means—

(A) 100 percent if the applicable value of the qualified corporation is less than $5,000,000, or

(B) 100 percent reduced by an amount which bears the same ratio to 100 percent as—

(i) the excess of the applicable value of the corporation over $5,000,000, bears to

(ii) $5,000,000.

(4) Applicable value.—For purposes of this subsection, the applicable value is the fair market value of all of the stock of the corporation on the date of the adoption of the plan of complete liquidation (or if greater, on August 1, 1986).

(5) Qualified corporation.—For purposes of this subsection, the term "qualified corporation" means any corporation if—

(A) on August 1, 1986, and at all times thereafter before the corporation is completely liquidated, more than 50 percent (by value) of the stock in such corporation is held by 10 or fewer qualified persons, and

(B) the applicable value of such corporation does not exceed $10,000,000.

(6) Definitions and special rules.—For purposes of this subsection—

(A) Qualified person.—The term "qualified person" means—

(i) an individual,

(ii) an estate, or

(iii) any trust described in clause (ii) or (iii) of section 1361(c)(2)(A) of the Internal Revenue Code of 1986.

(B) Attribution rules.—

(i) Entities.—Any stock held by a corporation, trust, or partnership shall be treated as owned proportionally by its shareholders, beneficiaries, or partners. Stock considered to be owned by a person by reason of the application of the preceding sentence shall, for purposes of applying such sentence, be treated as actually owned by such person.

(ii) Family members.—Stock owned (or treated as owned under clause (i)) by members of the same family (within the meaning of section 318(a)(1) of the Internal Revenue Code of 1986) shall be treated as owned by 1 person.

(C) Controlled group of corporations.—All members of the same controlled group (as defined in section 267(f)(1) of such Code) shall be treated as 1 corporation for purposes of this subsection.

(7) Section 338 transactions.—The provisions of this subsection shall also apply in the case of a transaction described in section 338 of the Internal Revenue Code of 1986 where the acquisition date (within the meaning of such section 338) is before January 1, 1989.

(8) Application of section 1374.—Rules similar to the rules of this subsection shall apply for purposes of applying section 1374 of the Internal Revenue Code of 1986 (as amended by section 632) in the case of a qualified corporation which becomes an S corporation for a taxable year beginning before January 1, 1989.

(d) Complete liquidation defined.—For purposes of this section, a corporation shall be treated as completely liquidated if all of the assets of such corporation are distributed in complete liquidation, less assets retained to meet claims.

* * *

Code Sections for Corporate Distributions Prior to Tax Reform Act of 1986

§ 311. Taxability of corporation on distribution

(a) General rule.—Except as provided in subsections (b), (c), and (d) of this section and section 453B, no gain or loss shall be recognized to a corporation on the distribution, with respect to its stock, of—

(1) its stock (or rights to acquire its stock), or

(2) property.

(b) LIFO inventory.—

(1) Recognition of gain.—If a corporation inventorying goods under the method provided in section 472 (relating to last-in, first-out inventories) distributes inventory assets (as defined in paragraph (2)(A)), then the amount (if any) by which—

(A) the inventory amount (as defined in paragraph (2)(B)) of such assets under a method authorized by section 471 (relating to general rule for inventories), exceeds

(B) the inventory amount of such assets under the method provided in section 472,

shall be treated as gain to the corporation recognized from the sale of such inventory assets.

(2) Definitions.—For purposes of paragraph (1)—

(A) Inventory assets.—The term "inventory assets" means stock in trade of the corporation, or other property of a kind which would properly be included in the inventory of the corporation if on hand at the close of the taxable year.

(B) Inventory amount.—The term "inventory amount" means, in the case of inventory assets distributed during a taxable year, the amount of such inventory assets determined as if the taxable year closed at the time of such distribution.

(3) Method of determining inventory amount.—For purposes of this subsection, the inventory amount of assets under a method authorized by section 471 shall be determined—

(A) if the corporation uses the retail method of valuing inventories under section 472, by using such method, or

(B) if subparagraph (A) does not apply, by using cost or market, whichever is lower.

(c) Liability in excess of basis.—If—

(1) a corporation distributes property to a shareholder with respect to its stock,

(2) such property is subject to a liability, or the shareholder assumes a liability of the corporation in connection with the distribution, and

(3) the amount of such liability exceeds the adjusted basis (in the hands of the distributing corporation) of such property,

then gain shall be recognized to the distributing corporation in an amount equal to such excess as if

the property distributed had been sold at the time of the distribution. In the case of a distribution of property subject to a liability which is not assumed by the shareholder, the amount of gain to be recognized under the preceding sentence shall not exceed the excess, if any, of the fair market value of such property over its adjusted basis.

(d) Distributions of appreciated property.—

(1) In general.—If—

(A) a corporation distributes property (other than an obligation of such corporation) to a shareholder in a distribution to which subpart A applies, and

(B) the fair market value of such property exceeds its adjusted basis (in the hands of the distributing corporation),

then gain shall be recognized to the distributing corporation in an amount equal to such excess as if the property distributed had been sold at the time of the distribution. This subsection shall be applied after the application of subsections (b) and (c).

(2) Exceptions and limitations.—Paragraph (1) shall not apply to—

(A) a distribution which is made with respect to qualified stock if—

(i) section 302(b)(4) applies to such distribution, or

(ii) such distribution is a qualified dividend;

(B) a distribution of stock or an obligation of a corporation if the requirements of paragraph (2) of subsection (e) are met with respect to the distribution;

(C) a distribution to the extent that section 303(a) (relating to distributions in redemption of stock to pay death taxes) applies to such distribution;

(D) a distribution to a private foundation in redemption of stock which is described in section 537(b)(2)(A) and (B); and

(E) a distribution by a corporation to which part I of subchapter M (relating to regulated investment companies) applies, if such distribution is in redemption of its stock upon the demand of the shareholder.

(e) Definitions and special rules for subsection (d)(2).—For purposes of subsection (d)(2) and this subsection—

(1) Qualified stock.—

(A) In general.—The term "qualified stock" means stock held by a person (other than a corporation) who at all times during the lesser of—

(i) the 5-year period ending on the date of distribution, or

(ii) the period during which the distributing corporation (or a predecessor corporation) was in existence,

held at least 10 percent in value of the outstanding stock of the distributing corporation (or predecessor corporation).

(B) Determination of stock held.—Section 318 shall apply in determining ownership of stock under subparagraph (A); except that, in applying section 318(a)(1), the term "family" includes any individual described in section 267(c)(4) and any spouse of any such individual.

(C) Rules for passthru entities.—In the case of an S corporation, partnership, trust, or estate—

(i) the determination of whether subparagraph (A) is satisfied shall be made at the shareholder, partner, or beneficiary level (rather than at the entity level), and

(ii) the distribution shall be treated as made directly to the shareholders, partners, or beneficiaries in proportion to their respective interests in the entity.

(2) Distributions of stock or obligations of controlled corporations.—

(A) Requirements.—A distribution of stock or an obligation of a corporation (hereinafter in this paragraph referred to as the "controlled corporation") meets the requirements of this paragraph if—

(i) such distribution is made with respect to qualified stock,

(ii) substantially all of the assets of the controlled corporation consists of the assets of 1 or more qualified businesses,

(iii) no substantial part of the controlled corporation's nonbusiness assets were acquired from the distributing corporation, in a transaction to which section 351 applied or as a contribution to capital, within the 5-year period ending on the date of the distribution, and

(iv) more than 50 percent in value of the outstanding stock of the controlled corporation is distributed by the distributing corporation with respect to qualified stock.

(B) Definitions.—For purposes of subparagraph (A)—

(i) Qualified business.—The term "qualified business" means any trade or business which—

(I) was actively conducted throughout the 5-year period ending on the date of the distribution, and

(II) was not acquired by any person within such period in a transaction in which gain or loss was recognized in whole or in part.

(ii) Nonbusiness asset.—The term "nonbusiness asset" means any asset not used in the active conduct of a trade or business.

(3) Qualified dividend.—The term "qualified dividend means any distribution of property to a shareholder other than a corporation if—

(A) such distribution is a dividend,

(B) such property was used by the distributing corporation in the active conduct of a qualified business (as defined in paragraph (2)), and

(C) such property is not property described in paragraph (1) or (4) of section 1221.

(Aug. 16, 1954, c. 736, 68A Stat. 94; Dec. 30, 1969, Pub.L. 91–172, Title IX, § 905(a), (b)(1), 83 Stat. 713, 714; Oct. 2, 1976, Pub.L. 94–452, § 2(b), 90 Stat. 1511; Oct. 4, 1976, Pub.L. 94–455, Title XIX, § 1901(a)(42)(A), (B)(i), (C), 90 Stat. 1771; Nov. 6, 1978, Pub.L. 95–600, Title VII, § 703(j)(2)(B), 92 Stat. 2941; Oct. 19, 1980, Pub.L. 96–471, § 2(b)(1), 94 Stat. 2253; Sept. 3, 1982, Pub.L. 97–248, Title II, § 223(a), 96 Stat. 483; July 18, 1984, Pub.L. 98–369, Title I, § 54(a), Title VII, § 712(j), 98 Stat. 568, 948.)

§ 333. Election as to recognition of gain in certain liquidations

(a) General rule.—In the case of property distributed in complete liquidation of a domestic corporation (other than a collapsible corporation to which section 341(a) applies), if—

(1) the liquidation is made in pursuance of a plan of liquidation adopted, and

(2) the distribution is in complete cancellation or redemption of all the stock, and the transfer of all the property under the liquidation occurs within some one calendar month,

then in the case of each qualified electing shareholder (as defined in subsection (c)) gain on the shares owned by him at the time of the adoption of the plan of liquidation shall be recognized only to the extent provided in subsections (e) and (f).

(b) Excluded corporation.—For purposes of this section, the term "excluded corporation" means a corporation which at any time between January 1, 1954, and the date of the adoption of the plan of liquidation, both dates inclusive, was the owner of stock possessing 50 percent or more of the total combined voting power of all classes of stock entitled to vote on the adoption of such plan.

(c) Qualified electing shareholders.—For purposes of this section, the term "qualified electing shareholder" means a shareholder (other than an excluded corporation) of any class of stock (whether or not entitled to vote on the adoption of the plan of liquidation) who is a shareholder at the time of the adoption of such plan, and whose written election to have the benefits of subsection (a) has been made and filed in accordance with subsection (d), but—

(1) in the case of a shareholder other than a corporation, only if written elections have been so filed by shareholders (other than corporations) who at the time of the adoption of the plan of liquidation are owners of stock possessing at least 80 percent of the total combined voting power (exclusive of voting power possessed by stock owned by corporations) of all classes of stock entitled to vote on the adoption of such plan of liquidation; or

(2) in the case of a shareholder which is a corporation, only if written elections have been so filed by corporate shareholders (other than an excluded corporation) which at the time of the adoption of such plan of liquidation are owners of stock possessing at least 80 percent of the total combined voting power (exclusive of voting power possessed by stock owned by an excluded corporation and by shareholders who are not corporations) of all classes of stock entitled to vote on the adoption of such plan of liquidation.

(d) Making and filing of elections.—The written elections referred to in subsection (c) must be made and filed in such manner as to be not in contravention of regulations prescribed by the Secretary. The filing must be within 30 days after the date of the adoption of the plan of liquidation.

(e) Noncorporate shareholders.—In the case of a qualified electing shareholder other than a corporation—

(1) there shall be recognized, and treated as a dividend, so much of the gain as is not in excess of his ratable share of the earnings and profits of the

corporation accumulated after February 28, 1913, such earnings and profits to be determined as of the close of the month in which the transfer in liquidation occurred under subsection (a)(2), but without diminution by reason of distributions made during such month; but by including in the computation thereof all amounts accrued up to the date on which the transfer of all the property under the liquidation is completed; and

(2) there shall be recognized, and treated as short-term or long-term capital gain, as the case may be, so much of the remainder of the gain as is not in excess of the amount by which the value of that portion of the assets received by him which consists of money, or of stock or securities acquired by the corporation after December 31, 1953, exceeds his ratable share of such earnings and profits.

(f) Corporate shareholders.—In the case of a qualified electing shareholder which is a corporation, the gain shall be recognized only to the extent of the greater of the two following—

(1) the portion of the assets received by it which consists of money, or of stock or securities acquired by the liquidating corporation after December 31, 1953; or

(2) its ratable share of the earnings and profits of the liquidating corporation accumulated after February 28, 1913, such earnings and profits to be determined as of the close of the month in which the transfer in liquidation occurred under subsection (a)(2), but without diminution by reason of distributions made during such month; but by including in the computation thereof all amounts accrued up to the date on which the transfer of all the property under the liquidation is completed.

(Aug. 16, 1954, c. 736, 68A Stat. 103; Feb. 26, 1964, Pub.L. 88–272, Title II, § 225(g), 78 Stat. 89; Oct. 4, 1976, Pub.L. 94–455, Title XIX, §§ 1901(a)(44), 1906(b)(13)(A), 1951(b)(6)(A), 90 Stat. 1772, 1834, 1838.)

§ 334. Basis of property received in liquidations

(a) General rule.—If property is received in a distribution in complete liquidation (other than a distribution to which section 333 applies), and if gain or loss is recognized on receipt of such property, then the basis of the property in the hands of the distributee shall be the fair market value of such property at the time of the distribution.

(b) Liquidation of subsidiary.—

(1) Distribution in complete liquidation.—If property is received by a corporation in a distribution in a complete liquidation to which section 332(a) applies, the basis of the property in the hands of the distributee shall be the same as it would be in the hands of the transferor.

(2) Transfers to which section 332(c) applies. —If property is received by a corporation in a transfer to which section 332(c) applies, the basis of the property in the hands of the transferee shall be the same as it would be in the hands of the transferor.

(3) Distributee defined.—For purposes of this subsection, the term "distributee" means only the corporation which meets the 80-percent stock ownership requirements specified in section 332(b).

(c) Property received in liquidation under section 333.—If—

(1) property was acquired by a shareholder in the liquidation of a corporation in cancellation or redemption of stock, and

(2) with respect to such acquisition—

(A) gain was realized, but

(B) as the result of an election made by the shareholder under section 333, the extent to which gain was recognized was determined under section 333,

then the basis shall be the same as the basis of such stock cancelled or redeemed in the liquidation, decreased in the amount of any money received by the shareholder, and increased in the amount of gain recognized to him.

(Aug. 16, 1954, c. 736, 68A Stat. 104; Nov. 13, 1966, Pub.L. 89–809, Title II, § 202(a), (b), 80 Stat. 1576; Oct. 4, 1976, Pub.L. 94–455, Title XIX, §§ 1901(a)(45), 1906(b)(13)(A), 90 Stat. 1772, 1834; Sept. 3, 1982, Pub.L. 97–248, Title II, §§ 222(e)(1)(C), 224(b), 96 Stat. 480, 488.)

§ 336. Distributions of property in liquidation

(a) General rule.—Except as provided in subsection (b) of this section and in section 453B (relating to disposition of installment obligations), no gain or loss shall be recognized to a corporation on the distribution of property in complete liquidation.

(b) LIFO inventory.—

(1) In general.—If a corporation inventorying goods under the LIFO method distributes inventory assets in complete liquidation, then the LIFO recapture amount with respect to such assets shall be treated as gain to the corporation recognized from the sale of such inventory assets.

(2) Exception where basis determined under section 334(b).—Paragraph (1) shall not apply to any liquidation under section 332 for which the basis of property received is determined under section 334(b).

(3) LIFO recapture amount.—For purposes of this subsection, the term "LIFO recapture amount" means the amount (if any) by which—

(A) the inventory amount of the inventory assets under the first-in, first-out method authorized by section 471, exceeds

(B) the inventory amount of such assets under the LIFO method.

(4) Definitions.—For purposes of this subsection—

(A) LIFO method.—The term "LIFO method" means the method authorized by section 472 (relating to last-in, first-out inventories).

(B) Other definitions.—The term "inventory assets" has the meaning given to such term by subparagraph (A) of section 311(b)(2), and the term "inventory amount" has the meaning given to such term by subparagraph (B) of section 311(b)(2) (as modified by paragraph (3) of section 311(b)).

(Aug. 16, 1954, c. 736, 68A Stat. 106; Apr. 2, 1980, Pub.L. 96–223, Title IV, § 403(b)(1), 94 Stat. 304; Oct. 19, 1980, Pub.L. 96–471, § 2(b)(1), (c)(1), 94 Stat. 2254; Sept. 3, 1982, Pub.L. 97–248, Title II, §§ 222(b), (e)(1)(D), 224(c)(4), 96 Stat. 478, 480, 489.)

§ 337. Gain or loss on sales or exchanges in connection with certain liquidations

(a) General rule.—If, within the 12-month period beginning on the date on which a corporation adopts a plan of complete liquidation, all of the assets of the corporation are distributed in complete liquidation, less assets retained to meet claims, then no gain or loss shall be recognized to such corporation from the sale or exchange by it of property within such 12-month period.

(b) Property defined.—

(1) In general.—For purposes of subsection (a), the term "property" does not include—

(A) stock in trade of the corporation, or other property of a kind which would properly be included in the inventory of the corporation if on hand at the close of the taxable year, and property held by the corporation primarily for sale to customers in the ordinary course of its trade or business,

(B) installment obligations acquired in respect of the sale or exchange (without regard to whether such sale or exchange occurred before, on, or after the date of the adoption of the plan referred to in subsection (a)) of stock in trade or other property described in subparagraph (A) of this paragraph, and

(C) installment obligations acquired in respect of property (other than property described in subparagraph (A)) sold or exchanged before the date of the adoption of such plan of liquidation.

(2) Nonrecognition with respect to inventory in certain cases.—Notwithstanding paragraph (1) of this subsection, if substantially all of the property described in subparagraph (A) of such paragraph (1) which is attributable to a trade or business of the corporation is, in accordance with this section, sold or exchanged to one person in one transaction, then for purposes of subsection (a) the term "property" includes—

(A) such property so sold or exchanged, and

(B) installment obligations acquired in respect of such sale or exchange.

(c) Limitations.—

(1) Collapsible corporations and liquidations to which section 333 applies.—This section shall not apply to any sale or exchange—

(A) made by a collapsible corporation (as defined in section 341(b)), or

(B) following the adoption of a plan of complete liquidation, if section 333 applies with respect to such liquidation.

(2) Liquidations to which section 332 applies. —In the case of any sale or exchange following the adoption of a plan of complete liquidation, if section 332 applies with respect to such liquidation, this section shall not apply.

(3) Special rule for affiliated group.—

(A) In general.—Paragraph (2) shall not apply to a sale or exchange by a corporation (hereinafter in this paragraph referred to as the "selling corporation") if—

(i) within the 12-month period beginning on the date of the adoption of a plan of complete liquidation by the selling corporation, the selling corpo-

ration and each distributee corporation is completely liquidated, and

(ii) none of the complete liquidations referred to in clause (i) is a liquidation with respect to which section 333 applies.

(B) Definitions.—For purposes of subparagraph (A)—

(i) The term "distributee corporation" means a corporation in the chain of includible corporations to which the selling corporation or a corporation above the selling corporation in such chain makes a distribution in complete liquidation within the 12-month period referred to in subparagraph (A)(i).

(ii) The term "chain of includible corporation" includes, in the case of any distribution, any corporation which (at the time of such distribution) is in a chain of includible corporations for purposes of section 1504(a) (determined without regard to the exceptions contained in section 1504(b)). Such term includes, where appropriate, the common parent corporation.

(d) Special rule for certain minority shareholders.—If a corporation adopts a plan of complete liquidation, and if subsection (a) does not apply to sales or exchanges of property by such corporation, solely by reason of the application of subsection (c)(2), then for the first taxable year of any shareholder (other than a corporation which meets the 80 percent stock ownership requirement specified in section 332(b)(1)) in which he receives a distribution in complete liquidation—

(1) the amount realized by such shareholder on the distribution shall be increased by his proportionate share of the amount by which the tax imposed by this subtitle on such corporation would have been reduced if subsection (c)(2) had not been applicable, and

(2) for purposes of this title, such shareholder shall be deemed to have paid, on the last day prescribed by law for the payment of the tax imposed by this subtitle on such shareholder for such taxable year, an amount of tax equal to the amount of the increase described in paragraph (1).

(e) Special rule for involuntary conversions. —If—

(1) There is an involuntary conversion (within the meaning of section 1033) of property of a distributing corporation and there is a complete liquidation of such corporation which qualifies under subsection (a),

(2) the disposition of the converted property (within the meaning of clause (ii) of section 1033(a)(2)(E)) occurs during the 60-day period which ends on the day before the first day of the 12-month period, and

(3) such corporation elects the application of this subsection at such time and in such manner as the Secretary may by regulations prescribe,

then for purposes of this section such disposition shall be treated as a sale or exchange occurring within the 12-month period.

(f) Special rule for LIFO inventories.—

(1) In general.—In the case of a corporation inventorying goods under the LIFO method, this section shall apply to gain from the sale or exchange of inventory assets (which under subsection (b)(2) constitute property) only to the extent that such gain exceeds the LIFO recapture amount with respect to such assets.

(2) Definitions.—The terms used in this subsection shall have the same meaning as when used in section 336(b).

(3) Cross reference.—

For treatment of gain from the sale or exchange of an installment obligation as gain resulting from the sale or exchange of the property in respect of which the obligation

was received, see the last sentence of section 453B(a).

(g) Title 11 or similar cases.—If a corporation completely liquidates pursuant to a plan of complete liquidation adopted in a title 11 or similar case (within the meaning of section 368(a)(3)(A))—

(1) for purposes of subsection (a), the term "property" shall not include any item acquired on or after the date of the adoption of the plan of liquidation if such item is not property within the meaning of subsection (b)(2), and

(2) subsection (a) shall apply to sales and exchanges by the corporation of property within the period beginning on the date of the adoption of the plan and ending on the date of the termination of the case.

(Aug. 16, 1954, c. 736, 68A Stat. 106; Sept. 2, 1958, Pub.L. 85–866, Title I, § 19, 72 Stat. 1615; Oct. 4, 1976, Pub.L. 94–455, Title XIX, §§ 1901(a)(46), 1906(b)(13)(A), Title XXI, § 2118(a), 90 Stat. 1772, 1834, 1912; Nov. 6, 1978, Pub.L. 95–600, Title VII, § 701(i)(1), 92 Stat. 2904; Nov. 10, 1978, Pub.L. 95–628, § 4(a), 92 Stat. 3628; Apr. 2, 1980, Pub.L. 96–223, Title IV, § 403(b)(2)(A), 94 Stat. 304; Oct. 19, 1980, Pub.L. 96–471, § 2(c)(2), 94 Stat. 2254; Dec. 24, 1980, Pub.L. 96–589, § 5(c), 94 Stat. 3405; Sept. 3, 1982, Pub.L. 97–248, Title II, § 224(c)(5), (6), 96 Stat. 489.)

TOPICAL INDEX

(References are to Code Sections)

TOPICAL INDEX

TOPICAL INDEX

†